A Dictionary of Official Titles
in Imperial China

A DICTIONARY OF
OFFICIAL TITLES
IN IMPERIAL CHINA

CHARLES O. HUCKER

*George Palmer Williams Emeritus Professor of
the College of Literature, Science, and the Arts
and Professor Emeritus of Chinese and of History
The University of Michigan*

STANFORD UNIVERSITY PRESS
Stanford, California   1985

Stanford University Press
Stanford, California
© 1985 by the Board of Trustees of the
Leland Stanford Junior University

Printed in the United States of America
ISBN 0-8047-1193-3
LC 82-62449

Published with the assistance of the National Endowment
for the Humanities. The preparation of this volume and costs
associated with its publication were supported by grants from
the Tools and Reference Works and Publications Programs of
the National Endowment for the Humanities.

A Dictionary of Official Titles in Imperial China

著　者：：Charles O. Hucker

發行所：：南 天 書 局 有 限 公 司
登記證字號：：行政院新聞局局版臺業字第一四三六號

出版者：：南 天 書 局 有 限 公 司
台北市羅斯福路三段二八一號三樓之二
電　話：：(○二)三九二○一九○
郵政劃撥帳戶：：○一○八○五三一八號

印刷者：：文 大 印 刷 有 限 公 司
台北市西園路二段二八一巷六弄二二號

中 華 民 國 七 十 四 年 十 月 景 印

SOUTHERN MATERIALS CENTER, INC.

P. O. Box 13-342 Taipei, Republic of China.

Preface

This is a reference aid for students and scholars who, from many disciplinary viewpoints, work with sources dating from or relating to premodern Chinese times, written principally in Literary or Classical Chinese (*wen-yen*). It identifies, defines, and places in their temporal and institutional contexts the official titles and agency names that abound in such materials. Items of unofficial (literary and colloquial) as well as official nomenclature are included, as are selected items of administrative terminology that seem especially relevant, particularly those in the realm of personnel administration. If less than absolutely comprehensive in its coverage, the Dictionary presses against the limits of practicality, and I am confident that it will serve most of the needs of its users.

My principal intent in undertaking the work was to relieve Sinologists who are not themselves institutional historians of the aggravations, confusions, and embarrassments they have endured in trying to cope with traditional China's ubiquitous governmental nomenclature. A secondary but important purpose was to provide a foundation, at least, for a history of China's governmental institutions. Acquaintances have suggested that the Dictionary may also prove to be a valuable source of data for social historians; if so, I shall naturally be gratified. I shall similarly be gratified if Sinologists generally accept my English renderings in their totality as a standard, since the troublesome and expensive use of Chinese characters in Sinological writings could thereby be reduced. However, I am aware that my work is not without imperfections, and that some Sinologists resist standardization of any sort as a matter of principle.

The work begins with a long Introduction that offers concise descriptions of governmental organization dynasty by dynasty from Chou to Ch'ing, including simple organizational charts for most dynasties. The main body of the Dictionary, prefaced with a User's Guide, consists of 8,291 individual entries for titles, agency names, and related terminology, in which differing usages are explained and pan-dynastic evolutions are traced. This is followed by a finding-list of suggested English renderings (English Index), another for Chinese characters and compounds (Chinese Index), and a conversion table from Pinyin romanizations currently endorsed by the People's Republic of China to the Wade-Giles romanizations used in the Dictionary, which have been standard in English-language and German writings about China for so long and are still preferred by so many Sinologists that for the foreseeable future no premodern China specialist can afford not to know them.

Suggested English renderings are based on principles long used by institutional historians of China in efforts to avoid the pitfalls of making traditional Chinese government seem either too much like a modern Western government or an otherworldly, Gilbert and Sullivan-like quagmire of nonsense. These principles as I use them can be summarized as follows:

1. The ideal is a rendering that reveals both the actual function of the office and the literal sense of the Chinese title, but if that ideal is unattainable a rendering suggesting the function is ordinarily preferred to one reflecting the literal sense.

2. The most notable exceptions to the preference for functional renderings tend to be in the nomenclature used for the military, eunuchs, and palace women. Army of Inspired Militancy (literal), for example, is preferred to Second Army or Third Army (terms that could only lead to ultimate confusion in a traditional Chinese con-

text); Eunuch of High Rank (literal) is preferred to some guess about the title-holder's usually undescribed function; and Lady of Bright Countenance (literal) is preferred to, say, Secondary Imperial Wife of the Fourth Rank.

3. Titles that are very familiar to English speakers and might be misleading are avoided: President, Prime Minister, Premier, Mayor, Sheriff, and the like. However, many familiar military terms not only seem unobjectionable, but are often unavoidable: General, Army, Regiment, Company, and the like.

4. Except in the cases of honorific or unofficial designations (Grandee of the Fourteenth Order, for example), bizarre renderings that are too foreign-sounding and esoteric neologisms are avoided.

5. Usages that are solidly established in the Sinological tradition, such as Chancellery, Secretariat, Department of State Affairs, Bureau of Military Affairs, Censorate, and Grand Secretariat, are not abandoned without good reason.

The making of this Dictionary has been possible only because Chinese scholars and Western Sinologists have alike realized the importance and the complexity of governmental nomenclature in imperial China and have long tried to make it understandable. The Chinese consequently have the world's most detailed histories and encyclopedias of governmental organization; and manuals of governmental organization in all major dynasties have been translated or compiled by Western scholars. In the former category, the imperially sponsored encyclopedia called *Li-tai chih-kuan piao* is the principal research source for this Dictionary, despite the distortions that result from its treating all agencies and posts of prior eras as antecedents of Ch'ing dynasty institutions. In the latter category, I have benefited enormously from the modern Western works that are cited by abbreviations in the entries, as is *Li-tai chih-kuan piao* (see Abbreviations on page 102): Edouard Biot's translation of the classic *Chou-li*; Hans Bielenstein's *The Bureaucracy of Han Times*; Robert des Rotours' *Traité des fonctionnaires et traité de l'armée* for T'ang; Chang Fu-jui's *Les Fonctionnaires des Song: Index des titres* for Sung; and Brunnert and Hagelstrom's *Present Day Political Organization of China* for Ch'ing. The

citation of *chüan* (chapters) of *Li-tai chih-kuan piao* and of renderings from Western-language manuals that are found in a large proportion of entries are not to be thought of as complete documentation of sources; they are merely cross-references to noteworthy works for the user's convenience.

Other materials used, which in general are less thorough and less readily available, are for those reasons not cited in the Dictionary entries. They are far too numerous to list here, but let me call special attention to the hitherto little-used *Ch'eng-wei lu* by the late Ch'ing scholar-official Liang Chang-chü, preserved in the collection of works on colloquialisms called *Ming-Ch'ing su-yü tz'u-shu chi-ch'eng*, which has been my principal source for unofficial usages through history; the abbreviated version of *Li-tai chih-kuan piao* by Huang Pen-chi, supplemented with brief dynasty-by-dynasty overviews of governmental structure, a considerable number of historical essays explaining individual titles, and a general index arranged by the four-corner system (Taipei, 1976); the *Chūgoku rekidai shokkan jiten* published by the Nitchū minzoku kagaku kenkyū-jo, a historical dictionary of 1,376 imperial Chinese titles, together with elaborate dynasty-by-dynasty charts of governmental structure (Tokyo, 1980); and the *Chung-kuo wen-kuan chih-tu shih* by Yang Shu-fan, my principal source for personnel-administration practices from Ch'in and Han through Ch'ing times, which has not received the attention from Western Sinologists that it deserves (Taipei, 1976).

While acknowledging my debt to all these and still other scholarly works, I must emphasize that the Dictionary is not merely a patchwork of data and English renderings easily plucked from the works of others. Both the introductory dynastic essays and the individual Dictionary entries are based largely on original research, and the suggested English renderings have been devised without obsessive adherence to those suggested by other Sinologists (or by myself in previous writings). My hope has been to achieve a coherent system of English nomenclature that accords with the continuities and discontinuities in Chinese usage over the long time span covered. Regardless of Ralph Waldo Emerson's famous pronouncement, I would like to have achieved absolute consistency in this regard. I have failed to do so because of the enduring attraction of some long-established Western renderings, some memory lapses or perhaps capricious aberrations on my part, and my inability to maintain concentration on such matters at a high level through the years that passed as a I drafted, revised, wordprocessed, copyread, and proofread the work. Now that the indexing has been done, I am sure I would do some things differently if I had the time—and the will—to go through it all again. However, I do not think my inconsistencies—mainly in such relatively petty matters as hyphenation and capitalization—detract significantly from the value of the work.

The Dictionary was originally conceived, as a vague project for some distant time, when I was a graduate student and in spare hours made an index to titles in the classic *Chou-li* for my own reference, and to an unusual and unanticipated degree it has been a one-man project. Actually initiated in 1976, the project has employed students of The University of Michigan and, at times in the past year, students of the University of Arizona as assistants with various kinds and levels of competence. But I alone wrote the Introduction, drafted and revised the entries, put the indexes in final form, tediously wordprocessed the English text and index on my personal computer for automated typesetting, contracted for the typesetting of Chinese characters throughout, supervised the cutting and pasting of Chinese characters into the English text, and did final proofreading of all parts of the Dictionary. Never before have I been so personally involved in the many stages of book-making. In consequence, putting the work between boards has taken far more time than I originally expected.

The principal reason for my personal absorption in the Dictionary for so long, and for the consequent delay in its publication, is that the process of compilation got under way just as personal computers came on the market, offering the possibility of automatically typesetting a work of this sort. My own infatuation with the new technology, coupled with the realization that rapidly rising publishing costs threatened to put the finished Dictionary completely out of the anticipated users' price range, led to an agree-

ment between the Stanford University Press and myself by which I would undertake to wordprocess the whole work and provide for the typesetting and insertion of Chinese characters into the text, and the Press would of necessity waive some of its normal editing prerogatives and keep the final published work at the lowest possible unit price. On both sides, it was an experiment whose consequences and complications could not be fully foreseen. In editorial and mechanical aspects alike, the result is perhaps less perfect than either of us would have liked; but what we have learned in the process should be of value to both of us, and others, in future.

In saying that preparation of the Dictionary has been largely a one-man process I do not wish to belittle the help, criticisms, and encouragement I have received from many others. Among the Sinologists who saw and commented usefully on sections of the work in draft form are Professors Hok-lam Chan of the University of Washington, John W. Dardess of the University of Kansas, Albert E. Dien of Stanford University, Edward L. Farmer of the University of Minnesota, A. F. P. Hulsewé of Leiden University, David N. Keightley of the University of California at Berkeley, James T. C. Liu of Princeton University, and Charles A. Peterson of Cornell University. Others who graciously contributed either published or unpublished materials of their own for my reference are Professors Priscilla Ching-Chung of the University of Hawaii at Manoa, R. R. C. de Crespigny of the Australian National University, Jack L. Dull of the University of Washington, David Farquhar of the University of California at Los Angeles, Penelope A. Herbert of Murdoch University, Igor de Rachewiltz of the Australian National University, and Daphne Lange Rosenzweig of the University of South Florida. If I have not fully profited from such help, the fault is mine alone, and I alone should be blamed for any factual errors as well as other flaws that may be found in the book.

Among the students who assisted in my research work for the Dictionary at The University of Michigan I owe special thanks to Thomas P. Massey (now Dr.), who gleaned data from *Li-tai chih-kuan piao* and other Chinese and Japanese sources, and to Chi-sheng (Jason) Kuo (now Dr.), who also worked in some of the Chinese sources; Maureen A. Flannery; and Cynthia Y. Ning. Alice Duan, Jennifer Lo, and Catherine Ehrlich at Michigan and Wayne Ten Harmsel and Lee Yi-ya of the University of Arizona also assisted, principally with indexing. I am heavily indebted to Barbara Congelosi and Diane Scherer, who far exceeded their obligations as members of the Publications Office of the Center for Chinese Studies at Michigan in helping me learn the fundamentals of word-processing and were always pleasant and helpful neighbors in Ann Arbor's memorable Corner House, where the Dictionary project was housed. In Tucson, Professor Stephen H. West, C. W. Fields, and Robert Arbogast sympathetically listened to my litany of technical problems and gave me knowledgeable advice that I greatly appreciate.

For encouragement and administrative support I am also greatly indebted to the successive chairmen of the Department of Far Eastern Languages and Literatures at Michigan, Professors Robert H. Brower and Luis O. Gómez, and their dedicated administrative assistant, Marjorie Petring; the successive directors of Michigan's Center for Chinese Studies, Professors Albert Feuerwerker and Robert F. Dernberger, and their administrative assistants, Rosalind Daly, Ann Detwiler, Eunice L. Burns, and Robert Eno; and the head of the Department of Oriental Studies at the University of Arizona, Professor Robert M. Gimello, and his administrative assistant, Salley Wallin. Among my faculty colleagues at Michigan, Professors James I. Crump and Kenneth DeWoskin were especially interested and encouraging, and Dr. Hilda Tao was helpful in checking substantial numbers of my romanizations for the accuracy of their tonal markings.

Not taking into account Stanford University Press's costs and my own working time and not-inconsequential expenses, preparation of the Dictionary has been supported primarily by two grants from the National Endowment for the Humanities and by cost-sharing funds and other kinds of contributions from The University of Michigan. Without the magnanimous financial support of both institutions, the project could never have been completed or undertaken at all. Supplementary grants from Michigan's College of Literature, Science, and the Arts, Horace H.

Rackham School of Graduate Studies, and Center for Chinese Studies have been invaluable in maintaining the momentum of the work at critical times, as have grants from the Committee on Studies of Chinese Civilization of the American Council of Learned Societies and its successor, the Joint Committee on Chinese Studies sponsored by the American Council of Learned Societies and the Social Science Research Council. The willingness of all these agencies to help bear the financial burden of such specialized work is of course greatly appreciated.

As for matters of technical production, I have wordprocessed the Dictionary on a TRS-80 Model III two-disk-drive microcomputer with an Okidata 82A microline printer attached, using a printer's special program built into the general wordprocessing program called Lazy Writer devised by David Welsh; both hardware and software have proved quite satisfactory. The English type used is New Times Roman, set by Edwards Brothers, Inc., of Ann Arbor, whose wordprocessing specialists, Nancy Firestone and Laurel Doty, have been consistently helpful. Chinese characters have been set by Asco Trade Typesetting Limited of Hong Kong, in its font called Basic Grotesk; its manager, Howard Wu, deserves great credit for the accuracy and promptness with which the work has been done. Keylining characters into the English text has been the work of Tucson Typographic Service; I appreciate the counsel and courtesies of its president, Larry Armstrong, and the always cheerful and resourceful help of its expert keyliner, José A. Fortuno. At Stanford University Press, Editor J. G. Bell and Associate Editor Barbara E. Mnookin have principally borne the heavy burden of collaborating with me in the publication process. Their professional expertise and, above all, their humane concern for my well-being, success, and gratification are greatly appreciated.

My wife, Myrl, has as always been understanding, tolerant, and supportive, at times in abnormally difficult circumstances, and I dedicate the work to her with all my love.

C.O.H.

Tucson
June 1984

Contents

INTRODUCTION:
GOVERNMENTAL ORGANIZATION ERA BY ERA
Some General Continuities / 3. Chou / 6. Ch'in / 8. Han / 11. Era of North-South Division / 17. Sui / 24. T'ang / 28. The Five Dynasties and Ten Kingdoms / 38. Sung / 40. Liao and Chin / 53. Yüan / 58. Ming / 70. Ch'ing / 83.

DICTIONARY OF OFFICIAL TITLES IN IMPERIAL CHINA
Guide to the Use of the Dictionary / 99. Abbreviations / 102.

THE DICTIONARY / 103-599

REFERENCE MATTER
Index to Suggested English Renderings / 601. Index to Chinese Terms / 645.
Conversion Table: Pinyin to Wade-Giles / 675.

INTRODUCTION: GOVERNMENTAL ORGANIZATION ERA BY ERA

Conventional Titles for Members of the Imperial Family

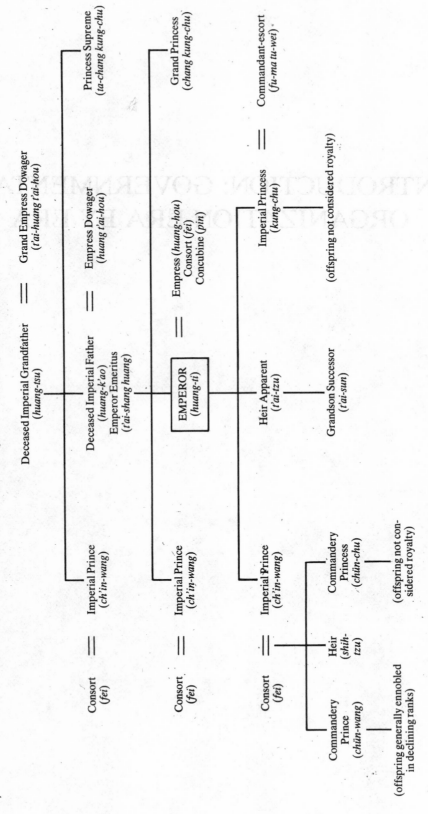

Some General Continuities

Some scholars seem to believe that the patterns of government in Imperial China never fundamentally changed. Dispelling that notion should be one of the principal achievements of this dictionary. Nevertheless, some aspects of Chinese government did persist almost unchanged throughout history, and others endured through very long stretches of time. To avoid unnecessary repetition in the era-by-era descriptions of governmental organization that follow, some of the most notable of these continuities are dealt with here at the outset.

Ruling Families Throughout History

Among the most stable patterns in traditional Chinese government was official nomenclature for the supreme ruler, his close relatives, and his places of residence. The single most significant change was made in 221 B.C., when the ancient but long depreciated title *wang* 王, which Westerners have traditionally rendered as King, was replaced as the designation of the supreme ruler by the newly coined title *huang-ti* 皇帝, translated as Emperor.

From 221 B.C. to the end of the Ch'ing dynasty in 1912, China was ruled by Emperors who lived in a walled compound or Palace (*kung* 宮), commonly known as the Great Within (*ta-nei* 大內) or the Forbidden City (*chin-ch'eng* 禁城), which contained many buildings called Halls (*tien* 殿, *ko* 閣) or individually named palaces. Around this core was a larger walled area commonly called the Imperial City (*huang-ch'eng* 皇城), enclosing the halls, or residences, of the intimate personal attendants of the Emperor and his immediate family. Buildings housing agencies of the central government were also clustered in the Imperial City or lay close outside it.

The larger city in which the Imperial City was located, itself normally walled, was designated the Capital (*ching* 京, *tu* 都; commonly with a hierarchical or directional prefix). A much larger area that was dominated by and administered directly from the capital, a special territorial jurisdiction as large as a modern Province (*sheng* 省), was the Metropolitan Area (*ching-shih* 京師, *ching-chao* 京兆, *chih-li* 直隸).

The Emperor had several categories of wives. There could be only one principal wife at any one time, the Empress (*huang-hou* 皇后); others were categorized as Consorts (*fei* 妃) and Concubines (*pin* 嬪)—designations normally prefixed with auspicious or laudatory epithets making such titles as Honored Consort (*kuei-fei* 貴妃). All such wives were known by their maiden surnames—as Empress Li, Honored Consort Yang, and the like. A child borne by any wife was considered legitimate and formally treated the Empress as its mother. The residence of the Empress was commonly called the Western Palace (*hsi-kung* 西宮).

Intimate personal attendants of the Emperor and his various wives were of two sorts. One was a group of lower-status palace women (*kung-nü* 宮女, *nü-kuan* 女官, and variants), who in principle could be promoted even to the status of Empress at the Emperor's whim, but who generally were servants of the Emperor and his wives. From T'ang times on, they were commonly organized hierarchically into Six Palace Services (*liu chü* 六局), each with a specified realm of responsibility, and each headed by one of the so-called Six Matrons (*liu shang* 六尚).

The other group of intimate attendants were eunuchs (*huan-kuan* 宦官, *nei-shih* 內侍, *t'ai-chien* 太監, and variants), among whom strong individuals or cliques sometimes exploited their close relations with the Emperors and their wives to such a degree that they gained great governmental authority—notably in Later Han, in late T'ang, and in Ming. Nominally, however, they were palace servants, organized—sometimes together with palace women—into a Palace Domestic Service (*ch'ang-ch'iu chien* 長秋監, *nei-shih chien* 內侍監, *nei-shih sheng* 內侍省) or a Court of Palace Attendants (*hsüan-hui yüan* 宣徽院).

Many members of the government who did not live in the palace nevertheless had important palace responsibilities. Perhaps most importantly, these included large numbers of Imperial Guardsmen (*shih-wei* 侍衛), whose duty it was to protect the imperial family and the palace. Others staffed such agencies as the Court of Imperial Entertainments (*hung-lu ssu* 鴻臚寺) and the Court of Imperial Sacrifices (*t'ai-ch'ang ssu* 太常寺), which had heavy responsibilities for provisioning and otherwise caring for the palace and the imperial family. Some central government agencies even had limited supervisory authority over the palace and its personnel. Such, for example, were the Han office of the Chamberlain for the Palace Revenues (*shao-fu* 少府), the T'ang–Sung Palace Administration (*tien-chung sheng* 殿中省), and the Ch'ing Imperial Household Department (*nei-wu fu* 內務府).

All sons of Emperors were Imperial Princes (*ch'in-wang* 親王), all daughters Imperial Princesses (*kung-chu* 公主). All other close relatives also had noble status, as shown in the accompanying table. The Emperor's most important offspring was the Heir Apparent (*t'ai-tzu* 太子), normally so designated during the father's reign and normally the eldest son by the Empress, except in the case of non-Chinese rulers such as the Mongols and the Manchus, who did not feel bound by traditional Chinese inheritance practices. Like the Empress, the Heir Apparent had his own establishment within the palace compound, commonly referred to as the Eastern Palace (*tung-kung* 東宮); it was managed by a large agency known from T'ang on as the Household Administration of the Heir Apparent (*chan-shih fu* 詹事府).

Other imperial offspring, especially sons, were usually enfeoffed with domains, real or nominal, named after ancient Chou feudal states, and had supporting staffs of officials constituting Princely Establishments (*wang-fu* 王府). Into T'ang times, Imperial Princes often served in important governmental posts, but in later

Chinese dynasties efforts were made to dissociate them from government and especially, as soon as they reached maturity if not before, to move them out of the palace and the capital into imposing residences scattered throughout the empire. All offspring of males descended from Emperors were normally granted noble status; eldest sons succeeded their fathers, and younger sons usually received lesser titles and emoluments. Descendants of Emperors through daughters, however, did not have such advantages. Since they did not bear the imperial surname, they were not considered members of the nobility and could not expect any special consideration from the state, especially if they were several generations removed from their imperial forebears.

The management of all imperial kinsmen's affairs, including the maintenance of strict genealogical records, was entrusted to an agency called the Court of the Imperial Clan (*tsung-cheng ssu* 宗正寺, *tsung-jen fu* 宗人府).

Official Ranks

Even in the ancient Chou dynasty there was a systematized gradation of government personnel into rank categories. Our understanding of such gradations becomes firm only with the Han dynasty, when officials were ranked in terms of annual salaries stated in grain payments, from fewer than 100 up to a maximum of 10,000 bushels. From Han on, officials were nominally paid at least partly in grain, although even the grain portions of their salaries were commonly converted to copper coins, bolts of silk, bulk silver, eventually paper currency, and other sorts of non-grain commodities—often at confusingly varied rates of exchange. In some regimes that followed close after Han, ranks continued to be stated in bushels of grain; but generally speaking, post-Han regimes to the end of Ch'ing used a system of gradations called the Nine Ranks (*chiu p'in* 九品).

The Nine Ranks system originated at the very end of Han, in A.D. 220. At first, ranks were specified in the following scheme:

1: upper-upper (*shang-shang*)
2: upper-middle (*shang-chung*)
3: upper-lower (*shang-hsia*)

4: middle-upper (*chung-shang*)
5: middle-middle (*chung-chung*)
6: middle-lower (*chung-hsia*)
7: lower-upper (*hsia-shang*)
8: lower-middle (*hsia-chung*)
9: lower-lower (*hsia-hsia*)

Later there were subgradations of various sorts, with as many as 36 categories. But the standard, enduring pattern that soon evolved provided for nine numbered ranks (*p'in* 品) from 1 down to 9, each divided into two grades, classes, or degrees (*teng* 等), namely, upper (*cheng* 正) and lower (*ts'ung* 從). Throughout this dictionary, as in most Sinological writings, such rank indicators are rendered 3a (*cheng san-p'in:* rank 3, upper class), 5b (*ts'ung wu-p'in:* rank 5, lower class), and the like. In some eras one further level of gradation was used, indicated here in the forms 6a1, 6a2, and so on.

In general, from the era when the Nine Ranks system was established, official posts were assigned ranks in the same fashion; and when a rank 4b post became vacant it was normally filled by an available rank 4b official or one ready for promotion to such rank. Ranks of posts and appointees did not always precisely match, however; and it is often very difficult to determine how an official's rank was affected when he was shifted from one post to another.

Salaries paid according to ranks were often supplemented by special allowances of many sorts, some determined by the specific posts that men occupied.

Lesser Functionaries

Officials with rank status (*kuan* 官) never comprised the entire body, or even the majority, of personnel in government service. In the military they constituted the officer corps that commanded multitudes of ordinary soldiers; similarly, in the civil service they were the executives, so to speak, who directed hordes of administrative, secretarial, and other assistants who did the drafting, record keeping, and menial labor required in all government agencies. These lesser functionaries (in Chinese called *li* 吏 or *hsü-li* 胥吏) are here referred to collectively by such designations as "unranked subofficials" and "nonofficial specialists." They were by no means be-

neath the notice of the central government, which commonly established quotas for them and prescribed their pay schedules; and they were usually differentiated by gradations similar to the ranks of their official superiors. Some of them—possibly very large numbers of them at times—were promoted to official status after meritorious service. But in general they were held in low esteem, considered to be "outside the current" (*liu-wai* 流外) that moved their betters up through the ranks of the hierarchy of officials. Traditional Chinese writers about governmental institutions tended to ignore them, so that they get little attention in the following descriptive essays and in individual dictionary entries; but students of Chinese government should always be aware of their presence and their influence.

"Avoidances"

From very early Han times if not earlier, Chinese rulers recognized the dangers of collusion among officials on the basis of kinship relations and bonds of geographic neighborliness. They consequently established principles that generally governed personnel administration throughout imperial history, generically known as "avoidances" (*hui-pi* 迴避), which eliminated or at least minimized opportunities for officials to collaborate with one another to their selfish advantage and to the disadvantage of the state.

One consequence was that lesser functionaries in units of territorial administration almost always were (and sometimes were rigidly required to be) natives of the jurisdictions in which they served, so that executive officials could not staff such agencies with personal hangers-on imported from their own native areas. On the other hand, officials were normally forbidden to serve in territorial jurisdictions of which they were themselves registered natives, or even at times in jurisdictions of which their wives were registered natives.

It was equally the rule, for the central government as well as for units of territorial administration, that no man could serve in any agency where a kinsman was already employed; the junior had to withdraw in deference to the senior, and if he failed to do so he could be punished severely.

Chou

1122(?)-256 B.C.

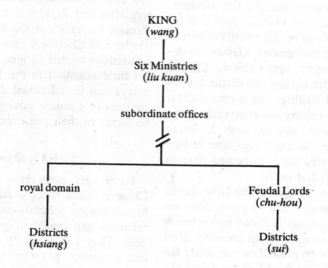

```
                        KING
                       (wang)

                   Six Ministries
                    (liu kuan)

                 subordinate offices
                        ─┼─

     royal domain                    Feudal Lords
                                      (chu-hou)

     Districts                        Districts
     (hsiang)                         (sui)
```

In Chou times the Chinese were organized under a King (*wang* 王) in a varying and changing feudal (*feng-chien* 封建) pattern, dominated by a hereditary aristocracy. Subsequent Chinese believed that Chou government conformed to a description found in the work called the *Chou Rituals* (*Chou-li* 周禮), although it is clearly an idealization drawn up perhaps as late as the third century B.C. Because of the great influence of this work on later Chinese thought about government, the structure of government it describes is briefly outlined here.

The Central Government

The Chou King was reportedly supported and advised by a council of trustworthy kinsmen called Elders (*chang-lao* 長老), with honorific titles in two categories. One category was the Three Dukes (*san kung* 三公): the Grand Preceptor (*t'ai-shih* 太師), Grand Mentor (*t'ai-fu* 太傅), and Grand Guardian (*t'ai-pao* 太保). The second category was the Three Solitaries (*san ku* 三孤): the Junior (*shao* 少) Preceptor, Junior Mentor, and Junior Guardian.

General administration (especially of the royal domain, but to some extent of the empire as a whole) was in the hands of Six Ministers (*liu ch'ing* 六卿, *liu kuan* 六官), namely, the Ministers of State (*chung-tsai* 冢宰), head of the Ministry of State (*t'ien-kuan* 天官, lit., "heavenly officials"), a kind of general agent or prime minister for the King; of Education (*ssu-t'u* 司徒), head of the Ministry of Education (*ti-kuan* 地官, "earthly officials"), principally responsible for civil administration and social welfare; of Rites (*tsung-po* 宗伯), head of the Ministry of Rites (*ch'un-kuan* 春官, "spring officials"); of War (*ssu-ma* 司馬), head of the Ministry of War (*hsia-kuan* 夏官, "summer officials"); of Justice (*ssu-k'ou* 司寇), head of the Ministry of Justice (*ch'iu-kuan* 秋官, "autumn officials"); and of Works (*ssu-k'ung* 司空), head of the Ministry of Works (*tung-kuan* 冬官, "winter officials").

Each Minister reportedly had a large staff of subordinates, many with narrowly specialized functions.

Territorial Administration

In the Chou feudal age, territories outside the directly controlled royal domain were allocated to Feudal Lords collectively known as "the various Marquises" (*chu-hou* 諸侯), whose fiefs were called States (*kuo* 國). There were five grades of lords, in descending order of eminence as follows: Dukes (*kung* 公), Marquises (*hou* 侯), Earls (*po* 伯), Viscounts (*tzu* 子), and Barons (*nan* 男). Each state, according to the *Chou Rituals*, had an administrative organization patterned after that of the royal domain but on a lesser scale. The lords were expected to appear for audience at the royal court regularly, and they were visited by royal overseers called Grand Master Inspectors (*ta-fu chien* 大夫監).

In theory, residents of both the royal and the lordly domains were organized for economic and fiscal purposes on 900-*mou* plots of agricultural land (one *mou* = one sixth of an English acre), each plot divided equally into 100-*mou* sections to resemble a tick-tack-toe design, or the Chinese character for a well, *ching*; hence the term well-field (*ching-t'ien* 井田) system. Eight families occupied each plot, communally working the central section to provide for their overlord and separately working the eight surrounding sections for themselves. For purposes of general administrative and military service, however, residents were reportedly organized in an overlapping hierarchy (terminology differing between areas in the royal domain and those elsewhere) in which five families constituted a Neighborhood (*pi* 比 in the royal domain, *lin* 鄰 elsewhere), five neighborhoods a Village (*lü* 閭, *li* 里), four villages a Precinct (*tsu* 族, *tsan* 酇), five precincts a Ward (*tang* 黨, *pi* 鄙), five wards a Township (*chou* 州, *hsien* 縣), and five townships a District (*hsiang* 鄉, *sui* 遂). At each of these levels of social organization, tradition holds, there was a popularly elected head, the hierarchy culminating in District Grand Masters (*hsiang ta-fu* 鄉大夫, *sui ta-fu* 遂大夫) in overall administrative control of 12,500 families.

The Military

The governing elite of Chou times was a chariot-riding class of warriors consisting of the King, the Feudal Lords, and the retainers who filled the posts in the royal and lordly courts. Serfs provided infantry support for the charioteering aristocrats.

According to the *Chou Rituals*, the hierarchical administrative organization of the agricultural population described above served also as a military organization. Five men, presumably chosen from the five families in a neighborhood, made a Squad (*wu* 伍), five squads a Platoon (*liang* 兩), four platoons a Company (*tsu* 卒), five companies a Battalion (*lü* 旅), five battalions a Regiment (*shih* 師), and five regiments an Army (*chün* 軍) of 12,500 men commanded by a General (*chiang* 將). The King maintained six armies; Feudal Lords were authorized from one to three armies similarly organized, depending on the size of their domains.

Personnel Administration

Although the *Chou Rituals* suggests that aristocratic officials were subject to a sophisticated system of personnel administration, few details are provided. Aristocrats in the service of the King or the Feudal Lords were graded in three large categories, in descending order of rank: Ministers (*ch'ing* 卿), Grand Masters (*ta-fu* 大夫), and Servicemen (*shih* 士). Grand Masters and Servicemen were subdivided into senior (*shang* 上), ordinary (*chung* 中), and junior (*hsia* 下) grades; and the whole aristocracy, including Feudal Lords, was overlaid with a complicated rank pattern called the Nine Honors (*chiu ming* 九命), ranging downward from 9. Available evidence indicates that virtually all official posts, like the status of Feudal Lords, were hereditary in practice.

Ch'in

221-206 B.C.

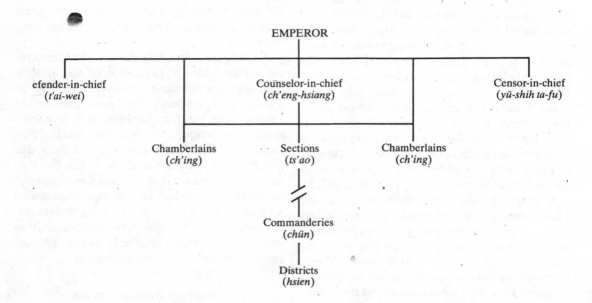

```
                              EMPEROR
                                 |
        ┌────────────────────────┼────────────────────────┐
  efender-in-chief        Counselor-in-chief          Censor-in-chief
    (t'ai-wei)             (ch'eng-hsiang)             (yü-shih ta-fu)
        └────────┬───────────────────────────────┬────────┘
                 |                                |
            Chamberlains    Sections         Chamberlains
              (ch'ing)       (ts'ao)           (ch'ing)
                                |
                                ╱
                                |
                          Commanderies
                             (chün)
                                |
                             Districts
                              (hsien)
```

Ch'in established China's first fully centralized, bureaucratic, nationwide empire. Its organization and workings are known only in sketchy outlines.

The Central Government

After King Cheng of Ch'in unified China in 221 B.C., he abandoned the traditional title King (*wang*) in favor of the new, more auspicious title that Westerners consistently render Emperor (*huang-ti*), which was used by all subsequent dynasties. His capital was at Hsien-yang near modern Sian, Shensi Province. His palace staff was a large one, made up of palace women, eunuchs, military guardsmen, a Supervisor of the Household (*chan-shih* 詹事) for the Empress and another for the Heir Apparent, various Receptionists (*yeh-che* 謁者) and Attendant Physicians (*shih-i* 侍醫), as many as 70 Erudites

(*po-shih* 博士), and a substantial corps of Court Gentlemen (*lang* 郎).

A kind of imperial household administration existed in the form of the so-called Nine Chamberlains (*chiu ch'ing* 九卿). There were actually eleven Chamberlains, each assisted by an Aide (*ch'eng* 丞) and various lesser subalterns: the Chamberlains for Ceremonials (*feng-ch'ang* 奉常, *t'ai-ch'ang* 太常); for Attendants (*lang-chung ling* 郎中令); for the Palace Garrison (*wei-wei* 衛尉); for Law Enforcement (*t'ing-wei* 廷尉); for the Capital (*nei-shih* 內史); for the National Treasury (*chih-su nei-shih* 治粟內史); for Dependencies (*tien-k'o* 典客); for the Imperial Clan (*tsung-cheng* 宗正); for the Imperial Stud (*t'ai-p'u* 太僕); for the Palace Revenues (*shao-fu* 少府); and for the Palace Buildings (*chiang-tso shao-fu* 將作少府).

Empire-wide administration was supervised by three central government dignitaries known collectively as the Three Dukes (*san kung* 三公). Of these, the most important was the Counselor-in-chief (*ch'eng-hsiang* 丞相). Two such appointees were authorized, one of the Left, the senior, and one of the Right. The Counselor-in-chief was the most esteemed and powerful official of the realm, an all-purpose deputy for the Emperor. His Office (*fu* 府) was subdivided by functions into various Sections (*ts'ao* 曹), staffed by Administrators (*yüan-shih* 掾史). The Censor-in-chief (*yü-shih ta-fu* 御史大夫), the second of this triumvirate, was an all-around assistant and consultant to the Counselor-in-chief and was the channel through which imperial orders were passed to him; the Censor-in-chief was also responsible for maintaining disciplinary surveillance over the whole officialdom. Subordinate to him was a Palace Aide to the Censor-in-chief (*yü-shih chung-ch'eng* 御史中丞), who in turn supervised a staff of Attendant Censors (*shih yü-shih* 侍御史). Attendant Censors were occasionally dispatched to inspect governmental units outside the capital and when on such duty were called Supervising Censors (*chien yü-shih* 監御史, *chien-ch'a shih* 監察史). The third of the Three Dukes was the Defender-in-chief (*t'ai-wei* 太尉), the empire's senior military officer and the Emperor's chief of military staff. Subordinate to him were field commanders throughout the empire, called Generals (*chiang-chün* 將軍).

Territorial Administration

Excluding the metropolitan area surrounding the imperial capital, which was administered by the Chamberlain for the Capital and was commonly referred to by his title (*nei-shih*), the Ch'in empire was divided into first 36 and ultimately more than 40 Commanderies (*chün* 郡), each having a Governor (*shou* 守) for general administration and a Defender (*wei* 尉) for supervision of the commandery's military garrisons. The Governor had an Aide (*ch'eng*) in charge of paperwork and a staff of subalterns divided into Sections (*ts'ao*) comparable to those in the Office of the Counselor-in-chief at the capital.

Commanderies were divided into Districts (*hsien* 縣), the lowest units in the regular administrative hierarchy. Each district was administered by a Magistrate (*ling* 令 where the population exceeded 10,000 households, *chang* 長 where the population was smaller). As in commanderies, principal subordinates were an Aide and a Defender, and lesser staff members were divided into Sections.

Districts were subdivided into residential groupings called Townships (*hsiang* 鄉), from among whose residents were chosen an Elder (*san-lao* 三老) to give moral leadership, a Husbander (*se-fu* 嗇夫) to manage local fiscal affairs, and a Patroller (*yu-chiao* 游徼) to keep the local peace. Each 1,000-household group within the township, generally, constituted a Neighborhood (*t'ing* 亭) with a designated Head (*chang* 長) in charge. Each 100-household group in the neighborhood was organized as a Village (*li* 里), also with a designated Head (*k'uei* 魁); and its member households were further organized into successively smaller mutual-responsibility groups, Tens (*shih* 什) and Fives (*wu* 伍).

The Military

Under Ch'in, all males aged twenty-three and older were required to participate in training exercises one month each year in district or commandery garrisons. Apparently once in his life every man was also called to serve for one year in the garrisons that guarded the dynastic capital and for another year in a frontier garrison. At any time while in service at the capital or at a frontier, a soldier could be assigned to a General (*chiang-chün*) for special campaigning. Some troops, such as the Imperial Guardsmen (*chin-ping* 禁兵) who served at the palace, must have been more nearly careerists than citizen-soldiers.

Personnel Administration

There was apparently no formal system for the recruitment, in-service evaluation, payment, promotion, demotion, and punishment of officials in Ch'in times. Appointments must have been based for the most part on recommendations, and tenure seems to have been indefinite. All regular officials down to the district level were appointed by the Counselor-in-chief and confirmed by the Emperor, but many subalterns in all agencies could probably be appointed by the various agency heads.

Rank-titles of what might be called a lay nobility, graded hierarchically from 20 (highest) to 1 (lowest), were awarded to officials and others for meritorious service to the Ch'in state. Such titles were not hereditary, and their recipients were not awarded fiefs. There is no clear evidence about how officials were otherwise ranked, or about how they were paid.

Han

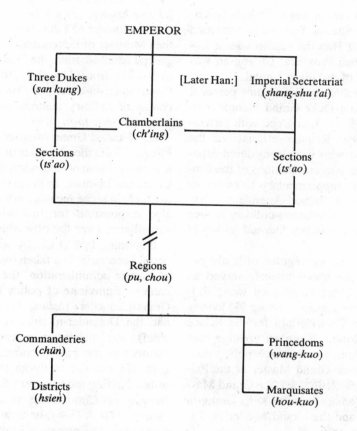

Han perpetuated and generally expanded the governmental structure instituted by Ch'in, but internal shifts in responsibilities paved the way for significant structural changes in later times. Government personnel, though of aristocratic social background, became a more systematized and professionally bureaucratic officialdom.

The Central Government

Han began with the Ch'in pattern of what is called a "strong prime ministership," in which the power of the Emperor was in some measure balanced by the collective influence of the officialdom under the leadership of a highly esteemed Counselor-in-chief (ch'eng-hsiang 丞相). But the powers of the Counselor-in-chief were gradually dissipated, especially under the autocratic Emperor Wu (r. 141–87 B.C.), until by the end of Former Han he was only one member of a triumvirate of state councilors called the Three Dukes (san kung 三公), and active administrative control of the government had passed out of their hands. This situation persisted throughout Later Han, although in the second century A.D. a long-threatened schism appeared between the imperial household and its agents, collectively known as the Inner Court (*chung-ch'ao* 中朝, *nei-ch'ao* 內朝), and on the other hand the regular officialdom, or Outer Court (*wai-ch'ao* 外朝). Empresses and their relatives, and then cliques of palace eunuchs, successively dominated the government; and in the end power was seized by generals who had become powerful regional warlords.

The Former Han capital was at Ch'in's Hsien-yang in modern Shensi Province, renamed Ch'ang-an. In Later Han the capital was at Lo-yang, modern Honan Province; Ch'ang-an was honored as a kind of auxiliary capital.

Each Emperor ordinarily chose some personal confidant as Superior Duke Grand Mentor (*t'ai-fu shang-kung* 太傅上公), charged with providing moral guidance. Regular officials of the central government who were considered especially worthy to serve as companions of the Emperor were granted supplementary titles (*chia-kuan* 加官), such as Palace Attendant (*shih-chung* 侍中), Palace Attendant-in-ordinary (*chung ch'ang-shih* 中常侍), or Palace Steward (*chi-shih-chung* 給事中).

Expectant officials, or regular officials between administrative appointments, served as courtiers entitled Court Gentlemen (*lang* 郎), organized under three Leaders (*chiang* 將) loosely subordinate to the Chamberlain for the Palace Revenues (see below). Of greater prestige than other Court Gentlemen were three policy consultants: the Superior Grand Master of the Palace (*t'ai-chung ta-fu* 太中大夫), the Grand Master of the Palace (*chung ta-fu* 中大夫, *kuang-lu ta-fu* 光祿大夫), and the Grand Master of Remonstrance (*chien ta-fu* 諫大夫, *chien-i ta-fu* 諫議大夫). Also in the Emperor's personal entourage, as in Ch'in times, were Erudites (*po-shih* 博士) noted for their scholastic learning.

The Emperor's paperwork was handled primarily by what was informally known as the Imperial Secretariat (*shang-shu t'ai* 尚書臺), formally a minor office under the Chamberlain for the Palace Revenues. Emperor Wu replaced it with a group of eunuchs, calling them Palace Secretaries (*chung-shu* 中書). Regular officials regained their former status in 29 B.C., and the Imperial Secretariat steadily gained control of the empire's administrative machinery at the expense of the Counselor-in-chief; throughout Later Han it was the dominant executive agency in the central government. It was headed by a Director (*shang-shu ling* 令), a Vice Director (*p'u-yeh* 僕射), and four, then five, and finally six Imperial Secretaries (*shang-shu*), each in charge of a function-specific Section (*ts'ao* 曹).

Formally if not always in practice, the central government officialdom continued to be headed by the Three Dukes: the Counselor-in-chief (*ch'eng-hsiang*; from 1 B.C. to A.D. 52 called Grand Minister of Education, *ta ssu-t'u* 大司徒, then Minister of Education, *ssu-t'u*) in charge of general administration; the Defender-in-chief (*t'ai-wei* 太尉; from 119 B.C. to A.D. 51 called Commander-in-chief, *ta ssu-ma* 大司馬), in charge of military matters; and the Censor-in-chief (*yü-shih ta-fu* 御史大夫; from 8 B.C. to A.D. 51 called Grand Minister of Works, *ta ssu-k'ung* 大司空, then Minister of Works *ssu-k'ung*), a general assistant and normal successor to the Counselor-in-chief. In Former Han, the Censor-in-chief, in some measure not wholly clear, was also responsible for maintaining disciplinary surveillance over the officialdom at large.

Beginning in 8 B.C., by which time the Imperial Secretariat had taken over de facto control of routine administration, the Three Dukes became a triumvirate of policy consultants called Grand Councilors (*hsiang* 相, *tsai-hsiang* 宰相); and the Defender-in-chief (or Commander-in-chief) was thereafter considered the senior member of the group, commonly a virtual regent. He was ordinarily an influential imperial in-law holding the two-tier title General-in-chief (serving as) Commander-in-chief (*ta ssu-ma ta chiang-chün* 大將軍), or a variant. To recapture a semblance of propriety in the relationship between the State Councilors and the Imperial Secretariat, Later Han Emperors beginning in 106 often put Defenders-in-chief, and sometimes Ministers of Works as well, in charge of the Imperial Secretaries.

After the warlord Tung Cho seized power in 189, he made himself first Minister of Works, then Defender-in-chief, and finally Counselor-in-chief (*hsiang-kuo* 相國), superior to the three Grand Councilors. In 208 the military dictator Ts'ao Ts'ao abolished all of the Grand Councilor posts and took for himself the old prestigious title *ch'eng-hsiang*.

During the first half of Former Han, when a

"strong prime ministership" prevailed in the form of the Counselor-in-chief, his staff swelled to more than 300 officials appointed by himself, including several secondary-level officials of various sorts and hosts of clerical subordinates divided among thirteen Sections (ts'ao), each assigned to a specific category of business. The Counselor-in-chief also supervised the Courts (ssu 寺) of the Nine Chamberlains (chiu ch'ing 九卿) inherited from Ch'in. As in Ch'in, the Chamberlains still had major roles in administering the imperial household, but they increasingly took on empire-wide responsibilities. The most influential of these offices were the Chamberlains for Ceremonials (t'ai-ch'ang 太常; under Wang Mang, chih-tsung 秩宗), under which after Emperor Wu's time a National University (t'ai-hsüeh 太學) became an important part of the government; for Attendants (lang-chung ling 郎中令; changed by Emperor Wu to kuang-lu hsün 光祿勳; also called nei-ch'ing 內卿); for the National Treasury (chih-su nei-shih 治粟內史), which in Emperor Wu's time (retitled ta ssu-nung 大司農) instituted and thereafter administered Han's famous ever-normal granary system and state monopolies of salt and iron; and for the Palace Revenues (shao-fu 少府), under which develop 1 the Imperial Secretariat discussed above.

There also were Chamberlains for the Palace Garrison (wei-wei 衛尉); for Law Enforcement (t'ing-wei 廷尉); for Dependencies (ta hung-lu 大鴻臚); for the Imperial Clan (tsung-cheng 宗正, tsung-po 宗伯; under Wang Mang merged with the chih-tsung); and for the Imperial Stud (t'ai-p'u 太僕).

Two other Chamberlains were not considered members of the group of Nine Chamberlains: the Chamberlain for the Imperial Insignia (chung-wei 中尉, chih chin-wu 執金吾), who was charged with responsibility for policing the capital and commanded one of the two grand armies garrisoned around the capital; and the Chamberlain for the Palace Buildings (chiang-tso shao-fu 將作少府, chiang-tso ta-chiang 將作大匠), who in Later Han came to be subordinated to the Chamberlain for Attendants.

The agency headed by the Censor-in-chief, commonly called the Censorate (yü-shih fu 御史府, yü-shih t'ai 御史臺), was a large and important establishment. As in Ch'in times, there was a Palace Aide to the Censor-in-chief (yü-shih chung-ch'eng 御史中丞), whose office was known as the Orchid Pavilion (lan-t'ai 蘭臺). In 8 B.C., when the Censor-in-chief became one of the Grand Councilors and was given the new title Minister of Works, the Palace Aide was transferred out of the palace to take charge of the whole Censorate; and thereafter through Later Han he was the de facto executive censor. Although this shift of personnel in the Censorate somewhat reduced the rank and prestige of its executive official, it effectively signaled a separation of the censorial institution from the general administrative hierarchy. Members of the Censorate were in large part divided among five or six Sections (ts'ao), each with a special functional responsibility; and they were sent out into localities outside the capital on both regular and unscheduled tours of inspection.

Territorial Administration

The Han founder restored a semifeudal character to government by dividing the empire about equally between areas directly controlled by the central government and areas granted as domains of allied generals and members of the imperial family. In centrally controlled areas, the Ch'in pattern was followed, the major regional unit being the Commandery (chün 郡), administered by a Governor (shou 守, t'ai-shou 太守, chün-chiang 郡將) with the assistance of a Defender (wei 尉, tu-wei 都尉). As in Ch'in, commanderies were subdivided into Districts (hsien 縣) in two grades, with Magistrates (ling 令 in more populous and chang 長 in less populous areas), Aides (ch'eng 丞, chang-shih 長史), and Defenders (wei). Principal clerical functionaries at the commandery and district levels, collectively called Senior Subalterns (chang-li 長吏), were largely organized into Sections (ts'ao), with special functional responsibilities.

Semifeudal domains were of two grades: Princedoms (wang-kuo 王國) corresponding in size to commanderies, and Marquisates (hou-kuo 侯國) corresponding in size to districts. During the early Han decades these domains were largely autonomous and had elaborate governmental structures on the pattern of the central government, but a series of imperial actions after 154 B.C. gradually brought them, by the end of Former Han, completely under central government control. Princedoms and marquisates then differed from commanderies and districts only in name; each domain was administered by a Counselor-delegate (*kuo-hsiang* 國相) appointed by and responsible to the central government.

Organization of the population below the district level nominally followed rigidly in the Ch'in pattern, including Townships (*hsiang* 鄉), Neighborhoods (*t'ing* 亭), and Villages (*li* 里) in descending order of size.

Aside from the revival of semifeudal domains, the major innovation in territorial government under Han was the evolution of intermediary administrative units between the central government and the commanderies. Until 106 B.C. intermediary supervision was provided unsystematically by touring Censors, but in that year Emperor Wu formally divided the empire into thirteen Regions (*pu* 部, later *chou* 州), each incorporating from five to ten commanderies and princedoms. To each was assigned a Censor from the staff of the Palace Aide to the Censor-in-chief to be a resident coordinator, or Regional Inspector (*tz'u-shih* 刺史). In the last years of Former Han these officials were replaced by higher-ranking and more influential Regional Governors (*chou mu* 州牧). Through Later Han, Regional Inspectors and Regional Governors were appointed in irregular alternation, until in A.D. 188 Regional Governors were appointed alongside existing Regional Inspectors. Regional Governors then quickly made themselves regional warlords who plunged into civil wars that brought the dynasty to an end in 220.

After 104 B.C. the specially administered Metropolitan Area surrounding the Han capital was governed by a triumvirate called the Three Guardians (*san fu* 三輔, a term by which the territory itself came to be known), whose individual titles were Metropolitan Governor (*ching-chao yin* 京兆尹), Guardian of the Left (*tso p'ing-i* 左馮翊), and Guardian of the Right (*yu fu-feng* 右扶風). These three dignitaries, who were considered more or less ex officio members of the Nine Chamberlains, had large staffs and great influence. Yet from 89 B.C. all came under the supervisory authority of a military officer responsible directly to the Emperor, the Metropolitan Commandant (*ssu-li hsiao-wei* 司隸校尉,

or simply *ssu-li*). In Later Han the Metropolitan Commandant shared with the Director of the Imperial Secretariat and the Palace Aide to the Censor-in-chief the popular collective designation the Three Venerables (*san tu-tso* 三獨坐), signifying the eminence of their posts in the national administration.

The Military

The Han military establishment consisted of a number of Armies (*chün* 軍). There was one army in each commandery or princedom under the command of a Defender (*wei, tu-wei*) or, in Later Han, of the Commandery Governor (*t'ai-shou*) himself. The most prestigious forces were at the dynastic capital: a Northern Army (*pei-chün* 北軍) commanded by the Chamberlain for the Imperial Insignia, which policed the capital city, and a Southern Army (*nan-chün* 南軍), which defended the palace proper. The Southern Army had two contingents, a troop of regular soldiers who guarded the palace walls and gates under the command of the Chamberlain for the Palace Garrison, and a kind of imperial bodyguard in which Court Gentlemen served under the command of the Chamberlain for Attendants. Beginning in the time of Emperor Wu, senior military officers were commonly entitled Commandants (*hsiao-wei* 校尉). As has been noted above, one among them, the Metropolitan Commandant (*ssu-li hsiao-wei*), soon became a kind of viceroy supervising the whole Metropolitan Area.

Commandery-level forces, especially those in frontier areas, were normally used for static defense. When special campaigns were undertaken, whether beyond the frontiers or in the interior, soldiers were assigned to them on temporary detached duty from appropriate commandery armies or from the Northern and Southern armies at the capital; the officers in command were given ad hoc designations as Generals (*chiang-chün* 將軍) or, in the case of large or especially important campaigns, Generals-in-chief (*ta chiang-chün* 大將軍). A Campaigning Army (*ying* 營) was normally organized in several Divisions (*pu* 部), each consisting of several Regiments (*ch'ü* 曲), which in turn comprised several Companies (*t'un* 屯). In early

Han times Counselors-in-chief sometimes led large military expeditions. In the latest Han decades, as has been noted, Regional Governors became dominant territorial warlords, and the capital forces waned in importance.

The Han military establishment was in theory manned by citizen-soldier militiamen. All males were registered for state service at twenty years of age and were eligible for active military duty between the ages of twenty-three and fifty-seven. Each male owed one month's service every year on labor or military duty in his local district, and twenty-four-year-olds were expected to provide one year's service in their home commandery armies or in the Southern Army at the dynastic capital. In theory, also, each male was required once in his life (or annually?) to serve for three days in a frontier garrison—a heritage presumably handed down from the small feudal states of the Chou era. In practice, payment of a fee relieved most males of this unrealistic requirement, and those who could not pay were sent to the frontier for a full year's service. The Northern Army at the capital came to be staffed in large part with specially recruited, indefinite-tenure guardsmen and thus resembled a professional standing army.

One special feature of the Han military system was the practice of settling soldier-farmers permanently beyond the frontiers in the North and Northwest in military colonies called State Farms (*t'un-t'ien* 屯田). Such colonies were expected to be self-sufficient, permanent extensions of Han's military and political presence in areas that could not be absorbed into the normal Han patterns of settlement and administration. It was with such scattered colonies, under a Protector-in-chief (*tu-hu* 都護), that Han eventually established its overlordship in Central Asia.

Personnel Administration

Han has been especially esteemed for introducing techniques of personnel administration that subsequently created in China an officialdom dominated by examination-recruited scholars, or literati. The Han officialdom was for the most part an aristocracy in which sons and favored friends of officeholders easily found placement, since the executive officials of every major agency down to the district level, though appointees of the central government themselves, could freely appoint their subordinates. But more bureaucratic principles came to be esteemed and put into practice in several ways.

The cornerstone of Han personnel recruitment was recommendation, commandery governors being the principal nominators of potential new officials. There were both regular and irregular systems of recommendation; beginning in Emperor Wu's reign every commandery and princedom was called on to nominate one or two men for appointment each year. Early in Later Han quotas were established according to population density, so that in general one man per 200,000 residents was nominated, and 200 or more nominees streamed into the capital annually. From 165 B.C. on, nominees in the irregular and later in the regular recommendation processes were commonly given written examinations to confirm their literacy and learning, administered by the Court of the Chamberlain for Ceremonials (or in Later Han the Imperial Secretariat) and at times presided over by the Emperors themselves. Nominees whose qualifications were approved were sometimes appointed directly to substantive offices. but they were more often appointed Court Gentlemen without active administrative assignments, from which status they could be assigned to substantive functional offices when opportunities arose.

An equally important path into the officialdom, also based on recommendations, was via the embryonic National University that Emperor Wu established in 124 B.C., with a faculty of five Erudites (*po-shih* 博士). Commandery Governors were called on to nominate promising youths as disciples of the Erudites, and 50 were chosen for the first student body. Commandery Governors later submitted nominations annually, and the student body steadily grew, until in the final years of Former Han, under Wang Mang's patronage, there were 3,000 students. In Later Han the number swelled to 30,000.

Students admitted to the National University pursued a standard curriculum of classical studies for one year and had to pass a written graduation examination. Some graduates were appointed Court Gentlemen in the same status as those discussed above. Others returned home to seek positions on the staffs of Commandery Governors or District Magistrates, in the hope that the regular or irregular recommendation process and the subsequent capital examinations might move them more rapidly into substantive official posts.

Once appointed, an official served for a year in probationary status. After he was off of probation he had indefinite tenure, but at three-year intervals each official was evaluated by his superior and could then be promoted, demoted, or dismissed.

Officials were ranked in terms of bushels of grain. The Three Dukes were ranked at 10,000, others from 2,000 down to 100 bushels per year. Ranks corresponded in only a relative way to annual salaries, which were paid partly in grain and partly in coin. In A.D. 106, for example, the salary schedule called for a 1,000-bushel official to receive a monthly stipend of 4,000 coins and 12 bushels of grain.

The Han rulers were especially strict in imposing "avoidances" on their territorial officialdom, and the rules steadily became more complex. The trend culminated in the second century A.D. with promulgation of the Law of Triple Avoidances (*san-hu fa* 三互法), which provided that an official not only could never be appointed Regional Inspector in an area of which he was a registered native but, in addition, could not so serve in the native area of his own native area's Regional Inspector, or even in the native area of the latter's wife.

Era of North-South Division

220-589

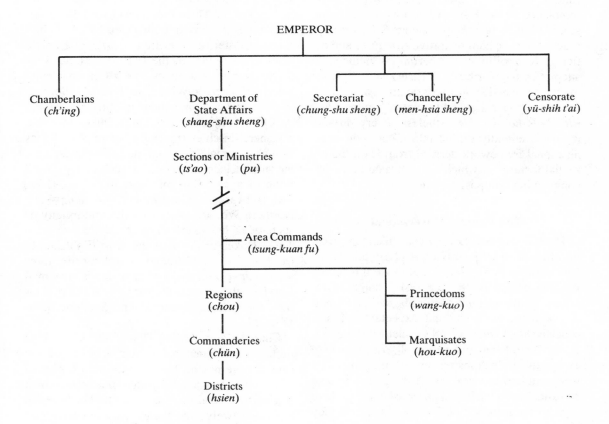

EMPEROR

Chamberlains (ch'ing)

Department of State Affairs (shang-shu sheng)

Secretariat (chung-shu sheng)

Chancellery (men-hsia sheng)

Censorate (yü-shih t'ai)

Sections or Ministries (ts'ao) (pu)

Area Commands (tsung-kuan fu)

Regions (chou)

Princedoms (wang-kuo)

Commanderies (chün)

Marquisates (hou-kuo)

Districts (hsien)

Three Kingdoms, 220–280
Chin, 266–316
Southern and Northern Dynasties
In the South:
Eastern Chin, 317–420
(Liu) Sung, 420–479
Southern Ch'i, 479–502
Liang, 502–557
Ch'en, 557–589
In the North:
Sixteen Kingdoms, 301–439
(Northern) Wei, 386–534
Eastern Wei, 534–550

Western Wei, 534–557
Northern Ch'i, 550–577
(Northern) Chou, 557–581

This long era of political disunion and cultural turbulence was a confusing transitional period in institutional history. The governmental structure inherited from Han was maintained by most regimes as a façade behind which a succession of militaristic rulers governed with personal aides and relatives, whose status was gradually regularized into a stable new structure, largely neofeudal in character. The Han offices that survived were retained largely as honorific appointments.

Every regime in the Era of Division had distinctive characteristics in its governmental structure. This was especially the case among the Sixteen Kingdoms and the Northern Dynasties, in which the normal pattern was for non-Chinese invaders to develop their original tribal organizations through several phases toward some semblance of the Han tradition as it was being modified in the contemporaneous Southern Dynasties. Ad hoc administrative structures and official titles proliferated. Aberrations included an attempt by the Northern (or Later) Chou dynasty to regularize and simplify its central government by reviving titles ascribed to antiquity in the *Chou Rituals* (*Chou-li*). Nevertheless, every durable regime eventually settled into a common organizational framework derived from Han, the essential features of which are indicated in the accompanying composite table.

The Central Government

The Han capitals, Loyang and Ch'ang-an, were the cities most frequently used as capitals by the later regimes in the North, and modern Nanking was the capital of the successive southern regimes. Emperors continued to be served by palace women, eunuchs, and expectant officials collectively known as Court Gentlemen (*lang* 郎). In the Three Kingdoms period all Princes (*wang*) except the Heir Apparent on reaching maturity were required to move out of the palace to take up residence in territorial bases assigned to them ("go to their fiefs"; *chih-kuo* 之國), and they were forbidden to visit the capital except when explicitly summoned. But the Chin dynasty reversed this policy, so that Princes often held important posts in the central government. This Chin policy prevailed during the rest of the era.

The top-echelon court titles inherited from Chou, Ch'in, and Han were perpetuated by almost all post-Han regimes, though they were now almost exclusively honorific and at times were used only as posthumous honors. They were normally referred to by the traditional collective designation the Three Dukes (*san kung* 三公) and included at least the Han triumvirate: a Counselor-in-chief (*ch'eng-hsiang* 丞相), a Defender-in-chief (*t'ai-wei* 太尉), and either a Censor-in-chief (*yü-shih ta-fu* 御史大夫) or a Minister of Works (*ssu-k'ung* 司空). The hoary Chou titles Grand Preceptor (*t'ai-shih* 太師), Grand Mentor (*t'ai-fu* 太傅), and Grand Guardian (*t'ai-pao* 太保) were often included as well, sometimes differentiated by such collective terms as the Three Grand Dukes (*san shang-kung* 三上公) or the Three Preceptors (*san shih* 三師). Sometimes there were both a Counselor-in-chief and a Minister of Education (*ssu-t'u* 司徒), or a Counselor-in-chief of the Left and Right. Similarly, there were at times both a Censor-in-chief and a Minister of Works, or both a Defender-in-chief and a Commander-in-chief (*ta ssu-ma* 大司馬). Sometimes the Three Dukes included a General-in-chief (*ta chiang-chün* 大將軍) as well as a Defender-in-chief; and sometimes, also, the term included men bearing such newly coined honorifics as Pillar of State (*chu-kuo* 柱國) and Bulwark of Government (*fu-cheng* 輔政). Northern Wei acknowledged the multiplicity of such titles by abandoning the collective term Three Dukes in favor of the term Eight Dukes (*pa kung* 八公). Although these honorific titles seldom involved any assigned duties, the men who held them normally had large staffs of their own appointees, organized into Sections (*ts'ao* 曹).

Chamberlains (*ch'ing* 卿) of the Ch'in-Han tradition continued as regular officials of the central government, but their Courts (*fu* 府, *ssu* 寺) were of less administrative importance than in Han times and fluctuated in number between eight and twelve. At their most numerous, under the Liang dynasty, there were twelve Chamberlains: for Ceremonials (*t'ai-ch'ang* 太常, *feng-ch'ang* 奉常); for Attendants (*lang-chung ling* 郎中令, *kuang-lu-hsün* 光祿勳); for the Palace Garrison (*wei-wei* 衛尉); for Law Enforcement (*t'ing-wei* 廷尉, *ta-li* 大理); for the National Treasury (*ssu-nung* 司農); for Dependencies (*ta hung-lu* 大鴻臚); for the Imperial Clan (*tsung-cheng* 宗正; lacking in Sung); for the Imperial Stud (*t'ai-p'u* 太僕); for the Palace Revenues (*shao-fu* 少府, *t'ai-fu* 太府); for the Palace Buildings (*chiang-tso ta-chiang* 將作大匠; only irregularly appointed beginning in Sung); for the

Palace Bursary (*ta-fu* 大府; originated in Liang); and for Waterways (*ta-chou* 大舟; originated in Liang).

The nominal Censor-in-chief seldom had anything to do with active surveillance in this era. Normally used for one of the honorific Three Dukes, the title was only occasionally assigned to the working head of the Censorate (*yü-shih t'ai* 御史臺). As in Later Han times, the Censorate was usually under the actual control of the nominal Palace Aide to the Censor-in-chief (*yü-shih chung-ch'eng* 御史中丞). The Censorate remained an active and sometimes became a domineering surveillance agency; there were Censors (*yü-shih*) with many specialized functions and designations, organized into from five to fifteen Sections (*ts'ao*).

In the major institutional development in the central governments of this era, the Imperial Secretariat (*shang-shu sheng* 尚書省 and variants) of Later Han times was gradually ousted from its paramount executive role as new dynastic founders entrusted executive powers to their personal favorites, while giving them titles appropriate to intimate court attendants. The agency inherited from Han slipped into a more routinely administrative role; beginning with this era, it might best be rendered Department of State Affairs. The department became the stable center of day-by-day communication between the central government and territorial units. Its staff was normally divided into functionally differentiated Sections (*ts'ao*), which evolved sporadically toward the status of the Ministries (*pu* 部) of later times. The number of Sections fluctuated greatly, from about a dozen to more than thirty. As in Later Han times, the whole agency was managed by a Director (*ling* 令), now commonly with two Vice Directors (*p'u-yeh* 僕射). The subordinate Sections, singly or in clusters, were more closely administered by Imperial Secretaries in process of becoming Ministers (*shang-shu* 尚書).

As each of the successive regimes of this era expanded its territorial control, it usually established Branch (*hsing* 行) Departments of State Affairs to administer newly incorporated areas. These were something in the nature of temporary proto-provincial administrations.

Although the prestige of the Department of State Affairs had waned, it was important to any new policy-formulating executives that they maintain supervisory control over the Department, which was still responsible for the implementation of policies. The custom arose, therefore, of appointing each de facto prime minister, whatever his principal status, also to be Overseer of the Department of State Affairs (*lu shang-shu shih* 錄尚書事). He was often an Imperial Prince. Consequently, important men commonly bore such multi-tiered titles as General-in-chief, Honorific (*chia* 加) Palace Attendant, Commander-in-chief of All Inner and Outer Armies, Overseer of the Department of State Affairs, and Bulwark of Government (*ta chiang-chün chia shih-chung tu-tu chung-wai chün-shih lu shang-shu shih fu-cheng*). At times more than one man held the title Overseer of the Department of State Affairs.

The new agency to which executive policy-formulating powers first shifted in this era was the Secretariat (*chung-shu sheng* 中書省 and variants), normally headed jointly by a Director (*ling* 令) and a Supervisor (*chien* 監). The staff included one or more Vice Directors (*shih-lang* 侍郎), several Secretariat Drafters (*chung-shu she-jen* 中書舍人), Secretarial Receptionists (*t'ung-shih she-jen* 通事舍人), and miscellaneous clerical aides. The great influence and prestige of the Secretariat derived from its being the channel through which all memorials and other government documents flowed to the Emperor and the agency that proposed and drafted all imperial rescripts and edicts. Although on occasion one man served as both Secretariat Director and Overseer of the Department of State Affairs, it seems to have been generally recognized that the policy-formulating executive functions of the Secretariat and the policy-implementing administrative functions of the Department of State Affairs should properly be kept separate.

Just as the Secretariat had encroached on and taken over the original functions of the Department of State Affairs, so in turn the Secretariat's influence and prestige were encroached on from the fourth and fifth centuries by yet another institution developing out of the Emperor's entourage of intimate attendants. Notable among these were bearers of such old Han honorific titles as Palace Attendant (*shih-chung* 侍中) and Palace Steward (*chi-shih-chung* 給事中). They were said to be in service "at the palace gate" (*men-hsia* 門下), and this term began to be used by the Chin dynasty as a new collective term for such policy consultants, institutionalized as a Chancellery (*men-hsia sheng* 門下省). Its principal function was to advise and remonstrate, but before the end of the Era of Division its officials were commonly so influential that they helped Emperors make decisions on proposals submitted by the Secretariat. The Chancellery was especially powerful in the Wei dynasties of the North.

Territorial Administration

Administrative geography is perhaps the most confusing aspect of history in the Era of Division, for two reasons. For one thing, whereas the Later Han administrative hierarchy of Regions (*chou* 州), Commanderies (*chün* 郡), and Districts (*hsien* 縣) was perpetuated throughout the period, post-Han rulers were so fearful that territorial magnates might usurp the throne that they systematically reduced the size and thus increased the number of all units of territorial administration. The proliferation of regions and particularly commanderies was especially pronounced during the great southward migrations of northern Chinese in the fourth century, when non-Chinese invaders took over the original Chinese homeland in the North. Whole communities often moved together into the South, where nostalgia and administrative convenience in combination brought about a transplanting of their original northern administrative organizations and nomenclature—not only in lands being brought under Chinese occupancy for the first time, but amidst already established systems of local administration as well. What had once been a single commandery often became four or five commanderies, each with only one or two subordinate districts. Thus, whereas there had been only thirteen regions in Later Han times and only twenty when Chin controlled most of China Proper, each of the Northern and Southern Dynasties had regions by the scores. In 580 the

northern dynasty Chou claimed 211 regions, 508 commanderies, and 1,124 districts. Not long before, the southern dynasty Liang tried to arrange its 170 regions into five ranks to reflect disparities in size and resident populations (Northern Ch'i arranged its 97 regions in nine ranks) and in the process discovered that some recognized regions had no territory at all; the locations of more than twenty recognized regions could not be identified.

The other consideration that makes the administrative history of this era so difficult is the fact that, under all regimes of the period, China was largely governed by neofeudal, hereditary local magnates including descendants of Han officials, large landowners, bandit chiefs, neighborhood bullies, and (especially in the North beginning in the fourth century) non-Chinese tribal leaders. Successive dynasties scattered their own favorites and imperial relatives about the countryside as new layers of local magnates. The domains of all these territorial power-wielders overlaid the pattern of regions, commanderies, and districts that dynasties counted as centrally controlled units. Some local magnates dominated several commanderies or even whole regions; others were formally recognized as members of the regular officialdom or the nobility. The most powerful were acknowledged, in Han fashion, as rulers of Princedoms (*wang-kuo* 王國) or Marquisates (*hou-kuo* 侯國) that coexisted alongside commanderies and districts.

In general, Han nomenclature was perpetuated in territorial administration. Regions had Regional Governors (*chou mu* 州牧) or Regional Inspectors (*tz'u-shih* 刺史), or both. Although they seem to have played censorial roles very seldom, they were collectively known as the Outer Censorate (*wai-t'ai* 外臺). Since in general Regional Governors were militarists and their functions were largely military, the most powerful ones commonly dominated a cluster of neighboring regions and were entitled Area Commanders (*tu . . . chün-shih* 督…軍事, with place-name inserts) or Area Commanders-in-chief (*tu-tu* 都督, *tsung-kuan* 總管).

Commanderies were administered by Governors (*t'ai-shou* 太守) and districts by Magistrates (*ling* 令, *chang* 長; occasionally *hsiang* 相). It became customary for all these units of territorial administration to be differentiated by ranks, from two to as many as nine, reflecting variations in size and population; and authorized members of the subordinate staffs varied accordingly.

Like Metropolitan Areas (*ssu-li* 司隸, *ssu-chou* 司州) surrounding dynastic capitals, princedoms and marquisates had special forms of organization; their Administrators (*nei-shih* 內史, *hsiang* 相) were responsible to the central government, at least in theory.

Below the district level the population was normally organized in two tiers: Townships (*hsiang* 鄉) and their constituent Villages (*li* 里). However, Northern Wei developed a new, three-tier pattern called the Three Elders (*san chang* 三長) system. In theory, every five families had a Neighborhood Elder (*lin-chang* 鄰長); every five neighborhoods had a Village Elder (*li-chang* 里長); and every five villages had a Ward Elder (*tang-chang* 黨長).

The Military

The general turbulence and neofeudal disunion of this era resulted in a fragmentation of military force throughout the empire, and especially the proliferation of small "private armies" (*pu-ch'ü* 部曲) employed by local magnates. In some cases, such private armies gained recognition as units of a dynasty's regular military establishment.

Each dynasty normally had a main military force garrisoned in and around its capital, called a Capital Army (*chung-chün* 中軍). Incorporating from four to many more separate Armies (*chün*), the Capital Army was customarily divided into two groups. One, commanded by a Capital Commandant (*chung ling-chün* 中領軍), guarded the palace and capital city; the other, commanded by a Capital Protector (*chung hu-chün* 中護軍), was a force in readiness for campaigning as needed. Each of the separate armies within the Capital Army had a commanding General (*chiang-chün* 將軍), and each was usually given a special directional designation: Army of the Left (*tso-chün*), Army of the Front (*ch'ien-chün*), Army of the Center (*chung-chün*; note the possible confusion with the Capital Army as a whole), and so forth.

Successive central governments tried to control, restrict, and even at times abolish regular military units in the hierarchy of territorial administration. In 280, for example, the Chin dynasty ordered the demobilization of all territorial military units except those of princedoms allocated to imperial clansmen. Such attempts were seldom successful. The general trend in the southern (that is, Chinese) regimes, in fact, was for military strength to gravitate steadily from the capital toward territorial warlords. At times the Capital Army had officers but no troops.

The non-Chinese northern rulers were generally more militarily alert than their southern counterparts. This was so in part because the northern regimes not only wanted to press aggressively southward but at the same time had to defend themselves against new non-Chinese nomadic empires that successively arose in their rear, in Mongolia. Beginning with Northern Wei, the northern regimes generally deployed strong defense forces along the Great Wall in zones that were designated Defense Commands (*chen* 鎮).

The Chinese dynasties of this era had no standard system by which men were called into military service. The governments relied primarily on voluntary recruits and, in emergencies, on draftees. Once in service, men normally became lifelong and even hereditary soldiers. It became common to make hereditary soldiers not only of convicts, but also of their relatives and in-laws. The post-Han Chinese dynasties greatly developed the system of State Farms (*t'un-t'ien* 屯田) introduced in China Proper in the last Han years; and they relied on similar state-owned civilian colonies (*min-t'un* 民屯) to resettle vagrants and migrants. Late in the Era of Division, as the South was increasingly under the threat of conquest by northerners, volunteer units were privately organized as "patriotic soldiers" (*i-ping* 義兵) to assist the long-deteriorated regular armies.

The non-Chinese dynasties of the North generally used their own and allied tribesmen as permanent, hereditary soldiers. The successive Wei dynasties thus segregated their own peoples in Garrisons (*fu* 府) scattered throughout their domain, leaving the subject Chinese as civilian, tax-paying agriculturalists organized in traditional Chinese administrative units. Gradually, however, ethnic differences blurred, and Chinese of the North came to be needed for military service as well as for agrarian production. They often welcomed opportunities for military service as a way to raise their social status. The Northern Ch'i dynasty thus came to have an integrated, multi-ethnic army, differentiated only as infantry (in Inner Sections, *nei-ts'ao* 內曹) and cavalry (in Outer Sections, *wai-ts'ao* 外曹), based on a Garrison Militia (*fu-ping* 府兵) system. Standardized in 564, this new system required all males to be available for military service between the ages of twenty and sixty.

Meanwhile, Western Wei was developing a somewhat different system. It required every family with more than two sons to give one son for lifelong, but not hereditary, military service in one of 100 garrisons, where they did agricultural work to support themselves while intermittently undergoing military training. Each garrison was commanded by a Commandant (*lang-chiang* 郎將). The garrisons were distributed for supervision among 24 armies, each under an Area Commander (*k'ai-fu* 開府). For every two armies there was a General-in-chief (*ta chiang-chün* 大將軍), and every two Generals-in-chief were supervised by a Pillar of State (*chu-kuo*). One specially favored Pillar of State was designated Commander-in-chief (*tu-tu* 都督).

Personnel Administration

The neofeudalism of the Era of Division manifested itself, among other ways, in the predominance of hereditary social status as the principal qualification for appointment to government office. Throughout the era, governments registered all families that rightfully belonged to the elite class of Servicemen (*shih* 士) and classified members of that class into ranks (*p'in* 品) theoretically reflecting their meritoriousness. All this was managed by specially chosen local dignitaries, often retired officials, called Rectifiers (*chung-cheng* 中正; sometimes with the added designation senior, *ta*, or junior, *hsiao*; sometimes *chou-tu* 州都 at the regional level) in every region, commandery, and district. The system was instituted in 220, at the very beginning of the era, in an effort to preserve social stability in a time of general turbulence, and it was perpetuated by all subsequent regimes of the era

with variations. A classification of all official posts into comparable ranks (*p'in* or *pan* 班) accompanied this classification of qualified appointees.

In addition to acquiring official personnel through the nominations-by-classification done by Rectifiers, all regimes of the Era of Division perpetuated in one form or another most of the recruitment practices inherited from Han: regular and irregular recommendations from current officeholders, followed by confirmatory examinations; direct inheritance of appointee status or of office; purchase of appointee status or of office; and graduation from state schools. Every regime maintained one or more National Universities (*t'ai-hsüeh* 太學 and variants). Some regimes attempted to establish state schools down to the commandery level. The Rectifier system was always predominant in official recruitment, however. It perpetuated the predominance in government of a hereditary elite.

The same end was achieved by an apparently unofficial but nonetheless very well-enforced classification of officials—and later of the offices in the government hierarchy—into "pure" (*ch'ing* 清) and "impure" (*cho* 濁) categories. The practice apparently began soon after the end of Han, and it became standard in both the Southern and the Northern Dynasties. Officials who were considered pure followed career patterns through clear sequences of pure offices, which took them into the top echelon of the officialdom; and officials who were considered impure found themselves stagnating in dead-end sequences of less prestigious offices. Quite clearly, one's degree of purity or impurity reflected one's hereditary standing in the aristocratic social order. Eventually a third category, "high expectations" (*ch'ing-wang* 清望), emerged as the most elite classification of personnel and offices. This practice persisted in the Sui dynasty and had echoes in T'ang times and perhaps later.

As in Han, officials in active service were evaluated by their superiors and occasionally by touring inspectors from the central government. It became common for such evaluations to be carried out every three years. There were no clear rules about tenure in office. Discreditable service could be punished and creditable service rewarded in various ways, including adjustments in one's rank, and promotions or demotions in office. A common reward was the granting of nominal noble status; the titular nobility expanded in every dynasty, including the traditional titles Prince (*wang* 王), Duke (*kung* 公), Marquis (*hou* 侯), Earl (*po* 伯), Viscount (*tzu* 子), and Baron (*nan* 男) and sometimes dozens of lesser titles. It became especially common to honor meritorious officials with grants of noble titles posthumously.

Sui

581-618

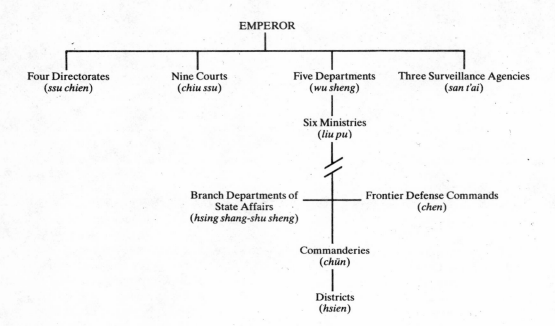

EMPEROR

Four Directorates (*ssu chien*) Nine Courts (*chiu ssu*) Five Departments (*wu sheng*) Three Surveillance Agencies (*san t'ai*)

Six Ministries (*liu pu*)

Branch Departments of State Affairs (*hsing shang-shu sheng*) Frontier Defense Commands (*chen*)

Commanderies (*chün*)

Districts (*hsien*)

The Central Government

The Sui capital was at Ch'ang-an, modern Sian in Shensi Province. There the two Sui rulers, Emperors Wen (r. 581–604) and Yang (r. 604–618), perpetuated the tradition of Chamberlains (*ch'ing* 卿), stabilized by now in a total of Nine Courts (*chiu ssu* 九寺) with large staffs divided among subordinate Offices (*shu* 署). These were the Courts of Imperial Sacrifices (*t'ai-ch'ang ssu* 太常寺), of the Palace Garrison (*wei-wei ssu* 衛尉寺), of Law Enforcement (*ta-li ssu* 大理寺), of Dependencies (*hung-lu ssu* 鴻臚寺), of the

Like Ch'in in the third century B.C., Sui was an important transitional period. The centralizing trends of the Northern Dynasties now culminated in Sui's reunification of the empire in 589 and paved the way for the more durable T'ang dynasty that followed.

Imperial Clan (*tsung-cheng ssu* 宗正寺), of the Imperial Stud (*t'ai-p'u ssu* 太僕寺), of the Palace Revenues (*t'ai-fu ssu* 太府寺), of Imperial Entertainments (*kuang-lu ssu* 光祿寺), and of the National Granaries (*ssu-nung ssu* 司農寺).

In early Sui there were two additional Courts (*ssu*) not headed by Chamberlains, which in mid-dynasty were redesignated and made part of a group of agencies called the Four Directorates (*ssu chien* 四監), all of which had special service roles rather than general administrative roles. One was the Directorate (originally Court) for the Palace Buildings (*chiang-tso chien* 將作監), headed by a Director (*ling* 令). It had two subordinate Offices (*shu*).

The other Court that became a Directorate was the Directorate of Education (*kuo-tzu chien* 國子監). At the beginning of Sui this was a subordinate agency in the Court of Imperial Sacrifices, but it soon became independent under a

Chancellor (*chi-chiu* 祭酒). He oversaw several schools: the National University (*t'ai-hsüeh* 太學), which accepted as many as 500 state-supported students from the official class; the School for the Sons of the State (*kuo-tzu hsüeh* 國子學), also for the sons of officials, which early limited enrollment to 140 students but later had no fixed quota; the School of the Four Gates (*ssu-men hsüeh* 四門學), whose quota of 360 students apparently included some gifted youths not of the official class; the Calligraphy School (*shu-hsüeh* 書學), with 40 students; and the Mathematics School (*suan-hsüeh* 算學), with 80 students.

The other two Directorates of the mature Sui central government were the Directorate for Imperial Manufactories (*shao-fu chien* 少府監), promoted out of subordinate status in the Court of the Palace Revenues, which thereafter concentrated on fiscal matters, and the Directorate of Waterways (*tu-shui chien* 都水監). Both of these Directorates were originally under Supervisors (*chien*) but ultimately under Directors (*ling*).

Another special group of central government organs were the Three Surveillance Agencies (*san t'ai* 三臺): the traditional Censorate (*yü-shih t'ai* 御史臺) under a Censor-in-chief (*yü-shih ta-fu* 御史大夫), responsible for disciplinary surveillance over the whole officialdom; and two supplementary agencies established by Emperor Yang, the Tribunal of Receptions (*yeh-che t'ai* 謁者臺) and the Tribunal of Inspectors (*ssu-li t'ai* 司隸臺), each under a Grand Master (*ta-fu*). The Tribunal of Receptions, while retaining its traditional function of managing the reception of important visitors at court, seems to have been charged with special ad hoc inquiries, whereas members of the Tribunal of Inspectors regularly made investigatory tours in the Metropolitan Area (*chi-nei* 畿內), the environs of the dynastic capital. Emperor Yang, in efforts to weaken the Censorate's power over the staff of the imperial household, reduced its corps of Palace Censors (*tien-nei shih yü-shih* 殿內侍御史) and terminated their traditional right to maintain a duty station within the palace.

National administration was concentrated at the capital in Five Departments (*wu sheng* 五省), and particularly in three of them. One was the Department of State Affairs (*shang-shu sheng* 尚書省), which incorporated the Six Ministries

(*liu pu* 六部) that were the administrative heart of the central government: the Ministries of Personnel (*li-pu* 吏部), of Rites (*li-pu* 禮部), of War (*ping-pu* 兵部), of Justice (*hsing-pu* 刑部), of Revenue (*min-pu* 民部), and of Works (*kung-pu* 工部). Each Ministry was subdivided into Sections (*ts'ao* 曹), later Bureaus (*ssu* 司), with specialized functions. The six Ministers (*shang-shu* 尚書) who headed the Ministries, together with the Director (*ling* 令) and Vice Director(s) (*p'u-yeh* 僕射) of the Department, were known collectively as the Eight Executives (*pa tso* 八座).

The two other particularly important Departments were the Secretariat (*chung-shu sheng* 中書省) and the Chancellery (*men-hsia sheng* 門下省). The Secretariat's staff received and processed memorials that the officialdom submitted for imperial consideration, and the Chancellery's staff consulted with the Emperor about his responses to such memorials, which established the policies that the Department of State Affairs carried out.

The remaining two Departments were the Palace Library (*pi-shu sheng* 祕書省) and the Palace Administration (*tien-nei sheng* 殿內省). The first was responsible for compiling historical and other scholarly works and supervised civil service recruitment examinations. The other was responsible for provisioning the imperial household; until Emperor Yang's time this was merely a subordinate agency in the Chancellery. It in effect replaced, in the top echelon of the central government, the earlier Palace Domestic Service (*nei-shih sheng* 內侍省) of eunuch attendants, which Emperor Yang downgraded in status to become the Directorate of Palace Domestic Service (*ch'ang-ch'iu chien* 長秋監).

Territorial Administration

The basic units of Sui territorial administration were the traditional Regions (*chou* 州), Commanderies (*chün* 郡), and Districts (*hsien* 縣), each category graded into nine ranks according to the importance and complexity of local administration. In the traditional pattern, regions were governed by Regional Inspectors (*tz'u-shih* 刺史), commanderies by Governors (*t'ai-shou* 太守), and districts by Magistrates (*ling* 令).

Below the district level, rural and urban groups

were organized differently. In theory at least, rural groups were organized into Villages (*li* 里) of ten families and Townships (*tang* 黨) of five villages. In urban areas five families constituted a Security Group (*pao* 保), five security groups a Neighborhood (*lü* 閭), four neighborhoods a Precinct (*tsu* 族), and five precincts a Ward (*hsiang* 鄉) of 500 families. At each level a non-official resident was designated Head (*chang* 長, *cheng* 正) and charged with the implementing of state policies.

Sui took major steps in China's institutional history by simplifying the complex hierarchy of territorial administration that developed during the Era of Division. First, in 586, Emperor Wen abolished the whole category of commanderies, leaving regions in direct control of districts. Then in about 605 Emperor Yang rearranged and consolidated territorial administration in two tiers; commanderies were revived in lieu of regions but reduced from nine ranks to three, and districts were also reduced to fewer ranks than previously. In late Sui there were in all 190 commanderies and 1,255 districts.

In the early Sui years it was not uncommon for powerful regional officials, as in the preceding long Era of Division, to be recognized as multi-region authorities called Area Commanders-in-chief (*tsung-kuan* 總管); but these semiautonomous warlords were gradually ousted as the dynasty gained power and confidence. It became more common, as new areas were brought under Sui control, for the central government to establish proto-provincial Branch Departments of State Affairs (*hsing t'ai-sheng* 行臺省) to administer them. Such Branch Departments were not full-bodied replicas of the metropolitan Department at the capital and were apparently intended to be only temporary agencies. It is not clear how many were established or when they were phased out of existence.

The Military

Sui military strength was based on a modified version of the Northern Dynasties' Garrison Militia (*fu-ping* 府兵) system, established in 583. In 590 Emperor Wen abolished all distinctions between military and civilian households; thereafter all male adults were registered in a single census category and were apparently subject to universal military conscription. Routine instruction and drill were carried on in urban Precinct Companies (*chün-fang* 軍坊) or rural Township Companies (*hsiang-t'uan* 鄉團) under Company Commanders (*fang-chu* 坊主 and *t'uan-chu*, respectively). Such local units in one area constituted a Garrison (*fu* 府). This was primarily an administrative agency, directed by an Area Commander (*k'ai-fu* 開府) with the aid of a large staff; it rotated troops to duty in the twelve Guards (*wei* 衛) that made up the Sui standing army, each Guard having a General-in-chief (*ta chiang-chün* 大將軍) and two Generals (*chiang-chün*). The Guards in turn contributed men to forces for special campaigning and to Palace Guards (*ch'in-wei* 親衛), which included the Imperial Body-guard (*pei-shen fu* 備身府) and the Palace Gate Guards (*chien-men fu* 監門府).

In strategic areas, especially along the Great Wall, special military commands were commonly superimposed on the basic administrative pattern of commanderies, districts, and garrisons. These were Defense Commands (*chen* 鎮), each under a Commander (*chiang* 將).

Emperor Yang changed the early Sui military nomenclature somewhat; the commanders of garrisons became Commandants (*lang-chiang* 郎將), and each Guard was placed under the command of a single General (*chiang-chün*). His most notable change was a reorganization of military units on campaign against Korea beginning in 612. The Garrison Militia system proved inadequate to fill his needs. Reportedly leading as many as 1.1 million men on campaign, he eventually had to rely on mercenary recruits (*mu-ping* 募兵) to supplement the regular forces. For his campaigns, he organized 24 Armies (*chün* 軍), each with a General-in-chief (*ta-chiang* 大將) and a Vice General (*ya-chiang* 亞將). Each such army consisted of four Divisions (*t'uan* 團) totaling 4,000 cavalrymen in 40 Companies (*tui* 隊), four divisions totaling 8,000 infantrymen in 80 companies, and four divisions of irregulars (*san-ping* 散兵) for logistical support. Each division was commanded by a Division Commander (*p'ien-chiang* 偏將).

Personnel Administration

Sui inherited the Rectifier-ranking system that had qualified men for office through most of the

Era of Division but quickly abandoned it in an effort to broaden the personnel base from which officials could be chosen. In 587 every region was ordered to nominate three men considered to have "cultivated talents" (*hsiu-ts'ai* 秀才) annually for confirmatory examinations at the capital, and in 599 all capital officials of rank 5 and above and a broader range of territorial officials were required to nominate men for consideration in several categories. In 607 Emperor Yang fixed ten categories of talents in which prospective officials should be nominated. One of these categories led to the confirmed status of Presented Scholar (*chin-shih* 進士). Particularly because this status became the principal gateway to officialdom in later dynasties, the year 607 is considered by many modern scholars to be the real beginning of China's famed system of recruitment examinations. Schools at the capital, to which sons of officials had easiest access, also produced candidates for appointments; and direct inheritance of official status (though not of office) was still practiced. Men of the merchant and artisan classes were commonly disqualified from careers as officials.

One of Sui's most notable developments in personnel administration was the result of Emperor Wen's efforts in his earliest years to accelerate the centralization of governmental authority. He ordered that all regular civil service officials down to the district level had to be appointed by the Department of State Affairs in the capital and be subject to its personnel-evaluation procedures, including annual merit ratings; that Regional Inspectors and District Magistrates had to be transferred every three years, and their subordinates at least every four years; and that no official on territorial duty could take his parents or adult children with him. Such measures, combined with the traditional "avoidances" (*hui-pi* 迴避) that forbade officials to hold offices in their native areas, made it almost impossible for any official to create a staff of hangers-on or otherwise build up a local, autonomous power base, and the groundwork was laid for a truly national officialdom.

Sui did not establish princedoms or marquisates of the Han sort, but it did award noble titles and emoluments lavishly. All uncles, brothers, and sons of an Emperor were Imperial Princes (*ch'in-wang* 親王), with substantial stipends and staffs. In addition, nine grades of nobility were awarded until the time of Emperor Yang, when only the three ranks of Prince (*wang* 王), Duke (*kung* 公), and Marquis (*hou* 侯) were retained.

Sui apparently carried on the unofficial but influential practice, begun in the preceding Era of Division, of classifying officials on the basis of their aristocratic pedigrees as "high expectations" (*ch'ing-wang* 清望), "pure" (*ch'ing* 清), and "impure" (*cho* 濁), and appointing them to sequences of offices similarly labeled, so that the highest-level aristocrats moved most rapidly up their career ladders whereas scions of the lesser aristocracy had few opportunities ever to rise into the most prestigious and influential positions. Sui also expanded a practice that seems to have been initiated in the southern courts during the sixth century, the granting of sinecure "prestige titles" (*san-kuan* 散官), to provide status and income for overaged or disabled officials. Sui also awarded large numbers of honorific titles (*chia-kuan* 加官) to members of the officialdom when they were not on active duty. A distinction thus arose between inactive or honorary officials, who had ranks (*chieh* 階) but no duty assignments, and functioning officials (*chih-kuan* 職官).

In Sui times there were also graded merit titles (*hsün* 勳), which were awarded in the fashion of modern Western military decorations to deserving suboffcial functionaries (*li* 吏, *hsü-li* 胥吏), who performed clerical and other lowly duties in government establishments, and even to members of the general population who were meritorious in the government's view. A careful distinction was always made, however, between men who were "of official status" (*liu-nei* 流內) and those who were "outside official status" (*liu-wai* 流外) or "not yet of official status" (*wei ju liu* 未入流).

T'ang
618-907

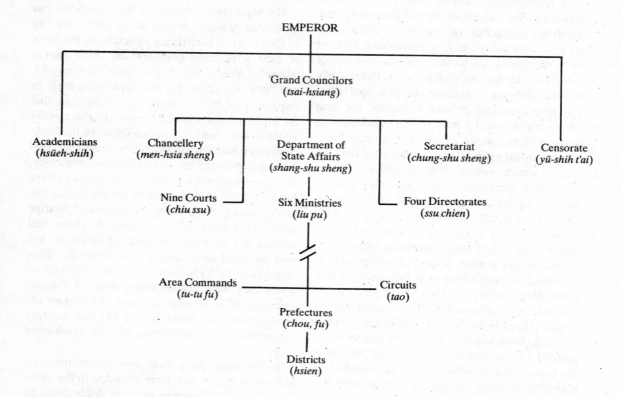

EMPEROR

Grand Councilors
(tsai-hsiang)

Academicians
(hsüeh-shih)

Chancellery
(men-hsia sheng)

Department of State Affairs
(shang-shu sheng)

Secretariat
(chung-shu sheng)

Censorate
(yü-shih t'ai)

Nine Courts
(chiu ssu)

Six Ministries
(liu pu)

Four Directorates
(ssu chien)

Area Commands
(tu-tu fu)

Circuits
(tao)

Prefectures
(chou, fu)

Districts
(hsien)

The T'ang government, culminating centuries of institution-building by the Northern Dynasties and Sui, was an effectively centralized one under which China attained political unity, international influence, and cultural grandeur to an extent not attained even in Han times. Heredity continued to be more important than ability in gaining entry to government service, but recruitment became more open, and personnel administration more sophisticated and bureaucratic. Although T'ang government was the model to which almost all subsequent dynasties aspired or claimed to aspire, it was stably centralized for less than a century and a half. After the famed rebellion of An Lu-shan beginning in 755, the T'ang empire was repeatedly on the brink of becoming a loose patchwork of virtually autonomous satrapies, and the greatly weakened central government was ultimately paralyzed by ministerial factions and dominated by eunuchs.

The Central Government

Like Sui, T'ang maintained its capital at Ch'ang-an in modern Shensi Province. Loyang in modern Honan was an auxiliary Eastern Capital (*Tung-tu* 東都), to which the whole imperial court often moved when supplies ran short in Ch'ang-an. To a greater degree than at any time since Later Han, palace eunuchs (*huan-kuan*

宦官, *nei-shih* 內侍) played major roles in the central government. Their organization, the Palace Domestic Service (*nei-shih sheng* 內侍省), was subdivided into many agencies with specialized functions. After middle T'ang one eunuch agency, the Palace Secretariat (*shu-mi yüan* 樞密院), became especially influential; it controlled the troops that guarded the capital, and occasionally its members became more powerful than any regular appointees in the central government.

The national administration. As in the past, the most esteemed members of the regular officialdom were the Three Preceptors (*san shih* 三師) and the Three Dukes (*san kung* 三公), dignitaries whose status, though not honorary, involved no special administrative functions. They were expected to give counsel to the Emperor on important matters of state, and they had the right to participate in major court deliberations. In practice, these exalted posts were often left vacant.

The real executive-administrative core of the central government, reflecting the evolution that had taken place during the centuries since Han, was the group of agencies called the Three Departments (*san sheng* 三省). The working administrative agency was the Department of State Affairs (*shang-shu sheng* 尚書省). A Director (*ling* 令) headed the Department's Executive Office (*tu-sheng* 都省, *tu-t'ang* 堂); but no Director was appointed after 626 in deference to Emperor T'ai-tsung (r. 626–649), who had held the post in his father's reign. Two nominal Vice Directors (*p'u-yeh* 僕射) then presided over the Department, supervising its subordinate Six Ministries (*liu pu* 六部), each headed by a Minister (*shang-shu* 尚書). Every Ministry was subdivided into four Bureaus (*ssu* 司) with specialized functions, each headed by a Director (*lang-chung* 郎中). The three Ministries of Personnel (*li-pu* 吏部), of Revenue (*min-pu* 民部, *hu-pu* 戶部), and of Rites (*li-pu* 禮部) were called the East Echelon (*tung-hang* 東行) of Ministries; the counterpart West Echelon (*hsi-hang* 西行) was made up of the Ministries of War (*ping-pu* 兵部), of Justice (*hsing-pu* 刑部), and of Works (*kung-pu* 工部). For prestige purposes the Ministries were considered to be divided into three other categories: a Front Echelon (*ch'ien-hang* 前行) comprising the Ministries of Personnel and War, a Middle Echelon (*chung-hang* 中行) of Revenue and Justice, and a Rear Echelon (*hou-hang* 後行) of Rites and Works. The Minister of Personnel was, at least for ceremonial purposes, the most prestigious of the Ministers.

The other two Departments were the Secretariat (*chung-shu sheng* 中書省) and the Chancellery (*men-hsia sheng* 門下省), which were not concerned with administrative routine, but handled the flow of government documents to and from the throne, giving counsel, drafting imperial edicts, and criticizing policy decisions. In comparison with the Department of State Affairs, each had a small staff. The Secretariat had two Directors (*ling*), two Vice Directors (*shih-lang* 侍郎), and six Secretariat Drafters (*chung-shu she-jen* 中書舍人). The Chancellery had two Directors (*shih-chung* 侍中), two Vice Directors (*shih-lang*), and four Supervising Secretaries (*chi-shih-chung* 給事中). Both Departments had staffs of Grand Masters of Remonstrance (*chien-i ta-fu* 諫議大夫), Rectifiers of Omissions (*pu-ch'üeh* 補闕), Reminders (*shih-i* 拾遺), Diarists (*ch'i-chü lang* 起居郎), and others. Directly subordinate to the Secretariat were the Academy of Scholarly Worthies (*chi-hsien tien shu-yüan* 集賢殿書院), an assemblage of litterateurs who compiled various scholarly works under imperial auspices, and the Historiography Institute (*shih-kuan* 史館), which prepared official histories. Subordinate to the Chancellery was the Institute for the Advancement of Literature (*hung-wen kuan* 弘文館), whose litterateurs assisted in drafting imperial pronouncements and instructed selected young men of the official class in literary skills.

The responsibilities of the Secretariat and the Chancellery overlapped substantially. In general, the Secretariat seems principally to have recommended policy decisions and drafted the documents in which imperial decisions were issued, whereas the Chancellery reviewed, revised, and polished the Secretariat's drafts. Various officials of both Departments technically had power to "veto" (*feng-po* 封駁) any imperial pronouncement on grounds either of substance or of form and style; and, at least in theory, no imperial pronouncement was considered valid without having been confirmed by the Secretariat and the Chancellery.

The Directors and Vice Directors of the Secretariat, the Chancellery, and the Department of State Affairs were, by virtue of their positions, Grand Councilors (*tsai-hsiang* 宰相). In this capacity they assembled daily in conference with the Emperor to discuss current problems and reach policy decisions, on a collegial basis. Their meeting place in the palace, the Administration Chamber (*cheng-shih t'ang* 政事堂), was originally a part of the Chancellery, but after the early T'ang years it was transferred to the jurisdiction of the Secretariat. Early in the eighth century, in confirmation of the fact that the Secretariat and the Chancellery had long been indistinguishable by their responsibilities, the two agencies became a combined Secretariat-Chancellery (*chung-shu men-hsia*), headquartered in the old Administration Chamber; and the new, unified executive agency was organized to encompass five Offices (*fang* 房): the Personnel Office (*li-fang* 吏房), the Central Control Office (*shu-chi fang* 樞機房), the War Office (*ping-fang* 兵房), the Revenue Office (*hu-fang* 戶房), and the Justice and Rites Office (*hsing-li fang* 刑禮房).

The Three Preceptors and the Three Dukes were theoretically entitled to participate with the Grand Councilors in their deliberations. From the early T'ang years, other officials were also co-opted to participate on a regular basis because of the personal esteem in which they were held. This supplementary duty was at first signified by the addition to an official's title of such suffixes as Participant in Deliberations about Court Policy (*ts'an-i ch'ao-cheng* 參議朝政, *ts'an-yü ch'ao-cheng* 參預朝政), Participant in Deliberations about Advantages and Disadvantages (*ts'an-i te-shih* 得失), or Participant in Determining Governmental Matters (*ts'an-chih cheng-shih* 參知政事). After the middle of the seventh century the standard terminology was Cooperating with Rank Three Officials of the Secretariat-Chancellery (*t'ung chung-shu men-hsia san-p'in* 同中書門下三品) or Jointly Manager of Affairs with the Secretariat-Chancellery (*t'ung chung-shu men-hsia p'ing-chang shih* 同中書門下平章事), commonly shortened to Manager of Affairs (*p'ing-chang shih*). Any of

these varied designations signified that, in addition to his regular appointment, a man was serving concurrently as a Grand Councilor. In the last half of the T'ang era, dozens of men at a time had such nominal status, including regional warlords, though the number of active Grand Councilors generally did not exceed four or five.

Other officials were often called on for regular supplementary duty in the Secretariat-Chancellery as concurrent Participants in the Drafting of Proclamations (*chih-chih-kao* 知制誥), Recipients of Edicts (*ch'eng-chih* 承旨), and even Sole Recipient of Secret Orders (*tu-ch'eng mi-ming* 獨承密命). These appointments were common stepping-stones to Grand Councilorships, but they did not themselves confer that status. This route to eminence was often taken by scholars and litterateurs patronized by the court, originally without regular appointments of any sort, who were generally known as Academicians (*hsüeh-shih* 學士) and were called on occasionally to add appropriate erudition or literary flair to official documents. In the 660s they were given official status as Academicians of the North Gate (*pei-men hsüeh-shih* 北門學士). Emperor Hsüan-tsung (r. 712–756) early in his reign transformed them into Academicians Awaiting Orders (*han-lin tai-chao* 翰林待詔) or Academicians in Attendance (*han-lin kung-feng* 供奉), thereby initiating the subsequently famous name Hanlin. In 738 he abolished these titles in favor of the traditional designation Academician (*hsüeh-shih*), creating the Institute of Academicians (*hsüeh-shih yüan* 學士院) to participate in the government's literary work. By that time a separate Hanlin Academy (*han-lin yüan* 院) was also in existence. From the late eighth century and through the ninth, Academicians attached to these agencies and to the Secretariat's Academy of Scholarly Worthies provided the Participants in the Drafting of Proclamations and similar secretarial assistants mentioned above. Their influence grew until they were popularly called Grand Councilors in the Palace (*nei-hsiang* 內相), and some Hanlin Academicians ultimately were appointed regular Grand Councilors.

The Censorate. Set apart from the executive-administrative agencies, but of great influence in T'ang government, was the Censorate (*yü-shih t'ai* 御史臺), charged with maintaining surveillance over the officialdom as a whole and submitting impeachments of wayward officials. It was headed by a Censor-in-chief (*yü-shih ta-fu* 御史大夫) and two Vice Censors-in-chief (*yü-shih chung-ch'eng* 御史中丞). Ordinary Censors (*yü-shih*) were distributed among three Bureaus (*yüan* 院): a Headquarters Bureau (*t'ai-yüan* 臺院) staffed with Attendant Censors (*shih yü-shih* 侍御史), a Palace Bureau (*tien-yüan* 殿院) staffed with Palace Censors (*tien-chung shih yü-shih* 殿中侍御史), and an Investigation Bureau (*ch'a-yüan* 察院) staffed with Investigating Censors (*chien-ch'a yü-shih* 監察御史). When making routine territorial tours of inspection, Investigating Censors were called Touring Censorial Inspectors (*hsün-an yü-shih* 巡按御史).

Special service agencies. The central government included two groups of more narrowly specialized service agencies, the Nine Courts (*chiu ssu* 九寺) and the Five Directorates (*wu chien* 五監). These had now become more stably established as central government agencies than the relatively shapeless staffs of the Ch'in–Han court dignitaries from whom most of their names derived, such as the old Nine Chamberlains (*chiu ch'ing* 九卿), and their administrative roles were by and large more clearly defined, so that they are commonly given somewhat different English renderings. Each Court was normally headed by a Chief Minister (*ch'ing* 卿) and two Vice Ministers (*shao-ch'ing* 少卿) and supervised several functionally differentiated Offices (*shu* 署). T'ang had Courts of Imperial Sacrifices (*t'ai-ch'ang ssu* 太常寺), of Imperial Entertainments (*kuang-lu ssu* 光祿寺), of the Imperial Regalia (*wei-wei ssu* 衛尉寺), of the Imperial Clan (*tsung-cheng ssu* 宗正寺), of the Imperial Stud (*t'ai-p'u ssu* 太僕寺), of Judicial Review (*ta-li ssu* 大理寺), of State Ceremonial (*hung-lu ssu* 鴻臚寺), of the National Granaries (*ssu-nung ssu* 司農寺), and of the Imperial Treasury (*t'ai-fu ssu* 太府寺).

The Five Directorates, each normally headed by one Supervisor (*chien* 監) and two Vice Directors (*shao-chien* 少監) and in supervisory charge of function-specific Offices (*shu*) or other agencies, included the Directorate for Imperial Manufactories (*shao-fu chien* 少府監), for the Palace Buildings (*chiang-tso chien* 將作監), for Armaments (*chün-ch'i chien* 軍器監), and of Waterways (*tu-shui chien* 都水監), the last headed by two Commissioners (*shih-che* 使者) rather than a Supervisor.

The fifth Directorate was the Directorate of Education (*kuo-tzu chien* 國子監), which was headed by a Chancellor (*chi-chiu* 祭酒). He, together with two Directors of Studies (*ssu-yeh* 司業) and their staffs, managed seven schools in the capital, each of which had a smaller counterpart in the auxiliary capital, Loyang. The seven schools were the School for the Sons of the State (*kuo-tzu hsüeh* 國子學), which normally enrolled 300 sons of the highest-ranking nobles and officials; the National University (*t'ai-hsüeh* 太學), which instructed some 500 sons of lesser nobles and middle-ranking officials; the Institute for the Extension of Literary Arts (*kuang-wen kuan* 廣文館), which annually tutored some 60 advanced students from the Directorate's schools to prepare them for the civil service recruitment examinations that emphasized literary skills; the School of the Four Gates (*ssu-men hsüeh* 四門學), which enrolled some 300 sons of low-ranking nobles and officials and some sons of non-officials; the Law School (*lü-hsüeh* 律學), which taught the T'ang law code and supplementary regulations to 20 sons of low-ranking officials and non-officials (at times this school was attached to the Court of Judicial Review, and it had no counterpart at Loyang until the early ninth century); the Calligraphy School (*shu-hsüeh* 書學), which enrolled 30 (later 10) sons of low-ranking officials and non-officials; and the Mathematics School (*suan-hsüeh* 算學), which enrolled 10 sons of low-ranking officials and non-officials. All these schools were staffed principally with Erudites (*po-shih* 博士) and Instructors (*chu-chiao* 助教).

Territorial Administration

Below the official government structure, the T'ang population theoretically was organized into Neighborhoods (*lin* 鄰) of five families each. Five neighborhoods constituted a Security Group (*pao* 保), and five security groups a rural Village or urban Community (*li* 里 in both cases) of 100 families. The villages and communities were the basic elements of subofficial organization, but in places they were in turn subordinated to rural Settlements (*ts'un* 村) or urban Precincts (*fang* 坊), and these were grouped into Townships (*hsiang* 鄉). The Heads (*chang* 長, *cheng* 正) of all these various groupings were expected to keep the peace, collect local taxes, organize local labor forces for government service, and perform such other services as were required by the officialdom, but they did not themselves have status as paid officials.

Units of local administration. T'ang perpetuated the two-tier system of local administration initiated by Sui. The lowest official unit, the District (*hsien* 縣), was administered by a Magistrate (*ling* 令), whose staff was largely distributed among six Sections (*ts'ao* 曹) corresponding in functions to the Six Ministries of the central government. Superior to the district was the Prefecture (ordinarily *chou* 州), headed by a Prefect (*tz'u-shih* 刺史), whose staff was also divided into Sections. Districts were graded in seven categories on the basis of their prestige and population size: imperial (*ch'ih* 赤), metropolitan (*chi* 畿), honored (*wang* 望), important (*chin* 緊), large (*shang* 上), middle (*chung* 中), and small (*hsia* 下). Prefectures were generally graded as large, middle, or small. On average, each prefecture supervised five districts. In 639 there were 358 prefectures and 1,551 districts; in 740, 328 and 1,473.

Three especially prestigious localities were distinguished by the designation Superior Prefecture (*fu* 府). These were the Ch'ang-an area, called Ching-chao fu; the Loyang area, called Ho-nan fu; and the homeland of the T'ang ruling family in modern Shansi Province, called T'ai-yüan fu. Each was nominally in the charge of an Imperial Prince (*ch'in-wang*) with the title Governor (*mu* 牧), but his assistant, the Administrator (*yin* 尹), was ordinarily the official in charge.

The normal pattern of local administration was also departed from in regions of critical military importance. For example, a Prefect might be given the title Commander-prefect (*tu-tu tz'u-shih* 都督刺史); or a unit that normally would have been a prefecture was designated an Area Command (*tu-tu fu* 都督府) under an Area Commander (*tu-tu*); or a few prefectures would be grouped either into a Superior Area Command (*ta tu-tu fu* 大都督府) under a Commander-in-chief (*ta tu-tu*) or into a Circuit (*tao* 道) under a Surveillance Commissioner for Military Training (*t'uan-lien kuan-ch'a shih* 團練觀察使). Yet another form of territorial administration was the Protectorate (*tu-hu fu* 都護府), headed by a Protector (*tu-hu*), which supervised the lands and tribes outside China's traditional borders that came under T'ang overlordship.

In the beginning, T'ang made no systematic effort to intrude coordinating officials into the intermediate zone between the empire's 300-odd prefectures and the central government, and throughout the dynasty routine administrative business appears to have been accomplished by direct communication between the central government and the prefectures that were under its effective control, supplemented by prescribed annual jaunts to the capital by prefectural Delegates to Court (*ch'ao-chi shih* 朝集使), sometimes Prefects themselves. As in Han times, however, there was a need for more regularized intermediary coordination, and T'ang efforts to fill that need eventually contributed, as had Han efforts, to the dissolution of the empire.

Commissioners. No sooner had the new dynasty pacified the country than the central government dispatched thirteen high-ranking officials separately throughout the empire to inspect local conditions and see that new policies were understood and implemented. Thereafter other central government officials were sent out to particular localities as ad hoc troubleshooters and expediters, to review and coordinate the efforts of Prefects who were coping with floods, famines, or other local disruptions. Such field representatives of the central government usually had at least nominal status in the Censorate (*yü-shih t'ai*), which gave them impeachment powers that added to their prestige. They bore the general title Commissioner (*shih* 使), with a more specific designation as varying circumstances warranted. Thus there were Touring Surveillance Commissioners (*hsün-ch'a shih* 巡察使), Pacification Commissioners (*an-fu shih* 安撫使), Relief Commissioners (*ts'un-fu shih* 存撫使), and so forth.

In 706 coordination between groups of prefectures and the central government was put on a somewhat more regularized basis. The whole empire was divided into ten Circuits (*tao*), which were of provincial size but were not organized with anything resembling provincial governments. Instead, the central government regularly assigned an itinerant Surveillance Commissioner (*an-ch'a shih* 按察使) to each circuit to visit the prefectures and districts of his jurisdiction checking on conditions in general and on the performance of the officials. Soon the designations became more awesome and cumbersome: Surveillance, Investigation, and Supervisory Commissioner (*an-ch'a ts'ai-fang ch'u-chih shih* 按察探訪處置使), then Investigation and Supervisory Commissioner (*ts'ai-fang ch'u-chih shih*), then concurrently Personnel Evaluation Commissioner (*ch'u-chih shih* 黜陟使), then Surveillance and Supervisory Commissioner (*kuan-ch'a ch'u-chih shih* 觀察處置使), and still other combinations.

Under Emperor Hsüan-tsung the number and variety of Commissioners increased, as men were appointed to oversee such matters as revenue, agriculture, and the suppression of banditry. Eight frontier Defense Commands (*chen* 鎮) were created in the North under Military Commissioners (*chieh-tu shih* 節度使), largely replacing Area Commanders. In 733 the ten early circuits were rearranged into fifteen, with Investigation Commissioners (*ts'ai-fang shih* 探訪使), soon replaced by Surveillance Commissioners (*kuan-ch'a shih* 觀察使), who served as more or less permanent overall coordinators of government in their jurisdictions. In response to the great An Lu-shan rebellion, many Circuit Commissioners and even Prefects of large prefectures were transformed into concurrent Military Commissioners (*chieh-tu shih*), and the number of circuits grew uncontrollably. After the rebellion the areas that remained under effective control of the central government normally had a Surveillance Commissioner as a kind of civil governor and a Military Commissioner as a kind of military governor. In many cases, however, warlords were virtually autonomous, and they used their status as Military Commissioners to become concurrent Surveillance Commissioners as well as Commissioners of many other sorts. Some acquired noble status as Marquises (*hou*) and even Princes (*wang*). They customarily appointed Prefects, District Magistrates, and all other officials in their domains and controlled their own revenues.

Two other types of Commissioners also became prominent in the last half of the T'ang dynasty. One type dealt with the transport of tax grain along the Grand Canal and the Yellow River to Loyang and Ch'ang-an, the other with the production and distribution of state-monopolized salt. In 712 Hsüan-tsung appointed a Water and Land Transport Commissioner (*shui-lu chuan-yün shih* 水陸轉運使) to expedite the forwarding of tax grain through the gorges between the two capitals. Then in 734 he appointed a Transport Commissioner-in-chief (*chuan-yün tu-shih* 轉運都使) to supervise grain transport to the capitals from the Yangtze delta, along the Grand Canal. After 763 an overall Transport Commissioner (*chuan-yün shih* 轉運使) based at Yangchow, at the junction of the Grand Canal and the Yangtze, became a still more essential provider of revenues for the central government as it lost control of many areas to autonomous Military Commissioners.

The state monopoly of salt, which had originated in Han times, was revived when the An Lu-shan rebellion forced the central government to seek new sources of revenue, and it kept the T'ang government solvent during the eighth and ninth centuries. The development of salt revenues in modern Shansi, Shensi, and Szechwan generally was managed by the Ministry of Revenue at Ch'ang-an. But in 758 exploitation of salt trade in the South was entrusted to a special appointee, a Salt Monopoly Commissioner (*chüeh yen-t'ieh shih* 榷鹽鐵使), whose headquarters subsequently stood alongside that of the Transport Commissioner at Yangchow. (The iron trade was not a state monopoly in T'ang times; the use of the term *t'ieh*, "iron," in the Chinese title was an anachronism derived from Han usage.)

Because the functions of the Transport Commissioner and the Salt Monopoly Commissioner were so closely related, and because they were both headquartered at Yangchow, it was inevitable that the two elaborate hierarchies of agencies would collaborate and to some extent overlap. Eventually the two functions merged under the direction of one official, the Salt and Transport Commissioner (*yen-t'ieh chuan-yün shih*

鹽鐵轉運使), whose role and importance in the late T'ang government was that of a de facto second Minister of Revenue.

The Military

Early T'ang stability and expansionism were made possible by military power, largely as organized in the Garrison Militia (*fu-ping* 府兵) system that had evolved through the Northern Dynasties and Sui eras. At its peak of effectiveness, in early T'ang, the system called for every six families to provide one capable young man for career service from the age of twenty-one to sixty in any of 634 Garrisons (*fu*) that were scattered about the empire and especially concentrated in the regions of Ch'ang-an, Lo-yang, and the northern and northwestern frontiers. Every garrison was assigned a tract of agricultural land on which its soldiers, numbering from 800 to 1,200, engaged in farming to support themselves, while also being regularly trained, drilled, and reviewed in the military arts. Each garrison had a Commandant (*tu-wei* 都尉), and was organized in 200-man Regiments (*t'uan* 團), 100-man Battalions (*lü* 旅), 50-man Companies (*tui* 隊), and 10-man Squads (*huo* 火). On a rotational schedule based on the distances between the garrisons and the duty stations, men were detached to serve one-month tours at the capital and three-year tours on the frontiers; and as needed they were mustered for special campaigns.

At the capital, rotated militiamen served in the Twelve Armies (*shih-erh chün* 十二軍) or, after 636, the Sixteen Guards (*shih-liu wei* 十六衛), each having a staff of officers including a Generalissimo (*shang chiang-chün* 上將軍), a General-in-chief (*ta chiang-chün* 大將軍), and two Generals (*chiang-chün*). The Sixteen Guards were responsible for the security of the palace, the capital, and the city gates, but they were largely ceremonial. They constituted what was called the Southern Command (*nan-ya* 南衙). The real imperial striking force was the Northern Command (*pei-ya* 北衙), made up originally of two and ultimately of ten Armies (*chün* 軍). These armies were also stationed in the Ch'ang-an area and had their own Generals-in-chief (*ta chiang-chün*). The Northern Command was the force with which the T'ang dynasty had been

founded, and it remained an elite force of hereditary professional soldiers, the sons and grandsons of the original T'ang supporters.

On frontier duty, militiamen were assigned to Area Commands (*tu-tu fu*), Superior Area Commands (*ta tu-tu fu*), or after 711, the circuits (*tao*) controlled by Military Commissioners (*chieh-tu shih*, sometimes called *ching-lüeh* 經略). For special campaigns, armies were made up of troops delegated from area commands or circuits, from the Northern and Southern Commands at the capital, and from conveniently located garrisons. Such armies were usually given ad hoc designations suggesting their purposes and areas of operations, and the officers assigned to command them were commonly designated Bandit-suppression Commissioners (*chao-t'ao shih* 招討使), Pacification Commissioners (*hsüan-wei shih* 宣慰使), Supervisory Commissioners (*ch'u-chih shih* 處置使), and the like. More specifically military titles used for the leaders of campaigns included Marshal (*yüan-shuai* 元帥), a title reserved solely for Imperial Princes; Vice Marshal (*fu yüan-shuai* 副元帥), Campaign Commander (*tu-t'ung* 都統), and Commander-in-chief (*ta tsung-kuan* 大總官).

By the early 700s the Garrison Militia system was losing its original effectiveness, and in 723 the rotation of militiamen to the capital was terminated. In their place a large force of paid volunteers was organized into a Permanent Palace Guard (*ch'ang-ts'ung su-wei* 長從宿衛, later *k'uo-chi* 彍騎), divided into twelve Guards (*wei*) in which five Squads (*huo*) of ten men each constituted Companies (*t'uan* 團). These new units, together with the hereditary soldiers of the Northern Command, thereafter served solely as an imperial bodyguard and capital-defense force; they did no campaigning. After the 760s it became common for palace eunuchs to control the capital armies, thereby intimidating the central government officialdom and manipulating Emperors to suit themselves, while ever stronger Military Commissioners dominated other areas with their Regional Armies (*ya-chün* 牙軍).

Personnel Administration

Traditional, somewhat feudalistic attitudes persisted in T'ang times to the extent that only men of good breeding, members of the great-family class called Servicemen (*shih* 士), were considered appropriate candidates for official appointments. Sons and grandsons of officials were predominant in the student bodies of all government schools that groomed men for service, and T'ang spelled out very systematically the so-called protection privileges (*yin* 蔭) that automatically and directly conferred official status (but not necessarily appointments) on the sons of officials, varying according to the ranks of the fathers. Moreover, the majority of middle- and low-ranking T'ang officials seem to have entered service (*ch'u-shen* 出身, lit., to have "come out" as a modern debutante does) by way of recommendations submitted by existing officials or by being promoted from the status of subofficial functionary (*hsü-li* 胥吏). Nevertheless, recruitment on the basis of merit as demonstrated in competitive examinations was developed to a new level of sophistication, and officials once in service were subjected to regularized, bureaucratic systems of evaluation. This remained the case throughout the dynasty in those areas that were under the effective control of the central government. After middle T'ang, however, the rise of autonomous regional warlords brought into being a number of varied regional personnel systems in which patron-client relations predominated.

Varieties of official titles. Elaborating on Sui beginnings, T'ang created a bewildering confusion of systems of official nomenclature. Although the title Prince (*wang*) was only rarely conferred outside the imperial family, both civil and military officials of outstanding merit were often granted noble status in the ranks of Duke (*kung* 公), Marquis (*hou* 侯), Earl (*po* 伯), Viscount (*tzu* 子), Baron (*nan* 男), or modifications of these. Nobles were graded in prescribed salary levels, ranging from the state taxes due from 10,000 families down to the revenue from 300 families; and they were paid stipends from general state funds that varied in proportion to their hypothetical salary levels. Eldest sons normally inherited noble status in perpetuity, but with declining salary levels.

The state also granted certain non-hereditary merit titles (*hsün* 勳) in recognition of extraordinary military service. The achievements by which one's merit was measured were defined precisely in many categories, for example, the

decapitation of such-and-such a number of enemy troops in battle; and regulations carefully spelled out how many achievements of what sorts entitled one to any particular level of merit. The merit ranks (*chuan* 轉) ranged from a low of 1 up to a high of 12, each conveying an honorary title. The highest was Supreme Pillar of State (*shang chu-kuo* 上柱國); lesser titles were mostly Commandants (*wei* 尉) differentiated by prefixes. Merit ranks also conveyed the privilege of wearing official costumes of different colors. Men granted merit titles who were not regular officials were entitled honorary officials (*hsün-kuan* 勳官); whether or not they received emoluments is not clear.

Another category of T'ang official nomenclature having no relevance to officials' assigned functions was that of prestige titles (*san-kuan* 散官), which were used to specify rank status finely and definitively. One set of prestige titles, comprising Grand Masters (*ta-fu* 大夫) and Court Gentlemen (*lang* 郎) with special prefixes, was for civil officials; it ranged from rank 1b down to 9b2 with 29 levels in all. Another set, comprising Generals (*chiang-chün*) and Commandants (*wei*) with special prefixes, was for military officers; it had a total of 42 levels. Prestige titles varied according to the manner in which men had entered service (*ch'u-shen*) at the time they were first deemed eligible for appointment; and the titles changed with seniority, achievement, and favor. All officials, active or inactive, had prestige titles at one level or another, and they assured (minimal?) state emoluments even for the inactive.

Functioning officials (*chih-kuan* 職官) were all those serving in the governmental posts described in the foregoing pages and many more not mentioned. Such officials were graded in nine ranks (*p'in* 品) subdivided into 30 classes (*teng* 等). The highest ranks, from 1 through 3, were each divided into two classes. a (*cheng* 正) and b (*ts'ung* 從), from 1a (*cheng-i p'in*) down to 3b (*ts'ung-san p'in*). In ranks 4 through 9, each class was further subdivided into an upper (*shang* 上) and a lower (*hsia* 下) grade, yielding, for example, 5a2 (*cheng-wu p'in hsia-teng*) and 8b1 (*ts'ung-pa p'in shang-teng*). A man's rank was indicated by the design and color of his official costume, and it determined his emoluments. These included grain allowances, money stipends, provisions of many sorts (fuel, cloth, writing materials, etc.), and so-called office-land (*chih-t'ien* 職田) income. In the earliest T'ang decade, for example, the scale of grain allowances for officials serving in the capital ran from 700 bushels down to 10 bushels a year; allowances for officials serving outside the capital were scaled down slightly. The scale of money stipends fixed in 736, for example, ranged from 31,000 coins down to 1,900 coins per month. As for office-land income, part was provided only while one was on active duty in the particular office for which lands were theoretically set aside, but the remainder became one's permanent income. This office-land income was defined as the state tax revenue from specified agricultural land—twelve *ch'ing* (one *ch'ing* was about fifteen acres) down to two and a half *ch'ing* for officials serving in the capital, with variations for officials serving elsewhere; but in fact the income was paid at a fixed rate of grain per *mou* (one *ch'ing* equalled 100 *mou*) of the prescribed land area.

Functioning officials did not always perform the functions associated with the titles they bore, but were detached on commissions or duty assignments (*ch'ai-ch'ien* 差遣) to perform wholly unrelated duties as needed. Also, an official might concurrently (*chien* 兼) hold two principal offices, or be responsible for (*chih* 知) a function unrelated to his principal office, or be assigned some other additional function (*chia-chih* 加職). Further, when newly appointed to any office, one was normally a probationary appointee (*shou* 守) for one year. Someone might therefore be referred to in Chinese sources, with all his appropriate designations, as the Grand Master of Correct Counsel (rank 4a prestige title), Probationary Minister of Personnel (rank 3a official title), Concurrently Minister of Justice (also rank 3a), Surveillance Commissioner of Chiang-nan (detached duty assignment), Grand Councilor (additional function), Grand Commandant of Light Chariots (1b merit title), Dynasty-founding Duke of Ying-ch'üan (noble title), Li Fu (personal name)—the complicated romanization being *cheng-i ta-fu shou li-pu shang-shu chien hsing-pu shang-shu chiang-nan kuan-ch'a shih t'ung chung-shu men-hsia p'ing-chang shih ch'ing-ch'e tu-wei k'ai-kuo kung* Li Fu.

Recruitment and appointment. The T'ang officialdom was recruited in a variety of ways, including promotion from subofficial status, on recommendation from officials in service, and inheritance of official status by the sons of existing officials. Students who completed prescribed curriculums in the government schools in the capital were considered eligible for appointment, that is, to have "entered service" (*ch'u-shen*). Men who had been granted merit titles (*hsün*) because of extraordinary military service similarly became eligible for appointments. In addition, there were several ways in which men could in effect purchase official status. But the most noteworthy path into officialdom was on the basis of merit as demonstrated in government-sponsored examinations at the capital.

Although most military officers seem to have attained their status by heredity, by recommendation, or by ad hoc appointments for many sorts of reasons, the Ministry of War conducted recruitment examinations for the military service in which candidates were tested on their abilities at archery, horsemanship, and so forth. More esteemed were the civil service recruitment examinations, of which there were two categories, irregular and regular. The special, irregular examinations (*chih-chü* 制舉) were ordered by Emperors in search of special talents. These flourished in the first half of the dynasty and especially under the famed eighth-century Emperor Hsüan-tsung. Candidates were normally nominated by high-ranking capital officials and by Prefects; they were always few in number; and no more than a dozen normally proved acceptable. These select few were either appointed directly to office or placed in the pool of unassigned officials (i.e., men bearing prestige titles but having no assigned duties) who were awaiting appointments. Many of the most notable officials of the first half of the dynasty were recruited in such irregular examinations.

In the regular examinations (*k'o-chü* 科舉), which were scheduled annually, as many as 2,000 candidates competed. The main body of candidates were so-called local tribute (*hsiang-kung* 鄉貢) candidates, that is, men nominated in accordance with prescribed quotas by Prefects, who were expected to choose their nominees on the basis of preliminary screening examinations. Other candidates at the capital examinations were new graduates of the government schools who chose to maximize their chances for good careers in this way. It also appears that functioning officials, unassigned officials, and even honorary officials had some sort of right to present themselves as candidates if they had not already passed recruitment examinations.

Almost 20 different kinds of examinations are known to have been given in T'ang times in the category of regular examinations. These even included an examination on Taoist literature given in Hsüan-tsung's reign. But the standard examinations were of five kinds. The two most prestigious led to the degrees of Classicist (*ming-ching* 明經), usually granted to only 10 or 20 percent of the candidates, and Presented Scholar (*chin-shih* 進士), usually granted to only 1 or 2 percent of the candidates. These examinations were based on the Confucian tradition and tested classical erudition and literary skill. They were written but sometimes included oral parts. The three less prestigious examinations were on calligraphy, mathematics, and law. By late T'ang times the irregular recruitment examinations had almost entirely been abandoned in favor of the regular annual examinations; the examination for the Presented Scholar degree had become preeminent, and men seldom had distinguished civil service careers without it.

The civil service recruitment examinations were supervised by the Ministry of Personnel until 736, when they were placed under the control of the Ministry of Rites. This transfer of responsibility clearly signaled that the recruitment of personnel for official status was a matter of ritual importance, wholly separate from the administrative business of appointing men to functioning offices, which remained the responsibility of the Ministry of Personnel.

Men who passed (*chi-ti* 及第) the recruitment examinations reported to the Ministry of Personnel to be assigned prestige titles (*san-kuan* 散官), and at prescribed intervals all unassigned officials and honorary officials were expected to report to the Ministry of Personnel for placement examinations (*k'ao-shih* 考試). This procedure emphasized bureaucratic capabilities and general demeanor, on the basis of which a man's prestige title might be changed for better or worse and he was considered for a substantive appointment in a suitable vacancy. After the earliest T'ang decades, the waiting period between attaining eligibility for office and getting a substantive appointment was often a very long one.

Once appointed, a junior official was given an annual merit rating (*k'ao* 考) by his administrative superior and was irregularly evaluated by touring censorial investigators; and an official's dossier containing all such ratings and evaluations was considered in his next placement evaluation at the Ministry of Personnel. There was no general rule limiting terms in office, but junior officials were commonly appointed for specified terms of three years or more. At the conclusion of one such term, a junior official often had another long wait before he was reappointed. Senior officials were irregularly evaluated by specially assigned investigators, usually censors, and normally served indefinitely at the pleasure of the Emperor.

The Five Dynasties and Ten Kingdoms
907-960

The Five Dynasties (North China)
    Later Liang, 907–923
    Later T'ang, 923–934
    Later Chin, 936–947
    Later Han, 947–951
    Later Chou, 951–960
The Ten Kingdoms (South China except the last)
    (Former) Shu, 907–925 (Szechwan)
    Later Shu, 934–965 (Szechwan)
    Nan-p'ing or Ching-nan, 907–963 (Hupei)
    Ch'u, 927–956 (Hunan)
    Wu, 902–937 (Nanking area)
    Southern T'ang or Ch'i, 937–975 (Nanking area)
    Wu-Yüeh, 907–978 (Chekiang)
    Min, 907–946 (Fukien)
    Southern Han or Yüeh, 907–971 (Canton area)
    Northern Han, 951–979 (Shansi)

A tumultuous era of transition followed the disappearance of the T'ang dynasty in a confusion of uprisings by contending Military Commissioners (*chieh-tu shih* 節度使) who dominated the ever more numerous Circuits (*tao* 道) into which the empire had been divided. In the Yangtze Valley and the farther South, power struggles led to the emergence of relatively durable regional kingdoms, each with dynastic pretensions but not much military power. On the North China Plain, however, a façade of unity was preserved through a succession of five short-lived dynasties based at Kaifeng or Loyang in modern Honan Province, where uneasy Emperors presided over a conglomeration of circuit satraps who were nominally their appointees. Upstart militaristic opportunists were supreme; it was an age of mutinies, massacres, usurpations, and assassinations. Emperors and Military Commissioners alike were commonly installed and deposed in coups engineered by their troops.

In all areas the T'ang pattern of governmental organization and personnel administration persisted, although affairs were actually managed by military leaders and their hangers-on. For a stable central government to emerge, with sufficient military and fiscal control to consolidate North China effectively and then bring fragmented South China again into a national polity, some structural innovations were required; and these awaited the following Sung dynasty (960–1279).

In the transitional era, the creation of reasonably effective central governments was facilitated by the fact that the founder of each new state or dynasty after T'ang was a warlord who had developed his own personal staff of relatives or dependents; they were hungry for prestige and power and had some measure of practical experience. They were normally military men, officers in the Regional Armies (*ya-chün* 牙軍) that had been recruited by all Military Commissioners of late T'ang times. Once a Military Commissioner became Emperor, he appointed his subalterns to posts in his capital guards or in traditional central government offices as sinecures; and then, in the pattern established by T'ang, he detached them on duty assignments or commissions (*ch'ai-ch'ien* 差遣) to serve in ad hoc capacities as needed. In this way there came into being as many as 26 special central government agencies, headed by what were generically called "the various palace commissioners" (*nei chu-ssu shih* 內諸司使), who actually administered the palace and the government.

Among these ad hoc appointees was a Commissioner of Palace Attendants (*hsüan-hui yüan shih* 宣徽院使), who controlled the formerly troublesome corps of palace eunuchs. Another effectively ousted eunuchs from their Palace

Secretariat (*shu-mi yüan* 樞密院), a base from which they had won ultimate control over the T'ang imperial armies. Now, without any change of its name, the old Palace Secretariat was transformed into a non-eunuch Bureau of Military Affairs, under a powerful Commissioner Participating in Control of Military Affairs (*ts'an-chang shu-mi shih* 參掌樞密事). In addition, someone close to the throne came to be designated Controller of the Armies and Guards (*p'an liu-chün chu-wei shih* 判六軍諸衛事), and eventually Emperors concentrated the best soldiers available to them in a Palace Army (*tien-ch'ien chün* 殿前軍) under their personal control, as the most powerful striking force in the state. Fiscal control was similarly consolidated, first under a Commissioner for State Revenue (*tsu-yung shih* 租庸使) and then under a State Finance Commissioner (*san-ssu shih* 三司使), who oversaw the activities of the three most important revenue-control agencies—the Census Bureau (*hu-pu ssu* 戶部司) and the Tax Bureau (*tu-chih ssu* 度支司), both in the Ministry of Revenue (*hu-pu* 戶部), and the Salt Transport Commission (*yen-t'ieh chuan-yün shih ssu* 鹽鐵轉運使司).

Emperors of the Five Dynasties tried to assert their control over the Military Commissioners by dispatching their personal agents into the hinterland, as Army-supervising Commissioners (*chien-chün shih* 監軍使) and Military Inspectors (*hsün-chien shih* 巡檢使). Meanwhile, at every opportunity, they attacked weak Military Commissioners and replaced them with their own relatives or dependents. North China was not yet stably consolidated, however, when the Sung dynasty began in 960; and the regional kingdoms of South China were still wholly autonomous.

As in T'ang times, the basic units of territorial administration during this transitional era were Districts (*hsien* 縣), grouped under Prefectures (*chou* 州) or Superior Prefectures (*fu* 府).

Sung

(NORTHERN) SUNG, 960-1127
SOUTHERN SUNG, 1127-1279

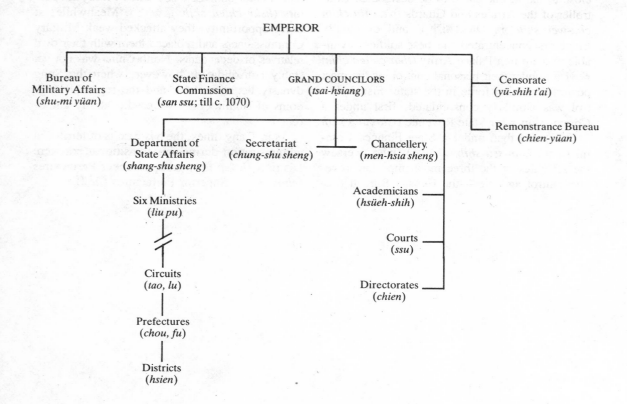

EMPEROR

- Bureau of Military Affairs (*shu-mi yüan*)
- State Finance Commission (*san ssu*; till c. 1070)
- GRAND COUNCILORS (*tsai-hsiang*)
- Censorate (*yü-shih t'ai*)
- Remonstrance Bureau (*chien-yüan*)

- Department of State Affairs (*shang-shu sheng*)
- Secretariat (*chung-shu sheng*)
- Chancellery (*men-hsia sheng*)

- Six Ministries (*liu pu*)
- Academicians (*hsüeh-shih*)
- Courts (*ssu*)
- Directorates (*chien*)

- Circuits (*tao, lu*)
- Prefectures (*chou, fu*)
- Districts (*hsien*)

After centuries of disorder and decentralized authority in the late T'ang and Five Dynasties eras, the Sung rulers determinedly consolidated power in their central government and, most particularly, in their own hands. Sung government was consequently more autocratic than government under previous national dynasties had been, establishing a trend that was subsequently to become more pronounced. At the same time, however, the civil service officialdom was esteemed as never before, education and recruitment for the civil service became increasingly open, and government generally became more professionalized and sophisticated. Among the most

professional statesmen of the dynasty was the famous, controversial "reform minister" Wang An-shih (1021–1086; in power 1069–1074, 1075–1076).

In order to centralize government effectively, the early Sung rulers perpetuated many institutional improvisations of the late T'ang and Five Dynasties periods and introduced more of their own. The result was the most complex and confusing pattern of nomenclature of China's whole imperial history. Especially in the first Sung century, what was in name a "regular" structure of governmental agencies and official posts that resembled the early T'ang structure was overlaid with networks of irregular, sometimes ad hoc agencies and commissions in which most officials actually served; and officials' formal titles had little relevance to their actual functions. Again in the confused transition from Northern Sung to Southern Sung, and in the final decades of Southern Sung, regular patterns of administration were disrupted, and ad hoc agencies and posts proliferated.

The Central Government

The original Sung capital was in the center of the North China Plain at modern Kaifeng city. It was formally designated the Eastern Capital (*Tung-ching* 東京), and Loyang in the western part of Honan was given honorific status as the Western Capital (*Hsi-ching* 西京). Two other cities were honored with the designations Northern Capital (*Pei-ching* 北京) and Southern Capital (*Nan-ching* 南京). The central government was nevertheless concentrated in Kaifeng. After Jurchen invaders took over North China in 1126–1127, the Sung court established itself in successive fall-back positions in the South and finally settled at Hangchow in modern Chekiang; the city was then called Lin-an and was known semiofficially as "the temporary imperial abode" (*hsing-tsai* 行在). It was the functioning capital of the Southern Sung era, although considerations of face and pride apparently prevented it from being so designated.

In the early Sung reigns, trusted eunuchs were dispatched in large numbers throughout the empire as Army Supervisors (*chien-chün* 監軍 and variants) or even at times as active Troop Commanders (*tien-ping* 典兵); but in general eunuchs played a considerably less important role outside the palace in Sung than in Han or T'ang times. As in T'ang, there was an elaborate nobility of imperial relatives and other favorites, and each noble nominally had a fief with a territorial identification. However, noble status did not endow men with real administrative authority; close imperial relatives in particular were effectively blocked from participation in government.

Grand Councilors. The preeminent offices in the working administration were those of Grand Councilors—men who supervised the central government and met regularly with the Emperor in an Administration Chamber (*cheng-shih t'ang* 政事堂) located inside the imperial palace grounds. Their titles changed repeatedly, but the one by which they are best known is *tsai-hsiang* 宰相. There were normally two Grand Councilors as well as several Vice Grand Councilors (*fu-hsiang* 副相) or Junior Grand Councilors (*shao-tsai* 少宰), so that the total of Councilors fluctuated between five and nine. Formally, Grand Councilors bore such cumbersome titles as Jointly Manager of Affairs with the Secretariat-Chancellery (*t'ung chung-shu men-hsia p'ing-chang shih* 同中書門下平章事); Vice Director of the Department of State Affairs (*shang-shu p'u-yeh* 尚書僕射) and Concurrent (*chien* 兼) Vice Director of the Secretariat (*chung-shu shih-lang* 中書侍郎); Senior Grand Councilor and Concurrent Vice Director of the Secretariat-Chancellery (*t'ai-tsai chien chung-shu men-hsia shih-lang* 太宰兼中書門下侍郎); Vice Director of the Department of State Affairs Jointly Manager of Affairs with the Secretariat-Chancellery (*shang-shu p'u-yeh t'ung chung-shu men-hsia p'ing-chang shih*); or in the last Sung century, Director of the Department of State Affairs (*shang-shu ling* 令) Jointly Manager of Affairs with the Secretariat-Chancellery. Their associates had equally variable and sometimes equally cumbersome formal titles, such as Executive Official Participant in Determining Governmental Matters (*chih-cheng kuan ts'an-chih cheng-shih* 執政官參知政事); Junior Grand Councilor and Concurrent Vice Director of the Secretariat-Chancellery (*shao-tsai chien chung-shu men-hsia shih-lang*); or Vice Director of the Secretariat-Chancellery Participating in Determining Governmental Matters (*chung-shu men-hsia shih-lang ts'an-chih cheng-shih*).

This confusion of Grand Councilor titles in part reflects the fact that until the 1070s the traditional Three Departments (*san sheng* 三省) that had long been the administrative core of Chinese central governments—the Secretariat (*chung-shu sheng* 中書省), the Chancellery (*men-hsia sheng* 門下省), and the Department of State Affairs (*shang-shu sheng* 尚書省)—were little more than nominal institutions. Only rarely was someone appointed to a top position in any of them, and the Vice Directorships (*shih-lang* 侍郎 in the

Secretariat and Chancellery, *p'u-yeh* 僕射 in the Department of State Affairs) were normally filled only by Grand Councilors and their associates. Commonly also, even after the 1070s, the hoary Three Departments were a single conglomerate agency and all but indistinguishable from the Administration Chamber, where the Grand Councilors presided over governmental operations.

Staff work for the Grand Councilors was provided primarily by several document-handling agencies and by Drafters (*chih-chih-kao* 知制誥) who were nominally members of the Secretariat, known collectively as Outer Drafters (*wai-chih* 外制), or by Hanlin Academicians (*han-lin hsüeh-shih* 翰林學士) assigned to palace duty from the Institute of Academicians (*hsüeh-shih yüan* 院), who were collectively called Inner Drafters (*nei-chih* 內制). The most esteemed Academicians were distinguished with the title Hanlin Academician Recipient of Edicts (*ch'eng-chih* 承旨). Until the 1080s, the Institute of Academicians also included Hanlin Academician Readers-in-waiting (*han-lin shih-tu hsüeh-shih* 翰林侍讀學士) and Hanlin Academician Lecturers-in-waiting (*han-lin shih-chiang hsüeh-shih* 翰林侍講學士). In addition to their staff work for the Grand Councilors, and as their primary regular function, members of the Institute of Academicians engaged in various editorial projects ordered by the Emperor.

The State Finance Commission and the Bureau of Military Affairs. The authority of the Grand Councilors in early Sung times was somewhat limited by the independent existence of a State Finance Commission (*san ssu* 三司), in which the Sung founder consolidated the direction of almost all important national fiscal activities. The Commission came to be divided into three Bureaus (*ssu* 司), initially a Salt and Iron Monopoly Bureau (*yen-t'ieh ssu* 鹽鐵司), a Tax Bureau (*tu-chih ssu* 度支司), and a Census Bureau (*hu-pu ssu* 戶部司, not to be confused with the traditional Ministry of Revenue, *hu-pu*), then a Census Bureau (*hu-pu*), a Tax Transport Bureau (*chuan-yün ssu* 轉運司), and a Stabilization Fund Bureau (*ch'ang-p'ing ssu* 常平司). Each Bureau was further divided into from five to eight specialized Sections (*an* 案).

For the first Sung century, the State Finance Commission was responsible for matters previously (and to some extent still, nominally) managed by the Ministry of Revenue, the Ministry of Works (*kung-pu* 工部), and various Courts and Directorates. Its Commissioner (*san-ssu shih* 三司使) and its three Vice Commissioners (*fu-shih* 副使), who directed the three subordinate Bureaus, were sometimes Grand Councilors or Vice Grand Councilors holding the fiscal offices concurrently, but for most of its existence the Commission was an autonomous agency of the central administration, organizationally of only slightly less prestige than the Grand Councilors. Wang An-shih created a still more prestigious Finance Planning Commission (*chih-chih san-ssu t'iao-li ssu* 制置三司條例司), which absorbed the functions of the State Finance Commission and even overshadowed the Grand Councilors. But in the regularization of government that followed Wang's fall from power in 1076, all this fiscal superstructure was swept away and the handling of state finances reverted to the traditional agencies, notably the Ministry of Revenue.

The most significant restriction on the authority of Sung Grand Councilors was the autonomous existence, and at the same organizational level, of a Bureau of Military Affairs (*shu-mi yüan* 樞密院), which under the Emperor's direct supervision controlled the state's military forces. It was normally headed by a Commissioner (*shih* 使), who was normally a civil official. If his principal nominal title was unrelated, he was additionally designated Manager of the Bureau of Military Affairs (*chih shu-mi yüan shih* 知樞密院使) or Jointly (*t'ung* 同) Manager of the Bureau of Military Affairs. The Bureau and the aggregation of Grand Councilors were commonly referred to as the Two Administrations (*erh fu* 二府), a term signifying the separation of powers between the two paramount civil and military agencies. Occasionally, however, in both Northern and Southern Sung times, influential Grand Councilors were made concurrent Managers of the Bureau of Military Affairs, thus becoming extraordinarily powerful leaders of the whole officialdom.

Censors, remonstrators, examiners, and evaluators. Yet another check on the Grand Councilors' authority was the independent existence of what were traditionally called surveillance officials (*ch'a-kuan* 察官) and remonstrance officials (*chien-kuan* 諫官). As in T'ang times, the supreme surveillance agency, the Censorate (*yü-shih t'ai* 御史臺), was divided into a Headquarters Bureau (*t'ai-yüan* 臺院), a Palace Bureau (*tien-yüan* 殿院), and an Investigation Bureau (*ch'a-yüan* 察院); and after 1080 the Investigation Bureau was further divided into six Investigation Sections (*ch'a-an* 察案) jurisdictionally parallel to the traditional Six Ministries. The staff of Censors, however, did not total more than a dozen or so through most of the eleventh century. The nominal Censor-in-chief (*yü-shih ta-fu* 御史大夫) was almost never appointed; the working head of the agency, the Vice Censor-in-chief (*yü-shih chung-ch'eng* 御史中丞), as often as not was a concurrent appointee based primarily in another agency; and at times there was neither a Censor-in-chief nor a Vice Censor-in-chief, and the Censorate was administered by a much less prestigious General Purpose Censor (*shih yü-shih chih tsa-shih* 侍御史知雜事). In general, explicit restrictions as well as their limited numbers confined Censors' surveillance to the capital area. Even when the Censorate staff expanded after the 1080s, Censors were not expected to make field inspections outside the capital, though they bore the traditional censorial obligation to impeach anyone in the whole officialdom who neglected or bungled his governmental responsibilities.

In the eleventh century the Censorate was sometimes given authority to remonstrate with the Emperor as well as to impeach wayward officials. Appointments as Remonstrating Censors (*yen-shih yü-shih* 言事御史) were authorized as early as 1017, and in 1045 a special Office of Remonstrating Censors (*chien-kuan yü-shih t'ing* 諫官御史廳) was created in the Censorate. But this arrangement did not long endure, and the remonstrance role of Censors was in general an unprecedented Sung experiment. Remonstrance generally remained a separate, specialized function. In early Sung, as in T'ang, it was the special responsibility of officials in the Secretariat and the Chancellery—Supervising Secretaries (*chi-shih-chung* 給事中), Secretariat Drafters (*chung-shu she-jen* 中書舍人), Rectifiers of Omissions (*pu-ch'üeh* 補闕), Reminders (*shih-i* 拾遺), and the like. In about 1020 the Reminders and Rectifiers of Omissions were shifted from the Secretariat and the Chancellery to a new, independent Remonstrance Bureau (*chien-yüan* 諫院), with new titles. The Rectifiers of Omissions became Remonstrators (*ssu-chien* 司諫), and the Reminders became Exhorters (*cheng-yen* 正言). In 1032 the Remonstrance Bureau was assigned a building of its own and began increasing in prestige. Later Sung officials commented that in the 1040s and 1050s Grand Councilors were little more than errand runners for the prestigious Censorate and Remonstrance Bureau; and modern scholars have suggested that the remonstrance officials' new organizational independence encouraged them to become critics primarily of Grand Councilors rather than of Emperors as in preceding dynasties, thus contributing to the rise of increasingly autocratic Emperors and the diminution of the powers of Grand Councilors.

In an obvious attempt to limit the influence of Grand Councilors, the early Sung Emperors also established special procedures for administering the recruitment and appointment of civil service personnel, which in T'ang times had been handled by the Ministry of Rites (*li-pu* 禮部) and the Ministry of Personnel (*li-pu* 吏部), respectively. Now recruitment by examinations was handled by imperially chosen court dignitaries given authority as ad hoc Examination Administrators (*chih kung-chü* 知貢舉), and the appointment evaluations of all but the highest-ranking civil officials were entrusted to a special, independent Bureau of Personnel Administration (*shen-kuan yüan* 審官院). All such responsibilities, however, were returned to the traditional organs in the 1080s.

Ministries, Courts, and Directorates. After the reorganization of the 1080s, the old Ministries (*pu* 部), Courts (*ssu* 寺), and Directorates (*chien* 監), previously reduced to almost nominal existence by the creation of such ad hoc agencies as the State Finance Commission, regained most of their T'ang-style functions and status. There were the traditional Six Ministries (*liu pu* 六部), each under a Minister (*shang-shu* 尚書): the Ministries of Personnel (*li-pu* 吏部), of Revenue (*hu-pu* 戶部), of Rites (*li-pu* 禮部), of War (*ping-pu* 兵部), of Justice (*hsing-pu*

刑部), and of Works (*kung-pu* 工部). The last two were combined into a single Ministry of Justice and Works (*hsing-kung pu*) during the last Southern Sung century. There were repeated requests that the full T'ang complement of 24 subordinate Bureaus (*ssu* 司) be reestablished in the Ministries, but there seem never to have been more than eighteen in all, three in each Ministry. Each Bureau was headed by a Director (*lang-chung* 郎中) and a Vice Director (*yüan-wai lang* 員外郎).

The Nine Courts (*chiu ssu* 九寺) of the Sung era were the Courts of Imperial Sacrifices (*t'ai-ch'ang ssu* 太常寺), of the Imperial Regalia (*wei-wei ssu* 衛尉寺), of Judicial Review (*ta-li ssu* 大理寺), of State Ceremonial (*hung-lu ssu* 鴻臚寺), of the Imperial Clan (*tsung-cheng ssu* 宗正寺), of the Imperial Stud (*t'ai-p'u ssu* 太僕寺), of the Imperial Treasury (*t'ai-fu ssu* 太府寺), of Imperial Entertainments (*kuang-lu ssu* 光祿寺), and of the National Granaries (*ssu-nung ssu* 司農寺). Each Court was headed by a Chief Minister (*ch'ing* 卿) and one or more Vice Ministers (*shao-ch'ing* 少卿).

The most important Directorates (*chien* 監) were the Directorates for Imperial Manufactories (*shao-fu chien* 少府監), for the Palace Buildings (*chiang-tso chien* 將作監), for Armaments (*chün-ch'i chien* 軍器監), and for Astronomy (*ssu-t'ien chien* 司天監), each headed by a Supervisor (*chien* 監), who was assisted principally by one or more Vice Directors (*shao-chien* 少監); and the Directorate of Education (*kuo-tzu chien* 國子監), headed by a Chancellor (*chi-chiu* 祭酒), who was principally assisted by a Director of Studies (*ssu-yeh* 司業). To a greater extent than in T'ang times, the Courts and Directorates came to be directly subordinate to the general central administration conglomerate, as were the Ministries. The prestige of the Ministries, however, seems to have risen above the T'ang level after the governmental reorganization of the 1080s, when the Department of State Affairs, of which they nominally remained parts, tended to lose its identity and become merely part of the staff of the Grand Councilors.

As in T'ang times, the Directorate of Education supervised a number of schools in the capital. The most important were the School for the Sons of the State (*kuo-tzu hsüeh* 國子學) and the National University (*t'ai-hsüeh* 太學), which in practice seem to have been consolidated into a relatively unified institution. The leading teachers were Erudites (*po-shih* 博士). Students increased in Northern Sung to a total of more than 4,000, distributed among as many as 80 Study Halls (*chai* 齋), some dedicated to classical studies and others to administrative studies. Wang An-shih organized the consolidated school (most commonly called the National University) into three Colleges (*she* 舍): the Outer College (*wai-she* 外舍), which sent about 20 percent of its graduates to the Inner College (*nei-she* 內舍), less than half of whose graduates were admitted to the Superior College (*shang-she* 上舍). Other schools supervised by the Directorate of Education most notably included the Military School (*wu-hsüeh* 武學) and the Law School (*lü-hsüeh* 律學). After the transition to Southern Sung, the Directorate of Education never flourished as in the eleventh century, but enrollment in the National University ultimately recovered to a total of 1,000 or so students.

Territorial Administration

At the level below the agencies of formal government, the Sung population was theoretically organized into rural Villages (*li* 里) and urban Precincts (*fang* 坊), both clustered in Townships (*hsiang* 鄉 in rural areas, *hsiang* 廂 in urban areas). The reformer Wang An-shih tried to organize the population more efficiently. For the collection of local taxes, from 10 to 30 neighboring households constituted a Tithing (*chia* 甲), and heads of well-to-do families in rotation served as Tithing Chiefs (*chia-t'ou* 頭). For local militia purposes, all families with two or more sons were required to provide one son for unpaid training and service. Ten families constituted a Small Security Group (*hsiao-pao* 小保) with a designated Head (*chang* 長); five small security groups constituted a Large Security Group (*ta-pao* 大保); and ten large security groups constituted a Superior Security Group (*tu-pao* 都保) of 500 families. Wang's system was abolished in 1085, but from the 1090s through the remainder of Sung times the system of villages and precincts and the system of tithings and security groups were both operating, intermixed.

Units of local administration. The lowest unit of formal government was the traditional District (*hsien* 縣), nominally headed by a Magistrate (*ling* 令) and staffed with a few low-ranking officials, many suboffical functionaries (*li* 吏) distributed among function-specific Sections (*ts'ao* 曹), and groups of militiamen, office flunkeys, and menials requisitioned, generally without pay, from the local population. Clusters of neighboring districts were supervised by T'ang-style Prefectures (*chou* 州), nominally headed by Prefects (*tz'u-shih* 刺史). On average, districts governed populations of 10,000 to 15,000, and four or five districts were subordinate to each prefecture. At the Sung empire's greatest extent, in the early 1100s, it had about 1,500 districts and about 300 prefectures.

Both districts and prefectures were classified on the basis of size and population, and also by prestige or functional specializations. The sites of capitals and a few other especially large or important cities were distinguished as Superior Prefectures (*fu* 府). Areas in which military garrisons accounted for most of the population were designated Military Prefectures (*chün* 軍), and a handful of areas in which mines and salterns were the preeminent economic enterprises were designated Industrial Prefectures (*chien* 監).

In order to suppress regional separatist inclinations and to establish firm control over local government units, the early Sung Emperors did not actually appoint Prefects or District Magistrates. Instead, they commissioned central government officials of appropriate qualities and characteristics, whatever their ranks and nominal titles, to administer these units, with the irregular designation Manager of the Affairs of such-and-such Prefecture or District (*chih* place-name *shih* 知...事). By the end of Sung, these irregular designations had become abbreviated and more regularized, Prefects being called *chih-chou, chih-fu, chih-chün*, or *chih-chien* and District Magistrates *chih-hsien*.

Also for the purpose of maintaining close control over the prefectures, the early Sung Emperors commissioned other central government officials as virtual spies on the prefectural Managers of Affairs, empowered to memorialize the throne directly without the knowledge or consent of their presumed prefectural superiors; and no prefectural directive was considered authentic unless countersigned by the so-called Prefectural Supervisor (*chien-chou* 監州). The official designation, supplementing the appointee's nominal central government title, was Controller-general (*t'ung-p'an* 通判) of such-and-such Prefecture.

Circuits. Like the Han and T'ang rulers before them, Sung Emperors additionally found it necessary to have coordinating officials in the intermediate zone between prefectures and the central government, which so repeatedly had been the breeding ground for regional warlordism. They inherited from T'ang the regional echelon of Circuits (*tao* 道; after 997 called *lu* 路). One of the most significant early acts of the Sung founder, however, was to summon to his capital all the Military Commissioners (*chieh-tu shih* 節度使) then in control of various circuits and persuade them to abandon their regional powers in exchange for valuable estates and eminent honorary status in the Sung central government—in effect, to retire in honor with princely pensions. He then replaced them with trusted civil officials from his own entourage (he was himself a Military Commissioner who had usurped the throne). The Sung pattern that soon evolved was to assign several Commissioners (*shih* 使) with different functional responsibilities and powers to the same area, sometimes with disparate but overlapping geographic jurisdictions. In consequence, no one man, however powerful, was able to dominate any region, and Sung was never troubled by regional warlordism.

The posts filled by these coordinating Commissioners were collectively called the Four Circuit Supervisorates (*ssu chien-ssu* 四監司). Appointments varied considerably on an ad hoc basis, but after the middle of the eleventh century the normal pattern included at least four Commissions—Military, Fiscal, Judicial, and Supply.

The Military Commission (informally called *shuai-ssu* 帥司) was headed by a Military Commissioner (*an-fu-shih* 安撫使 and variants). In the absence of other important Commissioners, as in some frontier regions, the Military Commissioner sometimes became overall coordinator of civil as well as military affairs, with a designation such as Commander-in-chief (*tu tsung-kuan* 都總管); and he was ordinarily concurrent Prefect of the military prefecture governed from his headquarters. In Southern Sung times, Military Commissioners became extraordinarily important, and it was not uncommon for Grand Councilors to be sent out on such assignments.

The Fiscal Commission (informally called *ts'ao-ssu* 漕司) was headed by a Fiscal Commissioner (*chuan-yün shih* 轉運使). His principal responsibility was to see that state revenues were collected and properly distributed, but he was often coordinator of general civil administration in his circuit. One such appointee sometimes coordinated two neighboring circuits; in such a case he was designated Fiscal Commissioner-in-chief (*tu chuan-yün shih* 都轉運使).

The Judicial Commission (informally called *hsien-ssu* 憲司) was headed by a Judicial Commissioner (*t'i-hsing an-ch'a shih* 提刑按察使, *t'i-tien hsing-yü kung-shih* 提點刑獄公事). He supervised the conduct of trials and the management of prisoners by the districts and prefectures of his jurisdiction.

The Supply Commission (informally called *ts'ang-ssu* 倉司) was headed by a Supply Commissioner (*fa-yün shih* 發運使, *t'i-chü ch'ang-p'ing kung-shih* 提舉常平公事). There were often several Supply Commissioners in one normal circuit with somewhat varied titles. They were primarily concentrated in the productive agricultural regions of the Yangtze Valley and along the Grand Canal. They supervised prefectural management of grain storage and transport, relief granaries, state-monopolized industries and trade, and agricultural-development activities. In areas without Supply Commissioners, their functions were normally performed by Fiscal Commissioners.

The normal circuit was identical with the geographic jurisdiction of a Fiscal Commissioner and a Judicial Commissioner. Sung began with ten such circuits. By the end of the Northern Sung era, the empire had been redivided into 26 circuits. In Southern Sung times, when first the Jurchen and then the Mongols dominated North China, the number of Sung's circuits dropped to sixteen. The circuits to which the Military and the Supply Commissioners were assigned fluctuated greatly in size and number.

The Military

The Sung military system was characterized by an extreme of centralized control, by reliance on professional career soldiers, by the development of a substantial navy, and by the stratification of forces at three levels—Imperial Armies, Prefectural Armies, and local militia units. The whole military establishment was dominated administratively by the Bureau of Military Affairs (*shu-mi yüan*) at the capital, with some assistance from the Ministry of War (*ping-pu*), though the Ministry was much weaker than in both earlier and later dynasties. The old T'ang Sixteen Guards (*shih-liu wei* 十六衛), with their Generals-in-chief (*ta chiang-chün* 大將軍), Generals (*chiang-chün*), and other officers, remained in existence only nominally; the titles were honors conferred on members of the imperial family and some other dignitaries.

The Imperial Armies (*chin-chün* 禁軍) were the first-line professional forces of Sung times. From them groups were rotated on a three-year basis to frontier garrisons under Military Commissioners (*an-fu shih*) of circuits, or on an ad hoc basis for special campaigning under the temporary control of Grand Marshals (*ta yüan-shuai* 大元帥) or Marshals (*yüan-shuai*), who were often designated Pacification Commissioners (*hsüan-fu shih* 宣撫使 and variants). The imperial armies were organized in two large groups of armies called the Two Commands (*erh ssu* 二司): the Palace Command (*tien-ch'ien shih-wei ssu* 殿前侍衛司), which played the major role in actually defending the capital and the palace, and the Metropolitan Command (*shih-wei ch'in-chün ma-pu ssu* 侍衛親軍馬步司), which was heavily involved in overseeing the Prefectural Armies (*hsiang-ping* 廂兵). In the middle of the eleventh century the Metropolitan Command was divided into a Metropolitan Cavalry Command (*ma-chün ssu* 馬軍司) and a Metropolitan Infantry Command (*pu-chün ssu*

步軍司); they and the Palace Command were then commonly referred to as the Three Capital Guards (*san wei* 三衛). Each of the two and then three commands was directly headed by a Commander-in-chief (*tu chih-hui shih* 都指揮使), several Commanders (*chih-hui shih*), and various other officers.

Prefectural armies, like the imperial armies, were made up of career professionals. They were scattered throughout the empire in garrisons, controlled by prefectural-level Commanders-in-chief (*tu chih-hui shih*) and subordinate officers. The best quality prefectural soldiers were routinely transferred into the units of the metropolitan commands, and soldiers in the imperial armies who grew old, became disabled, or became otherwise unsatisfactory were routinely transferred to prefectural units. The prefectural armies as a whole were not very reliable fighting units. They were commonly employed at menial labor and in general were less well treated than the imperial armies. Their soldiers often had military insignia tattooed on their faces, at least partly to discourage desertion.

The local militia (*hsiang-ping* 鄉兵) was a mixture of paid recruits and unpaid part-time soldiers provided by the villages and other local population organizations supervised by District Magistrates. The reform program of Wang An-shih in the 1070s included a plan to make the local militia units more efficient and ultimately to use their members in place of the costly, arrogant, often mutinous, and by no means fully effective professionals of the prefectural and imperial armies. Wang's effort was not successful and was quickly abandoned, partly because militiamen seldom wished to serve far from home and partly because careerists resisted being displaced.

In the confused withdrawal of the Sung government from North China in 1127, military organization was changed repeatedly, and irregular, semiofficial defense forces were raised in many areas. An emergency Imperial Defense Command (*yü-ying ssu* 御營司) was set up in the South to give overall direction to the remaining regular soldiery, now entitled the Five Inspired Armies (*shen-wu wu chün* 神武五軍). In 1130 conditions had stabilized enough to permit the Imperial Defense Command to be ab-

sorbed into the regular, transplanted Bureau of Military Affairs, and in 1131 the Five Inspired Armies were redesignated the Four Field Defense Armies (*hsing-ying ssu hu-chün* 行營四護軍); one of the four, the Central Defense Army (*chung hu-chün* 中護軍), was assigned to the central government's Palace Command. In 1141 the government ordered all the irregular defense forces that had sprung up, generally called Pacification Commissions (*hsüan-wei ssu* 宣慰司), to be regularized and placed under the control of the Bureau of Military Affairs, and such a reorganization had apparently been completed by about 1148. These forces were left in their original locations, however, and were given official names like the Palace Army Detached at such-and-such Prefecture (*chu-cha . . . chou yü-ch'ien chün* 駐箚 . . . 州御前軍). Their irregular commanders were removed, and the units came firmly under the control of the central government; but they were not made part of the Three Capital Guards (*san wei*) system. The importance of what remained of the original imperial armies organization consequently declined, and its soldiers were reduced to the status of menials doing labor and domestic service in the Southern Sung capital at Hangchow. To the end of the dynasty, the new professionals of the scattered palace armies in the prefectures were the principal Sung fighting force.

Since the Sung dynasty was on the defensive against northern invaders throughout its history, it maintained very large numbers of professional soldiers. The total strength of the imperial and prefectural armies exceeded 1,000,000 by the middle of the eleventh century, and similar strength was maintained throughout the Southern Sung era. In practice, reasonably effective combat-ready troops could hardly have made up half of the total at any time.

Sung Armies (*chün*) of all kinds theoretically comprised 2,500 men each, divided into five Regiments (*ying* 營 in garrison, *chen* 陣 on campaign) of 500 men each. The basic organizational unit was the Company (*tui* 隊), which seems to have varied in size between 25 and 50 men. The ideal sought in Wang An-shih's abortive reforms was a basic combat team consisting of one cavalryman, one archer, and three crossbowmen.

Sung was China's first dynasty to include a substantial naval arm in its regular military organization. In Northern Sung times every circuit was expected to maintain a fleet. Soon after the dynasty retreated into South China two large fleets were created to patrol the Yangtze and Huai Rivers, and eventually every prefecture was ordered to establish a fleet.

Personnel Administration

The aspect of Sung government that most confuses modern students is unquestionably the complexity of Sung personnel administration techniques. In no other time did Chinese governments manipulate their officials so flexibly, with the result that the many titles a man bore usually obscured what his actual function was and, conversely, his functional assignment often had little relevance to his rank or salary level.

Varieties of official titles. Sung made use of twelve grades of noble titles (*chüeh* 爵), which were almost automatically assigned to all males of the imperial family and sometimes were awarded to specially favored officials. Noble titles carried with them state-paid emoluments and various privileges, but they did not of themselves give one any governmental authority.

Merit titles (*hsün* 勳) of the T'ang type were entirely honorary and were in twelve ranks (*chuan* 轉). Each rank conveyed a special title, most commonly Commandant (*wei* 尉) with varying prefixes. In a departure from the T'ang system, Sung did not award merit titles for military achievements. Sung merit titles were earned automatically by achieving specified rank status in the regular officialdom. Whether or not merit titles were conferred on persons outside government service is not clear.

A man's titular office (*kuan* 官) in Sung times indicated his position in the regular, formal hierarchy of offices and originally determined his rank status and basic salary and allowances. For the first century or so of the Sung period, however, this titular office was almost never more than nominal. In those relatively rare cases in which an official actually performed the functions associated with his titular office, his official designation normally specified that he "performed his titular function" (*shou pen-kuan* 守本官).

Titular offices were distributed in nine ranks (*p'in* 品), each divided into two or four classes (*chieh* 階, *teng* 等). Until about 1080, the status of officials was graded even more finely. Protocol lists were regularly issued showing all offices in the titular hierarchy in the order of their prestige. It was thus possible to know how the officials in any single rank category stood in relation to one another—that in 1038, for example, the Chief Minister of the Court of the Imperial Stud (*t'ai-p'u ssu ch'ing*) took precedence over the Chief Minister of the Court of Judicial Review (*ta-li ssu ch'ing*), though the two officials were both of rank 5.

Titular officials were classified in still another way, into three groups: court officials (*ch'ao-kuan* 朝官), capital officials (*ching-kuan* 京官), and all others, called Selectmen (*hsüan-jen* 選人). It made little difference whether one's titular office was located close to the court, in the capital, or elsewhere; titular Prefects (*tz'u-shih*), for example, were classified as court officials. The classification was a matter of prestige, an echo of the old quasi-official categories "pure" (*ch'ing* 清) and "impure" (*cho* 濁) that had emerged in the Era of Division long before. The "court" and "capital" offices of Sung times were career ladders that officials climbed systematically, rung by rung, to ever more prestigious and influential positions; and men rarely moved into a high-ranking position without having served in what were by custom the approved prerequisite positions. It was not demeaning for an official serving in the capital to be promoted to a prefectural position, as was often the case in other periods; in fact, his prefectural service might be a necessary and desirable step up the career ladder into the highest-ranking positions in the capital.

Although in early Sung times titular offices determined rank status, the old T'ang-style prestige titles (*san-kuan* 散官) were also perpetuated. As in T'ang times, there were 29 such titles, mostly Grand Masters (*ta-fu* 大夫) and Court Gentlemen (*lang* 郎) with varying prefixes; and the titles were graded so that they corresponded precisely to the ranks and classes of the titular offices. Thus an early Sung official was likely to be identified formally, in order, by his merit title (*hsün*), then his prestige title (*san-kuan*), and then his titular post (*kuan*), although none of these was likely to have anything to do with the functions he actually performed.

In addition, an official might have what was technically called an assignment (*chih* 職). This could be at least a quasiofficial duty assignment, such as being some sort of Academician (*hsüeh-shih*), but for the most part such assignments were as nominal as the titular offices and served merely as additional honorary recognition. What really mattered in terms of functions was an official's commission or duty assignment (*ch'ai-ch'ien* 差遣). Whether or not he had an "assignment," almost every official had a commission, and the commission specified his duties. Since commissions were not ranked in any formal way, the system allowed the utmost flexibility in the use of an individual official's talents, so that a titular court official of very high rank could be dispatched to fill a lower-ranking post, for example, as an ad hoc Manager of the Affairs of a District, or conversely an official of relatively low rank but recognized talent could be put to work in a higher-ranking post than he technically deserved. Another element of flexibility was added by the fact that, whereas appointments to titular offices were generally for three-year terms, an official could be commissioned on an open-ended basis, for as long or as short a period as circumstances warranted. If a commission should endure for many years, the appointee's titular, merit, and prestige status categories could all change on schedule nevertheless, so that his opportunities for increases in salary and allowances were not jeopardized.

Through most of the Northern Sung period, in sum, officials were formally identified in very complex ways, for example, as Pillar of State (merit title), Grand Master for Splendid Happiness (prestige title), Hanlin Academician (nominal assignment), Minister of Justice (titular office), and Manager of the Affairs of such-and-such District (commission and actual function), the complex romanization of the whole being *chu-kuo kuang-lu ta-fu han-lin hsüeh-shih hsing-pu shang-shu chih . . . hsien*.

Since titular offices (*kuan*) among other things determined each official's basic salary and allowances, they were commonly referred to in Northern Sung times as salary ranks (*chi-lu chieh* 寄祿階) or salary offices (*chi-lu kuan* 寄祿官). In the 1080s the term prestige title (*san-kuan*)

was abolished in favor of the term salary office (*chi-lu kuan*). The categories were reduced from 29 to 24; then in the Southern Sung era they were increased to 40, distributed among the titular office ranks, which had been reduced to 18 by the abandonment of the earlier division of rank categories into grades (*teng*). Meantime, with the regularization of government beginning in 1080, titular offices generally regained status as functional offices, at least in the central government. During Southern Sung, therefore, commissions were less common than before, and officials more often did what their titular offices implied that they did; but basic salaries and allowances were no longer based on titular office status. They were based entirely on the former prestige titles, now called salary offices. If an appointee's titular and salary offices did not correspond in rank, then he was designated an acting appointee to the titular office (*hsing* 行 as a prefix if the titular post was higher, *shou* 守 or *shih* 試 as a prefix if the titular post was lower). As in earlier periods, appointments to most offices were probationary (*ch'üan* 權) for short periods.

In Sung times military officers and civil officials were not considered significantly different in status. The appointments of military officers followed the same complicated patterns just described; military and civil titles are intermixed on the Northern Sung protocol lists mentioned above; and it was not uncommon for men to transfer from one service to the other.

Recruitment. The process of recruiting officials was also more varied and complex than in previous times. It included all the traditional forms. For example, graduates of the technical schools supervised by the Directorate of Education seem commonly to have moved directly into low-ranking posts as technicians. The graduates of the National University's Superior College (*shang-she*) were ranked in three categories. The best graduates were sent to the general central administration for prompt appointment, the next-best were given the same status as passers of the recruitment examinations at the capital, and the rest were eligible to compete in the capital examinations without any other qualification. Men could be transferred to the civil service from the military service without much ado, and others could become officials by promotion out of the ranks of subofficial functionaries (men "outside official status," *liu-wai* 流外, or "not yet of official status," *wei ju liu* 未入流). Occasionally men entered service directly on the recommendation of local authorities, although without further qualifications their prospects for good careers were dim except in the very earliest Sung years. Also, the traditional protection privileges (*yin* 蔭) that enabled established officials to place one or more sons directly in official status were perpetuated and greatly extended, so that active officials could obtain official status for ever larger numbers of clients—for collateral relatives as well as direct heirs, for friends, and even for personal servants. It has been estimated that as many as half of all Sung officials could have originally entered service (*ch'u-shen* 出身) by this means.

For all this, however, Sung is renowned as the great age of personnel recruitment based on scholastic merit, and in Sung times the competitive written examinations were indeed more open, prestigious, and productive than ever before.

There were two systems of personnel recruitment by examinations, special and regular. The special, irregular recruitment (*chih-chü* 制舉) system was of lesser significance, though it had some interesting and important aspects. It involved examinations of many different sorts intended to seek out men of particular prescribed talents or moral qualities; the examinations were given irregularly on imperial order to candidates specially nominated by prefectural authorities. A man who had already passed the regular examinations and was an established official could apply to participate in certain special examinations, and passing gave his career a significant boost; passing a special examination seems at times to have been prerequisite to being made an Academician. In general, however, the special examinations do not seem to have been a productive way of recruiting new officials.

Sung began with a regular recruitment (*k'o-chü* 科舉) system that perpetuated the T'ang pattern of examinations conferring various types of "doctoral" degrees, then developed it into a two-stage and finally a three-stage process. The first stage was a qualifying examination (*chieh-shih* 解試) given in every prefectural city. How

men qualified to participate is not wholly clear; it is likely the examinations were not open to all who wished to participate but required nominations by local school administrators or other local dignitaries. Large numbers competed, however, and those deemed acceptable by the prefectural officials who served as examiners could proceed to the dynastic capital for the next stage of examinations.

Metropolitan examinations (*sheng-shih* 省試) at the capital were supervised by special, ad hoc groups of Examination Administrators (*chih kung-chü* 知貢舉) until the 1080s, and thereafter by the Ministry of Rites (*li-pu*). Examinees normally spent three full days writing their examination papers, spaced over a week. As in the prefectural examinations, they chose one of many varieties of examinations—on the Confucian classics, on selected historical texts, on ritual texts, on the law code, and so forth. By far the most esteemed examination was that leading to the degree Presented Scholar (*chin-shih* 進士), which originally emphasized literary ability but eventually, after reforms by Wang An-shih, was a relatively balanced test of literary ability, understanding of the classics, and the ability to apply classical precepts and historical precedents in discussions of practical governmental problems. The categories of degrees conferred were generally known as the Presented Scholar and "other examination" (*chu-k'o* 諸科) degrees.

The third stage of the examination process, introduced in 975, was the palace examination (*tien-shih* 殿試 and variants). This was imposed as a check on the validity and quality of the metropolitan examination and was theoretically, and sometimes in fact, conducted by the Emperor in person. After the palace examination all passers were listed in a straight-line order of quality, broken into broad categories (called *chia* 甲). The very best examinees were granted their degrees with honors (*chi-ti* 及第); the next-best with qualification to enter service (*ch'u-shen* 出身); and the rest with the notation that they shared in being qualified to enter service (*t'ung ch'u-shen* 同出身). The man whose name headed the list, besides being, for example, a Presented Scholar with Honors (*chin-shih chi-ti*), was called the Principal Graduate (*chuang-yüan* 狀元); and all concurrent graduates were thereafter referred to as graduates on the list headed by his name.

The T'ang doctoral examinations had been given annually. In the earliest Sung years examinations were not given on a prescribed schedule, although the annual ideal remained. Beginning in 1067, however, the whole system of regular recruitment examinations was placed on a three-year cycle, which characterized the system through the remainder of the Sung era and under later dynasties. The Sung system on average produced more than 200 doctoral graduates a year (more than 600 per examination), a substantially larger number than in any other dynasty, earlier or later. The number of graduates was perhaps sufficient to provide nearly half of all active Sung officials. Moreover, the Presented Scholar degree was held in such esteem that after the earliest Sung decades no one gained important status in government without having entered service in this fashion.

As compared with the civil service, admission to the Sung corps of military officers seems always to have been more dominated by hereditary privilege and otherwise more open to ad hoc appointments justified by demonstrated ability, usually by promotion from the lesser ranks of the military. Recruitment examinations for the military service (*wu-k'o* 武科) were also offered, however. They emphasized competitive demonstrations of ability in horsemanship and archery but in addition required some acquaintance with traditional writings that were considered military classics.

Appointments. In Sung, in a departure from T'ang practice, men who had entered service (*ch'u-shen*) were in general appointed to appropriate offices almost immediately, and waiting periods between appointments were not long. One consequence was that in time the Sung government had an overabundance of active officials, and complaints arose about the cost of supporting a large officialdom inflated by men who had only nominal functions.

The nature of an official's first appointment—indeed, of his whole career pattern—was very significantly influenced by the manner in which he had entered service. Presented Scholars generally got the best initial appointments, got the quickest promotions, and eventually moved into the most prestigious posts. Career progress,

however, was influenced by other factors as well. For one thing, annual merit ratings (*k'ao* 考) given by administrative superiors went into the files of the Bureau of Personnel Evaluation (*shen-kuan yüan*) or, after 1080, the Ministry of Personnel (*li-pu*), along with irregular evaluations submitted by others, and were taken into account when an "evaluation for reassignment" (*mo-k'an* 磨勘) was undertaken, normally at the end of each three-year term. Passing one of the special recruitment examinations mentioned above also earned special credit in the evaluation process. In the first Sung century, in addition, a man's progress up the career ladder came to be heavily dependent on the accumulation in his dossier of "guarantees" (*pao* 保) by his peers. These were recommendations that officials of designated categories were often—regularly or irregularly and variably in number—required to submit about men of their acquaintance, to the detriment of their own careers if their protégés did not perform adequately. By the middle of the eleventh century this sponsorship system had become very complicated, with rules specifying precisely how many guarantees from what kinds and ranks of officials were prerequisite to a man's being appointed to a particular office. Sponsorship served its purpose, yielding a harvest of high-ranking officials who as a group were among the most brilliant, most dedicated, and boldest statesmen of all Chinese history. The system was cumbersome, however, and after 1080 it gave way to a more bureaucratically satisfactory system of promotions based primarily on manner of entry into service, seniority, and regular merit ratings. Guaranteed recommendations were subsequently not systematically employed in personnel administration, although they were sporadically called for in special circumstances.

Another rare if not unique aspect of Sung personnel administration was that officials were free to nominate themselves for certain kinds of special treatment, and that such self-nominations were dealt with sympathetically and generously. For example, whenever any official believed he was qualified for promotion, he could request evaluation for reassignment (*mo-k'an*). Officials who for whatever reasons wished to escape the problems of active duty could request what was called a temple salary (*tz'u-lu* 祠祿)—that is, appointment to a sinecure as state Supervisor (*t'i-chü* 提舉 and variants) of a Taoist temple or monastery. Also, senior officials in capital ser-vice often sought respite in their later years by nominating themselves to be Prefects of rela-tively obscure and untroublesome prefectures.

Official salaries and allowances. Sung of-ficials were paid money salaries ranging from 400,000 coins (300,000 after 1080) down to 300 coins a month, depending, at first, on the ranks of their titular offices (*kuan*) and, later, on their salary offices (*chi-lu kuan*). Before 1080 these salaries were paid one third in coins and two thirds in other commodity equivalents. There-after they were nominally paid entirely in money, but especially in Southern Sung times the money was paper currency, which steadily declined in real value in the inflationary late Sung decades.

This basic pay was supplemented by duty pay (*chih-ch'ien* 職錢), which varied from 60,000 to 16,000 coins a month (or equivalents) depend-ing on the importance of each official's func-tional duty, whether or not his status was pro-bationary, and whether his basic rank was higher or lower than the rank of the office to which he was assigned for duty. In lieu of this duty pay, officials serving outside the capital received supplementary income from office land (*chih-t'ien* 職田) income, which was theoretically paid in grain on an annual schedule and was based on the state's rent revenues from agricultural tracts set aside for that purpose.

All officials were further entitled to regular allowances of goods such as clothing, fuel, and writing materials—and, most importantly, a basic grain allowance varying with ranks from 200 bushels to one bushel a month.

Liao and Chin

LIAO, 916-1125

CHIN, 1115-1234

The Liao state of the Khitan (*Ch'i-tan*) people and the Chin state of the Jurchen people, which successively dominated China's northern frontier from the end of T'ang to the late decades of Southern Sung, combined tribal elements with Chinese institutions patterned after those inherited from T'ang and modified by Sung. Both regimes were highly militarized, and in their encroachments on traditional Chinese territory they imposed on their Chinese subjects the humiliating and often cruel conditions of a military occupation. But both paid lip service to traditional Chinese principles of government and gave some Chinese opportunities to serve as government officials. In neither of these alien regimes was the borrowed Chinese official nomenclature fully understood; and it is clear from the descriptions of these regimes left to us that the Chinese writers did not fully understand the alien institutional usages. Such confusion on both sides requires that modern scholars exercise special caution in dealing with Liao and Chin nomenclature.

Liao

Liao incorporated modern Manchuria, eastern Mongolia, and a northern zone of modern Hopei and Shansi Provinces, including modern Peking. This large area was divided into five Circuits (*tao* 道), each governed from a Capital (*ching* 京): the Supreme Capital (*Shang-ching* 上京) in modern Jehol, the Eastern (*tung* 東) Capital in the area of Liao-yang in Manchuria, the Central (*chung* 中) Capital in southern Jehol, the Southern (*nan* 南) Capital at modern Peking, and the Western (*hsi* 西) Capital near Ta-t'ung of modern Shansi.

Each Liao capital, and the circuit under its jurisdiction, had a combined civil and military administration. All circuits except that dominated by the Supreme Capital were under the control of Regents (*liu-shou* 留守), who were members of the imperial clan. They were normally assisted by two Grand Councilors (*tsai-hsiang* 宰相), a military Commander-in-chief (*tu tsung-kuan* 都總管), an Inspector-in-chief (*tu yü-hou* 都虞侯), and some sort of fiscal official—a Tax Commissioner (*hu-pu shih* 戶部使) at the Eastern Capital, a Revenue Commissioner (*tu-chih shih* 度支使) at the Central Capital, a Finance Commissioner (*san-ssu shih* 三司使) and also a Fiscal Commissioner (*chuan-yün shih* 轉運使) at the Southern Capital, and an Accounting Commissioner (*chi-ssu* 計司) at the Western Capital.

The immediate environs of each capital constituted a Superior Prefecture (*fu* 府), over which the Regent concurrently presided as Governor (*yin* 尹). The rest of the circuit included a few other Superior Prefectures with Governors and some Military Prefectures (*chün* 軍), but was mostly made up of ordinary Prefectures (*chou* 州). The Prefectures were further differentiated into five categories depending on the designations of their heads as Military Commissioners (*chieh-tu shih* 節度使), Surveillance Commissioners (*kuan-ch'a shih* 觀察使), Military Training Commissioners (*t'uan-lien shih* 團練使), Defense Commissioners (*fang-yü shih* 防禦使), or plain Prefects (*tz'u-shih* 刺史). In all five categories, prefectures were further graded as large (*shang* 上), middle (*chung* 中), and small (*hsia* 下).

Prefectures were in turn divided into Districts (*hsien* 縣) headed by Magistrates (*ling* 令). On the same level of the administrative hierarchy, but not subject to District Magistrates, were walled settlements (*ch'eng* 城) and forts (*pao* 堡).

This generally Chinese-like pattern of organization, which was particularly well suited to a sedentary population, existed alongside, and was partially intermixed with, a decidedly non-Chinese structure of tribal organization, into which the Khitan themselves fitted, together with allied or subjugated nomadic groups of other ethnic identities. Their principal unit was an *ordo* (the Chinese rendered the sound as *wo-lu-to* 斡魯朵 and translated the word as *kung* 宮), from which the modern English word horde is derived. In Khitan usage, the *ordo* was the camp of a chief, including all his entourage; the group moved wherever he moved. After his death, *ordo* designated both his tomb and its attendants, his former followers. Each Liao ruler created a new *ordo*, and it survived him as a living, fighting group under a Commandant (*t'i-hsia-ssu* 提轄司).

The Khitan as a nation consisted of many kinship groups or tribes (*pu-tsu* 部族). Originally all Khitan seem to have been divided for administration into 10 tribes, but the number fluctuated and ultimately rose to a total of 44, 34 of them inside the Liao state and 10 outside it in allied or subjugated territories. Each tribe was headed by a Grand Prince (*ta-wang* 大王, originally called *i-li-chin* 夷離堇), apparently assisted by a Tribal Judge (*i-li-pi* 夷離畢), a Counselor (*yü-yüeh* 于越), and a Ritualist (*ti-lieh-ma-tu* 敵烈麻都). Tribes were divided into subtribes (*shih-lieh* 石烈), each headed by a Tribal Judge, and for military purposes were organized into armies called *t'e-man* 特滿, a term literally denoting 10,000 men, with variable designations for Generals (e.g., *hsiang-wen* 詳穩), all possibly derived from the Chinese title *chiang-chün* 將軍.

Tribal armies (*pu-tsu chün* 部族軍) were apparently organized territorially into Routes (*lu* 路), with supreme leaders whose variable designations the Chinese rendered as Campaign Commander (*chao-t'ao shih* 招討使), Army Commander (*t'ung-chün shih* 統軍使), Tribal Chief (*tu pu shu-ssu* 都部署司), and variants. At times overall control of the tribal forces seems to have been assigned to a Supreme Marshal of the Empire (*t'ien-hsia ping-ma tu yüan-shuai* 天下兵馬都元帥).

The dualistic nature of the Liao administrative structure most clearly appeared in the central government at the Supreme Capital in Jehol. Here there were two distinct structures, a Northern Administration (*pei-mien* 北面), which administered the Khitan and other non-Chinese tribes, and a Southern Administration (*nan-mien* 南面), which administered the sedentary peoples in the state, notably the subjugated Chinese of northern Hopei and Shansi.

The Northern Administration was in effect the Emperor's personal *ordo,* and many personages holding office in it followed the Emperor in regular, extended sojourns at various seasonal camps (*na-po* 捺鉢) in the mountains, on riverbanks, or on the steppes. The Northern Administration was a confusing mixture of Chinese-like and non-Chinese offices, further confused by a secondary dualism of Northern and Southern Establishments (*yüan* 院) within the Northern Administration itself. Why the Northern Administration was divided into these two Establishments or what the functional differences between them were is not clear.

Another thing that is not clear is the Liao system of ranks, but it appears that the most notable dignitaries of the Northern Administration were a Grand Counselor (*ta yü-yüeh* 大于越) and a Counselor (*yü-yüeh*), both no doubt quasi-honorary. The principal functioning agencies were two Bureaus of Military Affairs (*shu-mi yüan* 樞密院), a northern one that controlled military affairs and a southern one that controlled civil affairs. Lesser officials, all in northern and southern pairs, were two Grand Councilors (*tsai-hsiang* 宰相), two Grand Princes (*ta-wang*), and two Court Ceremonial Commissioners (*hsüan-hui shih* 宣徽使). The Northern Administration also included, apparently unidentified with either the Northern or the Southern Establishment, a Grand Clansman (*ta t'i-yin* 大惕隱) to look after affairs of the imperial clan, a Tribal Judge (*i-li-pi*), a Ritualist (*ti-lieh-ma-tu*), and numerous specialized offices charged with the care of the various dignitaries of the imperial clan, its herds and stables, and various other matters.

The Southern Administration of the central government had Three Preceptors (*san shih* 三師) and Three Dukes (*san kung* 三公), honorary dignitaries of the Chinese tradition; a Bureau of

Military Affairs (*shu-mi yüan*); Three Departments (*san sheng* 三省), as in T'ang consisting of the Secretariat (*chung-shu sheng* 中書省), the Chancellery (*men-hsia sheng* 門下省), and the Department of State Affairs (*shang-shu sheng* 尚書省), with six subordinate Ministries (*pu* 部); a Censorate (*yü-shih t'ai* 御史臺), Hanlin Academy (*han-lin yüan* 翰林院), Historiography Institute (*kuo-shih yüan* 國史院), and Court Ceremonial Institute (*hsüan-hui yüan* 宣徽院); and Courts (*ssu* 寺) and Directorates (*chien* 監) of traditional Chinese sorts.

Dominant personnel in both the Northern and the Southern Administration and in all agencies of territorial administration were Khitan of the tribal aristocracy. There seems to have been some social mobility based on individual competence among the Khitan, but many men simply inherited their positions. Chinese subjects were allowed to hold positions in the Southern Administration and in some cases even in the Northern Administration, as well as in territorial units in sedentary zones. Recruitment examinations for Chinese were conducted very irregularly, in sequence at the district, prefecture, and capital levels; but candidates and graduates were few. Most Chinese officeholders seem to have won their places as clients of influential Khitan aristocrats or, no doubt to a lesser extent, by the traditional Chinese protection privilege (*yin* 蔭) that enabled active officials to raise one or more of their sons to official status.

Chin

The Jurchen people admired Chinese culture more than the Khitan did and eventually became far more Sinicized. Their Chin state consequently grew into something more like a Chinese state than Liao was, especially after major reorganizations in 1138 and 1156. Nevertheless, it was, like Liao, essentially a military occupation regime in which the Jurchen tribal aristocracy was always dominant.

Before the Jurchen's overthrow of Liao in 1125, which led them on into a stable occupation of the whole North China Plain between 1127 and 1142, they were organized into tribal units of 100 families each under a hereditary chief called a *mou-k'o* 謀克, whom the Chinese re-

ferred to as a Company Commander (*po-hu* 百戶). Ten such units, nominally totaling 1,000 families, constituted the jurisdiction of a hereditary *meng-an* 猛安, whom the Chinese referred to as a Battalion Commander (*ch'ien-hu* 千戶). Leadership of larger groups was entrusted by the Jurchen Khan to hereditary nobles collectively called *po-chi-lieh* 勃極烈 (Chief), including a Supreme Chief (*tu po-chi-lieh* 都勃極烈). In 1134, by which time a Chinese-style government was coming into being, the whole stratum of *po-chi-lieh* was abolished. Nevertheless, Jurchen groups under hereditary *meng-an* and *mou-k'o*, like the later Manchu Banners, remained separate communities of Jurchen farmer-warriors or herder-warriors scattered as military occupation garrisons throughout the Chin state, not subject to the regular local authorities.

At its full extent, the Chin state incorporated Manchuria, most of Mongolia, and North China (excluding modern Kansu and western Shensi) down to a line approximately along the Huai River and the Tsinling Mountains. It was divided into nineteen Routes (*lu* 路), of which five were governed from Capitals (*ching* 京): a Supreme Capital (*Shang-ching* 上京) at Hui-ning in the north of modern Manchuria; an Eastern (*tung*) Capital at Liao-yang in southern Manchuria; a Western (*hsi*) Capital at Ta-t'ung in Shansi; Yen-ching (modern Peking); and Pien-ching (modern Kaifeng). At an early time, before Yen-ching and Pien-ching were made capitals, there was a Northern Capital in modern Jehol and a Central Capital (*Chung-tu* 中都) at modern Peking. The actual imperial capital was moved from northern Manchuria to Yen-ching in 1153, signaling a major step in the Sinicization of the Jurchen. In 1214, under pressure from the Mongols to the north, the Chin capital was moved farther southward, to Kaifeng.

The fourteen Routes not administered from capitals were controlled by Area Commands (*tsung-kuan fu* 總管府), and the capitals other than the site of the imperial court were each governed, as in Liao times, by Regents (*liu-shou* 留守). The staffs of a Route normally included a Fiscal Commissioner (*chuan-yün shih* 轉運使), who was in general charge of fiscal affairs, and a Judicial Commissioner (*t'i-hsing shih* 提刑使) or a Surveillance Commissioner (*an-ch'a shih*

按察使). One or another such Commissioner was often concurrently the Military Commissioner (*an-fu shih* 安撫使) or Agricultural Development Commissioner (*ch'üan-nung shih* 勸農使) of the Route.

Each Route supervised a prefecture-level jumble of agencies—Superior Prefectures (*san-fu* 散府), Defense Commands (*chieh-chen* 節鎮), Defense Commanderies (*fang-yü chün* 防禦郡), ordinary Commanderies (*tz'u-shih chün* 刺史郡), Military Prefectures (*chün* 軍), and plain Prefectures (*chou* 州). All such agencies were often headed by Military Commissioners (*chieh-tu shih* 節度使), Surveillance Commissioners (*kuan-ch'a shih* 觀察使), Defense Commissioners (*fang-yü shih* 防禦使), or officials of comparable status.

When the Jurchen began campaigning into the North China Plain they set up a special forward headquarters at modern Peking to direct the war against Sung, and from 1123 till 1140 this was the effective regional administration over the former Sung territories in North China. For this the Jurchen borrowed the Sung designation Bureau of Military Affairs (*shu-mi yüan* 樞密院) and gave it a staff of various Marshals (*yüan-shuai* 元帥), Vice Marshals (*fu yüan-shuai* 副元帥), Army Supervisors (*chien-chün* 監軍), and the like. In 1153 the new central government was installed at Peking. Meantime forward control of the expanded Chin domain in North China had been assured by the establishment in 1140 of a Branch (*hsing-t'ai* 行臺) Department of State Affairs at the old Sung capital, Kaifeng; but it disappeared when Yen-ching became the new imperial capital in the 1150s.

By then the Chin central government had taken on a durable Chinese look. There were the traditional honorary titles of the Three Preceptors (*san shih* 三師) and the Three Dukes (*san kung* 三公). The general civil administration was dominated by the traditional Three Departments (*san sheng* 三省). The Secretariat (*chung-shu sheng* 中書省) and the Chancellery (*men-hsia sheng* 門下省) of the Chinese tradition were never fully developed and were abolished in 1156, leaving the Department of State Affairs (*shang-shu sheng* 尚書省) and its six subordinate Ministries (*pu* 部) in full charge of general administration. The Department of State Affairs was headed by a traditional Director (*ling* 令), and

among his subordinates were officials bearing contemporary Sung titles, or variants of them, who in comparison with their Sung counterparts seem strangely out of place in the official hierarchy: for example, Grand Councilor (*ch'eng-hsiang* 丞相), Manager of Governmental Affairs (*p'ing-chang cheng-shih* 平章政事), and Participant in Determining Governmental Matters (*ts'an-chih cheng-shih* 參知政事).

In the mature Chin government the Bureau of Military Affairs (*shu-mi yüan*) was headed by a Commissioner (*shih* 使) and was apparently responsible only for military administrative matters. The direction of military campaigns was the responsibility of a Chief Military Command (*tu yüan-shuai fu* 都元帥府) headed by a Commander-in-chief (*tu yüan-shuai*). There is some confusion about this nomenclature, however; for the Bureau of Military Affairs was reportedly transformed into a Military Command (*yüan-shuai fu*) in 1206, presumably subordinate to the Chief Military Command, and then the Chief Military Command was retitled Bureau of Military Affairs two years later.

The rest of the Chin central government was a mixture of Liao and Sung agencies, including a Censorate (*yü-shih t'ai* 御史臺), a Remonstrance Bureau (*chien-yüan* 諫院), a Hanlin Academy (*han-lin hsüeh-shih yüan* 翰林學士院), the usual assortment of specialized Courts (*ssu* 寺) and Directorates (*chien* 監) with some modifications, a Court Ceremonial Institute (*hsüan-hui yüan* 宣徽院), and a Palace Inspectorate-general (*tien-ch'ien tu tien-chien ssu* 殿前都點檢司) in charge of troops in the capital and the palace. For relatively brief periods, separately, there also were such Sung-style agencies as a State Finance Commission (*san ssu* 三司) and a Bureau of Personnel Evaluation (*shen-kuan yüan* 審官院).

Chin adopted many Sung practices in personnel administration. Officials and their offices were all classified into nine ranks (*p'in* 品), each divided into two classes (*teng* 等). Officials were further classified into 42 grades (*chieh* 階) of civil service prestige titles (*san-kuan* 散官), a similar schedule of military prestige titles, and still other schedules for men in different specializations.

Most notably, Chin adopted the mature Sung

civil service recruitment examination system to bring into service the large numbers of educated men needed to help govern the North China masses who came under Jurchen control after 1127. Examinations were offered as early as 1123 and 1124, and beginning in 1129 they were regularly offered in the Sung-style three-year cycle, with sequences of examinations at the district, prefecture, and capital levels. In 1150 a palace examination was added. Jurchen educated in Chinese, eventually including some hereditary *meng-an* and *mou-k'o* aristocrats, flocked to the examinations alongside Chinese applicants. The need for officials remained so great that standards of grading examinations fell to notoriously low levels; it was not uncommon for one in three or even one in two candidates to pass. Degrees as Metropolitan Graduate (*chin-shih* 進士) were handed out freely, as many as 925 at a time; the average per year in Chin times was about 200, nearly as high as the average for the Sung dynasty, which ruled over a much larger population.

Although subject Chinese so recruited gained official appointments easily, a regional quota system generally assured that northerners (principally Jurchen) got easier examinations, passed them more consistently, and got promoted more quickly once in service. Some Chinese rose to high office in Chin times, but Chinese officials in general were discriminated against and sometimes physically abused, so that Jurchen always remained in unquestioned control of all aspects of Chin government.

The Sinicization of Jurchen proceeded so rapidly and extensively that in 1173 a special examination system based on the Jurchen language was instituted in a government effort to preserve the native language and customs. There were few candidates for such examinations and correspondingly few degrees; but those who won the status of Jurchen Metropolitan Graduate, apparently by demonstrating little more than Jurchen literacy, were promoted in service fastest of all.

The top ranks of the Chin government were naturally filled with Jurchen serving by hereditary privilege, sometimes also having won examination degrees. Inheritance of official status and appointment by recommendation were relied on to supplement examinations in the recruitment of Chinese for service.

Yüan

1264-1368

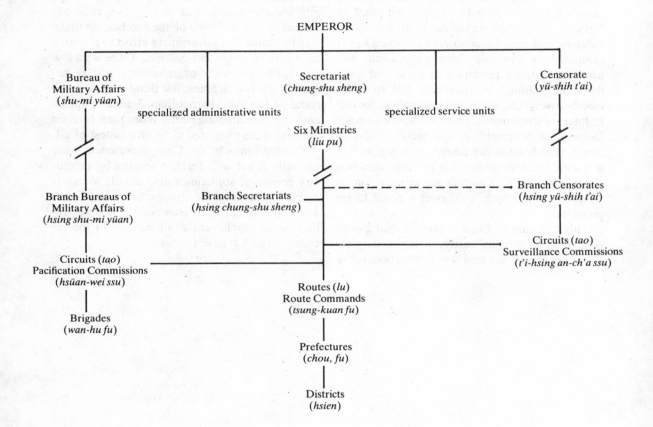

The Mongols, the most successful nomad conquerors of world history and the first aliens to subjugate all Chinese, first assaulted North China in 1212–1213. Thereafter they became overlords of the whole of China in several phases. In 1234 they destroyed the Jurchen Chin regime and won control of all North China. In 1259–1260 Kubilai, suspending his campaign against Southern Sung, returned to the ancestral capital in Outer Mongolia, Karakorum, and made himself Grand Khan. In 1264 he moved his capital to Peking and began a restrained Sinicization of

the Mongol governmental apparatus in China. In 1271, while his generals were still battling Sung armies in the South, he proclaimed the establishment of the Yüan dynasty; and at last, in 1279, his forces wiped out Sung resistance on the south coast, so that China Proper in its entirety was united under one Emperor for the first time since the T'ang era.

Until Kubilai's long reign (1260–1294), the Mongols controlled their subjects in China largely by leaving in place the existing Chin and Sung institutions and superimposing on them varying ad hoc supervisory offices staffed with Mongols or their Central Asian allies. For a time even the collection of Chinese taxes was farmed out to groups of Central Asian fiscal agents. To its end, the Yüan dynasty remained essentially a military occupation, dominated by Mongol nobles who were not always submissive to centralized leadership. Especially after Kubilai's time, real power was wielded by shifting coalitions of Mongol nobles and allied steppe chieftains, Empresses and Empress Dowagers, and Heirs Apparent, some of whom lived on the Mongolian steppes while nominally performing functions in China's government, and all of whom had personal armies and were supported in part by revenues from large land grants in China. Later Yüan Emperors were commonly the puppets of one or another clique of nobles, and sometimes they were deposed or assassinated by rival cliques. The decline and demise of Yüan rule can be blamed very largely on the incessant bickering and struggles for power among the Mongol elite.

It was Kubilai's achievement, during the 1260s and 1270s, to mask the unstable military occupation of China with a façade of Chinese-like institutions, organizing what was, at least from a broad structural point of view, the most centralized and best-articulated government yet developed in China. Thus the Mongols did not maintain a formal dualism in government as the Khitan had done in their Liao empire; but neither did they Sinicize the government as fully as the Jurchen. Users of Yüan materials must consequently be prepared to encounter some curious anomalies, since real authority seldom rested with the official whose title suggested he was in charge, but was usually exercised by some Mongol who remained behind the scenes.

The most common and pervasive example of this Mongol practice was the Yüan system of Overseers (*daruhachi*, transliterated into Chinese as *ta-lu-hua-ch'ih* 達魯花赤 and translated by the Chinese as *chang-yin kuan*, "seal-holding official"). With few exceptions, especially in the highest-ranking offices, almost every civil service agency had its Overseer in addition to its nominal head; and no document of importance issued from such an agency without the Overseer's approval. The Overseer was almost always a Mongol. At the District (*hsien* 縣) level,

for example, the general ideal seems to have been that the Overseer should be a Mongol, the Magistrate (*yin* 尹) a Chinese, and the Vice Magistrate (*ch'eng* 丞) a Moslem—that is, a Central Asian client of the Mongols. Unlike members of the ordinary officialdom, the Overseer often inherited his post directly from his father and had somewhat independent status as a notable in the Mongol military establishment.

The Central Government

The Mongols' early headquarters for East Asian affairs was at K'ai-p'ing in modern Chahar Province. In 1264, when Kubilai established a Chinese-style central government at Peking, K'ai-p'ing was entitled Supreme Capital (*Shang-tu* 上都) and placed under the administration of a Regency (*liu-shou ssu* 留守司). The official name for Peking was Grand Capital (*Ta-tu* 大都); Peking and its environs were administered by a Ta-tu Regency under the supervision of two agencies: a Chief Command (*tu tsung-kuan fu* 都總管府) and a Chief Military Commission (*ping-ma tu chih-hui shih ssu* 兵馬都指揮使司). In Peking Kubilai and his successors played their roles as Emperors with the staffs of palace women and eunuchs that were usual in the Chinese tradition.

The imperial household. The Yüan palace administration at Peking was extraordinarily large and complex. Its most influential unit was the Imperial Bodyguard or *kesig* (*ch'ieh-hsieh* 怯薛), a force of some 10,000 elite hereditary tribal warriors who recognized no superior other than the Emperor, who controlled all access to him, and who abused their authority as they pleased, virtually a law unto themselves. In addition to a host of service agencies that catered to each Emperor's personal needs, the imperial household notably included a Household Service for the Empress (*chung-cheng yüan* 中政院) and a Household Service for the Heir Apparent (*ch'u-cheng yüan* 儲政院), both elaborate complexes of agencies including revenue offices and military units.

In accordance with tribal custom, on the death of each adult Emperor his personal entourage, or *ordo*, including his widow along with her attendants, revenue agents, and military guards, continued in existence, theoretically in perpetuity. For each a special administering Court (*ssu* 寺) was created as something like an extension of the imperial household. Eventually there were six such Courts, beginning with the Court for Shih-tsu's (Kubilai's) Ordo (*ch'ang-hsin ssu* 長信寺), each headed by from four to six Chief Ministers (*ch'ing* 卿).

Nobles and honorary dignitaries. The Yüan nobility consisted of eight ranks (*chüeh*): Prince (*wang* 王, *wei-hsia* 位下), including Imperial Prince (*ch'in-wang* 親王, *yü wei-hsia* 御位下), Commandery Prince (*chün-wang* 郡王), Duke (*kuo-kung* 國公), Commandery Duke (*chün-kung* 郡公), Commandery Marquis (*chün-hou* 郡侯), Commandery Earl (*chün-po* 郡伯), District Viscount (*hsien-tzu* 縣子), and District Baron (*hsien-nan* 縣男). The affairs of each of the major Princes, who eventually numbered 46, were managed by a Princely Establishment (*ch'ang-shih fu* 常侍府).

The nobility was not restricted to the sons of Emperors and their descendants; the chieftains of nomad tribes participating in the original Mongol conquests held noble status, and eventually almost all middle- and high-ranking civil officials automatically earned at least nominal honorific titles of nobility. Noble status was not always hereditary, and for special achievements men could be promoted from one noble rank to another. The original tribal nobles received extensive land grants in China (known by such general terms as *fen-ti* 分地 and *t'ou-hsia* 投下), commonly appointed officials in the areas of their estates, and collected taxes as they pleased from peasants on their assigned lands, although the central government tried to impose standard tax schedules and ultimately to substitute state-paid annual salaries for the land revenues. Most of these land grants were in the North near Peking, but some nobles held tracts in the former Southern Sung domain. Virtually the whole of modern Yunnan province was the hereditary barony of one Mongol family throughout Yüan times, and Tibet was relatively autonomous under the control of two favored families.

The central government proper was nominally headed by nobles holding various hoary Chinese honorary titles, including the Three Dukes (*san kung* 三公)—the Grand Preceptor (*t'ai-shih* 太師), Grand Mentor (*t'ai-fu* 太傅), and Grand Guardian (*t'ai-pao* 太保)—and, in addition, Defender-in-chief (*t'ai-wei* 太尉), Grand Minister of Education (*ta ssu-t'u* 大司徒), and Minister of Education (*ssu-t'u*). These various dignitaries were not always appointed, and even when appointed they were not always active in the sense of having functioning Offices (*fu* 府) and staffs.

The Secretariat. The core unit of the central government was the Secretariat (*chung-shu sheng* 中書省). From time to time it was proposed that a Chancellery (*men-hsia sheng* 門下省) and a Department of State Affairs (*shang-shu sheng* 尚書省) should be activated so as to complete the T'ang-style battery of Three Departments (*san sheng* 三省); and intermittently through some 30 years from the late thirteenth century into the early fourteenth a Department of State Affairs existed alongside the Secretariat. When it existed, the Department was given most of the Secretariat's functions. But in general the Secretariat was the dominant institution of the central government, with overall responsibility for administering the Yüan state.

The Secretariat was nominally headed by a Director (*ling* 令), but in Kubilai's time this position came to be reserved for the Heir Apparent and was therefore no longer a functional position. The most prestigious and influential civil offices, consequently, were the nominal aides to the Director, two Grand Councilors (*tsai-hsiang* 宰相) and their associates, Managers of Governmental Affairs (*p'ing-chang cheng-shih* 平章政事). (Whereas the Chinese traditionally esteemed left over right, the Mongols had reversed values; the Grand Councilor of the Right, for example, was considered the senior.) Although in theory there should have been only two Grand Councilors and four Managers of Governmental Affairs, in fact their numbers fluctuated; at times there were five Grand Councilors.

Internally, the Secretariat did its work primarily through two agencies called the Left Office (*tso-ssu* 左司) and the Right Office (*yu-ssu* 右司), each headed by two Directors (*lang-chung* 郎中). The Left Office incorporated six Sections (*fang* 房) with different functions, which in turn were divided into from two to nine Subsections (*k'o* 科), each with a still more specialized function. The Right Office incorporated three Sections with a total of seventeen Subsections.

Directly subordinate to the Secretariat (or, at times, the Department of State Affairs) were China's traditional Six Ministries (*liu pu* 六部), each headed by three Ministers (*shang-shu* 尙書)—the Ministries of Personnel (*li-pu* 吏部), of Revenue (*hu-pu* 戶部), of Rites (*li-pu* 禮部), of War (*ping-pu* 兵部), of Justice (*hsing-pu* 刑部), and of Works (*kung-pu* 工部). The Ministries were probably less active and influential in the functioning of the Yüan government than the Secretariat's own regular Offices and their subsidiary units. The prescribed functions of the Ministries, at least, seem duplicated and more finely specified in the defined responsibilities of the Sections and Subsections. Moreover, the Ministries were not themselves divided into specialized bureaus.

The Bureau of Military Affairs. The Yüan Emperors controlled the Mongol military establishment through a Bureau of Military Affairs (*shu-mi yüan* 樞密院), headed by up to six Bureau Managers (*chih-yüan* 知院). The Bureau was primarily concerned with administering forces in the Peking area, the Imperial Armies (*ch'in-chün* 親軍). These incorporated both Palace Guards (*su-wei* 宿衛), notably including the largely independent Imperial Bodyguard or *kesig* already mentioned, and Imperial Guards (*shih-wei* 侍衛). The Imperial Guards came to be divided into five large units, each under two or three Chief Military Commissioners (*tu chih-hui shih* 都指揮使)—the Right Guard (*yu-wei* 右衛), the Left Guard (*tso-wei* 左衛), the Center Guard (*chung-wei* 中衛), the Front Guard (*ch'ien-wei* 前衛), and the Rear Guard (*hou-wei* 後衛). The Bureau of Military Affairs also supervised many other military agencies in the Peking area, including the Imperial Armies Support Commission (*wu-wei ch'in-chün tu chih-hui shih ssu* 武衛親軍都指揮使司), headed by one Overseer (*ta-lu-hua-ch'ih*) and three Chief Military Commissioners (*tu chih-hui shih*), which was responsible for the construction, maintenance, and repair of military installations; the Imperial Armies Tactical Defense Commission (*lung-chen wei ch'in-chün tu chih-hui shih ssu* 隆鎮衛親軍都指揮使司), headed by three Chief

Military Commissioners, which actively policed the Peking area and guarded the nearby passes through the Great Wall; two State Farm Brigades (*t'un-t'ien wan-hu fu* 屯田萬戶府), each headed by an Overseer and a Brigade Commander (*wan-hu*), which worked the farmlands set aside in the Peking area for the partial provisioning of the imperial armies; and a Chief Military Command (*ta tu-tu fu* 大都督府) under three Commanders-in-chief (*ta tu-tu*), which controlled notoriously fierce Turkic warriors who served in two Kipchak Guards (*ch'in-ch'a wei* 欽察衛) units, headed by Chief Military Commissioners.

Especially influential and favored Grand Councilors of the Secretariat were occasionally given concurrent supervisory control of the Bureau of Military Affairs, with the title Chief Councilor and Supervisor of Major Military Matters of State (*ch'eng-hsiang lu chün-kuo chung-shih* 丞相錄軍國重事).

The Censorate. The Yüan Censorate (*yü-shih t'ai* 御史臺) was responsible for maintaining disciplinary surveillance over the whole officialdom. For the first time in history, apparently, Censors were empowered to take direct punitive action against certain categories of offenders. In addition, since the Mongols did not establish specialized remonstrance officials of the traditional Chinese sorts, the Censorate was newly authorized to express criticisms of court policies and propose new policies. Because of its expanded functions, and also because the numbers of censorial officials were greater and their ranks higher than in earlier dynasties, the Censorate seems to have had more prestige and influence in the Yüan government than it had ever had before. It was directed by two Censors-in-chief (*yü-shih ta-fu* 御史大夫) with the assistance of two Vice Censors-in-chief (*yü-shih chung-ch'eng* 御史中丞). Two Attendant Censors (*shih yü-shih* 侍御史) and two Secretarial Censors (*chih-shu yü-shih* 治書御史) constituted a kind of headquarters staff. Other censorial officials were divided between two bureaus, a Palace Bureau (*tien-yüan* 殿院) with two Palace Censors (*tien-chung shih yü-shih* 殿中侍御史) and an Investigation Bureau (*ch'a-yüan* 察院) with 32 Investigating Censors (*chien-ch'a yü-shih* 監察御史).

Other central government agencies. Except for the Censorate, the Bureau of Military Affairs, and the numerous military units overseen by the Bureau, governmental agencies at the capital were almost entirely, directly or indirectly, under the control of the Secretariat; and there were hundreds of them. The Ministry of Works alone supervised 52 subordinate agencies, which in turn supervised 44 other agencies. Not only was there in consequence a very large number of officials in the capital; it was a peculiarity of the Yüan government that a high proportion of these officials were of very high rank, in grades 1, 2, and 3.

Service agencies that primarily looked after the needs of the imperial household were extraordinarily numerous. The largest by far was the Palace Provisions Commission (*hsüan-hui yüan* 宣徽院), which directed 28 subordinate agencies in providing food and drink for the palace, attending to the wants of the imperial in-laws and important visitors at court, and supplying and guarding the various Princes. Among the many other service agencies were the Directorate of the Imperial Treasury (*t'ai-fu chien* 太府監), the Imperial Academy of Medicine (*t'ai-i yüan* 太醫院), the Imperial Manufactories Commission (*chiang-tso yüan* 將作院), and the Palace Domestic Service (*shih-cheng fu* 侍正府) with fourteen Attendants-in-chief (*shih-cheng*).

Special advisory agencies included the Hanlin and Historiography Academy (*han-lin hsüeh-shih yüan chien kuo-shih yüan* 翰林學士院兼國史院); the Mongolian Hanlin Academy (*meng-ku han-lin yüan* 蒙古翰林院), which concerned itself with translation work; the Academy of Scholarly Worthies (*chi-hsien yüan* 集賢院), whose three Grand Academicians (*ta hsüeh-shih* 大學士) supervised various state schools and oversaw the Taoist clergy throughout the empire; the Academy in the Hall of Literature (*k'uei-chang ko hsüeh-shih yüan* 奎章閣學士院), which was in effect the Emperor's reference library; the Directorate of Astronomy (*ssu-t'ien chien* 司天監), which prepared the annual state-approved calendar; and the Directorate of Moslem Astronomy (*hui-hui ssu-t'ien chien* 回回司天監), which prepared annual calendars in the Moslem fashion.

Among other notable agencies were the Office for Religious Administration (*ta-hsi tsung-yin yüan* 大禧宗禋院); the Commission for Ritual Observances (*t'ai-ch'ang li-i yüan* 太常禮儀院); the Grand Agricultural Administration (*ta ssu-nung ssu* 大司農司), which promoted agriculture, sericulture, irrigation, famine relief, and local education; the Court of Imperial Armaments (*wu-pei ssu* 武備寺), with 29 subordinate agencies, which produced and issued weapons; the Directorate for the Mongolian Pastures (*ching-cheng chien* 經正監); the High Court of Justice (*ta tsung-cheng fu* 大宗正府), which until about 1312 had judicial jurisdiction over the whole empire; the Commission for Buddhist and Tibetan Affairs (*hsüan-cheng yüan* 宣政院), which in effect governed Tibet through 26 subordinate agencies; and the Commission for the Promotion of Religion (*ch'ung-fu ssu* 崇福司), which seems to have supervised Nestorians, Manichaeans, and other untraditional religious communities in China and had an astonishing total of 72 subordinate agencies scattered throughout the empire.

The message center of the central government was the Bureau of Transmission (*t'ung-cheng yüan* 通政院), through which memorials and petitions passed on their way to the Emperor and imperial proclamations were transmitted to government offices throughout the empire. It was apparently the headquarters of numerous Postal Relay Inspectors (*t'o-t'o-ho-sun* 脫脫禾孫), who supervised the functioning of Postal Relay Stations (*chan* 站, *i* 驛) maintained by the Ministry of War in a system that shuttled official documents rapidly back and forth across China.

Territorial Administration

The Yüan hierarchy of territorial administration units was a complex one, with more tiers of general administration jurisdictions than had ever existed in the past.

Provinces. In Yüan times China's modern administrative division into Provinces (*sheng* 省) began its development. When the Mongols originally brought ever larger regions of China under their control, it was common practice for Grand Councilors to be detached from the Secretariat as ad hoc, temporary regional administrators. Then in Kubilai's reign such temporary arrangements gradually settled into permanent, officially sanctioned patterns; and Branch Secretariats (*hsing chung-shu sheng* 行中書省 or simply *hsing-sheng*) emerged as the Emperor's all-purpose administrative agencies for large areas distant from Peking. Twelve provinces eventually developed, counting the large area directly governed from Peking, which incorporated modern Hopei, Shantung, Shansi, and Inner Mongolia, as a kind of Metropolitan Area (*chih-li* 直隸). The eleven Yüan provinces that were supervised by Branch Secretariats (hence generically known as *hsing-sheng* or *sheng*) were Ling-pei (Outer Mongolia and parts of Siberia), Liao-yang (Manchuria and northern Korea), Honan (Honan and Anhwei), Shensi (modern Shensi), Kansu (modern Kansu), Szechwan (western Szechwan), Hu-Kuang (Hupei, Hunan, Kwangsi, and Kweichow), Kiangsi (Kiangsi and Kwangtung), Chiang-Che (Kiangsu, Chekiang, and Fukien), Yunnan (modern Yunnan and eastern Szechwan), and Cheng-tung. Cheng-tung, meaning "punitive campaign eastward," referred to southern Korea, where Kubilai organized his naval assaults on Japan; after these ended in disasters for the Mongols, the area was left largely in the care of the King of Korea and was more a tributary state than a province.

The Branch Secretariats were at best only rudimentary provincial administrations. Although they were organized on the pattern of the metropolitan Secretariat at Peking, each was normally headed by two Managers of Governmental Affairs (*p'ing-chang cheng-shih*). Occasionally, but not often, one was headed by a Grand Councilor (*ch'eng-hsiang*), and no Branch Secretariat seems ever to have had more than one. Moreover, the Branch Secretariats did not have subordinate Ministries (*pu*), so that the effectiveness of their administration of the large territories they supervised is questionable. They did presumably control various agencies with specialized province-wide jurisdictions or specialized functions—for example, a Supervisorate for Confucian Schools (*ju-hsüeh t'i-chü ssu* 儒學提舉司) in every province; Supervisors of Mongolian Schools (*meng-ku t'i-chü hsüeh-hsiao kuan* 蒙古提舉學校官) in Chiang-Che, Hu-Kuang, and Kiangsi; Maritime Trade Supervisorates (*shih-po t'i-chü ssu* 市舶提舉司) on the

southeast coast in Chiang-Che; a Tea and Salt Monopoly and Tax Transport Commission (*ch'a-yen chuan-yün ssu* 茶鹽轉運司) in Szechwan; a Chief Transport Commission (*tu chuan-yün shih ssu* 都轉運使司) in Chiang-Che, which had a counterpart in the Metropolitan Area around Peking; and Salt Distribution Supervisorates (*yen-k'o t'i-chü ssu* 鹽課提舉司) in a number of areas. The revenue agencies, at least, were probably responsible ultimately to the metropolitan Secretariat, even if indirectly through Branch Secretariats.

On the other hand, it can be argued that the Branch Secretariats were only nominally supervised and coordinated by the metropolitan Secretariat at Peking—that they (and lower-level agencies as well) were the administrative bases from which entrenched Mongol nobles occasionally flouted Peking's authority and became autonomous warlords. In the formal structure of Yüan government, nevertheless, Branch Secretariats were not equal to or independent of the metropolitan Secretariat. Moreover, in some ways they were also subordinated to two types of intermediary agencies whose jurisdictions encompassed several provinces.

One of these agencies was the Branch Bureau of Military Affairs (*hsing shu-mi yüan* 行樞密院). Such Bureaus originated in the same fashion as the Branch Secretariats, to command military operations in specified regions during the protracted Mongol conquest of China, but they were more transitory. They fluctuated in number, had individually designed staffs normally headed by one or two Bureau Managers (*chih-yüan* 知院), and had vaguely defined territorial jurisdictions generally referred to as Regions (*ch'u* 處). When they existed, they presumably controlled military matters that otherwise were controlled by Branch Secretariats. The most durable was the Szechwan Branch Bureau of Military Affairs, headquartered at Chengtu, a forerunner of which was established in 1263 and which apparently lasted until 1338. Other relatively durable counterparts were the Ching-Hu (or Hu-Kuang), the Kiangsi, the Chiang-Huai, and the Ling-pei Branch Bureaus. Beginning in the 1350s, when the Mongols were seriously challenged by Chinese rebel leaders in the Yangtze Valley and elsewhere in the South, new Branch Bureaus of

Military Affairs were created to cope with the troubles—a Huai-nan and Chiang-pei Branch Bureau at Yangchow in 1355, a Chiang-Che Branch Bureau at Hangchow in 1356, a Honan and Shantung Branch Bureau in 1359, and a Fukien and Kiangsi Branch Bureau in 1366. Some of these were no more than nominal organizations that were actually controlled by rebel leaders, who occasionally found it expedient to accept appointments from the desperate Yüan government. As for the earlier period, it is unclear just how firmly the various Branch Bureaus were controlled by the Bureau of Military Affairs in Peking and how seriously they encroached on functions of the Branch Secretariats.

The other type of intermediate agency with specialized functional jurisdiction over several provinces was the Branch Censorate (*hsing yü-shih t'ai* 行御史臺). There were two of these. The first, a western one, was established about 1264 but had something of an intermittent, migratory existence in Shensi, Yunnan, and Szechwan until 1279, when it was permanently established as the Shensi Branch Censorate headquartered in Sian. The other, a Chiang-nan Branch Censorate for the South, was established at Yangchow in 1277 and moved to Hangchow in 1284. Each was headed by a Censor-in-chief and had a staff comparable to that of the metropolitan Censorate at Peking but without Palace Censors; as many as 28 Investigating Censors were authorized for Chiang-nan and 20 for Shensi. The Branch Censorates were explicitly directed to monitor the Branch Secretariats in their vicinities. They and the metropolitan Censorate thus divided Yüan China into three large surveillance spheres; but the Branch Censorates were responsible to the metropolitan Censorate. In 1365, as the dynasty was collapsing, the Chiang-nan Branch Censorate lost contact with various Yüan loyalist agencies in the South, whereupon the metropolitan Censorate set up a short-lived Branch Office (*fen-t'ai* 分臺) in Fukien, where communication with Peking was still maintained by sea.

Circuits. Below the provincial level in the governmental hierarchy were two types of jurisdictions called Circuits (*tao* 道) with agencies that coordinated matters between provincial-level

supervisors and lower-level administrators. In one pattern, provinces were divided into some 60 circuits with general administration or military responsibilities, or a combination of both. In a sense, they were outposts of the various Secretariats and Bureaus of Military Affairs (both metropolitan and branch, in both cases). Their staffs and their agency names varied greatly according to local circumstances. They were generically called Pacification Commissions (*hsüan-wei shih ssu* 宣慰使司), although only six bore this specific designation. In some circuits there was a combined Pacification Commission and Chief Military Command (*hsüan-wei shih ssu tu yüan-shuai fu* 宣慰使司都元帥府), in others a Pacification Commissioner and Concurrent Brigade Commander (*chien kuan-chün wan-hu fu* 兼官軍萬戶府), in others only a Chief Military Command (*tu yüan-shuai fu*) or a plain Military Command (*yüan-shuai fu*), and in still others Pacification Commissions under variant designations (*hsüan-fu ssu* 宣撫司, *an-fu ssu* 安撫司, *chao-t'ao ssu* 招討司).

The other type of circuit agency was the Surveillance Commission (*t'i-hsing an-ch'a ssu* 提刑按察司 until 1291; thereafter *su-cheng lien-fang ssu* 肅政廉訪司). At the fullest extent of the Yüan state, there were 24 such agencies. Each had a staff of censorial officials who monitored the various Pacification Commissions and lower-level administrative agencies in its territorial jurisdiction, and each reported either directly to the metropolitan Censorate or to a designated Branch Censorate any irregularities it discovered in governmental procedures.

Routes, prefectures, and districts. In Yüan times, the Route (*lu* 路) was a stable governmental region governed by one of 185 Route Commands (*tsung-kuan fu* 總管府), which in routine administrative matters seem to have communicated with the Secretariat and its Six Ministries in Peking, either directly or indirectly through an appropriate Branch Secretariat, while also being subject to the supervision of circuit agencies. For each Route Command there was an Overseer and a Commander (*tsung-kuan* 總管). Subordinate officials specialized in such matters as taxes and granaries; Confucian, Mongolian, and sometimes medical education; and the administration of justice and jails. Routes were ranked in two grades, large (*shang* 上) and small (*hsia* 下), depending primarily on whether the registered population exceeded or fell short of 100,000 households.

Below Route Commands in the hierarchy of territorial administration were approximately 400 prefectural-level units of three kinds: up to 33 Superior Prefectures (*fu* 府, *san-fu* 散府) in honored or strategic places, more than 350 ordinary Prefectures (*chou* 州), and four Military Prefectures (*chün* 軍) in frontier zones. Each was headed by an Overseer and a Prefect (*yin* 尹; sometimes *chih-fu* 知府 or *chih-chou*). A few prefectures were "directly attached" (*chih-li* 直隸) prefectures—that is, supervised by a Secretariat rather than by an intermediary Route Command. Ordinary prefectures were classified in three grades: large (*shang*), middle (*chung*), and small (*hsia*), depending on their registered populations. In North China the dividing lines between categories were drawn at 15,000 and 6,000 households, but in the much more densely populated former domain of Southern Sung the corresponding figures were 50,000 and 30,000. The four military prefectures were ranked on the same level as small prefectures of the ordinary sort.

Below the prefectures in the hierarchy, at the lowest level of the formal governmental structure, were 1,127 Districts (*hsien* 縣), each headed by an Overseer and a Magistrate (*yin* 尹). Like prefectures, districts were graded as large, middle, or small by their registered populations; the dividing lines were at 6,000 and 2,000 households in the North and at 30,000 and 10,000 households in the South. More than half of all districts were "directly attached" (*chih-li*) to a Route Command rather than to an intermediary prefecture; most of the others were supervised by prefectures that were in turn supervised by Route Commands. A relatively small number, 98, were supervised by prefectures that were "directly attached" to Secretariats rather than supervised by Route Commands.

The two Yüan capitals, Ta-tu and Shang-tu, and the cities in which other Route Commands were headquartered were not organized into districts. The headquarters city of the Ta-tu Route Command (i.e., Peking) was under the administration of two Police Commissions (*ching-hsün yüan* 警巡院), the Shang-tu city under one Po-

lice Commission. Most other Route Command headquarters cities were governed by Administration Offices (*lu-shih ssu* 錄事司), each under an Overseer.

A special system of nomenclature was designed for the unassimilated aboriginal tribes of southwestern China, to bring them into the formal governmental hierarchy. Interspersed among the routes, prefectures, and districts of modern Szechwan, Yunnan, and Kweichow were tribal units with varying official designations that for convenience might uniformly be rendered as Pacification Offices (*hsüan-fu ssu* 宣撫司, *chao-t'ao ssu* 招討司, *tsung-kuan fu* 總管府, *wan-hu fu* 萬戶府), under tribal chiefs given such titles as Overseer. All these aboriginal Pacification Offices had the same rank as small prefectures.

Below the district level, the Chinese population was theoretically organized in two systems. One was a system borrowed from T'ang, to facilitate the collection of taxes and the enforcement of the laws. For these purposes, four families constituted a Neighborhood (*lin* 鄰), five neighborhoods a Security Group (*pao* 保), and five security groups a rural Village or urban Precinct (both *li* 里) of 100 families, for which a designated Head (*li-chang* 長) was held responsible. The other, overlapping system organized every 50 or so neighboring families into a Community (*she* 社) with a designated Community Head (*she-chang* 長) to manage public services such as establishing elementary schools and charity granaries, controlling irrigation, and planting trees.

The Military

Because the Yüan dynasty was essentially an alien military occupation of China, its military dispositions were carefully guarded state secrets. It was commonly said that at any one time no more than two or three men had access to the military registers. Nevertheless, the basic structure of the Yüan military establishment is reasonably clear.

The standing army consisted of two principal groups, the Imperial Armies (*ch'in-chün* 親軍) and the Territorial Armies (*chen-shu chün* 鎮戍軍). Both were staffed with careerists conscripted from families designated as hereditary military families; they normally served between the ages of fifteen and seventy. The main force was the Mongol Army itself. It was supplemented by an Allied Army (*t'an-ma-ch'ih chün* 探馬赤軍) consisting, basically, of three elements: troops controlled by land-grant nobles and members of Khitan, Jurchen, and Chinese families who had joined the Mongol cause early in the assault on the Chin state in North China; a so-called Chinese Army (*han-chün* 漢軍), drawn from the families of Chin soldiers who had surrendered in North China; and ultimately a Newly Submitted Army (*hsin-fu chün* 新附軍), drawn from the families of surrendered Southern Sung soldiers. Although all these elements were in some measure intermingled in the various armies, the Mongols themselves and close nomad allies such as the Kipchak Turks dominated the imperial armies, which were garrisoned in and around Peking, and especially the Imperial Bodyguard (*kesig; ch'ieh-hsieh* 怯薛). The imperial armies were made up of a relatively small group of Palace Guards (*su-wei* 宿衛), among which the Imperial Bodyguard was by far the most influential unit, and a much larger number of what might be called Imperial Guards (*shih-wei* 侍衛, *chu-wei* 諸衛). The territorial armies consisted of all the military units that were scattered in other regions of the empire.

The basic Mongol military unit, normally both in garrison and in the field, was a nominal 10,000-man Brigade (*tumen;* Chinese *wan-hu fu* 萬戶府), led by a Brigade Commander (*wan-hu*). Units of the imperial armies stationed in the vicinity of Peking were given the traditional Chinese designation Guard (*wei* 衛) rather than brigade, perhaps for prestige purposes. In a strictly decimal progression, a brigade normally comprised ten 1,000-man Battalions (*ch'ien-hu so* 千戶所), led by Battalion Commanders (*ch'ien-hu*); a battalion comprised ten 100-man Companies (*po-hu so* 百戶所), led by Company Commanders (*po-hu*); and a company comprised ten 10-man Squads (*chia* 甲, *p'ai* 牌), led by Squad Commanders (*chia-chang* 長, *p'ai-t'ou* 頭). Brigades and battalions were graded as large, middle, or small (*shang, chung, hsia*) according to their actual troop strength—7,000, 5,000, or 3,000 in the case of brigades and 700, 500, or 300 in the case of battalions.

Outside the Peking area, brigades were normally garrisoned in or near the headquarters towns or cities of Route Commands, but their battalions were sometimes detached to subordinate prefectures or even districts. The chain of accountability ran from brigades at the Route Command level up through Military Commands (*yüan-shuai fu*), Chief Military Commands (*tu yüan-shuai fu*), or Pacification Commissions (*hsüan-wei shih ssu*) at the circuit level; and then through Branch Secretariats directly, or indirectly through appropriate Branch Bureaus of Military Affairs, to the Bureau of Military Affairs at the capital.

In order to provide grain for the military establishment, State Farms (*t'un-t'ien* 屯田) were created throughout the empire under the management of State Farm Brigades (*t'un-t'ien wan-hu fu*) or State Farm Battalions (*t'un-t'ien ch'ien-hu so*). These agricultural tracts were normally worked by Chinese civilians rather than by the soldiers who lived off their produce, although in the fourteenth century the Yüan government tried to increase the farming activity of its troops. Reportedly, there were more than 120 state farms in the empire, encompassing more than 2,500,000 acres, 23 in the Metropolitan Area around Peking alone. Thirteen of these were administered by the Bureau of Military Affairs, three each by the Secretariat and the Grand Agricultural Administration (*ta ssu-nung ssu*), and four by the Palace Provisions Commission (*hsüan-hui yüan*). Those outside the Metropolitan Area were administered by Branch Secretariats or by agencies subordinate to them.

Additional support for the military establishment came from more than a hundred horse herds organized into fifteen pasturages scattered across the North, managed by hereditary stockmen under the direction of the Court of the Imperial Stud (*t'ai-p'u ssu*). Occasionally, also, horses were requisitioned from civilians for military use.

Personnel Administration

The population of Yüan China was classified in a variety of ways—for example, in hereditary occupational classes. The most important classification scheme was based on a combination of ethnic and political considerations. It divided all residents into four great classes, and a man's status in this system determined, among other things, his suitability for government service. These four classes were (1) Mongols, (2) miscellaneous aliens (*se-mu jen* 色目人, lit., "special category men"), referring mostly to Central Asian Moslems, (3) North China residents (*han-jen* 漢人), including all the Khitan, Jurchen, and Chinese who had been subjects of Chin, and (4) Southern Chinese (*nan-jen* 南人, *man-tzu* 蠻子), meaning all former subjects of Southern Sung. Generally speaking, the Mongols entrusted important governmental posts only to themselves and their alien allies. The much more numerous "North China residents" got only meager consideration; and the Southern Chinese, who far outnumbered all the other groups combined, were trusted hardly at all, except to serve in local offices in their own areas.

Apparently, as the Mongol conquest of China passed through its early phases, submissive local officials, first in the Chin state and then even in the Southern Sung state, were mostly left in their posts, with Mongol Overseers (*ta-lu-hua-ch'ih*) assigned to each office down to the district level as representatives of the successive Mongol Khans. In the 1230s and 1240s a famous Khitan official, Yeh-lü Ch'ü-ts'ai, gained favor among the Mongols and helped lay the foundations for the later Yüan state; and after Kubilai came to power in 1259–1260, one of his advisers, a Chinese Taoist turned Ch'an monk named Liu Ping-chung, was instrumental in creating the institutional structure described above and the personnel administration procedures that were to characterize the Yüan officialdom.

Varieties of official titles and other status indicators. In the mature Yüan system, all officials and offices were graded in China's traditional hierarchy of nine ranks (*p'in*) and eighteen classes (*teng*), from 1a down through 9b. Subofficial functionaries (*li* 吏) did the bulk of paperwork and other routine administrative tasks in all agencies. On the basis of seniority, the highest-ranking officials were granted nominal status in the nobility. In addition, all officials of ranks 1a through 5b automatically earned merit titles (*hsün* 勳), mostly bearing the suffix Commandant (*wei* 尉); there were ten such titles, one for each of the ten classes of official ranks at the top of the hierarchy.

Every functioning official carried a state-issued seal (*yin* 印), which was the formal war-rant and symbol of his status and authority, and with which he authenticated documents. This was in accord with Chinese tradition. Yüan seals, however, were inscribed in Mongolian script and were of varying sizes and substances, which were minutely prescribed for all ranks. The larger the seal, the higher the rank; seals being equal in size, gold outranked silver, which in turn outranked brass. Finer distinctions, as among various Princes, were denoted by the designs and materials of the seals' handles (*niu* 紐). Military officers were additionally decorated with tallies (*fu* 符), which were granted as rewards for special service and varied in prestige according to the material they were made of and the number of pearls that adorned them. After the early Yüan years, civil officials also were sometimes so decorated.

As in the Chinese tradition, officials were further classified by prestige titles (*san-kuan* 散官), mostly bearing the suffixes Grand Master (*ta-fu* 大夫) or Court Gentleman (*lang* 郎). For normal civil service officials there were 42 prestige titles distributed among the regular ranks from 1a down through 8b; officials of rank 9 were not entitled to them. The assignment of prestige titles was a way of promoting men without creating imbalances between their personal status (and presumably their incomes) and the ranks of the offices they held. For example, fine distinctions could be drawn among all officials of rank 1a because there were six different prestige titles available for that high rank. Prestige titles were normally earned by seniority. Officials serving in the capital were supposed to be given merit ratings (*k'ao* 考) every 30 months and those serving outside the capital every 36 months, and after every satisfactory merit rating an official was promoted one degree in the prestige title hierarchy.

Yüan had several other schedules of prestige titles. In addition to 34 titles for military officers in general and 14 for officers of the Guards that were in closest attendance on the Emperor, there were prestige titles for various professional specialists—14 for members of the astronomical agencies (*ssu-t'ien kuan* 司天官), 15 for members of the Imperial Academy of Medicine (*t'ai-i yüan*), and 15 for musicians and other court entertainers (*chiao-fang kuan* 教坊官).

Building on a Chin practice, Yüan categorized certain types of officials in almost every agency, whatever their more specific titles, as Staff Supervisors (*shou-ling kuan* 首領官). Their characteristic role was to direct and be answerable for the clerical force of subofficial functionaries. Although available sources do not consistently specify which officials of a given agency belonged to the category, it is clear that contemporaries knew full well who was and who was not a Staff Supervisor. The category seems to have had something of the character of a caste; it may have been a carryover from the Era of Division distinction between "pure" and "impure" officials and offices. Officials of this category seem always to have belonged to the lower ranks and were perhaps limited forever to Staff Supervisor status; but this is by no means certain.

Recruitment and appointments. While taking for themselves the most important posts in the government, the conquering Mongols had to employ very large numbers of non-Mongols in less sensitive but essential administrative and clerical positions. At the outset they drew this pool of personnel from three sources. First, as has been noted above, they allowed many submissive officials of the Chin and Southern Sung to remain in their posts under supervision. Second, they thrust into office many Central Asian Moslem hangers-on, who were generally more literate and more familiar with Chinese ways than the Mongols were. Third, they recruited broadly among the Chinese on the basis of recommendations submitted by existing officeholders. In 1237 the Khitan aristocrat Yeh-lü Ch'ü-ts'ai even got permission to conduct examinations for the recruitment of North China residents, and it is reported that 4,030 new officials were brought into service through the one-year effort that he sponsored.

As the Yüan governmental system reached stable maturity under Kubilai, traditional Chinese recruitment procedures became routine, with the notable exception of examinations, which Kubilai mistrusted. Recruitment through recommendations continued on an ad hoc basis, and all existing officials became entitled to raise one or more sons into service by China's traditional "protection" privilege (*yin* 蔭). Military officers of all sorts commonly passed their positions directly to their sons, as did many Mongol Overseers throughout the government; and such direct inheritance of office was not unknown even among civil service officials.

Recruitment of officials through schools was also instituted in Kubilai's time. In 1261 he ordered Route Commands to open or restore schools, and in 1269 the establishment of state schools was ordered in all prefectures as well as routes. These were intended primarily for the training of sons and brothers of officials, but they admitted prescribed quotas of youths from non-official families. At the same time Route Commands were ordered to open Mongolian schools for the appropriate education of young Mongols in their jurisdictions. Then in 1271 (or also in 1269?) the School for the Sons of the State (*kuo-tzu hsüeh* 國子學) was established at the capital under the supervision of the Academy of Scholarly Worthies (*chi-hsien yüan*), with a mandate to give two or three years of training to sons of court officials and of members of the Imperial Bodyguard so that they might become suitable for official appointments. There was a quota of 100 regular students: 50 Mongols and 50 non-Mongol aliens or North China residents. In addition, 20 specially talented sons of non-official families were allowed to attend with secondary status as Fellows (*pan-tu* 伴讀). The quota of regular students was subsequently increased to 200 in 1287, to 300 in 1300, and to 400 in 1315, but the number of Fellows from non-official families did not change. After 1287 the school was divided into Study Halls (*chai* 齋) in the Sung pattern. The curriculum emphasized the traditional Confucian classics, and until 1315 graduates were appointed directly to office. It was the rule in 1287 that Mongol graduates got official status at rank 6a or 6b, non-Mongol aliens at rank 7a, and North China residents at rank 7b. At that time it appears there were no South China students; whether they were admitted later is not clear.

Officials were also produced by the Mongolian School for the Sons of the State in the capital, with a small enrollment including a few carefully chosen non-Mongols; and from a small branch of the School for the Sons of the State at the northern auxiliary capital, Shang-tu. Furthermore, there were private academies (*shu-yüan*

書院) in all areas of China, especially the South, and their students were regularly among those winning official status through recommendations.

Regular recruitment examinations for the civil service were at last authorized in 1313 and were first offered in 1314–1315. The regular procedure was for local officials to examine candidates every third year and recommend those showing promise for provincial examinations (*hsiang-shih* 鄉試) that were conducted by Branch Secretariats or, in the Metropolitan Area around Peking, by Route Commands. (When the examinations were instituted, graduates of the School for the Sons of the State no longer got direct appointments but moved into the stream of candidates for office via provincial examinations conducted by the Ta-tu Route Command at Peking.) Each province was assigned a quota of passers, based on its population; and a total of 300 candidates were then admitted to a metropolitan examination (*hui-shih* 會試) conducted in Peking by specially designated examiners, often Grand Councilors, under the supervision of the Ministry of Rites. The results were then confirmed in a brief follow-up palace examination (*tien-shih* 殿試), conducted under the Emperor's personal auspices for the purpose of ranking passers in order of quality; but not all passers regularly participated.

The rules allowed no more than one in three candidates at the capital to pass, totaling no more than 100; and passers were to be equally distributed among Mongols, non-Mongol aliens, North China residents, and Southern Chinese. (At all examination levels, Mongols and non-Mongol aliens were given different, easier examinations than native Chinese; and they were given favored treatment in subsequent official appointments.) All passers of the metropolitan examination were granted the status of Metropolitan Graduates (*chin-shih* 進士).

Except for an interlude from 1335 to 1340, the triennial cycle of civil service recruitment examinations continued to the end of the dynasty. In all, the examinations were offered 16 times, and they produced a total of 1,139 Metropolitan Graduates, an average of 71 per examination. The number of officials so recruited was consequently not an important factor in the staffing of the huge Yüan bureaucracy; and graduates of the examination system by no means displaced the hereditary Mongol nobility as the elite group in Yüan government.

Official salaries and allowances. Payment for service was unknown in the Mongol tradition but was standardized in the Chinese pattern in Kubilai's time. Salaries were then paid in silver, varying according to one's rank, one's prestige title, and one's functional appointment. The basic silver unit was an ingot (*ting* 錠) weighing 50 ounces (*liang* 兩; a tael), and the range of salaries ran from six ingots, or 300 ounces, to 35 ounces a month. Later the silver standard was abandoned in favor of China's traditional copper coins, counted at least in theory by strings of 1,000 each. Salaries then ranged from 166 strings to 10 strings of coins a month, and sometimes they were paid in paper money equivalents. Grain allowances were issued on the basis of rank, ranging from fifteen bushels to one bushel a month. In lieu of grain allowances, officials serving in the provinces received income from office land (*chih-t'ien*), the maximum being the state tax revenue from approximately 250 acres.

Ming

1368-1644

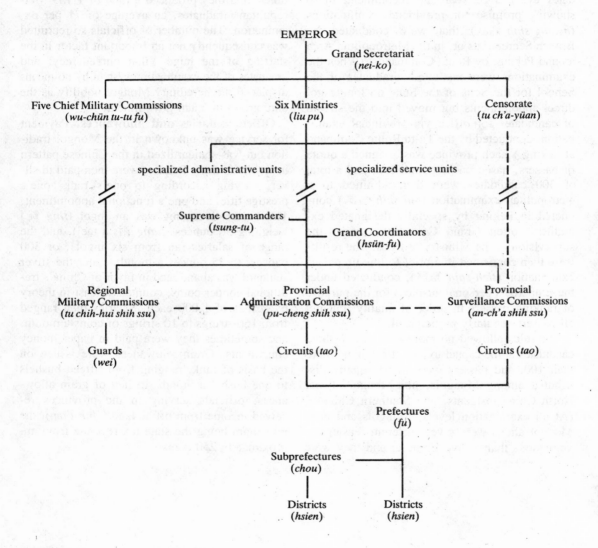

EMPEROR

Grand Secretariat
(*nei-ko*)

Five Chief Military Commissions
(*wu-chün tu-tu fu*)

Six Ministries
(*liu pu*)

Censorate
(*tu ch'a-yüan*)

specialized administrative units

specialized service units

Supreme Commanders
(*tsung-tu*)

Grand Coordinators
(*hsün-fu*)

Regional
Military Commissions
(*tu chih-hui shih ssu*)

Provincial
Administration Commissions
(*pu-cheng shih ssu*)

Provincial
Surveillance Commissions
(*an-ch'a shih ssu*)

Guards
(*wei*)

Circuits (*tao*)

Circuits (*tao*)

Prefectures
(*fu*)

Subprefectures
(*chou*)

Districts
(*hsien*)

Districts
(*hsien*)

Carrying forward and gradually modifying trends from both the alien tradition that culminated in Yüan and the native tradition of T'ang and Sung, the Ming government became a highly centralized, well-articulated autocracy. Everything was structured so that no one could challenge the authority of the Emperor, and the officialdom was less aristocratic than at any other time in Chinese history. After the earliest Ming years, intellectuals selected for government service in open, competitive, written recruitment examinations were the only significant elite group in both the state and the society. Although these scholar-officials dominated the workings of government, they were highly vulnerable to abusive treatment at the hands of the willful and capricious Ming Emperors and their favored eunuch attendants.

The Central Government

The original Ming capital was at Nanking. At the beginning of 1421, after many years of preparation, the central government was moved to modern Peking, where it remained. A skeletal auxiliary central government was maintained at Nanking, so that most of the agencies at Peking after 1420 had counterparts at Nanking, labeled with that place-name prefix; and the Nanking establishment continued to exercise some province-like functions in its environs.

Nomenclature is unfortunately confused for the period from 1425 to 1441, when it was anticipated that the functioning central government would be returned to Nanking. During those years the skeletal, largely ceremonial agencies at Nanking were referred to, for example, as "the" Ministry of Personnel, whereas the really functional central government agency at Peking was referred to as the Branch (*hsing-tsai* 行在) Ministry of Personnel, as had been the practice from 1403 to 1421, when Peking was the auxiliary capital.

Besides Peking and Nanking, there were two honorary capitals in the Ming empire. One was Chung-tu at Feng-yang in modern Anhwei, the ancestral home of the dynastic founder; the other was Hsing-tu at Chung-hsiang in modern Hupei, the ancestral home of Emperor Shih-tsung (r. 1521–1567). Neither had any semblance of a central government structure; both were administered by special Regencies (*liu-shou ssu* 留守司).

The imperial household. As prescribed by tradition, the Ming Emperors and their Empresses were attended intimately by large numbers of palace women and eunuchs. In the earliest Ming years, palace women were organized into seven specialized agencies, which supervised a total of 24 subordinate units. By the 1420s, however, eunuchs had taken over the women's domestic service functions to such an extent that they were left with only one agency, the Apparel Service (*shang-fu chü* 尚服局) with four subsidiary Offices (*ssu* 司). Eunuchs were originally organized in a single Directorate of Palace Attendants (*nei-shih chien* 內史監), but their number steadily increased, and they were successively reorganized until, by the 1420s, they staffed twelve Directorates (*chien* 監) concerned with such matters as ceremonial, staff surveillance, utensils, ritual regalia, document handling, stables, foodstuffs, and seals; four Offices (*ssu*) charged with providing fuel, music, paper, and baths; and eight Services (*chü* 局) responsible for weapons, silverwork, laundering, headgear, bronzework, textile manufacture, wineries, and gardens. In addition, eunuchs maintained numerous granaries and storehouses within the palace, collectively called the Palace Treasury (*nei-fu* 內府). The highest-ranking eunuchs were Directors (*t'ai-chien* 太監) of the eunuch Directorates, and one of them, the Director of Ceremonial (*ssu-li t'ai-chien* 司禮太監) became in effect chief of the palace staff.

Two other eunuch agencies became especially notorious. One was the Eastern Depot (*tung-ch'ang* 東廠), established in 1420 with special powers to investigate treasonable offenses. Under the supervision of powerful eunuch Directors of Ceremonial and in collaboration with the Imperial Bodyguard, eunuchs of the Eastern Depot and its later adjunct the Western Depot (*hsi-ch'ang* 西廠) served as a kind of imperial secret service that repeatedly harassed the officialdom. Recurringly, also, eunuchs were dispatched outside the palace as special imperial agents to carry out diplomatic missions abroad, supervise military operations, command armies and navies, oversee tax collections, and handle various other matters, with a bewildering variety of special designations.

During the first Ming reign, Imperial Princes (*ch'in-wang* 親王) were given important military commands. After the earliest years of the fifteenth century, however, they had no governmental functions. Other imperial relatives, imperial in-laws, and meritorious military officers were regularly granted lesser titles of nobility (*chüeh* 爵); but the nobility in general was an ornament on the Ming social scene, not a factor in government.

Nominally at the top of the civil service hierarchy, as in prior times, were the Three Dukes (*san kung* 三公) and the Three Solitaries (*san ku* 三孤). The Three Dukes were the Grand Preceptor (*t'ai-shih,* 太師), the Grand Mentor (*t'ai-fu* 太傅), and the Grand Guardian (*t'ai-pao* 太保). The Three Solitaries were the Junior (*shao* 少) Preceptor, the Junior Mentor, and the Junior Guardian. Except for brief periods early in the dynasty, these titles were only irregularly conferred as supplementary honorary titles for distinguished officials, entirely for prestige purposes.

The Grand Secretariat. Ming T'ai-tsu (r. 1368–1398), beginning as a rebel commoner, created the trappings of government on the basis of the Yüan model at hand as his rebellion progressed, and when the Ming dynasty was formally proclaimed at the beginning of 1368, its central government closely resembled that of Yüan. It included a Secretariat (*chung-shu sheng* 中書省) to supervise general administration, a Censorate (*yü-shih t'ai* 御史臺) to maintain disciplinary surveillance over the officialdom, and a Chief Military Commission (*tu-tu fu* 都督府) in control of the Ming armies.

This early Ming top echelon of central government was altered abruptly in 1380, when the Emperor put to death his senior Grand Councilor (*ch'eng-hsiang* 丞相) for conspiring to usurp the throne. The episode is generally referred to as "the abolition of the Secretariat." What the Emperor did abolish were all of the traditional executive posts in the Secretariat, leaving an uncoordinated, previously subordinate group of Six Ministries (*liu pu* 六部) as the general-administration core of his central government: the Ministries of Personnel (*li-pu* 吏部), of Revenue (*hu-pu* 戶部), of Rites (*li-pu* 禮部), of War (*ping-pu* 兵部), of Justice (*hsing-pu* 刑部), and of Works (*kung-pu* 工部). At the same time the unitary Chief Military Commission was splintered into five coequal, uncoordinated agencies, all with the former designation, collectively called the Five Commissions (*wu fu* 五府): the Chief Military Commission of the Center (*chung-chün tu-tu fu* 中軍都督府), of the Left, of the Right, of the Front, and of the Rear. The Censorate too was fragmented, losing all its executive-level posts; what was left was an uncoordinated group of low-ranking Investigating Censors (*chien-ch'a yü-shih* 監察御史). Whereas a relatively unified Censorate was soon reconstituted in somewhat modified form, the original Secretariat and the unified Chief Military Commission never reappeared; T'ai-tsu even left explicit instructions for his successors that the Secretariat must never be reconstituted and that anyone who proposed its reconstitution should be put to death.

T'ai-tsu's intention, clearly, was that no one official and no small group of officials should ever again have sufficient power to threaten the Emperor's personal authority. He himself undertook to be the sole coordinator of both the civil and the military establishments, whose supervision was now divided among the Six Ministries and the Five Commissions. The burden of paperwork that he thus imposed on himself was awesome, and before the end of his reign he was calling for secretarial help from the litterateurs of the Hanlin Academy.

The development of new governmental institutions was disrupted by T'ai-tsu's grandson and successor, Hui-ti (r. 1398–1402), who apparently had some idealistic notion of making the structure and nomenclature of government conform to models in the ancient text *Chou-li*. How institutions were actually affected is by no means clear, for after Hui-ti was deposed by an uncle who became the third Ming ruler, Ch'eng-tsu (r. 1402–1424), the record of Hui-ti's reign was compiled to reflect the biases of the usurper, and government was promptly restored to the format in which T'ai-tsu had left it.

Under Ch'eng-tsu the Emperor's reliance on secretarial aides from the Hanlin Academy became more regularized, and by the time of Hsüan-tsung (r. 1425–1435), the practice had produced an important new institution, the Grand Secretariat (*nei-ko* 內閣). The number of Grand Secretaries (*ta hsüeh-shih* 大學士) varied, but there were normally three or four. Although nominally low-ranking officials of the Hanlin Academy, they were regularly appointed concurrently to substantive (but inactive) posts as Ministers (*shang-shu* 尚書) or Vice Ministers (*shih-lang* 侍郎) in the Six Ministries for prestige purposes. In addition, they were often assured of preeminent civil service status by being given further concurrent appointments to theoretically substantive but actually honorary status as members of the Three Dukes or the Three

Solitaries. As coordinating aides to the Emperor, they were assigned to duty in different Halls (*tien* 殿 or *ko* 閣) in the palace and rendered individual service as ordered. Gradually, however, they developed collegial procedures for handling routine matters under the leadership of an informally designated Senior Grand Secretary (*shou-fu* 首輔), and came to be served by a Central Drafting Office (*chung-shu k'o* 中書科) staffed with numerous Secretariat Drafters (*chung-shu she-jen* 中書舍人). Even so, it was not until the late sixteenth century that the Grand Secretariat was formally recognized in state documents as an institution, and its members continued to be referred to by their individual titles as, for example, Grand Mentor (*t'ai-fu*), Minister of Rites (*lǐ-pu shang-shu*), and Grand Secretary of the Hall of Literary Profundity (*wen-yüan ko* 文淵閣).

The Ming Grand Secretariat was not by any means a revival of the "strong prime ministership" attributed to some earlier times. Grand Secretaries, however influential by force of individual personality, had weaker institutional foundations than the Grand Councilors of T'ang and Sung times. They attended and counseled the Emperor, remonstrated with him, screened documents submitted to him by all government agencies, and drafted the imperial rescripts in which decisions were promulgated. Of necessity, they worked closely with the palace eunuchs, who very often controlled all access to the throne. Moreover, their career patterns commonly led them into the Grand Secretariat through a succession of posts as academicians engaged in editing and compiling rather than through demanding administrative posts. For these reasons the officialdom in general, known as the "outer court" (*wai-t'ing* 外廷), did not find it easy to accept Grand Secretaries as its leaders and spokesmen; instead, officials commonly associated Grand Secretaries with the "inner court" (*nei-t'ing* 內廷) of palace women, eunuchs, and imperial kinsmen and in-laws. In their role as coordinating go-betweens, Grand Secretaries often found themselves distrusted and reviled both by irascible Emperors and by an indignant officialdom dedicated to opposing government by imperial whim.

Ministries, Courts, and Directorates. Under such coordination as the Grand Secretariat provided, the Six Ministries were the supreme administrative organs of the Ming government, more prestigious than any of their predecessors. Each was headed by a single Minister (*shang-shu*) and a single Vice Minister (*shih-lang*), and each incorporated several subordinate Bureaus (*ch'ing-li ssu* 清吏司), headed by Directors (*lang-chung* 即中) and Vice Directors (*yüan-wai lang* 員外郎). The Ministries of Personnel, Rites, War, and Works each had four Bureaus with functionally differentiated responsibilities and designations. The Ministries of Revenue and Justice both had thirteen Bureaus, each of which bore the name of the province that fell within its purview. The Ministries directly or indirectly supervised a large number of more specialized administrative and service agencies, including the Court of Imperial Sacrifices (*t'ai-ch'ang ssu* 太常寺), the Court of Imperial Entertainments (*kuang-lu ssu* 光祿寺), and the Court of State Ceremonial (*hung-lu ssu* 鴻臚寺), all supervised by the Ministry of Rites; and the Court of the Imperial Stud (*t'ai-p'u ssu* 太僕寺) and its several Branch Courts (*hsing-ssu* 行寺), supervised by the Ministry of War.

The more autonomous agencies of the central government included the Office of Transmission (*t'ung-cheng shih ssu* 通政使司), through which passed official documents circulating among the palace, the central government agencies, and the provinces; the Directorate of Astronomy (*ch'in-t'ien chien* 欽天監), which interpreted celestial and terrestrial irregularities and prepared the official state calendar, among other things; the Directorate of Imperial Parks (*shang-lin yüan-chien* 上林苑監); the Imperial Academy of Medicine (*t'ai-i yüan* 太醫院); and the Hanlin Academy (*han-lin yüan* 翰林院), which engaged in elaborate scholarly and historiographic projects and, at least in theory and sometimes in practice, tutored Emperors in continuing-education sessions called the Classics Colloquium (*ching-yen* 經宴).

Another major agency that was not subordinate to the Six Ministries was the Court of Judicial Review (*ta-li ssu* 大理寺), whose subordinate Left and Right Courts of Review (*ssu* 寺) provided a final check, short of imperial review in most of the important cases, on judicial findings and sentences throughout the empire. There was also a Directorate of Education (*kuo-tzu chien*

國子監), which under a Chancellor (*chi-chiu* 祭酒), aided by a Director of Studies (*ssu-yeh* 司業) dictated educational policy for all state-supported local schools. The Directorate was also an educational institution itself, in which capacity it was commonly known both as the School for the Sons of the State (*kuo-tzu hsüeh* 國子學) and as the National University (*t'ai-hsüeh* 太學). For instructional purposes, it was subdivided into six Colleges (*t'ang* 堂).

Censorial institutions. As has been noted above, the Censorate was a top-echelon agency of the Ming central government. After its original executive posts were abolished in 1380 along with those of the Secretariat, T'ai-tsu must have felt it was in his interest to reconstitute the Censorate as a unified surveillance organ. In 1382 eight Chief Investigating Censors (*chien-ch'a tu yü-shih* 監察都御史) were appointed, and the Censorate was named, literally, the Chief Surveillance Office (*tu ch'a-yüan* 都察院). Then in 1383 a whole new executive superstructure was appointed, notably including two Censors-in-chief (*tu yü-shih* 都御史), two Vice Censors-in-chief (*fu tu yü-shih* 副都御史), and four Assistant Censors-in-chief (*ch'ien tu yü-shih* 僉都御史).

Despite this reorganization, the 110 Investigating Censors (*chien-ch'a yü-shih*) who were the Emperor's front-line surveillance agents, so to speak, remained remarkably independent of their Censorate superiors except for the most routine sorts of personnel administration. They were appointed to office and assigned to special investigatory commissions only with the Emperor's personal approval, and their memorials went directly to the throne. For administrative purposes they were organized into offices called Circuits (*tao* 道) named after provinces, ultimately numbering thirteen; and their independence is reflected in the fact that they were always officially identified, not as officials of the Censorate, but as members of these circuits, for example, Investigating Censor of the Chekiang Circuit. It should be noted, however, that their duty stations were normally in the capital, not in the provinces for which the circuits were named. When sent outside the capital on special commission, a Censor might be sent to any area, regardless of the provincial designation of the circuit to which he belonged.

Of the many special commissions to which Investigating Censors were assigned, the most important was to serve as Regional Inspector (*hsün-an yü-shih* 巡按御史) in a province or some other well-defined strategic area for a one-year tour of duty. While on such duty, a Censor was not even formally identified with his Censorate circuit; he was merely designated, for example, Investigating Censor (serving as) Regional Inspector of Chekiang (*hsün-an che-chiang chien-ch'a yü-shih*). He was not, however, considered a member of the provincial staff; he was always an independent surveillance agent of the Emperor.

Except for the brief interval from 1380 to 1382, the Ming central government did not include a Remonstrance Bureau (*chien-yüan* 諫院). Instead, in accord with a Yüan precedent, Ming Censors were authorized to propose or criticize policies as well as to monitor the implementation of policy. In Ming times the Censorate was probably more active and influential, on balance, than in any other period of Chinese history.

Another prominent group of Ming censorial officials were Supervising Secretaries (*chi-shih-chung* 給事中), who were divided among six Offices of Scrutiny (*k'o* 科). Each Office monitored at close range the activities of one of the Six Ministries and was named accordingly—for example, the Office of Scrutiny for Personnel (*li-k'o* 吏科). Each Office had a Chief Supervising Secretary (*tu chi-shih-chung* 都給事中), one Left and one Right Supervising Secretary, and between four and eight ordinary Supervising Secretaries. The Offices of Scrutiny were not subordinate to either the Ministries or the Censorate, but they participated jointly with Censors in many investigatory undertakings and shared with Censors the prescribed duty of proposing and criticizing policies of every sort. It was the special duty of Supervising Secretaries to watch over the flow of official documents to and from the Ministries and to "veto" (*feng-po* 封駁) documents—that is, return them for reconsideration—if they were improper either in form or in substance.

Some common collective terms for central government offices. In addition to such terms as the Three Dukes, the Three Solitaries, the Six

Ministries, and the Five Chief Military Commissions already mentioned, Ming documents commonly refer to the Nine Chief Ministers (*chiu ch'ing* 九卿), a collective term for the active heads of the Six Ministries, the Censorate, the Office of Transmission, and the Court of Judicial Review. These were the officials who were regularly called on by the Emperor to assemble for court deliberations (*hui-i* 會議) on major policy problems. Another collective term commonly encountered is the Three Judicial Offices (*san fa-ssu* 三法司), signifying the Ministry of Justice, the Censorate, and the Court of Judicial Review, which were sometimes called on to act collegially on a judicial matter. The term Offices of Scrutiny and Circuits (*k'o-tao* 科道) was used to designate Supervising Secretaries and Censors in general, as were the terms "the avenues of criticism" (*yen-lu* 言路) and "the speaking officials" (*yen-kuan* 言官).

Territorial Administration

The lowest-echelon unit of regular administration in Ming times, as throughout China's imperial history, was the District (*hsien* 縣). Districts were supervised by Prefectures (*fu* 府), in some cases through intermediary Subprefectures (*chou* 州). Prefectures in turn were supervised by three cooperating agencies: a Provincial Administration Commission (*ch'eng-hsüan pu-cheng shih ssu* 承宣布政使司), a Provincial Surveillance Commission (*t'i-hsing an-ch'a shih ssu* 提刑按察使司), and a Regional Military Commission (*tu chih-hui shih ssu* 都指揮使司). A major Ming institutional innovation, corresponding to the development of the Grand Secretariat in the central government, was to provide for the coordination of these three provincial agencies under a Grand Coordinator and to provide further for their coordination across provinces under a Supreme Commander.

Grand Coordinators and Supreme Commanders. T'ai-tsu once sent his Heir Apparent to "tour and soothe" (*hsün-fu* 巡撫) the Shensi area. Subsequently other court dignitaries were occasionally dispatched on tours of inspection in the provinces, to "pacify and soothe" (*an-fu* 安撫) or "tour and inspect" (*hsün-shih* 巡視). Then in 1430 this makeshift practice fell into a stable

pattern. "Touring pacifiers" (*hsün-fu* 巡撫) began to appear as resident coordinators from the central government in the provinces as well as in special frontier zones and other strategic areas. Their tenure was indefinite and sometimes extended to 10 or even 20 years. Such Grand Coordinators, as the title might best be rendered, became prevalent in the middle of the fifteenth century with the specific charge of supervising and controlling (*chieh-chih* 節制) the triad of regular provincial agencies. A Grand Coordinator had no official staff, however, and cannot be considered a true provincial Governor. He always remained nominally an official of the central government, usually a Vice Minister of a Ministry, on special territorial assignment. After 1453 all Grand Coordinators were routinely given nominal concurrent appointments as Vice Censors-in-chief or Assistant Censors-in-chief, which conferred on them broad impeachment powers and presumably increased their prestige. Sometimes Grand Coordinators were explicitly given supervisory control over military affairs in their jurisdictions, with the designation Grand Coordinator and Concurrent Superintendent of Military Affairs (*hsün-fu chien t'i-tu chün-wu* 巡撫兼提督軍務), or a variant.

Because there was often a special need for cross-provincial coordination of military affairs, out of the Grand Coordinator system there eventually evolved the office of Supreme Commander (*tsung-tu* 總督). Like the Grand Coordinator, the Supreme Commander was an official of the central government delegated to territorial service, originally and normally on a temporary basis to deal with a particular crisis, especially military. The first such appointment was made in 1430, and appointments proliferated beginning in the second half of the fifteenth century. A few became more or less permanent fixtures in territorial administration.

A Supreme Commander was usually a nominal Minister of War and Concurrent Censor-in-chief, and often he was the Grand Coordinator of one of the provinces or other strategic areas in his broad jurisdiction. His military authority might extend over as many as five provinces. Sometimes Supreme Commanders were assigned non-military responsibilities, for example, overseeing the collection and transport of rice revenues from the Nanking area to Peking. (This was a continuing commission from 1451, involving a concurrent Grand Coordinatorship in the Huai-an region astride the Grand Canal.) Like Grand Coordinators, Supreme Commanders had no official staffs. They were special-purpose representatives of the central government, sent out to expedite the work of the Grand Coordinators and regular provincial authorities in their jurisdictions; they should consequently not be thought of as entrenched regional Governors-general.

Since Supreme Commanders and Grand Co-ordinators had no authorized assistants other than servants, by late Ming times they commonly assembled entourages of unofficial private aides with particular realms of administrative expertise. These were popularly referred to as Private Secretariats (*mu-fu* 幕府).

Provinces. The Ming dynasty brought to maturity the province-building efforts of Yüan times and stabilized most of China Proper's provinces in their modern forms. The thirteen Ming provinces were Shantung, Shansi, Shensi (incorporating Kansu), Honan, Szechwan, Hukwang (comprising modern Hupei and Hunan), Kiangsi, Chekiang, Fukien, Kwangtung, Kwangsi, Yunnan, and Kweichow. From 1407 to 1428 the northern part of Vietnam (Annam) was organized as a fourteenth province. In the earliest Ming years, modern Hopei was organized as Pei-p'ing Province, but in 1403 it was transformed into the Northern Metropolitan Area (*pei-ching* 北京 or *pei chih-li*), governed from the auxiliary capital then established at modern Peking. Then in 1421, when Peking became the paramount capital, the area's name was shortened to just the Metropolitan Area (*ching-shih* 京師, *chih-li* 直隸). At the same time the area dominated by Nanking, comprising most of modern Anhwei and Kiangsu Provinces and originally designated the Metropolitan Area, was changed to the Southern Metropolitan Area (*nan-ching* 南京 or *nan chih-li*). It should be noted that in Ming times the names Peking and Nanking were not properly used in reference to the cities so designated today; they referred to the province-size territories surrounding them. The cities and their immediate environs were officially known as Shun-t'ien Prefecture (Peking) and Ying-t'ien Prefecture (Nanking).

The Ming provinces were administered co-operatively by the three agencies mentioned above, called the Three Provincial Offices (*san ssu* 三司). The Provincial Administration Commission, until 1376 a Branch Secretariat, was headed by two Administration Commissioners (*pu-cheng shih* 布政使) who had general charge of all civil matters, and especially fiscal matters. A variable number of Administration Vice Commissioners (*ts'an-cheng* 參政) and Assistant Administration Commissions (*ts'an-i* 參議) individually staffed branch offices (*fen-ssu* 分司) from which they maintained closer, or more specialized, administrative supervision over jurisdictions called Circuits (*tao*); such officials were popularly known as Circuit Intendants (*tao-t'ai* 道臺). There were many different kinds of circuits, varying from province to province. Where the Intendant exercised all of the Provincial Administration Commission's authority in a limited geographic jurisdiction, there was a General Administration Circuit (*fen-shou tao* 分守道); each province had from three to eight such all-purpose branch offices. Other Intendants had authority in an unlimited territory coterminous with the province itself, but their authority was limited to specific functions. Every province had a Tax Intendant Circuit (*tu-liang tao* 督糧道) and several other function-specific circuits, depending on local needs. Circuit-level supervision in the two Metropolitan Areas was provided by Circuit Intendants assigned from the adjacent provinces.

The Provincial Surveillance Commission, headed by a single Surveillance Commissioner (*an-ch'a shih* 按察使), had local Censorate-like surveillance responsibilities, including a direct role in judicial administration. Although Provincial Surveillance Commissions were never Branch Censorates in Ming times, their working relationship with the Censorate was so close, and their functions so resembled those of the Censorate, that they were unofficially known collectively as the Outer Censorate (*wai-t'ai* 外臺); and their personnel shared with Censors such collective designations as "surveillance officials" (*ch'a-kuan* 察官) and "guardians of the customs and laws" (*feng-hsien kuan* 風憲官).

Variable numbers of Surveillance Vice Commissioners (*an-ch'a fu-shih* 副使) and Assistant Surveillance Commissioners (*an-ch'a ch'ien-shih* 簽事), like their counterparts in the Provincial Administration Commissions, were in charge of branch offices with prescribed geographic or functional jurisdictions called Circuits; they shared in the collective designation Circuit Intendants. In each province there were from three to nine General Surveillance Circuits (*fen-hsün tao* 分巡道), from two to seven Record Checking Circuits (*shua-chüan tao* 刷卷道), and from one to twelve Military Defense Circuits (*ping-pei tao* 兵備道). Most provinces also had an Education Intendant Circuit (*t'i-tu hsüeh tao* 提督學道), a Troop Purification Circuit (*ch'ing-chün tao* 清軍道), and a Postal Service Circuit (*i-ch'uan tao* 驛傳道). Like the Provincial Administration Commissions, the Surveillance Commissions of adjacent provinces assigned some Intendants to supervise the Metropolitan Areas.

The Regional Military Commissions, until 1375 called Branch Chief Military Commissions (*hsing tu-tu fu* 行都督府), were headed by Regional Military Commissioners (*tu chih-hui shih* 都指揮使), who administered all military garrisons in their provinces and were responsible to the five Chief Military Commissions in the capital. There were Commissions in every province and also in three vital defense zones along the northern frontier: in Liaotung, at Ta-ning in modern Jehol, and at Wan-ch'üan in modern Inner Mongolia. In addition, there were five Branch (*hsing* 行) Regional Military Commissions in Shensi, Shansi, Fukien, Szechwan, and Hukwang.

The Three Provincial Offices were sufficiently independent of each other that no one man or agency was able to gain control over a province, but they worked cooperatively, sending their senior officials to assemblies for discussion of major provincial problems and policies. The Censorate's Regional Inspectors (*hsün-an yü-shih*) and the senior provincial military officers usually participated, as did any palace eunuch assigned to the province as a special imperial agent, called a Grand Defender (*chen-shou*

鎮守, *shou-pei*). After the early 1400s, Grand Coordinators and Supreme Commanders normally took the lead in convening such assemblies.

Executive officials of the Three Provincial Offices were collectively known as Regional Overseers (*fang-mien* 方面). Circuit Intendancies were collectively called Supervisory Offices (*chien-ssu* 監司). The generic term for province was *sheng* 省, a holdover from the era of Branch Secretariats (*hsing-sheng*), and the term *chih-sheng* 直省 referred to all units of territorial administration, including those in the Metropolitan Areas (*chih*, from *chih-li*).

These more or less regular provincial agencies operated alongside many kinds of specialized administrative or service agencies that were directly responsible to the central government, notably: (1) four Branch Courts of the Imperial Stud (*hsing t'ai-p'u ssu*) and four Pasturage Offices (*yüan-ma ssu* 苑馬寺) supervised by the Ministry of War; (2) twelve domestic Customs Houses (*ch'ao-kuan* 鈔關), which collected transit duties along the Grand Canal, and many more Offices of Produce Levies (*ch'ou-fen chü* 抽分局), which collected in-kind revenues of forest products, both supervised by the Ministry of Revenue until 1471, when the Offices of Produce Levies were transferred to the jurisdiction of the Ministry of Works; (3) six Salt Distribution Commissions (*tu chuan-yün-yen shih ssu* 都轉運鹽使司) and fourteen branch offices (*fen-ssu*); (4) seven Salt Distribution Supervisorates (*yen-k'o t'i-chü ssu* 鹽課提舉司); (5) four Horse Trading Offices (*ch'a-ma ssu* 茶馬司) in western frontier areas, which traded state-owned tea to alien tribesmen for horses; (6) thirteen Iron Smelting Offices (*t'ieh-yeh so* 鐵冶所); and (7) three Maritime Trade Supervisorates (*shih-po t'i-chü ssu* 市舶提舉司), which under eunuch overseers supervised foreign trade at ports in Chekiang, Fukien, and Kwangtung.

Local units of administration. Below the level of provincial agencies, the general administration hierarchy descended from Prefectures (*fu* 府) to Subprefectures (*chou* 州) to Districts (*hsien* 縣). Some Subprefectures were "directly attached" (*chih-li*) to provinces, and some districts were similarly "directly attached" to prefectures. Both prefectures and districts were classified on the basis of their land-tax quotas as large (*shang*), middle (*chung*), and small (*hsia*). Officials of the prefectures embracing Peking and Nanking were singled out with special titles, such as Prefectural Governor (*fu-yin* 府尹). By the late Ming decades the empire was divided into 159 prefectures, 234 subprefectures, and 1,144 districts.

Whereas Prefects (*chih-fu* 知府) and Subprefectural Magistrates (*chih-chou* 知州) were essentially supervisory officials, the District Magistrate (*chih-hsien* 知縣), as at all other times in China's imperial history, was the all-purpose local representative of the Emperor, directly responsible for governing everyone in his geographic jurisdiction. District Magistrates were known collectively as "father-and-mother officials" (*fu-mu kuan* 父母官).

The aboriginal, still incompletely Sinicized tribespeople who occupied large tracts in Hukwang, Szechwan, and especially Yunnan and Kweichow Provinces were allowed a substantial measure of self-government under what was known as the "aboriginal offices" (*t'u-ssu* 土司) system. Their tribal chiefs, usually hereditary, were simply confirmed by the Emperor as "aboriginal" (*t'u*) Prefects, Subprefectural Magistrates, or District Magistrates. The most important and least assimilated chiefs were given such special designations as Pacification Commissioner (*hsüan-wei shih* 宣慰使, *hsüan-fu shih* 宣撫使, *an-fu shih* 安撫使, and variants).

Associated with all local units of government were swarms of low-level specialized agencies, such as Police Offices (*hsün-chien ssu* 巡檢司), Postal Relay Stations (*i* 驛), Transport Offices (*ti-yün so* 遞運所), Commercial Tax Offices (*hsüan-k'o ssu* 宣課司 and variants), Fishing Tax Offices (*ho-p'o so* 河泊所), Tea and Salt Control Stations (*p'i-yen so* 批鹽所), granaries, storehouses, manufactories, and schools.

Below the district level, the population, rural and urban, was organized into Communities (*li* 里), which were held responsible for maintaining local order, adjudicating local disputes, fostering morality and religion, establishing and maintaining essential communal services such as irrigation and schooling, and carrying out the laws in general. In theory 110 neighboring

households constituted a community, whose ten most prosperous households provided a Community Head (*li-chang* 長) in a ten-year rotation. The other 100 households were divided into ten Tithings (*chia* 甲), with a Head (*shou* 首) who represented his group of families to the Community Head. After the mid-Ming years some communities were redesignated Security Groups (*pao* 保), but the *li-chia* and *pao-chia* systems of local organization worked in essentially the same ways.

One responsibility of the Community Heads was to collect local land taxes. Into the sixteenth century these were delivered, not to district officials, but to specially designated Tax Captains (*liang-chang* 糧長). A Tax Captain was drawn from a designated prosperous household in a multi-community area broadly defined as one from which a standard 10,000 bushels of grain were owed as annual land taxes. The Tax Captain was responsible for delivering his collected tax grain annually to his District Magistrate, or directly to the capital, or to specified state granaries that were scattered throughout the empire. As population grew and the state fiscal system became steadily more monetized, the burden on Tax Captains became too complex and heavy. In the sixteenth century they gradually disappeared, and hired agents of District Magistrates were then relied on to collect taxes from Community Heads or directly from individual households.

The Military

The Ming military system provided for two organizational hierarchies, one administrative and the other tactical, or operational. Both extended throughout the empire, though they were naturally concentrated in areas of greatest military need—around the dynastic capital and along coastal and inland frontiers.

The outstanding characteristic of the Ming military system was that it was primarily a hereditary one. The population was divided and registered in hereditary classes based principally on occupation. The two largest classes were ordinary civilian families (*min-hu* 民戶) and military families (*chün-hu* 軍戶). The military family was largely exempted from the civilian family's obligations to the state—to pay land taxes and render service of non-military sorts—in return for providing, theoretically in perpetuity, one able-bodied male for career military service. Troops so obtained were assigned to administrative units or garrisons throughout the empire, where they received training while at least theoretically supporting themselves by part-time work on state-owned tracts called State Farms (*t'un-t'ien* 屯田). From their garrisons, troops were periodically rotated (*pan-chün* 班軍) to tactical or operational units—notably to special training divisions at the capital, to defense commands at the frontiers, or to special armies on campaign. In 1392 such regular troops (*kuan-ping* 官兵) were reported to total 1,198,442. The number fluctuated greatly thereafter. Because hereditary replacement did not work perfectly, the system had to be supplemented in late Ming by the recruitment of mercenaries (*mu-ping* 募兵). These swelled the military rolls to over four million, and the central government spent ever increasing amounts of money in annual military allocations (*nien-li* 年例). At all times, moreover, the regular troops were backed up by militiamen (*min-ping* 民兵) organized for home-guard duty by local civilian authorities.

As has already been noted, control over the Ming military establishment was divided among five Chief Military Commissions (*tu-tu fu*) in the capital. Each of these was responsible for a group of provincial-level Regional Military Commissions (*tu chih-hui shih ssu*), which in turn provided administrative supervision over local garrisons. The basic garrison unit was a Guard (*wei* 衛), headed by a Guard Commander (*chih-hui shih* 指揮使). Each Guard was normally named after the prefecture or subprefecture in which it was based and in theory consisted of 5,600 hereditary soldiers. A Guard theoretically had five Battalions (*ch'ien-hu so* 千戶所) of 1,120 men, each divided into ten Companies (*po-hu so* 百戶所). Companies and even battalions were often garrisoned apart from the Guards to which they belonged, and there were some Independent (*shou-yü* 守禦) Battalions that were controlled directly by Regional Military Commissions and were not parts of Guards.

Aside from the units scattered about the empire, there was an awesome assemblage of 74 Capital Guards (*ching-wei* 京衛) in the immediate vicinity of Peking (after 1420). Thirty-three of these were further distinguished as Imperial Guards (*shang-chih wei* 上直衛, *ch'in-chün wei* 親軍衛) and were charged with protecting the imperial palace. The most important of these was the Imperial Bodyguard (*chin-i wei* 錦衣衛, lit., "the embroidered-uniform Guard"). This unit cooperated with eunuchs of the Eastern and Western Depots (*tung-ch'ang, hsi-ch'ang*) in secret police activities; its officers exercised almost unlimited police and judicial authority, and its prison (*chen-fu ssu* 鎮撫司, *chao-yü* 詔獄) was a feared torture chamber. The Imperial Bodyguard also provided sinecures for various kinds of palace hangers-on and favorites, including court painters.

None of the Imperial Guards was under the supervision of the Five Chief Military Commissions, and fifteen other Capital Guards were similarly independent, solely under the Emperor's personal control.

Nanking, the auxiliary capital after 1420, had another large concentration of Capital Guards, 49 in all, including 17 Imperial Guards. All were subordinate to the Branch (*hsing*) Chief Military Commissions at Nanking. Actual military control at Nanking, however, was vested in three special dignitaries: the Grand Commandant (*shou-pei* 守備), normally a Duke, Marquis, or Earl, but often a eunuch; the Vice Commandant (*hsieh-t'ung shou-pei* 協同守備), usually a Marquis or Earl; and the Grand Adjutant (*ts'an-tsan chi-wu* 參贊機務), a post held concurrently by the Nanking Minister of War.

Troop training was undertaken in all local garrison units, but special tactical training was the responsibility of three Training Divisions (*ying* 營) at Peking, one of which was charged with training in firearms. At times their number was increased, including Integrated Divisions (*t'uan-ying* 團營) and other special organizations. Troops from all over the empire were rotated to the Training Divisions (or counterparts at Nanking), where they served as a sort of pool of combat-ready troops. By late Ming times the Training Divisions had deteriorated greatly, however, and their troops were used mostly as construction gangs.

In the Ming system there was no body of regular combat troops separate from the garrison forces of the Guards. When campaigns were mounted, troops were transferred to field commands out of appropriate local Guards units, or out of the Training Divisions, and high-ranking officers or nobles holding appointments as Military Commissioners-in-chief were specially delegated to lead them as Generals-in-chief (*ta chiang-chün* 大將軍) or Generals (*chiang-chün*). When campaigns were over, these special tactical commanders surrendered their temporary authority, and the troops returned to garrison duty.

Eventually, however, a system of permanent tactical commands developed, especially along the Great Wall and other inland frontiers where constant vigilance was required. There were exposed towns, forts, stockades, ports, passes, barriers, and other strategic locations that required permanent defenders. Troops from nearby Guards were rotated to such places, where they were commanded by specially delegated officers.

Such officers were on relatively temporary assignments; they held rank-titles or substantive appointments somewhere in the regular military administrative hierarchy. Those who directed defense operations in a province or some other large area were generally called Regional Commanders (*tsung-ping kuan* 總兵官) or Grand Defenders (*chen-shou* 鎮守), occasionally with the title of General as well. Officers who controlled smaller areas were called Regional Vice Commanders (*fu tsung-ping kuan* 副總兵官) and Assistant Regional Commanders (*ts'an-chiang* 參將). Every province normally also had a Mobile Corps Commander (*yu-chi chiang-chün* 遊擊將軍). Specialized local tactical commanders had many varying designations.

In the mature Ming system almost every province had a Regional Commander, and there were many others. The most important ones were the Regional Commanders of the nine so-called Defense Commands (*chen* 鎮) or Frontiers (*pien* 邊). These stretched across the northern land frontier, in some cases overlapping provinces. From east to west they were Liaotung, in modern Manchuria (which for civil administration was considered part of Shantung); Chi-chou, northeast of Peking; Hsüan-fu, northwest of Pe-

king; Ta-t'ung in northern Shansi; Shansi or T'ai-yüan, covering the central and western portions of Shansi Province; Yen-sui or Yü-lin in northern Shensi; Ku-yüan, covering the central and western portions of Shensi Province; Ning-hsia, outside the Great Wall north of Shensi; and Kansu in the far west.

After the development of Grand Coordinators and Supreme Commanders in the fifteenth century, all tactical commanders in the military service came under the supervision of these high-ranking civil service dignitaries.

Personnel Administration

Recruitment. Civil service officials were recruited primarily on the basis of educational qualifications. In T'ai-tsu's time, educated men were sought through repeated requests and even demands that existing officials recommend (*chien-chü* 薦舉) capable and virtuous men. Their nominees were promptly appointed to office, and many rose to very high posts. But after the reign of T'ai-tsu, the system of recruitment through recommendations was gradually superseded.

T'ai-tsu also utilized the empire's school system, which he extended to unprecedented levels, to recruit men for the civil service. State-supported Confucian Schools (*ju-hsüeh* 儒學) were ordered established in the headquarters cities and towns of every prefecture, subprefecture, and district, and they were regularly called on to produce prescribed quotas of "tribute students" (*kung-sheng* 貢生), who were examined by litterateurs of the Hanlin Academy (*han-lin yüan*) in the capital and then enrolled in the National University (*t'ai-hsüeh*)—unless they were found unfit, in which case the responsible school officials were punished. Upon completion of further study in the National University (in the student status called *chien-sheng* 監生), they were appointed to governmental posts. Like recommendees, these "tribute students" frequently went on to highly successful careers; but by the middle of the fifteenth century their prestige had seriously declined. They continued to enter service, but were almost completely overshadowed by men entering service through open, competitive examinations.

Recruitment through examinations (*k'o-chü*

科舉) was instituted at the beginning of the dynasty, suspended in 1373, and reinstituted in 1384. It flourished thereafter, quickly becoming the paramount system of recruitment. Eventually candidates had to write in a so-called "eight-legged essay" (*pa-ku wen* 八股文) style, with the result that in the second half of the dynasty the form of the examination became perhaps more important and rigid than in any preceding dynasty. As for subject matter, as in earlier times, the examinations emphasized thorough understanding of the classics and of history, the ability to relate classical precepts and historical precedents to fundamental ideological issues and current political problems, and skill in literary composition.

The "grand competition" (*ta-pi* 大比) of examinations was conducted every three years, in three phases. First there were provincial examinations (*hsiang-shih* 鄉試) in the provincial capitals or, for residents of the metropolitan areas, in Peking and Nanking. Candidates were qualified in advance by touring provincial Education Intendants (*t'i-tu hsüeh tao-t'ai*) and were called Cultivated Talents (*hsiu-ts'ai* 秀才, roughly comparable in esteem to a modern bachelor's degree). Some were students in the National University or graduates of the local schools, but entirely private scholars—often trained in private academies (*shu-yüan* 書院)—appear to have accounted for a steadily increasing proportion.

Men who successfully passed the provincial examinations were designated Provincial Graduates (*chü-jen* 舉人) and could next participate in a metropolitan examination (*hui-shih* 會試) at the capital. Those who passed it soon reassembled for a palace examination (*t'ing-shih* 廷試, *tien-shih* 殿試), nominally conducted by the Emperor, to be ranked by merit into three groups (*chia* 甲). All were generally designated Metropolitan Graduates (*chin-shih* 進士, often compared in esteem to a modern doctoral degree); they were assured of civil service careers.

Provincial Graduates who failed to pass the metropolitan examination were sometimes appointed directly to low-ranking offices in the civil service hierarchy, and sometimes they entered the National University for further training, after which they were eligible for appointments on the same basis as tribute students. After early Ming, however, neither Provincial Graduates nor tribute students could hope to rise as fast or as high in the service as Metropolitan Graduates. From the middle of the Ming period on, men who attained high rank without having entered service via the metropolitan and palace examinations were exceedingly rare.

The cycle of examinations was conducted 90 times during the Ming dynasty, producing a total of 24,874 Metropolitan Graduates. The average number of passers per metropolitan examination was thus 276; per year, 90. The smallest number of degrees granted at any metropolitan examination was 32; the largest was 472.

Of much less significance were two other systems of recruitment that were relied on sporadically. One was China's traditional "protection of sons" (*yin-tzu* 蔭子) or "employment of sons" (*jen-tzu* 任子) privilege. This was used rather extensively in the early Ming period, when civil officials of rank 7 or higher were able to "protect" one son each, by automatically attaining civil service status for them. This privilege, however, was subsequently restricted to officials of rank 3 and above, and the offices to which "protected" sons were appointed became steadily less important. In some cases sons were able to take office immediately on reaching maturity, but many had to be qualified through special examinations and then enrolled in the National University as "official students" (*kuan-sheng* 官生), later to enter service. When officials of any rank served the state with extraordinary merit—particularly if they gave their lives for the state—their sons could be specially entered in the National University as "students by grace" (*en-sheng* 恩生) and subsequently accepted into service.

The remaining system of recruitment, resorted to by many earlier dynasties, involved the purchase of official status. The Ming practice, initiated in 1450, seems to have had very little effect on the functioning officialdom, but served merely to confer honorific status and some exemptions from state obligations on generous contributors to the government in times of financial crisis.

Appointments. Before being actually appointed to offices, students of the National University were frequently and in great numbers assigned to various agencies of the government as novices (*li-shih* 歷事, *pan-shih* 辦事), usually for periods of one year. Metropolitan Graduates were sometimes so assigned as "observers" (*kuan-cheng* 觀政). Many posts at all rank levels were subject to probationary service (*li-cheng* 歷政) for periods of up to a year before substantive appointments (*shih-shou* 實授) were granted.

Once appointed to offices, officials were subject to continual surveillance by their superiors. The maximum tenure in a post was normally nine years. Every three years, however, each official was rated (*k'ao* 考) by his superiors and could be reassigned accordingly. When "ratings were completed" (*k'ao-man* 考滿)—that is, after an official had spent nine years in one post and received three ratings—he reported to the Ministry of Personnel at the capital for reconsideration of his status, which might result in his being promoted, demoted, or punished. The three-year ratings were supplemented by the evaluations (*k'ao-ch'a* 考察) of Magistrates of districts and subprefectures, who in monthly reports (*yüeh-chi* 月計) to their Prefects took note of personnel considered misfits or incompetents. Prefects submitted consolidated annual reports (*sui-chi* 歲計) of such special evaluations to the provincial authorities. Then every third year the provincial authorities submitted consolidated evaluation reports to the central government, triggering a large-scale "outer evaluation" (*wai-ch'a* 外察), for which all units of local administration sent representatives to a grand audience at the capital. For officials on duty at the capital, a comparable "capital evaluation" (*ching-ch'a* 京察) was conducted every sixth year. Capital officials of rank 4 and above were exempted from normal evaluation procedures but were expected to submit confessions of their own faults (*tzu-ch'en* 自陳). As a result of these great evaluations, large numbers of officials were downgraded, retired, or dismissed from the service.

Besides this routine system of merit ratings and evaluations, officials were subject to irreg-ular *k'ao-ch'a* evaluations by censorial officials or specially assigned investigators; and for especially noteworthy faults or offenses, officials might at any time be impeached by their superiors, by Censors, or by fellow officials—and might even be punished or dismissed summarily without having been impeached.

As in prior times, officials were entitled to merit titles (*hsün* 勳) and prestige titles (*san-kuan* 散官), automatically earned by attaining different rank levels and accumulating time in service. There were ten merit titles, one for each degree of rank from 1a down through 5b. They were mostly ornate titles such as Chief Minister (*ch'ing* 卿) or Governor (*yin* 尹) with special prefixes. Lesser civil officials did not receive merit titles, although all military officers received merit titles corresponding to their twelve degrees of rank—differing from those awarded civil officials.

Civil officials of all ranks were entitled to prestige titles, and officials in any one degree of rank could be promoted to a second- or even a third-level prestige title. In all, there were 42 prestige titles, mostly Grand Masters (*ta-fu* 大夫) and Court Gentlemen (*lang* 郎) with varying prefixes. For military officers there was a schedule of 30 prestige titles, mostly Generals (*chiang-chün* 將軍) and Commandants (*hsiao-wei* 校尉), with varying prefixes.

Official salaries and allowances. Officials received salaries and allowances according to their ranks (*p'in* 品), all nominally reckoned in bushels of grain, ranging from 1,044 to 60 a year. Parts of the salaries, however, were paid in silver, paper money, or other commodities, supposedly equivalent to the value of grain; and the commutation rates were arbitrarily changed from time to time, generally to the disadvantage of the recipients. The Ming salary scales have consequently been considered not very generous in comparison with other dynasties.

Military officers generally fared better than civil officials, principally because they were fairly readily given noble status (*chüeh* 爵), which could increase their stipends to as much as 5,000 bushels a year.

Ch'ing
1644-1912

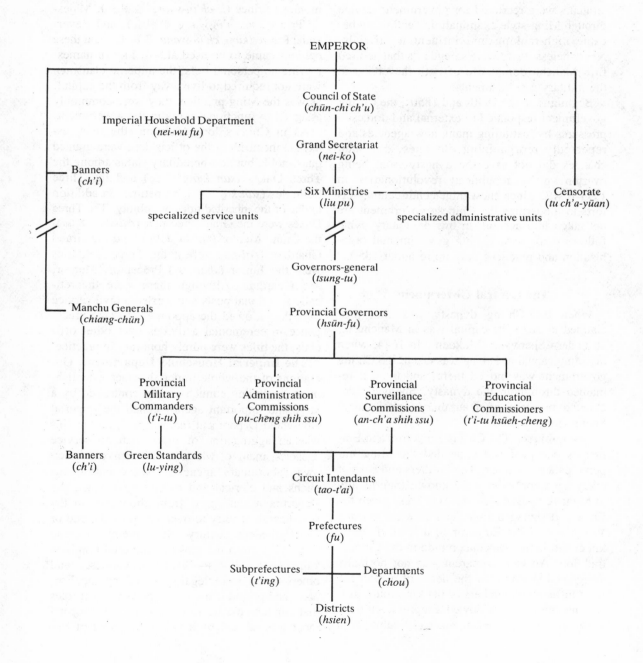

EMPEROR

Imperial Household Department
(*nei-wu fu*)

Council of State
(*chün-chi ch'u*)

Grand Secretariat
(*nei-ko*)

Banners
(*ch'i*)

Six Ministries
(*liu pu*)

Censorate
(*tu ch'a-yüan*)

specialized service units

specialized administrative units

Governors-general
(*tsung-tu*)

Manchu Generals
(*chiang-chün*)

Provincial Governors
(*hsün-fu*)

Provincial
Military
Commanders
(*t'i-tu*)

Provincial
Administration
Commissions
(*pu-cheng shih ssu*)

Provincial
Surveillance
Commissions
(*an-ch'a shih ssu*)

Provincial
Education
Commissioners
(*t'i-tu hsüeh-cheng*)

Banners
(*ch'i*)

Green Standards
(*lu-ying*)

Circuit Intendants
(*tao-t'ai*)

Prefectures
(*fu*)

Subprefectures
(*t'ing*)

Departments
(*chou*)

Districts
(*hsien*)

Like their Jurchen relatives before them, the Manchus greatly admired Chinese culture and institutions. In consequence, the government they fashioned for their Ch'ing dynasty was superficially a virtual replica of the Ming government it superseded. However, some important new elements were added that tightened the Emperors' autocratic control of the state. Chinese litterateurs were recruited for government service through Ming-style examinations, and many became high-ranking and influential officials. Nevertheless, there were safeguards that assured firm Manchu dominance of both the civil and the military establishments.

Beginning in the 1840s and 1850s, the Ch'ing government responded to external and domestic pressures by instituting many new agencies and repeatedly reorganizing old ones, but such changes did not save the dynasty from being overthrown by republican revolutionaries in 1911–1912. Since these nineteenth-century efforts to modernize the Chinese government are not taken into account in this dictionary, what follows deals with Ch'ing governmental organization and practices only up to about 1850.

The Central Government

When the Ch'ing dynasty was first proclaimed in 1635, its capital was in Manchuria, at modern Shenyang (Mukden). In 1644, when the Ming capital at Peking was taken, the Ch'ing government was moved there, and there it remained throughout the dynasty. Shenyang declined to the status of an auxiliary capital, called Sheng-ching.

The nobility. The Ch'ing Emperors and Empresses occupied and expanded the Ming imperial palace complex. The brothers and sons of every Emperor, who were known traditionally in Manchu as Beile (*pei-lo* 貝勒) and given the Chinese designation Imperial Prince (*ch'in-wang* 親王), joined the Emperor in a kind of ruling kin coalition that was uncommon in the Chinese tradition. An Heir Apparent was not normally designated. Rather, on the death of a ruler the most influential members of the kin group, usually including the widowed Empress, chose a successor. The successor normally came from among the deceased ruler's sons if any, but the eldest son was not necessarily chosen.

Members of the imperial family and other favored dignitaries were ennobled, but members of the Ch'ing nobility were not granted territorial fiefs, even nominally. The most esteemed Princes, however, bore and passed on to their heirs special laudatory epithets, such as Ceremonious Prince (*li ch'in-wang* 禮親王), Majestic Prince (*su ch'in-wang* 肅親王), and Reverential Prince (*kung ch'in-wang* 恭親王), and these epithets came to be used almost like surnames. Having no personal fiefs, the imperial clansmen were not required to live away from the capital, as was the Ming practice; they were commonly assigned to functional posts in the government.

As in China's long tradition, the most esteemed members of the officialdom were granted quasi-noble but non-hereditary status among the Three Dukes (*san kung* 三公) and the Three Solitaries (*san ku* 三孤), sometimes in addition to one of the inherited titles of nobility. The Three Dukes were the Grand Preceptor (*t'ai-shih* 太師), the Grand Mentor (*t'ai-fu* 太傅), and the Grand Guardian (*t'ai-pao* 太保); the Three Solitaries were the Junior (*shao* 少) Preceptor, Mentor, and Guardian. Although these were theoretically functional posts and carried a civil service rank that allowed the appointees to take precedence in ceremonial activities over other officials, the titles were purely honorary in practice.

The Imperial Household Department. Operations of the whole imperial palace establishment, including eunuchs, were controlled by a large and important agency called the Imperial Household Department (*nei-wu fu* 內務府). This was an aggregation of more than 50 service agencies, many of which in turn supervised their own subordinate agencies. Not counting eunuchs and clerical and menial underlings, the Department staff grew from about 400 in the seventeenth century to over 1,600 by the end of the eighteenth century. Staff members came principally from the ranks of imperial bondservants (*pao-i* 包衣)—Manchus, Chinese, and others—who were legally owned by the Emperor and played many of the governmental roles that eunuchs played in other eras. The Department was headed by a varying number of Supervisors-in-chief (*tsung-kuan* 總管), invariably chosen from among the Imperial Princes, other members of the nobility, and some other prestigious personages, all of whom were referred to generically as Grand Ministers (*ta-ch'en* 大臣).

The Grand Secretariat and the Council of State. The earliest "national" government of what was to become the Ch'ing dynasty was a group of Manchu nobles in three categories: the Grand Ministers Commanding the Eight Banners (*pa-ch'i tsung-kuan ta-ch'en* 八旗總管大臣), the Five Grand Ministers of the Deliberative Council (*i-cheng wu ta-ch'en* 議政五大臣), and the Ten Grand Ministers Administering Affairs (*li-shih shih ta-ch'en* 理事十大臣). When the Ch'ing dynasty was proclaimed in 1635, this unique Manchu central government was changed into a more Chinese-like one, headed by Three Palace Academies (*nei san yüan* 內三院), Six Ministries (*liu pu* 六部), and a Censorate (*tu ch'a-yüan* 都察院). The Three Palace Academies were the Palace Historiographic Academy (*nei kuo-shih yüan* 內國史院), the Palace Secretariat Academy (*nei pi-shu yüan* 內祕書院), and the Palace Academy for the Advancement of Literature (*nei hung-wen yüan* 內弘文院). The last named had the special charge of translating China's classical and historical writings into Manchu and tutoring the Emperor and his Princes in Chinese culture. Each Academy was headed by a Grand Academician (*ta hsüeh-shih* 大學士).

The Three Palace Academies combined the functions of the Ming dynasty Hanlin Academy (*han-lin yüan* 翰林院) and Grand Secretariat (*nei-ko* 內閣), and in 1658 they were reorganized in the Ming fashion. From that time on, the Grand Secretariat was a regular organ of government at the peak of the general administration hierarchy, and the Hanlin Academy was the government's paramount scholarly workshop and the training ground for officials who would ultimately become the ranking personages in that hierarchy, including the Grand Secretariat.

By the time the Grand Secretariat emerged in the Ch'ing government, a pattern had been established that, in general, required the appointment of Manchus and Chinese in equal numbers to all executive posts in central government offices. Thus the Grand Secretariat was headed by two Manchu and two Chinese Grand Secretaries (*ta hsüeh-shih*), each nominally assigned to one or another palace Hall (*tien* 殿 or *ko* 閣) as in Ming times. Manchu appointees were commonly Princes or other nobles. Each Grand Secretary normally served concurrently as a Minister (*shang-shu* 尚書) of one or another of the Six Ministries.

The Ch'ing Grand Secretariat had a large staff. Among others, it included one Manchu and one Chinese Assistant Grand Secretary (*hsieh-pan ta hsüeh-shih* 協辦大學士); varying numbers of Academicians (*hsüeh-shih* 學士), Readers-in-waiting (*shih-tu* 侍讀), and Archivists (*tien-chi* 典籍); and more than 100 Secretaries (*chung-shu* 中書). There were Manchu and Chinese appointees to each post, and Mongols as well in many posts; but the appointees were not ethnically paired below the level of the Assistant Grand Secretaries. Manchus greatly predominated.

Despite the Ch'ing Grand Secretariat's position atop the regular governmental hierarchy, it at no time attained much decision-making power. To be sure, its position in the hierarchy gave it status in the so-called outer court (*wai-t'ing* 外廷), so that Grand Secretaries could presume to represent the officialdom at large before the throne, as was not the case in Ming times. The converse, however, is that the Grand Secretariat was not part of the inner court (*nei-t'ing* 內廷) of the Emperor and his most intimate confidants, who really determined governmental policy. Determining policy on major issues remained the function of the leaders of the ruling kin group, known informally as Princes and Grand Ministers of the Deliberative Council (*i-cheng ch'u wang ta-ch'en* 議政處王大臣). Manchus serving as Grand Secretaries sometimes participated individually in such deliberations, and in time even Chinese Grand Secretaries were allowed to do so; but the Grand Secretariat as an institution was outside the circle of real power.

The influence of the Grand Secretariat was further weakened by a system of palace memorials (*tsou-che* 奏摺) instituted in the 1690s by the K'ang-hsi Emperor (r. 1661–1722) and made more systematic by his son, the Yung-cheng Emperor (r. 1722–1735). This system enabled imperial bondservants serving in the provinces and, eventually, even large numbers of nobles and officials serving in the capital to submit reports on nonroutine matters directly to the throne in sealed boxes, bypassing all normal avenues of administrative communication, including the Grand Secretariat.

By about 1730 the Yung-cheng Emperor had completely reduced the Grand Secretariat to a relatively impotent secretarial agency by transforming the previously unofficial Deliberative Council (*i-cheng ch'u*) into an official Council of State (*chün-chi ch'u* 軍機處). This was definitely an "inner court" institution, chaired by an Imperial Prince. Membership fluctuated at first, but settled in the nineteenth century into a standard group of five Grand Ministers of State (*chün-chi ta-ch'en*), made up of two Chinese and three Manchus, including the presiding Prince. Members normally held substantive appointments in the regular officialdom, most commonly in the Six Ministries, but they met as a body daily in conference with the Emperor, resolved current problems collegially, and countersigned all rescripts and edicts issued by or in the name of the Emperor. They came to be served by up to 60 Secretaries (*chang-ching* 章京), divided into two Manchu and two Chinese Duty Groups (*pan* 班). With this institutional change, the Grand Secretariat became for the most part a processor of paperwork concerning routine administrative business, subject to policy guidelines set by the Council.

Ministries, Courts, and Directorates. The Six Ministries duplicated their Ming predecessors in almost all respects, a major difference being that each was always headed jointly by one Manchu and one Chinese Minister (*shang-shu*). There were Ministries of Personnel (*li-pu* 吏部), of Revenue (*hu-pu* 戶部), of Rites (*li-pu* 禮部), of War (*ping-pu* 兵部), of Justice (*hsing-pu* 刑部), and of Works (*kung-pu* 工部). The Ministries of Personnel, Rites, War, and Works were each divided into four functionally differentiated Bureaus (*ch'ing-li ssu* 清吏司), and as in Ming times, the Ministries of Revenue and Justice were divided into Bureaus named after provinces or equivalent territories, totaling fourteen and eighteen, respectively.

Although the Ch'ing Ministries cannot all be considered major executive agencies, some retained much of their Ming authority and prestige. The Ministry of Revenue was the supreme fiscal agency of the state; the Ministry of Rites supervised activities that buttressed the religious authority of the Emperor and among other things administered civil service recruitment examinations; and the Ministry of Justice played an important role in supervising routine judicial and penal administration. Many of the traditional functions of the other Ministries—of Personnel, of War, and of Works—were lost to the Emperor and the Council of State, the Imperial Household Department, the military establishment, Grand Ministers on special commissions, and provincial authorities who were more powerful than their Ming predecessors.

A Ch'ing agency that was a seventh Ministry in all but name was the Court of Colonial Affairs (*li-fan yüan* 理藩院), which had its origins in a Mongol Agency (*meng-ku ya-men* 蒙古衙門) established during the Manchu conquest of China. Until 1861, when it was replaced by a Western-style Foreign Office (*tsung-li ya-men* 總理衙門), the Court of Colonial Affairs supervised all Ch'ing official relations with the various Mongol tribes that came under Manchu overlordship, Tibet, Russia, and the oasis statelets of Chinese Turkestan. Like a Ministry, it was headed by a Minister (*shang-shu*) and was divided into Bureaus (*ch'ing-li ssu*).

Among other noteworthy administrative agencies in the central government was the Office of Transmission (*t'ung-cheng shih ssu* 通政使司), which managed the government's routine communications. There also were five major Courts (*ssu* 寺) and two major Directorates (*chien* 監). These were the Court of Judicial Review (*ta-li ssu* 大理寺), which reviewed all important trials and sentences reported by local magistrates; the Court of Imperial Sacrifices (*t'ai-ch'ang ssu* 太常寺), which in collaboration with the Ministry of Rites managed the host of sacrificial ceremonies that were an essential part of traditional Chinese governance; the Court of Imperial Entertainments (*kuang-lu ssu* 光祿寺), which was a kind of banqueting and catering service for the whole central government; the Court of State Ceremonial (*hung-lu ssu* 鴻臚寺),

which supervised the ritual aspects of all state functions; the Court of the Imperial Stud (*t'ai-p'u ssu* 太僕寺), which managed the state horse pasturages; the Directorate of Astronomy (*ch'in-t'ien chien* 欽天監); and the Directorate of Education (*kuo-tzu chien* 國子監), a kind of national university whose state-supported students (*chien-sheng* 監生) were divided among six Colleges (*t'ang* 堂). Although the Courts and Directorates had regularly prescribed heads, such as the Chancellor (*chi-chiu* 祭酒) of the Directorate of Education, they were often under the supervision of dignitaries whose principal substantive appointments were as Grand Secretaries and Ministers and who were designated, for example, Concurrent Grand Minister Managing the Affairs of the Directorate (*chien kuan chien-shih ta-ch'en* 兼管監事大臣). Like the Ministries, the Courts and Directorates were regularly headed jointly by one Manchu and one Chinese, but the Directorate of Astronomy was distinctive in having one Manchu and one European Supervisor (*chien-cheng* 監正).

The Censorate. Until 1723, the Ch'ing central government's censorial establishment almost wholly duplicated its Ming counterpart. There was first of all the Censorate itself (*tu ch'a-yüan* 都察院), charged with maintaining disciplinary surveillance over the officialdom at large, impeaching wayward officials, and remonstrating with the Emperor about his personal or public misconduct. Its staff largely consisted of Investigating Censors (*chien-ch'a yü-shih* 監察御史), divided for administrative purposes into Circuits (*tao* 道) that were generally named after provinces. Independent of the Censorate were Six Offices of Scrutiny (*liu k'o* 六科) with designations paralleling those of the Six Ministries (e.g., the Office of Scrutiny for Personnel), staffed with Supervising Secretaries (*chi-shih-chung* 給事中), whose principal assignment was to monitor the flow of documents to and from the Ministries and to "veto" (*feng-po* 封駁)—that is, return for reconsideration—any memorial or imperial pronouncement judged to be improper either in style or in substance. As in Ming times, Investigating Censors and Supervising Secretaries were assigned to many sorts of special inspections and other duties, often jointly.

One striking difference from the Ming system, however, was that after 1661 Investigating Censors were not sent out on provincial commissions as Regional Inspectors (*hsün-an yü-shih* 巡按御史), in part because of the regularization of the appointments of the senior provincial officials, who consistently bore concurrent titles as Censor-in-chief of the Right (*yu tu yü-shih* 右都御史) or Vice Censor-in-chief of the Right (*yu fu tu yü-shih*). (The senior Censorate officials on duty in the capital were always designated "of the Left," *tso* 左).

The esteem and political sensitivity of the censorial offices are reflected in the fact that all Censors of every rank and all Supervising Secretaries were without exception appointed in exact ethnic pairings of Manchus and Chinese. Although the senior officials of almost every agency in the capital were appointed in such pairs, in no other agency was the principle of ethnic balance applied throughout virtually all ranks.

The Ming pattern of censorial organization was abruptly altered in 1723 by the Yung-cheng Emperor, who made the previously independent Offices of Scrutiny part of the Censorate. This reorganization subordinated the Supervising Secretaries (*chi-shih-chung*)—now better rendered into English as Supervising Censors—to the executive officials of the Censorate, at least for routine personnel administration purposes. It thus ended a long Chinese tradition separating remonstrance agencies from surveillance agencies and in some degree weakened the whole censorial establishment, already weakened by its lack of Regional Inspectors in the provinces. Of even more importance, probably, in the gradual weakening of the censorial establishment in Ch'ing times was the development under the K'ang-hsi and Yung-cheng Emperors of the secret palace memorial system mentioned above, which diffused the traditional censorial powers of secret reporting and impeaching among imperial bondservants and other noncensorial officials scattered throughout the empire.

At full strength after 1723, the Censorate was staffed principally by two Censors-in-chief of the Left, four Vice Censors-in-chief of the Left, 24 Supervising Censors divided among six Offices of Scrutiny, and 56 Investigating Censors divided among fifteen circuits. It should be noted that, as in Ming times, Investigating Censors had little direct connection with the provinces for which their circuits were named; they were stationed for normal duty in the dynastic capital.

Territorial Administration

The Manchus perpetuated the Ming division of China into Provinces (*sheng* 省). By 1850, there were eighteen provinces in China Proper. These were Chihli (the "directly attached" Metropolitan Area, *pei-ching* 北京), Shantung, Honan, Shansi, Shensi, Kansu, Szechwan, Hupei, Hunan, Kiangsu, Anhwei, Kiangsi, Chekiang, Fukien, Kwangtung, Kwangsi, Kweichow, and Yunnan. What Westerners call Manchuria was known as the Three Eastern Provinces (*tung san sheng* 東三省): Fengtien, Kirin, and Heilungkiang. Chinese Turkestan was organized into the modern Sinkiang Province in 1884, and Taiwan was made a twenty-third province in 1885 after having previously been dealt with as part of Fukien Province.

A province was normally administered by a Governor (*hsün-fu* 巡撫). This was now a substantive office rather than a duty assignment, or commission (*ch'ai-ch'ien* 差遣), as in Ming times, although Governors ordinarily held nominal additional posts as Vice Ministers of War (*ping-pu shih-lang* 兵部侍郎) and Vice Censors-in-chief of the Right. The institutional status of a Governor was nevertheless somewhat anomalous. Although all provincial agencies communicated with the central government through him, he had no authorized staff of assistants, as if he were still merely a Ming-style coordinator. In order to cope with their workloads, Governors commonly built up Private Secretariats (*mu-fu* 幕府) of non-official administrative specialists.

Only the Governors of Shansi, Shantung, and Honan were the paramount administrative authorities in their provinces. All others were subordinate to Governors-general (*tsung-tu* 總督). These posts also were now substantive ones, although appointees normally held nominal additional posts as Ministers of War (*ping-pu shang-shu*) and Censors-in-chief of the Right. Like Governors, Governors-general had to rely on personal staffs for assistance in coping with their responsibilities, which normally extended over two or three provinces.

There were nine Governors-general in 1850. Two administered only one province each, Chihli and Szechwan, as Governors-general Concurrently Managing the Affairs of the Governor (*tsung-tu chien-kuan hsün-fu shih* 總督兼管巡撫事). In six instances, Governors-general of two or three provinces were each concurrent Governors of one of the provinces under their jurisdiction (as shown in parentheses): for the Manchurian provinces of Fengtien, Kirin, and Heilungkiang (Fengtien); for Fukien and Chekiang (Fukien); for Hupei and Hunan (Hupei); for Shensi, Kansu, and Sinkiang (Kansu); for Kwangtung and Kwangsi (Kwangtung); and for Yunnan and Kweichow (Yunnan). Finally, the Governor-general of Liang-chiang (i.e., Kiangsu, Kiangsi, and Anhwei) was not a concurrent Governor but supervised Governors of each of these three provinces.

Although the Governor-general was clearly superior to the Governor in rank and in the administrative hierarchy, the relationship was usually one of close collaboration. The two dignitaries consulted together on all important matters and acted jointly in reporting to the central government and in issuing directives to subordinate agencies. They were popularly referred to by the combined term *tu-fu* 督撫 or as the Two Magnates (*liang yüan* 兩院).

From the provincial level on down there was no application of the principle of ethnic balance that applied so consistently in central government offices. The posts of Governors-general and Governors, and posts in lesser agencies, were not held jointly by Manchu and Chinese appointees. Indeed, in all of the provincial and local offices Chinese appointees substantially outnumbered Manchu appointees.

Provincial staff agencies. In the general administration hierarchy there were two kinds of agencies directly subordinate to the Governors: Provincial Administration Commissions (*ch'eng-hsüan pu-cheng shih ssu* 承宣布政使司; densely populated Kiangsu Province had two such Commissions, one at Nanking and one at Soochow) and Provincial Surveillance Commissions (*t'i-hsing an-ch'a shih ssu* 提刑按察使司). These were in effect the official staff agencies for the

Governors. The Provincial Administration Commissioner (*pu-cheng shih*) was a virtual lieutenant-governor and with his large staff bore especially heavy fiscal responsibilities. The Provincial Surveillance Commissioner (*an-ch'a shih*) supervised the administration of justice and with his staff provided Censorate-like surveillance over the provincial and local officials.

Not part of the general administration hierarchy but an important and prestigious official in every province was the Provincial Education Commissioner (*t'i-tu hsüeh-cheng* 提督學政). These were civil service officials with substantive appointments in the capital—most commonly as Vice Ministers, members of the Hanlin Academy, Supervising Secretaries (Supervising Censors), or Investigating Censors—who were assigned to serve three-year terms in the provinces, generally one per province, to supervise the schools and certify candidates for the civil service recruitment examinations. Originally this duty was performed by Assistant Surveillance Commissioners (*an-ch'a ch'ien-shih* 按察簽事) assigned to province-wide Education Intendant Circuits (*tu-hsüeh tao* 督學道), but the responsibility was upgraded in 1684 and again in 1726, into a commission for notably talented capital officials. However, despite their substantive appointments in the capital, they were not independent of the supervision of Governors and Governors-general.

Circuit Intendants. The next lower echelon in the general administration hierarchy consisted of Circuit Intendants (*tao-t'ai* 道臺) of several sorts. In the early Ch'ing period, as in Ming times, these were Administration Vice Commissioners (*pu-cheng ts'an-cheng* 布政參政), Assistant Administration Commissioners (*pu-cheng ts'an-i* 參議), Surveillance Vice Commissioners (*an-ch'a fu-shih* 按察副使), and Assistant Surveillance Commissioners (*an-ch'a ch'ien-shih*) assigned to General Administration Circuits (*fen-shou tao* 分守道), General Surveillance Circuits (*fen-hsün tao* 分巡道), and various more specialized circuits. In 1735 the Circuit Intendancies were all transformed from mere duty assignments to substantive posts in their own right, so that the Intendants thereafter were not considered representatives of the Provincial Commissions. Their function nevertheless continued to be coordinating the activities of groups of adjoining prefectures and serving as intermediaries between the prefectures and the Provincial Commissions. Most of the circuits were still called General Administration Circuits (*shou-tao*) or General Surveillance Circuits (*hsün-tao*) and were identified by territorial prefixes suggesting their geographic jurisdictions. But there were many other circuits whose names reflected their principal responsibilities: Waterways Circuits (*ho-tao* 河道), Grain Tax Circuits (*liang-ch'u tao* 糧儲道), and Salt Control Circuits (*yen-fa tao* 鹽法道). As local circumstances warranted, Intendants were sometimes given added responsibilities, such as for military defense, river maintenance, irrigation, education, or frontier horse trading. Most provinces had from three to six circuits; the total in mid-eighteenth-century China Proper was 89.

Units of local administration. The basic units of local administration, in descending rank order, were Prefectures (*fu* 府) headed by Prefects (*chih-fu* 知府), Subprefectures (*t'ing* 廳) headed by Subprefectural Magistrates (*t'ung-chih* 同知, *t'ung-p'an* 通判), Departments (*chou* 州) headed by Department Magistrates (*chih-chou* 知州), and finally Districts (*hsien* 縣) headed by District Magistrates (*chih-hsien*). Some subprefectures and departments were independent of prefectures, "directly attached" (*chih-li* 直隸) to circuits; some districts were directly supervised by prefectures without intervening subprefectures or departments; and some subprefectures and departments had no districts under their supervision but were directly in charge of the general population. The prefectures and districts in which provincial capitals were located were known as Principal (*shou* 首) Prefectures and Districts.

All agencies of local government, from the circuit down to the district, were ranked in four categories according to the importance and complexity of their activities: Most Important (*tsui-yao* 最要), Important (*yao-ch'üeh* 要缺), Ordinary (*chung-ch'üeh* 中缺), and Simple (*chien-ch'üeh* 簡缺). Many Circuit Intendants, Prefects, and District Magistrates with heavy responsibilities found it necessary to hire non-official Private Secretariats (*mu-fu*) to assist them, as Governors-general and Governors did, even though prefectures and lesser agencies had authorized staffs of subordinate officials and suboffical functionaries.

In the areas of the Southwest that were predominantly populated by largely unassimilated aboriginal tribes, the Manchus perpetuated the Ming practice of allowing the people a substantial measure of self-government under their customary chiefs; this was called the aboriginal-offices (*t'u-ssu* 土司) or aboriginal-officials (*t'u-kuan* 土官) system. Aboriginal chiefs were thus often designated Aboriginal Prefects (*t'u chih-fu*), Aboriginal Subprefects (*t'u t'ung-p'an*), and the like; others were given irregular but traditional titles, all with the meaning Pacification Commissioner (*hsüan-wei shih* 宣慰使 and variants).

In addition to these general administrative agencies, Ch'ing territorial administration abounded with many categories of multi-provincial or cross-provincial officials with special, limited functions. These notably included a single Director-general of Grain Transport (*ts'ao-yün tsung-tu* 漕運總督), based in the Huai-an area of Kiangsu; three Directors-general of the Grand Canal (*ho-tao tsung-tu* 河道總督), based in Kiangsu, Shantung, and Chihli; and five Salt Controllers (*tu chuan-yün-yen shih* 都轉運鹽使), based at Tientsin, Chi-nan, Yangchow, Hangchow, and Canton.

Below the district level, the general population was organized in two overlapping systems, perpetuating the Ming organizations called *li-chia* 里甲 and *pao-chia* 保甲. The *li-chia* system was intended to keep local order and to deliver taxes and requisitioned services to the responsible magistrates. In theory, at least, 110 neighboring households were grouped into a Community (*li* 里), in which the ten most prosperous households annually rotated the responsibility of Community Head (*li-chang* 長). The other 100 households were divided into ten Tithings (*chia*), each with a designated Tithing Head (*chia-shou* 首). After the earliest Ch'ing decades, the burdens on the Community Heads became so onerous that emphasis was placed increasingly on new ten-family groupings, each with a Tithing Head (*chia-chang*) who was responsible to the District Magistrate or his agents. Increasingly, such district hirelings became direct tax collectors in China's rural areas.

The overlapping *pao-chia* system was intended to be a self-policing, self-defense institution. Ten households constituted a Registration Unit (*p'ai* 牌) with a designated Registration Unit Head (*p'ai-t'ou* 頭); ten registration units a Tithing (*chia*) with a designated Tithing Head (*chia-chang*); and ten tithings a Security Group (*pao*) of 1,000 households, with a designated Security Group Head (*pao-chang* 保長 or *pao-cheng* 保正), who was accountable for the behavior of the local residents and the movements of suspicious strangers, and who organized local police patrols.

Peripheral dependencies. Relations between Ch'ing China and external areas that sooner or later became its dependencies—Mongolia, Chinese Turkestan, and Tibet—were generally supervised by the Court of Colonial Affairs (*li-fan yüan*) in the central government. On balance, the pattern was similar to that applied to the southwestern aborigines; the dependent peoples were allowed to follow their own way of life without much interference, under their customary chieftains, as long as they kept the peace and showed proper deference to the Manchu Emperor.

The Mongols were the earliest foreign people to accept Manchu overlordship, were in many cases allies of the Manchus in the conquest of China, and retained a large measure of autonomy. Many were organized in Manchu-style Banners. In Outer Mongolia, the native leaders of Banners or various tribal units (*pu* 部, *tsu* 族) normally organized themselves loosely into Leagues (*meng* 盟), which the Ch'ing government tried to hold accountable for the stability of the area. It was not until the nineteenth century that Outer Mongolia was subjected to somewhat tighter control under a Manchu General (*chiang-chün* 將軍), a Grand Minister Consultant (*ts'an-tsan ta-ch'en* 參贊大臣), and several Judicial Administrators (*pan-shih ssu-yüan* 辦事司員). Inner Mongolia was always dealt with more attentively, not only because it lay immediately beyond China's northern defenses and was the area in which the Ch'ing government maintained many of its horse pasturages, but also because it was an area into which Chinese agriculturalists migrated in increasing numbers. The Banners and tribes of Inner Mongolia were consequently subjected to supervision by the adjoining provincial administrations of Chihli and Fengtien Provinces and by a special Manchu General (*chiang-chün*).

Before Chinese Turkestan became Sinkiang Province in 1884, the local leaders of its mixed population of Mongols, Islamicized Turks, and Tangutans (Tibetans) were generally dealt with as tributary vassals and granted Chinese-style titles, usually of military sorts, in some cases as prestigious as Prince (*wang* 王, *pei-lo* 貝勒). The far northwestern region of Ili, an area of considerable turbulence in the seventeenth and eighteenth centuries, was ultimately placed under a Commander-general (*tsung-t'ung* 總統) and a corps of aides.

Tibet was relatively autonomous under its Lamaist religious leaders (*la-ma* 喇嘛) and its secular tribal chieftains, who were often enfeoffed as tributary Princes (*wang*), until the 1720s. Tibetan rebelliousness then prompted the Ch'ing government to place the area under the direct supervision of two Grand Minister Residents of Tibet (*chu-tsang ta-ch'en* 駐藏大臣), supported by Ch'ing military garrisons.

The Military

The most distinctive feature of the Ch'ing military system was its division into two wholly separate organizations, the famous Banner (*ch'i* 旗) units of Manchus, allied Mongols, and Chinese who had early joined the Manchu cause in the overthrow of the Ming dynasty, and the Green Standards (*lu-ying* 綠營) units of surrendered Ming soldiers. Membership in both was perpetuated hereditarily.

The Banners. The Banners were originally Manchu tribal groups transformed into living and fighting communities not unlike the *ordos* of the northern nomadic peoples who established the Liao and Chin dynasties. The earliest Manchu system organized all Manchus first into four Banners distinguished by the colors of their flags, yellow (*huang*), white (*po*), red (*hung*), and blue (*lan*), and then into eight Banners, the original four Plain (*cheng* 正) Banners being complemented with four Bordered (*hsiang* 鑲) Banners of the same colors. In 1635 allied Mongol tribesmen and collaborating Chinese were organized into eight similarly designated Mongol (*meng-ku* 蒙古) Banners and another eight similarly designated Chinese (*han-chün* 漢軍) Banners, so that the total Banner establishment consisted of 24 Banner units.

In general, each Banner was led by a Commander-in-chief (*tu-t'ung* 都統) and two Vice Commanders-in-chief (*fu tu-t'ung* 副都統). It incorporated five Regiments (only two in the case of the Mongol Banners), known in Manchu as *chalan* (*chia-la* 甲喇) and in Chinese as the command of, and by the title of, the Regimental Commander (*ts'an-ling* 參領), who was assisted by a Regimental Vice Commander (*fu ts'an-ling*). Each regiment, in turn, consisted of five Companies, known in Manchu as *niru* (*niu-lu* 牛彔) and in Chinese as the command of, and by the title of, the Company Commander (*tso-ling* 佐領), who was assisted by one or more Lieutenants (*hsiao* 校, with varying prefixes). Originally each company was intended to consist of 300 soldiers, so that a full Banner would number 7,500 soldiers; but eventually the standard strength was reduced to 100. Manchu Banners then had 70 or 80 Company Commanders, whereas Chinese Banners had only 30 or 40. At the time of the Manchu conquest of China in 1644, the Banners had an estimated strength of 200,000 men.

There was no overall coordinating command for the Banners. Three Manchu units—the Plain Yellow, Bordered Yellow, and Plain White Banners—were considered to be under the Emperor's direct supervision and were called the Three Superior Banners (*shang san ch'i* 上三旗). The remaining Manchu Banners, called the Five Lesser Banners (*hsia wu ch'i* 下五旗), were assigned to the various Imperial Princes.

Crosscutting all the Banners was a broad division between bannermen stationed in the capital (*ching-ch'i* 京旗) and those stationed throughout the empire (*chu-fang pa ch'i* 駐防八旗). The capital troops were further divided into Inner Banners (*nei-ch'i* 內旗) and Outer Banners (*wai-ch'i* 外旗). The Inner Banners guarded the imperial palace, and those of their members who belonged to the Three Superior Banners constituted the Imperial Bodyguard (*ch'in-chün ying* 親軍營). They were known as Imperial Guardsmen (*shih-wei ch'in-chün* 侍衛親軍) and were commanded by a variable number, nominally six, of Grand Ministers of the Palace Commanding the Imperial Body-

guard (*ling shih-wei nei ta-ch'en* 領侍衛
內大臣). Members of the Inner Banners who
were not Imperial Guardsmen were organized
into several Brigades (*ying* 營) with specialized
functions, including a Guards Brigade (*hu-chün
ying* 護軍營) that had principal responsibility for
guarding the environs of the imperial palace, a
Vanguard Brigade (*ch'ien-feng ying* 前鋒營), a
Firearms Brigade (*huo-ch'i ying* 火器營), and a
Scouting Brigade (*chien-jui ying* 健銳營). These
units were commanded by Commanders-general
(*t'ung-ling* 統領, *tsung-t'ung* 總統), often Imperial Princes. The Outer Banners, which in early
Ch'ing times were the main battle force of the
empire, were organized into a large Cavalry
Brigade (*hsiao-chi ying* 驍騎營), commanded
in annual rotation by the Commanders-in-chief
(*tu-t'ung*) of all the Banners.

Bannermen who were not stationed at the
capital, unlike the wholly autonomous military
establishment at Peking, were under the supervision of the Ministry of War (*ping-pu*). They
were more directly controlled by provincial-level
officers, designated either as Manchu Generals
(*chiang-chün*) or as Vice Commanders-in-chief
(*fu tu-t'ung*). Lesser local officers included Garrison Commandants (*ch'eng-shou wei* 城守尉),
Assistant Commandants (*hsieh-ling* 協領), Post
Commandants (*fang-shou wei* 防守尉), and Platoon Commanders (*fang-yü* 防禦). All these positions were substantive appointments, carrying
military ranks. However, all that a bannerman
passed along automatically to a son was apparently only his basic post in his home Banner,
with whatever rank was appropriate to it.

The Green Standards. Hereditary Chinese
soldiers of the Green Standards (*lu-ying*) served
principally as a kind of provincial constabulary,
or a ready reserve force. They too were under
the administrative jurisdiction of the Ministry of
War, but were subject (as bannermen were not)
to the control of Governors-general and Governors, and were supervised most particularly
by a Provincial Military Commander (*t'i-tu* 提督)
in each province. Their basic organizational units
were Brigades (*ying*) of 500 men under Brigade
Commanders (*yu-chi* 游擊). Theoretically a brigade comprised five 100-man Companies (*shao*
哨) under a Company Commander (*ch'ien-tsung*
千總). At intermediary levels between Pro-

vincial Military Commanders and Brigade Commanders, roughly equivalent to the civil service
Circuit Intendants, were from two to seven Regional Commanders (*tsung-ping* 總兵) in each
province, with subordinate Regional Vice Commanders (*fu-chiang* 副將) and Assistant Regional Commanders (*ts'an-chiang* 參將), all
outranking Brigade Commanders. At every level
in the hierarchy, the aggregate of troops under
the jurisdiction of a Green Standards officer was
known as his Command (*piao* 標; lit., his "flag");
thus, for example, one referred to the Command
of a Provincial Military Commander (*t'i-piao*) or
the Command of an Assistant Regional Commander (*ts'an-chiang piao*).

The Green Standards were not home guards;
they campaigned alongside the Banners. On
campaign, Green Standards detachments were
commanded by Grand Minister Commanders
(*ching-lüeh ta-ch'en* 經略大臣), assisted by
Grand Minister Consultants (*ts'an-i ta-ch'en*
參議大臣), all dignitaries specially delegated
from the court on an ad hoc basis.

When the Ch'ing dynasty was at its strongest,
in the eighteenth century, its permanent, hereditary soldiery totaled an estimated 200,000 bannermen and 660,000 Green Standards troops. All
soldiers were not treated alike in terms of pay
and grain allowances. Although all bannermen
(who were forbidden to engage in any occupation other than soldiering) seem to have received a monthly grain allowance of about two
and a half bushels, the capital troops received
monthly stipends of three or four taels, whereas
bannermen in the provinces received only one
and a half or two taels. Soldiers of the Green
Standards got only one or two taels and three
tenths of a bushel of grain a month. Their low
grain allowance was probably offset by the expectation that they would in some degree provide food for themselves and their families by
part-time farming on State Farms (*t'un-t'ien* 屯田)
set aside for their use.

District militia. The Ch'ing government required each District Magistrate to organize and
train a 50-man militia unit (*hsiang-yung* 鄉勇 or
variants) for subduing small-scale banditry. This
requirement seems not to have been very effective until the nineteenth century. When both the
Banners and Green Standards then proved in-

capable of dealing with imperialistic European intrusions and widespread domestic rebellions, the court permitted and encouraged provincial and local authorities to build new armies within the militia structure.

Personnel Administration

The most striking aspect of Ch'ing personnel administration, as would be expected in any alien dynasty, was the preferential treatment given the Manchu elite and, to a somewhat lesser extent, their Mongol allies in appointing and promoting men in the officialdom. However, as has been noted above, Chinese had opportunities to enter and rise high in the officialdom—greater opportunities by far than under any previous alien dynasty. It is not surprising that the Ch'ing Emperors saw to it that a Manchu appointee stood alongside every Chinese in virtually every executive position in the central government agencies; what is surprising is that Chinese shared these positions in the capital—even in the Grand Secretariat and the Council of State—and predominated in all provincial and lower-level positions.

Recruitment. In the recruitment of civil officials, except for the almost automatic rise to influence of scions of the Manchu elite and some Mongol leaders, the Ch'ing government relied most importantly on the Ming system of open, competitive examinations (*k'o-chü* 科舉). Special quotas were established so that some Manchu, Mongol, and Chinese bannermen could pass the examinations, but ordinary Chinese always dominated the pass lists.

It was the responsibility of the Provincial Education Commissioner (*t'i-tu hsüeh-cheng*) to give annual certification examinations that qualified educated men, including students of local government schools and private academies (*shu-yüan* 書院), to participate in provincial examinations (*hsiang-shih* 鄉試). These were held every three years in all provincial capitals under the supervision of dignitaries dispatched from the central government. Quotas were established for every province, according to the size of its population, both for candidates and for passers. Candidates who passed were entitled Provincial Graduates (*chü-jen* 舉人). This status exempted them from

certain tax and service obligations to the state and qualified them for lower-level official appointments. More important, they were eligible to participate in metropolitan examinations (*hui-shih* 會試) at the capital, conducted a few months following every round of provincial examinations. At the capital, as in the provinces, candidates were examined in three day-long sessions spaced over a week. As in the past, the emphasis was on explicating passages from the Confucian classics, applying classical precepts and historical precedents to ideological or political problems, and writing in prescribed literary forms. The examination questions were prepared and graded by distinguished capital officials—Grand Secretaries, Hanlin Academicians, and censorial officials. All passers then took a shorter, confirmatory palace examination (*tien-shih* 殿試), there to be ranked in order of excellence into groups (*chia* 甲), and all received the designation Metropolitan Graduate (*chin-shih* 進士). Those in the highest group were promptly appointed to offices in the Hanlin Academy, where they did advanced study and prepared themselves to become officials of the greatest responsibility and highest rank. Other Metropolitan Graduates were assured of successful careers in the officialdom.

In addition to this regular system of civil service recruitment examinations, Ch'ing Emperors often resorted to special, irregular examinations (*chih-k'o* 制科) to recruit men for service who might otherwise be overlooked. These special examinations were primarily of two types. One was an attempt to identify men of exceptional erudition and literary talent (*po-hsüeh hung-tz'u* 博學鴻詞). Officials who had already won the Metropolitan Graduate degree sometimes took advantage of these special opportunities in the hope of improving their career prospects. The other principal type of special examination was given by almost every Ch'ing Emperor; it was really a requirement that local officials submit guaranteed recommendations (*pao-chü* 保舉) of men who, though perhaps not erudite enough to compete in the regular examinations, deserved consideration for appointment to low-ranking posts by virtue of being "filial, incorrupt, straightforward, and upright" (*hsiao-lien fang-cheng* 孝廉方正). Both types of special examinations regularly yielded hundreds of new officials.

Government schools were used to recruit men for office, but as in the last Ming century they were not so much a direct channel into the officialdom as a means of preparation for the recruitment examinations. Every prefecture, subprefecture, department, and district was required to establish a state-supported Confucian School (*ju-hsüeh* 儒學) with a quota of students ranging from 70 to 120, of whom 20 to 40 received state stipends. Considerable preparation was prerequisite to admission, which was granted on the basis of competitive examinations, so that status as a government student (*sheng-yüan* 生員) was itself a symbol of achievement and of membership in the state-certified elite.

Status as a government student, however, was merely the first rung on the ladder of social and governmental esteem. The status could be withdrawn if a man failed to maintain his scholastic abilities sufficiently to pass tests regularly given by the itinerant Provincial Education Commissioner. The major step toward success was the next one—being chosen as a tribute student (*kung-sheng* 貢生). This meant gaining permanent status as a graduate, exempt from further certification by the Provincial Education Commissioner. It also entitled one to admission to the National University (*t'ai-hsüeh* 太學) in Peking. Every school had a quota for graduating its students: one a year in a prefecture school, two in three years in a department school, and one every two years in a district school. The pressure to become National University students (*chien-sheng* 監生) was so great that special arrangements were made to increase the number. On any occasion deemed worthy of national celebration, such as the accession of a new Emperor, the government commonly doubled the regular quotas; in such cases the supernumerary graduates were called "tribute students by grace" (*en kung-sheng* 恩貢生). By showing promise in special examinations students could also be added to the normal quota as "tribute students for excellence" (*yu kung-sheng* 優貢生). Eventually other kinds of examinations were given every twelve years to choose one or two students per school above the normal quota as "tribute students for preeminence" (*pa kung-sheng* 拔貢生).

After the early Ch'ing years, attaining the status of a National University student, in whatever fashion, did not mean that one in fact studied there. Relatively few did so. Attaining the status meant that one was qualified to take the provincial examination—or, in the case of tribute students "for excellence" and "for preeminence," that they could be considered for immediate low-level official appointments.

Beyond granting special inheritance privileges to members of the nobility, Ch'ing followed the Chinese tradition of allowing some civil service officials to "protect" (*yin* 蔭) sons, giving them automatic access to official status. The Ch'ing practice was restricted, however. Only officials of the top three ranks had the privilege, and it could normally be applied to only one son. Moreover, "protected" sons did not immediately become eligible for appointment; what they gained was automatic status as National University Students by Inheritance (*yin-chien*), which entitled them to participate in the provincial examinations without any other qualification.

The Manchus' one gross abuse of recruitment procedures was in regularly permitting the purchase of status as a National University student (Student by Purchase: *li chien-sheng* 例監生). In each case, the status exempted a man from certain kinds of tax and service obligations, enabled him to wear scholarly caps and gowns that were socially esteemed, and qualified him to compete in the provincial examinations. The sale of such status was a device by which the government raised enormous irregular revenues in the seventeenth century and again in the nineteenth.

Appointments. The "regular paths" (*cheng-t'u* 正途) for becoming an official (*ch'u-shen* 出身) were the examinations, the schools, and inheritance. Men might have normal official careers after entering service by "irregular paths" (*i-t'u* 異途), such as the purchase of degrees or even the purchase of offices, but only through special sponsorship by high-ranking dignitaries; and even though they might win transfer to regular-path status, they were forbidden ever to hold office in certain politically sensitive offices, notably the Hanlin Academy and the Censorate, and in general had small hope of attaining high office of any sort.

Dossiers on all men considered eligible for appointments were maintained by the Ministry of Personnel. The manner in which a man qualified to take the examinations combined with his performance in the examinations largely determined the category of offices to which he might first be appointed; and this determination in large part channeled his subsequent career through a fixed sequence of offices. From an early time, however, the number of men qualified for every position exceeded the number of vacancies, so that to be promoted, a man had to earn extraordinary merit ratings from his superiors; and even highly recommended men languished as expectant appointees for many years between active duty assignments.

Virtually all major appointments, both in the capital and in the provinces, were made directly by the Emperor in consultation with the Council of State. For the next echelon of posts, the Emperor and the Council of State selected among nominees submitted by the Ministry of Personnel. A few high-ranking executive officials were allowed to appoint men to some of the lesser posts in their agencies on a probationary basis. All appointments were generally for three-year, renewable terms. Every three years all officials on duty in the capital underwent a "capital evaluation" (*ching-ch'a* 京察), which resulted in promotions, demotions, and other changes of status including dismissal from the service. Officials of the top three ranks and all members of the Hanlin Academy and the Censorate were evaluated by the Emperor personally. Officials of ranks 4 and 5 were evaluated by specially assigned teams of Princes and Grand Ministers (*wang ta-ch'en*). Officials of lower ranks were evaluated by the executive officials of their agencies. Provincial officials were likewise subjected to three-year evaluations, called the Great Reckoning (*ta-chi* 大計), which were scheduled in between the capital evaluations. These evaluations were made by the superior officials of the local agencies, reviewed by Governors and Governors-general, and reported to the Ministry of Personnel for appropriate action. Governors and Governors-general, because of their high rank and their concurrent status as capital officials, were evaluated by the Emperor personally.

The Manchus failed notably to adhere to the merit principle in making appointments and pro-motions, and not merely because they naturally favored the Manchu elite and their Mongol allies. Because it was not easy for qualified men to get the limited number of active duty appointments, and because the Ch'ing government repeatedly found it necessary to raise extraordinary revenues, the Manchus recurringly sold official titles and functioning offices, eventually on a very large scale in the nineteenth century. National University students, whether or not they had bought that status to begin with, found it necessary to make special grain or monetary contributions to the state in order to gain even empty official titles, and considerably more for active appointments. Officials found that the only practical way to get a promotion, similarly, was to buy a higher office. Eventually even commoners were able to buy titles and offices—functioning offices as important, for example, as those of Circuit Intendants. Although the purchase of offices had been possible under some other dynasties, the practice had never been carried to as great an extreme as in the last half of the Ch'ing era.

Ch'ing followed the Ming system of grading both officials and offices in nine ranks (*p'in* 品), each divided into two degrees (*teng* 等), totaling eighteen categories from rank 1a down to 9b. Every official automatically received a sequence of prestige titles (*chieh* 階, *san-kuan* 散官) corresponding precisely to the ranks he gained; there were eighteen such titles, mostly Grand Masters (*ta-fu* 大夫) and Court Gentlemen (*lang* 郎) with varying prefixes. A different set of eighteen prestige titles was available to military officers, mostly Generals (*chiang-chün* 將軍) and Commandants (*wei* 尉) with varying prefixes.

Official salaries and allowances. Stipends for nobles of the imperial family were not fixed in a definite scale; most were rather arbitrarily determined by the Emperor. For nobles who were not members of the imperial family (most were Banner officers, but some were civil officials), there was a fixed scale of salaries and grain allowances, ranging from 700 taels and 350 bushels a year to 45 taels and 22.5 bushels. All civil officials received from 180 taels a year to 31 taels, depending on their rank. Officials on duty in the capital also received grain allowances from 90 to 15.75 bushels a year, but during the course of the dynasty these were converted to supplementary monetary payments, from 90 to 15 taels a year. Capital officials also regularly received so-called grace (*en* 恩) payments, from 540 to 46 taels a year according to rank, so that their real salaries ranged from 810 to 92 taels a year. Provincial officials received neither grain allowances nor "grace" payments. Instead, their salaries came to be supplemented by special allowances to suppress corrupting temptations (*yang-lien* 養廉; lit., "allowances to encourage honesty"). These varied not only according to an official's rank, but also according to his location and the burdens of his position; the disparity in such allowances was enormous, ranging from 20,000 taels to only 31 taels a year.

DICTIONARY OF OFFICIAL TITLES
IN IMPERIAL CHINA

Guide to the Use of the Dictionary

General Instructions and Suggestions

1. Entries are arranged in Wade-Giles alphabetical order. With minor modifications, this dictionary uses the Wade-Giles system of romanization offered in *A Chinese-English Dictionary* by Herbert A. Giles (2d ed. revised and enlarged, 2 vols.; Shanghai: Kelly & Walsh, Ltd., 1912), and entries appear in alphabetical order accordingly. Efforts have been made to place entries where the English-language reader is most likely to expect them, regardless of what might be deemed the technically correct pronunciation. For example, the common character found in Wade-Giles dictionaries under *ch'e* with such meanings as vehicle, carriage, and chariot is found here in that romanization even though its most frequent occurrence in titles is in military titles, where it was traditionally read *chü*.

Entries appear in the strictly alphabetical order that Wade-Giles users are accustomed to find in romanization indexes. That is, all entries beginning with *chang* are presented before any *ch'ang* entries begin, and all *ta* entries are presented before any *t'a* entries begin. In cases where umlauts are important, entries run, for example, through *chu* to *chun* to *ch'u* to *ch'un*, and so on, and only then to *chü* to *chün* to *ch'ü* to *ch'ün*, and so on. Thus, for example, a hypothetical sequence of entries would appear in the order *chi-chang, ch'ih, chin-pu, ch'ing-li ssu, chuang-yüan, chung-shih, chü-jan, ch'üan, fen-hsün, i, i-wei, jan-chih, ju-hsüeh*. Entries with identical initial-syllable romanizations are arranged in the alphabetical order of their second syllables, regardless of their Chinese characters. However, in any case where romanizations are completely identical, as in many single-syllable entries, the sequential arrangement is determined by the Chinese characters according to the standard Chinese practice of considering radicals plus supplemental strokes.

Hyphenation is used to group syllables into the most meaningful semantic units identifiable by the compiler.

Tones are indicated normally only in bold-faced romanized entry headings, where tone marks appear over principal vowels. First tone is indicated by a macron (ē), second tone by an acute accent (é), third tone by a haček (ě), and fourth tone by a grave accent (è). All tones are indicated in normal, isolated Mandarin usage, without consideration of elisions in combinations of syllables.

Readers who are most accustomed to Pinyin romanizations of Chinese will find a conversion table from Pinyin to Wade-Giles on pp. 675–76.

2. Entries present data in order of chronology and importance. Each entry normally begins with an indication of the era (fully capitalized) in which the nomenclature is known to have been used. If significant or especially interesting, the literal meaning or the etymology of the nomenclature is then briefly indicated. Most commonly, however, what immediately follows the dynasty or era indication is a bold-faced English rendering of the agency name or title, with explanations of numbers, hierarchical status or rank, organizational affiliations, functions, and important subordinates if any. (The equational symbol = immediately preceding a rank indicator signifies that, though nominally equivalent or comparable, the rank either was a courtesy rank or provided a stipend somewhat less than the regular rank indicated.) Each entry concludes with cross-references to other entries if appropriate, renderings found in standard Western-language manuals, and the relevant chapter number(s) in the standard Chinese source,

Li-tai chih-kuan piao (see list of abbreviations, below). A large proportion of entries explain multiple usages, which are numbered (1), (2), and so on; in such instances, usages are normally treated in the chronological order of their historical occurrence or in order of their importance, or in some combination of the two. In every entry where parenthetical numerals signal multiple usages, the reader is advised to scan the entire entry.

3. Do not expect comprehensive inclusiveness. The dictionary deals with official nomenclature from the *Chou-li* into the nineteenth century as comprehensively as possible within reasonable bounds. No attempt has been made, however, to include all governmental *terminology* beyond agency names and official titles. Within the realm covered, the dictionary is probably least comprehensive as regards the multitude of titles used in different dynasties for the military service, palace women and eunuchs, and non-official functionaries, especially in cases of designations that were clearly more on the order of descriptive labels than formal titles and are usually understandable in literal terms.

4. Be prepared to combine component elements. Every effort has been made to cover generic terms, even in such realms as the military service, that are among the components from which traditional nomenclature was constructed; but no effort has been made to include all combinations in which the components are found. For example, *shih-lang* is identified, among other things, as the second highest position (Vice Minister) in each of the Six Ministries (*liu pu*) of the central government from Sui to Ch'ing times, and in the entry for any one Ministry there is normally an indication that its staff included such a Vice Minister. However, separate entries are not provided for Vice Ministers by their full titles (*li-pu shih-lang, hu-pu shih-lang, ping-pu shih-lang,* etc.) Similarly, *chiang-chün* is identified as a common title for a military leader (General), and *chün* is identified, among other things, as what in English is called an Army. However, with rare exceptions of very special significance, the reader will not find individual entries for all the thousands of Generals of such-and-such Armies to be found in Chinese history.

Thus users of the dictionary are called on to use their ingenuity and imagination in combining the various components of titles. For such renderings as Vice Minister of Justice (*hsing-pu shih-lang*), for example, one must go to the entries for both *hsing-pu* and *shih-lang*. In searching for explanations of official nomenclature of all sorts, it will probably prove advantageous to work from the last component elements back to the first.

5. Be prepared to cross-reference. Because of efforts to avoid excessive repetition in entries, and in part for reasons explained immediately above, users may find it necessary to do extensive cross-referencing within the dictionary to understand the full significance of any particular item of nomenclature. In general, it can be assumed that every italicized romanization found in the body of an entry is a signal to look for a separate entry under such a romanization. For the most part, also, English renderings with initial capital letters found within an entry (or component elements) can be traced to separate entries indirectly through the appended Index to English Renderings. Thus, for example, when the text of one entry indicates that the term named identifies an aide to the Director (*lang-chung*) of the Bureau of Equipment (*chia-pu*) of the T'ang dynasty Ministry of War (*ping-pu*), the user will find separate entries in alphabetical order under *lang-chung, chia-pu,* and *ping-pu;* and serial numbers of those entries can be found in the Index to English Renderings under Director, Bureau of Equipment, and Ministry of War. (It is hoped that such indexing of English renderings will make it possible for many scholars to reduce romanizations and glossaries in their publications by introductory notations directing the specialist reader to this dictionary.) Users who want the larger institutional framework into which any particular agency fits will find a general treatment in the introductory descriptions of governmental organization era by era. Because both italicizations and English renderings can be thought of as cross-references, specific cross-reference notations such as q.v. are minimal. Where they occur, they suggest that cross-referencing should be particularly helpful.

6. Be prepared to extrapolate from one era to another. The dictionary attributes usages to those periods for which documentary evidence has been found; guesses and presumptions are noted with cautionary terms. However, since the compiler makes no claim to have exhausted all possible sources, users will undoubtedly find occurrences of nomenclature in periods not indicated here. Extrapolations backward and forward in time should be relatively safe; for example, a title found in a Three Kingdoms context that is identified here as a Han usage is likely to have been carried over into the Three Kingdoms era without significant change, as a T'ang usage is likely to have been carried over into early Sung. However, extrapolations of usages over longer spans of time might prove to be misleading. Thus, titles found in Ming or Ch'ing texts that are identified here only as Chou or Han or T'ang usages are likely to be unofficial, archaic references to Ming or Ch'ing officials who bore quite different formal titles but performed functions suggesting the archaic names. Special efforts have been made to include such unofficial designations in the dictionary, but those missed must be legion.

7. Do not expect to find entries for proper names. Place names and other proper names, with very rare exceptions, are not dealt with in this dictionary. In the case of specific descriptive elements in titles such as General of the Yunnan Army (*yün-nan chün chiang-chün*) or Kiangsi Provincial Administration Commissioner (*chiang-hsi ch'eng-hsüan pu-cheng shih*), no entries will be found under *yün-nan* or *chiang-hsi*. Similarly, though entries can be found for generic designations such as Prefecture (*chou, fu*) and District (*hsien*) as well as Province (*sheng*), individual entries are not provided for Hangchow Prefecture, K'un-shan District, and the like.

8. Note the nature and uses of the indexes. Two indexes are provided, beginning on page 601. The first is an Index to Suggested English Renderings, a finding-list of the English renderings suggested in the dictionary entries and of some English renderings that are often encountered in Sinological writings but are not suggested in this dictionary (for example, scholar-official); in the latter case the index directs the user to the dictionary's preferred renderings. Common generic or collective designations, both

official and unofficial, are generally indexed, but terms by which particular officials and agencies were known unofficially and that have no special interest of themselves are generally not indexed. In many instances index entries such as Director of . . . , Supervisor of . . . , and Vice Commandant of . . . do not lead to the commonest Chinese counterparts but lead to variants of standard titles, which themselves are found only in the respective agency entries and in generic index entries (Director, Supervisor, and the like). It should also be noted that the index is not arranged in absolute alphabetical order. Rather, it follows standard publishers' practice in ignoring most prepositions, conjunctions, and other particles. Thus the rendering Director of the Secretariat is alphabetized in the sequence Director, Secretariat; and Storehouse of Utensils for the Imperial Ancestral Temple is alphabetized in the sequence Storehouse, Utensils, Imperial Ancestral Temple. The user should consequently be prepared to find such a sequence as the following:

Office of Rivers and Canals
Office for Sacrifices at the Fen River
Office Scribe
Office of Scrutiny for Justice

Indexed renderings are followed by the serial numbers of the dictionary entries in which they are found. Some renderings are used for several variant Chinese terms. Where more than three or four entry numbers are given for one English rendering, italicized romanizations are added to aid in differentiating them. Any writer committed to using this dictionary's renderings will ordinarily be well advised to include parenthetical romanizations to specify unambiguously which of many Clerks he refers to, for example.

The compiler naturally regrets that considerations of time, complexity, and cost have prevented inclusion of a thorough analytical index of the dictionary by topics; but he hopes the desirability of such an index may be sufficiently strong to entice some other compiler to provide it in a separate (and inevitably bulky) volume.

The second index is a finding-list of entries by Chinese characters. It is organized in one of the standard patterns based on the K'ang-hsi system of radicals and strokes. The first character in each character-string found in a dictionary entry is placed in index sequence by its K'ang-hsi radical and the number of additional strokes it requires, running from least to most complex. Second and successive characters, however, place the character-string in sequence primarily by the total strokes they require and only secondarily by their radicals. As in the case of the Index to Suggested English Renderings, each indexed item is followed by the serial number of its dictionary entry. Although the Chinese Index is provided principally for the convenience of Chinese and other East Asian users, some Western users may find it the quickest way into the main body of the dictionary, especially if they are not thoroughly at ease with the Wade-Giles system of romanization.

Abbreviations

BH H. S. Brunnert and V. V. Hagelstrom, *Present Day Political Organization of China*, rev. by N. Th. Kolessoff, trans. from the Russian by A. Beltchenko and E. E. Moran. Peking, 1911.

CL [*Chou-li*]. *Le Tcheou-li ou Rites des Tcheou*, trans. by Edouard Biot. 3 vols. Paris, 1851.

HB Hans Bielenstein, *The Bureaucracy of Han Times*. Cambridge, Eng., 1980.

P *Li-tai chih-kuan piao* (Tables of Officialdom Through the Dynasties). Imperially sponsored compilation, 1780. Any edition. Numbers following P are chapter (*chüan*) numbers and are common to all editions.

RR Robert des Rotours, trans., *Traité des fonctionnaires et traité de l'armée* (from the *New T'ang History, Hsin T'ang-shu*, ch. 46–50). 2 vols. Leiden, 1948.

SP [Sung Project]. Chang Fu-jui, *Les Fonctionnaires des Song: Index des titres* (*Matériaux pour le Manuel de l'histoire des Song*, V). Paris, 1962.

The Dictionary

1 *ā-chiēn* 阿監

T'ANG: **Eunuch Attendant** upon the female Chief of Palace Surveillance (*kung-cheng*), apparently assigned from the Palace Domestic Service (*nei-shih sheng*); status =rank 7. RR: *grand eunuque.*

2 *ā-kó* 阿哥 or 阿格

CH'ING: **Prince,** unofficial reference to the son of an Emperor or of an Imperial Prince (*ch'in-wang*), especially used before his formal enfeoffment; differentiated by the prefix Eldest (*ta*) or by numerical prefix.

3 *ā-ssū-hā-ní hā-fān* 阿思哈尼哈番

CH'ING: Manchu word translated into Chinese as *nan* (**Baron**). P64.

4 *ā-tá-hā hā-fān* 阿達哈哈番

CH'ING: Manchu word translated into Chinese as *ch'ing-ch'e tu-wei* (**Commandant of Light Chariots**). P64.

5 *ā-tūn shìh-wèi* 阿敦侍衛

CH'ING: apparently an abbreviated reference to **Grand Ministers of the Imperial Household Department Concurrently Controlling the Imperial Guardsmen** (*ling shih-wei nei ta-ch'en*), 4 of whom from 1694 assisted in the management of the Palace Stud (*shang-ssu yüan*), steadily increasing in number to 21 and overseeing the work of 3 Directors of Saddles (*ssu-an chang*), 17 Chiefs of the Stables (*chiu-chang*), 5 Pasturage Directors (*mu-chang*), 5 Pasturage Vice Directors (*fu mu-chang*), and 45 Assistant Chiefs of Pasturages and Stables (*mu-chiu chang*). Generally responsible for the breeding, care, and training of the imperial horse herds, whereas administrative direction of the herds was the responsibility of the Operational Agents of the Two Offices (*pan-li erh-ssu shih-wu*) in the Palace Stud. See *shih-wei* (Imperial Guardsmen). BH: supervisors of droves. P39.

6 *ā-tūn yá-mén* 阿敦衙門

CH'ING: lit. meaning not clear; *ya-men* a common term meaning office, *a-tun* probably a transliteration of a Manchu word: from 1661 to 1677 the official designation of what after 1677 was known as the **Palace Stud** (*shang-ssu yüan*); prior to 1661 known by the Ming name *yü-ma chien* (Directorate of the Imperial Horses). Headed by Grand Ministers (*ta-ch'en*) of the Imperial Household Department (*nei-wu fu*) or Grand Ministers of the Imperial Household Department Concurrently Controlling the Imperial Guardsmen (*ling shih-wei nei ta-ch'en*). P39.

7 *ài-mǎ* 愛馬 or *ài-mǎ k'ò* 愛瑪克

Chinese transcriptions of Mongol word *aimaq* meaning **Tribe,** in some cases translated as *meng* (**League**). (1) YÜAN: one of 5 categories of fiefs granted to nobles. (2) CH'ING: a tribal group of Banners (*ch'i*).

8 *àn* 案

SUNG–CH'ING: lit., desk or table: **Section,** subordinate units in the Sung Salt and Iron Monopoly Bureau (*yen-t'ieh ssu*), Tax Bureau (*tu-chih ssu*), etc.; **Investigation Section** in the Sung Censorate (*yü-shih t'ai*); usually with prefix specifying function. In later eras came to be used, at least unofficially, as a designation for clerical groups in the headquarters of Prefectures (*fu*) and Districts (*hsien*), each dealing with business related to one of the Six Ministries (*liu pu*) in the central government. See *ch'a-an, ch'a-yüan, ts'ao.*

9 *àn-ch'á ch'iēn-shìh* 按察僉事 or 按察簽事

CHIN–CH'ING: **Assistant Surveillance Commissioner,** rank 5a, on the staff of a Surveillance Commissioner (*an-ch'a shih*) of Chin Route (*lu*), Yüan Circuit (*tao*), Ming–Ch'ing Province (*sheng*). From early Ming to 1735 number variable, assigned as Circuit Intendants (*tao-t'ai*) to Circuits (*tao*) with prescribed geographic or functional jurisdictions indicated by prefixes; in 1735 abolished, replaced with autonomous Circuit Intendants; see *tao, tao-t'ai.* P52.

10 *àn-ch'á fù-shìh* 按察副使

CHIN–CH'ING: **Surveillance Vice Commissioner,** rank 4a, principal aide to a Surveillance Commissioner (*an-ch'a shih*) of Chin Route (*lu*), Yüan Circuit (*tao*), Ming–Ch'ing Province (*sheng*). From early Ming to 1735 number variable, assigned as Circuit Intendants (*tao-t'ai*) to Circuits (*tao*) with prescribed geographic or functional jurisdictions indicated by prefixes; in 1735 abolished, replaced with autonomous Circuit Intendants; see *tao, tao-t'ai.* P52.

11 *àn-ch'á kuān* 按察官

SUNG: **Circuit Surveillance Official,** generic reference to Fiscal Commissioners (*chuan-yün shih*) and Judicial Commissioners (*t'i-hsing an-ch'a shih, t'i-tien hsing-yü kung-shih*).

12 *àn-ch'á shǐh* 按察使

(1) T'ANG: **Surveillance Commissioner,** in 711 delegated from the central government to each of 10 and later more Circuits (*tao*) as coordinators overseeing general conditions and the performance of local officials; in 714 retitled Surveillance, Investigation, and Supervisory Commissioner (*an-ch'a ts'ai-fang ch'u-chih shih*); in 720 restored with original title, but in 722 abolished. (2) SUNG: variant of *t'i-hsing an-ch'a shih* (**Judicial Commissioner**). SP: *intendant, inspecteur.* (3) CHIN–CH'ING: **Surveillance Commissioner,** rank 3a, overseer of judicial and surveillance activities in Chin Route (*lu*), Yüan Circuit (*tao*), Ming–Ch'ing Province (*sheng*). The agency he headed, the Surveillance Commission, usually bore the full name *t'i-hsing an-ch'a shih ssu.* BH: provincial judge, judicial commissioner. P52.

13 *àn-ch'á ssū* 按察司

Surveillance Commission. (l) CHIN: agency headed by a

Surveillance Commissioner (*an-ch'a shih*); created in 1199 to replace Judicial Commission (*t'i-hsing ssu*); in 1208 made concurrent Fiscal Commission (*chuan-yün ssu*). (2) YÜAN–CH'ING: common abbreviation of *t'i-hsing an-ch'a shih ssu*. P52.

14 *àn-ch'á … tào hsíng-yù shǐh* 按察···道刑獄使
LIAO: **Judicial Commissioner of … Circuit,** irregularly appointed in some Circuits (*tao*) to oversee judicial and surveillance activities. P52.

15 *àn-ch'á ts'ǎi-fǎng ch'ù-chìh shǐh* 按察探訪處置使
T'ANG: **Surveillance, Investigation, and Supervisory Commissioner** of a Circuit (*tao*); appointed 714–716 only, as replacement for Surveillance Commissioner (*an-ch'a shih*). P52.

16 *ān-fǔ chìh-chìh shǐh* 安撫制置使
SUNG: variant form of *an-fu shih* (**Military Commissioner**).

17 *ān-fǔ shìh* 安撫使
(1) T'ANG: **Pacification Commissioner,** delegated from the central government to bring order to a troubled area; often the concurrent title of the Military Commissioner (*chieh-tu shih*) of a Circuit (*tao*). (2) SUNG: **Military Commissioner** in charge of all military activities, and often many other activities, in a Circuit (*lu*). RR+SP: *commissaire impérial chargé de pacifier et de mettre en ordre une région.* P52. (3) YÜAN: **Pacification Commissioner** serving as overall coordinator of a Circuit (*tao*), commonly a non-Chinese noble. (4) MING–CH'ING: **Pacification Commissioner,** rank 5b, designation awarded chieftains of some southwestern aboriginal tribes. See *t'u-ssu*. P72.

18 *ān-fǔ shǐh ssū* 安撫使司 or ***ān-fǔ ssū***
(1) SUNG: **Military Commission,** agency headed by a Military Commissioner (*an-fu shih*). P52. (2) YÜAN–CH'ING: **Pacification Commission,** agency headed by a Pacification Commissioner (*an-fu shih*). P72.

19 *ān-fǔ tà-shǐh* 安撫大使
Pacification Commissioner-in-chief. (1) SUI: honorific title conferred on aboriginal chieftains in the South and Southwest. P72. (2) SUNG: variant of *an-fu shih* (Military Commissioner); used for court officials of rank 2a or higher. P50.

20 *ān-fǔ t'í-hsiá pīng-chiǎ* 安撫提轄兵甲
SUNG: **Military Commissioner and Superintendent of Troops** in an area such as a Circuit (*tao*).

21 *ān-hó shǔ* 安和署
YÜAN: **Office of Contented Music,** a unit in the Bureau of Musical Ritual (*i-feng ssu*); headed by 2 Directors (*ling*), rank 5b.

22 *àn-hsiéh shēng-lǜ kuān* 按協聲律官
SUNG: **Pitchpipe Player** in the Imperial Music Bureau (*t'ai-ch'eng fu*). SP: *fonctionnaire chargé d'harmoniser les tuyaux sonores.*

23 *ān-jén* 安人
SUNG–CH'ING: **Lady,** honorific title granted wives of certain officials; normally follows surname. In Sung granted wives of rank 6a1 officials; in Ming–Ch'ing, wives of rank 6a or 6b officials.

24 *àn-mó pó-shìh* 按摩博士
SUI–T'ANG: **Erudite for Massage,** one, rank 9b2, sub-

ordinate to the Masters of Masseurs (*an-mo shih*) in the Imperial Medical Service (*t'ai-i chü*); taught massage techniques and Taoist breathing exercises to disciples. P36.

25 *àn-mó shīh* 按摩師
SUI–T'ANG: **Master of Masseurs,** 4 in the Palace Medical Service (*shang-yao chü*), subordinate to the Palace Administration (*tien-chung sheng*); others in the Imperial Medical Service (*t'ai-i chü*), subordinate to the Court of Imperial Sacrifices (*t'ai-ch'ang ssu*). P36, 38.

26 *ān-p'èi chǘ* 鞍轡局
MING: **Saddlery Service** in the Ministry of Works (*kung-pu*), headed by a Commissioner-in-chief (*ta-shih*), rank 9a; abolished in 1567. P15.

27 *ān-p'èi k'ù* 鞍轡庫
SUNG: **Saddlery Storehouse** in the Court of the Imperial Stud (*t'ai-p'u ssu*). SP: *magasin de selles et de rênes.* P39.

28 *àn-shǒu* 案首
CH'ING: lit., one at the head of the table: **First Scholar,** unofficial reference to the top passer of a literary examination at the District (*hsien*) or Prefecture (*fu*) level.

29 *àn-yù yüàn* 案獄掾
HAN: **Judicial and Penal Administrator,** variable number of low-ranking or unranked personnel on the headquarters staffs of some Commanderies (*chün*). HB: prosecuting official.

30 *áng-pāng* 昂邦
CH'ING: abbreviation of *ku-shan ang-pang,* transliteration of a Manchu word translated into Chinese as *tu-t'ung* (**Commander-in-chief**); from 1723 replaced *ku-shan o-chen* as title of the leader of a Banner (*ch'i*) in the Eight Banner (*pa ch'i*) military organization. Also see *pao-i ang-pang, o-chen.* P44.

31 *aò-fēng* 鼇峯
SUNG–CH'ING: lit., the humped shell of a mythological leviathan, or the peak of a great mountain: one of several terms including *ao* that refer indirectly to the **Hanlin Academy** (*han-lin yüan*). Cf. *chan ao-t'ou.*

32 *aó-ts'āng* 敖倉
CH'IN–HAN: **Granary at Ao,** located at an ancient settlement named Ao near a hill called Mt. Ao in modern Honan; granary established by Ch'in, but the original purpose and organizational status is not clear; in Han overseen by the Director of Imperial Granaries (*t'ai-ts'ang ling*), a subordinate of the Chamberlain for the National Treasury (*ta ssu-nung*); headed by a Director (*chang*). During Han, Ao-ts'ang became a place-name itself. HB: Ao granary. P8.

33 *chá-ěrh-hū-ch'í* 札爾呼齊
YÜAN: Chinese transliteration of the Mongol word *jarhuchi,* translated as *tuan-kuan* (**Judge**); varying from 8 to 46, rank 1b, heads of the High Court of Justice (*ta tsung-cheng fu*). P1.

34 *chá-lǔ-hū-ch'í* 札魯呼齊
YÜAN: variant of *cha-erh-hu-ch'i* (**Judge**).

35 *chá-sà-k'ò* 札薩克
CH'ING: Chinese transliteration of a Mongol term roughly equivalent to such Chinese titles as General (*chiang-chün*) and Commander-in-chief (*tu-t'ung*): **Commander-in-chief** of each of the Eight Mongol Banners (*meng-ku pa-ch'i*), normally a hereditary chief.

36 *chá-shih* 蜡氏
CHOU: **Protector of Corpses,** 4 ranked as Junior Ser-

vicemen (*hsia-shih*), members of the Ministry of Justice (*ch'iu-kuan*) who made preliminary (?) burials so as to protect corpses from flies and other insects. CL: *préposé aux piqûres d'insectes*.

37   ch'á 察
Investigation Section. (1) T'ANG: from c. 805 an unofficial designation of subordinate units in the Censorate (*yü-shih t'ai*). (2) SUNG: variant of *ch'a-an*.

38   ch'a 差
See under *ch'ai*.

39   ch'á-àn 察案
SUNG: **Investigation Section,** units in the Censorate (*yü-shih t'ai*) staffed with Investigating Censors (*chien-ch'a yü-shih*); 6 created in 1080 out of the previously consolidated Investigation Bureau (*ch'a-yüan*) of the Censorate; differentiated by prefixes specifying realms of functional responsibility, e.g., Investigation Section for Revenue (*hu ch'a-an*), each corresponding to one of the Six Ministries (*liu pu*). Commonly abbreviated as either *ch'a* or *an*.

40   ch'á-àn 茶案
SUNG: **Tea Section,** one of 7 Sections in the Salt and Iron Monopoly Bureau (*yen-t'ieh ssu*) of the early Sung State Finance Commission (*san-ssu*); normally headed by an Administrative Assistant (*p'an-kuan, t'ui-kuan*); kept accounts concerning tea provisioning for the imperial palace. SP: *service de thé*.

41   ch'á-àn yù-shîh 察案御史
SUNG: generic reference to **Investigating Censors** (*chien-ch'a yü-shih*) of the 6 Investigation Sections (*ch'a-an*) in the Censorate (*yü-shih t'ai*) from 1080.

42   ch'á-fǎ t'ái 查法臺
MING: **Court of Judicial Inquiry,** unofficial reference to the Censorate (*yü-shih t'ai*), or possibly to the so-called Judicial Offices (*fa-ssu*): the Censorate, the Court of Judicial Review (*ta-li ssu*), and the Ministry of Justice (*hsing-pu*) collectively.

43   ch'á-fǎng shîh-chě 察訪使者 or **ch'á-fǎng shîh**
SUNG: **Investigation Commissioner** delegated from the court to a Circuit (*lu*) or comparable area. SP: *envoyé-inspecteur, inspecteur*.

44   ch'á-fēi yüàn 察非掾
T'ANG: **Investigator of Wrongs:** brief antecedent in 617–618 of the title *tien-chung shih yü-shih* (Palace Censor).

45   ch'ā-hsüǎn 插選
CH'ING: **Supplementary Selection,** part of the personnel appointment process conducted by the Ministry of Personnel (*li-pu*): the "insertio᾽" (*ch'a*) into appointment lists of Metropolitan Graduates (*chin-shih*) and Provincial Graduates (*chü-jen*) and others with special imperial favor; similar to but not identical with Expedited Selection (*chi-hsüan*).

46   ch'á-k'ù 茶庫
Tea Storehouse. (1) SUNG: a minor agency in the Court of the Imperial Treasury (*t'ai-fu ssu*). (2) CH'ING: one of 6 warehouses or vaults of valuables constituting the Storage Office (*kuang-ch'u ssu*) of the Imperial Household Department (*nei-wu fu*). BH: tea store. P37.

47   ch'á-kuān 察官
Surveillance Official, a generic term for Censors (*yü-shih*) and other officials whose prescribed duty was to keep watch over the officialdom and impeach or otherwise discipline

those who violated the law, proper administrative procedures, customary morality, etc., as distinguished from Speaking Officials (*yen-kuan*) or Remonstrance Officials (*chien-kuan*), whose prescribed duty was to monitor the making of policy decisions and to offer suggestions and policy criticisms to the throne.

48   ch'á-mǎ ssū 茶馬司
SUNG–CH'ING: **Horse Trading Office,** variable number in frontier areas where Chinese traded tea for horses; in Sung under the control of a Supervisor-in-chief of Horse Trading Offices (*tu-ta t'i-chü ch'a-ma ssu*); in Ming each headed by a Commissioner-in-chief (*ta-shih*), rank 9a, in Ch'ing by a Horse Trading Circuit Intendant (*ch'a-ma tao-t'ai*). P53.

49   ch'á-ts'āng yù-shîh 查倉御史
CH'ING: **Granary-inspecting Censor,** an Investigating Censor (*chien-ch'a yü-shih*) assigned to monitor delivery of tax grain at state granaries in the Peking area. See *hsün-ch'a yü-shih, hsün-ts'ang k'o-tao*.

50   ch'á-t'ūi 察推
SUNG: abbreviation of *kuan-ch'a t'ui-kuan* (**Surveillance Circuit Judge**).

51   ch'á-yén chìh-chìh shîh 茶鹽制置使
SUNG: **Tea and Salt Monopoly and Supervisory Commissioner** delegated from the central government to a Circuit (*lu*) or comparable area. See *ch'a-yen t'i-chü ssu*. SP: *régulateur-intendant du thé et du sel (de la gabelle)*. P61.

52   ch'á-yén chuǎn-yùn shîh 茶鹽轉運使
YÜAN: **Tea and Salt Monopoly and Tax Transport Commissioner,** rank 3b, subordinate of a Branch Secretariat (*hsing chung-shu sheng*).

53   ch'á-yén ssū 察言司
MING: **Office of Investigation and Remonstrance,** from 1370 to 1376 the variant title of the Office of Transmission (*t'ung-cheng ssu*). P21.

54   ch'á-yén t'í-chǔ ssū 茶鹽提舉司
SUNG: **Tea and Salt Supervisorate,** one established in each of 6 Circuits (*lu*) in tea and salt producing areas in 1111, to establish more firmly the central government's control over the tea and salt monopolies, which had previously been implemented on a part-time basis by Circuit Supervisors (*chien-ssu*); increased in 1121, and in S. Sung became a regular establishment in all Circuits; each headed by a Supervisor (*t'i-chü*) delegated from the central government and apparently functioning under guidelines issued by the Ministry of Revenue (*hu-pu*). Commonly abbreviated to *ch'a-yen ssu;* also called *t'i-chü ch'a-yen ssu*. SP: *régie du thé et du sel (de la gabelle)*. P61.

55   ch'á-yǐn p'ǐ-yèn sǒ 茶引批驗所 or **ch'á-yǐn sǒ**
MING–CH'ING: **Tea Control Station,** a local checkpoint to verify the certificates (*yin*) that were required to accompany all authorized commercial shipments of state-controlled tea in transit. See under *p'i-yen so*. P53.

56   ch'á-yüàn 察院
T'ANG–MING: **Investigation Bureau,** the unit of the Censorate (*yü-shih t'ai*) staffed by Investigating Censors (*chien-ch'a yü-shih*); in 1380–1382 was the sole element of the Censorate existing. The term is also used as a quasiofficial reference to Investigating Censors. See *tu ch'a-yüan, chien-yüan*. RR: *cour des enquêtes au dehors*. SP: *cour des enquêtes dehors, bureau d'administration du tribunal des censeurs*. P18.

57 *ch'á-yüán tū t'í-chǔ ssū* 茶園都提舉司
YÜAN: **Supervisorate of Tea Groves,** agencies subordinate to the Palace Provisions Commission (*hsüan-hui yüan*), normally with a place-name prefix; each headed by a Supervisor (*t'i-chü*), rank 4a. P62.

58 *chài* 寨 or 砦
SUNG–MING: **Stockade,** a minor administrative unit headed by an aboriginal chieftain in the Southwest; also occurs in its normal literal sense, as one kind of military post. See *t'u-ssu*. P72.

59 *chāi* 齋
SUNG, YÜAN: **Study Hall,** sections to which students were assigned in the Sung Directorate of Education (*kuo-tzu chien*) and the Yüan School for the Sons of the State (*kuo-tzu hsüeh*).

60 *chái-chiā* 宅家
T'ANG: **Your Majesty,** a term used for the Emperor in direct address.

61 *chái-chiā-tzǔ* 宅家子
N-S DIV (Ch'en): an unofficial designation for the residence, and thus indirectly for the person, of an **Imperial Princess** (*kung-chu*).

62 *chài-chǔ* 寨主 or 砦主
SUNG: **Stockade Commander,** an officer on staffs of many units of territorial administration.

63 *chāi-láng* 齋郎
Court Gentleman for Fasting. (1) N-S DIV (N. Wei): unspecified number, rank 7b2, on the staff of the Chamberlain for Ceremonials (*t'ai-ch'ang*). (2) SUI–SUNG: variable numbers of unranked personnel assigned to assist in imperial rituals supervised by the Office of the National Altars (*chiao-she chü, chiao-she shu*); also found in attendance at Imperial Ancestral Temples (*t'ai-miao*), temples honoring deceased Empresses (*hou-miao*), and perhaps elsewhere. See *ling chai-lang*. RR+SP: *chargé des préparatifs rituels*. P28.

64 *chāi-shīh* 齋師
Variant or erroneous form of *chai-shuai* (**Purification Guide**).

65 *chāi-shuài* 齋帥
N-S DIV (N. Ch'i)–T'ANG: **Purification Guide** in the Purification Service (*chai-shuai chü*) in the Secretariat of the Heir Apparent (*men-hsia fang, tso ch'un-fang*). In N. Ch'i 2 Purification Guides and 2 Palace Guides (*nei-ko shuai*) were the principal staff members of the Service; in Sui and T'ang Purification Guides were heads of the Service. In N. Ch'i also, 4 Purification Guides were staff members in each Princedom (*wang-kuo*). RR: *directeur des rites de l'abstinence*. P26, 37, 69.

66 *chāi-shuài chǔ* 齋帥局
N-S DIV (N. Ch'i)–T'ANG: **Purification Service,** a unit in the Secretariat of the Heir Apparent (*men-hsia fang, tso ch'un-fang*), presumably in charge of the abstinences and other preparations by the Heir Apparent that preceded his participation in major religious rituals. In Ch'i staffed with 2 Purification Guides (*chai-shuai*) and 2 Palace Guides (*nei-ko shuai*), in Sui with 4 Purification Guides, in T'ang with one (?) Purification Guide. In 662 retitled *tien-she chü* (Domestic Service of the Heir Apparent). RR: *service du directeur des rites de l'abstinence*. P26.

67 *ch'āi-ch'iěn* 差遣
Meaning "to be detached on commission or duty assignment," this term signifies that an official was not performing the function of his titular office but had been specially assigned to manage the affairs of another office; the title indicating his actual function was normally signaled by such a prefix as *chih* (lit., to know). The Sung dynasty from 960 to 1080 made especially notable use of "commissions" so as to assign officials to functions as flexibly as possible, regardless of considerations of rank, etc. P68.

68 *ch'āi-ch'iěn yüàn* 差遣院
SUNG: **Bureau of Commissions,** established in 981 to manage appointments of lower-ranking officials to duty assignments outside the capital; staffed with officials of the central administration on ad hoc duty assignments; in 991 or 992 merged with the Bureau of Capital and Court Officials (*mo-k'an ching-ch'ao kuan yüan*) into one agency called the Bureau of Minor Commissions (*mo-k'an ch'ai-ch'ien yüan*), which in 993 was retitled *shen-kuan yüan* (Bureau of Personnel Evaluation). SP: *chargé de faire des commissions*. P5.

69 *ch'āi-ì* 差役
Requisitioned Service: throughout history a common term for the assignment of residents on some kind of rotational basis to state service, e.g., as clerical aides, runners, transport workers, construction laborers; normally under the direction and supervision of District (*hsien*) authorities. The service obligation could sometimes be commuted to payments in money or goods, and members of the state officialdom were normally exempt. Often rendered corvée. Cf. *ch'ai-yao, ch'ai-ch'ien*.

70 *ch'ái-t'àn chǔ* 柴炭局
YÜAN: lit., service for firewood and charcoal or coal: **Fuels Service,** one each at the Mongol capitals Ta-tu and Shang-tu, supply units of the Palace Provisions Commission (*hsüan-hui yüan*; headed by a Commissioner (*shih*), rank 5b. P38.

71 *ch'ái-t'àn ssū* 柴炭司
MING: **Office of Fuels,** a minor agency subordinate to the Ministry of Works (*kung-pu*), headed by a Commissioner-in-chief (*ta-shih*), rank 9b, and an unranked Vice Commissioner (*fu-shih*). P15.

72 *ch'āi-tz'ǔ àn* 差次案
SUNG: **Assignment Section** in the Criminal Administration Bureau (*tu-kuan*) of the Ministry of Justice (*hsing-pu*), apparently responsible for monitoring criminals sentenced to state labor service. SP: *service de classement*.

73 *ch'āi-yáo* 差徭
Forced Labor: throughout history a common term for the assignment of residents to state service, particularly to hard labor in state construction gangs or as haulers or carriers of state goods; usually a more menial and physical type of labor than that called Requisitioned Service (*ch'ai-i*), and often (perhaps most commonly) a form of punishment; see *tsa-fan ch'ai-yao*. Administered by District (*hsien*) authorities. Sometimes rendered corvée. Cf. *ch'ai-ch'ien*.

74 *chàn* 站
YÜAN–CH'ING: **Postal Relay Station,** local message-relay post in system maintained by the military to transmit documents between the capital and distant agencies. Also see *i* and *p'u-ssu*. P17.

75 *chàn aò-t'óu* 占鰲頭
SUNG–CH'ING: lit., to have seized the head of the leviathan that in mythology supports the earth; or to have caught a giant sea-turtle, an allusion to an anecdote in the old text *Lieh-tzu* about a man who caught 6 giant sea-turtles on one

line: unofficial reference to the first-place passer of a major civil service recruitment examination, i.e., **Principal Graduate.** Cf. *chuang-yüan, tu-chan ao-t'ou.*

76 *chàn-ch'í* 站齊 or *chàn-ch'ìh* 站赤
YÜAN: **Manager of Postal Relay Stations** in the Bureau of Transmission (*t'ung-cheng yüan*). P17.

77 *chān-jén* 占人
CHOU: **Diviner** with tortoise shells, 8 ranked as Junior Servicemen (*hsia-shih*), members of the Ministry of Rites (*ch'un-kuan*). CL: *devin.*

78 *chān-mèng* 占夢
CHOU: **Interpreter of Dreams,** 2 ranked as Ordinary Servicemen (*chung-shih*), members of the Ministry of Rites (*ch'un-kuan*). CL: *devin des songes.*

79 *chān-shìh* 詹事
Lit., overseer of affairs: throughout imperial history, **Supervisor of the Household** of the Heir Apparent, sometimes one also appointed for the Empress. (1) HAN: one each for the Heir Apparent and the Empress, rank 2,000 bushels; in Later Han abolished, their functions absorbed by the Chamberlain for the Palace Revenues (*shao-fu*). (2) N-S DIV: rank generally 2 or 3; sometimes one prefixed Left and one Right. (3) SUI: existed only briefly, then his functions were absorbed by the Secretariat of the Heir Apparent (*men-hsia fang*). (4) T'ANG–CH'ING: head of the Household Administration of the Heir Apparent (*chan-shih fu, chan-shih yüan*), sometimes prefixed Left and Right, sometimes prefixed Senior (*cheng*) and Junior (*shao*); rank 3a (3b in Sung) till Ch'ing, then 3a (Senior) and 4a (Junior). HB: supervisor of the household. RR+SP: *intendant (général) de la maison de l'héritier du trône.* BH: (chief) supervisor of instruction. P26, 69.

80 *chān-shìh fŭ* 詹事府
T'ANG–CH'ING: **Household Administration of the Heir Apparent,** an agency of the central government in overall charge of administering the affairs of the Heir Apparent, public and private; headed by one or 2 Supervisors of the Household (*chan-shih*), rank 3a to 4a, with the principal help of a Junior (*shao*) Supervisor of the Household, 4a, and one or more Aides (*ch'eng*). Principal subunits were 2 Secretariats of the Heir Apparent (*ch'un-fang*) prefixed Left and Right, each headed by one or 2 Mentors (*shu-tzu*), 4a in T'ang, 5a in Ming and Ch'ing; also supervised various Services (*chü*), especially an Editorial Service (*ssu-ching chü*) headed by a Librarian (*hsien-ma*). In T'ang and Sung the Household Administration also supervised Ten Guard Commands (*shih shuai-fu*) that guarded the Heir Apparent's person and household. In Sung the Household Administration was established irregularly, only when considered appropriate, and was staffed by central government officials on temporary detached assignments. In Liao, Chin, and early Yüan called *chan-shih yüan;* in 1328–1329 known as the *ch'u-ch'ing shih ssu,* thereafter as the *ch'u-cheng yüan,* qq.v. Since the Manchu rulers customarily did not designate heirs, the Household Administration had no real functions in Ch'ing times, but its posts were held concurrently by members of the Hanlin Academy (*han-lin yüan*). RR+SP: *intendance générale de la maison de l'héritier du trône.* BH: supervisorate of imperial instruction. P26.

81 *chān-shìh yüàn* 詹事院
LIAO–YÜAN: variant of *chan-shih fu* (**Household Administration of the Heir Apparent**), headed by one or 2 Supervisors of the Household (*chan-shih*). From 1328 to 1329 retitled *ch'u-ch'ing shih ssu.* Also see *ch'u-cheng yüan.* P26.

82 *ch'án-jén* 廛人
CHOU: **Market Shop Supervisor,** 2 ranked as Ordinary Servicemen (*chung-shih*) and 4 ranked as Junior Servicemen (*hsia-shih*), subordinates of the Directors of Markets (*ssu-shih*) in the Ministry of Education (*ti-kuan*); allocated space in the marketplace(s) of the capital city to both resident and traveling merchants. CL: *officier des boutiques.*

83 *chăng* 掌
Lit., to hold in the palm of the hand; thus, "to manage" or "to be in control of." Most commonly used as a simple verb whose object indicates the things, functions, or agencies that one was responsible for. Often incorporated into an official title as a prefix. When used preceding an agency name, indicates the one among several officials with identical titles and ranks who was placed in charge of the agency they all served; or designates an official, whether or not a member of the named agency, who was not the normally prescribed head of it but had been put in charge of it on a temporary or other irregular basis; etc. E.g., *chang ho-nan tao chien-ch'a yü-shih* (Investigating Censor **in charge of** the Honan Circuit). See *erh-shih-ssu chang.* P14.

84 *chăng* 長
Lit., senior. (1) Common suffix indicating the chief official of whatever is designated by what precedes: **Head, Chief, Director, Magistrate,** etc. E.g., *li-chang* (Village Head), *hsien-chang* (District Magistrate). Also see under *ch'ang.* P32, 54. (2) CHOU: **Regional Administrator,** one of 9 Unifying Agents (*ou*) appointed in the Nine Regions (*chiu chou*) into which the kingdom was divided, as agents of the Minister of State (*chung-tsai*) overseeing geographical clusters of feudal states; special overseer of general administration (?). CL: *anciens, supérieures.*

85 *chăng-àn* 帳案
SUNG: **Accounts Section,** subordinate unit in the State Finance Commission (*san ssu*). SP: *service des comptes.*

86 *chăng-àn* 掌案
T'ANG: **File Clerk,** 20 subofficial functionaries in the Secretariat (*chung-shu sheng*). RR: *employé chargé des dossiers.*

87 *chăng-ch'á ssù-fāng* 掌察四方
CHOU: **Inspector of the Four Quarters,** 8 ranked as Ordinary Servicemen (*chung-shih*), members of the Ministry of Justice (*ch'iu-kuan*); functions not clear, but apparently relate to the administration of justice in domains of the Feudal Lords (*chu-hou*). CL: *agent inspecteur des quatre régions.*

88 *chăng-chàng* 掌仗
SUNG: **Ceremonial Regalia Maid,** 2 palace women, rank 8a, members of the Ceremonial Regalia Office (*ssu-chang ssu*) in the Wardrobe Service (*shang-i chü*).

89 *chăng-chēn* 掌珍
SUNG: **Jeweler,** 2 palace women, rank 8a, members of the Rarities Office (*ssu-chen ssu*) in the Workshop Service (*shang-kung chü*).

90 *chăng-chèng* 掌正
T'ANG: **Rectifier,** 3 palace women, rank 8a2, subordinate to the Directress of the Inner Quarters (*ssu-kuei*) in the establishment of the Heir Apparent; in charge of the receipt of correspondence and recommending punishments for violators of harem rules. RR: *chargé de la surveillance du harem de l'héritier du trône.*

91 *chăng-ch'eng* 長丞
A term signifying 2 categories of executive officials in an

agency, **the Head** (*chang*) **and his Aides** (*ch'eng*). Apparently does not occur as a 2-character title meaning, e.g., senior aide.

92 chǎng-chí 掌籍
SUNG: **Librarian,** 2 palace women, rank 8a, members of the Library Office (*ssu-chi ssu*) in the Ceremonial Service (*shang-i chü*).

93 chǎng-chì 掌計
SUNG: **Accounting Maid,** 2 palace women, rank 8a, members of the Accounts Office (*ssu-chi ssu*) in the Workshop Service (*shang-kung chü*).

94 chǎng-chì 掌記
Record Keeper. (1) T'ANG: non-official personal secretary for a territorial administrator. (2) SUNG: 2 palace women, rank 8a, members of the Records Office (*ssu-chi ssu*) in the General Palace Service (*shang-kung chü*).

95 chǎng-chí 掌集
SUNG: **Assembler,** 2 palace women, rank 8a, in the Music Office (*ssu-yüeh ssu*) of the Ceremonial Service (*shang-i chü*).

96 chàng-chí àn 帳籍案
SUNG: **Records Section,** one of 13 Sections directly subordinate to the executive officials of the S. Sung Ministry of Justice (*hsing-pu*); staffed with suboficial functionaries; handled documents relating to the rectification of deficiencies in state storehouses in the capital, modern Hangchow. SP: *service des registres de comptes*.

97 chàng-chí kào-shēn àn 帳籍告身案
SUNG: **Records and Warrants Section,** after 1129 one of 10 Sections in the Ministry of War (*ping-pu*) directly supervised by the Minister of War (*ping-pu shang-shu*); functions not wholly clear, but apparently related to maintaining personnel files on officers and issuing certificates of authority. SP: *service des registres de comptes et des titres de nomination*.

98 chǎng-ch'ì 掌饎
SUNG: **Banquets Maid,** 2 palace women, rank 8a, members of the Banquets Office (*ssu-ch'i ssu*) in the Food Service (*shang-shih chü*).

99 chǎng-chiāng 掌疆
CHOU: **Border Monitor,** 8 ranked as Ordinary Servicemen (*chung-shih*), members of the Ministry of War (*hsia-kuan*) responsible for delineating frontiers of the royal domain, domains of the Feudal Lords (*chu-hou*), and other administrative units. CL: *chargé des confins*.

100 chǎng-chiāo 掌交
CHOU: **Dissemination and Inquiry Officials,** 8 ranked as Ordinary Servicemen (*chung-shih*), members of the Ministry of Justice (*hsia-kuan*) charged to travel throughout the empire publicizing the royal virtue and gathering information for the throne; also, in conjunction with the Junior Messengers (*hsiao hsing-jen*), to make annual visits to each feudal domain to inquire into conditions. CL: *agents d'union*.

101 chǎng-chiào ssū 掌教司
YÜAN: **Religious Office,** 72 scattered about China under supervision of the Commission for the Promotion of Religion (*ch'ung-fu ssu*); responsible for overseeing Nestorian, Manichaean, and other untraditional religious communities; often prefaced by *yeh-li-k'o-wen*, a transcription from the Mongolian whose meaning is not clear.

102 chǎng-chiéh 掌節
CHOU: **Keeper of the Seal,** 2 ranked as Senior Servicemen (*shang-shih*) and 4 as Ordinary Servicemen (*chung-shih*), members of the Ministry of Education (*ti-kuan*) responsible for guarding the royal seal and supervising all its applications. CL: *préposé aux tablettes marquées du sceau impérial, ou passe-ports.*

103 chang-chien 長兼
See *ch'ang-chien*.

104 chǎng-chìh 掌製
SUNG: **Seamstress,** 2 palace women, rank 8a, members of the Sewing Office (*ssu-chih ssu*) in the Workshop Service (*shang-kung chü*).

105 chǎng-chīh k'ò-lòu 掌知刻漏
T'ANG: **Water Clock Supervisor,** until the early 700s an unranked appointee in the Bureau of Astronomy (*ssu-t'ien t'ai*), subordinate to the Palace Library (*pi-shu sheng*). RR: *chargé de surveiller la clepsydre.*

106 chǎng-chīn 掌津
N-S DIV (Chou): **Master of the Ford,** number variable, ranked as Ordinary Servicemen (*chung-shih*), appointed at appropriate water crossings by the Ministry of Works (*tung-kuan*).

107 chāng-chīng 章京
CH'ING: apparent transliteration of a Manchu word. (1) **Secretary** (civil) or **Adjutant** (military), variable numbers and ranks in the Council of State (*chün-chi ch'u*), the Court of Colonial Affairs (*li-fan yüan*), the late Ch'ing Foreign Office (*tsung-li ya-men*), etc. Prefixes often specify particular responsibilities or organizational affiliations, e.g., *chün-chi chang-ching*. P17. (2) **Banner Vice Commander-in-chief** (*mei-lo chang-ching*), **Regimental Commander** (*chia-la chang-ching*), or **Company Commander** (*niu-lu chang-ching*) in the Eight Banners (*pa ch'i*) military organization after 1634, replacing the earlier term *o-chen*, q.v. P44.

108 chàng-chiù 仗廄
T'ANG: **Stables of Trustworthy Mounts,** a collective reference to horses maintained in various palace stables for the use of the Emperor and his close attendants; divided into 2 groups prefixed Left and Right; under the control of the Palace Administration (*tien-chung sheng*). The Stables of the Left were also known as Stables of Meteoric Mounts (*pen-hsing chiu*) and Stables of the Palace Colts (*nei-chiü chiu*), and collectively as the Two Stables of the Palace (? *liang chang-nei*). RR: *écuries des gardes d'honneur.*

109 chǎng-chiù tū-hsiá 掌廄都轄
CHIN: **Stable Manager,** no fixed number, rank 9a, in the Livery Service (*shang-chiu chü*) of the Palace Inspectorate-general (*tien-ch'ien tu tien-chien ssu*). P39.

110 chǎng-ch'iú 掌囚
Jailor. (1) CHOU: 12 ranked as Junior Servicemen (*hsia-shih*), members of the Ministry of Justice (*ch'iu-kuan*), specifically responsible for strangling condemned criminals. (2) N-S DIV (Chou): one ranked as Ordinary Serviceman (*chung-shih*) and one as Junior Serviceman (*hsia-shih*), members of the Ministry of Justice (*ch'iu-kuan*). P13.

111 chang-ch'u 掌畜
See *chang-hsü*.

112 chǎng-chuàn t'īng 掌饌廳
MING: **Victualler's Office** in the Directorate of Education (*kuo-tzu chien*), headed by one or 2 Victuallers in charge of the Victualler's Office (*chang chang-chuan t'ing chang-chuan*). P34, 49.

113 *chǎng-ch'uán chú* 掌船局
SUI: **Water Transport Service,** subordinate unit in the Office of Waterways (*tu-shui t'ai*); headed by 2 Waterways Commandants (*tu-shui wei*).

114 *chǎng-ch'üèh àn* 掌闕案
SUNG: **Vacancies Section,** a unit of the Civil Appointments Process (*tso-hsüan*) in the Ministry of Personnel (*li-pu*). SP: *service des places vacantes des fonctionnaires civils.*

115 *chǎng-èrh* 長貳
Lit., senior (officials) and their seconds (i.e., assistants): **Executive Officials,** throughout imperial history a generic reference to the top 2 executive posts in an agency, e.g., the Chief Minister (*ch'ing*) and the Vice Minister (*shao-ch'ing*) of a Court (*ssu*); especially in Ming and Ch'ing, used primarily in collective reference to Prefects (*chih-fu*), Vice Prefects (*t'ung-chih*), possibly also Assistant Prefects (*t'ung-p'an*), and in addition to District Magistrates (*chih-hsien*) and Vice Magistrates (*hsien-ch'eng*); the group referred to possibly includes Assistant District Magistrates (*chu-pu*), but such an extension seems least likely. Cf. *ch'ing-erh* (Ministerial Executives).

116 *chǎng-fǎ àn* 掌法案
SUNG: **Law Section,** subordinate unit in the Court of Imperial Sacrifices (*t'ai-ch'ang ssu*) and the Imperial Music Bureau (*ta-sheng fu*); function not clear. SP: *service des règlements.*

117 *chǎng-féng* 掌縫
T'ANG: **Clothier,** 3 palace women, rank 8a2, subordinate to the Directress of Standards (*ssu-tse*) in the establishment of the Heir Apparent; in charge of spinning, weaving, and sewing to prepare and maintain the clothing of palace women. RR: *chargé des travaux de couture du harem de l'héritier du trône.*

118 *chǎng-hái shǔ* 掌醢署
SUI–SUNG, MING–CH'ING: **Spice Pantry,** one of 4 principal subunits in the Court of Imperial Entertainments (*kuang-lu ssu*); headed by a Director (*ling* through Sung; *shu-cheng* in Ming–Ch'ing), rank 8a through Sung, 6b in Ming–Ch'ing; in Ch'ing one Manchu and one Chinese Director. Staffed with Seasoners (*chang-hai*) in charge of salts, sauces, mincemeats, etc. RR+SP: *(office) chargé des hachis.* P30.

119 *chǎng-hán* 掌函
T'ANG: **Envelope Keeper,** 20 in the Secretariat (*chung-shu sheng*).

120 *chǎng-hàn* 掌翰
T'ANG: **Plume-bearer,** 30 authorized by the 680s in the Sedan-chair Service (*shang-lien chü*) of the Palace Administration (*tien-chung sheng*). RR: *chargé des insignes formés de plumes.*

121 *chàng-hsià tū* 帳下督
N-S DIV (San-kuo): **Camp Supervisor,** a designation commonly awarded to or assumed by officers commanding military units. See *men-hsia tu.*

122 *chǎng-hsièn* 掌憲
Unofficial reference to a **Censor-in-chief** (*yü-shih ta-fu, tu yü-shih*), perhaps from as early as T'ang times. See *hsien-kuan.*

123 *chǎng-hsién* 掌閑
T'ANG: **Groom,** 5,000 authorized in the Livery Service (*shang-sheng chü*) in the Palace Administration (*tien-chung sheng*). RR: *valets d'écurie.*

124 *chǎng-hsǜ* 掌畜
Keeper of Sacrificial Animals. (1) CHOU: 2 ranked as Junior Servicemen (*hsia-shih*), members of the Ministry of War (*hsia-kuan*). CL: *l'éléveur.* (2) HAN: headed by a Director (*ling*) of the Keepers of Sacrificial Animals, subordinate to the administrative official for the capital called Guardian of the Right (*yu fu-feng*). HB (*ling*): prefect in charge of sacrificial domestic animals.

125 *chǎng hùo-hùi* 掌貨賄
CHOU: **Tribute Monitors,** 6 ranked as Junior Servicemen (*hsia-shih*), members of the Ministry of Justice (*ch'iu-kuan*); kept watch over the domains of Feudal Lords (*chu-hou*) and were in charge of the tribute articles they submitted. CL: *agents des denrées et matières précieuses.*

126 *chǎng-í* 掌儀
Master of Ceremonies. (1) SUI: 20 in the Ceremonial Office (*ssu-i shu*) of the Court for Dependencies (*hung-lu ssu*). (2) T'ANG: 2 in the Secretariat of the Heir Apparent (*tso ch'un-fang*). RR: *fonctionnaire chargé de l'étiquette.* P33.

127 *chǎng-ī* 掌衣
SUNG: **Clothing Maid,** 2 palace women, rank 8a, members of the Clothing Office (*ssu-i ssu*) in the Wardrobe Service (*shang-i chü*).

128 *chǎng-ī* 掌醫
T'ANG: **Medical Attendant,** 3 palace women, rank 8a2, subordinate to the Directress of Foodstuffs (*ssu-chuan*) in the establishment of the Heir Apparent; in charge of medical care in the harem. RR: *chargé de la médecine du harem de l'héritier du trône.*

129 *chǎng-ī chiēn* 掌醫監
YÜAN: **Directorate of Medication,** a unit of the Palace Provisions Commission (*hsüan-hui yüan*); headed by a Concurrent Controller of the Directorate (*ling chien-kuan*), rank 5a. Agency retitled from *chang-i shu* in 1308–1309, then abolished in 1323–1324.

130 *chǎng í-lì* 掌夷隸
N-S DIV (Chou): **Warden of Captive Eastern Barbarians,** number not fixed, ranked as Ordinary Servicemen (*chung-shih;* 8a) and Junior Servicemen (*hsia-shih;* 9a), members of the Ministry of Justice (*ch'iu-kuan*). P13.

131 *chǎng-ī shǔ* 掌醫署
YÜAN: **Office of Medication,** a unit of the Palace Provisions Commission (*hsüan-hui yüan*); retitled from *tien-i shu* in 1294–1295, then changed to *chang-i chien* in 1308–1309.

132 *chǎng-í ssū* 掌儀司
CH'ING: **Office of Palace Ceremonial** in the Imperial Household Department (*nei-wu fu*); responsible for arranging sacrifices, ritual feasts, ritual music and dancing, etc.; headed by 2 Directors (*lang-chung*). Agency retitled from *li-i yüan* in 1677. BH: department of ceremonial.

133 *chǎng jǎn-ts'ǎo* 掌染草
CHOU: **Keeper of Dyes,** 2 ranked as Junior Servicemen (*hsia-shih*), members of the Ministry of Education (*ti-kuan*) who collected dye-yielding plants that had been submitted as taxes and distributed them to dye workers. CL: *préposé aux plantes de teinture.*

134 *chǎng júng-lì* 掌戎隸
N-S DIV (Chou): **Warden of Captive Western Barbarians,** number not fixed, ranked as Ordinary Servicemen (*chung-shih;* 8a) and Junior Servicemen (*hsia-shih;* 9a), members of the Ministry of Justice (*ch'iu-kuan*). P13.

135 *chǎng-kǎo ssū* 掌槁司
CH'ING: lit., office in charge of grain stalks, written drafts, printing proofs, etc.: **Office of Dies** (? meaning not wholly clear), a unit of the Ministry of Revenue's (*hu-pu*) Coinage Office (*ch'ien-fa t'ang*) established in 1761; staffed with one Chinese and one Manchu official delegated from the Ministry's subordinate Bureaus (*ch'ing-li ssu*). P16.

136 *chǎng-kó* 掌葛
CHOU: **Keeper of Fibers,** 2 ranked as Junior Servicemen (*hsia-shih*), members of the Ministry of Education (*ti-kuan*); collected fibrous plants submitted as taxes and distributed them to textile workers. CL: *préposé aux plantes textiles.*

137 *chǎng-k'ò* 掌客
Steward. (1) CHOU: 2 ranked as Senior Servicemen (*shang-shih*) and 4 as Ordinary Servicemen (*chung-shih*), members of the Ministry of Justice (*ch'iu-kuan*) responsible for ceremonious treatment of court visitors. CL: *agent des visiteurs.* (2) N-S DIV (Chou): number not clear, ranked as Senior Servicemen (*shang-shih;* 7a), members of the Ministry of Justice (*ch'iu-kuan*); with directional prefixes or inserts, e.g., *hsi chang-k'o* or *chang hsi-k'o* (Steward for Western Visitors). P11. (3) SUI: 10 on the staff of the Court for Dependencies (*hung-lu ssu*). (4) T'ANG: 15, rank 9a1, in the Office of State Visitors (*tien-k'o shu*), a unit in the Court of State Ceremonial (*hung-lu ssu*). RR: *fonctionnaire chargé des hôtes.* P9.

138 *chǎng ... k'ō* 掌⋯科
MING–CH'ING: prefix meaning **in charge of the Office of Scrutiny** (*k'o*) **for ...,** followed normally by Chief Supervising Secretary (*tu chi-shih-chung*) or Supervising Secretary (*chi-shih-chung*), or sometimes by another kind of title entirely. E.g., Chief Supervising Secretary in charge of the Office of Scrutiny for War (*chang ping-k'o tu chi-shih-chung*).

139 *chǎng-kù* 掌固
(1) CHOU: **Keeper of Security,** 2 ranked as Senior Servicemen (*shang-shih*) and 8 as Junior Servicemen (*hsia-shih*), members of the Ministry of War (*hsia-kuan*) responsible for maintaining defenses of the capital. CL: *préposé aux fortifications.* (2) T'ANG: **Clerk,** unranked suboffical; large numbers in Ministries (*pu*) and many other agencies. RR: *commis.* P30.

140 *chǎng-kù* 掌故
HAN: **Clerk,** 20 on the staff of the Grand Astrologer (*t'ai-shih ling*); rank and function not clear. HB: authority on ancient matters. P35.

141 *chǎng-k'ù* 掌庫
Keeper of the Storehouse. (1) SUNG: unranked subofficial, variable numbers in subordinate units of the Palace Administration (*tien-chung sheng*), e.g., the Palace Clothing Storehouse (*nei i-wu k'u*); and 14 in the Saddlery Storehouse (*an-p'ei k'u*) of the Court of the Imperial Stud (*t'ai-p'u ssu*). (2) CH'ING: several, apparently unranked, in the Office of Palace Construction (*ying-tsao ssu*) of the Imperial Household Department (*nei-wu fu*). See *k'u-chang.* P38.

142 *chàng-k'ù chú* 仗庫局
N-S DIV (N. Ch'i): **Armory Service,** headed by an Aide (*ch'eng*), subordinate to the Manager of Storehouses (*ssu-tsang*), an official of the Household Administration of the Heir Apparent (*chan-shih fu*). P26.

143 *chǎng-kuān* 長官
(1) **Senior Official,** a generic term specifying the head of any kind of agency. (2) YÜAN–CH'ING: **Chief,** leader of a southwestern aboriginal tribe officially designated a Chief's Office (*chang-kuan ssu*), normally with nominal rank 6a. P72.

144 *chǎng kuān-fáng* 掌關防
CH'ING: **Seal-holder,** a title suffix indicating official in charge of the ..., normally designating someone with a substantive office outside the indicated agency; e.g., *nei kuan-ling chang kuan-fang* (Seal-holder of the Overseers Office) in the Imperial Household Department (*nei-wu fu*); a concurrent appointment for the Director (*lang-chung*) of a Bureau (*ssu, ch'ing-li ssu*) in a Ministry (*pu*). Cf. *chang-yin* (Seal-holding ...). P37.

145 *chǎng kuān-fáng ch'ù* 掌關防處
CH'ING: variant designation of *nei kuan-ling ch'u* (**Overseers Office**), a unit of the Imperial Household Department (*nei-wu fu*). P37.

146 *chǎng kuān-fáng kuān* 掌關防官
(1) MING–CH'ING: **Seal-holding Official;** may be encountered as a generic reference to heads of agencies, or especially as a reference to the leader of a group of officials on a special mission. Cf. *chang-yin kuan.* (2) CH'ING: **Caretaker** of an imperial mausoleum (*ling*), rank 4a; commonly prefixed with the name of a particular mausoleum, as ... *ling chang kuan-fang kuan* (Caretaker of the ... Mausoleum). P29.

147 *chǎng kuān-fáng kuǎn-lǐ néi-kuǎn-lǐng shìh-wù ch'ù* 掌關防管理內管領事務處
CH'ING: variant designation of *nei kuan-ling ch'u* (**Overseers Office**), a unit of the Imperial Household Department (*nei-wu fu*). P37.

148 *chǎng kuān-fáng shìh-wù* 掌關防事務
CH'ING: lit., in charge of matters of the seal: variant designation of the *nei kuan-ling chang kuan-fang* (**Overseer of the Overseers Office**), an official of the Imperial Household Department (*nei-wu fu*). P37.

149 *chǎng-kuān ssū* 長官司
YÜAN–CH'ING: **Chief's Office,** one type of administrative agency created for southwestern aboriginal tribes, headed by a Chief (*chang-kuan*), rank 6a. See *t'u-ssu.* P72.

150 *chǎng kūng-chǔ* 長公主
Grand Princess: generally used as a title for a sister of a reigning Emperor; may be encountered as a reference to the eldest or most favored daughter (*kung-chu:* Princess) of an Emperor. See *ta-chang kung-chu.* HB: senior princess. P69.

151 *chǎng kùng-chǔ* 掌貢舉 or *chǎng kùng-pù* 掌貢部
T'ANG: **Chief Examiner** in a civil service recruitment examination.

152 *chǎng-kuǒ* 掌果
CH'ING: **Keeper of Fruits,** head of the Fruits Pantry (*kuo-fang*), a unit in the Office of Palace Ceremonial (*chang-i ssu*) of the Imperial Household Department (*nei-wu fu*). BH: controller of the fruit office.

153 *chǎng-lì* 長吏
Senior Subalterns. (1) Throughout history a generic term referring vaguely to the higher grades of suboffical functionaries (*li*), but may be encountered as an equivalent of *chang-kuan* (Senior Official). (2) HAN: specific generic reference to government personnel with stipends ranging

from 400 down to l00 bushels per year. Cf. *shao-li* (Junior Subaltern). P30, 68.

154 *chǎng-lì* 掌厤 or 掌曆
YÜAN–MING: **Calendar Clerk,** 2 or more, rank 8a or 9b, in the Astrological Commission (*t'ai-shih yüan*). P35.

155 *chǎng-liên* 掌輦
T'ANG–SUNG: **Sedan-chair Master,** rank 9b or unranked, in the Sedan-chair Service (*shang-lien chü*) of the Palace Administration (*tien-chung sheng*); variant of T'ang's *shang-lien*. RR+SP: *chargé des voitures (à bras).*

156 *chǎng-loù* 掌漏
T'ANG: **Keeper of the Water Clock,** 6 unranked technicians in the Court of the Watches (*lei-keng ssu*) in the household of the Heir Apparent. RR: *chargé de la clepsydre.* P26.

157 *chǎng-lù* 掌戮
CHOU: **Executioner,** 2 ranked as Junior Servicemen (*hsia-shih*), members of the Ministry of Justice (*ch'iu-kuan*). CL: *exécuteur.*

158 *chàng-mǎ* 仗馬
T'ANG: **Military Ceremonial Mounts,** a general reference to cavalry horses trained to participate quietly in imperial ceremonies, but more specifically the designation of horses maintained at the palace gates and at the frontiers for issuance to anyone bearing an urgent report or complaint for presentation to the Emperor. RR: *chevaux d'apparat.*

159 *chǎng mán-lì* 掌蠻隸
N-S DIV (Chou): **Warden of Captive Southern Barbarians,** number not clear, ranked as Ordinary Servicemen (*chung-shih;* 8a), members of the Ministry of Justice (*ch'iu-kuan*). P13.

160 *chǎng-mù* 掌墓
N-S DIV (Chou): **Gravetender,** number not clear, ranked as Junior Servicemen (*hsia-shih;* 9a), members of the Ministry of Rites (*ch'un-kuan*). P29.

161 *chǎng nán-yüàn t'oú-tzǔ* 掌南院頭子
LIAO: **Office Manager,** rank not clear but low, in the Southern Establishment (*nan-yüan*) of the Northern Administration (*pei-mien*). P5.

162 *chàng-nèi* 仗內
T'ANG: **Inner Quarters** of the imperial palace.

163 *chàng-nèi fǔ* 帳內府
T'ANG: **Escort Brigade,** theoretically consisting of 667 Escort Guardsmen (*chang-nei*) of Left and Right under 2 Escort Brigade Commanders (*tien-chün*), in each Princely Establishment (*wang-kuo fu*). RR: *garde du palais d'un prince.* P69.

164 *chàng-nèi liù hsién* 帳內六閑
T'ANG: **Six Palace Corrals** administered by the Livery Service (*shang-ch'eng chü*) of the Palace Administration (*tien-chung sheng*) for breeding and rearing horses inside the palace enclosure. Created in 696, by 700 came under the control of a Commissioner of the Palace Stables (*hsien-chiu shih*), a duty assignment for a Director (*chien*), rank 3a2, or an Assistant Director (*ch'eng*), 5b1, of the Palace Administration; also came jointly under the supervision of the Court of the Imperial Stud (*t'ai-p'u ssu*). The Six Corrals were the Flying Dragon Corral (*fei-lung chiu*), the Unicorn Corral (*hsiang-lin hsien*), the Phoenix Park (*feng-yün hsien*), the Pheasant Corral (*yüan-luan hsien*), the Mottled Bird (?) Corral (*chi-liang hsien*), and the Six Herds Corral (*liu-ch'ün*

hsien), the last also known as the Six Stables (*liu chiu*). Also see *wu fang, kuan-ma fang*. RR: *six parcs á chevaux de l'intérieur du palais de l'empereur.*

165 *chàng-nèi sàn-yüèh* 仗內散樂
T'ANG: **Secular Palace Musician,** 1,000 prescribed for the staff of the Imperial Music Office (*t'ai-yüeh shu*), subordinate to the Court of Imperial Sacrifices (*t'ai-ch'ang ssu*). RR: *musicien de musique profane de l'intérieur du palais.*

166 *chang-nien* 掌輦
See under the romanization *chang-lien*.

167 *chǎng-paǒ* 掌寶
T'ANG–SUNG: (1) **Keeper of Seals,** palace woman, rank 8a, in the Clothing Service (*shang-fu chü*) in the Palace Domestic Service (*nei-shih sheng*). (2) CHIN: **Keeper of Gems** in the household of the Heir Apparent, 2, rank and functions not clear. P26.

168 *chǎng pěi-yüàn t'oú-tzǔ* 掌北院頭子
LIAO: **Office Manager,** rank not clear but low, in the Northern Establishment (*pei-yüan*) of the Northern Administration (*pei-mien*). P12.

169 *chǎng-p'èi chiēn* 章佩監
YÜAN: **Directorate for the Imperial Accessories,** agency supervising the Emperor's eunuch valets, subordinate to the Palace Provisions Commission (*hsüan-hui yüan*); headed by a Supervisor (*chien*), rank 3a. P38.

170 *chǎng-p'í* 掌皮
CHOU: **Keeper of Hides,** 4 ranked as Junior Servicemen (*hsia-shih*), members of the Ministry of State (*t'ien-kuan*); collected hide and pelt tribute articles, delivered them to court leather and felt workers; collaborated with the Ministry of Works (*tung-kuan*) in supervising such manufactures. CL: *préposé aux peaux.*

171 *chǎng-pīn* 掌賓
SUNG: **Hostess,** 2 palace women, rank 8a, members of the Visitors Office (*ssu-pin ssu*) of the Ceremonial Service (*shang-i chü*).

172 *chǎng-pù* 掌簿
SUNG: **Registrar,** 2 palace women, rank 8a, members of the Registration Office (*ssu-pu*) in the General Palace Service (*shang-kung chü*).

173 *chàng-sāi wèi* 障塞尉
HAN: **Commandant of Fortifications,** rank 200 bushels, appointed in Later Han to the staffs of frontier Districts (*hsien*) in the North and Northwest as a special precaution against nomadic raids. HB: commandant of fortifications.

174 *chǎng-sǎn tsǔng-lǐng* 掌傘總領
CH'ING: **Supervisor of Umbrella-making** in the Court of Imperial Armaments (*wu-pei yüan*) of the Imperial Household Department (*nei-wu fu*). BH: supervisor of umbrella-making.

175 *chǎng sàn-yüèh* 掌散樂
N-S DIV (Chou): **Director of Secular Music,** number not clear, ranked as Ordinary Servicemen (*chung-shih;* 8a), members of the Ministry of Rites (*ch'un-kuan*). P10.

176 *chǎng-shàn* 掌膳
SUNG: **Table Maid,** 2 palace women, rank 7a, members of the Foods Office (*ssu-shan ssu*) in the Catering Service (*shang-shih chü*).

177 *chǎng-she* 掌舍
(1) CHOU: **Manager of Rest Stations,** 4 ranked as Junior

Servicemen (*hsia-shih*), members of the Ministry of State (*t'ien-kuan*) in charge of temporary camps used by the ruler on his travels. CL: *préposé aux stations de repos*. (2) SUNG: **Section Chief,** rank and function not clear, in the Three Institutes (*san kuan*). SP: *chargé des cabanes*.

178 *chǎng-shè* 掌設
SUNG: **Interior Maintenance Maid,** 2 palace women, rank 8a, members of the Interior Maintenance Office (*ssu-she ssu*) in the Housekeeping Service (*shang-ch'in chü*).

179 *chǎng-shèn* 掌蜃
CHOU: **Keeper of Clamshells,** 2 ranked as Junior Servicemen (*hsia-shih*), members of the Ministry of Education (*ti-kuan*); provided clamshells for powdering into a whitener for ceremonial uses. CL: *préposé aux huitres*.

180 *chàng-shǐh* 帳史
T'ANG: **Account Keeper,** unranked subofficial in Prefectures (*chou*) and Superior Prefectures (*fu*). RR: *scribe chargé du registre des contributions*. P53.

181 *chǎng-shǐh* 掌史
SUNG: **Account Keeper,** unranked subofficial in Prefectures (*chou*). SP: *chargé des registres*.

182 *chǎng-shíh* 掌食
T'ANG: **Provisioner,** 3 palace women, rank 8a2, subordinate to the Directress of Foodstuffs (*ssu-chuan*) in the establishment of the Heir Apparent; in charge of seasoned and other special dishes, wines, lamps, torches, firewood, vases, etc., in the harem. RR: *chargé de la nourriture du harem de l'héritier du trône*.

183 *chǎng-shìh* 掌飾
SUNG: **Adornments Maid,** 2 palace women, rank 8a, members of the Adornments Office (*ssu-shih ssu*) in the Wardrobe Service (*shang-i chü*).

184 *chǎng-shǐh* 長使
HAN: designation of one category of **Palace Woman,** rank =600 bushels. HB: senior maid.

185 *chǎng-shǐh* 長史
Lit., senior scribe. (1) CH'IN–SUNG: **Aide,** an official usually of executive status but of variable rank, found in many agencies both civil and military; e.g., in Princedoms (*wang-kuo*) and Commanderies (*chün*) in Han, in Regions (*chou*) in Sui, in Prefectures (*chou*) and Area Commands (*tu-tu fu*) in T'ang, in Prefectures (*chou*) in Sung. HB: chief clerk. RR: *administrateur en chef*. SP: *administrateur en chef, secrétaire en chef, secrétaire général, chef du bureau*. (2) N-S DIV–CH'ING: **Administrator,** chief executive official in a Princedom (*wang-kuo*) or, from T'ang on, a Princely Establishment (*wang-fu*); normally one, rank 4b1 in T'ang, 5a in Ming, 3a in Ch'ing, otherwise not clear. RR+SP: *administrateur en chef*. BH: commandant of a prince's palace. P69. (3) T'ANG, CH'ING: **Administrator,** chief executive official in a Princess' Establishment (*kung-chu fu*), rank 4b1 in T'ang, 3a or 4 in Ch'ing. RR: *administrateur en chef*. BH: commandant. P69. (4) T'ANG: **Administrator** of the Eastern Capital, Loyang, but early retitled *yin* (Governor). P49. (5) YÜAN: **Administrator,** occasionally a middle-level executive official on the staff of the Heir Apparent or the Empress. P26.

186 *chǎng-shǐh ssū* 長史司
Administrator's Office in a Princely Establishment (*wang-fu*), headed by an Administrator (*chang-shih*). P69.

187 *chǎng … shìh tà-ch'én* 掌⋯事大臣
CH'ING: lit., grand minister in charge of (commanding or managing) the affairs of such-and-such agency, civil or military; used as a designation when a Prince or other eminent nobleman was in service: **Grand Minister Managing** (or **Commanding**) **the …** (agency name).

188 *chǎng-shū* 掌書
Secretary. (1) T'ANG: 3 palace women, rank 8a2, subordinate to the Directress of the Inner Quarters (*ssu-kuei*) in the establishment of the Heir Apparent; in charge of seals, correspondence, and other paperwork. RR: *chargé des écrits du harem de l'héritier du trône*. (2) YÜAN: 4 officials or subofficial functionaries, status not clear, in the Institute of Interpreters (*hui-t'ung kuan*); another on the staff of the most direct descendant of Confucius, ennobled as Duke for Fulfilling the Sage (*yen-sheng kung*). (3) MING–CH'ING: one, rank 7a, on the staff of the Duke for Fulfilling the Sage. P66.

189 *chǎng shū-chì* 掌書記
T'ANG–SUNG: **Chief Secretary:** commonly on staffs of Surveillance Commissioners (*kuan-ch'a shih*) and Marshals of the Empire (*t'ien-hsia ping-ma yüan-shuai*), rank not clear, in T'ang; on staffs of Prefectures (*fu, chou, chün, chien*), rank 8b, in Sung. RR+SP: *secrétaire général*. See *chieh-tu chang shu-chi*. P52.

190 *chǎng sǒ-shìh kuàn-chūn shíh* 掌所事冠軍使
CH'ING: **Assistant Director** of the Standard-bearer Guard (*ch'i-shou wei*) of the Rear Subsection (*hou-so*) of the Imperial Procession Guard (*luan-i wei*), rank 5a. BH: assistant section chief.

191 *chǎng sǒ-shìh yún-hūi shíh* 掌所事雲麾使
CH'ING: **Assistant Director** of any Subsection (*so*) of the Imperial Procession Guard (*luan-i wei*), rank 4a; also of the Elephant-training Office (*hsün-hsiang so*) of the Rear Subsection (*hou-so*) of the same agency, rank 5a. BH: assistant sub-department chief, assistant section chief.

192 *chàng-ssū* 帳司
SUNG: **Accounts Office,** a unit in the Tax Transport Bureau (*chuan-yün ssu*), part of the early Sung State Finance Commission (*san ssu*); headed by a Manager of the Accounts Office (*chu-kuan chang-ssu*), a duty assignment for an official nominally established elsewhere in the central government.

193 *chǎng-t'àn* 掌炭
CHOU: **Keeper of Charcoal,** 2 ranked as Junior Servicemen (*hsia-shih*), members of the Ministry of Education (*ti-kuan*). CL: *préposé au charbon*.

194 *chǎng-té* 長德
N-S DIV (N. Wei): **Maturer of Virtue** (?), established in 400 as a prestige title (*san-kuan*) for tribal chiefs; traditionally compared to the later title Grand Master of Palace Leisure (*chung-san ta-fu*), rank 5a or 5b. P69.

195 *chǎng-tēng* 掌燈
SUNG: **Lantern Keeper,** 2 palace women, rank 8a, members of the Lanterns Office (*ssu-teng ssu*) in the Housekeeping Service (*shang-ch'in chü*).

196 *chǎng tí-lì* 掌狄隸
N-S DIV (Chou): **Warden of Captive Northern Barbarians,** number not clear, ranked as Ordinary Servicemen (*chung-shih*) and Junior Servicemen (*hsia-shih*), members of the Ministry of Justice (*ch'iu-kuan*). P13.

197 chǎng-ts'ái 掌材
N-S DIV (Chou): **Keeper of Lumber,** number not clear, ranked as Senior Servicemen (*shang-shih*) and Ordinary Servicemen (*chung-shih*), members of the Ministry of Works (*tung-kuan*). P14.

198 chǎng-ts'ǎi 掌綵
SUNG: **Silk Worker,** 2 palace women, rank 8a, members of the Rarities Office (*ssu-chen ssu*) in the Workshop Service (*shang-kung chü*).

199 chǎng-tsàn 掌贊
SUNG: **Ritual Receptionist,** 2 palace women, rank 8a, members of the Ritual Receptions Office (*ssu-tsan ssu*) in the Ceremonial Service (*shang-i chü*).

200 chǎng-tsàng 掌藏
T'ANG: **Storekeeper,** 3 palace women, rank 8a2, subordinate to the Directress of Standards (*ssu-tse*) in the establishment of the Heir Apparent; in charge of all gold, pearls, gems, and other precious objects in the harem. RR: *chargé du trésor du harem de l'héritier du trône.*

201 chǎng-tsò 掌座
Keeper of the Altars. (1) T'ANG: 24 unranked subofficials in the Office of the National Altars (*chiao-she shu*). RR: *chargé des autels des banlieues.* (2) SUNG: number not clear, unranked subofficials in the Ministry of Rites (*lǐ-pu*). SP: *fonctionnaire des rites.* P28.

202 chāng-tsoù fáng 章奏房
SUNG: **Memorials Office,** a unit in the Chancellery (*men-hsia sheng*). SP: *chambre d'adresses au trône.*

203 chǎng tsùi-lì 掌罪隸
N-S DIV (Chou): **Warden of Convicted Criminals,** number not clear, ranked as Ordinary Servicemen (*chung-shih*) and Junior Servicemen (*hsia-shih*), members of the Ministry of Justice (*ch'iu-kuan*). P13.

204 chǎng-t'ú 掌徒
N-S DIV (Chou): **Warden of Banished Criminals,** number not clear, ranked as Ordinary Servicemen (*chung-shih*) and Junior Servicemen (*hsia-shih*), members of the Ministry of Justice (*ch'iu-kuan*). P13.

205 chǎng-t'ú 掌荼
CHOU: **Keeper of Thistles,** 2 ranked as Junior Servicemen (*hsia-shih*), members of the Ministry of Education (*ti-kuan*); collected taxes in various plants used in funerals. CL: *préposé à la plante* tou.

206 chǎng-tzǔ 長子
Lit., eldest son; in most contexts used in that literal sense. CH'ING: **Heir of a Commandery Prince** (*chün-wang*), a title of imperial nobility. BH: son of a prince of the blood of the second degree.

207 chǎng-tz'ù 掌次
CHOU: **Tent Handler,** 4 ranked as Junior Servicemen (*hsia-shih*), members of the Ministry of State (*t'ien-kuan*) responsible for setting up tents and canopies for the ruler and other dignitaries outside the palace, using silk draperies provided by the Directors of Draperies (*mu-jen*). CL: *préposé au placement de la tente.*

208 chǎng-wáng 長王
CH'ING: variant form of *chang-tzu* (**Heir of a Commandery Prince**).

209 chǎng-wèi 掌闈
SUNG: **Gatekeeper,** 2 palace women, rank 8a, members of the Inner Gates Office (*ssu-wei ssu*) in the General Palace Service (*shang-kung chü*).

210 chǎng wèi-shìh tà-ch'én 掌衛事大臣
CH'ING: **Grand Minister Commanding the Guard,** abbreviation of the title Grand Minister Commanding the Imperial Procession Guard (see *luan-i wei*); might be used in reference to a dignitary commanding any other Guard (*wei*).

211 chǎng-yà 掌訝
CHOU: **Receptionist,** 8 ranked as Ordinary Servicemen (*chung-shih*), members of the Ministry of Justice (*ch'iu-kuan*); responsible for keeping a record of the status of feudal dignitaries and prescribing appropriate ceremonials for their visits to the royal court. CL: *agent de la rencontre.*

212 chǎng-yaò 掌藥
SUNG: **Pharmacist,** 2 palace women, rank 8a, members of the Medicines Office (*ssu-yao ssu*) in the Food Service (*shang-shih chü*).

213 chǎng-yěh shǔ 掌冶署
Foundry Office. (1) SUI: unit in the Court for the Palace Revenues (*t'ai-fu ssu*) headed by 2 Directors (*ling*); supervised imperial coinage. (2) T'ANG–SUNG: unit in the Directorate for Imperial Manufactories (*shao-fu chien*) staffed by Foundrymen (*chang-yeh*), responsible for casting metals and for producing paints, glass, jade objects, etc. RR+SP: *office des travaux de fonderie.*

214 chǎng-yén 掌嚴
T'ANG: **Manager of Decorum,** 3 palace women, rank 8a2, subordinate to the Directress of Standards (*ssu-tse*) in the establishment of the Heir Apparent; in charge of standards of dress, ornamentation, towels, combs, baths, toiletries, playthings, etc., in the harem. RR: *chargé du décorum du harem de l'héritier du trône.*

215 chǎng-yén 掌筵
T'ANG: **Manager of Furnishings,** 3 palace women, rank 8a2, subordinate to the Directress of the Inner Quarters (*ssu-kuei*) in the establishment of the Heir Apparent; in charge of bedding, tables, sedan chairs, parasols, etc., used by the palace women. RR: *chargé des nattes.*

216 chǎng-yén 掌言
SUNG: **Communicator,** 2 palace women, rank 8a, members of the Communications Office (*ssu-yen ssu*) in the General Palace Service (*shang-kung chü*).

217 chǎng-yìn 掌印
Lit., keeper of the seal or seal-holder, signifying the official in charge: normally precedes the title of an official who is the senior among equals in an office or who would not regularly be the head of the office in question. E.g., *hu-k'o chang-yin chi-shih-chung* (**Seal-holding** Supervising Secretary of the Office of Scrutiny for Revenue).

218 chǎng-yìn chiēn-tū t'ài-chiēn
掌印監督太監
MING: **Seal-holding Director,** eunuch head of the Directorate of the Imperial Horses (*yü-ma chien*); may be encountered in reference to other eunuch Directorates.

219 chǎng-yìn kuān 掌印官
Seal-holding Official, signifying the official in charge of an office. See *chang-yin.*

220 chǎng-yìn kuàn-chūn shǐh 掌印冠軍使
CH'ING: lit., seal-holding military commissioner: **Director** of any of the 5 Subsections (*so*) in the Imperial Procession Guard (*luan-i wei*), rank 3a; also used for heads of the

Elephant-training Office (*hsün-hsiang so*) and the Standard-bearers Guard (*ch'i-shou wei*), units of the Rear Subsection (*hou-so*). BH: sub-department chief.

221 *chǎng-yìn t'ài-chiēn* 掌印太監
MING: **Seal-holding Director,** designation of heads of various eunuch agencies.

222 *chǎng-yìn yǔn-hūi shǐh* 掌印雲麾使
CH'ING: lit., seal-holding flag assistant: **Director,** rank 4a, one in charge of each subordinate Office (normally *ssu*) in the 5 Subsections (*so*) of the Imperial Procession Guard (*luan-i wei*). BH: section chief.

223 *chǎng-yǔ* 掌輿
SUNG: **Transport Maid,** 2 palace women, rank 8a, members of the Transport Office (*ssu-yü ssu*) in the Housekeeping Service (*shang-ch'in chü*).

224 *chǎng yù t'āng-yaò* 掌御湯藥
CHIN: **Broth Cook,** from 1194 one or more non-official specialists on the staff of the Imperial Dispensary (*yü-yao yüan*), an agency associated with the Imperial Academy of Medicine (*t'ai-i yüan*).

225 *chǎng-yüán* 掌園
T'ANG: **Gardener,** 3 palace women, rank 8a2, subordinate to the Directress of Foodstuffs (*ssu-chuan*) in the establishment of the Heir Apparent; in charge of all fruit and vegetable production within the inner quarters. RR: *chargé des jardins du harem de l'héritier du trône.*

226 *chǎng-yüàn hsüéh-shìh* 掌院學士
CH'ING: **Chancellor of the Hanlin Academy,** 2, rank 5a but rose in accordance with concurrent appointments; senior officials of the Hanlin Academy (*han-lin yüan*), directed all its activities. First established in 1644, then recurringly merged with the Grand Secretariat (*nei-ko*) and its antecedents until 1670, when it was permanently re-established. P23.

227 *chǎng-yüèh* 掌樂
Musician. (1) T'ANG: 4 palace women, rank 8a, in the Ritual Service (*shang-i chü*) of the Palace Domestic Service (*nei-shih sheng*). RR: *chargé de la musique du harem.* (2) SUNG: unspecified number, unranked, attached to the Department of State Affairs (*shang-shu sheng*). SP: *préposé à la musique.*

228 *chǎng-yüèh kuān* 掌樂官
CH'ING: **Music Director** in the Imperial Procession Guard (*luan-i wei*). P10.

229 *chǎng-yùn* 掌醞
Wine Steward. (1) SUI–T'ANG: 50 in Sui, 20 in T'ang, unranked subofficials in the Office of Fine Wines (*liang-yün shu*) of the *kuang-lu ssu* (Court for Attendants in Sui, Court for Imperial Entertainments in T'ang). (2) T'ANG–SUNG: 2 palace women, rank 8a, members of the Wines Office (*ssu-yün ssu*) in the Food Service (*shang-shih chü*). RR: *chargé des boissons fermentées.* P30.

230 *chǎng-yùn shǔ* 掌醞署
MING–CH'ING: **Winery,** one of 4 provisioning agencies subordinate to the Court of Imperial Entertainments (*kuang-lu ssu*), headed by one or 2 Directors (*cheng*), rank 6b. Cf. *liang-yün shu* (Office of Fine Wines). P30.

231 *ch'ǎng* 廠
Depot or **Repository.** See *hsi-ch'ang, tung-ch'ang, pao-ch'üan ch'ang.*

232 *ch'áng* 常
See *ssu-ch'ang, t'ai-ch'ang.*

233 *ch'ǎng* 長
See *chǎng.*

234 *ch'áng-ch'én* 常臣
SUI–CH'ING: unofficial reference to personnel of the Court of Imperial Sacrifices (*t'ai-ch'ang ssu*).

235 *ch'áng-chì shìh* 常騎侍
HAN: **Cavalry Attendant-in-ordinary,** rank and function not clear.

236 *ch'áng-chiēn* 長兼
N-S DIV–T'ANG: a prefix originally meaning "probationary" (possibly for a longer period than normal) that apparently evolved gradually, during the era of N-S Division, into a component part of a regular, non-probationary title, e.g., *ch'ang-chien ts'an-chün* (Junior Adjutant); the practice seems to have died out in early T'ang.

237 *ch'áng-ch'iū chiēn* 長秋監
(1) HAN–T'ANG: **Palace Domestic Service,** a variant of the more common name *i-t'ing*, q.v.; staffed by palace women and eunuchs; prior to 104 B.C. called *yung-hsiang;* after A.D. 621 called *nei-shih chien.* RR: *direction de l'intendance du palais intérieur.* (2) SUI: **Directorate of Palace Domestic Service,** retitled from *nei-shih sheng* (Palace Domestic Service) c. 604, status changed from one of the Five Departments (*wu sheng*) to one of the Five Directorates (*wu chien*); headed by a Supervisor (*chien*). P38.

238 *ch'áng-ch'iū ssù* 長秋寺
N-S DIV (N. Ch'i): **Court of the Women's Chambers,** a eunuch agency responsible for attendance in the women's quarters in the palace, overseeing activities of the Palace Domestic Service (*i-t'ing*); headed by a eunuch Chamberlain (*ch'ing*) and Director (*chung-yin*).

239 *ch'áng-fú láng* 常服郎
N-S DIV (N. Wei): **Gentleman for the Ordinary Wardrobe,** status and organizational affiliation not clear, but traditionally understood to be a keeper of the Emperor's regular daily clothing.

240 *ch'áng-hó shǔ* 常和署
YÜAN: **Office of Moslem Music,** headed by a Director (*ling*), subordinate to the Bureau of Musical Ritual (*i-feng ssu*); until 1312 entitled *kuan-kou ssu.*

241 *ch'áng-hsìn chān-shìh* 長信詹事
HAN: **Steward of the Empress Dowager,** a eunuch; in 150 B.C. retitled *ch'ang-hsin shao-fu.*

242 *ch'áng-hsìn shaò-fǔ* 長信少府
HAN: **Steward of the Empress Dowager,** a eunuch; retitled from *ch'ang-hsin chan-shih* in 150 B.C., then in A.D. 1 retitled *ch'ang-lo shao-fu.*

243 *ch'áng-hsīng chūn* 長興車
T'ANG: **Long Flourishing Army,** 2, one Left and one Right, among many transitory military units organized under the Northern Command (*pei-ya*) during the An Lu-shan rebellion (755–763); apparently did not endure long if at all beyond the rebellion. RR: *armées de la prospérité éternelle.*

244 *ch'áng-hsíng jén* 長行人
CHIN: **Probationary Clerk,** 50 subofficial functionaries appointed to serve as *kuan-kou* (Clerk) in the Bureau of Astronomy (*ssu-t'ien t'ai*). P35.

245 *ch'áng-hsíng t'ài-ī* 長行太醫
CHIN: **Probationary Physician** in the Imperial Academy of Medicine (*t'ai-i yüan*); apparently gained regular status as Assistant Imperial Physician (*fu feng-sheng t'ai-i*) after successful apprenticeship.

246 *ch'áng-hsüăn kuān* 常選官
Ordinary Appointee: a categorical reference to personnel of the regular officialdom appointed in the normally prescribed way, in contrast to various types of irregular appointees, eunuchs, etc.

247 *ch'ǎng-jén* 場人
CHOU: **Gardener,** 2 ranked as Junior Servicemen (*hsia-shih*), members of the Ministry of Education (*ti-kuan*). CL: *jardinier*.

248 *ch'àng-jén* 鬯人
CHOU: **Keeper of Sacrificial Wines,** 2 ranked as Junior Servicemen (*hsia-shih*), members of the Ministry of Rites (*ch'un-kuan*); prepared aromatic millet wine for ancestral offerings. CL: *officier du vin odorant des sacrifices*.

249 *ch'áng-liú* 長流
CHOU: variant reference to the **Ministry of Justice** (*ch'iu-kuan*); may be encountered in later periods as an archaic reference to a comparable office.

250 *ch'áng-lò chiēn* 長樂監
T'ANG: **Directorate of the Park of Lasting Pleasure,** one of 4 Directorates in charge of maintaining the buildings and grounds of imperial parks in the 4 quadrants of the dynastic capital, Ch'ang-an, under the supervision of the Court of the Imperial Granaries (*ssu-nung ssu*); specifically in charge of the southern quadrant, which included ruins of the Han dynasty's Palace of Lasting Pleasure (*ch'ang-lo kung*). Headed by a Director (*chien*), rank 6b2. See *ssu-mien chien*. P40.

251 *ch'áng-lò shaò-fǔ* 長樂少府
HAN: **Steward of the Empress Dowager,** a eunuch; retitled from *ch'ang-hsin shao-fu* in A.D. 1.

252 *ch'áng-mǎn ts'āng* 常滿倉
HAN: **Ever Full Granary,** a Later Han variant of *ch'ang-p'ing ts'ang* (Ever Normal Granary). HB: ever full granary.

253 *ch'áng-p'íng àn* 常平案
SUNG: **Stabilization Fund Section.** (1) One of 8 Sections in the Tax Bureau (*tu-chih ssu*), one of 3 agencies that constituted the early Sung State Finance Commission (*san ssu*); normally headed by an Administrative Assistant (*p'an-kuan, t'ui-kuan*); monitored the operation of the Ever Normal Granary system (see *ch'ang-p'ing ts'ang*). When the State Finance Commission was discontinued in the 1080s, this Section became one of 6 Sections in the Right Section (*yu-ts'ao*) of the Ministry of Revenue (*hu-pu*), staffing not clear but bearing comparable responsibilities. (2) A subunit of Lin-an Prefecture (modern Hangchow) and probably other Prefectures (*chou, fu*) as well, administering Ever Normal Granaries in their territorial jurisdictions (only in S. Sung?). SP: *service chargé de maintenir l'uniformité du prix des grains*.

254 *ch'áng-p'íng kuān* 常平官
SUNG: **Supply Commissioner,** one of several terms used for the chief official of a Supply Commission (*ts'ang-ssu*) in a Circuit (*lu*). SP: *fonctionnaire chargé de maintenir l'uniformité du prix des grains*.

255 *ch'áng-p'íng shǔ* 常平署
T'ANG–SUNG: **Stabilization Fund Office** in the Court of the Imperial Treasury (*t'ai-fu ssu*), established 658; in general charge of the Ever Normal Granary system; from early Sung into the 1080s, its functions were largely handled by the State Finance Commission (*san ssu*), and after the 1080s they were shared with the Ministry of Revenue (*hu-pu*). RR+SP: *office chargé de maintenir l'uniformité du prix des grains*.

256 *ch'áng-p'íng ssū* 常平司
SUNG: **Stabilization Fund Bureau,** in charge of the Ever Normal Granary system; one of 3 agencies constituting the State Finance Commission (*san ssu*), succeeding the Tax Bureau (*tu-chih ssu*) in that role, date not clear; abolished in the 1080s.

257 *ch'áng-p'íng ts'āng* 常平倉
Ever Normal Granary: from Han on, a local unit in a system through which the state bought grain when and where it was in surplus for sale when and where it was in short supply, to stabilize prices and supplies. HB: ever level granary. RR+SP: *grenier pour maintenir l'uniformité du prix des grains*.

258 *ch'áng-p'íng ts'āng ssū* 常平倉司
SUNG: **Ever Normal Granary Office,** headed by a Supervisor (*t'i-chü kuan*); status not wholly clear, but apparently a local or regional agency directly or indirectly subordinate to the Supply Commissioner (*ts'ang-ssu*) of a Circuit (*lu*) or to the Ministry of Revenue (*hu-pu*), the Court of the Imperial Treasury (*t'ai-fu ssu*), or the State Finance Commission (*san ssu*). SP: *office des greniers chargé de maintenir l'uniformité du prix des grains*.

259 *ch'áng-pó* 常伯
Executive Attendant: unofficial reference to a high-ranking official having close access to the ruler, e.g., Palace Attendant (*shih-chung*), Cavalier Attendant-in-ordinary (*san-chi ch'ang-shih*). See *ta ch'ang-po, shao ch'ang-po*.

260 *ch'áng-shàng* 長上
T'ANG: lit., sent up (to the palace or possibly any higher agency) for continuing service: a prefix used with such descriptive terms as Entertainers (*san-yüeh*) to specify non-official specialists who were **permanent** or **career** members of the staff, as distinct from those who served temporarily on rotational requisitions from local units of government.

261 *ch'áng-shàng tì-tzǔ* 長上弟子
T'ANG: **Novice Career Musician** in the Imperial Music Office (*t'ai-yüeh shu*) of the Court of Imperial Sacrifices (*t'ai-ch'ang ssu*), required to pass various tests before being assigned to one of the palace orchestras. RR: *élève permanent*.

262 *ch'áng-shìh* 常侍
Attendant-in-ordinary. (1) HAN: eunuch director of the staff of palace eunuchs, in Later Han retitled *ch'ang-ch'iu chien* (?). (2) N-S DIV–T'ANG: member of the senior staff of a Princedom (*wang-kuo*) or Princely Establishment (*wang-fu*). RR: *fonctionnaire constamment à la disposition d'un prince*. P69. (3) SUNG: members of the Chancellery (*men-hsia sheng*), rank not clear, differentiated as Left and Right. SP: *grands conseillers politiques impériaux*. See *san-chi ch'ang-shih, chūng ch'ang-shih, nei ch'ang-shih*.

263 *ch'ǎng-shǐh* 敞史
Clerk. (1) LIAO: minor officials in both Northern and Southern Bureaus of Military Affairs (*shu-mi yüan*). (2) CH'ING: variant reference to Clerks called *pi-t'ieh-shih.* P5, l2.

264 *ch'áng-shìh chì* 常侍騎
HAN: **Mounted Attendant-in-ordinary,** an honorary office (*chia-kuan*) awarded to favored officials in Former Han, signifying their worthiness to be companions of the Emperor. HB: regular mounted attendant.

265 *ch'áng-shìh fǔ* 常侍府
Variant form of **Princely Establishment** (*wang-fu*), usually preceded by the title of the Prince, as … *wang ch'ang-shih fu* (Princely Establishment of …).

266 *ch'áng-shìh láng* 常侍郎
HAN: **Gentleman Attendant-in-ordinary,** one of several titles given to expectant officials, or officials awaiting reassignment, who were expected to be available for such service as the ruler required. HB: gentleman in regular attendance. P23.

267 *ch'áng-shìh ts'aó* 常侍曹
HAN: **Section for Attendants-in-ordinary,** one of 4 to 6 top-echelon units in the Imperial Secretariat (*chung-shu t'ai*), headed by an Imperial Secretary (*shang-shu*); handled the ruler's relations with the Counselor-in-chief (*ch'eng-hsiang*), the Censor-in-chief (*yü-shih ta-fu*), and other high dignitaries; reportedly also in charge of official appointments and of sacrificial ceremonies. Early in Later Han retitled *lì-pu ts'ao,* q.v. In later eras may be encountered as an unofficial reference to any agency responsible for civil service personnel matters, especially the Ming–Ch'ing Bureau of Appointments (*wen-hsüan ch'ing-li ssu*) in the Ministry of Personnel (*lì-pu*). HB: bureau of regular attendants. P5.

268 *ch'áng-shìh yèh-chě* 常侍調者
HAN: **Receptionist Attendant-in-ordinary,** 5, rank =600 bushels, subordinates of the Supervisor of Receptionists (*yeh-che p'u-yeh*) on the staff of the Chamberlain for Attendants (*kuang-lu-hsün*) in Later Han; assisted in organizing court audiences and other ceremonies, were also given various special assignments as needed. HB: internuncios in regular attendance.

269 *ch'áng-súi* 長隨
Lit., long-term (?) follower: **Member of the Regular Entourage,** a designation sometimes used for Palace Eunuchs (*huan-kuan,* etc.), in Ming for personal attendants attached to Palace Eunuchs, and in Ch'ing for personal servants of provincial and prefectural dignitaries.

270 *ch'áng-súi fèng-yǜ* 長隨奉御
MING: **Palace Groom,** the lowest-ranking eunuchs, rank 6a, in the Directorate of the Imperial Horses (*yü-ma chien*). P39.

271 *ch'áng-tsài* 常在
CH'ING: one of many titles designating **Palace Woman;** was considered eligible for promotion into the ranks of Consorts (*kuei-fei, kuei-jen,* etc.).

272 *ch'áng-ts'ān kuān* 常參官
Consultants-in-ordinary, a generic term for officials regularly expected to attend audiences. (1) T'ANG: refers to court officials of rank 5 and higher. RR: *fonctionnaires assistant toujours aux audiences.* (2) SUNG: variant form of *ch'ao-kuan* (Court Official). SP: *fonctionnaire titulaire de la cour.* See *chiu-ts'an kuan, liu-ts'an.*

273 *ch'áng-ts'úng* 常從
Attendant-in-ordinary: throughout history a generic reference to personal servants authorized for officials on a regular basis, as distinguished, e.g., from special retinues authorized for officials in travel status (see *tao-ts'ung*).

274 *ch'áng-ts'úng hǔ-pēn tū* 常從虎賁督
N-S DIV (Ch'i): **Commandant of the Bodyguard of the Heir Apparent,** rank not clear. P26.

275 *ch'áng-ts'úng láng* 常從郎
SUI: **Gentleman Attendant-in-ordinary,** a prestige title (*san-kuan*) for rank 9 officials under Emperor Yang. P68.

276 *ch'áng-ts'úng sù-wèi* 長從宿衛
T'ANG: **Permanent Palace Guard,** a body of paid volunteers established c. 723 as replacements for rotational militiamen controlling the gates to the inner quarters of the palace; c. 725 retitled *k'uo-chi.*

277 *ch'áng-yaò chiēn* 嘗藥監
HAN: **Supervisor of Medicine Tasting,** in Later Han a eunuch post attached to the Chamberlain for the Imperial Revenues (*shao-fu*), no doubt to test medications for the Emperor prepared by the office of the Imperial Physician (*t'ai-i ling*). HB: inspector of the medicine tasters.

278 *ch'áng-yíng k'ù* 常盈庫
MING: **Ever Full Haybarn,** a unit of the Court of the Imperial Stud (*t'ai-p'u ssu*) headed by an unranked subofficial Commissioner-in-chief (*ta-shih*). P31.

279 *chāo-ān shǐh* 招安使
SUNG: **Pacification Commissioner,** ad hoc assignment for an official who was, literally, "sent out to summon (rebels, bandits, other disaffected groups) to peace." SP: *commissaire chargé d'exiger la soumission des rebelles.*

280 *chāo-chièn pān* 招箭班
SUNG: **Targets and Arrows Section** in the Palace Command (*tien-ch'ien ssu*), a military unit headed by a Section Chief (*ya-pan*), probably unranked. SP: *compagnie chargée des cibles et des flèches.*

281 *chāo-fǔ ch'ù-chìh shǐh* 招撫處置使
SUNG: **Pacification and Supervisory Commissioner,** an eminent official sent out to deal with military and other disturbances on an ad hoc basis, usually in a multi-Circuit (*lu*) region suffering from invasion, rebellion, or natural disasters. SP: *commissaire chargé de prendre des mesures de pacification.*

282 *chāo-fǔ shǐh* 招撫使
SUNG: **Pacification Commissioner,** an eminent official sent out to deal with military disturbances on an ad hoc basis, usually in a multi-Circuit (*lu*) region suffering from invasion, rebellion, or other military disruptions. SP: *commissaire chargé de pacification, commissaire chargé de pacifier … (… areas).*

283 *chāo-hó shǔ* 昭和署
YÜAN: **Office of Western Music** in the Bureau of Musical Ritual (*i-feng ssu*), specializing in the music of northwestern China; established 1280, in 1313 retitled *t'ien-yüeh shu;* headed by 2 Directors (*ling*), rank 7a. P10.

284 *chāo-hsüān shǐh* 昭宣使
SUNG: **Commissioner of Clear Proclamations,** eunuch official, rank 6a, in the Palace Domestic Service (*nei-shih sheng*). See *kung-wei ta-fu.* SP: *commissaire tchao-siuan.*

285 *chāo-hsüán ssù* 昭玄寺
N-S DIV (N. Wei, N. Ch'i): **Office for the Clarification**

of Buddhist Profundities, an agency of the Court for Dependencies (*hung-lu ssu*) responsible for monitoring the teaching of Buddhism throughout the state; headed by a Controller-in-chief (*ta-t'ung*) with the assistance of a Controller (*t'ung*) and a Chief Buddhist Deacon (*tu wei-na*). Replaced an earlier Superintendency of Buddhist Happiness (*chien-fu ts'ao*) in the Court for Dependencies. Also see *seng-kuan*. P17.

286   *chāo-hsün* 昭訓
Lady of Clear Instruction. (1) N-S DIV (N. Ch'i): one of the 3 imperial concubines collectively known as the Superior Concubines (*shang-pin*). (2) T'ANG: 16 palace women of the 4th order, rank 7a, in the household of the Heir Apparent. RR: *femme d'une éducation remarquable*.

287   *chāo-huá* 昭華
N-S DIV: **Lady of Bright Loveliness,** a concubine title that apparently originated in San-kuo Wei; in Sung the designation of one of the Nine Concubines (*chiu-pin*); in N. Ch'i the designation of one of 27 imperial consorts collectively called Hereditary Consorts (*shih-fu*), rank =3b.

288   *chāo-í* 昭儀
HAN–SUNG: **Lady of Bright Deportment,** designation of one of the Nine Concubines (*chiu pin*), rank 2a in T'ang and Sung. HB: brilliant companion. RR: *femme d'une correction manifeste*.

289   *chāo-júng* 昭容
HAN–SUNG: **Lady of Bright Countenance,** designation of one of the Nine Concubines (*chiu pin*), rank 2a in T'ang and Sung. RR+SP: *femme d'une dignité manifeste*.

290   *chāo-kūng wàn-hù* 昭功萬戶
YÜAN: **Meritorious Brigade,** the personal bodyguard of the Heir Apparent, headed by a Commandant-in-chief (*tu tsung-shih*).

291   *chào-mó* 照磨
YÜAN–CH'ING: **Record Keeper,** lowly members, rank 8a to 9b, of the staffs of some Ministries (*pu*), the Censorate (*yü-shih t'ai, tu ch'a-yüan*), other capital agencies, and various agencies at the provincial and prefectural levels; sometimes head of a Records Office (*chao-mo so*).

292   *chào-mó chiēn ch'éng-fā chià-kó k'ù* 照磨兼承發架閣庫
YÜAN: **Record Keeper and Storekeeper,** rank 8a, in the Imperial Academy of Medicine (*t'ai-i yüan*) after 1322.

293   *chào-mó chiēn-chiào sŏ* 照磨檢校所
MING: **Records Office** in the very early Ming Secretariat (*chung-shu sheng*), headed by an Administrator (*tuan-shih kuan*), rank not clear but low; discontinued in 1369. P4.

294   *chào-mó chiēn kuǎn-kōu* 照磨兼管勾
YÜAN: **Record Keeper and Clerk,** rank 8b, in a Princely Establishment (*wang-fu*). P69.

295   *chào-mó chiēn kuǎn-kōu ch'éng-fā chià-kó* 照磨兼管勾承發架閣
YÜAN: **Record Keeper and Clerk-storekeeper,** one, rank not clear, in the Bureau of Transmission (*t'ung-cheng yüan*) at Peking from 1311 on. P12.

296   *chào-mó kuǎn-kōu* 照磨管勾
MING: **Record Keeper and Clerk** in the very early Ming Secretariat (*chung-shu sheng*), rank 7b, and Censorate (*yü-shih t'ai*), 8a; both discontinued in 1380.

297   *chào-mó sŏ* 照磨所
MING–CH'ING: **Records Office,** a unit for the maintenance of documentary files normally headed by a Record Keeper (*chao-mo*), rank 8a, 9a, or 9b, in such agencies as the Ministry of Revenue (*hu-pu*), Ministry of Justice (*hsing-pu*), Censorate (*tu ch'a-yüan*), Provincial Administration Commissions (*ch'eng-hsüan pu-cheng shih ssu*), and Provincial Surveillance Commissions (*t'i-hsing an-ch'a shih ssu*). P18, 52, 69.

298   *chāo-mù* 招募
Recruitment: from Sui on, a process of enlisting non-soldiers into military service for pay as Mercenary Recruits (*mu-ping*) to supplement Regular Troops (*kuan-ping*), especially in times of military crisis.

299   *chāo-nà ssū* 招納司
SUNG: **Capitulation Office,** an ad hoc agency for enticing rebels or invaders to surrender and for administering those who surrendered, established by Military Commissioners (*ching-lüeh*) on active campaign. SP: *bureau chargé de recevoir les rebelles soumis*.

300   *chāo-níng* 昭寧
N-S DIV (N. Ch'i): **Lady of Bright Tranquillity,** designation of one of 27 imperial consorts collectively called Hereditary Consorts (*shih-fu*); rank =3b.

301   *chǎo-shìh* 爪士
CH'ING: lit., soldiers (who serve as the ruler's) claws: unofficial reference to the most prestigious of the 3 groups of Imperial Guardsmen (*san-ch'i shih-wei*).

302   *chāo-shōu pù-shǔ* 招收部署
SUNG: **Recruiting Office,** an ad hoc agency established to recruit men for a campaigning army. SP: *directeur militaire de recrutement*.

303   *chāo-t'ǎo shǐh* 招討使
(1) T'ANG–SUNG: **Bandit-suppression Commissioner,** ad hoc appointee to bring order in a disrupted area, head of a Bandit-suppression Commission (*chao-t'ao ssu*). (2) MING–CH'ING: **Pacification Commissioner,** rank 5b, designation of a southwestern aboriginal chieftain heading a Pacification Commission (*chao-t'ao ssu*). P72.

304   *chāo-t'ǎo ssū* 招討司
(1) T'ANG–SUNG: **Bandit-suppression Commission,** an ad hoc military force headed by a Commissioner (*chao-t'ao shih*) sent to suppress disorders in an area normally specified in a prefix. RR: *commissaire impérial chargé d'exiger les soumissions et de châtier les rebelles*. SP: *commissaire chargé de faire soumettre et de châtier les rebelles dans ....* (2) YÜAN: 2 entirely different types of agencies with the same Chinese name. One was the **Pacification Commission,** overall coordinating agency for a Circuit (*tao*), headed by a Commissioner (*chao-t'ao shih*), normally a non-Chinese noble. Also **Pacification Office,** designating the headquarters of a southwestern aboriginal tribal chieftain, given variable rank as a titular Overseer (*ta-lu-hua-ch'ih*). See *t'u-ssu*. (3) MING–CH'ING: **Pacification Commission,** the headquarters of a southwestern aboriginal tribal chieftain designated Pacification Commissioner (*chao-t'ao shih*), rank 5b. See *t'u-ssu*. P72.

305   *chào-t'īng* 照廳
CH'ING: unofficial reference to a **Record Keeper** (*chao-mo*) in a Provincial Administration Commission (*ch'eng-hsüan pu-cheng shih ssu*).

306   *chāo-wén hsüéh-shìh* 昭文學士
Abbreviation of the title *chao-wen (ta) hsüeh-shih* ([**Grand**] **Academician of the Institute for the Glorification of Literature**). See *chao-wen kuan, ta hsüeh-shih, hsüeh-shih*.

307 *chāo-wén kuǎn* 昭文館
Institute for the Glorification of Literature. (1) T'ANG: from 705 to 706 and again from 711 to 719 the official variant designation of the agency most commonly called Institute for the Advancement of Literature (*hung-wen kuan*), staffed with 4 Senior Academicians (*ta hsüeh-shih*) and lesser Academicians (*hsüeh-shih*) who assisted in drafting imperial pronouncements and tutored young men of the official class; subordinate to the Chancellery (*men-hsia sheng*). RR: *collège pour la glorification de la littérature*. (2) SUNG: one of the Three Institutes (*san kuan*) constituting the Academy for the Veneration of Literature (*ch'ung-wen yüan*); Institute subordinate to the Chancellery (*men-hsia sheng*), with staff appointments granted only as supplementary honors for eminent court officials; in 1082 absorbed into the Palace Library (*pi-shu sheng*), appointments made substantive. SP: as RR above. (3) LIAO: existence as functional Institute not clear, but staff titles were granted as honorific supplements to those of eminent officials. P25.

308 *chāo-yáo chūn* 招搖軍
T'ANG: lit., the swaggering army (?): **Army of the Great Celestial Bear,** named after 2 stars in the Great Bear constellation; one of 12 regional supervisory headquarters for militia Garrisons (*fu*) called the Twelve Armies (*shih-erh chün*); existed only 620–623, 625–636. RR: *armée (de la constellation) du branlement des armes*. P44.

309 *chào-yù* 詔獄
Imperial Prison. (1) Most commonly, a prison in the palace to which were brought men whose arrests had been ordered (*chao*) by the Emperor. (2) HAN: a collective reference to prisons maintained by various central government agencies, at least some of which were intended for persons of certain status categories; e.g., the Convict Barracks at Sweet Spring Mountain (*kan-ch'üan chü-shih*) in modern Shensi for members of the imperial family, the Central Prison (*jo-lu yü*) for imperial relatives by marriage, the Prison for Palace Women (*i-t'ing pi-yü*), all apparently administered by the Chamberlain for the Palace Revenues (*shao-fu*); the Prison for Liaison Hostels for Commanderies (*chün-ti yü*; see *chün-ti*) administered by the Chamberlain for Dependencies (*ta hung-lu*). (3) MING: a common quasi-official designation of the Prison (*chen-fu ssu*) maintained by the Imperial Bodyguard (*chin-i wei*). P13, 37, 38.

310 *chāo-yüàn* 昭媛 or 昭苑
T'ANG–SUNG: **Lady of Bright Beauty,** designation of an imperial concubine, rank 2a in Sung. RR: *femme d'une beauté manifeste*. SP: *femme titré intérieure de 2ème rang*.

311 *chāo-yüàn ssù* 昭元寺
Variant of *chao-hsüan ssu* (**Office for the Clarification of Buddhist Profundities**).

312 *ch'áo* 朝
Throughout imperial history: (1) **Dynasty,** (2) **Court Audience,** especially spring audiences in contrast to autumn audiences (*ching;* see *ch'ao-ching lang*), and (3) **Court** in the sense of those who participated importantly in imperial audiences, e.g., Court Official (*ch'ao-kuan*).

313 *ch'āo* 超
See under *ch'ao-ch'ien, ch'ao-sheng, ch'ao-yüeh*.

314 *ch'áo-chí shǐh* 朝集使
SUI–T'ANG: **Territorial Representative,** a delegate from each Sui Region (*chou*) and Commandery (*chün*) and from each T'ang Prefecture (*chou*) sent to the dynastic capital annually to participate in New Year's audience and report on local conditions, normally the ranking official of the unit of territorial administration; revival of a Han tradition (see *chi-chieh*), and forerunner of regular assemblages of local officials for imperial audiences in later dynasties.

315 *ch'áo-ch'iēn* 超遷
Extraordinary Promotion, a term commonly used when an official, because of special merit or favor, was promoted more than the normal step up in rank.

316 *ch'āo-chǐh chú* 鈔紙局
MING: **Currency Supply Service,** a paper money printshop subordinate to the Ministry of Revenue (*hu-pu*), headed by a Commissioner-in-chief (*ta-shih*), rank not clear. P16.

317 *ch'āo-chǐh fāng* 鈔紙坊
CHIN: **Currency Printshop,** apparently subordinate to the Ministry of Works (*kung-pu*); headed by a Commissioner (*shih*), rank not clear. Cf. *yin-tsao ch'ao-yin k'u*. P16.

318 *ch'áo-chǐng láng* 朝請郎
SUI–YÜAN: **Gentleman for Court Audiences,** prestige title (*san-kuan*) for officials of rank 7a or 7a1; replaced the older term Audience Attendant (*feng ch'ao-ching*). In Han, *ch'ao* referred to spring audiences, *ching* (*sic;* not *ch'ing* in this use) to autumn audiences. P68.

319 *ch'áo-chǐng tà-fū* 朝請大夫
SUI–CH'ING: **Grand Master for Court Audiences,** prestige title (*san-kuan*) for officials of rank 5a in Sui, 5b1 in T'ang, 5b2 in Sung, 5b1 in Chin, 4b thereafter; replaced the older term Audience Attendant (*feng ch'ao-ching*). See comment on *ch'ao-ching* under *ch'ao-ching lang*. P68.

320 *ch'āo-fǎ* 鈔法
Normally used as a term meaning, literally, "the paper money laws." MING: apparently used, at least in 1468, as an unofficial designation for **Currency Tax Agents** collecting domestic customs duties at the 9 gates of Peking. P20.

321 *ch'áo-fèng láng* 朝奉郎
SUNG: **Gentleman for Court Service,** prestige title (*san-kuan*) for officials of rank 6a1 and 7a. P68.

322 *ch'áo-fèng tà-fū* 朝奉大夫
SUNG: **Grand Master for Court Service,** prestige title (*san-kuan*) for officials of rank 5a and 6b. P68.

323 *ch'áo-fú fǎ-wù k'ù* 朝服法物庫
SUNG: **Storehouse for Court Ritual Regalia,** which maintained special costumes and other regalia needed by officials in court audience; headed jointly by official and eunuch Supervisors (*chien-kuan*); established in 977 as a unit in the Court of Imperial Sacrifices (*t'ai-ch'ang ssu*), then in 1103 transferred to the jurisdiction of the Palace Administration (*tien-chung sheng*). Originally one storehouse, but increased to 3 in different parts of the palace grounds. SP: *magasin des vêtements d'audience et d'objets rituels*. P38.

324 *ch'áo-hóu* 朝侯
HAN: **Marquis** appointed for merit by the Emperor, with the privilege of participating in regular court audiences, ranking below the Nine Chamberlains (*chiu ch'ing*).

325 *ch'áo-ì láng* 朝議郎
SUI–T'ANG: **Gentleman for Court Discussion,** prestige title (*san-kuan*) for officials of rank 6a1. P68.

326 *ch'áo-ì tà-fū* 朝議大夫
SUI–SUNG, MING–CH'ING: **Grand Master for Court Discussion,** prestige title (*san-kuan*) for officials of rank 3b

in Sui, 5a1 in T'ang, 6a in Sung, 4b in Ming and Ch'ing. P68.

327 *ch'áo-k'ǎo* 朝考
CH'ING: **Court Examination,** the final stage of the Palace Examination (*tien-shih*), which recruited men into the civil service as Metropolitan Graduates (*chin-shih*).

328 *ch'áo-kuān* 朝官
Court Official, generic designation normally indicating all officials whose appointments and ranks entitled them to attend imperial audiences regularly; part of the larger category of Capital Officials (*ching-kuan*), including Court Officials and others serving in the capital who were not entitled to attend imperial audiences regularly. In Sung this was a more specific term, including officials serving in units of territorial administration who had court rank.

329 *ch'āo-kuān* 鈔關
MING: **Customs House,** 12 established along the Grand Canal to collect transit duties on all shipping; subordinate to the Ministry of Revenue (*hu-pu*), supervised by Investigating Censors (*chien-ch'a yü-shih*) commissioned as Customs House Censors (*ch'aò-kuan yü-shih*).

330 *ch'áo-lièh tà-fū* 朝列大夫
CHIN–MING: **Grand Master for Court Precedence,** prestige title (*san-kuan*) for officials of rank 5b2 in Chin (replacing the earlier Chin title Grand Master for Virtuous Service, *feng-te ta-fu*), 4b in Yüan and Ming. P68.

331 *ch'áo-p'ǐn* 超品
CH'ING: **Paramount Ranks** of the hereditary nobility not including Princes (*wang*): specifying Dukes (*kung*), Marquises (*hou*), and Earls (*po*). BH: eminent ranks.

332 *ch'áo-pù t'īng* 朝簿廳
MING–CH'ING: unofficial reference to the **General Services Office** (*ssu-wu t'ing*) of a Ministry (*pu*), the Censorate (*tu ch'a-yüan*), etc.

333 *ch'áo-sàn láng* 朝散郎
SUI–SUNG: **Gentleman for Closing Court,** prestige title (*san-kuan*) for officials of rank 7b in Sui, 7b1 in T'ang, 7b1 and 7a in Sung. P68.

334 *ch'áo-sàn tà-fū* 朝散大夫
SUI–YÜAN: **Grand Master for Closing Court,** prestige title (*san-kuan*) for officials of rank 4a then 5b in Sui, 5b2 in T'ang, 5b1 and 6b in Sung, 5b2 in Chin, 4b in Yüan. P68.

335 *ch'áo-shēng* 超升 or 超陞
Extraordinary Promotion, a term commonly used when an official, because of special merit or favor, was promoted more than the normal step up in rank.

336 *ch'áo-shìh* 抄事
CHIN: **Copyist,** unranked, on the staff of each Fiscal Commissioner (*chuan-yün shih*) and some Prefectures (*chou*). P53, 60.

337 *ch'áo-shìh* 朝士
CHOU: **Audience Monitor,** 6 ranked as Ordinary Servicemen (*chung-shih*), members of the Ministry of Justice (*ch'iu-kuan*) in charge of enforcing rules of conduct in audiences. CL: *prévôt d'audience.*

338 *ch'áo-shìh kūng-shìh* 抄事公使
CHIN: **Copyist Clerk,** unranked, 40 in each Salt Commission (*yen-shih ssu*). P61.

339 *ch'áo tà-fū* 朝大夫
CHOU: **Grand Master of Court Audience,** 2 ranked as Senior Servicemen (*shang-shih*) and 4 as Junior Servicemen (*hsia-shih*) for each feudal State (*kuo*); members of the Ministry of Justice (*ch'iu-kuan*) who oversaw administration of feudal domains and informed Feudal Lords (*chu-hou*) of decisions reached in daily audiences at court.

340 *ch'áo-tài* 朝代
Dynasty: throughout history a term more or less interchangeable with Dynasty (*ch'ao*), but especially referring to the era in which one dynastic family reigned.

341 *ch'áo-t'íng hóu* 朝廷侯
HAN: **Marquis for Audiences,** in Later Han the 2nd most prestigious of 3 designations awarded (see under *chia-kuan*) to Adjunct Marquises (*lieh-hou*) who were permitted to reside in the capital and were among those collectively called Audience Attendants (*feng ch'ao-ching*); the designation apparently imposed a responsibility to participate in regular court audiences. Cf. *t'e-chin* (specially advanced), *shih-tz'u hou* (Marquis Attending at Sacrifices). HB: marquis admitted to court.

342 *ch'áo-tuān* 朝端
N-S DIV–SUNG: **Prime Mover at Court,** an unofficial, awed reference to the executive officials of the Department of State Affairs (*shang-shu sheng*), most specifically its Director (*ling*) and its Vice Directors (*p'u-yeh*) of the Left and Right. Cf. *tuan-k'uei.*

343 *ch'áo-yüèh* 超越
Extraordinary Promotion, a term commonly used when an official, because of special merit or favor, was promoted more than the normal step up in rank, skipping over from one to as many as 5 grades in rank.

344 *che* 宅
See under the romanization *chai.*

345 *che* 澤
See under the romanization *tse.*

346 *ché-chūng ts'āng* 折中倉
SUNG: lit., storehouse where equity is attained or a fair exchange is struck: **Equitable Exchange Depot,** established in the late 900s to accept merchant deliveries of rice in the dynastic capital, Kaifeng, in exchange for certificates or vouchers entitling merchants to participate in the state-supervised domestic salt distribution; the system was called the Equitable Exchange of Rice for Salt (*chung-yen*). Also see *k'ai-chung.*

347 *ché-ch'ūng fǔ* 折衝府
Lit., agency for breaking the advance (of an enemy): **Assault-resisting Garrison.** (1) SUI: one of 2 types of units (see *kuo-i fu*, Courageous Garrison) created outside the regular establishment of Garrison Militia units (see *fu* and *fu-ping*) in 613, headed by a Commandant (*tu-wei*). Reasons for the creation of these units are not clear, nor is their fate, except that they were all apparently discontinued by the end of Sui in 618. (2) T'ANG: from 619 (623?) to 624 and again after 636, the formal name of each Garrison (*fu*) in the Garrison Militia system, each having one Commandant (*tu-wei*), rank 4a1, 4b2, or 5a2 depending on their classification as Large (*shang*), Medium (*chung*), or Small (*hsia*) according to the number of their militiamen contingents. Lesser officers included 2 Vice Commandants (*kuo-i tu-wei*), one of the Left and one of the Right, rank 5b2, 6a1, or 6a2; and

one Adjunct Commandant (*pieh-chiang*), rank 7a2, 7b1, or 7b2. For purposes of rotating personnel in and out of service at the dynastic capital, each Garrison was affiliated with or subordinate to one of the Sixteen Guards (*shih-liu wei*) at the capital. RR: *milice intrépide*.

348   *ché-fā* 謫發
MING: **Sentenced Soldiers,** one of several general descriptive terms for groups that, in the aggregate, constituted the early Ming armies and the *wei-so* military establishment (see *wei-so*); specifically refers to soldiers who were sentenced in judicial proceedings to military exile, especially in frontier units, and thus founded new hereditary military families (*chün-hu*). The category is differentiated from such other large contingents of soldiers as Old Campaigners (*ts'ung-cheng*), Adherents (*kuei-fu*), and Conscripts (*to-chi*).

349   *ché-kuèi jén* 折桂人
T'ANG–CH'ING: lit., one who has plucked a cassia tree: unofficial reference to one who had been nominated for or had passed a major civil service recruitment examination, especially in Ming and Ch'ing to a **Metropolitan Graduate** (*chin-shih*).

350   *ché-wēi chūn* 折威軍
T'ANG: **Fear-proof Army,** named after a group of stars in Virgo; one of 12 regional supervisory headquarters for militia Garrisons (*fu*) called the Twelve Armies (*shih-erh chün*); existed only 620–623, 625–636. RR: *armée de (la constellation) réprime-terreur*. P44.

351   *ch'e* 車
See *chin-ch'e*.

352   *ch'ē-chì chiāng-chūn* 車騎將軍
Chariot and Horse General. (1) HAN: until 87 B.C., one of many duty-assignment titles conferred on military officers on active campaign; thereafter awarded to favored courtiers without military significance until A.D. 77, when the imperial in-laws and other favorites who bore the title as often as not took part in active military campaigning. In the 150s the title began to be awarded to favored palace eunuchs, though not exclusively. HB: general of chariots and cavalry. (2) N-S DIV (San-kuo Wei): one of 3 Generals who shared command of the Imperial Guard (*chin-lü*); see *p'iao-chi chiang-chün, wu-wei chiang-chün*. (3) SUI–T'ANG: until 607, assistant to the Cavalry General (*p'iao-chi chiang-chün*) in the command echelon of each Garrison (*fu*) of the Garrison Militia system (*fu-ping*); by 607 the Garrisons had split into 2 types, a Cavalry Garrison (*p'iao-chi fu*) commanded by a Cavalry General and a Chariot and Horse Garrison (*ch'e-chi fu*) commanded by a Chariot and Horse General. In 607 the Garrisons were reorganized into a single type called the Soaring Hawk Garrison (*ying-yang fu*) headed by a Commandant (*lang-chiang*). In 618 the names Chariot and Horse Garrison, Chariot and Horse General, Cavalry Garrison, and Cavalry General were all revived for the T'ang Garrison Militia system, but very soon thereafter (619? 623?) they were all discontinued in favor of the consolidated-type designations Assault-resisting Garrison (*che-ch'ung fu*) and their Commandants (*tu-wei*). See separate entries. RR: *général des chars et des cavaliers*. P43.

353   *ch'ē-chì fǔ* 車騎府
SUI–T'ANG: **Chariot and Horse Garrison** in the Garrison Militia system (see *fu* and *fu-ping*), deriving from the title of its head, Chariot and Horse General (*ch'e-chi chiang-chün*). Usage established by the early 600s. In 607 all Garrisons (*fu*), including both Chariot and Horse Garrisons and Cavalry Garrisons (*p'iao-chi fu*), were given the standard title Soaring Hawk Garrison (*ying-yang fu*). At the begin-

ning of T'ang in 618, the names Chariot and Horse Garrison and Cavalry Garrison were reinstituted, only to be changed in 619 (623?) into one standard name, Assault-resisting Garrison (*che-ch'ung fu*) and then in 624 to Commander-general's Garrison (*t'ung-chün fu*). Finally, in 636, the terminology was stabilized with a change back to Assault-resisting Garrison. See separate entries. RR: *milice des chars et des cavaliers*. P43.

354   *ch'ē-chià* 車駕
Lit., the chariots and carriages: used as an indirect reference to the Emperor and his attendants, especially while traveling: **Imperial Entourage.**

355   *ch'ē-chià ch'īng-lì ssū* 車駕清吏司 or *ch'e-chia ssu*
(1) MING: **Bureau of Equipment and Communications** in the Ministry of War (*ping-pu*), headed by a Director (*lang-chung*), rank 5a; in charge of military regalia and the empire's postal relay system. (2) CH'ING: **Bureau of Communications** in the Ministry of War (*ping-pu*), headed by 4 Directors (*lang-chung*), 5a; in charge of the postal relay system and of pasturages that supplied it with horses. BH: remount department. P12.

356   *ch'ē-fǔ* 車府
SUNG: **Livery Office,** a unit in the Court of the Imperial Stud (*t'ai-p'u ssu*); staffing and specific functions not clear; cf. *ch'e-lu yüan*. SP: *office d'équipage*. P31.

357   *ch'ē-fǔ lìng* 車府令
HAN–N-S DIV: **Director of the Livery Office,** one of numerous subordinates of the Chamberlain for the Imperial Stud (*t'ai-p'u*). HB: prefect of the coachhouse for imperial equipages. P31.

358   *ch'ē-fǔ shǔ* 車府署
T'ANG: **Livery Office,** a subordinate unit in the Court of the Imperial Stud (*t'ai-p'u ssu*), headed by a Director (*ling*), rank 8a2. RR: *office des équipages des princes*.

359   *ch'è-hóu* 徹侯
CH'IN–HAN: lit., all-penetrating marquis: **Grandee of the Twentieth Order,** the highest of 20 titles of nobility (*chüeh*) awarded to deserving subjects; in the reign of Emperor Wu (141–87 B.C.) changed to *t'ung-hou*. P64, 65.

360   *ch'ē-láng* 車郎
HAN: **Court Gentleman for Carriages,** one of many duty-assignment titles for courtiers awaiting appointment or reappointment to substantive administrative positions. HB: gentleman of imperial equipages.

361   *ch'ē-láng chūng-chiàng* 車郎中將
HAN: **Center Leader of Court Gentlemen for Carriages,** head of the courtiers called Court Gentlemen for Carriages (*ch'e-lang*); see *chung-chiang*. HB (*chü lang-chung*): gentleman-of-the-palace of imperial equipages.

362   *ch'ē-lù yüàn* 車輅院
SUNG: **Carriage Livery,** a unit in the Court of the Imperial Stud (*t'ai-p'u ssu*); difference from *ch'e-fu* is not clear. SP: *cour des voitures*. P31.

363   *ch'ē-pù láng* 車部郎
N-S DIV (Chin): **Director of the Chariots Section,** a subordinate of the Defender-in-chief (*t'ai-wei*) only briefly in the 280s. May be encountered in later dynasties as an abbreviation of, or an archaic reference to, either the Vice Minister of War (*ping-pu shih-lang*) or the Director (*lang-chung*) of the *ch'e-chia ch'ing-li ssu* (Bureau of Equipment and Communications in Ming, Bureau of Communications in Ch'ing) of the Ministry of War (*ping-pu*). P12.

364 *ch'ē-pù ts'áo* 車部曹
N-S DIV (Chin): **Chariots Section,** existed only briefly in the 280s, apparently as a military-support agency subordinate to the Defender-in-chief (*t'ai-wei*), headed by a Director (*lang*). P12.

365 *ch'ē-p'ú* 車僕
CHOU: **Charioteer,** 2 ranked as Ordinary Servicemen (*chung-shih*) and 4 as Junior Servicemen (*hsia-shih*), members of the Ministry of Rites (*ch'un-kuan*); drivers of special ritual chariots. CL: *valet des chc*

366 *ch'ē ssū-mǎ* 車司馬
HAN: **Commander of Chariots,** one of many designations awarded military officers on active campaign.

367 *ch'é-ts'ù-shìh* 哲蔟氏
CHOU: **Destroyer of Malicious Birds,** one ranked as a Junior Serviceman (*hsia-shih*) in the Ministry of Justice (*ch'iu-kuan*). CL: *abatteur de nids.*

368 *ch'ē-yíng* 車營
SUNG: **Wagon Camp,** unit in the Court of the Imperial Stud (*t'ai-p'u ssu*). P31.

369 *ch'ē-yǚ chú* 車輿局
N-S DIV (N. Ch'i): **Livery Service** in the household of the Heir Apparent, headed by an Aide (*ch'eng*). P26.

370 *chèn* 朕
We: throughout imperial history, the Emperor's way of referring to himself in official pronouncements.

371 *chēn* 眞
(1) **Regular:** when prefixed to a title, signifies a normal substantive appointment in contrast to an honorary, probationary, acting, or otherwise qualified appointment. See *cheng, shih* (substantive); cf. *pen.* (2) **True:** when prefixed to a salary level stated in bushels in Han and some later times, signifies the exact amount stated (not necessarily as stated; normally partly converted to coins or other things) in contrast to Full (*chung*) meaning somewhat more than stated and Equivalent to (*pi*) meaning somewhat less than stated.

372 *chèn* 鎮
(1) N-S DIV–SUNG, MING: **Defense Command,** normally a territorial jurisdiction in a strategic area, especially along a dynastic frontier; headed by a Commander (*chiang*) in Sui, a Military Commissioner in T'ang (*chieh-tu shih*) and S. Sung (*chen-fu shih*), a Regional Commander (*tsung-ping kuan*) in Ming. Also see *chieh-chen, fang-chen, tu-tu fu.* (2) N-S DIV–SUNG: **Garrison,** usually in a frontier or other strategic area and easily confused with a Defense Command; in T'ang divided into 3 categories as Large (*shang*), Ordinary (*chung*), and Small (*hsia*), each headed by a Commander (*chiang*), rank 6a2, 7a1, or 7a2; the Sung command structure is not clear; perhaps such Garrisons were then located only in the area of the N. Sung dynastic capital, Kaifeng; but see under *keng-shu.* Also see *fu* (Garrison) and *wei* (Guard). RR+SP: *garnison.*

373 *chēn-fàn* 貞範
N-S DIV (N. Ch'i): **Lady of True Models,** designation of one of 27 imperial consorts collectively called Hereditary Consorts (*shih-fu*); rank =3b.

374 *chèn-fǔ* 鎮撫
YÜAN–MING: **Judge** in a military Guard (*wei*), 2, rank 5a in Yüan, 5b in Ming; also in Yüan Sea Transport Battalions (*hai-tao liang-yün ch'ien-hu so*), 2, rank 5a, and in Ming Battalions (*ch'ien-hu so*), 2, rank 6b. See *chen-fu ssu, chen-fu shih.* P60.

375 *chèn-fǔ shǐh* 鎮撫使
SUNG: **Military Commissioner,** delegated from the S. Sung court to take charge of military affairs in a shifting territorial jurisdiction along the northern frontier, called a Defense Command (*chen*). SP: *commissaire chargé de soumettre les bandits.*

376 *chèn-fǔ ssū* 鎮撫司
YÜAN–MING: **Prison** maintained by a military Guard (*wei*), under a Judge (*chen-fu*). P29.

377 *chēn-hsièn yüàn* 針線院
SUNG: **Tailoring Shop** staffed by eunuchs, a unit of the Palace Administration (*tien-chung sheng*). SP: *cour d'aiguille et de fil.*

378 *chēn-hsiū shǔ* 珍羞署
T'ANG–CH'ING: **Office of Delicacies,** a unit of the Court of Imperial Entertainments (*kuang-lu ssu*) in charge of providing special meat and fish dishes for court banquets; headed by a Director (*ling*) in T'ang, rank 8a2, a Commissioner (*shih*) in Sung, an Overseer (*ta-lu-hua-ch'ih*) in Yüan, one or 2 Directors (*cheng*) in Ming and Ch'ing, 6b. RR: *office des mets délicats.* SP: *office des mets exquis.* P30

379 *chēn-kuān shǔ* 甄官署
Pottery Office, a manufactory. (1) HAN: headed by Directors (*ling*) of the Front, Center, and Rear; subordinate to the Chamberlain for the Palace Buildings (*chiang-tso ta-chiang*). (2) N-S DIV: headed by a Director (*ling*); subordinate to the Chamberlain for the Palace Revenues (*shao-fu* or *t'ai-fu*). (3) SUI: headed by 2 Directors (*ling*); subordinate to the Court for the Palace Revenues (*t'ai-fu ssu*). (4) T'ANG–SUNG: headed by a Director (*ling*), rank 8b2 in T'ang, unclear for Sung; subordinate to the Directorate for the Palace Buildings (*chiang-tso chien*). RR+SP: *office des poteries et de la taille des pierres.* (5) CHIN: headed by a Director (*ling*), 6b; subordinate to the Ministry of Works (*kung-pu*). Functions continued by other agencies of the Ministry of Works in later dynasties.

380 *chēn-kūng* 針工
T'ANG: **Acupuncturist,** 20 unranked specialists in the Imperial Medical Office (*t'ai-i shu*) in the Court of Imperial Sacrifices (*t'ai-ch'ang ssu*). P36.

381 *chēn-kūng chú* 鍼工局
MING: **Sewing Service,** a minor agency of palace eunuchs headed by a eunuch Commissioner-in-chief (*ta-shih*) or Director (*t'ai-chien*); prepared and repaired clothing for palace use; see *pa chü* (Eight Services).

382 *chèn-kuó chiāng-chūn* 鎮國將軍
MING–CH'ING: **Defender-general of the State,** title of imperial nobility. In Ming, 3rd highest of 8 titles granted male descendants of Emperors; granted to younger sons of Commandery Princes (*chün-wang*). In Ch'ing, 11th highest of 14 titles, divided into 3 grades (*teng*); all sons including the heir were entitled to rank as Generals by Grace (*feng-en chiang-chün*). BH: noble of the imperial lineage of the 9th rank. P64.

383 *chèn-kuò chūng-wèi* 鎮國中尉
MING: **Defender-commandant of the State,** 6th highest of 8 titles of nobility granted to male descendants of Emperors; granted to younger sons of Supporters-general of the State (*feng-kuo chiang-chün*). P64.

384 *chèn-kuó kūng* 鎮國公
CH'ING: **Defender Duke,** 7th highest of 14 titles of nobility granted to male descendants of Emperors; granted to heirs of Beile Princes (*pei-tzu*). The heir of a Defender Duke

became a Bulwark Duke (*fu-kuo kung*); all other sons became Supporter-generals of the State (*feng-kuo chiang-chün*), and all daughters became Township Mistresses (*hsiang-chün*). BH: prince of the blood of the 5th degree. P64.

385   *chèn-kuó shàng chiāng-chūn* 鎮國上將軍
CHIN: **Defender-generalissimo of the State,** a prestige title (*san-kuan*) for rank 3b military officers, especially used to rank members of the imperial clan. P64.

386   *chèn-piāo* 鎮標
CH'ING: **Regional Command,** a group of Green Standards (*lu-ying*) military forces under the control of a Regional Commander (*tsung-ping*). BH: brigade.

387   *chèn-piéh* 甄別
CH'ING: lit., to distinguish: **Review of Probationers by Purchase,** a process conducted irregularly by the Ministry of Personnel (*lì-pu*) to evaluate the performance of Probationers (*shih-yung*) who had attained such status by contributing funds to the government; on the basis of these reviews, Probationers could be dismissed, retained, or promoted.

388   *chēn pó-shìh* 針博士
T'ANG: **Erudite for Acupuncture,** rank 8b1, instructor in the Imperial Medical Office (*t'ai-i shu*) of the Court of Imperial Sacrifices (*t'ai-ch'ang ssu*). RR: *maître acupuncteur au vaste savoir.* P36.

389   *chēn-shīh* 針師
T'ANG: **Acupuncture Master,** in charge of 20 authorized Acupuncture Students (*chen-sheng*) in the Imperial Medical Office (*t'ai-i shu*) of the Court of Imperial Sacrifices (*t'ai-ch'ang ssu*). RR: *maître acupuncteur.* P36.

390   *chèn-shoŭ* 鎮守
MING: **Grand Defender,** a special delegate from the central government to a large area such as a Province (*sheng*) or a Defense Command (*chen*) on the northern frontier, to be tactical commander of military forces; in general, an appointment equivalent to Regional Commander (*tsung-ping kuan*), sometimes used to identify a eunuch serving in such a capacity, occasionally used for commanders of relatively small areas of great military importance.

391   *chèn-t'ái* 鎮台
CH'ING: unofficial reference to a Regional Commander (*tsung-ping*).

392   *ch'én* 臣
Ety., apparently an eye in a head turned down, hence an underling, servant, or slave: **Minister,** throughout history the broadest generic term for persons holding positions in government, somewhat less specific than Official (*kuan*); commonly used by officials when referring to themselves in documents addressed to superiors, equivalent to "your minister" or "your humble servant." Especially in ancient texts, also sometimes used in the still broader sense of "subjects." See *nei hsiao-ch'en, ta-ch'en.*

393   *ch'én-fēi* 宸妃
MING: **Chamber Consort,** one of many titles for imperial concubines, number and rank not clear.

394   *chēng* 徵
A term used throughout history meaning **to summon** someone to the capital for an appointment. In Ch'in and Han, sometimes used when non-officials were summoned for appointment; thereafter normally used when able local or regional officials were summoned to take up central government positions, in some instances indicating special imperial action recognizing outstanding local or regional service.

395   *chèng* 政
Normally used with such meanings as administration, policy, to administer. On rare occasions used as the final character in a multi-character title, then usually in unofficial designations only. E.g., see *hsüeh-cheng* (Provincial Education Commissioner).

396   *chèng* 正
(1) Throughout history, a prefix commonly attached to titles with the following meanings: (a) **Principal,** used to differentiate, e.g., between a (Principal) Commissioner (see under *shih,* Commissioner) and a Vice Commissioner (*fu-shih*); (b) **Regular,** used to indicate a normal substantive appointment rather than one that was probationary, acting, or otherwise irregular (see *chen, pen*). (2) **Director, Supervisor, Head:** throughout history, a suffix commonly attached to an agency name as the title of the functioning leader, though sometimes designating a 2nd-tier executive under a leader of unusually high rank; e.g., see *t'ing-wei cheng.* (3) CHOU: **First Class Administrative Official,** the highest of 8 categories in which officials were classified in a hierarchy separate from the formal rank system called the Nine Honors (*chiu ming*), principally including Ministers (*ch'ing*); followed in prestige by the terms *shih* (Mentor, etc.), *ssu* (to be in charge; office), *lü* (Functionary), *fu* (Storekeeper), *shih* (Scribe), *hsü* (Assistant), and *t'u* (Attendant). CL: *le premier degré de la subordination administrative; chefs en titre.* (4) **Upright:** from Han on, one of several standard categories used in describing men nominated for recruitment or promotion in service; see *hsien-liang fang-cheng* (Worthy and Excellent, Straightforward and Upright). (5) **Upper Class:** from the era of N-S Division on, prefixed to a numeral specifying an official rank (*p'in*), in contrast to Lower Class (*ts'ung*); e.g., *cheng-san p'in* means rank 3 upper class (herein rendered 3a), *ts'ung-san p'in* means rank 3 lower class (herein rendered 3b).

397   *chèng-chāi* 正齋
CH'ING: unofficial reference to an **Instructor** (*chiao-yü*) in a local Confucian School (*ju-hsüeh*).

398   *chèng-chiàng* 正將
SUNG: **General,** apparently 16 appointees in a Grand Army (*ta-chün*), subordinate to a Vice Commander-general (*fu t'ung-ling*), SP: *général régulier.*

399   *chèng-chiēn-p'íng* 正監平
HAN–N-S DIV: abbreviated reference to the **Three Law Enforcement Aides** (*t'ing-wei san kuan*), the senior subordinates of the Chamberlain for Law Enforcement (*t'ing-wei*): the Supervisor (*cheng*), the Inspector (*chien*), and the Arbiter (*p'ing*). P22.

400   *chèng-chièn tà-fū* 正諫大夫
T'ANG: variant of *chien-i ta-fu* (**Grand Master of Remonstrance**) from 662 to 705.

401   *chèng chiēn-tsào* 正監造
CH'ING: **Foreman,** the senior member of the technical staff of the Imperial Printing Office (*wu-ying tien hsiu-shu ch'u*) in the Imperial Household Administration (*nei-wu fu*). BH: overseer of works.

402   *chèng chiēn-tsào ssū-k'ù* 正監造司庫
CH'ING: **Chief Librarian,** the senior member of the technical staff of the Imperial Library (*yü-shu ch'u*) in the Imperial Household Department (*nei-wu fu*). BH: librarian-in-chief, overseer of works.

403   *chèng-chìh ch'īng* 政治卿 or 正治卿
MING: **Chief Minister for Administration,** a merit title (*hsün*) granted to officials of rank 2b. P65.

404 *chèng-chìh shàng-ch'īng* 政治上卿
MING: **Supreme Chief Minister for Administration,** a merit title (*hsün*) granted to officials of rank 2a. P65.

405 *chèng-ch'ìh ... piēn-pèi* 整飭…邊備
MING: **Restorer of Frontier Defenses at ...:** a special ad hoc delegate from the central government to put in order defense preparations in a specified area; e.g., Grand Coordinator of the Area of Shun-t'ien and Other Prefectures and Concurrent Restorer of Frontier Defenses in Chi-chou and Other Locations (*hsün-fu shun-t'ien teng fu ti-fang chien cheng-ch'ih chi-chou teng ch'u pien-pei;* see under *hsün-fu* and *chien,* Concurrent). P50.

406 *chèng-ch'īng* 正卿
(1) HAN: **Regular Chamberlains,** 5th highest in a hierarchy of 10 status groups in the officialdom (see under *shang-kung*), including the officials commonly called the Nine Chamberlains (*chiu ch'ing*), i.e., Chamberlain for Ceremonials (*t'ai-ch'ang*), for Attendants (*lang-chung ling* or *kuang-lu hsün*), for the Palace Garrison (*wei-wei*), for the Imperial Stud (*t'ai-p'u*), for Law Enforcement (*t'ing-wei*), for Dependencies (*ta hung-lu*), for the Imperial Clan (*tsung-cheng* or *tsung-po*), for the National Treasury (*chih-su nei-shih* or *ta ssu-nung*), and for the Palace Revenues (*shao-fu*). Cf. *shang-ch'ing, p'ei-ch'ing, hsia-ch'ing.* P68. (2) T'ANG: from 662 to 670 the official title of all **Chief Ministers** (see *ch'ing*) heading the Nine Courts (*chiu ssu*).

407 *chēng-chūn* 徵君
Gentleman Summoned to Office: from Later Han if not earlier, a common unofficial reference to someone nominated by local authorities and summoned to court for possible placement in the officialdom, whether or not he responded. Equivalent to *p'ing-chün,* more polite than *cheng-shih.*

408 *chèng fèng-shàng t'ài-ī* 正奉上太醫
CHIN: **Imperial Physician** in the Imperial Academy of Medicine (*t'ai-i yüan*), rank not clear; attained such status only after 120 months of service as an Assistant Imperial Physician (*fu feng-sheng t'ai-i*), or perhaps combining service in that status and prior service as a Probationary Physician (*ch'ang-hsing t'ai-i*). P36.

409 *chèng-fèng tà-fū* 正奉大夫
SUNG–MING: **Grand Master for Proper Service,** a prestige title (*san-kuan*) for officials of rank 4a1 or 3a in Sung, 3b1 in Chin, 2b in Yüan and Ming. P68.

410 *chèng-fǔ* 政府
(1) **The Administration:** throughout history an unofficial reference to the top echelon of officials who were considered dominant in the central government, e.g., T'ang–Sung Grand Councilors (*tsai-hsiang*) or Ming–early Ch'ing Grand Secretaries (*ta hsüeh-shih*). (2) **The Government:** throughout history a vague unofficial reference to the whole governmental establishment or, occasionally, to some particular office or agency. See *kuan-fu.*

411 *chèng-fù* 正副
Principals and Assistants: a generic term designating the 2 or perhaps 3 top executive-echelon posts in an agency, e.g., in Ming–Ch'ing times, the Provincial Administration Commissioner (*pu-cheng shih*), the Administration Vice Commissioner (*ts'an-cheng*), and perhaps the Assistant Administration Commissioner (*ts'an-i*); similar to *chang-erh.* P49.

412 *chèng-hsiàng* 正相
SUNG–MING: an unofficial reference to a **Grand Councilor** (*tsai-hsiang*).

413 *chèng-hsuǎn* 政選 or 正選
CH'ING: **Regular Selection,** part of the personnel appointment process conducted by the Ministry of Personnel (*li-pu*): the appointment or promotion of regularly qualified candidates, i.e., those holding degrees as Provincial Graduates (*chü-jen*) and Metropolitan Graduates (*chin-shih*); normally conducted in even months, in contrast to Expedited Selections (*chi-hsüan*) normally conducted in odd months. Also known as *ta-hsüan.*

414 *chèng-huá* 正華
N-S DIV (N. Ch'i): **Lady of Proper Loveliness,** designation of one of 27 imperial consorts collectively called Hereditary Consorts (*shih-fu*); rank =3b.

415 *chèng-ī* 正一
MING: **Taoist Patriarch,** head of the Central Taoist Registry (*tao-lu ssu*), nominal rank 6a; responsible to the Ministry of Rites (*lǐ-pu*) for examining and certifying all Taoist priests through special local registries. See *tao-chi ssu, tao-cheng ssu, tao-hui ssu.*

416 *chèng-ī ssù-chiào chēn-jén* 正一嗣教眞人
or *cheng-i chen-jen*
CH'ING: **Taoist Patriarch,** nominal rank 3a, officially considered the direct-line hereditary successor of the First Century A.D. founder of religious Taoism, perpetuated by a Chang family of Kiangsi Province; responsible to the Ministry of Rites (*lǐ-pu*) for examining and certifying all Taoist priests through Taoist Registries (*tao-lu ssu*) at the capital and in all Prefectures (*fu*), Departments (*chou*), and Districts (*hsien*). See *cheng-i.*

417 *chèng-ì tà-fū* 正議大夫
SUI–MING: **Grand Master for Proper Consultation,** a prestige title (*san-kuan*) for officials of rank 4a1 in T'ang, 3b in Sung, 4a1 in Chin, 3a in Yüan and Ming. P68.

418 *chèng-ì t'áng* 正義堂
MING–CH'ING: **College for Moral Rectification,** one of the Six Colleges (*liu t'ang*) among which all students of the Directorate of Education (*kuo-tzu chien*) were distributed. P34.

419 *chěng-í wèi* 整儀尉 or 整宜尉
CH'ING: **Rectifier-commandant of Decorum,** rank 6a, officers in various units of the Imperial Procession Guard (*luan-i wei*). BH: controller of the 6th class.

420 *chèng-jèn* 正任
Principal, a prefix attached to a title to distinguish the appointee from another for whom the title did not represent his principal appointment. In Sung, used in the cases of various delegates from the central government such as Military Commissioners (*chieh-tu shih*) when the title indicated their principal function; they were considered the superiors of delegates with the same titles prefixed by Adjunct (*yao-chün*), which indicated that the title was supplementary to another, principal title held by the appointee. SP: *régulier.*

421 *chèng k'ǎo-kuān* 正考官
CH'ING: **Principal Examiner** at a Provincial Examination (*hsiang-shih*) in the civil service recruitment system; a temporary duty assignment for a senior official delegated from the central government.

422 *chèng-k'ō* 正科
CH'ING: **Principal of a Prefectural Medical School** (*i-hsüeh*), rank 9b, certified by the Ministry of Rites (*lǐ-pu*) and supervised by the Provincial Administration Commission (*ch'eng-hsüan pu-cheng shih ssu*). BH: prefectural physician.

423 *chèng-kuān* 政官
CHOU: **Executive Official,** a variant title for the Minister of War (*ssu-ma*).

424 *chèng-kuān* 正官
Principal Official: throughout history a common reference to the man in charge of any governmental unit; see under *cheng.*

425 *chèng-láng* 正郎
Principal Gentleman. (1) SUNG: a collective reference to holders of the 4 prestige titles (*san-kuan*) granted to officials of ranks 6a and 6b. (2) CH'ING: unofficial reference to a Bureau Director (*lang-chung*), rank 5a, in a Ministry (*pu;* see *liu pu*).

426 *chèng-lì* 正吏
CHOU: **Principal Functionary,** status attained with the first order (lowest rank) in the official hierarchy. CL: *officier régulier.*

427 *chèng lìng-shǐh* 正令史
N-S DIV (S. Dyn. and N. Ch'i): **Clerk,** a general term for minor government employees. See *ling-shih.*

428 *chèng-míng* 正名
Lit., a regular title: a reference to a ranked **regular official** (*kuan*) as distinct from, e.g., a suboffical functionary (*li*); see *pu cheng-ming.* Cf. *ssu-ming* (Probationer?).

429 *chèng-míng k'ǎi-shū* 正名楷書
SUNG: lit. meaning of the prefix *cheng-ming* not clear (to rectify names? regular ranked appointee?): **Copyist,** apparently unranked, 5 on the staff of the Imperial Archives (*pi-ko*). SP: *copiste en écriture régulière.*

430 *chèng-míng t'iēh-fáng* 正名帖房 or 貼房
SUNG: **Copyist,** unranked, 18 then 28 assigned to (each of?) the Twelve Sections (*shih-erh fang*) of the Bureau of Military Affairs (*shu-mi yüan*). SP: *employé-scribe.*

431 *chèng-míng tsàn-chě* 正名賛者
SUNG: **Ceremonial Assistant,** unranked, 7 in the Court of Imperial Sacrifices (*t'ai-ch'ang ssu*). SP: *héraut régulier.* P27.

432 *chēng-pǐ* 徵比
CH'ING: **Fiscal Secretary,** one of several types of Private Secretary (*mu-yu*) normally found on the staffs of Department and District Magistrates (*chih-chou, chih-hsien*), a non-official specialist in tax collecting and accounting.

433 *chèng-p'íng chiēn* 正平監
N-S DIV (Liang): **Police Superintendent,** a local official at the dynastic capital, modern Nanking. P32.

434 *chēng-shìh* 徵事
HAN: **Verifier** (?), a staff assistant to the Counselor-in-chief (*ch'eng-hsiang*), rank =600 bushels; functions not clear. HB: consultant.

435 *chēng-shìh* 徵士
Recruit for Office: from Later Han if not earlier, a common unofficial reference to someone nominated by local authorities and summoned to court for possible placement in the officialdom; less polite than *cheng-chün* or *p'ing-chün,* qq.v.

436 *chèng-shìh* 正侍
CH'ING: **Director** of the Palace Domestic Service (*kung-tien chien*), subordinate to the Supervising Commissioner (*tu-ling shih*); a eunuch, rank 4b; also called *tsung-kuan.*

437 *chèng-shìh* 正適
N-S DIV (Chin): unofficial reference to the **Heir Apparent.**

438 *chēng-shìh láng* 徵事郎 or 徵仕郎
T'ANG, CHIN–CH'ING: **Gentleman for Summoning,** a prestige title (*san-kuan*) for officials of rank 8a1 in T'ang, 8b1 in Chin, 7b in Yüan, Ming, and Ch'ing. P68.

439 *chèng-shìh láng* 正侍郎
SUNG: **Gentleman for Proper Attendance,** a prestige title (*san-kuan*) for officials of rank 7b. P68.

440 *chèng-shìh shěng* 政事省
LIAO: **Department of Administration,** predecessor from 950 to 1043 of the Secretariat (*chung-shu sheng*) in the top echelon of the central government. P4.

441 *chèng-shìh t'áng* 政事堂
T'ANG–SUNG: **Administration Chamber,** where Grand Councilors (*tsai-hsiang, ch'eng-hsiang,* etc.) met regularly with the Emperor to make policy decisions. In T'ang, part of the Chancellery until 683, then part of the Secretariat until the 720s, when it was reorganized as the Secretariat-Chancellery (*chung-shu men-hsia*). In Sung located in the imperial palace. RR: *grand salle du gouvernement des affaires.* SP: *grand salle des affaires de gouvernement.*

442 *chèng-shū* 正書
Proofreader. (1) N-S DIV: minor officials in the Palace Library (*pi-shu sheng*), apparently with some responsibility for instruction in calligraphy. (2) SUI: title replaced *cheng-tzu,* q.v., c. 604 in the Editorial Service (*ssu-ching chü*) of the Household Administration of the Heir Apparent (*chan-shih fu*). P26.

443 *chèng-shù* 正術
CH'ING: **Principal of a Prefectural Geomancy School** (*yin-yang hsüeh*), a nonofficial specialist certified by the Ministry of Rites (*lǐ-pu*) and supervised by the Provincial Administration Commission (*ch'eng-hsüan pu-cheng shih ssu*). Had some responsibility for the control of local fortune-tellers, entertainers, women dentists, midwives, etc. BH: prefectural inspector of petty professions.

444 *chèng-t'áng* 正堂
MING–CH'ING: a variant of the unofficial designation **Headquarters** (*t'ang*); commonly used by Prefects (*chih-fu*), Subprefectural or Department Magistrates (*chih-chou*), and District Magistrates (*chih-hsien*) when referring to their own positions.

445 *chèng-té* 正德
N-S DIV (N. Ch'i): **Lady of Proper Virtue,** designation of an imperial concubine, one of the group called the Three Consorts (*san fu-jen*).

446 *chèng-t'ǐ* 正體
Occasional unofficial reference to the **Heir Apparent.**

447 *chèng t'iēh-ssū* 正貼司
SUNG: **Principal Clerk,** unranked, 6 in the Imperial Archives (*pi-ko*) and variable numbers in units of the Ministry of Personnel (*lì-pu*). SP: *employé-scribe.*

448 *chèng-tsòu mǐng* 正奏名
SUNG: **Regularly Presented Graduates,** a collective designation of officials who had entered service through regular recruitment examinations and thus rose faster and higher in the officialdom than others.

449 *chèng-t'ú* 正途

MING–CH'ING: **Regular Paths** into officialdom; specifically, via regular recruitment examinations, via graduation from the hierarchy of state schools, and by reliance on inheritance privileges (*yin*); as distinguished from less esteemed and less promising paths, such as promotion from status as a subofficial functionary or purchase of official status. The term may be encountered in earlier dynasties with a similar sense.

450 *chèng-tzù* 正字

Proofreader. (1) N-S DIV (N. Ch'i): 4 minor officials in the Palace Library (*pi-shu sheng*), perhaps evolving from earlier *cheng-shu*, q.v. (2) SUI: 4 in the Palace Library and 2 in the Editorial Service (*ssu-ching chü*) of the Household Administration of the Heir Apparent (*chan-shih fu*) until c. 604, when the title was changed to *cheng-shu*, q.v. (3) T'ANG: 2, unranked, in the Secretariat of the Heir Apparent (*tso ch'un-fang*); 2, rank 9a2, in the Editorial Service (*chu-tso chü*) of the Palace Library; 2, rank 9b1, in the Secretariat (*chung-shu sheng*), apparently only from 792 to 807. RR: *rectificateur des caractères*. (4) SUNG: 2 or 4, rank 8b, in the Palace Library. SP: *correcteur des caractères*. (5) LIAO: minor officials in the Palace Library. (6) MING–CH'ING: 2 in Ming, 4 in Ch'ing, rank not clear, in the Editorial Service (*ssu-ching chü*) of the Household Administration of the Heir Apparent. BH: assistant librarian. P25, 26.

451 *chèng-yén* 正言

Exhorter, a category of remonstrance officials (*chien-kuan*) who monitored documents passing to and from the throne for propriety of form and content. (1) SUNG: one prefixed Left on the staff of the Chancellery (*men-hsia sheng*), one prefixed Right on the staff of the Secretariat (*chung-shu sheng*), both from 988, apparently replacing prior Reminders (*shih-i*), both rank 7b; about 1020 assigned to the newly formed Remonstrance Bureau (*chien-yüan*). SP: *rectificateur des paroles*. (2) MING: one each prefixed Left and Right, both 7b, in the Remonstrance Bureau until the Bureau was discontinued in the 1380s. P19.

452 *chèng-yén pó-shìh* 正言博士

N-S DIV (Liang): **Erudite of the True Word,** an instructor specializing in the teachings of the True Word sect of Buddhism on the staff of the National University (*t'ai-hsüeh, kuo-hsüeh*).

453 *chèng-yìn* 正印

CH'ING: lit., rectifier of certification: **Principal Priest,** a generic term for the heads of Buddhist Registries (*seng-lu ssu*) in Prefectures (*fu*), Departments (*chou*), and Districts (*hsien*); responsible for examining and certifying all Buddhist priests in the jurisdiction. under supervision of the Ministry of Rites (*lǐ-pu*).

454 *chèng-yìn kuān* 正印官

MING–CH'ING: **Principal Seal-holding Official,** a generic reference to the officials in charge of units of territorial administration, from the Provincial Administration Commission (*ch'eng-hsüan pu-cheng shih ssu*) down to the District (*hsien*) level. See *chang-yin kuan*.

455 *chèng-yüán* 正員

Regular Official: throughout history a reference to an appointee in any agency whose appointment was not temporary, provisional, acting, honorific, etc. See *yüan*.

456 *chèng-yüán ssū-mǎ* 正員司馬

N-S DIV (Liang): **Cavalry Commandant,** 4 in each of the 2 Guards (*wei*) in the establishment of the Heir Apparent, specifying regular appointees in normal service as distinct from honorific, provisional, acting, etc., appointees. P26.

457 *ch'éng* 丞

Aide. Lit., to assist, to help; oldest forms of the graph depict 2 hands lifting someone from a pit. The term is one of the commonest in Chinese official nomenclature, occurring in all eras, in many types of agencies, at virtually every level of rank. It very seldom appears as the first character in a title, but among such instances is a most important one: *ch'eng-hsiang* (Counselor-in-chief, Grand Councilor). Except in a context listing the various officials of an agency, it almost never occurs by itself as a complete title, although in S. Sung the prestigious title *ch'eng-hsiang* was formally shortened to the simple *ch'eng* alone. Normally *ch'eng* occurs as the final character in a title, preceded by the name of an agency or by a phrase suggesting a specialized function. Its sense is almost always Aide in ..., Aide to ..., or Aide for ...; the *ch'eng* was almost invariably at a secondary or tertiary level of authority, albeit sometimes with executive authority of importance. His rank was normally in the middle or lower ranges of the hierarchy. His role was normally that of an administrative assistant to the head of an agency, but his function may at times be better suggested by renderings such as Assistant Director, Assistant Magistrate, or even Vice .... E.g., *shang-hai hsien ch'eng* might literally mean Aide (to the Magistrate) of Shanghai District, but his function might be better suggested by the rendering Vice Magistrate of Shanghai District. Care is always called for to determine, e.g., that the *ch'ang-an shih ch'eng* of Han times was not an Aide *in* the Ch'ang-an Marketplaces but was Aide *for* the Ch'ang-an Marketplaces to the Metropolitan Governor (*ching-chao yin*), or that the *ku-ch'ui ch'eng* found in government from the era of N-S Division through Sung times was neither Aide to the Drummers and Fifers nor Aide for Drums and Fifes to someone, but in the Sung dynasty, e.g., was quite like an Assistant Director under a Director (*ling*) of the Drum and Fife Service (*ku-ch'ui chü*) in the Imperial Music Office (*ta-sheng fu*). Especially from Han through Sung times, *ch'eng* commonly played a secondary role below Directors (*ling*) and were often in pairs, prefixed Left and Right. Very few of the hundreds of titles that end with *ch'eng* are dealt with individually in this dictionary. HB: assistant. RR+SP: *assistant, exécutif assistant*.

458 *ch'éng* 城

Lit., a wall, walled settlement, town. See under *wu ch'eng* (Five Wards).

459 *ch'éng-ch'āi* 承差

CH'ING: lit., those who have received assignments: **Assignees,** an unofficial generic reference to unranked suboffical functionaries (*li*) and lesser servant personnel in government agencies.

460 *ch'éng-chèng* 承政

CH'ING: **Executive,** the pre-1644 counterpart of Minister (*shang-shu*) in the Ministries of Personnel (*lì-pu*) and Revenue (*hu-pu*). P5, 6.

461 *ch'éng-chiéh láng* 承節郎

SUNG: **Gentleman for Fostering Temperance,** a prestige title (*san-kuan*) for officials of rank 9b. P68.

462 *ch'éng-chíh* 丞直

SUI: **Duty Attendant,** 4 in the Inner Quarters (*nei-fang*), a unit in the Household Administration of the Heir Apparent (*chan-shih fu*), responsible for administering the personal apartment of the Heir Apparent; c. 604 the title was changed to *tien-chih*. See *nei ch'eng-chih*. P26.

463 ch'éng-chǐh 承旨
Recipient of Edicts. (1) T'ANG: a title and duty assignment granted as a supplement to one's regular position, enabling one to become a secretarial confidant of the Emperor and possibly later a Grand Councilor (*tsai-hsiang*); most commonly granted to Academicians (*hsüeh-shih*). (2) T'ANG: palace woman official, rank 5a. RR: *femme qui reçoit les ordres de l'empereur*. (3) SUNG: various regular appointees in the Institute of Academicians (*hsüeh-shih yüan*), the Historiography Office (*shih-kuan*), and the Bureau of Military Affairs (*shu-mi yüan*), e.g., as Hanlin Academician Recipient of Edicts (*han-lin hsüeh-shih ch'eng-chih*), Vice Recipient of Edicts for Military Affairs (*shu-mi fu ch'eng-chih*). SP: *transmetteur des directives*. (4) YÜAN: 6, rank 1b, established in 1318 in the Hanlin and Historiography Academy (*han-lin kuo-shih yüan*). See *tu ch'eng-chih*. P5, 23.

464 ch'èng-chíh 稱職
MING: lit., to fulfill one's function: **Adequate**, a term of approbation used when officials were being evaluated, generally every 3 years; meant to be deserving of promotion, as distinguished from Ordinary (*p'ing-ch'ang*) and Inadequate (*pu ch'eng-chih*).

465 ch'éng-chǐh hsüeh-shìh 承制學士
YÜAN: **Academician Recipient of Edicts**, an appointee in the Academy in the Hall of Literature (*k'uei-chang ko hsüeh-shih yüan*), rank not clear. P23.

466 ch'éng-chǐh kó-tzǔ 承旨閣子
T'ANG: in the 800s an unofficial reference to the **Director** (*yüan-chang*) **of the Hanlin Academy** (*han-lin yüan*). P23.

467 ch'éng-chǐh láng 承直郎
SUNG–MING: **Gentleman for Fostering Uprightness**, a prestige title (*san-kuan*) for officials of ranks 6a and 8b in Sung, 7a2 in Chin, 6a in Yüan and Ming. P68.

468 ch'éng-ch'ǐh chiēn 承勅監
MING: **Directorate for the Receipt of Edicts**, for a short time beginning in 1376 an autonomous agency of the central government to which Supervising Secretaries (*chi-shih-chung*) and Secretariat Drafters (*chung-shu she-jen*) were assigned to assist in the drafting of imperial rescripts and edicts; originally headed by a Director (*ling*), rank 6a then 7a, in 1377 replaced by 2 Directors (*lang*), 7b. In 1379 absorbed into the Office of Transmission (*t'ung-cheng ssu*). P19, 21.

469 ch'éng-chūng láng 成忠郎
SUNG: **Gentleman of Complete Loyalty**, a prestige title (*san-kuan*) granted to officials of rank 9a. P68.

470 ch'éng-ch'üán tà-fū 成全大夫
SUNG: **Grand Master for Complete Wholeness**, a prestige title (*san-kuan*) for officials of rank 7a. P68.

471 ch'éng-chūn chì-chiǔ 成均祭酒
T'ANG: from 684 to 705 the official variant of *kuo-tzu chien chi-chiu* (**Chancellor of the Directorate of Education**). P34.

472 ch'éng-chūn chiēn 成均監
T'ANG: from 684 to 705 the official variant of *kuo-tzu chien* (**Directorate of Education**). P34.

473 ch'éng-fā chià-kó k'ù 承發架閣庫
YÜAN: **Storekeeper**, rank 8b, on the staff of each Princely Administration (*nei-shih fu*). See *chao-mo chien ch'eng-fa chia-ko k'u*. P36, 69.

474 ch'éng-fā kuǎn-kōu chiēn yü-ch'éng
承發管勾兼獄丞
YÜAN: **Communications Clerk and Prison Aide**, one, rank 8a, on the staff of the Censorate (*yü-shih t'ai*). P18.

475 ch'éng-fā ssū 承發司
CHIN: **Communications Office**, a unit in the Ministry of War (*ping-pu*), headed by a Clerk (*kuan-kou*).

476 ch'éng-fēi 成妃
MING: **Complete Consort**, title of a relatively high-ranking palace woman.

477 ch'éng-fèng 承奉
MING: **Attendant**, from 1376 to 1380 the 3rd-ranking position in the Palace Ceremonial Office (*tien-t'ing i-li ssu*), antecedent of the Court of State Ceremonial (*hung-lu ssu*); rank 8b. P33.

478 ch'éng-fèng láng 承奉郎
SUI, T'ANG, SUNG: **Gentleman for Attendance**, a prestige title (*san-kuan*) granted to officials of rank 8b1. P68.

479 ch'éng-fèng pān tū-chīh 承奉班都知
General Manager of Attendants. (1) CHIN: member of the Palace Ceremonial Staff (*ko-men*), rank 7a. (2) YÜAN: member of the Palace Ceremonial Office (*shih-i ssu*), 7a. P33.

480 ch'éng-fú 承符
Bearer of Identification Certificates: in Sung and no doubt other periods as well, a common member of the retinue of a traveling official, carrying the seals and tallies (*fu*) with which the official's identity could be confirmed, or with which he could confirm the validity of documents presented or encountered en route. See under *tao-ts'ung*.

481 ch'éng-hó láng 成和郎
SUNG–YÜAN: **Gentleman for Perfect Health**, a prestige title (*san-kuan*) for medical officials of rank 7b in Sung, 6b in Yüan.

482 ch'éng-hó tà-fū 成和大夫
SUNG: **Grand Master for Perfect Health**, a prestige title (*san-kuan*) for rank 6b medical officials.

483 ch'éng-hsiàng 丞相
A title of great significance in Chinese history, normally indicating the most esteemed and influential member(s) of the officialdom, who was leader of and spokesman for the officialdom vis-à-vis the ruler and at the same time the principal agent for implementing the ruler's wishes in all spheres, civil and military; often abbreviated to *ch'eng* or *hsiang*. In all periods appointees were commonly prefixed Left and Right. (1) CH'IN–N-S DIV: **Counselor-in-chief**, one of the Three Dukes (*san kung*) among whom major responsibilities in the central government were divided; rank 10,000 bushels in Former Han, always chosen from among Marquises (*hou*) or made a Marquis on appointment. Immediate subordinates were divided among function-specific Sections (*ts'ao;* not itemized in sources), each headed by an Administrator (*yüan-shih*). In 1 B.C. changed to Grand Minister of Education (*ta ssu-t'u*), not revived until A.D. 208. In post-Han times mostly honorific. HB: chancellor. (2) T'ANG: from 713 to 741 replaced the title **Vice Direc-**

tor (*p'u-yeh*) **of the Department of State Affairs** (*shang-shu sheng*), the actual head of the agency; rank 2b. (3) SUNG–MING: **Grand Councilor.** In Sung a generic term for all participants in policy deliberations in the Administration Chamber (*cheng-shih t'ang*) until 1172, when it became the official title of the former Vice Director of the Department of State Affairs (as above), rank 1a. In Liao the 2nd executive post in the Secretariat (*chung-shu sheng*), under a Director (*ling*). In Chin 1b, the 2nd executive post in the Department of State Affairs. In Yüan 1a, active head of the Secretariat under an honorific Director (*ling*). In early Ming 1a, head of the Secretariat until the post was discontinued in 1380. Thereafter comparable prestige and power was not attainable by any official; the Ming and Ch'ing Emperors ruled more directly through a Grand Secretariat (*nei-ko*), whose Grand Secretaries (*ta hsüeh-shih*) lacked the institutional base required for exerting influence in the style of previous Grand Councilors. Also see *hsiang-kuo, t'ai-tsai, tsai-hsiang.* Common alternate English renderings are Chancellor, Imperial Chancellor, Lieutenant Chancellor. P2,4.

484 *ch'éng-hsiàng fǔ* 丞相府
HAN–N-S DIV: **Office of the Counselor-in-chief.**

485 *ch'éng-hsìn láng* 承信郎
SUNG: **Gentleman of Trust,** a prestige title (*san-kuan*) granted to officials of rank 9b.

486 *ch'éng-hsīn t'áng* 誠心堂
MING–CH'ING: **College for Making the Heart Sincere,** one of the Six Colleges (*liu t'ang*) among which all students of the Directorate of Education (*kuo-tzu chien*) were distributed. P34.

487 *ch'éng-hsüān pù-chèng shǐh ssū* 承宣布政使司
MING–CH'ING: lit., office of the commissioner for undertaking the promulgation (of imperial orders) and for disseminating governmental policies: **Provincial Administration Commission,** made specific by prefixing the name of a Province (*sheng*) or comparable area and commonly abbreviated to *pu-cheng ssu;* the principal agency at the provincial level for directing the routine general-administration business, especially fiscal, of Prefectures (*fu*) and lesser units of territorial administration, and for handling communications between the central government and regional and local administrative units. Created in 1376 by transformation of the early Ming Branch Secretariats (*hsing chung-shu sheng*) in the Yüan pattern, each sharing control over its jurisdiction with a Provincial Surveillance Commission (*t'i-hsing an-ch'a shih ssu*) and a Regional Military Commission (*tu chih-hui shih ssu*) and in a close cooperative relationship with a Regional Inspector (*hsün-an yü-shih*) delegated from the Censorate (*yü-shih t'ai* till 1380, then *tu ch'a-yüan*). From the 1400s these provincial authorities were gradually subordinated to the supervision of Grand Coordinators (*hsün-fu*) and then multi-province Supreme Commanders (*tsung-tu*) delegated from the central government on special duty assignments. In Ch'ing the Regional Military Commission was superseded by Manchu Generals (*chiang-chün*) of the Banner system (see *pa ch'i*) and Provincial Military Commanders (*t'i-tu*) of Green Standards (*lu-ying*) forces; and Ming's supervisory Grand Coordinators and Supreme Commanders evolved into Governors and Governors-general, respectively, entrenched in the regular territorial administration to such an extent that the Provincial Administration

Commissions became their staff agencies for administration, with less prestige than in Ming times. In the mature Ming system there were 13 such Commissions; none existed for the 2 Metropolitan Areas around the capitals Peking (*Chih-li* from 1421) and Nanking (*Nan Chih-li* from 1421), for which Administration Commission functions were extended from neighboring Provinces. Under Ch'ing, in 1661 2 Provincial Administration Commissions were established for the old Southern Metropolitan Area (since the fall of Ming called *Chiang-nan*) in the creation of modern Kiangsu and Anhwei Provinces; in 1663 old Shensi was similarly divided into Shensi and Kansu; in 1664 old Hukwang was divided into Hupei and Hunan; in 1724 a Provincial Administration Commission was established for the Metropolitan Area (*Chih-li*) around Peking; and in 1760 separate Commissions were established for the two natural parts of heavily populated, wealthy, and still united Kiangsu Province, one based at Soochow and called the Kiangsu Provincial Administration Commission, the other based at Nanking and called the Chiang-ning Provincial Administration Commission. Thus there were 20 such Commissions in the mature Ch'ing order. In both dynasties the principal post was that of Commissioner (*shih, pu-cheng shih*), rank 2b; there were normally 2 appointees, one prefixed Left and one prefixed Right, until 1667, but only one was appointed thereafter. In each Commission there were variable numbers of Administration Vice Commissioners (*ts'an-cheng*), 3b, and Assistant Administration Commissioners (*ts'an-i*), 4b; such supportive agencies as a Registry (*ching-li ssu*), a Records Office (*chao-mo so*), an Office of the Judicial Secretary (*li-wen so*), Granaries (*ts'ang*), and Storehouses (*k'u*); and in Ming but not Ch'ing a Miscellaneous Manufactures Service (*tsa-tsao chü*), a Weaving and Dyeing Service (*chih-jan chü*), and a Prison Office (*ssu-yü ssu*). Vice Commissioners and Assistant Commissioners were normally assigned to Branch Offices (*fen-ssu*) of the Commissions, given the generic designation Circuit Intendants (*tao-t'ai*). Commissions had from 3 to 8 all-purpose General Administration Circuits (*fen-shou tao*), each exercising all the authority of the Commissioner(s) in a geographically defined part of the Province; and there were many kinds of specialized, function-specific Circuits, e.g., Tax Intendant Circuits (*tu-liang tao*), Census Intendant Circuits (*tu-ts'e tao*). In 1735 all such Circuit Intendant duty assignments were transformed into regular, substantive positions in their own right, removed from their nominal associations with the Provincial Administration Commissions. For the most part, however, Circuit Intendants continued to function as intermediaries between Prefectures and the Commissions, as before. See separate entries; also see *chien-ssu, fan-ssu, fang-mien, liang ssu, san ssu.* BH: office of the lieutenant-governor or provincial treasurer. P52.

488 *ch'éng-hsüān shǐh* 承宣使
SUNG: **Pacification Commissioner,** from 1080 a salary office (*chi-lu kuan*) for officials with monthly salaries of 300,000 coins or equivalent, especially including Deputy Military and Surveillance Commissioners (*chieh-tu kuan-ch'a liu-hou*). Apparently c. 1117 also became a duty-assignment designation for some officials delegated to jurisdictions at the Circuit (*lu*) level to supervise military operations, but not a regular official appointment. P50, 52.

489 *ch'éng-huá chiēn* 承華監
HAN: **Directorate of the Ch'eng-hua Horses** under the Chamberlain for the Imperial Stud (*t'ai-p'u*), headed by a

Director (*chang*), rank not clear; the meaning of *ch'eng-hua* is not clear, but cf. *ch'eng-hua ling*. HB: chief inspector of the stables of the palace of continuing flowers. P31.

490 *ch'éng-huá lìng* 承華令
HAN: **Director of Palace Entertainments,** a subordinate of the Chamberlain for the Palace Revenues (*shao-fu*), in charge of the Palace Band (*huang-men ku-ch'ui*) and 27 theatrical Players (*hsi-shih*). P10.

491 *ch'éng-huáng* 乘黃
SUNG: **Imperial Coachman,** unranked, in the Court of the Imperial Stud (*t'ai-p'u ssu*). SP: *intendant des chars impériaux*. P31.

492 *ch'éng-huáng chiù* 乘黃廄
N-S DIV: **Stable of the Imperial Coachman,** from Chin on one of the agencies subordinate to the Chamberlain for the Imperial Stud (*t'ai-p'u ch'ing*) or sometimes the Chamberlain for Ceremonials (*t'ai-ch'ang ch'ing*); normally headed by a Director (*ling*); generally responsible for providing both vehicles and horses for imperial and court use, especially on ceremonial occasions. P31.

493 *ch'éng-huáng shǔ* 乘黃署
T'ANG: **Office of the Imperial Coachman,** one of the 4 principal units in the Court of the Imperial Stud (*t'ai-p'u ssu*); headed by a Director (*ling*), rank 9b2; provided both ordinary and ceremonial chariots and carriages for the Emperor's use in cooperation with the Livery Service (*shang-ch'eng chü*) of the Palace Administration (*tien-chung sheng*), which provided necessary horses. RR: *office des chars impériaux*. P31.

494 *ch'éng-hūi* 承徽
T'ANG: **Lady of Inherent Excellence,** title authorized for 10 concubines of the Heir Apparent, rank 5a. RR: *femme qui a reçu la vertu de naissance*.

495 *ch'éng-hūn* 成婚
CH'ING: **Dame-consort,** designation for consorts and concubines of imperial sons, grandsons, great-grandsons, etc., other than *fu-chin* (Princess-consort).

496 *ch'éng-ì* 乘驛
T'ANG: **Mounted Courier,** 20 authorized for the staff of the Secretariat (*chung-shu sheng*).

497 *ch'éng-í* 承衣
SUI: **Wardrobe Attendant,** designation for a category or palace women, rank =6 or lower.

498 *ch'éng-ì láng* 承議郎
SUI, T'ANG, SUNG: **Gentleman for Discussion,** a prestige title (*san-kuan*) granted to officials of rank 6a (?) in Sui, 6a2 in T'ang, 7b in Sung. P68.

499 *ch'éng-kuǎn* 承管
CH'ING: lit., hereditarily in charge: **Hereditary,** prefix to some titles of petty offices, especially in various Manchu agencies in Manchuria, that were apparently occupied in hereditary succession as sanctioned by custom.

500 *ch'éng-kuēi* 承閨
T'ANG: **Lady of the Inner Chamber,** a title for palace women of rank 4a, from 662 to 670 only. RR: *femme qui prend soin (?) du palais intérieur*.

501 *ch'éng-láng* 丞郎
From T'ang on, an unofficial reference to **Vice Ministers** (*shih-lang*) of Ministries (*pu*).

502 *ch'éng-lù shǔ* 承祿署
HAN: lit., office for receiving (containing?) stipends: **Office of the Palace Paymaster (?),** a unit of the Palace Storehouse (*chung-huang tsang*); staffing and specific functions not clear. HB: office for the receipt of salary.

503 *ch'éng-mén hóu* 城門侯
HAN: **Commandant of the Capital Gate,** one in charge of each of the 12 gates of the capital city, rank 600 bushels; under supervision of the Commandant of the Capital Gates (*ch'eng-men hsiao-wei*). BH: captain of a city gate.

504 *ch'éng-mén hsiào-wèi* 城門校尉
HAN: **Commandant of the Capital Gates,** rank 2,000 bushels in Former Han, =2,000 bushels in Later Han, supervisor of the military units that guarded the 12 gates of the capital city. BH: colonel of the city gates.

505 *ch'éng-mén láng* 城門郎
T'ANG, SUNG: **Gentleman of the Capital Gates,** an official of the Chancellery (*men-hsia sheng*), rank 6b1 in T'ang, not clear for Sung; in charge of the entry to the imperial residence. RR+SP: *secrétaire chargé des portes de la ville impériale*.

506 *ch'éng-mén lǐng* 城門領
CH'ING: **Gate Commandant,** one or 2 military officers with 4a rank stationed at each city gate of the dynastic capital, Peking. BH: captain of the gate.

507 *ch'éng-mén ssū-mǎ* 城門司馬
HAN: **Commander of the Capital Gates,** one, rank 1,000 bushels, assisting the Commandant of the City Gates (*ch'eng-men hsiao-wei*). HB: major of the city gates.

508 *ch'éng-míng lú* 承明廬
HAN: lit., a hut where one gains enlightenment: **Enlightenment Library,** a palace archive. May be encountered in later eras as an archaic reference to the Hanlin Academy (*han-lin yüan*).

509 *ch'éng-pàn shìh-wù yá-mén*
承辦事務衙門
CH'ING: **Imperial Mausolea Administration,** 2 agencies that oversaw Ch'ing tombs in the Peking area, headed by a Supervisor-in-chief (*tsung-kuan*) called Grand Minister Protector of the Imperial Mausolea (*shou-hu ling-ch'in ta-ch'en*). BH: office of the imperial mausolea. P29.

510 *ch'éng-pù* 丞簿
MING: **Horse Recorder,** an unranked subofficial representing the Court of the Imperial Stud (*t'ai-p'u ssu*) on the staff of each District (*hsien*) in which government horse herds were grazed. P31.

511 *ch'éng-shìh láng* 承事郎
SUNG–MING: **Gentleman for Managing Affairs,** a prestige title (*san-kuan*) for officials of rank 8a2 in Sung and Chin, 7a in Yüan and Ming; in Sung specially reserved for officials functioning as Case Reviewers (*p'ing-shih*) in the Court of Judicial Review (*ta-li ssu*). P68.

512 *ch'éng-shòu kuān* 承受官 or *ch'eng-shou*
SUNG: **Receptionist,** unranked subofficial, one each in the Palace Library (*pi-shu sheng*), the Historiography Institute (*kuo-shih yüan*), and the Visitors Bureau (*k'o-sheng*) of the Secretariat (*chung-shu sheng*); also the title of a eunuch on the staff of the Heir Apparent. From the early 1100s, eunuchs with this title were appointed to almost every civil and military office of any significance, becoming imperial

agents virtually dominating the regular officials; but from 1127 this practice was suppressed. SP: *employé chargé d'accepter les affaires; fonctionnaire chargé de recevoir les affaires.* P26.

513 ch'éng-shǒu wèi 城守尉
CH'ING: **Garrison Commandant,** a rank 3a military officer in the provincial Banner (see *pa ch'i*) hierarchy.

514 ch'éng-té láng 承德郎
CHIN–CH'ING: **Gentleman for Fostering Virtue,** a prestige title (*san-kuan*) for officials of rank 7a1 in Chin, 6a thereafter. P68.

515 ch'éng-wù 承務
T'ANG: **Director,** one each prefixed Left and Right, both rank 5b1; a variant title only during the period from 662 to c. 705 for the 2 *lang-chung*, q.v., who were directly subordinate to the Left and Right Assistant Directors (*ch'eng*) in the Department of State Affairs (*shang-shu sheng*) and helped the Assistant Directors supervise the work of the Department's 6 Ministries (*pu*); to be differentiated from the *lang-chung* who were Directors of the various Bureaus (*ssu*) in the Ministries. RR: *secrétaire supérieure.*

516 ch'éng-wù láng 成務郎 or 承務郎
(1) SUI: **Assistant Director,** apparently one each, rank not clear, subordinate to Directors (*lang*) and apparently also Vice Directors (*yüan-wai lang*) in Bureaus of Ministries, e.g., the Bureau of Equipment (*chia-pu*) and Bureau of Provisions (*k'u-pu*) in the Ministry of War (*ping-pu*) and the Bureau of Public Construction (*ch'i-pu*) in the Ministry of Works (*kung-pu*). P12, 14. (2) T'ANG–MING: **Gentleman for Rendering Service,** a prestige title (*san-kuan*) for officials of rank 8b2 until 1080, then 9b for the remainder of Sung, 7b1 in Chin, 6b thereafter. P68.

517 ch'éng-yìng hsiǎo-tǐ chú 承應小底局
LIAO: **Palace Domestic Service,** an agency staffed by menials, part of the Court Ceremonial Institute (*hsüan-hui yüan*). P38.

518 ch'éng-yú 乘輿
Lit., one who mounts a carriage: **His Majesty,** throughout history an indirect reference to the Emperor.

519 chí 畿
T'ANG–SUNG: **Metropolitan,** 2nd highest of 7 ranks into which Districts (*hsien*) were classified on the basis of their prestige and size; used as a prefix to *hsien.*

520 chí 級
Class: from Sui on a subdivision of a rank (*p'in*) in the official hierarchy, equivalent to *chieh* or *teng*, qq.v.; e.g., an office or official might have status as 3rd rank, 2nd class, rendered in this dictionary as rank 3b. Most commonly, the standard 9 ranks were subdivided into 2 classes each, but in some periods some ranks were subdivided into 4 classes: e.g., 8a1, 8a2, 8b1, 8b2. The term appears in many compounds referring to the general system of ranks, such as *p'in-chi, teng-chi, chieh-chi.* Also see *cheng* (Upper Class) and *ts'ung* (Lower Class).

521 chǐ 給
Occasional abbreviation of *chi-shih-chung* (**Supervising Secretary, Supervising Censor**).

522 chì 計
Account(s). (1) Throughout history occurs with the sense of account books in titles such as *k'uai-chi ssu* (Office of

Palace Accounts). (2) SUNG: from 993 to 994 referred to a division of the empire for fiscal purposes into 10 Circuits (*tao*), constituting 2 large regions called the Left Account (*tso-chi*) and the Right Account (*yu-chi*), for each of which there was a Commissioner (*shih*) and an Administrative Assistant (*p'an-kuan*), the whole apparatus supervised by a Supreme Commissioner of Accounts (*tsung chi-shih*). Before and after this short-lived arrangement, fiscal affairs were handled by the State Finance Commission (*san ssu*). Also see *kuo-chi shih.* P7.

523 chí-àn 騎案
SUNG: **Horses Section,** designation of units found in several central government agencies; e.g., one of 4 Sections in the Court of Palace Attendants (*hsüan-hui yüan*), one of 8 Sections in the Tax Bureau (*tu-chih ssu*) of the State Finance Commission (*san ssu*). Normally headed by an Administrative Assistant (*p'an-kuan, t'ui-kuan*). In all cases, the Sections seem to have been record-keeping units relating to the activities of the Court of the Imperial Stud (*t'ai-p'u ssu*) and its regional Directorates of Horse Pasturages (*mu-chien*) as well as other agencies charged with buying, breeding, and caring for horses and other state-owned animals. SP: *service de l'élevage et d'achat de chevaux.*

524 chī-ch'á 稽察
CH'ING: **Inspector,** designation of a Grand Secretary (*ta hsüeh-shih*) delegated to supervise the Office for Distribution of Imperial Pronouncements (*chi-ch'a ch'in-feng shang-yü shih-chien ch'u*).

525 chī-ch'á ch'ién-chú 稽查錢局
CH'ING: **Inspector of Provincial Coinage Services,** from 1680 to 1724 a duty assignment for Supervising Secretaries (*chi-shih-chung*) and Censors (*yü-shih*) sent out from the central government to investigate and report on the activities of Provincial Coinage Services (*ch'ien-chü*). P16.

526 chī-ch'á ch'īn-fèng shàng-yü shìh-chièn ch'ù 稽察欽奉上諭事件處
CH'ING: **Office for Distribution of Imperial Pronouncements,** established in 1730 as a subdivision of the Grand Secretariat (*nei-ko*) to apply imperial seals to imperial pronouncements, supervise their distribution to the appropriate central government agencies, and maintain a register of their distribution; no special staff; one Grand Secretary (*ta hsüeh-shih*) delegated to be in charge. BH: chancery for the publication of imperial edicts. P2.

527 chī-ch'á chūng-shū k'ǒ shìh-wù tà-ch'én 稽查中書科事務大臣
CH'ING: **Grand Minister Inspector of the Central Drafting Office,** designation of a junior member of the Grand Secretariat (*nei-ko*) delegated to supervise the subordinate unit called the Central Drafting Office (*chung-shu k'o*), staffed with Secretariat Drafters (*chung-shu she-jen*).

528 chī-ch'á fáng 稽察房
CH'ING: **Verification Office,** a subdivision of the Grand Secretariat (*nei-ko*) responsible for checking to ensure that central government agencies did not delay in carrying out imperial instructions and in submitting monthly reports on their activities to the Grand Secretaries (*ta hsüeh-shih*); no regular staff; functions performed by officials of the Hanlin Academy (*han-lin yüan*) and the Central Drafting Office (*chung-shu k'o*). P2.

529 *chī-ch'á kuān* 譏察官
CHIN: **Security Official**, concurrent title of 2 Monopoly Tax Commissioners (*chüeh-huo-wu shih*), rank 7a, stationed at the T'ung River frontier pass (T'ung-kuan, modern Shensi), signifying their special responsibility for detecting the infiltration of enemy spies and for generally controlling the frontier pass. P62.

530 *chī-ch'á nèi-kuǎn chiēn-tū* 稽察內館監督
CH'ING: **Supervisory Inspector of the Inner Hostel**, designation of a Censor (*yü-shih*), Supervising Censor (*chi-shih-chung*), or junior official of a Ministry (*pu*) assigned to keep watch over the functioning of the Inner Hostel (*nei-kuan*) maintained by the Court of Colonial Affairs (*li-fan yüan*) for visiting Mongol dignitaries. Also see *chi-ch'a wai-kuan chien-tu*. P17.

531 *chī-ch'á t'án-miào tà-ch'én* 稽查壇廟大臣
CH'ING: **Grand Minister Inspector of the Altars and Temples**, an ad hoc duty assignment for a senior member of the Imperial Household Department (*nei-wu fu*) prior to the undertaking of any sacrificial ceremonies at the Altar to Earth (*t'u-t'an*) or the Temple of Heaven (*t'ien-miao*) in the dynastic capital; assisted by a Grand Minister Preparer of the Altars and Temples (*pei-ch'a t'an-miao ta-ch'en*). BH: superintendent of altars and temples.

532 *chī-ch'á wài-kuǎn chiēn-tū* 稽察外館監督
CH'ING: **Supervisory Inspector of the Outer Hostel**, an exact counterpart of the Supervisory Inspector of the Inner Hostel (*chi-ch'a nei-kuan chien-tu*, q.v.); the difference in their functions is not clear. P17.

533 *chí-chèng* 集正
SUNG: **Registrar**, 2, rank not clear, in the Directorate of Education (*kuo-tzu chien*), responsible for keeping student records and investigating students who did not maintain standards. SP: *surveillant*. P34.

534 *chí-ch'éng* 棘丞
SUI–CH'ING: unofficial reference to the **Assistant Minister** (*ch'eng*) **of the Court of Judicial Review** (*ta-li ssu*). Also see *chi-shu*.

535 *chì-ch'ì ssū* 祭器司
SUNG: **Office of Sacrificial Utensils**, a unit in the Court of Imperial Sacrifices (*t'ai-ch'ang ssu*), staffed by 10 Provisioners (*kung-kuan*). SP: *bureau des objets de sacrifices chargé des offrandes*.

536 *chí-chiǎo tì* 急脚遞
SUNG: **Fast Courier**, a category of couriers in the postal relay system who reportedly could carry state documents from 300 to 500 Chinese miles (*li*) per day, used only for urgent military messages.

537 *chì-ch'iǎo* 技巧
HAN: **Skilled Workman**, subordinates of the Commandant of the Imperial Gardens (*shui-heng tu-wei*), headed by a Director (*ling*); functions not clear, but probably engaged in specialized craft workshops. HB (*ling*): prefect of the skilled workmen.

538 *chì-chiēh* 計偕
HAN: **Local Representative**, designation of one or more worthy citizens of each Commandery (*chün*) chosen to accompany an Accounts Assistant (*chi-yüan*) sent annually to the capital to report on local events and fiscal affairs; the written presentation came to be known as the *chi-chieh* report or account (*pu*). See *ch'ao-chi shih*. P53.

539 *chì-chièn* 給諫
MING–CH'ING: lit., submitter of remonstrance: unofficial reference to *chi-shih-chung* (**Supervising Secretary, Supervising Censor**). See *t'ai-chien* (Censors and Remonstrators). P19.

540 *chí-chíh chǎng* 籍直長
CHIN: **Director**, rank 8a, of the Department of Musicians (*yüeh-kung pu*) in the Court of Imperial Sacrifices (*t'ai-ch'ang ssu*). P10.

541 *chì-ch'īng* 棘卿
From T'ang on, an unofficial reference to the **Chief Minister** (*ch'ing*) **of the Court of Judicial Review** (*ta-li ssu*). P22.

542 *chì-chiǔ* 祭酒
Lit., **Libationer**. In Han and immediate post-Han times may be found used in this sense as an honorific designation for a distinguished older minister; otherwise, **Chancellor**. (1) HAN–CH'ING: head of the top-echelon educational agency in the dynastic capital, the National University (*t'ai-hsüeh, kuo-hsüeh*) or, from Sui on, the Directorate of Education (*kuo-tzu chien*). Originated late in Former Han as a function performed in rotation by the various Erudites (*po-shih*) of the National University, then during the era of N-S Division evolved into a regular official assignment, rank 3 or 4. Rank 3b in T'ang, 4b in Sung, 4a in Chin, 3b in Yüan, 4b in Ming and Ch'ing. In Yüan and again briefly in early Ch'ing, there were Chancellors of Mongolian (*meng-ku*) Directorates of Education as well as of the normal Directorates. In Ch'ing there were normally 2 appointees, one Chinese and one Manchu. The title was often given as *kuo-tzu chi-chiu*. HB: libationer. RR+SP: *recteur*. P34. (2) N-S DIV: head of the Department of Scholarly Counselors (*chi-shu sheng*), chosen from among its staff of Cavalier Attendants-in-ordinary (*san-chi ch'ang-shih*); existed from the mid-400s apparently to the beginning of Sui. Also see *liu-ching chi-chiu, wen-hsüeh chi-chiu, hsiao-kuan chi-chiu*. P23.

543 *chì-chó* 輯濯
HAN: **Imperial Oarsman**, subordinates of the Commandant of the Imperial Gardens (*shui-heng tu-wei*) headed by a Director (*ling*), in Later Han also (?) on the staff of the Loyang Market Director (*shih-chang*); presumably managed both cargo and pleasure boats. HB (*ling*): prefect of oarsmen and scullers.

544 *chì-chù àn* 記注案
SUNG: **Records Section**, units in the Secretariat (*chung-shu sheng*) and the Chancellery (*men-hsia sheng*). SP: *service chargé de rédiger le registre des actes*. P19.

545 *chì-chù kuān* 記注官
CH'ING: **Diarist**, duty assignment for Censors (*yü-shih*) and Supervising Censors (*chi-shih-chung*), normally 2 each, one Chinese and one Manchu, to compile the Imperial Diary (*ch'i-chü chu*) under supervision of the Hanlin Academy (*han-lin yüan*). P19, 24.

546 *chì-chù yüàn* 記注院
CHIN: **Institute of Imperial Diarists**, responsible for compilation of the Imperial Diary (*ch'i-chü chu*); established in 1135, staffed by various officials including Generals (*chiang-chün*) as a concurrent duty; in 1190 members of the Remonstrance Bureau (*chien-yüan*) were forbidden to serve; from 1215 Staff Supervisors (*shou-ling kuan*) from the Sec-

retariat (chung-shu sheng) or the Department of State Affairs (shang-shu sheng) were regularly delegated to serve. P24.

547 chì-chuāng k'ù 寄椿庫
SUNG: **Storehouse of Spices and Silks,** a unit of the Court of the Imperial Treasury (t'ai-fu ssu) that brought in revenue by selling state-owned medicinal spices and special silk fabrics; headed by 2 Supervisory Directors (chien-kuan t'i-ling). SP: bureau de vente du musc et de soie.

548 chì-chǔn 騎軍
Cavalry: throughout history a standard military term. See chi-ping. Cf. hsiao-chi.

549 chí-fǎ 畿法
N-S DIV (Chou): **Metropolitan Area Justice Bureau** in the Ministry of Justice (ch'iu-kuan); also title of its senior officials, the **Director,** ranked as a Senior Serviceman (shang-shih; 7a), and the **Vice Director,** ranked as an Ordinary Serviceman (chung-shih; 8a). P13.

550 chí-fǔ 畿輔
Metropolitan Area: throughout history a common reference to the dynastic capital (chi) and its "supporting" environs (fu). In Ming and Ch'ing, equivalent to chih-li. Also see chi-nei, ching-shih.

551 chì-hsiàng 計相
Lit., accounts minister. (1) HAN: **Minister of Finance,** a high-ranking keeper of imperial accounts, apparently appointed only in the earliest Han years; thereafter the term was used unofficially in reference to any official known as a skilled accounts keeper. (2) N-S DIV: **Local Representative** (from small area) or **Territorial Representative** (from larger area), delegated from units of territorial administration to carry annual fiscal reports to the capital; see chi-chieh, ch'ao-chi shih. (3) SUNG: a common variant designation of the **State Finance Commissioner** (san-ssu shih). After early Sung may be encountered as an unofficial reference to any dignitary whose principal charge was in the fiscal realm. SP: commissaire des finances, conseiller des comptes. P6.

552 chí-hsién shū-k'ù 集賢書庫
SUNG: **Library of the Academy of Scholarly Worthies** (see chi-hsien yüan).

553 chí-hsién tièn shū-yüàn 集賢殿書院
Lit., academy in the hall for assembling worthies: **Academy of Scholarly Worthies.** (1) T'ANG: name changed from Academy in the Hall of Elegance and Rectitude (li-cheng tien hsiu-shu yüan) in 725; staffed with Academicians (hsüeh-shih) and other court-patronized litterateurs who engaged in compiling imperially sponsored scholarly works; subordinate to the Secretariat (chung-shu sheng). RR: bibliothèque du palais où on assemble les sages. (2) SUNG: one of the Three Institutes (san kuan) constituting the Academy for the Veneration of Literature (ch'ung-wen yüan); staffed with Grand Academicians (ta hsüeh-shih) whose substantive posts were as Grand Councilors (tsai-hsiang) and other prestigious literati-officials of the central government; c. 980 name changed to chi-hsien yüan shu-k'u; in 1082 was absorbed into the Palace Library (pi-shu sheng). Commonly known in abbreviated forms as chi-hsien tien, chi-hsien yüan. SP: cour où l'on assemble les sages. P23, 25.

554 chí-hsién yüàn 集賢院
Academy of Scholarly Worthies. (1) T'ANG–SUNG: common abbreviation of chi-hsien tien shu-yüan. (2) CHIN:

existed, but responsibilities not clear. (3) YÜAN: staffed with Grand Academicians (ta hsüeh-shih), Academicians (hsüeh-shih), etc.; supervised the School for the Sons of the State (kuo-tzu hsüeh), oversaw the Taoist clergy, tried to entice reclusive scholars into state service; in 1283 merged into the Hanlin and Historiography Academy (han-lin hsüeh-shih yüan chien kuo-shih yüan), then in 1285 restored as an autonomous central government unit. P23, 25.

555 chí-hsüǎn 急選
CH'ING: **Expedited Selection,** part of the personnel appointment process conducted by the Ministry of Personnel (li-pu): the appointment or promotion of officials enjoying special imperial favor or otherwise in special status that entitled them to be considered for the 1st appropriate vacancy; normally conducted in odd months, in contrast to the Regular Selection (ta-hsüan, cheng-hsüan) normally conducted in even months.

556 chí-hsün ch'īng-lì ssū 稽勳清吏司 or **chi-hsün ssu**
MING–CH'ING: **Bureau of Records,** one of 4 principal units in the Ministry of Personnel (li-pu), headed by a Director (lang-chung); responsible for handling merit titles (hsün-kuan), prestige titles (san-kuan), retirements in mourning, etc. BH: record department. P5, 65.

557 chí-ī 疾醫
CHOU: **Royal Physician,** 8 ranked as Ordinary Servicemen (chung-shih), members of the Ministry of State (t'ien-kuan) responsible for looking after the health of the ruler and his ministers, for keeping watch over public health, and for recording and checking all death certificates. CL: médecin pour les maladies simples.

558 chì-ì kuān 計議官
SUNG: **Administrative Clerk,** 4, rank 8a, in the Bureau of Military Affairs (shu-mi yüan); variant designation of kan-pan kuan.

559 chī-í ssū 稽疑司
MING: **Religious Office,** in charge of divination and shamanism, headed by a Director (ling); established in 1384, apparently as an independent central government agency, but soon discontinued. P35.

560 chì-jén 迹人
CHOU: **Tracker,** 4 ranked as Ordinary Servicemen (chung-shih) and 8 as Junior Servicemen (hsia-shih), members of the Ministry of Education (ti-kuan) who were in charge of hunting in the royal hunting preserve. CL: officier des traces.

561 chì-jén 雞人
CHOU: **Master of the Chickens,** one ranked as a Junior Serviceman (hsia-shih), a member of the Ministry of Rites (ch'un-kuan) responsible for providing sacrificial chickens. CL: officier des coqs.

562 chí kōu-kuǎn 籍勾管
SUNG: **Registry Clerk,** apparently unranked, on the staff of a Circuit (lu) Supervisor of Education (t'i-chü hsüeh-shih). P51.

563 chì-kuān 計官
SUNG: **Accounts Clerk,** unranked, in the Palace Administration (tien-chung sheng). SP: fonctionnaire de compte.

564 chí-kuān chǔn 騎官軍
T'ANG: **Army of the Celestial Wolf,** named after a group of stars in the constellation called the Wolf: one of 12 regional supervisory headquarters for militia Garrisons (fu) called the Twelve Armies (shih-erh chün); existed only 620–

623, 625–636. RR: *armée de (la constellation de) la garde montée*. P44.

565 chì-láng 記郎

In Ch'ing and perhaps earlier times, an unofficial reference to **Vice Directors** (*yüan-wai lang*) of Bureaus (*ch'ing-li ssu*) in Ministries (*pu*).

566 chì-lì 計吏

HAN: **Accounts Clerk,** one sent annually to the capital from each Commandery (*chün*) as companion for an Accounts Assistant (*chi-yüan*) delegated to report on local events and fiscal affairs; also called *chi-shih*. Also see *chi-chieh*. HB: official in charge of accounts.

567 chí-lù 棘路

SUI–CH'ING: unofficial reference to the **Court of Judicial Review** (*ta-li ssu*). Also see *chi-shu*.

568 chì-lù chiēh 寄祿階 or **chì-lù kó** 寄祿格

SUNG: **Salary Ranks,** a term referring to the N. Sung system of paying salaries to officials on the basis of their titular positions, whatever their actual assigned functions.

569 chì-lù kuān 寄祿官

(1) SUNG: **Paymaster,** rank not clear, in the Court of the Imperial Clan (*tsung-cheng ssu*) during the early Sung decades, then replaced by a Court Gentleman-consultant (*feng-i lang*). (2) SUNG: **Salary Office,** a term referring to the N. Sung system of paying salaries to officials on the basis of their titular positions, whatever their actual assigned functions; in 1120 the term was made to apply to former prestige titles (*san-kuan*), and thereafter salary offices (with titles different than before) determined officials' salaries but had no direct relation to either titular or functional designations, which increasingly coalesced. P22, 23, 30.

570 chì-mǎ lìng 騎馬令

HAN: **Director of Cavalry Mounts,** one of numerous subordinates of the Chamberlain for the Imperial Stud (*t'ai-p'u*), rank 600 bushels. HB: prefect of the stables for riding horses. P31.

571 chī-mí chōu 羈縻州 or **chī-mí fǔ-chōu** 羈縻府州

T'ANG–SUNG: lit., prefecture under loose rein: **Subordinated Prefecture,** a category of administrative units into which submissive foreign and aboriginal groups were commonly organized to fit into the Chinese governmental hierarchy, usually headed by hereditary native chiefs and subordinated to a Chinese Area Command (*tu-tu fu*). P72.

572 chǐ-nà àn 給納案

SUNG: **Receipts and Payments Section** of the Granaries Bureau (*ts'ang-pu*) in the Ministry of Revenue (*hu-pu*). SP: *service de réceptions et de versements*.

573 chí-nèi 畿內

Metropolitan Area: throughout history a common designation of the dynastic capital and its environs. See *chi-fu*, *ching-shih*.

574 chì-pīng 騎兵

Cavalry or **Cavalryman:** throughout history a standard military term. See *chi-chün*. Cf. *hsiao-chi*.

575 chì-pīng ts'ān-chün shìh 騎兵參軍事

T'ANG: **Administrator for Cavalry,** a subaltern in various military Guard (*wei*) units, including the Sixteen Guards (*shih-liu wei*) at the dynastic capital, rank 8a2; c. 712 the post was reorganized into a Cavalry Section (*chi-ts'ao*) headed by 2 Administrators (*ts'an-chün-shih*). RR: *administrateur (du bureau) des chevaux et des armes*. P43.

576 chì-pīng ts'áo 騎兵曹

Cavalry Section. (1) N-S DIV: one of a fluctuating number of military Sections in transitional status toward becoming a Ministry of War in the developing Department of State Affairs (*shang-shu sheng*), especially in the S. Dynasties; normally headed by a Minister (*shang-shu*) and a Vice Minister (*lang*, *shih-lang*) or Director (*lang-chung*). (2) SUI–T'ANG: an agency in various kinds of military Guard (*wei*) units, e.g., the Sixteen Guards (*shih-liu wei*) at the dynastic capital; headed by an Administrator (*ts'an-chün shih*). Reorganized c. 712 as an Arms Section (*ping-ts'ao*). See *chi-ping ts'an-chün shih*. RR: *bureau des chevaux et des armes*. P12, 43.

577 chì-pù 計部

N-S DIV (Chou): **Ministry of Revenue,** headed by a Grand Master (*ta-fu*); subordinates irregularly included a *hu-pu*, *tu-chih*, *chin-pu*, and *ts'ang-pu*, qq.v. P6.

578 chì-p'ú 祭僕

CHOU: **Sacrificial Aide,** an official of the Ministry of War (*hsia-kuan*) who supervised sacrificial ceremonies conducted by a royal substitute. CL: *assistant des sacrifices*.

579 chí-sài 集賽

YÜAN: **Justiciar,** apparently a collective term for high-ranking Mongols assigned to the High Court of Justice (*ta tsung-cheng fu*) for the purpose of adjudicating disputes among Mongols; defined in some sources by the term *ch'ieh-hsieh*, name of the *kesig* or Imperial Bodyguard, suggesting that they might have been primarily members of the *kesig*, q.v.; the number varied from 13 to 46. P1.

580 chì-shàn 紀善

MING: **Moral Mentor,** one, rank 7a, till 1376, thereafter 2, rank 8a, constituting a Moral Mentors Office (*chi-shan so*) in a Princely Establishment (*wang-fu*). P69.

581 chì-shè 給舍

An abbreviated, combined reference to **Supervising Secretaries** (*chi-shih-chung*) and **Secretariat Drafters** (*chung-shu she-jen*). P19.

582 chì-shěng 計省

SUNG: lit., accounting department: common variant designation of the **State Finance Commission** (*san ssu*); may be encountered in later periods as an unofficial reference to the **Ministry of Revenue** (*hu-pu*).

583 chì-shìh 給事

Lit., to render service. N-S DIV: **Executive Assistant,** prefixed to names of agencies, e.g., *chi-shih pi-shu sheng*, (Executive Assistant in the Palace Library; see *pi-shu sheng*). In pre-Sui Chou, 60 were prescribed with rank as Ordinary Servicemen (*chung-shih*) in the Ministry of State (*t'ien-kuan fu*) to tend (and edit ?) classical and other writings Not to be confused with *chi-shih-chung*, although found in later periods as an abbreviated reference to *chi-chih-chung* (Supervising Secretary). Also cf. *chi-shih-chung chi-shih*. P19.

584 chì-shìh 計使

SUNG: **Commissioner of Accounts,** in 993–994 a reference to all or any of 3 posts: Commissioner of the Left Account (*tso chi-shih*), Commissioner of the Right Account (*yu chi-shih*), and Supreme Commissioner of Accounts (*tsung chi-shih*), in one stage in the development of the State Finance Commission (*san ssu*). SP: *commissaire aux comptes*. P7.

585 chì-shìh 計史

Accounts Clerk. (1) HAN: one sent annually to the dynastic capital from each Commandery (*chün*), as companion for an Accounts Assistant (*chi-yüan*) delegated to report on local events and fiscal affairs; also called *chi-li*. See *chi-chieh*. (2) T'ANG: 4 lowly appointees in the Court of the Imperial Treasury (*t'ai-fu ssu*); 7 also in the Directorate for Imperial Manufactories (*shao-fu chien*), but only from 685 to ç. 705 while the Directorate was called *shang-fang chien*. (3) SUNG: possibly a title used for lowly employees in the State Finance Commission (*san ssu*), but may be encountered as a variant of the homophonous *chi-shih* rendered here as Commissioner of Accounts. P7, 38, 53.

586 *chì-shìh* 記室
Record Keeper. (1) HAN–N-S DIV: a lowly clerical official on the staffs of Han's central government dignitaries called the Three Dukes (*san kung*), in groups each headed by a Clerk (*ling-shih*); after Han found among the central government personnel called Historiographers (*shih-kuan*), also in some Commanderies (*chün*). HB: secretary. P23, 57. (2) 5 DYN–YÜAN: one in each Princely Establishment (*wang-fu*), rank 8b in Sung, 6b in Yüan (2 appointees); also one unranked appointee in Sung's Chief Office of Imperial Clan Affairs (*ta tsung-cheng ssu*). SP: *secrétaire*. P69. (3) MING: found on the staffs of some provincial and prefectural dignitaries. P57.

587 *chì-shìh-chūng* 給事中
(1) CH'IN–N-S DIV: **Palace Steward,** originally an intimate attendant on the Emperor in Ch'in, officiating in a Palace Hall for Personal Service (*chi-shih kung-tien*); in Han became a supplementary honorific designation (*chia-kuan*) for variable numbers of eminent court officials; continued so into the era of N-S Division, sometimes coexisting with the substantive post of the same name rendered here as Supervising Secretary (see below). Since the title literally suggests one who provides service in the palace, it carried the implication that its bearer was a worthy companion and mentor of the Emperor. HB: serving within the palace. (2) N-S DIV–CH'ING: **Supervising Secretary** to 1723, thereafter **Supervising Censor,** officials normally charged to monitor the flow of documents to and from the throne, to return for revision any documents considered improper in form or substance, to check on the implementation of imperial orders, to criticize and propose imperial policies, and sometimes to assist in keeping the Imperial Diary (*ch'i-chü chu*); thus included among those collectively called "speaking officials" (*yen-kuan*), "remonstrance officials" (*chien-kuan*), and "the avenues of criticism" (*yen-lu*). In the era of N-S Division and some later periods, a concurrent duty assignment for men primarily appointed to other offices; but always of relatively high prestige and influence despite relatively low rank status. In Chin (266–420) no fixed number, normally imperial relatives or other noblemen, attached with rank 5 to the Department of Scholarly Counselors (*chi-shu sheng*). In both S. and N. Dynasties, commonly members of the Department of Scholarly Counselors; rank 7 (600 bushels) in Liang and Ch'en, 6b in N. Wei, 6b1 in N. Ch'i. In Sui sometimes called *chi-shih lang*; 20 appointees, in 605 transferred from the Ministry of Personnel (*lì-pu*) to the Chancellery (*men-hsia sheng*) and reduced to 4. Thereafter through Liao and Sung remained members of the Chancellery; 4, rank 5a1 in T'ang; 4, rank 4a in Sung (only concurrent appointments until 1078). In (Jurchen) Chin: one, rank 5b, on the staff of the Court Ceremonial Institute (*hsüan-hui yüan*), perhaps without the traditional "speaking official" functions. In Yüan: 2, rank 4a, attached to the Censorate (*yü-shih t'ai*), deprived of their traditional functions except keeping the Imperial Diary. In Ming and Ch'ing established independently in Six Offices

of Scrutiny (*liu k'o*) paralleling the Six Ministries (*liu pu*), 4 to 10 in each Office, rank fluctuating between 5a and 9a in the earliest Ming years, then 7b to 1729, then 5a; restored to their traditional "speaking officials" functions, especially focusing their attention on the activities of the Six Ministries. In Ming each Office of Scrutiny had an executive staff of one Chief Supervising Secretary (*tu chi-shih-chung*) and one each Left and Right Supervising Secretary (*tso, yu chi-shih-chung*); in Ch'ing each Office had two Seal-holding (*chang-yin*) Supervising Secretaries, one each Manchu and Chinese, as joint executives; and ordinary Supervising Secretary appointments were equally divided between Manchus and Chinese. In 1723 the Offices of Scrutiny were merged into the Censorate (*tu ch'a-yüan*) and made administratively subordinate to its senior officials; hence the suggested change of English rendering to Supervising Censor. See *chung chi-shih-chung, nei chi-shih-chung, feng-po ssu*. RR: *grand secrétaire du département de la chancellerie impériale*. SP: *grand secrétaire ou conseiller politique des projets politiques*. BH: metropolitan censor. P18, 19.

588 *chì-shìh-chūng chì-shìh* 給事中給事
N-S DIV·(N. Wei): **Senior Supervising Secretary,** rank 3b1 till 499; then title apparently changed to *chung chi-shih-chung*, rank 5b; functions and relations with major governmental agencies not clear.

589 *chì-shìh huáng-mén* 給事黃門
(1) HAN: **Palace Attendant:** a eunuch title; also a variant of *huang-men shih-lang* (Gentleman Attendant at the Palace Gate). HB: serving within the yellow gates. (2) N-S DIV–SUI: in alternation with *shih-chung* (Palace Attendants) and usually with the suffix *lang* or *shih-lang*, appointees gradually rose in influence as **Director** of the emerging Chancellery (*men-hsia sheng*), until c. 605 the prefix *chi-shih* was discontinued; see *huang-men shih-lang*. P3. (3) In later periods may be encountered as an unofficial, archaic reference to **Supervising Secretaries** (*chi-shih-chung*). P19.

590 *chì-shìh láng* 給事郎
(1) SUI–T'ANG: **Supervising Secretary,** 4, rank 5b, in the Chancellery (*men-hsia sheng*); in 620 retitled *chi-shih-chung*, q.v. P18, 19. (2) SUI–SUNG: **Gentleman for Service,** a prestige title (*san-kuan*) for officials of rank 8a1. P68.

591 *chì-shìh pěi-yüàn chīh shèng-chǐh t'óu-tzǔ shìh* 給事北院知聖旨頭子事
LIAO: **Handler of Imperial Edicts in the Northern Bureau of Military Affairs,** number and rank not clear. See *shu-mi yüan, pei-mien*. P12.

592 *chì-shìh shè-jén* 給事舍人
N-S DIV–CH'ING (?): contracted reference to **Supervising Secretaries** (*chi-shih-chung*) and **Secretariat Drafters** (*chung-shu she-jen*).

593 *chì-shìh ts'ān-chūn shìh* 記室參軍事 or *chi-shih ts'an-chün*
Secretarial Aide. (1) N-S DIV: number and ranks not clear; throughout the era found on the staffs of Princely Establishments (*wang-fu*) and various military headquarters. (2) T'ANG, SUNG, CHIN: on the staffs of Princely Establishments, 2 in T'ang, thereafter apparently only one; rank 6b1 in T'ang, not clear for Sung, 8a in Chin; from 618 to 626 also briefly established in all units of territorial administration. RR+SP: *administrateur du service des rédactions*. P69.

594 *chì-shìh yèh-chě* 給事謁者
HAN: **Receptionist in Attendance,** a dozen or so, rank 400 bushels, subordinates of the Supervisor of Reception-

ists (*yeh-che p'u-yeh*) on the staff of Later Han's Chamberlain for Attendants (*kuang-lu-hsün*). HB: serving internuncios.

595 *chí-shǔ* 棘署
SUI–CH'ING: lit., office of the jujube tree: an unofficial reference to the **Court of Judicial Review** (*ta-li ssu*), by allusion to a tradition that in high antiquity criminal cases dealt with at the royal court had to be conducted in the presence of eminent officials known collectively as the Three Locust Trees and Nine Jujube Trees (*san huai, chiu chi,* qq.v.).

596 *chí-shū shěng* 集書省
N-S DIV: **Department of Scholarly Counselors,** created in the mid-400s by Sung as an offshoot of and companion agency to the Chancellery (*men-hsia sheng*), with a staff of 4 to 6 Cavalier Attendants-in-ordinary (*san-chi ch'ang-shih*), one of whom was designated head with the title Chancellor (*chi-chiu*); soon other officials were added, notably Supervising Secretaries (*chi-shih-chung*) and Audience Attendants (*feng ch'ao-ching*); men holding the latter title numbered more than 600 by the 480s. The Department's functions were to provide personal attendance for the Emperor, to discuss state policies with him, to compile the Imperial Diary (*ch'i-chü chu*), to offer criticisms and remonstrances, to scrutinize all memorials, and to reject memorials judged to be improper in form or substance. In Liang the agency was considered one of the Five Departments (*wu sheng*) that constituted the top echelon of the central government and was known by the variant name *san-chi sheng*. In N. Wei and N. Ch'i the staff grew into a multitude. Sui abolished the agency, assigning its responsibility for maintaining the Imperial Diary to the Palace Domestic Service (*nei-shih sheng*) and restoring all its other functions to the Chancellery.

597 *chí-ssù* 棘寺
SUI–CH'ING: an unofficial reference to the **Court of Judicial Review** (*ta-li ssu*); also see *chi-shu*.

598 *chì-ssū* 計司
LIAO: **Accounting Commissioner,** responsible under a Regent (*liu-shou*) for all fiscal affairs in the Circuit (*tao*) governed from the Western Capital (*hsi-ching*) near modern Ta-t'ung, Shansi. P49.

599 *chì-ssù kūng-yìng kuān* 祭祀供應官
CH'ING: **Director of Sacrifices** at an Imperial Mausoleum (*ling, ling-ch'in*), rank 6a. BH: commissioner of sacrifices.

600 *chì-sù fáng* 機速房
SUNG: **Office for Emergencies,** an agency created by the Bureau of Military Affairs (*shu-mi yüan*) to help maintain security of the Emperor when he was campaigning. In 1127 superseded by the Imperial Defense Command (*yü-ying ssu*). SP: *chambre du camp impérial*.

601 *chí-tì* 及第
From T'ang on, a term meaning "to have passed" a civil service recruitment examination; in Sung limited to the top 2 of the 5 groups into which successful candidates at the Metropolitan Examination (*sheng-shih*) were grouped, hence suggesting **passed with distinction.** See *chin-shih chi-ti.*

602 *chí-t'ién* 籍田
This term designates the **sacred fields** outside the dynastic capital where Emperors traditionally performed ceremonial plowing at appropriate seasons. In Han there was a Director of the Sacred Fields (*chi-tien ling*). In N. Wei there was a Sacred Fields Office (*chi-t'ien shu*). In Sung the Han title Director of the Sacred Fields was revived for an official of the Court of Imperial Sacrifices (*t'ai-ch'ang ssu*), rank 9a. HB (*ling*): prefect of the sacred field. SP (*ling*): *chef de la cérémonie du labourage*.

603 *chí-t'íng* 棘庭
SUI–CH'ING: an unofficial reference to the **Court of Judicial Review** (*ta-li ssu*); also see *chi-shu*.

604 *chí-ts'áo* 集曹
HAN: **Accounts Section,** one of numerous clerical units on the staff of the Counselor-in-chief (*ch'eng-hsiang*), in Commanderies (*chün*), and in Districts (*hsien*); each headed by an Administrator (*yüan-shih*). HB: bureau of gathering.

605 *chì-ts'áo* 騎曹
SUI–T'ANG: **Mounts Section,** a common unit in all military Guard (*wei*) units—imperial Guards, Guards in the service of the Heir Apparent, and Guards assigned to Princely Establishments (*wang-fu*); normally headed by an Administrator (*ts'an-chün shih*). RR: *service des chevaux*.

606 *chì tū-wèi* 騎都尉
Commandant of Cavalry. (1) HAN–N-S DIV: a functional military title from the time of Han Wu-ti (r. 141–87 B.C.), apparently granted on an ad hoc basis. HB: chief commandant of cavalry. (2) T'ANG–MING: a merit title (*hsün*) awarded to government personnel of ranks 5a and 5b in T'ang, 5b in Sung and Chin, 4b in Yüan; in Ming explicitly restricted to rank 4b military officers. RR+SP: *directeur général de la cavalerie*. (3) CH'ING: 7th highest of 9 ranks of non-imperial nobility (*chüeh*), often inheritable, sometimes awarded posthumously. See *shang chi tu-wei, chüeh-yin*. P65.

607 *chì-wèi* 騎尉
Commandant of Cavalry: occasionally occurs, usually with a descriptive prefix, as the title of an active military officer. In addition, also usually with laudatory or descriptive prefixes, occurs from Sui on as a prestige title (*san-kuan, feng-tseng*), a merit title (*hsün*), or a rank of nobility (*chüeh*) awarded to military officers. P26, 65.

608 *chì-wèi fǔ* 騎尉府
SUI–T'ANG: apparently a scribal error for *hsiao-wei fu* (**Courageous Guard**), q.v.

609 *chì-yùng k'ù* 冀用庫
YÜAN: **Saddlery Storehouse,** a unit of the Household Service for the Heir Apparent (*ch'u-cheng yüan*), headed by a Superintendent (*t'i-tien*), rank not clear. P26.

610 *chì-yüàn* 計掾
HAN: **Accounts Assistant,** one sent annually to the dynastic capital from each Commandery (*chün*), together with one Accounts Clerk (*chi-shih* or *chi-li*), to report on local events and fiscal affairs. See *chi-chieh* and *ch'ao-chi shih*. P53.

611 *ch'í* 旗
CH'ING: **Banner,** the basic social-political-military organization of the Manchu people, and the core of hereditary soldiers in the imperial Ch'ing military organization. The Manchus originally organized themselves into 4 Banners named after the colors of their flags: yellow (*huang*), white (*po*), red (*hung*), and blue (*lan*). These Plain (*cheng*) Banners were early doubled by the addition of 4 Bordered (*hsiang*) counterparts. The forces under the Emperor's direct command were called the Three Superior Banners (*shang san ch'i*): the Plain Yellow, the Bordered Yellow, and the Plain White Banners; the others, called the Five Lesser Banners (*hsia wu ch'i*), were assigned to Imperial Princes

(*ch'in-wang*). Then in 1635 submissive Mongols and Chinese were organized into 8 similarly designated Mongol Banners (*meng-ku ch'i*) and 8 similarly designated Chinese Banners (*han-chün ch'i*). The number of Mongol Banners increased greatly later in the dynasty, as more Mongol groups submitted to Ch'ing authority. Each Banner theoretically consisted of 7,500 soldiers led by a Commander-in-chief (*tu-t'ung*) and 2 Vice Commanders-in-chief (*fu tu-t'ung*). See *ku-shan, pa ch'i*. P44.

612 *ch'ĭ* 起

Recall (to active service): from T'ang or perhaps an earlier time, a term indicating that someone of official status and with a record of prior service, having been out of active service in formal mourning for a parent or sometimes for other reasons, was recalled to service; often a procedure relied on by Emperors to exempt important or specially favored officials from the normal obligation imposed by the Confucian tradition to withdraw from active duty in mourning for 27 months. In turbulent times such recall could lead to the official's being denounced for a violation of moral standards. The term could be expanded with particularizing suffixes in such forms as *ch'i-fu* (recall and restore to the official's most recent post and rank) and *ch'i-chia* (recall and promote; see under *chia*, "to be promoted to").

613 *ch'ĭ* 騎

See under *chì*, the romanization used here except where the word is used in a clearly verbal sense, "to ride."

614 *ch'ĭ-chí ssū* 旗籍司

CH'ING: **Inner Mongolian Bureau**, one of 6 Bureaus in the Court of Colonial Affairs (*li-fan yüan*), headed by 3 Directors (*lang-chung*), 2 Manchus and one Mongol; responsible for supervising the Mongol Banners of Inner Mongolia. BH: department of the inner Mongols. P17.

615 *ch'ĭ-chì yüàn* 騏驥院

SUNG: **Mounts Service**, a unit in the Court of the Imperial Stud (*t'ai-p'u ssu*), headed by 2 Supervisors (*chien-kuan*) of the military services or a Commissioner (*shih*), rank 7a. SP: *cour des chevaux*. P31.

616 *ch'ĭ-ch'īng* 七卿

MING: **Seven Chief Ministers**, collective designation of the heads of the Six Ministries (*liu pu*) and the Censorate (*tu ch'a-yüan*), who were often called on to take part in special court deliberations. Also see *chiu ch'ing*.

617 *ch'ĭ-chū chù* 起居注

Imperial Diary, a daily record of the Emperor's activities and pronouncements, from which official histories were compiled; maintained erratically throughout history, apparently from beginnings in Han. The term may be encountered as if it were the title **Imperial Diarist**, but such usage was not normal. In early Ming 2 such officials were appointed in 1364, rank 4a, promoted to 5a in 1367, abolished c. 1368, reappointed 1381, rank 7a, again abolished before 1398; reappointments were proposed c. 1573, but the Imperial Diary was resurrected instead by members of the Hanlin Academy (*han-lin yüan*). P24.

618 *ch'ĭ-chū chù kuăn* 起居注館

CH'ING: **Imperial Diary Office**, a subsection of the Hanlin Academy (*han-lin yüan*) established in the K'ang-hsi reign (1662–1722) to maintain the Imperial Diary (*ch'i-chü chu*); staffed principally by 20 Imperial Diarists (*jih-chiang ch'i-chü chu kuan*). BH: office for keeping a diary of the emperor's movements. P24.

619 *ch'ĭ-chū chù pŭ-ch'üèh* 起居注補闕

YÜAN: **Imperial Diarist and Rectifier of Omissions**, one (?) each of Left and Right established in 1269 to keep records of all memorials submitted to the throne; in 1278 retitled Imperial Attendants of Left and Right and Concurrent Compilers of the Imperial Diary (*tso yu shih-i feng-yü chien hsiu ch'i-chü chu*). P24.

620 *ch'ĭ-chū láng* 起居郎

T'ANG–SUNG, LIAO: **Imperial Diarist**, staff members of the Chancellery (*men-hsia sheng*) charged with recording the activities of the Emperor for inclusion in the Imperial Diary (*ch'i-chü chu*); 2 in T'ang, otherwise numbers not clear; rank 6b1 in T'ang, 6b in Sung. Also see *lang she-jen*. RR+SP: *secrétaire chargé de noter les faits et gestes de l'empereur*. P19, 23, 24.

621 *ch'ĭ-chū lĭng-shĭh* 起居令史

Assistant Diarist. (1) N-S DIV (N. Wei): number not clear, rank 7b1; worked on materials for the Imperial Diary (*ch'i-chü chu*), apparently under 2 Imperial Diarists (*hsiu ch'i-chü chu*) appointed to concurrent service while holding primary posts of other sorts. (2) T'ANG: 3, rank not clear, apparently assistants to the Imperial Diarists (*ch'i-chü lang*) on the staff of the Chancellery (*men-hsia sheng*). P24.

622 *ch'ĭ-chū shè-jén* 起居舍人

SUI–SUNG: **Imperial Diarist**, 2 first appointed c. 605 in the Palace Domestic Service (*nei-shih sheng*); abolished in 628, reappointed in 659 in the Secretariat (*chung-shu sheng*), rank 6b1, sharing the duty of recording the Emperor's activities for inclusion in the Imperial Diary (*ch'i-chü chu*) with the Imperial Diarists called *ch'i-chü lang* on the staff of the Chancellery (*men-hsia sheng*); rank 6b in Sung; in Liao constituted an Imperial Diary Office (*ch'i-chü she-jen yüan*) in the Chancellery. Also see *lang she-jen*. RR+SP: *fonctionnaire chargé de noter les faits et gestes de l'empereur*.

623 *ch'ĭ-chū shĕng* 起居省

N-S DIV (N. Ch'i): **Imperial Diary Office**, staffed with a Cavalier Attendant-in-ordinary (*san-chi ch'ang-shih*), a Cavalier Attendant (*san-chi shih-lang*), etc., and with concurrent appointees primarily serving in other posts; responsible for preparing the Imperial Diary (*ch'i-chü chu*); subordinate to the Department of Scholarly Counselors (*chi-shu sheng*). P24.

624 *ch'ĭ-chū yüàn* 起居院

SUNG: **Imperial Diary Office**, apparently an autonomous agency staffed with officials who were primarily members of the Three Academies (*san kuan*), charged with compiling the Imperial Diary (*ch'i-chü chu*) until 1071; then the agency seems to have disappeared, replaced by a group of remonstrance officials (*chien-kuan*) serving as compilers. Also see *ch'i-chü she-jen*. SP: *cour impériale chargée de noter les faits et gestes de l'empereur*. P24.

625 *ch'ĭ-fù* 坼父 or 祈父

CHOU: lit., head of the royal domain or of the frontier: variant of *ssu-ma* (**Minister of War**).

626 *ch'ĭ-fù* 起復

Recall and Restore (to previously occupied post): from T'ang or perhaps an earlier time, a term indicating that someone of official status and with a record of prior service, having been out of active service in formal mourning for a parent or sometimes other reasons, was recalled to service and restored to his most recent post and rank. See *ch'i* (Recall).

627 *ch'ǐ-hsīn láng* 啓心郎

CH'ING: (1) lit., gentleman who opens up his heart or speaks his mind: an unofficial reference to a **Vice Director** (*tsung-cheng*) **of the Court of the Imperial Clan** (*tsung-jen fu*). (2) **Clerk**, variable numbers of low-ranking officials in the early Ch'ing Ministry of Personnel (*li-pu*) and other agencies; discontinued in 1658. P5, 6.

628 *ch'í-jén* 饎人

CHOU: **Cereals Chef**, 2 eunuch members of the Ministry of Education (*ti-kuan*), responsible for preparing grains for use in sacrificial ceremonies and in the royal household. See *nü-ch'i*. CL: *cuiseur de grains*.

629 *ch'í-mén láng* 期門郎

HAN: **Gate Guardsman**, as many as 1,000 Court Gentlemen (*lang*) led by a Supervisor (*p'u-yeh*) ranked at 1,000 bushels, participants in policing the palace under the control of the Chamberlain for Attendants (*lang-chung ling*); may have been members of the ordinary soldiery of the Southern Army (*nan-chün*). From A.D. 1, except intermittently in Later Han, retitled Gentlemen Brave As Tigers (*hu-pen lang;* see under *hu-pen*). HB: attendant at the gates.

630 *ch'í-p'ái kuān* 旗牌官

MING–CH'ING: lit., official with a bannered warrant: **Imperial Agent**, an unofficial generic reference to such specially delegated territorial authorities as *hsün-fu* (Grand Coordinator, Provincial Governor) and *tsung-tu* (Supreme Commander, Governor-general), who were accompanied with banners inscribed with the character *ling* (Director, etc.), signifying "by (imperial) command."

631 *ch'í-pèi k'ù* 器備庫

YÜAN: **Storehouse for Precious Valuables**, a rank 5b agency responsible for gold and silver objects in the imperial palace, subordinate to the Palace Maintenance Office (*hsiu-nei ssu*) of the Directorate of the Imperial Treasury (*t'ai-fu chien*); created in 1270 by retitling of the Service of the Imperial Ornaments (*yü-yung ch'i-wu chü*). P38.

632 *ch'í-p'ǐn àn* 七品案

SUNG: **Section for the Seventh Rank**, a subsection of the Ministry of Personnel's (*li-pu*) Bureau of Evaluations (*k'ao-kung ssu*); in charge of dealing with the cases of rank 7 officials in the Civil Appointments Process (*tso-hsüan;* see under *hsüan*). SP: *service des fonctionnaires de 7ème rang.*

633 *ch'í-pīng ts'áo* 七兵曹 or *ch'i-ping*

N-S DIV (N. Wei): lit., section for the 7 (categories of) troops. (1) **Ministry of War**, one of the major units under the developing Department of State Affairs (*shang-shu sheng*); headed by a Minister (*shang-shu*), rank 3a; supervised 7 Sections (*ts'ao*) that were evolving toward what would later be called Bureaus (*ssu, ch'ing-li ssu*): a Headquarters Section (also *ch'i-ping*) and Sections for Left Inner Troops (*tso chung-ping*), for Right Inner Troops (*yu chung-ping*), for Left Outer Troops (*tso wai-ping*), for Right Outer Troops (*yu wai-ping*), for Cavalry (*chi-ping*), and for the Capital (*tu-ping*). Cf. *wu-ping ts'ao, ping-pu*. P12. (2) **Headquarters Section** in the Ministry of War described above, headed by a Director (*lang-chung*), rank 6a2. P12.

634 *ch'í pó-shìh* 碁博士

T'ANG: **Erudite of Chess**, a specialist in the Chinese version of chess commonly called *hsiang-ch'i;* one of 18 Palace Erudites (*nei-chiao po-shih*) on the staff of the Palace Institute of Literature (*nei wen-hsüeh kuan*), where palace women were educated; from c. 741 a eunuch post. RR: *maître de jeu d'échecs*.

635 *ch'í-pù ts'áo* 起部曹 or *ch'i-pu*

(1) N-S DIV: **Section for Public Construction** or **Ministry of Public Construction**, in charge of building palaces and temples, an agency in the Department of State Affairs (*shang-shu sheng*) that was in transitional status; as a Ministry headed by a Minister (*shang-shu*) and a Vice Minister (*lang*), as a Section headed by a Director (*lang* or *lang-chung*); in Ch'i and Sung a Section under an intermediary Ministry of Revenue (*tu-chih*), in N. Ch'i a Section under an intermediary Ministry of Rites (*tz'u-pu*). (2) SUI: **Construction Bureau** in the Ministry of Works (*kung-pu*), headed by a Director (*lang*). (3) T'ANG: until 620 the name of the whole **Ministry of Works** (*kung-pu*). RR: *bureau des travaux publics*. P6, 14, 21, 30.

636 *ch'í-pù wèi* 七部尉

N-S DIV (N. Ch'i): **Commandant of the Capital Patrol**, divided into 7 Troops (*pu*), charged with maintaining peace and order in the streets of the dynastic capital. Cf. *liu-pu wei, wei wu-pu, ching-t'u wei*. P20.

637 *ch'í-p'ú* 齊僕

CHOU: **Ceremonial Charioteer**, 2 ranked as Ordinary Grand Masters (*chung ta-fu*), members of the Ministry of War (*hsia-kuan*), drivers of a gilded chariot used by the ruler in receptions for foreign visitors. CL: *conducteur du char d'apparat*.

638 *ch'í-shǒu wèi* 旗手衛

CH'ING: **Standard-bearer Guard**, one prefixed Left and one prefixed Right in the Rear Subsection (*hou-so*) of the Imperial Procession Guard (*luan-i wei*), each headed by a Director (*chang-yin kuan-chün shih*), rank 4a. BH: standard-bearer section. P42.

639 *ch'í-ts'áo* 起曹

SUI: variant of *kung-pu* (**Ministry of Works**); also see *ch'i-pu*.

640 *ch'ī tzǔ* 七子

HAN: lit. meaning not clear: **Lady**, designation of a category of palace women with rank =800 bushels. HB: seventh rank lady.

641 *ch'ì-wù chǘ* 器物局

YÜAN: **Service of the Imperial Utensils**, headed by a Commissioner-in-chief (*ta-shih*), rank 5b; responsible for the manufacture and maintenance of various ornamental goods, apparently mostly of iron; subordinate to the Palace Maintenance Office (*hsiu-nei ssu*) of the Directorate of the Imperial Treasury (*t'ai-fu chien*); created in 1270 when the former Service of the Imperial Ornaments (*yü-yung ch'i-wu chü*) was divided into 2 agencies, the other being the Storehouse for Precious Valuables (*ch'i-pei k'u*). P38, 49.

642 *ch'ī-yíng* 七營

T'ANG: **Seven Encampments**, from 627 the capital bases among which were distributed members of the Imperial Army of the Original Followers (*yüan-ts'ung chin-chün*); also known as the Seven Emcampments of the Northern Command (*pei-ya ch'i ying;* see under *pei-ya*). RR: *sept camps des "casernes du nord."*

643 *ch'í-yù* 齊右

CHOU: **Assistant Ceremonial Charioteer**, 2 ranked as Junior Grand Masters (*hsia ta-fu*), members of the Ministry of War (*hsia-kuan*) who participated in various sacrifices and ceremonial receptions. CL: *hommes de droite du char d'apparat*.

644 *ch'í-yù* 騎尉

See under the romanization *chi-wei*.

645 ch'ĭ-yüán chiēn 漆園監

T'ANG: **Directorate for the Temple to Chuang-tzu**, established for a short time beginning in 675 by the Office of Taoist Affairs (ch'ung-hsüan shu), a unit in the Court of the Imperial Clan (tsung-cheng ssu); apparently located at Ch'i-yüan in modern Shantung, traditionally associated with the ancient Taoist sage.

646 ch'ĭ-yüán k'ù 綺源庫

YÜAN: see wan-i ch'i-yüan k'u (**Imperial Cloth Vault**).

647 chiǎ 假

A term literally suggesting "false" or "simulated" but as a prefix to titles not normally used in that derogatory sense. (1) CH'IN–SUNG: **Acting**, as a prefix to a title suggesting that an official was serving in another's role temporarily for special reasons, not in a probationary status, and often with the sense that the acting appointee had special limitations on his authority or had specially augmented authority; see chia-chieh. (2) N-S DIV: **Honorary**, as a prefix to a title of nobility indicating that the status was not inheritable; as a prefix to an official title indicating that the appointee had no authority normally associated with the title. E.g., persons who made substantial contributions to the government were sometimes made honorary nobles, and respectable commoners on attaining advanced age might be named Honorary District Magistrates (hsien-ling) or even Commandery Governors (chün-shou). P50.

648 chiā 加

(1) Sometimes used as a verb meaning "to be promoted to." (2) Probably more often, at least through T'ang times, used in the sense of "added" preceding a title or other designation granted someone in addition to his principal substantive post, sometimes an additional substantive post but sometimes an honorific designation; hence, according to circumstances, meaning **Concurrent** or **Honorific**. See chia-kuan.

649 chiā 家

CHOU: **Administrative Region**, designation of those Regions (kuo) into which the royal domain was divided that were administered by official delegates from the court, differentiating them from those Regions that were hereditary fiefs of members of the royal family, called Inherited Regions (tu). Each Administrative Region was supervised by 2 Justiciars of the Administrative Region (chia-shih), ranking as Ordinary Servicemen (chung-shih), who reported to Justiciars of the Domain (fang-shih) in the Ministry of Justice (ch'iu-kuan). Cf. tu-shih. CL: domaine affecté.

650 chiǎ 甲

(1) An ordinal symbol indicating the **first** in a (usually short) series of things. (2) SUNG, MING–CH'ING: **Tithing**, a basic unit of organization among the people at the sub-District (hsien) level for rudimentary self-government purposes, led by a Tithing Chief (chia-t'ou) or Tithing Head (chia-chang) chosen on a rotational basis from among the well-to-do households of each group. In Sung Tithings numbered from 10 to 30 households apiece; in Ming and Ch'ing each theoretically numbered 10 households. See li-chia, pao-chia. (3) SUNG–CH'ING: groups or categories to which passers of the Metropolitan Examination (sheng-shih, hui-shih) in the civil service recruitment system were assigned on the basis of their excellence. (4) YÜAN: **Squad**, the basic unit in Mongol military organization, consisting normally of 10 soldiers under a Squad Commander (chia-chang); also called p'ài.

651 chiǎ-chǎng 甲長

(1) YÜAN: **Squad Commander**, leader of the basic unit of Mongol military organization, a Squad (chia) of 10 men. (2) **Tithing Chief**, leader of a rudimentary self-government organization at the sub-District (hsien) level, a Tithing (chia) theoretically consisting of 10 neighboring households.

652 chiǎ-chàng k'ù 甲仗庫

SUNG: **Armory**, storage depots for armor and arms in certain areas. SP: magasin des armes.

653 chiā-chèng chūng-shìh 嘉正中士

MING: lit., ordinary serviceman for admirable governance: an archaic substitute for the title chi-shih-chung (**Supervising Secretary**) used during the Chien-wen era (1399–1402). P68.

654 chiā-ch'éng 家丞

HAN: **Household Aide**, an assistant to the Administrator (hsiang) of a Princedom (wang-kuo) or a Marquisate (hou-kuo), theoretically one for every 1,000 households in the jurisdiction. HB: assistant of the household. P69.

655 chiǎ-chiéh 假節

N-S DIV: lit., with a warrant to represent (the Emperor)(?): **Commissioned with a Warrant**, the least prestigious of 3 prefixes appended to the titles of such territorial magnates as Area Commanders-in-chief (tu-tu or tsung-kuan), in effect giving them viceregal authority over all governmental agencies in their jurisdictions. Such commissioners commonly had authority to put to death any non-official who clearly violated military laws, whereas those designated Commissioned with Special Powers (ch'ih-chieh) could put to death any non-official on any pretext, and those designated Commissioned with Extraordinary Powers (shih ch'ih-chieh) could put to death anyone up to the status of officials with rank of 2,000 bushels. P50.

656 chiā-chíh 加職

T'ANG: **Supplemental Assignment**, carrying responsibilities over and above the functions associated with one's regular title, granted as a sign of special favor or trust; e.g., the designation p'ing-chang shih (Manager of Affairs), which entitled one to serve as a Grand Councilor (tsai-hsiang). Cf. chia-kuan.

657 chiǎ-fāng shǔ 甲坊署

T'ANG: **Swords Office**, a unit in the Directorate for Armaments (chün-ch'i chien) in charge of the manufacture of swords, armor, helmets, etc.; headed by a Director (ling), rank 8a2. Until 632 called chia-k'ai shu. Also see nu-fang shu. RR: office de l'atelier des cuirasses.

658 chiǎ-hòu 假候

HAN: **District Commandant**, in Later Han the head of local self-defense forces in an i (Fief, i.e., District, hsien?), controlling 110 (?) Aggregations (lien) each combining the fighting men of 4 Villages (li); the sources are not wholly clear. HB: acting captain.

659 chià-hsiàng 駕相

MING: **Imperial Carriageman**, unofficial reference to intimates of the Emperor, apparently especially to members of the Imperial Bodyguard (chin i wei).

660 chiā-ì tà-fū 嘉議大夫

(1) CHIN–MING: **Grand Master for Excellent Counsel**, a prestige title (san-kuan) for officials of rank 4a2 in Chin, 3a in Yüan and Ming. P68. (2) YÜAN: also an unofficial reference to the **Minister of Rites** (lǐ-pu shang-shu).

661 *chiā-jén-tzŭ* 家人子
HAN: **Woman of the Household,** a category of unranked palace women selected from reputable commoner families, differentiated as Senior (*shang*) and Ordinary (*chung*); also the general designation of wives and concubines of the eldest son of the Heir Apparent.

662 *chiă-k'ăi shŭ* 甲鎧署
T'ANG: until 632 the designation of the **Swords Office** (*chia-fang shu*).

663 *chià-kó k'ù* 架閣庫
SUNG–YÜAN: **Archives** found in the Sung Secretariat (*chung-shu sheng*), the Chin Department of State Affairs (*shang-shu sheng*), the Yüan Secretariat and Censorate (*yü-shih t'ai*), etc.; staffed with Archivists called *chia-ko kuan, wen-tzu, kuan-kou* (rank 8a in Chin and Yüan), etc. P18, 52.

664 *chià-kó kuān* 架閣官
Archivist: from Sung on, found in many agencies; also an unofficial reference to officials performing similar functions but with different titles, e.g., *tien-chi*. SP: *conservateur des archives*. P3.

665 *chiă-k'ù* 甲庫
(1) **Number One Storehouse:** may be encountered in many periods as the designation of one in a series of storehouses that were serially numbered by the Chinese "stems" *chia, i, ping, ting,* etc. (2) T'ANG–SUNG: **Archive of Personnel Records** called *chia,* a unit in the Chancellery (*men-hsia sheng*) and some Ministries (*pu*) of the Department of State Affairs (*shang-shu sheng*), normally headed by sub-official functionaries serving as Directors (*ling-shih*); in Sung one or more units in the Ministry of Personnel (*li-pu*), sometimes called *chia-k'u an.* RR: *archives*. SP: *bureau d'archives, service des archives.* (3) SUNG: **Armory,** a storehouse of military gear established at the headquarters of each Prefecture (*chou*); S. Sung also had an Imperial Armory (*yü-ch'ien chia-k'u*) where military gear and records were stored. (4) CH'ING: **Armory,** a unit of the Court of Imperial Armaments (*wu-pei yüan*) responsible for maintaining armor, weapons, flags, etc., required by the Emperor and his entourage.

666 *chiā-kuān* 加官
Additional Office, an appointment supplementing one's original, regular status, used primarily from Han through T'ang times; in Han most often denoted an honorific title granted in recognition of special merit without imposing any particular new responsibilities but sometimes conferring new privileges such as the right to attend court audiences; in T'ang most often denoted a substantive, functional post held concurrently in addition to one's regular post, usually conferring both new responsibilities and new privileges. P23.

667 *chiă-lă* 甲喇
CH'ING: **Regiment,** Chinese transliteration of the Manchu word *chalan;* created in 1615 as a group of 5 (later 2 to 5) Companies (*niru;* see *niu-lu*) in the development of the dynasty's Banner (*ch'i*) system; 5 Regiments constituted one Banner. Each Regiment was headed by a Regimental Commander (*chia-la o-chen,* in 1634 changed to *chia-la chang-ching*), translated into Chinese as *ts'an-ling,* also *hsiao-chi ts'an-ling,* qq.v. Also see *pa ch'i, o-chen, chang-ching.* BH: chalan or sub-division. P44.

668 *chiā-lì* 家吏
T'ANG: **Domestic Servant,** 2, rank 7a2, in each Princely

Administration (*wang-fu*); 2, unranked, in the household of each Princess (*kung-chu*). P69.

669 *chiā-lìng* 家令
Household Provisioner, in general charge of provisions, often also with some disciplinary authority, normally in the household of an Heir Apparent, sometimes also in that of a Princess (*kung-chu*). (1) CH'IN–N-S DIV: often subordinate to a Supervisor of the Household (*chan-shih*); rank from 300 to 1,000 bushels in Han, thereafter rank normally in the 7, 8, or 9 ranges. HB: prefect of the household. (2) SUI: one subordinate to the Supervisor of the Household of the Heir Apparent (*chan-shih*), after 605 retitled *ssu-fu ling;* one in the household of each Princess, rank 9a. (3) T'ANG: head of the Household Provisioner's Court (*chia-ling ssu*) in the Household Administration of the Heir Apparent (*chan-shih fu*), rank 4b1. RR: *chef de la cour du service domestique.* (4) SUNG, LIAO, CHIN: member(s) of the household of the Heir Apparent, rank not clear. SP: *maître de service du palais.* (5) YÜAN: head of the Household Provisioner's Office (*chia-ling ssu* or *chia-ssu*) in the household of the Heir Apparent; 2 appointees, rank not clear. (6) MING: head, rank 7a, of an Office of Domestic Affairs (*chia-nei ssu,* then *chung-shih ssu*) in the household of each Princess. Often occurs with the prefix *t'ai-tzu* (Heir Apparent). P26, 69.

670 *chiā-mă lìng* 家馬令
HAN: **Director of the Imperial Mares,** one of the numerous subordinates of the Chamberlain for the Imperial Stud (*t'ai-p'u*), rank 600 bushels; in 104 B.C. retitled *t'ung-ma ling.* HB: prefect of the stables for the imperial household mares. P31.

671 *chiā-nèi ssū* 家內司
MING: **Office of Domestic Affairs** in the household of each Princess (*kung-chu*), headed by a Household Provisioner (*chia-ling*); retitled *chung-shih ssu* in 1390. P69.

672 *chiă-nŭ fāng shŭ* 甲弩坊署
SUNG: **Crossbows Office,** headed by a Director (*ling*), rank not clear; apparently a unit in the Directorate for Armaments (*chün-ch'i chien*). SP: *office de l'atelier des arbalètes.*

673 *chiă-păng* 甲榜
Lit., list no. 1: in Ch'ing and perhaps earlier times referred to the Metropolitan Examination (*hui-shih*) pass-list and, indirectly, anyone who became a **Metropolitan Graduate** (*chin-shih*). Cf. *i-pang.*

674 *chiā-pīng* 家兵
Personal Troops, from antiquity, designation of irregular soldiers (or at times regular soldiers or militiamen drawn out of their regular units) recruited to serve as a private army for defense of a locality or a wealthy household in a time of troubles; usually considered a loyal supplement to beleaguered Regular Troops (*kuan-ping*) of the existing government, not an adversary. Commonly prefixed with the surname of the organizer and leader; e.g., the Chang (family) Troops (*chang-chia ping*). See *i-ping* (Patriotic Soldiers), *pu-ch'ü.*

675 *chià-pù* 稼部
Lit., ministry of agriculture; a common unofficial reference to the **Ministry of Revenue** (*hu-pu*).

676 *chià-pù* 駕部
(1) N-S DIV: **Ministry of War,** headed by a Minister (*shang-shu*), a unit in the Department of State Affairs (*shang-shu sheng*) in Chin only till the 280s, then briefly again in N.

Wei from 453. (2) N-S DIV: **Section for Communications and Horse-breeding** (most often *chia-pu ts'ao*), with a Director (*lang*); a unit in the Ministry of War (*wu-ping*) in San-kuo Wei and Chin from the 280s; with a Director (*lang-chung*) subordinate to the Left Minister of Revenue (*tso min shang-shu*) in Sung and S. Ch'i; with a Director (*shih-lang*) subordinate to the Minister of War (*wu-ping shang-shu*) in Liang and Ch'en; with a Director (*lang-chung*) subordinate to the Minister of Palace Affairs (*tien-chung shang-shu*) in N. Wei. (3) N-S DIV (Chou): **Bureau of Equipment** in the Ministry of War (*hsia-kuan*; also the title of its **Director**, ranked as an Ordinary Grand Master (*chung ta-fu*; 5a). (4) SUI–MING: **Bureau of Equipment,** a top-echelon unit in the Ministry of War (*ping-pu*); called *chia-pu ssu* (Court) in Sui, with a Director (*lang*); thereafter with a Director (*lang-chung*), rank 5b in T'ang, 6b in Sung; existed in Ming only from 1373 to 1396, then retitled *ch'e-chia ch'ing-li ssu,* q.v. RR: *bureau des équipages militaires.* P6, 12, 27.

677 *chiǎ-shìh* 假士
HAN: **Village Commandant,** in Later Han the head of a 10-man self-defense force in a rural Village (*li*), 4 of which combined into a unit called an Aggregation (*lien*) under an Aggregation Commandant (*chia-wu*). Also see *chia-hou.*

678 *chiā-shìh* 家士
CHOU: (1) **Household Serviceman,** a categorical reference to warrior-officials serving at the courts of feudal domains (*kuo*). (2) **Justiciar of the Administrative Region,** 2 ranked as Ordinary Servicemen (*chung-shih*) responsible for judicial and penal administration in each Administrative Region (*chia*); probably under the supervision of Justiciars of the Domain (*fang-shih*) in the Ministry of Justice (*ch'iu-kuan*), but possibly together with Justiciars of the Inherited Regions (*tu-shih*) known generically as Justiciars of the Domain. CL: *prévôts de justice des domaines affectés.*

679 *chiā-shìh* 駕士
T'ANG: **Coachman,** 140 authorized for the Livery Service for the Empress (*nei-p'u chü*), a unit in the Palace Domestic Service (*nei-shih sheng*). RR: *cocher.*

680 *chiǎ-shǒu* 甲首
MING–CH'ING: **Tithing Chief,** the rotating designated leader of a community of 10 households (*chia*) in the officially sponsored self-government system below the District (*hsien*) level. See *li-chia, pao-chia.*

681 *chiā-shū shǔ* 嘉蔬署
MING: **Office of Vegetables,** one of 4 subordinate Offices (*shu*) in the Directorate of Imperial Parks (*shang-lin yüan-chien*); headed by a Manager (*tien-shu*), rank 7a.

682 *chiā ssū-mǎ* 家司馬
CHOU: **Commandant of an Administrative Region** (see *chia*), an area in the royal domain administered by officials of the central government rather than an Inherited Region (*tu*) serving as the fief of a member of the royal family; no specific numbers or ranks, but responsible to the Ministry of War (*hsia-kuan*). CL: *commandant des chevaux, chef militaire dans un domain affecté aux offices.*

683 *chiǎ-t'óu* 甲頭
SUNG: **Tithing Chief,** the rotating designated leader of a community of from 10 to 30 households (*chia*) in the officially sponsored self-government system below the District (*hsien*) level.

684 *chiǎ-tsò* 假佐
(1) May be encountered in the sense of **Acting Assistant.** (2) HAN: **Clerical Aide,** 30 on the staff of the Chamberlain

for Law Enforcement (*t'ing-wei*); others normally on the staffs of Regional Inspectors (*tz'u-shih*). HB: acting accessory. P22, 52.

685 *chiǎ-tsú* 甲卒
HAN: **Militiaman,** generic reference in Former Han to males eligible for military service, who were expected to undergo training for one month every year and be available for active duty in emergencies. HB: militia.

686 *chiā tsūng-jén* 家宗人
CHOU: **Household Sacrificer,** numbers and ranks variable, members of the Ministry of Rites (*ch'un-kuan*) who assisted Ritualists of the Inherited Regions (*tu tsung-jen*) in religious ceremonies at the courts of feudal domains. CL: *officiers des cérémonies sacrées dans les domaines affectés.*

687 *chiǎ-wǔ* 假伍 or 假五
Aggregation Commandant, in Later Han the head of a local self-defense force called an Aggregation (*lien*), combining the fighting men of 4 neighboring Villages (*li*), each contingent led by a Village Commandant (*chia-shih*). Also see *chia-hou* (District Commandant).

688 *chiā-wū* 家巫
HAN: **Household Sorcerer,** 8 authorized for the staff of the Director (*ling*) of Sacrificers (*tz'u-ssu*); others perhaps found in the household of the Heir Apparent and in Princedoms (*wang-kuo*). HB: household shaman.

689 *ch'iǎ-kuān* 卡官
CH'ING: **Customs Collector,** unranked, in District (*hsien*) service. BH: keeper of a customs barrier.

690 *chiàng* 將
(1) A common abbreviation throughout history of *chiang-chün* (**General**). (2) CHOU: **General,** leader of a standard army (*chün*) of 12,500 men. (3) HAN: **Leader** of the expectant and unassigned officials who attended the Emperor as courtiers with the title Court Gentleman (*lang*), 3 differentiated with the prefixes Left, Right, and Middle. See under *lang, chung-lang chiang.* Cf. *lang-chung ling.* P37. (4) SUI: **Commander** of a Defense Command (*chen*) in a strategic frontier area. (5) T'ANG: **Commander** of a Garrison (also *chen*), usually in a frontier or other strategic area; rank 6a2, 7a1, or 7a2, depending on the number of troops commanded. Not to be confused with an Area Commander (*tu-tu*) or a Military Commissioner (*chieh-tu shih*) in control of a Circuit (*tao*) or Defense Command (*chen, fang-chen*). RR: *commandant de garnison.* (6) SUNG: **Area General**; see under *keng-shu.*

691 *chiàng-chiàng* 醬匠
T'ANG: **Sauce Maker,** unranked artisans employed in the Spice Pantry (*chang-hai shu*) of the Court of Imperial Entertainments (*kuang-lu ssu*). RR: *ouvrier pour la fabrication des condiments conservés dans le vinaigre.*

692 *chiǎng-chīng pó-shìh* 講經博士
T'ANG: **Erudites for Exposition of the Classics,** members of the Institute for the Advancement of Literature (*hung-wen kuan*) of the Chancellery (*men-hsia sheng*) from 628 to 823; rank not clear; principal function was teaching sons of the official class. RR: *maître du vaste savoir chargé d'expliquer les classiques.*

693 *chiàng-ch'īng* 匠卿
SUI: lit., chief minister of artisans: abbreviated reference to the **Chamberlain for the Palace Buildings** (*chiang-tso ta-chiang, ta-chiang ch'ing*).

694 *chiāng-chūn* 將軍
General: throughout history the most common term for the commander of a substantial body of troops, whether a regular officer of the standing army or the ad hoc commander of a special force organized for a campaign; occurs with many kinds of prefixes, including *shang* (Supreme), *ta* ([General]-in-chief), Left, Right, special functional and geographic designations, and the names of the Armies (*chün*), Guards (*wei*), etc., that Generals commanded. From T'ang on also used, with various prefixes, as prestige titles (*san-kuan*) for active military officers. In Ch'ing, in addition to traditional uses, also occurs among designations of the imperial nobility with various prefixes, e.g., *chen-kuo chiang-chün*. P26, 69, 72.

695 *chiàng-hsíng* 將行
HAN: Empress's Usher, eunuch attendant on the Empress; superseded in 144 B.C. by a Director of the Palace Domestic Service (*ta ch'ang-ch'iu*). HB: empress's usher.

696 *chiàng-hù* 匠戶
YÜAN–CH'ING: Artisan Family, one of numerous categories among which all residents were distributed in accordance with the kinds of social roles the state expected them to play; in the case of Artisan Families, some were assigned to permanent service in various agencies of the central government, whereas others were allowed to do business freely in their home areas but were subject to being called into temporary state service. Cf. *min-hu* (Civilian Family), *chün-hu* (Military Family).

697 *chiǎng-ì ssū* 講義司
SUNG: Advisory Office,, one in the Department of State Affairs (*shang-shu sheng*), one in the Bureau of Military Affairs (*shu-mi yüan*); role and status not clear. See *t'i-chü chiang-i ssu*. SP: *bureau de la réforme financière*.

698 *chiàng-jén* 漿人
CHOU: Eunuch Liquor Maker, 5 on the staff of the Ministry of State (*t'ien-kuan*) for overseeing the production of all liquors required by the ruler and his guests and for formal ceremonies. See *nü-chiang*. Cf. *chiu-jen*. CL: *employé aux extraits*.

699 *chiǎng-kuān* 講官
Lecturer. (1) May be encountered in reference to many kinds of educational officials. (2) SUNG–CH'ING: an ad hoc designation for officials participating with the Emperor in a Classics Colloquium (*ching-yen*, q.v.). P24.

700 *chiǎng-láng* 講郎
HAN: Court Gentleman for Lecturing, the Former Han antecedent of the Later Han title Expositor-in-waiting (*shih-chiang*), designation of a Court Gentleman (*lang*) chosen to give advice to the Emperor. May be encountered in later times as an archaic reference to members of the Hanlin Academy (*han-lin yüan*), especially for its Academician Expositors-in-waiting (*shih-chiang hsüeh-shih*). P23.

701 *chiàng-pīng chǎng-shǐh* 將兵長史
HAN: Aide-Commander, designation of certain Aides (*chang-shih*) on the staffs of frontier Commanderies (*chün*) or in campaigning areas, serving in active command of troops. HB: chief clerk in command of troops.

702 *chiàng-shīh* 匠師
N-S DIV (Chou): Director of Labor, ranked as an Ordinary Grand Master (*chung ta-fu;* 6a), head of the Office of Construction (*chiang-shih ssu*) in the Ministry of Works (*tung-kuan*). P14.

703 *chiāng-shìh láng* 將仕郎
SUI–MING: Court Gentleman for Ceremonial Service, a prestige title (*san-kuan*) for officials of rank 8b (?) in Sui, 9b2 in T'ang, 9b in Sung, 9a2 in Chin, 8a in Yüan, 9a in Ming. P68.

704 *chiāng-shìh tsò-láng* 將仕佐郎
CHIN–MING: Assistant Gentleman for Ceremonial Service, a prestige title (*san-kuan*) for officials of rank 9b2 in Chin, 8b in Yüan, 9b in Ming. P68.

705 *chiǎng-shū* 講書
(1) T'ANG–SUNG: occasional variant of *chih-chiang* (**Lecturer**). (2) SUNG: **Instructor,** 4 authorized in each Princely Establishment (*wang-fu*), unspecified numbers also in the Directorate of Education (*kuo-tzu chien*); rank not clear but low. SP: *lecteur*. P67.

706 *chiǎng-shū chiào-shòu* 講書教授
SUNG: Instructor, 12, rank not clear, in the Chief Office of Imperial Clan Affairs (*ta tsung-cheng ssu*). SP: *professeur*.

707 *chiǎng-shū shuō-shū* 講書說書
SUNG: Recitation Tutor, original designation of the rank 7b *shih-chiang* (Expositor-in-waiting) of the Institute of Academicians (*hsüeh-shih yüan*) assigned to the Directorate of Education (*kuo-tzu chien*). SP: *lecteur*.

708 *chiāng-tsò chiēn* 將作監
SUI–LIAO: Directorate for the Palace Buildings, responsible for construction and maintenance, normally loosely subordinated to and always cooperative with the Ministry of Works (*kung-pu*); headed by a Director (*ta-chien* then *ling* in Sui; *ta-chiang*, rank 3b, in T'ang; *chien*, 4b, in Sung); in Liao subordinated to the Court Ceremonial Institute (*hsüan-hui yüan*). Thereafter its responsibilities were borne more directly by the Ministry of Works. RR: *direction des travaux*. SP: *direction des travaux publics*. P14, 15, 38.

709 *chiāng-tsò shào-fǔ* 將作少府
CH'IN–HAN: Chamberlain for the Palace Buildings, responsible for construction and maintenance, including the planting of trees alongside roads; rank 2,000 bushels in Han; retitled *chiang-tso ta-chiang* in 151 B.C. HB: privy treasurer of architecture. P14.

710 *chiāng-tsò shào-fǔ chiēn* 將作少府監
SUNG: Directorate for the Palace Buildings, c. 1127 merged into the Ministry of Works (*kung-pu*), in 1133 reconstituted as the *chiang-tso chien*. P14, 38.

711 *chiāng-tsò ssū* 將作司
MING: Palace Buildings Office, from 1367 to 1368 a central government agency comparable to the traditional Directorate for the Palace Buildings (*chiang-tso chien*), with principal responsibility for construction of the palace at the new dynastic capital, Nanking; headed by a Chief Minister (*ch'ing*), rank 3a, and incorporating Left and Right Supervisorates (*t'i-chü ssu*) headed by Supervisors (*t'i-chü*), 6a; in 1368 subordinated to the Ministry of Works (*kung-pu*); in 1373 the Chief Minister was reduced to rank 6a, and the Office's Supervisorates were combined into a Supervisorate of Construction (*ying-tsao t'i-chü ssu*), which spawned Branch Supervisorates (*fen-ssu*), each alike headed by one Supervisor (*t'i-chü*). In 1392 the Office was reorganized as a Work Project Office (*ying-shan so*) in the Ministry of Works. P15.

712 *chiāng-tsò tà-chiàng* 將作大匠
HAN–SUI: Chamberlain for the Palace Buildings, re-

sponsible for construction and maintenance; rank 2,000 bushels in Han, 2b then 3b in N. Wei, otherwise not clear; created in 151 B.C. by retitling of the *chiang-tso shao-fu*. During the era of N-S Division the Chamberlain's agency gradually came to be known as the Court for the Palace Buildings (*chiang-tso ssu,*) and in Liang and Ch'en the Chamberlain was designated *chiang-tso ta-chiang ch'ing* (Chief Minister for the Palace Buildings). In the era of N-S Division, also, the Chamberlain and his Court gradually came to be subordinated to the Ministry of Works (most commonly *kung-pu*) in the developing Department of State Affairs (*shang-shu sheng*). Sui in 600 changed the Court into a Directorate for the Palace Buildings (*chiang-tso chien*) under a Director (*ta-chien*). In all these periods the Chamberlain and his agency were both often abbreviated as *chiang-tso*. HB: court architect. P14.

713   *chiāng-tsò ts'áo* 將作曹
HAN: **Construction Section,** a clerical unit found in some Commanderies (*chün*) and Districts (*hsien*), or established in such agencies when circumstances warranted. HB: bureau of architecture.

714   *chiāng-tsò yüàn* 將作院
YÜAN: **Imperial Manufactories Commission,** a rank 2a agency that supervised an abundance of artisans in the manufacture of gold, silver, jade, and other luxury utensils for palace use. P38.

715   *chiǎng-tú* 講讀
SUNG: an abbreviated, combined reference to *shih-chiang* and *shih-tu*, i.e., **Expositor-in-waiting and Reader-in-waiting.**

716   *chiǎng-tú kuān* 講讀官
SUNG: **Instructional Officials,** 4 in the Institute of Academicians (*hsüeh-shih yüan*), rank and specific functions not clear.

717   *chiàng yǔ-hòu* 將虞候
Inspector-general; see under *yü-hou.*

718   *chiào* 校
In addition to the following entries, also see under *hsiao.*

719   *chiao* 榷
See under *chüeh.*

720   *chiào-ch'ǎng* 窖廠
CH'ING: **Icehouse;** see under *ping-chiao.*

721   *chiāo-ch'āo* 交鈔
Lit., documents for exchange: i.e., **paper money:** from Chin if not earlier, a common term for state-authorized paper currency. Superseded the earlier terms *fei-ch'ien* (T'ang), *chiao-tzu* (see *chiao-tzu wu*) and *hui-tzu* (see *hui-tzu wu*) (both Sung). Also see *pao-ch'ao, ch'ao-chih, y :-ch'ao chü.* Cf. *pao-ch'üan, pao-yüan.* P16.

722   *chiāo-ch'āo k'u* 交鈔庫
CHIN: **Paper Money Storehouse,** one of several central government repositories (and print shops?) for paper currency, probably controlled by one or more Commissioners (*shih*) delegated from the Ministry of Revenue (*hu-pu*). P16.

723   *chiào-chèng hàn-wén kuān* 校正漢文官
CH'ING: **Editor of Chinese,** 2 on the staff of the Court of Colonial Affairs (*li-fan yüan*) for 3-year duty assignments, delegated from regular posts in the Grand Secretariat (*nei-ko*) or the Hanlin Academy (*han-lin yüan*). P17.

724   *chiào-chèng kuān* 校正官 or *chiao-cheng*
SUNG: **Editor,** low-ranking officials in the True Records Institute (*shih-lu yü.:n*) of the Palace Library (*pi-shu sheng*). SP: *rectificateur, correcteur.* P23.

725   *chiào-chìh* 教職
Educational Posts: a collective designation, usually denoting officials in charge of local schools.

726   *chiào-chù* 教助
T'ANG: **Educational Assistant,** rank 9a, assistant to the Medical Erudite (*i po-shih*) in the Imperial Medical Office (*t'ai-i shu*) of the Court of Imperial Sacrifices (*t'ai-ch'ang ssu*). RR: *professeur assistant.*

727   *chiào-fáng* 椒房
Lit., pepper chamber, deriving from an Empress's delight with imported Southeast Asian pepperwood used for paneling her bedchamber: from Han on, an indirect reference to the wife of a ruler.

728   *chiào-fáng ssū* 教坊司 or *chiao-fang*
Lit., office of instruction: **Music Office.** (1) T'ANG: one each prefixed Left and Right established in 714 under supervision of the Court of Imperial Sacrifices (*t'ai-ch'ang ssu*), soon made independent; specialized in the training of court entertainers including clowns, jugglers, etc.; came to be directed by one or more eunuch Commissioners (*shih*). See *nei chiao-fang.* (2) SUNG: a school in the Court of Imperial Sacrifices; see *ch'ien-hsia chiao-fang so.* RR + SP: *école pour l'enseignement de la musique.* (3) CHIN: headed by a Superintendent (*t'i-tien*). (4) YÜAN–CH'ING: a unit of the Ministry of Rites (*li-pu*), in Yüan headed by an Overseer (*ta-lu-hua-ch'ih*), rank 4a; in Ming and early Ch'ing headed by a Director (*feng-luan*), 9a; in 1729 divided into a Music Office (*ho-sheng shu*) and an Imperial Music Office (*shen-yüeh shu*). P10.

729   *chiào-hsí* 教習
CH'ING: **Instructor,** some Chinese, some Manchu, and some Mongolian in various schools established by Banners (*ch'i*), the Imperial Academy of Medicine (*t'ai-i yüan*), the Hanlin Academy (*han-lin yüan*), etc. P10, 36.

730   *chiào-hsí tà-ch'én* 教習大臣
CH'ING: **Grand Minister Instructor,** one Manchu and one Chinese dignitary assigned as senior staff members of the Institute of Advanced Study (*shu-ch'ang kuan*) in the Hanlin Academy (*han-lin yüan*), to supervise the studies of Hanlin Bachelors (*shu-chi-shih*). BH: senior professor.

731   *chiǎo-jén* 角人
CHOU: **Horn Collector,** 2 ranked as Junior Servicemen (*hsia-shih*), members of the Ministry of Education (*ti-kuan*) who gathered teeth and bones as well as horns from animals received in payment of hunters' taxes, for use in adorning the royal chariots and banners. CL: *officier des cornes.*

732   *chiǎo-k'àn kuān* 校勘官 or *chiao-k'an*
Proofreader. (1) T'ANG: low-ranking officials from 720 attached to the Academy in the Hall of Elegance and Rectitude (*li-cheng hsiu-shu yüan*), subordinate to the Secretariat (*chung-shu sheng*). (2) SUNG: unranked subofficials attached to the Palace Library (*pi-shu sheng*), the Historiography Institute (*kuo-shih yüan*), and the True Records Institute (*shih-lu yüan*). RR + SP: *correcteur vérificateur.* (3) CHIN: attached to the School for the Sons of the State (*kuo-tzu hsüeh*), rank 8b. P23, 25, 34.

733   *chiào-kuān* 教官
Educational Official. (1) A generic term for all officials engaged in instructional functions. (2) Occasionally a regular title, e.g., of school instructors in Princely Adminis-

trations (*wang-fu*) and in Military Prefectures (*chün*) in the Sung dynasty. P69. (3) A variant reference to the Minister of Education (*ti-kuan ssu-t'u*) ascribed to the Chou dynasty of antiquity.

734 *chiāo-lán pān* 椒蘭班
Lit., the pepper and orchid echelons (in court audience array?): an occasional unofficial reference to relatives of the ruler by marriage, i.e., **Imperial In-laws** (*wai-ch'i*). Also see *chiao-fang* and *lan-t'ai*.

735 *chiào-lǐ* 校理
Subeditor. (1) T'ANG: variable numbers of unranked subofficials attached to the Academy in the Hall of Elegance and Rectitude (*li-cheng hsiu-shu yüan*), the Academy of Scholarly Worthies (*chi-hsien tien shu-yüan*), and the Institute for the Advancement of Literature (*hung-wen kuan*). RR: *correcteur réviseur*. (2) SUNG: variable numbers in the Historiography Institute (*shih-kuan*), the Academy of Scholarly Worthies, the Institute for the Glorification of Literature (*chao-wen kuan*), etc.; often concurrent appointments for literati with nominal offices elsewhere in the central government. SP: *rédacteur-réviseur*. (3) CHIN: no specified number, rank 8a, in the Institute for the Advancement of Literature. (4) CH'ING: 16 authorized for the Hall of Literary Profundity (*wen-yüan ko*), normally concurrent appointments for literati with nominal offices elsewhere in the central government. *Chiao-li* were generally considered to rank below such personages as *hsiu-chuan* but above *chiao-k'an*, qq.v. P23, 25.

736 *chiāo-shè chǔ* 郊社局 or ***chiāo-shè shǔ*** 署
SUI–YÜAN: **Office of the National Altars** (*shu* in Sui and T'ang, *chü* in Sung, Chin, and Yüan), a unit of the Court of Imperial Sacrifices (*t'ai-ch'ang ssu*) responsible for preparing for and participating in rituals regularly conducted at the major sacrificial altars and temples at the dynastic capital; headed by a Director (*ling*), rank 7b2 in T'ang, 9a in Sung. RR: *office des temples des banlieues et du dieu du sol*. SP: *bureau des temples....* P28.

737 *chiào-shīh* 教師
YÜAN: **Music Master,** low-ranking instructors of music in various units of the Bureau of Musical Ritual (*i-feng ssu*). P10.

738 *chiāo-shìh chiēn* 交市監
T'ANG: **Directorate of Tributary Trade,** headed by a Director (*chien*), rank 6b2; supervised the procurement of horses, camels, mules, etc., in exchanges of goods with tributary states; a unit of the Directorate for Imperial Manufactories (*shao-fu chien*); in 632 redesignated *hu-shih chien*.

739 *chiào-shìh láng* 校事郎
Examiner. (1) YÜAN: 2 members of the educational staff of the Astrological Commission (*t'ai-shih yüan*), rank 8a; duties not clear. (2) MING: members of the pre-1367 Directorate of Astrology (*t'ai-shih chien*), antecedent of the Directorate of Astronomy (*ch'in-t'ien chien*); number, rank, and functions not clear. P35.

740 *chiào-shòu* 教授
SUNG–CH'ING: **Instructor,** a title with many uses, most commonly for the heads of Confucian Schools (*ju-hsüeh*) at the Prefecture (*chou, fu*) level; always low-ranking or unranked.

741 *chiào-shū* 校書
Editing Clerk. (1) SUI: 6, rank not clear, members of the Editorial Service (*ssu-ching chü*) in the Household Administration of the Heir Apparent (*chan-shih fu*). (2) T'ANG:

4, rank not clear, in the Secretariat of the Heir Apparent (*tso ch'un-fang*); also 4, rank 8a1 or 9a2, in the Academy of Scholarly Worthies (*chi-hsien tien shu-yüan*) from the 790s or 800s. RR: *réviseur de textes*. (3) SUNG: number and rank not clear; members of the Institute for the Veneration of Literature (*ch'ung-wen yüan*). (4) MING: 2, rank not clear, in the Editorial Service of the Household Administration of the Heir Apparent (as under #1 above). P25, 26.

742 *chiào-shū láng* 校書郎
Editor. (1) HAN: in Later Han a document-processing duty assignment for men with status as Court Gentlemen (*lang*) or Gentlemen of the Interior (*lang-chung*), referred to respectively as *chiao-shu lang* and *chiao-shu lang-chung*. HB: gentlemen collating books. (2) N-S DIV: from the Three Kingdoms era on, often appointed in the evolving Secretariat (*chung-shu sheng*) with special responsibility for compiling the Imperial Diary (*ch'i-chü chu*). (3) SUI: from 10 to 40 appointed in the Palace Library (*pi-shu sheng*), rank 9a. (4) T'ANG: 8, rank 9a1, appointed to work on the Imperial Diary in the Palace Library; appointments for men of great literary promise, considered the starting points for excellent careers; others with the same rank in the Institute for the Veneration of Literature (*ch'ung-wen kuan*) and the Institute for the Advancement of Literature (*hung-wen kuan*) from 719, when *ch'ou-chiao*, q.v., were so retitled. RR: *secrétaire réviseur de textes*. (5) SUNG: 2 then 4, rank 8b, in the Palace Library and the Institute for the Glorification of Literature (*chao-wen kuan*). SP: *réviseur-collationneur des textes*. (6) LIAO: appointed in the household of the Heir Apparent and in the Historical Archive (*chu-tso chü*). (7) CHIN: 2 then one assigned from among rank 7b officials of the Hanlin Academy (*han-lin yüan*). (8) YÜAN: 2, rank 8a, in the Directorate of the Palace Archives (*pi-shu chien*); also 2, rank not clear, on the staff of the Heir Apparent. P25, 26.

743 *chiào-ssù shǔ* 郊祀署
YÜAN: **Suburban Sacrifices Office,** one of 3 special sacrificial agencies in the central government (see *she-chi shu, t'ai-miao shu*); headed by 2 Directors (*ling*), rank 6b. P28.

744 *chiào-tùi* 校對
Proofreader. (1) SUNG: unspecified number of unranked clerical personnel serving in the Imperial Archives (*pi-ko*), more fully designated Proofreader of Imperial Documents (*chiao-tui huang-pen shu-chi kuan*). SP: *correcteur*. (2) CH'ING: 8 Manchu and 8 Chinese, unranked, in the Historiography Institute (*kuo-shih kuan*). BH: corrector.

745 *chiāo-tzǔ wù* 交子務
SUNG: **Paper Money Office,** opened at the Prefectural (*chou*) level beginning in the 1020s, apparently to control the production and distribution of paper currency (*chiao-tzu*); staffing not clear, but presumably subordinate to the Prefectural officials; after the transition to S. Sung, supplemented with similar offices called *hui-tzu wu*, etc. See *chiao-ch'ao, fei-ch'ien, yin-ch'ao chü*. P16.

746 *chiāo-yǐn k'ù* 交引庫
SUNG: **Paper Money Repository,** a unit in the Court of the Imperial Treasury (*t'ai-fu ssu*); staffing and exact functions not clear. SP: *caisse de billets d'échange (bons de monnaie)*.

747 *chiào-yù* 教諭
SUNG–CH'ING: **Instructor,** one of several terms that commonly occur in the sense of teacher. Especially found as head of the state-sponsored Confucian School (*ju-hsüeh*)

in a District (*hsien*), also in a Ch'ing dynasty Subprefecture (*t'ing*); normally unranked, but 8a in Ch'ing. Special uses include the designation of a Yüan dynasty medical specialist authorized in 1285 for every Circuit (*tao*), suggested rendering **Medical Inspector;** collected and annually reported information about physicians in the jurisdiction for the Instructor (*chiao-shou*) who headed the Medical School (*i-hsüeh*) of the Circuit. BH: district director of schools. P51.

748 *chiào-yù* 校尉
See *hsiao-wei*.

749 *chiào-yüèh fáng* 教閱房
SUNG: **Training and Monitoring Section** in the Bureau of Military Affairs (*shu-mi yüan*), one of 12 Sections created in the reign of Shen-tsung (1067–1085) to manage administrative affairs of military garrisons throughout the country, in geographic clusters, or to supervise specified military functions on a nationwide scale. This Section supervised the training and testing of troops, the establishment of military stations, the expediting of communication and transport services, and some personnel administration matters throughout the country and in addition supervised frontier defense in Hu-nan Circuit (*lu*). Headed by a Vice Recipient of Edicts (*fu ch'eng-chih*), rank 8b. Apparently abolished early in S. Sung. See *shih-erh fang* (Twelve Sections). SP: *chambre d'entraînement militaire*.

750 *chiào-yüèh kuān* 校閱官
SUNG: **Editorial Assistant,** unranked, in the Historiography Institute (*kuo-shih yüan*) and the True Records Institute (*shih-lu yüan*) of the Palace Library (*pi-shu sheng*). SP: *fonctionnaire chargé de correction des textes*.

751 *ch'iáo-tào shih* 橋道使
SUNG: **Commissioner for Bridges and Roads,** a specialized appointee presumably at the Circuit (*lu*) or lower levels.

752 *ch'iáo-tīng* 橋丁
T'ANG: **Bridge Tender,** unranked caretaker-guards assigned to bridges by the Directorate of Water Crossings (*chu-chin chien*), a unit in the Directorate of Waterways (*tu-shui chien*). RR: *gardien de pont*.

753 *chièh* 借
Acting: a common prefix to a title; especially in Sung times, signified that the appointee's regular official status was lower than the office to which he was temporarily appointed.

754 *chiēh* 階
From Sui on, a term used (1) to designate **class,** the subdivision of a rank (*p'in*) in the case of regular official appointments, e.g., 4b = 4th rank (*p'in*), 2nd class (*chieh*); or (2) to designate the **rank** of an official's prestige title (*san-kuan*). See *teng, chi, nei-shih chieh*. P68.

755 *chiēh-ch'á* 節察
SUNG: a common abbreviation combining the titles **Military Commissioner** (*chieh-tu shih*) and **Surveillance Commissioner** (*kuan-ch'a shih*).

756 *chiēh-chèn* 節鎮
(1) Variant of *chen* (**Defense Command**), normally a territorial administration in a frontier zone. (2) MING: unofficial reference to a **Grand Coordinator** (*hsün-fu*) or a **Supreme Commander** (*tsung-tu*), provincial and multiprovincial magnates who in areas or periods of military urgency commonly directed military affairs in their jurisdictions.

757 *chiēh-chèng chèn* 節政鎮
SUNG: **Defense Command,** specifying a territorial jurisdiction along the frontier headed by a Military Commissioner (*chieh-tu shih*). SP: *région d'une garnison militaire*.

758 *chiēh-chí* 階級
Especially from Sui on, a general term for the **ranks** of civil officials, incorporating both rank (*p'in*) and class or subdivision (*chieh*); e.g., 6a = 6th rank, first class, the entirety constituting a *chieh-chi*. Also see *chi, p'in-chi, teng-chi*.

759 *chiēh-fān* 价藩
Lit. meaning derived from the *chieh* of *chieh-tu shih* (Military Commissioner) and the sense of *fan* as frontier or boundary: **Territorial Administrator.** (1) SUNG: unofficial collective reference to both civil and military officials assigned to Circuits (*lu*) as Military Commissioners (*an-fu shih*), etc. (2) CH'ING: unofficial reference to a Provincial Administration Commissioner (*pu-cheng shih*).

760 *chiēh-fŭ shih* 節府使
CHIN: **Military Commissioner,** one of several titles used for the heads of Prefectures (*chou*), Military Prefectures (*chün*), Defense Commands (*chieh-chen*), and other Prefecture-level general-administration agencies.

761 *chiēh-fú shih* 節服氏
CHOU: **Royal Valet,** 8 ranked as Junior Servicemen (*hsia-shih*), members of the Ministry of War (*hsia-kuan*) responsible for selecting clothing for the ruler, especially on his outings from the palace, to suit the weather and other conditions he might encounter. CL: *régulateur de la convenance du costume*.

762 *chiēh-hsià* 節下
T'ANG: unofficial reference to the **Prefect** (*t'ai-shou, tz'u-shih*) of a Prefecture (*chou*).

763 *chiēh-hù* 解戶
MING–CH'ING: **Transporters,** a general term for commoners on state-requisitioned service transporting grains or money.

764 *chiēh-kuān* 階官
Rank Offices. (1) SUNG: refers to the system of paying official salaries on the basis of from 24 to 40 nominal positions such as Grand Masters (*ta-fu*) and Court Gentlemen (*lang*), differentiated by laudatory prefixes, regardless of officials' titular offices (*pen-kuan*) or the functions they actually performed. The system superseded the pre-1080 system of prestige titles (*san-kuan*) and by 1120 was in turn superseded by a system of salary offices (*chi-lu kuan*). (2) CHIN–CH'ING: interchangeable with *san-kuan* (prestige title).

765 *chiēh-pàn shih* 接伴使
SUNG: **Escort Commissioner,** an ad hoc assignment for officials regularly holding other appointments when they were charged to welcome and accompany foreign dignitaries during visits to China; often assisted by Escort Vice Commissioners (*chieh-pan fu-shih*). SP: *commissaire chargé de recevoir et d'accompagner les visiteurs étrangers*.

766 *chiēh-shèn k'ù* 節慎庫
MING–CH'ING: **Auditing Office,** a unit in the Ministry of Works (*kung-pu*) established in 1529; headed by a Commissioner-in-chief (*ta-shih*), rank 9b, until 1658, when the staff was made all Manchu under a Director (*lang-chung*), rank not clear.

767 chiĕh-shìh 解事
HAN: **Elucidator,** duty assignment for 2 Expectant Officials (*tai-chao*) on the staff of the Grand Astrologer (*t'ai-shih ling*); specific functions not clear. HB: elucidator.

768 chiĕh-shìh 解試
SUNG: **Prefectural Examination,** the lowest-level test in the formal civil service recruitment system, conducted by the officials of Prefectures (*chou*) and comparable-level agencies for the purpose of "forwarding" (*chieh*) successful candidates to the dynastic capital for further evaluation of their knowledge and promise.

769 chiĕh-tào ssū 街道司 or **chiĕh-tào t'īng** 廳
Office of Capital Streets, in charge of the repair and maintenance of streets and roads in the capital city. (1) SUNG (*ssu*): established in 1057 with a Commander (*chih-hui*) as head, in 1129 subordinated to the Directorate of Waterways (*tu-shui chien*). SP: *bureau des routes et des rues dans la capitale*. (2) CH'ING (*t'ing*): one in each of the Five Wards (*wu ch'eng*) into which both Peking and Nanking were administratively divided, supervised by Censors of the Five Wards (*wu-ch'eng yü-shih*). BH: roadway office. P15.

770 chiĕh-t'óu 解頭
Lit., first forwarded. (1) T'ANG: **First Graduate,** a quasi-official reference to the first-place passer of various civil service examinations other than that leading to the Presented Scholar (*chin-shih*) degree. (2) SUNG–CH'ING: **Prefectural (Provincial) Graduate with Highest Honors,** a variant of *chieh-yüan*, q.v.

771 chiĕh-tsú 街卒
HAN: **Street Patrolman,** apparently a guard or watchman employed in a small town or large village.

772 chiĕh-tù 節度
An introductory part of many important titles, especially *chieh-tu shih* (Military Commissioner), suggesting one who had special or irregular control of an area. Originally, in the era of N-S Division, seems derived from ancient usage meaning "to measure and regulate," but by T'ang times was clearly a somewhat corrupted abbreviation of the title Area Commander with Special Warrant (*shih ch'ih-chieh tu-tu*), corrupted because the 2 *tu* characters are different. In Sung and perhaps earlier times may be encountered as a prefix to the term Prefecture (*chou, fu,* or *chün*) specifying a Prefecture serving as the headquarters of a Military Commissioner (*chieh-tu shih*).

773 chiĕh-tù chăng shū-chì 節度掌書記
SUNG: **Prefectural Secretary,** rank 8b; unspecified numbers served in Prefectures (*chou*) and perhaps other Prefecture-level agencies. Also used as a prestige title (*sankuan*) for rank 9a1 officials until c. 1102, then combined with *ju-lin lang*, q.v. SP: *secrétaire général d'une préfecture*.

774 chiĕh-tù kuān-ch'á liú-hòu
節度觀察留後
SUNG: **Deputy Military and Surveillance Commissioner,** ranked at a salary level of 300,000 coins per month, often the senior official actually on duty in a Circuit (*lu*); from c. 1117 seems to have been superseded by ad hoc delegates called Pacification Commissioners (*ch'eng-hsüan shih*), which title seems to have fallen out of use as an active duty assignment in S. Sung. See *liu-hou*. SP: *délégué commandant et surveillant d'une région*.

775 chiĕh-tù mù 節度幕 or **chiĕh-tù tuān** 端
N-S DIV: occasional quasi-official or unofficial reference

to the **Supply Commission** (see under *chieh-tu shih*) for an army on campaign.

776 chiĕh-tù p'àn-kuān 節度判官
SUNG: **Administrative Assistant to the Military Commissioner,** either an ad hoc duty assignment or a nominal title for an official regularly appointed to another post. See *chieh-tu shih*.

777 chiĕh-tù shĭh 節度使
(1) N-S DIV: **Supply Commissioner,** in the Three Kingdoms era and perhaps later an ad hoc appointee responsible for provisioning an army on campaign. (2) T'ANG–CHIN: **Military Commissioner,** a military title of great historical importance. Originated in the late 600s as a common variant reference to Area Commanders (*tu-tu*), military officers in charge of frontier defenses. Beginning in 711, Military Commissioners were regularly appointed to head 8 Defense Commands (*chen*) along the northern frontier instead of Area Commanders, and soon some Prefects (*tz'u-shih*) also took the new title. Especially in consequence of the An Lu-shan rebellion beginning in 756, the number of Military Commissioners proliferated, and during much of the late T'ang period they were virtually autonomous regional governors. Theoretically, control over a Circuit (*tao*) came to be divided between a Military Commissioner and, for non-military affairs, a Surveillance Commissioner (*kuan-ch'a shih*); but in many Circuits a warlord took both functions for himself, as Military and Surveillance Commissioner (*chieh-tu kuan-ch'a shih*), and often in addition status as Revenue Commissioner (*tu-chih shih*), Agriculture Commissioner (*ying-t'ien shih*), Bandit-suppression Commissioner (*chao-t'ao shih*), etc. The Military Commissioners commonly designated their lieutenants Military Vice Commissioners (*chieh-tu fu-shih*). Princes (*wang*) were sometimes designated Military Commissioners-in-chief (*chieh-tu ta-shih*), often assisted by Military Vice Commissioners-in-chief (*chieh-tu fu ta-shih*), but they remained on duty in the capital. During the Five Dynasties era Military Commissioners continued as virtually autonomous satraps in their regions, but Sung gradually eliminated them and achieved a consolidation of authority in the central government. After the earliest Sung years, the title Military Commissioner was used only as an honorific designation for a few distinguished personages or as a title conferred on submissive aboriginal chieftains. In Liao there were Military Commissioners in charge of most Prefectures (*chou*) and Military Prefectures (*chün*), under the control of the Southern Administration (*nan-mien*). In Chin all civil and military affairs of Defense Commands (*chen*) were controlled by Military Commissioners, who held rank 3b. In Yüan times regional military authority was organized in new ways and divided among such dignitaries as Military Commanders (*yüan-shuai*) of Circuits (*tao*), Route Commanders (*...lu tsung-kuan*), etc. RR+SP: *commissaire impérial au commandement d'une région*. P50.

778 chiĕh-tù t'ūi-kuān 節度推官
SUNG: **Prefectural Judge,** rank not clear, in certain Superior Prefectures (*fu*) of S. Sung. SP: *juge*.

779 chiĕh-t'ūi 節推
SUNG: an abbreviated reference to *chieh-tu t'ui-kuan* (**Prefectural Judge**).

780 chiĕh-yú 婕妤 or 倢伃
Lady of Handsome Fairness. (1) HAN–N-S DIV: in Han and San-kuo Wei, the designation of a category of imperial concubines. (2) SUI: the designation given 12 imperial consorts, rank 3a, collectively called Hereditary Consorts (*shih-*

fu). (3) T'ANG–SUNG: a concubine title, rank 3a. RR+SP: *femme qui aide et assiste l'impératrice.*

781 *chiĕh-yüán* 解元
SUNG–CH'ING: lit., the first forwarded: **Prefectural (Provincial) Graduate with Highest Honors,** an unofficial reference to the highest-ranking passer of Sung's Prefectural Examination (*chieh-shih*) and the Provincial Examination (*hsiang-shih*) in Yüan, Ming, and Ch'ing in the civil service recruitment process. See *ching-k'uei.* P24.

782 *ch'iĕh-hsiēh* 怯薛
YÜAN: Chinese rendering of the Mongol word *kesig,* designation of the **Imperial Bodyguard,** comprising about 10,000 elite hereditary soldiers under the direct command of the Emperor.

783 *ch'iĕh-hú* 挈壺
CHOU: **Water-tester,** 6 ranked as Junior Servicemen (*hsia-shih*), members of the Ministry of War (*hsia-kuan*) responsible for drawing water from streams or wells to determine appropriate sites for military encampments and mess halls. CL: *officier qui érige le vase à eau.*

784 *ch'iĕh-hú chèng* 挈壺正
T'ANG–CH'ING: **Supervisor of Water Clocks,** associate members of the astrological group called the Five Offices (*wu kuan*). In T'ang, 2, rank 8a1, established in 702 (704?) in the Astrological Service (*t'ai-shih chü, ssu-t'ien t'ai*); by 758 shifted into association with the Five Offices of the Service. In Sung, one, rank not clear, in the Directorate of Astronomy (*ssu-t'ien chien*); also unspecified number, rank apparently 8a then 9a, in the Astrological Service (*t'ai-shih chü*). In Liao, members of the Directorate of Astronomy. Apparently not appointed in Chin. In Yüan, one, rank 8b, in the Astrological Commission (*t'ai-shih yüan*). In Ming, unspecified number and rank, members of the early Ming Directorate of Astrology (*t'ai-shih chien*); also 2 then one, rank 8b, in the Directorate of Astronomy (*ch'in-t'ien chien*). In Ch'ing, 4 senior officials, rank 8a, in the Water Clock Section (*lou-k'o k'o*) in the Directorate of Astronomy (*ch'in-t'ien chien*). RR+SP: *chef de service de la clepsydre.* BH: keeper of the clepsydra. P35.

785 *chiēn* 兼
Ety., one hand grasping 2 arrows: **Concurrent,** the most general term used throughout history connecting 2 titles borne by one appointee, e.g., *ping-pu shih-lang chien fu tu yü-shih* (Vice Minister of War and Concurrent Vice Censor-in-chief). The normal implication is that the appointee was equally responsible for 2 substantive posts; whether or not he enjoyed the salaries and other perquisites of both posts is seldom specified, but in most instances it can probably be assumed that he did. Only at times in the era of N-S Division was the term used, in addition to its normal usage, with the meaning "probationary" that was conveyed in most other periods by the term *shou,* q.v. Also see *ch'ang-chien.*

786 *chiēn* 監
Incorporated in many titles, commonly as the first character, in the verbal sense to oversee or supervise. As an independent noun or a noun suffix, occurs with several meanings: (1) **Directorate** in many varieties with both high and low status in the governmental hierarchy, e.g., *kuo-tzu chien* (Directorate of Education). (2) **Supervisor** or **Director** of a Directorate, e.g., *tu-shui (chien) chien* (Directorate of Waterways; in such instances, *chien* is often not duplicated and only context can suggest whether the Directorate or the Supervisor of the Directorate is intended), or **Direc-**

tor of some other kinds of agencies. (3) T'ANG: **Horse Pasturage** under the supervision of the Court of the Imperial Stud (*t'ai-p'u ssu*). See *chien-mu.* (4) SUNG: **Industrial Prefecture,** prefixed with a placename, identifying a Prefecture-level agency in an area where the preeminent economic enterprise was a mine, a saltern, or something of the sort that required the special attention of local officials.

787 *chiĕn* 諫
Incorporated in many titles, normally as the first character, in the verbal sense to remonstrate with the ruler. In addition to the following entries, see *ssu-chien, ta-chien, chung-chien, hsiao-chien.*

788 *chiĕn-ch'á ch'éng-shòu* 檢察承受
SUNG: **Caretaker,** unspecified number and rank, members of Offices for the Care of Imperial Mausoleums (*chien-ch'a kung-ling so*); under supervisory control of the Court of the Imperial Clan (*tsung-cheng ssu*). P29.

789 *chiĕn-ch'á kuān* 監察官
May be encountered as a variant of the generic term *ch'a-kuan* (**Surveillance Official**). P59.

790 *chiĕn-ch'á kŭng-líng sŏ* 檢察宮陵所
SUNG: **Office for the Care of Imperial Mausoleums,** one or more units in the Court of the Imperial Clan (*tsung-cheng ssu*) staffed by Caretakers (*chien-ch'a ch'eng-shou*). P29.

791 *chiĕn-ch'á lĭ-hsíng shĭh* 監察裏行使
T'ANG: **Acting Investigating Censor,** a designation for supernumerary Investigating Censors (*chien-ch'a yü-shih*) appointed for a short time beginning c. 719, when responsibilities of the Censorate (*yü-shih t'ai*) were expanded. RR: *commissaire impérial attaché aux censeurs de la cour des enquêtes au dehors.*

792 *chiĕn-ch'á shĭh* 監察使
Investigating Commissioner. (1) May be encountered in any period as a variant or unofficial reference to an Investigating Censor (*chien-ch'a yü-shih*). (2) T'ANG: from 784 on, designation of the Investigating Censor of longest service, who was assigned to maintain surveillance over the Ministries of Personnel (*li-pu*) and of Rites (*li-pu*). (3) SUNG: may be encountered in the T'ang sense or in reference to a central government official delegated to conduct special investigations in a Circuit (*lu*). RR+SP: *commissaire impérial chargé du contrôle et des enquêtes.* P18.

793 *chiĕn-ch'á shĭh* 監察史
CH'IN–HAN: **Supervising Censor,** designation of Attendant Censors (*shih yü-shih*) when dispatched to tour units of territorial administration, checking on the conduct of officials and the condition of the people; also known in Ch'in as *chien yü-shih* or *chien-chün yü-shih* (*chün:* Commandery) and in Han as *chih-chih shih* (lit., straight-pointing commissioner); generally comparable to *hsün-an yü-shih,* q.v., of later eras. The character *shih* (Commissioner) is sometimes found in place of the character *shih* (Scribe).

794 *chiĕn-ch'á tū yŭ-shĭh* 監察都御史
MING: **Chief Investigating Censor,** 8, rank 7a, appointed only in the 1382–1383 transitional period as senior officials of the Censorate (changing from *yü-shih t'ai* to *tu ch'a-yüan*); in 1383 superseded by a group of new executive officials entitled Censors-in-chief (*tu yü-shih*). P18.

795 *chiĕn-ch'á yŭ-shĭh* 監察御史
SUI–CH'ING: **Investigating Censor,** the most concentrated, broad-ranging investigative and impeaching officials, members of the Censorate (*yü-shih t'ai* to 1380, there-

after *tu ch'a-yüan*); generally empowered to gather complaints from the people, to review the handling of prisoners, to impeach any official for misconduct; from Yüan on also authorized to submit remonstrances or suggestions about the Emperor's conduct or policies. Normally assigned to routine surveillance over and checking of records in central government organs and as individuals dispatched to inspect territorial jurisdictions, e.g., as Regional Inspectors (*hsün-an yü-shih*), and on regular or irregular bases dispatched to inspect various categories of governmental activities, e.g., as Salt-control Censors (*hsün-yen yü-shih*). From T'ang to 1080 organized in a constituent unit of the Censorate called the Investigation Bureau (*ch'a-yüan*), thereafter during Sung in 6 Investigation Sections (*ch'a-an*), otherwise in the Investigation Bureau till 1382, thereafter in Circuits (*tao*) named after Provinces, varying but stabilizing at 13 in Ming and 15 in mid-Ch'ing. Appointees in Sui numbered 12–16, rank 7b; in T'ang 10–15, 8a2 (8a1?); in Sung variable but few, 7b; in Chin 12, 7a; in Yüan 32, 7a, mostly Mongols; in Ming 110, 7a; in Ch'ing 56, 7a with some variations, equally Manchus and Chinese. RR+SP: *censeur de la cour des enquêtes au (en) dehors, censeurs d'investigation.* BH: provincial censor. P18, 19, 20.

796 *chiēn-chǎng* 監長
HAN: **Director of the Directorate;** see *ch'eng-hua chien, hsien-chü chien, lung-ma chien, t'ao-t'u chien, t'o-ch'üan chien.* HB: chief inspector. P31, 39.

797 *chièn-chǎng* 諫長
A common unofficial reference to a **Grand Master of Remonstrance** (*chien-i ta-fu*).

798 *chièn-ch'āng yüàn* 建昌院
5 DYN (Liang): lit., office for the initiation of prosperity, derived from a palace building called the Initiation of Prosperity Palace (*chien-ch'ang kung*): **State Fiscal Commission,** a major agency of the central government, handling census reports and tax collections submitted by the dynasty's 4 proto-provincial Defense Commands (*chen*). Headed by an Initiation of Prosperity Palace Commissioner (*chien-ch'ang kung shih*), normally abbreviated to Palace Commissioner (*kung-shih*), who ordinarily was a Grand Councilor (*tsai-hsiang*), specifically a Vice Director of the Chancellery Managing Affairs (*men-hsia shih-lang p'ing-chang shih*) who was Commissioner of the Special Reserves Vault (*yen-tzu k'u shih*) and concurrently Supervisor (*p'an ... shih*) of the State Fiscal Commission. Established in 907; in 912 retitled *kuo-chi ssu* (see *kuo-chi shih*). P49.

799 *chiĕn-ch'ē tū* 檻車督
N-S DIV (N. Ch'i): **Supervisor of the Prisoner Cart,** 2 members of the Court of Judicial Review (*ta-li ssu*); presumably associated with the Prison (*yü*) maintained by the Court. P22.

800 *chiĕn-chèng kuān* 檢正官 or *chien-cheng*
SUNG: **Examiner,** 2 appointed for each of the Five Offices (*wu fang*) or Six Offices (*liu fang*) among which the business of the Secretariat (*chung-shu sheng*) was divided, apparently on special duty assignments from other central government posts, coordinated by a Chief Examiner (*tu chien-cheng*); initiated c. 1068, perhaps discontinued in 1070 but reappointed in 1129, then reduced to one for each Office in 1132. Precise functions are not clear. SP: *examinateur-contrôleur, fonctionnaire chargé d'examiner et de rectifier.* P3.

801 *chiĕn-chèng* 監正
Supervisor, normally of a Directorate, e.g., the Ming–

Ch'ing Directorate of Astronomy (*ch'in-t'ien chien*); in such cases the full sense would seem best suggested by the rendering *ch'in-t'ien chien chien-cheng,* but the superfluous *chien* is commonly omitted. P31, 35, 40.

802 *chiēn-ch'éng* 監丞
(1) May be encountered as an abbreviated, combined reference to the **Supervisor** or **Director** (*chien*) **and Vice Director** or **Aide** (*ch'eng*) of an agency. (2) MING–CH'ING: **Proctor** responsible for student discipline in the Directorate of Education (*kuo-tzu chien*); one, rank 8a, in Ming; one each Manchu and Chinese, rank 8a then 7a, in Ch'ing; in Ming headed a subsection of the Directorate called the Disciplinary Office (*sheng-ch'ien t'ing*). P34.

803 *chiēn-chì shǐh* 監祭使
SUNG: **Commissioner Supervising the Sacrifices,** an ad hoc duty assignment, not a regular post; delegated to represent the Emperor or to assist the Emperor in important sacrificial rituals.

804 *chiĕn-chiào* 檢校
(1) Often occurs in a straightforward verbal meaning such as to inspect, to compare, to verify. (2) N-S DIV–CHIN: **Acting.** Developed in the era of N-S Division from the ordinary verbal sense into a prefix to a title used when an official holding one regular post was assigned on an irregular, temporary basis to carry out the functions of (lit., to inspect) another post: A *chien-chiao* B. By T'ang the term was used very commonly in 3 ways: sometimes in the ordinary verbal sense, sometimes in the sense that an official holding post A also acted (still with some connotation of special or irregular status) with all the authority of post B, and sometimes to indicate that an official was Acting ... in an honorary status, without any real authority. By Sung and Chin times use of the term with titles seems predominantly to have signified honorary status: e.g., *chien-chiao t'ai-tzu pin-k'o chien chien-ch'a yü-shih* (Acting Adviser to the Heir Apparent and Concurrently Investigating Censor, *chien-ch'a yü-shih* in this case indicating the actual function). (3) YÜAN–CH'ING: **Proofreader,** a regular appointment. In Yüan: one in the Secretariat (*chung-shu sheng*) and one in each Branch Secretariat (*hsing chung-shu sheng*), all rank 7a. In Ming: one each, 9a, in the Records Office (*chao-mo so*) of the Ministry of Justice (*hsing-pu*) and of the Censorate (*tu ch'a-yüan*); also one each, 9b, on the staffs of Provincial Administration Commissions (*ch'eng-hsüan pu-cheng shih ssu*) and Provincial Surveillance Commissions (*t'i-hsing an-ch'a shih ssu*). In Ch'ing: unranked, included on the staffs of Provincial Administration Commissions and some Prefectures (*fu*), but not after the first Ch'ing century. (4) CH'ING: **Investigator,** unranked policemen-like personnel employed in most Prefectures and some other units of territorial administration. BH: police inspector.

805 *chiĕn-chiào p'ī-yèn kuān* 檢校批驗官
YÜAN: **Tea and Salt Inspector,** subordinates of Salt Distribution Commissioners (*tu chuan-yün yen shih*) who staffed Tea and Salt Control Stations (*chien-chiao p'i-yen so*) at strategic transport points to check on the weight of tea and salt bags in transit, to verify the government certificates accompanying them, and to catch traffickers in contraband tea and salt. See *p'i-yen so.* P53, 61.

806 *chiĕn-chiào sǒ* 檢校所
YÜAN: an abbreviation of *chien-chiao p'i-yen so* (**Tea and Salt Control Station**); see under *chien-chiao p'i-yen kuan.*

807 *chiĕn-chiào yù-shǐh* 檢校御史
N-S DIV (Chin, N. Dyn.): **Inspecting Censor,** apparently

an antecedent of the Sui–Ch'ing Investigating Censor (*chien-ch'a yü-shih*), though functions are not entirely clear; originated in 251; in the N. Dynasties, usually 12, rank 9. P18.

808   *chiēn-chìh*   監置
SUI: **Supervisor of Transport,** one appointed to the staff of the Hostel for Tributary Envoys (*ssu-fang kuan*) to inspect the camels, horses, carts, or boats of each tribute mission and to expose any violations of imperial instructions concerning transport; an ad hoc duty assignment, not a regular post. P11.

809   *chiēn chīh-nà kuān*   監支納官
CHIN–YÜAN: **Supervisor of Transactions** at government granaries, rank 8 in Chin, 7a in Yüan. P8.

810   *chiēn chīn-ch'ǘ ts'áo*   監津渠曹
HAN: **Section Supervising Fords and Drainways,** a clerical unit found in some Later Han Commanderies (*chün*). HB: bureau of the inspection of fords and canals.

811   *chiēn-chōu*   監州
SUNG: **Prefectural Supervisor,** designation of central government officials detached to monitor the administration of Prefectures (*chou*), one per Prefecture, until the 1080s; could submit reports and complaints about local affairs without the knowledge or consent of the Prefect (*chih-chou*); no prefectural directive was considered authentic without the Supervisor's mark of approval. The formal title, appended as a suffix to the appointee's central government title, was Controller-general (*t'ung-p'an*) of ... Prefecture (*chou*). P72.

812   *chiēn-chù*   監鑄
CHIN, CH'ING: **Director of Coinage,** a special duty assignment for an official with a substantive appointment that was normally specified by a suffix. In Chin used with the suffixes *lang-chung* (Director) and *yüan-wai lang* (Vice Director), signifying substantive posts in Bureaus (*ssu*) of the Ministry of Works (*kung-pu*). In Ch'ing used with suffixes such as *t'ung-chih* (Vice Prefect); each in charge of his Province's Coinage Service (*ch'ien-chü*). P16.

813   *chiēn-chǔ*   薦舉
Throughout history, used as the verb to recommend, signifying the process whereby men were brought into government service on the basis of nominations by existing officials—in contrast, e.g., to winning official status on the basis of inheritance or on the basis of competence demonstrated in recruitment examinations. May be encountered in cases when superior officials recommended subordinates for promotion.

814   *chiēn-ch'üēh*   簡缺
CH'ING: **Simple,** a descriptive term attached as a prefix to the titles of the heads of Prefectures (*fu*), Departments (*chou*), Subprefectures (*t'ing*), Districts (*hsien*), and General Surveillance Circuits (*fen-hsün tao*), signifying that the volume, importance, and complexity of administrative business in their jurisdictions justified ranking them below counterparts designated, in descending order of prestige, Most Important (*tsui-yao*), Important (*yao-ch'üeh*), and Ordinary (*chung-ch'üeh*). The practice of differentiating among territorial appointees in this way probably began in late Ming times.

815   *chiēn-chūn*   監軍
(1) HAN–N-S DIV (Chin): **Army Supervisor,** one of several designations of officers in command of armies on campaign, e.g., Supervisor of the ... Army (*chien ... chün*); less prestigious than Commander-in-chief (*tu-tu*) but more

so than Commander (*tu*). HB: inspector of the army. (2) 5 DYN: a common abbreviation of *chien-chün shih* (**Army-supervising Commissioner**), a representative of the central government dispatched in attempts to control semiautonomous regional Military Commissioners (*chieh-tu shih*). (3) CHIN: **Army Supervisor,** one of several designations for eminent Jurchen officers on the staff of the Bureau of Military Affairs (*shu-mi yüan*). (4) MING: a common abbreviation of *chien-chün yü-shih* (**Army-inspecting Censor**), designation of an Investigating Censor (*chien-ch'a yü-shih*) commissioned on an ad hoc basis to accompany an army on campaign, monitor its activities, and independently report to the throne. P50.

816   *chiēn-chùn*   監郡
CH'ING: unofficial reference to a **Departmental Magistrate** (*t'ung-p'an*).

817   *chiēn-chùn yù-shǐh*   監郡御史
CH'IN: **Commandery-inspecting Censor,** a variant of *chien-ch'a shih* (Supervising Censor).

818   *chiēn-fā*   揀發
CH'ING: lit., to select and send out or release; a prefix encountered before the titles of officials of the Wardens' Offices (*ping-ma ssu*) of the Five Wards (*wu ch'eng*) into which the capital was divided for police and fire-protection purposes, the meaning of which is not wholly clear; e.g., *chien-fa fu chih-hui* may mean Assistant to the Vice Commander, or possibly something akin to Acting Vice Commander.

819   *chiēn-fǎ*   檢法
SUNG, CHIN, YÜAN: **Legal Researcher,** one or more, unranked except rank 8b in Chin, on the staff of the Censorate (*yü-shih t'ai*) until 1282; also in Chin's Court of the Imperial Clan (*ta tsung-cheng fu*). P1, 6, 18.

820   *chiēn-fǎ àn*   檢法案
SUNG: **Legal Research Section,** a minor unit staffed with law specialists, one in each of the Six Ministries (*liu pu*), one in the Right Bureau (*yu-t'ing*) of the Court of Judicial Review (*ta-li ssu*). SP: *service du contrôle judiciaire (jurisprudence et lois)*.

821   *chiēn-fǎ kuān*   檢法官
SUNG: **Legal Researcher,** unranked or low-ranking official found in many offices including the Ministry of Revenue (*hu-pu*), Ministry of Justice (*hsing-pu*), Censorate (*yü-shih-t'ai*), Court of Judicial Review (*ta-li ssu*), State Finance Commission (*san ssu*), and that of the Judicial Commissioner (*t'i-tien hsing-yü kung-shih, t'i-hsing ssu*) in a Circuit (*lu*). SP: *fonctionnaire chargé du contrôle judiciaire (jurisprudence et lois)*. Also see *chien-fa*. P52.

822   *chiēn-fǔ*   監府
SUI: **Supervisor of Tribute Goods,** one appointed to the staff of the Hostel for Tributary Envoys (*ssu-fang kuan*) to receive and care for preferred articles of tribute whenever a tribute mission arrived; an ad hoc duty assignment, not a regular post. P11.

823   *chiēn-fú ts'áo*   監福曹
N-S DIV (N. Wei): **Superintendency of Buddhist Happiness,** a unit subordinate to the Chamberlain for Dependencies (*ta hung-lu*) that catered to the needs of foreign Buddhist priests during visits to China; staffing not clear. Before the end of the dynasty, superseded by the Office for the Clarification of Buddhist Profundities (*chao-hsüan ssu*). Also see *seng-kuan*. P17.

824 *chiēn-hòu* 監候

SUI–CH'ING: **Astronomical Observer,** members of Sui's astrological and calendar-calculating agency maintained by the Palace Library (*pi-shu sheng*) with the changing names Astrological Section (*t'ai-shih ts'ao*), Astrological Service (*t'ai-shih chü*), and Directorate of Astrology (*t'ai-shih chien*), in the early T'ang Astrological Service (*t'ai-shih chü*), Liao's Directorate of Astronomy (*ssu-t'ien chien*), Yüan's Astrological Commission (*t'ai-shih yüan*), and the Ming–Ch'ing Directorate of Astronomy (*ssu-t'ien chien* in early Ming, thereafter *ch'in-t'ien chien*); in Sui from 2 to 10, rank 9b; in T'ang one, 8a2; in Liao number and rank not clear; in Yüan 6, 8b; in early Ming 3, 8a; thereafter one, 9a. See *wu-kuan chien-hou*. RR: *directeur de l'observation des astres.* BH: *observer.* P35.

825 *chiēn-hòu fǔ* 監候府

SUI: **Office of Astronomical Observations,** a unit in an agency maintained by the Palace Library (*pi-shu sheng*) that was confusingly called either the Astrological Section (*t'ai-shih ts'ao*) or the Astrological Service (*t'ai-shih chü*) until c. 604, when it was redesignated Directorate of Astrology (*t'ai-shih chien*); consisted of 2 parts called the Left and Right Offices (*fu*) staffed with from 4 to 8 Timekeepers (*ssu-ch'en shih*), rank 9a, to whom were allocated 110 Students of the Water Clock (*lou-k'o sheng*) under the tutelage of 4 apparently non-official specialists called Erudites of the Water Clock (*lou-k'o po-shih*). P35

826 *chiěn-hsiáng fáng* 檢詳房 or *chiěn-hsiáng sǒ* 檢詳所

SUNG: **Editorial Office,** clerical units in the Bureau of Military Affairs (*shu-mi yüan*) and the Finance Planning Commission (*chih-chih san-ssu t'iao-li ssu*), staffed with Editorial Clerks (*chien-hsiang wen-tzu, chien-hsiang kuan*), rank 6B. SP: *chambre de contrôle, bureau de contrôle.*

827 *chiēn-hsiáng shǐh* 監香使

SUNG: **Commissioner for Incense Offerings,** a duty assignment for one or more Censors (*yü-shih*) to participate in imperial sacrifices; specific occasions and functions not clear. SP: *commissaire-surveillant de l'encens.*

828 *chiěn-hsiào* 檢校

See *chien-chiao.*

829 *chiēn-hsiū kuó-shǐh* 監修國史 or *chien-hsiu*

SUNG, LIAO, CHIN: **Chief Compiler of the Dynastic History,** nominal head of the Historiography Institute (*kuo-shih yüan*) and also, at least in Sung, of the True Records Institute (*shih-lu yüan*); in Sung commonly the responsibility of a Grand Councilor (*tsai-hsiang*). SP: *directeur de la rédaction de l'histoire de l'état.* P3, 23, 25.

830 *chiēn-hsüéh pó-shìh* 監學博士

SUNG: **Erudite Supervising Instruction,** one of the designations used for officials of the School for the Sons of the State (*kuo-tzu hsüeh*) and of the National University (*t'ai-hsüeh*). SP: *professeur.*

831 *chièn-ì tà-fū* 諫議大夫

Grand Master of Remonstrance, one of the category of prestigious officials called Remonstrance Officials (*chien-kuan*) or Speaking Officials (*yen-kuan*) whose principal function was to attend and advise the emperor, and especially to remonstrate with him about what they considered improper conduct or policy. (1) HAN–SUI: sometimes rendered *chien ta-fu* or simply *chien-i;* normally an honorific title awarded a particularly trusted high-ranking official,

considered to be loosely attached to the Chancellery (*men-hsia sheng*). HB: grandee remonstrant and consultant. (2) T'ANG: those prefixed Left were members of the Chancellery and those prefixed Right were members of the Secretariat (*chung-shu sheng*), all rank 5a till 843, then 4b; often simply called *chien-i,* from 662 to 705 called *cheng-chien ta-fu.* RR: *conseiller censeur de l'empereur.* (3) SUNG: prefixed Left and Right, both rank 4b, members of the Chancellery and Secretariat, respectively; were not reassigned to the new Remonstrance Bureau (*chien-yüan*) when it was created c. 1020 but shared in the great prestige accorded both Surveillance Officials (*ch'a-kuan*) and Remonstrance Officials, especially in N. Sung. SP: *conseiller censeur de l'empereur, conseiller politique.* (4) CHIN, MING: members of the Remonstrance Bureau, which was not perpetuated by Yüan and existed in Ming only from 1380 to 1382; rank not clear; in Yüan and again after 1382, in a departure from tradition, remonstrance functions were specifically assigned to Censors. P19, 21.

832 *chièn-jùi yíng* 健銳營

CH'ING: **Scouting Brigade,** one of the units into which members of the Inner Banners (*nei-ch'i*) were organized, normally commanded by a Prince (*wang*) serving as Commander-general (*t'ung-ling* or *tsung-t'ung*); created in 1749 particularly to assist in quelling revolts in Mongolia. BH: scouts, the light division.

833 *chièn-k'āng sān kuān* 建康三官

N-S DIV (Liang): **Three Wardens of Chien-k'ang,** police chiefs of Chien-k'ang District (*hsien*), the dynastic capital (modern Nanking); commonly cooperated with the Three Law Enforcement Aides (*t'ing-wei san kuan*) in conducting police investigations and trials regarding criminal offenses in the capital. P22.

834 *chiēn-k'ò yǔ-shǐh* 監課御史

MING: **Produce Levies Censor,** duty assignment for Investigating Censors (*chien-ch'a yü-shih*) to inspect the activities and audit the accounts of Offices of Produce Levies (*ch'ou-fen chu-mu chü*) in the Peking and Nanking vicinities.

835 *chiēn-kuān* 監官

SUNG: **Supervisory Official,** a designation used for the heads of many minor offices throughout the government subordinate to Ministries (*pu*), the Palace Administration (*tien-chung sheng*), the Court of the Imperial Stud (*t'ai-p'u ssu*), the Court of State Ceremonial (*hung-lu ssu*), etc. Sometimes used as a eunuch title. SP: *surveillant.*

836 *chiēn-kuān* 諫官

Remonstrance Official: from Han on, a generic term for officials appointed, on either a regular or an honorary basis, for the special purpose of keeping watch over documents flowing to and from the throne and to remonstrate with the ruler about conduct or policies that they considered improper. In Han times and through the era of N-S Division, most remonstrance titles were honorific, awarded to officials considered especially trustworthy. By T'ang the offices had become regular ones, divided between the Chancellery (*men-hsia sheng*) and the Secretariat (*chung-shu sheng*). In Sung, c. 1020, an independent Remonstrance Bureau (*chien-yüan*) was established; some modern historians interpret this development as an effort to deflect Remonstrance Officials' attention and efforts away from the ruler toward the Grand Councilors (*tsai-hsiang*), to whom they were no longer subordinate. From Yüan on, except for a brief revival of the Remonstrance Bureau in the 1380s, special Remonstrance Officials were not appointed and remonstrance functions became added responsibilities of Censors (*yü-shih*), who had previously been limited in general to maintaining watch over the officialdom and impeaching wayward officials, as Surveillance Officials (*ch'a-kuan*). Remonstrance Officials through history were also commonly referred to as Speaking Officials (*yen-kuan*). The most common specific remonstrance titles included *chien-i ta-fu*, *pu-ch'üeh*, and *shih-i*, qq.v. P18.

837 *chìen-kuān àn* 諫官案
SUNG: **Remonstrance Section** in the Chancellery (*men-hsia sheng*) and the Secretariat (*chung-shu sheng*), apparently the offices of the Grand Masters of Remonstrance (*chien-i ta-fu*). SP: *service de la réception des dépêches d'interpellation*.

838 *chiēn-kuān t'í-lǐng* 監官提領
SUNG: **Supervisory Director**, 2, rank not clear, heads of the Storehouse of Spices and Silks (*chi-chuang k'u*) in the Court of the Imperial Treasury (*t'ai-fu ssu*). See *t'i-ling*. SP: *surveillant administrateur*.

839 *chiēn-kuān yù-shǐh t'īng* 諫官御史廳
SUNG: **Office of Remonstrating Censors**, for a short time beginning in 1045 an agency of the Censorate (*yü-shih t'ai*) charged with remonstrance functions and staffed with Remonstrating Censors (*yen-shih yü-shih, yen-shih kuan, chien-kuan yü-shih*).

840 *chiēn-kúo* 監國
Lit., to supervise or oversee the state: throughout history used in the sense of **Regent** to prefix the title and name of a dignitary (commonly a member of the imperial family) to whom control over the central government was entrusted at periods when the ruler was traveling at a distance from the capital, or when the ruler was too young or otherwise unable to fulfill his normal functions.

841 *chiēn-lín* 監臨
MING–CH'ING: **Examiner,** collective reference to officials presiding over lower-level civil service recruitment examinations.

842 *chiēn-lìng* 監令
Director, normally of a Directorate, e.g., the early Ming Directorate of Astronomy (*ssu-t'ien chien*); in such cases the full sense would seem best suggested by the rendering *ssu-t'ien chien chien-ling*, but the superfluous *chien* was commonly omitted. P35.

843 *chiēn-mén* 監門
Gate Guard. (1) CHOU: unranked functionaries or soldiers, numbers unspecified, on duty at each of the capital gates, under the supervision of a Gatekeeper (*ssu-men*) on the staff of the Ministry of Education (*ti-kuan*). CL: *surveillant des portes*. (2) SUNG: unranked functionaries attached to the Palace Administration (*tien-chung sheng*), the establishment of the Heir Apparent, the Court of Imperial Entertainments (*kuang-lu ssu*), etc.; often occurs with a place-name or agency-name insert, e.g., *chien san sheng shu-mi yüan men* (Guards at the Gates of the Three Departments and the Bureau of Military Affairs). SP: *garde de la surveillance des portes*. (3) CHIN: one prefixed Left and one prefixed Right, in charge of the gates of the establishment of the Heir Apparent, i.e., the Eastern Palace (*tung-kung*). P26, 38.

844 *chiēn-mén fǔ* 監門府
Lit., garrison or office of gate supervisors: **Palace Gate**

Guard. (1) SUI: one of 2 units constituting the Palace Guards (*ch'in-wei*), elite troops drawn from the Twelve Guards (*shih-erh wei*) stationed in and around the dynastic capital, which in turn were staffed on a rotational basis by Garrison Militia units (see *fu-ping*) throughout the state; headed by a Commandant (*lang-chiang*) and a Vice Commandant (*chiang*). The other Palace Guards unit was the Imperial Bodyguard (*pei-shen fu*). (2) T'ANG: one prefixed Left and one prefixed Right; from 636, units in the group of Sixteen Guards (*shih-liu wei*) stationed at the capital; in 662 retitled *chien-men wei*. RR: *garde de la surveillance des portes*. P43.

845 *chiēn-mén kuān* 監門官
SUNG: **Gate Tender,** normally one unranked suboffical assigned to each important agency, e.g., the Six Ministries (*liu pu*), the Directorate of Education (*kuo-tzu chien*), the Court of the Imperial Granaries (*ssu-nung ssu*). See *chien-men*. SP: *fonctionnaire chargé de surveillance des portes*.

846 *chiēn-mén shuài-fǔ* 監門率府
SUI–SUNG: **Gate Guard Command,** one prefixed Left and one prefixed Right, military units assigned to the establishment of the Heir Apparent, each headed by a Commandant (*shuai*), rank 4a in T'ang, 7b in Sung. In c. 604 retitled *kung-men chiang-fu* (Palace Gates Guard Command); original Sui name revived in 622; from 662 to 670 variantly designated *ch'ung-i wei* (Guard Honoring the Inner Apartments). RR+SP: *garde de la surveillance des portes*. P26.

847 *chiēn-mén wèi* 監門衛
(1) T'ANG–SUNG: **Palace Gate Guard,** one prefixed Left and one prefixed Right, units in the Sixteen Guards (*shih-liu wei*) stationed at the dynastic capital; created in 662 by retitling of the *chien-men fu*; generally responsible for the defense of the imperial palace, especially for monitoring the comings and goings of authorized personnel and commodities. Each headed by a General-in-chief (*ta chiang-chün*), rank 3a1 in T'ang, 4a in Sung; from 786 to the end of T'ang occasionally under the control of Generalissimos (*shang chiang-chün*), rank 2a2. Troops were originally provided on a rotational basis by Garrison Militia units (see *fu-ping*), but the rotational system declined markedly in the 700s and was terminated in 750. Thereafter through Sung all of the Sixteen Guards became largely decorative, providing posts to which members of the imperial family and perhaps other favorites could be appointed. See *huan-wei, ch'in-wei, pei-shen fu*. RR+SP: *garde de la surveillance des portes*. (2) SUI–CHIN: 2 of the Ten Guard Commands (*shih shuai-fu*, q.v.) assigned to the establishment of the Heir Apparent. P26.

848 *chiēn-mù shǐh* 監牧使 or *chien-mu*
N-S DIV–SUNG: **Horse Pasturage Supervisor,** members of the Court of the Imperial Stud (*t'ai-p'u ssu*) delegated to monitor the activities of Horse Pasturages (*mu-chien*) in specified regions; in T'ang primarily bore the directional prefixes South, West, etc., coordinated by a Horse Pasturage Supervisor-in-chief (*tu chien-mu shih*); in Sung apparently more numerous and with smaller jurisdictions, reporting through intermediary Herds Offices (*ch'ün-mu ssu*) to the Bureau of Military Affairs (*shu-mi yüan*). See *chien, mu-ch'ang, mu-chien, mu-yüan, yüan-ma ssu*. RR: *commissaire impérial chargé de surveiller les élevages, commissaire impérial aux élevages*. SP: *commissaire à l'élevage des chevaux*. P31.

849 *chiēn-p'an* 兼判
SUNG: unofficial reference to a **Vice Minister** (see *t'ung-*

p'an ssu) of the Court of the Imperial Granaries (*ssu-nung ssu*). SP: *sous-directeur*.

850 *chiēn-p'íng* 監平
N-S DIV: variant of *cheng-chien-p'ing* (**Three Law Enforcement Aides**).

851 *chiēn-sǎo kuān* 監埽官
SUNG: **Dike Supervisor,** 135 unranked subofficials on the staff of the Directorate of Waterways (*tu-shui chien*), responsible to the State Finance Commission (*san ssu*). SP: *fonctionnaire chargé de la surveillance des chaussées*. P59.

852 *chiēn-shàn* 監膳
SUI–SUNG: **Head Cook,** 12 in Sui, 10 in T'ang, 15 in Sung, all non-official specialists on the staff of the Banquets Office (*ta-kuan shu*), a unit in the Court of Imperial Entertainments (*kuang-lu ssu*). RR+SP: *directeur des mets*. P30.

853 *chiēn-shàn shǐh* 監膳史
T'ANG: **Second Cook,** 15 non-official specialists serving under Head Cooks (*chien-shan*) in the Banquets Office (*ta-kuan shu*), a unit in the Court of Imperial Entertainments (*kuang-lu ssu*). RR: *sous-directeur des mets*. P30.

854 *chiēn-shè* 兼攝
Concurrent Temporary Appointment, a term used from Sung on if not earlier when an official was assigned, in addition to his normal duty, to assist in (but not take charge of) another agency at a busy time.

855 *chièn-shēn* 薦紳
CH'ING: one of many variants of *shen-shih* (**the elite**), q.v.

856 *chiēn-shēng* 監生
(1) SUNG–CH'ING: **National University Student,** the most common generic designation of students admitted to the National University (*t'ai-hsüeh*) maintained by the Directorate of Education (*kuo-tzu chien*). Normally subsidized by the state, all such students upon completion of their studies could be appointed directly to offices and were eligible to participate in the Metropolitan Examination (*sheng-shih, hui-shih*) stage of the civil service examination recruitment system. From mid-Ming on, the study body included Tribute Students (*kung-sheng*), Official Students (*kuan-sheng*), Students by Purchase (*li-chien*), and other categories. SP: *élève de l'université*. BH: collegian of the imperial academy of learning. (2) CH'ING: **Student by Purchase Fourth Class,** a subcategory of Students by Purchase (*li-chien*, q.v.) in the National University consisting of men who were admitted without having passed at any level of the civil service examination recruitment system, in recognition of their contributions of grain or money to the state; also called *min-sheng* (Civilian Student).

857 *chiēn-shìh* 監事
(1) T'ANG–CH'ING: **Office Attendant,** rank 8b in Ming, otherwise apparently unranked subofficials, appointees in various units of the Court of the Imperial Stud (*t'ai-p'u ssu*), Court of Imperial Entertainments (*kuang-lu ssu*), Court of the Imperial Granaries (*ssu-nung ssu*), Palace Administration (*tien-chung sheng*), etc. RR+SP: *surveillant des affaires*. (2) When the 2 characters envelop an agency name, in the form *chien … shih,* they indicate that an official not normally in charge of, or even associated with, the agency in question was on a temporary or some other special basis "supervising the affairs of" the named agency; hence concurrently (?) **Supervisor** of the named agency, or (e.g., censorial) **Inspector** of it.

858 *chiēn-shìh* 監試
T'ANG–CH'ING: **Examination Overseer,** duty assignment for a central government or, in Ming and Ch'ing, provincial official to assist as a proctor in a civil service recruitment examination.

859 *chiěn-shìh* 翦氏
CHOU: **Exterminator,** one ranked as a Junior Serviceman (*hsia-shih*) in the Ministry of Justice (*ch'iu-kuan*), responsible for keeping (the ruler's palace?) free of troublesome bugs and insects. CL: *destructeur*.

860 *chiēn-shōu* 監收
CH'ING: **Collection Superintendent,** a general reference to Circuit Intendants (*tao-t'ai*) and other regional and local officials who directed tax collections at various gates, passes, fords, etc. P62.

861 *chiēn-shǒu hsìn-p'ào kuān* 監守信礮官
CH'ING: **Commander of the Alarm Gun,** one, rank 5a, at each of the gates of the dynastic capital, subordinate to a Commander-in-chief of the Alarm Guns (*hsin-p'ao tsung-kuan*). BH: assistant controller of alarm-signal guns.

862 *chiēn-shū pó-shìh* 監書博士
YÜAN: **Literary Erudite,** designation of litterateurs assigned to the Hall for the Diffusion of Literature (*hsüan-wen ko*), established in 1340; charged to counsel the Emperor on the precepts of the classics and the precedents of history, especially as participants in the Classics Colloquium (*ching-yen*). P23, 24.

863 *chiēn-sōu yǜ-shǐh* 監搜御史
N-S DIV–T'ANG: **Censorial Gate Monitor,** a duty assignment for a Censor (*yü-shih*) to station himself at the entrance to the imperial palace and monitor all officials entering with memorials; the extent of this appointee's power is not clear, but no memorialist could enter the palace without permission of the Censor on duty. The practice did not end until the early 700s. P18.

864 *chiēn-ssū* 監司
(1) N-S DIV (Chin): unofficial reference to a **Regional Inspector** (*tz'u-shih*). (2) N-S DIV (Liang): **Supervisory Office,** variant designation of the Censorate (*yü-shih t'ai*) or its senior executive official, nominally the Palace Aide to the Censor-in-chief (*yü-shih chung-ch'eng*). (3) SUNG: **Circuit Supervisor,** a generic reference to coordinating commissioners of Circuits (*lu*); see *shuai-ssu, ts'ao-ssu, hsien-ssu, ts'ang-ssu*. SP: *intendant fiscal ou judiciaire de province*. (4) YÜAN: apparently a generic reference to the **Surveillance Commissions** (*t'i-hsing an-ch'a ssu, su-cheng lien-fang ssu*) of Circuits (*tao*) or to the executive officials of such agencies. (5) MING–CH'ING: **Provincial Intendant,** a generic reference to those provincial officials known as Circuit Intendants (*tao-t'ai*). Cf. *fang-mien*. P51, 62.

865 *chièn tà-fū* 諫大夫
HAN: **Grand Master of Remonstrance,** a subordinate of the Chamberlain for Attendants (*kuang-lu-hsün*); antecedent of *chien-i ta-fu*, q.v. HB: grandee remonstrant.

866 *chiēn t'ài-ts'āng shǐh* 監太倉使
T'ANG: **Inspector of the Imperial Granaries,** from 731 a special duty assignment for an Investigating Censor (*chien-ch'a yü-shih*) or a Palace Censor (*tien-chung shih yü-shih*) on the staff of the Censorate (*yü-shih t'ai*); see *t'ai-ts'ang*. RR: *commissaire impérial à la surveillance du grenier impérial*. P18.

867 *chiēn-tāng kuān* 監當官 or *chien-tang*
SUNG: **State Monopoly Agent,** a duty assignment for a Capital or Court Official (*ching-ch'ao kuan*), normally for a 3-year term, to administer the collection of taxes on state-monopolized commodities such as tea, salt, and wine in a particular jurisdiction at the Prefecture (*chou*) or lower level. SP: *gérant.* P62.

868 *chiēn-t'ǎo kuān* 檢討官 or *chien-t'ao*
Examining Editor, apparently with the principal function of checking the work of copyists. (1) T'ANG: normally a concurrent duty assignment for officials regularly holding other posts, one assigned to the Court of Imperial Sacrifices (*t'ai-ch'ang ssu*), unspecified numbers to the Academy of Scholarly Worthies (*chi-hsien tien shu-yüan*) and to the Secretariat (*chung-shu sheng*). RR: *fonctionnaire chargé d'examiner et de scruter les textes.* (2) SUNG: rank not clear, assignments scattered among the Institute for the Veneration of Literature (*ch'ung-wen yüan*) of the Secretariat of the Heir Apparent (*tso ch'un-fang*), the Department of State Affairs (*shang-shu sheng*), the Chancellery (*men-hsia sheng*), the Palace Library (*pi-shu sheng*), etc. SP: *rédacteur-assistant.* (3) CHIN: 2, rank 9b, usually sons and grandsons of high officials, in the Court of Imperial Sacrifices. (4) MING–CH'ING: rank 7b, 4 then 6 in Ming, no specified numbers in Ch'ing, staff members of the Hanlin Academy (*han-lin yüan*). BH: corrector. P4, 23, 25, 27.

869 *chiēn-tièn shè-jén* 監殿舍人
SUI: **Palace Secretary,** 4, rank not clear, members of the Palace Attendance Service (*nei-chih chü*) in the Secretariat of the Heir Apparent (*men-hsia fang*). P26.

870 *chiēn-tsào* 監造
Work Superintendent. (1) SUNG: 2, rank not clear, in the Armaments Office (*chün-ch'i so*) of the Ministry of Works (*kung-pu*). SP: *surveillant de fabrication.* (2) CH'ING: one, rank 6 or 7, in the Imperial Printing Office (*hsiu-shu ch'u*) in the Hall of Military Glory (*wu-ying tien*). BH: overseer of works. P37.

871 *chiēn-ts'áo* 監漕
T'ANG: **Director of Transport,** an unranked subofficial who was one of the less important staff members of the Office of Boats and Boatmen (*chou-chi shu*), which was the 632–738 equivalent of the Directorate of Waterways (*tu-shui chien*); also 10, rank 9b1, from c. 627 to the 760s or 770s in the Office of Rivers and Canals (*ho-ch'ü shu*), a unit of the Directorate of Waterways. RR: *directeur des transports par eau.* P60.

872 *chiēn-tsò* 監作
Work Supervisor. (1) SUI: 12 unranked subofficials in the Court for the Palace Buildings (*chiang-tso ssu*). (2) T'ANG: variable numbers, unranked, in units of the Directorate for the Palace Buildings (*chiang-tso chien*); 4 each, rank 9b2, in the Central Service Office (*chung-shang shu*) and the Foundry Office (*chang-yeh shu*), both units in the Directorate of Imperial Manufactories (*shao-fu chien*); one, rank 9b2, in the Office of Female Services (*i-t'ing chü*) of the Palace Domestic Service (*nei-shih sheng*). RR: *directeur des travaux.* (3) SUNG: one unranked subofficial in the Crossbows Office (*chia-nu fang shu*) of the Directorate for Armaments (*chün-ch'i chien*). SP: *surveillant.* P14, 15, 38.

873 *chiēn-tū* 監督
MING–CH'ING: **Superintendent,** normally very low rank or unranked, found in charge of various granaries, storehouses, post stations, stables, etc. BH: inspector.

874 *chiēn-wù wù* 監物務
SUNG: **Office of Monopolized Goods,** in charge of state-controlled exchanges in each Prefecture (*chou*); staffing not clear. SP: *surveillant d'échange monopolisé dans une préfecture.*

875 *chiēn-yā* 監押
SUNG: **Supervisor of Militia,** duty assignment of a staff member at the Prefecture (*fu, chou*) and lower levels; a common concurrent responsibility of a District Magistrate (*hsien-ling*). SP: *fonctionnaire militaire chargé de l'entraînement des troupes, commissaire à la surveillance générale.*

876 *chiēn-yìn* 監印
YÜAN: **Superintendent of Seals,** 2, probably of noble status but rank not clear, assigned as aides to the Director (*lîng*) of the Secretariat (*chung-shu sheng*) or of a Branch Secretariat (*hsing chung-shu sheng*). P4.

877 *chiēn-yù* 監獄
Prison: a term used irregularly throughout history. See *nei-chien, wai-chien, nan-chien, pei-chien.*

878 *chiēn yù-shǐh* 監御史
HAN: **Supervising Censor,** a term used for staff members of the Censorate (*yü-shih fu*) when sent out to tour and inspect Commanderies (*chün*); in 106 B.C. superseded by resident Regional Inspectors (*tz'u-shih*) in 13 Regions (*pu, chou*). HB: inspecting secretary. P18.

879 *chiēn-yüàn* 檢院
SUNG: abbreviated reference to *teng-wen chien-yüan* (**Public Petitioners Review Office**), q.v.

880 *chiēn-yüàn* 監院
SUNG: variant of *ch'a-yüan* (**Investigation Bureau**), q.v.

881 *chiēn-yüán* 諫垣
(1) SUNG: unofficial reference to the **Censorate** (*yü-shih t'ai*). (2) MING–CH'ING: may be encountered as an unofficial reference to the **Six Offices of Scrutiny** (*liu k'o*).

882 *chiēn-yüàn* 諫院
Remonstrance Bureau. (1) SUNG: nominally established c. 1020 (1017?), but without a significant staff until after 1032; thereafter an autonomous agency of the central government charged to scrutinize documents flowing to and from the throne and to criticize proposals and policy decisions considered improper; staffed with Remonstrators (*ssu-chien*), rank 7a, and Exhorters (*cheng-yen*), 7b. SP: *cour des remonstrances, bureau de critique politique.* (2) CHIN: staffed with Grand Masters of Remonstrance (*chien-i ta-fu*), Remonstrators, Rectifiers of Omissions (*pu-ch'üeh*), and Reminders (*shih-i*), ranks not clear. (3) MING: existed from 1380 to 1382 only, with a Grand Master of Remonstrance as head; thereafter remonstrance functions were assigned to members of the Censorate (*tu ch'a-yüan*), as in Yüan times, and also members of the Six Offices of Scrutiny (*liu k'o*). P19.

883 *chiēn-yüèh kuān* 檢閱官 or *chien-yüeh*
Editorial Examiner. (1) SUNG: unspecified numbers of low-ranking or unranked editorial clerks in the Historiography Institute (*kuo-shih yüan*), the True Records Institute (*shih-lu yüan*), and the Institute for the Veneration of Literature (*ch'ung-wen yüan*). SP: *examinateur.* (2) CHIN: one, rank 9b; in the Court of Imperial Sacrifices (*t'ai-ch'ang ssu*) from 1201 to 1204 only; also 5 Jurchen and 5 Chinese, 9b, in the Historiography Institute. (3) YÜAN: 4, 8a, in the

Hanlin Academy (*han-lin yüan*), normally designated *han-lin chien-yüeh*. (4) MING: Yüan pattern retained until 1381, then discontinued. (5) CH'ING: from 6 to 8, apparently unranked suboficials, assisted the Grand Secretary (*ta hsüeh-shih*) in charge of the Hall of Literary Profundity (*wen-yüan ko*). BH: inspector. P23, 25, 27.

884 chiēn-yǜn 監運
Supervisor of Transport, a common abbreviated reference to several types of officials responsible for the transport of tax commodities to the dynastic capital or for even broader fiscal affairs, such as T'ang's Transport Commissioners (*chuan-yün shih*), Sung–Chin Fiscal Commissioners (also *chuan-yün shih*), Yüan–Ming Salt Distribution Commissioners (*tu chuan-yün yen shih*), etc.

885 ch'iēn 僉 or 簽
A prefix found attached to official titles, literally suggesting and perhaps originally denoting a seal-keeper for or co-signatory with the official whose title follows, but ordinarily used to designate an **Assistant ...,** less prestigious than a Vice ... (*fu ...*); e.g., the Ming–Ch'ing Provincial Surveillance Commission (*t'i-hsing an-ch'a shih ssu*) was headed by a Surveillance Commissioner (*an-ch'a shih*), rank 3a, and usually included in its executive staff several Surveillance Vice Commissioners (*an-ch'a fu-shih*), 4a, and Assistant Surveillance Commissioners (*an-ch'a ch'ien-shih*), 5a.

886 ch'ién 鈐
SUNG: an abbreviated reference to the **Commandant** (*ch'ien-hsia*) on the staff of a Prefecture (*chou*).

887 ch'iēn chì 千騎
T'ANG: **Thousand Cavaliers,** an elite group of mounted archers who, in 2 shifts, escorted the Emperor on hunts and other outings; created in 689 by an expansion of the original Hundred Cavaliers (*po chi*), in 707 (710?) further transformed into the Myriad Cavaliers (*wan chi*), from which quickly evolved the Left and Right Militant as Dragons Armies (*lung-wu chün*) of the Northern Command (*pei-ya*). RR: *mille cavaliers.*

888 ch'ién-chiēn 錢監
CHIN: **Directorate of Coinage,** a generic term for several agencies; see *pao-fang ch'ien-chien, pao-yüan ch'ien-chien, li-yung ch'ien-chien, fu-t'ung ch'ien-chien.* P16.

889 ch'ién-chǘ 錢局
(1) MING: **Coinage Service,** an unofficial reference early in the dynasty to Provincial Coinage Services (*pao-ch'üan chü*); also see *pao-yüan chü.* (2) CH'ING: **Provincial Coinage Service,** a generic name for agencies in most Provinces and such closely dependent territories as Sinkiang that produced and circulated copper coins under the direction of the appropriate Provincial Administration Commissions (*ch'eng-hsüan pu-cheng shih ssu*) and under the relatively loose guidance of 2 Coinage Offices (*ch'ien-fa t'ang*) at the dynastic capital, one subordinate to the Ministry of Revenue (*hu-pu*), one to the Ministry of Works (*kung-pu*). Provincially-produced coins were separately identifiable, and each Provincial Coinage Service had a Province-specific, often archaic name in the pattern *pao*-(place-name) *chü*, e.g., *pao*-Chin *chü* (Shansi), *pao*-Che *chü* (Chekiang). However, all coins were produced from designs issued by the Ministry of Revenue. Provincial Services were staffed by generically-designated Coinage Officials (*chien-chu kuan;* see under *chien-chu*) on duty assignments from (or concurrently with) regular posts in appropriate Prefectures (*fu*)

as Vice Prefects (*t'ung-chih*) or Assistant Prefects (*t'ung-p'an*), ranks 5a and 6a, respectively; they were more specifically designated, e.g., as Vice Prefect of Pao-ting (serving as) Supervisor (*p'an ... shih*) of the Shansi Coinage Service. Cf. *ch'ien-chien, p'an.* P6, 16.

890 ch'ién-chūn 前軍
Army of the Front, one of the units into which Chinese military forces were traditionally divided, others at the same hierarchical level being the Army of the Left (*tso-chün*), Army of the Center (*chung-chün*), Army of the Right (*yu-chün*), and Army of the Rear (*hou-chün*), each normally commanded by a General (*chiang-chün*): e.g., General of the Front (*ch'ien chiang-chün*) or General of the Army of the Front (*ch'ien-chün chiang-chün*).

891 ch'ién-fǎ t'áng 錢法堂
Lit., monetary policy hall: **Coinage Office.** (1) MING: a quasi-official reference to the special Ministry of Revenue (*hu-pu*) post of Vice Minister Supervisory Manager of Coinage (*tu-li ch'ien-fa shih-lang*), established in the 1620s to expedite production of coins for emergency defense needs. See *pao-ch'üan chü.* (2) CH'ING: established in 1644 after the Ming example under the Ministry of Revenue with a Vice Minister of Revenue, either Chinese or Manchu, serving concurrently as Manager of the Coinage Office (*kuan-li ch'ien-fa t'ang*); but very quickly expanded into 2 Offices, one headed by a Vice Minister of Revenue and one by a Vice Minister of Works (*kung-pu shih-lang*), each designated Right Vice Minister Supervisory Manager of the Coinage Office (*tu-li ch'ien-fa t'ang yu shih-lang*). Originally in each case a Chinese official held the post, but in 1679 it was ordered that there should always be one Manchu and one Chinese Supervisory Manager. In 1761 the Ministry of Revenue's Coinage Office created a subordinate unit called the Office of Dies (*chang-kao ssu*) staffed with one Manchu and one Chinese official delegated from the Ministry's Bureaus (*ch'ing-li ssu*). The 2 Coinage Offices had top-level supervisory responsibility for the production and circulation of copper coins throughout the empire, but that responsibility seems to have been filtered in each case through a Metropolitan Coinage Service (*pao-ch'üan chü* in the Ministry of Revenue, *pao-yüan chü* in the Ministry of Works; see both entries). Also see *ch'ien-chü.* P6, 16.

892 ch'ién-fēng yíng 前鋒營
CH'ING: **Vanguard Brigade,** an elite military unit made up of members selected from all Manchu and Mongol Banners (*ch'i*), responsible for guarding the imperial palace in peacetime and for first engaging the enemy on campaign; not considered part of the Imperial Bodyguard (*ch'in-chün ying*); divided into Left and Right Wings (*i*), each led by a Commander-general (*t'ung-ling*); headed overall, by an Imperial Prince also entitled Commander-general (*t'ung-ling, tsung-t'ung*). BH: vanguard division.

893 ch'ién-fǔ 錢府
HAN: **Tax and Credit Office,** in the reign of Wang Mang (A.D. 9–23) established in official markets of the dynastic capital and 5 other major cities, subordinate to Market Masters (*shih-shih*); see under *wu chün-ssu shih-shih* (Five Market Masters).

894 ch'iēn-fū chǎng 千夫長 or **ch'ien-fu**
YÜAN–MING: lit., leader of 1,000 men: **Battalion Commander,** variant of *ch'ien-hu,* q.v. In Ming used principally as a title bestowed on southwestern aboriginal chieftains. P72.

895 ch'ién-háng 前行
(1) T'ANG–SUNG: **Front Echelon** of Ministries (*pu*) in the Department of State Affairs (*shang-shu sheng*), specifically meaning the Ministries of Personnel (*li-pu*) and of War (*ping-pu*), which were more prestigious than the Middle Echelon (*chung-hang*) comprising the Ministries of Revenue (*hu-pu*) and Justice (*hsing-pu*) and the Rear Echelon (*hou-hang*) comprising the Ministries of Rites (*li-pu*) and of Works (*kung-pu*). P38. (2) SUNG: **Senior Clerk** (?), an uncommon title coupled with Junior Clerk (? *hou-hang*), apparently unranked subofficials; found in the Court of Palace Attendants (*hsüan-hui yüan*), the Accounting Office (*shen-chi ssu*) of the Court of the Imperial Treasury (*t'ai-fu ssu*), etc. SP: *employé de rang avancé*.

896 ch'ién-háng chèng-láng 前行正郎
T'ANG: a collective reference to **Vice Ministers** (*shih-lang*) **of the Front Echelon** (*ch'ien-hang*), i.e., of the Ministries of Personnel (*li-pu*) and of War (*ping-pu*) in the Department of State Affairs (*shang-shu sheng*), who until c. 712 monopolized duty assignments as Participants in the Drafting of Proclamations (*chih-chih-kao*) in the Administration Chamber (*cheng-shih t'ang*), where Grand Councilors (*tsai-hsiang*) presided over general governmental affairs in consultation with the Emperor. RR: *secrétaire régulier de premier rang*.

897 ch'ién-háng yǐn 前行引
Forward Scout: possible variant romanization of *ch'ien hsing-yin*, q.v.

898 ch'ién-hsiá 鈐轄
SUNG–CHIN: lit., controller of the seal (?): (1) **Military Administrator** of a Circuit (*lu*), an army on campaign, etc.; not a combat commander, but apparently something like an administrative aide to a commander. Usually a concurrent title for either a civil official or a military officer with a substantive post elsewhere in the governmental establishment. Commonly expanded to the more explicitly military form *ping-ma ch'ien-hsia* (lit., Military Administrator of Infantry and Cavalry); prefixed variants include Chief (*tu*) and Vice (*fu*) Military Administrators. SP: *directeur militaire*. (2) **Administrative Aide,** a non-military assignment in such agencies as a Branch Directorate of Waterways (*wai tu-shui chien*), sometimes with eunuch appointees delegated from the Palace Domestic Service (*nei-shih sheng*). P59.

899 ch'ién-hsiá chiào-fāng sǒ 鈐轄教坊所
SUNG: **Office of Musical Instruction,** an agency of the Court of Imperial Sacrifices (*t'ai-ch'ang ssu*). SP: *direction de l'enseignement de la musique*.

900 ch'ién hsīng-yǐn 前行引
Forward Scout: designation of a common member of the retinue of an official in travel status, a guide to the route ahead.

901 ch'iēn-hù sǒ 千戶所
Lit., place (establishment) of 1,000 households: **Battalion,** a basic military unit normally comprising c. 1,000 men and headed by a Battalion Commander (*ch'ien-hu*). In Chin, the Chinese rendering (*ch'ien-hu*) of the Jurchen word *meng-an*, q.v. In Yüan, 10 such units, each with a Commander ranked 5a, constituted a Brigade (*wan-hu fu*) or Guard (*wei*). In Ming, 5 such units, each with a Commander ranked 5a, constituted a Guard (*wei*). In Ch'ing, used only as a designation for some submissive aboriginal tribes in the Southwest, whose chiefs were variably titled Battalion Com-

manders (*ch'ien-hu*), Battalion Vice Commanders (*fu ch'ien-hu*), or sometimes Battalion Heads (*ch'ien-hu chang*).

902 ch'ién-jén 傔人
T'ANG: **Retainer,** categorical reference to non-official clerks and messengers authorized for the staffs of central government officials on special assignments outside the capital.

903 ch'ién-jén 千人
HAN: **Battalion Commander,** an irregular military title apparently equivalent to the *ch'ien-hu* of later times. HB: millarian.

904 ch'ién-kuān 錢官
Common abbreviation of *chu-ch'ien kuan* (**Coins Officials**).

905 ch'ién-liáng kuān 錢糧官
SUNG: **Bursar,** one, probably an unranked suboffical, in the Prefectural School (*fu-hsüeh*) at K'ai-feng fu, the dynastic capital in N. Sung; presumably managed the issuance of stipends and allowances to staff members and students. SP: *percepteur*.

906 ch'ién-liáng yá-mén 錢糧衙門
CH'ING: **Office of the Paymaster,** an agency of the Imperial Household Administration (*nei-wu fu*) responsible for issuing pay and rations to members of the Inner Banners (*nei-ch'i*). BH: pay office.

907 ch'ién-mǎ 前馬
Variant form of *hsi-ma* (**Frontrider**).

908 ch'iēn-niú chiāng-chūn 千牛將軍
(1) T'ANG, SUNG, LIAO: **General of the Personal Guard** (*ch'ien-niu wei*), one of the Sixteen Guards (*shih-liu wei*) at the dynastic capital; 2nd or 3rd officer in the Guard's command echelon, rank 3 or 4; after mid-T'ang a sinecure for members of the imperial family or other favored dignitaries. (2) CHIN: **Personal Guard General,** a title of honor granted to favored courtiers, although no Personal Guard unit seems to have been established.

909 ch'iēn-niú pèi-shēn 千牛備身 or *ch'ien-niu*
SUI–SUNG: lit., a swordsman (*ch'ien-niu*) personal guard, the swordsman idea deriving from Chuang-tzu's anecdote about a butcher so skilled that he slaughtered several thousand oxen over 19 years without dulling the blade of his sword or knife: **Swordsman Guard,** 8 men authorized for service in the establishment of the Heir Apparent in Sui, after c. 604 retitled *ssu-chang tso-yu* (Swordsman Attendant). Restored in T'ang as members of various military units, principally the 2 Personal Guards (*ch'ien-niu wei*) of the Sixteen Guards (*shih-liu wei*) stationed at the dynastic capital; continuing at least nominally in Sung. RR+SP: *garde aux sabres tranchants*. P26, 43.

910 ch'iēn-niú wèi 千牛衛 or *ch'iēn-niú fǔ* 千牛府
T'ANG, SUNG, LIAO: **Personal Guard,** one prefixed Left and one prefixed Right, military units in the array at the dynastic capital called the Sixteen Guards (*shih-liu wei*) in T'ang and Sung; in cooperation with units of T'ang's Northern Command (*pei-ya*), responsible for maintaining security of the imperial palace; in Sung and Liao had merely nominal existence, officer posts being awarded to members of the imperial family and other favored dignitaries. Created in 660 by reorganization of the Left and Right Guards (*tso-fu, yu-fu;* cf. *tso-wei, yu-wei*); briefly in 662 given the

variant name *feng-ch'en wei*. Members of these Guards were commonly called Swordsmen Guards (*ch'ien-niu pei-shen*). Also see *pei-shen fu*. RR+SP: *garde aux sabres tranchants*. P43.

911   *ch'iēn-p'àn* 簽判
SUNG: abbreviated reference to the **Notary of the Administrative Assistant** (*ch'ien-shu p'an-kuan t'ing kung-shih*, q.v.) in a Prefecture (*chou*). P32.

912   *ch'iēn-p'àn t'ài-shǐh chiēn shìh*
     僉判太史監事
MING: **Assistant Director of Astrology** in the early Ming Directorate of Astrology (*t'ai-shih chien*), ranking below both the Director of Astrology (*t'ai-shih ling*) and the Vice Director of Astrology (*t'ung-p'an t'ai-shih chien shih*). P35.

913   *ch'ién-pó àn* 錢帛案
SUNG: **Coins and Silks Section,** one of 8 Sections in the early Sung Tax Bureau (*tu-chih ssu*), normally headed by an Administrative Assistant (*p'an-kuan, t'ui-kuan*); oversaw the provisioning of money and textiles required for the payment of official salaries and the issuance of military uniforms. In the 1080s transferred into the Treasury Bureau (*chin-pu*) of the Ministry of Revenue (*hu-pu*). SP: *service des monnaies et de tissus de soie*. P7, 52.

914   *ch'ién-pó ssū* 錢帛司
LIAO: **Tax Office,** a collection agency for a territory specified in a prefix, normally a Prefecture (*chou*); headed by a central government delegate designated Inspector-general (*tu tien-chien*), Superintendent-in-chief (*tu t'i-tien*), or Supervisor-general (*tsung-mu*), or sometimes a combination of *tsung-mu* as prefix and *tu tien-chien* as suffix. P52.

915   *ch'iēn-pù* 鉛部
T'ANG: lit., ministry of ores: a variant of *ch'üan-pu*, itself an unofficial reference to the **Ministry of Personnel** (*li-pu*).

916   *ch'ién-shěng* 前省
SUNG: **Front Section** of the Palace Domestic Service (*nei-shih sheng*), as distinguished from the Rear Section (*hou-sheng*); division of functions not clear. SP: *département antérieur du palais intérieur*.

917   *ch'iēn-shìh* 僉事 or 簽事
A suffix found attached to agency names, or a term sometimes enclosing an agency name in the form *ch'ien ... shih,* literally suggesting and perhaps originally denoting a seal-keeper for or co-signatory with the head of the named agency; normally designating a 3rd- or occasionally a 2nd-level executive official in the agency, as **Assistant ....** E.g., the Ming–Ch'ing Provincial Surveillance Commission (*t'i-hsing an-ch'a shih ssu*) was headed by a Surveillance Commissioner (*an-ch'a shih*), rank 3a, and usually included in its executive staff several Surveillance Vice Commissioners (*an-ch'a fu-shih*), 4a, and Assistant Surveillance Commissioners (*an-ch'a ch'ien-shih*), 5a. See under *ch'ien*.

918   *ch'iēn-shū* 簽書
SUNG: abbreviated reference to the **Notary of the Administrative Assistant** in some Military Commissions (see *ch'ien-shu chieh-tu p'an-kuan t'ing kung-shih*).

919   *ch'iēn-shū* 簽樞
SUNG: abbreviated reference to the **Notary of the Bureau of Military Affairs** (*ch'ien-shu shu-mi yüan shih*).

920   *ch'ién-shǔ* 錢署
N-S DIV (Sung): **Coinage Office,** established in 430, apparently subordinate to the Chamberlain for the Palace Rev-

enues (*shao-fu*); staffing not clear till 454, then staffed with Coins Officials (*chu-ch'ien kuan*). P16.

921   *ch'iēn-shū chiéh-tù p'àn-kuān t'īng kūng-shìh* 簽書節度判官廳公事
SUNG: **Notary of the Administrative Assistant to the Military Commissioner,** one, rank 8b, on the staff of some Military Commissions (*chieh-tu shih ssu*) in early Sung; in S. Sung on the staff of Lin-an Prefecture (Hangchow) and perhaps other units of territorial administration. SP: *signataire des dépêches officielles dans la salle des assistants*.

922   *ch'iēn-shū p'àn-kuān t'īng kūng-shìh* 簽書判官廳公事
SUNG: **Notary of the Administrative Assistant** in a Prefecture (*chou*) or Military Prefecture (*chün*), no specified number, rank 8b; presumably responsible for handling prefectural correspondence, especially with subordinate units. Also known as the Record Keeper (*ssu-lu*). SP: *signataire du personnel surveillant dans une préfecture*.

923   *ch'iēn-shū shěng-shìh* 簽書省事
SUNG: **Notary of the Palace Domestic Service** (*nei-shih sheng*); a eunuch post also known as *ya-pan* (Administrative Aide). SP: *signataire des affaires du département du palais intérieur*.

924   *ch'iēn-shū shū-mì yüàn shìh* 簽書樞密院事
SUNG–LIAO: **Notary of the Bureau of Military Affairs** (*shu-mi yüan*), a 2nd-level executive official of the Bureau, rank 2b; in Liao in the Northern Bureau of Military Affairs (*pei shu-mi yüan*) only. SP: *signataire des affaires du bureau des affaires militaires*. P12.

925   *ch'iēn-shū yüàn-shìh* 簽書院事
(1) SUNG: abbreviated reference to *ch'ien-shu shu-mi yüan shih* (**Notary of the Bureau of Military Affairs**). (2) YÜAN: found in a relatively important role on the executive staffs of various state Academies and Institutes in the form *ch'ien* (character lacking bamboo radical)-*shih ... (agency name) shih,* suggesting **Administrative Aide.** P3.

926   *ch'iēn-t'īng kuān* 簽廳官 or *ch'ien-t'ing*
SUNG: abbreviated reference to the *ch'ien-shu p'an-kuan t'ing kung-shih* (**Notary of the Administrative Assistant**).

927   *ch'iēn-tsǔng* 千總
CH'ING: lit., leader of 1,000 men: **Company Commander,** rank 6a, in the Chinese military establishment called the Green Standards (*lu-ying*); leader of a Company (*shao*) of 100 men, 5 of which theoretically constituted a Brigade (*ying*). BH: lieutenant. P37.

928   *ch'ién-ts'úng* 傔從
T'ANG: variant of *ch'ien-jen* (**Retainer**).

929   *ch'iēn tū yù-shǐh* 僉都御史
MING–CH'ING: **Assistant Censor-in-chief** of the Censorate (*tu ch'a-yüan*), ranking below Censor-in-chief (*tu yü-shih*) and Vice Censor-in-chief (*fu tu yü-shih*); in Ming 2 each prefixed Left or Right, rank 5a till 1384, then 4a; in Ch'ing a post (prefixed Left only) reserved for a Chinese but abolished in 1745. In Ming after 1453 the title was commonly granted as a concurrent appointment (for prestige purposes) to officials assigned as Grand Coordinators (*hsün-fu*) of some Provinces. P18, 49.

930   *ch'ién-yǐn tà-ch'én* 前引大臣
CH'ING: **Grand Minister of the Vanguard,** 10 hereditary dignitaries who led the Imperial Guardsmen (*shih-wei*).

subordinate to the Grand Minister of the Imperial Household Department Concurrently Controlling the Imperial Guardsmen (*ling shih-wei nei ta-ch'en*). BH: chamberlain of the van-guard.

931   *ch'iēn-yüàn* 僉院 or 簽院
(1) YÜAN: **Assistant Commissioner,** normally 2, rank 3b, in such agencies as the Imperial Academy of Medicine (*t'ai-i yüan*), the Astrological Commission (*t'ai-shih yüan*), Bureaus of Transmission (*t'ung-cheng yüan*), and the Household Service for the Heir Apparent (*ch'u-cheng yüan*); normally outranked by Commissioners (*shih*) and Vice Commissioners (*fu-shih*). P26, 35, 36. (2) MING–CH'ING: may be encountered as an abbreviated reference to *ch'ien tu yü-shih* (**Assistant Censor-in-chief**).

932   *ch'ién-yüán yüàn* 乾元院
T'ANG: **Academy of Heaven,** established in 717, then in 718 retitled Academy in the Hall of Elegance and Rectitude (*li-cheng tien hsiu-shu yüan*), which in 725 was retitled Academy of Scholarly Worthies (*chi-hsien tien shu-yüan*). RR: *cour céleste.* P25.

933   *chíh* 直
Lit., straight, direct, upright. (1) Commonly used, either as prefix or suffix, in the sense to take up duty in ..., to be on duty in ..., or a ... duty group, designating persons or groups who shared duties in some rotational scheme or functional distribution. E.g., Sui dynasty Bodyguards (*pei-shen*) of the Heir Apparent included *chih-ko* (those on duty in the Hall), *chih-ch'in* (those on duty in the Bedchamber), etc.; and Sung dynasty Palace Guards (*tien-ch'ien shih-wei*) were divided into 4 Duty Groups (see *ssu chih*), including Crossbowmen on Duty (*nu-chih*), Bowmen on Duty (*kung-chien chih*), etc. Cf. *fan* (on rotational duty). (2) T'ANG–SUNG: **Auxiliary,** originally designating someone, normally an Academician (*hsüeh-shih*), who was assigned to an agency without having nominal status in the agency, e.g., *chih chi-hsien yüan* (Auxiliary in the Academy of Scholarly Worthies), *chih shih-kuan* (Auxiliary in the Historiography Office). In time many such titles became regularized, with specified rank status. P23, 25, 26.

934   *chíh* 知
Lit., to know, to take notice of: from Han times on, commonly used as a prefix to an agency name in the sense to manage or to administer, often in the form *chih ... shih* (managing the affairs of ...), i.e., **Administrator** of .... Originally suggested a specially authorized appointment of someone with nominally different status to serve in a normally more prestigious post as administrator of an agency: e.g., *shih-chung chih tung-kung shih* (Palace Attendant and Administrator of the Eastern Palace) in Han, *chieh-tu fu-shih chih chieh-tu shih* (Vice Military Commissioner and Administrator of the Military Commission) in T'ang, *chi-shih-chung chih chien-yüan* (Supervising Secretary and Administrator of the Remonstrance Bureau) in Sung. Not later than Sung times, some titles of this sort became regularized: e.g., *chih-hsien* (District Magistrate). Although the term *chih* normally designated the official principally in charge of an agency, such was not always the case; e.g., see *chih-kuan* (Vice Superintendent) of Ch'ing times. P5, 6, 12, 15.

935   *chīh* 織
N-S DIV (Chou): **Weaver,** 4 categories in the Ministry of Works (*tung-kuan*): Weavers of Silks (*chih-ssu*), of Colors (*chih-ts'ai*), of Linens (*chih-hsi*), and of Tassels (*chih-tsu*), apparently divided equally between the ranks of Ordinary

Serviceman (*chung-shih;* 8a) and Junior Serviceman (*hsia-shih;* 9a). P14.

936   *chíh* 職
Assignment, a term normally referring to an official's functional duty regardless of his nominal rank status or other special circumstances. Thus a *chih-kuan* (assigned official) was differentiated from a *san-kuan* (unassigned official; prestige title). An official might nevertheless be detached from his assigned duty (*chih*) to provide a special service on commission (*ch'ai-ch'ien*), but this did not alter his basic status and rank in the service.

937   *chíh-ch'āi fáng* 支差房
SUNG: **Troop Disposition Section** in the Bureau of Military Affairs (*shu-mi yüan*); one of 12 Sections created in the reign of Shen-tsung (1067–1085) to manage administrative affairs of military garrisons throughout the country, in geographic clusters, or to supervise specified military functions on an empire-wide scale. This Section supervised the transfer of troops from Hu-pei Circuit (*lu*) to the frontiers and the environs of the capital and from Circuits south of the Yangtze River into the garrisons in the capital city. Headed by 3 to 5 Vice Recipients of Edicts (*fu ch'eng-chih*), rank 8b. Apparently discontinued early in S. Sung. See *shih-erh fang* (Twelve Sections). SP: *chambre de déplacement militaire.*

938   *chíh-chǎng* 直長
N-S DIV–MING: lit., chief of those who take up active duty, as in a rotational duty group, a shift, a watch, etc.: **Foreman, Chief:** originating late in the era of N-S Division, the title came to be applied to subalterns, usually of 7th or 8th rank, in many kinds of agencies where menial, manual, or routine military service was required on a rotational basis, including manufactories, provisioning agencies, park managements, etc.; especially prominent in Chin and Yüan times. Last known use was in the early Ming Directorate of the Palace Archives (*pi-shu chien*), which was discontinued in 1380, its functions absorbed by the Hanlin Academy (*han-lin yüan*). RR: *sous-chef de service, officier surveillant.* SP: *surveillant, officier-surveillant.*

939   *chíh-chèng kuān* 執政官 or *chíh-cheng*
SUNG: **Executive Official,** generic reference to all Vice Grand Councilors (*fu-hsiang*) serving in the Administration Chamber (*cheng-shih t'ang*), where the most important central government decisions were made; all held primary appointments in the Secretariat-Chancellery (*chung-shu men-hsia sheng*) or the Bureau of Military Affairs (*shu-mi yüan*). SP: *exécutif de gouvernement, conseiller-adjoint d'état.* P19.

940   *chíh chèng-shìh* 知政事
T'ANG: **Manager of Affairs,** a supplementary title granted to eminent officials who served as Grand Councilors (*tsai-hsiang*), regularly participating in deliberations about major governmental policies in the Administration Chamber (*cheng-shih t'ang*). Also see *ts'an-chih cheng-shih.* P3.

941   *chíh-chǐ* 執戟
T'ANG: **Halberdier,** 5, rank 9a, in each military Guard (*wei*) unit; considered one of the Officers of the Four Categories (*ssu-se kuan,* q.v.). RR: *officier des grandes lances.* P26.

942   *chíh chí-hsién yüàn* 直集賢院
SUNG: **Auxiliary in the Academy of Scholarly Worthies,** the designation of someone assigned to the Academy without having nominal status as a member. See under *chih.* SP: *lettré auxiliaire de la cour où on assemble les sages.* P25.

943 *chīh-chì kuān* 支計官
T'ANG–SUNG: **Account Keeper,** unranked subofficials found on the staffs of various units of territorial administration and military units. RR: *fonctionnaire chargé de la comptabilité.* SP: *chargé de compte.*

944 *chíh-chiǎng* 直講
Lecturer. (1) T'ANG: 4 each in the School for the Sons of the State (*kuo-tzu hsüeh*) and the School of the Four Gates (*ssu-men hsüeh*), both supervised by the Directorate of Education (*kuo-tzu chien*); rank not clear, but had less prestige than Erudites (*po-shih*) and Instructors (*chu-chiao*). RR: *répétiteur.* (2) SUNG: 8, rank 7b, on the staff of the Directorate of Education till c. 1068, then replaced with Erudites in the National University (*t'ai-hsüeh*). Also one, 7b, in the School for the Heir Apparent (*tzu-shan t'ang*) in the Eastern Palace (*tung-kung*). In 1117, one authorized in each Princely Establishment (*ch'in-wang fu*), rank not clear, replacing prior Lecturers-in-waiting (*shih-chiang*) and Readers-in-waiting (*shih-tu*). SP: *répétiteur, lecteur, chargé de l'explication.* P34, 69.

945 *chìh-chiàng fǎ* 置將法 or *chih-chiang*
SUNG: lit., to establish generals, the law to establish generals: refers to the establishment in 1074 of Area Generals (*chiang*). See under *chiang* (6) and under *keng-shu.*

946 *chīh chiēn-shìh* 知監事 or *chih-chien*
SUNG: **Prefect** of an Industrial Prefecture (*chien*), a duty assignment for someone with nominal status and rank in the central government. SP: *préfet de préfecture industrielle.*

947 *chíh-ch'ién* 職錢
SUNG: **Duty Pay,** a supplement to the basic salary of each official on active duty in the capital, a counterpart of supplementary income received by officials on duty outside the capital from Office Land (*chih-t'ien*); ranged from 60,000 down to 16,000 coins per month, or equivalents; amount determined by the importance of the duty post, whether or not the appointment was probationary, and whether the appointee's basic rank (*kuan, chi-lu kuan*) was higher or lower than the rank of the duty post.

948 *chíh ch'iēn-niú tāo pèi-shēn* 執千牛刀備身
SUI–T'ANG: **Saber-armed Guard,** members of various military units, principally the Palace Guard (*chin-nei shih-wei*) of the Heir Apparent in Sui and the Personal Guards (*ch'ien-niu wei*) at the imperial palace in T'ang. See *ch'ien-niu, pei-shen.* P26, 43.

949 *chìh-chìh* 制置
SUNG: lit., to regulate and arrange: **Supervisor of ...,** an introductory part of many designations of commissions or duty assignments (*ch'ai-ch'ien*) for officials nominally holding unrelated posts in the regular governmental hierarchy. Only a few examples are included among the following entries.

950 *chíh-chìh* 執秩
Lit., manager of ranks: from T'ang on, an unofficial reference to the **Ministry of Personnel** (*lì-pu*) or to its subordinate **Bureau of Honors** (*ssu-feng ssu, yen-feng ch'ing-li ssu*). P5.

951 *chíh-chíh* 直指
Straight-pointer: from Han on, an unofficial reference to Censors in general (*yü-shih*), and especially Investigating Censors (*chien-ch'a yü-shih*), apparently suggesting that they

were expected in court audiences to point out and denounce any violator of ceremonial regulations. See *ta chih-chih.*

952 *chìh-chìh ch'á-shìh* 制置茶事
SUNG: **Supervisor of the Tea Monopoly** in a region, an assignment often undertaken concurrently (*chien*) by the Supply Commissioner (*fa-yün shih*) of a Circuit (*lu*). SP: *régulateur du thé.*

953 *chìh-chìh fā-yün shìh* 制置發運使
SUNG: apparently an alternate rendering of *fa-yün shih* (**Supply Commissioner**). SP: *intendant des expéditions.*

954 *chìh-chìh fán-shùi* 制置礬稅
SUNG: **Supervisor of the Alum Monopoly** in a region, the geographic jurisdiction normally being designated by the insertion of place-names between *chih-chih* and *fan-shui;* a special duty assignment for someone with an unrelated regular post in the governmental hierarchy. SP: *intendant des revenues de l'alum.*

955 *chīh-chìh-kào* 知制誥
Lit., to be responsible for drafting imperial pronouncements. (1) T'ANG: **Participant in the Drafting of Proclamations,** supplementary designation for officials, most commonly Academicians (*hsüeh-shih*), who in addition to their regular duties were called on to assist in the drafting of imperial pronouncements; thus in some measure unofficial Grand Councilors (*tsai-hsiang*). (2) SUNG–CHIN: **Drafter,** supplementary designation for selected officials of the Secretariat (*chung-shu sheng*) and the Institute of Academicians (*hsüeh-shih yüan*) or the Hanlin Academy (*han-lin yüan*) assigned to drafting duties as in T'ang, but not as prestigious as in T'ang. May be encountered in later periods as an unofficial reference to members of the Hanlin Academy. RR+SP: *chargé de la rédaction des édits impériaux et des proclamations.* P19, 21, 23.

956 *chìh-chìh sān-ssū t'iáo-lì ssū* 制置三司條例司
SUNG: **Finance Planning Commission,** established in 1069 by the famous reform minister Wang An-shih, nominally as a unit of the Secretariat (*chung-shu sheng*), to reorganize the State Finance Commission (*san ssu*); promptly absorbed its functions and overshadowed even the Grand Councilors (*tsai-hsiang*) as the most powerful unit of the central government; abolished after Wang's fall from power in 1076. SP: *bureau chargé d'établir des réglements des finances, commission des réformes financières.*

957 *chìh-chìh shìh* 制置使 or *chìh-chìh tà-shìh* 制置大使
Military Commissioner or **Military Commissioner-in-chief,** ordinarily prefixed with the name of a geographic jurisdiction called a Circuit (*tao, lu*). (1) T'ANG: one of the titles granted to or assumed by Prefects (*tz'u-shih*) or regional warlords in the disruption following the rebellion of An Lu-shan in 756; equivalent to *chieh-tu shih,* q.v. (2) SUNG: one of several titles used for Military Commissioners (see *an-fu shih*) in Circuits (*lu*), e.g., Chiang-hsi (Kiangsi) *chih-chih shih; ta-shih* was a more prestigious variant. SP: *commissaire militaire, grand commissaire militaire, commissaire chargé de diriger les affaires militaires.* P50.

958 *chìh-ch'ìh fáng* 制勅房
MING: **Proclamations Office,** a drafting agency attached to the Grand Secretariat (*nei-ko*); established c. 1430, staffed with Drafters (*chung-shu she-jen*). P4.

959 *chìh-ch'ìh k'ù-fáng* 制敕庫房
SUNG: **Proclamations Archive,** one each in the Chancellery (*men-hsia sheng*), the Secretariat (*chung-shu sheng*), and the Department of State Affairs (*shang-shu sheng*). SP: *chambre de compilation des décrets et magasin des archives.*

960 *chìh-ch'ìh yüàn* 制勅院
SUNG: **Proclamations Office,** a drafting agency of the Secretariat (*chung-shu sheng*) subdivided into clerical units collectively known as the Five Offices (*wu fang*), staffed with Secretariat Clerks (*t'ang-hou kuan*), Scribes (*chu-shu*), and Office Managers (*lu-shih*) under the coordinating leadership of an executive official of the Secretariat or combined Secretariat-Chancellery (*chung-shu men-hsia*) with a duty assignment as Superintendent of the Five Offices (*t'i-tien wu fang*). The Offices were individually designated Clerks Office (*k'ung-mu fang;* see under *k'ung-mu kuan*), Personnel Office (*lì-fang*), Revenue Office (*hu-fang*), Justice Office (*hsing-fang*), and Rites Office (*lǐ-fang*). SP: *cour de la rédaction des édits et décrets impériaux.* P3.

961 *chīh-chìn* 織錦
YÜAN: **Embroiderer,** number not clear, probably non-official specialists; members of the Adornment Service (*wen-ch'i chü*). P28.

962 *chíh-chīn* 職金
CHOU: **Overseer of Treasures,** 2 ranked as Senior Servicemen (*shang-shih*) and 4 as Junior Servicemen (*hsia-shih*), members of the Ministry of Justice (*ch'iu-kuan*) responsible for administering laws relating to precious materials and for handling fines levied in gold or other precious objects. CL: *chargé de l'or.*

963 *chīh chìn-shìh chù-chiào* 知進士助教
T'ANG: **Instructor for the Preparation of Presented Scholars,** numbers and ranks not clear, members of the Institute for the Extension of Literary Arts (*kuang-wen kuan*) in the Directorate of Education (*kuo-tzu chien*) for a short time beginning in 750; then the prefix *chih chin-shih* was dropped. Responsible for the advanced tutoring of government students preparing to take the Presented Scholar (*chin-shih*) examination. RR: *professeur assistant chargé des (candidats à l')examen de lettré accompli.*

964 *chíh chīn-wú* 執金吾
HAN: **Chamberlain for the Imperial Insignia,** a dignitary commanding one of the 2 large armies that were stationed at the dynastic capital who was responsible for policing the capital; prior to 104 B.C. called *chung-wei,* q.v. Also see *chin-wu.* HB: bearer of the gilded mace.

965 *chìh-chōu* 知州
Lit., chief administrator of a unit of territorial administration called *chou.* (1) SUNG–YÜAN: **Prefect** of an ordinary Prefecture (*chou*), in Sung a duty assignment for someone whose rank derived from an unrelated nominal appointment, in Yüan rank 5b, sharing responsibilities with an Overseer (*ta-lu-hua-ch'ih*). (2) MING: **Subprefectural Magistrate,** 5b. (3) CH'ING: **Department Magistrate,** 5b.

966 *chìh chōu-chün shìh* 知州軍事
SUNG: collective reference to **Prefects** of all categories, specifically of ordinary Prefectures (*chou*) and of Military Prefectures (*chün*). P53.

967 *chìh-chūng* 治中
(1) From Han on, erratically used as a title for 2nd- or 3rd-level executive officials, i.e., **Vice ...** or **Assistant...,** in territorial units such as Commanderies (*chün*) or Regions (*chou*), and most commonly in the territorial administrations where dynastic capitals were located, under Governors or Metropolitan Governors (*yin*). (2) MING–CH'ING: **Vice Prefect,** rank 5a, at Peking (Shun-t'ien fu) and Nanking (Ying-t'ien fu), and in Ch'ing also at Feng-t'ien fu in Manchuria. Also had some military uses; see *tsan-chih* and *ssu-ma.* BH: sub-prefect. P32, 49, 50, 52, 53.

968 *chìh-chūng ts'áo* 治中曹
HAN: lit., section for governance of the center (?), a Later Han variant of *kung-ts'ao* (**Labor Section**) in some units of territorial administration. HB: bureau of headquarters.

969 *chìh-chǔ* 制舉
T'ANG–CH'ING: **Special Recruitment,** a designation for civil service recruitment examinations given "by decree," irregularly, in search of extraordinarily talented men from within or without the service, distinguished from regular, scheduled Examination Recruitment (*k'o-chü*). Also see *chih-k'o.*

970 *chìh-chün* 制軍
CH'ING: variant reference to a multi-Province **Governor-general** (*tsung-tu*).

971 *chìh-chün shìh* 知軍使 or *chih-chün*
SUNG: **Prefect** of a Military Prefecture (*chün*), a special duty assignment for a relatively high-ranking official nominally holding a regular post elsewhere in the governmental hierarchy.

972 *chìh-érh* 枝兒
YÜAN: Chinese transcription of a Mongol word meaning **Tribe;** one of 5 categories of fiefs granted to nobles.

973 *chíh-fǎ* 執法
HAN–N-S DIV: lit., to uphold or wield the law: the official variant designation of **Censors** (*yü-shih*) in the reign of Wang Mang and again in San-kuo Wei. May be encountered in later periods in unofficial reference to Censors. See *chung chih-fa.* P18.

974 *chīh-fǎ* 知法
CHIN: **Law Clerk,** one to 3, normally rank 8b, in each Prefecture (*chou*), in some Districts (*hsien*), and in various other specialized agencies such as Fiscal Commissions (*chuan-yün shih ssu*) and Salt Commissions (*yen-shih ssu*) of Routes (*lu*).

975 *chíh-fǎ láng* 執法郎
T'ANG–SUNG: **Legal Counselor,** apparently an ad hoc assignment for an official to assist in the nomination and appointment of officials under the supervision of the Ministry of Personnel (*lì-pu*).

976 *chīh fān-fǔ* 知藩府
SUNG: **Prefect** of a frontier Prefecture (*fan-fu*) in strategic areas such as those in which dynastic capitals were located, at Ch'eng-tu, at Yen-an, at Lin-an, etc.; a special duty assignment for a high-ranking official holding a nominal post elsewhere in the governmental hierarchy. SP: *grand préfet.*

977 *chíh-fāng* 執方
N-S DIV–SUI: unofficial collective reference to the Chamberlain for Law Enforcement (*t'ing-wei*) and his 2 principal subordinates. See *t'ing-wei san kuan.*

978 *chíh-fāng* 職方
N-S DIV (Chou)–SUNG: **Bureau of Operations,** a top-echelon agency in the Ministry of War (*hsia-kuan* in N.

Chou, *ping-pu* at other times); in N. Chou also the title of the **Director** of the Bureau, ranked as an Ordinary Grand Master (*chung ta-fu;* 5a). At other times the Director was entitled *lang* (in Sui) or *lang-chung*, rank not clear in Sui, 5b in T'ang, 6b in Sung. Responsible for maintenance of military maps, the manning of frontier fortifications and signal systems, etc. Functions performed by a differently organized Ministry of War (*ping-pu*) in Liao, Chin, and Yüan, then in Ming and Ch'ing by a *chih-fang ch'ing-li ssu*. RR: *bureau de l'organisation militaire des régions.* SP: *bureau de l'organisation militaire régionale.* P12.

979 *chíh-fāng ch'īng-lì ssū* 職方清吏司
MING–CH'ING: **Bureau of Operations,** one of 4 top-echelon Bureaus in the Ministry of War (*ping-pu*), with functions comparable to those of the earlier *chih-fang;* headed by a Director (*lang-chung*), rank 5a, in Ming, by 4 Manchu and 2 Chinese Directors, rank variable, in Ch'ing. BH: department of discipline. P12.

980 *chíh-fāng shìh* 職方氏
CHOU: **Overseer of Feudatories,** 4 ranked as Ordinary Grand Masters (*chung ta-fu*), 8 as Junior Grand Masters (*hsia ta-fu*), and 16 as Ordinary Servicemen (*chung-shih*), members of the Ministry of War (*hsia-kuan*) responsible for maintaining maps of feudatory regions and receiving tribute goods from them. CL: *agents de direction des régions.*

981 *chíh-fāng ssū* 職方司
MING–CH'ING: common abbreviation of *chih-fang ch'ing-li ssu* (**Bureau of Operations**), one of 4 Bureaus in the Ministry of War (*ping-pu*). P12, 16.

982 *chìh-fǔ* 制府
CH'ING: unofficial reference to a **Governor-general** (*tsung-tu*).

983 *chīh-fǔ* 知府
SUNG–CH'ING: **Prefect** of a Superior Prefecture (*fu*) from Sung through Yüan, of any Prefecture (also *fu*) in Ming and Ch'ing; a special duty assignment for a high-ranking official with a nominal post elsewhere in the governmental hierarchy in Sung; a regular post thereafter, rank 4a in Yüan, variable from 3b to 4b in early Ming, then 4a till 1753, then 4b. P32, 49, 53, 72.

984 *chīh-hòu* 祗候
SUNG: **Usher,** with or without suffixes specifying places or ranks: a title for eunuch attendants in the Palace Domestic Service (*nei-shih sheng*) serving at court audiences. With some suffixes, a rank title for eunuchs; see *nei-shih chieh.* SP: *huissier, intendant du palais intérieur.* P33, 36.

985 *chīh-hòu huáng-mén* 祗候黃門
SUNG: **Palace Gateman-usher,** 9th highest of 12 rank titles (*chieh*) granted to eunuchs from 1112; see *huang-men, nei-shih chieh.* P68.

986 *chīh-hòu kāo-p'ǐn* 祗候高品
SUNG: **Palace Eunuch Usher of High Rank,** variant of *chih-hou tien-chih* (**Palace Duty Officer-usher**). P68.

987 *chīh-hòu k'ù* 祗候庫
SUNG: **Storehouse of Gifts,** an agency of the Court of the Imperial Treasury (*t'ai-fu ssu*) that stored precious silks, fancy clothing, etc. Whether the goods it stored were those received by the Emperor on such occasions as his birthday or from tribute missions, or were those which the Emperor handed out, or were both, is not clear. SP: *magasin de gratifications.*

988 *chīh-hòu nèi-p'ǐn* 祗候內品
SUNG: **Palace Eunuch Usher,** 11th highest of 12 rank ti-

tles (*chieh*) awarded to eunuchs from 1112; see *nei-shih chieh.* P68.

989 *chīh-hòu nèi-t'íng* 祗候內廷
Palace Attendant, in Sung, Ch'ing, and perhaps other times, a generic reference to various kinds of eunuchs, palace women, and also civil service officials as well as other outsiders, e.g., Palace Painters (*hua-shih*), in Sung subordinate to the Palace Domestic Service (*nei-shih sheng*). In Ch'ing, the status was considered somewhat less prestigious than *kung-feng nei-t'ing* (also Palace Attendant).

990 *chīh-hòu shìh-chìn* 祗候侍禁
SUNG: **Palace Attendant-usher,** 7th highest of 12 rank titles (*chieh*) awarded to eunuchs from 1112; see *nei-shih chieh.* P68.

991 *chīh-hòu tièn-chíh* 祗候殿直
SUNG: **Palace Duty Officer-usher,** 8th highest of 12 rank titles (*chieh*) awarded to eunuchs from 1112; see *nei-shih chieh.* P68

992 *chìh-hsièn* 制憲
CH'ING: lit., regulator of the fundamental law: an unofficial reference to a multi-Province **Governor-general** (*tsung-tu*), reflecting his nominal status as an executive official of the Censorate (*tu ch'a-yüan*), which was commonly considered guardian of the fundamental laws.

993 *chīh-hsièn* 知縣
SUNG–CH'ING: **District Magistrate,** originating as a commission or duty assignment (*ch'ai-ch'ien*) for a central government official to "take charge of the affairs of a District" (*chih hsien shih*), but before the end of Sung becoming the standard designation of the senior local official. Rank variable in Sung, fluctuating from 6b to 7b in early Ming, then 7a through Ch'ing with some variations up to 6a in especially prestigious Districts. A common variant rendering is County Magistrate. P54.

994 *chīh hsüǎn-shìh* 知選事
T'ANG: **Administrator of Personnel Selections,** a designation attached to the titles of those officials who, in addition to their regular duties, made final decisions concerning evaluations and appointments of civil service personnel under the aegis of the Ministry of Personnel (*lì-pu*).

995 *chíh-hsüéh* 直學
(1) SUNG: **Registrar,** 2 in each College (*she*) under the Directorate of Education (*kuo-tzu chien*), responsible for maintaining student records. SP: *surveillant.* (2) YÜAN: **Bursar,** handlers of money and grain supplies in all government schools established by Routes (*lu*) and Prefectures (*fu, chou*), and in state-subsidized Private Academies (*shu-yüan*). P34, 51.

996 *chíh hsüéh-shìh* 直學士
T'ANG–MING: **Auxiliary Academician,** usually designating an official with nominal status elsewhere in the governmental hierarchy who was assigned to editorial duty in the T'ang Academy of Scholarly Worthies (*chi-hsien tien shu-yüan*) or Institute for the Advancement of Literature (*hung-wen kuan*), the Sung Bureau of Military Affairs (*shu-mi yüan*), Academy of Scholarly Worthies, Institute for the Glorification of Literature (*chao-wen kuan*), and various Halls (*ko*) of the Institute of Academicians (*hsüeh-shih yüan*), the Liao Institute for the Glorification of Literature, and Institute for the Veneration of Literature (*ch'ung-wen kuan*), and thereafter in the Hanlin Academy (*han-lin yüan*) until the early Ming post was discontinued in 1381. In T'ang the post was normally held by officials of rank 6 or below; in Sung it usually carried rank 3b; thereafter rank not clear.

RR: *lettré auxiliaire*. SP: *lettré ou académicien auxiliaire*. P23, 25, 26.

997 *chīh hsüéh-shìh yüàn* 直學士院

SUNG: abbreviated rendering of *chih han-lin hsüeh-shih yüan* (**Auxiliary Hanlin Academician**), designating an official with nominal status elsewhere in the governmental hierarchy when assigned to the Institute of Academicians (*hsüeh-shih yüan*) without being given outright the title Academician (*hsüeh-shih*); also sometimes rendered *chih-yüan hsüeh-shih*. SP: *lettré auxiliaire*. P23.

998 *chǐh-hūi* 指揮

SUNG, MING: **Commander,** a common designation for the leaders of Armies (*chün*) or various specialized kinds of troop units such as those guarding imperial mausoleums (*ling*), sometimes in charge of less clearly military agencies, e.g., the Sung Office of Capital Streets (*chieh-tao ssu*). May be encountered as an abbreviated reference to *chih-hui shih* or even *tu chih-hui shih*, qq.v. SP: *direction militaire*. P29, 31.

999 *chǐh-hūi ch'iēn-shìh* 指揮僉事

MING–CH'ING: **Assistant Commander,** normally ranking below the Commander (*chih-hui shih*) and Vice Commander (*chih-hui t'ung-chih*) in certain types of military units. In Ming 4, rank 4a, in each Guard (*wei*), the basic unit of military organization. In Ch'ing variable numbers, normally rank 4a; almost all were submissive chiefs of southwestern aboriginal tribes, technically subordinate to other chiefs called Pacification Commissioners (*hsüan-wei shih, an-fu shih, hsüan-fu shih*, etc.). P29, 72.

1000 *chih-hūi shǐh* 指揮使

T'ANG–CH'ING: **Commander** of a military organization, with various gradations indicated by such prefixes as *tu* and *ta* (both Commander-in-chief), *fu* (Vice Commander), etc. In T'ang and Sung, leader of one type of Army (*chün*), likely a smaller command than that, e.g., of a General (*chiang-chün*). In Sung and Ch'ing, a title awarded to some friendly southwestern aboriginal tribal chiefs. From Yüan through Ch'ing, one or more senior officers in Wardens' Offices (*ping-ma ssu*) in capital cities. In Ming one, rank 3a, in charge of each Guard (*wei*), the basic unit of military organization. RR: *commissaire impérial chargé de commander*. SP: *commissaire-commandant d'une armée, commissaire-adjoint chargé de commander l'armée, commissaire d'une direction militaire, commandant*. P29, 49, 72.

1001 *chǐh-hūi shǐh ssū* 指揮使司 or *chih-hui ssu*

T'ANG–CH'ING: **Military Command,** an agency headed by a Commander (*chih-hui shih*). P72.

1002 *chǐh-hūi t'úng-chīh* 指揮同知

MING–CH'ING: **Vice Commander,** normally ranking below the Commander (*chih-hui shih*) and above the Assistant Commander (*chih-hui ch'ien-shih*) in certain types of military units. In Ming 2, rank 3b, in each Guard (*wei*), the basic unit of military organization. In Ch'ing variable numbers, normally rank 3b; almost all were chiefs of submissive aboriginal tribes in the Southwest, technically subordinate to other chiefs called Commanders (*chih-hui shih*). P29, 72.

1003 *chìh-í chèng* 治儀正 or 治宜正

CH'ING: **Assistant Director,** one, rank 5a, in most Offices (*ssu*) subordinate to the various Subsections (*so*) of the Imperial Procession Guard (*luan-i wei*). BH: assistant section chief. P42.

1004 *chīh-jǎn chú* 織染局

YÜAN–CH'ING: **Weaving and Dyeing Service,** a professional craft shop operated by the state to supply the palace with silks. In Yüan, several in outer Routes (*lu*) as well as at the dynastic capital, all subordinate to the Ministry of Works (*kung-pu*). In Ming, commonly operated at provincial capitals by Provincial Administration Commissions (*ch'eng-hsüan pu-cheng shih ssu*), headed by a Commissioner-in-chief (*ta-shih*), rank 9b. In Ch'ing, an agency of the Imperial Household Department (*nei-wu fu*), headed by a dignitary of the category Grand Minister (*ta-ch'en*), with supervisory control over the Imperial Silk Manufactories (*chih-tsao chü*) at Nanking, Soochow, and Hangchow. BH: imperial weaving and dyeing office. P37, 52.

1005 *chīh-jǎn shǔ* 織染署

T'ANG, SUNG, CHIN: **Weaving and Dyeing Office,** an artisan workshop subordinate to the Directorate of Imperial Manufactories (*shao-fu chien*); headed by a Director (*ling*), rank 8a, in T'ang; staffing in Sung not clear; headed by a Foreman (*chih-chang*), rank 8a, in Chin. RR+SP: *office du tissage et de la teinture*. P38.

1006 *chīh-jǎn sǒ tsá-tsào chú* 織染所雜造局

MING: **Miscellaneous Weaving and Dyeing Service,** an agency of the Ministry of Works (*kung-pu*), headed by a Commissioner-in-chief (*ta-shih*), rank 9a; a possible variant understanding is Miscellany Service of the Weaving and Dyeing Office, but it is not clear that any such Office supervised any Services. P15.

1007 *chíh-jén* 質人

CHOU: **Mercantile Controller,** 2 ranked as Ordinary Servicemen (*chung-shih*) and 4 as Junior Servicemen (*hsia-shih*), members of the Ministry of Education (*ti-kuan*), responsible for regulating marketplace transactions, standardizing weights and measures, settling commercial litigations, fining dealers in contraband goods, etc. CL: *officier des contrats de garantie*. P6.

1008 *chih-jen* 饎人

See under the romanization *ch'i-jen*.

1009 *chìh-k'àn àn* 制勘案

SUNG: **Case Review Section,** one of 13 Sections (*an*) directly subordinate to the executive officials of the Ministry of Justice (*hsing-pu*); staffed with unranked subofficials; handled documents concerning the Ministry's review of judicial reports submitted by units of territorial administration throughout the empire. SP: *bureau de l'examen des affaires de province*.

1010 *chìh-kào àn* 制誥案

SUNG: **Proclamation Drafting Section,** an agency of the Secretariat (*chung-shu sheng*). SP: *service de la rédaction des édits impériaux*.

1011 *chìh-k'ō* 制科

T'ANG–CH'ING: **Special Examination,** designation of civil service recruitment examinations given "by decree," irregularly, in search of extraordinarily talented men within or without the ranks of the service; distinguished from regular, scheduled Examination Recruitment (*k'o-chü*). Also see *chih-chü*.

1012 *chīh-k'ò yā-yá* 知客押衙

SUNG: **Escort Officer,** apparently unranked military men, members of the Court of Palace Attendants (*hsüan-hui yüan*) and of the staff of the capital Prefecture, Kaifeng fu. SP: *huissier-gardien*.

1013 chīh-kuān 知觀
CH'ING: **Vice Superintendent** of the Imperial Music Office (*shen-yüeh kuan*), 2nd executive official under a Superintendent (*t'i-tien*); title changed to *chih-so* in 1743 when the Office was retitled *shen-yüeh so;* in 1755 changed again to *ch'eng* or *shu-ch'eng* (Vice Director) when the Office was retitled *shen-yüeh shu* and the Superintendent was redesignated Director (*cheng, shu-cheng*). This example illustrates that the term *chih* ("to know"), which normally designated the official principally in charge of an agency, did not always do so. P10.

1014 chìh-kuān 治官
CHOU: **Administrator,** variant designation of the Minister of State (*chung-tsai*), head of the Ministry of State (*t'ien-kuan*).

1015 chíh-kuān 職官
Functional Office or **Functioning Official,** a generic term for offices or office-holders with assigned functions, as distinguished from honorary and other kinds of purely nominal or otherwise irregular assignments and their recipients.

1016 chíh-kuǎn 直館 or 舘 or 官
Auxiliary. (1) T'ANG: from c. 750 designated new (probationary?) members of the Historiography Office (*shih-kuan*); from 811 applied to such members who did not participate in court audiences, then discontinued in 854. RR: *auxiliaire du collège des annalistes*. (2) SUNG: members of the Historiography Office and of the Institute for the Glorification of Literature (*chao-wen kuan*) until 1082, when all were absorbed with new titles into the new Palace Library (*pi-shu sheng*). SP: *fonctionnaire auxiliaire d'institut*. P25, 38.

1017 chíh-kuèi 執珪
HAN: lit., holder of a jade tablet symbolic of office: **Baton Holder,** a minor title of nobility granted irregularly. May be encountered in any later period as a statement elegantly indicating that someone took charge of an office. P65.

1018 chíh-kuěi shìh 知匭事 or 知匭使
T'ANG–LIAO: **Petition Box Commissioner,** from 686 a special assignment for selected Grand Masters of Remonstrance (*chien-i ta-fu*), Rectifiers of Omissions (*pu-ch'üeh*), and Reminders (*shih-i*), then in 781 made regular appointments in their own right, with title changed from "one who is in charge of petition-box affairs" (first form) to "commissioner in charge of the petition box" (2nd form). Tended 4 repositories for public petitions seeking redress of injustices, etc. In Liao, head of the Petition Box Office (*kuei-yüan*). Also see *li-kuei shih*. RR: *chargé du service des urnes*. P21.

1019 chíh-kùng àn 支供案
SUNG: **Bursary Section,** one of 5 Sections (*an*) in the Tax Bureau (*tu-chih ssu*) of the Ministry of Revenue (*hu-pu*) from c. 1080, when the Ministry was fully activated following discontinuance of the early Sung State Finance Commission (*san ssu*); staffed with unranked subofficials; apparently managed the issuance and distribution of tax receipts collected and stored by the Bureau. SP: *service des versements et des fournitures*. P6.

1020 chīh kùng-chǔ 知貢舉
Examination Administrator. (1) T'ANG–SUNG: one or more designated, on special assignment detached from their normal posts, to conduct the highest-level examinations of candidates for the civil service, specially delegated on each occasion; a prestigious assignment, in T'ang usually made only when the post of Vice Minister of Personnel (*li-pu*

shih-lang), who commonly conducted such examinations, was vacant. SP: *administrateur ou chargé d'examen de doctorat*. (2) CH'ING: a duty assignment for a regular official to participate on an ad hoc basis in supervising civil service recruitment examinations at any level.

1021 chīh-kuó 之國
Lit., to go to one's fief: from Han on, refers to the custom or dynastic law that required sons of Emperors other than the Heir Apparent, when they came of age, to "depart the palace" (*ch'u-ko*) and the capital city to take up residence in regional cities or towns in which, in name far more often than in reality, they reigned with designations such as Prince of Ch'u and Prince of Chin, imitating the nomenclature that prevailed in the Chou dynasty age of Feudal Lords (*chu-hou*). The purpose was to reduce the possibility of a junior prince's challenging the Heir Apparent for the throne when the reigning father died. See *wang, ch'in-wang, wang-fu*. P69.

1022 chìh kuó-yùng shǐh 制國用使
SUNG: lit., commissioner for the regulation of the state budget: **State Finance Commissioner,** in charge of the State Finance Office (*kuo-yung ssu*); normally after 1169 a concurrent appointment for a Grand Councilor (*tsai-hsiang*); also called *kuo-yung shih*. SP: *commissaire aux finances d'état (budget)*.

1023 chìh-lì 治曆
HAN: abbreviated reference to **Court Gentleman for Regulating the Calendar** (*chih-li lang*) or **Gentleman of the Interior for Regulating the Calendar** (*chih-li lang-chung*). HB: calendarist. P35.

1024 chìh-lì 直隸
YÜAN–CH'ING: (1) **Directly Attached** or **Independent,** a prefix used in the hierarchy of territorial administration units signifying, e.g., that a District (*hsien*) was directly under the administrative supervision of a Prefecture (*fu*) rather than under an intermediary Subprefecture (*chou*), or that a Prefecture was directly under the central government rather than under intermediary provincial-level agencies. (2) **Metropolitan Area,** designation of the area supervised directly by the central government without reliance on provincial-level agencies; equivalent to *ching-shih*. From predynastic Ming times till 1421, a period when the dynastic capital was at modern Nanking, *chih-li* designated the area, roughly, of modern Kiangsu and Anhwei Provinces. In 1402 what had been called Pei-p'ing Province (*pei-p'ing sheng*) was transformed into a Northern Metropolitan Area (*pei chih-li;* most properly, *Pei-ching*, i.e., Peking) around a newly established auxiliary capital at modern Peking; it corresponded roughly to modern Hopei Province. In 1421 Peking was made the dynastic capital and Nanking was made auxiliary capital; in consequence, what had been the Northern Metropolitan Area now became simply the Metropolitan Area (*chih-li*), and what had been the Metropolitan Area was redesignated the Southern Metropolitan Area (*nan chih-li*); and the terms Chih-li and Nan Chih-li gradually came to be used as proper names. In late Ming times the name Chiang-nan, "south of the (Yangtze) river," became a popular alternate reference to Nan Chih-li, and Ch'ing used the name Chiang-nan in preference to Nan Chih-li until 1664, when the area was divided into modern Anhwei and Kiangsu Provinces. Chih-li remained the name of modern Hopei throughout the Ch'ing era. P53.

1025 chìh-lì láng 治曆郎
HAN: **Court Gentleman for Regulating the Calendar,** a subordinate of the Grand Astrologer (*t'ai-shih ling*); some-

times abbreviated to *chih-li;* apparently had functions no different from those of the Gentleman of the Interior for Regulating the Calendar (*chih-li lang-chung*). P35.

1026　*chìh-lǐ láng* 治禮郎

(1) HAN–N-S DIV (N. Wei): **Court Gentleman for Regulating Rituals,** a subordinate of the Chamberlain for Ceremonials (*t'ai-ch'ang*) except in Later Han, when subordinate to the Chamberlain for Dependencies (*ta hung-lu*); as many as 47 appointees in Later Han, rank 200 bushels or below; in N. Wei numbers not clear, rank declined from 6b2 to 9b. HB: gentleman for ceremony. (2) SUI–T'ANG: **Vice Director for Rituals** in the Court of Imperial Sacrifices (*t'ai-ch'ang ssu*); reduced from 16 to 6 in Sui; in 649 changed to *feng-li lang,* q.v., to avoid imperial taboo. RR: *secrétaire directeur des rites.* P27, 33.

1027　*chìh-lì láng-chūng* 治曆郎中

HAN: **Gentleman of the Interior for Regulating the Calendar,** a subordinate of the Grand Astrologer (*t'ai-shih ling*); apparently had functions no different from those of the Court Gentleman for Regulating the Calendar (*chih-li lang*). P35.

1028　*chìh-lǐ lì* 治禮吏

N-S DIV (Chin, Ch'i): **Ritual Attendant:** in Chin 24 subordinate to the Chamberlain for Ceremonials (*t'ai-ch'ang*); in Ch'i 8 on the staff of the National University (*kuo-hsüeh*). P27, 34.

1029　*chīh lì-pù hsüǎn-shìh* 知吏部選事

T'ANG: **Administrator of Ministry of Personnel Selections,** additional duty for an official, whether or not based in the Ministry of Personnel (*lì-pu*), to supervise the Ministry's procedures in evaluating and appointing civil service personnel. See *chih-hsüan shih.*

1030　*chīh lǐ-pù kùng-chǔ* 知禮部貢舉

T'ANG: **Administrator of Ministry of Rites Examinations,** additional duty for an official, whether or not based in the Ministry of Rites (*lì-pu*), to supervise the Ministry's procedures in conducting civil service recruitment examinations; normally appointed when the post of Vice Minister of Rites (*lì-pu shih-lang*) was vacant. See *chih kung-chü.*

1031　*chìh-líng* 至靈

CH'ING: **Sacrificial Priest,** prefixed Left if in the Taoist priesthood and Right if in the Buddhist priesthood, both rank 8a; principally called on for "miracle-working" ceremonies at state temples in times of floods, drought, or other natural disasters. BH: thaumaturgist.

1032　*chíh-lú* 直廬

SUNG: lit., the chamber (*lu*) where one takes up duty (*chih*): **Imperial Study** in the Imperial Archives (*pi-ko*), designated c. 1000 as the place where the Emperor met regularly with Academicians (*hsüeh-shih*) for lessons in the classical literature—meetings eventually called Classics Colloquia (*ching-yen*); in 1023 such meetings were transferred to the Hall for the Veneration of Governance (*ch'ung-cheng tien*). P24.

1033　*chīh-lù* 知錄

SUNG: **Judicial Intendant,** a duty assignment (*ch'ai-ch'ien*) for men normally having nominal posts elsewhere in the government, to supervise the administration of justice in Prefectures (*chou, fu*). SP: *chargée des affaires judiciaires.*

1034　*chíh lúng-t'ú kó* 直龍圖閣

SUNG: **Auxiliary in the Hall of the Dragon Diagram,** from 1016 a designation used for men assigned to the Han-lin Academy (*han-lin yüan*) without having nominal status as a member, to assist in the drafting of imperial procla

mations; number not clear, rank 7a. SP: *lettré auxiliaire du pavillon Long-t'ou.*

1035　*chīh-mǎ fáng* 支馬房

SUNG: **Horse Management Section** in the Bureau of Military Affairs (*shu-mi yüan*); one of 12 Sections created in the reign of Shen-tsung (1067–1085) to manage administrative affairs of military garrisons throughout the country, in geographic clusters, or to supervise specified military functions on a country-wide scale. This Section, in cooperation with Directorates of Horse Pasturages (*mu-chien*) and other agencies of the Court of the Imperial Stud (*t'ai-p'u ssu*), supervised the breeding and care of government horses and their provision for military uses. Headed by a Vice Recipient of Edicts (*fu ch'eng-chih*), rank 8a. See *shih-erh fang.* Cf. *mu-ma fang* (Horse Pasturage Section). SP: *chambre d'administration des chevaux.*

1036　*chīh-miào shào-ch'īng* 知廟少卿

T'ANG: **Supervisor of the Imperial Ancestral Temple,** from c. 724 the designation of a Vice Minister (*shao-ch'ing*) of the Court of Imperial Sacrifices (*t'ai-ch'ang ssu*) who was assigned to supervise the Imperial Ancestral Temple (*t'ai-miao*). P28.

1037　*chíh-nèi* 職內

CHOU: **Keeper of Consumables,** 2 ranked as Senior Servicemen (*shang-shih*) and 4 as Junior Servicemen (*hsia-shih*), members of the Ministry of State (*t'ien-kuan*) charged with receiving, inventorying, and disbursing consumable goods among the palace revenues. CL: *chargé du dedans ou de l'entrée.*

1038　*chíh-nién* 值年

CH'ING: **On Annual Duty,** used as a prefix to various titles, often terminating in Grand Minister (*ta-ch'en*), indicating that the appointee was serving on a rotational basis for only a year; e.g., Grand Minister on Annual Duty as Supervisor-in-chief of the Imperial Household Department (*chih-nien tsung-kuan nei-wu fu ta-ch'en*). P37.

1039　*chīh-pān* 知班

Lit., to be in charge of ranks, or the order of precedence: **Master of Protocol.** (1) SUNG: 5 in the Censorate (*yü-shih t'ai*) and one in each of the Auxiliary Censorates (*liu-ssu yü-shih t'ai*) in the 3 auxiliary capitals of N. Sung—the Western, Northern, and Southern Capitals. SP: *employé.* (2) YÜAN: 4 in the Palace Bureau (*tien-chung ssu*) of the metropolitan Censorate, others in various agencies with important ceremonial functions. P18.

1040　*chíh-pì* 職幣

CHOU: **Keeper of Silks,** 2 ranked as Senior Servicemen (*shang-shih*) and 4 as Ordinary Servicemen (*chung-shih*), members of the Ministry of State (*t'ien-kuan*) responsible for checking the inventories and accounts of agencies that made use of silk goods owned by the state, and for collecting excess silk goods from such agencies. CL: *chargé des étoffes précieuses.*

1041　*chíh-pó* 執帛

HAN: **Holder of the Silks,** a minor title of nobility attributed to the ancient regional state of Ch'u and granted irregularly by Han; of less prestige than Baton Holder (*chih-kuei*). P65.

1042　*chíh-sáng* 職喪

CHOU: **Funeral Director,** 2 ranked as Senior Servicemen (*shang-shih*), members of the Ministry of Rites (*ch'un-kuan*) responsible for establishing rules of conduct at the funerals of important court officials and for monitoring the conduct of participants accordingly. Cf. *chung-jen* (Grave Maker), *mu ta-fu* (Grand Master of Cemeteries). CL: *directeur de funérailles*.

1043 *chǐh-shěng* 指省
CH'ING: lit., to designate a Province: refers to a custom that permitted men who had been qualified for office by the Ministry of Personnel (*lì-pu*) and wished to serve in a particular Province rather than participate in regular appointment procedures to pay a fee and become Expectant Appointees (*hou-pu*) in the Provinces (*sheng*) of their choice.

1044 *chǐh-shěng* 直省
MING–CH'ING: a collective reference to all units of territorial administration, lit., of **the Metropolitan Area(s)** (*chih-li*) **and Provinces** (*sheng*), normally referring to provincial and all lower-level agencies throughout the empire; e.g., *chih-sheng chu-kuan* (the various officials of the Metropolitan Area and the Provinces).

1045 *chǐh-shěng hsüéh-shìh* 直省學士
N-S DIV: **Academician on Duty in the Secretariat** (*chung-shu sheng, pi-shu sheng*), normally assigned to making copies of documents in or for the Imperial Archives (*pi-ko*). Whether or not the term *sheng* here refers to the Secretariat is not wholly clear; it might refer to the Department of State Affairs (*shang-shu sheng*) or the Chancellery (*men-hsia sheng*), or it might refer to all 3 *sheng* collectively. P23.

1046 *chǐh-shěng shè-jén* 直省舍人
YÜAN–MING: **Drafter on Duty in the Secretariat** (*sheng* referring to the *chung-shu sheng*), responsible for drafting imperial proclamations; in Yüan 33, rank not clear; in Ming 10, rank 8b, but only from 1374 to 1376, when the title was changed to *chung-shu she-jen*, q.v. P2, 4, 21.

1047 *chīh shěng-shìh* 知省事
T'ANG: **Administrator of the Department of State Affairs,** an additional duty for an official, whether or not based in the Department of State Affairs (*shang-shu sheng*), to take temporary charge of the Department; in this usage, *sheng* seems almost never to refer to the Secretariat (*chung-shu sheng*) or the Chancellery (*men-hsia sheng*).

1048 *chīh-shǐh* 支使
T'ANG–SUNG: **Commissioner's Agent,** a personal deputy in a local area for such regional dignitaries as Military Commissioners (*chieh-tu shih*), Surveillance Commissioners (*kuan-ch'a shih*), and Investigation Commissioners (*ts'ai-fang shih*); the title normally occurs with a specifying prefix, e.g., *kuan-ch'a chih-shih*. RR: *commissaire adjoint*. SP: *secrétaire ou commissaire adjoint*. P57.

1049 *chǐh-shǐh* 直史
MING: **Secretary,** one on the staff of each Commandery Prince (*chün-wang*), assisted by one each Left and Right Secretary (*tso, yu chih-shih*); all apparently unranked. P69.

1050 *chīh-shìh* 知事
CHIN–CH'ING: **Administrative Clerk,** normally a lowly official with rank between 7b and 9a, found in a great variety of agencies. N.B.: in earlier periods, *chih* (agency-name insert) *shih* was commonly used for important dignitaries serving as active heads of the agencies named; see under *chih* (to know).

1051 *chīh-shìh* 織室
HAN: **Weaving Shop,** an agency subordinate to the Chamberlain for the Palace Revenues (*shao-fu*), headed by a Director (*ling*); a consolidation of 2 early Han shops called the East and West Weaving Shops (*tung, hsi chih-shih*), each headed by a Director (*ling*). HB: weaving house. P37, 40.

1052 *chìh-shìh* 致仕
Throughout history, signified that an official had been **relieved of office** or had **retired from office;** it normally suggests a termination due to old age or illness rather than poor performance.

1053 *chǐh-shìh chiào-yǜ* 職事教諭
SUNG: **Instructor,** 2, unranked, in the Primary School (*hsiao-hsüeh*) maintained by the Directorate of Education (*kuo-tzu chien*). See the appropriate *chih-shih* entry. P34.

1054 *chīh shìh-i shìh* 知侍儀事 and 直侍儀使
YÜAN: executive officials of the Palace Ceremonial Office (*shih-i ssu*, q.v.) from 1271 to 1279. First form: **Vice Director,** normally the concurrent appointment of a Vice Minister of Rites (*lǐ-pu shih-lang*); one appointee, subordinate to 2 Directors (*shih-i feng-yü*). Second form: **Ceremonial Escort,** one each Left and Right, subordinate executives of the 3rd or 4th level. In 1279 both types of positions were apparently replaced by 14 Secretarial Receptionists (*t'ung-shih she-jen*) serving under 2 Directors (*shih-i*). Also see *yin-chin shih chih shih-i shih*. P33.

1055 *chǐh-shìh kuān* 職事官 or *chǐh-shìh*
Generally seems to be a generic term equivalent to *chih-kuan* (**Functioning Official**), but in Sung had 2 special additional uses: (1) *chih-shih kuan* occurs in the sense of **Administrative Official,** a collective term for 3 categories of officials—Rectifiers (*ssu-chih*) and Case Reviewers (*p'ing-shih*) of the Court of Judicial Review (*ta-li ssu*), Proofreaders (*cheng-tzu*) in the Palace Library (*pi-shu sheng*), and Erudites (*po-shih*) of the National University (*t'ai-hsüeh*). SP: *fonctionnaire-surveillant*. (2) *chih-shih* occurs as a prefix before some regular titles, e.g., *chih-shih hsüeh-lu* of the Directorate of Education (*kuo-tzu chien*); but how this differed from the regular post of *hsüeh-lu* (Provost) in the Directorate is not at all clear. SP: *surveillant ou chargé de faire observer les règlements scolaires*.

1056 *chǐh-shìh shìh* 執事侍
CH'ING: **Office Manager,** a eunuch official, rank 6, in the Directorate of Palace Domestic Service (*kung-tien chien*); considered in the category of Staff Supervisors (*shou-ling kuan*).

1057 *chǐh-shìh ts'áo* 直事曹
N-S DIV (N. Wei): **Section for Palace Service,** one of 4 Sections (*ts'ao*) in the Ministry of Palace Affairs (*tien-chung ts'ao*) of the developing Department of State Affairs (*shang-shu sheng*); headed by a Director (*lang-chung*), rank 6a2. P9.

1058 *chǐh-shǒu shìh* 執守侍
CH'ING: **Palace Guardian,** a eunuch official, rank 7, in the Directorate of Palace Domestic Service (*kung-tien chien*); considered in the category of Staff Supervisors (*shou-ling kuan*). P38.

1059 *chǐh-shū* 執書
N-S DIV (Ch'i): **Secretary,** a staff member in a Princedom (*wang-kuo*); number, rank, and specific functions not clear. P69.

1060 *chìh-shū* 治書
(1) HAN–N-S DIV (Chin): **Secretary** in a Princedom (*wang-kuo*); in Han number not clear, rank =600 bushels; in Chin 4 in each Princedom, rank not clear. HB: preparer of documents. (2) N-S DIV (San-kuo Wei): a prefix with document-handling significance appended to the censorial titles *chih-fa* and *yü-shih* to make Impeaching Censor (*chih-shu chih-fa*) and Secretarial Censor (*chih-shu yü-shih*), the for-

mer reportedly responsible for submitting impeachments, the latter "solely responsible for (interpreting?) codified laws." P18, 69.

1061 *chīh-shū* 知書
CHIN: **Record Keeper,** 2, probably unranked, assigned to each Storehouse (*k'u*) of imperial goods. P38.

1062 *chīh-shū kuān* 知書官
T'ANG: **Archivist,** 8, apparently unranked, attached to the Academy of Scholarly Worthies (*chi-hsien tien shu-yüan*); others perhaps in other, comparable agencies. RR: *fonctionnaire chargé des livres.* P25.

1063 *chìh-shū lìng-shǐh* 制書令史
T'ANG: **Secretarial Clerk,** variable numbers of subofficial functionaries (*li*) in Ministries (*pu*) and perhaps other agencies. See *ling-shih.* RR: *scribe chargé des édits impériaux.*

1064 *chīh shū-mì yüàn shìh* 知樞密院事
SUNG: **Administrator of the Bureau of Military Affairs,** rank 2a, one of the most common designations of senior officials assigned to head the Bureau of Military Affairs (*shu-mi yüan*) while nominally holding other positions. See *chih* (to know). SP: *administrateur de la cour des affaires militaires.*

1065 *chìh-shū shìh yǔ-shǐh* 治書侍御史
HAN–T'ANG, YÜAN–MING: **Secretarial Censor,** normally a high-ranking executive official of the Censorate (*yü-shih t'ai*), subordinate to a Censor-in-chief (*yü-shih ta-fu*) and a Vice Censor-in-chief (*yü-shih chung-ch'eng,* often the real head of the Censorate). In Former Han, 2; the term was also used in lieu of *yü-shih chung-ch'eng.* In Later Han, 2, rank 600 bushels; principally responsible for interpreting the laws. In the era of N-S Division numbered from one to 4, normally in ranks 5 or 6; often outranked in the Censorate only by its active head, whether a Censor-in-chief or a Vice Censor-in-chief. In Sui 2, became in effect vice censors-in-chief because the title *yü-shih chung-ch'eng* was discontinued. Then in T'ang, in 649, the title Secretarial Censor was discontinued and *yü-shih chung-ch'eng* was reinstituted. In Yüan 2 Secretarial Censors were re-established, rank 2b. In early Ming no fixed number, rank 3a, but disappeared in the 1380 reorganization of the Censorate. HB: attending secretary preparer of documents. RR: *vice-président du tribunal des censeurs.* P18.

1066 *chìh-shū ts'áo* 治書曹
N-S DIV: **Secretarial Section** of the Censorate (*yü-shih t'ai*), headed by from one to 4 Secretarial Censors (*chih-shu shih yü-shih*); apparently the administrative office for the Censorate's internal affairs, also sometimes responsible for handling Censorate funds. P18.

1067 *chìh-shū yǔ-shǐh* 治書御史
YÜAN: variant of *chih-shu shih yü-shih* (**Secretarial Censor**). P18.

1068 *chìh-ssū* 制司
SUNG: **Military Commission** in charge of a Circuit (*tao, lu*), the office of a Military Commissioner (*chih-chih shih,* q.v.). SP: *direction des affaires militaires.*

1069 *chìh-sù nèi-shǐh* 治粟內史
CH'IN-HAN: **Chamberlain for the National Treasury,** one of the major central government officials collectively called the Nine Chamberlains (*chiu ch'ing*), principally in charge of the palace granaries; in 143 B.C. changed to *ta-nung ling,* q.v. HB: clerk of the capital for grain. P8, 15.

1070 *chìh-sù tū-wèi* 治粟都尉
HAN: **Commandant-in-chief of the Granaries,** principally in charge of the capital granaries; apparently a variant of the early Han title *chih-su nei-shih* (Chamberlain for the National Treasury). In 143 B.C. retitled *ta-nung ling,* q.v. Cf. *sou-su tu-wei* (Commandant-in-chief for Foraging). HB: chief commandant for grain. P8.

1071 *chíh-sùi* 職歲
CHOU: **Controller of Accounts,** 4 ranked as Senior Servicemen (*shang-shih*) and 8 as Ordinary Servicemen (*chung-shih*), members of the Ministry of State (*t'ien-kuan*) responsible for disbursing state revenues and checking annually on all state expenditures. CL: *chargé des dépenses annuelles.*

1072 *chìh-t'ái* 制臺
MING-CH'ING: unofficial reference to a multi-Province **Supreme Commander** or **Governor-general** (*tsung-tu*), especially to the one appointed Director-general of Grain Transport (*ts'ao-yün tsung-tu*).

1073 *chīh t'ái-shìh* 知臺事
T'ANG: **Administrator of the Censorate,** a designation used in 2 senses: (1) to signify that an official was assigned to take active charge of the Censorate (*yü-shih t'ai*) in addition to his normal principal duty; and (2) to signify that a nominal Censor-in-chief (*yü-shih ta-fu*), after serving in a territorial assignment such as Surveillance Commissioner (*kuan-ch'a shih*), had returned to the capital to take active charge of the Censorate. P18.

1074 *chīh t'ái-tsá* 知臺襍
T'ANG: **Inspector of the Censorate,** a designation signifying that an official, in addition to his normal duty, had been assigned to conduct an evaluation of the Censorate (*yü-shih t'ai*).

1075 *chíh-tièn chiēn* 直殿監
MING-CH'ING: **Directorate for Palace Maintenance,** one of 12 major Directorates (*chien*) in which palace eunuchs were organized; headed by a eunuch Director (*t'ai-chien*); responsible for routine custodial services in the palace buildings. In Ch'ing existed only from 1656 to 1661; see under *shih-erh chien* (Twelve Directorates).

1076 *chíh-t'ién* 職田
Lit., **office fields:** From T'ang on, referred to government-owned land attached to various agencies outside the capital, the state income from which was allocated as supplementary compensation for the heads, and perhaps other officials, of the agencies.

1077 *chīh-tsá* 知雜
SUNG: (1) **General Clerk,** suboffical functionaries found in many agencies, e.g., the Ministry of Personnel (*li-pu*), the Ministry of Works (*kung-pu*), the Court of Judicial Review (*ta-li ssu*). (2) Abbreviated reference to an **Associate Censor** (*shih yü-shih chih tsa-shih*) of the Headquarters Bureau (*t'ai-yüan*) in the Censorate (*yü-shih t'ai*). SP: *service des affaires diverses.*

1078 *chīh-tsá àn* 知雜案
SUNG: **Miscellany Section,** an office for general routine administration found in Ministries (*pu*), Bureaus (*ssu*) subordinate to Ministries, etc.; also one of 4 Sections in the Right Bureau (*yu-t'ing*) of the Court of Judicial Review (*ta-li ssu*). Functions and staffing not clear. SP: *service des affaires diverses.*

1079   *chīh-tsá fáng* 知雜房
SUNG: **Miscellany Section** in the Bureau of Military Affairs (*shu-mi yüan*); one of 12 Sections created in the reign of Shen-tsung (1067–1085) to manage administrative affairs of military garrisons throughout the country, in geographic clusters, or to supervise specified military functions on a country-wide scale. This Section had general, routine administrative responsibilities. Headed by a Vice Recipient of Edicts (*fu ch'eng-chih*), rank 8b. Apparently abolished early in S. Sung. See *shih-erh fang*. SP: *chambre des affaires diverses*.

1080   *chīh-tsá yü-shǐh* 知雜御史
SUNG: lit., censor in charge of miscellany: an abbreviation of *shih yü-shih tsa-shih* (**Associate Censor**), q.v.

1081   *chīh-tsào* 織造
MING–CH'ING: **Superintendent of Imperial Silk Manufacturing,** an abbreviated reference to the Ming *t'i-tu chih-tsao t'ai-chien* (Eunuch Superintendent …) and the Ch'ing *chih-tsao chien-tu*, qq.v. P38.

1082   *chīh-tsào chiēn-tū* 織造監督
CH'ING: **Superintendent of Imperial Silk Manufacturing,** one Manchu notable, bondservant, or eunuch in charge of each Imperial Silk Manufactory (*chih-tsao chü*), at Nanking, Soochow, and Hangchow; at least nominally subordinate to the Imperial Household Department (*nei-wu fu*). P37.

1083   *chīh-tsào chǘ* 織造局
CH'ING: **Imperial Silk Manufactory,** an agency supervising the manufacture or purchase of fancy textiles for palace use, at least nominally subordinate to the Imperial Household Department (*nei-wu fu*) but normally closely monitored by the Emperor through Manchu notables, bondservants, or eunuchs who served as Superintendents of Imperial Silk Manufacturing (*chih-tsao chien-tu*); one each at Nanking, Soochow, and Hangchow.

1084   *chìh-tsào k'ù* 製造庫
CH'ING: **Storehouse of Leather and Metal,** a craft workshop in the Ministry of Works (*kung-pu*), headed by a Commissioner (*shih*) and 3 Vice Directors (*lang-chung*). BH: office of leather and metal works. P14.

1085   *chìh-tsào yü-ch'ién chün-ch'ì chú* 製造御前軍器局
SUNG: **Imperial Arsenal,** a manufactory of weapons for armies at the capital, apparently subordinate jointly to the Bureau of Military Affairs (*shu-mi yüan*) and the Ministry of Works (*kung-pu*). See *chün-ch'i chien*. SP: *bureau de la fabrication des armes*.

1086   *chìh-tsūn* 至尊
Most Venerated: from Han on, an indirect reference to the Emperor.

1087   *chīh-tsūng* 知宗
SUNG: **Administrator of the Office of Imperial Clan Affairs,** apparently an abbreviation of *chih ta tsung-cheng ssu shih* (see *ta tsung-cheng ssu*); one each at the metropolitan office in Kaifeng and at its western and southern branches (*hsi-wai tsung-cheng ssu, nan-wai tsung-cheng ssu*). SP: *chef de bureau des affaires de la famille impériale*.

1088   *chìh-tsūng* 秩宗
(1) HAN (Wang Mang era): a variant of the title *t'ai-ch'ang* (**Chamberlain for Ceremonials**), q.v. (2) T'ANG–CH'ING: **Sacrificial Commissioner,** an ad hoc assignment, often of a Minister (*shang-shu*), to supervise seasonal sacrifices at the suburban temple to Heaven (*chiao-miao*).

1089   *chīh tsūng-tzǔ piǎo-shū kuān* 知宗子表疏官
T'ANG: lit., official in charge of memorials submitted by imperial clansmen: **Memorial Processor** in the Court of the Imperial Clan (*tsung-cheng ssu*). RR: *fonctionnaire chargé des adresses envoyées à l'empereur par la famille impériale*.

1090   *chīh-tù shǐh* 支度使
T'ANG: **Fiscal Commissioner,** responsible for administering the finances of a group of military units along the frontier and submitting annual fiscal reports to the central government; in the late 700s became a supplementary title and responsibility of many Military Commissioners (*chieh-tu shih*). RR: *commissaire impérial aux finances*.

1091   *chìh-tù yüàn* 制度掾
HAN: **Inspector of Regulations,** duty assignment for Headquarters Clerks (*t'ing-yüan*) in Districts (*hsien*), to make fall and winter tours of the jurisdiction. HB: officials of regulations.

1092   *chīh t'ú-p'ǔ kuān* 知圖譜官
T'ANG: **Genealogist,** number and rank not clear, on the staff of the Court of the Imperial Clan (*tsung-cheng ssu*). RR: *fonctionnaire chargé des listes généalogiques*.

1093   *chīh-tùn shǐh* 知頓使 or 置頓使
T'ANG: **Commissioner for Arrangements,** an ad hoc duty assignment for a court official who, whenever the Emperor traveled, was sent ahead to make appropriate housing and eating arrangements.

1094   *chīh-tùng* 知洞   or   知峒
SUNG: **Chief of the Grotto,** an honorific title conferred on de facto heads of various aboriginal tribes in the Southwest. P18, 72.

1095   *chīh-yìn* 知印
CHIN–CH'ING: **Seal-keeper,** a lowly official or clerical suboofficial found in numerous offices in both the central government and units of territorial administration, especially in Yüan; apparently served as a notary to authenticate documents issued from an agency. Distinguish from *chang-yin*.

1096   *chīh-yìng chǘ* 支應局
CH'ING: **Bursary,** a provincial-level agency responsible for issuing money for public circulation. BH: treasury.

1097   *chīh-yìng ssū* 祗應司
CHIN–YÜAN: **Crafts Office,** headed by a Superintendent (*t'i-tien*), rank 5b; part of the imperial palace establishment, responsible for skilled carpentry, textile work, mounting scrolls, etc.; also often created for the establishments of Princes and other nobles. P38, 49.

1098   *chíh-yǜ* 執馭
T'ANG: **Coachman,** 100 unranked carriage drivers on the staff of the Office of the Imperial Stables (*tien-chiu ssu*), a unit in the Court of the Imperial Stud (*t'ai-p'u ssu*). RR: *conducteur d'attelages*.

1099   *chìh-yǜ ssū* 治獄司
SUNG: variant designation of the **Right Bureau** (*yu-t'ing*) of the Court of Judicial Review (*ta-li ssu*). SP: *bureau judiciaire*. P22.

1100   *chíh-yüàn* 直院
T'ANG–SUNG: **Auxiliary,** a collective term for various

clerical subofficials in the Academy of Scholarly Worthies (*chi-hsien tien shu-yüan*); initiated in 731 as a new title for Auxiliary Scribes (*shu-chih*), Auxiliary Illustrators (*hua-chih*), etc.; discontinued in 1082 when the Academy was absorbed into the Palace Library (*pi-shu sheng*). In Sung also members of the Court of Ceremonial Propriety (*li-i yüan*) in the Court of Imperial Sacrifices (*t'ai-ch'ang ssu*), and of the Medical Academy (*i-kuan yüan*) in the Hanlin Academy (*han-lin yüan*). RR+SP: *auxiliaire*. P25, 36.

1101   *chíh-yüàn hsüéh-shìh*   直院學士
SUNG: **Auxiliary in the Hanlin Academy,** variant form of *chih hsüeh-shih yüan*, q.v. SP: *lettré ou académicien auxiliaire*. P23.

1102   *chíh-yüàn kuān*   知院官
T'ANG: **Brokerage Official,** head of a regional Brokerage (*yüan*) in the late T'ang salt distribution system. See *chüeh yen-t'ieh shih* (Salt Monopoly Commissioner). P61.

1103   *chìh-yüǎn wù*   致遠務
SUNG: **Transport Service,** an agency of the Court of the Imperial Stud (*t'ai-p'u ssu*); function not clear. SP: *bureau d'élevage des animaux pour le transport*.

1104   *ch'ìh*   赤
T'ANG–SUNG: lit., red: **Imperial,** a prefix to District (*hsien*), signifying the highest of 7 categories in which Districts were ranked on the basis of prestige and size. May be encountered in various periods as a more general descriptive term signifying Imperial.

1105   *ch'íh-chiéh*   持節
HAN–N-S DIV: lit., bearing a warrant: **Commissioned with Special Powers,** the 2nd most prestigious of 3 prefixes appended, especially after Han, to the titles of such territorial magnates as Area Commanders-in-chief (*tu-tu, tsung-kuan*), in effect giving them viceregal authority over all governmental agencies in their jurisdictions. Early in the era of N-S Division, such Commissioners had authority to put to death anyone not of official status, whereas those with the more prestigious designation Commissioned with Extraordinary Powers (*shih ch'ih-chieh*) could put to death even officials up to the rank of 2,000 bushels, and those with the less prestigious designation Commissioned with a Warrant (*chia-chieh*) could put to death only commoners who clearly violated military law. P50.

1106   *ch'íh-chiéh tū*   持節督
N-S DIV: **Area Commander with Special Powers,** in the Three Kingdoms period a prefix sometimes added to the title Regional Governor (*chou mu*) or Regional Inspector (*tz'u-shih*), signifying that the appointee had been given special viceregal powers; see under *ch'ih-chieh*. P50.

1107   *ch'íh-ch'uáng*   癡牀
Lit., the couch of arrogance: from T'ang times on, an indirect reference to the **Censor-in-chief** (*yü-shih ta-fu, tu yü-shih*), deriving from the custom that senior Censors sat for meals on a couch that junior Censors were not permitted to use.

1108   *ch'ìh-fú shìh*   赤发氏
CHOU: **Exterminator** of insects in the royal palace; one Junior Serviceman (*hsia-shih*) in the Ministry of Justice (*ch'iu-kuan*). CL (*tchi-po*): *l'extracteur, enleveur*.

1109   *ch'ìh-k'ù*   敕庫
SUNG: lit., storehouse of proclamations: **Archives** of the Court of Judicial Review (*ta-li ssu*). SP: *magasin des archives*. P22.

1110   *ch'ìh-lì t'í-lǐng kuān*   赤曆提領官
SUNG: **Superintendent of the Imperial Calendar,** a member of the Court of the Imperial Granaries (*ssu-nung ssu*); rank and functions not clear. SP: *directeur Tch'e-li*.

1111   *ch'ìh-lìng*   赤令 ·
T'ANG–SUNG: abbreviated reference to the **Magistrate of an Imperial District** (*ch'ih-hsien ling*); see under *ch'ih* (Imperial).

1112   *ch'ìh-lìng sǒ* 敕令所 or *ch'ìh-lìng chú*   敕令局
SUNG: **Law Code Office,** apparently not a regular agency of the governmental hierarchy but one created occasionally with an ad hoc staff to revise the law code under the direction of a Grand Councilor (*tsai-hsiang*) serving as Supervisor (*t'i-chü*). See *pien-hsiu ch'ih-ling so*. SP: *bureau de la rédaction des décrets et des ordonnances*. P13.

1113   *ch'ìh-shū shìh yù-shǐh*   持書侍御史
T'ANG: after 649, a variant reference to a *chih-shu shih yü-shih* (**Secretarial Censor**). P18.

1114   *ch'ìh-t'óu*   敕頭
CHIN: lit., (at the) head of the proclamation: **Principal Graduate,** a quasi-official reference to the first-place passer of the Metropolitan Examination (*hui-shih*) in the civil service recruitment examination system; used interchangeably with *chuang-yüan*, q.v.

1115   *ch'ìh-t'óu*   螭頭
T'ANG: lit., (at the) dragon's head: an unofficial reference to an **Imperial Diarist** (*ch'i-chü lang, ch'i-chü she-jen*) deriving from the customary expectation that during court audiences such officials should take up positions in front of carved dragons at the palace gates. May be encountered in later periods in reference to anyone performing similar functions. P24.

1116   *chǐn*   緊
T'ANG–SUNG: **Important,** 4th highest of 7 categories in which Districts (*hsien*) were ranked on the basis of their prestige and size; used as a prefix to *hsien*.

1117   *chīn-chǎng*   津長
SUI: **Ford Master,** low-ranked or unranked; apparently 4 appointed at each ford under the jurisdiction of the Office of Waterways (*tu-shui t'ai*), each group subordinate to a director whose designation varied according to the importance of the ford, e.g., Commandant (*wei*), Director (*tien-tso*). P14.

1118   *chīn-ch'ē*   巾車
CHOU: **Master of the Royal Chariots,** 2 ranked as Junior Grand Masters (*hsia ta-fu*), 4 as Senior Servicemen (*shang-shih*), 8 as Ordinary Servicemen (*chung-shih*), and 16 as Junior Servicemen (*hsia-shih*), members of the Ministry of Rites (*ch'un-kuan*) responsible for the maintenance, allocation, and decoration of all chariots used by the royal entourage. CL: *decorateur des chars*. P16.

1119   *chìn-ch'én*   近臣
Lit., close underlings: **Members of the Imperial Coterie,** throughout history an unofficial, categorical reference to Emperors' most intimate attendants, especially palace eunuchs.

1120   *chīn-chèng*   金正
CHOU: lit. sense not clear; rectifier (with weapons of) metal (?): variant reference to the **Ministry of Justice** (*ch'iu-kuan*) or the **Minister of Justice** (*ta ssu-k'ou*). May be encoun-

tered in later periods as an archaic reference to eminent judicial officials. P16.

1121 *chìn-chiǎng* 進講
SUNG–CH'ING: **Attendant Lecturer,** one of several ad hoc designations for officials who participated with the Emperor in a Classics Colloquium (*ching-yen*). P24.

1122 *chīn-chǔ* 津主
N-S DIV (S. Dynasties): **Ford Guardian,** one each stationed in the western and eastern outskirts of the dynastic capital, modern Nanking, to watch for the import or export of prohibited goods, to catch fugitives, and to collect transit taxes on certain trade goods; rank and place in the governmental organization not clear. P62.

1123 *chìn-chūng* 禁中
Lit., the forbidden inside: **Imperial Palace,** throughout history a standard reference, especially to the residential quarters of the ruler, his wives and children, and his female and eunuch attendants. See *kung, ta-nei.*

1124 *chìn-chūn* 禁軍
Imperial Armies. (1) General reference to government troops in any era, especially from T'ang on; normally refers to military units stationed in or around the dynastic capital under the command of the ruler or of his personal delegate; cf. the broader terms *kuan-chün, kuan-ping* (Regular Troops). Also see *ch'in-chün, wei, chin-wei, su-wei.* (2) T'ANG: refers to the military units at the dynastic capital, divided into 2 types and differentiated as the Southern Command (*nan-ya*) and the Northern Command (*pei-ya*). RR: *armées de la défense de l'empereur.* (3) SUNG: refers to the 2 groups of military units collectively called the Palace Command (*tien-ch'ien shih-wei ssu*) and the Metropolitan Command (*shih-wei ch'in-chün ma-pu ssu*).

1125 *chìn-fáng yü-shǐh* 禁防御史
N-S DIV (San-kuo Wei–Chin): **Monitoring Censor,** rank 7, apparently associated with Palace Censors (*tien-chung shih yü-shih*) of the Censorate (*yü-shih t'ai*); perhaps guarded against intrusions into the forbidden precincts of the palace, but functions not clear. P18.

1126 *chìn-hsiēn pǔ-yùng* 儘先補用
CH'ING: **Expectant for Early Appointment,** designation given to men who had qualified for office and had been assigned to Provinces for miscellaneous duty pending regular appointment to vacant offices. See *hou-hsüan, yü-ch'üeh chi-pu.* BH: first candidate.

1127 *chìn-ī wèi* 錦衣衛
MING: lit., embroidered-uniform guard unit: **Imperial Bodyguard,** the most prestigious and influential of the Imperial Guards (*ch'in-chün wei*); functioned as the personal bodyguard of the Emperor; cooperated with influential eunuchs in maintaining an empire-wide, irregular police and judicial service; and provided sinecure appointments for palace hangers-on and favorites, including court painters. P21.

1128 *chīn-k'ō* 金科
(1) YÜAN: **Treasury Section,** one of 6 subordinate Sections (*k'o*) in the Ministry of Revenue (*hu-pu*), headed by a Clerk (*ling-shih*), unranked; specific responsibilities not clear. (2) MING: **Special Accounts Section,** one of 4 functionally differentiated units in each Bureau (*ch'ing-li ssu*) of the Ministry of Revenue (*hu-pu*); headed by a Manager (*kuan-li*). P6.

1129 *chīn-kuān* 金官
HAN: **Gold Factory,** a gold-producing agency located in Kuei-yang Commandery, modern Hunan Province; presumably supervised by the Chamberlain for the Palace Revenues (*shao-fu*). HB: office of gold.

1130 *chìn-lín* 禁林
SUNG: lit., forbidden grove: an unofficial designation for a member of the Hanlin Academy (*han-lin yüan*) or of various Institutes (*kuan*), or for the Academy or Institutes themselves. P23, 27.

1131 *chìn-luǎn* 禁臠
Lit., forbidden meat, thus indirectly one having access to forbidden delicacies: from the era of N-S Division on, an unofficial reference to the husband of an Imperial Princess (*kung-chu*).

1132 *chìn-mǎ* 進馬
T'ANG: lit., one who presents horses: **Ceremonial Horse Groom,** 5 or 6, rank 7a, members of the Livery Service (*shang-sheng chü*) of the Palace Administration (*tien-chung sheng*), others in the Court of the Imperial Stud (*t'ai-p'u ssu*); chosen from among the sons of such middle-ranking officials as the Vice Censor-in-chief (*yü-shih chung-ch'eng*), Supervising Secretaries (*chi-shih-chung*) of the Chancellery (*men-hsia sheng*), and Secretariat Drafters (*chung-shu she-jen*), assigned to tend horses that were used in important imperial ceremonies. See *chang-ma.* RR: *officiers chargés de présenter les chevaux d'apparat.*

1133 *chīn-mào chú* 巾帽局
MING: **Caps and Kerchiefs Service,** a minor agency of palace eunuchs headed by a eunuch Commissioner-in-chief (*ta-shih*) or Director (*t'ai-chien*); manufactured caps, kerchiefs, and some sorts of footwear for palace use; see *pa chü* (Eight Services).

1134 *chìn-nà ch'ū-shēn* 進納出身
SUNG: **Qualified by Contribution,** designation of men who had gained eligibility for official appointments by making voluntary contributions to the state in a time of emergency, e.g., by contributing grain for public relief during a famine. Men so qualified seldom gained more than titular or very low-ranking offices. See *ch'u-shen.* Cf. *li-chien* (Student by Purchase).

1135 *chìn-nèi shìh-wèi* 禁內侍衛
SUI: **Palace Guard,** a military unit under the Secretariat of the Heir Apparent (*men-hsia fang*), headed by 2 Palace Commandants (*nei-shuai*), one each designated Left and Right; incorporated the members of the Imperial Bodyguard (*ch'ien-niu wei*) and the Personal Bodyguard (*pei-shen wei*) who were attending the Heir Apparent. P26.

1136 *chìn-ní àn* 進擬案
SUNG: **Section for Submission of Recommendations,** one of 13 Sections directly subordinate to the executive officials of the Ministry of Justice (*hsing-pu*); handled all transmissions of judicial recommendations to the throne. SP: *service chargé de présenter les jugements proposés.*

1137 *chìn-pào shìh* 禁暴氏
CHOU: **Keeper of the Peace,** 6 ranked as Junior Servicemen (*hsia-shih*), members of the Ministry of Justice (*ch'iu-kuan*) charged with keeping people from harming one another. CL: *préveneurs de violences.*

1138 *chìn-pèi shǐh* 禁備史
N-S DIV (Chin): **Chief of the Guard,** a minor member of

the staff of each Imperial Mausoleum (*ling*), under a Manager (*ling*), all subordinate to the Chamberlain for Ceremonials (*t'ai-ch'ang*) of the central government. P29.

1139 *chìn-pīng* 禁兵

Imperial Guardsman: throughout imperial history a common designation for a member of the ruler's personal bodyguard.

1140 *chīn-pó fŭ-t'ăng* 金帛府帑

N-S DIV (Liang): **Fineries Storehouse,** established in 508 under the control of the Chamberlain for the Palace Revenues (*t'ai-fu ch'ing*, then archaically called *hsia-ch'ing*). The Fineries Storehouse, which apparently kept the imperial treasury of precious metals and fine silks, supervised a Left and Right Storehouse (*tso-yu tsang*) with a Director (*ling*) and a Superior Storehouse (*shang-tsang*) with a Vice Director (*ch'eng*). *Tso-yu tsang* may refer to a Left Storehouse (*tso-tsang*) and a Right Storehouse (*yu-tsang*), each with a Director (*ling*); but Chinese editors have decided that Liang in fact had no Right Storehouse, so that *tso-yu tsang* here is apparently an erroneous reference to a Left Storehouse alone. See *tso-tsang*. P7.

1141 *chìn-pŭ* 禁圃

HAN: **Imperial Garden,** designation of the park adjoining the capital commonly called *shang-lin yüan*, q.v.; under the supervision of a Director (*ling*) with the help of a Commandant (*wei*) and an Aide (*ch'eng*). HB: forbidden orchards.

1142 *chīn-pù ssū* 金部司 or *chīn-pù*

(1) N-S DIV (San-kuo)–MING: **Treasury Bureau,** a fiscal agency normally in the 2nd echelon of the central government, rather than a principal agency. In the era of N-S Division, one of several units in the developing Ministry of Revenue (*tu-chih*), most commonly headed by a Director (*lang, lang-chung*). In Sui and T'ang, one of 4 Bureaus in the Ministry of Revenue (*min-pu* to 649, thereafter *hu-pu*), headed by a Director (*lang*), rank 5b1; official variant designations *ssu-chen* 662–671, *ssu-chin* 752–758. In Sung, one of 5 Bureaus in the Ministry of Revenue (*hu-pu*), fully activated only from c. 1080, after discontinuance of the State Finance Commission (*san ssu*) of early Sung; headed by 2 Directors (*lang-chung*), 6b; supervised 6 subordinate Sections (*an*)—Left Storage Section (*tso-tsang an*), Right Storage Section (*yu-tsang an*), Coins and Silks Section (*ch'ien-po an*), Monopoly Exchange Section (*chüeh-i an*), Claims Section (*ch'ing-chi an*), and Miscellany Section (*chih-tsa an*). In Ming, one of 4 Bureaus in the Ministry of Revenue (*hu-pu*), headed by a Director (*lang-chung*), 5a; extant only from 1380 to 1390, when the Ministry was reorganized with territorially designated Bureaus (*ch'ing-li ssu*), one per Province (*sheng*). RR+SP: *bureau du trésor*. (2) N-S DIV (N. Wei): **Ministry of the Treasury** in the developing Department of State Affairs (*shang-shu sheng*), headed by a Minister (*shang-shu*); extant only from the 450s into the 460s. (3) MING: **Special Accounts Section,** one of 4 units under each Province-designated Bureau (*pu* till 1396, then *ch'ing-li ssu*) in the Ministry of Revenue (*hu-pu*), staffed with subofficial functionaries; discontinued at the end of Ming if not earlier. P6.

1143 *chìn-pù ts'áo* 金部曹

N-S DIV: **Treasury Section,** a common variant of Treasury Bureau (*chin-pu ssu*). P6.

1144 *chìn snā-lù* 禁殺戮

CHOU: **Preventer of Crimes of Violence,** 2 ranked as Junior Servicemen (*hsia-shih*), members of the Ministry of Justice (*ch'iu-kuan*) responsible for deterring murders and other physical violence. CL: *préveneur des meurtres et blessures*.

1145 *chìn-shēn* 搢紳 or 縉紳

Lit., one who had stuck (a tally symbolizing official status) in his sash: throughout history a generic reference to a member of **the official class,** particularly referring to members of the class not serving in office but residing at home and wielding great local influence; see *shen-chin, shen-shih*. Sometimes rendered as Gentry.

1146 *chìn-shěng* 禁省

T'ANG: lit., the confidential department: unofficial reference to a **Secretariat Drafter** (*chung-shu she-jen*), who prepared imperial pronouncements. P23.

1147 *chìn-shìh* 近侍

N-S DIV–CHIN: **Court Attendant,** a designation common in northern conquest dynasties for members of the ruler's personal entourage, chosen from among nobles of the ethnic ruling group; in the T'o-pa regimes, totaled almost 100 at times and were responsible for conveying government documents to and from the ruler; in the Jurchen Chin dynasty, constituted a Court Attendants Service (*chin-shih chü*) that sometimes wielded great political influence. P37.

1148 *chìn-shìh* 進士

SUI–CH'ING: **Presented Scholar** (into early Sung) or **Metropolitan Graduate** (from Sung on), a degree or status often compared to the academic doctorate in the modern West, conferred on successful candidates in the highest-level regular civil service recruitment examinations, qualifying them for appointment to government office. In Sui, T'ang, and early Sung this was only one of several "doctoral" degrees, and not necessarily the most esteemed; it emphasized talent in literary composition. In the 1060s the *chin-shih* examination was made more general, and thereafter it was the most esteemed, and normally the only, "doctoral" examination degree, without which entrants upon civil service careers had small hope of attaining high office. RR: *lettré accompli*. SP: *docteur des lettres*. BH: metropolitan graduate, doctor.

1149 *chìn-shìh chí-tì* 進士及第

SUNG–CH'ING: **Metropolitan Graduate with Honors,** designation of the few best graduates of the national civil service recruitment examinations, constituting the First Category (*i chia*), as contrasted to Regular Metropolitan Graduates (*chin-shih ch'u-shen*) in the Second Category (*erh chia*) and Associate Metropolitan Graduates (*t'ung chin-shih ch'u-shen*) in the Third Category (*san chia*) of successful candidates. See *chī-ti*.

1150 *chìn-shìh ch'ū-shēn* 進士出身

SUNG–CH'ING: **Regular Metropolitan Graduate,** designation of a graduate of the national civil service recruitment examinations listed in the Second Category (*erh chia*) of graduates, not as esteemed as a Metropolitan Graduate with Honors (*chin-shih chi-ti*) but more esteemed than an Associate Metropolitan Graduate (*t'ung chin-shih ch'u-shen*). See *ch'u-shen*.

1151 *chìn-shìh chú* 近侍局

CHIN: **Palace Attendants Service,** an assemblage of Jurchen nobles serving in the imperial entourage under supervision of the Palace Inspectorate-general (*tien-ch'ien tu tien-chien ssu*); as in the case of powerful eunuch groups in other periods, wielded much political influence in late Chin times because of its members' closeness to the ruler and his trusting reliance on them.

1152　*chīn ssū-tzǔ chú*　金絲子局
YÜAN: **Gold Thread Service**, a handicraft agency commonly subordinate to Supervisorates-in-chief of Metal Workers and Jewelers (*chin-yü jen-chiang tsung-kuan fu*) in Routes (*lu*), charged with the manufacture of precious ornaments for the court and the nobility.

1153　*chīn-ts'áo*　金曹
(1) HAN: **Revenues Section**, one of a dozen or more Sections (*ts'ao*) subordinate to the Defender-in-chief (*t'ai-wei*) and probably duplicated on the staff of the Counselor-in-chief (*ch'eng-hsiang*); headed by an Administrator (*yüan-shih*), rank =400 bushels; apparently handled matters concerning receipts from the state monopolies of salt, iron, etc. BH: bureau of metal. (2) SUI–SUNG: **Treasury Section**, variant of *chin-pu* (Treasury Bureau) in the Ministry of Revenue (*hu-pu*); subsequently may be encountered as an unofficial reference to the Ministry of Revenue itself.

1154　*chìn-tsèng*　晉贈
A term normally meaning **promoted posthumously** to such honorific status as Duke (*kung*) in recognition of outstanding achievement in government service.

1155　*chìn-tsòu kuān*　進奏官
(1) T'ANG: **Capital Liaison Representative** of a regional dignitary; see *chin-tsou yüan*. (2) SUNG: **Memorial Transmitter**, a general designation for Supervising Secretaries (*chi-shih-chung*) assigned to the Memorials Office (*chin-tsou yüan*) of the Chancellery (*men-hsia sheng*). RR+SP: *fonctionnaire chargé de présenter les adresses à l'empereur*. P21.

1156　*chìn-tsòu yüàn*　進奏院
(1) T'ANG: **Capital Liaison Office**, agencies maintained in the capital by such regional dignitaries as Surveillance Commissioners (*kuan-ch'a shih*) to present their reports to the court and, generally, to represent their interests in the capital; staffed with Capital Liaison Representatives (*chin-tsou kuan, liu-hou shih*) who were not necessarily members of the regular officialdom; often also referred to as Liaison Hostels (*ti, ti-she*). (2) SUNG: **Memorials Office**, an agency of the Chancellery (*men-hsia sheng*), staffed with Supervising Secretaries (*chi-shih-chung*) who were responsible for the transmission of government documents to and from the throne and from the central government to the various Circuit (*lu*) authorities; also called *tu chin-tsou yüan* (Chief Memorials Office). SP: *cour pour la présentation des adresses*. P21.

1157　*chìn-tsú pā-ch'í*　禁族八旗
CH'ING: **Metropolitan Bannermen**, a generic reference to members of the military Banner (*ch'i*) units who were stationed in and around the dynastic capital, Peking; a variant of *ching-ch'i*, q.v.

1158　*chìn-tzǔ*　金紫
CH'IN–HAN: **Lord of the Golden Seal and Purple Ribbon**, an unofficial reference to the Counselor-in-chief (*ch'eng-hsiang*) and ultimately to other dignitaries collectively called the Three Dukes (*san kung*, q.v.).

1159　*chìn-tzǔ kuāng-lù tà-fū*　金紫光祿大夫
N-S DIV–YÜAN: **Grand Master of the Palace with Golden Seal and Purple Ribbon**, from the Three Kingdoms era an honorific title (*chia-kuan*) conferred on officials of high distinction; from Sui through Yüan a prestige title (*san-kuan*) conferred on officials of rank 2b then 3a in Sui, 3a in T'ang, 2a or 3a in Sung (especially Ministers of Personnel, *li-pu shang-shu*), 2a1 in Chin, 1a in Yüan. From Sung on, may be encountered as an elegant reference to a Minister of Personnel. P68.

1160　*chìn-wèi*　禁衛
Palace Guard, a common unofficial reference to a unit or member of the military responsible for personal protection of the ruler.

1161　*chìn-wèi sǒ*　禁衛所
SUNG: a variant reference to the **Capital Security Office** (*huang-ch'eng ssu*) in S. Sung, commonly in the term *hsing-kung chin-wei so* (Capital Security Office at the Auxiliary Palace). See *hsing-kung, huang-ch'eng ssu*.

1162　*chìn-wú*　金吾
Lit. meaning not wholly clear; probably used interchangeably from Chou into Han times with a homophonous term for prison, but traditionally interpreted as a special weapon, or a gold-tipped baton, or the image of a bird called *chin-wu* that was believed to frighten away evil. From Han on, commonly used in reference to imperial insignia, as in *chih chin-wu* (Chamberlain for the Imperial Insignia). Eventually used in the sense of **Lord of the Imperial Insignia** in elegant reference to a distinguished military officer such as the Ch'ing dynasty *t'ung-ling* (Commander-general).

1163　*chīn-wú chàng-ssū*　金吾仗司
SUNG: **Armory of the Imperial Insignia Guard** (*chin-wu wei*), a unit of the imperial bodyguard.

1164　*chīn-wú chiēh-ssū*　金吾街司
T'ANG–SUNG: **Patrol Office of the Imperial Insignia Guard** (*chin-wu wei*), a unit of the imperial bodyguard. P20.

1165　*chīn-wú ssū*　金吾司
SUNG: abbreviated reference to the *chin-wu chieh-ssu* or the *chin-wu chang-ssu*, qq.v., or to both.

1166　*chīn-wú wèi*　金吾衛
T'ANG–MING: **Imperial Insignia Guard**, often one each of Left and Right, a distinguished unit of the imperial bodyguard, normally commanded by a General (*chiang-chün*), sometimes with prefixes creating titles such as General-in-chief (*ta chiang-chün*). See *shih-liu wei*. P43.

1167　*chīn-yín ch'ì-hó t'í-chǔ ssū*　金銀器盒提舉司
YÜAN: **Supervisorate of Gold and Silver Utensils**, a manufacturing unit subordinate to a Supervisorate-in-chief of Metal Workers and Jewelers (*chin-yü jen-chiang tsung-kuan fu*); created 1287 by renaming the *chin-yin chü*, q.v.

1168　*chīn-yín chú*　金銀局
Gold and Silver Service. (1) N-S DIV (Liang): one of 2 Craft Workshops (*tso-t'ang*) under the Chamberlain for the Palace Revenues (*shao-fu*); authorized to have a Director (*ling*), but actually headed by a nominal Assistant Director (*ch'eng*), rank 3. P14. (2) YÜAN: pre-1287 name of the *chin-yin ch'i-ho t'i-chü ssu* (Supervisorate of Gold and Silver Utensils).

1169　*chīn-yín tsò-fāng yüàn*　金銀作坊院
T'ANG: **Gold and Silver Workshop**, a manufacturing unit subordinate to the Directorate for Imperial Manufactories (*shao-fu chien*). RR: *cour des travaux en or et en argent*.

1170 *chīn-yǔ fǔ* 金玉府
YÜAN: **Metals and Jewels Workshop,** original name (1261–1266) of the *chin-yü jen-chiang tsung-kuan fu,* q.v.

1171 *chīn-yǔ jén-chiàng tsǔng-kuǎn fu* 金玉人匠總管府
YÜAN: **Supervisorate-in-chief of Metal Workers and Jewelers,** an agency of the Imperial Manufactures Commission (*chiang-tso yüan*) that supervised several artisan workshops; until 1266 called *chin-yü fu,* q.v.

1172 *chìn-yún* 縉雲 or *chìn-yún ssū* 縉雲司
Lit., clouds of red girdles: unofficial reference to the **Ministry of War** (*ping-pu*) or its officials.

1173 *ch'ǐn* 寢
Temple at an imperial mausoleum (*ling*): in Han normally autonomous units directly responsible to the throne, thereafter commonly supervised by the Director (*ling*) of the Imperial Ancestral Temple (*t'ai-miao*); in Han headed by a Director (*ling*) and an Assistant Director (*lang*). HB: funerary chamber.

1174 *ch'īn-ch'á wèi* 欽察衛
YÜAN: **Kipchak Guard,** one each Left and Right, military units made up of notoriously fierce Turkic warriors, controlled by a Chief Military Command (*ta tu-tu fu*) under the supervision of the Bureau of Military Affairs (*shu-mi yüan*).

1175 *ch'īn-chūn* 親軍
(1) YÜAN: **Imperial Armies,** the formal designation of the entire military establishment in and around the dynastic capital, distinguishing it from the Territorial Armies (*chen-shu chün*) garrisoned elsewhere. (2) A common unofficial designation of **Imperial Armies,** normally identifying those military units that were directly under the command of the ruler, or for common soldiers assigned to them, as **Imperial Guardsmen.**

1176 *ch'īn-chūn fǔ* 親軍府
T'ANG: **Personal Guard Garrison** of a Prince (*wang*), headed by a Commander (*t'ung-chün*); perhaps only in the first half of the dynasty and thereafter retitled *ch'in-shih fu,* q.v.

1177 *ch'īn-chūn wèi* 親軍衛
MING: **Imperial Guard,** designation of 33 of the 74 Capital Guard (*ching-wei*) military units garrisoned in and around the dynastic capital, Peking, also of 17 of the 49 Capital Guard units in the Nanking area; those at Peking were independent of the regular military hierarchy, not being under the control of the Five Chief Military Commissions (*wu-chün tu-tu fu*); each commanded by a Guard Commander (*chih-hui shih*), rank 3a; the most influential and notorious of the Imperial Guards was the Imperial Bodyguard (*chin-i wei*).

1178 *ch'īn-chūn yíng* 親軍營
CH'ING: **Imperial Bodyguard,** an elite military unit of Imperial Guardsmen (*shih-wei ch'in-chün*) drawn from the Three Superior Banners (*shang san ch'i*), supervised personally by the Emperor and commanded by 6 Grand Ministers of the Imperial Household Department Concurrently Controlling the Imperial Guardsmen (*ling shih-wei nei ta-ch'en*). P37.

1179 *ch'īn-fèng shàng-yǔ shìh-chièn ch'ù* 欽奉上諭事件處
CH'ING: abbreviation of *chi-ch'a ch'in-feng shang-yü shih-*

chien ch'u (**Office for Distribution of Imperial Pronouncements**), q.v.

1180 *ch'īn-fǔ* 親府
T'ANG: **Bodyguard Garrison,** designation of one of the Five Garrisons (*wu fu,* q.v.) in the Emperor's service, also of one of the Three Garrisons (*san fu*) in the service of the Heir Apparent. See *san wei.* RR: *milice proche.* P26.

1181 *ch'īn hsién-chái* 親賢宅
SUNG: **Peers School,** one established in each Princely Establishment (*wang-fu*) for the education of members of the imperial clan.

1182 *ch'īn-ī k'ù* 親衣庫
SUNG: **Minor Gifts Storehouse,** a unit in the Palace Administration (*tien-chung sheng*), headed jointly by 2 Supervisors (*chien-kuan*), one a civil official and one a eunuch; assembled and stored embroidered gowns for presentation to dependent states and clothes for issue to government laborers, soldiers, etc.. See *shang-i k'u, nei i-wu k'u, ch'ao-fu fa-wu k'u.* SP: *magasin de vêtements de brocart.* P38.

1183 *ch'īn-shìh* 親試
From Sung on, a variant reference to the **Palace Examination** (*tien-shih*), the final stage of national civil service recruitment examinations.

1184 *ch'īn-shìh fǔ* 親事府
T'ANG: **Personal Guard Garrison,** a military bodyguard, one in each Princely Establishment (*wang-fu*), each headed by a Commandant (*tien-chün*), rank 5a. P69.

1185 *ch'īn-t'iēn chiēn* 欽天監
MING–CH'ING: **Directorate of Astronomy,** an autonomous agency in the capital responsible for conducting astronomical observations, forecasting weather, interpreting natural phenomena, and preparing the annual state calendar, functions previously performed by the *ssu-t'ien chien, t'ai-shih ling,* qq.v., etc.; headed by a Director (*chien-cheng*), rank 5a (in Ch'ing, one each Chinese and Manchu), and staffed largely by hereditary professional astronomers-astrologers, including some Moslem (*hui-hui*) specialists; beginning in 1669 the Chinese Directorship was commonly occupied by a European Jesuit. In Ming there was a branch of the agency with the same name in Nanking. BH: imperial board of astronomy. P35, 49.

1186 *ch'īn-wáng* 親王
Throughout history, beginning not later than the era of N-S Division, **Imperial Prince,** a designation conferred on all sons of each reigning Emperor other than the Heir Apparent, who was normally the eldest. Imperial Princes were usually known by the names of territories with which they were (most often only nominally) enfeoffed, e.g. *Ch'in-kuo ch'in-wang* (Imperial Prince of the Princedom of Ch'in, or simply Prince of Ch'in); and on attaining maturity they were usually required to leave the dynastic capital and "go to their fiefs" (*chih-kuo*), i.e., take up residence elsewhere in the empire, where their household affairs were managed by Princely Establishments (*wang-fu*) staffed with members of the regular officialdom. The designated Heirs of Imperial Princes (*shih-tzu*) normally inherited the princely status in perpetuity; other sons were granted lesser titles of nobility, declining generation by generation. Imperial Princes as such had no specified official functions except when their Princedoms were actual governmental units, but at times some were appointed to high offices or given important military commands. See *wang.* P64.

1187 *ch'īn-wèi* 親衛 or *ch'īn-wèi fǔ* 親衛府
(1) SUI: **Palace Guard,** a general term encompassing both the Imperial Bodyguard (*pei-shen fu*) and the Palace Gate Guards (*chien-men fu*). (2) T'ANG–CH'ING: an unofficial reference to the Imperial Bodyguard or other special military units (*ch'in-chün, ch'in-chün fu, ch'in-chün wei, ch'in-chün ying,* etc.), or the personal bodyguards of Imperial Princes (*ch'in-wang*). SP: *garde proche.*

1188 *chīng* 京
Throughout history, the most common designation for a dynastic **Capital;** sometimes designating the **Metropolitan Area,** a large region administered directly from the capital. See *ching-chao* and *ching-shih.*

1189 *chīng-ch'á* 京察
MING–CH'ING: **Capital Evaluation,** a sweeping periodic assessment of the competence of all officials on duty in the capital, in contrast to the Outer Evaluation (*wai-ch'a*) of provincial and local officials; in consequence of the evaluations, officials were reappointed, promoted, demoted, retired, dismissed, etc. In Ming the capital evaluation was conducted every 6th year by the Ministry of Personnel (*li-pu*) with the aid of censorial officials; capital officials of rank 4 and above were exempt from the evaluation but were expected at the same time to submit "confessions" (*tzu-ch'en*) of their shortcomings. In Ch'ing the capital evaluation was conducted every 3rd year; officials of the top 3 ranks and all members of the Hanlin Academy (*han-lin yüan*) and the Censorate (*tu ch'a-yüan*) were evaluated by the Emperor personally, and officials of ranks 4 and 5 were evaluated by special teams of Princes and Grand Ministers (*ta-ch'en*).

1190 *chīng-chào* 京兆
Capital or **Metropolitan Area,** from Han on a common designation for the dynastic capital and its environs; eventually also an unofficial designation of the head of the Prefecture or comparable area in which the Capital was located, e.g., the Ch'ing dynasty Shun-t'ien *fu-yin* (Governor of Shun-t'ien Prefecture). See *ta ching-chao.*

1191 *chīng-chào fǔ* 京兆府
T'ANG: **Metropolitan Prefecture,** official designation of the dynastic capital, Ch'ang-an, and its environs. At other times may be encountered as an unofficial reference to the area of the capital, e.g., the Ch'ing dynasty Shun-t'ien Prefecture.

1192 *chīng-chào yǐn* 京兆尹
Metropolitan Governor. (1) HAN–SUI: administrative head of the dynastic capital and its environs; in Han considered one of the Three Guardians (*san fu,* q.v.), rank 2,000 bushels; in Sui rank 3a. HB: governor of the capital. (2) T'ANG–CH'ING: may be encountered as an unofficial reference to the administrative head of the Prefecture or comparable area in which the dynastic capital was located. P20, 32, 49.

1193 *chīng-ch'áo kuān* 京朝官
Metropolitan Officials, a generic designation normally indicating all members of the regular officialdom who were on duty at the dynastic capital, including both Court Officials (*ch'ao-kuan*) and Capital Officials (*ching-kuan*); the normal distinction was that Court Officials were entitled by their status to attend imperial audiences regularly, whereas Capital Officials were not.

1194 *chīng-chèng chiēn* 經正監
YÜAN: **Directorate for the Mongolian Pastures,** an agency at the capital that supervised the distribution of pasturing rights and resolved pertinent litigation among Mongol nobles; headed by an imperial clansman or other Mongol noble entitled Grand Minister (*t'ai-ch'ing*).

1195 *chīng-ch'éng* 經承
CH'ING: lit., to have received (assignment): **Assignee,** an unofficial generic reference to subofficial functionaries (*li*) and lesser servant personnel in government agencies.

1196 *chīng-ch'éng yú-chiǎo* 京城游徼
MING–CH'ING: unofficial reference to a **Chief of Police** (*li-mu*), unranked, in any of the Five Wards (*wu ch'eng*) into which the dynastic capital city was divided for policing and related purposes.

1197 *chīng-chí* 京畿
Metropolitan Region, from antiquity designating the area in which the ruler's capital was located; in T'ang, more specifically, the official name of the Circuit (*tao*) in which the dynastic capital, Ch'ang-an, was located.

1198 *chīng-chí àn* 經籍案
SUNG: **Books Section** in the Imperial Archives (*pi-ko*); staffing not clear, probably by clerical subofficials.

1199 *chīng-chí tào* 京畿道
Metropolitan Circuit. (1) T'ANG: name of the region in which the dynastic capital, Ch'ang-an, was located; designated a formal administrative unit in the reign of Hsüan-tsung (712–756). (2) MING: name of a Censorate (*tu ch'a-yüan*) unit existing solely as the collective designation of Investigating Censors (*chien-ch'a yü-shih*) on duty in the capital, who, in addition to their normal Province-oriented functions, had duty assignments to check records in agencies of the central government for evidence of malfeasance. (3) CH'ING: name of one of ultimately 20 Circuits (*tao*) in the Censorate, whose staff of 4 Investigating Censors were responsible for maintaining censorial surveillance over all administrative units in Chihli (modern Hopei) Province. See *chih-li, tao.*

1200 *chīng-ch'í* 京旗
CH'ING: **Metropolitan Bannermen,** a generic reference to members of the military Banner (*ch'i*) units who were stationed in and around the dynastic capital, Peking; subdivided into Inner Banners (*nei-ch'i*) and Outer Banners (*wai-ch'i*). BH: metropolitan banner forces.

1201 *chīng-ch'í-ní hā-fān* 精奇尼哈番
CH'ING: **Viscount,** Manchu title of nobility changed in the 18th century to the Chinese form *tzu,* q.v. P64.

1202 *chīng-chiéh kuān* 旌節官
SUNG: **Emblem Maker,** 2, probably unranked, on the staff of the Directorate for Imperial Manufactories (*shao-fu chien*). SP: *fonctionnaire chargé de la fabrication des bannières et des emblèmes de commandement.*

1203 *chīng-chiéh ssū* 旌節司
CH'ING: **Emblem Office,** subordinate to the Center Subsection (*chung-so*) of the Imperial Procession Guard (*luan-i wei*), headed by a Director (*chang-yin yün-hui shih*), rank 4a. BH: section chief.

1204 *chīng-chìh fā-yùn shǐh* 經制發運使
SUNG: **Fiscal and Supply Commissioner,** a delegate from the central government responsible for overseeing the collection of taxes in a Circuit (*lu*) and the transport of tax revenues and other state commodities to the capital; might be encountered as a combined reference to Fiscal Commissioners (*ching-chih shih*) and Supply Commissioners (*fa-*

yün shih). SP: *commissaire aux finances et à l'expédition des transports.* P60.

1205   *chīng-chìh … kàn-pàn ch'áng-p'íng kūng-shìh* 經制…幹辦常平公事
SUNG: **Supply Commissioner,** one of several terms used for the chief official of a Supply Commission (*ts'ang-ssu*) in a Circuit (*lu*); normally encloses a geographic name, e.g., such-and-such a Circuit. Often abbreviated to *ch'ang-p'ing kuan.* SP: *fonctionnaire chargé de maintenir l'uniformité du prix des graines.*

1206   *chīng-chìh mǎi-mǎ ssū* 經制買馬司
SUNG: **Horse Purchasing Office,** an agency subordinate to Chengtu Prefecture (*fu*), responsible for buying horses on the western frontier for state military use. SP: *bureau d'achat des chevaux.*

1207   *chīng-chìh piēn-fáng ts'ái-yùng ssū* 經制邊防財用司
SUNG: **Frontier Defense Supply Commission,** several established in frontier Circuits (*lu*) to maintain logistical support for frontier military forces; each headed by a delegate from the central government called a Commissioner (*shih*). SP: *bureau d'administration financière pour la défense des frontières.*

1208   *chīng-chìh ssū* 經制司
SUNG: apparently a variant reference to a **Fiscal Commission** (*ts'ao-ssu*) in a Circuit (*lu*), but may be encountered as an abbreviated reference to any of the *ching-chih … shih* or *ssu* listed above. SP: *bureau d'administration financière.*

1209   *chīng chǐng-hsún shìh* 京警巡使
LIAO: **Capital Police Commissioner,** head of the Police Commission (*ching-hsün yüan*) in each of the 5 Liao capitals; rank not clear. P20.

1210   *chīng-chú* 京局
CH'ING: abbreviated, unofficial reference to the **Metropolitan Coinage Service** (*pao-ch'üan chü*), a unit in the Ministry of Revenue (*hu-pu*).

1211   *chìng-fēi* 敬妃
MING: **Respectful Consort,** title conferred on selected palace women; rank not clear but relatively high.

1212   *chīng-fǔ* 京府
SUNG: **Capital Prefecture,** a common reference to the Superior Prefecture (*fu*) in which the dynastic capital was located.

1213   *chīng-fǔ* 京輔
HAN: variant reference to the **Metropolitan Area** (*ching-shih*), in which the dynastic capital was located. Also see under *san fu* (Three Guardians).

1214   *chīng-fǔ fáng* 經撫房
SUNG: **Frontier Defense Office,** a subsection of the Bureau of Military Affairs (*shu-mi yüan*); staffing and functions not clear. SP: *chambre des affaires militaires de la défense des frontières.*

1215   *chǐng-fú tièn shǐh* 景福殿使
SUNG: **Commissioner of the Hall of Abundant Happiness,** a title of honor but apparently no functions, carrying rank 5b.

1216   *chīng-fǔ tū-wèi* 京輔都尉
HAN: **Defender of the Capital,** one of the Three Defenders of the Metropolitan Area (*san-fu tu-wei*, q.v.). HB: chief commandant of the adjunct capital region.

1217   *chīng-hsièn* 京縣
MING–CH'ING: **Capital District,** unofficial reference to the Districts (*hsien*) constituting a dynastic capital.

1218   *chìng-hsìn* 敬信
N-S DIV (N. Ch'i): **Lady of Respectful Trustworthiness,** designation of one of 27 imperial consorts called *shih-fu,* q.v.; rank =3b.

1219   *chīng-hsüéh chù-chiào* 經學助教
T'ANG: **Classics Instructor,** 2 on the staff of the Metropolitan Governor (*ching-chao yin*), apparently unranked; functions not wholly clear. P32.

1220   *chīng-hsüéh pó-shìh* 經學博士
T'ANG: **Erudite of the Classics.** (1) Supervisor of state schooling in a unit of territorial administration; in a Metropolitan Prefecture (*fu*), rank 8b1; in an Area Command (*tu-tu fu*), 8b1 or 8b2; in a Prefecture (*chou*), 8b2, 9a1, or 9a2; in a District (*hsien*), unranked. P32, 51. (2) Five among the 18 Palace Erudites (*nei-chiao po-chih*) on the staff of the Palace Institute of Literature (*nei wen-hsüeh kuan*), where palace women were educated; from c. 741, a eunuch post. RR: *maître de la science des classiques.*

1221   *chìng-hsùn* 敬訓
N-S DIV (N. Ch'i): **Lady of Respectful Instruction,** designation of one of 27 imperial consorts called *shih-fu,* q.v.; rank =3b.

1222   *chìng-hsùn* 靜訓
N-S DIV (N. Ch'i): **Lady of Quiet Instruction,** designation of one of 27 imperial consorts called *shih-fu,* q.v.; rank =3b.

1223   *chǐng-hsún yüàn* 警巡院
LIAO–YÜAN: **Police Commission,** charged with maintaining control of the population in the dynastic capital, headed by a Police Commissioner (*ching-hsün shih*), rank 6a in Chin and Yüan, subordinate to an Overseer (*ta-lu-hua-ch'ih*) in Yüan. In Liao, one established in each of 5 capitals. Yüan divided the agency into 2, one each of Left and Right, and in 1305 created a 3rd called Police Commission of the Grand Capital (*ta-tu ching-hsün yüan*) to control the southern environs of Peking, whereupon the original 2 agencies were differentiated as being attached to the Ta-tu Route (*lu*). In some fashion not wholly clear, the Yüan agencies shared responsibility for policing the capital and its environs with 2 Wardens' Offices (*ping-ma ssu*). At the beginning of Ming, all Police Commissions were merged into a new structure of 5 Wardens' Offices. P20, 49, 53.

1224   *chīng-kuān* 京官
Capital Officials, an unofficial general designation of officials on duty in the dynastic capital. In Sung times, a more specific designation of those Metropolitan Officials (*ching-ch'ao kuan*) whose titular status was lower than Court Officials (*ch'ao-kuan*), who were entitled to attend imperial audiences regularly; the 2 categories had nothing to do with actual service in the capital or elsewhere, but were something like prescribed career ladders on which officials moved in accordance with their individual prestige, among other things.

1225   *chīng-k'uéi* 經魁
MING–CH'ING: lit., classics master: **Notable Graduate,** in early Ming a designation granted to the 5 best performers in a Provincial Examination (*hsiang-shih*) of the civil service recruitment system, one for each of the 5 classical texts

in which candidates were allowed to declare a specialization; subsequently (transition not clear, but not later than early Ch'ing) granted to those graduates who ranked 2nd, 3rd, 4th, and 5th either in a Provincial Examination, behind the Provincial Graduate with Highest Honors (*chieh-yüan*), or in the Metropolitan Examination (*hui-shih*), behind the Principal Graduate (*chuang-yüan*).

1226 *chīng-láng* 經郎
YÜAN: **Abundant Classicist,** a staff member of the Hall for the Diffusion of Literature (*hsüan-wen ko*), rank not clear; served concurrently as Translator for the Classics Colloquium (*ching-yen i-wen kuan*). P24.

1227 *chīng-lì* 經歷
YÜAN–CH'ING: **Registrar,** head of a Registry (*ching-li ssu*).

1228 *chīng-lì ssū* 經歷司
YÜAN–CH'ING: lit. meaning arguable, probably an office through which things pass, especially documents: **Registry,** an agency found in many agencies both in the central government and in the hierarchy of territorial administration, serving as a kind of central message center or internal management office for its agency; normally headed by a Registrar (*ching-li*), rank varying between 5a and 8b. P18, 21, 29, 72.

1229 *chīng-lì t'īng* 經歷廳
CH'ING: **Registry,** a variant of *ching-li ssu* found, e.g., in the Censorate (*tu ch'a-yüan*) and the Imperial Procession Guard (*luan-i wei*).

1230 *chīng-liǎng t'īng* 京糧廳
MING–CH'ING: **Office of the Capital Granaries,** an office staffed by ad hoc representatives of the Ministry of Revenue (*hu-pu*) who supervised the functioning of the many granaries in Peking and its environs that provided basic food supplies for the imperial palace and the central government establishment. P8.

1231 *chīng-lüèh* 經略 or *chīng-lüèh shǐh* 經略使
Lit., one who takes charge of and puts in order (an area): **Military Commissioner.** (1) T'ANG: variant designation of, or occasional supplementary prefix to, *chieh-tu shih* (Military Commissioner). RR: *commissaire impérial à la direction militaire d'une région.* (2) SUNG: one of several designations used for delegates from the capital in charge of Military Commissions (*shuai-ssu*) of Circuits (*lu*); also see *ching-lüeh an-fu shih.* SP: *commissaire militaire d'une préfecture.* (3) YÜAN: from 1358 dispatched on ad hoc basis into various regions to quell rebels and stabilize conditions. (4) MING: an ad hoc delegate from the central government sent to cope with urgent military matters, especially in frontier areas; comparable in prestige to the more stable and regular *tsung-tu* (Supreme Commander). P50.

1232 *chīng-lüèh ān-fù shǐh* 經略安撫使
SUNG: **Military Commissioner,** one of several designations used for delegates from the capital in charge of Military Commissions (*shuai-ssu*) of Circuits (*lu*), especially in frontier zones. Often abbreviated to *ching-lüeh shih.* P50.

1233 *chīng-lüèh ān-fù tū tsǔng-kuān* 經略安撫都總管
SUNG: **Commander-in-chief,** overall coordinator of civil and military affairs in a Circuit (*lu*), usually in a frontier zone; normally more prestigious and influential than a Military Commissioner (*ching-lüeh an-fu shih*). Also see *shuai-ssu.*

1234 *chīng-lüèh tà-ch'én* 經略大臣
CH'ING: **Grand Minister Commander,** designation of an ad hoc leader of a Green Standards (*lu-ying*) army on campaign.

1235 *chīng-pāng* 經邦
SUNG: **Manager of the State,** one of several special laudatory epithets for "meritorious ministers" (*kung-ch'en*), conferred occasionally on members of the Secretariat (*chung-shu sheng*) and the Bureau of Military Affairs (*shu-mi yüan*).

1236 *chīng-shàn ch'īng-lì ssū* 精膳清吏司
MING–CH'ING: **Bureau of Provisions,** one of 4 major constituent agencies in the Ministry of Rites (*li-pu*), headed by a Director (*lang-chung*), rank 5a; responsible for providing the food and drink used on ceremonial occasions. See *ch'ing-li ssu.* BH: banqueting department. P9.

1237 *chǐng-shān kuān-hsüéh* 景山官學
CH'ING: **Mount Prospect School,** a school in the imperial palace grounds for children of elite military men belonging to the Three Superior Banners (*shang san ch'i*), directed by Grand Minister Supervisors of the Imperial Household Department (*tsung-kuan nei-wu fu ta-ch'en*) designated as Managers of the Mount Prospect School (*kuan-li ching-shan kuan-hsüeh shih-wu*). BH: school at the red hill.

1238 *chīng-shàn ssū* 精膳司
MING–CH'ING: abbreviation of *ching-shan ch'ing-li ssu* **(Bureau of Provisions).**

1239 *chīng-shīh* 京師
Metropolitan Area, a term used from Han on for the region, whether large or small, that included the dynastic capital and its environs.

1240 *chīng-shīh* 經師
HAN: **Classics Teacher,** one ordered appointed to head a school (*hsüeh* or *hsiao*) in every unit of territorial administration by Emperor P'ing (r. A.D. 1–5). P51.

1241 *chǐng-t'ién k'ō* 井田科
CH'ING: **Banner Revenues Section,** established in 1734 as one of 3 agencies of the Ministry of Revenue (*hu-pu*) not subordinated to Bureaus (*ch'ing-li ssu*), responsible for reporting on income from lands set aside for support of the Eight Banners (*pa ch'i*) and payments to bannermen; staffing not clear. P6.

1242 *chīng-t'īng* 經廳
YÜAN–CH'ING: unofficial reference to **Registrars** (*ching-li*) or **Registries** (*ching-li ssu*), in Ch'ing especially the Registrar of a Provincial Administration Commission (*ch'eng-hsüan pu-cheng shih ssu*).

1243 *chīng-tū* 京都
The Capital, throughout history a common general reference to the capital city of an autonomous regional state or of the united empire, specifically indicating the city itself rather than the Metropolitan Area (*ching-shih*), of which it was the core. RR: *ville capitale.*

1244 *chīng-tù chìh-chìh shǐh* 經度制置使
SUNG: **Commissioner for Ceremonies,** an ad hoc assignment for an eminent official to be in charge of a major ritual ceremony. SP: *commissaire chargé des dispositions pour une grande cérémonie.*

1245 *chīng-t'ú wèi* 經途尉
N-S DIV (N. Wei, N. Ch'i): **Commandant of the Capital Street Patrol,** subordinate to the Commandant of the Capital Patrol (*liu-pu wei, ch'i-pu wei*), charged with maintaining peace and order in capital cities; each responsible

for 9 to 12 streets (*hang*), supervising from 74 to 135 urban Villages (*li*), whose Village Heads (*li-cheng*) were responsible for the conduct of the resident population. P20.

1246   *chīng-t'ūng ts'āng*   京通倉
MING–CH'ING: **Metropolitan Granaries,** an abbreviated, combined reference to the state granaries at the dynastic capital, Peking, and those nearby at T'ung-chou, the northern terminus of the Grand Canal. See *ts'ang-ch'ang*. P8.

1247   *chìng-wăn*   敬婉
N-S DIV (N. Ch'i): **Lady of Respectful Kindness,** designation of one of 27 imperial consorts called *shih-fu;* rank =3b.

1248   *chīng-wèi*   京衛
MING: **Capital Guards,** a collective designation of the Guard (*wei*) military units garrisoned in the immediate vicinities of the dynastic capital, Peking (74 *wei*), and the auxiliary capital, Nanking (49); except for those units called Imperial Guards (*ch'in-chün wei*) stationed near Peking, all were under the direction of the Five Chief Military Commissions (*wu-chün tu-tu fu*).

1249   *chīng-yén*   經筵
SUNG–CH'ING: **Classics Colloquium,** a gathering of the Emperor with eminent civil officials of the general administrative agencies in the capital, of the Hanlin Academy (*han-lin yüan*), of the Directorate of Education (*kuo-tzu chien*), etc., for the reading and discussion of classical and historical texts; irregular until Ming times, when sessions began to be scheduled every spring and autumn; participants were given ad hoc but prestigious designations as Lecturer (*chiang-kuan*), Attendant Lecturer (*chin-chiang*), Principal Expounder (*i-chu*), etc. In Yüan times the most prestigious participant was called the Translator (*i-wen kuan*). P24.

1250   *chīng-yén kuān*   經筵官
SUNG–CH'ING: **Participant in the Classics Colloquium,** an ad hoc generic designation for officials who participated with the Emperor in a Classics Colloquium (*ching-yen*). SP: *fonctionnaire chargé d'expliquer les textes devant l'empereur.* P24.

1251   *chīng-yĭn*   京尹
CH'ING: **Capital Governor,** unofficial reference to the Governor (*yin*) of Shun-t'ien Prefecture (*fu*), site of the dynastic capital, Peking.

1252   *chīng-yíng*   京營
MING: **Capital Training Divisions,** large military encampments at Peking and Nanking to which troops belonging to Guards (*wei*) throughout the empire were rotated for training and service as a kind of combat-ready reserve; in 1450 reorganized into Integrated Divisions (*t'uan-ying*) whose officers and troops remained together in both training and campaigning; in 1488 coordinated under a Superintendent (*t'i-tu*); in 1550 Integrated Divisions were discontinued, and thereafter the Training Divisions were coordinated by a Superintendent or a Supreme Commander (*tsung-tu*). In the last half of Ming, the Training Divisions ceased being effective fighting forces; their troops were normally used as tate construction gangs or assigned to other menial tasks. See *san ta-ying, jung-cheng t'ing, pan-chün, fan* (on rotational duty).

1253   *chĭng-yüèh chūn*   井鉞軍
T'ANG: **Army of the Celestial Twins,** named after a group of stars in Gemini called *ching-yüeh;* one of 12 regional supervisory headquarters for militia Garrisons (*fu;* see *fu-*

ping) called the Twelve Armies (*shih-erh chün*); extant only 620–623, 625–636. RR: *armée de (l'étoile) de la hache (près de la constellation) du puits.* P44.

1254   *ch'īng*   清
Beginning in the era of N-S Division very soon after the fall of Han, a term meaning **pure** used as an at least quasi-official designation for officials of esteemed genealogical status, who advanced through sequences of positions also designated "pure" into the top echelon of government; in contrast to the label "impure" (*cho*) for officials of less genealogical distinction and the less prestigious positions reserved for them. Such distinctions persisted into Sui times, when the label "high expectations" (*ch'ing-wang*) was used for the most elite group of "pure" officials; and there were echoes of these distinctions in later times. This traditional usage perhaps accounts for the name *ch'ing-li ssu* (lit., office of pure functionaries) given to Bureaus of Ministries (*pu*) in Ming and Ch'ing times.

1255   *ch'īng*   卿
From highest antiquity, a term used generically, or particularized with prefixes, for eminent officials. (1) CHOU: **Minister,** the highest rank category of officials serving the King and Feudal Lords, differentiated from Grand Master (*ta-fu*) and Serviceman (*shih*). (2) CH'IN–SUI: **Chamberlain,** in charge of a major service agency, e.g., Chamberlain for the Palace Revenues (*shao-fu*). (3) SUI–CH'ING: **Chief Minister,** designation of heads of various agencies including the Nine Courts (*chiu ssu*), e.g., Chief Minister of the Court of State Ceremonial (*hung-lu ssu ch'ing,* or simply *hung-lu ch'ing*). Also used unofficially for a Vice Minister (*shih-lang*) of a Ministry (*pu*), often with a descriptive prefix. Also see *chiu ch'ing, liu ch'ing, ch'i ch'ing.*

1256   *ch'īng-chào shĭh*   清詔使
HAN: **Imperial Commissioner,** a designation given various central government officials when sent on special, temporary investigatory missions away from the capital. HB: messenger with a pure edict.

1257   *ch'īng-ch'ē chiāng-chūn*   輕車將軍
HAN–T'ANG: **General of Light Chariots,** a title of nobility (*chüeh*) normally conferred on the eldest grandson of a Duke (*kung*) in direct line of succession. P65.

1258   *ch'īng-ch'ē tū-wèi*   輕車都尉
T'ANG–CH'ING: **Commandant of Light Chariots,** a merit title (*hsün*) through Ming, then a title of nobility (*chüeh*); in T'ang, Sung, and Chin, 6th highest of 12 grades, rank 4b; in Yüan and Ming, rank 3b; in Ch'ing, 6th highest of 9 ranks of non-imperial nobility. See *shang ch'ing-ch'e tu-wei, chüeh-yin.* RR: *directeur général des chars de guerre.* SP: *directeur des chars de guerre.* P64, 65.

1259   *ch'īng-ch'éng kūng-chiēn*   清城宮監
T'ANG: **Directorate of the Palace at Loyang,** in charge of maintaining buildings and grounds of imperial parks and gardens in the Eastern Capital (*Tung-tu*), Loyang, under the supervision of the Court of the Imperial Granaries (*ssu-nung ssu*); headed by a Director (*chien*), rank 6b2. In 657 renamed *tung-tu yüan pei-mien chien* (Directorate of Parks in the Eastern Capital, Northern Quadrant). P40.

1260   *ch'īng-chĭ àn*   請給案
SUNG: **Claims Section,** one of 6 Sections (*an*) in the Treasury Bureau (*chin-pu ssu*) of the Ministry of Revenue (*hu-pu*), staffed with subofficial functionaries; functions not clear, but apparently handled claims from local territorial administrative agencies for issuance of non-grain commodities under the jurisdiction of the Treasury Bureau. Estab-

lished c. 1080, when the State Finance Commission (*san ssu*) of early Sung was discontinued. SP: *service des réclamations*. P6.

1261 *ch'īng-chì láng* 清紀郎
MING: **Recorder of Misdeeds,** one in each Secretariat of the Heir Apparent (*ch'un-fang*), charged with criticizing and impeaching members of the Household Administration of the Heir Apparent (*chan-shih fu*); rank 8b. P26.

1262 *ch'īng-chiēn* 卿監
5 DYN–SUNG: **Chief Ministers and Directors,** a generic term—in the Five Dynasties era, for eminent officials assigned to superintend the Hostel for Tributary Envoys (*ssu-fang kuan*); in Sung, for officials with prestige titles (*san-kuan*) for ranks 5a to 6a. P21.

1263 *ch'īng-chīn tzǔ* 青衿子
T'ANG–CH'ING: **Blue Collar Graduate,** unofficial reference to a passer of a civil service recruitment examination; in Ming and Ch'ing most commonly denoted a Government Student (*sheng-yüan*).

1264 *ch'īng-chūn* 清軍
MING–CH'ING: **Troop Purification,** a process for maintaining the strength of the hereditary soldiery by finding appropriate replacements for the dead and overaged, tracking down deserters, etc.; abbreviation of *ch'ing-li chün-wu*. Used as a descriptive prefix for officials assigned to such duties, e.g., Troop-purifying Censors (*yü-shih*), Vice Prefects (*t'ung chih-fu*), Assistant Prefects (*t'ung-p'an*). P32.

1265 *ch'īng-chūn tào* 清軍道
MING–CH'ING: **Troop Purification Circuit,** the jurisdiction of a Surveillance Vice Commissioner (*an-ch'a fu-shih*) or an Assistant Surveillance Commissioner (*an-ch'a ch'ien-shih*) of a Provincial Surveillance Commission (*t'i-hsing an-ch'a shih ssu*) assigned to troop-purification duty. See *ch'ing-chün, tao*.

1266 *ch'īng-èrh* 鄉貳
Lit., ministers and their seconds (i.e., assistants): **Ministerial Executives,** an unofficial collective reference to high-level administrative officials in the central government, often not defined with precision. From Ch'in into the era of N-S Division, seems to refer primarily to Chamberlains (*ch'ing*, e.g., the Chamberlain for Ceremonials, *t'ai-ch'ang ch'ing*) and their Aides (*ch'eng*). From the era of N-S Division into Ch'ing times, may refer to the Chief Ministers (*ch'ing*), Vice Ministers (*shao-ch'ing*), and possibly even Assistant Ministers (*ch'eng*) of various Courts (*ssu*), e.g., the Court of Imperial Entertainments (*hung-lu ssu*); may be found referring to the Ministers (*shang-shu*) and Vice Ministers (*shih-lang*, sometimes unofficially called *ch'ing*) of the Six Ministries (*liu-pu*) that were the administrative core of the central government; and suggests a vaguely defined group representing Courts, Ministries, and even other agencies such as the Censorate (*yü-shih t'ai, tu ch'a-yüan*). Also see *chiu ch'ing, ch'i ch'ing, liu ch'ing*. Cf. *erh-ch'ing*.

1267 *ch'īng-fēng ssū* 慶豊司
CH'ING: lit., office of happy fertility: **Office of Imperial Pasturages,** an agency responsible for the administration of flocks and herds throughout the empire that belonged to the Emperor; autonomous till 1723, then subordinated to the Imperial Household Department (*nei-wu fu*); headed in annual rotation by a dignitary with the title Grand Minister (*ta-ch'en*). BH: pasturage department. P37.

1268 *ch'īng-hsüǎn* 清選
Lit., to purify the personnel selections: (1) SUI–CH'ING:

an unofficial reference to the **Vice Minister** (*shao-ch'ing*) **of the Court of Imperial Sacrifices** (*t'ai-ch'ang ssu*), apparently deriving from the popular epithet of an official who was noted for his honesty (*ch'ing*) in the selection of men for official appointments (*hsüan*). (2) MING–CH'ING: **Personnel Selection Staff,** an unofficial collective reference to the Director (*lang-chung*), the Vice Director (*yüan-wai lang*), and the Secretary (*chu-shih*) of Bureaus (*ch'ing-li ssu*) in Ministries (*pu*), probably most specifically the Ministry of Personnel (*li-pu*). P5.

1269 *ch'īng-kài ssū* 擎蓋司
CH'ING: **Umbrella Office,** one of 2 subordinate units in the Right Subsection (*yu-so*) of the Imperial Procession Guard (*luan-i wei*), headed by a Director (*chang-yin yün-hui shih*), rank 4a. BH: umbrella section.

1270 *ch'īng-kūng* 青宮
T'ANG: **Green Palace,** an unofficial reference to the residence, and thus indirectly to the person, of the Heir Apparent.

1271 *ch'īng-láng* 清郎
From T'ang on, an unofficial reference to a **Director** (*lang-chung*) of a Bureau (*ssu, ch'ing-li ssu*) in a Ministry (*pu*).

1272 *ch'īng-lǐ chūn-wù* 清理軍務
MING–CH'ING: **Troop Purification,** a process normally abbreviated to *ch'ing-chün*, q.v.

1273 *ch'īng-lì ssū* 清吏司
MING–CH'ING: lit., office of pure functionaries, perhaps derived from Han–T'ang distinctions between officials of "pure" and "impure" genealogies (see *ch'ing, cho*): **Bureau,** the generic name for top-echelon units in Ministries (*pu*) and some other agencies, succeeding the Bureaus (*ssu*) of T'ang–Sung times. In some Ministries prefixed with functionally descriptive terms, e.g., *ch'e-chia ch'ing-li ssu* (Bureau of Equipment and Communications in Ming, Bureau of Communications in Ch'ing) in the Ministry of War (*ping-pu*); in other Ministries prefixed with the names of Provinces for which they processed all Ministry business, e.g., the *shan-hsi ch'ing-li ssu* (Shansi Bureau) in the Ministry of Revenue (*hu-pu*); each headed by a Director (*lang-chung*), rank 5a. BH: department.

1274 *ch'īng-shāng shǔ* 清商署 or *ch'ing-shang*
N-S DIV–T'ANG: **Office of Bell Music,** deriving from the name of an ancient musical tune or style dominated by bell sounds and characteristically sad; responsible for preserving and performing such music; normally headed by a Director (*ling*); directly subordinate to the Chamberlain for Ceremonials (*t'ai-ch'ang ch'ing*) till very early T'ang, then absorbed into the Office of Drums and Pipes (*ku-ch'ui shu*) of the Court of Imperial Sacrifices (*t'ai-ch'ang ssu*). RR: *office de la musique*. P10.

1275 *ch'īng-shīh* 磬師
CHOU: **Master of the Musical Stones,** 4 ranked as Ordinary Servicemen (*chung-shih*) and 8 as Junior Servicemen (*hsia-shih*), in charge of a staff of musicians in the Ministry of Rites (*ch'un-kuan*). CL: *maître de king ou pierres sonores*.

1276 *ch'īng-tào* 清道
Clearer of the Way, designation of a lowly member of the retinue of an official in travel status, preceding the official so as to prevent any blocking of or interference with his progress.

1277 *ch'īng-tào shuài-fǔ* 清道率府
T'ANG–SUNG: **Police Patrol Guard Command,** one each

of Left and Right, military units assigned for general security in the palace of the Heir Apparent; created c. 713 by renaming the earlier *yü-hou shuai-fu*; first re-established in Sung in 995, thereafter established intermittently until the end of N. Sung. Each headed by a Commandant (*shuai*), rank 4a in T'ang, 7b in Sung; in Sung he was also concurrent Receptionist (*yeh-che*) of the Secretariat of the Heir Apparent (*ch'un-fang*). RR+SP: *garde de l'héritier du trône chargée de la sécurité des routes.* P26.

1278 *ch'īng-tào wèi* 清道衛
T'ANG: variant name from 662 to 705 of the **Police Patrol Guard Command** (*yü-hou shuai-fu*). Also see *ch'ing-tao shuai-fu*.

1279 *ch'īng-wàng* 清望
N-S DIV–T'ANG: a term signifying **high expectations or high repute,** used as a generic label for the most elite officials in terms of their genealogical pedigrees; see *ch'ing* (pure) and *cho* (impure). In subsequent eras the term may be encountered as a descriptive label of an official of great eminence and integrity.

1280 *ch'īng-yào* 清要
N-S DIV–T'ANG: **pure and important,** used as a generic label for various posts in both the central and territorial governments that were considered to require appointees of extraordinary intelligence and moral character; also a generic reference to expectant or active officials who were considered the elite members of the officialdom and could expect rapid advancement into the highest echelons of the government, their merit being defined largely in terms of their genealogical pedigrees. See *ch'ing* (pure) and *cho* (impure).

1281 *ch'ǐng-yǔ* 請雨
HAN: **Supplicant for Rain,** 2 minor subordinates of the Grand Astrologer (*t'ai-shih ling*) in Later Han. HB: supplicant for rain.

1282 *ch'ìng-yüǎn yù-mín ssū* 慶遠裕民司
MING: lit., office to reward the distant and be liberal toward the people: **Horse Trading Office,** an agency of the sort generally called *ch'a-ma ssu*, established in 1374 in Kwangsi to buy horses from aboriginal tribes; headed by a Commissioner-in-chief (*ta-shih*), rank 8b; abolished early, but date not clear. P53.

1283 *ch'īng-yún* 青雲
Lit., blue cloud. (1) CHOU: an unofficial reference to any official of the Ministry of Rites (*ch'un-kuan*). (2) May be encountered in any era in unofficial reference to any official of great eminence and prestige.

1284 *chio*
See under the romanization *chüeh*.

1285 *chiù* 廐
Stable: see *chiu-chang, chiu-ling, chiu-mu, liu chiu, nei-chiu*.

1286 *chiu* 救
See *ssu chiu*.

1287 *chiū-ch'á àn* 糾察案
SUNG: **Capital Punishment Section,** one of 13 Sections (*an*) directly subordinate to the executive officials of the S. Sung Ministry of Justice (*hsing-pu*); staffed with suofficial functionaries who handled documents relating to the Ministry's review of all death sentences recommended by magistrates throughout the empire. SP: *service d'enquête sur la peine capitale.*

1288 *chiū-ch'á hsíng-yù ssū* 糾察刑獄司 or *chiu-ch'a ssu*
SUNG: **Bureau of Judicial Investigation,** a unit in the Ministry of Justice (*hsing-pu*) staffed with 2 Judicial Investigators (*chiu-ch'a kuan*); apparently assisted senior officials of the Ministry in checking reports of judicial cases submitted by units of territorial administration. SP: *bureau de contrôle et de surveillance judiciaire.*

1289 *chiū-ch'á tsài-chīng hsíng-yù ssū* 糾察在京刑獄司
SUNG: **Bureau of Judicial Investigation for the Capital,** established in 1009 specially to review criminal cases in the dynastic capital, Kaifeng; staffed with 2 Judicial Investigators (*chiu-ch'a kuan*); in 1080 merged into the Ministry of Justice (*hsing-pu*). P13.

1290 *chiù-chái chiēn* 舊宅監
T'ANG: **Directorate of the Palace Ruins Park,** one of 4 Directorates in charge of maintaining the buildings and grounds of imperial parks in the 4 quadrants of the dynastic capital, Ch'ang-an, under the supervision of the Court of the Imperial Granaries (*ssu-nung ssu*); specifically in charge of the northern quadrant, which included ruins of the Han dynasty capital city. Headed by a Director (*chien*), rank 6b2. See *ssu-mien chien*. P40.

1291 *chiù-chǎng* 廐長
HAN–T'ANG, CH'ING: **Chief of the Stables,** from one to 17 per unit, normally in charge of the imperial stables and carriages, through Sui also commonly in the establishments of the Empress, the Heir Apparent, and other Princes; in T'ang rank 9a2. In Ch'ing, subordinate officials in the Palace Stud (*shang-ssu yüan*), an agency of the Imperial Household Department (*nei-wu fu*). See *chiu-mu*. HB: chief of the stables. BH: inspector of the stable. P26, 37, 39, 69.

1292 *chiù-chèng* 酒正
CHOU: **Supervisor of Wines,** 4 ranked as Ordinary Servicemen (*chung-shih*), members of the Ministry of State (*t'ien-kuan*) in general charge of the preparation and provision of all wines drunk by the royal family, used in official ceremonies at the capital, or offered distinguished visitors and other guests at the palace. Superior to Eunuch Wine-makers (*chiu-jen*). Also see *nü-chiu*. CL: *intendant des vins.*

1293 *chiǔ-ch'éng kūng tsǔng-chiēn* 九成宮總監
T'ANG: **Directorate-general of the Palace of the Perfect Cycle,** an agency under the Court of the Imperial Granaries (*ssu-nung ssu*); managed the imperial summer resort in Shensi not far from the dynastic capital, Ch'ang-an; until 631 called *jen-shou kung-chien* (Directorate of the Palace of Benevolence and Longevity), from 651 to 667 officially called *wan-nien kung-chien* (Directorate of the Palace of Longevity); headed by a Director-general (*tsung-chien*), rank 5b2. RR: *direction générale du palais de l'achèvement parfait.* P40.

1294 *chiǔ chí* 九棘
CHOU: lit., the 9 jujube trees: a collective reference to the high officials who stood in the front rank of attendants at court audiences. See *chi-ch'eng, chi-ch'ing, chi-ssu, chi-shu, ta-chi*.

1295 *chiǔ-chīng ch'ū-shēn* 九經出身
SUNG: **Graduate in the Nine Classics,** a degree earned in the highest-level examinations of the civil service re-

cruitment system, 2nd in prestige only to the degree of Presented Scholar (*chin-shih*); abolished in the 1080s. SP: *docteur de neuf classiques*.

1296 *chiǔ ch'īng* 九卿
(1) CH'IN–SUI: **Nine Chamberlains,** a collective reference to the heads of the top-echelon service agencies known as the Nine Courts (*chiu ssu*). (2) T'ANG–CH'ING: **Nine Chief Ministers,** a collective reference to high central government officials, with varying applications. In T'ang and Sung referred to the heads of the Courts of Imperial Sacrifices (*t'ai-ch'ang ssu*), of Imperial Entertainments (*kuang-lu ssu*), of the Imperial Regalia (*wei-wei ssu*), of the Imperial Clan (*tsung-cheng ssu*), of the Imperial Stud (*t'ai-p'u ssu*), of Judicial Review (*ta-li ssu*), of State Ceremonial (*hung-lu ssu*), of the Imperial Granaries (*ssu-nung ssu*), and of the Imperial Treasury (*t'ai-fu ssu*). In Ming referred to the Ministers (*shang-shu*) of the Six Ministries (*liu pu*), the Censors-in-chief (*tu yü-shih*) of the Censorate (*tu ch'a-yüan*), the Chief Minister (*ch'ing*) of the Court of Judicial Review, and the Transmission Commissioner (*t'ung-cheng shih*) of the Office of Transmission (*t'ung-cheng ssu*). Some sources say that Ch'ing followed the Ming pattern; others identify the group as the heads of the Censorate, the Office of Transmission, the Imperial Procession Guard (*luan-i wei*), and the Courts of Judicial Review, of Imperial Sacrifices, of Imperial Entertainments, of State Ceremonial, and of the Imperial Stud. In Ming and Ch'ing times the group was also known as the Nine Major Chief Ministers (*ta chiu ch'ing*); cf. *hsiao chiu ch'ing* (Nine Lesser Chief Ministers). Also see *ch'ing, p'ei-ch'ing*. P22, 68.

1297 *chiǔ chōu* 九州
Nine Regions: from high antiquity a reference to the 9 administrative areas into which the culture hero Yü was believed to have divided the Chinese world; hence used throughout history as an analog for the concept of China in its entirety. Names given to the Nine Regions vary somewhat in ancient texts, but probably the most common list is that given in "The Tribute of Yü" (*yü-kung*) section of the *Classic of Writings* (*shu-ching*): Chi, Yen, Ch'ing, Hsü, Yang, Ching, Yü, Liang, and Yung. See *mu*.

1298 *chiǔ ch'ùng* 九重
Lit., 9 to the 9th power, the most prestigious number in numerological lore; hence by analogy a traditional unofficial reference to the **Emperor.**

1299 *chiǔ chüéh* 九爵
SUNG: **Nine Orders of Nobility,** a collective reference to the 9 noble titles granted to distinguished officials not of the imperial family, sometimes posthumously; in declining order of prestige, Prince (*wang*), Commandery Prince (*chün-wang*), Duke (*kung, kuo-kung*), Commandery Duke (*chün-kung*), District Duke (*hsien-kung*), Marquis (*hou*), Earl (*po*), Viscount (*tzu*), and Baron (*nan*).

1300 *chiǔ-fāng* 酒坊
CHIN: **Imperial Winery,** a unit in the Court Ceremonial Institute (*hsüan-hui yüan*), headed by a Commissioner (*shih*), rank 8b; manufactured various kinds of wines for palace and court use, functions performed in other times by such agencies as the *nei chiu-fang, shang-yün chü*, qq.v. Also see *shang-yün shu, ch'ü-yüan*. P30.

1301 *chiǔ fǔ* 九府
(1) CHOU: **Nine Fiscal Agencies,** a collective reference to units in various Ministries (*kuan*) that bore responsibilities for coinage and other fiscal matters; specifically, the *ta-fu,*

yü-fu, nei-fu, wai-fu, kao-fu, t'ien-fu, chih-nei, chih-chin, and *chih-pi,* qq.v. (2) During and possibly after the era of N-S Division, a variant reference to the **Nine Courts** (*chiu ssu*).

1302 *chiǔ-ì lìng* 九譯令
HAN: **Director of Translations from Afar,** from 104 to 28 B.C. a subordinate of the Supervisor of Dependent Countries (*tien shu-kuo*) on the staff of the Chamberlain for Dependencies (*ta hung-lu*); responsible for relations between the court and distant peoples across Inner Asia, for which "multiple translation" (*chiu-i*) was necessary. See *i-kuan ling.* HB: prefect of the nine successive interpreters. P11, 17.

1303 *chiǔ-jén* 酒人
CHOU: **Eunuch Wine Maker,** 10 on the staff of the Ministry of State (*t'ien-kuan*) for overseeing the production of all wines required by the ruler and his guests, and for formal ceremonies, under the direction of the Supervisors of Wines (*chiu-cheng*). See *nü-chiu.* Cf. *hsiang-jen.* CL: *employé aux vins.*

1304 *chiǔ k'ō* 九科
SUNG: **Nine Sections,** a collective reference to training units to which were assigned Medical Students (*i-sheng*) of the Imperial Medical Service (*t'ai-i chü*), an agency in the Court of Imperial Sacrifices (*t'ai-ch'ang ssu*). SP: *neuves sections.*

1305 *chiù-kù-chái chiēn* 舊故宅監
T'ANG: variant reference to the *chiu-chai chien* (**Directorate of the Palace Ruins Park**).

1306 *chiǔ-kuān t'ūng-shìh shǐh* 九關通事使
MING: **Transmission Commissioner for the Capital Gates,** a member of the Palace Ceremonial Office (*tien-t'ing i-li ssu*) until 1377, then transferred to the staff of the Office of Transmission (*t'ung-cheng shih ssu*); presumably responsible for transmitting documents to and from the court within the capital. The position probably disappeared c. 1399. P21.

1307 *chiù-lìng* 厩令
HAN: **Director of the Stable** in the household of the Empress. In Later Han superseded by the Coachman of the Empress (*chung-kung p'u*). See *chiu-chang.* HB: prefect of the stables.

1308 *chiǔ mén* 九門
Lit., 9 gates: throughout history a symbolic reference to the imperial **Capital City.**

1309 *chiǔ miào* 九廟
T'ANG: **Nine Temples,** from 635 a collective reference to the Imperial Ancestral Temple (*t'ai-miao*), which was intended to be expanded from 4 to 9 rooms or halls, to match the size attributed by tradition to the ancient Chou dynasty ancestral temple; in fact, the T'ang temple was expanded only to 6 rooms.

1310 *chiǔ mìng* 九命
CHOU: **Nine Honors,** an array of official ranks ascribed to ancient times and often revived by subsequent Chou dynasties, in which the 9th honor (i.e., rank 9) was highest and the first honor was lowest. P68.

1311 *chiù-mù* 厩牧
N-S DIV–SUNG: **Stable Master,** a common reference to the head of a Stables Office (*chiu-mu shu*). P26.

1312 *chiù-mù shǔ* 厩牧署
N-S DIV–SUNG: **Stables Office,** an agency in the house-

hold of the Heir Apparent, normally headed by a Director (*ling*), rank 8b2 in T'ang; and in the households of other Princes, normally headed by a Director (*chang*), rank 9a2 in T'ang; apparently originated in N. Ch'i. SP: *bureau des écuries et des élevages de l'héritier du trône*. P26, 69.

1313 *chiŭ piēn* 九邊
MING: **Nine Frontiers,** regions along the northern and northwestern borders each organized as a Defense Area (*chen*): specifically, Liao-tung, Chi-chou, Hsüan-fu, Ta-t'ung, Yen-sui, Ning-hsia, T'ai-yüan, Ku-yüan, and Kansu.

1314 *chiŭ pín* 九嬪
Nine Concubines: throughout history a generic term for palace women ranking below principal wives (*fu-jen*) and consorts (*fei*). Specific designations of the Nine Concubines varied, but they commonly ranked 2a. See *pin, shang-pin, hsia-pin, hsüan-i*. CL: *neuf princesses, ou femmes de deuxième rang*. RR: *neuf concubines de second rang*.

1315 *chiŭ p'ĭn* 九品
N-S DIV (San-kuo)–CH'ING: **Nine Ranks,** categories into which all officials and the posts they occupied were divided for purposes of determining prestige, compensation, priority in court audience, etc. Ranks were commonly subdivided into 2 classes (*teng, chi, chieh*), first class (*cheng*) and 2nd class (*ts'ung*); and the lesser ranks from 4 through 9 were often further subdivided into upper grades (*shang*) and lower grades (*hsia*). Thus the normal number of gradations was 18, but 30 was common, and the number sometimes fluctuated as high as 36 or 45. The rank gradations are normally rendered, e.g., as 1a, 2b, 4a2, 7b, 9b2. P68.

1316 *chiŭ-p'ĭn àn* 九品案
SUNG: **Section for the Ninth Rank,** a unit of the Ministry of Personnel's (*li-pu*) Bureau of Evaluations (*k'ao-kung ssu*); dealt with the cases of rank 9 officials in the Civil Appointments Process (*tso-hsüan;* see under *hsüan*). SP: *service de 9ème degré*.

1317 *chiŭ ssù* 九寺
CH'IN–CH'ING: **Nine Courts,** a collective reference to top-echelon service agencies in the central government, membership in the group varying from time to time and before T'ang sometimes totaling more than 9; e.g., the Court of State Ceremonial (*hung-lu ssu*), the Court of the Imperial Clan (*tsung-cheng ssu*). Their heads were collectively known as *chiu ch'ing* (Nine Chamberlains through Sui, thereafter Nine Chief Ministers).

1318 *chiŭ-ts'ān kuān* 九參官
T'ANG: **Third Day Audience Officers,** a generic reference to military officers of rank 3 and higher who were on duty in the capital, because they were required to attend audience every 3rd day, i.e., 9 times a month. Cf. *liu-ts'an, ch'ang-ts'an kuan*. RR: *fonctionnaire assistant neuf fois par mois aux audiences*.

1319 *chiŭ-ts'ù-mièn chŭ* 酒醋麵局
MING: **Condiments Service,** a minor agency of palace eunuchs headed by a eunuch Commissioner-in-chief (*ta-shih*) or Director (*t'ai-chien*); prepared sauces and other condiments for palace use. See *pa chü* (Eight Services).

1320 *chiŭ yù* 九御
CHOU: lit., something like "the female nines": a collective reference to **Secondary Concubines** (*nü-yü*), who reportedly numbered 81 and attended upon the ruler in 9 groups of 9 women each; the equation 9 x 9 = 81 offers nothing but auspicious numbers in Chinese numerological lore.

1321 *ch'iū ch'īng* 秋卿
Autumn Chamberlain, an archaic reference deriving from Chou usage of the term *ch'iu-kuan,* q.v. (1) N-S DIV (Liang): a generic or collective reference to 3 of the central government officials called the Twelve Chamberlains (*shih-erh ch'ing,* q.v.). (2) SUI–CH'ING: an unofficial reference to a Minister of Justice (*hsing-pu shang-shu*).

1322 *ch'iū-fāng* 秋坊
Lit., the autumn workshop: from the era of N-S Division on, an unofficial reference to the **Household Administration of the Heir Apparent** (*chan-shih fu*).

1323 *ch'iū-hsièn* 秋憲
Lit., terms denoting "autumn" and "fundamental laws." (1) CHOU: a variant reference to the **Minister of Justice** (*ssu-k'ou*) or the **Ministry of Justice** (*ch'iu-kuan*), since autumn was deemed the appropriate season for imposing punishments in conformity with the fundamental laws. (2) HAN–CH'ING: an unofficial reference to Censors (*yü-shih*), since they were traditionally considered guardians of the fundamental laws (see *feng-hsien kuan*) and, reportedly, in Han times were most commonly appointed in autumn.

1324 *ch'iū-kuān* 秋官
Lit., official or office for autumn (a time of decaying and dying): (1) CHOU–T'ANG: **Ministry of Justice:** in Chou, 5th of 6 major agencies in the top echelon of the royal government, responsible for the administration of punishments; headed by a Minister of Justice (*ssu-k'ou*) ranked as a Minister (*ch'ing*). Revived by Chou of the era of N-S Division to replace what had been known as the *tu-kuan ts'ao* (Section for Justice); revived again from 684 to 705 in T'ang to replace the name *hsing-pu* (Ministry of Justice). May be encountered in any later period as an archaic reference to the *hsing-pu*. CL: *ministère de l'automne*. P13. (2) T'ANG–CH'ING: **Autumn Office,** one of 5 seasonal Offices, including one for Mid-year (*chung*), of calendrical specialists in the T'ang Astrological Service (*t'ai-shih chü*) and later Bureau of Astronomy (*ssu-t'ien t'ai*), the Sung Astrological Service, the Sung–Ming Directorate of Astronomy (*ssu-t'ien chien*), and the Ming–Ch'ing Directorate of Astronomy (*ch'in-t'ien chien*); headed by a Director (*ling* in early T'ang, otherwise *cheng*), rank 5a except 8a in Sung and 6b in Ming and Ch'ing; in Ch'ing one Manchu and one Chinese appointee. RR+SP: *administration de l'automne*. BH (*cheng*): astronomer for the autumn. P35. (3) MING: **Autumn Support,** from 1380 to 1382 one of 4 posts, each named after a season and open to more than one appointee, intended for the Emperor's closest and most trusted advisers; see *ssu fu-kuan* (Four Supports). P4, 67.

1325 *ch'iū-kuān tà-fù* 秋官大夫
(1) CHCU: variant reference to the **Vice Minister of Justice** (*hsiao ssu-k'ou*): (2) T'ANG–CH'ING: unofficial reference to a **Vice Director** (*yüan-wai lang*) of any Bureau (*ssu, ch'ing-li ssu*) in the Ministry of Justice (*hsing-pu*), especially one of the Bureau of Review (*pi-pu*) prior to Ming. P35.

1326 *ch'iū-tiĕn* 秋典
Unofficial reference to the **Ministry of Justice** (*ch'iu-kuan, hsing-pu*).

1327 *ch'iū-ts'áo* 秋曹
Unofficial reference to the **Ministry of Justice** (*ch'iu-kuan, hsing-pu*).

1328 *chiŭng-ch'īng* 囧卿
CH'ING: unofficial reference to a **Chief Minister of the**

Court of the Imperial Stud (*t'ai-p'u ssu ch'ing, t'ai-p'u ch'ing*).

1329 *chiǔng-t'ái* 冏臺
CH'ING: unofficial reference to the **Court of the Imperial Stud** (*t'ai-p'u ssu*).

1330 *chó* 濁
Beginning in the era of N-S Division very soon after the fall of Han, a term meaning **impure** used as an at least quasi-official designation of officials of lesser genealogical distinction and of the less prestigious positions available to them, in contrast to the label "pure" (*ch'ing*) used for officials of esteemed genealogical status and the governmental positions reserved for them. Such distinctions persisted into Sui times and were echoed in even later times.

1331 *chō-tséi chāo-ān ān-fǔ shǐh* 捉賊招安安撫使
SUNG: **Pacification Commissioner for the Suppression of Outlaws,** an ad hoc military commander campaigning against brigands or rebels. SP: *commissaire chargé de pacifier et de soumettre les rebelles et d'arrêter les voleurs.*

1332 *chōu* 州
Ety., a small island, as in a river: (1) CHOU: **Region,** generic designation of the 9 territories into which the culture hero Yü was thought to have divided the Chinese world in highest antiquity; see *chiu chou.* (2) CHOU: **Township,** a local administrative unit of 2,500 families, 5 of which constituted a District (*hsiang*). See *chou-chang.* (3) HAN–SUI: **Region,** a jurisdiction of intermediate coordination between the central government and a cluster of neighboring Commanderies (*chün*), recurringly becoming almost autonomous warlord domains; headed by a Regional Governor (*chou mu*) or Regional Inspector (*tz'u-shih*), or both; created c. 10 B.C. by a redesignation of 13 original Regions called *pu*, q.v., proliferated greatly in the era of N-S Division, then abolished by Sui in the 590s. HB: province. (4) T'ANG–YÜAN: **Prefecture,** successor of the former Commandery (*chün*) as the key unit of territorial administration overseeing several Districts (*hsien*), headed by a Prefect (*tz'u-shih* in T'ang and Sung, *chih-chou* or *yin* in Sung and Yüan), rank 3b1 to 4a2 in T'ang, generally 5b thereafter; graded according to strategic importance and size of population into the categories Large (*shang*), Middle (*chung*), and Small (*hsia*); in Sung considered ordinary Prefectures in contrast to Superior Prefectures (*fu*), Military Prefectures (*chün*), and Industrial Prefectures (*chien*). RR+SP: *préfecture, préfecture ordinaire.* (5) MING: **Subprefecture,** an intermediate agency of administrative supervision, normally between a Prefecture (*fu*) and its subordinate Districts (*hsien*), but sometimes an Independent Subprefecture (*chih-li chou; see chih-li*) responsible directly to provincial administrative authorities; headed by a Subprefectural Magistrate (*chih-chou*), rank 5b. (6) CH'ING: **Department,** a coordinating agency normally responsible for several Districts (*hsien*) but occasionally serving itself as the lowest-level unit of formal territorial administration, normally subordinate to a Prefecture (*fu*) and sometimes via an intermediary Subprefecture (*t'ing*); when directly subordinate to provincial administrative authorities, called an Independent Department (*chih-li chou*); headed by a Department Magistrate (*chih-chou*), rank 5b. In Ming and Ch'ing times, the original suffix *chou* had become so familiar that it was incorporated into the place-name prefixes of many newly "promoted" Prefectures (*fu*), e.g., Hang-chou *fu* (Hangchow Prefecture), Kuang-chou *fu* (Canton Prefecture). BH: department. P53, 54.

1333 *chòu-àn* 胄案
(1) SUNG: **Ceremonial Caps Section,** one of 4 units in the Court of Palace Attendants (*hsüan-hui yüan*), in charge of the various types of headgear prescribed for wear by the Emperor and his entourage at sacrifices and other rituals; staffing not clear, but likely by eunuchs. SP: *service des casques.* (2) SUNG: **Armaments Section,** one of 7 Sections in the Salt and Iron Monopoly Bureau (*yen-t'ieh ssu*) of the State Finance Commission (*san ssu*) of early Sung; normally headed by an Administrative Assistant (*p'an-kuan, t'ui-kuan*); monitored the production of military armor and the maintenance of dikes, breastworks, and other defense installations around the capital city. When the State Finance Commission was discontinued c. 1080, the Armaments Section was merged or transformed into the Directorate for Armaments (*chün-ch'i chien*) under the Ministry of Works (*kung-pu*). P15.

1334 *chōu-chǎng* 州長
CHOU: **Township Head,** one man with the rank of Ordinary Grand Master (*chung ta-fu*) in each Township (*chou*) of 2,500 families, theoretically responsible to representatives of the royal government for sacrifices, other rites, education, and general administration in his Township. May be encountered in later times as an archaic reference to the head of any agency called *chou* (Region, Prefecture, Subprefecture, Department). CL: *chef d'arrondissement.*

1335 *chōu-chí hó-ch'ǘ shǔ* 舟檝河渠署
SUNG: **River Transport Office,** a unit of the Directorate of Waterways (*tu-shui chien*), headed by a Director (*ling*), rank not clear; apparently responsible for providing boats and boatmen for official transport. SP: *office des bateaux et des voies fluviales.*

1336 *chōu-chí shǔ* 舟檝署
(1) SUI–T'ANG: **Office of Boats and Boatmen,** a unit of the Directorate of Waterways (*tu-shui chien*), in T'ang only from 632 to 738; headed by a Director (*ling*), rank 8b2. RR: *office des bateaux et des rames.* P14, 15, 60. (2) SUNG: abbreviation of *chou-chi ho-ch'ü shu* (River Transport Office).

1337 *chòu-chìn kūng* 咒禁工
SUI–T'ANG: **Spell Chanter,** 8 unranked specialists on the staff of the Imperial Medical Office (*t'ai-i shu*). RR: *incantateur.* P36.

1338 *chòu-chìn pó-shìh* 咒禁博士
SUI–T'ANG: **Erudite for Exorcism,** one master teacher of incantations and chanted spells, rank 9b2, on the staff of the Imperial Medical Office (*t'ai-i shu*); authorized to have 10 youths as Exorcism Students (*chou-chin sheng*). RR: *maître incantateur au vaste savoir.* P36.

1339 *chòu-chìn shīh* 咒禁師
SUI–T'ANG: **Master of Exorcism,** one each in the Imperial Medical Office (*t'ai-i shu*) and in the Palace Medical Service (*shang-yao chü*). RR: *maître incantateur.* P36, 38.

1340 *chōu-chūn-chiēn* 州軍監
SUNG: **the various Prefectures,** a common collective reference to ordinary Prefectures (*chou*), Military Prefectures (*chün*), and Industrial Prefectures (*chien*).

1341 *chōu-mù* 州幕
N-S DIV: **Regional Headquarters,** a quasi-official or unofficial reference to the headquarters office of a Region (*chou*). In later times may be encountered as an archaic reference to the headquarters of a Prefecture, Subprefecture, or Department (all *chou*).

1342 *chōu mù* 州牧
See under *mu*.

1343 *chōu p'àn* 州判
CH'ING: **Assistant Department Magistrate**, rank 7b, ranking behind the Magistrate (*chih-chou*) and the Vice Magistrate (*chou t'ung*). See *p'an-kuan*. BH: second class assistant department magistrate. P54, 59.

1344 *chōu tsăi* 州宰
HAN–N-S DIV: lit., steward of a Region (*chou*): unofficial reference to a **Regional Inspector** (*tz'u-shih*).

1345 *chòu-ts'áo* 胄曹
Helmets Section: (1) T'ANG: an agency in various military Guard (*wei*) units, normally headed by an Administrator (*ts'an-chün shih*), rank 8a2. See *shih-liu wei*, *k'ai-ts'ao*. RR: *service des casques*. (2) SUNG: variant of *chou-an*, q.v. P43.

1346 *chōu tū* 州都
N-S DIV: **Regional Rectifier**, a variant of the term Rectifier (*chung-cheng*, q.v.) used at the Regional (*chou*) level; responsible for identifying and classifying all males considered qualified for government office.

1347 *chōu-tuān* 州端
N-S DIV: **Regional Headquarters**, a quasi-official or unofficial reference to the headquarters office of a Region (*chou*). In later times may be encountered as an archaic reference to the headquarters of a Prefecture, Subprefecture, or Department (all *chou*).

1348 *chōu t'úng* 州同
CH'ING: **Department Vice Magistrate**, rank 6b, the principal assistant to a Department Magistrate (*chih-chou*). See *t'ung-chih*; cf. *chou p'an*. BH: first class assistant department magistrate. P54.

1349 *ch'óu-chiào* 讎校
T'ANG: **Editor**, stylistic revisers of imperially issued documents, on the staff of the Institute for the Veneration of Literature (*ch'ung-wen kuan*); in 719 renamed *chiao-shu lang*, q.v. RR: *réviseur chargé d'examiner (les textes)*. P25.

1350 *ch'óu-chiào ts'ò-wù* 讎校錯誤
T'ANG: **Proofreader**, rectifier of errors in imperially issued documents, on the staff of the Institute for the Advancement of Literature (*hung-wen kuan*). RR: *réviseur chargé d'examiner les fautes et erreurs*.

1351 *ch'ōu-fēn ch'ǎng t'í-lǐng sǒ*
　　　　抽分場提領所
YÜAN: **Office of Produce Levies**, 10 scattered about the empire, each headed by a Superintendent (*t'i-ling*), rank not clear; collected taxes on produce from public places, especially from fisheries. P62.

1352 *ch'ōu-fēn chú-mù chǔ* 抽分竹木局 or
　　　　ch'ou-fen chü
MING: **Office of Produce Levies**, variable but numerous, scattered throughout the empire at appropriate points to collect taxes on forest products in kind for use in official shipbuilding activities; headed by a Commissioner-in-chief (*ta-shih*), rank not clear; subordinate to the Ministry of Revenue (*hu-pu*) till 1471, thereafter to the Ministry of Works (*kung-pu*). P15, 62.

1353 *ch'óu-hsiāng* 仇香
CH'ING: lit., the scent of congeniality (?): unofficial reference to an **Assistant Magistrate** (*chu-pu*) of a District (*hsien*).

1354 *chǔ* 主
Lit., master, superior: (1) Throughout history a common reference to a **Ruler**, especially yoked for contrast with the term *ch'en* (Minister, subject). (2) Commonly occurs as a prefix in some titles with the meaning **in charge of**; e.g., see *chu-pu*, *chǔ-shih*. (3) Occurs as a suffix in some titles of female nobility; e.g., see *chün-chu*, *hsien-chu*, *kung-chu*. (4) CHOU: **Economic Overseer**, one of 9 Unifying Agents (*ou*, *liang*) appointed in the Nine Regions (*chiu chou*) of the kingdom as representatives of the Minister of State (*chung-tsai*) overseeing geographic clusters of feudal states; especially monitored the economic well-being of the populace in their Regions. CL: *maître*.

1355 *chù* 祝
Lit., one who prays, blesses, or invokes the deities: **Supplicant**. Normally occurs with clarifying prefixes, as in *nü-chu*, *ta-chu*, *hsiao-chu*, *sang-chu*, *tien-chu*, *tsu-chu*.

1356 *chù* 著
Compiler, a general reference to officials charged with preparing histories and other writings; e.g., see under *kuo-shih an* (Section for the History of the Dynasty).

1357 *chū* 諸
Lit., the various, used as a collectivizing prefix; e.g., *chu-hou* (the various Marquises), used in Chou times to refer to Feudal Lords in general. Although in such cases *chu* suggests "all," it must be noted that *chu* often occurs following a specifying antecedent to suggest "all other" or "the various other;" e.g., *ch'in-wang chu-wang* (Imperial Princes and other Princes).

1358 *chù-chá* 駐劄
A prefix signifying **Detached at:** e.g., the Sung dynasty *chu-cha ... chou yü-ch'ien chün* (Palace Army Detached at such-and-such Prefecture), the Ch'ing dynasty *chu-cha ... pan-li mu-ch'ang chu-shih* (Secretary for Managing Pasturages at such-and-such place). P31.

1359 *chū-chàn tū t'ǔng-líng shǐ*
　　　　諸站都統領使
YÜAN: **Controller-general of Postal Relay Stations**, an autonomous member of the central government appointed in 1270 to supervise Postal Relay Inspectors (*t'o-t'o ho-sun*), who directed the empire's postal relay system; in 1276 superseded by the Bureau of Transmission (*t'ung-cheng yüan*). P17.

1360 *chǔ-chāng chǎng* 主章長
HAN: **Chief of Lumber Supplies**, a subordinate of the Chamberlain for the Palace Buildings (*chiang-tso shao-fu*). HB: chief of large timbers. P14.

1361 *chū chǎng-shìh* 諸掌事
A common collective designation for **Palace Women** of low rank, who often were designated *chang ... shih* (in charge of such-and-such matters).

1362 *chǔ-chèng* 主政
CH'ING: a variant of *chu-shih* (**Secretary**).

1363 *chǔ-chì* 主計
HAN: **Fiscal Controller**, a term used only in early Han times for an eminent official assigned on an ad hoc basis to particular fiscal responsibilities. May be encountered in later eras as an archaic reference to any high fiscal official, e.g., the T'ang–Ch'ing Minister of Revenue (*hu-pu shang-shu*). P45.

1364 *chǔ-chì shìh* 主記室 or 主記史
HAN–N-S DIV: apparently an abbreviated reference to a *chu-chi shih-shih* (**Recording Secretary**). P53.

1365 *chǔ-chì shìh-shǐh* 主記室史
HAN–N-S DIV: **Recording Secretary,** minor staff members of Commanderies (*chün*) and Districts (*hsien*), apparently responsible for keeping records of the magistrates' appointments. HB: secretary clerk. P54.

1366 *chǔ ch'iāng-í lì-mín shàng-shū láng*
主羌夷吏民尚書郎
HAN: **Court Gentleman for Records Concerning the Western Barbarians,** a subordinate of the Director of the Imperial Secretariat (*shang-shu ling*); lit., in charge of matters concerning officials and commoners among the Ch'iang "barbarians." P17.

1367 *chù-chiào* 助教
N-S DIV–CH'ING: lit., assistant in instruction: **Instructor,** one of several common titles for educational officials assigned to the early National University (*t'ai-hsüeh*) or the later Directorate of Education (*kuo-tzu chien*), or sometimes to more specialized schools; normally ranked in the 7b-8a-8b range, of less prestige than an Erudite (*po-shih*); sometimes with specifying prefixes, e.g., *ching-hsüeh chu-chiao* (Classics Instructor). RR+SP: *professeur assistant.* BH: preceptor. P34, 36, 49, 51, 53.

1368 *chù-chiào t'īng* 助教廳
CH'ING: **Office of Instruction** in the Astronomical College (*t'ien-wen suàn-hsüeh*), headed by an Instructor (*chu-chiao*). BH: preceptory.

1369 *chù-chiēn* 鑄監
Minting Directorate, a common abbreviation of such terms as *chu-ch'ien chien*. In early Ming times, an occasional unofficial reference to a Provincial Coinage Service (*pao-ch'üan chü*; also see *pao-yüan chü*).

1370 *chù-ch'ién chiēn* 鑄錢監
T'ANG–SUNG: **Directorate of Coinage,** 7 in T'ang, 4 in Sung, subordinate to the Directorate for Imperial Manufactories (*shao-fu chien*), headed by Directors (*chien*) in T'ang, Supervisory Officials (*chien-kuan*) in Sung, ranks not clear; commonly supervised by a nearby regional dignitary such as the T'ang Area Commander (*tu-tu*). The relation between Directorates of Coinage and individual Mints (*chu-ch'ien fang, chu-ch'ien ssu*) is not clear. RR+SP: *direction de la fonte des monnaies.* P16.

1371 *chù-ch'ién fāng* 鑄錢坊
T'ANG: **Mint** for the coinage of money, one in each Circuit (*tao*); headed by a Coinage Commissioner (*chu-ch'ien shih*) subordinate to the Directorate for Imperial Manufactories (*shao-fu chien*). RR: *atelier de fonte des monnaies.*

1372 *chù-ch'ién kuān* 鑄錢官
Coins Officials: throughout history, a generic reference to officials responsible for minting coins, such as the Three Money Managers of the Court of the Imperial Parks (*shui-heng san kuan*) of Han and the Directors of Coinage (*chu-ch'ien chien*) of T'ang and Sung. Often abbreviated to *ch'ien-kuan.*

1373 *chù-ch'ién shǐh* 鑄錢使
T'ANG: **Coinage Commissioner;** see *chu-ch'ien fang* (Mint). P16.

1374 *chù-ch'ién ssū* 鑄錢司
SUNG: **Mint** for the coinage of money, established in various localities under the general supervision of the Direc-

torate for Imperial Manufactories (*shao-fu chien*); staffing and relation to Directorates of Coinage (*chu-ch'ien chien*) not clear. SP: *bureau de la fonte des monnaies.*

1375 *chù-ch'ién tū-chiàng* 鑄錢都將
N-S DIV (N. Wei): **Superintendent of Coinage,** status not clear. P16.

1376 *chu-chin* 祝禁…
See entries beginning with the romanization *chou-chin.*

1377 *chū-chīn chiēn* 諸津監
T'ANG: **Directorate of Water Crossings,** a unit of the Directorate of Waterways (*tu-shui chien*), headed by a Director (*ling*), rank 9a. RR: *direction des divers gués.* P15.

1378 *chù-chiū shìh* 祝鳩氏
Lit., master of wrens and pigeons, considered very filial birds: in Chou times occasionally used as a title equated with *ssu-t'u* (**Minister of Education**); may be encountered in later eras as an archaic reference to any official likened to the ancient *ssu-t'u.*

1379 *chǔ-chüéh* 主爵
Lit., to be in charge of noble titles. (1) HAN: a prefix found before *tu-wei* (Commandant-in-chief) and *chung-wei* (Commandant-in-ordinary), suggesting a dignitary responsible for supervising the titled nobility in the capital: **Commandant of the Nobles,** sometimes equated with the powerful capital official called Guardian of the Right (*yu fu-feng*). HB (*chu-chüeh chung-wei*): commandant over the nobility. (2) N-S DIV (N. Ch'i): a variant reference to the *tso chu-k'o* (**Manager of Visitors of the Left**), a member of the staff of the Chamberlain for Dependencies (*ta hung-lu*). See *chu-k'o.* (3) SUI–T'ANG: **Bureau of Honors,** a unit of the Ministry of Personnel (*li-pu*) charged with awarding noble titles; headed by a Vice Minister (*shih-lang*) in Sui, a Director (*lang-chung*), rank 5a, in T'ang; in 662 retitled *ssu-feng.* RR: *bureau des titres nobiliaires.* P5.

1380 *chù-chūn* 助軍
HAN: **Support Army,** one of 8 special capital-defense forces organized at the end of Han; see *pa hsiao-wei* (Eight Commandants).

1381 *chù-fáng pā-ch'í* 駐防八旗 or *chu-fang*
CH'ING: **Provincial Bannermen,** a general reference to military units in the Banner (*ch'i*) system that were stationed throughout the empire under the jurisdiction of the Ministry of War (*ping-pu*), in contrast to the Metropolitan Bannermen (*ching-ch'i*) stationed in and around Peking; normally commanded by provincial-level officers such as Manchu Generals (*chiang-chün*) or Vice Commanders-in-chief (*fu tu-t'ung*).

1382 *chù-hǎi* 主醢
T'ANG: **Spice Keeper,** 10, unranked, subordinate to Seasoners (*chang-hai*) in the Spice Pantry (*chang-hai shu*) of the Court of Imperial Entertainments (*kuang-lu ssu*). RR: *préposé aux hachis.* P30.

1383 *chū-hóu* 諸侯
Lit., the various Marquises. (1) CHOU: **Feudal Lords,** a collective term for all regional lords, regardless of their specific titles of nobility—Duke (*kung*), Marquis (*hou*), Earl (*po*), Viscount (*tzu*), and Baron (*nan*). (2) HAN: **Imperial Marquises,** a collective reference to all those sons of Princes (*wang*) who bore the noble title Marquis, i.e., those not expected to inherit their fathers' status as Princes. Cf. *lieh-hou* (Adjunct Marquis, Marquis-consort, Grandee of the First Order). P64.

1384 *chū-hóu wáng* 諸侯王
HAN: **Feudatory Prince,** a generic reference to all sons of Emperors other than Heirs Apparent, who were all given the title Prince; so referred to because of their similarity in status to the Feudal Lords (*chu-hou*) of Chou times.

1385 *chù-hsià shǐh* 柱下史
In Chou times, apparently, the designation of a kind of **Archivist.** Thereafter throughout history, an archaic reference to a **Censor** (*yü-shih*), especially an Attendant Censor (*shih yü-shih*) or a Palace Censor (*tien-chung shih yü-shih*). P18, 25.

1386 *chǔ-hsiá shōu-chīh ssū* 主轄收支司
SUNG: lit., office in charge of receipts and disbursements: **Money Transactions Office,** a unit of the Chief Accounting Office (*tu mo-k'an ssu*) in the State Finance Commission (*san ssu*) of early Sung. SP: *bureau des recettes et des dépenses.*

1387 *chǔ-hù* 主戶
SUNG: **Tribal Chief,** one of several titles awarded local chieftains of southwestern aboriginal peoples. P72.

1388 *chǔ-ī* 主衣
SUI–T'ANG: **Valet,** several on the staff of each Office of the Imperial Mausoleum (*ling-shu*), subordinate to the Court of Imperial Sacrifices (*t'ai-ch'ang ssu*) in Sui; in T'ang, 16 in the Clothing Service (*shang-i chü*) of the Palace Administration (*tien-chung sheng*), 4 in each Court of the Imperial Mausoleum (*ling-t'ai*) under the Court of the Imperial Clan (*tsung-cheng ssu*). RR: *préposé aux vêtements.* P29, 38.

1389 *chǔ-ī chǘ* 主衣局
N-S DIV (N. Ch'i): **Imperial Wardrobe Service,** a unit of the Chancellery (*men-hsia sheng*) responsible for maintaining the clothing of the imperial family; headed by 2 Supervisors (*tu-t'ung*), rank 5. P37.

1390 *chū-ī shǐh-chě* 朱衣使者
SUNG: lit., commissioners with vermilion gowns: unofficial reference to **Examining Officials** in civil service recruitment examinations. See *shih-kuan, chu-k'ao, lien-kuan, chien-shih.*

1391 *chǔ-kǎo* 主稿
CH'ING: **Drafter,** one or 2 in each Bureau (*ssu*) of the Court of Colonial Affairs (*li-fan yüan*), normally an ad hoc assignment for an official holding a regular post as Director (*lang-chung*) or Vice Director (*yüan-wai lang*) of a Bureau (*ch'ing-li ssu*) in a Ministry (*pu*). BH: keeper of drafts.

1392 *chǔ-k'ǎo* 主考
(1) **Examiner,** from T'ang on, an unofficial or quasi-official reference to the presiding official(s) at a civil service recruitment examination. (2) MING–CH'ING: **Provincial Examiner,** a court official delegated to preside over a triennial Provincial Examination (*hsiang-shih*) of candidates for civil service careers; normally assisted by one or more Assistant Provincial Examiners (*fu chu-k'ao*) and Department and District Magistrates (*chih-chou, chih-hsien*) serving as proctors and graders (see *lien-kuan*). Also see *shih-kuan, t'ung-k'ao.*

1393 *chū-k'ō* 諸科
SUNG: lit., other examinations: a general term denoting civil service recruitment examinations given at the capital other than that leading to the degree of Presented Scholar (*chin-shih*); nominally of equal status with the Presented Scholar examination, but of less prestige in practice. See *chu.*

1394 *chǔ-k'ò ch'īng-lì ssū* 主客清吏司
MING–CH'ING: **Bureau of Receptions,** one of 4 Bureaus in the Ministry of Rites (*lǐ-pu*), responsible for the reception of foreign dignitaries; headed by a Director (*lang-chung*), rank 5a; a counterpart of the earlier agency called *chu-k'o pu, chu-k'o ts'ao,* or simply *chu-k'o.* P9.

1395 *chǔ-k'ò lìng* 主客令
N-S DIV (N. Wei): **Director of Receptions,** a subordinate of the Supervisor of Dependencies (*tien-k'o chien*). P11.

1396 *chǔ-k'ò pù* 主客部 or *chu-k'o*
N-S DIV–SUI: **Ministry of Receptions,** one of a variable number of Ministries (*pu*) developing under the Department of State Affairs (*shang-shu sheng*), headed by a Minister (*shang-shu*); alternated from period to period with the name *chu-k'o ts'ao* (Section for Receptions), headed by a Director (*ling,* etc.), subordinate to a Ministry of Sacrifices (*tz'u shen-pu*) or a Ministry of Rites (*lǐ-pu*). In general, both types of agencies were antecedents of the later Bureau of Receptions (*chu-k'o ssu, chu-k'o ch'ing-li ssu*) in the Ministry of Rites. P9.

1397 *chǔ-k'ò ssū* 主客司 or *chu-k'o*
T'ANG–SUNG: **Bureau of Receptions,** one of 4 top-echelon units of the Ministry of Rites (*lǐ-pu*), responsible in collaboration with the Court of State Ceremonial (*hung-lu ssu*) for managing the reception of foreign dignitaries at court; headed by a Director (*lang-chung*), rank 5b in T'ang, 6b in Sung, and a Vice Director (*yüan-wai lang*), 6b in T'ang, 7a in Sung. Successor of the earlier Ministry of Receptions (*chu-k'o pu*) and antecedent of the Ming–Ch'ing *chu-k'o ch'ing-li ssu* (Bureau of Receptions). Also see *ssu-fan.* RR+SP: *bureau des hôtes.* P9.

1398 *chǔ-k'ò ts'áo* 主客曹 or *chu-k'o*
HAN–N-S DIV: **Section for Receptions,** one of 4 to 6 central government units headed by Imperial Secretaries (*shang-shu*), in the aggregate called the Imperial Secretariat (*shang-shu t'ai*); in collaboration with the Chamberlain for Dependencies (*ta hung-lu*), responsible for communications with foreign leaders and the reception of foreign dignitaries at court. Between Han and T'ang, regularly part of the developing Department of State Affairs (*shang-shu sheng*), alternating with a Ministry of Receptions (*chu-k'o pu*); as a Section headed by a Director (*ling, lang, shih-lang, lang-chung*), subordinate to a Ministry of Sacrifices (*tz'u-pu, shen-pu*) or a Ministry of Rites (*lǐ-pu*). In general, antecedent of the later Bureau of Receptions (*chu-k'o ssu, chu-k'o ch'ing-li ssu*) in the Ministry of Rites. See *ssu ts'ao, liu ts'ao, ssu-fan, tien-k'o shu, nan chu-k'o ts'ao, pei chu-k'o ts'ao, tso chu-k'o, yu chu-k'o.* HB: master of guests. P9, 11, 19.

1399 *chǔ-kuǎn* 主管
SUNG: lit., to be in charge of: a prefix found in many designations of official assignments, almost always in reference to low-ranking or unranked personnel; e.g., *chu-kuan hsüeh-shih* (Superintendent of Education), an assignment often borne by Prefects (*chih-chou*) and District Magistrates (*chih-hsien*); *chu-kuan chia-ko kuan* (Archivist in Charge), one in each Ministry (*pu*). P8, 20, 26, 29.

1400 *chù-kuó* 柱國
Pillar of State. (1) A designation of high merit apparently stemming from high antiquity, throughout history encountered as an unofficial reference to an eminent civil official such as a Counselor-in-chief (*ch'eng-hsiang*) or a Grand Councilor (*tsai-hsiang*), or to an eminent military officer. (2) SUI–MING: a merit title (*hsün*), usually 2nd in esteem

only to Supreme Pillar of State (*shang chu-kuo*), granted to either civil or military officials of rank 2b through Chin, thereafter 1b. In Ming, 2nd in esteem to Left and Right Pillars of State, each 1a. RR + SP: *pilier de l'état*. P63, 65.

1401 *chù-kuó tà chiāng-chūn* 柱國大將軍
N-S DIV (Chou): **Pillar of State and General-in-chief,** designation granted 8 supreme military leaders, one serving as commander-in-chief over all, one commanding the imperial bodyguard, and the others commanding 6 regional armies. May be encountered in other periods as a combination of the honorific title Pillar of State with the functional title General-in-chief. P65.

1402 *chǔ-lào* 主酪
T'ANG: **Milk Provisioner,** 74 unranked members of the Office of Herds (*tien-mu shu*) in the Court of the Imperial Stud (*t'ai-p'u ssu*). RR: *préposé aux laitages.*

1403 *chū-lì* 諸吏
(1) Lit., **the various functionaries:** may be encountered in any era as a collective reference to the imperial officialdom or to all suboffical functionaries (see *li*). (2) HAN: **Leader of the Officials** (?), a supplementary honorific title (*chia-kuan*) awarded to some eminent court officials who were deemed specially worthy companions of the Emperor. HB: inspector of officials.

1404 *chǔ-lǐn* 主廩
CHIN–YÜAN: **Commandant of Granaries,** in charge of supplying the imperial armies; in Chin a subordinate of the Court of the Imperial Regalia (*wei-wei ssu*); Yüan affiliation not clear.

1405 *chū-lù* 諸路
YÜAN: **the various Routes,** a prefix attached to central government agencies that had empire-wide authority in narrowly specified realms: e.g., the Supervisorate-in-chief of Precious Goods for (in?) the Various Routes (*chu-lu pao-ch'üan tu t'i-chü ssu*). It is important to note, however, that in other instances *chu-lu* is not properly part of the title but is merely a collectivizing term meaning "the various" or "all" Routes (see under *chu*), fulfilling its normal grammatical function. In Yüan materials it is not easy to determine whether a particular *chu-lu* ... construction signifies a central government agency with empire-wide authority or signifies agencies that were found in all or many Routes. In this dictionary, *chu-lu* ... (and similarly prefixed) agencies are entered under the immediately following words: i.e., in the example noted above, under *pao-ch'üan tu t'i-chü ssu*.

1406 *chú-mù wù* 竹木務
SUNG: **Bamboo and Lumber Service,** a unit in the Directorate for the Palace Buildings (*chiang-tso chien*), headed by an unranked Manager (*kou-tang kuan*). SP: *agence de bois et de bambou.* P15.

1407 *chù-nǐ àn* 注擬案
SUNG: **Nominations Section,** a unit in the Civil Appointments Process (*tso-hsüan*) in the Ministry of Personnel (*li-pu*). SP: *service chargé d'inscrire la nomination à une charge.*

1408 *chù-nǐ chǎng-ch'üèh* 注擬掌闕
SUNG: **Nominations and Vacancies Section,** a unit in the Military Appointments Process (*yu-hsüan*) in the Ministry of Personnel (*li-pu*). Might also be encountered as a combined reference to the Nominations Section (*chu-ni an*) and a Vacancies Section (*chang-ch'üeh an?*) in the Civil Appointments Process (*tso-hsüan*). SP: *service chargé d'in-*

scrire la nomination à une charge et de s'occuper des postes vacants.

1409 *chǔ-niěn* 主輦
SUI–T'ANG: **Sedan-chair Supervisor,** 4 unranked on the staff of each Office of the Imperial Mausoleum (*ling-shu*) and Court of the Imperial Mausoleum (*ling-t'ai*); in T'ang also members of the Sedan-chair Service (*shang-nien chü*) in the Palace Administration (*tien-chung sheng*). RR: *préposé aux voitures à bras.* P29.

1410 *chù-pǎn àn* 祝版案 or 祝板案
SUNG: **Prayer Tablet Section,** a unit of the Imperial Archives (*pi-ko*) presumably responsible for the preparation of inscribed tablets to be burned in sacrificial rites, or for storing copies of such texts. SP: *service des planches d'invocation ou service des prières des sacrifices.*

1411 *chǔ-p'àn kuān* 主判官 or *chu-p'an*
SUNG: lit., an official who is principally in charge, **Manager:** in the early Sung decades, a temporary assignment rather than a substantive appointment, commonly found in many agencies of the central government, sometimes even designating officials in active charge of Ministries (*pu*), no matter who might nominally be the Ministers (*shang-shu*). SP: *secrétaire ou directeur.* P13.

1412 *chù-p'ó* 駐泊
SUNG: lit., temporarily anchored: **Detached,** a prefix used with the names of military units to signify that they were not regular garrison forces of Prefectures (*chou*) but were assigned (temporarily?) to Area Commanders-in-chief (*tsung-kuan*). SP: *troupes impériales stationnées en province.*

1413 *chǔ-pù* 主簿
Lit., to be in charge of records. (1) HAN–CH'ING: **Recorder,** members of a great many agencies, normally handling the flow of documents in and out of their units, usually in ranks 7, 8, or 9; e.g., in the T'ang Court of Imperial Sacrifices (*t'ai-ch'ang ssu*), rank 7b1; in the Sung Censorate (*yü-shih t'ai*), 8b; in the Liao Directorate of Astronomy (*ssu-t'ien chien*), rank not clear; in the Ming Court of State Ceremonial (*hung-lu ssu*), 8b; in the Ch'ing Household Administration of the Heir Apparent (*chan-shih fu*), 7b. HB: master of records. RR + SP: *préposé aux registres.* BH: archivist. (2) HAN–CH'ING: **Assistant Magistrate** on the staff of various units of territorial administration, especially Districts (*hsien*); normally the 3rd ranking post, behind one or more Vice Magistrates (*ch'eng*) as well as the District Magistrate (*ling, chih-hsien*); rank from 9a2 to 9b1 in T'ang, 8b in Sung, 9a in Chin, Yüan, Ming, and Ch'ing. BH: registrar.

1414 *chǔ-pù t'īng* 主簿廳
Recorder's Office, especially in Ming and Ch'ing referring to the subunit in an agency that was headed by a Recorder; see *chu-pu* (1). P26.

1415 *chū-sè jén-chiàng tsǔng-kuǎn fǔ*
諸色人匠總管府
YÜAN: **Supervisorate-in-chief of All Classes of Artisans,** an agency in the Ministry of Works (*kung-pu*), responsible for supervising various manufactories of metal, wood, and stone products; headed by a Supervisor-in-chief (*tsung-kuan*), rank 3a, with the assistance of both 2 Associate Administrators (*t'ung-chih*) and 2 Vice Supervisors-in-chief (*fu tsung-kuan*). References may be found to a Supreme Supervisorate-in-chief of All Classes of Artisans (*chu-se jen-chiang tu tsung-kuan fu*), but this is probably no more than a variant form of the Supervisorate-in-chief. P15.

1416 *chŭ-shàn* 主膳

(1) N-S DIV (Chou): **Palace Provisioner,** head of the Catering Bureau (*hsiao shan-pu*) in the Ministry of State (*t'ien-kuan*), ranked as an Ordinary Grand Master (*chung ta-fu;* 5a); furnished drinks and delicacies for imperial banquets, receptions, sacrificial ceremonies, etc.; comparable to the head of the Court of Imperial Entertainments (*kuang-lu ssu*) of other periods. See *nei-shan.* P30. (2) T'ANG: **Waiter,** 840 unranked serving men authorized for the staff of the Food Service (*shang-shih chü*) of the Palace Administration (*tien-chung sheng*), for attendance at banquets and ceremonial occasions. RR: *serviteur préposé aux mets.* P38.

1417 *chŭ-shè tsŏ-yù* 主射左右

SUI: lit., archers on left and right: **Personal Bodyguard,** 8 men attached to the household of the Heir Apparent; a variant of *pei-shen tso-yu.* P26.

1418 *chŭ-shéng* 主乘

T'ANG: **Carriage Master,** 6 unranked personnel in the Office of the Imperial Stables (*tien-chiu shu*) in the Court of the Imperial Stud (*t'ai-p'u ssu*); supervised 100 Coachmen (*chih-yü*). RR: *préposé aux attelages.*

1419 *chū-shēng* 諸生

Throughout history, a collective reference to **Students** of almost any kind, sometimes made specific by preceding context. In Ming and Ch'ing, often used without any qualifying prefix as the equivalent of Government Student (*sheng-yüan*).

1420 *chŭ-shìh* 主事

Lit., one in charge of affairs: apparently originated as a military title, but early became a civil service title, ultimately a widespread one. (1) HAN–N-S DIV: **Administrative Aide** (?), a petty subordinate to the Chamberlain for Attendants (*lang-chung ling, kuang-lu-hsün*) and in certain military headquarters. HB: master of affairs. (2) N-S DIV–SUI: **Director,** head of a Section (*ts'ao*) in a Ministry (*pu*) in the developing Department of State Affairs (*shang-shu sheng*), rank apparently varying from 8b up to 5b; the title in this usage may have evolved from *chu-shih ling-shih* (Clerk); e.g., see under *chu-k'o.* (3) SUI–CH'ING: **Secretary** in a Bureau (*ssu, ch'ing-li ssu*) of a Ministry (*pu*) and in many other agencies of the central government; numbers variable; rank normally 8 or 9 in T'ang, 8b in Sung, 7b in Chin and Yüan, 6a in Ming and Ch'ing. See *t'ang chu-shih.* RR+SP: *préposé aux affaire.* BH: second class secretary, secretary.

1421 *chŭ-shíh* 主食

N-S DIV–T'ANG: **Cook,** 12 unranked in the N. Chou Catering Service (*hsiao shan-pu*) under the Ministry of State (*t'ien-kuan*); 16 unranked in the T'ang Food Service (*shang-shih chü*) of the Palace Administration (*tien-chung sheng*). RR: *préposé aux aliments.* P30, 38.

1422 *chù-shĭh* 柱史

Abbreviation of *chu-hsia shih* (**Archivist, Censor**).

1423 *chù-shíh* 柱石

Lit., pillar and plinth: throughout history, an unofficial reference to specially prominent ministers; in Ch'ing, particularly referred to Censors (*yü-shih*).

1424 *chù-shĭh* 祝史

N-S DIV (N. Wei)–T'ANG: **Supplication Scribe** in the Court of Imperial Sacrifices (*t'ai-ch'ang ssu*); rank 7b2 in N. Wei, thereafter apparently unranked; number not clear for N. Wei; 16 in Sui, 6 in T'ang. RR: *invocateur.* P27.

1425 *chŭ-shìh fáng* 主事房

SUI–CH'ING: **Secretary's Office,** a possible reference to the place of business of any *chu-shih* (Secretary). In Sung, particularly referred to the mail-handling section of the Secretariat (*chung-shu sheng*) called *k'ai-ch'ai fang.* SP: *chambre de la réception et de l'expédition des dépêches.*

1426 *chŭ-shìh kuān* 主試官

T'ANG–CH'ING: **Examining Official** in a civil service recruitment examination; an unofficial generic designation.

1427 *chŭ-shìh lìng-shĭh* 主事令史

N-S DIV (N. Wei)–SUI: **Clerk,** generally rank 8b or lower, found in various agencies, especially those subordinate to the Department of State Affairs (*shang-shu sheng*). See *chu-shih, ling-shih.*

1428 *chŭ-shū* 主書

N-S DIV–SUNG: **Scribe,** low-ranking or unranked personnel found in many agencies, especially the Secretariat (*chung-shu sheng*), often assisting Drafters (*chung-shu she-jen*); sometimes called *chu-shu ling-shih* (Scribal Clerks). SP: *scribe principal.* P2, 3.

1429 *chù-shū* 助書

N-S DIV: **Assistant Clerk,** suboffocial functionaries found in the Secretariat (*chung-shu sheng*) and perhaps other agencies. See *ling chu-shih.* P2.

1430 *chŭ-ssū* 主司

T'ANG: **Examiner,** a generic term for the officials who supervised civil service recruitment examinations. P24.

1431 *chū-ssū* 諸司

Lit., **the various offices:** throughout history a collective reference to categories of agencies often specified in the immediately preceding context; without such qualification, the term normally suggests all the agencies of the central government.

1432 *chū-ssū kuān* 諸司官

SUNG: **Officials of the Various Offices,** a collective reference to staff members (the heads?) of the various Offices (*ssu*) in the Historiography Institute (*kuo-shih yüan*), normally on assignment detached from the Palace Domestic Service (*nei-shih sheng*); hence may be encountered as a collective reference to palace eunuchs. In other eras as well as Sung, may be encountered as a collective reference to all officials of central government agencies. SP: *fonctionnaire chargé des affaires des divers services.*

1433 *chŭ-ssū lĭ-tsǎi* 主司里宰

N-S DIV (N. Wei): lit. meaning not clear; possibly a Chinese translation of an alien term: **Commander** (?), posts created, apparently throughout the domain, by Emperor Shih-tsu (r. 424–451) because of the prevalence of military disorders; status and specific functions not clear. P20.

1434 *chū ssū-shìh* 諸司事

SUI–MING: **the various Directresses,** a collective reference to 24 palace women individually known as Directress (*ssu*); rank 4a in T'ang, 6a from Sung on. See *erh-shih-ssu ssu.* RR: *directeur.*

1435 *chū-ssū shĭh* 諸司使

SUNG: **Commissioner of the Various Offices,** a collective reference to 2 groups of holders of honorific titles: one group designated Grand Masters (*ta-fu*), considered the principal Commissioners (*chéng-shih*); the other designated Court Gentlemen (*lang*), considered Vice Commissioners (*fu-shih*). SP: *commissaire des bureaux divers.*

1436 *chū-ssū ts'ān-chūn* 諸司參軍
SUNG: **Administrators of the Various Sections,** a collective reference to the officials in charge of clerical units in prefectural (*chou*) headquarters and some other agencies of territorial administration, rank 9b; e.g., Administrator of the Revenue Section (*hu-ts'ao ts'an-chün*), Administrator for Education (*wen-hsüeh ts'an-chün*). See *ts'an-chün.* SP: *administrateur des bureaux divers.*

1437 *chū tiĕn-shìh* 諸典事
SUI–MING: **the various Managers,** a collective reference to 24 palace women individually known as Manager (*tien*), rank 6a in T'ang, 7a in Sung. See *liu tien, erh-shih-ssu tien.* RR: *intendant.*

1438 *chù-tsàng tà-ch'én* 駐藏大臣
CH'ING: **Grand Minister Resident of Tibet,** a representative of the Court of Colonial Affairs (*li-fan yüan*) installed from 1709 to have full responsibility for the pacification and administration of Tibet. From 1729 he, the Grand Minister Assistant Administrator of Tibet (*pang-pan ta-ch'en*), and the Dalai Lama governed Tibet cooperatively. BH: imperial resident of Tibet.

1439 *chŭ-ts'áo* 主曹
CH'ING: an unofficial reference to a *chu-shih* (**Secretary**).

1440 *chù-tsò* 著作
N-S DIV–SUNG: lit., to write; a prefix in many titles suggesting **Editorial ....** Officials so designated often constituted an Editorial Service (*chu-tso chü*) and normally worked on the Imperial Diary (*ch'i-chü chu*) or other historical compilations in the *pi-shu sheng* (Secretariat, then Palace Library), the Historiography Office (*shih-kuan*), the Hanlin Academy (*han-lin yüan*), etc. Common titles include *chu-tso cheng-tzu* (Editorial Proofreader), *chu-tso chiao-shu lang* (Editor), *chu-tso chang-ku* (Editorial Clerk), and *chu-tso ling-shih* (Editorial Clerk). P23.

1441 *chù-tsò chú* 著作局
SUI–SUNG: **Editorial Service,** part of the Palace Library (*pi-shu sheng*), responsible for compilation of the Imperial Diary (*ch'i-chü chu*) and other historical materials till 630, when a Historiography Office (*shih-kuan*) was established to do so, whereupon the Editorial Service became increasingly devoted to preparation of the state-issued calendar; briefly after 661 known as *ssu-wen chü;* normally headed by one to 4 Editorial Directors (*chu-tso lang*). RR: *service des rédactions.* SP: *bureau de la rédaction·du calendrier.* P23.

1442 *chù-tsò láng* 著作郎
N-S DIV (San-kuo)–SUNG: **Editorial Director,** normally 2 but one to 4 in Sung, members of the Secretariat (*chung-shu sheng, pi-shu sheng*) or the Palace Library (*pi-shu sheng*) during the era of N-S Division, when the post was ordinarily filled by men with substantive posts elsewhere; from Sui on, head of the Editorial Service (*chu-tso chü*) of the Palace Library; responsible for compiling the Imperial Diary (*ch'i-chü chu*) and other historical materials till 630, thereafter responsible for preparing the state-issued calendar, etc.; rank 5a then 5b in Sui, 5b in T'ang, 7b in Sung. Normally aided by one or more Assistant Editorial Directors (*chu-tso tso-lang*), rank 6b1 in T'ang, 8a in Sung. RR+SP: *secrétaire, secrétaire assistant.* P23, 24.

1443 *chù-tsò shĕng* 著作省 or *chù-tsò ts'áo* 著作曹
N-S DIV–T'ANG: variant reference to the **Editorial Service** (*chu-tso chü*); *sheng* in San-kuo Wei and Chin, *ts'ao* in Sui and very early T'ang. P22, 23.

1444 *chŭ-tzŭ* 主子
Lit., a master or lord: occasionally used in unofficial reference to the **Emperor.** P64.

1445 *chū-tzŭ* 諸子
CHOU: **Royal Tutor,** 2 ranked as Junior Grand Masters (*hsia ta-fu*) and 4 as Ordinary Servicemen (*chung-shih*), members of the Ministry of War (*hsia-kuan*), responsible for the education of the Heir Apparent, other sons of the King, and sons of high officials. CL: *attaché aux fils.* In other contexts, of course, may refer to "the various (philosophical) masters" of antiquity or simply "the various sons."

1446 *chŭ-wén* 主文
T'ANG: unofficial reference to an **Examiner** in a civil service recruitment examination.

1447 *chŭ-wén chūng-sàn* 主文中散
N-S DIV (N. Wei): **Courtier-secretary,** one category of duty assignments for aristocratic Courtiers (*chung-san*, q.v.).

1448 *chŭ yā-kuān* 主押官
SUNG: **Chief Prison Custodian** in a Mail and Prison Office (*mo-k'an ssu*). SP: *préposé aux affaires.*

1449 *chŭ-yào* 主藥
SUI–T'ANG: **Pharmacist,** variable numbers of unranked personnel, probably professional specialists, assigned to the Imperial Medical Office (*t'ai-i shu*), the Medicines Service (*shang-yao chü*) of the T'ang Palace Administration (*tien-chung sheng*), and all Offices of the Imperial Mausoleum (*ling-shu*) and Courts of the Imperial Mausoleum (*ling-t'ai*). RR: *préposé aux remèdes.* P29, 36, 38.

1450 *chú-yào* 逐要
T'ANG: lit., to pursue what is important, to pursue with demands (?): **Inquiry Agent,** a minor member of the staff of a Military Commissioner (*chieh-tu shih*); specific functions not clear. RR: *fonctionnaire qui poursuit dans les cas importants.*

1451 *chū yĕh-shŭ lìng* 諸冶署令
N-S DIV (N. Ch'i): **Director of Coinage,** a subordinate in the Court of the Imperial Treasury (*t'ai-fu ssu*); one for the Eastern Circuit (*tung-tao*) and one for the Western Circuit (*hsi-tao*). P16.

1452 *chù-yìn chuàn-wén kuān* 鑄印篆文官
SUNG: **Seal Maker,** number not clear, unranked, on the staff of the Directorate for Palace Manufactories (*shao-fu chien*); made and inscribed imperial and other state seals. SP: *fonctionnaire chargé de la fabrication des sceaux et des caractères sigillaires.* P9.

1453 *chù-yìn chú* 鑄印局
YÜAN–CH'ING: **Seals Service,** an agency in the Ministry of Rites (*li-pu*), headed by a Commissioner-in-chief (*ta-shih*), responsible for casting all government seals. BH: office of seal-casting. P9.

1454 *chŭ-yüèh nèi-p'ĭn* 主樂內品
SUNG: **Eunuch Musician,** 30 authorized for the Bureau of Natural Harmony (*yün-shao pu*) in the Palace Domestic Service (*nei-shih sheng*). SP: *intendant de musique (eunuque).*

1455 *ch'ú* 儲
An adjective referring to the Heir Apparent: **the Heir Apparent's, of the Heir Apparent, for the Heir Apparent,** etc.

1456 *ch'ù* 處
Lit., a place or location. (1) YÜAN: **Region,** the territorial

jurisdiction of a Branch Bureau of Military Affairs (*hsing shu-mi yüan*); see *shu-mi yüan*. (2) CH'ING: **Office**, a common equivalent of the more traditional term *ssu*.

1457 *ch'ú* 除
(1) HAN–YÜAN: a common verb meaning **to appoint**. From Han into the era of N-S Division, used for appointments made by the heads of agencies rather than by the Emperor (see *pai*). From Han on, also, a more general term normally signifying appointment by the Emperor, but differentiated from *pai* in that *pai* was used for one's initial appointment as an official and *ch'u* was used for subsequent appointments or promotions. Thus a new Presented Scholar or Metropolitan Graduate (*chin-shih*) might be appointed (*pai*) a District Magistrate (*hsien-ling, chih-hsien*) and later appointed (*ch'u*, i.e., promoted) to Censor (*yü-shih*). In Yüan, *ch'u* differed from *pai* in specifying an appointment made on the basis of recommendations by superior officials. The use of both *ch'u* and *pai* waned in Ming; then and in Ch'ing the standard term "to appoint" was *shou*, qualified by prefixes in many ways. See *t'ang-chi*. (2) Throughout history, also used as the verb **to dismiss**. See *hsüeh-ch'u ming-chi*.

1458 *ch'ú-chèng yüàn* 儲政院
YÜAN: **Household Service for the Heir Apparent**, c. 1330 renamed from the more traditional Household Administration of the Heir Apparent (*chan-shih yüan*); a huge establishment controlling some territory, great wealth, and many subordinate agencies; headed by a Commissioner (*shih*), rank 2a. P26.

1459 *ch'ú-chí* 儲極
Unofficial reference to the status, hence indirectly to the person, of the **Heir Apparent**.

1460 *ch'ú-chí* 除籍
Lit., to be removed from the register, i.e., dismissed from service: abbreviation of *hsüeh-ch'u ming-chi*.

1461 *ch'ù-chìh shíh* 處置使
T'ANG–SUNG: lit., a delegate who arranges and disposes of matters: **Supervisory Commissioner**, one of the many titles commonly adopted by T'ang Military Commissioners (*chieh-tu shih*) when they became almost autonomous regional warlords beginning in the 750s; usually found in combinations such as Surveillance, Investigation, and Supervisory Commissioner (*an-ch'a ts'ai-fang ch'u-chih shih*); in Sung, one of the titles used for officials placed in charge of Military Commissions (*shuai-ssu*) of Circuits (*tao, lu*), or used for delegates from the central government to troubled areas with ad hoc assignments combining titles such as Pacification Commissioner Supervising ... (*ch'u-chih ... hsüan-fu shih*). SP: *commissaire-inspecteur*. P50.

1462 *ch'ū-chìh shíh* 黜陟使
T'ANG: lit., a delegate to demote and promote: **Personnel Evaluation Commissioner**, a concurrent title commonly taken by Military Commissioners (*chieh-tu shih*) as they became almost autonomous regional warlords beginning in the 750s; most often found in the combination Investigation and Personnel Evaluation Commissioner (*ts'ai-fang ch'u-chih shih*); implied the power to judge and deal with officials in the commissioner's jurisdiction on his own initiative and authority. RR: *commissaire impérial chargé de désigner à la disgrace et à l'avancement*. P50, 52.

1463 *ch'ú-ch'ìng shíh ssū* 儲慶使司
YÜAN: in 1328–1329 only, the official variant designation of the **Household Administration of the Heir Apparent** (*chan-shih yüan*); headed by a Supervisor of the Household

of the Heir Apparent (*ch'u-ch'ing shih*). Also see *ch'u-cheng yüan*. P26.

1464 *ch'ú-chún* 儲君
T'ANG–CH'ING: unofficial reference to the **Heir Apparent**.

1465 *ch'ú-èrh* 儲貳
N-S DIV–SUNG: unofficial reference to the **Heir Apparent**.

1466 *ch'ú-fēi* 儲妃
From antiquity, a general reference to a **Wife of the Heir Apparent**.

1467 *ch'ú-fù* 儲副
T'ANG: unofficial reference to the **Heir Apparent**.

1468 *ch'ú-huáng* 儲皇
An occasional unofficial reference to the **Heir Apparent**.

1469 *ch'ú-ì* 廚役
CH'ING: **Kitchen Helper**, 390 unranked personnel authorized for miscellaneous chores in the Court of Imperial Sacrifices (*t'ai-ch'ang ssu*). P27.

1470 *ch'ū-kó* 出閣 or 出閤
Lit., to depart the palace: from Han on, refers to the custom or dynastic law that required sons of Emperors other than the Heir Apparent, when they matured, to move out of the imperial palace and away from the dynastic capital city—"to go to their fiefs" (*chih-kuo*, q.v.), i.e., to take up residence in other cities from which, sometimes in reality but most often in name only, they reigned over territories with designations such as Prince of Ch'u (Ch'u-*wang*) or Prince of Chin (Chin-*wang*), imitating the nomenclature that prevailed in the Chou age of Feudal Lords (*chu-hou*). The custom was not followed at all times, e.g., in the latter half of T'ang and in Ch'ing. See *wang, ch'in-wang, wang-fu*. P69.

1471 *ch'ú-kūng* 儲宮
Throughout history an unofficial reference to the residence, hence indirectly to the person, of the **Heir Apparent**.

1472 *ch'ú-liǎng* 儲兩
N-S DIV (San-kuo): an unofficial reference to the **Heir Apparent**.

1473 *ch'ú-míng* 除名
Lit., to have one's name removed (from the register of officials), i.e., to be dismissed from service: an abbreviation of *hsüeh-ch'u ming-chi*. Also see *ch'u-chi*.

1474 *ch'ū-nà ch'ién-wù shíh* 出納錢物使
T'ANG: **Commissioner of Accounts**, supervisor of disbursements and receipts in the Court of the Imperial Granaries (*ssu-nung ssu*), from 746; rank not clear, but subordinate to the Chief Minister (*ch'ing*) and Vice Minister (*shao-ch'ing*) of the Court. P7.

1475 *ch'ū-nà shíh* 出納使
T'ANG: **Commissioner of Accounts**, supervisor of disbursements and receipts in the Court of the Imperial Treasury (*t'ai-fu ssu*), from 743; rank not clear, but subordinate to the Chief Minister (*ch'ing*) and Vice Minister (*shao-ch'ing*) of the Court. P7.

1476 *ch'ú shàn-ssū* 儲膳司
YÜAN: **Office of Food Supplies for the Heir Apparent**, part of the administrative establishment of the Eastern Palace (*tung-kung*), residence of the Heir Apparent; headed by a Chief Minister (*ch'ing*), rank not clear. P26.

1477 *ch'ū-shēn* 出身
T'ANG–CH'ING: lit., to produce the person, meaning to begin a career in government service; a term normally found with a prefix, e.g., *chin-shih ch'u-shen* (to enter government service via status as a Presented Scholar or Metropolitan Graduate). From Sung on, in addition to this general usage, the term also had a narrower one, specifying candidates who qualified in the highest-level civil service recruitment examinations as Regular Metropolitan Graduates (*chin-shih ch'u-shen*), with prestige below Metropolitan Graduates with Honors (*chin-shih chi-ti*) but above Associate Metropolitan Graduates (*chin-shih t'ung ch'u-shen*).

1478 *ch'ú-shǐh* 廚史
N-S DIV (Chin): **Kitchen Supervisor,** a subordinate of the Director of Banquets (*ta-kuan ling*) on the staff of the Chamberlain for Attendants (*kuang-lu-hsün*); rank not clear. P30.

1479 *ch'ú-tí* 儲嫡
Throughout history an unofficial reference to the eldest son of an Emperor's principal wife, who ordinarily became Heir Apparent.

1480 *ch'ú-tuān* 儲端
Especially in the last few dynasties, an unofficial reference to the **Supervisor of the Household of the Heir Apparent** (*chan-shih*).

1481 *ch'ú-wéi* 儲闈
T'ANG: an unofficial reference to the **Heir Apparent.**

1482 *chuǎn* 轉
Rank or **grade:** from T'ang on, most specifically, the rank of a merit title (*hsün*), hence **merit rank.**

1483 *chūan ch'éng-pó* 專城伯
SUNG: unofficial reference to a **Prefect** (*chün-shou*).

1484 *chuān-chīh* 專知
T'ANG–SUNG: **Specially-appointed Administrator,** prefix to an agency name indicating an official holding a different nominal position appointed by imperial order to take charge of the agency designated. See *chih* (to know).

1485 *chuān-chīh yǜ-shū chiěn-t'ǎo*
專知御書檢討
T'ANG: **Specially-appointed Examining Editor of Imperial Writings,** 8 serving in the Academy of Scholarly Worthies (*chi-hsien tien shu-yüan*) while holding nominal office elsewhere in the central government. P25.

1486 *chuān-kōu ssū* 專勾司
SUNG: **Special Control Office** in the Court of the Imperial Treasury (*t'ai-fu ssu*); staff and functions not clear.

1487 *chuān-shè* 傳舍
HAN: variant of *yu-t'ing* (**Postal Relay Station**).

1488 *chuàn-shǐh hsüéh-shìh* 撰史學士
N-S DIV: **Historiographer,** a compiler of historical works, subordinate to the Imperial Editor (*ta chu-tso*), apparently in the Secretariat (*pi-shu sheng*); rank not clear. P23.

1489 *chuàn-shū pó-shìh* 篆書博士
T'ANG: **Erudite of the Seal Script,** one of 18 Palace Erudites (*nei-chiao po-shih*) on the staff of the Palace Institute of Literature (*nei wen-hsüeh kuan*), where palace women were educated; from c. 741, a eunuch post. RR: *maître de l'écriture tchouan.*

1490 *chuǎn-yǜn shǐh* 轉運使
(1) T'ANG: **Transport Commissioner,** assignment for a court official in 712 to supervise transport of tax grain through the gorges of the Yellow River between Loyang and Ch'angan; in 734 a Transport Commissioner-in-chief (*tu chuan-yün shih*) was assigned to expedite transport of tax grain throughout the Chiang-Huai and Honan areas; after 763 headquartered at Yangchow to expedite the transport of tax grain throughout the Grand Canal system. Sometimes also established in a Circuit (*tao*) with concurrent responsibility for supervising the state monopoly of salt. (2) SUNG–CHIN: **Fiscal Commissioner,** one in each Circuit (*lu, tao*) with general responsibility for tax assessments and collections and all other fiscal matters. In Sung and Liao, a duty assignment for a nominal court official; in Chin, rank 3a. SP: *commissaire aux finances d'une province ou intendant fiscal ou commissaire des transports.* (3) YÜAN–CH'ING: unofficial reference to officials with responsibility for transport of tax grains along the Grand Canal, e.g., the Ch'ing dynasty Director-general of Grain Transport (*ts'ao-yün tsung-tu*). P60.

1491 *chuǎn-yǜn shǐh-fù t'í-tiěn hsíng-yǜ k'ò-chī yüàn* 轉運使副提點形獄課績院
SUNG: **Circuit Intendants Evaluation Bureau,** established in 1049 with a staff of court officials as ad hoc appointees, to conduct personnel evaluations of the supervisors of Circuits (*lu*), such as Fiscal Commissioners (*chuan-yün shih*) and Judicial Commissioners (*t'i-tien hsing-yü kung-shih*); apparently superseded not later than 1080 by evaluation procedures conducted by the Ministry of Personnel (*li-pu*).

1492 *chuǎn-yǜn ssū* 轉運司
Lit., the office of a *chuan-yün shih*. (1) T'ANG: **Transport Commission.** (2) SUNG: **Fiscal Commission.** (3) SUNG: **Tax Transport Bureau,** created (date not clear) in a reorganization of the Salt and Iron Monopoly Bureau (*yen-t'ieh ssu*), one of the 3 principal agencies in the State Finance Commission (*san ssu*) of early Sung; terminated c. 1080. SP: *bureau de transport ou des finances.* P52, 57, 59.

1493 *chuǎn-yǜn-yén shǐh ssū* 轉運鹽使司
YÜAN: **Tax Transport and Salt Monopoly Commission,** responsible to the metropolitan Secretariat (*chung-shu sheng*) for all transport and monopoly activities in the Metropolitan Area (*chih-li*) around Peking, after 1319 via the intermediary Ministry of Revenue (*hu-pu*); headed by a Commissioner (*shih*), rank not specified.

1494 *ch'uán-ch'ē* 傳車
HAN: unofficial reference to a **Regional Inspector** (*tz'u-shih*).

1495 *ch'uán-chìh* 傳制
T'ANG: **Proclamation Carrier,** 8 unranked personnel assisting Supervising Secretaries (*chi-shih-chung*) of the Chancellery (*men-hsia sheng*); apparently responsible for the delivery of imperial orders to or from the Supervising Secretaries. RR: *porteur d'édits impériaux.* P19.

1496 *ch'uán-fǎ yüàn* 傳法院
SUNG: **Institute for Propagation of the Tripitaka,** a group of scholarly officials subordinate to the Court of State Ceremonial (*hung-lu ssu*) responsible for translating and publishing Buddhist canonical works. SP: *cour de la propagation de la loi chargée de la traduction du canon bouddhique.*

1497 *ch'uān-héng* 川衡
Guardian of the Waterways. (1) CHOU: 12 assigned to

each major waterway, 6 to each middling waterway, and 2 to each minor waterway, all ranked as Ordinary Servicemen (*chung-shih*), subordinates of the Manager of Fisheries (*tse-yü*) in the Ministry of Education (*ti-kuan*) responsible for enforcing prohibitions regarding streams and ponds in the royal domain. CL: *inspecteur des cours d'eau.* (2) N-S DIV (Chou): number not clear, ranked as Ordinary Servicemen and Junior Servicemen (*hsia-shih*), members of the Ministry of Education. P14.

1498   *ch'uán-hsüān hó-t'úng ssū* 傳宣合同司
SUNG: **Registered Documents Office,** an agency of the Palace Eunuch Service (*ju-nei nei-shih sheng*) responsible for the issuance of blank registered documents (*ho-t'ung*) that government agencies were required to use in memorializing the throne. See *k'an-ho.* SP: *bureau de la délivrance des certificats pour les demandes du palais.*

1499   *ch'uán-lìng* 傳令
T'ANG: **Edict Carrier,** 4 unranked personnel on the staff of the Secretariat of the Heir Apparent (*tso ch'un-fang*). RR: *porteur des ordres de l'héritier du trône.* P26.

1500   *ch'uán-lú* 傳臚
CH'ING: **List Leader,** designation of those Metropolitan Graduates (*chin-shih*) whose names headed the lists of the 2nd and 3rd groups (*chia*) of passers in the palace examination (*tien-shih*), the culmination of the triennial civil service recruitment examination sequence. See *lu-ch'uan.* Cf. *chuang-yüan.*

1501   *ch'uān-shīh* 川師
CHOU: **Master of the Waterways,** 2 ranked as Ordinary Servicemen (*chung-shih*) and 4 as Junior Servicemen (*hsia-shih*), members of the Ministry of War (*hsia-kuan*) with overall responsibility for the management of streams, ponds, and other waterways. CL: *maître des cours d'eau.*

1502   *ch'uán-tsăi* 傳宰
Lit., manager of transmission: a common unofficial reference to personnel in charge of local Postal Stations (*i* or *yu*) in the state-maintained communications service.

1503   *chuāng-chái shìh* 莊宅使
SUNG: **Commissioner for Estates and Residences** (?), an early Sung antecedent of the prestige title (*san-kuan*) Grand Master for Military Tallies (*wu-chieh ta-fu*), awarded to rank 7a military officers. SP: *commissaire des colonies, commissaire des domaines et des résidences.*

1504   *chuāng chìh-ch'ìh chiàng* 裝制敕匠
T'ANG: **Mounter of Scrolls,** number not clear, unranked personnel on the staff of the Secretariat (*chung-shu sheng*) in charge of preparing imperial proclamations of all sorts in proper mountings. RR: *ouvrier chargé de relier les édits et décrets impériaux.*

1505   *chuāng-fēi* 莊妃
MING: **Sedate Consort,** one of a group of palace women ranking below the Imperial Honored Consort (*huang kuei-fei*) and the Honored Consort (*kuei-fei*).

1506   *chuāng-huàng chiàng* 裝潢匠
T'ANG: **Mounter of Scrolls,** 2 unranked specialists on the staff of the Institute for the Veneration of Literature (*ch'ung-wen kuan*). RR: *ouvrier relieur.*

1507   *chuāng-lǎo pó-shìh* 莊老博士
T'ANG: **Erudite of Chuang-tzu and Lao-tzu,** a teacher of Taoist texts; one of 18 Palace Erudites (*nei-chiao po-shih*) on the staff of the Palace Institute of Literature (*nei wen-hsüeh kuan*), where palace women were educated; from c.

741 a eunuch post. RR: *maître de la doctrine de Tchouang-tseu et de Lao-tseu.*

1508   *chuāng-shū chíh* 裝書直
T'ANG: **Scrollbinder,** 14 unranked specialists on the staff of the Secretariat's (*chung-shu sheng*) Academy of Scholarly Worthies (*chi-hsien tien shu-yüan*). RR: *relieur.* P25.

1509   *chuāng-shū lì-shēng* 裝書曆生
T'ANG: **Student Calendar Binder,** unranked, number not clear, on the staff of the Bureau of Astronomy (*ssu-t'ien t'ai*) in early T'ang, later discontinued; apparent apprentices in the skill of binding state-issued calendars. RR: *élève relieur du calendrier.*

1510   *chuàng-tīng* 壯丁
(1) **Able-bódied Male,** throughout history a common reference to adult men subject to military conscription and other kinds of government service in the rotational state service system normally called Requisitioned Service (*ch'ai-i*). (2) T'ANG–SUNG: **Policeman,** from late T'ang till 1075 (then abolished in Wang An-shih's reforms), a particular kind of Requisition Service assignment; assisted Local Elders (*ch'i-chang*) in peacekeeping activities.

1511   *chuàng-tīng chǘ* 粧釘局
YÜAN: **Bookbinding Service,** a workshop under the Supervisorate-in-chief of Metal Workers and Jewelers (*chin-yü jen-chiang tsung-kuan fu*), headed by a Commissioner (*shih*), rank 8b or 9b.

1512   *chuàng-t'óu* 狀頭
Unofficial reference to a **Principal Graduate** (*chuang-yüan*) in the highest civil service recruitment examination.

1513   *chuàng-t'óu ch'ù* 狀頭處
CH'ING: lit., estate manager's office (for the imperial lands): abbreviation of *san-ch'i yin-liang chuang-t'ou ch'u* (**Rents Office for Lands of the Inner Banners**).

1514   *chuāng-ts'ái chiàng* 裝裁匠
SUNG: **Scrollbinder,** 12 unranked specialists on the staff of the Imperial Archives (*pi-ko*). SP: *artisan relieur.*

1515   *chuàng-yüán* 狀元
T'ANG–CH'ING: **Principal Graduate,** designation of the candidate who stood first on the list of passers of the final examination in the civil service recruitment examination sequence. In Sung the top 3 passers were sometimes all called Principal Graduates, and in Yüan there were normally 2 Principal Graduates of each examination, one Chinese and one non-Chinese. The designation was highly coveted and esteemed, and it usually led to a prestigious initial appointment and subsequent career in the civil service. Sometimes rendered Primus or Optimus.

1516   *ch'uáng-chiàng* 幢將
N-S DIV (N. Wei): **Corps Leader** of the Imperial Bodyguard (*san-lang wei-shih*), made up of Courtiers (*chung-san*).

1517   *chūi-fēng* 追封
Posthumous enfeoffment, a personnel-administration term referring to the granting of noble titles (*chüeh*) to deceased officials of distinction.

1518   *chūi-hǔi àn* 追毀案
SUNG: **Section for Fines and Confiscations,** one of 13 Sections (*an*) directly subordinate to the executive officials of the S. Sung Ministry of Justice (*hsing-pu*); staffed with subofficial functionaries who handled documents relating to the implementation of judicial actions such as collecting fines,

confiscating property, and recovering stolen goods. SP: *service de reconsideration.*

1519   *chūi-shīh* 追師
See under the romanization *tui-shih.*

1520   *chúi-shìh* 箠氏
CHOU: **Handler of Divination Bamboo,** 2 ranked as Junior Servicemen (*hsia-shih*), members of the Ministry of Rites (*ch'un-kuan*) who made fires for divination purposes using a kind of bamboo named *chui.* CL: *préposé au bois de Tchoui.*

1521   *ch'úi-lién* 垂簾
Lit., to drop the curtain: a term used throughout history when Empresses or other palace women participated directly in court audiences, from which they were normally concealed behind a curtain.

1522   *chǔn-pèi* 準備
SUNG: **Reserve,** occasionally found as a prefix to a title, apparently signifying a supernumerary appointee or someone in a status preparatory to taking office without having formally been authorized to take office. SP: *... en réserve.*

1523   *ch'ūn-ch'īng* 春卿
Spring Chamberlain, an archaic reference deriving from the Chou usage of the term *ch'un-kuan* (Ministry of Rites). (1) N-S DIV (Liang): a generic or collective reference to 3 of the central government officials called the Twelve Chamberlains (*shih-erh ch'ing,* q.v.). (2) SUI–CH'ING: unofficial reference to the Minister of Rites (*lǐ-pu shang-shu*).

1524   *ch'ūn-fāng* 春坊
Lit., spring quarters. (1) N-S DIV–T'ANG: unofficial reference to the residence, hence indirectly to the person, of the **Heir Apparent.** (2) T'ANG–CH'ING: **Secretariat of the Heir Apparent,** one each Left and Right, in general charge of the household of the Heir Apparent, under the Supervisor of the Household of the Heir Apparent (*chan-shih*); each Secretariat normally headed by a Mentor (*shu-tzu*), rank 5a in Ch'ing. In T'ang till 662 the Left Secretariat was known as the *men-hsia fang,* and the Right Secretariat was known as the *tien-shu fang.* Also commonly rendered Directorate of Instruction. RR: *grand secrétariat de l'héritier du trône.* P4, 23, 26.

1525   *ch'ūn-kuān* 春官
Lit., official or office for spring, a season of renewals. (1) CHOU, N-S DIV, T'ANG: **Ministry of Rites.** In Chou, the 3rd of 6 top-echelon agencies in the royal government, headed by a Minister of Rites (*tsung-po*) ranked as a Minister (*ch'ing*); responsible for a wide range of ritual affairs and subordinate agencies. Revived by Chou in the era of N-S Division to replace what had been known as *tz'u-pu* (Ministry of Sacrifices); revived again from 684 to 705 in T'ang to replace the name *lǐ-pu* (Ministry of Rites). In all later eras may be encountered as an archaic reference to the *lǐ-pu.* CL: *ministère du printemps ou des rites.* P9. (2) T'ANG–CH'ING: **Spring Office,** one of 5 seasonal Offices (*kuan*), including one for Mid-year (*chung*), of calendrical specialists in the T'ang Astrological Service (*t'ai-shih chü*) and later Bureau of Astronomy (*ssu-t'ien t'ai*), the Sung Astrological Service, the Sung–Ming Directorate of Astronomy (*ssu-t'ien chien*), and the Ming–Ch'ing Directorate of Astronomy (*ch'in-t'ien chien*). Headed by a Director (*ling* in early T'ang, otherwise *cheng*), rank 5a in T'ang, 8a in Sung, 6b in Ming and Ch'ing; in Ch'ing one Manchu and one Chinese appointee. RR+SP: *administration du prin-*

temps. BH (*cheng*): astronomer for the spring. P35. (3) MING: **Spring Support,** from 1380 to 1382 one of 4 posts, each named after a season and open to more than one appointee, intended for the Emperor's closest and most trusted advisers; see *ssu fu-kuan* (Four Supports). P4, 67.

1526   *ch'ūn-kuān tà-fū* 春官大夫
T'ANG: variant designation from 684 to 705 of all **Directors** (*lang-chung*) of Bureaus (*ssu*) in the Ministry of Rites (*lǐ-pu*). P9.

1527   *ch'ūn-ssū* 春司
Unofficial reference to the **Ministry of Rites** (*lǐ-pu*).

1528   *ch'ūn-t'ái* 春臺
Unofficial reference to the **Ministry of Rites** (*lǐ-pu*).

1529   *ch'ūn-ts'áo* 春曹
Unofficial reference to the **Ministry of Rites** (*lǐ-pu*).

1530   *chūng* 中
Lit., center, central, middle. (1) In directional (or often combined directional-hierarchical) usage occurs, e.g., in Central Capital (*chung-tu, chung-ching*) as distinguished from Northern, Southern, Western, or Eastern Capitals, or in Inner Court (*chung-ch'ao;* more commonly *nei-ch'ao, nei-t'ing*) in contrast to Outer Court (*wai-ch'ao, wai-t'ing*). (2) In hierarchical usage occurs, e.g., in distinctions among Senior Servicemen (*shang-shih*), Ordinary Servicemen (*chung-shih*), and Junior Servicemen (*hsia-shih*); or among Large Districts (*ta-hsien*), Ordinary or Middle Districts (*chung-hsien*), and Small Districts (*hsiao-hsien*). (3) **Palace** or **Capital,** prefix to a title or agency name as in *chung-shu* (lit., palace writer), *chi-shih-chung* (lit., one who provides service within), etc. (4) **Full,** prefix to a salary notation stated in bushels in Han and some later times, signifying an amount actually somewhat greater than that stated; e.g., *chung erh-ch'ien shih* (full 2,000 bushels) in contrast to *erh-ch'ien shih* (ordinary or plain 2,000 bushels) or *chen erh-ch'ien shih* (true 2,000 bushels), and *pi erh-ch'ien shih* (equivalent to, i.e., somewhat less than, 2,000 bushels).

1531   *chūng ch'áng-ch'iū* 中長秋
HAN: **Domestic Service of the Empress,** a eunuch agency in the imperial palace, headed by a Director (*ling*). See *ch'ang-ch'iu chien, ch'ang-ch'iu ssu.* BH (*ling*): prefect of the empress's palace of prolonged autumn.

1532   *chūng ch'áng-shìh* 中常侍
HAN–N-S DIV: lit., a regular attendant in the palace: **Palace Attendant-in-ordinary.** (1) A supplementary honorific title (*chia-kuan*) granted to officials deemed especially worthy of being companions of the ruler. (2) Beginning c. A.D. 60 and continuing through most of the era of N-S Division, a title granted to 4 eunuchs in the domestic service of the Empress; in N. Ch'i members of the Palace Security Service (*chung shih-chung sheng*), which supervised all access to the inner chambers of the palace. P37.

1533   *chūng-ch'áo* 中朝
Inner Court, throughout history a variant of the more common terms *nei-ch'ao* and *nei-t'ing,* denoting imperial in-laws, palace eunuchs, and officials closely associated with the ruler, who were often thought to constitute a special interest group devoted to behind-the-scenes manipulation of the ruler to their selfish advantage, in contrast to the much larger body of officials, both in and outside the capital, who normally had very limited access to rulers and were occupied primarily with administering state affairs, referred to as the Outer Court (*wai-t'ing, wai-ch'ao*). Both groups were only vaguely definable, but factional disputes in government were

often described as struggles between the Inner and Outer Courts.

1534 *chūng-chèng* 中正

N-S DIV: lit., one who hits the mark and sets things right (?): **Rectifier,** from A.D. 220 local dignitaries appointed in each Region (*chou*), Commandery (*chün*), and District (*hsien*) to register and classify all males in their jurisdictions who were considered eligible for government office on the basis of their hereditary social status, assigning them to 9 ranks (*chiu p'in,* q.v.) theoretically reflecting their meritoriousness. Rectifiers were themselves often classified into grades as Senior Rectifiers (*ta chung-cheng*) and Junior Rectifiers (*hsiao chung-cheng*), and sometimes at the Regional level were called *chou-tu* (Regional Rectifier). Status ranks assigned by Rectifiers were the basis for civil service recruitment through most of the era of N-S Division, and the system had echoes in even later times. See *ch'ing, cho, ch'ing-wang, han-jen.* P53, 54.

1535 *chūng-chèng pǎng* 中正榜

CH'ING: **List of Expectant Appointees,** from 1761 refers to passers of the highest civil service recruitment examinations in relatively low status; normally 60, were appointed Secretaries (*chung-shu*) in the Grand Secretariat (*nei-ko*) or were presented to the Ministry of Personnel (*lì-pu*) for appointments as Instructors (*hsüeh-cheng, hsüeh-lu*) in the Directorate of Education (*kuo-tzu chien*) when vacancies occurred. P24.

1536 *chūng-chèng yüàn* 中政院

YÜAN: **Household Service for the Empress,** an enormous establishment with its own military and revenue-collecting agencies, headed by a Commissioner (*shih*) who must normally have been a Mongol noble; rank not specified.

1537 *chūng-ch'éng* 中丞

Abbreviated reference to *yü-shih chung-ch'eng* (**Palace Aide to the Censor-in-chief, Vice Censor-in-chief**).

1538 *chūng ch'éng-hsiàng* 中丞相

CH'IN: **Eunuch Counselor-in-chief,** a term used for the highest-ranking post in the officialdom (see *ch'eng-hsiang*) when it was held by a eunuch.

1539 *chūng chǐ-shìh* 中給事

N-S DIV (N. Wei): **Supervising Secretary,** rank 3b2; in 499 changed to traditional name *chi-shih-chung,* q.v. P18, 19.

1540 *chūng chǐ-shìh-chūng* 中給事中

(1) HAN–SUI: **Palace Attendant,** a eunuch title: in N. Ch'i, 4 were members of the Palace Security Service (*chung shih-chung sheng*); c. 605 renamed *nei ch'eng-chih,* q.v. (2) N-S DIV (N. Wei): **Senior Supervising Secretary,** changed from *chi-shih-chung chi-shih* in 499; functions and relations with major agencies of the central government not clear; rank 5b.

1541 *chūng-chiàng* 中將

HAN: **Center Leader** of a group of Court Gentlemen (*lang*), distinguished from a Left Leader (*tso-chiang*) and a Right Leader (*yu-chiang*). See *ch'e-lang chung-chiang.*

1542 *chūng-chièn* 中諫

T'ANG: unofficial reference to a **Rectifier of Omissions** (*pu-ch'üeh*).

1543 *chūng-chǐh* 中旨

Palace Edict: throughout history, referred to an imperial pronouncement of any sort that was initiated by the Emperor or his domestic agents rather than being a response from the Emperor to a proposal submitted by appropriate members of the officialdom; generally considered irregular and perhaps dangerous by the officialdom because from early Han it was state doctrine that Emperors would not initiate government action but instead would approve or disapprove proposals submitted by the officialdom, or choose among competing proposals; and because in the case of young or otherwise weak Emperors the officialdom commonly suspected that Palace Edicts were influenced by or issued directly from favored eunuchs or palace women for their own selfish purposes.

1544 *chūng chíh-fǎ* 中執法

HAN–N-S DIV (San-kuo): lit., one who maintains the law within the palace: an unofficial reference to the **Palace Aide to the Censor-in-chief** (*yü-shih chung-ch'eng*). P18.

1545 *chūng-ch'īng* 中卿

CHOU: **Ordinary Minister,** 2nd highest of 3 ranks among which Ministers (*ch'ing*) seem sometimes to have been distributed; see *shang-ch'ing, hsia-ch'ing.* Ministers were the highest category of officials serving the King (*wang*) and Feudal Lords (*chu-hou*), ranking above Grand Masters (*ta-fu*) and Servicemen (*shih*).

1546 *chūng chǔn-lìng* 中準令

HAN: **Eunuch Director of Standards,** in A.D. 175 replaced the Bureau of Standards (*p'ing-chun*) in control of the state's price-equalization system; at least nominally subordinate to the Chamberlain for the Palace Revenues (*shao-fu*). HB: palace prefect of standards.

1547 *chūng-chǔ* 中舉

MING–CH'ING: lit., to "hit the mark" in a civil service recruitment examination, meaning to pass the provincial examination (*hsiang-shih*) and become a **Provincial Graduate** (*chü-jen*).

1548 *chūng-ch'üán* 中銓

(1) T'ANG: **Vice Ministerial Selections,** a reference to the personnel evaluations supervised by the Vice Ministers of Personnel (*lì-pu shih-lang*) as distinguished from those supervised by the Minister of Personnel (*lì-pu shang-shu*), which were called *shang-shu ch'üan.* See *hsi-ch'üan, tung-ch'üan.* Cf. *chung-hsüan.* (2) T'ANG–CH'ING: unofficial reference to a **Vice Minister of Personnel.**

1549 *chūng-ch'üēh* 中缺

CH'ING: **Ordinary,** 3rd highest of 4 terms used in the classification of all units of territorial administration from Circuits (*tao*) down to Districts (*hsien*), reflecting the importance and complexity of the business transacted locally.

1550 *chūng-chūn* 中軍

(1) **Middle Army,** one of 8 special capital-defense forces organized at the end of Han; see *pa hsiao-wei* (Eight Commandants). (2) N-S DIV: **Capital Army** or **Army of the Center,** designation of a principal military force. (3) N-S DIV (N. Ch'i): **Adjutant,** one of Three Adjutants (*san chün*) assigned to a Princedom (*wang-kuo*); see *shang-chün, hsia-chün.* P69.(4) CH'ING: **Adjutant,** chief administrative officer on the staff of a field commander, or head of the Office of Military Affairs (*ying-wu ch'u*) under a Provincial Governor (*hsün-fu*) or Governor-general (*tsung-tu*), in the latter cases normally with the status of Vice General (*fu-chiang*), rank 2b. BH: adjutant.

1551 *chūng èrh-ch'iēn shíh* 中二千石

HAN–N-S DIV: **Full 2,000 Bushels,** in Han a designation of rank carrying a monthly stipend of 180 pecks (*hu*) of grain, compared to 120 pecks due to someone of ordinary

2,000 bushel rank (*erh-ch'ien shih*); in the era of N-S Division, also a general term for officials of ranks 2 and 3. See *chung* (4). HB: official ranking fully 2,000 *shih*. P60, 68.

1552 *chūng-fèng tà-fū* 中奉大夫
SUNG–MING: **Grand Master for Palace Attendance**, prestige title (*san-kuan*) for civil officials holding ranks 4a2 or 5b in Sung, 3b2 in Chin, 2b in Yüan and Ming P30, 68.

1553 *chūng-fù* 中傅
Palace Mentor, a title sometimes granted to esteemed eunuchs.

1554 *chūng-hàn* 中翰
MING–CH'ING: lit., palace penman: unofficial reference to secretarial personnel working in the Grand Secretariat (*nei-ko*), especially Secretaries (*chung-shu*) of the Grand Secretariat.

1555 *chūng-háng* 中行
T'ANG–SUNG: **Middle Echelon** of Ministries (*pu*) in the Department of State Affairs (*shang-shu sheng*), a general reference to the Ministries of Revenue (*hu-pu*) and Justice (*hsing-pu*), denoting their lesser prestige than the Ministries of the Front Echelon (*ch'ien-hang*), those of Personnel (*li-pu*) and War (*ping-pu*).

1556 *chūng-háng láng-chūng* 中行郎中
Middle Echelon Director. (1) T'ANG–SUNG: unspecific reference to a Director (*lang-chung*) of a Bureau (*ssu*) in either the Ministry of Revenue (*hu-pu*) or the Ministry of Justice (*hsing-pu*). (2) SUNG: variant reference to the prestige title (*san-kuan*) Grand Master for Closing Court (*ch'ao-san ta-fu*), granted to civil officials of ranks 5b1 and 6b.

1557 *chūng-háng yüán-wài láng* 中行員外郎
Middle Echelon Vice Director. (1) T'ANG–SUNG: unspecific reference to a Vice Director (*yüan-wai lang*) of a Bureau (*ssu*) in either the Ministry of Revenue (*hu-pu*) or the Ministry of Justice (*hsing-pu*). (2) SUNG: variant reference to the prestige title (*san-kuan*) Gentlemen for Closing Court (*ch'ao-san lang*), granted to civil officials of ranks 7b1 and 7a.

1558 *chūng-hòu* 中候
Watch Officer. (1) HAN: one Left and one Right on the staff of the Chamberlain for the Palace Buildings (*chiang-tso shao-fu*, *chiang-tso ta-chiang*); discontinued in 22 B.C. HB: captain of the central region. (2) From antiquity into Sung times if not later, a duty assignment for a military officer, to supervise the guarding of a central headquarters; in T'ang from 691 each Guard (*wei*) unit normally had 3 titular officers of this sort, rank 7b, the status being considered one among the Officers of the Four Categories (*ssu-se kuan*, q.v.). RR+SP: *officier de guet*. P14, 26.

1559 *chūng-hsiào* 中校
(1) HAN–SUNG: variant designation of the **Construction Office of the Center** (*chung hsiao-shu*; see *hsiao-shu*). (2) CH'ING: **Ordinary Lieutenant**, one category of military officers collectively called *hsiao* (Lieutenants), q.v.

1560 *chūng-hsièn tà-fū* 中憲大夫
CHIN–CH'ING: **Grand Master Exemplar**, prestige title (*san-kuan*) granted to civil officials of rank 5a2 in Chin, 4a thereafter. P68.

1561 *chūng-hsíng-p'íng-pó* 中行平博
MING–CH'ING: a collective abbreviated reference to Drafters (*chung-shu she-jen*), Messengers (*hsing-jen*), Case

Reviewers (*p'ing-shih*) of the Court of Judicial Review (*ta-li ssu*), and Erudites (*po-shih*) of the Court of Imperial Sacrifices (*t'ai-ch'ang ssu*), posts to which new Metropolitan Graduates (*chin-shih*) were commonly appointed. P5.

1562 *chūng-hsüän* 中選
T'ANG: **Central Appointer**, a reference to the Minister of War (*ping-pu shang-shu*) in terms of his role in personnel evaluations, as distinguished from Vice Ministers of War (*ping-pu shih-lang*), who were called *tung-hsüan* and *hsi-hsüan*. Cf. *chung-ch'üan*.

1563 *chūng-hù* 中護
T'ANG: from 662 to 670 the official redesignation of **Mentors** (*shu-tzu*) who headed the Secretariats of the Heir Apparent (see *ch'un-fang*). May be encountered in later periods as an unofficial reference to such Mentors. P26.

1564 *chūng hù-chūn* 中護軍
(1) HAN: **Army Supervisor**, apparently a court dignitary assigned to assist a General-in-chief (*ta chiang-chün*) during a campaign; in use from A.D. 25. HB: commissioner over the army of the centre. (2) N-S DIV (San-kuo Wei–Chin): **Capital Protector**, commander of one of 2 major military forces normally garrisoned around the dynastic capital; in contrast to the Capital Commandant (*chung ling-chün*), headed a force that was less a capital guard than an army held in readiness for campaigning if necessary. (3) T'ANG: **Palace Protector**, 2nd highest eunuch post in the Armies of Inspired Strategy (*shen-ts'e chün*) from the late 700s; subordinate to a Palace Commandant-protector (*hu-chün chung-wei*). RR: *protecteur d'armée*. P43. (4) SUNG: **Central Defense Army**, one of the Four Field Defense Armies (*hsing-ying ssu hu-chün*) that from 1131 comprised the S. Sung standing army under control of the Bureau of Military Affairs (*shu-mi yüan*); this was directly subordinated to the Palace Command (*tien-ch'ien ssu*) and was considered the mainstay of military defense around the capital at Hangchow. See *hu-chün*.

1565 *chūng huáng-mén* 中黃門
HAN: **Palace Attendant**, eunuch subordinates of the Chamberlain for the Palace Revenues (*shao-fu*); rank variable from =400 to =100 bushels. See *huang-men*. HB: palace attendant of (within) the yellow gates. P37.

1566 *chūng-huáng tsàng-fǔ* 中黃藏府 or
chung-huang tsang
HAN–N-S DIV (Chin): **Palace Storehouse**, headed by a Director (*ling*), in Later Han (created A.D. 147) rank 600 bushels; stored imperial valuables of all kinds under supervision of the Palace Treasurer (*shou-kung ling*) or the Chamberlain for the Palace Revenues (*shao-fu*); in Chin supervised by the Chamberlain for the Palace Revenues (then archaically called *hsia-ch'ing*). Often abbreviated to *chung-tsang fu*. In Chin grouped with Left and Right Storehouses (*tso-*, *yu-tsang*), constituting what was commonly called the Palace Treasury (*nei-fu*). HB: palace storehouse. P7, 37.

1567 *chūng-í* 中儀
T'ANG: lit., middle-size ritualist: unofficial reference to a **Vice Director** (*yüan-wai lang*) of the Headquarters Bureau (*li-pu*) in the Ministry of Rites (also *li-pu*). See *hsiao-i*, *shao-i*.

1568 *chūng-ì* 中議
YÜAN: **Counselor**, 2, rank not clear but considered Staff Supervisors (*shou-ling kuan*, q.v.), in the Household Administration of the Heir Apparent (*chan-shih yüan*). Perhaps equivalent to *ssu-i* (Counselor). P26.

1569 *chūng-ì tà-fū* 中議大夫
CHIN–CH'ING: **Grand Master for Palace Counsel,** a prestige title (*san-kuan*) for civil officials of rank 5a1 in Chin, 4a in Yüan and Ming, 3b in Ch'ing. P68.

1570 *chǔng-jén* 冢人
CHOU: **Grave Maker,** 2 ranked as Junior Grand Masters (*hsia ta-fu*), members of the Ministry of Rites (*ch'un-kuan*) responsible for preparing tombs for royal Princes resident in the capital, other dignitaries of the court, and Feudal Lords (*chu-hou*); also supervised funerals at such tombs, and in some sacrificial ceremonies there played the role of the dead recipient of the offerings. Cf. *chih-sang* (Funeral Director), *mu ta-fu* (Grand Master of Cemeteries). CL: *officier des sépultures.*

1571 *chūng-kēng* 中更
CH'IN–HAN: lit., a member of the 2nd (middle) watch: **Grandee of the Thirteenth Order,** the 8th highest of 20 titles of nobility (*chüeh*) awarded to deserving subjects. P65.

1572 *chūng-kǔ ssū* 鐘鼓司
MING: **Bells and Drums Office,** a minor agency of palace eunuchs, headed by a eunuch Director (*cheng, t'ai-chien*); provided musical signals at court audiences and accompaniment for intimate palace entertainments; see *ssu ssu* (Four Offices).

1573 *chūng-kǔ yüàn* 鐘鼓院
SUNG: **Bureau of Bells and Drums,** subordinate to or otherwise related to the Astrological Service (*t'ai-shih chü*); in charge of the bell and drum tower of the Hall of Civil Virtues (*wen-te tien*), which housed timekeeping mechanisms including a clepsydra. SP: *cour de clochettes et de tambours.* P35.

1574 *chūng-kuān* 中官
(1) Throughout history, one of many generic terms for **eunuch.** (2) T'ANG–CH'ING: **Mid-year Office,** one of 5 seasonal Offices of calendrical specialists in the T'ang Astrological Service (*t'ai-shih chü*) and later Bureau of Astronomy (*ssu-t'ien t'ai*), the Sung Astrological Service, the Sung–Ming Directorate of Astronomy (*ssu-t'ien chien*), and the Ming–Ch'ing Directorate of Astronomy (*ch'in-t'ien chien*); headed by a Director (*ling* in early T'ang, otherwise *cheng*), rank 5a in T'ang, 8a in Sung, 6b in Ming and Ch'ing; in Ch'ing one Manchu and one Chinese appointee. RR+SP: *administration du centre.* BH (*cheng*): astronomer for the mid-year. P35.

1575 *chūng-kuān lìng* 鐘官令
HAN: **Director of Minters,** in charge of the imperial household's coinage work, assisted by a Vice Director (*ch'eng*); subordinate first to the Chamberlain for the Palace Revenues (*shao-fu*), then from 115 B.C. to the Commandant of the Imperial Gardens (*shui-heng tu-wei*); in Later Han subordinate to the Chamberlain for the National Treasury (*ta ssu-nung*). HB: prefect of the office of coinage. P16.

1576 *chūng-kūng* 中宮
From Han on, a common unofficial reference to the residence, hence indirectly to the person, of the **Empress** (*huang-hou*).

1577 *chūng-kūng p'ú* 中宮僕
HAN: **Coachman of the Empress,** rank 1,000 bushels; replaced the Former Han Director of the Stables (*chiu-ling*). HB: coachman of the empress.

1578 *chūng-kūng shǔ* 中宮署
HAN: **Administrative Office of the Empress,** a Later Han

eunuch agency headed by a Director (*ling*), rank 600 bushels; his staff included an Aide (*ch'eng*) and an Aide for the Palace Walkways (*fu-tao ch'eng*). HB (*ling*): prefect recorder of the empress.

1579 *chūng-kūng yèh-chě* 中宮謁者
HAN: **Receptionist in the Empress's Palace,** 2 eunuch appointees in the Palace Domestic Service (*i-t'ing, ch'ang-ch'iu chien*); in Later Han, 3 eunuch appointees, rank 400 bushels, headed by a Director (*ling*), rank 600 bushels. HB: internuncios of the empress.

1580 *chūng-láng* 中郎
(1) CH'IN–HAN: **Inner Gentleman:** in Ch'in one of 3 categories to which expectant officials serving as courtiers were assigned, collectively called the Three Court Gentlemen (*san lang*); functional differentiations among the categories are not clear. In Han, the highest status accorded expectant officials serving as courtiers, rank =600 bushels. See under *lang.* HB: gentleman-of-the-household. (2) N-S DIV: **Palace Attendant** on the household staff of the Heir Apparent or a Prince. (3) SUNG: **Adjutant,** a civil or military official, rank 6a to 9a, found in various military headquarters, presumably as an administrative aide to the senior military officer(s). SP: *secrétaire-adjoint.* P5, 29, 69.

1581 *chūng-láng chiàng* 中郎將
(1) HAN–N-S DIV: **Leader of Court Gentlemen,** generic designation of the officials, rank =2,000 bushels, placed in charge of the Three Corps (*san shu*) of expectant officials in the imperial entourage who were collectively called Gentlemen (*lang*); differentiated by the prefixes *tso* (of the Left), *yu* (of the Right), and *wu-kuan* (for Miscellaneous Use). HB: general of the gentlemen-of-the-household. (2) T'ANG–SUNG: **Commandant,** one, rank 4b, in charge of each of the Five Garrisons (*wu fu*) that constituted the hereditary military elite corps of the Twelve Armies (*shih-erh chün*) or, after 636, the Sixteen Guards (*shih-liu wei*) at the capital. RR+SP: *colonel.* P5, 17, 26.

1582 *chūng-lěi lìng* 中壘令
HAN: **Director of the Capital Garrison,** a subordinate of the Chamberlain for the Imperial Insignia (*chung-wei*), assisted by a Vice Director (*ch'eng*) and associated with Commandants (*wei, hsiao-wei*) of the Capital Garrison. All these officials were in the command structure of the Northern Army (*pei-chün*) at the capital. HB: prefect of the capital rampart.

1583 *chūng-liàng láng* 中亮郎
SUNG: **Court Gentleman for Forthrightness,** a prestige title (*san-kuan*) for civil officials of rank 7b; also a variant reference to the Vice Commissioner of the Visitors Bureau (*k'o-sheng fu-shih*) in the Secretariat (*chung-shu sheng*).

1584 *chūng-liàng tà-fū* 中亮大夫
SUNG: **Grand Master of Forthrightness,** a prestige title (*san-kuan*) for civil officials of rank 5b; also a variant reference to the Commissioner of the Visitors Bureau (*k'o-sheng shih*) in the Secretariat (*chung-shu sheng*), or to the eunuch Congratulatory Commissioner (*hsüan-ch'ing shih*) in the Palace Domestic Service (*nei-shih sheng*).

1585 *chūng lǐng-chün* 中領軍
N-S DIV: **Capital Commandant,** commander of one of 2 major military forces normally garrisoned in and around the dynastic capital; his force was the principal guardian of the capital, whereas the 2nd force, under the command of the Capital Protector (*chung hu-chün*), was an army held in readiness for campaigning if necessary.

1586 *chūng lù-shìh ts'ān-chūn* 中錄事參軍
N-S DIV: **Adjutant for Household Records** in the establishments of the Heir Apparent and other Princes. P69.

1587 *chūng-lü láng* 鐘律郎
N-S DIV: **Court Gentleman for Bells and Pipes**, rank, organizational affiliation, and function not clear, but presumably had some involvement with formal court music.

1588 *chūng-pīng ts'áo* 中兵曹 or *chung-ping*
N-S DIV: **Section for Inner Troops**, normally one Left and one Right, units in the developing Ministry of War (*wu-ping ts'ao*, etc.) in the Department of State Affairs (*shang-shu sheng*); headed by a Director (*lang, lang-chung*), rank 6a2 in N. Wei. P12, 69.

1589 *chūng-sàn* 中散
N-S DIV (N. Wei): lit., unattached at court (?), apparently the Chinese translation of an alien term: **Courtier**, rank 5b, an aristocratic status normally awarded to sons of meritorious fathers, with functions much like those of the Han dynasty's Court Gentlemen (*lang*). From such status a man could be assigned to high office in the regular administration, central or regional, and even granted a title of nobility (*chüeh*). Eventually, Courtier status could be attained by promotion from status as a Student of the National University (*chung-shu hsüeh-sheng*) and was sometimes awarded even to Chinese commoners, especially those with specialized skills as physicians, diviners, astrologers, ritualists, etc. All Courtiers not on special duty assignments constituted an imperial bodyguard (*san-lang wei-shih*) commanded by a Corps Leader (*ch'uang-chiang*). While in Courtier status, a man could be assigned special tasks such as Courtier-attendant (*shih-yü chung-san;* unlike other Courtiers, rank 5a), Courtier for Memorials (*tsou-shih chung-san*), and Courtier-secretary (*chu-wen chung-san*); or he could be dispatched on special missions to investigate conditions in units of territorial administration up to Regions (*chou*) and Defense Commands (*chen*). Attendants in the households of Princes were also commonly awarded Courtier status. Meritorious Courtiers were apparently normally promoted from their rank 5 status to posts as Directors of Courtiers (*chung-san ling*), rank 4b, and thence to posts as Palace Stewards (*chi-shih-chung*), 3a. The term *chung-san* may be found, confusingly in reference to N. Wei times, as an abbreviation of *chung-san ta-fu* (Grand Master of Palace Leisure?), but the 2 titles were not interchangeable. Cf. *san-kuan* (prestige title).

1590 *chūng-sàn lìng* 中散令
N-S DIV (N. Wei): **Director of Courtiers**, several, rank 4b; functions not clear, but a stepping-stone from rank 5 status as a Courtier (*chung-san*) toward that of Palace Steward (*chi-shih-chung*), 3a.

1591 *chūng-sàn tà-fū* 中散大夫
HAN–YÜAN: **Grand Master of Palace Leisure** (?), initiated late in Former Han as a subordinate of the Chamberlain for Attendants (*lang-chung ling, kuang-lu-hsün*), thereafter carried a salary of 600 bushels; rank (*pan*) 10 in the era of N-S Division (Liang). From T'ang on, a prestige title (*san-kuan*) for civil officials of rank 5a or 5b. HB: palace attendant grandee. P68.

1592 *chūng-shàng* 中尚
SUNG: **Central Service Office** (?) in the Directorate for Imperial Manufactories (*shao-fu chien*); staff and functions not clear, but cf. *chung shang-fang shu*. SP: *office de l'atelier impérial du centre.*

1593 *chūng-shàng chiēn* 中尚監
YÜAN: **Directorate for Felt Manufactures,** a rank 3a agency responsible for providing felt goods of all sorts, including carpets, for the imperial household; staffing and organizational affiliation not clear. P38.

1594 *chūng shàng-fāng shǔ* 中尚方署
T'ANG: **Central Service Office** in the Directorate for Imperial Manufactories (*shao-fu chien*); established at the beginning of the dynasty in lieu of the Han–Sui *shang-fang, shang-fang ling, nei shang-fang shu;* then c. 680 renamed *chung-shang shu*. See separate entries. P38.

1595 *chūng shàng-shíh* 中尚食
N-S DIV (N. Wei): **Palace Provisioner,** number not clear, subordinates in the Department of Scholarly Counselors (*chi-shu sheng*) who were responsible for keeping the imperial palace supplied with food and drink. P30, 37.

1596 *chūng shàng-shū* 中尚書
HAN: lit., eunuch imperial secretary, a variant of *chung-shu* (**Palace Secretary**). Cf. *shang-shu* (Imperial Secretary). HB: palace master of writing.

1597 *chūng-shàng shǔ* 中尚署
T'ANG: **Central Service Office** in the Directorate for Imperial Manufactories (*shao-fu chien*), responsible for providing precious wares for ritual and ordinary palace use, clothing for the palace women, etc.; headed by a Director (*ling*), rank 7b2. Initiated c. 680 by renaming the earlier *shang-fang shu*. Also see *tso-shang shu, yu-shang shu*. RR: *office de l'atelier impérial du centre.* P38.

1598 *chūng-shè* 中舍
A common abbreviated reference to *chung-shu she-jen* (**Secretariat Drafter**).

1599 *chūng shè-jén* 中舍人
Secretary, a title more esteemed than *she-jen* alone, comparable to *nei she-jen*, both *chung* and *nei* suggestive of palace posts; commonly prefixed with *t'ai-tzu* (Heir Apparent). (1) N-S DIV (Chin)–T'ANG: irregularly, the 2nd-level executive post in the Secretariat of the Heir Apparent (*men-hsia fang*), aide to its head, the Mentor (*shu-tzu*); commonly 4, rank 600 bushels or rank 5; in 627 superseded by *chung-yün* (Companion). (2) T'ANG–LIAO: 2nd-level executive post in the Archive of the Heir Apparent (*tien-shu fang*), in 662–670 and again from 711 (707?) on called Right Secretariat of the Heir Apparent (*yu ch'un-fang*); in T'ang 2, rank 5a2; in Sung one, 7b. RR+SP: *vice-président du grand secrétariat de l'héritier du trône,* (SP only) *sous-secrétaire de ….* P26.

1600 *chūng-shǐh* 中使
Throughout history, a reference to anyone specially dispatched as a representative of the Emperor: **Imperial Commissioner.**

1601 *chūng-shìh* 中士
CHOU, N-S DIV (Chou): **Ordinary Serviceman,** next to lowest of the 7 (or 9) ranks into which all officials were classified, outranking only Junior Serviceman (*hsia-shih*); the rank indicator is normally a suffix appended to the functional title. In Northern Chou, equivalent to rank 8a. See *shih*. CL: *gradué du deuxième classe.*

1602 *chūng-shīh* 鐘師
CHOU: **Master of the Bells,** 4 ranked as Ordinary Servicemen (*chung-shih*) and 8 as Junior Servicemen (*hsia-shih*), subordinate to the Musicians-in-chief (*ta ssu-yüeh*) in the Ministry of Rites (*ch'un-kuan*). CL: *maître des cloches.*

1603 *chūng shìh-chūng* 中侍中
N-S DIV (N. Ch'i): **Palace Superintendent,** 2 eunuchs, heads of the Palace Security Service (*chung shih-chung sheng*), which controlled access to the inner chambers of the imperial palace. See *chung ssu-chung*. P37.

1604 *chūng shìh-chūng shěng* 中侍中省
N-S DIV (N. Ch'i): **Palace Security Service,** a eunuch agency that controlled access to the inner chambers of imperial palace, headed by 2 Palace Superintendents (*chung shih-chung*). Also see *chung ch'ang-shih, chung chi-shih-chung*. P37.

1605 *chūng-shǐh chǔ* 中使局
CHIN: **Supervisory Service** in the household of the Heir Apparent, in charge of all attendants; headed by a Director-in-chief (*tu-chien*). P26.

1606 *chūng-shū* 中書
(1) HAN: **Palace Secretary,** a eunuch post created late in the reign of Emperor Wu (r. 141–87 B.C.), perhaps with the famous historian Ssu-ma Ch'ien as the first appointee after his castration; such eunuchs took over the document-processing functions of Imperial Secretaries (*shang-shu*) until 29 B.C., when the eunuch appointments were apparently discontinued. Also called *chung shang-shu*. HB: palace writer. (2) HAN–MING: abbreviated reference to the **Secretariat** (*chung-shu sheng*) or, in Sung, the **Secretariat-Chancellery** (*chung-shu men-hsia*). (3) CH'ING: **Secretary,** 124, rank 7b, serving as clerical workers in the Grand Secretariat (*nei-ko*). Cf. *chung-shu she-jen*. P2.

1607 *chūng-shǔ* 中署
N-S DIV (Sung): **Central Office** in the Right Directorate for Imperial Manufactories (*yu shang-fang*), subordinate to the Chamberlain for the Palace Revenues (*shao-fu*); created in 464–465 by renaming *yü-fu* (Palace Wardrobe); apparently a eunuch agency headed by a Director (*ling*); specific functions not clear. P37.

1608 *chūng-shū chiēn* 中書監
N-S DIV: **Secretariat Supervisor,** recurringly the joint head of the Secretariat (*chung-shu sheng*) together with the Secretariat Director (*chung-shu ling*), thus the highest-ranking official in the most influential policy-formulating agency in the central government. P2, 23, 67.

1609 *chūng-shū chiěn-chèng* 中書檢正
SUNG: **Secretariat Examiner,** a variant of *chien-cheng kuan* (Examiner), q.v.

1610 *chūng-shū fáng* 中書房
MING: **Palace Secretariat,** from the 1430s or 1440s manned by palace eunuchs who handled the Emperor's paperwork as confidential secretaries. Also called *wen-shu fang*.

1611 *chūng-shū fǔ* 中書府
N-S DIV: common variant form of *chung-shu sheng* (**Secretariat**).

1612 *chūng-shū hòu-shěng* 中書後省
SUNG: **Secretariat Rear Section,** staffed with a Policy Adviser (*san-ch'i ch'ang-shih*), a Grand Master of Remonstrance (*chien-i ta-fu*), a Remonstrator (*ssu-chien*), and an Exhorter (*cheng-yen*), all prefixed Right; also 6 Drafters (*chung-shu she-jen*), and an Imperial Diarist (*ch'i-chü she-jen*); created c. 1080 as a special branch of the Secretariat (*chung-shu sheng*) charged with remonstrance functions; apparently abolished c. 1129. See *men-hsia hou-sheng*. SP: *grand secrétariat arrière*.

1613 *chūng-shū hsíng-shěng* 中書行省
See *hsing chung-shu sheng*.

1614 *chūng-shū hsüéh* 中書學
N-S DIV (N. Wei): variant reference to the **National University** (*kuo-tzu hsüeh*). P34.

1615 *chūng-shū k'ō* 中書科
MING–CH'ING: **Central Drafting Office,** responsible for drafting proclamations, staffed by an unspecified number of Drafters (*chung-shu she-jen*), rank 7b; originally subordinate to the Secretariat (*chung-shu sheng*), after 1380 autonomous but closely associated with the emerging Grand Secretariat (*nei-ko*); in Ch'ing headed by an Academician (*hsüeh-shih*) of the Grand Secretariat, rank 2b, commissioned as Grand Minister Inspector of the Central Drafting Office (*chi-ch'a chung-shu k'o shih-wu ta-ch'en*). BH: imperial patent office. P2.

1616 *chūng-shū lìng* 中書令
N-S DIV–YÜAN: **Secretariat Director:** promptly upon the fall of Han, became head of the former Palace Secretaries (*chung-shu*) in the Secretariat (*chung-shu sheng*), which evolved during the era of N-S Division into the most influential policy-formulating agency in the government; sometimes shared control with a Secretariat Supervisor (*chung-shu chien*); often bore the honorific status of Counselor-in-chief (*ch'eng-hsiang*); commonly ranked 2a. In T'ang rank 3a to 767, then 2a; as a Grand Councilor (*tsai-hsiang*) consulted regularly with the Emperor and participated in major governmental decisions; in Sung attained rank 1a. In Yüan the post was largely nominal, reserved for the Heir Apparent; not established in the early Ming Secretariat. RR: *président du grand secrétariat impérial*. SP: *secrétaire général du département du grand secrétariat impérial*. P2, 3, 4, 25, 32.

1617 *chūng-shū mén-hsià* 中書門下
T'ANG–SUNG: **Secretariat-Chancellery,** developed in the early 700s as a combination of the previously separate Secretariat (*chung-shu sheng*) and Chancellery (*men-hsia sheng*), in recognition of the fact that these two major agencies in the top echelon of the central government had long been virtually indistinguishable by their functions; replaced the Administration Chamber (*cheng-shih t'ang*) as the locus of Grand Councilors (*tsai-hsiang*); served by staff agencies generally comparable to the Six Ministries (*liu pu*) of the Department of State Affairs (*shang-shu sheng*), called Offices (*fang*): a Personnel Office (*li-fang*), a Central Control Office (*shu-chi fang*), a War Office (*ping-fang*), a Revenue Office (*hu-fang*), and a combined Justice and Rites Office (*hsing-li fang*). Sung perpetuated this late T'ang organization but with 6 subordinate administrative Offices: a Personnel Office, a Revenue Office, a Rites Office (*li-fang*), a War Office, a Justice Office (*hsing-fang*), and a Works Office (*kung-fang*). Together with the Bureau of Military Affairs (*shu-mi yüan*), known as the Two Administrations (*liang-fu*) that dominated the central administration. Nominally headed jointly by Vice Directors (*shih-lang*) of the Secretariat and Chancellery, who normally served principally as Grand Councilors, having cumbersome titles such as Vice Director of the Department of State Affairs Jointly Manager of Affairs with the Secretariat-Chancellery (*shang-shu p'u-yeh t'ung chung-shu men-hsia p'ing-chang shih*). See *men-hsia chung-shu shih-lang*. RR: *(la grande salle) du grand secrétariat impérial et de la chancellerie impériale*.

1618 *chūng-shū shè-jén* 中書舍人
N-S DIV–CH'ING: **Drafter** in the Secretariat (*chung-shu*

sheng) or **Secretariat Drafter**, principally a handler of central government documents; in the era of N-S Division their number was highly variable, and at times they were functioning heads of the Secretariat; in T'ang 6, rank 5a; in Sung 4, 4a; in Ming and Ch'ing 20 or more, 7b, staffing the Central Drafting Office (*chung-shu k'o*) that served the Grand Secretariat (*nei-ko*). Also see *she-jen, t'ung-shih she-jen, nan-kung she-jen, nan-sheng she-jen.* RR+SP: *grand secrétaire du département du grand secrétariat impérial.*

1619   *chūng-shū shěng*   中書省
N-S DIV–MING: **Secretariat,** a top-echelon agency of the central government, nominally responsible for promulgating the ruler's orders but usually having broader policy-formulating responsibilities. Deriving from the Han corps of Palace Secretaries (*chung-shu*), it evolved during the era of N-S Division as a major executive agency with shifting relationships with the simultaneously evolving Chancellery (*men-hsia sheng*) and Department of State Affairs (*shang-shu sheng*). In Sui, called *nei-shih sheng,* it was one of Five Departments (*wu sheng*) that dominated the central government. In T'ang known as the *nei-shu sheng* till 620; into Sung the Secretariat together with the Chancellery and the Department of State Affairs were the Three Departments (*san sheng*) that were the predominant central government agencies; their senior officials were the Grand Councilors (*tsai-hsiang, ch'eng-hsiang*) who advised the ruler on all important policies. In Yüan and early Ming the Secretariat alone was the core administrative unit of the central administration till 1380, when Ming T'ai-tsu (r. 1368–1398), in what has been considered a crucial advancement of imperial autocracy, "abolished" the Secretariat and left its subordinate Six Ministries (*liu pu*) uncoordinated except by himself. The Grand Secretariat (*nei-ko*) that subsequently evolved to provide intermediary coordination is considered to have had less authority and prestige than the earlier Secretariat. Through Yüan the nominal head of the Secretariat was a Director (*ling; see chung-shu ling*), although nominal Vice Directors (*shih-lang*) were often its functioning heads. In early Ming the Secretariat was headed by 2 Grand Councilors (*ch'eng-hsiang*). Often rendered Imperial Secretariat or Central Secretariat. RR+SP: *département du grand secrétariat impérial.* P2, 3, 4.

1620   *chūng-shū shìh-láng*   中書侍郎
See *shih-lang.*

1621   *chūng shù-tzǔ*   中庶子
CH'IN–N-S DIV, YÜAN: **Palace Cadet** in the household of the Heir Apparent, commonly prefixed *t'ai-tzu:* in earliest times number not clear, commonly 4 in the era of N-S Division, one in Yüan; rank =400 (=600?) bushels in Han, rank 4 common in the era of N-S Division, not clear in Yüan; in early centuries were perhaps the leaders (or most senior) of the companions and bodyguards of the Heir Apparent who were designated Cadets (*shu-tzu*), but functions were never clearly specified. HB: palace cadet of the heir-apparent. P26.

1622   *chūng-shū wài-shěng*   中書外省
SUNG: lit., secretariat outer section: meaning not wholly clear, but apparently an alternative reference to the **Secretariat** (*chung-shu sheng*) during the period 1080–1129, when its corps of remonstrance officials was separated into a Secretariat Rear Section (*chung-shu hou-sheng*). SP: *département extérieur du secrétariat impérial.*

1623   *chūng-shùn tà-fū*   中順大夫
CHIN–MING: **Grand Master of Palace Accord,** a pres-

tige title (*san-kuan*) for civil officials of rank 5a2 in Chin, 4a in Yüan and Ming. P68.

1624   *chūng-sǒ*   中所
CH'ING: **Center Subsection,** one of 5 divisions of the Imperial Procession Guard (*luan-i wei*), headed by a Director (*chang-yin kuan-chün shih*), rank 3a. BH: third sub-department.

1625   *chūng-ssū*   中司
T'ANG: lit., palace office: unofficial reference to a **Vice Censor-in-chief** (*yü-shih chung-ch'eng*), apparently because he was originally a representative of the Censor-in-chief (*yü-shih ta-fu*) inside the imperial palace.

1626   *chūng ssù-chūng*   中寺中
Variant rendering of *chung shih-chung* (**Palace Superintendent**), q.v.

1627   *chūng tà-fū*   中大夫
(1) CHOU, N-S DIV (Chou): **Ordinary Grand Master,** the 5th (or 3rd) highest of 9 (or 7) ranks into which all officials were classified, outranked by Ministers (*ch'ing*) and Senior Grand Masters (*shang ta-fu*); the rank indicator is normally a suffix appended to a functional title. In Northern Chou, equivalent to rank 5a. CL: *préfet de deuxième classe.* (2) HAN: **Ordinary Grand Master,** the 8th highest of 10 ranks into which all officials were classified, specifically designating officials with annual stipends between 1,000 and 2,000 bushels of grain. P68. (3) HAN: **Grand Master of the Palace,** a title granted to an eminent Court Gentleman (*lang*) serving as adviser to the imperial court; in 104 B.C. upgraded to Grand Master for Splendid Happiness (*kuang-lu ta-fu*), rank =2,000 bushels; also see *t'ai chung ta-fu.* HB: palace grandee. (4) N-S DIV: **Grand Master of the Palace,** variant of *kuang-lu ta-fu* and of *yü-shih chung-ch'eng* (**Palace Aide to the Censor-in-chief**), qq.v.; also a title of lowly attendants in the households of Princes, rank 8 or 9. (5) T'ANG–MING: **Grand Master of the Palace,** a prestige title (*san-kuan*) for civil officials of rank 4b2 in T'ang, Sung, and Chin and 3b in Yüan and Ming. P68.

1628   *chūng tà-fū lìng*   中大夫令
HAN: lit., director of grand masters of the palace: from c. 156 to 143 B.C., the official variant of *wei-wei* (**Chamberlain for the Palace Garrison**). HB: prefect of the palace grandees.

1629   *chūng-t'ái*   中臺
Central Pavilion. (1) T'ANG: from 662 to 671 and again from 703 to 705, the official variant name of the Department of State Affairs (*shang-shu sheng*). RR: *tribunal du centre.* (2) Unofficial reference, varying through history, to an Imperial Secretary (*shang-shu*) in Han, the developing Department of State Affairs in the era of N-S Division, the Minister (*shang-shu*) of any Ministry (*pu*) in Ming and Ch'ing.

1630   *chūng t'ài-p'ú*   中太僕
HAN: **Chamberlain for the Palace Stables,** in charge of the carriages and horses used by the Empress and other palace women. See *t'ai-p'u.* HB: palace grand coachman. P39.

1631   *chūng-t'áng*   中堂
YÜAN: **Central Hall.** (1) YÜAN: unofficial reference to a Grand Councilor (*ch'eng-hsiang*) of the Secretariat (*chung-shu sheng*). (2) MING–CH'ING: unofficial reference to a Grand Secretary (*ta hsüeh-shih*) of the Grand Secretariat (*nei-ko*).

1632   *chǔng-tsǎi*   冢宰
Minister of State. (1) CHOU: head of the Ministry of State

(*t'ien-kuan*), the paramount organ of the central administration, ranked as a Minister (*ch'ing*); was in effect chief of staff for the ruler in all matters, establishing administrative regulations, creating offices, appointing and disciplining official personnel, promulgating laws, directing tax collections, overseeing expenditures, etc.; supervised numerous directly subordinate agencies. CL: *grand administrateur.* P5. (2) Throughout history may be encountered as an unofficial, archaic reference to a central government dignitary such as a Counselor-in-chief (*ch'eng-hsiang*) or Grand Councilor (*tsai-hsiang*), or especially in the last few dynasties a Minister of Personnel (*li-pu shang-shu*).

1633   *chūng-tsāng fŭ* 中藏府
HAN–N-S DIV (Chin): variant reference to *chung-huang tsang* (**Palace Storehouse**). P7, 37.

1634   *chūng-ts'áo* 中曹
N-S DIV (N.Wei): **Palace Ministry,** in the 470s and 480s an agency nominally under the Department of State Affairs (*shang-shu sheng*), headed by an Attendant Minister (*shih-yü shang-shu*), a post occupied by a palace eunuch favored by the Empress Dowager (*t'ai-hou*); the Ministry was probably created for him and did not survive him. In 488 he was reportedly transferred to a (specially created?) Capital Ministry (*tu-ts'ao*) as Honorific (*chia*) Chancellor of Palace Attendants (*shih-chung chi-chiu*) while retaining concurrent status as Attendant Minister of the Palace Ministry. Cf. *nan-ts'ao, pei-ts'ao, hsi-ts'ao.*

1635   *chūng tū-kuān ts'áo* 中都官曹 or *chung-tu ts'ao*
HAN: variant reference to *tu-kuan ts'ao* (**Section for General Administration**), q.v.

1636   *chūng-tùn* 中盾
HAN–N-S DIV: **Palace Patrolman** in the household of the Heir Apparent, normally prefixed with *t'ai-tzu;* rank 400 bushels in Han; headed by a Director (*chang*) subordinate to the Supervisor of the Household of the Heir Apparent (*chan-shih*); often prefixed Left or Right. Also called *chung-yün,* q.v. HB: palace patroller. P26.

1637   *chūng-wài fŭ* 中外府
N-S DIV (Chou): **Branch Department of State Affairs,** name adopted in 553 to replace *hsing-t'ai,* q.v.

1638   *chūng-wèi* 中尉
(1) HAN: variant reference to the **Chamberlain for the Imperial Insignia** (*chih chin-wu,* q.v.). HB: commandant of the capital. (2) HAN: abbreviated reference to the **Commandant-in-ordinary of the Nobles** (*chu-chüeh chung-wei;* see *chu-chüeh*). (3) HAN–N-S DIV, YÜAN: **Commandant-in-ordinary,** a military officer actively entrusted with defense and police work in a Princedom (*wang-kuo*), a Marquisate (*hou-kuo*), or another noble fief; rank 2,000 bushels in Han, 6b to 9 in N. Wei, 3a in Yüan; normally 6 appointees in Yüan. In other periods encountered as a middle-level military officer serving in many capacities, often with functions indicated in a prefix. See *san ch'ing* (Three Ministers), *hu-chün chung-wei.* P13, 32, 65, 69.

1639   *chūng yèh-chě* 中謁者
HAN–N-S DIV: **Palace Receptionist,** a category of subordinates of the Chamberlain for the Palace Revenues (*shao-fu*) who were apparently eunuchs except for a brief interval beginning in 29 B.C.; headed by a Director (*ling*) or Supervisor (*p'u-yeh*) in Han, by a Director and one or more Vice Directors (*p'u-yeh*) in N. Wei and N. Ch'i. HB: palace internuncios. P37.

1640   *chūng-yén* 中鹽
SUNG: lit., being fair with salt: **Equitable Exchange of Rice for Salt,** a system instituted by T'ai-tsung (r. 976–997) to maintain a steady flow of rice into the populous capital city. The state established an Equitable Exchange Depot (*che-chung tsang*) in Kaifeng and there paid for merchant deliveries of rice with certificates or vouchers entitling the merchants, in theory always on a basis of fair exchange, to receive prescribed amounts of state-monopolized salt and to participate in the highly profitable domestic salt distribution. It is not clear how long and how effectively the system endured, or how important it was in the state fiscal system. The system was the source of inspiration, at least indirectly, for the Ming dynasty's Equitable Exchange of Grain for Salt (*k'ai-chung*). Cf. *t'i-chü chih-chih chieh-yen ssu* (Supervisorate of Grain and Salt Exchange).

1641   *chūng-yù fŭ* 中御府
(1) HAN–N-S DIV (San-kuo, S. Dyn.): **Palace Wardrobe,** normally a group of eunuchs and palace women responsible for mending and washing clothes in the household of an enfeoffed Prince (*wang*) or Marquis (*hou*); headed by a Director (*chang*). See *yü-fu.* P69. (2) T'ANG: from 662 to 670 the official variant name of the *tien-chung sheng* (**Palace Administration**). P38.

1642   *chūng-yŭn* 中允
(1) HAN: variant form of *chung-tun* (**Palace Patrolman**). (2) T'ANG–CH'ING: **Companion** for the Heir Apparent, often prefixed Left and Right and with *t'ai-tzu;* 2nd to the Mentor (*shu-tzu*) in the Secretariat of the Heir Apparent (*ch'un-fang*); number variable, rank 5a2 in T'ang, 8a in Sung, 6a in Ming and Ch'ing. From 616 to 620 and again from 652 to 656 called *nei-yün.* RR: *vice président du grand secrétariat de l'héritier du trône.* SP: *sous-secrétaire du secrétariat de la maison de l'héritier du trône.* BH: secretary of the supervisorate of imperial instruction. P26.

1643   *ch'ūng* 充
SUI–CH'ING: lit., to fill up; a term used in the sense "to take office as …" but often signifying a quasi-regular appointment taken in addition to one's regular position.

1644   *ch'ūng* 衝
CH'ING: lit., bustling: a category used in defining the importance of agencies of local government. See *ch'ung-fan-p'i-nan.*

1645   *ch'úng-chèng tièn* 崇政殿
SUNG: **Hall for the Veneration of Governance,** apparently a subsection of the Hanlin Academy (*han-lin yüan*) staffed with Lecturers (*shuo-shu*), rank 7b, who participated in tutoring the Emperor on classical texts. P24.

1646   *ch'úng-chèng yüàn* 崇政院
5 DYN (Liang): lit., office for the veneration of governance; a variant designation of the *shu-mi yüan* (**Bureau of Military Affairs**).

1647   *ch'úng-chìh t'áng* 崇志堂
MING–CH'ING: **College for Venerating Determination,** one of the Six Colleges (*liu t'ang*) among which all students of the Directorate of Education (*kuo-tzu chien*) were distributed. P34.

1648   *ch'úng-chìn* 崇進
CHIN–YÜAN: **Lord Advanced in Veneration,** a prestige title (*san-kuan*) for civil officials of rank 1b2 in Chin, 1a in Yüan. P68.

1649   *ch'ŭng-chŭ* 寵主
An elegant reference to an **Imperial Princess** (*kung-chu,* q.v.).

1650 *ch'ūng-fán-p'í-nán* 衝繁疲難
CH'ING: lit., bustling, complex, exhausting, and difficult: categories used in defining the importance of units of territorial administration, from Circuits (*tao*) down to Districts (*hsien*). Any one, 2, or 3 terms, or all 4, ranked the unit concerned, respectively, as Simple (*chien-ch'üeh*), Ordinary (*chung-ch'üeh*), Important (*yao-ch'üeh*), or Most Important (*tsui-yao*). Ranks of officials responsible for such units varied in accordance with these gradations.

1651 *ch'ūng-fēi* 充妃
MING: **Consort of Fulfillment,** title of a high-ranking palace woman.

1652 *ch'úng-fú ssū* 崇福司
YÜAN: **Commission for the Promotion of Religion,** a relatively autonomous agency of the central government responsible for supervising Nestorian, Manichaean, and other untraditional religious communities in China; staffing not clear; reportedly directed 72 local Religious Offices (*chang-chiao ssu*) scattered about the empire.

1653 *ch'úng-hsién kuǎn* 崇賢館
T'ANG: **Institute for the Veneration of Worthies,** predecessor from 639 to 675 of the Institute for the Veneration of Literature (*ch'ung-wen kuan*); during part of this interval, reportedly provided the Heir Apparent with a kind of censorial surveillance over his staff; headed by 2 Supervisors of the Household (*chan-shih*). RR: *collège pour l'exaltation de la sagesse.* P26.

1654 *ch'úng-hsū chú* 崇虛局
N-S DIV (N. Ch'i): lit., service for venerating emptiness: **Taoist Affairs Service,** responsible for supervising sacrifices and prayers to holy mountains and rivers and for registering and monitoring the Taoist clergy; headed by a Vice Director (*ch'eng*) of the Office for the Imperial Ancestral Temple (*t'ai-miao shu*) in the Court of Imperial Sacrifices (*t'ai-ch'ang ssu*); apparently a predecessor of the Office of Taoist Worship (*ch'ung-hsüan shu*).

1655 *ch'úng-hsüán hsüéh* 崇玄學
T'ANG: lit., school for venerating the (Taoist) mysteries: **Taoist School,** one in each capital city and one in each Prefecture (*chou, fu*) ordered established in 737 or 741, those in the capitals to be staffed with Erudites (*po-shih*) and Instructors (*chu-chiao*). In 743 those in the capitals were renamed *ch'ung-hsüan kuan* (Institute of Taoist Worship), and the Erudites were retitled *hsüeh-shih* (Academicians), the Instructors *chih hsüeh-shih* (Auxiliary Academicians); at the same time Prefecture-level Taoist Schools were renamed *t'ung-tao hsüeh.* Whether or not such schools existed until the end of the dynasty is not clear. RR: *école des études taoistes.*

1656 *ch'úng-hsüán shǔ* 崇玄署
SUI–SUNG: lit., office for venerating the (Taoist) mysteries: **Office of Taoist Worship,** headed by a Director (*ling*), rank 8b in T'ang; responsible for registering and generally monitoring the activities of all Taoist monks and nuns in the capital area; subordinate to the Court for Dependencies (*hung-lu ssu*) in Sui, the Court of State Ceremonial (*hung-lu ssu*) in T'ang till 694, then the Ministry of Rites (*li-pu*) till 736, then the Court of the Imperial Clan (*tsung-cheng ssu*) till 743, then the Ministry of Personnel (*li-pu*) till between 788 and 807, when the Office was apparently subordinated to special Commissioners for Merit and Virtue (*kung-te shih*) of several sorts, except that it was reassigned to the Ministry of Personnel for the era 842–846; the Sung

organizational relationships are not clear. RR+SP: *office du culte taoiste.*

1657 *ch'ūng-huá* 充華
SUI: **Lady of Complete Loveliness,** title of one of the Nine Concubines (*chiu pin*, q.v.); rank 2a.

1658 *ch'ūng-ī* 充依
HAN: **Favored Lady,** designation of a category of imperial concubines whose rank was equivalent to 1,000 bushels. HB: compliant lady.

1659 *ch'ūng-í* 充儀
SUI–SUNG: **Lady of Complete Deportment,** designation of one of the Nine Concubines (*chiu-pin*, q.v.); rank 2a. SP: *femme d'une correction accomplie.*

1660 *ch'úng-í shïh* 崇儀使
SUNG: **Commissioner for Fostering Propriety,** an early Sung antecedent of the prestige title (*san-kuan*) Grand Master for Military Strategy (*wu-lüeh ta-fu*), awarded to rank 7a military officers. P68.

1661 *ch'úng-ì wèi* 崇掖衛
T'ANG: **Guard Honoring the Inner Apartments,** from 662 to 670 the official redesignation of the Gate Guard Command (*chien-men shuai-fu*). P26.

1662 *ch'ūng-jén* 充人
CHOU: **Fattener of Sacrificial Animals,** 2 ranked as Junior Servicemen (*hsia-shih*), members of the Ministry of Rites (*ch'un-kuan*); received animals from the Breeders of Sacrificial Animals (*mu-jen*) and tended them in the final stages of their preparation as sacrificial victims in important state ceremonies. CL: *engraisseur.*

1663 *ch'úng-jén* 冲人
Lit., a young and weak man: **This Weakling,** throughout history a term used by rulers in direct reference to themselves; equivalent to the imperial We (*chen*).

1664 *ch'ūng-jén* 舂人
CHOU: **Eunuch Huller,** 2 attached to the Ministry of Education (*ti-kuan*), in charge of preparing rice required for sacrificial ceremonies, etc.; assisted by 2 Female Hullers (*nü ch'ung-wai*) and 5 convicts. CL: *officier de battage.* P6.

1665 *ch'ūng-júng* 充容
HAN, SUI–SUNG: **Lady of Complete Countenance,** designation of one of the Nine Concubines (*chiu-pin*, q.v.); rank 2a from Sui to Sung. RR+SP: *femme d'une dignité accomplie.*

1666 *ch'úng-lù ssù* 崇祿寺
LIAO: alternate designation of the *kuang-lu ssu* (**Court of Imperial Entertainments**), changed (date not clear) to avoid a name taboo. P30, 68.

1667 *ch'úng-shèng hòu* 崇聖侯
N-S DIV (N. Dyn.): **Marquis for Venerating the Sage,** a title conferred on successive heirs directly descended from Confucius; in 485 replaced Grand Master for Venerating the Sage (*ch'ung-sheng ta-fu*), which had served since 473 at the latest; was in turn changed in 550 to Marquis for Revering the Sage (*kung-sheng hou*); while in the S. Dynasties the counterpart title was Marquis for Honoring the Sage (*feng-sheng hou*). Enjoyed such perquisites as grants of land, was responsible for conducting appropriate sacrifices and other rituals for the spirit of Confucius. P66.

1668 *ch'úng-té* 崇德
N-S DIV (N. Ch'i): **Lady of Esteemed Virtue,** designation

of an imperial concubine considered one of the Three Consorts (*san fu-jen*, q.v.), ranking just below the Empress.

1669 *ch'úng-wén chiēn* 崇文監
YÜAN: **Directorate for the Reverence of Literature,** responsible for translating Confucian texts into Mongolian; subordinate to the combined Hanlin and Historiography Academy (*han-lin hsüeh-yüan chien kuo-shih yüan*); name changed from Directorate of Literature (*i-wen chien*) in 1340.

1670 *ch'úng-wén kuān* 崇文觀 or 崇文館
N-S DIV (San-kuo Wei), T'ANG, LIAO: **Institute for the Veneration of Literature,** a group of literati who did editorial and archival work for the imperial court in San-kuo Wei and for the household of the Heir Apparent in T'ang and Liao; in T'ang and Liao staffed with an Academician (*hsüeh-shih*) and unspecified numbers of Auxiliary Academicians (*chih hsüeh-shih*), and subordinate to the Left Secretariat of the Heir Apparent (*tso ch'un-fang*). From 639 to 675 called *ch'ung-hsien kuan* (Institute for the Veneration of Worthies). RR: *collège pour l'exaltation de la littérature.* P23, 26.

1671 *ch'úng-wén yüàn* 崇文院
SUNG: **Institute for the Veneration of Literature,** a palace building housing the Three Institutes (*san kuan*, q.v.) and the Imperial Archives (*pi-ko*); in 1082 absorbed into the Palace Library (*pi-shu sheng*). SP: *cour pour l'exaltation de la littérature.* P25.

1672 *ch'ūng-yüàn* 充媛
SUI-SUNG: **Lady of Complete Beauty,** designation of one of the Nine Concubines (*chiu pin*, q.v.); rank 2a. RR: *femme d'une beauté accomplie.*

1673 *ch'úng-yüán shǔ* 崇元署
SUI: **Bureau of Receptions** in the Court for Dependencies (*hung-lu ssu*), headed by a Director (*ling*); responsible for entertaining tributary delegations. P17.

1674 *chú* 局
Service: common term for an agency or office, normally a subordinate and relatively minor one; almost always with a descriptive prefix, e.g., *chih-tsao chü* (Imperial Silk Manufactory), *shang-i chü* (Clothing Service). P28, 38.

1675 *chù* 聚
HAN: **Community,** an unofficial reference to either a Neighborhood (*t'ing*) or a Village (*li*). HB: agglomeration.

1676 *chü-ch'i* 車騎
See *ch'e-chi chiang-cnün* (General of Chariots and Cavalry).

1677 *chǔ-chiēn* 舉監
MING: **University Student-initiate,** designation of a man who, having become a Provincial Graduate (*chü-jen*) in the civil service examination recruitment sequence, had been admitted to the Directorate of Education (*kuo-tzu chien*) for advanced study in preparation for attempting the highest-level examination leading to the degree of Metropolitan Graduate (*chin-shih*). Also see *chien-sheng, kung-sheng.*

1678 *chū-chiū shìh* 雎鳩氏
CHOU: lit., master osprey, master duck—both symbols of happiness in marriage: unofficial reference to a **Minister of War** (*ssu-ma*), head of the Ministry of War (*hsia-kuan*).

1679 *chú hsiù-ts'ái* 鞠秀才
Youthful Talent, an unofficial reference in the later dynasties to any student (*hsüeh-sheng*) preparing for the lowest-level examinations in the civil service examination recruitment sequence.

1680 *chǔ-hsù àn* 舉敘案
SUNG: **Recall Section,** one of 13 Sections (*an*) directly subordinate to the executive officials of the S. Sung Ministry of Justice (*hsing-pu*), staffed with clerical suboffiials; handled documents concerning the recall to duty of officials who had completed punitive absences. SP: *service de la restauration des fonctionnaires titrés.*

1681 *chǔ-jén* 屨人
CHOU: **Footwear Provisioner,** 2 ranked as Junior Servicemen (*hsia-shih*), members of the Ministry of State (*t'ien-kuan*) in charge of the many kinds of shoes and slippers required by the ruler and his household for various ritual and other functions. CL: *cordonnier.*

1682 *chǔ-jén* 舉人
(1) N-S DIV–T'ANG: **Recommendee,** a common quasi-official designation of men chosen by local authorities for submission to the capital as nominees for appointments in the civil service or, in Sui and T'ang, for participation in civil service recruitment examinations. (2) SUNG: **Prefectural Graduate,** quasi-official designation of men certified by heads of Prefectures (*chou, fu*) to participate in civil service recruitment examinations at the dynastic capital, normally on the basis of a Prefectural Examination (*chieh-shih*); not quite yet the official designation described below. See *te-chieh, mien-chieh.* (3) YUAN–CH'ING: **Provincial Graduate,** the official designation granted a passer of a Provincial Examination (*hsiang-shih*), entitling him to proceed further in the civil service recruitment examination sequence; lit., he was "offered up," in the sense that he was also available for immediate appointment, but after early Ming no Chinese could expect this status alone to lead to an eminent career.

1683 *chù-kūng* 鉅公
Lit., grand duke, "sir big": from Han on, an unofficial reference to the **Emperor.**

1684 *chū-shè* 居攝
Lit., to occupy (the throne) as an assistant: one of the terms used throughout history in reference to anyone serving as **Regent,** normally for an underaged ruler.

1685 *chū-shìh* 居室
HAN: **Palace Prison,** headed by a Director (*ling*), subordinate to the Chamberlain for the Palace Revenues (*shao-fu*); specific uses not clear; in 104 B.C. renamed *pao-kung.* HB: the convict barracks. P37.

1686 *chū-shōu ssū* 拘收司
SUNG: **Inventory Office,** one of many agencies that served the State Finance Commission (*san ssu*) of early Sung; headed by an Administrative Assistant (*p'an-kuan*), rank 8a or 8b; established in 1001 to keep inventory records for all granaries, storehouses, etc., under the Commission's control; discontinued c. 1080. SP: *bureau d'enregistrement et de contrôle.*

1687 *chù-ssū* 句司
N-S DIV–MING: lit., office for catching (?): unofficial reference to the **Bureau of Revision** (*pi-pu*) in the Ministry of Personnel (*li-pu*), the Ministry of General Administration (*tu-ts'ao*), or from T'ang to 1390 the Ministry of Justice (*hsing-pu*).

1688 *chù-ts'áo* 劇曹
Occasional unofficial reference to the **Ministry of Works** (*kung-pu*).

1689 *chǔ-tzǔ* 舉子
MING–CH'ING: unofficial reference to a **Provincial Graduate** (*chü-jen*).

1690 *ch'ǘ* 曲
HAN: **Regiment,** a military unit comprising several Companies (*t'un*). Any special campaigning force that was led by a General (*chiang-chün*) or General-in-chief (*ta chiang-chün*) was normally divided into Divisions (*pu*), each comprising several Regiments. See *pu-ch'ü*. HB: company.

1691 *ch'ǘ-àn* 麴案
SUNG: **Yeast Section,** one of 5 Sections in the Census Bureau (*hu-pu ssu*) in the State Finance Commission (*san ssu*) of early Sung; normally headed by an Administrative Assistant (*p'an-kuan, t'ui-kuan*); monitored the provisioning of the palace with yeasts and other fermenting agents needed for the preparation of vermicelli, liquors, etc. Discontinued c. 1080, its functions probably absorbed by the Ministry of Revenue (*hu-pu*). SP: *service de la vente monopolisée de farine*.

1692 *ch'ǘ-chǎng* 渠長
T'ANG: **Irrigation Chief,** a non-official designated to regulate the flow of water through irrigation canals in a prescribed locality in the vicinity of the capital; supervised by officials of the Directorate of Waterways (*tu-shui chien*). RR: *chef de canaux*.

1693 *ch'ǜ-mǎ* 趣馬
See *tsou-ma*.

1694 *ch'ǘ-mièn ts'āng-tū* 麴麵倉督
SUI–T'ANG: **Dough Pantry Supervisor,** 2 subordinates in the Office of Grain Supplies (*tao-kuan shu*) of the Court of the Imperial Granaries (*ssu-nung ssu*); responsible for providing the palace with yeast, flour, and dough; discontinued in the period 627–649. RR: *gouverneur de grenier des levures et des farines*.

1695 *ch'ǘ-mó àn* 驅磨案
SUNG: **Internal Accounts Section,** one of 4 Sections (*an*) in the Right Bureau (*yu-t'ing*) of the Court of Judicial Review (*ta-li ssu*); staffed with clerical suboffficials whose functions are not wholly clear but who apparently monitored the use of state funds, state commodities, and documents within both the Left and Right Bureaus of the Court. SP: *service de contrôle*. P22.

1696 *ch'ǘ-shǐh kuān* 驅使官
T'ANG–SUNG: **Express Courier,** unspecified number of unranked personnel under the supervision of the Northern Command (*pei-ya*) in T'ang, assigned to the Censorate (*yü-shih t'ai*), agencies of the Department of State Affairs (*shang-shu sheng*), etc., in Sung. RR+SP: *fonctionnaire chargé de porter les ordres impériaux*.

1697 *ch'ǘ-shǐh yüàn* 驅使院
SUNG: **Express Courier Office,** a subsection of the Institute of Academicians (*hsüeh-shih yüan*); staff and functions not clear. P23.

1698 *ch'ǔ-t'ái* 曲臺
HAN–CH'ING: unofficial reference to the **Chamberlain for Ceremonials** (*t'ai-ch'ang*) or the **Court of Imperial Sacrifices** (*t'ai-ch'ang ssu*).

1699 *ch'ǔ-wù tū-chiēn* 麴物都監
LIAO: **Director-in-chief of Brewing,** head of the Imperial Brewery (*ch'ü-yüan*); rank not clear. P30

1700 *ch'ǘ-yüàn* 麴院
Imperial Brewery. (1) LIAO: a unit of the Court of Im-

perial Entertainments (*kuang-lu ssu, ch'ung-lu ssu*), apparently headed by a Director-in-chief of Brewing (*ch'ü-wu tu-chien*). (2) CHIN: a unit of the Court Ceremonial Institute (*hsüan-hui yüan*); headed by a Director-in-chief of the Brewery (*ch'ü-yüan tu-chien*). Relations with such agencies as the Imperial Winery (*chiu-fang*) and the Wine Stewards Office (*shang-yün shu*) are not clear. Also see *nei chiu-fang, shang-yin chü, liang-yün shu*. P30, 49.

1701 *chüān* 捐
MING–CH'ING: lit., to contribute: a term used in a number of contexts referring to someone who had obtained his status, rank, or even office by contributing a prescribed amount, usually of grain, to the state in a time of emergency; i.e., **... by purchase.**

1702 *chüān-kùng* 捐貢
CH'ING: **Student by Purchase,** a student (*sheng-yüan*) in a state-operated Confucian School (*ju-hsüeh*) who had obtained the status and privileges by making a contribution to the state, in a prescribed amount. See *kung-sheng*.

1703 *chüān-shū* 捐輸
CH'ING: lit., to subscribe or contribute: used in the same sense as *chüan* (**... by purchase**).

1704 *ch'üán* 權
Lit., authority; hence, "with the authority of ...." (1) N-S DIV–SUNG: **Probationary,** a prefix indicating that the office-holder was appointed before attaining appropriate rank, pending regular substantive (*chen*) appointment or confirmation. (2) SUNG: **Provisional,** a prefix used during the early Sung decades especially to indicate that the office-holder was a court official detached on commission (*ch'ai-ch'ien*) to perform the functions of the post indicated, whether his rank was higher or lower than was appropriate, and particularly when the post already had a nominal appointee. Context must be relied on to determine which of these 2 senses is appropriate in any given case.

1705 *ch'üán* 銓
SUI–CH'ING: a term signifying "evaluation," one of the principal personnel-administration responsibilities normally borne by the Ministry of Personnel (*li-pu*). Cf. the term *hsüan*, meaning "selection for appointment." See *liu-nei ch'üan, liu-wai ch'üan, shang-shu ch'üan, chung-ch'üan, tung-ch'üan*.

1706 *ch'üán-fǔ* 泉府
CHOU: **Treasurer for Market Taxes,** 4 ranked as Senior Servicemen (*shang-shih*) subordinate to the Director of Markets (*ssu-shih*) in the Ministry of Education (*ti-kuan*); charged with receiving market-tax commodities and selling them at fair prices at times of low supply, apparently also responsible for minting coins for use in trade. Cf. *pao-ch'ao, pao-ch'üan, pao-feng, pao-yüan*, and various *p'ing-chun* entries. CL: *trésorier de la monnaie*. P16.

1707 *ch'üán-hsiěh* 詮寫 or 銓寫
YÜAN: **Evaluations Clerk,** 5 unranked personnel on the staff of the Ministry of Personnel (*li-pu*). P5.

1708 *ch'üán-hsüéh ts'úng-shìh* 勸學從事
N-S DIV: **Educational Assistant,** one of several school officials on the staffs of Regional Inspectors (*tz'u-shih*). See *tien-hsüeh ts'ung-shih*. P51.

1709 *ch'üǎn-jén* 犬人
CHOU: **Master of Hounds,** 2 ranked as Junior Servicemen (*hsia-shih*), members of the Ministry of Justice (*ch'iu-kuan*) in charge of dogs used in pursuing criminals and those offered as sacrificial victims. CL: *officier du chien*.

1710 *ch'üàn-núng kūng-shìh* 勸農公事
SUNG: **Agriculture Intendant,** a concurrent title for officials in units of territorial administration who were specially charged with encouraging agricultural development. SP: *chargé des affaires de l'exhortation agricole.*

1711 *ch'üàn-núng shìh* 勸農使
T'ANG–CHIN: **Agricultural Development Commissioner,** a special delegate from the central government to stimulate agriculture in a designated area; appointed as early as 723 in T'ang; after 1006 a concurrent title for officials of Circuits (*lu*) and sometimes smaller units of territorial administration who bore similar responsibilities. SP: *commissaire à l'agriculture.*

1712 *ch'üàn-núng yüàn* 勸農掾
HAN: **Agriculture Inspector,** a duty assignment for Headquarters Clerks (*t'ing-yüan*) of Districts (*hsien*) on spring and summer tours of the jurisdiction. HB: officials for the encouragement of agriculture.

1713 *ch'üán-pù* 泉布
Lit., wealth for distribution: in Ch'ing and perhaps earlier, a common reference to copper coins or, more generally, money. See *pao-ch'üan, pao-yüan.* P16.

1714 *ch'üán-pù* 銓部
Lit., ministry of evaluations: from T'ang on, a common unofficial reference to the **Ministry of Personnel** (*li-pu*).

1715 *chüēh* 爵
Nobility: throughout history, a general term referring to the titles and ranks of the nobility, whether substantive, honorific, or posthumous, whether hereditary or not. Titles normally indicated are Prince (*wang*), Duke (*kung*), Marquis (*hou*), Earl (*po*), Viscount (*tzu*), and Baron (*nan*), often in several gradations each indicated by prefixes, e.g., Commandery Duke (*chün-kung*). In Chou times *wang* was not included, being reserved for the King, and the titles Minister (*ch'ing*), Grand Master (*ta-fu*), and Servicemen (*shih*) were included.

1716 *chüēh-huò wù* 榷貨務
SUNG–CHIN: **Monopoly Tax Commission,** several established in 965 at the capital and elsewhere to supervise the collection of taxes on state-monopolized commodities including tea, salt, and liquor, each Commission apparently headed by an Overseer-general (*tsung-ling*), under whose supervision taxes were collected by local State Monopoly Agents (*chien-tang kuan*); the Overseers-general seem to have been responsible in part to the Department of State Affairs (*shang-shu sheng*) but also in part to the Court of the Imperial Treasury (*t'ai-fu ssu*). In Chin there seems to have been only one such Commission, headed by a Commissioner (*shih*). SP: *bureau des denrées monopolisées, bureau d'échange monopolisé.* P62.

1717 *chüēh-ì* 覺義
CH'ING: lit., perceiver of right: **Buddhist Rectifier,** one Left and one Right, both rank 8b, in the Buddhist Registry (*seng-lu ssu*). BH: principal clerk, secondary clerk.

1718 *chüēh-ì àn* 榷易案
SUNG: **Monopoly Exchange Section,** one of 6 units under the Treasury Bureau (*chin-pu ssu*) of the Ministry of Revenue (*hu-pu*), staffed with clerical suboffials who handled administrative details of the Bureau's supervision of transactions in non-grain commodities monopolized by the state. Established c. 1080, when the State Finance Commission (*san ssu*) of early Sung was discontinued. SP: *service des échanges monopolisés.* P6.

1719 *chüēh-ì k'ù* 榷易庫
SUNG: **Monopoly Exchange Storehouse,** headed by a Commissioner (*shih*); presumably a vault for storage of state-monopolized goods; existed only in the earliest years of the dynasty. P62.

1720 *chüēh-ì shìh* 榷易使
SUNG: **Monopoly Exchange Commissioner,** reportedly a prestige title (*san-kuan*) for rank 7a military officers, superseding Grand Master for the Preservation of Peace (*pao-an ta-fu*); a Vice Commissioner (*fu-shih*) title seems similarly to have superseded the rank 7b prestige title Gentleman for the Preservation of Peace (*pao-an lang*). These attributions seem unlikely; there may be errors in the sources. SP: *commissaire aux échanges monopolisés.*

1721 *chüēh-ì yüàn* 榷易院
SUNG: **Monopoly Exchange Bureau,** reportedly a unit in the Ministry of Revenue (*hu-pu*); staff and functions not clear; possibly the predecessor or successor of the Monopoly Exchange Section (*chüeh-i an*). SP: *cour des échanges monopolisés.*

1722 *chüēh-kuān yǜ-shìh* 榷關御史
MING: **Customs-collecting Censor,** one member of the Censorate (*tu ch'a-yüan*) assigned in 1429, together with a representative of the Ministry of Revenue (*hu-pu*) and another of the Imperial Bodyguard (*chin-i wei*), to collect customs duties on private boats arriving in Peking; soon discontinued when Customs Houses (*ch'ao-kuan*) were established along the Grand Canal. P62.

1723 *chüēh-ló kūng* 覺羅公
CH'ING: **Duke of the Collateral Line,** a title of nobility (*chüeh*) granted in perpetuity to Manchus descended collaterally from the founding Emperor, Nurhachi.

1724 *chüēh-pù* 榷部
MING–CH'ING: unofficial reference to a **Customs House** (*ch'ao-kuan*).

1725 *chüēh-ts'áo* 決曹
HAN: **Judicial Section,** one of a dozen or more Sections (*ts'ao*) subordinate to the Defender-in-chief (*t'ai-wei*) in the central government and probably duplicated on the staff of the Counselor-in-chief (*ch'eng-hsiang*); headed by an Administrator (*yüan-shih*), rank =400 bushels; functions not clear. BH: bureau of decisions.

1726 *chüēh-yén shìh* 榷鹽使
T'ANG: **Salt Commissioner,** after 808 one of several titles used for local or regional officials charged with collecting revenues on the state-monopolized salt trade. P61.

1727 *chüēh yén-t'ièh shìh* 榷鹽鐵使
T'ANG: **Salt Monopoly Commissioner,** established at Yangchow in 758 to exploit the salt trade to provide revenue for the central government; subsequently merged with the Transport Commissioner (*chuan-yün shih*), also at Yangchow, into one office, the Salt and Transport Commissioner (*yen-t'ieh chuan-yün shih*). Iron was not a state monopoly in T'ang times, but traditional usage of the combined term *yen-t'ieh* (salt and iron) was perpetuated in these titles. See *yen-t'ieh shih.*

1728 *chüēh-yìn* 爵廕
MING: **Hereditary Nobility,** a generic term for 9 ranks of hereditary nobility granted to men who were not members of the imperial family: Duke (*kung*), Marquis (*hou*), Earl (*po*), Viscount (*tzu*), Baron (*nan*), Commandant of Light Chariots (*ch'ing-ch'e tu-wei*), Commandant of Cavalry (*chi tu-wei*), Commandant of Fleet-as-clouds Cavalry (*yün-chi*

wei), Cavalry Commandant by Grace (*ên chi-wei*). The first 3 titles were subdivided into 3 grades (*teng*). Inheritance of such titles was only rarely indefinite; the privilege was normally prescribed, from one generation up to 26 generations.

1729 *chün* 君
Throughout history a broad generic term for rulers and other official superiors: **Lord,** often used in contrast to Minister (*ch'en*). Also used in direct address to any superior or respected elder, in the sense of **My Lord.**

1730 *chün* 軍
(1) Throughout history the most common term for **Army,** the largest military unit for operational purposes; commanded by dignitaries of many different titles, most commonly General (*chiang-chün*). Some Armies in some periods had specifically prescribed organizational patterns and sizes, but in normal usage such precision is not to be found. The term usually has some kind of identifying prefix. (2) **Military:** common prefix modifier in agency names and other nomenclature. (3) SUNG–YÜAN: **Military Prefecture,** designation of a Prefecture (otherwise commonly *chou* or *fu*) where military matters were the primary governmental concern; headed by a Prefect (*chih-chün*).

1731 *chün* 郡
(1) CH'IN–SUI: **Commandery,** a standard unit of territorial administration normally incorporating and coordinating several Districts (*hsien*), from late in the era of N-S Division differentiated on the basis of size of resident population so that in Sui there were 9 grades of Commanderies, from *shang-shang* (upper-upper) at the top to *hsia-hsia* (lower-lower) at the bottom, grouped into 3 categories of Large (*shang*), Middle (*chung*), and Small (*hsia*) Commanderies; headed by a Governor (*shou, t'ai-shou*), rank 2,000 bushels from Han into the era of N-S Division, then transformed into a range of ranks from 7 up to 3 according to population size of the units. As a formal unit of government, abolished at the beginning of T'ang. HB: commandery. P53. (2) SUNG–CH'ING: common quasi-official or unofficial reference to a **Prefecture** (*chou, fu*).

1732 *chün-chăng* 郡長
HAN: **Commandery Governor,** a title early superseded by *chün-shou*. P53.

1733 *chün-ch'éng* 郡丞
(1) CH'IN–SUI: **Commandery Aide,** principal assistant for non-military matters to a Commandery Governor (*chün-shou, t'ai-shou*). P53. (2) MING–CH'ING: unofficial reference to the **Vice Prefect** (*t'ung-chih*) of a Prefecture (*fu*).

1734 *chün-chī chăng-chīng* 軍機章京
CH'ING: **Secretary in the Council of State,** 60, rank not specified, divided into 4 Duty Groups (*pan*), each headed by a Duty Group Chief (*ling-pan*), rank 3a. See *chang-ching*.

1735 *chün-chī ch'ù* 軍機處
CH'ING: lit., office for military emergencies: **Council of State,** established in 1730 as successor to a previous quasi-official Deliberative Council (*i-cheng ch'u*); by taking over many functions previously performed by the Grand Secretariat (*nei-ko*), became the most prestigious and powerful agency in the policy-formulating procedures of the central government; normally, but with wide variations, consisted of 5 Grand Ministers of State (*chün-chi ta-ch'en*), 3 Manchus and 2 Chinese, who were all normally concurrent Grand Secretaries (*ta hsüeh-shih*) or senior officials of the Six Ministries (*liu pu*); often chaired by an Imperial

Prince. At the apex of the central government hierarchy, the Council deliberated with the Emperor on all policy matters, civil as well as military, and promulgated the Emperor's decisions.

1736 *chün-chī hsíng-tsŏu* 軍機行走
CH'ING: **Probationary Grand Minister of State,** common designation of a newly appointed *chün-chi ta-ch'en*.

1737 *chün-chī tà-ch'én* 軍機大臣
CH'ING: **Grand Minister of State,** designation of eminent dignitaries chosen to serve in the Council of State (*chün-chi ch'u*). BH: grand councillor.

1738 *chün-ch'ì chiēn* 軍器監
T'ANG–SUNG: **Directorate for Armaments,** in charge of the manufacture and storage of weapons; headed by a Director (*chien*), rank 4a in T'ang, 6a in Sung, under general supervision of the Ministry of Works (*kung-pu*). After mid-T'ang the Directorate gradually lost its functions to palace eunuchs. In the first Sung century its functions were mostly performed by units of the State Finance Commission (*san ssu*); after c. 1080 it became functionally important, but in S. Sung it again lost its functions, this time to an Armaments Office (*chün-ch'i so*) more tightly absorbed into the Ministry of Works. The relationship between these Sung agencies and the Imperial Arsenal (*chih-tsao yü-ch'ien chün-ch'i chü*) is not clear. Also see *wu-ch'i chien*. RR: *direction des armes de guerre.* SP: *direction des armes.*

1739 *chün-ch'ì chǔ* 軍器局
(1) SUNG: common abbreviation of *chih-tsao yü-ch'ien chün-ch'i chü* (**Imperial Arsenal**). (2) MING: **Provincial Arsenal,** commonly subordinate to a Provincial Administration Commission (*ch'eng-hsüan pu-cheng shih ssu*), headed by a Commissioner-in-chief (*ta-shih*), rank 9b. P15, 19, 52.

1740 *chün-ch'ì k'ù-shǐh* 軍器庫使
SUNG: **Commissioner of the Armory,** reportedly (though somewhat unlikely) an early Sung antecedent of the prestige title (*san-kuan*) Grand Master for Perfect Health (*ch'eng-ho ta-fu*), granted to rank 6b medical officials. SP: *commissaire du magasin des armes.*

1741 *chün-ch'ì kŭng-ch'iāng k'ù* 軍器弓槍庫
SUNG: **Armory for Bows and Lances,** a unit in the Court of the Imperial Regalia (*wei-wei ssu*). SP: *magasin des arcs et des lances.*

1742 *chün-ch'ì nŭ-chièn-chièn k'ù* 軍器弩箭劍庫
SUNG: **Armory for Crossbows, Arrows, and Swords,** a unit in the Court of the Imperial Regalia (*wei-wei ssu*). SP: *magasin des arbalètes, des épées et des flèches.*

1743 *chün-ch'ì sŏ* 軍器所
SUNG: **Armaments Office,** a unit in the S. Sung Ministry of Works (*kung-pu*). See *chün-ch'i chien*. SP: *service des armes.*

1744 *chün-ch'ì tsá-wù k'ù* 軍器雜物庫
SUNG: **Armory for Miscellaneous Weapons,** a unit in the Court of the Imperial Regalia (*wei-wei ssu*). SP: *magasin des armes diverses.*

1745 *chün-chiàng* 軍將
General of the Army: in Chou times, the commander of one of the armies maintained by the King or a Feudal Lord (*chu-hou*), a special duty assignment for someone ranked

as a Minister (ch'ing); in subsequent history, especially in Sung, an ad hoc designation for a military commander. CL+SP: général de l'armée.

1746 chừn chiāng-chừn 郡將軍 or chừn-chiàng
N-S DIV: **Commandery General,** a variant reference to the Governor (t'ai-shou) of a Commandery (chün).

1747 chừn-chiēn 軍監
SUNG: common combined reference to **Military and Industrial Prefectures;** see chün, chien.

1748 chừn-chǔ 君主
Throughout imperial history a common unofficial variant of kung-chu (**Imperial Princess**), to be distinguished carefully from the homonym signifying a Princess of lesser rank.

1749 chừn-chǔ 軍主
N-S DIV: **Army Commander,** common designation for an officer in control of a field army; sometimes prefixed with Chief (tu).

1750 chừn-chǔ 郡主
Commandery Princess: throughout history the most common noble title granted to daughters of Imperial Princes (ch'in-wang); in T'ang and early Sung restricted to daughters of Heirs Apparent. See chün kung-chu, hsien-chu, ko-ko.

1751 chừn-chừn 郡君
Commandery Mistress, title of honor or nobility granted to women. (1) T'ANG–SUNG: granted to mothers and wives of various members of the imperial clan and, until shortly after 1100, those of some other dignitaries. RR: dame de commanderie. (2) MING: granted to daughters of Defender-generals of the State (chen-kuo chiang-chün). (3) CH'ING: granted to daughters of Beile (pei-lo) and those of secondary wives or concubines of Imperial Princes (ch'in-wang).

1752 chừn-fāng 軍坊
SUI: **Precinct Company,** basic unit of urban militia in the Garrison Militia (fu-ping) system instituted in 583; headed by a Company Commander (fang-chu), subordinate to a Garrison (fu).

1753 chừn-fǔ 軍府
(1) **Armory,** throughout history a common designation for any storehouse of military gear. (2) **Army Headquarters** or **Military Command,** throughout history a common reference to the office and supporting staff of a General (chiang-chün) or a comparable military leader. (3) T'ANG: **Garrison,** common reference to the principal military unit in the Garrison Militia (fu-ping) system, most commonly abbreviated to fu. RR: milices pour l'armées (?). P43, 44. (4) T'ANG: possible antecedent of Sung dynasty Military Prefectures (chün)?. See shih-erh chün (Twelve Armies).

1754 chừn fū-jén 郡夫人
SUNG: **Commandery Mistress,** honorific designation awarded to wives and mothers of various high-ranking civil and military officials, e.g., Military Affairs Commissioner (shu-mi shih), Commissioner of the Court of Palace Attendants (hsüan-hui shih); not as prestigious as chün t'ai fu-jen, kuo fu-jen, kuo t'ai fu-jen, qq.v.

1755 chừn-hóu 君侯
From Han on, a collective or generic reference to **Marquises** (hou); also occasionally used as a form of direct address to a member of the nobility, in the sense of "my lord Marquis."

1756 chừn-hóu 郡侯
CHIN–YÜAN: **Commandery Marquis,** title of nobility (chüeh), rank 4a or 4b in Chin, 3a in Yüan; 4th highest of 7 noble grades in Chin, 6th highest of 10 in Yüan. See hou, chu-hou, kuo-hou, k'ai-kuo hou, k'ai-kuo hsien-hou, k'ai-kuo chün-hou. P65.

1757 chừn-hsiá chiēn hsừn-pǔ shǐh 軍轄兼巡捕使
CHIN: **Commandant and Police Commissioner,** rank 9b, on the staff of a Prefecture (chou). P53.

1758 chừn-hsièn 郡縣
Commanderies and Districts: from Ch'in on, a generic reference to the regional and local units administered by appointees of the central government in what eventually developed, through many transformations, into the territorial-administration hierarchy of Provinces (sheng), Prefectures (fu), and Districts (hsien) in the Ming–Ching era; regularly used as a shorthand reference to such a governmental system (centralized, bureaucratic, direct) in contrast to the ancient Chou dynasty system of regional and local administration by hereditary nobles "established by enfeoffment" (feng-chien; also see chu-hou, Feudal Lords) and by sub-infeudation (decentralized, feudal, indirect). These 2 patterns of governmental organization were the ideal polar opposites discussed throughout imperial history by Chinese political theorists, some of whom lamented the predominant chün-hsien system's lack of the benevolent, paternalistic qualities that they liked to think characterized the feng-chien system at its best. In Han the chün-hsien concept gained the added implication of government staffed with officials who were state-certified Confucian scholars and litterateurs.

1759 chừn-hsiù 俊秀
HAN–CH'ING: **Elegant Scholar,** unofficial polite reference to any student, especially in Ming and Ch'ing times to those admitted to the Directorate of Education (kuo-tzu chien); not used for anyone who had passed even the first examination in the civil service recruitment examination sequence.

1760 chừn-hsū k'ù 軍需庫
MING: **Armaments Storehouse,** an agency in the Ministry of Works (kung-pu), headed by a Commissioner-in-chief (ta-shih), rank 8b. P15.

1761 chừn-hsừn yüàn 軍巡院
SUNG–CHIN: **Police Office,** one established in each of the 4 Capital Townships (ssu hsiang) into which the successive Sung dynastic capitals, Kaifeng and Hangchow, were divided; each Police Office headed by a Left and a Right Military Inspector (chün-hsün shih), rank 8a, and a Left and a Right Administrative Assistant (p'an-kuan), 8b. In Chin, one established in each city designated a Capital (ching), headed by a Military Inspector or by a Commissioner (shih), rank not clear. SP: cour d'inspection militaire. P20, 49.

1762 chừn-hù 軍戶
YÜAN–CH'ING: **Military Family,** registration classification denoting a family that was obligated to provide males for hereditary, lifetime military service.

1763 chừn-jén 均人
CHOU: **Land Assessor,** 2 ranked as Ordinary Servicemen (chung-shih) and 4 as Junior Servicemen (hsia-shih), members of the Ministry of Education (ti-kuan) responsible for seeing that land taxes were equitable and that land tax and

state service obligations were fulfilled in the royal domain. See *t'u-chün.* CL: *égaliseur de l'impôt.*

1764   *chün-júng* 軍容
T'ANG: abbreviation of *kuan chün-jung shih* (**Inspector of the Armies**).

1765   *chün-júng chíh* 鈞容直
SUNG: **Military Band,** one each attached to the Palace Command (*tien-ch'ien ssu*) and the Office of Musical Instruction (*ch'ien-hsia chiao-fang so*) in the Court of Imperial Sacrifices (*t'ai-ch'ang ssu*). SP: *troupe de musique militaire.*

1766   *chün-kuān* 均官
HAN: **Fair Tax Office,** a unit under the Chamberlain for the Palace Revenues (*shao-fu*) apparently responsible for gathering taxes on mountain products in kind for palace use; headed by a Director (*chang*). HB: office of adjustment. P37.

1767   *chün-kūng* 郡公
T'ANG–YÜAN: **Commandery Duke,** title of nobility (*chüeh*), normally 4th highest, normally granted to sons of Imperial Princes (*ch'in-wang*) by secondary wives or concubines; in T'ang also granted to sons of Dukes of State (*kuo-kung*), Dynasty-founding Commandery Dukes (*k'ai-kuo chün-kung*), and Dynasty-founding District Dukes (*k'ai-kuo hsien-kung*). RR: *duc de commanderie.*

1768   *chün kūng-chǔ* 郡公主
N-S DIV (Chin): **Commandery Princess,** title of nobility (*chüeh*) granted to an Imperial Princess (*kung-chu*) who was actually enfeoffed with a Commandery (*chün*).

1769   *chün-kuó* 軍國
Lit., military matters and (other) state (affairs): **the Nation,** a term used throughout imperial history suggesting national security, national well-being, the national interest, etc.

1770   *chün-kuó* 郡國
HAN–T'ANG: **Territorial Administrations,** collective reference to Commanderies (*chün*), Princedoms (*wang-kuo*), and Marquisates (*hou-kuo*), i.e., to all regional units of territorial administration, of all categories.

1771   *chün-mǎ* 郡馬
N-S DIV–MING: lit., cavalry (commandant) of a Commandery (*chün*): unofficial reference to a **Commandant-escort** (*fu-ma tu-wei*), the husband of a Commandery Princess (*chün-chu*), deriving from the practice of enfeoffing some women of imperial descent with Commanderies. Cf. *hsien-ma.*

1772   *chün-mǎ lìng* 駿馬令
HAN: **Director of the Finest Steeds,** one of the numerous subordinates of the Chamberlain for the Imperial Stud (*t'ai-p'u*), rank 600 bushels. HB: prefect of the stables for fine horses. P31.

1773   *chün-mǎ mù* 軍馬牧
SUI: **Pasturage for Military Mounts,** 24 under supervision of the Court of the Imperial Stud (*t'ai-p'u ssu*), each headed by a Director (*i-ssu*). P31.

1774   *chün-mǎ tū-tū* 軍馬都督
SUNG: **Commander-in-chief of Infantry and Cavalry,** concurrent title sometimes granted to Grand Councilors (*tsai-hsiang*).

1775   *chün-mén* 軍門
CH'ING: lit., military gate, i.e., a military headquarters with an imposing entrance: unofficial reference to a **Provincial Military Commander** (*t'i-tu*).

1776   *chün-mín fǔ* 軍民府
YÜAN–MING: lit., office for soldiers and civilians: **Tribal Office,** one type of the agencies created to administer southwestern aboriginal groups; may also be encountered as an abbreviation of *chün-min tsung-kuan fu* or *chün-min wan-hu fu* (both Tribal Command); also see *t'u-ssu.* P72.

1777   *chün-mín tsǔng-kuǎn fǔ* 軍民總管府
YÜAN: **Tribal Command,** one type of the agencies created to administer southwestern aboriginal groups; see *tsung-kuan fu, t'u-ssu.*

1778   *chün-mín wàn-hù fǔ* 軍民萬戶府
YÜAN: **Tribal Command,** one type of the agencies created to administer southwestern aboriginal groups; see *wan-hu fu, t'u-ssu.*

1779   *chün-pó* 郡伯
(1) YÜAN: **Commandery Earl,** 6th highest of 8 grades of nobility (*chüeh*). (2) Throughout imperial history, an occasional indirect reference to a **Commandery Governor** (*chün-shou, t'ai-shou*) or a **Prefect** (*tz'u-shih, chih-chou, chih-fu*). Also see *ta chün-po.*

1780   *chün-shǐh* 軍使
SUNG: **Military Commander,** one for each 100 soldiers in the units under the Palace Command (*tien-ch'ien shih-wei ssu*) and the Metropolitan Command (*shih-wei ch'in-chün ma-pu ssu*). SP: *commissaire impérial d'une armée.*

1781   *chün-shǐh* 軍師
N-S DIV: **Army Supervisor,** variant of *chien-chün,* q.v.

1782   *chün-shǐh* 郡使
HAN: **Commandery Chief,** one of the titles granted to chiefs of southwestern aboriginal tribes. See *t'u-ssu.* P72.

1783   *chün-shìh chiēn-p'àn kuān* 軍事監判官
SUNG: **Military Supervisor,** rank 8b, on the staffs of such regional dignitaries as Military Commissioners (*chieh-tu shih*), Surveillance Commissioners (*kuan-ch'a shih*), and Military Training Commissioners (*t'uan-lien shih*). SP: *surveillant ou assistant ou régisseur militaire.*

1784   *chün-shìh t'ūi-kuān* 軍事推官
SUNG: **Military Judge,** rank 8b, on the staffs of such regional dignitaries as Military Commissioners (*chieh-tu shih*), Surveillance Commissioners (*kuan-ch'a shih*), and Military Training Commissioners (*t'uan-lien shih*). SP: *juge militaire.*

1785   *chün-shǒu* 郡守
(1) CH'IN–SUI: **Commandery Governor,** head of a Commandery (*chün*), rank 2,000 bushels in Han. HB: commandery administrator. (2) T'ANG–CH'ING: unofficial reference to a **Prefect** (*tz'u-shih, chih-fu, chih-chou*) or, in Ming–Ch'ing times, to a **Provincial Administration Commissioner** (*pu-cheng shih*). Also see *t'ai-shou.* P50, 53.

1786   *chün-shǒu* 郡首
Lit., Commandery head: throughout imperial history, an unofficial reference to a **Commandery Governor** (*chün-shou* homonym) or to a **Prefect** (*tz'u-shih, chih-chou, chih-fu*).

1787   *chün-shū* 均輸
HAN: **Office of Tax Substitutes,** one subordinate to the Chamberlain for the Palace Revenues (*shao-fu*) or the Chamberlain for the National Treasury (*ta ssu-nung*), in charge of collecting grain and other local products paid as taxes in lieu of cash and shipping them to places where they were in short supply (see *ch'ang-p'ing ts'ang, p'ing-chun*); another subordinate to the Commandant of the Imperial

Gardens (*shui-heng tu-wei*), sharing responsibility for the production of coins (see *shui-heng san kuan*, Three Money Managers of the Court of the Imperial Gardens). Each headed by a Director (*ling*) and an Aide (*ch'eng*). HB (*ling*): prefect of price adjustment and transportation. P16.

1788 chün-ssū 均司
HAN: **Economic Stabilization Office,** in the reign of Wang Mang (9–23) established in the dynastic capital and 5 other major cities under the control of Market Masters (*shih-shih*); see under *wu chün-ssu shih-shih* (Five Market Masters).

1789 chün-ssū 軍司
(1) HAN–SUNG: abbreviation of *hsing-chün ssu-ma* (**Adjutant**). (2) N-S DIV: variant of *chien-chün* (**Army Supervisor**).

1790 chün ssū-mǎ 軍司馬
(1) CHOU: **Cavalry Commander of the Army,** 4 ranked as Junior Grand Masters (*hsia ta-fu*), members of the Ministry of War (*hsia-kuan*), apparently of more importance than their rank would normally suggest, but specific functions not clear. CL: *commandant de chevaux en corps d'armée*. (2) HAN: **Division Commander,** title commonly assigned to the leader of a Division (*pu*), 5 of which were the normal components of a Campaigning Army (*ying*) under a General-in-chief (*ta chiang-chün*). HB: major of the army. (3) N-S DIV–SUNG: variant or unofficial designation of an **Adjutant** (*hsing-chün ssu-ma*). See *ssu-ma*, *chün-ssu*.

1791 chün-t'ái 郡台
CH'ING: **Post Station** on the 3 main routes from China into Mongolia; also served as places of banishment for some officials found guilty of crimes.

1792 chün t'ài-chūn 郡太君
SUNG: **Grand Lord** (or **Lady**) **of the Commandery,** honorific designation granted to antecedents, male and female, of various palace women and some eminent officials, e.g., Commissioners of the State Finance Commission (*san-ssu shih*).

1793 chün t'ài fū-jén 郡太夫人
SUNG: **Commandery Grand Mistress,** honorific designation granted to mothers and grandmothers of various high-ranking officials, e.g., a Military Affairs Commissioner (*shu-mi shih*), the Minister (*shang-shu*) of one of the Six Ministries (*liu pu*), or a Censor-in-chief (*yü-shih ta-fu*); also granted to the mothers and grandmothers of various secondary wives of the Emperor.

1794 chün-tǐ 郡邸
HAN: **Liaison Hostel for the Commandery,** a residence and office in the dynastic capital maintained by a Commandery Governor (*chün-shou*) to handle his communications with the central government and to house him and members of his staff on visits to the capital; headed by a Director (*chang*) and an Aide (*ch'eng*). HB (*chang*): chief of the commandery quarters. See *ti*.

1795 chün-t'óu 軍頭
SUNG: **Military Commander** of a small troop unit, found in some Guards (*wei*). SP: *chef de troupe*.

1796 chün-t'óu ssū 軍頭司
SUNG: **Office of Military Commanders,** a unit in the Court of Palace Attendants (*hsüan-hui yüan*); functions not clear. SP: *bureau des registres des chefs de troupes*.

1797 chün-tsò 郡佐
Commandery Assistant: from Han on, a generic reference

to the various 2nd- and 3rd-level assistants on the staff of a Commandery Governor (*chün-shou*) or his later counterpart, a Prefect (*tz'u-shih, chih-chou, chih-fu*).

1798 chün-ts'ùi 郡倅
Commandery Deputy: from Han on, a generic reference to subordinates of a Commandery Governor (*chün-shou*) or his later counterpart, a Prefect (*tz'u-shih, chih-chou, chih-fu*); in Ming and Ch'ing, referred more specifically to Assistant Prefects (*t'ung-p'an*). In general, this term seems to carry less prestige than does *chün-tso* (Commandery Assistant). See *ts'ui, p'in-ts'ui*.

1799 chün-t'ún 軍屯
Army Farm: throughout imperial history, state-owned land allocated to military garrisons in the expectation that soldiers would divide their time between farming and active military training or service, or that state revenues from tenant farmers on the land would be used to support the military. In Han, at least some such lands were under the control of a Supervisor (*p'u-yeh*) in the Northern Army (*pei-chün*) at the dynastic capital; in Ming, such lands were assigned to every unit in the *wei-so* system of hereditary soldiers. Also see *t'un-t'ien*. Cf. *min-t'un, shang-t'un*. HB: military garrison.

1800 chün-wáng 郡王
HAN–CH'ING: **Commandery Prince,** high title of nobility (*chüeh*), ordinarily prefixed with a place-name designating the noble's real or nominal fief; normally granted to sons of Imperial Princes (*ch'in-wang*) by their principal wives, except for the eldest son (see *shih-tzu*). RR+SP: *prince de commanderie*. BH: prince of the 2nd degree. P64, 65.

1801 chün-wáng shìh-tzǔ 郡王世子
MING: **Heir of the Commandery Prince,** normally with a place-name prefix: designation of the eldest son of the principal wife pending his succession to his father's title. See *shih-tzu*. P64.

1802 chün-wèi 軍衛
SUNG: **Army Guard,** one each of Left and Right, units in the Sixteen Guards (*shih-liu wei*); headed by one or more Generalissimos (*shang chiang-chün*), rank 2b, 3a, or 3b; functions not clear, particularly because the Sixteen Guard system inherited from T'ang had become largely decorative, providing posts to which members of the imperial family and perhaps other favorites could be appointed. A fuller, more formal name was *wei-kuan chün-wei* (lit., Army Guard of Guard Officers). SP: *garde militaire*. P43

1803 chün-wèi 郡尉
CH'IN-HAN, SUI: **Commandery Defender,** the principal assistant to a Commandery Governor (*chün-shou, t'ai-shou*), responsible for all military and police activities; in 148 B.C. retitled *tu-wei*, q.v., but original title revived in Sui. Han rank =2,000 bushels. Also see *wei, hsien-wei*. HB: commandery commandant. P53.

1804 ch'ún-chǎng 羣長
MING: **Herd Director,** one subofficial functionary in charge of each herd of horses overseen by the Court of the Imperial Stud (*t'ai-p'u ssu*). P31.

1805 ch'ún-mù chìh-chìh shīh 羣牧制置使
SUNG: apparently a variant form of *ch'ün-mu shih* (**Commissioner of Herds**). SP: *commissaire chargé de diriger l'élevage des chevaux*

1806 ch'ún-mù shīh 羣牧使
Commissioner of Herds. (1) T'ANG: number and orga-

nizational affiliation not clear; inspected herds of state horses and cattle that were overseen by Directorates of Horse Pasturages (*mu-chien*). Cf. *chien-mu shih* (Horse Pasturage Foreman). RR: *commissaire impérial aux troupeaux et aux élevages*. (2) SUNG–CHIN: the normal title of the head of a local Herds Office (*ch'ün-mu ssu*). SP: *commissaire du bureau des troupeaux et de l'élevage des chevaux*. P31.

1807 *ch'ün-mù sǒ* 羣牧所
CHIN–YÜAN: **Herds Office,** in charge of all state-owned horse herds; in 1279 changed to Directorate of Herds (*shang-mu chien*), which later was renamed Court of the Imperial Stud (*t'ai-p'u ssu*). P39.

1808 *ch'ün-mù ssū* 羣牧司
SUNG–CHIN: **Herds Office,** a local agency that looked after state horses in a designated area under the supervision of the Court of the Imperial Stud (*t'ai-p'u ssu*); commonly staffed with subofficial Commissioners (*shih*), Administrative Assistants (*p'an-kuan*), Herding Officials (*ch'ün-mu kuan*), etc. Cf. *ma-ch'ün ssu* (Horse Pasturage). SP: *bureau des troupeaux et de l'élevage des chevaux*. P31.

1809 *ch'ün-tài ch'īn* 裙帶親
Lit., apron-string relatives: in Sung and possibly other times, an unofficial generic reference to imperial relatives by marriage, i.e., **Imperial In-laws.**

1810 *ch'ün-tài kuān* 裙帶官
Lit., apron-string officials: in Sung and perhaps other periods, an unofficial reference to the husbands of Imperial Princesses (*kung-chu*), formally known as **Commandant-escorts** (*fu-ma tu-wei*).

1811 *ch'ün t'ài-pǎo* 羣太保
LIAO: **Grand Guardian of Herds,** head of the Herds Office (*ch'ün-mu ssu*) in each Route (*lu*). P31.

1812 *e*
See under the romanization *o*.

1813 *ēn chì-wèi* 恩騎尉
CH'ING: **Commandant of Cavalry by Grace,** the lowest of 9 ranks of hereditary nobility (*chüeh-yin*) granted to men not of the imperial family; from 1750 conferred in perpetuity on sons and grandsons of non-hereditary nobles who died in battle for the state. P64.

1814 *ēn-ch'ì chiā-tzǔ* 恩戚家子
SUNG: lit., descendant of a graciously chosen imperial in-law: **Imperial Distaff Nephew,** unofficial reference to a junior male relative of an Emperor by marriage.

1815 *ēn-ch'ǔ chiēn-shēng* 恩取監生
CH'ING: **Student by Grace** in the Directorate of Education (*kuo-tzu chien*), status gained by passing a special, irregular recruitment examination in celebration of some auspicious event. See *chien-sheng*.

1816 *ēn-k'ō ch'ū-shēn* 恩科出身
SUNG: **Qualified by Special Examination,** status making one eligible for an official appointment, gained by passing a special, irregular recruitment examination. See *t'e-tsou ming, ch'u-shen*.

1817 *ēn kùng-shēng* 恩貢生 or *en-kung*
MING–CH'ING: **Tribute Student by Grace,** status entitling one to participate in the Provincial Examination (*hsiang-shih*) in the civil service recruitment process and to be considered at least nominally a National University Student (*chien-sheng*) under the Directorate of Education (*kuo-tzu chien*), gained by passing a special, irregular recruitment

examination. See *kung-sheng*. BH: senior licentiate by imperial favor.

1818 *ēn-pǔ kùng-shēng* 恩補貢生
CH'ING: **Supplemental Tribute Student by Grace,** status entitling one to participate in the Provincial Examination (*hsiang-shih*) in the civil service recruitment process and to be considered at least nominally a National University Student (*chien-sheng*) under the Directorate of Education (*kuo-tzu chien*), awarded at times of national celebration to men who for 20 or more years had held the status of Stipend Student (*lin-sheng*) in government schools. Also see *kung-sheng, en kung-sheng*. BH: licentiate by imperial favor.

1819 *ēn-shēng* 恩生
MING: **National University Student by Grace** under the Directorate of Education (*kuo-tzu chien*), status awarded to sons of officials who served the state with extraordinary merit. See *chien-sheng, en-ch'ü chien-sheng, en-yin chien-sheng, nan-yin chien-sheng*.

1820 *ēn-shìh* 恩試
CH'ING: **Examination by Grace,** a special, irregular civil service recruitment examination given in celebration of some auspicious event. BH: examination held by imperial favor.

1821 *ēn-tì* 恩地
T'ANG: unofficial reference to an **Examiner** (*chu-ssu*) in a civil service recruitment examination.

1822 *ēn-tz'ù chiēn-shēng* 恩賜監生
CH'ING: **National University Student by Grace** under the Directorate of Education (*kuo-tzu chien*), status awarded to sons of prominent persons by special imperial decree. See *chien-sheng, en-sheng*.

1823 *ēn-tz'ù kùng-shēng* 恩賜貢生
CH'ING: **Tribute Student by Grace,** status entitling one to become at least nominally a National University Student (*chien-sheng*) under the Directorate of Education (*kuo-tzu chien*), attained by passing a special examination given by an Emperor at the Directorate. See *kung-sheng*. BH: licentiate by examination at the Pi Yung Hall.

1824 *ēn-yìn* 恩廕
CH'ING: **Hereditary by Grace,** prefix to a title of hereditary nobility (*chüeh-yin*) signifying that the status had been conferred on successive heirs of officials of extraordinary merit, e.g., *en-yin yün chi-wei* (Commandant of Cavalry Second Class Hereditary by Grace).

1825 *ēn-yìn chiēn-shēng* 恩廕監生
CH'ING: **National University Student Hereditary by Grace,** status awarded to sons of civil and military officials of rank 4 or higher in celebration of some auspicious event; comparable to *nan-yin chien-sheng* (National University Student Hereditary by Heroism), awarded to sons of officials who had lost their lives in state service, especially in battle. See *yin* (Protection Privilege), *sheng, chien-sheng, en-ch'ü chien-sheng, en-tz'u chien-sheng, kuan-sheng*.

1826 *èrh* 貳
Second: throughout history a generic reference to officials holding positions immediately subordinate to, or as the highest assistants of, the heads of various agencies; somewhat more specific than *tso* (Assistant). Also see *tso-erh*.

1827 *èrh chiǎ* 二甲
SUNG–CH'ING: **Second Category** of passers of the highest national civil service recruitment examination, who were awarded the status of Regular Metropolitan Graduate (*chin-*

shih ch'u-shen), less prestigious than passers in the First Category (*i chia*). BH: second class.

1828 *èrh-ch'iēn shíh* 二千石

Lit., 2,000 bushels of grain; by extension, an official entitled to an annual salary of that amount: a **Two Thousand Bushel Official.** (1) HAN–N-S DIV: generic reference to the highest-ranking officials of government below the Three Dukes (*san kung*), notably including Commandery Governors (*chün-shou, t'ai-shou*) because in Han they received annual salaries in money and various commodities reckoned to approximate the value of 2,000 bushels of grain; in Liang referred to officials of ranks (*p'in*) 4 and 5. (2) CH'ING: a term by which a Prefect (*chih-fu*), a near counterpart of the earlier Commandery Governor, might refer to his status or to himself. P68.

1829 *èrh-ch'iēn shíh ts'aó* 二千石曹

HAN–N-S DIV., lit., Section for 2,000-bushel officials: **Section for Commandery Governors,** one of 6 subdivisions of the Imperial Secretariat (*shang-shu t'ai*), headed by an Imperial Secretary (*shang-shu*) and with a staff including Court Gentlemen (*lang*) and Attendant Gentlemen (*shih-lang*); apparently originated as a unit in the Imperial Secretariat in charge of the court's relations with Commandery Governors (*chün-shou*); during the era of N-S Division occasionally became part of the emerging Ministry of Personnel (*lì-pu*) but for the most part seems to have been assigned judicial responsibilities as a unit of the emerging *tu-kuan* (Ministry of General Administration or Ministry of Justice). HB: bureau of officials ranking 2,000 *shih*. P5, l3.

1830 *èrh-ch'īng* 貳卿

T'ANG–CH'ING: unofficial generic reference to **Vice Ministers** (*shih-lang*) in the Six Ministries (*liu pu*).

1831 *èrh chù* 二著

SUNG: **Two Editors,** generic reference to Editorial Directors (*chu-tso lang*) and Assistant Editorial Directors (*chu-tso tso-lang*) on the staff of the Palace Library (*pi-shu sheng*).

1832 *èrh fù* 二傅

N-S DIV (San-kuo): **Two Mentors,** unofficial collective reference to the Grand Mentor of the Heir Apparent (*t'ai-tzu t'ai-fu*) and the Junior Mentor of the Heir Apparent (*t'ai-tzu shao-fu*). May be encountered in later periods with similar meaning. P67.

1833 *èrh fǔ* 二府

(1) HAN: **Two Ministries,** collective reference to the offices of the Counselor-in-chief (*ch'eng-hsiang*) and the Censor-in-chief (*yü-shih ta-fu*). (2) SUNG: **Two Administrations,** collective reference to the Bureau of Military Affairs (*shu-mi yüan*) and the office of Grand Councilor (*tsai-hsiang*) or the Secretariat (*chung-shu sheng*). See *liang fu*.

1834 *èrh-fǔ* 貳府

MING–CH'ING: unofficial reference to a **Vice Prefect** (*t'ung-chih*).

1835 *èrh-lìng* 貳令

T'ANG–CH'ING: unofficial reference to a **Vice Minister** (*shih-lang*) in one of the Six Ministries (*liu pu*).

1836 *èrh-mù kuān* 耳目官

Lit., ear and eye officials: throughout history, a common variant of the designation *t'ien-tzu erh-mu* (Ears and Eyes of the Emperor), applied categorically to all **Censors** (*yü-shih*) because their function was to report to the throne all cases of misconduct in the officialdom.

1837 *èrh-pǐ* 珥筆

Court Scribe: throughout history, a generic reference to officials who were responsible for recording the ruler's oral orders in court audience; e.g., in Ming and Ch'ing times, these were commonly Supervising Secretaries or Supervising Censors (*chi-shih-chung*).

1838 *èrh-p'ǐn* 二品

N-S DIV: lit., 2nd rank: sometimes used in a categorical reference to all men of, or eligible to attain, the highest official positions, or to their families; hence, the **Official Elite.**

1839 *èrh shǐh* 二史

SUNG: **Two Scribes,** collective reference to the Left Scribe (*tso-shih*) and Right Scribe (*yu-shih*) of the Chancellery (*men-hsia sheng*).

1840 *èrh-shíh-ssù chǎng* 二十四掌

SUI–MING: **Twenty-four Handlers,** collective reference to palace women, rank 9b in T'ang and 8a thereafter, who assisted the 24 Directresses (*ssu*) and the 24 Managers (*tien*) in the Offices (*ssu*) among which most palace women were divided; e.g., the Handler of Records (*chang-chi*).

1841 *èrh-shíh-ssù ssū* 二十四司

(1) SUI–MING: **Twenty-four Offices,** collective reference to the agencies among which most palace women were divided; e.g., the Office of Music (*ssu-yüeh ssu*). (2) SUI–MING: **Twenty-four Directresses,** collective reference to palace women, rank 4a in T'ang and 6a thereafter, who were senior members of the 24 Offices mentioned in (1) above; e.g., the Directress of Music (*ssu-yüeh*). (3) T'ANG–SUNG: **Twenty-four Bureaus,** collective reference to the principal subordinate agencies in the Six Ministries (*liu pu*); e.g., the Bureau of Operations (*chih-fang*) of the Ministry of War (*ping-pu*).

1842 *èrh-shíh-ssù tiěn* 二十四典

SUI–MING: **Twenty-four Managers,** collective reference to the palace women, rank 6a in T'ang and 7a thereafter, who were the principal assistants to the 24 Directresses (*ssu*) who presided over the 24 Offices (*ssu*) among which most palace women were divided; e.g., the Manager of Medicines (*tien-yao*).

1843 *èrh-shíh-ssù yá-mén* 二十四衙門

MING: **Twenty-four Agencies,** collective reference to the units of palace eunuchs known as the Twelve Directorates (*shih-erh chien*), the Four Offices (*ssu ssu*), and the Eight Services (*pa chü*).

1844 *èrh shoǔ* 貳守

MING–CH'ING: lit., secondary governor: unofficial reference to the **Vice Magistrate** (*t'ung-chih*) of a *chou* (Subprefecture in Ming, Department in Ch'ing).

1845 *èrh-shùi k'ō* 二税科

SUNG: **Semiannual Taxes Subsection,** one of 3 Subsections (*k'o*) in the Left Section (*tso-ts'ao*) of the Ministry of Revenue (*hu-pu*) from c. 1080, when the Ministry was fully activated following discontinuance of the State Finance Commission (*san ssu*) of early Sung; staffed with suboffidal functionaries who monitored the collection of both summer and autumn agricultural taxes. SP: *section de recette de l'impôt biannuel.* P6.

1846 *èrh ssū* 二司

SUNG: **Two Commands,** collective reference to the 2 headquarters units between which troops of the Imperial Armies (*chin-chün*) were divided, the Palace Command (*tien-*

ch'ien shih-wei ssu) and the Metropolitan Command (*shih-wei ch'in-chün ma-pu ssu*). May be encountered in any era, including Sung, as a coupling reference to any 2 agencies; the context should normally make the reference clear. See *san ya, liang ssu*. P43.

1847 *èrh yǐn* 貳尹
CH'ING: lit., to second the governor: unofficial, honorific reference to a **District Vice Magistrate** (*hsien-ch'eng*).

1848 *fā-chiěh* 發解
CHIN: lit., one who is sent forth: **Examination Graduate,** general designation of those passing civil service recruitment examinations, especially at the prefectural (*fu*) level.

1849 *fǎ-chíh kuān* 法直官
Lit., an official who straightens things out according to the law (?): **Legal Examiner.** (1) T'ANG: staff officials of late T'ang Military Commissioners (*chieh-tu shih*), prefixed with *fu-yüan*, suggesting that they were representatives "from the Offices and Courts," but the reference is by no means clear. RR: *fonctionnaire auxiliaire chargé de l'observation des règles dans les cours et administrations.* (2) 5 DYN–SUNG: from 931 in Later T'ang, 2 each in the Ministry of Justice (*hsing-pu*) and the Court of Judicial Review (*ta-li ssu*); rank and specific functions not clear. SP: *examinateur judiciaire, juge d'instruction.* P13.

1850 *fā-ch'ìh kuān* 發敕官
SUNG: **Order-promulgating Official,** number and rank not clear, staffing Order-promulgating Offices (*fa-ch'ih ssu*) in the Chancellery (*men-hsia sheng*) and the Bureau of Military Affairs (*shu-mi yüan*). SP: *fonctionnaire chargé de promulguer les décrets impériaux.*

1851 *fǎ-chiǔ k'ù* 法酒庫
SUNG: lit., storehouse for legally (-certified) wines (?): **Winery,** one of 3 subsections in the Office of Fine Wines (*liang-yün shu*) in the Court of Imperial Entertainments (*kuang-lu ssu*); staffing not clear; responsible for quality control of intoxicants used in court banquets and ceremonies. SP: *magasin du vin de sacrifice.* P30.

1852 *fǎ-ch'ǚ sǒ-ch'ù yüàn* 法曲所處院
T'ANG: **Bureau of Taoist Music,** staffed with court musicians who specialized in the Taoist music called *fa-ch'ü;* subordinate to the Imperial Music Office (*t'ai-yüeh shu*) in the Court of Imperial Sacrifices (*t'ai-ch'ang ssu*); in 838 renamed *hsien-shao yüan.* RR: *cour où on exécutait les airs taoistes.*

1853 *fā-fàng ssū* 發放司
SUNG: **Distribution Office,** one of many agencies that served the 3 bureaus constituting the State Finance Commission (*san ssu*) of early Sung; headed by an Administrative Assistant (*p'an-kuan*), rank 8a or 8b; established c. 980 to check and verify all goods issued by units of the Commission, discontinued c. 1080. SP: *bureau d'expédition.*

1854 *fǎ-ssū* 法司
(1) T'ANG–CH'ING: **Judicial Office,** a reference to any or all of the agencies collectively called the Three Judicial Offices (*san fa-ssu*, q.v.)—the Ministry of Justice (*hsing-pu*), the Censorate (*yü-shih t'ai, tu ch'a yüan*), and the Court of Judicial Review (*ta-li ssu*). In Sung may be found referring to the pre-1080 triad of the Ministry of Justice, the Court of Judicial Review, and the Judicial Control Office (*shen-hsing yüan*). (2) May be encountered as an unofficial reference to an official, especially the head, of any of the agencies mentioned in (1) above. (3) SUNG: **Laws Office,** a unit in the Left Bureau (*tso-t'ing*) of the Court of Judicial

Review; presumably checked the Court's decisions against the current law code. P22. (4) SUNG: **Judicial Offices Clerk,** suboficial functionary in the Ministry of Personnel (*lì-pu*) and the Censorate (*yü-shih t'ai*).

1855 *fǎ-ssù* 法寺
May be encountered as an unofficial reference to the **Court of Judicial Review** (*ta-li ssu*).

1856 *fǎ-ssū àn* 法司案
SUNG: **Section for Judicial Offices,** a unit in the Civil Appointments Process (*tso-hsüan*) of the Ministry of Personnel (*lì-pu*), which apparently handled administrative details concerning appointments of officials to the Judicial Offices (*fa-ssu*). SP: *service judiciaire.*

1857 *fǎ-ts'aó* 法曹
Lit., law section. (1) HAN: **Communications Section,** one of 3 agencies serving the Defender-in-chief (*t'ai-wei, t'ai-wei kung*); reportedly in charge of communications among military postal relay stations. HB: bureau of laws. P12. (2) N-S DIV–SUNG: **Law Section,** a clerical unit for the handling of legal affairs in Princely Establishments (*wang-fu*) and in units of territorial administration from Prefectures (*chou, fu*) down to Districts (*hsien*), commonly headed by an Administrator (*ts'an-chün-shih*), rank 7a or lower. Antecedent of the post-Sung Justice Section (*hsing-ts'ao*). Also see *liu ts'ao* (Six Sections). RR: *service judiciaire.* SP: *bureau judiciaire.* P53, 54, 69. (3) SUI–CH'ING: may be encountered as an unofficial, archaic reference to the **Ministry of Justice** (*hsing-pu*).

1858 *fǎ-wù àn* 法物案 or *fǎ-wù k'ù* 庫
SUNG, LIAO, YÜAN: **Ritual Regalia Section** (*an*) or **Ritual Regalia Storehouse** (*k'u*), a unit in the Court of Imperial Sacrifices (*t'ai-ch'ang ssu*); in Sung also a unit in the Imperial Music Bureau (*ta-sheng fu*); in charge of musical instruments, special costumes, vehicles, and other things used only for special ceremonies; in Sung headed by a Supervisor (*t'i-chü*), otherwise by a Commissioner (*shih*). SP: *service des vêtements de sacrifice.* P27.

1859 *fā-yùn àn* 發運案
SUNG: **Transport Section.** (1) One of 8 Sections (*an*) in the Tax Bureau (*tu-chih ssu;* later renamed Tax Transport Bureau, *chuan-yün ssu*) of the State Finance Commission (*san ssu*) of early Sung; normally headed by an Administrative Assistant (*p'an-kuan, t'ui-kuan*); monitored the receipt of various canal transport fees, etc.; transferred to the Ministry of Revenue (*hu-pu*) when the State Finance Commission was discontinued c. 1080. (2) One of 5 Sections in the Tax Bureau (*tu-chih ssu*) of the Ministry of Revenue from the 1080s; staffed with suboficial functionaries. SP: *service d'expédition.* P6, 60.

1860 *fā-yùn shǐh* 發運使
(1) T'ANG: **Transport Commissioner,** from 880 a duty assignment for a court official to supervise the gathering of tax grain throughout the Yangtze Valley for forwarding northward along the Grand Canal; apparently had a broader sphere of control than a *chuan-yün shih* (Transport Commissioner). (2) SUNG: **Supply Commissioner,** duty assignment for a court official to a specified geographic sphere called a Circuit (*tao, lu*), within which he supervised the forwarding to the dynastic capital of taxes and revenues from state monopolies, the operation of local storage granaries and relief granaries, and agricultural development activities; the post was one of 4 known collectively as the Four Circuit Supervisorates (*ssu chien-ssu*). Also see *tu-ta fa-yün shih.* SP: *intendant d'expédition ou commissaire des finances, du sel et du thé.* P60.

1861   *fā-yùn ssū* 發運司
SUNG: **Supply Commission,** the office of a Supply Commissioner (*fa-yün shih*). Also see *ts'ang-ssu*. SP: *bureau d'expédition.*

1862   *fān* 番
Lit., to take one's turn (of active service) in rotational sequence. (1) Throughout history, a descriptive term indicating that one was **on** (or **subject to**) **rotational duty,** e.g., when units of militiamen in the T'ang Garrison Militia (*fu-ping*) system were rotated up (*fan-shang*) from their home Garrisons (*fu*) to take tours of duty in the Southern Command (*nan-ya*) in the dynastic capital, or when groups of hereditary soldiers in the Ming *wei-so* military organization were rotated from their home Guards (*wei*) for tours of duty in Training Divisions (*ying*) at the dynastic capital. (2) T'ANG: **Duty Group,** designation of any team or shift that was rotating on (*fan-shang*) and off (*fan-hsia*) active duty on a daily or other short-term rotational schedule; the difference between (1) and (2) is comparable to that between soldiers who are assigned to guard duty (e.g., scheduled to be on actual watch at a guard post for 4 hours followed by 8 hours off such service) and those who constituted the watch or shift in active service at any particular time. (3) T'ANG: **Term of Service,** the length of time or units of time served in the Southern Command by Garrison Militia soldiers; according to the distance of the home Garrisons from the dynastic capital, the obligation of militiamen to take up rotational duty in the capital varied from one month every 5 months to one month per year. See *chih* (… on Duty), *fan-kuan, pan-chün, fan-man*. RR: *tour de service.*

1863   *fán* 繁
CH'ING: lit., complex: category used in defining the importance of units of territorial administration. See *ch'ung-fan-p'i-nan.*

1864   *fān* 藩
Lit., border or frontier: throughout history encountered as an unofficial reference to important agencies or officials with broad territorial authority delegated from the central government. E.g., see *fan-chen, fan-fang.*

1865   *fān-chèn* 藩鎮
Lit., frontier defense command. (1) T'ANG: from the early 8th century, a variant reference to **Military Commissioners** (*chieh-tu shih*). (2) MING–CH'ING: variant reference to a **Provincial Administration Commission** (*ch'eng-hsüan pu-cheng shih ssu*).

1866   *fān-fáng* 藩房
N-S DIV (N. Ch'i): unofficial reference to a **Princely Administration** (*wang-fu*).

1867   *fàn-fáng* 飯房
CH'ING: **Food Section,** one of 2 agencies constituting the Palace Larder (*yü ch'a-shan fang*), part of the Imperial Household Department (*nei-wu fu*); headed by 3 court attendants designated Overseers-general (*tsung-ling*), with a staff of 35 Food Provisioners (*fan-shang jen*); provided food for court banquets, imperial gifts, etc.; in 1689 changed into a Food Provisioners Office (*fan-shang jen-wei shu*) under a single Overseer-general. P37.

1868   *fān-fǔ* 藩府
Lit., frontier office or Prefecture. (1) T'ANG–CH'ING: unofficial reference to the headquarters of various territorial administrators such as a T'ang Military Commissioner (*chieh-tu shih*) or a Ming–Ch'ing Provincial Administration Commissioner (*pu-cheng shih*). (2) SUNG: **Frontier Prefecture,** designation granted a number of Prefectures (*fu*) lo-

cated in strategically important places as different as Chengtu and Hangchow, each headed by a Frontier Prefect (*chih fan-fu*).

1869   *fān-hsià* 番下
Rotated down (or **off**); see *fan* (on rotational duty), *fan-shang* (rotated up or onto).

1870   *fān-ì* 繙譯
CH'ING: lit., to translate: prefix meaning **in translation** appended to recruitment examination degrees awarded to Manchus who took examinations in their own language, e.g., Metropolitan Graduate in Translation (*fan-i chin-shih*).

1871   *fān-ì chīng jùn-wén shǐh* 翻譯經潤文使
SUNG: **Commissioner for Interpretation and Embellishment,** ad hoc duty assignment for a Grand Councilor (*tsai-hsiang*); the function is not clear. SP: *commissaire chargé d'embellir la traduction.*

1872   *fān-ì ch'ù* 番役處
CH'ING: lit., place of rotational duty: **Police Bureau** subordinate to the Office of Palace Justice (*shen-hsing ssu*) in the Imperial Household Department (*nei-wu fu*); headed by specially delegated Directors (*lang-chung*) and Vice Directors (*yüan-wai lang*) of the Department's various Offices (*ssu*) who while so assigned were called Supervisors of Police (*kuan-hsia fan-i*). The Bureau seems to have been staffed principally with imperial bondservants (*pao-i*) and was charged with maintaining order within the palace, especially among palace eunuchs.

1873   *fān-í tū chǐh-hūi shǐh* 番夷都指揮使
MING: **Commander-in-chief of Frontier Natives,** 3 posts in early Ming, apparently granted to important aboriginal chiefs. See *t'u-kuan*. P72.

1874   *fān-kuān* 番官
Official on Rotational Duty: see *fan* (on rotational duty).

1875   *fán-kuān àn* 蕃官案
SUNG: **Section for Submitted Tribes,** a unit in the Ministry of War (*ping-pu*), responsible for handling relations with friendly alien peoples on the northern and northwestern borders. SP: *service des officiers de la tribu soumise.*

1876   *fān-mǎn* 番滿
T'ANG: **Completion of a Tour of Duty,** referring principally to militiamen of the Garrison Militia (*fu-ping*) establishment who, having fulfilled their one-month service obligation in the Southern Command (*nan-ya*) at the dynastic capital, were released to return to their home Garrisons (*fu*). May also be encountered in the sense that a Duty Group (*fan*) was rotating off, or standing down from, its scheduled active service. See *fan* (on rotational duty). Cf. *k'ao-man.*

1877   *fān-nièh liǎng ssū* 藩臬兩司
CH'ING: **Two Provincial Offices,** collective reference to Provincial Administration Commissions (*ch'eng-hsüan pu-cheng shih ssu,* informally called *fan-ssu*) and Provincial Surveillance Commissions (*t'i-hsing an-ch'a shih ssu,* informally called *nieh-ssu*), or to their heads. BH: two chief commissioners of the provincial government.

1878   *fán-pīng* 蕃兵
SUNG: **Frontier Tribal Troops,** designation of military units formed with friendly alien peoples on the northern and northwestern borders. SP: *armée de la tribu soumise.*

1879   *fān-pó* 藩伯
Frontier Earl: from the era of N-S Division on, a common unofficial reference to a territorial magnate such as a Re-

gional Inspector (*tz'u-shih*) or, later, a Military Commissioner (*chieh-tu shih*).

1880   *fán-pù* 蕃部
N-S DIV (Chou): **Section for Foreign Relations** in the Ministry of Justice (*ch'iu-kuan*), in charge of the reception of tributary envoys; also the title of its **Director**, ranked as an Ordinary Grand Master (*chung ta-fu;* 5a). Cf. *pin-pu.* P11.

1881   *fān-shàng* 番上
Rotated up (or **onto**), referring (1) to men or groups taking their scheduled rotational terms on some particular active duty; or (2) in T'ang, more specifically, to militiamen of the Garrison Militia (*fu-ping*) establishment who, on a regular rotational schedule, were rotated from their home Garrisons (*fu*) into the Southern Command (*nan-ya*) at the dynastic capital. See *fan* (on rotational duty).

1882   *fàn-shàng jén-wěi shǔ* 飯上人委署
CH'ING: **Food Provisioners Office,** one of 2 agencies that constituted the Palace Larder (*yü ch'a-shan fang*), part of the Imperial Household Department (*nei-wu fu*); headed by an Overseer-general (*tsung-ling*), with a staff of 35 Food Provisioners (*fan-shang jen*); provided food for court banquets, imperial gifts, etc.; until 1689 called Food Section (*fan-fang*). P37.

1883   *fán-shū ì-yǔ* 蕃書譯語
T'ANG: **Translator of Foreign Writings,** 10, apparently unranked, on the staff of the Secretariat (*chung-shu sheng*). RR: *traducteur pour les écritures des pays étrangers.*

1884   *fān-ssū* 藩司
MING–CH'ING: **Regional Office,** unofficial reference to a Provincial Administration Commission (*ch'eng-hsüan pu-cheng shih ssu*).

1885   *fān-t'ái* 藩臺
MING–CH'ING: variant of **Regional Office** (*fan-ssu*), unofficial reference to a Provincial Administration Commission (*ch'eng-hsüan pu-cheng shih ssu*).

1886   *fān-t'óu* 番頭
T'ANG: **Duty Group Head,** in charge of a team or shift serving in a guard or other capacity on a short-term rotational schedule with other Duty Groups (*fan*).

1887   *fān-t'úng ssū* 旛幢司
CH'ING: **Flag Office,** one of 2 units in the Center Subsection (*chung-so*) of the Imperial Procession Guard (*luan-i wei*), headed by a Director (*chang-yin yün-hui shih*), rank 4a. BH: flags and signals section.

1888   *fān-wáng* 藩王
N-S DIV: **Regional Prince,** title of nobility (*chüeh*), rank 2, possibly originating in Liang, conferred on sons of Imperial Princes (*ch'in-wang*) other than the heirs (*ssu-wang,* Prince Presumptive); equivalent to T'ang status as Duke (*kung*) and Ming–Ch'ing status as Commandery Prince (*chün-wang*). P65.

1889   *fàn-yín ch'ù* 飯銀處
CH'ING: **Meal Allowance Office** in the Court of Colonial Affairs (*li-fan yüan*), responsible for auditing expense accounts of the Court's personnel. BH: mess allowance office.

1890   *fān-yù shǔ* 蕃育署
MING: **Office of Domestic Fowl,** one of 4 major Offices (*shu*) in the Directorate of Imperial Parks (*shang-lin yüan-chien*); headed by a Manager (*tien-shu*), rank 7a; respon-

sible for breeding and caring for all domestic fowl in the imperial parks. P40.

1891   *fān-yüán* 藩垣 or *fān-yüèh* 岳
T'ANG: lit., frontier wall or frontier peak: **Protector of State,** unofficial reference to almost any very powerful official, especially to a Military Commissioner (*chieh-tu shih*).

1892   *fāng* 坊
(1) Throughout history, a common designation for an area (perhaps normally enclosed) used as a **Shop, Workshop, Office,** or even **Cage** (see *wu fang*): e.g., *wei-fang* (Guards Office). The specific use or function is normally suggested by a prefix. (2) SUI–CH'ING: **Precinct,** a sub-District (*hsien*) unit of local organization of the population in large urban centers, especially capital cities, i.e., an urban counterpart of the rural Village (*li*); normally with a resident designated as Head (*chang, cheng*), who was responsible to the District Magistrate (*hsien-ling, chih-hsien*) for the Precinct's fulfillment of government-imposed obligations. P20.

1893   *fáng* 房
T'ANG–CH'ING: **Office** or **Section,** common designation for subordinate agencies, with prefixes suggesting their functions; e.g., the Central Control Office (*shu-chi fang*) in the combined Secretariat-Chancellery (*chung-shu men-hsia*) of T'ang times.

1894   *fāng-ch'ǎng àn* 坊場案
SUNG: **Shops and Yards Section,** a unit in the Right Section (*yu-ts'ao*) of the Ministry of Revenue (*hu-pu*). SP: *service d'ateliers et d'aires.*

1895   *fāng-chèn* 方鎮
T'ANG: variant of *chen* (**Defense Command**).

1896   *fāng-chèng* 方正
HAN–N-S DIV: **Straightforward and Upright,** recommendation category for men nominated by local officials to be considered at the dynastic capital for selection and appointment to office; usually only in combinations such as *hsiao-lien fang-cheng, hsien-ling fang-cheng,* qq.v.

1897   *fāng-ch'éng* 方丞
HAN: **Medical Treatment Aide** to the Imperial Physician (*t'ai-i ling*) on the staff of the Chamberlain for the Palace Revenues (*shao-fu*). Cf. *yao-ch'eng* (Pharmacist Aide). HB: assistant for prescriptions. P36.

1898   *fáng-chǐn shǐh* 防禁使
SUNG: **Defense Commissioner,** title occasionally granted to chiefs of southwestern aboriginal tribes. P72.

1899   *fāng-chǔ* 坊主
SUI: **Company Commander,** the militia chief in an urban Precinct (*fang*), i.e., a lowly officer in the Garrison Militia (*fu-ping*) system, abolished in a reorganization in 607. P20.

1900   *fáng-chǔ* 防主
N-S DIV: **Defense Chief,** ad hoc assignment for a military officer, normally to take charge of guarding a city specified in a prefix.

1901   *fǎng-chǔ* 訪舉
N-S DIV (Sung): **Examiner,** an official of the Library of Complete Discernment (*tsung-ming kuan*), serving under the Chancellor of the Eastern Library (*tung-kuan chi-chiu*); apparently responsible for examining and certifying the staff of Scholars (*hsüeh-shih*) selected to serve in the organization. P23.

1902 *fāng-hsiāng shìh* 方相氏
CHOU: **Shaman,** 4 non-official specialists attached to the Ministry of War (*hsia-kuan*) who led processions in seasonal purification ceremonies and funerals, wearing bearskin hoods with 4 golden eyes and red and black clothing, and brandishing lances and shields; believed to drive away pestilential demons. CL: *inspecteur de région.*

1903 *fāng-huá* 芳華
N-S DIV (N. Ch'i): **Lady of Fragrant Loveliness,** the designation of one of 27 imperial consorts called Hereditary Consorts (*shih-fu*), rank =3b.

1904 *fāng-huá yüàn* 芳華苑
T'ANG: lit., the park of fragrant flowers: **Imperial Capital Park,** from 618 to 657 the official name of the later *shen-tu yüan,* q.v. Also see *shang-lin yüan.* P40.

1905 *fāng-í* 芳儀
T'ANG: **Lady of Fragrant Deportment,** designation of an imperial concubine, rank 2a; one of the Six Ladies of Deportment (*liu i*). RR: *correction parfumée.*

1906 *fáng-k'ǎo kuān* 房考官
MING–CH'ING: **Examiner,** general designation for officials assigned to supervise civil service recruitment examinations.

1907 *fáng-kó* 防閣
N-S DIV (N. Ch'i): **Defender of the Hall,** members of the staffs of Princedoms (*wang-kuo*); no more than 4 on each staff. P69.

1908 *fāng-kuān* 坊官
CH'ING: unofficial reference to a **Vice Commander** (*fu chih-hui*) of one of the 5 Wardens' Offices (*ping-ma chih-hui ssu*) that policed the dynastic capital, Peking.

1909 *fāng-lüèh kuǎn* 方略館
CH'ING: **Military Archive,** a unit under the Grand Secretariat (*nei-ko*) that maintained records of military affairs; normally headed by a Grand Secretariat official with the designation Director-general (*tsung-ts'ai*). BH: military archives office.

1910 *fāng-mièn* 方面
MING: **Regional Supervisor,** general reference to executive officials of Provincial Administration Commissions (*ch'eng-hsüan pu-cheng shih ssu*), Provincial Surveillance Commissions (*t'i-hsing an-ch'a shih ssu*), and Regional Military Commissions (*tu chih-hui shih ssu*). Cf. *chien-ssu.*

1911 *fāng-pó* 方伯
Regional Earl. (1) CHOU: title of nobility (*chüeh*), perhaps specifying an Earl (*po*) enfeoffed with a territory that he administered, in contrast to Earls in service at the royal court. (2) HAN–N-S DIV: unofficial reference to a Regional Inspector (*tz'u-shih*). (3) MING–CH'ING: unofficial reference to a Provincial Administration Commissioner (*pu-cheng shih*). May be encountered in any period in unofficial reference to other territorial dignitaries. Also see *ta fang-po.*

1912 *fāng-shìh* 方士
CHOU: **Justiciar of the Domain,** title used ambiguously in the principal source; probably 16 with rank as Ordinary Servicemen (*chung-shih*), members of the Ministry of Justice (*ch'iu-kuan*) with supervisory responsibility over regional (*fang*) dignitaries called Justiciars of the Administrative Regions (*chia-shih*) and Justiciars of the Inherited Regions (*tu-shih*), but possibly a generic term including all these Justiciars. CL: *prévôt de région.*

1913 *fāng-shìh* 方氏
CHOU: **Regional Official,** common element in the titles of, and perhaps a generic reference to, 6 officials of the Ministry of War (*hsia-kuan*) who concerned themselves with various matters relating to fiefs and other dependent territories outside the royal domain. See *chih-fang shih, t'u-fang shih, huai-fang shih, ho-fang shih, hsün-fang shih, hsing-fang shih.*

1914 *fáng-shǒu wèi* 防守尉
CH'ING: **Post Commandant,** a rank 4a military officer commanding a minor garrison of bannermen (see *ch'i, pa ch'i*); responsible to the Vice Commander-in-chief (*fu tu-t'ung*) of a Province. BH: military commandant of the 2nd class.

1915 *fáng-tì k'ō* 房地科
SUNG: **State Properties Subsection,** one of 3 Subsections (*k'o*) in the Left Section (*tso-ts'ao*) of the Ministry of Revenue (*hu-pu*) from c. 1080, when the Ministry was fully activated following discontinuance of the State Finance Commission (*san ssu*) of early Sung; staffed with subofficial functionaries who monitored the management of state-owned buildings and nonagricultural lands and the receipt of regional specialty commodities submitted as nominal tribute (*kung*). SP: *section de taxe d'immeubles.* P6.

1916 *fáng-t'uán* 防團
SUNG: abbreviated collective reference to **Defense Commissioners** (*fang-yü shih*) **and Military Training Commissioners** (*t'uan-lien shih*), and to the system of military organization in which they served.

1917 *fāng-wǔ láng* 方舞郎
N-S DIV (N. Wei): **Regional Dance Director,** number unspecified, rank 5b or 6b, subordinates of the Palace Chief Musician (*hsieh-lü chung-lang;* see under *hsieh-lü lang*). P10.

1918 *fáng-yèh ch'éng* 坊鄴丞
N-S DIV (Chin): **Aide for Mercantile Taxes** (?), a subordinate of the Chamberlain for the Palace Revenues (*shao-fu*).

1919 *fāng-yú* 芳猷
N-S DIV (N. Ch'i): **Lady of Fragrant Excellence,** designation of one of 27 imperial consorts called Hereditary Consorts (*shih-fu*); rank =3b.

1920 *fáng-yù* 防禦
Lit., to defend against. (1) SUNG–CHIN: **Defense,** prefix attached to the term Prefecture (*fu, chou, chün*) when the area was dominated by a Defense Commissioner (*fang-yü shih*). (2) CH'ING: **Platoon Commander,** a rank 5a military officer commanding a minor garrison of bannermen (see *ch'i, pa ch'i*) at an imperial mausoleum, imperial horse pasturage, imperial hunting preserve, etc.; normally responsible to the Vice Commander-in-chief (*fu tu-t'ung*) of a Province. BH: captain.

1921 *fáng-yù hǎi-tào yùn-liáng wàn-hù fǔ* 防禦海道運糧萬戶府
YÜAN: **Sea Transport Defense Brigade,** created in 1355 by upgrading the prior Sea Transport Defense Battalion (*hai-tao hsün-fang ch'ien-hu so*) based at T'ai-chou (modern Chekiang); two months later established a Branch Office (*fen-ssu*) at P'ing-chiang (modern Kiangsu); headed by a Commander (*wan-hu*), apparently rank 2a. P60.

1922 *fáng-yù kuān-ch'á shih* 防禦觀察使
T'ANG: **Defense and Surveillance Commissioner,** a del-

egate from the central government on a nominally temporary duty assignment supervising a Prefecture (*chou*); less prestigious than a Military Commissioner (*chieh-tu shih*). P50.

1923 *fáng-yǜ shǐh* 防禦使
Defense Commissioner. (1) T'ANG: a delegate from the central government on ad hoc duty assignment supervising a Prefecture (*chou*), or a designation conferred on certain Prefects (*tz'u-shih*); after 762 displaced by the more prestigious title Military Commissioner (*chieh-tu shih*). (2) SUNG–LIAO: duty assignment (*ch'ai-ch'ien*) for a central government official to supervise the affairs of a Prefecture (*chou*) where military matters were of some importance; also a prestige title (*san-kuan*) for rank 5b military officers. RR+SP: *commissaire impérial à la défense.* P50, 57.

1924 *fáng-yü shǒu-chŏ shǐh* 防禦守捉使
T'ANG: **Defense and Security Commissioner,** a delegate from the central government on ad hoc duty assignment in charge of a Prefecture (*chou, chün*); originated in response to the rebellion of An Lu-shan in 755. RR: *commissaire impérial aux détachements militaires chargé de la défense de la région.*

1925 *fēi* 妃
(1) **Consort:** throughout history used generically in reference to wives of Emperors other than the principal wife designated Empress (*hou, huang-hou*), usually denoting the highest-ranking palace women excluding the Empress; commonly with several differentiating prefixes, e.g., *kuei-fei* (Honored Consort), *te-fei* (Virtuous Consort). RR: *concubine.* (2) **Consort:** throughout history the most common designation, without prefixes, of principal wives of Heirs Apparent and other Princes. HB: principal wife (of the heir apparent). (3) CH'ING: **Consort-in-ordinary,** used without prefixes as the designation of the 3rd-ranking Consort of the Emperor, after Imperial Honored Consort (*huang kuei-fei*) and Honored Consort. BH: imperial concubine of the 3d rank. See *san fei, ssu fei.*

1926 *fēi-chì* 飛騎
T'ANG: **Flying Cavalryman,** general designation of soldiers in the Left and Right Encampments (*t'un-ying*) established in 638 as bases for the Imperial Army of Original Followers (*yüan-ts'ung chin-chün*), supplemented with recruits from elite families; part of the Northern Command (*pei-ya*). The troops were regularly tested for archery, horsemanship, weight lifting, etc.; and those most skilled joined the elite imperial escort group called the Hundred Cavaliers (*po chi*). The term Flying Cavalryman was apparently not used officially after the Left and Right Encampments were transformed into the Left and Right Forest of Plumes Armies (*yü-lin chün*) in 662; but it may have been used even after T'ang as an unofficial reference to any group of elite cavalrymen. RR: *cavalier volant.* P43.

1927 *fēi-chì wèi* 飛騎尉
Commandant of Flying Cavalry. (1) SUI: the 5th highest of 8 Commandant (*wei*) titles conferred on inactive officials (see *san-kuan*), beginning in 586; the practice terminated c. 604. (2) T'ANG–MING: merit title (*hsün*) conferred on officials of rank 6b through Chin, thereafter 5b; in Ming conferred only on military officers. RR+SP: *directeur de la cavalerie volante.* P65.

1928 *fēi-ch'ién* 飛錢
T'ANG: lit., flying coins: common term for the various prototypes of paper money that circulated in the dynasty's last

years. See *pao-ch'ao, chiao-tzu wu, hui-tzu chien, chiao-ch'ao.* P16.

1929 *fēi-chiù* 飛廄
T'ANG: **Stable of Flying Mounts,** one Left and one Right, among the palace stable units collectively called the Six Stables (*liu chiu,* q.v.). RR: *écurie des chevaux volants.*

1930 *fēi-lúng chiù* 飛龍廄 or *fēi-lúng yüàn* 院
T'ANG–LIAO: **Flying Dragon Corral** (*chiu*) or **Flying Dragon Park** (*yüan*), from 696 the name of one of the Six Palace Corrals (*chang-nei liu hsien*), where horses were reared inside the palace grounds; headed by a eunuch Commissioner (*shih*); in Sung subordinate to the Court of the Imperial Stud (*t'ai-p'u ssu*) but early renamed Imperial Corral (*t'ien-chiu fang*). RR: *parc des dragons volants.* SP: *cour des écuries célestes.*

1931 *fēi-lúng shǐh* 飛龍使
Flying Dragon Commissioner. (1) T'ANG–LIAO: in T'ang a eunuch in charge of the Flying Dragon Corral (*fei-lung chiu*), thereafter a regular official, rank not clear, in charge of the Flying Dragon Park (fei-lung yüan). (2) CH'ING: unofficial reference to the Chief Minister (*ch'ing*) of the Palace Stud (*shang-ssu yüan*).

1932 *fēi-pó-shū pó-shìh* 飛白書博士
T'ANG: **Erudite of Fancy White Calligraphy,** a specialist in outline-like script originated by Ts'ai Yung of Later Han; one of 18 Palace Erudites (*nei-chiao po-shih*) on the staff of the Palace Institute of Literature (*nei wen-hsüeh kuan*), where palace women were educated; from c. 741 a eunuch post. RR: *maître de l'écriture fei-po.*

1933 *fēi-shíh* 肺石
T'ANG: **Resounding Stone,** suspended outside a palace gate to be struck by anyone who, having failed to get a satisfactory response from regular administrative agencies to a complaint about injustice or a disastrous state policy, wished to attract imperial attention to his complaint; members of the Palace Gate Guards (*chien-men wei*) were supposed to respond to such appeals and transmit the complaints to the throne. Also see *teng-wen ku* (Public Petitioners Drum).

1934 *fēn* 分
Common prefix to an agency name or official title meaning **Detached** or **Branch,** as in … *fen-ssu* (Branch Office of …). Normally such a branch agency or detached official carried the full range of the home office's responsibilities, but in a narrowly specified territorial jurisdiction. *Fen* differs from *hsing* (mobile) in that *fen* normally suggests a stably fixed establishment whereas *hsing* suggests a relatively impermanent, movable establishment.

1935 *fēn-ch'á shǐh* 分察使
5 DYN: variant reference to an **Investigating Censor** (*chien-ch'a yü-shih*). P18.

1936 *fēn-ch'āi liáng-liào yüàn* 分差糧料院
SUNG: **Branch Office for Provisions and Labor Services,** the local representative of an Overseer-general (*tsung-ling*), who managed the logistical support of armies. SP: *bureau des vivres, de fourrage, et des corvées.*

1937 *fēn chìh-chiēn* 分治監
CHIN: **Branch Directorate of Waterways,** a local agency representing the Directorate of Waterways (*tu-shui chien*) at the dynastic capital, headed by an Administrator (*yüan*), rank 8a; responsible for the management of rivers, marshes, ferries, bridges, and river boats. Apparently also known as

Outer Directorates (*wai-chien*); established 1153, in 1225 consolidated into two Outer Directorates. P59.

1938 *fēn-fŭ* 分府
CH'ING: lit., a detached representative of a Prefect (*chih-fu*): unofficial reference to a **Subprefectural Magistrate** (*t'ung-chih*).

1939 *fěn-hóu* 粉侯
Lit., powder Marquis, suggesting the Marquis-consort of a face-powdered lady: from Sung on, an unofficial reference to an **Imperial Son-in-law**, the husband of an Imperial Princess (*kung-chu*) officially entitled Commandant-escort (*fu-ma tu-wei*) or, in Ch'ing, Consort (*o-fu*).

1940 *fēn-hsún pīng-pèi tào* 分巡兵備道
CH'ING: **General Surveillance and Military Defense Circuit,** the jurisdiction of, and a quasi-official reference to, a Surveillance Vice Commissioner (*an-ch'a fu-shih*) or an Assistant Surveillance Commissioner (*an-ch'a ch'ien-shih*) detached from a Provincial Surveillance Commission (*t'i-hsing an-ch'a shih ssu*) to serve as a Circuit Intendant (*tao-t'ai*) in charge of a Branch Office (*fen-ssu*) of the Commission, with both censorial and military responsibilities. See *fen-hsün tao, ping-pei tao*. BH: military circuit taotai.

1941 *fēn-hsún tào* 分巡道
MING–CH'ING: **General Surveillance Circuit,** until 1753 a Branch Office (*fen-ssu*) of a Provincial Surveillance Commission (*t'i-hsing an-ch'a shih ssu*) headed by a Surveillance Vice Commissioner (*an-ch'a fu-shih*) or an Assistant Surveillance Commissioner (*an-ch'a ch'ien-shih*) detached from his home Commission with full authority to represent it in supervising the judicial and surveillance activities in a Circuit (*tao*) of 2 or more Prefectures (*fu*); the term is normally prefixed with geographical names suggesting the specific territorial jurisdiction. The official in charge was commonly called a Circuit Intendant (*tao-t'ai*). After 1753 Circuit Intendants of all sorts, while continuing to serve as intermediaries between the Prefectures of their jurisdictions and the Provincial Surveillance Commissions, were considered separate substantive appointees with rank 4a and no longer had titular appointments in Commissions. BH: circuit intendant. P52.

1942 *fēn-pù àn* 分簿案
SUNG: **Separating and Registering Section,** one of several Sections (*an*) in the Left Bureau (*tso-t'ing*) of the Court of Judicial Review (*ta-li ssu*); staffed with subofficial functionaries who recorded all trial reports received and distributed them to the appropriate units of the Court for review. SP: *service de la division des registres*. P22.

1943 *fēn-shŏu tào* 分守道
MING–CH'ING: **General Administration Circuit,** until 1753 a Branch Office (*fen-ssu*) of a Provincial Administration Commission (*ch'eng-hsüan pu-cheng shih ssu*) headed by an Administration Vice Commissioner (*pu-cheng ts'an-cheng*) or Assistant Administration Commissioner (*pu-cheng ts'an-i*) detached from his home Commission with full authority to represent it in supervising general administration activities in a Circuit (*tao*) of 2 or more Prefectures (*fu*); the term is normally prefixed with geographical names suggesting the specific territorial administration. The official in charge was commonly called a Circuit Intendant (*tao-t'ai*). After 1753 Circuit Intendants of all sorts, while continuing to serve as intermediaries between the Prefectures of their jurisdictions and the Provincial Administration Commissions, were considered separate substantive ap-

pointees with rank 4a and no longer had titular appointments in Commissions. BH: circuit intendant. P52.

1944 *fēn-shŭ* 粉署
T'ANG: lit., powder office: unofficial reference to a (any?) **Vice Director** (*yüan-wai lang*) of a Bureau (*ssu*) in the Ministry of Works (*kung-pu*).

1945 *fēn-ssū* 分司
Branch Office. (1) Throughout history, a term applied to units of many kinds that were detached from their base agencies; sometimes an indirect reference to the head of such a detached unit or even to a lone detached official. (2) SUNG: may be encountered as a clerical error for *san ssu* (State Finance Commission). (3) MING–CH'ING: most specifically refers to the office of a Circuit Intendant (*tao-t'ai*, q.v.), until 1753 nominally a member of a Provincial Administration Commission (*ch'eng-hsüan pu-cheng shih ssu*) or a Provincial Surveillance Commission (*t'i-hsing an-ch'a shih ssu*). P52.

1946 *fēn-t'ái* 分臺
YÜAN: **Branch Office** of the metropolitan Censorate (*yü-shih t'ai*), established in Fukien in 1365. Cf. *hsing-t'ai*.

1947 *fēn-tì* 分地
YÜAN: one of several general terms for **land grants** (often rendered as appanages) that were conferred on members of the nobility (*chüeh*); the recipients of larger tracts were virtually autonomous fief-holders who nominated men for official appointments in their domains, collected taxes, and exercised other governmental powers until about 1311, when the central government began exerting its direct control in all areas and nobles were given stipends in lieu of incomes derived from their tracts.

1948 *fēn-t'iáo* 分條
N-S DIV (Chin-S. Dyn.): a process of "dividing into groups" the Sections (*ts'ao*) of the evolving Department of State Affairs (*shang-shu sheng*), several Overseers (*lu … shih*) of the Department being assigned different groups (*t'iao*) so as to divide and limit their authority.

1949 *fén-tz'ú shŭ* 汾祠署
T'ANG: **Office for Sacrifices at the Fen River** (in modern Shansi Province, the original power base of the T'ang founders); established in 733 (whether in the dynastic capital or in Shansi is not clear) with principal sacrificial and custodial functions in the temple honoring the spirit of the river; apparently supervised by the Court of Imperial Sacrifices (*t'ai-ch'ang ssu*) and the Ministry of Rites (*li-pu*); headed by a Director (*ling, shu-ling*), rank 7b2. RR: *office du temple de la rivière Fen*. P28.

1950 *fèng-ān fŭ-păo sŏ* 奉安符寶所
SUNG: **Office of Tallies and Seals for Imperial Funerals,** relationship with other agencies not clear; probably headed by a dignitary entitled Court Gentleman (*lang*). SP: *bureau des insignes*.

1951 *fèng-ch'áng* 奉常
Lit., bearer of the flag, *ch'ang* in this usage denoting an imperial flag or banner decorated with the sun, the moon, and a dragon: occasional variant of or, more commonly, an unofficial reference to the Ch'in–Sui **Chamberlain for Ceremonials** (*t'ai-ch'ang*) or the Sui–Ch'ing **Chief Minister** (*ch'ing*) **of the Court of Imperial Sacrifices** (*t'ai-ch'ang ssu*). HB: upholder of ceremonies. SP: *intendant de rites et de musiques*. P27.

1952 *fèng-ch'áng ssù* 奉常寺
SUI–CH'ING: unofficial reference to the **Court of Imperial Sacrifices** (*t'ai-ch'ang ssu*); from 662 to 671, the official name of the Court. RR: *cour des sacrifices impériaux*. P27.

1953 *fèng-ch'áng tà-fū* 奉常大夫
CH'ING: unofficial reference to the **Vice Minister** (*shao-ch'ing*) **of the Court of Imperial Sacrifices** (*t'ai-ch'ang ssu*).

1954 *fèng ch'áo-chîng* 奉朝請
Audience Attendant: in Han, when *ch'ao* referred to spring audiences and *ching* (sic; not *ch'ing* in this use) referred to autumn audiences, a collective term for all members of the imperial clan, imperial in-laws, and retired officials who participated in court audiences. In the era of N-S Division (Sung), the official designation of numerous low-ranking members of the Department of Scholarly Counselors (*chi-shu sheng, san-chi sheng*). In Sui transformed into the prestige titles (*san-kuan*) *ch'ao-ching ta-fu* (Grand Master for Court Audiences) and *ch'ao-ching lang* (Gentleman for Court Audiences). HB: servant at the spring and autumn courts. P68.

1955 *fèng-ch'ē láng* 奉車郎
HAN: **Court Gentleman for Chariots,** apparently subordinate to the Commandant-in-chief of Chariots (*feng-ch'e tu-wei*). HB: gentleman of imperial equipages.

1956 *fèng-ch'ē tū-wèi* 奉車都尉
HAN: **Commandant-in-chief of Chariots,** honorific supplementary appointment (*chia-kuan*) carrying rank =2,000 bushels; in Later Han made a regular appointment at the same rank on the staff of the Chamberlain for Attendants (*kuang-lu-hsün*), but with no duties except when in active command of campaigning troops. HB: chief commandant of the imperial equipages.

1957 *fèng-ch'én k'ù* 奉宸庫
SUNG: **Jewelry Storehouse,** a unit under the Court of the Imperial Treasury (*t'ai-fu ssu*) in charge of precious objects received by the Emperor in tribute, etc. SP: *magasin d'or, de jade et de perles*.

1958 *fèng-ch'én tà-fū* 奉宸大夫
T'ANG: **Grand Master of the Palace Corral,** late T'ang designation for the head (or one of the heads) of horse-rearing and -training activities within the imperial palace grounds, under the supervision of the Palace Administration (*tien-chung sheng*); apparently replaced the Office of Heavenly Mounts (*t'ien-chi fu*), then in the 820s was absorbed into the pre-existing Flying Dragon Corral (*fei-lung chiu*). P39.

1959 *fèng-ch'én wèi* 奉宸衛
T'ANG: briefly in 662 the official variant designation of the **Personal Guards** (*ch'ien-niu wei, ch'ien-niu fu*) among the Sixteen Guards (*shih-liu wei*, q.v.) at the dynastic capital. P43.

1960 *fèng ch'én-yüàn* 奉宸苑
CH'ING: **Imperial Parks Administration,** one of Three Special Agencies (*san yüan*, q.v.) in the Imperial Household Department (*nei-wu fu*); supervised numerous imperial hunting grounds and gardens in the Peking area; headed by a Grand Minister of the Imperial Household Department (*nei ta-ch'en*) or a Prince serving as Manager (*kuan-li*), assisted by 2 Chief Ministers (*ch'ing*), rank 3a. Established 1684, but not fully staffed till 1728. HB: bureau of imperial gardens and hunting parks. P40.

1961 *fèng-chèng tà-fū* 奉政大夫
CHIN–CH'ING: **Grand Master for Governance,** prestige title (*san-kuan*) for civil officials of rank 6a1 in Chin, thereafter 5a. P68.

1962 *fèng-ch'éng* 奉乘
See under *feng-sheng*.

1963 *fèng-chì* 風紀
Customs and Regulations: from T'ang if not earlier, a combining abbreviation of *feng-hsien* (customs and laws) and *kang-chi* (disciplinary principles), qq.v., both references to the standards of official conduct that surveillance officials (*ch'a-kuan*) were expected to uphold; commonly occurs as an indirect reference to such officials.

1964 *fèng-chià chú* 奉駕局
T'ANG: lit., office for providing vehicles: from 662 to 670 the official variant of *shang-sheng chü* (**Livery Service**).

1965 *fèng-chià tà-fū* 奉駕大夫
T'ANG: **Grand Master of the Livery,** from 662 to 670 the official variant of *feng-yü* (Steward) of the Livery Service (*shang-sheng chü*). P39.

1966 *fèng-chiāng tà-lì* 封疆大吏
CH'ING: **Provincial Magnate,** unofficial reference to a Provincial Governor (*hsün-fu*) or a multi-Province Governor-general (*tsung-tu*), or collectively to officials of both sorts.

1967 *fēng-chièn* 封建
Lit., to install by enfeoffment or subinfeudation: **to enfeoff, feudal.** (1) CHOU: the procedure by which the Kings (*wang*) of early Chou governed those parts of their realm beyond the directly-administered royal domain, by ennobling their kinsmen and other associates (preferably linked by marriage to the royal family) as Dukes (*kung*), Marquises (*hou*), Earls (*po*), Viscounts (*tzu*), and Barons (*nan*), collectively called Feudal Lords (*chu-hou*), and installing them with oaths of fealty in geographic jurisdictions of varying size and strategic importance; to a lesser extent refers also to the subinfeudation of lesser members of the elite class (*shih*) as administrators within the royal domain and in the separate domains of the Feudal Lords. (2) CH'IN–CH'ING: used by political theorists throughout imperial history as the type of decentralized, indirect rule by hereditary dignitaries that was ascribed to antiquity and was the ideal polar opposite of the system of Commanderies and Districts (*chün-hsien*) instituted by the Ch'in dynasty (centralized, bureaucratic, direct). Often used in the sense of semifeudal, quasi-feudal, neofeudal, etc., in reference to the recurrence of Chou-like patterns of political decentralization and social stratification after Ch'in, especially in such periods as the era of N-S Division and the Mongol Yüan dynasty. In the 20th century, used by anti-tradition revolutionaries and polemicists, especially communists, in reference to the whole sociopolitical order of imperial times, mostly suggesting abuses of the peasantry by large landlords rather than particular patterns of political organization.

1968 *fèng-chíh* 奉職
CHIN: **Steward,** 30 authorized for the staff of the Palace Inspectorate-general (*tien-ch'ien tu tien-chien ssu*); created in 1172 by retitling the *wai-chang hsiao-ti* (Retainers of the Outer Chamber). Cf. *feng-yü* (Chief Steward). P38.

1969 *fèng-chìh* 奉觶
T'ANG: **Cupbearer,** 120 suboffical servants on the staff of the Office of Fine Wines (*liang-yün shu*) in the Court of

Imperial Entertainments (*kuang-lu ssu*), 30 additional in the Office of Foodstuffs (*shih-kuan shu*) in the Household Provisioner's Court (*chia-ling ssu*), part of the establishment of the Heir Apparent. RR: *serviteur chargé de présenter les coupes*. P30.

1970 *fèng-chíh láng* 奉直郎
SUNG: **Gentleman for Forthright Service,** prestige title (*san-kuan*) for civil officials of rank 6b1. SP: *dignitaire fong-tche*. P68.

1971 *fèng-chíh tà-fū* 奉直大夫
SUNG–CH'ING: **Grand Master for Forthright Service,** prestige title (*san-kuan*) for civil officials of rank 6a in Sung, 6b1 in Chin, 5b thereafter. SP: *grand dignitaire fong-tche*. P68.

1972 *fèng-chǐh ts'ān-chūn* 奉旨參軍
SUNG: **Correspondence Adjutant** on the staff of a Prefecture (*chou*), rank 9b, supplementing the Adjutants of the Six Sections (*liu ts'ao ts'an-chün*) among whom administrative responsibilities were divided. See *ts'an-chün, liu ts'ao*. P53.

1973 *fēng-ch'ú ts'āng* 豐儲倉
SUNG, YÜAN: **Reserve Granary,** in Sung local storage agencies under the supervisory control of the Court of the Imperial Granaries (*ssu-nung ssu*), in Yüan one under the Palace Provisions Commission (*hsüan-hui yüan*) headed by a subofficial Commissioner-in-chief (*ta-shih*). SP: *grenier de réserves abondantes*. P38.

1974 *fèng-chuāng ch'ién-wù k'ù* 封椿錢物庫
SUNG: lit., storehouse of savings in money and goods: **Treasury Reserve Storehouse,** maintained by the Department of State Affairs (*shang-shu sheng*) through both its Left Office (*tso-ssu*) and its Right Office (*yu-ssu*). SP: *magasin d'épargnes en argent et en nature*.

1975 *fèng-chuāng k'ù* 封椿庫
SUNG: **Emergency Reserves Storehouse,** a storehouse of fiscal reserves maintained by the Department of State Affairs (*shang-shu sheng*) for use in military emergencies and for famine relief. SP: *trésor d'épargnes pour les dépenses militaires et la famine*.

1976 *fèng-chüéh chìh-kào* 封爵制誥
CHIN: **Proclamation Drafter for Honors,** a member of the Ministry of Personnel (*lì-pu*), rank not clear; responsible for maintaining personnel dossiers concerning evaluations and the awarding of honors. P5.

1977 *fèng-ēn chèn-kuó kūng* 奉恩鎮國公
CH'ING: **Defender Duke,** the 5th highest title of imperial nobility (*chüeh*): (1) designation of the eldest son of a Beile Prince (*pei-tzu*); (2) inherited designation of a Commander-in-chief (*tu-t'ung*) of a Banner (*ch'i*) in the Mongol military organization. BH: prince (of the blood) of the 5th degree.

1978 *fèng-ēn chiāng-chūn* 奉恩將軍
CH'ING: **General by Grace,** the 12th and lowest title of imperial nobility (*chüeh*): designation of the eldest son of a General by Grace, any son of a Defender-general of the State (*feng-kuo chiang-chün*), or the adopted son of a Beile (*to-lo pei-lo*) or of a Beile Prince (*ku-shan pei-tzu*). BH: noble of the imperial lineage of the 12th rank.

1979 *fèng-ēn fǔ-kuó kūng* 奉恩輔國公
CH'ING: **Bulwark Duke,** the 6th highest title of imperial nobility (*chüeh*): (1) designation of the eldest son of a Defender Duke (*feng-en chen-kuo kung*); (2) inherited desig-

nation of a Commander-in-chief (*tu-t'ung*) of a Banner (*ch'i*) in the Mongol military organization. BH: prince (of the blood) of the 6th degree.

1980 *fèng-hsiǎng ch'ù* 俸餉處
CH'ING: **Commissary** in the Ministry of Revenue (*hu-pu*), independent of the Ministry's Bureaus (*ch'ing-li ssu*); responsible for the issuance of pay and rations to officers and troops of the Banners (*ch'i*). BH: office for issue of salaries and supplies. P6.

1981 *féng-hsiàng shìh* 馮相氏
CHOU: **Royal Astronomer,** 2 ranked as Ordinary Servicemen (*chung-shih*) and 4 as Junior Servicemen (*hsia-shih*), hereditary specialists on the staff of the Ministry of Rites (*ch'un-kuan*) who were responsible for charting the movements of celestial bodies, especially the planet Jupiter, in order to determine the correct times of the equinoxes and solstices, lunar cycles, etc., probably to assist in the preparation of the government-issued annual calendar. CL: *astronome impérial, officier chargé de monter et d'observer*.

1982 *fēng-hsièn kuān* 風憲官 or *feng-hsien*
Guardians of the Customs and Laws, throughout history an unofficial reference to members of the Censorate (*yü-shih t'ai, tu ch'a-yüan*) and regional counterpart agencies such as the Ming–Ch'ing Provincial Surveillance Commission (*t'i-hsing an-ch'a shih ssu*); also referred to generally as Surveillance Officials (*ch'a-kuan*).

1983 *fèng-hsìn láng* 奉信郎
SUI: **Gentleman for Trustworthy Service,** from c. 604 a prestige title (*san-kuan*) for civil officials apparently of rank 9b. P68.

1984 *fèng-hsūn ssū* 封勳司
CHIN: **Bureau of Honors,** one of 2 Bureaus (*ssu*) in the Ministry of Personnel (*lì-pu*) into which the more numerous traditional subsections of the Ministry were consolidated; each a petty agency managed by a Secretary (*chu-shih*), rank 7b. See *tzu-k'ao ssu* (Bureau of Evaluations). P5.

1985 *fèng-hsūn tà-fū* 奉訓大夫
CHIN–MING: **Grand Master for Admonishment,** prestige title (*san-kuan*) for civil officials of rank 6b2 in Chin, 5b thereafter. P68.

1986 *fèng-huà* 奉化
SUNG: **Promoter of Culture,** honorific designation conferred on various meritorious officials serving outside the capital, and on the parents of Emperors.

1987 *fèng-huáng ch'íh* 鳳凰池
Lit., phoenix pool: from early post-Han times on, an occasional unofficial reference to the **Secretariat** (*chung-shu sheng*).

1988 *fèng-í* 奉儀
T'ANG: **Lady of Decorous Service,** designation of 20 (24?) rank 9a concubines in the household of the Heir Apparent. RR: *femme qui présente les règles de l'étiquette*.

1989 *fèng-ǐ chǔ* 奉扆局
T'ANG: from 662 to 670 the official variant designation of the **Accommodations Service** (*shang-she chü*, q.v.).

1990 *fèng-ī chú* 奉醫局
T'ANG: from 662 to 670 the official variant designation of the **Palace Medical Service** (*shang-yao chü*, q.v.).

1991 *fèng-ì láng* 奉議郎
Court Gentleman Consultant. (1) T'ANG–SUNG: prestige title (*san-kuan*) for civil officials of rank 6b1 in T'ang, 8a in Sung. SP: *dignitaire fong-yi*. P68. (2) SUNG: 3rd-ranking executive official in the Court of the Imperial Clan (*tsung-cheng ssu*); after earliest Sung decades replaced the title Paymaster (*chi-lu kuan*); abolished in 1129, restored in 1135.

1992 *fèng-ì tà-fū* 奉議大夫
CHIN–MING: **Grand Master for Consultation,** prestige title (*san-kuan*) for civil officials of rank 6a2 in Chin, 5a thereafter. P68.

1993 *fèng-ī tà-fū* 奉醫大夫
T'ANG: from 662 to 670 the official variant designation of **Chief Stewards** (*feng-yü*) **of the Palace Medical Service** (*shang-yao chü*).

1994 *fēng-jén* 封人
CHOU: **Boundary Marker,** 4 ranked as Ordinary Servicemen (*chung-shih*) and 8 as Junior Servicemen (*hsia-shih*), members of the Ministry of Education (*ti-kuan*) responsible for building and protecting boundary embankments that defined the royal domain and separated the feudal states, and for participating in various major ceremonies. CL: *officier des levées aux frontières*.

1995 *féng-jén* 縫人
CHOU: **Royal Tailor,** 2 eunuchs and 8 palace women under direction of the Ministry of State (*t'ien-kuan*), who supervised 80 workers and 30 convicts in preparing and maintaining the wardrobes of the royal family. CL: *tailleur*.

1996 *fèng-kài yǔ-lín láng* 奉蓋羽林郎
HAN: **Umbrella-bearer of the Palace Guard,** number and rank not clear, members of the regular imperial entourage. See *yü-lin*.

1997 *fēng-kào k'ō* 封誥科
YÜAN: **Honors Section,** one of 3 minor Sections (*k'o*) in the Ministry of Personnel (*li-pu*), headed by one or more Clerks (*ling-shih*), rank not clear but low; responsible for preparing imperial proclamations awarding noble status. Comparable to the Bureau of Honors (*ssu-feng ssu, yen-feng ch'ing-li ssu*) in the Ministry in earlier and later periods. P5.

1998 *fèng-kó* 鳳閣
T'ANG: **Phoenix Hall,** from 684 to 705 the official variant designation of the Secretariat (*chung-shu sheng*). Subsequently an unofficial reference to the Secretariat. P3.

1999 *fèng-kuó chiāng-chūn* 奉國將軍
MING–CH'ING: **Supporter-general of the State,** title of nobility (*chüeh*) conferred on certain descendants of Emperors: in Ming, the 5th highest of 8 titles of imperial nobility, generally conferred on great-grandsons of Emperors other than the prospective heirs of Commandery Princes (*chün-wang*); in Ch'ing, the 11th highest of 12 titles of imperial nobility, conferred on all sons of Bulwark-generals of the State (*fu-kuo chiang-chün*), sons by concubines of Bulwark Dukes (*fu-kuo kung*), and adopted sons of Commandery Princes. BH: noble of the imperial lineage of the 11th rank. P64.

2000 *fèng-kuó chūng-wèi* 奉國中尉
MING: **Supporter-commandant of the State,** the lowest of 8 titles of imperial nobility (*chüeh*) conferred on males of imperial descent; normally conferred on all male descendants of Emperors in the 6th and later generations, ex-

cluding eldest sons who inherited their fathers' titles. P64.

2001 *fèng-kuó shàng chiāng-chūn* 奉國上將軍
CHIN: **Supporter-generalissimo of the State,** prestige title (*san-kuan*) for rank 3b military officers, especially used to rank members of the imperial clan. P64.

2002 *fèng-lǐ láng* 奉禮郎
(1) N-S DIV (N. Ch'i): **Court Gentleman for Ceremonials,** 30, rank not clear, on the staff of the Ceremonials Office (*ssu-i shu*). (2) SUI–CHIN: **Vice Director for Ceremonials** in the Court of Imperial Sacrifices (*t'ai-ch'ang ssu*), reduced from 16 to 8 in Sui, 2 in T'ang, one thereafter; rank 9b1 in T'ang, 8b thereafter. It should be noted that the Sui–early T'ang title was actually Vice Director for Rituals (*chih-li lang*) but it was changed in 649 to avoid a personal name taboo. SP: *secrétaire de la direction des rites ou surveillant des rites*. (3) YÜAN: **Vice Director for Ceremonials** in the Commission for Ritual Observances (*t'ai-ch'ang li-i yüan*), 2, rank 8b. P27, 33.

2003 *fèng-liěn chīh-yīng* 奉輦祇應
SUNG: **Palace Groom,** eunuch title. SP: *palefrenier des voitures impériales*.

2004 *fèng-luán* 奉鑾
MING–CH'ING: lit., provider of carriage bells: **Director of the Music Office** (*chiao-fang ssu*) in the Ministry of Rites (*li-pu*), rank 9a; in 1729 retitled Director (*shu-cheng*) of the Music Office (*ho-sheng shu*). P10.

2005 *fèng-mí kuān* 封彌官
SUNG: **Examination Sealer,** duty assignment of eminent court officials to inspect and keep under seal originals of Metropolitan Examination (*hui-shih*) papers that had been copied by the Bureau of Examination Copyists (*t'eng-lu yüan*) to help ensure objective grading; under the direction of the Ministry of Rites (*li-pu*). In Yüan retitled *mi-feng kuan*. P24.

2006 *fèng-miěn chǘ* 奉冕局
T'ANG: from 662 to 670 the official variant designation of the **Clothing Service** (*shang-i chü*) in the Palace Administration (*tien-chung sheng*).

2007 *fèng-pān tū-chīh* 奉班都知
MING: **Protocol Officer** under the Commissioner of Court Audiences (*shih-i shih*) from 1371 to 1376, rank 9a; functions subsequently performed by the Court of State Ceremonial (*hung-lu ssu*). P33.

2008 *fēng-pó* 封駁
Throughout history, a reference to sealing up and sending back for reconsideration a proclamation or other official document that was considered improper in form or substance (*feng*) and to annulling or correcting errors in such documents (*po*); a function most closely associated with Supervising Secretaries (*chi-shih-chung*). The term is often rendered "to veto," although the Chinese procedure was not as decisive and conclusive as the term veto normally suggests in modern American government. In Sung the process was institutionalized in 993 in an Office of Scrutiny (*feng-po ssu, feng-po fang, feng-po an*) subordinate to the Office of Transmission (*yin-t'ai ssu*), staffed with Supervising Secretaries of the Chancellery (*men-hsia sheng*) and with various Academicians (*hsüeh-shih*), all on special duty assignments detached from their nominal posts. In 1001 the Office of Scrutiny was shifted under the supervision of the Chancellery; then in 1059 it was shifted back to the Office

of Transmission, perhaps with dual status under the relatively new Remonstrance Bureau (*chien-yüan*). Its staff members were known officially or unofficially as Document Scrutinizing Officials (*feng-po kuan*). SP: *bureau de révision, bureau de critique, chambre de révision, service de révision*. P19.

2009 *fēng-shàn chú* 奉膳局
T'ANG: from 662 to 670 the official variant designation of the **Food Service** (*shang-shih chü*) in the Palace Administration (*tien-chung sheng*).

2010 *fèng-shàng t'ài-ī* 奉上太醫
CHIN: **Imperial Physician** in the Imperial Academy of Medicine (*t'ai-i yüan*); see *cheng feng-sheng t'ai-i*. P36.

2011 *fèng-shèng* 奉乘
T'ANG–SUNG: **Coachman** in the Palace Administration (*tien-chung sheng*); in T'ang 18, rank 9a2, in the Administration's Livery Service (*shang-sheng chü*); in Sung number and rank not clear. RR: *chef du personnel des écuries de l'empereur*. SP: *intendant de véhicule*. P39.

2012 *fèng-shèng hóu* 奉聖侯
N-S DIV: **Marquis for Honoring the Sage,** title of nobility (*chüeh*) conferred on successive heirs directly descended from Confucius; replaced Marquis for Exalting the Sage (*tsung-sheng hou*) in 267 and continued in use through the S. Dynasties; counterparts in the N. Dynasties were Grand Master for Venerating the Sage (*ch'ung-sheng ta-fu*) and after 485 Marquis for Venerating the Sage (*ch'ung-sheng hou*). The status carried various perquisites such as grants of land and imposed responsibility for conducting appropriate sacrifices and other rituals for the spirit of Confucius. P66.

2013 *fèng-shèng kūng* 奉聖公
SUNG: **Duke for Honoring the Sage,** official variant, for a very short time in (beginning in?) 1086, for the noble title Duke for Fulfilling the Sage (*yen-sheng kung*), granted to successive heirs directly descended from Confucius. SP: *duc fong-cheng*. P66.

2014 *fèng-shéng láng* 奉乘郎
N-S DIV (San-kuo Wei): **Court Gentleman for the Imperial Livery;** see under *tien-chung feng-sheng lang*.

2015 *fèng-shèng t'íng-hóu* 奉聖亭侯
N-S DIV: **Neighborhood Marquis for Honoring the Sage,** variant of *feng-sheng hou* (Marquis for Honoring the Sage). Also see *t'ing-hou*.

2016 *fèng-shǐh hsüān-fǔ* 奉使宣撫
YÜAN: **Pacification Commissioner,** occasional ad hoc duty assignment for unspecified officials to investigate local conditions and initiate the promotion or demotion of territorial officials. P52.

2017 *fèng-ssù* 奉祀
MING–CH'ING: **Sacrificer,** rank 7b, one appointed at each major altar and temple and at each imperial mausoleum (*ling*) to maintain appropriate ceremonials and head the local Sacrificial Office (*tz'u-chi shu*) under general supervision of the Bureau of Sacrifices (*tz'u-chi ch'ing-li ssu*) of the Ministry of Rites (*li-pu*). BH: priest. P28, 29.

2018 *fèng-ssù chūn* 奉祀君
HAN: **Lord Sacrificer,** reportedly a title of nobility (*chüeh*) awarded by the founding Emperor c. 200 B.C. to the 9th-generation direct male descendant of Confucius; if so, the first imperial ennoblement of the Confucian line; traditionally believed an unsupported tradition, not comparable to the ennoblement of the Praising Perfection Marquis (*pao-ch'eng hou*, q.v.) in A.D. 1. P66.

2019 *fēng-sú shǐh* 風俗使
T'ANG: **Inspector of Public Morality,** 8 delegated each spring from 684 to 705 by the Censorate (*yü-shih t'ai*, then divided into a Left and a Right *su-cheng t'ai*) to investigate and report on conditions in the empire's various regional and local administrations; counterparts of the Inspectors of Governmental Integrity (*lien-ch'a shih*) sent out each autumn to investigate the conduct of territorial officials. RR: *commissaire impérial chargé de surveiller les moeurs*.

2020 *fèng-tàng fáng* 俸檔房
CH'ING: **Stipends Office** in the Court of Colonial Affairs (*li-fan yüan*), staffing not clear. BH: treasury.

2021 *fèng-tè tà-fū* 奉德大夫
CHIN: **Grand Master for Virtuous Service,** prestige title (*san-kuan*) for officials of rank 5b2; before the end of Chin changed to Grand Master for Court Precedence (*ch'ao-lieh ta-fu*). P68.

2022 *fēng-ts'è piǎo-tsòu àn* 封冊表奏案
SUNG: **Section for Communication with the Nobility,** a unit in the Ministry of Rites (*li-pu*), apparently responsible for maintaining genealogical and other records concerning the nobility and for reporting matters concerning the nobility to the throne. SP: *service d'anoblissement et d'adresses au trône*.

2023 *fēng-tsèng* 封贈
CH'ING: lit., enfeoffments and posthumous honors: a term used, by and large, for what were called **Prestige Titles** (*san-kuan*) in prior periods. BH: titles of honour.

2024 *fèng-tz'ù sǒ* 奉祠所
MING: **Sacrificial Office,** an agency in each Princely Establishment (*wang-fu ch'ang-shih ssu*), headed by a Director (*cheng*), rank 8a. P69.

2025 *fēng-yìn yüàn* 封印院
SUNG: **Certification Office,** an ad hoc agency in which Metropolitan Examination (*hui-shih*) papers were collected after being inspected by Examination Sealers (*feng-mi kuan*); under the supervision of the Ministry of Rites (*li-pu*).

2026 *fèng-yù* 奉御
Chief Steward. (1) N-S DIV (N. Ch'i): 10 in the Office of Fine Steeds (*hua-liu shu*), which managed 12 horse corrals supervised by the Chamberlain for the Imperial Stud (*t'ai-p'u*). (2) SUI–CHIN: heads of the Services (*chü*) constituting the Palace Administration (*tien-chung sheng*), normally 2 or more per agency, rank 5a or 5b. RR+SP: *chef de service*. P36, 39.

2027 *fēng-yú* 奉輿
T'ANG: **Sedan-chair Bearer,** 15 unranked personnel in the Sedan-chair Service (*shang-lien chü*) of the Palace Administration (*tien-chung sheng*). RR: *porteur de chaise*.

2028 *fēng-yú chú* 奉輿局
T'ANG: from 662 to 670 the official variant name of the **Sedan-chair Service** (*shang-lien chü*) in the Palace Administration (*tien-chung sheng*).

2029 *fēng-yù wèi* 奉裕衛
T'ANG: **Good Fortune Guard,** one each Left and Right, from 662 to 671 the official variant name of the Inner Guard Commands (*nei shuai-fu*) in the establishment of the Heir Apparent. P26.

2030 *fèng-yüàn* 鳳苑

T'ANG: **Phoenix Park,** from 696 the name of one of the Six Palace Corrals (*chang-nei liu hsien*) where horses were reared inside the palace grounds. RR: *parc enclos des phénix males.*

2031 *fù* 傅

Lit., a teacher: **Mentor,** a tutor and adviser in a Princely Establishment (*wang-fu*), rank 2,000 bushels in Han, 3b in T'ang, 4a in Chin, 2b in Ming, otherwise not clear; may be encountered in household establishments of other dignitaries. Also see *t'ai-fu, shao-fu.* HB: tutor. RR+SP: *maître.* P69.

2032 *fù* 副

Vice: common designation, especially from T'ang on, of officials who were the principal assistants or deputies to the head of an agency. Most commonly occurs as a prefix, e.g., *fu-shih* (Vice Commissioner), *fu tu yü-shih* (Vice Censor-in-chief), but is occasionally found alone following an agency name, e.g., ... *chien fu* (Vice Director of the Directorate of ...).

2033 *fù* 婦

Generic term for certain categories of imperial concubines. See under *shih-fu, nei-ming fu, wai-ming fu.*

2034 *fǔ* 府

Ety., a man and a hand under a shelter; lit., to store or accumulate, a storehouse, an arsenal, etc. (1) **Storehouse** or **Stores Office,** throughout history found as an agency name, normally with a specifying prefix. (2) **Court** or **Office,** throughout history commonly appended as a suffix to official titles, usually of dignitaries, to designate their work places or official headquarters and in addition the staff of personnel that served them; e.g., the Han dynasty *ch'eng-hsiang fu* (Office of the Counselor-in-chief). Thus the term *k'ai-fu* (lit., to open an office), q.v., signified a dignitary's setting up a headquarters and staff. (3) CHOU: **Fifth Class Administrative Official,** 5th highest of 8 categories in which officials were classified in a hierarchy separate from the formal rank system called the Nine Honors (*chiu ming*); below those designated *cheng* (Principal, etc.), *shih* (Mentor, etc.), *ssu* (to be in charge; office), and *lü* (Functionary); above *shih* (Scribe), *hsü* (Assistant), and *t'u* (Attendant). CL: *le cinquième degré de la subordination administrative; garde-magasin.* (4) N-S DIV (N. Dyn.)– T'ANG: common abbreviated reference to **Garrison,** a unit of c. 1,000 soldiers in the Garrison Militia system (see *fu-ping*). The organizational development of these militia units, which were especially esteemed in the first T'ang century, was very complex but can be summarized as follows: The successive alien Wei dynasties that dominated North China in the 400s and 500s originally segregated their own peoples in such Garrisons scattered throughout their territories and eventually accepted (finally conscripted) Chinese as well into Garrison service. The Garrisons grew from an originally authorized 100 to more than 600 by early T'ang. In Sui each Garrison was controlled by a Cavalry General (*p'iao-chi chiang-chün*) assisted by a Chariot and Horse General (*ch'e-chi chiang-chün*), each subject to the control of one of Twelve Guards (*shih-erh wei*) at the dynastic capital, to which militiamen were rotated for service. By 607 the Garrisons had apparently split into 2 types, a Cavalry Garrison (*p'iao-chi fu*) and a Chariot and Horse Garrison (*ch'e-chi fu*), each with a correspondingly designated General; for in that year the 2 types were consolidated into a single standard type, a Soaring Hawk Garrison (*ying-yang fu*) with a Commandant (*lang-chiang*) and a Vice Commandant (*fu lang-chiang*). In 613, for reasons not clear, some additional Garrisons were separately established with the names Assault-resisting Garrison (*che-ch'ung fu*) and Courageous Garrison (*kuo-i fu*), each with a Commandant (*tu-wei*). At the beginning of T'ang in 618, briefly, the Commandants and Vice Commandants of the Soaring Hawk Garrisons were retitled Military Chief (*chün-t'ou*), rank 4a2, and Garrison Assistant (*fu-fu*), 5a1, respectively; but before year's end the Soaring Hawk Garrisons were all again named Cavalry Garrisons or Chariot and Horse Garrisons, each with a General (*chiang-chün*). At the same time similar military units were created in the household of the Heir Apparent, as Guard Commands (*shuai-fu*). In 619 (623?) the Cavalry Garrisons and Chariot and Horse Garrisons were consolidated into one type, Assault-resisting Garrisons, with Commandants (*tu-wei*) and Vice Commandants (*fu lang-chiang*). (The Assault-resisting and Courageous Garrisons established in 613 had apparently disappeared with Sui.) In 624 all Garrisons were renamed Commander-generals' Garrisons (*t'ung-chün fu*) and were headed by Commander-generals (*t'ung-chün*) and Adjunct Commandants (*pieh-chiang*, also called *fu t'ung-chün*). Finally, in 636 the militia Garrisons were renamed Assault-resisting Garrisons, each having one Commandant (*tu-wei*), rank 4a1, 4b2, or 5a2 depending on the number of militiamen in the Garrison; one each Left and Right Vice Commandant (*kuo-i tu-wei*), 5b2, 6a1, or 6a2; and one Adjunct Commandant (*pieh-chiang*), 7a2, 7b1, or 7b2. The Garrisons were graded as Large (*shang*), Medium (*chung*), or Small (*hsia*) according to the size of their militiamen contingents. For purposes of rotating personnel in and out of the military units at the dynastic capital, Garrisons were all affiliated with or subordinate to the Sixteen Guards (*shih-liu wei*, q.v.). RR: *milice.* (5) T'ANG–YÜAN: **Superior Prefecture,** a unit of territorial administration comparable to an ordinary Prefecture (*chou*) but in a specially honored or strategic location such as the environs of a capital city; normally headed by a high-ranking dignitary entitled Prefectural Governor (*mu* or *yin*). RR+SP: *préfecture supérieure.* (6) MING–CH'ING: **Prefecture,** a unit of territorial administration coordinating several Districts (*hsien*) and perhaps Subprefectures or Departments (both *chou*), and routinely communicating with major agencies of the central government, although increasingly subordinated to intermediary agencies at the provincial (*sheng*) level; headed by a Prefect (*chih-fu*), rank 4a or 4b. P53. Among many entries suffixed with *fu* in these varied meanings, see as examples *erh fu, san fu, shou-fu, shang-fu, ta-fu, nü-fu, wang-fu, nei-wu fu.*

2035 *fǔ* 輔

Ety., the side-props that prevent a chariot from turning over; hence, lit., to help, to support: **Bulwark.** (1) Used throughout history as a broad categorical reference to officials and subofficial functionaries in service under the head of an agency. (2) SUNG: quasi-official reference to a Grand Councilor (*tsai-hsiang, ch'eng-hsiang*) who was nominally a Director (*shih-chung*) of the Chancellery (*men-hsia sheng*). SP: *ministre d'état, premier ministre.* Also see *t'ai-fu, tsai-fu, yüan-fu, ting-fu.*

2036 *fù-chāi* 副齋

MING–CH'ING: lit., assistant purifier by fasting: unofficial reference to an **Assistant Instructor** (*hsün-tao*) in a local Confucian School (*ju-hsüeh*).

2037 *fù-ch'ē* 副車

CH'ING: lit., to help with the chariot: **Honorable Failure,** designation of a candidate in a Provincial Examination (*hsiang-shih*) in the civil service recruitment sequence whose merit was considered inadequate for status as a Provincial Graduate (*chü-jen*) but deserving of honorable mention; his name was therefore published on a Supplementary List (*fu-pang*) alongside the list of those who passed.

2038 *fù-chèng* 副正
May be encountered as the title of a **Vice Director** in an agency headed by a *cheng* (Director, Head, etc.).

2039 *fŭ-chèng* 輔政
N-S DIV: **Bulwark of Government,** honorific title of high esteem: one of many titles collectively referred to during this era as the Three Dukes (*san kung*) or, in N. Wei, the Eight Dukes (*pa kung*). P2.

2040 *fŭ-chèng tū-wèi* 輔正都尉
N-S DIV (San-kuo Wu): **Commandant for Rectitude,** one of several Commandants (*tu-wei*) who served as advisers to the Heir Apparent. P26.

2041 *fù-chiàng* 副將
(1) **Vice General,** a common military title ranking below that of General (*chiang-chün*), often used for the 2nd in command of a large military unit whether in garrison or on campaign. (2) MING: common reference to a **Regional Commander** (*tsung-ping kuan*). (3) CH'ING: title of 2b military rank in the Green Standards (*lu-ying*) organization, most commonly referring either to a **Regional Vice Commander** in charge of Green Standards forces in a relatively small area, subordinate to a Regional Commander (*tsung-ping*) and superior to Assistant Regional Commanders (*ts'an-chiang*), or to an **Adjutant** (*chung-chün fu-chiang* or simply *chung-chün*) serving as chief military aide to a Provincial Governor (*hsün-fu*) or a Governor-general (*tsung-tu*). BH: colonel, adjutant.

2042 *fú-chiéh lìng* 符節令
HAN: **Manager of Credentials,** rank 600 bushels, a subordinate of the Chamberlain for the Palace Revenues (*shao-fu*) in charge of tallies and other official symbols of authority; assisted by an Aide (*ch'eng*). HB: prefect of insignia and credentials. P37.

2043 *fù chiēn-shēng* 附監生
CH'ING: **Student by Purchase, Third Class,** under the Directorate of Education (*kuo-tzu chien*), a status attainable by men already entitled Supplementary Student (*fu-sheng*). See under *li chien-sheng, kung-sheng, sheng-yüan.*

2044 *fú-chìn* 福晉
CH'ING: **Princess-consort** of an Imperial Prince (*ch'in-wang*) or a Commandery Prince (*chün-wang*), i.e., the principal wife of an eldest son in direct descent from an Emperor. See *ts'e fu-chin.* BH: princess consort.

2045 *fù chīng-chào* 副京兆
From Han on, an unofficial reference to the 2nd-ranking official of the local administration unit in which the dynastic capital was located, e.g., the Ch'ing dynasty Vice Governor (*ch'eng* or *fu-ch'eng*) of Shun-t'ien Prefecture (Peking). See *ching-chao.*

2046 *fù-chŭ* 副主
Unofficial reference to the **Heir Apparent** (*t'ai-tzu*).

2047 *fŭ-chŭ* 府主
Unofficial reference to a **Commandery Governor** (*chün-shou, t'ai-shou*) or to a Prefect (*chih-chou, chih-fu*).

2048 *fù-chuăn* 副轉
CH'ING: unofficial reference to a **Second Assistant Salt Controller** (*yen-yün ssu yün-p'an*).

2049 *fŭ-chuăn* 輔轉
CH'ING: unofficial reference to a **Deputy Salt Controller** (*yen-yün ssu yün-t'ung*).

2050 *fù-chün* 副君
N-S DIV–T'ANG: unofficial reference to the **Heir Apparent** (*t'ai-tzu*).

2051 *fŭ-chün* 府郡
N-S DIV: unofficial reference to a **Commandery Governor** (*chün-shou, t'ai-shou*).

2052 *fŭ-chün* 撫軍
MING–CH'ING: unofficial reference to a *hsün-fu* (**Grand Coordinator** in Ming, **Provincial Governor** in Ch'ing).

2053 *fŭ-chün chiāng-chün* 撫軍將軍
N-S DIV (Chin): **General of the Pacification Army,** occasional designation of the overseer of military affairs in a specified area.

2054 *fŭ-fān* 輔藩
SUNG: **Frontier Bulwark,** occasional unofficial reference to a regional dignitary such as a Military Commissioner (*chieh-tu shih*), a Pacification Commissioner (*ch'eng-hsüan shih*), etc., whether of the civil or the military service.

2055 *fú-fēng* 扶風
See *yu fu-feng* (Guardian of the Right).

2056 *fŭ-hàn chiāng-chün* 輔漢將軍
N-S DIV (San-kuo Shu): **General Bulwark of the Han,** honorific title conferred on some chieftains of southwestern aboriginal tribes. P72.

2057 *fù-hòu* 副后
N-S DIV (Liang): unofficial reference to the **Heir Apparent** (*t'ai-tzu*).

2058 *fú-hsĭ láng* 符璽郎
(1) HAN: **Court Gentleman for the Imperial Seals,** rank and specific function not clear. (2) SUI–T'ANG: **Seals Secretary** in the Chancellery (*men-hsia sheng*), rank 6b1; official variant of *fu-pao lang* used to 694 and again from 705 to 713. RR: *secrétaire chargé des insignes en deux parties et de sceaux.*

2059 *fù-hsiàng* 副相
(1) From Han on, an unofficial reference to the **Censor-in-chief** (*yü-shih ta-fu, tu yü-shih*), deriving from his Ch'in–Han status as assistant to the Counselor-in-chief (*ch'eng-hsiang*). (2) SUNG: **Vice Grand Councilor,** abbreviated reference to members of the Secretariat (*chung-shu sheng*) and the Chancellery (*men-hsia sheng*) who, with the collective designation Executive Officials (*chih-cheng kuan*), served in the Administration Chamber (*cheng-shih t'ang*) together with Grand Councilors (*tsai-hsiang*) as chief policy advisers of the Emperor. P3.

2060 *fù-hsièn* 副憲
MING–CH'ING: unofficial reference to a **Vice Censor-in-chief** (*fu tu yü-shih*) in the Censorate (*tu ch'a-yüan*); see *hsien-t'ai.*

2061 *fŭ-hsièn* 撫憲
MING–CH'ING: unofficial abbreviated reference to a *hsün-fu* (**Grand Coordinator** in Ming, **Provincial Governor** in Ch'ing), combining the *fu* of *hsün-fu* with *hsien* suggesting the Censorate (*tu ch'a-yüan;* see *hsien-t'ai*), in which *hsün-fu* of Ming and early Ch'ing times held nominal high-ranking appointments.

2062 *fŭ-hsüéh* 府學
SUNG–CH'ING: **Prefectural School,** the state-operated

Confucian School (*ju-hsüeh*) in a prefectural capital city, though referring only to the school at K'ai-feng fu, the dynastic capital, in N. Sung; headed by an Erudite (*po-shih*) in Sung, thereafter by an Instructor (*chiao-shou*). SP: *école de préfecture*. P32.

2063 *fù hsüéh-shēng* 附學生
MING–CH'ING: **Supplementary Student,** admitted to government schools at the Prefecture (*fu*) and lower levels beyond the originally authorized quota; in early Ming understood to mean students not receiving state stipends, but gradually came to refer to all newly admitted students, with or without stipends; commonly abbreviated to *fu-sheng*.

2064 *fù-hsùn* 復訓
CH'ING: unofficial reference to an **Assistant Instructor** (*hsün-tao*) in a Confucian School (*ju-hsüeh*) in a District (*hsien*).

2065 *fǔ-ì tū-wèi* 輔義都尉
N-S DIV (San-kuo Wu): **Commandant Bulwark of Righteousness,** a counselor on the staff of the Heir Apparent. P26.

2066 *fū-jén* 夫人
(1) **Mistress,** a courteous reference to anyone's wife; more formally, a prestige title (*san-kuan*) officially conferred on the mother of the principal wife of an important dignitary, or an even more remote distaff relative; in Sung specifically indicated the wife or mother of a Grand Councilor (*tsai-hsiang*); in Ming and Ch'ing indicated the wife or mother of a civil or military dignitary of rank 1 or 2. Also see *chün fu-jen*, *kuo fu-jen*. (2) CHOU–MING: **Consort,** a title of nobility (*chüeh*) granted to women: in Chou the principal wife of a Feudal Lord (*chu-hou*); from Chou through T'ang a generic term for secondary wives of rulers, ranking immediately after the Queen or Empress (*hou, huang-hou*); in Ch'i of the S. Dynasties, more specifically, one of the Three Consorts (*san fu-jen*, q.v.); in Sui and T'ang till shortly after 700, a categorical reference to the Consorts entitled *kuei-fei, shu-fei, te-fei,* and *hsien-fei,* qq.v.; in Ming used with or without prefixes for secondary imperial wives, apparently esteemed less than the titles *fei* and *pin,* qq.v. RR: *femme de premier rang*. (3) CH'ING: **Dame-consort,** title of nobility granted to wives of Beile (*pei-lo*) and Beile Princes (*pei-tzu*), and occasionally wives of lesser members of the imperial nobility down to the rank of Supporter-general of the State (*feng-kuo chiang-chün*). BH: princess-consort.

2067 *fù-jén* 婦人
CH'ING: lit., woman or wife: **Priestess,** 3 assistants to the Petitioner (*ssu-chu*) in religious ceremonies of native Manchu shamanism, each prefixed with a function-indicator—Priestess for the Sacrifices (*ssu-tsu fu-jen*), for the Pestling (*ssu-tui fu-jen*), for the Incense (*ssu-hsiang fu-jen*); all normally wives of soldiers in palace service. BH: sub-priestesses.

2068 *fù-júng* 副戎
CH'ING: unofficial reference to a **Vice General** (*fu-chiang*), rank 2b.

2069 *fǔ-kuān* 府官
(1) Collective reference to all officials of any agency or group of agencies called *fu,* especially Prefectures from T'ang through Ch'ing. (2) N-S DIV (N. Wei, N. Ch'i)–T'ANG: **Officials of the Establishment,** a category of personnel in a Princely Establishment (*wang-kuo fu*), a Marquisate (*hou-kuo*), or other establishments of nobles, distinguished from other personnel called Officials of the Domain (*kuo-kuan*),

the first group serving in the noble's personal household, the 2nd group administering the territory allocated as his fief. E.g., the Administrator (*chang-shih*) of a Princely Establishment was an Official of the Establishment, whereas the Director of the Princedom (*wang-kuo ling*) was an Official of the Domain. These usages seem to have faded away in T'ang. P69.

2070 *fǔ-kūng* 府公
(1) N-S DIV: unofficial reference to a **Commandery Governor** (*chün-shou, t'ai-shou*); also used in direct address to a **Prince** (*wang*) by staff members of his Princely Establishment (*wang-fu*). (2) T'ANG: unofficial reference to a **Military Commissioner** (*chieh-tu shih*).

2071 *fù kùng-shēng* 副貢生
CH'ING: **Tribute Student, Second Class:** one of 4 categories of men certified in preliminary examinations by Provincial Education Commissioners (*t'i-tu hsüeh-cheng*) for at least nominal status as students under the Directorate of Education (*kuo-tzu chien*) and for participation in Provincial Examinations (*hsiang-shih*) of the civil service recruitment examination sequence; the status carried no stipend. It was sometimes granted to men who did not pass the Provincial Examination but did well enough to deserve honorable mention; see *fu-ch'e, fu-pang*. BH: senior licentiate of the second class.

2072 *fù kùng-shēng* 附貢生
CH'ING: **Tribute Student by Purchase, Third Class,** under the Directorate of Education (*kuo-tzu chien*), a status attainable by men already entitled Supplementary Students (*fu-sheng*), newly entitling them to compete in Provincial Examinations (*hsiang-shih*) in the civil service recruitment examination sequence. The status was lower than *lin kung-sheng* and *tseng kung-sheng* but higher than *li kung-sheng*.

2073 *fǔ-kuó chiāng-chūn* 輔國將軍
Bulwark-general of the State. (1) N-S DIV: common honorific designation conferred on chieftains of southwestern aboriginal tribes; see *fu-han chiang-chün*. (2) MING–CH'ING: a title of nobility (*chüeh*) conferred on males directly descended from an Emperor: in Ming, 4th highest of 8 such titles, conferred on grandsons of Commandery Princes (*chün-wang*) other than heirs in direct line of succession; in Ch'ing, 10th highest of 12 such titles, conferred on non-heir sons of Bulwark Dukes (*fu-kuo kung*), Lesser Defender Dukes (*pu-ju pa-fen chen-kuo kung*), Lesser Bulwark Dukes (*pu-ju pa-fen fu-kuo kung*), and Defender-generals of the State (*chen-kuo chiang-chün*), and on sons by concubines of Beile (*pei-lo*), Beile Princes (*pei-tzu*), and Defender Dukes (*chen-kuo kung*). BH: noble of imperial lineage of the 10th rank. P64.

2074 *fǔ-kuó chūng-wèi* 輔國中尉
MING: **Bulwark-commandant of the State,** 7th highest of 8 ranks of imperial nobility (*chüeh*), conferred on 4th-generation grandsons of Commandery Princes (*chün-wang*) other than heirs in direct line of succession. P64.

2075 *fǔ-kuó kūng* 輔國公
CH'ING: **Bulwark Duke,** 6th highest of 12 ranks of imperial nobility (*chüeh*), conferred on the eldest sons, i.e., the presumptive heirs, of Defender Dukes (*chen-kuo kung*). BH: prince of the 6th degree. P64.

2076 *fǔ-kuó shàng chiāng-chūn* 輔國上將軍
CHIN: **Bulwark-generalissimo of the State,** a rank 3b prestige title (*san-kuan*) granted to military officers, especially used to rank members of the imperial clan. P64.

2077 *fù-láng* 副郎
MING–CH'ING: unofficial reference to the **Vice Director** (*yüan-wai lang*) of a Bureau (*ch'ing-li ssu*) in a Ministry (*pu*).

2078 *fù-lǐ* 腹裏
YÜAN: **Metropolitan Area,** a Province-size region surrounding and directly administered from the dynastic capital at modern Peking, incorporating modern Hopei, Shansi, Shantung, and Inner Mongolia; most specifically, the area administered chiefly by the metropolitan Secretariat (*chung-shu sheng*).

2079 *fù-lǐ yìn-lì kuǎn-kōu* 腹裏印曆管勾
YÜAN: **Calendar Clerk for the Metropolitan Area,** one, rank 9b, in the Astrological Commission (*t'ai-shih yüan*). P35.

2080 *fù-liǎng* 副兩
T'ANG: unofficial reference to the **Heir Apparent** (*t'ai-tzu*).

2081 *fù-lìng* 傅令
N-S DIV (S. Dyn.): **Steward** in the household of a Princess (*kung-chu*). P69.

2082 *fù-mǎ* 副馬
Variant form of the *fu-ma* in *fu-ma tu-wei.*

2083 *fù-mǎ tū-wèi* 駙馬都尉
Lit., commander of the reserve horses accompanying a chariot or carriage: **Commandant-escort.** (1) HAN: from the time of Emperor Wu (r. 141–87 B.C.), an honor commonly conferred on imperial in-laws and the sons and grandsons of Dukes (*kung*); in Later Han a regular appointment ranked at =2,000 bushels for a subordinate of the Chamberlain for Attendants (*kuang-lu-hsün*), with no duties except when in active command of troops in campaigning armies. HB: chief commandant of attendant cavalry. (2) N-S DIV–MING: title conferred on the consorts of Imperial Princesses (*kung-chu*), in Ch'ing changed to *o-ma.* SP: *officier-surveillant; (fu-ma* alone): *gendre de l'empereur.* (3) T'ANG: title of either a functioning or an honorary military officer, rank 5b2, in the imperial bodyguard forces called the Left and Right Guards (*tso-, yu-wei*). RR: *officier des chevaux d'escorte.*

2084 *fǔ-mù* 府幕
N-S·DIV: **Headquarters,** quasi-official or unofficial reference to the principal office or quarters of any agency designated an Office (*fu*); in later times may be encountered as a reference to the headquarters of a Prefecture or Superior Prefecture (both *fu*).

2085 *fǔ-mù* 府牧
See under *mu.*

2086 *fù-mǔ kuān* 父母官
Lit., **Father-and-mother Officials,** i.e., officials who take parental care of the people: throughout history a common generic reference to officials in charge of local units of territorial administration, most particularly District Magistrates (*hsien-ling, chih-hsien*) but sometimes including even the heads of Prefectures (*chou, fu*).

2087 *fù-níng k'ù* 富寧庫
YÜAN: **Vault of Imperial Abundance,** a unit of the Ministry of Revenue (*hu-pu*) established in 1290 to manage receipts and disbursements at the Imperial Money Vault (*wan-i pao-yüan k'u*); headed by a Supervisor (*t'i-chü*), rank 5b. P7.

2088 *fù-nǔ* 負弩
CH'IN–HAN: lit., crossbow-bearer: variant designation of a **Neighborhood Head** (*t'ing-chang*).

2089 *fǔ-p'àn* 府判
Administrative Assistant. (1) CHIN: one, rank 5b, general staff assistant to the Governor (*yin*) of the Superior Prefecture (*fu*) in which the dynastic capital was located; specially responsible for maintaining discipline in the residential population. (2) YÜAN: number and rank not clear, found in the Commands (*tsung-kuan fu*) and Chief Commands (*tu tsung-kuan fu*) of Routes (*lu*). Also see *p'an-kuan.* P32.

2090 *fù-pǎng* 副榜
Supplementary List. MING: a rare bulletin published alongside the list of men who had passed a Provincial Examination (*hsiang-shih*) in the civil service recruitment examination sequence and were pronounced Provincial Graduates (*chü-jen*), announcing the extraordinary conferring of a Metropolitan Graduate (*chin-shih*) degree on an outstanding passer. (2) CH'ING: an announcement alongside the list of passers at a Provincial Examination, specially listing men who had not done well enough to become Provincial Graduates but were honored with the distinction of being Honorable Failures (*fu-ch'e*).

2091 *fú-paǒ láng* 符寶郎
T'ANG–SUNG: lit., court gentleman for tallies and seals: **Seals Secretary** in the Chancellery (*men-hsia sheng*), rank 6b1 in T'ang; 2, 7b, in Sung; in T'ang replaced *fu-hsi lang,* q.v., from 694 to 705 and again after 713. RR+SP: *secrétaire chargé des insignes en deux parties et de sceaux.*

2092 *fù-pěn k'ù* 副本庫
CH'ING: lit., storehouse for copies of documents: **Archive** of the Grand Secretariat (*nei-ko*), where the official copies of imperial documents were stored; apparently managed by 4 Manchu and 2 Chinese Grand Secretariat Archivists (*nei-ko tien-chi*). BH: archives office. P2.

2093 *fǔ-pīng* 府兵
N-S DIV (N. Dyn.)–T'ANG: **Garrison Militia,** a system of military organization originating with N. Wei settlements of non-Chinese troops, then gradually becoming a general military service in which men were career-long soldiers from the age of 21 to 60, stationed in Garrisons (*fu*) scattered throughout the country and being rotated in and out of training or tactical units at the dynastic capital and the frontiers. In late Sui and after the earliest T'ang decades, the system had to be supplemented with paid recruits, and it faded away in the 700s. See *fu.* Cf. *wei-so.*

2094 *fú-pù shìh* 服不氏
CHOU: lit., one who subjugates those that will not submit (?): **Animal Tamer,** a hereditary post carrying rank as Ordinary Serviceman (*hsia-shih*) with status in the Ministry of War (*hsia-kuan*); responsible for providing wild animals for sacrificial use and furs to be used as royal gifts. CL: *dompteur d'animaux féroces.*

2095 *fù-shēng* 附生
Supplementary Student. (1) MING–CH'ING: abbreviation of *fu hsüeh-sheng.* (2) CH'ING: sometimes used as a general reference to all candidates for Provincial Examinations (*hsiang-shih*) who had been certified in preliminary examinations by Provincial Education Commissioners (*t'i-tu hsüeh-cheng*), or to the better qualified of 2 categories of such candidates, distinguished from Added Students

(tseng-sheng); see *hsiu-ts'ai, kung-sheng*. BH: licentiates of the 1st class.

2096   *fù-shìh* 付事
CHIN: **Clerk** found in various offices of the central government, probably unranked. P5, etc.

2097   *fǔ-shǐh* 府史
SUI–SUNG: **Office Scribe,** a minor official or suboffical functionary found in many agencies such as the Nine Courts *(chiu ssu)* and the Five Directorates *(wu chien)*. SP: *scribe*. P5, etc.

2098   *fù-shīh* 父師
Lit., father-mentor: **Grand Master,** a term of direct address for aged degree-holders or retired officials of some repute; more prestigious than *shao-shih,* q.v.

2099   *fú-shìh* 覆試
CH'ING: **Confirmation Test,** a certification examination given to all Provincial Graduates *(chü-jen)* who appeared at the capital as candidates for the Metropolitan Examination *(hui-shih)* in the civil service recruitment examination sequence. BH: test examination.

2100   *fù-shǐh àn* 副使案
SUNG: **Section for Vice Commissioners,** a unit in the Military Appointments Process *(yu-hsüan)* in the Ministry of Personnel *(li-pu)*, headed by a Director *(lang-chung)*, rank 6a. SP: *service de commissaire-adjoint*.

2101   *fù-shǐh chèng* 副使正
SUNG: lit. sense and relevance not clear: **Assistant Music Master,** 2, probably unranked professional specialists, in the Imperial Music Service *(t'ai-yüeh chü)*. SP: *assistant de musique*. P10.

2102   *fú-shǐh ssū* 覆實司
CHIN–YÜAN: **Verification Office** for checking the measurements of materials acquired for construction: a unit in the Ministry of Works *(kung-pu)*; in Chin headed by a Clerk *(kuan-kou)*; Yüan staffing not clear but probably similar. P15.

2103   *fǔ-t'ái* 撫臺
MING–CH'ING: unofficial reference to a *hsün-fu* (**Grand Coordinator** in Ming, **Provincial Governor** in Ch'ing).

2104   *fù-taò ch'éng* 複道丞
HAN: **Aide for the Palace Walkways,** a eunuch subordinate in the Later Han Administrative Office of the Empress *(chung-kung shu)*; in some fashion supervised (use of?) the enclosed, elevated passageways that connected palace buildings in the establishment of the Empress. HB: assistant for the covered elevated passageways.

2105   *fù-ts'áo* 賦曹
N-S DIV (S. Dyn.): **Tax Collector,** one serving with a Ford Guardian *(chin-chu)* at each approach to Nanking, the dynastic capital. P62.

2106   *fù-tū* 副都
(1) SUNG–MING: common abbreviated reference to a *fu tu chih-hui shih* (**Vice Commander-in-chief, Military Vice Commissioner, Regional Vice Commissioner**); see *chih-hui shih*. (2) CHIN: also apparently stood alone as a title, **Assistant Commander;** see *ping-ma*.

2107   *fù tū-t'ǔng* 副都統
CH'ING: **Vice Commander-in-chief** of a Banner *(ch'i)* military organization, rank 2a; sometimes supervisor of all Banner garrisons in a Province *(sheng)* in lieu of a Manchu general *(chiang-chün)*. BH: deputy lieutenant-general.

2108   *fù tū yù-shǐh* 副都御史
MING–CH'ING: **Vice Censor-in-chief,** one each Left and Right comprising the 2nd echelon of executive officials of the Censorate *(tu ch'a-yüan)*, rank 3a; in Ch'ing one was Manchu, one Chinese. BH: vice-president of the censorate. P18.

2109   *fù-tuān* 副端
T'ANG: lit., **Vice Rectifier:** quasi-official reference to a Palace Censor *(tien-chung shih yü-shih)* who was performing the supervisory functions of an Attendant Censor *(shih yü-shih)* in the Headquarters Bureau *(t'ai-yüan)* of the Censorate *(yü-shih t'ai)*, or to the Attendant Censor assigned to review judicial decisions reported from the western half of the empire. RR: *sous-chef*. P18.

2110   *fǔ-tuān* 府端
N-S DIV: **Headquarters,** quasi-official or unofficial reference to the principal office or quarters of any agency designated an Office *(fu)*; in later times may be encountered as a reference to the headquarters of a Prefecture or Superior Prefecture (both *fu*).

2111   *fù-t'ūng ch'ién-chiēn* 阜通錢監
CHIN: lit., directorate of circulation-in-abundance coins (?): **Directorate of Money Circulation,** created in 1180 with a Director *(chien)*, rank 5a, by renaming the 2-year-old Tai-chou Directorate of Coinage *(tai-chou ch'ien-chien)* in modern Shansi, possibly because in addition to producing coins it began printing and circulating paper money (?); supervised from 1182 by a Controller of Coinage *(t'i-k'ung chu-ch'ien chien)* detached on special duty assignment from his regular post as Participant in Determining Governmental Matters *(ts'an-chih cheng-shih)* in the Department of State Affairs *(shang-shu sheng)* at the core of the central government, rank 2b, a virtual Grand Councilor *(tsai-hsiang)* of great influence and authority. The assignment of such a dignitary suggests that the Tai-chou monetary establishment required very special attention. See *li-yung ch'ien-chien*. P16.

2112   *fù-tzǔ chūn* 父子軍
T'ANG: lit., the father-to-son army: **Hereditary Army,** unofficial reference to the Imperial Army of Original Followers *(yüan-ts'ung chin-chün,* q.v.). RR: *armée héréditaire*.

2113   *fù-wèi* 傅尉 or 府尉
YÜAN: **Mentor-commandant,** one of 3 dignitaries on the household staff of every Prince *(wang)*, ranking below the Princely Mentor *(wang-fu)* and above the Commander *(ssu-ma)*; the first form of the title was used only on the staffs of the 3 most esteemed Princes. P69.

2114   *fū-wén kó* 敷文閣
SUNG: **Hall for the Diffusion of Literature,** an addition to the Hanlin Academy *(han-lin hsüeh-shih yüan)* in 1140, staffed with Academicians *(hsüeh-shih)*, rank 3a; Auxiliary Academicians *(chih hsüeh-shih)*, rank 3b; and Academicians-in-waiting *(tai-chih)*, rank 4b. SP: *pavillon Fou-wen*.

2115   *fù-yéh* 副爺
MING–CH'ING: unofficial reference to a **Squad Commander** *(pa-tsung)*.

2116   *fǔ-yǐn* 府尹
See under *yin*.

2117   *fǔ-yù chūn-mǎ* 撫諭軍馬
SUNG: **Military Commissioner,** one of many comparable titles for central government officials delegated to bring order to troubled areas, particularly in this case to restore or

improve discipline and morale among troops; usually prefixed with a geographic name, e.g., *liang-huai fu-yü chün-
ma* (Military Commissioner for Huai-tung and Huai-hsi).
SP: *commissaire chargé de consoler ou de réconforter les
armées.*

2118 *fŭ-yù shĭh* 撫諭使
SUNG: **Pacification Commissioner,** a central government
official delegated to bring order to a troubled area; usually
prefixed with a geographic name defining his territorial jurisdiction. SP: *commissaire chargé de consoler et de
réconforter le peuple.*

2119 *fŭ-yù ssū* 撫諭司
SUNG: **Pacification Office** subordinate to a Prefecture
(*chou*), staffed with or headed by regular prefectural officials with special assignments as Pacification Officials (*fu-
yü kuan*), responsible for maintaining social order and discipline. SP: *bureau chargé de consoler le peuple.*

2120 *fŭ-yüán* 府元
CHIN: **Graduate with Highest Honors,** designation
awarded the highest-ranking passer of a civil service recruitment examination at the Route (*lu*) level; comparable
to *chieh-yüan* of other periods.

2121 *fŭ-yüàn* 撫院
MING–CH'ING: unofficial reference to a Ming **Grand Coordinator** or a Ch'ing **Provincial Governor** (both *hsün-
fu*), combining the *fu* of *hsün-fu* with the *yüan* of *tu ch'a-
yüan* (Censorate), in which such provincial dignitaries commonly held nominal regular or concurrent appointments.

2122 *fŭ-yüàn fă-chíh kuān* 府院法直官
See under *fa-chih kuan.*

2123 *fù-yüán k'ù* 賦源庫
YÜAN: see *wan-i fu-yüan k'u* (**Imperial Silk Vault**).

2124 *fŭ-yüèh ssū* 斧鉞司
CH'ING: **Halberd Office,** one of 2 units constituting the
Forward Subsection (*ch'ien-so*) of the Imperial Procession
Guard (*luan-i wei*), headed by a Director (*chang-yin yün-
hui shih*), rank 4a. BH: halberd section.

2125 *hā-lă-lŭ wàn-hù fŭ* 哈喇魯萬戶府
YÜAN: **Karluk (Qarluk) Brigade,** a unit of the Palace
Guards (*su-wei*) under the control of the Chief Military
Command (*ta tu-tu fu*), headed by an Overseer (*ta-lu-hua-
ch'ih*) and a Brigade Commander (*wan-hu*).

2126 *hăi-fáng taò* 海防道
MING–CH'ING: **Coastal Defense Circuit,** the equivalent
in coastal areas of Military Defense Circuits (*ping-pei tao*);
supervisory jurisdictions of Vice Commissioners (*fu-shih*)
and Assistant Commissioners (*ch'ien-shih*) detached from
Provincial Surveillance Commissions (*t'i-hsing an-ch'a shih
ssu*) and commonly called Circuit Intendants (*tao-t'ai*); place-
name prefixes suggest the geographical extent of each Circuit. In 1753 all Circuit Intendants, while remaining intermediaries between provincial and prefectural (*fu*) administrations, were dissociated from their original Commissions
and transformed into autonomous regular appointments, rank
4a.

2127 *hăi-jén* 醢人
CHOU: **Spiceman,** a eunuch chef attached to the Ministry
of State (*t'ien-kuan*) for the preparation of relishes, minced
meats, and other condiments for the royal table and for important state sacrifices. CL: *employé aux hachis ou aux pâtes.*

2128 *hăi-tào hsŭn-fáng ch'iēn-hù sŏ*
海道巡防千戶所
YÜAN: **Sea Transport Defense Battalion,** 5 based along
China's southeast coast to protect government grain being
shipped northward by sea, from piracy; each headed by an
Overseer (*ta-lu-hua-ch'ih*) and a Battalion Commander
(*ch'ien-hu*), both rank 5a; subordinate to the Sea Transport
Brigade (*hai-tao liang-yün wan-hu fu*). P60.

2129 *hăi-tào hsŭn-fáng kuān* 海道巡防官
YÜAN: **Coastal Defense Commander,** 2 appointed in 1345
under the Chief Grain Transport Commission for the Metropolitan Area (*ching-chi tu ts'ao-yün ssu*) to organize troops
and sailors to protect government shipping on the Grand
Canal from banditry; assisted by 2 Vice Commanders
(*hsiang-fu kuan*). P60.

2130 *hăi-tào liáng-yùn wàn-hù fŭ*
海道糧運萬戶府
YÜAN: **Sea Transport Brigade,** from 1283 responsible
for transporting tax grain by sea from the Yangtze delta and
the southeast coast to the area of modern Peking, the dynastic capital; directed by an Overseer (*ta-lu-hua-ch'ih*) and
a Brigade Commander (*wan-hu*), both rank 3a; supervised
5 Sea Transport Battalions (*hai-tao liang-yün ch'ien-hu so*).
P60.

2131 *hăi-tzŭ* 海子
CH'ING: lit., little sea: unofficial reference to the **Southern Park** (*nan-yüan*) maintained by the Imperial Household Department (*nei-wu fu*).

2132 *han* 漢
From Han times on, used to refer to China or Chinese; under alien dynasties, used as a prefix to titles reserved for
Chinese appointees. N.B.: in Yüan times, the term *han-jen*
(normally meaning a Chinese or the Chinese people) officially designated those residents of North China including
Jurchen and Khitan as well as Chinese who prior to the
Mongol conquest had been subjects of the Jurchen Chin
dynasty, whereas *nan-jen* (Southerner) officially designated
the wholly Chinese population of South China that had been
governed by the S. Sung state.

2133 *hàn-chăng* 翰長
Common unofficial abbreviated reference to any executive
head of the Hanlin Academy (*han-lin yüan*), usually Academician Recipient of Edicts (*hsüeh-shih ch'eng-chih*) or
simply Academician (*hsüeh-shih*).

2134 *hàn-chūn* 漢軍
(1) YÜAN: **Chinese Army,** a collective reference to those
members of the military organization who prior to the Mongol conquest had been residents of North China, governed
by the Chin dynasty. (2) CH'ING: **Chinese Banners,** an
abbreviation of the term *han-chün pa ch'i.*

2135 *hàn-chūn pā ch'í* 漢軍八旗
CH'ING: lit., the Chinese army of 8 banners: **Eight Chinese
Banners,** one of 3 groups in the Banner system of military
organization (see *ch'i, pa ch'i*). Cf. *man-chou pa ch'i, meng-
ku pa ch'i.*

2136 *hàn-chūn t'áng* 漢軍堂
CH'ING: **Chinese Soldiers Office,** a unit in the Court of
Judicial Review (*ta-li ssu*) for dealing with cases involving
Chinese soldiers; staffed with one Judge (*p'ing-shih*), rank
7a; abolished in 1699. P22.

2137 *hàn èrh-pān* 漢二班
CH'ING: **Second Chinese Duty Group,** one of 4 groups of Secretaries in the Council of State (*chün-chi chang-ching*). Also see *han t'ou-pan, man t'ou-pan, man erh-pan.*

2138 *hán-jén* 寒人 or *hán-kuān* 寒官
N-S DIV: lit., a cold or impoverished man or official: **Humble Man, Humble Official.** The term was used in connection with the Nine Ranks (*chiu p'in*) system of categorizing potential appointees to government office on the basis of their genealogical distinction or lack of it; it refers to men considered suitable only to serve as subofficial functionaries or in very low-ranking posts, to officials (*kuan*) of such status, and to the offices (also *kuan*) allocated to them. Humble may have been used as a synonym of Impure (*cho*), but it appears probably to have denoted a category below Impure. Whether or not this *han* was used disparagingly in lieu of the homophonous name of the Han dynasty is not clear. See under *chung-cheng.*

2139 *hàn-jén ssū* 漢人司
CHIN: **Chinese Assistant,** 3, rank not clear, serving as administrative aides to the Vice Directors (*yüan-wai lang*) of Sections (*ts'ao*) in the Ministry of Revenue (*hu-pu*). P6.

2140 *hán-kūng* 函工
N-S DIV (Chou): **Armorer** in the Ministry of Works (*tung-kuan*), number not specified, with rank as Ordinary Servicemen (*chung-shih;* =7a). P14.

2141 *hàn-lín* 翰林
Lit., a grove or forest of brush-points, suggesting a group of litterateurs: from the 700s on, occurs as a prefix to numerous titles of literary and editorial workers and even other specialists such as physicians, most commonly but not solely members of the Hanlin Academy (*han-lin yüan*); normally rendered simply **Hanlin.** Also see *pei-men.* P23.

2142 *hàn-lín hsüéh-shìh* 翰林學士
T'ANG–CH'ING: **Hanlin Academician,** a member of the T'ang–Sung Institute of Academicians (*hsüeh-shih yüan*) and head of the Ming–Ch'ing Hanlin Academy (*han-lin yüan*). The title originated in the reign of T'ang Hsüantsung (r. 712–756) as a duty assignment (drafting, editing, compiling, etc.) for officials holding substantive posts elsewhere in the central government. In Sung became a substantive post, rank 3a; 3a in Chin; 3a then 2b, after 1318 2a in Yüan; 3a then 3b, but generally 5a in Ming; 2a in Ch'ing; in Ch'ing one each Chinese and Manchu appointee. Also see *shih-chiang hsüeh-shih, shih-tu hsüeh-shih.* RR+SP: *lettré.* P23.

2143 *hàn-lín hsüéh-shìh ch'éng-chìh*
翰林學士承旨
T'ANG–YÜAN: **Hanlin Academician Recipient of Edicts,** from the 800s normally one or more senior members of the group of Hanlin Academicians (*han-lin hsüeh-shih*) in the T'ang–Sung Institute of Academicians (*hsüeh-shih yüan*) and the Yüan Hanlin and Historiography Academy (*han-lin kuo-shih yüan*), who apparently organized and supervised the work of the group. Also see *ch'eng-chih.* P23.

2144 *hàn-lín hsüéh-shìh yüàn* 翰林學士院
T'ANG–CH'ING: **Hanlin Academy,** a common variant designation of the Institute of Academicians (*hsüeh-shih yüan*) in T'ang and Sung, and of the Hanlin Academy (*han-lin yüan*) in Yüan, Ming, and Ch'ing. P23.

2145 *hàn-lín ī-kuān yüàn* 翰林醫官院
5 DYN–CHIN: **Medical Institute,** staffed with profes-

sional physicians with greatly varying titles, in Sung headed by a Commissioner (*shih*); provided medical service for the imperial household. Comparable to the earlier Imperial Medical Office (*t'ai-i yüan*); apparently unrelated to the Hanlin Academy (*han-lin yüan*) or the Imperial Medical Service (*t'ai-i chü*), a unit in the Court of Imperial Sacrifices (*t'ai-ch'ang ssu*), but may have merged with the latter by the end of Sung. SP: *cour de médecine.* P36.

2146 *hàn-lín kūng-fèng* 翰林供奉
T'ANG: **Academician in Attendance,** literary and editorial aides to the Emperor; initiated c. 712 jointly with Academicians Awaiting Orders (*han-lin tai-chao*) as new titles replacing Academicians of the North Gate (*pei-men hsüeh-shih*); c. 738 both new titles consolidated into the single title Hanlin Academician (*han-lin hsüeh-shih*); appointees assigned to the Institute of Academicians (*hsüeh-shih yüan*) but apparently worked in a separate office unofficially called the Hanlin Academy (*han-lin yüan*). Not a substantive post, but a duty assignment (*ch'ai-ch'ien*) for officials holding substantive posts elsewhere in the central government. Also see *kung-feng hsüeh-shih, kung-feng kuan.* RR: *académicien à la disposition de l'empereur.* P23.

2147 *hàn-lín kuō-shìh yüàn* 翰林國史院
YÜAN: **Hanlin and Historiography Academy,** abbreviation of *han-lin hsüeh-shih yüan chien* (concurrently) *kuo-shih yüan:* designation for what in other periods was simply called the Hanlin Academy (*han-lin yüan*). Sometimes found in the further variant *han-lin kuo-shih chi-hsien yüan* (Hanlin, Historiography, and Scholarly Worthies Academy; see *chi-hsien yüan*). P23.

2148 *hàn-lín shìh-shū* 翰林侍書
SUNG: **Court Calligrapher,** a professional specialist (?) in the Court of Imperial Calligraphy (*han-lin yü-shu yüan*); no apparent relationship with the Hanlin Academy (*han-lin yüan*). SP: *lettré-calligraphe.*

2149 *hàn-lín ssū* 翰林司
SUNG: **Office of Fruits and Tea,** a unit under the Court of Imperial Entertainments (*kuang-lu ssu*); no relationship with the Hanlin Academy (*han-lin yüan*).

2150 *hàn-lín tài-chào* 翰林待詔
T'ANG–MING: **Academician Awaiting Orders,** a duty assignment in the T'ang Institute of Academicians (*hsüeh-shih yüan*) for officials of literary talent holding substantive posts elsewhere in the central government (see *han-lin kung-feng*); from Sung on, a substantive post in the Institute of Academicians, i.e., the Hanlin Academy (*han-lin yüan*); rank 9b in Ming. See *tai-chao.* RR: *académicien attendant les ordres de l'empereur.* P23.

2151 *hàn-lín tài-chìh* 翰林待制
CHIN–MING: **Academician Awaiting Instructions,** literary and editorial aides to the Emperor, members of the Hanlin Academy (*han-lin yüan*), rank 5a or 5b; discontinued in 1381. P23.

2152 *hàn-lín t'ú-huà yüàn* 翰林圖畫院
SUNG: **Imperial Painting Academy,** apparently an alternate reference to the Painter Service (*t'u-hua chü*) in the Artisans Institute (*han-lin yüan*) of the Palace Domestic Service (*nei-shih sheng*), but suggesting the inclusion of regular officials on special duty assignments as well as professional specialists. See under *hua-yüan.*

2153 *hàn-lín yù-shū yüàn* 翰林御書院
SUNG: **Imperial Academy of Calligraphy,** organizational

status, staff, and functions not clear, but apparently not connected with the Imperial Library (*yü-shu ch'u*) or the Institute of Academicians (*hsüeh-shih yüan*); likely a variant reference to the Calligraphy Service (*shu-i chü*) in the Artisans Institute (*han-lin yüan*) of the Palace Domestic Service (*nei-shih sheng*).

2154 *hàn-lín yüàn* 翰林院
(1) T'ANG–CH'ING: **Hanlin Academy,** a loosely organized group of litterateurs who did drafting and editing work in the preparation of the more ceremonious imperial pronouncements and the compilation of imperially sponsored historical and other works, principally designated Hanlin Academicians (*han-lin hsüeh-shih*). Originated c. 738 as the office of Academicians Awaiting Orders (*han-lin tai-chao*), who were soon retitled Hanlin Academicians and in the 800s gained governmental importance as palace counselors of Emperors, under leadership of a Hanlin Academician Recipient of Edicts (*han-lin hsüeh-shih ch'eng-chih*). In its early history, its staff held substantive posts elsewhere in the central government, and the Academy had no substantive status. In Yüan it had status as a regular central government agency titled the Hanlin and Historiography Academy (*han-lin kuo-shih yüan*), headed by 6 Hanlin Academicians Recipients of Edicts, rank 1b. In Ming headed by a Chancellor (*hsüeh-shih*), 3a then 3b, but generally 5a; was especially important as the career ladder by which men gained entry into the Grand Secretariat (*nei-ko*). In Ch'ing headed by 2 Academicians in Charge (*han-lin chang-yüan hsüeh-shih*), one Chinese and one Manchu, both 2b. RR: *académie*. BH: national academy. P23. (2) T'ANG–SUNG: common variant reference to the **Institute of Academicians** (*hsüeh-shih yüan*). SP: *bureau de la forêt des pinceaux*. (3) SUNG: **Artisans Institute,** a unit in the Palace Domestic Service (*nei-shih sheng*), staffed with astrologers, calligraphers, painters, and physicians who were mostly professional specialists, not members of the regular officialdom.

2155 *hàn luán-í shǐh* 漢彎輿使
CH'ING: **Chinese Commissioner of the Imperial Procession Guard,** one, rank 2a; paired with a Manchu Commissioner (*luan-i shih*) as 2nd in command under a Grand Minister in Charge of the Guard (*chang wei-shih ta-ch'en*). See *luan-i wei*.

2156 *hàn-pěn fáng* 漢本房
CH'ING: **Chinese Documents Section** in the Grand Secretariat (*nei-ko*), in charge of translating Manchu documents into Chinese. Cf. *man-pen fang, meng-ku pen-fang*. BH: Chinese copying office. P2.

2157 *hàn-p'iào ch'iēn-ch'ù* 漢票簽處
CH'ING: **Chinese Document Registry** in the Grand Secretariat (*nei-ko*), in charge of recording all Chinese documents handled. Cf. *man-p'iao ch'ien-ch'u.* BH: Chinese registry. P2.

2158 *hán-shǐh* 函使
Correspondence Clerk, one of many kinds of subofficial functionaries found in many periods of history.

2159 *hàn shìh-wèi* 漢侍衛
CH'ING: **Chinese Imperial Guardsman,** one of several categories of Imperial Guardsmen (*shih-wei*), who served as the Emperor's bodyguard. BH: Chinese corps of the imperial bodyguards.

2160 *hàn-tàng fáng* 漢檔房
CH'ING: **Chinese Archive** in the Court of Colonial Affairs

(*li-fan yüan*), a translation and archival agency. See *man-tang fang*. BH: translation office.

2161 *hàn t'óu-pān* 漢頭班
CH'ING: **First Chinese Duty Group,** one of 4 groups of Secretaries in the Council of State (*chün-chi chang-ching*). Also see *han erh-pan, man t'ou-pan, man erh-pan*.

2162 *hàn-yüàn* 翰苑
T'ANG–CH'ING: lit., garden of writing brushes: unofficial reference to the **Hanlin Academy** (*han-lin yüan*), comparable agencies such as the Sung dynasty **Institute of Academicians** (*hsüeh-shih yüan*) and the Yüan dynasty **Hanlin and Historiography Academy** (*han-lin kuo-shih yüan*), or their personnel. P23.

2163 *háng-shǒu* 行首
SUNG: **Column Leader,** subofficial functionaries serving as ushers in the Visitors Bureau (*k'o-sheng*) of the Secretariat (*chung-shu sheng*), or as heads of small squads in various military units. SP: *chef de troupe*.

2164 *háo-chài* 壕寨
CHIN–YÜAN: **Construction Foreman,** unranked, one in the Chin Southern Capital Construction Supervisorate (*nan-ching t'i-chü ching-ch'eng so*); 16 in the Yüan Directorate of Waterways (*tu-shui chien*), others in the Ta-tu (i.e., Peking) Regency (*liu-shou ssu*). P15, 49.

2165 *héng* 衡
See *ch'uan-heng, lin-heng, yü-heng*.

2166 *héng-háng shǐh* 橫行使
SUNG: **Commissioner of the Crosswise Ranks,** honorific designation of the man in charge of the highest-ranking military officers in court audience, assisted by a Vice Commissioner (*fu-shih*) in charge of the lowest-ranking officers.

2167 *héng-kuān* 衡官
HAN: **Weighmaster,** apparently several on duty in the Imperial Forest Park (*shang-lin yüan*) outside the capital city, presumably responsible for checking on hunting catches; headed by a Director (*chang*) subordinate to the Commandant of the Imperial Gardens (*shui-heng tu-wei*). HB (*chang*): chief of the office of the forest.

2168 *héng-tsǎi* 衡宰
HAN: lit., steward of the scales: unofficial reference to the **Counselor-in-chief** (*ch'eng-hsiang*).

2169 *hó-chì chú* 和劑局
SUNG: **Pharmacy Service,** a unit in the Court of the Imperial Treasury (*t'ai-fu ssu*). SP: *bureau pharmaceutique*.

2170 *hō-chǐh* 呵止
Lit., to call to a halt: **Shouter of Warnings,** in Sung and no doubt other periods as well, one of many types of men authorized to form the retinue of an official in travel status; see under *tao-ts'ung*.

2171 *hó-ch'ǘ shǔ* 河渠署
SUI–SUNG: **Office of Rivers and Canals,** a unit under the Directorate of Waterways (*tu-shui chien*), headed by a Director (*ling*), rank 8a. Temporarily in early Sung called Rivers and Canals Section (*ho-ch'ü an*), with a Manager (*kou-tang kung-shih*), subordinate to the State Finance Commission (*san ssu*). RR+SP: *office (bureau) des rivières et des canaux*. P14, 15.

2172 *hó-chüàn* 禾絹
Meaning and derivation not clear, but from the era of N-S Division on, an unofficial reference to the **Emperor.**

2173 *hó-fāng shìh* 合方氏
CHOU: **Region Unifier,** 8 ranked as Ordinary Servicemen (*chung-shih*), members of the Ministry of War (*hsia-kuan*) in charge of maintaining roads, monitoring trade, and overseeing visitors from afar. CL: *agents d'union des regions.*

2174 *hó-fáng t'í-chǔ ssū* 河防提舉司
YÜAN: **Supervisorate of River Defense,** each headed by a Supervisor (*t'i-chü*), rank 5b, established in 1351 under each Branch Directorate of Waterways (*hsing tu-shui chien*), to maintain security supervision along the Grand Canal and other important waterways. P59.

2175 *hó fèng-ssū* 合奉祀
MING: **Joint Sacrificer,** 8 constituting a Sacrificial Office (*tz'u-chi shu*), several of which were subordinate to the Court of Imperial Sacrifices (*t'ai-ch'ang ssu*) at Nanking. P49.

2176 *hó-hsī fáng* 河西房
SUNG: **Northwestern Defense Section** in the Bureau of Military Affairs (*shu-mi yüan*): one of 12 Sections created in the reign of Shen-tsung (1067–1085) to manage administrative affairs of military garrisons throughout the country, in geographic clusters, or to supervise specified military functions on a country-wide scale. This Section supervised the northwestern frontier, the core of which was Shan-hsi Circuit (*lu*), modern Shensi. Headed by 3 to 5 Vice Recipients of Edicts (*fu ch'eng-chih*), rank 8b. Apparently discontinued early in S. Sung. See *shih-erh fang* (Twelve Sections). SP: *chambre de défense de la frontière occidentale.*

2177 *hó-jù* 合入
SUNG: **Expectant,** a prefix indicating that one is qualified and certified to take up duty in the post named.

2178 *hó-k'ǒu chìh-chiàng* 合口脂匠
T'ANG: lit., maker of lard suitable for eating or, possibly, maker of lip ointments: **Medication Maker,** 2, probably professional specialists, on the staff of the Medicines Service (*feng-i chü*) of the Palace Administration (*tien-chung sheng*). RR: *ouvrier fabricant de graisse pour les lèvres.* P38.

2179 *hó-k'ù tào* 河庫道
CH'ING: **Grand Canal Storehouse Circuit,** in charge of paying laborers on the southern section of the Grand Canal, under the Director-general of the Grand Canal (*ho-tao tsung-tu*) based in Kiangsu; an abbreviated reference to the Circuit Intendant (*tao-t'ai*) in charge. P59.

2180 *hò-lì* 貉隸
See *mo-li* (Northeastern War Prisoners).

2181 *hó-piāo* 河標
CH'ING: lit., the river flag: **Waterways Command,** a general reference to the administrative structure and personnel subordinate to a Director-general of the Grand Canal (*ho-tao tsung-tu*); often occurs as prefix to a title, e.g., *ho-piao chung-chün fu-chiang* (Vice General serving as Adjutant of the Waterways Command; see *chung-chün*); also occurs as an indirect reference to a Director-general of the Grand Canal. See *piao.*

2182 *hó-p'ó sǒ* 河泊所
MING–CH'ING: **Fishing Tax Office,** headed by one or 2 Commissioners-in-chief (*ta-shih*), unranked; established in 1382 in all localities where fishing was of commercial importance, to collect taxes on the catch; in early Ming numbered more than 250, but in Ch'ing lost importance except in Kwangtung Province. BH: river police inspector. P54.

2183 *hó-shēng shǔ* 和聲署
CH'ING: **Music Office,** headed by 2 Directors (*cheng*), one each Chinese and Manchu; one of 2 agencies constituting the Music Ministry (*yüeh-pu*); established in 1729 to replace the traditional *chiao-fang ssu,* q.v. Also see *shen-yüeh shu.* P10.

2184 *hó-shíh ch'īn-wáng* 和碩親王
CH'ING: full designation of **Imperial Prince** (*ch'in-wang*); *ho-shih* is the transliteration of a Manchu word meaning fief or appanage, hence suggesting a Prince with territorial claims. BH: prince of the blood of the first degree.

2185 *hó-shíh kó-kó* 和碩格格
CH'ING: unofficial reference to a **Commandery Princess** (*chün-chu*).

2186 *hó-shíh kūng-chǔ* 和碩公主
CH'ING: **Imperial Princess,** specifying one borne by a secondary wife or concubine rather than by the Empress.

2187 *hó-shíh ó-fù* 和碩額駙
CH'ING: **Consort of the Imperial Princess** (i.e., of a *ho-shih kung-chu*), 2nd-ranking male consort in the nobility (*chüeh*). BH: husband of an imperial princess.

2188 *hó-shíh pèi-lò* 和碩貝勒
CH'ING: lit., fief-holding imperial kinsman: **Enfeoffed Beile,** a title of nobility (*chüeh*) awarded by the founder of the Manchu imperial line, Nurhachi, to his brothers, sons, and nephews, 8 of whom constituted the top-echelon advisory group serving Nurhachi until his death in 1626; soon thereafter transformed into a more formal Deliberative Council (*i-cheng ch'u*). See *pei-lo.* P64.

2189 *hó-t'ái* 河臺 or 河台
CH'ING: unofficial reference to a **Director-general of the Grand Canal** (*ho-tao tsung-tu*).

2190 *hō-tǎo* 呵導
Shouting Guide: in Sung and no doubt other periods as well, one of many types of men authorized to form the retinue of an official in travel status; see under *tao-ts'ung.*

2191 *hó-tào* 河道
MING–CH'ING: (1) **Waterways Circuit,** a branch office of a Provincial Administration Commission (*ch'eng-hsüan pu-cheng shih ssu*) or Provincial Surveillance Commission (*t'i-hsing an-ch'a shih ssu*) in charge of river maintenance, irrigation, etc.; commonly also an abbreviated reference to the Circuit Intendant (*tao-t'ai*) in charge; normally prefixed with a geographic name suggesting the jurisdiction of the Circuit. BH: river tao-tai. P59. (2) Unofficial reference to a **Director-general of the Grand Canal** (*ho-tao tsung-tu*) or his establishment.

2192 *hó-tào t'í-chǔ ssū* 河道提舉司
YÜAN: **Waterways Supervisorate,** variable number, established with place-name prefixes in appropriate areas to direct the maintenance of waterways, irrigation systems, etc., under supervision of the Directorate of Waterways (*tu-shui chien*) or one of its branches; each headed by a Supervisor (*t'i-chü*), rank 5b. Sometimes known as *ho-fang t'i-chü ssu* (Supervisorate of River Defense). P15, 59.

2193 *hó-tào tsǔng-tū* 河道總督
Director-general of the Grand Canal. (1) MING: variant reference to the *ts'ao-yün tsung-tu* (Director-general of Grain Transport). (2) CH'ING: number variable but commonly 3—one stationed at Huai-an and called Chiang-nan *ho-tao tsung-tu* or *nan-ho,* one stationed at Chi-ning and called

Shantung and Honan *ho-tao tsung-tu* or *tung-ho*, and one stationed at Ku-an and called Chihli *ho-tao tsung-tu* or *pei-ho*. Separate from the grain transport hierarchy (see *ts'ao-yün tsung-tu*), they controlled maintenance and operation of the Grand Canal and shipping on relevant sections of the Yellow River. They usually held nominal posts as Ministers of Works and concurrent Censors-in-chief (*kung-pu shang-shu chien tu yü-shih*). BH: director-general of the conservation of the Yellow River and the Grand Canal. P59.

2194 *hó-té* 和德
N-S DIV (N. Ch'i): **Lady of Harmonious Virtue,** designation of one of 27 Hereditary Consorts (*shih-fu*), rank =3b.

2195 *hó-tí ch'ǎng* 和糴場
SUNG: lit., place for harmonious purchases: **Grain Requisition Depot,** a local agency that purchased grain from the populace at a fixed low price to fulfill state needs, primarily military; subordinate to the Court of the Imperial Granaries (*ssu-nung ssu*). SP: *aire d'achat à l'amiable.*

2196 *hó-tī shih* 河隄使 or *hó-tī yeh-chě* 謁者
HAN–SUNG: **River Conservancy Commissioner,** supervisor of dike repairs, fishing practices, etc. Established in Former Han (*shih*) to coordinate and supervise various water-control (*tu-shui*) officials, in Later Han (*yeh-che*) superseded others; throughout Han, a duty assignment rather than a substantive post. See *hu tu-shui shih.* From the era of N-S Division through T'ang (primarily *yeh-che*, but both *shih* and *yeh-che* in T'ang), a substantive post in the Directorate of Waterways (*tu-shui t'ai, tu-shui chien*), rank 8a2 in T'ang; numbered as many as 60 in Sui. In Sung (*shih* or *p'an-kuan*) an added responsibility of senior functionaries in Prefectures (*chou*) around the dynastic capital, Kaifeng. RR (*shih*): *commissaire chargé des digues des fleuves;* (*yeh-che*): *visiteur des digues des fleuves.* SP: *commissaire des chaussées;* (*p'an-kuan*): *assistant des chaussées.* P14, 59.

2197 *hó-t'īng* 河廳
MING–CH'ING: unofficial reference to a **Fishing Tax Office** (*ho-p'o so*).

2198 *hó-t'īng* 鶴廳
Lit., crane pavilion: from T'ang on, an unofficial reference to the **Bureau of Evaluations** (*k'ao-kung ssu*) in the Ministry of Personnel (*lì-pu*), apparently because in T'ang times the office wall of the Bureau had a crane painted on it by a well-known artist.

2199 *hó-tū* 河督
MING–CH'ING: abbreviation of *ho-tao tsung-tu* (**Director-general of the Grand Canal**).

2200 *hó-t'úng* 合同
Lit., to match: one of several terms used for **registered document,** a form of paper used by officials for correspondence with the issuing agency, where the authenticity of the correspondence could be verified by matching the paper with a retained stub-book sheet, at the overlaid margins of which a seal had been impressed before the paper was issued. Sometimes called a tally. See *k'an-ho.*

2201 *hó-t'úng p'íng-yú ssū* 合同憑由司
SUNG: **Certificate Validation Office,** a unit in the Palace Eunuch Service (*ju-nei nei-shih sheng*) that prepared certificates needed by the appropriate authorities to issue commodities for palace use. SP: *bureau de délivrance des certificats des choses demandées par le palais.*

2202 *hó-wù tào* 河務道
CH'ING: **River Maintenance Circuit,** also a reference to the Circuit Intendant (*tao-t'ai*) in charge, rank 4a; used with place-name prefixes. See *tao, tao-t'ai.*

2203 *hó-yíng ts'ān-chiàng* 河營參將
CH'ING: **Assistant Brigade Commander,** highest-ranking military subordinate to a Director-general of the Grand Canal (*ho-tao tsung-tu*). See *ts'an-chiang.*

2204 *hó-yùng chién* 和用監
YÜAN: occasional variant reference, probably through scribal error, to the **Directorate for Leather and Fur Manufactures** (*li-yung chien*). P38.

2205 *hóu* 侯
(1) CHOU: **Marquis,** a title of nobility (*chüeh*) used by some regional lords and commonly granted to sons of Kings (*wang*). See *chu-hou* (Feudal Lords). (2) HAN–CH'ING: **Marquis,** a title of nobility, usually next in prestige only after Prince (*wang*) and Duke (*kung*), sometimes hereditary, sometimes conferred for special merit; usually prefixed with a geographic name designating the noble's real or hypothetical fief. Occurs with a variety of qualifying prefixes: e.g., *k'ai-kuo hou, hsien-hou, hsiang-hou, t'ing-hou, lieh-hou,* qq.v. P64, 65. (3) HAN: **Commandant,** a military title with many uses, commonly with rank of 600 bushels; less prestigious than *hsiao-wei* (also Commandant) and *ssu-ma* (Commander) but more prestigious than *ch'ien-hu* (Battalion Commander). HB: captain.

2206 *hòu* 后
(1) CHOU: **Queen,** principal wife of the King (*wang*). (2) CH'IN–CH'ING: **Empress:** throughout imperial history the most simple designation of an Emperor's principal wife, commonly prefixed with her maiden surname. See *huang-hou, huang t'ai-hou, t'ai-huang t'ai-hou.*

2207 *hòu-ch'ì* 候氣
HAN: **Observer of Air Currents,** a duty assignment for 12 Expectant Officials (*tai-chao*) in the Imperial Observatory (*ling-t'ai*). HB: watcher of the ethers. P35.

2208 *hòu chūng-lù* 候鐘律
HAN: **Observer of the Bell-like Pitchpipes,** a duty assignment for 7 Expectant Officials (*tai-chao*) in the Imperial Observatory (*ling-t'ai*). HB: watcher of the Chung pitchpipes. P35.

2209 *hòu-fēi ssù hsīng* 后妃四星
T'ANG: **The Empress and the Four Chief Consorts,** collective reference to the ranking palace ladies, including the consorts *kuei-fei, hui-fei, li-fei,* and *hua-fei,* qq.v.

2210 *hòu-fēng* 候風
HAN: **Observer of Winds,** a duty assignment for 3 Expectant Officials (*tai-chao*) in the Imperial Observatory (*ling-t'ai*). HB: watcher of the wind. P35.

2211 *hòu-háng* 後行
(1) T'ANG–SUNG: **Rear Echelon** of Ministries (*pu*) in the Department of State Affairs (*shang-shu sheng*), specifically designating the Ministries of Rites (*lǐ-pu*) and of Works (*kung-pu*), which were less prestigious than both the Front Echelon (*ch'ien-hang*) comprising the Ministries of Personnel (*lì-pu*) and of War (*ping-pu*) and the Middle Echelon (*chung-hang*) comprising the Ministries of Revenue (*hu-pu*) and of Justice (*hsing-pu*). P38. (2) SUNG: **Junior Clerk** (?), an uncommon title coupled with Senior Clerk (? *ch'ien-hang*), apparently subofficial functionaries; found in the Court of Palace Attendants (*hsüan-hui yüan*), the Accounting Office (*shen-chi ssu*) of the Court of the Imperial Treasury (*t'ai-fu ssu*), etc. SP: *employé de rang arrière.*

2212 *hòu-hsīng* 候星
HAN: **Observer of the Stars,** a duty assignment for 14 Expectant Officials (*tai-chao*) in the Imperial Observatory (*ling-t'ai*). HB: watcher of the stars. P35.

2213 *hòu-hsüăn* 候選
T'ANG–CH'ING: **Expectant Appointee,** designation of a qualified man awaiting appointment or reappointment by the Ministry of Personnel (*lì-pu*). BH: candidate.

2214 *hòu-hù tà-ch'én* 後扈大臣
CH'ING: **Grand Minister of the Rear Watch,** duty assignment in rotation for Grand Ministers of the Imperial Household Department Concurrently Controlling the Imperial Guardsmen (*ling shih-wei nei ta-ch'en*) to serve on active bodyguard duty. BH: chamberlain of the rear-guard.

2215 *hòu-jén* 候人
CHOU: lit., a watcher, or one who waits for people: **Scout,** 6 ranked as Senior Servicemen (*shang-shih*) and 6 as Junior Servicemen (*hsia-shih*), members of the Ministry of War (*hsia-kuan*) responsible for checking on road conditions and watching for travelers. CL: *attendants, vedettes.*

2216 *hòu-jìh* 候日
HAN: **Observer of the Sun,** a duty assignment for 2 Expectant Officials (*tai-chao*) in the Imperial Observatory (*ling-t'ai*). HB: watcher of the sun. P35.

2217 *hòu kuēi-yǐng* 候晷影
HAN: **Observer of the Sundial,** a duty assignment for 3 Expectant Officials (*tai-chao*) in the Imperial Observatory (*ling-t'ai*). HB: watcher of the sun's shadow. P35.

2218 *hóu-kuó* 侯國
Marquisate: throughout history, the domain of a Marquis (*hou*) on whom a fief (real or nominal) had been conferred. HB: marquisate.

2219 *hòu-miào* 后廟
Temple of the … Empress, common designation throughout history for buildings in which the spirits of Empresses were honored or worshipped by their descendants; each controlled by a civil service Temple Director (*shih-chang*), with the aid of Court Gentlemen for Fasting (*chai-lang*), Temple Attendants (*miao chih-kuan*), etc. The term is commonly prefixed with the posthumous designation of the Empress to whom the temple was dedicated. P28.

2220 *hòu-pǔ* 候補
CH'ING: **Expectant Appointee,** designation of qualified men for whom there were no vacant posts but who were assigned by the Ministry of Personnel (*lì-pu*) to appropriate central government or provincial agencies to occupy the first appropriate vacancy. See *hou-hsüan.*

2221 *hòu-pù láng* 候部郎 or *hòu-pù lì* 吏
N-S DIV (San-kuo Wei, Chin): **Astronomical Observer,** as many as 15 on the staff of the Grand Astrologer (*t'ai-shih ling*). P35.

2222 *hòu-pǔ pān* 候補班
CH'ING: **Corps of Expectant Appointees,** collective reference to all Expectant Appointees (*hou-pu*) on duty in an agency, where they might be given miscellaneous tasks pending substantive appointments to posts as they became vacant.

2223 *hóu-shé* 喉舌
Lit., throat and tongue, the speaking organs; hence **Spokesman for the Ruler:** from antiquity an unofficial reference to such dignitaries as the Chou dynasty Minister of State (*chung-tsai*), the Han dynasty Imperial Secretary (*shang-shu*), the Ming dynasty Transmission Commissioner (*t'ung-cheng shih*), etc. To be distinguished from the categorical designation Speaking Officials (*yen-kuan*), whose duty was to speak to the ruler, not for him.

2224 *hòu-shěng* 後省
SUNG: **Rear Section** of the Palace Domestic Service (*nei-shih sheng*), as distinguished from the Front Section (*ch'ien-sheng*); division of functions not clear. SP: *département postérieur du palais intérieur.* P19.

2225 *hòu-sǒ* 後所
CH'ING: **Rear Subsection,** one of 5 top-echelon units in the Imperial Procession Guard (*luan-i wei*), headed by a Director (*chang-yin kuan-chün shih*), rank 3a; with 8 subordinate Offices (mostly *ssu*). BH: fifth sub-department.

2226 *hòu-tsūng yüàn* 厚宗院
SUNG: lit., agency for generosity to clansmen: **Hostel for Imperial Kinsmen,** variant designation of *tun-tsung yüan,* q.v.; one each in the western and southern branches of the Court of the Imperial Clan (*tsung-cheng ssu*).

2227 *hòu-wèi* 候衛
SUI-T'ANG: **Reserve Guard,** one each Left and Right, created c. 604 as units of the Twelve Guards (*shih-erh wei*) at the dynastic capital; nomenclature apparently persisted in T'ang through the 636 reorganization of the Twelve Guards into the Sixteen Guards (*shih-liu wei*), but in 662 renamed Imperial Insignia Guards (*chin-wu wei*). RR: *garde de surveillance.* P43.

2228 *hòu-yüàn* 後苑
SUNG: **Rear Garden,** a reference to the inner quarters of the imperial palace, hence to eunuchs of the Palace Domestic Service (*nei-shih sheng*); prefixed to many eunuch titles. SP: *parc arrière.*

2229 *hsī* 奚
CHOU: lit., servant, perhaps derived from the name of an alien tribe in the far northeast: aside from use in common compounds such as *hsi-kuan* (slave) and *hsi-nu* (servant, slave), one of many terms used to designate a **eunuch** (see *huan-kuan*).

2230 *hsī* 西
West: common prefix in agency names and official titles, ordinarily paired with East (*tung*) but found in other directional combinations as well; in addition to the following entries, look for entries formed by the characters that follow *hsi* wherever encountered.

2231 *hsī-ch'ăng* 西廠
MING: **Western Depot,** a eunuch secret-service agency established in the 1470s on the pattern of the Eastern Depot (*tung-ch'ang*), under the control of the eunuch Director of Ceremonial (*ssu-li t'ai-chien*); collaborated with the Imperial Bodyguard (*chin-i wei*) in punishing those allegedly guilty of treason.

2232 *hsī-ch'ǐ wǔ* 喜起舞
CH'ING: lit., dancers who celebrate the ruler's achievements, derived from a passage in the ancient *Shu-ching* (*Classic of Writings*): **Palace Dancers,** supervised by one of the Grand Ministers (*ta-ch'en*) of the Imperial Household Department (*nei-wu fu*). BH: court ballet.

2233 *hsī-chiēn* 西監
(1) SUI-T'ANG: **Directorate of the Western Parks,** one of 4 Directorates in charge of maintaining the buildings and

grounds of imperial parks and gardens in the 4 quadrants of the dynastic capital, Ch'ang-an; in Sui under the Directorate-general of the Imperial Parks (*yüan tsung-chien*), in T'ang under the Court of the National Granaries (*ssu-nung ssu*); headed by a Supervisor (*chien*) in both periods, in T'ang rank 6b2. See *ssu-mien chien, tung-chien, pei-chien, nan-chien*. P40. (2) CHIN: abbreviated reference to the **Western Directorate of Coinage** (*pao-feng ch'ien-chien*).

2234   *hsī-chīh* 西織
HAN: **West Weaving Shop** under the Chamberlain for the Palace Revenues (*shao-fu*), headed by a Director (*ling*); eventually combined with the East Weaving Shop (*tung-chih*) into a single Weaving Shop (*chih-shih*). HB: western weaving house. P37.

2235   *hsī-ch'üān* 西銓
T'ANG: **Selector of the West,** unofficial reference to one of the Vice Ministers (*shih-lang*) of the Ministry of Personnel (*li-pu*), in contrast to the other Vice Minister's unofficial designation as Selector of the East (*tung-ch'üan*); reference is to the Ministry's role in selecting appointees for office. See *shang-shu ch'üan, chung-ch'üan*.

2236   *hsī-fǔ* 西府
SUNG: **West Administration,** unofficial reference to the Bureau of Military Affairs (*shu-mi yüan*) as contrasted to the East Administration (*tung-fu*), referring to the office of Grand Councilors (*tsai-hsiang, ch'eng-hsiang,* etc.) or the Secretariat (*chung-shu sheng*). These top-echelon agencies of the military and civil establishments in the central government were known collectively as the Two Administrations (*erh-fu*).

2237   *hsī-háng* 西行
T'ANG: **West Echelon** of Ministries (*pu*) in the Department of State Affairs (*shang-shu sheng*), consisting of the Ministries of War (*ping-pu*), of Justice (*hsing-pu*), and of Works (*kung-pu*), as distinguished from 3 others in an East Echelon (*tung-hang*); supervised by the Assistant Director of the Right (*yu-ch'eng*) in the Department.

2238   *hsī-hó* 義和
HAN: **Astrologer** (?) on the staff of the Grand Astrologer (*t'ai-shih ling*) (?). The term derives either from (a) a legend that families named Hsi and Ho were put in hereditary charge of calendrical calculations in high antiquity, or from (b) pre-Ch'in origins of the notion that a mythical being called Hsi Ho (or Hsi-ho) is charioteer of the sun. Han usage as a title is not clear.

2239   *hsī-hsīn ssū* 惜薪司
MING: **Firewood Office,** a minor agency of palace eunuchs headed by a eunuch Director (*cheng, t'ai-chien*); see *ssu ssu* (Four Offices).

2240   *hsī-hsüǎn* 西選
T'ANG: **Appointer of the West,** unofficial reference to one of the Vice Ministers (*shih-lang*) of the Ministry of War (*ping-pu*), as distinguished from the Appointer of the East (*tung-hsüan*); also see *chung-hsüan*. The usage derives from the role played by the Vice Minister in selecting appointees for military offices. Cf. *hsi-ch'üan*.

2241   *hsī-hsüéh kuān* 習學官
SUNG: **Apprentice,** variant of *hsi-hsüeh kung-shih*; 6 reportedly assigned to the Court of Judicial Review (*ta-li ssu*). SP: *fonctionnaire-stagiaire*.

2242   *hsī-hsüéh kūng-shìh* 習學公事
SUNG: **Apprentice** in the Secretariat (*chung-shu sheng*) or

the Court of Judicial Review (*ta-li ssu*); status not clear. SP: *stagiaire des affaires publiques*.

2243   *hsī-ì* 西掖
CH'ING: **West Chamber,** unofficial reference to the Central Drafting Office (*chung-shu k'o*).

2244   *hsī-ì kuān* 習藝館
T'ANG: **Institute for Study of the Polite Arts,** new name given the Palace Institute of Literature (*nei wen-hsüeh kuan*) in 692, then quickly changed again to Palace School in the Grove (*wan-lin nei chiao-fang*); responsible for educating palace women. RR: *collège où on apprend les arts*.

2245   *hsī-ì kuǎn-kōu kuān* 西驛管勾官
SUNG: **Clerk for Postal Relays in the West,** 2 unranked personnel on the staff of the Court of State Ceremonial (*hung-lu ssu*); in charge of travel arrangements for envoys from tribal groups on China's western frontier. P11.

2246   *hsī-jǎn yüàn* 西染院
SUNG: **West Dyeing Office,** a palace workshop headed by a (eunuch?) Commissioner (*shih*). SP: *cour occidentale de teinturerie*.

2247   *hsī-jén* 腊人
CHOU: **Keeper of Dried Meats,** 4 ranked as Senior Servicemen (*shang-shih*), members of the Ministry of State (*t'ien-kuan*) responsible for gathering from hunting expeditions and other sources various meats and other edibles to be preserved by drying, and for providing dried foods of all sorts needed for royal sacrifices, banquets, funeral rituals, etc. CL: *officier des pièces sèches, dessécheur*.

2248   *hsī-jén* 醢人
CHOU: **Vinegarman,** 2 eunuch members of the Ministry of State (*t'ien-kuan*), who prepared all foods preserved in vinegar for use in the royal palace, in sacrifices, in entertaining guests, etc. CL: *vinaigrier*.

2249   *hsī-júng shìh-chě* 西戎使者
SUI: **Commissioner for Western Tributaries,** a member of the Court for Dependencies (*hung-lu ssu*) designated on an ad hoc basis to set up an office (*shu*) to supervise arrangements for the treatment of envoys from tribes on China's western frontier; c. 610 superseded the consolidated Hostel for Tributary Envoys (*ssu-fang kuan*). P11.

2250   *hsī-kó chì-chiǔ* 西閤祭酒
SUI–T'ANG: **Master of Ceremonies in the West Hall,** a receptionist, rank 7b1, in a Princely Establishment (*wang-fu*); difference from *tung-ko chi-chiu* is not clear. RR: *maître des cérémonies de la salle de l'ouest de la maison d'un prince*. P69.

2251   *hsī-k'ù* 西庫
SUNG: **Western Storehouse,** one of several storage facilities constituting the Left Vault (*tso-tsang*), which stored general state revenues under the supervision of the Court of the Imperial Treasury (*t'ai-fu ssu*). See *tso-tsang, yu-tsang, nan-pei k'u*.

2252   *hsī-kuān* 西官
SUNG: lit., official of the west: unofficial reference to the husband of an Imperial Princess (*kung-chu*). See *fu-ma tu-wei*.

2253   *hsī-kuān chǘ* 奚官局
SUI–T'ANG: **Menials Service,** a eunuch agency in the Palace Domestic Service (*nei-shih sheng*), headed by 2 Directors (*ling*), rank 8b; in charge of palace slaves and laborers; also assigned titles and ranks to members of the palace staff

and provided medical and funeral services for palace women. RR: *service des esclaves du palais intérieur*.

2254 *hsī-kūng* 西宮
Western Palace: unofficial reference to the household, and indirectly the person, of the Empress, in contrast to the unofficial designation Eastern Palace (*tung-kung*), referring to the Heir Apparent.

2255 *hsì-láng* 夕郎
(1) HAN–N-S DIV: unofficial reference to a **Gentleman Attendant at the Palace Gate** (*chi-shih huang-men;* also see *huang-men shih-lang*). (2) T'ANG–CH'ING: archaic reference to a *chi-shih-chung* (**Supervising Secretary** or **Supervising Censor**). P19.

2256 *hsì-lǐn ssū* 餼廩司
YÜAN: **Victualling Office** of the combined Regency (*liu-shou ssu*) and Chief Route Command (*tu tsung-kuan fu*) at the auxiliary capital in modern Chahar called Shang-tu (Supreme Capital); responsible for providing victuals for members of the nobility and important visitors; headed by a Commissioner-in-chief (*ta-shih*), rank 5a. P49.

2257 *hsī líng-chǐn (ssū)* 西綾錦(司)
SUNG: **West Office of Embroidery,** a palace workshop headed by a (eunuch?) Commissioner (*shih*), rank 7a or higher. SP: *cour occidentale des brocarts*.

2258 *hsī liù pù* 奚六部
LIAO: **Six Hsi Tribes,** a group of (proto-Mongol?) tribes resident in modern Jehol, one of the Four Great Tribes (*ssu ta-pu*), each supervised from the dynastic capital by an Office of the Grand Prince (*ta-wang fu*), e.g., of the Six Hsi Tribes. P17.

2259 *hsǐ-mǎ* 冼馬
See under *hsien-ma* (Frontrider, Librarian).

2260 *hsí-mǎ hsiǎo-tǐ* 習馬小底
LIAO: **Horse Trainer** in the Palace Domestic Service (*ch'eng-ying hsiao-ti chü*). P39.

2261 *hsī-nán tū hsún-chiěn (shih)* 西南都巡檢(使)
CHIN: **Executive Police Chief for the Southwest,** rank 7a, in charge of suppressing banditry in the region of modern Pao-ting southwest of the Jurchen dynastic capital at modern Peking; based at Liang-hsiang District (*hsien*). P54.

2262 *hsī-nèi jǎn-yüàn* 西內染院
SUNG: **West Palace Dyeing Office,** probably a variant of *hsi jan-yüan* (West Dyeing Office). SP: *cour occidentale de teinturerie du palais*.

2263 *hsì-pài* 夕拜
Lit., to do homage in the evening; derivation not clear: from Han on, an unofficial reference to a *chi-shih-chung* (**Supervising Secretary, Supervising Censor**).

2264 *hsī-pù* 犀部
MING–CH'ING: lit., rhinoceros Ministry: unofficial reference to the **Ministry of War** (*ping-pu*).

2265 *hsì-pù* 西部
N-S DIV (N. Wei): **Ministry of Western Relations,** an agency of the Department of State Affairs (*shang-shu sheng*) responsible for overseeing administration along the western frontier and for the conduct of military operations against alien western tribes; headed by one or more Ministers (*shang-shu*), with a staff including Supervising Secretaries (*chi-shih-chung*) delegated for concurrent service from the De-

partment of Scholarly Counselors (*chi-shu sheng*); had one to 6 subordinate Sections (*ts'ao*); abolished in 493. See *man-pu, pei-pu*.

2266 *hsī-pù wèi* 西部尉
HAN: **Commandant of the Metropolitan Police, West Sector,** rank 400 bushels, a Later Han subordinate of the Metropolitan Commandant (*ssu-li hsiao-wei*) responsible for police supervision of the western quadrant of the dynastic capital, Loyang. See *yu-pu* (West Sector), *ming-pu wei*. P20.

2267 *hsī shàng kó-mén* 西上閣門
SUNG–CHIN: **Palace Audience Gate of the West;** see under *shang ko-men* (Palace Audience Gates). SP: *porte de pavillon supérieur de l'ouest, bureau des cérémonies de condoléance*. P33.

2268 *hsī-shēng sǒ* 犧牲所
MING: **Office of Animal Offerings,** a unit in the Court of Imperial Sacrifices (*t'ai-ch'ang ssu*) that provided animal victims for state sacrificial ceremonies; headed by a Clerk (*li-mu*), rank 9b. P27.

2269 *hsì-shīh* 戲師
HAN: **Players,** 27 professional (perhaps hereditary) theatrical performers under the Director of Palace Entertainments (*ch'eng-hua ling*), a subordinate of the Chamberlain for the Palace Revenues (*shao-fu*); apparently only in Later Han. May be referred to as *po-hsi shih*, q.v. P10.

2270 *hsī-shīh* 西使
(1) **West Commissioner:** may be encountered in any period referring to an east-west or a north-south-east-west differentiation among officials delegated from the central government to regional or local areas for special purposes, usually clarified by prefixes. (2) T'ANG: **Commissioner for the Western Pastures,** an official of the Court of the Imperial Stud (*t'ai-p'u ssu*) delegated to establish new horse pasturages or to inspect existing Directorates of Horse Pasturages (*mu-chien*) in the western parts of North China. RR: *commissaire impérial (aux élevages) de l'ouest*.

2271 *hsī-ssū* 西司
CH'ING: **Western Office,** one of 8 units of the Rear Subsection (*hou-so*) in the Imperial Procession Guard (*luan-i wei*), headed by a Director (*chang-yin yün-hui shih*), rank 4a. BH: western section.

2272 *hsī-t'ái* 西臺
Lit., western tower, terrace, or pavilion. (1) N-S DIV–T'ANG: unofficial reference to the **Secretariat** (*chung-shu sheng*). (2) T'ANG: from 662 to 670 only, the official designation of the **Secretariat.** (3) T'ANG–MING: unofficial reference to the **Ministry of Justice** (*hsing-pu*). (4) T'ANG–CH'ING: unofficial reference to the **Censorate** (*yü-shih t'ai, tu ch'a-yüan*) or a **Censor-in-chief** (*yü-shih ta-fu, tu yü-shih*). (5) SUNG: unofficial reference to the **Branch Censorate** (*hsing yü-shih t'ai*) in the Western Capital, Loyang. (6) CH'ING: unofficial reference to an **Investigating Censor** (*chien-ch'a yü-shih*). P16, 18, 49.

2273 *hsī-t'ái chūng-sàn* 西臺中散
N-S DIV (N. Wei): **Courtier of the Western Terrace,** i.e., of the Secretariat (*chung-shu sheng*): one of several categories of duty assignments for aristocratic Courtiers (*chung-san*, q.v.).

2274 *hsī-tǐ* 西邸
HAN: **West Residence,** a station outside the Later Han dynastic capital, Loyang, where from 178 on Emperors stored

for their personal use fees levied on all new appointees to office, ranging as high as 10,000,000 coins per person. HB: western quarters.

2275 *hsī-t'óu* 西頭
SUNG: unofficial reference to the **Clerks Office** (*k'ung-mu yüan*) in the Institute of Academicians (*hsüeh-shih yüan*). P23.

2276 *hsī-ts'aó* 西曹
(1) HAN: **Western Section,** one of a dozen or more Sections (*ts'ao*) subordinate to the Defender-in-chief (*t'ai-wei*) in the central government; headed by an Administrator (*yüan-shih*), rank =300 bushels; handled matters concerning personnel administration in the military service. Probably duplicated on the staff of the Counselor-in-chief (*ch'eng-hsiang*), but with different functions. HB: bureau of the west. (2) N-S DIV–SUI: **Western Section,** one of several units among which administrative work was divided in the headquarters of Regions (*chou*) and Commanderies (*chün*), probably responsible for paperwork concerning judicial matters; normally staffed with one or more Administrative Clerks (*shu-tso*). (3) CHIN: unofficial reference either to the **Ministry of War** (*ping-pu*) or to the **Ministry of Justice** (*hsing-pu*). (4) MING: unofficial reference to the **Ministry of Justice.** P52.

2277 *hsì-tsò shǔ* 細作署
N-S DIV: **Fineries Workshop** for the production of unspecified sorts of goods for palace use; headed by a Director (*ling*); in the S. Dynasties subordinate to the Chamberlain for the Palace Revenues (*shao-fu*), in the N. Dynasties to the Court of the Imperial Treasury (*t'ai-fu ssu*). P14, 37.

2278 *hsī-t'ūi* 西推
T'ANG: **West Surveillance Jurisdiction,** one of 2 jurisdictions defined for censorial surveillance; see under *ssu-t'ui yü-shih* (Four Surveillance Censors). RR: *examen judiciare des affaires de l'ouest.*

2279 *hsī-wài tsūng-chèng ssū* 西外宗正司
SUNG: **Western Office of Imperial Clan Affairs,** a branch of the Chief Office of Imperial Clan Affairs (*ta tsung-cheng ssu*) established at Loyang in 1104 to oversee imperial kinsmen resident in West China, headed by an Administrator (*chih*); incorporated a Hostel for Imperial Kinsmen (*tun-tsung yüan*); apparently disappeared in the flight of the Sung court southward in the 1120s. See *nan-wai tsung-cheng ssu, kuang-ch'in mu-ch'in chai.* Cf. *tsung-cheng ssu* (Court of the Imperial Clan). SP: *bureau extérieur des affaires de la famille impériale de la capital de l'ouest.* P1.

2280 *hsī-wáng fǔ* 奚王府
LIAO: **Office of the Grand Prince of the Hsi Tribes,** an agency at the dynastic capital charged with overseeing the Six Hsi Tribes (*hsi liu pu*); headed by 2 Generals (*hsiang-kun*). P17.

2281 *hsī-yěh* 西冶
N-S DIV (S. Dyn.): **Western Mint,** one of several coin-producing agencies, each with a Director (*ling*) or a Vice Director (*ch'eng*) in charge, subordinate to the Chamberlain for the Palace Revenues (*shao-fu*); see *yeh.* P16.

2282 *hsí-yù* 習馭
T'ANG: **Horse Trainer,** apparently several suboffical functionaries assigned, beginning in the 660s, to the Livery Service (*shang-sheng chü*) of the Palace Administration (*tien-chung sheng*). See *i-yü.* RR: *dresseur de chevaux.*

2283 *hsī-yù ī-yào ssū* 西域醫藥司
YÜAN: **Office of Western Medicine,** an agency apparently specializing in the medical and pharmaceutical lore of the Islamic world; organizational affiliation not clear.

2284 *hsī-yù tū-hū* 西域都護
HAN: **Protector-general of the Western Regions,** established in the reign of Hsüan-ti (r. 74–49 B.C.) as the duty assignment of a Commandant of Cavalry (*chi tu-wei*) and concurrent Grand Master of Remonstrance (*chien ta-fu*) to be China's proconsul in Inner Asia, supervising "the 36 states of the western regions." Discontinued in A.D. 107. HB: protector-general of the western regions.

2285 *hsī-yüàn* 西園
HAN: **West Garden,** an area of the capital city in which, at the end of Han, a special defense force was organized for the capital and the palace under the control of a mixture of regular officers and eunuchs known collectively as the Eight Commandants (*pa hsiao-wei*) of the West Garden.

2286 *hsī-yüán* 西垣
SUNG: lit., the west wall: unofficial collective reference to **Drafters** (*chung-shu she-jen*) of the Secretariat (*chung-shu sheng*).

2287 *hsī-yüàn* 西院
SUNG: **West Bureau,** abbreviation of *shen-kuan hsi-yüan* (West Bureau of Personnel Evaluation); see under *shen-kuan yüan.* Also a term apparently used in early Sung on some seals authorized for the Bureau of Military Affairs (*shu-mi yüan*) in contrast to others marked East Bureau (*tung-yüan*), although the terms had no relevance to the organizational structure of the unified Bureau.

2288 *hsià* 下
Lit., down, below, to go down. (1) In hierarchical usage occurs, e.g., in such combinations as Senior Serviceman (*shang-shih*), Ordinary Serviceman (*chung-shih*), and Junior Serviceman (*hsia-shih*); and in distinctions between, e.g., rank 6, 2nd class, grade 1 (6b1: *ts'ung-liu p'in shang-teng*) and rank 6, 2nd class, grade 2 (6b2: *ts'ung-liu p'in hsia-teng*). (2) **To send down,** often used as a verb referring to the transmission of a document from the throne to a particular agency for consideration, recommendation, or implementation. (3) **To demote,** sometimes used as a verb referring to the demotion of an official to an office of lower rank.

2289 *hsià-àn* 下案
SUNG: **Second Section,** one of 2 paired units (cf. *shang-an*) in such agencies as the Chancellery (*men-hsia sheng*) and the Secretariat (*chung-shu sheng*); the organization and specific functions of each are not clear, but it is possible the Second Section dealt with documents being "sent down" (*hsia*), i.e., transmitted to lesser administrative agencies. SP: *service de la réception et de l'expédition des dépêches officielles.*

2290 *hsià-chièh* 下界
SUNG: **Second Section,** one of 2 subdivisions of the Crafts Institute (*wen-ssu yüan*); a workshop for the production of ornamental goods in copper, iron, bamboo, and wood. See *shang-chieh.* SP: *bureau pour la fabrication des objets en cuivre, en fer, en bamboux et en bois.* P37.

2291 *hsià-chiēn* 下監
SUNG: **Second Veterinarian Directorate,** abbreviated reference to *mu-yang hsia-chien,* one of 2 units in the Court

of the Imperial Stud (*t'ai-p'u ssu*) charged with treating sick horses. See *shang-chien*. SP: *direction inférieure pour soigner les chevaux malades*.

2292 *hsià-ch'īng* 下卿
CHOU: **Junior Minister,** lowest of 3 Minister ranks (see *shang-ch'ing, chung-ch'ing*), the highest categories of officials serving the King (*wang*) and Feudal Lords (*chu-hou*), ranking above Grand Masters (*ta-fu*) and Servicemen (*shih*).

2293 *hsià-ch'īng* 夏卿
Summer Chamberlain, an archaic reference deriving from Chou usage of the term *hsia-kuan*, q.v. (1) N-S DIV (Liang): generic or collective reference to 3 of the central government officials called the Twelve Chamberlains (*shih-erh ch'ing*, q.v.). (2) SUI–CH'ING: unofficial reference to the Minister of War (*ping-pu shang-shu*). P37.

2294 *hsià-chūn* 下軍
HAN: **Lower Army,** one of 8 special capital-defense forces organized at the end of Han; see *pa hsiao-wei* (Eight Commandants). (2) N-S DIV (S. Ch'i): **Subordinate Adjutant,** one of Three Adjutants (*san chün*) assigned to a Princedom (*wang-kuo*); cf. *shang-chün, chung-chün*. P69.

2295 *hsià-hsièh ssū* 下卸司
SUNG: **Unloading Office,** an agency of the Court of the Imperial Granaries (*ssu-nung ssu*) responsible for the reception of grain taxes shipped to the dynastic capital along the Grand Canal; established in 988 in partial replacement of the former Supply Commissioner for the Capital (*ching-shih shui-lu fa-yün shih*). Also see *fa-yün shih, p'ai-an ssu*. SP: *bureau de la réception de convoi*. P60.

2296 *hsià-kuān* 夏官
Lit., official or office for summer, traditionally considered the season for war. (1) CHOU–CH'ING: **Ministry of War.** In Chou, 4th of the 6 major agencies in the royal government, responsible for aiding the ruler in all military matters, with 60 subordinate agencies; headed by a Minister of War (*ssu-ma*) ranked as a Minister (*ch'ing*). Revived by Chou of the era of N-S Division to replace what had been known as the *chia-pu* (Section for Communications and Horse-breeding); revived again from 684 to 705 in T'ang to replace the name *ping-pu* (Ministry of War). In all later eras may be encountered as an archaic reference to the *ping-pu*. CL: *ministère de l'été*. P12. (2) T'ANG–CH'ING: **Summer Office,** one of 5 seasonal offices, including one for Mid-year (*chung*), of calendrical specialists in the T'ang Astrological Service (*t'ai-shih chü*) and later Bureau of Astronomy (*ssu-t'ien t'ai*), the Sung Astrological Service, the Sung–Ming Directorate of Astronomy (*ssu-t'ien chien*), and the Ming–Ch'ing Directorate of Astronomy (*ch'in-t'ien chien*); headed by a Director (*ling* in early T'ang, otherwise *cheng*), rank 5a in T'ang, 8a in Sung, 6b in Ming and Ch'ing; in Ch'ing one each Manchu and Chinese appointee. RR+SP: *administration d'été*. BH (*cheng*): astronomer for the summer. P35. (3) MING: **Summer Support,** from 1380 to 1382 one of 4 posts, each named after a season and open to more than one appointee, intended for the Emperor's closest and most trusted advisers; see *ssu fu-kuan* (Four Supports). P4, 67.

2297 *hsià-pīn* 下嬪
N-S DIV (N. Ch'i): **Lesser Concubine,** categorical reference to 6 palace women equal in rank to the Six Chief Ministers (*liu ch'ing*). See *shang-pin, hsüan-hui, ning-hui, hsüan-ning, shun-hua, ning-hua, kuang-hsün*.

2298 *hsià-shìh* 下士
CHOU, N-S DIV (Chou): **Junior Serviceman,** the lowest of 9 (or 7) ranks into which all officials were classified, outranked by Ministers (*ch'ing*), Grand Masters (*ta-fu*), Senior Servicemen (*shang-shih*), and Ordinary Servicemen (*chung-shih*); the rank indicator is normally appended as a suffix to the functional title. In Chou of the era of N-S Division, equivalent to rank 9a. CL: *gradué de troisième classe*.

2299 *hsià tà-fū* 下大夫
Junior Grand Master. (1) CHOU, N-S DIV (Chou): 6th highest of 9 (or 4th of 7) ranks into which all officials were classified, following all Ministers (*ch'ing*) and both Senior Grand Masters (*shang ta-fu*) and Ordinary Grand Masters (*chung ta-fu*); the rank indicator is normally appended as a suffix to the functional title. In Chou of the era of N-S Division, equivalent to rank 6a. CL: *préfet de troisième classe*. (2) HAN: 9th highest in a hierarchy of 10 status groups in the officialdom (see under *shang-kung*), including all officials with annual salaries between 600 and 2,000 bushels of grain. P68.

2300 *hsià-ts'ǎi* 夏采
CHOU: lit., summer colors, deriving from an anecdote in the ancient *Shu-ching* (*Classic of Writings*): **Master of Mourning,** 4 ranked as Junior Servicemen (*hsia-shih*), members of the Ministry of State (*t'ien-kuan*) whose principal charge was to organize the funerals of members of the royal family and to try to summon back the soul of a newly dead King. CL: *assortisseur de couleurs*.

2301 *hsià wǔ ch'í* 下五旗
CH'ING: **Five Lesser Banners,** Manchu military organizations controlled by Imperial Princes (*ch'in-wang*), as distinguished from the Three Superior Banners (*shang san ch'i*) under the direct control of the Emperor; the Five Lesser Banners were the Bordered White, Plain Red, Bordered Red, Plain Blue, and Bordered Blue Banners. See *ch'i, pa ch'i*. BH: five lower banners.

2302 *hsiāng* 廂
(1) T'ANG–SUNG: **Township** (urban) in a large city; e.g., the N. Sung capital, Kaifeng, was divided for local administration into 2 each Right and Left Townships, each headed by a Magistrate (*ling*). See *ssu hsiang* (Four Capital Townships). SP: *arrondissement*. (2) T'ANG–SUNG: **Wing,** usually prefixed Left and Right: subsections of some agencies, commonly military; e.g., the Left and Right Wings of Inspired Strategy (*shen-ts'e hsiang*, q.v.). RR: *bâtiment*. SP: *aile*. (3) SUNG: occasional variant of *chün* (**Military Prefecture**).

2303 *hsiāng* 相
Ety., an eye beside (behind? peering from behind?) a tree; lit., to assist. (1) **Minister:** from high antiquity a title of distinction normally given only to senior officials in a ruler's central administration. (2) **Grand Councilor:** throughout imperial history a quasi-official reference to such top-echelon officials as Han Counselors-in-chief (*ch'eng-hsiang*), T'ang–Sung Grand Councilors (*tsai-hsiang*), and Ming–Ch'ing Grand Secretaries (*ta hsüeh-shih*). (3) HAN–MING: **Administrator:** in Han and early post-Han times the senior official in a Princedom (*wang-kuo*), Marquisate (*hou-kuo*), or other semifeudal domain; thereafter revived occasionally, as at the beginning of Ming for the senior official in a Princely Establishment (*wang-fu*), in 1380 changed to *chang-shih*. P69. (4) N-S DIV: occasional variant of **Dis-**

trict **Magistrate** (*hsien-ling, hsien-chang*), perhaps signifying that the District had been granted as a fief. P54. (5) T'ANG: from 662 to 671 and again from 742 to 758, the official redesignation of the **Director** (*shih-chung*) **of the Chancellery** (*chung-shu sheng*) and the **Director** (*ling*) **of the Secretariat** (*chung-shu sheng*), differentiated by the prefixes Left and Right, respectively. P2. (6) T'ANG: from 684 to 705 the official redesignation of the two **Vice Directors** (*p'u-yeh*) **of the Department of State Affairs** (*shang-shu sheng*), prefixed Left and Right. P2. (7) SUNG: variant of *hsiang* (urban **Township**).

2304　hsiāng 鄉
(1) Most generally, a somewhat derogatory reference to the suburbs or hinterland from the point of view of a city, or to "the provinces" from the point of view of a dynastic capital. (2) CHOU: **District**, in theory the largest grouping of people in the royal domain or the environs of the seat of a Feudal Lord (*chu-hou*), comprising 12,500 people subdivided in 5 Townships (*chou, hsien*); headed by a popularly elected Grand Master (*ta-fu*). CL: *district intérieur*. (3) CH'IN–CH'ING: **Township**, a sub-District (*hsien*) group of relatively self-governing families, subdivided in Villages (*li*). (4) SUI: **Ward**, a sub-District group of 500 relatively self-governing families in an urban area, subdivided in 5 Precincts (*tsu*).

2305　hsiáng-chèng hsüéh-shìh 詳正學士
T'ANG: **Academician Editor**, one or more members of the Institute for the Advancement of Literature (*hung-wen kuan*) from the 670s to 823; aided in drafting and revising government documents. RR: *lettré réviseur et correcteur*.

2306　hsiáng-chièn 鄉薦
MING–CH'ING: lit., recommended by the Provinces: unofficial reference to a **Provincial Graduate** (*chü-jen*) in the civil service recruitment examination system.

2307　hsiāng chìn-shìh 鄉進士
MING–CH'ING: lit., a scholar presented by the Provinces, or a Province-level counterpart of a Metropolitan Graduate (*chin-shih*): unofficial reference to a **Provincial Graduate** (*chü-jen*) in the civil service recruitment examination system.

2308　hsiāng-chǔ 鄉舉
SUNG: lit., an offering from the countryside (to the dynastic capital): unofficial reference to the **Prefectural Examination** (*chieh-shih*) in the sequence of civil service recruitment examinations; perhaps also to a **Prefectural Graduate** (see under *chü-jen, te-chieh*).

2309　hsiāng chūn 鄉君
T'ANG–CH'ING: **Township Mistress**, an honorific title for women, commonly with a place-name prefix: in T'ang–Sung granted to wives and mothers of officials with merit titles (*hsün*) of rank 4; in Ming to daughters of Supporter-generals of the State (*feng-kuo chiang-chün*); in Ch'ing to daughters of Defender Dukes (*chen-kuo kung*) and Bulwark Dukes (*fu-kuo kung*).

2310　hsiāng-chūn 鄉軍
May be encountered as a variant of *hsiang-ping* (**Local Militia**).

2311　hsiāng-fǎ 鄉法
N-S DIV (Chou): **Township Justice Bureau** in the Ministry of Justice (*ch'iu-kuan*); also the title of the Bureau's senior officials, the **Director**, ranked as a Senior Serviceman (*shang-shih;* 7a), and the **Vice Director**, ranked as an Ordinary Serviceman (*chung-shih;* 8a). P13.

2312　hsiáng-fú àn 詳覆案
SUNG: **Capital Punishments Section**, one of 13 Sections (*an*) directly subordinate to the executive officials of the S. Sung Ministry of Justice (*hsing-pu*); staffed with suboffical functionaries; reviewed capital punishment sentences submitted from Circuits (*lu*). SP: *service de révision*.

2313　hsiàng-fù kuān 相副官
YÜAN: **Assistant** in various agencies, usually found 3rd in a hierarchy after a Commissioner-in-chief (*ta-shih*) and a Vice Commissioner (*fu-shih*).

2314　hsiáng-fú kuān 詳覆官
SUNG: **Review Evaluator**, one of several categories of duty assignments in the Judicial Control Office (*shen-hsing yüan*) of early Sung; also found in the Bureau of Military Affairs (*shu-mi yüan*). SP: *fonctionnaire de révision*. P13.

2315　hsiáng-hó shǔ 祥和署
YÜAN: **Bureau of Sacrificial Music**, one of 2 major units in the Music Office (*chiao-fang ssu*); headed by 2 Directors (*ling*), rank 6b. See *hsing-ho shu* (Bureau of Joyful Music). P10.

2316　hsiāng-hóu 鄉侯
HAN–T'ANG: **Township Marquis**, a title of nobility (*chüeh*): in Han the lord of a Marquisate (*hou-kuo*) smaller that that of a District Marquis (*hsien-hou*); from the Three Kingdoms era on, the designation of the heir to a Princedom (*wang-kuo*); the usage was discontinued in T'ang.

2317　hsiāng-hsién 鄉賢
MING–CH'ING: **Local Worthy**, unofficial reference to members of the official class living at home on mourning leave or in retirement or awaiting reappointment; collectively constituted a recognizable local elite from which leadership in various kinds of semiofficial activities such as public sacrifices could be expected.

2318　hsiāng hsiēn-shēng 鄉先生 or **hsiāng hsiēn-tá** 鄉先達
MING–CH'ING: variant forms of *hsiang-hsien* (**Local Worthy**).

2319　hsiáng-hsíng àn 詳刑案
SUNG: **Sentence Review Section**, one of 5 Sections (*an*) constituting the Left Bureau (*tso-t'ing*) of the Court of Judicial Review (*ta-li ssu*); functions not clear. P22.

2320　hsiáng-hsíng ssù 祥刑寺 or 詳刑寺
T'ANG: lit., court for reviewing punishments: from 662 to 670, the official name of the *ta-li ssu* (**Court of Judicial Review**). P22.

2321　hsiàng-hsǖ 象胥
CHOU: **Interpreter**, one ranked as a Senior Serviceman (*shang-shih*), 2 as Ordinary Servicemen (*chung-shih*), and 8 as Junior Servicemen (*hsia-shih*)—in all, 11 specialists in the languages or dialects of each of the 4 quadrants of the empire; subordinates of the Senior Messenger (*ta hsing-jen*) in the Ministry of Justice (*ch'iu-kuan*), charged with interpreting in dealings with emissaries from frontier peoples. According to the ancient *Li-chi* (*Ritual Records*), *hsiang-hsü* was a collective term; there was a special title for Interpreters responsible for each quadrant. CL: *interprète*.

2322 *hsiāng-hsüéh* 鄉學
CH'ING: **Township School,** a sometime District School (*hsien-hsüeh*) whose District administration had been eliminated but which remained in operation. P51.

2323 *hsiāng-huǒ nèi-shǐh* 香火內使
SUNG: **Eunuch Sacrificer,** one assigned to each Imperial Mausoleum (*ling*) to make sacrificial offerings. See *nei-shih*. SP: *intendant de sacrifice*. P29.

2324 *hsiáng-ì kuān* 詳議官 or *hsiang-i*
(1) SUNG: **Recommendation Evaluator,** one of several categories of duty assignments in the Judicial Control Office (*shen-hsing yüan*) of early Sung. (2) SUNG: **Consultant,** a duty-assignment category in the Ritual Service (*i-li chü*) and the Ritual Regulations Service (*li-chih chü*) established shortly after 1100 by the Department of State Affairs (*shang-shu sheng*). SP: *chargé de délibérer en détail*. (3) MING: **Evaluator,** 3, rank 7a, in the Punishment Reviewing Office (*shen-hsing ssu*) of early Ming. P22.

2325 *hsiáng-ì ssū* 詳議司
SUNG: **Office of Recommendation Evaluators,** collective reference to the Recommendation Evaluators (*hsiang-i kuan*) in the Judicial Control Office (*shen-hsing yüan*) of early Sung. SP: *bureau de la délibération en détail, bureau de la réforme législative*.

2326 *hsiāng-kuān* 廂官
Township Officials or **Capital Township Officials.** (1) SUNG: generic reference to personnel, civil or military, assigned to police or judicial duty in the Four Capital Townships (*ssu hsiang*) into which each of the successive capital cities, Kaifeng and Hangchow, was divided for local administration; e.g., *chün-hsün shih, chün-hsün p'an-kuan, kung-shih kan-tang shih*. During Sung may itself have become a quasi-official title. SP: *juge d'arrondissement de la capitale*. P20. (2) CHIN: 2 each Left and Right, rank 8a, in the Ministry of Works (*kung-pu*); supervised laborers engaged in construction and maintenance of the dynastic capital. P15.

2327 *hsiāng-k'uéi* 鄉魁
MING–CH'ING: **Provincial Graduate with Distinction,** unofficial reference to those who ranked from 6th to 18th on the pass list of a Provincial Examination (*hsiang-shih*) in the civil service recruitment examination sequence. See *chü-jen, chieh-yüan, ching-k'uei*.

2328 *hsiáng-kǔn* 詳袞
General. (1) LIAO: apparently a Khitan rendering of the Chinese *chiang-chün*, but explained by Chinese to mean an official who was in charge of affairs (*li-shih kuan*); ranked below Commissioners (*shih*) and Vice Commissioners (*fu-shih*) in many agencies of the Northern Administration (*pei-mien*). P38, 40. (2) CHIN: title granted chieftains of some subordinate tribes. P17.

2329 *hsiāng-kǔn* 鄉袞
MING–CH'ING: lit., a local (wearer of) official garb: variant of *hsiang-hsien* (**Local Worthy**).

2330 *hsiāng-kūng* 廂公
N-S DIV: **Duke of the Household,** common unofficial reference to an imperial relative while on official duty.

2331 *hsiāng-kūng* 相公
Minister Duke, throughout history an unofficial reference to a paramount executive official in the central government such as a Han Counselor-in-chief (*ch'eng-hsiang*), a T'ang–Sung Grand Councilor (*tsai-hsiang*), or a Ming–Ch'ing Grand Secretary (*ta hsüeh-shih*).

2332 *hsiāng-kūng* 鄉公
N-S DIV (San-kuo Wei): **Township Duke,** a title of nobility (*chüeh*) initiated in 222 for the sons of Princes (*wang*) other than their heirs, who were called Township Marquises (*hsiang-hou*).

2333 *hsiāng-kùng* 鄉貢
T'ANG: lit., local tribute: **Prefectural Nominee,** unofficial reference to a man nominated by a Prefect (*tz'u-shih*) to participate in the regular civil service recruitment examinations.

2334 *hsiāng kūng-chǔ* 鄉公主
HAN: **Township Princess,** a title of nobility (*chüeh*) awarded to daughters of some Princes (*wang*); the basis for the distinction between them and Neighborhood Princesses (*t'ing kung-chu*) is not clear. See *kung-chu*. P69.

2335 *hsiāng-kùng láng* 鄉貢郎
MING–CH'ING: unofficial reference to a **Provincial Graduate** (*chü-jen*).

2336 *hsiāng-kùng shǒu* 鄉貢首
MING–CH'ING: unofficial reference to a **Provincial Graduate with Highest Honors** (*chieh-yüan*).

2337 *hsiāng-kuó* 相國
(1) CH'IN–N-S DIV: **Counselor-in-chief,** a title alternating with *ch'eng-hsiang*, q.v., but held in higher esteem; in Han made a Marquis (*hou*) if not already one, with rank of 10,000 bushels. HB: chancellor of state. (2) MING: **Grand Councilor,** highest-ranking official of the central government as head of the Secretariat (*chung-shu sheng*), one each Left and Right, rank 1a; existed only from 1364 to 1368, then changed to *ch'eng-hsiang*. (3) **Minister of State:** from T'ang on, an unofficial reference to the highest-ranking officials of the central government, e.g., a T'ang–Sung Grand Councilor (*tsai-hsiang*) or a Ming–Ch'ing Grand Secretary (*ta hsüeh-shih*). P2, 4.

2338 *hsiāng-lǎo* 鄉老
(1) CHOU: **District Elder,** 3 appointed among members of the Ministry of Education (*ti-kuan*), each to supervise 2 of the 6 Districts (*hsiang*) surrounding the royal capital; each bore the nominal title Duke (*kung*) and was among the intimate advisers of the ruler; each cooperated with the Grand Masters (*ta-fu*) of the Districts in his jurisdiction to recommend at court men of merit and ability. See *hsiang* (District). CL: *ancien de district intérieur*. (2) **Local Elder,** throughout history an unofficial reference to a man of age and distinction in his locality, with whom local officials were expected to consult.

2339 *hsiāng-lì* 廂吏
SUNG: **Township Supervisor,** 8 appointed in 1008 to provide police-like supervision of the 8 Townships (*hsiang*) outside the new city wall of the dynastic capital, Kaifeng, under the jurisdiction of the Kaifeng Superior Prefecture (*fu*); in 1021 the number was increased to 9. P20.

2340 *hsiāng-lì* 鄉吏
CH'IN–HAN: **Township Guardian,** a sub-District (*hsien*) dignitary sharing with the Elder (*san-lao*) supervision of a Township (*hsiang*, q.v.), principally responsible for police work; also known as *yu-chiao*, q.v. P20.

2341 *hsiāng-pīng* 廂兵
SUNG: **Prefectural Army,** garrisons of professional career soldiers stationed away from the capital, considered of poorer quality than troops in the Imperial Armies (*chin-chün*) stationed in and around the capital; headed by prefectural-level

Commanders-in-chief (*tu chih-hui shih*). SP: *armée provinciale*.

2342 hsiǎng-pīng 鄉兵
Local Militia: beginning in Sung if not earlier, a general term for civilian-soldiers recruited, trained, and assigned to patrol and other police duties in their home areas, at a sub-District (*hsien*) level of organization. See *hsiang-chün, hsiang-yung, min-ping, pao-chia, pao-wu*. Cf. *kuan-ping*.

2343 hsiǎng-pīng àn 廂兵案
SUNG: **Prefectural Armies Section,** a major unit in the Ministry of War (*ping-pu*), through which affairs of the various Prefectural Armies (*hsiang-ping*) were dealt with. SP: *service de l'armée provinciale*.

2344 hsiǎng-pó 巷伯
Lit., elder of the palace corridors. (1) May be encountered in any period as an archaic reference to a **senior eunuch.** (2) N-S DIV (Chou): **Senior Palace Attendant,** a eunuch title carrying rank as Ordinary Serviceman (*chung-shih*).

2345 hsiǎng-pó 鄉伯
N-S DIV (Chou): **District Earl,** an ancient title resurrected, status and functions not clear; sometimes has the prefix *hsiao* (Junior), usually has a rank-title suffix, e.g., Ordinary Grand Master (*chung ta-fu*), Senior Serviceman (*shang-shih*). P32.

2346 hsiǎng-shēn 鄉紳
Lit., rural (wearers of) sashes, a collective reference to all those who had status as officials (*kuan*) but, while unassigned or retired, lived in their home areas, where they constituted the most influential class in Chinese society: **rural elite,** commonly rendered alternatively as the **rural gentry.** Cf. *shen-shih* (the elite), *shen-chin* (the elite), *shih ta-fu* (the official class).

2347 hsiǎng-shēng 庠生
MING–CH'ING: archaic reference to a **Government Student** (*sheng-yüan*) in a Confucian School (*ju-hsüeh*) at the Prefecture (*fu*) or lower level.

2348 hsiǎng-shēng 餉生
CH'ING: lit., student (who had donated) troop rations: **Student by Purchase** in a government school; a variant of *li-sheng*, q.v. Also see *sheng-yüan*.

2349 hsiǎng-shìh 相室
HAN: lit., minister's office: unofficial reference to the office, hence indirectly the person, of a **Counselor-in-chief** (*ch'eng-hsiang*).

2350 hsiǎng-shìh 鄉士
CHOU: **District Judge,** 8 with rank as Senior Servicemen (*shang-shih*), members of the Ministry of Justice (*ch'iu-kuan*) with special responsibility for the administration of justice in the Districts (*hsiang*) in the immediate environs of the royal capital. CL: *prévôt de justice des districts intérieurs*.

2351 hsiǎng-shīh 鄉師
CHOU: **District Preceptor,** 4 with rank as Junior Grand Masters (*hsia ta-fu*) and 8 as Senior Servicemen (*shang-shih*), members of the Ministry of Education (*ti-kuan*), half appointed for each 3 of the 6 Districts (*hsiang*) in the immediate environs of the royal capital; responsible for giving moral instruction, taking the census, requisitioning labor service, commanding militia, participating in local rituals, sharing in the settlement of litigations among the people, etc. See *sui-shih*. CL: *chef de district*. P6.

2352 hsiǎng-shìh 鄉試
YÜAN–CH'ING: **Provincial Examination** in the civil service recruitment examination sequence; in Yüan managed by provincial authorities, in Ming–Ch'ing by ad hoc examiners delegated from the central government; candidates who passed, designated Provincial Graduates (*chü-jen*), were eligible for minor appointments or for participation in a subsequent Metropolitan Examination (*hui-shih*) at the dynastic capital. The recruitment examination sequence was authorized in 1313, and beginning in 1314 Provincial Examinations were conducted every 3 years with minor interruptions.

2353 hsiǎng tà-fū 鄉大夫
CHOU: **District Grand Master,** one for each of the 6 Districts (*hsiang*) in the immediate environs of the royal capital with rank as Minister (*ch'ing*), members of the Ministry of Education (*ti-kuan*) who served as general administrative heads of their Districts, specially charged, in collaboration with District Elders (*hsiang-lao*), to seek out and bring to attention at court men of merit suitable for holding office. See *sui ta-fu*. CL: *préfet de district intérieur*.

2354 hsiǎng-tào ch'ù 嚮導處
CH'ING: **Escort Office,** an ad hoc agency providing an entourage for each imperial outing, consisting of Bannermen (see *ch'i*) chosen from the Vanguard Brigade (*ch'ien-feng ying*) and the Guards Brigade (*hu-chün ying*), commanded by an ad hoc Commander-general (*tsung-t'ung*) with regular status normally as Vice Commander-in-chief (*tu-t'ung*) of one of the Eight Banners (*pa ch'i*) or as Commander-general (*t'ung-ling*) of the Vanguard Brigade or the Guards Brigade. BH: the guides.

2355 hsiǎng-tìng 詳定
SUNG: **Editor** in the Office for Compilation of Imperial Pronouncements (*pien-hsiu ch'ih-ling so*), apparently affiliated with the Chancellery (*men-hsia sheng*). SP: *chargé de codification*.

2356 hsiǎng-tìng chàng-chí sǒ 詳定帳籍所
SUNG: **Records Editing Office,** staffing and organizational affiliation not clear; possibly a variant reference to the Records Section (*chang-chi an*) of the Ministry of Justice (*hsing-pu*). SP: *bureau de vérification des registres*.

2357 hsiǎng-tìng ch'ǐh-lìng sǒ 詳定勅令所
SUNG: **Office for the Editing of Imperial Pronouncements,** possibly a variant reference to the Office for the Compilation of Imperial Pronouncements (*pien-hsiu ch'ih-ling so*). SP: *bureau de la codification des décrets et des ordonnances*.

2358 hsiǎng-tìng kuān 詳定官
SUNG: **Editor,** a duty assignment for variable numbers of officials in such agencies as the Law Code Office (*ch'ih-ling so*) and the Office for the Compilation of Imperial Pronouncements (*pien-hsiu ch'ih-ling so*). SP: *fonctionnaire chargé de codification*.

2359 hsiǎng-tìng kuān-chìh sǒ 詳定官制所
SUNG: **Office for the Editing of Regulations on the Officialdom (?),** staffing and organizational affiliation not clear. SP: *bureau de l'établissement du régime des fonctionnaires*.

2360 hsiǎng-tìng sǒ 詳定所
SUNG: **Editorial Office,** organizational affiliation and principal function not clear; presumably staffed with Editors (*hsiang-ting, hsiang-ting kuan*). SP: *bureau de codification*.

2361 hsiǎng-tuàn àn 詳斷案
SUNG: **Sentence Evaluators Section,** a special Section (*an*)

in addition to the 3 ordinary Sections (see *mo-k'an an, hsüan-huang an, fen-pu an*) in the Left Bureau (*tso tuan-hsing*) of the Court of Judicial Review (*ta-li ssu*), consisting of 8 Subsections (*fang*) that routinely reviewed trial records submitted from all Circuits (*lu*); staffed with Sentence Evaluators (*hsiang-ting kuan*, etc.). SP: *service de révision* P22.

2362   *hsiáng-tuàn kuān*   詳斷官
SUNG: **Sentence Evaluator.** (1) One ot several categories of duty assignments in the Judicial Control Office (*shen-hsing yüan*) of early Sung. (2) A title found in the Grand Court of Revision (*ta-li ssu*) for members of the Sentence Evaluators Section (*hsiang-tuan an*). Originally a catch-all designation of outsiders detached from their regular central government posts for either long-term or short-term duty in the Court, the former officially designated Concurrent Supervisor (*chien-cheng*), the latter Concurrent Aide (*chien-ch'eng*) in the Court; a total of 6 such duty assignments were originally authorized, later increased to 11. In 999 *hsiang-tuan kuan* was itself made an official title, with 8 authorized appointees who often thereafter filled vacancies among the executive officials of the Court, while principally overseeing the work of the 8 Subsections (*fang*) of the Sentence Evaluators Section, reviewing trial results reported by Circuits (*lu*) throughout the country. SP: *fonctionnaire chargé de révision*. P13, 22.

2363   *hsiáng-tuàn ssū*   詳斷司
SUNG: **Office of Sentence Evaluators,** a collective reference to Sentence Evaluators (*hsiang-tuan kuan*) in the Judicial Control Office (*shen-hsing yüan*) of early Sung. SP: *bureau de révision*. P13.

2364   *hsiāng-t'uán*   鄉團
SUI: **Township Company,** an urban militia unit in the Garrison Militia (*fu-ping*) system, headed by a Company Commander (*t'uan-chu*); several such units in an area constituted a Garrison (*fu*).

2365   *hsiáng-wáng*   相王
N-S DIV: **Minister Prince,** unofficial reference to a Prince (*wang*) when serving as Counselor-in-chief (*ch'eng-hsiang*).

2366   *hsiáng-wèi*   香尉
HAN: unofficial reference to a **District Defender** (*hsien-wei*).

2367   *hsiáng-wěn*   詳穩
LIAO: **General,** a tribal dignitary; one of several terms that seem to be Khitan renderings of the Chinese title *chiang-chün*. Also see *hsiang-kun*.

2368   *hsiāng wēng-chǔ*   鄉翁主
HAN: **Township Princess-ordinary,** designation of the daughter of a Prince (*wang*) not of the imperial family; outranked Neighborhood Princess-ordinary (*t'ing weng-chu*), but the basis for the distinction is not clear.

2369   *hsiáng-yào k'ù*   香藥庫
SUNG: **Musk Storehouse,** one of the imperial storehouses maintained by the Court of the Imperial Treasury (*t'ai-fu ssu*). SP: *magasin de musc*.

2370   *hsiáng-yèn àn*   詳讞案
SUNG: **Precedent Review Section** (?), one of 5 Sections (*an*) constituting the Left Bureau (*tso-t'ing*) of the Court of Judicial Review (*ta-li ssu*); functions not clear. P22.

2371   *hsiáng-yǔng*   鄉勇
CH'ING: lit., township braves: **Company,** a 50-man militia unit organized by a District Magistrate (*chih-hsien*). See *min-chuang, t'uan-lien*.

2372   *hsiāng-yüán*   鄉元
CHIN: **Principal Graduate,** the first man listed on the pass list for a Prefectural Examination (*hsiang-shih*) in the civil service recruitment examination sequence; equivalent to *chieh-yüan* of other periods.

2373   *hsiāng-yüēh*   鄉約
SUNG–CH'ING: **Community Compact,** a kind of constitution for local self-government initiated by N. Sung Neo-Confucians with imperial approval, in early Ming imposed by the government on all officially recognized Communities (*li*) in the Community Self-monitoring System (*li-chia*); basically a statement of principles for proper conduct, proper family and community relationships, proper community cooperation on projects such as irrigation systems, etc., incorporating moral admonitions promulgated by Ming T'ai-tsu (r. 1368–1398) and expanded by the Ch'ing K'ang-hsi Emperor (r. 1661–1722); known to many Westerners as the Sacred Edict. Members of the Community were expected to gather together for regular meetings at which the Community Compact was read aloud, something like a lay sermon was delivered by a local dignitary, complaints were aired and discussed, etc. Eventually the term came to refer to the group as well as to the written document. See *li-chia, pao-chia*.

2374   *hsiǎo*   小
Frequently occurs as a prefix to titles or agency names meaning small, lesser, junior, etc. In all instances, in addition to the following entries, see entries under the terminology that follows *hsiao* or comparable entries prefixed with *ta* (large, grand, senior, etc.). Cf. *shao*.

2375   *hsiào*   校
(1) HAN–SUI: **Construction Foreman** on the staff of the Chamberlain for the Palace Buildings (*chiang-tso ta-chiang*), commonly prefixed Left, Right, Front, and Rear. HB: enclosure. P14. (2) SUNG: **Construction Office,** a variant of *hsiao-shu*. SP: *office des travaux*. P14. (3) CH'ING: **Lieutenant,** a mid-rank military officer found in many units comprised of Bannermen (see *ch'i*); the unit and function are sometimes specified in a prefix; rank commonly 6, sometimes 7 or 8. Status modified by prefixes as in *shang-hsiao* (Senior Lieutenant), *chung-hsiao* (Ordinary Lieutenant), *shao-hsiao* (Junior Lieutenant), *fu-hsiao* (Vice Lieutenant). BH: lieutenant, sub-lieutenant, sergeant, colonel. P37. Also see under the common alternate romanization *chiao*.

2376   *hsiào-chǎng*   校長
HAN: **Guard Commander,** rank 200 bushels; one stationed at each Imperial Mausoleum (*ling*) with a detachment of troops to prevent looting and other abuses. HB: chief of a regiment. P29.

2377   *hsiǎo-ch'én*   小臣
CHOU: **Servant,** 4 ranked as Senior Servicemen (*shang-shih*), members of the Ministry of War (*hsia-kuan*) who valeted the King within his palace. See *nei hsiao-ch'en*. CL: *petit serviteur*.

2378   *hsiāo-chì*   驍騎
Lit., a mounted soldier, cavalryman, cavalier. (1) HAN–N-S DIV: from the early years of Later Han, the official designation of the **Imperial Guard.** Cf. *hsiao-chi ying, hsiao-wei, hsiao wei-fu, chin-chün, ch'in-chün, ch'ien-niu, su-wei, shih-wei, chin-i wei, ch'ieh-hsieh, nei hu-chün ying, huan-wei*. HB: resolute cavalry. (2) SUI–CHIN, CH'ING: **Courageous Guard,** designation of an ordinary soldier (*ping*) or imperial guardsman (*chin-chün, ch'in-chün*, etc.) in such

units as the Sui–Chin Courageous Guards (*hsiao-wei, hsiao wei-fu*) and the Ch'ing Imperial Guardsmen Command (*ch'in-chün ying*), but not limited to them. RR: *cavalier courageux*. BH: private of the 1st class. (3) Occurs as a prefix before military titles, e.g., *hsiao-chi ts'an-ling* (lit., commander of regimental troops?: Regimental Commander), *hsiao-chi hsiao* (lieutenant of troops?: Lieutenant); sometimes with a prefix of its own, e.g., *niao-ch'iang hsiao-chi ts'an-ling* (Regimental Commander of Mounted Musketeers?) in the Firearms Brigade (*huo-ch'i ying*) of the Ch'ing dynasty Inner Banners (*nei-ch'i*). The literal sense of *hsiao-chi* as a prefix in military titles is not clear; certainly by Ch'ing times the literal sense of cavalryman must have been lost, as was (or was beginning to be) the case described in (2) above. P43.

2379 *hsiāo-chì fǔ* 驍騎府 or *hsiāo-chì wèi-fǔ* 驍騎衛府
SUI–T'ANG: **Courageous Guard,** one Left and one Right, military units in the Sui and early T'ang Twelve Guards (*shih-erh wei*) serving at the dynastic capital. Created in 607 as the *hsiao-chi wei* or *hsiao-chi wei-fu;* at the founding of T'ang retained with the same confusion of names, but in 622 formally named *hsiao-wei*. RR: *garde courageuse*. P43.

2380 *hsiǎo chǐ-shǐh hsüéh-shēng* 小給使學生
T'ANG: **Eunuch Apprentice,** designation of young eunuchs being trained for palace service in the Palace Domestic Service (*nei-shih sheng*). RR: *élève jeune eunuque serviteur du palais intérieur*.

2381 *hsiǎo-chì wèi* 驍騎尉
Commandant of Courageous Guards. (1) SUI: 3rd highest of 8 Commandant titles conferred as prestige titles (*san-kuan*) on rank 7a officials, beginning in 586; the practice was discontinued c. 604. (2) T'ANG–MING: merit title (*hsün*) conferred on officials of rank 6a through Chin, thereafter 5a; in Ming conferred only on military officers. RR+SP: *directeur de la cavalerie courageuse*. P65.

2382 *hsiǎo-chì yíng* 驍騎營
(1) N-S DIV: from Chin on, a common variant of *hsiao-chi* (**Imperial Guard**), commanded by a General (*chiang-chün*). (2) CH'ING: **Cavalry Brigade,** collective reference to the Outer Banners (*wai-ch'i*) stationed in or near Peking; coordinated by a Commander-general (*t'ung-ling*) chosen in annual rotation (*chih-nien*) from among the Commanders-in-chief (*tu-t'ung*) of all the Banners. Cf. *nei hsiao-chi ying*. BH: banner corps of the line.

2383 *hsiǎo-ch'í* 小旗
MING: **Squad Commander,** subofficial leader of 10 soldiers; 5 such Squads constituted a Platoon under a Platoon Commander (*tsung-ch'i*) in a Guard (*wei*), the standard Ming military garrison.

2384 *hsiǎo-ch'í* 驍騎
See under the romanization *hsiao-chì*. Cf. *ch'í*.

2385 *hsiǎo chià-pù* 小駕部
N-S DIV (Chou): title shared by 2nd-level executive officials in the Bureau of Equipment (*chia-pu*) in the Ministry of War (*hsia-kuan*): **Vice Director,** ranked as a Junior Grand Master (*hsia ta-fu;* 6a), and **Assistant Director,** ranked as a Senior Serviceman (*shang-shih;* 7a). P12.

2386 *hsiǎo chiàng-shīh* 小匠師
N-S DIV (Chou): title shared by 2nd-level executive officials of the Office of Construction (*chiang-shih ssu*) in the Ministry of Works (*tung-kuan*): the **Vice Director,** ranked

as a Junior Grand Master (*hsia ta-fu;* 6a), and **Assistant Director,** ranked as a Senior Serviceman (*shang-shih;* 7a). P14.

2387 *hsiǎo chiào-hsí* 小教習
CH'ING: collective unofficial reference to **Instructors** (*hsün-k'o*) in charge of training Hanlin Bachelors (*shu-chi shih*) in the Hanlin Academy (*han-lin yüan*).

2388 *hsiǎo-chiēn* 小監
MING: **Boy Eunuch,** a generic reference rather than a title, apparently in contrast to the eunuch title *t'ai-chien* (Director), which came to be a generic reference to palace eunuchs of all sorts.

2389 *hsiǎo-chièn* 小諫
Junior Remonstrator: from T'ang on, an unofficial reference to a Reminder (*shih-i*) or, after Sung, to any "speaking official" (*yen-kuan*) other than the most senior ones.

2390 *hsiǎo chíh-fāng* 小職方
N-S DIV (Chou): title shared by 2nd-level executive officials of the Bureau of Operations (*chih-fang*) in the Ministry of War (*hsia-kuan*): the **Vice Director,** ranked as a Junior Grand Master (*hsia ta-fu;* 6a), and the **Assistant Director,** ranked as a Senior Serviceman (*shang-shih;* 7a). P12.

2391 *hsiào-chīng shīh* 孝經師
HAN–N-S DIV: lit., master of the *Classic of Filial Piety:* **Instructor** in a sub-District (*hsien*) school (*hsiang, hsü*); rank not clear, but quite low. HB: master of the classic of filial piety. P51.

2392 *hsiǎo chiǔ ch'īng* 小九卿
Nine Lesser Chief Ministers; cf. *chiu ch'ing* (Nine Chief Ministers). (1) MING: collective reference to the heads of the Courts of Imperial Sacrifices (*t'ai-ch'ang ssu*), of the Imperial Stud (*t'ai-p'u ssu*), of Imperial Entertainments (*kuang-lu ssu*), and of State Ceremonial (*hung-lu ssu*), and the heads of the Household Administration of the Heir Apparent (*chan-shih fu*), the Hanlin Academy (*han-lin yüan*), the Directorate of Education (*kuo-tzu chien*), the Pasturage Office (*yüan-ma ssu*), and the Seal Office (*shang-pao ssu*). (2) CH'ING: collective reference to the heads of the 4 Courts mentioned in (1) above, the Imperial Clan Office (*tsung-jen fu*), the Household Administration of the Heir Apparent, the Directorate of Education, the Left and Right Secretariats of the Heir Apparent (*tso, yu ch'un-fang*), and the Governor (*yin*) of Shun-t'ien Prefecture (*fu*), site of the dynastic capital, Peking.

2393 *hsiǎo-ch'iū* 小秋
T'ANG–CH'ING: lit., junior autumn (officials), deriving from the Chou dynasty name *ch'iu-kuan* (Ministry of Justice): collective reference to the **Vice Directors** (*yüan-wai lang*) of Bureaus (*ssu, ch'ing-li ssu*) in the Ministry of Justice (*hsing-pu*).

2394 *hsiǎo-chù* 小祝
CHOU: **Junior Supplicator,** 8 ranked as Ordinary Servicemen (*chung-shih*) and 16 as Junior Servicemen (*hsia-shih*), members of the Ministry of Rites (*ch'un-kuan*) who prayed at minor sacrifices and assisted at major ones. CL: *officier intérieur des prières ou sous-invocateur*.

2395 *hsiǎo-chù* 小著
SUNG: **Junior Writer,** counterpart in the earliest Sung years of the later Assistant Editorial Director (*chu-tso tso-lang;* see under *chu-tsō lang*) in the Palace Library (*pi-shu sheng*); cf. *ta-chu*. P23.

2396 *hsiăo-ch'ú míng-chí* 削除名籍
See under *hsüeh-ch'u ming-chi*.

2397 *hsiăo-ch'üán* 小銓
T'ANG–CH'ING: unofficial reference to a **Vice Minister of Personnel** (*lì-pu shih-lang*). See *ch'üan*.

2398 *hsiăo chūn-chī* 小軍機
CH'ING: **Secretary**, 60 unranked personnel in the service of the Council of State (*chün-chi ch'u*); divided into 4 Duty Groups (*pan*), each headed by a Duty Group Chief (*ling-pan*), rank 3a. Also called *chang-ching*, q.v.

2399 *hsiăo făn-pù* 小蕃部
N-S DIV (Chou): title shared by 2nd-level executive officials in the Section for Foreign Relations (*fan-pu*) of the Ministry of Justice (*ch'iu-kuan*): the **Vice Director**, ranked as a Junior Grand Master (*hsia ta-fu;* 6a), and the **Assistant Director,** ranked as a Senior Serviceman (*shang-shih;* 7a). P11.

2400 *hsiăo-făng* 小方
HAN: occurs in the last century of Later Han as a title used in at least one rebel movement, apparently in the sense of being junior boss (*hsiao*) in a region (*fang*), or boss of a smaller region than one dominated by a *ta-fang*, q.v.: **Vice General.**

2401 *hsiăo hsíng-jén* 小行人
CHOU: **Junior Messenger,** 4 ranked as Junior Servicemen (*hsia-shih*), members of the Ministry of Justice (*ch'iu-kuan*) who handled rituals and communications in relations between the King and lesser Feudal Lords (*chu-hou*); see *ta hsing-jen*. CL: *sous-voyageurs*.

2402 *hsiăo hsíng-pù* 小刑部
N-S DIV (Chou): title shared by 2nd-ranking executive officials of the Bureau of Punishments (*hsing-pu*) in the Ministry of Justice (*ch'iu-kuan*): the **Vice Director**, ranked as a Junior Grand Master (*hsia ta-fu;* 6a), and the **Assistant Director,** ranked as a Senior Serviceman (*shang-shih;* 7a). P13.

2403 *hsiăo-hsǖ* 小胥
CHOU: **Junior Dancing Master,** 8 ranked as Junior Servicemen (*hsia-shih*), members of the Ministry of Rites (*ch'un-kuan*) who examined and punished the court's dancing students and arranged the musical stones in accordance with the rank of the personage before whom dancing was performed. See *ta-hsü*. CL: *sous-aide*.

2404 *hsiăo-hsüăn* 小選
T'ANG–CH'ING: unofficial reference to a **Vice Minister of Personnel** (*lì-pu shih-lang*); see *hsüan*.

2405 *hsiăo-hsüăn yüàn* 小選院
SUNG: lit., office of the lesser selections (for appointments): **Office of the Vice Minister of Personnel** (*lì-pu shih-lang*) (?), probably referring to the fact that appointments of lesser-ranking personnel were handled by the Vice Minister, whereas appointments of higher-ranking personnel were handled by the Minister of Personnel (*lì-pu shang-shu*). See *hsüan, shih-lang tso-hsüan, shih-lang yu-hsüan*. SP: *petite cour du choix des fonctionnaires*.

2406 *hsiăo-hsüéh* 小學
Elementary School. (1) Throughout history the most common designation of schools for children up to about the age of 14. SP: *école primaire*. P34, 69. (2) N-S DIV (N. Wei)–SUNG: common variant designation of, or unofficial reference to, the School of the Four Gates (*ssu-men hsüeh*). P34.

2407 *hsiăo huáng-mén* 小黃門
Palace Attendant: one of many terms designating eunuchs. (1) HAN: 10 then 20 eunuchs, ranked at 400 then 600 bushels, from c. A.D. 30 regularly appointed as general-service flunkeys for the Emperor and Empress. HB: junior attendant at the palace gates. (2) SUNG: members of the Palace Domestic Service (*nei-shih sheng*). SP: *petite porte jaune, petit intendant du palais (eunuque)*.

2408 *hsiăo-í* 小儀
T'ANG: lit., little ritualist: unofficial reference to a **Secretary** (*chu-shih*) in the Headquarters Bureau (*lǐ-pu*) of the Ministry of Rites (also *lǐ-pu*). See *chung-i, shao-i*.

2409 *hsiào-jén* 校人
CHOU: **Commandant of the Royal Stud,** 2 ranked as Ordinary Grand Masters (*chung ta-fu*), members of the Ministry of War (*hsia-kuan*) who supervised the 12 Stables (*chiu*) that constituted the Royal Stud; a principal responsibility was classifying all the royal horses in 6 categories: for breeding, for war, for ceremonial display, for travel, for hunting, and the weak—the last category being used within the royal palace. CL: *inspecteur ou directeur des haras*.

2410 *hsiăo-kuān* 小官
CHOU: variant of *shih* (**Serviceman**).

2411 *hsiào-kuān* 校官
Education Official: throughout history a collective designation of teachers in local schools.

2412 *hsiào-kuān chì-chiŭ* 校官祭酒
HAN: **Director of Education,** head of a state school at the Commandery (*chün*) or lower level; apparently interchangeable with *wen-hsüeh chi-chiu*.

2413 *hsiăo-lì* 小吏
Suboffical functionary, a somewhat deprecatory variant of *li* (suboffical functionary).

2414 *hsiao-li* 校理
See under *chiao-li*.

2415 *hsiăo-lì fáng* 小吏房
SUNG: **Appointments Section** in the Bureau of Military Affairs (*shu-mi yüan*); one of 12 Sections (*fang*) created in the reign of Shen-tsung (r. 1067–1085) to manage administrative affairs of military garrisons throughout the country, in geographic clusters, or to supervise specified military functions on a country-wide scale. This Section, presumably in cooperation with both the Ministry of War (*ping-pu*) and the Ministry of Personnel (*lì-pu*), contributed to the evaluation for reassignment of officials with status as Minister Commissioner-in-chief (*ta-shih ch'en*), i.e., rank 8, and higher; and administered the promotions and transfers of military officers with status as Commandant (*hsiao-wei*), i.e., rank 9, and higher. Headed by a Vice Recipient of Edicts (*fu ch'eng-chih*), rank 8b. Apparently discontinued early in S. Sung. See *shih-erh fang* (Twelve Sections). SP: *chambre de contrôle*.

2416 *hsiăo lì-pù* 小吏部
N-S DIV (Chou): **Vice Director of the Bureau of Appointments,** ranked as a Junior Grand Master (*hsia ta-fu;* 6a), in the Ministry of War (*hsia-kuan*); see *lì-pu*. P5.

2417 *hsiăo liăng-shĕng kuān* 小兩省官
SUNG: **Junior Officials of the Two Departments,** collective reference to the Imperial Diarists (*ch'i-chü lang, ch'i-chü she-jen*) of the Chancellery (*men-hsia sheng*) and the Secretariat (*chung-shu sheng*). P24.

2418 *hsiào-lién* 孝廉
(1) HAN–N-S DIV: **Filial and Incorrupt,** a recommendation category for men nominated by local officials to be considered at the capital for selection and appointment; usually the most prestigious such category. (2) SUNG–CH'ING: unofficial reference to graduates in Prefectural Examinations (*chieh-shih*) or Provincial Examinations (*hsiang-shih*) in the civil service recruitment examination sequence; equivalent to the Yüan–Ch'ing **Provincial Graduate** (*chü-jen*).

2419 *hsiào-lién-fāng-chèng* 孝廉方正
CH'ING: **Filial, Incorrupt, Straightforward, and Upright,** a recommendation category instituted in 1722 for subofficials and commoners of great promise, whom successive Emperors irregularly ordered to be nominated by local units of territorial administration; being nominated in this way became a minor path of entry to official status and appointment to low-level posts, up to rank 6. BH: filial, disinterested, straightforward, and upright.

2420 *hsiào-lién láng* 孝廉郎
YÜAN–CH'ING: lit., a filial and incorrupt gentleman: unofficial reference to a **Provincial Graduate** (*chü-jen*) in the civil service recruitment examination sequence.

2421 *hsiào-lién tsǒ-wèi* 孝廉左尉 and *yù-wèi* 右尉
HAN: **Filial and Incorrupt Defender of the Left** and **of the Right,** rank 400 bushels, Later Han police officers in the capital city, Loyang; see *ssu wei* (Four Defenders). HB: commandant of the left (of the right) of the filially pious and incorrupt. P20.

2422 *hsiào-lìng* 校令
HAN–SUNG: variant reference to the **Director of a Construction Office** (*hsiao-shu ling;* see under *hsiao-shu, hsiao*). HB: prefect of the enclosure.

2423 *hsiǎo mén-hsià* 小門下
N-S DIV (N. Ch'i): lit., junior Chancellery (official): variant designation of a **Supervising Secretary** (*chi-shih-chung*) in the Chancellery (*men-hsia sheng*).

2424 *hsiǎo mù-chǘ* 小木局
YÜAN: **Carpentry Service,** a unit in the Palace Maintenance Office (*hsiu-nei ssu*) of the Peking Regency (*liu-shou ssu*), established in 1263 to work on carriages, boats, and furniture for palace use; headed by 2 Superintendents (*t'i-ling*), unranked; functions continued in Ming and Ch'ing by subsections of the Ministry of Works (*kung-pu*). P15.

2425 *hsiǎo-pǎo* 小保
SUNG: **Small Security Group,** a unit in sub-District (*hsien*) organization of the populace; consisted of 10 families with a Head (*chang*), 5 such units constituting a Large Security Group (*ta-pao*).

2426 *hsiǎo pīn-pù* 小賓部
N-S DIV (Chou): title shared by 2nd-level executive officials of the Section for Tributary Relations (*pin-pu*) in the Ministry of Justice (*ch'iu-kuan*): the **Vice Director,** ranked as a Junior Grand Master (*hsia ta-fu;* 6a), and the **Assistant Director,** ranked as a Senior Serviceman (*shang-shih;* 7a). Cf. *fan-pu.* P17.

2427 *hsiǎo pīng-pù* 小兵部
N-S DIV (Chou): title shared by 2nd-level executive officials of the Bureau of Military Personnel (*ping-pu*) in the Ministry of War (*hsia-kuan*): the **Vice Director,** ranked as a Junior Grand Master (*hsia ta-fu;* 6a), and the **Assistant**

Director, ranked as a Senior Serviceman (*shang-shih;* 7a). P12.

2428 *hsiǎo sān-ssū* 小三司
T'ANG: **Junior Three Judicial Offices,** designation of a court tribunal consisting of the 2nd-level executive officials of the Ministry of Justice (*hsing-pu*), the Censorate (*yü-shih t'ai*), and the Court of Judicial Review (*ta-li ssu*). See *san ssu, ta san-ssu.*

2429 *hsiǎo shàn-pù* 小膳部
N-S DIV (Chou): **Catering Bureau** in the Ministry of State (*t'ien-kuan*), headed by a Palace Provisioner (*chu-shan*) ranked as an Ordinary Grand Master (*chung ta-fu;* 5a); furnished drinks and delicacies for imperial banquets, receptions, sacrificial ceremonies, etc. See *nei-shan.* The counterpart of Bureaus in the Court of Imperial Entertainments (*kuang-lu ssu*) of other periods. P30.

2430 *hsiǎo-shǐh* 小史
Junior Scribe. (1) CHOU: 8 ranked as Ordinary Servicemen (*chung-shih*) and 16 as Junior Servicemen (*hsia-shih*), members of the Ministry of Rites (*ch'un-kuan*) who assisted Grand Scribes (*ta-shih*) in maintaining genealogies of Princes and historical records of the feudal states. CL: *annaliste inférieur ou sous-annaliste.* (2) From the era of N-S Division on, occasionally used for a minor clerical functionary, normally unranked. See *kan.* SP: *employé.* P53, 54.

2431 *hsiǎo-shīh* 小師
CHOU: **Junior Preceptor,** 4 ranked as Senior Servicemen (*shang-shih*), members of the Ministry of Rites (*ch'un-kuan*) who assisted Grand Preceptors (*ta-shih*) in instructing court musicians and participating musically in sacrifices and other ceremonials. CL: *sous-instructeur.*

2432 *hsiǎo shìh-kuān* 小試官
SUNG: **Metropolitan Examiner,** duty assignment for eminent officials of the central government to supervise the Metropolitan Examinations (*sheng-shih*) in the civil service recruitment examination sequence.

2433 *hsiǎo shīh-shìh* 小師氏
N-S DIV (Chou): lit., junior preceptor: **Vice Chancellor of the National University** (*t'ai-hsüeh, lu-men hsüeh*), ranked as an Ordinary Grand Master (*chung ta-fu;* 6a). P34.

2434 *hsiào-shǔ* 校署
HAN–T'ANG: **Construction Office** headed by one or more Directors (*ling*), rank 600 bushels in Han, 8b2 in T'ang, subordinate to the Chamberlain for the Palace Buildings (*chiang-tso ta-chiang, chiang-tso shao-fu*) or the Directorate for the Palace Buildings (*chiang-tso chien*); 5 in Han prefixed Left, Right, Center, Front, and Rear; thereafter commonly 3 prefixed Left, Right, and Center. At least in T'ang, the Construction Office of the Center provided boats, chariots, and various other military equipment; that of the Left did woodworking of all sorts; and that of the Right built walls of tamped earth. Also see *hsiao.* HB: enclosure. RR+SP: *office des travaux.* P14.

2435 *hsiǎo ssū-chīh* 小司織
N-S DIV (Chou): **Vice Director of the Bureau of Textiles** (*ssu-chih*) in the Ministry of Works (*tung-kuan*), ranked as a Senior Serviceman (*shang-shih;* 7a). P14.

2436 *hsiǎo ssū-chīn* 小司金
N-S DIV (Chou): title shared by 2nd-level executive officials of the Bureau of Metalwork (*ssu-chin*) in the Ministry of Works (*tung-kuan*): the **Vice Director,** ranked as a Junior Grand Master (*hsia ta-fu;* 6a), and the **Assistant Di-**

rector, ranked as a Senior Serviceman (*shang-shih;* 7a). P14.

2437 *hsiǎo ssū-hùi* 小司卉
N-S DIV (Chou): title shared by 2nd-level executive officials of the Bureau of Gardens (*ssu-hui*) in the Ministry of Works (*tung-kuan*): the **Vice Director,** ranked as a Junior Grand Master (*hsia ta-fu;* 6a), and the **Assistant Director,** ranked as a Senior Serviceman (*shang-shih;* 7a). P14.

2438 *hsiǎo ssū-k'òu* 小司寇
(1) CHOU: **Vice Minister of Justice,** 2 ranked as Ordinary Grand Masters (*chung ta-fu*) in the Ministry of Justice (*ch'iu-kuan*); administered justice for lesser personnel of the central government and for the general population of the royal domain. CL: *sous-préposé aux brigands.* (2) N-S DIV (Chou): **Vice Minister of Justice** in the Ministry of Justice (*ch'iu-kuan*), ranked as a Senior Grand Master (*shang ta-fu;* 4a). P13.

2439 *hsiǎo ssū-k'ūng* 小司空
(1) N-S DIV (Chou): **Vice Minister of Works** in the Ministry of Works (*tung-kuan*), ranked as a Senior Grand Master (*shang ta-fu;* 4a). P14. (2) T'ANG–CH'ING: may be encountered as an archaic reference to a **Vice Minister of Works** (*kung-pu shih-lang*).

2440 *hsiǎo ssū-lì* 小司隸
N-S DIV (Chou): title shared by 2nd-level executive officials in the Bureau of Convict Labor (*ssu-li*) of the Ministry of Justice (*ch'iu-kuan*): the **Vice Director,** ranked as a Junior Grand Master (*hsia ta-fu;* 6a), and the **Assistant Director,** ranked as a Senior Serviceman (*shang-shih;* 7a). P13.

2441 *hsiǎo ssū-mǎ* 小司馬
Vice Minister of War. (1) CHOU: 2nd highest post in the Ministry of War (*hsia-kuan*), 2 appointees ranked as Ordinary Grand Masters (*chung ta-fu*). CL: *sous-commandant des chevaux.* (2) N-S DIV (Chou): same as in (1) above, but with rank of Senior Grand Master (*shang ta-fu;* 4a). P12. (3) T'ANG–CH'ING: may be encountered as an archaic reference to a Vice Minister of War (*ping-pu shih-lang*).

2442 *hsiǎo ssū-mù* 小司木
N-S DIV (Chou): title shared by 2nd-level executive officials in the Bureau of Carpentry (*ssu-mu*) of the Ministry of Works (*tung-kuan*): the **Vice Director,** ranked as a Junior Grand Master (*hsia ta-fu;* 6a), and the **Assistant Director,** ranked as a Senior Serviceman (*shang-shih;* 7a). P14.

2443 *hsiǎo ssū-nèi* 小司內
N-S DIV (Chou): **Junior Palace Attendant,** a eunuch title with rank of Ordinary Serviceman (*chung-shih;* 8a).

2444 *hsiǎo ssū-p'í* 小司皮
N-S DIV (Chou): **Vice Director of the Bureau of Leatherwork** (*ssu-p'i*) in the Ministry of Works (*tung-kuan*), ranked as a Senior Serviceman (*shang-shih;* 7a). P14.

2445 *hsiǎo ssū-sè* 小司色
N-S DIV (Chou): **Vice Director of the Bureau of Paints** (*ssu-se*) in the Ministry of Works (*tung-kuan*), ranked as a Senior Serviceman (*shang-shih;* 7a). P14.

2446 *hsiǎo ssū-shì* 小司市
N-S DIV (Chou): **Vice Director of the Markets Office** (*ssu-shih*) in the dynastic capital administration, ranked as a Senior Serviceman (*shang-shih;* 7a); specific functions and organizational affiliation not clear. P32.

2447 *hsiǎo ssū-shǔi* 小司水
N-S DIV (Chou): title shared by 2nd-level executive officials in the Bureau of Waterways (*ssu-shui*) of the Ministry of Works (*tung-kuan*): the **Vice Director,** ranked as a Junior Grand Master (*hsia ta-fu;* 6a), and the **Assistant Director,** ranked as a Senior Serviceman (*shang-shih;* 7a). P14.

2448 *hsiǎo ssū-t'ǔ* 小司土
N-S DIV (Chou): title shared by 2nd-level executive officials of the Bureau of Excavation (*ssu-t'u*) (?) in the Ministry of Works (*tung-kuan*): the **Vice Director,** ranked as a Junior Grand Master (*hsia ta-fu;* 6a), and the **Assistant Director,** ranked as a Senior Serviceman (*shang-shih;* 7a). P14.

2449 *hsiǎo ssū-t'ú* 小司徒
CHOU: **Vice Minister of Education,** 2 ranked as Ordinary Grand Masters (*chung ta-fu*), 2nd-level executive officials of the Ministry of Education (*ti-kuan*); primarily in charge of censuses, land registers, and requisitioned service assignments; also supervised education in the feudal states. See *sui-jen.* CL: *sous-directeur des multitudes.* P6.

2450 *hsiǎo ssū-yù* 小司玉
N-S DIV (Chou): **Vice Director of the Bureau of Jade Work** (*ssu-yü*) in the Ministry of Works (*tung-kuan*), ranked as a Senior Serviceman (*shang-shih;* 7a). P14.

2451 *hsiǎo ssū-yüeh* 小司樂
N-S DIV (Chou): **Junior Music Director,** number unspecified in the Ministry of Rites (*ch'un-kuan*), ranked as Ordinary Grand Master (*chung ta-fu;* 5a) and Senior Serviceman (*shang-shih;* 7a). Cf. *ssu-yüeh, ta ssu-yüeh.* P10.

2452 *hsiǎo-tǐ* 小底
LIAO–CHIN: **Retainer,** servant of low status comparable to a bondservant, found in the households of most nobles and in the Palace Domestic Service (*ch'eng-ying hsiao-ti chü*); commonly prefixed with descriptive terms, e.g., *hsima hsiao-ti* (Retainer for Training Horses), *wai-chang hsiao-ti* (Retainer of the Outer Chamber). P38.

2453 *hsiào-tì lì-t'ién* 孝弟力田
HAN: lit., filial, brotherly, and industrious farmer: **Social Exemplar,** designation of a category of men whom local officials were called on to recommend as potential official appointees, beginning c. 190 B.C.; by the reign of Wen-ti (r. 180-157 B.C.) had become regular appointees in the sub-District (*hsien*) system of local administration, specially charged with educational functions; cooperated with other local dignitaries called Elders (*san-lao*).

2454 *hsiǎo tsǎi-hsiàng* 小宰相
N-S DIV (N. Dyn.): **Junior Grand Councilor,** unofficial reference to Palace Attendants (*shih-chung*) and eunuch Imperial Gatekeepers (*huang-men*) because of their great influence on Emperors, potential or actual. See *tsai-hsiang.* P2.

2455 *hsiáo-tsàng shǔ* 餚藏署
N-S DIV (N. Ch'i)–SUI: **Office of Delicacies,** a unit in the Court of Imperial Entertainments (*kuang-lu ssu*) that prepared special meat and fish dishes for court banquets; headed by a Director (*ling*). In T'ang retitled *chen-hsiu shu.* P30.

2456 *hsiào-wèi* 校尉
Commandant, normally prefixed with functionally descriptive or laudatory terms. (1) HAN–SUNG: title of functioning military officers in a wide range of ranks; see under prefix. (2) T'ANG–MING: prestige title (*san-kuan*) or merit

title (*hsün*) for military officers, commonly in ranks 6 or 7; see under prefix.

2457   *hsiāo wèi-fŭ* 驍衛府 or *hsiao-wei*

SUI–CHIN: **Courageous Guard,** one of many terms used from Sui on to designate an imperial palace or bodyguard unit, normally paired with prefixes Left and Right; included among the Twelve Guards (*shih-erh wei*) in Sui and early T'ang and among the Sixteen Guards (*shih-liu wei*) from 636 to the end of T'ang and in Sung. Created c. 604 by renaming *pei-shen fu* (Imperial Guard). Till 662 the names *hsiao-wei fu* and *hsiao-chi wei* were almost interchangeable with *hsiao-wei*, which then was made the single official name. In 685 renamed *wu-wei wei* (Militant and Awesome Guard); from 705 again called *hsiao-wei*. RR+SP: *garde courageuse*. P43.

2458   *hsiăo wŭ-tsàng* 小武藏

N-S DIV (Chou): **Vice Director of the Bureau of Provisions** (*wu-tsang*) in the Ministry of War (*hsia-kuan*), ranked as a Junior Grand Master (*hsia ta-fu;* 6a). P12.

2459   *hsiăo yŭ́-pù* 小虞部

N-S DIV (Chou): **Vice Director of the Bureau of Forestry** (*yü-pu*) in the Ministry of Works (*tung-kuan*), partly affiliated with the Ministry of Education (*ti-kuan*); ranked as a Senior Serviceman (*shang-shih;* 7a). P14.

2460   *hsiéh* 協

Common prefix, or part of a prefix, to titles suggesting "to assist with"; hence **Vice, Associate,** or **Assistant.**

2461   *hsiéh-chèn* 協鎮

CH'ING: unofficial reference to a **Vice General** (*fu-chiang*).

2462   *hsiéh-chèng shŭ-yĭn* 協正庶尹

MING: **Governor Companion in Rectitude,** a merit title (*hsün*) for civil officials of rank 5b. P65.

2463   *hsiéh-chūng láng* 協忠郎 and *hsiéh-chūng tà-fū* 大夫

SUNG: **Gentleman (Grand Master) Companion in Loyalty,** merit titles (*hsün*) for civil officials of ranks 7b and 5a, respectively, beginning in 1116.

2464   *hsiéh-hsiū* 協脩

CH'ING: **Assistant Proofreader,** 10 unranked personnel in the Imperial Printing Office (*hsiu-shu ch'u*) in the Hall of Military Glory (*wu-ying tien*).

2465   *hsiéh-júng* 協戎

CH'ING: unofficial reference to a **Vice General** (*fu-chiang*).

2466   *hsiéh-k'uĕi* 協揆

CH'ING: unofficial reference to a **Grand Secretary** (*ta hsüeh-shih*).

2467   *hsiĕh kuó-shĭh k'ăi-shū* 寫國史楷書

T'ANG: **Standard Script Calligrapher for the Dynastic History,** 18 unranked personnel in the Academy of Scholarly Worthies (*chi-hsien tien shu-yüan*). RR: *fonctionnaire à l'écriture régulière chargé d'écrire l'histoire de l'état.*

2468   *hsiéh-lĭ* 協理

MING–CH'ING: **Assistant Manager** or **Vice Director,** a common prefix to a title, normally suggesting that an official holding a position elsewhere in the government had been delegated temporarily to help oversee the affairs indicated in the terminology that follows.

2469   *hsiéh-lĭ ch'īn-t'iēn chiēn t'iēn-wén-suàn hsüéh shìh-wù* 協理欽天監天文算學事務

CH'ING: **Vice Director of the Astronomical College in**

the Directorate of Astronomy, a post normally held concurrently by the Director (*chien-cheng*) of the Directorate, rank 5a. BH: assistant superintendent.

2470   *hsiéh-lĭ kuān-fáng shìh-wù* 協理關防事務

CH'ING: **Vice Director,** 2 in the Overseers Office (*chang kuan-fang ch'u*) in the Imperial Household Department (*nei-wu fu*). BH: assistant chancellor. P37.

2471   *hsiéh-lĭ shìh-wù láng-chūng* 協理事務郎史

CH'ING: abbreviation of *hsieh-li yüan-ming yüan shih-wu lang-chung,* **Vice Director** in a Bureau of the Imperial Household Department (*nei-wu fu*) **serving as Assistant Director of the Summer Palace;** under the jurisdiction of the Imperial Household Department. P40.

2472   *hsiéh-lĭ shìh-wù tà-ch'én* 協理事務大臣

CH'ING: abbreviation of *hsieh-li hsien-an kung kuan-hsüeh shih-wu ta-ch'en,* **Grand Minister** of the Imperial Household Department (*nei-wu fu*) **serving as Assistant Director of the Official School in the Palace of Complete Contentment;** subordinate to a Grand Minister Manager (*kuan-li shih-wu ta-ch'en*); under the jurisdiction of the Imperial Household Department. P37.

2473   *hsiéh-lĭ shìh-wù yŭn-hūi shĭh* 協理事務雲麾使

CH'ING: abbreviation of *hsieh-li luan-i wei shih-wu yün-hui shih,* **Flag Assistant Serving as Assistant Director of the Imperial Procession Guard,** 2, rank 4a; subordinate to 2 Directors (*tsung-li shih-wu kuan-chün shih*), in turn subordinate to 3 Imperial Procession Commissioners (*luan-i shih*), and ultimately to a Grand Minister in Command of the Guard (*chang wei-shih ta-ch'en*). BH: assistant chief marshal.

2474   *hsiéh-lĭng* 協領

CH'ING: **Assistant Commandant** in the hierarchy of Provincial Bannermen (*chu-fang*), normal rank 3b; subordinate to a Vice Commander-in-chief (*fu tu-t'ung*) in charge of provincial forces, superior to Garrison Commandants (*ch'eng-shou wei*), Company Commanders (*tso-ling*), etc. BH: colonel of a regiment.

2475   *hsiéh-lù* 協律

YÜAN: **Assistant for Pitchpipes,** professional musicians attached to the Office of Western Music (*t'ien-yüeh shu*) and the Office of Contented Music (*an-ho shu*). P10.

2476   *hsiéh-lù hsiào-wèi* 協律校尉

N-S DIV (Chin-Liang): **Director of Imperial Music,** a subordinate of the Chamberlain for Ceremonials (*t'ai-ch'ang*); provided classical music for important state rituals. Successor to the *hsieh-lü tu-wei* of Han times and predecessor of the *hsieh-lü lang* of later times. P10.

2477   *hsiéh-lù láng* 協律郎

N-S DIV (N. Wei)–CH'ING: **Chief Musician,** normally hereditary professionals attached to the Court of Imperial Sacrifices (*t'ai-ch'ang ssu*); successors of earlier *hsieh-lü hsiao-wei.* Number variable, rank 5b1 in N. Wei, 8a in T'ang, 8b in Chin, 8a in Ming and Ch'ing. In N. Wei subordinate to a Palace Chief Musician (*hsieh-lü chung-lang*), rank 4b2. In Ch'ing members of both the Music Office (*ho-sheng shu*) and the Imperial Music Office (*shen-yüeh so, shen-yüeh shu*), both in the Music Ministry (*yüeh-pu*). RR+SP: *préposé à l'harmonie des tuyaux sonores.* BH: chief musician. P10.

2478   *hsiéh-lǜ tū-wèi* 協律都尉
HAN–N-S DIV (San-kuo Wei): **Director of Imperial Music**, rank 2,000 bushels, head of the Music Office (*yüeh-fu*) established in 121 B.C.; apparently outlived the abolition of the Music Office under Emperor Ai (r. 7–1 B.C.), continued as a subordinate of the Chamberlain for the Palace Revenues (*shao-fu*). HB: chief commandant of harmony. P10.

2479   *hsiéh-pàn tà hsüéh-shìh* 協辦大學士
CH'ING: **Assistant Grand Secretary** in the Grand Secretariat (*nei-ko*), one each Manchu and Chinese, rank 1b; established in the 1730s to increase the Grand Secretariat's executive staff; normally retained principal status and rank as, e.g., Minister (*shang-shu*), and concurrently served as members of the Council of State (*chün-chi ch'u*); regularly filled vacancies among the Grand Secretaries (*ta hsüeh-shih*). P2.

2480   *hsiéh-pàn yüàn-shìh* 協辦院事
CH'ING: **Assistant Administrator of the Hanlin Academy,** 2 appointed after 1729 to assist newly established Administrators of the Hanlin Academy (*pan yüan-shih*); a duty assignment rather than a regular post, assignees reportedly chosen from among the 4 Chancellors of the Hanlin Academy (*chang-yüan hsüeh-shih*) although the Chancellors ranked higher than their colleagues serving as Administrators and were often appointed to concurrent service in the Academy while principally serving as Grand Secretaries (*ta hsüeh-shih*) or Ministers (*shang-shu*) or Vice Ministers (*shih-lang*) of Ministries (*pu*). P23.

2481   *hsiéh-p'í chú* 斜皮局
YÜAN: **Striped Hides Service,** a manufacturing unit under the Directorate of Leather and Fur Manufactures (*li-yung chien*); staffing not clear; produced finished goods from the hides of wild horses. P38.

2482   *hsiéh-piāo* 協標
CH'ING: **Command of a Regional Vice Commander** or **Command of an Assistant Regional Commander** (*fu-chiang* or *ts'an-chiang*), a military jurisdiction incorporating several Brigades (*ying*) in the Green Standards (*lu-ying*) military establishment. See *piao*. BH: territorial regiment.

2483   *hsiéh shēng-lǜ kuān* 協聲律官
SUNG: **Assistant for the Resonant Pitchpipes,** unspecified number of professional musicians in the Imperial Music Bureau (*ta-sheng fu*). SP: *fonctionnaire chargé de l'harmonie des tuyaux sonores.*

2484   *hsiéh-t'ái* 協台
CH'ING: lit., assistant dignitary: unofficial reference to a **Regional Vice Commander** (*fu-chiang*) in the Green Standards (*lu-ying*) military establishment.

2485   *hsiéh-t'úng kuān* 協同官
CH'ING: **Assistant,** 15 then 10 professional musicians of low status attached to the Music Office (*chiao-fàng ssu*) of early Ch'ing, subordinate to the Ministry of Rites (*lǐ-pu*). P10.

2486   *hsiéh-t'úng shǒu-pèi* 協同守備
MING: **Vice Commandant,** usually the duty assignment of a Marquis (*hou*) or an Earl (*po*), from the 1420s one of 3 men who constituted a military regency council in control of the auxiliary capital, Nanking. See *shou-pei* (Grand Commandant), *ts'an-tsan chi-wu* (Grand Adjutant).

2487   *hsiéh-t'úng tú-yùn ts'ān-chiāng* 協同督運參將
MING: **Assistant Grain Transport Commander,** one authorized in 1457 to help the Grain Transport Commander (*ts'ao-yün tsung-ping kuan*) supervise the Tax Transport Leaders (*pa-tsung*) of various areas in organizing and directing the fleets of boats that brought tax grain from the Yangtze delta up the Grand Canal to provision the dynastic capital, Peking. See *ts'an-chiang*. P60.

2488   *hsiéh-yīn* 協音
YÜAN: **Assistant for Tones,** professional musicians attached to the Office of Contented Music (*an-ho shu*) and the Office of Western Music (*t'ien-yüeh shu*). Cf. *hsieh-lü*. P10.

2489   *hsiéh-yīn láng* 諧音郎
CHIN: **Musician,** variable number, rank 9b, in the Music Office (*chiao-fang*). P10.

2490   *hsiěh yù-shū jén* 寫御書人
T'ANG: **Copyist of Imperial Books** in the Academy of Scholarly Worthies (*chi-hsien tien shu-yüan*), an assignment for talented sons and grandsons of officials pending their being considered for official appointments. RR: *écrivain des textes impériaux.*

2491   *hsièn* 憲
Fundamental laws: throughout history, a vague reference to the uncodified teachings, rules, and precedents on which government was based; a common element in unofficial and sometimes official references to Censors (*yü-shih*), who were considered guardians of the fundamental laws, and sometimes other kinds of officials as well. See *feng-hsien*.

2492   *hsièn* 縣
(1) CHOU: **Township,** a local self-government unit under an elected Head (*cheng*), comprising 5 Wards (*pi*) in the outer regions of the royal domain, corresponding to *chou* in the immediate environs of the royal capital; responsible for properly classifying people and lands, adjudicating disputes, promoting agriculture and morality, and raising a local militia when called on. CL: *arrondissement extérieur.* (2) **District:** throughout imperial history, the basic formal unit in the hierarchy of territorial administration, several neighboring Districts being clustered under the supervision of a Commandery (*chün*), a Region (*chou*), or a Prefecture (*chou* or *fu*); graded by size of the resident population or prestige of location, e.g., in Ch'in and Han in larger Districts producing more than 10,000 bushels of tax grain and smaller Districts producing less; in T'ang in 7 grades indicated by the prefixes *ch'ih* (Imperial), *chi* (Metropolitan), *wang* (Honored), *chin* (Important), *shang* (Large), *chung* (Middle), and *hsia* (Small). District heads were Magistrates (*ling* and *chang* in Ch'in and Han, rank 1,000 to 600 bushels or 500 to 300 bushels, respectively; *ling* continuing into Sung, rank normally from 7a to 5a; *chih-hsien* from Sung through Ch'ing, rank normally 7a); they were consistently aided by Vice Magistrates (*ch'eng*, 7a to 9a) and had clerical staffs divided by functions into Sections (*ts'ao*); they were all-around representatives of the Emperor and the central government in their localities, commonly referred to as Father-and-mother Officials (*fu-mu kuan*). A common variant rendering is **County.** HB: prefecture. RR+SP: *sous-préfecture.* BH: district. P54.

2493   *hsién* 銜
A troublesome term, often loosely used; most commonly the equivalent of **rank** (*p'in, chieh*) or **nominal office** (i.e.,

an office not actually held); sometimes used specifically to indicate that an official's rank (on the basis of which he was paid) was not appropriate to, and normally was lower than, the office he actually occupied (*kuan*); sometimes used, e.g., when an official had been promoted to a higher post but his promotion had not yet been confirmed by the appropriate authorities. Often rendered "brevet rank."

2494 *hsién-ān kūng kuān-hsüéh* 咸安宮官學
CH'ING: **School at the Palace of Universal Peace,** a school established within the imperial palace for educating the sons of senior officers of the Eight Banners (*pa ch'i*), headed by Grand Ministers (*ta-ch'en*) of the Imperial Household Department (*nei-wu fu*) designated Managers of the School … (*kuan-li hsien-an kung kuan-hsüeh shih-wu*).

2495 *hsién-ch'á* 賢察
Customs Collector: common reference to any official assigned to collect fees at a customs barrier or market.

2496 *hsièn-chǎng* 憲長 or *hsièn-ch'én* 臣
From Sung or earlier, an unofficial reference to the senior executive official of the Censorate (*yü-shih t'ai, tu ch'a-yüan*), normally the Censor-in-chief (*yü-shih ta-fu, tu yü-shih*). See *hsien* (fundamental laws).

2497 *hsién-chǎng* 閑長
N-S DIV (Chou): **Stable Keeper,** rank 9a, a member of the Ministry of War (*hsia-kuan*). P35.

2498 *hsién-chíh* 閑職
Lit., assignment in an enclosure: from T'ang on, an unofficial reference to **Educational Officials** (*hsiao-kuan*). Also see *leng-kuan* (lit., cold officials).

2499 *hsién-chiù shíh* 閑廏使
T'ANG: **Commissioner for the Palace Corrals and Stables,** created c. 700 to replace the Livery Service (*shang-sheng chü*) of the Palace Administration (*tien-chung sheng*) as supervisor of all corrals and stables within the palace grounds, specifically the Six Palace Corrals (*chang-nei liu hsien*), Six Stables (*liu chiu*), and Five Cages (*wu fang*). Normally had nominal status as Director (*chien*), rank 3a2, or Assistant Director (*ch'eng*), 5b1, of the Palace Administration. RR: *commissaire impérial chargé des parcs à chevaux et des écuries.* P38.

2500 *hsièn-chǔ* 縣主
(1) **District Princess,** a title of nobility (*chüeh*). In Han granted to daughters of Emperors who were enfeoffed with Districts (*hsien*); from the era of N-S Division through Yüan, regularly granted to daughters of all Princes (*wang*); in Ming and Ch'ing granted to daughters of Commandery Princes (*chün-wang*). (2) Occasionally encountered as an unofficial reference to a **District Magistrate** (*hsien-ling, chih-hsien*).

2501 *hsièn-chǔ chiēn* 閑駒監長
HAN: **Directorate of Horse Corrals** under the Chamberlain for the Palace Stud (*t'ai-p'u*), headed by a Director (*chang*), rank and specific functions not clear but possibly in charge of training colts for palace use. HB: chief inspector of the pens for training colts. P31.

2502 *hsièn-chūn* 縣君
District Mistress, a title of nobility (*chüeh*) or honor granted to women: in Han to wives of some officials (category not clear); in T'ang to mothers and wives of officials of ranks 3, 4, and 5; in Sung to wives of Chief Secretaries (*shu-tzu*) in the household of the Heir Apparent; in Ming to daughters of Defender-generals of the State (*chen-kuo chiang-chün*);

in Ch'ing to daughters of Beile Princes (*pei-tzu*). RR: *dame de sous-préfecture.*

2503 *hsièn-fǎ* 縣法
N-S DIV (Chou): **District Justice Bureau** in the Ministry of Justice (*ch'iu-kuan*), functions not clearly specified; also a title shared by the Bureau's executive officials—the **Director,** ranked as a Senior Serviceman (*shang-shih;* 7a), and the **Vice Director,** ranked as an Ordinary Serviceman (*chung-shih;* 8a). P13.

2504 *hsién-fēi* 賢妃
SUI–MING: **Worthy Consort,** one of several secondary imperial wives; in T'ang and Sung seems to have ranked 4th among the major consorts, behind Honored Consort (*kuei-fei*), Pure Consort (*shu-fei*), and Virtuous Consort (*te-fei*); rank =1a. RR: *concubine sage.*

2505 *hsièn-fǔ* 憲府
Common unofficial reference to the **Censorate** (*yü-shih t'ai, tu ch'a-yüan*). See *hsien* (fundamental laws).

2506 *hsièn-hóu* 縣侯
HAN–N-S DIV (San-kuo Wei): **District Marquis,** title of nobility (*chüeh*) for someone enfeoffed with a District (*hsien*). P64.

2507 *hsién-í* 賢儀
T'ANG: **Lady of Worthy Deportment,** designation of an imperial concubine, rank 2a; one of the category called the Six Ladies of Deportment (*liu i*). RR: *correction sage.*

2508 *hsièn-kāng* 憲綱
MING: **Fundamental Laws and Regulatory Principles,** title of a code governing the collaboration of Censors (*yü-shih*) and members of Provincial Surveillance Commissions (*t'i-hsing an-ch'a shih ssu*) in maintaining disciplinary surveillance over local officials; first issued in 1371 and repeatedly revised. Sometimes used as an indirect generic reference to surveillance officials (*ch'a-kuan*). See *feng-hsien, kang-chi.*

2509 *hsièn-kuān* 憲官
Lit., official responsible for the fundamental laws (see *hsien*): **Censorial Official,** a common generic or collective reference to Censors (*yü-shih*); in Sung may be encountered as an honorific concurrent title awarded to favored officials. SP: *fonctionnaire de justice.*

2510 *hsièn-kuān* 縣官
District Official: generic reference to officials of Districts (*hsien*); in Han, for reasons not clear, sometimes an indirect reference to the Emperor.

2511 *hsién-kuān* 閑官
T'ANG–SUNG: **Official at Leisure,** an unofficial reference to subordinate officials in Prefectures (*chou*) and Districts (*hsien*), whose duties were commonly considered not burdensome.

2512 *hsièn-kūng* 縣公
N-S DIV (Chin)–SUI, SUNG: **District Duke,** title of nobility (*chüeh*); in Sui and Sung, 5th highest of 9 noble ranks; in Sui abolished c. 604 when the array of noble titles was reduced to Prince (*wang*), Duke (*kung*), and Marquis (*hou*), all without prefixed qualifications; in Sung may be found only as an abbreviation of *k'ai-kuo hsien-kung* (Dynasty-founding District Duke). Also see *k'ai-kuo kung, k'ai-kuo chün-kung, kuo-kung, chün-kung, kung.* SP: *duc du sous-préfecture.* P65.

2513 *hsièn kūng-chǔ* 縣公主

HAN: **Imperial Princess of … District,** title of nobility (*chüeh*) awarded to daughters of Emperors, prefixed with the names of Districts (*hsien*) whose tax receipts were allocated as stipends for the women—i.e., Districts with which they were "enfeoffed." Cf. *kung-chu, hsien-chu*.

2514 *hsièn-láng* 仙郎

T'ANG: lit., reclusive gentleman: unofficial reference to a **Supernumerary Director** (see *yüan-wai*) of a Bureau (*ssu*) in a Ministry (*pu*). Cf. *yüan-wai lang*.

2515 *hsièn-liáng* 賢良

HAN: **Worthy and Excellent,** a recommendation category for men nominated by local officials to be considered at the capital for selection and appointment to government posts. HB: capable and good.

2516 *hsièn-liáng fāng-chèng* 賢良方正

Worthy and Excellent, Straightforward and Upright, a recommendation category. (1) HAN: one of several categories for men nominated by local officials to be considered at the capital for selection and appointment to government posts. (2) SUNG: the most common term used for men within and without the civil service who were promoted or appointed on the basis of guaranteed recommendations (*pao-chü*) from eminent officials and success in subsequent special examinations (*chih-k'o*) presided over by the Emperor.

2517 *hsién-liáng wén-hsüéh* 賢良文學

HAN: **Worthy, Excellent, and Learned,** a recommendation category for men nominated by local officials to be considered at the capital for selection and appointment to government posts.

2518 *hsièn-lìng* 縣令

CH'IN–CHIN: **District Magistrate,** standard designation of the head of a District. See under *hsien* and *ling*.

2519 *hsièn-mǎ* 先馬 or 洗馬

(1) CHOU–N-S DIV: **Frontrider,** an attendant and mentor in the entourage of an Heir Apparent and also of a Marquis (*hou*) in Han and probably the early part of the era of N-S Division; in part responsible for riding before his master on any outing to clear the way or, less likely, for leading afoot his master's horse on an outing; in Han rank 600 bushels. In Han the 2nd form above (then no doubt homophonous) displaced the first, original form, for reasons that are not clear, but possibly to avoid some taboo or some ambiguity of the time. HB: forerunner. (2) N-S DIV–LIAO, MING–CH'ING (2nd form): **Librarian** in the Editorial Service (*ssu-ching chü*) of the Heir Apparent, such responsibilities growing out of the tutorial duties of the Frontrider described above and becoming the dominant responsibilities as early as the 4th century; rank 5b in N. Wei, 5b2 in T'ang, 8a in Sung, 5b in Ming and Ch'ing. In Chin and Yüan his functions were no doubt borne generally by the staffs of the Secretariats of the Heir Apparent (*ch'un-fang*). RR+SP: *bibliothécaire*. BH: librarian. P26.

2520 *hsièn-mǎ* 縣馬

HAN–MING: unofficial reference to a **Commandant Escort** (*fu-ma tu-wei*), the husband of an Imperial Princess (*hsien-chu, kung-chu*), originating with the Han practice of enfeoffing Imperial Princesses with Districts (*hsien*).

2521 *hsièn-méi shìh* 銜枚氏

CHOU: **Silencer,** 2 ranked as Junior Servicemen (*hsia-shih*), members of the Ministry of Justice (*ch'iu-kuan*) responsible for applying gags to soldiers sent on secret missions and for shouting for silence at state ceremonials. CL: *préposé au bâillon*.

2522 *hsiēn-mín* 先民

Lit., one who goes before (leads, sets an example for) the people: from antiquity, an indirect reference to a **King** (*wang*) or **Emperor.**

2523 *hsièn-nà shìh* 獻納使

Lit., one who makes a presentation (to the throne). (1) T'ANG: **Petition Box Commissioner,** from 742 to 756 the official redesignation of *li-kuei shih*, to avoid using a homophone of the *kuei* character meaning demon or ghost. See *chih-kuei shih*. RR: *commissaire impérial pour la réception et la présentation (des requêtes)*. P21. (2) MING–CH'ING: unofficial reference to a **Transmission Commissioner** (*t'ung-cheng shih*).

2524 *hsièn-nán* 縣男

CHIN–YÜAN: **District Baron,** title of nobility (*chüeh*), rank 5b; in Chin the lowest of 7 noble grades, in Yüan the lowest of 10. See *nan, k'ai-kuo nan, k'ai-kuo hsien-nan*. P65.

2525 *hsièn-pèi* 先輩

MING–CH'ING: lit., senior colleague: a respectful form of direct address to or between **Metropolitan Graduates** (*chin-shih*); may also be encountered as a form of direct address in other circumstances.

2526 *hsièn-pó* 縣伯

N-S DIV–CHIN: **District Earl,** 4th highest of 6 ranks of nobility (*chüeh*) normally awarded men unrelated to the imperial family; ranked below Marquis (*hou*) and above District Viscount (*hsien-tzu*). See *k'ai-kuo hsien-po*.

2527 *hsièn-pù* 縣簿

SUNG: abbreviated reference to an **Assistant District Magistrate** (see *chu-pu*).

2528 *hsièn-pù* 憲部

Lit., ministry of fundamental laws. (1) SUI–T'ANG, MING: **Bureau of Punishments,** a major unit of the Ministry of Justice (*hsing-pu*), changed from *hsing-pu* c. 604, changed back to *hsing-pu* in 620; in Ming changed from *tsung-pu* (Bureau of Supervision) in 1389, then abolished in 1390. (2) T'ANG–CH'ING: unofficial reference to the **Ministry of Justice.** Cf. *hsien-kuan, hsien-ssu, hsien-t'ai*. (3) T'ANG: from 752 to 757 the official redesignation of the **Ministry of Justice.** RR: *bureau de la justice*. P13.

2529 *hsièn-sàn* 閑散

CH'ING: translation of a Manchu word: **Unassigned Bannerman,** a hereditary soldier in the Banner system (see *ch'i, pa ch'i*) without position or pay. How a man came to this status is not clear. BH: bannerman at large.

2530 *hsiēn-sháo yüàn* 仙韶院

T'ANG: **Bureau of Taoist Music,** before 838 called *fa-ch'ü so-ch'u yüan;* a unit of the Imperial Music Office (*t'ai-yüeh shu*) in the Court of Imperial Sacrifices (*t'ai-ch'ang ssu*). RR: *cour où on exécutait les airs taoistes*.

2531 *hsièn-shěn ch'ù* 現審處

CH'ING: **Judicial Office,** established in 1748 in the Ministry of Revenue (*hu-pu*), independent of its Bureaus (*ch'ing-li ssu*), to settle litigations among officers and troops of the Banner establishment (see *ch'i, pa ch'i*), in coordination with the Ministry of Justice (*hsing-pu*). P6.

2532 *hsièn-shěn ssū* 現審司

CH'ING: **Interrogation Office,** one each Left and Right

in the Ministry of Justice (*hsing-pu*), independent of its Bureaus (*ch'ing-li ssu*); established in 1723 to coordinate interrogations of prisoners awaiting sentencing; in 1737 the Right Interrogation Office was transformed into a Metropolitan Area Bureau (*chih-li ch'ing-li ssu*) to supervise judicial matters of the Province-size region surrounding Peking; in 1742 the Left Interrogation Office was transformed into a Fengtien Bureau to supervise judicial matters of Fengtien Province in modern Manchuria. Always, like Bureaus, the Offices were headed by Directors (*lang-chung*), one each Chinese and Manchu, rank 5a. P13.

2533 *hsièn-shìh* 縣士
CHOU: **Township Justiciar,** 32 ranked as Ordinary Servicemen (*chung-shih*), under supervision of the Ministry of Justice (*ch'iu-kuan*) responsible for judicial and penal matters in regions distant from the royal capital that were called Townships (*hsien*). CL: *prévôt de justice d'une dépendance.*

2534 *hsièn-shīh* 縣師
CHOU: **Township Preceptor,** 2 ranked as Senior Servicemen (*shang-shih*) and 4 as Ordinary Servicemen (*chung-shih*), under supervision of the Ministry of Education (*ti-kuan*) responsible for general administrative, fiscal, and military controls in those regions distant from the royal capital that were called Townships (*hsien*). CL: *préposé à dépendance.*

2535· *hsièn-shíh fèng-lù* 現食俸祿
CH'ING: lit., currently receiving a salary: **On active duty,** used in reference to officials in regular service with substantive appointments.

2536 *hsièn-shū* 賢書
CH'ING: lit., worthy writer: unofficial reference to a **Provincial Graduate** (*chü-jen*) in the civil service recruitment examination sequence.

2537 *hsièn-ssū* 憲司
(1) SUNG: **Judicial Commission,** common reference to the office of a Judicial Commissioner (*t'i-hsing an-ch'a shih, t'i-tien hsing-yü kung-shih*) of a Circuit (*lu*), responsible for the supervision of judicial and penal affairs in his jurisdiction. (2) YÜAN: unofficial reference to a **Surveillance Commission** (*t'i-hsing an-ch'a ssu, su-cheng lien-fang ssu*) in a Circuit (*tao*). (3) MING–CH'ING: unofficial reference to a Provincial Surveillance Commission (*t'i-hsing an-ch'a shih ssu*).

2538 *hsièn-ssū mù* 憲司幕 or *hsièn-ssū tuān* 憲司端
N-S DIV: occasional quasi-official or unofficial reference to the **Censorate** (*yü-shih t'ai*).

2539 *hsièn tà-fū* 縣大夫
SUNG: unofficial reference to a **District Magistrate** (*chih-hsien*).

2540 *hsièn-t'ái* 憲臺
Lit., pavilion of the fundamental laws. (1) Throughout imperial history, an unofficial reference to the **Censorate** (*yü-shih t'ai, tu ch'a-yüan*) or any sort of **Censor** (*yü-shih*), considered a guardian of the fundamental laws (see *hsien, feng-hsien;* cf. *hsien-kuan*). (2) T'ANG: from 662 to 671, the official name of the **Censorate,** then headed by a Censorate Director (*hsien-t'ai chang*), rank 4a2. P18.

2541 *hsièn t'ài-chün* 縣太君
SUNG: **District Grand Mistress,** title of honor granted to

mothers of Worthy Ladies (*kuei-jen*), lesser imperial wives with rank =5a.

2542 *hsièn-tsǎi* 縣宰
Throughout history, an occasional archaic reference to a **District Magistrate** (*hsien-ling, chih-hsien*). See *tsai, tsai-hsiang, chung-tsai.*

2543 *hsiēn-ts'áo* 仙曹
T'ANG: unofficial reference to the **Director** (*lang-chung*) of a Bureau (*ssu*) in a Ministry (*pu*).

2544 *hsièn-tsò* 縣佐
Throughout history, an unofficial reference to a principal secondary official in a District (*hsien*), such as a **Vice Magistrate** (*ch'eng*) or an **Assistant Magistrate** (*chu-pu*); or a generic reference to all such officials: **District Assistants.**

2545 *hsièn-tsūn* 縣尊
Throughout history, an unofficial reference to a **District Magistrate** (*hsien-ling, chih-hsien*).

2546 *hsièn-tzǔ* 縣子
CHIN–YÜAN: **District Viscount,** title of nobility (*chüeh*); 6th highest of 7 noble grades in Chin, 9th highest of 10 in Yüan; rank 5a in both periods. See *tzu* (Viscount), *k'ai-kuo tzu, k'ai-kuo hsien-tzu.* P65.

2547 *hsièn-wǎng* 憲網
Calligraphic variant of *hsien-kang* (**Fundamental Laws and Regulatory Principles**).

2548 *hsièn-wáng* 縣王
N-S DIV: **District Prince,** title of nobility (*chüeh*) created by Wei in 224 with rank of 3,000 bushels for imperial sons in recognition of the constriction of the realm as compared to Han, when imperial sons were known as unqualified Princes (*wang*); the term was used intermittently through the rest of the era of N-S Division. P65.

2549 *hsièn-wèi* 縣尉
CH'IN–YÜAN: **District Defender,** status comparable to the Vice Magistrate (*ch'eng*), with special responsibility for police activities in the District. From T'ang on, duties became more varied. In lieu of a Defender, Ming entrusted police responsibilities to local Police Offices (*hsün-chien ssu*) and miscellaneous administrative work to Clerks (*tien-shih*). See *wei.* RR: *commandant.* SP: *directeur militaire, chef de police, commandant.* P49.

2550 *hsièn-wén kó* 縣文閣
SUNG: **Hall for Making Literature Illustrious,** one section of the Hanlin Academy (*han-lin yüan*), staffed with Academicians (*hsüeh-shih*).

2551 *hsièn-yǐn* 縣尹
District Governor, throughout history an unofficial (in T'ang, quasi-official) reference to a District Magistrate (*hsien-ling, chih-hsien*). See *yin.* P54.

2552 *hsìn* 信
Lit., someone who is trusted (?): occasionally encountered as a variant of *shih* (**Commissioner**), especially in reference to an envoy.

2553 *hsīn-fù chǖn* 新附軍
YÜAN: **Newly Submitted Army,** the component of Yüan military forces comprising officers and soldiers of the former S. Sung state who surrendered to the Mongols; distinguished from the Chinese Army (*han-chün*) comprising surrendered members of the Chin dynasty forces in North China,

and the Allied Army (*t'an-ma-ch'ih chün*) of Khitan, Jurchen, and some Chinese who joined the Mongol cause early in the assault on the Chin empire.

2554   *hsīn-ī k'ù* 新衣庫
SUNG: **Storehouse of New Clothes** in the Palace Administration (*tien-chung sheng*). SP: *nouveau magasin de vêtements.*

2555   *hsìn-p'ào tsǔng-kuǎn* 信礮總管
CH'ING: **Commander-in-chief of the Alarm Guns,** rank 4a, in charge of security at the various gates of the dynastic capital. See *chien-shou hsin-p'ao kuan* (Commander of the Alarm Gun). BH: controller of the alarm-signal guns.

2556   *hsìn-shìh* 信使
HAN–T'ANG: lit., a trusted commissioner: used occasionally as the designation of an **Envoy,** e.g., to a foreign ruler.

2557   *hsīn-tzù hsüéh-shìh* 新字學士
YÜAN: **New Script Academician,** one or more appointed in 1271 in the Historiography Institute (*kuo-shih yüan*), apparently specialists in writing Mongolian in the new alphabetic script devised by the Tibetan lama 'Phags-pa; in 1275 expanded into a complete and autonomous Mongolian Hanlin Academy (*meng-ku han-lin yüan*). P23.

2558   *hsīn yüèh-fǔ* 新樂府
T'ANG: **New Music Office,** status and functions not clear. See *huang-t'ou lang.*

2559   *hsīn yùn-liáng t'í-chǔ ssū* 新運糧提舉司
YÜAN: **New Grain Transport Supervisorate,** established in 1284 under the Chief Grain Transport Commission (*tu ts'ao-yün shih ssu*) for the Metropolitan Region (*ching-chi*), to supervise the use of 250 land transport wagons based at postal relay stations (*chan*) in north central China; headed by a Supervisor (*t'i-chü*), rank 5a, 2 Associate Supervisors (*t'ung t'i-chü*), and one Vice Supervisor (*fu t'i-chü*). P8, 60.

2560   *hsìng* 幸
Abbreviated variant of *hsün-hsing* (**Imperial Progress**).

2561   *hsíng* 行 or *hsíng ... shìh* 行···事
(1) (either form, the 2nd enclosing an agency name or official title) HAN–YÜAN: lit., to carry out the duties of ..., to act as ..., in an office where there was a temporary vacancy: **Acting,** usually but not always used when the appointee was of lower rank than was appropriate for the office. SP: *chargé en outre.* (2) (first form only, prefix to an agency name) Lit., moving: **Branch,** throughout history normally denoting a temporary, to some extent movable detachment or representative of the main agency indicated. Cf. *fen, hsing-tsai.*

2562   *hsíng-àn* 刑案
Justice Section: a unit attached to both the Census Bureau (*hu-pu ssu*; cf. *hu-pu*) and the Tax Bureau (*tu-chih ssu*) in the State Finance Commission (*san ssu*) of early Sung; apparently created in 1005 by a merging of the Military Section (*ping-an*) of the Salt and Iron Monopoly Bureau (*yen-t'ieh ssu*) with a Tax Section (*tu-chih an*; cf. *tu-chih ssu*), prior affiliation not clear. Subsequent history also not clear except that in the 1080s, with the discontinuance of the State Finance Commission, merged into or was transformed into the Tax Bureau (also *tu-chih ssu*) of the Ministry of Revenue (*hu-pu*). The name also occurs as a variant or unofficial reference to a Justice Section (*hsing-ts'ao*) on the staff of a territorial unit of administration; see *liu ts'ao* (Six Sections). SP: *service de justice.*

2563   *hsíng-ch'ièh ssū-yào chú* 行篋司藥局
YÜAN: **Medication Transport Service,** headed by a Commissioner (*shih*), rank 5b; provided medications for the imperial entourage (while traveling?); hierarchical relationships not clear. Abolished in 1323–1324.

2564   *hsíng-chìh* 星置
N-S DIV–CH'ING: lit. meaning not clear: unofficial reference to a **Secretary** (*chu-shih*).

2565   *hsíng chūng-shū shěng* 行中書省
YÜAN–MING: **Branch Secretariat,** a replica of, and responsible to, the metropolitan Secretariat (*chung-shu sheng*) in the dynastic capital; the paramount administrative agency in a provincial area; in Yüan headed by a Grand Councilor (*ch'eng-hsiang*), rank 1b (compared to 1a for his metropolitan counterpart); in Ming headed by a Chief Administrator (*p'ing-chang cheng-shih*), 1b; in 1376 abolished, provincial military direction being assigned to Regional Military Commissions (*tu chih-hui shih ssu*) and provincial civil direction being assigned to Provincial Administration Commissions (*ch'eng-hsüan pu-cheng shih ssu*). Also see *hsing-sheng, hsing shu-mi yüan.* P50, 52.

2566   *hsíng-chūn chǎng-shǐh* 行軍長史
T'ANG: **Army Aide,** a duty assignment, normally for a civil official, to accompany an army on campaign as a senior administrative aide to the campaign commander (*chiang-chün, yüan-shuai,* etc.). RR: *administrateur en chef de l'armée en campagne.*

2567   *hsíng-chūn ssū-mǎ* 行軍司馬 or *hsíng-chūn*
HAN–SUNG: **Adjutant** in the headquarters of an army on campaign or in the headquarters of a Military Commissioner (*chieh-tu shih*); originally had relatively unimportant status as an administrative aide to a commander (*chiang-chün,* etc.), but in T'ang was commonly a man of military abilities, who often succeeded to command; in Sung, again primarily an administrative subordinate to a military commander, rank 8b. See *ssu-ma, chün ssu-ma, chün-ssu.* RR: *administrateur supérieur de l'armée en campagne.* SP: *administrateur de l'armée d'expédition.*

2568   *hsíng-chūn ts'ān-móu* 行軍參謀
T'ANG: **Army Counselor,** one of several titles for senior but 2nd-level officers in armies on campaign. RR: *grand conseiller de l'àrmée en campagne.*

2569   *hsíng-fáng* 刑房
(1) SUNG: **Office of Justice** in the combined Secretariat-Chancellery (*chung-shu men-hsia sheng*). See *liu fang* (Six Offices). (2) SUNG: **Justice Section** in the Proclamations Office (*chih-ch'ih yüan*) of the Secretariat (*chung-shu sheng*). See *wu fang* (Five Sections). SP: *chambre de justice.* (3) From T'ang on, may be encountered as an unofficial reference to the **Ministry of Justice** (*hsing-pu*).

2570   *hsíng-fāng shìh* 形方氏
CHOU: **Supervisor of Territories,** 4 ranked as Ordinary Servicemen (*chung-shih*), members of the Ministry of War (*hsia-kuan*) who dealt with foreign envoys, determined the extent of dependent territories, and sought to harmonize foreign groups. CL: *préposé à la configuration des régions.*

2571   *hsíng-fū* 行夫
CHOU: **Courier,** 38 ranked as Junior Servicemen (*hsia-shih*), members of the Ministry of Justice (*ch'iu-kuan*) who carried messages to foreign leaders and welcomed and aided

important visitors at the royal court; subordinate to the Senior Messenger (*ta hsing-jen*). CL: *aide-voyageur*.

2572 *hsíng-hó shǔ* 興和署
YÜAN: **Bureau of Joyful Music,** one of 2 major units constituting the Music Office (*chiao-fang ssu*); headed by 2 Directors (*ling*), rank 6b. See *hsiang-ho shu* (Bureau of Sacrificial Music). P10.

2573 *hsīng-hsí* 刑席
CH'ING: variant of *hsing-ming* (**Legal Secretary**).

2574 *hsíng-jén* 行人
Messenger. (1) HAN: designation of couriers subordinate to the Chamberlain for Dependencies (*ta-hsing* till 104 B.C., then *ta hung-lu*), headed by a Director (*ling*); together with a counterpart group of Interpreters (*i-kuan*), maintained communication with enfeoffed Princes (*wang*) and Marquises (*hou*) and with foreign tributary chiefs. In Former Han also found on the staffs of Marquisates (*hou-kuo*). HB: usher. P17, 69. (2) MING: see under *hsing-jen ssu*. Also see *ta hsing-jen* (Senior Messenger).

2575 *hsíng-jén ssū* 行人司
MING: **Messenger Office,** a central government agency attached to the Ministry of Rites (*lǐ-pu*), headed by a Director (*cheng*), rank 7a, and staffed with Messengers (*hsing-jen*), 8a; its principal function was to deliver formal, non-routine documents to important dignitaries such as Princes (*wang*) and foreign chiefs. The Office was commonly staffed with new Metropolitan Graduates (*chin-shih*) who, despite its low rank, considered it a good stepping-stone to more prominent appointments. The Office was not perpetuated in Ch'ing, which used ad hoc duty assignments to fulfill its functions. Cf. *ta hsing-jen* (Senior Messenger).

2576 *hsíng-k'ō* 刑科
MING–CH'ING: **Office of Scrutiny for Justice,** one of the Six Offices of Scrutiny (*liu k'o*); staffed with Supervising Secretaries (*chi-shih-chung*) who principally monitored the functioning of the Ministry of Justice (*hsing-pu*). P18.

2577 *hsíng-kuān* 刑官
CHOU: variant reference to the **Minister of Justice** (*ssu-k'ou; also see *ch'iu-kuan*).

2578 *hsīng-kuān* 星官
Astronomical Official: throughout history a generic reference to officials responsible for astronomical observations and calculations. P35.

2579 *hsíng-kuān lì* 餳官吏 or *hsíng-kuān*
N-S DIV (Chin): **Provisioner of Sweets,** 2 subordinate to the Director of Banquets (*ta-kuan ling*) under the Chamberlain for Attendants (*kuang-lu-hsün*). P30.

2580 *hsíng-kūng* 行宮
Lit., mobile palace, i.e., a temporary residence of the ruler in travel status; from antiquity: **Auxiliary Palace.** During Sung's withdrawal from North China in the 1120s, used as a prefix for various central government agencies, especially close-support agencies for the imperial palace. In Liao used as a prefix for agencies in the dynasty's various branch capitals. In Ch'ing referred to the court's summer resort at Ch'eng-te, modern Jehol; also called *li-kung* (Detached Palace). See *hsing, hsing-tsai*. P37.

2581 *hsíng-kūng pù* 刑工部
(1) May be encountered in any period as an abbreviated reference to the **Ministries of Justice** (*hsing-pu*) **and of Works** (*kung-pu*). (2) SUNG: **Ministry of Justice and Works,** a combined agency in the last S. Sung century, displacing the two separate Ministries of other times.

2582 *hsíng-kūng shǐh* 行宮使
SUNG: **Commissioner of the Auxiliary Palace,** a central government dignitary during and perhaps after the transition from N. Sung to S. Sung in the 1100s; status and functions not clear, but likely a personage specially assigned to arrange quarters and provisions for the Emperor and his entourage in travel status. Cf. *tu tsung-kuan, tu pu-shu*. SP: *commissaire de palais mobile*.

2583 *hsīng-láng* 星郎
T'ANG–CH'ING: unofficial reference to the **Director** (*lang-chung*) of a Bureau (*ssu, ch'ing-li ssu*) in a Ministry (*pu*).

2584 *hsíng-lǐ fáng* 刑禮房
T'ANG: **Justice and Rites Office,** a clerical unit in the combined Secretariat-Chancellery (*chung-shu men-hsia*) from the early 700s; maintained liaison with the Ministries of Justice and of Rites (*hsing-pu, lǐ-pu*) in the Department of State Affairs (*shang-shu sheng*), and to some extent performed the functions these Ministries performed earlier.

2585 *hsīng-lì shēng* 星曆生
YÜAN: **Astrological Apprentice,** 44 authorized for the Astrological Commission (*t'ai-shih yüan*). P35.

2586 *hsíng-míng* 刑名
CH'ING: **Legal Secretary,** one of several private secretaries (*mu-yu*) normally found on the staffs of Department and District Magistrates (*chih-chou, chih-hsien*); a non-official specialist adviser on judicial matters.

2587 *hsíng-mù* 刑幕
CH'ING: variant of *hsing-ming* (**Legal Secretary**).

2588 *hsíng-nèi* 行內
HAN: lit., the palace (*nei, ta-nei*) where the ruler currently resided (*hsing-tsai*): a variant of **Imperial Palace** (*kung, chin-chung*).

2589 *hsíng-ŏ* 娙娥
HAN: **Lady of Graceful Beauty,** designation of an imperial consort, rank =2,000 bushels. HB: graceful lady.

2590 *hsíng-pù* 刑部
(1) N-S DIV: **Bureau of Punishments,** one of several major units in the Section for Justice (*tu-kuan*) that was evolving under the Department of State Affairs (*shang-shu sheng*); normally headed by a Director (*lang*). (2) SUI–CH'ING: **Ministry of Justice,** one of the Six Ministries (*liu pu*) that were the administrative core of the central government, from T'ang through Chin a unit in the Department of State Affairs, in Yüan and early Ming a unit in the Secretariat (*chung-shu sheng*), then from 1380 relatively autonomous. Headed by one or more Ministers (*shang-shu*), rank 3a in T'ang, 2b in Sung, 3a in Chin and Yüan, 2a in Ming, 1b in Ch'ing after 1720; in Ch'ing one Manchu and one Chinese appointee. In general, the Ministry supervised the administration of justice and the management of prisons and convicts throughout the empire, often collaborating with the Censorate (*yü-shih t'ai, tu ch'a-yüan*) and the Court of Judicial Review (*ta-li ssu*); these 3 agencies were known collectively as the Three Judicial Offices (*san fa-ssu*). Late in S. Sung the Ministry was combined with the Ministry of Works (*kung-pu*) into a single Ministry of Justice and Works (*hsing-kung pu*). In early Yüan there were many organizational changes: in 1260 there was established a combined Ministry of War, Justice, and Works (*ping-hsing-kung pu*),

also called the Right Ministry (*yu-pu*); in 1264 the Ministry of Works was made independent, leaving a combined Ministry of War and Justice (*ping-hsing pu*); in 1266 the 3-unit Right Ministry was re-established; in 1270 the Ministry of Justice was made independent; in 1271 it was reincorporated into a 3-unit Right Ministry; and finally in 1276 it was stably established as one of 6 separate Ministries coordinated by the Secretariat (*chung-shu sheng*). The Ministry was subdivided into Bureaus (*ssu*) in Sui, T'ang, and Sung, with minor variations: e.g., in T'ang a Bureau of Judicial Administration (*hsing-pu, hsing-pu ssu*), a Criminal Administration Bureau (*tu-kuan, tu-kuan pu, tu-kuan ssu*), a Bureau of Review (*pi-pu, pi-pu ssu*), and a Bureau of Frontier Control (*ssu-men, ssu-men ssu*), each headed by a Director (*lang, lang-chung*), rank 5b. The Ministry had no subordinate Bureaus in Liao, Chin, and Yüan, although Directors often remained on the staff, simply as Directors in the Ministry of Justice (*hsing-pu lang-chung*). The T'ang–Sung organizational pattern was restored at the beginning of Ming, but from 1390 through Ch'ing Bureaus had territorial jurisdictions and names, one per Province (*sheng*), each with a Director (*lang-chung*), 5a, through which the Ministry supervised judicial and penal affairs in the various Ming-Ch'ing Provinces. RR+SP: *ministère de la justice*. BH: ministry (board) of justice or of punishments. (3) T'ANG–SUNG: **Bureau of Judicial Administration,** one of 4 Bureaus in the Ministry of Justice; responsible for preparing and revising laws and various judicial regulations and for confirming the propriety of sentences in judicial cases presented to the Emperor for final decisions; headed by a Director (*lang-chung*), rank 5b or 6b. RR: *bureau de la justice*. P13.

2591 *hsíng sháng-shū shĕng* 行尙書省
N-S DIV: **Branch Department of State Affairs,** a kind of proto-provincial administrative unit commonly established temporarily to administer a territory being newly incorporated into the domain of a dynastic regime of this era. See *shang-shu ta hsing-t'ai, hsing-t'ai*.

2592 *hsíng-shĕng* 行省
YÜAN–MING: abbreviation of *hsing chung-shu sheng* (**Branch Secretariat**); may also be encountered in reference to a senior provincial-level official, especially a Yüan dynasty Overseer (*ta-lu-hua-ch'ih*).

2593 *hsīng-shĭh* 星使
Lit., a star-like delegate, apparently suggesting that the ruler was comparable to the sun and his representatives to the stars: throughout history a common unofficial reference to a **Commissioner** or **Envoy** sent from the court on a special mission, and sometimes used in directly addressing such an official. See *shih, shih-hsing*.

2594 *hsíng-shŏu* 行首
See *hang-shou*.

2595 *hsíng shū-mì yüàn* 行樞密院
YÜAN: **Branch Bureau of Military Affairs,** a transitory regional military headquarters representing the metropolitan Bureau of Military Affairs (*shu-mi yüan*) at the dynastic capital, normally headed by a central government dignitary on temporary duty assignment as Manager (*chih-yüan*); established to administer an area newly subjugated by the Mongols, eventually yielded authority to a more stable Branch Secretariat (*hsing chung-shu sheng*). Also established in various regions to coordinate military activities against domestic rebels in the 1350s and 1360s.

2596 *hsíng shū-tsò* 行書佐
SUI–T'ANG: **Field Investigator** (?), apparently an Administrative Clerk (*shu-tso*) in the Law Section (*fa-ts'ao*) of a Princely Establishment (*wang-fu*) dispatched on a tour of investigation in the jurisdiction; from 618 to 626 entitled *ts'an-chün-shih*. RR: *administrateur ambulant*.

2597 *hsíng ssū-mă* 行司馬
Cavalry Commander on Campaign. (1) CHOU: 16 ranked as Ordinary Servicemen (*chung-shih*) reportedly on the regular staff of the Minister of War (*ta ssu-ma*). CL: *commandant de chevaux de marche*. (2) HAN: occasionally encountered as a designation; hierarchical status not clear.

2598 *hsíng-t'ái* 行臺
(1) N-S DIV: abbreviation of *shang-shu ta hsing-t'ai* (**Branch Department of State Affairs**); also see *hsing shang-shu sheng*. (2) T'ANG: **Branch Department of State Affairs,** a regional replica of the Department of State Affairs at the dynastic capital, established temporarily at the beginning of the dynasty to administer each newly subjugated area, headed by a Director (*ling*), rank 2a; reappeared after the 780s designating the headquarters of various Military Commissioners (*chieh-tu shih*). Also see *ta hsing-t'ai*. P50, 52. (3) YÜAN: abbreviation of *hsing yü-shih t'ai* (**Branch Censorate**).

2599 *hsíng-t'ái shàng-shū shĕng* 行臺尙書省
CHIN: **Branch Department of State Affairs,** established in 1140 at Kaifeng to govern the newly subjugated North China portion of the Sung empire, replacing the Bureau of Military Affairs (*shu-mi yüan*) stationed at modern Peking during the military conquest; discontinued in the 1150s when a new central government became effective at Peking, chosen dynastic capital in 1153.

2600 *hsíng t'ái-shĕng* 行臺省
SUI: **Branch Department of State Affairs,** several created transitorily early in the dynasty, each under a Director (*ling*), to administer newly subjugated regions as branches of the Department of State Affairs (*shang-shu sheng*) at the dynastic capital. Each normally supervised only 2 Ministries, a Ministry of War (*ping-pu*) and a Ministry of Revenue (*tu-chih*), and a few locally appropriate Directorates (*chien*). See *hsing shang-shu sheng, t'ʾu -sheng*. P50.

2601 *hsíng-tsài* 行在
Lit., located or resident at .... while traveling. (1) **Imperial Encampment,** from antiquity a common designation of locations where the ruler and his entourage made temporary stops while touring the country; see *hsün-hsing*. (2) **Imperial Palace,** from Han times an infrequent designation deriving from the doctrine that "the Son of Heaven considers all within the four seas as his household (*chia*), and wherever he resides is called *hsing-tsai*" (i.e., a temporary abode). (3) **Imperial Capital,** an extended meaning of (2) above in S. Sung times, when the Sung court resettled at modern Hangchow after abandoning North China; *hsing-tsai* suggested the hope that the southern relocation would be temporary, and iş reflected in the European rendering Quinsai. (4) **Auxiliary,** a prefix attached to the names of various central government agencies and to official titles when found in places other than the legitimate, principal dynastic capital (*ching, ching-shih, tu*). E.g., applied to various S. Sung central government agencies and posts, from which the usage described in (3) above derived. In Ming, applied to agencies and posts at modern Peking (then Pei-p'ing) through 1420, while modern Nanking was the offi-

cial dynastic capital, and applied again to Peking agencies and posts from 1425 to 1441 even though Peking had become the official dynastic capital in 1421, because of a lingering feeling that Nanking, the founding Emperor's capital, should again in time be made the official capital. E.g., during these years the Ministry of Rites at Peking, the real seat of government, was confusingly designated the Auxiliary Ministry of Rites (*hsing-tsai lǐ-pu*), whereas the skeletal replica left at Nanking, now merely an auxiliary capital, was officially designated Ministry of Rites (*lǐ-pu*) without any qualifying prefix. After 1441 the prefix *hsing-tsai* was at last dropped from the names of Peking agencies and posts, whereas all agencies and posts at Nanking were clearly so identified, e.g., as the Nanking Ministry of Rites (*nan-ching lǐ-pu*). Good usage might well be to ignore the 1425–1441 aberration and from 1421 on to refer, e.g., to the Ministry of Rites without qualification (or, if greater precision is required by the context, the Ministry of Rites at Peking) and to the Nanking Ministry of Rites.

2602 *hsíng-ts'áo* 刑曹
Justice Section. (1) SUI–CH'ING: may be encountered as an archaic reference to the **Ministry of Justice** (*hsing-pu*) or possibly to the Ministry's **Bureau of Judicial Administration** (*hsing-pu, hsing-pu ssu*). (2) MING–CH'ING: a clerical agency in each unit of territorial administration from Prefectures (*fu*) down to Districts (*hsien*), staffed entirely with subofficial functionaries who handled paperwork concerning judicial matters. Successor of the *fa-ts'ao* (Law Section) of earlier times. Also see *liu ts'ao*.

2603 *hsíng-tsǒu* 行走
CH'ING: a suffix appended to the names of agencies or to titles suggesting "serving in ...," "concurrently assigned to ...," etc.: **Concurrently Serving.** Most commonly, but not exclusively, used for members of the Hanlin Academy (*han-lin yüan*) assigned to duty in the Council of State (*chün-chi ch'u*). E.g., Hanlin Academy Examining Editor Concurrently Serving in the Southern Study (*han-lin chien-t'ao nan shu-fang hsing-tsou*), Vice Minister of Personnel Concurrently Serving in the Council of State (*lǐ-pu shih-lang chün-chi ch'u hsing-tsou*), Secretary of the Council of State Concurrently Serving As Duty Group Chief (*ling-pan chang-ching shang hsing-tsou*, an honorary status sometimes awarded favored Secretaries).

2604 *hsīng-wén shǔ* 興文署
YÜAN: **Supply and Printing Office** in the Mongolian Directorate of Education (*meng-ku kuo-tzu chien*), responsible for provisioning all students in units of the Directorate and for printing government-sponsored publications; headed by a Director (*ling*), rank 6b, and an Assistant Director (*ch'eng*), posts normally occupied concurrently by a Senior Compiler (*hsiu-chuan*), 6b, and a Provisioner (*ying-feng*), 7b, both members of the Hanlin Academy (*han-lin yüan*). P23.

2605 *hsíng-yíng* 行營
T'ANG: lit., mobile encampment: **Mobile Brigade,** a military unit detached from the Armies of Inspired Strategy (*shen-ts'e chün;* also see *shen-ts'e hsiang*). See *ying*. P43.

2606 *hsíng-yíng ssù hù-chūn* 行營四護軍
SUNG: lit., 4 defense armies in mobile encampments: **Four Field Defense Armies,** a military organization created in 1131 encompassing all of the Sung imperial armies remaining after Sung's withdrawal from North China; especially included a Central Defense Army (*chung hu-chün*) based near the S. Sung capital, Hangchow; all steadily declined in importance as Sung relied more heavily on scat-

tered Palace Armies (*yü-ch'ien chün*) directed by the Bureau of Military Affairs (*shu-mi yüan*). Also see *yü-ying ssu*.

2607 *hsíng-yǜ àn-ch'á shíh* 刑獄按察使
LIAO: **Penal Commissioner,** a court official on an ad hoc duty assignment supervising the management of prisons and judicial processes in units of territorial administration. See *an-ch'a shih, t'i-hsing an-ch'a shih*.

2608 *hsíng yü-shíh t'ái* 行御史臺
YÜAN: **Branch Censorate,** 2 established to assist the metropolitan Censorate (*yü-shih t'ai*) at Peking in providing censorial surveillance over provincial-level Branch Secretariats (*hsing chung-shu sheng*), dividing China in effect into 3 large surveillance spheres. One established in Shensi in 1279 after an intermittent, somewhat migratory existence in the Northwest from 1264; one established at Yangchow in 1277 and moved to Hangchow in 1284 to monitor the South (Chiang-nan), disappearing amid rebel uprisings in 1365. Each organized like the metropolitan Censorate, headed by a Censor-in-chief (*yü-shih ta-fu*), rank 1a, but responsible to the metropolitan Censorate. Also see *hsing-t'ai*. P18.

2609 *hsíng-yüàn* 行院
YÜAN: abbreviation of *hsing shu-mi yüan* (**Branch Bureau of Military Affairs**).

2610 *hsiū-chèng chǘ* 修政局
SUNG: **Governmental Reform Service,** a short-lived autonomous agency created in 1132 during the confusion of the dynastic government's withdrawal to South China, to facilitate reorganization and stabilization, but abolished after only 3 months; headed by the notorious Grand Councilor (*tsai-hsiang*) Ch'in Kuei as Supervisor (*t'i-chü*). SP: *bureau politique, bureau de la réforme politique*.

2611 *hsiū-chíh láng* 修職郎
SUNG, MING: **Gentleman for Good Service,** prestige title (*san-kuan*) for civil officials of rank 9a in Sung, 8a in Ming; c. 1117 superseded *teng-shih lang* (Court Gentleman for Promoted Service); in Ming an appointee could be advanced to *ti-kung lang* (Gentleman for Meritorious Achievement) without a change of rank. P68.

2612 *hsiū ch'ìh-lìng ssū* 修敕令司
SUNG: **Decree Drafting Office,** staffing and organizational affiliation not clear; presided over by State Councilors (*tsai-hsiang*) serving as Supervisors (*t'i-chü*). SP: *bureau de la rédaction des décrets et des ordonnances*.

2613 *hsiū-chù* 修注
SUNG: variant of *lang she-jen* (**Imperial Diarist**).

2614 *hsiū-chùan kuān* 修撰官 or *hsiu-chuan*
Senior Compiler. (1) T'ANG–SUNG (either form): designation for litterateurs, ranks not clear, appointed to the Academy in the Hall of Elegance and Rectitude (*li-cheng tien hsiu-shu yüan*) in T'ang from 720, to the Historiography Institute (*kuo-shih yüan*) in Sung; responsible for the drafting of official compilations, especially the dynastic history. RR: *rédacteur compilateur*. SP: *fonctionnaire chargé de rédaction*. (2) YÜAN–CH'ING (2nd form): 3 or more appointed in the Hanlin Academy (*han-lin yüan*), rank 6b; a common appointment for top-ranking new Metropolitan Graduates (*chin-shih*); responsible for historical compilations. BH: compiler of the 1st class. P23.

2615 *hsiū-chūn huáng-hó ssū* 修濬黃河司
SUNG: lit., office for repairing (dikes) and dredging the

Yellow River: **Yellow River Conservation Office,** established in 1073 to keep the river open for transport in the area of its mouth; headed by a Supervisor-in-chief (*tu-ta t'i-chü*); apparently subordinate to the Directorate of Waterways (*tu-shui chien*). Also see *t'i-chü ho-ch'ü ssu*. P59.

2616   *hsiū-hó ssū* 修河司
SUNG: abbreviation of *hsiu-chün huang-ho ssu* (**Yellow River Conservation Office**).

2617   *hsiū-hó ssū-yào ssū* 修合司藥司
YÜAN: **Imperial Pharmacy,** responsible for the preparation of medications for the court; headed by a Commissioner (*shih*), rank 5b; hierarchical relationships not clear. Discontinued in 1323–1324. Cf. *hsing-ch'ieh ssu-yao chü*.

2618   *hsiū-hsùn* 修訓
N-S DIV (N. Ch'i): **Lady of Cultivated Instruction,** designation of one of 27 imperial wives called Hereditary Consorts (*shih-fu*); rank =3b.

2619   *hsiū-huá* 修華
N-S DIV–SUI: **Lady of Cultivated Loveliness,** designation of one of the Nine Concubines (*chiu pin*); rank 2a in Sui.

2620   *hsiū-í* 修儀
N-S DIV–SUNG: **Lady of Cultivated Deportment,** through T'ang the designation of one of the Nine Concubines (*chiu pin*), in Sung one of a group of minor concubines; rank 2a in T'ang and Sung. RR: *femme d'une correction raffinée.* SP: *femme titrée intérieure de 2e rang.*

2621   *hsiù-ī chíh-chǐh* 繡衣直指 or *hsiù-ī shǐh* 繡衣使
HAN: variant reference to a *hsiu-i yü-shih* (**Bandit-suppressing Censor**); also (2nd form) **Bandit-suppressing Commissioner,** a duty-assignment for an official other than a Censor to suppress banditry in an area normally specified in a prefix. HB: special commissioner clad in embroidered garments. P18, 52.

2622   *hsiù-ī yù-shǐh* 繡衣御史
HAN: lit., embroidered-uniform Censor: **Bandit-suppressing Censor,** a special imperially ordered duty assignment for a Censor (*yü-shih*) to supervise the suppression of banditry in an area normally specified in a prefix. HB: secretary clad in embroidered garments. P18.

2623   *hsiū jìh-lì sǒ* 修日曆所
SUNG: **Calendar Preparation Office,** a unit in the Palace Library (*pi-shu sheng*), headed by a Supervisor (*t'i-chü*). SP: *bureau de la rédaction du calendrier.*

2624   *hsiū-júng* 修容
N-S DIV–SUNG: **Lady of Cultivated Countenance,** designation of one of the Nine Concubines (*chiu pin*) through T'ang, of one of a group of minor concubines in Sung; rank 2a in T'ang and Sung. RR: *femme d'une dignité raffinée.* SP: *femme titrée intérieure de 2e rang.*

2625   *hsiū kūng-té shìh* 脩功德使
T'ANG: **Commissioner for the Cultivation of Merit and Virtue,** from about the 780s one of several titles granted to eminent Buddhist monks who, under supervision of the Court of State Ceremonial (*hung-lu ssu*), were charged with regulating the issuance of ordination certificates and the state obligations of Buddhist monks throughout the country. These were apparently antecedents of the Buddhist Registries (*seng-lu ssu*) of later dynasties. Also see *ta kung-te shih, kung-te shih*. RR: *commissaire chargé de pratiquer les mérites et la vertu.* P17.

2626   *hsiū kuó-shǐh* 修國史
SUNG, LIAO, CHIN: **State Historiographer,** a senior litterateur in the Historiography Institute (*kuo-shih yüan*), apparently without formal official status; in Chin was administrator of the Institute. SP: *rédacteur de l'histoire d'état.* P23.

2627   *hsiū lèi-p'ǔ kuān* 修類譜官
SUNG: **Imperial Genealogist,** number and rank not clear, in the Imperial Genealogy Office (*yü-t'ieh so*) in the Court of the Imperial Clan (*tsung-cheng ssu*). SP: *fonctionnaire chargé de rédiger la généalogie.*

2628   *hsiū lǘ shìh* 脩閭氏
CHOU: **Commandant of the City Gates** that separated areas within the royal capital; 2 ranked as Junior Servicemen (*hsia-shih*), members of the Ministry of Justice (*ch'iu-kuan*) who supervised the guarding of these internal barriers in any emergency. CL: *surveillant des portes de quartiers.*

2629   *hsiū-nèi ssū* 修內司
SUNG, CHIN, YÜAN: **Palace Maintenance Office** responsible for the construction and repair of palace buildings, subordinate to the Directorate for the Palace Buildings (*chiang-tso chien*) in Sung, the Ministry of Works (*kung-pu*) in Chin, and the Regency (*liu-shou ssu*) at Peking in Yüan; thereafter its functions were carried out by an enlarged Ministry of Works. Headed by 2 Directors (*chien-kuan*), one a court official and one a palace eunuch, in Sung; by a Commissioner (*shih*), rank 5b, in Chin; by a Superintendent (*t'i-tien*), rank 5b, in Yüan. Normally supervised 2 Repair Offices (*pa-tso ssu*) prefixed East and West. SP: *bureau de réparation du palais et du temple des ancêtres de l'empereur.* P15, 38.

2630   *hsiū-shū ch'ù* 修書處
CH'ING: **Imperial Printing Office** located in the Hall of Military Glory (*wu-ying tien*) within the palace grounds at Peking; printed and kept printing blocks of imperially sponsored compilations of many sorts; headed by a Manager (*kuan-li ... shih-wu*) who was normally a Prince (*wang*) or Grand Minister (*ta-ch'en*) under the authority of the Imperial Household Department (*nei-wu fu*). BH: printing office and bookbindery at the throne hall.

2631   *hsiū-shū hsüéh-shìh* 修書學士
T'ANG: **Compiler Academician,** unspecified number established in 723 in the Academy in the Hall of Elegance and Rectitude (*li-cheng hsiu-shu yüan*). RR: *lettré rédacteur de textes.*

2632   *hsiū-tào t'áng* 修道堂
MING–CH'ING: **College for Cultivating the Way,** one of the Six Colleges (*liu t'ang*) among which all students of the Directorate of Education (*kuo-tzu chien*) were distributed. P34.

2633   *hsiù-ts'ái* 秀才
Cultivated Talent. (1) From antiquity a categorical rubric under which talented men were nominated to be considered for official appointments. (2) T'ANG: originally one of several degrees awarded to men nominated for office by local authorities who passed qualifying examinations given by the Department of State Affairs (*shang-shu sheng*); discontinued by 650, thereafter becoming a common unofficial reference to a Presented Scholar (*chin-shih*). (3) SUNG: unofficial designation of all candidates in a Metropolitan Examination (*sheng-shih*) in the civil service recruitment examination sequence. (4) MING–CH'ING: unofficial reference to all men qualified to participate in Provincial Ex-

aminations (*hsiang-shih*) in the civil service recruitment examination sequence, having real or nominal status as Government Students (*sheng-yüan*) in Confucian Schools (*ju-hsüeh*) at the prefectural (*fu*) or lower level. BH: licentiate.

2634 *hsiū-ts'āng sǒ* 修倉所
Abbreviation of *t'i-hsia hsiu-ts'ang so* (**Office of Granary Repairs**).

2635 *hsiū-tsào àn* 修造案 or *hsiū-tsào ssū* 司
(1) SUNG (*an*): **Palace Construction Section,** one of 5 Sections in the Census Bureau (*hu-pu ssu;* cf. *hu-pu*), one of 3 agencies constituting the State Finance Commission (*san ssu*) in early Sung; normally headed by an Administrative Assistant (*p'an-kuan, t'ui-kuan*); managed palace construction projects, the construction of bridges and weirs, and storehouses for various pottery and wood products used in the palace; c. 1080, when the Commission was discontinued, was absorbed or transformed into the Directorate for the Palace Buildings (*chiang-tso chien*). (2) SUNG (*ssu*): **Palace Construction Office,** established in S. Sung as a unit of Lin-an Prefecture (*fu*), site of the new dynastic capital, modern Hangchow; staffing not clear. SP: *bureau (service) de réparation et de construction dans la capitale.* P15.

2636 *hsiū-tsuǎn* 修纂
SUNG: **Compiler,** number and rank not clear, in the Calendar Preparation Office (*hsiu jih-li so*) of the Palace Library (*pi-shu sheng*); also in the Imperial Genealogy Office (*yü-t'ieh so*) of the Court of the Imperial Clan (*tsung-cheng ssu*). SP: *rédacteur.*

2637 *hsiū-wén kuǎn* 修文館
T'ANG: **Institute for the Cultivation of Literature,** from 621 to 626 and again from 706 to 710 the official variant name of the *hung-wen kuan* (Institute for the Advancement of Literature). RR: *collège pour le perfectionnement de la littérature.*

2638 *hsiū-wǔ àn* 修武案
SUNG: **Section for the Cultivation of Militancy,** an ad hoc unit of the Ministry of Personnel (*li-pu*) that participated in the Military Appointments Process (*yu-hsüan*).

2639 *hsiū yù-t'iéh kuān* 修玉牒官
T'ANG–SUNG: **Compiler of the Imperial Genealogy,** number and rank not clear in T'ang, one or 2 but rank not clear in Sung; subordinates of the Court of the Imperial Clan (*tsung-cheng ssu*). RR: *fonctionnaire chargé de la généalogie impériale.* SP: *fonctionnaire chargé d'établir la généalogie impériale.*

2640 *hsiū-yüàn* 修媛
N-S DIV (N. Ch'i)–SUNG: **Lady of Cultivated Beauty,** designation of an imperial wife; in T'ang one of the group called the Nine Concubines (*chiu pin*); rank 2a in both T'ang and Sung. RR: *femme d'une beauté raffinée.* SP: *femme titrée intérieure de 2e rang.*

2641 *hsū* 胥
(1) **Assistant:** throughout history, one of several terms used in reference to suboffical functionaries in government service, especially found in such combinations as *hsü-li,* q.v. (2) CHOU: **Seventh Class Administrative Official,** 7th highest of 8 categories in which officials were classified in a hierarchy separate from the formal rank system called the Nine Honors (*chiu ming*); below those designated *cheng* (Principal, etc.), *shih* (Mentor, etc.), *ssu* (to be in charge; office), *lü* (Functionary), *fu* (Storekeeper), and *shih* (Scribe);

above only *t'u* (Attendant). CL: *le septième degré de la subordination administrative; aide.*

2642 *hsǖ-chǎng* 胥長 胥
SUNG: **Chief of Assistants,** unranked leader of subofficial functionaries in the Court of the Imperial Clan (*tsung-cheng ssu*), the Court of Judicial Review (*ta-li ssu*), etc. SP: *scribe en chef.*

2643 *hsǜ-chíh* 敍職
SUI: **Protocol Official,** one subordinate to each Commissioner (*shih-che*), e.g., Commissioner for Western Tributaries (*hsi-jung shih-che*), in the Court for Dependencies (*hung-lu ssu*); in charge of placing foreign envoys in correct order of rank for imperial audiences, etc. P11.

2644 *hsǖ-hsíng* 恤刑
MING–CH'ING: lit., to pity (those enduring) punishments: **Prison-inspecting,** a prefix to titles of members of the Ministry of Justice (*hsing-pu*) delegated at 5-year intervals or oftener to inspect and report on conditions in the empire's prisons; e.g., Prison-inspecting Bureau Director (*hsü-hsing lang-chung*); the practice was discontinued in 1666. P13.

2645 *hsǜ-í* 敍儀
SUI: **Ritual Official,** one subordinate to each Commissioner (*shih-che*), e.g., Commissioner for Western Tributaries (*hsi-jung shih-che*), in the Court for Dependencies (*hung-lu ssu*); in charge of monitoring the deportment of foreign envoys at imperial audiences and other functions. P11.

2646 *hsǜ-k'o* 序客
HAN: lit., (one who) places guests in proper order: unofficial reference to the **Chamberlain for Dependencies** (*ta hung-lu*). May be encountered in later times in reference to the personnel of the Court of State Ceremonial (*hung-lu ssu*).

2647 *hsǖ-k'uéi* 胥魁
One of many terms used in general reference to a **Subofficial Functionary.** See *li, hsü-li.*

2648 *hsǖ-lì* 胥吏
Throughout history, one of the most general generic designations for **Subofficial Functionary,** a class of personnel who performed the more menial tasks in all governmental units and had no ranked civil service status, though at times they could be promoted into official status for meritorious service. See *li.*

2649 *hsǜ-pān* 序班
N-S DIV (Ch'i), MING–CH'ING: **Usher** on the staff of the early Chamberlain for Dependencies (*hung-lu*) and in the later Court of State Ceremonial (*hung-lu ssu*), in charge of greeting officials and guests and positioning them at court audiences and other important ceremonies; in Ming and Ch'ing, rank 9b; in Ming commonly numbered almost 100 plus 9 at the auxiliary capital, Nanking; in Ch'ing gradually reduced from 22 to only 4, filled by Chinese appointees, aided by from 8 to 12 Apprentice Ushers (*hsüeh-hsi hsü-pan*). BH: ceremonial usher. P33.

2650 *hsǖ-shǐh* 胥史
Variant of *hsü-li* (**Subofficial Functionary**), either a scribal error or a specific indicator of clerical functions.

2651 *hsǖ-shīh* 胥師
CHOU: **Chief of Assistants,** one for every 20 clusters of merchant shops in the capital marketplace, representing the

Director of Markets (*ssu-shih*) in monitoring sales, prices, disputes, etc.; subordinate to the Ministry of Education (*ti-kuan*); each helped by 2 Scribes (*shih*). CL: *prévôt des aides.* P6.

2652   *hsü-tsò* 胥佐
One of many terms used as general designations of **Sub-official Functionaries** (see *li, hsü-li*).

2653   *hsüǎn* 選
(1) T'ANG–CH'ING: **Selection,** used principally in reference to the Ministry of Personnel's (*li-pu*) evaluation and selection of inactive officials for reappointment. See *ch'üan* (evaluation). (2) SUNG: **Appointments Process,** a formal designation for the process by which the Ministry of Personnel chose men for appointment or reappointment, qualified in several ways: Civil Appointments Process (*tso-hsüan*) and Military Appointments Process (*yu-hsüan*), also Senior Appointments Process (*shang-shu sheng*) and Junior Appointments Process (*shih-lang hsüan*). See separate entries. P5.

2654   *hsüǎn-chèng yüàn* 宣政院
YÜAN: **Commission for Buddhist and Tibetan Affairs,** originally named *tsung-chih yüan* (Supreme Control Commission) but renamed in 1288; a large agency with 26 branches throughout China to supervise the Buddhist clergy and in Tibet, where 18 of the branches were located, to provide general civil administration; headed by 2 Commissioners (*shih*) till 1329, when the number increased to 11; rank 1b; assisted by 2 Vice Administrators (*t'ung-chih yüan-shih*), 2a. P17.

2655   *hsüǎn-chiào láng* 宣教郎
SUNG: **Court Gentleman for Instruction,** prestige title (*san-kuan*) for civil officials of rank 8b in S. Sung.

2656   *hsüǎn-ch'ìng shìh* 宣慶使
SUNG: **Congratulatory Commissioner,** a eunuch post, rank 6a, in the Palace Domestic Service (*nei-shih sheng*); specific functions not clear, but presumably delivered imperial messages of congratulations to imperial kinsmen and perhaps other personages on suitable occasions such as birthdays. Also known as *chung-liang ta-fu* (Grand Master of Forthrightness).

2657   *hsüǎn-fān* 宣藩
MING–CH'ING: may be encountered as an unofficial reference to a **Provincial Administration Commissioner** (*ch'eng-hsüan pu-cheng shih*).

2658   *hsüǎn-fèng láng* 宣奉郎
SUNG: **Court Gentleman for Service,** until 1080 a prestige title (*san-kuan*) for civil officials of rank 7b.

2659   *hsüǎn-fèng tà-fū* 宣奉大夫
SUNG: **Grand Master for Court Service,** after 1080 a prestige title (*san-kuan*) for civil officials of rank 3a.

2660   *hsüǎn-fù* 宣父
T'ANG: **All-encompassing Father,** from 627 a title bestowed on Confucius; probably derived from *hsüan-ni kung* (Duke of Supreme Sageliness), q.v.

2661   *hsüǎn-fǔ shìh* 宣撫使 or *hsüǎn-fǔ ssū* 司
Pacification Commissioner or **Pacification Commission.**
(1) T'ANG (*shih*): originated as the designation of imperial delegates responsible for military or diplomatic action to restore order in areas disrupted by banditry, or among disruptive alien tribes outside China Proper; time not clear. (2) SUNG (*shih*): common designation of officers leading units of the Imperial Armies (*chin-chün*) on campaign. SP:

commissaire-inspecteur chargé de propager la majesté. (3) YÜAN–CH'ING: title conferred on some tribal chiefs (and their tribal organizations) among the unassimilated aboriginal peoples of southwestern China, in the system of Aboriginal Offices (*t'u-ssu*). Also see *an-fu shih, chao-t'ao shih.* P50, 72.

2662   *hsüǎn-huáng àn* 宣黄案
SUNG: **Sentence Promulgating Section,** one of 5 Sections (*an*) in the Left Bureau (*tso-t'ing*) of the Court of Judicial Review (*ta-li ssu*). SP: *service chargé des directives sur les fonctionnaires titrés.* P22.

2663   *hsüǎn-hūi* 宣徽
N-S DIV (N. Ch'i): **Lady of Manifest Excellence,** designation of one of 6 Lesser Concubines (*hsia pin*).

2664   *hsüǎn-hūi yüàn* 宣徽院
(1) T'ANG–SUNG: **Court of Palace Attendants,** headed by one or more Commissioners (*shih*), one of 2 organizational bases (see *shu-mi yüan*) from which palace eunuchs gained dictatorial power in the late T'ang decades; whereas the *shu-mi yüan* was transformed into a non-eunuch Bureau of Military Affairs in the Five Dynasties era, the Court of Palace Attendants retained its status as an agency supervising palace eunuchs and existed intermittently through Sung in competition with the Palace Domestic Service (*nei-shih sheng*); from the beginning divided into a Northern Court (*pei-yüan*) and a Southern Court (*nan-yüan*), functional distinction not clear, each with at least one Commissioner. SP: *cour chargée des registres des intendants militaires du palais.* (2) LIAO–CHIN: **Court Ceremonial Institute,** still divided into Northern and Southern Courts, each with one or more Commissioners, rank 3a in Chin; with broadened responsibilities for supervising court activities, combining the functions that in other eras were supervised by the Court of State Ceremonial (*hung-lu ssu*) and the Court of Imperial Entertainments (*kuang-lu ssu*). (3) YÜAN–CH'ING: **Palace Provisions Commission,** a very large agency in Yüan, headed by 6 Commissioners, rank 3a, supervising both the Court of Imperial Entertainments and the Palace Ceremonial Office (*shih-i ssu*); in 1375 terminated, yielding its functions to the more traditional Court of Imperial Entertainments and Court of State Ceremonial. In 1660 revived to replace the early Ch'ing Directorate of Palace Eunuchs (*nei-kuan chien*), then in 1677 transformed into the Office of Palace Accounts (*k'uai-chi ssu*) in the Imperial Household Department (*nei-wu fu*). P15, 17, 30, 37, 38.

2665   *hsüǎn-í* 宣儀
T'ANG: **Lady of Manifest Rectitude,** designation of rank 2a imperial concubines. RR: *femme qui manifeste la correction.*

2666   *hsüǎn-ì láng* 宣義郎 or 宣議郎
T'ANG–CH'ING: **Court Gentleman for Manifesting Rightness** (the 2nd form seems very likely a corruption of the first), prestige title (*san-kuan*) for civil officials of rank 7b2 in T'ang; for Assistant Ministers or Assistant Directors (both *ch'eng*) of the Court of Imperial Entertainments (*kuang-lu ssu*), the Directorate for the Palace Buildings (*chiang-tso chien*), and the Court of the Imperial Regalia (*wei-wei ssu*) in Sung; and for civil officials of rank 7a who entered the service from status as suboffici al functionaries (*li*) in Ming and Ch'ing.

2667   *hsüǎn-jén* 選人
Selectman. (1) T'ANG: general designation of unassigned officials—men who, having been selected for appointment or reappointment, were awaiting appropriate vacancies. (2)

SUNG: categorical reference to low-ranking members of the civil service, as distinguished from Court Officials (*ch'ao-kuan*) and Capital Officials (*ching-kuan*). SP: *fonctionnaire exécutif.*

2668 *hsüan-kŏ chūn* 玄戈軍
T'ANG: **Army of the Celestial Black Lance,** named after a star called *hsüan-ko;* one of 12 regional supervisory head-quarters for militia Garrisons (*fu*) called the Twelve Armies (*shih-erh chün*); existed only 620–623, 625–636. RR: *armée de (l'étoile) de la lance noire.* P44.

2669 *hsüan-k'ò ssū* 宣課司 or *hsüan-k'ò chú* 宣課局
YÜAN–CH'ING: **Commercial Tax Office,** one estab-lished at the dynastic capital and each significant market city or town to collect mercantile transaction taxes under the general direction of the Ministry of Revenue (*hu-pu*); each headed by a Supervisor (*t'i-chü*) or Superintendent (*t'i-ling*), rank 5b, in Yüan; by a Commissioner-in-chief (*ta-shih*), 9b, in Ming and Ch'ing. Often called *shui-k'o ssu, shui-k'o chü.* BH: examiner of taxes. P53, 62.

2670 *hsüän-kùng* 選貢
MING: **Selected Student,** designation of students admitted to the Directorate of Education (*kuo-tzu chien*) from the late 1400s on the basis of special recruitment examinations con-ducted throughout the empire every 3 or 5 years by Edu-cation Intendants (*t'i-tu hsüeh tao-t'ai*), in addition to those regularly admitted by nomination of local schools, etc. Cf. *kung-sheng* (Tribute Student).

2671 *hsüan-lìng shè-jén* 宣令舍人
SUI: **Transmission Secretary,** a member of the staff of the Heir Apparent; title changed from *t'ung-shih she-jen* c. 604. P26.

2672 *hsüän-míng* 宣明
N-S DIV (N. Ch'i): **Lady of Manifest Intelligence,** des-ignation of one of 6 imperial wives called Lesser Concu-bines (*hsia-pin*).

2673 *hsüän-ní kūng* 宣尼公
HAN: **Duke of Supreme Sageliness,** abbreviation of the title of nobility (*chüeh*) conferred on Confucius in 48 B.C. See *pao-ch'eng hsüan-ni kung.*

2674 *hsüän-p'àn* 宣判
SUNG: abbreviated reference to an **Administrative As-sistant** (*p'an-kuan*) **to a Pacification Commissioner** (*hsüan-fu shih*).

2675 *hsüän-pù ts'áo* 選部曹 or *hsüan-pu*
(1) HAN–SUI, MING: **Appointments Section,** an agency responsible for managing the appointments and reappoint-ments of officials, principally civil officials; one of a vari-able number of units in the Ministry of Personnel (*li-pu*) that gradually evolved between Han and Sui times; some-times replacing, sometimes co-existing with a Personnel Section (*lì-pu ts'ao, li-pu*). In Sui c. 604 replaced the Per-sonnel Section (*lì-pu*), but after Sui not used except for the interval 1389–1396 in early Ming. Normally headed by a Director (*lang, shih-lang, lang-chung,* or *yüan-wai lang*). After Sui the Section was succeeded by a Bureau of Ap-pointments (*wen-hsüan ssu, wen-hsüan ch'ing-li ssu*) headed by a Director (*lang-chung*), one of 4 Bureaus (*ssu, ch'ing-li ssu*) in the Ministry of Personnel. (2) From the era of N-S Division on, a common unofficial reference to the **Min-istry of Personnel** itself. P5.

2676 *hsüän-shèng* 宣聖
All-encompassing Sage: from Ming if not earlier, a com-mon reference to Confucius.

2677 *hsüän-shǐh* 宣使
YÜAN: **Courier,** designation of unranked subofficials found in large numbers in many agencies, especially in the central government.

2678 *hsüan-shìh* 宣室
Lit., promulgation room or office, i.e., the office from which imperial pronouncements of all sorts were issued: from an-tiquity, one of many unofficial references to the **Imperial Palace.** See *kung.*

2679 *hsüän-shìh* 選侍
MING: **Chosen Attendant,** a title granted to otherwise un-titled palace women, especially in the early 1600s, when the Wan-li Emperor (r. 1572–1620) had a group of healthy and attractive palace women assigned to attend his mature but childless Heir Apparent.

2680 *hsüan-té láng* 宣德郎
Court Gentleman of Manifest Virtue. (1) SUI–SUNG: prestige title (*san-kuan*) for civil officials of rank 7a. (2) MING–CH'ING: prestige title for civil officials of rank 6b who had entered service from status as suboffical func-tionaries (*li*). P68.

2681 *hsüan-tsàn shè-jén* 宣贊舍人
SUNG: **Audience Attendant,** 10, rank 7b, on the staff of the Commissioner for Audience Ceremonies (*ko-men shih*); introduced visitors. Also called *t'ung-shih she-jen.* SP: *in-troducteur des visiteurs et des affaires aux audiences.* P33.

2682 *hsüän-wèi ssū* 宣慰司
(1) YÜAN: **Pacification Commission,** headed by 2 Com-missioners (*shih*), rank 2b; one or an equivalent agency (see *yüan-shuai fu, tu yüan-shuai fu*) established in each Circuit (*tao*) as an intermediary for general administration between Prefectures (*fu*) and Brigades (*wan-hu fu*) at the local level and proto-provincial Branch Secretariats (*hsing chung-shu sheng*); essentially a unit of military occupation throughout China. P52. (2) YÜAN–CH'ING: **Pacification Office,** headed by a nominal Commissioner (*shih*), rank 3b; one of the most prestigious titles granted aboriginal tribes in south-western China and their natural, mostly hereditary chiefs. See *t'u-ssu.* P72.

2683 *hsüän-wēi tū chǐh-hūi shih* 宣威都指揮使
SUNG: **Majestic Commander-in-chief,** head of the Im-perial Armies (*chin-chün*) in the Palace Command (*tien-ch'ien ssu*), which was chiefly responsible for defending the dynastic capital and the imperial palace; relationship with the Militant Commander-in-chief (*hsüan-wu tu chih-hui shih*) not clear. SP: *commissaire général au commandement, commandant en chef.*

2684 *hsüän-wén kó* 宣文閣
YÜAN: **Hall for the Diffusion of Literature,** reorganized in 1340 from the Hall of Literature (*k'uei-chang ko*), staffed only with Attendant Classicists (*ching-lang*) and Literary Erudites (*chien-shu po-shih*), all litterateurs who counseled the Emperor about classical precepts and historical prece-dents, especially as participants in the Classics Colloquium (*ching-yen*). P23, 24.

2685 *hsüän-wǔ tū chǐh-hūi shǐh* 宣武都指揮使
SUNG: **Militant Commander-in-chief,** head of the Im-

perial Armies (*chin-chün*) in the Palace Command (*tien-ch'ien ssu*), which was chiefly responsible for defending the dynastic capital and the imperial palace; relationship with the Majestic Commander-in-chief (*hsüan-wei tu chih-hui shih*) not clear. SP: *commandant en chef.*

2686   *hsüan-yèh* 宣業
T'ANG: lit., (one who) emanates a sense of professional (scholarly) commitment: from 662 to 671 the official variant of the title **Erudite** (*po-shih*) in the central government's Directorate of Education (*kuo-tzu chien*) while it was called *ssu-ch'eng kuan.* Also called *ssu-ch'eng hsüan-yeh.* P34.

2687   *hsüan-yü shih* 宣諭使 or *hsüan-yü kuān* 宣諭官
SUNG: **Pacification Commissioner** or **Pacification Official,** an ad hoc delegate from the central government to help maintain or restore order in an area troubled by famine or banditry, lit., by promulgating imperial pronouncements. SP: *commissaire chargé de proclamer la bienfaisance impériale (ou la faveur impériale).*

2688   *hsüan-yüàn* 選院
T'ANG: unofficial reference to the **Ministry of Personnel** (*li-pu*), to its subordinate **Bureau of Appointments** (*wen-hsüan ssu*), or in a general way to the process of evaluating and selecting unassigned officials for appointment or reappointment. See *hsüan, hsüan-pu ts'ao.* P5.

2689   *hsüéh-chǎng* 學長
SUNG: **Monitor,** 2, rank not clear, in the Elementary School (*hsiao-hsüeh*) maintained by the Directorate of Education (*kuo-tzu chien*); responsible for maintaining the order of precedence among students according to age. SP: *surveillant.* P34.

2690   *hsüéh-chèng* 學政
(1) MING: unofficial reference to a provincial-level **Education Intendant** (*t'i-tu hsüeh-tao*). (2) CH'ING: unofficial reference to a **Provincial Education Commissioner** (*t'i-hsüeh tao, t'i-tu hsüeh-yüan, t'i-tu hsüeh-cheng*). BH: provincial director of education, literary chancellor.

2691   *hsüéh-chèng* 學正
(1) CHOU: **Instructor** in the Ministry of Education (*ti-kuan*); number and rank not clear. (2) SUNG–CH'ING: **Instructor Second-class,** in various units of the Directorate of Education (*kuo-tzu chien*), especially in charge of enforcing school regulations; 6, rank 9a, in Sung; 2, rank not clear, and another 2 then 4 in the Mongol (*meng-ku*) Directorate of Education, in Yüan; 10 at Peking and 5 at Nanking, 9a, in Ming; 4, 9a then 8a, in Ch'ing. Cf. *chu-chiao, hsüeh-lu.* SP: *chargé d'exécuter les règlements de l'école.* BH: director of studies. P34. (3) YÜAN–CH'ING: **Instructor** in a Confucian School (*ju-hsüeh*) at the *chou* level (Yüan Prefecture, Ming Subprefecture, Ch'ing Department), rank 9b in Yüan, 9a in Ming, 8a in Ch'ing. BH: departmental director of schools. P51.

2692   *hsüéh-chèng kuān-ī t'í-lǐng* 學正官醫提領
MING: **Superintendent of Medical Education,** rank 9b, only in the predynastic Supervisorate of Medicine (*i-yao t'i-chü ssu*), which after several reorganizations was transformed in 1364 into the Imperial Academy of Medicine (*t'ai-i yüàn*). P36.

2693   *hsüéh-chiù* 學究
T'ANG: **Single Classic Specialist,** designation of one of 4

examinations offered to candidates seeking the recruitment status of Classicist (*ming-ching*), and a reference to candidates taking this examination. Soon became a general reference to all students, and in later dynasties became a common, somewhat derisive reference to elderly scholars and teachers of only local reputation.

2694   *hsüéh-ch'ú míng-chí* 削除名籍
Throughout history, a term meaning **to erase the name from the register** (of certified officials), i.e., to dismiss from the service. Abbreviated as *ch'u-chi* and *ch'u-ming.* Also see *ch'u.*

2695   *hsüéh-hsí* 學習
CH'ING: **Apprentice,** prefixed to various lowly titles such as Clerk (*pi-t'ieh-shih*), denoting someone studying to become a Clerk, and sometimes authorized to wear some emblem of rank, normally rank 9. See *hsi-hsüeh kung-shih, hsi-hsüeh kuan.*

2696   *hsüéh-kuān* 學官
(1) **Educational Official,** a generic reference to all officials engaged in school instruction, especially in Confucian Schools (*ju-hsüeh*) in local governmental units. See *hsiao-kuan* (Education Official). (2) HAN: variant reference to an **Erudite** (*po-shih*). P34.

2697   *hsüéh-kuān chǎng* 學官長
SUI–T'ANG: **Chief of Instruction** in a Princedom (*wang-kuo*), rank 9a2, responsible for supervising the tutoring of women in a Prince's establishment. RR: *chef des fonctionnaires de l'enseignement.* P69.

2698   *hsüéh-kuān chì-chiǔ* 學官祭酒
HAN: **Director of Education** in a local school in Later Han; apparently a general term referring both to *wen-hsüeh chi-chiu* and to *hsiao-kuan chi-chiu,* or used interchangeably with them. P51.

2699   *hsüéh-kuān lìng* 學官令
N-S DIV (S. Dyn.): **Chief of Instruction** in a Princedom (*wang-kuo*); apparently antecedent of the Sui–T'ang title *hsüeh-kuan chang.* P69.

2700   *hsüéh-lù* 學錄
(1) SUNG: **Provost,** from 2 to 5 in the Directorate of Education (*kuo-tzu chien*), responsible for the enforcement of scholastic regulations. SP: *chargé d'appliquer les règlements de l'école.* (2) SUNG–CH'ING: **Instructor, Third Class,** from 2 to 7 in the Directorate of Education, in Yüan also in many local schools; rank 9b in Ming, 9b then 8a in Ch'ing. BH: sub-registrar. P34.

2701   *hsüéh-pó* 學博
(1) Polite generic reference to all **Educational Officials.** (2) CH'ING: unofficial reference to an **Instructor** (*chiao-shou*) in the Confucian School (*ju-hsüeh*) of a Prefecture (*fu*). See *po-shih.*

2702   *hsüéh-shēng* 學生
Throughout history, the most common generic term for **Student,** especially denoting students with state stipends in local government schools.

2703   *hsüéh-shìh* 學事
HAN: **Apprentice,** generic designation of very lowly appointees found in many offices. HB: apprentice.

2704   *hsüéh-shìh* 學士
(1) HAN: **Graduate** of a school; a descriptive term, not a title. (2) HAN–T'ANG: **Scholar,** a descriptive term for men of learning, often sought out by the government to give

counsel, engage in compilation projects, etc., but not a regular title. (3) N-S DIV (San kuo): **Instructor** in a Marquisate (*hou-kuo*) and possibly other agencies. (4) T'ANG–CH'ING: **Academician**, from c. 707 a duty assignment for an official called on to give special counsel, assist in drafting imperial pronouncements, participate in official compilation projects, etc.; usually assigned to a non-administrative agency such as the Institute of Academicians (*hsüeh-shih yüan*) or the Hanlin Academy (*han-lin yüan*), with concurrent status as Academician while holding a substantive post elsewhere in the central government until Sung times, when Academician became a regular substantive post itself. Normally has a descriptive prefix. RR+SP: *lettré*. (5) MING–CH'ING: **Chancellor** of the Hanlin Academy, rank falling from 3a to 3b to 5a in Ming; 2, one each Chinese and Manchu, in Ch'ing, rank 5a but rising with concurrent appointments to 2a; the senior appointee in the Academy and supervisor of all its activities. In Ch'ing the title was normally rendered *chang-yüan hsüeh-shih* (lit., Academician in Charge of the Academy). Also see *ta hsüeh-shih, han-lin, shih-tu hsüeh-shih, shih-chiang hsüeh-shih*. BH chancellor. P23, 25, 26.

2705 *hsüéh-shīh* 學師
Schoolmaster, a common unofficial reference to the head or senior instructor in a government school.

2706 *hsüéh-shìh* 穴氏
CHOU: **Supervisor of Hunting**, one ranked as a Junior Serviceman (*chung-shih*), a member of the Ministry of Justice (*ch'iu-kuan*) who established and enforced rules for the hunting of animals that made their lairs in caves. CL: *préposé aux tanières*.

2707 *hsüéh-shìh ch'éng-chǐh* 學士承旨
T'ANG–YÜAN: **Academician Recipient of Edicts**, abbreviated form of *han-lin hsüeh-shih ch'eng-chih* (Hanlin Academician Recipient of Edicts); also see *ch'eng-chih* (Recipient of Edicts). RR: *lettré recevant les décisions de l'empereur*.

2708 *hsüéh-shìh yüàn* 學士院
T'ANG–SUNG: **Institute of Academicians**, established in 738 as the home agency of various officials holding concurrent appointments as Academicians (*hsüeh-shih*), who assisted in the drafting and revising of imperial pronouncements and imperially sponsored compilations, in collaboration with the Hanlin Academy (*han-lin yüan*) and the Academy of Scholarly Worthies (*chi-hsien yüan*). In Sung, especially, housed many Academicians with the prefix Hanlin, but had no organizational affiliation with the Hanlin Academy and especially none with the *han-lin yüan* (Artisans Institute) subordinate to the Palace Domestic Service (*nei-shih sheng*). Often, however, used confusingly in reference to the Hanlin Academy, and sometimes confusingly referred to as *han-lin hsüeh-shih yüan*. After Sung, a variant reference to the Hanlin Academy. RR: *cour de lettrés*. SP: *cour des académiciens*. P23.

2709 *hsüéh-t'ái* 學臺 or *hsüéh-tào* 道 or *hsüéh-yüàn* 院
CH'ING: unofficial reference to a **Provincial Education Commissioner** (*t'i-tu hsüeh-cheng*).

2710 *hsüéh-yǜ* 學諭
SUNG: **Instructor**, about 30, rank 9a, in various schools administered by the Directorate of Education (*kuo-tzu chien*); one non-official specialist in the Painting School (*hua-hsüeh*) maintained by the Calligraphy Service (*shu-i chü*) of the Artisans Institute (*han-lin yüan*), subordinate to the Palace

Domestic Service (*nei-shih sheng*). SP: *professeur-assistant, instructeur*. P34.

2711 *hsǖn* 勳
SUI–MING: **Merit Title**, a category of honors awarded to both civil officials and military officers, nominally for meritorious service but usually earned simply by seniority; graded in accordance with recipients' regular ranks, but ordinarily extending only through the top 5 or 7 ranks; including such titles as Supreme Pillar of State (*shang chu-kuo*), variously prefixed Commandants (*wei*) for military officers, and Governors (*yin*) for civil officials. Cf. *san-kuan* (prestige title). RR: *titres honorifiques*. SP: *dignité*.

2712 *hsǖn* 巡
T'ANG: lit., to tour; hence, an area that was toured, also an official who toured the area: **Patrol** or **Patrolling Inspector**; both prefixed Left and Right. (1) The 2 parts into which the main north-south avenue divided the dynastic capital, Ch'ang-an; patrolled and supervised on a monthly rotation by Investigating Censors (*chien-ch'a yü-shih*) or Palace Censors (*tien-chung shih yü-shih*), who were expected to memorialize about all illegalities and irregularities observed; antecedents of the Ward-inspecting Censors (*hsün-ch'eng yü-shih*) of Ming–Ch'ing times. (2) The capital city proper (*tso*) and its environs (*yu*), through which Investigating Censors and other members of the Censorate (*yü-shih t'ai*) annually made tours inspecting government prisons and in spring and winter made tours inspecting imperial hunting preserves. Also see *hsün-shih* (Inspector). RR: *inspecteur*. P20.

2713 *hsǖn-àn yǜ-shìh* 巡按御史 or *hsün-an*
(1) T'ANG: **Touring Censorial Inspector**, designation of Investigating Censors (*chien-ch'a yü-shih*) when dispatched from the dynastic capital on routine inspection tours of government agencies in specified areas of the empire. (2) MING–CH'ING: **Regional Inspector**, the most important duty assignment or commission (*ch'ai-ch'ien*) in the censorial system, an activity of Investigating Censors; one per Province (*sheng*) and Defense Command (*chen*), more for the Peking and Nanking regions; each on a one-year assignment to tour all localities in his defined jurisdiction, observing all governmental activities, checking files, auditing accounts, interrogating officials, accepting complaints from the people, especially inspecting all prisons and trial records, regularly participating in policy deliberations of provincial-level authorities; submitted memorials directly to the Emperor denouncing unfit officials, criticizing inappropriate policies, or proposing new policies. In early Ch'ing officials of Ministries (*pu*) shared these assignments with Censors, bearing concurrent censorial titles. In both Ming and early Ch'ing times, supplemented with other kinds of censorial commissions, especially for more specialized purposes. In 1661, on the accession of the K'ang-hsi Emperor, Regional Inspectors were terminated "forever"; the Emperor preferred relying on his own bondservants for reports on conditions in the Provinces. His successor in 1725 restored the censorial function (see *hsün-ch'a k'o-tao*), but for intermittent and narrower assignments. P18.

2714 *hsǖn-ch'á k'ō-tào* 巡察科道 or *hsün-ch'a*
CH'ING: **Regional Inspector**, from 1725 intermittently a duty assignment for Investigating Censors (*chien-ch'a yü-shih*), Supervising Censors (*chi-shih-chung*), and other central government officials with concurrent censorial titles to tour the Metropolitan Area (*chih-li*) and multi-provincial regions (e.g., Shantung and Honan) with the special charge of assisting in the suppression of banditry; a partial resto-

ration of the Ming dynasty Regional Inspector (*hsün-an yü-shih*) tradition. See *k'o-tao, hsün-ch'a yü-shih*. P18.

2715 *hsǘn ch'á-mǎ yǜ-shíh* 巡茶馬御史
MING: **Horse Trade Censor,** regular duty assignment for an Investigating Censor (*chien-ch'a yü-shih*) to tour and check on the activities of Horse Trading Offices (*ch'a-ma ssu*) in the northwest, which traded Chinese tea to friendly Mongol tribes for horses needed by the Chinese military establishment.

2716 *hsǘn-ch'á shǐh* 巡察使
T'ANG: **Touring Surveillance Commissioner,** from 627 a central government official, often a member of the Censorate (*yü-shih t'ai*), delegated to tour a multi-prefectural (*chou*) region, investigating and reporting on conditions among the people, the conduct of officials, etc.; one of several such duty assignments (see *an-fu shih, ts'un-fu shih*). In 706, 20 men of rank 5 or higher in various central government and prefectural agencies, recommended for their integrity, chosen to tour 10 newly defined multi-prefectural Circuits (*tao*) with the same designation, each for a 2-year term; in 711 replaced by *an-ch'a shih* (Surveillance Commissioners). RR: *commissaire impériale chargé de visiter et d'inspecter une région*. P50, 52.

2717 *hsǘn-ch'á yǜ-shǐh* 巡察御史 or 巡查御史
(1) CHIN (first form): **Touring Censor,** from 1217 a duty assignment for Investigating Censors (*chien-ch'a yü-shih*) twice a year to tour and inspect governmental operations in regions not clear, to provide data for consideration in the promotion and demotion of local officials. (2) CH'ING (2nd form): **Regional Investigator** for the Metropolitan Area (*chih-li*), from 1726 a duty assignment for 6 censorial officials, counterparts of *hsün-ch'a k'o-tao* elsewhere. P18.

2718 *hsǖn-ch'én* 勳臣
Meritorious Ministers: from T'ang on, a collective reference to civil officials and military officers awarded merit titles (*hsün*). Also occurs in a narrower sense, referring collectively to the most distinguished personages at court with a flavor equivalent to "peers of the realm"; e.g., in Ming times the hereditary military nobles descended from generals of the early reigns. Cf. *hsün-kuan*.

2719 *hsǘn-chèng t'īng* 巡政廳
CH'ING: a polite, unofficial reference to a **Police Chief** (*hsün-chien*).

2720 *hsǘn-ch'éng k'ō-tào* 巡城科道
CH'ING: quasiofficial collective reference to **Ward-inspecting Censors** (*hsün-ch'eng yü-shih*), reflecting the participation of Supervising Censors (*chi-shih-chung*) as well as Investigating Censors (*chien-ch'a yü-shih*) in this type of assignment; see *k'o-tao*.

2721 *hsǘn-ch'éng yǜ-shǐh* 巡城御史
MING–CH'ING: **Ward-inspecting Censor,** a one-year duty assignment for one Investigating Censor (*chien-ch'a yü-shih*) in each of the 5 Wards (*ch'eng*) into which Peking and (in Ming only) Nanking were divided for police surveillance; in Ch'ing one each Chinese and Manchu assigned per Ward; closely supervised and directed the Wardens' Offices (*ping-ma ssu*) that policed the Wards. Also called *wu-ch'eng hsün-shih yü-shih*. BH: censors of the 5 districts. P20.

2722 *hsǖn-ch'ì* 勳戚
Distinguished Imperial Relative, a common generic term for men related to Emperors by marriage, often granted titles of nobility (*chüeh*) or merit titles (*hsün*).

2723 *hsǘn-chiāng yǜ-shǐh* 巡江御史
MING–CH'ING: **River-patrol Censor,** a duty assignment for Investigating Censors (*chien-ch'a yü-shih*); in Ming based at the auxiliary Censorate (*tu ch'a-yüan*) at Nanking, to maintain surveillance over the shipping and storage of tax grains along the lower Yangtze River; one stationed at An-ch'ing west of Nanking, one at Chen-chiang to the east at the juncture of the Yangtze and the Grand Canal; continued in Ch'ing, but terminated c. 1662. P18.

2724 *hsǘn-chiěn ssū* 巡檢司
(1) 5 DYN–SUNG: **Military Inspectorate,** headed by a delegate from the dynastic capital called Military Inspector (*hsün-chien, hsün-chien shih*), or in very important areas Chief Military Inspector (*tu hsün-chien*); primarily located in frontier areas but eventually in most units of territorial administration; responsible for local militia training, suppression of banditry, etc.; subordinate to the regular military hierarchy. Modified by geographic or function-specific prefixes and suffixes, e.g., *ping-ma hsün-chien*, q.v. SP: *bureau d'inspection, d'entrainement militaire, et d'arrestation de bandit; (shih:) commissaire-inspecteur*. (2) CHIN–CH'ING: **Police Office** for a small area distant from a District (*hsien*) town, extending the police and sometimes more general authority of the District Magistrate (*chih-hsien*) down to the lowest level; headed by a Police Chief (*hsün-chien*), normally rank 9b, sometimes staffed entirely by subofficial functionaries (*li*). BH: sub-district magistrate. P54.

2725 *hsǘn-chō* 巡捉
SUNG: **Arresting Agent** with a suffix such as "for tea smugglers" (*ssu-ch'a*), "for salt smugglers" (*ssu-yen*), or "for bandits" (*tsei-tao*); an ad hoc duty assignment for a staff member of a District (*hsien*) or a Military Inspectorate (*hsün-chien ssu*). SP: *inspecteur chargé d'arrêter ....*

2726 *hsǖn erh-fu* 勳二府
T'ANG: **Second Distinguished Garrison,** one of the Five Garrisons (*wu fu*) at the dynastic capital in which militiamen assigned to the Sixteen Guards (*shih-liu wei*) were apparently quartered. See *hsün i-fu, san fu, san wei*. Cf. *hsün-fu* (Distinguished Garrison). RR: *deuxième milice méritante*. P43.

2727 *hsǘn-fáng kuān* 巡防官
See under *hai-tao hsün-fang kuan*.

2728 *hsǜn-fāng shìh* 訓方氏
CHOU: **Mentor of All Regions,** 4 ranked as Ordinary Servicemen (*chung-shih*), members of the Ministry of War (*hsia-kuan*) responsible for moral instruction of the people and informing the ruler of conditions and morale among the people and local officials. CL: *préposé à l'instruction des régions*.

2729 *hsǖn-fēng k'ō* 勳封科
YÜAN: **Section for Honors and Enfeoffments,** a unit in the Ministry of Personnel (*li-pu*), headed by a Clerk (*ling-shih*), rank not clear; apparently combined the functions of the later Bureau of Honors (*yen-feng ch'ing-li ssu*) and Bureau of Records (*chi-hsün ch'ing-li ssu*) in handling paperwork concerning the awarding or inheriting of honorific and noble titles. P5.

2730 *hsǖn-fǔ* 勳府
T'ANG: **Distinguished Garrison,** one of the Three Garrisons (*san fu*) in the service of the Heir Apparent. Cf. *hsün i-fu, hsün erh-fu, san wei*. RR: *milice méritante*. P26.

2731 *hsún-fǔ* 巡撫

MING–CH'ING: lit., touring pacifier: **Grand Coordinator** in Ming, **(Provincial) Governor** in Ch'ing. From 1430 sent out as delegates from the central government to coordinate and supervise provincial-level agencies, the term being used as a prefix followed by the name of the Province or other region that defined the jurisdiction, e.g., *hsün-fu* Shantung. In Ming always a duty assignment for a court dignitary normally with the substantive title Vice Minister (*shih-lang*) of a Ministry (*pu*), and from 1453 normally given the nominal concurrent title Vice Censor-in-chief (*fu tu yü-shih*) or Assistant Censor-in-chief (*ch'ien tu yü-shih*) to increase the esteem and influence of the appointee by giving him impeachment powers and direct access to the throne. Appointees had no formal supporting staff of officials but in the latter half of Ming developed Private Secretariats (*mu-fu*) of non-official specialists. Early in Ch'ing, *hsün-fu* was transformed into a substantive post itself, rank 2b, still with nominal concurrent status as Vice Minister of War (*ping-pu shih-lang*) and Vice Censor-in-chief for prestige purposes; still had no official staff, as if appointees were still Ming-style special commissioners; the title now appears as a suffix, e.g., Shantung *hsün-fu*. In both Ming and Ch'ing, *hsün-fu* who had more than regular coordinating authority over general civil administration were identified with specifying suffixes, e.g., *hsün-fu* Shantung (or Shantung *hsün-fu* in Ch'ing) *chien tsan-li chün-wu* (Grand Coordinator [or Governor] and Concurrent Associate in Military Affairs). After mid-Ming and through Ch'ing, each *hsün-fu* commonly became militarily subordinate to a multi-Province *tsung-tu* (Supreme Commander in Ming, Governor-general in Ch'ing). P50.

2732 *hsún-fǔ shih* 巡撫使 or *hsún-fǔ tà-shǐh* 巡撫大使

SUNG: **Pacification Commissioner (-in-chief)**, a delegate from the central government to direct stabilization measures in a region that had experienced war, domestic uprisings, or natural disasters. SP: *(grand) commissaire-inspecteur chargé de s'informer de la souffrance du peuple.*

2733 *hsūn-fǔ yù t'à* 勳府右闈

T'ANG–SUNG: lit., right-hand door of the merits office: unofficial reference to the **Bureau of Records** (*ssu-hsün*) in the Ministry of Personnel (*li-pu*), or to its Director (*lang-chung*).

2734 *hsún-hǎi tào* 巡海道

MING: **Coastal Patrol Circuit**, one or more established in Fukien Province, apparently from the 1420s, to assist in subjugating coastal piracy; normally, concurrently in charge of storing tax grains for sea transport to the north; the Circuit Intendant (*tao-t'ai*) in charge was normally an Administration Vice Commissioner (*pu-cheng ts'an-cheng*), rank 3b, or a Surveillance Vice Commissioner (*an-ch'a fu-shih*), 4a.

2735 *hsún-hó kuān* 巡河官 or *hsún-ho*

SUNG–CHIN: **River Patroller**, a subordinate of a Sung Military Inspectorate (*hsün-chien ssu*) or a Chin Chief River Patroller (*tu hsün-ho kuan*) under the Directorate of Waterways (*tu-shui chien*); in both cases, in charge of maintaining dikes, supervising river traffic, and when necessary organizing river defenses. SP: *inspecteur de la rivière.* P59.

2736 *hsún-hó yù-shǐh* 巡河御史

MING: **Transport-control Censor**, duty assignment for 2 Investigating Censors (*chien-ch'a yü-shih*) to maintain surveillance over functioning of the Grand Canal grain transport system, one in the canal's northern sector, one in its southern sector; from the 1420s (?) to 1472, when their functions were absorbed by Salt-control Censors (*hsün-yen yü-shih*) in the area. Their function was separately established again later in the form of Transport-control Censors (*hsün-ts'ao yü-shih*) and Transport-control Supervising Secretaries (*hsün-ts'ao chi-shih-chung*).

2737 *hsún-hsiá mǎ p'ū* 巡轄馬鋪 or *hsún-hsiá mǎ-tì p'ū* 巡轄馬遞鋪

SUNG: **Supervisor of Postal Relay Stations**, duty assignment for a member of a District (*hsien*) staff. See *hsün ma-ti p'u.* SP: *inspecteur des relais de poste.*

2738 *hsún-hsiàng sǒ* 馴象所

CH'ING: **Elephant-training Office**, one each prefixed East and West in the Rear Subsection (*hou-so*) of the Imperial Procession Guard (*luan-i wei*), each headed by a Director (*chang-yin kuan-chün shih*), rank 4a. BH: elephant-training section. P42.

2739 *hsún-hsíng* 循行

HAN–N-S DIV (Chin): **Escort** (?), menials in large numbers attached to units of regional and local administration; functions not clear. HB: patrolman. P32, 53.

2740 *hsún-hsìng* 巡幸

Lit., to tour bringing blessings, good fortune, prosperity, etc.: **Imperial (Royal** for the Chou era) **Progress**, a term used from antiquity for a ruler's journeying away from his capital for almost any purpose. Sometimes abbreviated to *hsing.* Cf. *hsün-shou.*

2741 *hsūn ī-fǔ* 勳一府

T'ANG: **First Distinguished Garrison**, one of the Five Garrisons (*wu fu*) at the dynastic capital in which militiamen assigned to the Sixteen Guards (*shih-liu wei*) were apparently quartered. See *hsün erh-fu, san fu, san wei.* Cf. *hsün-fu* (Distinguished Garrison). RR: *première milice méritante.* P43.

2742 *hsùn-k'ō* 訓科

CH'ING: **Principal of a District Medical School** (*i-hsüeh*), certified by the Ministry of Rites (*li-pu*) and supervised by the Provincial Administration Commission (*ch'eng-hsüan pu-cheng shih ssu*). BH: district physician.

2743 *hsùn-k'ò* 訓課

CH'ING: **Instructor** of Hanlin Bachelors (*shu-chi shih*) in the Hanlin Academy (*han-lin yüan*); duty assignments of Grand Ministers (*ta-ch'en*) entitled Academician Expositor-in-waiting (*shih-chiang hsüeh-shih*) or Academician Reader-in-waiting (*shih-tu hsüeh-shih*).

2744 *hsún-k'ù* 巡庫

MING: **Storehouse-inspecting ...**, prefixed to Censors (*yü-shih*) or Supervising Secretaries (*chi-shih-chung*) with duty assignments to check on receipts and disbursements at the imperial treasury in the palace; by the 1620s a monopoly of Supervising Secretaries.

2745 *hsūn-kuān* 勳官

SUI–T'ANG: **Honorary Official**, a commoner or subofficial functionary awarded a merit title (*hsün*) for outstanding service, usually in battle; did not convey status as a regular official (*kuan*). Cf. *hsün, hsün-ch'en.*

2746 *hsún-kuān* 巡官

T'ANG–SUNG: **Inspector**, a lowly official, functions not

clear, found on the staffs of the T'ang Ministry of Revenue (*hu-pu*), Military Commissioner (*chieh-tu shih*), etc., and the State Finance Commission (*san ssu*) of early Sung. RR+SP: *inspecteur*.

2747 *hsùn-lièn ch'ién-hsiá* 訓練鈐轄
SUNG: **Director of Military Training** in a Circuit (*lu*); apparently a duty assignment rather than a substantive office. SP: *éducateur militaire*.

2748 *hsùn-mǎ ssū* 馴馬司
CH'ING: **Horse-training Office,** one of 2 units in the Left Subsection (*tso-so*) of the Imperial Procession Guard (*luan-i wei*), headed by a Director (*chang-yin yün-hui shih*), rank 4a. BH: equestrian section.

2749 *hsún-mǎ-tì p'ū* 巡馬遞鋪
SUNG: **Supervisor of Postal Relay Stations,** a duty assignment for a subordinate in a Military Inspectorate (*hsün-chien ssu*). See *hsün-hsia ma p'u*. SP: *inspecteur des relais de poste*.

2750 *hsún-núng yǜ-shǐh* 巡農御史
CH'ING: **Agricultural Inspector,** a Censor (*yü-shih*) on special assignment touring the Metropolitan Area (*chih-li*) around Peking; initiated in 1729 but quickly discontinued. P18.

2751 *hsùn-shìh* 訓士
N-S DIV (N. Wei): **Admonishing Serviceman** (?), established in 400 as a prestige title (*san-kuan*) for tribal chiefs, rank 5a or 4b; comparable to the later title Grand Master of Remonstrance (*chien-i ta-fu*).

2752 *hsún-shǐh* 巡使 or 巡史
(1) T'ANG: **Patrolling Inspector:** see under *hsün*. (2) SUNG: **Capital Inspector,** duty assignments for Censors (*yü-shih*), one to maintain disciplinary surveillance over civil officials in the capital, prefixed Right; one to maintain disciplinary surveillance over military officials in the capital, prefixed Left. SP: *commissaire-inspecteur*. (3) MING–CH'ING: unofficial reference to a **Ward-inspecting Censor** (*hsün-ch'eng yü-shih*). P20.

2753 *hsún-shìh* 巡視
MING–CH'ING: lit., to tour and observe: a prefix used primarily for Censors (*yü-shih*) on traveling duty assignments: **Censor Inspecting ...** or **...-inspecting Censor,** e.g., *hsün-shih shan-tung ho-hu kung-wu yü-shih* (Censor Inspecting River and Lake Conservancy Work in Shantung). Also see *hsün* (Patrol, Patrolling Inspector).

2754 *hsún-shìh huáng-ch'éng yǜ-shǐh* 巡視皇城御史
MING–CH'ING: **Ward-inspecting Censors of the Imperial Capital Wards,** collective designation of Ward-inspecting Censors (*hsün-ch'eng yü-shih*) in the dynastic capital. P20.

2755 *hsún-shìh ... ts'áo wù* 巡視…漕務
MING–CH'ING: **Canal Transport-inspecting ...:** prefix to Censor (*yü-shih*) or Supervising Secretary (*chi-shih-chung*), the place-name insert indicating each inspector's headquarters town. See *hsün-ts'ao yü-shih* (Transport-control Censor).

2756 *hsún-shìh yén-chèng yǜ-shǐh* 巡視鹽政御史
Variant of *hsün-yen yü-shih* (**Salt-control Censor**).

2757 *hsún-shìh ... yǜ-shǐh* 巡視…御史
MING–CH'ING: **Ward-inspecting Censor for the (Central, Eastern, Western, Southern, Northern) Ward,** sector specified by insert of *chung-*, *tung-*, *hsi-*, *nan-*, or *pei-ch'eng*. See *hsün-ch'eng yü-shih*. P20.

2758 *hsún-shǒu* 巡守 or 巡狩
Lit., to tour places that are guarded, held, cared for, etc.; interpreted to mean a ruler's making the rounds of feudatories or other territorial administrators to see how they have fulfilled their responsibilities as his regional representatives: **Imperial (Royal** for the Chou era) **Tour of Inspection,** from antiquity used in reference to a ruler's journeying away from his capital for almost any purpose; sometimes abbreviated to *shou*. Cf. *hsün-hsing*.

2759 *hsùn-shù* 訓術
CH'ING: **Principal of a District Geomancy School** (*yin-yang hsüeh*), a non-official certified by the Ministry of Rites (*lǐ-pu*) and supervised by the Provincial Administration Commission (*ch'eng-hsüan pu-cheng shih ssu*); had some control over local fortune-tellers, entertainers, women dentists, etc., at the District (*hsien*) level. BH: district inspector of petty professions.

2760 *hsún-ssū* 巡司
CH'ING: unofficial reference to a local **Police Chief** (*hsün-chien*), head of a sub-District (*hsien*) Police Office (*hsün-chien ssu*).

2761 *hsùn-tǎo* 訓導
(1) YÜAN: **Teacher** in a local Confucian School (*ju-hsüeh*); hierarchical status not clear. (2) MING–CH'ING: **Assistant Instructor,** from one to 4, in Confucian Schools in Districts (*hsien*), Subprefectures or Departments (*chou*), and Prefectures (*fu*); apparently unranked in Ming, ranked as high as 7a in Ch'ing. BH: sub-director of schools. P51.

2762 *hsún-tào* 巡道
MING–CH'ING: especially after 1753, a variant of *fen-hsün tao* (**General Surveillance Circuit**). Also see *tao*.

2763 *hsún-ts'āng k'ō-tào* 巡倉科道
CH'ING: **Granary-inspecting Censor,** one-year duty assignment for 14 Investigating Censors (*chien-ch'a yü-shih*) and Supervising Censors (*chi-shih-chung*) to watch over receipts and disbursements at the government granaries at Peking and nearby T'ung-chou, the northern terminus of the Grand Canal; apparently an 18th-century change from the title *ch'a-ts'ang yü-shih*. Also see *k'o-tao*. P18.

2764 *hsún-ts'āng yǜ-shǐh* 巡倉御史
MING: **Granary-inspecting Censor,** duty assignment for 2 Investigating Censors (*chien-ch'a yü-shih*), one to supervise receipts and disbursements at state granaries in Peking, one to do the same at nearby T'ung-chou, the northern terminus of the Grand Canal; the latter also to oversee operation of the whole northern sector of the Grand Canal transport system from 1529 to 1626, when the assignment was superseded by the establishment of Transport-control Censors (*hsün-ho yü-shih*). Antecedent of the Ch'ing *hsün-ts'ang k'o-tao*.

2765 *hsún-ts'áo yǜ-shǐh* 巡漕御史 or ***hsún-ts'áo k'ō-tào*** 巡漕科道
MING–CH'ING: **Transport-control Censor,** duty assignment for Censors (*yü-shih*) and in Ch'ing also for Supervising Secretaries or Supervising Censors (*chi-shih-chung*) to maintain surveillance over the handling of state tax grain shipments along the Grand Canal; established by the 1620s in lieu of part-time surveillance by Salt-control Censors (*hsün-yen yü-shih*); 4, one each at Huai-an in Kiangsu, Chi-ning

in Shantung, Tientsin in modern Hopei, and T'ung-chou outside Peking. Abolished by Ch'ing in 1650, such duties being turned over to Circuit Intendants (*tao-t'ai*) of appropriate Provincial Administration Commissions (*ch'eng-hsüan pu-cheng shih ssu*); in 1729 re-established at Huai-an and T'ung-chou, 2 each; in 1737 all 4 original posts were re-established, but later the Huai-an post was moved to Kuai and the Tientsin post to Yang-ts'un. See *k'o-tao*. P18, 60.

2766 *hsún-yén chíh-chǐh* 巡鹽直指 or *hsün-yen*
Variant forms of *hsün-yen yü-shih* (**Salt-control Censor**). Also see *chih-chih*.

2767 *hsún-yén yǔ-shǐh* 巡鹽御史
MING–CH'ING: **Salt-control Censor,** from 1416 a duty assignment for Investigating Censors (*chien-ch'a yü-shih*); 4, one assigned in annual rotation to supervise salt production in each major producing area—the Chekiang coast, the Nanking area, the Peking area, and the dry salt-bed sections of Shansi. They were expected to ensure that salt was issued only to licensed salt merchants and that the salt revenues were promptly remitted to the dynastic capital. Soon, as salt production and distribution were further developed, such Censors were assigned to every Province except Fukien and Shantung, where the function of preventing the distribution of contraband salt was entrusted to delegates from Provincial Surveillance Commissions (*t'i-hsing an-ch'a shih ssu*). In early Ch'ing the title was changed to *yen-cheng*, q.v. BH: salt censor. P61.

2768 *hsún yǔ-shǐh* 巡御史
T'ANG: variant of *hsün* (**Patrolling Inspector**).

2769 *hsún-yüàn* 巡院
T'ANG: **Touring Brokerage,** 13 established after 758 as touring collection agencies to control salt distribution in large areas not supervised by permanent Brokerages (*yüàn*); in effect, a mobile branch of the Salt Monopoly Commission (*chüeh yen-t'ieh ssu*) based at Yangchow on the Yangtze River. P52, 61.

2770 *hù-chí p'àn-kuān* 戶籍判官
CHIN: **Tax Assistant,** one or 2, rank 6b, on the staff of each Fiscal Commissioner (*chuan-yün shih*), in charge of tax collections. P60.

2771 *hù-chiàng* 戶將
HAN: **Gate Commander,** supervisor of Gate Gentlemen-attendants (*men shih-lang*) of Left and Right in the household of the Heir Apparent; in A.D. 25 superseded by Grand Masters of the Gates (*men ta-fu*). HB: general of the doors. P26.

2772 *hǔ-ch'iāng yíng* 虎槍營
CH'ING: **Tiger-hunting Brigade,** an elite group of Bannermen (see *ch'i, pa ch'i*) organized to attend the Emperor on hunts; headed by a Commander-general (*tsung-t'ung*); included 21 Chief Tiger Hunters (*hu-ch'iang chang*), 260 Associate Tiger Hunters (*hu-ch'iang fu-chang*), and 600 ordinary Tiger Hunters (*hu-ch'iang*). BH: marksman for tiger hunts.

2773 *hù chíh-láng* 戶直郎
HAN: lit., court gentleman on duty at the gate: **Gate Gentleman-attendant** in the household of the Heir Apparent, supervised by one or more Gate Commanders (*hu-chiang*). P26.

2774 *hú-chó shìh* 壺涿氏
CHOU: **Water Sprinkler,** one ranked as a Junior Serviceman (*hsia-shih*), a member of the Ministry of Justice (*ch'iu-kuan*); traditionally understood to be a man who beat on an earthen jug to frighten away insects and worms. CL: *frappeur de tambour en terre cuite*.

2775 *hù-chūn* 護軍
(1) HAN: **Military Protector,** briefly from A.D. 1, an official on the staff of the Defender-in-chief (*ta ssu-ma*), one of the eminent Three Dukes (*san kung*); rank apparently 2,000 bushels, but functions not clear; not continued in Later Han. Abbreviated from the Ch'in–early Han title *hu-chün tu-wei* (Protector Commander-in-chief), which was changed to the archaic *ssu-k'ou* (Minister of Justice) in 8 B.C. before becoming *hu-chün*. HB: commissioner over the army. (2) N-S DIV: **Capital Protector:** from San-kuo Wei on, intermittently, an eminent officer who shared with a Capital Commandant (*ling-chün*) command of the Imperial Guardsmen (*chin-ping*) who were depended on for defense of the capital city, the palace, and the ruler. Equivalent to *chung hu-chün;* also see *chung ling-chün*. (3) SUI: variant of *fu lang-chiang* (**Vice Commandant**), 2nd in command of each Soaring Hawks Garrison (*ying-yang fu*), from 607 to 618 the basic unit in the Garrison Militia system (see *fu-ping, fu*). (4) T'ANG–MING: **Military Protector,** a merit title (*hsün*) for military officers of rank 3b from T'ang to Chin, 2b in Yüan and Ming; replacing the earlier merit title General-in-chief (*ta chiang-chün*). RR+SP: *protecteur d'armée*. P65. (5) T'ANG, MING: **Military Protector,** commander of the Defense Brigade (*hu-chün fu*) assigned to each Princely Establishment (*wang-fu*); discontinued in 1376. P69. (6) CH'ING: **Guardsman,** designation of common soldiers in the Guards Brigade (*hu-chün ying*) and the Summer Palace Guard Brigade (*yüan-ming yüan hu-chün ying*). Also see *shang hu-chün, chung hu-chün*. P37.

2776 *hù-chūn chiāng-chūn* 護軍將軍
N-S DIV: **Protector-general,** from San-kuo Wei on, intermittently, the designation of a military dignitary who is reported to have controlled all military appointments in some periods and in others to have commanded military units beyond the environs of the dynastic capital; also in some uses seems to have been honorific.

2777 *hù-chūn chūng-wèi* 護軍中尉
(1) HAN: **Protector Commandant of the Center,** a title sometimes conferred on leaders or assistants to leaders of armies on campaign. HB: commissioner over the army and commandant of the capital. (2) T'ANG: **Palace Commandant-protector,** a high eunuch post in the Armies of Inspired Strategy (*shen-ts'e chün*) from the late 700s, one of the organizational bases from which palace eunuchs gained dictatorial control over the imperial armies, the court, and the throne in the 9th century. RR: *chef et protecteur d'armée*.

2778 *hù-chūn fǔ* 護軍府
Defense Brigade. (1) T'ANG: one of 3 types of military units authorized for Princely Establishments (*wang-fu*), one each Left and Right led by a Military Protector (*hu-chün*). RR: *garde des protecteurs d'armées*. (2) MING: authorized for Princely Establishments, staffing not clear; in 1376 superseded by Escort Guards (*hu-wei*). P69.

2779 *hù-chūn tū-wèi* 護軍都尉
(1) CH'IN–HAN: **Chief Commandant-protector,** status and functions not clear, but from 119 B.C. apparently a subordinate of the Defender-in-chief (*t'ai-wei*), one of the eminent Three Dukes (*san kung*). BH: commissioner over the army and chief commandant. (2) T'ANG: **Chief Palace Commandant-protector,** one of the very highest eunuch posts in the Armies of Inspired Strategy (*shen-ts'e chün*)

from the late 700s, one of the posts from which palace eunuchs gained dictatorial control over the imperial armies, the court, and the throne in the 9th century. RR: *chef protecteur d'armée*. P43.

2780   *hù-chūn yíng* 護軍營
CH'ING: **Guards Brigade,** a unit of elite Bannermen drawn from all Banners (*ch'i*) to provide guard duty for the imperial palace under a Commander-general (*t'ung-ling*). Each section of the Brigade was normally prefixed with the designation of one of the Eight Banners (*pa ch'i*). Also see *nei hu-chün ying*. BH: guards division.

2781   *hù-fáng* 戶房
(1) T'ANG–SUNG: **Revenue Office,** one of 5 (in Sung 6) Offices (see *liu fang*) in the combined Secretariat-Chancellery (*chung-shu men-hsia*) that developed in the early 700s as a counterpart of the Ministry of Revenue (*hu-pu*) in the Department of State Affairs (*shang-shu sheng*). (2) SUNG: **Revenue Section,** one of 5 Sections (see *wu fang*) in the Proclamations Office (*chih-ch'ih yüan*) of the Secretariat (*chung-shu sheng*); also one of 4 Sections (see *ssu fang*) in the Bureau of Military Affairs (*shu-mi yüan*), headed by a Vice Recipient of Edicts (*fu ch'eng-chih*), rank 8b; the channel through which, in collaboration with the Revenue Office mentioned in (1) above and the Ministry of Revenue, the Bureau managed fiscal administration for the military establishment; dissolved c. 1074 in a reorganization of the Bureau into 10 and later 12 Sections (see *shih-erh fang*). SP: *chambre des finances*. (3) From Sung on, may be encountered as an unofficial reference to the **Ministry of Revenue** (*hu-pu*).

2782   *hù-fāng* 鶻坊
T'ANG: **Hawk Cage,** one of the Five Cages (*wu fang*) of animals used in imperial hunts, supervised by the Commissioner for the Imperial Stables (*hsien-chiu shih*) in the Palace Administration (*tien-chung sheng*). RR: *le quartier des vautours*. P38.

2783   *hù-fáng* 鶻房
CH'ING: **Imperial Hawk Aviary,** one of 3 subsections of the Office of the Imperial Hunt (*tu-yü ssu*) in the Imperial Household Department (*nei-wu fu*).

2784   *hù-k'ō* 戶科
MING–CH'ING: **Office of Scrutiny for Revenue,** staffed with Supervising Secretaries (*chi-shih-chung*) charged with keeping censorial watch over activities of the Ministry of Revenue (*hu-pu*); headed by a Chief Supervising Secretary (*tu chi-shih-chung*) in Ming, by one Manchu and one Chinese Seal-holding Supervising Secretary (*chang-yin chi-shih-chung*) in Ch'ing. One of the Six Offices of Scrutiny (*liu k'o*), independent until absorbed into the Censorate (*tu ch'a-yüan*) in 1723. P18, 19.

2785   *hù-k'ǒu àn* 戶口案
SUNG: **Census Section,** one of 3 subsections in the Left Section (*tso-ts'ao*) of the Ministry of Revenue (*hu-pu*) from c. 1080, when the Ministry was fully activated following discontinuance of the State Finance Commission (*san ssu*) of early Sung; staffed with subofficial functionaries who monitored records pertaining to population and state labor requisitions. SP: *service de population*. P6.

2786   *hù-láng* 戶郎
HAN: **Court Gentleman at the Doors,** status and functions not wholly clear. BH: gentleman of the doors.

2787   *hǔ-pēn* 虎賁
Brave as Tigers: throughout history occurs as a prefix to

military titles associated with guarding the ruler, especially such Han–T'ang titles as *chung-lang chiang* (Leader of Court Gentlemen) and *hsiao-wei* (Commandant); the Yüan dynasty had a *hu-pen ch'in-chün* (Brave as Tigers Imperial Army).

2788   *hǔ-pēn láng* 虎賁郎
HAN: **Gentleman Brave as Tigers,** designation of as many as 1,000 Court Gentlemen (*lang*) led by a Leader of Palace Gentlemen (*lang-chung liang*) ranked at 2,000 bushels; in A.D. 1 replaced the title Gate Guardsman (*ch'i-men lang*); may have been members of the ordinary soldiery of the Southern Army (*nan-chün*). HB: gentlemen rapid as tigers.

2789   *hù-pù* 戶部
(1) CHOU: variant reference to the **Ministry of Education** (*ti-kuan*). CL: *ministère de la population*. (2) T'ANG–CH'ING: **Ministry of Revenue,** one of the Six Ministries (*liu pu*) that were the general-administration core of the central government, subordinate to the T'ang–Sung Department of State Affairs (*shang-shu sheng*) and the Yüan–early Ming Secretariat (*chung-shu sheng*), but relatively autonomous after 1380, though from the mid-1400s coordinated by the Grand Secretariat (*nei-ko*). Successor of the *tu-chih* (Ministry of Revenue) of the era of N-S Division and of the Sui–early T'ang *min-pu*, retitled c. 650 to avoid the personal name of T'ang T'ai-tsung (Li Shih-min); T'ang writers extended this taboo back to Sui, erroneously referring to Sui's *min-pu* as a *hu-pu*. The Ministry was in general charge of population and land censuses, assessment and collection of taxes, and storage and distribution of government revenues. Usually divided into specialized Bureaus (*ssu, ch'ing-li ssu*; also see *ts'ao*): a Census Bureau (*hu-pu, ssu-yüan, ti-kuan*), a General Accounts Bureau (*tu-chih, ssu-tu*), a Treasury Bureau (*chin-pu, ssu-chen, ssu-chin*), and a Granaries Bureau (*ts'ang-pu, ssu-yü, ssu-ch'u*). Chin and Yüan had no Bureaus, but in Yüan the Ministry had 6 much diminished Sections (*k'o*): a Treasury Section (*chin-k'o*), a Granaries Section (*ts'ang-k'o*), a Special Accounts Section (*nei-tu k'o*), a General Accounts Section (*wai-tu k'o*), a Fodder Section (*liang-ts'ao k'o*), and a Budget Section (*shen-chi k'o*). In Ming and Ch'ing, Bureaus were named on the basis of territorial jurisdictions, one per Province (*sheng*), each Bureau directing and monitoring fiscal administration in the Province for which it was named. In Ming each such Bureau had 4 subsidiary Sections (*k'o*) with functional specializations: a Statistics Section (*min-k'o*), a General Accounts Section (*tu-chih k'o*), a Special Accounts Section (*chin-k'o*), and a Granaries Section (*ts'ang-k'o*). The Ministry was always headed by a Minister (*shang-shu*), rank 3a to 1b; Bureaus were headed by Directors (*lang-chung*), 6b to 5a; Sections were normally headed by Clerks (*ling-shih*), unranked. For the early Ming transitional organization of the Ministry, see under *hu-pu wu k'o* (Five Sections of the Ministry of Revenue). RR+SP: *ministère des finances*. BH: ministry (board) of finance or revenue. P6. (3) T'ANG–SUNG: common abbreviation of *hu-pu ssu* (**Census Bureau**). Also see *ssu-t'u, ssu-nung, tso-ts'ao, yu-ts'ao*.

2790   *hù-pù chú* 戶部局
CH'ING: abbreviated, unofficial reference to the **Metropolitan Coinage Service** (*pao-ch'üan chü*), a unit in the Ministry of Revenue (*hu-pu*).

2791   *hù-pù shíh-ssū* 戶部使司
LIAO: **Tax Commission,** a regional fiscal agency located at the dynasty's Eastern Capital (*tung-ching*). P7.

2792 *hù-pù ssū* 戶部司
Census Bureau. (1) T'ANG–SUNG: one of 4 main sub-sections of the Ministry of Revenue (*hu-pu*); headed by a Director (*lang-chung*), rank 5b in T'ang, 6a or 6b in Sung; collected and maintained all registers of population, land, etc.; kept records concerning special taxes, remittances, and exemptions. In Sung existed only nominally. RR+SP: *bureau des finances*. (2) SUNG: one of the 3 agencies that constituted the State Finance Commission (*san ssu*) of early Sung, with functions essentially the same as those of the Ministry of Revenue at other times; headed by a Vice Commissioner (*fu-shih*) or, when the 3 agencies functioned separately, by a Commissioner (*shih*). Supervised 5 subordinate Sections (*an*): Summer Tax Section (*hu-shui an*), Prefectural Remittances Section (*shang-kung an*), Palace Construction Section (*hsiu-tsao an*), Yeast Section (*ch'ü-an*), Clothing and Rations Section (*i-liang an*). Discontinued c. 1080, its functions thereafter being divided among the Ministry of Revenue and other agencies. SP: *bureau des finances*. P6.

2793 *hù-pù wǔ k'ō* 戶部五科
MING: **Five Sections of the Ministry of Revenue,** a reference to the organization of the early Ming Ministry from 1368 to 1380, during which period, instead of traditional Bureaus (*ssu*), it supervised 5 subsidiary Sections (*k'o*): First Section (*i-k'o*), Second Section (*erh-k'o*), Third Section (*san-k'o*), Fourth Section (*ssu-k'o*), and General Section (*tsung-k'o*), each headed by a Director (*lang-chung*). In 1373, because of an increase in its activity, the Ministry was restaffed with a Minister (*shang-shu*) and a Vice Minister (*shih-lang*) for each of these subsidiary Sections. In a general reorganization of the central government in 1380, the Ministry's 5 Sections were transformed into 4 Bureaus (*ssu*) differentiated by functions; and finally in 1390 a Bureau (*ch'ing-li ssu*) was established for and named after each Province (*sheng*). See under *hu-pu*. P6.

2794 *hǔ-shìh* 虎士
CHOU: **Royal Guardsman,** 800 constituting the personal bodyguard of the King, commanded by officers of the Ministry of War (*hsia-kuan*) normally prefixed Brave as Tigers (*hu-pen*). CL: *guerriers tigres*.

2795 *hù-shìh chiēn* 互市監
SUI–T'ANG: **Directorate** (also **Director**) **of Tributary Trade,** in Sui one in each Hostel for Tributary Envoys (*ssu-fang kuan*), in T'ang subordinate to the Directorate for Imperial Manufactories (*shao-fu chien*); supervised trade carried on by tributary delegations. RR: *direction des marchés d'échange avec les pays étrangers*. P11.

2796 *hù-shùi àn* 戶稅案
SUNG: lit., Section for levies on households: **Summer Tax Section,** one of 5 Sections in the Census Bureau (*hu-pu ssu;* cf. *hu-pu*) in the State Finance Commission (*san ssu*) of early Sung, normally headed by an Administrative Assistant (*p'an-kuan, t'ui-kuan*); monitored the distribution among government agencies of revenues from summer tax collections. Discontinued in the 1080s, its functions absorbed by the Semiannual Taxes Subsection (*erh-shui k'o*) of the Ministry of Revenue (*hu-pu*). SP: *service de la taxe d'été*.

2797 *hù-tǒu àn* 斛斗案
SUNG: lit., Section for bushels and pecks: **State Grain Section,** one of 8 Sections in the Tax Bureau (*tu-chih ssu*), one of the 3 agencies constituting the State Finance Commission (*san ssu*) of early Sung, normally headed by an

Administrative Assistant (*p'an-kuan, t'ui-kuan*); responsible for keeping accounts concerning the amounts of grain in the capital granaries and for monitoring the payment of salary grain to officials. Discontinued c. 1080, its functions taken over by the Ministry of Revenue (*hu-pu*) and the Court of the National Granaries (*ssu-nung ssu*). SP: *service des greniers*.

2798 *hù-ts'áo* 戶曹
(1) HAN: **Civil Affairs Section,** one in the Imperial Secretariat (*shang-shu t'ai*), one on the staff of the Defender-in-chief (*t'ai-wei*), and probably one on the staff of the Counselor-in-chief (*ch'eng-hsiang*), all apparently headed by Administrators (*yüan-shih*), rank =300 bushels; concerned with census records, petitions from commoners, etc., but precise functions not clear; may be a calligraphic change from *min-ts'ao* (Census Section) traceable to T'ang writers (see under *hu-pu*). HB: bureau of households. (2) HAN–CH'ING: **Revenue Section,** a staff agency in each unit of territorial administration down to the District (*hsien*) level, responsible for overseeing regional or local fiscal management, after Han under the supervision of and in correspondence with the Ministry of Revenue (*hu-pu*) in the central government. May have been known as *min-ts'ao* until early T'ang. See *liu ts'ao* (Six Sections). HB: bureau of households. RR: *bureau des finances*. SP: *service des finances*. (3) N-S DIV: **Revenue Section,** alternating with *hu-pu* (Ministry of Revenue) as the name of a major agency of fiscal administration in the central government, subordinate to the evolving Department of State Affairs (*shang-shu sheng*). May have been known as *min-ts'ao;* see under (1) and (2) above. (4) SUI–CH'ING: may be encountered as an archaic, unofficial reference to the **Ministry of Revenue** (*hu-pu*) or to the Ministry's **Headquarters Bureau** (also *hu-pu*). P6.

2799 *hù-ts'áo tū-wèi* 護漕都尉
HAN: **Commandant-protector of Transport,** in charge of guarding tax grains shipped by water to the dynastic capital; abolished A.D. 31. HB: chief commandant protecting grain transport by water. P60.

2800 *hù tū-shǔi shǐh* 護都水使
HAN: **River Conservancy Commissioner,** variant reference to *ho-ti yeh-che;* see under *ho-ti shih*. P59.

2801 *hū-t'ú-k'ò-t'ú* 呼圖克圖
CH'ING: **Living Buddha,** designation of several heads of the Mongolian branch of Lamaism, distinguished by prefixes. BH: pontiff.

2802 *hù-wèi* 護衛
(1) LIAO: **Imperial Bodyguard,** established in both the Northern Establishment (*pei-yüan*) and the Southern Establishment (*nan-yüan*) of the Northern Administration (*pei-mien*) at the dynastic capital in modern Jehol; often called *hu-wei fu* (Imperial Bodyguard Office). (2) MING: **Escort Guard,** one assigned for the protection of each Princely Establishment (*wang-fu*), headed by a Guard Commander (*chih-hui shih*), rank 3a. (3) CH'ING: **Commandant** in 3 grades (*teng*), rank 3b to 5b, in charge of the troops in a Princely Establishment. P69.

2803 *huà-chíh* 畫直
T'ANG: **Auxiliary Illustrator,** 6 professional specialists in the Academy of Scholarly Worthies (*chi-hsien tien shu-yüan*); in 731 retitled Auxiliary (*chih-yüan*). RR: *dessinateur auxiliaire*.

2804 *huá-ch'iū yüàn* 華秋苑
N-S DIV (Chin): **Autumn Park,** one of several imperial parks and gardens under the supervision of the Chamberlain for Attendants (*kuang-lu-hsün*); managed by a Director (*ling*).

2805 *huà-chǘ* 畫局
CH'ING: **Painting Service,** an artisan workshop under the Supervisorate-in-chief of Metal Workers and Jewelers (*chin-yü jen-chiang tsung-kuan fu*); established 1278.

2806 *huá-fāng* 華坊
Lit., flower shop: apparently beginning in the era of N-S Division, an unofficial reference to the **Household Administration of the Heir Apparent** (*chan-shih fu*).

2807 *huá-fēi* 華妃
T'ANG: **Splendid Consort,** from the time of Hsüan-tsung (r. 712–756) one of the high-ranking palace women known collectively as the Three Consorts (*san fei*). See *hui-fei, li-fei.* RR: *concubine jolie.*

2808 *huà-hsüéh* 畫學
SUNG: **Painting School,** a training unit in the Hanlin Painting Service (*han-lin t'u-hua chü*) or the Hanlin Calligraphy Service (*han-lin shu-i chü*), or possibly both; headed by a Director (*cheng*). SP: *école de peinture.*

2809 *huà-kūng* 畫工
Artisan Painter, in Sung and perhaps later times a generic designation of craftsmen (possibly hereditary) who assisted Court Painters (*hua-shih*) of the Painting Academy (*hua-yüan*) or were given less prestigious, more menial artistic tasks. Normally associated in some fashion with the Hanlin Academy (*han-lin yüan*) or, in Sung, with the Artisans Institute (also *han-lin yüan*).

2810 *huā-liú mù* 驊騮牧
SUI: **Pasturage for Fine Steeds,** a unit under the Office of Fine Steeds (*hua-liu shu*) in the Court of the Imperial Stud (*t'ai-p'u ssu*); kept separate from 24 Pasturages for Military Mounts (*chün-ma mu*); headed by a Director (*i-ssu*). P31, 39.

2811 *huā-liú shǔ* 驊騮署
N-S DIV (N. Ch'i)–SUI: **Office of Fine Steeds,** in charge of some imperial horse corrals under supervision of the Court of the Imperial Stud (*t'ai-p'u ssu*); headed by a Director (*ling*), assisted by Chief Stewards (*feng-yü*). P31, 36, 39.

2812 *huā-mù chǘ* 花木局
CHIN: **Botanical Service,** a unit under the Superintendency of Imperial Parks (*shang-lin shu t'i-tien*); headed by a Director-in-chief (*tu-chien*).

2813 *huà-shěng* 畫省
From Han times, an uncommon official designation of the **Imperial Secretariat** (*shang-shu t'ai*) or of the post-Han **Department of State Affairs** (*shang-shu sheng*).

2814 *huà-shìh* 畫士
SUNG–CH'ING: **Court Painter,** the most common generic reference to notable painters, especially those in government service assigned to the Sung or Ch'ing Painting Academy (*hua-yüan*) or in other periods to the Hanlin Academy (*han-lin yüan*). Cf. *hua-kung* (Artisan Painter).

2815 *huà-shìh shǔ* 畫室署
HAN: **Portraiture Office** in the imperial palace, apparently responsible for painting portraits of palace women and perhaps Emperors themselves; headed by a eunuch Director (*chang*). Cf. *yü-t'ang shu* (Office of Imperial Portraiture?). HB: office of the house of painting.

2816 *huà-yüàn* 畫院
SUNG, CH'ING: **Painting Academy,** common unofficial reference to the Sung Painter Service (*t'u-hua chü;* also see *han-lin t'u-hua yüan*) or to such Ch'ing agencies as the Southern Study (*nan shu-fang*) and the later Institute of Indulgences (*ju-i kuan*); the group consisted in part of regular civil service officials with artistic talents who were detached from their regular administrative posts to serve as court painters within the palace, and in part of talented non-official professional specialists brought into such service. The Painting Academy always had close ties with the Hanlin Academy (*han-lin yüan*); in Yüan and Ming times court painters were commonly placed in the Hanlin Academy or, in Ming, in the Imperial Bodyguard (*chin-i wei*). The most common generic term for court painters was *hua-shih;* the term *hua-kung* (Artisan Painter) normally referred to less distinguished artisans or technicians who assisted the *hua-shih.* Court painters were commonly considered to belong to the category of Palace Attendants (*kung-feng nei-t'ing, nei-t'ing kung-feng, chih-hou nei-t'ing, nei-t'ing chih-hou*).

2817 *huái-fāng shìh* 懷方氏
CHOU: **Cherisher of Those Afar,** 8 ranked as Ordinary Servicemen (*chung-shih*), members of the Ministry of War (*hsia-kuan*) responsible for keeping the peace with distant peoples and causing them to send representatives to the royal court. CL: *agent de venue des régions.*

2818 *huái-huà chiāng-chūn* 懷化將軍
T'ANG–SUNG: **Civilizing General,** in T'ang an honorific title conferred on military officers of rank 3b, in Sung a title conferred on submitted alien chieftains. RR: *général qui aime la civilisation.* P72.

2819 *huái-t'īng* 槐廳
SUNG: lit., locust tree pavilion: unofficial reference to the **Institute of Academicians** (*hsüeh-shih yüan*).

2820 *huái-yüǎn ì* 懷遠驛
SUNG: **Relay Station for Cherishing Those Afar,** several maintained at appropriate points by the Court of State Ceremonial (*hung-lu ssu*) for showing hospitality to envoys from non-Chinese peoples of the South and West; each administered by 2 Directors (*chien-kuan*). SP: *relai de poste pour la contribution des pays suivants ....* P11.

2821 *huàn* 宦
Ety., an underling under a roof, hence a menial household servant (?). (1) **Eunuch:** throughout history one of the most common terms for castrated males in palace service. See under *nei-shih sheng, tien-chung sheng, tien-nei sheng, tien-nei chü, ch'ang-ch'iu chien, hsüan-hui yüan.* P37, 38. (2) **Official:** an uncommon but not rare reference to a non-eunuch appointee in government; comparable to *ch'en* (Minister).

2822 *huàn-chě* 宦者
Common generic term for **Eunuch.**

2823 *huàn-chě lìng* 宦者令
HAN: **Director of Eunuchs** under the Chamberlain for the Palace Revenues (*shao-fu*). HB: prefect of the eunuchs. P37.

2824 *huán-hún hsiù-ts'ái* 還魂秀才
MING–CH'ING: lit., a man of talent returned from status as a ghost: **Consolation Graduate,** a term used unofficially for a scholar who, having failed in the Provincial Examination (*hsiang-shih*) in the civil service recruitment examination sequence, succeeded on his second effort.

2825 *huǎn-ī chǘ* 浣衣局
MING: **Palace Laundry Service,** a minor agency of palace eunuchs, headed by a eunuch Commissioner-in-chief (*ta-shih*) or Director (*t'ai-chien*); directed overaged or expelled palace women (see *kung-jen*) who did the palace laundry; located outside the imperial palace. See *pa chü* (Eight Services).

2826 *huán-jén* 環人
CHOU: **Surveillance Agent,** 6 ranked as Junior Servicemen (*hsia-shih*) in the Ministry of War (*hsia-kuan*) and 4 as Ordinary Servicemen (*chung-shih*) in the Ministry of Justice (*ch'iu-kuan*), the former charged with circulating among the royal troops for purposes of disciplinary surveillance, the latter with surrounding and guarding foreign visitors at court, including surrendered chiefs. CL: *circulant, entoureur.*

2827 *huàn-jén* 宦人 or *huàn-kuān* 宦官
Common variants throughout history of *huan* (**Eunuch**).

2828 *huàn-nǚ* 宦女
(1) **Palace Woman,** from antiquity one of several generic terms used for the secondary wives, consorts, and concubines of rulers. See *kung-nü, nü-kuan.* (2) **Eunuchs and Palace Women,** an occasional usage combining terms for Eunuchs (*huan, huan-kuan,* etc.) and for Palace Women (*kung-nü, nü-kuan*) in abbreviated form.

2829 *huàn-ssù* 宦寺
Unofficial reference to a **Eunuch** (see *huan, huan-kuan*).

2830 *huán-wèi* 環衛
T'ANG–SUNG: lit., a surrounding or encircling guard: **Imperial Guards,** a quasiofficial reference to the Sixteen Guards (*shih-liu wei*), in T'ang constituting the Southern Command (*nan-ya*) at the dynastic capital; especially after 749 and on into Sung were largely decorative, providing posts (*huan-wei kuan*) to which members of the imperial family and perhaps other favorites could be appointed, as Generals (*chiang-chün*), Generals-in-chief (*ta chiang-chün*), etc. Cf. *chin-chün, ch'in-chün, chin-wei, wu fu* (Five Garrisons).

2831 *huán-wèi kuān* 環衛官
T'ANG–SUNG: **Officers of the Imperial Guards** (see *huan-wei*); in Sung the term encompassed a range of titles from Generalissimo (*shang chiang-chün*) down to Commandant (*lang-chiang*).

2832 *huáng chǎng-sūn* 皇長孫
Imperial Heir Once Removed: common reference to the eldest son of the Heir Apparent.

2833 *huáng-ch'éng ssū* 皇城司
5 DYN–SUNG: **Capital Security Office,** a kind of secret service agency entrusted with maintaining peace and order in the dynastic capital, headed by a military officer or a eunuch having the Emperor's personal trust, variably entitled Capital Security Commissioner (*huang-ch'eng shih*), Administrator (*kan-tang kuan*), Commander (*chih-hui*), Supervisor (*t'i-chü*), Superintendent (*t'i-tien*), etc. See *wu chih-hui* (Five Commanders). At the beginning of S. Sung named the Mobile Imperial Guard (*hsing-ying chin-wei so*), but soon retitled Auxiliary Capital Security Office (*hsing-tsai huang-ch'eng ssu*). SP: *bureau de la ville impériale.*

2834 *huáng-ch'ú* 皇儲
Variant reference to the **Heir Apparent** (*t'ai-tzu*).

2835 *huáng-fēi* 黃扉
N-S DIV–CH'ING (?): lit., (those having access to) the yellow (i.e., imperial) door: unofficial combined reference to **Supervising Secretaries** (*chi-shih-chung*) **and (Secretariat) Drafters** (*chung-shu she-jen*).

2836 *huáng-hòu* 皇后
Empress, throughout imperial history the standard official title of the Emperor's principal wife; mostly used posthumously, with many flattering descriptive prefixes.

2837 *huáng-k'ǎo* 黃考
Deceased Imperial Father, throughout imperial history the normal reference to the deceased father of a reigning Emperor, whether or not he himself had reigned.

2838 *huáng-kó* 黃閣
HAN–CH'ING: lit., the yellow (i.e., imperial) hall, indicating any hall or room in which the Emperor met with his senior officials, or indirectly referring to such officials: **Imperial Council, Imperial Councilor.**

2839 *huáng-kó ts'áo* 黃閣曹
HAN: **Archives Section,** one of a dozen or more Sections (*ts'ao*) subordinate to the Defender-in-chief (*t'ai-wei*), and probably also to the Counselor-in-chief (*ch'eng-hsiang*); headed by an Administrator (*yüan-shih*), rank =400 bushels. HB: bureau of the yellow door.

2840 *huáng kuèi-fēi* 皇貴妃
MING–CH'ING: **Imperial Honored Consort,** designation of the most esteemed secondary wife of the Emperor, outranked only by the Empress; introduced by Ming Hsientsung (r. 1464–1487). BH: imperial concubine of the first rank.

2841 *huáng-mén* 黃門
Lit., the yellow (i.e., imperial) gate, hence someone serving at the palace gate. (1) HAN–N-S DIV: **Imperial Gatekeeper,** 8 at each Imperial Mausoleum (*ling*), others subordinate to the Director of Imperial Gatekeepers (*huang-men ling*), who in turn was subordinate to the Chamberlain for the Palace Revenues (*shao-fu*). (2) SUNG: **Palace Gateman,** 6th highest of 12 rank titles (*chieh*) granted to eunuchs from 1112; see *nei-shih chieh.* SP: *intendant de la porte jaune.* (3) CH'ING: unofficial reference to *chi-shih-chung* (**Supervising Secretaries, Supervising Censors**) in the Censorate (*tu ch'a-yüan*). P21, 68.

2842 *huáng-mén kǔ-ch'ūi* 黃門鼓吹
HAN: **Palace Bandsman,** 135 headed by the Director of Palace Entertainments (*ch'eng-hua ling*), subordinate to the Chamberlain for the Palace Revenues (*shao-fu*). HB: drummers and pipers of the yellow gates. P10.

2843 *huáng-mén láng* 黃門郎
Gentleman of the Palace Gate. (1) HAN: a supplementary honorific title (*chia-kuan*) awarded to officials deemed worthy of attending closely upon the Emperor. HB: gentleman of the yellow gates. (2) N-S DIV (San-kuo Wei): a minor official assisting the Transmission Gentleman (*t'ung-shih lang*), who supervised the issuance and receipt of state documents at the palace; a member of the developing Secretariat (*chung-shu sheng*). P2.

2844 *huáng-mén líng* 黃門令
HAN: **Director of Eunuch Attendants,** a eunuch with rank of 600 bushels under the Chamberlain for the Palace Revenues (*shao-fu*); directed eunuchs in close attendance upon the Emperor, largely organized in Offices (*shu*), some merely

numbered serially in the stem-and-branch sequence of "stems" (*chia-shu, i-shu, ping-shu,* etc.). HB: prefect of the yellow gates.

2845 *huáng-mén pěi-ssù* 黃門北寺
HAN: lit., north office of the imperial gatekeepers: **Palace Prison** maintained by eunuchs under the Chamberlain for the Palace Revenues (*shao-fu*); specific uses not clear. Also see *chao-yü* (Imperial Prison), *jo-lu yü* (Central Prison). HB: northern office of the yellow gates. P37.

2846 *huáng-mén shěng* 黃門省
N-S DIV–T'ANG: alternate official designation of the **Chancellery** (*men-hsia sheng*), e.g., in T'ang from 713 to 717; headed by a Director (*huang-men shih-lang* in Sui, *huang-men chien* in T'ang). RR: *département de la porte jaune.* P3.

2847 *huáng-mén shìh-láng* 黃門侍郎
(1) HAN–SUI: **Gentleman Attendant at the Palace Gate,** originally a supplementary honorific title (*chia-kuan*) that gradually evolved into the title of the **Director of the Chancellery** (*huang-men sheng, men-hsia sheng*); 4 appointees in Sui. HB: gentleman-in-attendance of the yellow gates. (2) N-S DIV: late in the era, an archaic reference to a **Supervising Secretary** (*chi-shih-chung*). (3) T'ANG: **Vice Director of the Chancellery** (*men-hsia sheng, huang-men sheng*), 2 appointees; alternating with the form *men-hsia shih-lang,* used before 662, from 671 to 685, from 705 to 742, and from 758 to 767. RR: *vice-président de la porte jaune.* P3.

2848 *huáng mù-ch'ǎng* 皇木廠
CH'ING: **Imperial Lumber Depot,** one each at T'ung-chou and Chang-chia-wan near Peking, managed by Clerks (*pi-t'ieh-shih*) detached from the Ministry of Works (*kung-pu*) till 1687, when the T'ung-chou Depot was put under control of the Chihli Director-general of the Grand Canal (*ho-tao tsung-tu*), later to be transferred to the jurisdiction of the Circuit Intendant (*tao-t'ai*) of the Waterways Circuit (*ho-tao*) for T'ung-yang, and the Chang-chia-wan Depot was put under control of a Superintendent (*chien-tu*), one Manchu official detached from the Ministry of Works. In both cases, whenever a lumber shipment arrived, members of the Ministry of Works were dispatched to check on the amount and quality of the shipment and, if they approved it, to authorize its acceptance and eventual delivery to the Central Lumberyard (*mu-ts'ang*) at Peking, for use in the construction, repair, and general maintenance of palace and central government buildings. P14.

2849 *huáng-nǚ* 皇女
Imperial Princess: throughout history an unofficial reference to the daughters of Emperors.

2850 *huáng pāo-ī* 皇包衣
CH'ING: **Imperial Bondservant** assigned to one of the Three Superior Banners (*shang san ch'i*); see *pao-i.* BH: imperial household bondservant.

2851 *huáng-pó* 皇伯
Imperial Uncle: throughout history an unofficial reference to an elder brother of a reigning Emperor's father.

2852 *huáng-shàng* 皇上
Common indirect reference to the Emperor: **His Majesty.**

2853 *huáng-shú* 皇叔
Imperial Uncle: throughout history an unofficial reference to a younger brother of a reigning Emperor's father.

2854 *huáng-sūn* 皇孫
Imperial Heir Once Removed: a common unofficial reference to the eldest son of the Heir Apparent; less explicit than *huang chang-sun,* but identical in meaning.

2855 *huáng-sūn fǔ* 皇孫府
T'ANG: **Office of the Imperial Descendants,** an agency established in the palace in 691 to care for the families of Imperial Princes (*ch'in-wang*) resident in the capital. Cf. *tsung-cheng ssu.* RR: *maison des descendants de l'empereur.*

2856 *huáng-t'à* 黃闥
Lit., the yellow (i.e., imperial) apartments, throughout history a common indirect reference to the Emperor: **His Majesty.**

2857 *huáng tài-tzǔ* 黃帶子
CH'ING: lit., (wearers of) yellow girdles: **Imperial Clansmen,** the official designation of all male descendants of the founding Emperor.

2858 *huáng t'ài-fēi* 皇太妃
SUNG: **Imperial Mother:** occasional variant of the designation Empress Dowager (*huang t'ai-hou*).

2859 *huáng t'ài fū-jén* 皇太夫人
N-S DIV: **Imperial Mother:** occasional variant of the designation Empress Dowager (*huang t'ai-hou*).

2860 *huáng t'ài-hòu* 皇太后
Empress Dowager: from Ch'in on, the standard official designation of the mother of a reigning Emperor.

2861 *huáng t'ài-hòu lín-ch'áo* 皇太后臨朝
Lit., Empress Dowager participating in court audience (during her reigning son's minority): **Empress Dowager Regent.**

2862 *huáng t'ài-sūn* 皇太孫
Imperial Grandson-heir: normally the official designation of the eldest son of an Heir Apparent whose father had died and who had been named heir to the throne in his place; may be encountered as a variant of Imperial Heir Once Removed (*huang-sun, huang chang-sun*).

2863 *huáng t'ài-tzǔ* 皇太子
Common variant of **Heir Apparent** (*t'ai-tzu*), normally the eldest son of a reigning Emperor.

2864 *huáng-tàng fáng* 黃檔房
CH'ING: lit., office of the yellow (i.e., imperial) archive: **Imperial Genealogy Section** in the Court of the Imperial Clan (*tsung-jen fu*). BH: genealogical record office.

2865 *huáng-t'áng* 黃堂
(1) HAN–SUI: unofficial reference to a **Commandery Governor** (*chün-shou, t'ai-shou*). (2) T'ANG–CH'ING: unofficial reference to a **Prefect** (*tz'u-shih, chih-chou, chih-fu*).

2866 *huáng-tì* 皇帝
Lit., a combination of terms designating legendary sage kings of highest antiquity: **Emperor,** from Ch'in on the standard official designation of a dynastic ruler; instituted by the First Emperor of Ch'in to supersede the earlier term King (*wang*).

2867 *huáng-tì lí-yüán tì-tzǔ* 皇帝黎園弟子
T'ANG: lit., disciples in the Emperor's pear garden: **Members of the Palace Theater.** See *li-yüan.*

2868 *huáng tí-sūn* 皇嫡孫
SUNG: lit., imperial grandson in the line of principal wives:

variant reference to the **Heir Apparent Once Removed** (*t'ai-sun*), the eldest son of the Heir Apparent.

2869   *huáng-t'óu láng* 黄頭郎
Yellow-helmeted Gentleman. (1) HAN: one of many designations of members of the Palace Guard (*yü-lin*). (2) T'ANG: member of the New Music Office (*hsin yüeh-fu*), status and function not clear.

2870   *huáng-tsàng shǔ* 黄藏署
N-S DIV (N. Ch'i)–SUI: **Office of the Imperial Storehouse,** one of 3 storehouse offices under the Court of the Imperial Treasury (*t'ai-fu ssu*); headed by a Director (*ling* till c. 604, then *chien*), rank 8a. See *tso-tsang, yu-tsang.* P7.

2871   *huáng-tsǔ* 皇祖
Deceased Imperial Grandfather: throughout imperial history the standard ceremonial reference to the dead paternal grandfather of a reigning Emperor.

2872   *huáng-tzǔ* 皇子
Quasiofficial variant of *ch'in-wang* (**Imperial Prince**), or a reference to sons of Emperors before their formal installation as Imperial Princes.

2873   *huáng yüǎn-sūn* 皇元孫
Heir Apparent Twice Removed: common reference to the eldest son of an Heir Apparent Once Removed (*huang chang-sun*), who was eldest son of the Heir Apparent.

2874   *hùi-ch'ǎng àn* 會場案
SUNG: **Collections Section** in the Granaries Bureau (*ts'ang-pu*) of the Ministry of Revenue (*hu-pu*), presumably supervising collection points for shipments of tax grains to the capital granaries. SP: *service des places de collecte.*

2875   *hūi-chèng yüàn* 徽政院
YÜAN: **Household Administration of the Empress Dowager,** established on an ad hoc basis, normally whenever an Emperor took the throne while his mother was alive; established 1294, abolished 1324, re-established 1334. P26.

2876   *hùi-chì ssū* 會計司
See *k'uai-chi ssu* (Office of Accounts).

2877   *hūi-fàn* 暉範
N-S DIV (N. Ch'i): **Lady of Brilliant Models,** designation of one of 27 imperial wives called Hereditary Consorts (*shih-fu*); rank =3b.

2878   *hùi-fēi* 惠妃
T'ANG–MING: **Gracious Consort,** title of a high-ranking imperial wife; in T'ang, beginning in the reign of Hsüan-tsung (712–756), one of the esteemed group called the Three Consorts (*san fei*). Also see *hua-fei, li-fei.* RR: *concubine bienveillante.*

2879   *húi-húi* 回回
Moslem, Muslim: prefix to many titles indicating that they were reserved for Moslem appointees or specialized in Moslem affairs; especially prevalent in Yüan times. Apparently derived from references to early Uighurs.

2880   *húi-húi lìng-shǐh* 回回令史
YÜAN: **Moslem Clerk,** found in many agencies, e.g., various Ministries (*pu*), the Court of the Imperial Stud (*t'ai-p'u ssu*), the Directorate of Waterways (*tu-shui chien*); may be encountered in later dynasties as well.

2881   *húi-húi ssū-t'iēn chiēn* 回回司天監
YÜAN: **Directorate of Moslem Astronomy,** a central government agency principally charged with preparing an annual calendar in the Islamic mode.

2882   *húi-húi yào-wù yüàn* 回回藥物院
YÜAN: **Moslem Pharmacy,** for the preparation of medications in the Islamic tradition; established in 1292–1293 in both Mongol capitals Ta-tu (Peking) and Shang-tu (Chahar); in 1322–1323 was appended to the Moslem Medical Office (*kuang-hui ssu*); headed by an Overseer (*ta-lu-hua-ch'ih*) and a Commissioner-in-chief (*ta-shih*), rank 5b.

2883   *hùi-ì* 會議
Court Conference: throughout imperial history, a gathering of court officials under imperial orders to consider a proposal about policy, a criticism of policy, or an important judicial action, with the expectation of achieving a consensus about what imperial reaction to recommend.

2884   *hùi-k'uéi* 會魁
MING–CH'ING: **Metropolitan Graduate with Distinction,** unofficial reference to a candidate in the Metropolitan Examination (*hui-shih*) of the civil service recruitment examination sequence who ranked from 6th to 18th place on the pass list. See *sheng-k'uei, hui-yüan, pang-yüan, chuang-yüan, chin-shih.*

2885   *hùi-mín yào-chú* 惠民藥局 or *hui-min chü*
SUNG–MING: lit., pharmacy for the benefit of the people: **Public Pharmacy,** established both in the central government and in units of territorial administration for the sale or sometimes free distribution of medicines to the poor; commonly headed by Commissioners-in-chief (*ta-shih*); under the Court of the Imperial Treasury (*t'ai-fu ssu*) in Sung, the Imperial Academy of Medicine (*t'ai-i yüan*) in Yüan and Ming. SP: *bureau des medicaments au profit du peuple.* P36.

2886   *hùi-pàn* 會辦
CH'ING: **Manager** or **Commander,** a prefix used in late Ch'ing; e.g., *hui-pan ch'ang-chiang fang-shou shih-i* (Commander of Yangtze River Defense).

2887   *húi-pì* 廻避
Avoidance: from Han on, a principle relating to personnel assignments in the civil service, principally forbidding relatives to serve in the same government agency (the junior must withdraw in deference to the senior) or to accept appointments in units of territorial administration where they were themselves registered natives. The intent in both cases was to minimize collusion among relatives to the disadvantage of the state. The principle varied from dynasty to dynasty in its details and in the rigidity of its enforcement. See *san-hu fa* (Law of Triple Avoidances).

2888   *hùi-shìh* 會試
YÜAN–CH'ING: **Metropolitan Examination** in the civil service recruitment examination sequence, given at the capital to candidates for the degree of Metropolitan Graduate (*chin-shih*), normally already Provincial Graduates (*chü-jen*); normally followed by a confirmatory Palace Examination (*t'ing-shih, tien-shih*) presided over by the Emperor or his surrogate; successor of the Sung dynasty *sheng-shih.*

2889   *hùi-t'úng kuǎn* 會同館
Interpreters Institute. (1) YÜAN: the principal agency for receiving tributary envoys; established in 1276, discontinued in 1288, re-established in 1292; in 1295 put under supervision of the Minister of Rites (*lǐ-pu shang-shu*); headed by 2 Commissioners-in-chief (*ta-shih*), rank 4a. (2) MING–

CH'ING: the principal state hostelry for foreign envoys, headed by a Commissioner-in-chief, 9a; in 1492 placed under the concurrent control of a Secretary (*chu-shih*), 6a, of the Bureau of Receptions (*chu-k'o ssu*) in the Ministry of Rites; in 1657 put under an Administrator (*t'ung-shih*) with nominal status as Vice Director (*yüan-wai lang*), 5b, of a Bureau (*ch'ing-li ssu*) in a Ministry (*pu*); in 1748 combined with the Translators Institute (*ssu-i kuan*) into a single Interpreters and Translators Institute (*hui-t'ung ssu-i kuan*) under the Ministry of Rites. Cf. *ssu-fang kuan*. P11.

2890 *hùi-t'úng ssù-ì kuǎn* 會同四譯館
CH'ING: **Interpreters and Translators Institute,** primarily a hostel for foreign tributary envoys; headed by a Commissioner-in-chief (*ta-shih*), rank 9a, supervised by a Superintendent (*t'i-tu*) delegated from the Ministry of Rites (*li-pu*); created in 1748 by combining the previously separate Interpreters Institute (*hui-t'ung kuan*) and Translators Institute (*ssu-i kuan*). Also cf. *ssu-fang kuan*. BH: residence for envoys of the four tributary states. P11.

2891 *hùi-t'ūng yüàn* 會通苑
SUI: **Imperial Capital Park,** designation of the imperial park at the Eastern Capital (*tung-tu*), Loyang; late in the dynasty renamed *shang-lin yüan*. Also see *shen-tu yüan*. P40.

2892 *hūi-tsé* 暉則
N-S DIV (N. Ch'i): **Lady of Brilliant Patterns,** designation of one of 27 imperial wives called Hereditary Consorts (*shih-fu*); rank =3b.

2893 *hùi-tzǔ chiēn* 會子監 or *hùi-tzǔ wù* 務
SUNG: **Paper Money Office;** see under *chiao-tzu wu*.

2894 *hùi-wèn àn* 會問案
SUNG: **Section for Major Trials,** one of 13 Sections (*an*) directly subordinate to the executive officials of the S. Sung Ministry of Justice (*hsing-pu*); staffed with suboffical functionaries who handled documents concerning assemblages of judicial dignitaries for major trials and the rectification of criminal penalties not in accord with law. SP: *service des interrogatoires*.

2895 *hùi-yào sǒ* 會要所
SUNG: **Office of Collected Regulations,** a subsection of the Palace Library (*pi-shu sheng*) apparently responsible for maintaining and compiling documents setting forth major policies of the sort preserved in works known, e.g., as *T'ang hui-yao;* headed by a Supervisor (*t'i-chü*). SP: *office de la compilation des documents importants*.

2896 *hùi-yüán* 會元
MING–CH'ING: **Principal Graduate,** designation of the man whose name stood first on the pass list issued after a Metropolitan Examination (*hui-shih*) in the civil service recruitment examination sequence. Cf. *chuang-yüan*.

2897 *hún-í chiēn* 渾儀監
T'ANG: **Directorate of the Armillary Sphere,** from 700 to 710 the official name of the Directorate of Astrology (most commonly *t'ai-shih chien*), headed by a Director (*chien*); changed from *hun-t'ien chien,* changed to *t'ai-shih chü*. P35.

2898 *hún-í t'ái* 渾儀台
SUNG: **Armillary Sphere Office,** a subsection of the Astrological Service (*t'ai-shih chü*); staffing not clear. P35.

2899 *hūn-jén* 閽人
(1) CHOU: **Doorkeeper,** 4 unranked personnel of the Ministry of State (*t'ien-kuan*) stationed at each door to the royal palace, each entrance to a royal park or garden, etc. CL: *concierge*. (2) Throughout imperial history, one of many terms occasionally used to refer to a **eunuch.**

2900 *hùn-t'áng ssū* 混堂司
MING: **Bathing Office,** a minor agency of palace eunuchs, headed by a Director (*cheng, t'ai-chien*); prepared and assisted with the Emperor's baths; see *ssu ssu* (Four Offices).

2901 *hún-t'iēn chiēn* 渾天監
T'ANG: **Directorate of the Armillary Sphere,** official variant of the name Directorate of Astrology (most commonly *t'ai-shih chien*), possibly used as early as 684 but probably used for only a month in 700; changed from *t'ai-shih chü;* changed to *hun-i chien*. P35.

2902 *húng-ch'én* 鴻臣
HAN: lit., minister for loud announcements: abbreviated reference to the **Chamberlain for Dependencies** (*ta hung-lu*), who introduced tributary envoys at court audiences. May be encountered in later times as an abbreviated reference to the Court of State Ceremonial (*hung-lu ssu*) or members of its staff.

2903 *húng-fù* 宏父
CHOU: lit., great father: variant reference to the **Minister of Works** (*ssu-k'ung*).

2904 *húng-hūi* 宏徽
N-S DIV (N. Ch'i): **Lady of Vast Excellence,** designation of one of 27 imperial wives called Hereditary Consorts (*shih-fu*); rank =3b.

2905 *húng-lú ch'īng* 鴻臚卿
Lit., chief minister for making loud announcements. (1) N-S DIV (S. Dyn.): **Chief Minister for Dependencies,** in charge of the reception at court of tributary envoys; retitled from the earlier Chamberlain for Dependencies (*ta hung-lu*). P33. (2) SUI: **Chief Ceremonial Minister,** occasional honorary designation granted to a southwestern aboriginal chief. P72. (3) SUI–CH'ING: **Chief Minister of the Court for Dependencies** (Sui) or **of the Court of State Ceremonial** (T'ANG–CH'ING); see *hung-lu ssu*. P33.

2906 *húng-lú ssù* 鴻臚寺
(1) N-S DIV (N. Ch'i)–SUI: **Court for Dependencies,** a central government agency responsible for managing the reception at court of tributary envoys, continuing the tradition of the Han era Chamberlain for Dependencies (*ta hung-lu*); headed by a Chief Minister (*ch'ing*). (2) T'ANG–SUNG, MING–CH'ING: **Court of State Ceremonial,** in charge of court receptions of foreign dignitaries, state funerals, and other important court rituals, generally under supervision of the Ministry of Rites (*li-pu*); headed by a Chief Minister (*ch'ing*), rank 3b in T'ang, 4b in Sung, 4a in Ming and Ch'ing. For Yüan, see *shih-i ssu*. RR+SP: *cour du cérémonial envers les étrangers,* (SP also:) *cour de la réception diplomatique.* BH: court of state ceremonial. P33.

2907 *húng tài-tzǔ* 紅帶子
CH'ING: lit., (wearers of) red girdles: formal designation of men descended in the collateral line from the founding emperor: **Imperial In-law.** Imperial Clansmen (*huang tai-tzu*) could be degraded to this status for misconduct. See *chüeh-lo kung*.

2908 *húng-té* 宏德
N-S DIV (N. Ch'i): **Lady of Vast Virtue,** designation of one of 3 imperial wives called Three Consorts (*san fu-jen*).

2909 *húng-tū mén hsüéh* 鴻都門學
HAN: **School at the Gate of the Great Capital,** estab-

lished by an imperial summons of A.D. 178 for students of literary and calligraphic talents; later considered by some the origin of the term Academician (*hsüeh-shih*), but no clear evidence of this seems to exist. HB: school at the gate of the vast capital. P23.

2910 *húng-tz'ú* 宏詞
T'ANG–CH'ING: common abbreviated reference to *po-hsüeh hung-tz'u* (**Erudite Literatus**).

2911 *húng-wén kuǎn* 弘文館
T'ANG: **Institute for the Advancement of Literature**, established in 626 as a replacement for the Institute for the Cultivation of Literature (*hsiu-wen kuan*), in 705 renamed Institute for the Glorification of Literature (*chao-wen kuan*), in 719 renamed *hung-wen kuan* again; subordinate to the Chancellery (*men-hsia sheng*); managed literary and other compilation projects under imperial sponsorship and tutored talented sons of capital officials of rank 5 and above; staffed with various Academicians (*hsüeh-shih*) under administrative leadership of a Supervising Secretary (*chi-shih chung*) of the Chancellery assigned as Supervisor of the Institute (*p'an kuan-shih*). RR: *collège pour le développement de la littérature*. P25.

2912 *húng-wén yüàn* 宏文院
CHIN: **Office for the Advancement of Literature**, responsible for translating, proofreading, and reproducing Chinese classical and historical works; staffed with Subeditors (*chiao-li*), rank 8a, under a Director (*chih-yüan*), 5b, and an Associate Administrator (*t'ung … chih-shih*), 6b; apparently subordinate to the Directorate of the Palace Archives (*pi-shu chien*). P25.

2913 *húng-yú* 宏猷
N-S DIV (N. Ch'i): **Lady of Vast Counsel**, designation of one of 27 imperial wives called Hereditary Consorts (*shih-fu*); rank =3b.

2914 *huǒ* 火
T'ANG: lit., fire, campfire: **Squad**, the smallest unit in the dynastic military organization, comprising 10 soldiers; five Squads constituted a Company (*t'ui*, *t'uan*).

2915 *huǒ-ch'ì yíng* 火器營
CH'ING: **Firearms Brigade**, a unit of the Inner Banners (*nei-ch'i*) comprising Guardsmen (*hu-chün*) selected from various Banners and armed with muskets (*niao-ch'iang*) and artillery (see *p'ao hsiao-chi*), divided into an inner group stationed in Peking and an outer group stationed near the summer palace; commanded by 6 Commanders-general (*tsung-t'ung*), often Imperial Princes. See *shen-chi ying*. BH: artillery and musketry division.

2916 *huǒ-chiǎ* 火甲
MING: **Fire Captain**, head of a local fire defense organization in an urban Precinct (*fang*).

2917 *huò-ch'üán chú* 貨泉局
MING: **Coinage Service**, established in 1364 in immediate predynastic times in Kiangsi Province; at the beginning of the dynasty in 1368 superseded by Coinage Services (*pao-ch'üan chü*) established in all Provinces. P16.

2918 *huǒ-p'ō* 火坡
T'ANG: lit. sense and derivation not clear: unofficial reference to a **Censor-in-chief** (*yü-shih ta-fu*).

2919 *huǒ-yaò ssū* 火藥司
MING: **Gunpowder Office**, a unit under the palace eunuch agency called the Palace Armory (*ping-chang chü*).

2920 *ì* 役
Requisitioned Service; see *ch'ai-i*.

2921 *ǐ* 擬
See under the romanization *ni*.

2922 *ì* 易
HAN: **Exchange Manager**, established in the reign of Wang Mang (9–23) as a controller of price stabilization in the official markets of the dynastic capital and 5 other major cities, subordinate to Market Masters (*shih-shih*); see under *wu chün-ssu shih-shih* (**Five Market Managers**).

2923 *ì* 翼
Wing. (1) Common designation of flanking groups in military arrays, normally with a particularizing prefix, e.g., Left Wing (*tso-i*), Right Wing (*yu-i*). (2) CH'ING: a unit of Imperial Guardsmen (*ch'in-chün shih-wei*), 2 of which constituted a Duty Group (*pan*), 6 of which in rotation undertook guard duty in the imperial palace.

2924 *ì* 譯
Interpreter, used almost entirely with modifying prefixes or suffixes. E.g., see *i-kuan ling*.

2925 *ì* 邑
(1) **Fief**: from antiquity a small territory granted to a favored personage for his maintenance. HB: estate (*of a princess*). (2) Occasional unofficial reference to a **District** (*hsien*).

2926 *ì* 驛
Postal Relay Station: see under *chan, i-chan, i-ch'uan tao*.

2927 *ì-chàn* 驛站
CH'ING: **Postal Relay Station**, units scattered along main communications routes throughout the empire under general supervision of the Ministry of War (*ping-pu*); maintained by local units of territorial administration such as Districts (*hsien*), staffed with runners and mounted couriers drawn from the local population, each unit managed by a Station Master (*i-ch'eng, chan-kuan*); principally in charge of dispatching state documents between the central government and provincial and lower units of territorial administration; could sometimes be used for transporting officials on state business. See *chan, p'u-ssu*. BH: military post station. P72.

2928 *ì-chǎng* 翼長
Wing Commander, a common military designation. E.g., in Ch'ing there were Wing Commanders in both the Scouting Brigade (*chien-jui ying*) and the Firearms Brigade (*huo-ch'i ying*), rank 3a, and in the horse pasturage establishment operated by the Court of the Imperial Stud (*t'ai-p'u ssu*), 5a. BH: brigadier.

2929 *ì-chǎng* 譯長
HAN: **Chief of Interpreters**, a eunuch responsible for greeting and assisting foreign envoys in court audiences; apparently associated either with the Director of Imperial Gatekeepers (*huang-men ling*) or the Chamberlain for Dependencies (*ta hung-lu*). HB: chief interpreter. P11.

2930 *ì-chǎng* 邑長
HAN: lit., head of a fief: **Chieftain**, honorific title sometimes granted to tribal leaders of southern and southwestern aborigines. P72.

2931 *i chàng-fū* 一丈夫
Throughout history an unofficial reference to the ruler: **the solitary fellow**.

2932 *i-chàng kōu-tāng* 儀仗勾當
SUNG: **Bearers of the Imperial Insignia** in processions; see *kou-tang*. SP: *chargé des emblèmes et des armes d'apparat*.

2933 *i-chàng shǐh* 儀仗使
SUNG: **Imperial Regalia Commissioner** for ceremonies at the imperial mausoleums south of the dynastic capital, Kaifeng; assisted by a Chief Administrator (*tu pu-shu*) and a Vice Administrator (*fu pu-shu*); all duty assignments for capital officials under supervision of the Court of Imperial Sacrifices (*t'ai-ch'ang ssu*). See *liu chün i-chang ssu*. SP: *commissaire des emblèmes et des armes d'apparat*.

2934 *i-chàng ssū* 儀仗司
MING: **Insignia Office** in a Princely Establishment (*wang-fu*), only during the reign of Hui-ti (r. 1398–1402); staffed by a single Clerk (*li-mu*). See *liu chün i-chang ssu*. P69.

2935 *i-chēn pó-shìh* 醫針博士
SUNG: **Acupuncture Master**, organizational affiliation not clear but probably a member of the Imperial Medical Service (*t'ai-i chü*); one or more unranked professional specialists. SP: *docteur acuponcteur*.

2936 *i-chèng* 醫正
SUI–T'ANG, YÜAN: **Principal Practitioner** in the Sui–T'ang Imperial Medical Office (*t'ai-i shu*) and the Yüan Imperial Academy of Medicine (*t'ai-i yüan*); in T'ang 8, rank 9b2. P36.

2937 *i-chèng ch'ù* 議政處
CH'ING: **Deliberative Council**, an informal policy-advising group of Princes and Grand Ministers (*wang ta-ch'en*), the most influential shaper of policy in early Ch'ing; c. 1730 transformed into an official Council of State (*chün-chi ch'u*). Also see *i-cheng wu ta-ch'en, pei-lo*.

2938 *i-chèng láng* 醫正郎
YÜAN: **Court Gentleman for Medical Practice**, prestige title (*san-kuan*) for rank 7b members of the Imperial Academy of Medicine (*t'ai-i yüan*).

2939 *i-chèng wáng* 議政王
CH'ING: **Prince of the Deliberative Council**, a reference to a Prince who participated in the early Ch'ing Deliberative Council (*i-cheng ch'u*). Also occurs as a designation of the famous Prince Kung, personal name I-hsin, who was regent during the 1860s. BH: prince regent.

2940 *i-chèng wǔ tà-ch'én* 議政五大臣
CH'ING: **Five Grand Ministers of the Deliberative Council**, a predynastic group of Manchu nobles who counseled the Manchu ruler on policy matters; after 1635 transformed into the informal Deliberative Council (*i-cheng ch'u*) with less rigidly limited membership.

2941 *i-chèng yüàn* 益政院
CHIN: **Institute for Improving Governance**, a practice rather than an agency, initiated in 1226; a daily meeting of the ruler with an eminent official, normally the Minister of Rites (*li-pu shang-shu*), serving as Lecturer (*shuo-shu kuan*) on the classics, the lessons of history, governmental precedents, etc. Equivalent to the Classics Colloquium (*ching-yen*) in earlier and later periods. P24.

2942 *i-ch'í shìh* 伊耆氏
CHOU: **Attendant for Elders**, one ranked as a Junior Serviceman (*hsia-shih*) in the Ministry of Justice (*ch'iu-kuan*); provided canes for old officials participating in ceremonies, removed the canes at times out of respect for the spirits. CL: *officier de l'illustre viellard*.

2943 *i-chiǎ* 一甲
MING–CH'ING: **First Category** of Palace Examination (*tien-shih*) graduates in the sequence of civil service recruitment examinations, referring to the top 3 men on the final pass list, all of whom received the degree Metropolitan Graduate with Honors (*chin-shih chi-ti*): the Principal Graduate (*chuang-yüan*), the Second Graduate (*pang-yen*), and the Third Graduate (*t'an-hua*). See *chia*. BH: 1st class.

2944 *i-chiēn* 醫監
SUI–T'ANG: **Medical Supervisor** in the Imperial Medical Office (*t'ai-i shu*); 5 in Sui; 4, rank 8b2, in T'ang. RR: *directeur en chef de la médecine*. P36.

2945 *i-chìh ch'īng-lì ssū* 儀制清吏司 or *i-chih ssū*
MING–CH'ING: **Bureau of Ceremonies**, the most prestigious of 4 Bureaus (*ch'ing-li ssu, ssu*) in the Ministry of Rites (*li-pu*), headed by a Director (*lang-chung*), rank 5a; in charge of major court ceremonies and civil service recruitment via schools and examinations. BH: department of ceremonies. P9.

2946 *i-ch'íng chāng-chīng* 夷情章京
CH'ING: **Secretary for Native Affairs**, unspecified number, apparently unranked specialists, on the staffs of the 2 Grand Minister Residents of Tibet (*chu-tsang ta-ch'en*). See *chang-ching*.

2947 *i-chù* 儀注
MING: **Principal Expounder** at the Classics Colloquium (*ching-yen*); a duty assignment for a meritorious minister (*hsün-ch'en*) to serve as the leader in such meetings of officials with the Emperor to discuss classical precepts and historical precedents. P24.

2948 *i-ch'uán tào* 驛傳道
MING: **Postal Service Circuit** monitoring the maintenance and functioning of Postal Relay Stations (*i, chan*); one Circuit per Province with few variations, supervised by Intendants (*tao-t'ai*) delegated from Provincial Surveillance Commissions (*t'i-hsing an-ch'a shih ssu*) with substantive status as Surveillance Vice Commissioner (*an-ch'a fu-shih*) or Assistant Surveillance Commissioner (*an-ch'a ch'ien-shih*), ranks 4a and 5b.

2949 *i-ch'uán láng* 醫痊郎
YÜAN: **Court Gentleman for Medical Healing**, prestige title (*san-kuan*) for rank 8b officials of the Imperial Academy of Medicine (*t'ai-i yüan*).

2950 *i-chūn* 邑君
HAN: lit., lord of the fief: **Chieftain**, honorific title sometimes granted to tribal leaders of southern and southwestern aborigines. P72.

2951 *i-chūn hsiào-wèi* 翊軍校尉
N-S DIV (S. Dyn.): **Commandant of Standby Troops**, i.e., of a force presumably in combat readiness, on the staff of the Heir Apparent; at least in Sung, 7 appointees were authorized; in Ch'en they were of rank 6, with salary of 1,000 bushels. One of the group collectively known as the Three Commandants (*san hsiao-wei*). P26.

2952 *i èrh-fǔ* 翊二府
T'ANG: **Second Standby Garrison**, one of the Five Garrisons (*wu fu*) at the dynastic capital in which militiamen assigned to the Sixteen Guards (*shih-liu wei*) were apparently quartered. See *i i-fu, san fu, san wei, fu-ping*. Cf. *i-fu* (Standby Garrison). RR: *deuxième milice des ailes*. P43.

2953 *i-fèng ssū* 儀鳳司
YÜAN: **Bureau of Musical Ritual,** originally named *yü-ch'en yüan* (Office for the Imperial Quarters); originally subordinate to the Palace Provisions Commission (*hsüan-hui yüan*), then to the Ministry of Rites (*lǐ-pu*); headed by 5 Commissioners-in-chief (*ta-shih*), rank 3b. Supervised a group of agencies that provided music for state ceremonies: Office of Ancient Music (*yün-ho shu*), Office of Contented Music (*an-ho shu*), Office of Moslem Music (*ch'ang-ho shu*), Office of Western Music (*chao-ho shu*), and Music Office (*chiao-fang ssu*) with 2 subordinate units of its own, a Bureau of Joyful Music (*hsing-ho shu*) and a Bureau of Sacrificial Music (*hsiang-ho shu*). P10.

2954 *i-fŭ* 翊府
T'ANG: **Standby Garrison,** one of the Three Garrisons (*san fu*) in the service of the Heir Apparent. Cf. *i i-fu, i erh-fu, san wei.* RR: *milice des ailes.* P26.

2955 *i-hó* 義和
Lord Astrologer, a title ascribed to the reign of the legendary sage Yao in highest antiquity; occasionally encountered in polite, archaic reference to any astrological or astronomical official.

2956 *i-hóu láng* 醫侯郎
YÜAN: **Court Gentleman for Medical Attendance,** a prestige title (*san kuan*) for rank 8a officials of the Imperial Academy of Medicine (*t'ai-i yüan*).

2957 *i-hsiào láng* 醫效郎
YÜAN: **Court Gentleman for Medical Service,** prestige title (*san-kuan*) for rank 8a officials of the Imperial Academy of Medicine (*t'ai-i yüan*).

2958 *i-hsüéh* 醫學
(1) SUNG–CH'ING: **Medical School** under local units of territorial administration, supervised by the regular civil authorities but manned by unranked professional physicians; in Sung headed by a Director (*cheng*), in Yüan by a Supervisor (*t'i-chü*); normally staffed principally by Instructors (*chiao-shou*), but in Sung also had Erudites (*po-shih*). Medical students (*i hsüeh-sheng*) were normally not subsidized by the state. Medical Schools in all localities were apparently under the authority of the Imperial Medical Service (*t'ai-i chü*) or the Imperial Academy of Medicine (*t'ai-i yüan*). Also see *han-lin i-kuan yüan.* (2) SUNG: common abbreviation of *i hsüeh-sheng* (**Medical Student**).

2959 *i-hsüéh t'í-chǚ ssū* 醫學提舉司
YÜAN: **Supervisorate of Medical Schools,** a unit in the Imperial Academy of Medicine (*t'ai-i yüan*) headed by a Supervisor (*t'i-chü*), apparently responsible for overseeing all Medical Schools (*i-hsüeh*) in units of territorial administration; also examined the qualifications of prospective Medical Instructors in the Imperial Academy (*t'ai-i chiao-kuan*).

2960 *ì ǐ-fŭ* 翊一府
T'ANG: **First Standby Garrison,** one of the Five Garrisons (*wu fu*) at the dynastic capital in which militiamen assigned to the Sixteen Guards (*shih-liu wei*) were apparently quartered. See *i erh-fu, san fu, san wei, fu-ping.* Cf. *i-fu* (Standby Garrison). RR: *première milice des ailes.* P43.

2961 *i-jén* 宜人
SUNG–CH'ING: **Lady of Suitability:** honorific title granted wives of certain officials; normally follows the surname. In Yüan, granted to wives of rank 7 officials; in Ming and Ch'ing, to wives of rank 5 officials.

2962 *i-jén* 遺人
CHOU: **Almoner,** 2 ranked as Ordinary Servicemen (*chung-shih*), members of the Ministry of Education (*ti-kuan*) responsible for distributing royal aid to the aged, orphans, victims of natural calamities, visitors from afar, etc. CL: *officiers des gratifications et secours publics.*

2963 *i-k'ù* 衣庫
Clothing Storehouse in the imperial palace. (1) SUNG: organizational affiliation not clear, but probably a unit in the Palace Domestic Service (*nei-shih sheng*). SP: *magasin de vêtements.* (2) CH'ING: one of 6 storehouses constituting the Storage Office (*kuang-ch'u ssu*) of the Imperial Household Department (*nei-wu fu*). BH: imperial wardrobe.

2964 *i-kuān* 醫官
Medical Official, normally a professional, often hereditary specialist rather than a member of the civil service; a generic reference to members of such agencies as the Imperial Medical Service (*t'ai-i chü*) or the Imperial Academy of Medicine (*t'ai-i yüan*). From Sung on, awarded prestige titles (*san-kuan*) giving them honorific status comparable to the various ranks of civil officials.

2965 *i-kuān chú* 醫官局
SUNG: **Physician Service,** one of 4 assemblages of professional specialists in the Artisans Institute (*han-lin yüan*) of the Palace Domestic Service (*nei-shih sheng*); headed by a Manager (*kou-tang kuan*). Relationship with the Imperial Medical Service (*t'ai-i chü*) not clear. SP: *bureau des médecins.*

2966 *i-kuān lìng* 譯官令
HAN: **Director of Interpreters,** a subordinate of the Chamberlain for Dependencies (*ta hung-lu*); participated in the reception of foreign visitors at court. Apparently not perpetuated in Later Han. Cf. *i-chang* (Chief of Interpreters). HB: prefect of the office of interpreters. P11.

2967 *i-kuān shǔ* 衣冠署
T'ANG: **Valeting Office** in the Court of Imperial Sacrifices (*t'ai-ch'ang ssu*), headed by a Director (*ling*), rank 8a; discontinued in 627. RR: *office des vêtements et des coiffures.*

2968 *i-kuān yüàn* 醫官院
SUNG: abbreviation of *han-lin i-kuan yüan* (**Medical Institute**).

2969 *i-kūng* 遺公
T'ANG: unofficial reference to a **Reminder** (*shih-i*).

2970 *i-kūng* 醫工
T'ANG–SUNG: **Medical Apprentice** in the Imperial Medical Office (*t'ai-i shu*) of T'ang and the Imperial Medical Service (*t'ai-i chü*) of Sung, sometimes numbering as many as 100. In Sung, by showing merit, one could be promoted to the status of Medical Student (*i-hsüeh*). RR: *médecin.* P36.

2971 *i-kūng chǎng* 醫工長
HAN: **Chief of Physicians** on the staff of a Princedom (*wang-kuo*) and possibly on that of the Imperial Physician (*t'ai-i ling*); rank =400 bushels. HB: chief of the physicians. P36, 69.

2972 *i-láng* 議郎
HAN–N-S DIV (San-kuo Wei): **Court Gentleman for Consultation,** one of many duty assignments for officials without regular administrative appointments, to serve at court under guidance of the Chamberlain for Attendants (*lang-*

chung ling, kuang-lu-hsün); in Former Han 12, rank =600 bushels; in Later Han as many as 50, rank =400 bushels, then again =600 bushels. HB: gentleman consultant.

2973 *i-lì* 夷隸
CHOU: **Eastern War Prisoner,** 120 apparently authorized for service guarding the palace and tending state herds under supervision of the Directors of Convict Labor (*ssu-li*) in the Ministry of Justice (*ch'iu-kuan*) and also the Commandants of the Royal Stud (*hsiao-jen*) in the Ministry of War (*hsia-kuan*); these easterners were thought able to talk with birds. See *tsui-li*. CL: *condamné de l'est.*

2974 *i-lí-chin* 夷离堇
LIAO: Chinese rendering of a Khitan word meaning **Chief** of a tribe (*pu-tsu*) or subtribe (*shih-lieh*); in the period 925–947 changed to the more Chinese-like title *ta-wang* (Grand Prince); always among the most eminent Khitan nobles.

2975 *i-lǐ chú* 儀禮局
SUNG: **Ritual Service,** created in 1107 in the Department of State Affairs (*shang-shu sheng*) to supervise court rituals; headed concurrently by high-ranking Executive Officials (*chih-cheng kuan*) of the Administration Chamber (*cheng-shih t'ang*). SP: *bureau des rites.*

2976 *i-lǐ chú* 議禮局
SUNG: **Ritual Revision Service,** an agency of the Department of State Affairs (*shang-shu sheng*), possibly an ad hoc agency of the Wang An-shih era that led to the establishment in 1107 of the Ritual Service (*i-li chü*). SP: *bureau de délibérations sur le rétablissement des anciens rites.*

2977 *i-lí-pì* 夷离畢
Chinese rendering of a Khitan word meaning **Tribal Judge:** one of the most important aides to the Chief (*i-li-chin*) of a Khitan tribe (*pu-tsu*); at some date not clear (c. 940?) all gathered into a Tribal Judiciary (*i-li-pi yüan*), with various modified designations such as Tribal Judge of the Left; part of the Northern Administration (*pei-mien*), which governed nomadic tribes in the Liao empire.

2978 *i-liáng àn* 衣糧案
SUNG: **Clothing and Rations Section,** one of 5 Sections (*an*) in the Census Bureau (*hu-pu ssu*; cf. *hu-pu*), one of 3 agencies constituting the State Finance Commission (*san ssu*) of early Sung; normally headed by an Administrative Assistant (*p'an-kuan, t'ui-kuan*); responsible for monitoring the provisioning of officials with salary grain and seasonal clothing issues. Discontinued in the 1080s, its functions absorbed by the Ministry of Revenue (*hu-pu*). SP: *service de vêtement et de nourriture des fonctionnaires.*

2979 *i-lǐng* 翼領
CH'ING: **Wing Commander,** a military title equivalent to *i-chang,* q.v., especially common among officers assigned to command garrisons at imperial mausoleums.

2980 *i-lìng* 邑令
SUNG: **Administrator** of the household of an Imperial Princess (*kung-chu*). See *kung-chu i-ssu, chia-ling.* P69.

2981 *i ling-shih* 譯令史
N-S DIV (N. Wei): **Interpreter-clerk,** a minor member of the staffs of many agencies of the central government.

2982 *i-lò-hsī-pā yüàn* 伊勒希巴院
LIAO: Chinese rendering of a Khitan word equivalent to **Ministry of Justice** (*hsing-pu*); many posts in the Ministry had Khitan titles beginning with *i-lo*. P13.

2983 *i-luán ssū* 儀鸞司 or *i-luán chú* 儀鸞局
Lit., office of the presented phoenix (?), derived from the name of a T'ang palace hall, the *i-luan tien:* **Imperial Regalia Office (Service),** presumably responsible for assembling, maintaining, and providing gear used in important state ceremonies. (1) 5 DYN–SUNG: a unit of the Court of the Imperial Regalia (*wei-wei ssu*), headed by a Commissioner (*shih*). SP: *bureau du phénix.* (2) YÜAN: attached to the Regency (*liu-shou ssu*) at the principal dynastic capital, Ta-tu (Peking), and to various Route Commands (*tsung-kuan fu*); each headed by 2 Commissioners-in-chief (*ta-shih*), rank 5a. (3) MING: attached to the Imperial Guardsmen Command (*ch'in-chün tu-wei fu*) in the earliest years but promptly (date not clear) absorbed into the Imperial Bodyguard (*chin-i wei*). Cf. *luan-i wei.*

2984 *i-pǎng* 乙榜
Lit., list no. 2: in Ch'ing and perhaps earlier times a reference to the pass list issued after each Provincial Examination (*hsiang-shih*) in the civil service recruitment examination sequence and, indirectly, anyone who was named on the list and thus became a **Provincial Graduate** (*chü-jen*). Cf. *chia-pang.*

2985 *i-pīn* 儀賓
MING: **Ceremonial Companion,** a title of nobility (*chüeh*) bestowed on husbands of those women of the imperial clan who were designated Commandery Princess (*chün-chu*), District Princess (*hsien-chu*), Commandery Mistress (*chün-chün*), District Mistress (*hsien-chün*), and Township Mistress (*hsiang-chün*), i.e., women from the 2nd to 6th generations of descent from an Emperor.

2986 *i-pīng* 夷兵
MING: **Alien Soldier,** generic designation of friendly Mongol, Uighur, and other Inner Asian cavalrymen who were recruited from their settlements along the northern and northwestern borders for temporary service in Chinese armies. Cf. *i-ping* (Patriotic Soldier).

2987 *i-pīng* 役兵
Conscripted Troops: throughout history a designation of citizen-soldiers conscripted for active military duty. In Sung, differentiated on one hand from both Imperial Troops (*chin-ping*) and Prefectural Troops (*hsiang-ping*), who were professional career soldiers, and on the other hand from Local Militiamen (*hsiang-ping, min-ping*), who were part-time home-guard forces. Conscripted Troops in Sung apparently served for relatively long periods of time, continuously, amidst Imperial and Prefectural Troops; but whether they were self-supporting or state-supported is not clear.

2988 *i-pīng* 義兵
Patriotic Soldier: from Han on a flexible, generic term for armed forces outside the regular military establishment (see *kuan-ping*), rallied by local leaders to suppress banditry, to support a tottering dynasty, or to challenge the dynastic establishment in the name of "righteousness"; may be encountered in reference to local militia forces. Cf. *i-ping* (Alien Soldier).

2989 *ī pó-shìh* 醫博士
SUI-T'ANG: **Erudite for General Medicine,** one or more, rank 8a; instructional members of the Imperial Medical Service (*t'ai-i chü*) maintained by the Court of Imperial Sacrifices (*t'ai-ch'ang ssu*). RR: *maître au vaste savoir de la médecine.* P36.

2990 *i-pù* 儀部
(1) MING: **Bureau of Ceremonies** in the Ministry of Rites

(*li-pu*), from 1389 to 1396 only; previously called General Bureau (*tsung-pu*), later called Bureau of Ceremonies (*i-chih ch'ing-li ssu*). (2) MING–CH'ING: unofficial reference to the **Ministry of Rites.**

2991   *i-shàn* 翊善
SUNG: **Moral Mentor,** one, rank 7b, in each Princely Establishment (*wang-fu*) and in the household of the Heir Apparent, the Eastern Palace (*tung-kung*), to provide tutoring and remonstrances about moral principles. SP: *lecteur*. P69.

2992   *i-shēng* 佾生
CH'ING: **Ritualist** at a local temple dedicated to Confucius; normally assigned by the Provincial Education Commissioner (*hsüeh-cheng*) from among aspirants who had not been admitted to local Confucian Schools (*ju-hsüeh*).

2993   *i-shēng* 醫生
SUI–CH'ING: **Student of General Medicine,** 40 prescribed for the Imperial Medical Office (*t'ai-i shu*) in T'ang, as many as 300 in the Imperial Medical Service (*t'ai-i chü*) of Sung, numbers not prescribed for the Imperial Academy of Medicine (*t'ai-i yüan*) in Ming and Ch'ing. BH: medical assistant. P36.

2994   *i-shēng* 議生
N-S DIV (Chin): **Adviser** (?), one of many subofficial functionaries on the staffs of Commanderies (*chün*) and Districts (*hsien*); functions not clear. P53, 54.

2995   *i-shēng* 譯生
CH'ING: **Foreign Language Student,** variable numbers attached for training to the Interpreters Institute (*hui-t'ung kuan*), the Translators Institute (*ssu-i kuan*), and, from 1748, the combined Interpreters and Translators Institute (*hui-t'ung ssu-i kuan*). P11.

2996   *i-shìh* 易筮
HAN: **Diviner by the Classic of Changes,** 3 unranked specialists (?) on the staff of the Grand Astrologer (*t'ai-shih ling*) in Later Han; interpreted events according to the *Classic of Changes* (*I-ching*). HB: diviner by the book of changes.

2997   *i-shìh* 醫士
CH'ING: **Physician,** from 10 to 30 with nominal 9b rank but without civil service status, serving in the Imperial Academy of Medicine (*t'ai-i yüan*). P36.

2998   *i-shìh* 醫師
Master Physician. (1) CHOU: 2 ranked as Senior Servicemen (*shang-shih*) and 4 as Junior Servicemen (*hsia-shih*), members of the Ministry of State (*t'ien-kuan*) responsible for treating illnesses among members of the royal court and annually evaluating all medical officials in the kingdom, recommending that they be promoted or demoted. CL: *supérieur de médecins*. (2) SUI–SUNG: in Sui, 40 authorized for the Palace Medical Service (*shang-yao chü*), 200 for the Imperial Medical Office (*t'ai-i shu*); in T'ang number not clear but authorized for the Imperial Medical Service (*t'ai-i chü*); in Sung number not clear but attached to the Palace Medical Service, and specialists with the same title assigned as headmasters in state medical schools. Ranks never clear; no doubt were largely hereditary specialists unrelated to the civil service. RR+SP: *maître médecin*. P36, 38.

2999   *i-shìh* 譯史
Translator, a minor functionary serving in many government agencies in N. Wei (N-S DIV), Chin, and Yüan and in the Court of State Ceremonial (*hung-lu ssu*) in T'ang.

3000   *i-shìh chǎng* 醫師長
CH'ING: **Veterinarian,** 3 unranked specialists in treating horses and camels on the staff of the Palace Stud (*shang-ssu yüan*) in the Imperial Household Department (*nei-wu fu*). BH: veterinary surgeon.

3001   *i-shìh p'íng-chāng* 議事平章
YÜAN: lit., to deliberate about affairs and manage them: variant of *p'ing-chang cheng-shih* (**Manager of Governmental Affairs**), 4 established in 1270 to assist Grand Councilors (*ch'eng-hsiang*) in top-echelon policy deliberations. P4.

3002   *i-shíh pù* 伊實部
LIAO: **I-shih Tribes,** a group of (Uighur?) allied tribes in the Khitan confederation, in the aggregate considered one of the Four Great Tribes (*ssu ta-pu*); represented at the dynastic capital by an Office of the Grand Prince of the I-shih Tribes (*i-shih ta-wang fu*). P17.

3003   *i-ssū* 儀司
SUI: lit. meaning and derivation not clear: **Director** of the Pasturage for Fine Steeds (*hua-liu mu*) under supervision of the Court of the Imperial Stud (*t'ai-p'u ssu*). P31, 39.

3004   *i-ssū* 議司
CH'ING: lit., office for proposals (counsel, discussion, etc.): unofficial reference to an **Assistant Minister** (*ch'eng*) in the Court of Judicial Review (*ta-li ssu*).

3005   *i-ssū* 邑司
T'ANG–SUNG: lit., the fief office: **Household of an Imperial Princess** (*kung-chu*), managed by an Administrator (*ling*), rank 7b. See *kung-chu i-ssu, i-ling, chia-ling, kung-chu fu*. P69.

3006   *i tài-chào* 醫待詔
HAN: **Expectant Physician,** one or more men officially chosen but not yet formally appointed to serve as Attending Physicians (*shih-i*) on the staff of the Imperial Physician (*t'ai-i ling*). See *tai-chao*. HB: physician expectant appointee. P36.

3007   *i-t'ái* 儀臺
MING–CH'ING: lit., pavilion of decorum: unofficial reference to the **Court of State Ceremonial** (*hung-lu ssu*).

3008   *i-tì hǔn-tzǔ* 一第溷子
T'ANG–CH'ING: lit. sense not clear: unofficial reference to someone who did well in civil service recruitment examinations, especially Sung–Ch'ing **Metropolitan Graduates** (*chin-shih*).

3009   *i-tiěn-ch'īng* 一點青
SUNG: lit. sense not clear: unofficial reference to an **Imperial Diarist** (*ch'i-chü lang, ch'i-chü she-jen*). P24.

3010   *i-t'íng* 掖庭
Lit., the side apartments (in the palace). (1) From antiquity a general reference to **Palace Women** (*kung-nü*), especially those of relatively high status. (2) HAN–N-S DIV: **Palace Discipline Service,** name changed from *yung-hsiang* in 104 B.C.; a eunuch agency with a Director (*ling*) and several Aides (*ch'eng*) subordinate to the Chamberlain for the Palace Revenues (*shao-fu*), responsible for administering and monitoring the activities of the staff of palace women. In Later Han the Director was ranked at 600 bushels, and one of his Aides managed a Palace Isolation Building (*pu-shih*), where palace women who fell ill were cared for and where those who committed crimes were detained. During the S. Dynasties the Director was titled *chien* at times; at other

times all that remained of the agency was the Palace Isolation Building under a Director (*ling*), and it was sometimes superseded by, or its functions were shared with, the
Chamberlain for Attendants (*kuang-lu-hsün*). At the beginning of Sui it was made an Office of Female Services (*i-
t'ing chü*) in the Palace Domestic Service (*nei-shih sheng*).
Cf. *i-t'ing pi-yü, jo-lu yü*. HB: the lateral courts. P37.

3011　*i-t'íng chāo-yü* 掖庭詔獄
HAN: **Prison for Palace Women,** a variant reference to
the *i-t'ing pi-yü*.

3012　*i-t'íng chú* 掖庭局
SUI–T'ANG: **Office of Female Services,** a unit of the Palace Domestic Service (*nei-shih sheng*), headed by a eunuch
Director (*ling*), rank 7b2; kept registers of palace women,
directed their work, provided all supplies required by the
palace, specially supervised the nurturing of mulberry trees
and silkworms within the palace. RR: *service des
dépendances du palais intérieur*. P37.

3013　*i-t'íng líng-chiàng* 掖庭綾匠
T'ANG: **Palace Sericulturist,** designation of 150 women
(?) workers, unranked, who produced brocades and other
fine silk goods for palace use under supervision of the Directorate for Imperial Manufactories (*shao-fu chien*). RR:
artisans pour les soieries des dépendances du palais intérieur.
P38.

3014　*i-t'íng pì-yü* 掖庭祕獄
HAN: **Prison for Palace Women,** maintained by the
Chamberlain for Palace Revenues (*shao-fu*) with a eunuch
Director (*ling*); also known as *i-t'ing chao-yü* or simply *i-
t'ing yü*. See *i-t'ing*. HB: imperial prison of the lateral courts.

3015　*i-tsǎi* 邑宰
MING–CH'ING: lit., fief steward: unofficial reference to
a **District Magistrate** (*chih-hsien*).

3016　*i-ts'āng* 義倉
SUI–CH'ING: **Charity Granary,** from 583 ordered established in all Districts (*hsien*) for storage of grain surpluses
in anticipation of future bad harvests; in Sui and T'ang
overseen by the Granaries Section (*ts'ang-pu*) of the Ministry of Revenue (*min-pu, hu-pu*); in T'ang each District
had 3 Supervisors (*tu*), unranked, to encourage the establishment of such granaries, to establish prices, to account
for receipts and disbursements at each granary, etc. In later
times such granaries remained under the general supervision of the Ministry of Revenue, but at the local level supervision became one of the many obligations of the District Magistrate's (*chih-hsien*) staff. RR: *grenier de
prévoyance*.

3017　*i-ts'áo* 儀曹
(1) N-S DIV–T'ANG: alternated with, and to some extent
was interchangeable with, the term *li-pu* as the designation
of the **Section for (Bureau of) Ministry Affairs** in the developing Ministry of Rites (also *li-pu*, sometimes *tz'u-pu*);
headed by a Director (*lang, lang-chung*); c. 604 *i-ts'ao*
(Section) was settled upon, but in 620 that agency name
was terminated and superseded by *li-pu* (Bureau). RR: *bureau des rites*. P9. (2) N-S DIV (Ch'i): **Ritualist** (?), 2 on
the staff of the National University (*kuo-tzu hsüeh*). P34.
(3) N-S DIV (N. Wei): **Ministry of Rites** in the evolving
Department of State Affairs (*shang-shu sheng*), temporarily
displacing the term *li-pu*; headed by a Minister (*shang-shu*);
supervised several sections or bureaus including a Section
for Ministry Affairs (*i-ts'ao*) as described in (1) above. P9.
(4) T'ANG–CH'ING: occasional unofficial reference to the
Ministry of Rites (*li-pu*). (5) SUNG–CH'ING: a variant of

li-ts'ao (**Section for Rites**), one of 6 clerical subsections in
local units of territorial administration; dealt with ceremonial matters in correspondence with superior agencies at the
regional or provincial level and in the central government,
especially the Ministry of Rites (*li-pu*). SP: *bureau des rites*.

3018　*i-ts'áo* 議曹
HAN: **Consultation Section,** one of a dozen or more Sections (*ts'ao*) subordinate to the Defender-in-chief (*t'ai-wei*)
in the central government, and probably duplicated on the
staff of the Counselor-in-chief (*ch'eng-hsiang*); headed by
an Administrator (*yüan-shih*), rank =400 bushels; functions
not clear. Also found among the clerical units of some
Commanderies (*chün*) in Later Han. HB: bureau of consultation.

3019　*i-ts'áo* 醫曹
HAN: **Medical Section,** a unit on the staffs of some Commanderies (*chün*) in Later Han. HB: bureau of medicine.

3020　*i-tsò yüán* 醫佐員 or *i-tso*
SUI–SUNG: **Medical Assistant,** number not clear, rank 8b2
in T'ang, in the Palace Medical Service (*shang-yao chü*),
an agency of the Palace Administration (*tien-nei sheng, tien-
chung sheng*). RR: *aide médecin de l'empereur*. SP: *aide-
médecin du palais*.

3021　*i-tsūn* 邑尊
MING–CH'ING: lit., the most venerable one in the fief:
unofficial reference to a **District Magistrate** (*chih-hsien*).

3022　*i-t'ú* 異途
MING–CH'ING: **Irregular Paths** of entry into the officialdom, e.g., by purchase of a title or rank, as compared
to Regular Paths (*cheng-t'u*) such as passing the sequence
of civil service recruitment examinations. Entering the service by an Irregular Path meant that, even if a man subsequently "regularized" his entry by passing the recruitment examinations, he was forever barred from appointment
to such sensitive agencies as the Hanlin Academy (*han-lin
yüan*) and the Censorate (*tu ch'a-yüan*).

3023　*i-t'úng* 儀同
SUI: variant form (or calligraphic error) for *i-ssu* (**Director**
of a pasturage), q.v.

3024　*i-t'úng sān-ssū* 儀同三司
SUI, CHIN–YÜAN: lit., with prestige equal to that of the
3 offices, but reference not clear: **Unequaled in Honor,**
merit title (*hsün*) in Sui, prestige title (*san-kuan*) in Chin–
Yüan; 7th highest of 11 merit titles in Sui; awarded to civil
service officials of rank 1b in Chin, 1a in Yüan. See *shang
i-t'ung san-ssu, k'ai-fu i-t'ung san-ssu, shang k'ai-fu i-t'ung
san-ssu*. P65, 68.

3025　*i-tzù shēng* 譯字生
MING: **Apprentice Translator** in the Translators Institute
(*ssu-i kuan*), subordinate to the Court of Imperial Sacrifices
(*t'ai-ch'ang ssu*); could be promoted into the Court of State
Ceremonial (*hung-lu ssu*). P11.

3026　*i-tzù wáng* 一字王
YÜAN: lit., a Prince prefixed with only a single character,
e.g., *ch'in-wang* (Prince of Ch'in), as distinguished from
the less prestigious Princes whose titles bore 2-character
prefixes, e.g., *lo-yang wang* (Prince of Loyang): **First-class
Prince.** See *liang-tzu wang* (Second-class Prince). P64.

3027　*i-tz'ù* 曳刺
T'ANG (?)–MING: lit., one who grabs and stabs: **Sentry**
at the office of a District Magistrate (*hsien-ling, chih-hsien*).

3028 *ì-wèi* 儀衛

MING: **Ceremonial Guard,** a military unit assigned to each Princely Establishment (*wang-fu*), headed by a Director (*cheng*), rank 5a, equal to that of a Battalion Commander (*ch'ien-hu*) rather than to that of an ordinary Guard Commander (*chih-hui shih*); seems to have had ceremonial duties only, leaving an active military role to the Escort Guard (*hu-wei*) assigned to each Prince. P69.

3029 *ì-wèi* 翊衛

SUI–SUNG: **Standby Guard:** common name for a military unit at the dynastic capital. See *shih-erh wẹi* (Twelve Guards), *po chi* (Hundred Cavaliers), *san wei* (Three Guards). RR+SP: *garde des ailes.*

3030 *ì-wèi* 邑尉

CH'ING: **Defender of the Fief,** an archaic, unofficial reference to a suboficial functionary serving as District Jailor (*tien-shih*).

3031 *ì-wén chiēn* 藝文監

YÜAN: **Directorate of Literature,** established in 1329 primarily to translate Chinese classics into Mongolian; staffing not clear, but presumably had several Academicians (*hsüeh-shih*); subordinate to the Hanlin and Historiography Academy (*han-lin hsüeh-yüan chien kuo-shih yüan*); in 1340 renamed Directorate for the Reverence of Literature (*ch'ung-wen chien*). P23.

3032 *ì-wén kuān* 譯文官

YÜAN: **Translator** for the Classics Colloquium (*ching-yen*). P24.

3033 *ì-yàng chú* 異樣局

YÜAN: **Service of Rare Textiles,** headed by a Superintendent (*t'i-tien*) from 1261 to 1269, thereafter by a Supervisor-in-chief (*tsung-kuan*), rank 3a; one of many manufacturing agencies under the Supervisorate-in-chief of Metal Workers and Jewelers (*chin-yü jen-chiang tsung-kuan fu*); in turn supervised 4 workshops: Service of Rare Embroideries (*i-yang wen-hsiu chü*), Brocade Weaving and Dyeing Service (*ling-chin chih-jan chü*), Gauze Service (*sha-lo chü*), and Chief Storehouse of Gauze, Gold, and Dyestuffs (*sha-chin yen-liao tsung-k'u*).

3034 *ì-yàng wén-hsiù chú* 異樣紋繡局

YÜAN: **Service of Rare Embroideries,** established in 1261, then in 1287 reorganized as a Supervisorate of Rare Embroideries (*i-yang wen-hsiu t'i-chü ssu*) with a Supervisor (*t'i-chü*), rank 5b; one of many manufacturing agencies under the Supervisorate-in-chief of Metal Workers and Jewelers (*chin-yü jen-chiang tsung-kuan fu*).

3035 *ì-yào t'í-chǔ ssū* 醫藥提舉司

MING: **Supervisorate of Medicines** in immediate predynastic times, but before 1367 reorganized into a Directorate of Imperial Medicine (*t'ai-i chü*), which in 1367 became the Imperial Academy of Medicine (*t'ai-i yüan*); originally headed by a Supervisor (*t'i-chü*), rank 5b. P36.

3036 *ì-yào t'í-lǐng sŏ* 醫藥提領所

YÜAN: **Superintendency of Medicine,** apparently a provincial-level agency; headed by a Superintendent (*t'i-ling*), rank 5a.

3037 *ì-yào yüàn* 醫藥院

YÜAN: **Academy of Moslem Medicine,** staffed with professional, probably hereditary Islamic physicians from Central Asia; headed by several Supervisors (*t'i-chü*), status and rank not clear; in 1293 reorganized into a Moslem Medical Office (*kuang-hui ssu*), still with Supervisors, rank lowered from 3a to 5a in 1320–1321, raised to 3a again in 1322–1323; under general authority of the Imperial Academy of Medicine (*t'ai-i yüan*).

3038 *ì-yén tào* 驛鹽道

CH'ING: **Transport and Salt Control Circuit,** the jurisdiction of a Circuit Intendant (*tao-t'ai*) nominally based in a provincial-level agency in Chekiang beginning in the K'ang-hsi (1662–1722) era; in areas other than Chekiang, the same dual functions of monitoring the state transport service and overseeing the production and distribution of state-monopolized salt were entrusted to Salt Control Circuits (*yen-fa tao*). See *tao*. P61.

3039 *ì-yù* 翼馭

T'ANG: **Groom,** 10 suboficial functionaries in the Stables Office (*chiu-mu ssu*) in the household of the Heir Apparent; responsible for training horses and guiding them on any excursion of the Heir Apparent. RR: *dresseur de chevaux.*

3040 *ì-yù láng* 醫愈郎

YÜAN: **Court Gentleman for Medical Healing,** prestige title (*san-kuan*) for rank 8b officials of the Imperial Academy of Medicine (*t'ai-i yüan*).

3041 *ì-yǔ t'ūng-shìh* 譯語通事

SUNG: **Interpreter-clerk,** number not clear, probably suboficial functionaries; members of the Office for Foreign Tribute Envoys (*ssu-i kung-feng shih ssu*). SP: *interprète-traducteur.*

3042 *ì-yüán* 醫員

CH'ING: **Apprentice Physician,** 30 Chinese; non-official specialists authorized for the Imperial Academy of Medicine (*t'ai-i yüan*) from 1729; salaried (see the variant *shih-liang i-yüan*). BH: assistant physician. P36.

3043 *jǎn-jén* 染人

CHOU: **Dyer,** 2 ranked as Junior Servicemen (*hsia-shih*), members of the Ministry of State (*t'ien-kuan*) in charge of the dyeing of silk and other textiles. CL: *teinturier.*

3044 *jǎn-shǔ* 染署

N-S DIV (Sung): **Dyeing Office,** new name of the earlier Bureau of Standards (*p'ing-chun*); headed by a Director (*ling*) under the Chamberlain for the Palace Revenues (*shao-fu*); supervised the dyeing of textiles and the buying and selling (of textiles only?) to stabilize prices in the marketplaces. P40.

3045 *jǎn-yüàn* 染院

SUNG: **Dyeing Service,** one of the workshops under the Directorate for Imperial Manufactories (*shao-fu chien*). SP: *teinturerie.*

3046 *jǎo-tièn léi* 繞殿雷

SUNG–CH'ING: lit., thunder in the winding hall: unofficial reference to those named on the pass-list of Metropolitan Graduates (*chin-shih*) posted after the Palace Examination (*tien-shih*), which terminated each cycle of civil service recruitment examinations: **Palace Examination Graduate.**

3047 *jèn* 任

HAN: **Imperial Princess,** a designation used only in the reign of Wang Mang (A.D. 9–23).

3048 *jén-chǔ* 人主

Lit., master of men: throughout history an indirect reference to a ruler: **King** in Chou, thereafter **Emperor.**

3049 *jén-pù* 人部

(1) SUI: **Census Bureau,** one of 5 principal units in the Ministry of Revenue (*min-pu, hu-pu*); created c. 605 by

renaming the previous Census Bureau (also *min-pu, hu-pu*); in charge of all census matters; headed by a Director (*lang*). P6. (2) CH'ING: unofficial reference to the **Ministry of Revenue** (*hu-pu*).

3050 *jén-shòu kūng-chiēn* 仁壽宮監
SUI–T'ANG: **Directorate of the Palace of Benevolence and Longevity,** in charge of the maintenance and management of the imperial summer resort in modern Shensi, not far from the dynastic capital, Ch'ang-an; headed by a Director-general (*tsung-chien*), rank 5b2. In 631 renamed *chiu-ch'eng kung-chien* (Directorate-general of the Palace of the Perfect Cycle). RR: *palais de la bonté et de la longévité.* P40.

3051 *jén-shù yüàn* 仁恕掾
HAN: lit., a functionary who is human-hearted and merciful: **Jailor** in charge of the prison (*yü*) maintained by some Commanderies (*chün*) in Later Han. HB: merciful official. P32.

3052 *jén-ts'áo* 人曹
T'ANG: **Census Section,** variant of *hu-pu* (Census Bureau), q.v.; subsequently an unofficial reference to the **Ministry of Revenue** (also *hu-pu*).

3053 *jén-ts'úng k'àn-hsiáng àn* 人從看詳案
SUNG: **Personnel Verification Section,** one of 10 Sections (*an*) established in 1129 as top-echelon agencies in the Ministry of War (*ping-pu*); headed by a Director (*lang-chung*), rank 6b; apparently supervised personnel administration in the military service. SP: *service d'examination.* P12.

3054 *jèn-tzŭ* 任子
Employment of Sons: throughout history, one of the important paths (*t'u;* see *cheng-t'u, i-t'u*) by which men entered government service; also known as Protection of Sons (*yin-tzu*). Practices varied, but the general principle was that on completing a probationary period in a middle- or higher-level office, an official earned the privilege of "protecting" one or more sons, i.e., opportunities for sons to enter service at ranks determined by the fathers' status, without having to earn eligibility, e.g., by passing recruitment examinations. This was an important aspect of recruitment through T'ang and only slightly less so in Sung, but after early Ming "employment of sons" became so low in prestige and career potentiality that men with the privilege often chose instead to compete for the more prestigious status offered by the recruitment examination system.

3055 *jìh-chě* 日者
N-S DIV (N. Wei): **Astrologer** on the staff of the Chamberlain for Ceremonials (*t'ai-ch'ang*), rank 7b2; functions not clear, but probably related to weather forecasting. P27.

3056 *jìh-chiăng ch'ĭ-chū chù kuăn*
日講起居注館
CH'ING: **Imperial Diary Office,** part of the Hanlin Academy (*han-lin yüan*); resulted from combining the functions of Lecturers (*chiang-kuan*) in the Classics Colloquium (*ching-yen*) with those of Imperial Diarists (see *ch'i-chü chu, ch'i-chü chu kuan*) in the early 1700s; staffed with officials temporarily detached from their regular posts in the Hanlin Academy and the Household Administration of the Heir Apparent (*chan-shih fu*), normally 8 Manchus and 12 Chinese; responsible for recording all that occurred in the Emperor's public life to provide source materials for later official historians. BH: office for keeping a diary of the emperor's movements. P24.

3057 *jìh-kuān* 日官
Astrologer on the staffs of rulers in antiquity; throughout imperial history an unofficial, archaic reference to astrological or astronomical officials such as the Grand Astrologer (*t'ai-shih ling*) of Han and the Director (*chien*) of the Ming–Ch'ing Directorate of Astronomy (*ch'in-t'ien chien*).

3058 *jìh-lì sŏ* 日曆所
SUNG: **Court Calendar Office,** normally headed by from one to 4 Editorial Directors (*chu-tso lang*), rank 7b, of the Palace Library (*pi-shu sheng*); responsible for taking reports from Imperial Diarists (*ch'i-chü chu*) and editing them into daily accounts of events at court that could subsequently be made into a *True Record* (*shih-lu*) of each reign and could also be used in the periodic preparation of histories of the dynasty (*kuo-shih*). See *kuo-shih shih-lu yüan, shih-kuan, pien-hsiu kuan.* SP: *office du calendrier.* P23.

3059 *jìh-shìh* 日時
HAN: **Sun Time Specialist,** a duty assignment for 3 Expectant Officials (*tai-chao*) on the staff of the Grand Astrologer (*t'ai-shih ling*). HB: expert in the phases of the sun.

3060 *jò-k'ù* 箬庫
N-S DIV (Liang–Ch'en): **Bamboo-leaf Storehouse** for the storage of broad bamboo leaves used in making mats, screens, fans, etc.; supervised by an Aide (*ch'eng*) to the Chamberlain for the National Treasury (*ssu-nung*). P8.

3061 *jò-lú yù* 若盧獄
HAN: lit. meaning not clear: **Central Prison,** one of several Later Han Imperial Prisons (*chao-yü*), with a eunuch Director (*ling*) under the Chamberlain for the Palace Revenues (*shao-fu*); reportedly used for the imprisonment and interrogation of imperial relatives by marriage and other dignitaries, also as a storehouse of military weapons and gear. Reported successor of the Ch'in dynasty *ling-wu* and antecedent of the San-kuo Wei *ssu-k'ung,* qq.v. HB: hunting dog prison. P13, 37.

3062 *jóu-yüăn ssū* 柔遠司
CH'ING: lit., office for being gracious to those afar: **Outer Mongolian Reception Bureau,** one of 6 Bureaus in the Court of Colonial Affairs (*li-fan yüan*), headed by a Manchu Director (*lang-chung*); handled the reception of Outer Mongolian chieftains, collected their tribute goods, and issued gifts for presentation to them at court. In the K'ang-hsi era (1622–1722) divided into a Front Office (*jou-yüan ch'ien-ssu*) and a Rear Office (*jou-yüan hou-ssu*); in 1757 the Front Office was restored as the Outer Mongolian Bureau and the Rear Office was split away to become a separate Inner Mongolian Bureau (*ch'i-chi ssu*). BH: department for receiving princes of Outer Mongolia. P17.

3063 *jú* 儒
(1) CHOU: **Moral Instructor,** one of 9 Unifying Agents (*liang;* also see *ou*) who oversaw clusters of feudal states under supervision of the Ministry of State (*t'ien-kuan*); studied and taught the people the moral and ritual Way (*tao*), thereby consolidating the power of the King over all the people in the feudal states. CL: *lettrée.* (2) CHOU–CH'ING: **Confucian** in both nounal and adjectival uses, referring to scholars (and scholar-officials) of a moralistic and ritualistic bent who considered themselves followers of Confucius.

3064 *jŭ-chēn* 女眞
CHIN: **Jurchen,** the most common Chinese transliteration of the tribal name of the northern aliens who established the Chin dynasty; sometimes used as a prefix to a title or agency name. See *nü-chen, nü-chih.*

3065 *jǔ-chíh* 女直
Common alternate romanization of *nü-chih* (**Jurchen**).

3066 *jù ch'ǐn-tièn hsiǎo-tǐ* 入寢殿小氐
CHIN: **Retainer in the Bedchamber,** 16 on the staff of the Palace Inspectorate-general (*tien-ch'ien tu tien-chien ssu*); in 1172 retitled Chief Steward (*feng-yü*). See *hsiao-ti*. Cf. *pu ju ch'in-tien hsiao-ti*. P38.

3067 *jú-hsüéh* 儒學
YÜAN–CH'ING: **Confucian School** for the preliminary training of young men, principally those hoping to become officials. In Yüan such schools were ordered established in all units of territorial administration down to the District (*hsien*) level, but in practice the educational establishment probably did not extend below the Prefecture (*chou*) level. In Ming and Ch'ing such schools were established at all levels down to the District and also in units of the military hierarchy down to the Guard (*wei*) level, alongside Military Schools (*wu-hsüeh*). Through these 3 dynastic periods, students in Confucian Schools were largely subsidized by the state. Each school was headed by an Instructor (*chiao-shou*). P49, 51.

3068 *jú-hsüéh t'í-chǔ* 儒學提擧
YÜAN–MING: **Supervisor of Confucian Schools,** rank 5a, established in each Province-level Branch Secretariat (*hsing chung-shu sheng*) but terminated during early Ming governmental reorganizations, not later than 1380; responsible for overseeing, encouraging, and checking the achievements of all local schools. P51.

3069 *jú-ì kuǎn* 如意館
CH'ING: lit., the as-one-pleases establishment: **Institute of Indulgences,** established in the Ch'ien-lung era (1736–1796) as a center within the palace where Court Painters (see *hua-shih*) and other kinds of artisans worked. Superseded the earlier Southern Study (*nan shu-fang*). Often referred to unofficially as the Painting Academy (*hua-yüan*).

3070 *jú-jén* 孺人
SUNG, CH'ING: **Child Nurturess,** title of honor awarded to the mothers and wives of both civil officials and military officers; in Ch'ing, 7th highest of 9 such titles, followed by *pa-p'in ju-jen* (Rank 8 Child Nurturess) and *chiu-p'in ju-jen* (Rank 9 Child Nurturess).

3071 *jú-kuān* 儒官
Confucian Official, collective term for officials of esteemed scholarly attainments or moral qualities; also, in Han, an unofficial reference to **Erudites** (*po-shih*). P34.

3072 *jù-liěn chīh-yìng* 入輦祇應
SUNG: **Carriage Attendant,** a eunuch post in the Palace Domestic Service (*nei-shih sheng*). SP: *palefrenier des voitures impériales*.

3073 *jú-lín chì-chiǔ* 儒林祭酒
N-S DIV (Chin, S. Dyn.): **Chancellor of Confucian Education,** in charge of schools in a Chin dynasty Commandery (*chün*) or a Ch'i dynasty Region (*chou*). See *chi-chiu*. P51.

3074 *jú-lín láng* 儒林郎
SUI–CH'ING: **Gentleman-Confucian,** prestige title (*san-kuan*) for civil officials of rank 9a1 from Sui through Sung, 7b2 in Chin, 6b from Yüan through Ch'ing. P68.

3075 *jú-lín ts'ān-chün* 儒林參軍
N-S DIV (S. Dyn.): **Administrator** of a School (*hsüeh, wen-hsüeh*) in a unit of territorial administration; apparently

of higher status than, e.g., a Chancellor (*chi-chiu*) in the educational hierarchy. P51.

3076 *jú-lào yüàn* 乳酪院
SUNG: **Milk Products Office,** a unit in the Court of Imperial Entertainments (*kuang-lu ssu*). SP: *cour de lait et de crème*.

3077 *jù-nèi* 入內
SUNG: lit., (one who) entered the inner apartments (of the palace): **Eunuch,** commonly used as a prefix to identify a eunuch agency or post until 1160; see *ju-nei nei-shih sheng*.

3078 *jù-nèi huáng-mén pān yüàn*
入內黃門班院
SUNG: variant designation of the **Palace Eunuch Service** (*ju-nei nei-shih sheng*). See *huang-men*.

3079 *jù-nèi nèi-pān yüàn* 入內內班院
SUNG: variant designation of the **Palace Eunuch Service** (*ju-nei nei-shih sheng*).

3080 *jù-nèi nèi-shìh shěng* 入內內侍省 or
ju-nei sheng
SUNG: **Palace Eunuch Service,** until 1160 a eunuch-staffed subsection of the generally non-eunuch Palace Domestic Service (*nei-shih sheng*) in which most palace eunuchs were organized, with titles such as *ju-nei kao-pan* (Palace Eunuch of Rank Five), *ju-nei kao-p'in* (Palace Eunuch of Rank Four), *ju-nei nei-p'in* (Palace Eunuch of Rank Seven), and *ju-nei hsiao huang-men* (Junior Palace Eunuch). Early in the dynasty (date of change not clear) the eunuch agency was named *nei-chung kao-p'in pan yüan*, and in 1160 the *ju-nei* nomenclature was abolished and the *nei-shih sheng* itself, as in pre-Sung times, became primarily a eunuch-staffed agency. SP: *département de l'intendance du palais intérieur*. P38.

3081 *jù-p'ǐn* 入品 or *jù-těng* 入等
T'ANG–SUNG: prefixed to a title when a post normally held by a subofficial functionary (*li*) was held by a regular ranked official (*kuan*); e.g., **Rank-classified** Master of Protocol (*ju-p'in chih-pan*). See *chih-pan*.

3082 *jú-t'úng* 儒童
MING–CH'ING: **Confucian Apprentice,** a young man who had some education but had not yet been authorized to enter a government school. See *t'ung-sheng, wen-t'ung*.

3083 *jú-tzǔ* 孺子
HAN: **Child-bearing Concubine,** one of several titles granted secondary wives of the Heir Apparent. HB: young lady.

3084 *juǎn-p'í chú* 軟皮局
YÜAN: **Soft Leather Service,** a manufacturing unit under the Directorate for Leather and Fur Manufactures (*li-yung chien*); worked with silver squirrel and other wild animal pelts of particularly fine coloring; staffed with non-official artisans. P38.

3085 *jùi-chǐn k'ō* 瑞錦窠
SUNG–CH'ING: lit., someone in a nest of finery (?): unofficial reference to a **Vice Director** (*yüan-wai lang*) of a Bureau (*ssu, ch'ing-li ssu*) in the Ministry of Rites (*lǐ-pu*).

3086 *jùn-wén kuān* 潤文官
SUNG: **Reviser,** title held concurrently by a Hanlin Academician (*han-lin hsüeh-shih*) assigned to give a literary gloss to government documents. SP: *fonctionnaire chargé d'embellir le style de traduction*.

3087 *júng-chèng t'īng* 戎政廳 or *júng-chèng fŭ* 府

MING: **Military Headquarters** for the Capital Training Divisions (*ching-ying*) at Peking; established in 1550 as a coordinating agency for the several Training Divisions; headed by a Superintendent (*t'i-tu*) or a Supreme Commander (*tsung-tu*).

3088 *júng-ch'īng* 容卿

T'ANG–CH'ING: lit., chief minister of elegance: unofficial reference to a **Minister of Rites** (*lĭ-pu shang-shu*). See *jung-t'ai*.

3089 *júng-huá* 容華

HAN–N-S DIV (San-kuo Wei): **Lady of Lovely Countenance,** one of several designations for imperial consorts; in Han rank =2,000 bushels.

3090 *júng-lù tà-fū* 榮祿大夫

CHIN–CH'ING: **Grand Master for Glorious Happiness,** prestige title (*san-kuan*) for civil officials of rank 2b2 in Chin, 1b thereafter. P68.

3091 *júng-p'ú* 戎僕

CHOU: **Royal Charioteer,** 2 ranked as Ordinary Grand Masters (*chung ta-fu*), members of the Ministry of War (*hsia-kuan*) specially assigned to drive the King's war chariot. CL: *conducteur du char de guerre.*

3092 *júng-ssū* 戎司

SUNG: **Military Office** of a Prefecture (*chou*), apparently responsible for organizing and training militiamen. SP: *bureau militaire.*

3093 *júng-t'ái* 容臺

Lit., pavilion of elegance: from Han-on, an unofficial reference to the **Chamberlain for Ceremonials** (*t'ai-ch'ang*) or the **Court of Imperial Sacrifices** (*t'ai-ch'ang ssu*) or the **Ministry of Rites** (*lĭ-pu*). See *jung-ch'ing.*

3094 *jŭng-ts'úng* 冗從

HAN–N-S DIV: **Supernumerary Follower,** a term attached to a normal title, either as prefix or suffix, granted to a member of the imperial family or the son of an eminent noble so as to legitimate his being part of the imperial entourage. HB: extra retinue. P19.

3095 *jŭng-ts'ūng p'ú-yèh* 冗從僕射

HAN–N-S DIV (S. Dyn.): **Supervisor of the Entourage,** a title awarded distinguished military officers; in Han ranked 600 bushels, leader of Supernumerary Followers (*jung-ts'ung*) who served as imperial bodyguards and escorts; in the S. Dynasties, referred to bodyguards of the Heir Apparent. See *p'u-yeh, t'ai-tzu p'u.* HB: supervisor of the extra retinue. P26.

3096 *júng-wèi* 戎衛

T'ANG: **Martial Guard,** from 662 to 671 a pair of military units, prefixed Left and Right, included among the Sixteen Guards (*shih-liu wei*) at the dynastic capital, temporarily superseding the Metropolitan Guards (*ling-chün wei*). P43.

3097 *júng-yù* 戎右

CHOU: **Chariot Defenseman,** 2 ranked as Ordinary Grand Masters (*chung ta-fu*) in the Ministry of War (*hsia-kuan*); responsible, one at a time, for riding at the right side of the ruler in his chariot during battles or hunts, wielding a lance to protect the ruler (in the center position) and the driver (on the ruler's left side); also transmitted the ruler's orders to the troops. CL: *homme de droite du char de guerre.*

3098 *k'ă-lún shìh-wèi* 卡倫侍衛

CH'ING: **Frontier Guardsmen,** designation of detachments of Imperial Guardsmen (*shih-wei*) stationed at strategic places on the northwestern frontier, modern Sinkiang.

3099 *k'āi-ch'āi àn* 開拆案

SUNG: **Mail Distribution Section,** found in many agencies of the central government for receiving or issuing routine communications among agencies; sometimes named Offices (*fang* or *ssu*). See *chu-shih fang, mo-k'an ssu.* SP: *service* (*chambre* in the case of *fang, bureau* in the case of *ssu*) *chargé d'ouvrir et d'expédier les dépêches.*

3100 *k'āi-chūng* 開中

MING: lit., to strike a balance, attain a happy medium: **Equitable Exchange of Grain for Salt,** from 1370 a practice whereby the government increased and (at least from its own viewpoint) facilitated the delivery of grain to military units posted on the northern frontier, where soil conditions made the effective development of Army Farms (*chün-t'un*) difficult if not impossible. The state transferred the burden of acquiring and delivering grain to the frontier onto the merchant class, by restricting trade in salt (a state monopoly) only to those merchants who made deliveries of grain at the frontier garrisons. For each unit of grain delivered, a merchant received a salt certificate worth a specified amount of salt, payable principally at state Salt Depots (*yen-ts'ang*) in the central coastal region of East China. Since salt distribution was highly profitable, and since transporting grain from the rich Yangtze delta area to the northern frontier was no easier for private merchants than for the government, enterprising merchants soon lured farmers into tenancy on Merchant Farms (*shang-t'un*) close behind the frontier garrisons, which produced the grain needed to obtain salt certificates. The system was an important element in Ming fiscal arrangements into the 1420s, after which the development of a state transport system based on the newly reconstructed Grand Canal, together with gradual resettlement and economic development in the northern provinces, made the Equitable Exchange less important; but it remained an element of the frontier supply system into the 1600s. The Ming system was inspired by, though not directly copied from, the Sung dynasty Equitable Exchange of Rice for Salt (*chung-yen;* also see *che-chung ts'ang*) instituted in the reign of Sung T'ai-tsung (976–997), involving state payments in salt for the delivery of rice to the capital.

3101 *k'āi-fān* 開藩

SUNG: lit., to open (a headquarters) in a frontier zone: **Regional Supervisor,** a general term referring to Military Commissioners (*chieh-tu shih*), Pacification Commissioners (*ch'eng-hsüan shih, hsüan-yü shih*), etc.

3102 *k'āi-fāng* 開坊

MING–CH'ING: lit., to break free of the Secretariat, referring to the Secretariat of the Heir Apparent (*ch'un-fang*); officials promoted out of the Secretariat commonly moved steadily into high ministerial posts in the central government, so that "breaking free of the Secretariat" was considered desirable.

3103 *k'āi-fŭ* 開府

Lit., to open an office, implying the creation of one's own staff. (1) HAN: **Executive,** an honorific title (*chia*) originally reserved for the Three Dukes (*san kung*), i.e., the Defender-in-chief (*t'ai-wei*), the Counselor-in-chief (*ch'eng-hsiang*), and the Censor-in-chief (*yü-shih ta-fu*). At the end of Han, when regional warlords became dominant, they also "opened offices" on the same basis as the Three Dukes, and gradually the honorific title was clarified by expansion into the term *k'ai-fu i-t'ung san-ssu* (Area Commander Unequalled in Honor; lit., opening an office and being equal in prestige to the Three Dignitaries). (2) N-S DIV: **Area Commander,** a usage derived from Han, signifying a relatively autonomous regional warlord. (3) N-S DIV–SUI: **Commander,** also deriving from Han usage but a more regular, specific title for a military officer, often one in command of an Army (*chün*). In the Garrison Militia (*fu-ping*) system of the last N. Dynasties and Sui, normally indicated the commander of an army of 2,000 or so men drawn from several neighboring Garrisons (*fu*). (4) CH'ING: **Area Commander,** unofficial reference to a Governor-general (*tsung-tu*) of several Provinces or a Provincial Governor (*hsün-fu*).

3104 *k'āi-fǔ chì-chiǔ* 開府祭酒
N-S DIV (N. Wei): **Junior Administrator** (?) on the staff of an Imperial Prince (*huang-tzu*), rank 6b; functions not clearly indicated. Cf. *k'ai-fu, chi-chiu.* P69.

3105 *k'āi-fǔ í-t'úng sān-ssū* 開府儀同三司
N-S DIV–YÜAN: **Commander Unequalled in Honor,** first an honorific title (*chia*) for eminent generals, then from Sui a prestige title (*san-kuan*) for both civil officials and military officers of rank 1b; 1a in Yüan. This tradition was terminated at the beginning of Ming. See under *k'ai-fu.*

3106 *k'āi-kuó* 開國
N-S DIV–SUNG: **Dynasty-founding ...,** prefix to titles of nobility (*chüeh*) signifying that the bearer (and, by extension, his heirs) were considered worthy and capable enough to found a dynasty of their own or, especially in Sung, that the original noble had played a major role in the founding of the reigning dynasty; e.g., *k'ai-kuo chün-kung* (Dynasty-founding Commandery Duke). P65.

3107 *k'āi-kuó chün-hóu* 開國郡侯
N-S DIV (S. Dyn.): **Dynasty-founding Commandery Marquis,** 9th (?) highest of 15 normal titles of nobility (*chüeh*), rank 3b. See *k'ai-kuo, chün-hou, hou, k'ai-kuo hou.* P65.

3108 *k'āi-kuó chün-kūng* 開國郡公
N-S DIV–SUNG: **Dynasty-founding Commandery Duke,** title of non-imperial nobility (*chüeh*); in T'ang, 4th highest of 9 noble ranks, 2a, with income allocated from the taxes on 2,000 households; in Sung, 7th highest of 12 noble ranks, 2a. See *k'ai-kuo, chün-kung, kung, k'ai-kuo kung.* RR: *duc de commanderie fondateur de principauté.* SP: *duc de préfecture de la fondation d'état.* P65.

3109 *k'āi-kuó chün-pó* 開國郡伯
N-S DIV (S. Dyn.): **Dynasty-founding Commandery Earl,** 12th (?) highest of 15 normal titles of nobility (*chüeh*), rank 4b. See *k'ai-kuo, chün-po, po, k'ai-kuo po.* P65.

3110 *k'āi-kuó hóu* 開國侯
N-S DIV (Chou), SUNG: **Dynasty-founding Marquis,** title of nobility (*chüeh*); in Sung, 9th highest of 12 noble ranks, 3b. See *k'ai-kuo, hou, kuo-hou.* SP: *marquis de la fondation d'état.* P65.

3111 *k'āi-kuó hsièn-hóu* 開國縣侯
N-S DIV, T'ANG: **Dynasty-founding District Marquis,** title of nobility (*chüeh*); in T'ang, 6th highest of 9 noble ranks, 3b, awarded to dignitaries not of the imperial family, with income allocated from the taxes on 1,000 households.

See *k'ai-kuo, hsien-hou, hou, kuo-hou, k'ai-kuo hou.* RR: *marquis de sous-préfecture fondateur de principauté.* P65.

3112 *k'āi-kuó hsièn-kūng* 開國縣公
N-S DIV–SUNG: **Dynasty-founding District Duke,** title of nobility (*chüeh*), rank 2b; in T'ang, 5th highest of 9 noble ranks, with income allocated from taxes on 1,500 households; in Sung, 8th highest of 12 noble ranks. See *k'ai-kuo, hsien-kung, kung, kuo-kung, k'ai-kuo kung.* RR: *duc de sous-préfecture fondateur de principauté.* SP: *duc de sous-préfecture de la fondation d'état.* P65.

3113 *k'āi-kuó hsièn-nán* 開國縣男
N-S DIV (N. Dyn.), T'ANG–5 DYN: **Dynasty-founding District Baron,** title of nobility (*chüeh*); in T'ang, the lowest of 9 noble ranks, 5b1, with income allocated from the taxes on 300 households. See *k'ai-kuo, hsien-nan, nan, k'ai-kuo nan.* RR: *baron de sous-préfecture fondateur de principauté.* P65.

3114 *k'āi-kuó hsièn-pó* 開國縣伯
N-S DIV, T'ANG–5 DYN: **Dynasty-founding District Earl,** title of nobility (*chüeh*); in T'ang, 7th highest of 9 noble ranks, 4a1, with income allocated from the taxes on 700 households. See *k'ai-kuo, hsien-po, po, k'ai-kuo po.* RR: *comte de sous-préfecture fondateur de principauté.* P65.

3115 *k'āi-kuó hsièn-tzǔ* 開國縣子
N-S DIV, T'ANG–5 DYN: **Dynasty-founding District Viscount,** title of nobility (*chüeh*); in T'ang, 8th highest of 9 noble ranks, 5a1, with income allocated from the taxes on 500 households. See *k'ai-kuo, hsien-tzu, tzu, k'ai-kuo tzu.* RR: *vicomte de sous-préfecture fondateur de principauté.* P65.

3116 *k'āi-kuó kūng* 開國公
N-S DIV (Chou), SUNG: **Dynasty-founding Duke,** title of nobility (*chüeh*); in Sung, 6th highest of 12 noble ranks, 1b. See *k'ai-kuo, kung, kuo-kung.* SP: *duc de la fondation d'état.* P65.

3117 *k'āi-kuó nán* 開國男
N-S DIV (S. Dyn., Chou), SUNG: **Dynasty-founding Baron,** title of nobility (*chüeh*); in Sung, the lowest of 12 noble ranks, 5b. See *k'ai-kuo, nan.* SP: *baron de la fondation d'état.* P65.

3118 *k'āi-kuó pó* 開國伯
N-S DIV (Chin, Chou), SUNG: **Dynasty-founding Earl,** title of nobility (*chüeh*); in Sung, 10th highest of 12 noble ranks, 4a. See *k'ai-kuo, po.* SP: *comte de la fondation d'état.* P65.

3119 *k'āi-kuó tzǔ* 開國子
N-S DIV (S. Dyn., Chou), SUNG: **Dynasty-founding Viscount,** title of nobility (*chüeh*); in Sung, 11th highest of 12 noble ranks, 5a. See *k'ai-kuo, tzu.* SP: *vicomte de la fondation d'état.* P65.

3120 *k'āi-pǎo t'ūng-lǐ* 開寶通禮
SUNG: **Metropolitan Graduate with Ritual Specialization,** one of several degrees awarded in the early Sung civil service recruitment examination system, deriving from an imperial compilation with the same name (*Comprehensive Rituals of the K'ai-pao Era*, i.e., 968–976), in which candidates could choose to be examined rather than, e.g., in classics or history or literary composition. SP: *docteur des rites de 973.*

3121 *k'āi-shū* 楷書
SUNG: **Clerkly Calligrapher,** designation of subofficial

functionaries found in many agencies of the central government, e.g., the Ministry of Personnel (*lì-pu*), the Court of the Imperial Clan (*tsung-cheng ssu*), and the Court of Judicial Review (*ta-li ssu*). SP: *copiste en écriture régulière.*

3122   *k'ǎi-shū láng* 楷書郎
SUI: **Clerkly Calligrapher,** 20, rank 9b, in the Palace Library (*pi-shu sheng*). P25.

3123   *k'ǎi-shū pó-shìh* 楷書博士
T'ANG: **Erudite of the Clerical Script,** 2 of 18 Palace Erudites (*nei-chiao po-shih*) on the staff of the Palace Institute of Literature (*nei wen-hsüeh kuan*), where palace women were educated; from c. 741, a eunuch post. RR: *maître de l'écriture régulière.*

3124   *k'ǎi-shū shǒu* 楷書手
T'ANG: **Clerkly Calligrapher,** 80 suboffical functionaries in the Palace Library (*pi-shu sheng*) and 4 in the Secretariat (*chung-shu sheng*) as clerical assistants to the Imperial Diarists (*ch'i-chü she-jen*). RR: *copiste à l'écriture régulièr°.* P24, 25.

3125   *k'ǎi-shū yüán* 楷書員
SUI: variant of *k'ai-shu lang* (**Clerkly Calligrapher**). P25.

3126   *k'ǎi-ts'áo* 鎧曹
T'ANG: **Armor Section,** responsible for insignia and weapons, one in each of the Sixteen Guards (*shih-liu wei*) of the Southern Command (*nan-ya*) at the dynastic capital, also in each Princely Establishment (*wang-fu*); headed by an Administrator (*tṣan-chün-shih*), rank 7b or 8a. Those in the Princely Establishments were abolished in the era 627–649. Those in the Sixteen Guards were renamed Helmets Sections (*chou-ts'ao*) c. 701, Armor Sections again in 705, then Helmets Sections again in 712. RR: *service des casques.* P43, 69.

3127   *kàn* 幹
HAN–N-S DIV: variant of *kan-shih* (**Administrative Clerk**).

3128   *kān-ch'éng* 甘丞
HAN: **Assistant for Sweets** to the Provisioner (*t'ai-kuan ling*) in the office of the Chamberlain for the Palace Revenues (*shao-fu*). P37.

3129   *kān-ch'üán chū-shìh* 甘泉居室
HAN: **Convict Barracks at Sweet Spring Mountain** (*kan-ch'üan shan*), administered by a Director (*ling*) under the Chamberlain for the Palace Revenues (*shao-fu*); apparently a place of detention for imperial relatives and other dignitaries, located in or near the detached summer retreat called the Sweet Spring Palace (*kan-ch'üan kung*) in modern Shensi. Name changed to *k'un-t'ai* (Pavilion of Kinsmen?) in 104 B.C. See *chü-shih.* HB: convict barracks of the palace of sweet springs. P37.

3130   *kān-ch'üán shàng-lín ch'éng* 甘泉上林丞
HAN: **Assistant for the Sweet Spring Palace** (*kan-ch'üan kung*) **and the Imperial Forest Park** (*shang-lin yüan*), apparently a subordinate of the Chamberlain for the Palace Revenues (*shao-fu*). The Sweet Spring Palace was an imperial summer resort at Kan-ch'üan shan (mountain), modern Shensi.

3131   *kān-ch'üán ts'āng* 甘泉倉
HAN: **Granary at the Sweet Spring Palace** (*kan-ch'üan kung*), a detached summer retreat at Kan-ch'üan shan (mountain), modern Shensi; managed by a Director (*chang*) under the Chamberlain for the National Treasury (*ta ssu-nung*). P8.

3132   *kān-ch'üán tū-shǔi chǎng* 甘泉都水長
HAN: **Director of Waterways at the Sweet Spring Palace** (*kan-ch'üan kung*), a detached summer resort at Kan-ch'üan shan (mountain), modern Shensi; a subordinate of the Directorate of Waterways (*tu-shui chang*), responsible for collecting taxes from fishermen at Kan-ch'üan. HB: chief director of waters at the palace of sweet springs.

3133   *kān-ch'üán wèi-wèi* 甘泉衛尉
HAN: **Garrison Commandant at the Sweet Spring Palace** (*kan-ch'üan kung*), a detached summer resort at Kan-ch'üan shan (mountain), modern Shensi; subordinate to the Chamberlain for the Palace Garrison (*wei-wei*). HB: commandant of the guards of the palace of sweet springs.

3134   *kàn-kuān chǎng* 幹官長
HAN–N-S DIV (Chin): **Chief Administrative Clerk** in units of territorial jurisdiction; *kan-kuan* was perhaps interchangeable with *kan* and *kan-shih.* HB: chief of the controlling office.

3135   *kàn-pàn kuān* 幹辦官 or *kan-pan*
SUNG–YÜAN: **Office Manager,** a suboffical functionary who served as a kind of chief clerk in the Armaments Office (*chün-ch'i so*) of the Ministry of Works (*kung-pu*), the headquarters of Fiscal Commissioners (*ṭhuan-yün shih*) and Judicial Commissioners (*ṭ'i-tien hsing-yü kung-shih*), and many other agencies. Used only briefly in Chin, then changed to *kou-tang kuan* (Manager). SP: *gérant, administrateur, régisseur.*

3136   *kàn-pàn kǔng-shìh* 幹辦公事
SUNG: **Administrator,** a suboffical functionary with police or judicial powers in the urban Townships (*hsiang*) into which the dynastic capital was divided for sub-District (*hsien*) administration; also found on the staffs of Military Commissioners (*chih-chih shih*), Pacification Commissioners (*hsüan-fu shih*), and various military units; also in the Stabilization Fund Bureau (*ch'ang-p'ing ssu*), part of the State Finance Commission (*san ssu*) of early Sung. SP: *chargé des affaires, chargé des affaires publiques, chargé de gérer les affaires publiques.*

3137   *kàn-pàn yǔ-tiéh sǒ tièn* 幹辦玉牒所殿
SUNG: **Building Administrator for the Imperial Genealogy Office** (*yü-tieh so*), 4 suboffical functionaries apparently serving as building custodians. SP: *administrateur de la salle du bureau de la généalogie impériale.*

3138   *kàn-shìh* 幹事
HAN–N-S DIV: **Administrative Clerk,** a minor suboffical functionary (likely a bondservant or slave) in a unit of territorial administration; sometimes, e.g., in charge of a Section (*ts'ao*) in a District (*hsien*) headquarters. Often lumped together with Junior Scribes (*hsiao-shih*) in general reference to lowly clerical functionaries. Commonly abbreviated to *kan.* Also see *miao-kan.* HB (*kan-hsiao-shih*): capable junior clerk. P32, 53, 54.

3139   *kàn-tāng kǔng-shìh* 幹當公事 or *kan-tang*
SUNG: **Administrator,** suboffical functionaries found in varying numbers in many agencies, e.g., the Capital Security Office (*huang-ch'eng ssu*), the headquarters of Pacification Commissioners (*an-fu shih*) and Supply Commissioners (*fa-yün shih*), the Ministry of Revenue (*hu-pu*), and the State Finance Commission (*san ssu*) of early Sung. Also see *kung-shih kan-tang kuan.* SP: *régisseur, administrateur, exécutif, régisseur-inspecteur.*

3140 *k'ān-chèng kuān* 刊正官 or *k'an-cheng*
T'ANG: **Copyreader,** suboffical functionary; 4 in the Academy of Heaven (*ch'ien-yüan yüan*), established 717, renamed Academy in the Hall of Elegance and Rectitude (*li-cheng tien hsiu-shu yüan*) in 718, renamed Academy of Scholarly Worthies (*chi-hsien tien shu-yüan*) in 725. RR: *correcteur rectificateur.*

3141 *k'àn-hó* 勘合
Lit., to compare and match: one of several terms used for **registered documents,** i.e., sheets of paper bearing official communications between agencies. Before issuing a supply of such sheets to an agency with which it regularly communicated, the issuing agency laid each sheet across a page in a stub-book that it retained and imprinted its official seal along the overlap. Thus, on receipt of a document, the original issuing agency could authenticate it by matching the 2 parts of its seal, one on the document received and one on a stub-book page. Sometimes rendered as tally. See *ho-t'ung.*

3142 *k'àn-pān* 看班
SUNG: **Apprentice,** one of several designations of on-the-job trainees in various government agencies, e.g., *ko-men k'an-pan chih-hou* (Apprentice Audience Attendant). SP: *stagiaire.*

3143 *kǎo-jén* 橐人
CHOU: **Banquet Caterer,** 8 eunuchs attached to the Ministry of Education (*ti-kuan*) who prepared banquets celebrating victorious military officers and foods offered in various state ceremonies. CL: *officier des rations de récompense.*

3144 *kāo-pān* 高班
See *nei-shih kao-pan* (**Eunuch of the High Duty Group**).

3145 *kāo-p'ǐn* 高品
See *nei-shih kao-p'in* (**Eunuch of High Rank**).

3146 *kào-shēn* 告身
T'ANG–SUNG: **Appointment Certificate,** appointment-verification documents issued to new appointees or reappointees by the Ministry of Personnel (*li-pu*) and until c. 1080 by the Ministry of War (*ping-pu*). See *kuan-kao chü.* SP: *titre des nominations.*

3147 *kāo-tì* 高第
Customs Collector: common reference to an official assigned to collect fees at a customs barrier or marketplace.

3148 *k'ǎo* 考
Merit rating: from T'ang on and perhaps earlier, an evaluation of an official's performance written by his immediate administrative superior and accumulated by the central government's Ministry of Personnel (*li-pu*) pending triennial determinations about promoting, retaining in rank, or demoting officials; ratings were usually prepared annually. In Ming and perhaps other times, *k'ao* was also used to refer to a 3-year term of appointment, so that when an official survived 3 triennial evaluations it was said that his merit ratings were completed or fulfilled (see *k'ao-man*), and his appointment terminated. See *sui-chi, wai-ch'a, ching-ch'a, yüeh-chi, chu-k'ao.*

3149 *k'ǎo-ch'á* 考察
MING: **Evaluation** of officials on duty in provincial and lower units of territorial administration, irregularly prepared by touring Censors (*yü-shih*), especially by Regional Inspectors (*hsün-an yü-shih*) delegated to each Province from the Censorate (*tu ch'a-yüan*) on annual tours. These cen-

sorial evaluations supplemented the annual merit ratings (*k'ao*) prepared for each official by his immediate superior, broadening the range of opinion available when an official was being considered for promotion, demotion, etc.

3150 *k'ǎo-hsüǎn k'ō* 考選科
YÜAN: **Evaluations and Selections Section,** one of 3 functionally differentiated Sections (*k'o*) in the Ministry of Personnel (*li-pu*), handling promotions, demotions, etc., of both civil officials and military officers in both the central government and units of territorial administration; for routine administrative work headed by a Clerk (*ling-shih*), unranked. Comparable to the Bureau of Personnel (*li-pu ssu*), Bureau of Appointments (*wen-hsüan ssu*), and Bureau of Evaluations (*k'ao-kung ssu*) of earlier and later times. P5.

3151 *k'ǎo-k'ō chīng-ch'áo-kuān yüàn* 考課京朝官院
SUNG: **Office for the Evaluation of Capital and Court Officials,** part of the Ministry of Personnel (*li-pu*); apparently an ad hoc gathering of Ministry personnel, Censors (*yü-shih*), and others to rate the performances in office of the highest-ranking officials and recommend their promotion, retention in office, demotion, or dismissal from service. SP: *cour du contrôle des fonctionnaires de la capitale et de la cour.*

3152 *k'ǎo-k'ò ssū* 考課司
SUNG: **Bureau of Evaluations,** a unit of the Censorate (*yü-shih t'ai*) that accumulated censorial evaluations of active officials and collaborated with the Ministry of Personnel (*li-pu*) at intervals in determining which officials should be promoted, which retained in rank, which demoted, etc. SP: *bureau du contrôle des hauts fonctionnaires de province.*

3153 *k'ǎo-k'ò yüàn* 考課院
SUNG: **Bureau of Personnel Assignments,** from c. 990 to 1072 a rather autonomous agency staffed by central government dignitaries on ad hoc duty assignments, charged with evaluating and reassigning lower-ranking officials on duty outside the capital; in 1072 this function was given to the Ministry of Personnel (*li-pu*). Cf. *shen-kuan yüan.* SP: *cour d'examen des mérites.* P5.

3154 *k'ǎo-kuān* 考官
T'ANG–CH'ING: **Examining Official,** a generic reference to officials detached from their regular posts on duty assignments to supervise examinations in the civil service recruitment examination sequence.

3155 *k'ǎo-kūng chiēn* 孝功監
MING: **Directorate of Personnel Evaluation,** from 1375 to 1385 an autonomous agency of the central government reportedly established to assist in drafting imperial rescripts and edicts (?) but apparently to manage personnel administration, in an imperial effort to diminish the influence of the Secretariat (*chung-shu sheng*) and Ministry of Personnel (*li-pu*); headed by a Director (*ling*), rank 6a then 7a.

3156 *k'ǎo-kūng ch'īng-lì ssū* 考功清吏司
MING–CH'ING: **Bureau of Evaluations,** a major unit in the Ministry of Personnel (*li-pu*), responsible for maintaining personnel records for the whole civil service pending decisions on promotions, demotions, retentions in office, dismissals from service, etc. Headed by a Director (*lang-chung*), rank 5a; in Ch'ing one Chinese and 3 Manchu appointees. Commonly abbreviated to *k'ao-kung ssu.* BH: department of scrutiny (in the ministry). P5.

3157 *k'ǎo-kūng shìh* 攷工室 or *k'ao-kung*
HAN: **Imperial Workshop** headed by a Director (*ling*), in Former Han apparently produced equipment for palace use under supervision of the Chamberlain for the Palace Revenues (*shao-fu*); in Later Han apparently produced weapons under supervision of the Chamberlain for the Imperial Stud (*t'ai-p'u*). HB: complete workman office, complete workshop. P37.

3158 *k'ǎo-kūng sǒ* 考功所
MING: **Office of Personnel Evaluation,** a unit in the predynastic Secretariat (*chung-shu sheng*), established in 1364 to coordinate the rating of officials in preparation for promoting, demoting, etc.; headed by a Director (*lang*), rank 7a; terminated in 1368, soon replaced by the Bureau of Evaluations (*k'ao-kung ch'ing-li ssu*) in the Ministry of Personnel (*li-pu*). P4.

3159 *k'ǎo-kūng ssū* 考功司 or *k'ao-kung*
(1) N-S DIV (San-kuo Wei)–SUNG: **Bureau of Evaluations,** through the era of N-S Division evolved from a Section (*ts'ao*) of the developing Department of State Affairs (*shang-shu sheng*) into a Bureau (*ssu*) in a fully organized Ministry of Personnel (*li-pu*); responsible for maintaining personnel records on all officials pending decisions on promotions, demotions, retentions in office, dismissals from service, etc. Originally headed by a Court Gentleman for Evaluations (*k'ao-kung lang*), rank 4; in Sui by a Vice Minister (*shih-lang*); thereafter by a Director (*lang-chung*), 5b in T'ang, 6b in Sung. In Ming renamed *k'ao-kung ch'ing-li ssu*. RR+SP: *bureau de l'examen des mérites.* P5. (2) MING–CH'ING: abbreviation of *k'ao-kung ch'ing-li ssu* (also **Bureau of Evaluations**).

3160 *k'ǎo-mǎn* 考滿
MING: lit., **ratings fulfilled** or completed, signifying that an official had remained in a post through 3 triennial merit ratings (*k'ao*), i.e., for a total of 9 years, and that he was relieved of his duties and expected to report to the Ministry of Personnel (*li-pu*) for possible reassignment.

3161 *k'ǎo-shìh* 考試
T'ANG: **Placement Examination** given qualified men applying for appointment or reassignment, emphasizing their appearance, mannerisms, and professional capabilities; administered by the Ministry of Personnel (*li-pu*).

3162 *ke*
See under the romanization *ko*.

3163 *k'e*
See under the romanization *k'o*.

3164 *kēng-jén* 更人
SUNG: **Night Watchman,** a patroller who called out changes (*keng*) in the watch; provided in urban settings by members of sub-District (*hsien*) self-government organizations.

3165 *kēng-shù* 更戍
SUNG: **Changing the Frontier Guards,** a system relied on in early Sung to staff military garrisons in frontier zones, by dispatching both officers and soldiers in rotational shifts, normally at 3-year intervals, from units of the Imperial Armies (*chin-chün*) stationed in or around the dynastic capital, Kaifeng, to active duty posts in Defense Commands (*chen*) in strategic areas. An advantage of the system from the central government's viewpoint was that it mingled officers and soldiers who had no prior or future personal affiliations that might lead to regional warlordism. It was claimed, however, that the result was low morale and poor leadership in the field. In 1074 the system was discontin-

ued. It was replaced with a network of permanent garrisons, ideally with about 3,000 soldiers each, established in all strategic places, each under the control of a permanently assigned Area General (*chiang*) who was responsible for training his professional career soldiers and, as necessary, leading them in battle. Such garrisons quickly totaled 92. The Area Generals were commonly called Circuit Generals (*lu-chiang*) and were apparently prefixed with the names of the Circuits (*lu*) in which their garrisons were located; but the number of such garrisons far exceeded that of the normal Sung administrative realms called Circuits, so that, e.g., the Ho-pei Circuit included the garrisons of 17 Area Generals. The Area Generals were under the supervisory jurisdiction of the Bureau of Military Affairs (*shu-mi yüan*); their organizational relationship with various Circuit authorities (see *chien-ssu*) is not clear. The system of Area Generals naturally changed when Sung had to withdraw into the South, but the principle remained dominant in S. Sung times. See *yü-ch'ien chün* (Palace Armies). Cf. *fan, pan-chün.*

3166 *k'ēng-yěh ssū* 坑冶司
SUNG: **Foundry,** a local agency probably staffed with nonofficial technicians, under direction of the Ministry of Works (*kung-pu*) and probably subject to the immediate supervision of Supervisors of Foundries (*t'i-chü k'eng-yeh ssu*). SP: *bureau de fonderie.*

3167 *kó* 閣
Hall: throughout history, one of the terms used to designate buildings in the palace; often used for storage of books and other valuables, or as offices for litterateurs doing literary or editorial work for the ruler. Normally given auspicious prefixes, e.g., Hall of Profound Erudition (*wen-yüan ko*). See *nei-ko.*

3168 *kó-chǎng* 閣長
CH'ING: unofficial reference to a **Reader-in-waiting** (*shih-tu*) on the staff of the Grand Secretariat (*nei-ko*).

3169 *kō-chǐ ssū* 戈戟司
CH'ING: **Spears Office,** one of 8 units comprising the Rear Subsection (*hou-so*) of the Imperial Procession Guard (*luan-i wei*); headed by a Director (*chang-yin yün-hui shih*), rank 4a. BH: spear section.

3170 *kó-chíh* 閣職
SUNG: **Audience Steward,** generic reference to Audience Attendants (*hsüan-tsan she-jen*) and Audience Ushers (*ko-men chih-hou*).

3171 *kó-hsüéh* 閣學
MING–CH'ING: abbreviated reference to a **Grand Secretary** (*ta hsüeh-shih*) in Ming, an **Academician of the Grand Secretariat** (*nei-ko hsüeh-shih*) in Ch'ing. P2.

3172 *kó-kó* 格格
CH'ING: **Imperial Clanswoman,** unofficial general reference to any daughter of a male noble descended from an Emperor through not more than 6 generations, including all women entitled Commandery Princess (*chün-chu*), District Princess (*hsien-chu*), Commandery Mistress (*chün-chün*), District Mistress (*hsien-chün*), and Township Mistress (*hsiang-chün*).

3173 *kō-kūng* 歌工
CH'ING: **Singer,** 98 authorized for the Music Office (*chiao-fang ssu*) of the Ministry of Rites (*li-pu*). P10.

3174 *kó-lǎo* 閣老
Lit., oldster of the imperial hall. (1) T'ANG–SUNG: unofficial reference to **Secretariat Drafters** (*chung-shu she-*

jen) and **Supervising Secretaries** (*chi-shih-chung*) or even more senior members of the Chancellery (*men-hsia sheng*) and the Secretariat (*chung-shu sheng*), used especially in direct address among themselves. RR: *doyen d'âge du bureau*. (2) MING–CH'ING: unofficial reference to a **Grand Secretary** (*ta hsüeh-shih*).

3175   *kó-mén* 閣門
T'ANG: **Memorial Reception Staff,** various officials assigned on an ad hoc basis to position themselves at the east and west gates into the palace at audiences, and to collect all memorials submitted either from central government agencies or units of territorial administration; in late T'ang the function was taken over by palace eunuchs. See *tung-shang ko-men, hsi-shang ko-men*. P21.

3176   *kó-mén chīh-hòu* 閣門祇候
SUNG: **Audience Usher,** rank 8b, member of the Office for Audience Ceremonies (*ko-men ssu*). SP: *huissier audiencier des cérémonies d'audience*. P33.

3177   *kó-mén hsüān-tsàn shè-jén* 閣門宣贊舍人
SUNG: **Audience Attendant,** 10, rank 7b, members of the Office for Audience Ceremonies (*ko-men ssu*); originally titled *t'ung-shih she-jen*, retitled in 1116; responsible for tutoring visitors in audience behavior, introducing them in audience, and proclaiming imperial edicts in audience. SP: *introducteur des visiteurs et des affaires aux audiences*. P33.

3178   *kó-mén shè* 閣門舍
SUNG: **Audience Guide,** 10 subofficial functionaries attached to the Office for Audience Ceremonies (*ko-men ssu*). SP: *chargé des cérémonies du palais*. P33.

3179   *kó-mén shè-jén* 閣門舍人
SUNG: abbreviation of *ko-men hsüan-tsan she-jèn* (**Audience Attendant**) or *ko-men t'ung-shih she-jen* (**Secretarial Receptionist**). SP: *introducteur des visites*. P33.

3180   *kó-mén ssū* 閣門司
SUNG, CHIN: **Office for Audience Ceremonies,** headed by a central government dignitary on duty assignment as Commissioner (*shih*); in Sung under the Chancellery (*men-hsia sheng*), in Chin under the Court Ceremonial Institute (*hsüan-hui yüan*); responsible for presenting at audience all foreign envoys, but to some extent retained the older function of collecting memorials being submitted. See *ko-men*. SP: *bureau des affaires d'audience*. P33.

3181   *kó-mén t'ūng-shìh shè-jén* 閣門通事舍人
SUNG: **Secretarial Receptionist,** 10, rank 7b, members of the Office for Audience Ceremonies (*ko-men ssu*); in 1116 retitled *ko-men hsüan-tsan she-jen*. Also see *t'ung-shih she-jen*. SP: *introducteur des visiteurs et des affaires aux audiences*. P33.

3182   *kó-shīh* 閣師
CH'ING: **Secretariat Mentor,** a reference to Grand Secretaries (*ta hsüeh-shih*) used in direct address, especially by junior members of the Hanlin Academy (*han-lin yüan*).

3183   *kó-shìh* 閣試
SUNG: **Palace Examination,** the first of 2 levels of examinations given nominees in the Special Recruitment process (see *chih-chü*), the 2nd level being an Imperial Examination (*yü-shih*).

3184   *kō-shīh-hā* 戈什哈 or *ko-shih*
CH'ING: Chinese transcription of a Manchu word meaning

Personal Guard, used in reference to soldiers or military officers assigned as intimate bodyguards of the Emperor and, in addition, of Governors-general (*tsung-tu*), Provincial Governors (*hsün-fu*), Generals (*chiang-chün*), Regional Commanders (*tsung-ping*), and other such high officials.

3185   *kó-shuài* 閣帥
T'ANG: **Chief Eunuch,** 6 in the Domestic Service of the Heir Apparent (*t'ai-tzu nei-fang chü*). RR: *chef des eunuques du palais intérieur de l'héritier du trône*.

3186   *k'ò* 客
CHOU: **Visitor,** designation of a member of the retinue of a Feudal Lord (*chu-hou*) or an alien tribal chief visiting at the royal court, or to a diplomatic representative of such a dignitary; differentiated from *pin* (Guest), a designation reserved for visiting Feudal Lords or comparable dignitaries themselves. Also see *chu-k'o*. CL: *officier d'un prince (en visite)*.

3187   *k'ō* 科
(1) SUNG–CH'ING: **Section** or **Subsection,** common designation of subordinate units within an agency, normally at the 2nd or 3rd level in an organizational hierarchy; e.g., a Section subordinate to a Bureau (*ssu*) in a Ministry (*pu*). (2) MING–CH'ING: **Office of Scrutiny,** common designation of 6 groups in which *chi-shih-chung* (Supervising Secretaries, Supervising Censors) were organized, paralleling but not subordinate to the Six Ministries (*liu pu*) of the central government; primarily charged with receiving imperial pronouncements, distributing them to appropriate Ministries for action, and monitoring the resulting action. Also see *liu k'o* (Six Offices of Scrutiny), *k'o-tao* (Offices of Scrutiny and Circuits). (3) CH'ING: groups or categories to which passers of Provincial Examinations (*hsiang-shih*) in the civil service recruitment examination sequence were assigned on the basis of their excellence, hence an indirect general reference to all **Provincial Graduates** (*chü-jen*).

3188   *k'ō-chǎng* 科長
CH'ING: **Section Chief,** common designation of heads of Sections (*k'o*) in various agencies.

3189   *k'ò-chī yüàn* 課績院
SUNG: abbreviation of *chuan-yün shih-fu t'i-tien hsing-yü k'o-chi yüan* (**Circuit Intendants Evaluation Bureau**). SP: *bureau de mérite*.

3190   *k'ō-chiǎ* 科甲
CH'ING: **Examination Graduates,** a collective term referring to Provincial Graduates (*chü-jen*) and Metropolitan Graduates (*chin-shih*) in the civil service recruitment examination sequence; *k'o* was an indirect reference to Provincial Graduates, *chia* to Metropolitan Graduates.

3191   *k'ō-chiǎ ch'ū-shēn* 科甲出身
CH'ING: **Official by Examination,** descriptive term signifying that one had entered the civil service (*ch'u-shen*) with status as either a Provincial Graduate (*chü-jen, k'o*) or a Metropolitan Graduate (*chin-shih, chia*).

3192   *k'ò-ch'īng* 客卿
T'ANG–CH'ING: **Chief Minister for Visitors,** unofficial reference to the Chief Minister (*ch'ing*) of the Court of State Ceremonial (*hung-lu ssu*).

3193   *k'ō-chǔ* 科舉
T'ANG–CH'ING: **Recruitment by Examination** or **Regular Recruitment** via regularly scheduled civil service recruitment examinations, as distinguished from Special Re-

cruitment (*chih-chü*) via irregular Special Examinations (*chih-k'o*) conducted in response to special imperial decrees.

3194   *k'ò-kuān* 客館
N-S DIV (San-kuo Wei, Ch'i): lit., a hostel for visitors: **Visitors Bureau,** a redesignation of the Han dynasty Messenger Office (*ta-hsing*), subordinate to the Chamberlain for Dependencies (*ta hung-lu*); headed by a Director (*ling*); responsible for tending to the needs of envoys from foreign chiefs. This function was subsequently carried out by such agencies as the Bureau of Receptions (*tien-k'o kuan*), the Office of Receptions (*tien-k'o shu*), the Directorate of Receptions (*tien-k'o chien*), the Bureau of Receptions (*chu-k'o*), etc.

3195   *k'ò-kūng láng-chūng* 課功郎中
N-S DIV (N. Ch'i): **Court Gentleman for Personnel Evaluations,** a member of the evolving Ministry of Personnel (*li-pu*) in the Department of State Affairs (*shang-shu sheng*); examined nominations of potential officials submitted by regional and local authorities, then made his recommendations for appointment. His functions later became more regularized in the Ministry of Personnel's Bureau of Evaluations (*k'ao-kung ssu*). Also see under *lang-chung*.

3196   *k'ò-lì k'ō* 課利科
SUNG: **Wine Tax Subsection,** one of 3 Subsections in the Left Section (*tso-ts'ao*) of the Ministry of Revenue (*hu-pú*) from c. 1080, when the Ministry was fully activated following discontinuance of the State Finance Commission (*san ssu*) of early Sung; staffed with subofficial functionaries (*li*); monitored the taxing of state-monopolized wine and perhaps some other kinds of trade commodities. SP: *section des taxes de vin*. P6.

3197   *k'ò-lì ssū* 課利司
SUNG: **Merchant Tax Office,** an agency subordinate to the State Finance Commission (*san ssu*) of early Sung; staffing and more specific organizational affiliation not clear, but likely a variant designation of the Merchant Tax Section (*shang-shui an*) in the Salt and Iron Monopoly Bureau (*yen-t'ieh ssu*). SP: *bureau de recette des taxes des temples et des boutiques dans la capitale*.

3198   *k'ò-lò-mù-ěrh-ch'í* 克埒穆爾齊
YÜAN: transliteration of a Mongolian word: **Interpreter-clerk,** designation of subofficial functionaries found in all Ministries (*pu*), the Bureau of Military Affairs (*shu-mi yüan*), the Censorate (*yü-shih t'ai*), and other agencies at the dynastic capital. See *t'ung-shih* (Interpreter-clerk).

3199   *k'ò-lòu* 刻漏
See entries beginning *lou-k'o*, for which this is a common variant.

3200   *k'ò-shěng* 客省
T'ANG–CHIN: **Visitors Bureau:** from late T'ang, normally a unit subordinate to the Secretariat (*chung-shu sheng*), in charge of welcoming foreign envoys and arranging for them to have court audiences, presumably collaborating with the Palace Visitors Bureau (*nei k'o-sheng*) of the Palace Eunuch Service (*ju-nei nei-shih sheng*) and the Court of State Ceremonial (*hung-lu ssu*); headed by one or 2 Commissioners (*shih*), rank 5b in Sung, 5a in Chin. Supervised the Hostel for Tributary Envoys (*ssu-fang kuan*). SP: *bureau des visites, des audiences et des contributions des étrangers*. P11.

3201   *k'ō-tào* 科道
MING–CH'ING: **Supervising Secretaries and Censors,**

an abbreviated collective reference to Supervising Secretaries (*chi-shih-chung*), who were organized in Offices of Scrutiny (*k'o*), and Investigating Censors (*chien-ch'a yü-shih*), who were organized in Circuits (*tao*). Supervising Secretaries and Investigating Censors collaborated in many investigative activities.

3202   *k'ò-tì ts'áo* 課第曹
N-S DIV (San-kuo Wei): **Evaluations Section,** one of several Sections among which the personnel of the Censorate (*yü-shih t'ai*) were distributed; shared in the process of evaluating officials. P18.

3203   *k'ò-ts'ān* 科參
MING–CH'ING: lit., intervention by an Office of Scrutiny (*k'o*): one of several terms referring to the normal requirement that Supervising Secretaries (*chi-shih-chung*) of the Offices of Scrutiny monitor the flow of documents to and from the throne and "veto" any document, whatever its origin, that they deemed improper either in style and form or in substance. See *feng-po*.

3204   *k'ò-ts'áo* 客曹
HAN: variant of *chu-k'o ts'ao* (**Section for Receptions**), a unit in the Imperial Secretariat (*shang-shu t'ai*). Also see *nan chu-k'o ts'ao, pei chu-k'o ts'ao*. HB: bureau of guests.

3205   *kǒu-chiēn* 狗監
HAN: **Directorate of the Palace Kennels,** in charge of breeding and caring for imperial hunting dogs; headed by a Director (*chien*) under the Chamberlain for the Palace Revenues (*shao-fu*). HB: inspector of kennels. P37.

3206   *kǒu-fáng* 狗坊
T'ANG: **Dog Cage,** one of the Five Cages (*wu fang*) where birds and animals used in imperial hunts were cared for under supervision of the Commissioner of the Imperial Stables (*hsien-chiu shih*) in the Palace Administration (*tien-chung sheng*); headed by a Chief Steward (*feng-yü*). P38.

3207   *kǒu-fáng* 狗房
CH'ING: **Imperial Kennels,** charged with breeding and caring for dogs used in imperial hunts; part of the Office of the Imperial Hunt (*tu-yü ssu*) in the Imperial Household Department (*nei-wu fu*). P37.

3208   *kōu-fù kuān* 勾覆官
SUNG: **Investigator** (?), 4 on the staff of the State Finance Commission (*san ssu*) of early Sung and one on the staff of each of its 3 constituent Bureaus (*ssu*). Functions and ranks not clear. SP: *fonctionnaire chargé du contrôle des enquêtes*.

3209   *kōu-fù lǐ-ch'ièn p'íng-yú àn* 勾覆理欠憑由案
SUNG: **Investigation Section for Certificates and Fees** (?) in the Bureau of Review (*pi-pu*) of the Ministry of Justice (*hsing-pu*); functions and staffing not clear. SP: *service du contrôle des certificats de redevances*.

3210   *kōu-hó ssū* 溝河司
SUNG: **Waterways Office,** presumably responsible for supervising dredging, etc.; staffing and organizational relationships not clear, but likely subordinate to either the Ministry of Works (*kung-pu*) or the Directorate of Waterways (*tu-shui chien*). SP: *bureau chargé de draguer les égouts et les rivières*.

3211   *kōu-hsiāo fáng* 勾銷房
SUNG: **Cancellations Office** in the Secretariat (*chung-shu sheng*); staffing and functions not clear. SP: *chambre d'annulation*.

3212 *kōu-kuǎn* 勾管
SUNG: **Manager,** common title for relatively low-ranking officials who were normally in charge of minor governmental agencies such as storehouses (*k'u*); perhaps interchangeable with *kuan-kou*, q.v.; sometimes might refer to subofficial functionaries. SP: *régisseur*.

3213 *kōu-pù ssū* 勾簿司
SUNG: **Accounting Office** in the State Finance Commission (*san ssu*) of early Sung; staffing and function not clear. SP: *bureau du contrôle des cahiers de compte*.

3214 *kōu-tàng kuān* 勾當官 or *kou-tang*
SUI–CHIN: **Manager,** a term used in the sense "to take office as …," often signifying a quasi-regular appointment taken in addition to one's regular position; e.g., *kou-tang yü-yao yüan* (Manager of the Imperial Dispensary), *chu-mu wu kou-tang kuan* (Manager of the Bamboo and Lumber Service). SP: *administrateur, régisseur, contrôleur*.

3215 *kōu-tàng kūng-shìh kuān* 勾當公事官
SUNG: **Office Manager** on the staff of the State Finance Commission (*san ssu*) of early Sung, the Court of the Imperial Granaries (*ssu-nung ssu*), a Supply Commission (*fa-yün ssu*), etc. SP: *vérificateur-contrôleur*.

3216 *kōu-tàng sān-pān yüàn* 勾當三班院
SUNG: **Manager of the Bureau of Lesser Military Assignments** (*san-pan yüan*) in the Ministry of Personnel (*li-pu*). SP: *administrateur du bureau des nominations militaires*.

3217 *kōu-tsò ssū* 勾鑿司
SUNG: **Accounting Office** subordinate to the State Finance Commission (*san ssu*) of early Sung. SP: *bureau de la vérification des comptes*.

3218 *kōu-tùn shǔ* 鈎盾署 or *kou-tun*
HAN–CHIN: lit. meaning not clear: **Office of Imperial Parks Products,** responsible for providing the imperial household and the court with firewood, lumber, water birds, etc., from the imperial parks and gardens; in early history often staffed with eunuchs; headed by one or more Directors (*chien*, rank 600 bushels, in Han; *ling*, rank 8a, in T'ang); subordinate to the Chamberlain for the Palace Revenues (*shao-fu*) in Han, the Court of the Imperial Granaries (*ssu-nung ssu*) in T'ang and Sung. In 1192 reorganized by Chin into a Provisions Office (*tien-chi shu*), with no direct concern for any imperial parks, under the Directorate of the Imperial Treasury (*t'ai-fu chien*). HB (*kou-shun*): intendant of the imperial palace gardens. RR+SP: *office des produits recueillis dans les marécages et dans les bois*. P37, 38.

3219 *kōu-yā kuān* 勾押官
SUNG: **Administrative Clerk,** a category of subofficial functionaries found in many agencies, e.g., the Court of Palace Attendants (*hsüan-hui yüan*), Herds Offices (*ch'ün-mu ssu*). SP: *régisseur*.

3220 *kōu-yüàn p'àn-kuān* 勾院判官
SUNG: **Comptroller,** one in each of the 3 agencies that constituted the State Finance Commission (*san ssu*) of early Sung. Also see *p'an-kuan*. SP: *contrôleur des comptes*.

3221 *k'ǒu-pěi tào* 口北道
CH'ING: lit., circuit north of the passes: **Intendant for Chahar,** a representative of the Governor-general (*tsung-tu*) of the Metropolitan Area (*chih-li*) based at Hsüan-hua Prefecture (*fu*), with specific responsibility for dealing with the Mongols of Chahar. See *tao, tao-t'ai*.

3222 *kū* 孤
CHOU: **Solitaries:** collective reference to all Ministers (*ch'ing*) at the royal court and in the service of Feudal Lords (*chu-hou*). See *san ku* (Three Solitaries). CL: *vice-conseiller, ministre*.

3223 *kǔ* 瞽
CHOU: **Blind Musician** in the office of the Music Master (*ta-shih*) in the Ministry of Rites (*ch'un-kuan*), divided into 3 classes: Senior (*shang*), 40; Ordinary (*chung*), 100; Junior (*hsia*), 100. CL: *aveugle*.

3224 *kǔ* 賈
CHOU: **Merchant,** large numbers in quasiofficial status in a number of agencies; functions not clear. CL: *marchand*.

3225 *kǔ-ch'í chǖn* 鼓旗軍
T'ANG: **Army of the Celestial Herdboy,** named after a constellation of stars: one of 12 regional supervisory headquarters for militia Garrisons (*fu*) called the Twelve Armies (*shih-erh chün*); existed only 620–623, 625–636. RR: *armée (de la constellation) des étendards (près) du tambour*. P44.

3226 *kū-ch'īng* 孤卿
From Han on, a variant or unofficial reference to the **Three Solitaries** (*san ku*). P68.

3227 *kǔ-chù chú* 鼓鑄局
YÜAN: **Metropolitan Mint,** a copper coin production agency in the central government, under the Supervisorate-in-chief of Coinage (*pao-ch'üan tu t'i-chü ssu*); staffing not clear, but rank of the head was apparently 7a. P16.

3228 *kǔ chū-hóu* 古諸侯
Lit., Feudal Lord of old; see *chu-hou*. (1) N-S DIV: common unofficial reference to a **Commandery Governor** (*chün-shou*). (2) MING–CH'ING: unofficial reference to a provincial **Grand Coordinator** or **Governor** (*hsün-fu*) or to a multi-Province **Supreme Commander** or **Governor-general** (*tsung-tu*).

3229 *kǔ-chū kūng-shǔ* 鼓鑄公署
MING: **Coinage Office,** during the Chia-ching reign (1522–1566) imposed atop the pre-existing Metropolitan Coinage Service (*pao-yüan chü*), whose Commissioner-in-chief (*ta-shih*) now became subordinate to the Office; headed by a Superintendent (*chien-tu*) based in the Ministry of Works (*kung-pu*) as Vice Director (*yüan-wai lang*), rank 5b, of the Ministry's Bureau of Forestry and Crafts (*yü-heng ch'ing-li ssu*). P16.

3230 *kǔ-ch'ūi chú* 鼓吹局 or *kǔ-ch'ūi àn* 案
SUNG: **Drum and Fife Service (Section)** in the Imperial Music Bureau (*ta-sheng fu*) under the Court of Imperial Sacrifices (*t'ai-ch'ang ssu*); headed by a Director (*ling*); initiated in 1103; apparently equivalent to the Office of Drums and Fifes (*ku-ch'ui shu*) of other periods. SP: *bureau des tambours et des instruments à vent*. P10.

3231 *kǔ-ch'ūi shǔ* 鼓吹署
N-S DIV–CHIN: **Office of Drums and Fifes,** headed by a Director (*ling*), under a Director of Imperial Music (*hsieh-lü hsiao-wei*) or one or more Chief Musicians (*hsieh-lü lang*), both in turn subordinate to the Court of Imperial Sacrifices (*t'ai-ch'ang ssu*); apparently not established in early Sung, but in 1103 Sung established a counterpart, the Drum and Fife Service or Section (*ku-ch'ui chü, ku-ch'ui an*). RR: *office des tambours et des instruments à vent*. P10.

3232 *kǔ-jén* 鼓人
CHOU: **Royal Drummer,** 6 ranked as Ordinary Service-

men (*chung-shih*), members of the Ministry of Education (*ti-kuan*) responsible for teaching the public the meaning of various drum signals in battles, hunts, and sacrifices, and for giving the official drum signals in such situations. CL: *officier de tambour*.

3233   *kù-lún* 固倫
CH'ING: Chinese transliteration of the Manchu word *gu-run*, meaning state or country: a prefix appended to some titles of nobility (*chüeh*) to indicate that the noble was of high enough status to deserve having a state (*kuo*) as his fief.

3234   *kù-lún kūng-chǔ* 固倫公主
CH'ING: **Imperial Princess of the First Degree**, noble designation of imperial daughters borne by the official Empress. P69.

3235   *kù-lún ó-fù* 固倫額駙
CH'ING: **Consort** of an Imperial Princess of the First Degree (*ku-lun kung-chu*); title conferred only after the birth of a son. See *o-fu*. P69.

3236   *kǔ-méng* 瞽矇
CHOU: variant of *ku* (**Blind Musician**). CL: *aveugle musicien*.

3237   *kù-shān* 固山
CH'ING: Chinese transliteration of a Manchu word apparently meaning excellent, beautiful, etc.: (1) Manchu term for a **Banner** (*ch'i* in Chinese) in the Eight Banners (*pa ch'i*) military organization, led by a Banner Commander (*ku-shan o-chen* till 1723, thereafter *ku-shan ang-pang*), in Chinese called Commander-in-chief (*tu-t'ung*) or sometimes General Commander-in-chief (*chiang-chün tu-t'ung*). Five Banners constituted a Regiment (*chia-la*). P44. (2) Prefix appended to some titles of nobility (*chüeh*), e.g., *ku-shan pei-tzu* (Beile Prince), *ku-shan ko-ko* (District Mistress, daughter of a Beile Prince); less prestigious than the prefixes *ku-lun*, *ho-shih*, and *to-lo*, qq.v.

3238   *kù-shān áng-pāng* 固山昂邦
CH'ING: **Banner Commander** in the Eight Banners (*pa-ch'i*) military organization from 1723 on, superseding the earlier Manchu title *ku-shan o-chen;* commonly abbreviated as *ang-pang*. Officially translated into Chinese as *tu-t'ung* (Commander-in-chief); sometimes called *chiang-chün tu-t'ung* (General Commander-in-chief). P44.

3239   *kù-shān kó-kó* 固山格格
CH'ING: colloquial reference to a **District Mistress** (*hsien-chün*), daughter of a Beile Prince (*ku-shan pei-tzu*). See *ku-shan, ko-ko, ku-shan o-fu*.

3240   *kù-shān ó-chēn* 固山額眞
CH'ING: **Banner Commander** in the Eight Banners (*pa ch'i*) military organization; Manchu title changed to *ku-shan ang-pang* in 1723. From 1660 on, officially translated into Chinese as *tu-t'ung* (Commander-in-chief); sometimes known in Chinese as *chiang-chün tu-t'ung* (General Commander-in-chief). BH: lieutenant-general. P44.

3241   *kù-shān ó-fù* 固山額駙
CH'ING: **Consort of a District Mistress** (*hsien-chün*), i.e., of the daughter of a Beile Prince (*ku-shan pei-tzu*). See *ku-shan, fu-ma*.

3242   *kù-shān pèi-tzǔ* 固山貝子
CH'ING: the full formal title of nobility (*chüeh*) normally used in the abbreviated form *pei-tzu* (**Beile Prince**).

3243   *kù-shān-tà* 固山大
CH'ING: unofficial reference to an **Assistant Commander**

(*hsieh-ling*) in the hierarchy of Provincial Bannermen (*chu-fang*).

3244   *kǔ-shīh* 賈師
CHOU: **Overseer of Merchants**, number and rank not clear, representatives of the Directors of Markets (*ssu-shih*) on the staff of the Ministry of Education (*ti-kuan*) who monitored quantities, quality, and prices in the capital marketplaces; one for each cluster of 20 shops. Relationship with the Chiefs of Assistants (*hsü-shih*), one of whom was also appointed for each cluster of 20 shops, is not clear. Also cf. *chen-jen* (Market Shop Supervisor), *ssu-pao* (Market Shop Policeman), and *ssu-chi* (Market Shop Examiner). CL: *prévôt des marchands*.

3245   *kǔ-ssū* 鼓司
SUNG: **Complaint Drum Office**, an agency at the dynastic capital in charge of a drum that could be sounded by anyone having a grievance about judicial or administrative matters or a suggestion about an important matter of state; staffed by various officials of the central government on duty assignments, detached temporarily from their normal posts. In 1007 superseded by a Public Petitioners Drum Office (*teng-wen ku yüan*). SP: *cour des tambours pour annoncer pétitions et doléances*. P21.

3246   *kǔ-ts'āng tū* 穀倉督
SUI: **Supervisor of the Cereals Granary**, 2 members of the Imperial Granaries Office (*t'ai-ts'ang shu*). P8.

3247   *kǔ-yüàn* 鼓院
SUNG: abbreviation of *teng-wen ku yüan* (**Public Petitioners Drum Office**).

3248   *k'ù* 庫
Common designation throughout history for any kind of **Storehouse**; normally occurs with a particularizing prefix.

3249   *k'ù-pù ssū* 庫部司 or *k'u-pu*
Bureau of Provisions. (1) N-S DIV: recurringly, a major subsection of several agencies evolving under the Department of State Affairs (*shang-shu sheng*)—the Ministry of War (*wu-ping ts'ao, ch'i-ping ts'ao*), the Section for Justice (*tu-kuan ts'ao*), and the Ministry of Revenue (*tu-chih ts'ao*); headed by one or more Directors (*lang, shih-lang, lang-chung*). (2) SUI–MING: a major unit of the Ministry of War (*ping-pu*), headed by a Director (*lang-chung*), rank 5b1 in T'ang, 6b in Sung, 5a in Ming; in 1396 retitled *wu-k'u ch'ing-li ssu* (also Bureau of Provisions). RR+SP: *bureau des magasins militaires*. P12.

3250   *k'ù-pù ts'áo* 庫部曹 or *k'u-pu*
N-S DIV: **Storehouse Section**, occasional major unit in the Department of State Affairs (*shang-shu sheng*), headed by a Minister (*shang-shu*).

3251   *k'ù-shīh* 庫使
Storehouse Commissioner, common title for an official in charge of a government storehouse at any level, usually a subofficial functionary. BH: treasury overseer, inspector.

3252   *k'ù-shǒu* 庫守
CH'ING: **Storehouse Keeper**, subofficial functionary in charge of a government storehouse at any level.

3253   *k'ù tà-shǐh* 庫大使
Storehouse Commissioner-in-chief, common variant of *k'u-shih* (Storehouse Commissioner), likely to be used when the appointee was a regular official (ranked from 8a to 9b) rather than a subofficial functionary. BH: treasury keeper.

3254   *k'ù-tièn* 庫典
SUNG: **Storehouse Manager**, designation of numerous

suboofficial functionaries (and possibly some eunuchs) in the Palace Administration (*tien-chung sheng*). P38.

3255 *k'ù-t'īng* 庫廳
CH'ING: unofficial reference to a **Storehouse Commissioner-in-chief** (*k'u ta-shih*) in a Provincial Administration Commission (*ch'eng-hsüan pu-cheng shih ssu*).

3256 *k'ù-ts'áo* 庫曹
N-S DIV: variant of *k'u-pu ts'ao* (**Storehouse Section**).

3257 *k'ù-ts'áo yù-shǐh* 庫曹御史
N-S DIV (S. Dyn.): **Market Tax Censor,** duty assignment of one Attendant Censor (*shih yü-shih*), to supervise collecting and storing state taxes on sales in the animal markets (of the capital?) under the Chamberlain for the Palace Revenues (*shao-fu*). P7, 62.

3258 *k'ù-tzǔ* 庫子
SUNG, YÜAN: **Storehouseman,** designation of numerous suboofficial functionaries tending government storehouses under the Sung Court of Imperial Sacrifices (*t'ai-ch'ang ssu*) and the Yüan Censorate (*yü-shih t'ai*), and in both eras in many local storehouses. SP: *magasinier.*

3259 *k'uā-lán-tà* 夸蘭大
CH'ING: Chinese transliteration of a Manchu word, lit. meaning not clear but used as a military title: **Commandant** (?), occurs in some units serving in the imperial palace, often rank 3a and coupled with a Regimental Commander (*ts'an-ling*), also 3a.

3260 *k'uài-chì ssū* 會計司
(1) SUNG: common abbreviation of *san-ssu k'uai-chi ssu* (**State Finance Commission Accounting Office**). (2) CH'ING: **Office of Palace Accounts,** one of 7 top-echelon agencies in the Imperial Household Department (*nei-wu fu*), in charge of receipts and disbursements at the palace treasury; headed by one or more Directors (*lang-chung*), rank 5a; created in 1677 by renaming the earlier Palace Provisions Commission (*hsüan-hui yüan*). BH: accounts department. P37.

3261 *k'uài-ts'áo* 會曹
SUNG: **Accounts Section** in the headquarters of a Prefecture (*chou, fu*); in the case of the dynastic capital at Kaifeng, headed by an Administrator (*ts'an-chün*), elsewhere apparently staffed with suboofficial functionaries. SP: *bureau des comptes.*

3262 *kuān* 官
(1) Throughout history the most common general term for **Official,** whether civil (*wen-kuan*) or military (*wu-kuan*); also used as a term for the regular **Office** (i.e., position; see *pen-kuan*) and sometimes even the residence of an official; most commonly has a prefix describing or indirectly suggesting the function or status of an official, e.g., *tsung-ping kuan* (Regional Commander). (2) N-S DIV (San-kuo Wei-Chin, S. Dyn.): unofficial reference to the **Emperor.**

3263 *kuān* 關
Frontier pass or barrier, usually guarded by a military unit; often a **domestic customs-house** for the collection of taxes on goods in transit.

3264 *kuǎn* 館
Lodging, Academy, or **Office,** as indicated by a particularizing prefix. E.g., see *san kuan, ssu-fang kuan, ssu-i kuan, hui-t'ung kuan, kuo-shih kuan, fang-lüeh kuan.*

3265 *kuān-ch'á* 觀察
(1) SUNG: **Surveillance,** a prefix to the term Prefecture (*chou, fu, chün*) indicating that the area was under the ju-

risdiction of a Surveillance Commissioner (*an-ch'a shih*). (2) CH'ING: unofficial reference to a **General Administration Circuit** (*fen-shou tao*) or a **General Surveillance Circuit** (*fen-hsün tao*).

3266 *kuān-ch'á chīh-shǐh* 觀察支使
SUNG: **Surveillance Commissioner's Agent,** the deputy of a Surveillance Commissioner (*kuan-ch'a shih*) at the headquarters of a Prefecture (*chou, fu, chün*); rank 8b. See *chih-shih* (Commissioner's Agent). SP: *secrétaire de préfecture.*

3267 *kuān-ch'á ch'ù-chìh shǐh* 觀察處置使
T'ANG: **Surveillance and Supervisory Commissioner,** one of many delegates from the central government to province-size Circuits (*tao*) from the early 700s; in 758 Investigation and Supervisory Commissioners (*ts'ai-fang ch'u-chih shih*) were given this title. During the An Lu-shan rebellion (755–763) many holders of the title were transformed into Military Commissioners (*chieh-tu shih*). Later Surveillance and Supervisory Commissioners came to be civil governors of their Circuits, alongside Military Commissioners serving as military governors. In late T'ang, as central authority deteriorated, autonomous Military Commissioners took this title concurrently, as well as various other prestigious titles. See *ch'u-chih shih, kuan-ch'a shih*. RR: *commissaire impérial à l'organisation et à la surveillance (d'une région)*. P50, 52.

3268 *kuān-ch'á liú-hòu* 觀察留後
SUNG: **Deputy Surveillance Commissioner:** see *chieh-tu kuan-ch'a liu-hou* (Deputy Military and Surveillance Commissioner). SP: *surveillant d'une région.*

3269 *kuān-ch'á shǐh* 觀察使
T'ANG–LIAO: **Surveillance Commissioner,** originally one of many delegates from the central government to province-size Circuits (*tao*), from the late 700s sharing regional authority as civil governors with Military Commissioners (*chieh-tu shih*) as military governors. In late T'ang superseded by the title *kuan-ch'a ch'u-chih shih* (Surveillance and Supervisory Commissioner). In Sung, one of several types of Commissioners supervising Circuits (*tao, lu*), but steadily transformed into Military Commissioners (*an-fu shih*). In Liao, coordinating agents overseeing groups of Prefectures (*chou, chün*). RR+SP: *commissaire impérial à la surveillance d'une région*. P50, 52.

3270 *kuān-ch'á t'ūi-kuān* 觀察推官
SUNG: **Surveillance Circuit Judge,** one commonly on the staff of a Surveillance Circuit Commissioner (*kuan-ch'a shih*). SP: *juge*. P32.

3271 *kuān-ch'āi* 關差
Customs Collector: common reference to an official assigned to collect fees at a customs barrier or market.

3272 *kuān-chèng* 觀政
MING: **Observer,** designation of a new Metropolitan Graduate (*chin-shih*) assigned to a central government agency as a trainee, pending regular appointment to office.

3273 *kuān-ch'éng* 關丞
SUI–T'ANG: **Assistant Director of the Pass,** one or 2 at each frontier pass or domestic customs barrier (*kuan*), rank 9b1 or 9b2 in T'ang; assisted Directors of the Passes (*kuan-ling*) in monitoring the comings and goings of people at strategic places. P62.

3274 *kuān-chì shè-jén* 管記舍人
SUI: **Secretary** in the Right Secretariat of the Heir Apparent (*yu ch'un-fang*), in T'ang retitled *t'ai-tzu she-jen* (Palace

Secretary of the Heir Apparent). RR: *secrétaire du grand secrétariat de droite de l'héritier du trône.*

3275 *kuǎn-chiā* 官家
From the era of N-S Division if not earlier, an unofficial reference to the **Emperor.**

3276 *kuǎn-chiàng* 管匠
MING: **Crafts Foreman,** one, probably a subofficial functionary, on the staff of Shun-t'ien Prefecture (*fu*), i.e., modern Peking; apparently in general charge of construction workers controlled by the Prefecture. In 1581 abolished; in 1583 revived with the title *kuan chün-chiang* (Director of Troops and Craftsmen). P32.

3277 *kuǎn-chiàng tū t'í-lǐng sǒ* 管匠都提領所
YÜAN: **Superintendency-in-chief for Artisans,** a woodworking shop, one of several workshops under the Supervisorate-in-chief of Metal Workers and Jewelers (*chin-yü jen-chiang tsung-kuan fu*) in the dynastic capital at modern Peking; established 1276; headed by a Superintendent-in-chief (*tu t'i-ling*), rank 7b.

3278 *kuǎn ch'iēn-tīng* 管千丁
CH'ING: **Labor Crew Foreman,** members of the staffs that maintained imperial mausoleums (*ling*) and of some auxiliary Ministries (*pu*) in the auxiliary capital called Shengching, at Shenyang (Mukden) in modern Manchuria; rank 4 or 6. P29, 49.

3279 *kuǎn chīh-jǎn chú tà-ch'én*
管織染局大臣
CH'ING: **Grand Minister in Charge of the Weaving and Dyeing Service** (*chih-jan chü*) under the Imperial Household Administration (*nei-wu fu*); sometimes the assignment of an Imperial Prince. BH: director of the weaving and dyeing office.

3280 *kuǎn-chǔ* 管主
Manager, throughout history one of many terms used to designate the head of an agency; normally used only for concurrent (*chien*) appointments or special duty assignments (*ch'ai-ch'ien*) rather than a regular office (see under *pen-kuan*). Also see *chu-kuan.*

3281 *kuǎn-chǔ* 館主
(1) **Manager of the Hostel:** in T'ang and perhaps earlier times, designation of the ad hoc head of the Hostel for Tributary Envoys (*ssu-fang kuan*), which received memorials and gifts from foreign visitors and arranged for their audiences at court. (2) **Director of the Academy** or **Institute:** in T'ang, designation of the head of the Institute of Literary Attendants (*wen-hsüeh chih-kuan*), a concurrent appointment for a Grand Councilor (*tsai-hsiang*). Also an unofficial reference to the administrative head of the Institute for the Cultivation of Literature (*hsiu-wen kuan*) in T'ang, and after T'ang to the administrative head of the Hanlin Academy (*han-lin yüan*). RR: *chef du collège.*

3282 *kuān-chūng hóu* 關中侯
N-S DIV (San-kuo Wei), T'ANG: **Marquis of Kuan-chung** (a regional name referring to the passes through which the Yellow River moves from the highland northwest out onto the North China Plain), 11th highest of 12 ranks of nobility (*chüeh*). P65.

3283 *kuǎn-ch'üán chǔ-shìh* 管泉主事
MING: **Waterways Manager,** apparently a duty assignment (regular post and rank not clear), responsible for maintaining and operating the Grand Canal in southwestern Shantung, principally by collecting fees in lieu of labor from the local populace. P59.

3284 *kuàn-chün* 冠軍
Lit., the top army or the top or head of an army. (1) CHOU–HAN: **Army Commander,** one of many ad hoc titles awarded personages assigned to conduct an army on campaign; found in such combinations as Army-commanding Marquis (*kuan-chün hou*); can be expected to have a prefix indicating the army's purpose or area of operations. The term is equivalent to General (*chiang-chün*). (2) T'ANG–CH'ING: **First Chosen,** unofficial designation of the man heading the pass list after almost any kind or level of civil service recruitment examination, or of the first new graduate to be chosen for an official appointment. The rationale for this usage of the term is not clear.

3285 *kuān-chün* 官軍
Regular Troops: throughout history a standard reference to regular government soldiers, differentiated from many kinds of irregular troops. See *kuan-ping.* Cf. *chia-ping, san-ping.*

3286 *kuǎn-chün* 管軍
YÜAN: **Commanding the Troops,** a common prefix to regular military titles such as Brigade Commander (*wan-hu*), Battalion Commander (*ch'ien-hu*), and Company Commander (*po-hu*); perhaps indicating that the appointment was substantive rather than nominal, or that the appointee was engaged in campaigning rather than administering a garrison.

3287 *kuàn-chün chiāng-chün* 冠軍將軍
General Commanding the Troops. (1) HAN–N-S DIV (S. Dyn.): a title regularly conferred on officers in charge of campaigns. (2) N-S DIV: one of many titles conferred on chieftains of friendly southwestern aboriginal tribes. P72.

3288 *kuān chün-júng hsüān-wèi ch'ù-chìh shǐh* 關軍容宣尉處置使
T'ANG: lit., commissioner to arrange and dispose of matters concerning conditions in the armies and manifestations of imperial conciliation: **Inspector of the Armies,** commonly abbreviated to *kuan chün-jung shih;* from the 760s the most influential military appointment, commonly granted to a palace eunuch; inspected all armies going on campaigns and controlled the 2 Armies of Inspired Strategy (*shen-ts'e chün*), the base from which eunuchs gained dominance in the capital. RR: *commissaire impérial chargé de surveiller la tenue de l'armée et de répandre les consolations.* P43.

3289 *kuàn-chün shǐh* 冠軍使
CH'ING: **Military Commissioner,** a duty assignment for a noble or an eminent military officer, prefixed with functionally descriptive terms, e.g., *tsung-li shih-wu kuan-chün shih* (Military Commissioner Director of the Imperial Procession Guard), q.v.

3290 *kuān chün-shǐh* 關軍使
5 DYN (Liang): **Guard Commander at the Customs House,** with a place-name prefix. P62.

3291 *kuān-chün tà chiāng-chün* 冠軍大將軍
T'ANG, SUNG, LIAO: **General-in-chief Commanding the Troops,** prestige title (*san-kuan*) for military officers of rank 3a. Cf. *kuan-chün chiang-chün.* RR: *grand général de l'armée dominante.* SP: *grand général Kouan-kiun.* P68.

3292 *kuān-fáng shìh-wù ch'ù* 關防事務處 or *kuan-fang ch'u*
CH'ING: common abbreviations of *chang kuan-fang kuan-li nei kuan-ling shih-wu ch'u* (**Overseers Office**) in the Imperial Household Department (*nei-wu fu*); supervised use of

the imperial seals and controlled individual access to the Emperor; headed by an Overseer (*nei kuan-ling chang kuan-fang*) who had status as a Grand Minister (*ta-ch'en*). Also see *chang kuan-fang ch'u*. BH: chancery of the imperial household. P37.

3293 *kuān-fáng tsū-k'ù* 官房租庫
CH'ING: **Government Property Rental Agency,** a central government unit responsible for collecting rents on buildings in Peking and its environs that had been confiscated from the Ming dynasty rulers or private owners in the 1640s; originally directly subordinate to the Office of Palace Construction (*ying-tsao ssu*), which received the Rental Agency's revenues; in 1731 became directly subordinate to the Imperial Household Department (*nei-wu fu*), headed by the Department's Grand Ministers (*ta-ch'en*) in annual rotation. BH: office for collecting rent on confiscated property. P37.

3294 *kuān-fǔ* 官府
Throughout history a very general reference to **the government** as a whole, or to those officials who collectively were considered to be **the administration** in power, or to particular government agencies. See *cheng-fu*.

3295 *kuǎn-hó* 管河
MING–CH'ING: **Controller of Waterways,** a duty assignment of Vice Prefects (*t'ung-chih*), Assistant Prefects (*t'ung-p'an*), and other provincial and local officials delegated to provide local assistance to the Director-general of the Grand Canal (*ho-tao tsung-tu*); the designation occurs as a prefix to the regular titles of the appointees, e.g., *kuan-ho t'ung-chih* (Vice Prefect Controller of Waterways). P52, 59.

3296 *kuǎn-hsiá fān-ì* 管轄番役
CH'ING: **Supervisor of Police,** head of the Police Bureau (*fan-i ch'u*) attached to the Office of Palace Justice (*shen-hsing ssu*) in the Imperial Household Department (*nei-wu fu*); a rotational duty assignment for Directors (*lang-chung*) and Vice Directors (*yüan-wai lang*) of Bureaus (*ch'ing-li ssu*) in Ministries (*pu*), or for lesser officials at the capital. BH: controller of the police bureau.

3297 *kuǎn-hsiá kuān* 管轄官
SUNG: **Supervisor,** an uncommon title apparently indicating an ad hoc assignment to a special duty; full implications not clear. E.g., see under *ya-pan* (Service Allocation Office).

3298 *kuān-hsüéh* 官學
(1) **Government School,** a generic term for all kinds of state-established schools as distinct from Private Academies (*shu-yüan*) and other schools not established by the state. (2) CH'ING: **Palace Schools,** collective reference to 3 schools established by the Imperial Household Department (*nei-wu fu*)—the School at the Palace of Universal Peace (*hsien-an kung kuan-hsüeh*), the Mt. Prospect School (*ching-shan kuan-hsüeh*), and the Court Theatrical School (*nan-fu kuan-hsüeh*). BH: schools of the imperial household.

3299 *kuān hsüéh-shēng* 官學生
N-S DIV (Chin), MING–CH'ING: **Official Student** in the National University (*t'ai-hsüeh, kuo-tzu hsüeh*) or in one of the Ch'ing dynasty Palace Schools (*kuan-hsüeh*); admitted without normal qualification certification, solely by entitlement as the son or younger brother of a noble or high-ranking official. P24, 37.

3300 *kuān-ī* 官醫
HAN: **Government Physician,** apparently non-official

specialists; found on the staffs of various central government agencies. HB: official physician. P22.

3301 *kuǎn-ì hsŭn-kuān* 館驛巡官
T'ANG: **Inspector of Postal Relay Stations,** 4 authorized on the staff of each Military Commissioner (*chieh-tu shih*) from the 750s, apparently focusing on the postal system more closely than was possible for the Censorate's (*yü-shih t'ai*) Postal Inspectors (*kuan-i shih*). RR: *inspecteur des relais de poste.*

3302 *kuǎn ī-jén t'óu-mù* 管醫人頭目
YÜAN: **Head of Physician Families,** probably a descriptive term rather than a title, indicating the chief and spokesmen for all physician families (*i-hu*) in a locality; in cooperation with local officials, resolved disputes between physician families and others.

3303 *kuǎn-ì shǐh* 館驛使
T'ANG: **Postal Inspector,** from 779 the duty assignment of an Investigating Censor (*chien-ch'a yü-shih*) in the Censorate (*yü-shih t'ai*) located at each dynastic capital, Ch'ang-an and Loyang, to oversee the operations of the postal relay system. Cf. *kuan-i hsün-kuan*. RR: *commissaire impérial aux services de poste.* P18.

3304 *kuān-ī t'í-chǔ ssū* 官醫提舉司
YÜAN: **Supervisorate of Physicians,** one in the dynastic capital, one in each Province (*hsing-sheng*), and one in each lower unit of territorial administration down to the District (*hsien*) level, headed by a Supervisor (*t'i-chü*), rank 5b at the capital, 6b elsewhere; normally attached to the Medical School (*i-hsüeh*) at each administrative level. Primarily responsible for overseeing the affairs of hereditary physician families (*i-hu*), arranging for their state service, settling disputes among them, and nominating young men of talent who might be admitted to the Medical Schools. Cf. *kuan-i t'i-ling so*.

3305 *kuān-ī t'í-lǐng sǒ* 官醫提領所
YÜAN: **Superintendency of Physician Families,** a central government agency (?) that shared responsibility, in some fashion not clear, with Supervisorates of Physicians (*kuan-i t'i-chü ssu*; or only the Supervisorate in the capital?) for overseeing the affairs of hereditary physician families (*i-hu*) and the medical care provided imprisoned criminals; also assigned physicians to prison duty; headed by a Superintendent (*t'i-ling*).

3306 *kuǎn-kàn* 管幹
SUNG: **Administrative Clerk,** title of numerous suboffi-cial functionaries on the staffs of Ministries (*pu*) and many other agencies, e.g., *kuan-kan chia-ko k'u kuan* (Administrative Clerk of the Archives), *kuan-kan wen-tzu* (Administrative Clerk for Correspondence). SP: *administrateur, gérant.*

3307 *kuǎn-kàn chiāo-miāo chì-ch'ì sǒ*
管幹郊廟祭器所
SUNG: **Office of Sacrificial Regalia for the Suburban Temple,** a unit of the Court of Imperial Sacrifices (*t'ai-ch'ang ssu*); headed by a Superintendent (*t'i-tien*). SP: *bureau des objets de sacrifice des temples de la banlieue.* P27.

3308 *kuān-kào chú* 官告局 or 官誥局
SUNG: **Appointment Verification Service,** an agency in charge of issuing appointment certificates (*kao-shen*) to newly appointed or reappointed officials; an ad hoc arrangement within the Ministries of Personnel (*li-pu*) and of War (*ping-pu*) until c. 1080, thereafter solely in the Ministry of Per-

sonnel; headed by a Secretariat Drafter (*chung-shu she-jen*) serving as Supervisor (*t'i-chü*). SP: *cour des titres des nominations*. P3.

3309   *kuān-kào yüàn* 官告院 or 官誥院
SUNG: **Appointment Verification Office:** variant of *kuan-kao chü*.

3310   *kuǎn-kó* 館閣
(1) T'ANG–SUNG: **Academies and Institutes:** common collective reference to the Institute of Academicians (*hsüeh-shih yüan*), Academy of Scholarly Worthies (*chi-hsien yüan*), Institute for the Glorification of Literature (*chao-wen kuan*), Historiography Institute (*shih-kuan*), etc.; and especially to eminent officials who held nominal supernumerary appointments (*t'ieh-chih*) as **Academicians** (*hsüeh-shih*), etc., in these agencies. SP: *fonctionnaires des divers collèges littéraires*. P23. (2) MING–CH'ING: unofficial reference to the **Hanlin Academy** (*han-lin yüan*). P25.

3311   *kuǎn-kó chiào-k'àn* 館閣校勘
SUNG: **Proofreader in the Academy** or **Institute,** designation of subofficial functionaries found on the staffs of various agencies that had compiling and editorial functions, e.g., the Historiography Institute (*shih-kuan*). See *chiao-k'an*.

3312   *kuǎn-kōu* 管勾 or *kuǎn-kōu … shìh* 事
(1) SUNG: **Concurrently Serving as …** or **Concurrently Managing …,** used when an official's nominal post was of lower rank and status than the post held concurrently, in such forms as nominal post + *kuan-kou* + concurrent post: … *kuan-kou t'ai-shih* (Concurrently Managing the Censorate, *yü-shih t'ai*), … *kuan-kou chien shih* (Concurrently Managing the Directorate of Education, *kuo-tzu chien*). (2) SUNG–CHIN: **Clerk,** a title sometimes held by eunuchs of the Palace Domestic Service (*nei-shih sheng*). SP: *régisseur*. (3) SUNG–CH'ING: **Clerk,** found in many agencies, rank from 7a to 9b, sometimes apparently subofficial functionaries; e.g., *kuo-shih yüan ch'eng-fa chia-ko k'u kuan-kou* (Clerk Storekeeper in the Historiography Institute), one, rank 9a. Especially common in Chin and Yüan; little used after 1380 in Ming. See *kou-kuan*.

3313   *kuǎn-kōu ssū* 管勾司
YÜAN: **Clerks Office** in the Bureau of Musical Ritual (*i-feng ssu*); in 1312 changed into the Office of Moslem Music (*ch'ang-ho shu*). P10.

3314   *kuǎn-kōu wǎng-lái kuó-hsìn sǒ* 管勾往來國信所
SUNG: **Concurrent Manager of the Office of Diplomatic Correspondence,** a unit of the Court of State Ceremonial (*hung-lu ssu*); a special assignment for the eunuch Office Manager (*tu-chih*) or Administrative Aide (*ya-pan*) of the Palace Eunuch Service (*ju-nei nei-shih sheng*), rank 6a; took part in the management of early Sung diplomatic exchanges with the Khitan state of Liao. See *wang-lai kuo-hsin so*. Cf. *kuo-hsin fang*. SP: *administrateur des missions diplomatiques (relations avec les K'i-tan)*.

3315   *kuǎn-lǐ* 管理
Manager. (1) MING: head of a Section (*k'o*) in a Bureau (*ch'ing-li ssu*) in the Ministry of Revenue (*hu-pu*) and perhaps elsewhere; rank not clear, possibly unranked. See *min-k'o, tu-chih k'o, chin-k'o, ts'ang-k'o*. P6. (2) CH'ING: duty assignment or concurrent appointment, most commonly of a Grand Minister (*ta-ch'en*) of the Imperial Household Department (*nei-wu fu*); e.g., *kuan-li chieh-tao t'ing* (Manager of the Office of Capital Streets), a duty assignment for Cen-

sors (*yü-shih*), officials of the Ministry of Works (*kung-pu*), and officers representing the Commander-general of Metropolitan Bannermen (*pu-chün t'ung-ling*); or *kuan-li wu-ying tien hsiu-shu ch'u shih-wu* (Manager [lit., of the affairs] of the Imperial Printing Office in the Hall of Military Glory).

3316   *kuǎn-liáng* 管糧
(1) MING: **Tax Manager,** one, rank not clear, on the staff of Shun-t'ien Prefecture (*fu*), modern Peking. P32. (2) CH'ING: **Manager of Tax Transport,** a duty assignment for Vice Prefects (*t'ung-chih*) and Assistant Prefects (*t'ung-p'an*) along the route of the Grand Canal from 1667. P32.

3317   *kuān-lìng* 關令
SUI–T'ANG: **Director of the Pass,** one at each significant border, pass, ford, etc.; responsible for collecting mercantile taxes on goods in transit, watching for contraband goods, and verifying the credentials of all travelers. Ranked in 3 categories: Senior (*shang*), Ordinary (*chung*), and Junior (*hsia*), from 8b2 to 9b2. P54, 62.

3318   *kuǎn-lǐng* 管領 or *kuǎn-lǐng … kuān* 官
(1) YÜAN: **Supervisor, Supervising …:** overseer of the staff in various agencies, especially in the households of Empresses and Princes, e.g., *kuan-ling chu-tzu min-chiang kuan* (Supervisor of Pearl Fishing) under the Supervisorate-in-chief of Metal Workers and Jewelers (*chin-yü jen-chiang tsung-kuan fu*), *kuan-ling sui-lu jen-chiang tu t'i-ling so* (Supervisor of the Supervisory Directorate of Artisans in the Various Routes) under the Supervisorate-in-chief of All Classes of Artisans (*chu-se jen-chiang tsung-kuan fu*). (2) CH'ING: **Chief Clerk** in the establishments of Imperial Princes (*ch'in-wang*) and Commandery Princes (*chün-wang*), 4 and 3 respectively, rank 6a; in charge of correspondence and personnel matters. Also see *nei kuan-ling*. P69.

3319   *kuān-mǎ fāng* 官馬坊
T'ANG: **Palace Grazing Grounds,** apparently a reference to areas in the imperial parks and gardens reserved for grazing by the thousands of horses reportedly kept within the imperial palace; see *chang-nei liu hsien* (Six Palace Corrals), *liu chiu* (Six Stables). RR: *quartiers pour les chevaux du gouvernement*.

3320   *kuǎn-mín tsǔng-kuān fù* 管民總管府
YÜAN: **Civil Administration Command** for Pien-liang (Kaifeng) and other Routes (*lu*), a unit of the Household Service for the Heir Apparent (*ch'u-cheng yüan*); staffing and functions not clear.

3321   *kuán-nèi hóu* 關內侯
CH'IN–N-S DIV (San-kuo Wei): **Marquis of Kuan-nei** (a regional designation: lit., within the passes, referring to the northern part of modern Shensi Province), the 19th of 20 (i.e., 2nd highest) titles of nobility (*chüeh*) awarded to exceptionally meritorious personages. P65.

3322   *kuǎn p'ào hsiāo-chí hsiào* 管礮驍騎校
CH'ING: **Artillery Lieutenant,** 10, rank 6a, from 1764 (?) junior officers in the Firearms Brigade (*huo-ch'i ying*), in command of Artillerymen (*p'ao hsiao-chi*). Also see *hsiao-chi, hsiao*. BH: lieutenant of artillery.

3323   *kuān-pīng* 官兵
Regular Troops: throughout history a reference to regular government soldiers as distinguished from many kinds of irregular troops. See *kuan-chün*. Cf. *chia-ping, san-ping*.

3324   *kuān-shēng* 官生
MING–CH'ING: **Official Student** under the Directorate of

Education (*kuo-tzu chien*), admitted without normal certification of qualifications but solely by entitlement as the son of a noble or official who had been awarded the protection privilege (*yin-tzu*) that guaranteed one or more of his sons direct admission into student status or direct appointment to office. The category of Official Students included those admitted "by grace" (see *en-sheng*), as sons of officials who had rendered extraordinary state service, especially those who had lost their lives in battle. In Ch'ing the status was often awarded in celebration of various auspicious events. Sons of foreign rulers who studied in the Directorate of Education were also considered Official Students. Also see *en-ch'ü chien-sheng, en-tz'u chien-sheng, en-yin chien-sheng, nan-yin chien-sheng*.

3325 *kuăn … shìh* 管⋯事
In charge of the affairs of …: a term commonly found enclosing an agency name or official title, indicating that the named official was in active charge of the designated agency or post, which may or may not have been his nominal status; used to differentiate such an official from one bearing a title but not actively performing its functions.

3326 *kuān-shǐh* 關使
CHIN: **Gate Commissioner,** many, rank 7a and 7b, in charge of opening and closing city gates, monitoring travelers, and collecting taxes on goods in transit. P62.

3327 *kuăn shìh-wù tà-ch'én* 管事務大臣
CH'ING: **Grand Minister Supervisor** of the Palace Stud (*shang-ssu yüan*) under the Imperial Household Department (*nei-wu fu*). Also see *ta-ch'en*. P39.

3328 *kuān-shùi chiēn-tū* 關稅監督
CH'ING: **Superintendent of Domestic Customs Barriers,** normally a concurrent duty assignment for a Provincial Governor (*hsün-fu*), a representative of the Court of Colonial Affairs (*li-fan yüan*), or another central government official of rank 4 or 5; arranged for and supervised the collection of mercantile taxes on goods in transit throughout the empire. P62.

3329 *kuăn-sŏ chiēn-tū* 館所監督
CH'ING: **Superintendent of Postal Relay Stations** (*i-chan*), one Manchu appointed from 1651, one Chinese from 1753; apparently special duty assignments for members of the Ministry of War (*ping-pu*). P12.

3330 *kuăn tà-fū* 官大夫
CH'IN–HAN: lit., official grand master: **Grandee of the Sixth Order,** 6th lowest of 20 ranks of honorary nobility (*chüeh*) awarded to meritorious personages. P65.

3331 *kuăn-tài* 管帶
CH'ING: variant reference to a **Brigade Commander** (*yu-chi*) in the Green Standards (*lu-ying*) military organization. BH: battalion commander.

3332 *kuān-t'ién* 官田
State Land: throughout history a common designation of arable lands belonging to the government, howsoever acquired—by state-sponsored reclamation, by confiscation, by takeover of the preceding dynasty's holdings, etc. The term normally encompasses imperial gardens, etc., in the vicinity of the dynastic capital and, on a much larger scale, lands rented to tenant farmers whose rent payments were used to help maintain nearby government offices and garrisons, lands sometimes given to favored religious establishments or favored families (e.g., the most direct descendants of Confucius) as endowments, and lands sometimes given to groups of landless peasants in State Farms (*t'un-*

t'ien) located in regions where the government was trying to encourage agricultural development, usually in frontier zones or areas that had been devastated by wars. See *chih-t'ien, min-t'un, chün-t'un*.

3333 *kuān tū-wèi* 關都尉
CH'IN–HAN: **Commandant-in-chief of the Customs Barrier,** assignments to supervise customs collections at major strategic places in the empire, commonly awarded to nobles, sons of eminent officials, and other favorites. HB: chief commandant of a pass. P62.

3334 *kuān-wài hóu* 關外侯
N-S DIV (San-kuo Wei, S. Dyn.): **Marquis of Kuan-wai** (regional designation: beyond the passes, reference not specific), 5th lowest of 20 titles of nobility (*chüeh*) conferred on meritorious personages. P65.

3335 *kuàn yèh-chĕ láng-chūng* 灌謁者郎中
HAN: **Gentleman of the Interior Serving as Receptionist,** about a dozen junior members of the staff of the Later Han Chamberlain for Attendants (*kuang-lu-hsün*), rank =300 bushels; after a year of satisfactory service could be promoted to Receptionist in Attendance (*chi-shih yeh-che*), rank 400 bushels. See *lang-chung*. HB: gentleman-of-the-palace serving as probationary internuncio.

3336 *kuàn-yù chú* 瓘玉局
YÜAN: **Jade Service,** one of many artisan workshops under the Supervisorate-in-chief of Metal Workers and Jewelers (*chin-yü jen-chiang tsung-kuan fu*).

3337 *kuāng-chèng* 光正
N-S DIV (N. Ch'i): **Lady of Bright Rectitude,** one of 27 imperial wives collectively called Hereditary Consorts (*shih-fu*); rank =3b.

3338 *kuăng-chì t'í-chŭ ssū* 廣濟提舉司
YÜAN: **Supervisorate of Medical Relief,** a public health agency established in each Capital and Province, headed by a Supervisor (*t'i-chü*), rank 7b; organizational affiliation and specific functions not clear.

3339 *kuăng-ch'īn mù-ch'īn chái* 廣親睦親宅
SUNG: lit., residence for the expansive and friendly treatment of relatives: **Hostel for Imperial Clansmen** maintained by the Chief Office of Imperial Clan Affairs (*ta tsung-cheng ssu*) from c. 1000 as a residence and school for the male descendants of the founding Emperors, T'ai-tsu and T'ai-tsung. Possibly located at the dynastic capital, Kaifeng; but there was apparently one such Hostel in each Princely Establishment (*wang-fu*), some of whose officials, in addition to their normal administrative duties, concurrently served as Instructors (*chiao-shou*) in the Hostel. Commonly found in the variant forms *mu-ch'in kuang-ch'in ssu, mu-ch'in ssu;* also called the Southern Palace (*nan-kung*). Cf. *tun-tsung yüan* (Hostel for Imperial Kinsmen), one each at Loyang and at Yangchow from 1104 into the 1120s. SP: *maison de la propagation de l'harmonie de la famille impériale*.

3340 *kuăng-ch'ú ssū* 廣儲司
CH'ING: **Storage Office,** one of 7 major units in the Imperial Household Department (*nei-wu fu*), an aggregation of Six Storehouses (*liu k'u*): the Silver Vault (*yin-k'u*) and the Hides (*p'i-k'u*), Porcelain (*tz'u-k'u*), Silks (*tuan-k'u*), Clothing (*i-k'u*), and Tea (*ch'a-k'u*) Storehouses; headed by 2 Directors (*lang-chung*) of the Storage Office, also called Supervisors-in-chief of the Six Storehouses (*tsung-kuan liu-k'u shih-wu*). BH: department of the privy purse. P37.

3341 *kuǎng-hsī fáng* 廣西房
SUNG: **Southwestern Defense Section** in the Bureau of Military Affairs (*shu-mi yüan*); one of 12 Sections created in the reign of Shen-tsung (r. 1067–1085) to manage administrative affairs of military garrisons throughout the country, in geographic clusters, or to supervise specified military functions on a country-wide scale. This Section supervised the raising of troops to suppress banditry in the frontier zone of Kuang-nan-hsi Circuit (*lu*) and the distributing of consequent rewards and punishments; generally supervised garrisons of Liang-Che Circuit, and established quotas for the rotation of personnel into the Imperial Armies (*chin-chün*) at the dynastic capital. Headed by 3 to 5 Vice Recipients of Edicts (*fu ch'eng-chih*), rank 8b. Apparently abolished early in S. Sung. See *shih-erh fang* (Twelve Sections). SP: *chambre de recrutement et de la défense de Kouang-nan Ouest*.

3342 *kuāng-hsùn* 光訓
N-S DIV (N. Ch'i): **Lady of Bright Instruction,** designation of one of 6 imperial wives called Lesser Concubines (*hsia-pin*).

3343 *kuǎng-hsùn* 廣訓
N-S DIV (N. Ch'i): **Lady of Broad Instruction,** designation of one of 27 imperial wives collectively called Hereditary Consorts (*shih-fu*); rank =3b.

3344 *kuǎng-hùi k'ù* 廣惠庫
MING: common abbreviation of *pao-ch'ao kuang-hui k'u* (**Treasury for the Benevolent Issuance of Paper Money**).

3345 *kuǎng-hùi ssū* 廣惠司
YÜAN: lit., broadening benevolence office: **Moslem Medical Office,** a unit of the Imperial Academy of Medicine (*t'ai-i yüan*) staffed with Moslem physicians who provided treatment for the Emperor, military officers, and the needy in the dynastic capital; headed by a Supervisor (*t'i-chü*), rank 3a to 1319, then 5a, then back to 3a in 1322–1323.

3346 *kuǎng-hùi ts'āng* 廣惠倉
SUNG: lit., broadening benevolence granary: **Public Welfare Granary,** in 1057 ordered established in all Prefectures (*chou*) and Districts (*hsien*) to store grains for issuance to widows, widowers, and others who could not provide for themselves. Cf. *pao-ch'ao kuang-hui k'u* (Treasury for the Benevolent Issuance of Paper Money).

3347 *kuāng-lù-hsūn* 光祿勳
Lit. meaning not wholly clear: (one who) enhances (the ruler's) happiness and meritorious achievements? (1) HAN–N-S DIV: **Chamberlain for Attendants,** c. 104 B.C. superseded the title *lang-chung ling*; in Han one of the major officials of the central government, ranked at 2,000 bushels; was in overall charge of all Court Gentlemen (*lang*), whom he examined annually, and of the Emperor's personal counselors and bodyguards; gradually became a purely honorary post in the era of N-S Division. HB: superintendent of the imperial household. P37. (2) N-S DIV–CH'ING: occasional unofficial reference to the **Chief Minister** (*ch'ing*) **of the Court of Imperial Entertainments** (*kuang-lu ssu*).

3348 *kuǎng-lù ssù* 光祿寺
N-S DIV (N. Ch'i)–CH'ING: **Court of Imperial Entertainments,** in charge of catering for the imperial household, court officials, and imperial banquets honoring foreign envoys and other dignitaries; normally had 4 subordinate Offices (*shu*) specializing in various kinds of foodstuffs; headed by a Chief Minister (*ch'ing*), rank 3b in T'ang, 4b in Sung, 3a in Yüan, 3b in Ming and Ch'ing; always had a huge staff of cooks, servingmen, etc. Normally under general supervision of the Ministry of Rites (*lǐ-pu*); in Sung from 1127 absorbed into the Ministry. In Liao from the era 927–947 retitled *ch'ung-lu ssu* to avoid a name taboo. In Chin and Yüan subordinate to the *hsüan-hui yüan* (Court Ceremonial Institute in Chin, Palace Provisions Commission in Yüan). Ming followed the Yüan pattern till 1375, when the Court was re-established with relative autonomy, loosely supervised by the Ministry of Rites. RR+SP: *cour des banquets impériaux*. BH: banqueting court. P37.

3349 *kuāng-lù tà-fū* 光祿大夫
Grand Master for Splendid Happiness. (1) HAN–N-S DIV: an intimate imperial aide and adviser, resident in the palace; under supervision of the Chamberlain for Attendants (*kuang-lu-hsün*); rank =2,000 bushels in Han. HB: imperial household grandee. (2) SUI–CH'ING: prestige title (*san-kuan*) for civil officials of rank 1a then 1b in Sui; 2b in T'ang, Sung, and Chin; 1b in Yüan and Ming, 1a in Ch'ing. Sometimes occurs with prefixes Left and Right. See *chin-tzu kuang-lu ta-fu*, *yin-ch'ing kuang-lu ta-fu*. P68.

3350 *kuǎng-pù wèi* 廣部尉
HAN: **Commandant of the Metropolitan Police, East and South:** 2 ranked at 400 bushels, responsible for police supervision over the eastern and southern quadrants of the Former Han dynastic capital, Ch'ang-an, a jurisdiction known in the aggregate as the Left Sector (*tso-pu*); from 91 B.C. subordinate to the Metropolitan Commandant (*ssu-li hsiao-wei*); in Later Han made separate offices entitled Commandant of the Metropolitan Police, East Sector (*tung-pu wei*) and Commandant of the Metropolitan Police, South Sector (*nan-pu wei*). P20.

3351 *kuǎng-wén* 廣文
T'ANG–CH'ING: **Litterateur,** an unofficial reference to scholarly men and especially to educational officials (*hsüeh-kuan*) such as Instructors (*chiao-shou*) in regional and local schools.

3352 *kuǎng-wén kuǎn* 廣文館
T'ANG–SUNG: **Institute for the Extension of Literary Arts,** one of the advanced schools maintained by the Directorate of Education (*kuo-tzu chien*), responsible (at least in T'ang) for the training of students in the School for the Sons of the State (*kuo-tzu hsüeh*) to take the civil service recruitment examinations that led to the degree of Presented Scholar (*chin-shih*); staffed with 4 Erudites (*po-shih*) and 2 Instructors (*chu-chiao*). Established in 750 to handle 60 students annually; in Sung grew to have 2,400 students. RR: *collège pour la propagation de la littérature*. SP: *collège de la littérature*. P34.

3353 *kuǎng-yèh t'áng* 廣業堂
MING–CH'ING: **College for Broadening Academic Scope,** one of the Six Colleges (*liu t'ang*) among which students of the Directorate of Education (*kuo-tzu chien*) were distributed. P34.

3354 *kuāng-yú* 光猷
N-S DIV (N. Ch'i): **Lady of Bright Counsel,** designation of one of 3 Superior Concubines (*shang-pin*).

3355 *kuǎng-yūan k'ù* 廣源庫
YÜAN: abbreviation of *wan-i kuang-yüan k'u* (**Imperial Treasures Vault**).

3356 *kuǎng-yùeh k'ù* 廣樂庫
YÜAN: **Office of Musical Supplies,** one directly subordinate to the Bureau of Musical Ritual (*i-feng ssu*) and one subordinate to the Music Office (*chiao-fang ssu*), a con-

stituent unit of the Bureau; each headed by a Commissioner-in-chief (*ta-shih*), rank 9b; apparently responsible for storing and repairing court musical instruments. P10.

3357 *k'uāng-chèng* 匡政
T'ANG: **Rectifier of Governance,** from 662 to 671 the official variant of the title Vice Director (*p'u-yeh*) of the Department of State Affairs (*shang-shu sheng*); 2 prefixed Left and Right, both rank 2b.

3358 *k'uáng-fū* 狂夫
CHOU: lit., madman: **Eccentric,** 4 non-official appointees associated with the Shamans (*fang-hsiang shih*) in the Ministry of War (*hsia-kuan*), responsible for various ceremonies; it has been speculated that they were court jesters. CL: *insensés*.

3359 *k'uāng-jén* 匡人
CHOU: **Rectifier,** 4 ranked as Ordinary Servicemen (*chung-shih*), members of the Ministry of War (*hsia-kuan*) responsible for monitoring conduct of the Feudal Lords (*chu-hou*). CL: *rectificateur*.

3360 *kuèi* 貴
(1) Throughout history incorporated into titles as a descriptive prefix denoting high social or moral status; e.g., honored, worthy. (2) CHOU: **Regional Mentor,** one of 9 Unifying Agents (*ou*) appointed in the Nine Regions (*chiu chou*) into which the kingdom was divided, as agents of the Minister of State (*chung-tsai*) overseeing geographic clusters of feudal states, to monitor the dignity (?) of regional and local lords and other leaders. CL: *instructeur*.

3361 *kuēi-ān hóu* 歸安侯
N-S DIV (Ch'in): lit., Marquis who has reverted to peace: **Allied Marquis,** an honorary title apparently conferred on unrelated tribal chiefs who accepted tributary status.

3362 *kuèi-chiēh* 貴階
T'ANG: **Honored Ranks,** collective reference to civil service ranks 1 through 5.

3363 *kuèi-chièh kūng-tzǔ* 貴介公子
Noble Scion, common generic reference to sons of the nobility (*chüeh*).

3364 *kuèi-chǔ* 貴主
Elegant variant of *kung-chu* (**Imperial Princess**).

3365 *kuèi-fāng* 桂坊
T'ANG: lit., cassia area: from 662 to 670 the official variant of *ssu-ching chü* (**Editorial Service**) in the household of the Heir Apparent; during its short life, its head, rank 5b2, was called *kuei-fang ta-fu* (Grand Master of the Editorial Service) and it had strongly censorial functions (see *yü-shih*) not characteristic of the agency in other periods. See *kuei-hsia shih*. RR: *secrétariat des censeurs de la maison de l'héritier du trône.* P26.

3366 *kuèi-fēi* 貴妃
N-S DIV (Ch'i)–CH'ING: **Honored Consort,** generally the most esteemed palace woman after the Empress until the era 1464–1487, when Imperial Honored Consort (*huang kuei-fei*) was introduced as a still more prestigious title. In Sui, first of the Three Consorts (*san fu-jen*); in T'ang, first of the Four Principal Consorts (*ssu fei*); rank 1a till the late 1400s, thereafter not clear. RR+SP: *concubine précieuse.* BH: imperial concubine of the 2nd rank.

3367 *kuēi-fù* 歸附
MING: **Adherents,** one of several categories of troops that constituted the early Ming armies and the hereditary military establishment called *wei-so,* q.v.; specifically refers to

soldiers who originally served the Yüan dynasty or regional warlords of late Yüan times but surrendered and joined the Ming challenge to Yüan; also refers to villagers of areas newly subjugated by Ming armies who, given a choice to be registered as hereditary civilian or military families (*min-hu, chün-hu*), chose to become soldiers. Cf. *ts'ung-cheng* (Old Campaigners), *che-fa* (Sentenced Soldiers), and *to-chi* (Conscripts).

3368 *kuèi-hsià shǐh* 桂下史
Lit., scribe under the cassia tree, a description of the Taoist sage Lao-tzu. (1) CHOU: **Royal Archivist,** in charge of the royal library. (2) In later times an unofficial reference to **Censors** (*yü-shih*) or to **members of the Hanlin Academy** (*han-lin yüan*).

3369 *kuèi-í* 貴儀
SUNG: **Lady of Noble Deportment,** from 1033 the designation of an imperial consort, rank 1b or 2a.

3370 *kuēi-ì hóu* 歸義侯
HAN: lit., Marquis who has reverted to righteousness or duty: **Allied Marquis,** an honorary title conferred on chiefs of some aboriginal tribes. P72.

3371 *kuèi-jén* 貴人
Worthy Lady. (1) HAN: in Later Han, a collective designation of one group of imperial wives ranking just below the Empress. HB: honourable lady. (2) SUNG–CH'ING: generic reference to rank 5 palace women, less prestigious than consorts (*fei*) and concubines (*pin*). BH: imperial concubine of the fifth rank

3372 *kuēi-jén* 龜人
CHOU: **Tortoise Keeper,** 2 ranked as Ordinary Servicemen (*chung-shih*), members of the Ministry of Rites (*ch'un-kuan*) who provided tortoises for divination ceremonies. CL: *préposé aux tortues.*

3373 *kuēi-míng* 歸明
Lit., (one who) returns to the light, i.e., turns as if homeward to Chinese civilization: **Alien Defector** or **Surrendered Forces.** E.g., see *po-hai ch'i-tan kuei-ming* (Surrendered Po-hai and Khitan Forces) in Sung times. Cf. *kuei-fu.*

3374 *kuèi-pīn* 貴嬪
N-S DIV: **Honored Concubine,** in Ch'i one of the Three Consorts (*san fu-jen*), the 3 ranking secondary wives of the Emperor; also occurs in Liang and Sung.

3375 *kuēi-pǔ* 龜卜
HAN: **Tortoiseshell Diviner,** duty assignment for 3 Expectant Officials (*tai-chao*) on the staff of the Grand Astrologer (*t'ai-shih ling*). HB: diviner by tortoise shell.

3376 *kuěi-shǐh* 匭使
CH'ING: lit., commissioner of the petition box: unofficial reference to the **Transmission Commissioner** (*t'ung-cheng shih*), head of the Office of Transmission (*t'ung-cheng shih ssu*), which received memorials bound for the throne. See *kuei-yüan.*

3377 *kuèi-yú tzǔ-tì* 貴遊子弟
Noble Scion, common general reference to sons and younger brothers of members of the nobility (*chüeh*).

3378 *kuěi-yüàn* 匭院
SUNG: **Petition Box Office** maintained by the Chancellery (*men-hsia sheng*) to receive complaints by commoners about official misconduct or about government policies; in 984 superseded by the Public Petitioners Office (*teng-wen yüan*). SP: *cour du dépôt des pétitions.* P21.

3379 *⁐kuēi-yùn ssū* 規運司
YÜAN: **Religious Support Office,** an agency that transmitted revenues from endowment lands to the monasteries and temples for which they were created; a unit of the Office for Religious Administration (*ta-hsi tsung-yin yüan*).

3380 *k'uěi* 揆
T'ANG–SUNG: lit., mastermind: unofficial reference to a **Vice Director** *(p'u-yeh)* **of the Department of State Affairs** (*shang-shu sheng*). See *tuan-k'uei, tso-k'uei, yu-k'uei.*

3381 *k'uéi* 魁
(1) CH'IN: **Head** of a Village *(li)* of about 100 households; part of the sub-District *(hsien)* organization of mutual-help and mutual-surveillance groups. (2) SUNG–CH'ING: **Exemplar:** quasiofficial reference to a Principal Graduate *(chuang-yüan)* in a Metropolitan Examination (*sheng-shih, hui-shih*) in the civil service recruitment examination sequence; also from Yüan on (?) a reference to the 6th through 18th men on the pass list for a Provincial Examination *(hsiang-shih)*. See *ching-k'uei, hsiang-k'uei, hui-k'uei, k'uei-chia, k'uei-chien, ta-k'uei.*

3382 *k'uéi-chāng kó* 奎章閣
YÜAN: **Hall of Literature,** created in 1329 as a group of Academicians *(hsüeh-shih)* attending the Emperor; very quickly (1329–1332) redesignated the Academy in the Hall of Literature (*k'uei-chang ko hsüeh-shih yüan*), then in 1340 renamed the Hall for the Diffusion of Literature (*hsüan-wen ko*). Staff included Grand Academicians (*ta hsüeh-shih*), Academicians Recipients of Edicts (*ch'eng-chih hsüeh-shih*), etc.; they organized and participated in the Classics Colloquium *(ching-yen)*, at which the Emperor was tutored in the Confucian classics and Chinese history, and in general they served as a kind of literary reference service for the Emperor. P23, 24.

3383 *k'uéi-chiǎ* 魁甲
MING–CH'ING: **Chief on the List,** popular reference to the candidate at the head of the pass list after a Metropolitan Examination *(hui-shih)* in the civil service recruitment examination sequence. See under *k'uei.*

3384 *k'uéi-chièn* 魁薦
MING–CH'ING: **Chief Recommendee,** popular reference to the candidate at the head of the pass list after a Provincial Examination *(hsiang-shih)* in the civil service recruitment examination sequence. See under *k'uei.*

3385 *k'uéi-wén kó* 奎文閣
CH'ING: **Library** of the Confucian family estate at Ch'ü-fu, Shantung; headed by a Librarian *(tien-chi)*, rank 7a. P66.

3386 *k'ūn-t'ái* 昆臺
HAN: **Pavilion of Kinsmen** (?), place of detention for imperial relatives and other dignitaries at the Sweet Spring Palace (*kan-ch'üan kung*) in modern Shensi; name changed from *kan-ch'üan chü-shih* (Convict Barracks at Sweet Spring Mountain) c. 146 B.C. Subordinate to the Chamberlain for the Palace Revenues *(shao-fu)*; headed by a Director *(ling)*. HB *(ling)*: prefect of the K'un terrace. P37.

3387 *k'ūn-t'í yüàn* 騉蹄苑
CH'IN–HAN: **Prime Horse Pasturage,** one of many scattered horse pasturages supervised by the Chamberlain for the Imperial Stud *(t'ai-p'u)*; headed by a Director *(ling)*; special function not clear, though the name ("hooves so hard they can clamber over high mountains") suggests fine quality horses. HB *(ling)*: prefect of flinty-hoofed horses. P31.

3388 *kūng* 公
(1) **Duke,** from high antiquity the highest title of nobility *(chüeh)* after *wang* (King in Chou, thereafter Prince), normally reserved for members of the ruling family; commonly but not always inheritable by the eldest son. Into T'ang, denoted a member of a "real" feudal-like nobility with land grants for support, but in native dynasties from Sung on was an honorary status normally conferred on distinguished military officers. Commonly prefixed with territorial names, but see *chen-kuo kung, chün-kung, fu-kuo kung, hsiang-kung, hsien-kung, k'ai-kuo chün-kung, k'ai-kuo hsien-kung, k'ai-kuo kung, kuo-kung, pi-kung, san kung, shang-kung.* From Sung on, also, commonly conferred posthumously on eminent civil officials prefixed with laudatory terms, e.g., *wen-chung kung* (Cultured and Loyal Duke); not inheritable. P65. (2) **The Honorable** or **His Honor,** polite term of indirect address applied to someone considered deserving of respect, used either alone or as a suffix appended to the surname, e.g., Li-kung (the Honorable Li; His Honor, Li).

3389 *kūng* 宮
Palace. (1) Throughout history the most common designation for the residence of the supreme ruler, his wives, and other members of the ruling family; usually used with a directional, laudatory, or auspicious prefix as the name of a building or cluster of buildings in the ruler's residence. See *hsi-kung, hsing-kung, tung-kung, nü-kung, wu kung.* (2) Sometimes used unofficially in reference to an important government agency, e.g., *nan-kung* (Southern Palace), a common reference to the Han–T'ang Department of State Affairs (*shang-shu sheng*) or the Sung Ministry of Rites (*li-pu*). (3) Occasionally encountered as the designation of the tomb of a ruler. Cf. *ling.* (4) LIAO–YÜAN: Chinese translation of the Khitan-Mongolian word *ordo* (see *wo-lu-to*), designation of the camp of a tribal chief including all his entourage, which moved wherever the chief moved and after his death endured as a living and fighting unit.

3390 *kūng-àn* 工案
SUNG–CH'ING: **Works Section,** a subsection in a unit of territorial administration that processed local documents pertaining to the sphere of authority of the central government's Ministry of Works *(kung-pu)*; staffed with subofficial functionaries.

3391 *kūng-chān* 宮詹
T'ANG–CH'ING: unofficial reference to the **Supervisor of the Household of the Heir Apparent** *(chan-shih)*.

3392 *kūng-ch'ē* 公車
(1) HAN–N-S DIV: abbreviation of *kung-ch'e ssu-ma men* **(Gate Traffic Control Office).** (2) CH'ING: unofficial reference to **Provincial Graduates** *(chü-jen)* in the civil service recruitment examination sequence, especially when they appeared at the gates of the dynastic capital to participate in the Metropolitan Examination *(hui-shih)*.

3393 *kūng-ch'ē shǔ* 公車署
N-S DIV (N. Ch'i): **Grievance Office,** in charge of receiving public complaints about injustice and memorializing accordingly; headed by a Director *(ling)*, but organizational affiliations not clear. Traditionally considered an antecedent or variant of the Public Petitioners Office (*teng-wen yüan*) of later dynasties, and quite different from the Gate Traffic Control Offices (*kung-ch'e ssu-ma men*) of Han times. P21.

3394 *kūng-ch'ē ssū-mǎ mén* 公車司馬門
HAN–N-S DIV: lit., the Commander's *(ssu-ma)* gates for

government vehicles (*kung-ch'e*): **Gate Traffic Control Office,** one at each of the 4 gates of the imperial palace, responsible for accepting certain kinds of memorials and tribute articles intended for the Emperor and for maintaining vehicles in readiness to fetch personages summoned to court; each headed by 2 Directors (*k'ung-ch'e ssu-ma ling, kung-ch'e ling*), rank 600 bushels in Han; subordinate to the Chamberlain for the Palace Garrison (*wei-wei, wei-wei ch'ing*) in Han, thereafter to Palace Attendants or Directors (both *shih-chung*) of the developing Chancellery (*men-hsia sheng*), in Ch'i to the Bureau of Public Instruction (*ch'i-pu*). Traditionally considered the antecedent of later dynasties' Offices of Transmission (*t'ung-cheng shih ssu*). HB (*ling*): prefect of the majors in charge of official carriages. P21.

3395 *kūng-ch'én* 功臣
T'ANG, SUNG, MING: **Meritorious Minister,** a generic designation of eminent civil officials and military officers; in Sung, especially those who were awarded laudatory epithets in 2-character combinations, e.g., *ching-pang* (Manager of the State).

3396 *kūng-ch'én pīn-k'ò* 宮臣賓客
YÜAN: **Palace Companion,** 2 in the Household Administration of the Heir Apparent (*chan-shih yüan*); rank and precise function not clear. P26.

3397 *kūng-chèng* 宮正
(1) CHOU: **Palace Steward,** 2 ranked as Senior Servicemen (*shang-shih*), 4 as Ordinary Servicemen (*chung-shih*), and 8 as Junior Servicemen (*hsia-shih*), members of the Ministry of State (*t'ien-kuan*) in charge of maintaining security, discipline, and decorum in the palace during great state ceremonials and whenever the royal capital might come under military attack. CL: *commandant du palais*. (2) N-S DIV: variant designation of, or unofficial reference to, the senior official of the Censorate (*yü-shih t'ai*), especially the **Censor-in-chief** (*yü-shih ta-fu*). (3) T'ANG–MING: **Chief of Palace Surveillance,** title of the palace woman who headed the Office of Palace Surveillance (*kung-cheng ssu*), in charge of keeping watch over and disciplining the whole staff of palace women; in T'ang and Sung rank 5a. RR: *chef de la surveillance du harem*. SP: *directeur de palais*. (4) CH'ING: unofficial reference to the **Supervisor of the Household of the Heir Apparent** (*chan-shih*).

3398 *kūng-chèng* 工正
T'ANG, MING: **Construction Foreman** in a Princely Establishment (*wang-fu*); rank 8a in Ming. Cf. *ssu-chiang*. P69.

3399 *kūng-ch'éng* 公乘
CH'IN–HAN: see *kung-sheng* (**Grandee of the Eighth Order**).

3400 *kūng-chí chiēn* 宮籍監
CHIN: **Directorate of Palace Accounts,** a unit under the Palace Inspectorate-general (*tien-ch'ien tu tien-chien ssu*); headed by a Superintendent (*t'i-tien*), rank 5a. P38.

3401 *kūng-chiào pó-shìh* 宮教博士
T'ANG: **Erudite for Palace Instruction,** 2 in the Office of Female Services (*i-t'ing chü*) of the Palace Domestic Service (*nei-shih sheng*), rank 9b2; in charge of the training and education of palace women. RR: *maître au vaste savoir pour l'instruction des femmes du palais*.

3402 *kùng-chiēn* 貢監
MING: variant of *kung-sheng* (**Tribute Student**).

3403 *kūng-chièn chíh* 弓箭直
SUNG: **Archer on Duty,** a soldier in the Palace Command (*tien-ch'ien ssu*), apparently when on active guard assignment. SP: *garde, porteur d'arcs et de flèches*.

3404 *kūng-chièn k'ù* 弓箭庫
SUNG: **Archery Storehouse:** staffing and organizational affiliation not clear, but probably an armory under the Palace Command (*tien-ch'ien ssu*). See *nei kung-chien k'u*. SP: *magasin d'arcs et de flèches*.

3405 *kūng-chíh* 宮直
CH'ING: **On Palace Duty,** added as prefix or suffix to titles of members of the Imperial Academy of Medicine (*t'ai-i yüan*) assigned to clinical service inside the palace, as distinguished from those assigned to provide medical services to members of the Outer Court (*wai-t'ing*), i.e., the body of civil officials and military officers serving in the capital. P36.

3406 *kūng-chìn pǐ* 供進筆
T'ANG: **Provisioner of Writing Brushes,** suboffical functionaries on the staff of the Chancellery (*men-hsia sheng*). RR: *serviteur chargé d'apporter les pinceaux*.

3407 *kūng-ch'īng* 宮卿
Palace Minister. (1) CHOU: 2 ranked as Senior Servicemen (*shang-shih*), members of the Ministry of State (*t'ien-kuan*); functions not clear. CL: *commandant du palais*. (2) HAN: unofficial reference to a eunuch **Director** (*ta ch'ang-ch'iu*) **of the Palace Domestic Service** (*ch'ang-ch'iu chien*), specially responsible for administering the household of the Empress. (3) From Han on, a common unofficial reference to the **Mentor of the Heir Apparent** (*t'ai-tzu shu-tzu*).

3408 *kūng-chǔ* 公主
Princess or **Imperial Princess:** throughout history the standard designation of daughters of Emperors; modified with various prefixes, e.g., *chang kung-chu, hsien kung-chu, ku-lun kung-chu, ho-shih kung-chu,* qq.v. P69.

3409 *kūng-chǔ chiā-lìng* 公主家令
CH'IN–N-S DIV: **Household Provisioner for the Princess,** normally with a particularizing prefix; see under *chia-ling*.

3410 *kūng-chǔ fǔ* 公主府
Princess' Establishment. (1) T'ANG: established briefly in the early 700s with a staff comparable to that of a Princely Establishment (*wang-fu*), headed by an Administrator (*chang-shih*), rank 4b1. RR: *maison d'une princesse*. (2) CH'ING: regularly established, with an Administrator, rank 3a or 4, as head. BH: *commandant*. P69.

3411 *kūng-chǔ ì-ssū* 公主邑司 or *kung-chu i*
T'ANG–SUNG: **Administration of the Princess' Estate,** in T'ang headed by a Director (*ling*), rank 7b2; Sung staffing not clear. RR: *administration du domaine d'une princesse*. P69.

3412 *kūng-chùng* 宮衆
CHOU: **Palace Army,** an ad hoc assemblage of elite troops and the sons of officials in a time of emergency, e.g., when the royal capital was attacked. CL: *troupes du palais*.

3413 *kūng-chūng kuān* 宮中官
Variant of *kung-kuan* (**Palace Eunuch, Palace Personnel**).

3414 *kung-chü* 公車
See under *kung-ch'e*.

3415 *kùng-chǔ àn* 貢舉案
SUNG: **Recruitment Section,** one of 5 top-echelon Sections (*an*) established in 1129 in the Ministry of Rites (*li-pu*); headed by a Director (*lang-chung*), rank 6b; principally responsible for organizing and administering civil service recruitment examinations. SP: *service des examens de doctorat.* P9.

3416 *kūng-fāng* 宮坊
MING: a combination of abbreviations suggesting **Heir Apparent** (*t'ai-tzu*) **and his staff;** derived from terms relating to the Heir Apparent such as Eastern Palace (*tung-kung*), Green Palace (*ch'ing-kung*), and Secretariat of the Heir Apparent (*ch'un-fang*). P4.

3417 *kūng-fáng* 工房
(1) SUNG: **Office of Works,** one of Six Offices (*liu fang*), comparable in their spheres of responsibility to the Six Ministries (*liu pu*) in the central government, that served as staff agencies in the combined Secretariat-Chancellery (*chung-shu men-hsia sheng*); the 6 Offices were administered by 4 Supervising Secretaries (*chi-shih-chung*). SP: *chambre des travaux publics.* (2) SUNG–CH'ING: may be encountered as a variant or unofficial reference to the **Ministry of Works** (*kung-pu*).

3418 *kūng-fèng* 供奉 or *kūng-fèng kuān* 官
Lit., (those who) provide for, wait upon, serve. (1) T'ANG: **Lady for Service,** from 662 to 670 the designation of a palace woman of rank 7a. RR: *femme à la disposition de l'empereur.* (2) T'ANG (*kung-feng* only): **Auxiliary** (?), from the early 700s an appendix to titles apparently signifying that the officials were fully qualified for the posts indicated but were supernumerary, awaiting vacancies that they might fill. (3) T'ANG–CH'ING (?) (*kung-feng* only): **For Court Service,** an appendix to titles signifying that the officials had been chosen on a rotational basis to be on duty as close attendants of the Emperor; e.g., *kung-feng hsüeh-shih* (Academician for Court Service). RR: *fonctionnaire à la disposition de l'empereur.* (4) SUNG: **Palace Servitor,** highest of 12 rank titles (*chieh*) granted to eunuchs from 1112; see *nei-shih chieh.* Also see *nei kung-feng.*

3419 *kūng-fèng hsüéh-shìh* 供奉學士
YÜAN: **Academician for Court Service,** designation of members of the Hall of Literature (*k'uei-chang ko*) assigned to participate in the Classics Colloquium (*ching-yen*), at which Emperors were tutored about the Confucian classics and Chinese history. P23.

3420 *kūng-fèng kūng-chièn pèi-shēn*
      供奉弓箭備身
SUI: **Personal Archer Guard,** 20 included among the Personal Guards (*pei-shen*) in the establishment of the Heir Apparent; apparently superseded in T'ang by Guards in Personal Attendance (*pei-shen tso-yu*). P26.

3421 *kūng-fèng kūng-yùng* 供奉供用
CH'ING: **Administrative Aide** (?): indefinite numbers authorized for the Music Office (*ho-sheng shu*), concurrent duty assignments for officials of the Court of Imperial Sacrifices (*t'ai-ch'ang ssu*), the Court of State Ceremonial (*hung-lu ssu*), and the Imperial Household Department (*nei-wu fu*); functions not clear. P10.

3422 *kūng-fèng nèi-t'íng* 供奉內廷
SUNG–CH'ING: **Palace Attendant,** from Sung on (perhaps not continuously) a collective reference to various kinds of eunuchs, palace women, officials, and specially talented outsiders in painting, etc.; in Sung subordinate to the Palace Domestic Service (*nei-shih sheng*). In Ch'ing the status was considered somewhat more prestigious than *chih-hou nei-t'ing* (also Palace Attendant). Special functions of the post are not clearly defined, but in general such personnel offered social companionship and entertainment for the Emperor in his private quarters. Sometimes the elements of the term are reversed, making *nei-t'ing kung-feng.*

3423 *kūng-fèng shè-shēng kuān* 供奉射生官
T'ANG: variant of *ya-ch'ien she-sheng ping* (**Bowmen Shooters at Moving Targets**).

3424 *kùng-fèng shǐh* 貢奉使
Tributary Envoy, a descriptive reference to a representative of a foreign ruler, not an official title.

3425 *kūng-fèng shìh-wèi* 供奉侍衛
T'ANG: **Imperial Bodyguard,** duty assignment for various members of Palace Guard (*su-wei*) units, serving in a rotational pattern. RR: *garde à la disposition de l'empereur.*

3426 *kūng-fǔ* 公府
(1) From Han on, an unofficial collective reference to the **Three Dukes** (*san kung*). (2) N-S DIV–CH'ING: **Ducal Establishment,** the household establishment of a dignitary ennobled as a Duke (*kung*). See *kung-kuo.* P65.

3427 *kūng-fù* 宮傅
SUNG–CH'ING: unofficial reference to the **Junior Mentor of the Heir Apparent** (*t'ai-tzu shao-fu*); also see *kung-hsien.*

3428 *kung-fu* 宮輔
See *ta kung-fu.*

3429 *kūng-fù* 工副
MING: **Assistant Construction Foreman,** one, rank 8b, in each Princely Establishment (*wang-fu*), aide to the Construction Foreman (*kung-cheng*); discontinued in 1565. P69.

3430 *kūng-fǔ ssù* 宮府寺
T'ANG: from 662 to 670 the official variant of *chia-ling ssu* (**Household Provisioner's Court**) in the establishment of the Heir Apparent; headed by a Grand Master Provisioner (*kung-fu ta-fu*) rather than the traditional Household Provisioner (*chia-ling*).

3431 *kūng-hó* 共和
HAN: **Lady of Reverent Gentleness,** designation of palace women with rank =100 bushels. HB: tender maid.

3432 *kūng-hsiàng* 公相
Counselor Duke. (1) HAN–T'ANG: abbreviated reference to a Counselor-in-chief (*ch'eng-hsiang*) concurrently bearing the honorific designation Grand Preceptor (*t'ai-shih*), one of the Three Dukes (*san kung*). (2) SUNG: a title especially revived for the controversial minister Ts'ai Ching when he was Grand Councilor (*tsai-hsiang*) and concurrently honorific Grand Guardian (*t'ai-pao*), also one of the Three Dukes. SP: *duc-ministre, directeur des 3 départements.*

3433 *kūng-hsiàng* 宮相
T'ANG: lit., palace minister: unofficial reference to the **Mentor of the Heir Apparent** (*t'ai-tzu shu-tzu*).

3434 *kūng-hsién* 宮銜
SUNG–CH'ING: lit., ranks in the (eastern) palace: **Counselors of the Heir Apparent,** unofficial collective reference to the 6 eminent semi-honorary posts called the Three Preceptors of the Heir Apparent (*t'ai-tzu san-shih*) and the Three Junior Counselors of the Heir Apparent (*t'ai-tzu san-shao*); i.e., the Grand Preceptor of the Heir Apparent (*t'ai-tzu t'ai-shih*), etc.

3435 *kŭng-hsìng* 公姓
From antiquity, a polite reference to the surname of the reigning family, hence indirectly to a member of the imperial family: **Surname of State.** See *kuo-hsing*.

3436 *kŭng-hsüéh* 宮學
SUNG: **Palace School,** the primary school section of the School for the Imperial Family (*tsung-hsüeh*). SP: *école supérieure et primaire du palais royale.*

3437 *kŭng-jén* 宮人
(1) CHOU: **Palace Servant,** 4 ranked as Ordinary Servicemen (*chung-shih*), members of the Ministry of State (*t'ien-kuan*) who provided water for the King's ablutions and torches and braziers for his personal quarters; not eunuchs. CL: *homme du palais, attaché aux appartements de l'empereur.* (2) Throughout history a general reference to **Palace Women,** but sometimes used only for servant-status women, not including the Empress, Consorts (*fei*), or Concubines (*pin*). See *kung-kuan, kung-nü, nü-kuan.* HB: palace maid.

3438 *kŭng-jén* 卅人
CHOU: **Mining Superintendent,** 2 ranked as Ordinary Servicemen (*chung-shih*), members of the Ministry of Education (*ti-kuan*) responsible for the care and exploitation of all mineral deposits of value. CL: *officier des métaux.*

3439 *kŭng-jén* 恭人
Respectful Lady, honorific title awarded to wives of nobles and officials. (1) SUNG: awarded to wives of officials of rank 5 and above. (2) YÜAN: awarded to wives of rank 6 officials. (3) MING: awarded to wives of rank 4 officials. (4) CH'ING: awarded to wives of rank 4 officials and of low-ranking nobles entitled General-by-grace (*feng-en chiang-chün*).

3440 *kŭng-k'ō* 工科
MING–CH'ING: **Office of Scrutiny for Works,** one of the Six Offices of Scrutiny (*liu k'o*) staffed with *chi-shih-chung* (Supervising Secretaries, Supervising Censors). P18, 19.

3441 *kŭng-kuān* 供官
SUNG: **Provisioner,** 12 subofficial functionaries in the Sacrifices Service (*tz'u-chi chü*) or Sacrifices Section (*tz'u-chi an*), 10 in the Office of Sacrificial Utensils (*chi-ch'i ssu*), all subordinate to the Court of Imperial Sacrifices (*t'ai-ch'ang ssu*). P27.

3442 *kŭng-kuān* 宮官
(1) Throughout history a common reference to **Palace Eunuchs** (see *huan-kuan, nei-shih*). (2) May occasionally be found referring collectively to Palace Eunuchs and Palace Women, as **Palace Personnel.** (3) T'ANG–MING: **Palace Woman,** large numbers divided among various Services (*chü*) and Offices (*ssu*); in T'ang and Sung organized under the Palace Domestic Service (*nei-shih sheng*). The basic organization consisted of 6 Services: General Palace Service (*shang-kung chü*), Ceremonial Service (*shang-i chü*), Wardrobe Service (*shang-fu chü*), Food Service (*shang-shih chü*), Housekeeping Service (*shang-ch'in chü*), and Workshop Service (*shang-kung chü*); each Service was normally subdivided into more specialized units, and each was headed by one or more Matrons (*shang …*), rank 5a; e.g., Matron of General Palace Service (*shang-kung*), Matron of the Wardrobe (*shang-fu*). See *kung-nü, nü-kuan.* RR: *chargé du harem.*

3443 *kŭng-kuān* 工官
HAN: **State Laborer,** categorical designation of personnel on the staffs of Commanderies (*chün*) and Princedoms (*wang-*

kuo), headed either by a Chief (*chang*), rank 300 to 400 bushels, or a Director (*ling*), rank 600 to 1,000 bushels. BH: office of workmen.

3444 *kŭng-kuān shih* 宮觀使
SUNG: **Palace and Temple Custodian,** a sinecure to which eminent officials entering retirement were sometimes appointed, or a concurrent assignment for an active official; tended detached imperial villas or favored Taoist temples. See *tz'u-lu*. SP: *commissaire des palais et des temples taoistes.*

3445 *kŭng-kuān tū-chiēn* 宮觀都監
SUNG: **Director-in-chief of Palaces and Temples,** a concurrent appointment or duty assignment for an eminent official, normally in retirement; apparently oversaw individual custodians of detached imperial villas and Taoist temples (see *kung-kuan shih*); organizational affiliation not clear, but probably under the Ministry of Rites (*li-pu*). See *tz'u-lu*. SP: *surveillant général des palais et des temples taoistes.*

3446 *kùng-kūng* 共工
HAN: **Director of Works,** an archaic title equivalent to *ssu-k'ung* (Minister of Works); Han status and functions not clear, but probably bore water-control responsibilities.

3447 *kŭng-kùng* 功貢
CH'ING: **Tribute Student for Merit,** collective designation of those Tribute Students (*kung-sheng*) who were admitted to the Directorate of Education (*kuo-tzu chien*) for advanced education as members of military families (*chün-hu*) who were credited with extraordinary achievements.

3448 *kŭng-kuó* 公國
Dukedom: throughout history, the domain of a Duke (*kung*) on whom a fief (real or nominal) was conferred. Cf. *wang-kuo* (Princedom), *hou-kuo* (Marquisate). See *kung-fu* (Ducal Establishment). HB: duchy. P65.

3449 *kŭng-lùn láng* 功論郎
N-S DIV (Sung): **Court Gentleman for Evaluations,** initiated in 441 (426?) as a subordinate of the Ministry of General Administration (*tu-kuan*) in lieu of the traditional *k'ao-kung lang*, q.v.; apparently terminated with the dynasty in 479, when development resumed toward the Sui–Ch'ing Directors (*lang-chung*) of the Bureau of Evaluations (*k'ao-kung ssu*) in the Ministry of Personnel (*li-pu*); in charge of annual merit ratings (*k'ao*) for officials of Regions (*chou*) and Commanderies (*chün*). See under *k'ao-kung*. P5.

3450 *kŭng-mén chiàng-fŭ* 宮門將府
SUI–T'ANG: **Palace Gates Guard Command,** prefixed Left and Right, military units assigned to the establishment of the Heir Apparent; each headed by a Commander (*chiang*). Superseded units called *chien-men shuai-fu* (Gate Guard Commands) c. 605; in 622 reverted to the former name. P26.

3451 *kŭng-mén chŭ* 宮門局
SUI–LIAO: **Gatekeepers Service,** a unit of the (Left) Secretariat of the Heir Apparent (*men-hsia fang, tso ch'un-fang*), staffed with eunuchs. In Sui headed by one Commandant (*shuai*), c. 604 renamed General (*chiang*), and 2 Grand Masters (*ta-fu*), c. 604 renamed Directors (*chien*); in T'ang by 2 Directors till 662, then by 2 Directors (*lang*), rank 6b2; thereafter ranks not clear, but the title Director of Gatekeepers (*kung-men lang*) endured. Generally responsible for gatekeeping duty in the household of the Heir Apparent. Cf. *kung-wei chü*. RR+SP: *service des portes du palais de l'héritier du trône.* P26.

3452 *kŭng-mén p'ú* 宮門僕
N-S DIV (N. Wei): **Palace Gatekeeper,** indefinite number, rank 6b; members of the Palace Administration (*tien-chung chien*); probably eunuchs. P37.

3453 *kŭng-mén ssū* 宮門司
(1) SUI–YÜAN: possible variant reference to *kung-men chü* (**Gatekeepers Service**). (2) CHIN: **Palace Gates Office,** in 1210 renamed Palace Gates Service (*kung-wei chü*).

3454 *kŭng-nŭ shŭ* 弓弩署
T'ANG: **Bows Office** in the Directorate of the Palace Buildings (*chiang-tso chien*); in 632 renamed *nu-fang shu*.

3455 *kŭng-nŭ tsào-chièn yüàn* 弓弩造箭院
or *kung-nu yüàn*
SUNG: **Bow and Arrow Workshop,** staffing and organizational affiliation not clear, but probably subordinate, at least indirectly, to the Directorate for Armaments (*chün-ch'i chien*) and the Ministry of Works (*kung-pu*). SP: *cour de la fabrication d'arcs et de flèches.*

3456 *kŭng-nŭ* 宮女
Throughout history a general reference to female residents of the palace: **Palace Women.** See *kung-jen, kung-kuan, nü-kuan.*

3457 *kŭng-p'ái* 功牌
CH'ING: **Medal for Merit,** awarded to military officers and soldiers for excellence in reviews and inspections; could be awarded by Governors-general (*tsung-tu*), Provincial Governors (*hsün-fu*), and Regional Commanders (*tsung-ping kuan*). BH: soldier's medal.

3458 *kŭng-păo* 宮保
SUNG–CH'ING: unofficial reference to the **Junior Guardian of the Heir Apparent** (*t'ai-tzu shao-pao*); also see *kung-hsien.*

3459 *kŭng-pèi k'ù* 供備庫
SUNG: **Imperial Larder,** a unit of the Imperial Kitchen (*yü-ch'u*) operated by the Court of Imperial Entertainments (*kuang-lu ssu*); headed by a Commissioner (*shih*), rank 7a. In c. 1080 (?) renamed *nei-wu liao-k'u.* SP: *magasin de provisions pour la cuisine impériale.*

3460 *kŭng-pīn* 宮嬪
Uncommon generic reference to secondary imperial wives, i.e., Consorts (*fei*) and Concubines (*pin*).

3461 *kŭng-pó* 宮伯
CHOU: **Master of the Palace Militia,** rank not clear; member of the Ministry of State (*t'ien-kuan*) in charge of training and evaluating selected Servicemen (*shih*) and Cadets (*shu-tzu*) on guard duty in the royal palace. Junior to the Palace Steward (*kung-cheng*); shared with him supervision of the palace militia. CL: *préfet du palais.*

3462 *kŭng-pù* 工部
(1) N-S DIV (Chou)–CH'ING: **Ministry of Works,** one of the top-echelon agencies (from Sui on collectively called the Six Ministries, *liu pu*) under the Department of State Affairs (*shang-shu sheng*) through Sung and Chin, then under the Secretariat (*chung-shu sheng*) in Yüan and early Ming, and after 1380 directly subordinate to the Emperor, though from the early 1400s under the supervisory coordination of the Grand Secretariat (*nei-ko*). Headed in Chou of the N. Dynasties by a (Grand) Minister of Works (*ssu-k'ung, ta ssu-k'ung*) ranked as an Ordinary Grand Master (*chung ta-fu*), thereafter by one or more Ministers of Works (*kung-pu shang-shu*): in T'ang one, rank 3b; in Sung one, 2b; in Chin one, 3a; in Yüan 3, 3a; in Ming one till the

mid-1500s then 2, 3a till 1380 then 2a; in Ch'ing one each Manchu and Chinese, 1b. In general charge of government construction projects, the conscription of artisans and laborers for periodic state service, the manufacture of government equipment of all sorts, the maintenance of waterways and roads, the standardization of weights and measures, the production of coins and other forms of money, the exploitation of mountains, lakes, marshes, etc. Originated as a coordinating superstructure for the Bureau of Public Construction (*ch'i-pu*), the Chamberlain for the Palace Buildings (*chiang-tso ta-chiang*), and the Directorate of Waterways (*tu-shui chien*); from Sui through Yüan had to share its functions with other agencies, e.g., the strengthened Directorates for the Palace Buildings (*chiang-tso chien, chiang-tso shao-fu chien*) and of Waterways (*tu-shui chien*); then lost some of its functions to powerful eunuchs in Ming and to Provincial Governors (*hsün-fu*) and Governors-general (*tsung-tu*) in Ch'ing. Usually considered the weakest of the Ministries; was sometimes consolidated with the Ministry of Justice (*hsing-pu*) into a single agency. From Sui and T'ang on, normally had 4 major subordinate Bureaus (*ssu, ch'ing-li ssu*): in T'ang a Headquarters Bureau (*kung-pu, kung-pu ssu*), a State Farms Bureau (*t'un-t'ien ssu*), a Bureau of Forestry (*yü-pu*), and a Bureau of Waterways (*shui-pu*); in Ming a Bureau of Construction (*ying-shan ssu*), a Bureau of Forestry and Crafts (*yü-heng ssu*), a Bureau of Irrigation and Transportation (*tu-shui ssu*), and a State Farms Bureau; etc. Each Bureau was headed by one or more Directors (*lang-chung*). In addition, the Ministry normally supervised a large array of storehouses, supply agencies, manufactories, mints, etc., throughout the empire. RR+SP: *ministère des travaux publics.* BH: ministry (board) of works. P14, 15. (2) T'ANG–YÜAN: **Headquarters Bureau,** one of 4 Bureaus in the Ministry of Works, in charge of the general administrative management of the Ministry's affairs, primarily responsible for overseeing the construction of walls and buildings and making arrangements for providing needed labor in all Ministry projects; headed by one or more Directors (*lang-chung*), rank 5b in T'ang, 6b in Sung, 5b in Yüan. RR+SP: *bureau des travaux publics.* P15.

3463 *kùng-pù* 貢部
SUNG: **Recruitment Bureau,** an ad hoc group of officials on detached duty assignments from the Ministry of Rites (*li-pu*) and other agencies to make arrangements for all civil service recruitment examinations. See *chang kung-pu.* SP: *bureau d'examen.*

3464 *kŭng-shàn* 供膳
T'ANG: **Meat Server,** as many as 2,400 suboficial functionaries so designated in the Banquets Office (*t'ai-kuan shu*) of the Court of Imperial Entertainments (*kuang-lu ssu*) and the Office of Foodstuffs (*shih-kuan shu*) in the household of the Heir Apparent. RR: *serviteur chargé des mets.* P30.

3465 *kŭng-shéng* 公乘
CH'IN–HAN: lit., one in charge of government chariots: **Grandee of the Eighth Order,** 13th highest of 20 titles of honorary nobility (*chüeh*) awarded to exceptionally meritorious personages. P65.

3466 *kŭng-shěng* 宮省
Palace Establishment(s): unofficial and vague reference to any agency headquartered within the imperial palace, or to all such agencies, e.g., the Chancellery (*men-hsia sheng*) and the Secretariat (*chung-shu sheng*) of T'ang times.

3467 *kùng-shēng* 貢生
MING–CH'ING: **Tribute Student,** designation of students

under the Directorate of Education (*kuo-tzu chien*) who had been admitted as nominees of local Confucian Schools (*ju-hsüeh*), for advanced study and subsequent admission to the civil service; until the 1440s could expect good official careers; then the status of civil service recruitment examination graduates, especially that of Metropolitan Graduates (*chin-shih*), became so esteemed that Tribute Students could no longer expect good official careers as a matter of course and began trying to enhance their opportunities by competing in the Metropolitan Examination (*hui-shih*) along with other candidates. The Tribute Student status nevertheless remained one of those considered Regular Paths (*cheng-t'u*) into officialdom, as distinguished from Irregular Paths (*i-t'u*) such as purchase of student status. See *sui-kung, pa kung-sheng, fu kung-sheng, yu kung-sheng, en-tz'u kung-sheng, en-pu kung-sheng, lin kung-sheng, tseng kung-sheng, li kung-sheng*. BH: senior licentiate.

3468 *kūng-shèng hóu* 恭聖侯
N-S DIV (N. Ch'i): **Marquis for Revering the Sage,** title of nobility (*chüeh*) granted from 550 to direct heirs descended from Confucius; changed from Marquis for Venerating the Sage (*ch'ung-sheng hou*); under N. Chou the title was changed to Duke of (the Dukedom) of Tsou (*tsou-kuo kung*). P66.

3469 *kūng-shìh* 供事
CH'ING: **Hired Employee,** non-officials and non-functionaries hired for relatively unimportant tasks in many governmental agencies; after experience could be promoted into the lowest ranks of the officialdom. BH: clerk.

3470 *kūng-shìh* 公事 or 宮使
SUNG: **Supervisor,** usually of a quasi-public establishment such as a Taoist temple or monastery, prefixed with the name of the establishment; normally a sinecure for an eminent official in semi-retirement. SP: *chargé d'affaires.*

3471 *kūng-shǐh* 公使
(1) SUNG: **Envoy,** duty assignment for a capital official chosen on an ad hoc basis; specific functions or area of responsibility suggested by prefix. (2) CHIN: **Agent,** sub-official functionaries who served in large numbers on the staffs of Prefectures (*chou, fu*) and many other agencies, e.g., Fiscal Commissions (*chuan-yün shih ssu*) in the various Routes (*lu*), Transport Offices (*ts'ao-yün ssu*) in various localities. P53, 60.

3472 *kūng-shìh* 公士
Lit., state serviceman. (1) CH'IN–HAN: **Grandee of the First Order,** the lowest of 20 titles of honorary nobility (*chüeh*) awarded to exceptionally meritorious personages. (2) SUNG: **Public Worthy,** honorific status awarded the very elderly and those who had fought successfully against bandits. P65.

3473 *kūng-shìh* 宮師
SUNG–CH'ING: unofficial reference to the **Junior Preceptor of the Heir Apparent** (*t'ai-tzu shao-shih*); also see *kung-hsien.*

3474 *kùng-shìh* 貢士
(1) **Nominee for Office:** from antiquity a general reference to men of virtue and talent recommended to the ruler by regional or local authorities, as if in tribute (*kung*), to be considered for appointment as officials (*shih*); from Han on, specially referred to regional or local recommendees considered for admission to schools at the dynastic capital, equivalent to the Ming–Ch'ing term Tribute Student (*kung-sheng*). (2) CH'ING: **Passed Scholar,** specific designation of a civil service examination candidate who had passed the

Metropolitan Examination (*hui-shih*) administered by the Ministry of Rites (*li-pu*) but had not yet taken the follow-up, confirmatory Palace Examination (*tien-shih, t'ing-shih*).

3475 *kūng-shīh fǔ* 宮師府
CHIN–YÜAN: **Administration of the Heir Apparent,** an agency comprising all of the dignitaries assigned to tutor, assist, and protect the Heir Apparent, e.g., the Grand Preceptor of the Heir Apparent (*t'ai-tzu t'ai-shih*), the Junior Guardian of the Heir Apparent (*t'ai-tzu shao-pao*), the Supervisor of the Household of the Heir Apparent (*chan-shih*) and his large service staff. P67.

3476 *kūng-shīh kàn-tāng kuān* 公事幹當官
SUNG: **Police Executive,** normally prefixed Left and Right, one in each of the Four Capital Townships (*ssu hsiang*) into which the successive capital cities, Kaifeng and Hangchow, were divided for administration; responsible for keeping order, investigating crimes, and punishing minor offenders. See *wu ch'eng* (Five Wards). SP: *inspecteur de police.* P20.

3477 *kūng-shǐh ssū* 弓矢司
CH'ING: **Bow and Arrow Office,** one of 2 units comprising the Right Subsection (*yu-so*) of the Imperial Procession Guard (*luan-i wei*); headed by a Director (*chang-yin yün-hui shih*), rank 4a. BH: bow and arrow section.

3478 *kūng-shù* 宮庶
CH'ING: unofficial reference to a **Mentor** (*shu-tzu*) in one of the Secretariats of the Heir Apparent (*ch'un-fang*).

3479 *kūng-ssū lìng* 宮司令
SUNG: **Mistress of the Palace,** one, rank 4a; from 1013 designation of a palace woman who had overall responsibility for the proper functioning of palace women agencies; created to honor a particular palace woman for her many years of service as Chief of Palace Surveillance (*kung-cheng*). See under *liu shang* (Six Matrons).

3480 *kūng tà-fū* 公大夫
CH'IN–HAN: lit., grand master of state: **Grandee of the Seventh Order,** 14th highest of 20 titles of honorary nobility (*chüeh*) awarded to exceptionally meritorious personages. P65.

3481 *kūng t'ài-fù* 宮太傅
SUNG–CH'ING: unofficial reference to the **Grand Mentor of the Heir Apparent** (*t'ai-tzu t'ai-fu*); also see *kung-hsien.*

3482 *kūng t'ài-pǎo* 宮太保
SUNG–CH'ING: unofficial reference to the **Grand Guardian of the Heir Apparent** (*t'ai-tzu t'ai-pao*); also see *kung-hsien.*

3483 *kūng t'ài-shīh* 宮太師
SUNG–CH'ING: unofficial reference to the **Grand Preceptor of the Heir Apparent** (*t'ai-tzu t'ai-shih*); also see *kung-hsien.*

3484 *kūng-t'áng* 公堂
MING–CH'ING: variant of the informal designation **Headquarters** (*t'ang*, q.v.).

3485 *kūng-té shǐh* 功德使
T'ANG–YÜAN: **Commissioner of Merit and Virtue,** sometimes with directional or other prefixes; first appointed in the period 788–807 to supervise the Buddhist establishments in the 2 dynastic capitals, Ch'ang-an and Loyang; gradually evolved into a supervisory controller of adherents of other religions as well, e.g., Islam, Manichaeism. Commonly the duty assignment of an Imperial Prince in Sung. Loosely subordinated to the Court of State Ceremonial (*hung-*

lu ssu) in T'ang and Sung, to the Commission for Buddhist and Tibetan Affairs (*hsüan-cheng yüan*) in Yüan, and in 1329 absorbed into that Commission. See *hsiu kung-te shih, ta kung-te shih*. SP: *commissaire des mérites*. P17.

3486　*kŭng-tièn chièn* 宮殿監
CH'ING: **Directorate of Palace Domestic Service,** a eunuch agency loosely supervised by the Imperial Household Department (*nei-wu fu*) and more directly overseen by senior eunuchs generically called Eunuch Supervisors-in-chief (*tsung-kuan t'ai-chien*), a term prefixed to such specific titles as Supervising Attendant (*tu-ling shih*), rank 4a, the working head of the Directorate. P38.

3487　*kŭng-tièn fŭ hsíng kŭng-pù*
宮殿府行工部
YÜAN: **Palace Branch of the Ministry of Works,** apparently primarily occupied with the construction of the Yüan palace at the Grand Capital (*ta-tu*, i.e., modern Peking); in 1282 was changed into the Grand Capital Regency (*ta-tu liu-shou ssu*), generally responsible for administering the capital city. See *liu-shou ssu*. P15.

3488　*kŭng-tsàn* 宮贊
CH'ING: unofficial reference to the **Admonisher** (*tsan-shan*) in the Secretariat of the Heir Apparent (*ch'un-fang*).

3489　*kŭng-ts'áo* 功曹
Lit., meritorious service section. (1) HAN–N-S DIV: **Labor Section,** designation of staff agencies in Regions (*chou*), Commanderies (*chün*), and Districts (*hsien*) in charge of assembling and overseeing labor gangs as needed; in Later Han sometimes called *chih-chung ts'ao*, q.v. Headed by Administrative Clerks (*shu-tso*) in Regions, Scribes (*shih*) in Commanderies, and Administrators (*yüan-shih*) in Districts. Monitoring the work of labor gangs gradually transformed the unit into that described under (2) below. HB: bureau of merit. (2) N-S DIV–SUNG: **Personnel Evaluation Section,** staff agencies in units of territorial administration down to the District; in the era of N-S Division also found in various central government agencies, e.g., the Court of Imperial Sacrifices (*t'ai-ch'ang ssu*), the Court of State Ceremonial (*hung-lu ssu*). Responsible for preparing and processing merit ratings (*k'ao*) of subordinate officials, also generally for monitoring all government activities in their jurisdictions. Commonly headed by Record Keepers (*chi-shih*) in the N. Dynasties and Sui, by Administrators (*ts'an-chün-shih*), rank 8b or below, in T'ang and Sung. Antecedents of the Ming–Ch'ing units called *lì-ts'ao* (Personnel Section). Also see *liu ts'ao*. RR: *bureau des mérites*. SP: *service des mérites*. (3) SUI: **Palace Guard,** a renaming of *ch'in-wei* c. 605; changed back to that at the beginning of T'ang. (4) SUI–CH'ING: may be encountered as an unofficial reference to the **Ministry of Personnel** (*lì-pu*). P6, 26, 27, 30, etc.

3490　*kŭng-ts'áo* 工曹
Works Section. (1) SUI–CH'ING: may be encountered as an unofficial, archaic reference to the Ministry of Works (*kung-pu*) or to the Ministry's Headquarters Bureau (*kung-pu, kung-pu ssu*). (2) MING–CH'ING: a clerical agency in each unit of territorial administration from the Prefecture (*fu*) down to the District (*hsien*), staffed entirely with suboffical functionaries; managed all local matters that fell under the jurisdiction of the central government's Ministry of Works; successor of the earlier *shih-ts'ao* (Levied Service Section).

3491　*kŭng-tsò àn* 工作案
SUNG: **Labor Section,** one of 6 subsections in the Ministry of Works (*kung-pu*), apparently subordinate to one or more of the Ministry's Bureaus (*ssu*) and responsible for overseeing the assembling of labor gangs to work on state projects; probably staffed with suboffical functionaries. SP: *service des travaux*. P15.

3492　*kŭng-tsŭ* 公祖
CH'ING: **Local Authority,** unofficial general reference to civil officials serving in Departments (*chou*) and Districts (*hsien*); derived from the Ming term *tsu-kung*.

3493　*kŭng-tuàn* 宮端
T'ANG–CH'ING: unofficial reference to the **Supervisor of the Household of the Heir Apparent** (*chan-shih*). See *ch'u-tuan, tuan-yin*.

3494　*kŭng-tzŭ* 公子
CHOU–HAN: **Noble Scion,** an unofficial general reference to sons of members of the nobility (*chüeh*).

3495　*kŭng-wéi chŭ* 宮闈局
SUI–SUNG, CHIN: **Palace Gates Service,** in Sui and T'ang one of 6 eunuch agencies in the Palace Domestic Service (*nei-shih sheng*), responsible primarily for keeping the keys for entrances into the inner quarters of the imperial palace and for opening and closing the gates at proper times; headed by a Director (*ling*), rank 7b2. In Sung apparently subordinate to the Court of Imperial Sacrifices (*t'ai-ch'ang ssu*); whether staffed with eunuchs is not clear; headed by a Director, rank also not clear. In Chin, a eunuch agency under the Court Ceremonial Institute (*hsüan-hui yüan*); headed by a Superintendent (*t'i-tien*), rank 5a, a Commissioner (*shih*), 5b, and a Vice Commissioner (*fu-shih*), 6a. Cf. *kung-men chü, kung-men ssu*. RR: *service des portes du palais intérieur*. SP (*kung-wei ling*): *chargé de maintenir la propreté dans le palais intérieur*. P38.

3496　*kŭng-yĭn* 宮尹
Palace Governor for the Heir Apparent. (1) N-S DIV (Chou): chief administrator of the household establishment of the Heir Apparent, the counterpart of other dynasties' Supervisor of the Household of the Heir Apparent (*chan-shih*); assisted by a Vice Governor (*hsiao-yin*). (2) T'ANG: from 684 to 705 the official variant of *chan-shih* (as above), whose office was known as the *kung-yin fu* (Household Administration of the Heir Apparent; see *chan-shih fu*). (3) SUNG–CH'ING: from late T'ang, an unofficial reference to the **Supervisor of the Household of the Heir Apparent** (*chan-shih*). P26.

3497　*kùng-yüàn* 貢院
SUNG: **Examination Office** in the Ministry of Rites (*lì-pu*); functions not clearly specified, but probably an ad hoc group of Ministry officials and others charged with organizing and doing paperwork about civil service recruitment examinations as they occurred. See *ling kung-yüan*. SP: *bureau des examens*.

3498　*kŭng-yüàn shĭh* 宮苑使
SUNG–CHIN: **Commissioner of Palace Halls and Parks,** apparently one stationed at each of several locations in or near the imperial palace that required continuing maintenance; rank 7a in Sung, not clear in Chin; apparently subordinate to the Directorate-general of the Imperial Parks (*kung-yüan tsung-chien*) in the Court of the Imperial Granaries (*ssu-nung ssu*). SP: *commissaire du parc du palais*.

3499　*kŭng-yüàn tsŭng-chiēn* 宮苑總監
Directorate-general of the Imperial Parks. (1) SUI–CHIN: under supervision of the Court of the Imperial Granaries (*ssu-nung ssu*), managed all imperial buildings, parks, and

gardens outside the imperial palace proper, through subordinate Directorates (*chien*) in charge of particular installations; headed by a Director (*chien*), in T'ang rank 5b2. RR: *direction générale des parcs des palais impériaux*. P40. (2) CH'ING: unofficial reference to the Imperial Parks (*feng-ch'en yüan*) managed by the Imperial Household Department (*nei-wu fu*).

3500 *kūng-yǔn* 宮允
CH'ING: unofficial reference to the **Companion** for the Heir Apparent (*chung-yün*) on the staff of the Household Administration of the Heir Apparent (*chan-shih fu*).

3501 *k'ūng-fáng* 空房
CH'ING: lit., the empty room: **Imperial Clan Prison** maintained by the Court of the Imperial Clan (*tsung-jen fu*). BH: prison of the imperial clan court.

3502 *k'ùng-hó* 控鶴
Lit., (one who) reins in the cranes, i.e., controls the imperial mounts. (1) T'ANG: **Groom**, 20 prefixed Left and 20 prefixed Right appointed in 699 in a Directorate of Imperial Mounts (*k'ung-ho chien*), in 700 renamed Office of Heavenly Mounts (*t'ien-chi fu*); whether the posts endured to the end of the dynasty is not clear. RR: *fonctionnaire chargé de diriger les grues*. (2) CHIN: **Groom** (?), 200 authorized for the Court Ceremonial Institute (*hsüan-hui yüan*). P38. (3) YÜAN: **Household Guard** of the Heir Apparent; 135 assigned in 1282, 65 more authorized in 1293; under the Office of Household Guards (*wei-hou ssu*) of the Heir Apparent, a unit of the Household Provisioner's Office (*chia-ling ssu*) in the establishment of the Heir Apparent.

3503 *k'ùng-mù kuān* 孔目官 or *k'ung-mu*
T'ANG–CH'ING: lit., something like "every hole and item," i.e., one whose work touches all aspects of an agency's responsibilities (?): **Clerk** in charge of files or a book collection, a subofficial functionary except in very rare cases. In T'ang found in a few agencies, e.g., the Academy of Scholarly Worthies (*chi-hsien tien shu-yüan*), the Armies of Inspired Strategy (*shen-ts'e chün*). In Sung found in many kinds of agencies both in the central government and in units of territorial administration; in the Proclamations Office (*chih-ch'ih yüan*) in the Secretariat (*chung-shu sheng*) there was a whole Clerks Office (*k'ung-mu yüan, k'ung-mu fang*), headed by a Chief Clerk (*tu k'ung-mu kuan*). In Chin also widespread, but apparently not used in Yüan, and in Ming and Ch'ing found only in the Hanlin Academy (*han-lin yüan*). RR: *fonctionnaire mettant en ordre les livres*. SP: *fonctionnaire chargé de mettre en ordre les livres et les registres*. BH: junior archivist.

3504 *kuó* 國
(1) CHOU: **Region,** designation of territories within the royal domain, whether fiefs awarded to members of the royal family or territories administered entirely by non-hereditary officials delegated from the royal court. Some early texts refer to the existence of 93 such Regions, divided into 3 categories on the basis of size. See *fang-shih, chia-shih, tu-shih*. (2) **State,** from antiquity the most common designation of China as a whole or any area in or outside China that had a defined, reasonably autonomous political identity, even if it were only nominal; e.g., a Princedom (*wang-kuo*), a Marquisate (*hou-kuo*). Often used in place of Dynasty (*ch'ao, ch'ao-tai*) in reference to a currently reigning dynasty.

3505 *kuó-ch'aó* 國朝
Our Dynasty: throughout imperial history, a common reference to the currently reigning dynasty (*ch'ao, ch'ao-tai*)

or sometimes to China as organized under the currently reigning dynasty.

3506 *kuǒ-ch'éng* 果丞
HAN: **Aide for Fruits,** one subordinate to the Provisioner (*t'ai-kuan ling*), a member of the staff of the Chamberlain for the Palace Revenues (*shao-fu*); another (a eunuch) a member of the Office of Imperial Parks Produce (*kou-tun shu*). HB: assistant for fruits. P37.

3507 *kuó-chì shìh* 國計使
5 DYN (Liang): lit., commissioner for state accounts: **State Fiscal Commissioner,** in charge of taxation and the storing of state revenues; in 912 superseded the previous *chien-ch'ang yüan*. P7.

3508 *kuó-ch'ì chāng-chīng* 國戚章京
CH'ING: **Imperially Related Secretary** (civil official) or **Imperially Related Adjutant** (military officer), imperial in-laws assigned to the curatorial staff of an imperial mausoleum (*ling*), in some cases numbering 65. See *chang-ching*. P29.

3509 *kuó-chiù* 國舅
Dynastic Elder: unofficial reference to a maternal uncle of an Emperor.

3510 *kuó-chūn* 國君
HAN: variant designation of a **Counselor-delegate** (*kuo-hsiang*), the central government's administrator in charge of a Princedom (*wang-kuo*) or a Marquisate (*hou-kuo*). P69.

3511 *kuǒ-fáng* 果房
CH'ING: **Fruits Pantry,** a subsection of the Office of Palace Ceremonial (*chang-i ssu*) in the Imperial Household Department (*nei-wu fu*); responsible for providing fruits needed in sacrificial ceremonies; headed by a Keeper of the Fruits (*chang-kuo*). BH: fruit office.

3512 *kuó fū-jén* 國夫人
T'ANG–SUNG: **Consort of State,** title of nobility (*chüeh*) for women. In T'ang conferred on mothers and wives of the nobles entitled Duke of State (*kuo-kung*) and of rank 1 officials; or, according to some sources, conferred on the mothers and principal wives of Princes (*wang*). In Sung conferred on the wives of Princes, the Three Dukes (*san kung*), Grand Councilors (*tsai-hsiang*), etc. RR: *épouse de principauté*. See *fu-jen*.

3513 *kuó-hóu* 國侯
YÜAN: **Marquis of State,** 5th highest of 10 titles of nobility (*chüeh*), rank 3A. See *hou, chu-hou*. P65.

3514 *kuó-hsiàng* 國相
HAN–N-S DIV: **Counselor-delegate,** the central government's representative in a Princedom (*wang-kuo*) or a Marquisate (*hou-kuo*), equivalent to a Commandery Governor (*chün t'ai-shou*) and a District Magistrate (*hsien-ling*), respectively; rank 2,000 and 1,000 bushels, respectively; interchangeable with *hsiang* (Administrator). Apparently coexisted with Administrators (*nei-shih*) from the 140s B.C. to 8 B.C., when the latter post was discontinued. Thereafter the Counselor-delegate was the unchallenged manager of a Prince's or a Marquis's domain. Early in the era of N-S Division superseded by Administrators (*chang-shih*) in Princely Establishments (*wang-fu*). Sometimes mistakenly written *hsiang-kuo* (Counselor-in-chief), q.v. P53, 69.

3515 *kuó-hsìn fáng* 國信房
SUNG: **Diplomacy Section,** a unit in the Bureau of Military Affairs (*shu-mi yüan*) that handled correspondence and diplomatic exchanges between the throne and foreign peo-

ples including, most notably, the Khitan, the Jurchen, and the Mongols; headed by an executive official of the Bureau on duty assignment as Administrator (*tu-hsia*) of the Section. The Section was apparently discontinued c. 1074 when the support staff of the Bureau was reorganized into Twelve Sections (*shih-erh fang*). SP: *bureau des lettres de créance*.

3516 *kuó-hsìn shǐh* 國信使
SUNG: **State Courier-envoy,** apparently a representative of the throne in international dealings with such peoples as the Jurchen; no doubt an ad hoc duty assignment for a trusted central government official. SP: *envoyé muni de lettres de créance (ambassadeur)*.

3517 *kuó-hsìn ssū* 國信司 or *kuó-hsìn sǒ* 所
SUNG: **Diplomacy Office,** variant references to the Diplomacy Section (*kuo-hsin fang*) of the Bureau of Military Affairs (*shu-mi yüan*).

3518 *kuó-hsìng* 國姓 or *kuó-hsìng-ā* 阿
Surname of State, throughout history a reference to the surname of the ruling dynasty, hence an indirect reference to a member of the ruling family or, as in the case of the famous 17th century pirate-loyalist Cheng Ch'eng-kung (Koxinga), to someone formally granted the imperial surname for extraordinary merit. See *kung-hsing*.

3519 *kuó-hsù* 國婿
SUNG: **Imperial Son-in-law,** unofficial reference to the husband of an Imperial Princess, formally ennobled as Commandant-escort (*fu-ma tu-wei*).

3520 *kuó-hsüéh* 國學
N-S DIV: one of several designations of the **National University** (*kuo-tzu hsüeh, t'ai-hsüeh*) at the dynastic capital.

3521 *kuó-hūn* 國婚
N-S DIV: **Imperial Son-in-law,** common unofficial reference to the husband of an Imperial Princess.

3522 *kuǒ-ì fǔ* 果毅府
SUI: **Courageous Garrison,** one of 2 special types of military units (see *che-ch'ung fu,* Assault-resisting Garrison) created outside the regular establishment of Garrison Militia units (see *fu* and *fu-ping*) in 613; headed by 2 Commandants (*tu-wei*) prefixed Left and Right, rank 5b2, 6a1, or 6a2. Reasons for the creation of these units are not clear, nor is their fate, except that they were apparently discontinued by the end of Sui in 618. In 636, however, T'ang resurrected the title *kuo-i tu-wei* for the 2 Vice Commandants of each newly standardized Assault-resisting Garrison. RR: *milice intrépide*.

3523 *kuó-kuān* 國官
N-S DIV (N. Wei, N. Ch'i)–T'ANG: **Official of the Domain,** a generic reference to official personnel of a Princedom (*wang-kuo*), a Marquisate (*hou-kuo*), and other domains of nobles, charged with administering the territory allocated to the nobles as their fiefs. Distinguished from Officials of the Establishment (*fu-kuan*) serving in the noble's personal headquarters or household, e.g., a Princely Establishment (*wang-fu*). Thus the Director of the Princedom (*wang-kuo ling*) was an Official of the Domain, whereas the Administrator (*chang-shih*) of a Princely Establishment was an Official of the Establishment. These usages seem to have faded away in T'ang. P69.

3524 *kuó-kuān* 果官
N-S DIV (Chin): **Fruit Provisioner,** a subordinate of the Director of Banquets (*ta-kuan ling*) under the Chamberlain for Attendants (*kuang-lu-hsün*). See *kuo-ch'eng, chang-kuo, kuo-fang*. P30, 37.

3525 *kuó-kūng* 國公
SUI–YÜAN: **Duke of State,** normally the 3rd highest of 9 titles of nobility (*chüeh*), following Prince (*wang*) and Commandery Prince (*chün-wang*), but 3rd of 3 in Liao, 2nd of 7 in Chin, and 3rd of 10 in Yüan; rank normally 1b, but 2a in Yüan; discontinued by Sui c. 604, when the nobility was restructured with only the 3 titles Prince, Duke (*kung*), and Marquis (*hou*); restored in T'ang. Normally conferred on the heirs (usually eldest sons) of Commandery Princes, but in Sung conferred only on selected descendants of the first 2 Sung Emperors. Seldom found without territorial prefixes indicating real or nominal ducal domains; e.g., *liang-kuo kung* (Duke of Liang, i.e., of the "state" of Liang; not Liang Duke of State). Also see *k'ai-kuo kung, k'ai-kuo chün-kung, k'ai-kuo hsien-kung, chün-kung, hsien-kung*. RR+SP: *duc de principauté*. P65.

3526 *kuó-lǎo* 國老
CHOU: **Elders of the State,** a reference to retired officials who had held rank as Minister (*ch'ing*) or Grand Master (*ta-fu*), distinguished from retired Servicemen (*shih*), who were called Elders of the People (*shu-lao*). CL: *vieillards de l'état*.

3527 *kuó-mǔ* 國母
CH'ING: **Mother of the State,** a respectful reference to the Empress.

3528 *kuó-shēng* 國甥
Imperial Nephew, at least in the later dynasties if not earlier, an unofficial reference to the son of an Empress' sister.

3529 *kuó-shǐh* 國史
(1) **History of the Dynasty,** a common general reference to compilations of historical data prepared while a dynasty reigned, ideally organized after each Emperor's reign; not to be confused with what Westerners refer to as the dynastic histories, beginning with *Shih-chi* by Ssu-ma Ch'ien, which the Chinese call Standard Histories (*cheng-shih*). (2) N-S DIV (San-kuo Wu): **State Historiographer,** one each prefixed Left and Right; status and organizational affiliation not clear. P23.

3530 *kuó-shīh* 國師
(1) **Preceptor of State,** occasional unofficial reference to a Grand Preceptor (*t'ai-shih*) or to all of the court dignitaries known collectively as the Three Preceptors (*san shih*). (2) N-S DIV: unofficial reference to the **Chancellor of the National University** (*kuo-hsüeh chi-chiu*). (3) YÜAN: **Preceptor of State,** head of the Supreme Control Commission (*tsung-chih yüan*) in general charge of the Buddhist priesthood, in 1288 retitled *hsüan-cheng yüan* (Commission for Buddhist and Tibetan Affairs).

3531 *kuō-shìh* 蝈氏
CHOU: **Master of Crickets,** ranked as a Junior Serviceman (*hsia-shih*), a member of the Ministry of Justice (*ch'iu-kuan*) apparently responsible for dealing with harmful cricket swarms, but functions not clear. CL: *préposé aux grenouilles*.

3532 *kuó-shǐh àn* 國史案
SUNG: **Section for the History of the Dynasty,** an agency in the Palace Library (*pi-shu sheng*) responsible for compiling dynastic historical materials; headed by a Grand Compiler (*ta-chu*). Replaced (date not clear) the early Sung Bureau of Compilation (*pien-hsiu yüan*) of the Chancellery (*men-hsia sheng*). SP: *service de l'histoire d'état*. P23.

3533 *kuó-shǐh jìh-lì sǒ* 國史日曆所
SUNG: **Office of History and the Calendar,** part of the

Palace Library (*pi-shu sheng*); probably a variant reference to the Section for the History of the Dynasty (*kuo-shih an*). SP: *bureau du calendrier (et?) de l'histoire d'état.* P23.

3534 *kuó-shǐh kuǎn* 國史館
SUNG–CH'ING: **Historiography Institute,** responsible for preparing the reign-by-reign chronicles of important events called the *True Records* (*shih-lu*); in Sung headed by a Chief Compiler (*chien-hsiu*) whose principal post commonly was Grand Councilor (*tsai-hsiang*); nominally under the Palace Library (*pi-shu sheng*), the Institute was housed in the Institute for the Veneration of Literature (*ch'ung-wen yüan*) and was one of the so-called Three Institutes (*san kuan,* q.v.). In Ch'ing the Institute was loosely attached to the Hanlin Academy (*han-lin yüan*), headed by a Grand Secretary (*ta hsüeh-shih*) or the Minister (*shang-shu*) of a Ministry (*pu*) on concurrent assignment as Director-general (*tsung-ts'ai*) of the Institute. BH: state historiographer's office.

3535 *kuó-shǐh shíh-lù yüan* 國史實錄院
SUNG: **Historiography and True Records Institute,** an umbrella-like superstructure for 2 agencies, nominally subordinate to the Palace Library (*pi-shu sheng*) but more or less autonomous units in the central government: the Historiography Institute (*kuo-shih kuan*) headed by a Chief Compiler (*chien-hsiu*), which was responsible for preparing contemporary histories reign by reign, and the True Records Institute (*shih-lu yüan*) headed by a Supervisor (*t'i-chü*), which was responsible for preparing a day-by-day narrative of important events; both agencies were staffed largely by officials of the central government concurrently assigned as Senior Compilers (*hsiu-chuan*), Examining Editors (*chien-t'ao kuan*), Compilers (*pien-hsiu kuan*), Proofreaders (*chiao-k'an*), Editors (*chiao-cheng*), Editorial Examiners (*chien-yüeh*), etc.; the Chief Compiler of the Historiography Institute was commonly the concurrent assignment of a Grand Councilor (*tsai-hsiang*). How functions were divided among the Historiography and True Records Institute, the Section for the History of the Dynasty (*kuo-shih an*) of the Palace Library, the Court Calendar Office (*jih-li so*) of the Palace Library, the Dynastic History Office (*kuo-shih yüan*) of the Chancellery (*men-hsià sheng*), and the Editorial Service (*chu-tso chü*) of the Palace Library, if all coexisted simultaneously, is not clear. All these agencies performed functions that, for the most part, were performed in prior times by the Editorial Service and in later times by the Hanlin Academy (*han-lin yüan*). SP: *cour de la rédaction de l'histoire d'état et des annales véridiques.*

3536 *kuó-shǐh yüàn* 國史院
SUNG–YÜAN: **Historiography Academy,** generally responsible for preparing the reign-by-reign chronicles of important events called the *True Records* (*shih-lu*). In Sung subordinate to the Chancellery (*men-hsia sheng*); had a recurrent, unstable existence; probably abandoned most of its functions to the Historiography Institute (*kuo-shih kuan*) that was nominally subordinate to the Palace Library (*pi-shu sheng*). In Liao, Chin, and Yüan increasingly associated with the Hanlin Academy (*han-lin yüan*) until in Yüan the 2 units were combined as the Hanlin and Historiography Academy (*han-lin kuo-shih yüan*); after Yüan its functions were absorbed into the Hanlin Academy alone. SP: *cour de l'histoire d'état.* P23.

3537 *kuó tà-fū* 國大夫
HAN: **Grand Master of State,** a title of honorary nobility (*chüeh*) awarded to meritorious subjects; perhaps equivalent to *kuan ta-fu* (Grandee of the Sixth Order), q.v. P65.

3538 *kuó t'ài-fū jén* 國太夫人
SUNG: **Master (Mistress) of State,** a title of merit and honor awarded to mothers and maternal grandparents of Grand Councilors (*tsai-hsiang*), the Three Dukes (*san kung*), and some other dignitaries.

3539 *kuó-tzǔ* 國子
CHOU, HAN: **Scions of State,** a collective designation of the sons and younger brothers of Feudal Lords (*chu-hou*), Ministers (*ch'ing*), and Grand Masters (*ta-fu*) in Chou and in Han those of officials corresponding to Chou Ministers and Grand Masters. CL: *fils de l'état.*

3540 *kuó-tzǔ chì-chiǔ* 國子祭酒
From Han on, designation of the **Chancellor of the National University** (*t'ai-hsüeh, kuo-hsüeh*) or **Chancellor of the Directorate of Education** (*kuo-tzu chien*). See *chi-chiu.* P34, 49.

3541 *kuó-tzǔ chiēn* 國子監
SUI–CH'ING: **Directorate of Education,** a central government agency headed by a Chancellor (*chi-chiu*) that oversaw several schools at the dynastic capital, chiefly the National University (*t'ai-hsüeh*), the School for the Sons of the State (*kuo-tzu hsüeh*), and the School of the Four Gates (*ssu-men hsüeh*); at times the Directorate also provided loose supervision over regional and local schools. From Sung through Yüan there was a steady consolidation until in Ming and Ch'ing there was only one school under the Directorate, the *kuo-tzu hsüeh* (now best rendered National University). Throughout, the instructional staff consisted primarily of Erudites (*po-shih*), often bearing prefixes specifying the classical works in which they individually specialized, and Instructors (*chu-chiao, hsüeh-cheng, hsüeh-lu*). Students, who regularly numbered in the thousands, were called National University Students (*kuo-tzu chien sheng* or simply *chien-sheng*). Prior to c. 605, the capital schools developed under such designations as *t'ai-hsüeh, kuo-hsüeh, kuo-tzu hsüeh, kuo-tzu ssu.* In Ming from 1421 there was a Nanking Directorate of Education as well as the principal Directorate at Peking. From the outset, schools in the capital existed primarily to prepare qualified students for official careers, but from Sung on this route into the officialdom lost esteem as the system of civil service recruitment examinations (see *k'o-chü*) leading to status as Metropolitan Graduates (*chin-shih*) matured and gained dominance in recruitment. Also see *ssu chien* (Four Directorates) and *wu chien* (Five Directorates). RR+SP: *l'université des fils de l'état.* BH: national college, imperial academy of learning. P34.

3542 *kuó-tzǔ hsüéh* 國子學
(1) HAN: occasional variant of *t'ai-hsüeh* (**National University**). (2) N-S DIV: **National University,** from the 200s on alternated with *t'ai-hsüeh* as the official designation; headed by a Chancellor (*chi-chiu*); normally supervised by the Chamberlain for Ceremonials (*t'ai-ch'ang*), but in N. Ch'i gained an autonomous status in the central government organized as a Court for Education (*kuo-tzu ssu*). (3) SUI–CH'ING: **School for the Sons of the State,** one of several capital schools under the Directorate of Education (*kuo-tzu chien*); in Sung and again from Ming on, consolidated into the sole school under the Directorate, its name becoming almost interchangeable with that of the Directorate as well as with the name National University (*t'ai-hsüeh*). Headed collectively by Erudites (*po-shih*) until Yüan, then by the Chancellor (*chi-chiu*) of the Directorate through Ming, then in Ch'ing by a Grand Minister Managing the Directorate of Education (*kuan-li kuo-tzu chien ta-ch'en*). From Sui into

early Sung was specially charged with educating sons of the most eminent nobles and officials in the Confucian classics. Always closely affiliated with the Court of Imperial Sacrifices (*t'ai-ch'ang ssu*) and the Ministry of Rites (*li-pu*), and in Yüan subordinated to the Academy of Scholarly Worthies (*chi-hsien yüan*). RR: *section des fils de l'état*. P34.

3543 *kuó-tzŭ pó-shìh* 國子博士
Erudite of the National University; see under *po-shih* (Erudite).

3544 *kuó-tzŭ shēng* 國子生
National University Student, variant of *chien-sheng*.

3545 *kuó-tzŭ shīh* 國子師
T'ANG: unofficial reference to the **Director of Studies** (*ssu-yeh*) in the Directorate of Education (*kuo-tzu chien*).

3546 *kuó-tzŭ ssū* 國子寺
N-S DIV–T'ANG: **Court for Education,** a relatively autonomous central government agency created during N. Ch'i to supersede the National University (*kuo-tzu hsüeh, t'ai-hsüeh*); c. 605 changed to Directorate of Education (*kuo-tzu chien*); revived at the beginning of T'ang but in 627 again changed to *kuo-tzu chien*. P34.

3547 *kuŏ-tzŭ tū-chiēn* 果子都監
CHIN: **Directorate-in-chief of Fruits,** a unit of the Court Ceremonial Institute (*hsüan-hui yüan*) responsible for keeping the Emperor stocked with fresh fruits; headed by a Director-in-chief (*tu-chien*), rank not clear. P30.

3548 *kuó-wáng* 國王
Prince of the State: from Han on, the equivalent of *wang* (Prince); used only as a collective or generic reference to Princes enfeoffed with real or nominal Princedoms (*wang-kuo*) to distinguish them, e.g., from Commandery Princes (*chün-wang*). In the case of a particular Prince, *kuo* was normally omitted, e.g., Lu-*wang* (Prince of Lu) rather than Lu-*kuo wang* (Prince of the State of Lu). At times a personal name was inserted, e.g., Lu Hsing-*wang* (Prince Hsing of Lu) as distinct from his father, Lu Ching-*wang* (Prince Ching of Lu).

3549 *kuó-wèi* 國尉
CH'IN: **Defender-in-chief,** variant of *tu-wei*, the Emperor's chief of military staff and one of the Three Dukes (*san kung*).

3550 *kuó-yīn* 國姻
Imperial In-laws: throughout history a collective reference to the ruler's relatives by marriage.

3551 *kuó-yùng ssū* 國用司
SUNG: **State Finance Office,** a late Sung agency responsible directly to the Emperor for the state budget and all related fiscal matters; created not later than 1169; headed by a State Finance Commissioner (*kuo-yung shih, chih kuo-yung shih*), normally a concurrent appointment for a Grand Councilor (*tsai-hsiang*). SP: *bureau des finances d'état (budget)*.

3552 *kuó-yùng ts'ān-chì sŏ* 國用參計所
SUNG: **Accounting Office,** a constituent unit in the State Finance Office (*kuo-yung ssu*) of late Sung times; headed by an Accountant (*ts'an-chi kuan*), normally a concurrent appointment for a Vice Minister (*shih-lang*), presumably of the Ministry of Revenue (*hu-pu*). SP: *bureau de comptabilité des finances d'état (budget)*.

3553 *k'uò-chí* 躓騎
T'ANG: lit., cavalryman with a fully drawn bow: **Perma-**

nent **Palace Guard,** from c. 725 a corps of paid volunteer soldiers charged with controlling the gates of the private quarters of the palace; superseded the name *ch'ang-ts'ung su-wei*. RR: *cavalier aux arcs tendus*.

3554 *la-jen* 腊人
See *hsi-jen* (Keeper of Dried Meats).

3555 *lă-má yìn-wù ch'ù* 喇嘛印務處
CH'ING: **Lama Office** in the Court of Colonial Affairs (*li-fan yüan*) in charge of all court relations with priests of Tibetan Lamaism; staffing and organizational history not clear. BH: lama office.

3556 *lài-yüăn chūn* 來遠軍 or 徠遠軍
CHIN: lit., Military Prefecture intended to win the allegiance of outsiders: **Frontier-defense Military Prefecture,** a type of unit of territorial administration; staffing not clear. See *chün* (Military Prefecture). P53.

3557 *lài-yüăn ssū* 徠遠司
CH'ING: lit., bureau for causing distant peoples to' come, i.e., to submit: **Eastern Turkestan Bureau** in the Court of Colonial Affairs (*li-fan yüan*); abbreviation of *lai-yüan ch'ing-li ssu* (see *ch'ing-li ssu*); headed by one Manchu Director (*lang-chung*). Not established until 1761, then charged with managing relations with the dependent peoples of Hami, Turfan, and nearby regions. BH: department of eastern Turkestan. P17.

3558 *lán-líng shìh-wèi* 藍翎侍衛
CH'ING: lit., guardsman wearing blue feathers: **Junior Guardsman,** 90, rank 6a: one category of members of the Imperial Bodyguard (*ch'in-chün ying*) consisting of low-ranking officers granted the honor of wearing blue plumes. See *shih-wei ch'in-chün*. BH: junior body-guards.

3559 *lán-líng tsŭng-ch'éng* 藍翎總承
CH'ING: **Junior Guardsman-gamekeeper,** 2 delegated from the Imperial Bodyguard (*ch'in-chün ying*) to serve as principal gamekeepers in the Imperial Game Preserve (*yü niao-ch'ing ch'u*); supervised by a Manager (*kuan-li … shih-wu*) with status as a Grand Minister of the Imperial Household Department (*nei-wu fu ta-ch'en*). BH: senior gamekeeper (subaltern of the guards).

3560 *lán-t'ái* 蘭臺
Orchid Pavilion. (1) HAN–CH'ING: originally a palace archive or library, headed until 8 B.C. by the Palace Aide to the Censor-in-chief (*yü-shih chung-ch'eng*); hence throughout subsequent history a common unofficial reference to the *yü-shih chung-ch'eng*, q.v., to the Censorate (*yü-shih t'ai, tu ch'a-yüan*), to Censors (*yü-shih*) in general, and most particularly to Supervising Secretaries or Supervising Censors (*chi-shih-chung*). HB: orchid terrace. (2) HAN–N-S DIV: from late Han, a common official variant of *yü-shih t'ai* (Censorate). (3) T'ANG: from 662 to 670 the official variant of *pi-shu sheng* (Palace Library), headed by a Grand Scribe (*t'ai-shih*) and staffed with a Vice Director (*shih-lang*), a Grand Master (*ta-fu*), and a Gentleman-attendant (*lang*). RR: *terrace des orchidées*. (4) CH'ING: unofficial reference to the Hanlin Academy (*han-lin yüan*), whereas the Censorate (*tu ch'a-yüan*) was unofficially called *lan-t'ai ssu* (Court of the Orchid Pavilion). (5) Because from 8 B.C., when the *yü-shih chung-ch'eng* was shifted out of his palace office to become active head of the Censorate (*yü-shih t'ai, yü-shih fu*), the *lan-t'ai* was headed by a Clerk (*ling-shih*) and because the noted Later Han historian Pan Ku at one time held this post, *lan-t'ai* was subsequently used as an unofficial reference to Historiographers (*shih-kuan*). P5, 18, 25.

3561 *lán-t'ái ssù* 蘭臺寺
HAN–CH'ING: **Court of the Orchid Pavilion,** unofficial reference to the Censorate (*yü-shih t'ai, tu ch'a-yüan*).

3562 *lán-tièn ch'ǎng* 藍靛廠
MING: **Blue Dye Shop,** a workshop in western Peking subordinate to the eunuch agency named the Palace Weaving and Dyeing Service (*nei chih-jan chü*).

3563 *láng* 郎
Court Gentleman, Gentleman-attendant, Gentleman. (1) CH'IN: generic term for court attendants, divided in 3 categories: Inner Gentlemen (*chung-lang*), Outer Gentlemen (*wai-lang*), and Standby Gentlemen (*san-lang*). All were presumably officials awaiting appointment or reappointment; special functional differentiations are not clear. See *san lang* (Three Court Gentlemen). (2) HAN–N-S DIV: generic term for court attendants from various sources including sons of eminent officials, men specially recommended by regional and local authorities, experienced officials awaiting reappointment, and from 124 B.C. graduates of the National University (*t'ai-hsüeh*); all regular participants in court audiences and used as door guards, ushers, etc., but principally constituted a pool of qualified men available for appointments when vacancies occurred or special needs arose. Differentiated into 3 salary ranks: Inner Gentlemen (*chung-lang*), rank =600 bushels; Attendant Gentlemen (*shih-lang*), =400 bushels; and Gentlemen of the Interior (*lang-chung*), =300 bushels. Organized under Leaders (*chiang*) subordinate to the Chamberlain for Attendants (*lang-chung ling* until c. 104 B.C., thereafter *kuang-lu-hsün*). In Later Han grouped into Three Corps (*san shu*). These Han practices continued into the post-Han era but gradually changed as indicated under (3) below. HB: gentleman. (3) N-S DIV–YÜAN: used almost interchangeably with the title *lang-chung,* to designate regular official appointees in various agencies, especially in the era of N-S Division in the developing Department of State Affairs (*shang-shu sheng*), its subordinate Ministries (*pu*), and their constituent Bureaus (*ssu*) or Sections (*ts'ao*), sometimes denoting Vice Minister of a Ministry, sometimes Director of a Ministry Bureau or Section. By Sui these usages yielded to *shih-lang* (Vice Minister) and *lang-chung* (Director of a Bureau); but the term *lang* was perpetuated in the usage just described continuously through Yüan times, e.g., in the case of *pi-shu lang* (Assistant in the Palace Library, *pi-shu sheng*). (4) SUI–CH'ING: used extensively, as descriptive or laudatory prefixes (*san-kuan*) for civil officials, e.g., *ch'eng-te lang* (Gentleman for Fostering Virtue), *ch'ao-feng lang* (Gentleman for Court Service). In Sui, when one series of prestige titles was available for both civil and military personnel, *lang* corresponded to the upper degree (*shang-teng*) of a rank-class (e.g., 6a1, 6b1) whereas *wei* corresponded to the lower degree (*hsia-teng*) of a rank-class (e.g., 6a2, 6b2); but from T'ang on, *wei* occurred in prestige titles for military officers and *lang* was used for civil officials. RR: *secrétaire.* SP: *secrétaire, sous-directeur, vice-commissaire.* P68.

3564 *láng-chiàng* 郎將
(1) HAN–N-S DIV: **Leader of Court Gentlemen,** equivalent to *chiang* and *chung-lang chiang,* qq.v. (2) N-S DIV (N. Wei): **Commandant** of a Garrison (*fu*) in the early development of the Garrison Militia (*fu-ping*) system. (3) SUI–T'ANG: **Commandant** of a Soaring Hawks Garrison (*ying-yang fu*), the basic local unit in the Garrison Militia system from 607 to 618. RR: *colonel.* (4) T'ANG: **Vice Commandant,** 2 prefixed Left and Right, under the Commandant (*chung-lang chiang*) in charge of each of the Five Gar-

risons (*wu fu*) that constituted the hereditary elite corps of troops at the dynastic capital. RR: *lieutenant-colonel.* (5) SUNG: **Commandant,** a title occasionally granted to aboriginal chiefs of the West and Southwest; also an officer in various Guards (*wei*) and other military units at the dynastic capital; rank not clear, but apparently below *chung-lang chiang* (also Commandant). SP: *colonel.* P26, 72.

3565 *láng-chūng* 郎中
(1) HAN–N-S DIV: **Gentleman of the Interior,** the lowest of 3 rank categories (=300 bushels) into which most expectant appointees serving as court attendants were divided; see under *lang.* HB: gentleman-of-the-palace. (2) N-S DIV–CH'ING: **Director** of a Section (*ts'ao*) or Bureau (*pu, ssu, ch'ing-li ssu*) in a Ministry (*pu*) or in some agency of comparable status, e.g., in all Yüan Branch Secretariats (*hsing-sheng*), the Ch'ing Court of Colonial Affairs (*li-fan yüan*); rank 5b in T'ang, 6a or 6b in Sung, 5b in Chin and Yüan, 5a in Ming and Ch'ing; sometimes more than one appointee. In T'ang, this post and Vice Directors of Bureaus (*yüan-wai lang*), though of relatively low rank, were considered "pure and important" (*ch'ing-yao*), i.e., part of the hierarchic tracks through which extraordinarily influential or promising men were speeded into the status of Grand Councilor (*tsai-hsiang*); see *ch'ing* (pure). Cf. *t'ung lang-chung.* RR+SP: *secrétaire supérieur, directeur de bureau.* BH: department director.

3566 *láng-chūng ch'ē-chiàng* 郎中車將
HAN: **Gentleman of the Interior Serving as Chariot Commander,** reportedly with rank =1,000 bushels but apparently a duty assignment, probably ad hoc, for a Gentleman of the Interior (*lang-chung*); specific functions not clear. Discontinued in Later Han. HB: general of the gentlemen-of-the-palace of imperial equipages.

3567 *láng-chūng chí-chiàng* 郎中騎將
HAN: **Gentleman of the Interior Serving as Cavalry Commander,** reportedly with rank =1,000 bushels but presumably an ad hoc duty assignment for a Gentleman of the Interior (*lang-chung*); specific functions not clear. Discontinued in Later Han. BH: general of the gentlemen-of-the-palace of the cavalry.

3568 *láng-chūng chù-hsià lìng* 郎中柱下令
HAN: **Gentleman of the Interior Serving as Director of Archivists,** apparently an ad hoc duty assignment for a Gentleman of the Interior (*lang-chung*); specific functions not clear. P25.

3569 *láng-chūng hù-chiàng* 郎中戶將
HAN: **Gentleman of the Interior Serving as Gate Commander,** apparently an ad hoc duty assignment for a Gentleman of the Interior; specific functions not clear. Discontinued in Later Han. HB: general of the gentlemen-of-the-palace of the doors.

3570 *láng-chūng lìng* 郎中令
Chamberlain for Attendants. (1) CH'IN–HAN: a major executive official of the central government, rank 2,000 bushels; in charge of all Court Gentlemen (*lang*), in a large number of specialized groups including the Emperor's personal guard; responsible for monitoring activities in the public part of the palace and for protecting the Emperor when he went out of the palace; c. 104 B.C. retitled *kuang-lu-hsün.* HB: prefect of the gentlemen-of-the-palace. P37. (2) HAN–N-S DIV: in charge of the bodyguards in Princedoms (*wang-kuo*), Marquisates (*hou-kuo*), and other noble fiefs; rank 1,000 bushels in late Han, then not clear except 5b, 7b, or 8b in N. Wei. P69.

3571 *láng-chūn* 郎君

(1) LIAO: **Court Attendant,** designation of lowly officials in most Services (*chü*) subordinate to the Northern Court Ceremonial Institute (*hsüan-hui pei-yüan*); provided companionship for the Emperor and Heir Apparent; other functions not clear, rank not clear. P38. (2) MING–CH'ING: unofficial reference to a new **Metropolitan Graduate** (*chin-shih*).

3572 *láng-hsià shìh-shǐh* 廊下食使 or *láng-hsià shǐh*

T'ANG–SUNG: **Supervisor of Post-audience Banquets,** duty assignment of 2 Palace Censors (*tien-chung shih yü-shih*) to attend and monitor the conduct of high officials at meals they took together with the Emperor in one of the side galleries (*lang-hsia*) of the audience hall on the first and 15th days of each month. RR+SP: *commissaire (impérial) chargé des repas sous la galerie.*

3573 *láng-kuān* 郎官

(1) CH'IN–HAN: variant of *lang* (**Court Gentleman**). (2) T'ANG–CH'ING: unofficial reference to the **Director** (*lang-chung*) of a Bureau (*ssu, ch'ing-li ssu*) or sometimes the **Vice Minister** (*shih-lang*) in a Ministry (*pu*).

3574 *láng p'ú-yèh* 郎僕射

HAN: **Supervisor of Court Gentlemen** (?): status, functions, and organizational affiliation not clear. See *p'u-yeh.*

3575 *láng shè-jén* 郎舍人

SUNG: **Imperial Diarist** in the Chancellery (*men-hsia sheng*), also in the Secretariat (*chung-shu sheng*); in early Sung (date not clear) retitled *ch'i-chü lang* and *ch'i-chü she-jen,* qq.v.; thereafter possibly an unofficial reference to these 2 groups of officials. Also called *hsiu-chu,* q.v. SP: *secrétaire chargé de noter les faits et gestes de l'empereur.*

3576 *láng shìh-chiǎng* 郎侍講

HAN: variant of *shih-chiang* (**Expositor-in-waiting**); also see *chiang-lang* (Court Gentleman for Lecturing). P23.

3577 *lǎo-chiā* 老家

MING: **Oldster,** generic designation of soldiers in Training Divisions (*ying*) who were deemed unfit for active military duties and were commonly assigned to construction gangs or other menial status.

3578 *lǎo-fèng* 老鳳

SUNG: lit., old phoenix: unofficial reference to a **Grand Councilor** (*tsai-hsiang*).

3579 *lǎo hsiù-ts'ái* 老秀才

MING: lit., old man of cultivated talents: **Honored Student,** collective designation of 37 National University Students (*chien-sheng*) of outstanding erudition and intelligence who were chosen in 1381 to lecture before the Emperor on matters of government policy. See *hsiu-ts'ai.*

3580 *lǎo-kūng* 老公

CH'ING: a term somewhat like **His Honor:** deferential reference to a palace eunuch.

3581 *lǎo-yéh* 老爺

CH'ING: **Venerable Sir,** unofficial reference to any official dignitary, especially a District Magistrate (*chih-hsien*).

3582 *le*

See under the romanization *lo.*

3583 *léi-fēng* 雷封

SUNG–CH'ING: unofficial reference to a **District Magistrate** (*chih-hsien*), derived from a poetic allusion by Po Chü-i of late T'ang.

3584 *lèi-kēng lìng* 率更令

HAN–SUNG, LIAO: **Director of the Watches** or, from N. Ch'i on, **Director of the Court of the Watches** (*lei-keng ssu*), an important member of the staff of the Supervisor of the Household of the Heir Apparent (*chan-shih*); commonly prefixed with *t'ai-tzu.* From the beginning was apparently responsible for the functioning of the household's water clock(s) (*lou-k'o*), in accordance with which he directed the rotation of guard watches maintained by attendants called Cadets (*shu-tzu*) and Housemen (*she-jen*), and his authority seems to have increased gradually to include the routine functioning of the household. In the era of N-S Division was clearly responsible for rewarding and punishing members of the household, and by Sui if not earlier was also in charge of household entertainments. By T'ang was reportedly in charge of rites, music, punishments, etc., in the household of the Heir Apparent and in addition was charged with establishing the order of precedence among all imperial clansmen in state ceremonies, while including on his staff large numbers of water clock specialists. In Han and the S. Dynasties ranked 1,000 bushels; from N. Wei on, 4b. His title is not to be confused with various military titles that include the character *lei* with its more common pronunciation *shuai,* e.g., *t'ai-tzu shuai-fu shuai* (Commandant of the Heir Apparent's Guard Command). HB: prefect stationer of the watches of the heir-apparent. RR: *chef de la cour de la direction des veilles.* SP: *directeur de la garde de l'héritier du trône.* P26.

3585 *lèi-kēng ssù* 率更寺

N-S DIV (N. Ch'i)–SUNG, LIAO: **Court of the Watches,** headed by a Director (*ling*), rank 4b, in the Household Administration of the Heir Apparent (*chan-shih fu*); responsible for maintaining water clocks and accordingly directing changes in household guard watches, and more generally for supervising the routine activities of the household. Developing out of the Han dynasty Director of the Watches (*lei-keng ling*), by T'ang times the Court had a large staff including 6 Erudites of the Water Clock (*lou-k'o po-shih*), 6 Keepers of the Water Clock (*chang-lou*), 60 Tenders of the Water Clock (*lou-t'ung*), and 24 Time Drummers (*tien-ku*) in addition to an administrative staff; and its Director arranged the order of precedence among all imperial clansmen for state ceremonies in addition to supervising ceremonial rites and maintaining discipline in the Heir Apparent's household. In Sung the Court was established irregularly, as needed, and staffed largely with concurrent appointees from among central government dignitaries. At all times the name was commonly prefixed with *t'ai-tzu* (Heir Apparent). RR: *cour de la direction des veilles.* P26.

3586 *lì* 吏

Throughout history the most common generic term used for **Suboffical Functionary,** a category of state employees who performed the clerical and more menial tasks in all governmental agencies at all levels and had no ranked civil service status, though at times they could be promoted into official status (*kuan*) for meritorious service. See *hsü-li, liu-wai, liu-wai ch'u-shen.* (2) CHOU: **Local Agent,** one of 9 types of Unifying Agents (*ou*) who, as representatives of the Minister of State (*chung-tsai*), supervised geographic clusters of feudal states while apparently living in and administering villages or small towns. CL: *officier secondaire.*

3587 *lǐ* 里

(1) **Village:** from antiquity the most common term designating a small rural settlement. (2) T'ANG–CH'ING: **Com-**

munity, a mutual-responsibility, mutual-help grouping of neighboring families under state auspices. Also see *fang, hsiang, chia, pao.*

3588 *lǐ-chǎng* 禮長
SUNG: lit., director of rituals: unofficial reference to the **Minister of Rites** (*lǐ-pu shang-shu*) or to the **Director of the Headquarters Bureau** (*lǐ-pu lang-chung*) in the Ministry of Rites (*lǐ-pu*).

3589 *lǐ-chǎng* 里長
MING–CH'ING: **Community Head,** locally appointed administrative, judicial, and to some extent fiscal chief of a group of neighboring households, responsible to his District Magistrate (*chih-hsien*) for maintaining peace and order and for providing state-service laborers from among the families of his group. Used in earlier times as an unofficial or quasiofficial variant of *li-cheng.* Also see *li-k'uei, li-chia, pao-chia.*

3590 *lì chàng-mǎ* 立仗馬
T'ANG: variant reference to *chang-ma* (**Military Ceremonial Mounts**).

3591 *lì-chèng* 歷政
MING: lit., to experience governance: **Probationary Service,** normally required for up to one year in any office or rank before the appointee could be considered for a regular substantive appointment (*shih-shou*). See *shih-chih* (Acting Appointment).

3592 *lǐ-chèng* 里正
N-S DIV–YÜAN: **Village Head,** locally appointed chief of a neighboring group of households, responsible to the District Magistrate (*hsien-ling, chih-hsien*) for fulfilling all state requirements imposed on the families of his group. See *li-chang, li-k'uei, pao-chia.*

3593 *lì-chèng tièn hsiū-shū yüàn* 麗正殿修書院 or *li-cheng hsiu-shu yüan*
T'ANG: **Academy in the Hall of Elegance and Rectitude,** an agency of literary and scholastic support for the court, subordinate to the Secretariat (*chung-shu sheng*); headed by a Commissioner (*shih*), staffed with Academicians (*hsüeh-shih*), various editorial officials (*chien-chiao kuan*), Senior Compilers (*hsiu-chuan kuan*), Subeditors (*chiao-li kuan*), etc.; created in 718 by renaming the Academy of Heaven (*ch'ien-yüan yüan*); in 725 renamed the Academy of Scholarly Worthies (*chi-hsien tien shu-yüan*); often abbreviated to *li-cheng yüan.* RR: *palais des embellissements et des rectifications.* P25.

3594 *lì-chí àn* 吏籍案
SUNG: **Personnel Records Section,** a subdivision of the Criminal Administration Bureau (*tu-kuan*) in the Ministry of Justice (*hsing-pu*); probably staffed with subofficial functionaries; functions not entirely clear. SP: *service des registres des fonctionnaires.*

3595 *lǐ-chiǎ* 里甲
MING–CH'ING: lit., Communities and Tithings: **Community Self-monitoring System,** one important type of sub-District (*hsien*) local self-government organizations. Prescribed by the government during the founding reign of Ming, the system in theory designated every 110 households a Community (*li*), whose 10 most affluent households provided a Community Head (*li-chang*) in annual rotation while the remaining 100 households were divided into 10 clusters each with 10 neighboring households constituting a Tithing (*chia*), for which one of the households provided a Tithing Head (*chia-shou*). Both Community Heads and Tithing Heads

were responsible to their District Magistrates (*chih-hsien*) for the proper conduct of their charges, for settling local disputes, and to some extent for the collection of local land taxes. In the last Ming years the system was largely superseded by the Community Self-defense System (*pao-chia*). Ch'ing perpetuated the *li-chia* system for tax-collection purposes, but by the 1700s it was losing its effectiveness and giving way to the use of tax collectors employed by the Districts. Also see *liang-chang, hsiang-yüeh.*

3596 *lì chiēn-shēng* 例監生 or *li-chien*
MING–CH'ING: **Student by Purchase** in the Directorate of Education (*kuo-tzu chien*); originated in 1450 when, at a time of military and financial crisis, the Ming government offered student status in the Directorate to anyone who contributed rice or horses in specified amounts, up to a limit of 1,000 men; during the late 1500s and especially in Ch'ing times the numbers swelled as governments exploited this practice as a regular source of revenue. In Ch'ing such students provided a substantial number of active officials in low-ranking posts. From the beginning, however, it appears that men bought student status principally because of the social esteem and the exemption from state-requisitioned labor service that it gave them. In Ch'ing, Students by Purchase came to have 4 major subcategories: First Class (*lin chien-sheng*), Second Class (*tseng chien-sheng*), Third Class (*fu chien-sheng*), and Fourth Class (*chien-sheng* with no prefix), the latter also known as Civilian Students (*min-sheng*). It should be kept in mind that *chien-sheng* without a prefix was also used as a common generic designation of all students under the Directorate.

3597 *lǐ-chiěn yüàn* 理檢院
SUNG: **Complaint Review Office,** a central government agency that received and considered complaints by officials and commoners about official misconduct or major state policies, monitored by a Vice Censor-in-chief (*yü-shih chung-ch'eng*) serving as Complaint Review Commissioner (*li-chien shih*); one of 3 agencies that accepted public petitions and complaints; see *teng-wen chien-yüan* (Public Petitioners Review Office), *teng-wen ku-yüan* (Public Petitioners Drum Office). Established in 991, apparently abolished c. 995, re-established in 1029, apparently terminated during the hectic transition to S. Sung in the 1120s, then re-established in 1176. SP: *cour d'administration du dépôt des pétitions.* P21.

3598 *lǐ-ch'ièn ssū* 理欠司
SUNG: **Deficits Monitoring Office,** normally headed by an Administrative Assistant (*p'an-kuan*), rank 8a or 8b. From 985 to 987, one subordinate to each of the 3 agencies collectively called the State Finance Commission (*san ssu*); in 987 consolidated as a General Deficits Monitoring Office (*tu li-ch'ien ssu*); responsible for expediting the remittance of tax arrearages from Prefectures (*chou*); discontinued c. l080. Also, probably from c. 1080, a subsection of the Bureau of Review (*pi-pu*) in the Ministry of Justice (*hsing-pu*); functions not clear, but likely continued the work of its predecessor. SP: *bureau pour le règlement des dettes.*

3599 *lǐ-chìh chǘ* 禮制局
SUNG: **Ritual Regulations Service,** established in 1112 in the Department of State Affairs (*shang-shu sheng*); probably an ad hoc group of officials on duty assignments detached from their regular posts; functions not clear. SP: *bureau de règlement des rites.*

3600 *lǐ-chíh kuān* 禮直官 or *li-chih*
Lit., suggests a ritual specialist who was on rotational ser-

vice or perhaps available to take up active service in court or elsewhere when summoned: **Ritual Duty Official.** (1) T'ANG: 5, rank and range of functions not clear, members of the Court of Imperial Sacrifices (*t'ai-ch'ang ssu*); abolished c. 758, restored c. 791 with the new designation *li-i chih*, q.v. (2) SUNG: found in various units subordinate to the Court of Imperial Sacrifices; normally 4 in a set, 2 Principals (*cheng*) and 2 Assistants (*fu*); all suboffical functionaries, perhaps hereditary specialists. SP: *chargé des rites.* P27.

3601 *li chù-chiào* 曆助教
SUI: **Calendar Instructor,** apparently existed only briefly, probably as a subordinate in the Astrological Section (*t'ai-shih ts'ao*) of the Palace Library (*pi-shu sheng*). P35.

3602 *li-fān* 理藩
CH'ING: **Frontier-regulating,** one of many prefixes indicating special functions of Subprefectural Magistrates (*t'ung-chih*); signifying responsibility for maintaining order among alien frontier tribes or aboriginal tribes.

3603 *li-fān yüàn* 理藩院
CH'ING: **Court of Colonial Affairs,** a top-echelon agency in the central government managing relations with the Mongols, Tibet, Kokonor, and tribal chiefs of Eastern Turkestan; organized like a Ministry (*pu*) and headed by a Minister (*shang-shu*). Originated in 1637 as the transformation of an earlier Mongol Office (*meng-ku ya-men*); from 1661 had 4 subordinate Bureaus (*ssu, ch'ing-li ssu*): Honors Bureau (*lu-hsün ssu*), Receptions Bureau (*pin-k'o ssu*), Outer Mongolian Reception Bureau (*jou-yüan ssu*), and Judicial Bureau (*li-hsing ssu*), each with several Manchu and Mongol Directors (*lang-chung*), rank 5a. In the early 1700s the Outer Mongolian Reception Bureau was split in 2: a Front Office (*jou-yüan ch'ien-ssu*) and a Rear Office (*jou-yüan hou-ssu*). In 1757 the Honors Bureau became the Outer Mongolian Bureau (*tien-shu ssu*), the Receptions Bureau became the Inner Mongolian Reception Bureau (*wang-hui ssu*), the Rear Office of the Outer Mongolian Reception Bureau became the Inner Mongolian Bureau (*ch'i-chi ssu*), and the Front Office was redesignated the Outer Mongolian Reception Bureau (*jou-yüan ssu*). In 1761 the latter 2 agencies were consolidated into a single Mongolian Reception Bureau (*ch'i-chi jou-yüan ssu*), and a new Eastern Turkestan Bureau (*lai-yüan ssu*) was established. The next year the consolidated Mongolian Reception Bureau was redivided into its 2 earlier Bureaus, but in 1764 the Inner Mongolian Bureau and the Outer Mongolian Bureau exchanged names. After these changes, there were 6 continuing Bureaus: Inner Mongolian Bureau (*ch'i-chi ssu*), Inner Mongolian Reception Bureau (*wang-hui ssu*), Outer Mongolian Bureau (*tien-shu ssu*), Outer Mongolian Reception Bureau (*jou-yüan ssu*), Eastern Turkestan Bureau (*lai-yüan ssu*), and Judicial Bureau (*li-hsing ssu*), each with one or more Manchu and Mongol Directors (*lang-chung*), rank 5a. In its early years the Court's executive posts were held as concurrent assignments by outside Ministers (*shang-shu*) and Vice Ministers (*shih-lang*), especially of the Ministry of Rites (*li-pu*), but from the 1720s they were commonly concurrent assignments for Princes (*wang*), Dukes (*kung*), and Grand Secretaries (*ta hsüeh-shih*), without fixed numbers. See separate entries. P17.

3604 *li-fáng* 吏房
(1) T'ANG–SUNG: **Personnel Office,** one of 5 Offices (*fang*) in the combined Secretariat-Chancellery (*chung-shu men-hsia sheng*) in T'ang, one of 6 in Sung; counterpart of the Ministry of Personnel (*li-pu*) in the Department of State Affairs (*shang-shu sheng*). See *liu fang*. RR+SP: *chambre*

des fonctionnaires. (2) SUNG: **Personnel Section,** one of 5 Sections (see *wu fang*) in the Proclamations Office (*chih-ch'ih yüan*) of the Secretariat (*chung-shu sheng*); also one of 4 Sections (see *ssu fang*) in the Bureau of Military Affairs (*shu-mi yüan*), headed by a Vice Recipient of Edicts (*fu ch'eng-chih*), rank 8b: the channel through which, in collaboration with the Personnel Office mentioned in (1) above and the Ministry of Personnel, the Bureau managed personnel administration for the military establishment till c. 1074, when the Bureau's administrative staff was reorganized into 10 (later 12) Sections (see *shih-erh fang*). SP: *chambre des fonctionnaires.* (3) SUNG: **Directors-in-chief Section,** one of 12 Sections (*shih-erh fang*) created c. 1074 in the Bureau of Military Affairs; supervised the assignments of military officers to serve as Directors-in-chief (*tu-chien*) of Prefectures (*chou, fu*), Military Prefectures (*chün*), and subdivisions of Circuits (see *lu-fen tu-chien*); also supervised the assignments of palace eunuchs to such duties. Headed by 3 to 5 Vice Recipients of Edicts (*fu ch'eng-chih*), rank 8b. Apparently terminated early in S. Sung. SP: *chambre des fonctionnaires.* (4) From Sung on, may be encountered as an unofficial reference to the **Ministry of Personnel.**

3605 *li-fáng* 禮房
(1) SUNG: **Rites Office,** one of 6 administrative agencies (see *liu fang*) organized under the combined Secretariat-Chancellery (*chung-shu men-hsia sheng*), counterpart of the Ministry of Rites (*li-pu*) in the Department of State Affairs (*shang-shu sheng*). (2) SUNG: **Rites Section,** one of 5 Sections (see *wu fang*) in the Proclamations Office (*chih-ch'ih yüan*) of the Secretariat (*chung-shu sheng*); also in the Bureau of Military Affairs (*shu-mi yüan*) till c. 1074, when the Bureau's administrative staff was reorganized in 10 (later 12) Sections (see *shih-erh fang*). SP: *chambre des rites.* (3) From Sung on may be encountered as an unofficial reference to the **Ministry of Rites.**

3606 *li-fēi* 麗妃
T'ANG, MING: **Elegant Consort,** a high-ranking palace woman; in T'ang, beginning in the reign of Hsüan-tsung (r. 712–756), one of the esteemed group called the Three Consorts (*san fei*). See *hua-fei, hui-fei.* RR: *concubine belle.*

3607 *li-hsíng shíh* 裏行使 or *li-hsing*
T'ANG–MING: **Probationary,** a suffix or prefix appended to some titles signifying that the official named was an acting or probationary appointee rather than a regular substantive one (*shih-shou*); e.g., the T'ang and Sung *yü-shih li-hsing* (Probationary Censor), the Ming *li-hsing chih-hsien* (Probationary District Magistrate). RR+SP: *attaché.* P18.

3608 *li-hsíng ssū* 理刑司
CH'ING: **Judicial Bureau,** one of 6 major subdivisions in the Court of Colonial Affairs (*li-fan yüan*), responsible for supervising litigations arising among peripheral peoples overseen by the Court; headed by one Manchu and one Mongol Director (*lang-chung*), rank 5a. BH: judicial department. P17.

3609 *li-hsù* 里胥
SUNG–CH'ING: **Village (Community) Functionaries,** generic reference to commoners chosen or designated to bear responsibilities of leadership in sub-District (*hsien*) organizations. See *li* (Village, Community), *hsü-li* (Suboffical Functionaries).

3610 *li-hù-li pù* 吏戶禮部
(1) SUI–CH'ING: combining reference to the separate **Ministries of Personnel** (*li-pu*), **of Revenue** (*hu-pu*), **and**

of Rites (*lǐ-pu*). (2) YÜAN: **Personnel, Revenue, and Rites Ministry,** from 1260 to 1264 and 1266 to 1268 a consolidation of the normally separate Ministries of Personnel, of Revenue, and of Rites into a single Ministry, known in the aggregate as the Three Ministries of the Left (*tso san-pu*); headed by 2 Ministers (*shang-shu*), rank 3a. Also see *li-li pu.*

3611 *lǐ-í àn* 禮儀案
SUNG: **Section for Ceremonial Propriety,** reportedly a subdivision of the Court of Imperial Sacrifices (*t'ai-ch'ang ssu*), but institutional affiliation, staffing, and functions not wholly clear; possibly one of the 5 Sections into which the early Sung *t'ai-ch'ang li-yüan* (also Court of Imperial Sacrifices) was divided when retitled *t'ai-ch'ang ssu* c. 1080; possibly a variant form of *li-i yüan* (Court of Ceremonial Propriety), an agency that was originally independent of the Court of Imperial Sacrifices but c. 1030 was incorporated into it and thereafter known as the Ritual Academy (*li-yüan*). SP: *service des rites et des cérémonies.* P27.

3612 *lǐ-í chiēn* 禮儀監
CH'ING: **Directorate of Ceremonial Propriety,** a major subdivision of the Imperial Household Department (*nei-wu fu*), headed by 2 or 3 Directors (*lang-chung*), rank 5a, and 8 Vice Directors (*yüan-wai lang*), 5b; responsible for arranging sacrifices, ritual feasts, ritual music and dancing, etc.; in 1660 retitled Court of Ceremonial Propriety (*li-i yüan*), then in 1677 further retitled Office of Palace Ceremonial (*chang-i ssu*). P37.

3613 *lǐ-í chíh* 禮儀直
T'ANG: **Attending Ritualist,** 2, rank not clear, in the Court of Imperial Sacrifices (*t'ai-ch'ang ssu*); a renaming c. 791 of *li-chih kuan* (Ritual Duty Official). P27.

3614 *lǐ-í shǐh* 禮儀使
T'ANG–SUNG: **Commissioner for Ceremonial Propriety,** from 750 apparently a special, ad hoc court delegate to be in charge of various rituals; relationship with the Ministry of Rites (*lǐ-pu*) and the Court of Imperial Sacrifices (*t'ai-ch'ang ssu*) not clear. SP: *commissaire aux rites et aux cérémonies.* P9.

3615 *lǐ-í yüàn* 禮儀院
Court of Ceremonial Propriety. (1) SUNG: originally independent of both the Ministry of Rites (*lǐ-pu*) and the Court of Imperial Sacrifices (*t'ai-ch'ang ssu*), headed by a Grand Councilor (*tsai-hsiang*) with a concurrent duty assignment as Supervisor of the Court (*p'an-yüan*), assisted by one of the officials collectively called the Two Regulators (*liang chih*, q.v.) with a concurrent duty assignment as Administrator of the Court (*chih-yüan*). About 1030 absorbed into the Court of Imperial Sacrifices. SP: *cour des rites et des cérémonies.* P27. (2) CH'ING: originated in 1660 as a replacement for the Directorate of Ceremonial Propriety (*li-i chien*); a major subdivision of the Imperial Household Administration (*nei-wu fu*), headed by 2 or 3 Directors (*lang-chung*), rank 5a, and 8 Vice Directors (*yüan-wai lang*), 5b. In 1677 renamed Office of Palace Ceremonial (*chang-i ssu*). P37.

3616 *lǐ-k'ō* 吏科
MING–CH'ING: **Office of Scrutiny for Personnel,** one of the Six Offices of Scrutiny (*liu k'o*, q.v.). Also see *chi-shih-chung* (Supervising Secretary, Supervising Censor). P18, 19.

3617 *lǐ-k'ō* 禮科
MING–CH'ING: **Office of Scrutiny for Rites,** one of the Six Offices of Scrutiny (*liu k'o*, q.v.). Also see *chi-shih-*

chung (Supervising Secretary, Supervising Censor). P18, 19.

3618 *lǐ-kuān* 理官
Regulatory Official. (1) CHOU–HAN: common generic reference to officials charged with judicial functions. (2) HAN: more specifically, an unofficial reference to the Chamberlain for Law Enforcement (*t'ing-wei, ta-li*). P22.

3619 *lǐ-kuān* 禮官
(1) CHOU: variant reference to the **Minister of Rites** (*ch'un-kuan tsung-po*). CL: *supérieur des hommages respectueux ou des cérémonies sacrées.* (2) HAN: variant reference to **Erudites** (*po-shih*) of the National University (*t'ai-hsüeh*). P34.

3620 *lǐ-kuěi shǐh* 理匭使·
T'ANG–SUNG: **Petition Box Commissioner,** one of several posts responsible for maintaining a station where commoners and officials alike could submit complaints about official misconduct and major policy issues; originally a duty assignment for a Vice Censor-in-chief (*yü-shih chung-ch'eng*) and a Grand Master of Remonstrance (*chien-i ta-fu*); from 742 to 756 bore the alternate designation *hsien-na shih*, q.v.; in 762 the assignment was given to a Supervising Secretary (*chi-shih-chung*) and a Secretariat Drafter (*chung-shu she-jen*) under supervision of an official specially selected for his integrity by the combined Secretariat-Chancellery (*chung-shu men-hsia sheng*) to serve as *chih-kuei shih* (also Petition Box Commissioner); in 781 full responsibility was restored to a Vice Censor-in-chief as *li-kuei shih* and a Grand Master of Remonstrance as *chih-kuei shih*. After the earliest Sung years, in 991 retitled Complaint Review Commissioner (*li-chien shih*) in charge of a Complaint Review Office (*li-chien yüan*). Also see *teng-wen chien-yüan, teng-wen ku-yüan, kuei-yüan, teng-wen yüan.* RR: *commissaire impérial à la direction des urnes.* P21.

3621 *lǐ-k'uéi* 里魁
CH'IN–N-S DIV (S. Dyn.): **Village Head,** designated chief of 100 households in the sub-District (*hsien*) administrative organization of the people; in the S. Dynasties was gradually replaced by *li-cheng*. HB: headman of a hamlet.

3622 *lǐ-kūng* 離宮
CH'ING: **Detached Palace,** variant of *hsing-kung* (Auxiliary Palace), referring to the court's summer resort at Ch'eng-te, Jehol.

3623 *lì kùng-shēng* 例貢生
(1) MING: **Tribute Student by Purchase** in the Directorate of Education (*kuo-tzu chien*), having purchased such status after becoming a regular Government Student (*sheng-yüan*) in a Confucian School (*ju-hsüeh*), as distinguished from Students by Purchase (*li chien-sheng*), who bought status in the Directorate directly, without any previous qualification. Also known as *na-kung* (Student by Contribution). (2) CH'ING: **Tribute Student by Purchase, Fourth Class,** in the Directorate of Education, a status attainable by men already entitled Student by Purchase, Fourth Class (*chien-sheng*), newly entitling them to compete in Provincial Examinations (*hsiang-shih*) in the civil service recruitment examination sequence. The status was lower than *lin kung-sheng, tseng kung-sheng,* and *fu kung-sheng,* qq.v.

3624 *lǐ-lǎo* 里老
(1) **Village Elder:** throughout history an unofficial or quasi-official reference to the heads of important families in a natural village, who provided leadership in organizing communal defense against bandits, management of local irrigation systems, etc. (2) MING: **Community Elder,** from

the late 1300s designated by District Magistrates (*chih-hsien*) for each officially recognized Community (*li*), to be responsible for local legal and judicial proceedings alongside the already operational Community Self-monitoring System (*li-chia*, q.v.).

3625 *lǐ-lǐ pù* 吏禮部

(1) Normally, from Sung on, an abbreviated reference to the separate **Ministries of Personnel and of Rites** (*li-pu, lǐ-pu*). (2) YÜAN: **Personnel and Rites Ministry,** from 1264 to 1266 and 1268 to 1270 a combination of the normally separate Ministries of Personnel and of Rites into a single consolidated Ministry, headed by 3 then 2 Ministers (*shang-shu*), rank 3a. See *li-hu-li pu.*

3626 *lì-mù* 吏目

(1) YÜAN–CH'ING: **Clerk,** rank variable at levels 7, 8, and 9, but often suboffical functionaries; found in many agencies, both central and territorial; often prefixed with a particularizing term, e.g., *kuan-ho li-mu* (Clerk Controller of Waterways) in territorial administrations. BH: secretary. (2) MING–CH'ING: **Medical Secretary** in the Imperial Academy of Medicine (*t'ai-i yüan*), from one to 10 in Ming, from 10 to 30 in Ch'ing, rank 9b in Ming, 8 or 9 in Ch'ing. P36. (3) MING–CH'ING: **Chief of Police** in various units of territorial administration, especially in Ming Subprefectures and Ch'ing Departments (both *chou*), and one each in the 5 Wardens' Offices (*ping-ma chih-hui ssu*) that bore public security responsibilities in Peking.

3627 *lǐ-pīn yüàn* 禮賓院

SUNG: **Foreign Relations Office,** one of several subordinate units in the Court of State Ceremonial (*hung-lu ssu*), specially in charge of the administrative management of diplomatic and trade relations with the Uighurs and other peoples of Eastern Turkestan; headed by 2 rank 8b military officers (?) serving as Audience Ushers (*ko-men chih-hou*) in the Office for Audience Ceremonies (*ko-men ssu*), on special duty assignments as Supervisory Officials (*chien-kuan*); assisted by a Vice Commissioner (*fu-shih*). In other periods its functions were the responsibility of such agencies as the Visitors Bureau (*k'o-sheng*), the Interpreters Institute (*hui-t'ung kuan*), etc. SP: *bureau des relations diplomatiques et commerciales, bureau du protocole.* P11.

3628 *lì pó-shìh* 曆博士

SUI–T'ANG: **Erudite of the Calendar,** number not clear, probably non-official professional specialists; in the Sui–T'ang Astrological Section (*t'ai-shih ts'ao*) and the T'ang Directorate of Astrology (*t'ai-shih chien*) till 704, then replaced by Directors of Calendrical Calculations (*pao-chang cheng*). RR: *maître au vaste savoir rédacteur du calendrier.* P35.

3629 *lì-pù* 例部

Lit., ministry of rules or regulations: a common unofficial reference to the **Ministry of Personnel** (*lǐ-pu*).

3630 *lì-pù* 吏部

(1) N-S DIV (San-kuo Wei)–CH'ING: **Ministry of Personnel,** one of several major agencies in the Department of State Affairs (*shang-shu sheng*) as it developed through the era of N-S Division; then one of the Department's Six Ministries (see *liu pu*), which with some variations were the administrative core of the central government through Chin; then under the Secretariat (*chung-shu sheng*) in Yüan and early Ming; then from 1380 responsible directly to the throne though from the mid-1400s coordinated by the Grand Secretariat (*nei-ko*). Prior to Sui often named Personnel Section (*lì-pu ts'ao*). For a time in the late 1200s, in Yüan, when

traditional Ministries were consolidated in new forms, was absorbed first into a Personnel and Rites Ministry (*li-li pu*) and then into a Ministry of Personnel, Revenue, and Rites (*li-hu-li pu*), also known in the aggregate as the Left Ministry (*tso-pu; also see yu-pu*); but by 1294 regained its separate identity, though tightly coordinated by the metropolitan Secretariat. In general charge of the appointments, merit ratings, promotions, demotions, titles, and honors of civil officials (*wen-kuan*) and suboffical functionaries (*li*); in early Sung also handled appointments, etc., of military officers (*wu-kuan*), who in other times were the responsibility of the Ministry of War (*ping-pu*). From the outset headed by one or more Ministers (*shang-shu*), rank 3a in T'ang, 2b in Sung, 3a in Chin and Yüan, 2a in Ming and Ch'ing till 1730, thereafter 1b; in Ch'ing one Manchu and one Chinese appointee; commonly took ceremonial precedence over all other Ministry heads. In the era of N-S Division the Ministry was subdivided into Bureaus (*ssu*) or Sections (*ts'ao*): e.g., in San-kuo Wei an Appointments Section (*li-pu ts'ao, li-pu;* see #2 below), a Discipline Section (*shan-ting ts'ao*), a Section for the Three Dukes (*san-kung ts'ao;* see *san kung*), and a Review Section (*pi-pu ts'ao*). Thereafter the subordinate agencies varied greatly in number and designations, and when designated Bureaus they often had numerous Sections subordinate to them. From Sui on, however, the standard organization of the Ministry included 4 Bureaus (*ssu, ch'ing-li ssu*): Bureau of Appointments (*li-pu ssu, wen-hsüan ssu*), Bureau of Honors (*ssu-feng ssu, yen-feng ssu*), Bureau of Merit Titles (*ssu-hsün ssu, chi-hsün ssu*), and Bureau of Evaluations (*k'ao-kung ssu*). Each Sui–Ch'ing Bureau was normally headed by a Director (*lang-chung, lang*), rank 6b to 5a. In Chin all Bureaus of the Ministry were consolidated into 2, a Bureau of Evaluations (*tzu-k'o ssu*) and a Bureau of Honors (*feng-hsün ssu*), each a petty agency managed by a Secretary (*chu-shih*), rank 7b, although a pretence was maintained that the traditional 4 Bureaus still existed. In Yüan the Ministry's nominal Bureaus were inactive, their traditional work being done by 3 Sections (*k'o*) of much lesser status: an Honors Section (*feng-kao k'o*), a Section for Honors and Enfeoffments (*hsün-feng k'o*), and an Evaluations and Selections Section (*k'ao-hsüan k'o*), each managed by an unranked Clerk (*ling-shih*). Until 1380 in Ming, the Ministry was considered so dependent on the Secretariat that its head was commonly referred to as Minister of Personnel in the Secretariat (*chung-shu li-pu shang-shu*); after 1380 its relative autonomy was indicated by the simpler title Minister of Personnel (*li-pu shang-shu*). Also see *hsüan-pu, wen-pu, t'ien-kuan, ch'üan, hsüan, ts'ao, ssu* (Bureau), *ch'ing-li ssu.* RR+SP: *ministère des fonctionnaires.* BH: ministry (board) of personnel. P5. (2) N-S DIV (*li-pu, li-pu ts'ao*): **Appointments Section,** one of a variable number of functionally specialized agencies in the developing Ministry of Personnel or Personnel Section in the Department of State Affairs. P5. (3) SUI–YÜAN (*li-pu, li-pu ssu*): **Bureau of Appointments,** one of a normal cohort of 4 Bureaus in the Ministry of Personnel, headed by a Director (*lang-chung, lang*), rank 5b to 6b. In charge of routine administrative matters in the Ministry and especially appointments, promotions, demotions, and ranks. After early Yüan the Bureau's functions were performed by the Evaluations and Selections Section described under (1) above. In Ming and Ch'ing the Bureau's functions were performed by the Bureau of Appointments (*wen-hsüan ch'ing-li ssu*). RR: *bureau des fonctionnaires.* P5.

3631 *lǐ-pù* 禮部

(1) SUI–CH'ING: **Ministry of Rites,** one of the Six Min-

istries (*liu pu*) that were the administrative core of the central government, subordinate to the Department of State Affairs (*shang-shu sheng*) through Sung, then under the Secretariat (*chung-shu sheng*) in Yüan and early Ming, then from 1380 autonomous though coordinated from the mid-1400s by the Grand Secretariat (*nei-ko*). For a time in the late 1200s, in Yüan, when Ministries were being consolidated in new ways, was first absorbed into a Personnel and Rites Ministry (*li-li pu*) and later into a Ministry of Personnel, Revenue, and Rites (*li-hu-li pu*), also known in the aggregate as the Left Ministry (*tso-pu;* also see *yu-pu*); but in 1294 regained its separate identity, though tightly coordinated by the Secretariat. The Ministry carried on functions that since Han times had been performed by such other agencies as the Foreign Relations Section (*k'o-ts'ao*) and the Ministry of Sacrifices (*tz'u-pu*) in the developing Department of State Affairs (*shang-shu sheng*), the Section of Ministry Affairs (*i-ts'ao*) in the Ministry of Sacrifices, and various subordinate agencies in the developing Court of Imperial Sacrifices (*t'ai-ch'ang ssu*) and Court of State Ceremonial (*hung-lu ssu*), with both of which the Ministry continued to have a loosely supervisory relationship. The Ministry was generally responsible for overseeing all imperial and court rituals, for codifying rituals, for managing visits by foreign dignitaries, for supervising state-sponsored education, for monitoring Taoist and Buddhist communities, and from 736 for managing the civil service examination recruitment system (*k'o-chü*). Headed by one or more Ministers (*shang-shu*), rank 3a in T'ang, 2b in Sung, 3a in Chin and Yüan, 2a in Ming and Ch'ing till 1730, thereafter 1b; in Ch'ing one Manchu and one Chinese appointee. Normally had 4 constituent Bureaus (*ssu, ch'ing-li ssu*): e.g., in T'ang a Headquarters Bureau (also *li-pu* or *li-pu ssu*), a Bureau of Sacrifices (*tz'u-pu, tz'u-pu ssu*), a Bureau of Receptions (*chu-k'o, chu-k'o ssu*), and a Bureau of Provisions (*shan-pu, shan-pu ssu*), each with a Director (*lang-chung*), rank 5b; in Ming a Bureau of Ceremonies (*li-pu ch'ing-li ssu*), a Bureau of Sacrifices (*tz'u-chi ch'ing-li ssu*), a Bureau of Receptions (*chu-k'o ch'ing-li ssu*), and a Bureau of Provisions (*ching-shan ch'ing-li ssu*), each with a Director (*lang-chung*), 5a. In Ming and Ch'ing there was a close relationship between the Ministry and the Grand Secretariat; some executive officials of the Ministry were concurrently made Grand Secretaries (*ta hsüeh-shih*), and many Grand Secretaries bore nominal concurrent titles of Ministers and Vice Ministers (*shih-lang*) of Rites. Also see *tsung-po, k'o-ts'ao, ch'un-kuan*. RR+SP: *ministère des rites*. BH: ministry (board) of rites. P9. (2) N-S DIV (Chou)–YÜAN: **Headquarters Bureau,** one of a normal cohort of 4 Bureaus (*ssu*) in the Ministry of Rites; in Chou of the era of N-S Division the name alternated with *ssu-tsung*, q.v., headed by a Grand Master of Rites (*li-pu ta-fu;* also see *ta ssu-li*); in later periods the head was entitled Director (*lang, lang-chung*), rank 5a to 6b. The Bureau was particularly in charge of the Ministry's routine internal administrative work. It was perpetuated in the Ming–Ch'ing Bureau of Ceremonies (*i-chih ch'ing-li ssu*). RR: *bureau des rites*. BH: department of ceremonies. P9.

3632 *li-pù ts'áo* 吏部曹
Personnel Section. HAN–N-S DIV (S. Dyn.): created by a renaming of the earlier Section for Attendants-in-ordinary (*ch'ang-shih ts'ao*) shortly after the establishment of Later Han in A.D. 25; one of 6 Sections (*ts'ao*) of Imperial Secretaries (*shang-shu*) in the steadily more important Imperial Secretariat (*shang-shu t'ai*), the dominant executive agency in the central government; responsible for the selection and appointment of officials. After Han, became one of many top-level agencies under the developing Department of State Affairs (*shang-shu sheng*), evolving into the Sui–Ch'ing Ministry of Personnel (*li-pu*) headed by a Minister (*shang-shu*). Also from the 400s on, the designation of a principal subdivision of the emerging Ministry of Personnel, staffed with Clerks (*ling-shih*) with many particularizing prefixes. Also see *li-pu, li-pu ssu*. Cf. *hsüan-pu ts'ao*. P5.

3633 *li-p'ú* 隸僕
CHOU: **Domestic Servant,** 2 ranked as Junior Servicemen (*hsia-shih*), members of the Ministry of War (*hsia-kuan*); assigned as orderlies to clean the inner quarters of the royal palace. CL: *assistant-valet*.

3634 *li-shēng* 例生
CH'ING: **Local Student by Purchase** in a Confucian School (*ju-hsüeh*) in a unit of territorial administration; status and privileges awarded to men who responded to state appeals for emergency contributions of money or goods, but only for a short period in the K'ang-hsi reign (1662–1722). Cf. *li-chien.*

3635 *li-shēng* 曆生
SUNG: **Calendrical Apprentice,** 4, unranked, authorized for the Directorate of Astronomy (*ssu-t'ien chien*). SP: *élève-intendant du calendrier.*

3636 *li-shēng* 禮生
(1) T'ANG: **Ritual Apprentice,** 35 authorized for the Ritual Academy (*li-yüan*) under the Court of Imperial Sacrifices (*t'ai-ch'ang ssu*); unranked. RR: *étudiant des rites à la cour des sacrifices impériaux*. P27. (2) SUNG: **Calendrical Apprentice** in the Directorate of Astronomy (*ssu-t'ien chien*); 4, unranked. A scribal error for *li* (calendar)-*sheng*. SP: *élève-intendant des rites.*

3637 *li-shìh* 吏士
N-S DIV (N. Wei): **Guardsmen** assigned to various Commanders (see *chu-ssu li-tsai*) by Shih-tsu (r. 424–451) to help quell military disorders in various localities; exact status not clear. P20.

3638 *li-shìh* 歷事
MING: **Novice,** designation of National University Students (*chien-sheng*) serving apprenticeships in government agencies, especially in the central government; such status might endure from 3 months to 3 years before one attained a substantive appointment (*shih-shou*) in the officialdom. See *li-cheng, pan-shih, kuan-cheng.*

3639 *li ... shìh* 理…事 or *li ... shìh-wù* 務
CH'ING: **Administering the Affairs of ...,** enclosing a functional or territorial designation, prefixed to many titles such as Assistant Prefect (*t'ung-p'an*) to particularize their duty assignments.

3640 *li-shìh kuān* 理事官
CH'ING: **Administrator,** in predynastic times a common designation of 2nd-level officials in many central government agencies, including the Six Ministries (*liu pu*); associated with Assistant Administrators (*fu li-shih kuan*). After 1644 these designations were replaced with the Ming titles *lang-chung* (Director) and *yüan-wai lang* (Vice Director), except that the Court of the Imperial Clan (*tsung-jen fu*) maintained on its staff both Administrators, rank 5a, and Assistant Administrators, 5b, in subsections such as its Registry (*ching-li ssu*):

3641 *li-shìh shíh tà-ch'én* 理事十大臣
CH'ING: **Ten Grand Ministers Administering Affairs,**

one of 3 groups of Manchu nobles that constituted the Manchu central government in predynastic times, alongside the Grand Ministers Commanding the Eight Banners (*pa-ch'i tsung-kuan ta-ch'en*) and the Five Grand Ministers of the Deliberative Council (*i-cheng wu ta-ch'en*); in 1635 all these groups were abolished when the Manchus began a transition to a more Ming-like governmental structure. See *ta-ch'en*.

3642 *lǐ-ssū kuān* 里司官
SUI: lit., official(s) of the Precinct office: **Precinct Official,** in 607 replaced Company Commander (*fang-chu*) in all Precincts (formerly *fang,* now *li*) in the dynastic capital; each responsible for maintaining order in his jurisdiction. P20.

3643 *lǐ-tsǎi* 里宰
CHOU: **Village Head,** chief of 25 households outside the royal domain, ranked as a Junior Serviceman (*hsia-shih*); charged with promoting agriculture, collecting taxes, etc. Through a hierarchy of a Precinct (*tsan*), a Ward (*pi*), and a Township (*hsien*), was responsible to a District Grand Master (*sui ta-fu*), who in turn was responsible to one of 2 Supervisors of Exterior Districts (*sui-jen*) on the staff of the Ministry of Education (*ti-kuan*). CL: *administrateur de hameau.*

3644 *lì-ts'áo* 吏曹
(1) HAN: **Personnel Section,** one of 6 Sections (*ts'ao*) of Imperial Secretaries (*shang-shu*) in the Imperial Secretariat (*shang-shu t'ai*); in charge of selections and appointments in the officialdom, also responsible for managing fasts and sacrifices; apparently had a supervisory role over the Section for the Three Dukes (*san-kung ts'ao*). Also called *lì-pu ts'ao;* also see *liu ts'ao.* HB: bureau of personnel. P9. (2) N-S DIV: alternated with *lì-pu* as the designation of the evolving **Ministry of Personnel.** (3) SUI–CH'ING: unofficial, archaic reference to the **Bureau of Appointments** (*lì-pu, wen-hsüan ssu*) in the Ministry of Personnel (*lì-pu*). (4) MING–CH'ING: **Personnel Section,** a clerical agency in each unit of territorial administration from Prefectures (*fu*) down to Districts (*hsien*), staffed entirely with suboficial functionaries; managed clerical work within the purview of the central government's Ministry of Personnel. Successor of the earlier Personnel Evaluation Section (*kung-ts'ao*). Also see *liu ts'ao.*

3645 *lǐ-ts'áo* 禮曹
Rites Section. (1) SUI–CH'ING: unofficial, archaic reference to the Ministry of Rites (*lǐ-pu*) or possibly to the Ministry's Bureau of Ceremonies (*i-chih ssu*). (2) MING–CH'ING: a clerical agency in each unit of territorial administration from Prefectures (*fu*) down to Districts (*hsien*), staffed entirely with suboficial functionaries; managed clerical work within the purview of the central government's Ministry of Rites. See *liu ts'ao.*

3646 *lì-ts'úng kuān* 吏從官
HAN: **Foreman,** 6 suboficial functionaries assigned to the Palace Storehouse (*chung huang-tsang*). P7.

3647 *lǐ-wèi* 里尉
N-S DIV: abbreviation of *liu-pu li-wei,* itself a variant of *liu-pu wei* (**Commandant of the Capital Patrol**).

3648 *lǐ-wèn* 理問
YÜAN–CH'ING: **Judicial Secretary,** 2 in Yüan, rank not clear, on the staff of each Branch Secretariat (*hsing chung-shu sheng*); one in Ming and Ch'ing, rank 6b, head of the Office of the Judicial Secretary (*li-wen so*) in a Provincial Administration Commission (*ch'eng-hsüan pu-cheng shih*

ssu); responsible for monitoring and in some cases conducting judicial proceedings and punishments. BH: law secretary. P49, 52.

3649 *lì-yùng chiēn* 利用監
YÜAN: lit., Directorate for making advantageous use (of goods): **Directorate for Leather and Fur Manufactures,** an apparently autonomous agency of the central government, but loosely supervised by the Directorate of the Imperial Treasury (*t'ai-fu chien*); headed by a Director (*chien*), rank 3a; supervised a number of subsidiary manufacturing Services (*chü*), e.g., the Striped Hides Service (*hsieh-p'i chü*). P38.

3650 *lì-yùng ch'ién-chiēn* 利用錢監
CHIN: lit., Directorate for (making) coins of advantageous usefulness: **Directorate of Coinage,** established c. 1158 in the principal dynastic capital near modern Peking to mint copper coins and supervise their circulation; headed by a Director of Coinage (*chien-chu*) on duty assignment from a regular substantive post in the Ministry of Works (*kung-pu*). See *tai-chou ch'ien-chien, fu-t'ung ch'ien-chien, pao-yüan ch'ien-chien, pao-feng ch'ien-chien.* Cf. *pao-yüan chü.* P16.

3651 *lì-yüán* 吏員
(1) Throughout history a common generic term for suboficial **Clerk.** See *li* (Suboficial Functionary). (2) CH'ING: **Clerical Official,** generic term for men who gained official status (*ch'u-shen*) on the basis of guaranteed recommendations (*pao-chü*) by existing officials after serving as Archivists (*shu-pan*); became eligible for the prestige titles (*san-kuan*) Court Gentleman of Manifest Virtue (*hsüan-te lang*), rank 6b, and Court Gentleman for Manifesting Rightness (*hsüan-i lang*), 7a. P68.

3652 *lí-yüán* 梨園
T'ANG: lit., pear garden: **Palace Theater,** established by Hsüan-tsung (r. 712–756) as a resident troupe of actors, singers, acrobats, etc., in the palace for his personal entertainment; apparently did not survive him. Its personnel were chosen from among skilled professionals, reportedly 300 in total, and also included large numbers of palace women; all participants were known as Members of the Palace Theater (*huang-ti li-yüan ti-tzu:* lit., disciples in the Emperor's pear garden). It was the Emperor's personal institution, not considered an agency of the government.

3653 *lǐ-yüàn* 禮院
T'ANG–SUNG: **Ritual Academy,** an autonomous agency of the central government till 1040, then subordinated to the Court of Imperial Sacrifices (*t'ai-ch'ang ssu*); staffed principally with 4 Erudites (*po-shih*), rank 7b in T'ang, 8a in Sung; in Sung overseen by a Supervisor (*p'an-yüan*) on detached duty assignment from a regular nominal office elsewhere in the central government. Responsible for compiling ritual regulations and training Ritual Apprentices (*li-sheng*). Commonly called *t'ai-ch'ang li-yüan.* Also see *li-i yüan.* RR: *service des rites.* SP: *bureau des rites.* P27.

3654 *lì-yüán ssū* 栗園司
LIAO: **Office of the Chestnut Park** in the Court Ceremonial Institute (*hsüan-hui yüan*) at the Southern Capital (*nan-ching*), modern Peking; staffing and functions not clear; possibly in charge of the Peking palace grounds. P49.

3655 *lǐ-yüèh àn* 禮樂案
SUNG: **Ritual and Music Section** in the Ministry of Rites (*lǐ-pu*); staffing not clear. SP: *service des rites et de la musique.*

3656 *lǐ-yüèh chǎng* 禮樂長
HAN: **Director of Ceremonial Music,** rank =400 bushels, in charge of musicians in each Princedom (*wang-kuo*). HB: chief of ritual music. P69.

3657 *liǎng* 兩
CHOU: (1) **Unifying Agent,** representative of the Minister of State (*chung-tsai*) supervising a geographical cluster of Feudal Lords (*chu-hou*); see under *ou*. (2) **Platoon** of 25 militiamen under a Commander (*ssu-ma*), comprising 5 Squads (*wu*); 4 Platoons constituted a Company (*tsu*). Apparently was the militia unit provided by a Village (*lü* in the royal domain, *li* elsewhere). CL: *peloton*.

3658 *liáng-chǎng* 糧長
MING: lit., one in charge of (collecting) tax grains: **Tax Captain,** from 1371 designated by District Magistrates (*chih-hsien*), one for each area, whatever its size or population, on which an aggregate annual land tax of 10,000 bushels of grain was assessed; each chosen from among the more affluent residential families, responsible for collecting tax grains from all Community Heads (*li-chang*) in his area and for delivering his receivables, in early Ming to the dynastic capital at Nanking or elsewhere as directed, after 1420 to many designated agencies or depots, some to be forwarded to the new dynastic capital at Peking. In early Ming Tax Captains seem to have prospered by abusing those in their jurisdictions, but by the 16th century being a Tax Captain was a burden that bankrupted many families, and tax-collecting responsibilities were gradually transferred to hired agents of District Magistrates.

3659 *liǎng chàng-nèi* 兩伏內
T'ANG: **Two Stables of the Palace,** collective reference to 2 groups of stables in the imperial palace grounds: Stables of Trustworthy Mounts of the Left (*tso chang-chiu*; see *chang-chiu*), also called Stables of Meteoric Mounts (*pen-hsing chiu*), and Stables of Trustworthy Mounts of the Right (*yu chang-chiu*), also called Stables of the Palace Colts (*nei-chü chiu*).

3660 *liǎng chìh-kuān* 兩制官 or *liang chih*
SUNG: **Two Drafting Groups** on duty in the Administration Chamber (*cheng-shih t'ang*), where Grand Councilors (*tsai-hsiang*, etc.) presided over the central government; one group consisted of Hanlin Academicians (*han-lin hsüeh-shih*) of the Institute of Academicians (*hsüeh-shih yüan*), collectively called Inner Drafters (*nei-chih*); the other consisted of nominal members of the Secretariat (*chung-shu sheng*), collectively called Outer Drafters (*wai-chih*). The collective designation of both groups was Drafters (*chih-chih-kao*). SP: *fonctionnaire chargé des édits*. P21.

3661 *liǎng-chīng chū-shìh shǔ* 兩京諸市署
T'ANG: **Offices for Marketplaces in the Two Capitals** in the Court of the Imperial Treasury (*t'ai-fu ssu*), one based at the dynastic capital, Ch'ang-an, and another at the auxiliary Eastern Capital, Loyang; each headed by a Director (*ling*), rank 6b1; charged with monitoring activities in the official marketplaces in the 2 cities; checked the accuracy of weights and measures, and every 10 days adjusted the officially authorized price ranges for various commodities. RR: *offices des marchés des deux capitales*.

3662 *liǎng-chīng wǔ-k'ù shǔ* 兩京武庫署
T'ANG: **Armories of the Two Capitals,** one based at the dynastic capital, Ch'ang-an, and from 737 another at the auxiliary Eastern Capital, Loyang; each headed by 2 Directors (*ling*), rank 6b2, subordinate to the Court of the Imperial Regalia (*wei-wei ssu*). Each Armory was appar-

ently stocked with all the weapons, armor, and other gear needed by an army on campaign. RR: *offices des magasins des armes des deux capitales*. P12.

3663 *liáng-ch'ú tào* 糧儲道
CH'ING: **Grain Tax Circuit,** headed by an executive official of a Provincial Surveillance Commission (*t'i-hsing anch'a shih ssu*) commonly called a Circuit Intendant (*tao-t'ai*), but in 1735 made independent without any formal affiliation with the Commission, with rank 4a. Established wherever necessary to organize, facilitate, and generally supervise the shipment of grain tax revenues along the Grand Canal. Counterpart of the Tax Intendant Circuits (*tu-liang tao*) established by Provincial Administration Commissions (*ch'eng-hsüan pu-cheng shih ssu*); both commonly abbreviated to *liang-tao*. Prior to 1735, the Grain Tax Circuit Intendant was commonly concurrent head of a General Surveillance Circuit (*fen-hsün tao*). BH: grain intendant.

3664 *liǎng fǔ* 兩府
Lit., the 2 offices. (1) HAN: **Two Administrators,** a reference to the 2 top-level civil authorities in the central government, the Counselor-in-chief (*ch'eng-hsiang*) and the Censor-in-chief (*yü-shih ta-fu*). P18. (2) SUNG: **Two Administrations,** a reference to the 2 top-level executive agencies in the central government, the Secretariat (*chung-shu sheng*) or the consolidated Secretariat-Chancellery (*chung-shu men-hsia sheng*) and the Bureau of Military Affairs (*shu-mi yüan*). See *erh fu*.

3665 *liǎng-ì* 兩翼
CH'ING: **Two Pasturelands** for the imperial horse herds, prefixed Left and Right, in Mongolia; each headed by a Supervisor-in-chief (*tsung-kuan*), rank 4a, and a Wing Commander (*i-chang*), 5a; subordinate to a Supervisor-in-chief in Command of Pasturages in the Two Pasturelands (*t'ung-hsia liang-i mu-ch'ang tsung-kuan*), a post normally held concurrently by the Vice Commander-general (*fu tu-t'ung, tso-ling*) of Chahar; ultimately responsible to the Court of the Imperial Stud (*t'ai-p'u ssu*) in the central government at Peking. P31.

3666 *liáng-ī sǒ* 良醫所
MING: **Medical Office** in a Princely Establishment (*wang-fu*), staffed with a Director (*cheng*), rank 8a, and a Vice Director (*fu*), 8b. P69.

3667 *liáng-jén* 良人
HAN–N-S DIV (S. Dyn.): **Virtuous Lady,** designation of a group of imperial concubines, rank =800 bushels; abolished in Later Han but revived in the era of N-S Division. HB: sweet lady.

3668 *liàng-jén* 量人
CHOU: **Surveyor,** 2 ranked as Junior Servicemen (*hsia-shih*), members of the Ministry of War (*hsia-kuan*) in charge of outlining sites for capital walls and royal palaces, determining locations and borders of newly created states, and land measuring in general. CL: *mesureur*.

3669 *liáng-liào àn* 糧料案
SUNG: **Supplies Section,** one of 8 Sections (*an*) in the Tax Bureau (*tu-chih ssu*), one of 3 agencies that constituted the State Finance Commission (*san ssu*) of early Sung times; normally headed by an Administrative Assistant (*p'an-kuan, t'ui-kuan*); monitored the issuance of uniforms, food rations, and paper money to military units in the area of the dynastic capital. Discontinued c. 1080, its functions being absorbed by the Ministry of Revenue (*hu-pu*) and the Court of the Imperial Treasury (*t'ai-fu ssu*). SP: *service des vivres, du transport des grains et des bons de monnaie*. P6.

3670 *liǎng-liào yüǎn* 糧料院
SUNG: **Bursary** in the Court of the Imperial Treasury (*t'ai-fu ssu*), an early Sung agency staffed by members of the State Finance Commission (*san ssu*) on special duty assignments; stocked grains and hay for issuance as official stipends and allowances and for the support of armies as needed; eventual fate not clear. SP: *cour des grains et de foin pour la subvention aux fonctionnaires civils et militaires et aux armées.*

3671 *liǎng-mù shǔ* 良牧署
MING: **Office of Husbandry,** one of 4 Offices (*shu*) in the Directorate of Imperial Parks (*shang-lin yüan-chien*); headed by a Manager (*tien-shu*), rank 7a; responsible for the breeding and care of domestic animals in the imperial parks. P40.

3672 *liǎng pān* 兩班
T'ANG: **Two Ranks,** a reference to gatherings at court in which civil officials (*wen-kuan*) and military officers (*wu-kuan*) took positions in separate groups.

3673 *liǎng pǎng* 兩榜
MING–CH'ING: lit., 2 lists: unofficial reference to a scholar who, having achieved success in the Provincial Examination (*hsiang-shih*) in the civil service recruitment examination sequence, subsequently passed the Metropolitan Examination (*hui-shih*) and won status as a **Metropolitan Graduate** (*chin-shih*); i.e., one whose name had appeared on both the provincial and the metropolitan pass lists (*i-pang, chia-pang*).

3674 *liǎng shěng* 兩省
T'ANG–SUNG: **Two Departments,** unofficial collective reference to the Secretariat (*chung-shu sheng*) and the Chancellery (*men-hsia sheng*) or to the consolidated Secretariat-Chancellery (*chung-shu men-hsia sheng*). SP: *les deux départements.*

3675 *liǎng-shěng kuān* 兩省官
SUNG: **Remonstrance Officials of the Two Departments,** i.e., the Secretariat (*chung-shu sheng*) and the Chancellery (*men-hsia sheng*), specifically designating Policy Advisers (*san-chi ch'ang-shih*) and Exhorters (*cheng-yen*) of both agencies. SP: *fonctionnaires des deux départements.*

3676 *liǎng shǐh* 兩使
SUNG: **Two Commissioners:** might refer to any combination of 2 Commissioners (*shih*) depending on context, but likely refers most commonly to a Defense Commissioner (*fang-yü shih*) and a Military Training Commissioner (*t'uan-lien shih*).

3677 *liǎng shǐh* 兩史
SUNG: **Two Categories of Diarists,** collective reference to *ch'i-chü lang* and *ch'i-chü she-jen* (both Imperial Diarists) on the staff of the Chancellery (*men-hsia sheng*). SP: *deux annalistes.*

3678 *liǎng-shǐh* 良使
HAN: **Lady of Excellent Employment,** designation of a lowly palace woman, rank =100 bushels. HB: sweet maid.

3679 *liǎng ssū* 兩司
(1) **Two Offices:** may be encountered as a reference to any 2 agencies called *ssu* that are mentioned in the preceding context, in any era. (2) SUNG: **Two Commands,** a common unofficial reference to the Cavalry Command (*ma-chün ssu*) and the Infantry Command (*pu-chün ssu*), the 2 subsidiary headquarters controlled by the Metropolitan Command (*shih-wei ssu*). (3) CH'ING: **Two Provincial Of-**fices, collective reference to the Provincial Administration Commission (*ch'eng-hsüan pu-cheng shih ssu*) and the Provincial Surveillance Commission (*t'i-hsing an-ch'a shih ssu*). See *fan-nieh liang ssu, erh ssu.* P52.

3680 *liǎng ssū-mǎ* 兩司馬
CHOU: **Platoon Commander,** ranked as an Ordinary Serviceman (*chung-shih*). See *liang, ssu-ma.* CL: *chef de peloton.*

3681 *liǎng t'ái* 兩臺
T'ANG: **Two Censorates,** a reference to the Censorate (*yü-shih t'ai*) from 684 to 713; when it was entitled *su-cheng t'ai* and was divided into 2 sections, one designated Left to maintain censorial surveillance over the court and capital and one designated Right to extend surveillance empire-wide to all units of territorial administration. P18.

3682 *liáng-t'ái* 糧臺 or 糧台
Paymaster. (1) SUNG: ad hoc designation of an officer who (obtained and?) issued rations, horse fodder, etc., to the personnel of an army on campaign; the usage probably persisted after Sung. Such pre-Sung agencies as the Bursary (*liang-liao yüan*) in the T'ang Court of the Imperial Treasury (*t'ai-fu ssu*) no longer provided these services regularly. (2) CH'ING: from the 1750s, 3 posted in different parts of Tibet to pay Ch'ing soldiers stationed there; rank not clear; subordinate to, and general deputies for, the Grand Minister Resident of Tibet (*chu-tsang ta-ch'en*), a representative of the Court of Colonial Affairs (*li-fan yüan*). BH: commissary.

3683 *liáng-tào* 糧道
CH'ING: **Tax Circuit,** common abbreviation of both *liang-ch'u tao* (Grain Tax Circuit) and *tu-liang tao* (Tax Intendant Circuit).

3684 *liǎng-tì* 良娣
HAN–T'ANG: lit., excellent sister-in-law: **Related Lady of Excellence,** designation of a category of concubines of the Heir Apparent; in T'ang, the most esteemed of 5 such categories, 2 appointees, rank 3a, subordinate only to the principal wife, the Princess-consort (*fei*). HB: sweet little lady. RR: *bonne soeur cadette de la femme principale.*

3685 *liáng-ts'ǎo k'ō* 糧草科
YÜAN: **Fodder Section,** one of 6 major subsections of the Ministry of Revenue (*hu-pu*); headed by one or more Clerks (*ling-shih*), rank not clear but low. Probably in charge of supplies that provided stipends and allowances for officials of the central government; comparable to the Sung dynasty Supplies Section (*liang-liao an*) or Bursary (*liang-liao yüan*). P6.

3686 *liǎng-tū lù-yùn t'í-chǔ ssū* 兩都陸運提舉司
YÜAN: **Supervisorate of Land Transport to the Two Capitals,** in 1317 replaced the Supervisorate of Grain Tax Transport (*yün-liang t'i-chü ssu*); headed by 2 Supervisors (*t'i-chü*), rank 5b; under supervision of the Ministry of War (*ping-pu*), directed the transport of grain supplies to the Grand Capital (Ta-tu; modern Peking) and the Supreme Capital (Shang-tu; K'ai-p'ing in modern Chahar). P60.

3687 *liǎng-tzù wáng* 兩字王
YÜAN: lit., 2-character Prince: **Second-class Prince,** differentiated from First-class Prince (*i-tzu wang*, q.v.). P64.

3688 *liáng-wù tào* 糧務道
CH'ING: variant form of *liang-tao* (**Grain Tax Circuit**). Also see *liang-ch'u tao.*

3689 *liǎng yá-mén* 兩衙門
MING: **Two Censorial Offices,** unofficial collective reference to Supervising Secretaries (*chi-shih-chung*) of the Six Offices of Scrutiny (*liu-k'o*) and Investigating Censors (*chien-ch'a yü-shih*), who constituted the Investigation Bureau (*ch'a-yüan*) of the Censorate (*tu ch'a-yüan*).

3690 *liǎng yüàn* 兩院
MING–CH'ING: **Two Magnates,** unofficial collective reference to *tsung-tu* (Supreme Commander in Ming, Governor-general in Ch'ing) and *hsün-fu* (Grand Coordinator in Ming, Provincial Governor in Ch'ing), probably deriving from the practice of granting such provincial authorities concurrent nominal status in the Censorate (*tu ch'a-yüan*).

3691 *liáng-yüàn* 良媛
T'ANG: **Lady of Excellent Beauty,** designation of 6 palace women in the household of the Heir Apparent; rank 4a, below Related Ladies of Excellence (*liang-ti*) and above Ladies of Inherited Excellence (*ch'eng-hui*). RR: *femme bonne et belle.*

3692 *liáng-yün shǔ* 良醞署
SUI–CH'ING: **Office of Fine Wines,** one of 4 principal agencies in the Court of Imperial Entertainments (*kuang-lu ssu*), in Sung subordinated to the Court's Imperial Kitchen (*yü-ch'u*). Headed in T'ang by 2 Directors (*ling*), rank 8b; in Sung by 2 Supervisory Officials (*chien-kuan*), rank not clear; in Yüan by a Superintendent (*t'i-tien*), 5b, and a Commissioner-in-chief (*ta-shih*), 6a; in Ming by a Director (*shu-cheng*), 6b; in Ch'ing by one Manchu and one Chinese Director (*shu-cheng*), 6b. In Yüan created in 1274 to replace the Wine Storehouse (*yü-chiu k'u*), then in 1279 renamed the Wine Stewards Service (*shang-yün chü; cf. shang-yün shu*). Counterpart agencies in Liao and Chin were the Imperial Brewery (*ch'u-yüan*) in the Liao Court of Imperial Entertainments and the Chin Court Ceremonial Institute (*hsüan-hui yüan*) and the Chin Wine Stewards Office (*shang-yün shu*), also a unit in the Institute. In Sung the Office supervised 3 more specialized agencies: a Palace Winery (*nei chiu-fang*), a Winery (*fa chiu-k'u*), and a Yeast Office (*tu mien-yüan*). The Office was always responsible for producing, storing, and providing wine for palace and sacrificial uses. RR+SP: *office des boissons fermentées excellentes, bureau de vin.* P30.

3693 *liào-kū sǒ* 料估所
CH'ING: **Office of Estimates** in the Ministry of Works (*kung-pu*); a function more than a substantive agency, to estimate materials, labor, and other costs required for each construction project, and on completion to confirm actual costs; a duty assignment for 3 Manchus and 3 Chinese officials of the Ministry, to serve in rotation one year at a time. BH: department of estimates. P14.

3694 *liáo-shěn tào* 遼瀋道
CH'ING: **Liao-Shen Circuit,** one of the Circuits (*tao*, q.v.) in the Censorate (*tu ch'a-yüan*) among which Investigating Censors (*chien-ch'a yü-shih*) were distributed, comparable to those named after Provinces (*sheng*); handled routine surveillance concerning the 3 Manchurian Provinces; name abbreviated from Liao-yang and Shen-yang, major cities of the area.

3695 *liáo-shǔ* 僚屬
Staff Officers: from the Three Kingdoms era a generic term for men serving in lower-level posts in units of territorial administration, e.g., *chang-shih* (Aide), *ssu-ma* (Commander). P50.

3696 *liào-yüàn* 料院
SUNG: abbreviated reference to the *liang-liao yüan* (**Bursary**) in the Court of the Imperial Treasury (*t'ai-fu ssu*).

3697 *lièh* 列
A prefix commonly meaning **array of, group of, the various,** e.g., *lieh-pu* (the various Ministries), *lieh-ts'ao* (the various Sections); also used to suggest **separate, different, other** in contrast to some group similarly named; e.g., *lieh-hou* (meaning "marquises other than those called *chu-hou*").

3698 *lièh-hóu* 列侯
HAN–N-S DIV (San-kuo): (1) **Adjunct Marquis,** a title of nobility (*chüeh*) awarded for extraordinary merit in state service, distinguished from an Imperial Marquis (*chu-hou*), who inherited noble status as the son of a Prince (*wang*). See *lieh.* HB: full marquis. (2) **Marquis-consort,** a title granted to husbands of Imperial Princesses (*kung-chu*). (3) **Grandee of the First Order,** variant of *ch'e-hou* and *t'ung-hou,* the 20th (i.e., the highest) of 20 titles of honorary nobility (also *chüeh*) awarded to deserving subjects; in San-kuo Wei the highest of 6 categories of Marquises. P64, 65.

3699 *lièh-kūng* 列宮
Lit., other palaces (see *lieh*), i.e., palatial residences in addition to that occupied by the Empress: **Imperial Women,** an unofficial reference to all imperial wives excluding the Empress.

3700 *lièh tà-fū* 列大夫
HAN: **Adjunct Grand Master,** a title of honorary nobility (*chüeh*) awarded to deserving subjects; perhaps equivalent to *kung ta-fu* (Grandee of the Fourteenth Order). P65.

3701 *lién* 廉
CH'ING: **Incorruptible:** a form of direct address, used in addressing a District Magistrate (*chih-hsien*). See *hsiao-lien.*

3702 *lién* 連
Lit., to connect, join: **Aggregation.** (1) CHOU: according to one ancient source (*Li-chi*), 10 states (*kuo*) organized under a Leader (*shuai;* see *lien-shuai*); according to another ancient source (*Kuo-yü*), 4 Villages (*li*) constituted an Aggregation and 200 of its fighting men constituted a Company (*tsu*) led by the Aggregation Head (*lien-chang*). Neither report is corroborated by the *Chou-li.* (2) HAN: in Later Han a local self-defense force comprising 40 men (?) gathered from 4 neighboring Villages (*li*), led by an Aggregation Commandant (*chia-wu*); 110 (?) Aggregations further constituted a District (*i*) whose combined forces were led by a District Commandant (*chia-hou*). The sources are not wholly clear.

3703 *lién-ch'á shǐh* 廉察使   or *lien-ch'a*
T'ANG: **Inspector of Governmental Integrity,** from 684 to 705 a designation of members of the Two Censorates (*liang t'ai*) dispatched every autumn to investigate the conduct of officials in units of territorial administration; usually 8 assigned each year; counterparts of the censorial Inspectors of Public Morality (*feng-su shih*) sent out every spring. RR: *commissaire impérial enquêteur.*

3704 *lién-ch'ē* 廉車
T'ANG: lit., inspector's carriage (?): unofficial reference to a **Surveillance Commissioner** (*an-ch'a shih*).

3705 *lién-chèn* 廉鎮
T'ANG: lit., to inspect frontier areas: unofficial reference to a **Surveillance Commissioner** (*kuan-ch'a shih*).

3706 *lién-făng* 廉訪
CH'ING: lit., to conduct investigations: unofficial reference to a **Provincial Surveillance Commissioner** (*an-ch'a shih*). Also see *su-cheng lien-fang shih*.

3707 *lién-făng kuān* 廉訪官
SUNG: **Investigatory Official,** unofficial reference to an Investigation Commissioner (*lien-fang shih*).

3708 *lién-făng shĭh* 廉訪使
(1) SUNG: **Investigation Commissioner:** from 1116 to the end of N. Sung, a duty assignment of a court official to maintain liaison between the dynastic capital and the northern frontier. SP: *commissaire chargé de la transmission des alertes à la frontière*. (2) YÜAN: abbreviation of *su-cheng lien-fang shih* (**Surveillance Commissioner**).

3709 *lién-hsièn* 廉憲
MING–CH'ING: lit., to investigate (implementation of) the fundamental laws: unofficial reference to a **Provincial Surveillance Commissioner** (*an-ch'a shih*). Also see *hsien, feng-hsien*.

3710 *lién-kuān* 廉官
YÜAN–CH'ING: **Examination Aides,** collective reference to District Magistrates (*chih-hsien*) and other officials in units of territorial administration who were chosen to assist Provincial Examiners (*chu-k'ao*) in triennial Provincial Examinations (*hsiang-shih*) of candidates for civil service careers. One group, called Outer Aides (*wai-lien*: lit., those outside the screen) helped proctor the examinations; another group, called Inner Aides (*nei-lien*: lit., those inside the screen) helped read and grade examination papers. See *shih-kuan* (Examination Officials).

3711 *lièn-láng* 輦郎
HAN: **Court Gentleman Driver of the Imperial Hand-drawn Carriage,** reportedly an honor conferred on the sons of officials of distinction, at the age of 12.

3712 *lién-mù* 蓮幕
From the era of N-S Division if not earlier, a reference to the personal retainers, i.e., the **Private Secretariat** (see *mu-fu*), of an eminent official, especially a Regional Inspector (*tz'u-shih;* also see *chou*) or a later provincial-level counterpart; lit., a lotus-leaf tent, deriving from early comments that such retainers constituted a lotus-flower pool (connotations not clear).

3713 *lién-pó ch'ăng* 廉箔場
SUNG: **Lattice and Trellis Factory,** one of the workshops under the Directorate for the Palace Buildings (*chiang-tso chien*); headed by 2 Supervisory Officials (*chien-kuan*), unranked. SP: *aire de treillis*. P15.

3714 *lién-pŭ* 廉捕
CH'ING: lit., (one who) investigates and arrests: unofficial reference to a **District Jailor** (*tien-shih*), unranked member of a District (*hsien*) staff.

3715 *lién-shĭh* 廉使
T'ANG: **Investigation Commissioner,** unofficial reference to a Surveillance Commissioner (*kuan-ch'a shih, an-ch'a shih*).

3716 *lién-shuài* 連率 or 連帥
(1) CHOU: **Aggregation Leader;** see under *lien*. (2) HAN (first form): unofficial reference to a **Commandery Governor** (*chün t'ai-shou*). (3) MING–CH'ING (2nd form): unofficial reference to a **Provincial Surveillance Commissioner** (*an-ch'a shih*).

3717 *lín* 鄰
Neighborhood, a unit in officially recognized sub-District (*hsien*) organizations of local populations. (1) CHOU: a group of 5 households outside the royal domain (cf. *pi*, a comparable unit within the royal domain) with a Head (*chang*); 5 such units constituted an official Village (*li*). CL: *voisinage*. (2) N-S DIV (N. Wei): part of a 3-tier sub-District organization called the Three Elders (*san chang*) system; 5 households with a Neighborhood Elder (*lin-chang*), 5 of which constituted a Village, 5 of which in turn constituted a Ward (*tang*), all units headed by Elders (*chang*). (3) T'ANG: a unit of 5 households with a Head (*chang*), 5 of which constituted a Security Group (*pao*). (4) YÜAN: a unit of only 4 families with a Head (*chang*), 5 of which constituted a Security Group.

3718 *lín-ch'áo* 臨朝
Lit., (one who) oversees the court, participating in or directing court audiences, normally suggesting a period when the ruler was absent or otherwise unable to participate: **Regent,** more a descriptive term than a formal title, used particularly in reference to a widowed Empress who presided in court during the minority of the reigning Emperor; i.e., Empress Dowager Regent (*huang t'ai-hou lin-ch'ao*).

3719 *lĭn chiēn-shēng* 廩監生
CH'ING: **Student by Purchase, First Class,** under the Directorate of Education (*kuo-tzu chien*), a status attainable by men already entitled Stipend Students (*lin-sheng*), i.e., Government Students (*sheng-yüan*) considered best qualified for Provincial Examinations (*hsiang-shih*) in the civil service recruitment examination sequence. Also see *chien-sheng, lin kung-sheng*.

3720 *lín-chĭh tièn* 麟趾殿
N-S DIV (Chou): lit., unicorn hooves hall, deriving from a passage in the ancient *Classic of Songs* (*Shih-ching*), signifying a wish for many worthy sons and grandsons: **Institute of Litterateurs,** charged with writing and compiling efforts for the court, staffed with as many as 80 personnel including Academicians (*hsüeh-shih*). P23.

3721 *lín-hàn chiēn* 臨漢監
T'ANG: lit. relevance ("Directorate overlooking the Han River"?) not clear: **Directorate of Herds,** in charge of horse breeding; staffing and organizational affiliation not clear, but likely attached to the Court of the Imperial Stud (*t'ai-p'u ssu*).

3722 *lín-héng* 林衡
CHOU: lit., forest measurer (?): **Supervisor of Public Lands,** large numbers ranked as Junior Servicemen (*hsia-shih*), members of the Ministry of Education (*ti-kuan*) delegated to enforce royal prohibitions concerning catching and killing wildlife caught or killed in mountains, forests, streams, or marshes—areas traditionally considered public (i.e., royal) lands—and to collect taxes from hunters, trappers, and fishers in such areas. See *ch'uan-heng, yü-heng, shan-yü, tse-yü*. CL: *inspecteur forestier*.

3723 *lín-héng shŭ* 林衡署
MING: **Office of Fruits and Flowers,** one of 4 Offices (*shu*) under the Directorate of Imperial Parks (*shang-lin yüan-chien*); headed by a Manager (*tien-shu*), rank 7a. P40.

3724 *lĭn-hsī* 廩犧
HAN, T'ANG–SUNG: **Section (Office) of Sacrificial Grains and Animals,** in Han (Section) headed by a Director (*ling*) subordinate to the Left Chamberlain for the Capital (*tso nei-shih*) till 104 B.C., thereafter to the Guard-

ian of the Left (*tso p'ing-i*); in T'ang (*lin-hsi shu:* Office) headed by a Director (*ling*), rank 8b2, in Sung (*lin-hsi an:* Section) staffing not clear; in both T'ang and Sung under the Court of Imperial Sacrifices (*t'ai-ch'ang ssu*). Always responsible for providing materials to be sacrificed in important state ceremonies, including live animals. HB: office of sacrificial oblations and victims. RR+SP: *office des approvisionnements et des victimes pour les sacrifices.* P27.

3725 *lǐn-jén* 廩人
CHOU: **Granary Master,** 2 ranked as Junior Grand Masters (*hsia ta-fu*), members of the Ministry of Education (*ti-kuan*) who monitored the amount and condition of grain in state granaries and administered its distribution through subordinate Granary Managers (*ts'ang-jen*). CL: *officiers des greniers.*

3726 *lǐn kùng-shēng* 廩貢生
CH'ING: **Tribute Student by Purchase, First Class,** under the Directorate of Education (*kuo-tzu chien*), a status attainable by men already entitled Stipend Student (*lin-sheng*), i.e., Government Students (*sheng-yüan*) considered best qualified candidates for Provincial Examinations (*hsiang-shih*) in the civil service recruitment examination sequence. Also see *kung-sheng, lin chien-sheng.*

3727 *lǐn-shàn shēng* 廩膳生
MING–CH'ING: variant of *lin-sheng* (**Stipend Student**).

3728 *lǐn-shēng* 廩生
MING–CH'ING: **Stipend Student,** designation of students in government schools (*sheng-yüan*) who were paid stipends; certified as best qualified to participate in Provincial Examinations (*hsiang-shih*) in the civil service recruitment examination sequence by the Ming Education Intendant (*t'i-tu hsüeh tao-t'ai*) or the Ch'ing Provincial Education Commissioner (*t'i-tu hsüeh-cheng*). BH: stipendiaries.

3729 *lín-shíh chèng-fǔ* 臨時政府
Provisional Government: throughout history (?) a reference to an ad hoc central government trying to govern the country during an interregnum or in some other time of irregularities or emergency; normally headed by someone designated Executive Official (*chih-cheng*).

3730 *lín-t'ái* 麟臺
Lit., the unicorn pavilion. (1) T'ANG: from 685 to 712, the official redesignation of the **Palace Library** (*pi-shu sheng*). (2) CH'ING: unofficial reference to the **Hanlin Academy** (*han-lin yüan*).

3731 *lín-wǔ* 鄰伍
CHOU: **Local Units of Organization,** a combination of the terms *lin* (Neighborhood) and *wu* (Squad), in an abbreviated reference to the sub-District (*hsien*) organization of the population. Cf. *pao-chia, li-chia.*

3732 *lín-yá* 林牙 or 林㕛
LIAO: **Secretary,** Chinese rendering of a Khitan word similar to *han-lin* (Hanlin); occurs throughout the Liao government with a variety of particularizing prefixes and suffixes, e.g., *pei-mien lin-ya ch'eng-chih* (Secretary Recipient of Edicts in the Northern Administration), *han-lin tu lin-ya* (Supreme Secretary of the Hanlin Academy). P5, 12, 23.

3733 *lìng* 令
Lit., to order, (one who) gives orders: **Director:** throughout history one of the commonest titles given to administrative or executive heads of agencies large or small, ranging from District Magistrate (*hsien-ling*) up to Secretariat Director (*chung-shu ling*) and Director of the Department of State

Affairs (*shang-shu ling*). Normally prefixed with an agency name; often part of a binome incorporating the generic term designating the agency, e.g., *hsien-ling, chen-kuan shu shu-ling* (Director of the Pottery Office), *yen-ch'ang ssu ssu-ling* (Director of a Saltern Office). In Ming and Ch'ing, *ling* by itself was an archaic unofficial reference to a District Magistrate (then *chih-hsien*). Sometimes best rendered **Manager,** e.g., of an imperial mausoleum (*ling*) or **Magistrate,** as in *hsien-ling.* HB: prefect.

3734 *líng* 陵
Throughout history the most common general term for **Imperial Mausoleum** or **Imperial Tomb,** normally prefixed with a laudatory expression, e.g., *i-ling* (Righteousness Tomb), *hsiao-ling* (Filial Piety Tomb), *yung-ling* (Eternity Tomb). See *ling-ch'in, ling-yüan, ling-shu, ling-t'ai.* Cf. *miao* (Temple). P29.

3735 *lǐng* 領 or *lǐng ... shìh* 領···事
Lit., to lead, control, control the affairs of ...: **Concurrent** or **Concurrent Controller:** throughout history, especially from Han through Sung, the designation of an official who, in addition to performing the duties of his principal regular post, was assigned to serve concurrently in charge of another agency or in another post, often signifying that his regular titular post was of lesser status and rank than the post he was newly assigned to; e.g., *ling i-chou mu* (Concurrent Governor of I-chou), *ling chung-shu chien* (Concurrent Secretariat Supervisor), *ling hui-t'ung kuan shih* (Concurrent Controller of the Interpreters Institute), *ling shu-mi yüan shih* (Concurrent Controller of the Bureau of Military Affairs). Cf. other terms with similar functions: *chien, lu, p'ing, tai.* Also see *yao-ling* (Remote Controller).

3736 *lǐng chāi-láng* 領齋郎
N-S DIV (Sung): **Concurrent Court Gentleman for Fasting,** 24 ad hoc appointees having substantive posts elsewhere in government, subordinate to the Director (*ling*) of the Imperial Ancestral Temple (*t'ai-miao*). See *chai-lang.* P28.

3737 *lìng-chǎng* 令長
District Magistrate: throughout history a common combined reference to *ling* and *chang;* from Sung on, an unofficial generic reference.

3738 *líng-chǎng* 陵長
N-S DIV (N. Ch'i): **Director of Tombs,** one, rank not clear, in each Princedom (*wang-kuo*), charged with the building and maintenance of all tombs of Princes and their relatives. P69.

3739 *lìng-ch'éng* 令丞
Administrators: throughout history an unofficial generic, combined reference to the Directors (*ling*) and Vice Directors (*ch'eng*) of many kinds of agencies and most particularly to District Magistrates (*ling, chang, chih-hsien*) and Vice Magistrates (*ch'eng*).

3740 *lìng-ch'éng àn* 令丞案
SUNG: **Section for Administrators,** an agency of the Bureau of Evaluations (*k'ao-kung*) in the Ministry of Personnel (*li-pu*); staffing not clear, likely unranked. See *ling, ch'eng, ling-ch'eng.* SP: *service des directeurs et des assistants.*

3741 *líng-chiēn* 陵監
N-S DIV: variant of *ling-ling* (**Director of the ... Imperial Mausoleum**).

3742 *lǐng-chiēn kuān* 領監官
YÜAN: lit., official (serving as) concurrent controller of

the Directorate; variant of *ling* (Concurrent, Concurrent Controller); specifically, but perhaps not exclusively, **Concurrent Controller of the Directorate of Medication** (*chang-i chien*), rank 5a.

3743 *líng-chīh yüán-chiēn* 靈芝園監
N-S DIV (San-kuo Wei): **Director of the Magnificent Iris Garden,** rank 7, probably subordinate to the Chamberlain for the National Treasury (*ssu-nung*). P40.

3744 *líng-chǐn chīh-jǎn chú* 綾綿織染局 or *líng-chǐn chīh-jǎn t'í-chǔ ssū* 提舉司
YÜAN: **Brocade Weaving and Dyeing Service** (*chü*), in 1287 renamed **Supervisorate** (*t'i-chü ssu*) **of Brocade Weaving and Dyeing;** one of 4 subsection workshops in the Service of Rare Textiles (*i-yang chü*); headed by a Supervisor (*t'i-chü*), rank 5b.

3745 *líng-chǐn fāng* 綾錦坊 or *líng-chǐn yüàn* 院
T'ANG, SUNG: **Silk Brocade Workshop** (*fang* in T'ang) or **Office** (*yüan* in Sung), a subsection of the Directorate for Imperial Manufactories (*shao-fu chien*); in T'ang reportedly employed as many as 365 palace artisans, in Sung headed by a Commissioner (*shih*), rank 7a. RR: *atelier des brocarts et des soieries.* SP: *cour des ....* P38.

3746 *líng-ch'ǐn* 陵寢
Common variant of *ling* (Imperial Mausoleum, Imperial Tomb).

3747 *líng-ch'ǐn chù-fáng* 陵寢駐防
CH'ING: **Garrison of the ... Imperial Mausoleum,** normally with a particularizing prefix; one at each of the Ch'ing Imperial Mausolea, commanded by 2 Wing Commanders (*i-chang, i-ling*), rank 4a, and 16 or more Platoon Commanders (*fang-yü*), 5a. See *chu-fang.* P29.

3748 *líng-ch'ǐn kuǎn-lǐ shāo-tsào chuān-wǎ kuān* 陵寢管理燒造磚瓦官
CH'ING: **Director of Brick and Tile Making for the Imperial Mausolea** in the Peking area, rank 5a; probably only one establishment serving both of the Imperial Mausolea Administrations (see *ling-ch'in tsung-kuan*). BH: overseers of brick and tile making for the imperial mausolea.

3749 *líng-ch'ǐn ssū kūng-chiàng* 陵寢司工匠
CH'ING: **Maintenance Director at the ... Imperial Mausoleum,** rank 4a; normally with a particularizing prefix. BH: overseer of works at ....

3750 *líng-ch'ǐn tsǔng-kuǎn* 陵寢總管
CH'ING: **Supervisor-in-chief of the Imperial Mausolea Administration,** one, rank 3a, in charge of each group of Ch'ing imperial tombs in the Peking area. See *ch'eng-pan shih-wu ya-men, shou-hu ling-ch'in ta-ch'en.* BH: controller-general of the banner garrison at....

3751 *lǐng chǔ-shìh* 領主事
N-S DIV (Ch'en): **Chief Clerk,** 10, rank not clear but low, in the Secretariat (*chung-shu sheng*); apparently assisted 5 Secretariat Drafters (*chung-shu she-jen*) in supervising 200 Clerks (*shu-li*) and an unspecified number of Assistant Clerks (*chu-shu*) divided among 21 Services (*chü*). P2.

3752 *lìng-chün* 令君
Throughout history, an occasional unofficial reference to a **District Magistrate** (*hsien-ling, chih-hsien*).

3753 *lǐng-chün* 領軍
HAN–N-S DIV: **Commandant,** number and rank not clear,

occasionally found on the staff of the Director of Banquets (*ta-kuan ling*), a subordinate of the Chief Minister for Dependencies (*hung-lu ch'ing*), also on the staff of Gate Traffic Control Offices (*kung-ch'e ssu-ma men*); functions not clear, but perhaps a patrol or police security officer. Also (San-kuo Shu) a title conferred on chieftains of southwestern aboriginal tribes. Also see *chung ling-chün* (Capital Commandant). HB: intendant of the army. P21, 30, 43, 72.

3754 *lǐng-chün chiáng-chūn* 領軍將軍
N-S DIV: lit., general commanding the army: **General of the Palace Guard,** at times a sinecure for a court favorite, at times actively in charge of the palace guard. P43.

3755 *lǐng-chün tà tū-tū* 領軍大都督
T'ANG: **Commander-in-chief of the Armies,** 2 prefixed Left and Right, commanders of the 6 armies, 3 prefixed Left and 3 prefixed Right, with which the founding Emperor, as General-in-chief (*ta chiang-chün*), established the dynasty; posts held by his sons Li Chien-ch'eng and Li Shih-min. This organizational system faded away when the dynasty was securely established. RR: *grand gouverneur général de gauche et de droite dirigent les armées.*

3756 *lǐng-chün wèi* 領軍衛
T'ANG: **Metropolitan Guard,** 2 prefixed Left and Right, included among the Sixteen Guards (*shih-liu wei*, q.v.) at the dynastic capital; created in 622 as successors of the Left and Right Protective Guards (*yü-wei*) inherited from the Sui dynasty's Twelve Guards (*shih-erh wei*, q.v.) system; in 662 retitled the Martial Guards (*jung-wei*), in 671 resumed the name Metropolitan Guards, in 684 retitled Guards of the Jade Strategy (*yü-ch'ien wei*), in 705 again named Metropolitan Guards. Members of the Metropolitan Guards were commonly called Bowmen Shooters by Sound (*she-sheng*) and were sometimes referred to as the Fierce as Leopards Cavaliers (*pao-chi*). RR: *garde guide des armées.* P43.

3757 *líng-hsiá* 鈴轄 or 鈴下
(1) T'ANG: unofficial reference to the **Prefect** (*t'ai-shou, tz'u-shih*) of a Prefecture (*chou*). (2) SUNG: **Circuit (Prefectural) General,** head of all regular army forces in his jurisdiction, a Circuit (*lu*) or a Prefecture (*chou*); often the concurrent duty assignment of a Prefect (*tz'u-shih, chih-chou, chih-fu, chih-chün, chih-chien*); the military headquarters of such an appointee was called the General's Office (*ling-hsia ssu*). (3) SUNG: **Supervisor,** common prefix to agency names, normally signifying an official put in charge on some irregular basis, e.g., *ling-hsia chu-tao tu chin-tsou yüan* (Supervisor of the Memorials Office for All The Circuits; see *chin-tsou yüan*).

3758 *líng-jén* 凌人
CHOU: **Royal Iceman,** 2 ranked as Junior Servicemen (*hsia-shih*), members of the Ministry of State (*t'ien-kuan*) responsible for gathering, cutting, storing, and issuing ice for use by the King and the court, especially for the chilling of various foods and drinks for banquets, receptions for foreigners, and sacrifices; distributed ice to officials by royal command on particularly hot days; also packed royal corpses in ice for preservation. CL (*ping-jen?*): *employé aux glacières.*

3759 *líng kó-shìh* 領閣事
CH'ING: lit., concurrent controller of the Hall (of Literary Profundity; see *wen-yüan ko*), but actually 2 **Concurrent Assistant Directors** of the Hall of Literary Profundity, subordinate to a Supervisor (*t'i-chü ko-shih*) who in turn was subordinate to the Grand Secretary (*ta hsüeh-shih*) of the

Hall of Literary Profundity. The posts were assigned to nominal members of various court agencies. BH: assistant director. P23, 25.

3760 *lĭng ... kuān* 領…官
Lit., official concurrently controlling ...: variant of *ling* (**Concurrent, Concurrent Controller**).

3761 *lĭng-kuān shīh* 伶官師 or 泠官師
T'ANG: **Master of Musical Entertainments**, 2, rank not clear, reportedly members of the Court of the Watches (*lei-keng ssu*) of the Heir Apparent. There is disagreement among the sources as to the existence and organizational affiliation of this post, and no explanation is provided for the seemingly strange affiliation given above. RR: *maître des musiciens.* P26.

3762 *lìng kùng-yüàn* 令貢院
SUNG: **Concurrent Controller of the Examination Office** (*kung-yüan*) in the Ministry of Rites (*lĭ-pu*). See *ling.* SP: *chargé de diriger le bureau d'examen.*

3763 *lĭng-lìng* 陵令
N-S DIV: **Director of the ... Imperial Mausoleum** (*ling*, q.v.), normally with a particularizing prefix; supervised by the Chamberlain for Ceremonials (*t'ai-ch'ang*). May be encountered as an abbreviation of *ling-shu ling, ling-t'ai ling, ling-yüan ling*, qq.v. Also see *ling-chien, miao-chang.*

3764 *lĭng-lù* 令錄
SUNG: **Local Administrators**, apparently a generic reference to officials of significant authority and responsibility below Prefects (*chih-chou*) in the hierarchy of regional and local administration; specifically seems an abbreviated, combined reference to District Magistrates (*hsien-ling*) and Administrative Supervisors (*lu-shih ts'an-chün*) in Prefectures (*chou*). Also see *ling-chang, ling-ch'eng.*

3765 *lĭng-pān* 領班
CH'ING: **Duty Group Chief**, one for each Duty Group (*pan*) of Secretaries (*chang-ching*) in the Council of State (*chün-chi ch'u*), rank 3a. See *man t'ou-pan, man erh-pan, han t'ou-pan, han erh-pan.* BH: chief of section.

3766 *lĭng-pān chāng-chīng shàng hsíng-tsŏu* 領班章京上行走
CH'ING: **Secretary of the Council of State Concurrently Serving as Duty Group Chief**, variant of Duty Group Chief (*ling-pan*), also commonly awarded as an honorary title to Secretaries of the Council of State (*chün-chi chang-ching*). Also see *chang-ching, hsing-tsou.* BH: chief of section.

3767 *lìng-shìh* 令事
Occasional variant of *ling* (**Director**) or *ling* (**Concurrent, Concurrent Controller**).

3768 *lĭng-shĭh* 令史
(1) HAN–YÜAN: **Clerk**, generally a very low-level official or suboffficial functionary, found in many agencies both in the central government and in units of territorial administration; in Han had official status one rank below Secretarial Court Gentleman (*shang-shu lang*), in Former Han could be promoted after satisfactory service to Secretarial Court Gentleman, in Later Han was promotable to Magistrate (*ling*) of a small District (*hsien*); in Sung could have 8b rank. Occurs with many particularizing prefixes: e.g., *chih-shu ling-shih, chu-shih ling-shih, shang-shu ling-shih.* Also see *ch'i-chü ling-shih* (Assistant Diarist). HB: foreman clerk. RR+SP: *scribe de première classe.* (2) **Director**, occasionally an appropriate rendering, when a *ling-shih* (even with low or suboffficial status) was in fact the senior ap-

pointee in a minor agency: e.g., the T'ang dynasty *chia-k'u* (Archives).

3769 *lĭng ... shìh* 領…事
Lit., concurrent controller of the affairs of ...: variant of *ling* (**Concurrent, Concurrent Controller**); e.g., *ling san-sheng shih* (Concurrent Controller of the Three Departments; see *san sheng*) of Chin times. P4.

3770 *lĭng shìh-wèi fŭ* 領侍衛府
CH'ING: **Headquarters of the Imperial Bodyguard**, a unit of the Imperial Household Department (*nei-wu fu*). See *ling shih-wei nei ta-ch'en.* BH: office of the imperial bodyguard.

3771 *lĭng shìh-wèi nèi tà-ch'én* 領侍衛內大臣
CH'ING: **Grand Minister of the Imperial Household Department Concurrently Controlling the Imperial Guardsmen**, 6, rank 1a, in charge of the Imperial Bodyguard (*ch'in-chün ying*); 2 always on rotational duty as active leaders of the bodyguard, entitled Grand Ministers of the Rear Watch (*hou-hu ta-ch'en*). BH: chamberlain of the imperial bodyguard. P37.

3772 *lĭng-shŭ* 陵署
N-S DIV (N. Ch'i), SUI–T'ANG, CHIN–YÜAN: **Office of the ... Imperial Mausoleum**, normally with a particularizing laudatory prefix such as *ting* (Determination), *hsiao* (Filial Piety); each managed by a Director (*ling*), rank 7b2 to 5b1 in T'ang, 6b in Chin; subordinate to a Superintendent (*t'i-tien*), 5a, in Chin and Yüan. Generally subordinate to the Court of Imperial Sacrifices (*t'ai-ch'ang ssu*), but in T'ang subordinate to the Court of the Imperial Clan (*tsung-cheng ssu*) from the 730s (?) to 753 and again from 757 to 767. The agency name seems to have been interchangeable with Court of the ... Imperial Mausoleum (*ling-t'ai*), which seems to have predominated after the 750s till *ling-shu* was revived by Chin, also managed by a Director (*ling*). RR: *office du tombeau impérial.* P29.

3773 *lĭng-t'ái* 陵臺
T'ANG–SUNG: **Court of the ... Imperial Mausoleum**, normally with a particularizing laudatory prefix (see under *ling, ling-shu*); each managed by a Director (*ling*) in T'ang, rank 7b2 to 5b1, in Sung by a Director, 6b, or a Commissioner (*shih*), rank deriving from the appointee's regular, nominal post elsewhere. The agency name alternated with Office of the ... Imperial Mausoleum (*ling-shu*) in T'ang until about the 750s; thereafter *ling-t'ai* seems to have been standard through the remainder of T'ang and in Sung. In T'ang normally under the supervision of the Court of Imperial Sacrifices (*t'ai-ch'ang ssu*), but under the Court of the Imperial Clan (*tsung-cheng ssu*) from the 730s (?) to 753 and again from 757 to 767; in Sung supervised by the Court of the Imperial Clan. RR+SP: *administration du tombeau impérial.* P29.

3774 *lĭng-t'ái* 靈臺
Lit., spiritual or inspirational terrace or pavilion, i.e., a location suffused with spiritual, extraterrestrial force: **Imperial Observatory**: from Han on, with minor lapses (in the sources, but not likely in reality) in the N. Dynasties and in Chin, generally responsible for maintaining steady astronomical observation, keeping records of stellar activity, predicting weather, and participating in the preparation and occasional revision of the state-authorized calendar. A major unit in the central government's Directorate of Astrology (see *t'ai-shih ling, ssu-t'ien t'ai, t'ai-shih chü, ssu-t'ien chien*) through Sung and Liao, in the Yüan Astrological Commission (*t'ai-shih yüan*), in the Ming–Ch'ing Directorate of Astronomy (*ch'in-t'ien chien*). Headed by

unranked Expectant Officials (*tai-chao*) in Former Han; by a Director (*ch'eng*, "aide": note the rare use of *ch'eng* for an agency head rather than for the principal assistant to a *ling*, Director) from Later Han through the era of N-S Division, rank 200 bushels in Later Han; by a Director (*lang*) thereafter: rank 7b in T'ang, 7a (in *ssu-t'ien chien*) or 8b (in *t'ai-shih chien*) in Sung, 7a in Yüan and Ming, 7b in Ch'ing; one Director common till T'ang, then one for each of the Five Offices (*wu kuan*, q.v.) in the agency; 8 then 4 distributed among the Five Offices again in Ming; 8 in Ch'ing. HB: spiritual terrace. RR+SP: *la terrasse des esprits*. BH: the observatory. P35.

3775 *lǐng tsǒ-yù fǔ* 領左右府
SUI: lit., office for the supervision of attendants (? *tso-yu*): **Palace Military Headquarters,** a unit of the Left and Right Guard (*tso-yu wei*) that rotated troops of the Garrison Militia system (see *fu, fu-ping*) in and out of the various military units at the dynastic capital, and also rotated select members of these units in and out of duty assignments in the personal guard of the Emperor. Headed by an Aide (*chang-shih*) to the General-in-chief of the Left and Right Guard. In c. 604 transformed into 2 units, the Left and Right Imperial Bodyguards (*pei-shen fu*), in the new Twelve Guards (*shih-erh wei*) military organization at the capital. P43.

3776 *líng-wǔ* 囹圄
(1) CH'IN: **Central Prison,** organizational affiliation and staffing not clear; reportedly the antecedent of the Han prison called *jo-lu yü*, q.v. (2) From Han on, a common generic term for **Prison, Jail.**

3777 *líng-yǜ* 淩玉
T'ANG: lit., ice-clear jade: unofficial reference to a **Hanlin Academician** (*han-lin hsüeh-shih*). P23.

3778 *lǐng-yǜn* 領運
CH'ING: **Transport Station Commandant,** head of a small Transport Station (*so*, with place-name prefix) that manned tax-grain transport boats along the Grand Canal; a military officer of low rank on special duty assignment in the tax-grain transport establishment. See under *ts'ao-yün tsung-tu* (Director-general of Grain Transport). BH: lieutenant charged with the conduct of grain squadrons. P60.

3779 *liù ch'á* 六察
SUNG: **Six Investigators,** a collective reference to the 6 Investigating Censors (*chien-ch'a yü-shih*) authorized for the Investigation Bureau (*ch'a-yüan*) of the Censorate (*yü-shih t'ai*). SP: *six censeurs de la cour des enquêtes en dehors*. P18.

3780 *liù-chái shǐh* 六宅使
SUNG: **Commissioner of the Six Residences** (?), an early Sung antecedent of the prestige title (*san-kuan*) Grand Master for Military Tallies (*wu-chieh ta-fu*), awarded to rank 7a military officers. P68.

3781 *liù-chīng chì-chiǔ* 六經祭酒
HAN: lit., chancellor (libationer) of the 6 classics: **Exalter of the Six Classics,** one for each classical work, teachers in the National University (*t'ai-hsüeh*), ranked as a Senior Minister (*shang-ch'ing*) in the Chou dynasty system of ranks; also called *po-shih liu-ching chi-chiu* (Erudite Exalter of the Six Classics) or in a particular case specifying the particular classic intended, as in *po-shih chiang-shu chi-chiu* (Erudite Exalter of the Classic of Writings, *Shu-ching*; *chiang* meaning to expound upon). This nomenclature was used only during the reign of Wang Mang (r. A.D. 9–23), replacing

the standard Han term Erudite of the Five Classics (*wu-ching po-shih*). P34.

3782 *liù ch'īng* 六卿
CHOU: variant of *liu kuan* (**Six Ministers**).

3783 *liù chiù* 六廄
Six Stables. (1) HAN: collective reference to various horse herds maintained in the Imperial Forest Park (*shang-lin yüan*) by a Director (*ling*), rank 600 bushels, and his Aide (*ch'eng*) under the Commandant of the Imperial Gardens (*shui-heng tu-wei*). Abolished in 31 B.C. HB: the six stables. (2) T'ANG: collective reference after 739 to 6 horse stables inside the palace grounds: the Left and Right Stables of Flying Mounts (*fei-chiu*), the Left and Right Stables of Myriad Mounts (*wan-chiu*), the Inner Stable of the Southeast (*tung-nan nei-chiu*), and the Inner Stable of the Southwest (*hsi-nan nei-chiu*), all under a Commissioner for the Palace Stables (*hsien-chiu shih*), nominally a member of the Palace Administration (*tien-chung sheng*), who also supervised the Six Palace Corrals (*chang-nei liu hsien*) and the Five Cages (*wu fang*), which provided animals used in imperial hunts. In the mid-700s the Six Stables and the Six Palace Corrals reportedly cared for as many as 10,000 horses and additionally camels, cattle, and elephants. Administrative relations among these various units and with many other pasturages, especially those controlled by the Court of the Imperial Stud (*t'ai-p'u ssu*), are not clear. See *nei-chiu, chien-mu, mu-chien, mu-ch'ang, mu-yüan, yüan-ma ssu*. RR: *les six écuries*. (3) T'ANG: prior to 739, a variant reference to the Six Palace Corrals (*chang-nei liu hsien*).

3784 *liù chǘ* 六局
(1) N-S DIV–SUNG: **Six Services,** collective reference to agencies of the central government that served the personal needs of the Emperor and the imperial household, deriving from the collective term Six Chief Stewards (*liu shang*, q.v.); in the era of N-S Division, with varying patterns of nomenclature, subordinate to the Chamberlain for the Palace Revenues (*shao-fu*); in Sui subordinated to the Directorate of Palace Administration (*tien-nei chien*), thereafter to the T'ang–Sung Palace Administration (*tien-nei sheng, tien-chung sheng*). From Sui through Sung the heads of the agencies were titled *feng-yü* (Chief Steward), and the standard Services in the group were the Clothing Service (*shang-i chü*), Food Service (*shang-shih chü*), Palace Medical Service (*shang-yao chü*), Accommodations Service (*shang-she chü*), Sedan-chair Service (*shang-lien chü*), and Livery Service (*shang-ch'eng chü*), the latter replaced in Sung by a Wine Stewards Service (*shang-yün chü*). After Sung the functions of these Services were scattered among several central government agencies, especially the Yüan dynasty Palace Provisions Commission (*hsüan-hui yüan*), the Ming dynasty Ministry of Works (*kung-pu*) and Court of Imperial Entertainments (*kuang-lu ssu*), and the Ch'ing dynasty Imperial Household Department (*nei-wu fu*). RR: *six services*. SP: *six services de l'empereur*. P37, 38. (2) T'ANG–MING: **Six Palace Services,** collective reference to the chief agencies in which palace women were organized; see under *liu shang* (#2: Six Matrons).

3785 *liù chǖn* 六軍
Six Imperial Armies. (1) Throughout history, beginning with the *Chou-li* assertion that only the King was allowed 6 armies, a general term for the major fighting forces of a domain or a dynasty; usually garrisoned in the vicinity of the dynastic capital and in some degree under the ruler's personal control; synonymous with such terms as Imperial

Armies (*chin-chün*). (2) T'ANG: from 757 till 807, a specific reference to the Forest of Plumes Armies (*yü-lin chün*), the Militant as Dragons Armies (*lung-wu chün*), and the Armies of Inspired Militancy (*shen-wu chün*), all in Left and Right pairs; from 807 on, a specific reference to the Forest of Plumes Armies, the Militant as Dragons Armies, and the Armies of Inspired Strategy (*shen-ts'e chün*); the term Six Armies was almost synonymous with the term Northern Command (*pei-ya*). Aiso see *ssu chün* (Four Imperial Armies), *shih chün* (Ten Imperial Armies). (3) SUNG: perpetuated the T'ang pre-807 nomenclature, but apparently only for honorific uses; the real equivalent of the Six Imperial Armies was the aggregation of troops in the Three Capital Guards (*san wei*). RR+SP: *six armées*. P43.

3786   *liù chūn í-chàng ssū* 六軍儀仗司
SUNG: **Bureau of Ceremonial Insignia and Arms for the Six Imperial Armies,** staffing not clear; a supply unit under the Court of the Imperial Insignia (*wei-wei ssu*). See *i-chang ssu*, *i-chang shih*. SP: *bureau des emblêmes et des armes d'apparat pour les six armées*.

3787   *liù ch'ún* 六群
T'ANG: **Six Herds,** collective designation of one of the 6 units that in turn were collectively called the Six Palace Corrals (*chang-nei liu hsien*), attached to the Palace Administration (*tien-chung sheng*). Also see *liu chiu*. RR: *le parc de chevaux des six troupeaux*.

3788   *liù fáng* 六房
SUNG: **Six Offices,** collective designation of administrative support agencies serving the combined Secretariat-Chancellery (*chung-shu men-hsia sheng*), counterparts of the Six Ministries (*liu pu*) in the Department of State Affairs (*shang-shu sheng*); administered collectively (?) by 4 Supervising Secretaries (*chi-shih-chung*) under supervision of 2 Examiners (*chien-cheng*). The Six Offices were the Personnel Office (*li-fang*), Revenue Office (*hu-fang*), Rites Office (*li-fang*), War Office (*ping-fang*), Justice Office (*hsing-fang*), and Works Office (*kung-fang*). SP: *six chambres*. P3.

3789   *liù fǔ* 六府
CHOU: **Six Tax Supervisors,** according to one source (*Li-chi*), 6 agencies subordinate to the Ministry of Education (*ti-kuan*) that oversaw tax collections of separate categories: Land Tax Supervisor (*ssu-t'u*), Forest Tax Supervisor (*ssu-mu*), River Tax Supervisor (*ssu-shui*), Grain Tax Supervisor (*ssu-ts'ao*), Crafts Tax Supervisor (*ssu-ch'i*), Market (?) Tax Supervisor (*ssu-huo*).

3790   *liú-hòu shǐh* 留後使 or *liu-hou*
Lit., an agent left behind, a deputy. (1) T'ANG–SUNG: **Capital Liaison Representative,** an agent in the dynastic capital charged with maintaining communication between the central government and his superior in a territorial base, such as a Prince or Military Commissioner (*chieh-tu shih*). (2) SUNG: **Deputy Commander,** an agent of a Military Commissioner (*chieh-tu shih*) in a region not personally supervised by the Commissioner. The title was also sometimes conferred on chieftains of southwestern aboriginal tribes. SP: *délégué-commandant*.

3791   *liù hsién* 六閑
T'ANG: abbreviation of *chang-nei liu hsien* (**Six Palace Corrals**).

3792   *liù í* 六儀
T'ANG: **Six Ladies of Deportment,** a collective reference to 6 imperial concubines of rank 2a: *shu-i, te-i, hsien-i, shun-i, wan-i, fang-i,* qq.v.

3793   *liù k'ō* 六科
(1) T'ANG–SUNG: **Six Categories** of examinations given in the civil service recruitment examination process, a standard term that seems never to have been a very accurate description of the number of examination fields actually permitted. In T'ang, although there were variations, the most important examinations seem always to have been those leading to the degrees Classicist (*ming-ching*) and Presented Scholar (*chin-shih*); the degree of Cultivated Talent (*hsiu-ts'ai*) was also awarded, and examinations were given in law, history, rituals, and mathematics. In Sung fields of specialization were much more numerous; the Presented Scholar degree predominated, the term "other examinations" (*chu-k'o*) supplementing it to permit subspecializations in the general fields of law, history, rituals, and classics; and the Presented Scholar examination became so predominant from the 1070s that Metropolitan Graduate seems a more suitable rendering for the term *chin-shih* thereafter. (2) MING–CH'ING: **Six Offices of Scrutiny,** a cluster of major central government agencies staffed with Supervising Secretaries or Supervising Censors (both *chi-shih-chung,* q.v.) who were responsible for maintaining censorial surveillance over the Six Ministries (*liu pu*), especially for monitoring the flow of documents between the throne and the Ministries; generally independent agencies until 1723, then made constituent units in the Censorate (*tu ch'a-yüan*), after which Supervising Censor seems a more appropriate rendering than Supervising Secretary. Named after the Ministries for which they were separately responsible: Office of Scrutiny for Personnel (*li-k'o*), for Revenue (*hu-k'o*), for Rites (*li-k'o*), for War (*ping-k'o*), for Justice (*hsing-k'o*), for Works (*kung-k'o*). Created in 1373 as the agencies among which Supervising Secretaries were distributed, stabilized at 12 (10 from 1376), rank 7a. In 1377 made subordinate to the Directorate of Proclamations (*ch'eng-ch'ih chien*), in 1379 transferred to the Office of Transmission (*t'ung-cheng ssu*). In 1393 each Office of Scrutiny was reorganized with one Chief Supervising Secretary (*tu chi-shih-chung*), 8a, and one each Left and Right Supervising Secretary, 8b, providing administrative supervision over a total of 40 Supervising Secretaries, 9a. From 1399 till 1402 ranks were raised for Chief Supervising Secretaries and Supervising Secretaries to 7a and 7b, respectively, and Left and Right Supervising Secretaries were discontinued; c. 1402 Left and Right Supervising Secretaries were re-established, with rank 7b. Thereafter each Office was staffed with one Chief Supervising Secretary, 7a, one each Left and Right Supervising Secretary, 7b, and from 4 to 10 Supervising Secretaries, 7b (dwindling to from 4 to 7 in the late Ming decades). Ch'ing perpetuated the Ming system till 1660, when one each Manchu and Chinese Chief Supervising Secretary, one each Manchu and Chinese Left and Right Supervising Secretaries, and two Chinese Supervising Secretaries were prescribed in each Office. In 1665 all these posts were abolished except for one each Manchu and Chinese Supervising Secretary in each Office; but the next year one each Manchu and Chinese Seal-holding Supervising Secretary (*chang-yin chi-shih-chung*) were authorized as the new administrative leaders of each Office with rank at the 4 level. They were quickly dropped to the 7 level, then in 1667 restored to the 4 level, then in 1670 made 7a and in 1729 raised to 5a. Left and Right Supervising Secretaries were no longer appointed. In 1729, after being absorbed into the Censorate, Supervising Censors rose from 7b to 5a. Thus from

1729 each of the Offices of Scrutiny, integrated into the Censorate, had one each Manchu and Chinese Seal-holding Supervising Censors and one Supervising Censor in each Office. Also see *shu-chi-shih*. BH: senior (*chang-yin*) and junior metropolitan censors. P18, 19.

3794 *liù k'ù* 六庫
CH'ING: **Six Storehouses,** collective reference to the warehouses or vaults of valuables that constituted the Storage Office (*kuang-ch'u ssu*) of the Imperial Household Department (*nei-wu fu*). The Six Storehouses were the Silver Vault (*yin-k'u*), Hides Storehouse (*p'i-k'u*), Porcelain Storehouse (*tz'u-k'u*), Silks Storehouse (*tuan-k'u*), Clothing Storehouse (*i-k'u*), and Tea Storehouse (*ch'a-k'u*). P37.

3795 *liù kuān* 六官
CHOU: **Six Ministries,** a collective reference to the 6 top-echelon agencies in the royal government: Ministry of State (*t'ien-kuan*), Ministry of Education (*ti-kuan*), Ministry of Rites (*ch'un-kuan*), Ministry of War (*hsia-kuan*), Ministry of Justice (*ch'iu-kuan*), and Ministry of Works (*tung-kuan*). Often also used as a collective reference to the **Six Ministers** (*liu ch'ing*) who headed the Ministries.

3796 *liú-kuān* 流官
(1) SUI–CH'ING: lit., officials in the current (of ranked officials): equivalent of *liu-nei* (**Of Official Status**), q.v. (2) MING: **Circulating Offices,** a collective reference to all posts in the military hierarchy above Guard Commander (*wei chih-hui shih*), rank 3a. The higher-ranking and more prestigious offices at the provincial and central government levels were "circulating" (lit., in the current) in the sense that they were not inheritable but were filled by appointments made by the Ministry of War (*ping-pu*) or directly by the Emperor from among Guard Commanders or officers of lesser rank, whose status was in general hereditary, or from the hereditary nobility. Both Circulating Offices and Hereditary Offices (*shih-kuan*) were regular, substantive posts. When an officer was promoted from a Hereditary Office to a Circulating Office, or even to a higher Hereditary Office, he retained hereditary rights only to his original Hereditary Office; but for exceptional merit he could be awarded expanded hereditary rights, so that his heir (normally the eldest son) might enter service at a higher-level Hereditary Office than his father's, or an additional Hereditary Office might be made available to a second son. No military heir outside the nobility, however, was able to enter service in a Circulating Office.

3797 *liú-kuǎn* 留館 or 留官
CH'ING: **Retained in the Institute** or (in the irregular 2nd form) **Retained Official,** terms referring to a change in status from that of Hanlin Bachelor (*shu-chi-shih*). Hanlin Bachelors, selected from among promising new Metropolitan Graduates (*chin-shih*), were assigned to the Institute of Advanced Study (*shu-ch'ang kuan*) in the Hanlin Academy (*han-lin yüan*) for careful nurturing of their talents. After completing 3 years of intense literary studies, they were "released from the Institute" (*san-kuan*) to take a special imperial examination. Those who did well were "retained in the Institute" as Senior Compilers (*hsiu-chuan*) and Junior Compilers (*pien-hsiu*) of the Hanlin Academy, the term *kuan* (first form only) in this instance apparently used in archaic reference to a long nonexistent Historiography Institute (*shih-kuan*, *kuo-shih kuan*); others were "released from the Institute" (same terminology) in another sense—to take up careers outside the Hanlin Academy in the regular administrative hierarchy. Confusion may arise from the use of *san-kuan* in these different ways: a Hanlin Bachelor who

was "released from the Institute" to take the special examination may actually have been "retained in the Institute" (i.e., the Hanlin Academy) in consequence. All Hanlin Bachelors were "released" but, confusingly, the best were "retained." Cf. *liu-yüan kuan*. BH: retained at the academy. P23.

3798 *liù kūng* 六宮
CHOU: lit., the 6 palaces, but used to refer to the bedchambers of the King's six principal wives, hence to these wives personally, including the Queen: **Six Principal Wives** of the King.

3799 *liú-lí chú* 琉璃局
YÜAN: **Porcelain Service,** one of many workshops under the Peking Regency (Ta-tu *liu-shou ssu*); established in 1267; headed by a Commissioner-in-chief (*ta-shih*), rank not clear. P15.

3800 *liú-lí yáo* 琉璃窯
CH'ING: **Porcelain Works,** one of many workshops under the Ministry of Works (*kung-pu*); headed by 2 Superintendents (*chien-tu*), one Manchu and one Chinese, on rotational duty assignment for one year at a time, detached from regular staff posts in the Ministry; originally had only one Superintendent, a Chinese; reorganized in 1662. Produced tiles and other pottery required in imperial construction projects. Cf. *wa-kuan shu, yao-wu chien, t'ao-kuan*. P14.

3801 *liú-mǎ yüàn* 流馬苑
HAN: **Roaming Horse Pasturage,** established early in Later Han at Han-yang in modern Honan Province under the jurisdiction of the Chamberlain for the Imperial Stud (*t'ai-p'u ch'ing*), but soon transferred under the Supervisor of the Palace Guard (*yü-lin lang-chien*); more closely managed by a Director (*chien*). Reportedly consolidated or superseded a number of previous pasturages. HB: pasture of roaming horses. P31.

3802 *liú-nèi* 流內
SUI–CH'ING: lit., within the current (of ranked officials), contrasted with subofficial functionaries and others who were "outside the current" (*liu-wai*): **Of Official Status,** a reference to all government personnel who had status with rank (*p'in*) in the officialdom. Also see *shih liu-nei*. RR+SP: (*fonctionnaires*) *dans le courant*. P68.

3803 *liú-nèi ch'üān* 流內銓
SUNG: variant designation of the **Bureau of Personnel Assignments** (*k'ao-k'o yüan*), independent of though nominally subordinate to the Ministry of Personnel (*li-pu*); from c. 993 controlled evaluations and appointments for the lowest but most numerous category of civil service officials, those called Selectmen (*hsüan-jen*). In 1080 the Bureau was abolished, and its functions reverted to the Ministry of Personnel, specifically to its Senior and Junior Civil and Military Appointments Processes (see under *hsüan*). Cf. *shen-kuan yüan*. SP: *bureau des nominations civiles*. P5.

3804 *liù-p'ǐn àn* 六品案
SUNG: **Section for the Sixth Rank,** a subsection of the Ministry of Personnel's (*li-pu*) Bureau of Evaluations (*k'ao-kung ssu*); dealt with the cases of rank 6 officials in the Civil Appointments Process (*tso-hsüan; see under hsüan*). SP: *service du sixième grade*.

3805 *liù pù* 六部
(1) SUI–CH'ING: **Six Ministries** comprising the administrative core of the central government: the Ministries of Personnel (*li-pu*), of Revenue (*tu-chih,* in Sui changed to

min-pu, in T'ang changed to *hu-pu*), of Rites (*lǐ-pu*), of War (*ping-pu*), of Justice (*tu-kuan*, in Sui changed to *hsing-pu*), and of Works (*kung-pu*); evolved gradually during the era of N-S Division, when the numbers varied greatly and the term *pu* (Ministry) only gradually predominated over *ts'ao* (Section). From the outset, the Ministries were constituent units of the Department of State Affairs (*shang-shu sheng*); in Yüan the Department alternated with the Secretariat (*chung-shu sheng*) as the supreme central government agency housing the Ministries. Ming in 1380 abolished the superstructure of the Secretariat inherited from Yüan, leaving the Six Ministries in the top echelon of the central government without coordination except by the Emperor; but in the 15th century the Ministries came to be subordinated in practice to a new coordinating institution, the Grand Secretariat (*nei-ko*); this situation was perpetuated by Ch'ing. Each Ministry normally had an executive staff including one Minister (*ch'ing;* 3 in Yüan, one each Manchu and Chinese in Ch'ing), rank 3a in T'ang, 2b in Sung, 3a in Chin and Yüan, 2a in Ming, fluctuating between 1 and 2 in early Ch'ing, then 2 from 1670, 1b from 1730; and one or, most often, 2 Vice Ministers (*shih-lang*), 4a2 in T'ang except that the Vice Minister of Personnel was 4a1, 3b in Sung, 4a in Chin and Yüan, 3a in Ming, from 3a to 2a in Ch'ing. The Minister of Personnel was considered the senior Minister, taking ritual precedence over his counterparts in other Ministries. Each Ministry normally had 4 or more constituent Bureaus (*ssu;* in Ming and Ch'ing, *ch'ing-li ssu* but commonly abbreviated to *ssu*); the Bureaus normally had functional designations, e.g. *k'ao-kung ssu* (Bureau of Evaluations) in the Ministry of Personnel, *chu-k'o ssu* (Bureau of Receptions) in the Ministry of Rites; but in Ming and Ch'ing times Bureaus of the Ministries of Revenue and of Justice were increased in number and given territorial designations, generally one per Province (*sheng*), e.g., a Shantung Bureau (*shan-tung ch'ing-li ssu*) in each of those 2 Ministries. Each Bureau was headed by a Director (*lang-chung*), occasionally more than one per Bureau, 5b in T'ang, 6a or 6b in Sung, 6b in Chin and Yüan, 5a in Ming and Ch'ing; each Bureau Director was assisted by one or more Vice Directors (*yüan-wai lang*), 6b1 in T'ang, 7a in Sung, 7b in Chin and Yüan, 6a in Ming and Ch'ing. The Ministries in Yüan times did not always have constituent Bureaus but, rather, had Sections (*k'o*) of lesser status, designated according to functions; and the Ming Ministry of Revenue's constituent Bureaus, with territorial designations, each had 4 subsidiary Sections (*k'o*) with functional specializations (see *hu-pu*). Various Ministries in all eras also directly controlled or indirectly supervised other agencies; e.g., the Ministry of War normally supervised the Court of the Imperial Stud (*t'ai-p'u ssu*). Each Ministry also had a headquarters staff for general administrative support, including an Office Manager (*tu-chih* through Yüan, thereafter *ssu-wu*). RR+SP: *six ministères*. BH: six ministries (boards). P5–16. (2) N-S DIV (S. Dyn., N. Wei): **Six Troops,** a group of military units responsible for patrolling the streets of the capital city; antecedents of the T'ang *hsün* (Patrols), the Sung *ssu hsiang* (Four Capital Townships), and the Ming–Ch'ing *wu-ch'eng ping-ma ssu* (Wardens' Offices of the Four Capital Wards). Also see *liu-pu wei* (Commandant of the Capital Patrol). P20

3806 *liù pù chià-kó* 六部架閣
SUNG: **Archives of the Six Ministries,** a consolidated records office in the Department of State Affairs (*shang-shu sheng*) serving all of the Ministries, which in S. Sung were housed within the Department's office compound. SP: *archives des six ministères.* P5

3807 *liù pù chiēn-mén* 六部監門
SUNG: **Gate Tender for the Six Ministries,** established in 1132 by the Department of State Affairs (*shang-shu sheng*) to serve as a kind of receptionist for all of the Ministries, which in S. Sung were housed in the Department's office compound. SP: *surveillant des portes des six ministères, fonctionnaire chargé de surveiller les portes des six ministères.* P5, etc.

3808 *liù-pù lǐ-wèi* 六部里尉
N-S DIV (N. Wei): variant of *liu-pu wei* (**Commandant of the Capital Patrol**).

3809 *liù-pù wèi* 六部尉
N-S DIV (S. Dyn., N. Wei): **Commandant of the Capital Patrol,** divided into 6 Troops (*pu*), charged with maintaining peace and order in the streets of the dynastic capital. See under *liu pu.* Cf. *ching-t'u wei, ch'i-pu wei.* P20.

3810 *liù shàng* 六尙
A common and uncommonly ambiguous term; possibilities of confusion among the following usages should be noted with care. (1) CH'IN–SUNG: **Six Chief Stewards,** collective reference to 6 middle-level officials of the central government who were responsible for providing goods and services required by the Emperor and other members of the imperial household. In Ch'in the group consisted of Chief Stewards for Headgear (*shang-kuan*), for the Wardrobe (*shang-i*), for Food (*shang-shih*), for the Bath (*shang-mu*), for the Bedchamber (*shang-hsi*), and for Writing (*shang-shu*), all under the Chamberlain for the Palace Revenues (*shao-fu*). In Han there were only 5 such posts (see under *wu shang*); the *shang-shu,* q.v., developed separately into Imperial Secretaries. In the following era of N-S Division the Ch'in nomenclature was revived intermittently with many variations; and by the end of the era the Chief Stewards had become heads of agencies called Services (*chü*), e.g., the Food Service (*shang-shih chü*), collectively known as the Six Services (*liu chü*), still subordinate to the Chamberlain for the Palace Revenues. In Sui these agencies came under the Directorate of Palace Administration (*tien-nei chien*), later called the Palace Administration (*tien-nei sheng, tien-chung sheng*), and the titles of the Chief Stewards were changed from *shang-...* to *feng-yü,* q.v. However, through Sung the collective term *liu shang* continued in use as a quasiofficial reference to the Six Chief Stewards. RR: *chefs des six services.* SP: *chefs des six services de l'empereur.* P37. (2) T'ANG–MING: **Six Matrons,** heads of the Six Palace Services (*liu chü*) to which ordinary palace women were assigned: the General Palace Service (*shang-kung chü*), Workshops Service (*shang-kung chü*), Ceremonial Service (*shang-i chü*), Wardrobe Service (*shang-fu chü*), Food Service (*shang-shih chü*), and Housekeeping Service (*shang-ch'in chü*). The Matrons normally had 5a rank, and each (or each pair identically titled) supervised a staff including Directresses (*ssu* as a prefix), Managers (*tien* as a prefix), and Leaders (*chang* meaning to hold, as prefix) in subordinate Offices (*ssu*), normally 4 per Service; e.g., under the Matron(s) for Ceremonies (*shang-i*) were 4 Offices, one of which was the Music Office (*ssu-yüeh ssu*), headed by one or 2 Directresses of Music (*ssu-yüeh*), assisted by one or more Managers of Music (*tien-yüeh*) and one or more Leaders of Music (*chang-yüeh*). In Ming, the Six Palace Services came to be dominated in the 15th century by palace eunuch organizations; there ultimately remained only the Wardrobe Service with its 4 subsidiary Offices: Seals Office (*ssu-pao ssu*), Clothing Office (*ssu-i ssu*), Adornments Office (*ssu-shih ssu*), and Ceremonial Regalia Office

(*ssu-chang ssu*). (3) Occasional variant reference to the **Six Ministers** (*liu shang-shu*) of the Six Ministries (*liu pu*).

3811   *liù shàng-chǘ* 六尙局
CH'IN–SUNG: **Six Palace Services,** collective reference to the principal agencies under the Chamberlain for the Palace Revenues (*shao-fu*) or the Directorate of Palace Administration (*tien-nei chien, tien-nei sheng, tien-chung sheng*). Also see *liu shang* (Six Chief Stewards).

3812   *liù shàng-shū* 六尙書
SUI–CH'ING: **Six Ministers,** collective reference to the Ministers (*shang-shu*) who headed the Six Ministries (*liu pu*): of Personnel (*lì-pu*), of Revenue (*hu-pu*), of Rites (*lǐ-pu*), of War (*ping-pu*), of Justice (*hsing-pu*), and of Works (*kung-pu*).

3813   *liú-shǒu ssū* 留守司
T'ANG–MING: lit., an office left on guard: **Regency,** an agency ordinarily found in each auxiliary capital and established in the principal dynastic capital whenever the Emperor was not present, with a Regent (*liu-shou*) representing him in all matters. This was normally a duty assignment for a Prince, some other noble, or rarely an eminent official. In Yüan, perhaps because the Mongol rulers were so often away from the dynastic capital, Ta-tu (Peking), a Regency was established there as a regular agency of the central government with a corps of 5 Regents; it seems to have served as an imperial household administration, including such units as a Crafts Office (*chih-yung ssu*), an Imperial Regalia Service (*i-luan chü*), an Office of Imperial Parks (*shang-lin shu*), and military guards. RR+SP (*liu-shou*): *fonctionnaire chargé de garder la capitale pendant l'absence de l'empereur.* P49.

3814   *liù ssū* 六司
T'ANG–MING: **Six Directresses,** categorical reference to the palace women, generally rank 6a, who headed specialized Offices (*ssu*) under the Six Services (*liu chü*) presided over by the Six Matrons (see under *liu shang*); assisted by the Six Managers (*liu tien*). Since each Service normally incorporated 4 Offices, and since Offices commonly had from 2 to 6 Directresses, there were actually many more than 24 posts as Directress, all encompassed by the term *liu ssu*. E.g., the Food Service (*shang-shih chü*) staff included Directresses of Foods (*ssu-shan*), of Wines (*ssu-yün*), of Medicine (*ssu-yao*), and of Cooking (*ssu-ch'ih*); the Offices were designated, e.g., the Foods Office (*ssu-shan ssu:* lit., the Office of the Directresses of Foods).

3815   *liú-ssū yǜ-shǐh t'ái* 留司御史臺
SUNG: **Auxiliary Censorate,** one skeletal replica of the metropolitan Censorate (*yü-shih t'ai*) based at each of N. Sung's 3 auxiliary capitals: the Western, Northern, and Southern Capitals.

3816   *liú-t'ái* 留臺
T'ANG: **Branch Censorate,** a skeletal replica of the Censorate (*yü-shih t'ai*) at the dynastic capital, Ch'ang-an, established at the Eastern Capital, Loyang; the staff normally consisted of one Vice Censor-in-chief (*yü-shih chung-ch'eng*), one Attendant Censor (*shih yü-shih*), 2 Palace Censors (*tien-chung shih yü-shih*), and 3 Investigating Censors (*chien-ch'a yü-shih*); but on occasion a Censor-in-chief (*yü-shih ta-fu*) was also posted there.

3817   *liù t'áng* 六堂
MING–CH'ING: **Six Colleges,** study units into which all students (*chien-sheng*) of the Directorate of Education (*kuo-tzu chien*) were divided: the Colleges for Guiding Human Nature (*shuai-hsing t'ang*), for Cultivating the Way (*hsiu-tao t'ang*), for Making the Heart Sincere (*ch'eng-hsin t'ang*), for Moral Rectification (*cheng-i t'ang*), for Venerating Determination (*ch'ung-chih t'ang*), and for Broadening Academic Scope (*kuang-yeh t'ang*). Each College was headed by one Instructor (*chu-chiao*), rank 8b to 7b, assisted by one Instructor Second-class (*hsüeh-cheng*), 9a to 8a, or one Instructor Third-class (*hsüeh-lu*), 9b to 8a, or one of both. P34.

3818   *liù tiěn* 六典
T'ANG–MING: **Six Managers,** categorical reference to palace women, generally rank 7a, who assisted the Six Directresses (*liu ssu*) who were in charge of the specialized Offices (*ssu*) under the Six Services (*liu chü*) presided over by the Six Matrons (see under *liu shang*). Since each Service normally incorporated 4 Offices, and since Offices commonly had from 2 to 4 Managers, there were actually many more than 24 posts as Manager, all encompassed by the term *liu tien*. E.g., the Managers of Seals (*tien-pao*) assisted the Directresses of Seals (*ssu-pao*) in the Seals Office (*ssu-pao ssu*) under the Matrons of the Wardrobe (*shang-fu*), heads of the Wardrobe Service (*shang-fu chü*).

3819   *liù-ts'ān kuān* 六參官   or   *liù-ts'a..*
T'ANG–SUNG: **Fifth Day Audience Officers,** generic reference to military officers of ranks 4 and 5 on duty in the dynastic capital, who were required to attend audience every 5th day, i.e., 6 (*liu*) times a month. Cf. *chiu-ts'an kuan, ch'ang-ts'an kuan.* RR+SP: *fonctionnaires assistant à l'audience six fois par mois.*

3820   *liù ts'áo* 六曹
Six Sections. (1) HAN: collective reference to the functionally differentiated groups in which Imperial Secretaries (*shang-shu*) served under the Chamberlain for the Palace Revenues (*shao-fu*); in Later Han emerged as top-echelon administrative agencies in the central government, unofficially designated the Imperial Secretariat (*shang-shu t'ai*), headed by a Director (*ling*) ranked at 600 bushels. Consisted originally of 4, then 5, and finally 6 Sections (*ts'ao*): Personnel Section (*lì-pu ts'ao*), Section for Commandery Governors (*erh-ch'ien shih ts'ao*), Section for the People (*min-ts'ao*), Section for Receptions (*chu-k'o ts'ao*), Section for the Three Dukes (*san-kung ts'ao*), and Section for Justice (*tu-kuan ts'ao*). Each Section was headed by an Imperial Secretary, rank 600 bushels, eventually assisted by a Gentleman of the Interior (*lang-chung*), 300 bushels, or an Attendant Gentleman (*shih-lang*), =400 bushels, but apparently not both. Some sources do not include the Section for Justice among the Six Sections but list both a Northern and a Southern Section for Receptions; this confusion no doubt reflects changes in the shape of the evolving Imperial Secretariat. HB: six bureaus. (2) N-S DIV: common collective reference to units of the continuously evolving Department of State Affairs (*shang-shu t'ai, shang-shu sheng*), the term *ts'ao* being used alternatively with *pu* (Ministry) and the units fluctuating in number to more than 30; a common grouping of Six Sections during this period included the Personnel Section, Census Section (*tso-min ts'ao*), Section for Receptions, Revenue Section (*tu-chih ts'ao*), War Section (*wu-ping ts'ao*), and Rites Section (*tz'u-pu ts'ao*), each headed by a *shang-shu* (evolving from Imperial Secretary to Director to Minister, with much overlapping). Other occasionally prominent Sections of this era were the Palace Affairs Section (*tien-chung ts'ao*), Personnel Selection Section (*hsüan-pu ts'ao*, a variant of *lì-pu ts'ao*), Rites Section (*i-ts'ao*), Storehouse Section (*k'u-pu ts'ao*), and Music Sec-

tion (*yüeh-pu ts'ao, yüeh-ts'ao*). As the Department of State Affairs became more regularized, the term Ministry (*pu*) predominated over the term Section, and the title *shang-shu* is better rendered Minister than Director. However, it was not until c. 605 in Sui times that the organizational structure of the Department became durably fixed, with a cohort of Six Ministries (*liu pu*) headed by Ministers (*shang-shu*). (3) SUI–CH'ING: collective reference to clerical staff agencies in units of territorial administration from Districts (*hsien*) up to Prefectures (*chou, fu*) or higher, through which territorial executive officials administered their jurisdictions; functionally designated Personnel Evaluation Section (*kung-ts'ao*), Granaries Section (*ts'ang-ts'ao*), Revenue Section (*hu-ts'ao*), War Section (*ping-ts'ao*), Law Section (*fa-ts'ao*), and Levied Service Section (*shih-ts'ao*) through Sung; thereafter designated correspondingly with the Six Ministries of the central government, as the Personnel Section (*li-ts'ao*), Revenue Section (*hu-ts'ao*), Rites Section (*li-ts'ao*), War Section (*ping-ts'ao*), Justice Section (*hsing-ts'ao*), and Works Section (*kung-ts'ao*). Through Sung, the Sections were commonly headed by Administrators (*ts'an-chün-shih*), rank 7a or lower; thereafter they were normally staffed entirely with subofficial functionaries. (4) SUI–CH'ING: occasional archaic reference to, or rare variant designation of, the Six Ministries (*liu pu*) of the central government. Also see under *ts'ao*.

3821   *liù t'ǔng-chūn* 六統軍
T'ANG–SUNG: **Six Commander-generals,** secondary-level officers in the Six Imperial Armies (see under *liu chün*) constituting, at least in theory, the main fighting force of the empire, normally encamped around the dynastic capital. In T'ang, the units that came to be called the Six Imperial Armies were created in Left and Right pairs in 662, 739, and 757 as the core of the professional troops called the Northern Command (*pei-ya*). Sung perpetuated the nomenclature, but how it related to Sung's Imperial Armies (*chin-chün*) or to the S. Sung Palace Command (*tien-ch'ien ssu*) is not clear. See *t'ung-chün*. RR+SP: *six directeurs d'armées*.

3822   *liú-wài* 流外
N-S DIV–CH'ING: lit., outside the current (of ranked officials): **Not of Official Status,** a categorical reference to all persons in government service other than officials (*kuan*) with ranks (*p'in*), most abundantly including suboffical functionaries (see *li, hsü-li*) but also including honorary officials (*hsün-kuan*), artisans, physicians, and various other persons who were employed by state agencies without being Of Official Status (*liu-nei*). Also see *wei ju liu*.

3823   *liú-wài ch'ū-shēn* 流外出身
T'ANG–CH'ING: **Promoted Functionary,** someone who had attained status as a ranked official (*kuan*) for serving meritoriously as a suboffical functionary (see *li, hsü-li*); men with such backgrounds could seldom expect distinguished official careers. In Ming and Ch'ing times entry to the service in this fashion was not considered a Regular Path (*cheng-t'u*) into the officialdom. Also see *liu-wai, liu-nei, ch'u-shen*.

3824   *liú-wài ch'üān* 流外銓
(1) N-S DIV: **Selection of Suboffical Functionaries,** apparently a procedure for appointing, reappointing, and promoting men who were "outside the current" (*liu-wai*) of the regular officialdom, including the promotion of such functionaries (*li, hsü-li*) into regular official status (*kuan*). (2) T'ANG–SUNG: **Bureau for Functionaries** in the Ministry of Personnel (*li-pu*), from 735 into or through Sung times; its staffing, its history, and its relationship to other con-

stituent units of the Ministry are not clear. See *liu-nei ch'üan, hsüan, k'ao-kung*. SP: *bureau chargé de choisir les fonctionnaires "en dehors du courant" ou bureau des clercs*.

3825   *liù yā* 六押
T'ANG–SUNG: lit., the 6 (keepers of) seals: unofficial reference to **Secretariat Drafters** (*chung-shu she-jen*).

3826   *liù yüàn* 六院
(1) SUNG: **Six Offices,** an early Sung collective reference to the Bureau of Personnel Evaluation (*shen-kuan yüan*), the Appointment Verification Office (*kuan-kao yüan*) of the Ministry of Personnel (*li-pu*), the Memorials Office (*chin-tsou yüan*), the Bursary (*liang-liao yüan*) in the Court of the Imperial Treasury (*t'ai-fu ssu*), the Public Petitioners Review Office (*teng-wen chien-yüan*), and the Public Petitioners Drum Office (*teng-wen ku-yüan*). It is not clear what these agencies had in common other than the designation *yüan*, which they shared with many other agencies, e.g., the Hanlin Academy (*han-lin yüan*). SP: *les six cours*. (2) LIAO: **Six Groups,** one of the categories into which the founding Emperor, A-pao-chi, divided his tribal followers; its civil affairs were administered by the Office of the Southern Grand Prince (*nan ta-wang yüan*), its military affairs by the Office of the Northern Grand Prince (*pei ta-wang yüan*), both agencies of the Northern Administration (*pei-mien*), through which the dynastic government managed the affairs of the Khitan tribes and allied northern nomads. See *wu yüan* (Five Groups). P17.

3827   *liú-yüàn kuān* 留院官
T'ANG: lit., officials retained in the academy, i.e., in contrast to others who served in the academy only on short-term duty assignments while holding regular substantive posts elsewhere: **Permanent Academician** in the Academy of Scholarly Worthies (*chi-hsien yüan*); status apparently not prominent, but awarded only by special imperial decree. Cf. *liu-kuan*. RR: *fonctionnaire permanent de la bibliothèque*. P23, 25.

3828   *lò-shìh* 羅氏
CHOU: **Bird Netter,** ranked as a Junior Serviceman (*hsia-shih*), a member of the Ministry of War (*hsia-kuan*) responsible for catching (and probably destroying) birds that were harmful nuisances. CL: *preneur d'oiseaux au filet*.

3829   *lò-yáng núng-pǔ chiēn* 洛陽農圃監
T'ANG: **Directorate of Agricultural Production for the Loyang Palace,** in charge of imperial gardens at Loyang, the dynasty's auxiliary Eastern Capital (*tung-tu*), under the Court of the Imperial Granaries (*ssu-nung ssu*); headed by a Director (*chien*), rank 6b2. In 657 retitled *tung-tu yüan tung-mien chien* (Directorate of Parks in the Eastern Capital, Eastern Quadrant), q.v. P40.

3830   *lò-yüàn shìh* 洛苑使
SUNG: **Commissioner of the Loyang Gardens,** an early Sung antecedent of the prestige title (*san-kuan*) Grand Master for Military Strategy (*wu-lüeh ta-fu*), awarded to rank 7a military officers. P68.

3831   *lóu-ch'uán kuān* 樓船官
HAN: **Office of Towered Warships,** a local agency in Lu-chiang Commandery (*chün*); presumably built and maintained a fleet of river and coastal defense warships; staffing and relationship to central government agencies not clear. HB: office of towered warships.

3832   *lóu-fán chiàng* 樓煩將
HAN: **Bowmen Leader,** in early Han put in charge of an army of expert archers. The title was derived either from a

Hsiung-nu tribe in modern Shansi whose name, Lou-fan in Chinese transliteration, meant expert archer, or from the name of an early Han man who was renowned as a skilled archer.

3833   *lòu-k'ò k'ō* 漏刻科
Water Clock Section, responsible for maintaining and teaching use of the palace water clocks and for proclaiming each of the watches (*keng*) in the night and the time by day. (1) CHIN: a unit in the Directorate of Astronomy (*ssu-t'ien t'ai*), staffed with 25 officials; specific titles and ranks not clear. (2) YÜAN: a unit in the Directorate of Astronomy (*ssu-t'ien-chien*), headed by 2 Clerks (*kuan-kou*), rank 9b. (3) CH'ING: a unit in the Directorate of Astronomy (*ch'in-t'ien chien*) with a staff of 6 Chinese Erudites (*po-shih*), non-official specialists. BH: section of the clepsydra. P35.

3834   *lòu-k'ò pó-shìh* 漏刻博士
Erudite of the Water Clock, specialists in training disciples to maintain and use the palace water clocks. (1) SUI: 4, probably non-official specialists, in the Office of Astrological Observations (*chien-hou fu*) under the Astrological Section (*t'ai-shih ts'ao*), later renamed Directorate of Astrology (*t'ai-shih chien*). (2) T'ANG: 6, rank 9b2, in the Directorate of Astrology (*ssu-t'ien chien, t'ai-shih chien*, etc.); and 2, apparently non-official specialists, in the Court of the Watches (*lei-keng ssu*) of the Heir Apparent. RR: *maître au vaste savoir du service de la clepsydre*. (3) LIAO: number and status not clear; in the Directorate of Astronomy (*ssu-t'ien chien*). (4) MING: 6 then 1, rank 9b, in the Directorate of Astronomy (*ch'in-t'ien chien*). Also see *t'ai-shih, wu kuan, po-shih*. P35.

3835   *lòu-k'ò sǒ* 漏刻所
SUNG: **Water Clock Office,** staffing not clear, one unit each under the Bureau of Astronomy (*t'ien-wen yüan*) and the Directorate of Astronomy (*ssu-t'ien chien*), both subordinate to the Palace Library (*pi-shu sheng*); independent of the Astrological Service (*t'ai-shih chü*). P35.

3836   *lòu-k'ò tiěn-shìh* 漏刻典事
T'ANG: **Manager of the Water Clock,** 16, probably non-official specialists, on the staff of the Supervisor of Water Clocks (*ch'ieh-hu cheng*) in the Directorate of Astrology (*t'ai-shih chien*). P35.

3837   *lòu-láng chiàng* 漏郎將 or *lou-lang*
N-S DIV (Sung): **Keeper of the Water Clock,** number and rank not clear, on the staff of the Grand Astrologer (*t'ai-shih*), a subordinate of the Chamberlain for Ceremonials (*t'ai-ch'ang*). P35.

3838   *lòu-t'úng* 漏童
T'ANG: **Tender of the Water Clock,** 60 youths, unranked, authorized for the Court of the Watches (*lei-keng ssu*) of the Heir Apparent (*t'ai-tzu*); apparently responsible for keeping watch over the water clocks and announcing changes in the night watches. RR: *veilleurs de la clepsydre*. P26.

3839   *lù* 路
(1) SUNG: **Circuit,** in 997 superseded *tao* as the generic name of the largest territorial administrative jurisdictions: a clustering of neighboring Prefectures (*chou, fu, chün, chien*), each Circuit headed by one or more Circuit Supervisors (see *chien-ssu, shuai-ssu, ts'ao-ssu, hsien-ssu, ts'ang-ssu*) and bearing an appropriate geographic prefix; the coordinating link between Prefectures and the central government. SP: *province*. (2) LIAO: **Route,** the territorial base or jurisdiction of a tribal army (*pu-tsu chün*). (3) CHIN: a

proto-Province, 19 in all at dynastic maturity; one administered directly from the dynastic capital, 4 by Regents (*liu-shou*) stationed at auxiliary capitals, and 14 by Area Commands (*tsung-kuan fu*), all agencies coordinating clusters of different sorts of Prefecture-level units of territorial administration, e.g., Defense Commanderies (*fang-yü chün*), Superior Prefectures (*san-fu*), ordinary Prefectures (*chou*). The Routes were normally headed by Commissioners (*shih*) of various sorts, e.g., Fiscal Commissioners (*chuan-yün shih*), Judicial Commissioners (*t'i-hsing shih*). (4) YÜAN: a stably defined territory administered by a Route Command (*lu tsung-kuan-fu*, with place-name prefix); 185 at maturity, supervising c. 360 Prefectures (*fu, chou, chün*), subordinate either to the metropolitan Secretariat (*chung-shu sheng*) or one of at most 11 Branch Secretariats (*hsing chung-shu sheng*); also under the military control of Circuit (*tao*) Pacification Commissions (*hsüan-wei ssu*, etc., with place-name prefixes) and the surveillance jurisdiction of Circuit (also *tao*) Surveillance Commissions (*t'i-hsing an-ch'a ssu, su-cheng lien-fang ssu*). Each Route Command was headed by an Overseer (*ta-lu-hua-ch'ih*) and a Commander (*tsung-kuan*). The Route was an all-purpose civil administration branch, in effect, of the central government. Routes were graded as Large (*shang*) or Small (*hsia*) on the basis of their resident populations, 100,000 being the dividing line.

3840   *lù* 錄
See under *lu … shih*.

3841   *lù-ch'én* 祿臣
HAN: variant of *kuang-lu-hsün* (**Chamberlain for Attendants**).

3842   *lù-chì chiù* 騄驥廄
HAN: lit., a stable for (horses such as) Lu (name of a famous horse belonging to King Mu of Chou times) and (other) magnificent steeds (*chi*): **Special Stable** established in A.D. 181 to collect in the dynastic capital horses for army use that were then being requisitioned from units of territorial administration throughout the empire; headed by an Aide (*ch'eng*), presumably to the Chamberlain for the Imperial Stud (*t'ai-p'u*). HB: stables for thoroughbreds.

3843   *lù-chiàng* 路將
SUNG: **Circuit General,** common but misleading reference to Area General (see under *chiang #6*).

3844   *lù-ch'ién* 路鈐
SUNG: abbreviated, unofficial reference to *lu-fen ch'ien-hsia* (**Military Administrator**).

3845   *lú-ch'uán* 臚傳
SUNG–CH'ING: **Palace Examination Graduate,** variant of *jao-tien lei*. Also see *ch'uan-lu* (List Leader), which has a more restricted meaning.

3846   *lù-fēn* 路分
SUNG: abbreviated reference to *lu-fen tu-chien* (**Director-in-chief** of Circuit military forces).

3847   *lù-fēn ch'ién-hsiá* 路分鈐轄
SUNG: **Military Administrator** of a part of the military forces available in a Circuit (*lu*), a post normally held concurrently by an executive official at the Prefecture (*chou*) level. See *lu, chou, ch'ien-hsia*. SP: *directeur militaire provincial*.

3848   *lù-fēn tū-chiēn* 路分都監
SUNG: **Director-in-chief** of part of the military forces available in a Circuit (*lu*), a post normally held concurrently by a senior official of a Military Commission (*shuai-*

ssu), presumably coordinating and supervising the Military Administrators (*lu-fen ch'ien-hsia*) in the Commission's jurisdiction. See *lu, tu-chien, li-fang* (Director-in-chief Section). SP: *surveillant général militaire provincial chargé de la défense et de l'entrainement de l'armée impériale.*

3849 *lù-hsūn ssū* 錄勳司
CH'ING: **Honors Bureau,** established in 1661 as one of 4 Bureaus (full designation *lu-hsün ch'ing-li ssu;* see *ch'ing-li ssu*) that constituted the principal administrative echelon in the Court of Colonial Affairs (*li-fan yüan*); each headed by several Manchu and Mongol Directors (*lang-chung*), rank 5a; functions not entirely clear, but probably focused on maintaining records concerning the ceremonial status of tributary chiefs. In 1757 changed to *tien-shu ssu* (Outer Mongolian Bureau), then one of 6 Bureaus, charged with handling relations with peoples on the outer periphery of the empire, in Outer Mongolia, modern Sinkiang, and Tibet. P17.

3850 *lú-jén* 臚人
N-S DIV: unofficial reference to the **Chief Minister for Dependencies** (*hung-lu ch'ing*).

3851 *lù-kūng* 錄公
N-S DIV: variant of *lu shang-shu shih* (**Overseer of the Department of State Affairs**).

3852 *lù-líng lìng* 路軨令 or 輅軨令
HAN: **Director of the Imperial Hunting Chariots,** one of numerous subordinates of the Chamberlain for the Imperial Stud (*t'ai-p'u*), rank 600 bushels. HB: prefect of the coachhouses for imperial chariots. P31.

3853 *lù-lù* 陸路
CH'ING: **Land Forces** of the Green Standards (*lu-ying*), the Chinese soldiery in provincial bases, as distinguished from the *shui-lu* (Naval Forces); while in garrison, normally under the direction of a Provincial Military Commander (*t'i-tu*).

3854 *lù-mén hsüéh* 露門學 or *lù-mén kuǎn* 館
N-S DIV (Chou): lit., school (institute) at the innermost gate: **Palace School,** established in 567 with an authorized student corps of 72; apparently for children of the imperial family including the Heir Apparent; not to be confused with the National University (*t'ai-hsüeh*); in 571 (first?) staffed with a Palace School Erudite (*lu-men po-shih*) ranked as a Junior Grand Master (*hsia ta-fu*). The 2nd form is apparently a variant. P34.

3855 *lù-pù shíh* 鹵簿使 or *lu-pu*
Lit. meaning is a matter of controversy: **Escort Carriage Rider,** from Ch'in on, a dignitary who accompanied the Emperor in all public appearances; in T'ang the duty assignment of a Vice Minister of War (*ping-pu shih-lang*), in Sung of a Minister of War (*ping-pu shang-shu*). SP: *commissaire de l'escorte d'honneur.*

3856 *lù-shíh* 錄事
N-S DIV–CH'ING: lit., (one who) manages affairs: **Office Manager,** one or more found in many agencies, both in the central government and in units of territorial administration; sometimes ranked from 7a to 9b, sometimes unranked. The title was most extensively used in ''ang–Sung times. RR+SP: *greffier.*

3857 *lù ... shíh* 錄⋯事 or *lù ...*
Lit., to record the activities of ..., to keep records of .... (1) HAN–N-S DIV (S. Dyn.): **Overseer,** from Later Han a duty assignment rather than a regular post, mostly used in the case of a noble or eminent official assigned concurrently to be in charge of Han's Imperial Secretariat (*shang-shu t'ai*) and later the evolving Department of State Affairs (*shang-shu sheng*); a powerful post even when the Department was losing status to the Secretariat (*chung-shu sheng*) and Chancellery (*men-hsia sheng*), since agencies of the Department of State Affairs remained the channel of routine administration between the central government and units of territorial administration. The normal full form is, e.g., *lu shang-shu shih* (Overseer of Imperial Secretariat Affairs in Han, thereafter Overseer of the Department of State Affairs), displacing earlier titles such as *ling ... shih, shih ... shih, p'ing ... shih.* The most eminent dignitaries were sometimes designated Chief Overseers (*tsung-lu*) of the Department of State Affairs. In Sung and perhaps other periods of the era of N-S Division, some Emperors tried to prevent consolidation of administrative authority in one man's hands by appointing more than one Overseer simultaneously; from the 330s 3 Overseers were regularly appointed, each responsible for a specified group (*t'iao*) of Sections (*ts'ao*) in the Department of State Affairs. Also see *fen-t'iao, lu-kung.* P2. (2) N-S DIV (San-kuo Wei–N. Dyn.): **Overseer,** gradually became the title of the regular head of the Department of State Affairs rather than a concurrent duty assignment: e.g., *lu* (or *tsung-lu*) *shang-shu sheng shih* (Overseer, or Chief Overseer, of the Department of State Affairs), *lu san-shih-liu. ts'ao shih* (Overseer of the Thirty-six Sections [into which the Department was divided]). P2. (3) SUNG (*lu* alone): **Office Manager,** from 2 to 5, rank 9a, in the Directorate of Education (*kuo-tzu chien*); also probably one unranked in the Court Calligraphy Service (*han-lin shu-i chü*). Cf. *lu-shih.*

3858 *lù-shìh shǐh* 錄事史
Lit., scribe in charge of affairs: **Secretary.** (1) N-S DIV (Chin): one of many types of lowly or unranked personnel on the staffs of Commandery Governors (*chün-shou*) and District Magistrates (*hsien-ling*). P53, 54. (2) T'ANG: one each attached to the Western Commissioner (*hsi-shih*) and the Southern Commissioner (*nan-shih*) of the various Directorates of Horse Pasturages (*mu-chien*) subordinate to the Court of the Imperial Stud (*t'ai-p'u ssu*). RR: *scribe greffier.*

3859 *lù-shìh ssū* 錄事司
YÜAN: **Administration Office,** the equivalent of a District (*hsien*) in the headquarters city of a Route Command (*lu tsung-kuan fu*), except that in the dynastic capital, modern Peking, its functions were divided among 3 Police Commissions (*ching-hsün yüan*) and 2 Wardens' Offices (*ping-ma ssu*); normally headed by an Office Manager (*lu-shih*), rank 8a, but after 1283 under an Overseer (*ta-lu-hua-ch'ih*). The former capital of S. Sung, modern Hangchow Prefecture, was so populous that 4 Administration Offices were created there, later reduced to 2, prefixed Left and Right. P53.

3860 *lù-shìh ts'ān-chūn-shìh* 錄事參軍事 or *lu-shih ts'an-chün*
N-S DIV (Liang)–SUNG, LIAO: **Administrative Supervisor,** one or more found most commonly on the staffs of Prefectures (*chou, fu*) and Princely Establishments (*wang-fu*), but also in some military units, especially Guards (*wei*) in T'ang times; ranked from 5b down to 8a. See *lu-shih, ts'an-chün.* RR: *administrateur greffier.* SP: *inspecteur exécutif, administrateur-greffier, chargé d'enregistrer des expéditions.* P53, 69.

3861 *lù-ts'ān* 錄參
SUNG: unofficial abbreviation of *lu-shih ts'an-chün-shih* (**Administrative Supervisor**).

3862 *lù-yīng* 綠營
CH'ING: **Green Standards**, collective designation for hereditary Chinese military men outside the Banner (*ch'i*) system, stationed throughout the country as a kind of provincial constabulary, the core being former Ming hereditary officers and soldiers who surrendered early to the Manchus during their conquest of China. Green Standards officers and soldiers were under the general control of the Ministry of War (*ping-pu*) and, unlike Bannermen, were under the jurisdiction of regular provincial authorities, the Governors-general (*tsung-tu*), Governors (*hsün-fu*), and especially Provincial Military Commanders (*t'i-tu*). Within each Province military control was subdivided among Regional Commanders (*tsung-ping*), Regional Vice Commanders (*fu-chiang*), and Assistant Regional Commanders (*ts'an-chiang*). Below them in the hierarchy were the basic Green Standards units, Brigades (*ying*), each with approximately 500 men under a Brigade Commander (*yu-chi*), comprising 5 Companies (*shao*), each subdivided further into 100-man Squads (*p'eng*). The Green Standards were not home-guard militia forces but were "regular" army forces; when called on, they campaigned alongside Bannermen. While on campaign away from their garrisons or other regular stations, they were commanded by dignitaries delegated from the court as ad hoc Grand Minister Commanders (*ching-lüeh ta-ch'en*) with assistants called Grand Minister Consultants (*ts'an-i ta-ch'en*). See *piao, t'un-t'ien, ta-ch'en*. Cf. *pao-chia, hsiang-yung, min-chuang, t'uan-lien*. BH: army of the green standard, Chinese army.

3863 *lù yùn-shǐh* 陸運使
T'ANG: abbreviation of *shui-lu chuan-yün shih* (**Water and Land Transport Commissioner**).

3864 *lù-yùn t'í-chǔ ssū* 陸運提舉司
YÜAN: **Supervisorate of Land Transport**, responsible under the Ministry of War (*ping-pu*) for the land transport of tax grains and military rations in the area of the dynastic capital, Ta-tu (Peking); headed by 2 Supervisors (*t'i-chü*), rank 5b. P8, 60.

3865 *luán-í wèi* 鑾儀衛
CH'ING: **Imperial Procession Guard**, a largely ceremonious aggregation of Bannermen (see *ch'i, pa ch'i*), hereditary Chinese troops, and even civil officials who escorted the Emperor whenever he emerged from his palace; commanded by a Prince (*wang*) or Duke (*kung*) of the imperial family designated Grand Minister in Command of the Guard (*chang wei-shih ta-ch'en*), rank 1a, assisted by one Manchu and one Chinese Commissioner of the Imperial Procession Guard (*luan-i shih*), rank 2a, 2 Directors of the Imperial Procession Guard (*tsung-li shih-wu kuan-chün shih*), and 2 Flag Assistants serving as Assistant Directors (*hsieh-li shih-wu yün-hui shih*). The Directors and Assistant Directors were specially responsible for overseeing the various units into which the Guard was divided: Subsections (*so*) further divided into Offices (*ssu*), each Subsection headed by a Director (*chang-yin kuan-chün shih*), rank 3a, and each Office by a Director (*chang-yin yün-hui shih*), rank 4a. The Subsections were prefixed Left, Right, Center, Forward, and Rear. The Offices were the Carriage (*luan-yü ssu*) and Horse-training (*hsün-ma ssu*) Offices under the Left Subsection, the Umbrella (*ch'ing-kai ssu*) and Bow and Arrow (*kung-shih ssu*) Offices under the Right Subsection, the Emblem (*ching-chieh ssu*) and Flag (*fan-t'ung ssu*) Offices under the

Center Subsection, the Fan Bearers (*shan-shou ssu*) and Halberd (*fu-yüeh ssu*) Offices under the Forward Subsection, and the Spear (*ko-chi ssu*) and Sword (*pan-chien ssu*) Offices under the Rear Subsection. Separately, with slightly different patterns of organization, there were 2 Elephant-training Offices (*hsün-hsiang so*) prefixed East and West and 2 Standard-bearer Guards (*ch'i-shou wei*) prefixed Left and Right; these 4 units were headed by Directors (*chang-yin kuan-chün shih*). Still lesser units of many sorts were headed by Managers (*kuan-li*), e.g., of the Livery Stable (*chia-k'u*), of the Jade-adorned Carriage (*yü-lo*). In 1909, to avoid an imperial name taboo, the Imperial Procession Guard was renamed *luan-yü wei*. Cf. *i-luan ssu*. BH: imperial equipage department. P42.

3866 *luán-p'ō* 鑾坡
Lit., the bell slope, an abbreviation of the slope (*p'o*) down from the Hall of Golden Bells (*chin-luan tien*): from T'ang on, an unofficial reference to **members of the Hanlin Academy** (*han-lin yüan*), which was once housed in the Hall of Golden Bells, within the imperial palace.

3867 *luán-t'ái* 鑾臺
T'ANG: lit., the phoenix (pheasant?) pavilion: from 685 to 705 the official name of the **Chancellery** (*men-hsia sheng*). RR: *tribunal des phénix*. P3.

3868 *luán-yǔ ssū* 鑾輿司
CH'ING: **Carriage Office**, one of 2 agencies under the Left Subsection (*tso-so*) of the Imperial Procession Guard (*luan-i wei*), headed by a Director (*chang-yin yün-hui shih*), rank 4a. BH: carriage section. P3.

3869 *luán-yǔ wèi* 鑾輿衛
CH'ING: from 1909, in a change to avoid an imperial name taboo, the new name of the *luan-i wei* (**Imperial Procession Guard**).

3870 *lui*
See under the romanization *lei*.

3871 *lún* 輪
In rotation: throughout history, one of the terms signifying that an official had taken a temporary duty assignment (e.g., for a year) that he shared on a rotational basis with other officials; normally occurs as a prefix to an official's principal substantive title; e.g., *lun-ch'ien ch'eng* (Assistant Director [of the Directorate of Waterways, *tu-shui chien*] delegated in rotation …) in Sung, *lun-kuan tso-ling* (Company Commander in the Banner [*ch'i*] forces, not by hereditary right, but chosen on a rotational basis from among other types of officers, possibly subalterns in the same Company) in Ch'ing.

3872 *lún-kó* 綸閣
T'ANG: lit., the hall of silk threads, i.e., the hall of imperial utterances: unofficial reference to the **Secretariat** (*chung-shu sheng*). See *ssu-lun ko*.

3873 *lúng* 龍
Dragon. (1) Throughout history a term equivalent to Royal (in Chou) or Imperial, e.g., *lung-wei* (Dragon Throne), and having many other connotations of good fortune, extraordinary strength, vigorous militancy, etc.; e.g., *lung-ma chien* (Directorate of the Dragon Horses) in Han, *lung-wu chün* (Militant as Dragons Army) in Sung, *lung-hsiang chün* (Soaring Dragon Army) in Chin. (2) SUNG: also an unofficial reference to Academicians (*hsüeh-shih*) of the Dragon Diagram Hall (*lung-t'u ko*), differentiated by prefixes: *chia* (Acting? Probationary?), *hsiao* (Junior), *ta* (Senior), and *lao* (Venerable).

3874 *lúng-chèn wèi ch'īn-chūn tū chǐh-hūi ssū* 隆鎮衛親軍都指揮司
YÜAN: **Imperial Armies Tactical Defense Commission,** one of the major military commands at the dynastic capital, responsible for policing the Peking area and guarding nearby passes through the Great Wall; headed by 3 Chief Military Commissioners (*tu chih-hui shih*) under supervision of the Bureau of Military Affairs (*shu-mi yüan*).

3875 *lúng-hūi* 隆徽
N-S DIV (N. Ch'i): **Lady of Exalted Excellence,** designation of one of 3 Superior Concubines (*shang-pin*) in the imperial harem.

3876 *lúng-mǎ chiēn* 龍馬監
HAN: **Directorate of the Dragon Horses** under the Chamberlain for the Imperial Stud (*t'ai-p'u*), headed by a Director (*chang*), rank not clear; apparently in charge of the 1,000 "blood-sweating" (Arabian?) horses brought to the Han capital from Ferghana in 101 B.C. HB: stables for tall horses. P31.

3877 *lúng-shǒu* 龍首 or *lúng-t'óu* 龍頭
SUNG–CH'ING: lit., chief of dragons, head of dragons: unofficial reference to the **Principal Graduate** (*chuang-yüan*) in the Metropolitan Examination (*sheng-shih, hui-shih*) in the civil service recruitment examination sequence.

3878 *lúng-t'ú kó* 龍圖閣
SUNG: **Dragon Diagram Hall,** established between 1008 and 1016 to house official documents from the 2nd reign (976–997); staffed with various ranks of Academicians (*hsüeh-shih*); parallel with (subordinate to?) the Imperial Archives (*pi-ko*) in the archival-editorial complex called the Academy for the Veneration of Literature (*ch'ung-wen yüan*); in 1082 incorporated into the Palace Library (*pi-shu sheng*). The title Dragon Diagram derives from an ancient legend about a dragon emerging from a river with markings on its back that inspired the 8 trigrams that became the basis of the *Classic of Changes* (*I-ching*). SP: *pavillon Long-t'ou*. P25.

3879 *lúng-wèi* 龍位
Dragon Throne, common unofficial reference to the imperial institution.

3880 *lúng-wèi ssù hsiàng* 龍衛四廂
SUNG: **Four Dragon Guard Wings,** one of the major military units of the Imperial Armies (*chin-chün*) stationed at the dynastic capital, one of those known collectively as the Four Elite, Armies (*shang ssu chün*); headed by a Commander-in-chief (*tu chih-hui shih*); each of its Wings (*hsiang*) reportedly included 3 armies (*chün*). From the middle of the 11th century belonged to the Metropolitan Cavalry Command (*ma-chün ssu*). SP: *garde de dragon*. P47.

3881 *lúng-wǔ chūn* 龍武軍
T'ANG–SUNG: **Militant as Dragons Army,** 2 prefixed Left and Right, units of the Imperial Armies (*chin-chün*) that constituted the Northern Command (*pei-ya*) at T'ang's dynastic capital. Created in only a quasiofficial status in 710 with elite troops formerly known as the Myriad Cavaliers (*wan chi*; also see *po chi*), then in 738 placed on a regular basis alongside the Forest of Plumes Armies (*yü-lin chün*). Until 757 shared with the Forest of Plumes Armies the collective designation Four Imperial Armies (*ssu chün*); from 757 considered 2 of the Six Imperial Armies (*liu chün*), a term almost synonymous with the Northern Command; later also units of the Ten Imperial Armies (*shih chün*). Through the 800s, like all other units of the Northern Command,

fell under the dominance of the eunuch-led Armies of Inspired Strategy (*shen-ts'e chün*). The nomenclature was perpetuated in Sung, but apparently only for honorific uses. RR: *armée guerrière comme les dragons*. SP: *armée de la bravoure du dragon*. P43.

3882 *lǚ* 旅
(1) **Functionary:** throughout history, one of several terms used for unranked subofficials (see *li, hsü-li*) in government service. (2) **Troops:** throughout history, a very general reference to almost any military group. (3) CHOU: **Fourth Class Administrative Official,** 4th highest of 8 categories in which officials were classified in a hierarchy separate from the formal rank system called the Nine Honors (*chiu ming*); below those designated *cheng* (Principal, etc.), *shih* (Mentor, etc.), and *ssu* (to be in charge; office); above *fu* (Storekeeper), *shih* (Scribe), *hsü* (Assistant), and *t'u* (Attendant). CL: *le quatrième degré de la subordination administrative, officier ordinaire*. (4) CHOU, T'ANG: **Battalion,** in Chou a military unit of 500 men constituting 5 Companies (*tsu*), 5 Battalions making up a Regiment (*shih*); headed by a Battalion Commander (*lü-shuai*). In the T'ang Garrison Militia system (see *fu-ping, fu*), a unit of 100 men comprising 2 Companies (*t'ui*), 2 Battalions making up a 200-man Regiment (*t'uan*); headed by a Battalion Commander, rank 6b1 or 7b2. The term may have persisted into Sung times.

3883 *lǘ* 閭
(1) CHOU: **Village,** a unit in state-prescribed local organization of the population in the royal domain, counterpart of *li* in other areas; consisting of 5 Neighborhoods (*pi*), each an artificial administrative group of 5 families; 4 Villages in turn constituted a Precinct (*tsu*). (2) SUI: **Neighborhood,** a unit in sub-District (*hsien*) organization of the population in urban areas, comprising 5 Security Groups (*pao*) of 5 families each; 4 Neighborhoods constituted a Precinct. Cf. *li* (Village), a rural group of 10 families.

3884 *lǘ-hsū̄* 閭胥
CHOU: **Village Assistant,** one in each Village (*lü*) in the royal domain, ranked as as Ordinary Serviceman (*chung-shih*) and considered a member of the Ministry of Education (*ti-kuan*); the actual head of a Village (*lü*), responsible to one of 2 Supervisors of Villages (*lü-shih*) for such matters as census, taxes, state service assignments, and public morality. Cf. *li-tsai*. CL: *assistant de section*.

3885 *lǜ-hsüéh* 律學
SUI–SUNG: **Law School,** one of several schools in the dynastic capital, where sons of low-ranking officials and some commoners studied the dynastic law code in preparation for specialized careers in legal and judicial agencies; subordinate to the Court of Judicial Review (*ta-li ssu*) in Sui, thereafter to the Directorate of Education (*kuo-tzu chien*); abolished c. 626, re-established in 632, abolished again in 658, re-established again in 662, attached again to the Court of Judicial Review (now called *hsiang-hsiang ssu*) in 663, reattached to the Directorate of Education by 739, probably in 671 or 705. In T'ang staffed with 3 Erudites (*po-shih*), rank 8b2, and one Instructor (*chu-chiao*), 9b2. In Sung headed by a Director (*cheng*), 9a; included one or 2 Erudites, 8b, and one Instructor, unranked. The student corps seems to have been limited to c. 20 in Sung. RR: *section du droit*. SP: *école de droit*. P34.

3886 *lǜ-lì kuǎn* 律例館
CH'ING: **Codification Office** under the Ministry of Justice (*hsing-pu*) from 1742, responsible for preparing and issuing

a revised law code at 5-year intervals; headed nominally by a Prince (*wang*) or Grand Minister (*ta-ch'en*), with a staff of officials chosen for their judicial experience and knowledge. BH: commission of laws. P13.

3887 *lǜ-lìng pó-shìh* 律令博士
T'ANG: **Erudite of Law,** non-official specialist on the staff of the Palace Institute of Literature (*nei wen-hsüeh kuan*), where palace women were educated; from c. 741 a eunuch post. RR: *maître de droit*.

3888 *lǜ-lìng shīh* 律令師
HAN: **Master of Laws,** special duty assignment, on an annual rotation, for Clerical Aides (*chia-tso*) on the staff of the Chamberlain for Law Enforcement (*t'ing-wei*), probably detached for service under the Metropolitan Commandant (*ssu-li hsiao-wei*) to monitor the fairness of judicial actions; others found (similarly detached?) on the staffs of Commanderies (*chün*). HB: master of statutes and ordinances.

3889 *lǚ-pēn* 旅賁
HAN–T'ANG: lit. meaning not clear, but derived from *lüpen shih* (Royal Foot Escort), a group of military men who jogged alongside the royal chariot in Chou times: **Imperial Escort,** a small group of privileged soldiers assigned to flank the imperial carriage during all imperial outings, bearing arms and armor in military situations but not in sacrificial, funeral, and other ceremonial situations. Led by a Director (*ling*) in Han, a Leader of Palace Gentlemen (*chung-lang chiang*) or simply a Court Gentleman (*lang*) thereafter. HB: emergency cohort. P26.

3890 *lǚ-pēn shìh* 旅賁氏
CHOU: **Royal Foot Escort,** a small group of soldiers responsible for jogging alongside the royal chariot on all royal outings, bearing arms and armor except in sacrificial, funeral, and other ceremonial situations; consisted of 16 Junior Servicemen (*hsia-shih*) under the leadership of one Ordinary Serviceman (*chung-shih*), all members of the Ministry of War (*hsia-kuan*). CL: *coureurs en troupe*.

3891 *lǜ pó-shìh* 律博士
N-S DIV: **Legal Erudite,** one or more on the staff of the Chamberlain for Law Enforcement (*t'ing-wei*), presumably participating as law specialists in judicial cases; normally outranked by Judicial Supervisors (*cheng chien-p'ing*). P22.

3892 *lǚ-shīh* 旅師
CHOU: **Superintendent of Grain Supplies,** 4 ranked as Ordinary Servicemen (*chung-shih*) and 8 as Junior Servicemen (*hsia-shih*), members of the Ministry of Education (*ti-kuan*) who were responsible, through many subordinates, for distributing to and disbursing from royal granaries taxes collected in grain, presumably from areas within the royal domain. CL: *préposé aux quantités*.

3893 *lǚ-shīh* 閭師
CHOU: **Supervisor of Villages,** 2 ranked as Ordinary Servicemen (*chung-shih*), members of the Ministry of Education (*ti-kuan*) responsible for assigning people of the royal capital and the 6 Districts (*hsiang*) of the royal domain to state-requisitioned services (or determining appropriate kinds of vocations for them?), supervising the census, collecting taxes, etc. CL: *préposé aux habitations*.

3894 *lǚ-shuài* 旅帥
Battalion Commander. (1) CHOU: leader of a militia-like unit of 500 men in 5 Companies (*tsu*), ranked as a Junior Grand Master (*hsia ta-fu*). CL: *chef de bataillon*. (2) T'ANG: 20, rank 6b1, in each of the Five Garrisons (*wu fu*) that constituted the hereditary elite corps of the Twelve Armies

(*shih-erh chün*) or, after 636, the Sixteen Guards (*shih-liu wei*) at the dynastic capital; also in the Personal Guard Garrison (*ch'in-shih fu*) of each Princely Establishment (*wang-fu*), number variable, rank 7b2; and in still other military units, including those of the Garrison Militia system (see *fu-ping, fu*). Ranked below Commandants (*hsiao-wei*) but above Company Commanders (*tui-cheng*). RR: *capitaine*. (3) SUNG: number, ranks, and hierarchical status not clear. SP: *capitaine*.

3895 *mǎ* 馬
See *chang-ma, ssu-ma, tsou-ma, wu ma*, etc.

3896 *mǎ-chiēn* 馬監
SUNG: **Directorate of Horses,** staffing and hierarchical relationships not clear, but likely a subordinate unit of the Court of the Imperial Stud (*t'ai-p'u ssu*) or the Bureau of Military Affairs (*shu-mi yüan*). SP: *direction des chevaux*.

3897 *mǎ-ch'ién* 馬前
Variant of *hsi-ma* (**Frontrider**).

3898 *mǎ-chíh* 馬質
CHOU: **Horse Appraiser,** 2 ranked as Ordinary Servicemen (*chung-shih*), members of the Ministry of War (*hsia-kuan*) responsible for buying horses for the central government and through negotiation fixing the prices of various types of horses. CL: *estimateur de chevaux*.

3899 *mǎ-chūn ssū* 馬軍司
SUNG: **Metropolitan Cavalry Command,** created in the middle of the 11th century by a division of the prior Metropolitan Command (*shih-wei ch'in-chün ma-pu ssu*) into a Metropolitan Cavalry Command and a Metropolitan Infantry Command (*pu-chün ssu*); these 2 units and the pre-existing and unchanged Palace Command (*tien-ch'ien shih-wei ssu*) controlled military forces at the dynastic capital and were known collectively as the Three Capital Guards (*san wei*); each was headed by a Commander-in-chief (*tu chih-hui shih*), rank 5a. SP: *bureau de cavalerie*.

3900 *mǎ-ch'ǘn ssū* 馬羣司
LIAO: **Horse Pasturage,** local agencies responsible to the Court of the Imperial Stud (*t'ai-p'u ssu*) in the Southern Administration (*nan-mien*) at the dynastic capital; had geographic prefixes, e.g., *mo-pei* (north of the Gobi); headed by Commissioners (*shih*), apparently unranked, with the assistance of Keepers of Horse Herds (*t'ai-pao*), et al. Cf. *ch'ün-mu ssu* (Herds Office), which coexisted in the same hierarchy, and *mu-ch'ang*. P31.

3901 *mǎ-hsiēn* 馬先
Variant of *hsi-ma* (**Frontrider**).

3902 *mǎ-k'uài* 馬快
CH'ING: **Mounted Courier,** one of many sorts of requisitioned state-service personnel in all Prefectures (*fu*), Departments (*chou*), and Districts (*hsien*). Cf. *pu-k'uai* (Runner).

3903 *mǎ-kuǎn* 馬館
CH'ING: **Horses Office** under the Ministry of War (*ping-pu*), headed by an unranked Superintendent (*chien-tu*) with the assistance of 2 Office Managers (*lu-shih*); apparently had supervisory responsibilities over the state's postal courier system; relations with such agencies as the Court of the Imperial Stud (*t'ai-p'u ssu*) are not clear. BH: depot of military horses.

3904 *mǎ-mù shǐh* 馬牧使
T'ANG: **Commissioner for Horse Pasturages,** apparently a (regular?) duty assignment for officials of the Court of

the Imperial Stud (*t'ai-p'u ssu*), to inspect and implement policies relevant to Directorates of Horse Pasturages (*mu-chien*) scattered throughout the empire. RR: *commissaire impérial aux élevages de chevaux.*

3905   *mǎ-nǎo chǘ* 瑪瑙局
YÜAN: **Agate Service,** antecedent from 1272 to 1278 of the Supervisorate of Agate Workers (*ma-nao t'i-chü ssu*), one of several manufacturing agencies under the Supervisorate-in-chief of Metal Workers and Jewelers (*chin-yü jen-chiang tsung-kuan fu*).

3906   *mǎ-pù chūn* 馬步軍
SUNG: lit., army of cavalry and infantry: **Army,** a general term for many kinds of military units, including both the Imperial Armies (*chin-chün*) garrisoned around the N. Sung dynasty capital, Kaifeng, and the Prefectural Armies (*hsiang-ping*) scattered throughout the country; normally headed by a Commander-in-chief (*tu chih-hui shih*), rank 5a, or a Circuit Commander-in-chief (... *lu tu tsung-kuan*), but often the concurrent post of a prefectural Administrator (*chih ... fu shih*) or, in an especially strategic area along the frontier, the concurrent post of a Circuit Military Commissioner (... *lu an-fu shih*). SP: *la cavalerie et l'infanterie.*

3907   *mǎ-pù tū yǔ-hòu* 馬步都虞候
5 DYN–SUNG: **Inspector-general of the ... Army** or **Associate Commander of the ... Army:** originally an officer responsible for maintaining discipline in an army at the frontier, but not later than early Sung evolved into a second in command. See *ma-pu chün, tu yü-hou.* SP: *surveillant général de l'armée.*

3908   *mǎ-pù yüàn* 馬步院
5 DYN: unofficial reference to the headquarters, hence indirectly to the person, of an **Inspector-general of the ... Army** (*ma-pu tu yü-hou*). Also see *tu yü-hou.*

3909   *má-p'ǔ* 麻普
LIAO: lit. meaning not clear; probably a Chinese transliteration of a Khitan word: quasiofficial reference to a **District Vice Magistrate** (*hsien-ch'eng*).

3910   *mǎ-ts'áo* 馬曹
N-S DIV (Chin): apparently an unofficial reference to the **Cavalry Section Adjutant** (*chi-ping ts'an-chün*) in the developing Department of State Affairs (*shang-shu sheng*). May be encountered in later eras as an unofficial reference to lesser officials of the Ministry of War (*ping-pu*).

3911   *mài-chián ch'ǎng* 麥麹場
SUNG: **Threshing Office** under the Directorate for the Palace Buildings (*chiang-tso chien*), headed by a Director (*chien-kuan*), apparently unranked; received annual submissions of wheat-straw from areas near the dynastic capital, then threshed and mixed it with lime to produce mortar used in constructing and maintaining the palace buildings. SP: *aire de la paille de blé.* P15.

3912   *mǎn* 滿
CH'ING: common abbreviation of **Manchu** (*man-chou*), especially as a title prefix indicating that the office was normally held by a Manchu.

3913   *mǎn-chōu pā ch'í* 滿洲八旗
CH'ING: **Eight Manchu Banners,** one of 3 groups in the Banner (*ch'i*) military organization. See under *pa ch'i.* Cf. *han-chün pa ch'i, meng-ku pa ch'i.*

3914   *mǎn èrh-pān* 滿二班
CH'ING: **Second Manchu Duty Group,** one of 4 groups of Secretaries in the Council of State (*chün-chi chang-ching*).

Also see *man t'ou-pan, han t'ou-pan, han erh-pan, chang-ching.*

3915   *mán-í chǎng-kuān ssū* 蠻夷長官司
MING: **Aboriginal Chiefs' Offices,** a general reference to the administrative units in which friendly aboriginal tribes of the Southwest were organized, absorbed at least nominally into the Chinese state hierarchy. See *chang-kuan ssu, t'u-ssu.* P68, 72.

3916   *mán-í kuān* 蠻夷官
YÜAN–MING: **Tribal Chief,** one of many designations conferred on friendly southwestern aboriginal chieftains. P72.

3917   *mán-lì* 蠻隸
CHOU: **Southern War Prisoner,** 120 apparently authorized for service as horse grooms, palace guards, or local police under supervision of the Manager of War Prisoners (*ssu-li*) in the Ministry of Justice (*ch'iu-kuan*) and also the Inspectors of Horses (*hsiao-jen*) in the Ministry of War (*hsia-kuan*). See *tsui-li.* CL: *condamné du midi.*

3918   *mǎn-pèn fáng* 滿本房
CH'ING: **Manchu Documents Section** in the Grand Secretariat (*nei-ko*), in charge of translating Chinese documents into Manchu. Cf. *han-pen fang, meng-ku pen-fang.* BH: Manchu copying office. P2.

3919   *mǎn-p'iào ch'iēn-ch'ù* 滿票簽處
CH'ING: **Manchu Document Registry** in the Grand Secretariat (*nei-ko*), in charge of recording all Manchu documents handled, and in some instances making abstracts for the files. See *han-p'iao ch'ien-ch'u.* BH: Manchu registry. P2.

3920   *mǎn-tàng fáng* 滿檔房
CH'ING: **Manchu Archive,** one each in the Court of Colonial Affairs (*li-fan yüan*), the Ministry of War (*ping-pu*), the Ministry of Rites (*li-pu*), and perhaps other agencies; a translation agency as well as an archive. See *han-tang fang.* BH: record and registry office.

3921   *mǎn t'óu-pān* 滿頭班
CH'ING: **First Manchu Duty Group,** one of 4 groups of Secretaries in the Council of State (*chün-chi chang-ching*). Also see *man erh-pan, han t'ou-pan, han erh-pan, chang-ching.*

3922   *mán-tzǔ* 蠻子
The Chinese name for a large group of non-Han aboriginal tribespeople in South China, and occasionally used as an abbreviated general reference to all non-Han aborigines in the South and Southwest. In Yüan times, used by the Mongols as an unofficial and quite humiliating reference to Southern Chinese (officially *nan-jen*), former subjects of S. Sung. Rendered Manzi by Marco Polo and others. See *han.*

3923   *máo-jén* 旄人
CHOU: lit., man with a wild ox tail, i.e., a dancer carrying an oxtail with which to signal changes or emphases in the accompanying music: **Master of Foreign Dances,** 4 ranked as Junior Servicemen (*hsia-shih*), members of the Ministry of Rites (*ch'un-kuan*) who learned the dances performed at the courts of alien rulers of East China and taught them to a corps of special court dancers; such dances were performed at the Chou court at receptions for chiefs of eastern tribes and also at various sacrifices and funerals. Cf. *mei-shih.* CL: *porteur d'étendard à queue de boeuf.*

3924   *máo-kuǎng* 茂光
N-S DIV (N. Ch'i): **Lady of Elegant Brightness,** designation of one of 27 imperial wives called Hereditary Consorts (*shih-fu*); rank =3b.

3925 *māo-shíh* 貓食

Lit., cat food: in late Ming if not other times, a derisive categorical reference to a **dependent of a palace eunuch.**

3926 *máo-t'óu láng* 髦頭郎 or *máo-t'óu chì* 騎

CH'IN–HAN: **Oxtail-haired Court Gentleman** (*lang*) or **Cavalryman** (*chi*), a court attendant assigned on an ad hoc basis to ride horseback at the head of an imperial procession with disheveled hair hanging down his back resembling an oxtail, to invoke the spirit of a legendary ox that awed horses. HB (*mao-t'ou*): standard bearer.

3927 *máo-ts'ái* 茂才

In Han an official variant of, and in later times an unofficial reference to, a **Cultivated Talent** (*hsiu-ts'ai,* q.v.). HB: abundant talent.

3928 *máo-ts'ái ì-těng* 茂材異等

SUNG: **Extraordinary Talent,** one of several designations given to examinations and the degrees earned in them; the examinations were given rarely, as Special Examinations (*chih-k'o*) scheduled only by imperial edict; more commonly examinations of and degrees awarded to men already in service for purposes of promotion than recruitment examinations and degrees.

3929 *me*

See under the romanization *mo.*

3930 *měi-jén* 美人

HAN–SUNG: **Beauty,** common designation of secondary imperial wives or consorts (15 in Sui, 4 in T'ang, otherwise number not clear), rank =2,000 bushels in Han, thereafter normally 4a but 3a from the early 700s to the end of T'ang. In Sui considered members of the group called Hereditary Consorts (*shih-fu*). In T'ang specifically charged with making preparations for sacrificial ceremonies, receptions, etc. HB: beautiful lady. RR: *belle personne.* SP: *femme titré intérieure.*

3931 *měi-lò ó-chēn* 梅勒額眞

CH'ING: **Banner Vice Commander,** one each prefixed Left and Right in each Banner (*ch'i*) in the Eight Banner (*pa ch'i*) military organization, ranking below only Banner Commanders-in-chief (*ku-shan o-chen, ku-shan ang-pang, tu-t'ung*); originated in 1615, in 1634 changed to *ku-shan chang-ching;* from 1660 equated with the Chinese title *fu* (Vice) *tu-t'ung.* Also see *o-chen.* P44.

3932 *méi-shìh* 媒氏

CHOU: **Marriage Monitor,** 2 ranked as Ordinary Servicemen (*chung-shih*), members of the Ministry of Education (*ti-kuan*) responsible for keeping records concerning marriages within the royal domain, regularly assembling unmarried young people and punishing those considered guilty of improper liaisons, and encouraging marriage not later than the age of 30 for men, 20 for women. Described in a section of the *Chou-li* considered by some to be a late addition to the text in the time of the mid-Han usurper Wang Mang. CL: *officier des mariages.*

3933 *méi-shīh* 韎師

CHOU: **Master of Foreign Music,** 2 ranked as Junior Servicemen (*hsia-shih*), members of the Ministry of Rites (*ch'un-kuan*) who presumably learned and taught musicians to play alien music that accompanied performances of court dancers under the Masters of Foreign Dancers (*mao-jen*). CL: *maître de la musique orientale.*

3934 *mén-hsià* 門下

HAN–N-S DIV: lit., at the gate, denoting service at the palace; used as a prefix to various titles indicating a rela-tionship with the imperial palace; e.g., *men-hsia shu-tso* (Palace Clerk) in the establishment of the Heir Apparent. May also be encountered as an abbreviation of *men-hsia shěng* (Chancellery; lit., the agency at the [palace] gate); or in non-governmental use referring to one's disciples, e.g., *men-hsia shěng,* lit., students at one's gate.

3935 *mén-hsià chūng-shū shíh-láng* 門下中書使郎

SUNG: **Vice Director of the Secretariat-Chancellery,** 2, nominally rank 3b but in fact the most senior executive of-ficials in the combined Secretariat-Chancellery (most often occurs as *chung-shu men-hsia sheng*), with status equiva-lent to rank 1a, almost always serving as Grand Councilors (*tsai-hsiang, ch'eng-hsiang,* etc.) and thus the dominant civil service officials in the central government; filled the void created by the Sung practice of not appointing traditional Secretariat Directors (*chung-shu ling*), 1a, and Chancellery Directors (*men-hsia shih-chung*), 1a. Often had such spe-cific designations as Vice Director of the Secretariat-Chan-cellery Participating in Determining Governmental Matters (... *ts'an-chih cheng-shih*), signaling status as a Grand Councilor or Vice Grand Councilor (*fu-hsiang, shao-tsai*). Also see *chung-shu sheng, men-hsia sheng.* SP: *vice-président de la chancellerie et du secrétariat impériaux.* P2, 3, 4.

3936 *mén-hsià fāng* 門下坊

N-S DIV (N. Ch'i)–T'ANG: **Secretariat of the Heir Ap-parent,** a constituent unit of the Household Administration of the Heir Apparent (*chan-shih fu*) with general adminis-trative control over the household; headed by 4 then 2 Men-tors (*shu-tzu*), rank 4a in T'ang; in 662 renamed *tso ch'un-fang,* q.v.; from 670 to 711 again known as *men-hsia fang,* thereafter again as *tso ch'un-fang.* Oversaw the functioning of 6 subordinate Services (*chü*) in the Heir Apparent's household: see *ssu-ching chü, tien-shan chü, yao-tsang chü, nei-chih chü, tien-she chü, kung-men chü.* Also see *chung-yün, ssu-i lang.* RR: *grand secrétariat de gauche de l'héritier du trône.* P26.

3937 *mén-hsià fēng-pó ssū* 門下封駁司

SUNG: **Chancellery Office of Scrutiny;** see under *feng-po.*

3938 *mén-hsià hòu-shěng* 門下後省

SUNG: **Chancellery Rear Section,** staffed with a Left (*tso*) Policy Adviser (*san-ch'i chang-shih*), a Left Grand Master of Remonstrance (*chien-i ta-fu*), a Left Remonstrator (*ssu-chien*), a Left Exhorter (*cheng-yen*), and an indefinite num-ber of Supervising Secretaries (*chi-shih-chung*); established c. 1080 together with a Secretariat Rear Section (*chung-shu hou-sheng,* q.v.), apparently to keep alive remonstrance and "veto" (see *feng-po*) traditions at a time when the Chancellery (*men-hsia sheng*), the Secretariat (*chung-shu sheng*), and the Department of State Affairs (*shang-shu sheng*) had become a single conglomerate central admin-istration whose executive officials were in fact Grand Councilors (*tsai-hsiang, ch'eng-hsiang*) and Vice Grand Councilors (*fu-hsiang, shao-tsai*). Within the Chancellery Rear Section were 6 functionally specialized Sections (*an*) named in the pattern of the Six Ministries (*liu pu*) under the Department of State Affairs. After Sung's retreat to the South, the Chancellery Rear Section was re-established in 1129 with 4 Supervising Secretaries as its executive offi-cials, overseeing 4 functionally differentiated Sections. The organizational structure, the purpose, and the specific func-tions of this agency are not wholly clear. SP: *arrière-chan-cellerie impériale.* P19.

3939 *mén-hsià shĕng* 門下省

N-S DIV (Chin)–CHIN: **Chancellery,** an executive agency in the central government's top echelon, commonly responsible for advising rulers about proposals submitted through the Secretariat (*chung-shu sheng*), remonstrating with rulers about the practicality and morality of policy decisions, and serving as the channel through which imperial pronouncements were put in final form and transmitted to the Department of State Affairs (*shang-shu sheng*) for implementation. Deriving from a late Han practice of gathering trusted advisers into a Court of Palace Attendants (*shih-chung ssu*) with titles that formerly were entirely honorary, such as Palace Steward or Supervising Secretary (both *chi-shih-chung*) and Gentleman Attendant at the Palace Gate (*huang-men shih-lang*), the Chancellery developed in the 4th and 5th centuries to contend with the evolving Secretariat for influence over imperial decision making; by Sui it had become one of the Five Departments (*wu sheng*) that dominated the central government, and in T'ang it became, with the Secretariat and the Department of State Affairs, the Three Departments (*san sheng*) that handled the general administration of government in the patterns described above. In early Sung, executive officials of the Chancellery and the Secretariat normally served as Grand Councilors (*tsai-hsiang, ch'eng-hsiang*) or Vice Grand Councilors (*fu-hsiang, shao-tsai*); other posts in the two agencies were collapsed into an almost functionless, combined Secretariat-Chancellery (*chung-shu men-hsia sheng*), and remonstrance functions were perpetuated by the creation of an autonomous Chancellery Rear Section (*men-hsia hou-sheng*) and a separate Remonstrance Bureau (*chien-yüan*). In Liao's Southern Administration (*nan-mien*) the T'ang-style Three Departments were retained, but in Chin both the Chancellery and the Secretariat faded in importance and were formally abolished in 1156, the Chancellery never to be re-established despite occasional proposals in Yüan times that all of T'ang's Three Departments be restored. In its early history, in the N. Dynasties and Sui, the Chancellery was a large organization including 6 subordinate Sections (*chü*): see *ch'eng-men chü, shang-shih chü, shang-yao chü, fu-hsi chü, yü-fu chü,* and *tien-nei chü.* In late Sui this large agency was reorganized into 2 units, an Office of Palace Attendants (*men-hsia ssu*) and an Office of the Imperial Coachman (? *t'ai-p'u ssu*). In T'ang the reunited Chancellery was given new names several times, from 662 to 670 being called the Eastern Pavilion (*tung-t'ai*), from 685 to 705 the Phoenix Pavilion (*luan-t'ai*), and from 713 to 717 Pavilion of Imperial Gatekeepers (*huang-men t'ai*), which had been an intermittent variant of *men-hsia sheng* in earlier times. The Chancellery originally was headed by an Adviser (*na-yen;* lit., [one who] submits statements) and staffed with Palace Attendants (*shih-chung*), Supervising Secretaries (*chi-shih-chung*), Imperial Gatekeepers (*huang-men*), Attendant Gentlemen (*shih-lang*), etc. In mid-Sui the post of Adviser was terminated; thereafter the Chancellery was headed by 2 *shih-chung,* now appropriately rendered Directors; the name of the post was occasionally changed in the late 7th and during the 8th centuries. The Directors' rank was raised from 3a to 2a in 767 and was 1a in Sung. There was normally one Vice Director (*shih-lang*), rank 3a in T'ang, 3b in Sung; lesser officials in T'ang included counterparts of those in the Secretariat, but prefixed Left rather than Right as in the Secretariat: 2 Policy Advisers (*san-chi ch'ang-shih*), 3b till 764, then 3a through Sung; 4 Grand Masters of Remonstrance (*chien-i ta-fu*), 5a then 4b; 4 Supervising Secretaries (*chi-shih-chung* without any prefix; Secretariat counterparts were Secretariat Drafters, *chung-shu she-jen*), 5a in T'ang, 4a in Sung; 4 Imperial Diarists (*ch'i-chü lang*), 6b1; 4 Gentlemen of the Palace Gates (*ch'eng-men lang*), 6b1; 6 Rectifiers of Omissions (*pu-ch'üeh*), 7b1; 6 Reminders (*shih-i*), 8b1; Supervisors of Rites (*tien-i*), 9b2; etc. The Chancellery normally had general supervisory authority over various lesser agencies but did not have significant constituent units after Sui. RR+SP: *département de la chancellerie impériale.* P2, 3, 4.

3940 *mén-hsià shĭh* 門下史

N-S DIV (Chin): **Headquarters Clerk** on the staff of the Governor (*t'ai-shou*) of a Commandery (*chün*). P53.

3941 *mén-hsià shìh-chūng* 門下侍中

Director of the Chancellery; see under *men-hsia sheng, shih-chung.* RR+SP: *président (du département) de la chancellerie impériale.*

3942 *mén-hsià shìh-láng* 門下侍郎

Vice Director of the Chancellery; see under *men-hsia sheng, shih-lang.* RR+SP: *vice-président (du département) de la chancellerie impériale.*

3943 *mén-hsià shū-tsò* 門下書佐

N-S DIV (Chin): **Palace Clerk,** one of low rank on the staff of the Supervisor of the Household of the Heir Apparent (*chan-shih*). Also see *shu-tso.* P26.

3944 *mén-hsià ssū* 門下司

SUI: **Office of Palace Attendants,** one of 2 agencies created c. 605 out of the previous Chancellery (*men-hsia sheng*), assigned supervisory responsibility over 6 Services (*chü*) formerly under the Palace Administration (*tien-nei sheng*) and staffed with palace eunuchs. The other new agency was the *t'ai-p'u ssu* (Office of the Imperial Coachman?); staffing, functions, and organizational relationships not clear. Cf. *men-hsia fang, t'ai-p'u ssu* (Court of the Imperial Stud). P37.

3945 *mén-hsià t'íng-chăng* 門下亭長

N-S DIV (Chin): **Managing Clerk in the Palace,** one of low rank in each Section (*ts'ao*) under the Supervisor of the Household of the Heir Apparent (*chan-shih*). See *t'ing-chang.* P26.

3946 *mén-hsià tū* 門下督

(1) N-S DIV (San kuo): **Palace Supervisor,** designation commonly awarded to or assumed by dominant military commanders. P32. (2) N-S DIV (N. Ch'i): **Headquarters Supervisor,** a clerical post in establishments of Regional Inspectors (*tz'u-shih*) and perhaps elsewhere in government. Also see *chang-hsia tu.* P52.

3947 *mén-hsià wài-shĕng* 門下外省

SUNG: **Outer Chancellery,** a branch of the central government's Chancellery (*men-hsia sheng*), probably created during the Sung court's retreat from North China in the 1120s, but its location, duration, and functions are not clear. SP: *département extérieur de la chancellerie impériale.*

3948 *mén-hsià wăn-shēng* 門下晚生

CH'ING: lit., a tardy disciple at the gate: **Your Disciple,** a polite, deprecatory reference to oneself when addressing a civil service recruitment Examiner (*tso-chu*) under whom one's own Examiner had graduated, or the father of one's own Examiner.

3949 *mén-p'ú* 門僕

SUI–T'ANG: **Gatekeeper** on the staff of the Office for the National Altars (*chiao-she shu*) in the Court of Imperial Sacrifices (*t'ai-ch'ang ssu*); unranked, number in T'ang reportedly varying from 8 to 32. Also see *chai-lang* (Court Gentleman for Fasting). RR: *portier.* P28.

3950 *mén-shēng* 門生
Lit., student at the gate: **Disciple,** a traditional term signifying that one's relationship to another was, even metaphorically, that of student to teacher; in the civil service, all who had passed a recruitment examination under any official serving as examiner were expected to consider themselves his disciples and to support him in any partisan struggles or controversies. Cf. *t'ien-tzu men-tzu* (Disciples of the Son of Heaven).

3951 *mén tà-fū* 門大夫
HAN–N-S DIV: **Grand Master of the Gates,** an official commonly serving in the household of the Heir Apparent, in Former Han also in Marquisates (*hou-kuo*); as many as 5, rank 600 bushels in Han and the S. Dynasties; one or 2, rank 6b, in the N. Dynasties. More than an ordinary gatekeeper; likened to Leader of the Palace Gentlemen (*lang-chiang*) and Receptionist (*yeh-che*). HB: grandee at the gate. P26, 67, 69.

3952 *mén t'íng-chǎng* 門亭長
HAN–N-S DIV (Chin): **Managing Clerk at the Gate,** apparently one or more at each gate of a Commandery (*chün*) headquarters city or town, serving as administrators of civil matters dealt with in the vicinity of the gate; of low official status. See *t'ing-chang*. HB: chief of the check point at the gate. P52.

3953 *mén-tsú* 門卒
HAN: **Gateman,** numerous unranked subofficials on the staff of the Counselor-in-chief (*ch'eng-hsiang*), headed by one or more Directors (*ling*). No doubt found in other offices and in other eras. HB: conscripts at the gates.

3954 *mén-wèi* 門尉
HAN: **Commandant of the Gates** in the household of an Imperial Princess (*kung-chu*), responsible to the Chamberlain for the Imperial Clan (*tsung-cheng*) in the central government. HB: commandant of the gates.

3955 *méng* 盟
Throughout history refers to a covenant or sworn agreement, normally made by potentially hostile political entities, or by several political entities threatened by a common enemy; hence, a **League** with a chosen or designated Head (*chang*), a form of tribal organization used by Mongols of Outer Mongolia in Ch'ing times. See *ai-ma* (Tribe). BH: league.

3956 *měng-ān* 猛安
CHIN: **Battalion,** also **Battalion Commander:** Chinese transliteration of a Jurchen title that the Chinese equated with their traditional title *ch'ien-fu* or *ch'ien-hu*, qq.v.; the hereditary, aristocratic leader of a tribal military unit of 1,000 or more households, many of which settled in North China after the Jurchen conquest as military garrisons independent of the normal administrative hierarchy. In theory comprised 10 Companies (*po-hu*, the Chinese translation of the Jurchen word transliterated as *mou-k'o*, q.v.). In Ch'ing times *meng-an* was newly transliterated as *ming-an*. Also see *po-chin, po-chi-lieh*.

3957 *méng-kǔ* 蒙古
YÜAN, CH'ING: **Mongol, Mongolian:** common prefix indicating that the agency or official so designated had a realm of responsibility relating principally if not entirely to Mongols or that the agency staff or title holder was Mongolian, or both.

3958 *méng-kǔ chāng-chīng* 蒙古章京
CH'ING: **Mongolian Secretary,** from 1650 a minor official in the Bureau of Ceremonies (*i-chih ch'ing-li ssu*) of the Ministry of Rites (*lǐ-pu*), which managed ceremonial aspects of relations between the Manchu court and those Mongols with whom the court had relations; 4 till 1670, then reduced to 2, the 3rd being transformed into a Mongol Director (*lang-chung:* Co-director?) of the Bureau and the 4th being made Mongol Vice Director (*yüan-wai lang*) of the Bureau; ranks not clear. See *chang-ching*. P9.

3959 *méng-kǔ ch'éng-chèng* 蒙古承政
CH'ING: **Mongolian Executive,** till 1644 shared with a Chinese Executive (*han ch'eng-cheng*) the active direction of the Ministry of Revenue (*hu-pu*), then abolished in favor of one Manchu and one Chinese Minister (*shang-shu*), the traditional Chinese title. See *ch'eng-cheng*. P6.

3960 *méng-kǔ chūn* 蒙古軍
YÜAN: **Mongol Army,** generic reference to all Mongol military units controlled by the central government's Bureau of Military Affairs (*shu-mi yüan*), distinguishing them from other military units in 3 main generic categories—the Allied Army (*t'an-ma-ch'ih chün*), the Chinese Army (*han-chün*), and the Newly Submitted Army (*hsin-fu chün*). Personnel of the Mongol Army dominated the Imperial Armies (*ch'in-chün*) stationed in and around the dynastic capital, especially the Imperial Bodyguard (*kesig: ch'ieh-hsieh*) and the Palace Guards (*su-wei*). The Mongol Army's officers and soldiers were organized in nominal 10,000-man Brigades (*wan-hu fu*) administered overall by a Chief Brigade (*tu wan-hu fu*) headquartered at the capital. At times some were organized into other Brigades, e.g., the Mongol Army Chief Brigade for Ho-nan and Huai-pei (*ho-nan huai-pei meng-ku chün tu wan-hu fu*) headquartered at Loyang.

3961 *méng-kǔ fān-ì fáng* 蒙古繙譯房
CH'ING: **Mongolian Translation Office,** a small unit in the Court of Colonial Affairs (*li-fan yüan*) responsible for translating into Manchu official documents submitted to the throne in Mongolian; staffed principally by a nominal Vice Director (*yüan-wai lang:* of a Bureau in a Ministry), rank apparently 5b, and a nominal Secretary (*chu-shih:* of a Bureau in a Ministry), rank apparently 6a. See *meng-ku fang*. P17.

3962 *méng-kǔ fáng* 蒙古房
CH'ING: (1) Abbreviation of *meng-ku fan-i fang* (**Mongolian Translation Office**). (2) Abbreviation of *meng-ku pen-fang* (**Mongolian Documents Section**) serving the Grand Secretariat (*nei-ko*). See *man-pen fang, han-pen fang*. P2.

3963 *méng-kǔ hàn-lín yüàn* 蒙古翰林院
YÜAN: **Mongolian Hanlin Academy,** an autonomous central government agency that drafted all imperial pronouncements in Mongolian and translated state documents from Mongolian into the various languages represented in the Mongol empire, and vice versa. Originated in 1275 as an enlargement of the post of the New Script Academician (*hsin-tzu hsüeh-shih*) in the Historiography Institute (*kuo-shih yüan*); by the early 1300s had a prescribed staff of 28 officials and 24 subofficial functionaries; headed at first by one Auxiliary Academician (*chih hsüeh-shih*), then from 1281 by 3 Academicians (*hsüeh-shih*), rank 2b, then from 1301 rank 2a, finally from c. 1320 rank 1b. The staff included Readers-in-waiting (*shih-tu hsüeh-shih*), Edict Attendants (*tai-chih*), Senior Compilers (*hsiu-chuan*), etc., with ranks the same as counterparts in the Hanlin and Historiography Academy (*han-lin kuo-shih yüan*). P23.

3964 *méng-kǔ ī-shēng t'óu-mù* 蒙古醫生頭目
CH'ING: **Mongolian Head Veterinarian,** 3, rank 6, at-

tached to the Palace Stud (*shang-ssu yüan*), a unit of the Imperial Household Department (*nei-wu fu*). P39.

3965 *méng-kǔ kuó-tzǔ chiēn* 蒙古國子監
YÜAN: **Mongolian Directorate of Education,** under supervision of the Hanlin Academy (*han-lin yüan*) directed the Mongolian School for the Sons of the State (*meng-ku kuo-tzu hsüeh*); established in 1267 with a Director of Studies (*ssu-yeh*) as head; in 1292 reorganized with a Chancellor (*chi-chiu*), rank 3b, as head and a staff including 2 Directors of Studies, 5a. A similarly organized Directorate of Education (*kuo-tzu chien*) coexisted under supervision of the Academy of Scholarly Worthies (*chi-hsien yüan*); it directed a School for the Sons of the State (*kuo-tzu hsüeh*). P34.

3966 *méng-kǔ kuó-tzǔ hsüéh* 蒙古國子學
YÜAN: **Mongolian School for the Sons of the State,** one of several units subordinate to the Mongolian Directorate of Education (*meng-ku kuo-tzu chien*); established in 1287; taught sons of Mongol nobles and officials, in the 1300s preparing them for participation in the civil service recruitment examinations; headed by 2 Erudites (*po-shih*), rank 7a. This was a smaller school than the School for the Sons of the State (*kuo-tzu hsüeh* without prefix) under the Directorate of Education (*kuo-tzu chien* without prefix); its student body included only a very small quota of non-Mongols. P34.

3967 *méng-kǔ pā ch'í* 蒙古八旗
CH'ING: **Eight Mongol Banners,** one of 3 groups in the Banner (*ch'i*) system of military organization. Also see *pa ch'i*. Cf. *han-chün pa ch'i, man-chou pa ch'i*.

3968 *méng-kǔ pěn-fáng* 蒙古本房
CH'ING: **Mongolian Documents Section** in the Grand Secretariat (*nei-ko*), in charge of translating Manchu documents into Mongolian. See *han-pen fang, man-pen fang, meng-ku fang*. BH: Mongolian copying office. P2.

3969 *méng-kǔ pǐ-ch'ièh-ch'í* 蒙古筆且齊
YÜAN: **Mongolian Clerk,** unranked functionary found in many agencies of the central government, apparently to translate government documents from Mongolian into Chinese and vice versa. See *pi-ch'ieh-ch'i, pi-ch'e-ch'ih*.

3970 *méng-kǔ shū-hsiéh* 蒙古書寫
YÜAN: **Mongolian Scribe,** unranked functionary found in agencies of the central government; seemingly not as numerous or as widespread as Mongolian Clerks (*meng-ku pi-ch'ieh-ch'i*); the distinction between these two titles is not clear.

3971 *méng-kǔ t'í-chǔ hsüéh-hsiào kuān* 蒙古提舉學校官
YÜAN: **Supervisor of Mongolian Schools,** delegated from Branch Secretariats (*hsing chung-shu sheng*) in the Chiang-Che, Hu-Kuang, and Kiangsi Provinces, presumably to supervise the activities of Mongolian Schools in their Provinces; supplementary to each Province's Supervisorate for Confucian Schools (*ju-hsüeh t'i-chü ssu*).

3972 *méng-kǔ yá-mén* 蒙古衙門
CH'ING: **Mongol Agency,** an important unit of the predynastic central government, responsible for relations with Mongol allies; superseded by the Court of Colonial Affairs (*li-fan yüan*).

3973 *méng-yǎng* 蒙養
N-S DIV (N. Wei): **Tutor of the Young,** established in 400 as a prestige title (*san-kuan*) for tribal chiefs; compa-

rable to the later title Grand Master for Splendid Happiness (*kuang-lu ta-fu*), rank 1b.

3974 *mi* 祕 or 秘
See under the romanization *pi*.

3975 *mì-chǔ* 覓舉
N-S DIV–T'ANG: lit., to search out and nominate: unofficial reference to a **Recommendee** (*chü-jen*), i.e., someone nominated by local or regional officials for consideration as a potential appointee in the civil service.

3976 *mí-fēng kuān* 彌封官
YÜAN: **Examination Sealer;** counterpart of the Sung dynasty *feng-mi kuan*, q.v.

3977 *mì-jén* 羃人
CHOU: **Provisioner of Sacrificial Wine Covers,** a eunuch charged with preparing and providing various kinds of cloth covers or spreads used atop wine goblets in sacrificial ceremonies; attached to the Ministry of State (*t'ien-kuan*); assisted by 10 palace women and 20 criminals who had been sentenced to be palace slaves. CL: *employé aux toiles pour couvrir*.

3978 *mǐ-lǐn tū* 米稟督
SUI: **Supervisor of the Rice Granary,** 2 subordinates in the Imperial Granaries Office (*t'ai-ts'ang shu*). P8.

3979 *mì-yüàn* 密院
SUNG: common abbreviation of *shu-mi yüan* (**Bureau of Military Affairs**).

3980 *miào* 廟
Temple, common generic reference to a building where ancestral spirits were honored or worshipped. See *tsung-miao, t'ai-miao, hou-miao, chiu miao*. Cf. *ling* and *ling-ch'in* (Imperial Mausoleum).

3981 *miào-chǎng* 廟長
HAN–N-S DIV: **Director of the ... Temple,** normally prefixed with the name of a particular ancestral temple; most commonly established in each Princely Establishment (*wang-fu*). Also see *chang, miao-ling*. Cf. *ling-ling*.

3982 *miào chíh-kuān* 廟直官
SUNG: **Temple Attendant,** one on duty at each ancestral temple of members of the imperial lineage (see *tsung-miao, t'ai-miao*); in early Sung a eunuch of the Palace Domestic Service (*nei-shih sheng*), but from c. 1080 a regular civil service official, rank 9a. SP: *assistant du temple des ancêtres de l'empereur*.

3983 *miào-hsüéh* 廟學
SUNG: **Temple School** established near the Confucian temple at Ch'ü-fu, Shantung, in the era 1008–1016 by imperial order, to educate descendants of Confucius and, later, those of the Confucian disciple Yen Hui and of Mencius; in the era 1086–1093 supplemented with separate schools for the descendants of Yen Hui and Mencius. Headed by one or more Instructors (*chiao-shou*), rank 8a, chosen from among Metropolitan Graduates (*chin-shih*) or staff members of a Circuit Supervisor (*chien-ssu*) having local jurisdiction. The staff apparently included members of the Confucian clan serving as Instructors Second-class (*hsüeh-cheng*) and Instructors Third-class (*hsüeh-lu*). The name Temple School was no doubt used for many other schools attached to temples, differentiated with place-name or family-name prefixes. See *san-shih hsüeh, ssu-shih hsüeh*. P66.

3984 *miào-kān* 廟幹
T'ANG: **Temple Clerk,** normally in pairs, unranked, found

on the curatorial staffs of most temples established by Emperors and other members of the imperial family, chiefly to honor their ancestors, but also found at the principal temple in the School for the Sons of the State (*kuo-tzu hsüeh*), in the Office for Sacrifices at the Fen River (*fen-tz'u shu*), etc. Principal function was to do menial custodial work, especially "sprinkling and sweeping." See *kan*. RR: *serviteur attaché au temple*. P28.

3985 *miào-lìng* 廟令
Temple Director, from Han on the common designation of officials in charge of temples in which the spirits of deceased Emperors were honored or worshipped, each normally assisted by a Vice Director (*ch'eng*) and others. Cf. *t'ai-miao, ling-t'ai* (Court of the ... Imperial Mausoleum). Also see *miao-chang*. HB: prefect of the ancestral temple. SP: *chef de temple*.

3986 *miáo-mín kuān* 苗民官
MING: **Chief of the Miao Tribes,** one of many types of leaders of southern and southwestern aboriginal tribes considered more or less as wards of the Ming state; commonly a staff member in an Aboriginal Chief's Office (*man-i chang-kuan ssu*). See *t'u-kuan, t'u-ssu, chang-kuan ssu, man-i kuan*. P72.

3987 *miào-pù* 廟簿
SUNG: **Temple Registrar,** apparently an account keeper for any temple sponsored by the state: e.g., temples celebrating famous mountains, great rivers, and the Eastern and Southern Oceans; post normally held as an added function by a lesser official of an appropriate District (*hsien*). SP: *préposé aux registres d'un temple*.

3988 *miào-ssù lìng* 廟祀令
Director of Temple Sacrifices, from Han on the designation of an official on the staff of (any?) temple sponsored by the state. HB: prefect ancestral temple invocator.

3989 *miěn-chiěh jén* 免解人
SUNG: lit., someone excused from being forwarded: **Already Certified Candidate** for the Metropolitan Examination (*sheng-shih*) in the civil service recruitment examination sequence, i.e., someone already submitted (*chieh*) with approval by prefectural (*chou, fu*) authorities, who remained eligible to take the Metropolitan Examination even though he had missed or failed it one or more times since being so certified. See *te-chieh*.

3990 *miěn-ì àn* 免役案
SUNG: **Section for Labor Exemptions,** one of 6 Sections (*an*) under the Right Section (*yu-ts'ao*) of the Ministry of Revenue (*hu-pu*); in S. Sung, also a unit of Lin-an Prefecture (*fu*), modern Hangchow, site of the new dynastic capital; apparently responsible for considering appeals from people called into state service as runners, general flunkeys, etc. SP: *service de l'exemption des corvées*.

3991 *mín-chiàng tsŭng-kuǎn fǔ* 民匠總管府
YÜAN: **Supervisorate-in-chief of Civilian Artisans,** an agency of the central government supervising numerous workshops that wove cloth and did tailoring for the imperial wardrobe; headed by a Supervisor-in-chief (*tsung-kuan*), rank 3b. Relationship with presumably similar agencies such as the Supervisorate-in-chief of Metal Workers and Jewelers (*chin-yü jen-chiang tsung-kuan fu*) not wholly clear, but all were probably subordinate to the Imperial Manufactories Commission (*chiang-tso yüan*).

3992 *mín-chuàng* 民壯
CH'ING: **Militia Company,** a 50-man militia unit orga-

nized by a District Magistrate (*chih-hsien*). May also be encountered as a general term for Militiamen. See *hsiang-yung, t'uan-lien*. Cf. *min-ping, kuan-ping*.

3993 *mín-hù* 民戶
YÜAN–CH'ING: **Civilian Family,** one of several categories among which all residents of China were distributed in accordance with the kinds of social roles the state expected them to play; it was the role of Civilian Families to pay land taxes and provide occasional state labor service when called on. Cf. *chiang-hu, chün-hu*.

3994 *mín-k'ō* 民科
MING: **Statistics Section,** one of 4 functionally designated Sections created in 1390 as constituent units of each Bureau (*ssu, ch'ing-li ssu*) in the Ministry of Revenue (*hu-pu*); headed by a Manager (*kuan-li*). See *tu-chih k'o, chin-k'o, ts'ang-k'o*. P6.

3995 *mín-kūng* 民公
CH'ING: **Commoner Duke,** a title of nobility (*chüeh*) with inheritance rights granted, albeit rarely, to non-official Chinese for extraordinary service to the state; sometimes conferred posthumously.

3996 *mìn-lì* 閩隸
CHOU: **Southeastern War Prisoner,** 120 authorized for service in the establishment of the Heir Apparent, charged with breeding various kinds of birds for use in sacrificial ceremonies and as delicacies for the Heir Apparent's table; supervised by the Manager of War Prisoners (*ssu-li*) in the Ministry of Justice (*ch'iu-kuan*). The name Min specifies the region of modern Fukien Province, whose residents were anciently thought able to converse with birds, as were some aboriginal tribesmen of the East (the *I*) and the North (the *Ti*). See *tsui-li*. CL: *condamné de Sud-Est*.

3997 *mín-pīng* 民兵
SUNG, MING: **Militiaman,** designation of part-time home-guard soldiers organized for local defense by officials of Districts (*hsien*), supplementing Regular Troops (*kuan-ping*) of the Sung Imperial Armies (*chin-chün*) and Prefectural Armies (*hsiang-ping*) and of the Ming dynasty Guards (*wei*; see *wei-so*). May be encountered as a general term for militiamen in any era. Also see *ping, chün, pao-chia, hsiang-ping* (Local Militia), *hsiang-yung, min-chuang, t'uan-lien*. SP: *milice*.

3998 *mín-pīng fáng* 民兵房
SUNG: **Militia Section** in the Bureau of Military Affairs (*shu-mi yüan*); originally one of 4 Sections (*fang*), then in the reign of Shen-tsung (r. 1067–1085) reorganized as one of 12 Sections in the Bureau that managed administrative affairs of military garrisons throughout the country, in geographic clusters, or supervised specified military functions on an empire-wide scale. The Militia Section supervised matters relating to archers serving in the Palace Command (*tien-ch'ien ssu*) at the dynastic capital on rotational assignment from locally organized militia units (?) called *pao-chia*, q.v., of the Three Circuits (*san lu*), i.e., those surrounding the capital, Kaifeng: Ching-chi, Ching-tung, Ching-hsi. Headed by 3 to 5 Vice Recipients of Edicts (*fu ch'eng-chih*), rank 8b. Apparently discontinued early in S. Sung. See *shih-erh fang* (Twelve Sections). SP: *chambre de milice*.

3999 *mín-pīng wèi-àn* 民兵衛案
SUNG: **Militia Guard Section,** one of numerous constituent units in the Ministry of War (*ping-pu*), responsible for overseeing the operation of locally organized militia forces, presumably in collaboration with the Militia Section (*min-*

ping fang) of the Bureau of Military Affairs (*shu-mi yüan*); headed by a Director (*lang-chung*), rank 6a or 6b, with the aid of a Vice Director (*yüan-wai lang*), 7a. See *hsiang-ping*. SP: *service des gardes de milice*.

4000   *mín-pù* 民部

(1) N-S DIV–T'ANG: **Ministry of Revenue,** one of a variable number of top-echelon units in the developing Department of State Affairs (*shang-shu sheng*), alternating from period to period with such names as *tu-chih, min-ts'ao, tso-min*, qq.v. Normally headed by a Minister (*shang-shu*). In c. 583 Sui changed the inherited name *tu-chih* to *min-pu;* then in c. 650 T'ang changed *min-pu* to *hu-pu* to avoid use of the personal name of T'ang T'ai-tsung (Li Shih-min). Thereafter *hu-pu* remained the standard name of the Ministry, and T'ang writers often substituted *hu-pu* for the unacceptable *min-pu* even in writing of Sui or earlier times. RR: *ministère des finances*. P6. (2) MING: revived in 1389 to replace *tsung-pu* (**General Bureau**) as one of 4 functionally differentiated Bureaus in the Ministry of Revenue (*hu-pu*), then in 1390 discontinued when the Ministry was reorganized into more numerous Bureaus (*ssu, ch'ing-li ssu*), one per Province (*sheng*). P6. (3) CH'ING: unofficial, archaic reference to the **Ministry of Revenue** (*hu-pu*).

4001   *mín-shēng* 民生

MING–CH'ING: **Civilian Student,** designation of "elegant scholars" (*chün-hsiu*, q.v.) in the general population who, without passing any examination in the civil service recruitment examination sequence, were admitted to the National University (*t'ai-hsüeh*) maintained by the Directorate of Education (*kuo-tzu chien*) in the status of Student by Purchase Fourth Class (*chien-sheng* without prefix). Also see *li-chien, kung-sheng, kuan-sheng, en-sheng*.

4002   *mín-ts'áo* 民曹

HAN–N-S DIV: **Section for the People,** one of 4 then 5 then 6 top-echelon units headed by Imperial Secretaries (*shang-shu*), in the aggregate called the Imperial Secretariat (*shang-shu t'ai*); originally established in the time of Emperor Wu (r. 141–87 B.C.) to handle governmental communications from low-ranking officials and commoners; in Later Han concurrently assigned to provision the palace with fine foodstuffs as well as to supervise palace construction work, salterns, parks, and gardens. Imperial Secretaries were commonly assisted by officials with such designations as *lang* (Court Gentleman), *shih-lang* (Attendant Gentleman), and *lang-chung* (Gentleman of the Interior). After Han the name *min-ts'ao* was used sporadically, alternating with *tu-chih, min-pu*, and other names, for a unit of the gradually developing Department of State Affairs (*shang-shu sheng*) that can be considered the antecedent of the Sui–Ch'ing Ministry of Revenue (*hu-pu*, q.v.); headed by a *shang-shu* who was gradually evolving from an Imperial Secretary to a Director to a Minister. Also see *tso-min, yu-min, ssu ts'ao, wu ts'ao, liu ts'ao*. HB: *bureau of the common people*. P6.

4003   *mín-t'ún* 民屯

Civilian State Farm, from Han or soon thereafter the designation of a settlement of civilian farmers on state-owned land, to populate and bring under cultivation a wilderness or in frontier areas to help provide food supplies for frontier military units; sometimes created to transfer landless families from overpopulated areas to relatively underpopulated and underdeveloped areas. See *t'un-t'ien, chün-t'un*.

4004   *mìng* 命

CHOU: **Honor,** any of the Nine Honors (*chiu ming*, q.v.) by which the Chou aristocracy including Feudal Lords (*chu-*

hou) was ranked, ranging from the 9th Honor at the top to the first Honor at the bottom of the governmental hierarchy.

4005   *míng-ān* 明安

CH'ING: new transliteration of a Jurchen-Manchu title used by the Chinese in Chin times in the sense **Battalion** or **Battalion Commander** (*meng-an*, q.v.). P17.

4006   *míng-chí àn* 名籍案

SUNG: **Nominations Section,** one each serving the Ministry of Personnel's (*li-pu*) Civil Appointments Process (*tso-hsüan*) and Military Appointments Process (*yu-hsüan*); staffing and precise functions not clear. Also see *hsüan*. SP: *service des registres nominatifs*.

4007   *míng-chīng* 明經

Classicist. (1) HAN, MING: one of several categories in which local authorities were called on to submit nominees to be considered for official appointments; in Ming an archaic revival used only in the founder's reign. (2) T'ANG–SUNG: one of several degrees awarded to men nominated by local authorities to participate in the regular civil service recruitment examination system (see *k'o-chü*), who passed an examination with the same name; in T'ang a highly popular, very competitive examination, 2nd among the regular examinations after only the Presented Scholar (*chin-shih*) examination in prestige; after early Sung lost esteem and became one of many "other examinations" (*chu-k'o*) conferring status far less prestigious than the *chin-shih* degree, now better rendered Metropolitan Graduate, which after Sung was the only significant examination degree awarded. In Sung *ming-ching* was in a group of Classics degrees of generally equal status, such as the *chiu ching* (Graduate in the Nine Classics) and the *wu ching* (Graduate in the Five Classics); all emphasized rote memorization, whereas the *chin-shih* examination after the 1060s was much broader, emphasizing more mental and literary creativity, after having originated as an examination in literary composition in T'ang times. (3) CH'ING: an unofficial, archaic reference to one group of students in the National University (*t'ai-hsüeh*), who had formal status as Tribute Students (*kung-sheng*).

4008   *mìng-ch'īng* 命卿

HAN: **District Minister,** generic reference to principal officials on the staffs of District Magistrates (*hsien-ling, hsien-chang*), specifically those titled Aide (*ch'eng*) and Defender (*wei*); literal meaning and derivation not clear, but probably related to the Chou rank system called the Nine Honors (*chiu ming*) and the rank category *ch'ing* (Minister).

4009   *míng-fǎ* 明法

T'ANG–SUNG: **Law Examination** or **Law Graduate,** designation of one type of civil service recruitment examination and of those who passed it to gain entry to the officialdom; in T'ang one of 5 examinations given regularly; in early Sung lost esteem and became one of many "other examinations" (*chu-k'o*) of far less prestige than the *chin-shih* (Presented Scholar, Metropolitan Graduate) examination and degree. The examination was narrowly focused on the dynastic law code and normally did not attract many good candidates. It faded out of use after the 1060s, when the *chin-shih* examination and degree became the standard gateway to a successful official career.

4010   *míng-fǎ yüàn* 明法掾

N-S DIV: **Law Clerk,** a specialist in judicial matters serving as a professional, non-official aide to an official with heavy judicial responsibilities, such as the Chamberlain for Law Enforcement (*t'ing-wei*); in N. Ch'i an official in the Court of Judicial Review (*ta-li ssu*). P22.

4011 *míng-fàn* 明範
N-S DIV (N. Ch'i): **Lady of Bright Models,** designation of one of 27 imperial wives collectively called Hereditary Consorts (*shih-fu*); rank =3b.

4012 *míng-fān* 名藩
T'ANG: lit., famous frontier region; from c. 750 an unofficial reference to a **Military Commissioner** (*chieh-tu shih*).

4013 *mìng-fū* 命夫 or 命婦
(1) CHOU: titles of nobility (*chüeh*); see under *nei ming-fu, wai ming-fu*. (2) SUNG (2nd form only): **Court Lady,** uncommon reference to a palace woman or a category of palace women; status and functions not clear. SP: *femme titrée*.

4014 *míng-fǔ* 明府
Lit., enlightened office, an unofficial form of direct address. (1) HAN: used in reference to a **Commandery Governor** (*chün t'ai-shou*). (2) T'ANG, MING–CH'ING: used in reference to a **District Magistrate** (*hsien-ling, chih-hsien*). See *ming-t'ing, shao-fu*.

4015 *míng-hào hòu* 名號侯
N-S DIV (San-kuo Wei): lit., a named Marquis (*hou*), i.e., one with a laudatory or other prefix appended to his title: **Grandee of the Third Order,** the 18th (3rd highest) of 20 titles of honorary nobility (*chüeh*) awarded to subjects for extraordinary military achievements. Cf. *lieh-hou, kuan-nei hou*. P65.

4016 *míng-hsìn* 明信
N-S DIV (N. Ch'i): **Lady of Bright Trustworthiness,** designation of one of 27 imperial wives collectively called Hereditary Consorts (*shih-fu*); rank =3b.

4017 *míng-piǎo láng* 名表郎
SUNG: **Director of the Rosters Bureau** (?) in the Ministry of Rites (*li-pu*); established c. 1080, with *lang* the equivalent of *lang-chung*, q.v.; probably supervised preparations for civil service recruitment examinations and posted rosters of examination passers.

4018 *míng-pù wèi* 明部尉
HAN: **Commandant of the Metropolitan Police, West and North,** 2, rank 400 bushels, responsible for police supervision over the western and northern quadrants of the Former Han dynastic capital, Ch'ang-an, a jurisdiction known in the aggregate as the Right Sector (*yu-pu*); from 91 B.C. subordinate to the Metropolitan Commandant (*ssu-li hsiao-wei*); in Later Han separately retitled Commandant of the Metropolitan Police, West Sector (*hsi-pu wei*) and Commandant of the Metropolitan Police, North Sector (*pei-pu wei*). P20.

4019 *míng-shìh* 冥氏
CHOU: **Nighttime Trapper,** 2 ranked as Junior Servicemen (*hsia-shih*), members of the Ministry of Justice (*ch'iu-kuan*) responsible for setting nets and snares in which to catch night-prowling wild animals. CL: *officier de l'obscurité*.

4020 *míng-shú* 明淑
N-S DIV (N. Ch'i): **Lady of Clear Purity,** designation of one of 27 imperial wives collectively called Hereditary Consorts (*shih-fu*); rank =3b.

4021 *míng-t'áng* 明堂
Hall of Enlightened Rule: from high antiquity a special building in or near the ruler's palace, serving as a symbol of dynastic legitimacy and sovereignty; its prescribed dimensions and uses are variably described in ancient texts.

In Chou times reportedly used as an audience hall for the reception of Feudal Lords (*chu-hou*) and for other ritual purposes. Later an archaic reference to the Imperial Ancestral Temple (*t'ai-miao*), sometimes even to the National University (*t'ai-hsüeh*). Sometimes rituals that according to legend were appropriate for the Hall of Enlightened Rule, long after such a structure had actually existed, were carried out on a concurrent-duty basis by officials of the Office of the National Altars (*chiao-she chü, chiao-she shu*) or the Court of Imperial Sacrifices (*t'ai-ch'ang ssu*). In Han and the S. Dynasties there was a special staff for the Hall, headed by a Director (*ling*) and an Aide (*ch'eng*) or sometimes by a *ch'eng* alone as Director, rank 200 bushels. In Han the Hall and its staff were under the jurisdiction of the Grand Astrologer (*t'ai-shih ling*). HB: bright hall. P35.

4022 *míng-té kūng-chiēn* 明德宮監
T'ANG: **Directorate of the Palace of Bright Virtue,** in charge of maintaining the buildings and grounds of one of several auxiliary palaces in the Eastern Capital (*tung-tu*), modern Loyang, under supervision of the Court of the Imperial Granaries (*ssu-nung ssu*); headed by a Director (*chien*), rank 6b2. In 657 retitled Directorate of Parks in the Eastern Capital, Southern Quadrant (*tung-tu yüan nan-mien chien*). See *ssu-mien chien*. RR: *direction du palais de la vertu éclatante*. P40.

4023 *míng-t'íng* 明廷
Lit., enlightenment pavilion: from Han on, a common unofficial reference to a **District Magistrate** (*hsien-ling, hsien-chang, chih-hsien*), especially used as a form of direct address; may be encountered in some eras in reference to a Commandery Governor (*chün t'ai-shou*) or a Prefect (*chih-fu*). See *ming-fu*.

4024 *míng-tsàn* 鳴贊
MING–CH'ING: **Herald,** official responsible for making announcements at ceremonial functions; in Ming, 4 each in the Court of State Ceremonial (*hung-lu ssu*) and in the Nanking Court of State Ceremonial, rank 9b, also 2 in the early Ming Palace Ceremonial Office (*tien-t'ing i-li ssu*), 9a; in Ch'ing, 16 then 14 Manchu appointees, 8 then 2 Chinese appointees, all 9b, in the Court of State Ceremonial. P33, 49.

4025 *míng-t'ūng păng* 明通榜
CH'ING: **Roster of Lesser Scholastics,** a supplementary list (*wai-pang*) posted after Metropolitan Examinations (*hui-shih*) in the civil service recruitment examination sequence, naming men who, though not having passed the examination, were considered well educated; they were commonly assigned to their home Provinces as Instructors or Instructors Second-class (see *chiao-yü, hsüeh-cheng*) in local Confucian Schools (*ju-hsüeh*); the practice began in 1737 and eventually was extended so that Provinces could nominate Provincial Graduates (*chü-jen*) for such employment, with quotas based on the size and population density of the Provinces, from 40 down to 20 Lesser Scholastics (*ming-t'ung*).

4026 *míng-tzū chiàng* 明資匠
T'ANG: **Specially Gifted Artisan,** 260 permanently authorized for the Directorate of the Palace Buildings (*chiang-tso chien*); apparently non-official personnel requisitioned for state service from the civilian population. RR: *artisan d'un talent remarquable*.

4027 *mo*
Also see under *mai*.

4028 *mo* 幕
See under the romanization *mu*.

4029 *mò-fŭ* 莫府
Variant of *mu-fu* (**Private Secretariat**).

4030 *mó-k'àn* 磨勘
Lit., to grind up and examine, hence to examine thoroughly. (1) SUNG: **evaluation for reassignment,** the designation of a procedure whereby, normally at 3-year intervals, the Bureau of Personnel Evaluation (*shen-kuan yüan*) or, after the 1070s, the Ministry of Personnel (*li-pu*) together with Censors (*yü-shih*) and other specially assigned officials reviewed the service records of active civil officials on duty outside the capital and recommended promotions, terminations, reappointments, etc.; officials were entitled to request such evaluations of themselves at any time. (2) SUNG: **judicial review,** a procedure whereby the Ministry of Justice (*hsing-pu*) and the Court of Judicial Review (*ta-li ssu*) regularly screened reports of judicial cases from units of territorial administration so that inappropriate sentences might be reconsidered and others forwarded to the throne for ultimate confirmation. (3) SUNG: **reconfirmation,** a procedure whereby examination papers generated at regional and metropolitan examinations in the civil service recruitment examination sequence were sent to the Hanlin Academy (*han-lin yüan*) for review and verification. See *tu mo-k'an ssu*. P5, 22.

4031 *mó-k'àn àn* 磨勘案
SUNG: **Records Reviewing Section:** one in the Criminal Administration Bureau (*tu-kuan*) of the Ministry of Justice (*hsing-pu*), staffed with subofficial functionaries whose precise functions are not clear; another under the Left Bureau (*tso-t'ing*) of the Court of Judicial Review (*ta-li ssu*), also staffed with unranked subofficials, charged with monitoring personnel changes made by the Ministry of Personnel (*li-pu*). SP: *service de révision*. P5, 22.

4032 *mó-k'àn ch'āi-ch'iĕn yüàn* 磨勘差遣院
SUNG: **Bureau of Minor Commissions,** created in 991 or 992 by merging the Bureau of Commissions (*ch'ai-ch'ien yüan*) and the Bureau of Capital and Court Officials (*mo-k'an ching-ch'ao kuan yüan*); in 993 retitled Bureau of Personnel Evaluation (*shen-kuan yüan*). Originally an agency with considerable autonomy, staffed with officials of the regular central administration on ad hoc duty assignments to consider relatively low-ranking officials for commissions or duty assignments (*ch'ai-ch'ien*) outside the capital and to evaluate and reassign such personnel on completion of their commissions. Sometimes used as a variant reference to the *k'ao-k'o yüan* (Bureau of Personnel Assignments). SP: *cour d'examen des mérites*. P5.

4033 *mó-k'àn chīng-ch'áo kuān yüan* 磨勘京朝官院
SUNG: **Bureau of Capital and Court Officials,** from 991 or 992 a relatively autonomous agency staffed with officials of the central administration on ad hoc duty assignments to evaluate merit ratings of all but the very highest officials and recommend that they be retained in rank, promoted, demoted, or dismissed from service. Promptly merged with the Bureau of Commissions (*ch'ai-ch'ien yüan*) into a united agency called Bureau of Minor Commissions (*mo-k'an ch'ai-ch'ien yüan*), which in 993 was retitled Bureau of Personnel Evaluation (*shen-kuan yüan*). Also see *ching-kuan* (Capital Official) and *ch'ao-kuan* (Court Official). SP: *cour de révision ou de contrôle des fonctionnaires de la cour et de la capitale*. P5.

4034 *mó-k'àn chū-lù t'í-tiĕn hsíng-yü ssū* 磨勘諸路提點刑獄司
SUNG: **Bureau for Judicial Commissioners,** a relatively autonomous agency under the jurisdiction of the combined Secretariat-Chancellery (*chung-shu men-hsia sheng*) established in 1036 to evaluate the performances of Judicial Commissioners (*t'i-tien hsing-yü kung-shih*) and recommend their retention in office, promotion, demotion, or dismissal from the service; staffed by officials of the central administration on ad hoc duty assignments; in 1049 authorized in addition to evaluate Fiscal Commissioners (*chuan-yün shih*) and Fiscal Vice Commissioners (*chuan-yün fu-shih*), and renamed Circuit Intendants Evaluation Bureau (*chuan-yün shih-fu t'i-tien hsing-yü k'o-chi yüan*); in the 1080s this disappeared, its functions being taken over by the Ministry of Personnel (*li-pu*). SP: *bureau de la révision des intendants judiciaires.*

4035 *mó-k'àn ssū* 磨勘司
(1) SUNG: **Mail and Prison Office,** in S. Sung a lowly unit in Lin-an Prefecture (modern Hangchow), the dynastic capital, possibly also found in some other units of territorial administration; apparently oversaw the receipt and issuance of government mail and in addition oversaw the prefectural prison; headed by a Chief Prison Custodian (*chu ya-kuan*), a Principal Mail Handler (*cheng k'ai-ch'ai kuan*), and an Associate Mail Handler (*fu k'ai-ch'ai kuan*), all unranked subofficials who supervised small numbers of Mail Handlers (*k'ai-ch'ai kuan*) and Prison Custodians (*ya-kuan, ya-ssu kuan*). See *k'ai-ch'ai an*. SP: *bureau de révision ou de contrôle*. P32. (2) MING: **Office of Judicial Review,** in 1370 superseded the traditional Court of Judicial Review (*ta-li ssu*) in the central administration as a reviewing agency for judicial cases arising throughout the empire; headed by a Director (*ling*), 2 from 1374, rank not clear; supervised 4 constituent Sections (*k'o*), presumably differentiated by functions; abolished in 1377, re-established in 1381, again abolished in 1387, its functions carried on by an already (1381) re-established Court of Judicial Review. P22.

4036 *mò-lì* 貉隸
CHOU: **Northeastern War Prisoner,** 120 apparently authorized for service as patrol guards, palace guards, and handlers of captured wild animals, with which the Mo tribesmen were thought able to converse; under the control of the Ministry of Justice (*ch'iu-kuan*) but normally assigned to the supervision of the Animal Tamer (*fu-pu shih*) in the Ministry of War (*hsia-kuan*). See *tsui-li*. CL: *condamné de Nord-Est.*

4037 *mò-pān* 末班
Rear Ranks: from early post-Han times if not earlier, a collective reference to officials of unspecified but very low rank, who in court audience formed the unprestigious rear ranks of officials in attendance.

4038 *mò-ts'áo* 墨曹
T'ANG–CH'ING: lit., the tattooing section: unofficial reference to the **Ministry of Justice** (*hsing-pu*), deriving from the traditional practice of tattooing criminals.

4039 *móu-k'ò* 謀克
CHIN: **Company,** also **Company Commander,** a Chinese transliteration of a Jurchen title that the Chinese equated with their traditional title *po-hu*, q.v.: the hereditary, aristocratic leader of a tribal military unit of 100 or more households, many of which settled in North China after the Jurchen conquest as military garrisons independent of the normal administrative hierarchy. In theory, 10 such Companies constituted a Battalion (*ch'ien-hu*, from Jurchen *meng-an*). Also see *po-chin, po-chi-lieh.*

4040 *mù* 幕
N-S DIV: lit., tent, living quarters: **Headquarters,** quasi-

official or unofficial designation of the principal office or quarters of certain agencies or officials; e.g., see *chieh-tu mu* (Supply Commission), *hsien-ssu mu* (Censorate), *chou-mu* (Regional Headquarters).

4041 *mù* 牧

Lit., shepherd, pastor. (1) CHOU: **Regional Representative,** one of 9 Unifying Agents (*ou* or *liang*) appointed in the Nine Regions (*chiu chou*) into which the kingdom was divided, as agents of the Minister of State (*chung-tsai*) overseeing geographical clusters of feudal states; special overseer of land assignments (?). CL: *pasteur.* (2) HAN–N-S DIV: **Regional Governor** of one of the natural areas called Regions (*chou*) as a coordinator and supervisor representing the central government; originated in 7 B.C. with rank status of 2,000 bushels, superseding less prestigious Regional Inspectors (*tz'u-shih*); thereafter the two titles alternated irregularly. In Later Han Regional Governors eventually became almost autonomous regional warlords. By the end of the era of N-S Division the title was displaced by *tz'u-shih.* HB: shepherd. P50, 52, 53. (3) SUI–SUNG: **Metropolitan Governor** of a Region (*chou*) in Sui or, later, a Superior Prefecture (*fu*), in all cases the site of a dynastic capital, principal or auxiliary; rank 2b, but often a sinecure for a member of the imperial family, in which case an Administrator (*yin*), nominally his assistant, actually bore his responsibilities. See *tsung-kuan.* RR+SP: *gouverneur.* P32, 49. (4) SUNG: **Prefectural Governor,** used in early Sung for court dignitaries delegated to administer ordinary Prefectures (*chou*); after the early Sung decades displaced by the term Prefect (*tz'u-shih,* then *chih-chou*). SP: *préfet.* (5) SUNG–CH'ING: commonly encountered as an archaic, unofficial reference to a **Prefect** (*chih-fu*) or a comparable regional administrator. (6) CH'ING: **Department Magistrate** of an Independent Department (*chih-li chou*), rank 5a. P53.

4042 *mù-chǎng* 牧長

N-S DIV–T'ANG, CH'ING: **Pasturage Director,** in charge of a horse or cattle herd under supervision of the Chamberlain for the Imperial Stud (*t'ai-p'u ch'ing*) or, from Sui on, the Court of the Imperial Stud (*t'ai-p'u ssu*); through T'ang, found principally on the staffs of Princes with establishments separated from the dynastic capital; in Ch'ing 5 in the Palace Stud (*shang-ssu yüan*), 4 in the establishment of each Imperial Prince (*ch'in-wang*), 3 in the establishment of each Commandery Prince (*chün-wang*), and others in provincial-level agencies subordinate to the Palace Stud. Rank 9b2 in T'ang, 8b in Ch'ing. See *mu-chien, chiu-chang.* RR: *chef d'élevage.* BH: inspector of droves. P31, 39, 69.

4043 *mù-ch'ǎng* 木場

YÜAN: **Lumberyard,** established in 1263 as one of many service agencies in the dynastic capital under the Grand Capital Regency (Ta-tu *liu-shou ssu*), headed by a Superintendent (*t'i-ling*) and a Commissioner-in-chief (*ta-shih*), ranks not clear. In 1267 separate agencies with identical names were established for the South (*nan mu-ch'ang*) and for the East (*tung mu-ch'ang*); they were consolidated into a single Lumberyard for the South and East (*nan-tung mu-ch'ang*) in 1280; the locations of these supplementary agencies are not clear, but all the various Lumberyards were responsible for providing lumber required for the building and maintenance of the imperial palace. P15.

4044 *mù-ch'ǎng* 牧場

Pasturage, a descriptive term used throughout history in reference to areas set aside for the rearing of state horse

and cattle herds. In Ch'ing concentrated primarily in Mongolia, each headed by a Supervisor-in-chief (*tsung-kuan*), under the ultimate authority of the Court of the Imperial Stud (*t'ai-p'u ssu*). See *liang i* (Two Pasturelands). P31.

4045 *mù-chèng* 牧正

MING: **Pasturage Director,** one, rank 8a, on the staff of each Princely Establishment (*wang-fu*). See *mu-chang.* P69.

4046 *mù-chiēn* 牧監

SUI–SUNG, MING: **Directorate of Horse Pasturages,** also the title of its head, the **Pasturage Director:** regional agencies scattered across North China to supervise local horse pasturages under jurisdiction of the Court of the Imperial Stud (*t'ai-p'u ssu*), sometimes through its constituent Office of Herds (*tien-mu shu*), or in Ming under the direct control of Pasturage Offices (*yüan-ma ssu*) responsible to the Ministry of War (*ping-pu*); normally prefixed with place-names. In T'ang the Directorates were classified into 3 grades: Large (*shang*) with 5,000 or more horses, Ordinary (*chung*) with from 3,000 to 5,000 horses, and Small (*hsia*) with fewer than 3,000 horses; the Directors varied in rank accordingly: 5b2, 6a2, 6b2. In Ming the Directors had rank 9a. RR+SP: *direction des élevages.* P31.

4047 *mù-chíh kuān* 幕職官

SUNG: lit., one functioning behind a screen, i.e., behind the scenes: **Ancillary,** categorical reference to a group of officials within the major category called Selectmen (*hsüan-jen*) found in the central government serving, e.g., as Case Reviewers (*p'ing-shih*) in the Court of Judicial Review (*ta-li ssu*) and Editors (*chiao-shu lang*) in such agencies as the Palace Library (*pi-shu sheng*), both posts rank 8b; and in 2nd-echelon posts in Prefectures (*chou*), e.g., Judges (*t'ui-kuan*) and Administrative Assistants (*p'an-kuan*), also normally 8b; sometimes appointed District Magistrates (*chih-hsien*). SP: *fonctionnaire-assistant.* P52.

4048 *mù-ch'īn chái* 睦親宅

SUNG: abbreviation of *kuang-ch'in mu-ch'in chai* (**Hostel for Imperial Clansmen**); also see *ta tsung-cheng ssu* (Office of Imperial Clan Affairs). SP: *maison de l'harmonie de la famille royale.*

4049 *mù-ch'īn kuǎng-ch'īn chái* 睦親廣親宅

SUNG: variant of *kuang-ch'in mu-ch'in chai* (**Hostel for Imperial Clansmen**); also see *ta tsung-cheng ssu* (Office of Imperial Clan Affairs). SP: *maison de l'harmonie et de la propagation de la famille royale.*

4050 *mù-chǘ* 木局

N-S DIV (Liang): **Woodworking Service,** one of 2 Craft Workshops (*tso-t'ang*) under the Chamberlain for the Palace Revenues (*shao-fu*); authorized a Director (*ling*) but actually headed by a nominal Assistant Director (*ch'eng*), rank 3. P14.

4051 *mù-ch'ǘn* 牧羣

YÜAN: **Horse Herd** under at least nominal jurisdiction of the Court of the Imperial Stud (*t'ai-p'u ssu*) in the central government; organized in military fashion, headed by a Battalion Commander (*ch'ien-hu*) or a Company Commander (*po-hu*), rank 5a or 5b. P31.

4052 *mù-fǔ* 幕府

Lit., tent office, i.e., field office, originally denoting the headquarters of a military leader on campaign: **Private Secretariat,** from the Three Kingdoms era on, unofficial designation of subordinate officials attached to a military commander, a Regional Inspector (*chou tz'u-shih*), or a T'ang Military Commissioner (*chieh-tu shih*); in Sung became a common generic designation of the official subordinates of a Prefect (*chih-chou*). In late Ming and Ch'ing, designated the staff of any regional or local dignitary from provincial-level Grand Coordinators or Governors (both *hsün-fu*) and multi-Province Supreme Commanders or Governors-general (both *tsung-tu*) on down, especially in Ch'ing, to the District (*hsien*) level. Such staff members had no official status but were hired professional specialists who served as advisers or other kinds of helpers recruited and paid by the regional or local dignitaries personally. Known collectively as Private Secretaries (*mu-yu*), they commonly included such specialists as Legal Secretaries (*hsing-ming*), Fiscal Secretaries (*cheng-pi*), and personal servants (*ch'ang-sui*). Also see *k'ai-fu, lien-mu, pin-liao*. P50.

4053 *mǔ-hòu* 母后
From Han on, an unofficial reference to the principal wife of an Emperor: **Empress** (*huang-hou*).

4054 *mù-jén* 幕人
CHOU: **Director of Draperies,** 2 ranked as Junior Servicemen (*hsia-shih*), members of the Ministry of State (*t'ien-kuan*) responsible for maintaining and handling the silk curtains that secluded the ruler when he went out of his palace, when he received foreign dignitaries and Feudal Lords (*chu-hou*), and when he participated in important funerals and other ceremonies. Cf. *chang-tz'u* (Tent Handler). CL: *préposé au ciel de tente*.

4055 *mù-jén* 牧人
CHOU: **Breeder of Sacrificial Animals,** 6 ranked as Junior Servicemen (*hsia-shih*), members of the Ministry of Education (*ti-kuan*) responsible for maintaining a supply of animals suitable for the many ceremonial offerings made by the King and his court, in some cases delivering them to Fatteners of Sacrificial Animals (*ch'ung-jen*). Cf. *niu-jen* (Breeder of Sacrificial Cattle). CL: *pâtre*.

4056 *mù-kuān tū-wèi* 牧官都尉
N-S DIV (San-kuo Wei): **Commandant of Horse Pasturages,** number and rank not clear; apparently one in charge of all breeding and care of imperial horses in a defined territory under loose direction of the central government's Chamberlain for the Imperial Stud (*t'ai-p'u*). Apparent antecedents of *mu-chang* and *mu-chien*. P31.

4057 *mù-k'ūn* 穆昆
CHIN: Chinese transliteration of a Jurchen word meaning both **Tribe** and **Tribal Chief,** comparable to *mou-k'o* (Company, Company Commander); a force of 300 households united in peace and war.

4058 *mù-kūng* 木工
HAN: **Woodworker,** post created in 104 B.C. through retitling of Woodsmen of the Eastern Park (*tung-yüan chu-chang*); headed by a Director (*ling*) under the Chamberlain for the Palace Buildings (*chiang-tso ta-chiang*), in turn under the Chamberlain for Attendants (*kuang-lu-hsün*); specially responsible for making coffins for members of the imperial family and perhaps other dignitaries. HB: workmen in timber. P14.

4059 *mù-lán* 木蘭
CH'ING: Chinese transliteration of the Manchu word *muran*, an unofficial reference to the **Imperial Summer Resort** (*wei-ch'ang*) at Jehol city (modern Ch'eng-te) north of the Great Wall, where Emperors hunted and received distinguished visitors from China's peripheral areas, from Mongolia to Tibet.

4060 *mù-lǐng* 牧領
N-S DIV (Yen): variant of *mu* (**Regional Governor**).

4061 *mù-mǎ chiēn* 牧馬監
SUNG: variant of *mu-chien* (**Directorate of Horse Pasturages**).

4062 *mù-mǎ fáng* 牧馬房
SUNG: **Horse Pasturage Section** under the Bureau of Military Affairs (*shu-mi yüan*), presumably responsible for maintaining appropriate liaison between the Bureau and the Directorates of Horse Pasturages (*mu-chien*) directed by the ·Court of the Imperial Stud (*t'ai-p'u ssu*). Apparently in c. 1074 disappeared in the creation of the Bureau's Twelve Sections (*shih-erh fang*, q.v.). Staffing not clear. Cf. *chih-ma fang* (Horse Management Section).

4063 *mù-pīng* 募兵
Mercenary Recruit: from Sui on a general reference to irregular soldiers recruited and paid as auxiliaries to assist Regular Troops (*kuan-ping*) in times of military crises. See *chao-mu*.

4064 *mù-pó* 牧伯
Combined abbreviation of *chou-mu* (Regional Governor) and *fang-po* (Regional Earl), titles attributed to high antiquity: **Regional Dignitary,** used as an unofficial reference to such officials as the Han–Sui Regional Inspector (*tz'u-shih*), the T'ang–Sung Prefect (also *tz'u-shih*), and the Ming–Ch'ing Provincial Administration Commissioner (*pu-cheng shih*). P50.

4065 *mù-shìh* 幕士
T'ANG–SUNG: **Tapestry Weaver,** unranked, many probably hereditary professional artisans, employed in the Accommodations Service (*shang-she chü*) of the Palace Administration (*tien-chung sheng*) and the Tents Office (*shou-kung shu*) of the T'ang Court of the Imperial Regalia (*wei-wei ssu*); manufactured tapestries for use in the palace and ornamented cloth for various ceremonial uses. RR+SP: *tapissier*. P38.

4066 *mù-shīh* 牧師
CHOU: **Horse Trainer,** 4 ranked as Junior Servicemen (*hsia-shih*), members of the Ministry of War (*hsia-kuan*) responsible for overseeing horse training in the royal pasturages. CL: *chef de pacage*.

4067 *mù-shīh yüàn* 牧師苑
HAN: **Imperial Horse Pasturage,** 36 locations along the northern frontier, each with a Director (*ling*) and 3 Assistant Directors (*ch'eng*); presumably subordinate to the Chamberlain for the Imperial Stud (*t'ai-p'u*). Early sources indicate a total horse count in the Pasturages of 300,000. HB: master herdsman's pasture.

4068 *mù-sù yüàn* 苜蓿苑
HAN: **Clover Pasturage,** generic reference to horse pasturages under the Director of the Inner Compound Stable (*wei-yang chiu*), on the staff of the Chamberlain for the Imperial Stud (*t'ai-p'u*). HB: clover pasture. P31.

4069 *mù tà-fū* 幕大夫
CHOU: **Grand Master of Cemeteries,** 2 ranked as Junior Grand Masters (*hsia ta-fu*), members of the Ministry of Rites (*ch'un-kuan*) responsible for establishing and managing cemeteries serving commoners, including determining the proper positions and proportions of graves; oversaw agents stationed in all such cemeteries. Cf. *chung-jen* (Grave Maker), *chih-sang* (Funeral Director). CL: *préfet des tombes*.

4070   *mù-t'iēn* 木天
Lit., a heaven made of wood. (1) SUNG: unofficial reference to the **Imperial Archives** (*pi-ko*), a building with a very high ceiling supported by great arched beams. (2) SUNG–CH'ING: unofficial reference to the **Hanlin Academy** (*han-lin yüan*).

4071   *mù-t'ó* 牧橐
HAN: **Camel Herd,** a pasturage agency headed by a Director (*ling*) on the staff of at least one Imperial Horse Pasturage (*mu-shih yüan*); location not clear. HB: camel herdsmen.

4072   *mù-ts'āng* 木倉
(1) **Lumberyard,** general descriptive reference to storage buildings or areas where wood supplies were kept. (2) CH'ING: **Central Lumberyard,** a wood storage area near the imperial palace in Peking, to which provincial authorities annually delivered, through intermediary Imperial Lumber Depots (*huang mu-ch'ang*) at T'ung-chou and Chang-chia-wan on the Grand Canal, wood to be used in the construction, repair, and maintenance of the palace and central government buildings, and possibly as firewood for the palace and for officials on duty in Peking; headed by one Chinese and one Manchu Superintendent (*chien-tu*), members of the Ministry of Works (*kung-pu*) on special 2-year duty assignments. BH: fire-wood store. P14.

4073   *mù-wèi* 牧尉
T'ANG: **Assistant Director of the Cattle Pasturage;** see under *mu-chang*. RR: *chef des employés d'élevage.* P31.

4074   *mù-yăng chiēn* 牧養監
SUNG: **Veterinarian Directorate,** 2 units under the Court of the Imperial Stud (*t'ai-p'u ssu*) called First and Second Directorates (*shang-chien, hsia-chien*); staffing and ranks not clear, but *mu-yang chien* may have served as designation of the head (**Director of Veterinarians**) as well as of the agency; responsible for treating sick horses in the imperial herds. SP: *direction pour soigner les chevaux malades.*

4075   *mù-yŭ* 幕友
MING–CH'ING: **Private Secretary,** generic reference to non-official specialists hired to serve in the Private Secretariats (*mu-fu*) of provincial-level Grand Coordinators or Governors (both *hsün-fu*), multi-Province Supreme Commanders or Governors-general (both *tsung-tu*), and especially in Ch'ing on down the hierarchy of territorial administrators to District Magistrates (*chih-hsien*). The most common and influential Private Secretaries were Legal Secretaries (*hsing-ming*) and Fiscal Secretaries (*cheng-pi*).

4076   *mù-yŭ* 牧圉
T'ANG: unofficial reference to a **Commissioner of Herds** (*ch'ün-mu shih*).

4077   *nà-kùng* 納貢
MING: **Student by Contribution,** categorical designation of students admitted to the National University (*t'ai-hsüeh*) because of their monetary contributions to the government; essentially identical to Student by Purchase (*li-chien*) but with somewhat greater esteem. Reasons for the differentiation of these 2 statuses are not clear. Also see *chüan-kung.*

4078   *nà-pō* 捺鉢
LIAO: Chinese transliteration of a Khitan word meaning **seasonal camp;** refers to various sites to which the Emperor and his entourage moved in a regular, seasonal rotation.

4079   *nà-yén* 納言
Lit., to make statements (to the ruler): **Adviser.** (1) HAN: designation of one of many types of attendants collectively known as Court Gentlemen (*lang*), perhaps one through whom memorials from the officialdom were submitted to the throne. (2) N-S DIV–T'ANG: head of the evolving Chancellery (*men-hsia sheng*), but in 620 terminated and replaced by the title *shih-chung* (Director); revived from 684 to 705. RR: *celui qui expose son opinion.* P2, 3. (3) CH'ING: unofficial reference to the head of the Office of Transmission (*t'ung-cheng ssu*), entitled Transmission Commissioner (*t'ung-cheng shih*). Also see *ta na-yen.*

4080   *nà-yén lìng* 納言令
N-S DIV (Yen): **Adviser-Director,** apparently a variant of *na-yen* (**Adviser**).

4081   *nán* 南
On any encounter, see entry under the following character(s).

4082   *nán* 男
Baron, a title of nobility (*chüeh*). (1) CHOU: nominally the lowest of 5 titles of hereditary nobility conferred by the King on Feudal Lords (*chu-hou*), in declining order of prestige: Duke (*kung*), Marquis (*hou*), Earl (*po*), Viscount (*tzu*), and Baron. Cf. *nei-ming nan, wai-ming nan.* (2) N-S DIV–SUNG: one of a varying number of noble titles, always low in the hierarchy; most commonly with prefixes such as *k'ai-kuo nan* (Dynasty-founding Baron) or *k'ai-kuo hsien-nan* (Dynasty-founding District Baron). (3) CHIN–YÜAN: occurs only in the form District Baron (*hsien-nan*, q.v.). (4) MING: conferred only in the founding reign, after which both Viscount and Baron were discontinued. (5) CH'ING: 5th highest of 9 grades of nobility, subdivided into 3 degrees (*teng*): Baron First Class (*i-teng nan*), Baron Second Class (*erh-teng nan*), Baron Third Class (*san-teng nan*), inheritable for 8 to 11 generations. P65.

4083   *nán* 難
CH'ING: difficult, a category used in defining the importance of units of territorial administration. See *ch'ung-fan-p'i-nan.*

4084   *nán-ān k'ù* 南鞍庫
CH'ING: **Southern Storehouse,** a unit of the Court of Imperial Armaments (*wu-pei yüan*) responsible for maintaining fur trappings required by the Emperor and his entourage. Cf. *pei-an k'u.*

4085   *nán-chái* 南宅
SUNG: **Southern Residence Hall,** one of 2 units into which the School for the Imperial Family (*tsung-hsüeh*) was divided. See *nan-pei chai.*

4086   *nán-chāi* 南齋
CH'ING: variant designation of the Emperor's **Southern Study** (*nan shu-fang*).

4087   *nán-ch'éng* 南丞
SUNG: abbreviated reference to the **Assistant Director of Southern Outer Waterways** (*nan-wai tu-shui ch'eng*) in the Directorate of Waterways (*tu-shui chien*); stationed at Shang-ch'iu, modern Honan, to supervise waterways maintenance in the South.

4088   *nán-chiāo chì-ch'ì k'ù* 南郊祭器庫
SUNG: **Utensil Storehouse for the Southern Suburban Sacrifices** that were conducted annually at the Altar of Heaven (*t'ien-t'an*) south of the dynastic capital; subordinate to the Directorate for Imperial Manufactories (*shao-fu*

chien). Unless this was a manufacturing workshop, the difference between it and the Utensil Storehouse for the Southern Suburban and the Imperial Ancestral Temple Sacrifices (*nan-chiao t'ai-miao chi-ch'i k'u*) is not clear. Cf. *chiao-she chü*. SP: *magasin des objets de sacrifice de la banlieue du sud.*

4089 *nán-chiāo shíh-wù k'ù* 南郊什物庫
SUNG: **Miscellaneous Storehouse for the Southern Suburban Sacrifices** that were conducted annually at the Altar of Heaven (*t'ien-t'an*) south of the dynastic capital; subordinate to the Court of Imperial Sacrifices (*t'ai-ch'ang ssu*). SP: *magasin des objets divers de la banlieue du sud.*

4090 *nán-chiāo t'ài-miào chì-ch'ì k'ù*
南郊太廟祭器庫
SUNG: **Utensil Storehouse for the Southern Suburban and the Imperial Ancestral Temple Sacrifices,** subordinate to the Court of Imperial Sacrifices (*t'ai-ch'ang ssu*), perhaps through the intermediary Office of the National Altars (*chiao-she chü*). See *nan-chiao chi-ch'i k'u, t'ai-miao chi-ch'i fa-wu k'u, t'ai-miao ling.* SP: *magasin des vases de sacrifice aux temples des ancêtres impériaux dans la banlieue du sud.*

4091 *nán-chiēn* 南監
(1) SUI: **Directorate of the Southern Park,** one of 4 Directorates (*chien*) in charge of maintaining the buildings and grounds of imperial parks and gardens in the 4 quadrants of the dynastic capital under supervision of the Directorate-general of the Imperial Parks (*yüan tsung-chien*); headed by a Director (*chien*). See *hsi-chien, tung-chien, pei-chien.* P40. (2) CH'ING: variant reference to the **South Prison** (*nan-so*) maintained by the Ministry of Justice (*hsing-pu*). Also see *pei-chien.* P13.

4092 *nán chǔ-k'ò ts'áo* 南主客曹
HAN–N-S DIV: **Section for Southern Relations,** created early in Later Han when the Section for Receptions (*chu-k'o ts'ao,* q.v.) was divided into northern and southern agencies; part of the evolution of the Department of State Affairs (*shang-shu t'ai, shang-shu sheng*); sometimes a top-echelon agency in the evolving Department, sometimes a 2nd-level agency subordinate to an intermediate Ministry (*pu*), e.g., the Ministry of Personnel (*li-pu*). In collaboration with the Chamberlain for Dependencies (*ta hung-lu*), responsible for the reception of foreign envoys from beyond the southern frontier. Sometimes headed by a Minister (*shang-shu*), but most commonly by a Director (*lang*). Also see *pei chu-k'o ts'ao, tso chu-k'o, yu chu-k'o, nan-pu, pei-pu.* HB: southern bureau in charge of guests. P9.

4093 *nán-ch'uáng* 南牀
Lit., the southern couch: **Senior Censor:** from T'ang on, because of a customary seating arrangement at meals, an unofficial reference to the Censor-in-chief (*yü-shih ta-fu, tu yü-shih*) or other senior personnel in the Censorate (*yü-shih t'ai, tu ch'a-yüan*).

4094 *nán-chǖn* 南軍
HAN: **Southern Army,** a collective reference to units of military conscripts encamped in the capital cities of Commanderies (*chün*) and Marquisates (*hou-kuo*), from which they were detached on rotational duty in the dynastic capital, where they were primarily responsible for defense of the imperial palace; one contingent, made up of regular conscripts, was under the command of the Chamberlain for the Palace Garrison (*wei-wei*); a 2nd contingent, made up of Court Gentlemen (*lang*) and commanded by the Chamberlain for Attendants (*lang-chung ling, kuang-lu-hsün*),

served as a kind of elite personal bodyguard for the Emperor. In contrast to the Southern Army, there was a Northern Army (*pei-chün*) of career professional soldiers encamped outside the capital city under the command of the Chamberlain for the Imperial Insignia (*chung-wei, chih chin-wu*), which patrolled the city streets and was responsible for defense of the city. The Southern Army nomenclature and organization seems to have disappeared in the transition from Former to Later Han. Also see *nan-ya, pei-ya, chin-wei, ch'in-wei.* HB: southern army.

4095 *nán-fǔ* 南府
CH'ING: variant reference to the *sheng-p'ing shu* (**Court Theatrical Office**), a eunuch agency responsible for providing theatrical entertainments for the imperial family and for supervising the Court Theatrical School (*nan-fu kuan-hsüeh*), where young eunuchs were trained as performers; subordinate to the Office of Palace Ceremonial (*chang-i ssu*) of the Imperial Household Department (*nei-wu fu*). BH: court theatrical bureau.

4096 *nán-hó* 南河
CH'ING: unofficial reference to the **Director-general of the Grand Canal** (*ho-tao tsung-tu*) who, from a base at Huai-an, modern Kiangsu Province, supervised the maintenance and functioning of the southern segments of the Grand Canal; cf. *tung-ho, ts'ao-yün tsung-tu.* P59.

4097 *nán-hsiāng* 南廂
SUNG: **South Township,** one of 2 Townships (*hsiang*) into which the S. Sung capital city, modern Hangchow, was divided for sub-District (*hsien*) local administration; probably headed by a Magistrate (*ling*). Also see *pei-hsiang.* SP: *région du sud.*

4098 *nán-hsüǎn ts'áo* 南選曹
T'ANG: lit., southern selections section: unofficial reference to the **Bureau of Military Appointments** (*ping-pu, ping-pu ssu*), one of 4 top-echelon Bureaus (*ssu*) in the Ministry of War (*ping-pu*); also a reference to a **Director** (*lang-chung;* 2, rank 5b) of the Bureau.

4099 *nán-jén* 南人
Southerner, an identifying label rather than an official title throughout most of Chinese history, with varying implications. In Yüan times it was an official category of the population, designating all subjects who before the Mongol conquest had been subjects of S. Sung; the least privileged of the 4 major population groups in Yüan China (see *meng-ku, se-mu jen, han*). Often called *man-tzu* (Manzi by Marco Polo and others), the traditional Chinese general designation of all aboriginal tribespeople in South and Southwest China.

4100 *nán k'ò-kuǎn* 南客館
N-S DIV (Sung): **South Visitors Bureau,** created c. 420 by division of the office of the Chamberlain for Dependencies (*ta hung-lu*) into 2 Visitors Bureaus, one for the South and one for the North (*pèi k'o-kuan*); headed by a Director (*ling*); responsible for the reception of chiefs or envoys of the aboriginal tribes of South China and from Southeast Asian states. See *k'o-kuan.* P11.

4101 *nán-k'ù* 南庫
SUNG: **Southern Storehouse;** see under *nan-pei k'u* (Southern and Northern Storehouses).

4102 *nán-kūng* 南宮
Southern Palace. (1) HAN–T'ANG: quasiofficial reference to the developing Department of State Affairs (*shang-shu sheng*) and its senior officials. (2) T'ANG: unofficial

reference to the Ministry of Rites (*lĭ-pu*), especially those of its staff who were delegated to serve as editorial aides to the senior officials of the Department; see *nan-kung she-jen*, *nan-sheng*. (3) SUNG: unofficial reference to the Ministry of Rites, because of the tradition described under (2) above. (4) SUNG: unofficial reference to the Hostel for Imperial Clansmen (*kuang-ch'in mu-ch'in chai*) maintained by the Office of Imperial Clan Affairs (*ta tsung-cheng ssu*).

4103　*nán-kūng shè-jén* 南宮舍人
Drafters in the Southern Palace: from late Han on, an unofficial reference to officials of the Ministry of Rites (*lĭ-pu*) delegated to be editorial aides to senior officials of the Department of State Affairs (*shang-shu sheng*). Cf. *chung-shu she-jen* (Secretariat Drafter), *nan-sheng she-jen*.

4104　*nán-kūng tì-ī jén* 南宮第一人
SUNG: lit., number one man in the Southern Palace: **Principal Graduate** of the Metropolitan Examination (*hui-shih*) in the civil service recruitment examination sequence, i.e., the man whose name topped the pass list posted after the examination; apparently so referred to because the examination was managed by the Ministry of Rites (*lĭ-pu*), commonly called the Southern Palace. See *hui-yüan*, *chuang-yüan*.

4105　*nán-mán hsiào-wèi* 南蠻校尉
N-S DIV (Chin): **Commandant of Southern Aborigines**, the name of one group of aboriginal tribes in the South, the Man, being extended into a general designation of all aboriginal tribes in the South; actually in charge of Ching Region (*chou*), approximately modern Hunan and Hupei; rank and status in the military hierarchy not clear.

4106　*nán-mán shĭh-chě* 南蠻使者
SUI: **Commissioner for Southern Tributaries,** a member of the Court for Dependencies (*hung-lu ssu*) designated on an ad hoc basis to set up an office (*shu*) to supervise arrangements for the reception of chiefs or envoys of friendly aboriginal tribes of the South; c. 610 superseded the consolidated Hostel for Tributary Envoys (*ssu-fang kuan*). P11.

4107　*nán-mièn* 南面
LIAO: **Southern Administration,** designation of that part of the central government that administered the sedentary peoples of the Liao empire, notably the subjugated Chinese of northern Hopei and Shansi Provinces, in contrast to the Northern Administration (*pei-mien*), which administered the affairs of the Khitan tribes and their nomadic allies; organized generally in the T'ang fashion, with an upper echelon consisting of a Secretariat (*chung-shu sheng*), Chancellery (*men-hsia sheng*), Department of State Affairs (*shang-shu sheng*), Bureau of Military Affairs (*shu-mi yüan*), and Censorate (*yü-shih t'ai*). Cf. *nan-yüan* (Southern Establishment). P4.

4108　*nán-pān kuān* 南班官
SUNG: **Official of the South Rank,** generic reference to educational officials serving the imperial family, perhaps especially those of the School for the Imperial Family (*tsung-hsüeh*); reference is to the positions they took for court audiences. Cf. *pei-pan nei-p'in*. SP: *fonctionnaire de la classe du sud*, *fonctionnaire de la maison d'éducation de la famille royale*.

4109　*nán-pĕi chái* 南北宅
SUNG: **Southern and Northern Residence Halls,** the 2 units into which the School for the Imperial Family (*tsung-hsüeh*) was divided, each staffed with Instructors (*chiao-shou*). Details of their organization and their functional differences are not clear. SP: *maisons du sud et celles du nord*.

4110　*nán-pĕi k'ù* 南北庫
SUNG: **Southern and Northern Storehouses,** variant designations of the Western and Eastern Storehouses (*hsi-k'u, tung-k'u*), respectively, of the Left Vault (*tso-tsang*, q.v.; cf. *yu-tsang*), which stored general state revenues under supervision of the Court of the Imperial Treasury (*t'ai-fu ssu*). SP: *magasin du sud et celui du nord*. P7.

4111　*nán-pĕi shĕng-ts'āng* 南北省倉
SUNG: **Southern and Northern Granaries of the Department of State Affairs** (?), administered by the Court of the Imperial Granaries (*ssu-nung ssu*). SP: *greniers de la capitale du nord et celle du sud*.

4112　*nán-pĕi wài tū-shŭi ch'éng ssū* 南北外都水丞司
SUNG: **Offices of Assistant Directors for Southern and Northern Outer Waterways,** subordinate to 2 Commissioners of Outer Waterways (*wai tu-shui shih-che*) in the Directorate of Waterways (*tu-shui chien*), who were Assistant Directors (*ch'eng*) of the Directorate on special duty assignments to supervise maintenance of waterways south and north, respectively, of the dynastic capital (?). SP: *bureau des assistants de la direction extérieure du contrôle des eaux de la capitale du sud and celle du nord*.

4113　*nán-pĕi yüàn* 南北院
SUNG: **Southern and Northern Bureaus** in the Princely Establishments (*wang-fu*) of Imperial Princes (*ch'in-wang*); functions and staffing not clear. SP: *cour du sud et celle du nord*.

4114　*nán-pù* 南部
N-S DIV (N. Wei): **Ministry of Southern Relations,** an important agency in the Department of State Affairs (*shang-shu sheng*), headed by one or more Ministers (*shang-shu*); established in c. 400, abolished in 493; had 4 to 6 constituent Sections (*ts'ao*). Responsible for overseeing administration along the southern frontier and for the conduct of any military operations against the S. Dynasties. The staff included Supervising Secretaries (*chi-shih-chung*) delegated for concurrent service from the Department of Scholarly Counselors (*chi-shu sheng*). See *hsi-pu*, *pei-pu*.

4115　*nán-pù wèi* 南部尉
HAN: **Commandant of the Metropolitan Police, South Sector,** one, rank 400 bushels, a Later Han subordinate of the Metropolitan Commandant (*ssu-li hsiao-wei*) responsible for police supervision of the southern quadrant of the dynastic capital, Loyang. See *tso-pu* (Left Sector), *kuang-pu wei*. P20.

4116　*nán-shĕng* 南省
Lit., the southern department. (1) N-S DIV–T'ANG: unofficial reference to, or rarely the official designation of, the **Ministry of Rites** (*lĭ-pu*), whose personnel were often assigned as editorial aides to senior officials of the Department of State Affairs (*shang-shu sheng*; see #2 below) and consequently were called Drafters in the Southern Department (*nan-sheng she-jen*). (2) N-S DIV–SUNG: unofficial reference to the **Department of State Affairs** (*shang-shu sheng*) and its senior officials, because it was the dominant agency in the southern part of the imperial palace grounds. Cf. *nan-kung*, *nan-kung she-jen*.

4117　*nán-shĕng shè-jén* 南省舍人
N-S DIV–T'ANG: **Drafters in the Southern Department,** unofficial reference to officials of the Ministry of Rites (*lĭ-pu*) delegated to be editorial aides to senior officials in the Department of State Affairs (*shang-shu sheng*), which was

known unofficially as the Southern Department (*nan-sheng*). Cf. *nan-kung, nan-kung she-jen, chung-shu she-jen*.

4118   *nán-shĭh* 南使
(1) **South Commissioner:** may be found in any period referring to a north-south or a north-south-east-west differentiation among officials delegated from the dynastic capital with jurisdictions denoted by such prefixes and possibly functions by others. (2) T'ANG: **Commissioner for the Southern Pasturages,** an official of the Court of the Imperial Stud (*t'ai-p'u ssu*) delegated to establish new horse pasturages or to inspect existing Directorates of Horse Pasturages (*mu-chien*) in the southern parts of North China. RR: *commissaire impérial (aux élevages) du sud.*

4119   *nán shū-fáng* 南書房
CH'ING: **Southern Study,** originally the personal study of the K'ang-hsi Emperor; from 1659 members of the Hanlin Academy (*han-lin yüan*) served there as writers, calligraphers, copyists, etc., for a time enjoying great influence as the group through which imperial pronouncements were issued; lost such influence after establishment of the Council of State (*chün-chi ch'u*) in 1730. Often called *nan-chai*. Also see *hsing-tsou*; cf. *chung shu-fang, wen shu-fang.*

4120   *nán shū-mì yüàn* 南樞密院
LIAO: **Bureau of Military Affairs in the Southern Establishment** (*nan-yüan*), a top-echelon agency in the Northern Administration (*pei-mien*) of the central government, responsible for appointments, taxes, etc., of the Khitan tribesmen; commonly compared to the Ministry of Personnel (*lì-pu*) in the Southern Administration (*nan-mien*), which dealt with Chinese subjects of Liao; headed by one or more Commissioners of Military Affairs (*shu-mi shih*). Confusion may arise from the fact that this Bureau was commonly abbreviated in the form *nan-yüan* (Southern Bureau), the same term that designated the whole Southern Establishment in the Northern Administration; and any use of the term Southern (*nan*) naturally suggests the Southern Administration. See *shu-mi yüan*. P5.

4121   *nán-sŏ* 南所
CH'ING: **South Prison,** one of 2 prisons maintained in the capital by the Prison Office (*t'i-lao t'ing*) of the Ministry of Justice (*hsing-pu*); staffed with Warders (*ssu-yü*), 2 Manchu and 2 Chinese, rank 9b; a facility for holding persons accused of serious crimes presented by units of territorial administration throughout the empire for sentence reviews, pending resolution of their cases. Also known as *chien-yü*. Also see *pei-so, ssu-yü ssu*. P13.

4122   *nán-ssū* 南司
(1) N-S DIV: unofficial reference to the **Censorate** (*yü-shih t'ai*), to its actual head during this period, nominally the **Palace Aide to the Censor-in-chief** (*yü-shih chung-ch'eng*), or to the nominal **Censor-in-chief** (*yü-shih ta-fu*) when, rarely, such an appointee was actual head of the Censorate. Also see *nan-t'ai*. (2) T'ANG: **Southern Offices,** unofficial reference to those top-echelon agencies of the central government that had headquarters in the southern part of the imperial palace grounds, most notably the Secretariat (*chung-shu sheng*), Chancellery (*men-hsia sheng*), Department of State Affairs (*shang-shu sheng*), Censorate (*yü-shih t'ai*), and various Courts (*ssu*) and Directorates (*chien*), in contrast to the Palace Domestic Service (*nei-shih sheng*), staffed largely with eunuchs, which was housed in the northern part of the palace grounds and was consequently called the Northern Office (*pei-ssu*).

4123   *nán-ssù* 南寺
CH'ING: lit., the southern Court: unofficial reference to the **Censorate** (*tu ch'a-yüan*). See *nan-t'ai.*

4124   *nán tà-wáng yüàn* 南大王院
LIAO: **Southern Office of the Grand Princes,** a top-echelon agency in the Southern Establishment (*nan-yüan*) of the Northern Administration (*pei-mien*), responsible for civil administration of the Five Groups (*wu yüan*) and the Six Groups (*liu yüan*) in the ordo (*kung*) of the dynastic founder, A-pao-chi; the counterpart *pei ta-wang yüan* (Northern Office of the Grand Princes), responsible for military administration of these tribesmen, was part of the Northern Establishment (*pei-yüan*) of the Northern Administration. Headed by an Administrator (*chih yüan-shih*). P17.

4125   *nán-t'à* 南榻
Lit., the southern couch: **Senior Censor:** from T'ang on, an unofficial reference to a Censor-in-chief (*yü-shih ta-fu, tu yü-shih*); comparable to *nan-ch'uang,* q.v.

4126   *nán-t'ái* 南臺
N-S DIV (Sung)–CH'ING: lit., southern pavilion or terrace: unofficial reference to the **Censorate** (*yü-shih t'ai, tu ch'a-yüan*) or occasionally to a **Censor-in-chief** (*yü-shih ta-fu, tu yü-shih*). See *nan-ssu, hsi-t'ai*. P18.

4127   *nán-ts'áo* 南曹
T'ANG–SUNG: lit., the southern Section: unofficial reference to the **Bureau of Appointments** (*hsüan-ssu, hsüan-pu, wen-hsüan ch'ing-li ssu*) in the Ministry of Personnel (*lì-pu*); in T'ang used quasiofficially when a Vice Director (*yüan-wai lang*) was in charge of the Bureau pending appointment of a Director (*lang-chung*). Cf. *nan-hsüan ts'ao*. SP: *service du sud, service du choix des fonctionnaires.*

4128   *nán-wài tsūng-chèng ssū* 南外宗正司
SUNG: **Southern Office of Imperial Clan Affairs,** a branch of the Chief Office of Imperial Clan Affairs (*ta tsung-cheng ssu*) established at Yangchow in 1104 to oversee imperial kinsmen resident in South China, headed by an Administrator (*chih*); incorporated a Hostel for Imperial Kinsmen (*tun-tsung yüan*); apparently disappeared in the flight of the Sung court southward in the 1120s. See *hsi-wai tsung-cheng ssu, kuang-ch'in mu-ch'in chai*. Cf. *tsung-cheng ssu* (Court of the Imperial Clan). SP: *bureau extérieur des affaires de la famille impériale de la capitale du sud*. P1.

4129   *nán-wài tū-shŭi ch'éng-ssū* 南外都水丞司
SUNG: **Office of the Assistant Director of Southern Outer Waterways,** subordinate to 2 Commissioners of Outer Waterways (*wai tu-shui shih-che*) in the Directorate of Waterways (*tu-shui chien*); organizational relationships and ranks not wholly clear. Located at Ying-t'ien Prefecture (modern Shang-ch'iu District, Honan); apparently oversaw the maintenance of waterways in the southern approaches to the dynastic capital, Kaifeng. See *nan-pei wai tu-shui ch'eng-ssu, nan-ch'eng*. SP: *assistant du contrôle des eaux de la capital du sud.*

4130   *nán-wú* 南巫
CHOU: **Sorcerer,** unprescribed number of non-official specialists led by 4 Ordinary Servicemen (*chung-shih*) under jurisdiction of the Director of Sorcery (*ssu-wu*) in the Ministry of Rites (*ch'un-kuan*); together with Sorceresses (*nü-wu*), at appropriate times summoned spirits to be honored or reprimanded, preceded the King on his visits of condolence, prayed for rain and for cessation of epidemics,

and participated in many royal sacrificial and other ceremonies. CL: *sorcier*.

4131   *nán-yá* 南衙
(1) T'ANG: **Southern Command,** collective designation of the Twelve Armies (*shih-erh chün*) and after 636 the Sixteen Guards (*shih-liu wei*) stationed at the dynastic capital for security of the capital city and the palace; personnel drawn principally from Garrison Militia units (see *fu-ping, fu*) on rotational duty till 712, then staffed with paid volunteers organized into a Permanent Palace Guard (*ch'ang-ts'ung su-wei*). The Southern Command soldiers were distributed among 5 base areas in the capital and thus were also known as the Five Garrisons (*wu fu*). Cf. *pei-ya* (Northern Command), a group of largely hereditary soldiers who were the main striking force of the early T'ang military system. Also see *ch'in-chün, chin-chün, chin-wei, wei*. (2) T'ANG: **Southern Offices,** unofficial reference to the main agencies of the central government, which were headquartered in the southern sector of the imperial palace grounds; a variant of *nan-ssu*.

4132   *nán-yáng tà-ch'én* 南洋大臣
CH'ING: **Grand Minister for the Southern Seas,** quasi-official designation of the Governor-general (*tsung-tu*) of Kwantung and Kwangsi Provinces, headquartered at Canton. P50.

4133   *nán-yěh* 南冶
N-S DIV (San-kuo Wu, S. Dyn.): **Southern Mint,** one of several coin-producing agencies, each with a Director (*ling*) or Assistant Director (*ch'eng*) in charge, under supervision of the Chamberlain for the Palace Revenues (*shao-fu*); see *yeh*. P16.

4134   *nán-yìn chiēn-shēng* 難廕監生
CH'ING: **National University Student Hereditary by Heroism,** status awarded sons of officials who had lost their lives in state service, principally in battle (lit., because of difficulty, hardship, suffering, etc.); comparable to *en-yin chien-sheng* (National University Student Hereditary by Grace), a status awarded sons of eminent officials in celebration of some auspicious event. See *yin* (protection privilege), *sheng, chien-sheng, kuan-sheng*.

4135   *nán-yüàn* 南苑
CH'ING: **Southern Park,** one of several parks and gardens in or near the dynastic capital, collectively known as the Imperial Parks (*feng-ch'en yüan*); administered by an Aide (*ch'eng*), rank 6 or 7, of the Manager of the Imperial Parks (*kuan-li feng-ch'en yüan shih-wu*) in the Imperial Household Department (*nei-wu fu*); tended and protected by a Guards Brigade (*hu-wei ying*) drawn from the Three Superior Banners (*shang san ch'i*) under a Supervisor-in-chief (*tsung-kuan*), rank 4a. The Southern Park was also called *hai-tzu* (lit., little sea). P40.

4136   *nán-yüàn* 南院
Lit., southern agency or office. (1) T'ANG: variant of *nan-ts'ao* (**Evaluation Section**), established in 734 in the Bureau of Appointments (*lì-pu*) of the Ministry of Personnel (also *lì-pu*); responsible for determining seniority and reputation as elements considered in the reappointment or dismissal of an official; headed by a Vice Director (*yüan-wai lang*) of the Bureau, rank 6b1; traditionally considered the antecedent of the later Bureau of Appointments (*wen-hsüan ssu*) in the Ministry. May also be encountered in unofficial reference to the Evaluation Section (also *nan-ts'ao*) in the Bureau of Military Appointments (*ping-pu*) of the Ministry of War (also *ping-pu*). (2) T'ANG-CHIN: **Southern Court,**

together with a Northern Court (*pei-yüan*) constituting the *hsüan-hui yüan* (Court of Palace Attendants in T'ang and Sung, Court Ceremonial Institute in Liao and Chin), each headed by one or more Commissioners (*shih*); division of responsibilities not clear. (3) SUNG: **Southern Court,** a unit in each Princely Establishment (*wang-fu*), paired with a Northern Court (*pei-yüan*); the significance of this division is not clear. SP: *cour du sud*. P69. (4) LIAO: **Southern Establishment,** one of 2 major segments of the Northern Administration (*pei-mien*) of the central government, dominated by a Bureau of Military Affairs (*shu-mi yüan*). (5) LIAO: abbreviation of *nan shu-mi yüan* (**Bureau of Military Affairs in the Southern Establishment**) in the Northern Administration (*pei-mien*). P5, 16.

4137   *nèi* 內
Inner, contrasted with *wai* (Outer); comparable to *chung* (palace), but more consistently and unmistakably equated with *ta-nei* (imperial residence). Most commonly used as a prefix, e.g., *nei-kuan* (palace official, i.e., eunuch), *nei-t'ing* (inner court).

4138   *nèi-chàng* 內仗
T'ANG: **Palace Guard,** common designation of members of the Left and Right Forest of Plumes Armies (*yü-lin chün*), especially those elite mounted archers of the Armies who escorted the Emperor on hunts and other outings. See *po chi* (Hundred Cavaliers), a term that perhaps displaced *nei-chang* in normal use after 689. RR: *garde d'honneur intérieure*.

4139   *nèi chăng-shàn* 內掌扇
T'ANG: **Eunuch Fan-bearer,** principally assigned to the Empress; members of the Gates Service (*kung-wei chü*) of the Palace Domestic Service (*nei-shih sheng*). RR: *chargé des éventails du palais intérieur*.

4140   *nèi chăng-shìh* 內掌侍
T'ANG: variant of, or possibly scribal error for, *nei ch'ang-shih* (**Palace Eunuch Attendant-in-ordinary.**) RR: *sous-chef de l'intendance du palais intérieur*.

4141   *nèi ch'áng-shìh* 內常侍
T'ANG-SUNG: **Palace Eunuch Attendant-in-ordinary,** title created in 621 to replace *nei ch'eng-feng*, q.v.; in 743 retitled Vice Director (*shao-chien*) but promptly changed back; although always nominally outranked by a Director (*chien*), rank 3a2, reportedly was the actual head of the Palace Domestic Service (*nei-shih chien, nei-shih sheng*); rank 4b1 in T'ang, 8a in Sung; commonly abbreviated to *nei-shih*. RR+SP: *sous-chef de l'intendance du palais intérieur*. P38.

4142   *nèi-ch'áo* 內朝
Inner Court, throughout imperial history a collective reference to residents of the imperial palace (imperial family, palace women, eunuchs) and a few eminent persons or institutions having close relations with the Emperor as administrators of the imperial household, intimate counselors, etc.; in contrast to Outer Court (*wai-ch'ao*), the established hierarchy of administrative, military, censorial, and other agencies that managed the empire for the ruler. Tensions, and sometimes open power struggles, between the Inner and Outer Courts (neither clearly defined except in the eyes of the other) arose from the Inner Court's fears that dominant Outer Court personages might try to overthrow the dynasty, and from the Outer Court's fears that Inner Court personages (especially empresses, their relatives, and eunuchs) might win such favor with or influence over the Emperor that they might overthrow him in a palace coup, or might

block the Outer Court's normal communication with the Emperor, might usurp the Emperor's authority in such a way as to interfere with normal established governmental activities, or might in other ways disrupt the normal practices of the officialdom for their own selfish advantage. The early Han relationship between unaggressive Emperors and their Counselors-in-chief (*ch'eng-hsiang*), who were acknowledged leaders of and spokesmen for the officialdom and especially the Outer Court, was later praised as an appropriately balanced ruler-minister relationship. See *chung-ch'ao, nei-t'ing, wai-ch'ao, wai-t'ing.* P38.

4143   *nèi-chě* 內者
HAN: **Palace Servant,** 20 eunuchs principally in charge of caring for the clothing of the imperial family; headed by a (eunuch?) Director (*ling*), rank 600 bushels, under the Chamberlain for the Palace Revenues (*shao-fu*). HB: valet. P37.

4144   *nèi-ch'én* 內臣
(1) **Eunuch,** a common general designation throughout history, comparable to *huan-kuan* and *nei-shih.* (2) CH'ING: abbreviation of *nei ta-ch'en,* itself an abbreviation of *nei-wu fu ta-ch'en* (**Grand Minister of the Imperial Household Department**).

4145   *nèi-chèng ssū* 內正司
MING–CH'ING: **Eunuch Rectification Office,** an agency of palace eunuchs responsible for punishing offending members of the eunuch staff. In Ch'ing existed only from 1656 to 1661.

4146   *nèi ch'éng-chíh* 內承直
SUI–T'ANG: **Palace Attendant,** title of a eunuch with secretarial duties (?); 8 in Sui from c. 604, when the title was changed from *chung chi-shih-chung;* T'ang in 621 changed it to *nei chi-shih,* q.v.; members of the Palace Domestic Service (*nei-shih sheng*). RR: *secrétaire de l'intendance du palais intérieur.* P38.

4147   *nèi ch'éng-fèng* 內承奉
T'ANG: **Palace Provisioner,** eunuch member of the Palace Domestic Service (*ch'ang-ch'iu chien*) until the Service was renamed *nei-shih sheng* in 621, when *nei ch'eng-feng* was changed to the title *nei ch'ang-shih* (Palace Eunuch Attendant-in-ordinary). RR: *sous-chef de l'intendance du palais intérieur.* P38.

4148   *nèi ch'éng-fèng pān yā-pān* 內承奉班押班
CHIN: **Eunuch Chief of Palace Attendants** in the Office for Audience Ceremonies (*ko-men*), rank 7a; led members of his group (*pan*) in their work. P33.

4149   *nèi chǐ-shìh* 內給事
T'ANG: **Eunuch Ceremonial Secretary,** 8 to 10, rank 5b2, in the Palace Domestic Service (*nei-shih chien, nei-shih sheng*); created in 621 by retitling *nei ch'eng-chih* (Palace Attendant); principally responsible for accepting and delivering communications for the Empress, e.g., on her birthday or on New Year's Day; also kept account of the clothing and other expenditures for lesser palace women and assisted the Director (*chien*) in administering the Palace Domestic Service. Cf. *nei-shih, chung chi-shih-chung.* RR: *secrétaire de l'intendance du palais intérieur.* P38.

4150   *nèi chǐ-shǐh* 內給使
SUI–T'ANG: **Eunuch Gate Monitor,** number indefinite, attached to the Gates Service (*kung-wei chü*) of the Palace Domestic Service (*nei-shih sheng*), responsible for opening the entrances to the imperial residence in the morning and locking them at night, and for checking on the legitimacy of all comings and goings through the gates. RR: *eunuque serviteur du palais intérieur.* P37.

4151   *nèi-ch'í* 內旗
CH'ING: **Inner Banners,** one of 2 large groups of military units stationed in the dynastic capital, the other being the Outer Banners (*wai-ch'i*), both groups made up of Bannermen drawn from all Eight Manchu Banners (*man pa-ch'i*); generally responsible for guarding the imperial palace. Some Bannermen of the Inner Banners, called Imperial Guardsmen (*shih-wei ch'in-chün, san-ch'i shih-wei*), constituted the Imperial Bodyguard (*ch'in-chün ying*), commanded by 6 Grand Ministers of the Palace Commanding the Imperial Bodyguard (*ling shih-wei nei ta-ch'en*). Others were organized into a Guards Brigade (*hu-chün ying*), a Vanguard Brigade (*ch'ien-feng ying*), a Firearms Brigade (*huo-ch'i ying*), a Scouting Brigade (*chien-jui ying*), etc., each unit under a Commander-general (*t'ung-ling, tsung-t'ung*), often an Imperial Prince. Cf. *chu-fang pa ch'i, shang san ch'i, hsia wu ch'i, ching-ch'i, chin-tsu pa ch'i.* BH: household or inner banners.

4152   *nèi-chiàng* 內匠
N-S DIV (Chou): **Palace Artisan,** one or more ranked as Senior Servicemen (*shang-shih;* 7a) and others as Ordinary Servicemen (*chung-shih;* 8a); members of the Ministry of Works (*tung-kuan*) apparently responsible for construction and maintenance within the palace. See *wai-chiang.* P14.

4153   *nèi-chiào fāng* 內教坊
T'ANG: **Palace Music School,** created in the 620s to train musicians for the Emperor's private entertainment; from 692 to 714 called *yün-shao fu,* q.v.; loosely supervised by the Palace Domestic Service (*nei-shih sheng*). Originally staffed with professional, non-official Erudites (*po-shih*), but in 692 these were replaced with eunuchs. See *chiao-fang, li-yüan, yin-sheng po-shih, t'ai-yüeh shu, nei wen-hsüeh kuan.* RR: *école pour l'enseignement (de la musique) de l'intérieur du palais.*

4154   *nèi-chiào pó-shìh* 內教博士
(1) T'ANG: **Erudite of the Palace Music School,** unspecified number of unranked specialists who taught Novice Career Musicians (*ti-tzu ch'ang-chiao-che*) in the Palace Music School (*nei-chiao fang*) for service in one of the palace orchestras or to become Instructors (*chu-chiao*) in the School. They and their students were allowed to live in the palace; but from 692 eunuchs served as teachers, and whether the students were still allowed to live in the palace is not clear. RR: *maître au vaste savoir chargé de donner l'instruction à l'intérieur du palais.* (2) T'ANG: **Palace Erudite,** 18 unranked specialists in the Palace Institute of Literature (*nei wen-hsüeh kuan*), where palace women were educated; had various particularizing prefixes, e.g., *ching-hsüeh po-shih, k'ai-shu po-shih;* from c. 741, a eunuch post. RR: *maître au vaste savoir chargé de l'enseignement à l'intérieur du palais.*

4155   *nèi-chiēn* 內監
(1) T'ANG–CH'ING: **Eunuch,** a general reference apparently deriving from the name of the T'ang Palace Domestic Service (*nei-shih sheng*). P28. (2) CH'ING: **Inner Prison,** one of 2 sections into which Prisons (*chien-yü*) were commonly divided: an Inner Prison for the detention of serious criminals and an Outer Prison (*wai-chien*) for the detention of persons accused of lesser crimes.

4156   *nèi-chiēn kuǎn-lǐ* 內監管理
CH'ING: **Eunuch Manager,** e.g., of the Southern Park (*nan-yüan*), one of the Imperial Parks (*feng-ch'en yüan*).

4157   *nèi ch'ien-fēng yíng* 內前鋒營
CH'ING: **Palace Vanguard Brigade,** an elite force chosen only from members of the Three Superior Banners (*shang san ch'i*) in the Vanguard Brigade (*ch'ien-feng ying*) for service as Imperial Guardsmen (*shih-wei ch'in-chün*); commanded by one or more Grand Ministers of the Palace Commanding the Imperial Bodyguard (*ling shih-wei nei ta-ch'en*). Also see *nei-ch'i, nei hu-chün ying, nei hsiao-chi ying.* BH: household vanguard. P37.

4158   *nèi-chìh* 內制
SUNG: **Inner Drafters,** unofficial collective reference to Hanlin Academicians (*han-lin hsüeh-shih*) of the Institute of Academicians (*hsüeh-shih yüan*) who were detached to do writing and other staff work in the Administration Chamber (*cheng-shih t'ang*), where Grand Councilors (*tsai-hsiang,* etc.) presided over the central government; in contrast to Outer Drafters (*wai-chih*), a comparable duty assignment for members of the Secretariat (*chung-shu sheng*). The unofficial collective reference to both groups combined was Drafters (*chih-chih-kao*). Also see *liang chih-kuan* (Two Drafting Groups). SP: *chargé de la rédaction des édits intérieurs.*

4159   *nèi-chíh* 內直
Lit., to take a tour (turn, shift) of active service in the palace. (1) N-S DIV (N. Ch'i)–CHIN: **Palace Attendant,** large numbers of unranked personnel (apparently not eunuchs) attached to the Palace Attendance Service (*tien-nei chü, nei-chih chü*) in the Secretariat of the Heir Apparent (*men-hsia fang, tso ch'un-fang*); in the Jurchen Chin era attached to the Court Ceremonial Institute (*hsüan-hui yüan*). (2) SUNG: **Palace Attendance Service,** abbreviated reference to the agency (*nei-chih chü*) rather than to its personnel. RR+SP: *service des fournitures intérieures du palais de l'héritier du trône.* P26, 38.

4160   *nèi-chíh* 內職
SUNG: **Inner Posts,** collective reference to 3 powerful agencies in the early Sung central government: the Bureau of Military Affairs (*shu-mi yüan*), Court of Palace Attendants (*hsüan-hui yüan*), and State Finance Commission (*san ssu*). Cf. *nei-kuan, nei-shih.* P38.

4161   *nèi-chíh chiēn* 內直監
N-S DIV (N. Ch'i)–T'ANG: **Director of Palace Attendants,** 2, rank 6b2 in T'ang, heads of the Palace Attendance Service (*tien-nei chü, nei-chih fang*) under the Secretariat of the Heir Apparent (*men-hsia fang*); in 662 the title Director was changed to *nei-chih lang* and the name Secretariat of the Heir Apparent was changed to *tso ch'un-fang.* RR: *chef du service des fournitures intérieures du palais de l'héritier du trône.* P26.

4162   *nèi-chíh chú* 內直局
SUI–SUNG: **Palace Attendance Service,** a non-eunuch unit in the Secretariat of the Heir Apparent (*men-hsia fang, tso ch'un-fang*) responsible for maintaining the tallies, seals, insignia, clothing, accessories, and furnishings in the household of the Heir Apparent; name changed from *tien-nei chü* (N. Ch'i); headed by 2 Directors of Palace Attendants (*nei-shih chien* till 662, then *nei-shih lang*), rank 6b2 in T'ang. RR: *service des fournitures intérieures du palais de l'héritier du trône.* P26.

4163   *nèi chīh-jǎn chú* 內織染局
MING: **Palace Weaving and Dyeing Service,** a minor agency of palace eunuchs, headed by a eunuch Commissioner-in-chief (*ta-shih*) or Director (*t'ai-chien*); prepared

textiles for palace use; supervised a Blue Dye Shop (*lan-tien ch'ang*); also see *pa chü* (Eight Services).

4164   *nèi-chíh láng* 內直郎
T'ANG–SUNG: **Director of Palace Attendants,** in 662 replaced *nei-chih chien* as title of the head of the Palace Attendance Service (*nei-chih chü, nei-chih*), part of the Secretariat of the Heir Apparent (*tso ch'un-fang*). RR+SP: *chef du service des fournitures intérieures du palais de l'héritier du trône.* P26.

4165   *nèi-chīng pó-shìh* 內經博士
SUNG: **Erudite of the Yellow Emperor's Classic of Medicine,** a professional teacher of Taoist medicine; number and organizational affiliation not clear.

4166   *nèi-ch'īng* 內卿
HAN: lit., palace minister: variant reference to the **Chamberlain for Attendants** (*kuang-lu-hsün*).

4167   *nèi-chiù* 內廏
Inner Stables. (1) SUI–T'ANG: in charge of vehicles in the establishment of the Heir Apparent; in Sui subordinate to the Secretariat of the Heir Apparent (*men-hsia fang*), in T'ang to the Domestic Service of the Heir Apparent (*t'ai-tzu nei-fang chü*); headed by 2 Commandants (*wei*). RR: *écuries du palais intérieur.* P26. (2) T'ANG: one prefixed Southeast (*tung-nan*) and one prefixed Southwest (*hsi-nan*) among the palace stable units collectively called the Six Stables (*liu chiu*). RR: *écurie du ... dans l'intérieur du palais.* (3) CH'ING: stables maintained in the dynastic capital by the Palace Stud (*shang-ssu yüan*), part of the Imperial Household Department (*nei-wu fu*), in contrast to Outer Stables (*wai-chiu*) scattered in the Provinces. BH: stables at the capital. Also see *chiu-chang, chiu-ling, chiu-mu.*

4168   *nèi chiǔ-fāng* 內酒坊
SUNG: **Palace Winery** under the Office of Fine Wines (*liang-yün shu*) in the Court of Imperial Entertainments (*kuang-lu ssu*), in close relationship with the Court's Imperial Kitchen (*yü-ch'u*); headed by a Commissioner (*shih*), unranked. SP: *distillerie de vin fermenté.*

4169   *nèi chū-ssū shǐh* 內諸司使
5 DYN: **The Various Palace Commissioners,** collective reference to numerous personal agents of Emperors who assisted in gradual efforts to bring under imperial control the corps of palace eunuchs, the military establishment, and fiscal administration, all of which had been allowed to get out of imperial control in the late T'ang years; including a Commissioner of Palace Attendants (*hsüan-hui yüan shih*), a Commissioner Participating in Control of Military Affairs (*ts'an-chang shu-mi shih*), a Controller of the Armies and Guards (*p'an liu-chün chu-wei shih*), a Commissioner for State Revenue (*tsu-yung shih*), and a State Finance Commissioner (*san-ssu shih*).

4170   *nèi-chūng kāo-p'ǐn-pān yüàn* 內中高品班院
SUNG: lit., court of high rank palace (workers): **Palace Eunuch Service,** counterpart of the Directorate of Palace Domestic Service (*ch'ang-ch'iu chien*), the Directorate of Palace Attendants (*nei-shih chien*), etc., of other periods; in early Sung renamed *ju-nei nei-shih sheng* (Palace Eunuch Service). See under *ju-nei.* SP: *cour de l'intendance du palais intérieur.*

4171   *nèi-chù chiù* 內駒廏
T'ANG: **Stables of the Palace Colts,** collective reference to the Stables of Trustworthy Mounts on the Right (*yu chang-*

chiu; see *chang-chiu*) maintained by the Palace Administration (*tien-chung sheng*). RR: *écuries des chevaux rapides du palais.*

4172 *nèi fān-shū fáng* 內繙書房
CH'ING: **Sino-Manchu Translation Office** attached to the Grand Secretariat (*nei-ko*) to translate state documents from Chinese into Manchu; staffing not clear. BH: Manchu-Chinese translation office.

4173 *nèi-fāng* 內坊
N-S DIV (N. Ch'i)–SUNG: **Inner Quarters,** one of many units of the Household Administration of the Heir Apparent (*chan-shih fu*) till 739, then assigned to the Palace Domestic Service (*nei-shih sheng*) though still responsible for serving the Heir Apparent; headed by a Director (*ling*) in N. Ch'i, a Palace Manager (*tien-nei*) in Sui and T'ang till 739, thereafter a Director again, rank 5b2. The title Palace Manager was restored during Sung, rank not clear. The agency was probably staffed with eunuchs and probably provided personal servant-like service for the Heir Apparent. In T'ang after 739 it was named *nei-fang chü* (Inner Quarters Service), and a common alternate name was *t'ai-tzu nei-fang chü* (Domestic Service of the Heir Apparent). RR+SP: *service du palais intérieur de la maison de l'héritier du trône.* P26.

4174 *nèi fēi-lúng shǐh* 內飛龍使
T'ANG: **Eunuch Commissioner of the Flying Dragon Corral,** one of the Six Palace Corrals (*chang-nei liu hsien*); also see *liu hsien, fei-lung chiu.* RR: *commissaire impérial chargé des dragons volants de l'intérieur du palais.*

4175 *nèi-fǔ* 內府
Palace Treasury, sometimes an official designation but more often an unofficial reference to various storehouses and vaults where rulers kept their personal fortunes in money and goods in the palace or, if elsewhere, under direct palace control. (1) CHOU: an agency in the Ministry of State (*t'ien-kuan*), also the title of its 2 Directors, ranked as Ordinary Servicemen (*chung-shih*). CL: *magasin intérieur.* (2) CH'IN-N-S DIV: refers to the Chamberlain of the Palace Revenues (*shao-fu, shao-fu chien, shao-fu ch'ing*), late in the period alternating with *t'ai-fu, t'ai-fu ssu.* (3) SUI–T'ANG: refers to the Palace Treasury Service (*nei-fu chü*) under the Palace Domestic Service (*nei-shih sheng*). RR: *service du trésor du palais intérieur.* (4) SUNG: refers to the Palace Storehouses (*nei tsang-k'u*) supervised by the Court of the Imperial Treasury (*t'ai-fu ssu*). SP: *magasin du trésor du palais.* (5) YÜAN: refers to the Directorate of the Imperial Treasury (*t'ai-fu chien*) under the Palace Provisions Commission (*hsüan-hui yüan*). (6) MING: refers to storehouses controlled by palace eunuchs. (7) CH'ING: refers to the Office of the Palace Treasury (*kuang-ch'u ssu*) under the Imperial Household Department (*nei-wu fu*). P37, 38.

4176 *nèi-fǔ chiēn* 內府監
T'ANG: from 662 to 685, the official variant of *shao-fu chien* (**Directorate for Imperial Manufactories**). P38.

4177 *nèi fú-pǎo láng* 內符寶郎
SUNG: **Eunuch Seals Secretary,** rank 7b; established in 1107 to be responsible for keeping the imperial seals (*pao*) and tallies (*fu*) and possibly responsible for issuing appropriate seals and insignia to civil officials and military officers; organizational affiliation not clear. Apparently a eunuch counterpart of the Seals Secretary (*fu-pao lang*) in the Chancellery (*men-hsia sheng*), 2, also rank 7b. Seems to correspond to *ssu-pao* (Seal-keeper) or *ssu-pao ssu* (Seals Office) in the eunuch-staffed Wardrobe Service (*shang-fu*

chü), or to the civil service Seals Office (*shang-pao ssu*), of other eras. SP: *secrétaire du palais chargé des insignes en deux parties et des sceaux.*

4178 *nèi-hàn* 內翰
Lit., inner (i.e., palace) writing brush (wielders): **Palace Writers.** (1) SUNG–CH'ING: unofficial reference to members of the Hanlin Academy (*han-lin yüan*). (2) CH'ING: in addition, an unofficial reference to secretarial staff members of the Grand Secretariat (*nei-ko*).

4179 *nèi hsī-t'óu kūng-fèng kuān* 內西頭供奉官
(1) SUNG: **Court Service Official on the West,** a title for some palace eunuchs, rank 6 or 7, members of the Palace Eunuch Service (*ju-nei nei-shih sheng*). (2) SUNG: variant reference to *tso shih-chin* (**Left Palace Attendant**), 2nd highest of 12 rank titles granted to eunuchs from 1112; see *nei-shih chieh.* Cf. *nei tung-t'ou kung-feng kuan.* SP: *intendant à la disposition de l'empereur à l'ouest du palais intérieur.*

4180 *nèi-hsiāng* 內廂
SUNG: **Inner Capital Townships;** see *ssu hsiang* (Four Capital Townships).

4181 *nèi-hsiàng* 內相
Grand Councilor in the Palace. (1) T'ANG: common unofficial reference to Academicians (*hsüeh-shih*) in the Institute of Academicians (*hsüeh-shih yüan*). (2) T'ANG: unofficial collective reference to those Hanlin Academicians (*han-lin hsüeh-shih*) and members of the Institute of Academicians and the Academy of Scholarly Worthies (*chi-hsien tien shu-yüan*) who were called into detached service as Participants in the Drafting of Proclamations (*chih-chih-kao*) under Grand Councilors (*tsai-hsiang*), some of whom ultimately became Grand Councilors themselves. RR: *grand ministre de l'intérieur.* (3) CH'ING: unofficial reference to the Academician in Charge of the Hanlin Academy (*chang-yüan hsüeh-shih*). P23.

4182 *nèi hsiǎo-ch'én* 內小臣
CHOU: **Palace Attendant,** designation of palace eunuchs awarded nominal rank as Senior Servicemen (*shang-shih*) and attached to the Ministry of State (*t'ien-kuan*) to attend and escort the Queen (*hou*) in her public appearances. See *hsiao-ch'en.* CL: *petit officier de l'intérieure.*

4183 *nèi hsiǎo-chì yíng* 內驍騎營
CH'ING: **Palace Cavalry Brigade,** an elite force chosen only from members of the Three Superior Banners (*shang san ch'i*) in the Cavalry Brigade (*hsiao-chi ying*) for service as Imperial Guardsmen (*shih-wei ch'in-chün*); commanded by one or more Grand Ministers of the Palace Commanding the Imperial Bodyguard (*ling shih-wei nei ta-ch'en*). Also see *wai-ch'i, nei ch'ien-feng ying, nei hu-chün ying.* BH: household brigade of the line. P37.

4184 *nèi-hsíng ch'ǎng* 內行廠
MING: lit. meaning not clear; repository concerning palace conduct (?): **Palace Depot,** a eunuch agency existing only during the era 1505–1521, apparently created to dominate the notorious eunuch secret police agencies, the Eastern and Western Depots (*tung-ch'ang, hsi-ch'ang*).

4185 *nèi hù-chūn yíng* 內護軍營
CH'ING: **Palace Guards Brigade,** an elite force selected only from members of the Three Superior Banners (*shang san ch'i*) in the Guards Brigade (*hu-chün ying*) for service as Imperial Guardsmen (*shih-wei ch'in-chün*); commanded by one or more Grand Ministers of the Palace Commanding

the Imperial Bodyguard (*ling shih-wei nei ta-ch'en*). Also see *nei-ch'i; nei ch'ien-feng ying, nei hsiao-chi ying*. BH: imperial guards. P37.

4186 *nèi-hùi tsǔng-k'ō chǔ-shìh* 內會總科主事
MING: **Internal Accounts Secretary in the Headquarters Section of the Ministry of Revenue** (*hu-pu*), 6, rank 6a; created in 1373, discontinued in 1380; supplemented Secretaries (*chu-shih*) in the Section. Also see *tsung-k'o, wai ch'ien-chao k'o*. P6.

4187 *nèi hūn-kuān* 內閣官
N-S DIV: **Palace Doorman,** common title for palace eunuchs.

4188 *nèi hūn-shǐh* 內閣史
T'ANG: **Palace Doorman,** unspecified number of eunuchs in the Palace Gates Service (*kung-wei chü*) of the Palace Domestic Service (*nei-shih sheng*). RR: *portier du palais intérieur*.

4189 *nèi húng-wén yüàn* 內弘文院
CH'ING: **Palace Academy for the Advancement of Literature,** one of the Three Palace Academies (*nei san yüan*), each supervised by a Grand Secretary (*ta hsüeh-shih*); specially charged with translating China's classical and historical writings into Manchu and tutoring the Emperor and Heir Apparent in the Chinese cultural tradition. Established in 1635; in 1658 regrouped into Ming-style agencies, the Hanlin Academy (*han-lin yüan*) and Grand Secretariat (*nei-ko*). Also see *hung-wen kuan, nei kuo-shih yüan, nei pi-shu yüan*. P2.

4190 *nèi hǔo-yào k'ù* 內火藥庫
CH'ING: **Palace Gunpowder Depot,** headed by 2 Directors (*chang*), unranked (eunuchs?); one of several units under the Imperial Game Preserve (*niao-ch'iang ch'u*) maintained by the Imperial Household Department (*nei-wu fu*). BH: ammunition-store.

4191 *nèi ī-wù k'ù* 內衣物庫
SUNG: **Special Gifts Storehouse,** established in 977, from 1008 under both the Palace Administration (*tien-chung sheng*) and the Palace Domestic Service (*nei-shih sheng*), headed jointly by one civil service and one eunuch Supervisor (*chien-kuan*); received fine silks, brocades, and other materials, principally to be used as gifts for members of the imperial family, imperial in-laws, civil and military officials, and foreign envoys at suitable times, e.g., the Emperor's birthday. See *shang-fu chü, shang-i chü, shang-i k'u*. SP: *magasin de vêtements et d'objets du palais intérieur*. P38.

4192 *nèi-jén* 內人
CHOU: **Palace Woman,** members of one of the Nine Concubine Groups (*chiu yü*) resident in the royal palace in the service of the ruler and his principal wives. Also see *nü-yü*. CL: *femme de l'intérieur*.

4193 *nèi-kó* 內閣
Lit., the palace halls and, by extension, those who served in them: **Grand Secretariat.** (1) N-S DIV (San-kuo Wei): unofficial reference to the Palace Library (*pi-shu; see pi-shu chien*), in contrast to the Orchid Pavilion (*lan-t'ai*), called *wai-t'ai* (Outer Pavilion). P18. (2) SUNG: unofficial reference to the Hanlin Academy (*han-lin yüan*). (3) MING–CH'ING: from the 1420s to 1730, the most distinguished and influential body in the central government, like a collective prime ministership; staffed with Grand Secretaries (*ta hsüeh-shih*) of the Hanlin Academy detached to establish offices within the imperial palace to handle the Em-

peror's paperwork, recommend decisions in response to memorials received from the officialdom, and draft and issue imperial pronouncements. Created as a small, loosely organized body of secretarial consultants after the Ming founder's abolition in 1380 of the Secretariat's (*chung-shu sheng*) executive posts, which made himself sole coordinator of the Six Ministries (*liu pu*) that were the administrative core of the central government. The secretarial establishment gradually grew in importance until in the 1420s it attained durable form and status. The members remained loosely organized, each designated by the Hall to which he was assigned, e.g., Grand Secretary of the Hall of Literary Profundity (*wen-yüan ko ta hsüeh-shih*); but collegial procedures were evolved among them, and leadership of the Grand Secretaries, commonly numbering from 2 to 6, fell to a so-called Senior Grand Secretary (*shou-fu*). Since the ranks associated with their Hanlin titles were low (5a), it became standard practice for each Grand Secretary to be given concurrent nominal status as Minister (*shang-shu*), 2a, or Vice Minister (*shih-lang*), 3a, in one of the Six Ministries, especially the Ministry of Rites (*li-pu*); and particularly esteemed Grand Secretaries eventually were awarded status among the Three Dukes (*san kung*), honorific posts carrying rank 1a. As the Grand Secretaries grew in importance, the former Secretariat's Drafters (*chung-shu she-jen*) were attached to them as a staff agency, the Central Drafting Office (*chung-shu k'o*); and by 1600 the Grand Secretariat had been acknowledged in state documents as a regular, formal agency of the central government. Because, beginning in the 1400s, top-ranking Metropolitan Graduates (*chin-shih*) were regularly assigned to the Hanlin Academy on track ultimately to become Grand Secretaries, and because Grand Secretaries with few exceptions never had experience in the line administrative agencies of government, the officialdom at large (see *wai-ch'ao*, Outer Court) naturally considered the Grand Secretaries with a certain hostility as members of the Inner Court (*nei-ch'ao, nei-t'ing*); and this feeling grew as Grand Secretaries found it necessary, especially in the reigns of the more reclusive Ming Emperors, to collaborate with powerful palace eunuchs to maintain contact and influence with the ruler. Hostility between the officialdom in general and the Grand Secretariat became seriously disruptive after the tenure of Chang Chü-cheng (1525–1582) as Senior Grand Secretary and interfered with the operation of the central government to the end of the Ming dynasty. Some subsequent historians have argued that the abolition of the early Ming Secretariat and the consequent rise of the Grand Secretariat were the most important institutional changes in late imperial history and foredoomed the dynasty to collapse in undisciplined partisan feuding. The Manchus originally structured the central government of their Ch'ing dynasty with Three Palace Academies (*nei san yüan*), the traditional Six Ministries, and the traditional Censorate (*tu ch'a-yüan*) in its top echelon, but in 1658 the Three Palace Academies were organized into a Hanlin Academy and a Grand Secretariat of the Ming sorts. The Ch'ing Grand Secretariat was headed by 2 Manchu and 2 Chinese Grand Secretaries (*ta hsüeh-shih*), commonly Princes or other nobles; and the agency was formally established at the top of the official hierarchy, as unchallengeable head of the Outer Court. But the Grand Secretariat gradually lost prestige and influence, because the determining of policy was entrusted to an unofficial organization of the Manchu ruling group, called the Deliberative Council (*i-cheng ch'u*), staffed with Princes and Grand Ministers (*ta-ch'en*) of the Imperial Household Department (*nei-wu fu*). When in 1730 this Deliberative Council was reorganized and formalized as an official top-echelon Council of State (*chün-chi ch'u*), although some Grand Secretaries as individuals became members of the Council, the Grand Secretariat as an institution slipped into the secondary role of processing paperwork concerning routine administrative business under guidelines established by the Council. P2.

4194   *nèi-kó chūng-shū* 內閣中書
MING-CH'ING: **Secretaries in the Grand Secretariat,** originally in Ming a group of writers organized in a Central Drafting Office (*chung-shu k'o*) attached to the Secretariat (*chung-shu sheng*); after central government reorganizations in the 1380s, this became relatively autonomous, and it soon came to be attached loosely to the evolving Grand Secretariat (*nei-ko*); number not prescribed, rank 7b. In Ch'ing still organized in a Central Drafting Office, still 7b, but number grew remarkably to include 70 Manchus, 8 Chinese Bannermen (*han-chün*), and 30 Chinese civil officials. Selected triennially from among the most promising new Metropolitan Graduates (*chin-shih*), after those chosen to enter the Hanlin Academy (*han-lin yüan*) as Hanlin Bachelors (*shu-chi-shih*); after a fixed term of years (3?) had to transfer out to be staff members of Departments (*chou*) or, in the 18th century, to be Secretaries in the Council of State (*chün-chi chang-ching*). During tours of the South made by the K'ang-hsi and Ch'ien-lung Emperors, men with status as Provincial Graduates (*chü-jen*) and Government Students (*sheng-yüan*) who presented meritorious petitions were commonly appointed Secretaries in the Grand Secretariat. In Ch'ing the Central Drafting Office was headed by an Academician of the Grand Secretariat (*nei-ko hsüeh-shih*), 2b, with the duty-assignment designation Grand Minister Inspector of the Central Drafting Office (*chi-ch'a chung-shu k'o shih-wu ta-ch'en*). P2.

4195   *nèi-kó hsüéh-shìh* 內閣學士
CH'ING: **Academician of the Grand Secretariat,** 6 Manchus and 4 Chinese with nominal status as Vice Ministers (*shih-lang*) of one of the Six Ministries (*liu pu*), most often the Ministry of Rites (*lǐ-pu*); rank 2b. Subordinate to the Grand Secretaries (*ta hsüeh-shih*) in the Grand Secretariat. BH: sub-chancellor of the grand secretariat. P2.

4196   *nèi-kó shìh-tú* 內閣侍讀
CH'ING: **Grand Secretariat Reader-in-waiting,** transformation of a traditional title for academicians (see *shih-tu*) to designate an undistinguished corps of copyreaders who examined all documents issued from the palace; 10-14 Manchus, 2 each Mongols, Chinese Bannermen (*han-chün*), and Chinese civil officials; rank 4 then 6a. BH: assistant readers of the grand secretariat. P2.

4197   *nèi-kó shìh-tú hsüéh-shìh*
           內閣侍讀學士
CH'ING: **Grand Secretariat Academician Reader-in-waiting,** transformation of a traditional title for academicians (see *hsüeh-shih, shih-tu*) to designate an undistinguished group of editors and translators of documents issued from the palace; 4-6 Manchus, 2 Chinese, originally also 2 Mongols (later discontinued); rank 3 then 5 then 4b. On the Grand Secretariat staff of regular officials, these ranked above only Grand Secretariat Readers-in-waiting (*nei-ko shih-tu*), rank 4 then 6a, Certification Clerks (*tien-chi*), 7a, and Secretaries (*chung-shu*), 7b; but early held concurrent nominal appointments as Chief Ministers (*ch'ing*), 3a, in the Court of Imperial Sacrifices (*t'ai-ch'ang ssu*); date of discontinuance not clear. BH: readers of the grand secretariat. P2.

4198   *nèi-kó shuài* 內閣帥
N-S DIV (N. Ch'i): **Palace Guide** in the Purification Service (*chai-shuai chü*) in the Secretariat of the Heir Apparent, (*men-hsia fang;* antecedent of *tso ch'un-fang*); 2, rank not clear; paired with 2 Purification Guides (*chai-shuai*); functions not wholly clear, though clearly related to supervision of fasting, other abstinences, and other types of preparation by the Heir Apparent for participation in important religious rituals. P26.

4199   *nèi-kó tà hsüéh-shìh* 內閣大學士
MING-CH'ING: **Grand Secretary of the Grand Secretariat,** from 2 to 6 in Ming, in Ch'ing 2 Manchus and 2 Chinese; in Ming a special duty assignment, in Ch'ing a regular official post, rank 1a. See *nei-ko, ta hsüeh-shih, hsüeh-shih*.

4200   *nèi-kó tiěn-chí* 內閣典籍
CH'ING: **Certification Clerk in the Grand Secretariat,** 4 Manchus and 2 Chinese, rank 7a; apparently supervised the Archive (*fu-pen k'u*) of the Grand Secretariat (*nei-ko*); also kept the only seals that could be used on behalf of the Grand Secretariat, hence were called on to certify and authorize all incoming and outbound documents. See *tien-chi*. P2.

4201   *nèi-k'ò shěng* 內客省
SUNG: **Palace Visitors Bureau** under the Palace Eunuch Service (*ju-nei nei-shih sheng*), headed by a eunuch Commissioner (*shih*), rank 5b; in charge of palace receptions for foreign dignitaries, collaborating with the Visitors Bureau (*k'o-sheng*) of the Secretariat (*chung-shu sheng*) and probably also the Court of State Ceremonial (*hung-lu ssu*). SP: *commissaire du palais chargé des relations diplomatiques (visites, audiences, et contributions des étrangers) (eunuque)*.

4202   *nèi-k'ù* 內庫
Palace Storehouses: from the era of N-S Division if not earlier, a common collective reference to all storehouses or vaults under the direct control of the imperial palace and at the disposition of the ruler only, i.e., those buildings that constituted what was called the Palace Treasury (*nei-fu*).

4203   *nèi-kuān* 內官
(1) From antiquity, one of many terms for **eunuch;** see *huan-kuan, nei-shih, t'ai-chien.* (2) From antiquity, a variant of *nü-kuan* (**Palace Woman**). (3) Throughout history may be encountered in reference to personnel in palace service as opposed to central government personnel, or to personnel serving in the dynastic capital as opposed to those in units of territorial administration. Cf. *nei-ch'ao, wai-ch'ao, nei-t'ing, wai-t'ing.* (4) HAN: **Palace Manager,** 2 appointed from 144 B.C. under the Chamberlain for the Palace Revenues (*shao-fu*); possibly chief eunuchs. HB: inner palace office. P37. (5) HAN: **Inner Officials,** collective reference to all personnel in the Imperial Guards (*shih-wei*), others being referred to as Outer Officials (*wai-kuan*). (6) SUI: **Inner Officials,** collective reference to all personnel in the Imperial Guards and all others on active service in the imperial palace, others being referred to as Outer Officials.

4204   *nèi-kuǎn* 內館
CH'ING: **Inner Hostel,** one of 2 capital residences maintained by the Court of Colonial Affairs (*li-fan yüan*) to house visiting Mongol dignitaries; the other was the Outer Hostel (*wai-kuan*). Differences in functions between the 2 Hostels not clear; each under the surveillance of a Supervisory Inspector (*chi-ch'a nei-kuan [wai-kuan] chien-tu*) chosen from the ranks of Censors (*yü-shih*), Supervising Censors (*chi-shih-chung*), or junior officials of Ministries (*pu*). BH: inner inn. P17.

4205 *nèi-kuān chiēn* 內官監
MING–CH'ING: **Direcrorate of Palace Eunuchs,** one of 12 eunuch Directorates (*chien*) in the imperial palace, each headed by a eunuch Director-in-chief (*t'ai-chien*); apparently supervised the care and use of all imperial seals and controlled access to the Emperor. From 1395 to 1398 may have been given authority over the 11 other eunuch Directorates, but in the 1400s the Directorate of Ceremonial (*ssu-li chien*) gained primacy among the eunuch agencies. Ch'ing originally did not establish eunuch Directorates; all palace affairs came under the control of the Imperial Household Department (*nei-wu fu*). From 1656 to 1661 the Department was superseded by Ming-style Directorates, but then they were discontinued and the Imperial Household Department was re-established. Previously, in 1660, the Directorate of Palace Eunuchs had been transformed into a non-eunuch Palace Provisions Commission (*hsüan-hui yüan*), which in 1677 became the Office of Palace Accounts (*k'uai-chi ssu*) under the Imperial Household Department. See under *shih-erh chien*. P37, 38.

4206 *nèi kuǎn-lǐng* 內管領
CH'ING: **Overseer,** designation of many mid-level officials (ranks 5a to 6a) in the Imperial Household Department (*nei-wu fu*), normally supervising menial custodial work in the various Halls (*ko, tien, kung*) of the palace, at Imperial Mausolea (*ling, ling-ch'in*), in the Imperial Dispensary (*yü-yao fang*), etc. Those serving in the imperial palace were organized into an Overseers Office (*nei kuan-ling ch'u*). P29, 37, 49.

4207 *nèi kuǎn-lǐng ch'ù* 內管領處
Overseers Office in the Imperial Household Department (*nei-wu fu*) with an authorized staff of 30 Overseers (*nei kuan-ling*), 30 Assistant Overseers (*fu nei kuan-ling*), and 8 Clerks (*pi-t'ieh-shih*) under leadership of a Director (*chang kuan-fang*) and 2 Vice Directors (*hsieh-li kuan-fang shih-wu*) chosen for these duty assignments from among the Directors (*lang-chung*) and Vice Directors (*yüan-wai lang*) of Bureaus (*ssu, ch'ing-li ssu*) in the Six Ministries (*liu pu*). Responsible for menial custodial services in the palace, maintaining and providing wines, foodstuffs, and dining utensils, etc. BH: chancery of the imperial household. P37.

4208 *nèi-kūng* 內宮
CHOU: variant reference to the **Six Principal Wives** (*liu kung*) of the King.

4209 *nèi kūng-chiēn k'ù* 內弓箭庫
SUNG: **Palace Archery Storehouse,** a unit of the Court of the Imperial Regalia (*wei-wei ssu*), headed by a Superintendent (*t'i-tien*). Cf. *kung-chien k'u.* SP: *magasin des arcs et des flèches du palais.*

4210 *nèi kūng-fèng* 內供奉
T'ANG: lit., to provide service or be on duty within (the palace); relevance not clear: **Auxiliary,** from the early 700s a term appended as a suffix to various titles, especially those of censorial officials (*ch'a-kuan, chien-kuan*), signifying that the title-holders were fully qualified for the posts indicated but were supernumeraries awaiting regular appointments when vacancies occurred; performed most of the functions of the posts indicated but did not enjoy all their perquisites. E.g., Auxiliary Attendant Censor (*shih yü-shih nei kung-feng*), Auxiliary Palace Censor (*tien-chung yü-shih nei kung-feng*), and such Secretariat (*chung-shu sheng*) and Chancellery (*men-hsia sheng*) posts as Auxiliary Rectifier of Omissions (*pu-ch'üeh nei kung-feng*) and Auxiliary Reminder (*shih-i nei kung-feng*). The difference in T'ang usage between *nei kung-feng* and the term *kung-feng*, q.v., is not

clear. RR: *fonctionnaire devant rester à la disposition de l'empereur à l'intérieur du palais.* P18.

4211 *nèi kūng-pù* 內工部
CH'ING: **Palace Ministry of Works,** from 1661 to 1677 a specialized agency concerned with construction and maintenance of the imperial palace, then superseded by the Office of Palace Construction (*ying-tsao ssu*) of the Imperial Household Department (*nei-wu fu*).

4212 *nèi kuó-shǐh yüàn* 內國史院
CH'ING: **Palace Historiographic Academy,** from 1635 to 1658 one of the Three Palace Academies (*nei san yüan*) in the top echelon of the early Ch'ing central government, providing counsel and editorial assistance in ways similar to those of the Ming Hanlin Academy (*han-lin yüan*) and Grand Secretariat (*nei-ko*); each headed by a Grand Academician (*ta hsüeh-shih*). Kept records, edited imperial pronouncements, produced historical documents, etc. In 1658 split into a Hanlin Academy and a Grand Secretariat. Cf. *kuo-shih kuan, kuo-shih yüan.* P2.

4213 *nèi-lién kuān* 內簾官 or *nei-lien*
YÜAN–CH'ING: lit., within (i.e., behind) the screen: **Inner Examiners,** unofficial collective reference to Provincial Examiners (*chu-k'ao*) and Assistant Provincial Examiners (*t'ung-k'ao, fu chu-k'ao*) in the civil service recruitment examination sequence, who were sequestered "within the screen" in private quarters of the examination hall and participated primarily in reading and grading examination papers; also **Inner Aides,** officials of units of territorial administration who were detached to help grade papers in the Provincial Examination (*hsiang-shih*). See *lien-kuan, wai-lien kuan.*

4214 *nèi mìng-fū* 內命夫
Variant of *nei ming-nan* (**Inner Nobleman**).

4215 *nèi mìng-fù* 內命婦
Inner Noblewoman. (1) CHOU: categorical designation of a large group of palace women considered secondary wives of the ruler, including those known collectively as *chiu pin, shih-fu,* and *nü-yü*, qq.v., in contrast to the wives of royal officials, called Outer Noblewomen (*wai ming-fu*). CL: *femme titrée de l'intérieur du palais.* (2) T'ANG: categorical designation of palace women of the first 3 ranks, not including the Empress. RR: *femme titrée de l'intérieur du palais.*

4216 *nèi mìng-nán* 內命男
CHOU: **Inner Nobleman,** categorical reference to officials serving in the royal capital with ranks of Minister (*ch'ing*), Grand Master (*ta-fu*), and Serviceman (*shih*); cf. *wai ming-nan.* CL: *homme titré de l'intérieur.*

4217 *nèi mìng-nǔ* 內命女
CHOU: variant of *nei ming-fu* (**Inner Noblewoman**).

4218 *nèi-nǔ* 內女
CHOU: **Royal Clanswoman,** categorical reference to all females of the reigning family, presumably only those bearing the ruler's surname. Cf. *nei-tsung.* CL: *femme de l'intérieur.*

4219 *nèi pā-fǔ tsǎi-hsiàng* 內八府宰相
YÜAN: **Grand Councilors of the Eight Palace Offices,** 8, rank =2; an informal, irregular assembly of imperial in-laws and sons and younger brothers of the nobility, gathered on an ad hoc basis to constitute a distinguished entourage when the Emperor received Princes in audience; had no role in normal governance. P4.

4220   *nèi pàn-shìh ch'ǎng* 內辦事廠
MING: variant of *nei-hsing ch'ang* (**Palace Repository**).

4221   *nèi-pān yüàn* 內班院
SUNG: **Palace Personnel Office,** an early Sung agency of palace eunuchs, quickly superseded by the Palace Domestic Service (*nei-shih sheng*). SP: *cour de l'intendance du palais intérieur.*

4222   *nèi pāo-ī niú-lù chāng-chīng* 內包衣牛条章京
CH'ING: **Palace (Department of) Bondservants, Bannermen, and Secretaries,** an unofficial reference to the Imperial Household Department (*nei-wu fu*); also see *pao-i, niu-lu, chang-ching.*

4223   *nèi pì-shū shěng* 內祕書省
N-S DIV (N. Wei): **Inner Palace Library,** sometimes with the prefix *chung* (central, inner) rather than *nei,* sometimes called a *chien* (Directorate) or a *ssu* (Court) rather than a *sheng* (Department); resulted from a division of the traditional Palace Library (*pi-shu sheng*) into Inner and Outer (*wai*) units. The Inner unit was responsible for handling the flow of documents into and out of the imperial palace. Its head was sometimes an eminent official with principal duty elsewhere in the central government serving as Concurrent Controller (see under *ling, ling ... shih*) of the Inner Palace Library; sometimes it was a palace eunuch entitled Director (*ling*). The staff consisted principally of aristocrats designated Courtiers (*chung-san*), including Courtier-attendants (*shih-yü chung-san*), Courtiers for Memorials (*tsou-shih chung-san*), and Courtier-secretaries (*chu-wen chung-san*). Cf. *pi-shu nei-sheng* (Inner Branch of the Palace Library). P19.

4224   *nèi pì-shū yüàn* 內祕書院
CH'ING: **Palace Secretariat Academy,** one of the Three Palace Academies (*nei san yüan*) that from 1635 to 1658 constituted the top echelon of the early Ch'ing central government, providing counsel and editorial assistance in ways similar to those of the Ming Hanlin Academy (*han-lin yüan*) and Grand Secretariat (*nei-ko*); each headed by a Grand Academician (*ta hsüeh-shih*). The Palace Secretariat Academy specialized in writing or editing imperial pronouncements, especially those requiring literary elegance such as diplomatic correspondence and funerary testimonials. In 1658 the Three Palace Academies were transformed into a Hanlin Academy and Grand Secretariat. Cf. *pi-shu chien, pi-shu sheng.* P2.

4225   *nèi-p'ǐn* 內品
SUNG: lit., palace rank: **Palace Eunuch.** One of several designations of eunuchs used in the Palace Eunuch Service (*ju-nei nei-shih sheng*), often with prefixes specifying functional assignments, e.g., *hsi-ching nei-p'in* (Palace Eunuch of the Western Capital); also 10th highest of 12 rank titles granted eunuchs from 1112; see *nei-shih chieh.* Also see *chih-hou nei-p'in, t'ieh chih-hou nei-p'in, nei-pan nei-p'in.* P68.

4226   *nèi pù-pīng ts'áo* 內步兵曹
N-S DIV (N. Ch'i): **Inner Section,** designation of infantry, apparently in battle formation; distinguished from the Outer Section (*wai chi-ping ts'ao*) of cavalrymen, which might be expected to enwrap the infantry in battle formation.

4227   *nèi-p'ú chǘ* 內僕局
SUI–T'ANG: **Livery Service for the Empress** in the eunuch-staffed Palace Domestic Service (*nei-shih sheng*), responsible for maintaining horses and carriages used by the

Empress; headed by 2 Directors (*ling*), rank 8b, and 2 Assistant Directors (*ch'eng*), 9b. The staff included 140 authorized Coachmen (*chia-shih*). The Director and Assistant Directors escorted the Empress's carriage on any outing. RR: *service des équipages du palais intérieur.*

4228   *nèi sān ch'í* 內三旗
CH'ING: **Three Inner Banners,** collective reference to those military units called Banners (*ch'i*) that were directly under the Emperor's control: the Bordered Yellow (*hsiang-huang*), Plain Yellow (*cheng-huang*), and Plain White (*cheng-po*) Banners. The Three Inner Banners provided the Imperial Bodyguard (*ch'in-chün ying*) and also the following units: Palace Guards Brigade (*nei hu-chün ying*), Palace Vanguard Brigade (*nei ch'ien-feng ying*), Palace Cavalry Brigade (*nei hsiao-chi ying*), Summer Palace Guards Brigade (*yüan-ming yüan nei ch'i hu-chün ying*), and the Southern Park Guards Brigade (*nan-yüan hu-wei ying*). The Three Inner Banners were also called the Three Superior Banners (*shang san ch'i*); they were administered under the Imperial Household Department (*nei-wu fu*). Also see *pa ch'i.* Cf. *hsia wu ch'i.* BH: three imperial banners. P37.

4229   *nèi sān yüàn* 內三院
CH'ING: **Three Palace Academies,** collective reference to the Palace Historiographic Academy (*nei kuo-shih yüan*), the Palace Secretariat Academy (*nei pi-shu yüan*), and the Palace Academy for the Advancement of Literature (*nei hung-wen yüan*), each headed by a Grand Academician (*ta hsüeh-shih*). From 1635 to 1658 the Three Palace Academies, which generally provided counsel and editorial assistance to the Emperor, were in the top echelon of the early Ch'ing central government, along with the Six Ministries (*liu pu*) and the Censorate (*tu ch'a-yüan*); but in 1658 they were reorganized into a Grand Secretariat (*nei-ko*) and Hanlin Academy (*han-lin yüan*) in the Ming pattern P2, 23.

4230   *nèi-shàn* 內膳
N-S DIV (Chou): **Palace Vice Provisioner,** number not specified, ranked as Senior Servicemen (*shang-shih;* 7a); and **Assistant Palace Provisioner,** number not specified, ranked as Ordinary Servicemen (*chung-shih;* 8a); aides of the Palace Provisioner (*chu-shan*) in the Ministry of State (*t'ien-kuan*), who furnished drinks and delicacies for imperial banquets, receptions, sacrificial ceremonies, etc. The counterpart of junior executive officials in the Court of Imperial Entertainments (*kuang-lu ssu*) in other periods. See *hsiao shan-pu* (Catering Bureau). P30.

4231   *nèi shàng-fāng shǔ* 內尚方署
HAN–SUI: variant of *shang-fang shu* (**Central Service Office**) under the Chamberlain for the Palace Revenues (*shao-fu*), presumably so named when the agency was staffed principally by eunuchs. At the beginning of T'ang renamed *chung shang-fang shu.* Also see *shang-fang, shang-fang ling, chung-shang shu.* P38.

4232   *nèi-shè* 內舍
(1) SUI–T'ANG: abbreviation of *nei she-jen* (**Secretary**). (2) SUNG: **Inner College,** 2nd highest of 3 Colleges (*she*) in the National University (*t'ai-hsüeh*) from c. 1070; selected about 20% of students in the Outer College (*wai-she*) for further training, then promoted about half of its students into the Superior College (*shang-she*) for final training. SP: *collège intérieur.*

4233   *nèi shè-jén* 內舍人
(1) SUI: **Secretary,** 4, rank not clear; 2nd-level executive officials in the Secretariat of the Heir Apparent (*men-hsia fang*); at the beginning of T'ang retitled *chung she-jen.* (2)

T'ANG: from 652 to 662 the official variant of *chung she-jen* (**Secretary**) in the Archive of the Heir Apparent (*tien-shu fang*). P26.

4234 *nèi-shěng* 內省

(1) SUNG: abbreviation of *nei-shih sheng* (**Palace Domestic Service**). P38. (2) LIAO: **Palace Domestic Service**, considered part of the Southern Administration's (*nan-mien*) corps of court officials (*ch'ao-kuan*); staffed by eunuchs, including a Commissioner (*shih*), a Vice Commissioner (*fu-shih*), etc. Possibly also an abbreviated reference to the Palace Service Office (*nei-sheng ssu*) at Liao's Eastern Capital near modern Liaoyang, Manchuria. P49.

4235 *nèi-shěng ssū* 內省司

LIAO: **Palace Service Office**, a eunuch agency at the Eastern Capital near modern Liaoyang, Manchuria; provided domestic service that was provided elsewhere by palace women, who were not posted in the Eastern Capital palace; headed by a Vice Commissioner (*fu-shih*) and an Administrative Assistant (*p'an-kuan*). P49.

4236 *nèi-shǐh* 內史

Lit., palace scribe. (1) CHOU: **Royal Secretary,** one ranked as an Ordinary Grand Master (*chung ta-fu*), a member of the Ministry of Rites (*ch'un-kuan*) who prepared all royal documents with the help of a large staff of subordinates; the work reportedly became so important and the post so influential that the original Royal Secretary was retitled Director of Royal Secretaries (*nei-shih ling*) and became something like a chief of the royal staff. CL: *annaliste de l'intérieur*. (2) CH'IN–SUI: **Chamberlain for the Capital,** the administrative executive for local government in the metropolitan area in which the dynastic capital was located, rank =2,000 bushels in Han; c. 140 B.C. divided into 2 posts prefixed Left and Right; later the Right Chamberlain was redesignated Metropolitan Governor (*ching-chao yin*), the Left Chamberlain was redesignated Guardian of the Left (*tso p'ing-i*), and the post Guardian of the Right (*yu fu-feng*) was added to create a triumvirate in charge of the metropolitan area, known collectively as the Three Guardians (*san fu*); all ranked at 2,000 bushels. During the era of N-S Division the term *nei-shih* alternated with *yin* (Metropolitan Governor) and by Sui yielded to *yin*. HB: clerk of the capital. P53, 54. (3) HAN–SUI, LIAO, YÜAN: **Administrator** delegated from the central government to serve as chief executive official of a Princedom (*wang-kuo*) or Marquisate (*hou-kuo*); in 8 B.C. superseded by *hsiang* (Administrator) and *kuo-hsiang* (Counselor-delegate), but revived in post-Han times to alternate with the titles *hsiang* and *chang-shih* (Administrator); in T'ang *chang-shih* became the standard, though *nei-shih* was revived again by Liao and Yüan. In its early history, *nei-shih* was the counterpart in a quasi-official fief of a Commandery Governor (*chün t'ai-shou*). P32, 69. (4) SUI: **Director of the Secretariat** (*nei-shih sheng*), changed from *chung-shu ling* in early Sui to avoid a personal-name taboo, then in 616 changed to *nei-shu ling* (see *nei-shu sheng*). In T'ang from 618 to 620 and again from 684 to 705, *nei-shih* and *nei-shih sheng* were revived to replace *chung-shu ling* (Secretariat Director) and *chung-shu sheng* (Secretariat). P3. (5) MING–CH'ING: unofficial reference to the **Hanlin Academy** (*han-lin yüan*). (6) CH'ING: unofficial reference to a **Secretary in the Grand Secretariat** (*nei-ko chung-shu*). P3. (7) In any era may be encountered as the equivalent of *nèi-shìh* (Palace Attendant), specifically meaning a **eunuch.**

4237 *nèi-shìh* 內侍

Lit., to serve (be in attendance) in the palace: **Palace At-**tendant. (1) N-S DIV: common designation for civil officials with duty stations inside the imperial palace, especially those organized into the Palace Administration (*tien-chung chien, tien-chung chü*) or under supervision of the Chamberlain for the Palace Revenues (*shao-fu*). (2) T'ANG–CH'ING: common quasiofficial designation of eunuchs. (3) T'ANG–SUNG: official title of some eunuchs in the Palace Administration (*tien-chung chien, tien-chung sheng*). RR: *chef de l'intendance du palais intérieur*. SP: *intendant du palais intérieur*. P37, 38. (4) CH'ING: prestige title (*san-kuan*) for eunuchs of rank 9.

4238 *nèi-shìh chǎng* 內侍長

N-S DIV (N. Wei): **Director of Palace Attendants,** 4, rank and organizational affiliation not clear; responsible for giving counsel to the Emperor, reminding him of things omitted, responding to his questions, etc. P37.

4239 *nèi-shìh chiēh* 內侍階

SUNG: **Eunuch rank titles,** corresponding to prestige titles (*san-kuan*) awarded to civil and military appointees; a scale of 12 titles was created in 1112, prior to which eunuchs shared the prestige titles used for civil officials. The 12 eunuch rank titles, in descending order of prestige, were *kung-feng kuan, tso shih-chin, yu shih-chin, tso-pan tien-chih, yu-pan tien-chih, huang-men, chih-hou shih-chin, chih-hou tien-chih, chih-hou huang-men, nei-p'in, chih-hou nei-p'in,* and *t'ieh chih-hou nei-p'in,* qq.v. P68.

4240 *nèi-shìh chiēn* 內侍監

(1) T'ANG: **Palace Domestic Service,** the agency in which palace eunuchs were organized; created in 621 by renaming the *ch'ang-ch'iu chien* inherited from Sui, then in 662 more durably named *nei-shih sheng*. In 743 renamed *nei-shih chien* again, but only very briefly. RR: *département de l'intendance du palais intérieur*. P38. (2) T'ANG–SUNG: **Director of the Palace Domestic Service** (in Sung the Service was called *nei-shih sheng* or *ju-nei nei-shih sheng*), normally 2, rank 3b or 3a. RR+SP: *directeur de l'intendance du palais intérieur*. P38.

4241 *nèi-shǐh chiēn* 內史監

MING: **Directorate of Palace Attendants,** the organization of palace eunuchs in the founding reign (1368–1398); in the early 1400s disappeared as eunuch numbers grew, yielding to the emergence of 12 Directorates (see *shih-erh chien*), 4 Offices (*ssu*), and 8 Services (*chü*) staffed by eunuchs. See *t'ai-chien.*

4242 *nèi-shǐh fǔ* 內史府

YÜAN: **Princely Administration,** one created to manage the establishment of each Prince, headed by an Administrator (*nei-shih*), rank 2a; also used in reference to the administrative unit that managed the 4 ordos that originated as the personal entourage of Chingis Khan. Cf. *ssu* (Court). P69.

4243 *nèi-shǐh hsiàng* 內史相

N-S DIV: **Administrative Counselor,** delegated from the central government to administer a Princedom (*wang-kuo*) or a Marquisate (*hou-kuo*); alternating with the titles *hsiang* (Administrator) and *kuo-hsiang* (Counselor-delegate). P53.

4244 *nèi-shìh kāo-pān* 內侍高班

SUNG: **Eunuch of the High Duty Group** (?), variant of *yu-pan tien-chih* (Eunuch of the Right Duty Group), 5th highest of 12 rank titles granted eunuchs from 1112; see *nei-shih chieh*. P68.

4245 *nèi-shìh kāo-p'ín* 內侍高品

SUNG: **Eunuch of High Rank,** variant of *tso-pan tien-chih*

(Eunuch of the Left Duty Group), 4th highest of 12 rank titles granted eunuchs from 1112; see *nei-shih chieh*. P68.

4246   *nèi-shìh kuān* 內侍官
Palace Attendant. (1) N-S DIV: common designation of civil officials with duty stations inside the imperial palace, especially those organized into the Palace Administration (*tien-chung chien, tien-chung chü*) or under supervision of the Chamberlain for the Palace Revenues (*shao-fu*). (2) T'ANG–CH'ING: common quasiofficial generic reference to palace eunuchs. Cf. *nei-shih*.

4247   *nèi-shìh pān* 內侍班
SUNG: **Eunuch Duty Group,** categorical reference to eunuchs in active attendance on the Emperor, in the sense of a day shift and a night shift, or a morning shift and an evening shift; some particularizing prefix should be expected; may refer only to eunuchs bearing the highest 6 of 12 eunuch rank titles (*nei-shih chieh*). Also see *pan*. SP: *classe des intendants du palais.*

4248   *nèi-shìh pó* 內侍伯
T'ANG: variant of the eunuch title *nei-ssu po* (**Senior Steward**).

4249   *nèi-shìh shěng* 內使省
SUI–SUNG: **Palace Domestic Service,** agency of palace eunuchs (from this era commonly called *nei-shih;* also called *nei-ch'en, huan-kuan, t'ai-chien*) and to a lesser extent palace women (*kung-nü, nü-kuan*), who in general were the only persons outside the Emperor's immediate family who were allowed in the innermost living quarters of the palace, where they provided intimate personal service for the Emperor, his Empress, and his various lesser wives. Created at the beginning of Sui by combining 2 units formerly subordinate to the Chamberlain for the Palace Revenues (*shao-fu, t'ai-fu*), the Palace Treasury Service (*nei-fu chü*) and the Palace Discipline Service (*i-t'ing chü*); became one of the top-echelon agencies in the central government called the Five Departments (*wu sheng*), but in 607 demoted to Directorate (*chien*) status as Directorate of Palace Domestic Service (*ch'ang-ch'iu chien*). In its early years the T'ang dynasty, in an apparent shift from Sui policy, rigidly confined eunuchs to this agency, requiring a special imperial warrant for any eunuch to take up a post outside the palace; and it gave eunuchs no rank higher than 4. In 621 the name *ch'ang-ch'iu chien* was changed to *nei-shih chien,* and from 662 the standard name was *nei-shih sheng*. Official variant names existed briefly: *ssu-kung t'ai* from 685 to 705 and *nei-shih chien* again very briefly in 754, or perhaps a year longer. From the 750s the early T'ang restrictions on eunuch activities loosened, and through the 800s eunuchs gained almost paramount power in the central government by their dominance of such agencies as the Palace Secretariat (*shu-mi yüan*) and the Armies of Inspired Strategy (*shen-ts'e chün*), and in outlying territories with status as Military Commissioners (*chieh-tu shih*). In late T'ang a eunuch-dominated Court of Palace Attendants (*hsüan-hui yüan*) overshadowed the Palace Domestic Service in the routine administration of the palace. This trend continued during the Five Dynasties era and into Sung times, when the Palace Domestic Service became a non-eunuch, civil service agency that substantially encroached on the authority of the non-eunuch Palace Administration (*tien-chung sheng*) inherited from T'ang, in which some eunuchs were assigned to collaborate with civil officials. The non-eunuch Palace Domestic Service included among its constituent agencies a Palace Eunuch Service (*ju-nei nei-shih sheng*) in which eunuchs were organized, coexisting alongside the

Court of Palace Attendants. In 1160 the Palace Eunuch Service was absorbed into the Palace Domestic Service, and this again was made a wholly eunuch organization; but it came to be overshadowed by the Court of Palace Attendants, and after Sung the name *nei-shih sheng* was not officially restored. Throughout its history, the Palace Domestic Service was normally headed by one or more Directors (*chien*), rank 3b1 in T'ang, 3a in Sung, with the aid of Vice Directors (*shao-chien*); and in Sui–T'ang times its eunuch members were distributed among 6 Services (*chü*). In Sui this battery included a Palace Food Service (*nei shang-shih chü*), an Office of Female Services (*i-t'ing chü*), a Palace Gates Service (*kung-wei chü*), a Menials Service (*hsi-kuan chü*), a Livery Service for the Empress (*nei-p'u chü*), and a Palace Treasury Service (*nei-fu chü*). The T'ang battery differed only slightly, not including a Palace Food Service but including an Inner Quarters Service (*nei-fang* till 739, then *nei-fang chü*). Such Services were normally headed by one or 2 Directors (*ling*), but the Inner Quarters Service did not get a Director until 739, after having been headed by a Palace Manager (*tien-nei*). The Directors of these Services were normally in pairs and ranked either 7b2 or 8a2, but the Director of the Inner Quarters Service ranked 5b2. In Sung the Palace Domestic Service did not have such constituent Services but did supervise an Imperial Dispensary (*yü-yao yüan*) operated jointly with the Palace Administration, a Monitors Office at the East Palace Gate (*nei tung-men ssu*), a Certificate Validation Office (*ho-t'ung p'ing-yu ssu*), a Manufactory (*tsao-tso so*), etc. Another of its subordinate agencies was an Artisans Institute (*han-lin yüan*) staffed with astrologers, calligraphers, painters, and physicians, not to be confused with the Hanlin Academy (also *han-lin yüan*) staffed with Academicians (*hsüeh-shih*). RR: *département de l'intendance du palais intérieur.* SP: *cour de l'inten-dance du palais intérieur.* P37, 38.

4250   *nèi-shǐh shěng* 內史省
SUI–T'ANG: possible variant of *chung-shu sheng* (**Secretariat**); also see *nei-shu sheng*.

4251   *nèi-shìh tièn-t'óu* 內侍殿頭
SUNG: variant of *yu shih-chin* (**Chief Eunuch of the Right**), 3rd highest of 12 rank titles granted eunuchs from 1112. P68.

4252   *nèi-shìh tū-chīh* 內侍都知
SUNG: **Office Manager** (eunuch) in the Palace Domestic Service (*nei-shih sheng*); also attached to some other agencies, e.g., the Office of Musical Instruction (*ch'ien-hsia chiao-fang so*). SP: *intendant ou administrateur général.* P59.

4253   *nèi-shìh yā-pān* 內侍押班
SUNG: **Administrative Aide,** variant designation of the eunuch Notary of the Palace Domestic Service (*ch'ien-shu sheng-shih*), rank 4 or 5; the variant was apparently used primarily when such a eunuch was delegated for special duty outside the palace or even the capital, e.g., to the Directorate of Waterways (*tu-shui chien*) for service in one of its Branch Directorates (*wai tu-shui chien*), or in S. Sung to the military headquarters called the Palace Command (*tien-ch'ien ssu*) for service in its subordinate units, e.g., as Targets and Arrows Section Chief (*chao-chien ya-pan;* see *chao-chien pan*). Also see *nei-shih, ya-pan*. SP: *signataire pour les affaires du département du palais intérieur, adminis-trateur.*

4254   *nèi-shù* 內豎
CHOU: **Junior Eunuch,** designation of castrated boys who

had not yet reached maturity, number indefinite; served in the royal palace as messengers, etc., under the Ministry of State (*t'ien-kuan*). CL: *jeunes de l'intérieur*.

4255   *nèi shū-mì shǐh* 內樞密使
T'ANG: variant of the eunuch title *shu-mi shih* (**Palace Secretary**).

4256   *nèi-shū shěng* 內書省
T'ANG: only from 618 to 620, the official designation of the top-echelon central government agency known at other times as *chung-shu sheng* (**Secretariat**). There is some confusion about this in the sources. It is possible that in early Sui the *chung-shu sheng* was renamed *nei-shih sheng* (Secretariat) and that in 616 this was renamed *nei-shu sheng*, a name perpetuated by T'ang till 620. Some sources contend that in the late Sui years the traditional Secretariat (*chung-shu sheng*) was headed by Directors called both *nei-shih ling* and *nei-shu ling*, or that in 618 the T'ang founder chose the designations *nei-shih sheng* and *nei-shih ling* and then in 620 changed them to *chung-shu sheng* and *chung-shu ling*. RR: *département du grande secrétariat impérial*. P3.

4257   *nèi shū-t'áng* 內書堂
MING: **Eunuch School** established in the palace in 1429 to train young eunuchs to be literate. This violated the founding Emperor's principle that eunuchs should be kept illiterate to minimize their influence on governmental affairs and has been denounced by later historians as the seed from which eunuch dominance over the court grew notoriously in subsequent years.

4258   *nèi shuài-fǔ* 內率府
SUI-SUNG: **Inner Guard Command,** 2 prefixed Left and Right; military units assigned to the establishment of the Heir Apparent, each headed by a Commandant (*shuai*), rank 4a in T'ang, 7b in Sung. From 662 to 670 redesignated the Good Fortune Guards (*feng-yü wei*). P26.

4259   *nèi-ssū* 內司
Inner Offices. (1) May be encountered in any era as a reference to eunuch offices or palace women offices, but should be interpreted with careful attention to context. (2) SUNG: collective reference to 3 powerful agencies in the early Sung central government: the Bureau of Military Affairs (*shu-mi yüan*), Court of Palace Attendants (*hsüan-hui yüan*), and State Finance Commission (*san ssu*). Cf. *nei-kuan, nei-shih*. P38.

4260   *nèi ssū-fú* 內司服
CHOU: **Eunuch Master of the Wardrobe** under the Ministry of State (*t'ien-kuan*), in charge of the palace women who prepared and maintained the formal gowns of the Queen (*hou*) and of secondary royal wives as well. Antecedent of later agencies such as the *shang-fu chü* (Wardrobe Service) in T'ang and Ming times. Cf. *ssu-fu*. CL: *directeur des habillements à l'intérieur*.

4261   *nèi-ssù pó* 內寺伯
T'ANG: **Senior Steward,** a rank 7b eunuch post in the Palace Domestic Service (*nei-shih sheng*); 2 till 788, then 6; maintained police-like scrutiny over residents in the palace, mainly palace women. RR: *chargé du police du palais intérieur*.

4262   *nèi tà-ch'én* 內大臣
(1) CH'ING: **Grand Minister of the Imperial Household Department,** abbreviated from *nei-wu fu ta-ch'en*, a general reference to members of the imperial family, nobles, and other eminent personages who staffed the Imperial

Household Department (*nei-wu fu*). (2) CH'ING: **Grand Minister Assistant Commander of the Imperial Guardsmen,** 6, rank 1b; a command echelon 2nd only to 6 Grand Ministers of the Imperial Household Department Concurrently Controlling the Imperial Guardsmen (*ling shih-wei nei ta-ch'en*), 1a; also see *ch'in-chün wei* (Imperial Bodyguard). BH: senior assistant chamberlain of the imperial bodyguard. P37.

4263   *nèi-t'ái* 內臺
(1) N-S DIV (Sung, N. Wei): lit., inner pavilion: one of many variant designations of the evolving **Department of State Affairs** (see *shang-shu sheng*); inner because located at the dynastic capital, in contrast to Branch Departments of State Affairs (*hsing-t'ai, shang-shu ta hsing-t'ai*) set up to administer newly absorbed territory. Also see *shang-shu t'ai, shang-shu ssu, tu-sheng, pei-sheng, chung-t'ai*. P50. (2) YÜAN: variant reference to the metropolitan **Censorate** (*yü-shih t'ai*) located at the dynastic capital, in contrast to Branch Censorates (*hsing yü-shih t'ai*) generically called Outer Censorates (*wai-t'ai*), a term sometimes denoting all surveillance agencies outside the capital, including Surveillance Commissions (*t'i-hsing an-ch'a ssu*). P18.

4264   *nèi-tièn ch'éng-chìh* 內殿承制
SUNG: **Palace Courier,** rank and organizational affiliation not clear; likely a member of the eunuch-staffed Palace Domestic Service (*nei-shih sheng*). SP: *courrier impérial de la salle intérieure*.

4265   *nèi-tièn chíh* 內殿直
SUNG: **Palace Duty Group,** reference to personnel of the Palace Command (*tien-ch'ien ssu*) on rotational active duty within the palace; apparently used most commonly as a suffix (or possibly a prefix) attached to a regular military title. SP: *service ou garde du palais intérieur*.

4266   *nèi tièn-yǐn* 內典引
T'ANG: **Palace Presenter,** eunuch member(s) of the Palace Domestic Service (*nei-shih sheng*) who announced the introduction of anyone into the imperial presence; number not clear. RR: *intendant chargé d'introduire les visiteurs au palais intérieur*.

4267   *nèi-t'íng* 內廷
Common variant throughout history of *nei-ch'ao* (**Inner Court**).

4268   *nèi-t'íng chīh-hòu* 內廷祗候
SUNG, CH'ING: variant of the generic term *chih-hou nei-t'ing* (**Palace Attendant**).

4269   *nèi-t'íng kūng-fèng* 內廷供奉
(1) SUNG: common variant of the generic term *kung-feng nei-t'ing* (**Palace Attendant**). (2) CH'ING: **Palace Provisioner,** from 1726 a rank 7 eunuch member of the Directorate of Palace Domestic Service (*kung-tien chien*); considered a Staff Supervisor (*shou-ling kuan*).

4270   *nèi-t'íng kūng-yùng* 內廷供用
CH'ING: **Palace Supplier,** from 1726 a rank 8 eunuch member of the Directorate of Palace Domestic Service (*kung-tien chien*); considered a Staff Supervisor (*shou-ling kuan*).

4271   *nèi-t'íng shìh* 內廷侍
CH'ING: **Chief of Domestic Service,** from 1726 a rank 5b eunuch member of the Directorate of Palace Domestic Service (*kung-tien chien*); considered a Staff Supervisor (*shou-ling kuan*), but not the head of the Directorate, which had both a Supervisory Commissioner (*tu-ling shih*), 4a, and a Commissioner (*shih, cheng-shih*), 4b.

4272 *nèi-t'íng tài-chào* 內廷待詔
CH'ING: **Palace Editorial Assistant,** from 1726 a rank 6 eunuch member of the Directorate of Palace Domestic Service (*kung-tien chien*); considered a Staff Supervisor (*shou-ling kuan*).

4273 *nèi-tsăi* 內宰
CHOU: **Palace Administrator,** 2 ranked as Junior Grand Masters (*hsia ta-fu*), members of the Ministry of State (*t'ien-kuan*) responsible for managing the affairs of all palace women including the Queen (*hou*), monitoring the productivity of those palace women with assigned craft duties, and supervising those palace eunuchs assigned to the women's quarters. Controlled a number of subsidiary agencies and personnel, e.g., Palace Attendants (*nei hsiao-ch'en;* attended the Queen), Doorkeepers (*hun-jen*), Junior Eunuchs (*nei-shu*), Royal Tailors (*feng-jen*). The title may be encountered in the following imperial age as an archaic reference to the head of any agency responsible for management of the palace, e.g., the Sui–T'ang Palace Administration (*tien-nei sheng, tien-chung sheng*), the Sui–Sung Palace Domestic Service (*nei-shih sheng*), the Ch'ing Imperial Household Department (*nei-wu fu*). Also see *kung-cheng* (Palace Steward), *kung-po* (Master of the Palace Militia). CL: *administrateur de l'intérieur.* P37, 38.

4274 *nèi tsăi-hsiàng* 內宰相
Grand Councilor in the Palace: from T'ang on an occasional unofficial and no doubt sardonic reference to any high official who won unusual favor with the ruler.

4275 *nèi-tsăi ssū* 內宰司
YÜAN: **Commissary,** a provisioning agency established whenever there was a Household Service for the Heir Apparent (*ch'u-cheng yüan*) or a Household Administration of the Empress Dowager (*hui-cheng yüan*), to supply its needs; staffing not regularly prescribed. P26.

4276 *nèi tsàng-k'ù* 內藏庫 or *nei-tsang*
Palace Storehouse, a storage vault for goods considered the Emperor's personal property. (1) SUNG: one of 3 treasuries or vaults supervised by the Court of the Imperial Treasury (*t'ai-fu ssu*), headed by a Commissioner (*shih*), rank 7a; received state surplus goods at the end of each year, to be held for times of emergency needs. Cf. *feng-chen k'u* (Jewelry Storehouse), *chih-hou k'u* (Storehouse for Gifts), *tso tsang-k'u* (Left Storehouse), *yu tsang-k'u* (Right Storehouse). SP: *magasin du trésor du palais pour les dépenses extraordinaires.* (2) LIAO: maintained by the Palace Domestic Service (*nei-sheng*) in the Southern Administration (*nan-mien*) but apparently functioned as part of the Northern Administration (*pei-mien*), probably much the same as the Sung counterpart; headed by a eunuch Superintendent (*t'i-tien*). P38. (3) CHIN: a unit of the Court Ceremonial Institute (*hsüan-hui yüan*) headed by a Commissioner, 5b; in 1162 divided into 4 storehouses, differentiating names not clear. P38. (4) YÜAN: a unit of the Directorate of the Imperial Treasury (*t'ai-fu chien*), headed by a Superintendent, 5b. P38.

4277 *nèi-ts'ăng* 內倉
CH'ING: **Palace Granary,** 8 in the Peking area for supplying the imperial household with grain and horse fodder; originally managed by eunuchs but in 1653 transferred to the Ministry of Revenue (*hu-pu*); each managed by 2 Superintendents (*chien-tu*) detached for such duty from regular posts in the Ministry's Kwangsi Bureau (*kuang-hsi ch'ing-li ssu*), both Manchu and Chinese; in 1693 Superintendents were ordered chosen from among the Manchu, Mongol, and Chinese Bannermen members of (all?) the

Ministry's Bureau(s) who had earned eligibility for minor commissions (*hsiao-ch'ai;* see *ch'ai-ch'ien*) and the Bureaus' (Bureau's?) elderly officials, one per Granary; in 1763 it was fixed that each Granary should have 2 Superintendens̆, both Manchu, chosen for 2-year duty assignments from the personnel of the Ministry's Bureau(s). Cf. *ts'ang-ch'ang* (Capital Granary). BH: court granary. P6.

4278 *nèi-ts'áo* 內曹
N-S DIV (N. Ch'i): abbreviation of *nei pu-ping ts'ao* (**Inner Section** of infantry).

4279 *nèi-tsò ch'iăo-érh* 內作巧兒
T'ANG: **Palace Artisan,** 42 non-official craftsmen authorized for the Directorate of Imperial Manufactories (*shao-fu chien, nei-fu chien, shang-fang chien*). See *ling-chin fang.* RR: *garçon habile pour les fabrications de l'intérieur du palais.* P38.

4280 *nèi tsŏ-k'ù* 內左庫
N-S DIV: **Inner Storehouse of the Left,** one of 2 storehouses established in Chin times by splitting up the earlier Storehouse Section (*k'u-ts'ao*) established in the Yangtze delta region and staffed with Censors (*yü-shih*), the 2nd known as the Outer Storehouse of the Left (*wai tso-k'u*); specific functions not clear. In Sung the 2nd unit was abolished in the era 424–451 and the *nei tso-k'u* was renamed Left Storehouse (*tso-k'u*), then in c. 460 both units were re-established only to be abolished finally in c. 465. P7.

4281 *nèi-tsò shĭh* 內作使
T'ANG: **Palace Construction Commissioner,** irregularly assigned from the staff of the Directorate for the Palace Buildings (*chiang-tso chien*) as the on-site director of a major construction project in the imperial palace. Sources are confusing about this title, linking it only with *nei-tso shih ling-chiang* (Palace Silk Worker) of the Directorate for Imperial Manufactories (*shao-fu chien*) and suggesting that it had no independent existence. P38.

4282 *nèi-tsò shĭh líng-chiàng* 內作使綾匠
T'ANG: **Palace Silk Worker,** 83 non-official craftsmen authorized for the Directorate for Imperial Manufactories (*shao-fu chien, nei-fu chien, shang-fang chien*) to produce silk goods for palace use. Sources are confusing about this title, which appears to suggest literally that the silk workers had a special relationship with Palace Construction Commissioners (? *nei-tso shih*). RR: *artisan chargé des soieries des fabrications de l'intérieur du palais.* P38.

4283 *nèi-tsūng* 內宗
CHOU: **Royal Kinswoman,** general reference to women of the royal family who bore the royal surname, all of whom were awarded titles of nobility (*chüeh*); supervised by the Ministry of Rites (*ch'un-kuan*). Cf. *wai-tsung.* CL: *honorable de l'intérieur.*

4284 *nèi tū-chĭh ssū* 內都知司
SUNG: **Headquarters Bureau,** one of several Bureaus (*ssu*) in the Palace Eunuch Service (*ju-nei nei-shih sheng*), part of the Palace Domestic Service (*nei-shih sheng*); apparently the Service's internal administration unit, with a eunuch Office Manager (*tu-chih*), rank 6a, in charge. SP: *bureau de l'administration générale du palais intérieur.*

4285 *nèi-tù k'ō* 內度科
YÜAN: **Special Accounts Section,** one of 6 Sections (*k'o*) through which the Ministry of Revenue (*hu-pu*) carried out its principal functions of gathering and expending the government's tax income; presumably handled receipts that were considered due to the Emperor, in contrast to a General

Accounts Section (*wai-tu k'o*), which presumably dealt with more general revenues and expenditures. Headed by a Clerk (*ling-shih*), unranked. Comparable to the *chin-k'o*, q.v., of earlier and later times; also see *tu-chih k'o*. P6.

4286 *nèi tūng-mén ch'ǔ-sǒ ssū* 內東門取索司
or *nei tung-men ssu*
SUNG: **Monitors Office at the East Palace Gate,** staffed by the Palace Eunuch Service (*ju-nei nei-shih sheng*), part of the Palace Domestic Service (*nei-shih sheng*); accepted memorials and petitions while carefully scrutinizing those who submitted them. SP: *bureau de la porte de l'est du palais intérieur chargé de recevoir les dépêches secrètes.*

4287 *nèi tūng-mén tū-chīh ssū* 內東門都知司
SUNG: **Headquarters Bureau at the East Palace Gate,** staffed by the Palace Eunuch Service (*ju-nei nei-shih sheng*), part of the Palace Domestic Service (*nei-shih sheng*); presumably headed by an Office Manager (*tu-chih*), rank 6a. Apparently superior to the Monitors Office at the East Palace Gate (*nei tung-men ch'ü-so ssu*), but the division of responsibilities between the 2 agencies is not clear. Also see *nei tu-chih ssu* (Headquarters Bureau of the Palace Eunuch Service), which might easily, but no doubt erroneously, be considered an abbreviation of *nei tung-men tu-chih ssu*. SP: *bureau de l'administration générale de la porte de l'est du palais intérieur.*

4288 *nèi tūng-t'óu kūng-fèng kuān* 內東頭供奉官
SUNG: **Court Service Official on the East,** a title for some rank 5 or 6 palace eunuchs, members of the Palace Eunuch Service (*ju-nei nei-shih sheng*); also a variant of *kung-feng kuan* (**Palace Servitor**), highest of 12 rank titles granted to eunuchs from 1112; see *nei-shih chieh*. Cf. *nei hsi-t'ou kung-feng kuan*. SP: *intendant à la disposition de l'empereur.*

4289 *nèi-wén àn* 內文案
CH'ING: **Personal Staff,** common unofficial reference to those members of the Private Secretariats (*mu-fu*) of provincial Governors (*hsün-fu*) and multi-Province Governors-general (*tsung-tu*) in whom these dignitaries had most confidence, and who consequently enjoyed very close relationships with their superiors. Often abbreviated to *wen-an*.

4290 *nèi wén-hsüéh kuǎn* 內文學館
T'ANG: **Palace Institute of Literature,** an agency charged with the Confucian education of palace women under supervision of the Secretariat (*chung-shu sheng*); in c. 692 renamed *hsi-i kuan* (Institute for Study of the Polite Arts), shortly again renamed *wan-lin nei chiao-fang* (Palace School in the Grove), then quickly restored to its original name but terminated in c. 740. Headed by 2 Erudites for Palace Instruction (*kung-chiao po-shih*), rank 9b2, with a large staff including 12 Erudites of General Instruction in the Palace (*nei-chiao po-shih*) and professional specialists in the regular educational core of classical, historical, philosophical, and literary works and, in addition, in both standard and fancy calligraphy, in law, in mathematics, and in the game called Chinese chess (*ch'i*). After the 740s the education of palace women was entrusted to eunuchs of the Office of Female Services (*i-t'ing chü*) in the Palace Domestic Service (*nei-shih sheng*). RR: *collège des études littéraires du palais intérieur.*

4291 *nèi-wù fǔ* 內務府
CH'ING: **Imperial Household Department,** a multi-agency administrative organization responsible for serving the personal needs of the Emperor, his immediate family, and his intimate attendants in the private residential quarters of the imperial palace; had no functions relating to the general national administration, but was the supreme Inner Court (*nei-ch'ao, nei-t'ing*) organ corresponding to such Outer Court (*wai-ch'ao, wai-t'ing*) organs as the Grand Secretariat (*nei-ko*) and, from 1730, the Council of State (*chün-chi ch'u*), which supervised the national administration. Created in 1661 to absorb and supersede eunuch agencies inherited from Ming, e.g., the Directorate of Ceremonial (*ssu-li chien*), the Department was the Ch'ing counterpart of such earlier agencies as the staff of the Han dynasty Chamberlain for the Palace Revenues (*shao-fu*), the T'ang–Sung Palace Administration (*tien-chung sheng*) and Palace Domestic Service (*nei-shih sheng*), but greatly expanded. The Department was staffed almost entirely by Imperial Bondservants (*huang pao-i*), overwhelmingly Manchus; it was headed by an unprescribed but large number of Supervisors-in-chief (*tsung-kuan*) selected from among the Imperial Princes (*ch'in-wang*), other members of the nobility, and various prestigious personages; all were known generically as Grand Ministers (*ta-ch'en*) or, more fully, Grand Ministers Supervisors-in-chief of the Imperial Household Department (*tsung-kuan nei-wu fu ta-ch'en*), commonly abbreviated to Grand Ministers Supervisors-in-chief (*tsung-kuan ta-ch'en*) or Grand Ministers of the Imperial Household Department (*nei-wu fu ta-ch'en, nei ta-ch'en*). These dignitaries were often detached from the Department's headquarters (*t'ang*) to be in charge of some of the agencies directly subordinate to the Department and some unrelated to it, even agencies of the Outer Court: e.g., as Manager of the Court of Imperial Armaments (*kuan-li wu-pei yüan*), Manager of the Palace Larder (*kuan-li yü ch'a-shan fang shih-wu*), Grand Minister in Command of the Imperial Procession Guard (*chang luan-i wei shih ta-ch'en*), Imperial Household Department Supervisor-in-chief of the ... Imperial Mausoleum (... *ling-ch'in nei-wu fu tsung-kuan*). Top-echelon agencies directly subordinate to the Department were the following 7 Offices (*ssu*): Storage Office (*kuang-ch'u ssu*), Office of Palace Accounts (*k'uai-chi ssu*), Office of Palace Ceremonial (*chang-i ssu*), Office of the Imperial Hunt (*tu-yü ssu*), Office of Palace Justice (*shen-hsing ssu*), Office of Palace Construction (*ying-tsao ssu*), and Office of Imperial Pasturages (*ch'ing-feng ssu*; from 1723), each headed by from one to 4 Directors (*lang-chung*) and from one to 12 Vice Directors (*yüan-wai lang*), except that the Office of Imperial Pasturages was under a Grand Minister on Annual Duty (*chih-nien ta-ch'en*; see *chih-nien*). Major agencies that were subordinate to the Department, but less directly controlled by it, included the Palace Stud (*shang-ssu yüan*), the Court of Imperial Armaments (*wu-pei yüan*), and the Imperial Parks Administration (*feng-ch'en yüan*). Most of the larger, top-echelon agencies in the Department had their own subordinate agencies. The staff of the Department headquarters included one Headquarters Director (*t'ang lang-chung*), 2 Headquarters Secretaries (*t'ang chu-shih*), and many Headquarters Clerks (*t'ang pi-t'ieh-shih*). BH: imperial household. P37, 38, 39.

4292 *nèi-wù liào-k'ù* 內物料庫
SUNG: **Imperial Larder,** a renaming of the *kung-pei k'u*; date not clear. SP: *magasin des provisions du palais intérieur.*

4293 *nèi yǎng-kǒu ch'ù* 內養狗處
CH'ING: **Palace Kennel** maintained at the Auxiliary Palace (*hsing-kung*) in Jehol by the Imperial Household Department (*nei-wu fu*) to provide hunting dogs for the court on its visits; with 2 Heads (*t'ou-mu*), one with rank as Imperial Guardsman Third Class (*san-teng shih-wei*) and one as Junior Guardsman (*lan-ling shih-wei*). The difference

between this kennel and the Outer Kennel (*wai yang-kou ch'u*) is not clear. P37.

4294 *nèi yèh-chě* 內謁者
SUI–T'ANG: **Palace Receptionist,** 12 palace eunuchs, rank 8b2, subordinate to 6 eunuch Directors (*chien*), rank 6a2, in the Palace Domestic Service (*nei-shih sheng*); specially responsible for attending the Empress, but to some extent apparently received memorials submitted to the palace and delivered imperial pronouncements to the central government. See *yeh-che.* RR: *introducteur des visiteurs du palais intérieur; (nei yeh-che chien:) directeur de la réception des visites du palais intérieur.* P38.

4295 *nèi-yūng* 內饔
CHOU: **Grand Chef of the Palace,** 4 ranked as Ordinary Servicemen (*chung-shih*) and 8 as Junior Servicemen (*hsia-shih*), members of the Ministry of State (*t'ien-kuan*) responsible for preparing food for the royal meals, sacrifices, and receptions of dignitaries. Cf. *wai-yung* (Grand Chef for External Ceremonies). CL: *cuisinier de l'intérieur.*

4296 *nèi-yüán* 內園
SUNG: **Palace Garden,** supervised by a Commissioner (*shih*), rank not clear; organizational relationships also not clear. See *nei-yüan* (Palace Park). SP: *jardins du palais intérieur.*

4297 *nèi-yüàn* 內掾
YÜAN: **Clerk,** found in central government agencies; counterpart of *yüan-shih* (Clerk).

4298 *nèi-yüàn* 內苑
T'ANG–SUNG: **Palace Park,** combined designation of a group of small parks within or adjacent to the imperial palace. In T'ang these were divided into 2 sections, West and East, each apparently having a Director (*chien*), rank 6b2; under the Directorate-general of the Imperial Parks (*kung-yüan tsung-chien*), which in turn was subordinate to the Court of the Imperial Granaries (*ssu-nung ssu*). In Sung the Palace Park was managed by a Commissioner (*shih*), rank 7a, but its organizational affiliations are not clear. In particular, the relationships between *kung-yüan* (Imperial Park, Palace Park) and *nei-yüan,* and between this *nei-yüan* (Palace Park) and *nei-yüan* (Palace Garden), are not clear. RR: *parc à l'intérieur du palais.* SP: *parc du palais intérieur.*

4299 *nèi-yǔn* 內允
T'ANG: lit., palace confidant: **Companion** for the Heir Apparent, 2nd ranking post in the Left Secretariat of the Heir Apparent (*men-hsia fang, tso ch'un-fang*), below only the Mentor (*shu-tzu*); rank 5a2. Alternated with the title *chung-yün; nei-yün* was used from 618 to 620 and again from 652 to 656; in other periods *chung-yün* was used. Also see *nei she-jen.* RR: *vice-président du grand secrétariat de gauche de l'héritier du trône.* P26.

4300 *niáng-niáng* 娘娘 or 孃孃
(1) Throughout history a common unofficial reference to an **Empress,** usually with qualifying prefixes, e.g., *t'ai-hou niang-niang* (Empress Dowager). (2) **Consort,** a less common unofficial usage, also with qualifying prefixes, e.g., *hsiao* (little) *niang-niang* for a *fei* (Consort).

4301 *niàng-shíh tiěn-chūn* 釀食典軍
N-S DIV (N. Ch'i): **Commandant-steward,** 2, rank and organizational affiliation not clear, but apparently found on the staffs of Ducal Establishments (*kung-fu*) in charge of providing fine wines and delicacies for banquets. See *tien-chün.* P30.

4302 *niǎo-ch'iāng chǎng* 鳥槍長
CH'ING: **Director of the Gun Room,** 5 unranked personnel (eunuchs?), in charge of the muskets used in imperial hunting in the Imperial Game Preserve (*niao-ch'iang ch'u, yü niao-ch'iang ch'u*). Cf. *nei huo-yao k'u* (Palace Gunpowder Depot). BH: keeper of the gunroom.

4303 *niǎo-ch'iāng ch'ù* 鳥槍處
CH'ING: **Imperial Game Preserve,** an autonomous agency closely related to the Imperial Household Department (*nei-wu fu*), supervised by a Prince or a Grand Minister (*ta-ch'en*) serving as Manager (*kuan-li … shih-wu*). Also called *yü* (Imperial) *niao-ch'iang ch'u.*

4304 *niǎo-ch'iāng hsiāo-chí* 鳥槍驍騎
CH'ING: **Musketeer** of the Firearms Brigade (*huo-ch'i ying*) of the Inner Banners (*nei-ch'i*); headed by a Regimental Commander (*ts'an-ling*), rank 3a. Cf. *niao-ch'iang hu-chün, p'ao hsiao-chi.* See *hsiao-chi.*

4305 *niǎo-ch'iāng hù-chūn* 鳥槍護軍
CH'ING: **Musketeer Guardsman** of the Firearms Brigade (*huo-ch'i ying*), from 1764 a unit of the Inner Banners (*nei-ch'i*); headed by a Regimental Commander (*ts'an-ling*), rank 3a. Cf. *niao-ch'iang hsiao-chi, hu-chün.* BH: imperial regiment of the artillery and musketry division.

4306 *nièh-fǔ* 臬府 or *nièh-ssū* 司 or *nièh-t'ái* 臺
Law Office, unofficial generic reference to Circuit (*tao*) or Province-level (*sheng*) agencies with judicial responsibilities. (1) YÜAN (*fu* or *ssu*): reference to a (Circuit) Surveillance Commission (*t'i-hsing an-ch'a shih ssu, an-ch'a ssu, su-cheng lien-fang shih ssu*). (2) MING–CH'ING (*ssu* or *t'ai*): reference to a Provincial Surveillance Commission (*t'i-hsing an-ch'a shih ssu, an-ch'a ssu*). Also see *fan-fu, fan-ssu, fan-t'ai.*

4307 *nien* 輦
See under the romanization *lien.*

4308 *nièn-chū ts'āo* 念珠曹
T'ANG: lit., rosary section; an unofficial reference to the **Ministry of Revenue** (*hu-pu*), reportedly because that Ministry's officials received a daily cash allowance of 108 copper coins, the number corresponding to the number of beads in a Buddhist rosary.

4309 *nién-lì* 年例
MING: **Annual Military Subsidy,** an aggregation of payments from central government reserves to sustain military organizations, usually paid in silver ingots; an unbudgeted expense, since the early Ming rulers theorized that the hereditary soldiers of the *wei-so* system (see *wei-so*) could support themselves by part-time farming on state-allocated lands (see *chün-t'un, t'un-t'ien*). Probably from the first Ming reign, and certainly not later than the 1450s, the *wei-so* units could neither maintain an adequate national defense nor maintain themselves in their garrisons. Central government subsidies were gradually institutionalized to revive the deteriorating *wei-so* units and increasingly in the 1500s and 1600s to supplement them with paid recruits (*mu-ping*). Through the 1500s the annual subsidy averaged more than 2 million taels and then more than 3 million taels; and from 1618 through 1627 Ming attempts to repel the Manchus cost the central government a cumulative total of some 60 million taels in unbudgeted subsidies.

4310 *níng-fēi* 寧妃
MING: **Restful Consort,** one of the titles granted secondary wives of the Emperor; see *fei.*

4311 *nīng-huā* 凝華
N-S DIV (N. Ch'i): **Lady of Perfect Loveliness,** title granted one of 6 Lesser Concubines (*hsia-pin*) of the Emperor.

4312 *níng-hūi* 凝暉
N-S DIV (N. Ch'i): **Lady of Perfect Radiance,** title granted one of 6 Lesser Concubines (*hsia-pin*) of the Emperor.

4313 *niú-jén* 牛人
CHOU: **Cowherd,** 3 ranked as Ordinary Servicemen (*chung-shih*) and 4 as Junior Servicemen (*hsia-shih*), members of the Ministry of Education (*ti-kuan*) responsible for overseeing the royal oxen herds and providing oxen for sacrificial ceremonies, etc. CL: *bouvier.*

4314 *niú-lù* 牛錄
CH'ING: **Company** (military), Chinese transliteration of the Manchu word *niru,* which served also as the abbreviated title of the **Company Commander** (*tso-ling* in Chinese translation); regularized in 1601 as the basic tribal living-fighting group consisting of 300 people controlled by a Company Commander called *niu-lu o-chen* in Chinese transliteration, earlier the designation of the leader of a 10-man hunting or fighting group. When the Banner system (see *ch'i, pa ch'i*) was established in 1615, each Banner incorporated from 2 to 5 Regiments (*chalan* in Manchu, *chia-la* in Chinese transliteration, *ts'an-ling* in Chinese translation), each of which was a consolidation of 5 Companies, each large enough in theory to provide 300 active fighting men. In 1634 the designation *niu-lu o-chen* was changed to *niu-lu chang-ching* (*tso-ling* in Chinese). At about the same time, Companies were reorganized to be able to provide only 70 to 100 fighting men. P44.

4315 *niú-yáng kūng-yìng sŏ* 牛羊供應所
SUNG: lit., office for the provisioning of cattle and sheep: apparently a variant of *niu-yang ssu* (**Cattle and Sheep Office**). SP: *bureau chargé de fournir les boeufs et les moutons.*

4316 *niú-yáng shŭ* 牛羊署
SUI: **Cattle and Sheep Office,** one of several Offices (*shu*) directly subordinate to the Court of the Imperial Stud (*t'ai-p'u ssu*), headed by a Director (*ling*); responsible for maintaining cattle, oxen, and sheep in the imperial herds. Cf. *tien-mu shu, ssu-yang shu.*

4317 *niú-yáng ssū* 牛羊司
T'ANG–SUNG: **Cattle and Sheep Office,** in T'ang apparently existed only in the dynasty's final century or even its final decades, apparently one each at the 2 capitals, Ch'ang-an and Loyang; organizational affiliation not clear; probably headed by a Commissioner (*shih*); responsible for providing sheep and calves for the imperial table. In Sung probably had similar functions, under the Court of Imperial Entertainments (*kuang-lu ssu*); staffing not clear. SP: *bureau des boeufs et des moutons.* P38.

4318 *nŭ-fāng shŭ* 弩坊署
T'ANG: **Bows Office,** one of 2 subordinate units in the Directorate for Armaments (*chün-ch'i chien*); headed by a Director (*ling*), rank 8a2. Until 632 called *kung-nu shu;* from 723 to 728 the Office or its function was shifted under the Directorate for the Palace Buildings (*chiang-tso chien*). Responsible for the manufacture of bows, crossbows, arrows, various kinds of lances, etc. See *chia-fang shu.* RR: *office de l'atelier des arbalètes.*

4319 *nŭ-shŏu pān* 弩手班
SUNG: **Company of Crossbowmen,** a category of military units controlled by the Palace Command (*tien-ch'ien shih-*

wei ssu) into the 1140s, then in a general reorganization subordinated to the Bureau of Military Affairs (*shu-mi yüan*); special function not clear. SP: *compagnie d'arbalétriers.*

4320 *nú-ts'ái* 奴才
CH'ING: **Slave,** a term with which the Manchus referred to themselves ("your slave," "this slave") when addressing the Emperor; comparable to the traditional Chinese usage of *ch'en* (Minister, "your humble servant")

4321 *nuăn-ch'īng* 煖卿
SUNG–CH'ING: **Intimate Minister,** unofficial reference to certain officials in close attendance on the Emperor such as the Sung dynasty's Chief Minister (*ch'ing*) of the Court of the Imperial Regalia (*wei-wei ssu*) or the Ch'ing dynasty's Grand Minister in Command of the Imperial Procession Guard (*chang luan-i wei shih ta-ch'en*).

4322 *núng-fù* 農父
From high antiquity, a title used for someone of importance with responsibility for improving agriculture through popular education: **Agriculture Master.** May be encountered in any era as an unofficial, archaic reference to such officials as the Minister of Revenue (*hu-pu shang-shu*) in the later dynasties. Often equated with *ssu-t'u* (Minister of Education).

4323 *núng-kuān* 農官
HAN: **Office of Agriculture,** staffing and organizational affiliations not clear; possibly under the Chamberlain for the National Treasury (*ta ssu-nung*), possibly the office of a Commandant of Agriculture (*nung tu-wei*); functions apparently related to the collection of agricultural revenues.

4324 *núng-pŭ chiēn* 農圃監
T'ANG: **Director of Food Production,** one on the staff of each Area Command (*tsung-kuan fu* till 624, then *tu-tu fu*), responsible for monitoring the use of cultivated fields and gardens, maintaining appropriate granaries and stores of firewood, charcoal, and hay, and supervising overland and river transport of such materials. RR: *directeur de l'agriculture et des potagers.*

4325 *núng-pù ts'áo* 農部曹 or *nung-pu*
(1) N-S DIV (San-kuo Wei): **Agriculture Section,** one of several units with specialized functions in the Ministry of Revenue (see *tu-chih, min-pu, hu-pu*) in the evolving Department of State Affairs (*shang-shu sheng*); headed by a Director (*lang-chung, lang*). P6. (2) T'ANG–CH'ING: common unofficial, archaic reference to the **Ministry of Revenue** (*hu-pu*).

4326 *núng-t'ién àn* 農田案
SUNG: **Agriculture Section,** one of 3 Sections (*an*) in the Left Section (*tso-ts'ao*) of the Ministry of Revenue (*hu-pu*) from c. 1080, when the Ministry was fully activated following discontinuance of the State Finance Commission (*san ssu*) of early Sung; staffed with unranked subofficials; monitored the management of state-owned agricultural lands. SP: *service des champs agricoles.* P6.

4327 *núng-ts'āng* 農倉
HAN: **Granary,** designation of state grain depots under the Commandant of the Imperial Gardens (*shui-heng tu-wei*) or, in Later Han, under the Director (*ling*) of the Imperial Forest Park (*shang-lin yüan*), a favorite imperial resort adjoining the dynastic capital. Each Granary was in the charge of a Director (*chang*) and his Aide(s) (*ch'eng*). HB: agricultural granary. P8.

4328 *núng tū-wèi* 農都尉
HAN: **Commandant of Agriculture,** rank not clear, one

appointed to supervise State Farms (*t'un-t'ien*) in each frontier Commandery (*chün*). HB: chief commandant of agriculture.

4329 *nǔ-chēn* 女眞

See the more common romanization *ju-chen* (**Jurchen**); also see *nü-chih*.

4330 *nǔ-ch'ì* 女饎

CHOU: **Female Cook**, 8 employed under 2 eunuch Cereals Chefs (*ch'i-jen*) of the Ministry of Education (*ti-kuan*) to prepare cereals for the royal table and otherwise as required. CL: *femme pour cuire*.

4331 *nǔ-chiāng* 女漿

CHOU: **Female Liquor Maker,** 15 women of the general populace chosen for employment under 5 Eunuch Liquor Makers (*chiang-jen*) of the Ministry of State (*t'ien-kuan*), to produce all liquors required by the ruler and his guests and for formal ceremonies. Cf. *nü-chiu*. CL: *femme aux liquors*.

4332 *nǔ-chíh* 女直

CHIN: variant of the more common tribal name *ju-chen* (**Jurchen**), used as a prefix in some titles, e.g., *nü-chih. ling-shih* (Jurchen Clerk). Also see *ju-chih*.

4333 *nǔ-chiǔ* 女酒

CHOU: **Female Wine Maker,** 30 chosen from the general populace to serve under 10 Eunuch Wine Makers (*chiu-jen*) of the Ministry of State (*t'ien-kuan*) in the preparation of various wines for the royal table and for ceremonial occasions. Each reportedly supervised 12 convicts, who did the most strenuous work. Cf. *nü-chiang* (Female Liquor Maker). CL: *femme aux vins*.

4334 *nǔ-chù* 女祝

CHOU: **Female Supplicant,** 4 women subordinates in the Ministry of State (*t'ien-kuan*), attendants on the Queen (*hou*) especially responsible for praying on her behalf when appropriate and for arranging sacrificial ceremonies in which she participated. Apparently under general supervision of the Palace Administrators (*nei-tsai*). CL: *femme chargée des prières*.

4335 *nǔ ch'ūng-wǎi* 女舂扰

CHOU: lit., woman thresher and grinder: **Female Huller,** 2 women who assisted 2 Eunuch Hullers (*ch'ung-jen*) of the Ministry of Education (*ti-kuan*) and directed 5 convicts in preparing rice required for sacrificial ceremonies. CL: *femme pour battre et vider le mortier*. P6.

4336 *nǔ-fǔ* 女府

CHOU: **Female Storekeeper,** 2 in the service of each of the six Principal Wives (*liu kung*) of the ruler, in each instance under the supervision of 2 eunuch Ministers of Hereditary Consorts (*shih-fu ch'ing*), attached to the Ministry of Rites (*ch'un-kuan*); responsible for provisioning the Queen or one of the 5 other Principal Wives. CL: *femme garde-magasin*.

4337 *nǔ-hǎi* 女醢

CHOU: **Spicewoman,** 20 subordinate to the eunuch Spiceman (*hai-jen*) of the Ministry of State (*t'ien-kuan*), assisting in the preparation of relishes, minced meats, and similar condiments for the royal table and for ceremonial occasions. CL: *hacheuse, femme aux hachis*.

4338 *nǔ-hsī* 女醯

CHOU: **Vinegar Woman,** 20 subordinate to 2 eunuch Vinegarmen (*hsi-jen*) of the Ministry of State (*t'ien-kuan*), assisting in the preparation of all food preserved in vinegar for the royal table or ceremonial occasions. CL: *vinaigrière, femme au vinaigre*.

4339 *nǔ-kǎo* 女稾

CHOU: **Female Banquet Caterer,** 2 assistants to each of 8 eunuch Banquet Caterers (*kao-jen*) of the Ministry of Education (*ti-kuan*), responsible for preparing banquets celebrating victorious military officers and foods offered in various official ceremonies. CL: *femme des rations de récompense*.

4340 *nǔ-kuān* 女官

Palace Woman: throughout history one of the most common general references to imperial consorts, concubines, and some others, though not itself a title.

4341 *nǔ-kūng* 女宮

CHOU: **Female Palace Attendant,** large numbers chosen from the general populace, not to be consorts and concubines, but to be working women subordinate to the eunuchs (*ssu-jen*) who oversaw the activities of the royal consorts and concubines. Some traditional Chinese understood that these were female criminals sentenced to service as slaves in the palace. CL: *femme attachée au service du palais réservé*.

4342 *nǔ-mì* 女冪

CHOU: **Female Provisioner of Sacrificial Wine Covers,** 10 subordinate to the eunuch Provisioner of Sacrificial Wine Covers (*mi-jen*) in the Ministry of State (*t'ien-kuan*). CL: *femme aux toiles pour couvrir*.

4343 *nǔ-piēn* 女籩

CHOU: **Female Basket Handler,** 10 subordinate to the eunuch Basket Handler (*pien-jen*) of the Ministry of State (*t'ien-kuan*), responsible for providing baskets for various foods required for the royal table or for important ceremonies. CL: *femme aux paniers*.

4344 *nǔ shàng-shū* 女尚書

T'ANG: variant reference to any of the Six Matrons (*liu shang*, q.v.).

4345 *nǔ-shǐh* 女史

Female Scribe, a formal title rather than a general descriptive term like *kung-nü* (Palace Woman). (1) CHOU: numerous lowly female attendants in the ruler's palace; particularly handled paperwork in the establishments of the ruler's wives, consorts, and concubines. Cf. *shih* (Scribe). CL: *femme chargée des écritures, femme annaliste*. (2) T'ANG–MING: regularly found on the staffs of the Six Matrons (*liu shang*, q.v.); also a common title of honor added to the principal duty designation of a palace woman. RR: *femme secrétaire*.

4346 *nǔ shìh-chūng* 女侍中

Lady in Palace Attendance. (1) N-S DIV (N. Wei): designation of one category of palace women of high rank (=2) but not a consort or concubine; apparently served as a palace hostess, a mistress of ceremonies in the inner quarters of the palace, or even a chaperone for the Emperor's various wives; at times such a post was held by the mother of a Grand Councilor (*tsai-hsiang*). (2) CH'ING: title of honor conferred on wives of favored eminent officials, especially those chosen to be ladies in waiting on the Empress. See *shih-chung*.

4347 *nǔ shìh-shǐh* 女侍史

HAN: **Female Attendant,** 2 palace women so designated when they accompanied the Emperor on a visit to the Imperial Secretariat (*shang-shu t'ai*), keeping his costume in proper adjustment and carrying incense-burners. HB: female clerk-in-attendance.

4348 *nǚ-t'iāo* 女祧

CHOU: **Chambermaid,** 2 assigned to each of the 8 palace chambers that were dedicated to important (female?) ancestors of the royal family, each such chamber being supervised by a eunuch Caretaker (*shou-t'iao*) of the Ministry of Rites (*ch'un-kuan*). CL: *femme attachée au service du dépôt.*

4349 *nǚ-wū* 女巫

Sorceress, unspecified number, together with male Sorcerers (*nan-wu*) led by 4 Ordinary Servicemen (*chung-shih*) under jurisdiction of the Director of Sorcery (*ssu-wu*) in the Ministry of Rites (*ch'un-kuan*); at appropriate times summoned spirits to be honored or reprimanded, preceded the King on his visits of condolence, prayed for rain and for cessation of epidemics, and participated in many royal sacrifices and other ceremonies. CL: *sorcière.*

4350 *nǚ-yén* 女鹽

CHOU: **Salt Maid,** 20 palace women subordinate to 2 eunuch Salt Stewards (*yen-jen*) of the Ministry of State (*t'ien-kuan*); prepared and provided salt for use by members of the royal family and in appropriate ceremonies. CL: *femme au sel.*

4351 *nǚ-yù* 女御

Secondary Concubine. (1) CHOU: 81 authorized in this category of palace women, considered affiliated with the Ministry of State (*t'ien-kuan*), apparently known collectively as the Hereditary Consorts (*shih-fu*, q.v.); ranked below the Nine Concubines (*chiu pin*) and above the Lesser Wives (*yü-ch'i*), though sometimes equated with the Lesser Wives category. Also called *nei-jen, yü-nü, chiu yü.* CL: *concubine impériale.* (2) SUI–T'ANG: rank 7a then 6a in Sui, 7a1 in T'ang; number fluctuated in Sui from 38 to 81 to 24, in T'ang stabilized at 27. In T'ang not only ranked below the Empress, 4 Consorts (*fei, fu-jen*), and the Nine Concubines, but also ranked below 4 other categories of concubines with ranks from 3a1 down to 6a1. RR: *femme du service de l'empereur.*

4352 *ó-chēn* 額眞

CH'ING: **Commander,** Chinese transliteration of a Manchu word of importance in the early development of the Banner military establishment (see *pa ch'i, ch'i*): originally the informal designation of the leader of a 10-man hunting-fighting unit, in 1611 became the name of newly created Companies (*niru,* Chinese transliteration *niu-lu*) differentiated by the colors of their flags into 4 Banners (*ch'i*); in 1615, when the Eight Banner system was instituted, became the title of leaders at all organizational levels, prefixed with the unit designation—*niu-lu o-chen* (Company Commander), 5 under a Regimental Commander (*chia-la o-chen*), 5 in turn under a Banner Commander (*ku-shan o-chen*); in 1634 all except Banner Commander changed to *chang-ching*—*chia-la chang-ching, niu-lu chang-ching.* In 1660 Banner Commanders (still *ku-shan o-chen*) were given the officially authorized Chinese title *tu-t'ung* (Commander-in-chief); and in 1723 their Manchu title was changed to *ku-shan ang-pang.* See *chang-ching, ang-pang.* P44.

4353 *ó-ěrh-ch'í-mù* 額爾奇木

CHIN: Chinese transliteration of a Jurchen word equated with the Chinese titles *tsung-kuan* (**Area Commander-in-chief**) and *chieh-tu shih* (**Military Commissioner**), referring to chiefs given control over all Jurchen tribes (*pu-tsu*) in areas called Routes (*lu*) other than the Routes controlled directly from the dynastic capital. P17.

4354 *ó-fù* 額駙

CH'ING: **Consort** (i.e., husband) of a noblewoman of imperial descent, equivalent of the titles *fu-ma* and *fu-ma tu-wei* (Commandant-escort) used in earlier times; in 9 grades, from Consort of the ... Imperial Princess of the First Degree (Princess: *ku-lun kung-chu,* Consort: *ku-lun o-fu*) down to Consort of the ... Township Mistress (noblewoman: *hsiang-chün,* Consort: *hsiang-chün o-fu*). Also see *ho-shih o-fu, to-lo o-fu, ku-shan o-fu, chün-chu o-fu, hsien-chu o-fu, chün-chün o-fu, hsien-chün o-fu.* BH: husband of an imperial princess. P69.

4355 *ó-wài* 額外

CH'ING: lit., beyond the quota: **Supernumerary,** prefix attached to titles whenever appointees exceeded the authorized quota (*o*), whether in the central government or in units of territorial administration; e.g., *o-wai ching-li* (Supernumerary Registrar) in a Registry (*ching-li t'ing*), *o-wai shih-lang* (Supernumerary Vice Minister) of the Court of Colonial Affairs (*li-fan yüan*). BH: supernumerary.

4356 *ǒu* 耦 or 偶

CHOU: **Unifying Agent,** categorical reference to 9 types of personages appointed by the Minister of State (*chung-tsai*) as intermediaries or liaison officials between the central government and the Feudal Lords (*chu-hou*); apparently lived in and administered villages or small towns in their jurisdictions. The 9 types were Regional Representative (*mu*), Regional Administrator (*chang*), Regional Mentor (*shih*), Moral Instructor (*ju*), Family Unifier (*tsung*), Economic Overseer (*chu*), Exemplar of Virtue (*shih*), Local Agent (*li*), Friend (*yu*), and Manager of Cultivated Marshes (*sou*). Also known categorically as *liang,* q.v. CL: *couple ou lien d'association.*

4357 *pà* 霸

Hegemon. (1) CHOU: leader of Feudal Lords (*chu-hou*) of the Yellow River drainage area in league or alliance against military threats posed by non-Chinese tribes of the North and East and especially by the great Yangtze River Valley state, Ch'u; first chosen in 678 B.C. by a gathering of lords dedicated to preserving peace and the honor of the Chou King. Under successive Hegemons, the league was active almost to 400 B.C., giving way then to unrestrained warfare among the regional lords that eventually annihilated the Chou dynasty and its feudal organization of China. (2) From late Chou on throughout imperial history, an unofficial term of disparagement applied to those who seized power and ruled by force, in contrast to "true Kings" (*wang*) who were considered legitimate in the eyes of the people and of Heaven because of their personal commitments to peace and benevolent rule.

4358 *pā ch'í* 八旗

CH'ING: **Eight Banners,** collective reference to the system of social-political-military organization of the Manchu people, gradually extended to include 8 Mongol and 8 Chinese Banners, making a total of 24 tribe-like Banners of hereditary troops garrisoned along the frontiers and at strategic places throughout the country. See *ch'i.*

4359 *pā-ch'í kuān-hsüéh* 八旗官學

CH'ING: **Bannermen's School,** one of several types of schools operated by the Directorate of Education (*kuo-tzu chien*); for sons of officers in the Manchu and Mongol Banners; staffed by 16 Manchu and 8 Mongol Instructors (*chu-chiao*), rank 7b. BH: government schools for bannermen. P34.

4360 *pā-ch'í kūng* 八旗公
CH'ING: **Duke of the Eight Banners,** a title of nobility (*chüeh*) awarded to military heroes, subject to perpetual inheritance. Cf. *tsung-shih kung, chüeh-lo kung.*

4361 *pā-ch'í tsŭng-kuăn tà-ch'én*
八旗總管大臣
CH'ING: **Grand Ministers Commanding the Eight Banners,** from predynastic times till 1635, when the dynastic name Ch'ing was adopted and a somewhat more Chinese-like central government was established, a group of military leaders who participated in deliberations and policy formulation at the Manchu court together with 2 other groups, the Five Grand Ministers of the Deliberative Council (*i-cheng wu ta-ch'en*) and the Ten Grand Ministers Administering Affairs (*li-shih shih ta-ch'en*). In 1635 these groups of Manchu noblemen were superseded by another triad, which constituted the top echelon of Ch'ing government until the establishment of a Ming-style Grand Secretariat (*nei-ko*) in 1658. This triad included Three Palace Academies (*nei san yüan*), Six Ministries (*liu pu*), and a Censorate (*tu ch'a-yüan*).

4362 *pá-chiĕh* 拔解
T'ANG: lit., to pluck up and release, i.e., send to the capital: **Irregular Candidate,** categorical reference to candidates at civil service recruitment examinations given in the dynastic capital who had not taken qualifying tests in their home Prefectures (*chou*). Sources suggest that such candidates were not discriminated against.

4363 *pā-chiéh hsüéh-shìh* 八節學士
T'ANG: **Academician of the Eight Solar Seasons,** 8 appointed from 708 to 710 in the Institute for the Advancement of Literature (*hung-wen kuan*) of the Chancellery (*men-hsia sheng*); the Eight Solar Seasons refers to the principal points in the solar year, i.e., equinoxes, solstices, etc. RR: *lettré à l'image des huit divisions de l'année.*

4364 *pā chú* 八局
MING: **Eight Services,** collective reference to 8 minor agencies of palace eunuchs, each headed by a eunuch Commissioner-in-chief (*ta-shih*) or Director (*t'ai-chien*): the Palace Armory (*ping-chang chü*), Jewelry Service (*yin-tso chü*), Palace Laundry Service (*huan-i chü*), Caps and Kerchiefs Service (*chin-mao chü*), Sewing Service (*chen-kung chü*), Palace Weaving and Dyeing Service (*nei chih-jan chü*), Condiments Service (*chiu-ts'u-mien chü*), and Garden Service (*ssu-yüan chü*).

4365 *pā fáng* 八房
SUNG: **Eight Review Sections** in the Court of Judicial Review (*ta-li ssu*); status and staffing not clear. SP: *huit chambres chargées de juger les rapports sur les causes criminelles de province.*

4366 *pā fēn* 八分
CH'ING: **Eight Privileges,** collective term for rights awarded to the upper echelon of the imperial nobility (*chüeh*), including the ranks of Imperial Prince (*ch'in-wang*), Commandery Prince (*chün-wang*), Beile (*pei-lo*), Beile Prince (*pei-tzu*), Defender Duke (*chen-kuo kung*), and Bulwark Duke (*fu-kuo kung*). The special privileges referred to the use of purple buttons, 3-eyed peacock feathers, and dragon squares on costumes; red-painted spears at entrances of residences; breast-tassels and purple reins on horses; a special type of teapot; and sitting on yellow or red rugs (BH, p. 6). Lesser members of the imperial nobility were designated "not to encroach on the 8 privileges" (*pu ju pa-fen*); e.g., Lesser Defender Duke (*pu ju pa-fen chen-kuo kung*).

4367 *pā-fù tsăi-hsiàng* 八付宰相
Variant of *nei pa-fu tsai-hsiang* (**Grand Councilors of the Eight Palace Offices**).

4368 *pā hsiào-wèi* 八校尉
HAN: **Eight Commandants,** collective reference to 8 military leaders including both regular officers and eunuchs who at the end of Han were entrusted with defense of the dynastic capital city and the palace. Their separate forces were called the Upper Army (*shang-chün*), Middle (*chung*) Army, Lower (*hsia*) Army, Control (*tien*) Army, Support (*chu*) Army, Secondary (*tso*) Army, Left (*tso*) Army, and Right (*yu*) Army.

4369 *pă-júng* 把戎
MING–CH'ING: unofficial reference to a military officer entitled *pa-tsung* (**Squad Leader**), q.v.

4370 *pā-kŭ wén* 八股文
MING–CH'ING: **Eight-legged Essay,** from the 1500s a prescribed form in which papers were required to be written in civil service recruitment examinations, hence taught in all schools that prepared men for the examinations; came to be a rigid control over the sequence of rhetorical steps in organizing a paper and over the total number of words as well. Commonly considered a rhetorical straitjacket that led to overly disciplined, too uncreative writing and thinking among all educated Chinese.

4371 *pā kūng* 八公
N-S DIV (N. Wei): **Eight Dukes,** from 414 a collective reference to an ever-enlarged group of eminent personages considered the topmost echelon of the officialdom, each with a large staff though without any prescribed function except to give counsel when called on; derived from the earlier term Three Dukes (*san kung,* q.v.), instituted in acknowledgment that the number 3 was no longer adequate. The group commonly included several kinds of Counselors-in-chief (*ch'eng-hsiang, tso ch'eng-hsiang, yu ch'eng-hsiang, hsiang-kuo*) and such titles as Minister of Education (*ssu-t'u*), Minister of Works (*ssu-k'ung*), Censor-in-chief (*yü-shih ta-fu*), Commander-in-chief (*ta ssu-ma*), Defender-in-chief (*t'ai-wei*), General-in-chief (*ta chiang-chün*), Pillar of State (*chu-kuo*), and Bulwark of Government (*fu-cheng*). Sometimes interpreted as the equivalent of *pa kuo* (Eight Statesmen), *pa pu ta-fu* (Eight Grand Masters of the Ministries), and even *pa pu ta-jen* (Eight Tribal Overseers), though no such equivalences seem likely. P2.

4372 *pá kùng-shēng* 拔貢生 or *pa-kung*
CH'ING: lit., a student plucked up and offered as tribute: **Graduate for Preeminence,** designation of students sent from Confucian Schools (*ju-hsüeh*) throughout the empire every 12th year for admission to the National University (*t'ai-hsüeh*) maintained at the dynastic capital by the Directorate of Education (*kuo-tzu chien*), as distinguished supernumeraries beyond the more regular presentation of Tribute Students (*kung-sheng*); the Directorate on such occasions prescribed a supplementary quota of one or 2 students from each Confucian School. BH: senior licentiate of the first class.

4373 *pā kuó* 八國
N-S DIV (N. Wei): lit., 8 states, traditionally explained as referring to the 4 sides (*fang*) of the capital city plus the 4 cardinal points (*wei*) of the compass: **Eight Statesmen,** traditionally interpreted as a variant of *pa pu ta-fu* (Eight Grand Masters of the Ministries) and even *pa kung* (Eight Dukes), but more likely a variant of *pa pu ta-jen* or *pa ta-jen kuan* (both Eight Tribal Overseers). Also probably unrelated to

pa tso (Eight Executives). Also see *ta jen* (Tribal Overseer).

4374 *pă-mén* 把門
SUNG: **Palace Doorman** in the innermost quarters of the imperial residence; eunuchs (*nei-p'in*), number indefinite, rank 8, members of the Palace Eunuch Service (*ju-nei nei-shih sheng*).

4375 *pā-p'ĭn àn* 八品案
SUNG: **Section for Eighth Rank Personnel,** a unit in the Ministry of Personnel's (*li-pu*) Junior Appointments Process (*shih-lang hsüan; see hsüan*), subordinate to the Director (*lang-chung*) of the Bureau of Evaluations (*k'ao-kung ssu*). SP: *service des fonctionnaires de 8ème rang.* P5.

4376 *pā pù tà-fū* 八部大夫
N-S DIV: **Eight Grand Masters of the Ministries,** occasional variant of *pa tso* (Eight Executives). Cf. *pa kung, pa kuo, pa pu ta-jen.*

4377 *pā pù tà-jén* 八部大人
N-S DIV (N. Wei): **Eight Tribal Overseers,** fullest development of the institution of Tribal Overseers (*ta-jen*), originally 2, then 4, then 8. The terminology is confusing because *pu* is commonly used in the sense of Tribe (*pu-lo, pu-tsu*) and also for the agencies translated here as Ministries, consolidated into a Department of State Affairs (*shang-shu sheng*), from which derive the terms *pa tso* (Eight Executives), *pa pu ta-fu* (Eight Grand Masters of the Ministries), and perhaps *pa kuo* (Eight Statesmen). It is possible that *pa kuo* was in fact a variant of the tribal term *pa pu ta-jen* rather than of the term *pa pu ta-fu.*

4378 *pā tà-chiā* 八大家
CH'ING: **Eight Great Families,** unofficial collective reference to a group of Imperial Princes (*ch'in-wang*) and Commandery Princes (*chün-wang*) descended directly from men considered founders of the Manchu nation and dynasty, formally known collectively as the Iron-helmet Princes (*t'ieh mao-tzu wang*); their status was guaranteed perpetual inheritance. These included the Imperial Princes prefixed Li, Jui, Su, Cheng, Chuang, and Yü and the Commandery Princes prefixed Shun-ch'eng and K'o-ch'in. BH: 8 great or princely houses.

4379 *pā tà-jén kuān* 八大人官
N-S DIV (N. Wei): **Eight Tribal Overseers,** deriving from the early title *ta-jen* (Tribal Overseer); probably a variant of *pa pu ta-jen* (Eight Tribal Overseers). Some traditional interpretations link the term *pa ta-jen kuan* into the development of the Department of State Affairs (*shang-shu sheng*) and its Ministries (*pu*), suggesting it was a variant of *pa pu ta-fu* (Eight Grand Masters of the Ministries); but it is likely that *pa ta-jen kuan* was actually a variant of *pa kuo* (Eight Statesmen).

4380 *pā tiāo* 八貂
T'ANG: **Eight Sabled Dignitaries,** collective reference to the incumbents in 8 central government posts that most consistently provided Grand Councilors (*tsai-hsiang*): the 2 Directors (*ling*) and 2 Policy Advisers (*san-chi ch'ang-shih*) of the Secretariat (*chung-shu sheng*) and the 2 Directors (*shih-chung*) and 2 Policy Advisers of the Chancellery (*men-hsia sheng*); from 658 the incumbents in these posts were authorized to wear sable adornments on their caps. The Chancellery members of the group attended on the Emperor's left side, wore their sable ornaments over their left eyes (i.e., away from the Emperor), and were consequently called the Left Sabled Dignitaries (*tso-tiao*); those who were

members of the Secretariat were called Right Sabled Dignitaries (*yu-tiao*) for similar reasons. RR: *huit zibelines.*

4381 *pā tsò* 八座
Lit., 8 thrones, daises, or seats of honor or authority, hence those who occupied such seats: **Eight Executives,** from Han to Ch'ing times an unofficial reference to 8 important posts in the central government. (1) HAN–T'ANG: from Later Han, except during the Chin, Liang, and Ch'en dynasties in the era of N-S Division, normally referred to the Director (*ling*), the one or 2 Vice Directors (*p'u-yeh*), and the 5, 6, or more Ministers (*shang-shu*) of Ministries (*pu*) in the Department of State Affairs (*shang-shu t'ai, shang-shu sheng*), which between Han and T'ang became the administrative core of the central government. (2) T'ANG–CH'ING: collective reference to the Ministers (*shang-shu*) of the Six Ministries (*liu pu*). P2, 3.

4382 *pā-tsŏ ssū* 八作司 or *pā-tsŏ yüàn* 院
Lit., office of the 8 crafts, i.e., plastering (*ni*), painting (? *ch'ih-po*: red and white), varnishing (*t'ung-yu:* tung oil), stonework (*shih*), tilework (*wa*), bamboo work (*chu*), masonry (? *chuan*), and well work (*ching*). (1) SUNG, YÜAN: **Repair Office,** one each Left and Right; in Sung each headed by 3 Managers (*kou-tang kuan*), in Yüan by an Overseer (*ta-lu-hua-ch'ih*), a Superintendent (*t'i-ling*), and a Commissioner-in-chief (*ta-shih*), with identical offices at the 2 capitals Shang-tu and Ta-tu (Peking). SP: *bureau de construction et de réparation.* (2) CHIN (*pa-tso yüan*): **Armory,** a storehouse for military gear including weapons; one each Left and Right, staffing not clear; under the Ministry of Works (*kung-pu*). P15, 49.

4383 *pá-ts'ùi* 拔萃
(1) T'ANG–SUNG: lit., plucked from the thicket, i.e., the crowd: **Preeminent Talent,** one of many high-prestige examination degrees, awarded for success in a civil service recruitment examination known by the same name; the examination was a Special Examination (*chih-k'o*) given irregularly by imperial decree and administered by the Ministry of Personnel (*li-pu*) rather than a regularly scheduled recruitment examination administered by the Ministry of Rites (*lǐ-pu*); it was especially difficult, concentrating on candidates' judgment as well as literary skill. It was first authorized in 673 and from 701 gave its graduates the right to immediate appointment to office; terminated by Sung in 1034. Also known as *shu-p'an pa-ts'ui.* Also see *chih-chü, k'o-chü, po-hsüeh hung-tz'u, shen-yen-shu p'an.* (2) CH'ING: occasional variant reference to *pa kung-sheng* (**Graduate for Preeminence**).

4384 *pă-tsŭng* 把總
Lit., to take hold of and manage (?). (1) MING–CH'ING: **Squad Leader,** military commandant of a minor place such as a fort (*pao*) with a small party of soldiers often referred to as a *ssu* (lit., his office, charge, or responsibility: a Squad); cf. the more important title *shou-pei* (Defender) and the less important title *t'i-t'iao kuan* (Officer in Charge). In Ming, a duty assignment in the tactical hierarchy headed by a Regional Commander (*tsung-ping kuan*), the appointee having rank status in a nearby Guard (*wei*) in the administrative hierarchy headed by a provincial-level Regional Military Commissioner (*tu chih-hui shih*) in what was called the *wei-so* system (see *wei-so*). In Ch'ing, the title was transformed into a regular appointment, rank 7a, in the Green Standards (*lu-ying*); in command of 10 men called a Squad (*p'eng*). Such Squad Leaders were reportedly very numerous, e.g., 137 in Shansi, 283 in Fukien, 309 in Chekiang; as in Ming, they were scattered in charge of forts, etc., throughout the

Provinces. BH: sub-lieutenant. P58. (2) MING: **Tax Transport Leader,** from 1457 the lowest-ranking officer in the military organization that transported tax revenues to the dynastic capital via the Grand Canal (see *tsung-tu ts'ao-yün, ts'ao-yün tsung-tu*), but nevertheless had significant authority and responsibility. There were 8 large regions that fed tax receipts into the Grand Canal transport system, and for tax transport purposes all military units in each region were supervised and directed by the one or 2 Tax Transport Leaders assigned to each, totaling 12. As in (1) above, they were on duty assignments away from their nominal posts in the *wei-so* establishment. In Ch'ing, tax transport duties were regularly handled by Brigades (*ying*) of the Green Standards (*lu-ying*), organized into a Waterways Command (*ho-piao*) and a Transport Command (*ts'ao-piao*). P59, 60.

4385 *pā tzǔ* 八子
CH'IN–HAN: lit., 8 children (?); relevance not clear: **Consort,** normally prefixed by the surname, a title granted to one or more secondary wives of the Emperor, rank = 1,000 bushels in Han; equated with the male title of honorary nobility (*chüeh*) Grandee of the Eighth Order (*chung-keng*). HB: eighth rank lady.

4386 *pà-wáng* 霸王
Hegemons and Kings: from late Chou on throughout history, especially among moralistic philosopher-statesmen of the Confucian tradition, a combination of contrasting terms referring on one hand to tyrants who ruled by force (Hegemons) and on the other hand to "true Kings" who ruled benevolently and manifested personal virtue. May be encountered at times in the sense of a Hegemon-King, i.e., a ruler who was not a "true King" as defined above and whose rule was harsh. See *pa, wang.*

4387 *pai*
Also see under the romanization *po.*

4388 *pài* 拜
Ety., 2 arms upraised in salute, hence to honor: from Han on, a common term meaning **to appoint.** In Han and through most of the era of N-S Division, differed from *ch'u* (also: to appoint) in that *pai* was used when an appointment was made by an Emperor whereas *ch'u* was used when an appointment was made by some dignitary on his own authority to a post on his staff. Before the end of the era of N-S Division, however, *pai* and *ch'u* were being used interchangeably. In T'ang both terms meant an imperial appointment, but *pai* was used only for an initial appointment to office and *ch'u* was used only for subsequent appointments. In Sung *pai* continued to denote appointment by the Emperor whereas *ch'u* had a broader, more flexible meaning, including appointments made by the Department of State Affairs (*shang-shu sheng*) without involvement of the Emperor. In Chin and Yüan the terms continued in use generally in the Sung pattern. Thereafter the two terms were used more or less interchangeably, but the term *shou,* with many qualifying prefixes, took their place as the most common term in use meaning to appoint.

4389 *pai-kuan* 百官
See under the romanization *po-kuan* (**All Officials, the Officialdom**).

4390 *pài-kuān* 稗官
Petty Official: not a title, but a descriptive term for officials of low rank.

4391 *p'ái* 牌
(1) YÜAN: **Squad,** the basic unit of Mongol military organization, consisting normally of 10 soldiers under a Squad Commander (*p'ai-chang*); 10 Squads constituted a Company (*po-hu so*). Also called *chia,* q.v. (2) MING–CH'ING: a unit in sub-District (*hsien*) organization of the population: in Ming a **Subprecinct** of urban organization, subordinate to a Precinct (*fang*); in Ch'ing a **Registration Unit,** the smallest unit in the local security system called *pao-chia* (lit., Security Groups and Tithings), consisting ideally of 10 neighboring households with a designated Head (*p'ai-t'ou*), 10 such units constituting a Tithing (*chia*) of 100 households.

4392 *p'ái-àn ssū* 排岸司
SUNG: **River Transport Bureau,** apparently 4 created in 988, each headed by a River Transport Director (*p'ai-an*), to replace Supply Commissioners (*fa-yün shih*) in supervising the transport of tax grain revenues to the dynastic capital, Kaifeng, in cooperation with an Unloading Office (*hsia-hsieh ssu*) and under supervision of the Court of the Imperial Granaries (*ssu-nung ssu*); in 1008 Supply Commissioners were re-established in several Circuits (*lu*) to manage the transport system, and the River Transport Bureaus might then have been abolished. SP: *bureau de transport fluvial.* P60.

4393 *p'ái-chǎng* 俳長
MING–CH'ING: **File Leader,** number not limited but 20 or so unranked hereditary professionals; members of the Music Office (*chiao-fang ssu*), presumably responsible for keeping marching musicians in straight ranks and files while the 17 or so Appearance Monitors (? *se-chang*) checked on their dress and overall visual impression; in 1723 all hereditary musicians were liberated from their service obligations, and court musicians were chosen from among gifted amateurs. Whether or not the title *p'ai-chang* survived the 1729 division of the Music Office into a Music Office (*ho-sheng shu*) and an Imperial Music Office (*shen-yüeh shu*) is not clear. P10.

4394 *p'ái-chèn shǐh* 排陣使
SUNG: **Formation Monitor,** one or more (per army?) low-ranking or unranked military personnel responsible for organizing and keeping under scrutiny a military array on parade, on campaign, and in battle. SP: *commissaire chargé d'aligner les troupes pendant l'expédition.*

4395 *p'ái-mǎ* 排馬
T'ANG: lit., (one who) deploys horses, but more likely: **Horse Trainer,** one or more attached to each Directorate of Horse Pasturages (*mu-chien*); apparently an unranked professional specialist. P31.

4396 *p'ái-mén jén* 排門人
T'ANG: lit., men who open gates: **Gate Watcher,** a duty assignment for soldiers of the Garrison Militia system (see *fu-ping*) during tours of duty in the capital, responsible for opening the city gates each morning and through the daylight hours keeping under surveillance all who entered or exited, ready to sound alarms if disturbances occurred. RR: *gens chargés d'ouvrir les portes.*

4397 *p'ài-pàn ch'ù* 派辦處
CH'ING: **Office for Duty Assignments,** a minor agency in the Ministry of War (*ping-pu*); staffing and specific functions not clear, but probably responsible for keeping records of special duty assignments of military officers. BH: office for deputation of officials for special duty.

4398 *p'ái-t'óu* 牌頭 or *p'ái-tzǔ t'óu* 牌子頭
(1) YÜAN: **Squad Commander,** head of the basic unit of

Mongol military organization, a Squad (*p'ai*) of 10 men; 10 such Squads constituted a Company (*po-hu so*). (2) CH'ING: **Registration Unit Head,** leader of a group of 10 neighboring households, a Registration Unit, the smallest group in the sub-District (*hsien*) local security system called *pao-chia* (lit., Security Groups and Tithings); 10 Registration Units ideally constituted a Tithing (*chia*). See *chia-t'ou, chia-chang*.

4399 *păn* 板 or 版
N-S DIV (San-kuo)–T'ANG: lit., a board, plank, placard, etc.; hence, to have a placard designating official status: **by Courtesy,** a common suffix to titles of many sorts signifying that the appointee was not a regular functioning official legitimated by an appropriate seal and sash, e.g., *hsien-ling pan* (District Magistrate by Courtesy). Originally such titles, which entitled appointees to reduced ranks and stipends but no authority, were awarded principally to leaders of unofficial military groups as rewards for disbanding their forces and submitting to the reigning dynasty, but they quickly came to be awarded to aged men among the general population in recognition of their merits or to other men of merit who were unqualified for regular status as officials. By Sui and T'ang times such appointments were purely honorific and were awarded sparingly to aged men of good repute.

4400 *pān* 班
Lit., a kind, class, row, rank (and file), group of people with similarities, etc. (1) May be encountered in any period in a straightforward descriptive sense, e.g., a group of officials who took positions in the same row in court audiences, or the Sung term Company of Crossbowmen (*nu-shou pan*); often with directional prefixes such as Front, Rear, Left, Right, East, West, etc. (2) N-S DIV (Liang, Ch'en): **Class,** from 1 (lowest) to 20 (highest), granted to officials as indicators of status, particularly reflecting the relative purity or impurity (see *ch'ing, cho*) of their social pedigrees; coexisted with the system of Nine Ranks (*chiu p'in*) that arose in the Three Kingdoms era, which endured through the rest of imperial history. The difference between the 2 systems in Liang and Ch'en is not clear. Cf. *p'in* (Rank), *chieh* (Class, Rank), *teng* (Grade, Class, Degree). (3) CH'ING: **Duty Group,** 6 groups into which Imperial Guardsmen (*ch'in-chün*) were divided, each group responsible for taking up active guard service in its rotational turn under an Imperial Guard Duty Group Commander (*shih-wei pan-ling*). Each Duty Group was divided into 2 Wings (*i*). BH: relief.

4401 *pàn-chiăng* 伴講
MING: **Lecturer-companion,** a minor official on the staff of each Princely Establishment (*wang-fu*), in the Chien-wen era (1399–1402) only. P69.

4402 *pān-chiàng àn* 頒降案
SUNG: **Section for Promulgations,** one of 13 Sections (*an*) directly subordinate to the executive officials of the S. Sung Ministry of Justice (*hsing-pu*); staffed with suofficial functionaries; handled the distribution of imperial pronouncements concerning new or changed laws and imperial amnesties. SP: *service de promulgation des lois*.

4403 *pān-chièn ssū* 班劍司
CH'ING: lit., office of the arrayed swords: **Swords Office,** one of 8 Offices in the Rear Subsection (*hou-so*) of the Imperial Procession Guard (*luan-i wei*); headed by a Director (*chang-yin yün-hui shih*), rank 4a. BH: sword section.

4404 *pān-chūn* 班軍
MING: **Rotational Troops,** referring to the practice of dispatching soldiers from their regular assignments in garrisons throughout the country (see under *wei-so*) in rotational patterns to serve in Training Divisions (*ying*) at the dynastic capital, or from garrisons near the Great Wall to active defense posts along the Wall. Cf. *fan, keng-shu*.

4405 *păn-hù* 版戶
N-S DIV–CH'ING: lit., (office that) registered households (?): unofficial reference to the **Ministry of Revenue** (*hu-pu*).

4406 *pàn-kò tsò-lĭng* 半箇佐領
CH'ING: **Half Company Commander,** also **Half Company** in reference to the unit in the Banner military organization (see *ch'i, pa-ch'i*): occasionally used when the total strength of a Company Commander's (*tso-ling*) Company (also *tso-ling*) was less than 100 men.

4407 *pàn-lĭ èrh-ssū shìh-wù* 辦理二司事務
CH'ING: **Operational Agents of the Two Offices** (*ssu*, one each Left and Right) through which the Palace Stud (*shang-ssu yüan*) managed its affairs; 2 for each Office established in 1694, 7 more added soon, and in 1736 another 6 added, making a total authorization of 17 positions. Presumably responsible for administrative supervision of the steadily increasing horse pasturages, corrals, and stables that were under the Imperial Household Department (*nei-wu fu*). P39.

4408 *pān-lĭng* 班領
CH'ING: abbreviated reference to the **Officer in Charge** (*ling*) **of a Duty Group** (*pan*) in rotational active service as imperial bodyguards; i.e., either or both (1) an Imperial Guard Duty Group Commander (*shih-wei pan-ling*, q.v.) or (2) an Imperial Guard Duty Group Acting (? see under *shu*) Assistant Duty Group Commander (*shu pan-ling*, q.v.). Also see *pan, shih-wei, ling, shih-wei ch'in-chün, san-ch'i shih-wei*. BH: commander of a relief of the body-guards, second in command of a relief ....

4409 *păn-pù* 版部
Lit., ministry of registers (census, tax registers, etc.): from Sui on if not earlier, an unofficial reference to the **Ministry of Revenue** (*min-pu, hu-pu*).

4410 *pān-pù fáng* 班簿房
SUNG: **Section for Personnel Registers,** a unit of the Secretariat (*chung-shu sheng*); staffing, ranks, and specific functions not clear. SP: *chambre des registres nominatifs des fonctionnaires*.

4411 *păn-shĭh* 版使
Lit., commissioner of registers (census, tax registers, etc.): from Sui on if not earlier, an unofficial reference to a senior post in the Ministry of Revenue (*min-pu, hu-pu*), either the **Minister of Revenue** (*min-pu* or *hu-pu shang-shu*) or a **Supervisor** (*p'an*, q.v.), the latter usually having a nominal appointment elsewhere in the government but detached for temporary duty in charge of the Ministry, or at times having rank status too low for a regular appointment as Minister.

4412 *pàn-shìh* 辦事
MING: **Apprentice,** designation of a National University Student (*chien-sheng*) who, prior to completing his studies, was detached to gain experience in actual government as staff member of an agency, especially in the central government; such status might endure from 3 months to 3 years before one attained a substantive appointment (*shih-shou*)

in the officialdom. See *li-shih, li-cheng, kuan-cheng.* Cf. *pan-shih ssu-yüan.*

4413 *pàn-shìh ssū-yüán* 辦事司員
CH'ING: **Judicial Administrator,** several appointed to various jurisdictions in Outer Mongolia under a Manchu General (*chiang-chün*) in the 1800s, specially responsible for supervising Manchu and Chinese traders and visitors in their jurisdictions, resolving disputes among them, and resolving disputes between the Mongol residents and such visitors. Commonly abbreviated to *ssu-yüan;* also called *ssu-kuan, pu-yüan, t'ung-p'an.* BH: judicial commissioner for Chinese affairs.

4414 *pàn-shìh tà-ch'én* 辦事大臣
CH'ING: variant reference to the **Grand Minister Superintendent of Ch'ing-hai** (*tsung-li ch'ing-hai shih-wu ta-ch'en*).

4415 *pǎn-shòu* 版授 or 板授
N-S DIV (San-kuo)–T'ANG: **Appointment by Courtesy;** see *pan* (by Courtesy).

4416 *pàn-shū* 伴書
MING: **Secretary-companion,** a minor official on the staff of each Princely Establishment (*wang-fu*), in the Chien-wen era (1399–1402) only. P69.

4417 *pān tièn-chíh* 班殿直
SUNG: **Palace Duty Officer,** prefixed Left and Right; 4th and 5th highest rank titles for eunuchs; see *nei-shih chieh.* P68.

4418 *pǎn-ts'áo* 版曹
From Sui or T'ang on, an unofficial (in Sung perhaps quasi-official) reference to the **Ministry of Revenue** (*hu-pu*); see *pan-hu, pan-pu.*

4419 *pàn-tú* 伴讀
(1) SUNG, LIAO, MING: **Reader-companion,** a minor official in each Princely Establishment (*wang-fu*). In Sung number not fixed, rank not clear; first appointed in 1020, how long persisted is not clear; prefixed South or North to denote affiliation with the Princely Establishment's Southern or Northern Court (*nan-yüan, pei-yüan*). In Ming 4, rank 9a, first appointed in 1376, apparently abolished in 1380, revived in the Chien-wen era (1399–1402) but apparently survived no longer. SP: *compagnon d'études.* P69. (2) YÜAN: **Fellow** in the School for the Sons of the State (*kuo-tzu hsüeh*); 20 posts authorized for specially talented sons of non-official families.

4420 *pàn-tz'ù* 半刺
Lit., half a Prefect (*tz'u-shih,* q.v.)? From Sui or T'ang on, apparently an unofficial reference to any official from the Prefecture (*chou, fu*) down to the District (*hsien*) level, or a collective reference to all such officials. In Ch'ing usage, seems to designate such territorial officials who had not been appointed in normal evaluation and appointment procedures in the central government, but instead were appointed on the basis of recommendations from active officials, who at the end of each year were authorized to nominate for appointment men who had not been dealt with in regular proceedings.

4421 *pān-yā t'ūi-ssū* 般押推司
SUNG: **Interrogator,** 4, status not clear but probably unranked, attached to the Right Prison (*yu chih-yü*) of the Court of Judicial Review (*ta-li ssu*); assisted by 4 Writers (*t'ieh-shu*). SP: *greffier.*

4422 *pàn-yèn shū-huà chíh-chǎng* 辦驗書畫直長
YÜAN: **Foreman Curator of Calligraphy and Painting,** rank 8a, in the Directorate of the Palace Archives (*pi-shu chien*). P25.

4423 *pàn yüàn-shìh* 辦院事
CH'ING: **Administrator of the Hanlin Academy** (*han-lin yüan*), from 1729 2 Manchus and 2 Chinese chosen from among talented and conscientious Junior Compilers (*pien-hsiu*) and Examining Editors (*chien-t'ao*) on the Academy staff to provide administrative leadership under supervision of Chancellors of the Hanlin Academy (*chang-yüan hsüeh-shih*), this innovation intended to counter a growing belief that the Academy was corrupt and useless. The title Administrator was a duty assignment, not a substantive post, and carried no rank. See *hsieh-pan yüan-shih* (Assistant Administrator ...). P23.

4424 *p'àn* 判
See under *p'an ... shih* (**Supervisor**).

4425 *p'àn-kuān* 判官
Lit., a decision-making official, from antiquity inheriting the connotation of judging. (1) T'ANG–YÜAN: **Administrative Assistant,** from the 700s the manager of official paperwork on the staff of a Military Commissioner (*chieh-tu shih*) or comparable regional dignitary, a duty undertaken by military officers as well as civil officials, apparently regardless of rank. From Sung through Yüan, a very common title at all levels of government with status seldom higher than rank 6, normally prefixed with the appropriate agency name and sometimes with a functional responsibility also indicated; e.g., *chün-hsün p'an-kuan* (Administrative Assistant in a metropolitan Police Office; see *chün-hsün yüan*), *hsüan-fu p'an-kuan* (Administrative Assistant to a Pacification Commissioner; see *hsüan-fu shih*). Very seldom found designating the head of an agency; almost always a 2nd-level or more commonly a 3rd-level post, e.g., below a Commissioner (*shih*) and a Vice Commissioner (*fu-shih*). RR: *fonctionnaire chargé des affaires ....* (2) SUNG–MING: **Assistant,** a suffix serving as a standard designation of a 3rd-level executive official in a unit of territorial administration; meaning essentially the same as in (1) above, but better rendered, e.g., as Assistant Prefect (*fu p'an-kuan*), Assistant District Magistrate (*hsien p'an-kuan*). Normally prefixed with the name of the territorial unit, sometimes also with the designation of a special function; e.g., ...-*chou ho-ti p'an-kuan* (Assistant Prefect for Water Conservancy in ... Prefecture). Status normally rank 6 or below. In Ming used almost exclusively as Assistant Prefect, below Prefect (*chih-fu*) and Vice Prefect (*fu t'ung-chih*); number not fixed, rank 7b. In Ch'ing changed to *t'ung-p'an,* q.v. Also see *chou p'an.* SP: *fonctionnaire chargé des affaires courantes, assistant.*

4426 *p'àn kuǎn-shìh* 判館事
T'ANG: abbreviation of *p'an hung-wen kuan shih* (**Supervisor of the Institute for the Advancement of Literature**); see *hung-wen kuan.* Sometimes appears as *p'an yüan-shih.*

4427 *p'àn-kuān ssū* 判官司
SUNG: **Office of the Administrative Assistant** to the Commissioners of the State Finance Commission (*san-ssu shih*); probably had specialized functions, but not clear. SP: *bureau de fonctionnaire chargé des affaires courantes.*

4428 *p'àn-kūng* 泮宮
SUNG–CH'ING: lit., a palace or hall with an adjacent cres-

cent-shaped bathing pool, reportedly in ancient Chou times an exercise yard or field established in the capital of each Feudal Lord (*chu-hou*): an archaic reference to any **local school** or any **local school teacher** (*p'an-kung hsien-sheng*). In Ming and Ch'ing, when candidates in the civil service examination sequence became eligible to participate as Cultivated Talents (*hsiu-ts'ai*) in Provincial Examinations (*hsiang-shih*), it was said they had entered (*ju*) the *p'an-kung*.

4429 *p'àn liù-chūn chū-wèi shìh*
判六軍諸衛事
5 DYN: **Controller of the Armies and Guards**, designation of a favored general made chief of a ruler's military staff.

4430 *p'àn liú-nèi ch'üān shìh* 判流內銓事
SUNG: **Supervisor of the Bureau of Personnel Assignments**; see *liu-nei ch'üan*. SP: *chargé de juger les fonctionnaires "dans le courant."*

4431 *p'àn mén-hsìà shěng shìh* 判門下省事
SUNG: **Supervisor of the Chancellery**, an ad hoc duty assignment for a Grand Councilor (*tsai-hsiang*), either in the absence of a regular Director of the Chancellery (*men-hsia shih-chung*) or as an overseer with greater authority than an incumbent Director. SP: *chargé de décider les affaires du département de la chancellerie impériale.*

4432 *p'àn nán-yá* 判南衙
SUNG: lit., supervisor of the Southern Command (see *nan-ya*); an anachronistic reference in S. Sung to the **Governor** (*yin*) **of Lin-an Prefecture** (modern Hangchow).

4433 *p'àn pù* 判部 or *p'àn pù-shìh* 事
SUNG: **Supervisor of the Ministry**, designation of a court official who, regardless of his principal appointment, was delegated to oversee one of the Six Ministries (*liu pu*) in the absence of a regular Minister (*shang-shu*) or, probably less commonly, with authority over an incumbent Minister. SP: *chargé de décider les affaires du ministère.*

4434 *p'àn sān-ssū* 判三司
T'ANG–SUNG: **Supervisor of the Three Fiscal Agencies** (T'ang, Five Dynasties), **Supervisor of the State Finance Commission** (early Sung): a specific or collective reference to eminent officials of the central government who, as concurrent appointments added to their regular posts, were placed in charge of the 3 vital fiscal organs of the central government, which eventually came to be considered a separate, consolidated agency (see *san ssu*). The pattern emerged in the latter half of T'ang, not later than 818, and persisted through the first Sung century to c. 1080, when responsibility for fiscal affairs was restored to more traditional agencies, principally the Ministry of Revenue (*hu-pu*). The 3 offices referred to were the Census Bureau (*hu-pu ssu*) and the Tax Bureau (*tu-chih ssu*), both normally subordinate to the Ministry of Revenue, and the Salt (and Iron) Monopoly Bureau (*yen-t'ieh ssu*). Also see *kuo-chi, tsu-yung shih, tsung-chi shih, chi* (Account). P7.

4435 *p'àn shěng-shìh* 判省事
N-S DIV–SUNG: abbreviation of **Supervisor (of the Affairs) of the Department**, e.g., of the Department of State Affairs (*shang-shu sheng*). In Sung seems to have been used solely in the case of the Palace Administration (*tien-chung sheng*), and only in the earliest decades of the dynasty. SP: *chargé de diriger les affaires du département.* P38.

4436 *p'àn ... shìh* 判⋯事 or *p'an*
N-S DIV–CH'ING: **Supervisor** (of the affairs of ... agency),

signifying that an official holding a regular post was assigned on a temporary or otherwise irregular basis to take charge of an agency, sometimes his own, as a special duty assignment; e.g., *hu-pu shih-lang p'an pen-pu* (Vice Minister of Revenue serving as Supervisor of His Ministry), *kung-pu ...-ssu yüan-wai lang p'an tu-shui chien shih* (Vice Director of the Bureau of ... in the Ministry of Works serving as Supervisor of the Directorate of Waterways), *tu-shui shao-chien p'an chien shih* (Vice Director of the Directorate of Waterways serving as Supervisor of the Directorate, i.e., a Vice Director in charge of his own Directorate). Normally the term indicates that the official was serving (in an emergency, temporarily, or provisionally) in a higher-ranking post than he was qualified for. Much less commonly it indicates the reverse, as when a T'ang or Sung Grand Councilor (*tsai-hsiang*) was delegated in an emergency situation to take charge of a Prefecture (*chou, fu*). See *tien* (Manager). The term was also used to identify who was actually in charge of an agency with 2 or more nominal heads with identical titles and ranks; e.g., *t'ai-ts'ang shu ling p'an shu shih* (Director of the Office of Imperial Granaries serving as Supervisor of the Office, which normally had 3 Directors). RR: (*fonctionnaire*) *dirigeant* (*une charge*). SP: *chargé des affaires de ....*

4437 *p'àn-ssū* 判司 or 判寺
T'ANG–SUNG: **Supervisor of the Bureau** (or **Office** or **Court**), abbreviation of such titles as Supervisor of the Bureau of Operations (*p'an chih-fang ssu*) in the Ministry of War (*ping-pu*) and Supervisor of the Court of State Ceremonial (*p'an hung-lu ssu*). See *p'an ... shih.*

4438 *p'àn-ssū kuān* 判司官
SUNG: common variant of *p'an-kuan* (**Administrative Assistant, Assistant**).

4439 *p'àn-t'ái* 判台
SUNG: abbreviation of **Supervisor of the Censorate** (*yü-shih t'ai*), an eminent court official delegated to take charge of the Censorate in the absence of its regular executives, or perhaps to oversee the performance of the regular executives. Cf. *kuan-kou*. SP: *administrateur des affaires du censorat.*

4440 *p'àn yüàn-shìh* 判院事 or *p'an-yüan*
T'ANG–SUNG: **Supervisor (of the Affairs) of the ...**; see *p'an ... shih*. In T'ang may be found referring to the Institute for the Advancement of Literature (*hung-wen kuan;* also see *p'an kuan-shih*), but most commonly refers to the Academy of Scholarly Worthies (*chi-hsien tien shu-yüan*). In Sung most commonly refers to the Appointment Verification Office (*kuan-kao yüan*) of the Ministry of Personnel (*li-pu*), the Court of Ceremonial Propriety (*li-i yüan*) or the Ritual Academy (*li-yüan*), and the Public Petitioners Drum Office (*teng-wen ku-yüan*) or Public Petitioners Review Office (*teng-wen chien-yüan*). RR: *fonctionnaire chargé de décider des affaires de la bibliothèque.* SP: *chargé de décider des affaires de la cour.* P5, 21, 25, 27.

4441 *pāng lǐng-pān* 帮領班
CH'ING: **Assistant Duty Group Chief**, rank 4a, one each in 4 Duty Groups (*pan*) among which Secretaries (*chang-ching*) of the Council of State (*chün-chi ch'u*) were distributed for rotational service. See *ling-pan*. BH: assistant chief of section.

4442 *pāng lǐng-pān chāng-chīng shàng hsíng-tsǒu* 帮領班章京上行走
CH'ING: **Secretary of the Council of State Concurrently Serving as Assistant Duty Group Chief**, variant desig-

nation of Assistant Duty Group Chief (*pang ling-pan*), also commonly awarded as an honorary title to Secretaries of the Council of State (*chün-chi chang-ching*). See *chang-ching, hsing-tsou*. BH: assistant chief of section.

4443 *păng-pàn tà-ch'én* 帮办大臣
CH'ING: lit., grand minister assisting in management: **Grand Minister Assistant Administrator of Tibet,** established in 1727 to assist the Grand Minister Resident of Tibet (*chu-tsang ta-ch'en*), in 1792 joined the Grand Minister Resident and the Dalai Lama in a triumvirate charged with governing Tibet. BH: assistant resident (of Tibet).

4444 *păng-pó* 邦伯
Earl of Subordinate States: title of nobility (*chüeh*) attributed to high antiquity; throughout imperial history an archaic, unofficial reference to territorial administrators whose jurisdictions were large enough to include several states (*pang*), i.e., Princedoms (*wang-kuo*), Marquisates (*hou-kuo*), or comparable units of civil administration; e.g., Regional Governors (*chou mu*), Prefects (*tz'u-shih, chih-chou, chih-fu, yin*). See *fang-po, kuo-po, chün-po, hsien-po*.

4445 *păng-shìh* 榜式
CH'ING: lit. relevance not clear; possibly a Chinese transliteration of a Manchu word: (1) **Clerk,** a term early superseded by *pi-t'ieh-shih*, q.v. (2) **Grand Academician** (?), possibly a variant of *ta hsüeh-shih*, the title of heads of the Three Academies (*nei san yüan*) in early Ch'ing.

4446 *păng-shŏu* 榜首
Lit., at the head of the placard, i.e., the topmost name on the pass list posted after a civil service recruitment examination. (1) SUNG: equivalent of *chuang-yüan* (**Principal Graduate** in a Palace Examination, *t'ing-shih*). (2) MING: equivalent of *chieh-yüan* (**Provincial Graduate with Highest Honors**).

4447 *păng-tsò* 邦佐
Lit., helper in a subordinate state: in Han and the era of N-S Division, an unofficial reference to a **Commandery Aide** (*chün-ch'eng*); in later times an archaic, unofficial reference to a **Vice Prefect** (*t'ung-chih*).

4448 *păng-yĕn* 榜眼
Lit. sense not clear: at the eye of the placard? Cf. *pang-shou*. (1) SUNG: unofficial reference to both the **Second and Third Graduates** in the highest-level civil service recruitment examination, following immediately after the Principal Graduate (*chuang-yüan*) on posted pass lists. (2) MING–CH'ING: unofficial designation of the **Second Graduate** in a Palace Examination (*tien-shih*) in the civil service recruitment examination sequence, following the Principal Graduate (*chuang-yüan*) and preceding the Third Graduate (*t'an-hua*), these 3 constituting the topmost category of passers (*i-chia*), collectively called Metropolitan Graduates with Honors (*chin-shih chi-ti*). Normally appointed promptly to posts as Junior Compilers (*pien-hsiu*), rank 7a, in the Hanlin Academy (*han-lin yüan*).

4449 *păng-yüán* 榜元
YÜAN: **Principal Graduate,** designation sometimes used for the man in first place on the pass-list placard following the Metropolitan Examination (*hui-shih*) in the civil service recruitment examination sequence. Cf. *chuang-yüan*.

4450 *păo* 保
Lit., to protect. (1) **Guardian,** from antiquity a title of high honor awarded to specially meritorious or favored dignitaries, prefixed in various forms. E.g., see *t'ai-pao, shao-*

pao, t'ai-tzu t'ai-pao, t'ai-tzu shao-pao. (2) SUNG–CH'ING: **Security Group,** a unit in sub-District (*hsien*) organization of the population. See *pao-chia, pao-wu*. Cf. *li-chia*. (3) SUNG–CH'ING: **Guaranteed Recommendation,** a nomination by a relatively higher-rank official of a relatively lower-rank official, often given in response to an imperial order and sometimes a fixed requirement of various officials at specified intervals; used as one kind of data taken into account in considering officials for promotion. The sponsor was held accountable for the duty performance and the whole conduct of his nominees and could be made to suffer if any of his nominees proved inadequate. The system of Guaranteed Recommendations was relied on most heavily in the first Sung century. See *pao-chü*. Cf. *k'ao* (merit rating).

4451 *păo-chăng* 保長
SUNG, MING–CH'ING: **Security Group Head,** leader of a unit in the sub-District (*hsien*) local self-government organization known as *pao-chia*, q.v. In Sung, the title of a leader of a Small Security Group (*hsiao-pao*) and of a Large Security Group (*ta-pao*), which ideally encompassed 5 Small Security Groups of 10 families each, whereas the leader of a Superior Security Group (*tu-pao*) encompassing 10 Large Security Groups was entitled *tu-pao cheng* or *pao-cheng* (Superior Security Group Head). In Ming and Ch'ing the designations *pao-chang* and *pao-cheng* were equivalent variants, a Security Group (*pao*) being at the top of a hierarchy in which 10 households constituted a Registration Unit (*p'ai*), 10 Registration Units constituted a Tithing (*chia*), and 10 Tithings ideally included 1,000 households constituting a Security Group.

4452 *păo-chăng chèng* 保章正
T'ANG–CH'ING: lit., possibly be understood as director (*cheng*) of guarding (*pao*, i.e., keeping the state-issued annual calendar in accord with) the 19-year lunar cycle (*chang*); but, taking into account the Chou dynasty title Royal Astrologer (*pao-cheng shih*), seems more likely to have the less specific meaning of director (*cheng*) of guarding (*pao*, i.e., keeping close watch on) celestial manifestations (*chang*) of many sorts, even though in later times the term *pao-chang* was importantly related to the preparation of the calendar: **Director of Calendrical Calculations,** associate members of the astrological group called the Five Offices (*wu kuan*), specifically charged with keeping records of movements of the sun, moon, planets, stars, etc., so as to contribute to the preparation of the state-issued annual calendar; also charged with noting and reporting any celestial irregularities that might be considered omens. In T'ang 2, rank 7b1; created in 702 (704?) to replace Erudites of the Calendar (*li po-shih*) on the staff of the Supervisor of Water Clocks (*ch'ieh-hu cheng*) in the Astrological Service (*t'ai-shih chü, ssu-t'ien t'ai*), which was sometimes subordinated to the Palace Library (*pi-shu cheng, lin-t'ai*) and sometimes an autonomous agency of the central government. In Sung one, 7b, associated with the Five Offices of the Astrological Service (*t'ai-shih chü*); one, 8b, also authorized for the Directorate of Astronomy (*ssu-t'ien chien*). In Liao an unspecified number, rank not clear, in the Directorate of Astronomy. Apparently not appointed in Chin. In Yüan 5, 7a, and in addition 5 Assistant Directors (*pao-chang fu*), 8a, in the Astrological Commission (*t'ai-shih yüan*). In Ming 2 then one, 8a, in the Directorate of Astronomy (*ch'in-t'ien chien*). In Ch'ing 2 appointed in the Directorate's Astronomy Section (*t'ien-wen k'o*) till 1675, then discontinued. Commonly called *wu kuan pao-chang cheng* (Directors of Calendrical Calculations in the Five Offices). RR: *maître*

au vaste savoir rédacteur du calendrier. SP: *rédacteur du calendrier.* P35.

4453 *păo-chāng shìh* 保章氏
CHOU: lit., apparently to be understood as a hereditary official (*shih*, i.e., keeping close watch on) celestial manifestations (*chang*); not likely to have any relation to the sense of *chang* referring to the 19-year lunar cycle that had to be accounted for in Chinese calendars: **Royal Astrologer,** 2 ranked as Ordinary Servicemen (*chung-shih*) on the staff of the Ministry of Rites (*ch'un-kuan*), hereditary specialists responsible for observing and interpreting celestial phenomena, e.g., correlating celestial changes in any of the 12 spheres into which the Chinese divided the sky with events in the 12 regions into which the earth was considered to be divided, at equinoxes and solstices reporting that celestial conditions, the colors of clouds, and the qualities of winds foretold good or bad things to come. CL: *astrologue impérial; officier chargé de préserver et d'éclaircir.*

4454 *păo-ch'āo* 寶鈔 or 寶抄
YÜAN–MING: lit., precious currency: a common designation of **paper money,** which had originated in T'ang with the designation "flying coins" (*fei-ch'ien*) and had greatly proliferated in Sung with such designations as *chiao-tzu* (see under *chiao-tzu wu*), *hui-tzu* (see under *hui-tzu wu*), and many others. The terms *pao-ch'ao* and *chiao-ch'ao* became relatively standard in Yüan and remained in use through Ming, though *t'ung-pao* (circulating valuable) was the term printed on the actual paper currency. In Ch'ing the production and circulation of paper money was banned. P16.

4455 *păo-ch'āo kuăng-hùi chūn* 寶鈔廣惠軍
MING: common scribal error for *pao-ch'ao kuang-hui k'u* (**Treasury for the Benevolent Issuance of Paper Money**).

4456 *păo-ch'āo kuăng-hùi k'ù* 寶鈔廣惠庫
MING: **Treasury for the Benevolent Issuance of Paper Money,** nominally subordinate to the Ministry of Revenue (*hu-pu*) but located inside the imperial palace and used for relatively small receipts in copper coins as well as paper money, which were commonly disbursed as gifts to officials and military officers on occasions for celebration such as the Emperor's birthday; headed by a Commissioner-in-chief (*ta-shih*), rank not clear but low, possibly a eunuch. Discontinued in the Chia-ching era (1522–1566). A counterpart was subordinate to the Nanking Ministry of Revenue and presumably survived to the end of the dynasty. P16.

4457 *păo-ch'āo ssū* 寶鈔司
MING: **Paper Office,** a minor agency of palace eunuchs headed by a eunuch Director (*cheng, t'ai-chien*); prepared paper for palace use. See *ssu ssu* (Four Offices).

4458 *păo-ch'āo t'í-chŭ ssū* 寶鈔提舉司
Supervisorate of Paper Money. (1) YÜAN: a central government agency headed by an Overseer (*ta-lu-hua-ch'ih*) and a Supervisor-in-chief (*tu t'i-chü*), rank not clear; apparently relatively autonomous though at least nominally subordinate through the weak Ministry of Revenue (*hu-pu*) to the Secretariat (*chung-shu sheng*). In Yüan regional varieties of paper money abounded, but there was also an empire-wide form called *t'ung-hsing* (universal circulation); and paper money was the dominant form of money in circulation. About 1308 the central government ordered the circulation of coins (to supplement paper money?) but soon abandoned it because of its lack of acceptance in domestic trade. In the 1350s and 1360s, when Yüan was steadily losing ground to rebel movements, another attempt to cir-

culate coins failed. Nevertheless, the Supervisorate of Paper Money was apparently overshadowed after 1350 by the Supervisorate-in-chief of Coinage (*pao-ch'üan t'i-chü ssu*), which oversaw a much larger establishment including branches throughout the country. Both agencies, despite the specificity of their names, seem to have been authorized to handle both paper money and coins. The Supervisorate of Paper Money probably oversaw other agencies in the dynastic capital, the Chief Paper Money Depository (*pao-ch'ao tsung-k'u*), the Paper Money Printshop (*yin-tsao pao-ch'ao k'u*), and 2 Paper Money Incinerators (*shao-ch'ao k'u*) prefixed Eastern and Western, all with Overseers and Commissioners-in-chief (*ta-shih*) in charge. (2) MING: established in 1374 under the Ministry of Revenue (*hu-pu*); headed originally by a Supervisor (*t'i-chü*) but later (from 1380?) by a Commissioner-in-chief; probably had some authority over the Currency Supply Service (*ch'ao-chih chü*) and the Plate Engraving Service (*yin-ch'ao chü*). The chief agent of the central government's early efforts to circulate paper money successfully, but no doubt declined in importance as these efforts failed and particularly after the mid-1500s, when taels of silver became the unchallenged standard medium of account, of taxes, and of trade. Cf. *pao-ch'üan t'i-chü ssu, pao-yüan chü, ch'ien-chien.* P16, 49.

4459 *păo-ch'āo tsŭng-k'ù* 寶鈔總庫
YÜAN: **Chief Paper Money Depository,** managed by an Overseer (*ta-lu-hua-ch'ih*) and a Commissioner-in-chief (*ta-shih*), ranks not clear; presumably the central government's treasury of paper money, subordinate to the Supervisorate of Paper Money (*pao-ch'ao t'i-chü ssu*) and the Ministry of Revenue (*hu-pu*). Also see *yin-tsao pao-ch'ao k'u, shao-ch'ao k'u.* P16.

4460 *păo-chèng* 保正
(1) SUNG: abbreviation of the designation *tu pao-cheng* (**Superior Security Group Head**). (2) MING–CH'ING: **Security Group Head,** leader of a group in the sub-District (*hsien*) self-government organization called *pao-chia,* q.v.; the Security Group ideally encompassed 10 Tithings (*chia*), which in turn encompassed 10 Registration Units (*p'ai*), each consisting of 10 households. A common variant was *pao-chang.*

4461 *păo-ch'éng chün kuān-nèi hóu* 襃成君關內侯
HAN: lit., the lord favored for completion (of his tutorship, now ennobled as) Marquis of the area within the pass, Kuan-nei being a proper area name: **Lord Praised for Fulfillment, Marquis of Kuan-nei,** title of nobility (*chüeh*) awarded to a direct descendant of Confucius in 48 B.C. by Emperor Yüan (r. 49–33 B.C.) in gratitude for his work as a tutor prior to the Emperor's enthronement; charged with perpetuating sacrificial rites at the tomb of Confucius in modern Shantung Province. Traditional scholars did not consider this ennoblement the origin of the noble status borne throughout later history by each generation's most direct descendant of Confucius, which they assigned to the year A.D. 1; see under *pao-ch'eng hou.* Also see *kuan-nei hou.* P65, 66.

4462 *păo-ch'éng hóu* 襃成侯
HAN: lit., Marquis favored for completion (see under preceding entry), appropriate under the circumstances of 48 B.C., but later likely to have been understood as Marquis charged with honoring the perfection of Confucius in sacrificial rites at Confucius's grave: **Praising Perfection Marquis,** a special title of nobility (*chüeh*) awarded in A.D. 1 by Emperor P'ing (r. 1 B.C.–A.D. 5) to the contempo-

rary generation's most direct descendant of Confucius, with perpetual inheritance rights, for the purpose of offering sacrifices at the tomb of Confucius in modern Shantung Province. Although descendants of Confucius had been dignified in earlier Han times with such titles as Lord Sacrificer (*feng-ssu chün*) and Lord Praised for Fulfillment, Marquis of Kuan-nei (*pao-ch'eng chün kuan-nei hou*), traditional scholars have assigned to the ennoblement of A.D. 1 the true origin of the noble status borne throughout later history by successive most direct male descendants of Confucius. Some sources report that the title was changed in A.D. 29 to Duke for the Abundant Perpetuation of Excellence (? see *yin-shao-chia kung*), then in 37 to Duke of Sung (*sung-kung;* Sung the name of a specific area), then in 38 back to Praising Perfection Marquis, and finally in 92 to Marquis for Worshipping at the Temple (*pao-t'ing hou*). But in stele of Han date the title Praising Perfection Marquis was used until very late in the dynasty; it was perhaps not changed until 220, when Han collapsed and the regional state of Wei changed the title to Marquis for Honoring the Sage (*tsung-sheng hou*). Also see *yen-sheng kung*. P66.

4463 ***pǎo-ch'éng hsüan-ní kūng*** 襃成宣尼公
Lit. sense not entirely clear and seemingly inappropriate; Duke who promulgates (the teachings of Chung)-ni, (ennobled on the occasion of) praising for the completion (of tutorship) (?); see under *pao-ch'eng chün kuan-nei hou*: **Duke of Supreme Sageliness** (rendered without relation to possible literal meanings), a posthumous title awarded to Confucius in 48 B.C. by Emperor Yüan of the Han dynasty on taking the throne, when he ennobled the current most direct male descendant of Confucius as Marquis of Kuan-nei (*kuan-nei hou*) in recompense for the completion (*pao-ch'eng*) of his tutorial work with Emperor Yüan when he was Heir Apparent. The word *ni* undoubtedly derives from Confucius's appelation Chung-ni, alluding to a hill called Ni-ch'iu near his birthplace, as does his formal name (K'ung) Ch'iu. P66.

4464 ***pào-chì*** 豹騎
SUI–T'ANG: **Fierce as Leopards Cavaliers,** a common name for members of the Courageous Guards (*hsiao-wei, hsiao-wei fu*), prefixed Left and Right, units in the Sui-early T'ang Twelve Guards (*shih-erh wei*) and the T'ang Sixteen Guards (*shih-liu wei*) stationed at the dynastic capital. RR: *cavalier aux peaux de léopard.* P43.

4465 ***pǎo-chiǎ*** 保甲
SUNG, MING–CH'ING: lit., Security Groups and Tithings: **Community Self-defense System,** one important type of sub-District (*hsien*) self-government organizations, originated by Wang An-shih in N. Sung, revived with modifications in the early 1500s by Wang Yang-ming and others, revived again in early Ch'ing. In Sung, from 10 to 30 neighboring households were grouped administratively as a Tithing (*chia*) with a Tithing Chief (*chia-t'ou*) who had heavy responsibilities concerning the collection of local taxes; concurrently, neighboring households were also organized into 3 levels of Security Groups (*pao*) to provide local self-defense forces. In Ch'ing, this system coexisted with the Ming-style *li-chia* (Community Self-monitoring System), being specially responsible for local police and militia work. Ten households constituted a Registration Unit (*p'ai*), 10 such units constituted a Tithing, and 10 Tithings constituted a Security Group, in theory encompassing 1,000 households residing, ideally, in a cohesive, natural geographic area. See *ta-pao, hsiao-pao, tu-pao, chang* (Head), *chia* (Tithing), *li* (Village, Community). Cf. *kuan-ping, pao-wu, t'uan-lien.*

4466 ***pǎo-chiéh*** 保節
SUNG: **Preserver of Temperance,** laudatory epithet added to titles awarded to the parents of Emperors and of the favored officials who were known as Meritorious Ministers (*kung-ch'en*).

4467 ***pǎo-ch'īng*** 飽卿
Lit., chief minister for feeding to the full: from T'ang on, an unofficial reference to a senior official of the Court of Imperial Entertainments (*kuang-lu ssu*), especially its head, the **Chief Minister of Imperial Entertainments** (*kuang-lu ch'ing*).

4468 ***pǎo-chǔ*** 保舉
Guaranteed Recommendation, variant of *pao* (Guardian, etc.; see under #3): from Sung if not earlier, refers to nominations of deserving subordinates by their official superiors, to be considered for promotion; the patrons were normally held accountable for any misconduct by their nominees. In Ming and Ch'ing, guaranteed recommendations were relied on heavily to assure that officials in the lowest ranks, 8 and 9, would not be overlooked in normal evaluation and promotion deliberations. By mid-Ming times, officials generally had little hope of good careers without accumulating such recommendations in their dossiers maintained by the Ministry of Personnel (*li-pu*); but the system was abused by both clique-building patrons and sycophantic clients; thus from 1530 the recommendation system fell into disfavor and gradually lost its importance in personnel administration. In Ch'ing, recommendations were restored to their earlier prominence in general; in addition, they were used to bring men into the officialdom from status as National University Students (*chien-sheng*) or as unranked subofficials.

4469 ***pǎo … chǔ*** 寶⋯局
CH'ING: with place-name insert, **Coinage Service,** the place-name ordinarily being abbreviated or suggested by an archaic equivalent, e.g. *pao-Chin chü* (Shansi Coinage Service), *pao-Che chü* (Chekiang Coinage Service). The generic name for all Provincial Coinage Services was *ch'ien-chü,* q.v. P16.

4470 ***pǎo-ch'üan*** 寶泉
Lit., source or spring of wealth or precious things: from Yüan if not earlier, a common reference to coins. See *pao-yüan, ch'üan-fu, ch'üan-pu.* Cf. *pao-ch'ao.* P16.

4471 ***pǎo-ch'üan ch'ǎng*** 寶泉廠
CH'ING: **Coinage Depot,** 4 established in 1726 as immediately subordinate units of the Ministry of Revenue's (*hu-pu*) Metropolitan Coinage Service (*pao-ch'üan chü*). BH: mint. P16.

4472 ***pǎo-ch'üan chǔ*** 寶泉局
(1) MING: **Provincial Coinage Service,** from 1368 established in each Province, superseding the sole predynastic Kiangsi Coinage Service (*huo-ch'üan chü*); headed by Commissioners-in-chief (*ta-shih*), rank 9b, sometimes supervised by 2nd-level executive officials of Provincial Administration Commissions (*ch'eng-hsüan pu-cheng shih ssu*). Produced copper coins on order of the central government and according to designs issued by the Ministry of Works (*kung-pu*), which maintained a counterpart Metropolitan Coinage Service (*pao-yüan chü*) at the dynastic capital; from 1380 coinage was specifically made the responsibility of the Ministry of Works, whereas the production and circulation of paper money was assigned to the Ministry of Revenue (*hu-pu*); see *pao-ch'ao t'i-chü ssu* (Supervisorate of Paper Money). The early history of the Ming coinage organizations was confused even in contemporary

sources; the terms *pao-yüan* and *pao-ch'üan* were often used interchangeably, and agencies were often referred to vaguely as the Service (*chü* without any prefix) or by descriptive terms such as Coinage Services (*ch'ien-chü*) and Minting Directorates (*chu-chien*). In both the dynastic capital and the Provinces, the Services seem to have had ad hoc existences, being activated when they were needed but otherwise lapsing. It is clear that there was a continuing shortage of coins through the 1400s, and in the 1500s counterfeiting became a serious problem. The people and eventually the state moved to the use of unminted silver as the principal monetary standard, in units of taels (Chinese ounces). Coins were always needed, however, and in 1576 all Provincial Administration Commissions were ordered to reactivate their Coinage Services. Coins were minted at the capital and in the Provinces to the end of the dynasty, though such production was overshadowed from 1625 by that undertaken by the Ministry of Revenue (see #2 following). (2) MING: **Coinage Service of the Ministry of Revenue,** established at Peking in 1625 to increase the money supply needed for the costly Ming defense efforts against the Manchus, and probably also for the personal advantage of the notorious eunuch dictator Wei Chung-hsien and his henchmen. Headed by a special, supernumerary Right Vice Minister of Revenue (*hu-pu yu shih-lang*), rank 3a, with the duty designation Vice Minister Supervisory Manager of Coinage (*tu-li ch'ien-fa shih-lang*), whose post was commonly called the Coinage Office (*ch'ien-fa t'ang*); he substantially increased the number of mints in the capital and vigorously sought raw materials throughout the country. (3) CH'ING: **Metropolitan Coinage Service** in the pattern of (2) preceding; an agency of the Ministry of Revenue which, in cooperation with the Metropolitan Coinage Service (*pao-yüan chü*) maintained by the Ministry of Works, was expected to oversee the production and circulation of copper coins throughout the country. Each of the 2 Ministries for this purpose set up a Coinage Office (*ch'ien-fa t'ang*). (For the Ministry of Works agency, see under both *ch'ien-fa t'ang* and *pao-yüan chü*.) The Ministry of Revenue's Service was headed originally by one Chinese and one Manchu Superintendent (*chien-tu*), assisted by one Chinese technician called Commissioner-in-chief (*ta-shih*). Posts as Superintendents were filled in 2-year rotations by officials on special duty assignments from substantive posts in Bureaus (*ch'ing-li ssu*) of any of the Six Ministries (*liu pu*), but the Commissioners-in-chief were always chosen from among the unranked Clerks (*pi-t'ieh-shih*) of the Ministry of Revenue itself to serve 5-year terms on rotational schedules monitored by the Ministry of Personnel (*li-pu*); a successful term might lead to promotion into the civil service officialdom. In 1726 the Service created 4 immediately subordinate Coinage Depots (*pao-ch'üan ch'ang*), each staffed with one Chinese Commissioner-in-chief. From 1729 on, however, only Manchus were approved for service as Commissioners-in-chief in the Service. The Metropolitan Coinage Services of both Ministries of Revenue and Works seem to have cooperated in giving some leadership if not specific direction to Provincial Coinage Services (generic name *ch'ien-chü*). However, these were more closely associated with the various Provincial Administration Commissions (*ch'eng-hsüan pu-cheng shih ssu*) and were staffed with 2nd-level executive officials of appropriate Prefectures (*fu*). Province-level identification of coins was the practice, but the general designs were established by the Ministry of Revenue. P6, 16.

4473 *păo-ch'üán t'í-chŭ ssū* 寶泉提舉司
YÜAN: **Supervisorate of Coinage,** from 1351 established in several provincial areas to produce and circulate copper coins as the central government tried to restrain the circulation of paper money (see under *pao-ch'ao t'i-chü ssu,* Supervisorate of Paper Money); each staffed with a Superintendent (*t'i-ling*), rank 8a, and a Commissioner-in-chief (*ta-shih*), 8b. Subordinate to the Supervisorate-in-chief of Coinage (*pao-ch'üan tu t'i-chü ssu*) established at the dynastic capital in 1350. See *pao-ch'üan chü.* Cf. *pao-yüan ch'ien-chien, pao-yüan chü.* P16.

4474 *păo-ch'üán tū t'í-chŭ ssū* 寶泉都提舉司
YÜAN: **Supervisorate-in-chief of Coinage,** established in 1350 in the central government to have empire-wide control over the production and circulation of money, paper money as well as coins despite the specificity of its name; staffing not clear, but probably headed by a Supervisor-in-chief (*tu t'i-chü*). In 1351 began establishing subordinate Supervisorates of Coinage (*pao-ch'üan t'i-chü ssu*) in various provincial areas; in 1352 opened Copper Smelters (*t'ung-yeh ch'ang*) in 3 localities. Directly supervised a Metropolitan Mint (*ku-chu chü*) and a Paper Money Treasury (*yung-li k'u*) at the dynastic capital. Also see *pao-ch'üan chü, pao-yüan chü, pao-yüan ch'ien-chien.* P16.

4475 *păo-ch'úng tà-fū* or *tài-fū* 保冲大夫
YÜAN: lit., grand master for protecting the weak, i.e., the ruler: **Grand Master Preserver of the Emperor's Health,** prestige title (*san-kuan*) for rank 4a officials of the Imperial Academy of Medicine (*t'ai-i yüan*). See *ch'ung-jen* (This Weakling).

4476 *păo-fēng ch'ién-chiēn* 寶豐錢監
CHIN: **Western Directorate of Coinage,** one of 2 agencies (see *pao-yüan ch'ien-chien*) established in 1158 at Chung-tu (the Central Capital) in Manchuria to supervise the production and distribution of copper coins in that region; staffed on (part-time?) duty assignments by officials of the regular governmental establishment at Chung-tu. Also known simply as the Western Directorate (*hsi-chien*). The counterpart at the principal dynastic capital in the area of modern Peking was the *li-yung ch'ien-chien* (Directorate of Coinage); another important production agency was at Tai-chou in modern Shansi (*tai-chou ch'ien-chien*). See *ch'ien-chien, pao-ch'üan chü, pao-yüan chü, chu-ch'ien chien.* P16.

4477 *păo-fù* 保傅
Throughout history, an occasional combined reference to the honorary titles *t'ai-pao* and *t'ai-fu* (**Grand Guardian and Grand Mentor**), normally members of the group of dignitaries collectively called the Three Dukes (*san kung*).

4478 *păo-hó tièn* 保和殿
SUNG: **Hall for the Preservation of Harmony,** a unit in the Institute of Academicians (*hsüeh-shih yüan*), staffed with Grand Academicians (*ta hsüeh-shih*) and Academicians (*hsüeh-shih*), both rank 3a, Edict Attendants (*tai-chih*), 4b, etc. SP: *pavillon Pao-ho.*

4479 *păo-hsiàng* 保相
N-S DIV (Chin): variant of *t'ai-tzu t'ai-fu* (**Grand Mentor of the Heir Apparent**).

4480 *păo-hsüăn* 保選
Guaranteed Selection (for appointment): from Yüan if not earlier, the designation of an appointment made by a supervisory official accepting the same responsibility for the conduct of his appointee that was taken by those giving Guaranteed Recommendations (see *pao-chü, pao*).

4481 *păo-hsüéh-ī* 保學醫
N-S DIV (S. Ch'i): lit. sense not clear; texts possibly gar-

bled: **Medical Instructor** (?), 2, rank not clear, in the National University (*kuo-hsüeh, kuo-tzu hsüeh*). P34.

4482 *pāo-ī* 包衣
CH'ING: Chinese rendering of a Manchu word meaning enslaved prisoner of war or simply slave: **Bondservant** or **Imperial Bondservant,** members of Manchu families (eventually others including Chinese) that were attached as hereditary personal servants to the Emperor and Imperial Princes (*ch'in-wang*); together with eunuchs and palace women, did many menial tasks. Administered by the Imperial Household Administration (*nei-wu fu*) and staffed most of its posts; Supervisors-in-chief (*tsung-kuan*) of the Administration were commonly called Commandant of Bondservants (*pao-i ang-pang*). Also largely comprised the Inner Banners (*nei-ch'i*) and Outer Banners (*wai-ch'i*) of the military establishment stationed in the capital, the former attached to the Emperor and the latter to Imperial Princes. Beginning not later than the K'ang-hsi era (1662–1722), Imperial Bondservants were commonly appointed to sensitive posts throughout the empire as personal reporting agents of the Emperor, somewhat in the fashion some Emperors of earlier dynasties, e.g., Ming, had utilized trusted palace eunuchs. See under *huang pao-i* and *wang pao-i*.

4483 *pāo-ī áng-pāng* 包衣昂邦
CH'ING: **Commandant of Bondservants,** unofficial reference to a Supervisor-in-chief of the Imperial Household Department (*nei-wu fu tsung-kuan*). Also see *pao-i, ang-pang*. P19.

4484 *pāo-ī ts'ān-lǐng* 包衣參領
CH'ING: **Regimental Commander of Bondservants,** a rank 3b officer on the staff of a Princely Establishment (*wang-fu*) commanding Bondservants (*pao-i*) of the Outer Banners (*wai-ch'i*) who were hereditarily attached to the agency. Also see *ts'an-ling*. BH: chief controller of bondservants.

4485 *pāo-ī tsò-lǐng* 包衣佐領
CH'ING: **Company Commander of Bondservants,** a rank 4b officer on the staff of a Princely Establishment (*wang-fu*) commanding Bondservants (*pao-i*) of the Outer Banners (*wai-ch'i*) who were hereditarily attached to the agency. Also see *tso-ling*. BH: department controller of bondservants.

4486 *pǎo-jèn* 保任
SUNG: **Sponsored Appointment,** designation of an appointment made on the basis of Guaranteed Recommendations (*pao-chü, pao*) submitted by official sponsors, who were punishable for any misconduct by their nominees. Also see *pao-hsüan*. SP: *nomination des fonctionnaires par recommandation*.

4487 *pǎo-kūng* 保宮
HAN: lit., building or hall for guarding or protecting: **Palace Prison,** renamed in 104 B.C. from *chü-shih* (Palace Prison); headed by a Director (*ling*) under the Chamberlain for the Palace Revenues (*shao-fu*); specific uses not clear. HB: protective enclosure. P37.

4488 *pǎo-lín* 保林
HAN: **Lady Who Could Comfort a Multitude,** title of a palace woman, rank =100 bushels. HB: soothing maid.

4489 *pǎo-lín* 寶林
SUI–T'ANG: **Lady of the Precious Bevy,** 20 in Sui, rank 5a; 17 in T'ang, 6a; in Sui one of the groups of palace women considered Secondary Concubines (*nü-yü*), in T'ang ranked below those called the Nine Concubines (*chiu pin*); part of the palace harem from c. 604 to 662 and again from 670 probably to the 740s. RR: *forêt des joyaux*.

4490 *pào-ló shǐh* 報羅使
Lit., one sent to find recompense in the great canopy of Heaven: **Examination Casualty,** from T'ang on a common term applied to any civil service recruitment candidate who died promptly after issuance of the highest examination pass list.

4491 *pǎo-mǎ* 保馬
SUNG: **Security Group Horses,** reference to one of the reforms of the 11th century Grand Councilor (*tsai-hsiang*) Wang An-shih, which required each local self-government Security Group (see under *pao-chia*) to accept, care for, and breed government horses to be ready for military use when needed.

4492 *pǎo-mò kó* 寶謨閣
SUNG: **Hall for Treasuring the Heritage,** from 1202 one of the palace buildings served by members of the Institute of Academicians (*hsüeh-shih yüan*).

4493 *pǎo-shèng hóu* 襃聖侯
T'ANG: **Marquis for Praising the Sage,** title of nobility (*chüeh*) awarded to the most direct descendant of Confucius in each generation, charged with maintaining the Confucian grave, temple, and estate at Ch'ü-fu, Shantung; changed from Marquis for Perpetuating the Sage (*shao-sheng hou*) in 626, in 739 changed to Duke for the Propagation of Culture (*wen-hsüan kung*). P66.

4494 *pǎo-shìh* 保氏
CHOU: **Palace Protector,** ranked as a Junior Grand Master (*hsia ta-fu*), a member of the Ministry of Education (*ti-kuan*); together with the Palace Mentor (*shih-shih*) guarded the ruler and his sons against wrong-doing, keeping watch over all royal audiences and accompanying the King on all his outings; tutored the royal princes in ritual, music, archery, charioteering, writing, mathematics, and deportment. CL: *protecteur*.

4495. *pao-shih* 暴室
HAN: see *p'u-shih* (**Palace Isolation Building**).

4496 *pǎo-shùn láng-chiàng* 保順郎將
SUNG: **Maintaining Submission Commandant,** laudatory title conferred on friendly alien military chiefs. *Pao-shun* was a laudatory epithet commonly prefixed to titles of nobility (*chüeh*), etc. See *lang-chiang*. SP: *colonel Pao-chouen*.

4497 *pào-t'āo wèi* 豹韜衛
T'ANG: **Guard of the Leopard Strategy,** from 684 to 705 the name of 2 military units, prefixed Left and Right, temporarily replacing the name Awesome Guards (*wei-wei*) units in the Sixteen Guards (*shih-liu wei*) at the dynastic capital. P43.

4498 *pǎo-té hóu* 襃德侯
T'ANG: **Marquis for Praising Virtue,** briefly from 705 a variant of Marquis for Praising the Sage (*pao-sheng hou*), the title awarded the current most direct descendant of Confucius; discontinued before 739. P66.

4499 *pǎo-tīng* 保丁
SUNG: **Security Guard,** principal serviceman in the local self-defense system called *pao-chia*, q.v. Cf. *ting, yü-ting, chuang-ting*.

4500 *pǎo-t'íng hóu* 襃亭侯
HAN: **Marquis for Worshipping at the Temple** (to Confucius), reported in some sources to be awarded from A.D. 92 to the most direct descendant of Confucius; but see *pao-ch'eng hou* (Praising Perfection Marquis). P66.

4501   *pào-tùn* 鉋盾

HAN–CHIN: variant of *kou-tun* (**Office of Imperial Parks Products**). P38, 40.

4502   *păo-wén kó* 寶文閣

SUNG: **Hall for Treasuring Culture,** from 1067 a palace building served by members of the Institute of Academicians (*hsüeh-shih yüan*).

4503   *păo-wŭ* 保伍

SUNG: **Local Militia Squad,** throughout the dynasty referred to a self-defense unit organized under direction and supervision of District (*hsien*) authorities, most commonly structured in a hierarchy of units called Security Groups (*pao*); commonly referred to in the aggregate as *hsiang-ping* (Local Militia). Coexisted with, and often confused with, militiamen of the *pao-chia* system (see *pao-chia*) instituted by Wang An-shih in the 1070s.

4504   *păo-yüán* 寶源

Lit., as in the case of *pao-ch'üan*, q.v., a source or spring of wealth or precious things: from Chin times if not earlier, a common reference to copper coins. Cf. *pao-ch'ao*. P16.

4505   *păo-yüán ch'ién-chiēn* 寶源錢監

CHIN: **Eastern Directorate of Coinage,** one of 2 agencies (see *pao-feng ch'ien-chien*) established in 1158 at Chung-tu (Central Capital) in Manchuria to supervise the production and distribution of copper coins in that region; staffed on (part-time?) duty assignments by officials of the regular governmental establishment there. Also known simply as the Eastern Directorate (*tung-chien*). The counterpart at the principal dynastic capital in the area of modern Peking was the *li-yung ch'ien-chien* (Directorate of Coinage); another important production agency was at Tai-chou in modern Shansi (see *tai-chou ch'ien-chien*). Also see *ch'ien-chien, pao-ch'üan chü, pao-yüan chü, chu-ch'ien chien*. P16.

4506   *păo-yüán chü* 寶源局

MING–CH'ING: **Metropolitan Coinage Service,** established in 1361 even before the new national dynasty was created; from 1380 directly subordinate to the Ministry of Works (*kung-pu*), which until 1625 (see below) was the central government's principal agency for the minting and circulation of copper coins, whereas the Ministry of Revenue (*hu-pu*) was responsible for the printing and circulation of paper money; see *pao-ch'ao t'i-chü ssu* (Supervisorate of Paper Money). Counterpart provincial-level agencies that were established as early as 1364 and were standardized as Provincial Coinage Services (*pao-ch'üan chü*) beginning in 1368 were subordinate to the Provincial Administration Commissions (*ch'eng-hsüan pu-cheng shih ssu*) rather than the Metropolitan Coinage Service; but they normally minted copper coins only on order from the central government and followed designs provided by the Ministry of Works, presumably through its Metropolitan Coinage Service. The early Ming history of all the *pao-yüan* and *pao-ch'üan* Services was confused even in contemporary sources; the two terms were often used interchangeably, and the agencies were often referred to vaguely as the Services (*chü* without any prefix) or by descriptive terms such as Coinage Services (*ch'ien-chü*) and Minting Directorates (*chu-chien*). In both the capital and the Provinces, the Services seem to have had ad hoc existences, being activated only when they were needed but otherwise lapsing (see under *pao-ch'üan chü*). When actively minting, they were managed by Commissioners-in-chief (*ta-shih*), rank 9b, usually under the general supervision of officials on special duty assignments from regular posts in the Provincial Admin-

istration Commissions or, in the case of the Metropolitan Service, from the Ministry of Works. In the Chia-ching era (1522–1566) the Ministry of Works established a new subordinate agency, the Coinage Office (*ku-chu kung-shu*), which was imposed atop the Metropolitan Coinage Service with a Superintendent (*chien-tu*) on duty assignment from a regular post in the Ministry, rank 5b. Thereafter the Metropolitan Coinage Service declined in importance, but it remained operational on its normal irregular basis throughout the rest of the dynasty. Despite government recognition of unminted silver as the monetary standard in the mid-1500s, the need for coins remained, and severe shortages of coins were regularly reported. In 1576 all Coinage Services, Metropolitan and Provincial, were ordered into active operation. After 1625, however, the Ministry of Works' primacy in coinage matters was undermined by the Ministry of Revenue's establishment of its own Coinage Service (*pao-ch'üan chü*) with a special, supernumerary Vice Minister of Revenue (*hu-pu shih-lang*), 3a, serving as Supervisory Manager of Coinage (*tu-li ch'ien-fa*). From 1421 to the end of Ming, there was another Metropolitan Coinage Service (*pao-yüan chü*) at Nanking under the Nanking Ministry of Works, intended to serve the coinage needs of the Province-size region around Nanking. In Ch'ing, the late Ming situation was perpetuated; the Ministry of Revenue's Metropolitan Coinage Service (*pao-ch'üan chü*) was established in 1644, the Ministry of Works' counterpart (*pao-yüan chü*) soon thereafter. Each of these Ministries maintained a Coinage Office (*ch'ien-fa t'ang*) to which the 2 Metropolitan Coinage Services were subordinate. The Ministry of Works' Office was headed by a Right Vice Minister Supervisory Manager (*tu-li ch'ien-fa t'ang yu shih-lang*), originally a Chinese but from 1679 on supplemented by a Manchu equal. The 2 Metropolitan Coinage Offices gave loose leadership to Provincial Coinage Services (generic name *ch'ien-chu*) throughout the country. P6, 16.

4507   *păo-yüán k'ù* 寶源庫

YÜAN: abbreviation of *wan-i pao-yüan k'u* (**Imperial Money Vault**).

4508   *p'áo-chèng* 庖正

Kitchen Director, a title used in antiquity and occasionally found in unofficial, archaic reference to the Han and post-Han Chamberlain for Attendants (*kuang-lu-hsün*) or the later Chief Minister (*ch'ing*) of the Court of Imperial Entertainments (*kuang-lu ssu*).

4509   *p'ào hsiāo-chí* 礮驍騎

CH'ING: **Artilleryman** of the Firearms Brigade (*huo-ch'i ying*) of the Inner Banners (*nei-ch'i*); headed by 10 Artillery Lieutenants (*kuan p'ao hsiao-chi hsiao*), rank 6a; apparently not numerous enough to constitute a Regiment (*chia-la*) with a Regimental Commander (*ts'an-ling*). Cf. *niao-ch'iang hsiao-chi*. See *hsiao-chi*.

4510   *p'áo-jén* 庖人

CHOU: **Palace Cook,** 4 ranked as Ordinary Servicemen (*chung-shih*) and 8 as Junior Servicemen (*hsia-shih*), members of the Ministry of State (*t'ien-kuan*) charged with the preparation of meals for the King, Queen, and Heir Apparent and specialty foods for sacrifices, funerals, receptions for visitors, etc. CL: *officier de la tuerie.*

4511   *p'áo-jén* 胞人

HAN: **Palace Butcher** or **Palace Butchery,** headed by a Director (*chang*) under the Chamberlain for the Palace Revenues (*shao-fu*). Clearly derived from the Chou *p'ao-jen* (Palace Cook), but the existence of other palace food agencies such as the *t'ai-kuan* (Provisioner), the *t'ang-kuan* (Office of Drinks and Delicacies), and the *tao-kuan* (Rice Hulling Office) suggests that Han's replacement of the Chou "shelter" radical with the "meat" radical was a deliberate denotation of butchering, and early commentators so understood the term. HB: chef, chief of the chefs. P37.

4512 *pěi* 北
North: on any encounter, see entry under the following terminology.

4513 *pěi-ān k'ù* 北鞍庫
CH'ING: **Northern Storehouse,** a unit of the Court of Imperial Armaments (*wu-pei yüan*) responsible for maintaining saddlery, sunshades, and various carriage drapes required by the Emperor and his entourage. Cf. *nan-an k'u*.

4514 *pèi-ch'á t'án-miào tà-ch'én* 備查壇廟大臣
CH'ING: **Grand Minister Preparer of the Altars and Temples,** an ad hoc duty assignment of a senior member of the Imperial Household Department (*nei-wu fu*) prior to the undertaking of any sacrificial ceremonies at the Altar to Earth (*t'u-t'an*) or the Temple of Heaven (*t'ien-miao*) in the dynastic capital; assisted a Grand Minister Inspector of the Altars and Temples (*chi-ch'a t'an-miao ta-ch'en*). BH: assistant superintendent of altars and temples.

4515 *pěi-chái* 北宅
SUNG: **Northern Residence Hall,** one of 2 units into which the School for the Imperial Family (*tsung-hsüeh*) was divided. See *nan-pei chai*. SP: *maison du nord*.

4516 *pèi-chāng tsǔng-yüàn* 備章總院
YÜAN: **Chief Office for the Imperial Costume,** a tailoring agency staffed with artisans requisitioned from the general populace, headed by a Commissioner (*shih*) or Commissioner-in-chief (*ta-shih*), rank 6a. Created in 1276 by aggregating 8 earlier workshops (see *yang lin chü*); subordinate to the Supervisorate-in-chief of Civilian Artisans (*min-chiang tsung-kuan fu*), but division of labor with similar agencies under the Supervisorate-in-chief is not wholly clear. See *shang-i chü, yü-i chü*.

4517 *pěi-ch'éng* 北丞
SUNG: abbreviation of *pei wai tu-shui ch'eng* (**Assistant Director of Northern Outer Waterways**); see *nan-pei wai tu-shui ch'eng ssu*.

4518 *pěi-chiēn* 北監
T'ANG: **Directorate of the Northern Parks,** one of 4 Directorates (*chien*) in charge of maintaining the buildings and grounds of imperial parks and gardens in the 4 quadrants of the dynastic capital, Ch'ang-an, under supervision of the Directorate-general of the Imperial Parks (*yüan tsung-chien*); headed by a Director (*chien*). See *hsi-chien, tung-chien, nan-chien*. P40.

4519 *pěi chíh-lì* 北直隸
MING: **Northern Metropolitan Area,** variant of *pei-ching*, designation of the Province-size territory surrounding and governed from the post-1420 dynastic capital, modern Peking. See *chih-li*.

4520 *pěi chǔ-k'ò ts'áo* 北主客曹
HAN–N-S DIV: **Section for Northern Relations** in the Imperial Secretariat (*shang-shu t'ai*) of Later Han or the Department of State Affairs (*shang-shu sheng*) that evolved in the era of N-S Division; created early in Later Han when the Section for Receptions (*chu-k'o ts'ao*) was divided into northern and southern agencies. Sometimes headed by a Minister (*shang-shu*), but most commonly by a Director

(*lang*). In collaboration with the Chamberlain for Dependencies (*ta hung-lu*), responsible for the reception of foreign envoys from beyond the northern frontier. See *nan chu-k'o ts'ao* for more detail. HB: northern bureau in charge of guests. P9.

4521 *pěi-chūn* 北軍
(1) HAN: **Northern Army,** an elite force charged with policing and defending the dynastic capital city, outside which it was garrisoned; headed by the Chamberlain for the Imperial Insignia (*chung-wei, chih chin-wu*) assisted by several Commandants (*wei*). (2) T'ANG: unofficial variant of *pei-ya* (**Northern Command**). Cf. *nan-chün, chin-chün, chin-wei, ch'in-wei*. P43.

4522 *pěi-hsiāng* 北廂
SUNG: **North Township,** one of 2 Townships into which the Southern Sung capital, Lin-an (modern Hangchow), was divided for local administration; probably headed by a Magistrate (*ling*). See *hsiang* (Township), *nan-hsiang* (South Township). SP: *région du nord*.

4523 *pěi k'ò-kuǎn* 北客館
N-S DIV (Sung): **North Visitors Bureau,** created in c. 420 by division of the office of the Chamberlain for Dependencies (*ta hung-lu*) into 2 Visitors Bureaus, one for the North and one for the South (*nan k'o-kuan*); headed by a Director (*ling*); responsible for the reception of chiefs or envoys of alien tribes north of the dynastic frontier. See *k'o-kuan*. P11.

4524 *pěi-k'ù* 北庫
SUNG: **Northern Storehouse;** see under *nan-pei k'u*.

4525 *pěi-kūng* 北宮
HAN: **North Palace,** designation of the imperial palace complex at Ch'ang-an in Former Han, built by Kao-tsu (r. 202–195 B.C.) and expanded by Wu-ti (r. 141–87 B.C.); also that at Loyang in Later Han, built by Ming-ti (r. A.D. 57–75). The palace at Ch'ang-an was destroyed by rebels who in A.D. 23 assassinated the usurper Wang Mang; that at Loyang was destroyed by rebels as Han approached its extinction in A.D. 220.

4526 *pèi-lò* 貝勒
Beile. (1) CHIN: Manchu "correction" of the proto-Manchu Jurchen title *po-chi-lieh*, q.v. (2) CH'ING: title of imperial nobility, originally a descriptive term for a tribal chief but awarded by the founder of the imperial line, Nurhachi, to his own brothers, sons, and nephews. Until Nurhachi's death 8 such Beiles prefixed *ho-shih* (meaning fief-holding or appanage-holding; see various entries beginning with this prefix) served as an intimate advisory group. Subsequently this group was semi-institutionalized as a Deliberative Council (*i-cheng ch'u*) staffed by 5 Grand Ministers (*ta-ch'en*) including Princes, and after the Ch'ing dynasty was formally proclaimed in 1635 a schedule of noble ranks was established, in which Beile became the 3rd highest of 12 titles of imperial nobility, formally prefixed *to-lo*, q.v., awarded to Manchus and Mongols in direct imperial descent as sons other than heirs of Commandery Princes (*chün-wang*). The wife of a Beile was entitled Dame-consort (*fu-jen*), the heir inherited the lesser title Beile Prince (*pei-tzu*), other sons by the Dame-consort inherited the title Defender-general of the State (*chen-kuo chiang-chün*), 2nd grade (*teng*), sons by lesser wives inherited the title Bulwark-general of the State (*fu-kuo chiang-chün*), first grade, and adopted sons inherited the title General by Grace (*feng-en chiang-chün*); daughters of a Beile inherited noble status

as Commandery Mistresses (*chün-chün*). BH: prince of the blood of the third degree. (3) CH'ING: honorary title sometimes conferred on foreign dignitaries such as dependent Moslem tribal chiefs of Central Asia. P64.

4527 *pěi-mén* 北門
North Gate. (1) T'ANG: from 666–667 the collective designation of a group of litterateurs entitled Academicians of the North Gate (*pei-men hsüeh-shih*), who were charged with drafting imperial pronouncements and composing literary works on imperial order; in c. 713 the designation was changed to *han-lin tai-chao* (Academician Awaiting Orders; also see *han-lin kung-feng*), apparently the first step in official nomenclature toward the famous Hanlin Academy (*han-lin yüan*). RR: *porte du nord, lettré de la porte du nord*. (2) T'ANG–CH'ING: continued in use as an unofficial, archaic reference to the Hanlin Academy, apparently because the Hanlin Academy of T'ang times was located north of a Silver Pavilion (*yin-t'ai*) in the palace grounds, where imperial pronouncements were customarily issued; but later dynasties had other explanations for the term. See *hsüeh-shih, han-lin, yin-t'ai ssu*. P23.

4528 *pěi-mén ssù chün* 北門四軍
T'ANG: **Four Imperial Armies of the North Gates,** from 713 to 742 a collective reference to the units that constituted the Northern Command (*pei-ya*)—the 2 Forest of Plumes Armies (*yü-lin chün*) and the 2 Militant as Dragons Armies (*lung-wu chün*). Also see *ssu chün*.

4529 *pěi-mièn* 北面
LIAO: **Northern Administration,** that part of the central government that administered the affairs of the Khitan tribes and their nomadic allies, in contrast to the Southern Administration (*nan-mien*), which governed the sedentary peoples of the Liao empire, notably the subjugated Chinese of modern Shansi and northern Hopei. The Northern Administration was a confusing mixture of Chinese-like and non-Chinese agencies, further confused by a secondary dualism of Northern and Southern Establishments (*yüan*) within the Northern Administration itself. Why these 2 Establishments existed and how functions were divided between them cannot adequately be explained. The principal agencies of the Northern Administration were 2 Bureaus of Military Affairs (*shu-mi yüan*), a Northern Bureau with military responsibilities and a Southern Bureau with civil responsibilities. Many lesser offices were also in Northern and Southern pairs: 2 Grand Councilors (*tsai-hsiang*), 2 Grand Princes (*ta-wang*), 2 Court Ceremonial Commissioners (*hsüan-hui shih*), etc. Also see *ta t'i-yin, i-li-chin, i-li-pi, ti-lieh-matu*. P4.

4530 *pěi-mièn fáng* 北面房
SUNG: **Northern Defense Section** in the Bureau of Military Affairs (*shu-mi yüan*); one of 12 Sections (see *shih-erh fang*) created in the reign of Shen-tsung (r. 1067–1085) to manage administrative affairs of military garrisons throughout the country, in geographic clusters, or to supervise specified military functions on a country-wide scale. This Section generally supervised 2 Circuits (*lu*), Ho-pei and Ho-tung. Headed by 3 to 5 Vice Recipients of Edicts (*fu ch'eng-chih*), rank 8b. Apparently discontinued early in S. Sung. SP: *chambre chargée de la défense de frontière du nord*.

4531 *pěi-pān nèi-p'ǐn* 北班內品
SUNG: **Palace Eunuch of the North Rank,** the designation apparently reflecting the position taken by eunuchs in court audiences; a rank title (*chieh*) awarded to eunuchs,

dates not clear; equivalent both to the 8th highest (*chih-hou tien-chih*) and to the lowest (*t'ieh chih-hou nei-p'in*) of 12 such rank titles awarded beginning in 1112; see *nei-shih chieh*. Possibly a general quasiofficial reference to the whole eunuch staff of the Palace Eunuch Service (*ju-nei nei-shih sheng*). Also see *nei-p'in, pan* (kind, class, rank, etc.; see under #1), *nan-pan kuan*. SP: *intendant du palais intérieur de 12e ou 8e rang (eunuque)*. P⸱⸱

4532 *pèi-pǎng* 備榜
YÜAN: **List of Adequates** (?), lit. sense not entirely clear, but refers either to candidates in Provincial Examinations (*hsiang-shih*) in the civil service recruitment examination sequence who stood low on the pass list or, more likely, those who were named on a list supplementary to the pass list indicating adequate albeit unsuccessful performance; candidates named on this list were commonly assigned immediately to teaching posts in schools maintained by units of territorial administration. Cf. *fu-pang, fu-ch'e, chü-jen*.

4533 *pèi-pèi* 輩輩
CH'ING: colloquial term for the **perpetual inheritance** (*shih-hsi wang-t'i*) of noble status (*chüeh*).

4534 *pèi-piēn k'ù* 備邊庫
T'ANG: **Frontier Defense Vault,** a special storehouse for coins and other valuables in the dynastic capital to provide for emergency military expenditures on the frontier, supervised by a Grand Councilor (*tsai-hsiang*) designated as Commissioner (*shih*) of the Vault. Originated c. 845; by 860 renamed *yen-tzu k'u* (Special Reserves Vault). P7.

4535 *pěi-pù* 北部
N-S DIV (N. Wei): **Ministry of Northern Relations** in the Department of State Affairs (*shang-shu sheng*); established c. 400 as one of 6 (4?) Ministries (*pu*) in the top echelon of the Department's agencies, responsible for overseeing the Regions (*chou*) and Commanderies (*chün*) along the northern frontier and for defending against tribal groups beyond it; discontinued in governmental reorganizations of 493. Headed by one or more Directors (*chang*) or Ministers (*shang-shu*); supervised 4 to 6 Sections (*ts'ao*) headed by Directors (*lang-chung*) and staffed by Clerks (*ling-shih*). The staff also included Supervising Secretaries (*chi-shih-chung*) delegated for concurrent service from the Department of Scholarly Counselors (*chi-shu sheng*). The name *pei-pu* has sometimes been written *pi-pu* by clerical error; it is not to be confused with the agencies properly named *pi-pu* (Bureau of Revision) and *pi-pu ts'ao* (Review Section). Also see *nan-pu, hsi-pu*.

4536 *pěi-pù wèi* 北部尉
HAN: **Commandant of the Metropolitan Police, North Sector,** rank 400 bushels, a Later Han subordinate of the Metropolitan Commandant (*ssu-li hsiao-wei*), responsible for police supervision of the northern quadrant of the dynastic capital, Loyang. See *yu-pu* (Right Sector), *ming-pu wei*. P20.

4537 *pèi-shēn* 備身
(1) N-S DIV (N. Wei, N. Ch'i)–SUI: **Personal Guard** in the establishment of the Heir Apparent, with many differentiating prefixes: *ch'ien-niu pei-shen* (Swordsman Guard), *chih ch'ien-niu tao pei-shen* (Saber-armed Guard), *chi-kuan pei-shen* (Mounted Guard), *nei-chih pei-shen* (Palace Station Guard), *wu-chih pei-shen* (Guard of the Five Posts?), etc.; headed by Commanders-in-chief (*tu-tu* as prefix, e.g., *tu-tu chi-kuan pei-shen*), Marshals (*shuai*), Generals (*chiang*), Commandants (*lang-chiang*), etc. (2) T'ANG–SUNG: **Im-**

perial Bodyguard, with varying prefixes (e.g., *ch'ien-niu* as above) and suffixes (e.g., *pei-shen tso-yu*, q.v.), members of the Left and Right Personal Guards (*ch'ien-niu wei*), 2 of the Sixteen Guards (*shih-liu wei*) that constituted the Southern Command (*nan-ya*) at the T'ang dynastic capital. Perpetuated at least nominally in Sung times, but later superseded by such terms as *shih-wei, ch'in-chün*. RR: *garde personnel*. P26, 43.

4538   *pèi-shēn fǔ* 備身府
Lit., garrison or office of personal guards. (1) SUI: **Imperial Bodyguard,** one of 2 units constituting the Palace Guards (*ch'in-wei*), elite troops drawn from the Twelve Guards (*shih-erh wei*) stationed in and around the dynastic capital, which in turn were staffed on a rotational basis by Garrison Militia units (see *fu-ping*) throughout the country; headed by a Commandant (*lang-chiang*) and a Vice Commandant (*chiang*). The 2nd Palace Guards unit was the Palace Gate Guard (*chien-men fu*). (2) T'ANG: **Personal Guard,** prefixed Left and Right, 2 of the original Twelve Guards stationed at the dynastic capital; in 622 renamed the Left and Right Guards (*tso-fu, yu-fu*, qq.v.). Also see *ch'ien-niu pei-shen*. RR: *garde personnel*.

4539   *pèi-shēn tsǒ-yù* 備身左右
SUI–T'ANG: **Guard in Personal Attendance,** normally an archer (cf. *ch'ien-niu pei-shen,* Swordsman Guard), principally in the Palace Guard (*chin-nei shih-wei*) of the Heir Apparent in Sui and in the Personal Guards (*ch'ien-niu wei*) at the imperial palace in T'ang. RR: *garde personnel de gauche et de droite*. P26, 43.

4540   *pěi-shěng* 北省
N-S DIV (Liang, N. Ch'i)–SUNG: **Northern Department,** unofficial reference to the Department of State Affairs (*shang-shu sheng*), apparently because in early times it was located in the northern portion of the outer palace grounds.

4541   *pěi-shǐ* 北使
(1) **North Commissioner:** may be found in any period referring to a north-south or a north-south-east-west differentiation among officials delegated from the dynastic capital with functions possibly clarified by prefixes. (2) T'ANG: **Commissioner for the Northern Pasturages,** an official of the Court of the Imperial Stud (*t'ai-p'u ssu*) delegated to establish new horse pasturages or to inspect existing Directorates of Horse Pasturages (*mu-chien*) in the northernmost parts of North China. RR: *commissaire impérial (aux élevages) du nord*.

4542   *pěi-sǒ* 北所
CH'ING: **North Prison,** one of 2 prisons maintained in the dynastic capital by the Prison Office (*t'i-lao t'ing*) of the Ministry of Justice (*hsing-pu*); see *nan-so* (South Prison). Staffing presumably similar; functions presumably similar, shared on some basis not clear.

4543   *pěi-ssū* 北司
T'ANG: **Northern Office,** unofficial reference to the Palace Domestic Service (*nei-shih sheng*), located in the northern section of the central government quarters in the palace grounds.

4544   *pěi tà-wáng yüàn* 北大王院
LIAO: **Northern Office of the Grand Princes** in the Northern Establishment (*pei-yüan*) of the central government's Northern Administration (*pei-mien*), headed by an Administrator (*chih yüan-shih*); see under *nan ta-wang yüan* (Southern Office of the Grand Princes). P17.

4545   *pěi-tí shǐh-chě* 北狄使者
SUI: **Commissioner for Northern Tributaries,** a member of the Court for Dependencies (*hung-lu ssu*) designated on an ad hoc basis to set up an Office (*shu*) to supervise arrangements for the treatment of envoys from tribes on China's northern frontier; in c. 610 superseded the consolidated Hostel for Tributary Envoys (*ssu-fang kuan*). P11.

4546   *pèi-tzǔ* 貝子
CH'ING: **Beile Prince,** 4th highest of 12 titles of imperial nobility (*chüeh*), formally prefixed *ku-shan*, q.v.; awarded to the heirs of Beiles (*pei-lo*) whereas lesser sons inherited the 8th highest title, Lesser Bulwark Duke (*pu-ju pa-fen fu-kuo kung*), 2nd grade (*teng*). The principal wife of a Beile Prince was entitled Dame-consort (*fu-jen*), his heir became a Defender Duke (*chen-kuo kung*), other sons by the Dame-consort became Lesser Defender Dukes (*pu-ju pa-fen chen-kuo kung*), 2nd grade, sons by lesser wives became Lesser Bulwark Dukes (*pu-ju pa-fen fu-kuo kung*), 2nd grade, and adopted sons inherited the title General by Grace (*feng-en chiang-chün*); daughters of a Beile Prince inherited noble status as District Mistresses (*hsien-chün*). BH: prince of the blood of the 4th degree. P64.

4547   *·pěi-wài tū-shǔi ch'éng ssū* 北外都水丞司
SUNG: **Office of the Assistant Director for Northern Outer Waterways,** subordinate to 2 Commissioners of Outer Waterways (*wai tu-shui shih-che*); see *nan-pei wai tu-shui ch'eng ssu*. SP: *assistant du contrôle des eaux du nord*.

4548   *pěi-yá* 北衙
(1) T'ANG: **Northern Command,** collective designation of a group of Imperial Armies (*chin-chün*) based at the dynastic capital, the principal striking force of the T'ang state, primarily composed of specially chosen soldiers descended from those who helped found the dynasty or could otherwise be counted on to be loyal; created as a counterweight to the militiamen who served in rotation in the Sixteen Guards (*shih-liu wei*) collectively called the Southern Command (*nan-ya*), but ultimately determined the fate of Emperors under the command of palace eunuchs. Originally a personal bodyguard (*su-wei*) of the founding Emperor called the Imperial Army of Original Followers (*yüan-ts'ung chin-chün*) or, more informally, the Hereditary army (*fu-tzu chün*), the Northern Command was created in 627 with the title Seven Encampments of the Northern Command (*pei-ya ch'i ying*). These 7 groups undertook one month of active guard duty at a time, in rotation, apparently serving alongside various units of the Southern Command. In 638, renamed the Left and Right Encampments (*t'un-ying*), they were restaffed with men chosen from elite families who could pass rigorous tests in archery, horsemanship, weight lifting, etc., and were called the Flying Cavalrymen (*fei-chi*), led by Generals (*chiang-chün*) of the Sixteen Guards organization. Then in 662 a new reorganization transformed the Encampments into the Left and Right Forest of Plumes Armies (*yü-lin chün*), reviving an ancient name derived from a celestial constellation; these were staffed with expert archers chosen at least in part from among the militiamen of the Southern Command. In 710 Left and Right Militant as Dragons Armies (*lung-wu chün*) were established, and in 738–739 they were placed on par with the Forest of Plumes Armies, the Northern Command aggregation now being given the collective designation Four Imperial Armies (*ssu chün*). In 757, during the An Lu-shan rebellion of 755–763, Left and Right Armies of Inspired Militancy (*shen-wu chün*) were added, making a total of Six Imperial Armies (*liu chün*), a

designation that became almost synonymous with Northern Command. These 6 units, all but destroyed during the rebellion, were soon restored at the capital as T'ang regained strength, and they remained the core of the capital's military establishment, commonly under the overall control of one or more Army Commissioners of the Northern Command (*pei-ya chün-shih*). In c. 763 Left and Right Armies of Inspired Strategy (*shen-ts'e chün*) were initiated as garrisons in the imperial palace grounds under the unified control of a palace eunuch entitled Palace Commissioner (*chung-shih*); these quickly became the special military forces of a series of influential eunuchs who, through the 800s, dominated the court and deposed Emperors as they pleased. Meantime, during the great rebellion, many transitory units were added to the Northern Command, notably including the Left and Right Awesome and Militant Armies (*wei-wu chün*) and the Left and Right Long Flourishing Armies (*ch'ang-hsing chün*); and in 787 were established the Left and Right Armies of Inspired Awesomeness (*shen-wei chün*). Before 800 the Northern Command was said to consist of Ten Imperial Armies (*shih chün*), counting the earlier Six Imperial Armies and the newer Armies of Inspired Strategy and Armies of Inspired Awesomeness. In 807 the Armies of Inspired Militancy were disbanded. Thereafter the term Six Imperial Armies was commonly understood to refer collectively to the 2 Forest of Plumes Armies, the 2 Militant as Dragons Armies, and the 2 Armies of Inspired Strategy, the latter pair remaining paramount under eunuch control almost without interruption until the end of the dynasty, despite occasional efforts to put all defense forces in the capital under the control of members of the imperial family. In both T'ang and later times, various Imperial Armies were confusingly referred to as Guards (*wei*), but they are to be differentiated from the Sixteen Guards of the Southern Command. In general, each of the Imperial Armies was headed by one General-in-chief (*ta chiang-chün*), rank 3a1 till 784 (787?), then 2a2, assisted by 2 Generals (*chiang-chün;* normally 3 after the mid-700s), 3a2. From 784 (787?) each was additionally assigned a Commander-general (*t'ung-chün*), 3a1, as principal aide to the General-in-chief. The eunuchs who controlled the Armies of Inspired Strategy from the later 700s had themselves awarded a variety of different, impressive, sometimes archaic titles; see under *shen-ts'e chün*. Cf. the Han dynasty term *pei-chün* (Northern Army), also *shih-erh chün* (Twelve Armies). RR: *casernes du nord*. (2) LIAO: variant or unofficial reference to the **Northern Bureau of Military Affairs** (see under *pei-mien, shu-mi yüan*).

4549 *pěi-yěh* 北冶
N-S DIV (S. Dyn.): **Northern Mint,** one of several coin-production agencies, each with a Director (*ling*) or a Vice Director (*ch'eng*) in charge, subordinate to the Chamberlain for the Palace Revenues (*shao-fu*); see *yeh*. P16.

4550 *pěi-yüàn* 北院
Lit., northern bureau or office. (1) T'ANG–CHIN: **Northern Court,** together with a Southern Court (*nan-yüan*) constituting the *hsüan-hui yüan* (Court of Palace Attendants in T'ang and Sung, Court Ceremonial Institute in Liao and Chin), each headed by one or more Commissioners (*shih*); division of responsibilities not clear. (2) SUNG: **Northern Court,** part of each Princely Establishment (*wang-fu*), together with a Southern Court; the significance of this division is not clear. P69. (3) LIAO: **Northern Establishment,** one of 2 major aggregations of agencies (cf. *nan-yüan*) in the Northern Administration (*pei-mien*) of the Khitan central government, dominated by a Bureau of Military Affairs

(*shu-mi yüan*). P5, 15. (4) LIAO: abbreviation of *pei shu-mi yüan* (**Bureau of Military Affairs in the Northern Establishment**), part of the Northern Administration (*pei-mien*).

4551 *p'éi-chīng* 陪京
Auxiliary Capital: equivalent of *p'ei-tu*, q.v. SP: *capitale annexe*.

4552 *p'éi-ch'īng* 陪卿
HAN: **Adjunct Chamberlains,** 6th highest in a hierarchy of 10 status groups in the officialdom (see under *shang-kung*), including the following: Chamberlain for the Imperial Insignia (*chih chin-wu*), Grand Mentor of the Heir Apparent (*t'ai-tzu t'ai-fu*), Chamberlain for the Palace Buildings (*chiang-tso shao-fu*), Supervisor of the Household of the Empress Dowager (*chan-shih ta ch'ang-ch'iu*), Commandant of the Imperial Gardens (*shui-heng tu-wei*), and both Guardian of the Left (*p'ing-i*) and Guardian of the Right (*fu-feng*) of the Metropolitan Area (*ching-chao*). Also see *shang-ch'ing* (Superior Chamberlains), *cheng-ch'ing* (Regular Chamberlains), *hsia-ch'ing* (Junior Minister). Cf. *chiu ch'ing* (Nine Chamberlains). P68.

4553 *p'éi-júng fù-wèi* 陪戎副尉
T'ANG, SUNG, LIAO: **Vice Commandant Tending the Western Frontier** (?), prestige title (*san-kuan*) for military officers of the 9th rank. RR: *vice-commandant qui soutient ses soldats*. SP: *commandant-adjoint P'ei-jong*. P68.

4554 *p'éi-júng hsiào-wèi* 陪戎校尉
T'ANG, SUNG, LIAO: **Commandant Tending the Western Frontier** (?), prestige title (*san-kuan*) for military officers of the 9th rank. RR: *commandant qui soutient ses soldats*. SP: *commandant P'ei-jong*. P68.

4555 *p'èi-lì àn* 配隸案
SUNG: **Criminal Residency Section,** one of 4 (in S. Sung 5) units staffed with clerical subofficials in the Criminal Administration Bureau (*tu-kuan*) of the Ministry of Justice (*hsing-pu*); arranged for and monitored the residency and work assignments of criminals sentenced to banishment or exile. SP: *service chargé d'assigner la résidence des condamnés*. P22.

4556 *p'éi-shìh* 陪侍
Lit., to accompany and attend upon: **Companion,** throughout history a generic reference to those officials whom the ruler regularly associated with for purposes of relaxation rather than business; not a disparaging term.

4557 *p'éi-ssù kuàn-chün shǐh* 陪祀冠軍使
CH'ING: **Military Commissioner for Participating in Sacrifices,** 2 important Grand Ministers (*ta-ch'en*) of the Imperial Household Department (*nei-wu fu*), directly responsible to the Directors of the Department (*tsung-li shih-wu kuan-chün shih*). BH: sacrificial marshals.

4558 *p'éi-t'áng shěng* 陪堂生
YÜAN: **Adjunct Student** in the School for the Sons of the State (*kuo-tzu hsüeh*) under the Directorate of Education (*kuo-tzo chien*), 20 authorized in addition to a quota of 300 regular students (*kuo-tzu sheng, chien-sheng*).

4559 *p'éi-tū* 陪都
Auxiliary Capital, from antiquity a reference to one or more cities recognized as secondary seats of dynastic authority, sometimes having at least a skeletal replica of the central government, sometimes presided over by a Regent (*liu-shou*), sometimes a place of refuge for a ruler when the principal dynastic capital was threatened or occupied by invaders or rebels, sometimes a place to which the court moved for

special seasonal activities such as hunting or to be closer to available food supplies in times of shortages. An equivalent term is *p'ei-ching*.

4560 *pěn* 本

Lit., basic, original, one's own: when encountered as a prefix to agency names such as Offices, Bureaus, Ministries, Courts, Armies, etc., means "the same," "the one mentioned above," etc.; almost never used as the beginning of an agency name or official title such as "the Basic Office." Cf. *chen, cheng.*

4561 *pěn-fáng* 本房

CH'ING: see *man-pen fang* (Manchu Documents Section), *han-pen fang* (Chinese Documents Section), *meng-ku pen-fang* (Mongolian Documents Section).

4562 *pēn-hsīng chiù* 奔星廐

T'ANG: **Stables of Meteoric Mounts,** variant of *tso chang-chiu* (Stables of Trustworthy Mounts of the Left; see *chang-chiu*) maintained by the Palace Administration (*tien-chung sheng*). RR: *écuries des étoiles rapides.*

4563 *pěn-kuān* 本官

Titular Office, throughout history the designation of one's regular post in the officialdom, civil or military, by which one's rank was determined or signified. This sense was carried by the term *kuan* alone, but *pen-kuan* was used to differentiate most specifically between regular posts or titles and, on the other hand, assignments, commissions, prestige titles, merit titles, honorific assignments, acting or probationary or temporary or concurrent appointments, etc. E.g., a Vice Minister of Justice (*pen-kuan*) might (in the absence of his normal superior) be Acting Minister of Justice, Concurrent Minister of Works, temporarily commissioned as Chief Examiner in a Provincial Examination, holder of the prestige title (*san-kuan*) Grand Master for Thorough Counsel, etc.

'564 *pěn-pǎ* 本把

CHIN–YÜAN: **Stock Clerk,** apparently subofficials in clerical service; found in various kinds of storehouses granaries, etc.

4565 *pēng* 伻

Messenger: sometimes found in the sense of ambassador or envoy, or equivalent to *shih* (Commissioner).

4566 *p'éng* 棚

CH'ING: lit., a tent, hence those who shared a tent: **Squad** of 10 men under a Squad Commander (*pa-tsung*), the smallest command unit in Brigades (*ying*) of the army of hereditary Chinese soldiers called the Green Standards (*lu-ying*); 10 Squads normally constituted a Company (*shao*).

4567 *p'ēng-jén* 烹人

CHOU: **Stove Attendant,** 4 ranked as Junior Servicemen (*hsia-shih*), members of the Ministry of State (*t'ien-kuan*) in charge of cooking under direction of the Grand Chefs of the Palace (*nei-yung*) and the Grand Chefs for External Ceremonies (*wai-yung*). CL: *cuiseur.*

4568 *p'ěng-jīh ssù hsiāng* 捧日四廂

SUNG: **Four Sun-sustaining Wings,** one of the major military aggregations of Imperial Armies (*chin-chün*) in the Palace Command (*tien-ch'ien ssu*) at the dynastic capital, one of those known collectively as the Four Elite Armies (*shang ssu chün*); headed by a Commander-in-chief (*tu chih-hui shih*); each of its Wings (*hsiang*) reportedly included 3 Armies (*chün*). P47.

4569 *pì* 弼

Lit., supporter; see *yu-pi* (Supporter on the Right), *yu-pi tu-wei* (Commandant Supporter on the Right).

4570 *pǐ* 比

(1) CHOU: **Neighborhood,** a basic 5-family unit in which residents of the royal domain were organized for local sacrificial, fiscal, and security purposes, equivalent to units called *lin* outside the royal domain; with a leader called Head (*chang*), ranked as a Junior Serviceman (*hsia-shih*), responsible to the Ministry of Education (*ti-kuan*). Five such units comprised an official Village (*lü*, equivalent to *li*). CL: *groupe.* (2) **Adjunct,** throughout history an occasional prefix to a title indicating somewhat lesser status than the main title alone (i.e., used like *p'ei* in *p'ei-ch'ing*), or indicating equivalent status without substantive duties or emoluments, as in the cases of some honored palace ladies and palace eunuchs (used like *shih* in *shih liu-nei*). (3) **Equivalent to:** when prefixed to rank indicators, normally refers to cases in which, like those of women and eunuchs mentione ʻn (2), equivalent ranks had been awarded to signify ceremonial status; when prefixed to salaries, or to salaries representing ranks as in Han times, normally signifies a salary somewhat less than stated. In Han times, e.g., every salary level expressed in bushels of grain (*shih;* probably never paid wholly in grain; partly converted to coins in ratios established by the government) actually had 3 grades: the level as stated (if necessary for clarification, prefixed with *chen,* True), a variably higher level (prefixed with *chung:* middle, center; here meaning heaped up, Full), and a variably lower level (prefixed with *pi,* Equivalent to). In this dictionary such uses of *pi* are normally indicated with the equivalence symbol (=): e.g., rank =4b, rank =2,000 bushels.

4571 *pǐ* 鄙

(1) CHOU: **Ward,** a unit of local organization outside the royal domain, counterpart of *tang* in the royal domain; theoretically comprised 500 families distributed among 5 Precincts (*tsan*); 5 Wards constituted a Township (*hsien*). Headed by a Preceptor (*shih*) responsible to the Ministry of Education (*ti-kuan*), ranked as a Senior Serviceman (*shang-shih*). CL: *canton extérieur.* (2) In later times used as an archaic reference to various sub-District (*hsien*) units in which local populations were organized, e.g., the Ming dynasty Precinct (*fang*).

4572 *pì-chǎng* 陛長

HAN: **Chief of the Throne Steps,** in Later Han one each prefixed Left and Right, rank =600 bushels, in charge of those Court Gentlemen (*lang*) who served as imperial bodyguards and took up positions at the center of the throne hall during audiences. HB: chief of the throne steps.

4573 *pǐ-chèng* 筆政

CH'ING: unofficial variant of *pi-t'ieh-shih* (**Clerk**).

4574 *pǐ-chiàng* 筆匠

T'ANG: **Writing-brush Maker,** 3 unranked artisans in the Institute for the Advancement of Literature (*hung-wen kuan*) under the Chancellery (*men-hsia sheng*). RR: *ouvrier fabricant de pinceaux.* P25.

4575 *pì-chiào* 祕校

SUNG–CH'ING: **Palace Library Editor,** originally an abbreviation of the title *chiao-shu lang* (Editor in the Palace Library, *pi-shu sheng*), became (time not clear) an unofficial reference to new Metropolitan Graduates (*chin-shih*) who expected or received first appointments to editorial posts in the Hanlin Academy (*han-lin yüan*) as Senior Compilers (*hsiu-chuan*) or Junior Compilers (*pien-hsiu*).

4576 *pǐ-ch'iěh-ch'í* 筆且齊
YÜAN: **Mongolian Clerk,** Chinese transcription of a Mongolian title also called *meng-ku pi-ch'ieh-ch'i* and *pi-she-ch'ih*.

4577 *pì-hsià* 陛下
Your Majesty, throughout history the standard form of direct address when an official spoke to the ruler; lit., (those of you) at the bottom of the steps, traditionally explained as the only polite way to address the ruler, by seeming to speak to the attendants at the foot of his throne or dais.

4578 *pì-kó* 秘閣
Imperial Archives. (1) SUNG: established in 988 as the archive or library commonly serving the Three Institutes (*san kuan*), i.e., the Institute for the Glorification of Literature (*chao-wen kuan*), the Academy of Scholarly Worthies (*chi-hsien yüan*), and the Historiography Institute (*shih-kuan*), which in the aggregate were called the Academy for the Veneration of Literature (*ch'ung-wen yüan*). Staffed with eminent litterateur-officials chosen in special examinations and granted such titles as Auxiliary in the Imperial Archives (*chih pi-ko*), Subeditor (*chiao-li*), etc. It became the practice that after the death of each Emperor all official documents of his reign were deposited in a newly established Hall (*ko*), presumably a section of the Imperial Archives; e.g., the Dragon Diagram Hall (*lung-t'u ko*) established to store and use documents of the 2nd Sung reign (976–997), staffed with Academicians (*hsüeh-shih*), Auxiliary Academicians (*chih hsüeh-shih*), etc.; and the prestige of all archival appointments rose so that distinguished officials were given nominal archival status. In 1082 the imperial editorial and archival services were reorganized. The Institute for the Glorification of Literature and the Academy of Scholarly Worthies were discontinued; the Historiography Institute was subordinated to the Editorial Service (*chu-tso chü*); and the Imperial Archives, which in time included 10 Halls, were incorporated into the Palace Library (*pi-shu sheng*). SP: *bibliothèque ou archives impériales*. P25. (2) MING–CH'ING: unofficial reference to the **Hanlin Academy** (*han-lin yüan*).

4579 *pì-kó chǘ* 祕閣局
T'ANG: **Astrological Service,** headed by a Director (*lang-chung*); from 662 (661?) to 670 the official name of the eventual Directorate of Astrology (*t'ai-shih chien,* q.v.) in the dynastic capital; name changed from and then back to *t'ai-shih chü,* q.v. Sources are confused about this name; some report *pi-shu ko chü* instead. Both names suggest Imperial Archives (*pi-ko*) or Palace Library (*pi-shu sheng*); at times the Astrological Service was indeed subordinate to the Palace Library. P35.

4580 *pì-kó lìng* 祕閣令
N-S DIV (N. Wei): **Director of the Palace Library,** an official variant of *pi-shu chien.*

4581 *pǐ-kūng* 比公
HAN: **Adjunct Dukes,** 3rd highest in a hierarchy of 10 status groups in the officialdom (see under *shang-kung*), including the following: General-in-chief (*ta chiang-chün*), Cavalry General (*p'iao-chi chiang-chün*), and Chariot and Horse General (*ch'e-chi chiang-chün*). P68.

4582 *pǐ-pù ssū* 比部司 or *pi-pu*
Bureau of Review. (1) N-S DIV–SUI: a subsection of the Ministry of Personnel (*li-pu*) or the Section for Justice (*tu-kuan ts'ao*) in the evolving Department of State Affairs (*shang-shu sheng*), normally headed by a Director (*lang*); responsible for conducting audits of state accounts and disciplinary investigations of officials, but not empowered to try, sentence, or punish. (2) SUI–T'ANG, SUNG, MING: from 583, when Sui transformed the traditional *tu-kuan ts'ao* into the *hsing-pu* (Ministry of Justice), the *pi-pu ssu* became a subsection of it, one of 4 Bureaus in Sui and T'ang, one of 3 in Sung, and again one of 4 in early Ming. The Bureau was consistently headed by a Director (*lang-chung*), rank 5b in T'ang, 6b in Sung; with a Vice Director (*yüan-wai lang*), 6b in T'ang, 7a in Sung. At times there were 2 appointees at each level, prefixed Left and Right. The Bureau continued to have the broad range of responsibilities suggested in (1) above. It disappeared in 1390, when Ming reorganized the Ministry of Justice to have 13 constituent Bureaus (now *ch'ing-li ssu*), one for each Province, which supervised all aspects of judicial administration in the Province for which it was named. The term *pi-pu* may occasionally be encountered in later years, however, as an archaic reference to the Ministry of Justice. RR+SP: *bureau du contrôle judiciaire*. SP also: *bureau de verification des comptes*. P13.

4583 *pǐ-pù ts'áo* 比部曹
N-S DIV: **Review Section,** occasional official variant of *pi-pu ssu* or *pi-pu* (Bureau of Review); e.g., in Sung of the S. Dynasties, a subsection of the Ministry of Personnel (*li-pu*), in N. Wei a subsection of the Section for Justice (*tu-kuan ts'ao*). P5, 13.

4584 *pì-shé-ch'ih* 必闍赤
YÜAN: **Mongolian Clerk,** Chinese transcription of a Mongolian title of some importance in predynastic times, but later abounded in many agencies of government, equated with unranked Chinese functionaries called *ling-shih* (Clerk). Sometimes prefixed *meng-ku* (Mongolian). Variant of *pi-ch'ieh-ch'i*. Also see *meng-ku pi-ch'ieh-ch'i.*

4585 *pǐ-shīh* 鄙師
CHOU: **Ward Preceptor,** ranked as a Senior Serviceman (*shang-shih*) in the Ministry of Education (*ti-kuan*), responsible for maintaining peace, propriety, and law among the 500 families constituting his jurisdiction, a Ward (*pi*) outside the royal domain. CL: *chef de canton extérieur.*

4586 *pì-shū* 祕書 or 秘書
Lit., secret writings. (1) Abbreviated reference to the **Palace Library** (*pi-shu chien, pi-shu sheng*), or prefix to the title of officials in such agencies. (2) MING–CH'ING: archaic reference to the **Hanlin Academy** (*han-lin yüan*).

4587 *pì-shū ch'éng* 祕書丞
Lit., aide to (the director of) the Palace Library (*pi-shu chien, pi-shu sheng*). (1) N-S DIV (San-kuo Wei)–SUI: **Vice Director of the Palace Library,** principal executive aide to the Director (*chien*) from the 220s to c. 604. (2) SUI–YÜAN: **Assistant Director of the Palace Library,** 3rd ranking executive official in the agency from c. 604, outranked both by the Director (*chien*) and by one or 2 Vice Directors (*shao-chien*); rank 5a in Sui, 5b1 in T'ang, 7b in Sung, 6a in Chin. In Yüan 2 eunuch posts, rank 5b, outranked by 4 Chief Ministers (*ch'ing*), 2 Directors (*t'ai-chien*), and 2 Vice Directors (*shao-chien*). RR: *assistant du département de la bibliothèque de l'empereur.* SP: *assistant-executif de la bibliothèque impériale.* P25.

4588 *pì-shū chiēn* 祕書監
(1) HAN–MING: **Director of the Palace Library:** origi-

nated in Later Han as a subordinate of the Chamberlain for Ceremonials (*t'ai-ch'ang*), rank 600 bushels; maintained all imperial documents and books. In the Three Kingdoms period, Wei had an eminent official entitled *pi-shu ling* (also Director ...) who managed general administrative affairs and at the same time maintained the imperial archives, but by 227 this post was split into 2, one a *chung-shu ling* (Secretariat Director) to assist in administration, the other a *pi-shu chien* to maintain the archives under supervision of the Chamberlain for the Palace Revenues (*shao-fu*). The first Chin ruler, Wu-ti (r. 265–290), gave control of the archives to the developing Secretariat, but his successor, Hui-ti (r. 290–306), appointed a *pi-shu chien* to oversee archival materials in 3 Halls (*ko*) in the outer palace grounds; it was traditionally considered that this marked the beginning of a governmental rather than a personal imperial institution. The Director soon was in charge of a substantial agency called Court of the Palace Library (*pi-shu ssu*), normally having a Vice Director (*ch'eng:* aide) and 4 specially esteemed Assistants (*lang* or *lang-chung*), each in charge of a Hall (*ko*) or Bureau (*pu*) with a subordinate staff of Clerks (*ling-shih*) and Proofreaders (*cheng-shu*). Although from time to time both the names and the functions of the Palace Library and the Secretariat seem to have been interchangeable, the Palace Library was increasingly devoted to archival-editorial work. Under the S. Dynasty Sung, which in 464–465 changed the agency's name to *pi-shu sheng* (Department of ...) and apparently turned it again into a personal imperial institution, the staff began regularly producing bibliographies called *ssu pu mu-lu* (Catalogs of the Four Bureaus) and inaugurated the enduring bibliographic division of Chinese books into the categories commonly called the Four Classifications or Four Treasuries (*ssu pu*). By the end of the S. Dynasties in the 580s the Palace Library was regularly considered one of the major, top-echelon agencies at the dynastic capital called the Five Departments (*wu sheng*). Meantime N. Wei had adopted the institution (*pi-shu sheng*) and had given its Director (*chien*) the high rank of 2 and a large staff still including 4 Assistants (*lang*); but the title Director seems to have changed back and forth among the terms *pi-shu chien*, *pi-shu ling*, and *pi-ko ling*. Sui's Director (*chien*) was initially rank 3a; but in c. 607 the post was reduced to rank 3b and shortly thereafter was renamed *ling*. T'ang re-established the title *chien* and fixed the agency name as *pi-shu sheng*. Except for the intervals from 662 to 670, when the Palace Library was called Orchid Pavilion (*lan-t'ai*) and its Director was known as Grand Scribe (*t'ai-shih*), and from 684 to 712, when the agency name was Unicorn Pavilion (*lin-t'ai*), the title *pi-shu chien* prevailed till 1380; then the first Ming Emperor reduced the Palace Library institution to the single post of Librarian (*tien-chi*) in the Hanlin Academy (*han-lin yüan*). The Director's rank was 3b in T'ang, 4a in Sung, 3b in Chin, and 6a in early Ming. In Yüan, executive posts in the Palace Library were held by palace eunuchs with the titles Chief Minister (*ch'ing*), 4, rank 3a; Director (*t'ai-chien*), 2, 3b; Vice Director (*shao-chien*), 2, 4b; and Assistant Director (*ch'eng* or *chien-ch'eng*), 2, 5b. From mid-T'ang on, the Directorship generally declined in importance, at times becoming little more than a sinecure; for the compiling and editing work on which it had flourished was taken over increasingly by a variety of new Institutes and Academies, of which the Hanlin Academy (*han-lin yüan*) is best known; also see, e.g., *chi-hsien yüan*, *ch'ung-wen yüan*, *hsüeh-shih yüan*. Cf. *pi-ko*. HB: inspector of the imperial library. RR: *directeur (du département) de la bibliothèque de l'empereur*. SP: *directeur de la bibliothèque impériale*. P25. (2) N-S DIV, LIAO–

YÜAN: **Palace Library** or (if differentiation from *pi-shu sheng* is desired), **Directorate of the Palace Library:** unofficially a reference to the agency or staff represented by the Director of the Palace Library (*pi-shu chien*) for the brief period in the mid-200s before the agency names *pi-shu ssu* and *pi-shu sheng* were established; the official name in Liao, Chin, and Yüan, headed by a Director (*chien*) in Liao and Chin, rank 3b in Chin; by 4 eunuch Chief Ministers (*ch'ing*), 3a, in Yüan. P25. (3) N-S DIV: especially when headed by a *ling* (Director), a common official variant of *chung-shu sheng* (**Secretariat**). Also see *chung-shu fu, hsi-t'ai*.

4589 *pì-shū chūng-sǎn* 祕書中散
N-S DIV (N. Wei): **Courtier in the Palace Library,** one category of aristocratic Courtiers (*chung-san*, q.v.). P25.

4590 *pì-shū kó* 祕書閣
Possible reference to *pi-ko, pi-ko chü, pi-shu sheng*, or (?) one of the Halls (*ko*) that constituted the Sung dynasty Imperial Archives (*pi-ko*).

4591 *pì-shū kó chǚ* 祕書閣局
T'ANG: variant or confused reference to *pi-ko chü* (**Astrological Service**).

4592 *pì-shū láng* 祕書郎
N-S DIV–YÜAN: **Assistant in the Palace Library** (see *pi-shu chien, pi-shu sheng*), normally 4, rank 7a then 5b in Sui, 6b1 (9b1?) in T'ang, 8a in Sung, 7a in Chin and Yüan; generally responsible for the Halls (*ko*) or Bureaus (*pu*) among which the Palace Library's materials were divided, and for cataloging such materials. In the S. Dynasties an especially esteemed post, to which scions of important families were appointed for short tenure before being moved up in the governmental hierarchy. Sometimes, officially or unofficially, called *lang-chung*. RR+SP: *secrétaire de la bibliothèque de l'empereur*. P25.

4593 *pì-shū lìng* 祕書令
N-S DIV–SUI: **Director of the Palace Library:** in Wei of the Three Kingdoms era established in predynastic times as principal administrative aide to the Emperor, dealing both with general administration and with archival record keeping; by 227 divided into 2 posts, one *chung-shu ling* (Secretariat Director) and one *pi-shu chien* (Director of the Palace Library, but possibly originally *chung-shu chien*) for archival-editorial service. In N. Wei the term seems to have alternated with *pi-shu chien* and *pi-ko chien*. In Sui resurrected in c. 607 to replace *pi-shu chien*, but from T'ang on *pi-shu chien* was the standard title. Cf. *pi-shu ling-shih*. P25.

4594 *pì-shū lìng-shǐh* 祕書令史
N-S DIV (San-kuo Shu Han): apparently a variant of *pi-shu ling* (**Director of the Palace Library**) under Wei of the Three Kingdoms era. See *ling-shih*. P25.

4595 *pì-shū nèi-shěng* 祕書內省
SUI-T'ANG: **Inner Branch of the Palace Library** (see *pi-shu sheng, pi-shu chien*), established in 593, reason not clear; apparently discontinued at the end of Sui. Revived in 629 for the specific purpose of compiling histories of the 5 immediately preceding dynasties (Liang, Ch'en, Ch'i, Chou, Sui), apparently terminated when that task was completed in 636. Located inside the imperial palace as a unit of the Secretariat (*chung-shu sheng*), whereas the Palace Library proper was located outside the imperial palace alongside other agencies of the central government. Staffing not clear, probably litterateurs with only quasiofficial status. Cf. *nei*

pi-shu sheng (Inner Palace Library). RR: *département intérieur de la bibliothèque de l'empereur.*

4596 *pì-shū shào-chiēn* 祕書少監
Vice Director of the Palace Library. (1) SUI–CHIN: normally one (2 in T'ang), 2nd ranking member of the Palace Library (*pi-shu sheng*) staff; rank 4b in Sui, 4b1 in T'ang, 5b in Sung, 5a in Chin; principal aide to the Director (*chien*). RR+SP: *sous-directeur.* (2) YÜAN: 2 eunuchs, rank 4b, 3rd ranking post in the Palace Library, after 4 Chief Ministers (*ch'ing*) and 2 Directors (*t'ai-chien*). See *pi-shu shao-ling, pi-shu ch'eng.* P25.

4597 *pì-shū shào-lìng* 祕書少令
SUI: **Vice Director of the Palace Library,** changed in c. 607 from *pi-shu shao-chien.* Also see *pi-shu ling.* P25.

4598 *pì-shū shěng* 祕書省
N-S DIV–SUNG, MING: **Palace Library** or (if differentiation from *pi-shu chien,* q.v., is desired) **Department of the Palace Library.** Originated in 464–465 as a new name for the *pi-shu chien,* a relatively autonomous agency of the central government generally in charge of maintaining the collection of the Emperor's official documents and at times compiling and editing historical records based on its archives. N. Wei split it into 2 agencies to separate its functions, an Inner Palace Library (*nei pi-shu sheng*) and an Outer Palace Library (*wai pi-shu sheng*). The former had an at least quasiadministrative role in that it handled documents flowing into and out of the imperial palace, reflecting the fact that the Palace Library and the Secretariat (*chung-shu sheng*) were virtually interchangeable or alternating agencies at times during the era of N-S Division; the latter was charged with archival and editorial responsibilities. Before the end of the era of N-S Division the Palace Library was officially considered among the top-echelon agencies of the central government called the Five Departments (*wu sheng*), as was the separate Secretariat. In Sui and early T'ang, for different purposes than in N. Wei (certainly in T'ang, possibly not in Sui), the Palace Library spawned an Inner Branch (*pi-shu nei-sheng*). In T'ang, this was housed in and subordinate to the Secretariat in the inner precincts of the palace, whereas the Palace Library proper was located among other general-administration agencies in the outer precincts; and the sole purpose of the Inner Branch was to compile some historical records, upon the completion of which in 636 it was apparently terminated. After mid-T'ang the functions of the Palace Library were gradually taken over by other agencies. As early as 630 the Editorial Service (*chu-tso chü*), long a constituent unit of the Palace Library, was assigned to the preparation of the official state calendar and became relatively autonomous, while Palace Library members called Historiographers (*shih-kuan*) were transferred out to constitute a separate Historiography Institute (*shih-kuan*). Before long the archival functions of the Palace Library were taken over by various Academies and Institutes such as the Academy of Scholarly Worthies (*chi-hsien yüan*), the Hanlin Academy (*han-lin yüan*), etc. From the early 700s through the Sung era, consequently, the Palace Library ceased functioning; but eminent members of the central government continued to be given Palace Library sinecure appointments for prestige purposes, including Supervisor (*t'i-chü*). Liao, Chin, and Yüan restored the old agency name *pi-shu chien.* Ming revived the *pi-shu sheng* as a functioning institution but in 1380 reduced it to the single post of Librarian (*tien-chi*) in the Hanlin Academy. Official variant names of the *pi-shu sheng* included Orchid Pavilion (*lan-t'ai*) from 662 to 670 and Unicorn Pavilion (*lin-t'ai*) from 684 to 712. The head

of the agency was regularly entitled Director (*chien, pi-shu chien*), rank 3b in Sui and T'ang, 4a in Sung, 6b in early Ming. There was normally a Vice Director (*shao-chien*), 4b in Sui and T'ang, 5b in Sung; an Assistant Director (*ch'eng*), 5a in Sui, 5b1 in T'ang, 7b in Sung; and 4 Assistants (*lang*), 5b in Sui, 6b1 in T'ang, 8a in Sung. The Assistants in the Palace Library were responsible (at least nominally) for managing the Halls (*ko*) or Bureaus (*pu*) among which the agency's materials were divided for storage and maintenance. Also see *pi-ko, pi-shu ssu.* RR: *département de la bibliothèque de l'empereur.* SP: *département de la bibliothèque impériale.* P25.

4599 *pì-shū ssù* 祕書寺
N-S DIV (Chin, Sung): lit., Court of the Palace Library: official name of the **Palace Library** (see *pi-shu chien, pi-shu sheng*) from c. 300 to 464-465, then changed to the long-enduring name *pi-shu sheng.* P25.

4600 *pǐ-té-chēn* 比德眞
N-S DIV (N. Dyn.): lit. meaning not clear; perhaps a transcription of a Hsien-pi or other non-Chinese word: **Clerk,** equated with *shu-li,* an unranked subofficial.

4601 *pǐ-t'iēh-shìh* 筆帖式
CH'ING: Chinese transcription of a Manchu word: **Clerk,** found in large, usually unspecified numbers in virtually all agencies of the central government, rank from 7 to 9 levels; available to Manchus, Mongols, and Chinese, but only to members of the Banner (*ch'i*) organization; in the Imperial Clan Office (*tsung-jen fu*) available only to Manchus, and after 1755 only to members of the imperial clan.

4602 *pǐ-t'iēh-shìh shǔ* 筆帖式署
CH'ING: **Clerks Office,** the aggregation of *pi-t'ieh-shih* (Clerks) in the Seals Service (*chu-yin chü*) and perhaps in many other agencies of the central government; headed by a Manchu chosen from among the staff Clerks, tentatively called Secretary of the Clerks Office (*chu-shih, shu chu-shih,* or *pi-t'ieh-shih shu chu-shih*), who after 2 years of satisfactory service could formally become Secretary (*chu-shih*) of the Seals Service itself (?). P9.

4603 *pì-yù* 祕獄
HAN: lit., secret prison: abbreviation of *i-t'ing pi-yü* (**Prison for Palace Women**).

4604 *pì-yūng* 辟雍
Lit., to withdraw and be at peace. (1) CHOU: **Royal Learning Retreat,** a general reference to any place where the ruler commonly studied or was tutored. (2) Throughout imperial history an archaic reference to the **National University** (*t'ai-hsüeh,* etc.), where men were prepared to become officials. (3) SUNG: **Preparatory Branch of the National University,** established in 1102 just outside the capital city to house and train new Nominees for Office (*kung-shih*) and other students in the lowest-level unit, the Outer College (*wai-she*), of the National University; had its own staff of Erudites (*po-shih*), etc.; supervised by the central government's Directorate of Education (*kuo-tzu chien*). Apparently not continued in S. Sung. SP: *université.*

4605 *pì-yūng shěng* 辟雍省
From Sung times or earlier, an archaic reference to the **Directorate of Education** (*kuo-tzu chien*). See *pi-yung.*

4606 *p'í* 疲
CH'ING: lit., exhausting: one of the categories used in defining the importance of units of territorial administration; see *ch'ung-fan-p'i-nan.* BH: wearisome.

4607 *p'i-chiàng* 裨將
Assistant General: from Han on, used occasionally as the title of a military officer on temporary campaign assignment or as an unofficial reference to any officer in the command echelon subordinate to a General (*chiang-chün*). Equivalent to *fu-chiang*, q.v.

4608 *p'i-chiǎo ch'ǎng* 皮角場
SUNG: **Leather and Horns Warehouse,** a unit of the Directorate for Armaments (*chün-ch'i chien*) in the Ministry of Works (*kung-pu*). SP: *bureau de la réception des cuirs et des cornes.*

4609 *p'ì-jèn* 辟任
HAN: lit., one excused from (or summoned to) public service (?): **Imperial Princess,** official designation of daughters of the Emperor, only during the reign of Wang Mang (A.D. 9–23). See *kung-chu.*

4610 *p'í-k'ù* 皮庫
CH'ING: **Hides Storehouse,** one of 6 warehouses or vaults of valuables in the Storage Office (*kuang-ch'u ssu*) of the Imperial Household Department (*nei-wu fu*). BH: fur store. P37.

4611 *p'ī-pěn ch'u* 批本處
CH'ING: **Endorsement-copying Office,** a minor unit under the Grand Secretariat (*nei-ko*); staffed with clerical workers, details not clear. BH: office for copying the emperor's endorsements of documents.

4612 *p'í-pō sǒ* 皮剝所
SUNG: **Horse-skinning Office,** 2 minor agencies, one under the Court of the Imperial Stud (*t'ai-p'u ssu*), the other under the Bureau of Military Affairs (*shu-mi yüan*); possibly a consolidated agency serving both the Court and the Bureau; staffing not clear, but probably manned by unranked, possibly hereditary specialists. SP: *bureau chargé d'enlever les peaux des chevaux.*

4613 *p'í-tsò chú* 皮作局
MING: **Leatherwork Service,** a craft workshop in the Ministry of Works (*kung-pu*), headed by a Commissioner-in-chief (*ta-shih*), rank 9a. Antecedent of the Ch'ing dynasty *chih-tsao k'u*, q.v. P15.

4614 *p'ī-yèn sǒ* 批驗所
YÜAN–CH'ING: lit., investigating and verifying post: **Tea and Salt Control Station,** full name *chien-chiao p'i-yen so* in Yüan, could be specified as Tea Control Station (*ch'a-yin p'i-yen ṣo, ch'a-yin so*) or Salt Control Station (*yen-yin p'i-yen so, yen-yin so*) in Ming; came to have no responsibility for tea in Ch'ing. A checkpoint maintained on a principal road or waterway for the verification of certificates (*yin*) that were required to accompany all authorized commercial shipments of state-controlled salt (and tea to a lesser extent) in transit. Responsible to a regional or provincial-level Salt Distribution Commissioner (*tu chuan-yün yen shih*) or Salt Distribution Supervisor (*yen-k'o t'i-chü*) and also, in Ming and Ch'ing, to a Salt Control Censor (*hsün-yen yü-shih*). In Yüan headed by a Superintendent (*t'i-ling*), rank 7a; in Ming and Ch'ing by a Commissioner-in-chief (*ta-shih*), unranked in Ming, 8a in Ch'ing. BH (*ta-shih*): salt examiner. P53, 61.

4615 *piāo* 標
Lit., flag, banner, standard: throughout history used in reference to identification banners; in Ch'ing, more specifically, **Command,** the designation of any military unit in the Chinese armies called the Green Standards (*lu-ying*), prefixed with an abbreviated reference to the commander,

e.g., the Command of a Provincial Military Commander (*t'i-piao*, i.e., the *piao* of a *t'i-tu*). BH: regiment.

4616 *piǎo-tsòu-ì ssū* 表奏議司
SUNG: **Decision Expediting Office,** one of several units in the Left Bureau (*tso-t'ing*) of the Court of Judicial Review (*ta-li ssu*); staffed with subofficial functionaries who monitored action by the 8 Subsections (*fang*) of the Sentence Evaluators Section (*hsiang-tuan an*) and the submission of resulting memorials to the throne. SP: *bureau chargé de presser le jugement et de présenter les adresses au trône.* P22.

4617 *piǎo-tsòu kuān* 表奏官
T'ANG–SUNG: **Memorial Presenter,** both a generic and a specific designation, apparently denoting a member of an agency staff responsible for the proper submission of his agency's communications to the throne; in T'ang seems to occur only in the eunuch-dominated Armies of Inspired Strategy (*shen-ts'e chün*); in Sung occurs with such variants as *piao-tsou ssu* (Office of the Memorial Presenter) and *piao-tsou-i ssu* (Decision Expediting Office) in such varied agencies as the Palace Library (*pi-shu sheng*), the Regalia Office (*ssu-chang ssu*) of the Imperial Insignia Guards (*chin-wu wei*), the Three Institutes (*san kuan*), and the Court of Judicial Review (*ta-li ssu*); apparently of low rank or unranked. Cf. *ch'eng-chih* (Recipient of Edicts). RR+SP: *(fonctionnaire, bureau) chargé de présenter les adresses au trône.*

4618 *p'iāo-chì chiāng-chūn* 驃騎將軍
Cavalry General. (1) HAN: until 87 B.C., one of many duty-assignment titles conferred on military officers on active campaign; thereafter awarded to favored courtiers, often in combinations such as General-in-chief and Cavalry General (*ta chiang-chün p'iao-chi chiang-chün*), and had no military significance. HB: general of agile cavalry. (2) N-S DIV (San-kuo Wei): one of 3 Generals who shared command of the Imperial Guard (*chin-lü*); see *ch'e-chi chiang-chün, wu-wei chiang-chün*. (3) SUI–T'ANG: before 607, the designation of the head of each Garrison (*fu*) in the Garrison Militia system (see *fu-ping*), assisted by a Chariot and Horse General (*ch'e-chi chiang-chün*); by 607 the Garrisons had split into 2 types, a Cavalry Garrison (*p'iao-chi fu*) commanded by a Cavalry General and a Chariot and Horse Garrison (*ch'e-chi fu*) commanded by a Chariot and Horse General. In 607 the Garrisons were reorganized into a single type called the Soaring Hawk Garrison (*ying-yang fu*) headed by a Commandant (*lang-chiang*). In 618 the names Cavalry Garrison, Cavalry General, Chariot and Horse Garrison, and Chariot and Horse General were all revived for the T'ang Garrison Militia system, but very soon thereafter (619? 623?) they were all discontinued in favor of the standard designations Assault-resisting Garrison (*che-ch'ung fu*) and their Commandants (*tu-wei*). RR: *général de la cavalerie hardie.* P43, 44.

4619 *p'iāo-chì fǔ* 驃騎府
SUI–T'ANG: **Cavalry Garrison** in the Garrison Militia system (see *fu* and *fu-ping*), deriving from the title of its head, Cavalry General (*p'iao-chi chiang-chün*); the usage was established by the early 600s. In 607 all Garrisons (*fu*) in the system, including Chariot and Horse Garrisons (*ch'e-chi fu*) as well as Cavalry Garrisons, were given the standard name Soaring Hawk Garrison (*ying-yang fu*). At the beginning of T'ang in 618 the former names were revived, only to be changed in 619 (623?) into one standard name, Assault-resisting Garrison (*che-ch'ung fu*) and then in 624 to Commander-general's Garrison (*t'ung-chün fu*). Finally,

in 636, the nomenclature was stabilized with a change back to Assault-resisting Garrison. RR: *milice de la cavalerie hardie.* P43.

4620 *p'iǎo-chì tà chiāng-chūn* 驃騎大將軍
T'ANG–SUNG: **Cavalry General-in-chief,** prestige title (*san-kuan*) for military officers of rank 1b. RR+SP: *grand général de la cavalerie hardie.* P68.

4621 *p'iào-ch'iēn ch'ù* 票籤處
CH'ING: **Registry,** one each Manchu (*man*) and Chinese (*han*) unit under the Grand Secretariat (*nei-ko*), responsible for recording digests of all official documents handled.

4622 *p'iào-k'ò* 票客
HAN: common scribal error for *su-k'o,* a variant of *chih-su tu-wei* (**Commandant-in-chief of the Granaries**). P8.

4623 *piéh-chià* 別駕
Lit., to ride apart, an outrider. (1) HAN–N-S DIV: **Mounted Escort,** an official who accompanied Regional Inspectors (*tz'u-shih*) on tours of their Regions (*chou*); specific functions not clear. HB: aide-de-camp attendant. (2) N-S DIV–SUNG: **Administrative Aide** to the heads of Regions (*chou*) and Commanderies (*chün*), then in T'ang and Sung in Prefectures (*chou*); evolved from the status noted in (1) above, from Sui on alternated with such titles as *chang-shih, tsan-chih, t'ung-p'an;* rank 4b in Sui, 4b2, 5a2, 5b1 in T'ang, 9a in Sung. RR: *fonctionnaire adjoint.* SP: *assistant ou fonctionnaire-associé de préfecture ou administrateur des affaires courantes.* (3) CH'ING: unofficial reference to a **Department Vice Magistrate** (*chou t'ung-chih, chou-t'ung*), 6b, or an **Assistant Department Magistrate** (*chou p'an-kuan, chou-p'an*), 7b. P32, 49, 50, 53, 54.

4624 *piéh-chiàng* 別將
T'ANG–SUNG: **Adjunct Commandant,** from 624 to 636 the designation of the 2nd in command, under a Commander-general (*t'ung-chün*), in each Garrison of the Garrison Militia organization (see *fu* and *fu-ping*), then called Commander-generals' Garrisons (*t'ung-chün fu*); from 636, the 3rd ranking post in Garrisons, then called Assault-resisting Garrisons (*che-ch'ung fu*); rank 7a2, 7b1, or 7b2 according to the number of troops in the Garrisons; subordinate each to one Commandant (*tu-wei*), 4a1, 4b2, or 5a2, and 2 Vice Commandants (*kuo-i tu-wei*), 5b2, 6a1, 6a2. The title seems to have been retained into early Sung, but its post-T'ang usage is not clear. RR+SP: *adjoint au chef de milice.*

4625 *piéh-chiào yüàn* 別教院
T'ANG: **Court of Special Instruction,** a unit of the Imperial Music Office (*t'ai-yüeh shu*); staffing and functions not clear, but possibly a section of the Office in which temporary instructors with specialized skills were housed, supplementing the regular, permanent staff. RR: *cour des professeurs spéciaux.*

4626 *piéh-huǒ lìng* 別火令
HAN: lit. meaning not clear, and supporting evidence inadequate: **Director of Fire Renewal,** probably a transmitter of new ritual fire from the imperial palace to regional or foreign dignitaries at seasonal changings of the fires (*kai-huo*). Traditionally understood, however, to have been a kind of jailor-adjudicator in the court's relations with peripheral dependencies and tributary groups, possibly dealing with tribal groups split into separate campfires, i.e., camps (?). Established in 104 B.C. as one of 3 major subordinates of the Chamberlain for Dependencies (*ta hung-lu*); see *hsing-jen* (Messenger) and *i-kuan ling* (Director of

Interpreters). Seconded by an Aide (*ch'eng*). HB: prefect of the fresh fire.

4627 *piēh-jén* 鼈人
CHOU: **Turtle Catcher,** 4 ranked as Junior Servicemen (*hsia-shih*), members of the Ministry of State (*t'ien-kuan*) responsible for collecting and keeping turtles, spearfish, oysters, etc., and providing them to the Ministry's Spiceman (*hai-jen*) for use in sacrifices. CL: *preneur de tortues.*

4628 *piéh-pīng ts'áo* 別兵曹
N-S DIV (San-kuo Wei, Chin, S. Dyn.): **Allied Troops Section,** one of 5 or more units under the Minister of War (*wu ping shang-shu*) in the developing Department of State Affairs (*shang-shu sheng*); dealt with subjugated or surrendered alien or aboriginal soldiers; headed by a Director (*lang*). P12.

4629 *piéh-shīh-pā-lǐ chú* 別失八里局
YÜAN: **Bishbalik Service,** 2 agencies of this name under the elaborate Bureau of Works (*kung-pu*) having something to do with the Central Asian city, Bishbalik, which served as capital of the Chagatai Khanate; possibly construction workers from Bishbalik skilled in Islamic architectural styles or construction methods.

4630 *piéh-t'óu* 別頭
SUNG: lit., another head, another director: **Avoidance Examination,** a special examination, administered separately from regular civil service recruitment examinations, given to candidates who were related to any of the regularly appointed examiners, to avoid possible favoritism; probably limited to the earliest Sung decades.

4631 *piēn* 邊
Frontier, occasionally used as a variant of *chen* (Defense Command); also see *chiu pien* (Nine Frontiers).

4632 *piēn-chiào kuān* 編校官 or *pien-chiao*
SUNG: **Editorial Assistant,** one of several designations for unranked subofficials employed in the Historiography Institute (*kuo-shih kuan*) and the True Records Institute (*shih-lu yüan*). Cf. *pien-hsiu, hsiu-chuan, chien-t'ao, hsiu-cheng, chiao-k'an, chiao-cheng, chien-yüeh.* SP: *rédacteur-correcteur.* P23.

4633 *piēn-hsiū ch'ìh-lìng sǒ* 編修勅令所
SUNG: **Office for the Compilation of Imperial Pronouncements,** apparently an agency of the Chancellery (*men-hsia sheng*) but not a regular, continuing one; staffing and specific functions not clear. Cf. *ch'ih-ling so.* SP: *bureau de la compilation des décrets et des ordres impériaux.*

4634 *piēn-hsiū chūng-shū t'iáo-lì sǒ* 編修中書條例所
SUNG: **Office for the Compilation of Secretariat Regulations,** affiliation and status not clear; likely an ad hoc group of central government dignitaries given the task of regularizing administrative procedures in the Secretariat (*chung-shu sheng*), date(s) not clear. SP: *bureau de la compilation des règlements du grand secrétariat impérial.*

4635 *piēn-hsiū kuān* 編修官 or *pien-hsiu*
SUNG–CH'ING: **Junior Compiler** in the Historiography Institute (*kuo-shih yüan*), the True Records Institute (*shih-lu yüan*), the Academy of Scholarly Worthies (*chi-hsien yüan*), and even the Bureau of Military Affairs (*shu-mi yüan*) in Sung, number variable, rank 8a; thereafter members of the Hanlin Academy (*han-lin yüan*)—in Chin 4 Jurchen and 4 Chinese, 8a; in Yüan 3 to 10, 8a then 6b; in Ming 4 to 6, 7a; in Ch'ing unlimited, 7a. Participants in historio-

graphic and other compilations under imperial sponsorship, in association with Senior Compilers (*hsiu-chuan*) and others. In Ming and Ch'ing times, the 2nd and 3rd ranking new Metropolitan Graduates (*chin-shih*) were normally appointed to this post in the expectation they would rapidly move into higher Hanlin positions and finally into the Grand Secretariat (*nei-ko*). SP: *compilateur, compilateur rédacteur.* BH: compiler of the second class. P23.

4636 *piēn-hsiū shíh-chèng chì fáng* 編修時政記房
SUNG: **Office for Maintaining a Record of Current Policies,** a unit of the Bureau of Military Affairs (*shu-mi yüan*); staffing and specific functions not clear. SP: *chambre de la rédaction des notes sur les èvènements politiques.*

4637 *piēn-hsiū wén-tzù* 編修文字
SUNG: lit., compiler of writings: **Clerk,** unranked or of very low rank, found in many central government agencies; eventually (date not clear) superseded by the title *shou-tang kuan.*

4638 *piēn-hsiū yüàn* 編修院
SUNG: **Bureau of Compilation,** established as a unit of the Chancellery (*men-hsia sheng*) to prepare successive, periodically updated histories of the dynasty, True Records (*shih-lu*) of each reign, and a daily calendar (*jih-li*) of events at court. Apparently discontinued very early, the Chancellery retaining a Dynastic History Office (*kuo-shih yüan*) but most compilation functions being taken over by relatively autonomous agencies nominally constituting the Palace Library (*pi-shu sheng*)—Historiography and True Records Institute (*kuo-shih shih-lu yüan*), Court Calendar Office (*jih-li so*), Editorial Service (*chu-tso chü*)—and the Historiography Institute (*shih-kuan*) in the Institute for the Veneration of Literature (*ch'ung-wen yüan*). Duplication and overlapping were apparently avoided because none of these was more than a titular agency, brought into functioning existence only when court officials were assigned, commonly as concurrent Academicians (*hsüeh-shih*), to specific compilation tasks. SP: *cour de la compilation de l'histoire d'état, des annales véridiques et du calendrier.* P23.

4639 *piēn-jén* 邊人
CHOU: **Basket Handler,** a eunuch assigned to the Ministry of State (*t'ien-kuan*) to supervise 10 Female Basket Handlers (*nü-pien*) assisted by 20 convicts in preparing baskets of food for the ruler, his wives, and his heir, for various sacrifices and receptions, etc. CL: *employé aux paniers.*

4640 *piēn-kǔ chǘ* 編估局
SUNG: **Classifications and Estimates Section** under the Court of the Imperial Treasury (*t'ai-fu ssu*); staffing and specific functions not clear, but presumably handled, recorded, and distributed all commodities of value submitted to the palace. SP: *bureau de classement et d'estimation.*

4641 *piēn-lèi shèng-chèng sǒ* 編類聖政所
SUNG: **Office for the Compilation by Category of Imperial Policy Pronouncements,** a unit of the Historiography Institute (*kuo-shih yüan*) that apparently drafted treatises on topics concerning governmental regulations in all realms; staffing not clear. SP: *bureau de la compilation des édits impériaux.*

4642 *piēn-lèi yù-pǐ sǒ* 編類御筆所
SUNG: **Office for the Compilation by Categories of Imperial Pronouncements,** organizational affiliation not clear, but likely related to one of the many Institutes and Academies at the dynastic capital; probably active only inter-

mittently when court officials undertook, probably as concurrent Academicians (*hsüeh-shih*), to prepare a specific imperial publication. SP: *bureau de la compilation des écrits impériaux.*

4643 *piēn-lù kuān* 編錄官
T'ANG: **Recorder,** from 786 members of the Academy of Scholarly Worthies (*chi-hsien yüan*); number, rank, and specific functions not clear. RR: *fonctionnaire chargé de classer et d'inscrire.* P25.

4644 *pièn-shīh* 弁師
CHOU: **Master of the Royal Headgear,** 2 ranked as Junior Servicemen (*hsia-shih*), members of the Ministry of War (*hsia-kuan*) who maintained and as was appropriate provided the 5 kinds of headgear worn by the King. CL: *maître du bonnet.*

4645 *piēn-tìng shū-chí kuān* 編定書籍官
SUNG: **Compilation Clerk,** 2 in the Palace Library (*pi-shu sheng*), apparently unranked suboficials. SP: *fonctionnaire chargé de réviser les ouvrages.*

4646 *pièn-t'úng lìng* 辨銅令 or 辯銅令
HAN: **Director of Grading and Sorting Raw Copper** to be used in the production of copper coins, a subordinate originally of the Chamberlain for the Palace Revenues (*shao-fu*), then from 115 B.C. of the Commandant of the Imperial Gardens (*shui-heng tu-wei*); in Later Han subordinate to the Chamberlain for the National Treasury (*ta ssu-nung*), in some degree also to the Metropolitan Governor (*ching-chao yin*). Considered one of the Three Money Managers of the Court of the Imperial Gardens (*shui-heng san kuan*), also referred to generically as Coins Officials (*ch'ien-kuan, chu-ch'ien kuan*). Beginning under Emperor Wu (r. 141–87 B.C.), there were repeated efforts to suppress the minting of coins in regions such as Princedoms (*wang-kuo*) and Commanderies (*chün*) and to consolidate money supply controls in these central government agencies. HB: prefect of the office for assorting copper. P16.

4647 *p'iēn* 偏
CHOU: lit., to be on a side, a one-side part of something: **Squadron** of 25 chariots.

4648 *p'iēn chiāng-chūn* 偏將軍 or *p'ien-chiang*
Lit., a general on one side, a general leading part of a military force. (1) HAN (first form): **Deputy General,** normally subordinate to a General (*chiang-chün*) and perhaps also a General-in-chief (*ta chiang-chün*) in a Campaigning Army (*ying*), all on ad hoc duty assignments, detached from their regular posts. This title was not common and may have been used only in the wars preceding the establishment of Later Han. HB: lieutenant general. (2) SUI (2nd form): **Division Commander,** from 612 the designation of the leader of a Division (*t'uan*) of 4,000 cavalrymen; 4 Divisions constituted an Army (*chün*).

4649 *pín* 嬪
Lit., female guest: **Concubine,** throughout history a categorical designation of palace women ranking below the Queen or Empress and the secondary wives of rulers called Consorts (*fei*). Most commonly found in the form *chiu pin* (Nine Concubines), q.v. Also see *san pin, shang-pin, hsia-pin, kuei-pin, kung-nü*. BH: imperial concubine of the 4th rank.

4650 *pīn* 賓
CHOU: **Guest,** designation of a Feudal Lord (see *chu-hou*) or an alien tribal chief while visiting the royal court, in contrast to Visitor (*k'o*), designation used for diplomatic

representatives or members of the retinue of such a dignitary. CL: *prince en visite.*

4651   *pīn-fù* 嬪婦
Supplementary Secondary Wives, from Chou times on a collective designation of all ranked palace women, a combined abbreviation of the terms *chiu pin* (Nine Concubines) and *shih-fu* (Hereditary Consorts).

4652   *pīn-fǔ* 賓輔
MING: **Companion,** 2 appointed in the service of the Heir Apparent in the era 1398–1402, but not perpetuated. P69.

4653   *pīn-k'ò* 賓客
See *t'ai-tzu pin-k'o* (**Adviser to the Heir Apparent**); also see *ta pin-k'o* and separate entries *pin* and *k'o.*

4654   *pīn-k'ò ssū* 賓客司
CH'ING: **Receptions Bureau,** one of the original 4 Bureaus (*ch'ing-li ssu*) in the Court of Colonial Affairs (*li-fan yüan*), headed by a variable number of Directors (*lang-chung*), some Manchu, some Mongolian, normally on concurrent duty assignments from regular posts elsewhere; established in 1661, in 1757 renamed *wang-hui ssu* (Inner Mongolian Reception Bureau). P17.

4655   *pīn-liáo* 賓僚
MING–CH'ING: variant of *mu-yu* (**Private Secretaries**), q.v., collective reference to members of a Private Secretariat (*mu-fu*).

4656   *pīn-mù* 賓幕
SUNG: **Private Secretary,** early counterpart of the term *mu-yu,* q.v. SP: *assistant.*

4657   *pīn-pù* 賓部
N-S DIV (Chou): **Section for Tributary Relations,** a unit in the Ministry of Justice (*ch'iu-kuan*) in charge of communications with foreign peoples; also the title of its Director, ranked as an Ordinary Grand Master (*chung ta-fu;* 5a). See *hsiao pin-pu.* Cf. *fan-pu.* P17.

4658   *pīn-p'ú* 賓僕
T'ANG: **Receptionist,** 18 unranked subofficials in the Office of State Visitors (*tien-k'o shu*), a unit of the Court of State Ceremonial (*hung-lu ssu*). P11.

4659   *pīn-yǔ* 賓友
MING: **Companion,** 2 on the staff of each Commandery Prince (*chün-wang*), only in the era 1398–1402. P69.

4660   *p'ĭn* 品
N-S DIV (San-kuo)–CH'ING: **Rank,** the status categories among which officials and the posts they occupied were distributed; see *chiu p'in* (Nine Ranks), *chi* (Class), *chieh* (Class, Rank), *teng* (Degree, Grade, Class).

4661   *p'ĭn-ch'áng kuān* 品嘗官
Lit., an official who tastes all kinds, i.e., all kinds of foods before presenting them to the ruler, deriving from a practice attributed to the Food Steward (*shan-fu*) by the ancient text *Chou-li:* **Food Taster,** unofficial reference to any official charged with serving the ruler's meals, e.g., a member of the Provisioner's Office (*t'ai-kuan shu*) or the Court of Imperial Entertainments (*kuang-lu ssu*).

4662   *p'ĭn-láng* 品郎
Lit., gentleman who classifies things (?): **Customs Collector,** common reference to an official assigned to collect fees at a customs barrier or marketplace.

4663   *p'ín-ts'ùi* 貧倅
SUNG: lit., an impoverished secondary official in a Prefecture (*fu*) or District (*hsien*), now retired; from a poem by Lu Yu: **Retired Helper,** a literary reference to such an official, probably used only by himself in a self-deprecating fashion. See *ts'ui, chün-ts'ui.*

4664   *p'ĭn-tzǔ* 品子
T'ANG–CH'ING: **Kinsmen of Officials,** unofficial collective reference to younger brothers and sons of ranked (see *p'in*) officials.

4665   *pīng* 兵
Throughout history, one of the most common terms for **Soldier,** contrasting with *chün* (Army) although they were sometimes used almost interchangeably; used both as a prefix (e.g., *ping-pu, ping-ma* ...) and as a suffix (e.g., *kuan-ping, fu-ping*)..

4666   *pīng-àn* 兵案
SUNG: **Military Section,** designation of units found in several central government agencies; e.g., one of 4 Sections in the Court of Palace Attendants (*hsüan-hui yüan*), one of 7 in the Salt and Iron Monopoly Bureau (*yen-t'ieh ssu;* see *tu-chih an*); normally headed by an Administrative Assistant (*p'an-kuan, t'ui-kuan*), such Sections seem to have been relatively routine account-keeping agencies monitoring a range of governmental fiscal affairs broader than the name suggests, but among other things concerning the provisioning of the military establishment with accouterments and funds, the handling of military personnel matters, etc. In addition, a variant or unofficial reference to one type of Sections (*ts'ao*) into which the clerical staffs of units of territorial administration were divided, which handled paperwork under the purview of the central government's Ministry of War (*ping-pu*). SP: *service de l'armée.*

4667   *pīng-chàng chǘ* 兵仗局
MING: **Palace Armory,** a minor agency of palace eunuchs, headed by a eunuch Commissioner-in-chief (*ta-shih*) or Director (*t'ai-chien*); manufactured weapons and supervised a subsidiary Gunpowder Office (*huo-yao ssu*). See *pa chü* (Eight Services).

4668   *pīng-chí fáng* 兵籍房
SUNG: **Officer Assignments Section** in the Bureau of Military Affairs (*shu-mi yüan*); one of 12 Sections created under Shen-tsung (r. 1067–1085) to monitor the administrative affairs of military garrisons throughout the country, in geographic clusters, or to manage specified military functions on an empire-wide scale; this Section handled the rotational assignments of military officers from Circuits (*lu*) to service in the military establishment at the dynastic capital. Headed by from 3 to 5 Vice Recipients of Edicts (*fu ch'eng-chih*), rank 8b. Apparently not perpetuated in S. Sung. See *shih-erh fang* (Twelve Sections). SP: *chambre des registres militaires.*

4669   *pīng-chiàng àn* 兵匠案
SUNG: **Military Artisans Section,** one of numerous Sections under the Ministry of Works (*kung-pu*), probably in the Ministry's Bureau of State Farms (*t'un-t'ien ssu*); supervised the government's use of military personnel in construction, water control work, etc.; staffed with suboffical functionaries. SP: *service des artisans militaires.* P15.

4670   *pīng-chiào* 冰窖
CH'ING: **Icehouse** maintained by the Bureau of Waterways (*tu-shui ssu*) of the Ministry of Works (*kung-pu*) to provide ice for court use; also called *chiao-ch'ang,* q.v.; headed by a Supervisor (*chien-tu*), apparently an unranked suboffical.

4671 *pīng-chǐng wù* 冰井務
SUNG: **Service for the Capital Approaches** (?) under the Capital Security Office (*huang-ch'eng ssu*); apparently in charge of the glacis, the sloping approaches to the city wall at the dynastic capital. SP: *agence des glacières.*

4672 *pīng-fáng* 兵房
(1) T'ANG–SUNG: **War Office**, in T'ang one of 5 Offices in the combined Secretariat-Chancellery (*chung-shu men-hsia sheng*) that developed from the early 700s; equivalent to the Ministry of War (*ping-pu*) in the Department of State Affairs (*shang-shu sheng*); in Sung one of 6 Offices in the combined Secretariat-Chancellery. See *liu fang, chung-shu men-hsia sheng chien-cheng chu-fang kung-shih* (Examiner of the Offices of the Secretariat-Chancellery). RR: *chambre de l'armée.* SP: *chambre militaire.* (2) SUNG: **War Section,** one of 4 Sections in the Bureau of Military Affairs (*shu-mi yüan*); headed by a Vice Recipient of Edicts (*fu ch'eng-chih*), rank 8b; the channel through which, in collaboration with the War Office mentioned in (1) above and the Ministry of War, the Bureau directed training and tactical operations of military units throughout the empire. Dissolved in c. 1074 in a reorganization of the Bureau into 10 and later 12 Sections (see *shih-erh fang*). SP: *chambre de guerre.* (3) SUNG–CH'ING: occasional unofficial reference to the **Ministry of War** (*ping-pu*).

4673 *pīng-hsíng-kūng pù* 兵刑工部
(1) Normally, from Sui on, an unofficial or quasiofficial abbreviated reference to the **Ministries of War, of Justice, and of Works** (*ping-pu, hsing-pu, kung-pu*). (2) YÜAN: **War, Justice, and Works Ministry,** from 1260 to 1264 and again from 1266 to 1268 a consolidation of the normally separate Ministries of War, of Justice, and of Works into a single Ministry, known in the aggregate as the Three Ministries of the Right (*yu san-pu*); headed by 2 Ministers (*shang-shu*), rank 3a. See *ping-hsing pu, tso san-pu.*

4674 *pīng-hsíng pù* 兵刑部
(1) Normally, from Sui on, an unofficial or quasiofficial abbreviated reference to the **Ministries of War and of Justice** (*ping-pu, hsing-pu*). (2) YÜAN: **War and Justice Ministry,** from 1264 to 1266, 1268 to 1270, and 1271 to 1276, a consolidation of the normally separate Ministries of War and of Justice into a single Ministry, headed by 3 Ministers (*shang-shu*), rank 3a. See *ping-hsing-kung pu, yu san-pu.*

4675 *pīng-hsǔn tào* 兵巡道
MING: **Military Defense and General Surveillance Circuit,** a branch office (*fen-ssu*) of a Provincial Surveillance Commission (*t'i-hsing àn-ch'a shih ssu*) combining the functions of normally separate branch offices called a Military Defense Circuit (*ping-pei tao*) and a General Surveillance Circuit (*fen-hsün tao*); apparently existed only in Kwangsi Province, where there were 3 headquartered at Kuei-lin, Nan-ning, and Pin-chou.

4676 *pīng-k'ō* 兵科
MING–CH'ING: **Office of Scrutiny for War,** one of the Six Offices of Scrutiny (*liu k'o*, q.v.); also see *chi-shih-chung.* P18, 19.

4677 *pīng-lǐ fáng* 兵禮房
SUNG: **Office for War and Rites,** a combined administrative agency through which the Secretariat (*chung-shu sheng*), when separated from the Chancellery (*men-hsia sheng;* see under *chung-shu men-hsia sheng,* Secretariat-Chancellery), provided coordinating supervision over the Ministries of War (*ping-pu*) and of Rites (*lǐ-pu*) in the De-partment of State Affairs (*shang-shu sheng*); probably staffed by Secretariat Drafters (*chung-shu she-jen*). SP: *chambre de l'armée et celle de rites.*

4678 *pīng-liáng tào* 兵糧道
MING: **Military Defense and Tax Intendant Circuit,** a combination of a Military Defense Circuit (*ping-pei tao*) of a Provincial Surveillance Commission (*t'i-hsing an-ch'a shih ssu*) and a Tax Intendant Circuit (*tu-liang tao*) of a Provincial Administration Commission (*ch'eng-hsüan pu-cheng shih ssu*); one established in the Ning-hsia region, dates and staffing not clear. Also see *tao, tao-t'ai.*

4679 *pīng-mǎ* 兵馬
See under *ping-ma shih.*

4680 *pīng-mǎ chiēn-yā* 兵馬監押
SUNG: variant of *chien-ya* (**Supervisor of Militia**). SP: *directeur des soldats et des chevaux pour arrêter des bandits.*

4681 *pīng-mǎ ch'ién-hsiá* 兵馬鈐轄
SUNG: **Military Administrator of Infantry and Cavalry;** see under *ch'ien-hsia.* SP: *directeur des soldats et des chevaux.*

4682 *pīng-mǎ chǐh-hūi ssū* 兵馬指揮司
YÜAN–CH'ING: **Warden's Office** in charge of a Ward (*ch'eng*) of a capital city; commonly abbreviated to *ping-ma ssu,* q.v.

4683 *pīng-mǎ hsǔn-chiěn* 兵馬巡檢
SUNG: **Military Inspector,** designation of a concurrent duty assignment for some Prefects (*chih-fu*). Cf. *hsün-chien ssu.* SP: *contrôleur-inspecteur des soldats et des chevaux.*

4684 *pīng-mǎ shǐh* 兵馬使
(1) T'ANG–SUNG: **Commander,** common designation for military officers on duty assignments in troubled frontier zones or in armies on campaign, with varying prefixes and other forms. E.g., T'ang regularly used such directional prefixes as *ch'ien-chün* (Vanguard), *hou-chün* (Rearguard), and *chung-chün* (Center Army), and such variants as *ping-ma ta-shih* (Commander-in-chief) and *tu-chih ping-ma shih* (Supreme Commander), although all forms of *ping-ma shih* seem to have been less prestigious than the term *chiang-chün* (General) in its various forms. In Sung *ping-ma shih* was used in units of the Palace Command (*tien-ch'ien ssu*) with laudatory prefixes, e.g., *ch'in-jung fu ping-ma shih* (Barbarian-capturing Vice Commander). RR: *commissaire impérial des soldats et des chevaux.* SP: *commissaire des soldats et des chevaux.* (2) CHIN: **Military Commandant,** from 1179 each (total unspecified) in command of 60 troops charged with defending and policing the capital city; rank 4a, promoted from the low (but unclear) status of *ping-ma;* further promoted to Commander-in-chief (*tu chih-hui shih*), 3b; in each case seconded by one or more Assistant Commandants or Assistant Commanders (*fu-tu,* q.v.). (3) MING: **Military Commandant,** originally several in charge of military guards at each of the gates of the capital city, no rank indicated, subordinate to the Wardens' Offices (*ping-ma chih-hui ssu*) that provided police protection for the Five Wards (*wu ch'eng*) into which the city was divided for local administration. Then from 1398 to 1402 replaced the title Commander (*chih-hui, chih-hui shih*) for the head of each Warden's Office, seconded by a Vice Commander (*fu ping-ma*); apparently discontinued after 1402. P20.

4685 *pīng-mǎ ssū* 兵馬司
Warden's Office, a military unit responsible for police patrols, fire watchers, and general peace and order in a Ward

(ch'eng) of a capital city; full name commonly ping-ma chih-hui ssu. (1) YÜAN (ping-ma chih-hui ssu, ping-ma tu chih-hui ssu): one established at the dynastic capital, Ta-tu (modern Peking), in 1272, replacing a Battalion (ch'ien-hu so) that had previously borne capital police responsibilities; headed by a Commander (chih-hui shih), rank 4a1; subordinate both to the metropolitan area administration called the Ta-tu Route Chief Command (see lu, tu tsung-kuan fu) and, for judicial purposes, to the High Court of Justice (ta tsung-cheng fu). In 1292 reorganized into 2 more elaborate agencies, one each for the North and South Wards, each with 2 Mongol nobles serving as Commanders-in-chief (tu chih-hui shih), assisted by 5 Vice Commanders (fu chih-hui shih), an Administrative Clerk (chih-shih), a Record Keeper (t'i-k'ung an-tu), etc. Each also supervised a Prison (ssu-yü ssu) headed by a Warder (ssu-yü); a 3rd capital prison was maintained directly under the Ta-tu Route Chief Command. In some fashion not wholly clear, the Wardens' Offices shared police responsibilities in the capital with 3 Police Commissions (ching-hsün yüan). In 1292 a single Warden's Office was established at the auxiliary capital Shang-tu in modern Chahar, under the Shang-tu Regency (liu-shou ssu), headed by 3 Commanders (chih-hui shih). (2) MING (ping-ma chih-hui shih ssu): 5 established at Nanking at the founding of the dynasty, another 5 established at Peking in 1403, both capitals being divided into 5 Wards (see under wu ch'eng). Each Office headed by a Commander (chih-hui shih), rank 6a, having various aides, but dominated by a Ward-inspecting Censor (hsün-ch'eng yü-shih) delegated from the Censorate (tu ch'a-yüan) on a one-year rotational assignment. For administrative purposes, the Offices were subordinate to the Ministry of War (ping-pu). (3) CH'ING (ping-ma ssu): perpetuated the Ming pattern but only at Peking and with each Office supervised by 2 Ward-inspecting Censors, one each Manchu and Chinese. BH: (office of the?) police magistrate. P20.

4686   *pīng-mǎ ts'áo* 兵馬曹
HAN: **Cavalry Section,** one of many Sections (ts'ao) constituting the staff of the Governor (t'ai-shou) of a Commandery (chün); sometimes coexistent with a more common Military Section (ping-ts'ao). HB: bureau of arms and horses. P12.

4687   *pīng-mǎ tū-chiēn* 兵馬都監
SUNG: **Military Director-in-chief,** a duty assignment, or a nominally concurrent (chien) appointment, for officials of units of territorial administration from District Magistrates (hsien-ling, chih-hsien) up to Circuit Supervisors (chien-ssu), giving them authority over military forces in their jurisdictions for the suppression of banditry or other pacification activities; also for various officials in the central government occasionally assigned to oversee police activities of the 4 urban Townships (hsiang) into which the dynastic capital, Kaifeng, was divided for local administration. Commonly abbreviated as tu-chien. Cf. ping-ma ssu. SP: surveillant général des soldats et des chevaux pour arrêter des bandits.

4688   *pīng-mǎ tū ch'ién-hsiá* 兵馬都鈐轄
SUNG: **Chief Military Administrator of Infantry and Cavalry;** see under ch'ien-hsia. SP: directeur général des soldats et des chevaux.

4689   *pīng-mǎ yüán-shuài* 兵馬元帥
SUNG: **Marshal,** probably the most prestigious category of ad hoc military duty assignments, sometimes reserved for members of the imperial family; used for leaders of armies on campaign, with such varying prefixes as ta (Grand Mar-

shal) and fu (Vice Marshal). Also see t'ien-hsia ping-ma ta (or tu) yüan-shuai and yüan-shuai. SP: maréchal des soldats et des chevaux.

4690   *pīng-pèi tào* 兵備道
MING–CH'ING: **Military Defense Circuit,** a multi-Prefecture (fu) jurisdiction, from one to 12 per Province (sheng) in Ming times, numbers generally comparable in Ch'ing; under the special military supervision of an official commonly called Circuit Intendant (tao-t'ai) who until 1753 was a Vice Commissioner (fu-shih), rank 4a, or an Assistant Commissioner (ch'ien-shih), 5a, of a Provincial Surveillance Commission (t'i-hsing an-ch'a shih ssu); in 1753 the special duty assignment was made a regular post, 4a, formally independent of the Provincial Surveillance Commission. See tao. BH: military taotai. P52.

4691   *pīng-pù* 兵部
(1) N-S DIV (Chou): **Bureau of Military Personnel,** one of 4 Bureaus in the Ministry of War (hsia-kuan); also the title of the Bureau **Director,** ranked as an Ordinary Grand Master (chung ta-fu; 5a). (2) SUI–YÜAN (ordinarily with suffix ssu, Office, etc.): **Bureau of Military Appointments,** one of a normal battery of 4 Bureaus in the Ministry of War (also ping-pu; see #3 below). Alternately named ping-ts'ao from c. 604 to 620, wu-pu from 752 to 756; permanently changed at the beginning of Ming to wu-hsüan ch'ing-li ssu. Existed only nominally in Sung and omitted in Liao. Responsible for all aspects of military personnel administration. Headed by a Director (shih-lang to c. 604, lang to 620, then lang-chung), generally rank 5b; seconded by a Vice Director (yüan-wai lang), generally 6b. RR: bureau de l'armée. (3) SUI–CH'ING: **Ministry of War,** part of the core administrative complex in the central government called the Six Ministries (liu pu); through Chin subordinate to the Department of State Affairs (shang-shu sheng), then to the Secretariat (chung-shu sheng) in Yüan and early Ming; from 1380 directly responsible to the throne though from the early 1400s coordinated ever more tightly by the developing Grand Secretariat (nei-ko). In T'ang, closely affiliated with the Ministries of Justice (hsing-pu) and of Works (kung), these 3 being known as the West Echelon (hsi-hang) of Ministries in the Department of State Affairs; for prestige purposes also considered to join the Ministry of Personnel (li-pu) in a Front Echelon (ch'ien-hang) of Ministries. In Yüan, intermittently, combined with other Ministries into a War and Justice Ministry (ping-hsing pu) and even a War, Justice, and Works Ministry (ping-hsing-kung pu), known in the aggregate as the Three Ministries of the Right (yu san-pu). Following in the tradition of such prior agencies or officials as the t'ai-wei, ssu-ma or ta ssu-ma, wu ping or ch'i ping, chia-pu, etc., the Ministry in all eras from Sui on was at least nominally in charge of all personnel management, troop dispositions, strategic planning, installations, weapons, and supplies for the whole regular military establishment (see kuan-ping), and for the operation of a postal relay system for handling government communications. It usually supervised, directly or indirectly, other agencies that served essential military needs, e.g., the Court of the Imperial Stud (t'ai-p'u ssu) and its pasturages, from which the Ministry requisitioned the horses needed by the military. From the mid-700s the Ministry lost its prominence in military matters to Imperial Armies (chin-chün) based at the dynastic capital and to regional Military Commissioners (chieh-tu shih). Then in Sung the Ministry became little more than an administrative support agency for the Bureau of Military Affairs (shu-mi yüan), which directed all military operations; in Ming it generally super-

vised the major operational agencies, the 5 Chief Military Commissions (*tu-tu fu;* also see *wu fu*); in Ch'ing it oversaw the Chinese forces called the Green Standards (*lu-ying*) but had no control over the Banner (see *ch'i, pa ch'i*) military establishment. From the 1400s Provice-level Grand Coordinators or Provincial Governors (*hsün-fu*) and multi-Province Supreme Commanders or Governors-general (*tsung-tu*) were commonly granted concurrent status as executive officials of the Ministry for prestige purposes. From Sui on, the Ministry's executive echelon consisted of a Minister (*shang-shu*), rank 3a from T'ang through Yüan, then 2a, in Ch'ing one each Manchu and Chinese; and normally 2 Vice Ministers (*shih-lang*), 4a through Yüan, then 3a, in Ch'ing one each Manchu and Chinese. In Ming and Ch'ing these executives were served by a General Services Office (*ssu-wu t'ing*) headed by an Office Manager (*ssu-wu*), 9b then 8a. The normal business of the Ministry was carried on through 4 subsidiary Bureaus (*ssu, ch'ing-li ssu*), each headed by a Director (*lang-chung*), 5b in T'ang, 6a or 6b in Sung, 5b in Chin and Yüan, 5a in Ming and Ch'ing, seconded by a Vice Director (*yüan-wai lang*), normally 6b. The T'ang–Sung battery of Bureaus included the Bureau of Military Appointments (*ping-pu ssu; see #2 above*), Bureau of Operations (*chih-fang ssu*), Bureau of Equipment (*chia-pu ssu*), and Bureau of Provisions (*k'u-pu ssu*). The Ming–Ch'ing battery included the Bureau of Military Appointments (*wu-hsüan ch'ing-li ssu*), Bureau of Operations (*chih-fang ch'ing-li ssu*), Bureau of Equipment and Communications or (Ch'ing) Bureau of Communications (*ch'e-chia ch'ing-li ssu*), and Bureau of Provisions (*wu-k'u ch'ing-li ssu*). RR: *ministère de l'armée*. SP: *ministère de l'armée ou de guerre*. BH: ministry (or board) of war. P12.

4692 *pīng-pù ssū* 兵部司
SUI–YÜAN: **Bureau of Military Appointments** in the Ministry of War (*ping-pu*); see (2) under *ping-pu*.

4693 *pìng-shěng* 并省
N-S DIV (N. Ch'i): lit., Department (of State Affairs, *shang-shu sheng*) in Ping (Region, *chou*): **Auxiliary Department of State Affairs** established at Ping-chou (modern T'ai-yüan, Shansi), the base from which the dynastic founder arose and which was considered a ceremonial second capital; had a skeletal staff including a Director (*ling*), an Overseer (*lu ... shih*), and various subordinate Ministries (*pu*). P49.

4694 *pīng-shǔ* 兵署
Lit., military office: from T'ang on an uncommon unofficial reference to the **Ministry of War** (*ping-pu*).

4695 *pīng-t'īng* 冰廳
Lit., office of icy (resolve), i.e., of determined austerity: from T'ang an unofficial reference to the **Bureau of Sacrifices** (*tz'u-pu ssu, tz'u-chi ch'ing-li ssu*) in the Ministry of Rites (*li-pu*). P9.

4696 *pīng-ts'áo* 兵曹
(1) HAN: **Military Section,** one of at least 13 Sections (*ts'ao*) among which the headquarters staff of the Defender-in-chief (*t'ai-wei*) and possibly also of the Counselor-in-chief (*ch'eng-hsiang*), both members of the eminent Three Dukes (*san kung*), was divided; headed by an Administrator (*yüan-shih*), rank 300 bushels; functions not clear, but presumably the administrative channel through which the central government executives dealt with military matters. HB: bureau of arms. P12. (2) HAN–CH'ING: **War Section,** one of several Sections constituting the headquarters administrative staff of a territorial dignitary such as a Han Commandery Governor (*chün-shou*), the Administrator (*chang-shih*) of a Princely Establishment (*wang-fu*) from Sui on or earlier, a

Prefect (*chih-chou, chih-fu*) from Sung on or earlier, and eventually any territorial administrator down to the District (*hsien*) level. From Sui on, one of 6 standard Sections corresponding in names and functional specializations to the Six Ministries (*liu pu*) in the central government. From Sui through Sung, the Section was normally headed by an Administrator (*ts'an-chün-shih, ts'an-chün*), rank 7a or lower; thereafter by unranked suboficials. See *ping-ma ts'ao, liu ts'ao*. HB: bureau of arms. RR: *service des troupes*. SP: *service de l'armée*. P69. (3) SUI–T'ANG: from c. 604 to 620, the official variant of *ping-pu ssu* (**Bureau of Military Appointments**). (4) T'ANG: **Military Service Section,** one in each of the major units of militiamen stationed at the dynastic capital: the Sixteen Guards (*shih-liu wei*), the Five Garrisons (*wu fu*), and the Ten Guard Commands of the Heir Apparent (*shih shuai-fu*); in each case the Section was apparently in charge of personnel matters including the rotation of Garrison Militia troops (see *fu* and *fu-ping*) in and out of capital service and in and out of specific duty assignments; each Section was headed by an Administrator (*ts'an-chün-shih*), rank 8a2, 9a1, or 8b2, respectively. RR: *service des troupes*. P26, 43. (5) T'ANG–CH'ING: occasional unofficial, archaic reference to the **Ministry of War** (*ping-pu*) or to its executive personnel.

4697 *pīng-yù* 兵右
CHOU: **Chariot Lancer,** 2 ranked as Ordinary Grand Masters (*chung ta-fu*) and 2 as Senior Servicemen (*shang-shih*), members of the Ministry of War (*hsia-kuan*) responsible, on some basis of selection not now clear, for serving as 3rd man in the ruler's chariot on campaigns or hunts, wielding a lance from the right side of the chariot. CL: *homme de droite du char de guerre.*

4698 *p'íng* 平 or 評
Lit., to equalize, settle, decide, make decisions for or about .... HAN–N-S DIV: **Arbiter:** in the first form, a duty assignment rather than a regular post, designating an official who, regularly appointed to one office, was concurrently put in charge of another; used principally for concurrent Arbiters of the Imperial Secretariat (*shang-shu t'ai*), commonly found in the form *p'ing shang-shu shih* (lit., Arbiter of the Affairs of the Imperial Secretariat). Perhaps originated in Ch'in times; comparable to, and eventually superseded by, the designation Overseer (*lu, lu ... shih*). In both forms, from 66 B.C. used for one to 4 members of the staff of the Chamberlain for Law Enforcement (*t'ing-wei*), sometimes called *t'ing-wei p'ing;* rank 600 bushels in Han, rank 6 then 5 in N. Wei. Dispatched from the capital to review judicial case records in units of territorial administration; also in charge of the Imperial Prison (*chao-yü*) maintained by the Chamberlain for Law Enforcement. HB: referee. P22.

4699 *p'íng-chāng* 平章
Lit., to deliberate and decide. (1) T'ANG–MING: common abbreviated reference to the most eminent officials of the central government, those who served as **Grand Councilors** (*tsai-hsiang, ch'eng-hsiang*) overseeing all governmental activities in collaboration with the Emperor, who commonly bore titles for which *p'ing-chang* was a prefix (*p'ing-chang shih, p'ing-chang cheng-shih,* etc.); all such usages terminated in 1380. (2) YÜAN–MING: **Administrator,** a more specific usage designating an apparent mid-level executive of the Secretariat (*chung-shu sheng*) and of each Branch (*hsing*) Secretariat; terminated in 1380. P2, 3, 4.

4700 *p'íng-chāng chèng-shìh* 平章政事
Manager of Governmental Affairs. (1) SUNG: one of

several common designations of central government dignitaries chosen to serve as Grand Councilors (*tsai-hsiang*); technically, an abbreviation of the title *t'ung chung-shu men-hsia p'ing-chang cheng-shih* (Jointly Manager of Governmental Affairs with the Secretariat-Chancellery), also abbreviated as *t'ung p'ing-chang shih;* a duty-assignment suffix to a regular title (*pen-kuan*), e.g., as in Vice Director of the Department of State Affairs and Jointly Manager of Governmental Affairs with the Secretariat-Chancellery (*shang-shu p'u-yeh t'ung chung-shu men-hsia p'ing-chang cheng-shih*). (2) LIAO: designation of one or more eminent central government officials on the executive staff of the Grand Councilor (*tsai-hsiang*), at each auxiliary capital as well as at the principal dynastic capital. (3) CHIN: nominal title of 2 heads of the Department of State Affairs, who served as Grand Councilors (*tsai-hsiang*). (4) YÜAN: 4 or more, rank 1b; the 2nd ranking regular post in the Secretariat (*chung-shu sheng*), after 2 or more Grand Councilors (*ch'eng-hsiang*). (5) MING: 2, rank 1b, subordinate to 2 Grand Councilors (*ch'eng-hsiang*) in the Secretariat until 1380, when the entire executive echelon of the Secretariat was discontinued; one also the senior official of each Province-level Branch (*hsing*) Secretariat until 1376, when all Branch Secretariats were reorganized as Provincial Administration Commissions (*ch'eng-hsüan pu-cheng shih ssu*). P3, 4.

4701 *p'ing-chāng chün-kuó chùng-shìh*
平章軍國重事
Manager of Important National Security Matters. (1) T'ANG–SUNG: the most prestigious title awarded those serving as Grand Councilors (*tsai-hsiang*), appended as a suffix to their regular titles (*pen-kuan*) in the fashion of *p'ing-chang cheng-shih* or *p'ing-chang shih*, qq.v. SP: *ministre des affaires d'état importantes.* (2) YÜAN: from 1295 to 1309 only, the official variant title of a mid-level executive official in the Secretariat (*chung-shu sheng*), earlier called *shang-i sheng-shih* (Discussant of Secretariat Affairs), later changed to *p'ing-chang* (Administrator). P3, 4.

4702 *p'ing-chāng chün-kuó shìh* 平章軍國事
SUNG: **Manager of National Security Matters,** a S. Sung variant of *p'ing-chang chün-kuo chung-shih* (Manager of Important National Security Matters); reportedly instituted by a Grand Councilor (*tsai-hsiang*) who wanted his authority not to be limited to important matters only, but extended to all matters. SP: *ministre des affaires d'état.* P3.

4703 *p'ing-chāng shìh* 平章事
Manager of Affairs. (1) T'ANG–SUNG: from the mid-600s through Sung a common general designation of central government dignitaries chosen to serve as Grand Councilors (*tsai-hsiang*); technically, an abbreviation of the title *t'ung chung-shu men-hsia p'ing-chang shih* (Jointly Manager of Affairs with the Secretariat and the Chancellery; after the early 700s, with the Secretariat-Chancellery), also abbreviated as *t'ung p'ing-chang shih;* a duty-assignment suffix to a regular title (*pen-kuan*), e.g., Vice Director of the Department of State Affairs and Jointly Manager of Affairs with the Secretariat-Chancellery (*shang-shu p'u-yeh t'ung chung-shu men-hsia p'ing-chang shih*). RR: *fonctionnaire chargé d'examiner et régler les affaires.* SP: *premier ministre chargé d'examiner et de régler les affaires.* (2) CHIN–MING: a regular post (*pen-kuan*) of middling status in the executive echelon of the Department of State Affairs (*shang-shu sheng*) in Chin, of the Secretariat (*chung-shu sheng*) in Yüan and early Ming till 1380, when the entire executive echelon of the Secretariat was discontinued. P3.

4704 *p'ing-ch'áng* 平常
MING: **Ordinary,** one of 3 evaluation categories to which officials were assigned in evaluations given ordinarily every 3 years; not as good as Adequate (*ch'eng-chih*) and deserving of promotion, but better than Inadequate (*pu ch'eng-chih*) and in danger of demotion.

4705 *p'ing-chǔn* 平準
CH'IN–N-S DIV: **Bureau of Standards,** responsible for the functioning of a system whereby the state bought grain (and at times other commodities as well) when and where there was a surplus, to be sold when and where there was a short supply, to maintain stable prices and supplies. In Ch'in and early Han to c. 110 B.C. probably had narrower responsibilities, possibly involved with the dyeing of silks as traditionally reported. Headed by a Director (*ling*), rank 600 bushels in Han; originally under the Chamberlain for the Palace Revenues (*shao-fu*), from 110 B.C. under the Chamberlain for the National Treasury (*ta-nung ling*, from 104 B.C. *ta ssu-nung*); after Han, again under the Chamberlain for the Palace Revenues into the S. Dynasties. HB: bureau of equalization and standards. P37, 40.

4706 *p'ing-chǔn àn* 平準案
SUNG: **Price Stabilization Section,** one of 6 Sections (*an*) in the Right Section (*yu-ts'ao*) of the Ministry of Revenue (*hu-pu*) from the 1080s, apparently continuing functions previously carried out by units of the State Finance Commission (*san ssu*) of early Sung, i.e., monitoring state efforts to regulate the prices of commodities other than grain (see *ch'ang-p'ing an, ch'ang-p'ing ts'ang*); staffing not clear. Also a unit in the Court of the Imperial Treasury (*t'ai-fu ssu*), staffing not clear; either cooperated with the work of the Ministry of Revenue just described or superseded the Ministry in this realm in S. Sung; relationship not clear. SP: *service de l'équilibre des prix; bureau chargé de maintenir l'équilibre des prix.*

4707 *p'ing-chǔn wù* 平準務
SUNG: **Price Stabilization Agency,** from 1100 the name of the Market Exchange Offices (*shih-i ssu*) instituted in 1072 by the reform minister Wang An-shih.

4708 *p'ìng-chūn* 聘君
Gentleman Summoned to Office: from early in the S. Dynasties if not before, a common unofficial reference to a man nominated by territorial administrators and summoned to court for possible placement in the officialdom; equivalent to *cheng-chün.* The term was applicable whether or not the nominee responded to his summons.

4709 *p'ing-hsiāng shìh* 馮相氏
CHOU: lit., one who mounts (*p'ing*) to a topographic height and observes (*hsiang*) the sky: **Astronomical Observer,** 4 ranked as Ordinary Servicemen (*chung-shih*) and 4 as Junior Servicemen (*hsia-shih*), members of the Ministry of Rites (*ch'un-kuan*) who reported celestial phenomena to the Grand Astrologer (*ta-shih, t'ai-shih*). CL: *officier chargé de monter et d'observer.*

4710 *p'ing-shìh* 萍氏
CHOU: lit., duckweed man: **River Patroller,** 2 ranked as Junior Servicemen (*hsia-shih*), members of the Ministry of Justice (*ch'iu-kuan*) who supervised efforts to keep waterways of the royal domain free of floating weeds and debris; also reportedly checked on the quality of wines available for river festivals and warned residents against overindulgence in wine, and tried to prevent damage from flooding. CL: *préposé aux lentilles d'eau ou plantes flottantes.*

4711 *p'íng-shìh* 平事
See under *p'ing* (**Arbiter**).

4712 *p'íng-shìh* 評事
(1) N-S DIV: occasional unofficial variant of *p'ing* (**Arbiter**). (2) SUI–SUNG, CHIN, MING–CH'ING: **Case Reviewer,** established in c. 607 in the Court of Judicial Review (*ta-li ssu*); 48 in Sui, 8 in T'ang, 12 in Sung, 6 then 3 in Chin, 2 in Ming and Ch'ing, one each Left and Right; rank 8b2 in T'ang, 8b in Sung, 8a in Chin, 7a in Ming and Ch'ing. In Sui and T'ang toured the empire inspecting judicial records and impeaching officials for mishandling judicial cases, but later in their capital office handled judicial paperwork received from units of territorial administration and recommended approval or disapproval of trial procedures and sentences. In Ch'ing their jurisdiction came to be limited to cases involving the death penalty. RR+SP: *enquêteur judiciaire.* BH: assistant secretary of the court of judicature and revision. P22.

4713 *p'íng-shìh shìh* 評事史
T'ANG: **Case Reviewer's Clerk,** 24 unranked subofficials attached to Case Reviewers (*p'ing-shih*) of the Court of Judicial Review (*ta-li ssu*). RR: *scribe d'enquêteur judiciaire.* P22.

4714 *p'íng-tào chǖn* 平道軍
T'ANG: lit., army of the way of equality, possibly understood commonly as army to pacify the Circuits (*tao*): **Army of the Celestial Cornucopia,** named after two stars in Virgo; one of 12 regional supervisory headquarters for militia Garrisons (*fu*) called the Twelve Armies (*shih-erh chün*); existed only from 620 to 623 and again from 625 to 636. RR: *armée (de la constellation) de la route de l'égalité.* P44.

4715 *p'íng-tuàn kuān* 評斷官
SUNG: **Sentence Evaluator,** one of several categories of duty assignments in the Judicial Control Office (*shen-hsing yüan*) of early Sung, established from 991 to 1080 to review judicial cases processed by the Ministry of Justice (*hsing-pu*) and the Court of Judicial Review (*ta-li ssu*); number variable, service limited to 3 years (?). Apparently also called *hsiang-tuan kuan,* q.v. SP: *examinateur judiciaire.*

4716 *p'íng-yú ssū* 憑由司
SUNG: abbreviation of *ho-t'ung p'ing-yu ssu* (**Certificate Validation Office**).

4717 *po*
Also see under the romanization *pai.*

4718 *pó* 伯
Earl: a title of nobility (*chüeh*), normally awarded to men not members of the ruling family, normally inheritable by the eldest son. In Chou, 3rd most prestigious of the 5 noble titles held by Feudal Lords (*chu-hou*), following Duke (*kung*) and Marquis (*hou*) and preceding Viscount (*tzu*) and Baron (*nan*). Not used in Ch'in and Han. From the era of N-S Division through the remainder of imperial history the ancient Chou noble nomenclature generally prevailed, but Earl was seldom used without qualifying prefixes, e.g., *chün-po* (Commandery Earl), *k'ai-kuo po* (Dynasty-founding Earl). Cf. *kung-po, tsung-po, fang-po.* CL: *prince feudataire du troisième rang.* RR+SP: *comte.* BH: earl. P65.

4719 *pǒ-chǎng* 百長
CH'ING: lit., leader of 100 men: **Assistant Commander,** a petty military title used in western frontier regions such as Ch'ing-hai and Tibet, for aides to either Battalion Heads (*ch'ien-hu chang*) or Company Heads (*po-hu chang*). P72.

4720 *pǒ chí* 百騎
T'ANG: **Hundred Cavaliers,** an elite group of mounted archers selected from the Imperial Army of Original Followers (*yüan-ts'ung chin-chün*) and, after 661, from the Forest of Plumes Armies (*yü-lin chün*), all of the Northern Command (*pei-ya*), to escort the Emperor on hunts and other outings. Also referred to as the Standby Guard (*i-wei*). In 689 the Hundred Cavaliers were expanded somewhat and retitled the Thousand Cavaliers (*ch'ien chi*), and in 707 (710?) they were retitled the Myriad Cavaliers (*wan-chi*), although it is likely they never exceeded 1,000 at most. In 710 the unit was transformed into 2 new units of the Northern Command, the Left and Right Militant as Dragons Armies (*lung-wu chün*). RR: *cent cavaliers.*

4721 *pó-chí-lièh* 勃極烈
CHIN: **Chief,** Chinese rendering of a Jurchen word used from predynastic times to designate hereditary leaders of Jurchen groups leagued under a Supreme Chief (*tu po-chi-lieh*). As the Jurchen gradually developed a Chinese-style state organization, such nobles became heads of all important state agencies, resembling Yüan dynasty *ta-lu-hua-ch'ih* (Overseers), with a wide variety of qualifying prefixes. In Ch'ing times the term was said to be equivalent to the Manchu noble title Beile (*pei-lo*). The whole category of *po-chi-lieh* was abolished in 1134, as Chin began adopting Chinese titles.

4722 *pó-chíh* 白直
T'ANG: lit. meaning not clear, probably a commoner (*po*) who undertook governmental duty on a requisitioned basis and in some rotational pattern (*chih*): **Attendant,** petty subofficials found in groups of 16, 18, 20, 24, etc., in Prefectures (*chou, fu*); specific functions not clear. P49, 53.

4723 *pó-chǐn* 勃董
CHIN: **Clan Leader,** Chinese rendering of a Jurchen word; from predynastic times the basic leaders of Jurchen society, in war assigned as Company Commanders (*mou-k'o;* Chinese *po-hu*) or Battalion Commanders (*meng-an;* Chinese *ch'ien-hu*). Abolished in the 1130s, melded into the continuing sociomilitary groups *mou-k'o* and *meng-an* (Companies, Battalions). Also see *po-chi-lieh.*

4724 *pō-fā ch'uán-yùn kuān* 撥發船運官
SUNG: **Cargo Dispatcher,** designation of officials on duty assignments delegated from regular posts in local administrative units, probably on short-term ad hoc bases, to direct the unloading and distributing of cargo from military cargo boats under a Director-general of Military Supplies (*tsung-ling*), possibly only in Szechwan during active military campaigning. SP: *fonctionnaire chargé de distribuer la cargaison des bateaux de transport.*

4725 *pō-fā ts'ūi-kāng* 撥發催綱
SUNG: **Dispatcher and Expediter,** duty assignment of an official serving in the river transport system, probably delegated on an ad hoc basis from a local administrative unit. SP: *chargé de distribuer les expéditions et d'activer les convois.*

4726 *pó-fǔ* 柏府 or 栢府
From Han on, an unofficial reference to the **Censorate** (*yü-shih t'ai, tu ch'a-yüan*), whose quarters in Han times were distinguished by a large cedar tree (*po*) frequented by large numbers of birds. See *po-t'ai.*

4727 *pó-fū chǎng* 百夫長
Lit., leader of 100 men, normally implying laborers: **Foreman:** throughout imperial history an occasional variant ref-

erence to *po-hu* (Company Commander). Also cf. *po-hu chang.*

4728 *pó-hǎi ch'ì-tān kuēi-míng*
渤海契丹歸明
SUNG: **Surrendered Po-hai and Khitan Forces,** a military group of surrendered or defected soldiers from the Khitan Liao state and its northeastern neighbor, Po-hai; incorporated into the Sung armies (period not clear) under the Palace Command (*tien-ch'ien ssu*). SP: *armée de ... soumis.*

4729 *pǒ-hsì shīh* 百戲師
HAN: **Player,** 26 professional (perhaps hereditary) theatrical performers under the Director of Palace Entertainments (*ch'eng-hua ling*), a subordinate of the Chamberlain for the Palace Revenues (*shao-fu*); apparently only in Later Han. The name literally suggests "masters of 100 (i.e., a wide variety of) theatrics," implying variety show or vaudeville performers. May be encountered in the abbreviated form *hsi-shih.* P10.

4730 *pó-hsüéh húng-jú* 博學鴻儒
CH'ING: **Erudite Scholasticus,** name of an extraordinary Special Examination (*chih-k'o*) given only once, in 1679, to entice reclusive Chinese scholars into the officialdom, but also open to Chinese already serving the Manchus; also the designation of the degree awarded to passers. It was a very difficult general literary examination, and the 50 men who passed were promptly assigned to the Historiography Office (*shih-kuan*) of the Hanlin Academy (*han-lin yüan*) and set to work compiling the official history of the Ming dynasty.

4731 *pó-hsüéh húng-ts'ái* 博學宏材
LIAO: **Erudite of Promise,** one of several Special Examinations (*chih-k'o*) offered irregularly to recruit Chinese scholars into the officialdom.

4732 *pó-hsüéh húng-tz'ú* 博學宏詞 or 鴻詞
T'ANG, SUNG, CH'ING: **Erudite Literatus,** name of a Special Examination (*chih-k'o*) given to recruit men of extraordinary literary talents, whether in or out of the officialdom, to serve in such compiling agencies as the Hanlin Academy (*han-lin yüan*). Initiated in 717, when only 2 candidates passed. In 731 given relatively regular status as a Special Examination. Revived in S. Sung and again in Ch'ing times. In examinations of 1733 and 1735 no candidate passed. Commonly abbreviated to *hung-tz'u.* Not to be confused with *po-hsüeh hung-ju* (Erudite Scholasticus).

4733 *pǒ-hù* 百戶
CHIN–CH'ING: lit., 100 (military) households: **Company Commander,** a regular military officer, rank 6a, theoretically in charge of 100 soldiers; in Yüan and Ming his command was called a *po-hu so* (Company). In Ch'ing the title was apparently used only for aboriginal tribal chieftains in the Southwest. Often rendered as Centurion.

4734 *pó-hù chǎng* 百戶長
Lit., leader of 100 households: **Company Commander,** an occasional variant of *po-hu;* in Ch'ing times one of many titles awarded aboriginal tribal chieftains of the Southwest. Cf. *po-fu chang.*

4735 *pǒ-hù sǒ* 百戶所
YÜAN–MING: lit., locality, place, or base of 100 (military) households: **Company** theoretically comprising 100 soldiers quartered in one place or camp (*so*); used principally in reference to troops in garrison, not as a unit of tactical organization. Normally occurs as a place-name followed simply with *so.* In both dynasties the troops were

hereditary and, with their families, constituted a residential unit, 10 of which made a Battalion (*ch'ien-hu so*). The Company Commander (*po-hu*) was assisted by Squad Commanders (*chia-chang, p'ai-t'ou*) in Yüan, by Platoon Commanders (*tsung-ch'i*) and Squad Commanders (*hsiao-ch'i*) in Ming. Also see *wei-so.* Cf. *tsu, t'un, t'ui, t'uan, niu-lu, tso-ling, shao.*

4736 *pó-ī ch'īng-hsiàng* 白衣卿相
SUNG–CH'ING: lit., a high minister in plain clothes, i.e., someone not yet in high office but having the qualification and potentiality for attaining it: **Potential Dignitary,** an unofficial laudatory reference to a new Metropolitan Graduate (*chin-shih*) in the civil service recruitment examination sequence.

4737 *pó-ī lǐng-chíh* 白衣領職
N-S DIV: lit., to hold a post in plain clothes, i.e., without wearing the costume prescribed by regulations: **Appointee on Punitive Probation,** one kind of punishment for officials, depriving them of formal status and rank but authorizing them to remain in office, hence having an opportunity to redeem themselves by their future conduct.

4738 *pó-k'ò* 伯克
CH'ING: Chinese transcription of **Beg** or **Bey,** a generic term for chiefs of Moslem groups in Central Asia, especially those in modern Sinkiang, with gradations in status indicated by prefixes also transcribed from foreign words. BH: Beg. P70.

4739 *pǒ-kuān* 百官
Lit., 100 officials: **All Officials** or **the Officialdom,** throughout history a common collective reference to all officials serving in the governmental hierarchy, from top to bottom, including both civil and military services.

4740 *pǒ-kuān àn* 百官案
SUNG: **Officials Section,** one of 8 Sections (*an*) in the Tax Bureau (*tu-chih ssu*), one of the 3 agencies that constituted the State Finance Commission (*san ssu*) of early Sung; normally headed by an Administrative Assistant (*p'an-kuan, t'ui-kuan*); monitored the receipt and issuance of funds needed for officials' salaries, various state ceremonies, maintenance of the postal relay system, etc. SP: *service des fonctionnaires.*

4741 *pǒ-k'uěi* 百揆
Lit., one who takes care of all (the 100) things: **Chief Executive,** from antiquity an unofficial reference to an extraordinarily influential and powerful executive in the central government such as a Counselor-in-chief (*ch'eng-hsiang*), a Grand Councilor (*tsai-hsiang*), a Senior Grand Secretary (*shou-fu*), etc.

4742 *pǒ-kūng chiēn* 百工監
T'ANG: **Directorate of General Production,** one under each regional military Area Command (*tu-tu fu*), responsible for the production of boats and carriages and for various construction projects; headed by a Director (*chien*), rank 8a2; one also under the Directorate for the Palace Buildings (*chiang-tso chien*) from 618 till terminated in the era 627–649; located in modern Shansi Province, specialized in the production of boats and carriages; headed by a Director, probably 7a2. RR: *directeur des cent travaux.*

4743 *pǒ lǐ* 百里
Lit., 100 Chinese miles: from Han times, a self-deprecatory term used by **District Magistrates** (*hsien-ling, chih-hsien*), traditionally explained as reflecting the attitude "How can

100 miles be the road of a great worthy?" The implications are not wholly clear.

4744 *pó-p'áo-tzŭ* 白袍子
SUNG–CH'ING: lit., those in plain (white?) gowns, signifying a confusing abundance of people: an unofficial reference to **Examination Candidates** at a civil service recruitment examination.

4745 *pó-shēn* 白身 or *pó-shìh* 白士
Commoner: throughout history, an ordinary person with no official status, but in the case of *po-shih* having social standing as a man of good repute.

4746 *pó-shìh* 博士
Erudite, an official of special, broad skill and knowledge. (1) Throughout imperial history, a staff member of the Chamberlain for Ceremonials (*t'ai-ch'ang*) or, from N. Ch'i on, the Court of Imperial Sacrifices (*t'ai-ch'ang ssu*); a ritual specialist, early held in considerable esteem, in Han ranked at 600 bushels, but thereafter gradually sank in esteem, to rank 7b in N. Wei; 6, 7b1, in T'ang; 4, 8a, in Sung; 2, 7a, in Chin and Yüan; in Ming one, 7a, relegated to the Archives (*tien-pu t'ing*) of the Court of Imperial Sacrifices; in Ch'ing 3, 7a. In Ch'in and Han reportedly guided the imperial carriage, participated in major court policy deliberations, particularly recommended appropriate posthumous epithets for distinguished officials. In Sung the post was again highly esteemed if of low rank; Grand Councilors (*tsai-hsiang*) sometimes held such appointments concurrently. Otherwise, the Erudites were not highly esteemed and were apparently limited to the handling of detailed preparations for state ritual ceremonies. In Ming their traditional responsibility for recommending posthumous epithets was taken over by the Grand Secretariat (*nei-ko*). In many eras the post was a sinecure. It is often found in the more specific form *t'ai-ch'ang po-shih* (Erudite of the Court of Imperial Sacrifices), which differentiates it from the title Erudite of the National University (*kuo-tzu po-shih*; see #2 below). P27. (2) From Han on throughout imperial history, the designation of a teacher in an organized state school, almost without exception a school located in the dynastic capital; especially, from 124 B.C., a principal teacher in the National University (*t'ai-hsüeh*), commonly specified by the title *kuo-tzu po-shih* (Erudite of the National University). Through Han and much of the era of N-S Division, few distinctions were made between these and the Erudites described under (1) above; it was not until N. Wei or perhaps Sui that a clear differentiation was made between the ritual Erudites of the Court of Imperial Sacrifices and the teaching Erudites, from Sui on principally in schools supervised by the Directorate of Education (*kuo-tzu chien*). In T'ang, e.g., these schools were the National University (*t'ai-hsüeh*), the School for the Sons of the State (*kuo-tzu hsüeh*), the School of the Four Gates (*ssu-men hsüeh*), the Law School (*lü-hsüeh*), the Calligraphy School (*shu-hsüeh*), and the Mathematics School (*suan-hsüeh*). Other teaching Erudites were on the staffs of the Sung dynasty Directorate of Education's Military School (*wu-hsüeh*); the Medical School (*i-hsüeh*) maintained at the capital by the T'ang–Sung Imperial Medical Service (*t'ai-i chü*) including an Erudite for General Medicine (*i po-shih*), an Erudite for Acupuncture (*chen po-shih*), an Erudite for Massage (*an-mo po-shih*), and an Erudite for Exorcism (*chou-chin po-shih*); various Sui–Ch'ing astrological and astronomical services (see *t'ai-shih chü, t'ai-shih chien, ssu-t'ien t'ai, ssu-t'ien chien, ch'in-t'ien chien*) including Erudites of the Water Clock (*lou-k'o po-shih*); and various institutes and acade-

mies such as the Court of Imperial Calligraphy (*han-lin yü-shu yüan*) maintained by the Sung dynasty Artisans Institute (*han-lin yüan*). Usage of the title Erudite for teachers in schools outside the dynastic capital (and some auxiliary capitals such as Loyang in T'ang and Nanking in Ming) was a temporary aberration. Erudites served in some Princedoms (*wang-kuo*) during the first Han reigns, no doubt more ritual than teaching Erudites. N. Wei ordered the appointment of Erudites in schools at Region (*chou*) and Commandery (*chün*) levels, and this practice reoccurred in very limited ways at the Prefecture (*chou, fu*) level in Sui, T'ang, and Liao. Emperor Yang of Sui even ordered that Erudites be appointed in District Schools (*hsien-hsüeh*). By Ming and Ch'ing times the teaching title was restricted to the Directorate of Education and the Directorate of Astronomy (*ch'in-t'ien chien*) in the central government. Originally, in Han, teaching Erudites were more fully identified as Erudites of the Five Classics (*wu-ching po-shih*), a title perpetuated throughout history for Erudites in the National University; and other Erudites, such as the Erudites of the Water Clock mentioned above, were normally identified by specifying prefixes. Erudites of the Five Classics from the beginning were specialists in a single classic each and were sometimes even more specifically designated, e.g., as Erudite of the Five Classics (Specializing in) the Mao (Version of the Classic of) Songs (*wu-ching mao-shih po-shih*). Erudites of the Five Classics originally shared the relatively high 600-bushel rank of their ritual counterparts on the staff of the Chamberlain for Ceremonials, and occasionally in Han a post as teaching Erudite was filled by an official of the very high 2,000-bushel category. Erudites' status declined after Han, although Ch'en of the S. Dynasties gave them regular rank at the 1,000-bushel level. From T'ang through Ch'ing they held low ranks from 7b to 9b. The original Han number was 14. As the National University grew from an enrollment of 50 to 1,000 to an astonishing 30,000 (Later Han), the number of Erudites swelled to as many as 70. They probably never approached that number again after Han, even in the multiple schools maintained at the capital especially in T'ang and Sung times. By Ming, when the Directorate of Education in fact constituted a single National University, it had an authorized staff of only 5 Erudites; and Ch'ing reduced that number first to 3 and then to 2. Such Erudites were administratively subordinate throughout history to a Chancellor (*chi-chiu*), originally a post filled by the Erudites in rotation, but from the era of N-S Division a regular post itself; in Ming the Erudites constituted an Office of Erudites (*po-shih t'ing*) within the National University. From the era of N-S Division the Erudites were assisted by various categories of Instructors (*chu-chiao, hsüeh-cheng, hsüeh-lu*). Also cf. *hsüeh-shih, po-hsüeh* .... HB: erudit. RR: *maître au vaste savoir*. SP: *professeur*. BH: doctor, (in the Directorate of Astronomy:) mathematician. P34.

4747 *pŏ shíh* 百石
HAN–N-S DIV: **Hundred Bushels,** very low category of rank as measured in annual salary grain; sometimes used as if it were the title of a subofficial functionary of such salary status. P68.

4748 *pò-shīh* 鎛師
CHOU: **Master of Metal Bells,** 2 ranked as Ordinary Servicemen (*chung-shih*), members of the Ministry of Rites (*ch'un-kuan*) who specialized in the use of a type of bell called po, the tone of which was used in tuning other metal instruments. Cf. *chung-shih* (Master of the Bells). CL: *maître des cloches* po.

4749 *pó-shìh chì-chiŭ* 博士祭酒
HAN: **Chancellor of the Erudites,** administrative director of the National University (*t'ai-hsüeh*), rank 600 bushels; revival in Later Han of the Former Han post called *po-shih p'u-yeh*. Also see *chi-chiu*. HB: libationer of the erudits. P34.

4750 *pó-shìh liù-chīng chì-chiŭ* 博士六經祭酒
HAN: **Erudite Exalter of the Six Classics,** a variant of *liu-ching chi-chiu*, q.v.

4751 *pó-shìh p'ú-yeh* 博士僕射
HAN: **Chief Administrator of the Erudites** in the National University (*t'ai-hsüeh*) in Former Han; in Later Han changed to Chancellor of the Erudites (*po-shih chi-chiu*); in both cases, normally filled on a concurrent basis by one of the Erudites (*po-shih*). Also see *p'u-yeh*. HB: supervisor of the erudits. P34.

4752 *pó-shìh shīh* 博士師
HAN: from A.D. 1 an official variant of *po-shih* (**Erudite**). P34.

4753 *pó-shìh tì-tzŭ* 博士弟子
HAN: lit., disciple of the Erudites (*po-shih*), first appointed in 124 B.C.: **National University Student,** a promising man admitted to the National University (*t'ai-hsüeh*) at the dynastic capital on the basis of a recommendation by a territorial administrator; pursued studies of classical texts for one year; if successful in examinations given then, became a qualified member of the official class and might join the pool of expectant appointees to office called Court Gentlemen (*lang*) at the capital or might seek an appointment on the staff of a District Magistrate (*hsien-ling*) or a higher territorial administrator. Comparable to *chien-sheng* of the late imperial dynasties. Commonly abbreviated to *ti-tzu*. P34.

4754 *pó-shìh tì-tzŭ yüán* 博士弟子員
CH'ING: unofficial reference to a **Government Student** (*sheng-yüan*) in a state-established Confucian School (*ju-hsüeh*) from the District (*hsien*) up to the Prefecture (*fu*) level.

4755 *pó-shìh t'īng* 博士廳
MING: **Office of Erudites** in the Directorate of Education (*kuo-tzu chien*), i.e., the National University; merely the collective designation of the Erudites of the Five Classics (*wu-ching po-shih*), rank 8b, who directed the teaching of National University Students (*chien-sheng*). P34.

4756 *pŏ-ssū shù-fŭ* 百司庶府
Lit., the 100 offices and the multitude of agencies: from antiquity an unofficial general reference to **the whole governmental establishment.**

4757 *pŏ-ssū wèn-shìh yèh-chĕ* 百司問事謁者
T'ANG: **Receptionist for All Inquiries,** rank 7a2, in each Princely Establishment (*wang-fu*) until abolished between 690 and 705; functions not clear, since *wen-shih* was a T'ang title for functionaries who interrogated offenders and beat them with the bamboo; possibly used less specifically here, designating the doorman of a Prince's private residence (?). RR: *fonctionnaire chargé d'introduire les visiteurs et les affaires de tous les services (?)*. P69.

4758 *pó-t'ái* 柏臺 or 栢臺
Lit., cedar-tree pavilion. (1) From Han on, an unofficial reference to the **Censorate** (*yü-shih t'ai, tu ch'a-yüan*); see under *po-fu*. (2) CH'ING: also an unofficial reference to a **Provincial Surveillance Commission** (*t'i-hsing an-ch'a shih ssu*).

4759 *pó-wàng yüàn-shìh* 博望苑使
HAN: **Commissioner of the Park of Broad Vistas** (?): sources are confusing, but apparently someone so designated was appointed to be a companion to the Heir Apparent who became Emperor Wu (r. 141–87 B.C.); considered an antecedent of the later title *t'ai-tzu pin-k'o* (Adviser to the Heir Apparent). P67.

4760 *pó-yǘn* 白雲
Lit., white clouds: from high antiquity an unofficial reference to judicial agencies and officials, especially to the Sui-Ch'ing **Minister of Justice** (*hsing-pu shang-shu*).

4761 *pŭ* 卜
Lit., to divine, a diviner: from the Shang dynasty of high antiquity, the designation of a **Diviner** at the ruler's court. See *ta-pu, t'ai-pu*.

4762 *pù* 簿
LIAO, YÜAN: occasional variant of *chu-pu* (**Recorder** or **Assistant Magistrate**), q.v. P27, 54.

4763 *pŭ* 補
Lit., to patch, to repair; hence, to fill a vacancy: one of the common terms meaning **to appoint,** normally used throughout history to indicate that the position in question had been unoccupied for some time, so that the new appointee could not go through the ritual and practical procedures of relieving a predecessor. The term normally did not suggest any special, temporary, or probationary conditions of appointment.

4764 *pù* 部
Ety. not at all clear; combination of a graph meaning fief or a comparably important locality (right side: *i*) with another (left side: *pu*) with the only recorded early meaning to spit out (?); likely a late-developing graph derived from an unidentifiable homophone, perhaps meaning to cut apart, to divide (?); the post-Chou text *Chou-li* used the graph for the central ring from which the arc-like ribs of a chariot canopy spread outward. Lit., principally suggests a part, section, or division of a whole, a sense that underlies all of the usages described below. (1) Throughout history, the designation of a **Tribe** of non-Chinese peoples, most commonly in such compounds as *pu-tsu* and *pu-lo*, qq.v. (2) HAN–N-S DIV: **Division** of a Campaigning Army (*ying*), variable in number but according to an old saying 5 under the command of a General-in-chief (*ta chiang-chün*), presumably fewer normally in an Army (*chün*) under a General (*chiang-chün*); each led by a Commandant (*hsiao-wei*) and subdivided into several Regiments (*ch'ü*). This usage persisted through the S. Dynasties and even into N. Wei, but with a less specific hierarchical sense, perhaps best rendered **Troop;** see *liu-pu wei* (Commandant of the Capital Patrol). Also see *pu-ch'ü*. HB: regiment. (3) HAN: **Region,** generic designation of 13 province-size areas into which the empire was divided from 106 B.C. to c. 10 B.C. for administrative supervision and coordination of Commanderies (*chün*), Princedoms (*wang-kuo*), etc., by Regional Inspectors (*tz'u-shih, pu tz'u-shih, chou tz'u-shih*), who were itinerant Censors (*yü-shih*) delegated from the central government and accountable to the Palace Aide to the Censor-in-chief (*yü-shih chung-ch'eng*); in c. 12 B.C. the name *pu* was changed to the very durable name *chou*, q.v. HB: regional division, province (?). (4) From late Han on, **Ministry,** in mature Sui-Ch'ing government the generic term for the Six Ministries (*liu pu*) that were the core general administration units in the central government; apparently originated as part of the name Personnel Section (*lì-pu ts'ao*),

the designation of one of 6 units among which Imperial Secretaries (*shang-shu*) were divided in the steadily more important Imperial Secretariat (*shang-shu t'ai*) of Later Han, but did not itself gain currency until the Three Kingdoms period, when it began to compete interchangeably with the older term *ts'ao* (Section) as the generic name of major constituent units in the developing Department of State Affairs (*shang-shu sheng*). RR+SP: *ministère*. BH: ministry, board. (5) CH'ING: **League** of Outer Mongolian Banners (*ch'i*); see under *ai-ma-k'o*. (6) CH'ING: **Province,** 4 established in Tibet under this generic name by the Manchus, no doubt related to the uses rendered above as Tribe and League. Cf. *sheng* (Province).

4765 *pù-chǎng* 部長
N-S DIV–CH'ING: unofficial reference to a **Minister** (*shang-shu*), the head of a Ministry (*pu*); see under *liu pu* (Six Ministries).

4766 *pǔ-ch'én* 逋臣
Lit., a fleeing minister or subject: **Defector,** traditional term for a man who had left one regime to serve another or who had repudiated his ruler and become a recluse; the usage normally had strong pejorative implications. Cf. *pu-k'o.*

4767 *pù-ch'én* 部臣
N-S DIV–CH'ING: **Ministry Officials,** common collective reference to the official personnel, especially executive officials, of the Ministries (*pu*) of the central government (see under *liu pu*, Six Ministries) or of any single Ministry.

4768 *pǔ-chèng* 卜正
T'ANG–SUNG: **Divination Director:** in T'ang 2, rank 9b2, in the Imperial Divination Office (*t'ai-pu shu*) of the Court of Imperial Sacrifices (*t'ai-ch'ang ssu*); in Sung apparently non-official specialists attached to the Imperial Diviner (*t'ai-pu*) in the same Court; number not clear. RR+SP: *directeur de la divination*. P27.

4769 *pǔ chèng-míng* 補正名
SUNG: lit., to fill a vacancy among the regular titles, i.e., **Promoted to Official Status:** a term used when someone "outside the current" (*liu-wai*), specifically a subofficial functionary (*li*), upon recommendation of his official superiors, took and passed an examination qualifying him to be a regular, ranked official (*kuan*); a device used to help fill the lower ranks of the officialdom, such appointees apparently having little hope of more distinguished careers.

4770 *pù-chèng ssū* 布政司 and *pù-chèng shìh* 使
MING–CH'ING: common abbreviated references to a **Provincial Administration Commission** and its head, a **Provincial Administration Commissioner** (see under *ch'eng-hsüan pu-cheng shih ssu*).

4771 *pù-ch'éng* 部丞
HAN: **Regional Assistant** to the Chamberlain for the National Treasury (*ta ssu-nung*), 13 appointed under Emperor P'ing (r. A.D. 1–5), each to (go out and?) stimulate agriculture and sericulture in one of Han's 13 province-size Regions (*pu, chou*), the name of which was presumably prefixed to his title. In Later Han the number shrank to one, and the function changed to being in charge of the Chamberlain's treasury. Then the term *pu* cannot have had any meaning beyond the possible sense of dealing with revenues submitted by the various Regions; it was perhaps retained in the title principally to differentiate the *pu-ch'eng* from the single ordinary Aide (*ch'eng*, q.v.) to the Chamberlain, who was apparently of higher status. HB: divisional assistant.

4772 *pù ch'ēng-chíh* 不稱職
MING: **Inadequate,** one of 3 evaluation categories to which officials were assigned in evaluations given generally every 3 years, as distinguished from Ordinary (*p'ing-ch'ang*) and Adequate (*ch'eng-chih*); to be rated Inadequate meant to be deserving of demotion, dismissal, or other punishment.

4773 *pù-chí* 部集
HAN: **Divisional Gatherer** (?), an officer in a military Division (*pu*), apparently responsible for keeping the commander informed of conditions among the troops and units of the Division, but status and functions not at all clear. HB: regimental gatherer.

4774 *pù-chiàng* 部將
(1) HAN: **Divisional Subaltern,** unofficial reference to officers subordinate to the Commandant (*hsiao-wei*) of a Division (*pu*), the principal subdivision of an Army (*chün, ying*). Cf. *chiang-chün, chiang*. (2) SUNG: **Troop Commander,** one of several quasiofficial titles that emerged in the confused transition between N. Sung and S. Sung, denoting the leader of a relatively small loyalist military force. SP: *général-assistant*.

4775 *pǔ chù-chiào* 卜助教
T'ANG: **Divination Instructor,** 2 unranked specialists in the Imperial Divination Office (*t'ai-pu shu*) of the Court of Imperial Sacrifices (*t'ai-ch'ang ssu*). See *pu po-shih, pu-shih*. RR: *professeur assistant de la divination*.

4776 *pù-ch'ǔ* 部曲
(1) HAN: lit., **Divisions and Regiments** (see *pu* and *ch'ü*), an unofficial, synecdochic reference to a campaigning Army (*chün, ying*). Cf. *pu-tui, pu-wu*. (2) HAN–N-S DIV, MING: **Private Army,** a common borrowing of the normal Han usage of (1) above to refer to assemblages of irregular or quasiregular troops, often bondservants or otherwise indentured retainers, under the control of regional warlords or local great families. See *chia-ping, i-ping*. (3) HAN–MING: **Private Retainer,** a reference to an individual member of such an assemblage as is described under (2) above or, apparently from late in the era of N-S Division until the usage faded out in early Sung, a reference to one category of indentured peasants close to the status of serfs or slaves working the agrarian lands of great families who formed the social elite.

4777 *pǔ-ch'üeh* 補闕
Lit., to fill a vacancy or an omission. (1) Throughout history, one of many terms used with the meaning **to appoint;** see under *pu* (to appoint). (2) T'ANG–MING: **Rectifier of Omissions,** one of several titles used for officials known generically as Remonstrance Officials (*chien-kuan, yen-kuan*), whose prescribed function was to remonstrate with rulers about their deviations from honored traditions or from laws and administrative regulations, whether in their public or private lives, in contrast to Censors (*yü-shih*) and other Surveillance Officials (*ch'a-kuan*), whose traditionally prescribed function was to keep watch over the officialdom and impeach officials for misconduct. Rectifiers of Omissions were specifically responsible for checking drafts of proclamations and other documents flowing from the throne so as to return for reconsideration any that they considered inappropriate in form or substance, or to propose corrections; this procedure is commonly referred to as exercise of a veto power (see under *feng-po*), although no Remonstrance Official had any legal authority over his ruler or any legal immunity from punishment at the hands of an irate ruler. The position of Rectifier of Omissions was created in 685; thereafter there was an authorized staff of 12. rank

7b1, divided equally between the Chancellery (*men-hsia sheng*) and the Secretariat (*chung-shu sheng*) in the top echelon of the central government, prefixed Left and Right, respectively. In Sung, perhaps as early as 988 and probably not later than c. 1020, the title was changed to *ssu-chien* (Remonstrator) and the position was transferred from the then combined Secretariat-Chancellery (*chung-shu men-hsia sheng*) to an autonomous Remonstrance Bureau (*chien-yüan*). Some sources suggest that the title *pu-ch'üeh* was re-established in the Chancellery and the Secretariat in 1183, but the circumstances are not clear. In Chin there was a Sung-style Remonstrance Bureau with both Rectifiers of Omissions and Remonstrators, numbers and ranks not clear. In 1269 Yüan established Left and Right Rectifiers of Omissions, but only to assist Supervising Secretaries (*chi-shih-chung*) keep records of memorials submitted to the throne and compile the Imperial Diary (*ch'i-chü chu*); in 1278 the title was changed to the more appropriate Imperial Attendant and Concurrent Compiler of the Imperial Diary (*shih-i feng-yü chien hsiu ch'i-chü chu*). In Yüan remonstrance functions were explicitly shifted to the Censorate (*yü-shih t'ai*). In early Ming a Remonstrance Bureau was revived briefly from 1380 to 1382, but without Rectifiers of Omission; this title reappeared once more, however, in the 1399–1402 era, at least one each Left and Right, on the staff of the Transmission Commissioner (*t'ung-cheng shih*). But during Ming and Ch'ing, in general, the remonstrance function was carried on by Censors and Supervising Secretaries. Also see *chien-i ta-fu, shih-i, cheng-yen, ch'i-chü chu pu-ch'üeh*. RR+SP: *fonctionnaire chargé de reprendre les omissions de l'empereur*. P19.

4778   *pù-chün ssū* 步軍司
SUNG: **Metropolitan Infantry Command,** created in the mid-1000s by a division of the original Metropolitan Command (*shih-wei ch'in-chün ma-pu ssu*) into a Metropolitan Infantry Command and a Metropolitan Cavalry Command (*ma-chün ssu*); these 2 units together with the pre-existing and unchanged Palace Command (*tien-ch'ien shih-wei ssu*) were known collectively as the Three Capital Guards (*san wei*); each was headed by a Commander-in-chief (*tu chih-hui shih*), rank 5a. SP: *bureau de l'infanterie*.

4779   *pù-hsièn* 布憲
CHOU: lit., disseminator of fundamental policies or laws: **Promulgator of the Laws,** 2 ranked as Ordinary Servicemen (*chung-shih*) and 4 as Junior Servicemen (*hsia-shih*), members of the Ministry of Justice (*ch'iu-kuan*) who regularly disseminated announcements of punishments to the public, and information about new laws to both Feudal Lords (*chu-hou*) and local administrators in the royal domain. CL: *publicateur général*.

4780   *pù-ī* 布衣
Lit., plain cotton clothes: throughout imperial history a reference to **the common people;** sometimes used by men of learning without official status in humble reference to themselves, or by officials in reference to their pre-official status.

4781   *pù-ī* 部醫
YÜAN: **Ministry Physician,** one or more professional, probably hereditary, physicians attached to the Ministry of Justice (*hsing-pu*) to provide necessary medical care for state prisoners. P13.

4782   *pù-ì kuān* 部役官 or *pu-i*
CHIN–YÜAN: lit., (official in charge of) laborers requisitioned by the Ministry (of Works?): **Labor Foreman,** 4,

rank 8a, in Chin; 7, rank not clear, in Yüan; in the Palace Maintenance Office (*hsiu-nei ssu*); directed gangs of construction workers requisitioned from the general populace for work on the imperial palace. P15, 38.

4783   *pǔ-jén* 卜人
CHOU: **Diviner,** 8 ranked as Ordinary Servicemen (*chung-shih*) on the staff of the Grand Diviner (*ta-pu*) in the Ministry of Rites (*ch'un-kuan*); specialists in tortoiseshell divination. Also see *pu-shih*. CL: *augures ordinaires*.

4784   *pù jù ch'ǐn-tièn hsiǎo-tǐ* 不入寢殿小氏
CHIN: lit., retainer not allowed into the imperial bedchamber: variant of *wai-chang hsiao-ti* (**Retainer of the Outer Chamber**), in 1172 retitled *feng-chih* (Steward). Also see *hsiao-ti*. P38.

4785   *pù jù pā-fēn* 不入八分
CH'ING: lit., not to encroach on the Eight Privileges (see *pa fen*): **Lesser,** a prefix to certain middle-echelon titles of imperial nobility (*chüeh*). E.g., the title rendered herein as Lesser Defender Duke (*pu ju pa-fen chen-kuo kung*) has the literal sense Defender Duke (see *chen-kuo kung* without prefix) "not to encroach on the Eight Privileges."

4786   *pù-kēng* 不更
CH'IN–HAN: lit., one who does not take a tour or shift of active service, apparently signifying one exempted from labor service requisitioned by the state: **Grandee of the Fourth Order,** the 4th lowest of 20 titles of honorary nobility (*chüeh*) conferred on meritorious subjects. P65.

4787   *pū-k'ò* 逋客
MING–CH'ING: lit., a fleeing guest: **Evader,** a term for a recluse trying to avoid political and social involvements; the usage does not seem to have pejorative implications. Cf. *pu-ch'en*.

4788   *pù-k'ù* 布庫
SUNG: **Cloth Storehouse,** one of 25 or more units under the Court of the Imperial Treasury (*t'ai-fu ssu*) in N. Sung, apparently not re-established in S. Sung; staffing not clear, probably unranked subofficials; a storehouse for cloth of all sorts submitted as tax receipts from units of territorial administration, classified by type pending disposition by the court. SP: *magasin de toile*.

4789   *pù-k'uài* 步快
CH'ING: **Runner,** one of many kinds of menial posts on the staffs of magistrates up to the Prefecture (*fu*) level, provided by requisition from among the general populace.

4790   *pǔ-kǔn* 補袞
T'ANG: lit., patched gown, derivation and relevance not clear: unofficial reference to a **Censor-in-chief** (*yü-shih ta-fu*).

4791   *pǔ-lǐn* 補廩
MING–CH'ING: lit., supplementary stipend: variant of *lin-sheng* (**Stipend Student**).

4792   *pǔ-lò* 部落
Tribe or **Tribal Domain:** throughout history a common reference to any non-Chinese group and the territory it occupied. Cf. *pu-tsu*. In the Yüan dynasty, one of several terms (see *fen-ti, t'ou-hsia*) for lands in China granted to chiefs of Mongol and some allied tribes as relatively autonomous domains, commonly rendered **land grants** or appanages.

4793   *pù-pàn* 部辦
MING–CH'ING: abbreviated collective or generic refer-

ence to **Clerical Subofficials** (*shu-pan*) **of the Six Ministries** (*liu pu*).

4794 *pù-pīng hsiào-wèi* 步兵校尉

Infantry Commandant. (1) May be encountered in almost any period as an unofficial or quasiofficial title of a military officer. (2) HAN–N-S DIV (S. Dyn.): under Emperor Wu of Han (r. 141–87 B.C.), one of 5 Commandants (*hsiao-wei*) who shared command of the Northern Army (*pei-chün*), the principal military force at the dynastic capital; had the high rank of 2,000 bushels and the responsibility of guarding the entrances to the renowned Imperial Forest Park (*shang-lin yüan*). However, even before the end of Former Han the title seems to have become a sinecure to be awarded imperial favorites, and it continued in such use through Later Han and on to the end of the S. Dynasties, when the prefix *t'ai-tzu* was sometimes added for retainers of the Heir Apparent. HB: colonel of foot soldiers. P23, 40.

4795 *pǔ pó-shìh* 卜博士

T'ANG–SUNG: **Erudite of Divination,** 2, rank 9b2, in T'ang; number and rank status not clear in Sung; in both dynasties under the Court of Imperial Sacrifices (*t'ai-ch'ang ssu*), in T'ang through the intermediary Imperial Divination Office (*t'ai-pu shu*), in Sung through the intermediary Imperial Diviner (*t'ai-pu*); ritual specialists in divination arts, probably at all times hereditary professionals without normal civil service qualifications. See *po-shih*. RR: *maître au vaste savoir de la divination*. SP: *professeur de la divination*.

4796 *pǔ-shìh* 卜師

Divination Master. (1) CHOU: 4 ranked as Senior Servicemen (*shang-shih*) on the staff of the Grand Diviner (*ta-pu*) in the Ministry of Rites (*ch'un-kuan*); specialists in tortoiseshell divination. Also see *pu-jen*. CL: *maître d'auguration*. (2) T'ANG: 20, apparently unranked hereditary professionals, in the Imperial Divination Office (*t'ai-pu shu*) of the Court of Imperial Sacrifices (*t'ai-ch'ang ssu*). Also see *pu po-shih*, *pu chu-chiao*. RR: *maître de la divination*.

4797 *pù-shìh* 暴室

HAN–N-S DIV (S. Dyn.): lit., a house (enclosure) for drying in the sun: **Palace Isolation Building,** a place in the imperial palace where palace women were sent to be cured of illnesses or in punishment for misbehavior; a eunuch agency created in Later Han, headed by a eunuch Aide (*ch'eng*) to the eunuch Director (*ling*) of the Palace Discipline Service (*i-t'ing*) under the general supervision of the Chamberlain for the Palace Revenues (*shao-fu*). In the S. Dynasties this was at times the only remnant of the Palace Discipline Service, and the eunuch in charge was titled Director (*ling*); it was then commonly under the joint supervision of the Chamberlain for the Palace Revenues and the Chamberlain for Attendants (*kuang-lu-hsün*), or under the latter alone. HB: drying house. P37.

4798 *pǔ-shīh shēng* 卜筮生

T'ANG: **Divination Student,** 45 authorized for the Imperial Divination Office (*t'ai-pu shu*) of the Court of Imperial Sacrifices (*t'ai-ch'ang ssu*), to study divination with tortoiseshells and with milfoil stalks under the Office's Erudites of Divination (*pu po-shih*), Divination Instructors (*pu chu-chiao*), Divination Masters (*pu-shih*), etc. RR: *élève de la divination par l'écaille de tortue et l'achillée*.

4799 *pù-shìh yù* 暴室獄

HAN: variant of *pu-shih* (**Palace Isolation Building**), emphasizing its penal aspect. See *yü*, *chao-yü*. HB: prison of the drying house.

4800 *pǔ-shòu* 補授

Lit., **to appoint to fill a vacancy** (see under *pu*, *shou*, and *pu-ch'üeh*): most commonly used in that literal verbal sense, but occasionally encountered in noun form as if for a title, meaning **Supplementary Appointee,** the post or agency being indicated by a prefix or by the preceding context.

4801 *pù-shǔ* 部署

(1) From Han on, may be encountered as a term meaning "to divide up and assign matters (to the appropriate offices)." (2) Also from Han on, may be encountered as a term meaning "to establish offices or agencies (for the handling of) divided-up and distributed (affairs or business matters)." (3) **Ministries and Offices:** from the era of N-S Division may be encountered as a generic reference to all the agencies of the central government. (4) SUNG: **Administrator,** in very early Sung used as a designation for the head of a Superior Prefecture (*fu*) and in some military units, in the latter cases traditionally equated with the titles *tsung-kuan* (Area Commander-in-chief) and *tu tsung-kuan* (Supreme Area Commander). SP: *commandant en chef*.

4802 *pù-t'áng* 部堂

MING–CH'ING: lit., (one who occupies) the principal hall, room, or (judge's) bench in a Ministry (*pu*): **Ministry Executive,** unofficial reference to an executive official, primarily the Minister (*shang-shu*) but not uncommonly the Vice Minister (*shih-lang*) as well, of any of the Six Ministries (*liu pu*) in the central government; or to a Ming dynasty Supreme Commander or a Ch'ing dynasty Governor-general (both *tsung-tu*) of 2 or more contiguous Provinces, who normally had nominal status as a Minister or Vice Minister.

4803 *pǔ-tào àn* 捕盗案

SUNG: **Section for the Arrest of Bandits,** one of 13 Sections (*an*) directly subordinate to the executive officials of the S. Sung Ministry of Justice (*hsing-pu*); staffed with subofficial functionaries who handled documents relating to bandit-suppression activities in units of territorial administration throughout the empire. SP: *service de l'arrêtation des bandits*.

4804 *pǔ-t'īng* 捕廳

CH'ING: lit., pavilion or office of a catcher (of lawbreakers): unofficial reference to a **District Jailor** (*tien-shih*).

4805 *pù-ts'áo* 簿曹

HAN: **Records Section,** one of several Sections that formed the staff of the Metropolitan Commandant (*ssu-li hsiao-wei*); also commonly on the staff of each Regional Inspector (*tz'u-shih*); in both cases, the Section was headed or manned alone by a Retainer Clerk (*ts'ung-shih shih*). HB: bureau of records.

4806 *pù-ts'áo* 部曹

MING–CH'ING: lit., a combination of traditional names for important central government agencies, Ministries (*pu*) and Sections (*ts'ao*): a common, partly archaic general reference to **the central government.**

4807 *pǔ-tséi kuān* 捕賊官

Lit., thief-catching official. (1) Throughout history an unofficial reference to officials, subofficial functionaries, or hirelings charged with **local police** functions. (2) T'ANG: **Metropolitan Police Official,** a quasiofficial generic reference to the District Defenders (*hsien-wei*; also see *wei*) of the 2 Districts (*hsien*) seated at the dynastic capital. P20.

4808 *pù-tsú* 部族

Tribe: throughout history, one of several common designations of groups of non-Chinese peoples; does not seem to carry as clearly the additional sense of tribal domain that was associated with the term *pu-lo*, but seems to emphasize kinship ties within the group. Also see under *pu*.

4809 *pù ts'úng-shìh* 部從事
Regional Retainer; see under *ts'ung-shih* (Retainer) and *pu* (Region; equivalent to *chou*).

4810 *pù-tùi* 部隊
Divisions and Companies: from Han on, a shorthand, synecdochic reference to any large military force divisible into smaller units. From high antiquity, *tui* was a designation of a military unit of 100 or so men, and in Han a *pu* (Division) was the largest constituent unit in an Army (*chün, ying*). Cf. *pu-wu*.

4811 *pù tz'ù-shìh* 部刺史
HAN–N-S DIV: **Regional Inspector;** see under *tz'u-shih* (Regional Inspector) and *pu* (Region).

4812 *pù-wǔ* 部伍
Divisions and Squads: from Han on, a synecdochic combination of terms for the largest and smallest units in a military force to refer generally to the whole Army (*chün, ying*). See under *pu* and *wu*. Also see *pu-tui*.

4813 *pù-yüán* 部員
CH'ING: variant reference in treaties to **Judicial Administrator** (*pan-shih ssu-yüan*), a category of officials in Outer Mongolia.

4814 *pù-yüàn* 部院
(1) MING–CH'ING: collective reference to the **Ministries** (*pu;* see *liu pu*) **and the Censorate** (*tu ch'a-yüan*), the top echelon of civil agencies in the central government. (2) MING–CH'ING: unofficial reference to a **Grand Coordinator** or **Provincial Governor** (both *hsün-fu*), who normally had nominal status both in one of the Six Ministries and in the Censorate of the central government, usually as a Vice Minister (*shih-lang*) and Vice Censor-in-chief (*fu tu yü-shih*) or Assistant Censor-in-chief (*ch'ien tu yü-shih*). Use of the term *pu-yüan* to refer to any Vice Minister seems to be a very late Ch'ing practice, possibly originating as late as 1901.

4815 *p'ú* 僕
(1) Ety. not clear; in antiquity used principally in the senses charioteer, servant, slave; hence through later history a term of derogation, including a conventionally polite reference to oneself. (2) HAN–N-S DIV: **Royal Coachman,** important retainer of a Princess (*kung-chu*), rank 600 bushels, and from 104 B.C. in a Princedom (*wang-kuo*), rank from 1,000 down to 600 bushels, in the latter case after demotion from the same 2,000-bushel stipend and the identical title of the central government counterpart, the Chamberlain for the Imperial Stud (*t'ai-p'u*), in efforts to weaken the Princedoms by Emperor Wu (r. 141–87 B.C.). Responsible for the management of horses and carriages. The Han pattern was continued under Wei of the Three Kingdoms and possibly later. Also see *t'ai-tzu p'u* (Coachman of the Heir Apparent), *ch'e-p'u, ch'i-p'u, jung-p'u, li-p'u, ta-p'u, tao-p'u, t'ien-p'u, yü-p'u ssu*. HB: coachman. P69.

4816 *p'ù* 舖
Lit., a building, shed, mercantile shop. (1) MING–CH'ING: **Post Station,** a small, often isolated building housing horses and runners by which government dispatches were relayed between agencies. See *i-chan*. (2) MING–CH'ING: **Neighborhood,** a unit of quasiofficial sub-District (*hsien*) organization of the population in an urban setting such as Pe-

king, subordinate to a Precinct (*fang*), sometimes through an intermediate Subprecinct (*p'ai*); led by a Head (*t'ou*) designated among the residents. The usage apparently died out in early Ch'ing. See *pao-chia*. Cf. *li-chia*.

4817 *p'ú-chǎng* 僕長
Head of the Livery Service; see under *t'ai-tzu p'u-ssu* (Livery Service of the Heir Apparent).

4818 *p'ú-ch'én* 僕臣
SUI–CH'ING: unofficial reference to **officials of the Court of the Imperial Stud** (*t'ai-p'u ssu*).

4819 *p'ú-chèng* 僕正
CHIN: abbreviated reference to *t'ai-tzu p'u-cheng* (**Director of the Livery Service of the Heir Apparent**); see under *t'ai-tzu p'u-ssu*.

4820 *p'ǔ-chì t'áng* 普濟堂 or *p'ǔ-chì yüàn* 院
CH'ING: lit., hall for aiding everyone: **State Refuge** for the care of the ill and the poor, by law established in each District (*hsien*), normally with the help of private contributors.

4821 *p'ú-fū* 僕夫
CHOU: **Aide in the Royal Stud,** number and rank not clear, each in charge of from one to 12 royal stables (*chiu*); supervised by 2 Commandants (*hsiao-jen*) in the Ministry of War (*hsia-kuan*). CL: *aide-conducteur*.

4822 *p'ú-jén shīh* 僕人師
Lit., master of the grooms: throughout imperial history an unofficial, archaic reference to the **Chamberlain for the Imperial Stud** (*t'ai-p'u*) or to any **Executive Official of the Court of the Imperial Stud** (see under *t'ai-p'u ssu*).

4823 *p'u-she* 僕射
See under the romanization *p'u-yeh*.

4824 *p'ú-ssù* 僕寺
Abbreviation of *t'ai-tzu p'u-ssu* (**Livery Service of the Heir Apparent**).

4825 *p'ù-ssū* 舖司
YÜAN: **Local Courier Station,** established throughout the country under supervision of the Ministry of War (*ping-pu*), staffed at least in part by Courier Soldiers (*p'u-ping*); also called Postal Relay Station (*chan* or *i*, qq.v.).

4826 *p'ú-yèh* 僕射
Lit. charioteering archer (suggesting the pronunciation *p'u-she*), one of the most interesting and important titles in Chinese government through the Sung dynasty; traditionally believed to have originated in the early military-dominated society's custom of letting the best archers take charge of things. (1) CH'IN–N-S DIV: **Supervisor** or **Chief Administrator,** an ad hoc concurrent assignment to take charge of something, used commonly among all kinds of groups—civil, military, eunuch, etc., often designating one man in a group of equals to be the administrative coordinator, or designating someone to take active charge under a nominal but inactive head such as a Director (*ling*). E.g., Chief Administrator of the Erudites (*po-shih p'u-yeh*), Supervisor of an Army Farm (*chün-t'un p'u-yeh*), 2 Chief Administrators of the Music Office (*yüeh-fu p'u-yeh*) under a Director (*ling*), eunuch Chief Administrator of the Palace Discipline Service (*yung-hsiang chü*) under a Director (*ling*). This usage faded in Later Han with the rise to power of the Imperial Secretariat, as noted below, but recurred intermittently through the era of N-S Division. (2) HAN–SUNG: **Vice Director** of the Later Han Imperial Secretariat (*shang-shu t'ai*), thereafter of the Department of State Affairs (*shang-shu*

sheng), in both cases under a Director (*ling*). During the era of N-S Division, the appointment of Left and Right Vice Directors became the normal practice. Rank 2b in T'ang, 1b in Sung. The post was initiated in 32 B.C. The next most important date in its history is A.D. 626, when the Imperial Prince Li Shih-min, who had been serving in his father's government as Director of the Department of State Affairs, took the T'ang throne, to become the renowned ruler known posthumously as T'ang T'ai-tsung. In deference to him, no one accepted the directorship during his reign, and thereafter through Sung times the Director was an inactive post and the Vice Directors were in fact joint heads of the Department. As such, they joined the Director of the Secretariat (*chung-shu ling*) and the Director of the Chancellery (*men-hsia shih-chung*) as senior Grand Councilors (*tsai-hsiang*), at least in theory attending daily conferences with the Emperor to make decisions about state policies. In recognition of their importance, the Vice Directors were officially retitled Rectifiers of Governance (*k'uang-cheng*) from 662 to 671; from 684 to 705 Ministers (*hsiang*) of the Pavilion of Culture and Prosperity (*wen-ch'ang t'ai, wen-ch'ang tu-sheng*); from 713 to 741 Counselors-in-chief (*ch'eng-hsiang*); and they were commonly known by the supplementary title Manager of Affairs (*p'ing-chang shih*). In Sung the Vice Director of the Left was commonly Concurrent Vice Director of the Chancellery (*chien men-hsia shih-lang*), and the Vice Director of the Right was commonly Concurrent Vice Director of the Secretariat (*chien chung-shu shih-lang*); and the pair were normally de facto heads of the government under the Emperor. From the time of Hui-tsung (r. 1100–1125) the Vice Directors of the Left and Right bore the awesome archaic titles *t'ai-tsai* (Senior Grand Councilor) and *shao-tsai* (Junior Grand Councilor), respectively, and they were known by such cumbersome full designations as Senior Grand Councilor Vice Director of the Department of State Affairs Jointly Manager of Affairs with the Secretariat-Chancellery (*t'ai-tsai shang-shu p'u-yeh t'ung chung-shu men-hsia p'ing-chang shih*). In the era 1162–1189 the title Counselor-in-chief (*ch'eng-hsiang*) was again revived. Throughout its history the title *p'u-yeh* was commonly rendered *shang-shu p'u-yeh*. After Sung it dropped from use. RR+SP: *vice-président du département des affaires d'état*. P2, 3.

4827   *sā-mǎn t'ài-t'ài*   薩滿太太
CH'ING: **Shamaness,** collective or generic reference to 12 priestesses of Shamanism, one of the religions officially patronized by the court; members of the Shamanism Office (*shen-fang*) in the Office of Palace Ceremonial (*chang-i ssu*) of the Imperial Household Administration (*nei-wu fu*); normally wives of Manchu Imperial Guardsmen (*shih-wei*) and officially entitled Petitioners (*ssu-chu*). Shared with palace eunuchs responsibility for conducting regular Shamanistic services in the palace of the Empress (the *k'un-ming kung*) and at the Shamanistic Temple (*t'ang-tzu*) in the dynastic capital. The designation is found in several variant, similar-sounding Chinese transliterations. BH: shamanic priestess.

4828   *sā-pǎo*   薩寶
N-S DIV (N. Ch'i)–T'ANG: one of several Chinese transcriptions of a Persian word: **Persian Priest,** devotees of Manichaeism or Mazdaism established in temples at the dynastic capital and at various headquarters towns of territorial administration; treated as responsible heads of resident Persian communities.

4829   *sài-ts'áo*   塞曹
HAN: **Border Section,** one of a varying number of Sec-

tions (*ts'ao*) normally headed by Administrators (*yüan-shih*) that constituted the staff of a Commandery Governor (*chün-shou*); documented only for the northwestern frontier region; functions not specified but clearly related to local contacts, military or otherwise, between Chinese authorities and adjoining non-Chinese groups. HB: bureau of the frontier.

4830   *sān*   三
CHOU: **The Three,** collective reference to the Three Ministers (*san ch'ing*). CL: *trois grands ministres*.

4831   *sàn*   散
Lit., separate, unattached, dispersed; hence inactive or irregular. This is a troublesome term used as a prefix to titles. In one usage it has the sense of **detached** as in the case, e.g., of a branch office of some agency (see *san hsün-chien shih;* cf. *san-chi*). From the early 500s if not earlier, it began to be used also in the sense of **inactive** prefixed to official titles and even such titles of nobility as Duke (*kung*) when they were awarded to men without official status or prescribed duties, or when added to a man's official title for honorific purposes only, in neither case providing a stipend or increasing one's established stipend. At the same time *san* began to be appended to the titles of officials when they were not in active service—between appointments, when disabled or overaged, etc.—apparently in an effort to give some social status (and stipends?) to sometime officials in such conditions. In Sui this practice was transformed into grants of Prestige Titles (*san-kuan*, q.v.) for officials in active service, to pinpoint their ranks and seniority within any rank, which regular titles (*kuan, pen-kuan*) did not do. The term *san* was not itself incorporated into such prestige titles, but it occasionally reappeared in the other usages described above, often seeming to denote irregular, supernumerary, but not merely honorific status, as in the case of several Sung dynasty titles, e.g., *san chih-hui*. Whether *san chih-hui* meant Supernumerary (active and salaried) Commander or Honorary (inactive and unsalaried) Commander can often be clarified only by reference to the particular context.

4832   *sān cháng*   三長
N-S DIV: **Three Elders,** collective reference to the Heads (*chang*) of Neighborhoods (*lin*), Villages (*li*), and Wards (*tang*) in one common quasiofficial hierarchy of units of sub-District (*hsien*) organization of the population; also a reference to that pattern of organization.

4833   *sàn-chì*   散騎
HAN: **Cavalier Attendant,** an honorific title (*chia-kuan*) conferred on favored officials entitling them, in addition to their normal functions and privileges, to ride alongside (lit., detached from, apart from) the imperial carriage or chariot on outings, ceremonial and otherwise, and thus to be available as companions and advisers to the Emperor. Apparently used only in Former Han.

4834   *sàn-chì ch'áng-shìh*   散騎常侍
(1) N-S DIV: **Cavalier Attendant-in-ordinary,** an honorific title (*chia-kuan*) conferred on favored officials giving them status as companions and advisers of the ruler, reportedly more prestigious than the honorific title *chi-shih-chung* (Palace Steward, Supervising Secretary); common in the 300s, both in Chin and in the Sixteen Kingdoms of the Hsiung-nu tribes. P19. (2) N-S DIV: **Senior Recorder,** a regular official post no doubt growing out of that described in (1) above, having some responsibility (perhaps as early as Chin and certainly not later than 480 in S. Ch'i) for com-

pilation of the Imperial Diary (*ch'i-chü chu*) and considered a member of the group called Historiographers (*shih-kuan*). P23. (3) SUI–SUNG, LIAO: **Policy Adviser,** normally 2 to 4, rank 3a, those prefixed Left in the Chancellery (*men-hsia sheng*) and those prefixed Right in the Secretariat (*chung-shu sheng*); discontinued in 607 but re-established in 627; perhaps only one in Liao, a member of the Chancellery. Responsible for attending the Emperor daily, for responding to questions, and principally for criticizing the Emperor's faults; among the eminent officials collectively called the Eight Sabled Dignitaries (*pa tiao*) in T'ang. RR: *grand conseiller de l'empereur.* SP: *grand conseiller politique impérial ou censeur.* P19.

4835   *sàn-chì láng* 散騎郎
CH'ING: **Gentleman Cavalier Attendant,** variable numbers of hereditary retainers on the staffs of some Princely Establishments (*wang-fu*). P69.

4836   *sàn-chì shěng* 散騎省
N-S DIV: quasiofficial variant of *chi-shu sheng* (**Department of Scholarly Counselors**).

4837   *sàn-chì shìh-láng* 散騎侍郎
N-S DIV: **Gentleman Cavalier Attendant,** then **Senior Recorder:** a title whose history paralleled that of *san-chi ch'ang-shih* (#1 and #2), q.v. P24.

4838   *sān ch'í* 三旗
CH'ING: see *nei san ch'i* (Three Inner Banners) and *shang san ch'i* (Three Superior Banners).

4839   *sān-ch'í chuāng-t'óu ch'ù* 三旗莊頭處
CH'ING: lit., office of the estate manager for the Three Banners; abbreviation of *san-ch'i yin-liang chuang-t'ou ch'u* (**Rents Office for Lands of the Inner Banners**).

4840   *sān-ch'í pāo-ī t'ǔng-lǐng* 三旗包衣統領
CH'ING: **Commander-general of the Bondservants of the Three Banners,** rank 3a, a Grand Minister (*ta-ch'en*) of the Imperial Household Department (*nei-wu fu*) in charge of those units of the Three Superior Banners (*shang san ch'i*) that were staffed with imperial bondservants (*pao-i*).

4841   *sān-ch'í shìh-wèi* 三旗侍衛
CH'ING: **Imperial Guardsmen of the Three (Superior) Banners,** one of several designations of the elite military unit constituting the Imperial Bodyguard (*ch'in-chün ying*). See *shang san ch'i.* P37.

4842   *sān-ch'í tsūng-shìh shìh-wèi* 三旗宗室侍衛
CH'ING: **Imperial Clansmen Guards of the Three (Superior) Banners,** a unit of Imperial Guardsmen (*shih-wei*) made up of members of the imperial family rather than the predominant imperial bondservants (*pao-i*). BH: clansmen corps of the imperial bodyguards.

4843   *sān-ch'í yín-liáng chuāng-t'óu ch'ù* 三旗銀糧莊頭處
CH'ING: lit., office of the (imperial) estate manager (responsible for collecting) silver and grain taxes (due from members of) the Three Banners (resident thereon): **Rents Office for Lands of the Inner Banners,** a unit of the Imperial Household Department (*nei-wu fu*), headed by one or more of the Department's Grand Ministers (*tà-ch'en*). BH: office for collecting rents of imperial lands.

4844   *sān-chiǎ* 三甲
SUNG–CH'ING: **Third Category,** designation on the pass list posted after national civil service recruitment exami-

nations, identifying all those called Associate Metropolitan Graduates (*t'ung chin-shih ch'u-shen*). Also see *chin-shih.*

4845   *sān-ch'iēn yíng* 三千營
MING: **Division of the Three Thousand,** one of the Three Great Training Divisions (*san ta-ying*) at Peking, with counterparts at Nanking; originated in the founding reign as a unit of 3,000 surrendered aliens (mostly Mongols), but eventually seems to have become, like the Division of the Five Armies (*wu-chün ying*), a training unit for troops rotated to one of the capitals from Guard (*wei*) garrisons throughout the country.

4846   *sàn-chìh tà-ch'én* 散秩大臣
CH'ING: lit., grand minister without rank, or out of normal rank order (sense not clear): **Grand Minister Assistant Commander** of Imperial Guardsmen (*shih-wei*), number unprescribed, rank 2b; aides to the Grand Minister Controlling the Imperial Guardsmen (*ling shih-wei nei ta-ch'en*), in charge of the Imperial Bodyguard (*ch'in-chün ying*). The title was often held by hereditary privilege. BH: junior assistant chamberlain of the imperial bodyguard.

4847   *sān ch'īng* 三卿
Three Ministers. (1) CHOU: collective reference to the 3 eminent officials at the royal court entitled Minister of Education (*ssu-t'u*), of War (*ssu-ma*), and of Works (*ssu-k'ung*), especially when they concurrently held the 3 other posts included among the top-level Six Ministers (*liu ch'ing*) at court: Minister of State (*chung-tsai*), of Rites (*tsung-po*), and of Justice (*ssu-k'ou*). Commonly abbreviated to *san* (The Three). CL: *trois grands ministres.* (2) CHOU: reference to the 3 officials with rank as Minister (*ch'ing*) who were authorized to assist the most eminent group of Feudal Lords (*chu-hou*); in the largest tributary states all 3 were reportedly appointed by the King, whereas in the next largest states only 2 of the 3 were so appointed, the 3rd being appointed by the local lords. (3) N-S DIV (S. Dyn.): collective reference to 3 eminent officials in Princedoms (*wang-kuo*): Chamberlain for Attendants (*lang-chung ling*), Commandant-in-ordinary (*chung-weì*), and Minister of Agriculture (*ta-nung*). P69.

4848   *sàn-chōu* 散州
CH'ING: lit., detached Department (territorial unit), i.e., one not directly under the supervision of a Circuit Intendant (*tao-t'ai*) but part of a Prefecture (*fu*) or even part of a Sub-prefecture (*t'ing*): **Ordinary Department** as distinguished from an Independent Department (*chih-li chou*), which was not part of a Prefecture but was directly supervised by a Circuit Intendant. Also called *shu-chou,* q.v.

4849   *sān chūn* 三軍
(1) **Three Armies,** from antiquity a common pattern of organizing troops for battle, into Left, Right, and Center Armies; by extension, a common general reference to a state's or a dynasty's total military establishment, suggesting the alternate rendering **the armed forces.** (2) CHOU: **Three Armies,** the reported authorized military force of the largest tributary states, theoretically totaling 37,500 soldiers. (3) N-S DIV (S. Dyn.): **Three Adjutants,** common collective reference to the 3 most eminent military officers in a Princedom (*wang-kuo*): the Senior (*shang*), the Ordinary (*chung*), and the Junior (*hsia*) Adjutants (*chün*). P69.

4850   *sān fǎ-ssū* 三法司
MING–CH'ING: **Three Judicial Offices,** collective reference to the Censorate (*tu ch'a-yüan*), the Ministry of Justice (*hsing-pu*), and the Court of Judicial Review (*ta-li ssu*),

whose executive officials cooperated in conducting or supervising major judicial actions. BH: three high courts of judicature.

4851 *sān fēi* 三妃

T'ANG: **Three Consorts,** after Hsüan-tsung (r. 712–756) a collective reference to the secondary imperial wives entitled Gracious Consort (*hui-fei*), Elegant Consort (*li-fei*), and Splendid Consort (*hua-fei*), the most esteemed such titles following the disgrace and execution of the previously most esteemed Honored Consort (*kuei-fei*), née Yang. Cf. *ssu fei*.

4852 *sān fŭ* 三府

Lit., the 3 offices. (1) Throughout imperial history, a common unofficial reference to the **Three Dukes** (*san kung*). (2) N-S DIV: **Three Departments,** an unofficial collective reference to the top-echelon agencies of the central government later called *san sheng*, q.v.; most commonly referred to the Secretariat (*chung-shu sheng*), the Department of State Affairs (*shang-shu sheng*), and the Chancellery (*men-hsia sheng*). (3) T'ANG: **Three Garrisons,** collective reference to military units under the Left and Right Defense Guard Commands (*wei shuai-fu*) of the Heir Apparent: the Bodyguard Garrison (*ch'in-fu*), the Distinguished Garrison (*hsün-fu*), and the Standby Garrison (*i-fu*), each under a Commandant (*chung-lang chiang*), rank 4b1. Cf. *san wei*. P26. (4) CH'ING: polite unofficial reference to a **Subprefectural Magistrate** (*t'ung-p'an*).

4853 *sàn-fŭ* 散府

CHIN–YÜAN: **Superior Prefecture,** one category of administrative units directly subordinate to Routes (*lu*), ordinarily in locations of special strategic or other importance; in Chin each headed by some sort of Commissioner (*shih*), e.g., Military Commissioner (*chieh-tu shih*); in Yüan each headed by a Prefect (*yin*), often the designation given a southwestern aboriginal tribe. P72.

4854 *sān fŭ* 三輔

(1) HAN: **Three Guardians,** collective reference to the 3 officials who from 104 B.C. administered the Metropolitan Area (*ching-shih*), in which the dynastic capital was located: the Metropolitan Governor (*ching-chao yin, yu nei-shih*), the Guardian of the Left (*tso p'ing-i, tso nei-shih*), and the Guardian of the Right (*yu p'ing-i, yu fu-feng*), each with the high rank of 2,000 bushels. They superseded the early Han Chamberlain for the Capital (*nei-shih*) and in turn after 91 B.C. were overshadowed in importance and authority by the Metropolitan Commandant (*ssu-li hsiao-wei*). HB: three adjuncts. P32. (2) HAN: unofficial reference to the jurisdiction of the Three Guardians identified above, i.e., the **Metropolitan Area** (*ching-shih*).

4855 *sān fū-jén* 三夫人

Three Consorts, from antiquity a generic designation of the most esteemed secondary wives of the ruler. (1) CHOU: number actually flexible, specific titles not identified, perhaps not assigned; status higher than that of the Nine Concubines (*chiu pin*). CL: *trois épouses légitimes.* (2) N-S DIV: variably referred to the 3 titles Lady of Vast Virtue (*hung-te*), Lady of Proper Virtue (*cheng-te*), and Lady of Esteemed Virtue (*ch'ung-te*) or to Honored Concubine (*kuei-pin*), Honored Consort (*fu-jen*), and Honored Consort (*kuei-fei*). (3) SUI: referred to Honored Consort (*kuei-fei*), Pure Consort (*shu-fei*), and Virtuous Consort (*te-fei*).

4856 *sān fú-kuān* 三服官 or *san fu*

HAN: **Three Seasonal Tailoring Groups,** apparently un-ranked suboffical artisans, possibly slaves or eunuchs, each with a specific charge: one to make imperial headgear for spring use, one to make imperial gowns for winter, and one to make imperial gowns for summer, all presumably subordinates in the large establishment of the Chamberlain for the Palace Revenues (*shao-fu*). P37.

4857 *sān-fŭ tū-wèi* 三輔都尉

HAN: **Three Defenders of the Metropolitan Area,** collective reference to the leaders of units of the Northern Army (*pei-chün*) that policed the dynastic capital and its environs; the Metropolitan Area (*ching-shih*) was divided into 3 parts (see *san fu*), known by the titles of their separate military overseers: Defender of the Capital (*ching-fu tu-wei*), Left (*tso*) Defender of the Capital, and Right (*yu*) Defender of the Capital, all under the coordination of the Chamberlain for the Imperial Insignia (*chih chin-wu*). These arrangements evolved early in Later Han; relations between the Three Defenders and the powerful Metropolitan Commandant (*ssu-li hsiao-wei*) are not clear. Also see *tu-wei*.

4858 *sān hsiàng* 三相

SUNG: **Three Ministers,** collective reference to 3 categories of academicians and litterateurs whose posts commonly led to, or were concurrently occupied by men with, status as Grand Councilors (*tsai-hsiang*): Grand Academician (*ta hsüeh-shih*) in the Institute for the Glorification of Literature (*chao-wen kuan*) and in the Academy of Scholarly Worthies (*chi-hsien tien shu-yüan*), and Chief Compiler of the Dynastic History (*chien-hsiu kuo-shih*). P3.

4859 *sān hsiào-wèi* 三校尉

N-S DIV (S. Dyn.): **Three Commandants,** collective reference to military officers on the personal staff of the Heir Apparent: Commandant of Garrison Cavalry (*t'un-chi hsiao-wei*), Commandant of Infantry (*pu-ping hsiao-wei*), and Commandant of Standby Troops (*i-chün hsiao-wei*). At least in Sung, 7 appointees were authorized for each post; in Ch'en all were of rank 6, salary 1,000 bushels. P26.

4860 *sān-hsüăn shìh-láng* 三選侍郎

SUNG: **Vice Ministers of the Three Appointments Processes,** collective reference to Vice Ministers of Personnel (*li-pu shih-lang*) who participated in any or all of 3 types of appointment processes (see under *hsüan*): for Civil Appointments (*tso-hsüan*), for Military Appointments (*yu-hsüan*), for Temporary Concurrent Appointments (*chien-she*).

4861 *sān hsŭn-chiĕn shĭh* 散巡檢使 or *san hsün-chien*

CHIN: **Detached Police Chief,** one, rank 9a, in each Prefecture (*chou*); presumably in a branch office located in the part of the jurisdiction that was least accessible from the Prefectural headquarters town, since each Prefecture was also authorized an Executive Police Chief (*tu hsün-chien shih*) as well as an Assistant Executive Police Chief (*fu tu hsün-chien shih*), both of higher rank. The Detached Police Chief was also authorized to have an Assistant (*fu san hsün-chien shih*). Both Detached posts were sometimes occupied by suboffical Clerks (*kuan-kou*). Detached Police Chiefs were commonly not policemen alone, but in some degree were representatives of the Prefect for all purposes; it appears that one of their principal charges was to keep disciplinary watch over District (*hsien*) authorities in their jurisdictions. P54.

4862 *sān-hù fă* 三互法

HAN: lit., triple mutual law: **Law of Triple Avoidances,** a rule established in the 2nd century A.D. expanding earlier policies taking account of native places and marriage connections in making appointments in units of territorial administration. From the 2nd century B.C. it had been the practice that imperial appointees, excepting those in the Metropolitan Area (*ching-chao*) including the dynastic capital, could not serve in territorial jurisdictions of which they were registered natives. Moreover, if an official native to area A were married to a woman of area B, he could not be appointed to an executive post in area B, and no native of area B could be made an executive of area A; or if an area A man were the executive official of area B, then no area B man could be appointed executive of area A. These were the first 2 "mutual" or "reciprocal" exclusionary rules. The 3rd, added in Later Han, provided that if an area A man were the executive official of area B and an area B man were the executive of area C, then no area C man could be appointed executive of either area B or area A; and further that if the executive official of area A were married to a woman of area B, then no area A man could be appointed executive of area B. The purpose of these bans was to prevent collusion among relatives, even by marriage, that might gain them personal advantage of any sort, and the rules were apparently enforced with increasing rigidity during Later Han. They initiated so-called "rules of avoidance" (*hui-pi*) that were standard practices throughout later history.

4863 *sān huái* 三槐
Lit., 3 locust trees: from Chou on, an unofficial reference to the **Three Dukes** (*san kung*) or others of comparable eminence such as Grand Councilors (*tsai-hsiang*); from a *Chou-li* notation that the Three Dukes' positions in audiences outside the palace were opposite 3 locust trees in the courtyard. Cf. *chiu chi* (9 jujube trees).

4864 *sān kū* 三孤
Lit., 3 orphans, i.e., 3 who are alone, special, unique, etc.: **Three Solitaries**, irregularly used throughout history as an official collective designation for 3 posts in the topmost echelon of the central government, in the last dynasties ranking 1b, secondary in rank and prestige only to a similar group of 3 known as the Three Dukes (*san kung*). As in the case of the Three Dukes, they were considered to be regular functional posts (*chih-kuan*), each with grave responsibilities vis-a-vis the Emperor; and in fact they were not honorific titles (*chia-kuan*, etc.). But they were titles awarded only to the most eminent officials in the central government in recognition of their great achievements and merit. The 3 titles were Junior Preceptor (*shao-shih*), Junior Mentor (*shao-fu*), and Junior Guardian (*shao-pao*). The same titles prefixed with *t'ai-tzu* designated the Three Solitaries of the Heir Apparent, rank normally 2a. SP: *trois précepteurs*. P67.

4865 *sān-k'ù* 三庫
Three Storehouses. (1) SUI: collective reference to the Left Storehouse Office (*tso tsang-shu*), the Imperial (*huang*) Storehouse Office, and the Right (*yu*) Storehouse Office, each with a Director (*chien*); the principal treasuries of the central government, units of the Ministry of Revenue (*min-pu*). (2) CH'ING: collective reference to the Silver Vault (*yin-k'u*), Piece Goods Vault (*tuan-hsü k'u*), and Miscellany Vault (*yen-liao k'u*) supervised by the Ministry of Revenue (*hu-pu*), each under a Director (*lang-chung*), rank 5a, but collectively overseen by a Grand Minister (*ta-ch'en*) of the Imperial Household Department (*nei-wu fu*). P7.

4866 *sān kuān* 三官
(1) **The Three … Officials**, a common collective designation prefixed with specifying terms; e.g., see *shui-heng san kuan*, *t'ing-wei san kuan*, *chien-k'ang san kuan*. (2) Occasional variant of *san kung* (**Three Dukes**).

4867 *sān kuǎn* 三館
SUNG: **Three Institutes,** collective reference to the Historiography Institute (*shih-kuan*), the Institute for the Glorification of Literature (*chao-wen kuan*), and the Academy of Scholarly Worthies (*chi-hsien yüan*), which in the aggregate constituted what was called the Academy for the Veneration of Literature (*ch'ung-wen yüan*). SP: *trois collèges*. P25.

4868 *sàn-kuān* 散官
SUI–CH'ING: **Prestige Title,** a title in a hierarchy of up to several dozens having no literal relation to one's actual functional activity but awarded solely to fix one's rank status and indicate one's seniority within a particular rank category such as 5b; used in the civil service, the military service, the corps of palace eunuchs, groups of specialized professionals such as physicians and astrologers, etc. Growing out of the Ch'in–Han practice of awarding honorific titles (see *chia*, *chia-kuan*) through usage in the era of N-S Division to give status to officials while not serving on active duty and to some other persons entirely outside the officialdom (see *san*, detached), the term passed through a transition in Sui to become the names, so to speak, of official ranks, which were not always revealed by the titles of whatever posts one happened to occupy. Into the Sung period prestige titles continued to be used as indicators of rank status, regardless of either the nominal office (*pen-kuan*) or the duty assignment (*ch'ai-ch'ien*), from late T'ang allowing great disparities among ranks, nominal posts, and actual functions. Reforms of 1080 greatly reduced the extravagant use of prestige titles by redesignating them nominal offices (*chieh-kuan*) and, apparently for the first time, making them rather than nominal offices the basis on which official salaries were paid. In 1120 this change was made more emphatic with the adoption of a new set of titles under the generic designation salary offices (*chi-lu kuan*). From Chin through Ch'ing the early *san-kuan* practices were stabilized; salaries were again determined by nominal offices, nominal offices increasingly reflected actual functions, and the terms *san-kuan*, *chieh-kuan*, and the combination *san-chieh* were all used synonymously for standardized prestige titles that most specifically denoted rank and seniority within ranks. From the outset, prestige titles were generally variably-prefixed Grand Masters (*ta-fu*) from ranks 1 through 5 and variably-prefixed Gentlemen (*lang*) from ranks 6 through 9 in the civil service, and their counterparts in the military service were normally Generals (*chiang-chün*) and Commandants (*hsiao-wei*). There were enough prestige titles so that an official could be promoted in the hierarchy of prestige titles without a change of actual rank (*p'in*) or nominal office. In Ming and Ch'ing an official was entitled to an appropriate prestige title after completing his initial 3-year term of active duty, and he could request that the same title be conferred (posthumously if need be) on his father and grandfather. In formal documentation prestige titles took precedence over nominal offices; e.g., a Ming official might be designated Grand Master for Excellent Counsel (*chia-i ta-fu*, the first or lowest of 3 prestige titles awarded to officials of rank 3a), Vice Minister of War and Concurrent Vice Censor-in-chief (*ping-pu shih-lang chien fu tu yü-shih*, both nominal offices of rank 3a); and so cumbersome a designation might in addition be preceded or followed by reference to a detached duty assignment such as Grand Coordinator of Kiangsi Province (*hsün-fu chiang-hsi*).

RR: *titre qui ne comporte pas de fonction.* SP: *titre de prestige ou fonctionnaire ne comportant pas de fonction.* P68.

4869   *sàn-kuǎn* 散館 or 散官

CH'ING: **Released from the Institute** or **Released into Officialdom** (the 2nd form is aberrant and not to be confused with *san-kuan*, Prestige Title), terms referring to a change in status from that of Hanlin Bachelor (*shu-chi-shih*). Selected from among promising new Metropolitan Graduates (*chin-shih*), Hanlin Bachelors were assigned for careful nurturing of their talents to the Institute of Advanced Study (*shu-ch'ang kuan*) in the Hanlin Academy (*han-lin yüan*). After completing 3 years of intense literary studies, they were "released from the Institute" to take a special imperial literary examination. Those who did well were "retained in the Institute" (*liu-kuan*) as Senior Compilers (*hsiu-chuan*) and Junior Compilers (*pien-hsiu*) in the Hanlin Academy, the term *kuan* in this instance apparently used as an archaic reference to the long nonexistent Historiography Institute (*shih-kuan, kuo-shih kuan*). The others were "released from the Institute" (the same *san-kuan,* confusingly used in a 2nd sense) to begin careers in the administrative hierarchy as appointees in Ministries (*pu*) and other agencies of the central government or, commonly, as District Magistrates (*chih-hsien*). Cf. *san* (separate, unattached, etc.). P23.

4870   *sān kuǎn shū-yüàn* 三館書院

SUNG: lit., library of the 3 institutes; quasiofficial reference to the **Academy for the Veneration of Literature** (*ch'ung-wen yüan,* q.v.). SP: *bibliothèque des trois collèges.*

4871   *sān kūng* 三公

Three Dukes: from antiquity a collective reference to dignitaries who were officially considered the 3 paramount aides to the ruler and held the highest possible ranks in the officialdom, though from N. Wei to Yüan commonly superseded or overshadowed by the term Three Preceptors (*san shih,* q.v.). The posts were seldom conferred capriciously and were considered regular substantive posts throughout history; until Sui each was provided with subordinate officials constituting an Office (*fu*). However, from mid-Han on appointees as such had no functional responsibilities except to attend audiences and provide counsel to rulers when called on. Nevertheless, appointees were almost always officials with additional functional appointments that gave them effective supervisory authority over the central government, e.g., as Grand Councilors (*tsaihsiang*) or Grand Secretaries (*ta hsüeh-shih*). From Chou on, the individual titles of the Three Dukes were ordinarily Grand Preceptor (*t'ai-shih*), Grand Mentor (*t'ai-fu*), and Grand Guardian (*t'ai-pao*). Notable exceptions included the Ch'in–Former Han era, when the Three Dukes consisted of the Counselor-in-chief (*ch'eng-hsiang*), the Censor-in-chief (*yü-shih ta-fu*), and the Defender-in-chief (*t'ai-wei*) and their variants. In Later Han the old-style Three Dukes were restored with the collective designation Superior Dukes (*shang-kung*). After Han, in Chin and the S. Dynasties, Grand Preceptor was commonly replaced with Grand Steward (*ta-tsai*). From Sui till 1122 in Sung and Liao, while the designation Three Preceptors prevailed, the term Three Dukes also continued in use, referring to the Defender-in-chief (*t'ai-wei*), the Minister of Education (*ssu-t'u*), and the Minister of Works (*ssu-k'ung*), of equal rank but slightly less prestige than the Three Preceptors. In Chou the Three Dukes ranked as Feudal Lords (*chu-hou*); in Han their rank swelled to 10,000 bushels; from the era of N-S Division they normally ranked 1a. A group of related titles of slightly less prestige was the Three Solitaries (*san ku*), e.g., Junior Preceptor (*shao-*

shih), likewise derived from ancient Chou usage and revived in Sung; and complete sets of Three Dukes and Three Solitaries were also commonly assigned to the Heir Apparent and prefixed accordingly, e.g., as Grand Preceptor of the Heir Apparent (*t'ai-tzu t'ai-shih*). HB: three excellencies. RR+SP: *trois ducs.* P67.

4872   *sān-kūng ts'áo* 三公曹

HAN–N-S DIV: **Section for the Three Dukes,** from 29 B.C. one of 5 (later 6) Sections comprising the Imperial Secretariat (*shang-shu t'ai*), each headed by an Imperial Secretary (*shang-shu*); handled correspondence pertaining to judicial and other business between the Emperor and his chief ministers (see under *san kung*). In the post-Han development of the eventual Department of State Affairs (*shang-shu sheng*), this Section was in effect a Ministry of Justice headed by a Minister (*shang-shu*) until the 280s, when the Ministry of Personnel (*li-pu*) took over its functions. It promptly reappeared and persisted through the S. Dynasties as a unit in the Ministry of Personnel, still concerned principally with judicial matters, headed by a Director (*lang*); it was adopted by the N. Dynasties as a unit of the Ministry of Palace Affairs (see *tien-chung ts'ao*), headed by a Director (*lang-chung*), but it was not continued by Sui. HB: bureau of the three excellencies. P13.

4873   *sān láng* 三郎

CH'IN: **Three Court Gentlemen,** collective reference to the 3 categories into which most expectant appointees and officials awaiting reappointment were assigned: Inner Gentlemen (*chung-lang*), Outer Gentlemen (*wai-lang*), and Standby Gentlemen (? *san-lang*). See under *lang.*

4874   *sàn-láng* 散郎

Standby Gentleman (?). (1) CH'IN: a member of one of 3 categories into which expectant appointees serving as courtiers were assigned, collectively called the Three Court Gentlemen (*san lang*). Also see *lang.* (2) HAN: occasional variant of *wai-lang* (Outer Gentleman).

4875   *sān-láng wèi-shìh* 三郎衛士

N-S DIV (N. Wei): lit., guardsmen of the Three Court Gentlemen: **Imperial Bodyguard** staffed by aristocratic Courtiers (*chung-san*), an intimate guard unit commanded by a Corps Leader (*ch'uang-chiang*) under the supervision of 4 Directors of Palace Attendants (*nei-shih chang*). Cf. *san lang, san shu.*

4876   *sān-lǎo* 三老

CH'IN-HAN: lit., the 3 stages of old age, presumably the 50s, 60s, and 70s; hence someone in one of these age groups: **Elder,** one of 3 appointees from among the resident population in the quasiofficial sub-District (*hsien*) administration of a Township (*hsiang*); normally a man of good character more than 50 years old, responsible for providing moral leadership and discipline. From among the Township Elders, one was commonly designated District Elder (*hsien san-lao*); and at least in Later Han there were some Commandery (*chün*) Elders, presumably chosen from among the District Elders. HB: thrice venerable.

4877   *sān-lì* 三吏

Lit., 3 functionaries: throughout history an occasional unofficial reference to the **Three Dukes** (*san kung*).

4878   *sàn-lì* 散吏

N-S DIV (Chin): **Irregular Functionary,** designation of a commoner used (requisitioned from the resident population?) on the headquarters staff of a District (*hsien*), differentiated from regular subofficial functionaries (*li, hsü-*

li)—lit., "functioning suboffical functionaries" (*chih-li;* cf. *chih-kuan,* Functioning Official). Even though irregular, they were officially authorized on a quota basis: from 18 regulars and 4 irregulars in the smallest Districts, with fewer than 300 households, to 88 regulars and 26 irregulars in the largest Districts, with 3,000 or more households. P54.

4879 *sàn-liáo* 散僚
T'ANG: **Unoccupied Placeman,** an unofficial derisive reference to an appointee of very low rank or to any official who did little if any actual work. Cf. *san-pei.*

4880 *sàn-lìng* 散令
N-S DIV (N. Wei): apparently a variant of *chung-san ling* (**Director of Courtiers**)

4881 *sān lù* 三路
SUNG: **Three Circuits,** collective reference to the protoprovincial Circuits (*lu*) surrounding the N. Sung dynastic capital, Kaifeng: i.e., Ching-chi, Ching-tung, Ching-hsi.

4882 *sān mèi* 三昧
SUNG: lit., the 3 mysteries, a Buddhist term; hence a master of the 3 mysteries (?): **Savant,** unofficial reference to an Academician (*hsüeh-shih*) of the Hanlin Academy (*hanlin yüan*). On leaving their duty stations, Academicians commonly exited from the imperial palace via the Silver Pavilion Gate (*yin-t'ai men*); those who left afoot were called the Junior (*hsiao*) Savants, whereas those who left on horseback were called the Senior (*ta*) Savants.

4883 *sān pàn* 三伴
MING: **Three Companions,** collective reference to Reader-companions (*pan-tu*), Lecturer-companions (*pan-chiang*), and Secretary-companions (*pan-shu*), lowly members of Princely Administrations (*wang-fu*) during the 1398–1402 period only. P69.

4884 *sān pān* 三班
SUNG: **Three Ranks,** a reference to positions taken by participants in court audiences, specifically in order of eminence from high to low: the Left Rank (*tso-pan*), the Right Rank (*yu-pan*), and the Crosswise Rank (*heng-pan*), all as seen from the Emperor's viewpoint. Most commonly used in reference to lowly military officers of ranks 8 and 9, and particularly to those of rank 9b, who bore prestige titles (*san-kuan*) as Attendant of the Three Ranks (*san-pan feng-chih*) or Gentleman for Fostering Temperance (*ch'eng-chieh lang*). SP: *trois classes d'intendance dans le palais.*

4885 *sān-pān chièh-chíh* 三班借職
SUNG: **Attendant of the Three Ranks,** prestige title (*san-kuan*) awarded to officials of rank 9b, mainly those in military service; superseded by the title *ch'eng-hsin lang* (Gentleman of Trust), date not clear. SP: *stagiaire de l'intendant inférieur du palais.* P68.

4886 *sān-pān fèng-chíh* 三班奉職
SUNG: **Attendant of the Three Ranks,** prestige title (*san-kuan*) awarded to officials of rank 9b, mainly those in military service; superseded by the title *ch'eng-chieh lang* (Gentleman for Fostering Temperance), date not clear. SP: *intendant inférieur du palais.* P68.

4887 *sān-pān nèi-shìh* 三班內侍
SUNG: lit., inner attendants of the 3 (lowest?) ranks (in assemblies for court audiences): common general reference to **Eunuchs** under the Court of Palace Attendants (*hsüanhui yüan*); not to be confused with junior military officers commonly known by the prefix *san-pan,* or with agencies known as Inner Offices (*nei-ssu*). P38.

4888 *sān-pān shǐh-ch'én* 三班使臣
SUNG: **Commissioners of the Three Ranks,** common designation of military officers of the low 8th and 9th ranks (see *san pan*) when on temporary duty assignments; e.g., often found among military personnel expediting water transport of grain to the dynastic capital. P60.

4889 *sān-pān yüàn* 三班院
SUNG: **Bureau of Lesser Military Assignments,** an element in the Ministry of Personnel (*li-pu*) appointments process (see under *hsüan*), by which the selection of men for appointments or reappointments was delegated to different executive officials of the Ministry according to the ranks and the services (civil or military) of the appointees. This Bureau, presided over by the Vice Minister (*shih-lang*) of the Ministry, dealt with military appointees of ranks 8 and 9. In 1080 the Bureau was abolished, but the process continued under the name Junior Military Appointments Process (*shih-lang yu-hsüan*). Also see *yu-hsüan* (Military Appointments Process), *shih-lang hsüan* (Junior Appointments Process). SP: *bureau de nomination militaire.* P5.

4890 *sān-pèi* 三輩
HAN: **In unoccupied status,** a term used, apparently not derisively, in reference to a vacant office or to a position requiring little activity. Cf. *san-liao.*

4891 *sān pīn* 三嬪
SUI: **Three Concubines,** collective reference to 3 secondary or tertiary wives of the Emperor, rank =3a; of lesser standing than the traditional Nine Concubines (*chiu pin*), 2a. Specific titles not clear.

4892 *sàn-pīng* 散兵
Irregular Troops: from Sui on if not earlier, a common reference to loyal military groups not part of the regular governmental military organization (see *kuan-ping, kuan-chün*), though sometimes enjoying quasiofficial recognition. See *i-ping, chia-ping.*

4893 *sān pù* 三部
SUNG: lit., the 3 Ministries: variant of *san ssu* (**State Finance Commission**) in early Sung.

4894 *sān-pù kōu-yüàn* 三部勾院
SUNG: **Comptroller's Office,** one in each of the 3 agencies constituting the State Finance Commission (*san ssu*) of early Sung, each headed by a mid-level central government official on special duty assignment as concurrent Comptroller (*kou-yüan p'an-kuan*). SP: *cour du contrôle des trois offices.*

4895 *sān-sè jén* 三色人
SUNG: **Men of the Three (Lesser) Categories,** collective reference to candidates for official appointments who had only temporary status as officials, or who sought transfer or had been transferred from status as suboffical functionaries (*li*), or who were "qualified by contribution" (*chienna ch'u-shen*), i.e., who had made voluntary contributions of money or grain to the state in a time of emergency. Except in the earliest years of the dynasty, candidates in these categories had no hope of successful careers in government.

4896 *sān shàng-fāng* 三尚方
N-S DIV (San-kuo Wei)–SUI: **Three Service fficials,** prefixed Central (*chung*), Left (*tso*), and Right (*yu*) a collective reference to the heads of artisan units tha produced handicraft goods of all sorts for the imperial household, succeeding Han's unified Directorate for Imperial Manufactories (*shang-fang*) and eventually superseded by the T'ang (possibly Sui) Directorate for Imperial Manufactories (*shao-*

fu chien). Normally subordinate to the Chamberlain for the Palace Revenues (*shao-fu*, at times *t'ai-fu*). Separation of responsibilities not always clear, but collectively produced silk goods, vehicles, fans, and some weapons, and made minor construction and building repairs. P37, 38.

4897   *sān shàng-shǔ* 三尙署
T'ANG: **Three Service Offices,** a collective reference to the Central, Left, and Right Service Offices (*shang-shu*) of the Directorate for Imperial Manufactories (*shao-fu chien*), each headed by a Director (*ling*), rank 7b2. RR: *trois ateliers impériaux.* P38.

4898   *sān shào* 三少
Three Juniors: from T'ang on if not earlier, a sometimes official, sometimes unofficial collective reference to the dignitaries otherwise known as the Three Solitaries (*san ku*) or, particularly if prefixed *t'ai-tzu*, the Three Solitaries of the Heir Apparent (*t'ai-tzu san ku*). RR: *trois seconds (précepteurs).* SP: *trois précepteurs, maître et gardien seconds (de l'héritier du trône).* P67.

4899   *sān shè* 三舍
SUNG: **Three Colleges,** a reference to the 3 divisions of the National University (*t'ai-hsüeh*) among which students were divided according to their ability from the 1070s; about 20% of the graduates of the Outer College (*wai-she*) continued in the Inner College (*nei-she*), and less than half of its graduates continued in the Superior College (*shang-she*). SP: *trois collèges.* P34.

4900   *sān shěng* 三省
N-S DIV–YÜAN: **Three Departments,** a quasiofficial collective reference to the Department of State Affairs (*shang-shu sheng*), the Chancellery (*men-hsia sheng*), and the Secretariat (*chung-shu sheng*), traditionally the 3 topmost agencies of the central government. SP: *trois départements.*

4901   *sān shěng shū-mì yüàn* 三省樞密院
SUNG: **The Three Departments and the Bureau of Military Affairs,** a combined reference to the top-echelon administrative agencies of the central government collectively called the Three Departments (*san sheng*), i.e., the Department of State Affairs (*shang-shu sheng*), the Chancellery (*men-hsia sheng*), and the Secretariat (*chung-shu sheng*), and the central government's paramount military agency, the Bureau of Military Affairs (*shu-mi yüan*); in S. Sung all these were virtually a single conglomerate supervised by Grand Councilors (*tsai-hsiang*), with some subordinate officials and agencies serving the conglomerate as a whole, e.g., Archivists of the Three Departments and the Bureau of Military Affairs (... *chia-ko kuan*), appointed from 1215.

4902   *sān shìh* 三事
Lit., the 3 (in charge of) affairs: from antiquity an occasional unofficial reference to the **Three Dukes** (*san kung*); occurs especially in poetry. Also see *san-shih ta-fu.*

4903   *sān shìh* 三使
SUNG: **Three Commissioners,** collective reference to the heads of the 3 early Sung agencies known in the aggregate as the State Finance Commission (*san ssu*); see *yen-t'ieh ssu, tu-chih ssu, hu-pu ssu.* Cf. *san-ssu shih.* SP: *trois commissaires.*

4904   *sān shìh* 三師
Three Preceptors. (1) N-S DIV (N. Wei, N. Ch'i)–YÜAN: alternate collective reference to the eminent central government dignitaries known in other periods from antiquity as the Three Dukes (*san kung*): Grand Preceptor (*t'ai-shih*), Grand Mentor (*t'ai-fu*), and Grand Guardian (*t'ai-pao*). The

term *san-shih* was used in Sui only to c. 604, in T'ang from 632 or 637, in Sung and Liao to 1122. RR+SP: *trois précepteurs de l'empereur.* P67. (2) MING–CH'ING: occasional unofficial reference to the Three Dukes.

4905   *sān-shìh hsüéh* 三氏學
SUNG–CH'ING: **Schools of the Three Sage Clans,** from the 1080s a collective reference to state schools established near the Confucian Temple (*k'ung-miao, hsüan-sheng miao*) in modern Shantung for educating descendants of Confucius, his disciple Yen Hui, and his later admirer Mencius. In Ch'ing a temple to the Confucian disciple Tseng-tzu was added, making Schools of the Four Sage Clans (*ssu-shih hsüeh*).

4906   *sān-shìh k'ō* 三式科
YÜAN: **Section for Astrological Interpretation,** one of 5 Sections (*k'o*) in the Directorate of Astronomy (*ssu-t'ien t'ai, ssu-t'ien chien*), headed by 2 Clerks (*kuan-kou*), rank 9b; probably under the intermediary supervision of the Directorate's Superintendent of Training (*t'i-hsüeh*), as a training unit. The term *san-shih* refers to 3 types of celestial phenomena, but identifications differ. P35.

4907   *sān shìh shàng-kūng* 三師上公
N-S DIV (N. Wei, N. Ch'i): **Three Superior Duke Preceptors,** common variant of *san shih* (Three Preceptors) as a collective reference to the Grand Preceptor (*t'ai-shih*), Grand Mentor (*t'ai-fu*), and Grand Guardian (*t'ai-pao*). Also see *san kung, shang-kung, t'ai-fu shang-kung.* P67.

4908   *sān-shìh tà-fū* 三事大夫
Lit., the 3 grand masters of affairs: from antiquity an occasional unofficial reference to the **Three Dukes** (*san kung*); occurs especially in poetry; sometimes abbreviated to *san shih.*

4909   *sān shǔ* 三署
HAN: **Three Corps,** a reference, possibly not common until Later Han, to the 3 categories in which expectant appointees called Court Gentlemen (*lang*) were differentiated by rank; comparable to the Ch'in dynasty term Three Court Gentlemen (*san lang*). The 3 groups were the Inner Gentlemen (*chung-lang*), the Attendant Gentlemen (*shih-lang*), and the Gentlemen of the Interior (*lang-chung*), each loosely organized under a Leader of Court Gentlemen (*chung-lang chiang*) under overall supervision of the Chamberlain for Attendants (*lang-chung ling, kuang-lu-hsün*). HB: three corps. P5, 26.

4910   *sān-shǔ láng* 三署郎
HAN: **Court Gentlemen of the Three Corps,** collective reference to all expectant appointees known as Court Gentlemen (*lang*); also see *san lang, san shu.* P5.

4911   *sān shuài* 三帥
SUNG: **Three Marshals,** unofficial reference to the 3 senior posts in the N. Sung Palace Command (*tien-ch'ien ssu*): Commander-in-chief (*tu chih-hui shih*), Vice Commander-in-chief (*fu tu chih-hui shih*), and Inspector-in-chief (*tu yü-hou*). SP: *trois généraux.*

4912   *sān ssū* 三司
Lit., 3 Offices; it should be kept in mind that in any particular context the term might refer to 3 previously mentioned agencies of any sort. (1) HAN: **Three Dignitaries,** from A.D. 52 a collective reference to the Minister of Education (*ssu-t'u*), the Defender-in-chief (*t'ai-wei*), and the Minister of Works (*ssu-k'ung*), more commonly known as the Three Dukes (*san kung*). (2) T'ANG: **Three Monitoring Offices,** collective reference to Attendant Censors (*shih*

yü-shih) of the Censorate (*yü-shih t'ai*), Supervising Secretaries (*chi-shih-chung*) of the Chancellery (*men-hsia sheng*), and Secretariat Drafters (*chung-shu she-jen*), who on a rotational basis attended all court audiences to note any breach of prescribed conduct among the participants, to accept complaints lodged against officials, and to accept for investigation any appeals from persons who believed they had been wronged by officials and had found no redress in the regular administrative hierarchy. (3) T'ANG–5 DYN: **Three Judicial Agencies,** collective reference to the Ministry of Justice (*hsing-pu*), the Censorate, and the Court of Judicial Review₁ (*ta-li ssu*), the executive officials of which were summoned irregularly into a tribunal that considered legal cases of great importance and made recommendations for imperial decision; comparable to the later term *san fa-ssu*, q.v. When the heads of the 3 agencies formed such a tribunal, it was called the Senior Three Judicial Offices (*ta san-ssu*); when 2nd-level executive officials were convened, the tribunal was called the Junior Three Judicial Offices (*hsiao san-ssu*). (4) T'ANG–5 DYN: **Three Fiscal Agencies:** during the last T'ang century and into the Five Dynasties era, a collective reference to the office of the Salt Monopoly Commissioner (*yen-t'ieh shih*), the Tax Bureau (*tu-chih ssu*), and the Census Bureau (*hu-pu ssu*). In T'ang all were commonly headed by Grand Councilors (*tsai-hsiang*); in the Five Dynasties era, commonly coordinated by a State Fiscal Commissioner (*san-ssu shih*). (5) SUNG: **State Finance Commission,** the most important fiscal agency in the central government until the 1070s; then discontinued, its functions being taken over primarily by the Ministry of Revenue (*hu-pu*) from c. 1080. Developing out of the T'ang–Five Dynasties institutions described under (4) above, this was an aggregation of the Salt and Iron Monopoly Bureau (*yen-t'ieh ssu*), the Tax Bureau (*tu-chih ssu*), and the Census Bureau (*hu-pu ssu*); sometimes a consolidated agency under one Commissioner (*shih*), sometimes fragmented into 3 autonomous agencies each with a Commissioner. From 993 to 994 consolidated under a Supreme Commissioner of Accounts (*tsung-chi shih*) and divided into 2 large regional jurisdictions called the Left and Right Accounts (*tso-chi, yu-chi*), sharing supervision over 10 territorial Circuits (*tao*); but in 994 the 3 separate commissions were reinstated. A late reorganization (date not clear) transformed the Salt and Iron Monopoly Bureau into a Tax Transport Bureau (*chuan-yün ssu*) and the Tax Bureau into a Stabilization Fund Bureau (*ch'ang-p'ing ssu*). Each of the constituent Bureaus had subsidiary Sections (*an*), and there were various minor offices that served the 3 Bureaus collectively, normally each headed by an Administrative Assistant (*p'an-kuan*): General Accounting Office (*tu mo-k'an ssu*), General Money Circulating Office (*tu chu-hsia chih-shou ssu*), Inventory Office (*ch'ü-shou ssu*), General Deficits Monitoring Office (*tu li-ch'ien ssu*), General Wastage Monitoring Office (*tu p'ing-yu ssu*), Mail Distribution Office (*k'ai-ch'ai ssu*), Distribution Office (*fa-fang ssu*), Storage Monitoring Office (*ts'ui-ch'ü ssu*), Receiving Office (*shou-shih ssu*), and Service Allocation Office (*ya-ssu*). Also see *p'an san-ssu*, *chih-chih san-ssu t'iao-li ssu*. SP: *commission des finances ou tri-commissariat*. P7. (6) MING: **Three Provincial Offices,** collective generic reference to Provincial Administration Commissions (*ch'eng-hsüan pu-cheng shih ssu*), Provincial Surveillance Commissions (*t'i-hsing an-ch'a shih ssu*), and Regional Military Commissions (*tu chih-hui shih ssu*). (7) CH'ING: **Three Provincial Offices,** collective generic reference to Provincial Administration Commissions, Provincial Surveillance Commissions, and Provincial Education Commissioners (*t'i-tu hsüeh-cheng*).

4913   *sān ssù*   三寺

N-S DIV (N. Ch'i), SUI–T'ANG: **Three Courts,** collective reference to 3 service agencies under the Supervisor of the Household (*chan-shih*) of the Heir Apparent or, for part of Sui, the Secretariat of the Heir Apparent (*men-hsia fang*): specifically, the Household Provisioner's Court (*chia-ling ssu*), the Court of the Watches (*lei-keng ssu*), and the Livery Service of the Heir Apparent (*p'u-ssu*). RR: *trois cours*. P26.

4914   *sān-ssū k'uài-chì ssū*   三司會計司

SUNG: **State Finance Commission Accounting Office,** designation of a consolidation of the 3 formerly rather autonomous Bureaus (*ssu*) of the Commission (see *san ssu*) into a single agency in 1074, headed by one Grand Councilor (*tsai-hsiang*) as Supervisor (*t'i-chü*); abolished in a general governmental reorganization in 1080. SP: *bureau des comptes des finances*. P7.

4915   *sān-ssū shǐh*   三司使

Lit.; commissioner(s) of the 3 Offices; a reference to any of the officials noted in the *san ssu* (3 Offices) entry above and to some others as well, especially: (1) T'ANG: **Three Monitoring Surrogates,** a term used in lieu of Three Monitoring Offices (see *san ssu* under #2) when the Heir Apparent was serving as Regent (*chien-kuo*) in the absence of the Emperor from the capital, indicating 3 members of the Heir Apparent's household staff who undertook to receive and analyze memorials to the throne—the Supervisor of the Household (*chan-shih*) and the Mentors (*shu-tzu*) in charge of the Left and Right Secretariats of the Heir Apparent (*tso, yu ch'un-fang*). RR: *commissaires des trois services*. (2) T'ANG: **Three Judicial Commissioners,** collective reference to members of the Three Judicial Agencies (see *san ssu* under #3), including a Senior (*ta*) and a Junior (*hsiao*) group. (3) 5 DYN, LIAO: **State Fiscal Commissioner:** in Later T'ang head of 3 Bureaus (*ssu*) as described in the *san ssu* entry (#4); in Liao an all-around manager of Khitan financial interests in North China from his base at modern Peking, which Liao called its Southern Capital, Nan-ching. P8. (4) SUNG: **State Finance Commissioner,** briefly in 993 and then from 1003 to 1069 the single head of the State Finance Commission (see *san ssu* under #5). SP: *commissaire des finances*. P7.

4916   *sān-ssū t'iáo-lì ssū*   三司條例司

SUNG: abbreviation of *chih-chih san-ssu t'iao-li ssu* (**Finance Planning Commission**), q.v.

4917   *sān tà*   三大

Three Greats: occasional unofficial reference to the Three Preceptors (*san shih*) or Three Dukes (*san kung*); less common than *san t'ai* (Three Supremes). P68.

4918   *sān tà-chèng*   三大政

CH'ING: **Three Great Administrations,** unofficial collective reference to the Salt Administration (*yen-cheng*), the Grand Canal Administration (see under *ho-tao tsung-tu*), and the Grain Transport Administration (see under *ts'ao-yün tsung-tsu*).

4919   *sān tà-hsièn*   三大憲

CH'ING: lit., 3 great (defenders of) the fundamental laws: **Three Provincial Authorities,** unofficial collective reference to the Provincial Governor (*hsün-fu*), Provincial Administration Commissioner (*pu-cheng shih*), and Provincial Surveillance Commissioner (*an-ch'a shih*); also see *hsien, feng-hsien*.

4920   *sān tà-yíng*   三大營

MING: **Three Great Training Divisions,** also called Capital Training Divisions (*ching-ying*): military encampments established in 1424 at Peking with auxiliary counterparts at Nanking. Specifically named Division of the Five Armies (*wu-chün ying*), Division of the Three Thousand (*san-ch'ien ying*), and Firearms Division (*shen-chi ying*). Troops of Guard (*wei*) garrisons throughout the empire were rotated to these units for training and service as a kind of combat-ready reserve, under a Superintendent (*t'i-tu*) or Supreme Commander (*tsung-tu*). From 1450 to 1550 these Divisions were overshadowed by a newer type of organization called Integrated Divisions (*t'uan-ying*); and by the late 1550s if not earlier all troops at the capital had been allowed to degenerate into little more than construction gangs. Also see *wei-so, pan-chün.*

4921   sān t'ài 三太
Three Supremes: throughout history a common unofficial collective reference to the central government dignitaries known as the Three Dukes (*san kung*) or Three Preceptors (*san-shih*); also see *san ta* (Three Greats).

4922   sān t'ái 三臺
(1) HAN: **Three Communicating Agencies,** collective reference to 3 agencies that were intended to keep the Emperor in contact with the central administration, the officialdom at large, and foreign states: respectively, the Imperial Secretariat (*shang-shu t'ai;* known unofficially as *chung-t'ai,* Central Pavilion), the Censorate (*yü-shih t'ai;* known unofficially as *hsien-t'ai,* Pavilion of the Fundamental Laws), and the Tribunal of Receptions (*yeh-che t'ai;* known unofficially as *wai-t'ai,* Outer Pavilion). (2) SUI: **Three Surveillance Agencies,** collective reference from c. 604 to the Censorate, the Tribunal of Receptions, and the Tribunal of Inspectors (*ssu-li t'ai*). P16.

4923   sàn-t'īng 散廳
CH'ING: lit., detached Subprefecture, i.e., one not directly under the supervision of a Circuit Intendant (*tao-t'ai*) but part of a Prefecture (*fu*): **Ordinary Subprefecture** as distinguished from an Independent Subprefecture (*chih-li t'ing*), which was not part of a Prefecture but was directly supervised by a Circuit Intendant. Also called *shu-t'ing,* q.v.

4924   sān-t'óu 三頭
T'ANG: **Triple First,** unofficial reference to a man who stood at the head of pass lists in 3 civil service recruitment examinations: a prefectural-level examination at the dynastic capital (*ching-chao chieh-shih*), a Presented Scholar (*chin-shih*) examination, and a special Erudite Literatus (*hung-tz'u*) examination for accelerated advancement. Comparable in prestige to the status of *san-yüan* (Triple First) in later dynasties.

4925   sàn ts'úng-kuān 散從官
Detached as a Retinue Official: in Sung and no doubt other periods as well, referred to a staff member of a unit of territorial administration such as a Prefecture (*chou, fu*), usually not a regular member of the ranked officialdom, who was released from his ordinary duties and assigned temporarily to the retinue of a traveling official from a higher agency; considered in the general category of Guides and Followers (*tao-ts'ung*). SP: *coureur pour les affaires publiques.*

4926   sān tū-tū 三都督
N-S DIV (N. Wei)–SUI: **Three Area Commanders-in-chief,** collective reference to 3 military leaders among whom supervisory responsibility for the state's various Regions (*chou*) was divided: the Commanders-in-chief of Nan-Yü; of Chi-chou, Ting-chou, and Hsiang-chou; and of Chi-ch'ing

(all place-names). N. Ch'i formally changed the title *tu-tu* to *tsung-kuan,* q.v., but the collective term *san tu-tu* continued in use. In Sui the 3 titles were used as honorific or prestige titles (*san-kuan*) for eminent military officers till c. 604, then discontinued. P50.

4927   sān tú-tsò 三獨坐
HAN: lit., 3 who sit alone, i.e., separate from other participants assembled in court audience, at least in part so as to keep all under observation and to impeach or reprimand any who conducted themselves improperly: **Three Venerables,** from about 8 B.C. through Later Han a collective reference to the Director of the Imperial Secretariat (*shang-shu ling*), the de facto head of the Censorate (*yü-shih t'ai*) officially entitled Palace Aide to the Censor-in-chief (*yü-shih chung-ch'eng*), and the Metropolitan Commandant (*ssu-li hsiao-wei*). Also see *tu-tso.*

4928   sàn-tuān 散端
T'ANG: lit., separate from the leader(s) (?): unofficial reference to those **Attendant Censors** (*shih yü-shih*) of the Censorate (*yü-shih t'ai*) who were not authorized to exercise unrestricted censorial powers (?); sources not entirely clear. See *tuan-kung, tsa-tuan.* RR: *chefs détachés (qui n'étaient pas chargés des affaires diverses).* P18.

4929   sān wèi 三衛
Three Capital Guards. (1) T'ANG: collective reference to the categories of personnel who were garrisoned in the palace to provide close personal security for the Emperor, i.e., members of the Bodyguard Garrison (*ch'in-fu*), the 2 Distinguished Garrisons (*hsün-fu*), and the 2 Standby Garrisons (*i-fu*), administered by the Left and Right Guards (*tso-wei, yu-wei*) of the capital's Sixteen Guards (*shih-liu wei*). Since the Garrisons themselves numbered 5, they were commonly referred to as the Five Garrisons (*wu fu*), as in the expression "the Three Capital Guards of the Five Garrisons" (*wu fu chih san wei*). RR: *trois espèces de gardes.* P43. (2) T'ANG: a common but misleading reference to the Three Garrisons (*san fu,* q.v.) in the establishment of the Heir Apparent. P26. (3) SUNG: collective reference to the Palace Command (*tien-ch'ien shih-wei ssu*), the Metropolitan Cavalry Command (*shih-wei ma-chün ssu*), and the Metropolitan Infantry Command (*shih-wei pu-chün ssu*). These 3 were also commonly referred to as the Three Commands (*san ya*). SP: *trois espèces de gardes.* P43.

4930   sàn-wèi 散位
SUI–CH'ING: **Rank Status,** variant of *san-kuan* (Prestige Title).

4931   sān yá 三衙
SUNG: **Three Commands,** collective reference to the Palace Command (*tien-ch'ien shih-wei ssu*), the Metropolitan Cavalry Command (*shih-wei ma-chün ssu*), and the Metropolitan Infantry Command (*shih-wei pu-chün ssu*). These 3 were also commonly referred to as the Three Capital Guards (*san wei*). Also see *erh ssu* (Two Commands). SP: *trois bureaux militaires.* P43.

4932   sān yĭn 三尹
CH'ING: lit., 3rd (in rank order) Governor (?): unofficial reference to the **Assistant Magistrate** (*chu-pu*) of a District (*hsien*), who ordinarily ranked below both a Magistrate (*chih-hsien*) and a Vice Magistrate (*ch'eng*).

4933   sān-yüán 三元
SUNG–CH'ING: **Triple First,** quasiofficial reference to the extremely rare man who stood first on the pass lists of each of the 3 levels of civil service recruitment examinations: in

Sung and Chin, the Prefectural Examination (*chieh-shih*), the Metropolitan Examination (*sheng-shih*), and the Palace Examination (*t'ing-shih*); from Yüan to Ch'ing, the Provincial Examination (*hsiang-shih*), the Metropolitan Examination (*hui-shih*), and the Palace Examination (*t'ing-shih* or *tien-shih*). See *san-t'ou, chieh-yüan, hui-yüan, chuang-yüan.*

4934 *sān yüàn* 三院
(1) T'ANG–YÜAN: **Three Bureaus** of the Censorate (*yü-shih t'ai*): Headquarters Bureau (*t'ai-yüan*), Palace Bureau (*tien-yüan*), and Investigation Bureau (*ch'a-yüan*). RR+SP: *trois cours.* P18. (2) CH'ING: **Three Special Agencies** of the Imperial Household Department (*nei-wu fu*): the Palace Stud (*shang-ssu yüan*), Court of Imperial Armaments (*wu-pei yüan*), and Imperial Parks Administration (*feng-ch'en yüan*).

4935 *sàn-yüèh* 散樂
Lit., separate music, in the sense that it was folk or popular music rather than music in the formal, classical style; apparently as early as Han referred to all sorts of vaudeville-like court entertainments including but not restricted to musical ones, and throughout history designated, not only such entertainments, but also the **Entertainers** who performed in them. In T'ang 100 such Entertainers were authorized for the Imperial Music Office (*t'ai-yüeh shu*) in the Court of Imperial Sacrifices (*t'ai-ch'ang ssu*) as permanent (*ch'ang-shang*) staff specialists, and 1,000 more were authorized to be requisitioned on rotational service from Prefectures (*chou*) throughout the empire. RR: *musicien de musique profane.*

4936 *sàng-chù* 喪祝
CHOU: **Funerary Chanter,** 2 ranked as Senior Servicemen (*shang-shih*); members of the Ministry of Rites (*ch'un-kuan*), responsible primarily for escorting funeral carriages. See *chih-sang.* CL: *officier des prières faites dans les cérémonies funèbres, invocateur des funérailles*

4937 *sǎo-sǎ yüàn-tzǔ* 掃洒院子
SUNG: **Palace Sweeper,** unspecified number of eunuchs of the Palace Domestic Service (*nei-shih sheng*). SP: *chargé de balayer la cour.*

4938 *sè-cháng* 色長
Appearance Monitor, apparently in charge of checking on the costumes and the overall visual impression given by court musicians and dancers; cf. *p'ai-chang* (File Leader). (1) SUNG: 3 non-official, probably hereditary professionals in the Office of Musical Instruction (*ch'ien-hsia chiao-fang so*) of the Court of Imperial Sacrifices (*t'ai-ch'ang ssu*). SP: *chef de section (musique).* (2) MING–CH'ING: 17 in the Music Office (*chiao-fang ssu*), at least by early Ch'ing. In 1723 all hereditary musicians were liberated from their service obligations, and thereafter court musicians were chosen from among gifted amateurs. Whether or not the title *se-chang* survived the 1729 division of the Music Office into a Music Office (*ho-sheng shu*) and an Imperial Music Office (*shen-yüeh shu*) is not clear. P10.

4939 *sè-ch'én* 穡臣
Minister of Husbandry: from the era of N-S Division, an unofficial reference to any fiscal official of high status such as a Minister of Revenue (*hu-pu shang-shu*).

4940 *sè-fū* 嗇夫
Lit., a collector, keeper, miser; occurs from high antiquity in titles apparently relating to fiscal matters, but of low status. (1) Throughout history a common unofficial reference, normally derisive, to very lowly members of the official-

dom: **Functionary.** (2) CH'IN–N-S DIV (S. Dyn.): **Husbander,** one of a group of personages chosen to deal with affairs of their home Townships (*hsiang*) in the system of sub-District (*hsien*) organization of the population; principally responsible for tax collections, but also listened to people's complaints; sometimes described traditionally as having been a local police authority. (3) HAN: **Bailiff,** found in lowly status in agencies of all sorts, apparently responsible principally for maintaining supplies. HB: bailiff. P37, 40.

4941 *sè-mù jén* 色目人
YÜAN: **Special Category Men,** 2nd highest of 4 social castes ordained by the Mongol government; an amalgam of non-Mongol, non-Chinese peoples from Central and Western Asia and even Europe, whose social and political privileges were exceeded only by those of the Mongols themselves; below them in the hierarchy came all former subjects of the Jurchen Chin dynasty in North China—Chinese, Jurchen, and Khitan alike—all called *han-jen* (Chinese); and at the bottom were former subjects of S. Sung in South China, called *nan-jen* (Southerners). The term *se-mu* is a compound of words meaning kind, sort, category, etc.; what might seem to be its literal meaning, "colored eyes," is of no relevance.

4942 *sēng-chèng* 僧正
Lit. head or rectifier (? of Buddhists. (1) N-S DIV: **Buddhist Chief,** a state-designated monk responsible for the whole Buddhist clergy in Later Ch'in (384–417), under supervision of the Chamberlain for Dependencies (*ta hung-lu*), possibly continuing through the N. Dynasties till N. Wei (see *seng-t'ung*). (2) MING–CH'ING: **Buddhist Superior** in a Subprefecture or Department (both *chou*); see *seng-cheng ssu.* Also see *seng-kuan.*

4943 *sēng-chèng ssū* 僧正司
MING–CH'ING: **Subprefectural** (in Ch'ing **Departmental**) **Buddhist Registry,** an agency in each Subprefecture or Department (both *chou*) responsible for monitoring the numbers, qualifications, and conduct of all Buddhist monks in its jurisdiction; headed by a senior resident monk designated by the state as Buddhist Superior (*seng-cheng*), without official rank. Supervised by a Prefectural Buddhist Registry (*seng-kang ssu*), a Central Buddhist Registry (*seng-lu ssu*) in the dynastic capital, and ultimately the Ministry of Rites (*li-pu*).

4944 *sēng-chīh-pù ch'éng* 僧祇部丞
N-S DIV (N. Ch'i): **Aide for the Mahāsanghikāh Sect** (of Buddhism), on the staff of the Supervisorate of Monasteries (*tien-ssu shu*) in the Court for Dependencies (*hung-lu ssu*); *seng-chih* is the Chinese transcription of the Sanskrit term *sānghikāh,* meaning a monastic establishment. P17.

4945 *sēng-hùi ssū* 僧會司
MING–CH'ING: **District Buddhist Registry,** an agency in each District (*hsien*) responsible for monitoring the numbers, qualifications, and conduct of all Buddhist monks in its jurisdiction; headed by a senior resident monk designated by the state as Buddhist Superior (*seng-hui*), without official rank. Supervised by a Prefectural Buddhist Registry (*seng-kang ssu*), a Central Buddhist Registry (*seng-lu ssu*) in the dynastic capital, and ultimately the Ministry of Rites (*li-pu*).

4946 *sēng-kāng ssū* 僧綱司
MING–CH'ING: **Prefectural Buddhist Registry,** an agency in each Prefecture (*fu*) responsible for monitoring the numbers, qualifications, and conduct of all Buddhist monks in

its jurisdiction; headed by a senior resident monk designated by the state as Buddhist Superior (*seng-kang*), without official rank. Supervised by the Central Buddhist Registry (*seng-lu ssu*) at the dynastic capital, and ultimately by the Ministry of Rites (*lǐ-pu*).

4947   *sēng-kuān* 僧官
Buddhist Authorities, collective reference to Buddhist monks recognized by the state as heads of all Buddhist monastic establishments within a specified jurisdiction, whether a District (*hsien*) or the state as a whole; responsible for monitoring the numbers, qualifications, and conduct of Buddhist monks and nuns. Specific titles originated in the era of N-S Division with *seng-cheng* (Buddhist Chief), *seng-t'ung* (Buddhist Controller), etc.; the practice culminated in the establishment of Buddhist Registries (see under *seng-lu ssu*) from late T'ang through Ch'ing times.

4948   *sēng-lù ssū* 僧錄司
Central Buddhist Registry, a central government agency responsible for monitoring the numbers, qualifications, and conduct of Buddhist monks and nuns, normally staffed with senior monks of the capital monasteries recognized by the state as leaders of the empire-wide Buddhist clergy, sometimes given nominal official ranks. (1) T'ANG–SUNG: from 807 an agency subordinate to the Court of State Ceremonial (*hung-lu ssu*), a revival of institutions originated in the era of N-S Division, e.g., the N. Wei *chien-fa ts'ao* (Section for the Supervision of Buddhism). More fully known as the Buddhist Registry for the Avenues of the Capital (*tso-yu chieh seng-lu ssu*). SP: *bureau d'enregistrement des moines et des nonnes des grandes rues de droite et de gauche.* (2) MING–CH'ING: under the Ministry of Rites (*lǐ-pu*), supervised Buddhist Registries at Prefectural or Subprefectural or Departmental (both *chou*), and District (*hsien*) levels of territorial administration; see, respectively, *seng-kang ssu, seng-cheng ssu, seng-hui ssu.* BH: superior of the Buddhist priesthood.

4949   *sēng-t'ǔng* 僧統
N-S DIV (N. Wei, N. Ch'i): **Buddhist Controller,** collective reference to the Controller-in-chief (*ta-t'ung*) and the Controller (*t'ung*) of the Office for the Clarification of Buddhist Profundities (*chao-hsüan ssu*, q.v.). Also see *seng-kuan.*

4950   *shā-chīn yén-liào tsǔng-k'ù* 紗金顏料總庫
YÜAN: **Chief Storehouse of Gauze, Gold, and Dyestuffs,** a unit of the Service of Rare Textiles (*i-yang chü*). P38.

4951   *shā-ló chǘ* 紗羅局
YÜAN: **Gauze Service,** a unit of the Service of Rare Textiles (*i-yang chü*); after 1275 called **Gauze Supervisorate** (*sha-lo t'i-chü ssu*); headed by a Supervisor (*t'i-chü*), rank 5b.

4952   *shān-chǎng* 山長
5 DYN–MING: lit., chief of the mountain (retreat): **Dean,** common designation of the head of an instructional Academy (*shu-yüan*), private or state-sponsored. P51, 66.

4953   *shàn-chūn chiǔ-k'ù* 瞻軍酒庫
SUNG: **Army Wine Storehouse;** local agency in some areas.

4954   *shàn-fū* 膳夫
CHOU: **Food Steward,** 2 ranked as Senior Servicemen (*shang-shih*), 4 as Ordinary Servicemen (*chung-shih*), and 8 as Junior Servicemen (*hsia-shih*), members of the Ministry of State (*t'ien-kuan*) who supervised the preparation

of, and personally tasted and served, all food and drink consumed by the King, the Queen, and the Heir Apparent. CL: *intendant des mets.*

4955   *shàn-hsiěh* 繕寫
CH'ING: **Copyist,** 6 to 8 Bannermen Clerks (*pi-t'ieh-shih*) on duty assignment in each Bureau (*ssu*) of the Court of Colonial Affairs (*li-fan yüan*); commonly prefixed *cheng* (Principal) or *fu* (Assistant). BH: senior writer, junior writer.

4956   *shàn-jén* 繕人
CHOU: **Marksmen,** 2 ranked as Ordinary Servicemen (*chung-shih*) and 4 as Junior Servicemen (*hsia-shih*), members of the Ministry of War (*hsia-kuan*) assigned to the King's personal service as expert archers. CL: *excellents.*

4957   *shàn-kūng* 膳工
SUNG: **Provisioner,** one category of personnel, apparently subofficial functionaries, in the Food Service (*shang-shih chü*) of the Palace Administration (*tien-chung sheng*). SP: *travailleur d'approvisionnement pour les sacrifices.* P38.

4958   *shàn-kūng chiēn* 繕工監
T'ANG: lit., directorate of skilled workmen: from 662 to 670 the official variant name of the **Directorate for the Palace Buildings** (*chiang-tso chien*). P15.

4959   *shàn-pù* 膳部
N-S DIV (N. Ch'i, Chou)–SUNG: **Catering Bureau** in the N. Ch'i Section for Justice (*tu-kuan*), in the Chou Ministry of State (*t'ien-kuan*), thereafter one of 4 Bureaus (*ssu*) in the Ministry of Rites (*lǐ-pu*); headed in Chou by a Palace Provisioner (*chu-shan*) ranked as Ordinary Grand Master (*chung ta-fu;* 5a), at other times by a Director (*lang-chung;* in Sui temporarily *shih-lang*), rank 5b1 in T'ang, 6b in Sung; shared with such agencies as the Court of State Ceremonial (*hung-lu ssu*) and the Food Service (*shang-shih chü*) of the Palace Administration (*tien-chung sheng*) responsibility for presenting foodstuffs for use in major state sacrificial ceremonies. RR+SP: *bureau des approvisionnements pour les sacrifices.* P9.

4960   *shàn-shìh* 善世
MING–CH'ING: **Buddhist Patriarch,** 2 prefixed Left and Right, rank 6a but without stipends, principal members of the Central Buddhist Registry (*seng-lu ssu*) in the central government, under general supervision of the Ministry of Rites (*lǐ-pu*); recognized by the state, at least nominally, as heads of the empire-wide Buddhist clergy and held accountable for the authenticity and proper conduct of all Buddhist monks and nuns. BH: preceptor.

4961   *shān-shīh* 山師
CHOU: **Mountain Tax Master,** 4 ranked as Ordinary Servicemen (*chung-shih*) and 4 as Junior Servicemen (*hsia-shih*), members of the Ministry of War (*hsia-kuan*) responsible for the supervision of noted mountains and lakes excluded from fiefs granted to the Feudal Lords (*chu-hou*), and for the collection of royal taxes on timber, game, and fish taken from them. CL: *maître des montagnes.*

4962   *shàn-shǒu ssū* 扇手司
CH'ING: **Fan Bearers Office,** one of 2 units in the Forward Subsection (*ch'ien-so*) of the Imperial Procession Guard (*luan-i wei*), headed by a Director (*chang-yin yün-hui shih*), rank 4a. BH: fan section.

4963   *shàn-ssū* 膳司
YÜAN: abbreviation of *ch'u shan-ssu* (**Office of Food Supplies for the Heir Apparent**).

4964   *shān-tìng kuān* 刪定官
SUNG: **Reviser,** no definite number, rank 8a officials of

various central government agencies on duty assignments in the Law Code Office (*ch'ih-ling so*); also see *chih-shih, chih-shih kuan.* SP: *reviseur.* P13.

4965 *shān-tīng shĭh* 刪定使
T'ANG: **Disciplinary Commissioner,** number, rank, and status not clear; apparently an ad hoc continuation of the earlier Disciplinary Section (*shan-ting ts'ao*) tradition; among other things, apparently reviewed the situations of civil officials who had completed sentences of banishment, etc. P13.

4966 *shān-tīng ts'áo* 刪定曹
N-S DIV (S. Dyn.)–SUI: **Discipline Section,** a unit of the Ministry of Personnel (*li-pu*) concerned with the disciplining of civil officials, headed by a Director (*lang*). Its functional relationship with such surveillance and judicial agencies as the Censorate (*yü-shih t'ai*) and the Ministry of Justice (*hsing-pu*) is not clear; it was likely the administrative agency through which the Ministry of Personnel implemented and monitored the disciplining of civil officials. P5, P13.

4967 *shàn-tsăi* 膳宰
CHOU: variant of *shan-fu* (**Food Steward**).

4968 *shán-yǘ* 單于
CH'IN–N-S DIV: Chinese transcription of a Hsiung-nu title: **Khan** of the Hsiung-nu or other non-Chinese tribes to the north.

4969 *shān-yǘ* 山虞
Supervisor of Forestry and Hunting. (1) CHOU: 4 ranked as Ordinary Servicemen (*chung-shih*) and 8 as Junior Servicemen (*hsia-shih*), members of the Ministry of Education (*ti-kuan*) responsible for supervising the felling of timber and all hunting and trapping activities at each major mountain region in the royal domain; lesser numbers of lower ranks assigned to each such region considered ordinary, fewer still to those considered minor. CL: *inspecteur des montagnes.* (2) N-S DIV (Chou): one or more ranked as Ordinary Servicemen and one or more as Junior Servicemen, members of the Ministry of Education (*ti-kuan*), presumably with responsibilities similar to those described under (1) above. P14.

4970 *shàng* 上
Lit., above, upper, superior, to go up. (1) Throughout history used as a polite reference to the supreme ruler, i.e., the Chou dynasty **King** or a later **Emperor**; see such variants as *huang-shang, chin-shang.* In some contexts the rendering **Your Majesty** or **His Majesty** may be appropriate. (2) In hierarchical usage occurs, e.g., in Supreme Capital (*Shang-tu*) as distinct from auxiliary capitals, which were normally directionally designated; in such combinations as Senior Serviceman (*shang-shih*), Ordinary Serviceman (*chung-shih*), and Junior Serviceman (*hsia-shih*); and in distinctions between, e.g., rank 6, 2nd class, grade 1 (6b1: *ts'ung-liu p'in shang-teng*) and rank 6, 2nd class, grade 2 (6b2: *ts'ung-liu p'in hsia-teng*). (3) **To submit,** often used as a verb referring to the presentation of memorials or other documents to the throne. (4) **To promote,** sometimes used as a verb referring to the formal advancement of an official to a higher post or rank.

4971 *shàng* 尚
(1) **Chief Steward;** see *liu shang* (Six Palace Stewards). (2) **Matron,** designation of one category of palace women; see *liu shang* (Six Matrons). (3) Common abbreviation of *shang-shu* (**Minister,** etc.). Also see *tso-shang, yu-shang.*

4972 *shàng-àn* 上案
SUNG: **First Section,** one of 2 paired subordinate units (cf. *hsia-an*) in such agencies as the Chancellery (*men-hsia sheng*) and the Secretariat (*chung-shu sheng*); the organization and specific functions of each are not clear, but it is possible the First Section dealt with documents being forwarded to the throne. SP: *service des rites.*

4973 *shàng-ch'á* 尚茶
CH'ING: **Tea Server,** designation of Imperial Guardsmen (*shih-wei*) assigned to the Palace Larder (*yü ch'a-shan fang*) of the Imperial Household Department (*nei-wu fu*), 3 called Principal (*cheng* as suffix) Tea Server, one Secondary (*fu* as suffix) Tea Server, and 6 ordinary (no prefix or suffix) Tea Servers; also found on the staff at each Imperial Mausoleum (*ling*). BH: cup-bearer, chief cup-bearer, assistant chief cup-bearer. P29, 37.

4974 *shàng-chàng* 尚帳
HAN: **Chief Steward for Accommodations,** one of the Five Chief Stewards (see *wu shang*) on the staff of the Chamberlain for the Palace Revenues (*shao-fu*), presumably responsible for providing and caring for the tents used by the Emperor while traveling and, possibly, for some of his ordinary bedding gear. Also see *liu shang* (Six Chief Stewards). Cf. *shang-she chü* (Accommodations Service). P30.

4975 *shàng-chēn shǔ* 尚珍署
YÜAN: **Office of Delicacies** in the Court of Imperial Entertainments (*kuang-lu ssu*); established 1276, in 1288 renamed *chen-hsiu shu,* q.v. P30.

4976 *shàng-ch'éng chǘ* 尚乘局
T'ANG–SUNG: **Livery Service,** one of many constituent units of the Palace Administration (*tien-chung sheng*), headed by 2 Chief Stewards (*feng-yü*), rank 5a or 5b; managed the use of horses by personnel of the imperial household, including those maintained in the Six Stables (*liu chiu*) and Six Palace Corrals (*liu hsien*). RR: *service des attelages de l'empereur.* SP: *écuyers impériaux.*

4977 *shàng-ch'éng ssù* 尚乘寺
YÜAN: **Court of the Imperial Saddlery,** an autonomous agency of the central government responsible for manufacturing and maintaining carriages, saddles, and other riding gear for the imperial household; established in 1287 independent of the Court of the Imperial Stud (*t'ai-p'u ssu*), which retained control over the imperial horse herds. Headed by a Chief Minister (*ch'ing*), rank not clear. P39.

4978 *shăng-chǐ àn* 賞給案
SUNG: **Gifts and Presentations Section,** one of 8 Sections (*an*) in the Tax Bureau (*tu-chih ssu*) of early Sung, normally headed by an Administrative Assistant (*p'an-kuan, t'ui-kuan*); made available to the Emperor goods to be given as rewards, etc.; also reportedly provided paper, inks, and medicines, and oversaw the collection of taxes on trade at public markets and on maritime trade. SP: *service de récompense.*

4979 *shàng-chì lì* 上計吏
HAN: lit., functionary who submits an accounting (to the throne): variant of *chi-li, chi-shih* (both **Accounts Clerk**). Also see *chi-chieh.* HB: official who hands up accounts.

4980 *shàng chì tū-wèi* 上騎都尉
T'ANG–MING: **Senior Commandant-in-chief of Cavalry,** merit title (*hsün*) awarded to government personnel of rank 5a through Chin, 4a in Yüan; in Ming explicitly

restricted to rank 4a military officers. RR+SP: *grand directeur général de la cavalerie*. P65.

4981   *shàng-chì yüàn* 上計掾
HAN: lit., official who submits an accounting (to the throne): variant of *chi-yüan* (**Accounts Assistant**). Also see *chi-chieh*.

4982   *shàng chiāng-chūn* 上將軍
Generalissimo. (1) T'ANG–SUNG: from 786, designation of the head of each of the major military units at the dynastic capital collectively called the Sixteen Guards (*shih-liu wei*, q.v.); rank 2b in T'ang, 2b or 3a in Sung. RR: *général supérieur*. SP: *général supérieur, grand général*. (2) SUNG: also the head of any Guard (*wei*) not included in the Sixteen Guards; rank 3b. (3) CHIN: title of nobility (*chüeh*); see *chen-kuo shang chiang-chün, feng-kuo shang chiang-chün, fu-kuo shang chiang-chün*. P64.

4983   *shàng-chièh* 上界
SUNG: **First Section**, one of 2 subdivisions of the Crafts Institute (*wen-ssu yüan*), originally part of the Directorate for Imperial Manufactories (*shao-fu chien*), later under the Ministry of Works (*kung-pu*); staffed with non-official hereditary specialists who did craft work with gold, silver, and pearls. See *hsia-chieh*. SP: *bureau pour la fabrication des objets en or, argent et en perles*. P37.

4984   *shàng-chièn* 上監
SUNG: **First Veterinarian Directorate**, one of 2 units fully designated *mu-yang chien*, subordinate to the Court of the Imperial Stud (*t'ai-p'u ssu*); also see *hsia-chien*. SP: *direction supérieure pour soigner les chevaux*.

4985   *shàng-chíh wèi* 上直衛
MING: lit., guard unit that takes up active duty: **Imperial Guard**, a categorical designation of 33 of the 74 major military units called Capital Guards (*ching-wei*) stationed in the Peking area after 1420, also of 17 of the 49 Capital Guards stationed in the area of the auxiliary capital, Nanking; the most notable of the Imperial Guards at Peking was the Imperial Bodyguard (*chin-i wei*). The Imperial Guards at Peking were directly responsible to the Emperor; those at Nanking, like all other Guards (*wei*) throughout the empire, were distributed for supervision among the Five Chief Military Commissions (*wu-chün tu-tu fu*) in the central government. Also see *wei-so*. P43.

4986   *shàng-ch'ìn chǘ* 尚寢局
T'ANG–SUNG, MING: **Housekeeping Service**, one of 6 agencies among which palace women were distributed; headed by 2 Matrons (*shang-ch'in*), rank 5a, who supervised 4 subordinate Offices: Interior Maintenance Office (*ssu-she ssu*), Transport Office (*ssu-yü ssu*), Gardens Office (*ssu-yüan ssu*), and Lanterns Office (*ssu-teng ssu*); the Matrons also kept records concerning the Emperor's sexual relations with the females of his household. See *liu shang* (Six Matrons). RR: *service des appartements particuliers*.

4987   *shàng-ch'īng* 上卿
(1) CHOU: **Senior Minister**, highest of 3 Minister ranks (see *chung-ch'ing, hsia-ch'ing*), the highest category of officials serving the King and Feudal Lords (*chu-hou*), ranking above Grand Masters (*ta-fu*) and Servicemen (*shih*). (2) HAN: **Superior Chamberlains**, 4th highest in a hierarchy of 10 status groups in the officialdom (see under *shang-kung*), including only the titles General of the Front (*ch'ien chiang-chün*), General of the Rear (*hou*), General of the Left (*tso*), and General of the Right (*yu*). Also see *cheng-ch'ing* (Regular Chamberlains), *p'ei-ch'ing* (Adjunct Chamberlains), *ch'ing*. Cf. *chiu ch'ing* (Nine Chamberlains). P68.

4988   *shàng ch'īng-ch'ē tū-wèi* 上輕車都尉
T'ANG–SUNG: **Senior Commandant of Light Chariots**, the 5th highest merit title (*hsün*), awarded to rank 4a military officers. See *ch'ing-ch'e tu-wei*. RR+SP: *grand directeur général des chars de guerre*. P65.

4989   *shàng-chiù chǘ* 尚廐局
CHIN: **Livery Service**, in charge of horses and carriages used by the imperial household, a unit of the Palace Inspectorate-general (*tien-ch'ien tu tien-chien ssu*); counterpart of the T'ang–Sung *shang-ch'eng chü*.

4990   *shàng chù-kuó* 上柱國
N-S DIV (Chou)–YÜAN: **Supreme Pillar of State**, honorific designation of great prestige from high antiquity, reportedly derived from usage in the ancient southern state of Ch'u: the highest merit title (*hsün*), awarded to officials of rank 2a; in Ming superseded by the titles Left and Right Pillars of State (*tso, yu chu-kuo*). RR+SP: *grand pilier de l'état*. P65.

4991   *shàng-chūn* 上軍
(1) HAN: **Upper Army**, one of 8 special capital-defense forces organized at the end of Han; see *pa hsiao-wei* (Eight Commandants). (2) N-S DIV (S. Dyn.): **Senior Adjutant**, one of the eminent military officers called the Three Adjutants (*san chün*) assigned to each Princedom (*wang-kuo*); see *chung-chün, hsia-chün*. P69. (3) SUNG: **Elite Army;** see *shang ssu chün* (Four Elite Armies).

4992   *shàng-fāng* 尚方
CH'IN–SUI: **Directorate for Imperial Manufactories**, a workshop normally under the Chamberlain for the Palace Revenues (*shao-fu*), headed by a Director (*ling*), rank 600 bushels in Han, an office apparently filled by a eunuch in Later Han and perhaps then even overseen by a eunuch Supervisor (*chien*); manufactured commodities of many sorts used in the imperial palace, in Han times reportedly including weapons. At least as early as San-kuo Wei, and perhaps late in Later Han, divided into 3 units prefixed Central, Left, and Right, whose heads were collectively known as the Three Service Officials (*san shang-fang*). In T'ang (Sui?) the organization was renamed *shao-fu chien*, q.v. HB: prefect (*ling*), inspector (*chien*) of the masters of techniques. P37, 38.

4993   *shàng-fāng chièn* 尚方監
(1) HAN: **Supervisor of the Imperial Manufactories**, apparently a eunuch appointee in Later Han; oversaw the Directorate for Imperial Manufactories (*shang-fang*). HB: inspector of the masters of techniques. P38. (2) T'ANG: from 685 to 705 the official redesignation of the *shao-fu chien* (**Directorate for Imperial Manufactories**), q.v. Also see *nei-fu chien*. P38.

4994   *shàng-fāng shǔ* 尚方署
CHIN: **Gold and Silver Workshop**, one of 6 artisan craft agencies under the Directorate for Imperial Manufactories (*shao-fu chien*), headed by a Director (*ling*), rank 6b. P38.

4995   *shàng-fāng ssū* 尚方司 or *shàng-fāng yüàn* 院
CH'ING: early names of the **Office of Palace Justice** (see *shen-hsing ssu*); *shang-fang ssu* to 1655, then *yüan* till 1677. P37.

4996   *shàng-fú chǘ* 尚服局
T'ANG–SUNG, MING: **Wardrobe Service**, one of 6 major agencies among which palace women were distributed; headed by 2 Matrons (*shang-fu*), rank 5a, who supervised

4 subordinate Offices: Seals Office (*ssu-pao ssu*), Clothing Office (*ssu-i ssu*), Adornments Office (*ssu-shih ssu*), and Ceremonial Regalia Office (*ssu-chang ssu*). Also see *liu shang* (Six Matrons). RR: *service de l'habillement du harem*.

4997   *shàng-hsí* 尚席
CH'IN–N-S DIV: **Chief Steward for the Bedchamber** under the Chamberlain for the Palace Revenues (*shao-fu*), responsible for furnishing and maintaining the Emperor's sleeping quarters; see under *liu shang* (Six Chief Stewards), *wu shang* (Five Chief Stewards). P30, 37.

4998   *shàng-hsiàng* 上相
SUNG: **Supreme Councilor,** a variant of *tsai-hsiang* (Grand Councilor), especially in the case of such an eminent dignitary when he bore the supplementary titles Grand Academician of the Institute for the Glorification of Literature (*chao-wen kuan ta hsüeh-shih*) and Chief Compiler of the Dynastic History (*chien-hsiu kuo-shih*).

4999   *shàng hù-chün* 上護軍
T'ANG–MING: **Senior Military Protector,** superseding the Sui–early T'ang merit title Senior General-in-chief (*shang ta chiang-chün*), 3rd highest merit title (*hsün*) awarded for extraordinary military service; rank 3a through Chin, 2a in Yüan and Ming; in Ming reserved solely for rank 2a military officers. See *hu-chün*. RR+SP: *grand protecteur d'armée*. P65.

5000   *shàng-ī* 尚衣
(1) CH'IN–N-S DIV: **Chief Steward for the Wardrobe** under the Chamberlain for the Palace Revenues (*shao-fu*), responsible for providing and maintaining the Emperor's clothing; see under *liu shang* (Six Chief Stewards), *wu shang* (Five Chief Stewards), *liu chü* (Six Services). P30, 37. (2) CH'ING: unofficial reference to a **Superintendent of Imperial Silk Manufacturing** (*chih-tsao chien-tu*).

5001   *shàng-ī chiēn* 尚衣監
MING–CH'ING: **Directorate for Imperial Apparel,** one of 12 major Directorates (*chien*) in which palace eunuchs were organized, headed by a eunuch Director (*t'ai-chien*); responsible for the Emperor's personal headgear, gowns, shoes, boots, stockings, etc. In Ch'ing existed only from 1656 to 1661; see under *shih-erh chien* (Twelve Directorates).

5002   *shàng-ī chiēn* 尚醫監
YÜAN: **Imperial Directorate of Medicine,** from 1283 to 1285 the official redesignation of the Imperial Academy of Medicine (*t'ai-i yüan*), during which time its head was retitled Director (*chien, t'ai-chien*) and lowered in rank from 3a to 4a.

5003   *shàng-í chű* 尚儀局
T'ANG–SUNG, MING: **Ceremonial Service,** one of 6 major agencies among which palace women were distributed; headed by 2 Matrons (*shang-i*), rank 5a, who supervised 4 subordinate Offices: Library Office (*ssu-chi ssu*), Music Office (*ssu-yüeh ssu*), Visitors Office (*ssu-pin ssu*), and Ritual Receptions Office (*ssu-tsan ssu*). See *liu shang* (Six Matrons). RR: *service de l'étiquette du harem*.

5004   *shàng-í chű* 尚衣局
Clothing Service. (1) T'ANG–YÜAN: one of 6 Services (*chü*) in the T'ang–Sung Palace Administration (*tien-chung sheng*), headed by 2 Chief Stewards (*feng-yü*), rank 5a or 5b; in the Chin dynasty Court Ceremonial Institute (*hsüan-hui yüan*), headed by a Superintendent (*t'i-tien*), 5a; and in the Yüan dynasty Supervisorate-in-chief of Civilian Arti-

sans (*min-chiang tsung-kuan fu*), headed by an Overseer (*ta-lu-hua-ch'ih*) and a Supervisor (*t'i-chü*), 5b. Generally responsible for providing and maintaining the clothing and other items required by the Emperor for his public appearances. This function, which must always have involved palace eunuchs to some extent, was apparently taken over completely by eunuchs in Ming times. Cf. *shang-fu chü*. RR+SP: *service des vêtements de l'empereur*. P37. (2) CH'ING: unofficial reference to an Imperial Silk Manufactory (*chih-tsao chü*); see under *chih-tsao chien-tu*.

5005   *shàng-ī k'ù* 尚衣庫
SUNG: **Imperial Wardrobe,** a personal valeting service for the Emperor headed by a eunuch Commissioner (*shih*), under supervision of the Palace Administration (*tien-chung sheng*). SP: *magasin des vêtements de l'empereur*. P38.

5006   *shāng-ì shěng-shìh* 商議省事
YÜAN: **Discussant of Secretariat Affairs,** from 1292 a middle-level executive post in the Secretariat (*chung-shu sheng*); in 1295 retitled Manager of Important National Security Affairs (*p'ing-chang chün-kuo chung-shih*, q.v.). P4.

5007   *shàng-kāng* 上綱
HAN: lit., the ruler's net (?): occasional unofficial reference to any official position, signifying **in government service.**

5008   *shàng kó-mén* 上閣門
SUNG–CHIN: **Palace Audience Gate,** two prefixed East and West, through which officials and foreign envoys entered the palace for audience; each staffed with ushers, heralds, etc., under 3 Commissioners of the Palace Audience Gate (*shang ko-men shih*), rank 6a; the staffs were apparently subordinate to the Secretariat (*chung-shu sheng*), in Sung possibly to the Court of State Ceremonial (*hung-lu ssu*). SP: *portes du pavillon supérieur*. P33.

5009   *shàng-kuàn* 尚冠
CH'IN–N-S DIV: **Chief Steward for Headgear** under the Chamberlain for Palace Revenues (*shao-fu*), responsible for providing and maintaining the variety of caps worn in public by the Emperor; see under *liu shang* (Six Chief Stewards), *wu shang* (Five Chief Stewards). P30, 37.

5010   *shàng-kūng* 上公
HAN: **Superior Dukes,** the highest in a hierarchy of 10 status groups in the officialdom, limited to the Grand Preceptor (*t'ai-shih*), Grand Mentor (*t'ai-fu*), and Grand Guardian (*t'ai-pao*). The lesser status groups were as follows: 2. Three Dukes (*san kung*). 3. Adjunct Dukes (*pi-kung*). 4. Superior Chamberlains (*shang-ch'ing*). 5. Regular Chamberlains (*cheng-ch'ing*). 6. Adjunct Chamberlains (*p'ei-ch'ing*). 7. Senior Grand Masters (*shang ta-fu*). 8. Ordinary Grand Masters (*chung ta-fu*). 9. Junior Grand Masters (*hsia ta-fu*). 10. Servicemen (*shih*). This Han system of categorization was in part carried on into the Three Kingdoms era. Part of the terminology was borrowed from ancient Chou usage. P68.

5011   *shàng-kūng àn* 上供案
SUNG: **Prefectural Remittances Section,** one of 5 Sections (*an*) in the Census Bureau (*hu-pu ssu*; cf. *hu-pu*), one of 3 agencies that constituted the State Finance Commission (*san ssu*) of early Sung; in c. 1080 shifted under the Granaries Bureau (*ts'ang-pu*) of the Ministry of Revenue (*hu-pu*); monitored payments of various kinds made by Prefectures (*chou*) throughout the empire to the central government and the imperial palace; normally headed by an Administrative Assistant (*p'an-kuan, t'ui-kuan*). SP: *service de contribution*.

5012 *shàng-kūng chú* 尚功局
T'ANG–SUNG, MING: **Workshop Service,** one of 6 major agencies among which palace women were distributed; headed by 2 Matrons (*shang kung*), rank 5a, who supervised 4 subordinate Offices: Sewing Office (*ssu-chih ssu*), Rarities Office (*ssu-chen ssu*), Silks Office (*ssu-ts'ai ssu*), and Accounts Office (*ssu-chi ssu*). Also see *liu shang* (Six Matrons). RR: *service des travaux du harem.*

5013 *shàng-kūng chú* 尚宮局
T'ANG–SUNG, MING: **General Palace Service,** one of 6 major agencies among which palace women were distributed; headed by 2 Matrons (*shang-kung*), rank 5a, who generally supervised the other 5 Services and directly controlled 4 immediately subordinate Offices: Records Office (*ssu-chi ssu*), Communications Office (*ssu-yen ssu*), Registration Office (*ssu-pu ssu*), and Inner Gates Office (*ssu-wei ssu*). Also see *liu shang* (Six Matrons). RR: *service des affaires générales du harem.*

5014 *shàng-liěn* 尚輦
T'ANG: **Sedan-chair Foreman,** 2, rank 9b, on the staff of the Sedan-chair Service (*shang-lien chü*) in the Palace Administration (*tien-chung sheng*). RR: *chef du personnel du service des voitures à bras.*

5015 *shàng-liěn chú* 尚輦局
T'ANG–SUNG: **Sedan-chair Service,** one of 6 Services (*chü*) in the Palace Administration (*tien-chung sheng*); headed by 2 Chief Stewards (*feng-yü*), rank 5a or 5b. RR+SP: *service des voitures à bras de l'empereur.* P37.

5016 *shàng-lín* 上林
Imperial Forest: the name given by the First Emperor of Ch'in to a park reserved for his recreational use west of his capital near modern Sian, greatly expanded by Emperor Wu of Han, the subject of a famous long poem (*Shang-lin fu*) by the Han poet Ssu-ma Hsiang-ju; subsequently throughout history used in unofficial or quasiofficial reference to any comparable imperial park or garden, and prefixed to many titles of officials with responsibilities relating to such parks and gardens. HB: supreme forest. P40.

5017 *shàng-lín chào-yù* 上林詔獄
HAN: **Imperial Prison in the Imperial Forest,** one of the many prisons (see under *chao-yü*) in the capital area, probably for the imprisonment of anyone who violated the prohibitions in force; headed by one or more Directors (*chang*) under the Commandant of the Imperial Gardens (*shui-heng tu-wei*); abolished in 32 B.C. HB: imperial prison of the park of the supreme forest. P40.

5018 *shàng-lín chiēn* 上林監
CH'ING: unofficial reference to both the **Chief Ministers of the Imperial Parks Administration** (*feng-ch'en ch'ing*) and to the **Imperial Parks Administration** (*feng-ch'en yüan*) itself.

5019 *shàng-lín chūng shíh-ch'íh chiēn* 上林中十池監
HAN: **Supervisor of the Ten Ponds in the Imperial Forest,** a category of assistants to the Director of the Imperial Forest (*shang-lin ling*), but on the staff of the Chamberlain for the Palace Revenues (*shao-fu*) and apparently responsible for the collection of taxes or fees from licensed fishermen in the park. HB: inspector of the ten ponds in the park of the supreme forest. P37, 40.

5020 *shàng-lín láng* 上林郎
HAN: **Court Gentleman of the Imperial Forest,** assis-

tants to the Director of the Imperial Forest (*shang-lin ling*); specific functions not clear. See *lang*. P37.

5021 *shàng-lín lìng* 上林令
HAN–N-S DIV (San-kuo Wei): **Director of the Imperial Forest,** in charge of the recreational area near the capital called the Imperial Forest (*shang-lin*) or the Imperial Forest Park (*shang-lin yüan*), under the Commandant of the Imperial Gardens (*shui-heng tu-wei*); assisted by 8 Aides (*ch'eng*), 12 Commandants (*wei*), and various others such as Court Gentlemen of the Imperial Forest (*shang-lin lang*), Supervisors of the Ten Ponds in the Imperial Forest (*shang-lin chung shih-ch'ih chien*), and Bailiffs of the Imperial Forest (*shang-lin se-fu*). HB: prefect of the park of the supreme forest. P40.

5022 *shàng-lín shǔ* 上林署
T'ANG–MING: **Office of Imperial Parks** under the Court of the Imperial Granaries (*ssu-nung ssu*) till Chin, then under the Ministry of Works (*kung-pu*); headed by 2 Directors (*ling*), rank 7b1, in T'ang, by a Superintendent (*t'i-tien*), 5b, in Chin; in 1407 transformed into a Directorate of Imperial Parks (*shang-lin yüan-chien*); responsible for gathering fruits, vegetables, winter ice, etc., from the various imperial parks and gardens for use in the imperial palace, in great state ceremonies, etc. RR+SP: *office des bosquets impériaux.* P40.

5023 *shàng-lín yüàn* 上林苑
Imperial Forest Park, intermittently throughout imperial history, the official or unofficial designation of one or more great parks or gardens in the vicinity of the dynastic capital; the tradition began with the creation of a hunting preserve and playground adjacent to the capital by the First Emperor of Ch'in, called the Imperial Forest (*shang-lin*); also see *feng-ch'en yüan, shen-tu yüan.* P40.

5024 *shàng-lín yüàn-chiēn* 上林苑監
MING: **Directorate of Imperial Parks,** in 1407 superseded the traditional Office of Imperial Parks (*shang-lin shu*) in charge of all imperial parks, gardens, menageries, etc., in the area of the dynastic capital; headed by 2 Directors (*cheng*), rank 5a; originally with more than 10 subsidiary Offices (*shu*), in 1435 fixed at 4: Office of Husbandry (*liang-mu shu*), Office of Domestic Fowl (*fan-yü shu*), Office of Fruits and Flowers (*lin-heng shu*), and Office of Vegetables (*chia-shu shu*), each with a Manager (*tien-shu*), rank 7a. Superseded in early Ch'ing by the Imperial Parks Administration (*feng-ch'en yüan*). P40.

5025 *shàng-mù* 尚沐
CH'IN: **Chief Steward for the Bath,** one of Six Chief Stewards (*liu shang*, q.v.) who tended to the needs of the imperial household under supervision of the Chamberlain for the Palace Revenues (*shao-fu*). Perhaps revived intermittently in the era of N-S Division. P37.

5026 *shàng-mù chiēn* 尚牧監
YÜAN: **Directorate of Herds,** changed from Herds Office (*ch'ün-mu so*) in 1279, in 1282 renamed Court of the Imperial Stud (*t'ai-p'u yüan*, later *t'ai-p'u ssu*). P39.

5027 *shàng-pǎo chiēn* 尚寶監
MING: **Directorate of Palace Seals,** a palace eunuch agency in charge of the numerous imperial seals, originally in cooperation with the civil service Seals Office (*shang-pao ssu*), but after the founder's reign with almost complete control itself; established in 1367 with a eunuch head called Chief Steward of Seals (*shang-pao*), rank 6a then 6b then 7a; from 1384 headed by a eunuch Director (*ling;* from 1395 *t'ai-chien*); size of staff not fixed.

5028 *shàng-pǎo chú* 尚寶局

MING: **Seals Service,** variant name of the palace women agency most commonly called *ssu-pao ssu* (Seals Office).

5029 *shàng-pǎo ssū* 尚寶司

MING: **Seals Office,** an autonomous agency of the central government headed by a Chief Minister (*ch'ing*), rank 5a, charged with the monitoring of a large number of seals, tallies, and stamps used by the Emperor, each having special, specified uses; in the tradition of *fu-pao lang, fu-hsi lang,* etc., of prior times. After the founder's reign came to be overshadowed, dominated, and often humiliated by palace eunuchs of the Directorate of Palace Seals (*shang-pao chien*).

5030 *shàng-pīn* 上嬪

N-S DIV (N. Ch'i): **Superior Concubines,** collective reference to 3 imperial concubines individually entitled Lady of Bright Counsel (*kuang-yu*), Lady of Exalted Excellence (*lung-hui*), and Lady of Clear Instruction (*chao-hsün*). See *hsia-pin.*

5031 *shàng sān ch'í* 上三旗

CH'ING: **Three Superior Banners,** collective designation of those military units called Banners (*ch'i*) that were under the personal control of the Emperor: specifically, the Bordered Yellow Banner (*hsiang-huang ch'i*), Plain Yellow Banner (*cheng-huang ch'i*), and Plain White Banner (*cheng-po ch'i*); also called the Three Inner Banners (*nei san ch'i*). Cf. *hsia wu ch'i* (Five Lesser Banners).

5032 *shàng-shàn* 尚膳

CH'ING: **Meal Server,** designation of Imperial Guardsmen (*shih-wei*) assigned to the Palace Larder (*yü ch'a-shan fang*) of the Imperial Household Department (*nei-wu fu*), 3 called Principal (*cheng* as suffix) Meal Server, one Secondary (*fu* as suffix) Meal Server, and 12 Ordinary (no prefix or suffix) Meal Servers; also found on the staff of each Imperial Mausoleum (*ling*). BH: trencher-knight, serving-man, chief trencher-knight, assistant chief trencher-knight. P29, 37.

5033 *shàng-shàn chiēn* 尚膳監

MING–CH'ING: **Directorate for Palace Delicacies,** one of 12 major Directorates (*chien*) in which palace eunuchs were organized; headed by a eunuch Director (*t'ai-chien*) in Ming, apparently staffed with Manchus in early Ch'ing; responsible for providing special foods from the palace gardens; in Ch'ing existed only from 1656 to 1661. See under *shih-erh chien.*

5034 *shàng-shè* 上舍

(1) SUNG: **Superior College,** highest of 3 Colleges (*she*) in the National University (*t'ai-hsüeh*) from c. 1070; some 10% of students admitted to the University eventually advanced into the Superior College for advanced training before beginning official careers or undertaking civil service recruitment examinations. SP: *collège supérieur.* (2) CH'ING: unofficial reference to a **National University Student** (*chien-sheng*).

5035 *shàng-shè chú* 尚舍局

T'ANG–SUNG: **Accommodations Service,** one of 6 Services (*chü*) in the Palace Administration (*tien-chung sheng*); headed by 2 Chief Stewards (*feng-yü*), rank 5b; in charge of the Emperor's personal quarters in the imperial palace, his baths, special imperial accommodations for great ceremonial occasions, and tents and other accommodations required by the Emperor while traveling away from the capital. RR+SP: *service des appartements de l'empereur.*

5036 *shang-sheng chü* 尚乘局

See under *shang-ch'eng chü* (**Livery Service**).

5037 *shàng-shìh* 上士

CHOU, N-S DIV (Chou): **Senior Serviceman,** 5th highest of 7 (or 7th of 9) ranks into which all officials were divided, following Junior Grand Master (*hsia ta-fu*) and outranking Ordinary Serviceman (*chung-shih*) and Junior Serviceman (*hsia-shih*); the rank indicator is normally a suffix appended to the functional title. In Later Chou, equivalent to rank 7a. CL: *gradué de première classe.*

5038 *shàng-shíh* 尚食

(1) CH'IN–N-S DIV: **Chief Steward for Food** under the Chamberlain for the Palace Revenues (*shao-fu*) or, in N. Wei, in the Chancellery (*men-hsia sheng*); responsible for provisioning the imperial palace with food and drink; see under *liu shang* (Six Chief Stewards), *wu shang* (Five Chief Stewards), *liu chü* (Six Services). HB: master of food. P30, 37. (2) T'ANG–SUNG, MING: **Matron for Food,** 2, rank 5a, heads of the palace women agency called the Food Service (*shang-shih chü*); also see under *liu shang* (Six Matrons).

5039 *shàng-shíh chiēn* 尚食監

HAN: **Director of Provisions** on the staff of a Princedom (*wang-kuo*), apparently responsible for supervising the preparation and serving of food and drink for the Prince and his princely household. HB: inspector of the masters of food. P69.

5040 *shàng-shíh chú* 尚食局

Food Service. (1) SUI–YÜAN: one of Six Services (*liu chü*) through which such agencies as the T'ang–Sung Palace Administration (*tien-chung sheng*), the Chin Court Ceremonial Institute (*hsüan-hui yüan*), and the Yüan Provisions Commission (also *hsüan-hui yüan*) provided necessities for the imperial palace, often in collaboration with eunuchs and palace women and with such central government agencies as the Court of Imperial Entertainments (*kuang-lu ssu*). Responsible, among other things, for preliminary tastings of foods served at the imperial table. In T'ang and Sung headed by 2 Chief Stewards (*feng-yü*), rank 5a; in Chin and Yüan by a Superintendent (*t'i-tien*), 5a or 5b. RR+SP: *service de la nourriture de l'empereur.* P30. (2) T'ANG–SUNG, MING: one of 6 major agencies among which palace women were distributed; headed by 2 Matrons (*shang-shih*), rank 5a, who supervised 4 subordinate Offices: Foods Office (*ssu-shan ssu*), Wines Office (*ssu-yün ssu*), Medicines Office (*ssu-yao ssu*), and Banquets Office (*ssu-ch'i ssu*). See *liu shang* (Six Matrons). RR: *service de la nourriture du harem.*

5041 *shàng-shōu sǒ* 尚收所

YÜAN: **Collections Office** (?), a unit of the Palace Provisions Commission (*hsüan-hui yüan*), apparently headed by a Commissioner (*shih*), rank 5b; specific functions not clear. P38.

5042 *shàng-shū* 尚書

Lit., in charge of writing; one of the most important titles of imperial history, a key to the evolution of the central government. (1) CH'IN–HAN: **Chief Steward for Writing,** one of the Six Chief Stewards (*liu shang*) under the Chamberlain for the Palace Revenues (*shao-fu*), responsible for the Emperor's personal secretarial work. Not later than the time of Emperor Wu of Han (r. 141–87 B.C.), normally 4 appointees, each in charge of a functionally differentiated Section (*ts'ao;* see under *ssu ts'ao*); functionally if not nominally, had become a more important category of officials, now appropriately rendered Imperial Secretaries (see under #2 following). P37. (2) HAN–N-S DIV: **Imperial Secretary**, rank 600 bushels, 4 from the time of Emperor Wu of Han, 5 from 29 B.C., 6 in Later Han, each in charge of a Section with functionally differentiated responsibilities, controlling all documents flowing in and out of the imperial palace. Appointees were required to pass a vocabulary test involving 9,000 characters and came to be assisted in each Section by an Aide (*ch'eng*) and a Secretarial Court Gentleman (*shang-shu lang*). Late in Emperor Wu's reign the Imperial Secretaries were overshadowed if not superseded by palace eunuchs appointed as Palace Secretaries (*chung-shu*), the great historian Ssu-ma Ch'ien being perhaps the first such appointee after his castration; but in 29 B.C. the Palace Secretaries were withdrawn from formal administrative duties and probably abolished, whereupon the Imperial Secretaries resumed their earlier functions and were increased to 5 (see under *wu ts'ao*). In Later Han the number was further increased to 6 (see under *liu ts'ao*). From Former Han times the group was known unofficially by the collective designation Imperial Secretariat (*shang-shu t'ai*), which in its full Later Han maturity had an executive superstructure consisting of a Director (*ling*), rank 1,000 bushels, a Vice Director (*p'u-yeh*), 600 bushels, and one each Left and Right Aide (*tso-ch'eng, yu-ch'eng*), 400 bushels. This pattern of organization was perpetuated in the following era of N-S Division, gradually becoming a stable top-level organ commonly called *shang-shu sheng* (lit., Department of Imperial Secretaries, but normally rendered Department of State Affairs); and the Imperial Secretaries were gradually transformed into formally recognized executives of the central government (see #3 following). HB: master of writing. P5. (3) N-S DIV–CH'ING: **Minister**, head of a top-level administrative agency in the central government's Department of State Affairs (*shang-shu sheng*) till Yüan times, then in the Secretariat (*chung-shu sheng*) till 1380 in early Ming, when the Secretariat was abolished; thereafter the Ministers were the most eminent members of the general administration hierarchy, directly responsible to the Emperor, although from the 1420s through Ch'ing times they came to be increasingly subordinate to a coordinating group of Grand Secretaries (*ta hsüeh-shih*) collectively known as the Grand Secretariat (*nei-ko*), stably institutionalized in Ch'ing. Throughout the era of N-S Division the units headed by Ministers were called either Sections (*ts'ao*) or Ministries (*pu*); the term Ministry predominated late in the era and was the standard from Sui through Ch'ing. Their number fluctuated greatly at first; a cluster of 12 was common, and at times the number grew to more than 30; but from Sui through Ch'ing 6 was the standard (see under *liu pu*): Ministries of Personnel (*li-pu*), of Revenue (*hu-pu*), of Rites (*li-pu*), of War (*ping-pu*), of Justice (*hsing-pu*), and of Works (*kung-pu*). The rank of Ministers was 3a in T'ang, 2b in Sung, 3a again in Chin, Yüan, and early Ming, 2a from 1380 till 1730 in Ch'ing, thereafter 1b; though ranks were equal, the Minister of Personnel was always considered preeminent in the group. There was normally only one Minister for each Ministry through Sung and Chin; Yüan appointed 3 in each Ministry; Ming reverted to a single appointee; Ch'ing commonly appointed one Manchu and one Chinese. In the mature organization of Ministries, the Minister was assisted by one or more Vice Ministers (*shih-lang*) and supervised 4 or more subordinate Bureaus (*ssu; ch'ing-li ssu* in Ming and Ch'ing) with function-specific or, in some Ming–Ch'ing Ministries, region-specific responsibilities. See *chung shang-shu*. RR: *président de ministère.* SP: *président*

de ministère, ministre. BH: president of the ministry. P5, 6, 9, 12, 13, 14, 15. (4) T'ANG: may be encountered as a variant of the palace women title **Matron** (see under *liu shang,* Six Matrons).

5043 *shang shu* 尙署
See under *tso-shang shu* and *yu-shang shu.*

5044 *shàng-shū ch'éng* 尙書丞
HAN: **Aide to the Imperial Secretary**, one assistant for each Imperial Secretary (*shang-shu*) in Former Han, rank not clear; in Later Han and thereafter, may be found as a reference to the Left or Right Assistant Director (*tso-ch'eng, yu-ch'eng*) of Han's Imperial Secretariat (*shang-shu t'ai*) or the later Department of State Affairs (*shang-shu sheng*). HB: assistant. P37.

5045 *shàng-shū ch'üán* 尙書銓
(1) T'ANG: **Ministerial Selections,** reference to the personnel evaluations supervised by the Minister of Personnel (*li-pu shang-shu*), as distinguished from those supervised by the Vice Ministers of Personnel (*li-pu shih-lang*), which were called *chung-ch'üan, hsi-ch'üan.* Also see *tung-ch'üan, hsi-ch'üan.* Cf. *chung-hsüan, tung-hsüan, hsi-hsüan.* (2) From T'ang on, a common unofficial reference to the **Minister of Personnel,** derived from the function described in (1) above.

5046 *shàng-shū hsüǎn* 尙書選
SUNG: lit., selections by the Minister: **Senior Appointments Process,** a reference to the Ministry of Personnel's (*li-pu*) appointments process (see under *hsüan*), in which the selection of men for appointments and reappointments was allocated to different executive officials of the Ministry according to the ranks and services (civil or military) of the appointees. The Minister (*shang-shu*) presided over selections of both civil (see *shang-shu tso-hsüan*) and military (see *shang-shu yu-hsüan*) officials for appointments in the categories called Capital Officials (*ching-kuan*) and Court Officials (*ch'ao-kuan*). Cf. *shih-lang hsüan* (Junior Appointments Process), *shen-kuan yüan* (Bureau of Personnel Evaluation), *tso-hsüan, yu-hsüan.*

5047 *shàng-shū láng* 尙書郎
HAN–N-S DIV: **Secretarial Court Gentlemen,** men of the court retinue generically called Court Gentlemen (*lang*) assigned for duty in the Imperial Secretariat (*shang-shu t'ai;* also see *shang-shu*), normally prefixed with a function indicator beginning with *chu* (in charge of), e.g., in charge of correspondence with the Hsiung-nu chieftain, in charge of the transport of money and valuables. The general practice was for a new assignee to be made Probationary (*shou*) Secretarial Court Gentleman of the Interior (*shang-shu lang-chung*) for one year with rank of 300 bushels; then after 3 years of satisfactory service he was given the higher status of Attendant Gentleman (*shih-lang*) with rank of 400 bushels. In Former Han some Clerks (*ling-shih*) with good service records were also given such Probationary appointments. In San-kuo Wei and perhaps later in the era of N-S Division, the appointees were designated as being attached to one of the Sections (*ts'ao*) in the Imperial Secretariat, e.g., as *shang-shu hu-ts'ao lang* (Secretarial Court Gentleman of the Revenue Section; see *hu-ts'ao*). During the era of N-S Division the title *shang-shu lang* was also a common collective reference to both *shih-lang* and *lang-chung,* which became executive posts in the Department of State Affairs (*shang-shu sheng*) as it evolved out of Han's Imperial Secretariat. HB: gentleman of the masters of writing. P5, 6, 9, 14, 22.

5048 *shàng-shū lǐ-hsíng* 尚書裏行
SUNG: lit., Probationary Minister (see *li-hsing*): variant reference to the **Chief Minister for Imperial Sacrifices** (*t'ai-ch'ang ch'ing*), i.e., Chief Minister (*ch'ing*) of the Court of Imperial Sacrifices (*t'ai-ch'ang ssu*).

5049 *shàng-shū lìng* 尚書令
(1) HAN–N-S DIV: **Director of the Imperial Secretariat** (*shang-shu t'ai;* also see *shang-shu*), rank 1,000 bushels in Later Han. HB: prefect of the masters of writing. (2) N-S DIV–CHIN: **Director of the Department of State Affairs** (*shang-shu sheng*), one of the most powerful posts in the central government; rank 2 in N. Wei, 2a in Sui and T'ang, 1a in Sung and Chin. In early T'ang held by Li Shih-min, the future T'ai-tsung, and subsequently not filled in deference to him. In Sung withdrawn from use in 1172, replaced with the archaic title *ch'eng-hsiang* (Grand Councilor). RR+SP: *président de département des affaires d'état*. P2, 3, 4.

5050 *shàng-shū lìng-shǐ* 尚書令史
HAN–SUI: **Clerk in the Imperial Secretariat** (Han: *shang-shu t'ai*) or **Clerk in the Department of State Affairs** (post-Han: *shang-shu sheng*); a relatively lowly official or unranked subofficial; cf. *ling-shih, shang-shu.* P6, 9, 12, 13, 14.

5051 *shàng-shū pó-shìh* 尚書博士
SUNG: **Erudite of the Classic of Writings** (*Shu-ching,* also called *Shang-shu*), one category of Erudites (*po-shih*) in the Directorate of Education (*kuo-tzu chien*). Also see *po-shih.*

5052 *shàng-shū p'ú-yèh* 尚書僕射
HAN–CHIN: **Vice Director of the Imperial Secretariat** (Han: *shang-shu t'ai*) or **Vice Director of the Department of State Affairs** (post-Han: *shang-shu sheng*), a common variant of *p'u-yeh*, q.v.

5053 *shàng-shū shěng* 尚書省
N-S DIV–YÜAN: **Department of State Affairs,** an outgrowth of the Han dynasty's Imperial Secretariat (*shang-shu t'ai*) and known throughout the era of N-S Division by a variety of names (including *shang-shu ssu, tu-sheng, pei-sheng, chung-t'ai, nei-t'ai*); early became the agency through which the general administrative business of the central government was carried on, coordinating function-specific Sections (*ts'ao*) or Ministries (*pu*), varying in number to more than 30; from Sui on stood alongside the Chancellery (*men-hsia sheng*) and the Secretariat (*chung-shu sheng*) in the central government's executive core, called the Three Departments (*san sheng*), presiding over a standardized group of Six Ministries (*liu pu,* q.v.); and its senior officials commonly served among the Grand Councilors (*tsai-hsiang*) who joined the Emperor in formulating policies; in Chin from 1156 served as a consolidated central administration, the Chancellery and Secretariat being abolished; in Yüan replaced in this role by the Secretariat but intermittently called into existence alongside the Secretariat until the early 1300s. Its head was normally a single Director (*ling;* see under *shang-shu ling*); other senior officials normally included Vice Directors (*p'u-yeh*) and Assistant Directors (*ch'eng;* see under *shang-shu ch'eng*). RR+SP: *département des affaires d'état.* P2, 3, 4.

5054 *shàng-shū ssū* 尚書寺
N-S DIV (Sung): variant of *shang-shu sheng* (**Department of State Affairs**).

5055 *shàng-shū ssū ts'áo* 尚書四曹
HAN: **Four Sections of Imperial Secretaries;** see under *shang-shu* and *ssu ts'ao.*

5056 *shàng-shū tà hsíng-t'ái* 尚書大行臺
N-S DIV: **Branch Department of State Affairs,** common variant of *hsing shang-shu t'ai* or *hsing-t'ai* late in the N. Dynasties, when such proto-provincial regional administrations, structured like the metropolitan Department of State Affairs (*shang-shu sheng*) at the dynastic capital, were becoming semi-autonomous governments capable of challenging the central government. P50.

5057 *shàng-shū t'ái* 尚書臺
HAN–N-S DIV: lit., pavilion of the chief stewards of writing (see *shang-shu*): **Imperial Secretariat,** from Former Han a quasiofficial designation of the aggregation of 4, then 5, then 6 Sections (*ts'ao*) to which Imperial Secretaries (*shang-shu*) and various other officials were assigned to handle the Emperor's paperwork under supervision of a Director (*ling;* see *shang-shu ling*); in Later Han became the effective administrative core of the central government, continued so in the era of N-S Division with a varying number of constituent Sections, then often called Ministries (*pu*); gradually yielded to the designation *shang-shu sheng* (Department of State Affairs), but occurred as late as S. Ch'i.

5058 *shàng-shū tsǒ-hsüǎn* 尚書左選
SUNG: **Senior Civil Appointments Process,** a reference to the Ministry of Personnel's (*li-pu*) appointments process (see under *hsüan*), in which the selection of men for appointments and reappointments was allocated to different executive officials of the Ministry according to the ranks and services (civil or military) of the appointees. The Minister (*shang-shu*) presided over selections of both civil and military categories in the categories called Capital Officials (*ching-kuan*) and Court Officials (*ch'ao-kuan*), the term Left denoting civil service appointees. This Process acquired its name in 1080, superseding the Left Bureau of Personnel Evaluation (see under *shen-kuan yüan*).

5059 *shàng-shū tū-shěng* 尚書都省
T'ANG: from 684 to 703, an unofficial reference to *wen-ch'ang tu-sheng* or *tu-sheng,* themselves official variants of *shang-shu sheng* (**Department of State Affairs**). P3.

5060 *shàng-shū yù-hsüǎn* 尚書右選
SUNG: **Senior Military Appointments Process,** a reference to the Ministry of Personnel's (*li-pu*) appointments process (see under *hsüan*), in which the selection of men for appointments and reappointments was allocated to different executive officials of the Ministry according to the ranks and services (civil or military) of the appointees. The Minister (*shang-shu*) presided over selections of both civil and military officials in the categories called Capital Officials (*ching-kuan*) and Court Officials (*ch'ao-kuan*), the term Right denoting military appointees. This Process acquired its name in 1080, superseding the Right Bureau of Personnel Evaluation (see under *shen-kuan yüan*). SP: *bureau des nominations militaires.*

5061 *shāng-shùi àn* 商稅案 or *shāng-shùi yüàn* 院
SUNG: **Merchant Tax Section,** one of 8 constituent units of the Salt and Iron Monopoly Bureau (*yen-t'ieh ssu*) in early Sung; normally headed by an Administrative Assistant (*p'an-kuan, t'ui-kuan*); oversaw the collection and distribution of mercantile taxes. SP: *service des taxes commerciales.* P62.

5062 *shāng-shùi wù* 商稅務
SUNG: **Commercial Tax Office** in the Court of the Imperial Treasury (*t'ai-fu ssu*), responsible for collecting taxes from merchants doing business in the dynastic capital. SP: *bureau de recette des taxes commerciales dans la capitale.*

5063　*shàng ssù chūn*　上四軍
SUNG: **Four Elite Armies,** collective reference to 4 major elements of the Imperial Armies (*chin-chün*) stationed at the dynastic capital: the Four Sun-sustaining Wings (*p'eng-jih ssu hsiang*) and Four Wings of Heaven-endowed Militancy (*t'ien-wu ssu hsiang*) of the Palace Command (*tien-ch'ien ssu*), the Four Dragon Guards Wings (*lung-wei ssu hsiang*) of the Metropolitan Cavalry Command (*ma-chün ssu*), and the Four Inspired Guard Wings (*shen-wei ssu hsiang*) of the Metropolitan Infantry Command (*pu-chün ssu*). P47.

5064　*shàng-ssù yüàn*　上駟院
CH'ING: **Palace Stud,** one of the Three Special Agencies (*san yüan*) of the Imperial Household Department (*nei-wu fu*); oversaw a large and steadily increasing number of horse pasturages, corrals, and stables throughout the empire in which the Emperor's horses were bred and cared for; originally patterned and named after the Ming dynasty Directorate of the Imperial Horses (*yü-ma chien*), in 1661 renamed *a-tun ya-men*, q.v., then in 1677 renamed *shang-ssu yüan*. Headed by an indefinite number of Grand Ministers (*ta-ch'en*) of the Imperial Household Department assisted by 2 Chief Ministers (*ch'ing*); supervised 2 subordinate divisions, a Left Office and a Right Office (*tso-ssu, yu-ssu*). Cf. *t'ai-p'u ssu.* P39.

5065　*shàng tà chiāng-chūn*　上大將軍
SUI–T'ANG: **Senior General-in-chief,** 3rd highest military merit title (*hsün*) awarded for extraordinary military service, rank 3a; superseded in early T'ang by Senior Military Protector (*shang hu-chün*). P65.

5066　*shàng tà-fū*　上大夫
Senior Grand Master. (1) CHOU: highest of 3 grades of Grand Master (*ta-fu*) categories, the 2nd highest of 3 categories of officials in the service of the King and Feudal Lords (*chu-hou*); ranked above Ordinary Grand Masters (*chung ta-fu*) and Junior Grand Masters (*hsia ta-fu*), below all Minister (*ch'ing*) categories, and above all Serviceman (*shih*) categories. (2) HAN: 6th highest in a hierarchy of 10 status groups in the officialdom (see under *shang-kung*), denoting all officials with annual salaries of 2,000 bushels of grain. P68.

5067　*shàng-tsào*　上造
CH'IN–HAN: lit., producer for the ruler (?): **Grandee of the Second Order,** next to lowest of 20 titles of honorary nobility (*chüeh*) awarded to distinguished personages. P65.

5068　*shàng-tsǒ*　尚左
SUNG: common abbreviation of *shang-shu tso-hsüan* (**Senior Civil Appointments Process**).

5069　*shàng-tsò kuān*　上佐官 or *shang-tso*
HAN–SUNG: **Principal Territorial Aide,** generic reference to 2nd- and 3rd-level assisting officials in major units of territorial administration such as Regions (*chou*) or Prefectures (*chou, fu*), including those bearing titles such as *pieh-chia, ssu-ma, chang-shih,* qq.v. RR: *grand fonctionnaire de la préfecture.* SP: *assistant-supérieur.*

5070　*shàng-tsǒ láng-kuān*　尚左郎官
SUNG: unofficial reference to the **Vice Minister of the Left** (*tso shih-lang*) of the **Ministry of Personnel** (*lì-pu*). See *lang-chung.*

5071　*shàng-tsūng*　上宗
Supervisor of the Imperial Clan, throughout imperial history an unofficial reference to the senior official who kept genealogical records on, and in general monitored the conduct of, members of the ruling family, such as the Han

dynasty Chamberlain for the Imperial Clan (*tsung-po*) and later Chief Ministers (*ch'ing*) or Directors (*ling*) of the Court of the Imperial Clan (*tsung-cheng ssu, tsung-jen ssu*).

5072　*shàng tū-hù fǔ*　上都護府
T'ANG–SUNG: **Superior Protectorate,** 2nd most eminent military administration (cf. Grand Protectorate, *ta tu-hu fu*) established to govern submitted non-Chinese peoples in Mongolia and Central Asia, headed by a Superior Protector (*shang tu-hu*), rank 3a1; the title was perpetuated in Sung, but probably a non-functional post. RR: *protectorat général de première classe.* SP: *protecteur supérieure.* P50.

5073　*shǎng-t'ún*　商屯
MING: **Merchant Farm,** generic designation of agricultural settlements sponsored by salt merchants in the vicinity of the northern frontier, from which the merchants produced grain for delivery to the state's frontier military garrisons, in exchange for certificates entitling them to allocations of state-monopolized salt for general distribution throughout the empire. See under *k'ai-chung* (Equitable Exchange of Grain for Salt); cf. *t'un-t'ien* (State Farm).

5074　*shǎng-tz'ù àn*　賞賜案
SUNG: **Gifts Section,** one of 5 Sections in the Tax Bureau (*tu-chih ssu*) of the Ministry of Revenue (*hu-pu*), staffed with unranked suboffficials who oversaw the collection, storage, and issuance of goods with which the Emperor rewarded officials for special achievements or on special occasions; established c. 1080, when the State Finance Commission (*san ssu*) of early Sung was discontinued. P6.

5075　*shàng-yào chiēn*　尚藥監 or *shang-yao*
(1) HAN–N-S DIV: **Director of Palace Medications,** in Later Han apparently replaced the title Palace Physician (*t'ai-i*), thereafter a common concurrent title for Palace Physicians; in N. Ch'i 4 appointees in the Palace Medical Service (*shang-yao chü*). P36. (2) CH'ING: unofficial reference to the **Imperial Academy of Medicine** (*t'ai-i yüan*).

5076　*shàng-yào chú*　尚藥局
N-S DIV (N. Wei)–YÜAN: **Palace Medical Service,** a unit of the Chancellery (*men-hsia sheng*) to c. 605, then under the Palace Administration (*tien-nei sheng, tien-chung sheng*), in Yüan apparently made an autonomous agency of the central government; relations with institutions stemming from the Han dynasty Imperial Physician (*t'ai-i ling*) such as the *t'ai-i shu, t'ai-i chü,* and *t'ai-i yüan* are not clear, but the *shang-yao chü* never seems to have had the teaching functions of these agencies; after Yüan its functions may have been absorbed by the Imperial Academy of Medicine (*t'ai-i yüan*) and the Imperial Dispensary (*yü-yao chü, yü-yao fang*). Normally headed by Chief Stewards (*tien-yü, feng-yü*), rank 5a or 5b, in Yüan with an Overseer (*ta-lu-hua-ch'ih*) and a Superintendent (*t'i-tien*), rank 5a, superimposed. RR+SP: *service des remèdes de l'empereur.* P36.

5077　*shàng-yǐn chú*　尚飲局
YÜAN: **Imperial Winery** that produced wines for the Emperor's table; one unit in the Palace Provisions Commission (*hsüan-hui yüan*) headed by a Commissioner-in-chief (*ta-shih*), rank 6b; another in the Court of Imperial Entertainments (*kuang-lu ssu*) headed by a Superintendent (*t'i-tien*), 5b. P30, 38.

5078　*shàng-yù*　尚右
SUNG: abbreviation of *shang-shu yu-hsüan* (**Senior Military Appointments Process**).

5079　*shāng-yù láng-kuān*　尚右郎官
SUNG: unofficial reference to the **Vice Minister of the Right** (*yu shih-lang*) of the **Ministry of Personnel** (*lì-pu*).

5080 *shàng-yǘ pèi-yùng ch'ù* 上虞備用處
CH'ING: **Imperial Hunting Office,** a military unit responsible for the organization and conduct of imperial hunts; staffing and organizational affiliation not clear. BH: imperial hunting department.

5081 *shàng-yūn chú* 尚醞局
Wine Stewards Service. (1) SUNG: a unit of the Palace Administration (*tien-chung sheng*) headed by 2 Chief Stewards (*feng-yü*), rank 5a or 5b. SP: *service du vin de l'empereur*. (2) YÜAN: a unit of the Palace Provisions Commission (*hsüan-hui yüan*) headed by a Commissioner-in-chief (*ta-shih*), 6b. P38.

5082 *shàng-yūn shǔ* 尚醞署
(1) CHIN: **Wine Stewards Office,** a unit of the Court Ceremonial Institute (*hsüan-hui yüan*) responsible for preparing and serving the Emperor's wines; headed by a Director (*ling*), rank 6b. P30. (2) YÜAN: from 1283 to 1286 the official redesignation of the **Court of Imperial Entertainments** (*kuang-lu ssu*). P30.

5083 *shào* 哨
CH'ING: **Company,** a military unit of approximately 100 soldiers in the forces called the Green Standards (*lu-ying*), commanded by a Company Commander (*ch'ien-tsung*); 5 such Companies normally constituted a Brigade (*ying*).

5084 *shào* 少
Lit., small, lesser: a common prefix to titles throughout history. (1) **Vice,** e.g., in *shao-ch'ing* (Vice Minister); normally denoting a 2nd-tier executive official in an agency, e.g., ranking after a *ch'ing* (Chief Minister). (2) **Junior,** in contrast to the prefixes *ta* and especially *t'ai*, e.g., in *shao-pao* (Junior Guardian) paired with Grand Guardian (*t'ai-pao*).

5085 *shào chān-shìh* 少詹事
T'ANG–CH'ING: **Vice Supervisor of the Household** of the Heir Apparent, 2nd highest post in the Supervisorate of the Household of the Heir Apparent (*chan-shih fu, chan-shih yüan*), after the Supervisor of the Household (*chan-shih*); often designated *t'ai-tzu shao chan-shih*. Rank 4a in T'ang, 6a in Sung; 2, 4a, in Ming and Ch'ing; in Ch'ing one Manchu and one Chinese appointee; in Yüan retitled *fu* (Vice) *chan-shih*. RR: *sous-intendant général de la maison de l'héritier du trône*. SP: *intendant-adjoint de la maison de l'héritier du trône*. BH: supervisor of instruction. P26.

5086 *shào ch'áng-pó* 少常伯
T'ANG–CH'ING: **Junior Executive Attendant,** from 662 to 671 the official designation of all Vice Ministers (*shih-lang*) of Ministries (*pu*); after 671 a common unofficial reference to the Vice Minister of a Ministry, in Ch'ing especially a Left (*tso*) Vice Minister.

5087 *shāo-ch'āo k'ù* 燒鈔庫
YÜAN: **Paper Money Incinerator,** 2 prefixed East and West, each headed by an Overseer (*ta-lu-hua-ch'ih*) and a Commissioner-in-chief (*ta-shih*), under the Supervisorate of Paper Money (*pao-ch'ao t'i-chü ssu*); disposed of paper money in bad condition or otherwise withdrawn from use. P16.

5088 *shào-chiàng* 少匠
T'ANG–5 DYN: **Vice Director,** 2, rank 4b2, 2nd highest executive official in the Directorate for the Palace Buildings (*chiang-tso ssu, chiang-tso chien*); after 662, with some fluctuation, called *shao-chien* (Vice Director). RR: *petit artisan*. P14, 15.

5089 *shào-chiēn* 少監
N-S DIV–MING: **Vice Director,** a common title for 2nd-tier executive officials of various agencies, especially those designated Directorates (*chien*) and headed by Supervisors or Directors (both also *chien*), e.g., the Directorate of Astronomy (*ssu-t'ien chien*). Cf. *t'ai-chien, hsiao-chien*. RR+SP: *sous-directeur*.

5090 *shào-chìh* 少秩
SUNG: lit., lesser (determiner of) precedence: unofficial reference to the **Vice Minister** (*shao-ch'ing*) **of the Court of Imperial Sacrifices** (*t'ai-ch'ang ssu*).

5091 *shào-ch'īng* 少卿
N-S DIV–CH'ING: **Vice Minister,** common title for 2nd-tier executive officials of central government agencies headed by Chief Ministers (*ch'ing*), e.g., the various Courts (*ssu*) such as the Court of the Imperial Stud (*t'ai-p'u ssu*); ordinarily with relatively high rank 4 or 5. RR+SP: *vice-président*. BH: sub-director, vice president.

5092 *shào ch'īng-chiēn* 少卿監
SUNG: abbreviated, collective reference to **Vice Ministers and Vice Directors** (*shao-ch'ing* and *shao-chien*).

5093 *shāo-chū sǒ* 燒朱所
SUNG: **Burnt Vermilion Office,** an agency of palace eunuchs commonly prefixed *hou-yüan* (rear garden), q.v.; functions not clear, possibly a workshop where vermilion was produced for use in imperial inks, paints, etc. SP: *bureau chargé de fabriquer du vermilion*.

5094 *shào chūng tà-fū* 少中大夫
CHIN–YÜAN: **Junior Grand Master of the Palace,** prestige title (*san-kuan*) for civil officials of rank 4b2 in Chin, 3b in Yüan; c. 1314 changed to Lesser Grand Master of the Palace (*ya chung ta-fu*). P68.

5095 *shāo-fǎ* 稍法
N-S DIV (Chou): **Assessor of Lesser Penalties** (?), number unspecified, ranked as Senior Servicemen (*shang-shih; 7b*) and Ordinary Servicemen (*chung-shih; 8a*), members of the Ministry of Justice (*ch'iu-kuan*). P13.

5096 *shào-fù* 少傅
Junior Mentor: irregularly from Chou into Ch'ing times, a title of great prestige conferred on officials of the central government, one of the 3 posts collectively called the Three Solitaries (*san ku*); in the mid-Han reign of Wang Mang, considered one of the Four Supports (*ssu fu*); in the later dynasties carried rank 1b. SP: *second maître*. BH: junior tutor. P67.

5097 *shào-fǔ* 少府
Lit., lesser office or storehouse, contrasted with *ta-fu* or *t'ai-fu*. (1) CH'IN–N-S DIV: **Chamberlain for the Palace Revenues,** an important post in the central government, considered one of the prestigious Nine Chamberlains (*chiu-ch'ing*), rank 2,000 bushels in Han, rank 3 during most of the following era of N-S Division; throughout its history, shared control over governmental revenues with the Chamberlain of the National Treasury (*ta ssu-nung, ssu-nung*), being charged with providing for the Emperor's personal needs, maintaining and provisioning the imperial palace, etc. His staff included many Aides (*ch'eng*) and other assistants who managed imperial parks, artisan workshops, prisons, etc.; some eventually developed into such influential separate agencies as the Imperial Secretariat (*shang-shu t'ai*) and the Palace Library (*pi-shu sheng*). He normally also had supervisory jurisdiction over both palace eunuchs and palace women. In N. Wei the post was absorbed into

the newly developing Court for the Palace Revenues (*t'ai-fu ssu*) as Vice Minister (*shao-ch'ing*), but in Sui it regained its independence as Director (*chien*, then *ling*) of the Directorate of Palace Provisions (*shao-fu chien*). HB: privy treasurer. P37. (2) T'ANG–YÜAN: unofficial reference to a **District Defender** (*hsien-wei*). (3) CH'ING: unofficial reference to a **Grand Minister** (*ta-ch'en*) **of the Imperial Household Department** (*nei-wu fu*). (4) CH'ING: unofficial reference to a **District Jailor** (*tien-shih*). Cf. *ch'ang-hsin shao-fu, ch'ang-lo shao-fu.*

5098 shào-fǔ chiēn 少府監
SUI–YÜAN: **Directorate for Imperial Manufactories**, a 2nd-level agency of the central government supervising a variety of artisan workshops producing goods for palace use, created c. 604 by being split off from the early Sui Court for the Palace Revenues (*t'ai-fu ssu*); normally headed by a Director (*chien*), rank 3b in T'ang, 4b in Sung. In T'ang incorporated a Central Service Office (*chung-shang shu*), Left Service Office (*tso-shang shu*), Right Service Office (*yu-shang shu*), Weaving and Dyeing Office (*chih-jan shu*), and Foundry Office (*chang-yeh shu*) and supervised various Foundry Directorates (*yeh-chien*), Directorates of Coinage (*chu-ch'ien chien*), and Directorates of Tributary Trade (*hu-shih chien*) in scattered localities. By Sung times the Directorate had been subordinated to the Ministry of Works (*kung-pu*), but it still directed such subsidiary agencies as a Crafts Institute (*wen-ssu yüan*), a Silk Brocade Office (*ling-chin yüan*), an Embroidery Office (*wen-hsiu yüan*), an Ornaments Office (*ts'ai-tsao yüan*), and a Dyeing Service (*jan-yüan*) and supervised Directorates of Coinage based in various Prefectures (*chou*). The much broader responsibilities of the Han dynasty Chamberlain for the Palace Revenues (*shao-fu*), after whom the Directorate was named, had long been divided with other agencies such as the Palace Administration (*tien-chung sheng*) and the Palace Domestic Service (*nei-shih sheng*); the Directorate had no authority over palace eunuchs or palace women. In Liao, Chin, and Yüan the Directorate existed only intermittently, finally in Yüan yielding all its functions to the Palace Provisions Commission (*hsüan-hui yüan*). It was apparently resurrected at the very beginning of Ming but was promptly abolished, its functions being absorbed by the Ministry of Works and the corps of palace eunuchs. RR+SP: *direction des ateliers impériaux*. P37, 38.

5099 shào-fǔ ch'īng 少府卿
N-S DIV: common variant of *shao-fu* (**Chamberlain for the Palace Revenues**).

5100 shào-fǔ ssù 少府寺
HAN–N-S DIV: **Court for the Palace Revenues**, official or quasiofficial designation of the agency headed by the Chamberlain for the Palace Revenues (*shao-fu, shao-fu ch'ing*). P37.

5101 shào-hào ssū 少皞司
Lit., office of lesser brilliance, deriving from the title assumed by a legendary ruler of highest antiquity: throughout history an unofficial reference to a **Minister of Justice** (*ch'iu-kuan, hsing-pu shang-shu*, etc.).

5102 shào-hsiēn 少仙
T'ANG–YÜAN: lit., junior immortal, deriving from a poem by Tu Fu involving a punning play on the word *hsien* meaning District: unofficial reference to a **District Defender** (*hsien-wei*), the 2nd ranking official of a District.

5103 shào hsíng-jén 少行人
CH'ING: lit., junior messenger: unofficial reference to the Vice Minister (*shao-ch'ing*) **of the Court of State Ceremonial** (*hung-lu ssu*).

5104 shào-í 少儀
T'ANG: lit., lesser ritualist: unofficial reference to a **Vice Director** (*yüan-wai lang*) **of the Headquarters Bureau** (*li-pu*) **in the Ministry of Rites** (also *lǐ-pu*). See *chung-i, hsiao-i.*

5105 shāo-jén 稍人
CHOU: **Area Inspector**, 4 with rank as Junior Servicemen (*hsia-shih*), members of the Ministry of Education (*ti-kuan*) who made inspection tours of small areas distant from the capital called *shao*, divisions of Townships (*hsien*), under the direction of the Ministry's Township Preceptors (*hsien-shih*); also assisted in the conduct of great military or funeral assemblages. CL: *officier des terres affectées aux offices.*

5106 shào-kūng 少公
T'ANG–YÜAN: lit., little Duke: unofficial reference to a **District Defender** (*hsien-wei*).

5107 shào-lì 少吏
HAN: **Junior Subaltern**, generic reference to government personnel with stipends below 100 bushels a year. Cf. *chang-li* (Senior Subaltern). P68.

5108 shào-lìng 少令
Vice Director: occasionally occurs as the title of, or unofficial reference to, the 2nd ranking official of an agency headed by a Director (*ling*) in lieu of the much more common title Aide (*ch'eng*), e.g., in the Palace Library (*pi-shu sheng*) of early T'ang. P37.

5109 shào-nèi 少內
HAN: unofficial reference to the **Chamberlain for the Palace Revenues** (*shao-fu*) (?); usage rare and not clear. P37.

5110 shào-pǎo 少保
Junior Guardian: irregularly from Chou into Ch'ing times, a title of great prestige conferred on officials of the central government, one of the 3 posts collectively called the Three Solitaries (*san ku*); in the later dynasties carried 1b rank. SP: *second gardien*. BH: junior guardian. P67.

5111 shào shàng-tsào 少上造
CH'IN–HAN: lit., junior producer for the ruler (?): **Grandee of the Fifteenth Order**, 6th highest of 20 titles of honorary nobility (*chüeh*) conferred on deserving subjects. P65.

5112 shào-shèng hóu 紹聖侯
SUI–T'ANG: **Marquis for Perpetuating the Sage**, title of nobility (*chüeh*) awarded to the most direct male descendant of Confucius, in 608 changed from Duke of (the Dukedom of) Tsou (*tsou-kuo kung*), then in 626 changed to Marquis for Praising the Sage (*pao-sheng hou*); responsible for maintaining the Confucian grave, temple, and estate at Ch'ü-fu, Shantung. P66.

5113 shào-shīh 少師
(1) **Junior Preceptor:** irregularly from Chou into Ch'ing times, a title of great prestige conferred on officials of the central government, one of the 3 posts collectively called the Three Solitaries (*san ku*); in the later dynasties carried 1b rank. SP: *second précepteur*. BH: junior preceptor. P67. (2) **Junior Master**, a term of direct address for aged degree-holders or retired officials of some repute; less prestigious than *fu-shih* (Grand Master).

5114 shào-shǐh 少使
(1) HAN: **Junior Maid**, categorical reference to palace

women with rank =400 bushels. HB: junior maid. (2) **Vice Commissioner:** may be encountered in any period as a quasi-official or unofficial reference to a 2nd ranking official of an agency headed by a Commissioner (*shih*) or Commissioner-in-chief (*ta-shih*), in lieu of the more common title *fu-shih*.

5115 *shào ssū-ch'éng* 少司成
T'ANG: lit., lesser official in charge of success or of maturing: from 662 to 671 the official redesignation of the **Director of Studies** (*ssu-yeh*) in the Directorate of Education (*kuo-tzu chien*). P34.

5116 *shào ssū-lǐ* 少司禮
Lit., 2nd official in charge of rites: from T'ang on, unofficial reference to a **Vice Minister of Rites** (*lǐ-pu shih-lang*).

5117 *shào ssū-mǎ* 少司馬
CHOU: variant of *hsiao ssu-ma* (**Vice Minister of War**).

5118 *shào ssū-núng* 少司農
CH'ING: archaic, unofficial reference to a **Vice Minister of Revenue** (*hu-pu shih-lang*), especially to one serving as **Superintendent of the Capital Granaries** (*tsung-tu ts'ang-ch'ang*).

5119 *shào ssū-p'ú* 少司僕
CH'ING: unofficial reference to a **Vice Minister** (*shao-ch'ing*) **of the Court of the Imperial Stud** (*t'ai-p'u ssu*).

5120 *shào ssū-shàn* 少司膳
CH'ING: unofficial reference to a **Vice Minister** (*shao-ch'ing*) **of the Court of Imperial Entertainments** (*kuang-lu ssu*).

5121 *shào ssū-t'ú* 少司徒
CH'ING: archaic, unofficial reference to a **Vice Minister of Revenue** (*hu-pu shih-lang*), especially to one serving as **Superintendent of the Capital Granaries** (*tsung-tu ts'ang-ch'ang*).

5122 *shào-tsǎi* 少宰
(1) T'ANG–CH'ING: **Junior Steward,** unofficial reference to a Vice Minister of Personnel (*lì-pu shih-lang*). (2) SUNG: in addition, briefly in the early 1100s, **Vice Grand Councilor,** the official redesignation of the Right Vice Director (*yu p'u-yeh*) of the Department of State Affairs (*shang-shu sheng*), one of the Grand Councilors (*tsai-hsiang*), and thereafter in S. Sung an unofficial reference to the same post, commonly known as *fu-hsiang*. Also see *ta-tsai, t'ai-tsai*. SP: *conseiller d'état en chef*. P3.

5123 *shào-ts'ān* 少參
MING–CH'ING: unofficial reference to an **Assistant Administration Commissioner** (*ts'an-i*) of a Provincial Administration Commission (*ch'eng-hsüan pu-cheng shih ssu*). Cf. *ta-ts'an* (Administration Vice Commissioner).

5124 *shào-wèi* 少尉
CH'ING: unofficial reference to a **District Jailor** (*tien-shih*).

5125 *sháo-wǔ* 韶舞
MING–CH'ING: **Ceremonial Dancer,** 2 prefixed Left and Right, rank 9b, in the Music Office (*chiao-fang ssu*); terminated in 1729. P10.

5126 *shào-yǐn* 少尹
(1) T'ANG–CHIN: **Vice Governor,** 2nd ranking post in a Superior Prefecture (*fu*); one or 2, rank 4b2 in T'ang, 6b in Sung, 5a in Chin. RR+SP: *vice-préfet*. P32, 49, 53. (2) T'ANG–CH'ING: from 662 to 670 and again from 684 to 705 the official redesignation of the **Vice Supervisor of the Household** of the Heir Apparent (*shao chan-shih;* see un-

der *chan-shih*); thereafter irregularly an unofficial reference to the post. (3) CH'ING: unofficial reference to a **Police Chief** (*hsün-chien;* see *hsün-chien ssu*) or a **District Jailor** (*tien-shih*), both in a District (*hsien*).

5127 *shè* 攝
Acting: throughout imperial history, a term used whenever someone without appropriate rank status was temporarily put in charge of a vacant office to which he might subsequently be regularly appointed, or when an official already on duty was given additional temporary responsibility for a vacant post of higher rank status.

5128 *shè* 社
YÜAN–CH'ING: **Community:** a unit in state-sponsored sub-District (*hsien*) organization of the population; apparently originated in Yüan times as a cluster of 50 or so neighboring families designated as a unit to establish elementary schools and charity granaries, control irrigation, plant trees, bring vacant land under cultivation, promote morality, agriculture, sericulture, fishing, etc., existing alongside law-enforcement and tax-collecting units called *li* (rural Village, urban Community); after Yüan, intermittently appeared in regional variations of the local administrative systems commonly called *li-chia* and *pao-chia*. Normally had a chosen or designated leader called Community Head (*she-chang*).

5129 *shè* 舍
SUNG: **College,** designation of a unit in the National University (*t'ai-hsüeh*) from c. 1070; see *wai-she* (Outer College), *nei-she* (Inner College), *shang-she* (Superior College).

5130 *shè-àn* 設案
SUNG: **Special Preparations Section,** one of 7 Sections (*an*) in the Salt and Iron Monopoly Bureau (*yen-t'ieh ssu*) of early Sung, normally headed by an Administrative Assistant (*p'an-kuan, t'ui-kuan*); oversaw provisioning of the imperial palace with seasonal fresh foods, foods used in periods of fasting, mutton, pork, firewood, and pottery. SP: *service de préparation des frais de l'abstinence, mouton, porc, bois de chauffage, poterie*.

5131 *shè-chèng* 攝政
Lit., to be in acting charge of government: **Regent** or **Regency,** a term normally used when a child had succeeded to the throne and one or more persons had been designated to run the government during his minority. Cf. *liu-shou, chien-kuo*.

5132 *shè-chí shǔ* 社稷署
YÜAN: **Office for the Altar of the Soil and Grain,** one of 3 special sacrificial agencies in the central government (see *t'ai-miao, chiao-ssu shu*); headed by 2 Directors (*ling*), rank 6b. Cf. *chiao-she shu* (Office of the National Altars). P28.

5133 *shè-chí t'án* 社稷壇
Altar of the Soil and Grain: throughout history, an altar symbolizing the land and its contributions to life, which served as one of the important national altars; Emperors normally offered sacrifices there in spring and autumn; commonly maintained by an Office for the Altar … (*she-chi shu*) or a Director of the Altar … (*she-chi ling*). Also see *chiao-she shu* (Office of the National Altars), *ti-t'an*. P28.

5134 *shè-jén* 射人
CHOU: **Expert Archer,** 2 ranked as Junior Grand Masters (*hsia ta-fu*), 4 as Senior Servicemen (*shang-shih*), and 8 as

Junior Servicemen (*hsia-shih*), members of the Ministry of War (*hsia-kuan*) who competed in archery contests on important royal ceremonial occasions including sacrifices. CL: *officier du tir d'arc, grand archer.*

5135 *shé-jén* 舌人
CHOU: lit., tongue-man: variant of *hsiang-hsü* (**Interpreter**).

5136 *shè-jén* 舍人
Lit., man in or of the lodgings; hence a retainer. (1) **Houseman:** throughout history, a general reference to, or a quasi-official title for, kinsmen and others who were squire-like dependents of dignitaries. In Chou times, the title of 4 Ordinary Servicemen (*chung-shih*) and 8 Junior Servicemen (*hsia-shih*) in the Ministry of Education (*ti-kuan*) whose principal duty was to distribute grain to inhabitants of the royal palace. In Ming times, a salaried but unranked status for younger brothers, sons, cousins, and unrelated hangers-on of hereditary military officers, from among whom vacancies in the officer corps were commonly filled. During the era of N-S Division, persons of such status who took on secretarial functions gradually established a category of officials as indicated in (2) below. CL: *officier de logement.* HB: member of the suite. (2) N-S DIV–T'ANG: **Secretary,** officials of low rank or unranked subofficials attached to the establishments of Heirs Apparent, Princes, Princesses, and some other dignitaries, generally acting as receptionists and document handlers. RR: *secrétaire.* P69. (3) N-S DIV–CH'ING: **Drafter,** also developing from the Houseman status described in (1) above; abbreviation of *chung-shu she-jen* or *t'ung-shih she-jen.* Also see *ch'i-chü she-jen.*

5137 *shè-jén shěng* 舍人省
N-S DIV (N. Ch'i): **Department of Drafters** under the developing Secretariat (*chung-shu sheng*), staffed with 10 Secretariat Drafters (*chung-shu she-jen*) and 10 Scribes (*chu-shu*); responsible for the issuance of imperial pronouncements. P2.

5138 *shè-jén yüàn* 舍人院
SUNG: **Document Drafting Office,** in early Sung an agency of the central government responsible for the preparation of all state documents; staffing and history not clear, but apparently subordinated at least loosely to the combined Secretariat-Chancellery (*chung-shu men-hsia sheng*) and probably staffed with Secretariat Drafters (*chung-shu she-jen*). SP: *bureau des fonctionnaires-rédacteurs, bureau des secrétaires.*

5139 *shè-kuān* 設官
To establish officials: a term consistently used with the sense of authorizing such-and-such posts with so-and-so many appointees at such-and-such ranks. Occurs commonly in descriptions of government following the names of agencies, introducing their authorized posts in order of ranks, suggesting the rendering **with authorized posts (as follows:).**

5140 *shè-niǎo shìh* 射鳥氏
CHOU: **Bird Killer,** one with hereditary rank as a Junior Serviceman (*hsia-shih*) in the Ministry of War (*hsia-kuan*), primarily responsible for shooting and killing birds of ill omen that were sighted during royal sacrificial ceremonies; also in charge of retrieving arrows during royal archery tournaments. CL: *tireur d'oiseaux.*

5141 *shè-shēng* 射生
Lit., one who shoots the living (i.e., moving targets); see

ya-ch'ien she-sheng ping, tien-ch'ien she-sheng shou, tien-ch'ien she-sheng hsiang, tien-ch'ien she-sheng chün, kung-feng she-sheng kuan.

5142 *shè-shēng* 射聲
Lit., one who shoots at or by sound: **Bowmen Shooter by Sound,** from Han on a common reference to an archer so skilled that he could stalk and shoot his prey in the dark of night, relying only on sounds to guide him. In T'ang, referred to members of the Left and Right Metropolitan Guards (*ling-chün wei*). HB: archer who shoots by sound. RR: *archer habile.* P43.

5143 *shěn-chì k'ō* 審計科
YÜAN: **Budget Section** in the Ministry of Revenue (*hu-pu*), a minor office headed by a Clerk (*ling-shih*).

5144 *shěn-chì ssū* 審計司
SUNG: **Accounting Office,** a minor agency found in the Court of the Imperial Treasury (*t'ai-fu ssu*), in military units, and in some units of territorial administration. SP: *bureau de vérification des comptes.*

5145 *shén-chī yíng* 神機營
MING: **Firearms Division,** one of the Three Great Training Divisions (*san ta-ying*) at Peking, with counterparts at Nanking; reportedly originated in the early 1400s as a unit in which troops of the 2 other Divisions (*wu-chün ying, san-ch'ien ying*) were trained in the use of firearms of types acquired in the Ming annexation of Annam (modern North Vietnam). Also called Division of the Five Thousand (*wu-ch'ien ying*).

5146 *shěn-chì yüàn* 審計院
SUNG: variant of *shen-chi ssu* (**Accounting Office**).

5147 *shēn-ch'í chūn* 參旗軍
T'ANG: **Army of the Celestial Lion's Pelt,** named after a star in Orion called *shen-ch'i;* one of 12 regional supervisory headquarters for militia Garrisons (*fu;* also see *fu-ping*) called the Twelve Armies (*shih-erh chün*); existed only 620–623, 625–636. RR: *armée (de la constellation) des Étendard Chen.* P44.

5148 *shēn-chīn* 紳衿
Lit., (wearers of) sashes and collars: **the elite,** a collective reference to all those who were, were entitled to become, or had been officials in government service and in consequence constituted the most influential group in Chinese society; commonly used as the equivalent of *hsiang-shen* (rural elite). Whether or not Government Students (*sheng-yüan*) were included in such a class has been a matter of controversy. Also see *shih ta-fu* (the official class) and *shen-shih* (the elite). Commonly rendered alternatively as **the gentry** or **the ruling class.**

5149 *shén-chìng chūn* 神勁軍
SUNG: **Army of Inspired Power,** designation of a military force armed with explosive weapons. SP: *artillerie de force transcendante.*

5150 *shén-ch'ú yüàn* 神廚院
T'ANG: **Office of Sacrificial Foods,** one of 4 minor service agencies in the Court of Imperial Sacrifices (*t'ai-ch'ang ssu*); maintained grain and utensils for imperial sacrificial ceremonies; apparently staffed solely by state slaves. RR: *service de la cuisine des esprits.*

5151 *shén-fáng* 神房
CH'ING: **Shamanism Office** in the Office of Palace Ceremonial (*chang-i ssu*) of the Imperial Household Depart-

ment (*nei-wu fu*); directed palace eunuchs and Shamanesses (*sa-man t'ai-t'ai*) in offering prayers for the deceased Manchu rulers. BH: office of shamanism.

5152 *shěn-hsíng ì-kuān* 審刑議官
SUNG: **Consultant in the Review of Sentences,** a duty assignment in the Ministry of Justice (*hsing-pu*); status details not clear. SP: *chargé de déliberation dans les investigations judiciaires.*

5153 *shěn-hsíng ssū* 審刑司
(1) MING: **Punishment Reviewing Office,** from 1381 to 1386 only, an autonomous agency of the central government that reviewed judgments recommended by the Court of Judicial Review (*ta-li ssu*); headed by 2 Punishment Reviewers (*shen-hsing*), rank 6a, assisted by 3 Evaluators (*hsiang-i*), 7a. P22. (2) CH'ING: **Office of Palace Justice,** one of 7 major units of the Imperial Household Department (*nei-wu fu*), charged with the judicial disciplining of the Department's own personnel as well as Bannermen (see under *ch'i,* Banner) and palace eunuchs under its supervision. Name changed from *shang-fang yüan* in 1677. BH: judicial department. P37.

5154 *shěn-hsíng yüàn* 審刑院
SUNG: **Judicial Control Office,** a special agency under the combined Secretariat-Chancellery (*chung-shu men-hsia sheng*) from 991 to 1080; scrutinized and evaluated recommendations about judicial cases submitted by the Ministry of Justice (*hsing-pu*) and the Court of Judicial Review (*ta-li ssu*); staffed with mature central government officials on duty assignments limited to 3 years, bearing such designations as Recommendation Evaluator (*hsiang-i kuan*), Sentence Evaluator (*hsiang-tuan kuan, p'ing-tuan kuan*), Review Evaluator (*hsiang-fu kuan*), etc., under leadership of an Administrator of the Judicial Control Office (*chih shen-hsing yüan shih*). After 1080 the Office's functions generally reverted to the Ministry of Justice. SP: *cour des investigations judiciaires chargée de réviser les cas importants.* P13.

5155 *shěn-kuān yüàn* 審官院
Bureau of Personnel Evaluation. (1) SUNG: an early Sung agency that periodically evaluated and recommended for appointment or reappointment both civil and military officials of the categories called Capital Officials (*ching-kuan*) and Court Officials (*ch'ao-kuan*), i.e., those of middling and high rank; staffed by central government officials on special duty assignments, principally those having nominal status in the Ministry of Personnel (*li-pu*). Established in 993 to replace 2 earlier agencies, the Bureau of Commissions (*ch'ai-ch'ien yüan*) and the Bureau of Capital and Court Officials (*mo-k'an ching-ch'ao kuan yüan*), apparently in an imperial effort to weaken the great powers of the State Finance Commission (*san ssu*). Technically, divided into an East Bureau of Personnel Evaluation (*shen-kuan tung-yüan*) for dealing with civil officials and a West Bureau of Personnel Evaluation (*shen-kuan hsi-yüan*) for dealing with military officers. Abolished in the general governmental reorganization of 1080, its functions reverting to the Ministry of Personnel, specifically to what were known as the Ministry's Senior Civil Appointments Process (*shang-shu tso-hsüan*) and Senior Military Appointments Process (*shang-shu yu-hsüan*); also see *hsüan.* SP: *cour du personnel administratif.* P16. (2) CHIN: established in 1199 for the specific purpose of checking on the propriety of memorials submitted by officials, in the absence of a Chinese-style Chancellery (*men-hsia sheng*), which traditionally performed this function among others. Staffing and organizational affiliations not clear. P19.

5156 *shén-kūng chiēn* 神宮監
MING–CH'ING: **Directorate for Imperial Temples,** one of 12 major Directorates (*chien*) into which palace eunuchs were organized; headed by a eunuch Director (*t'ai-chien*); responsible for maintaining the imperial ancestral temple and other temples as ordered. In Ch'ing existed only from 1656 to 1661. See under *shih-erh chien* (Twelve Directorates).

5157 *shěn-lǐ sǒ* 審理所
MING: **Disciplinary Office,** an agency in each Princely Establishment (*wang-fu*) charged with judicial control over the Prince's staff; headed by a Director (*cheng*), rank 6a.

5158 *shēn-lièh shìh-pǎn* 身列仕版
CH'ING: lit., **personally on active service:** reference to an official on normal duty in a regular substantive appointment, as distinguished from acting, honorific, and other nonsubstantive appointments.

5159 *shén-miào fū-jén* 神廟夫人
SUNG: **Mistress of the Ancestral Temple,** apparently a specialized duty assignment for some noblewoman; see under *fu-jen.* SP: *dame du temple.*

5160 *shén-pù* 神部
N-S DIV (N. Wei): variant of *tz'u-pu* (**Ministry of Sacrifices**). P27.

5161 *shén-shìh* 神士
CHOU: **Religious Devotee,** a general term for persons devoted to local or special cults who were recognized by the Ministry of Rites (*ch'un-kuan*) and granted official rank according to the extent of their religious knowledge. CL: *officier attaché au service des esprits surnaturels.*

5162 *shēn-shìh* 紳士
Lit., **girdled servicemen,** i.e., servicemen (wearing) sashes: **the elite,** a collective reference to all those who were, were entitled to be, or had been officials in government service and in consequence constituted the most influential group in Chinese society; commonly used as the equivalent of *hsiang-shen* (rural elite). Whether or not Government Students (*sheng-yüan*) were included in such a class has been a matter of controversy. Also see *shih ta-fu* (the official class) and *shen-chin* (the elite). Commonly rendered alternatively as **the gentry** or **the ruling class.**

5163 *shén-ts'è chūn* 神策軍
T'ANG: **Army of Inspired Strategy,** 2 designated Left and Right in the Imperial Armies (*chin-chün*) stationed at the dynastic capital and known in the aggregate as the Northern Command (*pei-ya*); from 807 on, considered units of the Six Imperial Armies (*liu chün*). Initiated c. 753 as a Wing of Inspired Strategy (*shen-ts'e hsiang*), renamed in 786. Stationed in the imperial parks at the capital, came under the influence of palace eunuchs; by the late 790s had a reported strength of 150,000 troops at the capital and numerous Mobile Brigades (*hsing-ying, shen-ts'e hsing-ying*) stationed at strategic locations under eunuch Military Commissioners (*chieh-tu shih*). Leaders of the Armies of Inspired Strategy bore impressive titles not used in other Imperial Armies: *kuan chün-jung shih* (Inspector of the Armies), *hu-chün chung-wei* (Palace Commandant-protector), *chung hu-chün* (Palace Protector), *chien kou-tang* (Supervisory Manager), *chih-hui shih* (Commander), *ma-chün chih-hui shih* (Cavalry Commander), *pu-chün chih-hui shih* (Infantry Commander), etc., as well as more regular titles such as General-in-chief (*ta chiang-chün*) and Commander-general (*t'ung-chün*). Through the 800s eunuch leaders of the

Armies of Inspired Strategy dominated the capital city, the palace, and the Emperors, installing and deposing Emperors as they pleased. In 885 the Armies of Inspired Strategy spawned 10 so-called Armies (*chün;* see *shih chün*), now constituting what was called the New Army of Inspired Strategy (*shen-ts'e hsin-wei*), that were scattered through the domain controlled by T'ang in an effort to reassert court control throughout the empire. The effort failed, and in 898 the Left and Right Armies of Inspired Strategy were reconstituted, with a total force of some 6,000 men. They existed at least in name until the end of the dynasty in 907. Meantime, particularly during and after the great rebellion of 875–884 led by Huang Ch'ao, regional warlords bearing the title Military Commissioner (*chieh-tu shih*) or variants ruled autonomously in many parts of the empire. In 903 one of them captured the capital city and slaughtered eunuchs in the hundreds. RR: *armée de la strategie transcendante.* P43.

5164 *shén-ts'è hsiāng* 神策廂
T'ANG: **Wing of Inspired Strategy,** created c. 753 as a unit of the Imperial Armies (*chin-chün*) in the far Northwest (modern Kansu) after T'ang's retreat from Central Asia; in 760–761, because of the march of Islam across Central Asia and the problems created in China by the An Lu-shan rebellion (755–763), transferred to a base in modern Honan; c. 765 divided into Left and Right Wings stationed inside the imperial parks at the dynastic capital and began falling under the influence of palace eunuchs; quickly grew to a total force of perhaps 150,000 men, and in 783 began spawning Mobile Brigades (*hsing-ying, shen-ts'e hsing-ying*), each under a eunuch Military Commissioner (*chieh-tu shih*) or a variant, which increased greatly in the 790s. Meantime, in 786, the Left and Right Wings of Inspired Strategy were renamed the Left and Right Armies of Inspired Strategy (see *shen-ts'e chün*). P43.

5165 *shén-ts'è hsíng-yíng* 神策行營
T'ANG: **Mobile Brigade of the Wing of Inspired Strategy** (from 786, **Army of Inspired Strategy**); see *shen-ts'e hsiang, shen-ts'e chün.*

5166 *shén-tū yüàn* 神都苑
T'ANG: **Imperial Capital Park,** one each east of the dynastic capital, Ch'ang-an, and east of the auxiliary Eastern Capital, Tung-tu (modern Loyang); managed by a Supervisor (*chien*) under the Court of the Imperial Granaries (*ssu-nung ssu*); created c. 657 by renaming the *fang-hua yüan,* q.v. P40.

5167 *shén-wèi chūn* 神威軍
T'ANG: **Army of Inspired Awesomeness,** 2 designated Left and Right in the Imperial Armies (*chin-chün*) of the Northern Command (*pei-ya*) at the dynastic capital; also known as the *tien-ch'ien* (palace) *shen-wei chün* because by 800 they were under the control of palace eunuchs with such grandiose titles as Supervisory Commissioner (*chien ... shih*) of the Left or Right Army of Inspired Awesomeness, Palace Protector (*chung hu-chün*) of the Left or Right Army of Inspired Awesomeness, etc. Initiated in 787 by a renaming of the Left and Right Armies of Bowmen Shooters at Moving Targets (*tien-ch'ien she-sheng chün;* see *ya-ch'ien she-sheng ping*); terminated in 813, when all their troops were absorbed into the increasingly dominant Armies of Inspired Strategy (*shen-ts'e chün*). RR: *armée de la majesté transcendante.* P43.

5168 *shén-wèi ssù hsiāng* 神衛四廂
SUNG: **Four Inspired Guard Wings,** one of the major

military organizations in the Imperial Armies (*chin-chün*) stationed at the dynastic capital, one of those known collectively as the Four Elite Armies (*shang ssu chün*); headed by a Commander-in-chief (*tu chih-hui shih*); each of its Wings (*hsiang*) reportedly included 3 Armies (*chün*). From the mid-l000s belonged to the Metropolitan Infantry Command (*pu-chün ssu*). SP: *garde transcendante, armée de mer.* P47.

5169 *shén-wŭ chūn* 神武軍
Army of Inspired Militancy. (1) T'ANG: 2 military units, designated Left and Right, in the Northern Command (*pei-ya*) of Imperial Armies (*chin-chün*) stationed at the dynastic capital; included in the groups called the Six Imperial Armies (*liu chün*) and later the Ten Imperial Armies (*shih chün*). Perhaps created in 738 concurrently with the Militant as Dragons Armies (*lung-wu chün*), but if so promptly terminated; in 757 created or restored by splitting some troops off from the Forest of Plumes Armies (*yü-lin chün*), especially incorporating a force of skilled archers previously called the Left and Right Armies of Heroic Militancy (*ying-wu chün*). RR: *armée de la guerre transcendante.* (2) SUNG: generic reference to the Five Inspired Armies (*shen-wu wu chün*).

5170 *shén-wŭ t'iēn-chì* 神武天騎
T'ANG: **Heavenly Horsemen of Inspired Militancy,** quasi-official reference to personnel of the 2 Armies of Inspired Militancy (*shen-wu chün*).

5171 *shén-wŭ wŭ chūn* 神武五軍
SUNG: **Five Inspired Armies,** from 1129 to 1131 the collective designation of Sung's armies during the central government's retreat to the South, supervised by an emergency Imperial Defense Command (*yü-ying ssu*); differentiated by the directional terms Left, Right, Center, Front, and Rear; each commanded by a General (*chiang-chün*). Superseded the Five Imperial Armies (*yü-ch'ien wu chün*), superseded in turn by the Four Field Defense Armies (*hsing-ying ssu hu-chün*). Cf. *shen-wu chün.* SP: *cinq armées de la bravoure transcendante.* P43.

5172 *shén-yüèh kuān* 神樂觀
MING–CH'ING: **Imperial Music Office** under the Court of Imperial Sacrifices (*t'ai-ch'ang ssu*), staffed with hereditary musicians and dancers considered Taoists, led by a Superintendent (*t'i-tiao*); performed for sacrificial and other imperial ceremonies; in a reorganization of 1729 paired with the Music Office (*chiao-fang ssu*) under the Ministry of Rites (*lĭ-pu*) with the new name *shen-yüeh so.* P10.

5173 *shén-yüèh sŏ* 神樂所 or *shén-yüèh shŭ* 署
CH'ING: **Imperial Music Office,** official redesignation of the *shen-yüeh kuan* in 1729, when it was paired with the Music Office (*chiao-fang ssu,* itself now renamed *ho-sheng shu*) under the Ministry of Rites (*lĭ-pu*). Headed by a Superintendent (*t'i-tien*). In 1755 *so* was changed to *shu;* thereafter headed by a Director (*cheng*), rank 6a. BH: office of sacred music. P10.

5174 *shēng* 升
To promote: a standard term throughout history, normally without any special qualifying implications.

5175 *shēng* 生
Student: throughout history a common generic term equivalent to *hsüeh-sheng,* q.v.; particular sense is normally denoted by a prefix.

5176 *shěng* 省
Ety. very confusing, but lit. meaning "to inspect"; hence, to oversee, supervise (?). (1) **Department:** from Han on,

a generic term for some major agencies of the central government, a usage that developed most extensively in the era of N-S Division; e.g., see *chung-shu sheng, men-hsia sheng, shang-shu sheng, pi-shu sheng, tien-chung sheng, nei-shih sheng.* (2) YÜAN–CH'ING: **Province,** generic designation of the largest units of territorial administration under the central government, growing out of the Yüan practice of establishing Branch Secretariats (*hsing chung-shu sheng,* commonly abbreviated to *hsing-sheng*) as territorial administrations, e.g., *ho-nan hsing-sheng,* lit., Branch Secretariat for (the region) South of the Yellow River, by Ming times firmly entrenched as the name of the territory itself, Honan Province (*sheng*).

5177 *shēng ch'áo-kuān* 升朝官
SUNG: variant of *ch'ao-kuan* (**Court Official**), but apparently of lesser status than those Court Officials who were called Consultants-in-ordinary (*ch'ang-ts'an kuan*); perhaps denotes those newly promoted (*sheng*) to Court Official status, hence in the lower ranks of that category. SP: *fonctionnaire titulaire de la cour.*

5178 *shèng-chì tièn* 聖濟殿
MING: lit., hall for sagely (i.e., imperial) relief from suffering: from 1536, the official redesignation of the **Imperial Dispensary** (*yü-yao chü*). P36.

5179 *shèng-chì yüàn* 聖濟院
MING: lit., office for sagely (i.e., imperial) relief from suffering: from the mid-1500s, an unofficial reference to the **Imperial Academy of Medicine** (*t'ai-i yüan*).

5180 *shèng-chiěn ssū* 省減司
SUNG: **Cost-reduction Office,** from 1058 to c. 1080 a special agency apparently staffed by officials of regular central government organs on temporary duty assignments; cooperated with the State Finance Commission (*san ssu*) in eliminating unnecessary state expenditures.

5181 *shéng-ch'iēn t'īng* 繩愆廳
MING: lit., office for correcting faults: **Disciplinary Office** in the Directorate of Education (*kuo-tzu chien*), responsible for enforcing rules of conduct and maintaining scholastic standards; headed by a Proctor (*chien-ck'eng*), rank 8a. Although Ch'ing perpetuated the post of Proctor, it did not continue the agency name. P34.

5182 *shèng-chǔ* 聖主
Lit., sage master: a common reference to the **Emperor.**

5183 *shèng-ì* 聖裔
CH'ING: lit., descended from the Sage, i.e., Confucius: prefix to a title denoting that the post was hereditarily reserved for a descendant of Confucius and normally filled by appointment of the most direct descendant, ennobled as the Duke for Fulfilling the Sage (*yen-sheng kung*); usually found in the Confucian family establishment at Ch'ü-fu, Shantung, but also in the Directorate of Education (*kuo-tzu chien*) at the dynastic capital. P66.

5184 *shěng-k'uéi* 省魁
SUNG: **Metropolitan Graduate with Distinction,** unofficial reference to the best passers of the Metropolitan Examination (*sheng-shih*) in the civil service recruitment examination sequence, but the precise group referred to is not clear. Cf. *hui-k'uei.*

5185 *shèng-miào* 聖廟
Lit., temple to the Sage: **Confucian Temple,** common reference to the state-recognized temple honoring Confucius at the Confucian family estate at Ch'ü-fu, Shantung.

5186 *shēng-p'íng shǔ* 昇平署
CH'ING: lit., office of tranquillity and peace: **Court Theatrical Office,** a unit of the Office of Palace Ceremonial (*chang-i ssu*) in the Imperial Household Department (*nei-wu fu*); supervised entertainments provided by palace eunuchs; headed by one of the Department's Grand Ministers (*ta-ch'en*) serving as Concurrent Manager (*chien-li sheng-p'ing shu shih-wu*). BH: court theatrical bureau.

5187 *shěng-shìh* 省事
N-S DIV: lit., (dealing with) business of the Department (*sheng*): **Departmental Clerk,** a minor post found in both the Chancellery (*men-hsia sheng*) and the Department of State Affairs (*shang-shu sheng*), with status comparable to Clerk (*ling-shih*); neither the post nor appointees to it were considered in the "pure" category (see under *ch'ing*). P5, 26.

5188 *shěng-shìh* 省試
T'ANG–SUNG: lit., examination in the Department (*sheng*), i.e., under supervision of the Department of State Affairs (*shang-shu sheng*): **Metropolitan Examination,** 2nd-stage examination in the civil service recruitment examination sequence, following qualifying examinations (*chieh-shih*) in Prefectures (*chou, fu*); given at the dynastic capital by officials of the central government on ad hoc duty assignments as Examination Administrators (*chih kung-chü*) until the 1080s, thereafter by the Ministry of Rites (*lǐ-pu*); consisted of a variety of examinations, the most prestigious leading to the Presented Scholar (*chin-shih*) degree; from 975 followed by a confirmatory Palace Examination (*tien-shih*). Cf. *hui-shih.*

5189 *shēng-shīh* 笙師
CHOU: **Master of the Panpipe,** 2 ranked as Ordinary Servicemen (*chung-shih*) and 4 as Junior Servicemen (*hsia-shih*), members of the Ministry of Rites (*ch'un-kuan*) responsible for instructing players of an instrument resembling a mouth organ and for conducting them in court ceremonial performances. CL: *maître des orgues, jeux de tuyaux.*

5190 *shēng-yào k'ù* 生藥庫
MING: lit., storehouse of raw medicines: **Herbs Repository** under the Imperial Academy of Medicine (*t'ai-i yüan*), headed by a Commissioner-in-chief (*ta-shih*), probably a non-official specialist. P36.

5191 *shěng-yěn* 省眼
T'ANG–SUNG: lit., the eye of the Department (*sheng*), i.e., the Department of State Affairs (*shang-shu sheng*) (?): unofficial reference to a **Vice Director** (*yüan-wai lang*) **of the Bureau of Appointments** (*lì-pu*) in the Ministry of Personnel (also *lì-pu*).

5192 *shèng-yüán* 剩員
Lit., surplus appointee: throughout history an unofficial reference to a **sinecure** or an appointee to a sinecure, a **placeholder.**

5193 *shēng-yüán* 生員
SUI–CH'ING: **Government Student,** generic designation of students entitled to state stipends; in early usage referred to students of many kinds, including Sui dynasty students of calendar-making, astrology, water clocks, etc.; but in Ming and Ch'ing normally referred to fully subsidized students in Confucian schools (*ju-hsüeh*) at prefectural (*fu*) and lower levels of territorial administration, hence a common variant of Cultivated Talent (*hsiu-ts'ai*), i.e., anyone eligible to participate in the Provincial Examinations (*hsiang-*

shih), the first major stage in the civil service recruitment examination sequence. BH: licentiate. P35, 51.

5194 *shěng-yüán* 省元
SUNG: **Principal Graduate** in the Metropolitan Examination (*sheng-shih*) in the civil service recruitment examination sequence; cf. *chuang-yüan.*

5195 *shěng-yüan* 省掾
YÜAN: **Secretariat Clerk,** common designation of suboffcial functionaries assigned to do scribal work in the Secretariat (*chung-shu sheng*); also see *yüan, yüan-shih.*

5196 *shih* 什
(1) **File:** throughout history a common designation for a unit of 10 soldiers. (2) CH'IN: **Ten,** designation of 10 neighboring households in the sub-District (*hsien*) organization of the population for mutual surveillance and accountability; each Ten was subdivided into 2 Fives (*wu*), and 10 Tens constituted an official Village (*li*).

5197 *shih* 使
Lit., sent as a representative: **Commissioner,** one of the most common Chinese titles, almost invariably found with a prefix suggesting his function or designating the agency he headed; his principal aide was most commonly a Vice Commissioner (*fu-shih*). In T'ang, Sung, and Liao times, the term was used almost solely for duty assignments (*ch'ai-ch'ien*) of officials with regular status elsewhere in the officialdom; from Chin through Ch'ing, however, Commissioners were normally substantive appointees. In any contexts, the use of *shih* in its normal verbal sense is a possibility to be kept in mind. In this dictionary, *shih* titles are to be found under their prefixes.

5198 *shih* 侍
Attendant or **Attending,** normally referring to palace service: a term occurring only in compounds, e.g., *nei-shih* (Palace Attendant), *ch'ang-shih* (Attendant-in-ordinary), *shih yü-shih* (Attendant Censor).

5199 *shih* 史
(1) **Scribe:** throughout history occurs as a lowly or unranked post identifiable only by a prefixed agency name, but most commonly incorporated into compounds such as *yü-shih, t'ai-shih, chang-shih, nei-shih.* CL: *écrivain.* (2) CHOU: **Sixth Class Administrative Official,** 6th highest of 8 categories in which officials were classified in a hierarchy separate from the formal rank system called the Nine Honors (*chiu ming*); below those designated *cheng* (Principal, etc.); *shih* (Mentor, etc.), *ssu* (to be in charge; office), *lü* (Functionary), and *fu* (Storekeeper); above only *hsü* (Assistant) and *t'u* (Attendant). CL: *sixième degré de la subordination administrative.*

5200 *shih* 士
(1) **Elite:** throughout history a broad generic reference to the group dominant in government, which also was the paramount group in society; originally a warrior caste, it was gradually transformed into a non-hereditary, ill-defined class of bureaucrats among whom litterateurs were most highly esteemed. From the era of N-S Division into T'ang times, status in the group was authenticated by the state and jealously guarded by powerful families. (2) CHOU, N-S DIV (Chou): **Serviceman,** lowest of 3 broad categories in which officials were ranked, below Minister (*ch'ing*) and Grand Master (*ta-fu*); subdivided into the grades of Senior (*shang*), Ordinary (*chung*), and Junior (*hsia*) Servicemen. CL: *gradué.* (3) CHOU: **Elite Soldier,** generic reference to sons of meritorious officials chosen for guard duty within the royal pal-

ace or to form the vanguard, under command of the Heir Apparent, in an emergency defense force or a campaigning army. CL: *guerrier d'élite qui garde un poste.* (4) HAN: **Servicemen,** lowest of 10 status groups for regular officials; see under *shang-kung* (Superior Dukes). P68. Also see *hsüeh-shih, chin-shih, shu-chi-shih,* and other variously prefixed *shih* entries.

5201 *shih* 實
Substantive, prefix used with terms of appointment or promotion meaning that the appointment was not, or was no longer, acting, probationary, temporary, or in any other way irregular. See *chen.*

5202 *shih* 師
(1) CHOU: **Regiment,** a standard military unit, 5 of which constituted an Army (*chün*); consisted of 5 Battalions (*lü*) theoretically totaling 2,500 soldiers; led by a Regimental Commander (*shih-shuai*) with rank as Ordinary Grand Master (*chung ta-fu*). CL: *régiment.* (2) CHOU: **Second Class Administrative Official,** 2nd highest of 8 categories in which officials were classified in a hierarchy separate from the formal rank system called the Nine Honors (*chiu ming*); below only those designated *cheng* (Principal, etc.), and above *ssu* (to be in charge; office), *lü* (Functionary), *fu* (Storekeeper), *shih* (Scribe), *hsü* (Assistant), and *t'u* (Attendant). CL: *deuxième degré de la subordination administrative; directeur.* (3) CHOU: **Regional Mentor,** one of 9 types of liaison officials between the central government and the Feudal Lords (*chu-hou*); see under *ou* (Unifying Agent). CL: *instructeur.* (4) N-S DIV–T'ANG: **Preceptor** in a Princely Establishment (*wang-fu*), rank not clear, till the early 790s, then retitled Mentor (*fu*). P69. Also see under *t'ai-shih, shao-shih, san shih,* and variously prefixed *shih* entries.

5203 *shih* 視
(1) **Equivalent to:** when prefixed to rank status or salary, normally indicates honorific or ceremonial but not substantive status, or a salary somewhat less in substance than indicated; in this dictionary *shih* in this sense is indicated with the equivalence symbol (=): rank =4b, rank =1,000 bushels. Interchangeable with *pi* (equivalent to). (2) **Acting:** irregularly prefixed to a title when the appointee was not of appropriate rank status. In Sung, used when an official's assignment (*chih*) was of higher rank status than his titular office (*kuan*); in Ming, used when the head of an agency was additionally fulfilling the duties of the 2nd highest post in the same agency, in a construction concluding with the term *shih* (affairs), e.g., Minister of Revenue (*hu-pu shang-shu*) and Acting Vice Minister (*shih shih-lang shih*).

5204 *shih* 試
(1) **Probationary:** irregularly throughout history prefixed to titles when an appointee, if fully qualified, was first appointed subject to reconsideration, commonly after a year's service in his post; or when an appointee, if not qualified, was appointed on an emergency basis pending the appointment of a qualified official or his own transformation, upon evaluation, into a regular appointee. (2) SUNG: **Acting:** prefixed to a title in S. Sung if the titular office (*pen-kuan*) was lower in rank than the appointee's salary office (*chi-lu kuan*); cf. *hsing* and *shou* (both Acting). SP: *stagiaire.* (3) **Examination:** see under *hsiang-shih, chieh-shih, sheng-shih, tien-shih, hui-shih, t'ing-shih, ta-pi.*

5205 *shih-chǎng* 室長
T'ANG–SUNG: **Temple Director,** members of the Office of the National Altars (*chiao-she chü, chiao-she shu*) as-

signed to care for different chambers (*shih*) of the temples in which ancestral spirits of the imperial clan, the spirits of deceased Empresses, etc., were honored or worshipped; number and rank not specified. P28.

5206   *shìh-chǎng* 市長
Variant of *shih-ling* (**Market Director**), sometimes used for less important markets such as those in the headquarters towns of Districts (*hsien*). HB: chief of a market.

5207   *shīh-chǎng* 師長
CHOU: **Master,** generic reference to the Palace Mentor (*shih-shih*), the Palace Protector (*pao-shih*), and various other officials with teaching responsibilities. CL: *maître.*

5208   *shìh-chě* 使者
Lit., someone sent as a representative. (1) HAN: **Envoy,** occasional designation of a diplomatic representative from China to a foreign state or chief. HB: messenger. (2) T'ANG–SUNG: **Commissioner,** head of the Directorate of Waterways (*tu-shui chien*); 2, rank 5a in T'ang. RR: *commissaire.* SP: *commissaire chargé de la direction du contrôle des eaux.*

5209   *shìh-ch'én* 使臣
it., minister sent as a representative. (1) **Envoy:** throughout history a common designation of a diplomatic representative from one state to another. (2) SUNG: **Policeman,** a soldier assigned to police duty at the imperial palace or in the capital. SP: *policier chargé d'arrêter les bandits dans la ville.*

5210   *shìh-chèng fǔ* 侍正府
YÜAN: **Palace Domestic Service,** headed with 14 Attendants-in-chief (*shih-cheng*); status and functions not clear, but probably not eunuchs.

5211   *shìh-ch'éng* 市丞
(1) HAN–T'ANG: **Assistant Market Director,** principal aide to a Market Director (*shih-ling, shih-chang*). RR: *assistant du service des marchés.* P20, 52, 62. (2) CH'ING: unofficial reference to a **Vice Commander** (*fu chih-hui*) of a **Warden's Office** (*ping-ma ssu*) in the dynastic capital city.

5212   *shìh-chí* 侍極
T'ANG: lit., attending the supreme, i.e., the Emperor: from 662 to 671 the official redesignation of **Policy Advisers** (*san-chi ch'ang-shih*) in the Chancellery (*men-hsia sheng*), specifically Policy Advisers of the Left.

5213   *shìh-chiā láng* 勢家郎
HAN: lit., court gentleman from a powerful or important family: **Court Gentleman by Influence,** unofficial reference to those Court Gentlemen (*lang*) who won their positions merely as sons of influential personages.

5214   *shíh-chiàng* 什將
File Leader: throughout history a not uncommon designation for the commander of a military squad of 10 soldiers. SP: *chef de troupe.*

5215   *shìh-chiǎng* 侍講
Expositor-in-waiting, an attendant skilled in explaining classical texts. (1) HAN–T'ANG: a prestigious title added to a regular title (see under *chia-kuan*) to signify that the appointee was worthy, and sometimes expected, to serve as companion and classical tutor of the Emperor; the title had no rank of its own and carried no salary. (2) SUNG–CH'ING: regular members of the Hanlin Academy (*han-lin yüan*); unspecified number, rank 7a, in Sung; 2 then 3, rank 6a, in Ming; 3 Manchu and 3 Chinese in Ch'ing, rank

6a till 1725, then 5b. SP: *chargé de l'explication.* BH: sub-expositor. (3) SUNG: one, rank 7a, assigned to the household of the Heir Apparent and to each Princely Establishment (*wang-fu*). Cf. *shih-tu* (Reader-in-waiting). P23, 26, 69.

5216   *shìh-chiàng* 豉匠
T'ANG: **Bean Sauce Maker,** 12 non-official employees in the Spice Pantry (*chang-hai shu*) in the Court of Imperial Entertainments (*kuang-lu ssu*). RR: *ouvrier pour la fabrication de la sauce de farine de haricot.*

5217   *shìh-chiǎng hsüéh-shìh* 侍講學士
Academician Expositor-in-waiting, a title of greater prestige than Expositor-in-waiting alone. (1) T'ANG–SUNG: from the 700s, designation of non-official litterateurs invited to attend upon the Emperor as tutorial companions, with nominal status in the Academy of Scholarly Worthies (*chi-hsien tien shu-yüan*), later in the Sung Hanlin Academy (*han-lin yüan*). Often prefixed Hanlin, even in T'ang. RR: *lettré chargé d'expliquer les textes à l'empereur.* SP: *lettré chargé d'expliquer les textes, académicien-conférencier.* (2) CHIN–CH'ING: eminent regular members of the Hanlin Academy; unspecified number, rank 3b, in Chin; 2, 2b, in Yüan; 2, 5b, in Ming; 3 Manchus and 3 Chinese in Ch'ing, 5b till 1725, then 4b. BH: expositor of the academy. P23.

5218   *shìh-chiào* 侍教
SUNG: **Attendant Tutor,** one or more, rank not clear, assigned to each Princely Establishment (*wang-fu*) for instruction of the Prince's children. SP: *chargé d'enseignement.* P69.

5219   *shìh-chiéh* 使節
Lit., sent as a representative with credentials (?): **Envoy,** traditional designation of a diplomatic representative from one state to another.

5220   *shìh-chiéh* 侍櫛
T'ANG: **Coiffure Attendant,** from 662 to 670 the official redesignation of the category of imperial wives otherwise called Ladies of Elegance (*ts'ai-nü*), rank 8a. RR: *femme chargée de peigner les chevelures.*

5221   *shìh-chiēn* 侍監
CH'ING: **Chief of Service,** a rank 8 palace eunuch in the Directorate of Palace Domestic Service (*kung-tien chien*); considered to belong to the category of Staff Supervisors (*shou-ling kuan*). P38.

5222   *shíh-chiēn* 食監
HAN: **Supervisor of Food,** 2, rank not clear, on the staff of the Chamberlain for the Palace Revenues (*shao-fu*), one under the Provisioner (*t'ai-kuan ling*) and one tending to the palace of the Empress; in Later Han one also posted at each imperial mausoleum (*ling*), rank 600 bushels, to provide twice-monthly food offerings; also known as *shih-kuan ling.* HB: inspector of food, inspector of offerings. P29.

5223   *shìh ch'íh-chiéh* 使持節
HAN–T'ANG: lit., sent holding a warrant: **Commissioned with Extraordinary Powers,** the most prestigious of 3 prefixes appended, especially after Han, to the titles of such territorial magnates as Area Commanders-in-chief (*tu-tu* or *tsung-kuan*), in effect giving them viceregal authority over all governmental agencies in their jurisdictions. Early in the era of N-S Division, such commissioners had the authority to put to death any official up to the rank of 2,000 bushels, whereas those designated Commissioned with Special Powers (*ch'ih-chieh*) could put to death anyone not of official status, and those designated Commissioned with a Warrant

(*chia-chieh*) could put to death only commoners who clearly violated military law. Out of this tradition eventually grew the T'ang regional warlords called *chieh-tu shih* (Military Commissioner). RR: *commissaire impérial tenant les emblèmes de commandement.* P50.

5224 *shìh-chìn* 仕進
Lit., advanced for service: a common general reference to all **officials.**

5225 *shìh-chīn* 侍巾
T'ANG: **Towel Attendant,** from 662 to 670 the designation of imperial wives of rank 9a; apparently had no counterpart in other eras. RR: *femme chargée des serviettes.*

5226 *shìh-chìn* 侍禁
SUNG: **Palace Attendant,** prefixed Left and Right, respectively the 2nd and 3rd highest of 12 rank titles (*chieh*) granted to palace eunuchs from 1112; see under *nei-shih chieh.* SP: *intendant du palais (eunuque).* P68.

5227 *shìh-chìn* 眡祲
CHOU: lit., observer of encroachments (of Yang and Yin forces upon one another): **Reporter of Ill Omens,** 2 with rank as Ordinary Servicemen (*chung-shih*), members of the Ministry of Rites (*ch'un-kuan*). CL: *observateur des phénomènes d'envahissement.*

5228 *shìh-ch'īng* 士卿
Lit., chief minister for the elite (?): occasional variant reference to the **Chief Minister of the Court of the Imperial Clan** (*tsung-cheng ch'ing;* i.e., *tsung-cheng ssu ch'ing*).

5229 *shìh-chūng* 侍中
Lit., serving in the palace. (1) HAN–N-S DIV: **Palace Attendant,** supplementary title (*chia-kuan*) awarded to officials of the central government chosen by the Emperor as his confidential advisers, led by one among them known as Supervisor of the Palace Attendants (*shih-chung p'u-yeh*); from Later Han on, regular officials ranked at 2,000 then =2,000 bushels, headed by one among them designated Chancellor of the Palace Attendants (*shih-chung chi-chiu*), all on the staff of the Chamberlain for the Palace Revenues (*shao-fu*). In the era of N-S Division sometimes served as officers of the Imperial Bodyguard (*san-lang nei-shih*) under 4 Directors of Palace Attendants (*nei-shih chang*), but steadily gained status as 4, 5, or 6 autonomous counselors at court associated with the emerging Chancellery (*men-hsia sheng*) and known colloquially as Junior Grand Councilors (*hsiao tsai-hsiang*). HB: palace attendant. P2. (2) N-S DIV (Ch'en): **Princely Attendant,** senior appointee in a Princely Establishment (*wang-fu*). P69. (3) SUI–CHIN: **Director of the Chancellery** (*men-hsia sheng*), 2, rank 2a, in T'ang; one, rank 1a, in Sung; one of the most powerful posts in the central government, always with concurrent status as Grand Councilor (*tsai-hsiang*). RR+SP: *président du département de la chancellerie impériale.* P3, 4. (4) LIAO: **Attendant,** one of the senior officials found in Herds Offices (*ch'ün-mu ssu*) at the Route (*lu*) level. P31.

5230 *shìh-chūng chì-chiŭ* 侍中祭酒
HAN–N-S DIV: **Chancellor of the Palace Attendants;** see under *shih-chung* and *chi-chiu,* also *shih-chung p'u-yeh* and *chung-ts'ao* (Palace Ministry). HB: libationer of the palace attendants.

5231 *shìh-chūng p'ú-yèh* 侍中僕射
HAN: **Supervisor of the Palace Attendants,** designation of one Palace Attendant (*shih-chung*) chosen to be leader of and spokesman for the group in Former Han; superseded in Later Han by *shih-chung chi-chiu* (Chancellor of the Pal-

ace Attendants); see under *shih-chung* and *p'u-yeh.* HB: supervisor of the palace attendants.

5232 *shìh-chūng shìh-láng* 侍中侍郎
HAN: **Gentleman Attendant at the Palace Gate,** official redesignation c. A.D. 200 of *chi-shih huang-men shih-lang.*

5233 *shìh-chūng ssù* 侍中寺
HAN–N-S DIV: **Court of Palace Attendants,** quasiofficial designation of the group of Palace Attendants (*shih-chung*); antecedent of the *men-hsia sheng* (Chancellery).

5234 *shìh-chüéh* 世爵
CH'ING: variant of *chüeh-yin* (**Hereditary Nobility**).

5235 *shíh-ch'üēh* 實缺
CH'ING: **substantively appointed to fill a vacancy:** a term used for the initial substantive appointment of an Expectant Appointee (*hou-pu*).

5236 *shíh chün* 十軍
T'ANG: **Ten Imperial Armies.** (1) From 787 to 807, when the 2 Armies of Inspired Militancy (*shen-wu chün*) were terminated, a collective designation of all the Imperial Armies (*chin-chün*) constituting the Northern Command (*pei-ya*) at the dynastic capital: i.e., the 2 Forest of Plumes Armies (*yü-lin chün*), the 2 Militant as Dragons Armies (*lung-wu chün*), the 2 Armies of Inspired Militancy (these 6 units being known till 807 as the Six Imperial Armies, *liu chün*), the 2 Armies of Inspired Awesomeness (*shen-wei chün*), and the 2 Armies of Inspired Strategy (*shen-ts'e chün*), all in Left and Right pairs. (2) Established in 885, when the 2 Armies of Inspired Strategy, then the only effective fighting forces at the capital, were divided into 10 Armies, which were further subdivided into a total of 54 Area Commands (*tu*); the result of this reorganization was called the New Army of Inspired Strategy (*shen-ts'e hsin-wei*). The term Ten Imperial Armies was now of no significance, but out of the 54 new Area Commands emerged the regional warlords who soon tore the T'ang empire apart. RR: *dix armées.* P43.

5237 *shíh-èrh chiēn* 十二監
MING–CH'ING: **Twelve Directorates,** collective reference to major units in which palace eunuchs were organized, more important than other eunuch agencies such as the Four Offices (*ssu ssu*) and the Eight Services (*pa chü*); each headed by a eunuch Director (*t'ai-chien*). The 12 units were the Directorates of Palace Eunuchs (*nei-kuan chien*), for Palace Accouterments (*yü-yung chien*), for Imperial Regalia (*ssu-she chien*), of the Imperial Horses (*yü-ma chien*), for Imperial Temples (*shen-kung chien*), for Palace Delicacies (*shang-shan chien*), of Palace Seals (*shang-pao chien*), for Credentials (*yin-shou chien*), for Palace Maintenance (*chih-tien chien*), for Imperial Apparel (*shang-i chien*), for Intimate Attendance (*tu-chih chien*), and of Ceremonial (*ssu-li chien*); the last became the paramount palace administrative agency from the early 1400s. In Ch'ing the Directorates were reconstituted only from 1656 to 1661 and then were replaced by agencies of the Imperial Household Department (*nei-wu-fu*).

5238 *shíh-èrh ch'īng* 十二卿
N-S DIV (Liang): **Twelve Chamberlains,** from 508 a collective reference to central government officials previously known as the Nine Chamberlains (*chiu ch'ing*), newly expanded: the Chamberlains for Ceremonials (*t'ai-ch'ang*), for the Imperial Clan (*tsung-cheng*), and for the National Treasury (*ssu-nung*) now collectively called the Spring Chamberlains (*ch'un-ch'ing*); the Chamberlains for the Pal-

ace Bursary (*ta-fu*), for the Palace Revenues (*shao-fu*), and for the Imperial Stud (*t'ai-p'u*) now collectively called the Summer Chamberlains (*hsia-ch'ing*); the Chamberlains for the Palace Garrison (*wei-wei*), for Law Enforcement (*t'ing-wei*), and for the Palace Buildings (*chiang-tso ta-chiang*) now collectively called the Autumn Chamberlains (*ch'iu-ch'ing*); and the Chamberlains for Attendants (*kuang-lu-hsün*), for Dependencies (*hung-lu*), and for Waterways (*ta-chou*) now collectively called the Winter Chamberlains (*tung-ch'ing*).

5239 *shíh-èrh chūn* 十二軍
Twelve Armies. (1) SUI: originally an apparent collective reference to groups of Garrisons (*fu*) in the Garrison Militia system (see *fu-ping*), subject for personnel administration to the Palace Military Headquarters (*ling tso-yu fu*). Not to be confused with the Twelve Guards (*shih-erh wei*) created c. 604 at the capital, in and out of which militiamen were rotated for capital service. (2) T'ANG: created in 620 by transformation of the Twelve Military Circuits (*shih-erh tao*) that had been established c. 618, each in charge of a cluster of Garrison Militia Garrisons; each Army headed by a General (*chiang-chün*). This structure of Armies was suspended from 623 to 625 and finally seems to have disappeared in a reorganization of the militia system (see especially under *fu*, Garrison) in 636. The Twelve Armies were not the same as units called Imperial Armies (*chin-chün*), which constituted the Northern Command (*pei-ya*) at the capital. They were regional administrative headquarters supervising geographical clusters of units in the Garrison Militia system; sources repeatedly state that they supervised the agricultural work of their subordinate Garrisons as well as directed them in combat. They were commonly called *chün-fu*, a term that seems to suggest Armies and Garrisons (an Army and its Garrisons?) but perhaps was nearly equivalent to the Sung dynasty Military Prefecture (see *chün*). The Armies were named after zodiacal constellations, rendered as follows in only rough equivalence to traditional Western zodiacal terms: Army of the Celestial Lion's Pelt (*shen-ch'i chün*), Army of the Celestial Herdboy (*ku-ch'i chün*), Army of the Celestial Black Lance (*hsüan-ko chün*), Army of the Celestial Twins (*ching-yüeh chün*), Army of the Celestial Water Bearer (*yü-lin chün*), Army of the Celestial Wolf (*chi-kuan chün*), Fear-proof Army (*che-wei chün*), Army of the Celestial Cornucopia (*p'ing-tao chün*), Army of the Great Celestial Bear (*chao-yao chün*), Army of the Celestial Parks and Gardens (*yüan-yu chün*), Army of the Celestial Serpent (*t'ien-chi chün*), and Army of the Celestial Bull (*t'ien-chieh chün*). P44.

5240 *shíh-èrh fáng* 十二房
SUNG: **Twelve Sections,** collective reference to 12 (originally 10) subdivisions created in the Bureau of Military Affairs (*shu-mi yüan*) under Shen-tsung (r. 1067–1085), each of which served as a channel through which the Bureau administered military units in a designated area of the country or supervised specified military functions on a country-wide scale. The Twelve Sections replaced 4 prior Sections: War Section (*ping-fang*), Personnel Section (*li-fang*), Revenue Section (*hu-fang*), and Rites Section (*li-fang*). They apparently also superseded another 4 Sections with specialized, empire-wide functions: Diplomacy Section (*kuo-hsin fang*), Militia Section (*min-ping fang*), Horse Pasturage Section (*mu-ma fang*), and Transport Supervision Section (*tsung-ling fang*). The new Twelve Sections were staffed with various clerical officials of rank 8b; their number increased several times from an original authorization of 38 in each Section, including from 3 to 5 Vice Recipients of

Edicts (*fu ch'eng-chih*) who were apparently in charge, 5 Secretaries (*chu-shih*), 2 Acting Secretaries (*shou-ch'üeh chu-shih*), 13 or 14 Clerks (*ling-shih*), 15 to 19 Clerical Scribes (*shu ling-shih*), and 3 Acting (*shou-ch'üeh*) Clerical Scribes; there were also unranked Copyists (*cheng-ming t'ieh-fang*), increasing from 18 to 28. The Twelve Sections were titled as follows: Northern Defense Section (*pei-mien fang*), Northwestern Defense Section (*ho-hsi fang*), Southwestern Defense Section (*kuang-hsi fang*), Palace Defense Section (*tsai-ching fang*), Troop Dispositions Section (*chih-ch'ai fang*), Training and Monitoring Section (*chiao-yüeh fang*), Officer Assignments Section (*ping-chi fang*), Militia Section (*min-ping fang*), Directors-in-chief Section (*li-fang*), Miscellany Section (*chih-tsa fang*), Horse Management Section (*chih-ma fang*), and Appointments Section (*hsiao-li fang*).

5241 *shíh-èrh tào* 十二道
T'ANG: **Twelve Military Circuits,** 12 regional military headquarters supervising local units of the Garrison Militia system (see *fu* and *fu-ping*); all established in 618 (619?) in the area of early T'ang territorial jurisdiction, called Kuan-chung, and each identified by a place-name prefix, e.g., the Ch'ang-an Circuit, the T'ung-chou Circuit. In 620 the Twelve Military Circuits were transformed into Twelve Armies (*shih-erh chün,* q.v.). Not to be confused with T'ang's proto-provincial 10 then 15 Circuits (*tao*), the jurisdictions of many kinds of supervisory officials called Commissioners (*shih*), e.g., Military Commissioners (*chieh-tu shih*).

5242 *shíh-èrh wèi-fǔ* 十二衛府 or *shih-erh wei*
SUI–SUNG: **Twelve Guards,** collective reference to the military units at the dynastic capital in and out of which Sui and T'ang militiamen of the Garrison Militia system (see *fu* and *fu-ping*) were rotated for service guarding the capital and the imperial palace; each headed by a General (*chiang-chün*), rank normally 3a. The term continued in use even after 636, when the original array was reorganized into Sixteen Guards (*shih-liu wei*, q.v.) and even into the Sung dynasty, although from mid-T'ang the Guards had only nominal existence, providing grandiose military titles for members of the imperial family and other favored dignitaries. The Twelve Guards were created in 607 out of the early Sui Left and Right Guards (*tso-wei, yu-wei*) and 2 Palace Military Headquarters (*ling tso-yu fu*). The late Sui–early T'ang units, with few changes, were 2 Standby Guards (*i-wei*), 2 Courageous Cavalry Guards (*hsiao-chi wei*), 2 Militant Guards (*wu-wei*), 2 Encampment Guards (*t'un-wei*), 2 Protective Guards (*yü-wei*), and 2 Reserve Guards (*hou-wei*), all in Left and Right pairs. It should be noted that the term Twelve Guards may be found in several sources confused with the term Twelve Armies (*shih-erh chün,* q.v.). P43, 44.

5243 *shīh-fàn* 師範
CHIN: **National Exemplar,** honorific title of great prestige, apparently on the same level as the Three Dukes (*san kung*); probably awarded to a religious leader, but circumstances not clear. P67.

5244 *shìh-fèng ts'áo* 侍奉曹
HAN: **Attendants Section,** in Later Han found among the staff Sections of some Commandery Governors (*chün-shou, t'ai-shou*); personnel and functions not clear. HB: bureau of attendance.

5245 *shìh-fù* 世婦
CHOU, N-S DIV (N. Ch'i), SUI: **Hereditary Consort,**

categorical designation of 2nd or 3rd level imperial wives, ideally numbering 27, who were expected to counsel the Empress and participate in important ceremonies including receptions; rank =3b in N. Ch'i, 3a in Sui. Meaning of the title not clear, but traditionally explained as a mark of the ladies' high esteem. CL: *femmes de troisième rang.*

5246 *shìh-fù ch'īng* 世婦卿
CHOU: **Ministers of Hereditary Consorts,** 2 eunuchs for each of the Six Principal Wives (*liù kung*) of the ruler, attached to the Ministry of Rites (*ch'un-kuan*); each 2 assisted by 5 eunuchs ranked as Junior Grand Masters (*hsia ta-fu*) and 8 as Ordinary Servicemen (*chung-shih*). CL: *attaché aux femmes impériales.*

5247 *shìh-hsí* 世襲
CH'ING: **Hereditary,** prefixed to titles of hereditary nobility (*chüeh-yin*) to indicate that the status was inheritable; the number of generations through which a title could be inherited was normally established at the time of the original enfeoffment.

5248 *shìh-hsí wăng-t'ì* 世襲罔替
CH'ING: **Perpetual Inheritance,** a term referring to titles of nobility (*chüeh*) that were awarded without any limit to the number of generations through which they could be inherited.

5249 *shíh-hsiàng* 使相
Commissioner-Councilor. (1) T'ANG: unofficial reference to a Military Commissioner (*chieh-tu shih*) who concurrently held one of the central government posts included under the generic term Grand Councilor (*tsai-hsiang*). (2) SUNG: quasiofficial reference to an Imperial Prince (*ch'in-wang*), a Commissioner of the Bureau of Military Affairs (*shu-mi shih*), a Military Commissioner (*chieh-tu shih*), etc., who concurrently was a Grand Councilor (*tsai-hsiang*). (3) SUNG: unofficial reference to a Grand Councilor who, on leaving that office, had been given nominal status as Military Commissioner. SP: *commissaire-conseiller.* P3. (4) CH'ING: unofficial reference to a Governor-general (*tsung-tu*) with concurrent status as Grand Secretary (*ta hsüeh-shih*).

5250 *shīh-hsiàng* 師相
SUNG: variant of the prestigious title **Grand Preceptor** (*t'ai-shih*), reportedly used to indicate the post's pre-eminence over Grand Councilor (*tsai-hsiang*).

5251 *shíh-hsièn k'ō* 時憲科
CH'ING: **Calendar Section** in the Directorate of Astronomy (*ch'in-t'ien chien*), responsible for defining the 24 periods of the solar year and the 5 seasons (including *chung,* Mid-year) and for compiling the official state calendar; an aggregation of the calendrical agencies known as the Five Offices (*wu kuan*), one named after each season, each headed by one Manchu and one Chinese Director (*cheng*), rank 6b. BH: calendar section. P35.

5252 *shìh-hsīng* 使星
Lit., sent as a star: throughout history a common unofficial reference to a **Commissioner** or **Envoy** representing the ruler; sometimes used in directly addressing such an official. See *hsing-shih.*

5253 *shíh-huò chiēn* 食貨監
T'ANG: **Director of Commerce,** staff member of an Area Command (*tsung-kuan fu*) responsible for provisioning the headquarters with mercantile goods. RR: *directeur des vivres et du commerce.*

5254 *shìh-ì* 侍儀
YÜAN: from 1279, an official abbreviated reference to *shih-i feng-yü* (**Imperial Attendant**).

5255 *shìh-ī* 侍醫
Attending Physician, irregularly throughout history a designation for personal physicians of Emperors or Heirs Apparent, alternating in use with the more common title *yü-i,* q.v. P26, 36.

5256 *shíh-i* 拾遺
T'ANG–MING: **Reminder,** a remonstrance official (*chien-kuan*) responsible for catching and correcting errors of substance or style in state documents; one or more prefixed Left in the Chancellery (*men-hsia sheng*), one or more prefixed Right in the Secretariat (*chung-shu sheng*); both rank 8b in T'ang. Initiated in 685; in 988 retitled *cheng-yen* (Exhorter); reinstituted in 1183. In Chin members of the Remonstrance Bureau (*chien-yüan*). Existed in Ming only in the era 1399–1402. RR: *chargé de reprendre les oublis.* SP: *chargé de reprendre les oublis de l'empereur.* P19.

5257 *shíh-ī* 食醫
Lit., (responsible for) food and medication: **Dietician.** (1) CHOU: 2 ranked as Ordinary Servicemen (*chung-shih*), members of the Ministry of State (*t'ien-kuan*) who determined that food offered the ruler was appropriate to the season and to his state of health. CL: *médecin pour les aliments.* (2) SUI–SUNG: 4, rank 9a2 in T'ang, members of the Food Service (*shang-shih chü*) of the Palace Administration (*tien-chung sheng*). RR+SP: *médecin pour les aliments de l'empereur.* Also see *shih-i shih-yü* (Imperial Attendant Dietician). P37.

5258 *shíh-ì* 食邑
YÜAN: lit., to feed off a fief: a general reference to **land-grant nobles,** who had broad political, military, and fiscal control over tracts awarded them; see under *fen-ti* and *t'ou-hsia.*

5259 *shìh-í fèng-yù* 侍儀奉御
YÜAN: **Imperial Attendant.** (1) From 1271 to 1320, one each Left and Right, rank 4a, headed the Palace Ceremonial Office (*shih-i ssu*); from 1279 title abbreviated to *shih-i;* in 1320 replaced by 4 Commissioners (*shih*), 3a. (2) From 1278, one each Left and Right, rank not clear, replaced Rectifiers of Omissions (*pu-ch'üeh*) as collaborators with Supervising Secretaries (*chi-shih-chung*) in compiling the Imperial Diary (*ch'i-chü chu*). P24, 33.

5260 *shìh-ì hsià-chièh* 市易下界
SUNG: lit., 2nd realm or jurisdiction for commercial exchange: variant designation of the **Monopoly Tax Commission** (*chüeh-huo wu*) in the Court of the Imperial Treasury (*t'ai-fu ssu*). SP: *deuxième section de l'agence des échanges commerciaux chargée des versements et des mandats.*

5261 *shìh-ì shàng-chièh* 市易上界
SUNG: lit., first realm or jurisdiction for commercial exchange: variant designation of the **Market Exchange Office** (*shih-i wu*) in the Court of the Imperial Treasury (*t'ai-fu ssu*). SP: *première section de l'agence des échanges commerciaux chargée d'achats pour equilibrer les prix.*

5262 *shíh-ī shìh-yù* 食醫侍御
SUNG: **Imperial Attendant Dietician,** rank not clear, member(s) of the Palace Administration (*tien-chung sheng*); see *shih-i* (Dietician). SP: *chef de nourriture et de médecine de l'empereur.*

5263 *shìh-í ssū* 侍儀司
YÜAN–MING: **Palace Ceremonial Office,** from 1271 to 1376 a central government agency loosely subordinated to the Ministry of Rites (*li-pu*) and in Yüan also to the Court Ceremonial Institute (*hsüan-hui yüan*), responsible for the

conduct of court audiences, especially those involving receptions of foreign dignitaries—functions at other times of the Court of State Ceremonial (*hung-lu ssu*). Headed by 2 Imperial Attendants (*shih-i feng-yü*; from 1279 *shih-i*), rank 4a, till 1320, then by 4 Commissioners (*shih*), 3a. In early Ming there was apparently a solitary Commissioner, 5b till 1371, then 7b. In 1376 the agency was renamed *tien-t'ing i-li ssu*, and in 1397 it became the Court of State Ceremonial. P33.

5264   *shìh-ì ssū*   市易司
SUNG: variant of *shih-i wu* (**Market Exchange Office**).

5265   *shìh-ì tǐ-tàng k'ù*   市易抵當庫
SUNG: **Market Exchange Mortgage Storehouse**, apparently depositories of documents pertaining to state loans; established in some Huai River regions under Overseers-general (*tsung-ling*); possibly depots from which annual tribute payments were made by S. Sung to the Jurchen Chin state (?). SP: *magasin hypothécaire du troc étatique*.

5266   *shìh-ì wù*   市易務
SUNG: **Market Exchange Office**, in 1072 established in the dynastic capital, in border areas, and in major cities and towns throughout the empire to implement the price control system for mercantile goods instituted by the reform minister Wang An-shih; set market prices, bought and sold to stabilize markets, made loans to small merchants, etc.; each headed by a Supervisor (*chien-kuan, t'i-chü*); in 1100 renamed *p'ing-chun wu* (Price Stabilization Agency). SP: *agence des échanges commerciaux*.

5267   *shìh-jén*   筮人
CHOU: **Diviner with Stalks**, 2 ranked as Ordinary Servicemen (*chung-shih*), members of the Ministry of Rites (*ch'un-kuan*); specialists in divining by use of the stalks of plants. CL: *officier de la plante divinatoire*.

5268   *shíh-k'ù*   石庫
HAN: **Stoneyard**, a construction supply unit under the Chamberlain for the Palace Buildings (*chiang-tso ta-chiang*), headed by a Director (*ling*). HB: stoneyard. P14.

5269   *shíh-k'ū ch'éng*   石窟丞
N-S DIV (N. Ch'i): **Aide for Stone Quarries** in the Pottery Office (*chen-kuan shu*) of the Court for the Palace Revenues (*t'ai-fu ssu*). P14.

5270   *shìh-kuān*   世官
Hereditary Office: throughout history, designated a post reserved for a particular family, to be occupied by its eldest sons generation after generation. In Ming, a special reference to military posts in the Guards (*wei*) and lesser units—garrison posts that were inheritable as distinguished from supervisory posts of higher rank that were not inheritable, called circulating offices (*liu-kuan*).

5271   *shíh-kuān*   史官
N-S DIV–CH'ING: **Historiographer**, occasionally a temporary duty assignment, but generally a generic reference to officials engaged in compilation of the Imperial Diary (*ch'i-chü chu*), True Records (*shih-lu*), and similar historical records; originally referred to Editorial Directors (*chu-tso lang*), then to personnel of the T'ang–Sung Historiography Institute (*shih-kuan*), eventually to Senior Compilers (*hsiu-chuan*) and their associates in the Hanlin Academy (*han-lin yüan*). P23.

5272   *shǐh-kuǎn*   史館
T'ANG–SUNG: **Historiography Institute**, from 630 a special group of Senior Compilers (*hsiu-chuan*), Academicians

(*hsüeh-shih*), etc., on ad hoc duty assignments to compile or revise dynastic histories; in T'ang under the Chancellery (*men-hsia sheng*) and the Secretariat (*chung-shu sheng*), in Sung one of the Three Institutes (*san kuan*) that constituted the Academy for the Veneration of Literature (*ch'ung-wen yüan*). RR: *collège des annalistes*. SP: *collège des annalistes, institut d'histoire*. P23.

5273   *shìh-kuān*   試官
T'ANG–CH'ING: **Examination Official**, generic reference to officials who participated as examiners, proctors, and readers in recruitment examinations for candidates for civil service careers, primarily in Prefectural or Provincial examinations (*chieh-shih, hsiang-shih*) but also in Metropolitan Examinations (*sheng-shih, hui-shih*). See *chu-k'ao, lien-kuan, chien-shih*.

5274   *shíh-kuān*   食官
HAN–T'ANG: **Food Provisioner**, generic reference to officials responsible for providing foodstuffs for the Empress, the Heir Apparent, Princely Establishments (*wang-fu*), etc.; in Han also posted at each imperial mausoleum (*ling*). Commonly a lowly post under the Chamberlain for the Palace Revenues (*shao-fu*), the Chamberlain for Ceremonials (*t'ai-ch'ang*), or their successor agencies. In the era of N-S Division commonly constituted a Foodstuffs Service (*shih-kuan chü*), in T'ang an Office of Foodstuffs (*shih-kuan shu*). At the capital or a mausoleum normally headed by a Director (*ling*), rank 600 bushels in Han, 8b2 in T'ang; in Princely Establishments commonly had Heads (*chang*), rank 600 bushels in Han, 9b2 in T'ang. P26, 29, 30, 69.

5275   *shíh-kuān chǎng*   食官長
HAN–T'ANG: **Head of Food Provisioners** in a Princely Establishment (*wang-fu*), also in Han in the household of the Empress; rank 600 bushels in Han, 9b2 in T'ang. HB: chief of the office of offerings, chief of the office of food. RR: *chef des fonctionnaires chargés de la nourriture de la maison des princes*. P69.

5276   *shíh-kuān lìng*   食官令
HAN–T'ANG: **Director of Food Provisioners** in the household of the Heir Apparent or at an imperial mausoleum (*ling*), under the Chamberlain for the Palace Revenues (*shao-fu*), the Chamberlain for Ceremonials (*t'ai-ch'ang*), or their successor agencies; rank 600 bushels in Han, 8b2 in T'ang. HB: prefect of the office of offerings, prefect of the office of food. P26, 29.

5277   *shíh-kuān shǔ*   食官署
T'ANG: **Office of Foodstuffs**, a minor provisioning agency in the Household Provisioner's Court (*chia-ling ssu*) in the establishment of the Heir Apparent; headed by a Director (*ling*), rank 8b2. RR: *office des aliments de la maison de l'héritier du trône*. P26.

5278   *shìh-láng*   侍郎
(1) HAN–T'ANG: **Attendant Gentleman**, in Han the 2nd highest of 3 categories in which Court Gentlemen (*lang*) were divided, with status below Inner Gentlemen (*chung-lang*) but above Gentlemen of the Interior (*lang-chung*); rank =400 bushels. In Later Han 36 Attendant Gentlemen were distributed equally among the Six Sections (*liu ts'ao*) of the Imperial Secretariat (*shang-shu t'ai*), as assistants to the Imperial Secretaries (*shang-shu*) who headed the Sections. During the era of N-S Division began to be used in the ways described under (2) and (3) following, but until T'ang continued in use as a relatively lowly secretarial post in Princely Establishments (*wang-fu*). HB: gentleman-in-attendance. RR: *secrétaire au service d'un prince*. P5, 69.

(2) N-S DIV–SUNG: **Vice Director,** 2nd executive post in the Secretariat (*chung-shu sheng*) and in the Chancellery (*men-hsia sheng*), in each case ranking after a Director (*ling* in the Secretariat, *shih-chung* in the Chancellery), in T'ang and Sung included among the officials serving as Grand Councilors (*tsai-hsiang*). In T'ang one each of Left and Right in each of the great departments, rank 3a; in Sung one in each, 3b. RR+SP: *vice-président.* P3. (3) N-S DIV–CH'ING: **Vice Minister,** from late in the era of N-S Division, 2nd executive post in each of the Ministries (*pu*) that quickly became the administrative core of the central government, consolidated in a Department of State Affairs (*shang-shu sheng*); from Sui through Ch'ing 2nd executive post in each of the standard Six Ministries (*liu pu*) of the central government, assisting Ministers (*shang-shu*); normally 2 in each Ministry prefixed Left and Right, rank 4a in T'ang, 3b in Sung, 4a in Chin and Yüan, 3a in Ming and early Ch'ing, then 2b in 1730, then 2a from 1749. In Ch'ing 2 each Left and Right, one Manchu and one Chinese. RR: *vice-président.* SP: *vice-président, vice-ministre.* BH: vice-president. P5, 6, 9, 12, 13, 14, 15.

5279   shìh-láng 士郎
N-S DIV (Chin, N. Wei): **Caterer** (?), one each of Left and Right in the Chin Ministry of Sacrifices (*tz'u-pu*); in the N. Wei Ministry of General Administration (*tu-kuan*), number and status not clear; functions also not clear, but traditionally believed to have been providers of foodstuffs. P9.

5280   shìh-láng hsüăn 侍郎選
SUNG: lit., selections by the Vice Minister: **Junior Appointments Process,** a reference to the Ministry of Personnel's (*li-pu*) appointments process (see under *hsüan*), in which the selection of men for appointments or reappointments was delegated to different executive officials of the Ministry according to the ranks and services (civil or military) of the appointees. The 2 Vice Ministers (*shih-lang*) presided over appointments to the lower ranks, the Vice Minister of the Left handling the Junior Civil Appointments Process (*shih-lang tso-hsüan*), prior to 1080 known as the Bureau of Personnel Assignments (*k'ao-k'o yüan*), and the Vice Minister of the Right handling the Junior Military Appointments Process (*shih-lang yu-hsüan*), prior to 1080 known as the Bureau of Lesser Military Assignments (*san-pan yüan*).

5281   shìh-láng tsŏ-hsüăn 侍郎左選
SUNG: **Junior Civil Appointments Process;** see under *shih-lang hsüan.* Also see *hsüan, liu-nei ch'üan.* SP: *bureau des nominations civiles.*

5282   shìh-láng yù-hsüăn 侍郎右選
SUNG: **Junior Military Appointments Process;** see under *shih-lang hsüan.* Also see *hsüan.* SP: *bureau des nominations militaires.*

5283   shìh-lì hsiū-chù kuān 侍立修注官
SUNG: lit., official who stands in attendance and makes notes: **Court Diarist,** duty assignment for a member of the Chancellery (*men-hsia sheng*); relationship to Imperial Diarists (*ch'i-chü she-jen*) not clear. SP: *fonctionnaire chargé d'inscription.* P24.

5284   shíh-liáng ī-yüán 食糧醫員
CH'ING: variant of *i-yüan* (**Salaried Apprentice Physician** in the Imperial Academy of Medicine, *t'ai-i yüan*). P36.

5285   shih-liáo 眂瞭
CHOU: lit., those of clear sight: **Guides for Blind Musi-**

cians, 300 equipped with small hand-drums, one unranked functionary for each blind musician under control of the Music Master (*ta-shih*) in the Ministry of Rites (*ch'un-kuan*). CL: *clairvoyants, conducteurs d'aveugles.*

5286   shìh-lièh 石烈
LIAO: **Subtribe,** Chinese transcription of a Khitan word for a social and military unit smaller than a Tribe (*pu-tsu*) but, like a Tribe, led by a Grand Prince (*i-li-chin, ta-wang*).

5287   shìh-lín kuăn 士林館
N-S DIV (Liang): lit., institute of the elite or of servicemen: **Elite Academy,** created by Emperor Wu (r. 502–549), who reportedly appointed as Scholars (*hsüeh-shih*) of the Elite Academy those who used, or were skilled in using, litchi nuts (?). P23.

5288   shìh-lîng 市令
(1) HAN–T'ANG: **Market Director,** one or more appointed to oversee commercial activities and collect commercial taxes, originally in marketplaces in the dynastic capitals but by T'ang times on the staff of all Prefectures (*chou*); rank as high as 5b in N. Wei, but 9b at best in T'ang. Sometimes called *shih-chang,* q.v. Also see *shih-shu* (Market Office). RR: *directeur des marchés.* P20, 57, 62. (2) CH'ING: unofficial reference to a **Commander** (*chih-hui*) **of a Warden's Office** (*ping-ma ssu*) in the dynastic capital.

5289   shìh liú-nèi 視流內
SUI–T'ANG: lit., equivalent to being within the current, i.e., equivalent to official status: **Adjunct,** prefix added to titles of persons who were not regular officials (*kuan*) but were granted equivalent status for ceremonial purposes: e.g, honorably retired officials, palace women, palace eunuchs. In this dictionary such status is indicated by the equivalence symbol (=); thus *shih* 6a (rank) is rendered =6a. See *shih, pi.*

5290   shíh-liù wèi-fŭ 十六衛府 or shih-liu wei
T'ANG–SUNG: **Sixteen Guards,** collective reference to an important group of military units stationed at the dynastic capital. In 636 units previously called the Twelve Guards (*shih-erh wei*) were reorganized into the Sixteen Guards; at least in theory they were the principal defense force for the dynastic capital city, the palace, and the Emperor, in the aggregate called the Southern Command (*nan-ya*) in contrast to the Northern Command (*pei-ya*) of Armies (*chün*) that was the main striking force of the early T'ang rulers. The Guards consisted principally of militiamen called up from their local Garrisons (see *fu*) in rotational patterns, each Guard having an assigned geographic grouping of Garrisons under its jurisdiction, at least for the management of such troop rotations (see under *fan,* Term of Service; cf. *pan-chün*). Each Guard was commanded by a General-in-chief (*ta chiang-chün*), rank 3a1, and 2 Generals (*chiang-chün*), 3a2. From 786 an even more prestigious Generalissimo (*shang chiang-chün*), 2a2, was normally the Guard leader. Each Guard had administrative and logistical support agencies largely headed by civil service officials: an Administrative Aide (*chang-shih*), 6b1; an Administrative Supervisor (*lu-shih ts'an-chün-shih*), 8a1; an Administrator for Granaries (*ssu-ts'ang ts'an-chün-shih*), 8a2; an Administrator for Arms (*ssu-ping ts'an-chün-shih*), 8a2; an Administrator for Cavalry (*chi-ping ts'an-chün-shih*), 8a2; etc. In the early 700s these support services were reorganized into Sections (*ts'ao*): the Administrator for Granaries was replaced by 2 Administrators of a Granaries Section (*ts'ang-ts'ao ts'an-chün-shih*), the Administrator for Arms by 2 Administrators of an Arms Section (*ping-ts'ao*), the Admin-

istrator for Cavalry by 2 Administrators of a Cavalry Section (*chi-ts'ao*); and by 705 there was added an Armor Section (*k'ai-ts'ao*), in c. 712 renamed Helmets Section (*chou-ts'ao*), with 2 Administrators. Meantime, the Garrison Militia system (*fu-ping*) and its troop rotations deteriorated significantly, so that by 749 the Guards ceased calling up militiamen. Thereafter into Sung the Sixteen Guards were decorative, militarily unimportant units existing almost solely to provide grandiose titles and appropriate perquisites for members of the imperial family and occasionally other favored dignitaries; and active defense of the Emperor and his palace was managed with other forces such as the late T'ang Permanent Palace Guard (*ch'ang-ts'ung su-wei, k'uo-chi*) and the Sung Palace Command (*tien-ch'ien shih-wei ssu*), counterpart of the early T'ang Southern Command. In Sung the general officers of the Sixteen Guards ranked 2b, 3a, or 3b (Generalissimos), 3a or 4a (Generals-in-chief), and 3b or 4b (Generals); and such titles became prestige titles (*san-kuan*) conferred automatically on military officers according to the ranks of their substantive posts. In both T'ang and Sung, names of the individual Guards changed from time to time, but the most common names in T'ang were the Left and Right Guards (*tso-wei, yu-wei*), 2 Courageous Guards (*hsiao-wei*) prefixed Left and Right as in all following cases, 2 Militant Guards (*wu-wei*), 2 Awesome Guards (*wei-wei*), 2 Metropolitan Guards (*ling-chün wei*), 2 Imperial Insignia Guards (*chin-wu wei*), 2 Palace Gate Guards (*chien-men wei*), and 2 Personal Guards (*ch'ien-niu wei*). The Sung array similarly included the Left and Right Guards, the Courageous Guards, the Militant Guards, the Imperial Insignia Guards, the Palace Gate Guards, and the Personal Guards, and in addition 2 Encampment Guards (*t'un-wei*) and 2 Army Guards (*chün-wei*). In both T'ang and Sung times the Sixteen Guards were commonly referred to as the Imperial Guards (*huan-wei*), and some of their names, prefixed *t'ai-tzu*, appeared in the establishment of the Heir Apparent. Cf. *chin-chün* (Imperial Armies), the Ming dynasty *chin-i wei*, the Ch'ing dynasty *luan-i-wei*. P43.

5291 *shih-lù yüan* 實錄院

SUNG: **True Records Institute,** one of 2 largely autonomous agencies that were nominally subordinate to the Palace Library (*pi-shu sheng*); responsible for recording day-by-day activities at court; headed by a Grand Councilor (*tsai-hsiang*) serving as Supervisor (*t'i-chü*). See under *kuo-shih shih-lu yüan* (Historiography and True Records Institute). SP: *cour des annales veridiques*. P23.

5292 *shih-măi ssū* 市買司

SUNG: lit., office for purchases in the market: official variant (dates not clear) for *tsa-mai wu* (**Office of Miscellaneous Purchases**) in the Court of the Imperial Treasury (*t'ai-fu ssu*).

5293 *shih-nèi* 侍內

SUI-T'ANG: from c. 604 to 618, the official variant of *shih-chung* (**Director of the Chancellery**). P3.

5294 *shih-nü* 使女

CH'ING: **Palace Serving Women,** a low class of palace women requisitioned annually from families of members of the Imperial Household Department (*nei-wu fu*) to provide menial service in the imperial palace for a specified term of years. BH: serving women of the imperial family.

5295 *shih-pò shih* 市舶使

T'ANG–SUNG: lit., commissioner for seagoing junks: **Maritime Trade Commissioner,** from 763 established at

modern Canton to collect customs duties on overseas trade; in early Sung (date not clear) retitled Maritime Trade Supervisor (*shih-po t'i-chü*). P62.

5296 *shih-pò t'i-chŭ ssū* 市舶提舉司

SUNG–MING: **Maritime Trade Supervisorate,** a category of agencies subordinate to the Ministry of Revenue (*hu-pu*) established along the southeast and south seacoasts to regulate overseas commerce, collect customs duties, prevent the smuggling of contraband goods, etc.; headed by a Supervisor (*t'i-chü*) on special duty assignment in Sung; a regular post, rank 5b, in Ming. Original numerous agencies reduced to 3 in Ming: at modern Ningpo in Chekiang, Ch'üan-chou in Fukien, and Canton in Kwangtung; came to be dominated by palace eunuchs and centers of friction between Chinese and Japanese and early modern European traders. In 1522 all but the Canton agency were closed. After Ming, control over coastal trade reverted to provincial authorities. SP: *bureau de douane*. P62.

5297 *shih-sān ssū* 十三司

MING: **Thirteen Bureaus,** collective reference to the 13 Bureaus (*ch'ing-li ssu*), each named after a Province (*sheng*), that were the major subordinate units in both the Ministry of Revenue (*hu-pu*) and the Ministry of Justice (*hsing-pu*).

5298 *shih-sān tào* 十三道

MING: **Thirteen Circuits,** collective reference to the 13 units called Circuits (*tao*), each named after a Province (*sheng*), among which Investigating Censors (*chien-ch'a yü-shih*) were distributed in the Censorate (*tu ch'a-yüan*). Each Circuit handled routine paperwork relating to judicial affairs of the Province for which it was named but otherwise had no special relationship with the Province; e.g., Investigating Censors of any Circuit were freely assigned to tours of duty as Regional Inspectors (*hsün-an*) of any Province. It was considered a badge of their independence in action that Investigating Censors were officially identified only as members of their Circuits, not as subordinates of the Censorate or its executive officials. P18.

5299 *shih-shīh* 士師

CHOU: lit., master of the elite: **Chief Judge,** 3rd ranking executive post in the Ministry of Justice (*ch'iu-kuan*); 4 appointees ranked as Junior Grand Masters (*hsia ta-fu*), responsible for the enforcement of criminal laws. CL: *grand prévôt criminel, prévôt de justice*.

5300 *shih-shīh* 室史

See under *chu-chi shih-shih* (**Recording Secretary**).

5301 *shih-shīh* 市師

HAN: **Market Master,** in the reign of Wang Mang (r. A.D. 9–23) replaced Former Han's Market Directors (*shih-ling*) in the dynastic capital and 5 other major cities; see *wu chün-ssu shih-shih* (Five Market Masters) and *chün-ssu* (Economic Stabilization Office).

5302 *shih-shīh* 師氏

Palace Master. (1) CHOU: one ranked as an Ordinary Grand Master (*chung ta-fu*) and 2 as Senior Servicemen (*shang-shih*), members of the Ministry of Education (*ti-kuan*) responsible for accompanying the ruler in all public appearances and rectifying his mistakes in conduct; collaborated with the Palace Protector (*pao-shih*) in tutoring the ruler's kinsmen and other nobles who did not yet have administrative appointments. CL: *instructeur, professeur*. (2) N-S DIV (Chou): one ranked as an Ordinary Grand Master in the Ministry of Education, believed to have directed both the Palace School (*lu-men hsüeh*) and the National University (*t'ai-hsüeh*). P34.

5303 *shìh-shìh* 筮仕
New Official, throughout history an unofficial, literary reference to a man newly entering on an official career, from an ancient practice of divining (first *shih*) to determine good or bad auspices before undertaking an appointment.

5304 *shìh-shìh* 翟氏
CHOU: **Bird Catcher,** 2 ranked as Junior Servicemen (*hsia-shih*), members of the Ministry of Justice (*ch'iu-kuan*) responsible for destroying birds of prey that must be caught by the wings. CL: *préposé aux ailes.*

5305 *shìh-shòu* 實授
Substantive appointment, in contrast to any form of acting, probationary, or otherwise irregular, temporary appointment. See *chen* (regular, true), *cheng* (regular), *pen-kuan* (titular office).

5306 *shìh-shū* 侍書
SUNG, MING: **Court Calligrapher,** members of the Hanlin Academy (*han-lin yüan*); status in Sung not clear; 2, rank 9a, in Ming. SP: *lettré-calligraphe.* P23.

5307 *shìh-shǔ* 市署
N-S DIV–T'ANG: **Market Office,** one established in each dynastic capital to supervise and control trade in the officially designated market(s); headed by a Director (*ling*), in T'ang rank 6b1; institutional affiliation not clear, possibly subordinate to the Court of the Imperial Treasury (*t'ai-fu ssu*). Not to be confused with *shih-ling* (Market Director). See *liang-ching chu-shih shu.* P62.

5308 *shìh-shū hsüéh-shìh* 侍書學士
YÜAN: **Attendant Academician** in the Hanlin Academy (*han-lin yüan*), number and rank not clear; charged with tutoring and evaluating the ruler in accordance with classical and historical texts; abolished in 1269. P23.

5309 *shìh-shū lìng-shìh* 史書令史
HAN: **Calligraphy Clerk,** unspecified numbers of specialists on the staff of the Palace Aide to the Censor-in-chief (*yü-shih chung-ch'eng*); qualified for appointment by passing tests involving knowledge of 9,000 characters and all standard styles of calligraphy. HB: foreman clerk of clerkly writing.

5310 *shìh-shū shìh yù-shìh* 侍書侍御史
T'ANG: variant of *chih-shu shih yü-shih* (**Secretarial Censor**), used to avoid a name taboo. P18.

5311 *shìh-shuài* 師帥
CHOU: **Regimental Commander,** with rank as Ordinary Grand Master (*chung ta-fu*); leader of a standard military unit of 2,500 soldiers called a *shih* (Regiment). CL: *chef de regiment.*

5312 *shìh shuài-fǔ* 侍率府
SUI–T'ANG: **Attendant Guard Command,** one designated Left and one Right, from c. 605 to 622 the official redesignation of the military units previously and later known as Defense Guard Commands (*wei shuai-fu*) in the establishment of the Heir Apparent. P26.

5313 *shìh shuài-fǔ* 十率府
SUI–SUNG: **Ten Guard Commands,** collective reference to military units organized similarly to Guards (*wei*) that were assigned to the establishment of the Heir Apparent, each normally headed by a Commandant (*shuai*), rank 4a in T'ang, 7b in Sung. The units always appeared in Left and Right pairs and were prefixed with *t'ai-tzu* or *tung-kung* (Eastern Palace). The names of the individual units repeatedly changed; some of the more durable were Defense Guard Command (*wei shuai-fu*), Protective Guard Command (*ssu-yü shuai-fu*), Gate Guard Command (*chien-men shuai-fu*), Police Patrol Guard Command (*ch'ing-tao shuai-fu*), and Inner Guard Command (*nei shuai-fu*). RR+SP: *dix gardes de l'héritier du trône.* P26.

5314 *shìh-sūn* 世孫
MING: **Grandson-heir,** designation of the eldest son by the principal wife of a deceased Heir (*shih-tzu*), i.e., the eldest son of an Imperial Prince (*ch'in-wang*); prefixed with the place-name associated with the Princedom. P64.

5315 *shìh tà-fū* 士大夫
Lit., Servicemen (*shih*) and Grand Masters (*ta-fu*): **the official class,** throughout history a collective reference to all those who were, were entitled to be, or had been officials (*kuan*) in government service and in consequence constituted the elite group in Chinese society. Cf. *shen-shih* (the elite).

5316 *shíh-t'àn ch'ǎng* 石炭場
SUNG: **Coalyard,** a unit under the Court of the Imperial Treasury (*t'ai-fu ssu*). SP: *aire de la réception et de la vente de l'anthracite.*

5317 *shíh tào-ān chú* 史道安局
YÜAN: **Service of Shih Tao-an,** an agency providing clothing for the imperial family, from its establishment in 1265 known by the name of the official authorized to make appointments in it. Subsequently regularized as an agency under the Supervisorate-in-chief of Civilian Artisans (*min-chiang tsung-kuan fu*) and staffed with artisans in obligatory service; headed by a Commissioner (*shih*) or Commissioner-in-chief (*ta-shih*), rank 6b. Also called *yü-i* (imperial clothes) *shih tao-an chü;* but not to be confused with *yü-i chü* (Imperial Wardrobe Service).

5318 *shìh-tào hóu* 式道侯
HAN: **Commandant of the Imperial Escort,** 3 distinguished as Central, Left, and Right Commandants, each with rank of 600 bushels, under the Chamberlain of the Imperial Insignia (*chih chin-wu*); cleared the way for the Emperor on any outing from the palace, and on his return waved flags that called for the opening of the appropriate gate. HB: captain of the standard bearers.

5319 *shìh-ts'ái ch'ǎng* 事材場
SUNG: **Materials Yard,** a storage area for construction materials maintained by the Directorate for the Palace Buildings (*chiang-tso chien*), headed by 2 Supervisors (*chien-kuan*), probably unranked. SP: *aire de matériaux de construction.*

5320 *shìh-ts'áo* 士曹
Levied Service Section. (1) SUI–SUNG: a clerical agency found in such units of territorial administration as Princely Establishments (*wang-fu*) and Superior Prefectures (*fu*), normally headed by an Administrator (*ts'an-chün-shih*), rank 7a or lower; managed local construction and maintenance projects in correspondence with the central government's Ministry of Works (*kung-pu*). Antecedent of the Ming–Ch'ing *kung-ts'ao* (Works Section). Also see *liu ts'ao* (Six Sections). RR+SP: *service des travaux.* P49, 59, 69. (2) SUI–CH'ING: may be encountered as an unofficial, archaic reference to the Ministry of Works.

5321 *shìh-ts'áo* 市曹
HAN: **Market Section,** a staff agency commonly found at the Commandery (*chün*) and District (*hsien*) levels of territorial administration, headed by an Administrator (*yüan-shih*); apparently supervised commercial activities and collected mercantile taxes in official markets in its jurisdiction. HB: bureau of markets.

5322 *shĭh-ts'áo* 時曹

HAN: **Seasons Section,** apparently found as a staff agency in some Commanderies (*chün*), headed by an Administrator (*yüan-shih*); responsible for monitoring seasonal cosmological activities. HB: bureau of the seasons.

5323 *shìh-tsŏ* 侍左

SUNG: abbreviation of *shih-lang tso-hsüan* (**Junior Civil Appointments Process**).

5324 *shìh-ts'úng* 侍從

Attendant, throughout history a vague generic reference to officials who had personal contact with the Emperor; may be encountered as a prefix to a title.

5325 *shìh-tú* 侍讀

Reader-in-waiting, an attendant skilled in reciting classical texts. (1) N-S DIV–T'ANG, MING: a prestigious title added to a regular title (see under *chia-kuan*) when an official was delegated to provide tutorial services in the establishment of the Heir Apparent or in another Princely Establishment (*wang-fu*). RR: *lecteur, lecteur d'un prince.* P23, 26, 69. (2) SUNG–CH'ING: regular members of the Hanlin Academy (*han-lin yüan*); status in Sung not clear; 2 then 3, rank 6a, in Ming and early Ch'ing, then 5b from 1725; in Ch'ing 3 each Manchu and Chinese appointees. SP: *lecteur.* BH: sub-reader. P23. (3) CH'ING: designation given lowly copyreaders of documents issued from the imperial palace, on the staff of the Grand Secretariat (*nei-ko*); see *nei-ko shih-tu.* P2. Cf. *shih-chiang* (Expositor-in-waiting).

5326 *shìh-tú hsüeh-shìh* 侍讀學士

Academician Reader-in-waiting, a title of greater prestige than *shih-tu* alone. (1) T'ANG–SUNG: from 725, designation of non-official litterateurs invited to attend the Emperor as tutorial companions, with nominal status in the Academy of Scholarly Worthies (*chi-hsien tien shu-yüan*), later in the Sung Hanlin Academy (*han-lin yüan*). Often prefixed Hanlin, even in T'ang. (2) CHIN–CH'ING: eminent regular members of the Hanlin Academy; unspecified number, rank 3b, in Chin; 2 then 3 then 2, 2b, in Yüan; 2, 5b, in Ming and early Ch'ing, then 4b from 1725; in Ch'ing 3 each Manchu and Chinese. BH: reader. P23. (3) CH'ING: designation given editors and translators of documents on the staff of the Grand Secretariat (*nei-ko*); see *nei-ko shih-tu hsüeh-shih.* P2. Cf. *shih-chiang hsüeh-shih.*

5327 *shìh-t'ú* 仕途

Lit., (to have entered upon) the path of service: common general reference to **officials.**

5328 *shìh-tzŭ* 世子

Heir: from antiquity a common unofficial reference to the eldest son of anyone of noble status, sometimes including even the Heir Apparent; in Ming and Ch'ing times, the formal designation of the eldest son by the principal wife of an Imperial Prince (*ch'in-wang*), with ceremonial rank between Imperial Princes and Commandery Princes (*chün-wang*). P64.

5329 *shìh-tzŭ* 士子

CH'ING: **Examination Candidate,** general reference to candidates at Provincial Examinations (*hsiang-shih*). BH: scholar.

5330 *shìh-tzŭ* 適子

Son by the Principal Wife, a kinship term used throughout history, sometimes of significance in reference to the sons of rulers or members of the nobility, specifying the legal heir.

5331 *shǐh-tzŭ-chí chùi-wén pó-shìh*
史子集綴文博士

T'ANG: **Erudite of History, the Masters, Belles Lettres, and Narrative,** 3 of 18 Palace Erudites (*nei-chiao po-shih*) on the staff of the Palace Institute of Literature (*nei wen-hsüeh kuan*), where palace women were educated; from c. 741, eunuch posts. RR: *maître pour l'enseignement des historiens, des philosophes, des oeuvres littéraires et des compositions littéraires.*

5332 *shìh-tz'ú hóu* 侍祠侯

HAN: **Marquis Attending at Sacrifices,** in Later Han the least prestigious of 3 designations awarded (see under *chia-kuan*) to Adjunct Marquises (*lieh-hou*) who were permitted to reside in the capital and were among those collectively called Audience Attendants (*feng ch'ao-ching*); the designation imposed a responsibility to participate in certain sacrificial ceremonies but not to participate in regular court audiences. Cf. *t'e-chin* (specially advanced), *ch'ao-t'ing hou* (Marquis for Audiences). HB: marquis attending at sacrifices.

5333 *shìh-wèi* 侍衛

Imperial Guard or **Imperial Guardsman,** throughout history a recurring general designation of those military units and personnel that were responsible for the security of the Emperor and the imperial palace; prefixes must be relied on to determine identities more precisely.

5334 *shìh-wèi ch'īn-chūn* 侍衛親軍

Imperial Bodyguard, throughout history a common designation of Imperial Guardsmen (*shih-wei, ch'in-chün*) entrusted with the personal protection of the Emperor.

5335 *shìh-wèi ch'īn-chūn mă-pù ssū*
侍衛親軍馬步司

SUNG: **Metropolitan Command,** one of 2 major headquarters units under which the Imperial Armies (*chin-chün*) of professional soldiers were organized, each headed by a Commander-in-chief (*tu chih-hui shih*); generally responsible for overseeing the Prefectural Armies (*hsiang-ping*) garrisoned throughout the empire, whereas the counterpart Palace Command (*tien-ch'ien shih-wei ssu*) was responsible for defense of the dynastic capital and the imperial palace. In the mid-1000s divided into 2 headquarters units, a Metropolitan Cavalry Command (*ma-chün ssu*) and a Metropolitan Infantry Command (*pu-chün ssu*). Often abbreviated as *shih-wei ssu.* See *erh ssu* (Two Commands), *san wei* (Three Capital Guards).

5336 *shìh-wèi ch'ù* 侍衛處

CH'ING: variant of *ling shih-wei fu* (**Headquarters of the Imperial Bodyguard**).

5337 *shìh-wèi mă-chūn pù-chūn ssū*
侍衛馬軍步軍司

SUNG: combined reference to the **Metropolitan Cavalry Command** (*ma-chün ssu*) **and the Metropolitan Infantry Command** (*pu-chün ssu*), into which the originally unified Metropolitan Command (*shih-wei ch'in-chün ma-pu ssu*) was divided in the mid-1000s. SP: *bureau de la cavalerie et de l'infanterie de la garde de l'empereur.*

5338 *shìh-wèi pān-lìng* 侍衛班領

CH'ING: **Imperial Guard Duty Group Commander,** leader of any of the 6 Duty Groups (*pan*) into which Imperial Guardsmen (*ch'in-chün*) were divided for active service on a rotational basis. BH: commander of a relief of the bodyguards.

5339 *shìh-wèi ssū* 侍衛司
SUNG: abbreviation of *shih-wei ch'in-chün ma-pu ssu* (**Metropolitan Command**).

5340 *shìh-wǔ tào* 十五道
CH'ING: **Fifteen Circuits,** collective reference to the 15 units called Circuits (*tao*), each named after a Province (*sheng*), among which Investigating Censors (*chien-ch'a yü-shih*) were distributed in the Censorate (*tu ch'a-yüan*); see *shih-san tao* (Thirteen Circuits). P18.

5341 *shìh-yù* 師友
SUNG: abbreviation of *shih-lang yu-hsüan* (**Junior Military Appointments Process**).

5342 *shìh-yǔ* 侍右
N-S DIV (Chin, S. Dyn.): **Tutorial Companion,** a dignitary on the staffs of Princely Establishments (*wang-fu*). P69.

5343 *shìh-yù láng-kuān* 侍右郎官
SUNG: **Bureau Executive in the Military Appointments Process,** reference to a Director (*lang-chung*) or Vice Director (*yüan-wai lang*) of a Bureau (*ssu*) in the Ministry of Personnel (*lì-pu*) when assigned to participate in the selection of military personnel for appointments or reappointments (see under *yu-hsüan*). SP: *secrétaire du bureau des nominations militaires*.

5344 *shìh-yù shìh-láng* 侍右侍郎
SUNG: **Vice Minister in the Military Appointments Process,** reference to a Vice Minister (*shih-lang*) of the Ministry of Personnel (*lì-pu*) when assigned to participate in the selection of military personnel for appointments or reappointments (see under *yu-hsüan*). SP: *director du bureau des nominations militaires*.

5345 *shìh-yùng* 試用
CH'ING: **Probationer,** designation appended to all new appointees in units of territorial administration below the level of Circuit Intendant (*tao-t'ai*) for periods of from one to 2 years until, after evaluation of service, their appointments were made substantive (*shih, shih-shou*).

5346 *shìh-yù* 侍御
Common abbreviation of *shih yü-shih* (**Attendant Censor**), but sometimes used in unofficial reference to any kind of Censor (*yü-shih*).

5347 *shìh-yù chūng-sàn* 侍御中散
N-S DIV (N. Wei): **Courtier-attendant,** rank 5a; one of many special duty assignments for aristocratic Courtiers (*chung-san*, q.v.).

5348 *shìh yù-ī* 侍御醫
SUI–SUNG: **Imperial Physician-in-attendance,** 4, rank 6b, in the Palace Medical Service (*shang-yao chü*) of the Palace Administration (*tien-nei sheng, tien-chung sheng*). RR: *médecin du service de l'empereur*. P36, 37.

5349 *shìh-yù shàng-ī* 侍御尚醫
T'ANG: **Medical Attendant,** 2, rank 6a1, on the staff of the Commissioner for the Palace Corrals and Stables (*hsien-chiu shih*). RR: *médecin chef du service de l'empereur*. P38.

5350 *shìh yǔ-shìh* 侍御史
CH'IN–MING: **Attendant Censor,** a prominent post in the central government until its abolition in 1376, beginning as the designation of the core staff of the Censorate (*yü-shih t'ai*) and finally becoming the Censorate's 3rd ranking executive post. In general, maintained surveillance over the officialdom and impeached wayward officials. In Ch'in and Han times, dispatched on regional tours of inspection with the special designation Supervising Censors (*chien-ch'a shih, chien yü-shih*). The Han staff reportedly totaled 45 men ranked at 600 bushels, 30 of them distributed among 5 function-specific Sections (*ts'ao*) under the Censor-in-chief (*yü-shih ta-fu*) and 15 assigned to the staff of the Palace Aide to the Censor-in-chief (*yü-shih chung-ch'eng*). Their number fluctuated in the era of N-S Division; the Sections in which they functioned grew to 13, but the authorized quota for Attendant Censors early stabilized at 8. By Sui times other categories of Censors had been established, Palace Censors (*tien-nei shih yü-shih*) and Investigating Censors (*chien-ch'a yü-shih*); and in T'ang the Censorate was formally organized in 3 units, one a Headquarters Bureau (*t'ai-yüan*) staffed with 4 then 6 Attendant Censors, rank 6b2 then 6a, who had the most general surveillance and impeachment powers, regularly participated in court audiences, and joined with members of the Ministry of Justice (*hsing-pu*) and the Court of Judicial Review (*ta-li ssu*) in conducting major court trials. The T'ang form of Censorate organization persisted into early Ming, but the number of Attendant Censors was reduced to one in Sung and 2 thereafter; the rank was 6b in Sung, 5b in Chin, and 2b in Yüan and Ming till 1376, when the post was terminated. Also see *chih-shu shih yü-shih, tien-chung shih yü-shih*. HB: attending secretary. RR: *censeur de la cour des affaires générales*. SP: *censeur général-assistant*. P18.

5351 *shìh yǔ-shīh* 侍御師
N-S DIV (N. Ch'i): **Imperial Physician-in-attendance,** 4 members of the Palace Medical Service (*shang-yao chü*) under the Chancellery (*men-hsia sheng*). See *shih yü-i*. P36, 37.

5352 *shìh yù-shìh chīh tsá-shìh* 侍御史知雜事
5 DYN–SUNG: lit., Attending Censor for miscellaneous affairs: **General Purpose Censor,** a member of the headquarters staff of the Censorate (*yü-shih t'ai*), apparently the counterpart of Secretarial Censors (*chih-shu shih yü-shih*) of other times; rank not clear; became acting head of the Censorate whenever the offices of Censor-in-chief (*yü-shih ta-fu*) and Vice Censor-in-chief (*yü-shih chung-ch'eng*) were vacant. SP: *censeur-assistant des affaires diverses*. P18.

5353 *shìh-yüàn* 使院
SUNG: abbreviated reference to a **Police Office** (*chün-hsün yüan*) in the dynastic capital or to a **Military Inspector** (*chün-hsün shih*) of such an agency.

5354 *shǐh-yüàn* 史院
CH'ING: unofficial reference to **Junior Compilers** (*pien-hsiu*) in the Hanlin Academy (*han-lin yüan*).

5355 *shǒu* 守
(1) HAN–SUNG: **Probationary,** prefix to a title during the appointee's first year in service, only after which he was normally entitled to substantive (*shih, chen*) status and full salary. (2) T'ANG–SUNG: **Acting,** in addition to the meaning given under (1) above, sometimes prefixed to a title when the appointee's rank was lower than was appropriate for the post, or when there was already a nominal appointee for the post. (3) Common abbreviation of *t'ai-shou* (**Governor**). (4) Common abbreviation of *hsün-shou* (**Imperial Tour of Inspection**). (5) CH'ING: unofficial reference to a **Prefect** (*chih-fu*).

5356 *shòu* 授
T'ANG–CH'ING: one of the most common terms meaning **to appoint;** often with a prefix indicating the type of state document used in making the appointment, varying with the rank of the post and the appointee.

5357 *shòu* 狩
See under *hsün-shou* (**Imperial Tour of Inspection**).

5358 *shōu-chǎng* 收掌
CH'ING: **Archivist,** unranked clerical functionaries, 4 assigned to the Military Archive (*fang-lüeh kuan*) in the Grand Secretariat (*nei-ko*), 4 to the Codification Office (*lü-li kuan*) in the Ministry of Justice (*hsing-pu*).

5359 *shǒu-chèng* 守正
SUNG: **Guardian of Rectitude,** a laudatory epithet bestowed on meritorious officials of the Secretariat (*chung-shu sheng*), the Bureau of Military Affairs (*shu-mi yüan*), etc.

5360 *shòu-chǐ* 受給 or *shòu-chǐ kuān* 官
SUNG–CHIN: lit., officials who receive and disburse: **Monitor,** one, rank not clear, in charge of the Sung Armaments Office (*chün-ch'i so*); 2, rank 8a, in the Chin Palace Maintenance Office (*hsiu-nei ssu*), and 2, 8a, in the Chin Construction and Maintenance Office (*tu-ch'eng so*). SP: *chargé des affaires.* P15, 38, 49.

5361 *shòu-chǐ k'ù* 受給庫
YÜAN: **Construction Storehouse,** a unit of the Ministry of Works (*kung-pu*) that stored and issued various building materials for construction projects in the palace and the capital city; headed by a Superintendent (*t'i-ling*), rank 8a. P15.

5362 *shōu-chīh chū-wù k'ù* 收支諸物庫
YÜAN: **Storehouse** of the Interpreters Institute (*hui-t'ung kuan*), which apparently collected and appropriately disbursed goods received in tribute; headed by a Commissioner-in-chief (*ta-shih*), rank 9b. P11.

5363 *shōu-chīh k'ù* 收支庫
CHIN: **Materiel Storehouse,** a unit of the Palace Maintenance Office (*hsiu-nei ssu*) that stored and issued construction materials needed for palace maintenance; headed by a Supervisor-in-chief (*tu-chien*), rank not clear. P38.

5364 *shǒu-chō* 守捉
T'ANG: lit., to guard and catch: **Defense Detachment,** an early T'ang generic term for military units along the northern frontier too small to be considered Armies (*chün*), each commanded by a Commissioner (*shih*). RR: *détachement militaire (de milice locale).*

5365 *shǒu-chō shǐh* 守捉使
T'ANG: **Defense Commissioner,** in early T'ang the head of a small frontier military unit called a Defense Detachment (*shou-cho*); from the 750s one of the many types of central government delegates with supervisory authority over a cluster of Prefectures (*chou*) called a Circuit (*tao*), normally subordinate to a Surveillance Commissioner (*kuan-ch'a shih*) or the equivalent. P52.

5366 *shǒu-chù yüàn* 守助掾
HAN: **Aid Provider,** several lowly appointees found on the staffs of Commanderies (*chün*) in Later Han, but functions not clear. HB: official in charge of aid.

5367 *shǒu-ch'üèh* 守闕
T'ANG–SUNG: **Acting,** prefix denoting a temporary appointment, especially when the appointee's rank was lower than was appropriate for the post.

5368 *shòu-ēn* 受恩
N-S DIV (N. Wei): **Recipient of Grace,** from 400 a prestige title (*san-kuan*) for major tribal chiefs, comparable to the later titles Specially Promoted Grand Master for Splendid Happiness (*t'e-chin kuang-lu ta-fu*) or Specially Promoted Grand Master for Glorious Happiness (*t'e-chin jung-lu ta-fu*), both rank 1a.

5369 *shōu-fā húng-pěn ch'ù* 收發紅本處
CH'ING: lit., place for the receipt and issuance of documents with imperial notations: **Imperial Documents Office,** one of several clerical agencies attached to the Grand Secretariat (*nei-ko*). BH: receiving and forwarding office.

5370 *shǒu-fǔ* 守府
CH'ING: unofficial reference to an **Assistant Brigade Commander** (*shou-pei*) in the Chinese military forces called the Green Standards (*lu-ying*).

5371 *shǒu-fǔ* 首府
CH'ING: **Principal Prefect,** designation of the Prefect (*chih-fu*) of a Prefecture (*fu*) that was a provincial capital.

5372 *shǒu-fǔ* 首輔
MING: lit., principal bulwark or support (of the Emperor): **Senior Grand Secretary,** quasiofficial designation of the Grand Secretary (*ta hsüeh-shih*) with longest tenure in the Grand Secretariat (*nei-ko*), who organized the work of the Grand Secretariat and did final editing of rescripts submitted for imperial approval.

5373 *shǒu-hsiàng* 首相
SUNG: **Principal Grand Councilor,** designation of a senior or a sole Grand Councilor (*tsai-hsiang*). SP: *premier ministre.*

5374 *shǒu-hsièn* 首縣
CH'ING: **Principal Magistrate,** designation of a District Magistrate (*chih-hsien*) whose District (*hsien*) was a provincial capital.

5375 *shǒu-hsún tào* 守巡道
MING–CH'ING: combined reference to **General Administration Circuits** (*fen-shou tao*) **and General Surveillance Circuits** (*fen-hsün tao*).

5376 *shǒu-hù líng-ch'ǐn tà-ch'én* 守護陵寢大臣
CH'ING: **Grand Minister Protector of the Imperial Mausolea,** an official of the Imperial Household Department (*nei-wu fu*) delegated as Supervisor-in-chief (*tsung-kuan*) of the 2 Imperial Mausolea Administrations (*ch'eng-pan shih-wu ya-men*) that supervised the imperial Ch'ing tombs in the Peking area.

5377 *shòu-ī* 獸醫
Veterinarian. (1) CHOU: 4 ranked as Junior Servicemen (*hsia-shih*), members of the Ministry of State (*t'ien-kuan*) who apparently tended domestic animals in the royal palace. CL: *médecin pour les animaux, vétérinaire.* (2) T'ANG: 600 authorized for the Court of the Imperial Stud (*t'ai-p'u ssu*), 2 for each park controlled by the Directorate-general of the Imperial Parks (*kung-yüan tsung-chien*), and others for the Livery Service (*shang-ch'eng chü*) in the Palace Administration (*tien-chung sheng*), all apparently non-official specialists. RR: *vétérinaire.* P31, 39, 40.

5378 *shòu-ī pó-shǐh* 獸醫博士
SUI–T'ANG: **Erudite of Veterinary Medicine,** non-official specialists attached to the Court of the Imperial Stud (*t'ai-p'u ssu*); 120 reported for Sui, 4 for T'ang; in T'ang had 100 authorized students, not counting 600 Veterinarians (*shou-i*) in active service. RR: *maître vétérinaire au vaste savoir.* P31.

5379 *shòu-jén* 獸人
CHOU: **Hunter,** 4 ranked as Ordinary Servicemen (*chung-shih*) and 8 as Junior Servicemen (*hsia-shih*) in the Ministry

of State (*t'ien-kuan*); supervised all hunting except for imperial hunts; during imperial hunts generally supervised the catching of game with nets; provided both live and dead animals for sacrifices. CL: *preneurs d'animaux, chasseurs*.

5380 shǒu-kuān 守關
SUNG: common variant of *shou-ch'üeh* (**Acting**).

5381 shòu-kuāng shěng 壽光省 or **shòu-kuāng tièn** 殿
N-S DIV (Liang): **Institute of Eternal Splendor,** apparently a palace organization to which favored litterateurs were appointed as Academicians (*hsüeh-shih*). P23.

5382 shǒu-k'uěi 首揆
MING: lit., principal calculator or arranger: unofficial reference to a **Senior Grand Secretary** (*shou-fu*).

5383 shǒu-kūng lìng 守宮令
HAN: **Palace Stationer,** in Later Han under the Chamberlain of the Palace Revenues (*shao-fu*), rank 600 bushels; provided paper, brushes, ink, and other writing materials for Imperial Secretaries (*shang-shu*); after A.D. 157, a palace eunuch post. HB: prefect of the palace stationery. P7.

5384 shǒu-kūng shǔ 守宮署
T'ANG–SUNG: **Canopies Office** in the Court of the Imperial Regalia (*wei-wei ssu*), responsible for supplying the Emperor and other dignitaries with canopies, screens, and mats needed on ceremonial occasions; headed by a Director (*ling*), rank 8a2 in T'ang. RR+SP: *office des tentures du palais*. P29.

5385 shǒu-lìng 守令
MING–CH'ING: a combined, archaic, generic reference to **Prefects** (*chih-fu;* see *t'ai-shou*) **and District Magistrates** (*chih-hsien;* see *hsien-ling*).

5386 shǒu-líng 守陵
N-S DIV (Chou), MING: **Mausoleum Manager,** in charge of an imperial mausoleum (*ling*); ranked as Senior Serviceman (*shang-shih*) in Chou, rank in Ming not clear. P29.

5387 shǒu líng-ch'ǐn tsǔng-pīng kuān 守陵寢總兵官
CH'ING: **Regional Commander for the Protection of Imperial Mausolea,** one appointed at each of 2 locations in Manchuria where there were ancestral graves of the Manchu monarchs; special duty assignments for Grand Ministers (*ta-ch'en*) of the Imperial Household Department (*nei-wu fu*). P29.

5388 shǒu-lǐng kuān 首領官
Staff Supervisor. (1) CHIN–MING: generic reference to officials of various central government agencies who were considered responsible for the internal clerical functioning of the agencies; e.g., Registrars (*ching-li*) and Office Managers (*tu-shih, shih-wu*). (2) CH'ING: categorical reference to various senior eunuchs of the Directorate of Palace Domestic Service (*kung-tien chien*).

5389 shǒu-líng t'ài-chiēn 守陵太監
MING: **Eunuch Protector of the Mausoleum,** one posted at each imperial mausoleum (*ling*) to supervise the local Escort Guard (*hu-wei*). P29.

5390 shǒu-lìng t'ài-chiēn 首令太監
CH'ING: **Eunuch Director,** prefix to the titles of 2nd-tier eunuch personnel of the Directorate of Palace Domestic Service (*kung-tien chien*), especially including the Palace Guardian (*chih-shou shih*), rank 7. BH: chief of the office of eunuch affairs. P38.

5391 shǒu-lǐng t'īng 首領廳
(1) CHIN–MING: may be encountered in the sense of **Staff Supervisors Office;** see under *shou-ling kuan*. (2) MING–CH'ING: **Administrative Office** in the Imperial Academy of Medicine (*t'ai-i yüan*), headed by 2 Medical Secretaries (*li-mu*). BH: office of administration.

5392 shǒu-nà p'ī-tuàn k'ù 受納匹段庫
SUNG: **Storehouse of Silk Bolts** under the Palace Administration (*tien-chung sheng*); staffing not clear, probably unranked. SP: *magasin de la réception d'étoffe de soie*.

5393 shǒu-pèi 守備
(1) MING–CH'ING: **Commandant,** common designation of the duty assignment of a military officer placed in charge of troops in a particular locality, especially an active defense post or a military station along the Grand Canal; normally with a function-specific prefix. (2) MING: **Grand Commandant,** from the 1420s the senior of 3 dignitaries who constituted a military regency council in control of the auxiliary capital, Nanking; nominally a duty assignment for a Marquis (*hou*) or an Earl (*po*), but early became an assignment for favored eunuchs. (3) CH'ING: **Assistant Brigade Commander,** rank 5b, in the Chinese military forces called the Green Standards (*lu-ying*); commonly the officer in active control of a Brigade (*ying*). BH: second captain.

5394 shǒu-pèi t'ài-chiēn 守備太監
MING: (1) **Eunuch Protector-general of the Mausolea,** overseer of the Eunuch Protectors of the Mausolea (*shou-ling t'ai-chien*) posted at the Ming imperial tombs west of Peking. P29. (2) **Eunuch Grand Commandant,** senior member of the triumvirate in military control of the auxiliary capital, Nanking; see under *shou-pei*

5395 shǒu pěn-kuān 守本官
SUNG: **serving in his titular office,** a term encountered in early Sung in the relatively unusual case of an official who actually performed the duties associated with his title. See under *ch'ai-ch'ien*.

5396 shǒu-p'íng 守屏
Lit., to defend and protect: unofficial reference to a **Regional Governor** or **Metropolitan Governor** (both *chou mu;* see under *mu*).

5397 shòu-shìh ssū 受事司
SUNG: **Receiving Office,** one of many agencies that served the 3 bureaus that constituted the State Finance Commission (*san ssu*) of early Sung; headed by an Administrative Assistant (*p'an-kuan*), rank 8a or 8b; received all kinds of registers and reports dispatched from units of territorial administration throughout the empire and distributed them within the Commission; terminated c. 1080. SP: *bureau des registres divers*.

5398 shòu-shìh yù-shǐh 受事御史
T'ANG: **Receptionist Censor,** from 726 the duty assignment of a Censor (*yü-shih*) to accept accusations against officials submitted by non-Censors and to record the names of the accusers. RR: *censeur chargé de la réception des affaires*.

5399 shǒu-tāng kuān 守當官
SUNG: lit., official who keeps records (?): **Clerk,** unranked or of very low rank, found in many central government agencies; superseded *pien-hsiu wen-tzu*, date not clear. SP: *assistant aux affaires, scribe-assistant*. P4, 9, 12, 13, 14.

5400 *shǒu-tào* 守道
MING–CH'ING: variant of *fen-shou tao* (**General Administration Circuit**). Also see *tao*.

5401 *shǒu-t'iào* 守祧
CHOU: **Caretaker,** 8 eunuchs attached to the Ministry of Rites (*ch'un-kuan*), one for each of the 8 palace chambers that were dedicated to important (female?) ancestors of the royal family, each assisted by 2 Chambermaids (*nü-t'iao*). CL: *garde des tablettes de la famille régnante.*

5402 *shǒu-tsǎi* 守宰
N-S DIV: lit., protector and steward: **Territorial Administrator,** generic reference to members of units of territorial administration.

5403 *shǒu-ts'ān* 首參
SUNG: lit., chief participant (in state affairs): **Senior Grand Councilor,** unofficial reference to the senior or sole Grand Councilor (*tsai-hsiang*).

5404 *shǒu-ts'ùi* 守倅
SUNG: lit., governors and their deputies: unofficial collective reference to the personnel of Circuits (*lu*). See *chien-ssu*.

5405 *shǒu wéi-ch'ǎng pīng* 守圍場兵
CH'ING: **Guards of the Hunting Preserve,** a special detachment of some 900 officers and soldiers stationed in the Imperial Hunting Preserve (*wei-ch'ang*) at Jehol, modern Ch'eng-te; instituted by the K'ang-hsi Emperor (r. 1661–1722); commanded by a Supervisor-in-chief (*tsung-kuan*).

5406 *shǒu-yù* 守禦
CH'ING: **Commandant** of a Transport Command (*wei*), a military officer normally of rank 5b on special duty assignment with the tax-grain transport establishment; see under *ts'ao-yün tsung-tu* (Director-general of Tax Transport). BH: first lieutenant on garrison duty. P60.

5407 *shǒu-yù ch'iēn-hù sǒ* 守禦千戶所
MING: **Independent Battalion,** a military unit of approximately 1,000 men organized like a normal Battalion (*ch'ien-hu so*) under a Battalion Commander (*ch'ien-hu*), but directly subordinate to a Regional Military Commission (*tu chih-hui ssu*) rather than part of a Guard (*wei*); see *wei-so*.

5408 *shǒu-yù ch'iēn-tsǔng* 守禦千總
CH'ING: **Assistant Gate Commandant,** 2 ranked as Company Commanders (*ch'ien-tsung*) stationed at each city gate of the dynastic capital, Peking; subordinate to 2 Gate Commandants (*ch'eng-men ling*). BH: lieutenant of the gate.

5409 *shǔ* 屬
(1) **Subordinate to,** throughout history normally used in its verbal sense, indicating the affiliation of one agency with another. (2) HAN: **Subsidiary Clerk,** rank 100 or 200 bushels, status between *yüan-shih* (Administrator) and *ling-shih* (Clerk), found in many agencies of both central and territorial governments, especially in Later Han. HB: associate. (3) T'ANG: **Clerical Supervisor,** rank 6a, oversaw the various clerical Sections (*ts'ao*) in which the paperwork of a Princely Establishment (*wang-fu*) was done. RR: *deuxième administrateur des services de la maison d'un prince.*

5410 *shǔ* 署 or *shù* 署
(1: 3rd tone): **Office,** throughout history a common suffix in an agency name, especially of an agency of middle or low status; comparable to *ssu* (Office). (2: 4th tone): N-S DIV–CH'ING: **Acting** or **Acting Concurrent,** irregularly used as prefix to a title awarded on a more or less temporary basis to an official already on duty in another post; also, in Ch'ing times, **Deputy,** appended as prefix to a title in some cases, denoting a regular appointee junior to an appointee without the prefix.

5411 *shù* 豎
CHOU: **Juniors,** categorical reference to expectant officials who had not yet attained their majority.

5412 *shù-chǎng* 庶長
(1) CH'IN–HAN: **Militia General,** a title of honorary nobility (*chüeh*) awarded to deserving subjects; see entries with prefixes *ta, tso, yu, ssu-ch'e*. (2) N-S DIV (N. Wei): **Group Leader,** a rank 5a2 official subordinate to the Palace Chief Musician (*hsieh-lü chung-lang*); functions not clear; may have been a prefix to the title *hsieh-lü lang* (Chief Musician). P10.

5413 *shǔ-chǎng* 署長
Office Chief. (1) May be encountered in any era in reference to the head of any Office (*shu*). (2) HAN: used with the prefix *chung-lang* (Inner Gentleman), but whether it signifies a Chief of the Office of Inner Gentlemen, i.e., some kind of administrator of Inner Gentlemen, or an Office Chief for Inner Gentlemen on the staff of some dignitary is not clear; also used in Later Han as the title of numerous eunuchs on the staff of the eunuch Director of Imperial Gatekeepers (*huang-men ling;* see under *huang-men*); e.g., *huang-men shu-chang* (Chief of the Imperial Gatekeepers Office). HB: chief of the office of ....

5414 *shù-ch'áng* 庶常
CH'ING: unofficial reference to a **Hanlin Bachelor** (*shu-chi-shih*) in the Hanlin Academy (*han-lin yüan*).

5415 *shù-ch'áng kuǎn* 庶常館
CH'ING: **Institute of Advanced Study** in the Hanlin Academy (*han-lin yüan*), in which Hanlin Bachelors (*shu-chi-shih*) improved their education under Grand Minister Instructors (*chiao-hsi ta-ch'en*) and Junior Instructors (*shao hsiao-hsi*). See under *liu-kuan* (retained in the Institute) and *san-kuan* (released from the Institute). BH: department of study of the national academy. P23.

5416 *shǔ-chèng* 署正
Office Director, common reference to the head of any Office (*shu*).

5417 *shǔ-chí àn* 屬籍案
SUNG: **Genealogy Section** in the Court of the Imperial Clan (*tsung-cheng ssu*). SP: *service des registres généalogiques.*

5418 *shū-chī fáng* 樞機房
T'ANG: **Central Control Office,** from the early 700s one of 5 staff agencies in the combined Secretariat-Chancellery (*chung-shu men-hsia sheng*); specific responsibilities and staffing not clear.

5419 *shù-chí-shìh* 庶吉士
Lit., a host of fortunate scholars. (1) MING: **Bachelor,** till 1404 a category of new Metropolitan Graduates (*chin-shih*) in the civil service recruitment examination sequence who were assigned as unranked Observers (*kuan-cheng*) in the Six Offices of Scrutiny (*liu k'o*), the Hanlin Academy (*han-lin yüan*), and other central government agencies as trainees pending substantive appointments. (2) MING–CH'ING: **Hanlin Bachelor,** from 1404 a category of new Metropolitan Graduates with special literary promise who were assigned as unranked Observers to the Hanlin Academy for

advanced study, then after 3 years given special examinations, on the basis of which they were retained for regular appointments in the Academy or released for appointments elsewhere. In Ch'ing the Hanlin establishment in which they pursued their studies was organized as an Institute of Advanced Study (*shu-ch'ang kuan*). Also see *liu kuan* (retained in the Institute) and *san-kuan* (released from the Institute). BH: bachelor. P23.

5420   *shū-chíh* 書直
T'ANG–SUNG: lit., writer on duty: **Auxiliary Scribe,** unranked copyist in the Academy of Scholarly Worthies (*chi-hsien tien shu-yüan*); from 731 to the end of T'ang superseded by the title *chih-yüan* (Auxiliary). RR: *écrivain auxiliaire.* SP: *copiste.* P25.

5421   *shú-chíh chiàng* 熟紙匠
T'ANG: **Glossy Paper Maker,** one non-official specialist on the staff of the Institute for the Veneration of Literature (*ch'ung-wen kuàn*). RR: *ouvrier chargé de la fabrication du papier lisse.*

5422   *shú-chíh chuāng-huàng chiàng*
熟紙裝潢匠
T'ANG: **Glossy Paper Maker and Mounter of Scrolls,** 8 non-official specialists on the staff of the Institute for the Advancement of Literature (*hung-wen kuan*). RR: *ouvrier chargé de la fabrication du papier lisse et des relieures.* P25.

5423   *shū-chíh hsiěh yù-shū shǒu*
書直寫御書手
T'ANG: **Copiers of Imperial Documents,** 90 unranked clerks on the staff of the Academy of Scholarly Worthies (*chi-hsien tien shu-yüan*). RR: *écrivain auxiliaire et copiste chargé d'écrire les documents impériaux.* P25.

5424   *shǔ-chōu* 屬州
CH'ING: unofficial reference to a **Department Magistrate** (*chih-chou*).

5425   *shù-chǔ* 戍主
N-S DIV–SUNG: **Frontier Post Commander,** common designation for petty military leaders on frontier duty; in T'ang categorized as Major (*shang*), Ordinary (*chung*), and Minor (*hsia*), rank 8a2 down. RR+SP: *chef de poste frontière.*

5426   *shū-chǔn huáng-hó ssū* 疏濬黃河司
SUNG: **Office for Dredging the Yellow River,** probably a field agency of the Directorate of Waterways (*tu-shui chien*), possibly also subordinate to the Bureau of Waterways and Irrigation (*shui-pu*) in the Ministry of Works (*kung-pu*). SP: *bureau chargé de draguer le fleuve jaune.*

5427   *shú-fēi* 淑妃
N-S DIV–MING: **Pure Consort,** irregularly the designation of a high-ranking imperial concubine, normally 2nd only to Honored Consort (*kuei-fei*). RR: *concubine pure.* SP: *concubine de l'empereur de premier rang.*

5428   *shū-fù* 樞副
SUNG: unofficial reference to a **Vice Commissioner** (*fu-shih*) of the Bureau of Military Affairs (*shu-mi yüan*).

5429   *shū-fǔ* 樞府
SUNG: unofficial reference to the **Bureau of Military Affairs** (*shu-mi yüan*).

5430   *shū-fǔ* 樞輔
SUNG: unofficial reference to the **Commissioner** (*shih*) of the Bureau of Military Affairs (*shu-mi yüan*).

5431   *shū-hsiàng* 樞相
SUNG: unofficial reference to the **Commissioner** (*shih*) of the Bureau of Military Affairs (*shu-mi yüan*).

5432   *shū-hsiěh* 書寫
CHIN–CH'ING: **Copier,** lowly or unranked staff member of the Hanlin Academy (*han-lin yüan*) and many other agencies of both the central and territorial governments. P23, 34, 66, etc.

5433   *shū-hsiěh chī-í wén-tzù* 書寫機宜文字
SUNG: **Confidential Copier,** unranked personnel on the staffs of various military and regional dignitaries, perhaps private hirelings. SP: *fonctionnaire chargé des écritures confidentielles.*

5434   *shū-hsüéh* 書學
SUI–SUNG: **Calligraphy School,** one of the schools at the capital maintained by the Directorate of Education (*kuo-tzu chien*), staffed with Erudites (*po-shih*), Provosts (*hsüeh-lu*), etc.; in Sung eventually downgraded to a unit of the Calligrapher Service (*shu-i chü*) of the Artisans Institute (*han-lin yüan*). RR: *section de l'écriture.* SP: *école d'écriture.*

5435   *shú-í* 淑儀
Lady of Chaste Deportment, designation of a minor imperial wife. (1) N-S DIV (Chin, Sung): one of the palace women called the Nine Concubines (*chiu pin*). (2) T'ANG–SUNG: one of the Six Ladies of Deportment (*liu i*), rank 2a in T'ang, 1b in Sung. RR: *correction pure.* SP: *concubine de l'empereur de second rang.*

5436   *shū-ì chǘ* 書藝局
SUNG: **Calligrapher Service,** one of 4 assemblages of non-official specialists in the Artisans Institute (*han-lin yüan*) of the Palace Domestic Service (*nei-shih sheng*); headed by a Manager (*kou-tang kuan*). SP: *office de calligraphie, service de l'art d'écriture.*

5437   *shù-jén* 庶人
CHOU: lit., commoner: **Suboffical Functionary,** categorical reference to government employees below the status of Servicemen (*shih*); specifically, those designated *fu, shih* (scribe), *hsü,* and *t'u,* qq.v. CL: *officier subalterne.*

5438   *shú-jén* 淑人
(1) SUNG–CH'ING: **Lady of Virtue,** a title of honor sometimes conferred on the wives and mothers of officials. (2) CH'ING: **Princess-consort,** designation of the principal wife of a member of the imperial family ennobled as Supporter-general of the State (*feng-kuo chiang-chün*).

5439   *shú-júng* 淑容
N-S DIV, SUNG: **Lady of Chaste Countenance,** designation of a minor imperial wife; in the era of N-S Division, one of those called the Nine Concubines (*chiu-pin*); in Sung rank 1b. SP: *femme titrée intérieure du 2ème rang.*

5440   *shù-kǔ tièn chíh hsüéh-shìh*
述古殿直學士
SUNG: unofficial reference to an **Auxiliary Academician of the Bureau of Military Affairs** (*shu-mi chih hsüeh-shih*).

5441   *shū-k'ù* 書庫
SUNG: **Publications Office,** one each in the Directorate of Education (*kuo-tzu chien*), the Imperial Archives (*pi-ko*), and the True Records Institute (*shih-lu yüan*).

5442   *shǔ-kuó* 屬國
Dependent State, throughout history a categorical reference to non-Chinese states or peoples that accepted China's overlordship and submitted tribute to the Chinese ruler.

5443 *shǔ-kuó tū-wèi* 屬國都尉
HAN: **Defender of the Dependent State of ...** (see prefix), designation of the principal Chinese dignitary representing the Emperor in a tributary state. HB: chief commandant of a dependent state.

5444 *shù-lǎo* 庶老
CHOU: **Elders of the People,** designation of retired officials who had held rank as Servicemen (*shih*), distinguishing them from retired Ministers (*ch'ing*) and Grand Ministers (*ta-fu*), who were called Elders of the State (*kuo-lao*). CL: *vieillards du peuple.*

5445 *shū-lì* 書吏
N-S DIV–YÜAN: **Clerk,** common designation of subofficial functionaries in many state agencies.

5446 *shū lìng-shǐh* 書令史
N-S DIV–SUNG: **Clerical Scribe,** common designation of suboffical functionaries found in many agencies and in great numbers; status generally lower than *ling-shih* (Clerk).

5447 *shū-mì* 樞密
Lit., of primary importance and confidential, i.e., great affairs of state. (1) T'ANG–YÜAN: prefix to titles of members of the *shu-mi yüan* (Palace Secretariat, Bureau of Military Affairs). (2) CH'ING: unofficial reference to a **Grand Minister of State** (*chün-chi ta-ch'en*).

5448 *shū-mì ch'éng-chǐh* 樞密承旨
SUNG: **Recipient of Edicts in the Bureau of Military Affairs,** rank 6a; received and distributed imperial pronouncements directed to the Bureau of Military Affairs (*shu-mi yüan*). SP: *transmetteur des directives de la cour des affaires militaires.*

5449 *shū-mì chíh hsüéh-shìh* 樞密直學士
SUNG: **Auxiliary Academician of the Bureau of Military Affairs,** 6 litterateurs, rank 3a, general aides to the executive officials of the Bureau (*shu-mi yüan*); authorized to act in routine matters in the absence of the executive officials. SP: *lettré auxiliaire de la cour des affaires militaires.* P23.

5450 *shū-mì shǐh* 樞密使
(1) T'ANG: **Palace Secretary,** a eunuch post created in 765 to coordinate and supervise the Emperor's paperwork; gradually grew in importance until from the 870s eunuchs of the Palace Secretariat (*shu-mi yüan*) dominated and manipulated the palace and central government. (2) 5 DYN–CHIN: **Military Affairs Commissioner,** one of the senior executive officials of the Bureau of Military Affairs (*shu-mi yüan*), rank 1b; transformed by those who terminated the T'ang dynasty from the eunuch secretaryship described under (1) above into a regular official post with chief military responsibility. SP: *commissaire aux affaires militaires.*

5451 *shū-mì yüàn* 樞密院
Lit., agency for the important and confidential, i.e., great affairs of state. (1) T'ANG: **Palace Secretariat,** from 765 an agency in which eunuch Palace Secretaries (*shu-mi shih*) coordinated and supervised the Emperor's paperwork and from which by the 870s they gained dictatorial power over the palace and the central government. (2) 5 DYN–YÜAN: **Bureau of Military Affairs,** reconstituted after the fall of T'ang as the paramount central government agency in control of the state's military forces, headed by one or more Military Affairs Commissioners (*shu-mi shih*), commonly rank 1b, or by Grand Councilors (*tsai-hsiang*) or similar

dignitaries on special concurrent assignments as Bureau Managers (*chih-yüan*), or in Sung sometimes by both kinds of appointees at one time. The agency was always large and its organization complex, and its division of responsibilities with the Ministry of War (*ping-pu*) was seldom clear; but the Bureau generally directed military operations and the Ministry generally consulted on military policy and provided supportive administrative services. In Sung the Bureau's principal subordinate units grew from 4 to 10 and finally, in the 1080s, to 12 Sections (*fang*; see *shih-erh fang*, Twelve Sections), some of which disappeared in S. Sung. The Yüan Bureau had as many as 35 subordinate agencies, and there were 5 transitory Branch Bureaus of Military Affairs (*hsing shu-mi yüan*), like the metropolitan Bureau headed by Bureau Managers; each at a given time was responsible for Mongol military activities in a vaguely defined jurisdiction called a Region (*ch'u*), which once stabilized came under the control of one or more Branch Secretariats (*hsing chung-shu sheng*) as the Branch Bureaus were deactivated. The Ming founder originally copied the Yüan Bureau but in 1361, still in predynastic times, transformed it into a Chief Military Commission (*tu-tu fu*, then *ta tu-tu fu*). SP: *cour des affaires militaires.* P21.

5452 *shū-pàn* 書辦
MING–CH'ING: **Clerical Subofficial,** generic reference to a category of workers in government offices at all levels without any officially recognized status, hence of lower status than unranked subofficial functionaries (*li*); apparently did the bulk of government paperwork. Those in local units of territorial administration such as Districts (*hsien*) were normally requisitioned for service from among the general populace, without compensation. However, those in central government agencies such as the Six Ministries (*liu pu*) seem often to have been well qualified, specialized careerists entrenched in their posts because of their detailed technical knowledge of their agencies' workings; they must have had reasonable compensation, and it seems not to have been difficult for them to pass their posts on to their sons at retirement.

5453 *shú-p'í chű* 熟皮局
YÜAN: **Finished Leather Goods Service,** a manufacturing unit of the Directorate of Leather and Fur Manufactures (*li-yung chien*); headed by a Superintendent (*t'i-tien*), rank 8b (?); worked on each year's harvest of wild animal hides. P38.

5454 *shū-piǎo* 書表 or *shū-piǎo ssū* 司
SUNG–CHIN: **Clerk,** unranked subofficial found in the Sung Court of Imperial Sacrifices (*t'ai-ch'ang ssu*) and the Office of Receptions (*tien-k'o shu*) of Chin's Court Ceremonial Institute (*hsüan-hui yüan*). SP: *employé aux écritures.* P11, 27.

5455 *shū-shěng* 樞省
Lit., department for matters of primary importance: common unofficial reference to the **Ministry of War** (*ping-pu*).

5456 *shū-shìh* 庶氏
CHOU: **Worm Specialist,** one ranked as Junior Serviceman (*hsia-shih*) in the Ministry of Justice (*ch'iu-kuan*); traditionally understood to be responsible for studying worms and establishing rules for their preservation, but to what end is not clear. CL: *préservateur des vers.*

5457 *shū-shǐh* 書史
SUNG–YÜAN: **Scribe,** designation of some unranked subofficials. SP: *scribe.*

5458 *shū-shǐh* 樞使
SUNG: common abbreviated reference to *shu-mi shih* (**Military Affairs Commissioner**).

5459 *shū-shǒu* 書手
Copyist, common designation for some unranked subofficials.

5460 *shū tài-chào* 書待詔
SUNG: **Editorial Assistant for Calligraphy,** non-official specialist in the Imperial Academy of Calligraphy (*han-lin yü-shu yüan*). SP: *attendant des décrets pour la calligraphie.*

5461 *shǔ-t'īng* 屬廳
CH'ING: lit., subordinate Subprefecture, i.e., not directly under the supervision of a Circuit Intendant (*tao-t'ai*) but part of a Prefecture (*fu*): **Ordinary Subprefecture** as distinguished from an Independent Subprefecture (*chih-li t'ing*), which was not part of a Prefecture but was directly supervised by a Circuit Intendant. Also called *san-t'ing.*

5462 *shū-t'óu fū-jén* 梳頭夫人
SUNG: **Imperial Hairdresser,** designation of a palace woman, unranked.

5463 *shū-t'óu kuǎn-lǐ* 梳頭管理
CH'ING: **Manager of Combs,** an officer of the Imperial Procession Guard (*luan-i wei*). BH: overseer of combs.

5464 *shū-tsò* 書佐
HAN–T'ANG: **Administrative Clerk,** lowly or unranked aide in many Sections (*ts'ao*) of various government agencies, especially units of territorial administration down to the District (*hsien*) level. HB: accessory clerk for documents. RR: *administrateur.* P26, 52, etc.

5465 *shū-tsòu* 書奏
SUNG: **Memorial Scribe,** 4 unranked subofficials in the Department of State Affairs (*shang-shu sheng*), shared by or divided between the Department's Left and Right Offices (*tso-ssu, yu-ssu*). SP: *scribe.*

5466 *shù-tsú* 戍卒
HAN: **Active Duty Conscript,** designation of a militiaman serving a year of active duty in the Southern Army (*nan-chün*) at the dynastic capital, in a Commandery (*chün*), or at a frontier post. HB: garrison conscript.

5467 *shù-tsūng* 庶宗
MING: **Ordinary Imperial Clansman,** apparently a general designation of male descendants of Emperors with status lower than Commandery Prince (*chün-wang*), or of those borne by women of lesser status than principal and secondary wives; in some instances may refer to all imperial clansmen regardless of their titled status.

5468 *shù-tzǔ* 庶子
(1) **Son by a Secondary Wife,** throughout history a common kinship term, especially as applied to members of the ruling family and members of the nobility; but also used with special meanings as indicated below. (2) **Non-inheriting Son,** in ancient Chou times a standard reference to all sons of Feudal Lords (*chu-hou*) other than Heirs (*shih-tzu*), and encountered subsequently in the same sense applied to sons of Emperors even by the principal wife. (3) CHOU–N-S DIV: **Cadet,** young men sometimes in the hundreds assigned to be companions and bodyguards of the Heir Apparent; also found in Chou on staff assignments in the Ministry of Justice (*ch'iu-kuan*), in Han on the staffs of some Marquises (*hou*). In earliest times such appointees were chosen from among the sons and younger brothers of court officials, and the tradition may have persisted through the era of N-S Division. In Chou studied under a Royal Tutor (*chu-tzu*); in Han under the control of the Director of the Watches (*lei-keng ling*), subsequently under various subordinates of the Supervisor of the Household of the Heir Apparent (*chan-shih*), and numbers gradually dwindled to 4 or 5. CL+HB: *cadet.* (4) SUI–CH'ING: **Mentor,** prefixed Left and Right, heads of the 2 major subdivisions of the Supervisorate of the Household of the Heir Apparent (*chan-shih fu*)—in Sui the Secretariat of the Heir Apparent (*men-hsia fang*) and the Archive of the Heir Apparent (*tien-shu fang*), thereafter the Left and Right Secretariats of the Heir Apparent (*tso-yu ch'un-fang;* see *ch'un-fang*); 2 each Left and Right, rank 4a, in T'ang; one each, 5b, in Sung; one each, 5a, in Ming; one Manchu and one Chinese in each, 5a, in Ch'ing. Appointees were the major administrative officials of the Heir Apparent's residence, the Eastern Palace (*tung-kung*), supervising numerous subordinate agencies. RR+SP: *président du grand secrétariat de l'héritier du trône.* BH: deputy supervisor of instruction. See *chung shu-tzu.* P26.

5469 *shú-yào k'ù* 贖藥庫
SUNG: **Storehouse for Drugs Acquired by Redemption,** an agency under the Director-general of Military Supplies (*tsung-ling*) in the modern Szechwan area; apparently collected medicinal herbs in lieu of punishments, probably for forwarding to the Pharmacy (*shu-yao so*) of the Court of the Imperial Treasury (*t'ai-fu ssu*). SP: *magasin du rachat de médicaments.*

5470 *shú-yào sǒ* 熟藥所
SUNG: lit., location for prepared medications: **Pharmacy** of the Court of the Imperial Treasury (*t'ai-fu ssu*); staffing not clear. SP: *bureau des remèdes préparés.*

5471 *shū-yüàn* 書院
T'ANG–CH'ING: **Academy,** generic designation of establishments where litterateurs gathered to study, assemble collections of books, confer on scholarly issues, and teach; commonly believed to have originated in 718 with T'ang Hsüan-tsung's (r. 712–756) creation of an Academy in the Hall of Elegance and Rectitude (*li-cheng tien hsiu-shu yüan*); from Sung on, widely established by private scholars, often with some state support, becoming important centers for the development of Neo-Confucian thought; in Ch'ing gradually transformed into elements of a national system of state-controlled education and preparation for civil service recruitment examinations. For the Sung–Ch'ing era, commonly rendered **Private Academy** to contrast with such official establishments as the Hanlin Academy (*han-lin yüan*) in the central government.

5472 *shú-yüàn* 淑媛
N-S DIV: **Lady of Chaste Beauty,** in San-kuo Wei the designation of a high-ranking imperial consort, in Sung one of the Nine Concubines (*chiu pin*).

5473 *shuā-chüàn tào* 刷卷道
MING: **Record Checking Circuit,** from 2 to 7 per Province (*sheng*), function-specific jurisdictions in regions identified by place-name prefixes, staffed by personnel of Provincial Surveillance Commissions (*t'i-hsing an-ch'a shih ssu*) who periodically checked the files in all government agencies to determine if assigned responsibilities had been carried out, if deadlines had been met, etc., and to impeach responsible officials for malfeasance or inefficiency.

5474 *shuā-chüàn yù-shǐh* 刷卷御史
MING: **Record Checking Censor,** one of the duty assignments for Investigating Censors (*chien-ch'a yü-shih*): to check the files of central government and provincial-level agencies periodically and to impeach officials for malfeasance or inefficiency accordingly. P19.

5475 *shuài* 帥
Commander. (1) Throughout history a common designation of the head of a military unit or post, normally of relatively low status. (2) CH'ING: common unofficial reference to both a Provincial Governor (*hsün-fu*) and a Governor-general (*tsung-tu*).

5476 *shuài* 率
(1) **Commandant,** a common military title, especially in Sui–Sung times; see under prefixes. (2) Also see under the romanization *lei*, as in *lei-keng ling* (Director of the Watches).

5477 *shuài-ch'én* 帥臣
SUNG: **Military Commissioner,** one of many designations used for the heads of Military Commissions (*shuai-ssu*) in Circuits (*lu*). SP: *directeur militaire de province.*

5478 *shuài-fǔ* 率府
SUI–SUNG: lit., office of a Commandant (*shuai*): **Guard Command,** generic reference to military units organized like Guards (*wei*) that were assigned to the Eastern Palace (*tung-kung*), the establishment of the Heir Apparent. See *shih shuai-fu* (Ten Guard Commands). P26.

5479 *shuài-fǔ shuài* 率府率
SUI–SUNG: **Commandant of the Guard Command,** commonly abbreviated to *shuai*, q.v.; also see *shuai-fu*.

5480 *shuài-fǔ t'ūng-p'àn* 帥府通判
SUNG: **Vice Prefect for Militia,** from 1135 appointed in many Prefectures (*chou*); see *t'ung-p'an*. P53.

5481 *shuài-hsìng t'áng* 率性堂
MING–CH'ING: **College for Guiding Human Nature,** one of the Six Colleges (*liu t'ang*, q.v.) among which students of the Directorate of Education (*kuo-tzu chien*) were distributed. P34.

5482 *shuai-keng* 率更
See under the romanization *lei-keng.*

5483 *shuài-ssū* 帥司
SUNG: **Military Commission,** one of the protoprovincial agencies used to coordinate groups of Prefectures (*chou*) in jurisdictions called Circuits (*lu*), known collectively as the Four Circuit Supervisorates (*ssu chien-ssu*); headed by a Military Commissioner variably designated *shuai-ch'en, an-fu shih*, etc. Usually the predominant regional authority; especially in frontier regions, commonly coordinated all civil as well as military affairs; increasingly important in S. Sung, when Grand Councilors (*tsai-hsiang*) were sometimes delegated as Military Commissioners. Also see *tu tsung-kuan.* SP: *autorité militaire de province.*

5484 *shuài-ts'áo-hsièn-ts'āng* 帥漕憲倉
SUNG: abbreviated collective reference to the **Four Circuit Supervisorates** (*ssu chien-ssu*): Military Commission (*shuai-ssu*), Fiscal Commission (*ts'ao-ssu*), Judicial Commission (*hsing-ssu*), and Supply Commission (*ts'ang-ssu*).

5485 *shuài tū-tū* 帥都督
(1) N-S DIV (Chou): **Area Commander-in-chief,** one of several titles awarded Regional Governors (*chou mu*) of special power and influence; apparently more prestigious than *tù-tu* alone and less prestigious than *ta tu-tu*. Before

the end of the dynasty, all such titles were apparently changed to *tsung-kuan*. P50. (2) SUI: **Assistant Commander,** subordinate officials found in Pasturages (*mu-ch'ang*) overseen by the Court of the Imperial Stud (*t'ai-p'u ssu*). P31, 39.

5486 *shuǎng-chiū shìh* 爽鳩氏
CHOU: lit., kingfisher man, gatherer (?): unofficial reference to the **Minister of Justice** (*ta ssu-k'ou*).

5487 *shuāng-hsièn chǘ* 雙線局
YÜAN: **Double Sewing Service,** a manufacturing unit under the Directorate for Leather and Fur Manufactures (*li-yung chien*); headed by a Superintendent (*t'i-tien*), rank 8b; produced leather falcon hoods, etc., for imperial use. P38.

5488 *shuāng-t'ái* 霜臺
Lit., frosty terrace; derivation not clear: unofficial reference to the **Censorate** (*yü-shih t'ai*) or to a **Censor-in-chief** (*yü-shih ta-fu*).

5489 *shui* 瑞
See under the romanization *jui.*

5490 *shǔi-chèng* 水正
CHOU: lit., rectifier of the waters (?): unofficial reference to the **Ministry of Works** (*tung-kuan*).

5491 *shùi-ch'īng* 睡卿
T'ANG: lit., minister (who provides visitors with) sleep (?): unofficial reference to the **Chief Minister** (*ch'ing*) **of the Court of State Ceremonial** (*hung-lu ssu*), which among other things provided accommodations for visiting foreign rulers and envoys.

5492 *shǔi-chūn* 水軍
Throughout history a common designation of military units prepared to fight on water in riverine or coastal engagements, i.e., a **Navy.**

5493 *shǔi-héng chiēn* 水衡監
T'ANG: lit., directorate for (taxing things taken from) the water by weight (?): from 685 to 705, the official redesignation of the **Directorate of Waterways** (*tu-shui chien*), the head then being known by the ancient title *shui-heng tu-wei* (Commandant of the Imperial Gardens).

5494 *shǔi-héng lìng* 水衡令
N-S DIV: beginning with Sung of the S. Dynasties, a common official variant of *tu-shui shih-che* (**Commissioner of Waterways**), a usage terminated by Sui. P14.

5495 *shǔi-héng sān kuān* 水衡三官
HAN: **Three Money Managers of the Court of the Imperial Gardens,** collective reference to 3 subordinates of the Commandant of the Imperial Gardens (*shui-heng tu-wei*) who were involved in the production and circulation of copper coins: the Director of Tax Substitutes (*chün-shu ling*), the Director of Minters (*chung-kuan ling*), and the Director of Grading and Sorting Raw Copper (*pien-t'ung ling*), each seconded by an Aide (*ch'eng*). P16.

5496 *shǔi-héng tiěn-yǘ* 水衡典虞
N-S DIV (San-kuo Wei): apparently a variant of *shui-heng tu-wei* (**Commandant of Waterways**). P37.

5497 *shǔi-héng tū-wèi* 水衡都尉
(1) HAN–N-S DIV: **Commandant of the Imperial Gardens,** from 115 B.C. a major official of the central government, in Han rank =2,000 bushels; in general supervisory control of the Imperial Forest Park (*shang-lin yüan*) and many revenue-producing and manufacturing activities associated with it; his subordinate Directors (*ling*) controlled such disparate things as coinage, granaries, stables,

and steel manufacturing. In Later Han the position was irregularly filled, its functions often being absorbed by the Chancellor of the Palace Revenues (*shao-fu*); it was revived in the Three Kingdoms era, but after Han its functions steadily narrowed to those described under (2) below. HB: chief commandant of waters and parks. P37, 40. (2) N-S DIV: **Commandant of Waterways,** exercised state-wide control over the construction and maintenance of dikes, boats, etc., alternating or coexisting with a Commissioner of Waterways (*tu-shui shih-che*); variably under the Chamberlain for the Palace Revenues (*shao-fu*), the Chamberlain for the Palace Buildings (*chiang-tso ta-chiang*), and the developing Ministry of Works (*kung-pu*); in N. Wei ranked 5b2. From Sui on its functions were absorbed by the Ministry of Works and the Directorate of Waterways (*tu-shui chien*). P14, 37. (3) T'ANG: from 685 to 705, the official redesignation of the **Commissioner** (*shih-che*) **of the Directorate of Waterways** (then called *shui-heng chien*). P59.

5498   *shùi-k'ò ssū*   稅課司 or *shùi-k'ò chú* 局
YÜAN–CH'ING: **Commercial Tax Office,** agencies of units of territorial administration down to the District (*hsien*) level, responsible for overseeing trade, issuing trading permits, and collecting various kinds of tax ; imposed on merchants; headed by a Supervisor (*t'i-c *) in Yüan, a Commissioner-in-chief (*ta-shih*) in Ming an 'h'ing; ranks ranged from 5b down to subofficial function, depending on the burden of responsibility of particular Offices. See *hsüan-k'o ssu, t'ung-k'o ssu*. P53, 54, 62.

5499   *shùi-k'ù ssū*   稅庫司
MING: occasional variant of, or scribal error for, *shui-k'o ssu* (**Commercial Tax Office**).

5500   *shǔi-lì tào*   水利道
MING–CH'ING: **Irrigation Circuit,** also a reference to its **Irrigation Intendant,** rank 4a, found with place-name prefixes. See *tao, tao-t'ai*.

5501   *shǔi-lù chuǎn-yùn shǐh*   水陸轉運使
T'ANG: **Water and Land Transport Commissioner,** designation of a court dignitary delegated from 712 to supervise the moving of state grain supplies through the difficult gorges of the Yellow River to the dynastic capital, Ch'ang-an. P60.

5502   *shǔi-lù fā-yùn shǐh*   水陸發運使
(1) T'ANG: variant of *shui-lu chuan-yün shih* (**Water and Land Transport Commissioner**). (2) SUNG: variant of *fa-yün shih* (**Supply Commissioner**). SP: *commissaire d'expédition par voie fluviale et terrestre*. P60.

5503   *shǔi-lù shǐh t'í-tū*   水陸師持督
CH'ING: **Provincial Military and Naval Commander,** a variant of Provincial Military Commander (*t'i-tu*) found in Chekiang and Fukien Provinces.

5504   *shǔi-lù tū hsǔn-chǐen shǐh*   水陸都巡檢使
SUNG: **Chief Military and Naval Inspector,** a variant of Chief Military Inspector (*tu hsün-chien; see hsün-chien ssu*). SP: *inspecteur général des voies fluviales et terrestres*.

5505   *shǔi-lù yùn-shǐh*   水陸運使
T'ANG: variant of *shui-lu chuan-yün shih* (**Water and Land Transport Commissioner**).

5506   *shǔi-mó wù*   水磨務
SUNG: **Water Mill Office** under the Court of the Imperial Granaries (*ssu-nung ssu*); staffing not clear. SP: *bureau de moulins*.

5507   *shǔi-pù*   水部
(1) N-S DIV–MING: abbreviated reference to *shui-pu ssu* or *shui-pu ts'ao* (**Bureau of Waterways and Irrigation**). (2) CH'ING: unofficial reference to the **Ministry of Works** (*kung-pu*).

5508   *shǔi-pù ssū*   水部司 or *shǔi-pù ts'áo* 曹
N-S DIV–MING: **Bureau of Waterways and Irrigation,** from N. Wei if not earlier a major unit in the developing Ministry of General Administration (*tu-kuan*) or Ministry of Works (*kung-pu*); headed by a Director (*lang-chung*), rank 6a in N. Wei, 5b in T'ang, 6a or 6b in Sung. Responsible for the construction and maintenance of fords, boats, bridges, dikes, dams, irrigation canals, grain mills, etc., and for supervision of state grain transportation by water. In 1396 renamed *tu-shui ch'ing-li ssu*. RR+SP: *bureau des eaux*. P14, 15.

5509   *shǔi-shīh*   水師
CH'ING: **Naval Forces** of the Green Standards (*lu-ying*), organized by Provinces under Provincial Commanders (*t'i-tu*); cf. *lu-shih* (Land Forces). BH: marine forces.

5510   *shǔi-shīh yíng*   水師營
CH'ING: **Naval Brigade,** designation of Banner (*ch'i*) units assigned to riverine or coastal patrol duties. BH: marine battalion.

5511   *shǔi ssū-k'ūng chǎng*   水司空長
HAN: **Director of Hydraulic Works** in the Imperial Forest Park (*shang-lin yüan*); one of numerous subordinates of the Commandant of the Imperial Gardens (*shui-heng tu-wei*). HB: chief of the office of the director of water works.

5512   *shǔi-ts'áo*   水曹
Waterways Section. (1) HAN: one of numerous agencies found on the staffs of some Commanderies (*chün*) and Districts (*hsien*), headed by Administrators (*yüan-shih*); probably reappeared in later times where and when waterways and irrigation were particular problems. HB: bureau of waters. (2) T'ANG: until 649 or somewhat earlier, found on the staffs of Princely Establishments (*wang-fu*), headed by Administrators (*ts'an-chün-shih*); supervised the use of boats, fishing, and apparently some irrigation. RR: *service des eaux*. (3) Occasional abbreviation of *shui-pu ts'ao* (Bureau of Waterways and Irrigation).

5513   *shǔi-tz'ù ts'āng-shǔ*   水次倉署
N-S DIV (N. Ch'i): **Riverside Granary Office,** established at several locations under supervision of the Court for the National Treasury (*ssu-nung ssu*); each headed by a Director (*ling*). P8.

5514   *shùi-wù ssū*   稅務司
YÜAN: **Commercial Tax Office** under a Route Command (*tsung-kuan fu*), headed by a Superintendent (*t'i-ling*) with the assistance of a Commissioner-in-chief (*ta-shih*); see *shui-k'o ssu, hsüan-k'o ssu*. P53.

5515   *shùn-ch'áng*   順常
HAN: **Lady of Complaisant Constancy,** designation of a palace woman with rank =200 bushels. HB: constant maid.

5516   *shùn-ch'éng*   順成
N-S DIV (San-kuo Wei): **Lady of Complete Complaisance,** designation of a palace woman.

5517   *shùn-fēi*   順妃
MING: **Complaisant Consort,** designation of a secondary wife of the Emperor.

5518 *shùn-huá* 順華
Lady of Complaisant Loveliness. (1) N-S DIV (N. Ch'i): designation of one of 6 Lesser Concubines (*hsia-pin*). (2) SUI: designation of one of the Nine Concubines (*chiu pin*), rank 2a.

5519 *shùn-i* 順儀
Lady of Complaisant Deportment. (1) SUI: designation of one of the Nine Concubines (*chiu pin*), rank 2a. (2) T'ANG: designation of one of the Six Ladies of Deportment (*liu i*), 2a. RR: *correction obéisante*. (3) SUNG: designation of a rank 1b secondary wife of the Emperor. SP: *concubine de second rang de l'empereur*.

5520 *shùn-júng* 順容
Lady of Complaisant Countenance. (1) SUI: designation of one of the Nine Concubines (*chiu pin*), rank 2a. (2) SUNG: designation of a rank 1b secondary wife of the Emperor. SP: *concubine de second rang de l'empereur*.

5521 *shuō-shū* 說書
SUNG–CHIN: lit., to speak about or explain writings: **Lecturer**, in Sung, low-ranking appointees found in Princely Establishments (*wang-fu*) as well as in such central government agencies as the Hanlin Academy (*han-lin yüan*), the School for the Heir Apparent (*tzu-shan t'ang*), and the Hall for the Veneration of Governance (*ch'ung-cheng tien*), in the last case rank 7b; those in the central government presumably participated in the Classics Colloquium (*ching-yen*) with the Emperor. In Chin served comparable functions, but a duty assignment for the Minister of Rites (*lǐ-pu shang-shu*). SP: *lecteur*. P24, 69.

5522 *shuō-shū kŭng* 說書宮 or *shuō-shū sŏ* 所
SUNG–CHIN: **Lecture Hall**, the location where Classics Colloquia (*ching-yen*) were conducted; in Sung called *so*, in Chin *kung*. SP: *lieu d'explication des textes*.

5523 *sŏ* 所
Lit., place, location. (1) **Office:** throughout history used to designate the station of a specified official or the location of a specified official activity, on balance less common and less prestigious than many comparable terms such as *ssu* (Office, Bureau, etc.), *pu* (Ministry, Region, Division, etc.), *ts'ao* (Section), *chien* (Directorate). Sometimes prefixed with an official title, e.g., the Ming–Ch'ing *chao-mo so* (Records Office) found in various agencies: lit., the office of the *chao-mo* (Record Keeper). Sometimes prefixed with a verbal construction suggesting the activity of the agency, e.g., the *ta-pu so* (Hunting Office) of the Yüan dynasty Bureau of Military Affairs (*shu-mi yüan*), and the *ying-shan so* (Construction Office) at Nanking under the Ming dynasty Ministry of Works (*kung-pu*). The term *so* as designation of such an agency is rarely used by itself unless the full title is well established in the preceding context. (2) YÜAN–MING: abbreviation of *ch'ien-hu so* (**Battalion**) or *po-hu so* (**Company**) in the military establishment; sometimes a generic reference to both. (3) CH'ING: **Subsection**, 5 top-echelon units of the Imperial Procession Guard (*luan-i wei*), each headed by a Director (*chang-yin kuan-chün shih*), rank 3a, each subdivided into from 2 to 8 Offices (*ssu*). See *tso-so, yu-so, chung-so, ch'ien-so, hou-so*. BH: sub-department. (4) CH'ING: **Transport Station**, designation of many small military units based along the Grand Canal to man tax-grain transport boats, prefixed with place-names; each headed by a military officer on duty assignment as Transport Station Commandant (*ling-yün*). Cf. *wei* (Transport Command). BH: second class transport station. P60.

5524 *sŏ* 鎖
SUNG: **Inspection Station**, 2 established in N. Sung in the vicinity of the dynastic capital to monitor and collect fees on upstream and downstream boat traffic on the Pien River, differentiated by the prefixes *shang* (up) and *hsia* (down). Supervised by the Court of the Imperial Treasury (*t'ai-fu ssu*). SP: *octroi*.

5525 *sŏ-ssū* 所司
In addition to its perhaps more normal sense of "what ... is in charge of," a common expression in governmental documents with the sense of "those in charge": **the responsible authorities.** Cf. *yu-ssu* (the authorities).

5526 *sŏ-t'īng* 瑣廳
SUNG: lit., pavilion of anxieties or of fidgets: **Expectant Examinee**, unofficial reference to someone in office waiting to achieve status as a Metropolitan Graduate (*chin-shih*) in the regular civil service recruitment examination sequence or to take a Special Examination (*chih-k'o*) in the hope of extraordinary advancement.

5527 *sŏ-wéi* 瑣闈
Imperial Palace, an unofficial reference derived from the practice of inscribing paired phrases (*so-wen*) on palace gates (*wei*).

5528 *sŏ-yú* 所由
T'ANG–CH'ING: lit., that through which or from which (governmental orders were promulgated): unofficial reference to a **Prefect** (*chih-chou, chih-fu*).

5529 *sŏu* 藪
CHOU: **Manager of Cultivated Marshes**, one of 9 categories of intermediaries between the central government and the Feudal Lords (*chu-hou*) called Unifying Agents (*ou*); members of the Ministry of State (*t'ien-kuan*). CL: *marais cultivé*.

5530 *sōu-chiĕn huài-hsièh kuān* 搜檢懷挾官
YÜAN: lit., official who searched for concealed notes (at civil service recruitment examinations): **Examination Monitor**, one soldier assigned to each examinee for constant surveillance during sessions of the Metropolitan Examination (*hui-shih*), to prevent the examinee's consulting notes. The designation is also abbreviated to *sou-chien kuan*.

5531 *sōu-jén* 廋人
CHOU: **Horse Trainer**, 2 ranked as Junior Servicemen (*hsiao-shih*), members of the Ministry of War (*hsia-kuan*) who supervised the training of horses in the 12 royal parks and chose horses for various royal uses. CL: *surveillant des troupes de chevaux*.

5532 *sōu-sù tū-wèi* 騪粟都尉
HAN: **Commandant-in-chief for Foraging**, one of the principal aides to the Chamberlain for the National Treasury (*chih-su nei-shih, ta ssu-nung*), apparently in charge of collections for the capital granaries. HB: chief commandant who searches for grain. P8.

5533 *ssū* 司
Lit., to be in charge of; office, bureau, etc.: one of the most common terms used in traditional official nomenclature; as indicated below, rarely used alone. (1) Verb: **to be in charge of,** throughout history found in titles with suffixes specifying the appointee's responsibility; e.g., *ssu-ma* (lit., in charge of horses), *ssu-i* (lit., in charge of medicines). May be found nominalized with the sense of "the person in charge," as in (4) and (6) below, but very rarely. (2) Noun: **Office** or **Bureau**, throughout history a very common des-

ignation for government agencies, normally less prestigious than such terms as *sheng* (Department), *pu* (Ministry, Division, etc.), and *ssu* (Court), but found at all levels of the governmental hierarchy with prefixes specifying the official whose office was designated or the responsibility of the office; e.g., *pu-cheng ssu* (lit., office for disseminating governmental policies), *ying-tsao ssu* (lit., office for planning and building), *shih-wei ssu* (lit., office of attendant guards), *ching-li ssu* (lit., office of a registrar of documents), *liu-shou ssu* (lit., office of a regent). The term "the various offices" (*chu-ssu*) was a common collective reference to all governmental agencies, especially those located at the dynastic capital. (3) CHOU: **Third Class Administrative Official,** 3rd highest of 8 categories in which officials were classified in a hierarchy separate from the formal rank system called the Nine Honors (*chiu ming*): below those designated *cheng* (Principal, etc.) and *shih* (Mentor, etc.) but above *lü* (Functionary), *fu* (Storekeeper), *shih* (Scribe), *hsü* (Assistant), and *t'u* (Attendant); notably included the Assistant Ministers (*tsai-fu*) of the Ministry of State (*t'ien-kuan*) and District Preceptors (*hsiang-shih*). CL: *troisième degré de la subordination administrative, préposés supérieurs.* (4) SUI–MING: **Directresses,** collective reference to 24 palace women individually known as Directress (also *ssu*); rank 4a in T'ang, 6a from Sung on. See *erh-shih-ssu ssu, chu ssu-shih.* (5) MING–CH'ING: **Squad,** a military unit headed by a Squad Leader (*pa-tsung*). (6) CH'ING: informal reference to a *hsün-chien* (**Police Chief**); see under *hsün-chien ssu.* In all occurrences, prefixes and suffixes should be noted carefully, including numerical prefixes, e.g., *san ssu, erh ssu, liang ssu.*

5534   *ssù* 寺
Court: throughout history, one of several terms commonly designating government agencies, differentiated by prefixes; e.g., the Court of Judicial Review (*ta-li ssu*). Especially associated with a group of agencies collectively called the Nine Courts (*chiu ssu*). Normally less prestigious than the term *sheng* (Department), about equal in prestige to *fu* (Court or Office), and more prestigious than such terms as *ssu* (Office), *ts'ao* (Section), and *k'o* (Section). See under the prefixed terms.

5535   *ssú* 食
Romanized *shih* throughout this dictionary.

5536   *ssū-ān chǎng* 司鞍長
CH'ING: **Director of Saddles,** 3 members of the Imperial Household Department (*nei-wu fu*), likely imperial bond-servants or Bannermen (see *ch'i*), assigned to the staff of the Department's Palace Stud (*shang-ssu yüan*). Also see *a-tun shih-wei.* BH: saddlery inspector. P39.

5537   *ssū-chàng* 司仗
(1) SUI: **Swordsman in Attendance,** commonly suffixed with *tso-yu* (left and right: attendant); number and rank not clear; part of the establishment of the Heir Apparent until c. 604, then retitled *ch'ien-niu pei-shen* (Swordsman Guard). P26. (2) T'ANG–SUNG, MING: **Directress of Ceremonial Regalia,** head of the Ceremonial Regalia Office (*ssu-chang ssu*), an agency of palace women. RR: *directeur des insignes.* (3) MING: **Swordsman,** 6 with rank equivalent to Company Commander (*po-hu*) authorized in 1370 for each Princely Establishment (*wang-fu*); in 1371 retitled *tien-chang* (Manager of Ceremonial Regalia). P69.

5538   *ssù-chǎng* 肆長
Market Shop Inspector. (1) CHOU: one of several duty assignments for members of the staff of the Market Shop

Supervisor (*ch'an-jen*) in the Ministry of Education (*ti-kuan*); one delegated to supervise each group (definition not specified) of market stalls or shops during business hours in the marketplace(s) of the capital city. CL: *chef de boutiques.* (2) SUI: 40, rank not clear, on the staff of the 2 Directors (*ling*) of the Market Office (*shih-ssu*) in the Court for the National Treasury (*ssu-nung ssu*); supervised activities in the 5 marketplaces of the dynastic capital and collected taxes on sales. Also see *shih-ling, shih se-fu.* P32, 62.

5539   *ssū-chàng ssū* 司仗司
Ceremonial Regalia Office. (1) T'ANG–SUNG, MING: one of 4 palace women agencies under the Wardrobe Service (*shang-fu chü*); headed by 2 Directresses (*ssu-chang*), rank 6a; in charge of ceremonial flags, emblems, etc., used by palace women. (2) SUNG: a unit of the Imperial Insignia Guards (*chin-wu wei*). P43.

5540   *ssū-ch'áng* 司常
CHOU: lit., in charge of the flags, *ch'ang* in this usage denoting a flag reportedly decorated with the sun, the moon, and a dragon: **Manager of the Royal Flags,** 2 ranked as Ordinary Servicemen (*chung-shih*) and 4 as Junior Servicemen (*hsia-shih*), members of the Ministry of Rites (*ch'un-kuan*) responsible for the maintenance and display of 9 types of flags or banners used by the King. CL: *préposé à l'étendard.*

5541   *ssū-ch'áng ssù* 司常寺
T'ANG: official variant from 684 to 705 of *t'ai-ch'ang ssu* (**Court of Imperial Sacrifices**).

5542   *ssù-ch'ē shù-chǎng* 馭車庶長
CH'IN–HAN: lit., militia general (see *shu-chang*) of 4-horse chariots: **Grandee of the Seventeenth Order,** 4th highest of 20 titles of honorary nobility (*chüeh*) awarded to deserving subjects. P65.

5543   *ssū-chēn* 司珍
Lit., in charge of rarities. (1) T'ANG: variant from 662 to 671 of *chin-pu* (**Treasury Bureau**) in the Ministry of Revenue, *hu-pu*). RR: *administration des objets précieux.* P6. (2) T'ANG–SUNG, MING: **Directress of Rarities,** 2 palace women, rank 6a, in charge of gems, pearls, and precious coins used by the Empress and other palace women; one of 4 major subordinate posts in the Workshop Service (*shang-kung chü*) of the Palace Domestic Service (*nei-shih sheng*). RR: *directeur des objets précieux du harem.*

5544   *ssū-chēn ssū* 司珍司
T'ANG–SUNG, MING: **Rarities Office,** one of 4 palace women agencies subordinate to the Workshop Service (*shang-kung chü*); headed by 2 Directresses (*ssu-chen*), rank 6a; in charge of pearls, gems, and coins used in the women's quarters of the imperial palace.

5545   *ssū-chēn tà-fū* 司珍大夫
T'ANG: official variant from 662 to 671 (?) of the **Director** (*lang-chung*) **of the Treasury Bureau** (*chin-pu,* then called *ssu-chen*), one of 4 principal agencies in the Ministry of Revenue (*hu-pu*). P6.

5546   *ssū-ch'én* 司辰
T'ANG–CH'ING: **Timekeeper,** normally 8, rank normally 9a; normally subordinate to Supervisors of Water Clocks (*ch'ieh-hu cheng*) in the T'ang Astrological Service (*t'ai-shih chü, ssu-t'ien t'ai*), the Sung–Liao Directorate of Astronomy (*ssu-t'ien chien*), the Yüan Astrological Commission (*t'ai-shih yüan*), the early Ming Directorate of Astrology (*t'ai-shih chien*), and the Ming–Ch'ing Directorate of Astronomy (*ch'in-t'ien chien*). Originated in 700, when the

title was abbreviated from *ssu-ch'en shih*. From c. 758 through Ch'ing, closely associated with the season-designated astronomical agencies known as the Five Offices (*wu kuan*). In Yüan the term Official (*kuan*) or Gentleman (*lang*) was commonly added as a suffix. RR+SP: *contrôleur des heures*. BH: assistant keeper of the clepsydra. P35.

5547   *ssū-ch'én shīh*   司辰師
SUI–T'ANG: **Timekeeper,** 4 till c. 604, thereafter 8, rank 9a; senior members of astrological and calendar-making agencies known in Sui as *t'ai-shih ts'ao* (Astrological Office), *t'ai-shih chü* (Astrological Service), and *t'ai-shih chien* (Directorate of Astrology) and in T'ang as *t'ai-shih chü* and *pi-shu ko* (both Astrological Service). Derived from pre-Sui titles such as *hou chung-lü, chung-lü lang*, qq.v. In 700 abbreviated to *ssu-ch'en*, q.v. RR: *contrôleur des heures*. P35.

5548   *ssū-chèng*   司正
(1) **Director:** throughout history a common reference to the head (see under *cheng*) of any government agency whose name ended in *ssu* (Office). (2) T'ANG–MING: **Directress of Palace Surveillance,** 2 palace women, rank 6a, principal assistants to the Chief of Palace Surveillance (*kung-cheng*), who was responsible for maintaining discipline among all palace women. RR: *directeur de la surveillance du harem*.

5549   *ssū-ch'éng*   司城
T'ANG: lit., in charge of the walls: from 662 to 670 the official variant of *chih-fang* (**Bureau of Operations**) in the Ministry of War (*ping-pu*), then officially named *ssu-jung;* the Director (*lang-chung*) of the Bureau during the same period was retitled *ta-fu* (Grand Master). RR: *administration des remparts*. P12.

5550   *ssū-ch'éng*   司成
Lit., in charge of maturation: **Rector.** (1) T'ANG: from 662 to 671, 2 designated as heads of the central government's Directorate of Education (*kuo-tzu chien*) while it bore the variant name *ssu-ch'eng kuan;* i.e., official variant of the normal title Chancellor (*chi-chiu*); one appointee prefixed *ta* (Senior), the other *shao* (Junior). (2) SUNG: from 1102 to the end of N. Sung (?), title of the head of the Preparatory Branch of the National University (*pi-yung*). SP: *directeur de l'université, recteur*. P34.

5551   *ssū-ch'éng*   司程
MING: **Monitor of Measurements,** rank 7a, in the Bureau of Construction (*chiang-tso ssu*) in the early Ming Ministry of Works (*kung-pu*). P15.

5552   *ssù-ch'éng*   祀丞
CH'ING: **Sacrificial Aide,** one Chinese official, rank 8b, subordinate to the Sacrificer (*feng-chi*) in each Sacrificial Office (*tz'u-chi shu*), e.g., those responsible for ceremonies at the Altar of Heaven (*t'ien-t'an*) and the Altar of Earth (*ti-t'an*). P28.

5553   *ssū-ch'éng hsüan-yèh*   司成宣業
T'ANG: from 662 to 671 the official variant of *po-shih* (**Erudite**) in the central government's Directorate of Education (*kuo-tzu chien*) while it was called *ssu-ch'eng kuan*. Also see *hsüan-yeh*. P34.

5554   *ssū-ch'éng kuǎn*   司成館
T'ANG: lit., academy of the Rector (see *ssu-ch'eng*), or academy in charge of maturation: official variant from 662 to 671 of *kuo-tzu chien* (**Directorate of Education**). P34.

5555   *ssū-ch'éng kuǎn*   司程官
YÜAN: lit., official in charge of measurements: **Assayer,**

4, rank not specified, on the staff of the Ministry of Works (*kung-pu*), presumably to inspect and approve materials used in construction projects at the dynastic capital. P15.

5556   *ssū-chí*   司寂
N-S DIV (Chou): lit., in charge of quiet seclusion: **Supervisor of the Buddhist Clergy** with rank as Senior Serviceman (*shang-shih*), a member of the Ministry of Rites (*ch'un-kuan*).

5557   *ssū-chǐ*   司戟
T'ANG: lit., in charge of halberds: from 662 (?) to 670 the official variant of *k'u-pu* (**Bureau of Provisions** in the Ministry of War, *ping-pu*).

5558   *ssū-chī*   司稽
CHOU: **Market Shop Examiner,** one of several duty assignments for members of the staff of the Market Shop Supervisor (*ch'an-jen*) in the Ministry of Education (*ti-kuan*); one delegated to enforce marketing regulations and catch marketplace thieves in each cluster of 5 groups (definition not specified) of market stalls or shops during business hours in the marketplace(s) of the capital city; immediately subordinate to a Market Shop Policeman (*ssu-pao*) overseeing 2 such Examiners. CL: *inspecteur*. P6.

5559   *ssū-chí*   司籍
(1) SUI: **Bureau of Receptions** in the developing Ministry of Rites (*lǐ-pu*); counterpart of the earlier Ministry of Receptions (*chu-k'o pu*) and the later Bureau of Receptions (*chu-k'o ssu*) in the Ministry of Rites; headed by a Director (*lang*). (2) T'ANG–SUNG: **Directress of the Library,** 2 palace women, rank 6a; see *ssu-chi ssu* (Library Office). RR: *directeur de la bibliothèque du harem*.

5560   *ssū-chī*   司績
T'ANG: lit., in charge of merit: from 662 to 670 the official variant of *k'ao-kung* (**Bureau of Evaluations** in the Ministry of Personnel, *lì-pu*).

5561   *ssū-chì*   司計
(1) T'ANG–SUNG: **Directress of Accounts,** 2 palace women, rank 6a; see *ssu-chi ssu* (Accounts Office). RR: *directeur des comptes*. (2) T'ANG: from 662 to 670 and again from 752 to 758 the official variant of *pi-pu* (**Bureau of Review**) in the Ministry of Justice (*hsing-pu*), which itself was known as *ssu-hsing* in the 660s and as *ssu-hsien* in the 750s. RR: *administration des comptes-rendus*. (3) YÜAN: **Account Keeper,** 4, rank not clear, minor members of the Ministry of Revenue (*hu-pu*); also called *ssu-chi kuan* (lit., official in charge of accounts). P6.

5562   *ssū-chì*   司記
T'ANG–SUNG, MING: **Directress of Records,** 2 palace women; see *ssu-chi ssu* (Records Office). RR: *directeur de l'enregistrement des pièces*.

5563   *ssū-chí sǒ*   司籍所
YÜAN: **Office of Fines and Confiscations,** a unit of the Ministry of Justice (*hsing-pu*) responsible for the collection of judicially imposed fines or the confiscation of possessions in lieu of fines; headed by a Superintendent (*t'i-ling*), rank not clear but low; established in 1283 to replace the Superintendency of Fines and Confiscations (*tuan-mo t'i-ling so*). Cf. *tsang-fa k'u*. P13.

5564   *ssū-chí ssū*   司籍司
T'ANG–SUNG, MING: **Library Office,** one of 4 palace women agencies subordinate to the Ceremonial Service (*shang-i chü*); headed by 2 Directresses (*ssu-chi*), rank 6a; in charge of the books available to the Empress and other

palace women, the education provided for such women, and the writing and study materials they used.

5565 *ssū-chì ssū* 司計司
T'ANG–SUNG, MING: **Accounts Office,** one of 4 palace women agencies subordinate to the Workshop Service (*shang-kung chü*); headed by 2 Directresses (*ssu-chi*), rank 6a; kept records of clothing, foodstuffs, firewood, etc., issued to women in palace service.

5566 *ssū-chì ssū* 司記司
T'ANG–SUNG, MING: **Records Office,** one of 4 palace women agencies in the General Palace Service (*shang-kung ssu*); headed by 2 Directresses (*ssu-chi*), rank 6a; provided secretarial services within the palace women's quarters, handling the transmission of correspondence and other documents within the palace and keeping records about the receipt and distribution of such documents.

5567 *ssū-chǐ tà-fū* 司戟大夫
T'ANG: from 662 (?) to 670 the official variant of *k'u-pu lang-chung* (**Director of the Bureau of Provisions** in the Ministry of War, *ping-pu*).

5568 *ssū-chī tà-fū* 司績大夫
T'ANG: from 662 to 670 the official variant of *k'ao-kung lang-chung* (**Director of the Bureau of Evaluations** in the Ministry of Personnel, *li-pu*).

5569 *ssū-chì tà-fū* 司計大夫
T'ANG: from 662 to 670 and again from 752 to 758 the official variant of *pi-pu lang-chung* (**Director of the Bureau of Review** in the Ministry of Justice, *hsing-pu*). P13.

5570 *ssū chī-yén* 司几筵
CHOU: **Supervisor of Ceremonial Seating,** 2 ranked as Junior Servicemen (*hsia-shih*), members of the Ministry of Rites (*ch'un-kuan*) responsible for arranging benches and mats for ceremonial occasions and seating dignitaries in appropriate positions according to their ranks. CL: *préposé aux bancs d'appui et aux nattes pour s'asseoir.*

5571 *ssū-ch'ì* 司器
CHOU: **Crafts Tax Supervisor,** one of 6 agencies in the Ministry of Education (*ti-kuan*) responsible for various tax collections, according to the ancient ritual treatise *Li-chi.* See *liu fu* (Six Tax Supervisors).

5572 *ssū-ch'ì ssū* 司饎司
T'ANG–SUNG, MING: **Banquets Office,** one of 4 palace women agencies subordinate to the Food Service (*shang-shih chü*); headed by 2 Directresses (*ssu-ch'i*), rank 6a; in charge of recording the receipt and distribution of foodstuffs and fuels in the women's quarters of the imperial palace. RR (*ssu-ch'i*): *directeur des repas.*

5573 *ssū-chiǎ* 司甲
CHOU: **Armorer,** 2 ranked as Junior Grand Masters (*hsia ta-fu*) and 8 as Ordinary Servicemen (*chung-shih*), members of the Ministry of War (*hsia-kuan*) in charge of maintaining the ruler's body armor and dressing him in it when appropriate. CL: *préposé aux cuirasses.* P16.

5574 *ssū-chià* 司稼
CHOU: **Seed Specialist,** 8 ranked as Junior Servicemen (*hsia-shih*), members of the Ministry of Education (*ti-kuan*) responsible for inspecting and classifying grain seeds, distributing information about seed varieties and their suitability for various soils, and determining seasonal yields of grain for tax assessment purposes. CL: *préposé aux semences.*

5575 *ssū-chià* 司駕
T'ANG: from 752 to 758 the official variant of *chia-pu* (**Bureau of Equipment** in the Ministry of War, *ping-pu*). P12.

5576 *ssū-chià ssù* 司稼寺
T'ANG: from 662 to 670 the official variant of *ssu-nung ssu* (**Court of the Imperial Granaries**). P8.

5577 *ssū-chiàng* 司匠
CH'ING: **Supervisor of Craftsmen,** a petty official ranking 8a or below found in various storehouses, workshops, and similar agencies, in charge of workmen engaged in construction or manufacturing projects. BH: overseer of works, inspector of works, clerk of works.

5578 *ssū-chiào* 司教
CH'ING: unofficial reference to an **Instructor** (*chiao-yü*), the head of a local Confucian School (*ju-hsüeh*).

5579 *ssū-chiāo* 司郊
N-S DIV (Chou): **Supervisor of the Suburban Sacrifices,** members of the Ministry of Rites (*ch'un-kuan*) ranked as Senior Servicemen (*shang-shih;* 7a), Ordinary Servicemen (*chung-shih;* 8a), and Junior Servicemen (*hsia-shih;* 9a); assisted in important state sacrificial rituals at the dynastic capital; counterparts of earlier staff members of the Hall of Enlightened Rule (*ming-t'ang*) or later officials of the Office of the National Altars (*chiao-she chü*), etc. P28.

5580 *ssū-chiēh* 司階
T'ANG–SUNG: **Guard of the Staircase,** 2 military officers of 6a rank in each of the Sixteen Guards (*shih-liu wei*); also in T'ang if not Sung, one in the Left Guard (*tso-wei*) and one in the Right Guard (*yu-wei*) in the establishment of the Heir Apparent. RR+SP: *officier des escaliers.* P26.

5581 *ssū chiēn* 四監
SUI: **Four Directorates,** collective reference to a group of 2nd-level agencies in the central government: Directorate of Waterways (*tu-shui chien*), Directorate for Imperial Manufactories (*shao-fu chien*), Directorate for the Palace Buildings (*chiang-tso chien*), and Directorate of Education (*kuo-tzu chien*). Cf. *wu chien* (Five Directorates).

5582 *ssū-chièn* 司諫
Remonstrator, one of the titles of officials generically called *chien-kuan* (Remonstrance Officials), q.v. (1) CHOU: 2 ranked as Ordinary Servicemen (*chung-shih*), members of the Ministry of Education (*ti-kuan*) responsible for fostering proper conduct among the people and rectifying improper conduct; played some role in evaluating the qualifications of men to be local chiefs and headmen. CL: *chargé des remonstrances, censeur.* (2) SUNG: one each Left and Right initiated in 988 by retitling of Rectifiers of Omissions (*pu-ch'üeh*), both rank 7a; the former on the staff of the Chancellery (*men-hsia sheng*), the latter on the staff of the Secretariat (*chung-shu sheng*); from c. 1020 members of the Remonstrance Bureau (*chien-yüan*); responsible for inspecting all imperial pronouncements and returning for reconsideration those deemed improper (see under *feng-po*). SP: *fonctionnaire chargé de remonstrance, censeur politique.* (3) CHIN: number and ranks not clear; members of the Remonstrance Bureau. (4) MING: one each Left and Right, both rank 7a, members of the Remonstrance Bureau with functions as in Sung, but only from 1380 to 1382, when the Bureau was abolished and its functions reassigned to the Censorate (*tu ch'a-yüan*). Also one each Left and Right, both rank 9b, members of the 2 Secretariats of the Heir Apparent (see *ch'un-fang*). P19, 26.

5583 *ssù-chīēn* 寺監
SUNG: **Courts and Directorates,** a common categorical reference to the Nine Courts (*chiu ssu*), the Palace Library (*pi-shu chien, pi-shu sheng*), and the Palace Administration (*tien-chung chien, tien-chung sheng*). P54.

5584 *ssù chiēn-ssū* 四監司
SUNG: **Four Circuit Supervisors** or **Four Circuit Supervisorates,** collective reference to the 4 most common types of Circuit (*lu*) administrators (or their agencies): Military Commissioners (see *shuai-ssu*), Fiscal Commissioners (see *ts'ao-ssu*), Judicial Commissioners (see *hsien-ssu*), and Supply Commissioners (see *ts'ang-ssu*). Often abbreviated to *ssu ssu* (lit., 4 offices). See under *chien-ssu*. P51, 62.

5585 *ssū-chíh* 司直
Rectifier. (1) HAN: from 118 B.C. to A.D. 35 the senior subordinate of the Counselor-in-chief (*ch'eng-hsiang*), to whom he was responsible for reporting wayward officials; rank =2,000 bushels. HB: director of uprightness. (2) N-S DIV–SUNG: 10 in N. Wei, 6 thereafter; rank 5 in N. Wei, 6b1 in T'ang, 8a in Sung; on the staff of the N. Wei Chamberlain for Law Enforcement (*t'ing-wei*) and the Sui-Sung Court of Judicial Review (*ta-li ssu*); commonly used as agents to conduct investigations or trials of officials on service outside the dynastic capital, in response to impeachments. RR+SP: *inspecteur judiciaire*. P22. (3) T'ANG, SUNG, LIAO: from 656, 2 (later 1?), rank 7a in T'ang but not clear thereafter, on the staff of the Heir Apparent, responsible for maintaining censorial surveillance over members of his staff; perpetuated in Ming by the *ssu-chih lang* (Rectifier). RR+SP: *inspecteur judiciaire*. P26. (4) YÜAN: initiated in 1305 by retitling all *tien-pu* (Archivists), in 1312 all further retitled *ching-li* (Registrars); found at all levels of government. P23.

5586 *ssū-chīh* 司織
N-S DIV (Chou): **Director of Textile Production,** ranked as a Junior Grand Master (*hsia ta-fu; 6a*), a member of the Ministry of Works (*tung-kuan*). P14.

5587 *ssù chíh* 四直
SUNG: **Four Duty Groups,** collective reference to 4 units of Palace Guards (*tien-ch'ien shih-wei*) that took up active duty in rotational shifts: Crossbowmen on Duty (*nu-chih*), Bowmen on Duty (*kung-chien chih*), Mace Bearers on Duty (*ku-to-tzu chih*), and Military Police on Duty (? *yü-lung chih*). See *chih*. Cf. *fan* (on rotational duty). SP: *quatre compagnies*.

5588 *ssū-chíh láng* 司直郎
MING: **Rectifier,** 2 each, rank 6b, in the Left and Right Secretariats of the Heir Apparent (see *ch'un-fang*); in the tradition of previous Rectifiers (see *ssu-chih*), maintained disciplinary surveillance over staff members of the household of the Heir Apparent. P26.

5589 *ssū-chíh shǐh* 司直史
T'ANG: **Rectification Clerk,** 12 unranked subofficials serving as aides to the Rectifiers (*ssu-chih*) of the Court of Judicial Review (*ta-li ssu*). RR: *scribe d'inspecteur judiciaire*.

5590 *ssū-chìh ssū* 司製司
T'ANG-SUNG, MING: **Sewing Office,** one of 4 palace women agencies subordinate to the Workshop Service (*shang-kung chü*); headed by 2 Directresses (*ssu-chih*), rank 6a; made and maintained clothing of the Empress and other palace women. RR: (*ssu-chih*): *directeur de la confection des vêtements*.

5591 *ssù-chíh tū yú-hòu* 四直都虞候
SUNG: **Inspector-in-chief of the Four Duty Groups,** duty assignment for a military officer to serve, at least nominally, as disciplinary supervisor of those members of the Palace Guards (*tien-ch'ien shih-wei*) who performed active guard duty at the imperial palace in rotational shifts; normally 2nd in command under a Commander-in-chief (*tu chih-hui shih*) of the Palace Guards. See *ssu chih* (Four Duty Groups), *yü-hou*. SP: *surveillant en chef des quatre compagnies*.

5592 *ssū-chīn* 司金
(1) N-S DIV: **Master of Metals,** principal court official in charge of metal-casting, perhaps including coinage; in San-kuo Wei had the status of Commandant (*tu-wei*), in San-kuo Shu that of Leader of Court Gentlemen (*chung-lang chiang*), but institutional affiliation not clear; in Chou was a major member of the Ministry of Works (*tung-kuan*), ranked as an Ordinary Grand Master (*chung ta-fu; 4a*). P14, 16. (2) T'ANG: from 752 to 758 the official variant of *chin-pu* (**Treasury Bureau** in the Ministry of Revenue, *hu-pu*), its Director (*lang-chung*) then being called *ta-fu* (Grand Master). RR: *administration de l'or*. P6.

5593 *ssū-chīn chiēn* 司津監
T'ANG: lit., Directorate in charge of fords: from 662 to 671 the official variant of *tu-shui chien* (**Directorate of Waterways**), its head then being called *chien* (Director) rather than the normal *shih-che* (Commissioner).

5594 *ssū-chīng* 司經
CHIN–YÜAN: **Librarian,** with the suffixes *cheng* (Principal) and *fu* (Assistant), in the household of the Heir Apparent; numbers and ranks not clear; counterparts of *hsien-ma* (Librarian) of other periods; also see *ssu-ching chü*. P26.

5595 *ssū-chīng chǘ* 司經局
SUI–T'ANG, LIAO, MING–CH'ING: **Editorial Service** in the household of the Heir Apparent, a new name for the era of N-S Division's *tien-ching chü* and *tien-ching fang*; responsible for maintaining the library and archive of the Heir Apparent, providing writing materials, and preparing compilations as desired; headed by one or more Librarians (*hsien-ma*), commonly rank 5b. Such Librarians existed in Sung without constituting a formally recognized Editorial Service; in Chin and Yüan there also were Librarians (*ssu-ching*), but there was no formalized Service. RR: *service de la bibliothèque de l'héritier du trône*. P26.

5596 *ssū-chīng tà-fū* 司經大夫
T'ANG: lit., grand master in charge of books: from 662 to 663 the official variant of *hsien-ma* (**Librarian**) of the Editorial Service (*ssu-ching chü*) in the household of the Heir Apparent; rank 5b2.

5597 *ssū-chiù* 司救
CHOU: **Welfare Supervisor,** 2 ranked as Ordinary Servicemen (*chung-shih*), members of the Ministry of Education (*ti-kuan*) responsible for monitoring the morality of the people and reprimanding transgressors, also for aiding people in times of natural disasters and epidemics. CL: *chargé de secourir ou sauveur*.

5598 *ssū-ch'iú* 司裘
CHOU: **Manager of Furs,** 4 ranked as Junior Servicemen (*hsia-shih*), members of the Ministry of State (*t'ien-kuan*) responsible for maintaining all furs and pelts used by the ruler for clothing, as gifts, etc. CL: *chef des habits de fourrure*.

5599 *ssū-chōu* 司州
HAN–N-S DIV: lit., in charge of the (capital) region: **Metropolitan Area,** a common designation, and from Chin on the official designation, of the large territorial jurisdiction surrounding the dynastic capital, under the dominant supervision of the Metropolitan Commandant (*ssu-li hsiao-wei* in Han, then *ssu-chou mu* or *ssu-chou tz'u-shih*). Comparable to the later terms *chih-li* and *ching-shih* (both Metropolitan Area). Also see *chou* (Region), *mu* (Governor), *tz'u-shih* (Regional Inspector). P32, 50, 51, 52.

5600 *ssū-chù* 司祝
CH'ING: **Petitioner,** 12 priestesses of Shamanism, one of the religions officially patronized by the court; members of the Shamanism Office (*shen-fang*) in the Office of Palace Ceremonial (*chang-i ssu*) of the Imperial Household Department (*nei-wu fu*); normally wives of Manchu Imperial Guardsmen (*shih-wei*). See under *sa-man t'ai-t'ai*. BH: shamanic priestess.

5601 *ssū-chú chǎng* 司竹長
HAN: **Director of Bamboo Crafts,** rank and hierarchical affiliation not clear; probably a middle-level official on the staff of the Chamberlain for the Palace Revenues (*shao-fu*).

5602 *ssū-chú chiēn* 司竹監
SUI–T'ANG: **Directorate of Bamboo Crafts,** one of many agencies under the Court of the Imperial Granaries (*ssu-nung ssu*); headed by a Director (*chien*), rank 6b2; responsible for cultivating bamboo and rattan and for making bamboo and rattan curtains, baskets, etc., for use in the palace and agencies of the central government. RR: *direction du service des bambous.*

5603 *ssū-chú tū-wèi* 司竹都尉
N-S DIV (N. Wei): **Commandant of Bamboo Crafts,** rank and hierarchical status not clear; probably a middle-level subordinate in the Ministry of Granaries (*k'u-pu* or *t'ai-ts'ang*) responsible for cultivation and manufacture of bamboo for palace and government use.

5604 *ssū-ch'ú* 司儲
T'ANG: from 752 to 758 the official variant of *ts'ang-pu* (**Bureau of Granaries** in the Ministry of Revenue, *hu-pu*); during the same period its Director (*lang-chung*) was retitled *ta-fu* (Grand Master). RR: *administration des provisions; bureau des greniers de l'empire.* P6.

5605 *ssū-chuàn* 司饌
T'ANG: **Directress of Foodstuffs,** 2 palace women, probably with rank 6a2, in the household of the Heir Apparent; supervised the preparation of meals for the female members of the household. RR: *directeur des mets du harem de l'héritier du trône.*

5606 *ssū-ch'uān* 司川
T'ANG: from 662 to 671 and again from 752 to 758 the official variant of *shui-pu* (**Bureau of Waterways** in the Ministry of Works, *kung-pu*); during the same period its Director (*lang-chung*) was retitled *ta-fu* (Grand Master). RR: *administration des fleuves; bureau des eaux.* P15.

5607 *ssū-ch'ūi* 司吹
N-S DIV (Chou): **Flutist,** number not specified, some ranked as Ordinary Servicemen (*chung-shih;* 8a) and some as Junior Servicemen (*hsia-shih;* 9a), subordinates of the Musicians-in-chief (*ta ssu-yüeh*) in the Ministry of Rites (*ch'un-kuan*). P10.

5608 *ssū-chǔn* 司準
N-S DIV (Chou): **Weighmaster,** number not specified,

ranked as Ordinary Servicemen (*chung-shih;* 8a), members of the Ministry of Works (*tung-kuan*). P14.

5609 *ssū-chūng* 司中
N-S DIV: lit., in charge of the palace: only in the reign of Wang Mang (r. A.D. 8–23), the official variant of *kuang-lu-hsün* (**Chamberlain for Attendants**).

5610 *ssū chūng-ch'ìng* 司鐘磬
N-S DIV (Chou): **Ringer of Bells and Musical Stones,** number not specified, some ranked as Ordinary Servicemen (*chung-shih;* 8a) and some as Junior Servicemen (*hsia-shih;* 9a); subordinates of the Musicians-in-chief (*ta ssu-yüeh*) in the Ministry of Rites (*ch'un-kuan*). P10.

5611 *ssū chú* 四局
SUNG: **Four Artisan Services,** collective reference to the 4 component units of the Artisans Institute (*han-lin yüan*) in the Palace Domestic Service (*nei-shih sheng*), all staffed with non-official specialists, some hereditary: the Astrologer Service (*t'ien-wen chü*), the Painter Service (*t'u-hua chü*), the Calligrapher Service (*shu-i chü*), and the Physician Service (*i-kuan chü*). SP: *quatre bureaux.*

5612 *ssū-chǔ ts'úng-shìh* 司舉從事
T'ANG: lit., assistants in charge of undertakings: **Regional Investigator,** a duty assignment comparable in functions and status to Attendant Censor (*shih yü-shih,* rank 6a2) in the Censorate (*yü-shih t'ai*); 2 appointed in 711 on the staff of each of 24 newly established Supervisors-in-chief (*tu-tu*), among whom all of the empire's Prefectures (*chou*) were allocated for surveillance supervision. One source confusingly reports that Regional Investigators were created by retitling Administrative Supervisors (*lu-shih ts'an-chün-shih*). Regional Investigators who failed to perform their surveillance and disciplinary functions effectively were to be impeached by the Censorate. How long the posts existed is not clear. RR: *enquêter adjoint.*

5613 *ssū-chǔn* 司軍
CHIN: **Commandant,** one or more, rank 9b, on the staff of the Prefect (*tz'u-shih*) of each Prefecture (*chou*); specific functions and relations with the regular military establishment not clear. P53.

5614 *ssù chūn* 四軍
T'ANG: **Four Imperial Armies,** from 738 or 739 a collective reference to the forces of the Northern Command (*pei-ya*): the Left and Right Forest of Plumes Armies (*yü-lin chün*) and the Left and Right Militant as Dragons Armies (*lung-wu chün*). The term was superseded in 757 by the term Six Imperial Armies (*liu chün*) on establishment of the Left and Right Armies of Inspired Militancy (*shen-wu chün*), but it occasionally reappeared as a specific reference to the Forest of Plumes Armies and the Militant as Dragons Armies. Also see *shih chün* (Ten Armies), *pei-men ssu chün.*

5615 *ssū-fǎ* 司法
T'ANG: lit., in charge of the laws: a prefix commonly attached to the titles of Administrators (*ts'an-chün-shih*) and lesser personnel of Law Sections (*fa-ts'ao*) in units of territorial administration. P53.

5616 *ssū-fān* 司著
SUI–T'ANG: **Bureau of Receptions,** one of 4 top-echelon units in the Ministry of Rites (*lǐ-pu*), in c. 607 replacing the name Ministry of Receptions (*chu-k'o*), in c. 620 replaced by *chu-k'o* meaning Bureau of Receptions, a usage that endured through Sung except during the period 661–670, when *ssu-fan* was revived; headed by a Director (*lang,*

lang-chung, ta-fu), rank 5b, and a Vice Director (ch'eng-wu lang, yüan-wai lang), 6b; in collaboration with the Court of State Ceremonial (hung-lu ssu), managed the reception of foreign rulers and envoys at court. RR: *administration des princes tributaires.* P9.

5617   *ssù fáng*   四房
SUNG: **Four Sections,** collective reference to 4 agencies of the Bureau of Military Affairs (shu-mi yüan) that were superseded c. 1080 by Twelve Sections (shih-erh fang); the 4 original agencies were the War Section (ping-fang), the Personnel Section (li-fang), the Revenue Section (hu-fang), and the Rites Section (li-fang). The collective term may also be found referring to 4 other agencies in the same Bureau, which apparently were also superseded by the Twelve Sections c. 1080: the Diplomacy Section (kuo-hsin fang), the Militia Section (min-ping fang), the Horse Pasturage Section (mu-ma fang), and the Transport Supervision Section (tsung-ling fang). Cf. *wu fang* (Five Sections).

5618   *ssù-fāng kuǎn*   四方館
N-S DIV–CHIN: **Hostel for Tributary Envoys,** an agency responsible for the greeting of foreign rulers and envoys, their preparation for presentation at court audience, the handling of their tributary gifts, etc. Originated possibly as early as Later Han, had intermittent existence during the era of N-S Division as a unit of the evolving Secretariat (chung-shu sheng), staffed as circumstances warranted by Receptionists (t'ung-shih she-jen) of the Secretariat under a court official designated Manager (kuan-chu); alternated or collaborated with various kinds of units subordinate to the Court for Dependencies (hung-lu ssu; also see ta hung-lu). In Sui attached to the Court for Dependencies, but from T'ang on was a unit of the Secretariat, staffed with Receptionists; in T'ang headed by a court official on duty assignment as Administrator (chih ... shih) or Supervisor (p'an ... shih) of the Hostel, in Sung and Liao by one or 2 Commissioners (shih), rank 6a. Chin attached the agency to the Ministry of War (ping-pu) with a Commissioner, 5a, as head, and gave it the principal function of transmitting official documents between the central government and Route (lu) territorial administrations, like a Bureau of Transmission (t'ung-cheng yüan) or Office of Transmission (t'ung-cheng ssu) of later dynasties or even the Ming dynasty Messenger Office (hsing-jen ssu). In Yüan, Ming, and Ch'ing times the reception of foreign dignitaries was managed by an Interpreters Institute (hui-t'ung kuan), first established in 1276. Also see k'o-kuan, chu-k'o ssu, li-fan yüan. RR+SP: *collège des quatre directions.* SP: *centre d'accueil des étrangers.* P11, 21.

5619   *ssù fēi*   四妃
T'ANG–SUNG: **Four Principal Consorts,** collective designation of the Emperor's most esteemed secondary wives, rank =1a: in the early T'ang order of precedence, the Honored Consort (kuei-fei), Pure Consort (shu-fei), Virtuous Consort (te-fei), and Worthy Consort (hsien-fei).

5620   *ssū-fēng ssū*   司封司
T'ANG–SUNG, MING: **Bureau of Honors,** one of 4 major units in the Ministry of Personnel (li-pu), originated in 661 as the new name of the chu-chüeh q.v.; in 1396 renamed yen-feng ch'ing-li ssu, q.v. Responsible for processing conferrals of noble titles, confirming the inheritance of noble titles, etc.; by Sung if not earlier expanded to include processing awards of posthumous titles to officials, claims for the inheritance of official status, etc. Headed by a Director (ta-fu till 684, thereafter lang-chung), rank 5b1 in T'ang, 6b in Sung; with a Vice Director (yüan-wai lang), 6b1 in

t'ang, 7a in Sung. A Yüan counterpart was designated feng-kao k'o (Honors Section). RR+SP: *bureau des titres nobiliaires.* P5.

5621   *ssū-fù*   司副 or 寺副
Common variants of fu (Vice), i.e., **Vice Director** of ... Office (first form) or **Vice Minister** of ... Court (2nd form).

5622   *ssū-fú*   司服
(1) CHOU: **Master of the Wardrobe,** 2 ranked as Ordinary Servicemen (chung-shih), members of the Ministry of Rites (ch'un-kuan) in charge of the production of gowns with which the ruler rewarded officials on their 2nd promotions. Cf. *nei ssu-fu, shang-fu, shih-fu.* CL: *préposé aux costumes.* (2) CH'ING: unofficial, archaic reference to a **Superintendent of Imperial Silk Manufacturing** (chih-tsao chien-tu).

5623   *ssù fǔ*   四輔 or *ssù fǔ-kuān*   官
Four Supports. (1) HAN (first form): collective reference in the time of Wang Mang (r. A.D. 9–23) to the eminent dignitaries entitled Grand Preceptor (t'ai-shih), Grand Mentor (t'ai-fu), Grand Guardian (t'ai-pao), and Junior Mentor (shao-fu). (2) MING (2nd form): from 1380 to 1382 only, duty assignments for Confucian literati who were concurrently Advisers to the Heir Apparent (t'ai-tzu pin-k'o) to assist the Emperor in ceremonies at the Imperial Ancestral Temple (t'ai-miao) and generally to be his intimate advisers; individually designated Spring Support (ch'un-kuan), Summer Support (hsia-kuan), Autumn Support (ch'iu-kuan), and Winter Support (tung-kuan), each post being available to more than one appointee at a time, although the last 2 posts were never filled. P4, 67.

5624   *ssū-fǔ*   私府
HAN: **Private Storehouse,** an agency in the household of the Empress and of each Princess; each supervised by a Director (ling in Former Han, chang in Later Han), rank 600 bushels, with an Aide (ch'eng). HB: private storehouse. P69.

5625   *ssū-fǔ lìng*   司府令
SUI: from c. 605, the official variant of chia-ling (**Household Provisioner** in the establishment of the Heir Apparent). P26.

5626   *ssū-fǔ ssù*   司府寺
T'ANG: from 684 to 705 the official variant of t'ai-fu ssu (**Court of the Imperial Treasury**). P7.

5627   *ssū-hán*   司函
CH'ING: **Armorer,** unspecified numbers of non-official specialists employed in the Court of Imperial Armaments (wu-pei yüan), an agency of the Imperial Household Department (nei-wu fu). BH: supervisor of armour-making.

5628   *ssū-hòu*   司候
CHIN–YÜAN: **Chief of Attendants,** one in charge of unranked subofficials in certain units of territorial administration, who were authorized in proportion to the number of households in the jurisdiction. In Chin rank 9a, commonly found in the headquarters of frontier Prefectures (chou); in Yüan rank not clear, authorized for Route Commands (tsung-kuan fu) until 1283, then replaced with Overseers (ta-lu-hua-ch'ih). P53.

5629   *ssù hsiá*   四轄
SUNG: **Four Controllers,** collective reference to officials charged with supervising the Chief Tea Markets (tu ch'a-ch'ang) of the Monopoly Tax Commission (chüeh-huo wu), the Market of Miscellanies (tsa-mai ch'ang) of the Office

of Miscellaneous Purchases (*tsa-mai wu*), and the Eastern and Western Storehouses (*tung-k'u, hsi-k'u*) of the Left Vault (*tso-tsang*), all fiscal agencies under the Court of the Imperial Treasury (*t'ai-fu ssu*); and the Crafts Institute (*wen-ssu yüan*) maintained by the Ministry of Works (*kung-pu*). SP: *quatres régisseurs*. P15.

5630   *ssū-hsiāng* 司香
CH'ING: **Incense Handler,** numerous subofficials of the Imperial Household Department (*nei-wu fu*) attached to the Department's Office of Palace Ceremonial (*chang-i ssu*) and to each imperial mausoleum (*ling*). BH: acolyte.

5631   *ssù hsiāng* 四廂
SUNG: **Four Capital Townships,** the units of local police and judicial administration into which both Kaifeng and Hangchow, the successive capital cities, were subdivided. Township organizations coexisted with the regular Prefecture (*fu*) and District (*hsien*) administrations, especially supplementing District Defenders (*hsien-wei*). In the case of Kaifeng 2 Capital Townships, one Left and one Right, supervised the area within the city walls as Inner Capital Townships (*nei-hsiang*), and 2 others, also differentiated as Left and Right, supervised the area immediately surrounding the walled city as Outer Capital Townships (*wai-hsiang*). The extramural population grew so rapidly that 8 additional Outer Townships were established in 1008 (or the existing 2 were increased to a total of 8?); and a 9th was added in 1021. In the case of Hangchow, where Four Capital Townships were established in the 1130s, there were similarly 2 Inner Townships differentiated as Left and Right, but the 2 Outer Townships were differentiated as South and North. In both capitals, all Capital Townships were supervised or directed by Censors (*yü-shih*) on rotational duty assignments as Capital Inspectors (*hsün-shih*), and the central government's Bureau of Military Affairs (*shu-mi yüan*) occasionally delegated senior officers as Military Directors-in-chief (*ping-ma tu-chien*) to oversee the military aspects of Township operations. The regular Township establishment was dominated by a Police Office (*chün-hsün yüan*) staffed by junior military officers serving as Military Inspectors (*chün-hsün shih*) and Administrative Assistants (*chün-hsün p'an-kuan*); there were also civil officials serving as Police Executives (*kung-shih kan-tang kuan*) or Managers (*kou-kuan*). Members of the Township staffs were generically referred to as Capital Township Officials (*hsiang-kuan*). Whether of the military or of the civil service, Township personnel had unusual powers to arrest and sentence troublemakers. Originally they were apparently subordinate to the Kaifeng Superior Prefecture (*fu*), but through most of the dynasty they seem to have enjoyed great independence of action, though under the close scrutiny of the central government. The Townships were roughly comparable to the earlier Commandant of the Capital Patrol (*liu-pu wei*) and the later (Ming–Ch'ing) Wardens' Offices of the Five Wards (*wu-ch'eng ping-ma chih-hui ssu, wu-ch'eng ping-ma ssu*). Also see *hsiang* and *pu-tsei kuan* (Metropolitan Police Officials). Cf. the T'ang–Sung *wei-wei ssu* (Court of the Imperial Regalia). P20.

5632   *ssū-hsièn* 司憲
(1) Throughout history a common unofficial reference to the **Censorate** (*yü-shih t'ai, tu ch'a-yüan*); cf. *feng-hsien kuan*. (2) N-S DIV (Chou): formal name of the traditional *yü-shih t'ai* (**Censorate**); its personnel were differentiated by rank designations—one Ordinary Grand Master (*chung ta-fu*; 5a) comparable to a Censor-in-chief (*yü-shih ta-fu*)

or Vice Censor-in-chief (*yü-shih chung-ch'eng*) of other times, 2 Senior Servicemen (*shang-shih;* 7a), an unspecified number of Ordinary Servicemen (*chung-shih;* 8a), and 18 Junior Servicemen (*hsia-shih;* 9a). P18. (3) T'ANG: from 752 to 758 the official variant of *hsing-pu* (**Ministry of Justice**). RR: *administration de la loi*.

5633   *ssū-hsiěn* 司險
(1) CHOU: **Director of Defense Works,** 2 ranked as Ordinary Servicemen (*chung-shih*) and 4 as Junior Servicemen (*hsia-shih*), members of the Ministry of War (*hsia-kuan*) responsible for planning and preparing ditches, lines of trees, etc., for purposes of military defense. CL: *préposé aux travaux de défense*. (2) SUNG: unofficial reference to a **Director of the Bureau of Waterways and Irrigation** (*shui-pu lang-chung*) in the Ministry of Works (*kung-pu*).

5634   *ssū-hsièn tà-fū* 司憲大夫
T'ANG: from 662 to 671 the official variant of *yü-shih chung-ch'eng* (**Vice Censor-in-chief**), during the period when the Censorate (*yü-shih t'ai*) was called *hsien-t'ai*. P18.

5635   *ssū-hsíng* 司刑
(1) CHOU: **Director of Corporal Punishments,** 2 ranked as Ordinary Servicemen (*chung-shih*), members of the Ministry of Justice (*ch'iu-kuan*). CL: *préposé aux supplices*. (2) T'ANG: from 662 to 670 the official variant of *hsing-pu* (both **Ministry of Justice** and the Ministry's **Bureau of Judicial Administration**); during this period the Minister (*shang-shu*) was retitled Grand Executive Attendant (*t'ai ch'ang-po*) and the Bureau Director (*lang-chung*) was retitled Grand Master (*ta-fu*). RR: *administration de la justice*. P13.

5636   *ssù hsīng* 四星
T'ANG: lit., the 4 stars: **Four Luminaries,** under Hsüan-tsung (r. 712–756) an unofficial collective reference to the Emperor and his secondary wives known as the Three Consorts (*san fei*): Gracious Consort (*hui-fei*), Elegant Consort (*li-fei*), and Splendid Consort (*hua-fei*). Cf. *ssu fei* (Four Principal Consorts).

5637   *ssū-hsíng ssù* 司刑寺
T'ANG: from 684 to 704 the official variant of *ta-li ssu* (**Court of Judicial Review**). P22.

5638   *ssù hsüān* 四選
SUNG: **Four Appointments Processes,** collective reference to the ways in which the Ministry of Personnel (*li-pu*) organized its staff, and to the procedures it followed, for the evaluation and selection of inactive officials for reappointment: Senior Civil Appointments Process (*shang-shu tso-hsüan*), Senior Military Appointments Process (*shang-shu yu-hsüan*), Junior Civil Appointments Process (*shih-lang tso-hsüan*), and Junior Military Appointments Process (*shih-lang yu-hsüan*). Also used in reference to the early Sung agencies entitled East Bureau of Personnel Evaluation (*shen-kuan tung-yüan*), West Bureau of Personnel Evaluation (*shen-kuan hsi-yüan*), Bureau of Personnel Assignments (*liu-nei ch'üan*), and Bureau of Lesser Military Assignments (*san-pan yüan*). Also see *shen-kuan yüan, hsüan*. SP: *quatre bureaux de nomination*.

5639   *ssū-hsüān shìh* 司烜氏
CHOU: **Light Tender,** 6 ranked as Junior Servicemen (*hsia-shih*), members of the Ministry of Justice (*ch'iu-kuan*) responsible for igniting ceremonial torches by mirrored sunlight or moonlight, providing torchlight for all important state occasions, and promulgating warnings and prohibitions about the use of fire. CL: *préposé à la lumière du feu*.

5640 *ssū-hsūn* 司勳

(1) CHOU, N-S DIV (Chou): **Director of Merit Awards,** 2 ranked as Senior Servicemen (*shang-shih*) and 4 as Junior Servicemen (*hsia-shih*), members of the Ministry of War (*hsia-kuan*) who processed grants of land and other awards to meritorious military personnel. CL: *préposé aux actions d'éclat.* P5. (2) SUI–SUNG: common alternate reference to the **Bureau of Merit Titles** (*ssu-hsün ssu*) in the Ministry of Personnel (*li-pu*).

5641 *ssū-hsùn* 司訓

MING–CH'ING: lit., in charge of admonishment: unofficial reference to an **Assistant Instructor** (*hsün-tao*) in a Confucian School (*ju-hsüeh*).

5642 *ssū-hsūn ssū* 司勳司

SUI–SUNG: **Bureau of Merit Titles,** one of 4 major agencies in the Ministry of Personnel (*li-pu*); headed by a Director (*lang, lang-chung*), rank 5b1 in T'ang, 6b in Sung; processed the awards of merit titles (*hsün*) to both civil and military personnel on the basis of their achievements combined with seniority. In Ming and Ch'ing replaced by a Bureau of Records (*chi-hsün ch'ing-li ssu*). RR+SP: *bureau des titres honorifiques.* P5.

5643 *ssū-hù* 司戶

T'ANG: lit., in charge of revenue: **Revenue Manager,** a prefix commonly attached to the titles of Administrators (*ts'an-chün-shih*) and lesser personnel of Revenue Sections (*hu-ts'ao*) in units of territorial administration. P53.

5644 *ssù hù* 四戶

N-S DIV: **Four Households,** common collective reference to Secretariat Drafters (*chung-shu she-jen*) or to Secretarial Receptionists (*t'ung-shih she-jen*), all members of the evolving Secretariat (*chung-shu sheng*). Especially in S. Ch'i, the 4 posts as Secretarial Receptionists were very powerful.

5645 *ssù-hù lìng* 寺互令

HAN: **Director of the Ssu-hu,** meaning and function not clear; on the staff of the Chamberlain for the Palace Revenues (*shao-fu*), then of the Commandant of the Nobles (*chu-chüeh tu-wei*), and ultimately (after 104 B.C.) of the Chamberlain for the Imperial Insignia (*chih chin-wu*); assisted by one Aide (*ch'eng*). HB: prefect of the Ssu-hu.

5646 *ssū-huán* 司圜

CHOU: **Jailor of the Central Prison,** 6 ranked as Ordinary Servicemen (*chung-shih*) and 12 as Junior Servicemen (*hsia-shih*), members of the Ministry of Justice (*ch'iu-kuan*); supervised the main prison in the royal capital. CL: *préposé à la prison centrale.*

5647 *ssū-hùi* 司卉

N-S DIV (Chou): **Chief Gardener,** ranked as Junior Grand Master (*hsia ta-fu; 6a*), a member of the Ministry of Works (*tung-kuan*) who supervised the care of flowers and other plants in the imperial palace. P14.

5648 *ssu-hui* 司會

See under *ssu-k'uai.*

5649 *ssū-hūn* 司闇

T'ANG: **Directress of the Inner Gates,** apparently a variant reference to the palace women entitled *ssu-wei,* q.v. RR: *directeur des portes du harem.*

5650 *ssū-huò* 司貨

CHOU: **Market (?) Tax Supervisor,** according to the ancient ritual record *Li-chi,* one of 6 agents in the Ministry of Education (*ti-kuan*) responsible for various tax collections. See *liu fu* (Six Tax Supervisors).

5651 *ssū-í* 司儀

Ceremonials Official. (1) CHOU: 8 ranked as Senior Servicemen (*shang-shih*) and 16 as Ordinary Servicemen (*chung-shih*) subordinate to the Senior Messengers (*ta hsing-jen*) of the Ministry of Justice (*ch'iu-kuan*); assisted in receptions for important court guests including foreign envoys. CL: *chef d'étiquette.* (2) N-S DIV (Chou): number not clear, ranks (7a, 8a) and status as in ancient Chou times, but apparently had broader responsibilities regarding court ceremonies. P33. (3) N-S DIV (N. Ch'i)–MING: lowly members of the Court of State Ceremonial (*hung-lu ssu*), counterparts of Ming–Ch'ing Ushers (*hsü-pan*); from N. Ch'i through T'ang belonged to the Court's Ceremonials Office (*ssu-i shu*), which principally conducted the funerals of officials. RR: *directeur des rites funéraires.* SP: *chargé des rites.* P33.

5652 *ssū-ī* 司衣

T'ANG–SUNG, MING: **Directress of Clothing,** 2 palace women, rank 6a, heads of the Clothing Office (*ssu-i ssu*) in the Wardrobe Service (*shang-fu chü*). RR: *directeur des vêtements du harem.*

5653 *ssū-ì* 司議

YÜAN: **Counselor,** 2, rank not clear, on the staff of the Household Service for the Heir Apparent (*ch'u-cheng yüan*); others in the Household Service for the Empress (*chung-cheng yüan*). Apparently redesignated *chung-i,* q.v., when the Household Service for the Heir Apparent was reorganized as the Household Administration of the Heir Apparent (*chan-shih yüan;* date not clear). Counterpart of *ssu-i lang* (Remonstrance Secretary) in earlier periods. P26.

5654 *ssū-ī* 司醫

SUI–T'ANG: **Palace Physician,** 4, rank 8a, members of the Palace Medical Service (*shang-yao chü*) in the Palace Administration (*tien-nei sheng, tien-chung sheng*); probably hereditary specialists. RR: *médecin du palais.* P36.

5655 *ssū-í chǎng* 司儀長

CH'ING: **Director of Ceremonials,** rank 4a; one on the staff of each Princely Establishment (*wang-fu*). BH: majordomo. P69.

5656 *ssù-ì kuǎn* 四譯館 or 四夷館

MING–CH'ING (2nd form a common unofficial variant): **Translators Institute,** an agency that handled correspondence between the court and foreign states; originally an integral part of the Hanlin Academy (*han-lin yüan*), but in 1496 placed under a Vice Minister (*shao-ch'ing*) of the Court of Imperial Sacrifices (*t'ai-ch'ang ssu*), rank 4a, assigned as Superintendent (*t'i-tu*) of the Institute; in 1748 merged with the Interpreters Institute (*hui-t'ung kuan*) into a single Interpreters and Translators Institute (*hui-t'ung ssu-i kuan*) under a Superintendent with status as Director (*lang-chung*) of the Bureau of Receptions (*chu-k'o ch'ing-li ssu*) and concurrent Vice Minister (*shao-ch'ing*) of the Court of State Ceremonial (*hung-lu ssu*), ranks 5a and 5b, each Superintendent serving a 3-year term of duty. BH: residence for envoys of the four tributary states. P21.

5657 *ssū-ì kuān* 司議官

CHIN: **Remonstrator,** number unlimited, rank 8a, members of the Academy of Scholarly Worthies (*chi-hsien yüan*); specific functions not clear, but likely the counterpart of earlier Remonstrance Secretaries (*ssu-i lang*) and later Counselors (*ssu-i*). P25.

5658 *ssù-í kùng-fèng ssū* 四夷貢奉司

SUNG: **Office for Foreign Tribute Envoys,** headed by one

or more Commissioners (*shih*); apparently a subsidiary of the Court of State Ceremonial (*hung-lu ssu*); probably a counterpart of the later Interpreters Institute (*hui-t'ung kuan*), but specific functions not clear. SP: *bureau des commissaires des tributs des barbares*.

5659   *ssū-í láng*   司議郎
T'ANG, SUNG, LIAO: **Remonstrance Secretary,** 4, rank 6a, in T'ang; number and rank not clear for Sung and Liao; members of the Left Secretariat of the Heir Apparent (*tso ch'un-fang;* see *ch'un-fang*); served as confidential advisers to the Heir Apparent and checked on the correctness of documents flowing to and from his palace. Cf. *ssu-i* (Counselor), *ssu-i kuan* (Remonstrator). RR: *secrétaire du grand secrétariat de gauche*. SP: *secrétaire du grand secrétariat de l'héritier du trône*. P26.

5660   *ssū-í shǔ*   司儀署
N-S DIV (N. Ch'i)–T'ANG: **Ceremonials Office,** a major subsection of the Court of State Ceremonial (*hung-lu ssu*); headed by one or 2 Directors (*ling*), rank 8a in T'ang; principally managed the funerals of officials. RR: *office des rites funéraires*. P33.

5661   *ssū-í ssū*   司衣司
T'ANG–SUNG, MING: **Clothing Office,** one of 4 palace women agencies in the Wardrobe Service (*shang-fu chü*); headed by 2 Directresses (*ssu-i*), rank 6a, who were responsible for making and maintaining all items of clothing required by the Empress and other female members of the imperial household.

5662   *ssū-jǎn shǔ*   司染署
N-S DIV (N. Ch'i): **Dyeing Office,** a craft workshop headed by a Director (*ling*), rank not clear, in the Left Directorate for Imperial Manufactures (*tso shang-fang*) under the Court of the Imperial Treasury (*t'ai-fu ssu*); the Director supervised 3 branches called Services (*chü*) located at the dynastic capital, at Ho-tung, and at Hsin-tu, each managed by an Aide (*ch'eng*). P37.

5663   *ssù-jén*   寺人
Lit., a variant of *shih* (Attendant). (1) **Eunuch,** one of several terms used as a generic reference to palace eunuchs; cf. *huan-kuan, yen-jen, nei-shih*. (2) CHOU: **Chief Steward,** 5 eunuch attendants in the royal palace specially responsible for overseeing and protecting the Empress and other palace women. CL: *assistant ou eunuque*. (3) T'ANG: **Eunuch Escort,** 6, rank 7b2, members of the Palace Domestic Service (*nei-shih sheng*) charged with guarding the entrance to the Empress's quarters and escorting her carriage on horseback whenever she left the palace. RR: *eunuque chargé d'escorter l'impératrice*.

5664   *ssū-júng*   司戎
T'ANG: lit., in charge of the military: from 662 to 670 the official variant of *ping-pu* (both **Ministry of War** and the Ministry's **Bureau of Military Appointments**); during this period the Minister (*shang-shu*) was retitled Grand Executive Attendant (*t'ai ch'ang-po*) and the Director of the Bureau was retitled Grand Master (*ta-fu*). RR: *administration des armes*. P12.

5665   *ssū-kān*   司干
CHOU: **Director of Shields,** 2 ranked as Junior Servicemen (*hsia-shih*), members of the Ministry of Rites (*ch'un-kuan*) who directed a ceremonial shield-dance traced back to the Chou founder, King Wu, in which dancers beat on their shields. CL: *préposé au bouclier*.

5666   *ssū-kēng ssù*   司更寺
T'ANG: from 662 to 670 the official variant of *lei-keng ssu* (**Court of the Watches**); during this period the Director (*ling*) was retitled Grand Master (*ta-fu*).

5667   *ssū-kō*   司戈
T'ANG–SUNG: **Manager of Lances,** a petty military officer, rank commonly 8a; 2 or more normally found in each Guard (*wei*) or comparable military unit at the dynastic capital. RR+SP: *officier des petites lances*. P26.

5668   *ssū-kō*   司歌
N-S DIV (Chou): **Singer,** number not specified, ranked as Ordinary Servicemen (*chung-shih;* 8a) and Junior Servicemen (*hsia-shih;* 9a); members of the Ministry of Rites (*ch'un-kuan*). P10.

5669   *ssū-kó*   司閣
T'ANG: **Gatekeeper,** rank 9b, in a Princely Establishment (*wang-fu*). RR: *directeur des palais (du prince)*.

5670   *ssū kō-tùn*   司戈盾
CHOU: **Director of Lances and Shields,** 2 ranked as Junior Servicemen (*hsia-shih*), members of the Ministry of War (*hsia-kuan*); provided lances and shields for men ranked as Grand Masters (*ta-fu*) and Servicemen (*shih*), a lesser responsibility than that of the Director of Arms (*ssu-ping*). Cf. *ssu kung-shih*. CL: *préposé aux lances et aux boucliers*.

5671   *ssū-k'òu*   司寇
(1) CHOU: variant of *ta ssu-k'ou* (**Minister of Justice**), one of the 6 great Ministers (*ch'ing*) at the royal court, head of the Ministry of Justice (*ch'iu-kuan*). (2) HAN: from 1 B.C. to A.D. 1 only, the official variant of *hu-chün tu-wei* (**Chief Commandant-protector**), a subordinate of the eminent Defender-in-chief (*t'ai-wei*). HB: director against brigands. (3) MING–CH'ING: unofficial reference to the **Minister of Justice** (*hsing-pu shang-shu*).

5672   *ssū-k'òu ts'ān-chūn*   司寇參軍
SUNG: **Administrator for Public Order,** a petty official or suboffical found on the staffs of many Prefects (*chih-fu, chih-chou*), responsible for supervising police activities at the prefectural seat. Also called *ssu-li ts'an-chün*. SP: *inspecteur-policier*.

5673   *ssū-kǔ*   司鼓
N-S DIV (Chou): **Drummer,** number not specified, ranked as Ordinary Servicemen (*chung-shih;* 8a) and Junior Servicemen (*hsia-shih;* 9a), members of the Ministry of Rites (*ch'un-kuan*). P10.

5674   *ssū-k'ù*   司庫
(1) T'ANG: from 662 to 670 and again from 752 to 757 the official variant of *k'u-pu* (**Bureau of Provisions** in the Ministry of War, *ping-pu*); during these periods the Bureau Director (*lang-chung*) was retitled Grand Master (*ta-fu*). RR: *administration des magasins*. P12. (2) T'ANG, YÜAN, CH'ING: **Warehouseman:** in T'ang one, rank 9a2, in the Livery Service (*shang-ch'eng chü*) of the Palace Administration (*tien-chung sheng*). In Yüan petty officials or subofficials associated with several storehouses in the dynastic capital. In Ch'ing number highly variable, rank from 6a down to subofficial status, found in storehouses of many sorts, e.g., those jointly supervised by the Ministry of Revenue (*hu-pu*) and the Imperial Household Department (*nei-wu fu*) and collectively called the Three Storehouses (*san k'u,* q.v.), that maintained by the Court of Imperial Sacrifices (*t'ai-ch'ang ssu*), those in Princely Establishments (*wang-fu*). RR: *directeur des selleries*. BH: treasurer, controller, inspector. P7, 14, 17, 30, 39, etc.

5675 *ssù k'ù* 四庫
Four Treasuries: from the era of N-S Division, a quasi-official name for the Palace Library (*pi-shu chien, pi-shu sheng*), in which books were stored according to the traditional division into Four Categories (*ssu pu*). In Sung times, each of the Four Treasuries was allocated 2 Librarians (*shu-kuan*), rank not clear. SP: *quatre collections de la littérature, quatre magasins de livres*.

5676 *ssū-k'uài* 司會
CHOU: **Accountant,** 2 ranked as Ordinary Grand Masters (*chung ta-fu*), 4 as Junior Grand Masters (*hsia ta-fu*), 8 as Senior Servicemen (*shang-shih*), and 16 as Ordinary Servicemen (*chung-shih*), members of the Ministry of State (*t'ien-kuan*) who conducted monthly and annual audits of fiscal records in all government agencies, maintained land and population registers, and kept other important government documents. CL: *chef des comptes généraux*. P6.

5677 *ssū-kuān* 司官
MING–CH'ING: lit., officials of Bureaus (*ssu*), but application widened; hence, **Administrative Associates.** Originally a generic term for Directors (*lang-chung*), Vice Directors (*yüan-wai lang*), and Secretaries (*chu-shih*) of the various Bureaus (*ch'ing-li ssu*) in the Six Ministries (*liu pu*) of the central government—an echelon of officials differentiated from higher ranking Senior Officials (*t'ang-shang, t'ang-kuan*) and lower ranking Staff Supervisors (*shou-ling kuan*) of Ministries. Later, especially in Ch'ing, usage expanded to include, e.g., Commanders (*chih-hui*) of Wardens' Offices (*ping-ma ssu*) in the capital, Judicial Administrators (*pan-shih ssu-yüan*) in the administrative regions of Mongolia, and Secretaries (*chang-ching*) in the late Ch'ing Foreign Office (*tsung-li ya-men*). BH: officers.

5678 *ssù-kuàn* 司爟
CHOU: **Fire Director,** 2 ranked as Junior Servicemen (*hsia-shih*), members of the Ministry of War (*hsia-kuan*) who promulgated regulations about the proper uses of fire, firewoods, etc.; in public ceremonies offered sacrifices to the discoverer of fire. CL: *préposé au feu, préposé au feu allumé*.

5679 *ssū-kuān* 司關
(1) CHOU: **Supervisor of Customs Duties,** 2 ranked as Senior Servicemen (*shang-shih*) and 4 as Ordinary Servicemen (*chung-shih*), members of the Ministry of Education (*ti-kuan*) responsible for collecting mercantile transit fees and dealing with related matters throughout the royal domain; in addition, 2 ranked as Junior Servicemen (*hsia-shih*) assigned to each frontier entry and exit point. CL: *préposé aux barrières*. (2) T'ANG: from 662 to 670 the official variant of *ssu-men* (**Transit Authorization Bureau** in the Ministry of Justice, *hsing-pu*). RR: *administration des barrières*.

5680 *ssù-kuān chāi-láng* 祀官齋郎
N-S DIV (N. Wei): **Court Gentleman for Sacrifices and Fasting,** number unspecified, rank 9b; organizational affiliation not clear, but apparently not identical with Court Gentlemen for Fasting (*chai-lang,* q.v.) on the staff of the Chamberlain for Ceremonials (*t'ai-ch'ang*). P28.

5681 *ssù-kuēi* 司閨
T'ANG: **Directress of the Inner Quarters,** 2 palace women, rank 6a2, principal attendants on the consort (*fei*) of the Heir Apparent and supervisors of other female attendants in his palace. RR: *directeur du service de l'administration du harem de l'héritier du trône*.

5682 *ssū-kūng* 司功
T'ANG: **Personnel Manager:** a prefix commonly found attached to the titles of Administrators (*ts'an-chün-shih*) and lesser members of Personnel Evaluation Sections (*kung-ts'ao*) in units of territorial administration. P53.

5683 *ssū-kūng* 司弓
CH'ING: **Bowmaker,** unspecified number, apparently non-official specialists employed in the Court of Imperial Armaments (*wu-pei yüan*). BH: supervisor of bow-making.

5684 *ssū kùng-chí* 司貢籍
T'ANG: **Chief Examiner** in a civil service recruitment examination.

5685 *ssū kūng-shǐh* 司弓矢
CHOU, N-S DIV (Chou): **Manager of Bows and Arrows,** in ancient Chou 2 ranked as Junior Grand Masters (*hsia ta-fu*) and 8 as Ordinary Servicemen (*chung-shih*); in later Chou numbers not clear, ranked as Ordinary Servicemen (8a) and Junior Servicemen (*hsia-shih;* 9a); in both eras members of the Ministry of War (*hsia-kuan*). CL: *préposé aux arcs et aux flèches*. P12.

5686 *ssū-kūng t'ái* 司宮臺
T'ANG: lit., office in charge of the palace: from 685 to 705 the official variant of the eunuch agency name *nei-shih sheng* (**Palace Domestic Service**). P38.

5687 *ssū-k'ūng* 司空
Lit., in charge of digging, e.g., the digging of canals. (1) **Minister of Works,** a title of great prestige from high antiquity. In Chou, as head of the Ministry of Works (*tung-kuan*), one of the 6 great Ministers (*ch'ing*) in the royal government; supervised all governmental construction and provisioning through many subordinate agencies and agents. In A.D. 51 in Han, revived in place of *ta ssu-k'ung* (Grand Minister of Works) as one of the Three Dukes (*san kung*) who were the paramount dignitaries of the central government, rank 10,000 bushels; continued in such usage intermittently till 1122 in Sung and Liao; thereafter through Ch'ing a common unofficial reference to the central government's Minister of Works (*kung-pu shang-shu*). CL: *ministre des travaux, ministre de l'hiver*. HB: minister of works. RR+SP: *directeur des travaux publics*. (2) HAN: **Capital Construction Office,** 2 prefixed Left and Right, each headed by a Director (*ling*); works agencies under the Chamberlain for the Palace Revenues (*shao-fu*). P37. (3) N-S DIV (San-kuo Wei): **Central Prison,** organizational affiliation and staffing not clear; reportedly successor of the prison for dignitaries previously called *ling-wu* and *jo-lu yü,* qq.v.

5688 *ssū-k'ūng kūng* 司空公
HAN: common Later Han variant of *ssu-k'ung* (**Minister of Works**).

5689 *ssū-k'ūng lìng* 司空令
HAN: **Director of Convict Labor,** in Former Han one subordinate to the Chamberlain for the Imperial Clan (*tsung-cheng*) and 2 to the Chamberlain for the Palace Revenues (*shao-fu*), the former prefixed *tu* (Chief) and the latter 2 prefixed Left and Right, in reference to the eastern and western sectors, respectively, of the capital city; rank and specific functions not clear, but apparently supervised convicted criminals (members of the imperial clan in the first instance) who were assigned to labor projects in the capital. Reference is also found to such an official title prefixed *chün* (Army), suggesting Director of Military Convict Labor. HB: prefect director of works.

5690 *ssū-lì* 司厲
CHOU, N-S DIV (Chou): **Manager of Criminal Gear**, 2 ranked as Ordinary Servicemen (*chung-shih*), members of the Ministry of Justice (*ch'iu-kuan*) in both eras; kept weapons and other instruments apparently confiscated from convicted thieves and robbers. CL: *préposé aux malfaiteurs.*

5691 *ssū-lì* 司吏
CHIN–YÜAN: **Staff Foreman**, rank very low or unranked, numbers highly variable; found in many agencies in which large numbers of unranked subofficials were employed.

5692 *ssū-lì* 司曆
SUI–YÜAN: **Manager of the Calendar**, in charge of astronomical-astrological calculations required for preparation of the state-issued calendar; in Sui 2, rank 9b, members of the Astrological Office (*t'ai-shih ts'ao*) in the Palace Library (*pi-shu sheng*); in T'ang 5, 8b1, members of the Astrological Service (*t'ai-shih chü, ssu-t'ien t'ai*); from 758 called *ssu-li wu-kuan*, q.v.; in Sung number not clear, 8a1, members of the Astrological Service (*t'ai-shih chü*); in Liao number and rank not clear, members of the Directorate of Astronomy (*ssu-t'ien chien*); in Yüan 12, 9a, one per Province, members of the Astrological Commission (*t'ai-shih yüan*). In Ming superseded by *wu-kuan ssu-li*. RR+SP: *contrôleur du calendrier.* P35.

5693 *ssū-lǐ* 司理
(1) Throughout history a common unofficial reference to the **Court of Judicial Review** (*ta-li ssu*) or its senior personnel. (2) SUNG: common quasiofficial reference to an **Administrator for Public Order** (*ssu-k'ou ts'an-chün, ssu-li ts'an-chün*) on the staff of a Prefecture (*fu, chou*). Also see *ssu-li yüan*. SP: *administrateur judiciaire.* P53.

5694 *ssū-lǐ* 司禮
T'ANG: from 662 to 684 the official variant of *lǐ-pu* (both **Ministry of Rites** and the Ministry's **Headquarters Bureau**); during this period the Minister (*shang-shu*) was titled Grand Executive Attendant (*t'ai ch'ang-po*) and the Bureau Director was titled Grand Master (*ta-fu*). Cf. *ssu-li ssu*. P9.

5695 *ssū-lì* 司隸
Lit., in charge of slaves, i.e., war prisoners or criminals sentenced to hard state labor. (1) CHOU–N-S DIV: **Director of Convict Labor**, in ancient Chou 2 ranked as Ordinary Servicemen (*chung-shih*) and 12 as Junior Servicemen (*hsia-shih*), members of the Ministry of Justice (*ch'iu-kuan*) who supervised the use of convict laborers on public works projects. In early Han one (?) supervised convict labor on roads and canals; in 89 B.C. superseded by the Metropolitan Commandant (*ssu-li hsiao-wei*); in 7 B.C. restored with original functions, rank =2,000 bushels, subordinate to the Minister of Works (*ssu-k'ung*). Apparently not continued in Later Han, but restored by later Chou in the ancient Chou pattern, number not clear, ranked as Junior Grand Masters (*hsia ta-fu; 5a*). CL: *préposé aux condamnés à des travaux ignominieux.* HB: director of the retainers. P13. (2) HAN–N-S DIV: common abbreviated reference to the **Metropolitan Commandant** or by analogy to the area of his jurisdiction, the **Metropolitan Area** (both *ssu-li hsiao-wei*).

5696 *ssū-lǐ chiēn* 司禮監
MING: **Directorate of Ceremonial**, one of 12 eunuch Directorates (*chien*) among which, together with 4 Offices (*ssu*) and 8 Services (*chü*), all palace eunuchs were distributed; quickly became by far the most prestigious and powerful of these agencies, its Director (*t'ai-chien*) being the de facto chief of the imperial household staff, supervisor of secret

police units called the Eastern and Western Depots (*tung-ch'ang, hsi-ch'ang*), and chief collaborator with the Imperial Bodyguard (*chin-i wei*) in recurrent terroristic purges of officials from the 1400s on.

5697 *ssū-lì hsiào-wèi* 司隸校尉
HAN–N-S DIV: **Metropolitan Commandant**, in 89 B.C. appointed to supersede the Director of Convict Labor (*ssu-li*), with expanded powers of investigation and impeachment over officials of the area around the dynastic capital (see under *ching-shih, ssu-chou, san fu*); directed a kind of personal censorial service for the Emperor. Stripped of some powers in 45 B.C. and abolished in 9 B.C.; revived in Later Han with rank reduced from 2,000 to =2,000 bushels, and again wielded great supervisory control over the capital officialdom; shared with the Director of the Imperial Secretariat (*shang-shu ling*) and the Palace Aide to the Censor-in-chief (*yü-shih chung-ch'eng*) the awesome collective designation Three Venerables (*san tu-tso*). Had a large staff including a Recorder (*chu-pu*) and many Retainer Clerks (*ts'ung-shih shih*), who were in charge of functionally differentiated Sections (*ts'ao*); e.g., see *tu-kuan ts'ao* (Capital Officials Section), *kung-ts'ao* (Labor Section). In the era of N-S Division perpetuated along with the variants Regional Governor (*mu*) or Regional Inspector (*tz'u-shih*) of the Metropolitan Area (*ssu-chou*). The tradition was apparently reflected in Sui's *ssu-li t'ai ta-fu* (Grand Master of the Tribunal of Inspectors). HB: colonel director of the retainers. P20, 50, 52.

5698 *ssū-lǐ ssū* 司禮寺
(1) T'ANG: from 684 to 705 the official variant of *t'ai-ch'ang ssu* (**Court of Imperial Sacrifices**). P27. (2) CH'ING: unofficial reference to the **Court of Imperial Sacrifices**. Cf. *ssu-li*.

5699 *ssū-lì t'ái* 司隸臺
SUI: **Tribunal of Inspectors**, created c. 605 with a Grand Master (*ta-fu*) as head, rank not clear, to conduct disciplinary investigations of officials on duty in the Metropolitan Area (*chi-nei*) including the dynastic capital and its environs; traditionally equated with Regional Inspectors (*tz'u-shih*) of other large areas; shared with the Censorate (*yü-shih t'ai*) and the Tribunal of Receptions (*yeh-che t'ai*) the collective designation Three Surveillance Agencies (*san t'ai*). P52.

5700 *ssū-lǐ ts'ān-chūn* 司理參軍
SUNG: official variant of *ssu-k'ou ts'an-chün* (**Administrator for Public Order**) in a Prefecture (*fu, chou*). SP: *administrateur du bureau judiciaire, officier de paix de préfecture, inspecteur de police.*

5701 *ssū-lì wǔ-kuān* 司曆五官
T'ANG: **Manager of the Calendar**, 5, rank 8b, members of the Astrological Service (*ssu-t'ien t'ai*); title changed from *ssu-li* in 758. Cf. *wu kuan* (Five Offices), *wu-kuan ssu-li.*

5702 *ssū-lǐ yüàn* 司理院
SUNG: **Office of Public Order**, designation of the headquarters of the Administrator for Public Order (*ssu-li ts'an-chün*) in the Prefecture (*fu*) in which the dynastic capital was located. SP: *cour judiciaire.*

5703 *ssū-liàng* 司量
N-S DIV (Chou): **Grain Measurer**, number not specified, ranked as Ordinary Servicemen (*chung-shih; 8a*), members of the Ministry of Works (*tung-kuan*). P14.

5704 *ssū-lièh* 司列
T'ANG: from 662 to 684 the official variant of *lǐ-pu* (both

Ministry of Personnel and the Ministry's **Bureau of Appointments**); during the same period the Minister (*shang-shu*) was titled Grand Executive Attendant (*t'ai ch'ang-po*) and the Bureau Director (*lang-chung*) was titled Grand Master (*ta-fu*). P5.

5705 *ssū-lĭn* 司廩
T'ANG–SUNG: **Granary Manager**, 2, rank 9a2, in the Livery Service (*shàng-ch'eng chü*) of the Palace Administration (*tien-chung sheng*) in T'ang; number, rank, and organizational affiliation not clear in Sung. RR: *directeur des greniers*. SP: *administrateur de grenier*. P39.

5706 *ssū-lìng* 司令
Abbreviation of ... *ssu ling* (**Director of the ... Office**); specific identification can be determined only by reference to prefix of *ssu* in preceding context.

5707 *ssū-lù* 司錄
Record Keeper. (1) CHOU: 4 ranked as Ordinary Servicemen (*chung-shih*) and 8 as Junior Servicemen (*hsia-shih*), members of the Ministry of Education (*ti-kuan*) who kept accounts concerning issuance of funds and supplies to various government agencies (?). CL: *préposé aux appointements ou fournitures affectées aux différentes charges.* (2) N-S DIV (Chou): normally ranked from 4a to 6b, found in units of territorial administration including Branch Departments of State Affairs (*chung-wai fu*) and Regions (*chou*), rank depending on the size of the resident population; functions not specified, but apparently responsible for handling unit correspondence and paperwork in general. P52. (3) SUNG: rank variable, commonly found in Prefectures (*chou, fu*), often as heads of the Six Sections (*liu ts'ao*) through which prefectural affairs were managed; equated with Notary of the Administrative Assistant (*ch'ien-shu p'an-kuan t'ing kung-shih*). SP: *fonctionnaire chargé d'enregistrer les expéditions, exécutif général, signataire de préfecture.* P32, 49, 53.

5708 *ssū lù-shìh* 司錄事
SUNG: **Record Keeper**, variant of *ssu-lu ts'an-chün* (**Administrator for Records**) in the Capital Prefecture (*ching-fu*). SP: *chargé d'enregistrer les expéditions.*

5709 *ssū-lù ssū* 司錄司
SUNG: **Records Office** in the Capital Prefecture (*ching-fu*), headed by an Administrator for Records (*ssu-lu ts'an-chün*). SP: *bureau chargé d'enregistrer les expéditions.*

5710 *ssū-lù ts'ān-chǔn-shìh* 司錄參軍事 or *ssu-lu ts'an-chün*
T'ANG–SUNG: **Administrator for Records**, 2 in T'ang and one in Sung, rank 7a, in charge of correspondence in Superior Prefectures (*fu*) and Capital Prefectures (*ching-fu*). See *ts'an-chün-shih*. RR: *administrateur inscrivant les expéditions*. SP: *administrateur chargé d'enregistrer les expéditions*. P49.

5711 *ssū-lún kó* 絲綸閣
T'ANG: lit., silk-thread hall, i.e., hall of imperial utterances: unofficial reference to the **Secretariat** (*chung-shu sheng*). See *lun-ko*.

5712 *ssū-lù chūng-láng chiàng* 司律中郎將
N-S DIV (Chin): **Leader of Court Gentlemen in Charge of Music**, variant reference to the Director of Imperial Music (*hsieh-lü hsiao-wei, hsieh-lü tu-wei*). P10.

5713 *ssū-mǎ* 司馬
Lit., to be in charge of horses, i.e., of cavalry; a title deriving from high antiquity and used through most of imperial history; prefixes are especially to be noted with care,

e.g., *ta ssu-ma, shao ssu-ma.* (1) CHOU: common abbreviated reference to the **Minister of War** (*ta ssu-ma*), head of the Ministry of War (*hsia-kuan*) and paramount military dignitary in the royal government. (2) CHOU: **Commander,** common generic reference to all, or an abbreviated reference to one, of the military officers serving under the Minister of War with such titles as Vice Minister of War (*shao ssu-ma*), Cavalry Commander of the Army (*chün ssu-ma*), Commander of Chariots (*yü ssu-ma*), and Cavalry Commander on Campaign (*hsing ssu-ma*). (3) HAN–N-S DIV: common abbreviated reference to the **Defender-in-chief** (*t'ai-wei, ta ssu-ma*), one of the eminent central government dignitaries collectively called the Three Dukes (*san kung*). (4) HAN–N-S DIV: **Commander,** title of a 2nd-level military officer found in many agencies, e.g., on the staff of the Chamberlain for the Imperial Insignia (*chung-wei, chih chin-wu*), who commanded the Northern Army (*pei-chün*) at the dynastic capital. HB: major. (5) N-S DIV–SUNG: erratically used as a title for 2nd- or 3rd-level executive officials, i.e., **Vice ...** or **Assistant ...,** in territorial units of administration such as Regions (*chou*), Area Commands (*tu-tu fu*), Princely Establishments (*wang-fu*), Commanderies (*chün*), Prefectures (*chou, fu*); normally rank 4b or lower; commonly alternating with the title *chih-chung*, q.v. RR: *administrateur supérieur*. SP: *administrateur supérieur, sous-directeur du bureau, surintendant-adjoint.* (6) SUI–T'ANG: **Adjutant,** a 2nd- or 3rd-level executive officer found in most military Guards (*wei*) stationed at the dynastic capital. RR: *administrateur supérieur*. (7) CHIN–YÜAN: **Adjutant,** rank 6b in Chin, 4 of rank 4a in Yüan, on the staff of each Princely Establishment (*wang-fu*), specifically in charge of police security. P69. (8) MING–CH'ING: deriving from the usage described in (5) above, an unofficial reference to a **Vice Prefect** (*t'ung-chih*) in a Prefecture (*fu*) and, in Ch'ing, also to a **Vice Magistrate** (also *t'ung-chih*) in a Department (*chou*). (9) MING–CH'ING: deriving from the usage described in (1) above, an unofficial reference to executive officials of the Ministry of War (*ping-pu*), with the prefix *ta* indicating a **Minister of War** (*ping-pu shang-shu*), with the prefix *shao* indicating a **Vice Minister of War** (*ping-pu shih-lang*)

5714 *ssū-mǎ chūng* 司馬中
HAN: lit., doors (under the control of) the Commander (*ssu-ma*): **Inner Palace Doors,** distinguished from the Outer Palace Gates (*ssu-ma men*); both under the military jurisdiction of the Chamberlain for the Palace Garrison (*wei-wei*). P21.

5715 *ssū-mǎ mén* 司馬門
HAN: lit., gates (under the control of) the Commander (*ssu-ma*): **Outer Palace Gates,** distinguished from the Inner Palace Doors (*ssu-ma chung*); under the direct military control of Gate Traffic Control Offices (*kung-ch'e ssu-ma men*), one at each of the 4 great palace entrances; supervised by the Chamberlain for the Palace Garrison (*wei-wei*). P21.

5716 *ssū-mǎ tà-fū* 司馬大夫
T'ANG: especially after 662, an occasional unofficial reference to the **Director** (*lang-chung*) **of the Bureau of Military Appointments** (*ping-pu*) in the Ministry of War (also *ping-pu*). Cf. *ssu-jung.*

5717 *ssū-mǎ tū* 司馬督
Commander: see under *tien-chung ssu-ma tu* (Palace Commander) and *yüan-wai ssu-ma tu* (Auxiliary Commander).

5718 *ssū-mén* 司門
(1) CHOU: **Gatekeeper,** 2 ranked as Junior Grand Masters

(hsia ta-fu), 4 as Senior Servicemen (shang-shih), 8 as Ordinary Servicemen (chung-shih), and 16 as Junior Servicemen (hsia-shih), members of the Ministry of Education (ti-kuan) who had charge of the locks on the gates of the royal capital, controlled the exit and entry of people and goods at the gates, informed the royal court of important arrivals, and collected gate fees with which the court supported dependents of those who had died in state service. CL: préposé aux portes. (2) SUI–MING: **Transit Authorization Bureau,** one of the 4 Bureaus (ssu) through which the Ministry of Justice (tu-kuan in early Sui, thereafter hsing-pu) conducted its business, headed by a Director (lang, lang-chung), rank 5b in T'ang, 6b in Sung; responsible for monitoring traffic in and out of the gates of the dynastic capital and through all recognized gateways or ports of entry into the empire. Terminated in 1390, when the Ministry of Justice was reorganized; see under hsing-pu, ch'ing-li ssu. RR+SP: bureau de la surveillance des barrières. P13.

5719　ssù-mén hsüéh　四門學
N-S DIV (N. Wei)–SUNG: **School of the Four Gates,** one of several schools located at the dynastic capital, from Sui on under the Directorate of Education (kuo-tzu chien); open to sons of lesser nobles and officials and to some specially gifted sons of commoners, enrollment reaching a high point of about 300 in T'ang times; staffed primarily with Erudites (po-shih). First established in the late 400s, probably not fully operational until Sui; existed only nominally in Sung. The name derived from the tradition that in ancient Chou times schools were established in all of the 4 suburban areas around the royal capital; the school was commonly known as the Elementary School (hsiao-hsüeh), in contrast to the National University (t'ai-hsüeh). RR: collège des quatre portes. SP: école de quatre sections. P34.

5720　ssū-méng　司盟
CHOU: **Sanctifier of Covenants,** 2 ranked as Junior Servicemen (hsia-shih), members of the Ministry of Justice (ch'iu-kuan) responsible for sanctifying agreements among Feudal Lords (chu-hou) by applying to them the blood of sacrificial animals, also for impeaching those who violated such agreements. CL: préposé aux serments solennels.

5721　ssū-mín　司民
CHOU: **Population Registrar,** 6 ranked as Ordinary Servicemen (chung-shih), members of the Ministry of Justice (ch'iu-kuan) responsible for making an annual census of teething babies and more generally, in collaboration with the Ministry of Education (ti-kuan), maintaining various demographic records. CL: préposé au peuple.

5722　ssù-mièn chiēn　四面監
T'ANG: **Directorates of Parks of the Four Quadrants,** collective reference to the 4 Directorates that supervised parks and gardens in the dynastic capital and its environs; see ch'ang-lo chien, chin-chai chien, tung-chien, hsi-chien. P40.

5723　ssū-míng　私名
SUNG: **Probationer** (?), 35 or so lowly or unranked personnel in the Ministry of Personnel (li-pu); status and functions not clear, but apparently differentiated from "regular" appointees; see under cheng-ming. SP: employé stagiaire.

5724　ssū-míng tsàn-chě　私名贊者
SUNG: **Probationary Ceremonial Assistant** (?), 7 authorized in the Court of Imperial Sacrifices (t'ai-ch'ang ssu); status and functions not clear, but differentiated from cheng-ming tsan-che (Ceremonial Assistant). SP: héraut-stagiaire. P27.

5725　ssū-mù　司木
(1) CHOU: **Forest Tax Supervisor,** according to the ancient ritual text Li-chi, one of 6 agencies in the Ministry of Education (ti-kuan) responsible for various tax collections. See liu fu (Six Tax Supervisors). (2) N-S DIV (Chou): **Director of Woodcraft Production** in the Ministry of Works (tung-kuan), ranked as an Ordinary Grand Master (chung ta-fu; 5a). P14.

5726　ssū-mù chú　司牧局
MING: **Horse Pasturage Service,** a local agency for maintenance of the palace horse herds under supervision of the Directorate of the Imperial Horses (yü-ma chien), headed by a eunuch Commissioner-in-chief (ta-shih), rank 9a. P39.

5727　ssū-nèi　司內
N-S DIV (Chou): **Palace Attendant,** a eunuch title with rank of Senior Serviceman (shang-shih). Cf. hsiao ssu-nei (Junior Palace Attendant).

5728　ssū-nièh　司臬
Variant of nieh-ssu (**Law Office**); see under nieh-fu.

5729　ssū-núng　司農
Lit., in charge of agriculture. (1) Throughout history a common variant of ta ssu-nung (**Chamberlain for the National Treasury**), q.v. (2) N-S DIV (Chou): **Manager of Agriculture,** one ranked as Senior Serviceman (shang-shih), a member of the Ministry of Education (ti-kuan). P8. (3) N-S DIV–SUI: common abbreviation of ssu-nung ssu (**Court for the National Treasury**) or ssu-nung ch'ing (**Chamberlain for the National Treasury**). (4) T'ANG–SUNG: common abbreviation of ssu-nung ssu (**Court of the Imperial Granaries**) or ssu-nung ch'ing (**Chief Minister of the Court of the Imperial Granaries**). (5) CH'ING: unofficial, archaic reference to a **Minister of Revenue** (hu-pu shang-shu).

5730　ssū-núng ch'īng　司農卿
(1) N-S DIV (Liang, Ch'en, N. Ch'i)–SUI: **Chamberlain for the National Treasury,** from 508 gradually displacing the former title ta ssu-nung, q.v., his establishment becoming known as the Court for the National Treasury (ssu-nung ssu); responsible for fostering agriculture, collecting grain revenues in granaries at the dynastic capital, and through a subsidiary Market Office (shih-shu) collecting mercantile taxes in the capital marketplaces. After the Market Office was transferred to the Court of the Imperial Treasury (t'ai-fu ssu) in 605, the Court for the National Treasury changed in character and had narrower responsibilities. P6, 8, 32, 40. (2) SUI–SUNG: common reference to the **Chief Minister** (ch'ing) of the Court of the National Granaries (ssu-nung ssu).

5731　ssū-núng ssū　司農寺
(1) N-S DIV (Liang, Ch'en, N. Ch'i)–SUI: **Court for the National Treasury,** from 508 a central government revenue agency headed by the Chamberlain for the National Treasury (ssu-nung ch'ing). (2) SUI–SUNG: **Court of the National Granaries,** from 605 evolving out of the Court for the National Treasury (see #1 above), with supervisory responsibility over receipts and disbursements of the central government's grain revenues, especially through subsidiaries such as the Imperial Granaries Office (t'ai-ts'ang shu) and Directorates (chien) of various other granaries. Headed by a Chief Minister (ch'ing), rank 3a in T'ang, 4b in Sung, aided by 2 Vice Ministers (shao-ch'ing), 4b1, in T'ang and one Vice Minister, 6a, in Sung. Although in early Sung the management of state revenues was dominated by the State Finance Commission (see san ssu), the Court retained su-

pervisory control over the Ever-normal Granary (*ch'ang-p'ing ts'ang*) system. RR+SP: *cour de la direction de l'agriculture*. P8.

5732 *ssū-p'àn* 司判
CHIN: **Disciplinarian of Attendants**, one, rank 9b, commonly an aide to the Chief of Attendants (*ssu-hou*) in charge of unranked subofficials assigned to frontier Prefectures (*chou*). P53.

5733 *ssū-pào* 司虣
CHOU: **Market Shop Policeman**, one assigned to each cluster of 10 shops in the capital marketplace(s) to publicize and enforce commercial prohibitions; unranked subordinates of the Market Shop Supervisors (*ch'an-jen*) of the Ministry of Education (*ti-kuan*). CL: *préposé aux violences*. P6.

5734 *ssū-pǎo ssū* 司寶司
T'ANG–SUNG, MING: **Seals Office**, one of 4 palace women agencies in the Wardrobe Service (*shang-fu chü*); headed by 2 Directresses (*ssu-pao*), rank 6a, who maintained and monitored the use of various precious seals and tallies used in the imperial palace and who recorded the departures and returnings of palace women. RR (*ssu-pao*): *directeur des sceaux*.

5735 *ssū p'ào-ǎo* 司袍襖
N-S DIV (Chou): **Manager of Outer Garments**, numbers not clear, ranked as Ordinary Servicemen (*chung-shih*; 8a) and Junior Servicemen (*hsia-shih*; 9a), members of the Ministry of War (*hsia-kuan*). P12.

5736 *ssū-p'ēng tà-fū* 司烹大夫
T'ANG: lit., grand master of cookery: unofficial reference to the Vice Director (*yüan-wai lang*) of the Catering Bureau (*shan-pu*) in the Ministry of Rites (*lǐ-pu*).

5737 *ssū-p'í* 司皮
N-S DIV (Chou): **Manager of Leatherwork**, number not clear, ranked as Junior Grand Master (*hsia ta-fu*; 6a) in the Ministry of Works (*tung-kuan*). P14.

5738 *ssū-pīn ssū* 司賓司
T'ANG–SUNG: **Visitors Office**, one of 4 palace women agencies in the Ceremonial Service (*shang-i chü*); headed by 2 Directresses (*ssu-pin*), rank 6a, who supervised and monitored all receptions of visitors in the women's quarters of the imperial palace. RR: *directeur des visites du harem*.

5739 *ssū-pīn ssù* 司賓寺
(1) T'ANG: from 684 to 705 the official variant of *hung-lu ssu* (**Court of State Ceremonial**). P33. (2) CH'ING: quasiofficial variant of *li-fan yüan* (**Court of Colonial Affairs**).

5740 *ssū-pīn tà-fū* 司賓大夫
Grand Master of Guests: may be encountered as an unofficial reference to the head of the Han dynasty Section for Receptions (*k'o-ts'ao*) in the Imperial Secretariat (*shang-shu t'ai*) or the head of the T'ang–Sung Bureau of Receptions (*chu-k'o ssu*) in the Ministry of Rites (*lǐ-pu*).

5741 *ssū-pīng* 司兵
(1) CHOU: **Manager of Arms**, 4 ranked as Ordinary Servicemen (*chung-shih*), members of the Ministry of War (*hsia-kuan*) who maintained and issued weapons and shields. CL: *préposé aux armes*. (2) T'ANG–SUNG: **Military**: a prefix commonly attached to the titles of Administrators (*ts'an-chün-shih*) and lesser personnel of War Sections (*ping-ts'ao*) in units of territorial administration, or in T'ang dynasty Military Service Sections (also *ping-ts'ao*) in military units at the dynastic capital. P26, 43, 53.

5742 *ssù pīng* 四兵
SUNG: **Four Categories of Troops**, collective reference to the various kinds of military groups in the national military establishment: Imperial Troops (*chin-ping*), Prefectural Troops (*hsiang-ping*), Conscripted Troops (*i-ping*), and Local Militiamen (*hsiang-ping, min-ping*).

5743 *ssū-pìng kuān* 司病官
YÜAN: **Military Coroner**, a duty assignment from 1278 for officials to investigate cases of death by illness in the military forces.

5744 *ssū-p'íng* 司平
T'ANG: from 662 to 670 the official variant of *kung-pu* (both **Ministry of Works** and the Ministry's **Headquarters Bureau**); during this period the Minister (*shang-shu*) was titled Grand Executive Attendant (*t'ai ch'ang-po*) and the Bureau Director (*lang-chung*) was titled Grand Master (*ta-fu*). RR: *administration de l'aplanissement*. P15.

5745 *ssù pù* 四部
Four Bureaus, also **Four Classifications**: see under *pi-shu chien* (Director of the Palace Library).

5746 *ssù-pù* 寺簿
SUNG: **Registrar of the Court ...**, one or more, rank 7a, in each of the central government agencies known collectively as the Nine Courts (*chiu ssu*, q.v.); apparently responsible for keeping registers of correspondence received and dispatched. SP: *préposé aux registres*.

5747 *ssū-pù ssū* 司簿司
T'ANG–SUNG: **Registration Office**, one of 4 palace women agencies in the General Palace Service (*shang-kung chü*); headed by 2 Directresses (*ssu-pu*), rank 6a, who kept registers of all palace women, their assigned duties, and their authorized remunerations. RR (*ssu-pu*): *directeur des registres du harem*.

5748 *ssū-p'ú* 司僕
T'ANG: from 662 to 670 the official variant of *tu-kuan* (**Bureau of Prisons** in the Ministry of Justice, *hsing-pu*); during this period the Bureau Director (*lang-chung*) was titled Grand Master (*ta-fu*). RR: *administration des esclaves*. P13.

5749 *ssū-p'ú ssū* 司僕寺
T'ANG–CH'ING: from 684 to 705 the official variant of *t'ai-p'u ssu* (**Court of the Imperial Stud**); thereafter a not uncommon unofficial reference to it. P31.

5750 *ssū-sè* 司色
N-S DIV (Chou): **Manager of Coloring Processes**, ranked as a Junior Grand Master (*hsia ta-fu*; 6a), a member of the Ministry of Works (*tung-kuan*). P14.

5751 *ssù-sè kuān* 四色官
T'ANG: **Officers of the Four Categories**, collective reference to 4 types of military officers established in 691 throughout the Sixteen Guards (*shih-liu wei*) at the dynastic capital: Managers of Lances (*ssu-ko*), Halberdiers (*chih-chi*), Watch Officers (*chung-hou*), and Guards of the Staircase (*ssu-chieh*). RR: *officers des quatre genres*.

5752 *ssū-shàn* 四膳
(1) T'ANG: from 662 to 670 the official variant of *shan-pu* (**Catering Bureau** in the Ministry of Rites, *lǐ-pu*). P9. (2) T'ANG–SUNG: **Directress of Foods**, 2 palace women, rank 6a, heads of the Foods Office (*ssu-shan ssu*) in the Food Service (*shang-shih chü*). RR: *directeur des mets exquis*. (3) YÜAN: **Cook**, unranked subofficials found in various agencies.

5753 *ssū-shàn ssū* 司膳司
T'ANG–SUNG: **Foods Office**, one of 4 palace women

agencies in the Food Service (*shang-shih chü*); headed by 2 Directresses (*ssu-shan*), rank 6a, who were in charge of table service for imperial banquets and other ceremonies.

5754 *ssū-shàn ssù* 司膳寺
T'ANG: from 684 to 705 the official variant of *kuang-lu ssu* (**Court of Imperial Entertainments**). P30.

5755 *ssū-shàn tà-fū* 司膳大夫
T'ANG: from 662 to 670 the official redesignation of the **Director** (*lang-chung*) **of the Catering Bureau** (*shan-pu*) in the Ministry of Rites (*lǐ-pu*). P9.

5756 *ssū-shè* 司社
N-S DIV (Chou): **Supervisor of Sacrifices to the Soil,** members of the Ministry of Rites (*ch'un-kuan*) ranked as Senior Servicemen (*shang-shih;* 7a), Ordinary Servicemen (*chung-shih;* 8a), and Junior Servicemen (*hsia-shih;* 9a); assisted in important state sacrifices at the dynastic capital; counterparts of earlier staff members of the Hall of Enlightened Rule (*ming-t'ang*) and later officials of the Office of the National Altars (*chiao-she shu*), etc. P28.

5757 *ssū-shè chiēn* 司設監
MING-CH'ING: **Directorate for Imperial Regalia,** one of 12 major Directorates (*chien*) among which, together with 4 Offices (*ssu*) and 8 Services (*chü*), palace eunuchs were distributed; responsible for the Emperor's personal insignia, ceremonial weapons, tents, etc. In Ch'ing existed only from 1656 to 1661. See under *shih-erh chien* (Twelve Directorates).

5758 *ssū-shè ssū* 司設司
T'ANG–SUNG: **Interior Maintenance Office,** one of 4 palace women agencies in the Housekeeping Service (*shang-ch'in chü*); headed by 2 Directresses (*ssu-she*), rank 6a, who were responsible for providing beds, blankets, pillows, nets, mats, etc., and for cleaning the imperial bedchambers. RR (*ssu-she*): *directeur de l'arrangement intérieur du harem.*

5759 *ssù shěng* 四省
SUI: **Four Departments,** collective reference to the Department of State Affairs (*shang-shu sheng*), the Secretariat (*chung-shu sheng*), the Chancellery (*men-hsia sheng*), and the Palace Library (*pi-shu sheng*). P5.

5760 *ssū-shēng chǘ* 司牲局 or *ssū-shēng ssū* 司牲司
MING–CH'ING: **Service** (*chü*) or **Office** (*ssu*) **of Sacrificial Animals,** a unit of the Court of Imperial Entertainments (*kuang-lu ssu*), headed by a Commissioner-in-chief (*ta-shih*), rank 9b; the two agencies apparently coexisted until 1528, when the Service was discontinued; the Office was eventually also discontinued in 1658; differences in functions are not clear. P30.

5761 *ssū-shìh* 司士
(1) CHOU: **Manager of Servicemen,** 2 ranked as Junior Grand Masters (*hsia ta-fu*), 6 as Ordinary Servicemen (*chung-shih*), and 12 as Junior Servicemen (*hsia-shih*), members of the Ministry of War (*hsia-kuan*) who maintained registers of all active military personnel classed as Servicemen (*shih*), processed reports on their conduct, positioned them appropriately at sacrificial and other ceremonies, etc. CL: *chef des gradués ou officiers secondaires.* P5. (2) T'ANG–SUNG: **Manager of Requisitioned Labor,** prefix attached to the titles of Administrators (*ts'an-chün-shih*) and lesser personnel of Levied Service Sections (*shih-ts'ao*) in units of territorial administration. P53.

5762 *ssū-shìh* 司市
Director of Markets. (1) CHOU: 2 ranked as Junior Grand

Masters (*hsia ta-fu*), 4 as Senior Servicemen (*shang-shih*), 8 as Ordinary Servicemen (*chung-shih*), and 16 as Junior Servicemen (*hsia-shih*), members of the Ministry of Education (*ti-kuan*) who supervised the marketplace and all mercantile transactions in the royal capital, establishing the physical layout of the marketplace, fixing rules governing transactions there, punishing violators of the rules, adjudicating disputes between merchants, fixing fair prices for commodities, issuing trading permits, even supervising coinage. CL: *prévôt du marché.* P6. (2) N-S DIV: established irregularly to supervise marketplaces in dynastic capitals, organizational relationships not clear; in later Chou ranked as Junior Grand Master (*hsia ta-fu*). P20, 32, 62.

5763 *ssū-shìh* 司矢
CH'ING: **Arrow Maker,** unspecified number of non-official specialists in the Court of Imperial Armaments (*wu-pei yüan*) of the Imperial Household Department (*nei-wu fu*). BH: supervisor of arrow-making.

5764 *ssū-shìh* 司筮
MING: **Augur,** number not clear, rank 9a, in the short-lived Religious Office (*chi-i ssu*) of early Ming. P35.

5765 *ssù-shìh* 嗣適
Lit., succession through the principal wife: throughout history an unofficial reference to the **Heir Apparent** (*t'ai-tzu*).

5766 *ssù-shīh* 肆師
CHOU: **Master of the Sacrifices,** 4 ranked as Junior Grand Masters (*hsia ta-fu*), members of the Ministry of Rites (*ch'un-kuan*) who assisted or represented the executive officials of the Ministry in many ways, especially in supervising the establishment and conduct of appropriate sacrificial rituals in feudatory realms. CL: *maître des sacrifices.*

5767 *ssù-shìh hsüéh* 四氏學
CH'ING: **School of the Four Sage Clans,** a state-sponsored school for educating pupils of families descended from the early thinkers considered founders of Confucianism: Confucius, Yen Hui, Tseng-tzu, and Mencius; located at the Confucian family estate at Ch'ü-fu, Shantung; staffed with one Instructor (*chiao-shou*), rank 7a, and one Instructor Third Class (*hsüeh-lu*), 8a, both originally appointed by the current most direct male descendant of Confucius, who was ennobled as Duke for Fulfilling the Sage (*yen-sheng kung*), but eventually so appointed only with the approval of the Provincial Governor (*hsün-fu*) of Shantung. See *san-shih hsüeh.* P66.

5768 *ssū-shìh ssū* 司飾司
T'ANG–SUNG, MING: **Adornments Office,** one of 4 palace women agencies in the Wardrobe Service (*shang-fu chü*); headed by 2 Directresses (*ssu-shih*), rank 6a; managed personal adornments worn by palace women, also supervised the palace women's baths. RR (*ssu-shih*): *directeur des parures du harem.*

5769 *ssū-shū* 司書
(1) CHOU: **Manager of Writings,** 2 ranked as Senior Servicemen (*shang-shih*) and 2 as Ordinary Servicemen (*chung-shih*), members of the Ministry of State (*t'ien-kuan*) who processed all major state documents, registers, and pronouncements. CL: *chef des écritures.* (2) CH'ING: **Compiler,** one non-official specialist in the Calendar Section (*shih-hsien k'o*) of the Directorate of Astronomy (*ch'in-t'ien chien*); editor of the official calendar issued by the central government. BH: compiler.

5770 *ssū-shǔ ssù* 司屬寺
T'ANG: lit., court in charge of dependents: from 684 to 705

the official variant of *tsung-cheng ssu* (**Court of the Imperial Clan**).

5771 *ssū-shǔi* 司水
(1) CHOU: **River Tax Supervisor,** according to the ancient ritual text *Li-chi,* one of 6 agencies in the Ministry of Education (*ti-kuan*) responsible for various tax collections. See *liu fu* (Six Tax Supervisors). (2) N-S DIV (Chou): **Manager of Waterways,** one or more ranked as Ordinary Grand Masters (*chung ta-fu*), members of the Ministry of Works (*tung-kuan*) who supervised the maintenance of waterways and perhaps even the water transport of grain to the dynastic capital. P14, 59, 60. (3) T'ANG: from 752 to c. 757 the official variant of *shui-pu* (**Bureau of Waterways and Irrigation** in the Ministry of Works, *kung-pu*); during this period the Bureau Director (*lang-chung*) was retitled Grand Master (*ta-fu*). P15.

5772 *ssū-shùi* 司稅
CH'ING: **Rent Collector,** number and status unspecified, members of the Office of Palace Ceremonial (*chang-i ssu*) in the Imperial Household Department (*nei-wu fu*) who collected rents from state lands controlled by the Office. BH: rent collector.

5773 *ssū-shuò* 司矟
N-S DIV (Chou): **Manager of Long Lances,** unspecified number ranked as Ordinary Servicemen (*chung-shih;* 8a) and Junior Servicemen (*hsia-shih;* 9a), members of the Ministry of War (*hsia-kuan*). P12.

5774 *ssù ssū* 四司
Four Offices. (1) SUNG: abbreviation of *ssu chien-ssu* (Four Circuit Supervisors or Supervisorates). (2) SUNG: collective reference to the 4 Bureaus of the Ministry of War (*ping-pu*): Bureau of Military Appointments (also *ping-pu*), Bureau of Equipment (*chia-pu*), Bureau of Operations (*chih-fang*), and Bureau of Provisions (*k'u-pu*); also to the 4 Bureaus of the Ministry of Works (*kung-pu*): Headquarters Bureau (also *kung-pu*), State Farms Bureau (*t'un-t'ien ssu*), Bureau of Forestry and Crafts (*yü-pu*), and Bureau of Waterways and Irrigation (*shui-pu*). SP: *quatre bureaux*. (3) MING: collective reference to 4 minor agencies of palace eunuchs, less important than those called Directorates (*chien;* see *shih-erh chien*), each headed by a Director (*cheng* or *t'ai-chien*): Firewood Office (*hsi-hsin ssu*), Bells and Drums Office (*chung-ku ssu*), Paper Office (*pao-ch'ao ssu*), and Bathing Office (*hun-t'ang ssu*).

5775 *ssù tà-pù* 四大部
LIAO: **Four Great Tribes,** collective reference to the 4 most esteemed tribal groups in the Khitan confederation: the Five Groups (*wu yüan*), the Six Groups (*liu yüan*), the I-shih Tribes (*i-shih pu*), and the Six Hsi Tribes (*hsi liu pu*); also see *ssu ta-wang fu*. P17.

5776 *ssù tà-wáng fǔ* 四大王府
LIAO: **Four Offices of the Grand Princes,** collective reference to the court agencies in the Northern Establishment (*pei-yüan*) of the Northern Administration (*pei-mien*) representing the interests of the 4 most esteemed tribal groups in the Khitan confederation (see under *ssu ta-pu*), each of which was represented in government by a headquarters unit called Office of the Grand Prince (*ta-wang fu*). Cf. *wang-fu* (Princely Establishment). P17.

5777 *ssū tāo-tùn* 司刀盾
N-S DIV (Chou): **Manager of Swords and Shields,** number unspecified, ranked as Ordinary Servicemen (*chung-shih;*

8a) and Junior Servicemen (*hsia-shih;* 9a), members of the Ministry of War (*hsia-kuan*). P12.

5778 *ssū-tēng ssū* 司燈司
T'ANG–SUNG, MING: **Lanterns Office,** one of 4 palace women agencies in the Housekeeping Service (*shang-ch'in chü*); headed by 2 Directresses (*ssu-teng*), rank 6a; in charge of lanterns, lamps, candles, kerosene supplies, etc., used in the women's quarters of the imperial palace. RR (*ssu-teng*): *directeur des lamps du harem.*

5779 *ssū-t'ién* 司田
T'ANG: from 662 to 671 the official variant of *t'un-t'ien ssu* (**State Farms Bureau** in the Ministry of Works, *kung-pu*); during this period the Bureau Director (*lang-chung*) was titled Grand Master (*ta-fu*). RR: *administration des champs.*

5780 *ssū-t'iēn chiēn* 司天監
(1) T'ANG, CHIN–YÜAN: **Director of Astronomy,** in T'ang one, rank 3a, head of the Bureau of Astronomy (*ssu-t'ien t'ai*); in Chin one (?), 5b, 2nd-level executive post in the Bureau of Astronomy under a Superintendent (*t'i-tien*), 5a; in Yüan 3, 4a, 2nd-level executive posts in the Directorate of Astronomy (*ssu-t'ien chien*) under a Superintendent, 4a or 3a. Commonly assisted by one or more Vice Directors of Astronomy (*ssu-t'ien shao-chien*). P35. (2) 5 DYN–MING: **Directorate of Astronomy,** an autonomous agency in the central government concerned with making and recording astronomical observations, preparing the official calendar issued annually by the state, and training students of astronomy; branched off from, and through Yüan partly coexisted with, a tradition of astrologically-oriented institutions stemming from the Grand Astrologer (*t'ai-shih, t'ai-shih ling*) of high antiquity. This name apparently originated in the Later Chou state (950–959) as a replacement for the T'ang Bureau of Astronomy (*ssu-t'ien t'ai*), which was headed by a Director (*chien*); in Later Chou the agency was headed by a Chief Minister of the Court of the Imperial Treasury (*t'ai-fu ssu ch'ing*) as concurrent Supervisor (*p'an*). Sung perpetuated the Later Chou institution and added a separate Bureau of Astronomy (*t'ien-wen yüan*) in the 1060s (?), but after 1078 both seem to have fallen under the dominance of a more traditional Astrological Service (*t'ai-shih chü*), which unlike the astronomical agencies indulged in weather forecasting and various astrological esoterica; all 3 agencies were in some degree subordinated to the Palace Library (*pi-shu sheng*). Consolidation of these different agencies was achieved by Liao in a *ssu-t'ien chien* headed by a *t'ai-shih ling*, for which Chin revived the T'ang name *ssu-t'ien t'ai.* In Yüan an original Bureau of Astronomy (*ssu-t'ien t'ai*) was renamed *ssu-t'ien chien* in the 1260s, and after 1271 there was at least one Branch Directorate of Astronomy (*hsing ssu-t'ien chien*), location not clear; the Directorate was headed by a Superintendent (*t'i-tien*) whose rank changed from 4a to 3a in 1314 and then back to 4a in 1320; he was aided by 3 Directors (*chien*), also rank 4a, and 5 Vice Directors (*shao-chien*), rank 5a. However, in 1267 the Directorate was effectively subordinated to a higher-ranking Astrological Commission (*t'ai-shih yüan*), which thereafter was principally responsible for preparation of the calendar while the Directorate became primarily an institution for the training of astronomers for service in the Commission. The Directorate's executive posts became almost sinecures, and its principal active officials were 2 Superintendents of Training (*t'i-hsüeh*), rank 9b, and 2 Instructors (*chiao-shou*) of equal rank, who oversaw subdivisions called the Section for Astronomy (*t'ien-wen k'o*),

the Section for Calendrical Calculations (*suan-li k'o*), the Section for Astrological Interpretation (*san-shih k'o*), the Section for Validations (*ts'e-yen k'o*), and the Water Clock Section (*lou-k'o k'o*), each administered by 2 Clerks (*kuan-kou*) of 9b rank. In early Ming, from 1368 to 1370, a *ssu-t'ien chien* existed under the leadership of a Director (*ling*), rank 3a; but it was then permanently renamed *ch'in-t'ien chien* (Directorate of Astronomy). Also see *hui-hui ssu-t'ien chien*. SP: *direction des observations astronomiques*. P35. (3) CH'ING: common unofficial reference to the **Directorate of Astronomy** (*ch'in-t'ien chien*).

5781 *ssū-t'iēn kuān* 司天官
T'ANG–CH'ING: **Astronomical Officials,** common generic reference to hereditary professional astronomical specialists utilized in such central government astronomical agencies as the *ssu-t'ien t'ai, ssu-t'ien chien, t'ai-shih chü, ch'in-t'ien chien*, qq.v.

5782 *ssū-t'iēn líng-t'ái láng* 司天靈臺郎
SUNG: **Director of the Imperial Observatory** (*ling-t'ai*), rank 8b or 7a2, a hereditary professional specialist known in other eras from T'ang through Ming as *wu-kuan ling-t'ai lang;* also see *ling-t'ai*. SP: *maître astronomique de la direction des observations astronomiques*. P35.

5783 *ssū-t'iēn t'ái* 司天臺
(1) T'ANG, CHIN–YÜAN: **Bureau of Astronomy,** a central government agency generally responsible for astronomical observations and preparation of the official calendar issued annually by the state; created in 758 by renaming the traditional Astrological Service (*t'ai-shih chü*), superseded in Sung and Liao by a Directorate of Astronomy (*ssu-t'ien chien*) but restored in Chin and Yüan till the 1260s, then again named Directorate of Astronomy; normally subordinated to the Palace Library (*pi-shu sheng, pi-shu chien*); staffed largely with hereditary professional specialists, principally clustered in seasonally-designated agencies collectively called the Five Offices (*wu kuan*). In T'ang headed by a Director (*chien*), rank 3a; in Chin and early Yüan by a Superintendent (*t'i-tien*), 5a, assisted by a Director (*chien*), 5b. RR: *tribunal des observations astronomiques*. P35. (2) CH'ING: common unofficial reference to the **Directorate of Astronomy** (*ch'in-t'ien chien*).

5784 *ssū-tǐng* 司鼎
T'ANG–CH'ING: lit., in charge of the tripod, i.e., of the symbol of sovereignty and state power: a common unofficial reference to the **Chief Minister** (*ch'ing*) of the Court of Imperial Entertainments (*kuang-lu ssu*).

5785 *ssū-tsǎi ssù* 司宰寺
T'ANG–CH'ING: lit., court in charge of slaughtering (?): from 662 to 671 the official variant of *kuang-lu ssu* (**Court of Imperial Entertainments**); thereafter into Ch'ing an unofficial reference to that Court. P30.

5786 *ssū-ts'ǎi ssū* 司綵司
T'ANG–SUNG, MING: **Silks Office,** one of 4 palace women agencies in the Workshop Service (*shang-kung chü*); headed by 2 Directresses (*ssu-ts'ai*), rank 6a; in charge of all raw materials used in the making of clothing for palace women. RR (*ssu-ts'ai*): *directeur des soieries*.

5787 *ssū-tsàn ssū* 司贊司
T'ANG–SUNG, MING: **Ritual Receptions Office,** one of 4 palace women agencies in the Ceremonial Service (*shang-i chü*); headed by 2 Directresses (*ssu-tsan*), rank 6a; directed palace women in various imperial processions and in great palace receptions. RR (*ssu-tsan*): *directeur des cérémonies du harem*.

5788 *ssū-tsàng* 司藏 or *ssū-tsàng shǔ* 署
N-S DIV (N. Ch'i)–T'ANG, CHIN: **Storehouse Office** in the establishment of the Heir Apparent, headed by one or more Household Provisioners (*chia-ling*) through Sui, one or more Directors (*ling*), rank 8b2, in T'ang, and one or more Directors (*cheng*) in Chin; managed the receipt, storage, and disbursement of the Heir Apparent's non-grain wealth; in T'ang subordinate to the Household Provisioner's Court (*chia-ling ssu;* see under *chia-ling*). RR: *office des magasins de la maison de l'héritier du trône*. P26.

5789 *ssū-ts'āng* 司倉
Lit., in charge of granaries. (1) N-S DIV (Chou): **Granary Master,** ranked as a Junior Grand Master (*hsia ta-fu;* 6a), a member of the Ministry of Education (*ti-kuan*) responsible for maintaining adequate grain supplies in the dynastic capital. P8. (2) T'ANG: **Director of Granaries,** a prefix commonly attached to the titles of Administrators (*ts'an-chün-shih*) and lesser personnel of Granaries Sections (*ts'ang-ts'ao*) in units of territorial administration. P53. (3) CHIN: **Director of Granaries** in the establishment of the Heir Apparent; rank not clear.

5790 *ssū-ts'ǎo* 司草
CHOU: **Grain Tax Supervisor,** according to the ancient ritual text *Li-chi*, one of 6 agencies in the Ministry of Education (*ti-kuan*) responsible for various tax collections. See *liu fu* (Six Tax Supervisors).

5791 *ssù ts'áo* 四曹
HAN: **Four Sections,** collective designation of the units, each headed by an Imperial Secretary (*shang-shu*), rank 600 bushels, that constituted what was informally called the Imperial Secretariat (*shang-shu t'ai*) until 29 B.C., when a 5th Section was added (see *wu ts'ao*). The original Four Sections were the Sections for Attendants-in-ordinary (*ch'ang-shih ts'ao*), for Commandery Governors (*erh-ch'ien shih ts'ao*), for the People (*min-ts'ao*), and for Receptions (*chu-k'o ts'ao*). Also see *liu ts'ao*. HB: four bureaus. P5.

5792 *ssū-tsé* 司則
T'ANG: **Directress of Standards,** 2 palace women, rank 8a2, in the establishment of the Heir Apparent; responsible for proper conduct in the harem and for the reception of visitors there. RR: *directeur du service des règlements du harem de l'héritier du trône*.

5793 *ssū-tsò kuān* 司胙官
CH'ING: **Sacrificing Official,** 4 or 5, rank 6a, members of the Office of Palace Ceremonial (*chang-i ssu*) in the Imperial Household Department (*nei-wu fu*); after the early Ch'ing years, retitled *ssu-tsu kuan*. BH: supervisor of sacrificial attributes. P37.

5794 *ssū-tsǔ kuān* 司俎官
CH'ING: **Sacrificing Official,** 5, rank 6a, members of the Office of Palace Ceremonial (*chang-i ssu*) in the Imperial Household Department (*nei-wu fu*); changed from *ssu-tso kuan* after the early Ch'ing years. BH: supervisor of sacrificial attributes. P37.

5795 *ssū-ts'uàn* 司爨
CH'ING: **Cook for Sacrifices,** number not specified, probably unranked subofficials, members of the Office of Palace Ceremonial (*chang-i ssu*) in the Imperial Household Department (*nei-wu fu*). BH: supervisor of preparation of eatables for sacrifices.

5796 *ssū tsūn-í* 司尊彝
CHOU: **Manager of the Wine Goblets,** 2 ranked as Junior Servicemen (*nsia-shih*), members of the Ministry of Rites

(*ch'un-kuan*) responsible for the preparation and handling of wine goblets of the forms called *tsun* and *i* in sacrificial and other ceremonial events. CL: *préposé aux vases tsun et i*.

5797 *ssū-tsūng* 司宗
(1) N-S DIV (Chou): **Headquarters Bureau** (the *li-pu* of later eras) of the Ministry of Rites (*ch'un-kuan;* later also *li-pu*); headed by a Grand Master (*ta-fu*) with rank as an Ordinary Grand Master (*chung ta-fu;* 5a). P9. (2) Throughout imperial history an archaic reference to a **Chamberlain for the Imperial Clan** (*tsung-cheng*) or the **head of the Court of the Imperial Clan** (see *tsung-cheng ssu, tsung-jen fu*).

5798 *ssū-tsūng ssù* 司宗寺
T'ANG: from 662 to 671 (684?) the official variant of *tsung-cheng ssu* (**Court of the Imperial Clan**).

5799 *ssū-tù* 司度
(1) N-S DIV (Chou): **Estimator,** number not specified, ranked as Ordinary Servicemen (*chung-shih;* 8a), members of the Ministry of Works (*tung-kuan*). P14. (2) T'ANG: from 662 to 671 the official variant of *tu-chih* (**Tax Bureau** in the Ministry of Revenue, *hu-pu*); during this period the Bureau Director (*lang-chung*) was titled Grand Master (*ta-fu*). RR: *administration des estimations*. P6.

5800 *ssū-t'ǔ* 司土
(1) CHOU: **Land Tax Supervisor,** according to the ancient ritual text *Li-chi*, one of 6 agencies in the Ministry of Education (*ti-kuan*) responsible for various tax collections. See *liu fu* (Six Tax Supervisors). (2) N-S DIV (Chou): **Manager of Earthwork** (?), number not specified, ranked as Ordinary Grand Masters (*chung ta-fu;* 5a), members of the Ministry of Works (*tung-kuan*); may have supervised state digging enterprises and the provision of earth for walls, etc. P14.

5801 *ssū-t'ú* 司徒
Lit., to be in charge of disciples or followers: **Minister of Education,** a title of great prestige from high antiquity. (1) CHOU: head of the Ministry of Education (*ti-kuan*), in general charge of training in and enforcement of proper moral and political values among the people, with special responsibility for overseeing commercial activities, through a large staff of subordinates. CL: *ministre de l'enseignement officiel, directeur des multitudes*. (2) HAN–LIAO: from A.D. 1 on, intermittently the title of one of the eminent central government officials called the Three Dukes (*san kung*); until 1122 in Sung and Liao used almost interchangeably with *ta ssu-t'u, ch'eng-hsiang,* etc. HB: minister over the masses. RR+SP: *directeur de l'instruction*. P2. (3) YÜAN: though not considered one of the Three Dukes, sometimes used for similar quasi-honorific appointments. P67. (4) CH'ING: common unofficial reference to the executive officials of the Ministry of Revenue (*hu-pu*).

5802 *ssū-t'ú kūng* 司徒公
HAN: after A.D. 51 a common variant of *ssu-t'u* (**Minister of Education**).

5803 *ssū-tùi* 司碓
CH'ING: **Bark Grinder,** number unspecified, apparently non-official artisans employed in the Office of Palace Ceremonial (*chang-i ssu*) of the Imperial Household Department (*nei-wu fu*); powdered bark used in the manufacture of incense. BH: supervisor of preparation of incense.

5804 *ssù-t'ūi yù-shǐh* 四推御史
T'ANG: **Four Surveillance Censors,** collective reference

to Censors (*yü-shih*) who, on the basis of seniority, were delegated in 2 pairs to be responsible for an East Surveillance Jurisdiction (*tung-t'ui*) and a West Surveillance Jurisdiction (*hsi-t'ui*); the nature of their responsibilities is not clear, except that the East Surveillance Jurisdiction included receipts and disbursements from the Imperial Granaries (*t'ai-ts'ang*) and that of the West included receipts and disbursements from the Left Vault (*tso-tsang*) in the Court of the Imperial Treasury (*t'ai-fu ssu*). RR: *quatre censeurs qui examinent judiciairement les affaires*.

5805 *ssū-tz'ù* 司刺
Executioner. (1) CHOU: 2 ranked as Junior Servicemen (*hsia-shih*), members of the Ministry of Justice (*ch'iu-kuan*); made arrests and conducted executions, also made inquiries among the people about their living conditions. CL: *chef des exécutions capitales*. (2) N-S DIV (Chou): number not clear, ranked as Senior Servicemen (*shang-shih;* 7a) and Ordinary Servicemen (*chung-shih;* 8a), members of the Ministry of Justice (*ch'iu-kuan*). P13.

5806 *ssù-wáng* 嗣王
N-S DIV (Liang)–SUNG: **Prince Presumptive,** title of nobility (*chüeh*) with rank 1a2 in T'ang, 1b in Sung; normally granted to the eldest son of an Imperial Prince (*ch'in-wang*) by his principal wife, other sons being granted the less prestigious title Commandery Prince (*chün-wang*); counterpart of *shih-tzu* (Heir). RR+SP: *prince successeur*.

5807 *ssù wèi* 四尉
HAN–N-S DIV (San-kuo Wei): **Four Defenders,** collective reference to 4 military officers with rank of 400 bushels among whom were divided responsibilities for policing the capital cities, capturing burglars and thieves, and investigating all sorts of wrongdoing; for purposes of police surveillance, each capital city was divided into a Left and a Right Division (*pu*), each having 2 such Defenders. The Defenders were traditionally considered counterparts of the Wardens' Offices (*ping-ma chih-hui ssu*) of later dynasties. P20.

5808 *ssū-wèi ssù* 司衛寺
T'ANG: from 662 to 671 and again from 684 to 704, the official variant of *wei-wei ssu* (**Court of the Imperial Regalia**).

5809 *ssū-wéi ssù* 司闈司
T'ANG–SUNG, MING: **Inner Gates Office,** one of 4 palace women agencies in the General Palace Service (*shang-kung chü*); headed by 2 Directresses (*ssu-wei*), rank 6a; supervised the locks and keys at the entrances to the inner quarters of the imperial palace and monitored passage in and out. RR (*ssu-wei*): *directeur des portes intérieures du harem*.

5810 *ssū-wén chiēn* 司文監
MING: **Directorate for Documents,** from 1377 to 1378 only, an autonomous agency of the central government responsible for assisting in drafting imperial rescripts and edicts; headed by a Director (*ling*), rank 6a then 7a.

5811 *ssū-wén chǔ* 司文局
T'ANG: from 662 to 670 the official variant of *chu-tso chü* (**Editorial Service** in the Palace Library, *pi-shu sheng*). P23.

5812 *ssū-wò* 司幄
CH'ING: **Tentmaker,** unspecified number of hereditary non-official artisans employed in the Court of Imperial Armaments (*wu-pei yüan*). BH: supervisor of tent-making.

5813 *ssū-wù* 司寤
CHOU: lit., in charge of the awake: **Night Patroller,** 2

ranked as Junior Servicemen (hsia-shih), members of the Ministry of Justice (ch'iu-kuan) who with a corps of underlings watched over all who were abroad at night in the royal capital, called out the time at night, and were expected to prevent nighttime thievery. CL: préposé aux éveillés.

5814 ssū-wū 司巫

CHOU: **Director of Sorcery,** 2 ranked as Ordinary Servicemen (chung-shih), members of the Ministry of Rites (ch'un-kuan) responsible for all sorcery at court including appeals for rain in times of drought and various activities in response to other sorts of calamities; participated in all court ceremonies and funerals. See wu, nan-wu, nü-wu. CL: chef des sorciers.

5815 ssū-wǔ 司舞

N-S DIV (Chou): **Dancer,** number not specified, with rank as Ordinary Servicemen (chung-shih; 8a) and Junior Servicemen (hsia-shih; 9a), members of the Ministry of Rites (ch'un-kuan). P10.

5816 ssù-wù ssū 寺務司

SUNG: **Temple Maintenance Office,** an agency of the capital prefecture at Kaifeng in N. Sung; staffing and functions not specified. SP: bureau de l'entretien des temples dans la capitale.

5817 ssū-wù t'īng 司務廳

MING–CH'ING: lit., office in charge of business: **General Services Office,** an internal management office in the executive structure of each of the Six Ministries (liu pu), the Censorate (tu ch'a-yüan), and the Court of Judicial Review (ta-li ssu) in the central government, also in the Ch'ing Court of Colonial Affairs (li-fan yüan) and the early Ch'ing Office of Transmission (t'ung-cheng ssu); headed in Ming by one Office Manager (ssu-wu), rank 9b, in Ch'ing by one Manchu and one Chinese appointee excepting one Manchu and one Mongol in the Court of Colonial Affairs; 9b till 1760, then 8a. The post was among those considered in the category of Staff Supervisors (shou-ling kuan). BH: chancery. P5, 6, etc.

5818 ssū-yáng shǔ 司羊署

N-S DIV (N. Ch'i): **Sheep Office** in charge of the imperial herds of sheep, under the Court of the Imperial Stud (t'ai-p'u ssu); headed by a Director (ling); supervised a Rams Service (t'e-yang chü) and a Ewes Service (tzu-yang chü).

5819 ssū-yào chǎng 司鑰長

CH'ING: **Keeper of the Palace Keys,** a Grand Minister (ta-ch'en) in the Imperial Household Department (nei-wu fu), perhaps serving on rotational assignment.

5820 ssū-yào ssū 司藥司

T'ANG–SUNG, MING: **Medicines Office,** one of 4 palace women agencies in the Food Service (shang-shih chü); headed by 2 Directresses (ssu-yao), rank 6a, in charge of all medicines and medical treatments in the quarters of the palace women. RR (ssu-yao): directeur des remèdes.

5821 ssū-yèh 司業

Lit., in charge of the (scholastic) inheritance or profession: **Director of Studies.** (1) SUI–CH'ING: from c. 605, the 2nd executive official of the central government's Directorate of Education (kuo-tzu chien), subordinate only to its Chancellor (chi-chiu); generally supervised the Directorate's instructional programs. Normally one, rank 4b2 in T'ang, 6a in Sung, 5a in Chin and Yüan, 6a in Ming and Ch'ing; but 2 appointees common in T'ang and Yüan; in Ch'ing originally 2 Manchus but after early Ch'ing one each

Manchu, Mongol, and Chinese. RR: vice-recteur. SP: sous-directeur d'éducation. BH: tutor. P34. (2) CH'ING: also one non-official specialist in the Tibetan School (t'ang-ku-t'e hsüeh) maintained by the Court of Colonial Affairs (li-fan yüan). P17.

5822 ssū-yén chiēn 司鹽監

N-S DIV (San-kuo Wei–Chin): **Directorate of Salt Distribution,** a central government agency apparently responsible for supervising the distribution of salt under state monopoly; headed by a Commandant-in-chief (tu-wei), rank 6. P61.

5823 ssū-yén ssū 司言司

T'ANG–SUNG, MING: **Communications Office,** one of 4 palace women agencies in the General Palace Service (shang-kung chü); headed by 2 Directresses (ssu-yen), rank 6a; received and distributed imperial orders affecting palace women. RR (ssu-yen): directeur de la transmission des ordres.

5824 ssū-yīn 司禋

T'ANG: lit., in charge of sacrifices: from 662 to 670 the official variant of tz'u-pu (**Bureau of Sacrifices** in the Ministry of Rites, li-pu); during this period the Bureau Director (lang-chung) was titled Grand Master (ta-fu). P9.

5825 ssū-yīn chiēn 司禋監

YÜAN: **Directorate of Sacrifices,** a relatively autonomous agency of the central government, apparently headed by a Director (chien) probably under an Overseer (ta-lu-hua-ch'ih), responsible for making appropriate offerings before images of the original 3 Grand Khans (Chingis, Ögödëi, and Mangu) in the Stone Buddha Temple (shih-fo ssu) at the dynastic capital. P28.

5826 ssū-yù 司右

CHOU: **Manager of the Royal Lancers,** 2 ranked as Senior Servicemen (shang-shih) and 4 as Junior Servicemen (hsia-shih), members of the Ministry of War (hsia-kuan) who scheduled appropriate military officers with rank as Junior Grand Masters (hsia ta-fu) and Senior Servicemen for duty as bodyguards of the King in the royal chariot, where one at a time was positioned with lance and shield at the right side of the King. CL: chef de droite.

5827 ssū-yù 司域

T'ANG: lit., in charge of the frontier: from 662 to 670 (?) the official variant of chih-fang (**Bureau of Operations** in the Ministry of War, ping-pu); during this period the Bureau Director (lang-chung) was titled Grand Master (ta-fu).

5828 ssū-yǔ 司庾

T'ANG: lit., in charge of grain stores: from 662 to 671 the official variant of ts'ang-pu (**Granaries Bureau** in the Ministry of Revenue, hu-pu); during this period the Bureau Director (lang-chung) was titled Grand Master (ta-fu). RR: administration des approvisionnements. P6.

5829 ssū-yù 司獄

CHIN–CH'ING: **Warder,** head of a Prison (ssu-yü ssu). BH: warder, jail warden.

5830 ssū-yù 司玉

N-S DIV (Chou): **Jadeworker,** probably one ranked as a Junior Grand Master (hsia ta-fu; 6a), a member of the Ministry of Works (tung-kuan) in charge of non-official specialist jade artisans. P14.

5831 ssū-yù 司禦

SUNG: **Protector,** head of a Protective Guard Command (ssu-yü shuai-fu); equivalent to shuai (Commandant); may have been used in T'ang times. SP: *chargé de la protection de l'héritier du trône.* P26.

5832 ssū-yǘ 司虞
T'ANG: from 662 to 671 and again from 752 to 758 the official variant of *yü-pu* (**Bureau of Forestry and Crafts** in the Ministry of Works, *kung-pu*); during the first of these periods the Bureau Director (*lang-chung*) was titled Grand Master (*ta-fu*). RR: *administration des forêts.* P15.

5833 ssū-yǘ 司輿
(1) T'ANG–SUNG, MING: D rectress of Transport, head of the palace women agency called the Transport Office (*ssu-yü ssu*), rank 6a. RR: *directeur des chaises à porter du harem.* (2) T'ANG: from 662 to 670 the official variant of *chia-pu* (**Bureau of Equipment** in the Ministry of War, *ping-pu*); during this period the Bureau Director (*lang-chung*) was titled Grand Master (*ta-fu*). RR: *administration des chars.* P12.

5834 ssū-yù shuài-fǔ 司禦率府
T'ANG–SUNG: **Protective Guard Command,** one each of Left and Right, military units assigned to the establishment of the Heir Apparent, each headed by a Protector (*ssu-yü*) or Commandant (*shuai*), rank 4a in T'ang, 7b in Sung. Founded in 622 by renaming the Clan Defense Guard Command (*tsung-wei shuai-fu*); resumed the former name from 705 to 711. P26.

5835 ssū-yù ssū 司獄司
CHIN–CH'ING: **Prison,** headed by from one to 6 Warders (*ssu-yü*), rank commonly 9a; maintained by various central government agencies, particularly including the Ministry of Justice (*hsing-pu*) and, in Ming, the Censorate (*tu ch'a-yüan*); provincial-level agencies such as the Yüan Route Commands (*tsung-kuan fu*), the Ming–Ch'ing Provincial Surveillance Commissions (*t'i-hsing an-ch'a shih ssu*), and in Ming the Provincial Administration Commissions (*ch'eng-hsüan pu-cheng shih ssu*) as well; and lesser units of territorial units especially including Prefectures (*chou, fu*) and in Ming some Districts (*hsien*), especially those at the dynastic capital. P13, 18, 20, 49, 52, 53.

5836 ssū-yǘ ssū 司輿司
T'ANG–SUNG, MING: **Transport Office,** one of 4 palace women agencies in the Housekeeping Service (*shang-ch'in chü*); headed by 2 Directresses (*ssu-yü*), rank 6a; in charge of vehicles, umbrellas, etc., used on outings by palace women.

5837 ssū-yù ssū 司馭寺
T'ANG: lit., court in charge of charioteering: from 662 to 671 the official variant of *t'ai-p'u ssu* (**Court of the Imperial Stud**). P31.

5838 ssū-yüán 司元
Lit., in charge of what is primary. (1) N-S DIV (Chou): **Taoist Administrator,** number unspecified, ranked as Ordinary Servicemen (*chung-shih;* 8a), members of the Ministry of Rites (*ch'un-kuan*) with apparent responsibility for regulating the Taoist clergy. P6. (2) T'ANG: from 662 to 670 the official variant of *hu-pu* (both **Ministry of Revenue** and the Ministry's **Census Bureau**); during this period the Minister (*shang-shu*) was titled Grand Executive Assistant (*t'ai ch'ang-po*) and the Bureau Director (*lang-chung*) was titled Grand Master (*ta-fu*).

5839 ssū-yüán 司員
CH'ING: (1) abbreviation of *pan-shih ssu-yüan* (**Judicial Administrator**). (2) **Secretary,** a reference to Secretaries (*chang-ching*) of various central government agencies de-

tached to serve in the Western-style Foreign Office (*tsung-li ya-men*) that was established in 1861. BH: secretary.

5840 ssū-yüán 四元
T'ANG, CHIN: **Quadruple First,** quasiofficial reference to the extremely rare man who in T'ang stood first on the pass lists of civil service recruitment examinations at both the prefectural level and the level presided over by the Ministry of Rites (*lǐ-pu*) and, in addition, on 2 subsequent Special Examinations (*chih-k'o*); and in Chin stood first on the pass lists of 2 prefectural examinations, the Metropolitan Examination (*sheng-shih*), and the Palace Examination (*t'ing-shih*). Cf. *san-yüan* (Triple First).

5841 ssū-yüàn chǘ 司苑局
CH'ING: **Garden Service,** a minor agency of palace eunuchs headed by a eunuch Commissioner-in-chief (*ta-shih*) or Director (*t'ai-chien*); provided vegetables, melons, and fruits for the imperial table; see *pa chü* (Eight Services).

5842 ssū-yüàn ssū 司苑司
T'ANG–SUNG, MING: **Gardens Office,** one of 4 palace women agencies in the Housekeeping Service (*shang-ch'in chü*); headed by 2 Directresses (*ssu-yüan*), rank 6a; in charge of parks and gardens in the women's quarters of the imperial palace. RR (*ssu-yüan*): *directeur des jardins du harem.*

5843 ssù yüán-yüàn t'í-chǔ kuān 四園苑提擧官
SUNG: **Supervisor of the Four Imperial Parks,** the duty assignment of an eminent court official or a palace eunuch, to oversee 4 imperial parks in the N. Sung capital, modern Kaifeng; eventually (date not clear) the parks came directly under the control of the Court of the Imperial Granaries (*ssu-nung ssu*). The parks were named the Jade Ford (*yü-chin*), Auspicious Sage (*jui-sheng*), Always Spring (*i-ch'un*), and Glorious Grove (*i-iung-lin*). SP: *intendant ou administrateur des quatre parcs impériaux.* P40.

5844 ssū-yüèh 司樂
(1) T'ANG–SUNG, MING: **Directress of Music,** 2 palace women, rank 6a, heads of the Music Office (*ssu-yüeh ssu*). RR: *directeur de la musique du harem.* (2) MING: **Music Director,** one prefixed Left and one Right, rank 9b, members of the Court of Imperial Sacrifices (*t'ai-ch'ang ssu*). P10. (3) MING–CH'ING: **Music Director,** one prefixed Left and one Right, rank 9b, members of the Music Office (*chiao-fang ssu*) maintained by the Ministry of Rites (*lǐ-pu*); retitled *ssu-yüeh lang* and became more numerous in 1729 when the Office was split into a Music Office (*ho-sheng shu*) and an Imperial Music Office (*shen-yüeh shu*). BH: bandmaster. P10. (4) MING–CH'ING: **Music Director,** also one, rank 7a, authorized for the Shantung establishment of the most direct male descendant of Confucius, ennobled as Duke for Fulfilling the Sage (*yen-sheng kung*). P66: Cf. *ta ssu-yüeh, hsiao ssu-yüeh.*

5845 ssū-yüēh 司約
CHOU: **Enforcer of Agreements,** 2 ranked as Junior Servicemen (*hsia-shih*), members of the Ministry of Justice (*ch'iu-kuan*) charged with preventing violations of responsibilities owed to the state or those undertaken between individuals. Cf. *ssu-meng* (Sanctifier of Covenants). CL: *préposé aux engagements.*

5846 ssū-yüèh láng 司樂郎
CH'ING: **Music Director,** number indefinite, rank 9b, from 1729 in both the Music Office (*ho-sheng shu*) and the Imperial Music Office (*shen-yüeh shu*) of the Ministry of Rites (*lǐ-pu*); previously titled *ssu-yüeh*, q.v. BH: bandmaster. P10.

5847 *ssū-yüèh ssū* 司樂司

T'ANG–SUNG, MING: **Music Office,** one of 4 palace women agencies in the Ceremonial Service (*shang-i chü*); headed by 2 Directresses (*ssu-yüeh*), rank 6a; supervised the musical instruments available to palace women.

5848 *ssū-yün ssū* 司醞司

T'ANG–SUNG, MING: **Wines Office,** one of 4 palace women agencies in the Food Service (*shang-shih chü*); headed by 2 Directresses (*ssu-yün*), rank 6a; in charge of all wines and liquors in the quarters of the palace women. RR (*ssu-yün*): *directeur des boissons fermentées.*

5849 *sù-chèng lién-fǎng ssū* 肅政廉訪司

YÜAN: lit., office to conduct investigations to make government respectable: **Surveillance Commission,** normally 22 but varying in number to a maximum of 24, each with a territorial jurisdiction called a Circuit (*tao*) particularized by its place-name prefix. Responsible for making interrogations and audits relating to the functioning of government at all levels from Pacification Commissions (*hsüan-wei ssu*) and Route Commands (*tsung-kuan fu*) down to Districts (*hsien*), and for submitting reports and impeachments accordingly either to the metropolitan Censorate (*yü-shih t'ai*) at the dynastic capital or to one of the 2 Branch Censorates (*hsing yü-shih t'ai*) at Sian and Hangchow, each Surveillance Commission being directly subordinate to, and something like a regional representative of, one of these Censorates, according to its geographical location. Until 1291 the Commissions were named *t'i-hsing an-ch'a ssu*. Each Commission had a staff of censorial officials headed by 2 Commissioners (*shih,* commonly called *lien-fang shih*), rank 3a; members of the staff reportedly toured their jurisdictions from the 2nd to 10th months each year. They were traditionally considered forerunners of the Ming dynasty's Regional Inspectors (*hsün-an yü-shih*), dispatched from the metropolitan Censorate (*tu ch'a-yüan*). P52.

5850 *sù-chèng t'ái* 肅政臺

T'ANG: lit., pavilion for making government respectable: from 684 to 713 the official variant of *yü-shih t'ai* (**Censorate**), from 685 divided into 2 units called the Left and Right *su-cheng t'ai,* each headed by a Censor-in-chief called *su-cheng t'ai ta-fu*. P18.

5851 *sù-chī* 肅機

Lit., engine of rectification. (1) T'ANG: from 662 to 705 (?) the official variant of *shang-shu ch'eng* (**Assistant Director of the Department of State Affairs,** *shang-shu sheng*). (2) T'ANG–CH'ING: unofficial reference to a **Vice Minister** (*shih-lang*) of any of the Six Ministries (*liu pu*).

5852 *sù-k'ò* 粟客

HAN: early Han variant of *chih-su tu-wei* (**Commandant-in-chief of the Granaries**) or *chih-su nei-shih* (**Chamberlain for the National Treasury**).

5853 *sū-lā* 蘇拉

CH'ING: **Office Boy,** a term for youths employed as general servants in Inner Court (*nei-t'ing*) agencies such as the Council of State (*chün-chi ch'u*); apparent Chinese transcription of a Manchu word.

5854 *sù-wèi* 宿衛

Lit., guard of the lodgings. (1) One of many terms used throughout history for military units serving as the **Imperial Bodyguard;** cf. *chin-wei, ch'in-wei, pei-shen.* (2) YÜAN: **Palace Guards,** one segment of the Imperial Armies (*ch'in-chün*) stationed at the dynastic capital, responsible for guarding the imperial palace in contrast to the Capital Guards (*shih-wei*) that were responsible for guarding the capital city; included the most elite military group, the Imperial Bodyguard (*kesig:* see *ch'ieh-hsieh*).

5855 *sù-wèi* 肅衛

SUNG: **Majestic Guardsman,** 10th in a hierarchy of laudatory epithets conferred on meritorious members of the Imperial Armies (*chin-chün*).

5856 *suàn-hsüéh* 算學

SUI–SUNG: **Mathematics School,** one of 5 schools organized by Sui's Directorate of Education (*kuo-tzu chien*), staffed with Erudites (*po-shih*) and Instructors (*chu-chiao*) and with an authorized quota of 80 enrolled students, chosen on the basis of special mathematical aptitude from among the sons of petty officials and commoners, who after their training could take regular civil service recruitment examinations in mathematics or move directly from the Mathematics School into the officialdom. T'ang did not duplicate the Sui school until 657, when it was added to the then normal complement of 6 schools supervised by the Directorate of Education; it had 2 Erudites, rank 9b2, and one Instructor, and its prescribed student enrollment was set at only 10. After only one year it was abolished. In 662 it was revived, only to be transferred the next year to the supervisory jurisdiction of the Astrological Service (*pi-ko chü;* also see *t'ai-shih chien*), but in 671 (705? not later than 739) it was durably restored to the Directorate of Education. In early Sung the school seems to have had only a nominal existence, but in 1084 the Ministry of Personnel (*li-pu*) won approval for a proposal that vacant posts as Erudites and Instructors (*chiao-yü*) of the Mathematics School be filled in current evaluations of officials for reappointment, on the basis of demonstrated mathematical skills. Such posts were abolished in 1086, revived in 1104, abolished again in 1106, but revived once more the same year. Until that time the school presumably remained under the Directorate of Education, but in the restoration of 1106 it was assigned to the Palace Library (*pi-shu sheng*), and from 1110 on it was a unit in the Astrological Service (*t'ai-shih chü*) again, apparently perpetuating the same staff titles and concentrating on calendrical calculations. After Sung such educational functions were performed by the Superintendent of Training (*t'i-hsüeh*) and his subordinates in the Yüan dynasty Directorate of Astronomy (*ssu-t'ien chien*), and in the Ming–Ch'ing Directorate of Astronomy (*ch'in-t'ien chien*). Also see *t'ien-wen suan-hsüeh*. RR+SP: *section des mathématiques.* P35.

5857 *suàn-lì k'ō* 算曆科

YÜAN: **Section for Calendrical Calculations,** one of 5 Sections in the Directorate of Astronomy (*ssu-t'ien t'ai, ssu-t'ien chien*), headed by 2 Clerks (*kuan-kou*), rank 9b; probably under the intermediary supervision of the Directorate's Superintendent of Training (*t'i-hsüeh*), as a teaching unit similar in functions to the Sui–Sung Mathematics School (*suan-hsüeh*). P35.

5858 *suàn pó-shìh* 算博士

T'ANG: **Erudite of Mathematics,** one of 18 Palace Erudites (*nei-chiao po-shih*) on the staff of the Palace Institute of Literature (*nei wen-hsüeh kuan*), where palace women were educated; from c. 741, a eunuch post. RR: *maître de calcul.*

5859 *sùi* 遂

CHOU: **District,** the largest unit of local organization of the population outside the royal domain, comparable to a *hsiang* (District) within the royal domain, each theoretically consisting of 12,500 families in 5 Townships (*hsien* or *chou*); headed, according to tradition, by a popularly elected District Grand Master (*sui ta-fu*).

5860 *súi-ch'áo pàn-kuān* 隨朝伴官
MING–CH'ING: **Escort for Court Audiences** on the staff of the Duke for Fulfilling the Sage (*yen-sheng kung*), i.e., the most direct male descendant of Confucius and head of the Confucian family estate in Shantung Province; made all arrangements for the Duke's visits to the dynastic capital; one to 6, rank 7a; normally members of the Confucian clan appointed upon recommendation of the Duke. P66.

5861 *súi-ch'áo t'ài-ī* 隨朝太醫
YÜAN: **Court Physician,** general reference to those members of the Imperial Academy of Medicine (*t'ai-i yüan*) who were medical practitioners in personal attendance on the Emperor; hereditary professionals, subject to qualifying examinations on entering service and periodic examinations thereafter.

5862 *sùi-chǐ* 歲計
MING: **Annual Personnel Evaluation,** a consolidated merit rating of all officials in his jurisdiction submitted by each Prefect (*chih-fu*) to his superior Provincial Administration Commission (*ch'eng-hsüan pu-cheng shih ssu*); based largely on monthly personnel evaluations (*yüeh-chi*) submitted to the Prefect by District and Subprefectural Magistrates (*chih-hsien, chih-chou*) in his jurisdiction; contributed to triennial Outer Evaluations (*wai-ch'a*) of officials on duty outside the dynastic capital, conducted by the Ministry of Personnel (*li-pu*), as a result of which officials were reassigned, promoted, demoted, dismissed, etc. Also see *ta-chi*.

5863 *sùi chìn-shìh* 歲進士
MING–CH'ING: lit., annual presented scholar: unofficial general reference to **Tribute Students** (*kung-sheng*) promoted annually from local Confucian Schools (*ju-hsüeh*) throughout the empire into the National University (*t'ai-hsüeh, kuo-tzu chien*). Cf. *chin-shih* (Metropolitan Graduate).

5864 *súi-chūn* 隨軍
T'ANG: **Attendant Officer,** 4 military officers authorized for duty assignments on the staff of each Military Commissioner (*chieh-tu shih*), to carry out whatever special orders they might be given. RR: *officier adjoint*. P57.

5865 *súi-chūn chuǎn-yùn shìh* 隨軍轉運使
SUNG: **Army Provisioning Commissioner,** responsible for ensuring logistical support for campaigning armies; apparently a duty assignment for staff members of the Fiscal Commissions (*chuan-yün ssu*) of appropriate Circuits (*lu*), sometimes those of Bandit-suppression Commissions (*chao-t'ao ssu*); cf. *liang-t'ai* (Paymaster). SP: *commissaire au transport chargé d'accompagner l'armée*. P60.

5866 *súi-chūn kàn-pàn kuān* 隨軍幹辦官
SUNG: **Manager for the Campaigning Army,** duty assignment for an administrative clerk with status as an unranked subofficial; see *kan-pan kuan*. SP: *régisseur chargé d'accompagner l'armée*.

5867 *sùi-fǎ* 遂法
N-S DIV (Chou): **Law Compliance Official,** number not clear, ranked as Senior and Ordinary Servicemen (*shang-shih, chung-shih;* 7a and 8a), members of the Ministry of Justice (*ch'iu-kuan*); functions not clear, but traditionally understood to be equivalent to a Vice Director (*yüan-wai lang*) of a Bureau (*ssu, ch'ing-li ssu*) in the later Ministry of Justice (*hsing-pu*). P13.

5868 *sùi-jén* 遂人
CHOU: **Supervisor of Exterior Districts,** 2 ranked as Ordinary Grand Masters (*chung ta-fu*), members of the Ministry of Education (*ti-kuan*) who served as general administrative supervisors of Districts (*sui*) outside the royal domain, with authority comparable to that of the Minister of Education (*ssu-t'u*) within the royal domain. CL: *grand officier des districts extérieurs*.

5869 *sùi-kùng* 歲貢 or *sùi kùng-shēng* 生
MING–CH'ING: **Tribute Student,** one of several variant references to students annually promoted into the National University (*t'ai-hsüeh, kuo-tzu chien*) at the dynastic capital from local Confucian Schools (*ju-hsüeh*) throughout the empire; most commonly called *kung-sheng*, q.v. BH: senior licentiate of the second class.

5870 *súi-lù tà-pǔ yīng-fáng chū-sè mín-chiàng tsǔng-kuǎn fǔ*
隨路打捕鷹房諸色民匠總管府
YÜAN: **Supervisorate-in-chief of Migratory Hunters, Falconers, and All Classes of Artisans,** organizational affiliation and functions not entirely clear, but apparently a central government agency headed by an Overseer (*ta-lu-hua-ch'ih*) and a Supervisor-in-chief (*tsung-kuan*) responsible for registering or otherwise keeping watch over persons of migratory occupations who by their nature were outside normal place-specific jurisdictions.

5871 *súi-shēn* 隨身
SUNG: **Escort,** prefix to the title of an official assigned to accompany a dignitary such as a Grand Councilor (*tsai-hsiang*) or a Prefect (*tz'u-shih*) in travel status. SP: *escorte*.

5872 *sùi-shìh* 遂士
CHOU: **District Judge,** 12 ranked as Ordinary Servicemen (*chung-shih*), members of the Ministry of Justice (*ch'iu-kuan*) with special responsibility for the administration of justice in the Districts (*sui*) beyond the immediate environs of the royal domain; cf. *hsiang-shih* (District Judge). CL: *prévôts de justice des districts extérieures*.

5873 *sùi-shīh* 遂師
CHOU: **District Preceptor,** 4 ranked as Junior Grand Masters (*hsia ta-fu*) and 8 as Senior Servicemen (*shang-shih*), members of the Ministry of Education (*ti-kuan*), half appointed for each 3 of the 6 Districts (*sui*) beyond the immediate environs of the royal domain; responsible for instruction, taking the census, assigning corvée duties, commanding militia, participating in various rituals, sharing in the settlement of litigations among the people; responsible to the Supervisors of Exterior Districts (*sui-jen*), supervised District Grand Masters (*sui ta-fu*). CL: *chefs des districts extérieures*.

5874 *sùi tà-fū* 遂大夫
CHOU: **District Grand Master,** one with rank as Ordinary Grand Master (*chung ta-fu*), member of the Ministry of Education (*ti-kuan*) serving as general administrative head for each of the 6 exterior Districts (*sui*) beyond the immediate environs of the royal domain; under the supervision of a designated District Preceptor (*sui-shih*), oversaw the moral and agrarian promotional efforts undertaken by the local heads of administrative units in his jurisdiction, from Townships (*hsien*) down to Neighborhoods (*lin*). Cf. *hsiang ta-fu*. CL: *préfet de district extérieur*.

5875 *sùng-hsùn* 誦訓
CHOU: **Travel Guide,** 2 ranked as Ordinary Servicemen (*chung-shih*) and 4 as Junior Servicemen (*hsia-shih*), mem-

bers of the Ministry of Education (*ti-kuan*) who accompanied the King on his travels and explained to him the history and mores of the areas through which he passed. CL: *lecteur démonstrateur.*

5876　*sùng-pàn shĭh* 送伴使
SUNG: **Commissioner-escort** for foreign visitors; organizational affiliation not clear, no doubt an ad hoc duty assignment for an appropriate official. SP: *commissaire chargé d'accompagner les visiteurs étrangers.*

5877　*szu*
See under the romanization *ssu.*

5878　*tà* 大
Used as·a prefix in titles to mean **Grand ...** or **...-in-chief**, as in Grand Master (*ta-fu*) and Commissioner-in-chief (*ta-shih*); normally not paired with a contrasting prefix such as *hsiao* (small, lesser) or *shao* (few, junior); rather, the difference most commonly is between a Commissioner-in-chief and an ordinary Commissioner (*shih*), or between a General-in-chief (*ta chiang-chün*) and an ordinary General (*chiang-chün*); not as prestigious as the prefix *shang* (upper, supreme). Also see under *t'ai.*

5879　*tà ch'án-tsūng* 大禪宗
CH'ING: unofficial reference to the **Central Buddhist Registry** (*seng-lu ssu*) in the central government.

5880　*tà chăng-hàn* 大掌翰
CH'ING: unofficial reference to a clerical **Secretary** (*chung-shu*) in the Grand Secretariat (*nei-ko*).

5881　*tà chăng-hóu* 大長侯
CH'ING: unofficial reference to a **Company Commander** (*ch'ien-tsung*) in the Chinese military establishment called the Green Standards (*lu-ying*).

5882　*tà-chăng kūng-chŭ* 大長公主
Princess Supreme: throughout imperial history the standard designation of a paternal aunt of an Emperor. RR+SP: *grande princesse impériale aînée.* P69.

5883　*tà chăng-lù* 大掌籙
CH'ING: unofficial reference to the **Central Taoist Registry** (*tao-lu ssu*) in the central government.

5884　*tà chăng-shū* 大掌樞
T'ANG–CH'ING: unofficial reference to the **Ministry of War** (*ping-pu*) or to a **Minister of War** (*ping-pu shang-shu*).

5885　*tà chăng-shù* 大掌術
CH'ING: unofficial reference to a **Principal of a Prefectural Geomancy School** (*cheng-shu*).

5886　*tà ch'áng-ch'iū* 大長秋
(1) HAN–N-S DIV (San-kuo Wei): **Director of the Palace Domestic Service** (see *ch'ang-ch'iu chien*), a eunuch agency primarily responsible for administering the household of the Empress; in 144 B.C. superseded the title *chiang-hsing* (Empress's Usher), then in 18 B.C. superseded the title *chan-shih* (Supervisor of the Household) as the ranking post on the Empress's staff; through Later Han had a substantial group of eunuch subordinates, including Directors (*ling*); rank 2,000 bushels. HB: grand prolonger of autumn. (2) CH'ING: unofficial reference to a **palace eunuch** (*t'ai-chien, huan-kuan*).

5887　*tà ch'áng-pó* 大常伯
CH'ING: **Executive Attendant-in-chief,** unofficial reference to a Minister (*shang-shu*) of any of the Six Ministries (*liu pu*). Also see *t'ai ch'ang-po* (Grand Executive Attendant).

5888　*tà-ch'én* 大臣
CH'ING: **Grand Minister,** common suffix to the duty assignments of Imperial Princes (*ch'in-wang*) and other nobles and dignitaries who served as senior officials of the Imperial Household Department (*nei-wu fu*), e.g., *tsung-kuan nei-wu fu ta-ch'en* (Grand Minister Supervisor of the Imperial Household Department); also a common generic reference to such officials.

5889　*tà ch'éng-hsiàng* 大丞相
N-S DIV, YÜAN: **Grand Counselor-in-chief, Grand Councilor-in-chief:** used irregularly, apparently to give special prestige to a favored Counselor-in-chief (*ch'eng-hsiang*) or Grand Councilor (*ch'eng-hsiang, tsai-hsiang*). P2, 4.

5890　*tà-chí* 大棘
CH'ING: lit., great jujube tree: unofficial reference to a **Chief Minister** (*ch'ing*) **of the Court of Judicial Review** (*ta-li ssu*); see *chi-shu.*

5891　*tà-chì* 大計
Great Reckoning. (1) CHOU: an evaluation of officials reportedly conducted every 3rd year. (2) MING–CH'ING: a general evaluation of all officials, referring primarily to the Outer Evaluation (*wai-ch'a*) of officials on duty outside the capital, conducted regularly every 3rd year, but sometimes referring also to the Capital Evaluation (*ching-ch'a*) of officials serving in the capital, which was conducted less regularly in Ming, more or less in a 6-year cycle, and regularly in a 3-year cycle in Ch'ing. These were evaluations in addition to merit ratings (*k'ao*) given individual officials in separate cycles. Every month each District Magistrate (*chih-hsien*) submitted a status report on officials in his jurisdiction to his Prefect (*chih-fu*); every year each Prefect submitted a consolidated status report to provincial authorities; and every 3rd year the Grand Coordinator or Provincial Governor (both *hsün-fu*), in Ming acting together with the Censorate's Regional Inspector (*hsün-an yü-shih*) in his Province, submitted a consolidated provincial personnel report. This was then supplemented with other information in the files of the Ministry of Personnel (*li-pu*) and the Censorate (*tu ch'a-yüan*), which joined in making recommendations concerning the promotion, demotion, reassignment, transfer, dismissal, etc., of provincial officials who had been summoned to the capital in thousands for the event. These evaluations focused on instances of malfeasance or shortcomings in 8 specific categories: avarice, cruelty, frivolity or instability, inadequacy, senility, ill health, weariness, and inattentiveness. Each official summoned to the capital for the triennial evaluations was required to submit in advance a self-evaluation that was taken into account in deliberations by the Ministry and the Censorate.

5892　*tà chĭ-chièn* 大給諫
CH'ING: unofficial reference to a *chi-shih-chung* (**Supervising Secretary, Supervising Censor**).

5893　*tà chí-mù* 大畿牧
CH'ING: unofficial reference to the **Governor** (*yin*) of Shun-t'ien **Prefecture,** site of the dynastic capital.

5894　*tà-chiā* 大家
Your Majesty: from the era of N-S Division, one of the terms irregularly used for the Emperor in direct address.

5895　*tà-chiàng* 大匠
SUI–SUNG: **Director of the Directorate for the Palace Buildings** (*chiang-tso chien*), replaced intermittently in Sui and T'ang by *ling* and *chien;* rank 3a2 in T'ang. RR: *grand artisan.* SP: *chef de la direction des travaux.*

5896 *tà-chiàng ch'īng* 大匠卿
N-S DIV (Liang, Ch'en): **Chief Minister for the Palace Buildings,** from 508 the official variant of *chiang-tso ta-chiang* (Chamberlain for the Palace Buildings). P14.

5897 *tà chiàng-chün* 大將軍 or *ta-chiang*
General-in-chief: throughout history a designation of military officers in command of armies; more prestigious than General (*chiang, chiang-chün*) alone, less prestigious than Generalissimo (*shang chiang-chün*); location- or task-specific prefixes should be noted. HB: general-in-chief. RR+SP: *grand général.*

5898 *tà chiàng-chün fǔ* 大將軍府
Headquarters (or Command) of the General-in-chief, an ad hoc name used from Han on during military campaigns. Cf. *chün-fu.* RR: *administration du grand général.*

5899 *tà-chiēn* 大監
SUI-YÜAN: occasional variant of *chien* (Director). Distinguish from the Ming-Ch'ing eunuch title *t'ai-chien.* RR+SP: *grand directeur.*

5900 *tà-chièn* 大諫
T'ANG–SUNG: unofficial reference to a **Grand Master of Remonstrance** (*chien-i ta-fu*).

5901 *tà chiēn-pù* 大監部
SUI: **Waterways Supervisor,** an official responsible for constructing a transport canal connecting the dynastic capital near modern Sian with the Yellow River; apparently unrelated to the Directorate of Waterways (*tu-shui chien*).

5902 *tà chíh-chǐh* 大直指
MING–CH'ING: unofficial reference to an **Investigating Censor** (*chien-ch'a yü-shih*), most particularly to one on duty assignment as **Ward-inspecting Censor** (*hsün-ch'eng yü-shih*) in the dynastic capital. See *chih-chih.*

5903 *tà chìh-tsūng* 大秩宗
CH'ING: unofficial reference to a **Minister of Rites** (*lǐ-pu shang-shu*). See *chih-tsung.*

5904 *tà chīn-wú* 大金吾
MING: unofficial reference in late Ming to the **Guard Commander** (*chih-hui shih*) of the Imperial Bodyguard (*chin-i wei*). See *chin-wu, chih chin-wu.*

5905 *tà chīng-chào* 大京兆
MING–CH'ING: unofficial reference to the **Governor** (*yin*) **of Shun-t'ien Prefecture,** site of the dynastic capital after 1420. See *ching-chao.*

5906 *tà chiǔ ch'īng* 大九卿
MING–CH'ING: **Nine Greater Chief Ministers,** collective reference to the heads of the Six Ministries (*liu pu*), the Censorate (*tu ch'a-yüan*), the Court of Judicial Review (*ta-li ssu*), and the Office of Transmission (*t'ung-cheng ssu*); Ch'ing usage not consistent. Cf. *chiu ch'ing, hsiao chiu ch'ing.*

5907 *tà-chiù lìng* 大廄令
HAN: **Director of the Palace Stable,** one of numerous subordinates of the Chamberlain for the Palace Stud (*t'ai-p'u*), rank 600 bushels. HB: prefect of the great stables. P31.

5908 *tà ch'iū-t'ái* 大秋臺
T'ANG–CH'ING: unofficial reference to the **Ministry of Justice** (*hsing-pu*). Cf. *ch'iu-kuan.*

5909 *tà chiūng-pó* 大冏伯
CH'ING: unofficial reference to the **Chief Minister** (*ch'ing*) **of the Court of the Imperial Stud** (*t'ai-p'u ssu*).

5910 *tà-chōu* 大舟 or *tà-chōu ch'īng* 卿
N-S DIV (Liang)–SUI: **Chamberlain for Waterways,** official variant of *tu-shui shih* (Commissioner for Waterways). P14, 17, 59.

5911 *tà chōu-mù* 大州牧
CH'ING: unofficial reference to a **Chief of Police** (*li-mu*) in an Independent Department (*chih-li chou*).

5912 *tà chōu-mù* 大州幕
CH'ING: unofficial reference to a **Department Magistrate** (*chih-chou*) of an Independent Department (*chih-li chou*).

5913 *tà-chù* 大祝
CHOU: **Senior Supplicator,** 4 ranked as Junior Grand Masters (*hsia ta-fu*) and 8 as Senior Servicemen (*shang-shih*), members of the Ministry of Rites (*ch'un-kuan*) who prayed for the ruler's good fortune, invoked the spirits during state sacrificial ceremonies, etc.; cf. *hsiao-chu, t'ai-chu.* CL: *grand officier des prières, grand invocateur.*

5914 *tà-chù* 大著
SUNG: **Senior Writer,** counterpart in the earliest Sung years of the later *chu-tso lang* (Editorial Director in the Palace Library, *pi-shu sheng*); cf. *hsiao-shu.* P23.

5915 *tà chǔ-k'ǎo* 大主考
CH'ING: unofficial reference to the **Principal Examiner** (*cheng k'ao-kuan*) in a Provincial Examination (*hsiang-shih*) in the civil service recruitment examination sequence.

5916 *tà chù-kuó* 大柱國
Grand Pillar of State: throughout history a common unofficial reference to paramount executive officials in the central government such as Counselors-in-chief (*ch'eng-hsiang*), Grand Councilors (*tsai-hsiang*), and Grand Secretaries (*ta hsüeh-shih*); in Ming also referred to a provincial-level Grand Coordinator (*hsün-fu*); cf. *chu-kuo, shang chu-kuo.*

5917 *tà chù-shǐh* 大柱史
MING–CH'ING: unofficial reference to a Censor (*yü-shih*) on duty assignment as **Regional Inspector** (*hsün-an yü-shih*).

5918 *tà chù-shíh* 大柱石
CH'ING: lit., great pillar stone: unofficial reference to a **Grand Secretary** (*ta hsüeh-shih*).

5919 *tà chù-tsò* 大著作
Imperial Editor. (1) N-S DIV: occasional variant of *chu-tso lang* (Editorial Director in the Palace Library, *pi-shu sheng*). P23. (2) CH'ING: unofficial reference to the Chancellor (*hsüeh-shih*) of the Hanlin Academy (*han-lin yüan*).

5920 *tà chǔ-yīn* 大主禋
CH'ING: lit., great master of sacrifices: unofficial reference to the *tz'u-chi ssu* (**Bureau of Sacrifices** in the Ministry of Rites, *lǐ-pu*).

5921 *tà ch'ú-tuān* 大儲端
CH'ING: lit., great exemplar for the Heir Apparent: unofficial reference to the *chan-shih* (**Supervisor of the Household of the Heir Apparent**).

5922 *tà ch'uán-chīng* 大傳經
CH'ING: lit., great transmitter of the classics: unofficial reference to an **Instructor** (*chiao-shou*), the head of a Confucian School (*ju-hsüeh*) at the Prefecture (*fu*) level.

5923 *tà chūng-ch'éng* 大中丞
MING–CH'ING: lit., great palace aide (to the Censor-in-chief); see *yü-shih chung-ch'eng:* unofficial reference to a **Censor-in-chief** (*tu yü-shih*), particularly one serving as a provincial-level **Grand Coordinator** (*hsün-fu*).

5924 *tà chūng-hù* 大中護
CH'ING: lit., great protector of the palace: unofficial reference to a **Mentor** (*shu-tzu*) in the Household Administration of the Heir Apparent (*chan-shih fu*).

5925 *tà chǔng-tsǎi* 大冢宰
Grand Minister of State. (1) N-S DIV (Chou): from 556 head of the Ministry of State (*t'ien-kuan*), considered the paramount executive official of the central government, comparable to a Counselor-in-chief (*ch'eng-hsiang*) or Grand Councilor (*tsai-hsiang*) of other times. P2. (2) MING–CH'ING: unofficial reference to a Minister of Personnel (*li-pu shang-shu*). See *chung-tsai*.

5926 *tà ch'üān-héng* 大銓衡
CH'ING: lit., great assayer and measurer: unofficial reference to the **Minister of Personnel** (*li-pu shang-shu*).

5927 *tà-chüěh shǒu* 大角手
T'ANG: **Blower of the Great Horn,** designation of 600 soldiers in the Imperial Insignia Guard (*chin-wu wei*). RR: *joueur de grande corne*.

5928 *tà chūn-chī* 大軍機
CH'ING: unofficial reference to a **Grand Minister of State.** (*chün-chi ta-ch'en*), i.e., a member of the Council of State (*chün-chi ch'u*).

5929 *tà chùn-hóu* 大郡侯
Lit., great Commandery Marquis: unofficial reference throughout history to a **Commandery Governor** (*chün-shou*) or to a **Prefect** (*chih-chou, chih-fu*).

5930 *tà chùn-pó* 太郡伯
Lit., great Commandery Earl: unofficial reference throughout history to a **Commandery Governor** (*chün-shou*) or to a **Prefect** (*chih-chou, chih-fu*).

5931 *tà èrh-hóu* 大貳侯
CH'ING: lit., great secondary Marquis: unofficial reference to a **Vice Prefect** (*t'ung chih-fu, t'ung-chih*).

5932 *tà fān-fǔ* 大藩府
SUNG: **Great Border Prefecture,** generic reference to a specific group of large and strategic Prefectures (*chou*): Ching-chao, Ch'eng-tu, T'ai-yüan, Ching-nan, Chiang-ning, Yen-chou, T'ai-chou, Yangchow, Hangchow, T'an-chou, Kuang-chou, and the Prefectures in which N. Sung's 3 auxiliary capitals were located. SP: *grande préfecture*.

5933 *tà fān-hóu* 大藩侯
MING–CH'ING: lit., great border Marquis: unofficial reference to a **Provincial Administration Commissioner** (*pu-cheng shih*).

5934 *tà-fāng* 大方
HAN: appeared in the last century of Later Han as a title used in at least one rebel movement, apparently in the sense of big boss (*ta*) of a region (*fang*), or perhaps boss of a large region; traditionally equated with **General** (*chiang-chün*). See *hsiao-fang*.

5935 *tà fāng-pó* 大方伯
MING–CH'ING: lit., great regional Earl: unofficial reference to a **Provincial Administration Commissioner** (*pu-cheng shih*).

5936 *tà fāng-yüèh* 大方岳
CH'ING: lit., great regional peak: unofficial reference to a **Provincial Administration Commissioner** (*pu-cheng shih*).

5937 *tà fēn-hūi* 大分麾
CH'ING: lit., great detached flag: unofficial reference to an **Assistant Regional Commander** (*ts'an-chiang*) or to a

Brigade Commander (*yu-chi*) in the Chinese military establishment called the Green Standards (*lu-ying*).

5938 *tà-fèng* 大鳳
SUNG: lit., great phoenix: unofficial reference to a **Hanlin Academician** (*han-lin hsüeh-shih*).

5939 *tà-fū* 大夫
(1) **Grand Master:** throughout history found as a suffix in many titles of relative importance, both functional such as Censor-in-chief (*yü-shih ta-fu*) and honorific such as Specially Promoted Grand Master for Splendid Happiness (*t'e-chin kuang-lu ta-fu*); see under prefixed terms. (2) CHOU: **Grand Master,** designation of the 2nd highest category of officials, below Minister (*ch'ing*) and above Serviceman (*shih*); subdivided into 3 grades: Senior Grand Master (*shang ta-fu*), Ordinary (*chung*) Grand Master, and Junior (*hsia*) Grand Master. CL: *préfet*. (3) CH'IN–HAN: **Grandee of the Fifth Order,** the 16th highest of 20 titles of honorary nobility (*chüeh*) conferred on meritorious subjects. HB: grandee. P65. (4) HAN–N-S DIV: **Grand Master,** found on the administrative staffs of Princely Establishments (*wang-fu*), functions not clear; rank =600 bushels in Han. P69. (5) T'ANG: **Grand Master,** from 662 to 671 the official variant title of various mid-level posts in the central government, including Directors (*lang-chung*) of all Bureaus (*ssu*) in the Six Ministries (*liu pu*), Vice Ministers (*shao-ch'ing*) in the Nine Courts (*chiu ssu*), various Aides or Assistant Directors (*ch'eng*), and Chief Stewards (*feng-yü*) of the Services (*chü*) that constituted the Palace Administration (*tien-chung sheng*). (6) SUNG: **Grand Master,** briefly in the early 1100s the official variant of *shih* (Commissioner) of the Palace Audience Gates (*shang ko-men*). P33.

5940 *tà-fǔ* 大府
(1) CHOU: **Grand Treasurer,** 2 ranked as Junior Grand Masters (*hsia ta-fu*) and 8 as Junior Servicemen (*hsia-shih*), members of the Ministry of State (*t'ien-kuan*) who supervised the palace storehouses and accepted payments of taxes, tribute, and fees. Traditionally considered comparable to the Han dynasty Chamberlain for the National Treasury (*ta ssu-nung*). CL: *grand trésorier*. (2) N-S DIV (Liang, Ch'en): **Chamberlain for the Palace Bursary,** responsible for supervising marketplace transactions in the dynastic capital city, probably among other things not specified, such as collecting fees and taxes from merchants. P62. Cf. *t'ai-fu*.

5941 *tà-fū àn* 大夫案
SUNG: **Section for Grand Masters,** a subdivision of the Senior Military Appointments Process (*shang-shu yu-hsüan*) in the Ministry of Personnel (*li-pu*); specific functions not clear. SP: *service des nominations des commissaires militaires*.

5942 *tà-fū chiēn* 大夫監
CHOU: **Grand Master Inspector,** a delegate of the King assigned to visit and inspect the domain of a Feudal Lord (*chu-hou*).

5943 *tà fǔ-fǔ* 大黼黻
CH'ING: lit., great (provider of) embroidered sacrificial gowns: unofficial reference to a **Superintendent of Imperial Silk Manufacturing** (*chih-tsao chien-tu*).

5944 *tà-hàn chiāng-chūn* 大漢將軍
MING: **Elite Guard,** designation of 1,500 members of the Imperial Bodyguard (*chin-i wei*) who attended the Emperor on all ceremonial occasions; chosen for their tallness.

5945 *tà hàn-pó* 大翰博
CH'ING: lit., abbreviation of great Hanlin Academy (*han-lin yüan*) Erudite (*po-shih*): unofficial reference to **Erudite**

of the Five Classics (*wu-ching po-shih*), a title awarded hereditarily to direct male descendants of noted Confucians or paragons of Confucian virtues.

5946   *tà hó-kēng* 大和羹
CH'ING: lit., great (provider of) mild broth: unofficial reference to a **Vice Minister** (*shao-ch'ing*) **of the Court of Imperial Entertainments** (*kuang-lu ssu*).

5947   *tà húng-lú* 大鴻臚
HAN–N-S DIV: lit., great maintainer of orderliness: **Chamberlain for Dependencies,** rank 2,000 bushels in Han, rank 3 in N. Wei, one of the Nine Chamberlains (*chiu ch'ing*) in the central government; responsible for supervising the receptions of Princes (*wang*) and Marquises (*hou*) at the capital, keeping genealogical records of nobles not of the imperial lineage, handling diplomatic relations with non-Chinese leaders, and ordering the conduct of all officials and visitors in imperial audiences. Initiated in 104 B.C. to supersede the Director of the Messenger Office (*ta-hsing ling*); in Former Han included among his subordinates a Director of Interpreters (*i-kuan ling*), a Director of Fire Renewal (*pieh-huo ling*), and a reconstituted Director of the Messenger Office (as above); in addition, supervised all Liaison Hostels for Commanderies (*chün-ti*) established in the capital. In Later Han some of these subordinates were redistributed to other agencies or downgraded to minor posts, but the Chamberlain remained an important part of the central government until reorganizations in Liang and N. Wei transformed the post into the Chief Minister (*ch'ing*) of the Court for Dependencies (*hung-lu ssu*). HB: grand herald. P11, 17, 33.

5948   *tà-hsǐ tsūng-yīn yüàn* 大禧宗禋院
YÜAN: **Office for Religious Administration,** a central government agency that supervised state-supported religious institutions such as temples and monasteries, monitoring the uses of their lands, endowment funds, and dependents; staffing not clear.

5949   *tà hsiàng-t'ái* 大相臺
MING–CH'ING: unofficial reference to an Investigating Censor (*chien-ch'a yü-shih*) on duty assignment as a **Regional Inspector** (*hsün-an yü-shih*).

5950   *tà-hsiǎo tiāo-mù chú* 大小彫木局
YÜAN: **Large and Small Woodworking Service,** one of numerous craft workshops under the Supervisorate-in-chief of Metal Workers and Jewelers (*chin-yü jen-chiang tsung-kuan fu*); probably 2 Services, one Large and one Small.

5951   *tà hsièn-ch'iēn* 大憲僉
MING–CH'ING: lit., assistant to the great (enforcer of) fundamental laws: unofficial reference to a provincial-level **Assistant Surveillance Commissioner** (*an-ch'a ch'ien-shih*).

5952   *tà hsièn-fù* 大憲副
MING–CH'ING: lit., vice great (enforcer of) fundamental laws: unofficial reference to a provincial-level **Surveillance Vice Commissioner** (*an-ch'a fu-shih*).

5953   *tà hsièn-nà* 大獻納
Lit., great presenter-submitter. (1) T'ANG: unofficial reference to a **Petition Box Commissioner** (*hsien-na shih*). (2) MING–CH'ING: unofficial reference to a **Transmission Commissioner** (*t'ung-cheng shih*).

5954   *tà hsièn-t'ái* 大憲臺
MING–CH'ING: lit., great pavilion of fundamental laws: unofficial reference to a nominal senior official of the Censorate (*tu ch'a-yüan*) serving as a Ming **Grand Coordi-**

nator or a Ch'ing **Provincial Governor** (both *hsün-fu*) or to an Investigating Censor (*chien-ch'a yü-shih*) serving as **Regional Inspector** (*hsün-an yü-shih*).

5955   *tà-hsíng* 大行
HAN–N-S DIV: **Messenger Office,** headed by a Director (*ling*) with rank of 600 bushels, at least one Aide (*ch'eng*), and a staff of Messengers (*hsing-jen*); maintained communications with enfeoffed Princes (*wang*) and Marquises (*hou*) and with non-Chinese leaders. Superseded the *tien-k'o* (Chamberlain for Dependencies) in 144 B.C., then in 104 B.C. superseded by the *ta hung-lu* (also Chamberlain for Dependencies), became one of its subsidiary units; perhaps did not endure beyond Chin times. HB: grand usher. P17.

5956   *tà-hsíng chìh-lǐ ch'éng* 大行治禮丞
HAN: **Aide for Ceremonial in the Messenger Office;** see *ta-hsing*.

5957   *tà hsíng-jén* 大行人
(1) CHOU: **Senior Messenger,** 2 ranked as Ordinary Grand Masters (*chung ta-fu*), members of the Ministry of Justice (*ch'iu-kuan*) who made arrangements for the visits and receptions of Feudal Lords (*chu-hou*) at the royal court; assisted by Junior Messengers (*hsiao hsing-jen*). CL: *grand voyageur*. (2) CH'ING: unofficial reference to the **Chief Minister** (*ch'ing*) **of the Court of State Ceremonial** (*hung-lu ssu*). Cf. *hsing-jen, hsing-jen ssu*.

5958   *tà hsíng-t'ái* 大行臺
N-S DIV: abbreviation of *shang-shu ta hsing-t'ai* (**Branch Department of State Affairs**).

5959   *tà-hsū* 大胥
CHOU: **Senior Dancing Master,** 4 ranked as Ordinary Servicemen (*chung-shih*), members of the Ministry of Rites (*ch'un-kuan*) who taught the children of central government officials the art of court dancing and helped direct the music and dance aspects of state ceremonies; assisted by Junior Dancing Masters (*hsiao-hsü*). CL: *grand aide*.

5960   *tà-hsüǎn* 大選
CH'ING: **Regular Selection,** part of the personnel appointment process conducted by the Ministry of Personnel (*li-pu*); principally referred to the consideration for appointments of new Metropolitan Graduates (*chin-shih*) and Provincial Graduates (*chü-jen*); normally conducted in even months, in contrast to Expedited Selection (*chi-hsüan*) normally conducted in odd months. Also known as *cheng-hsüan*.

5961   *tà-hsüéh* 大學
Variant of *t'ai-hsüeh* (**National University**).

5962   *tà hsüéh-shìh* 大學士
(1) T'ANG–YÜAN: **Grand Academician,** prefixed with the name of some Hall (*tien, ko*) in the palace such as the Hall of Scholarly Worthies (*chi-hsien tien*); a designation awarded to Grand Councilors (*tsai-hsiang*) suggesting a concurrent function, but actually given to enhance prestige without adding any functions. RR+SP: *grand lettré*. P3, 25. (2) MING: **Grand Academician,** one, rank 5a, shared with Mentors (*shu-tzu*) seniority in each of the 2 Secretariats of the Heir Apparent (*ch'un-fang*); a general counselor in charge of the Heir Apparent's communications to the throne. P26. (3) MING–CH'ING: **Grand Secretary,** officials of great power in the central government, comparable to Grand Councilors (*tsai-hsiang*) of earlier dynasties; originated in 1382 as a new category of posts in the Hanlin Academy (*han-lin yüan*), rank 5a, with the specific duties

of tutoring the Heir Apparent and assisting the Emperor with his paperwork, which had greatly increased after reorganizations of 1380 that included abolition of the Grand Councilorship. In the early 1400s their influence increased, and from 1424 they were regularly given concurrent nominal appointments as Vice Ministers (*shih-lang*) or Ministers (*shang-shu*) in the Six Ministries (*liu pu*), which raised their ranks to the level of 3a or 2a; in addition, they came to be given even more prestigious status in the officialdom with top-echelon but non-functioning posts among the Three Dukes (*san kung*) or Three Solitaries (*san ku*), with 1a or 1b rank. Each Grand Secretary was assigned to a Hall in the palace, e.g., Grand Secretary of the Hall of Military Glory (*wu-ying tien ta hsüeh-shih*); their numbers varied, normally in the range from 3 to 6, and their working procedures gradually stabilized under a Senior Grand Secretary (*shou-fu*) as recognized leader and decision-maker in the group. Their principal function came to be recommending imperial action on memorials and preparing edicts after an imperial decision was reached; they utilized the services of the Central Drafting Office (*chung-shu k'o*) but had no supporting staffs of their own. After the earliest years, appointees as Grand Secretaries came almost exclusively through a special channel from status as Metropolitan Graduates (*chin-shih*) in the civil service recruitment examination sequence into a series of positions in the Hanlin Academy, without ever having active service in regular administrative agencies, either in central or territorial administrations. Consequently, despite their nominal status as Ministers or Vice Ministers, which was intended to provide a linkage for them with the administrative hierarchy, Grand Secretaries inevitably came to be looked on as members of the Inner Court (*nei-t'ing, nei-ch'ao*) who were agents of the Emperor, not as leaders of the Outer Court (*wai-t'ing, wai-ch'ao*) comparable to Counselors-in-chief (*ch'eng-hsiang*) of antiquity; and from early in the 16th century they became focal points of controversies between the Inner and Outer Courts. Few Senior Grand Secretaries had successful, happy tenures. From the beginning the Grand Secretaries were referred to collectively as the *nei-ko* (lit., the inner or palace Halls), and by 1600 this term became at least a quasiofficial agency name, rendered as Grand Secretariat. In Ch'ing, after some institutional experimenting (see under *nei san yüan*, Three Palace Academies), the Grand Secretariat was formally constituted in 1658 as the paramount coordinating agency in the central government with a large staff headed by 2 Manchu and 2 Chinese Grand Secretaries, rank 1a, each nominally assigned to a palace Hall as in Ming times. Although the Grand Secretariat as an institution gradually yielded in influence to informal deliberative groups and eventually was formally subordinated to a Council of State (*chün-chi ch'u*) in 1730, individual Grand Secretaries remained prestigious and commonly served ex officio as members of the Council of State. P2.

5963 *tà hsün-hàn* 大訓翰
SUNG: lit., big counseling writing brush: unofficial reference to a member of the Hanlin Academy (*han-lin yüan*), hence **Hanlin Academician.**

5964 *tà hsün-hsüān* 大旬宣
CH'ING: lit., great thorough promulgator (?): unofficial reference to a **Provincial Administration Commissioner** (*pu-cheng shih*).

5965 *tà-ì* 大儀
Lit., great ritualist. (1) T'ANG: unofficial reference to a **Minister of Rites** (*lǐ-pu shang-shu*) or to the **Director** (*lang-*

chung) **of the Headquarters Bureau** (*lǐ-pu*) in the Ministry of Rites (also *lǐ-pu*). Also see *chung-i, hsiao-i, shao-i*. (2) SUNG: **Lady of Supreme Deportment,** from the late 990s a consort title, rank 1b, regularly awarded to surviving wives of deceased Emperors other than Empresses. (3) CH'ING: unofficial reference to the **Chief Minister** (*ch'ing*) **of the Court of Imperial Sacrifices** (*t'ai-ch'ang ssu*).

5966 *tà-ì* 大議
Great Court Conference: throughout imperial history an important assemblage of senior central government officials to consider a problem of policy and recommend a solution; distinguished from normal Court Conferences (*hui-i, t'ing-i*) by being presided over by the Emperor in person, or perhaps at times by an especially eminent surrogate.

5967 *tà-ì* 大醫
SUNG–CH'ING: **Grand Physician,** unofficial reference to a physician in palace service, such as a member of the Imperial Academy of Medicine (*t'ai-i yüan*).

5968 *tà ì-tsǎi* 大邑宰
CH'ING: lit., great steward of the fief: unofficial reference to a **District Magistrate** (*chih-hsien*).

5969 *tà-jén* 大人
N-S DIV (N. Wei): **Tribal Overseer,** originally 2 prefixed North and South, then 4, finally 8; responsible for supervising affairs of all tribes (*pu-lo*), i.e., presumably all non-Chinese groups within the domain. See *pa pu ta-jen*.

5970 *tà júng-pó* 大戎伯
CH'ING: lit., great military Earl: unofficial reference to a **Company Commander** (*ch'ien-tsung*) in the Chinese military establishment called the Green Standards (*lu-ying*).

5971 *tà-kuān* 達官
Lit., an official who had gained success. (1) Throughout history may be encountered in unofficial reference to an eminent official such as a Grand Councilor (*tsai-hsiang*), i.e., someone who had access to the ruler. (2) MING: **Mongol Official,** generic designation of Mongols who entered Ming service; apparently abbreviated from a Chinese transliteration of Tatar or some similar Mongol term.

5972 *tà-kuān lìng* 大官令
Variant of *t'ai-kuan ling* (**Provisioner**).

5973 *tà-kuān shǔ* 大官署
N-S DIV (N. Ch'i)–SUNG, MING–CH'ING: **Banquets Office,** one of a normal complement of 4 major subordinate Offices in the Court of Imperial Entertainments (*kuang-lu ssu*); headed by a Director (*ling* through Sung, *cheng* in Ming and Ch'ing), rank 7b2 in T'ang, 9a in Sung, 6b in Ming and Ch'ing; in Ch'ing one each Manchu and Chinese appointee. Responsible for preparing meals for the palace and the court, commonly supervising a huge staff of cooks, waiters, etc. In Sung subordinated to an intermediary supervising agency called the Imperial Kitchen (*yü-ch'u*), but limited to the preparation of sacrificial foodstuffs; the feeding of the palace and the court became the responsibility of the Food Service (*shang-shih chü*) of the Palace Administration (*tien-chung sheng*). No Banquets Office was established in Liao, Chin, or Yüan. RR: *office de la direction générale des banquets de l'empereur.* SP: *bureau d'approvisionnement.* P30.

5974 *tà-k'uéi* 大魁
T'ANG–CH'ING: lit., big chief: unofficial reference to a **Principal Graduate** (*chuang-yüan*) in the highest civil service recruitment examination.

5975 *tà kūng-fǔ* 大宮輔
Lit., great palace bulwark: common unofficial reference to the **Supervisor of the Household of the Heir Apparent** (*chan-shih*).

5976 *tà kūng-té shǐh* 大功德使
T'ANG: **Grand Commissioner for Merit and Virtue,** one appointed to supervise Buddhist establishments in the eastern half of the capital city, another appointed for the western half; see *kung-te shih*. RR: *grand commissaire pour la mérite et la vertu*. P17.

5977 *tà kūng-tsàn* 大宮贊
CH'ING: lit., great palace encourager: unofficial reference to an **Admonisher** (*tsan-shan*) in one of the 2 Secretariats of the Heir Apparent (*ch'un-fang*).

5978 *tà kūng-ts'áo* 大功曹
CH'ING: lit., great section for requisitioned labor: unofficial reference to a **Chief of Police** (*li-mu*) in an Independent Department (*chih-li chou*). See *kung-ts'ao*.

5979 *tà kūng-tuān* 大宮端
CH'ING: lit., great palace exemplar: unofficial reference to a **Supervisor of the Household of the Heir Apparent** (*chan-shih*).

5980 *tà kūng-yǔn* 大宮允
CH'ING: lit., great palace confidant: unofficial reference to a **Companion** (*chung-yün*) in one of the 2 Secretariats of the Heir Apparent (*ch'un-fang*).

5981 *tà kuó-ī* 大國醫
CH'ING: unofficial reference to the **Principal of a Prefectural Medical School** (*cheng-k'o*).

5982 *tá-lá-huǒ-ch'ìh* 答剌火赤
YÜAN: variant of *ta-lu-hua-ch'ih* (**Overseer**).

5983 *tà lǎo-yéh* 大老爺
CH'ING: lit., great old gentleman: **His Honor, Your Honor,** polite reference to, or form of direct address for, a Prefect (*chih-fu*), a Departmental Magistrate (*chih-chou*), or a District Magistrate (*chih-hsien*).

5984 *tà-lǐ* 大理
HAN–N-S DIV: intermittent official variant of *t'ing-wei* (**Chamberlain for Law Enforcement**). HB: grand judge.

5985 *tà-lǐ shǐh* 大禮使
SUNG: **Commissioner for Grand Ceremonials,** an ad hoc duty assignment for a court official; specific functions or occasions not clear. SP: *commissaire des grands cérémonies de sacrifice*.

5986 *tà-lǐ ssù* 大理寺
N-S DIV–CH'ING: **Court of Judicial Review,** an important central government agency, considered one of the Nine Courts (*chiu ssu*) and one of the Three Judicial Offices (*san fa-ssu*). Emerged out of the *ta-li* (Chamberlain for Law Enforcement) tradition, by N. Ch'i and Sui was a stable, large agency responsible for reviewing reports of judicial proceedings at all levels of territorial administration, recommending to the Emperor what cases involving major punishments should be returned for retrial, submitted to a gathering of court dignitaries for deliberation, or decided by the Emperor himself, and participating in important judicial proceedings at court along with the Censorate (*yü-shih t'ai, tu ch'a-yüan*) and the Ministry of Justice (*hsing-pu*). In general, the regular administrative hierarchy, under supervision of the Ministry, conducted trials and implemented sentences; the Censorate maintained surveillance over such activities for the purpose of impeaching officials for

misconduct; and the Court reviewed judicial proceedings from the point of view of law, justice, and equity. The Court was headed by a Chief Minister (*ch'ing*), rank 3b in T'ang, 4b in Sung, 4a in Chin, 3a in Ming and Ch'ing; in Ch'ing one Manchu and one Chinese appointee. Vice Ministers (*shao-ch'ing*) and Assistant Ministers (*ch'eng*) commonly supervised 2 Bureaus (*t'ing*) or Courts of Review (*ssu*), prefixed Left and Right, which had functional differences or divided the empire geographically into 2 jurisdictions, staffed with such officials as Rectifiers (*ssu-chih*) and Case Reviewers (*p'ing-shih*). In Yüan the Court existed only from 1283 to 1285, and then only as the redesignation of a Protectorate (*tu-hu fu*) headed by 4 Grand Protectors (*ta tu-hu*) who heard legal complaints submitted by Uighur and other non-Mongol nomadic peoples in the empire. RR+SP: *cour suprême de justice*. BH: court of judicature and revision. P22.

5987 *tà liáng-hsiàng* 大良相
Lit., great minister of excellence. (1) MING: unofficial reference to a **Commissioner** (*shih*) **of the Imperial Academy of Medicine** (*t'ai-i yüan*). (2) CH'ING: unofficial reference to a **Principal of a Prefectural Medical School** (*cheng-k'o*).

5988 *tà lién-hsièn* 大廉憲
CH'ING: lit., great (monitor of) integrity and fundamental laws: unofficial reference to a **Provincial Surveillance Commissioner** (*an-ch'a shih*).

5989 *tà lín-yá yüàn* 大林牙院
LIAO: **Secretarial Academy,** a unit of the Northern Administration (*pei-mien*), apparently responsible for documents in the Khitan language or documents concerning Khitan affairs; staffing not clear. See *lin-ya*. P23.

5990 *tà-lìng* 大令
CH'ING: unofficial reference to a **District Magistrate** (*chih-hsien*).

5991 *tá-lò-tá* 達勒達
YÜAN: variant of *ta-ta* (**Postal Relay Station**).

5992 *tà-lù chiù* 大輅廐
HAN: **Stable for Ceremonial Chariots,** one of numerous function-specific units under the Chamberlain for the Imperial Stud (*t'ai-p'u*). HB: coachhouses for great state chariots.

5993 *tá-lǔ-huā-ch'ìh* 達魯花赤
YÜAN: **Overseer,** Chinese transliteration of the Mongol word *daruhachi*, translated into Chinese as *chang-yin kuan* (Seal-holding Official); designation of Mongols who, with varying ranks, were appointed alongside the regular heads of many agencies in both central and territorial administrations as mandatory co-signers of all official documents issuing from the agencies; commonly hereditary posts for Mongols with status in the Mongol military hierarchy. The term appears in many variant transliterations.

5994 *tà mù-chèng* 大牧正
MING: lit., great pasturage director: unofficial reference to the **Supervisor** (*chien*) **of the Imperial Forest Park** (*shang-lin yüan*).

5995 *tà mù-ch'īn fǔ* 大睦親府
CHIN: lit., great office for the friendly treatment of relatives: the official variant of *ta tsung-cheng fu* (**Court of the Imperial Clan**) from 1206, to avoid an imperial name taboo; headed by a Supervisor (*p'an … shih*), no doubt of the imperial lineage. Cf. *kuang-ch'in mu-ch'in chai*. P1.

5996   *tà mù-chǚ* 大木局

YÜAN: **Carpentry Service,** a unit of the Palace Maintenance Office *(hsiu-nei ssu)*; headed by 7 Superintendents *(t'i-ling)*, apparently non-official specialists. P15.

5997   *tà nà-yén* 大納言

CH'ING: lit., great maker of statements (to the ruler): unofficial reference to the head of the Office of Transmission *(t'ung-cheng ssu)*, titled **Transmission Commissioner** *(t'ung-cheng shih)*. Cf. *na-yen.*

5998   *tà-nèi* 大內

(1) **Great Within,** from Han if not earlier a common quasi-official reference to the imperial palace, especially its innermost private quarters. (2) HAN: apparently a variant reference to the early Han **Chamberlain for the National Treasury** *(chih-su nei-shih)*, among whose subordinates were Palace Managers *(nei-kuan)* of Left and Right. HB: grand inner palace office.

5999   *tà nèi-shǐh* 大內史

·CH'ING: unofficial reference to a **Secretary** *(chung-shu)* on the staff of the Grand Secretariat *(nei-ko)*. See *nei-shih.*

6000   *tà-nèi tū-pù shǔ* 大內都部署

SUNG, LIAO: **Chief Administration Office of the Imperial Residence,** hierarchical status in Sung not clear; in Liao established in some auxiliary capitals as equivalents of Palace Service Offices *(nei-sheng ssu)* elsewhere; probably,staffed by eunuchs and headed by a Chief Administrator *(tu-pu)*, since some agencies were referred to as *fu-pu shu* (lit., vice administrator's office). SP: *directeur général du palais.* P49.

6001   *tà-núng* 大農

N-S DIV–SUNG: **Minister of Agriculture,** chief fiscal administrator in a Princely Establishment *(wang-fu)*, rank 6 in N. Wei, 8b2 in T'ang; in the era of N-S Division commonly appointed also in Marquisates *(hou-kuo)* and other neo-feudal fiefs. RR+SP: *directeur des travaux agricoles du fief d'un prince.* P69.

6002   *tà-núng lìng* 大農令

HAN: **Chamberlain for the National Treasury,** changed from *chih-su nei-shih* in 144 B.C., changed to *ta ssu-nung* in 104 B.C. HB: grand prefect of agriculture. P15.

6003   *tà-pài* 大拜

Lit., great (recipient of) homage: **His Eminence, Your Eminence:** throughout history a common unofficial reference to the most prestigious officials, e.g., Counselors-in-chief *(ch'eng-hsiang)*, Grand Councilors *(tsai-hsiang)*, and Grand Secretaries *(ta hsüeh-shih)* in direct address as well as in indirect reference.

6004   *tà pāng-pó* 大邦伯

CH'ING: lit., great Earl of the domain: unofficial reference to the **Governor** *(yin)* of Shun-t'ien Prefecture, site of the dynastic capital.

6005   *tà pǎo-lí* 大保釐

CH'ING: lit., abbreviation of Grand Guardian *(t'ai-pao)* of the Metropolitan Area *(chih-li)*: unofficial reference to the **Governor** *(yin)* of Shun-t'ien Prefecture, site of the dynastic capital.

6006   *tà-pǐ* 大比

Grand Competition. (1) CHOU: reportedly a search conducted every 3rd year by District Grand Masters *(hsiang ta-fu)* in collaboration with District Elders *(hsiang-lao)* to find worthy and capable men suitable for appointment to office. (2) T'ANG–CH'ING: quasiofficial reference to each sequence of civil service recruitment examinations, especially the qualifying examinations held at the prefectural or provincial levels.

6007   *tà pīn-k'ò* 大賓客

CHOU: **Grand Guest,** reference to a Feudal Lord *(chu-hou)* while visiting the royal court. CL: *grand visiteur.*

6008   *tà-pǔ* 大卜

CHOU: **Grand Diviner,** 2 ranked as Junior Grand Masters *(hsia ta-fu)*, members of the Ministry of Rites *(ch'un-kuan)* assisted by 4 Senior Servicemen *(shang-shih)* called Divination Masters *(pu-shih)*, 8 Ordinary Servicemen *(chung-shih)* called Diviners *(pu-jen)*, and 16 Junior Servicemen *(hsia-shih)*; specialists in tortoiseshell d·vination but in supervisory charge of other forms of divining, soothsaying, etc. Also called *t'ai-pu.* CL: *grand augure.*

6009   *tǎ-pǔ sǒ* 打捕所

YÜAN: **Hunting Office** under the Bureau of Military Affairs *(shu-mi yüan)*; apparently⤳ several field agencies, commonly prefixed with place-names plus *t'un-t'ien* (State Farm)—i.e., each in supervisory control of hunting on a specified domain of state lands; staffing not clear, probably ad hoc and transitory.

6010   *tǎ-pǔ tsǔng-kuǎn fǔ* 打捕總管府

YÜAN: **Area Command for Hunting** under the Bureau of Military Affairs *(shu-mi yüan)*; comparable to a Hunting Office *(ta-pu so)*, but more prestigious; presumably headed by an Area Commander-in-chief *(tsung-kuan)*.

6011   *tà-p'ú* 大僕

CHOU: **Royal Groom,** 2 ranked as Junior Grand Masters *(hsia ta-fu)*, members of the Ministry of War *(hsia-kuan)* who were principally responsible for assisting the King with his costume and serving as mounted escorts in all his public appearances. Cf. *p'u, t'ai-p'u.* CL: *assistant impérial.*

6012   *tà sān-ssū* 大三司

T'ANG: **Senior Three Judicial Offices,** designation of a court tribunal consisting of the heads of the Ministry of Justice *(hsing-pu)*, the Censorate *(yü-shih t'ai)*, and the Court of Judicial Review *(ta-li ssu)*. See *san ssu, hsiao san-ssu.*

6013   *tà shàng-shū* 大尚書

N-S DIV (Chin): **Grand Imperial Secretary,** probably not an official title but an unofficial reference to any Imperial Secretary *(shang-shu)*, or perhaps a reference to the Imperial Secretary of the Personnel Section *(li-pu ts'ao)*, who was usually the most esteemed of the group.

6014   *tà shàng-tsào* 大上造

CH'IN–HAN: lit., senior producer for the ruler (?): **Grandee of the Sixteenth Order,** the 5th highest of 20 titles of honorary nobility *(chüeh)* conferred on meritorious subjects. P65.

6015   *tà shào-fù* 大少府

CH'ING: unofficial reference to a **District Jailor** *(tien-shih)*.

6016   *tà-shèng fǔ* 大晟府

SUNG: **Imperial Music Bureau,** established from 1103 to 1120 in the Court of Imperial Sacrifices *(t'ai-ch'ang ssu)* to provide court music for ceremonial occasions; apparently staffed entirely with non-official specialists, headed by a Musician-in-chief *(ta ssu-yüeh)* with the assistance of a Grand Director of Music *(t'ai-yüeh ling)* who at other times was head of the Imperial Music Service *(t'ai-yüeh chü)*. The Bureau included 6 Sections *(an)*: Headquarters Section *(t'ai-yüeh an)*, Drum and Fife Section *(ku-ch'ui an)*, Banquet Music Section *(yen-an yüeh an)*, Regalia Section *(fa-wu an)*,

Miscellany Section (*chih-tsa an*), and Law Section (*chang-fa an*). SP: *bureau de musique impériale*. P10.

6017   *tà-shǐh* 大使
YÜAN–CH'ING: **Commissioner-in-chief** or simply **Commissioner**, common designation of the head of an agency, usually of low status; e.g., the Ming–early Ch'ing Auditing Office (*chien-shen k'u*) in the Ministry of Works (*kung-pu*), rank 9b; consistently seconded by a Vice Commissioner (*fu-shih*). Most common, and most likely to have relatively high rank, in Yüan; e.g., in the Music Office (*chiao-fang ssu*) of the Ministry of Rites (*lǐ-pu*), rank 4a.

6018   *tà-shǐh* 大史
CHOU: **Grand Scribe**, 2 ranked as Junior Grand Masters (*hsia ta-fu*) and 4 as Senior Servicemen (*shang-shih*), semi-autonomous advisers to the King attached to the Ministry of Rites (*ch'un-kuan*); responsible for informing Feudal Lords (*chu-hou*) and other territorial administrators of royal regulations and policies, monitoring the compliance of such dignitaries and reporting irregularities in their activities, maintaining duplicate copies of state documents sent to and received from them, preparing annalistic records of important state affairs, preparing the royal calendar, advising the King concerning astrological conditions for important sacrifices, funerals, and similar events, etc. Later Censors (*yü-shih*), Historiographers (*shih-kuan*), and state astrologers (see under *t'ai-shih ling*) were all considered to have had their origins in this office. Commonly also read *t'ai-shih*. CL: *grand annaliste*.

6019   *tà-shǐh* 大士
CHOU: **Jailor**, apparently a term in common use though it does not appear in the *Chou-li*.

6020   *tà-shǐh* 大師
CHOU: **Music Master**, 2 ranked as Junior Grand Masters (*hsia ta-fu*), members of the Ministry of Rites (*ch'un-kuan*) who took part in musical education at court and directed the musical aspects of state sacrifices, archery contests, troop reviews, funerals, etc. Cf. *t'ai-shih* (Grand Preceptor). CL: *grand instructeur*.

6021   *tà shìh-chǎng* 大世長
CH'IN–HAN: lit., senior member of his generation (?): **Grandee of the Eighteenth Order**, 3rd highest of 20 titles of honorary nobility (*chüeh*) awarded to meritorious subjects. P65.

6022   *tà-shǐh ch'én* 大使臣
SUNG: **Minister Commissioner-in-chief**, collective reference to military officers having prestige titles (*san-kuan*) of rank 8. SP: *grands envoyés militaires*.

6023   *tà shǒu-hóu* 大守侯
CH'ING: lit., great guardian Marquis: unofficial reference to an **Assistant Brigade Commander** (*shou-pei*) in the Chinese military forces called the Green Standards (*lu-ying*).

6024   *tà shù-chǎng* 大庶長
CH'IN–HAN: lit., great chief of a host, i.e., great militia leader: **Grandee of the Third Order**, the 18th highest of 20 titles of honorary nobility (*chüeh*) awarded to meritorious subjects.

6025   *tà shū-t'ái* 大樞臺
CH'ING: great pavilion of important matters: unofficial reference to a multi-Province **Governor-general** (*tsung-tu*).

6026   *tà-shuài* 大帥
Lit., great leader; see under *shuai*. (1) **Grand Marshal:** throughout history found occasionally as the ad hoc des-

ignation of a major military commander. (2) CH'ING: unofficial reference to a **Provincial Governor** (*hsün-fu*) or a multi-Province **Governor-general** (*tsung-tu*).

6027   *tà-shuài chiéh-tù shǐh* 大率節度使
T'ANG: **Grand Marshal Military Commissioner**, from the 780s the designation of a Military Commissioner (*chieh-tu shih*) who was also an active Prefect (*tz'u-shih*). P50.

6028   *tà ssū-ch'éng* 大司城
CH'ING: unofficial reference to a **Commander** (*chih-hui*) **of a Warden's Office** (*ping-ma chih-hui ssu*), a police-like agency responsible for one of the 5 Wards (*ch'eng*) into which the capital city was divided.

6029   *tà ssū-ch'éng* 大司成
Lit., great fulfiller or maturer; see *ssu-ch'eng*. (1) CHOU: variant of *shih-shih* (**Palace Master**). (2) T'ANG–CH'ING: from 662 to 670 the official variant of *chi-chiu* (**Chancellor** of the Directorate of Education, *kuo-tzu chien*); thereafter a common unofficial reference to a Chancellor. P34. (3) SUNG: **Rector**, from 1102 to c. 1111 head of the short-lived Preparatory Branch of the National University (*pi-yung*), considered to rank above Vice Ministers (*shih-lang*), rank 3b. SP: *grand recteur*. P34.

6030   *tà ssū-ch'ì* 大司戚
Lit., great supervisor of kinsmen: from Han on, a common unofficial reference to a **Chamberlain for the Imperial Clan** (*tsung-cheng*) or his later counterpart, a **Chief Minister** (*ch'ing*) of the Court of the Imperial Clan (*tsung-cheng ssu, tsung-jen fu*).

6031   *tà ssū-ch'ú* 大司儲
T'ANG–CH'ING: **Grand Storekeeper**, a common unofficial reference to an official of the Ministry of Revenue (*hu-pu*), especially its subordinate Granaries Bureau (*ts'ang-pu*) in T'ang–Sung times. Cf. *ssu-ch'u*.

6032   *tà ssū-fù* 大司賦
CH'ING: lit., great tax collector: unofficial reference to a **Salt Controller** (*yen-yün shih*).

6033   *tà ssū-hsièn* 大司憲
Lit., great keeper of the fundamental laws; cf. *ssu-hsien*. (1) T'ANG: from 662 to 671 the official variant of *yü-shih ta-fu* (**Censor-in-chief**). (2) CH'ING: unofficial reference to a **Censor-in-chief** (*tu yü-shih*), also to an **Investigating Censor** (*chien-ch'a yü-shih*) or a **Supervising Censor** (*chi-shih-chung*).

6034   *tà ssū-hsún* 大司巡
CH'ING: lit., great patroller: unofficial reference to a local **Police Chief** (*hsün-chien*).

6035   *tà ssū-í* 大司儀
CH'ING: lit., great ritualist: unofficial reference to a **Chief Minister** (*ch'ing*) **of the Court of State Ceremonial** (*hung-lu ssu*). Cf. *ssu-i* (Ceremonials Official).

6036   *tà ssū-k'òu* 大司寇
Lit., great manager of criminals: **Minister of Justice**. (1) CHOU: ranked as a Minister (*ch'ing*), head of the Ministry of Justice (*ch'iu-kuan*) in the royal government, responsible for publicizing and enforcing laws throughout the realm; principally aided by 2 Vice Ministers (*hsiao ssu-k'ou*) ranked as Ordinary Grand Masters (*chung ta-fu*) and 4 Chief Judges (*shih-shih*) ranked as Junior Grand Masters (*hsia ta-fu*); directed many other subordinates. CL: *grand préposé aux brigands, grand juge criminel*. (2) N-S DIV (Chou): head of the Ministry of Justice (as above), ranked as a Minister (*ch'ing*; 3a). P13. (3) T'ANG–CH'ING: may be encoun-

tered as an unofficial reference to a Minister of Justice (*hsing-pu shang-shu*).

6037 *tà ssŭ-k'ūng* 大司空
Grand Minister of Works. (1) CHOU: variant of *ssu-k'ung* (Minister of Works). (2) HAN: irregularly the title of one of the Three Dukes (*san kung*); superseded Censor-in-chief (*yü-shih ta-fu*) in 8 B.C., changed back to Censor-in-chief in 5 B.C., superseded Censor-in-chief again in 1 B.C., finally in A.D. 51 changed to Minister of Works (*ssu-k'ung*). HB: grand minister of works. P18. (3) N-S DIV (Chou): head of the Ministry of Works (*tung-kuan*), with rank as Minister (*ch'ing*; 3a). P14. (4) MING–CH'ING: unofficial reference to a Minister of Works (*kung-pu shang-shu*).

6038 *tà ssŭ-lǐ* 大司禮
N-S DIV (Chou): **Minister of Rites,** one of several titles used for the head of the Ministry of Rites (*ch'un-kuan*). Cf. *ssu-li*.

6039 *tà ssŭ-mǎ* 大司馬
Lit., great manager of mounts; cf. *ssu-ma*. (1) CHOU: **Minister of War,** ranked as a Minister (*ch'ing*), head of the Ministry of War (*hsia-kuan*), responsible for all military personnel and activities in the realm, including supervision of the 6 authorized royal Armies (*chün*); assisted principally by 2 Vice Ministers (*hsiao ssu-ma*) ranked as Ordinary Grand Masters (*chung ta-fu*) and 4 Cavalry Commanders of the Armies (*chün ssu-ma*) ranked as Junior Grand Masters (*hsia ta-fu*). CL: *grand commandant des chevaux*. (2) HAN–N-S DIV: **Commander-in-chief,** official variant of Defender-in-chief (*t'ai-wei*), one of the Three Dukes (*san kung*), from 119 B.C. to A.D. 51; from 87 B.C. was virtual regent. Perpetuated interchangeably with *t'ai-wei* as one of the Three Dukes in the era of N-S Division. HB: commander-in-chief. (3) N-S DIV (Chou): **Minister of War,** ranked as a Minister (*ch'ing*; 3a), head of the Ministry of War (*hsia-kuan*). P12. (4) CH'ING: unofficial reference to a **Minister of War** (*ping-pu shang-shu*).

6040 *tà ssŭ-mǎ ch'ē-chì chiāng-chūn*
大司馬車騎將軍
HAN: **Chariot and Horse General Serving as Commander-in-chief,** in Former Han a title used for a military officer who was virtual regent, dominating the central government.

6041 *tà ssŭ-mǎ tà chiāng-chūn* 大司馬大將軍
HAN: **General-in-chief Serving as Commander-in-chief,** in Former Han a title used for a military officer who was virtual regent, dominating the central government.

6042 *tà ssŭ-núng* 大司農
Lit., great supervisor of agriculture; cf. *ssu-nung*. (1) HAN–N-S DIV: **Chamberlain for the National Treasury,** initiated in 104 B.C. in a change from *ta-nung ling*; one of the Nine Chamberlains (*chiu ch'ing*) in the central government; had very broad responsibilities for the registration of agricultural lands, the collection of land taxes, the storage of state grain supplies, management of the state monopolies of such commodities as salt and iron, management of the state's price stabilization schemes including its Ever-normal Granaries (*ch'ang-p'ing ts'ang*), etc.; rank 2,000 bushels; assisted by an Aide (*ch'eng*) and numerous Directors (*ling*) of special-function agencies. In the era of N-S Division rank usually 3, sometimes 2; endured into N. Wei, but his responsibilities were steadily lost to other agencies, especially the emerging Ministry of Revenue (*min-pu, hu-pu*). HB: grand minister of agriculture. P6, 8. (2) T'ANG–

CH'ING: unofficial reference to a **Minister of Revenue** (*hu-pu shang-shu*).

6043 *tà ssŭ-núng ch'īng* 大司農卿
HAN–N-S DIV: common variant of *ta ssu-nung* (**Chamberlain for the National Treasury**). Cf. *ssu-nung ch'ing*.

6044 *tà ssŭ-núng ssŭ* 大司農司
YÜAN: **Grand Agricultural Administration,** a central government agency headed by an Overseer (*ta-lu-hua-ch'ih*) and 2 Chief Ministers (*ch'ing*); responsible for promoting agriculture, sericulture, irrigation, famine relief, local education, etc., and for managing some State Farms (*t'un-t'ien*). Continued by the Ming founder with one or more Chief Ministers, but quickly terminated; date not clear. Cf. *ssu-nung ssu*.

6045 *tà ssŭ-p'íng* 大司平
HAN: lit., great supervisor of peace: unofficial reference to a **Chamberlain for Law Enforcement** (*t'ing-wei*). Cf. *ssu-p'ing*.

6046 *tà ssŭ-p'ú* 大司僕
CH'ING: lit., great supervisor of coachmen: unofficial reference to a **Chief Minister** (*ch'ing*) **of the Court of the Imperial Stud** (*t'ai-p'u ssu*). Cf. *ssu-p'u*.

6047 *tà ssŭ-shàn* 大司膳
CH'ING: lit., great manager of delicacies: unofficial reference to a **Chief Minister** (*ch'ing*) **of the Court of Imperial Entertainments** (*kuang-lu ssu*). Cf. *ssu-shan*.

6048 *tà ssŭ-t'iēn* 大司天
CH'ING: unofficial reference to a **Director** (*chien-cheng*) **of the Directorate of Astronomy** (*ch'in-t'ien chien*).

6049 *tà ssŭ-ts'áo* 大司漕
CH'ING: lit., great supervisor of canal transport: unofficial reference to a **Director-general of Grain Transport** (*ts'ao-yün tsung-tu*).

6050 *tà ssŭ-tsú* 大司族
Lit., great supervisor of the lineage: throughout history an unofficial reference to a **Chamberlain for the Imperial Clan** (*tsung-cheng*) or his later counterpart, a **Chief Minister** (*ch'ing*) **of the Court of the Imperial Clan** (*tsung-cheng ssu, tsung-jen fu*).

6051 *tà ssŭ-tsūng* 大司宗
CH'ING: lit., great supervisor of the lineage: unofficial reference to an **Associate Director** (*tsung-cheng*) **of the Court of the Imperial Clan** (*tsung-jen fu*). Cf. *ssu-tsung*.

6052 *tà ssŭ-t'ú* 大司徒
Lit., great supervisor of disciples or followers: **Grand Minister of Education.** (1) CHOU: variant of *ssu-t'u* (Minister of Education). CL: *grand directeur des multitudes*. (2) HAN–N-S DIV: irregularly the title of one of the Three Dukes (*san kung*); revived in a change from *ch'eng-hsiang* (Counselor-in-chief) in 1 B.C., in A.D. 51 changed to *ssu-t'u* (Minister of Education); in the Three Kingdoms period reappeared irregularly (see under *ssu-t'u*). HB: grand minister of the masses. (3) YÜAN: an occasional variant of *ssu-t'u* (Minister of Education). P2, 6.

6053 *tà ssŭ-yǔ* 大司庾
Variant of *ta ssu-ch'u* (**Grand Storekeeper**).

6054 *tà ssŭ-yǔ* 大司籞
MING: lit., great manager of hedges: unofficial reference to a **Supervisor** (*chien*) **of the Imperial Forest Park** (*shang-lin yüan*).

6055 *tà ssū-yuán* 大司元
Lit., great supervisor of what is primary; cf. *ssu-yüan*. (1) CHOU: variant of *ssu-k'uai* (**Accountant**). (2) CH'ING: unofficial reference to a **Minister of Revenue** (*hu-pu shang-shu*).

6056 *tà ssū-yüèh* 大司樂
Musician-in-chief. (1) CHOU: 2 ranked as Ordinary Grand Masters (*chung ta-fu*), members of the Ministry of Rites (*ch'un-kuan*) who were in charge of all musical education and performances at court, supervising a corps of Music Masters (*yüeh-shih*). CL: *grand directeur de la musique*. (2) N-S DIV (Chou): number not clear; otherwise as in (1) above. P10. (3) SUNG: head of the short-lived Imperial Music Bureau (*ta-sheng fu*) established in 1103 under the Court of Imperial Sacrifices (*t'ai-ch'ang ssu*); unranked, probably a non-official specialist. SP: *chef du bureau musical*. P10. Cf. *ssu-yüeh*.

6057 *tà ssū-yǔn* 大司允
HAN–N-S DIV (S. Dyn.): unofficial reference to an **Arbiter** (*t'ing-wei p'ing*) on the staff of the Chamberlain for Law Enforcement (*t'ing-wei*).

6058 *tá-tá* 達達
YÜAN: **Postal Relay Station**, under supervision of the Office of Transmission (*t'ung-cheng yüan*); Chinese transliteration of a Mongolian word. P17.

6059 *tà t'ài-shǐh* 大太史
CH'ING: **Paramount Scribe:** unofficial reference to a member of the Hanlin Academy (*han-lin yüan*). See *ta-shih*, *t'ai-shih*.

6060 *tà-t'áng* 大堂
MING–CH'ING: **Headquarters**, a variant of *t'ang*, q.v.

6061 *tǎ-t'ào chǔ* 打套局
SUNG: **Scents Service**, a minor unit under the Court of the Imperial Treasury (*t'ai-fu ssu*). SP: *bureau de sélection du musc etc.*

6062 *tà t'è-lǐ-kǔn ssù* 大特哩袞司
LIAO: **Court of the Imperial Clan**, deriving from the Chinese transliteration *t'e-li-kun* of a Khitan word designating the head of the agency; counterpart of the T'ang–Sung *tsung-cheng ssu*. P1.

6063 *tà t'ì-yǐn ssū* 大惕隱司
LIAO: **Office of the Grand Clansman**, headed by a Grand Clansman (*t'i-yin*: Chinese transliteration of a Khitan word) or by an Administrator (*chih ... shih*); relationship with the Court of the Imperial Clan (*ta t'e-li-kun ssu*) not clear, possibly had more of a tutorial function relating to the Emperor and his family than an administrative function relating to the imperial clan; apparently transcended the organization of central government agencies in Northern and Southern Administrations (*pei-mien, nan-mien*), but is sometimes indicated to have been part of the Northern Administration.

6064 *tà tién-lǐ* 大典禮
CH'ING: lit., great manager of rituals: unofficial reference to a **Minister of Rites** (*li-pu shang-shu*) or a **Chief Minister** (*ch'ing*) **of the Court of Imperial Sacrifices** (*t'ai-ch'ang ssu*).

6065 *tà-t'iēn* 大天
T'ANG: unofficial reference to a **Minister of Personnel** (*li-pu shang-shu*); the lit. meaning, Great Heaven, probably suggested that the Minister of Personnel, by his control of or influence on appointments, had Heaven-like power over the fates of officials in their careers.

6066 *tà tǐng-hsiàng* 大鼎相
CH'ING: unofficial reference to a **Chief Minister** (*ch'ing*) **of the Court of Imperial Entertainments** (*kuang-lu ssu*).

6067 *tà-t'īng* 大廳
CH'ING: lit., great office: unofficial reference to an **Assistant Regional Commander** (*ts'an-chiang*) in the Chinese military forces called the Green Standards (*lu-ying*) when he was serving as head of the Command (*piao*) of a Provincial Governor (*hsün-fu*).

6068 *tà-tsǎi* 大宰
Grand Steward. (1) CHOU: variant of *chung-tsai* (**Minister of State**). (2) Throughout history may be encountered as an unofficial, archaic reference to a central government dignitary such as a Counselor-in-chief (*ch'eng-hsiang*) or a Grand Councilor (*tsai-hsiang*).

6069 *tà tsàn-chèng* 大賛政
CH'ING: lit., great participant in administration: unofficial reference to a **District Jailor** (*tien-shih*).

6070 *tà tsàn-chìh* 大賛治
CH'ING: lit., great participant in administration: unofficial reference to a **Vice Prefect** (*t'ung-chih*) or an **Assistant Prefect** (*t'ung-p'an*). Cf. *tsan-chih*.

6071 *tà tsàn-fǔ* 大賛府
CH'ING: lit., great assistant in the office (?): unofficial reference to a **Registrar** (*ching-li*) in a Provincial Administration Commission (*ch'eng-hsüan pu-cheng shih ssu*). Cf. *tsan-fu*.

6072 *tà tsàn-hóu* 大賛侯
CH'ING: lit., great assistant to the Marquis (?): unofficial reference to a **District Vice Magistrate** (*hsien-ch'eng*).

6073 *tà-ts'ān* 大參
MING–CH'ING: unofficial reference to an **Administration Vice Commissioner** (*ts'an-cheng*) in a Provincial Administration Commission (*ch'eng-hsüan pu-cheng shih ssu*). Cf. *shao-ts'an* (Assistant Administration Commissioner).

6074 *tà ts'ān-júng* 大參戎
CH'ING: great participant in military affairs: unofficial reference to an **Assistant Regional Commander** (*ts'an-chiang*) in the Chinese military forces called the Green Standards (*lu-ying*). Cf. *ts'an-jung*.

6075 *tà-ts'áo* 大漕
SUNG: lit., great transporter by water; unofficial reference to a **Supply Commissioner** (*fa-yün shih*). Cf. *ts'ao-ch'en*, *ts'ao-shuai*, *ts'ao-ssu*.

6076 *tà tsò-fù* 大佐賦
CH'ING: lit., great assistant in taxation; unofficial reference to a **Deputy Salt Controller** (*yün-t'ung*), an **Assistant Salt Controller** (*yün-fu*), or a **Second Assistant Salt Controller** (*yün-p'an*).

6077 *tà ts'ó-hóu* 大鹺侯
CH'ING: lit., great salt Marquis (?): unofficial reference to a **Salt Controller** (*yen-yün shih*) or a **Deputy Salt Controller** (*yün-t'ung*). Also see *ts'o-erh*.

6078 *tà ts'ó-hsièn* 大鹺憲
CH'ING: lit., great (enforcer) of salt laws: unofficial reference to a **Salt Controller** (*yen-yün shih*). Also see *ts'o-jen*.

6079 *tà-tsú chūn-chǔ* 大族軍主
SUNG: **Great Tribal Chief**, honorific title conferred on

heads of some southern and southwestern aboriginal tribes comprising more than 100 households. P72.

6080 *tà-tsūn* 大尊
N-S DIV (N. Dyn.): lit., greatly venerable: **His Majesty,** unofficial reference to the Emperor.

6081 *tà-tsūng* 大宗
Grand Clansman. (1) CHOU: variant of *tsung-po* (Minister of Rites). (2) Throughout history an occasional reference to the Emperor. (3) CH'ING: unofficial reference to the Minister of Rites (*lǐ-pu shang-shu*).

6082 *tà tsūng-chèng fǔ* 大宗正府
(1) CHIN: **Court of the Imperial Clan,** counterpart of the *tsung-cheng ssu* and *tsung-jen fu* of other periods; maintained genealogical records of the imperial clan and generally administered the affairs of its members; headed by a Supervisor (*p'an ... shih*), no doubt an eminent clansman. In 1206 renamed *ta mu-ch'in fu*. P1. (2) YÜAN: **High Court of Justice,** an autonomous agency of the central government headed by from 8 to 46 Judges (*cha-erh-hu-ch'i*); exercised judicial powers over the whole empire until c. 1312, thereafter remained the agency that dealt with all Mongols and all residents of the 2 principal Mongol capitals, Ta-tu (modern Peking) and Shang-tu (in modern Chahar), but yielded its jurisdiction over non-Mongols elsewhere to the Ministry of Justice (*hsing-pu*) and regular units of territorial administration. P1.

6083 *tà tsūng-chèng ssū* 大宗正司
SUNG: **Chief Office of Imperial Clan Affairs,** established in 1036 separate from but complementary to the traditional Court of the Imperial Clan (*tsung-cheng ssu*); headed by Imperial Princes (*ch'in-wang*) normally serving as Military Commissioners (*chieh-tu shih*) or in comparable posts, with the designations Administrator (*chih*) and Vice Administrator (*t'ung-chih*) prefixing the agency name. Whereas the Court routinely recorded genealogical data concerning the imperial clan, confirmed inheritances, etc., the Chief Office was specially charged with admonishing the clansmen about their responsibilities, hearing their grievances, exposing their transgressions, impeaching them for their misconduct, and in general recommending rewards and punishments for them; and it submitted annual reports to the Court accordingly. Civil officials served as Assistant Ministers (*ch'eng*) of the Chief Office and in its lesser administrative posts. From 1104 until the flight of the Sung court southward in the 1120s, the Chief Office had branch offices at Loyang and Yangchow (see *hsi-wai tsung-cheng ssu, nan-wai tsung-cheng ssu*). From c. 1000 it also maintained one and possibly more Hostels for Imperial Clansmen (*kuang-ch'in mu-ch'in chai*). SP: *grande cour des affaires de la famille impériale chargée d'instruction et de surveillance.* P1.

6084 *tà tsūng-chèng yüàn* 大宗正院
YÜAN–MING: quasiofficial variant of *t'ai tsung-cheng yüan* (**Office of the Imperial Clan**). Cf. *tsung-cheng ssu, tsung-jen fu*. P1.

6085 *tà tsǔng-chìh* 大總制
CH'ING: lit., great chief regulator: unofficial reference to a **Regional Commander** (*tsung-ping*) in the Chinese military forces called the Green Standards (*lu-ying*) or to a multi-Province **Governor-general** (*tsung-tu*). Cf. *tsung-chih*.

6086 *tà tsǔng-hóu* 大總侯
CH'ING: lit., great chief Marquis: unofficial reference to

a **Regional Commander** (*tsung-ping*) in the Chinese military forces called the Green Standards (*lu-ying*)

6087 *tà tsǔng-kuǎn fǔ* 大總管府
SUI–T'ANG: **Superior Area Command,** the headquarters of a Commander-in-chief (*ta tsung-kuan*) appointed in a frontier zone or some other strategic area, with a jurisdiction commonly called a Circuit (*tao*). In 624 the names were changed to *ta tu-tu fu* and *ta tu-tu*, but till 649 the earlier names continued to be used when military forces were on active campaign. See *tsung-kuan fu*. RR (*ta tsung-kuan*): *grand commandant en chef.* P50.

6088 *tà tsǔng-pó* 大宗伯
Lit., grand clansman Earl, apparently a change from the more ancient title Grand Clansman (*ta-tsung*). (1) CHOU: **Minister of Rites,** ranked as a Minister (*ch'ing*), head of the Ministry of Rites (*ch'un-kuan*); counseled and assisted the King in all sacrificial and other major ritual matters, established and enforced ritual regulations for the Feudal Lords (*chu-hou*), and supervised numerous agencies concerned with the preparation for and conduct of state rituals; principally assisted by 2 Vice Ministers (*hsiao tsung-po, shao-tsung*) ranked as Ordinary Grand Masters (*chung ta-fu*); Senior Supplicators (*ta-chu*), 4 ranked as Junior Grand Masters (*hsia ta-fu*) and 8 as Senior Servicemen (*shang-shih*); and 2 Grand Diviners (*ta-pu*) ranked as Junior Grand Masters. CL: *grand supérieur des cérémonies sacrées.* (2) N-S DIV (Chou): revival of the ancient Chou post, rank 3. Cf. *tsung-po*. P27.

6089 *tà tsūng-shīh* 大宗師
MING–CH'ING: lit. meaning not clear; see *tsung-shih:* unofficial reference to a *t'i-hsüeh*, i.e., a Ming–early Ch'ing **Education Intendant** (*tu-hsüeh tao-t'ai*) or a later Ch'ing **Provincial Education Commissioner** (*t'i-tu hsüeh-cheng*).

6090 *tà tsǔng-ts'ái* 大總裁
CH'ING: lit., great chief decider: unofficial reference to a principal **Examining Official** (*k'ao-kung*) in a civil service recruitment examination. Cf. *tsung-ts'ai*.

6091 *tà tū-hó* 大督河
CH'ING: unofficial reference to a **Director-general of the Grand Canal** (*ho-tao tsung-tu*) for the Shantung–Honan region.

6092 *tà tū-hsièn* 大都憲
(1) T'ANG: unofficial reference to a **Censor-in-chief** from 662 to 671, when his official title was *ta ssu-hsien* rather than the traditional *yü-shih ta-fu*. (2) MING: unofficial reference to a provincial-level **Grand Coordinator** (*hsün-fu*), who usually was a nominal Censor-in-chief (*tu yü-shih*). (3) CH'ING: unofficial reference to a Censor-in-chief of the Left (*tso tu yü-shih*), i.e., one in actual charge of the Censorate (*tu ch'a-yüan*).

6093 *tà tū-hù* 大都護
Grand Protector. (1) T'ANG–SUNG: nominal head of a Grand Protectorate (*ta tu-hu fu*), in T'ang rank 2a but commonly an Imperial Prince (*ch'in-wang*) not on active service, in Sung probably a non-functional post. RR: *grand protecteur général.* SP: *grand protecteur.* P50. (2) YÜAN: 4, rank 2b, each the head of a Protectorate (*tu-hu fu*) that supervised the affairs of Uighur and other non-Mongol nomadic peoples in the empire. See *tu-hu*. P22.

6094 *tà tū-hù fǔ* 大都護府
T'ANG–SUNG: **Grand Protectorate,** the most eminent type of military administration established to govern submitted

non-Chinese in Mongolia and Central Asia, nominally headed by a Grand Protector (*ta tu-hu*), rank 2a, who most commonly was an Imperial Prince (*ch'in-wang*) not on active service, so that the Vice Grand Protector (*fu ta tu-hu*), rank 3a, was the actual head. The title was perpetuated in Sung, but probably an entirely non-functional post. See *tu-hu fu*. RR: *grand protectorat général*. P50.

6095   *tà tū-k'ǔn*   大都闔
CH'ING: lit., great chief pacifier (?): unofficial reference to a **Brigade Vice Commander** (*tu-ssu*) in the Chinese military forces called the Green Standards (*lu-ying*), presumably when he was in actual command of a Brigade (*ying*). Cf. *tu-k'un*.

6096   *tà tū-tū*   大都督
(1) N-S DIV: **Area Commander-in-chief,** one of several titles awarded to or adopted by warlords who dominated clusters of Regions (*chou*), usually from power bases as Governors (*mu*) or Regional Inspectors (*tz'u-shih*) of single Regions; apparently less prestigious than the variant *tsung-tu* (Supreme Commander) but more or less interchangeable with *tsung-kuan* and *tu-tu*. P50. (2) SUI: **Area Commander-in-chief,** apparently interchangeable with Regional Inspector (*tz'u-shih*) until c. 607, then made a prestige title (*san-kuan*) divided into 9 grades, from upper-upper (*shang-shang*) down to lower-lower (*hsia-hsia*); also **Commander,** one of several terms used for the heads and even secondary officials of horse or cattle pasturages (*mu; see. mu-chang*) supervised by the Court of the Imperial Stud (*t'ai-p'u ssu*). P31, 39, 50. (3) T'ANG–YÜAN: **Commander-in-chief,** the common title of the senior official of a *ta tu-tu fu* (Superior Area Command, Chief Military Command). RR+SP: *grand gouverneur général*

6097   *tà tū-tū fǔ*   大都督府
(1) T'ANG–SUNG: **Superior Area Command,** the most prestigious type of Area Command (*tu-tu fu*), headed by a Commander-in-chief (*ta tu-tu*), in T'ang and perhaps Sung a nominal appointment for an Imperial Prince (*ch'in-wang*) or other dignitary who was not actively on military duty, so that actual control was exercised by a Commander-in-chief (*tu-tu*), rank 2a, with the help of an Aide (*chang-shih*), 3a. RR: *grand gouvernement général*. SP: *gouvernement du grand gouverneur général*. P50. (2) YÜAN: **Chief Military Command,** a unit of the Bureau of Military Affairs (*shu-mi yüan*) that controlled a special, notoriously fierce group of Turkic warriors organized into Left and Right Kipchak Guards (*ch'in-ch'a wei*). (3) MING: **Chief Military Command,** a predynastic central government agency in charge of all military forces, created in 1361 by redesignation of the Yüan-style Bureau of Military Affairs in the central government; headed by one Commander-in-chief (*ta tu-tu*) until 1367; then reorganized into a Chief Military Commission (*tu-tu fu*) with one Left and one Right Commissioner-in-chief (*tu-tu*), which in 1380 was divided into 5 Chief Military Commissions. Also see *wu fu*.

6098   *tà tuān-tsò*   大端佐
CH'ING: lit., great assistant exemplar: unofficial reference to an **Assistant Prefect** (*t'ung-p'an*).

6099   *tà-t'ǔng*   大統
N-S DIV (N. Wei, N. Ch'i): **Controller-in-chief,** head of the Office for the Clarification of Buddhist Profundities (*chao-hsüan ssu*). P17.

6100   *tà-tzū*   大資
SUNG: lit., great assistant: unofficial, abbreviated reference to a **Grand Academician** (*ta hsüeh-shih*) **of the Hall for Aid in Governance** (*tzu-cheng tien*).

6101   *tà tz'ú-hàn*   大詞翰
SUNG–CH'ING: lit., great brush-writer of phrases: **Grand Stylist,** unofficial reference to a member of the Hanlin Academy (*han-lin yüan*).

6102   *tà wài-hàn*   大外翰
CH'ING: lit., great outer brush-writer: unofficial reference to an **Instructor** (*chiao-shou*) in a Confucian School (*ju-hsüeh*) at the Prefecture (*fu*) level. Also see *wai-han*.

6103   *tà-wáng*   大王
LIAO: **Grand Prince,** Chinese translation of a Khitan term transliterated as *i-li-chin;* chief of a Tribe (*pu-tsu*). Cf. *wang*.

6104   *tà-wáng fǔ*   大王府
LIAO: **Office of the Grand Prince,** a court agency representing the interests of a major tribal group in the Northern Establishment (*pei-yüan*) of the Northern Administration (*pei-mien*). See under *ssu ta-wang fu* (Four Offices of the Grand Princes). Cf. *wang-fu* (Princely Establishment). P17.

6105   *tà wēi-wèi*   大威衛
CH'ING: lit., great august guardian: unofficial reference to a **Commissioner of the Imperial Procession Guard** (*luan-i shih;* see under *luan-i wei*). Cf. *wei-wei*.

6106   *tà wén-héng*   大文衡
CH'ING: lit., great arbiter of literature: unofficial reference to a **Provincial Education Commissioner** (*t'i-tu hsüeh-cheng*).

6107   *tà wén-tsūng*   大文宗
MING–CH'ING: lit., great literatus: unofficial reference to a Ming–early Ch'ing **Education Intendant** (*tu-hsüeh tao-t'ai*) or a later Ch'ing **Provincial Education Commissioner** (*t'i-tu hsüeh-cheng*). Cf. *wen-tsung*.

6108   *tà wū-t'ái*   大烏臺
MING–CH'ING: lit., great blackbird pavilion; see under *wu-t'ai* (Censorate): unofficial reference to a **Censor** (*yü-shih*) on duty assignment as a **Regional Inspector** (*hsün-an yü-shih*).

6109   *tà-yèh*   大業
Lit., the great vocation, i.e., governing: **His Majesty,** throughout history an unofficial reference to the ruler.

6110   *tà yèh-chě*   大謁者
HAN: lit., great receptionist: apparently a variant reference to a **Supervisor of Receptionists** (*yeh-che p'u-yeh*). P33.

6111   *tà-yǐn*   大尹
(1) HAN: official variant of *t'ai-shou* (**Governor** of a Commandery, *chün*) during the reign of Wang Mang (A.D. 9–23). (2) CH'ING: unofficial reference to a **District Magistrate** (*chih-hsien*). Cf. *yin*.

6112   *tà yín-t'ái*   大銀臺
CH'ING: lit., great silver pavilion, derived from the name of a Sung agency called *yin-t'ai ssu*, q.v.: unofficial reference to the **Office of Transmission** (*t'ung-cheng ssu*) or to its head, the **Transmission Commissioner** (*t'ung-cheng shih*).

6113   *tā-yìng*   答應
Responder. (1) MING: categorical designation of one low-status group of palace eunuchs. (2) CH'ING: categorical designation of one low-status group of palace women, ranking below Worthy Ladies (*kuei-jen*).

6114 *tà yú-jiàng* 大遊戎
CH'ING: great roving warrior: unofficial reference to a **Brigade Commander** (*yu-chi*) in the Chinese military forces called the Green Standards (*lu-ying*).

6115 *tà-yǜ* 大馭
CHOU: **Grand Charioteer**, 2 ranked as Ordinary Grand Masters (*chung ta-fu*), members of the Ministry of War (*hsia-kuan*) responsible for driving a jade (jade ornamented?) chariot in which the King rode to major state sacrificial ceremonies. CL: *grand cocher*.

6116 *tà yǔ-ch'īng* 大虞卿
MING: lit., great minister of precautions: unofficial reference to a **Supervisor** (*chien*) **of the Imperial Forest Park** (*shang-lin yüan*).

6117 *tà yǔ-yüèh* 大于越
LIAO: **Grand Counselor**, highest official post in the Northern Administration (*pei-mien*), qualifications and functions not clear but probably a quasi-honorary appointment for an imperial clansman or some other tribal dignitary. See *yü-yüeh*.

6118 *tà yüán-fǔ* 大元輔
CH'ING: lit., great principal bulwark: unofficial reference to a **Grand Secretary** (*ta hsüeh-shih*).

6119 *tà yüán-hóu* 大元侯
CH'ING: lit., great principal Marquis: unofficial reference to a **Provincial Military Commander** (*t'i-tu*).

6120 *tà yüán-shuài* 大元帥
SUNG: **Grand Marshal**, one of the most eminent duty assignment designations for military commanders on active campaign. See *yüan-shuai*.

6121 *tà yüán-tsǎi* 大元宰
CH'ING: lit., great principal steward: unofficial reference to a **Grand Secretary** (*ta hsüeh-shih*).

6122 *tà-yüèh àn* 大樂案
See under *t'ai-yüeh an*.

6123 *tà yüèh-mù* 大岳牧
MING–CH'ING: lit., great regional authority (see under *yüeh-mu*): unofficial reference to a **Provincial Administration Commissioner** (*pu-cheng shih*).

6124 *t'à-lín* 撻林
LIAO: apparently a transcription of a Khitan word: variant of both *p'u-yeh* (**Vice Director of the Department of State Affairs**) and *ssu-k'ung* (**Minister of Works**).

6125 *t'à-shū shǒu* 搨書手
T'ANG: **Rubbing Maker**, 3 (6?) non-official craftsmen on the staff of the Academy of Scholarly Worthies (*chi-hsien tien shu-yüan*), to make impressions from woodblocks or stone engravings. P25.

6126 *tài* 帶
N-S DIV–T'ANG: lit., to take charge of: **Concurrent**, prefix used with a title awarded as a quasi-honorary supplement to a regular title, often for no purpose other than to increase the prestige or income of a relatively lowly official; especially in pre-T'ang times, regularly used for favorites of dignitaries, creating personal factions.

6127 *tài-chào* 待詔
Lit., awaiting an edict. (1) HAN–T'ANG: **Expectant Official**, basically someone serving, or expecting to serve, in a post requiring an imperial appointment, when the imperial appointment had not yet been issued; sometimes occurs by itself, suggesting a recommendee awaiting a duty assignment probably of lower status than a Court Gentlemen (*lang*), but most commonly occurs with a prefix indicating the agency served in or the function performed; e.g., *t'ai-shih tai-chao* (Expectant Official under the Grand Astrologer), one of several instances in which *tai-chao* became an authorized, quota-limited status in itself even in Han times. HB: expectant appointee. P23, 35, etc. (2) SUNG, CH'ING: **Editorial Assistant,** lowly compilers found in such Sung agencies as the Institute of Academicians (*hsüeh-shih yüan*); in Ch'ing one Manchu and one Chinese, both rank 9b, in the Editorial Office (*tai-chao t'ing*) of the Hanlin Academy (*han-lin yüan*). SP: *attendant des décrets*. BH: compiler. P23.

6128 *tài-chào t'īng* 待詔廳
CH'ING: **Editorial Office** in the Hanlin Academy (*han-lin yüan*), staffed with one Manchu and one Chinese Editorial Assistant (*tai-chao*), rank 9b, and a number of Clerks (*pi-t'ieh-shih*); apparently responsible for making preliminary drafts of certain kinds of imperial pronouncements, but functions not wholly clear. BH: office for compilation of edicts (manifests). P23.

6129 *tài-chìh kuān* 待制官 *or tai-chih*
T'ANG–SUNG: **Edict Attendant**, litterateur apparently assigned to take notes on imperial pronouncements during the Emperor's meetings with officials; in T'ang members of the Academy of Scholarly Worthies (*chi-hsien tien shu-yüan*), unranked; in Sung members of the Hanlin Academy (*han-lin yüan*), 4b, prefixed with the name of one or another palace Hall (*ko*). RR: *fonctionnaire attendant les édits impériaux*. SP: *lettré attendant les édits impériaux du pavillon ....* P25.

6130 *tài-chōu ch'ién-chiēn* 代州錢監
CHIN: **Tai-chou Directorate of Coinage**, established in 1178 at Tai-chou in modern Shansi; in 1180 renamed *fu-t'ung ch'ien-chien* (Directorate of Money Circulation). Also see *li-yung ch'ien-chien*. P16.

6131 *tài-fèng* 帶俸
MING: **receiving salary,** a term sometimes prefixed to the title of a military officer, indicating that he received his pay in the status indicated but was on detached duty in another post and was not actually performing the duty suggested by his nominal title. Cf. *kuan ... shih* (in charge of the affairs ...).

6132 *tài-jén lìng-shǐh* 代人令史
N-S DIV (N. Wei): **Replacement Clerk,** one, probably unranked, in the Ministry of Personnel (*li-pu*) from 396 or 397; function not clear but, since the post was regularly authorized, may have handled the filling of vacancies rather than being a substitute. P5.

6133 *tài yù ch'ì-chièh* 帶御器械
SUNG: **Bearer of the Imperial Arms,** from 6 to 10 attached to the Bureau of Military Affairs (*shu-mi yüan*) with status above Editorial Clerks (*chien-hsiang wen-tzu; see chien-hsiang fang*); functions not clear. SP: *officier armé de carquois et d'épées impériaux*.

6134 *t'ài* 太
Lit., great, supreme: a common prefix in titles. In addition to the following entries, see under the common variant *ta* (large, grand).

6135 *t'ái* 臺
Lit., terrace, pavilion: a suffix in many agency names; identifiable only by preceding terminology, but in isolation

most likely refers in most periods to the *yü-shih t'ai* (Censorate).

6136　*t'ái-chăng* 臺長

Head of the Censorate: throughout history an unofficial reference to the senior executive official of the Censorate (*yü-shih t'ai, tu ch'a-yüan*), i.e., the Censor-in-chief (*yü-shih ta-fu, tu yü-shih*) or, in periods when the Censor-in-chief was dissociated from active duty in the Censorate, the Palace Aide to the Censor-in-chief or the Vice Censor-in-chief (both *yü-shih chung-ch'eng*).

6137　*t'ài-ch'áng* 太常

CH'IN–N-S DIV (Liang): lit., great flag bearer (see under *feng-ch'ang*): **Chamberlain for Ceremonials,** in charge of great state sacrificial ceremonies, especially at the Imperial Ancestral Temple (*tsung-miao, t'ai-miao*) and at imperial mausolea (*ling*); rank 2,000 bushels in Han; foremost of the Nine Chamberlains (*chiu ch'ing*) in prestige. Assisted principally by an Aide (*ch'eng*), rank 1,000 bushels in Han; supervised many subordinate units commonly headed by Directors (*ling*), rank 600 bushels. These included a Great Supplicator (*t'ai-chu*), a Great Sacrificial Butcher (*t'ai-tsai*), a Grand Director of Music (*t'ai-yüeh ling*), an Imperial Diviner (*t'ai-pu*), a Grand Astrologer (*t'ai-shih ling*), and the Chancellor (*chi-chiu*) of the National University (*t'ai-hsüeh*). In early Han if not thereafter, the Chamberlain for Ceremonials examined candidates for office nominated by officials in units of territorial administration. In Liang the Chamberlain's title was officially made *t'ai-ch'ang ch'ing*, and in N. Ch'i his agency was officially designated *t'ai-ch'ang ssu* (Court); both terms had been used quasiofficially since Chin times. HB: grand master of ceremonies. P27.

6138　*t'ài-ch'áng ch'īng* 太常卿

(1) N-S DIV: **Chamberlain for Ceremonials,** from Liang on, in both southern and northern regimes, the common official redesignation of *t'ai-ch'ang*. (2) N-S DIV (N. Ch'i): **Chief Minister of the Court of Imperial Sacrifices;** see under *t'ai-ch'ang ssu*. P27.

6139　*t'ài-ch'áng fŭ* 太常府

N-S DIV (Sung, Ch'i): **Office of the Chamberlain for Ceremonials,** antecedent of the name Court of Imperial Sacrifices (*t'ai-ch'ang ssu*). P27.

6140　*t'ài-ch'áng lĭ-í yüàn* 太常禮儀院

YÜAN: **Commission for Ritual Observances,** recurrent variant of *t'ai-ch'ang ssu* (Court of Imperial Sacrifices), dominant from 1329; headed by a Commissioner (*shih*), rank 2a. Distinguish from *li-i yüan* (Court of Ceremonial Propriety) of Sung and Ch'ing times. P27.

6141　*t'ài-ch'ăng lĭ-yüàn* 太常禮院

T'ANG–SUNG: common variant of *li-yüan* (**Ritual Academy**), normally a subordinate unit of the Court of Imperial Sacrifices (*t'ai-ch'ang ssu*). P27.

6142　*t'ài ch'áng-pó* 太常伯

T'ANG: **Grand Executive Attendant,** from 662 to 670 the official variant of *shang-shu* (Minister) in all of the Six Ministries (*liu pu*) of the central government. See *ch'ang-po, ta ch'ang-po*.

6143　*t'ài-ch'áng pó-shìh* 太常博士

Erudite of the Chamberlain for Ceremonials (Ch'in–era of N-S Division) or **Erudite of the Court of Imperial Sacrifices** (era of N-S Division–Ch'ing); see under *po-shih* (Erudite). P27.

6144　*t'ài-ch'áng ssū* 太常司

MING: **Office of Imperial Sacrifices,** from 1367 to 1397 the official variant of *t'ai-ch'ang ssu* (Court of Imperial Sacrifices); headed by a Chief Minister (*ch'ing*), rank 3a. P27.

6145　*t'ài-ch'áng ssù* 太常寺

N-S DIV (N. Ch'i)–CH'ING: **Court of Imperial Sacrifices,** one of the Nine Courts (*chiu ssu*) in the central government and foremost in prestige among the Courts until Ch'ing, when it yielded this status to the Court of Judicial Review (*ta-li ssu*); generally responsible for the conduct of major state sacrificial ceremonies according to ritual regulations prescribed by the Ministry of Rites (*lĭ-pu*), and through most of its history indirectly subordinated to the Ministry; through Sung also responsible for recommending posthumous titles of Emperors, a function then yielded to the Grand Secretariat (*nei-ko*) in Ming. Headed by one or 2 Chief Ministers (*ch'ing*), rank 3 in N. Wei, 3a in T'ang, 4a in Sung, 3a in Ming and Ch'ing; in Ch'ing one Manchu and one Chinese appointee. Aided by one or more Vice Ministers (*shao-ch'ing*) and Assistant Ministers (*ch'eng*). Commonly had several subordinate agencies: e.g., in T'ang an Office of the National Altars (*chiao-she shu*), an Imperial Music Office (*t'ai-yüeh shu*), an Office of Drums and Fifes (*ku-ch'ui shu*), an Imperial Medical Office (*t'ai-i shu*), an Imperial Divination Office (*t'ai-pu shu*), an Office of Sacrificial Grains and Animals (*lin-hsi shu*), an Office of Sacrificial Treasures (*t'ien-fu yüan*), an Office of Sacrificial Clothing (*yü-i yüan*), an Office of Sacrificial Music (*yüeh-hsien yüan*), and an Office of Sacrificial Foods (*shen-ch'u yüan*); in Sung 5 subordinate Sections (*an*); in Ming a Sacrificial Office (*tz'u-chi shu*) and an Office of Animal Offerings (*hsi-sheng so*). The staff usually included such officials as Erudites (*po-shih*), Chief Musicians (*hsieh-lü lang*), and Sacrificers (*feng-ssu*). RR+SP: *cour des sacrifices impériaux.* BH: court of sacrificial worship. P27.

6146　*t'ái-ch'éng* 臺丞

T'ANG–SUNG: unofficial reference to the **Vice Censor-in-chief** (*yü-shih chung-ch'eng*).

6147　*t'ài-ch'eng fu* 太晟府

See under *ta-sheng fu* (**Imperial Music Bureau**).

6148　*t'ài-chiēn* 太監

(1) **Director,** from Sung if not earlier a variant of *chien* (Director), used for heads of some agencies called Directorates (*chien*) and occasionally with other designations; in Ming and perhaps earlier referred to the eunuch chief of any palace agency called a Directorate, e.g., the Directorate of Ceremonial (*ssu-li chien*). (2) MING–CH'ING: **Palace Eunuch,** a generic term deriving from the usage described in (1) above.

6149　*t'ái-chièn* 臺諫

SUNG–MING: abbreviated combination of *yü-shih t'ai* (Censorate) and *chien-yüan* (Remonstrance Bureau): **Censors and Remonstrators,** a quasiofficial reference to members of the Censorate (*yü-shih t'ai, tu ch'a-yüan*) and the Sung dynasty Remonstrance Bureau or the Ming dynasty Offices of Scrutiny (see *liu k'o;* i.e., Supervising Secretaries, *chi-shih-chung*); from some mid-Ming point became primarily a reference to Censors (*yü-shih*), while *chi-shih-chung* came to be known separately as *chi-chien* (submitters of remonstrances). P19.

6150　*t'ài-ch'īng* 太卿

YÜAN: **Grand Minister,** variant of *ch'ing* (Minister, Chief Minister) found in some agencies designated *chien* (Directorate), *ssu* (Court), and *ssu* (Office), usually of relatively low status.

6151 *t'ài-chǔ* 太主

HAN: **Princess Supreme,** designation of the paternal aunt of an Emperor; comparable to *ta-chang kung-chu.*

6152 *t'ài-chù* 太祝

CH'IN–MING: **Great Supplicator,** chief specialist in ceremonial prayers at ancestral temples on the staff of the Ch'in–Han and early post-Han Chamberlain for Ceremonials (*t'ai-ch'ang*), then commonly titled *t'ai-chu ling,* and his institutional successor the Court of Imperial Sacrifices (*t'ai-ch'ang ssu*) or, in Yüan, the Commission for Ritual Observances (*t'ai-ch'ang li-i yüan*); derived from the ancient Chou *ta-chu* (Senior Supplicator). In T'ang 6, rank 9a1; in Sung and Chin one, 8b; in Yüan 10, 8b; in Ming existed only from 1399 to 1402, number and rank not clear. RR: *invocateur.* SP: *chef des invocations.* P27.

6153 *t'ái-chǔ* 臺主

N-S DIV: lit., chief of the pavilion, i.e., of the Censorate (*yü-shih t'ai*): common unofficial reference to the **Palace Aide to the Censor-in-chief** (*yü-shih chung-ch'eng*), then the senior executive official in the Censorate.

6154 *t'ài-chù lìng* 太祝令

HAN–N-S DIV: **Great Supplicator,** rank in Han 600 bushels, one of the chief subordinates of the Chamberlain for Ceremonials (*t'ai-ch'ang*); see *t'ai-chu.* HB: prefect grand supplicator. P27.

6155 *t'ài chūng tà-fū* 太中大夫

Superior Grand Master of the Palace. (1) HAN–N-S DIV (Chin): one of 3 or more eminent personages in the Emperor's personal service as counselors and remonstrators, in Han with rank of 2,000 (1,000?) bushels; see *chung ta-fu, chien ta-fu, kuang-lu-hsün.* HB: grand palace grandee. (2) T'ANG–MING: prestige title (*san-kuan*) for civil officials of rank 4b1 in T'ang, Sung, and Chin, rank 3b in Yüan and Ming. P68.

6156 *t'ài-chūn* 太君

SUNG: see *chün t'ai-chün* (**Grand Lord** or **Lady of the Commandery**).

6157 *t'ài-fēi* 太妃

Great Consort. (1) From Chin of the era of N-S Division on, a title or quasiofficial designation of the natural mother of a reigning Emperor who had not been his father's Empress, especially when the title Empress Dowager (*huang t'ai-hou*) was otherwise in use. (2) N-S DIV (N. Wei): official designation of the principal wife of a Prince. (3) T'ANG: from 790, designation of the mother of a Prince. See *fei.*

6158 *t'ài-fù* 太傅

Grand Mentor. (1) Throughout history one of the eminent court dignitaries known as the Three Preceptors (*san shih*) or the Three Dukes (*san kung*), ranked as a Feudal Lord (*chu-hou*) in Chou, at 10,000 bushels in Han, thereafter 1a. In Han, a special case, the Grand Mentor was esteemed as the paramount post in the officialdom, above the Three Dukes as then constituted, but it was seldom filled in Former Han. In Later Han it was ordinarily filled, and appointees were also normally designated Directors (*ling*) of the powerful Imperial Secretariat (*shang-shu t'ai*), becoming important actors in the political struggles of their times. HB: grand tutor. RR+SP: *grand maître.* BH: grand tutor. (2) HAN: designation given the most eminent adviser on the staff of a Princedom (*wang-kuo*), rank 2,000 bushels; from 8 B.C. reduced to the simpler title *fu* (Mentor). P67, 69.

6159 *t'ài-fù* 太府

N-S DIV: **Chamberlain for the Palace Revenues,** appar-

ently interchangeable with *shao-fu;* one of the so-called Nine Chamberlains (*chiu ch'ing*) in the central government; gradually became involved primarily with the central government's non-grain revenues whereas grain revenues were managed by the Chamberlain for the National Treasury (*ssu-nung*), and the *shao-fu* became increasingly involved with palace construction and manufacturing activities. From Liang on, coexisted with *ta-fu* (Chamberlain for the Palace Bursary), although the sources may be in error in differentiating between *t'ai-fu* and *ta-fu* in this era. P38.

6160 *t'ái-fǔ* 台輔

Chief Bulwark of the State: throughout imperial history an occasional unofficial reference to a paramount executive official of the central government such as a Counselor-in-chief (*ch'eng-hsiang*) or a Grand Councilor (*tsai-hsiang*).

6161 *t'ài-fǔ chiēn* 太府監

LIAO, CHIN, YÜAN: **Directorate of the Imperial Treasury,** headed by a Supervisor (*chien*), rank 4a, until Yüan, then by 6 Grand Ministers (*t'ai-ch'ing*), 2a or 3a; generally responsible, under guidelines established by the Ministry of Revenue (*hu-pu*), for managing the receipt and disbursement of the central government's non-grain revenues and the various storehouses in which such revenues were kept; counterpart of the earlier Court of the Imperial Treasury (*t'ai-fu ssu*). Not established in Ming, its functions taken over more directly by the Ministry of Revenue and palace eunuchs. P38.

6162 *t'ài-fǔ ch'īng* 太府卿

Common variant of *t'ai-fu* (**Chamberlain for the Palace Revenues**) and *t'ai-fu ssu ch'ing* (**Chief Minister of the Court of the Imperial Treasury**).

6163 *t'ài fū-jén* 太夫人

SUNG: see *chün t'ai fu-jen* (**Commandery Grand Mistress**).

6164 *t'ài-fù shàng-kūng* 太傅上公

HAN: **Superior Duke Grand Mentor,** a title of the highest eminence in the central government, awarded to a personal confidant of the Emperor who was expected to provide him moral guidance.

6165 *t'ài-fù ssù* 太府寺

(1) N-S DIV–SUI: **Court for the Palace Revenues,** from Liang interchangeable with *shao-fu ssu* till N. Wei, then absorbed or finally displaced the *shao-fu ssu* and became the central government's principal agency for the management of non-grain revenues, provisioning the palace, etc.; in Sui gradually transformed into a nationally-oriented fiscal agency (see #2 below). Headed by a Chamberlain (*ch'ing*), commonly rank 3. (2) T'ANG–SUNG: **Court of the Imperial Treasury,** a 2nd-tier central government agency responsible for managing the central government's non-grain receipts and disbursements; headed by a Chief Minister (*ch'ing*), rank 3a in T'ang, 4b in Sung, with the help of one or more Vice Ministers (*shao-ch'ing*) and various subalterns who managed an array of storehouses and vaults and in addition supervised trade in the capital city's marketplaces, where they presumably collected fees and taxes on mercantile transactions. In Sung dominated successively by the State Finance Commission (*san ssu*) and the Ministry of Revenue (*hu-pu*); in Liao, Chin, and Yüan superseded by the Directorate of the Imperial Treasury (*t'ai-fu chien*). In general, the Court was always subject to policies established by the Ministry of Revenue, and the central government's grain revenues were separately managed by the Court of the Imperial Granaries (*ssu-nung ssu*). RR+SP: *cour du trésor impérial.* P38. (3) CH'ING: unofficial reference to the **Imperial Household Department** (*nei-wu fu*).

6166 *t'ài-hòu* 太后
(1) HAN: **Consort Dowager,** designation of the mother of an Imperial Marquis (*chu-hou*), i.e., a son of a Prince who did not succeed to his father's title and status. (2) May be encountered occasionally as an abbreviation for *huang t'ai-hou* (**Empress Dowager**).

6167 *t'ài-hsī tsūng-yīn yüàn* 太禧宗禋院
YÜAN: **Office of Imperial Ancestral Worship,** a central government agency headed by a Commissioner (*shih*); supervised the offering of prayers and sacrifices at temples to all Mongol Emperors, each temple having a branch office called a Supervisorate-in-chief (*tsung-kuan fu*).

6168 *t'ài-hsüéh* 太學
Lit., supreme school: **National University.** (1) HAN–SUNG: created in 124 B.C., when 50 disciples or students were chosen and distributed among 5 pre-existing Erudites (*po-shih*) on the staff of the Chamberlain for Ceremonials (*t'ai-ch'ang*); thereafter was the paramount educational institution in dynastic capitals, staffed most importantly by Erudites supervised by a Chief Administrator (*p'u-yeh*) or, from late in Former Han, a Chancellor (*chi-chiu*). In Han the number of Erudites and students fluctuated considerably, enrollment rising to 3,000 under Wang Mang's patronage and to 30,000 in the 2nd century A.D. Post-Han dynasties perpetuated the University in coexistence with other educational agencies. The names *t'ai-hsüeh* and *kuo-hsüeh* (lit., school of the state) alternated and sometimes apparently coexisted, and in addition there was commonly a School for the Sons of the State (*kuo-tzu hsüeh*). In Sui the National University became one of 3 major schools now removed from traditional status in the Court of Imperial Sacrifices (*t'ai-ch'ang ssu*) and organized into a consolidated Directorate of Education (*kuo-tzu chien*) headed by a Chancellor with the assistance of a Director of Studies (*ssu-yeh*); the *t'ai-hsüeh* alone had some 500 students regularly enrolled. In T'ang the new Directorate of Education was expanded to incorporate 7 schools; the *t'ai-hsüeh* continued to enroll some 500 students under Erudites, its students being primarily the sons of lesser nobles and middle-rank officials. In early Sung the 2 principal schools in the Directorate were consolidated into a single institution, *t'ai-hsüeh* and *kuo-tzu hsüeh* both becoming variant references to the Directorate; some 4,000 students were divided among 80 Study Halls (*chai*). In reforms of the 1070s the school was reorganized into 3 Colleges (*she*): an Outer College (*wai-she*), about 20% of whose graduates continued their studies in an Inner College (*nei-she*), less than half of whose graduates were admitted to a Superior College (*shang-she*). In S. Sung the whole Directorate of Education declined in vitality, in part because of a burgeoning of private Academies (*shu-yüan*), but it retained a regular enrollment of some 1,000 students. Throughout its history, the National University served as a channel through which educated men were obtained for service as officials. Some of its graduates always moved directly into low-level official posts; others were good prospects for service as subalterns of regional and local authorities, from whom some could get recommendations that moved them up into regular office. From Sui on, graduates commonly competed in both regular and irregular civil service recruitment examinations with candidates qualified by other means such as recommendation. The rise in importance of relatively open recruitment examinations probably was most responsible for the decline of the National University in S. Sung. See separate entries, also *chien-chü* (recruitment by nomination) and *k'o-chü* (Recruitment by Examination). HB: academy. RR: *section des études*

supérieures. SP: *université*. P34. (2) MING–CH'ING: quasi-official reference to the Directorate of Education (*kuo-tzu chien*) and to the school it operated, officially named School for the Sons of the State (*kuo-tzu hsüeh*).

6169 *t'ài-huáng t'ài-hòu* 太皇太后
Grand Empress Dowager: throughout imperial history the standard official designation of the paternal grandmother of a reigning Emperor, normally having previously been Empress and then, during the reign of her son, Empress Dowager (*huang t'ai-hou*).

6170 *t'ài-í* 太儀
Lady of Supreme Deportment, a title granted to women. (1) T'ANG: awarded to mothers of Imperial Princesses (*kung-chu*) other than the Empress; prefixed with place-names identifying the daughters' assigned fiefs. (2) SUNG: variant of *ta-i*, q.v.

6171 *t'ài-ī* 太醫
Palace Physician: throughout history a common unofficial or quasiofficial designation of a physician in attendance on the ruler, normally a non-official specialist, often hereditary or selected from a social class of hereditary physicians. Similar generic designations include *i-kuan, i-shih, i-yüan, yü-i*. The principal agency in which such personnel served was the office of the Imperial Physician (*t'ai-i ling*) from Ch'in into the era of N-S Division, the Sui–T'ang Imperial Medical Office (*t'ai-i shu*), the Sung–Liao Imperial Medical Service (*t'ai-i chü*), and the Chin–Ch'ing Imperial Academy of Medicine (*t'ai-i yüan*). In early times medical practitioners were under the supervision of the Chamberlain for Ceremonials (*t'ai-ch'ang*) or the agency that superseded him, the Court of Imperial Sacrifices (*t'ai-ch'ang ssu*); but from Yüan through Ch'ing they constituted an independent central government institution. From Sung on, there was a special hierarchy of prestige titles (*san-kuan*) for physicians. P36, 37.

6172 *t'ái-ī* 臺醫
YÜAN: **Censorate Physician,** 2 non-official specialists on the staff of the Censorate (*yü-shih t'ai*); special functions if any not clear. P18.

6173 *t'ài-ī àn* 太醫案
SUNG: variant (official?) designation of the **Imperial Medical Service** (*t'ai-i chü*). SP: *service de la médecine impériale*.

6174 *t'ài-ī chèng* 太醫正
(1) N-S DIV (Liang): **Director of Palace Physicians** (?), probably the equivalent of *t'ai-i ling* (Imperial Physician) in other periods, but sources not clear. P36. (2) SUNG: variant, perhaps quasiofficial reference to the **Imperial Physician** (*t'ai-i ling*). SP: *directeur du bureau de la médecine impériale, directeur de l'office impérial de la médecine*. (3) CH'ING: unofficial reference to a **Medical Secretary** (*li-mu*) in the Imperial Academy of Medicine (*t'ai-i yüan*).

6175 *t'ài-ī ch'éng* 太醫丞
(1) CH'IN–N-S DIV: **Aide to the Imperial Physician,** commonly the 2nd executive official in the group of Palace Physicians (*t'ai-i*), assisting the Imperial Physician (*t'ai-i ling*). P36. (2) CH'ING: unofficial reference to a **Vice Commissioner** (*yüan-p'an*) **of the Imperial Academy of Medicine** (*t'ai-i yüan*)

6176 *t'ài-ī chiào-kuān* 太醫教官
YÜAN: **Medical Instructor,** non-official specialist(s) on the staff of the Imperial Academy of Medicine (*t'ai-i yüan*).

6177   *t'ài-ī chiēn* 太醫監
(1) HAN: **Imperial Medical Supervisor,** status not clear but apparently not a variant reference to the Imperial Physician (*t'ai-i ling*). HB: inspector of the grand physician. (2) MING: **Directorate of Imperial Medicine,** predynastic agency name, in 1367 changed to *t'ai-i yüan* (Imperial Academy of Medicine); earlier (date not clear) changed from Supervisorate of Medicines (*i-yao t'i-chü ssu*). P36.

6178   *t'ài-ī chù-chiào* 太醫助教
N-S DIV (N. Wei): **Medical Instructor,** one or more, rank 9b, assistants to the Medical Erudite(s) (*t'ai-i po-shih*) on the staff of the Imperial Physician (*t'ai-i ling*). P36.

6179   *t'ài-ī chü* 太醫局
SUNG–LIAO: **Imperial Medical Service,** a quasi-autonomous agency of the central government generally subordinated to the Court of Imperial Sacrifices (*t'ai-ch'ang ssu*), in Liao part of the Northern Administration (*pei-mien*); maintained a staff of Palace Physicians (*t'ai-i*) headed in Sung by a Supervisor (*t'i-chü*) or a Director (*ling* or *cheng*), in Liao by both a Supreme Secretary (*tu lin-ya*) and a Commissioner (*shih*); in Sung had a particularly erratic existence as one of several medical agencies in the palace and central government, repeatedly abolished and re-established, briefly from 1102 attached to the Directorate of Education (*kuo-tzu chien*). Successor of the Sui–T'ang *t'ai-i shu,* antecedent of the Chin–Ch'ing *t'ai-i yüan.* SP: *office impérial de la médecine.* P36.

6180   *t'ài-ī lìng* 太醫令
Imperial Physician. (1) CH'IN–N-S DIV: principal medical attendant on the Emperor and supervisor of a staff of Palace Physicians (*t'ai-i*); from Han on, commonly 2 or more in the central government, one attached to the Chamberlain for Ceremonials (*t'ai-ch'ang*), rank 1,000 bushels; another, rank 600 bushels, attached to the Chamberlain for the Palace Revenues (*shao-fu*) in Han and the Three Kingdoms era, thereafter gravitating to the emerging Chancellery (*men-hsia sheng*). Also, from Han on, commonly found on the staffs of Princes and various other central government or regional dignitaries. The Imperial Physicians were normally assisted by Aides (*ch'eng*) and at times large numbers of Palace Physicians. In Han the Imperial Physician attached to the Chamberlain for the Palace Revenues had 2 Aides, one Medical Treatment Aide (*fang-ch'eng*) and one Pharmacist Aide (*yao-ch'eng*), the latter possibly a practitioner of Taoist-type alchemical medicine. HB: prefect grand physician. P36. (2) SUNG: common reference to the Director (*ling*) of the Imperial Medical Service (*t'ai-i chü*). (3) CH'ING: unofficial reference to the Commissioner (*shih*) of the Imperial Academy of Medicine (*t'ai-i yüan*).

6181   *t'ài-ī pó-shìh* 太一博士
T'ANG: **Erudite of the Supreme Unity,** a teacher of Taoist doctrines; one of 18 Palace Erudites (*nei-chiao po-shih*) on the staff of the Palace Institute of Literature (*nei wen-hsüeh kuan*), where palace women were educated; from c. 741, a eunuch post. RR: *maître de la doctrine du suprême un.*

6182   *t'ài-ī pó-shìh* 太醫博士
N-S DIV (N. Wei): **Medical Erudite,** one or more, rank 7b, teachers of medical practices on the staff of the Imperial Physician (*t'ai-i ling*). P36.

6183   *t'ài-ī shü* 太醫署
SUI–T'ANG: **Imperial Medical Office,** a quasi-autonomous unit under the Court of Imperial Sacrifices (*t'ai-ch'ang ssu*), nominally responsible for medical care of the Emperor but after c. 605, when a Palace Medical Service (*shang-*

yao chü) was established in the Palace Administration (*tien-nei sheng*), increasingly became a teaching and certifying agency for professional physicians in government service. In Sui notably included a Director (*ling*), an Aide (*ch'eng*), 2 Pharmacists (*chu-yao*), 200 Master Physicians (*i-shih*), 2 Herbal Gardeners (*yao-yüan shih*), 2 Erudites for General Medicine (*i po-shih*), 2 Erudites for Massage (*an-mo po-shih*), and 2 Erudites for Exorcism (*chou-chin po-shih*). The T'ang agency was much the same, with 2 Directors, rank 7b2, and with the addition of one or more Erudites for Acupuncture (*chen po-shih*). The tradition was carried on during the Five Dynasties era principally by medical practitioners in the Hanlin Academy (*han-lin yüan*) and in Sung by an Imperial Medical Service (*t'ai-i chü*). RR: *office de la médecine suprême.* P36.

6184   *t'ài-ī yüàn* 太醫院
CHIN–CH'ING: **Imperial Academy of Medicine,** in Chin subordinate to the Court Ceremonial Institute (*hsüan-hui yüan*) but thereafter an autonomous agency of the central government; in general charge of establishing medical standards throughout the empire, training medical practitioners for government service, and at least nominally providing medical care for the Emperor. In Chin headed by a Superintendent (*t'i-tien*), rank 5a, and a Commissioner (*shih*), 5b, and divided into 10 Sections (*k'o*) with various ranks of Master Physicians (*i-shih*). In Yüan headed by 4 rank 2a Superintendents and from 2 eventually to 12 Commissioners, rank 3a then also 2a; among its constituent units was a Supervisorate of Medical Schools (*i-hsüeh t'i-chü ssu*). In Ming headed by a single Commissioner, rank 3a then 5a, assisted by several Administrative Assistants (*yüan-p'an*), 6a; and divided into 13 Sections (*k'o*) staffed with Imperial Physicians (*yü-i*); from 1381 to 1389 the head was a Director (*ling*). Ch'ing followed the Ming structure but superimposed atop it a member of the Imperial Household Department (*nei-wu fu*) as Manager (*kuan-li*). For antecedents of the Academy, see under *t'ai-i.* Cf. *yü-yao yüan* (Imperial Dispensary). BH: imperial medical department. P36.

6185   *t'ài-kuān* 太官 or *t'ài-kuān lìng* 令
(1) CH'IN–N-S DIV: **Provisioner,** one of the major subordinates of the Chamberlain for the Palace Revenues (*shao-fu*), rank from 600 to 1,000 bushels in Han; responsible for preparing meals for the palace and the court, at some point reportedly employed 3,000 state slaves and annually spent 200 million coins. By the end of the era of N-S Division, the Provisioner's staff had stabilized as one of the major agencies under the Court of Imperial Entertainments (*kuang-lu ssu*); see *ta-kuan ssu.* HB: prefect grand provisioner. P30. (2) CH'ING: unofficial reference to a **Chief Minister** (*ch'ing*) **of the Court of Imperial Entertainments.**

6186   *t'ài-kuān shü* 太官署
See *ta-kuan shu* (**Banquets Office**).

6187   *t'ài-láng* 臺郎
(1) HAN–N-S DIV: unofficial reference to a **Secretarial Court Gentleman** (*shang-shu lang*). (2) SUNG: unofficial reference to a **Bureau Director** (*lang-chung*) in a Ministry (*pu*) in the Department of State Affairs (*shang-shu sheng*). (3) May be encountered at any time as an unofficial reference to a **Censor** (*yü-shih*).

6188   *t'ài-miào* 太廟
Imperial Ancestral Temple: throughout history the family temple at which Emperors regularly worshipped; at times maintained by the Imperial Clan Court (*tsung-cheng ssu, tsung-jen fu*), at times by the Court of Imperial Sacrifices

(*t'ai-ch'ang ssu*), at times by a special Office of the Imperial Ancestral Temple (*t'ai-miao shu*) or Director of the Imperial Ancestral Temple (*t'ai-miao ling*). Cf. *chai-lang* (Court Gentleman for Fasting), *chiao-she chü* (Office of the National Altars), *she-chi t'an* (Altar of Land and Grain).

6189   *t'ài-miào chì-ch'ì fǎ-wù k'ù*
太廟祭器法物庫
SUNG: **Storehouse of Utensils for the Imperial Ancestral Temple,** a unit of the Directorate for Imperial Manufactories (*shao-fu chien*); staffing not clear, probably unranked suofficials. SP: *magasin des objets de sacrifice du temple des ancêtres de l'empereur.*

6190   *t'ài-miào chǚ* 太廟局
SUNG: **Imperial Ancestral Temple Service,** organizational affiliation not clear; headed by one Director (*ling*), probably a court official on ad hoc detached duty assignment from a regular central government agency; specific functions not clear, but no doubt organized to assist the Emperor in worship. SP: *bureau des temples des ancêtres de l'empereur.*

6191   *t'ài-miào lìng* 太廟令
N-S DIV–YÜAN: **Director of the Imperial Ancestral Temple,** sometimes a court dignitary on ad hoc duty assignment from a regular central government post for short-term assistance of the Emperor in his worship, commonly with an Aide (*ch'eng*); sometimes an abbreviated reference to the Director (*ling*) of the Imperial Ancestral Temple Service (*t'ai-miao chü*) or of the Imperial Ancestral Temple Office (*t'ai-miao shu*). P28.

6192   *t'ài-miào shǔ* 太廟署
Imperial Ancestral Temple Office. (1) N-S DIV (N. Ch'i): a unit under the Court of Imperial Sacrifices (*t'ai-ch'ang ssu*), headed by a Director (*ling*), rank not clear. (2) YÜAN: one of 3 special sacrificial agencies in the central government (see *chiao-ssu shu, she-chi shu*), headed by a Director (*ling*), rank 6b. P28.

6193   *t'ài-miào wèi* 太廟尉
CH'ING: **Commandant at the Imperial Ancestral Temple,** 10 Manchu military officers, 2 of rank 4, 8 of rank 5, under supervision of the Court of Imperial Sacrifices (*t'ai-ch'ang ssu*); in rotation took active command of soldiers guarding the temple, on sacrificial days monitored the comings and goings of authorized persons. P28.

6194   *t'ài-mǔ* 太母
(1) T'ANG–SUNG: **Imperial Mother,** one of many designations used for the natural mother of a reigning Emperor. (2) **Imperial Grandmother,** occasional reference to the mother of a reigning Emperor's mother, or possibly to a Grand Empress Dowager (*t'ai-huang t'ai-hou*).

6195   *t'ài-pǎo* 太保
(1) **Grand Guardian,** throughout history one of the eminent court dignitaries collectively known as the Three Preceptors (*san shih*) or the Three Dukes (*san kung*); ranked as a Feudal Lord (*chu-hou*) in Chou, at 10,000 bushels in Han, thereafter 1a. Cf. *t'ai-wei.* HB: grand guardian. RR: *grand gardien.* SP: *grand protecteur.* P67. (2) LIAO: **Keeper of Horse Herds,** apparently unranked underlings in Horse Pasturages (*ch'ün-ma ssu*).

6196   *t'ài-p'íng hùi-mín chǚ* 太平惠民局
SUNG: lit., service for favoring the people in an era of great peace: variant name of the **Pharmacy** (*shu-yao so*) maintained by the Court of the Imperial Treasury (*t'ao-fu ssu*).

6197   *t'ài-pǔ* 太卜
(1) CHOU: variant of *ta-pu* (**Grand Diviner**), from which subsequent *t'ai-pu* titles derived. (2) CH'IN, N-S DIV, SUNG: **Imperial Diviner,** generally in charge of divining about good and bad auspices concerning court and state activities; occurred irregularly in Ch'in, status not clear; in Chou of the era of N-S Division in the Ministry of Rites (*ch'un-kuan*) with rank as Junior Grand Master (*hsia ta-fu;* 6a); in Sung, rank not clear, in the Court of Imperial Sacrifices (*t'ai-ch'ang ssu*). Also see *t'ai-pu ling, t'ai-pu chü, t'ai-pu shu.* SP: *chef de divination.* P35.

6198   *t'ài-pǔ chǚ* 太卜局
N-S DIV: **Imperial Divination Service,** especially in N. Ch'i but probably in other periods as well, the office headed by the Imperial Diviner (*t'ai-pu ling*) under the Grand Astrologer (*t'ai-shih ling*). P35.

6199   *t'ài-pǔ lìng* 太卜令
Imperial Diviner. (1) HAN: established in 104 B.C. under the Chamberlain for Ceremonials (*t'ai-ch'ang*), with rank of 600 bushels and a staff including an Aide (*ch'eng*), one or more Erudites (*po-shih*), and sometimes Expectant Officials (*tai-chao*); in Later Han the title may have been perpetuated irregularly, but the functions were apparently wholly absorbed under the Grand Astrologer (*t'ai-shih ling*). HB: prefect grand augur. (2) N-S DIV–T'ANG: abbreviated reference to the Director (*ling*) of the Imperial Divination Service (*t'ai-pu chü*) or the Imperial Divination Office (*t'ai-pu shu*). P35.

6200   *t'ài-pǔ shǔ* 太卜署
T'ANG: **Imperial Divination Office** under the Court of Imperial Sacrifices (*t'ai-ch'ang ssu*), responsible for all forms of divination pertaining to imperial sacrifices, including the use of tortoiseshells and the ancient text *I-ching;* headed by a Director (*ling*), rank 7b2 then 8b2, with the assistance of 2 Aides (*ch'eng*), 2 Divination Directors (*pu-cheng*), 2 Erudites (*po-shih*), etc. Such divination responsibilities were subsequently shifted to the astrological-astronomical agencies that evolved into the Ming–Ch'ing Directorate of Astronomy (*ch'in-t'ien chien*). RR: *office de la divination suprême.* P35.

6201   *t'ài-p'ú* 太僕
(1) CHOU: variant of *ta-p'u* (**Royal Groom**). (2) CH'IN–N-S DIV: **Chamberlain for the Imperial Stud,** one of the 2nd-tier central government dignitaries collectively called the Nine Chamberlains (*chiu ch'ing*), in general charge of providing the Emperor and the court with horses and vehicles and maintaining the imperial horse herds; rank generally 2,000 bushels; supervised a large staff of subordinates ranging from Aides (*ch'eng*) ranked at 1,000 bushels down to state slaves reportedly numbering 30,000; managed stables, corrals, coachhouses, and pasturages where as many as 300,000 horses were reportedly maintained in Han. Subordinates of the Han Chamberlain included Directors (*ling*) of the Palace Stable (*ta-chiu ling*), of the Inner Compound Stable (*wei-yang ling*), of the Imperial Mares (*chia-ma ling, t'ung-ma ling*), of the Livery Office (*ch'e-fu ling*), of the Imperial Hunting Chariots (*lu-ling ling*), of Cavalry Mounts (*chi-ma ling*), and of the Finest Steeds (*chün-ma ling*); and Directors (*chang*) of the Directorates of Dragon Horses (*lung-ma chien*), of Horse Corrals (*hsien-chü chien*), of the T'o-ch'üan Pasturage (*t'o-ch'üan chien*), of the Wild Horse Pasturage (*t'ao-t'u chien*), and of the Ch'eng-hua Pasturage (*ch'eng-hua chien*). Late in the era of N-S Division the Chamberlain's agency became stably institutionalized as the Court of the Imperial Stud (*t'ai-p'u ssu*), a

name it retained through the Ch'ing dynasty. Cf. *p'u*. HB: grand coachman. P31. (3) HAN: **Royal Coachman,** one in charge of the horses and vehicles in each Princedom (*wang-kuo*), rank identical with the Chamberlain for the Imperial Stud; in 104 B.C. retitled *p'u* and demoted to the rank of 1,000 bushels; one also appointed in the establishments of all Empresses Dowager (*huang t'ai-hou*) briefly from 5 B.C. HB: grand coachman. P69.

6202   t'ài-p'ú ch'īng 太僕卿
(1) Common variant of *t'ai-p'u* (**Chamberlain for the Imperial Stud**). (2) N-S DIV–CH'ING: **Chief Minister of the Court of the Imperial Stud** (*t'ai-p'u ssu*, q.v.).

6203   t'ài-p'ú ssū 太僕司
SUI: **Office of the Imperial Coachman** (?), a central government agency created c. 605 by a division of the Chancellery (*men-hsia sheng*) into 2 agencies, the 2nd being an Office of Palace Attendants (*men-hsia ssu*); functions and staffing not clear; not perpetuated into T'ang.

6204   t'ài-p'ú ssù 太僕寺
N-S DIV–CH'ING: **Court of the Imperial Stud,** a 2nd-tier agency of the central government principally responsible, under policies determined by the Ministry of War (*ping-pu*), for managing state horse pasturages throughout the empire and maintaining related vehicles and gear; after T'ang shared management of stables and corrals at the dynastic capital, which provided horses and vehicles for use by the imperial household and members of the central government, with other agencies such as the Livery Service (*shang-ch'eng chü*) of the Sung Palace Administration (*tien-chung sheng*), the Yüan Court of the Imperial Saddlery (*shang-ch'eng ssu*), the Ming eunuch-staffed Directorate for Imperial Mounts (*yü-ma chien*), and the Ch'ing Imperial Household Department's (*nei-wu fu*) Palace Stud (*shang-ssu yüan*). Considered one of the Nine Courts (*chiu ssu*), headed by a Chief Minister (*ch'ing*), rank 3a in N. Wei, 3b in T'ang, 4b in Sung, 2b in Yüan (2 appointees), 3b in Ming and Ch'ing (2 appointees in Ch'ing), normally with the assistance of one or more Vice Ministers (*shao-ch'ing*) and Assistant Ministers (*ch'eng*). The Court normally supervised a large number of local horse pasturages (*mu-ch'ang*). Other subordinate units included, in T'ang, an Office of the Imperial Coachman (*ch'eng-huang shu*), an Office of the Imperial Stables (*tien-chiu shu*), an Office of Herds (*tien-mu shu*), and a Livery Office (*ch'e-fu shu*); in Sung, a Carriage Livery (*ch'e-lu yüan*), a Mounts Service (*ch'i-chi yüan*), a Left and a Right Directorate of Fine Steeds (*t'ien-ssu chien*), a Saddlery Storehouse (*an-p'ei k'u*), an Office for Elephant Care (*yang-hsiang so*), a Camel Corral (*t'o-fang*), and a Wagon Camp (*ch'e-ying*); in Ming, 4 Branch Courts of the Imperial Stud (*hsing t'ai-p'u ssu*) with staffs comparable to the metropolitan Court based in the good pasturelands along the northern frontier. RR+SP: *cour des équipages impériaux*. BH: court of the imperial stud. P31.

6205   t'ài-shàng 太上
Lit., great superior: from Han on, an unofficial reference to the **Emperor.**

6206   t'ài-shàng chūn 太上君
N-S DIV (San-kuo Wei): **Grand Princess-cognate,** designation of the principal wife of the father (but not necessarily the mother) of an Empress.

6207   t'ài-shàng huáng-hòu 太上皇后
SUNG: **Imperial Mother,** occasional variant of the normal designation *huang t'ai-hou* (Empress Dowager), possibly

used particularly when the Emperor's natural mother had never borne the title Empress.

6208   t'ài-shàng huáng-tì 太上皇帝 or t'ài-shàng huáng
(1) **Emperor Emeritus,** common designation of an abdicated Emperor during his remaining life, particularly during the reign of a son. (2) **Honorary Emperor,** common designation of the living father of an Emperor who had not himself reigned. Cf. *huang-k'ao* (Deceased Imperial Father).

6209   t'ài-shè chǘ 太社局
SUNG: **Service for the Altars of the Soil and Grain,** a unit of the Court of Imperial Sacrifices (*t'ai-ch'ang ssu*), headed by a Director (*ling*), rank 9a. SP: *bureau de l'autel du dieu du sol et des moissons*. P28.

6210   t'ài-shè lìng 太社令
N-S DIV: **Director of the Altar of the Soil and Grain** under the Chamberlain for Ceremonials (*t'ai-ch'ang*); in Sui the post was absorbed into the Office of the National Altars (*chiao-she shu*), but also see *t'ai-she chü*. P28.

6211   t'ái-shěng 臺省
(1) HAN–SUNG: common unofficial reference to the **Department of State Affairs** (*shang-shu sheng*), because from Han on it was also unofficially called *chung-t'ai* (lit., central or palace pavilion). (2) T'ANG: unofficial collective reference to the **Three Departments** (*san sheng*), i.e., the Department of State Affairs (*shang-shu sheng*), known as *chung-t'ai* (central or palace pavilion); the Secretariat (*chung-shu sheng*), known as *hsi-t'ai* (western pavilion); and the Chancellery (*men-hsia sheng*), known as *tung-t'ai* (eastern pavilion). Cf. *san t'ai*. (3) MING–CH'ING: unofficial collective reference to **Censors** (*yü-shih*) **and Supervising Secretaries** (*chi-shih-chung*), combining elements from the old names *yü-shih t'ai* (Censorate), to which Censors belonged, and *men-hsia sheng* (Chancellery), to which Supervising Secretaries belonged.

6212   t'ài-shǐh 太史
Lit., grand scribe. (1) CHOU: variant of *ta-shih* (**Grand Scribe**). (2) CH'IN–YÜAN: variant of *t'ai-shih ling* (**Grand Astrologer**); not later than very early Han lost its scribal functions, thereafter throughout imperial history was associated with the recording and interpreting of celestial and other remarkable natural phenomena, weather forecasting, and other esoteric aspects of astronomy, in contrast to the more rational and objective astronomical and calendrical work that, from T'ang on, was assigned to separate agencies (see under *ssu-t'ien chien*). (3) N-S DIV (Chou): **Grand Astrologer,** one ranked as an Ordinary Grand Master (*chung ta-fu;* 5a), in charge of calendrical calculations in the Ministry of Rites (*ch'un-kuan*). (4) T'ANG: **Grand Scribe,** from 662 to 670 the official designation of the head of the Orchid Pavilion (*lan-t'ai*), then the archaic official name of the Palace Library (*pi-shu sheng*). (5) CH'ING: unofficial reference to members of the Hanlin Academy (*han-lin yüan*), especially **Junior Compilers** (*pien-hsiu*). P35.

6213   t'ài-shīh 太師
Grand Preceptor: throughout history one of the eminent court dignitaries known as the Three Preceptors (*san shih*) or the Three Dukes (*san kung*), ranked as a Feudal Lord (*chu-hou*) in Chou, at 10,000 bushels in Han, thereafter 1a. In the post-Han Chin dynasty and the following S. Dynasties, commonly replaced by the equally archaic title *ta-tsai* (Grand Steward). HB: grand master. RR+SP: *grand précepteur*. P67.

6214 *t'ài-shǐh àn* 太史案
SUNG: **Astrological Section** in the Imperial Archives (*pi-ko*), apparently an early Sung variant of *t'ai-shih chü* or *pi-ko chü* (both Astrological Service). SP: *service des observations astronomiques.*

6215 *t'ài-shǐh chiēn* 太史監
(1) SUI–T'ANG, MING, CH'ING: **Directorate of Astrology**, changed from *t'ai-shih chü* (Astrological Service) in 604, changed back and subordinated to the Palace Library (*pi-shu sheng*) in 621; revived as an independent agency in 708–711, 714–726, 742–758, then transformed into an independent Bureau of Astronomy (*ssu-t'ien t'ai*) with an emphasis on objective celestial observation and calendrical calculations; thereafter not revived until formation of the original predynastic Ming government, but in 1367 renamed Astrological Commission (*t'ai-shih yüan*); in Ch'ing used only as an unofficial reference to the Directorate of Astronomy (*ch'in-t'ien chien*). RR: *direction des observations astronomiques.* P35. (2) SUI–T'ANG: **Supervisor of the Directorate of Astrology** (also *t'ai-shih chien*), rank apparently 3a in T'ang. P35.

6216 *t'ài-shǐh chǘ* 太史局
SUI–SUNG: **Astrological Service,** a unit of the Palace Library (*pi-shu sheng*) headed by one or 2 Directors (*ling*), rank 7b in Sui, not clear from T'ang to Sung; originated as a variant of the early Sui name Astrological Office (*t'ai-shih ts'ao*), renamed Directorate of Astrology (*t'ai-shih chien*) in 604; revived in 621, then from 662 to 758 alternated with *t'ai-shih chien* and other variants, appearing in 670–700, 702–708, and 726–742; thereafter not revived until c. 1080 and not continued after the end of Sung. Principal functions were interpreting celestial and other extraordinary natural phenomena, divining about auspicious days for state ceremonies, weather forecasting, and contributing to the preparation of the official state calendar. Subordinates included the Office of Celestial Understanding (*t'ung-hsüan yüan*), Five Offices (*wu kuan*, q.v.) of astrological interpreters, Directors of Calendrical Calculations (*pao-chang cheng*), the Imperial Observatory (*ling-t'ai*), Erudites of the Water Clock (*lou-k'o po-shih*) and other specialized teachers, the Armillary Sphere Office (*hun-i t'ai*), the Bureau of Bells and Drums (*chung-ku yüan*), and the Calendar Printing Office (*yin-li so*). From 758 the more rational and objective aspects of astronomical work were shifted to other agencies such as the T'ang Bureau of Astronomy (*ssu-t'ien t'ai*), the Sung Directorate of Astronomy (*ssu-t'ien chien*), and the Ming–Ch'ing Directorate of Astronomy (*ch'in-t'ien chien*). RR: *service des observations astronomiques.* SP: *bureau des ....* P35.

6217 *t'ài-shǐh kūng* 太史公
HAN: lit., the honorable *t'ai-shih:* not a title, but the honorfic way in which the great historian Ssu-ma Ch'ien referred to his dead father, from whom he inherited the official post of **Grand Astrologer** (*t'ai-shih ling*). P35.

6218 *t'ài-shǐh lìng* 太史令
(1) CH'IN–N-S DIV: **Grand Astrologer,** a subordinate of the Chamberlain for Ceremonials (*t'ai-ch'ang*) till N. Wei, then subordinated to the Palace Library (*pi-shu sheng*); rank 600 bushels in Han, commonly rank 7 thereafter; in very early Han apparently had some historiographic duties, but in general was in charge of observing celestial phenomena and irregularities in nature, interpreting portents, divining and weather forecasting as regards important state ceremonies, and preparing the official state calendar. His staff regularly consisted of one or more Aides (*ch'eng*); in Later

Han there was a specialized Aide for the Hall of Enlightened Rule (*ming-t'ang ch'eng*) and another for the Imperial Observatory (*ling-t'ai ch'eng*), both rank 200 bushels, supported by dozens of Expectant Officials (*tai-chao*) with specialized assignments, Gentlemen Observers (*wang-lang*), and Clerks (*chang-ku*). From Later Han on, the post of Imperial Diviner (*t'ai-pu*) was normally incorporated into the staff of the Grand Astrologer. HB: prefect grand astrologer. P35. (2) SUI–YÜAN: variant reference to the **Director** (*ling*) in a series of astrological agencies: the Sui Astrological Office (*t'ai-shih ts'ao*), 2, rank 7b; the T'ang–Sung Astrological Service (*t'ai-shih chü*), rank not clear; the Liao Directorate of Astronomy (*ssu-t'ien chien*); the Yüan Astrological Commission (*t'ai-shih yüan*), 3a then 2b then 2a; and the predynastic Ming Directorate of Astrology (*t'ai-shih chien*), rank not clear. RR+SP: *directeur.* P35. (3) CH'ING: unofficial reference both to a **Chancellor of the Hanlin Academy** (*han-lin yüan chang-yüan hsüeh-shih*) and a **Director** (*chien-cheng*) **of the Directorate of Astronomy** (*ch'in-t'ien chien*).

6219 *t'ài-shǐh ts'áo* 太史曹
SUI: **Astrological Office** in the Palace Library (*pi-shu sheng*); responsible for observing and interpreting celestial phenomena, weather forecasting, preparing the official state calendar, etc.; headed by 2 Directors (*ling*), rank 7b, and 2 Vice Directors (*ch'eng*), 9a; staffed additionally with specialists such as Managers of the Calendar (*ssu-li*), Astronomical Observers (*chien-hou*), Erudites of the Calendar (*li po-shih*), Erudites of Astronomy (*t'ien-wen po-shih*), Erudites of the Water Clock (*lou-k'o po-shih*), etc. Also called *t'ai-shih chü* (Astrological Service). In 604 reorganized as the Directorate of Astrology (*t'ai-shih chien*). P35.

6220 *t'ài-shǐh yüàn* 太史院
YÜAN: **Astrological Commission,** a large autonomous central government agency responsible for preparing and distributing the official state calendar, in contrast to the Directorate of Astronomy (*ssu-t'ien chien*), which was responsible for the training of astronomers and astrologers; headed by a Director (*ling*), rank 3a then 2b then 2a, and a Commissioner (*shih*) of equal rank, assisted by an executive staff including 2 Vice Directors (*t'ung-chih*), 3a, 2 Assistant Commissioners (*ch'ien-yüan*), 3b, 2 Deputies (*t'ung-ch'ien*), 4a, and 2 Administrative Assistants (*yüan-p'an*), 5a. Subordinate specialists included seasonal astrological interpreters in what were collectively called the Five Offices (*wu kuan*), 5 Directors of Calendrical Calculations (*pao-chang cheng*), 7a, and the Director of the Imperial Observatory (*ling-t'ai lang*), 7a. In each Province (*sheng*) the Commission was represented by a Manager of the Calendar (*ssu-li*), 9a. Revived briefly in predynastic Ming times by a renaming of the *t'ai-shih chien* (Directorate of Astrology) in 1367, then in 1368 reorganized as the Directorate of Astronomy (*ssu-t'ien chien*). P35.

6221 *t'ài-shǒu* 太守
(1) CH'IN–SUI: **Governor** of the territorial unit of administration called a Commandery (*chün*), normally with both military and civil responsibilities and often bearing the additional title General (*chiang-chün*); in Han rank 2,000 bushels, in the era of N-S Division rank from 3 down to 7 depending on the size of the resident population; discontinued with T'ang's abolition of the Commandery level of administration. (2) HAN–SUI: **Grand Protector,** a title commonly awarded chieftains of southern and southwestern aboriginal tribes. (3) SUNG–CH'ING: common quasiofficial or unofficial reference to a **Prefect** (*chih-chou, chih-*

fu). HB: grand administrator. RR: *préfet de commanderie*. P53, 72.

6222 *t'ài-sūn* 太孫
Grandson Successor: throughout imperial history the designation most commonly used for the eldest son of the Heir Apparent, especially used when the Heir Apparent had predeceased him before taking the throne, so that the *t'ai-sun* was expected to become the next Emperor.

6223 *t'ái-tsá* 臺雜
SUNG: unofficial abbreviation of *shih yü-shih chih tsa-shih* (General Purpose Censor) in the Censorate (*yü-shih t'ai*).

6224 *t'ái-tsǎi* 台宰
HAN: unofficial reference to a Counselor-in-chief (*ch'eng-hsiang*).

6225 *t'ài-tsǎi* 太宰
Great Steward. (1) Variant of *ta-tsai* (Grand Steward). Also see *shao-tsai*. (2) HAN: variant of *t'ai-tsai ling* (Great Sacrificial Butcher). (3) N-S DIV: from Chin on, commonly replaced *t'ai-shih* (Grand Preceptor) among the dignitaries known as the Three Dukes (*san kung*). P67. (4) T'ANG-CH'ING: unofficial reference to a Minister of Personnel (*li-pu shang-shu*). (5) SUNG: briefly in the early 1100s and again during S. Sung the official redesignation of the Vice Director of the Left (*tso p'u-yeh*) of the Department of State Affairs (*shang-shu sheng*), one of the senior Grand Councilors (*tsai-hsiang*). SP: *grand intendant, conseiller en chef de l'état*. P3.

6226 *t'ài-tsǎi lìng* 太宰令
HAN: Great Sacrificial Butcher, one of the principal subordinates of the Chamberlain for Ceremonials (*t'ai-ch'ang*), responsible for the preparation of meats for major state sacrificial ceremonies, rank 600 bushels; assisted by an Aide (*ch'eng*) and a large staff reportedly including more than 200 Butchers (*tsai*) and several dozen Meat Trimmers (*t'u-che*). The post seems not to have survived Later Han. HB: prefect grand butcher. P27.

6227 *t'ài-ts'āng* 太倉
Imperial Granaries: throughout history a quasiofficial or official collective designation for the principal state granaries located at the dynastic capital to provide for the imperial palace and the central government; individual granary units sometimes identified with place-name prefixes, function-specific descriptive prefixes, numerical prefixes based on the Chinese sequence of "stems" (*chia, i, ping, ting*, etc.), and perhaps others. Supervised by a Director (*ling*) from Ch'in until late in the era of N-S Division, then by an Office (*shu*) through T'ang, and by a Commissioner (*shih*) in Chin; in Sung, Yüan, Ming, and Ch'ing known formally by such other names as *t'i-ling ts'ang-chien, tso-ao t'ing, tso-liang t'ing*. HB: great granary. RR+SP: *grenier impérial*. P8.

6228 *t'ài-ts'āng ch'ū-nà shǐh* 太倉出納使
T'ANG: Inspector of Receipts and Disbursements at the Imperial Granaries, an irregular duty assignment for a Vice Minister (*shao-ch'ing*) of the Court of the National Granaries (*ssu-nung ssu*), apparently to check records maintained by the Imperial Granaries Office (*t'ai-ts'ang shu*) concerning the flow of grain in and out of the granaries at the dynastic capital. See *t'ai-ts'ang shih*. P8.

6229 *t'ài-ts'āng k'ù* 太倉庫
MING: National Silver Vault, the principal treasury maintained by the central government; under the Ministry of Revenue (*hu-pu*), managed by a Vice Minister of Revenue

(*hu-pu shih-lang*); established in 1442, by the late 1500s normally handled 4 million taels of silver annually, including many kinds of taxes, fines, and confiscations converted into silver. The original Vault eventually came to have 2 attached buildings, where receipt and disbursement were most convenient; the original building then was called the Inner Vault (*chung-k'u*) and the 2 added buildings were said to constitute the Outer Vault (*wai-k'u*). Because it only dealt with silver, the Vault was also known as the Silver Vault (*yin-k'u*).

6230 *t'ài-ts'āng lìng* 太倉令
CH'IN-N-S DIV: Director of the Imperial Granaries, a principal subordinate of the Chamberlain for the National Treasury (*ta-nung ling, ta ssu-nung, ssu-nung ch'ing*); responsible for the management of the state granaries at the dynastic capital and their receipts and disbursements; rank 600 bushels, assisted by an Aide (*ch'eng*) and an unspecified but no doubt large number of underlings. Late in the era of N-S Division the post was transformed into an agency called the Imperial Granaries Office (*t'ai-ts'ang shu*). HB: prefect of the great granary. P8.

6231 *t'ài-ts'āng shǐh* 太倉使
(1) T'ANG: Inspector of the Imperial Granaries, status not clear; probably an abbreviated reference to the *t'ai-ts'ang ch'u-na shih* (Inspector of Receipts and Disbursements at the Imperial Granaries). (2) CHIN: Commissioner of the Imperial Granaries, rank 6b, under the Directorate of the Imperial Treasury (*t'ai-fu chien*); responsible for managing the state granaries at the dynastic capital. P8.

6232 *t'ài-ts'āng shǔ* 太倉署
N-S DIV-T'ANG: Imperial Granaries Office under the National Treasury or Court of the National Granaries (both *ssu-nung ssu*); managed state granaries at the dynastic capital; an institutionalization of the earlier Director of the Imperial Granaries (*t'ai-ts'ang ling*), headed by 2 Directors (*ling*) in Sui, 3 ranked 7b2 in T'ang; in Sui had 3 subordinate Supervisors (*tu*)—Supervisors of the Salt Storehouse (*yen-ts'ang*), the Rice Granary (*mi-lin*), and the Grain Granary (*ku-ts'ang*). The Office was not perpetuated beyond T'ang. RR: *office du grenier impérial*. P8.

6233 *t'ài-ts'āng yín-k'ù* 太倉銀庫
MING: variant of *t'ai-ts'ang k'u* (National Silver Vault).

6234 *t'ài-tsūn* 太尊
CH'ING: lit., the great venerable: His Honor or Your Honor, an unofficial reference to a Prefect (*chih-fu*). Cf. *ta-tsun* (His Majesty).

6235 *t'ài-tsūng* 太宗
CHOU: lit., great clansman: variant of *tsung-po* (Minister of Rites). See *ta-tsung*.

6236 *t'ài tsūng-chèng* 太宗正
SUNG: variant reference to a Chief Minister (*ch'ing*) of the Court of the Imperial Clan (*tsung-cheng ssu*) or to anyone assigned to manage the Court without that title. See *ta tsung-cheng* entries. SP: *directeur de la grande maison des affaires impériales*.

6237 *t'ài tsūng-chèng yùàn* 太宗正院
YÜAN-MING: Office of the Imperial Clan, staffed with imperial relatives charged with maintaining the imperial genealogy, certifying inheritances within the imperial clan, etc.; in 1389 renamed Court of the Imperial Clan (*tsung-jen fu*). Commonly rendered *ta tsung-cheng yüan*.

6238 *t'ái-tuān* 臺端
T'ANG-SUNG: lit., leader or exemplar of the Censorate

(*yü-shih t'ai*), a common unofficial reference to an **Attendant Censor** (*shih yü-shih*) or by extension to any executive official of the Censorate. See *tsa-tuan, san-tuan*. RR: *chef du tribunal*. P18.

6239   *t'ài-tzǔ* 太子
Heir Apparent: throughout history the formal designation of a reigning ruler's son chosen to be successor on the throne, most commonly in Chinese dynasties the ruler's eldest son, especially the eldest son borne by the principal wife (Queen or Empress). His living quarters in imperial times were referred to as the Eastern Palace (*tung-kung*), and his affairs were generally managed by a Household Administration of the Heir Apparent (*chan-shih fu*; also see *chan-shih*). The term *t'ai-tzu* is commonly prefixed to the titles of all posts in his establishment, many duplicating posts elsewhere in the central government. In addition to the entries that follow, note should be taken of entries without the *t'ai-tzu* prefix.

6240   *t'ài-tzǔ kūng-fù fǔ* 太子宮傅府
YÜAN: official variant from 1346 to 1353 of *chan-shih fu* (**Household Administration of the Heir Apparent**); staffed with Advisers (*yü-te*), Admonishers (*tsan-shan*), etc., apparently for the most part constituting a school called the Hall of Fundamentals (*tuan-pen t'ang*). P26.

6241   *t'ài-tzǔ líng* 太子陵
T'ANG: **Mausoleum of the Heir Apparent,** headed by a Director (*ling*), rank 8b2, subordinate to the Court of the Imperial Clan (*tsung-cheng ssu*); one apparently created for each successive Heir Apparent, becoming his imperial mausoleum upon his accession to the throne. RR: *tombeau de l'héritier du trône*.

6242   *t'ài-tzǔ miào* 太子廟
T'ANG: **Temple of the Heir Apparent,** headed by a Director (*ling*), rank 8b1, under the Court of the Imperial Clan (*tsung-cheng ssu*), perhaps created only for Heirs Apparent who died before succeeding to the throne, but possibly built in anticipation of each successive Heir Apparent's eventual accession and death on the throne. RR: *temple de l'héritier du trône (décédé)*.

6243   *t'ài-tzǔ nèi-fāng chǘ* 太子內坊局
T'ANG: **Domestic Service of the Heir Apparent,** an agency of the Household Administration of the Heir Apparent (*chan-shih fu*) till 739, then assigned to the Palace Domestic Service (*nei-shih sheng*); probably staffed with eunuchs responsible for personal attendance on the Heir Apparent and his harem. Commonly called *nei-fang* (Inner Quarters). RR: *service du palais intérieur de la maison de l'héritier du trône*. P67.

6244   *t'ài-tzǔ pīn-k'ò* 太子賓客
T'ANG–MING: **Adviser to the Heir Apparent,** nominally a regular post with rank of 3a in T'ang, 3b in Sung, and 3a in Ming, but almost always a post held concurrently by a Grand Councilor (*tsai-hsiang*) or comparable court dignitary; expected to provide companionship and guidance in governmental affairs in preparing the Heir Apparent for his future role as Emperor; sometimes more than one appointee. RR: *moniteur de l'héritier du trône*. SP: *moniteur de l'héritier du trône, conseiller en chef de l'héritier du trône*. P67.

6245   *t'ài-tzǔ p'ú* 太子僕
HAN–SUNG: **Coachman of the Heir Apparent,** one of the dignitaries assigned to the household of the Heir Apparent, rank 1,000 bushels in Han, rank 4 or 5 in the era

of N-S Division, 4b1 in T'ang; in general charge of the horses and vehicles available to the Heir Apparent and his staff; from Sui if not earlier, head of an office called the Livery Service of the Heir Apparent (*t'ai-tzu p'u-ssu*). See *p'u*. HB: coachman of the heir apparent. RR: *chef de la cour des équipages de l'héritier du trône*. SP: *maître d'écurie de l'héritier du trône*. P26.

6246   *t'ài-tzǔ p'ú-ssù* 太子僕寺
SUI–CHIN: **Livery Service of the Heir Apparent,** in charge of all horses and vehicles assigned to the Heir Apparent's establishment; headed by the Coachman of the Heir Apparent (*t'ai-tzu p'u*) through Sung, but in Liao and Chin by a Director (*ling* in Liao, *cheng* in Chin). See *p'u, t'ai-p'u ssu*. RR: *cour des équipages de l'héritier du trône*. P26.

6247   *t'ài-tzǔ sān ch'īng* 太子三卿
N-S DIV: **Three Chamberlains of the Heir Apparent,** a collective reference to the Household Provisioner (*chia-ling*), the Director of the Watches (*lei-keng ling*), and the Coachman of the Heir Apparent (*t'ai-tzu p'u*), the 3 most important dignitaries assigned to the Heir Apparent's establishment to supplement the Household Administration of the Heir Apparent (*chan-shih fu*). Cf. *san ch'ing*. P26.

6248   *t'ài-tzǔ sān shào* 太子三少
Three Junior Counselors of the Heir Apparent: from the post-Han Chin dynasty on, counterparts on the staff of the Heir Apparent of the dignitaries at the imperial court known as the Three Solitaries (*san ku*): specifically, Junior Preceptor of the Heir Apparent (*t'ai-tzu shao-shih*), Junior Mentor of the Heir Apparent (*t'ai-tzu shao-fu*), and Junior Guardian of the Heir Apparent (*t'ai-tzu shao-pao*). Considered regular, substantive appointments, but normally awarded only as concurrent appointments to officials already in positions of considerable stature at court, solely for the purpose of enhancing their prestige and possibly their income. All normally ranked 2a. P67.

6249   *t'ài-tzǔ sān shīh* 太子三師
Three Preceptors of the Heir Apparent: from the post-Han Chin dynasty on, counterparts on the staff of the Heir Apparent of the eminent dignitaries at the imperial court known as the Three Dukes (*san kung*) or Three Preceptors (*san shih*). Considered regular, substantive appointments, but normally awarded only as concurrent appointments to officials already having considerable stature at court, solely for the purpose of enhancing their prestige and possibly their income. The standard individual titles were Grand Preceptor of the Heir Apparent (*t'ai-tzu t'ai-shih*), Grand Mentor of the Heir Apparent (*t'ai-tzu t'ai-fu*), and Grand Guardian of the Heir Apparent (*t'ai-tzu t'ai-pao*). All normally carried rank 1b. It is noteworthy that the term Three Dukes seems never to have carried the prefix *t'ai-tzu*. P67.

6250   *t'ài-tzǔ shào chān-shìh* 太子少詹事
Vice Supervisor of the Household of the Heir Apparent; see under *shao chan-shih*.

6251   *t'ài-tzǔ shào-fù* 太子少傅
HAN–CH'ING: **Junior Mentor of the Heir Apparent,** in Han shared with the Grand Mentor of the Heir Apparent (*t'ai-tzu t'ai-fu*) responsibility for the education of the Heir Apparent; both posts filled with distinguished scholars; rank 2,000 bushels. From the post-Han Chin dynasty on, one of the Three Junior Counselors of the Heir Apparent (*t'ai-tzu san shao*), rank normally 2a. HB: junior tutor of the heir-apparent. RR+SP: *second maître de l'héritier du trône*. BH: junior tutor of the heir apparent. P67.

6252 *t'ài-tzǔ shào-pǎo* 太子少保

N-S DIV (Chin)–CH'ING: **Junior Guardian of the Heir Apparent,** one of the Three Junior Counselors of the Heir Apparent (*t'ai-tzu san shao*), normal rank 2a. RR: *second gardien de l'héritier du trône.* SP: *second protecteur de l'héritier du trône.* P67.

6253 *t'ài-tzǔ shào-shīh* 太子少師

N-S DIV (Chin)–CH'ING: **Junior Preceptor of the Heir Apparent,** one of the Three Junior Counselors of the Heir Apparent (*t'ai-tzu san shao*), normal rank 2a. RR+SP: *second précepteur de l'héritier du trône.* P67.

6254 *t'ài-tzǔ shuài-kēng lìng* 太子帥更令

SUNG: commonly appears as a scribal error for *t'ai-tzu lei-keng ling;* see under *lei-keng ling* (**Director of the Watches** in the household of the Heir Apparent).

6255 *t'ài-tzǔ shuài-kēng ssù* 太子率更寺

See under *lei-keng ssu* (**Court of the Watches** in the household of the Heir Apparent).

6256 *t'ài-tzǔ t'ài-fù* 太子太傅

HAN–CH'ING: **Grand Mentor of the Heir Apparent,** in Han shared with the Junior Mentor of the Heir Apparent (*t'ai-tzu shao-fu*) responsibility for the education of the Heir Apparent; both posts filled only with distinguished scholars, rank 2,000 bushels. From the post-Han Chin dynasty on, one of the Three Preceptors of the Heir Apparent (*t'ai-tzu san shih*), rank normally 1b. HB: grand tutor of the heir-apparent. RR+SP: *grand maître de l'héritier du trône.* BH: grand tutor of the heir apparent. P67.

6257 *t'ài-tzǔ t'ài-pǎo* 太子太保

N-S DIV (Chin)–CH'ING: **Grand Guardian of the Heir Apparent,** one of the Three Preceptors of the Heir Apparent (*t'ai-tzu san shih*), normal rank 1b. RR: *grand gardien de l'héritier du trône.* SP: *grand protecteur de l'héritier du trône.* P67.

6258 *t'ài-tzǔ t'ài-shīh* 太子太師

N-S DIV (Chin)–CH'ING: **Grand Preceptor of the Heir Apparent,** one of the Three Preceptors of the Heir Apparent (*t'ai-tzu san shih*), normal rank 1b. RR+SP: *grand précepteur de l'héritier du trône.* P67.

6259 *t'ài-tzǔ yüèh-lìng* 太子樂令

HAN: common scribal error for the Later Han title *t'ai yü-yüeh ling* (**Grand Director of Music**). P10.

6260 *t'ài-wèi* 太尉

Defender-in-chief. (1) CH'IN–HAN: commander of the empire's armed forces, one of the Three Dukes (*san kung*) among whom major responsibilities in the central government were divided; rank 10,000 bushels in Han; supervised an Office (*fu*) subdivided into a dozen or more Sections (*ts'ao*): Eastern Section (*tung-ts'ao*) in charge of the Office's fiscal affairs, Western Section (*hsi-ts'ao*) in charge of personnel appointments in the military service, Civil Affairs Section (*hu-ts'ao*), Memorials Section (*tsou-ts'ao*), Complaints Section (*tz'u-ts'ao*), Communications Section (*fa-ts'ao*), Conscript Section (*wei-ts'ao*), Judicial Section (*chüeh-ts'ao*), Banditry Section (*tsei-ts'ao*), Military Section (*ping-ts'ao*), Revenues Section (*chin-ts'ao*), Granaries Section (*ts'ang-ts'ao*), Archives Section (*huang-ko ts'ao*), and Consultation Section (*i-ts'ao*), each headed by an Administrator (*yüan-shih*), rank =300 or =400 bushels. From 119 B.C. to A.D. 51 the title *t'ai-wei* was replaced by *ta ssu-ma* (**Commander-in-chief**). HB: grand commandant. (2) N-S DIV–YÜAN: in irregular alternation with *t'ai-pao* (Grand Guardian), one of the eminent posts in the central government collectively known as the Three Dukes (*san kung*) or the Three Preceptors (*san shih*), rank 1a or 2a. RR+SP: *grand chef des armées,* also (SP only) *grand maréchal.* P2, 12. (3) N-S DIV: occasionally occurs as the title of the senior military officer in a Princedom (*wang-kuo*). P69.

6261 *t'ài-wèi kūng* 太尉公

HAN: official variant of *t'ai-wei* (**Defender-in-chief**) in Later Han. P12.

6262 *t'ài yǔ-yüèh lìng* 太予樂令

HAN: lit. meaning traditionally disputed; *yü* may have been a term for musician in high antiquity: from A.D. 60 the official redesignation of *t'ai-yüeh ling* (**Grand Director of Music**). P10.

6263 *t'ái-yüàn* 臺院

(1) T'ANG–SUNG: **Headquarters Bureau,** one of 3 units among which Censors (*yü-shih*) were distributed in the Censorate (*yü-shih t'ai*); staffed with 4 to 6 Attendant Censors (*shih yü-shih*) in T'ang, only one in Sung; in T'ang its personnel regularly participated in court audiences and major judicial proceedings at court; in Sung the lone Attendant Censor became a junior executive official of the Censorate. RR+SP: *cour des affaires générales.* P18. (2) YÜAN: unofficial reference to the entire **Censorate** (*yü-shih t'ai*). P19.

6264 *t'ài-yüèh* 太樂

CHOU: quasiofficial variant of *ta ssu-yüeh* (**Musician-in-chief**).

6265 *t'ài-yüèh àn* 太樂案

SUNG: **Headquarters Section** of the short-lived Imperial Music Bureau (*ta-sheng fu*), one of its 6 subordinate units; very possibly a reorganization of what, except from 1103 to 1120, was the Imperial Music Service (*t'ai-yüeh chü*). P10.

6266 *t'ài yüèh-chèng* 太樂正

CHIN: **Music Master,** rank 9b, in the Imperial Music Office (*t'ai-yüeh shu*); the counterpart of *yüeh-cheng* in other periods. P10.

6267 *t'ài-yüèh chú* 太樂局

SUNG: **Imperial Music Service,** a major unit of the Court of Imperial Sacrifices (*t'ai-ch'ang ssu*) that provided music and dancing for state sacrificial and other ceremonies; headed by a Director (*ling*), rank not clear, perhaps a non-official specialist. From 1103 to 1120 apparently absorbed into a new Imperial Music Bureau (*ta-sheng fu*). SP: *bureau de musique.* P10.

6268 *t'ài-yüèh lìng* 太樂令

(1) CH'IN–N-S DIV: **Grand Director of Music,** one of the major subordinates of the Chamberlain for Ceremonials (*feng-ch'ang, t'ai-ch'ang*), rank 600 bushels in Han; headed a large staff, including 388 musicians incorporated from the terminated Music Bureau (*yüeh-fu*) in 7 B.C.; provided music and dancing for sacrificial and other ceremonial occasions at court. In A.D. 60 renamed *t'ai yü-yüeh ling;* restored by San-kuo Wei. At times in the era of N-S Division apparently under the intermediary supervision of the Director of Imperial Music (*hsieh-lü hsiao-wei*) or the Palace Chief Musician (*hsieh-lü chung-lang*), also subordinates of the Chamberlain for Ceremonials. By N. Ch'i evolved into the head of a more stably institutionalized Imperial Music Office (*t'ai-yüeh shu*). HB: prefect grand musician. P10. (2) N-S DIV (N. Ch'i)–YÜAN: abbreviated reference to the **Director** (*ling*) **of the Imperial Music Office** (*t'ai-yüeh shu*) or, in Sung, the Imperial Music Service (*t'ai-yüeh chü*). P10

6269 *t'ài-yüèh shǔ* 太樂署

N-S DIV (N. Ch'i)–YÜAN: **Imperial Music Office,** a major unit of the Court of Imperial Sacrifices (*t'ai-ch'ang ssu*) except in Sung times (see *t'ai-yüeh chü*), responsible for providing music and dancing for state sacrifices and other ceremonies; headed by one or 2 Directors (*ling*), rank 7b2 in T'ang, 6b in Chin and Yüan, responsible for supervising Erudites (*po-shih*) who selected and trained professional performers, usually hereditary, for palace service, and Music Masters (*yüeh-cheng*), who directed performances. In Ming the Office's functions were carried on by Chief Musicians (*hsieh-lü lang*) of the Court of Imperial Sacrifices. RR: *office de la musique suprême.* P10.

6270 *tān-ch'ē tz'ù-shǐh* 單車刺史

N-S DIV (San-kuo Wei–S. Dyn.): lit., single-chariot *tz'u-shih:* **Restricted Regional Inspector,** designation of the chief administrator of a Region (*chou*) who did not have status as a General (*chiang-chün*) and was limited to civil aspects of administration in his jurisdiction; suggests officials who were career bureaucrats rather than members of the military elite. P50.

6271 *tān-fěn sǒ* 丹粉所

SUNG: **Paint Production Office** in the Directorate for the Palace Buildings (*chiang-tso chien*); manufactured paint pigments for use in decorating the imperial palace; headed by a Supervisor (*chien-kuan*), probably a non-official technician. SP: *bureau de peinture pour décoration.* P15.

6272 *tān-pǎng chuàng-yüán* 擔榜壯元

SUNG–CH'ING: lit., "principal graduate" whose shoulders supported the list of graduates: **Bottom Graduate,** unofficial reference to a Metropolitan Graduate (*chin-shih*) whose name was last on the pass list promulgated after the Metropolitan Examination (*sheng-shih, hui-shih*) in the civil service recruitment examination sequence. Cf. *chuang-yüan.*

6273 *tān-yǘ* 單于

See under *shan-yü* (**Khan** of the Hsiung-nu).

6274 *t'àn-ch'ǎng* 炭場

SUNG: **Charcoal Yard** under the Court of the National Granaries (*ssu-nung ssu*); presumably a storage depot for charcoal used in the palace and the central government; staffing not clear. SP: *magasin de charbon.*

6275 *t'àn-huā lāng* 探花郎 or *t'an-hua*

SUNG–CH'ING: lit., to seek the garland (?): **Third Graduate,** quasiofficial designation of the Metropolitan Graduate (*chin-shih*) who ranked 3rd in the final pass list posted after the last stage of the civil service recruitment examinations, the Palace Examination (*tien-shih, t'ing-shih*), after the Principal Graduate (*chuang-yüan*) and the Second Graduate (*pang-yen*); in Ming and Ch'ing normally appointed directly as Junior Compiler (*pien-hsiu*) in the Hanlin Academy (*han-lin yüan*).

6276 *t'ǎn-jén* 撢人

CHOU: lit., hand-carrier (?): **Disseminator,** 4 ranked as Ordinary Servicemen (*chung-shih*), members of the Ministry of War (*hsia-kuan*) responsible for carrying royal decisions throughout the realm and explaining them to local authorities. CL: *teneur de main.*

6277 *t'àn-mǎ-ch'ìh chūn* 探馬赤軍

YÜAN: Chinese transliteration of a Mongol word: **Allied Army,** one of the military forces that constituted the regular Yüan army, made up of Khitan, Jurchen, and Chinese soldiers who joined the Mongol cause early during Chingis

Khan's assault on Chin, together with troops of land-grant nobles (see under *fen-ti* and *t'ou-hsia*).

6278 *t'àn-miào àn* 壇廟案

SUNG: **Section for Altars and Temples** under the Court of Imperial Sacrifices (*t'ai-ch'ang ssu*); specific functions and staffing not clear. SP: *service des autels, temples èt tombeaux impériaux.*

6279 *t'án-wěi* 壇壝

SUNG: **Caretaker of the Altar Mound,** number, status, and specific functions not clear; in the Court of Imperial Sacrifices (*t'ai-ch'ang ssu*). SP: *chargé de balayer les autels et tertres.*

6280 *t'àn-yā* 彈壓

CHIN–YÜAN: lit., to press down, repress: **Disciplinarian** (?), at least on one occasion in Chin a duty assignment for a Battalion Commander (*ch'ien-hu*) to quell rioting among construction workers; in Yüan commonly a regular staff officer in a military Company (*po-hu so*). P59.

6281 *tāng* 璫

Lit., earring, pendant: from Later Han on, one of many designations for **Palace Eunuch;** see *huan-kuan, nei-shih, t'ai-chien.*

6282 *tǎng* 黨

(1) CHOU: **Ward,** a local self-government unit in the royal domain with a Head (*cheng*) who was reportedly popularly elected; consisted of 5 Precincts (*tsu*) totaling 500 families; 5 Wards constituted a Township (*chou*). CL: *canton.* (2) N-S DIV (N. Wei): **Ward,** a unit of sub-District (*hsien*) organization of the population comprising 5 Villages (*li*) totaling 125 families, with a designated Head (*chang*); see *san chang* (Three Elders). (3) SUI: **Township,** a unit of sub-District organization of the population whose Head (*chang*) was responsible for 5 rural Villages (*li*) totaling 50 families.

6283 *tāng-chīn fó-yéh* 當今佛爺

CH'ING: **Present Day Buddha,** an unofficial reference to the Emperor.

6284 *tāng-chú* 當軸

Lit., a pivot, someone in control: from Han on, an unofficial reference to anyone on official duty.

6285 *tàng-fáng* 檔房

Archive: e.g., see *man-tang fang, huang-tang fang, han-tang fang, feng-tang fang.*

6286 *tāng-lù-tzǔ* 當路子 or *tang-lu*

Lit., one who is on the road, deriving from a passage in *Meng-tzu* reporting that when "the master was on the road to Ch'i ...": unofficial reference to anyone on official duty.

6287 *tāng-yüèh ch'ù* 當月處

CH'ING: lit., in (such-and-such) month office: **Seal Office** in the Court of Colonial Affairs (*li-fan yüan*), the name suggesting that the Court's documents were here dated and certified; staffing not clear. BH: record office.

6288 *t'áng* 堂

(1) MING–CH'ING: **Headquarters,** quasiofficial designation of the duty station for senior officials of an agency at any level of government. See *kung-t'ang, cheng-t'ang, ta-t'ang, t'ang-kuan, t'ang-shang.* (2) MING–CH'ING: **College,** generic designation of 6 study units among which students of the Directorate of Education (*kuo-tzu chien*) were distributed; see *liu t'ang* (Six Colleges). P34.

6289 *t'áng* 塘
CH'ING: **Postal Relay Station,** a Sinkiang variant of the term *i-chan;* each headed by a Station Master (*t'i-t'ang*). BH: military courier bureau.

6290 *t'áng-chiàng* 錫匠
T'ANG: **Confectioner,** 5 non-official specialists in the Office of Delicacies (*chen-hsiu shu*) of the Court of Imperial Entertainments (*kuang-lu ssu*). RR: *confiseur.*

6291 *t'āng-chiēn* 湯監
T'ANG: **Directorate of Hot Baths,** one established at each of several noted spas where the state had built special housing facilities to which dignitaries were invited for bathing, also responsible for growing special kinds of vegetables around the hot springs; subordinate to the Court of the National Granaries (*ssu-nung ssu*), each headed by a Supervisor (*chien*), rank 6b2. RR: *direction de la source chaude.*

6292 *t'áng chǔ-shìh* 堂主事
CH'ING: **Headquarters Secretary,** a title specifying a Secretary (*chu-shih*) on the executive staff of an agency rather than a member of a subsidiary unit; e.g., on the executive staff of a Ministry (*pu*) in contrast to a Secretary in a Bureau (*ch'ing-li ssu*) of a Ministry; rank generally 6a. BH: secretary, chief secretary, senior secretary. P1, 5, 6, 9, etc.

6293 *t'áng-ch'ú* 堂除
SUNG: **Departmental Appointment,** signifying the appointment (*ch'u*) of an official by the Executive Office (*tu-t'ang*) of the Department of State Affairs (*shang-shu sheng*) without recourse to normal Evaluation Processes (*hsüan*); the practice was terminated by imperial order in 1172. See *t'ang-hsüan.*

6294 *t'áng-hòu kuān* 堂後官
T'ANG–SUNG–LIAO: lit., officials serving behind the headquarters, i.e., members of the clerical units reportedly "arrayed behind" the combined Secretariat-Chancellery (*chung-shu men-hsia*) when it was reorganized in the 720s from the prior Administration Chamber (*cheng-shih t'ang*): **Secretariat Clerk,** unranked subofficials in the Five Offices (*wu fang*) and the Six Offices (*liu fang*) that served the Secretariat-Chancellery. In Liao considered to rank lower than Secretaries (*chung she-jen*). SP: *préposé aux affaires.* P3, 4.

6295 *t'áng-hsüǎn* 堂選
SUNG: variant of *t'ang-ch'u* (**Departmental Appointment**).

6296 *t'áng-kǔ-t'è hsüéh* 唐古忒學
CH'ING: **Tangutan** (i.e., **Tibetan**) **School** in the Court of Colonial Affairs (*li-fan yüan*), staffed with one Director of Studies (*ssu-yeh*), one Instructor (*chu-chiao*), and 4 Clerks (*pi-t'ieh-shih*). P17.

6297 *t'áng-kuān* 堂官
MING–CH'ING: **Senior Official(s),** generic reference to the heads of any governmental agencies, usually including the top 2 or 3 officials of any one agency; in contrast to *ssu-kuan* (Administrative Associates) and *shou-ling kuan* (Staff Supervisors); rarely used as a specific title (see under *shang-ssu yüan,* Palace Stud). P39, 52.

6298 *t'āng-kuān* 湯官
HAN: **Office of Drinks and Delicacies** under the Provisioner (*t'ai-kuan*) on the staff of the Chamberlain for the Palace Revenues (*shao-fu*); in charge of providing the palace with wines, cakes, and other sweets; headed by a Director (*ling*) assisted by 2 Aides (*ch'eng*), in control of 3,000 state slaves; abolished early in Later Han. HB: office of liquors. P37.

6299 *t'áng láng-chūng* 堂郎中
CH'ING: **Headquarters Bureau Director,** one, rank 5a, senior administrative aide to the Grand Minister Supervisors of the Imperial Household Department (*tsung-kuan nei-wu fu ta-ch'en*); another on the staff of the Palace Stud (*shang-ssu yüan*). BH: department director. P37.

6300 *t'áng-lǎo* 堂老
SUNG: **Your Honor,** a term by which Grand Councilors (*tsai-hsiang*) addressed one another.

6301 *t'āng-mù ì* 湯沐邑 or 湯木邑
Lit., fief (that provides) hot water for bathing. (1) HAN: **Fief,** a quasiofficial designation of a District (*hsien*) whose tax collections were assigned as private income to the Heir Apparent or the Empress. HB: town which provides hot water for washing the hair. (2) YÜAN: **Land Grant,** a territory awarded to a Prince or another noble in which, in the early Yüan years, he had broad political, military, and fiscal controls; see under *fen-ti* and *t'ou-hsia.*

6302 *t'áng pǐ-t'iēh-shìh* 堂筆帖式
CH'ING: **Headquarters Clerk,** many low-ranking or unranked Clerks (*pi-t'ieh-shih*) who directly served the Grand Minister Supervisors of the Imperial Household Department (*tsung-kuan nei-wu fu ta-ch'en*). BH: clerk.

6303 *t'áng-shàng* 堂上
MING–CH'ING: common variant of *t'ang-kuan* (**Senior Official**).

6304 *t'áng-tsàng* 帑藏
HAN: **Treasury of the Chamberlain for the National Treasury** (*ta ssu-nung*), directly supervised by an Aide (*ch'eng*) to the Chamberlain, rank 600 bushels; established in A.D. 82. HB: treasury of the grand minister of agriculture.

6305 *t'áng-tzǔ* 堂子
CH'ING: **National Temple** located outside the Left Ch'ang-an Gate of Peking, where the Emperor worshipped on New Year's Day and at times of dynastic crisis; overseen by 8 Manchu Commandants (*wei*), 2 ranked 7 and 6 ranked 8, under supervision of the Ministry of Rites (*lǐ-pu*). P28.

6306 *tào* 道
Lit., a path, a way, hence the rather loosely delineated jurisdiction of an itinerant supervisory official: **Circuit,** normally with a particularizing geographic prefix. (1) HAN: official designation of a District (*hsien*) in a strategic frontier area predominantly populated by non-Chinese. How its staffing differed from a normal District is not clear. HB: march. (2) T'ANG: from the earliest years of the dynasty, a frontier military jurisdiction encompassing several Armies (*chün*) supervised by a General-in-chief (*ta-chiang*), then a Commander-in-chief (*ta tsung-kuan*), then a Commander-in-chief (*ta tu-tu*); not to be confused with the Circuits described in (3) below, though in the 700s both became jurisdictions of Military Commissioners (*chieh-tu shih*). RR: *district.* (3) T'ANG–SUNG: from 706 a Province-size area supervised by a Commissioner (*shih*) specially delegated from the central government, each serving as a coordinating intermediary between a cluster of Prefectures (*chou, fu*) and the capital; originally 10, created as the jurisdictions of itinerant Surveillance Commissioners (*an-ch'a shih*), whose title soon developed such variants as Surveil-

lance, Investigation, and Supervisory Commissioner (*an-ch'a ts'ai-fang ch'u-chih shih*), Investigation and Supervisory Commissioner (*kuan-ch'a ch'u-chih shih*), and Bandit-suppression Commissioner (*chao-t'ao shih*). In 733 Circuits were increased to 15, each with an Investigation Commissioner (*ts'ai-fang shih*), soon retitled Surveillance Commissioner (*kuan-ch'a shih*); the Commissioners became more stable coordinators of territorial administration. In response to the great rebellion of An Lu-shan beginning in 755, many Surveillance Commissioners were made concurrent Military Commissioners (*chieh-tu shih*); soon Circuits had both Surveillance and Military Commissioners as civil and military supervisors, respectively. As regional warlordism escalated, Military Commissioners of this type and those described under (2) above commonly became almost autonomous regional satraps, and their number grew large. At the end of T'ang, Circuits in South China were transformed into the independent regimes known to historians as the Ten Kingdoms, and Military Commissioners succeeded one another in control of the North China Plain, establishing the Five Dynasties that followed T'ang. When most of China Proper was reconsolidated by Sung, it was again divided into 10 Circuits, but governmental powers in each Circuit were divided among several function-specific Commissioners; see under *ssu chien-ssu* (Four Circuit Supervisorates). In 997 such Circuits were all redesignated *lu*, q.v. RR: *province*. (4) LIAO: 5 Province-size areas into which the empire was divided, each governed from a Capital (*ching*) and prefixed accordingly: Supreme (*shang*), Eastern, Central, Southern, and Western. Except for the Circuit surrounding the Supreme Capital, which was governed by the dynastic central government, each Circuit was governed by a Regent (*liu-shou*) with a staff including 2 Grand Councilors (*tsai-hsiang*). (5) YÜAN: the jurisdiction of a Pacification Commission (*hsüan-wei ssu*), as many as 60 into which the empire was divided for administrative, military, or combined military and administrative supervision; each supervised a cluster of Route Commands (*lu tsung-kuan fu*) and in turn was responsible to the metropolitan Secretariat (*chung-shu sheng*) at Peking or to a Branch Secretariat (*hsing chung-shu sheng*) and, for military purposes, to the metropolitan Bureau of Military Affairs (*shu-mi yüan*) or one of its branches. In lieu of Pacification Commissions, some Circuits had comparable agencies named Pacification Commission and Chief Military Command (*hsüan-wei ssu tu yüan-shuai fu*), Chief Military Command (*tu yüan-shuai fu*), Military Command (*yüan-shuai fu*), or a further variant such as *hsüan-fu ssu, an-fu ssu*, or *chao-t'ao ssu* (all rendered Pacification Commission). (6) YÜAN: also the separate jurisdiction of a Surveillance Commission (*t'i-hsing an-ch'a ssu, su-cheng lien-fang ssu*), 24 at their peak, each a regional subordinate of the metropolitan Censorate (*yü-shih t'ai*) or one of its branches. (7) MING–CH'ING: the jurisdiction of a Branch Office (*fen-ssu*) of a Provincial Administration Commission (*ch'eng-hsüan pu-cheng shih ssu*) or a Provincial Surveillance Commission (*t'i-hsing an-ch'a shih ssu*), staffed by a Vice Commissioner (*ts'an-cheng, an-ch'a fu-shih*) or an Assistant Commissioner (*ts'an-i, an-ch'a ch'ien-shih*) of such a provincial agency. Officials on such duty were known generically as Circuit Intendants (*tao-t'ai*). Some Circuits were function-specific and had Province-wide responsibilities, such as Tax Intendant Circuits (*tu-liang tao*), Education Intendant Circuits (*t'i-tu hsüeh-tao*), Troop Purification Circuits (*ch'ing-chün tao*), and Postal Service Circuits (*i-ch'uan tao*). Others exercised full powers of their base agencies in limited areas; these were called General Administration Circuits (*fen-shou tao*) and General

Surveillance Circuits (*fen-hsün tao*). Circuit Intendants delegated from Provincial Surveillance Commissions also included several who were limited both in area and in function: Record Checking Circuits (*shua-chüan tao*) and Military Defense Circuits (*ping-pei tao*). This pattern persisted until 1735, when Circuits were given status as regular posts (*kuan*) rather than duty assignments (*ch'ai-ch'ien*); were dissociated, at least nominally, from the provincial agencies; and got more direct authority over the Prefectures in their jurisdictions. Most continued to be General Administration Circuits (*shou-tao*) or General Surveillance Circuits (*hsün-tao*), but function-specific Circuits also survived, especially Waterways Circuits (*ho-tao*), Grain Tax Circuits (*tu-liang tao*), Military Defense Circuits (*ping-pei tao*), River Maintenance Circuits (*ho-wu tao*), Irrigation Circuits (*shui-li tao*), Education Circuits (*hsüeh-cheng tao*), etc. In the middle 1700s the total number of all Circuits in the empire was 89. After the reorganization of 1735, the name of a Circuit and the title of its Intendant were generally identical, and the rank of all Intendants was 4a. BH: circuit. (8) MING–CH'ING: also subsections, one named for each Province (*sheng*), among which Investigating Censors (*chien-ch'a yü-shih*) were distributed for internal administrative purposes within the Censorate (*tu ch'a-kuan*), each headed by one member designated Investigating Censor in charge of the ... Circuit (*chang ... tao chien-ch'a yü-shih*). Two things are especially noteworthy about this mode of designation. On one hand, the individual authority and responsibility of each Censor, or his independence from the Censors-in-chief (*tu yü-shih*) and other executive officials of the Censorate, were emphasized by the official designation of Censors as members of their Circuits, never as members of the Censorate. On the other hand, although members of the Circuits were routinely responsible for auditing accounts and reviewing judicial proceedings emanating from the Provinces for which the Circuits were named, they were based in the dynastic capital, and when Censors were sent out from the capital on special investigatory assignments they were sent to Provinces without regard to the names of the Circuits of which they were members. In addition to its routine functions, each Circuit was assigned responsibility for maintaining disciplinary surveillance over a specified group of central government agencies, including the Censorate itself. In Ming all Investigating Censors on duty in the capital at any time were considered to constitute a Metropolitan Circuit (*ching-chi tao*), with responsibility for checking records in the capital agencies. In Ch'ing the Metropolitan Circuit became a Circuit like any other, with routine responsibilities regarding the Metropolitan Area (*chih-li*); and routine surveillance over the administration of Manchuria, which was eventually divided into 3 Provinces, was vested in a single Liao-Shen Circuit, i.e., Circuit for Liao-yang and Shen-yang. BH: circuit. P18, 19.

6307   *tào-chèng ssū*   道正司

MING–CH'ING: **Taoist Registry,** unit in a Ming Subprefecture or a Ch'ing Department (both *chou*) responsible for certifying and disciplining Taoist religious practitioners in the jurisdiction; headed by a non-official Taoist Registrar (*tao-cheng*). BH: superior of the Taoist priesthood.

6308   *tào-chì ssū*   道紀司

MING–CH'ING: **Taoist Registry,** unit in a Prefecture (*fu*) responsible for certifying and disciplining Taoist religious practitioners in the jurisdiction; headed by a non-official Taoist Registrar (*tao-chi*), nominal rank 9b. BH: superior of the Taoist priesthood.

6309 *tào-ch'iáo ts'áo* 道橋曹
HAN: **Section for Roads and Bridges,** clerical subdivision of some Commanderies (*chün*) and some Districts (*hsien*), probably headed by an Administrator (*yüan-shih*) concerned with the maintenance of transport and communication routes. HB: bureau of roads and bridges.

6310 *tào-chíh* 道職
SUNG: **Taoist Posts,** 8 degrees or categories of positions created by Hui-tsung (r. 1100–1125) for Taoist adepts, along with 26 degrees of prestige titles (*san-kuan*) for Taoists, collectively called *tao-kuan* (Taoist Offices).

6311 *tào-chǘ* 道舉
T'ANG: **Taoist Recruit,** designation created by Hsüan-tsung (r. 712–756) to be awarded to Taoist adepts after study in the Institute of Taoist Worship (*ch'ung-hsüan kuan*).

6312 *tào-hùi ssū* 道會司
MING–CH'ING: **Taoist Registry** in a District (*hsien*), responsible for certifying and disciplining Taoist religious practitioners in the jurisdiction; headed by a non-official Taoist Registrar (*tao-hui*). BH: superior of the Taoist priesthood.

6313 *tāo-jén* 刀人
SUI: **Beard Trimmer** (?), designation of a category of palace women, rank =6 or lower.

6314 *tào-jén* 稻人
CHOU: **Paddy Supervisor,** 2 ranked as Senior Servicemen (*shang-shih*), 4 as Ordinary Servicemen (*chung-shih*), and 8 as Junior Servicemen (*hsia-shih*), members of the Ministry of Education (*ti-kuan*) responsible for the cultivation of rice and other crops in flooded fields, providing goods for rain prayers in times of drought, etc. CL: *officier des semences en terrain inondé.*

6315 *tǎo-k'ò chǘ* 導客局
N-S DIV (Ch'i): **Reception Service** in the establishment of the Heir Apparent, responsible for guiding and assisting persons having audience with the Heir Apparent; headed by one Office Manager for Ceremonial (*tien-i lu-shih*). P33.

6316 *tǎo-k'ò shè-jén* 導客舍人
T'ANG: **Reception Secretary,** 6, rank not clear (possibly eunuchs), members of the Domestic Service of the Heir Apparent (*t'ai-tzu nei-fang chü*). RR: *introducteur des visiteurs de l'héritier du trône.*

6317 *tào-kuān* 道官
SUNG: **Taoist Offices,** general designation of 26 degrees or levels of prestige titles (*san-kuan*) for Taoist adepts created by Hui-tsung (r. 1100–1125); also see *tao-chih* (Taoist Posts).

6318 *tǎo-kuān shǔ* 稟官署 or *tao-kuan*
HAN–SUNG: **Office of Grain Supplies,** an agency for provisioning the imperial palace with dried foods and especially for the sorting and hulling of rice for palace use; originally under the Chamberlain for the Palace Revenues (*shao-fu*), from Later Han under the Chamberlain for the National Treasury (*ta ssu-nung, ssu-nung ch'ing*), in Sui under the Court for the National Treasury (*ssu-nung ssu*), in T'ang and Sung under the Court for the National Granaries (also *ssu-nung ssu*); headed by a Director (*ling*), rank 600 bushels in Han, thereafter 2 appointees with rank 8a1 in T'ang. HB: office for the selection of grain. RR+SP: *office du triage des grains.* P6, 37.

6319 *tào-lù ssū* 道錄司
MING–CH'ING: **Central Taoist Registry,** a central government agency responsible for certifying and disciplining Taoist religious practitioners throughout the empire through Taoist Registries (*tao-chi ssu, tao-cheng ssu, tao-hui ssu*) at all levels of territorial administration, under the general supervision of the Ministry of Rites (*li-pu*); headed by a Director (*cheng*) with nominal rank 6a. Cf. *seng-lu ssu* (Central Buddhist Registry). BH: superiors of the Taoist priesthood. P16.

6320 *tāo-pǐ lì* 刀筆吏
Lit., functionary using a knife (for erasing) and a brush: **Scribbler,** throughout history the designation of a petty subofficial with copying chores, often used contemptuously.

6321 *tào-p'ú* 道僕
CHOU: **Supplementary Charioteer,** 12 ranked as Senior Servicemen (*shang-shih*), members of the Ministry of War (*hsia-kuan*) who managed chariots used for informal purposes within the palace and for the ruler's guests in jaunts outside the palace. CL: *conducteur du char de route.*

6322 *tào-t'ái* 道臺
MING–CH'ING: **Circuit Intendant,** quasiofficial designation of an official in charge of a Circuit (*tao*) in the hierarchy of territorial administration.

6323 *tào-t'ién ch'ǎng* 稻田場
CH'ING: **Palace Garden,** used for growing rice and other garden products for the palace; a unit of the Imperial Parks Administration (*feng-ch'en yüan*). BH: imperial agricultural office.

6324 *tào-t'ién t'í-lǐng sǒ* 稻田提領所
YÜAN: **Superintendency of Palace Gardening** in the Palace Provisions Commission (*hsüan-hui yüan*); staffing not clear, but presumably headed by a Superintendent (*t'i-ling*). P40.

6325 *tǎo-ts'úng* 導從
Guides and Followers, generic reference to personnel authorized to constitute the retinue of an official in travel status. At least in Sung times, the category included men called Housemen (*she-jen*), Followers (*ts'ung-jen*), Shouters of Warnings (*ho-chih*), Clearers of the Way (*ch'ing-tao*), Shouting Guides (*ho-tao*), Front Scouts (*ch'ien hsing-yin*), Military Escorts (*ts'ung chün-shih*), and Bearers of Identification Certificates (*ch'eng-fu*), no doubt among many others varying from locality to locality and from situation to situation.

6326 *tào-yù* 道右
CHOU: **Assistant Supplementary Charioteer,** 2 ranked as Senior Servicemen (*shang-shih*), members of the Ministry of War (*hsia-kuan*) who occupied the right (protective) side of royal chariots driven by Supplementary Charioteers (*tao-p'u*). CL: *homme de droite du char de route.*

6327 *tào-yüán* 道員
MING–CH'ING: **Circuit Intendants,** quasiofficial collective reference to officials in charge of Circuits (*tao*) in the hierarchy of territorial administration, more commonly called *tao-t'ai.*

6328 *t'áo-kuān-wǎ shǔ* 陶官瓦署
N-S DIV (S. Dyn.): **Government Pottery Works,** one each prefixed Left and Right under the Chamberlain for the Palace Revenues (*shao-fu*), each headed by a Supervisor (*tu*) or a Director (*ling*), or both; ranks not clear. Cf. *wa-kuan shu.* P14.

6329 *t'áo-t'ú chiēn* 駒驗監
N-S DIV: **Directorate of the Wild Horse Pasturage** under the Chamberlain for the Imperial Stud (*t'ai-p'u*), in charge of horses brought from the far northeastern frontier, in modern Siberia; headed by a Director (*chang*). HB (*chang*): chief inspector of the stables for wild horses. P31.

6330 *té-chiěh* 得解 or *té-chiěh chǔ-jén* 舉人
SUNG: lit., to attain being forwarded (to the capital) as a recommendee (of prefectural-level authorities after succeeding in a Prefectural Examination, *chieh-shih*): **Prefectural Graduate,** someone qualified to participate in a Metropolitan Examination (*sheng-shih*) in the civil service recruitment examination sequence. The term *chieh* seems to refer both to the act of forwarding or submitting a graduate to the capital and also to the documentary material, a diploma or certificate, that evidenced his qualification; but the emphasis is on his being sent from, rather than on his being sent to or certified for. Cf. *mien-chieh, chü-jen*.

6331 *té-fēi* 德妃
SUI–SUNG: **Virtuous Consort,** 3rd ranking imperial consort after Honored Consort (*kuei-fei*) and Pure Consort (*shu-fei*); rank 1a in Sung. RR: *concubine vertueuse*. SP: *correction vertueuse*.

6332 *té-í* 德儀
T'ANG: **Lady of Virtuous Deportment,** a rank 2a imperial concubine of the group known collectively as the Six Ladies of Deportment (*liu i*). RR: *correction vertueuse*.

6333 *t'è-chǐh* 特旨
MING: **Special Edict,** reference to the announcement of an official appointment, usually to a high post, made by the Emperor without recourse to normal selection and appointment procedures; normally considered capricious, and resented by the officialdom.

6334 *t'è-chìh* 特置
T'ANG: **Specially Established,** reference to an office or post created outside the normal hierarchy or complement for some ad hoc purpose.

6335 *t'è-chìn* 特進
Lord Specially Advanced. (1) HAN–T'ANG, LIAO: a supplementary (*chia*) title, in early use apparently only as an honorific but in T'ang and Liao probably involving added responsibilities. At least in T'ang, perhaps increased rank to 2a. HB: specially advanced. (2) SUI, SUNG, CHIN–YÜAN: prestige title (*san-kuan*) for officials of rank 2a in Sui and Sung, 1b in Chin, 1a in Yüan. SP: *spécialement promu*. P68.

6336 *t'è-chìn júng-lù tà-fū* 特進榮祿大夫
MING: **Specially Promoted Grand Master for Glorious Happiness,** prestige title (*san-kuan*) for rank 1a civil officials; anyone so honored could subsequently be further advanced to the prestige title Specially Promoted Grand Master for Splendid Happiness (*t'e-chin kuang-lu ta-fu*). P68.

6337 *t'è-chìn kuāng-lù tà-fū* 特進光祿大夫
MING: **Specially Promoted Grand Master for Splendid Happiness,** the highest prestige title (*san-kuan*) for civil officials of rank 1a. P68.

6338 *t'è-chìn tzū-chèng shàng-chīng* 特進資政上卿
MING: **Specially Promoted Senior Minister for Aid in Governance,** a title conferred on all Ministers (*shang-shu*) of the Six Ministries (*liu pu*) in the central government by Hui-ti (r. 1398–1402). P68.

6339 *t'è-lì-kǔn ssū* 特哩衮司
LIAO: variant of *ta t'e-li-kun ssu* (**Court of the Imperial Clan**), headed by a Director (*t'e-li-kun*). P1.

6340 *t'è-mǎn* 特滿
LIAO: Chinese transliteration of a Khitan word literally meaning 10,000 men, related to the Mongol word *tümen*: **Army,** designation of a Khitan Tribe (*pu-tsu*) when in military formation.

6341 *t'è-p'ài-ch'āi shih* 特派差使
CH'ING: **Special Commissioner,** an official on ad hoc duty assignment (*ch'ai-ch'ien*), regardless of his regular position and rank. BH: specially deputed official.

6342 *t'è-tsòu míng* 特奏名
SUNG: lit., a specially submitted name: **Facilitated Candidate,** a civil service recruitment status sometimes granted to graduates of Prefectural Examinations (*chieh-shih*) who, despite repeated efforts, reached old age without having passed a Metropolitan Examination (*sheng-shih*); this nominally made them eligible for official appointments on the same basis as Metropolitan Graduates (*chin-shih*). Cf. *en-k'o ch'u-shen* (Qualified by Special Examination).

6343 *t'è-yáng chú* 特羊局
N-S DIV (N. Ch'i): **Rams Service** in the Sheep Office (*ssu-yang shu*) of the Court of the Imperial Stud (*t'ai-p'u ssu*); cf. *tzu-yang chü* (Ewes Service).

6344 *těng* 等
Grade, Class, or **Degree:** generic term for various categories in the official hierarchy, most commonly a subdivision of Rank (*p'in*), e.g., 2nd rank, 2nd degree (*erh p'in erh teng*), most commonly indicated as *ts'ung-erh p'in*: rank 2b.

6345 *tēng hsién-shū* 登賢書
CH'ING: lit., to ascend into the book of worthies: unofficial reference to a **Provincial Graduate** (*chü-jen*).

6346 *tēng-lòu chíh-chǎng* 燈漏直長
YÜAN: **Duty Chief for Lamps and Water Clocks,** a member of the Astrological Commission (*t'ai-shih yüan*), probably unranked; apparently in charge of a shift of servants who maintained the Commission's lights and timepieces at night. P35.

6347 *tēng-shìh láng* 登仕郎
SUI–CH'ING: **Court Gentleman for Promoted Service,** prestige title (*san-kuan*) for civil officials of rank 8a in Sui, 9a thereafter except 8a in Yüan. In Sung changed to *hsiu-chih lang* (Court Gentleman for Improved Functioning) in c. 1117; in Ming an official with this title could be advanced to Court Gentleman for Ceremonial Service (*chiang-shih lang*) without change of rank. P68.

6348 *tēng-shìh tsò-láng* 登仕佐郎
CHIN–CH'ING: **Secondary Gentleman for Promoted Service,** the lowest prestige title (*san-kuan*) for civil officials of rank 9b; in Ming an official with this title could be advanced to Secondary Gentleman for Ceremonial Service (*chiang-shih tso-lang*) without change of rank. P68.

6349 *tēng-tì* 登第
MING–CH'ING: **Raised to a Ranking,** reference to the practice of listing examination passers in rank order after the Metropolitan Examination (*hui-shih*); also a reference to anyone named on such a pass list.

6350 *tēng-wén chiěn-yüàn* 登聞檢院
SUNG–CHIN: **Public Petitioners Review Office,** received

and considered complaints from officials and commoners about official misconduct or major policy issues, theoretically only after petitioners had vainly sought to appeal to the Public Petitioners Drum Office (*teng-wen ku-yüan*); manned by officials of court rank (*ch'ao-kuan*) on temporary duty assignments under supervision of the Grand Master of Remonstrance (*chien-i ta-fu*). Created in 1007 by renaming the Public Petitioners Office (*teng-wen yüan*). Also see *li-chien yüan* (Complaint Review Office). SP: *cour du dépôt des pétitions*. P21.

6351 *tēng-wén kǔ* 登聞鼓
T'ANG–CH'ING: **Public Petitioners Drum,** a resounding drum set up outside various government buildings and at the palace, to be struck by persons who, after having failed to get satisfactory hearings in the regular administrative hierarchy, wished to appeal outside regular channels. In T'ang, originally not regularly attended at the palace, but when struck was supposed to be responded to by a member of the Palace Gate Guards (*chien-men wei*); later in T'ang, regularly attended by Censors (*yü-shih*) on rotational duty assignments. Subsequently served by regularly established agencies; see *teng-wen ku-yüan, teng-wen ku-t'ing*. Such attention-getting devices were apparently common at the headquarters of all units of territorial administration down to the office of the District Magistrate (*hsien-ling, chih-hsien*). P21.

6352 *tēng-wén kǔ-t'īng* 登聞鼓廳
CH'ING: **Public Petitioners Drum Office,** established in 1723 in the Office of Transmission (*t'ung-cheng ssu*) to receive and process complaints from officials and commoners who had failed to get satisfactory hearings about injustices and disastrous state policies in the regular administrative hierarchy; staffed by one Manchu and one Chinese Clerk (*pi-t'ieh-shih*). Replaced a system of attendance at a Public Petitioners Drum outside the Right Ch'ang-an Gate of Peking by either a Censor (*yü-shih*) or a Supervising Secretary (*chi-shih-chung*), which in 1656 had superseded an original Ch'ing system of assigning one Censor in daily rotation to monitor such a drum at the gate of the Censorate (*tu ch'a-yüan*). P21.

6353 *tēng-wén kǔ-yüàn* 登聞鼓院
SUNG–MING: **Public Petitioners Drum Office,** evolving from the T'ang *teng-wen ku;* an office to receive complaints from officials and commoners about injustices and major policy disasters after they had failed to get satisfactory hearings in the normal administrative hierarchy; established in 1007 by renaming the earlier Complaint Drum Office (*ku-ssu*); staffed by Remonstrators (*ssu-chien*) and Exhorters (*cheng-yen*); in 1129 subordinated to the Public Petitioners Review Office (*teng-wen chien-yüan*). In Chin subordinated to the Censorate (*yü-shih t'ai*). In Ming manned by one Investigating Censor (*chien-ch'a yü-shih*), one Supervising Secretary (*chi-shih-chung*), and one representative of the Imperial Bodyguard (*chin-i wei*); channeled complaints to the Office of Transmission (*t'ung-cheng ssu*) for distribution to appropriate central government agencies, or to the palace. Also see *li-chien yüan* (Complaint Review Office). SP: *cour des tambours pour annoncer des pétitions et des doléances*. P21.

6354 *tēng-wén lìng* 登聞令
N-S DIV (N. Wei): **Director of Public Petitions,** duty assignment of a Vice Director (*shih-lang*) of the Secretariat (*chung-shu sheng*), to receive and process complaints from officials and commoners who, having failed to get satisfactory responses in the regular administrative hierarchy,

desired special attention for complaints about injustices or disastrous state policies. P21.

6355 *tēng-wén yüàn* 登聞院
SUNG: **Public Petitioners Office,** created c. 995 by renaming the prior Complaint Review Office (*li-chien yüan*), c. 1007 renamed Public Petitioners Review Office (*teng-wen chien-yüan*). P21.

6356 *tēng yíng-chōu* 登瀛洲
T'ANG: lit., to ascend to the fairy isles in the ocean, or those who have done so: **Paragons,** unofficial reference to Academicians (*hsüeh-shih*) in the early T'ang Institute of Academicians (*hsüeh-shih yüan, hsüeh-shih kuan*), or to other persons of outstanding talents. P23.

6357 *t'éng-huáng yù t'ūng-chèng* 謄黃右通政
MING: **Vice Commissioner of the Right for Imperial Warrants,** one, rank 4a, in the Office of Transmission (*t'ung-cheng ssu*) from 1466 to 1581; apparently had the specific function of issuing on yellow paper notifications calling to duty the heirs of military officers. P21.

6358 *t'éng-lù kuān* 謄錄官
(1) SUNG–YÜAN: **Examination Copyist,** generic term for officials or subofficials assigned to transcribe the writings of candidates in civil service recruitment examinations, to prevent examiners from identifying candidates by their handwriting. In Sung, considered to constitute a Bureau of Examination Copyists (*t'eng-lu yüan*). (2) CH'ING: **Copyist,** 6 delegated from among Clerks (*pi-t'ieh-shih*) of the Ministry of Justice (*hsing-pu*) to serve, probably in rotation, in the Codification Office (*lü-li kuan*) from 1742. P13.

6359 *t'éng-lù yüàn* 謄錄院
SUNG: **Bureau of Examination Copyists,** an ad hoc group of officials or suboofficials assigned to transcribe the writings of candidates in civil service recruitment examinations, to prevent examiners from identifying candidates by their handwriting. SP: *cour des copistes des épreuves d'examen*.

6360 *tǐ* 邸
(1) **Liaison Hostel,** from Han on the common designation of agencies in the dynastic capital serving as representatives and document-forwarding channels for regional dignitaries in the hierarchy of territorial administration. See *chün-ti, chin-tsou yüan*. P21. (2) CH'ING: unofficial reference to an **Imperial Prince** (*ch'in-wang*); cf. *wang-ti*.

6361 *tǐ chīng-shīh* 邸京師
Liaison Hostel in the Capital: from Han on a variant of *ti* (Liaison Hostel). P21.

6362 *tì-ch'īng* 地卿
CH'ING: lit., minister of soil: unofficial reference to the **Minister of Revenue** (*hu-pu shang-shu*).

6363 *tì-fāng kuān* 地方官
Territorial Official: common generic reference to personnel in any unit of territorial administration.

6364 *tì-fū* 遞夫
T'ANG: **Courier,** a non-military carrier of state documents; unranked, probably a requisitioned commoner.

6365 *tí fú-chìn* 嫡福晉
CH'ING: variant of *fu-chin* (**Princess-consort**), the principal wife of an Imperial Prince (*ch'in-wang*) or a Commandery Prince (*chün-wang*).

6366 *tì-hsià* 第下
T'ANG: unofficial reference to the **Prefect** (*t'ai-shou, tz'u-shih*) of a Prefecture (*chou*

6367 *tǐ-hsüǎn* 抵選
CH'ING: **Selection by Substitution,** a process of appointing new Metropolitan Graduates (*chin-shih*) or Provincial Graduates (*chü-jen*) who made appropriate contributions to the state treasury when there was a shortage of regular candidates for the offices purchased.

6368 *tì-ī* 帝姬
SUNG: lit., imperial woman: from 1113, **Imperial Princess,** the title granted to all daughters, sisters, and aunts of Emperors, replacing the several titles *kung-chu, chang kung-chu, ta-chang kung-chu.*

6369 *tì-ī jén* 第一人
CH'ING: variant of *hui-yüan* (**Principal Graduate**), first on the pass list of new Metropolitan Graduates (*chin-shih*) after the Metropolitan Examination (*hui-shih*) in the civil service recruitment examination sequenc

6370 *tí-k'ù* 荻庫
N-S DIV (Liang, Ch'en): **Reed Storehouse** under the Chamberlain for the National Treasury (*ssu-nung*); managed by an Aide (*ch'eng*). P8.

6371 *tì-kuān* 地官
(1) CHOU: lit., office of earth: **Ministry of Education,** 2nd of 6 major agencies in the central government; headed by a Minister of Education (*ssu-t'u*) ranked as a Minister (*ch'ing*), in general charge of training in and enforcement of proper moral values, overseeing commercial transactions, fostering and regulating agriculture, forestry, and mining, and monitoring local self-government practices of District Elders (*hsiang-lao*) and Township Heads (*hsien-cheng*). The Ministry's emphasis on economic productivity led traditional Chinese to consider it the antecedent of later fiscal agencies such as the Ministry of Revenue (*hu-pu*). CL: *ministère de la terre, ministère de l'enseignement officiel.* (2) T'ANG: from 684 to 705 the official variant of *hu-pu* (**Ministry of Revenue**). P6.

6372 *tì-kuān* 邸官
T'ANG: **Liaison Hosteler,** variant reference to a Capital Liaison Representative (*chin-tsou kuan*) in charge of a Capital Liaison Office (*chin-tsou yüan*), sometimes entitled General-in-chief (*ta-chiang*). See *ti* (Liaison Hostel). P21.

6373 *tì-kuān ch'īng* 地官卿
T'ANG–SUNG: unofficial reference to a **Minister of Revenue** (*hu-pu shang-shu*).

6374 *tí-kǔng láng* 廸功郎
SUNG, MING: **Gentleman for Meritorious Achievement,** prestige title (*san-kuan*) for civil officials of rank 9b in Sung, 8a in Ming; c. 1117 superseded *chiang-shih lang* (Court Gentleman for Ceremonial Service); in Ming an official could be advanced to this from Gentleman for Good Service (*hsiu-chih lang*) without change of rank. P68.

6375 *tí-kǔng tsò-láng* 廸功佐郎
MING: **Secondary Gentleman for Meritorious Achievement,** prestige title (*san-kuan*) for civil officials of rank 8b; an official could be advanced to this from Secondary Gentleman for Good Service (*hsiu-chih tso-lang*) without change of rank. P68.

6376 *tí-lì* 邸吏
HAN: **Liaison Hosteler,** head of a Liaison Hostel (*ti*) in the dynastic capital, representing the interests and facilitating the communications of a regional dignitary. P21.

6377 *tí-lièh-má-tū* 敵烈麻都
LIAO: Chinese transliteration of a Khitan word, perhaps

tirämät, possibly meaning "pillar of the empire": **Ritualist,** an eminent post in the Northern Administration (*pei-mien*) of the central government in general charge of court ritual ceremonies and especially the conduct of prayers for rain. The term was "corrected" by the Manchus to *to-to-lun mu-t'eng,* q.v. P9.

6378 *tì-lù shìh* 鞮鞻氏
CHOU: **Master of Foreign Music,** 4 ranked as Junior Servicemen (*hsia-shih*), members of the Ministry of Rites (*ch'un-kuan*) in charge of court presentations of songs and dances of "the 4 barbarians," i.e., the non-Chinese tribes with which the Chinese had contact. CL: *préposé aux bottines de cuir.*

6379 *tì-mièn* 地面
MING: **Aboriginal Area,** formal designation of 7 administrative units for aboriginal tribes of the South and Southwest, each governed in traditional ways by a tribal chief. See *t'u-ssu.* P72.

6380 *tì-p'ì* 帝匹
CH'ING: lit., imperial mate: unofficial reference to an **Empress.**

6381 *tí-p'ièn ssū* 糴便司
SUNG: **Office for the Purchase of Cheap Grain** (?), probably a local agency to buy up grain when prices fell, part of the Ever Normal Granary (*ch'ang-p'ing ts'ang*) system; but precise functions, staffing, and hierarchical status not clear. SP: *bureau d'achat des grains á crédit*

6382 *tì-shè* 邸舍
T'ANG: variant of *ti* (**Liaison Hostel**). Also see *chin-tsou yüan.*

6383 *tì t'ài-hòu* 帝太后
HAN: **Imperial Mother,** a designation possibly used when the Emperor's mother had not been the principal wife of a reigning Emperor.

6384 *tì t'ài-t'ài-hòu* 帝太太后
HAN: variant reference to an Emperor's grandmother, normally *t'ai-huang t'ai-hou* (**Grand Empress Dowager**); possibly an Emperor's maternal grandmother, or mother of an Emperor's natural mother who had not officially been Empress.

6385 *tì-t'án* 地壇
MING–CH'ING: **Altar of Earth,** an altar in the northern suburbs of Peking where Emperors made sacrificial offerings to the spirit of Earth. Cf. *she-chi t'an.*

6386 *tì-t'án wèi* 地壇尉
CH'ING: **Commandant at the Altar of Earth,** 8 Manchu officers, one of rank 5 and 7 of rank 6; in rotation presided over the altar under supervision of the Court of Imperial Sacrifices (*t'ai-ch'ang ssu*). P28.

6387 *tí-tàng miěn-hsíng sǒ* 抵當免行所 or *ti-tang so*
SUNG: **Pawnbroking Office** under the Court of the Imperial Treasury (*t'ai-fu ssu*); in charge of state loans made to respectable citizens in emergency situations. SP: *bureau de prêt sur gage.*

6388 *tì-ts'áo* 地曹
N-S DIV–CH'ING: unofficial reference to the **Ministry of Revenue** (*min-pu, hu-pu*).

6389 *tì-ts'ě kuān* 第策官
T'ANG: **Examination Grader,** an ad hoc duty assignment for eminent officials on the occasions of civil service recruitment examinations.

6390 *tì-tzŭ ch'áng-chiào-chě* 弟子長教者
T'ANG: **Novice Career Musician,** designation of students with state stipends studying in the Palace Music School (*nei-chiao fang*). RR: *élève qui reçoit un enseignement d'une manière permanent.*

6391 *tì-tzŭ yüán* 弟子員
CH'ING: unofficial reference to a **Government Student** (*sheng-yüan*).

6392 *tì-yùn sǒ* 遞運所
MING: **Transport Office,** a local unit in the national state-transport system, subordinate to a District (*hsien*) and staffed largely with requisitioned commoners.

6393 *t'í-àn ssū* 堤岸司
SUNG: abbreviation of *t'i-chü pien-ho t'i-an ssu* (**Supervisorate of the Pien River Dikes**). SP: *bureau chargé d'aménager des berges.*

6394 *t'í-chiěn àn-tú* 提檢案牘
YÜAN: **Supervisor of Archives,** 4, rank not clear, members of the Supreme Supervisorate-in-chief (*tu tsung-kuan fu*) of Ta-tu Route (*lu*), i.e., the environs of the dynastic capital at Peking. P32.

6395 *t'í-chǔ* 提舉
SUNG–CH'ING: lit., to take up and undertake, i.e., to be responsible for: **Supervisor** or **Supervisorate,** a common title or agency name, normally of middling rank; usually occurs prefixed to function-descriptive terms, sometimes followed by *ssu* (Office), when used as an agency name; when used as a title sometimes occurs prefixed to function-descriptive terms, sometimes as a suffix following an agency name. Cf. *t'i-tien* and *t'i-ling* (both Superintendent).

6396 *t'í-chǔ ch'á-mǎ ssū* 提舉茶馬司
SUNG: **Supervisorate of Horse Trading;** see under *ch'a-ma ssu* (Horse Trading Office). SP: *intendance chargée d'échanger les chevaux contre le thé.*

6397 *t'í-chǔ ch'á-yén ch'áng-p'íng těng kūng-shìh* 提舉茶鹽常平等公事
SUNG: lit., supervisor of public business concerning trade in tea and salt, ever normal granaries, etc.: variant title of the **Supervisor** (*t'i-chü*) **of a Tea and Salt Supervisorate** (*ch'a-yen t'i-chü ssu*) in a Circuit (*lu*). SP: *intendant des affaires de la régie du thé, du sel et des greniers régulateurs.*

6398 *t'í-chǔ ch'á-yén kūng-shìh* 提舉茶鹽公事
SUNG: **Tea and Salt Supervisor,** one title used for the head of a Tea and Salt Supervisorate (*ch'a-yen t'i-chü ssu*) in a Circuit (*lu*). SP: *intendant de monopole du thé et du sel.*

6399 *t'í-chǔ ch'á-yén ssū* 提舉茶鹽司
SUNG: variant of **Tea and Salt Supervisorate** (*ch'a-yen t'i-chü ssu*) in a Circuit (*lu*). P61.

6400 *t'í-chǔ chàng ssū* 提舉帳司
SUNG: **Supervisorate of Accounts,** one in the Left Section (*tso-ts'ao*) of the Ministry of Revenue (*hu-pu*), one in the Bureau of Review (*pi-pu*); staffing of the former not clear; the latter headed by a Director (*lang-chung*), rank 6b. SP: *directeur du bureau des comptes.*

6401 *t'í-chǔ ch'áng-p'íng ch'á-yén kūng-shìh* 提舉常平茶鹽公事
SUNG: variant title of a **Tea and Salt Supervisor** (see *ch'a-yen t'i-chü ssu*) in a Circuit (*lu*). SP: *intendant des greniers régulateurs et de la régie du thé et du sel.*

6402 *t'í-chǔ ch'áng-p'íng ssū* 提舉常平司
SUNG: lit., supervisorate of ever normal granaries: **Stabilization Fund Supervisorate,** one of the Four Circuit Supervisorates (*ssu chien-ssu*), the name alternating with *ts'ang-ssu* (Supply Commission) and others; each in a jurisdiction called a Circuit (*lu*) including several Prefectures (*chou*); supervised grain storage and transport, relief granaries, state-monopolized industries and trade, and agricultural development activities; headed by a Stabilization Fund Supervisor (*t'i-chü ch'ang-p'ing kung-shih*). SP: *bureau des greniers régulateurs.* P52.

6403 *t'í-chǔ ch'áng-p'íng ts'āng ssū* 提舉常平倉司
SUNG: variant of *t'i-chü ch'ang-p'ing ssu* (**Stabilization Fund Supervisorate**). SP: *intendant de greniers régulateurs.*

6404 *t'í-chǔ chiǎng-ì ssū* 提舉講義司
SUNG: **Supervisor of the Advisory Office** in the Department of State Affairs (*shang-shu sheng*), from 1102 a concurrent duty assignment for a Grand Councilor (*tsai-hsiang*). See *chiang-i ssu* (Advisory Office). SP: *directeur du bureau du conseil politique et financier.*

6405 *t'í-chǔ chiěh-yén pǎo-chiǎ* 提舉解鹽保甲
SUNG: **Supervisor of Grain and Salt Exchange and of Community Self-defense,** a commission combining the functions of a Supervisorate of Grain and Salt Exchange (*t'i-chü chih-chih chien-yen ssu*) and a Supervisorate of Community Self-defense (*t'i-chü pao-chia ssu*).

6406 *t'í-chǔ chìh-chìh chiěh-yén ssù* 提舉制置解鹽司
SUNG: **Supervisorate of Grain and Salt Exchange,** number and status in the governmental hierarchy not clear; apparently established only in regions with extensive salt flats; responsible for enforcing the state monopoly on salt production, for regulating salt prices, and for adjusting the amount of paper currency in circulation, apparently by requiring merchants to deliver grain to the frontiers for military support and in return giving merchants paper money with which (and only with which?) they could buy salt from the state salterns. When and how this system functioned is not wholly clear, nor is its relation to the system called the Equitable Exchange of Grain for Salt (*chung-yen*). SP: *directeur de la régie du sel de Kiai.* P61.

6407 *t'í-chǔ chìn-tsòu yüàn* 提舉進奏院
SUNG: **Supervisor of the Memorials Office,** a unit in the Chancellery (*men-hsia sheng*) traditionally considered the counterpart of the later Office of Transmission (*t'ung-cheng ssu*); post normally held by a eunuch Palace Servitor (*kung-feng kuan*); see *chin-tsou yüan.* P21.

6408 *t'í-chǔ chū-ssū k'ù-wù ssū* 提舉諸司庫務司
SUNG: **Supervisorate of the Various State Storehouses,** an agency of Kaifeng Prefecture (*fu*). SP: *intendance des agences et des magasins des divers bureaus.*

6409 *t'í-chǔ chüēh-huò ssū* 提舉権貨司
CHIN: **Supervisorate of Monopoly Taxes,** one located at the Southern Capital (*Nan-ching*), rank 5b or 6b, in charge of collecting taxes on state-monopolized trade. P62.

6410 *t'í-chǔ chùn-hsièn-chǔ těng chái kuān* 提舉郡縣主等宅官
SUNG: **Supervisor of Residences for Commandery and District Princesses,** duty assignment of a member of the Office of the Imperial Clan (*ta tsung-cheng yüan*). See *chün-*

chu, hsien-chu. SP: *intendant des maisons de princesses de commanderie et de celle de sous-préfecture.*

6411 *t'í-chǔ hó-ch'ǚ ssū* 提舉河渠司
SUNG: **Supervisorate of Waterways,** an ad hoc local agency established under supervision of the Directorate of Waterways (*tu-shui chien*) to repair breaks in river and canal embankments. SP: *intendance des rivières et des canaux.* P59.

6412 *t'í-chǔ hsiāng-ch'á-fán shìh ssū* 提舉香茶礬事司
SUNG: **Supervisorate of Incense, Tea, and Alum,** probably an agency at the Circuit (*lu*) level to manage trade in the state-monopolized commodities named. SP: *bureau de l'intendance des affaires de l'encens, du thé et de l'alun.*

6413 *t'í-chǔ hsiū-hó ssū* 提舉修河司
SUNG: reference to the **Supervisor of the Yellow River Conservancy Office** (*hsiu-chün huang-ho ssu,* q.v.). P59.

6414 *t'í-chǔ hsiū-nèi ssū* 提舉修內司
SUNG: **Supervisor of the Palace Maintenance Office** (*hsiu-nei ssu,* q.v.). SP: *directeur du bureau de la réparation des palais.*

6415 *t'í-chǔ hsüéh-hsiào sǒ* 提舉學校所
YÜAN: **Supervisor of Schools,** rank 6a, on the staff of the Ta-tu Route (*lu*), the unit for territorial administration of the environs of the dynastic capital, modern Peking. P32.

6416 *t'í-chǔ hsüéh-shìh ssū* 提舉學事司
SUNG: **Supervisorate of Education,** an agency at the Circuit (*lu*) level to foster and monitor state-subsidized education in Prefectures (*chou*) and Districts (*hsien*); apparently not established until 1103, perhaps did not survive into S. Sung times. SP: *directeur des affaires d'éducation, bureau d'éducation provinciale.* P51.

6417 *t'í-chǔ huáng-ch'éng ssū* 提舉皇城司
SUNG–CHIN: **Supervisor of the Capital Security Office** (*huang-ch'eng ssu,* q.v.). P49.

6418 *t'í-chǔ k'ēng-yěh shìh-pò* 提舉坑冶市舶
SUNG: **Supervisor of Foundries and Maritime Trade,** a commission found in 9 Circuits (*lu*), normally the concurrent duty of a Supply Commissioner (*fa-yün shih*). SP: *directeur de fonderie et de douane.*

6419 *t'í-chǔ k'ēng-yěh ssū* 提舉坑冶司
SUNG: **Supervisor of Foundries,** apparently a commission at the Circuit (*lu*) level in appropriate regions. SP: *intendant du bureau des mines, des fonderies et des monnaies.*

6420 *t'í-chǔ kó-shìh* 提舉閣事
CH'ING: **Administrative Supervisor of the Hall,** a Grand Minister (*ta-ch'en*) of the Imperial Household Department (*nei-wu fu*) delegated to administer the Hall of Literary Profundity (*wen-yüan ko*), where from the late 1700s was kept the great collectanea called *Ssu-k'u ch'üan-shu;* under the nominal headship of a Grand Secretary (*ta hsüeh-shih*) identified with the Hall in the palace. BH: director of the library.

6421 *t'í-chǔ kuǎn-kàn kuān* 提舉管幹官
SUNG: **Supervisor of Administrative Clerks,** number and rank not clear, in the Ministry of Revenue (*hu-pu*) and perhaps other central government agencies. See *kuan-kan.* SP: *directeur-administrateur.*

6422 *t'í-chǔ kuǎn-kōu hsüéh-shìh* 提舉管勾學事
SUNG: **Supervisor of Education,** from c. 1111 a concurrent duty decreed for all officials of Prefectures (*chou*) and Districts (*hsien*). SP: *directeur des affaires d'éducation.* P51.

6423 *t'í-chǔ kūng-chièn-shǒu ssū* 提舉弓箭手司
SUNG: **Supervisorate of Archery,** an agency found in units of territorial administration, especially in frontier regions, presumably in charge of militia training; headed by a Supervisor (*t'i-chü*). SP: *bureau d'organisation et d'entraînement des archers.*

6424 *t'í-chǔ ... kūng* 提舉…宮 or *t'í-chǔ ... kuān* 觀
SUNG: **Supervisor of the ... Palace, Supervisor of the ... Taoist Temple** (with proper-name inserts), a sinecure awarded to a retired official, normally of high rank; presumably subordinate, directly or indirectly, to the Ministry of Rites (*li-pu*). SP: *intendant des palais et des temples taoistes.*

6425 *t'í-chǔ kuó-shǐh* 提舉國史
SUNG: **Supervisor of the Dynastic History,** one of the designations used for the head of the Historiography Institute (*kuo-shih kuan*) in the Palace Library (*pi-shu sheng*). SP: *directeur de la rédaction de l'histoire d'état.*

6426 *t'í-chǔ liù shàng-chǚ chí kuǎn-kàn kuān* 提舉六尚局及管幹官
SUNG: **Supervisor of the Six Palace Services and of Administrative Clerks,** one, rank not clear, member of the Palace Administration (*tien-chung sheng*). See *liu shang-chü, kuan-kan.* SP: *administrateur dirigeant les six services de l'empereur.* P38.

6427 *t'í-chǔ mǎi-mǎ* 提舉買馬
SUNG: **Supervisor of Horse Purchases,** duty assignment associated with a local Herds Office (*ch'ün-mu ssu*) responsible to the Court of the Imperial Stud (*t'ai-p'u ssu*). SP: *intendant d'achat des chevaux.*

6428 *t'í-chǔ pièn-hó t'í-àn ssū* 提舉汴河堤岸司
SUNG: **Supervisorate of the Pien River Dikes,** a unit under the Directorate of Waterways (*tu-shui chien*) responsible for maintaining the embankments of the Pien River at the N. Sung capital, Kaifeng; headed by a Supervisor (*t'i-chü*), rank not clear. SP: *bureau de la navigation sur la rivière Pien.*

6429 *t'í-chǔ pǎo-chiǎ ssū* 提舉保甲司
SUNG: **Supervisorate of Community Self-defense,** an agency apparently at the Circuit (*lu*) level overseeing the organizing and working of the system called *pao-chia,* q.v. SP: *directeur de l'organisation et de l'entraînement militaire du peuple.*

6430 *t'í-chǔ piēn-hsiū kuó-ch'áo hùi-yào* 提舉編修國朝會要
SUNG: **Supervisor of Preparation of the Dynastic Administrative Regulations,** a duty assignment in the Palace Library (*pi-shu sheng*) normally filled concurrently by the Vice Director of the Right (*yu p'u-yeh*) of the Department of State Affairs (*shang-shu sheng*); responsible for preparation of the collected dynastic administrative rules and precedents called the *Hui-yao.* SP: *directeur de la rédaction des documents importants d'état.*

6431 *t'í-chǔ pīng-mǎ* 提舉兵馬
SUNG: **Supervisor of the Military,** a common concurrent duty assignment for officials at the Prefecture (*chou*) level. SP: *directeur de l'entraînement militaire et de l'arrestation des bandits.*

6432 *t'í-chǔ pīng-mǎ hsún-chiēn tū-chiēn* 提舉兵馬巡檢都監
SUNG: **Chief Military Inspector,** a concurrent duty assignment of prefectural (*chou*) officials, acting under the supervision of regional military authorities such as Circuit (*lu*) Commanders-in-chief (*tu tsung-kuan*); responsible for local military training, defense against banditry, etc. SP: *directeur de l'entraînement militaire et de l'arrestation des bandits, inspecteur policier et surveillant général.*

6433 *t'í-chǔ shìh-pò ssū* 提舉市舶司
SUNG: variant of *shih-po t'i-chü ssu* (**Maritime Trade Superintendency**).

6434 *t'í-chǔ t'í-tiěn chù-ch'ién těng kùng-shìh* 提舉提點鑄錢等公事
SUNG: **Supervisory Superintendent of Coinage,** a special duty assignment for officials in several southern and western Circuits (*lu*), presumably where copper was most extensively mined. SP: *intendant des affaires de la frappe des monnaies, intendant de la fonte des monnaies etc.*

6435 *t'í-chǔ tsài-chīng chū-ssū k'ù-wù ssū* 提舉在京諸司庫務司
SUNG: **Supervisorate of Storehouses in the Capital Agencies,** status in the governmental hierarchy not clear; possibly a temporary, ad hoc agency during the transition from N. to S. Sung. SP: *intendance des agences et des magasins des divers bureaux dans la capitale.*

6436 *t'í-chǔ ts'āng-ch'ǎng ssū* 提舉倉場司
CHIN: **Supervisorate of Grain Supplies,** created in 1217 in the Directorate of the Imperial Treasury (*t'ai-fu chien*) to oversee the various officials in charge of specific granaries, including the Commissioner (*shih*) of the Imperial Granaries (*t'ai-ts'ang*); headed by a Commissioner (*shih*), rank 5b, and a Vice Commissioner (*fu-shih*), 6b. P8.

6437 *t'í-chǔ tsūng-tzǔ hsüéh shìh* 提舉宗子學事
SUNG: **Supervisor of the School for the Imperial Family,** duty assignment for a member of the Chief Office of Imperial Clan Affairs (*ta tsung-cheng ssu*); also see *tsung-hsüeh.* SP: *directeur des affaires d'éducation des fils de la famille impériale.* P1.

6438 *t'í-chǔ tū-ch'éng sǒ* 提舉都城所
YÜAN: **Supervisorate for Capital Construction,** created in 1337 as a unit in the Ministry of Works (*kung-pu*) in charge of extensive repairs of the capital city walls and state buildings; headed by 2 Supervisors (*t'i-chü*), rank 5b, and 2 Vice Supervisors (*fu t'i-chü*), rank not clear. P15.

6439 *t'í-hsiá chiěn-ch'á kuān* 提轄檢察官
SUNG: **Controller of Inspections,** duty assignment for one member of the Court of the Imperial Treasury (*t'ai-fu ssu*), apparently principally responsible for overseeing operations of the Southern Storehouse (*nan-k'u;* see under *nan-pei k'u*) of the Left Vault (*tso-tsang*). SP: *régisseur-contrôleur.* P7.

6440 *t'í-hsiá chìn-tsòu yüàn* 提轄進奏院
SUNG: **Controller of the Memorials Office,** a unit in the Chancellery (*men-hsia sheng*) traditionally considered the counterpart of the later Office of Transmission (*t'ung-cheng ssu*); post normally held by a eunuch Palace Servitor (*kung-feng kuan*); see *chin-tsou yüan.* P21.

6441 *t'í-hsiá hsiū-ts'āng sǒ* 提轄修倉所
SUNG: **Office of Granary Repairs** under the Court of the National Granaries (*ssu-nung ssu*); headed by a Controller (*t'i-hsia*), status not clear. SP: *bureau de la réparation des greniers.*

6442 *t'í-hsiá kuān* 提轄官 or *t'i-hsia*
SUNG: **Controller,** designation of one type of supervisory officials, normally of middling status; in addition to entries so prefixed, see *ssu hsia* (Four Controllers). SP: *contrôleur, intendant, gérant, régisseur.*

6443 *t'í-hsiá pīng-chiǎ tào-tséi kūng-shìh* 提轄兵甲盜賊公事
SUNG: **Controller of Military Training and Banditry Suppression,** duty assignment for a Military Administrator (*ch'ien-hsia*) in a frontier area and sometimes for an official of a Prefecture (*chou*). SP: *responsable de l'entraînement militaire et de l'arrestation des bandits.*

6444 *t'í-hsiá ssū* 提轄司
LIAO: lit., office of a controller, possibly the Chinese rendering of a Khitan word: **Commandant** of a tribe-like fighting unit called an *ordo* (see under *wo-lu-to, kung*) comprising the entourage of a deceased Liao ruler.

6445 *t'í-hsíng* 提刑
SUNG: variant or abbreviation of *t'i-tien hsing-yü kung-shih* (**Judicial Commissioner**). SP: *intendant judiciaire.* P52.

6446 *t'í-hsíng àn-ch'á shìh ssū* 提刑按察使司
MING–CH'ING: lit., office of the commissioner in charge of judicial matters and investigations: **Provincial Surveillance Commission,** one per Province (*sheng*) totaling 13 in the mature Ming system and 18 in Ch'ing, commonly abbreviated to *an-ch'a ssu*; the principal provincial-level agency for supervisory administration of judicial and penal matters and for censorial surveillance over the sub-provincial officialdom. Created in 1367 alongside Branch Secretariats (*hsing chung-shu sheng*) to administer provincial areas captured from the disintegrating Yüan state, then from 1376 shared provincial authority with Provincial Administration Commissions (*ch'eng-hsüan pu-cheng shih ssu*) and Regional Military Commissions (*tu chih-hui shih ssu*). Abolished in 1380 but revived in 1381. During the 1400s the triad of provincial agencies came to be coordinated by central government dignitaries delegated as Grand Coordinators (*hsün-fu*) of Provinces and further by multi-Province Supreme Commanders (*tsung-tu*). As Grand Coordinators and Supreme Commanders became more stably entrenched in late Ming, and especially when they were transformed into regular posts as Governors and Governors-general, respectively, in Ch'ing times, the Surveillance Commissions became in effect provincial-level staff agencies for judicial and penal administration, and their role in censorial surveillance declined without disappearing. The Commissions were collectively called the Outer Censorate (*wai-t'ai*), and their personnel shared with Censors (*yü-shih*) such traditional collective designations as Surveillance Officials (*ch'a-kuan*) and Guardians of the Customs and Fundamental Laws (*feng-hsien kuan*); moreover, the Censorate (*yü-shih t'ai* till 1380, then *tu ch'a-yüan*) was the central government channel for all communications between the Commissions and the throne. Nevertheless, the Commissions were not branch Censorates, nor were they directly controlled by the Censorate. [In Ming times the Censorate

had its own representatives in the Provinces, principally Investigating Censors (*chien-ch'a yü-shih*) serving as Regional Inspectors (*hsün-an yü-shih*), who participated importantly in all decision-making assemblages of provincial officials.] Each Surveillance Commission was headed by a Surveillance Commissioner (*an-ch'a shih*), rank 3a, with a support staff including a Registry (*ching-li ssu*), a Records Office (*chao-mo so*), and a Prison (*ssu-yü ssu*). There were variable numbers of Surveillance Vice Commissioners (*an-ch'a fu-shih*), 4a, and Assistant Surveillance Commissioners (*an-ch'a ch'ien-shih*), 5a; they were assigned to Branch Offices (*fen-ssu*), each with a jurisdiction called a Circuit (*tao*), and were generically called Circuit Intendants (*tao-t'ai*), a designation they shared with counterparts in Branch Offices of Provincial Administration Commissions. In each Ming Province there were from 3 to 9 General Surveillance Circuits (*fen-hsün tao*), from 2 to 7 Record Checking Circuits (*shua-chüan tao*), and from one to 12 Military Defense Circuits (*ping-pei tao*), all with specified geographic jurisdictions encompassing several Prefectures (*fu*). Each Province also had function-specific Circuits: one Troop Purification Circuit (*ch'ing-chün tao*), one Postal Service Circuit (*i-chuan tao*), and one Education Intendant Circuit (*t'i-tu hsüeh tao*). As local circumstances warranted, there were also such function-specific Circuits as Irrigation Circuits (*shui-li tao*), State Farms Circuits (*t'un-t'ien tao*), Waterways Circuits (*kuan-ho tao*), and Salt Control Circuits (*yen-fa tao*) with limited territorial jurisdictions. This Ming pattern was perpetuated with minor changes into mid-Ch'ing times. Then in 1735 Circuit Intendants were all made regular posts (*kuan*) in their own right with 4a rank, dissociated at least nominally from the Surveillance Commissions, becoming formal intermediaries between Provinces and Prefectures rather than representatives of the Surveillance Commissions. Also see *san ssu, liang ssu, chien-ssu, fang-mien, nieh-fu, nieh-ssu, nieh-t'ai*. BH: judicial commission. P52.

6447   *t'í-hsíng àn-ch'á ssū*   提刑按察司
Lit., office in charge of judicial matters and investigations. (1) SUNG: **Judicial Commission** in a Circuit (*lu;* see *t'i-tien hsing-yü kung-shih*). (2) YÜAN: **Surveillance Commission** in a Circuit (*tao*) until 1291; see under *su-cheng lien-fang ssu*. (3) MING–CH'ING: common variant of *t'i-hsing an-ch'a shih ssu* (**Provincial Surveillance Commission**). P52.

6448   *t'í-hsíng ch'á-yén ssū*   提刑茶鹽司
SUNG: **Judicial and Tea and Salt Commission,** a common combined agency in those Circuits (*lu*) that were not important tea and salt production areas and thus had no separate Tea and Salt Supervisorate (*ch'a-yen t'i-chü ssu*). P61.

6449   *t'í-hsíng ssū*   提刑司
Judicial Commission. (1) SUNG: abbreviation of *t'i-hsing an-ch'a ssu.* (2) CHIN: one of the major administrative posts at the Route (*lu*) level, with supervisory responsibility for judicial operations in the territorial units of its jurisdiction. In 1199 redesignated *an-ch'a ssu* (Surveillance Commission) and given broader, censorial responsibilities—not merely to oversee judicial activities, but actively to tour and investigate the conduct of officials and consequently to denounce corrupt or ineffective territorial personnel. P52.

6450   *t'í-hsüéh*   提學
YÜAN: **Superintendent of Training,** 2, rank 9b, members of the Directorate of Astronomy (*ssu-t'ien chien*) in general charge of the Directorate's educational functions. P35.

6451   *t'í-hsüéh tào*   提學道
MING–CH'ING: variant of *t'i-tu hsüeh tao* (**Education Intendant Circuit**). BH: taotai of education. P52.

6452   *t'í-hsüéh yǜ-shǐh*   提學御史
MING: **Education-intendant Censor,** from 1436 a duty assignment for Investigating Censors (*chien-ch'a yü-shih*) delegated from the capital to serve as the equivalent of provincial Education Intendants (see *ti-tu hsüeh tao*) in the 2 Metropolitan Areas dominated by Peking and Nanking, approving students for admission to state schools, testing and classifying them periodically, and certifying those considered qualified to undertake civil service recruitment examinations; each assignment was for a 3-year term. This was considered one of the major assignments for Censors, comparable in importance and prestige to assignments as Regional Inspectors (*hsün-an yü-shih*). P51.

6453   *t'í-k'ùng àn-tú*   提控案牘 or *t'i-k'ung*
YÜAN: lit., in charge of files: **Record Keeper,** a lowly or unranked clerical worker commonly found in both central government agencies and units of territorial administration. P15, 20, 53, 60, etc.

6454   *t'í-k'ùng chù-ch'íén chiēn*   提控鑄錢監
CHIN: **Controller of Coinage** at the major foundry at Taichou, modern Shansi; a temporary concurrent appointment in 1182 for a Participant in Determining Governmental Matters (*ts'an-chih cheng-shih*) of the Department of State Affairs (*shang-shu sheng*). See *fu-t'ung ch'ien-chien, tai-chou ch'ien-chien*. P16.

6455   *t'í-k'ùng chū wū-lǔ-kǔ*   提控諸烏魯古
CHIN: **Controller of Herds Offices,** 2, rank 4a, served in lieu of Chief Ministers (*ch'ing*) of a traditional Chinese Court of the Imperial Stud (*t'ai-p'u ssu*), with supervisory authority over all Herds Offices (*ch'ün-mu so*) that managed the state horse herds. See *wu-lu-ku*. P31.

6456   *t'í-k'ùng ts'áo-hó shìh*   提控漕河事
CHIN: **Controller of Waterways,** a concurrent duty assignment for officials of Prefectures (*chou*) and other units of territorial administration; responsible for keeping waterways in good repair and otherwise expediting water transport. P59.

6457   *t'í-láo t'īng*   提牢廳
CH'ING: **Prison Office** in the Ministry of Justice (*hsing-pu*) for the detention of persons awaiting trial; managed by one Manchu and one Chinese Secretary (*chu-shih*), rank 6a. P13.

6458   *t'í-liáng àn*   體量案
SUNG: **Section for Confirmations,** one of 13 Sections (*an*) directly subordinate to the executive officials of the S. Sung Ministry of Justice (*hsing-pu*), reportedly responsible for physical or factual investigations (*t'i-chiu*), probably to confirm reports of judicial findings submitted by units of territorial administration. SP: *service des investigations*.

6459   *t'í-lǐng*   提領
SUNG–MING: lit., to be in charge of: **Superintendent,** one of several common titles used for the senior official of an agency, usually of middling status; the term is found either as prefix or suffix to an agency name. SP: *directeur*.

6460   *t'í-lǐng chù-ch'íén ssū*   提領鑄錢司
SUNG: **Superintendent of Mints,** a concurrent duty for a Vice Minister of Revenue (*hu-pu shih-lang*), to oversee the operations of state-wide coinage production; on the staff of the Tax Transport Bureau (*chuan-yün ssu*) of early Sung.

SP: *fonctionnaire chargé de diriger la fonte des monnaies dans les provinces.* P16.

6461   *t'í-lǐng sǒ* 提領所 or *t'í-lǐng ssū* 司
SUNG–MING: lit., the location or office of a Superintendent: **Superintendency,** a designation for offices of sundry sorts, identifiable only from the prefixed terminology. SP: *bureau de directeur.*

6462   *t'í-lǐng ts'ù-chìh ·hù-pù ts'ái-yùng* 提領措置戶部財用
SUNG: **Superintendent of the Disposition of the Ministry of Revenue's Monies,** apparently a duty assignment for an executive official of the Ministry of Revenue (*hu-pu*), to manage the Ministry's finances. SP: *directeur chargé de disposer des moyens financiers du ministère des finances.*

6463   *t'í-lǐng tù-tiéh sǒ* 提領度牒所
SUNG: **Superintendency of Ordination Certificates,** an agency of the Ministry of Rites (*lǐ-pu*) headed by a staff member on duty assignment as Superintendent (*t'i-ling*); managed the issuance of ordination certificates for Buddhist monks. From the early decades of the 11th century, such certificates were sold by the government in large numbers in efforts to raise funds for military expenses. SP: *bureau des certificats de moines.*

6464   *t'í-piāo* 提標
CH'ING: **Provincial Command,** designation of the aggregate forces under the control of a Provincial Military Commander (*t'i-tu*) of the Chinese military forces called the Green Standards (*lu-ying*).

6465   *t'ì-shìh* 薙氏
CHOU: **Weed Burner,** 2 ranked as Junior Servicemen (*hsia-shih*), members of the Ministry of Justice (*ch'iu-kuan*). The burning of weeds or stalks left after the harvest seems to have been an autumnal activity, hence appropriately under the jurisdiction of the Ministry of Justice ("autumn officials"). CL: *sarcleur de plantes ou d'herbes.*

6466   *t'í-shǔ* 題署
CH'ING: **Reports Office** in the Court of Colonial Affairs (*li-fan yüan*), staffed by 3 Manchu and 5 Mongolian Clerks (*chu-shih*); presumably inscribed materials for submission to the throne. P17.

6467   *t'í-t'ái* 提台
CH'ING: unofficial reference to a **Provincial Military Commander** (*t'i-tu*) of the Chinese military forces called the Green Standards (*lu-ying*).

6468   *t'í-t'áng* 提塘
(1) MING–CH'ING: **Provincial Courier,** designation of someone delegated to carry documents to the dynastic capital from a *hsün-fu* (Grand Coordinator, Provincial Governor) or a *tsung-tu* (Supreme Commander, Governor-general). Cf. *chin-tsou yüan.* (2) CH'ING: **Station Master,** unranked, manager of a Postal Relay Station (*t'ang*).

6469   *t'í-tiào hsüéh-hsiào kuān* 提調學校官
MING: **Supervisor of Education,** irregularly from the early 1400s a duty assignment for a provincial-level official to inspect local schools, test students enrolled in state schools, and certify candidates for provincial-level civil service recruitment examinations; comparable to, and probably a variant of, Education Intendants of Education Intendant Circuits (*t'i-tu hsüeh tao*). Cf. *t'i-hsüeh yü-shih.*

6470   *t'í-tiào kuān* 提調官 or *t'i-tiao*
YÜAN–CH'ING: **Supervisor,** an ad hoc duty assignment for a regular official detached to undertake special functions, not always as the official in charge; used in both civil and military services. Specifically identifiable by prefixes.

6471   *t'í-tiěn ch'áo-fú fǎ-wù k'ù sǒ* 提點朝服法物庫所
SUNG: **Superintendency of Court Clothing and Regalia,** a unit in the Court of Imperial Sacrifices (*t'ai-ch'ang ssu*) responsible for the storing of gowns, headgear, and other accouterments used by the Emperor and other dignitaries in court audiences and sacrificial ceremonies. SP: *dirigeant du magasin des vêtements d'audience et des objets rituels.* P27.

6472   *t'í-tiěn chù-ch'ién shìh* 提點鑄錢事
SUNG: **Coinage Commissioner** at the Circuit (*lu*) level, first established in 1038; oversaw the operation of local Mints (*chu-ch'ien ssu*); commonly a concurrent assignment for a Supply Commissioner (*fa-yün shih*). SP: *intendant de la fonte des monnaies.* P16.

6473   *t'í-tiěn hsíng-yù kūng-shìh* 提點刑獄公事
SUNG: lit., Superintendent of penal affairs: **Judicial Commissioner,** one of the major Circuit (*lu*) posts known collectively as the Four Circuit Supervisorates (*ssu chien-ssu, ssu ssu*); first delegated in 991 as subordinates of Fiscal Commissioners (*chuan-yün shih*), in 1007 established independently, from 1020 to 1026 were concurrent Agricultural Development Commissioners (*ch'üan-nung shih*), abolished from 1028 to 1033 and again from 1064 to 1069; responsible for supervising the judicial and penal operations of Prefectures (*chou*) and Districts (*hsien*), and joined with Fiscal Commissioners in awarding merit ratings (*k'ao*) to all officials serving in subsidiary units of territorial administration. In N. Sung the post was sometimes held by a military officer, but this practice was not continued in S. Sung. The title was commonly abbreviated to *t'i-tien hsing-yü; t'i-hsing an-ch'a shih* was a quasiofficial variant. SP: *intendant judiciaire, intendant des affaires judiciaires.* P52.

6474   *t'í-tiěn k'āi-fēng fǔ-chièh kūng-shìh* 提點開封府界公事
SUNG: **Commissioner-general for Kaifeng,** a central government official assigned specially to oversee the fiscal, judicial, transport, and supply operations of Districts (*hsien*) and other units of territorial administration within Kaifeng Prefecture (*fu*), site of the N. Sung dynastic capital. SP: *surveillant des affaires dans le territoire de la capitale.*

6475   *t'í-tiěn kuān* 提點官 or *t'i-tien*
SUNG–YÜAN, CH'ING: **Superintendent,** comparable to and sometimes interchangeable with *t'i-chü* (Supervisor); a title occurring as either prefix or suffix to an agency name in a middle-level agency or to a functional description, normally outside the regular hierarchy of routine administration. Also cf. *t'i-ling.*

6476   *t'í-tiěn ... kūng* 提點⋯宮 or *t'í-tiěn ... kuān* 觀
SUNG: **Superintendent of the ... Palace** or **Superintendent of the ... Taoist Temple,** variants of *t'i-chü ... kung, t'i-chü ... kuan.* SP: *directeur des palais et des temples taoistes.*

6477   *t'í-tiěn mǎ-chiēn* 提點馬監
SUNG: **Superintendent of the Directorate(s) of Horses,** probably a special duty assignment for one or more members of the Court of the Imperial Stud (*t'ai-p'u ssu*); see under *ma-chien.* SP: *dirigeant de la direction des chevaux.*

6478   *t'í-tiěn shān-líng* 提點山陵
CHIN–CH'ING: **Superintendent of the Mausoleum,** one in charge of each Imperial Mausoleum (*ling*), rank 5a in Chin. P29.

6479   *t'í-tiěn sǒ* 提點所 or *t'í-tiěn ssū* 司
SUNG–YÜAN, CH'ING: **Superintendency,** the standard designations of agencies headed by Superintendents (*t'i-tien kuan*).

6480   *t'í-tiěn tsài-chīng ts'āng-ch'ǎng sǒ*
提點在京倉場所
SUNG: **Superintendent of the Capital Granaries,** status in the governmental hierarchy not clear; possibly a temporary, ad hoc post during the transition from N. to S. Sung. Cf. *t'i-chü tsai-ching chu-ssu k'u-wu ssu*. SP: *directeur du bureau des greniers et des fenils.*

6481   *t'í-tiěn wǔ fáng* 提點五房
SUNG: **Superintendent of the Five Offices,** a duty assignment for an executive official of the Secretariat (*chung-shu sheng*) or the combined Secretariat-Chancellery (*chung-shu men-hsia*), to supervise and coordinate the clerical agencies that conducted the routine business of the Secretariat's Proclamations Office (*chih-ch'ih yüan*), known collectively as the Five Offices (*wu fang*). SP: *chargé de diriger les cinq chambres du secrétariat.* P3.

6482   *t'í-tū* 提督
CH'ING: **Provincial Military Commander,** rank 1b, one in each of the Provinces (*sheng*) of China Proper and in some other especially strategic places; leaders in their jurisdictions of the Chinese military forces called the Green Standards (*lu-ying*). BH: provincial commander-in-chief, general-in-chief. P56.

6483   *t'í-tū chīng-t'ūng èrh ts'āng yù-shǐh*
提督京通二倉御史
MING: lit., Censor superintending the granaries at Peking and T'ung-chou: variant reference to a **Granary-inspecting Censor** (*hsün-ts'ang yü-shih*). P18.

6484   *t'í-tū chūn-wù* 提督軍務
MING: **Military Superintendent,** supplementary designation for a provincial Grand Coordinator (*hsün-fu*) when he was specially authorized concurrently to deal with military matters; from 1662 also a concurrent duty designation of the Supreme Commander of Grain Transport (*tsung-tu ts'ao-yün*). Cf. *tsan-li chün-wu* (Associate Military Superintendent). P50, 60.

6485   *t'í-tū hsüéh-chèng* 提督學政
CH'ING: **Provincial Education Commissioner,** from 1684 a duty assignment at the provincial level for such members of the central government as Vice Ministers (*shih-lang*), Supervising Censors (*chi-shih-chung*), Investigating Censors (*chien-ch'a yü-shih*), and dignitaries of the Hanlin Academy (*han-lin yüan*); each for a 3-year term assigned to tour and inspect schools in his provincial jurisdiction, certifying students for subsidies in state schools, encouraging educational and cultural activities in general, and most importantly selecting candidates for triennial Provincial Examinations (*hsiang-shih*) in the civil service recruitment examination sequence. Superseded Education Intendants (see under *t'i-tu hsüeh-tao*) delegated from Provincial Surveillance Commissions (*t'i-hsing an-ch'a shih ssu*). BH: provincial director of education. P51.

6486   *t'í-tū hsüéh-tào* 提督學道
MING–CH'ING: **Education Intendant Circuit,** designation of the jurisdiction (and indirectly of the Intendant as well), one per province, of a Surveillance Vice Commissioner (*an-ch'a fu-shih*) or an Assistant Surveillance Commissioner (*an-ch'a ch'ien-shih*) assigned for 3 years to approve the subsidized admission of students to state-supported local schools, test them regularly, evaluate their teachers, and select students to undertake triennial Provincial Examinations (*hsiang-shih*) in the civil service recruitment examination sequence. Superseded in 1684 by Provincial Education Commissioners (*t'i-tu hsüeh-cheng*) delegated from the central government. See under *tao* (Circuit). P51.

6487   *t'í-tū hsüéh-yüàn* 提督學院
CH'ING: variant of *t'i-tu hsüeh-cheng* (**Provincial Education Commissioner**).

6488   *t'í-tū hùi-t'úng kuǎn* 提督會同館
MING: **Superintendent of the Interpreters Institute,** concurrent post from 1492 for a Secretary (*chu-shih*) of the Bureau of Receptions (*chu-k'o ssu*) of the Ministry of Rites (*lǐ-pù*); see *hui-t'ung kuan*. P11.

6489   *t'í-tū hùi-t'úng ssù-ì kuǎn*
提督會同四譯館
CH'ING: **Superintendent of the Interpreters and Translators Institute,** from 1748 the concurrent post of a Director (*lang-chung*) of a Bureau (*ch'ing-li ssu*) in the Ministry of Rites (*lǐ-pù*), who additionally bore the title Vice Minister (*shao-ch'ing*) of the Court of State Ceremonial (*hung-lu ssu*). See *hui-t'ung ssu-i kuan*. BH: superintendent. P11.

6490   *t'í-tū kuǎn-wù* 提督館務
CH'ING: abbreviated reference to the **Superintendent of the Interpreters and Translators Institute** (*t'i-tu hui-t'ung ssu-i kuan*).

6491   *t'í-tū ssù-í kuǎn* 提督四夷館
MING: **Superintendent of the Translators Institute,** concurrent assignment for a Vice Minister (*shao-ch'ing*) of the Court of Imperial Sacrifices (*t'ai-ch'ang ssu*). P11.

6492   *t'í-tū t'éng-huáng yù t'ūng-chèng*
提督謄黄右通政
MING: **Vice Commissioner of the Right Superintending Imperial Warrants,** apparently a variant of *t'eng-huang yu t'ung-cheng* (Vice Commissioner of the Right for Imperial Warrants) in the Office of Transmission (*t'ung-cheng ssu*). P21.

6493   *tiāo* 貂
See under *pa tiao* (Eight Sabled Dignitaries).

6494   *tiāo-fāng* 鵰坊
T'ANG: **Eagle Cage,** one of the Five Cages (*wu fang*) of animals used in imperial hunts, under supervision of the Commissioner for the Imperial Stables (*hsien-chiu shih*) in the Palace Administration (*tien-chung sheng*). RR: *quartier des aigles de Mongolie.* P38.

6495   *tiào-lién* 調廉
YÜAN–CH'ING: **Examination Aide,** generic reference to local officials who were assigned to help proctor Provincial Examinations (*hsiang-shih*) in the civil service recruitment examination sequence; see *lien-kuan, nei-lien, wai-lien.*

6496   *tiāo-mù chú* 彫木局
YÜAN: **Woodworking Service;** see under *ta-hsiao tiao-mu chü* (Large and Small Woodworking Service).

6497   *t'iáo* 條
N-S DIV (Chin–S. Dyn.): **Group,** a variable number of

Sections (*ts'ao*) in the Department of State Affairs (*shang-shu sheng*), at times supervised by Overseers of the Department (*lu ... shih*) who divided Sections among themselves in such Groups. See *fen-t'iao*. P2.

6498   *t'iáo-jén* 調人
CHOU: **Arbitrator,** 2 ranked as Junior Servicemen (*hsia-shih*), members of the Ministry of Education (*ti-kuan*) responsible for mediating quarrels among commoners and determining appropriate action when someone was accidentally injured or killed by another or by another's domestic animals, etc. CL: *officier de paix, conciliateur.*

6499   *t'iáo-láng shìh* 條狼氏
CHOU: **Excoriator of Evil,** 6 ranked as Junior Servicemen (*hsia-shih*), members of the Ministry of Justice (*ch'iu-kuan*) who accompanied the King on all public outings, using whips to chase away commoners who threatened distractions. CL: *expurgateur, enleveur d'impurités.*

6500   *t'iáo-lì ssū* 條例司
SUNG: abbreviation of *chih-chih san-ssu t'iao-li ssu* (**Finance Planning Commission**).

6501   *t'iào-tí àn* 糶糴案
SUNG: **Grain Transactions Section,** one of 6 Sections (*an*) in the Granaries Bureau (*ts'ang-pu ssu*) of the Ministry of Revenue (*hu-pu*), staffed with unranked subofficials; oversaw the purchasing and selling of grain, presumably grain handled by Ever Normal Granaries (*ch'ang-p'ing ts'ao*) throughout the empire, apparently in cooperation with units of the Ministry's Right Section (*yu-ts'ao*); established c. 1080, when the State Finance Commission (*san ssu*) of early Sung was discontinued. SP: *service de vente et d'achat des grains.* P6.

6502   *t'iěh-àn* 鐵案
SUNG: **Iron Section,** one of 7 Sections (*an*) in the Salt and Iron Monopoly Bureau (*yen-t'ieh ssu*) of early Sung, normally headed by an Administrative Assistant (*p'an-kuan, t'ui-kuan*); kept records on the production and distribution of iron and the manufacture of various ironwares. SP: *service de fer.*

6503   *t'iěh-chíh* 貼職
SUNG: **Nominal Supernumerary Appointment,** reference to the appointment of an eminent official to such status as Auxiliary in the Historiography Office (*chih shih-kuan*), Auxiliary in the Academy of Scholarly Worthies (*chih chi-hsien yüan*), etc. See under *chih* (Auxiliary).

6504   *t'iěh chīh-hòu nèi-p'ǐn* 貼祇候內品
SUNG: **Supernumerary Palace Eunuch Usher,** lowest of 12 rank titles (*chieh*) awarded to eunuchs from 1112; see *nei-shih chieh, chih-hou nei-p'in.* SP: *intendant du palais de 4ème rang.* P68.

6505   *t'iěh-chù* 鐵柱
Lit., an iron-ribbed hat, suggesting unyielding sternness: occasional unofficial reference to a **Censor** (*yü-shih*).

6506   *t'iěh-hsiěh chūng-shū* 貼寫中書
CH'ING: lit., Secretary (*chung-shu*) for pasting-up and writing: **Scribe,** 40 Manchus and 6 Mongols, rank 7b, responsible for keeping records, making translations and transcriptions, etc., on the staff of the Grand Secretariat (*nei-ko*). P2.

6507   *t'iěh-hsíng kuān* 貼刑官
MING: lit., official dedicated to punishment: unofficial reference to **eunuchs of the Eastern Depot** (*tung-ch'ang*).

6508   *t'iěh-kuān* 鐵官
HAN: **Iron Monopoly Office,** an agency commonly found in Commanderies (*chün*) and Princedoms (*wang-kuo*) for management of the state-controlled production and distribution of iron; headed by a Director (*ling*), rank from 600 to 1,000 bushels or from 300 to 400 bushels. HB: office of iron. P16.

6509   *t'iěh mào-tzǔ wáng* 鐵帽子王
CH'ING: **Iron-helmet Prince,** generic reference to any of 8 nobles distinguished for their outstanding service in the founding of the dynasty and to their successive heirs, whose hereditary status was guaranteed: Imperial Princes (*ch'in-wang*) prefixed Li, Jui, Su, Cheng, Chuang, and Yü, and Commandery Princes (*chün-wang*) prefixed Shun-ch'eng and K'o-ch'in. Also called the Eight Great Families (*pa ta-chia*). BH: iron-capped prince.

6510   *t'iěh-shìh* 鐵市
HAN: **Iron Market,** apparently a unit subordinate to the Chamberlain for the National Treasury (*ta ssu-nung*), headed by a Director (*chang*); specific functions not clear. HB: market of iron.

6511   *t'iěh-shū* 貼書
SUNG: **Writer,** unranked, varying numbers found in the Court of the Imperial Clan (*tsung-cheng ssu*) and the Court of Judicial Review (*ta-li ssu*). SP: *scribe assistant, employé.*

6512   *t'iěh-ssū* 帖司
5 DYN: **Clerk,** one in charge of official seals in the Censorate (*yü-shih t'ai*). P18.

6513   *t'iěh-ssū* 貼司
SUNG: **Clerk,** apparently unranked, found in varying numbers in the Censorate (*yü-shih t'ai*), the Court of Imperial Sacrifices (*t'ai-ch'ang ssu*), and other agencies. SP: *employé, scribe.*

6514   *t'iěh-yěh sǒ* 鐵冶所
MING: **Iron Smelting Office,** 13 scattered throughout the empire in appropriate locations, presumably under the supervision of the Ministry of Works (*kung-pu*); staffing not clear.

6515   *tiěn* 典
(1) **Manager,** prefixed to nouns including some agency names, as Manager of .... In addition to the following entries, see *liu tien, erh-shih-ssu tien, chu tien-shih.* RR: *intendant.* SP: *régisseur.* (2) **Clerk,** uncommon designation of unranked office personnel.

6516   *tièn* 殿
Hall, one of several terms used to designate palace buildings; e.g., *wu-ying tien* (Hall of Military Glory).

6517   *tièn-chái wù* 店宅務
SUNG: **Building Maintenance Office,** a unit of the Court of the Imperial Treasury (*t'ai-fu ssu*); staffing and specific functions not clear. SP: *agence de location (et de construction) des magasins et des maisons d'état.*

6518   *tiěn-chàng* 典仗
Manager of Ceremonial Regalia. (1) T'ANG–SUNG: 2 palace women, rank 7a, under the Directresses of Ceremonial Regalia (*ssu-chang*) in the Ceremonial Regalia Office (*ssu-chang ssu*) of the Wardrobe Service (*shang-fu chü*). RR: *intendant des insignes.* (2) MING: 6 military officers, rank 6a, in the Ceremonial Guard (*i-wei*) of each Princely Establishment (*wang-fu*). P69.

6519 *tiěn-chǎng-í wèi* 典掌儀衛
CH'ING: lit., guard in charge of ritual: unofficial reference to the **Imperial Procession Guard** (*luan-i wei*).

6520 *tiěn-chēn* 典珍
T'ANG–SUNG: **Manager of Rarities**, 2 palace women, rank 7a, under the Directresses of Rarities (*ssu-chen*) in the Rarities Office (*ssu-chen ssu*) of the Workshop Service (*shang-kung chü*). RR: *intendant des objets précieux du harem*.

6521 *tiěn-chèng* 典正
T'ANG–SUNG, MING: **Manager of Palace Surveillance**, 2 palace women, rank 7a, under the Directresses of Palace Surveillance (*ssu-cheng*). RR: *intendant de la surveillance du harem*.

6522 *tiěn-chí* 典籍
(1) T'ANG–SUNG: **Manager of the Library**, 2 palace women, rank 7a, under the Directresses of the Library (*ssu-chi*) in the Ceremonial Service (*shang-i chü*). RR: *intendant de la bibliothèque du harem*. (2) YÜAN: **Archivist**, 2, rank 8a, in the Hanlin Academy (*han-lin yüan*). P23. (3) MING–CH'ING: **Archivist**, one, rank 9b, head of the Archives (*tien-chi t'ing*) in the Directorate of Education (*kuo-tzu chien*); others found in such agencies as the Ming dynasty's Left Secretariat of the Heir Apparent (*tso ch'un-fang*). P23, 34, 49. (4) CH'ING: **Certification Clerk**; see under *nei-ko tien-chi* (Certification Clerk in the Grand Secretariat).

6523 *tiěn-chì* 典計
T'ANG–SUNG: **Manager of Accounts**, 2 palace women, rank 7a, under the Directresses of Accounts (*ssu-chi*) in the Accounts Office (*ssu-chi ssu*) of the Workshop Service (*shang-kung chü*). RR: *intendant des comptes*.

6524 *tiěn-chì* 典記
T'ANG–SUNG: **Manager of Records**, 2 palace women, rank 7a, under the Directresses of Records (*ssu-chi*) in the Records Office (*ssu-chi ssu*) of the General Palace Service (*shang-kung chü*). RR: *intendant de l'enregistrement des pièces*.

6525 *tiěn-chǐ kuān* 典給官 or *tien-chi*
YÜAN: **Provisioner**, manager of food supplies; 8 in the Interpreters Institute (*hui-t'ung kuan*), one in the Directorate of Education (*kuo-tzu chien*), and one in the Mongolian Directorate of Education (*meng-ku kuo-tzu chien*); all lowly or unranked. P11, 34.

6526 *tiěn-chǐ shǔ* 典給署
CHIN: **Provisions Office**, a unit of the Directorate of the Imperial Treasury (*t'ai-fu chien*) responsible for supplying fuel, torches, etc., for the palace; created in 1192 by renaming of the *kou-tun shu* (Office of Imperial Parks Products); staffing not clear. P38, 40.

6527 *tiěn-chí t'īng* 典籍廳
MING–CH'ING: **Archives** in the Directorate of Education (*kuo-tzu chien*), headed by one Archivist (*tien-chi*), rank 9b; cf. *tien-pu t'ing*. P34.

6528 *tiěn-ch'ì* 典饎
T'ANG–SUNG: **Manager of Banquets**, 2 palace women, rank 7a, under the Directresses of Banquets (*ssu-ch'i*) in the Banquets Office (*ssu-ch'i ssu*) of the Food Service (*shang-shih chü*). RR: *intendant des repas*.

6529 *tiěn-chiěn fāng* 點檢房
SUNG: **Office of Inspection**, one each in the Chancellery (*men-hsia sheng*) and the Secretariat (*chung-shu sheng*), staffed by Inspectors (*tien-chien*); functions not clear. SP: *chambre d'examen et de contrôle*.

6530 *tiěn-chiěn ī-yào fàn-shíh* 點檢醫藥飯食
SUNG: **Inspector of Medicine and Food**, duty assignment in the imperial palace for one officer each of the Palace Command (*tien-ch'ien shih-wei ssu*), the Metropolitan Cavalry Command (*ma-chün ssu*), and the Metropolitan Infantry Command (*pu-chün ssu*), probably serving on some rotational basis. SP: *contrôleur de médecine et de nourriture*.

6531 *tiěn-chiěn kuān* 點檢官
SUNG: **Inspector**, 20 in the Ministry of Rites (*li-pu*); what they specifically inspected is not clear. Cf. *tien-chien fang*. SP: *examinateur-contrôleur*.

6532 *tiěn-chiěn wén-tzù* 點檢文字
SUNG: **Calligraphy Inspector**, one in the Historiography and True Records Institute (*kuo-shih shih-lu yüan*), one in the S. Sung capital Prefecture, Lin-an fu (modern Hangchow). SP: *examinateur-contrôleur des écritures*.

6533 *tiěn-ch'iēn* 典籤
N-S-DIV–MING: lit., manager of bamboo slips: **Document Clerk**, a lowly or unranked staff member in units of territorial administration; specific functions not clear. RR+SP: *intendant des pièces officielles*. P25, 52, 69.

6534 *tiěn-ch'ién chūn* 殿前軍
Palace Army. (1) 5 DYN: common designation of the main military force of a regime, directly under the control of the ruler. (2) SUNG: abbreviation of *tien-ch'ien ma-pu chün* (Palace Cavalry and Infantry Armies).

6535 *tiěn-ch'ién kāo-p'ǐn* 殿前高品
SUNG: **Palace Eunuch of High Rank**, variant of *chih-hou kao-p'in* (Palace Eunuch Usher of High Rank). P68.

6536 *tiěn-ch'ién mǎ-pù chūn* 殿前馬步軍
SUNG: **Palace Cavalry and Infantry Armies**, designation of that part of the Imperial Armies (*chin-chün*) that was responsible for active defense of the capital and palace under the Palace Command (*tien-ch'ien shih-wei ssu*). SP: *cavalerie et infanterie devant le palais*.

6537 *tiěn-ch'ién pān* 殿前班
SUNG: **Palace Army Duty Group**, assemblages of personnel or units of the Palace Cavalry and Infantry Armies (*tien-ch'ien ma-pu chün*), apparently organized into a Left and a Right Duty Group (*pan*), which in rotation shared responsibility for active guard service in the capital and at the palace; officers in active charge were on duty assignments as Commandants (*tu-t'ou*), Commanders (*chih-hui shih*), Inspectors (*yü-hou*), etc. SP: *compagnie devant le palais*.

6538 *tiěn-ch'ién shè-shēng chūn* 殿前射生軍
T'ANG: **Army of Bowmen Shooters at Moving Targets**, a pair of military units prefixed Left and Right, created in 786 by being split off from the Left and Right Armies of Inspired Militancy (*shen-wu chün*), among the Imperial Armies (*chin-chün*) in the Northern Command (*pei-ya*). See under *ya-ch'ien she-sheng ping*. P43.

6539 *tiěn-ch'ién shè-shēng hsiāng* 殿前射生廂
T'ANG: **Wing of Bowmen Shooters at Moving Targets**, a pair of military units prefixed Left and Right, created in 757 as a special imperial bodyguard; see under *ya-ch'ien she-sheng ping*.

6540 *tiěn-ch'ién shè-shēng shǒu* 殿前射生手
T'ANG: variant of *ya-ch'ien she-sheng ping* (**Bowmen Shooters at Moving Targets**).

6541 *tièn-ch'ién shén-wēi chūn* 殿前神威軍
T'ANG: **Army of Inspired Awesomeness,** normally abbreviated to *shen-wei chün,* q.v.

6542 *tièn-ch'ién shìh-wèi ssū* 殿前侍衛司
SUNG: **Palace Command,** commonly abbreviated to *tien-ch'ien ssu,* administrative headquarters of one of the 2 large groups of armies known in the aggregate as the Imperial Armies (*chin-chün*), the first-line professional forces of the state (see under *shih-wei ch'in-chün ma-pu ssu,* Metropolitan Command). Created at the beginning of the dynasty to avoid the decentralization of military power among regional warlords commonly called Military Commissioners (*chieh-tu shih*), who now were absorbed into the central government as Commanders-in-chief (*tu chih-hui shih*), rank 2b, or Vice Commanders-in-chief (*fu tu chih-hui shih*), 4a, in collective control of the Palace Command, while former Prefects (*tz'u-shih*) were similarly co-opted into the lesser posts of Commanders (*chih-hui shih*) or Vice Commanders (*fu chih-hui shih*), ranks not clear. These various officers seem to have constituted a pool of military talent from which the Emperor picked leaders of active attack or defense actions, then bearing such commissions as Palace Command Commander-general (*t'ung-ling kuan*), Controller-general (*t'ung-chih kuan*), Supervisory General (*chiang yü-hou*), or Inspector (*yü-hou*). Such field commanders dispatched from the Palace Command were commonly known also as Marshals (*yüan-shuai*), Grand Marshals (*ta yüan-shuai*), or, more formally, Pacification Commissioners (*hsüan-fu shih*). The headquarters of the Palace Command seems to have been staffed principally by Administrative Aides (*ya-pan*), probably palace eunuchs of the 4th and 5th ranks. The Palace Command was under the joint supervisory jurisdiction of the Bureau of Military Affairs (*shu-mi yüan*) and the Ministry of War (*ping-pu*), and from c. 1084 the Ministry of Personnel (*li-pu*) administered the appointments of military officers as well as civil officials (see under *hsüan, yu-hsüan*). The Palace Command existed through S. Sung, but it declined in importance as the original Imperial Armies gradually lost their primary role in Sung military organization and became little more than labor gangs at the disposal of the central government or those who dominated it, while the burden of active military defense against the Jurchen and then the Mongols was borne principally by regionally-based forces (see under *yü-ch'ien chün*). SP: *bureau devant le palais.*

6543 *tièn-ch'ién ssū* 殿前司
SUNG: abbreviation of *tien-ch'ien shih-wei ssu* (**Palace Command**).

6544 *tièn-ch'ién tū tièn-chiěn ssū*
殿前都點檢司
CHIN: **Palace Inspectorate-general,** the chief central government agency in charge of military protection of the palace and the capital city, staffed with Jurchen noblemen; comparable to the Sung dynasty Palace Command (*tien-ch'ien shih-wei ssu*).

6545 *tièn-chìh* 典彘
N-S DIV (Chou): **Manager of Swine,** ranked as an Ordinary Serviceman (*chung-shih*), a member of the Ministry of Works (*tung-kuan*) apparently responsible for the provisioning of pigs for eating in the palace and the central government. P14.

6546 *tièn-chíh* 典直
SUI–SUNG: **Duty Attendant,** 4 in T'ang, rank 9a1, status thereafter not clear; members of the household staff of the Heir Apparent who monitored the coming and going of visitors, transmitted communications in and out, and apparently maintained a kind of censorial surveillance over all those who dealt with the Heir Apparent. Established c. 604 to replace the title *ch'eng-chih* (Duty Attendant). RR+SP: *intendant de l'étiquette du palais intérieur de l'héritier du trône.*

6547 *tièn-chìh* 典製
T'ANG–SUNG, MING: **Manager of Sewing,** 2 palace women, rank 7a, under the Directresses of Sewing (*ssu-chih*) in the Sewing Office (*ssu-chih ssu*) of the Workshop Service (*shang-kung chü*). RR: *intendant de la confection des vêtements.*

6548 *tièn-chíh* 殿直
SUNG: lit., to be on palace duty: one of several generic references to **Palace Eunuchs;** see *huan-kuan, nei-shih, tso-pan tien-chih, yu-pan tien-chih, chih-hou tien-chih.* P68.

6549 *tièn-chīng chǘ* 典經局 or *tièn-chīng fāng* 坊
N-S DIV: **Editorial Service** in the household of the Heir Apparent, staffed with 8 Librarians (*hsien-ma*) in Liang and N. Ch'i; antecedent of the Sui and later *ssu-ching chü.* P26.

6550 *tièn-chiù* 典廄
SUNG: **Manager of Stables** in the Court of the Imperial Stud (*t'ai-p'u ssu*), number and status not clear, but presumably counterpart(s) of the T'ang Directors (*ling*) of the Office of the Imperial Stables (*tien-chiu shu*). SP: *intendant des écuries.*

6551 *tièn-chiù shǔ* 典廄署
T'ANG: **Office of the Imperial Stables,** one of 4 major Offices (*shu*) in the Court of the Imperial Stud (*t'ai-p'u ssu*), responsible for managing the horses, cattle, and other domestic animals kept at the capital by the Court for palace use; headed by 2 Directors (*ling*), rank 7b2. RR: *office de l'intendance des écuries de l'empereur.*

6552 *tièn-chù* 甸祝
CHOU: **Offeror of Hunting Prayers,** 2 ranked as Junior Servicemen (*hsia-shih*), members of the Ministry of Rites (*ch'un-kuan*) who conducted sacrifices and prayers at the beginning of royal hunting expeditions. CL: *officier des prières faites aux chasses impériales, invocateur des chasses.*

6553 *tièn-chuàn* 殿撰
MING–CH'ING: lit., abbreviated from *tien-shih* (Palace Examination) and *hsiu-chuan* (Senior Compiler): unofficial reference to a **Principal Graduate** (*chuang-yüan*) in the Palace Examination, the final stage of the triennial civil service recruitment examination sequence, who was commonly appointed Senior Compiler in the Hanlin Academy (*han-lin yüan*).

6554 *tièn-chuàn t'īng* 典饌廳
MING: **Provisioning Office,** a foods service in the Directorate of Education (*kuo-tzu chien*), also authorized for each Princely Administration (*wang-fu*); headed by one or more Managers of Provisions (*tien-chuan*), possibly unranked. P23, 69.

6555 *tièn-chūng* 典鐘
T'ANG, LIAO: lit., in charge of bells or clocks: **Time Keeper** in the T'ang Bureau of Astronomy (*ssu-t'ien t'ai*) and the Liao Directorate of Astronomy (*ssu-t'ien chien*); unranked, totaling more than 300 at times in T'ang; specific functions not clear, but were associated with clepsydras or water clocks and with Time Drummers (*tien-ku*). RR: *intendant des cloches.* P35.

6556 *tièn-chūng* 殿中

LIAO: **Palace Administrator,** head of the Palace Administration Office (*tien-chung ssu*); also see *tien-chung ts'ao*. P38.

6557 *tièn-chūng chiāng-chūn* 殿中將軍

N-S DIV (Ch'i–Liang): **General of the Palace,** 10 appointed under each of 2 Commandants (*shuai*) who controlled the military forces in the establishment of the Heir Apparent; antecedents of the later Commandants of the Ten Guard Commands (*shih shuai-fu*) of the Heir Apparent. P26.

6558 *tièn-chūng chiēn* 殿中監

(1) N-S DIV (San-kuo Wei–S. Dyn.): **Palace Directorate,** a minor unit in the central government established in the last years of Later Han by the warlord-dictator Ts'ao Ts'ao and continued through the S. Dynasties, headed by a Director (also *chien;* see under #2 below); responsible for supervising and provisioning the imperial household, staffed with non-eunuch dignitaries; gradually subordinated to the developing Department of State Affairs (*shang-shu sheng*). (2) N-S DIV: **Director of the Palace,** non-eunuch head of the Palace Directorate described under (1) above, commonly assisted by a Vice Director (*lang*). In Ch'i and Liang both Inner (*nei*) and Outer (*wai*) Directors were appointed, perhaps indicating a division of the Palace Directorate into eunuch and non-eunuch segments; but during this era palace women and eunuchs were most commonly under the general supervision of the Chamberlain for Palace Revenues (*shao-fu*) through various subordinates. (3) N-S DIV (N. Ch'i): **Director of the Palace Attendance Service** (*tien-chung chü,* q.v.). (4) T'ANG–SUNG: **Director of the Palace Administration** (*tien-chung sheng,* q.v.). (5) CH'ING: unofficial, archaic reference to the Imperial Household Department (*nei-wu fu*). P9, 37.

6559 *tièn-chūng chü* 殿中局

N-S DIV (N. Ch'i): **Palace Administration,** a non-eunuch unit in the Chancellery (*men-hsia sheng*) in general charge of administering and provisioning the imperial palace; headed by 4 Directors (*chien*); apparently successor of the earlier *tien-chung shang-shu* and *tien-chung lang* and antecedent of the Sui *tien-nei chü*. P37.

6560 *tièn-chūng fèng-ch'èng láng* 殿中奉乘郎

N-S DIV (San-kuo Wei): **Court Gentleman for the Imperial Livery,** rank 5b2, under the Director of the Palace (*tien-chung chien*); apparently in charge of all horses and carriages used by palace personnel. P37.

6561 *tièn-chūng shěng* 殿中省

Lit., department for (those) inside the palace halls: **Palace Administration,** a central government agency generally responsible for administering and provisioning the imperial palace, to be distinguished from organizations of palace eunuchs, e.g., those described in various *nei-shih* entries. (1) N-S DIV (San-kuo Wei): occasionally found as a variant or unofficial reference to the Palace Directorate (*tien-chung chien*) established by the dictator Ts'ao Ts'ao in the waning Han years. (2) T'ANG–SUNG: originated in 618 as a renamed *tien-nei sheng,* q.v., inherited from Sui; from 622 to 670 variantly named *chung-yü fu.* Headed by a Director (*chien*), rank 3a, with the aid of 2 Vice Directors (*shao-chien*), 4b, and 2 Assistant Directors (*ch'eng*), 5b. In Sung these ranks slipped, e.g., to 4b for the Director, and the agency was often overseen by a Supervisor (*p'an sheng-shih*). The Palace Administration included 6 subsidiary Services (*chü*), each headed by 2 Chief Stewards (*feng-yü*), 5a, and several Foremen (*chih-chang*), 7a, in T'ang; in Sung the whole battery was controlled by a Supervisor of the Six

Services (*t'i-chü liu shang-chü*) and a Manager (*kou-tang kuan*). The Six Services (*liu chü, liu shang-chü, liu shang*) were the Food Service (*shang-shih chü*), Medicines Service (*shang-yao chü*), Clothing Service (*shang-i chü*), Accommodations Service (*shang-she chü*), Sedan-chair Service (*shang-lien chü*), and Livery Service (*shang-ch'eng chü*); in Sung the last of these was replaced by a Wines Service (*shang-yün shü*). Until 735 the Palace Administration also managed an Imperial Treasury (*t'ien-fu tsang*). In Sung various other agencies were assigned to the Administration for supervision: a Minor Gifts Storehouse (*ch'in-i k'u*) managed jointly by official and eunuch Supervisors (*chien-kuan*); an Imperial Wardrobe (*shang-i k'u*) managed jointly by a Commissioner (*shih*) and 2 eunuch Supervisors; from 976 a Special Gifts Storehouse (*nei i-wu k'u*) managed jointly by official and eunuch Supervisors; from 1103 an Imperial Dispensary (*yü-yao yüan*) managed by a eunuch Manager (*kou-tang kuan*) and a Storehouse of Court Ritual Regalia (*ch'ao-fu fa-wu k'u*) managed jointly by official and eunuch Supervisors. Nevertheless, in Sung the executive posts in the Palace Administration were normally sinecures for imperial in-laws and other palace favorites, and active supervision of palace administration became increasingly the responsibility of the Court of Palace Attendants (*hsüan-hui yüan,* q.v.). In S. Sung the various *tien-chung* titles fell into disuse. RR+SP: *département du service domestique de l'empereur.* P37, 38.

6562 *tièn-chūng shìh yǜ-shǐh* 殿中侍御史

N-S DIV (Chin)–MING: **Palace Censor,** members of the Palace Bureau (*tien-yüan*) of the Censorate (*yü-shih t'ai*), deriving from the Attendant Censors (*shih yü-shih*) under the Han dynasty's Palace Aide to the Censor-in-chief (*yü-shih chung-ch'eng*), who maintained a duty station in the palace called the Orchid Pavilion (*lan-t'ai*); responsible for maintaining censorial surveillance over palace personnel and members of the outer officialdom who had occasion to enter the palace. In the era of N-S Division fluctuated in number from 2 to as many as 14 in N. Wei, also in rank between 5b and 8b. Sui changed the designation to *tien-nei shih yü-shih,* and in c. 604 Emperor Yang deprived the Censorate of its traditional palace outpost and strengthened its surveillance over the outer officialdom. In T'ang Palace Censors increased from 6 to 9 in number, had rank 7a, and exercised broad surveillance powers over the conduct of officials in court audience and over the management of imperial finances in the Imperial Granaries (*t'ai-ts'ang*) and the Left Vault (*tso-tsang*). In Sung and Yüan they numbered 2 and rose in rank from 7a to 4a. In early Ming their number was not specified and they ranked 5a, but only till 1376, when the Palace Bureau and its personnel were finally discontinued. RR+SP: *censeur de la cour des affaires du palais.* P18.

6563 *tièn-chūng ssū* 殿中司

(1) LIAO: **Palace Administration Office,** apparently a non-eunuch agency of the Southern Administration (*nan-mien*) responsible for overseeing general service administration of the imperial palace; headed by a Palace Administrator (*tien-chung*) and a Palace Administration Aide (*tien-ch'eng*); supervised 6 subsidiary Services (*chü*) in the pattern of T'ang's Palace Administration (*tien-chung sheng*). P38. (2) YÜAN: variant of *tien-yüan* (**Palace Bureau** in the Censorate, *yü-shih t'ai*).

6564 *tièn-chūng ssū-mǎ tū* 殿中司馬督

N-S DIV: **Palace Commander,** a subaltern of the Capital Commandant (*chung ling-chün*).

6565 *tièn-chūng ts'áo* 殿中曹 or *tien-chung*
(1) N-S DIV (Ch'i, Liang, N. Wei): **Section for Palace Affairs,** one of 3 or 4 Sections (*ts'ao*) in the Ministry of Sacrifices (*tz'u-pu*) in the developing Department of State Affairs (*shang-shu sheng*); headed by a Director (*lang, lang-chung*). P9. (2) N-S DIV (N. Wei): **Ministry of Palace Affairs,** one of the more important units in the dynasty's unstable Department of State Affairs; headed by a Minister (*shang-shu*); early in the 400s had great influence over military affairs and revenues as well as administration of the imperial palace, but by the end of the 400s had lost most of this influence and was in charge of palace ceremonial matters; supervised Sections (also *ts'ao*) for Palace Affairs (also *tien-chung*), for Palace Service (*chih-shih*), for the Three Dukes (*san kung*), and for Communications and Horse Breeding (*chia-pu*), each headed by a Director (*lang, lang-chung*). P9. (3) N-S DIV (N. Wei): one of 4 major Sections in the Ministry of Palace Affairs (see #2 above). P9.

6566 *tièn-chūng yù-shǐh* 殿中御史
Common variant of *tien-chung shih yü-shih* (**Palace Censor**).

6567 *tièn-chǔ* 典學
T'ANG: **Examination Manager,** a duty assignment for a Vice Director (*yüan-wai lang*) of the Evaluations Bureau (*k'ao-kung*) in the Ministry of Personnel (*li-pu*), to participate in administering civil service recruitment examinations.

6568 *tièn-chūn* 典軍
(1) HAN: **Control Army,** one of 8 capital-defense forces organized at the end of Han; see *pa hsiao-wei* (Eight Commandants). (2) T'ANG–YÜAN: **Escort Brigade Commander,** 2, rank 5a1 in T'ang, not clear in Sung, 7b in Yüan, leaders of the Personal Guard Garrison (*ch'in-shih fu*) in a Princely Establishment (*wang-fu*). RR+SP: *colonel de la garde d'un prince.* P69.

6569 *tièn-chūn* 典郡
HAN: lit., manager of a Commandery: unofficial reference to a **Regional Inspector** (*tz'u-shih*) or a **Commandery Governor** (*t'ai-shou*).

6570 *tièn-chūn ssū* 典軍司
YÜAN: variant of *ch'in-shih fu* (**Personal Guard Garrison** in a Princely Establishment, *wang-fu*). P69.

6571 *tièn-fǎ tà-ch'én* 典法大臣
HAN: lit., grand minister manager of the law: unofficial reference to a **Censor-in-chief** (*yü-shih ta-fu*).

6572 *tièn-fǎ ts'áo* 典法曹
HAN: **Section for Laws** under the Chamberlain for Law Enforcement (*t'ing-wei*); specific functions not clear, but presumably headed by an Administrator (*yüan-shih*). HB: bureau for the direction of laws.

6573 *tièn-fān shǔ* 典蕃署
SUI: briefly from c. 604 the official variant of *tien-k'o shu* (**Office of Receptions** in the Court of State Ceremonial, *hung-lu ssu*). P11.

6574 *tièn-fǔ* 典府
N-S DIV–T'ANG: **Manager of Supplies,** more than one suboficial on the staff of each Princely Establishment (*wang-fu*), normally led by a Director (*chang*), in T'ang rank 9a2. RR: *intendant des magasins.* P69.

6575 *tièn-fú* 典服
T'ANG: **Clothier,** 12 (or 30?) non-official workers in the Palace Attendance Service (*nei-chih chü*) in the household of the Heir Apparent. RR: *intendant des vêtements.*

6576 *tièn-fú chèng* 典服正
MING: **Director of the Wardrobe,** rank 7a, in a Princely Establishment (*wang-fu*). P69.

6577 *tièn fù-kūng* 典婦功
CHOU: **Manager of Palace Women's Work,** 2 ranked as Ordinary Servicemen (*chung-shih*) and 4 as Junior Servicemen (*hsia-shih*), members of the Ministry of State (*t'ien-kuan*) responsible for directing the craft work of palace women, who produced clothing and other objects for use by the ruler and his principal wives. CL: *directeur du travail des femmes.*

6578 *tièn-hàn* 典翰
T'ANG: **Plume Maker** (?), 8 or 10 non-official workers in the Palace Attendance Service (*nei-chih chü*) in the household of the Heir Apparent. RR: *intendant des insignes en plumes.*

6579 *tièn-hsǐ* 典枲
CHOU: **Manager of Hemp,** 2 ranked as Junior Servicemen (*hsia-shih*), members of the Ministry of State (*t'ien-kuan*) who received and stored hempen and coarser cloth paid as taxes. CL: *directeur du chanvre en fil.*

6580 *tièn-hsǐ* 典璽
T'ANG: **Seal Keeper,** 4 non-official workers in the Palace Attendance Service (*nei-chih chü*) in the household of the Heir Apparent; abolished in the early 700s. RR: *intendant des sceaux.*

6581 *tièn-hsià* 殿下
Lit., below the Hall; variant of *pi-hsia* (**Your Majesty**). (1) N-S DIV (S. Dyn.): form used in speaking to the ruler. (2) T'ANG: form used in speaking to the Empress or the Heir Apparent.

6582 *tièn-hsīng* 典星
HAN: **Star Watcher,** number and rank not clear, on the staff of the Grand Astrologer (*t'ai-shih ling*); from A.D. 89 assisted by Expectant Star Watchers (*tien-hsing tai-chao*). P35.

6583 *tièn hsiū-chuàn* 殿修撰
SUNG: **Senior Compiler of the Academy,** quasiofficial reference to an Academician (*hsüeh-shih*) of the Academy of Scholarly Worthies (*chi-hsien tien shu-yüan*). SP: *rédacteur du palais, lettré du palace où l'on rassemble les sages.*

6584 *tièn-hsüéh* 典學
N-S DIV–T'ANG: **Teaching Aide,** 2 to 4, apparently unranked suboficials, members of the Directorate of Education (*kuo-tzu chien*) or its predecessor the National University (*t'ai-hsüeh*); in T'ang reportedly responsible for copying study materials. RR: *intendant des études.* P34.

6585 *tièn-hsüéh ts'úng-shìh* 典學從事
N-S DIV: **Educational Aide** on the staff of a Regional Inspector (*tz'u-shih*), with general responsibility for all educational activities in the Region (*chou*); also found in some Commanderies (*chün*). See *ch'üan-hsüeh ts'ung-shih.* P51, 67.

6586 *tièn-hù* 典護
SUI: **Manager of Security,** one appointed for each tributary chief or envoy under the jurisdiction of the Court for Dependencies (*hung-lu*); an ad hoc duty assignment, not a regular post. P11.

6587 *tiĕn-í* 典儀
(1) SUI–T'ANG: **Supervisor of Rites,** 2, rank 9b2, ceremonial escorts and ushers on the staff of the Tribunal of Receptions (*yeh-che t'ai*); introduced important visitors to the Emperor in court audiences and other ceremonies. RR: *intendant des cérémonies officielles.* P3. (2) CH'ING: **Manager of Ceremonies,** one or 2, rank 4b to 8a, on the staff of each Princely Establishment (*wang-fu*) and Princess's Establishment (*kung-chu fu*). BH: assistant majordomo. P69.

6588 *tiĕn-ī* 典衣
T'ANG–SUNG: **Manager of Clothing,** 2 palace women, rank 7a, under the Directresses of Clothing (*ssu-i*) in the Clothing Office (*ssu-i ssu*) of the Wardrobe Service (*shang-fu chü*). RR: *intendant des vêtements du harem.*

6589 *tiĕn-ī ch'éng* 典醫丞
N-S DIV (Liang, Ch'i): **Medical Aide** in a Princely Establishment (*wang-fu*). P69.

6590 *tiĕn-í chiēn* 典儀監
N-S DIV (N. Wei): **Supervisor of Ceremonies,** rank 5b1, in the Court for Dependencies (*hung-lu ssu*). P33.

6591 *tiĕn-ī chiēn* 典醫監
YÜAN: **Directorate of Medicine** in the establishment of the Heir Apparent, staffed with non-official Palace Physicians (*t'ai-i*); headed by a Supervisor (*chien*), rank 3a; created in 1294 (1307?) in a reorganization of the Office of Medication (*tien-i shu*); abolished in 1311, re-established in 1329. P36.

6592 *tiĕn-í lù-shìh* 典儀錄事
N-S DIV (S. Dyn.): **Office Manager for Ceremonial,** head of the Reception Service (*tao-k'o chü*) in the establishment of the Heir Apparent. P33.

6593 *tiĕn-ī shǔ* 典醫署
YÜAN: **Office of Medication** in the establishment of the Heir Apparent, staffed with non-official Palace Physicians (*t'ai-i*); head ranked 5b, title not clear; absorbed into the new Directorate of Medicine (*tien-i chien*) in 1294 (1307?); re-established in 1326, in 1329 again absorbed into the Directorate of Medicine. P36.

6594 *tiĕn-í sǒ* 典儀所
MING: **Ceremonies Office** in a Princely Establishment (*wang-fu*), headed by a Director (*cheng*), rank 9a. P69.

6595 *tiĕn í-yüèh* 典夷樂
N-S DIV (Chou): **Foreign Music-master,** number unspecified, ranked as Ordinary Servicemen (*chung-shih;* 8a) and Junior Servicemen (*hsia-shih;* 9a), under Musicians-in-chief (*ta ssu-yüeh*) in the Ministry of Rites (*ch'un-kuan*). P10.

6596 *tiĕn-jáng* 典禳
HAN: **Exorcist,** 2, probably non-officials, on the staff of the Grand Astrologer (*t'ai-shih ling*), in charge of prayers and sacrifices intended to drive off unfavorable influences. HB: director of sacrifices to expel evil influences.

6597 *tiĕn-jùi* 典瑞
Manager of Seals. (1) CHOU: 2 ranked as Ordinary Servicemen (*chung-shih*), members of the Ministry of Rites (*ch'un-kuan*), apparently responsible for management of the royal seals. CL: *conservateur des tablettes marquées des sceaux officiels.* (2) N-S DIV (Chou): number unspecified, ranked as Ordinary Servicemen and Junior Servicemen (*hsia-shih*), members of the Ministry of Rites. P9.

6598 *tiĕn-jùi yüàn* 典瑞院
YÜAN: **Imperial Seals Commission,** apparently an autonomous agency of the central government in charge of keeping and authorizing use of the imperial seals; staffing not clear.

6599 *tiĕn-júng wèi* 典戎衛
T'ANG: **Militant Guard,** from 662 to 670 the official redesignation of the Defense Guard Command (*wei shuai-fu*) in the establishment of the Heir Apparent. P26.

6600 *tiĕn-k'ò* 典客
(1) CH'IN–HAN: **Chamberlain for Dependencies,** one of the Nine Chamberlains (*chiu ch'ing*) of the central government, rank 2,000 bushels in Han; managed relations with submitted alien tribes and in early Han with enfeoffed Princes (*wang*) and Marquises (*hou*); in 144 B.C. retitled *ta-hsing ling,* then in 104 B.C. *ta hung-lu.* HB: director of guests. P33. (2) T'ANG–SUNG: **Custodian of Foreign Visitors,** as many as 13 apparently unranked subofficials in the Office of Receptions (*tien-k'o shu*) of the Court of State Ceremonial (*hung-lu ssu*), who looked after the needs of important foreign visitors at court. RR+SP: *intendant des hôtes.* P11. (3) CH'ING: unofficial reference to the **Minister** (*shang-shu*) **of the Court of Colonial Affairs** (*li-fan yüan*). BH: president of the court of colonial affairs.

6601 *tiĕn-k'ō* 典科
CH'ING: **Principal of a Departmental Medical School,** head of a Medical School (*i-hsüeh*) established by a Department (*chou*), certified by the Ministry of Rites (*lǐ-pu*) and under supervision of the Provincial Administration Commission (*ch'eng-hsüan pu-cheng shih ssu*). BH: departmental physician.

6602 *tiĕn-k'ò chiēn* 典客監
N-S DIV (N. Wei): **Supervisor of Dependencies,** rank 5b1, a central government official; organizational affiliations not clear, but apparently supervised a Director of Receptions (*chu-k'o ling*). P11.

6603 *tiĕn-k'ò kuǎn* 典客館
N-S DIV (Liang, Ch'en): **Bureau of Receptions** under the Chamberlain for Dependencies (*ta hung-lu*); headed by a Director (*ling*), rank 7b (?). See *k'o-kuan.* P11.

6604 *tiĕn-k'ò lìng* 典客令
N-S DIV (Chin): **Manager of Receptions** on the staff of the Chamberlain for Dependencies (*ta hung-lu*); assisted by an Aide (*ch'eng*). P11.

6605 *tiĕn-k'ò shǔ* 典客署
N-S DIV (N. Ch'i)–T'ANG, CHIN: **Office of Receptions** under the Court of State Ceremonial (*hung-lu ssu*) through T'ang, in Chin under the Court Ceremonial Institute (*hsüan-hui yüan*); responsible for attending to the needs of important foreign visitors; headed by one or 2 Directors (*ling*), rank 7b in T'ang, 6b in Chin. RR: *office de l'intendance des hôtes.* P11.

6606 *tiĕn-kǔ* 典鼓
T'ANG, LIAO: **Time Drummer,** unspecified numbers, unranked, in the T'ang Bureau of Astronomy (*ssu-t'ien t'ai*) and the Liao Directorate of Astronomy (*ssu-t'ien chien*), also 12 in the T'ang Court of the Watches (*lei-keng ssu*) in the establishment of the Heir Apparent; gave time signals with drums in conformity with the operation of clepsydras. See *tien-chung* (Time Keeper). RR: *intendant des tambours.* P26, 35.

6607 *tiĕn kùng-chǔ* 典貢舉
T'ANG: **Chief Examiner,** duty assignment for a court official to supervise a civil service recruitment examination.

6608 *tiĕn-lì* 典曆
N-S DIV: **Calendar Maker,** variable number, rank not specified, on the staff of the Grand Astrologer (*t'ai-shih ling*). P35.

6609 *tiĕn-lì* 典吏
YÜAN: **Clerk,** unranked subofficials found in large numbers both in central government agencies and in units of territorial administration. P5, 6, 12, 13, etc.

6610 *tiĕn-lù* 典路
CHOU: **Manager of the Royal Chariots,** 2 ranked as Ordinary Servicemen (*chung-shih*) and 4 as Junior Servicemen (*hsia-shih*), members of the Ministry of Rites (*ch'un-kuan*) who looked after the 5 special types of chariots (called *lu*) in which the King and his Queen rode on ceremonial occasions. CL: *conservateur des chars.*

6611 *tiĕn-mìng* 典命
CHOU: **Manager of Titles of Honor,** 2 ranked as Ordinary Servicemen (*chung-shih*), members of the Ministry of Rites (*ch'un-kuan*) who apparently handled paperwork concerning the award of titles known as the Nine Honors (*chiu ming*), which determined the kinds, numbers, and sizes of residences, chariots, gowns, etc., to which nobles and officials were entitled. CL: *conservateur des brevets.*

6612 *tiĕn-mŭ* 典牡
N-S DIV (Chou), SUNG: **Manager of Herds,** ranked a. Senior Servicemen (*shang-shih*) and Ordinary Servicemen (*chung-shih*) in Chou of the era of N-S Division, members of the Ministry of War (*hsia-kuan*); in Sung rank not clear, members of the Court of the Imperial Stud (*t'ai-p'u ssu*). Cf. *tien-p'in.* SP: *intendant des élevages.* P31.

6613 *tiĕn-mù shŭ* 典牧署
SUI-T'ANG: **Office of Herds,** one of 4 major units in the Court of the Imperial Stud (*t'ai-p'u ssu*), headed by 3 Directors (*ling*), rank 8a; nominally in overall charge of all imperial herds and the provisioning of the palace and central government with meat and milk products, but the herds were under the direct control of Directorates of Horse Pasturages (*mu-chien*) throughout North China. RR: *office de l'intendance des élevages.* P31.

6614 *tiĕn-nèi* 典內
SUI-T'ANG, SUNG: **Palace Manager,** head of the Inner Quarters (*nei-fang*), apparently a eunuch agency providing intimate services for the Heir Apparent; also see *nei-shih sheng.* SP: *chef de service du palais intérieur de la maison de l'héritièr du trône.* P26.

6615 *tiĕn-nèi chiēn* 殿內監
SUI: **Director of the Palace Administration;** see *tien-nei sheng,* at the beginning of T'ang (618) renamed *tien-chung sheng,* q.v. Sometimes mistaken as an agency name rather than the title of the agency head. RR: *direction du service domestique de l'empereur.* P37, 38.

6616 *tiĕn-nèi chŭ* 殿內局
(1) N-S DIV (N. Ch'i): **Palace Attendance Service,** a non-eunuch agency in the Secretariat of the Heir Apparent (*men-hsia fang*), headed by 2 Directors of Palace Attendants (*nei-chih chien*); subsequently renamed *nei-chih chü,* q.v. Distinguish from the N. Ch'i *tien-chung chü* (Palace Administration) serving the imperial palace. P26. (2) SUI: **Palace Administration,** a revival of the N. Ch'i agency described in (1) above as a non-eunuch subdivision of the Chancellery (*men-hsia sheng*) in general charge of administering and provisioning the imperial palace; headed by 2 Directors (*chien*), rank 5a or 5b; in 607 raised to the status of a De-

partment (*sheng*), replacing the Palace Domestic Service (*nei-shih sheng*) as one of the Five Departments (*wu sheng*) in the top echelon of the central government, although it remained under the supervision of the Chancellery. Also see *tien-chung sheng.* P37.

6617 *tiĕn-nèi shĕng* 殿內省
SUI: **Palace Administration,** changed from *tien-nei chü,* q.v., in 607, then in 618 renamed *tien-chung sheng,* q.v.; under the jurisdiction of the Chancellery (*men-hsia sheng*), generally responsible for administering and provisioning the imperial palace; a non-eunuch agency headed by 2 Directors (*chien*), rank 5a or 5b, and including 6 subsidiary Services (*chü*): Food Service (*shang-shih chü*), Medicines Service (*shang-yao chü*), Clothing Service (*shang-i chü*), Accommodations Service (*shang-she chü*), Livery Service (*shang-ch'eng chü*), and Sedan-chair Service (*shang-lien chü*), each headed by 2 Chief Stewards (*feng-yü*) assisted by several Foremen (*chih-chang*). Cf. *nei-shih sheng.* P37.

6618 *tiĕn-nèi shìh yŭ-shĭh* 殿內侍御史
SUI: variant of the standard designation *tien-chung shih yü-shih* (**Palace Censor**). P18.

6619 *tiĕn-núng shŭ* 典農署
N-S DIV (N. Wei): **Agriculture Office,** one of 3 provisioning agencies at the capital under the Chamberlain for the Palace Revenues (*t'ai-fu*), headed by a Director (*ling*), rank 8 or 9. P37.

6620 *tiĕn-păo* 典寶
T'ANG-MING: **Manager of Seals,** 2 to 4 palace women, rank 7a, under the Directresses of Seals (*ssu-pao*) in the Seals Ofice (*ssu-pao ssu*) of the Wardrobe Service (*shang-fu chü*). RR: *intendant des sceaux.*

6621 *tiĕn-păo sŏ* 典寶所
MING: **Seals Office** in a Princely Establishment (*wang-fu*), headed by a Director (*cheng*), rank 8a. P69.

6622 *tiĕn-p'áo* 典庖
N-S DIV (Chou): **Manager of the Kitchen,** ranked as an Ordinary Serviceman (*chung-shih;* 8a); organizational affiliation not clear.

6623 *tiĕn-pīn* 典賓
(1) T'ANG-SUNG: **Manager of Visitors,** 2 palace women, rank 7a, under the Directresses of Visitors (*ssu-pin*) in the Visitors Office (*ssu-pin ssu*) of the Ceremonial Service (*shang-i chü*). RR: *intendant des visites du harem.* (2) Unofficial reference to the **Bureau of Receptions** (*chu-k'o ssu*) in the Ministry of Rites (*lĭ-pu*).

6624 *tiĕn-p'ìn* 典牝
N-S DIV (Chou): **Manager of Mares,** number not specified, ranked as Senior Servicemen (*shang-shih*) and Ordinary Servicemen (*chung-shih*), members of the Ministry of War (*hsia-kuan*); apparently responsible for the breeding of military mounts. Cf. *tien-mu.* P31.

6625 *tiĕn-pīng* 典兵
SUNG: **Troop Commander,** an active military duty assignment sometimes awarded to eunuchs in the early reigns of the dynasty.

6626 *tiĕn-pù* 典簿
(1) T'ANG-SUNG: **Manager of Registration,** 2 palace women, rank 7a, under the Directresses of Registration (*ssu-pu*) in the Registration Office (*ssu-pu ssu*) of the General Palace Service (*ssu-kung chü*). RR: *intendant des registres du harem.* (2) YÜAN-CH'ING: **Archivist,** rank 7 or lower, found in both agencies of the central government and units

of territorial administration; in Ming and Ch'ing was commonly head of a subdivision called an Archive (*tien-pu t'ing*); not significantly different from *tien-chi* (Archivist). BH: senior archivist. P15, 23, 25, etc.

6627 *tiĕn-pù t'īng* 典簿廳
MING–CH'ING: **Archive,** a subdivision in many central government agencies, headed by an Archivist (*tien-pu*), rank 7 or lower. BH: record office. P23, 27, 30, etc.

6628 *tiĕn-shàn* 典扇
T'ANG: **Fan Maker,** 8 or 10 unranked subofficials or non-official specialists in the Palace Attendance Service (*nei-chih chü*) in the household of the Heir Apparent. RR: *intendant des éventails.*

6629 *tiĕn-shàn* 典膳
Manager of Foods. (1) T'ANG–SUNG: 2 palace women, rank 7a, under the Directresses of Foods (*ssu-shan*) in the Foods Office (*ssu-shan ssu*) of the Food Service (*shang-shih chü*). RR: *intendant des mets exquis.* (2) SUNG–MING: rank 6 or lower officials found in the Sung establishment of the Heir Apparent and in Ming Princely Establishments (*wang-fu*), also in the Ming Directorate of Education (*kuo-tzu chien*) till 1380, then retitled *tien-chuan* (Manager of Provisions; see *tien-chuan t'ing*). P34, 69.

6630 *tiĕn-shàn chiēn* 典膳監
N-S DIV (N. Ch'i)–T'ANG: **Supervisor of Foods,** until 662 title of the head of the Foods Service (*tien-shan chü*) in the establishment of the Heir Apparent; thereafter titled *lang* (Director).

6631 *tiĕn-shàn chǘ* 典膳局
N-S DIV (N. Ch'i)–T'ANG: **Foods Service** in the establishment of the Heir Apparent, headed by one or 2 Supervisors (*chien*) till 662, thereafter by 2 Directors (*lang*), rank 6b2. RR: *service de la nourriture de l'héritier du trône.* P26.

6632 *tiĕn-shàn sŏ* 典膳所
MING: **Foods Office** in a Princely Establishment (*wang-fu*), headed by a Director (*cheng*), rank 8a. P69.

6633 *tiĕn-shè* 典設
T'ANG–SUNG: **Manager of Interior Maintenance,** 2 palace women, rank 7a, under the Directresses of Interior Maintenance (*ssu-she*) in the Interior Maintenance Office (*ssu-she ssu*) of the Housekeeping Service (*shang-ch'in chü*). RR: *intendant de l'arrangement intérieur du harem.*

6634 *tiĕn-shè chǘ* 典設局
Household Affairs Service. (1) T'ANG, LIAO: a unit of the Left Secretariat of the Heir Apparent (*tso ch'un-fang*), headed by a Director (*lang*), rank 6b2 in T'ang; in charge of preparing hot baths, providing lanterns, and making other domestic arrangements for the Heir Apparent's quarters. RR: *service de l'arrangement intérieur du palais de l'héritier du trône.* P26. (2) YÜAN: a unit of the Regency (*liu-shou ssu*) at Shang-tu; renamed from *tien-she shu* in 1311; apparently headed by a Commissioner-in-chief (*ta-shih*), rank not clear; responsible for preparing the Emperor's quarters at the Mongol summer capital. P49.

6635 *tiĕn-shè shŭ* 典設署
YÜAN: **Household Affairs Office,** a unit of the Regency (*liu-shou ssu*) at Shang-tu; in 1311 renamed *tien-she chü.* P49.

6636 *tiĕn-shèng* 典乘
T'ANG: **Manager of Chariot Horses,** 4, rank 9b2, members of the Stables Office (*chiu-ma shu*) in the Livery Ser-

vice of the Heir Apparent (*t'ai-tzu p'u-ssu*); managed the Heir Apparent's chariot horses whenever he appeared in public. RR: *intendant des attelages.*

6637 *tiĕn-shìh* 典事
(1) T'ANG: **Manager** or **Foreman,** middling or lowly officials found in many agencies of the central government and in specialized territorial agencies, e.g., in the Office of Female Services (*i-t'ing chü*) of the Palace Domestic Service (*nei-shih sheng*), at various Imperial Mausolea (*ling*), at frontier passes (*kuan*), in the Weaving and Dyeing Office (*chih-jan shu*) of the Directorate of Imperial Manufactories (*shao-fu chien*). RR: *intendant des affaires.* P10, 28, 29, etc. (2) CHIN–YÜAN: **Office Manager,** 2, rank 7b, in the Censorate (*yü-shih t'ai*); in 1270 retitled *tu-shih.* P18.

6638 *tiĕn-shĭh* 典史
(1) YÜAN–CH'ING: **Clerk,** unranked subofficial; in Yüan found at all levels of the governmental hierarchy, thereafter normally found only at the District (*hsien*) level, sometimes with function-specifying prefixes such as *kuan-ho* (Controller of Waterways), but probably most commonly in the sense indicated in (2) below. P9, 20, 32, etc. (2) MING–CH'ING: **District Jailor,** unranked subofficial who served as the District Magistrate's (*chih-hsien*) police agent and presided over the District jail. BH: jail warden. P54.

6639 *tiĕn-shìh* 典飾
T'ANG–SUNG: **Manager of Adornments,** 2 palace women, rank 7a, under the Directresses of Adornments (*ssu-shih*) in the Adornments Office (*ssu-shih ssu*) of the Wardrobe Service (*shang-fu chü*). RR: *intendant des parures du harem.*

6640 *tiĕn-shìh* 殿試
SUNG–CH'ING: **Palace Examination,** the final stage in any sequence of civil service recruitment examinations beginning in 975, normally a one-day examination that confirmed and listed in order of excellence all passers of the Metropolitan Examination (*sheng-shih, hui-shih*); until 1057 also eliminated some such passers. This examination was prepared and presided over by the Emperor in person or, more commonly, by a special surrogate. In Ming and Ch'ing times, the degree Metropolitan Graduate (*chin-shih*) was awarded only after completion of the Palace Examination.

6641 *tiĕn-shĭh* 甸師
CHOU: **Master of the Hinterland,** 2 ranked as Junior Servicemen (*hsia-shih*), members of the Ministry of State (*t'ien-kuan*) who generally supervised the administration of the royal domain beyond the environs of the capital, especially overseeing the cultivation of the King's own lands; also reportedly responsible for executing members of the royal family who were sentenced to death. CL: *préposé au territoire hors banlieue.*

6642 *tiĕn-shū* 典書
T'ANG–MING: **Library Clerk,** unranked subofficials found in many specialized agencies such as the Institute for the Advancement of Literature (*hung-wen kuan*), the Imperial Archives (*pi-ko*), and the Directorate of Education (*kuo-tzu chien*); not appointed after very early Ming. RR: *intendant des livres.* SP: *préposé aux livres.* P23, 25, 30, 34.

6643 *tiĕn-shŭ* 典署
MING: **Manager,** rank 7a, head of each Office (*shu*) under the Directorate of Imperial Parks (*shang-lin yüan-chien*), e.g., Office of Husbandry (*liang-mu shu*). P40.

6644 *tiĕn-shù* 典術
CH'ING: **Principal of a Department Geomancy School**

(*yin-yang hsüeh*), unranked; certified by the Ministry of Rites (*lǐ-pu*) and supervised by the Provincial Administration Commission (*ch'eng-hsüan pu-cheng shih ssu*). Had some responsibility for the control of fortune-tellers, entertainers, women dentists, midwives, etc., in a Department (*chou*). BH: departmental inspector of petty professions.

6645 *tiěn-shù fāng* 典書坊
N-S DIV (N. Ch'i)–T'ANG: **Archive of the Heir Apparent**, a major unit in the Household Administration of the Heir Apparent (*chan-shih fu*) headed by 4 then 2 Mentors (*shu-tzu*); from 652 to 670 retitled *yu ch'un-fang* (Right Secretariat of the Heir Apparent), then in 711 (707?) given that title permanently. The staff included Secretaries (*chung she-jen, she-jen*), Advisers (*yü-te*), Admonishers (*tsan-shan*), etc. P26.

6646 *tiěn shǔ-kuó* 典屬國
CH'IN–HAN, N-S DIV (N. Wei): **Supervisor of Dependent Countries**, an autonomous member of the central government, rank 2,000 bushels in Han, responsible for relations with non-Chinese peoples who accepted Chinese overlordship; terminated in 28 B.C., his functions being taken over by the Chamberlain for Dependencies (*ta hung-lu*). In N. Wei the title reappeared, but possibly only as an unofficial reference to the Chamberlain for Dependencies. HB: director of dependent states. P17.

6647 *tiěn-shū lìng* 典書令
N-S DIV: **Archivist**, rank 7 or 8, in Princely Establishments (*wang-fu*) and some other administrative establishments of members of the nobility such as Princess's Establishments (*kung-chu fu*). P65, 69.

6648 *tiěn-shǔ ssū* 典屬司
CH'ING: lit., office for managing dependencies: **Outer Mongolian Bureau** in the Court of Colonial Affairs (*li-fan yüan*), principally responsible for China's relations with the Dzungars and Tibetans; cf. *ch'i-chi ssu* (Inner Mongolian Bureau). BH: department of the outer Mongols. P17.

6649 *tiěn-shuài* 殿帥
SUNG: abbreviated reference to a **Commander-in-chief** (*tu chih-hui shih*) **of the Palace Command** (*tien-ch'ien shih-wei ssu*). SP: *maréchal du palais*.

6650 *tiěn-ssū* 典祀
(1) CHOU: **Manager of Sacrifices**, 2 ranked as Ordinary Servicemen (*chung-shih*) and 4 as Junior Servicemen (*hsia-shih*), members of the Ministry of Rites (*ch'un-kuan*) responsible for the Altar of Earth, preserving it from improper uses and presiding over the execution of sacrificial victims there. CL: *conservateur des sacrifices*. (2) N-S DIV (Chou): **Sacrificer**, unspecified number ranked as Ordinary Grand Masters (*chung ta-fu*; 5a), members of the Ministry of Rites (*ch'un-kuan*); specific functions not clear. P9.

6651 *tiěn-ssū* 典絲
CHOU: **Manager of Silk**, 2 ranked as Junior Servicemen (*hsia-shih*), members of the Ministry of State (*t'ien-kuan*) responsible for receiving, storing, and distributing silk goods received in taxes, for overseeing craft workers manufacturing silk products for court use, and for providing silk goods used in sacrifices, in funerals, and as royal gifts. CL: *directeur de la soie en fil*.

6652 *tiěn-ssù shǔ* 典寺署
N-S DIV (N. Ch'i): **Supervisorate of Monasteries** under the Court for Dependencies (*hung-lu ssu*), responsible for the supervision of all Buddhist monasteries (in the state? in

the capital?), headed by a Director (*ling*); included on the staff an Aide for the Māhāsanghikāh Sect (*seng-chih-pu ch'eng*). Certified and registered monks, sharing responsibility in some fashion not clear with the Office for the Clarification of Buddhist Profundities (*chao-hsüan ssu*). Also see *seng-kuan*. P17.

6653 *tiěn-tēng* 典燈
T'ANG–SUNG: **Manager of Lanterns**, 2 palace women, rank 7a, under the Directresses of Lanterns (*ssu-teng*) in the Lanterns Office (*ssu-teng ssu*) of the Housekeeping Service (*shang-ch'in chü*). RR: *intendant des lampes du harem*.

6654 *tiěn-t'íng í-lǐ ssū* 殿庭儀禮司
MING: **Palace Ceremonial Office**, headed by a Commissioner (*shih*), rank 7a; in charge of all major state ceremonial functions; created in 1376 by renaming of the *shih-i ssu*, in 1379 subordinated to the Office of Transmission (*t'ung-cheng ssu*), then in 1397 reorganized as the Court of State Ceremonial (*hung-lu ssu*). P21, 33.

6655 *tiěn-t'óu* 殿頭
SUNG: (1) **Palace Foreman**, a eunuch title, rank 9a, found in the Palace Domestic Service (*nei-shih sheng*). (2) **Eunuch of Fifth Rank**, apparently a categorical reference to all palace eunuchs of rank 5. Cf. *nei-shih tien-t'ou*. SP: *intendant de la compagnie de l'intendance du palais*.

6656 *tiěn-ts'ǎi* 典綵
T'ANG–SUNG: **Manager of Silks**, 2 palace women, rank 7a, under the Directresses of Silks (*ssu-ts'ai*) in the Silks Office (*ssu-ts'ai ssu*) of the Workshop Service (*shang-kung chü*). RR: *intendant des soieries*.

6657 *tiěn-tsàn* 典贊
T'ANG–SUNG: **Manager of Ritual Receptions**, 2 palace women, rank 7a, under the Directresses of Ritual Receptions (*ssu-tsan*) in the Ritual Receptions Office (*ssu-tsan ssu*) of the Ceremonial Service (*shang-i chü*). RR: *intendant des cérémonies du harem*.

6658 *tiěn-ts'āng lìng* 典倉令
N-S DIV (N. Ch'i)–SUI: **Manager of Granaries** in the household of the Heir Apparent, subordinate to the Household Provisioner (*chia-ling*), rank not clear; aided by an Assistant Manager of Granaries (*tien-ts'ang ch'eng*). P26.

6659 *tiěn-ts'āng shǔ* 典倉署
T'ANG–SUNG: **Granaries Office** in the household of the Heir Apparent, a unit in the Household Provisioner's Court (*chia-ling ssu;* see under *chia-ling*); headed by a Director (*ling*), rank 8b in T'ang. RR: *office des approvisionnements de la maison de l'héritier du trône*. SP: *bureau des .... P26.

6660 *tiěn-ts'ǎo* 典艸
N-S DIV (Chou): **Manager of Hay**, several ranked as Ordinary Servicemen (*chung-shih*) and Junior Servicemen (*hsia-shih*), members of the Ministry of Works (*tung-kuan*). P14.

6661 *tiěn-tsò* 典作
SUI: **Director**, one, rank not clear; supervised some fords under the jurisdiction of the Directorate of Waterways (*tu shui-t'ai*), each ford normally managed by 4 Ford Masters (*chin-chang*). P14, 59.

6662 *tiěn-tsò chú* 典作局
N-S DIV (N. Ch'i): **Construction Service** (?) under the Storehouses Office (*ssu-tsang*) in the household of the Heir Apparent, headed by an Aide (*ch'eng*), rank not clear. P26.

6663 *tiěn-t'úng* 典同

CHOU: lit., manager of female (i.e., imperfect) tones: **Tone Monitor,** 2 ranked as Ordinary Servicemen (*chung-shih*), members of the Ministry of Rites (*ch'un-kuan*) responsible for keeping musical instruments in tune, harmonizing what were called the male and female tones. CL: *régulateur des tons femelles.*

6664 *tiěn-tz'ù lìng* 典祠令

N-S DIV: **Manager of Sacrifices,** rank 9 in N. Wei; commonly found on the staffs of Princely Establishments (*wang-fu*). P69.

6665 *tiěn-wéi* 典闈

T'ANG–SUNG: **Manager of the Inner Gates,** 2 palace women, rank 7a, under the Directresses of the Inner Gates (*ssu-wei*) in the Inner Gates Office (*ssu-wei ssu*) of the General Palace Service (*shang-kung chü*). RR: *intendant des portes intérieures du harem.*

6666 *tiěn-wèi lìng* 典衛令 or *tien-wei*

N-S DIV–T'ANG: **Commandant of the Guard** in a Princely Establishment (*wang-fu*), as many as 8 in Sui and T'ang, rank 9 in N. Wei, otherwise not clear. RR: *intendant des gardes.* P69.

6667 *tiěn-wò shǔ* 典幄署

YÜAN: **Tents Office** in the establishment of the Heir Apparent, headed by 2 Directors (*ling*), rank not clear; presumably in charge of the yurts or tents used by the Heir Apparent and his entourage while traveling. P26.

6668 *tiěn-yào* 典藥

(1) T'ANG–SUNG: **Manager of Medicines,** 2 palace women, rank 7a, under the Directresses of Medicines (*ssu-yao*) in the Medicines Office (*ssu-yao ssu*) of the Food Service (*shang-shih chü*). RR: *intendant des remèdes.* (2) T'ANG–SUNG, MING: **Pharmacist,** one each in the T'ang Imperial Medical Office (*t'ai-i shu*), the household of the Sung Heir Apparent, and the household of each Ming Commandery Prince (*chün-wang*). SP: *intendant des remèdes.* P36, 69.

6669 *tiěn-yào chú* 典藥局

YÜAN: **Pharmacy** staffed with non-official specialists under the Directorate of Medicine (*tien-i chien*) in the establishment of the Heir Apparent.

6670 *tiěn-yèh* 典謁

T'ANG: **Escort,** 10 unranked subofficials assigned to the staff of Secretarial Receptionists (*t'ung-shih she-jen*) in the Secretariat (*chung-shu sheng*). RR: *intendant des visiteurs.*

6671 *tiěn-yén* 典言

T'ANG–SUNG: **Manager of Communications,** 2 palace women, rank 7a, under the Directresses of Communications (*ssu-yen*) of the Communications Office (*ssu-yen ssu*) in the General Palace Service (*shang-kung chü*). RR: *intendant à la transmission des ordres.*

6672 *tiěn-yén* 殿巖

SUNG: lit., palace eminence: unofficial reference to a **Commander-in-chief** (*tu chih-hui shih*) **of the Palace Command** (*tien-ch'ien shih-wei ssu*). Cf. *tien-shuai.*

6673 *tiěn-yìn* 典印

MING: **Seal Keeper,** one authorized for each Commandery Prince (*chün-wang*), rank not clear. P69.

6674 *tiěn-yūng* 典壅

N-S DIV (Chou): **Director of Embankments,** several ranked as Senior Servicemen (*shang-shih;* 7a) and Ordinary Servicemen (*chung-shih;* 8a), members of the Ministry of Works

(*tung-kuan*); functions not clear, perhaps maintained ponds where fish were cultivated to serve the needs of the palace and the central government. P14.

6675 *tiěn yūng-ch'ì* 典庸器

Manager of Trophies. (1) CHOU: 4 ranked as Junior Servicemen (*hsia-shih*), members of the Ministry of Rites (*ch'un-kuan*) responsible for engraved trophies of various sorts made from melted-down weapons of vanquished troops; such trophies reportedly adorned musical instruments in some cases. CL: *conservateur des pièces de mérite.* (2) N-S DIV (Chou): number not clear, ranked as Ordinary Servicemen (*chung-shih;* 8a) and Junior Servicemen (*hsia-shih;* 9a), members of the Ministry of Rites (*ch'un-kuan*); functions not specified in sources. P10.

6676 *tiěn-yù* 典御

N-S DIV (N. Ch'i)–SUI, SUNG: variant of *feng-yü* (**Chief Steward**). P36, 37, 38.

6677 *tiěn-yù* 典獄

T'ANG, CHIN: **Jailor,** variable numbers of unranked suboficials in units of territorial administration; in Chin on the staff of Prisons (*ssu-yü ssu*); also cf. *tien-shih* (District Jailor). RR: *intendant des prisons.* P49, 53, 54.

6678 *tiěn-yü* 典虞

See *shui-heng tien-yü* (**Commandant of Waterways**).

6679 *tiěn-yü* 典輿

T'ANG–SUNG: **Manager of Transport,** 2 palace women, rank 7a, under the Directresses of Transport (*ssu-yü*) of the Transport Office (*ssu-yü ssu*) in the Housekeeping Service (*shang-ch'in chü*). RR: *intendant des chaises à porteur du harem.*

6680 *tiěn-yú* 典魚

N-S DIV (Chou): **Manager of Fish,** ranked as an Ordinary Serviceman (*chung-shih;* 8a), a member of the Ministry of Works (*tung-kuan*); functions not clear, but perhaps provided the palace and central government with supplies of edible fish. P14.

6681 *tiěn-yüàn* 典苑

T'ANG–SUNG: **Manager of Gardens,** 2 palace women, rank 7a, under the Directresses of Gardens (*ssu-yüan*) of the Gardens Office (*ssu-yüan ssu*) in the Housekeeping Service (*shang-ch'in chü*). RR: *intendant des jardins du harem.*

6682 *tiěn-yüán* 殿元

YÜAN–CH'ING: variant of *chuang-yüan* (**Principal Graduate** of a Palace Examination, *tien-shih*).

6683 *tiěn-yüàn* 殿院

T'ANG–MING: **Palace Bureau,** an agency in the Censorate (*yü-shih t'ai*) composed of Palace Censors (*tien-chung shih yü-shih*); the unit designation may have antedated T'ang, as the title Palace Censor did. The Palace Bureau and its Palace Censors were discontinued in 1376. RR+SP: *cour des affaires du palais,* (SP only:) *bureau du palais.* P18.

6684 *tiěn-yüèh* 典樂

Manager of Music. (1) T'ANG–SUNG: 2 palace women, rank 7a, under the Directresses of Music (*ssu-yüeh*) of the Music Office (*ssu-yüeh ssu*) in the Ceremonial Service (*shang-i chü*). RR+SP: *intendant de la musique du harem.* (2) MING: one, rank 9a, senior official in charge of music in a Princely Establishment (*wang-fu*). P69.

6685 *tiěn-yùn* 典醞

T'ANG–SUNG: **Manager of Wines,** 2 palace women, rank 7a, under the Directresses of Wines (*ssu-yün*) of the Wines

Office (*ssu-yün ssu*) in the Food Service (*shang-shih chü*). RR: *intendant des boissons fermentées*.

6686 *t'iēn-ch'āng kó* 天章閣
SUNG: **Hall of Heavenly Manifestations,** one of the palace buildings to which Hanlin Academicians (*han-lin hsüeh-shih*) were assigned; built in 1020.

6687 *t'iēn-chí* 天騎
T'ANG: **Heavenly Horseman,** unofficial reference to personnel of the 2 Armies of Inspired Militancy (*shen-wu chün*). Also see *shen-wu t'ien-chi*.

6688 *t'iēn-chǐ chūn* 天紀軍
T'ANG: **Army of the Celestial Serpent,** named after stars in the Hydra and Hercules constellations; one of 12 regional supervisory headquarters for militia Garrisons (*fu*) called the Twelve Armies (*shih-erh chün*); existed only 620–623, 625–636. RR: *armée (de la constellation) de l'ordonnateur céleste*. P44.

6689 *t'iēn-chì fǔ* 天驥府
T'ANG: **Office of Heavenly Mounts,** a unit of the Palace Administration (*tien-chung sheng*) responsible for horses stabled within the palace; in 700 superseded the Directorate of Imperial Mounts (*k'ung-ho chien;* see under *k'ung-ho*); staffing not clear; subsequently superseded by the post of the Grand Master of the Palace Corral (*feng-ch'en ta-fu*). P39.

6690 *t'iēn-chiā* 天家
Lit., (head of) the Heaven-favored family: unofficial reference to the **Emperor.**

6691 *t'iēn-chiéh chūn* 天節軍
T'ANG: **Army of the Celestial Bull,** named after a group of stars in Taurus; one of 12 regional supervisory headquarters for militia Garrisons (*fu*) called the Twelve Armies (*shih-erh chün*); existed only 620–623, 625–636. RR: *armée de la tablette céleste*. P44.

6692 *t'iēn-chiù fāng* 天廄坊
SUNG: **Imperial Corral,** one prefixed Left and one Right, each headed by a Commissioner (*shih*), perhaps a eunuch; units of the Court of the Imperial Stud (*t'ai-p'u ssu*) that cared for horses used within the palace grounds. Superseded the T'ang–early Sung name Flying Dragon Park (*fei-lung yüan*). SP: *quartier des écuries célestes*.

6693 *t'iēn-chù* 天柱
N-S DIV (N. Wei): **Pillar of Heaven,** a title of honor derived from the name of a celestial constellation; awarded in 529, perhaps for the only time in history; precise rank, etc., not clear.

6694 *t'iēn-chù kuān* 添注官
CH'ING: **Supplementary Official,** a categorical reference to officials appointed to posts on ad hoc bases, beyond the normal quota; how their status and stipends differed from those of regular (*cheng*) officials is not clear and perhaps was specified in each instance.

6695 *t'iēn-fǔ* 天府
CHOU: **Keeper of the Temple Treasures,** one ranked as a Senior Serviceman (*shang-shih*) and 2 as Ordinary Servicemen (*chung-shih*), members of the Ministry of Rites (*ch'un-kuan*) responsible for keeping precious objects that were considered national treasures and used in ceremonies at the ancestral temple of the ruling house. CL: *trésorier céleste, chef du magasin céleste*.

6696 *t'iēn-fǔ tsàng* 天府藏
T'ANG: variant of *t'ien-tsang fu* (**Imperial Treasury**).

6697 *t'iēn-fǔ yüàn* 天府院
T'ANG: **Office of Sacrificial Treasures,** one of 4 minor agencies in the Court of Imperial Sacrifices (*t'ai-ch'ang ssu*); maintained good omens such as materiel captured from non-Chinese enemies in battle, displayed during some imperial sacrifices; apparently staffed solely by state slaves (prisoners of war?). RR: *service du magasin céleste*.

6698 *t'iēn-hòu* 天后
(1) N-S DIV: occasional variant of *huang t'ai-hou* (**Empress Dowager**). (2) T'ANG: from 675 (till ?) the official designation of the **Empress** (normally *huang-hou*).

6699 *t'iēn-hsià mǔ* 天下母
CH'ING: unofficial reference to an **Empress** (*huang-hou*).

6700 *t'iēn-hsià pīng-mǎ yüán-shuài*
天下兵馬元帥
T'ANG, SUNG, LIAO: **National Commander-in-chief,** ad hoc designation of a general put in charge of a major military campaign, sometimes with added honorifics such as … *ta yüan-shuai* (Grand National Commander-in-chief), … *tu yüan-shuai* (Supreme National Commander-in-chief). See *yüan-shuai*. RR: *généralissime des soldats et des chevaux de l'empire*. SP: *maréchal*.

6701 *t'iēn-hsià tsūng-shīh* 天下宗師
HAN: lit., most honored mentor in the empire: unofficial reference to an **Erudite** (*po-shih*).

6702 *t'iēn-huáng* 天皇
T'ANG: from 675 (to 705?), the official designation of the **Emperor** (normally *huang-ti*).

6703 *t'iēn-ī* 天姬
Lit., a heavenly (i.e., imperial) beauty: unofficial reference to an **Imperial Princess** (*kung-chu*).

6704 *t'iēn-kuān* 天官
Lit., minister of Heaven. (1) CHOU: **Ministry of State,** most esteemed of the Six Ministries (*liu kuan*) of the central government; aided the King in establishing all governmental policies applicable both to the royal domain and to the domains of regional Feudal Lords (*chu-hou*), with special responsibilities in personnel administration; headed by a Minister of State (*chung-tsai, ta-tsai*) with rank as a Minister (*ch'ing*). CL: *ministère du ciel, ministère du gouvernement*. (2) T'ANG: from 684 to 705 the official designation of the **Ministry of Personnel** (*li-pu*). (3) CH'ING: unofficial reference to a **Minister of Personnel** (*li-pu shang-shu*).

6705 *t'iēn-kuān chǐ-shìh* 天官給事
N-S DIV (Chou): variant reference to an **Executive Assistant in the Ministry of State** (see *chi-shih*).

6706 *t'iēn-kūng* 天公
Lit., Heaven-ordained duke or ruler: from Han on, an indirect reference to the **Emperor.**

6707 *t'iēn-lǎo* 天老
T'ANG: lit., Heaven-favored elder: unofficial reference to a **Grand Councilor** (*tsai-hsiang*).

6708 *t'iēn-nǔ* 天女
HAN: unofficial reference to an **Imperial Princess** (*kung-chu*).

6709 *t'iēn-pù* 天部
Ministry of Heaven: occasional unofficial reference to such astrological-astronomical agencies as the Directorate of Astrology (*t'ai-shih chien*), Bureau of Astronomy (*ssu-t'ien t'ai*), and Directorate of Astronomy (*ch'in-t'ien chien*).

6710 *t'ién-p'ú* 田僕
CHOU: **Hunting Charioteer,** 12 ranked as Senior Servicemen (*shang-shih*), members of the Ministry of War (*hsia-kuan*) who drove the royal chariot on travels and hunts. CL: *conducteur du char de chasse.*

6711 *t'iēn-shè* 添設
YÜAN: **Supplementary,** a prefix commonly attached to titles associated with the Secretariat (*chung-shu sheng*), denoting appointments made in excess of the normal quota of appointees; difference from regular (*cheng*) appointees in status, stipend, etc., not clear. P4.

6712 *t'iēn-shēng hsiēn* 天生仙
MING: lit., immortal born of Heaven: unofficial reference to a **Metropolitan Graduate** (*chin-shih*) **of the First Class** (*chia*), i.e., any of the 3 graduates at the top of the pass list after a Palace Examination (*tien-shih*) in the civil service recruitment examination sequence. See *chia.*

6713 *t'iēn-ssù chiēn* 天馴監
SUNG: **Directorate of Fine Steeds,** 2 prefixed Left and Right under the Court of the Imperial Stud (*t'ai-p'u ssu*); staffing and specific functions not clear. SP: *direction des chevaux célestes.* P31.

6714 *t'iēn-sūn* 天孫
Occasional unofficial reference to a **Grandson Successor** (*t'ai-sun*), the eldest son of an Heir Apparent, especially of a deceased Heir Apparent.

6715 *t'iēn-t'án* 天壇
MING–CH'ING: **Altar of Heaven,** an elaborate altar in the southern suburbs of Peking, where Emperors made sacrificial offerings to Heaven. Cf. *she-chi t'an, ti-t'an.*

6716 *t'iēn-t'án wèi* 天壇尉
CH'ING: **Commandant at the Altar of Heaven,** 8 Manchu officers, one of rank 5 and 7 of rank 6; in rotation presided over the Altar of Heaven under supervision of the Court of Imperial Sacrifices (*t'ai-ch'ang ssu*). P28.

6717 *t'iēn-tsàng fǔ* 天藏府
T'ANG: **Imperial Treasury,** a unit of the Palace Administration (*tien-chung sheng*) until 735; staffing and specific functions not clear. RR: *trésor du palais impérial.*

6718 *t'ién-ts'áo* 田曹
HAN–T'ANG: **Section for Cultivated Fields,** in Han an administrative unit in a Commandery (*chün*), presumably headed by an Administrator (*yüan-shih*); in T'ang a staff agency in a Princely Establishment (*wang-fu*) in charge of the Establishment's lands and buildings, headed by an Administrator (*ts'an-chün-shih*), rank 7a2. HB: bureau of cultivated land. RR: *service des champs.* P69.

6719 *t'iēn-tzǔ* 天子
Son of Heaven: from Chou on, a standard reference to the supreme ruler of China.

6720 *t'iēn-tzǔ chīn-chün* 天子禁軍
In T'ang and perhaps other eras, a variant of *chin-chün* (**Imperial Armies**).

6721 *t'iēn-tzǔ ěrh-mù* 天子耳目
Lit., the ears and eyes of the Son of Heaven, i.e., of the ruler: from early times a common unofficial reference to **Censors** (*yü-shih*), especially Investigating Censors (*chien-ch'a yü-shih*), suggesting their function as specialized surveillance officials (*ch'a-kuan*) with the traditional right, as individuals, to submit impeachments directly to the Emperor.

6722 *t'iēn-tzǔ mén-shēng* 天子門生
T'ANG–CH'ING: **Disciple of the Son of Heaven,** unofficial reference to all passers of a Palace Examination (*tien-shih, t'ing-shih*), the final stage of a civil service recruitment examination sequence; equivalent to Metropolitan Graduate (*chin-shih*).

6723 *t'iēn-wáng* 天王
Lit., Heaven-appointed King: indirect reference to an **Emperor.**

6724 *t'iēn-wèi chūn* 天威軍
T'ANG: **Army of Heavenly Awesomeness,** a single unit of the Imperial Armies (*chin-chün*) of the Northern Command (*pei-ya*) at the dynastic capital, created in 808 by a consolidation of the prior Left and Right Armies of Inspired Awesomeness (*shen-wei chün*), but terminated in 813, all its personnel being absorbed into the increasingly dominant Armies of Inspired Strategy (*shen-ts'e chün*). RR: *armée de la majesté céleste.* P43.

6725 *t'iēn-wén chǘ* 天文局
SUNG: **Astrologer Service,** one of 4 assemblages of non-official specialists in the Artisans Institute (*han-lin yüan*) of the Palace Domestic Service (*nei-shih sheng*); headed by a Manager (*kou-tang kuan*). SP: *office d'astronomie.*

6726 *t'iēn-wén k'ō* 天文科
CH'ING: **Astronomical Section,** a unit of the Directorate of Astronomy (*ch'in-t'ien chien*) in charge of astronomical and meteorological observations; staffed principally by 8 Directors of the Imperial Observatory (*ling-t'ai lang*), rank 7b. BH: astronomical section.

6727 *t'iēn-wén pó-shìh* 天文博士
SUI–T'ANG: **Erudite of Astronomy,** number unspecified, non-official specialists in the Sui Astrological Section (*t'ai-shih ts'ao*) and the T'ang Astrological Service (*t'ai-shih chü*); in 704 superseded by the office of Director of the Imperial Observatory (*ling-t'ai lang*). RR: *maître astronome au vaste savoir.*

6728 *t'iēn-wén suàn-hsüéh* 天文算學
CH'ING: **Astronomical College,** teaching unit in the Directorate of Astronomy (*ch'in-t'ien chien*), headed by a Director (*kuan-li*). BH: astronomical college.

6729 *t'iēn-wén yüàn* 天文院
SUNG: **Bureau of Astronomy,** a unit in the Palace Library (*pi-shu sheng*) in charge of water clocks and astronomical observations, cooperating with the separate Directorate of Astronomy (*ssu-t'ien chien*); unlike the Astrological Service (*t'ai-shih chü*), did not engage in weather forecasting, interpretation of omens, etc. SP: *bureau d'astronomie.* P35.

6730 *t'iēn-wǔ ssù hsiāng* 天武四廂
SUNG: **Four Wings of Heaven-endowed Militancy,** one of the major military units of the Imperial Armies (*chin-chün*) in the Palace Command (*tien-ch'ien ssu*) stationed at the dynastic capital, one of those known collectively as the Four Elite Armies (*shang ssu chün*); headed by a Commander-in-chief (*tu chih-hui shih*); each of its Wings (*hsiang*) reportedly included 3 Armies (*chün*). P47.

6731 *t'iēn-yüèh chì-ch'ì k'ù* 天樂祭器庫
SUNG: **Storehouse for Musical and Sacrificial Instruments,** a unit of the Court of Imperial Sacrifices (*t'ai-ch'ang ssu*). SP: *magasin des objets rituels et de la musique céleste.*

6732 *t'iēn-yüèh shǔ* 天樂署
YÜAN: **Office of Western Music** in the Bureau of Musical

Ritual (*i-feng ssu*), specializing in the music of northwestern China; headed by 2 Directors (*ling*), rank 5b; created in 1313 by renaming the *chao-ho shu*. P10.

6733 *tīng* 丁
See under *chuang-ting* (Able-bodied Male), *pao-ting* (Security Guard), and *yü-ting* (Supplementary Security Guard, Surplus Man).

6734 *tǐng-ch'én* 鼎臣
Lit., minister for the tripods (symbols of sovereignty), minister (standing as stably as a) tripod: **Executive Official of State,** occasional unofficial reference to a paramount central government official such as a Counselor-in-chief (*ch'eng-hsiang*) or a Grand Councilor (*tsai-hsiang*).

6735 *tǐng-chiǎ* 鼎甲
T'ANG–CH'ING: lit., a combination of tripod (symbol of sovereignty) and class or category, referring to the groups into which examination passers were divided: unofficial reference to a **Metropolitan Graduate** (*chin-shih*) **of the First Class** (*chia*), especially in Ming and Ch'ing to the 3 men whose names stood at the top of the pass list after a Palace Examination (*tien-shih*), the culmination of a triennial civil service recruitment examination sequence. See *chia.*

6736 *tǐng-fǔ* 鼎輔
Lit., a combination of tripod (symbol of sovereignty) and support or bulwark: variant of *ting-ch'en* (**Executive Official of State**).

6737 *tǐng-hsí* 鼎席
Lit., a combination of tripod (symbol of sovereignty) and mat (something to rely on): variant of *ting-ch'en* (**Executive Official of State**).

6738 *tìng-k'ō ts'áo* 定科曹 or 定課曹
N-S DIV (San-kuo Wei): **Law Codification Section,** a unit of the developing Ministry of Personnel (*li-pu*) (?) responsible for drafting laws and administrative regulations, headed by a Director (*lang*); traditionally understood to have been coupled with the Discipline Section (*shan-ting ts'ao*), which implemented laws in disciplining officials. P5, 13.

6739 *tǐng-k'uéi* 鼎魁
SUNG–CH'ING: **Third Ranking Metropolitan Graduate,** unofficial reference from S. Sung times to the new Metropolitan Graduate (*chin-shih*) whose name stood in 3rd place on the pass list issued after a Palace Examination (*tien-shih, t'ing-shih*), the culmination of a triennial civil service recruitment examination sequence. Cf. *ta-k'uei, ting-chia.*

6740 *tìng-piēn* 定邊
CH'ING: **Pacifier of the Frontier,** prefix commonly added to the titles of Generals (*chiang-chün*) or Grand Minister Adjutants (*ts'an-tsan ta-ch'en*) who were assigned to supervise tribal affairs in far northern Mongolia. BH: warden of the marches.

6741 *tǐng-ssū* 鼎司
Lit., a combination of tripod (symbol of authority) and office: variant of *ting-ch'en* (**Executive Official of State**).

6742 *tǐng-tài* 頂戴 or *tǐng-tzǔ* 頂子
CH'ING: **Rank Button,** insignia of rank worn atop an official's headgear, ranging from a ruby (rank 1) down to a silver-plated button (rank 9).

6743 *tìng-tó àn* 定奪案
SUNG: **Section for Terminations,** one of 13 Sections (*an*) directly supervised by the executive officials of the S. Sung Ministry of Justice (*hsing-pu*); reportedly dealt with charges

of cruelty that led to the removal of officials from office. SP: *service de reconsidération.*

6744 *tǐng-wèi* 鼎位
Lit., combination of a tripod (symbol of sovereignty) and position: variant of *ting-ch'en* (**Executive Official of State**).

6745 *tǐng-yüán* 鼎元
T'ANG–CH'ING: variant of *chuang-yüan* (**Principal Graduate** in a civil service recruitment examination sequence), deriving from the term *ting-chia* (Metropolitan Graduate of the First Class).

6746 *tìng-yüǎn chiāng-chūn* 定遠將軍
T'ANG–SUNG: **General for Pacifying Faraway Lands,** prestige title (*san-kuan*) awarded to military officers of rank 5a. RR: *général qui fait des conquêtes au loin.* SP: *général faisant les conquêtes au loin.*

6747 *t'íng* 亭
CH'IN–HAN: **Neighborhood,** a unit in sub-District (*hsien*) organization of the population theoretically comprising 1,000 households; several such units constituted a Township (*hsiang*). Led by a non-official Head (*chang*), the unit performed local police functions and also maintained one or more Postal Relay Stations (*yu-t'ing*), which among other things served as hostels for traveling officials. HB: commune, officials' hostel. P20.

6748 *t'īng* 廳
(1) **Hall,** one of the common terms used in naming palace buildings; not as common as *tien* and *ko*. (2) **Office** or **Bureau,** a not overly common suffix in an agency name; e.g., see *po-shih t'ing* (Office of Erudites), *ssu-wu t'ing* (General Services Office). (3) CH'ING: **Subprefecture,** a unit of territorial administration normally intermediating between a Prefecture (*fu*) and its subordinate Districts (*hsien*), but in some cases directly responsible to provincial authorities, also in some cases without any subordinate Districts; headed by a Subprefectural Magistrate (*t'ung-chih, t'ung-p'an*), rank 5a and 6a, respectively. BH: sub-prefecture.

6749 *t'íng* 廷
Audience Chamber or **Court,** not normally a reference to a specific building in the palace; rather, referred to a place where officials and visitors assembled for audience, or to the Emperor and his close attendants as a group. See *nei-t'ing, wai-t'ing.*

6750 *t'íng-chǎng* 亭長
(1) CH'IN–HAN: **Neighborhood Head;** see under *t'ing.* HB: chief of a commune, chief of an officials' hostel. P20.
(2) N-S DIV–T'ANG: **Managing Clerk,** unranked subofficial found in many agencies of the central government; e.g., see *men-hsia t'ing-chang* (Managing Clerk of the Palace). RR: *huissier.* P5, 19, 25, etc.

6751 *t'íng-fù* 亭父
HAN: variant of *t'ing-chang* (**Neighborhood Head**). HB: father of a commune.

6752 *t'íng-hóu* 亭侯
N-S DIV: **Neighborhood Marquis,** from the Three Kingdoms period a title of nobility (*chüeh*) commonly awarded to Non-inheriting Sons (*shu-tzu*) of a Prince Presumptive (*ssu-wang*); i.e., awarded to sons other than the eldest sons of the eldest sons of Imperial Princes (*ch'in-wang*); in Liang was apparently the lowest rank of nobility entitled to a fief. P64, 65.

6753 *t'íng-hòu ch'āi-shǐh* 聽候差使
SUNG: **Messenger Awaiting Assignment,** 6 apparently

unranked subofficials authorized for the staff of the S. Sung capital Prefecture (*fu*), Lin-an (modern Hangchow); specific functions not clear. SP: *fonctionnaire attendant à être envoyé pour un service officiel.*

6754 *t'íng-ì* 廷議
Variant of *hui-i* (**Court Conference**).

6755 *t'íng-k'uéi* 廷魁
SUNG–CH'ING: lit., the best at court: unofficial reference to the **Principal Graduate** (*chuang-yüan*) in a Palace Examination (*t'ing-shih, tien-shih*), final stage in the triennial civil service recruitment examination sequence.

6756 *t'íng kūng-chǔ* 亭公主
HAN: **Neighborhood Princess,** title of nobility (*chüeh*) awarded to the daughters of some Princes (*wang*); the basis of distinction between this and Township Princess (*hsiang kung-chu*) is not clear. See *kung-chu.* P69.

6757 *t'íng-lì wén-hsüéh* 廷吏文學
HAN: **Judicial Clerk,** 12 ranked at 200 bushels and 16 at 100 bushels on the staff of the Chamberlain for Law Enforcement (*t'ing-wei*), probably divided among Sections (*ts'ao*); specific functions not clear. HB: literary scholars who are officers of justice. P22.

6758 *t'íng-p'íng* 廷平 or 廷評
HAN–N-S DIV (S. Dyn.): abbreviation of *t'ing-wei p'ing* (**Arbiter**).

6759 *t'íng-pó* 亭伯
N-S DIV (San-kuo Wei): **Neighborhood Earl,** title of nobility (*chüeh*) commonly awarded to Non-inheriting Sons (*shu-tzu*) of Dukes (*kung*), i.e., sons other than the eldest sons, who were expected to inherit their fathers' status. P64.

6760 *t'íng-shìh* 庭氏
CHOU: **Protector of the Palace,** one ranked as a Junior Serviceman (*hsia-shih*), a member of the Ministry of Justice (*ch'iu-kuan*) charged with shooting birds of ill omen that appeared in the palace grounds. CL: *préposé à l'intérieur du palais.*

6761 *t'íng-shǐh* 廷史
HAN: abbreviation of *t'ing-wei shih* (**Clerk for the Chamberlain for Law Enforcement**). P22.

6762 *t'íng-shìh* 廷試
SUNG–CH'ING: **Palace Examination,** from 975 on, the final stage in a civil service recruitment examination sequence, nominally presided over by the Emperor in person; see under the synonym *tien-shih.*

6763 *t'íng-tài hsiéh-p'í chǔ* 鞓帶斜皮局
YÜAN: **Belt and Leatherwork Service,** from 1278 a unit of the Supervisorate-in-chief of Metal Workers and Jewelers (*chin-yü jen-chiang tsung-kuan fu*).

6764 *t'íng-tsé* 廷則
CH'ING: lit., court arbiter or rule-setter: unofficial reference to the **Chief Minister** (*ch'ing*) **of the Court of Judicial Review** (*ta-li ssu*).

6765 *t'íng-tùi* 廷對
SUNG: lit., palace confrontation: unofficial reference to the **Palace Examination** (*t'ing-shih, tien-shih*), final stage in a civil service recruitment examination sequence.

6766 *t'íng-t'ūi* 廷推
MING: **Audience Nomination,** a nomination for high office produced by a gathering of all officials entitled to participate in regular court audiences, especially involving

nominations for posts as Grand Secretaries (*ta hsüeh-shih*) and Ministers of Personnel (*lì-pu shang-shu*).

6767 *t'íng-wèi* 廷尉
CH'IN–N-S DIV: **Chamberlain for Law Enforcement,** one of the eminent central government officials collectively called the Nine Chamberlains (*chiu ch'ing*), ranked at 2,000 bushels; responsible for recommending decisions in questionable judicial cases reported by units of territorial administration and for conducting major trials at the capital; aided by a Supervisor (*cheng*), one or 2 Inspectors (*chien*), and one or more Clerks (*shih*) or, in lieu of Clerks after 66 B.C., one or 2 Arbiters (*p'ing*); a staff of lesser personnel was apparently distributed among various Sections (*ts'ao*), each headed by lowly or unranked Administrators (*yüan-shih*). From Later Han the Chamberlain came to be called *t'ing-wei ch'ing* (Chief Minister for Law Enforcement), and during the ensuing era of N-S Division his staff was gradually institutionalized as the Court of Judicial Review (*ta-li ssu*), an agency that endured throughout the rest of imperial history. HB: commandant of justice. P22.

6768 *t'íng-wèi chēng* 廷尉正
HAN–N-S DIV: **Supervisor of Law Enforcement,** ranked at 1,000 bushels in Han, chief aide to the Chamberlain for Law Enforcement (*t'ing-wei*). HB: director (under the commandant of justice). P22.

6769 *t'íng-wèi chiēn* 廷尉監
CH'IN–N-S DIV: **Inspector of Law Enforcement,** one or 2 subordinates of the Chamberlain for Law Enforcement (*t'ing-wei*), rank 1,000 bushels in Han; originally 2 differentiated by prefixes Left and Right, from Later Han commonly only one, rank 5 then 6 in N. Wei; specific functions not clear. HB: inspector. P22.

6770 *t'íng-wèi ch'īng* 廷尉卿
HAN–N-S DIV: **Chief Minister for Law Enforcement,** from Later Han an irregular variant of *t'ing-wei* (Chamberlain for Law Enforcement); rank 2,000 bushels in Han, rank 2 then 3 in N. Wei; antecedent of the Sui–Ch'ing Chief Minister (*ch'ing*) of the Court of Judicial Review (*ta-li ssu*). P22.

6771 *t'íng-wèi ch'iū-ch'īng* 廷尉秋卿
N-S DIV (Liang–Ch'en): lit., combination of the titles *t'ing-wei* (Chamberlain for Law Enforcement) and *ch'iu-kuan ch'ing* (Minister of Justice): variant of *t'ing-wei ch'ing* (**Chief Minister for Law Enforcement**). P22.

6772 *t'íng-wèi fǔ* 廷尉府
N-S DIV (Ch'i): lit., office of the Chamberlain for Law Enforcement: **Office for Law Enforcement.** P22.

6773 *t'íng-wèi lǜ pó-shìh* 廷尉律博士
N-S DIV (San-kuo Wei, S. Dyn.): **Legal Erudite for the Chamberlain for Law Enforcement** (*t'ing-wei*); specific functions not clear, but presumably instructed junior staff members in legal matters. P22.

6774 *t'íng-wèi míng-fǎ yüān* 廷尉明法掾
N-S DIV (Chin): **Law Clerk** on the staff of the Chamberlain for Law Enforcement (*t'ing-wei*); see under *ming-fa yüan.* P22.

6775 *t'íng-wèi p'íng* 廷尉平 or 廷尉評
HAN–N-S DIV: **Arbiter** on the staff of the Chamberlain for Law Enforcement (*t'ing-wei*); normally 2 prefixed Left and Right. Also see under *p'ing.*

6776 *t'íng-wèi sān kuān* 廷尉三官
N-S DIV (San-kuo Wei, Chin): **Three Law Enforcement**

Aides to the Chamberlain for Law Enforcement (*t'ing-wei*): collective reference to the senior members of the Chamberlain's staff, the Supervisor (*cheng*), Inspectors (*chien*), and Arbiters (*p'ing*).

6777   t'íng-wèi shǐh 廷尉史
HAN: **Clerk for the Chamberlain for Law Enforcement** (*t'ing-wei*), one or two, rank not clear but low; regularly dispatched from the dynastic capital to assist officials of territorial administration in adjudicating law cases; in 66 B.C. superseded by Arbiters (*p'ing*) with higher prestige and rank. HB: clerk. P22.

6778   t'íng-wèi ssū-chíh 廷尉司直
N-S DIV (N. Wei): **Rectifier for the Chamberlain for Law Enforcement** (*t'ing-wei*), 10, rank 5; see under *ssu-chih*. P22.

6779   t'íng wēng-chǔ 亭翁主
HAN: **Neighborhood Princess-ordinary,** title of nobility (*chüeh*) awarded to daughters of a Prince (*wang*) not of the imperial blood; outranked by the Township Princess-ordinary (*hsiang weng-chu*), but the basis of the distinction is not clear. Also see *weng-chu*. Cf. *t'ing kung-chu*.

6780   t'íng-yüán 亭員
Variant of *t'ing-chang* (**Neighborhood Head**).

6781   t'íng-yüàn 廷掾
HAN–N-S DIV (Chin): **Headquarters Clerk** in a District (*hsien*), probably unranked suboffical; in Han constituted a Miscellaneous Section (*wu-kuan ts'ao*) in the District headquarters and seasonally toured the jurisdiction, in spring and summer assigned as Agricultural Inspectors (*ch'üan-nung yüan*) and in fall and winter assigned as Inspectors of Regulations (*chih-tu yüan*). HB: official of justice. P54.

6782   tǒ-chí 垛集
MING: lit., piled up, accumulated: **Conscript,** designation of one category of soldiers in the predynastic and early Ming armies. Cf. *ts'ung-cheng, kuei-fu, che-fa*.

6783   tō-ěrh-chí yá-mén 多爾吉衙門
CH'ING: Manchu name for the **Grand Secretariat** (*nei-ko*).

6784   tō-ló 多羅
CH'ING: Chinese transliteration of a Manchu word apparently derived from the Sanskrit word *pattra*, the name of the palm tree; a laudatory term prefixed to some titles of nobility (*chüeh*), carrying less prestige than the prefixes *ku-lun* and *ho-shih*, qq.v.

6785   tō-ló chùn-wáng 多羅郡王
CH'ING: full title of a **Commandery Prince** (see *chün-wang*), a title of nobility (*chüeh*) awarded sons other than the eldest son of each Imperial Prince (*ch'in-wang*). BH: prince of the blood of the second degree. P64.

6786   tō-ló kó-kó 多羅格格
CH'ING: unofficial reference to a **District Princess** (*hsien-chu*) or a **Commandery Mistress** (*chün-chün*). P64.

6787   tō-ló-lún mù-t'éng 多囉倫穆騰
LIAO: Manchu "correction" of the earlier Chinese transliteration of the Khitan word *ti-lieh-ma-tu* (**Ritualist**). P9.

6788   tō-ló ò-fù 多羅額駙
CH'ING: **Consort of a District Princess** (*hsien-chu*) or **Consort of a Commandery Mistress** (*chün-chün*), title of nobility (*chüeh*) conferred on husbands of daughters of Commandery Princes (*chün-wang*) and of Beile (*pei-lo*). P64.

6789   tō-ló pèi-lō 多羅貝勒
CH'ING: full title of a **Beile** (*pei-lo*), a title of nobility (*chüeh*) conferred on sons other than heirs of Commandery Princes (*chün-wang*). BH: prince of the blood of the third degree. P64.

6790   t'ó-ch'üán chiēn 橐泉監
HAN: **Directorate of the T'o-ch'üan Horses** under the Chamberlain of the Imperial Stud (*t'ai-p'u*), headed by a Director (*chang*), rank not clear; T'o-ch'üan was the name of a suburban palace south of the dynastic capital. HB: stables of the T'o Spring Palace. P31.

6791   t'ó-fāng 駝坊
SUNG: **Camel Corral** under the Court of the Imperial Stud (*t'ai-p'u ssu*); staffing not clear. SP: *quartier des chameaux*. P31.

6792   t'ō-k'ò-t'ō hó-ssū 托克托和斯
YÜAN: Manchu "correction" of the Chinese transcription of the Mongol term *t'o-t'o ho-sun* (**Postal Relay Inspector**). P17.

6793   t'ó-niú shǔ 駝牛署
N-S DIV (N. Ch'i): **Camel and Cattle Office** under the Court of the Imperial Stud (*t'ai-p'u ssu*), subdivided into various Services (*chü*); staffing not clear.

6794   t'ō-shā-lā hā-fān 拖沙喇哈番
CH'ING: Manchu form of the title of nobility (*chüeh*) transcribed in Chinese as *yün chi-wei* (**Commandant of Cavalry Second Class**). P64.

6795   t'ǒ-t'ǒ hó-sūn 脫脫禾孫
YÜAN: **Postal Relay Inspector,** originally number not specified, scattered throughout the empire to supervise operation of the postal relay system, organizational affiliation not clear; in 1270 number fixed at 6, subordinated to a Controller-general of Postal Relay Stations (*chu-chan tu t'ung-ling shih*), whose office in 1276 was transformed into the Bureau of Transmission (*t'ung-cheng yüan*). P17.

6796   tǒu-shíh 斗食
HAN: lit., eaters by the peck: **Personnel Paid in Pecks,** a rank indicator for petty suboffical appointees paid less than 100 bushels a year, one grade higher than Accessory Clerks (*tso-shih*). HB: officials whose salaries are in terms of *tou*. P68.

6797   t'óu-hsià 投下
YÜAN: one of several general terms for **land grants** (often rendered appanages) conferred on members of the nobility; the recipients of larger tracts were virtually autonomous fiefholders who nominated men for official appointments in their domains, collected taxes, and exercised other governmental powers until c. 1311, when the central government began exerting its direct control in all areas and nobles were given stipends in lieu of incomes derived from their tracts.

6798   t'óu-lǐng 頭領
CH'ING: **Leader,** a military title used by Junior Guardsmen (*lang-ling shih-wei*) on special duty assignments, e.g., 5 assigned to the Gerfalcon and Hawk Aviary (*yang ying-yao ch'u*) of the Imperial Household Department (*nei-wu fu*). P37.

6799   t'óu-mù 頭目
CH'ING: **Head,** title of a principal official rarely encountered, e.g., in the case of the Mongolian Head Veterinarian (*meng-ku i-sheng t'ou-mu*) of the Palace Stud (*shang-ssu yüan*) or that of the head of the Palace Kennel (*nei yang-kou ch'u*). P37.

6800   *t'óu-shàng yǐn* 頭上尹
Unofficial reference to a **Metropolitan Governor** (*ching-chao yin*).

6801   *tsá-chíh* 雜職
MING–CH'ING: lit., miscellaneous post: **Suboffical Post**, a categorical reference to offices commonly held by un-ranked suboffical functionaries (*li*), but sometimes includ-ing those held by officials of the 9th rank as well.

6802   *tsá-fàn ch'āi-yáo* 雜犯差徭
Forced Labor for a Minor Offense: in the last several dynasties and perhaps earlier, a sentence normally assigned by District (*hsien*) authorities, requiring the offender to serve for a specified time in state construction gangs, as a hauler or carrier of state goods, etc.; more explicitly a judicial sentence than *ch'ai-yao* without a prefix, also meaning forced labor but perhaps more nearly a rotational service obliga-tion such as Requisitioned Service (*ch'ai-i*).

6803   *tsá-mài ch'áng* 雜賣場
SUNG: **Market of Miscellanies** maintained for the sale of various (surplus?) commodities by both the Palace Admin-istration (*tien-chung sheng*) and the Court of the Imperial Treasury (*t'ai-fu ssu*). SP: *place de vente d'objets divers*.

6804   *tsá-mǎi wù* 雜買務
SUNG: **Office of Miscellaneous Purchases** in the Court of the Imperial Treasury (*t'ai-fu ssu*); staffing and specific purpose not clear. SP: *agence d'achats divers*.

6805   *tsá-tsào chú* 雜造局
MING: **Miscellaneous Manufactures Service**, a unit in each Provincial Administration Commission (*ch'eng-hsüan pu-cheng shih ssu*), headed by a Commissioner-in-chief (*ta-shih*), rank 9b. P52.

6806   *tsá-tuān* 雜端
T'ANG: lit., chief of miscellaneous matters; both a general unofficial reference to those **Attendant Censors** (*shih yü-shih*) who bore the title-suffix "in charge of miscellaneous matters" (*chih tsa-shih*), which apparently authorized them to exercise unrestricted censorial powers (? sources not clear); and a specific reference to the most senior Attendant Cen-sor, who was de facto **Head of the Headquarters Bureau** (*t'ai-yüan*) of the Censorate (*yü-shih t'ai*). Cf. *tuan-kung, san-tuan*. RR: *chef des affaires diverses*. P18.

6807   *tsá-tuān chièn-ì* 雜端諫議
T'ANG: lit., chief of miscellaneous matters and remonstra-tor: unofficial reference to a **Censor-in-chief** (*yü-shih ta-fu*).

6808   *tsá-wù k'ù* 雜物庫
SUNG: **Miscellaneous Storehouse**, found in such agencies as the Court of the Imperial Treasury (*t'ai-fu ssu*), the Court of Imperial Sacrifices (*t'ai-ch'ang ssu*), and the Court of the Imperial Regalia (*wei-wei ssu*); functions sometimes made explicit by preceding terminology, e.g., *t'ai-miao tsa-wu k'u* (Miscellaneous Storehouse for the Imperial Ancestral Temple). SP: *magasin d'objets divers*.

6809   *tsǎi* 宰
(1) **Steward**, in high antiquity the overseer of a fief; sub-sequently used as an element in many titles. In addition to the following entries, see *ta-tsai, shao-tsai, chung-tsai, hsiao-tsai, nei-tsai, li-tsai*. (2) HAN: **Butcher**, more than 200 non-official workers on the staff of the Great Sacrificial Butcher (*t'ai-tsai ling*). HB: butcher.

6810   *tsǎi-chíh* 宰執
SUNG: **State Councilor**, a collective term combining ele-ments from Grand Councilor (*tsai-hsiang*) and Executive Official (*chih-cheng*) to denote all those who regularly served in the Administration Chamber (*cheng-shih t'ang*), where major decisions of state policy were made in consultation with the Emperor; normally totaled from 5 to 9. SP: *con-seiller d'état*.

6811   *tsài-chīng jén-shìh* 在京人事
SUNG: **Palace Assistant**, title of palace eunuchs in the Pal-ace Domestic Service (*nei-shih sheng*). SP: *intendant as-sistant du palais*.

6812   *tsài-chīng fáng* 在京房
SUNG: lit., Section (for those) at the capital: **Palace De-fense Section** in the Bureau of Military Affairs (*shu-mi yüan*), one of 12 Sections created by Shen-tsung (r. 1067–1085) to manage administrative affairs of military garrisons throughout the country, in geographic clusters, or to su-pervise specified military functions on a country-wide scale. This Section supervised the Palace Command (*tien-ch'ien ssu*) and the Metropolitan Infantry Command (*pu-chün ssu*), the dispatching of troops and weapons to the western fron-tier (modern Shensi and Szechwan), and the use of troops from Chi-nei and Fukien Circuits (*lu*) in the forces of the Capital Security Office (*huang-ch'eng ssu*). Headed by 3 to 5 Vice Recipients of Edicts (*fu ch'eng-chih*), rank 8b. Ap-parently abolished early in S. Sung. See *shih-erh fang* (Twelve Sections). SP: *chambre de la capitale*.

6813   *tsái-chùng t'í-chǔ ssū* 裁種提舉司
YÜAN: **Supervisorate of Agriculture**, a category of agen-cies in scattered localities and prefixed with place-names, subordinate to the Palace Provisions Commission (*hsüan-hui yüan*); staffing not clear, but no doubt headed by a Su-pervisor (*t'i-chü*). P40.

6814   *tsái-chūn* 宰君
Lit., something like His Lordship the Steward: unofficial reference to a **District Magistrate** (*hsien-ling, chih-hsien*).

6815   *tsài chūn-chī tà-ch'én shàng hsüéh-hsí hsíng-tsǒu* 在軍機大臣上學習行走
CH'ING: lit., student among the Grand Ministers of State: variant of *chün-chi hsing-tsou* (**Probationary Grand Min-ister of State**); also see *chün-chi ta-ch'en*. BH: probation-ary grand councillor.

6816   *tsǎi-fū* 宰夫
CHOU: **Assistant Minister of State**, 4 ranked as Junior Grand Masters (*hsia ta-fu*), general aides in the Ministry of State (*t'ien-kuan*) to the Minister (*ta-tsai*) and Vice Min-isters (*hsiao-tsai*) in all matters pertaining to administrative regulations, the conduct of officials, state ceremonies, fis-cal affairs, etc. CL: *aide-administrateur général*. P5.

6817   *tsǎi-fǔ* 宰輔
Steward-bulwark of State: unofficial reference to a par-amount executive official of the central government such as a Counselor-in-chief (*ch'eng-hsiang*) or a Grand Coun-cilor (*tsai-hsiang*).

6818   *tsǎi-héng* 宰衡
Steward-regulator of State. (1) HAN: title awarded the influential minister Wang Mang by Emperor P'ing (r. 1 B.C.–A.D. 5). (2) From Later Han on, an unofficial ref-erence to a paramount executive official of the central gov-ernment such as a Counselor-in-chief (*ch'eng-hsiang*) or a Grand Councilor (*tsai-hsiang*).

6819   *tsǎi-hsiàng* 宰相
Lit., steward and minister: **Grand Councilor.** (1) From 8

B.C., when the Three Dukes (*san kung*) were collectively so designated, if not earlier, a quasiofficial reference to a paramount executive official who shared power in the central government such as a Counselor-in-chief (*ch'eng-hsiang*), a T'ang–Sung personage bearing the title Jointly Manager of Affairs with the Secretariat-Chancellery (*t'ung chung-shu men-hsia p'ing-chang shih*) or an equivalent, and a Ming–Ch'ing Grand Secretary (*ta hsüeh-shih*). Cf. *hsiang, hsiang-kuo*. RR: *grand ministre*. SP: *conseiller d'état, chef ministre, premier ministre*. (2) LIAO: 2 prefixed Left and Right, senior administrative officials in both the Northern and Southern Establishments (*pei-yüan, nan-yüan*) in the Northern Administration (*pei-mien*); rank not clear. Similar pairs were established in each auxiliary capital under a Regent (*liu-shou*) of the imperial clan. P4, 49.

6820 *tsǎi-hsiàng fǔ* 宰相府
LIAO: **Office of the Grand Councilors,** designation of the headquarters agency headed by each pair of Grand Councilors (*tsai-hsiang*). P4, 49.

6821 *tsǎi-hsiàng p'àn-kuān* 宰相判官
SUNG: lit., decision-making official for the Grand Councilors: unofficial reference to a **Secretariat Drafter** (*chung-shu she-jen*).

6822 *tsǎi-hsièn* 宰縣
Lit., to take stewardship of a District, to be appointed head of a District: from Han on, an unofficial reference to **being appointed a District Magistrate** (*hsien-ling, chih-hsien*).

6823 *tsǎi-lì* 宰歷
CHOU: variant of *ta-tsai* (**Grand Steward**), i.e., Minister of State (*chung-tsai*).

6824 *tsài-shǐh* 載師
CHOU: **Mentor of Labor,** 2 ranked as Senior Servicemen (*shang-shih*) and 4 as Ordinary Servicemen (*chung-shih*), members of the Ministry of Education (*ti-kuan*) responsible for determining what uses were appropriate for different lands and directing the collection of taxes from workers on the land. See *ts'ao-jen* (Planting Manager). CL: *préposé au travail*.

6825 *ts'ǎi-fǎng ch'ù-chìh shǐh* 探訪處置使
T'ANG: **Investigation and Supervisory Commissioner,** one of several designations used for central government delegates in charge of territorial Circuits (*tao*) in the 700s, coordinating civil administration in a cluster of Prefectures (*chou, fu*). RR: *commissaire impérial organisateur et enquêteur*. P18, 52.

6826 *ts'ǎi-fǎng shǐh* 探訪使
T'ANG–SUNG, LIAO: **Investigation Commissioner,** one of several designations used for central government delegates in charge of territorial Circuits (*tao*); in Sung and Liao apparently used only for special, ad hoc investigatory missions. RR: *commissaire impérial enquêteur*. SP: *commissaire chargé d'enquêter sur les souffrances du peuple*. P52.

6827 *ts'ǎi-fù ssū* 財賦司
SUNG: **Revenues Office,** an agency of Lin-an Prefecture (*fu*), i.e., modern Hangchow, and perhaps found in some other units of territorial administration; staffing not clear. SP: *bureau des finances*.

6828 *ts'ǎi-fù tū tsǔng-kuǎn fǔ* 財賦都總管府
YÜAN: **Supreme Supervisorate-in-chief for Revenues,** established in the Chiang-Huai region, apparently to arrange for the collection and transport of tax income allocated to the Empress; specific functions not clear.

6829 *ts'ǎi-huà kuān* 彩畫官
SUNG: **Decorator,** non-official specialist in the Bureau of Nomination Certificates (*yü-ts'e yüan*) of the Secretariat (*chung-shu sheng*). SP: *fonctionnaire chargé de dessiner*.

6830 *ts'ǎi-jén* 才人
HAN–MING: **Lady of Talents,** a designation occasionally awarded to an imperial consort; in San-kuo Wei ranked from 1,000 bushels down; in Sui, 15, rank 4a, considered in the category of Hereditary Consorts (*shih-fu*); in T'ang 5a then 4a; in Sung 5a. RR+SP: *personne de talent*.

6831 *ts'ǎi-kuān* 材官
Skilled Soldier: one category of Han dynasty militiamen serving on active training duty in their home Commanderies (*chün*), specifying ordinary infantrymen in contrast to cavalrymen and naval forces; subsequently used unofficially in reference to personnel as eminent as Generals (*chiang-chün*) and Ch'ing dynasty Governors-general (*tsung-tu*). HB: skilled soldier.

6832 *ts'ǎi-kuān chiàng-chūn* 材官將軍
N-S DIV (Chin, S. Dyn.): **Construction Supervisor,** in general charge of central government activities in building with wood, normally subordinate to the Bureau of Public Construction (*ch'i-pu*); the use of military terminology perhaps signifies that military forces were commonly employed in such construction projects. The term may have originated in Han, perhaps in the military sense of leader of the militiamen called Skilled Soldiers (*ts'ai-kuan*). HB: general of skilled soldiers. P14.

6833 *ts'ǎi-kuān hsiào-lìng* 材官校令 or *ts'ai-kuan ling*
N-S DIV (San-kuo Wei, Chin): variant of *ts'ai-kuan hsiao-wei* (**Director of Construction**). P14, 37.

6834 *ts'ǎi-kuān hsiào-wèi* 材官校尉
HAN–N-S DIV (San-kuo Wei): **Director of Construction** on the staff of the Chamberlain for the Palace Revenues (*shao-fu*); antecedent of the Construction Supervisor (*ts'ai-kuan chiang-chün*) of Chin and the S. Dynasties. P13.

6835 *ts'ǎi-kuān ssū-mǎ* 材官司馬
N-S DIV (S. Dyn.): **Assistant Construction Supervisor,** aide to the *ts'ai-kuan chiang-chün* (Construction Supervisor) in the Bureau of Public Construction (*ch'i-pu*). P14.

6836 *ts'ǎi-kuān wǎn-ch'iáng* 材官挽強
HAN: **Skilled Archer,** apparently one category of those militiamen on active training service who were known as Skilled Soldiers (*ts'ai-kuan*); specific status not clear.

6837 *ts'ǎi-liào àn* 材料案
SUNG: **Section for Building Materials** under the Headquarters Bureau (*kung-pu*) of the Ministry of Works (also *kung-pu*), probably staffed by non-official specialists. SP: *service des matériaux*.

6838 *ts'ǎi-nǔ* 彩女
HAN: **Pleasure Girl,** one of 3 categories of unranked palace women in Later Han.

6839 *ts'ǎi-nǔ* 采女
HAN–SUNG: **Lady of Elegance,** designation for some imperial concubines; in Han ranked below Worthy Lady (*kuei-jen*); in Sui 37, rank 7a; in T'ang rank 8a. HB: chosen lady. RR: *femme élégante*. SP: *dame du palais*.

6840 *ts'ǎi-pǔ yá-mén* 探捕衙門
CH'ING: **Harvesting Office** in the Imperial Household Department (*nei-wu fu*); supervised the Southern Park (*nan-*

yüan) from 1661, superseding a Eunuch Manager (*nei-chien kuan-li*); then in 1684 superseded by subordinates of the Manager of the Imperial Parks (*kuan-li feng-ch'en yüan shih-wu*). P40.

6841 *ts'ǎi-shā sǒ* 探沙所
YÜAN: **Sand Gathering Office** established in 1279 in Ta-t'ung Route (*lu*) under authority of the Supervisorate-in-chief of Metal Workers and Jewelers (*chin-yü jen-chiang tsung-kuan fu*) at the dynastic capital; staffing and specific purpose not clear.

6842 *ts'ái-shìh chiēn-mào* 才識兼茂
SUNG: **Understanding and Knowledge Both Excellent,** a scholastic degree awarded to passers of Special Recruitment (*chih-chü*) examinations in 1034, 1042, 1057, and 1061.

6843 *ts'ái-tsào shǔ* 裁造署 or *ts'ái-tsào yüàn* 院
SUNG–CHIN: **Ornaments Office,** one of several workshops under the Directorate for Imperial Manufactories (*shao-fu chien*), headed by a Director (*ling*), rank 6b in Chin; another under the Palace Administration (*tien-chung sheng*) in Sung. SP: *cour de confection de vêtements et d'ornements.* P38.

6844 *ts'ǎi-yào shīh* 採藥師
T'ANG: **Master of Medications,** one delegate from the Imperial Medical Service (*t'ai-i chü*) assigned to each Prefecture (*chou*) noted for its varieties of medicinal herbs, etc., to see that the Service was regularly supplied with medications. RR: *maître chargé de recueillir les remèdes.*

6845 *tsàn* 酇
CHOU: **Precinct,** a unit of local government outside the royal domain comprising 4 neighboring Villages (*li*) each theoretically consisting of 25 households; comparable to the Precinct called *tsu* within the royal domain; each with a Head (*chang*) responsible to the Ministry of Education (*ti-kuan*) for general administration of local ceremonial, military, agricultural, and craft activities, reportedly elected but carrying the rank of Ordinary Serviceman (*chung-shih*). CL: *village, comprenant cent feux.*

6846 *tsàn-chě* 贊者
SUI–T'ANG: **Court Herald,** 12 apparently unranked subofficials in the Sui Court for Dependencies (*hung-lu ssu*) and the T'ang Chancellery (*men-hsia sheng*), serving in two rotational shifts as announcers in court ceremonial activities. RR: *héraut.* P33.

6847 *tsàn-chìh* 贊治
Administrative Aide. (1) SUI: one, rank 4b, in a Region (*chou*) till 586; revived c. 605 as the principal 2nd-level official in a Commandery (*chün*), rank 5a to 6a depending on the size and importance of the jurisdiction. P49, 53. (2) SUNG: laudatory epithet (see under *kung-ch'en*) awarded to members of the Bureau of Military Affairs (*shu-mi yüan*), to imperial parents, and to officials serving outside the capital.

6848 *tsàn-chìh shǎo-yǐn* 贊治少尹
MING: **Vice Governor Participating in Administration,** a merit title (*hsün*) for rank 4b civil officials. P65.

6849 *tsàn-chìh yǐn* 贊治尹
MING: **Governor Participating in Administration,** a merit title (*hsün*) for rank 4a civil officials. P65.

6850 *tsàn-fǔ* 贊府
T'ANG–CH'ING: lit., assistant's office: unofficial reference to a **District Vice Magistrate** (*hsien-ch'eng*).

6851 *tsàn-hsiǎng* 贊饗
HAN: **Sacrificial Aide,** rank 600 bushels, under the Chamberlain for Ceremonials (*t'ai-ch'ang*); assisted the Emperor in sacrificial rites. HB: assistant at sacrifices. P27.

6852 *tsàn-kūng* 贊公
T'ANG: lit., honorable assistant: unofficial reference to a **District Vice Magistrate** (*hsien-ch'eng*).

6853 *tsàn-lǐ chǖn-wù* 贊理軍務
MING: **Associate Military Superintendent,** supplementary designation for a Grand Coordinator (*hsün-fu*) when, in an area under the jurisdiction of a Regional Commander (*tsung-ping kuan*), he was authorized concurrently to share responsibility for military matters. Cf. *t'i-tu chün-wu* (Military Superintendent). P50.

6854 *tsàn-lǐ láng* 贊禮郎
MING–CH'ING: **Ceremonial Assistant** assignable to highly varied chores; in Ming from 9 to 33, rank 9a, in the Court of Imperial Sacrifices (*t'ai-ch'ang ssu*); in Ch'ing ranged from rank 4 down, found in large numbers in the Office of Palace Ceremonial (*chang-i ssu*) and at each Imperial Mausoleum (*ling*) as well as in the Court of Imperial Sacrifices. BH: herald, ceremonial usher. P27, 29, 37, 49.

6855 *tsàn míng-piēn* 贊鳴鞭
CH'ING: **Whip-cracker,** from 1772 (till ?) a special duty assignment in the Imperial Procession Guard (*luan-i wei*) for 2 Ceremonial Assistants (*tsan-li lang*) of the Court of Imperial Sacrifices (*t'ai-ch'ang ssu*), presumably to assist in maintaining public order during imperial processions. P27.

6856 *tsàn-niǎo* 簪裊
CH'IN–HAN: lit., a horse-girdler: **Grandee of the Third Order,** the 3rd lowest of 20 titles of honorary nobility (*chüeh*) conferred on meritorious subjects. P65.

6857 *tsàn-pù* 贊部
CH'ING: **Headquarters Aide,** unofficial reference to an Office Manager (*ssu-wu*) in a Ministry (*pu*) or other central government agency; see *ssu-wu t'ing.*

6858 *tsàn-shàn* 贊善
T'ANG–CH'ING: lit., to assist toward goodness: **Admonisher,** 2 each prefixed Left and Right in the Left and Right Secretariats of the Heir Apparent (*ch'un-fang*), responsible for giving moral and social guidance to the Heir Apparent; in T'ang and Sung known most commonly as Grand Master Admonishers (*tsan-shan ta-fu*); in Ming and Ch'ing rank 6b; in Ch'ing shared equally by Manchus and Chinese. BH: assistant secretary of the supervisorate of imperial instruction. P4, 26.

6859 *tsàn-shàn tà-fū* 贊善大夫
T'ANG, SUNG, LIAO: **Grand Master Admonisher,** 2 prefixed Left and Right, members of the Left and Right Secretariats of the Heir Apparent (*ch'un-fang*), respectively; rank 5a in T'ang, 8a in Sung; originated as the official redesignation of the Companion (*chung-yün*) of the Heir Apparent from 662 to 679, then separately established. RR+SP: *conseiller censeur de l'héritier du trône.* P26.

6860 *tsàn-té* 贊德
T'ANG: lit., to assist toward virtue: **Lady for Admonishment,** from 662 to 670 the official redesignation of all rank 1a secondary imperial wives otherwise known collectively as Consorts (*fu-jen*). RR: *femme qui exhorte à la vertu.*

6861 *tsàn-tú* 贊讀
SUNG: **Reading Assistant,** rank 7b, in the School for the Heir Apparent (*tzu-shan t'ang*); also from 1117 the official

redesignation of Readers-in-waiting (*shih-tu*) in Princely Establishments (*wang-fu*). SP: *lecteur auxiliaire*. P26, 69.

6862 *tsàn-wù* 贊務
SUI: variant of *tsan-chih* (**Administrative Aide**), probably in avoidance of a personal name taboo. P32.

6863 *tsàn-yǐn shǐh* 贊引使 or *tsan-yin*
SUI–SUNG, LIAO: **Ceremonial Escort,** unranked subofficials in the Court of Imperial Sacrifices (*t'ai-ch'ang ssu*); 60 in Sui, 20 in T'ang, 2 in Sung. RR+SP: *chargé d'introduire et de guider les visiteurs*. P27.

6864 *tsǎn-yùn yù-shǐh* 儹運御史
MING–CH'ING: **Transport-control Censor,** a duty assignment for Investigating Censors (*chien-ch'a yü-shih*), to patrol and inspect operations of the state tax grain transport system along the Grand Canal; intermittent from the early 1400s, but regular beginning in the Wan-li era (1573–1620). P60.

6865 *ts'ān* 參
Lit., to counsel, take part in; three. (1) CHOU: quasiofficial reference to the **Three Ministers** (*ch'ing*) authorized for the regional governments of major Feudal Lords (*chu-hou*). (2) N-S DIV: variant of *ts'an-chang* (**Administrator**).

6866 *ts'ān-chǎng* 參掌
N-S DIV: **Administrator** assigned on a special basis to take charge of an office other than his regular post; used as a prefix to a title or agency name; equivalent of *chih* (to know).

6867 *ts'ān-chǎng shū-mì shìh* 參掌樞密事
5 DYN: **Commissioner Participating in Control of Military Affairs,** duty assignment for a powerful member of the court to head the Bureau of Military Affairs (*shu-mi yüan*) and wield administrative authority over a regime's armed forces.

6868 *ts'ān-chèng* 參政
Lit., to take part in governance. (1) SUNG: quasiofficial abbreviation of *ts'an-chih cheng-shih* (**Participant in Determining Governmental Matters**), i.e., a Vice Grand Councilor (*fu-hsiang, shao-tsai*). (2) YÜAN: **Assistant Grand Councilor,** normally 2, rank 2b, in the Secretariat (*chung-shu sheng*) and also, during its irregular existence, in the Department of State Affairs (*shang-shu sheng*). P4. (3) MING–CH'ING: **Administration Vice Commissioner,** variable number, rank 3b, 2nd executive post in a Provincial Administration Commission (*ch'eng-hsüan pu-cheng shih ssu*); like Assistant Administration Commissioners (*ts'an-i*), normally detached from the Commission headquarters to head a function-specific or region-specific Branch Office (*fen-ssu*); see under *tao* (Circuit). Officially, an abbreviation of *pu-cheng ts'an-cheng*. Abolished in 1735, when all heads of Branch Offices were separated from their Commissions and made autonomous Circuit Intendants (*tao-t'ai*). P52. (4) CH'ING: **Vice Minister,** variable numbers prefixed Left and Right, from 1631 to 1644 in each Ministry (*pu*) of the predynastic central government, then retitled *shih-lang*. P5, 6.

6869 *ts'ān-chì kuān* 參計官
SUNG: **Accountant** in the late Sung Accounting Office (*kuo-yung ts'an-chi so*), a post normally held concurrently by a Vice Minister (*shih-lang*). SP: *commissaire préposé aux comptes d'état*.

6870 *ts'ān-chiàng* 參將
MING–CH'ING: **Assistant Regional Commander,** normally several military officers on the staff of a Province-

level Regional Commander (*tsung-ping kuan*), in control of troops in a segment of the Regional Commander's jurisdiction; in Ming a duty assignment rather than a regular post (*kuan*), in the early decades for various nobles, then for officers of the regular hereditary hierarchy (see under *wei-so*), finally for some civil officials and even eunuchs; in Ch'ing a regular post, rank 3a, in the hierarchy of Chinese military forces called the Green Standards (*lu-ying*). The title was usually prefixed with a place-name defining the jurisdiction. BH: lieutenant-colonel.

6871 *ts'ān-chǐh* 參知
CH'ING: unofficial reference to a **Grand Secretary** (*ta hsüeh-shih*), deriving from the earlier title *ts'an-chih cheng-shih* (Participant in Determining Governmental Matters).

6872 *ts'ān-chǐh chèng-shìh* 參知政事
(1) T'ANG–SUNG: **Participant in Determining Governmental Matters,** originally a supplementary title conferred on eminent officials entitling them to participate in policy discussions in the Administration Chamber (*cheng-shih t'ang*) as members of the group known collectively by the quasiofficial term Grand Councilors (*tsai-hsiang*); after the mid-600s was generally superseded by the term Manager of Affairs (*p'ing-chang shih*); revived in 964, then in 973 made a regular post (*kuan*) of rank 2a, normally with from one to 3 appointees, in effect Vice Grand Councilors (*shao-tsai, fu-hsiang*). Included among those collectively known as Executive Officials (*chih-cheng kuan*) and State Councilors (*tsai-chih*). (2) LIAO–CHIN: **Vice Grand Councilor,** 2nd executive post in the Liao Secretariat (*chung-shu sheng*) and the Chin Department of State Affairs (*shang-shu sheng*); in Chin 2, rank 2b. (3) YÜAN–MING: **Assistant Administrator,** 2, rank 2b, 4th executive post in the Secretariat (*chung-shu sheng*), after Grand Councilor (*ch'eng-hsiang*), Manager of Governmental Affairs (*p'ing-chang cheng-shih*), and Aide (*ch'eng*); duplicated in Yüan Branch Secretariats (*hsing chung-shu sheng*), but early Ming Branch Secretariats had only single appointees, 3rd executive post since Ming Branch Secretariats had no Grand Councilors. Terminated in 1376 in Branch Secretariats, which were then transformed into Provincial Administration Commissions (*ch'eng-hsüan pu-cheng shih ssu*), and in 1380 in the metropolitan Secretariat, which was then abolished. Considered the antecedent of the Ming–Ch'ing Administration Vice Commissioner (*ts'an-cheng*) in a Provincial Administration Commission. SP: *participant à la direction des affaires gouvernementales, grand conseiller assistant d'état*. P3, 4.

6873 *ts'ān-chǐh chī-wù* 參知機務
T'ANG: variant of *ts'an-chih cheng-shih* (**Participant in Determining Governmental Matters**).

6874 *ts'ān-chó yüàn* 參酌院
T'ANG: **Consultative Office,** unofficial reference to a Secretariat Drafter (*chung-shu she-jen*) sent out to participate in a major trial conducted by local officials; from c. 821.

6875 *ts'ān-ch'í chūn* 參旗軍
See under *shen-ch'i chün* (**Army of the Celestial Lion's Pelt**).

6876 *ts'ān-chūn-shìh* 參軍事 or *ts'an-chün*
Adjutant or **Administrator.** (1) N-S DIV–MING: originating at the very end of Han as a designation used by retainers of the militarist Ts'ao Ts'ao, quickly became regularized as the title of aides to regional military authorities, to Regional Inspectors (*chou tz'u-shih*), and in Princely Establishments (*wang-fu*), rank varying from 7 to 9. In T'ang also found in Guards (*wei*) and Guard Commands (*wei shuai-*

fu) at the capital; in Sung normally restricted to Prefectures (*chou*) and Superior Prefectures (*fu*), thereafter to Princely Establishments. From late in the era of N-S Division, commonly distributed among Sections (*ts'ao*) with functional specializations: Personnel Evaluation Section (*kung-ts'ao*), Law Section (*fa-ts'ao*), Revenue Section (*hu-ts'ao*), Levied Service Section (*shih-ts'ao*), War Section (*ping-ts'ao*), etc., accordingly prefixed *ssu-kung, ssu-fa, ssu-hu*, etc. Taking note of such prefixes is necessary for proper identification and understanding. The title seems to have been terminated in 1376, when the *ts'an-chün* in Princely Establishments were retitled *chang-shih* (Administrator). RR+SP: *administrateur*. P26, 32, 49, 52, 53, 69. (2) CH'ING: unofficial reference to an Assistant Department Magistrate (*chou-p'an, p'an-kuan*). (3) CH'ING: unofficial reference to a Registrar (*ching-li*) in a Provincial Administration Commission (*ch'eng-hsüan pu-cheng shih ssu*).

6877   *ts'ān-chǖn tū-hù*   參軍都護
N-S DIV (Liang, N. Wei): **Adjutant-protector,** rank from 5b down to 9b, on the staff of the Heir Apparent and staffs of various Princely Establishments (*wang-fu*); specific functions not clear. P69.

6878   *ts'ān-chǖn tuàn-shìh kuān*   參軍斷事官
MING: **Judicial Administrator,** rank 3b, in the predynastic Secretariat (*chung-shu sheng*); established 1364, apparently terminated in 1368. P4.

6879   *ts'ān-fǔ*   參府
CH'ING: unofficial reference to an **Assistant Regional Commander** (*ts'an-chiang*) in the Chinese military forces called the Green Standards (*lu-ying*).

6880   *ts'ān-hsiáng kuān*   參詳官
SUNG: **Consultant,** duty assignment for a central government official to serve in various special agencies such as the Advisory Office (*chiang-i ssu*) of the Department of State Affairs (*shang-shu sheng*) and the Ministry of Rites (*lǐ-pu*). SP: *fonctionnaire participant à la révision*.

6881   *ts'ān-ì*   參議
(1) SUNG–YÜAN: **Consultant,** duty assignment for an official serving in an ad hoc or somewhat irregular agency such as the Sung Advisory Office (*chiang-i ssu*) of the Department of State Affairs (*shang-shu sheng*) or on the staff of a temporary Commissioner (*shih*). SP: *prenant part aux délibérations, conseiller*. (2) MING–CH'ING: **Assistant Administration Commissioner,** 3rd executive post in a Provincial Administration Commission (*ch'eng-hsüan pu-cheng shih ssu*), number variable, rank 4b; like Administration Vice Commissioners (*ts'an-cheng*), normally detached from the Commission headquarters as head of a function-specific or region-specific Branch Office (*fen-ssu*); see under *tao* (Circuit). Officially, an abbreviation of *pu-cheng ts'an-i*. Abolished in 1735, when all heads of Branch Offices were separated from their Commissions and made autonomous Circuit Intendants (*tao-t'ai*). P52. (3) MING–CH'ING: **Assistant Transmission Commissioner** in the Office of Transmission (*t'ung-cheng ssu*), in Ch'ing one each Manchu and Chinese, rank 5a; 3rd executive post in the Office, after the Commissioner (*shih*) and the Vice Commissioner (*t'ung-cheng* or *fu-shih*). BH: secretary of the transmission office. P21.

6882   *ts'ān-ì ch'áo-chèng*   參議朝政
T'ANG: **Participant in Deliberations about Court Policy,** a supplementary title conferred on eminent officials entitling them to participate in policy discussions in the Administration Chamber (*cheng-shih t'ang*) as members of the group

known collectively by the quasiofficial term Grand Councilors (*tsai-hsiang*); after the mid-600s generally superseded by the title Manager of Affairs (*p'ing-chang shih*). P3.

6883   *ts'ān-ì chūng-shū shěng shìh*
參議中書省事
YÜAN: **Consultant in the Secretariat** (*chung-shu sheng*), 4, rank 4a; supervised the Left and Right Offices (*tso-ssu, yu-ssu*) and the 6 Sections (*ts'ao*) in which the administrative business of the Secretariat was handled. P4.

6884   *ts'ān-ì kuān*   參議官
SUNG: variant of *ts'an-i* (**Consultant**).

6885   *ts'ān-ì tà-ch'én*   參議大臣
CH'ING: **Grand Minister Consultant,** designation of a court dignitary assigned to assist the Grand Minister Commander (*ching-lüeh ta-ch'en*) of a contingent of campaigning soldiers from the Chinese forces called the Green Standards (*lu-ying*). Cf. *ts'an-tsan ta-ch'en* (also Grand Minister Consultant).

6886   *ts'ān-ì té-shīh*   參議得失
T'ANG: **Participant in Deliberations about Advantages and Disadvantages,** a supplementary title conferred on eminent officials entitling them to participate in policy discussions in the Administration Chamber (*cheng-shih t'ang*) as members of the group known collectively by the quasiofficial term Grand Councilors (*tsai-hsiang*); after the mid-600s generally superseded by the title Manager of Affairs (*p'ing-chang shih*). P3.

6887   *ts'ān-júng*   參戎
CH'ING: unofficial reference to an **Assistant Regional Commander** (*ts'an-jung*) in the Chinese military forces known as the Green Standards (*lu-ying*).

6888   *ts'ān-lǐng*   參領
CH'ING: (1) **Regimental Commander,** rank 3a, in the Manchu military organization called the Eight Banners (*pa ch'i*), identifiable by prefixed terminology, e.g., *hu-chün ts'an-ling* (Regimental Commander in the Guards Brigade), *ch'ien-feng ts'an-ling* (Regimental Commander in the Vanguard Brigade); usually aided by one or more Regimental Vice Commanders (*fu ts'an-ling*), 4a. BH: colonel. P37. (2) **Commandant,** 5, rank 3b, one for each of the Banner (*ch'i*) groups of families under the jurisdiction of a Princely Establishment (*wang-fu*) or Ducal Establishment (*kung-fu*), each aided principally by 7 Assistant Commandants (*tso-ling*), 4b. P69.

6889   *ts'ān-móu kuān*   參謀官 or *ts'an-mou*
T'ANG–YÜAN: **Counselor,** common designation for aides to military commanders; probably originated in reference to non-official personal aides of T'ang Military Commissioners (*chieh-tu shih*) and comparable militarists; in Sung became a recognized duty assignment for officials on the staff of campaign commanders such as Pacification Commissioners (*hsüan-fu shih*) or of Superior Area Commands (*ta tu-tu fu*). SP: *conseiller, grand conseiller*.

6890   *ts'ān-shìh*   蠶室
Lit., room for rearing silkworms: **Castration Chamber,** at least from Han on a quasiofficial designation of a prison where castration was performed; traditionally explained as deriving from the warmth required for survival of castration, comparable to that required for the nurturing of silkworms. HB: silkworm house.

6891   *ts'ān-tsàn chī-wù*   參贊機務
MING: **Grand Adjutant,** 3rd in a triumvirate to whom

military control of the auxiliary capital at Nanking was entrusted after 1420, normally a concurrent appointment for the Nanking Minister of War (*nan-ching ping-pu shang-shu*); ranked after the Grand Commandant (*shou-pei*) and the Vice Commandant (*hsieh-t'ung shou-pei*). P49.

6892 *ts'ān-tsàn chǔn-shìh* 參贊軍事
SUNG: **Military Consultant,** a post in the Imperial Defense Command (*yü-ying ssu*) normally held by an imperial favorite. SP: *conseiller des affaires militaires.*

6893 *ts'ān-tsàn tà-ch'én* 參贊大臣
CH'ING: **Grand Minister Consultant,** 2 representatives of the central government who assisted the Manchu General (*chiang-chün*) of Outer Mongolia; others sometimes assigned to assist the commanders of campaigning armies. See *ta-ch'en.* Cf. *ts'an-i ta-ch'en* (also Grand Minister Consultant). BH: assistant military governor, councillor.

6894 *ts'ān-yù ch'áo-chèng* 參預朝政
T'ANG: variant of *ts'an-i ch'ao-cheng* (**Participant in Deliberations about Court Policy**).

6895 *ts'ān-yǔ chèng-shìh* 參與政事
T'ANG: variant of *ts'an-chih cheng-shih* (**Participant in Determining Governmental Matters**).

6896 *tsàng* 藏
Storehouse; see under *tso-tsang, yu-tsang, huang-tsang shu,* and other prefixes as encountered.

6897 *tsāng-fá k'ù* 贓罰庫
CH'ING: **Depository** in the Ministry of Justice (*hsing-pu*) for the collection of money confiscated from criminals and levied in fines, which the Depository periodically transferred to the Ministry of Revenue (*hu-pu*); headed by 2 Manchu Treasurers (*ssu-k'u*) and one or more Commissioners (*shih*). BH: treasury. P13.

6898 *tsāng-fú* 藏府
HAN: **Storehouse:** variant of *ssu-fu;* also see *chung-huang ssu-fu.*

6899 *ts'āng* 倉
Granary: throughout history the standard designation of repositories of state grain supplies at all levels of government, normally with a Head (*chang*), Director (*ling*), Supervisor (*chien*), or Commissioner (*shih*), often an unranked subofficial; specifically identifiable only by place-name or other prefixes. In addition to the following entries, see *ch'ang-p'ing ts'ang, i-ts'ang, nei-ts'ang.*

6900 *ts'āng-àn* 倉案
SUNG: **Granary Section,** one of 4 subsidiary units in the Court of Palace Attendants (*hsüan-hui yüan*), responsible for maintaining the palace food stores and providing special meals for the Emperor and his entourage at birthday celebrations, important sacrifices, and other ceremonial occasions. SP: *service des greniers ou service des banquets et des sacrifices.*

6901 *ts'āng-ch'áng* 倉場
(1) **Granaries and Yards:** may be encountered as a collective or generic reference to granaries and other storage facilities, e.g., for hay or lumber. (2) MING–CH'ING: **Capital Granaries,** collective reference to state granaries originally at Nanking when it was the early Ming capital, from 1421 to those at Peking, later also including those built at nearby T'ung-chou, the northern terminus of the Grand Canal; each managed by officials of the Ministry of Revenue (*hu-pu*) in Ming, in Ch'ing by one Manchu and one Chinese Superintendent (*chien-tu*) chosen for 3-year duty

assignments from among members of the Central Drafting Office (*chung-shu k'o*) and various other central government agencies under supervision of the Imperial Household Department (*nei-wu fu*); all under the general supervision of a Director-general of the Capital Granaries (*tsung-tu ts'ang-ch'ang*), duty assignment for a Minister (*shang-shu*) or Vice Minister (*shih-lang*) of the Ministry of Revenue in Ming, in Ch'ing for one Manchu and one Chinese Vice Minister of the Ministry. BH: government granary at the capital. P8.

6902 *ts'āng-huò chiēn* 倉貨監
T'ANG: (1) **Directorate of Granaries and Commerce,** from 657 the official redesignation of the former Directorate of the West Imperial Park at the Eastern Capital (*tung-tu yüan hsi-mien chien*), i.e., at Loyang; a unit of the Court of National Granaries (*ssu-nung ssu*), headed by an Office Manager (*lu-shih*). RR: *direction des greniers et des valeurs d'échange.* (2) Occasional variant of *shih-huo chien* (**Director of Commerce**).

6903 *ts'āng-jén* 倉人
CHOU: **Granary Manager,** 4 ranked as Ordinary Servicemen (*chung-shih*) and 8 as Junior Servicemen (*hsia-shih*), members of the Ministry of Education (*ti-kuan*) who oversaw granaries located throughout the royal domain under supervision of the Ministry's Granary Masters (*lin-jen*). CL: *officier des dépôts.*

6904 *ts'āng-k'ō* 倉科
YÜAN–MING: **Granaries Section,** in Yüan one of 6 function-specific Sections in the Ministry of Revenue (*hu-pu*), headed by an unranked subofficial Director (*ling-shih*); in Ming one of 4 function-specific Sections in each Bureau (*ch'ing-li ssu*) of the Ministry of Revenue, headed by an unranked subofficial Manager (*kuan-li*). P6.

6905 *ts'āng-k'ù shǔ* 倉庫署
YÜAN: **Office for Granaries and Storehouses** in the establishment of the Heir Apparent, headed by 2 Directors (*ling*), probably unranked. P26.

6906 *ts'āng-núng chiēn* 倉農監
HAN: **Supervisor of Granaries and Agriculture** on the staff of a Commandery (*chün*) or a Princedom (*wang-kuo*); status and precise functions not clear. P8.

6907 *ts'āng-pù ssū* 倉部司 or *ts'ang-pu*
(1) N-S DIV (San-kuo Wei)–SUI: **Granaries Section,** one of several specialized units in the Ministry of Revenue (*tu-chih*) of the evolving Department of State Affairs (*shang-shu sheng*), headed by a Director (*lang, lang-chung*); generally administered the receipt and disbursement of state grain revenues. P6. (2) SUI–SUNG, MING: **Granaries Bureau,** from 583 one of 4 specialized units in the Ministry of Revenue (*min-pu; hu-pu*), headed by a Director (*lang* in Sui, thereafter *lang-chung*), rank 5b in T'ang, 6b in Sung; revived in Ming only from 1380 till 1390, when the Ministry was reorganized with a Bureau (*ch'ing-li ssu*) for each Province. In Sung had 6 subordinate Sections (*an*): Collection Section (*hui-ch'ang an*), Prefectural Remittances Section (*shang-kung an*), Grain Transactions Section (*t'iao-ti an*), Receipts and Payments Section (*chi-na an*), Miscellany Section (*chih-tsa an*), and Mail Distribution Section (*k'ai-ch'ai an*). RR: *bureau des greniers de l'empire.* SP *bureau des greniers.* P6.

6908 *ts'āng-pù ts'áo* 倉部曹
N-S DIV (S. Dyn.): variant of *ts'ang-pu* (**Granaries Section**); not to be confused with *ts'ang-ts'ao.* P6.

6909   *ts'āng-ssū* 倉司
SUNG: **Supply Commission,** variant of *t'i-chü ch'ang-p'ing ssu* (Stabilization Fund Supervisorate), one of the Four Circuit Supervisorates (*ssu chien-ssu*). SP: *office provincial des greniers.*

6910   *ts'āng-ts'áo* 倉曹
Granaries Section. (1) HAN: one of a dozen or more Sections (*ts'ao*) subordinate to the Defender-in-chief (*t'ai-wei*) in the central government, probably duplicated on the staff of the Counselor-in-chief (*ch'eng-hsiang*); headed by an Administrator (*yüan-shih*), rank =400 bushels; precise functions not clear. HB: bureau of granaries. P12. (2) HAN: a common staff unit in a Commandery (*chün*), staffed with Scribes (*shih*), probably unranked. P53. (3) N-S DIV–SUNG: a staff agency in such units of territorial administration as Princely Establishments (*wang-fu*) and Superior Prefectures (*fu*), normally headed by an Administrator (*ts'an-chün-shih*), rank 7a or lower; managed local provisioning under supervision of the central government's Ministry of Revenue (*tu-chih, min-pu, hu-pu*). See *liu ts'ao.* RR+SP: *service des greniers.* P69. (4) T'ANG: a provisioning unit in each of the Sixteen Guards (*shih-liu wei*) at the dynastic capital and in Guard Commands (*shuai-fu*) in the establishment of the Heir Apparent, each headed by 2 Administrators, 8b. RR: *service des greniers.* (5) T'ANG–CH'ING: occasional unofficial reference to the Ministry of Revenue (*hu-pu*).

6911   *ts'āng-tū* 倉督
N-S DIV (N. Ch'i)–T'ANG: **Granary Supervisor,** unranked staff aides in Commanderies (*chün*) in N. Ch'i, Regions (*chou*) in Sui, and Prefectures (*chou*) and Districts (*hsien*) in T'ang. RR: *contrôleur des greniers.* P52, 53, 54.

6912   *tsào-chú* 造局
MING: **Manufactory,** a workshop attached to a District (*hsien*) government, more precisely identifiable only by prefixes.

6913   *tsào-pàn huó-chì ch'ù* 造辦活計處
CH'ING: **Workshop** within the palace headed by an unspecified number of Managers (*kuan-li*) assigned from the staff of the Imperial Household Department (*nei-wu fu*); in 1759 renamed *yang-hsin tien tsao-pan ch'u.* BH: workshop of the imperial household. P37.

6914   *tsào-pì chíh* 造筆直
T'ANG: **Auxiliary for Making Writing-brushes,** 4 unranked craftsmen on the staff of the Academy of Scholarly Worthies (*chi-hsien tien shu-yüan*). RR: *fonctionnaire auxiliaire fabricant de pinceaux.* P25.

6915   *tsào-tsò sǒ* 造作所
SUNG: **Palace Workshop,** a unit of the Palace Eunuch Service (*ju-nei nei-shih sheng*) that produced articles for use in the palace and especially for wedding ceremonies involving members of the imperial family. SP: *bureau de fabrication des objets pour le palais et pour le mariage de la famille impériale.*

6916   *ts'áo* 曹
Section: throughout history a common generic term for specialized units among which the clerical or administrative staffs of larger agencies were distributed, found at all levels of government, in the military as well as the civil service; precisely identifiable only by their descriptive prefixes. It is especially noteworthy that during the era of N-S Division such Sections were top-echelon subordinate units in the developing Department of State Affairs (*shang-shu sheng*), gradually being transformed into Ministries (*pu*); and that from Sui–T'ang on the suboffical clerical staffs of units of territorial administration were commonly distributed among Six Sections (*liu ts'ao*) that corresponded in names with, and processed routine business in the realms of, the Six Ministries (*liu pu*) of the central government.

6917   *ts'áo-chǎng* 曹長
T'ANG: lit., Section head: unofficial reference to a **Vice Director** (*ch'eng*) **of the Department of State Affairs** (*shang-shu sheng*), rank 4a, or a **Bureau Director** (*lang-chung*) in a Ministry (*pu*), 5a.

6918   *ts'ǎo-ch'áng* 草場
SUNG: **Hay Yard,** 12 in the dynastic capital controlled by the Court of the National Granaries (*ssu-nung ssu*). Also see *ts'ao-liao ch'ang.* SP: *place de réception de la paille dans le territoire de la capitale.*

6919   *ts'áo-ch'én* 漕臣
SUNG: **Transport Intendant,** variant designation of a Fiscal Commissioner (*chuan-yün shih*) in a Circuit (*lu*). SP: *intendant fiscal.* P59, 60.

6920   *ts'áo-chēng* 漕正
T'ANG: **Transport Director,** 2 apparently non-official specialists in the Office of Boats and Boatmen (*chou-chi shu*) in the Directorate of Waterways (*tu-shui chien*). RR: *chef des transports par eau.* P60.

6921   *ts'āo-chiāng* 操江
MING: **River Controller,** duty assignment for Vice Censors-in-chief (*fu tu yü-shih*) and Assistant Censors-in-chief (*ch'ien tu yü-shih*) of the Nanking Censorate (*nan-ching tu ch'a-yüan*); maintained surveillance over operation of transport along the upper and lower reaches of the Yangtze River. P49.

6922   *ts'áo-hsièn* 漕憲
MING–CH'ING: **Transport Censor-in-chief,** unofficial reference to a nominal Censor-in-chief (*tu yü-shih*) serving as Director-general of Grain Transport (*ts'ao-yün tsung-tu*). Also see *hsien.*

6923   *ts'ǎo-jén* 草人
CHOU: **Planting Manager,** 4 ranked as Junior Servicemen (*hsia-shih*), members of the Ministry of Education (*ti-kuan*) who classified cultivated lands in the environs of the royal capital, prescribed treatments to improve the soil, and determined what crops should be planted where. See *tsai-shih* (Master of Labor). CL: *officier des herbes.*

6924   *ts'áo-liào ch'áng* 草料場
SUNG: **Fodder Yard,** a fodder-storage unit in the dynastic capital, subordinate to the Court of the National Granaries (*ssu-nung ssu*). Also see *ts'ao-ch'ang.* SP: *place des fourrages.*

6925   *ts'áo-piāo* 漕標
CH'ING: **Transport Command,** a special organization of Green Standards (*lu-ying*) troops for moving tax grains from Southeast China along the Grand Canal to Peking, consisting of detachments based in Guards (*wei*) and Battalions (*so*) along the waterway, sectors of such detachments headed by Regional Vice Commanders (*fu-chiang*), Brigade Commanders (*yu-chi*), etc., under overall supervision of the Director-general of Grain Transport (*ts'ao-yün tsung-tu*). Also see *piao.* P60.

6926   *ts'áo-shǐh* 漕史
T'ANG: **Transport Clerk,** 2 unranked subofficials on the staff of the Office of Boats and Boatmen (*chou-chi shu*) in the Directorate of Waterways (*tu-shui chien*). RR: *scribe chargé des transports par eau.* P60.

6927 *ts'áo-shuài* 漕帥
SUNG: **Transport Commander,** variant designation of a Fiscal Commissioner (*chuan-yün shih*) in a Circuit (*lu*). SP: *commissaire aux finances.* P50, 60.

6928 *ts'áo-shǔi ts'áo* 漕水曹
HAN: **Section for Water Transport,** in Later Han a clerical staff unit in some Commanderies (*chün*), headed by an Administrator (*yüan-shih*). HB: bureau of grain transport by water.

6929 *ts'áo-ssū* 漕司
SUNG: **Fiscal Commission,** quasiofficial reference to the office of a Fiscal Commissioner (*chuan-yün shih*) or comparable authority responsible for collecting grain taxes in a Circuit (*lu*) and forwarding them to the dynastic capital. SP: *autorité fiscale de province.* P52.

6930 *ts'áo-tū* 漕督
CH'ING: abbreviated reference to a **Director-general of Grain Transport** (*ts'ao-yün tsung-tu*).

6931 *ts'áo-yüàn* 曹掾
HAN–SUNG: **Section Clerk,** generic reference to the personnel of clerical and administrative Sections (*ts'ao*) in units of territorial administration, especially the Administrators (*yüan-shih, yüan*) who normally headed them.

6932 *ts'áo-yüàn àn* 曹掾案
SUNG: **Section for Section Clerks** in the Bureau of Evaluations (*k'ao-kung ssu*) of the Ministry of Personnel (*li-pu*); processed merit ratings and other evaluations of lowly personnel serving in units of territorial administration. SP: *service des administrateurs des services.*

6933 *ts'áo-yün shǐh* 漕運使
Transport Commissioner. (1) CHIN: head of a Transport Office (*ts'ao-yün ssu*). (2) MING: head of the Chief Transport Office (*tu ts'ao-yün ssu*) at the capital during the Hung-wu reign (1368–1398), in charge of the transport of state grain to modern Nanking, then the dynastic capital. P60.

6934 *ts'áo-yün ssū* 漕運司
CHIN–YÜAN: **Transport Office,** established at crucial points on major waterways to manage the transport of state grain to the dynastic capital, in Chin headed by a Commissioner (*shih*), in Yüan by a Supervisor (*t'i-chü*), rank 5a; in both eras apparently subordinate to a Chief Transport Office (*tu ts'ao-yün ssu*) in the capital; in Chin co-existed with Fiscal Commissioners (*chuan-yün shih*), who also had some grain transport responsibilities in their Route (*lu*) jurisdictions. P60.

6935 *ts'áo-yün tsǔng-pīng kuān* 漕運總兵官
MING: **Grain Transport Commander,** from 1404 a duty assignment for a noble or eminent military officer, originally to organize the coastal transport of tax grain from Southeast China to the Peking area in support of military operations in the North and in preparation for the transfer of the dynastic capital from Nanking to Peking in 1421, then from 1411 concurrently to reconstruct the Grand Canal and subsequently direct the shipment of tax grain inland along the canal from the Yangtze delta to Peking, from 1450 in cooperation with a civil service Director-general of Grain Transport (*ts'ao-yün tsung-tu*). Neither was specifically subordinate to the other: the Commander focused his attention on controlling the troops to whom transport duties were assigned, and the Director-general had broader scope, being concurrently Grand Coordinator (*hsün-fu*) of the Huai-an region in the middle sector of the canal. P60.

6936 *ts'áo-yün tsǔng-tū* 漕運總督
MING–CH'ING: **Director-general of Grain Transport,** in Ming from its inception in 1450 a duty assignment for a Censor-in-chief (*tu yü-shih*), in Ch'ing a regular post (*kuan*) of rank 2a or, if held concurrently by a Minister (*shang-shu*) in the central government, 1b; in Ming cooperated with a military Grain Transport Commander (*ts'ao-yün tsung-ping kuan*); in both eras importantly assisted by Transport-control Censors (*hsün-ts'ao yü-shih*). Had general supervisory responsibility for the transport of tax grains from the Yangtze delta to the Peking area along the Grand Canal. Commonly occurs transposed as *tsung-tu ts'ao-yün.* Also see *ho-tao tsung-tu* (Director-general of the Grand Canal). BH: director of grain transport. P60.

6937 *tsé-yǔ* 澤虞
Supervisor of Marshes. (1) CHOU: 4 ranked as Ordinary Servicemen (*chung-shih*) and 8 as Junior Servicemen (*hsia-shih*), members of the Ministry of Education (*ti-kuan*) responsible for collecting plants and rushes from watery areas not suitable for cultivation for use in sacrifices, receptions, and funerals; also assisted in imperial hunts in such areas, and supervised the imposition of taxes or punishments on unauthorized persons who gathered or hunted there. CL: *inspecteur des étangs.* (2) N-S DIV (Chou): one or more ranked as Ordinary Servicemen (8a) and Junior Servicemen (9a) in the Ministry of Education, presumably with responsibilities as described in (1) above. P14.

6938 *ts'è fǔ-chìn* 側福晉
CH'ING: **Princely Lady,** designation of secondary wives of Imperial Princes (*ch'in-wang*), 4 authorized for each; ranked after the principal wife, titled Princess-consort (*fu-chin*).

6939 *ts'è-shìh* 側室
CH'ING: lit., side chamber: **Princely Lady,** designation of secondary wives of members of the imperial family titled Heir (*shih-tzu*) and Commandery Prince (*chün-wang*), 3 authorized for each, and those titled Heir of a Commandery Prince (*chang-tzu*) and Beile (*pei-lo*), 2 authorized for each; ranked after the principal wives, designated Princess-consorts (*fu-chin, fu-jen*).

6940 *ts'è-yèn hún-í k'ò-lòu sǒ*
　　　　　　　測驗渾儀刻漏所
SUNG: **Office for Testing Armillary Spheres and Water Clocks** in the Bureau of Astronomy (*t'ien-wen yüan*) of the Palace Library (*pi-shu sheng*). Cf. *hun-i t'ai, lou-k'o so.* SP: *bureau de la clepsydre.*

6941 *tséi-pǔ yüàn* 賊捕掾
HAN: **Police Clerk** on the staff of the Metropolitan Governor (*ching-chao yin*) at the dynastic capital; perhaps not a title but a descriptive term akin to *pu-tsei kuan* (thief-catching officials). P32.

6942 *tséi-ts'áo* 賊曹
Police Section. (1) HAN: one of a dozen or more Sections (*ts'ao*) on the staffs of the Counselor-in-chief (*ch'eng-hsiang*) and the Defender-in-chief (*t'ai-wei*) in the central government, headed by an Administrator (*yüan-shih*), rank =300 bushels; probably supervised the jailing as well as the capturing of thieves and bandits. HB: bureau of banditry. (2) HAN: quasiofficial reference to the Section for Commandery Governors (*erh-ch'ien shih ts'ao*) in the Imperial Secretariat (*shang-shu t'ai*). P13. (3) N-S DIV: one of several Sections among which the subordinates of Regional Inspectors (*tz'u-shih*) and lesser territorial administrators were

distributed; normally headed by a suboffical Clerk (*yüan*). P32.

6943　*tsēng chiēn-shēng* 增監生
CH'ING: **Student by Purchase, Second Class** in the Directorate of Education (*kuo-tzu chien*) at the dynastic capital; see under *li chien-sheng* (Student by Purchase).

6944　*tsèng-kuān* 贈官
Posthumous Office: apparently beginning in the post-Han Chin dynasty and systematically used from T'ang on, a title awarded to a deceased official or to deceased forebears of officials, commonly extending back to grandparents. From Sung on, the posthumous title commonly awarded to eminent civil officials was Duke (*kung*), prefixed with laudatory terms.

6945　*tsēng-kuǎng shēng-yüán* 增廣生員
Added Student: in Ming and Ch'ing, and perhaps from as early as the era of N-S Division, a designation of students admitted to state schools at the Prefecture (*chou, fu*) and lower levels of territorial administration, beyond the quota normally authorized; in Ming and Ch'ing the status was above that of Supplementary Student (*fu hsüeh-sheng, fu-sheng*) and below that of Stipend Student (*lin-sheng*). Such students at times were granted state stipends somewhat less than those of Stipend Students.

6946　*tsēng kùng-shēng* 增貢生
CH'ING: **Tribute Student by Purchase, Second Class,** a category of men qualified to take Provincial Examinations (*hsiang-shih*) in the civil service recruitment examination sequence by having purchased promotion from status as Added Students (*tseng-kuang sheng-yüan*). The status was lower than *lin kung-sheng* but higher than *fu kung-sheng* and *li kung-sheng*.

6947　*tsēng-shēng* 增生
MING–CH'ING: abbreviation of *tseng-kuang sheng-yüan* (**Added Student**).

6948　*tsǒ* 佐
Assistant. (1) Throughout history a collective reference to the 2nd and 3rd tiers of officials in an agency, and especially to very low-ranking or unranked personnel serving in the clerical and administrative Sections (*ts'ao*) in which the routine business of units of territorial administration was conducted, down to the District (*hsien*) level. (2) HAN–T'ANG: a low-ranking or unranked member of a minor agency, ranking after both its head and his Aide (*ch'eng*). RR: *secrétaire, administrateur*. (3) Occasional prefix to such a title as Editorial Director (*chu-tso lang*), signifying Assistant Editorial Director.

6949　*tsǒ* 左
(1) **Left, of the Left, Senior:** throughout history (except as noted in #2 below) a common prefix to a title when a pair of appointees was authorized, both normally of the same rank, or to an agency name when a pair of identically named agencies existed; in prestige, Left took precedence over Right (*yu*); geographically, Left indicated East (*tung*) whereas Right indicated West (*hsi*). (2) YÜAN: **Left, of the Left, Junior:** used as above but with reversed order of prestige among the Mongols.

6950　*tsò-aó t'īng* 坐廠廳
MING: **Granaries Office,** variant of *ching-liang t'ing* (Office of the Capital Granaries). P8.

6951　*tsǒ-ch'éng* 左丞
(1) **Left Aide,** throughout history may be encountered in

reference to a 2nd or 3rd executive official of an agency; see under *ch'eng*. (2) HAN: **Assistant Director of the Left,** one of a pair of 3rd-tier officials of the Imperial Secretariat (*shang-shu t'ai*), rank 400 bushels, ranking after the Director (*ling*) and Vice Director (*p'u-yeh*). HB: assistant of the left. P5. (3) N-S DIV–YÜAN: **Assistant Director of the Left** in the Department of State Affairs (*shang-shu sheng*), one of a pair normally ranking after the Director and one or more Vice Directors (both as in #2 above), rank commonly 4a till Sung, then advanced to 2a; in T'ang had supervisory jurisdiction over the Ministries of Personnel (*ti-pu*), Revenue (*hu-pu*), and Rites (*lǐ-pu*); from Sung on were commonly members of the elite central government group collectively known as Grand Councilors (*tsai-hsiang*), with the specific added designation Participant in Determining Governmental Matters (*ts'an-chih cheng-shih*). RR: *assistant de gauche*. SP: *grand conseiller assistant de gauche*. (4) T'ANG–CH'ING: common unofficial reference to the **Vice Minister** (*shih-lang*) of a Ministry (*pu*).

6952　*tsǒ-chí* 佐棘
CH'ING: unofficial reference to a **Vice Minister** (*shao-ch'ing*) **of the Court of Judicial Review** (*ta-li ssu*); see *ta-chi, chi-shu*.

6953　*tsǒ-chì* 左計
SUNG: **Left Account,** one of 2 large regional jurisdictions into which the empire was divided for fiscal purposes in 993–994, under a Commissioner of the Left Account (*tso chi-shih*), supervised by a Supreme Commissioner of Accounts (*tsung chi-shih*), in one stage in the development of the State Finance Commission (*san ssu*). SP: *comptes de gauche*. P7.

6954　*tsǒ-chiàng* 左將
HAN: **Left Leader** of a group of Court Gentlemen (*lang*), distinguished from those led by the Right Leader (*yu-chiang*) and the Center Leader (*chung-chiang*).

6955　*tsǒ-ch'iēn* 左遷
Lit., shifted to the left, presumably referring to positions in a list of personnel: throughout history a term meaning **to demote.**

6956　*tsǒ chíh-fá* 左執法
N-S DIV (San-kuo Wu): unofficial reference to the *yü-shih chung-ch'eng* (nominally **Palace Aide to the Censor-in-chief,** but at the time de facto head of the Censorate, *yü-shih t'ai*); see *chung chih-fa*.

6957　*tsǒ chīng-fǔ tū-wèi* 左京輔都尉
HAN: **Left Defender of the Capital,** one of the Three Defenders of the Metropolitan Area (*san-fu tu-wei*). HB: chief commandant of the eastern adjunct capital region.

6958　*tsò-chǔ* 座主
T'ANG: lit., chairman: **Examination Master,** polite term used by graduates of a civil service recruitment examination for a chief examiner at the examination.

6959　*tsǒ chǔ-k'ò* 左主客
N-S DIV (N. Wei): **Left Section for Foreign Relations,** from c. 400 a component of the Ministry of Rites (*i-ts'ao*) in the evolving Department of State Affairs (*shang-shu sheng*), headed by a Director (*lang-chung*); shared dealings with foreign states (and dependencies?) with a Right Section for Foreign Relations (*yu chu-k'o*), but basis for division not clear.

6960　*tsǒ-chūn* 佐軍
HAN: **Secondary Army,** one of 8 special capital-defense

forces organized at the end of Han; see *pa hsiao-wei* (Eight Commandants).

6961 *tsǒ-chūn* 左軍
Left Army. (1) Throughout history a common designation for one of 3 or 5 military forces in battle array, others normally prefixed right and center (sometimes also front and rear). (2) HAN: one of 8 special capital-defense forces organized at the end of Han; see *pa hsiao-wei* (Eight Commandants).

6962 *tsǒ-èrh* 佐貳
Lit., assistants and seconds: **Associate,** throughout history a collective reference to the 2nd and lower tiers of executive officials in any agency, especially a unit of territorial administration such as a District (*hsien*).

6963 *tsò-fāng ssū* 作坊司
SUNG: **Palace Workshop,** a generic reference to various kinds of craft production units prefixed only with direction words: Eastern, Western, Northern, and Southern, each headed by a Commissioner (*shih*), probably an unranked artisan foreman; organizational affiliation not clear, but most likely under the Directorate for the Palace Buildings (*chiang-tso chien*) and responsible for general construction and repair work in quadrants of the palace grounds as indicated by the prefixes. SP: *ateliers.*

6964 *tsò-fāng wù-liào k'ù* 作坊物料庫
SUNG: **Warehouse for the Palace Workshops** (*tso-fang ssu*), a general supply depot for workshop units of the Directorate for the Palace Buildings (*chiang-tso chien*), headed by 3 Supervisors (*chien-kuan*), probably unranked subofficials; apparently divided into sections (*chieh;* lit., boundaries) by category of materials stored. SP: *magasin des matériaux pour les ateliers de fabrication.* P15.

6965 *tsǒ-fǔ* 左府
T'ANG: **Left Guard,** one of the Twelve Guards (*shih-erh wei*) stationed at the dynastic capital; created in 622 by renaming the Left Personal Guard (see *pei-shen fu*), then in 660 renamed Left Personal Guard (see *ch'ien-niu wei*). Cf. *tso-wei.* P43.

6966 *tsǒ-fǔ tū-wèi* 左輔都尉
N-S DIV (San-kuo Wei): **Commandant Bulwark on the Left,** one of several Commandants (*tu-wei*) serving as advisers to the Heir Apparent. P26.

6967 *tsò-hsién* 坐銜
CH'ING: lit., to occupy nominal office, a nominal office occupied; a term sometimes used, e.g., to indicate that Right Censor-in-chief (*yu tu yü-shih*) was the nominal office occupied by a Governor-general (*tsung-tu*). P18.

6968 *tsǒ hsién-wáng* 左賢王
HAN–N-S DIV: lit., (one who) assists the worthy King: (1) **Prince,** a title commonly granted chiefs of northern alien tribes that were subordinate to the Hsiung-nu Khan (*shan-yü*). (2) **Crown Prince,** a title bestowed on the heir apparent of a Khan of the Hsiung-nu or other northern tribal confederation.

6969 *tsò-hsüǎn* 左選
CH'ING: lit. meaning not clear: **Special Reappointment,** referring to the Ministry of Personnel's (*lì-pu*) procedure for placing officials who had been absent in mourning or on sick leave, etc., back in their original positions or, with imperial authorization, in new positions.

6970 *tsǒ-hsüǎn* 坐選
SUNG: lit., selections of the left: **Civil Appointments Pro-**
cess, a reference to the Ministry of Personnel's (*lì-pu*) appointments procedures (see under *hsüan*), by which the selection of men for appointments and reappointments was delegated to different executive officials of the Ministry according to the ranks and services (civil or military) of the appointees. The term Left (*tso*) referred to civil service appointments. See *shang-shu tso-hsüan, shih-lang tso-hsüan.* Cf. *yu-hsüan.* SP: *bureau des nominations civiles.*

6971 *tsǒ-hù ts'áo* 左戶曹 or *tso-hu*
N-S DIV: **Census Section** in the developing Department of State Affairs (*shang-shu sheng*), perhaps originating in very late Han; headed by a Minister (*shang-shu*) or Director (*lang, lang-chung*); apparently a variant form of *tso-min ts'ao,* perhaps reflecting a tampering with original terminology in T'ang times to avoid the tabooed personal name Li Shih-min (T'ang T'ai-tsung). Also see *yu-hu ts'ao, hu-ts'ao, min-ts'ao.* P6.

6972 *tsǒ-ì* 左弋
HAN: **Duck Hunter,** unspecified number under the Chamberlain for the Palace Revenues (*shao-fu*); shot ducks and geese in the capital parks for the Emperor's table and sacrificial uses; headed by a Director (*ling*); in 104 B.C. retitled *tz'u-fei.* Some traditional scholars understood *tso-i* to be a place-name, apparently the location of a palace prison (see *chü-shih*). HB: bird shooting aide. P37.

6973 *tsǒ-ì ch'ién-fēng* 左翼前鋒
CH'ING: **Vanguard Brigade Left Wing,** a seemingly transposed term commonly used as a prefix to the titles of officers of the Brigade; see under *ch'ien-feng ying* and *i.*

6974 *tsǒ-kēng* 左更
CH'IN–HAN: lit., member of the left (3rd) watch: **Grandee of the Twelfth Order,** 9th highest of 20 titles of honorary nobility (*chüeh*) conferred on meritorious subjects. P65.

6975 *tsǒ-k'ù* 左庫
N-S DIV (Sung): **Left Storehouse,** official redesignation of the Inner Storehouse of the Left (*nei tso-k'u*) from the era 424–451 till c. 460. P7.

6976 *tsǒ-k'uéi* 左揆
T'ANG–SUNG: lit., left mastermind: unofficial reference to the **Vice Director of the Left** (*tso p'u-yeh*) **of the Department of State Affairs** (*shang-shu sheng*), in contrast to his counterpart the Vice Director of the Right (*yu p'u-yeh*). See *tuan-k'uei.*

6977 *tsǒ-láng* 佐郎
SUI: **Adjunct,** 4, rank 6b, established late in the dynasty as aides to the Assistants in the Palace Library (*pi-shu lang;* see *pi-shu sheng*. This is apparently the only occurrence of this combination as a title. P25.

6978 *tsǒ-lì* 佐吏
HAN–T'ANG: variant of the generic designation *tso* (**Assistant**), used especially for minor personnel in units of territorial administration; in Han reportedly specified the Assistant (*chih-chung*) Governor (*shou*) of a Commandery (*chün*) or Assistant Regional Inspector (*tz'u-shih*) of a Region (*chou*), and in addition Mounted Escorts (*pieh-chia*) on the staffs of such Governors and Regional Inspectors. P54.

6979 *tsò-liáng t'īng* 坐糧廳
MING–CH'ING: **Supervisorate of the T'ung-chou Terminus of the Grand Canal** or **Supervisor of the T'ung-chou Terminus of the Grand Canal,** serving both as an

agency name and as the title of those in charge of it; responsible for overseeing maintenance of the Grand Canal embankments and the operation of its transport facilities, private as well as state; collected any transit taxes or fees due at T'ung-chou. Persons in charge were assigned for 2-year tours of duty from among officials serving as Supervising Secretaries (*chi-shih-chung*), Censors (*yü-shih*), and Directors (*lang-chung*) and Vice Directors (*yüan-wai lang*) of Bureaus (*ch'ing-li ssu*) in the Six Ministries (*liu pu*); in Ch'ing there was one Manchu and one Chinese appointee. Such assignees were also known as Supervisors (*chien-tu*) of the Supervisorate. BH: supervisors of the government granaries at the capital. P8.

6980 *tsŏ-lĭng* 佐領
(1) MING: **Staff Administrator,** a collective reference to all those officials of units of territorial administration who were in the categories called Associates (*tso-erh*) and Staff Supervisors (*shou-ling kuan*). (2) CH'ING: **Company Commander** in the Eight Banners (*pa ch'i*) military system, rank 4a; Chinese translation of the Manchu titles transliterated as *niu-lu o-chen* and *niu-lu chang-ching;* see under *niu-lu.* BH: major commander of a company of the provincial Manchu garrison, or captain. (3) CH'ING: **Assistant Commandant,** rank 4b, in a Princely Establishment (*wang-fu*) or Ducal Establishment (*kung-fu*), 2nd in command under a Commandant (*ts'an-ling*). P69. (4) CH'ING: **Vice Commander-general** of Chahar; see under *tu-t'ung* (Commander-general) and *liang-i* (Two Pasturelands). P31.

6981 *tsŏ-mín ts'áo* 左民曹 or *tso-min*
N-S DIV: **Census Section,** from the Three Kingdoms era into N. Wei one of the major units in the developing Department of State Affairs (*shang-shu sheng*), principally responsible for processing census reports submitted by units of territorial administration but occasionally having a broader scope including supervision of grain tax receipts and even state construction projects; at times headed by a Minister (*shang-shu*), at times by a Director (*lang, lang-chung*) and subordinated to a Ministry of Revenue (*tu-chih*); sometimes paired with a Land Tax Section (*yu-min ts'ao*), at times not so paired and grouped with such agencies as the Treasury Bureau (*chin-pu*), Granaries Section (*ts'ang-pu*), Ministry of Revenue (*tu-chih*), and Transport Section (*yün-ts'ao*). Also see *tso-hu ts'ao, hu-ts'ao, min-ts'ao.* P6, 14.

6982 *tsŏ-pān tièn-chīh* 左班殿直
SUNG: **Palace Eunuch of the Left Duty Group,** 4th highest of 12 rank titles (*nei-shih chieh*) granted eunuchs from 1112. P68.

6983 *tsŏ-pān tū-chīh* 左班都知
SUNG: **Office Manager of the Left Duty Group,** rank 1 eunuch in the Palace Domestic Service (*nei-shih sheng*), aided by a rank 2 eunuch entitled Assistant Office Manager of the Left Duty Group (*tso-pan fu tu-chih*). SP: *administrateur général des compagnies de gauche, intendant du palais de 1er rang (eunuque).*

6984 *tsŏ-păng* 左榜
YÜAN: **Chinese Pass List** issued at the conclusion of civil service recruitment examinations conducted in the dynastic capital, distinguished from the Non-Chinese Pass List (*yu-pang*); the men named at the top of each list were both considered Principal Graduates (*chuang-yüan*). Note that in Yüan times Right was more esteemed than Left.

6985 *tsŏ p'íng-ì* 左馮翊
HAN: **Guardian of the Left,** from 104 B.C. one of the Three Guardians (*san-fu*) who were responsible for super-

vising administration of the Metropolitan Area (*ching-shih*) around the dynastic capital, from 89 B.C. under the supervisory control of the Metropolitan Commandant (*ssu-li hsiao-wei*); ranked at 2,000 bushels; subordinates included an Aide (*ch'eng*), a Director of the Four Markets (*ssu-shih chang*) at Ch'ang-an, a Prison of the West Market (*hsi-shih yü*), and an Office of Sacrificial Grains and Animals (*lin-hsi*). HB: eastern supporter. P32, 68.

6986 *tsŏ-pù* 左部
(1) HAN: **Left Sector,** designation of the south and east quadrants of the dynastic capitals, Ch'ang-an and Loyang; in Former Han the jurisdiction of 2 Commandants of the Metropolitan Police, East and South (*kuang-pu wei*); in Later Han the jurisdiction of the Commandant of the Metropolitan Police, East Sector (*tung-pu wei*) and the Commandant of the Metropolitan Police, South Sector (*nan-pu wei*). Cf. *yu-pu* (Right Sector). P20. (2) YÜAN: **Ministries of the Left,** a variant of *tso san-pu* (Three Ministries of the Left).

6987 *tsŏ sān-pù* 左三部
YÜAN: **Three Ministries of the Left,** from 1260 to 1264 and again from 1266 to 1268 a combination of the normally separate Ministries of Personnel (*li-pu*), Revenues (*hu-pu*), and Rites (*li-pu*) into a single agency, with 2 Ministers (*shang-shu*), rank 3a. Also see *li-hu-li pu, li-li pu, yu san-pu.*

6988 *tsŏ-shàng shŭ* 左尚署
T'ANG–SUNG: **Left Service Office** in the Directorate for Imperial Manufactories (*shao-fu chien*), responsible for preparing fans, parasols, carriages, sedan-chairs, and painted or sculpted decorations for the imperial palace; headed by a Director (*ling*), rank 7b2. See *chung-shang shu, yu-shang shu.* RR+SP: *office de l'atelier impérial de gauche.* P38.

6989 *tsŏ-shĭh* 佐史
HAN: **Accessory Clerk,** a rank indicator for petty subofficial appointees at the very bottom of the officialdom, paid considerably less than 100 bushels per year. HB: accessory clerk. P68.

6990 *tsŏ-shĭh* 左史
T'ANG–SUNG: **Left Scribe,** from 662 to 671 and again from 690 to 705 the official variant designation of Imperial Diarists (*ch'i-chü lang*) in the Chancellery (*men-hsia sheng*); thereafter an unofficial reference to the same post. Cf. *yu-shih* (Right Scribe). RR+SP: *annaliste de gauche.*

6991 *tsŏ-shīh* 左師
T'ANG: variant of *ssu-yeh* (**Director of Studies** in the Directorate of Education, *kuo-tzu chien*).

6992 *tsò-shīh* 座師
MING–CH'ING: **Examination Mentor,** a reference by Provincial Graduates (*chü-jen*) and Metropolitan Graduates (*chin-shih*) to the senior officials who had presided over the examinations in which they succeeded. Cf. *tso-chu.*

6993 *tsò-shìh* 柞氏
CHOU: **Uprooter of Trees,** 2 ranked as Junior Servicemen (*hsia-shih*), members of the Ministry of Justice (*ch'iu-kuan*); specific functions not clear, but probably responsible for the removal of diseased or damaged trees from royal property, a duty assigned to the Ministry of Justice for symbolic reasons. CL: *arracheur d'arbres.*

6994 *tsŏ shìh-chìn* 左侍禁
SUNG: **Left Palace Attendant,** 2nd highest of 12 rank titles (*chieh*) granted to palace eunuchs from 1112; see *nei-shih chieh.* Cf. *yu shih-chin.* SP: *intendant du palais du 6e ou 7e rang (eunuque).* P68.

6995 *tsŏ-shìh ts'áo* 左士曹
N-S DIV: **Left Section of Servicemen,** intermittently a unit in the developing Department of State Affairs (*shang-shu sheng*), apparently responsible for handling personnel matters relating to officials of middling to low rank; in Chin apparently a major unit in the Department, headed by a Minister (*shang-shu*); in N. Wei one of 6 subordinate units in the Section for Justice (*tu-kuan*), headed by a Director (*lang-chung*). In N. Ch'i reportedly transformed into the functionally quite different Catering Bureau (*shan-pu*) in the Section for Justice. See *yu-shih ts'ao*.

6996 *tsŏ-shŭ* 左署
HAN: **Left Corps,** a variant reference to one of the Three Corps (*san shu*) into which Court Gentlemen (*lang*) were organized.

6997 *tsŏ shù-chăng* 左庶長
CH'IN–HAN: lit., left chief of a host: **Grandee of the Tenth Order,** the 11th highest of 20 titles of honorary nobility (*chüeh*) conferred on meritorious subjects. P65.

6998 *tsŏ-sŏ* 左所
CH'ING: **Left Subsection** of the Imperial Procession Guard (*luan-i wei*), headed by a Director (*chang-yin kuan-chün shih*), rank 4a; subdivided into a Carriage Office (*lüan-yü ssu*) and a Horse-training Office (*hsün-ma ssu*). BH: first sub-department.

6999 *tsŏ-ssū* 左司
Lit., left office, normally paired with a Right Office (*yu-ssu*). (1) N-S DIV–CH'ING: **Left Office of the ...,** common unofficial or quasiofficial collective reference to all personnel whose titles were prefixed with Left in agencies of many sorts whose members were titled in Left and Right pairs. (2) N-S DIV–SUNG, CHIN: **Left Office** of the Department of State Affairs (*shang-shu sheng*), a common quasiofficial and sometimes official designation of the aggregation of Ministries of Personnel (*li-pu*), Revenue (*hu-pu*), and Rites (*li-pu*), commonly supervised by the Left Vice Director (*tso shih-lang*) of the Department with the support of a staff comparable to that of a Bureau (*ssu*) in a Ministry, especially including a Bureau Director (*lang-chung*) and Vice Director (*yüan-wai lang*). RR+SP: *bureau de gauche*. P5. (3) YÜAN: **Left Office** of the Secretariat (*chung-shu sheng*), a variant reference to *tso-pu* (Ministries of the Left) or *tso san-pu* (Three Ministries of the Left). (4) CH'ING: **Left Office,** one of 8 units in the Rear Subsection (*hou-so*) of the Imperial Procession Guard (*luan-i wei*), headed by a Director (*chang-yin yün-hui shih*), rank 4a; also one of a pair of Offices into which the Court of the Imperial Clan (*tsung-jen fu*) and the Palace Stud (*shang-ssu yüan*) were each divided. BH: first department.

7000 *tsŏ-ssù* 左寺
MING–CH'ING: **Left Court of Review,** one of a pair of subsections in the Court of Judicial Review (*ta-li ssu*), each staffed with Case Reviewers (*p'ing-shih*); until the 1690s (?) headed by a Director (*cheng*), rank 6a; thereafter headed by a Left Assistant Minister (*tso-ch'eng; see ch'eng*) of the Court, 5a or 6a. P22.

7001 *tsŏ-t'ái* 左臺
T'ANG: **Left Tribunal,** abbreviation of *tso yü-shih t'ai* or *tso su-cheng t'ai* from 684 to 712, when the traditionally unified Censorate (*yü-shih t'ai, su-cheng t'ai*) was split into Left and Right units; the Left Tribunal was principally responsible for maintaining disciplinary surveillance over the central government and the military, whereas the Right Tribunal was principally concerned with standards of territo-

rial administration and local conditions throughout the empire. RR: *tribunal de gauche*. P18.

7002 *tsò-t'áng* 作堂
N-S DIV (Liang): **Craft Workshop,** apparently a generic reference to the Gold and Silver Service (*chin-yin chü*) and the Woodworking Service (*mu-chü*) under the Chamberlain for the Palace Revenues (*shao-fu*), each authorized a Director (*ling*) but actually headed by a nominal Assistant Director (*ch'eng*), rank 3. P14.

7003 *tsŏ-t'áng* 左堂
CH'ING: unofficial reference to a **District Vice Magistrate** (*hsien-ch'eng*); cf. *yu-t'ang, t'ang*.

7004 *tsŏ-t'īng* 左廳
SUNG: **Left Bureau,** one of 2 major subdivisions of the Court of Judicial Review (*ta-li ssu*), headed by a Vice Minister (*shao-ch'ing*), rank 6a; cf. *yu-t'ing* (Right Bureau). Also called *tuan-hsing ssu, tso tuan-hsing*. Supervised a variety of lesser units: Records Reviewing Section (*mo-k'an an*), Sentence Promulgating Section (*hsüan-huang an*), Separating and Registering Section (*fen-pu an*), Decision Expediting Office (*piao-tsou-i ssu*), Mail Distribution Office (*k'ai-ch'ai ssu*), Miscellany Office (*chih-tsa ssu*), Laws Office (*fa-ssu*), Sentence Evaluators Section (*hsiang-tuan an*), and Archives (*ch'ih-k'u*). SP: *bureau judiciaire de gauche chargé des révisions*. P22.

7005 *tsŏ-tsá* 佐雜
Variant of *tso* (**Assistant**); in Ch'ing a general reference to personnel of ranks 8 and 9 in units of territorial administration. Cf. *tsa-chih* (Suboffical Post). BH: petty officials.

7006 *tsŏ-tsàng* 左藏
N-S DIV–YÜAN: **Left Storehouse** or **Left Vault,** one of a pair of major units under the early Chamberlain for the Palace Revenues (*t'ai-fu*) or later agency counterparts such as the Sui Court for the Palace Revenues (*t'ai-fu ssu*), the Sui–Sung Court of the Imperial Treasury (*t'ai-fu ssu*), and the Yüan Directorate of the Imperial Treasury (*t'ai-fu chien*). In Sung subdivided into a Southern Storehouse (*nan-k'u*) and a Northern Storehouse (*pei-k'u*), alternatively called the Western and Eastern Storehouses (*hsi-k'u, tung-k'u*), respectively; functional specializations not clear. Normally headed by 2 or more Directors (*ling*), rank 8a in Sui, 7b in T'ang, or from Sung on by Commissioners (*shih*). Originally shared with a Palace Storehouse (*chung-huang tsang, nei-tsang*) or an Imperial Storehouse (*huang-tsang*) responsibility for the receipt, storage, and disbursement of valuables used in the palace; but from Sung on became principally responsible for handling general state revenues. In Ming superseded by clusters of storehouses subordinate to the Ministries of Revenue (*hu-pu*), War (*ping-pu*), and Works (*kung-pu*), collectively known as the Palace Storehouses (*nei-k'u*). Also see *yu-tsang, t'ai-tsang k'u, san k'u*. RR+SP: *trésor de gauche*. P7.

7007 *tsŏ-tsàng àn* 左藏案
SUNG: **Left Storage Section,** one of 6 Sections (*an*) in the Treasury Bureau (*chin-pu ssu*) of the Ministry of Revenue (*hu-pu*), staffed with unranked suboffials; division of functions beween this and the Right Storage Section (*yu-tsang an*) is not clear; both presumably oversaw the receipt, storage, and issuance of the non-grain commodities with which the Treasury Bureau dealt; established c. 1080, when the State Finance Commission (*san ssu*) of early Sung was discontinued. SP: *service du trésor de gauche*. P6.

7008 *tsŏ-tsàng ch'ū-nà shĭh* 左藏出納使
T'ANG: **Commissioner Supervising the Left Storehouse,**

from the early 740s a special duty assignment for an imperial favorite; monitored receipts and disbursements from the Left Storehouse (*tso-tsang*), aided by an Administrative Assistant (*p'an-kuan*). P7.

7009 *tsŏ-tsàng k'ù* 左藏庫
SUNG–CHIN: variant of *tso-tsang* (**Left Storehouse, Left Vault**). SP: *magasin du trésor pour les dépenses ordinaires.* P7.

7010 *tsŏ-tsàng shŭ* 左藏署
N-S DIV–T'ANG: **Left Storehouse Office** under the Court for the Palace Revenues or the Court of the Imperial Revenues (both *t'ai-fu ssu*); in charge of the palace depository for valuables called the Left Storehouse (*tso-tsang*), headed by 2 or 3 Directors (*ling*), rank 8a in Sui, 7b2 in T'ang, except during the interval from c. 604 to the end of Sui, when it was headed by a Supervisor (*chien*). RR: *office du trésor de gauche.* P7, 37.

7011 *tsŏ-tsàng t'í-tiĕn* 左藏提點
YÜAN: **Superintendent of the Left Storehouse,** 4, rank not clear, appointed from 1282 to oversee the 2 Commissioners-in-chief (*ta-shih*) who were nominal heads of the Left Storehouse (*tso-tsang*), which shared with the Right Storehouse (*yu-tsang*) the receipt and disbursement of general government revenues. P7.

7012 *tsŏ-ts'áo* 左曹
(1) HAN: **Head of the Left Section,** rank 2,000 bushels, nominally under the Chamberlain for Attendants (*kuang-lu-hsün*); presented to the Emperor paperwork completed by the Imperial Secretaries (*shang-shu*), but apparently a sinecure for one or more favored companions of the Emperor; discontinued in Later Han. BH: bureau head of the left. (2) SUNG: **Left Section,** one of 5 Sections in the Ministry of Revenue (*hu-pu*) from the 1080s, when the Ministry was fully activated after being little more than a nominal office while its traditional functions were carried on by the State Finance Commission (*san ssu*) in early Sung; headed by 2 Directors (*lang-chung*), rank 6b, and 2 Vice Directors (*yüan-wai lang*), 7b. Consisted of 3 (originally 5?) Sections (*an*) and 3 Subsections (*k'o*), staffing and status vis-à-vis each other not clear: Census Section (*hu-k'ou an*), Agriculture Section (*nung-t'ien an*), Legal Research Section (*chien-fa an*), Semiannual Taxes Subsection (*erh-shui k'o*), House and Land Tax Subsection (*fang-ti k'o*), Wine Tax Subsection (*k'o-li k'o*). Also see *yu-ts'ao, hu-pu ssu, chin-pu ssu, ts'ang-pu ssu.* SP: *bureau de gauche chargé de registres des impôts et des contributions.* (3) SUNG: **Left Section,** one of 2 Sections into which the Ministry of Justice (*hsing-pu*) was divided from 1103 (till the mid-1100s only?), presided over by the Left Vice Minister (*tso shih-lang*); shared the work of the Ministry with a Right Section (*yu-ts'ao*) in some pattern not clear. SP: *service de gauche.*

7013 *tsŏ tuàn-hsíng* 左斷刑
SUNG: variant of *tso-t'ing* (**Left Bureau** in the Court of Judicial Review, *ta-li ssu*).

7014 *tsŏ-t'ūi àn* 左推案
SUNG: **Investigative Section of the Left,** one of 5 Sections (*an*) that constituted the Right Bureau (*yu-t'ing*) in the Court of Judicial Review (*ta-li ssu*); functions not clear. SP: *bureau judiciaire de gauche (réception et expédition des dépêches officielles).* See *t'ui.* P22.

7015 *tsŏ-wèi* 左衛
SUI–SUNG: **Left Guard,** a military unit at the dynastic capital; see *tso-yu wei, shih-erh wei, shih-liu wei, yu-wei.*

7016 *tsŏ-yù* 左右
Lit., left and right. (1) **Attendants,** those positioned on the ruler's left and right sides; from antiquity a common reference in audience situations. (2) Combined reference to the prefixes **Left and Right,** commonly used for officials appointed in pairs to one office; see under separate entries prefixed *tso* and *yu,* as well as under nomenclature so prefixed.

7017 *tsŏ-yù chiēh sēng-lù ssū* 左右街僧錄司
T'ANG–SUNG: **Buddhist Registry for** (Monasteries Situated Along) **the Avenues of the Capital;** see under *seng-lu ssu* (Central Buddhist Registry)

7018 *tsŏ-yù ssū* 左右司
Left and Right Offices: see separate entries for *tso-ssu* and *yu-ssu.*

7019 *tsŏ-yù ssù-àn* 左右寺案
SUNG: **Sentence Fulfillment Section,** one of 4 Sections (*an*) in the Right Bureau (*yu-t'ing*) of the Court of Judicial Review (*ta-li ssu*); staffed with unranked subofficials who monitored the implementation of approved punishments, assessments of fines, etc. SP: *services chargés des poursuites contre la corruption.* P22.

7020 *tsŏ-yù wèi* 左右衛
(1) SUI: **Left and Right Guard,** apparently a single consolidated military unit in early Sui, headed by one General-in-chief (*ta chiang-chün*) and 2 Generals (*chiang-chün*), ranks not clear; in overall charge of palace security, personal bodyguards of the Emperor, etc. Included various subdivisions called Sections (*ts'ao*), each with a specialized responsibility and headed by Adjutants (*ts'an-chün*) or Acting Adjutants (*hsing ts'an-chün*); also included a Palace Military Headquarters (*ling tso-yu fu*), which managed military assignments, rotating militiamen of the Garrison Militia system (see *fu* and *fu-ping*) to the capital and rotating selected men in the capital forces to duty shifts in the imperial bodyguard, etc. In c. 604 the Left and Right Guard was reorganized into 2 units, the Left and Right Standby Guards (*i-wei*), of the new Twelve Guards (*shih-erh wei*) organization. (2) T'ANG–SUNG: abbreviated reference to the **Left Guard and the Right Guard,** 2 of the Sixteen Guards (*shih-liu wei*) of the Southern Command (*nan-ya*) in T'ang, perpetuated in Sung but in honorific use only. P43. (3) **Left and Right Guards:** may be encountered in any era from Sui on as an abbreviated reference to any 2 Guards making a Left and Right pair, depending on context.

7021 *tsŏ-yù* 左御
T'ANG: **Left Charioteer,** unofficial reference to a Chief Minister of the Imperial Stud (*t'ai-p'u ch'ing*).

7022 *tsò-yüàn* 作院
SUNG: **Armory** maintained by the Ministry of Works (*kung-pu*). SP: *cour de fabrication des armes.*

7023 *tsŏ-yüàn* 左院
MING: **Left Tribunal,** one of a pair of units into which Investigating Censors (*chien-ch'a yü-shih*) were reorganized from 1400 to 1402, temporarily replacing the Circuits (*tao*) of the Censorate (*tu ch'a-yüan*). P18.

7024 *ts'ò-chiàng* 酢匠
T'ANG: **Vinegar Maker,** 12 non-official specialists in the Spice Pantry (*chang-hai shu*) of the Court of Imperial Entertainments (*kuang-lu ssu*). RR: *ouvrier pour la fabrication du vinaigre.*

7025 *ts'ó-èrh* 鹾貳
CH'ING: **Salt Aide,** unofficial reference to a Deputy Salt

Controller (*yün-t'ung*), an Assistant Salt Controller (*yün-fu*), or a Second Assistant Salt Controller (*yün-p'an*).

7026 *ts'ó-jèn* 鹺任
CH'ING: unofficial reference to a **Salt Controller** (*yen-yün shih*).

7027 *ts'ó-shǐh* 鹺使
CH'ING: unofficial reference to a **Salt Controller** (*yen-yün shih*).

7028 *ts'ó-wù* 鹺務
CH'ING: quasi-official reference to the **State Salt Monopoly,** a fragmented enterprise directed by various Salt Controllers (*yen-yün shih*) under supervision of the Ministry of Revenue (*hu-pu*).

7029 *ts'ó-yǐn* 鹺尹
CH'ING: unofficial reference to a **Salt Distribution Commissioner** (*yen-k'o t'i-chü*).

7030 *tsòu-ch'ài* 奏差
YÜAN–CH'ING: **Agent** available for special assignments as needed, particularly as a courier; numerous in Yüan as unranked subofficials both in central government agencies and in units of territorial administration; in Ming and Ch'ing apparently retained solely as a staff member, rank 7a, in the Ducal Establishment (*kung-fu*) in Shantung presided over by the current most direct male descendant of Confucius, ennobled as Duke for Fulfilling the Sage (*yen-sheng kung*). P6, 13, 15, 30, 66, etc.

7031 *tsòu-ché* 奏摺
CH'ING: **Palace Memorial,** a confidential communication to the Emperor from an imperial bondservant (*pao-i*) or other personal agent stationed in the provinces, providing the Emperor with information about local weather, crops, prices, public sentiment, etc., not reliably obtainable through regular bureaucratic channels.

7032 *tsòu-chièn shǎng-kūng àn* 奏薦賞功案
SUNG: **Merit Recommendation Service** in the Ministry of Personnel (*li-pu*), part of the Military Appointments Process (*yu-hsüan*); apparently prepared dossiers on military officers deserving rewards for meritorious service. SP: *service des adresses et des recommandations pour la récompense des mérites des fonctionnaires militaires.*

7033 *tsòu-chièn shǎng-kūng ssū* 奏薦賞功司
SUNG: **Merit Recommendation Office** in the Ministry of Personnel (*li-pu*), part of the Civil Appointments Process (*tso-hsüan*); apparently prepared dossiers on civil officials deserving rewards for meritorious service. SP: *bureau des adresses et des recommandations pour la récompense des mérites des fonctionnaires civils.*

7034 *tsǒu-ch'īng* 走卿
SUNG: lit., traveling minister (?): unofficial reference to the **Chief Minister of the Court of the Imperial Granaries** (*ssu-nung*).

7035 *tsōu-kuǒ kūng* 鄒國公
N-S DIV (Chou)–SUI: **Duke of Tsou,** archaic title conferred on the successive most direct male descendants of Confucius, who presided over the Confucian estate in Shantung; replaced the N. Ch'i title *kung-sheng hou* (Marquis for Revering the Sage), then in 608 was replaced by *shao-sheng hou* (Marquis for Perpetuating the Sage). P66.

7036 *tsòu-mǎ* 趣馬
CHOU: **Horse Trainer,** one ranked as a Junior Serviceman (*hsia-shih*) assigned by the Ministry of War (*hsia-kuan*) for each 12-horse, 3-chariot team in the royal stables; directly subordinate to the Horse Team Supervisor (*yü-fu*) on the staff of the Commandant of the Royal Stud (*hsiao-jen*). CL: *presse-chevaux, écuyer*

7037 *tsǒu-mǎ ch'éng-shòu kūng-shìh*
走馬承受公事
SUNG: **Mounted Courier,** duty assignment for a Circuit (*lu*) official to maintain liaison between the dynastic capital and military commanders on the frontier. SP: *commissaire provincial chargé de la transmission des alertes à la frontière.*

7038 *tsòu-piǎo àn* 奏表案
SUNG: **Memorializing Section,** one of 5 Sections (*an*) in the Left Bureau (*tso-t'ing*) of the Court of Judicial Review (*ta-li ssu*); staffing not clear, but presumably handled the Court's communications to the throne.

7039 *tsōu p'ú-yèh* 騶僕射
HAN: **Supervisor of Grooms,** rank not clear, found on the staffs of some Temples (*miao*) dedicated to imperial ancestors, probably under the supervision of the Chamberlain for the Imperial Stud (*t'ai-p'u*). HB: supervisor of the grooms. P28.

7040 *tsòu-shìh ch'ù* 奏事處
CH'ING: **Office for Provincial Memorials** staffed by personnel of the Imperial Household Department (*nei-wu fu*), divided into one unit for Chinese and Manchu language materials and another for Mongolian materials; received memorials submitted from outside the capital, scanned them for improprieties, and delivered them to the Council of State (*chün-chi ch'u*); supervised by a Grand Minister in Attendance (*yü-ch'ien ta-ch'en*). The Office's functional relationship with the Office of Transmission (*t'ung-cheng shih ssu*) is not clear. BH: chancery of memorials to the emperor.

7041 *tsòu-shìh chūng-sǎn* 奏事中散
N-S DIV (N. Wei): **Courtier for Memorials,** one category of aristocratic Courtiers (see *chung-san*).

7042 *tsòu-shìh kuān* 奏事官
CH'ING: **Memorial Processors,** a generic designation for members of the Imperial Household Department (*nei-wu fu*) assigned to the Office for Provincial Memorials (*tsou-shih ch'u*). BH: chancellors of memorials to the emperor.

7043 *tsòu-shìh lìng* 奏事令
N-S DIV (N. Wei): **Director of the Receipt of Grievances,** rank and organizational affiliation not clear, possibly a temporary duty assignment; traditionally considered a counterpart of the earlier Gate Traffic Control Office (*kung-ch'e ssu-ma men*) and the later Grievance Office (*kung-ch'e shu*).

7044 *tsòu-ts'áo* 奏曹
HAN: **Memorials Section,** one of a dozen or more Sections (*ts'ao*) under the Defender-in-chief (*t'ai-wei*) and probably also the Counselor-in-chief (*ch'eng-hsiang*) in the central government; headed by an Administrator (*yüan-shih*), rank =400 bushels; apparently responsible for preparing the office's submissions to the throne. HB: bureau of memorials.

7045 *tsòu-yèn ts'áo* 奏讞曹
HAN: **Section for Memorials Requesting Judicial Decisions** under the Commandant for Law Enforcement (*t'ing-wei*), headed by an Administrator (*yüan-shih*). HB: bureau of memorials requesting judicial decisions.

7046   *tsòu-yìn* 奏蔭

CHIN: lit., to submit a claim to inheritance: **Official by Inheritance,** a categorical reference to all men who had entered government service (*ch'u-shen*) by virtue of their fathers' official status; a reputable status 2nd in esteem only to that of Metropolitan Graduates (*chin-shih*) in civil service recruitment examinations.

7047   *tsú* 卒

(1) **Soldier,** throughout history a general reference to military men or to others with comparable functions such as policemen and jailors. (2) CHOU: **Company,** a military organization of 100 men under a Head (*chang*) ranked as a Senior Serviceman (*shang-shih*); each Company consisted of 2 Platoons (*liang*), and 5 Companies constituted a Battalion (*lü*). CL: *compagnie*.

7048   *tsú* 族

(1) **Tribe,** throughout history a term by which the Chinese designated cohesive groups of non-Chinese peoples. (2) CHOU, SUI: **Precinct,** a unit of 100 families in local self-government organization of the populace; in Chou a unit in the royal domain headed by a Mentor (*shih*) ranked as a Senior Serviceman (*shang-shih*), in Sui an urban unit with a non-official Head (*chang, cheng*); in Chou responsible to the Ministry of Education (*ti-kuan*) for local defense, reporting data about the census and stored supplies, informing the people about state regulations, etc. CL: *commune*. Cf. *lü* (Functionary, etc.).

7049   *tsŭ-chù* 詛祝

CHOU: **Fulminator,** 2 ranked as Junior Servicemen (*hsia-shih*), members of the Ministry of Rites (*ch'un-kuan*) who apparently offered threatening prayers at oath-taking ceremonies, various court assemblages, ancestral sacrifices, the departure of campaigning armies, etc. CL: *officier des prières faites dans les prestations de serment, invocateur des serments*.

7050   *tsū-hǎi chiàng* 菹醢匠

T'ANG: **Pickler,** 8 non-official specialists, members of the Spice Pantry (*chang-hai shu*) in the Court of Imperial Entertainments (*kuang-lu ssu*); preserved vegetables and fruits for display in ancestral worship and perhaps for consumption at court. RR: *ouvrier pour la fabrication des légumes conservés dans le vinaigre et des hachis*.

7051   *tsú-ī* 族姬

SUNG: official variant from 1113 of *hsien-chu* (**District Princess**).

7052   *tsŭ-kūng* 祖公

MING: lit., honorable grandfather: **Local Authority,** an unofficial, general reference to officials serving in Subprefectures (*chou*) and Districts (*hsien*). See *kung-tsu*.

7053   *tsú-shǐh* 卒史

HAN: **Clerk,** normally ranked at 100 bushels, in numerous Later Han agencies. HB: clerk.

7054   *tsú-shīh* 族師

CHOU: **Precinct Mentor,** ranked as a Senior Serviceman (*shang-shih*) and considered a member of the Ministry of Education (*ti-kuan*); head of 100 families constituting a Precinct (*tsu*) in local self-government organization of the populace. CL: *chef de commune*.

7055   *tsú-tsōu* 卒騶

HAN: **Groom,** unranked subofficials found in various palace stables (*chiu*). HB: groom. P39.

7056   *tsū-yūng shìh* 租庸使

(1) T'ANG: **Special Supply Commissioner,** one or more appointed c. 756, after the outbreak of the An Lu-shan rebellion, to sell off court valuables in the wealthy Huai and Yangtze River basins in exchange for grain for army rations; a duty assignment for Investigating Censors (*chien-ch'a yü-shih*). P60. (2) 5 DYN: **Commissioner for State Revenue,** in Liang and Later T'ang till 926 a special appointee to coordinate all fiscal affairs under central government control; antecedent of later State Finance Commissioners (*san-ssu shih*). P60.

7057   *ts'ù-chìh tí-pièn ssū* 措置糴便司

SUNG: **Office for Arranging Grain Purchases on Credit,** organizational affiliation and specific purpose not clear; possibly a temporary agency created during the central government's withdrawal from North China in the 1120s. SP: *bureau d'organisation de l'achat des grains à crédit*.

7058   *tsuǎn-hsiū kuān* 纂修官 or *tsuan-hsiu*

CH'ING: **Compiler,** varying numbers, usually under a Director-general (*tsung-ts'ai*), found in the imperial publishing organ known as the Hall of Military Glory (*wu-ying tien*), the Military Archive (*fang-lüeh kuan*), the Historiography Institute (*kuo-shih kuan*), and the Ministry of Justice's (*hsing-pu*) Codification Office (*lü-li kuan*); a duty assignment for officials of the Hanlin Academy (*han-lin yüan*) or, in the last case, for regular Ministry of Justice personnel. BH: proof reader, compiler. P13, 23, 37.

7059   *tsuàn-tiěn* 攢典

YÜAN: **Keeper of Accounts,** a lowly or unranked clerk found on the staffs of many storehouses, granaries, and other places of storage.

7060   *tsùi-lì* 罪隸

CHOU: **War Prisoners** who were assigned to hard labor as state slaves under supervision of the Ministry of Justice (*ch'iu-kuan*), perhaps including relatives of convicted criminals who were also made state slaves; divided into 4 categories: Southern War Prisoners (*man-li*), Southeastern War Prisoners (*min-li*), Eastern War Prisoners (*i-li*), and Northeastern War Prisoners (*mo-li*). CL: *criminels condamnés à des travaux ignominieux*.

7061   *tsùi-yào* 最要

CH'ING: **Most Important,** highest of 4 ratings assigned to units of territorial administration from Circuits (*tao*) down to Districts (*hsien*), indicating fulfillment of all 4 qualifications: bustling, complex, exhausting, and difficult; see under *ch'ung-fan-p'i-nan*. BH: most important.

7062   *ts'ùi* 倅

MING–CH'ING: unofficial reference to an **Assistant Prefect** (*t'ung-p'an*). Cf. *chün-i ts'ui, p'in-ts'ui*.

7063   *ts'ūi-chǎng* 催長

CH'ING: **Foreman,** rank 8 or unranked, found on the staffs of various imperial gardens, the Workshop (*tsao-pan ch'u*), the Court of Imperial Armaments (*wu-pei yüan*), the Office of the Imperial Hunt (*tu-yü ssu*), and the Office of Palace Accounts (*k'uai-chi ssu*)—all managed by the Imperial Household Department (*nei-wu fu*). BH: overseer. P37, 40.

7064   *ts'ùi-ch'ē* 倅車

Lit., assistant in the chariot: **Deputy,** from antiquity an unofficial reference to anyone serving in a secondary post in a unit of territorial administration, e.g., as *t'ung-p'an, chang-shih, ssu-ma*.

7065 *ts'ūi-ch'ū̄ àn* 催驅案
SUNG: **Expediting Section,** a unit in the Civil Appointments Process (*tso-hsüan*) of the Ministry of Personnel (*li-pu*); specific functions not clear. SP: *service chargé d'activer les dépêches retardées.*

7066 *ts'ūi-ch'ū̄ fáng* 催驅房
SUNG: **Expediting Office,** one each in the Department of State Affairs (*shang-shu sheng*), the Secretariat (*chung-shu sheng*), and the Outer Chancellery (*men-hsia wai-sheng*); specific functions and staffing not clear; perhaps all created during the withdrawal of the central government from North China in the 1120s for short-lived transitional purposes. SP: *chambre de contrôle pour activer les dépêches retardées.*

7067 *ts'ūi-ch'ū̄ ssū* 催驅司
SUNG: **Storage Monitoring Office,** one of many agencies that served the 3 bureaus that constituted the State Finance Commission (*san ssu*) of early Sung; headed by an Administrative Assistant (*p'an-kuan*), rank 8a or 8b; oversaw the storage of goods by the various agencies in the capital and certified the issuance of salary payments to palace and central government personnel; terminated c. 1080. SP: *bureau chargé d'activer les dépêches retardées ou bureau de contrôle.*

7068 *ts'ùi-èrh* 倅貳
SUNG–CH'ING: **Associate,** a vague generic reference to secondary and lower officials in units of territorial administration, especially from the Prefecture (*chou, fu*) down.

7069 *ts'ùi-huá chiù* 翠華廐
HAN: lit., stable for (horses with) kingfisher-feather adornments, referring to kingfisher-feather banners that escorted a ruler on tour outside his capital: **Stable for Imperial Processions,** presumably a stable supervised by the Chamberlain for the Imperial Stud (*t'ai-p'u*). HB: stables of the imperial banner ornamented with kingfisher's feathers.

7070 *ts'ūi-kāng kuān* 催綱官
SUNG: **Expediter of Shipments,** an ad hoc duty assignment for an official subject to the Superintendency-general of Foundries (*tu-ta t'i-tien k'eng-yeh ssu*); oversaw and expedited the water transport of coins and perhaps other foundry products. SP: *fonctionnaire chargé d'activer les convois.*

7071 *ts'ūi-kāng pō-fā* 催綱撥發
SUNG: **Expediter of Shipment and Distribution,** an ad hoc duty assignment for an official subject to the Superintendency-general of Foundries (*tu-ta t'i-tien k'eng-yeh ssu*); probably a variant of Expediter of Shipments (*ts'ui-kang kuan*). SP: *fonctionnaire chargé d'activer la distribution et l'expédition des convois.*

7072 *ts'ūi-tsǎn yùn-ch'uán* 催趲運船
MING: **Expediter of Canal Transport Boats,** from 1567 the special assignment of an Investigating Censor (*chien-ch'a yü-shih*), to oversee and speed up the organization of state tax grain in the Yangtze delta for shipment north along the Grand Canal; from 1571 to 1578 joined by a Bureau Director (*lang-chung*) of the Ministry of Revenue (*hu-pu*). P18.

7073 *ts'ūi-tsǔng* 催總
CH'ING: **Foreman,** early Ch'ing antecedent of *ts'ui-chang* and *tsung-ling*, qq.v. P37, 40.

7074 *ts'ūn* 村
T'ANG–CH'ING: **Settlement,** a term occasionally used in systems of sub-District (*hsien*) self-government organizations of the populace, especially in rural areas and com-

monly an intermediary unit incorporating several Villages (*li*).

7075 *ts'ūn chǎng-kuān* 村長官
SUNG: **Settlement Head,** unofficial, deprecatory reference to a District Magistrate (*hsien-ling, chih-hsien*).

7076 *ts'ún-fǔ shǐh* 存撫使
T'ANG: **Relief Commissioner,** one of several types of central government officials specially dispatched into the hinterland to cope with region-wide floods or droughts in early T'ang, antecedent to Circuit Commissioners (see under *tao*). RR: *commissaire impérial chargé de secourir et de mettre en ordre une région.* P50.

7077 *tsūng* 宗
CHOU: **Family Unifier,** one of 9 categories of Unifying Agents (*ou*) who represented the Minister of State (*chung-tsai*) as a liaison official between the central government and the Feudal Lords (*chu-hou*); see under *ou*. CL: *ancêtre.*

7078 *tsǔng-chāng* 總章
HAN–N-S DIV (S. Dyn.): **Music Master,** one of several titles granted to directors of court music, often a concurrent title (*chia-kuan*) of the Grand Director of Music (*t'ai-yüeh ling*). P10.

7079 *tsǔng-chèn* 總鎮
CH'ING: unofficial reference to a **Regional Commander** (*tsung-ping*); also see *chen.*

7080 *tsǔng-chēng* 宗正
(1) CH'IN–HAN: **Chamberlain for the Imperial Clan,** one of the Nine Chamberlains (*chiu ch'ing*) in the central government, always a member of the imperial family; in Han ranked at 2,000 bushels; maintained the genealogy of the imperial family and monitored the conduct of imperial relatives. In A.D. 4 retitled *tsung-po*, in Later Han called *tsung-cheng ch'ing.* HB: director of the imperial clan. (2) N-S DIV–SUI: common variant of *tsung-cheng ch'ing* (**Chamberlain for the Imperial Clan**). (3) MING–CH'ING: **Associate Director of the Court of the Imperial Clan** (*tsung-jen fu*), 2 prefixed Left and Right, 2nd executive officials after the Director (*ling*), all ranked 1a and members of the imperial family. BH: assistant controller of the imperial clan court. P1. (4) MING: **Imperial Family Monitor,** rank not clear, in the Wan-li era (1573–1620) one established in each Princely Establishment (*wang-fu*), presumably to provide liaison with the Court of the Imperial Clan at the capital. P69.

7081 *tsūng-chēng ch'īng* 宗正卿
(1) HAN: **Minister for Imperial Clansmen,** in A.D. 5 one ordered established in each Commandery (*chün*) or territorial equivalent to monitor and regulate the conduct of resident imperial clansmen, also to report genealogical data to the Chamberlain for the Imperial Clan (*tsung-cheng*) at the dynastic capital. P1. (2) N-S DIV–SUI: **Chamberlain for the Imperial Clan,** alternating with *tsung-cheng* as the title of one of the Nine Chamberlains (*chiu ch'ing*) of the central government; responsible for maintaining the imperial genealogy and monitoring the conduct of all members of the imperial family; usually an Imperial Prince (*ch'in-wang*), assisted by one or more Vice Ministers (*shao-ch'ing*) and Assistant Ministers (*ch'eng*). P1. (3) T'ANG–SUNG: **Chief Minister** (*ch'ing*) **of the Court of the Imperial Clan** (*tsung-cheng ssu*). RR+SP: *président de la cour des affaires de la famille impériale.* P1. (4) MING–CH'ING: may be encountered as an unofficial reference to the **Director** (*ling*) **of the Court of the Imperial Clan** (*tsung-jen fu*).

7082 *tsūng-chēng fèng-shǐh chàng-àn*
宗正奉使帳案
SUNG: **Accounts Section for Imperial Envoys,** a unit of the Ministry of Rites (*lǐ-pu*); staffing and specific functions not clear. SP: *service des registres des envoyés à l'étranger*.

7083 *tsūng-chēng fǔ* 宗正府
YÜAN: from c. 1311 to 1336, the official variant of *ta tsung-cheng fu* (**High Court of Justice**). P1.

7084 *tsūng-chēng ssū* 宗正司
SUNG: **Office of Imperial Clan Affairs,** 2 branches of the central government's Chief Office of Imperial Clan Affairs (*ta tsung-cheng ssu*); see *hsi-wai tsung-cheng ssu, nan-wai tsung-cheng ssu*. P1.

7085 *tsūng-chēng ssù* 宗正寺
N-S DIV–SUNG: **Court of the Imperial Clan,** one of the Nine Courts (*chiu ssu*) in the central government, responsible for maintaining the imperial genealogy and monitoring activities of all imperial relatives; originated late in the N. Dynasties as the name of the agency headed by the Chamberlain for the Imperial Clan (*tsung-cheng ch'ing*), standardized in T'ang, superseded in Chin by a *ta tsung-cheng fu;* antecedent of the Ming–Ch'ing *tsung-jen fu* (also Court of the Imperial Clan). Staffed principally with imperial relatives, headed by a Chief Minister (*ch'ing*), rank 3a2 in T'ang, 4a in Sung; with one or 2 Vice Ministers (*shao-ch'ing*), 4b1 in T'ang, 5b in Sung; and one or 2 Assistant Ministers (*ch'eng*), 6b1 in T'ang, from 5b to 7b in Sung. In S. Sung there was an identically named branch of the Court in Shao-hsing Prefecture (*fu*), modern Chekiang Province, where displaced clansmen from North China had presumably gathered in large numbers. Also see *tsung-cheng ssu* (Office of Imperial Clan Affairs), *ta tsung-cheng ssu* (Chief Office of Imperial Clan Affairs). RR+SP: *cour des affaires de la famille impériale*. P1.

7086 *tsūng-ch'éng* 宗丞
CH'ING: unofficial reference to an **Assistant Director** (*ch'eng*) **of the Court of the Imperial Clan** (*tsung-jen fu*).

7087 *tsǔng-ch'éng* 總承
CH'ING: abbreviated reference to a **Junior Guardsman-gamekeeper** (*lan-ling tsung-ch'eng*) in the Imperial Game Preserve (*yü niao-ch'iang ch'u*).

7088 *tsǔng chì-shǐh* 總計使
SUNG: **Supreme Commissioner of Accounts,** in 993–994 the central government's chief fiscal officer, supervising 2 regional jurisdictions into which the empire was divided for fiscal purposes, a Left Account (*tso-chi*) and a Right Account (*yu-chi*), in one stage in the development of the State Finance Commission (*san ssu*). SP: *commissaire général des comptes*. P7.

7089 *tsǔng-ch'í* 總旗
MING: **Platoon Commander,** 2 unranked military officers in each Company (*po-hu so*) in the Ming military organization; see *wei-so*.

7090 *tsǔng-chiǎ* 總甲
MING–CH'ING: occasional variant designation of the head of an urban Precinct (*fang*) or Neighborhood (*p'u*), or the equivalent of Fire Captain (*huo-chia*), in sub-District (*hsien*) self-government organization of the populace. P20.

7091 *tsǔng-chiēn* 總監
Supervisor-general: a relatively uncommon title, but especially in Sui and T'ang found in petty posts responsible for stables or pastures under the Court of the Imperial Stud (*t'ai-p'u ssu*). P31, 39.

7092 *tsǔng-chìh* 總制
Regulator-general. (1) SUNG: from 1172 an assignment for an Executive Official (*chih-cheng*) of the central government to coordinate fiscal (water transport?) affairs in a Circuit (*lu*). SP: *directeur des finances*. (2) MING: an early form, used from the late 1400s, of the title given a multi-Province military coordinator, best known as Supreme Commander (*tsung-tu*).

7093 *tsǔng-chìh* 總知
N-S DIV: **Administrator-general,** variant of *chih* (Administrator).

7094 *tsǔng-chīh ch'áo-t'íng lǐ-í*
總知朝廷禮儀
LIAO: **Administrator-general of Court Rituals,** 3rd-tier official under the Ritualist (*ti-lieh-ma-tu*) in the Northern Administration (*pei-mien*) of the central government. P9.

7095 *tsǔng-chīh chūn-kuó shìh* 總知軍國事
LIAO: **Administrator-general of National Affairs,** principal assistant to the Grand Councilors (*tsai-hsiang*), one each in the Northern Administration (*pei-mien*) and the Southern Administration (*nan-mien*) of the central government. P4.

7096 *tsǔng-chìh hó-fáng shǐh* 總治河防使
YÜAN: **Director-general of River Defense,** duty assignment given a Minister of Works (*kung-pu shang-shu*) in 1351, to oversee the repair of flood damage to river and canal embankments in the Shantung-Honan region. Cf. *ho-fang t'i-chü ssu, hsing tu-shui chien*. P59.

7097 *tsǔng-chìh yüàn* 總制院
YÜAN: **Supreme Control Commission** in charge of all Buddhist monks and the administration of some near Central Asian areas, headed by the Mentor of State (*kuo-shih*); established c. 1264, in 1288 reorganized as the Commission for Buddhist and Tibetan Affairs (*hsüan-cheng yüan*). P17.

7098 *tsǔng-ch'īng* 宗卿
SUNG–CH'ING: occasional unofficial reference to a **Chief Minister** (*ch'ing*) or **Director** (*ling*) **of the Court of the Imperial Clan** (*tsung-cheng ssu, tsung-jen fu*), or to a **Minister of Rites** (*lǐ-pu shang-shu*), or to a **Chief Minister** (*ch'ing*) **of the Court of Imperial Sacrifices** (*t'ai-ch'ang ssu*).

7099 *tsǔng-fǔ* 總府
MING: unofficial reference to a multi-Province **Supreme Commander** (*tsung-tu*) or to his office. P50.

7100 *tsǔng-hó* 總河
MING–CH'ING: abbreviation of *ho-tao tsung-tu* (**Director-general of the Grand Canal**). P50, 59.

7101 *tsǔng-hsièn* 宗憲
MING–CH'ING: lit., general controller of the fundamental laws: unofficial reference to a **Censor-in-chief** (*tu yü-shih*). Also see *feng, feng-hsien*.

7102 *tsǔng-hsüeh* 宗學
SUNG: **School for the Imperial Family,** established in 1083 as a unit of the Directorate of Education (*kuo-tzu chien*), later subordinated to the Court of the Imperial Clan (*tsung-cheng ssu*); headed by an eminent member of the central government on duty assignment as Supervisor (*t'i-chü*), together with a representative of the Chief Office of Imperial Clan Affairs (*ta tsung-cheng ssu*) as Director (*cheng*); staffed with one or more Erudites (*po-shih*), one Office Manager (*lu*), etc. SP: *école de la famille impériale*.

7103 *tsŭng-ī* 宗姬
SUNG: official variant from 1113 of *chün-chu* (**Commandery Princess**).

7104 *tsūng-jén* 宗人
(1) CHOU: **Ancestral Intendant,** 2 ranked as Junior Grand Masters (*hsia ta-fu*) and 4 as Ordinary Servicemen (*chung-shih*), members of the Ministry of Rites (*ch'un-kuan*) responsible for the construction of royal tombs; also acted as the spirit of the dead in certain funeral ceremonies. CL: *officier des sépultures.* (2) MING–CH'ING: **Assistant Director of the Court of the Imperial Clan** (*tsung-jen fu*), 2 prefixed Left and Right, rank 1a; normally Imperial Princes (*ch'in-wang*) or other members of the imperial family; technically subordinate to the Director (*ling*) and Associate Directors (*tsung-cheng*) of the Court. BH: director. P1.

7105 *tsūng-jén fŭ* 宗人府
MING–CH'ING: **Court of the Imperial Clan,** counterpart of the traditional *tsung-cheng ssu,* established in 1389 to replace a Yüan-style Office of the Imperial Clan (*t'ai tsung-cheng yüan*); headed by members of the imperial family designated Director (*ling*), Associate Directors (*tsung-cheng*), and Assistant Directors (*tsung-jen*); maintained the imperial genealogy, kept records on births, marriages, deaths, and all other matters pertaining to imperial kinsmen. BH: imperial clan court. P1.

7106 *tsūng-jén lìng* 宗人令
MING–CH'ING: **Director of the Court of the Imperial Clan** (*tsung-jen fu*), rank 1a. P1.

7107 *tsŭng-júng* 總戎
CH'ING: lit., in general charge of martial matters: unofficial reference to a **Regional Commander** (*tsung-ping*).

7108 *tsŭng-k'ó* 總科
MING: **General Section,** one of 5 Sections in the early Ming Ministry of Revenue (*hu-pu*), the other 4 simply being numbered, as Section One (*i-k'o*), Section Two (*erh-k'o*), etc.; headed by 2 Directors (*lang-chung*) with 2 Vice Directors (*yüan-wai lang*); in 1373, in recognition of their heavy load of important business, each of the Sections was authorized a Minister (*shang-shu*) and a Vice Minister (*shih-lang*); then in 1380 the Ministry was reorganized with 4 subordinate Bureaus (*pu*), only to be further reorganized in 1390 with one Bureau (*ch'ing-li ssu*) per Province (*sheng*), named accordingly. P6.

7109 *tsŭng-kuān* 宗官
CHOU: **Ritual Official,** generic reference to personnel of the Ministry of Rites (*ch'un-kuan*).

7110 *tsŭng-kuăn* 總管 or *tsŭng-kuān* 總官
Lit., to be in general charge; the 2nd form is a rare aberration. (1) N-S DIV–CHIN: **Area Commander-in-chief,** originally a common designation of a powerful Regional Governor (*chou mu*) who militarily dominated a cluster of neighboring Regions (*chou*); gradually suppressed by Sui; reinstituted in T'ang as military coordinators in important frontier areas, but in 624 generally retitled *tu-tu;* occasionally revived by Sung and Chin. RR+SP: *commandant en chef.* P49, 50. (2) YÜAN: **Assistant Brigade Commander,** until 1284 the senior aide to a Brigade Commander (*wan-hu*) in the military hierarchy, rank not clear; in 1284 abolished. (3) YÜAN: **Route Commander,** rank 3a or 3b; in collaboration with an Overseer (*ta-lu-hua-ch'ih*), headed a unit of territorial administration called a Route (*lu*), each supervising the governance of about 100,000 residents; for routine administration communicated directly with the Secretariat (*chung-shu sheng*) at the dynastic capital or the Branch (*hsing*) Secretariat to which it was assigned, but was subject to both administrative and surveillance Circuits (*tao*) as well. P50. (4) CH'ING: **Supervisor-in-chief,** a common designation for military officers of rank 3 or 4 assigned to duty at Imperial Mausolea (*ling*), with the Palace Stud (*shang-ssu yüan*), in various palace gardens, etc.; also in units of Mongol tribes. BH: commandant, controller-general. P29, 37, 39. (5) CH'ING: abbreviation of *tsung-kuan nei-wu fu ta-ch'en* (**Grand Minister Supervisor of the Imperial Household Department**). (6) CH'ING: variant reference to a eunuch **Commissioner** (*cheng-shih*) **of the Directorate of Palace Domestic Service** (*kung-tien chien*).

7111 *tsŭng-kuăn ch'iēn-hsiá ssū* 總管鈐轄司
SUNG: **Office of General Military Administration** (?), place in the governmental hierarchy not clear; possibly a jumble or confusing combination of the titles *tsung-kuan* and *ch'ien-hsia,* qq.v. SP: *bureau général d'entraînement, de cantonnement et de défense militaires.*

7112 *tsŭng-kuăn fŭ* 總管府
(1) N-S DIV–CHIN: **Area Command,** the headquarters (also the jurisdiction) of an Area Commander-in-chief (*tsung-kuan*). (2) YÜAN: **Route Command,** the headquarters of a Route Commander (*tsung-kuan*); the jurisdiction was a Route (*lu*). (3) YÜAN: **Supervisorate-in-chief,** an agency headed by a Supervisor-in-chief (*tsung-kuan*); in addition to following entries, see under prefixes.

7113 *tsŭng-kuăn kuān-hsüéh shìh-wù*
總管官學事務
CH'ING: **Supervisor-in-chief of Palace Schools,** designation of members of the Imperial Household Department (*nei-wu fu*) who assisted the Managers of the Palace Schools (*kuan-li kuan-hsüeh shih-wu*) in administering 3 Palace Schools (*kuan-hsüeh*) operated by the Department. BH: superintendent of government (imperial household) schools.

7114 *tsŭng-kuăn liù-k'ù shìh-wù*
總管六庫事務
CH'ING: **Supervisor-in-chief of the Six Storehouses** (*liu k'u*), 2 with nominal status as Bureau Directors (*lang-chung*) of the Ministry of Revenue (*hu-pu*), heads of the Storage Office (*kuang-ch'u ssu*) of the Imperial Household Department (*nei-wu fu*) and the 6 storehouses it controlled (see under *kuang-ch'u ssu*). BH: superintendent of the six imperial storehouses. P37.

7115 *tsŭng-kuăn nèi-wù fŭ tà-ch'én*
總管內務府大臣
CH'ING: **Grand Minister Supervisor of the Imperial Household Department** (*nei-wu fu*), unspecified number, posts occupied by Imperial Princes (*ch'in-wang*) and other Manchu dignitaries; commonly divided among themselves close supervision of the many function-specific agencies spawned by the Department; commonly abbreviated to *tsung-kuan* (Supervisor-in-chief) or *ta-ch'en* (Grand Minister), with agency-name prefixes. BH: minister of the household. P37, 38, 39.

7116 *ısŭng-kuăn ssū* 總管司
SUNG: variant of *tsung-kuan fu* (**Area Command**).

7117 *tsŭng-kuăn tà-ch'én* 總管大臣
CH'ING: abbreviation of *tsung-kuan nei-wu fu ta-ch'en* (**Grand Minister Supervisor of the Imperial Household Department**); see *nei-wu fu.*

7118 *tsǔng-kuǎn t'ài-chiēn* 總管太監
CH'ING: **Eunuch Supervisor-in-chief,** prefix to the titles of senior eunuchs of the Directorate of Palace Domestic Service (*kung-tien chien*), especially including a Supervising Commissioner (*tu-ling shih*), rank 4a, and a Commissioner (*cheng-shih, shih*), 4b. BH: chief eunuch. P38.

7119 *tsǔng-k'ǔn* 總閫
MING–CH'ING: lit., in general charge of the women's quarters (?); relevance not clear: unofficial reference to a multi-Province **Supreme Commander** or **Governor-general** (*tsung-tu*).

7120 *tsūng-kúng* 宗工
CHOU: unofficial reference to a **Minister of Works** (*ssu-k'ung*).

7121 *tsǔng-lǐ* 總理
Superintendent, commonly followed by a function designation or agency name plus *shih-wu* (the affairs of). (1) MING: variant of *tsung-tu* (Supreme Commander). P50. (2) CH'ING: common designation of duty assignments for Grand Ministers (*ta-ch'en*) of the Imperial Household Department (*nei-wu fu*). P37, 38, 39, 40.

7122 *tsūng-lǐ chiēn-wù* 宗理監務
CH'ING: **Superintendent of the Directorate of Astronomy,** from 1745 a special duty assignment for an Imperial Prince (*ch'in-wang*) or another Grand Minister (*ta-ch'en*) of the Imperial Household Department (*nei-wu fu*). P35.

7123 *tsǔng-lǐ ch'īng-hǎi shìh-wù tà-ch'én* 總理青海事務大臣
CH'ING: **Grand Minister Superintendent of Ch'ing-hai,** a Mongol or Manchu, nominally an executive of the Imperial Household Department (*nei-wǔ fu*), with viceregal authority over the Mongol and Tangutan tribes of Ch'ing-hai, based at Hsi-ning; commonly called *pan-shih ta-ch'en*. BH: imperial controller-general.

7124 *tsǔng-lǐ hó-tào* 總理河道
MING: **Superintendent of the Grand Canal,** variant of *ts'ao-yün tsung-tu* (Director-general of Grain Transport); also see *tsung-tu ho-tao, ho-tao tsung-tu*. P59.

7125 *tsǔng-lǐ hó-ts'áo* 總理河漕
MING: **Superintendent of the Grand Canal and of Grain Transport,** a combined duty assignment for a Minister of Works (*kung-pu shang-shu*) briefly from 1587, temporarily substituting for the appointment of a Censor-in-chief (*tu yü-shih*) as Director-general of the Grand Canal (*ho-tao tsung-tu*). P59.

7126 *tsǔng lǐ-í shìh* 總禮儀事
LIAO: **Superintendent of Ceremonies,** 4th-tier official under the Ritualist (*ti-lieh-ma-tu*) in the Northern Administration (*pei-mien*) of the central government. P9.

7127 *tsǔng-lǐ kò-kuó shìh-wù yá-mén* 總理各國事務衙門
CH'ING: **Foreign Office,** from 1861 in charge of China's foreign relations, previously shared by the Court of Colonial Affairs (*li-fan yüan*) and the Ministry of Rites (*lǐ-pu*); headed by one or more Imperial Princes (*ch'in-wang*) and other Grand Ministers (*ta-ch'en*) of the Imperial Household Department (*nei-wu fu*). Commonly abbreviated as *tsung-li ya-men* or as *tsung-shu*. BH: office of foreign affairs.

7128 *tsǔng-lǐ kūng-ch'éng ch'ù* 總理工程處
CH'ING: **Palace Construction Office** in the Imperial Household Department (*nei-wu fu*); responsible for the construction and major maintenance of large palace buildings;

headed by a Grand Minister (*ta-ch'en*) of the Department serving as Superintendent (*tsung-li*). BH: imperial construction office.

7129 *tsǔng-lǐ shìh-wù kuān-chūn shìh* 總理事務冠軍使
CH'ING: **Director,** 2 among the executive officers of the Imperial Procession Guard (*luan-i wei*); members of the Imperial Household Department (*nei-wu fu*) assigned to assist the Grand Minister in Command of the Guard (*chang wei-shih ta-ch'en*) and his principal associates, 2 Commissioners of the Guard (*luan-i shih*). BH: chief marshal.

7130 *tsǔng-lǐ yá-mén* 總理衙門
CH'ING: common abbreviation of *tsung-li ko-kuo shih-wu ya-men* (**Foreign Office**).

7131 *tsǔng-lǐ yén-chèng* 總理鹽政
CH'ING: **Superintendent of Salt Distribution,** a concurrent title given various Governors-general (*tsung-tu*) and Provincial Governors (*hsün-fu*), signifying their authority and responsibility in their jurisdictions to implement and enforce the state monopoly of the distribution of salt through control of local Salt Control Stations (*p'i-yen so*).

7132 *tsǔng-lǐ yüèh-pù tà-ch'én* 總理樂部大臣
CH'ING: **Grand Minister Superintendent of the Music Ministry,** no fixed number, members of the Imperial Household Department (*nei-wu fu*) assigned to oversee the Music Ministry (*yüeh-pu*). BH: director-general of the board of music. P10.

7133 *tsūng-lìng* 宗令
CH'ING: variant of *tsung-jen ling* (**Director of the Court of the Imperial Clan**).

7134 *tsǔng-lǐng* 總領
Lit., general leader or controller. (1) HAN: unofficial reference to a **Chamberlain for Attendants** (*kuang-lu-hsün*). (2) SUNG: **Overseer-general,** duty assignment for an official in an agency of the fiscal hierarchy, normally in charge of collecting and transporting military supplies in a designated area; see under *tsung-ling … ts'ai-fu*. SP: *directeur-général chargé de transport des vivres de l'armée, directeur-général des finances*. (3) CH'ING: **Wing Commander,** 6, rank not clear, leaders of Wings (*i*) in the Tiger Hunting Brigade (*hu-ch'iang ying*). BH: brigadier. (4) CH'ING: **Foreman,** from 1752 to 1759 a title used in the Imperial Parks Administration (*feng-ch'en yüan*), superseding *ts'ui-tsung*, then superseded by *yüan-ch'eng*. P40.

7135 *tsǔng-lǐng fáng* 總領房
SUNG: **Transport Supervision Section,** a subdivision of the Bureau of Military Affairs (*shu-mi yüan*) responsible for administrative liaison between the Bureau and Overseers-general (*tsung-ling*) who coordinated the transport of military supplies to garrisons or field armies as needed, presumably relying on the provision of labor and supplies by Fiscal Commissioners (*chuan-yün shih*) of Circuits (*lu*). Headed by a Vice Recipient of Edicts (*fu ch'eng-chih*), rank 8a. Apparently superseded c. 1074 when the Bureau was reorganized with Twelve Sections (*shih-erh fang*).

7136 *tsǔng-lǐng nèi-wài chiù-mǎ chú* 總領內外廄馬局
LIAO: **Service of the Imperial Stud,** an agency of the Northern Administration (*pei-mien*) in the central government, headed by an Overseer-general (*tsung-ling*); apparently supervised all of the imperial horse herds. The contemporaneous Court of the Imperial Stud (*t'ai-p'u ssu*), an agency of the Southern Administration (*nan-mien*), appar-

ently had responsibility only for horses pastured among the regime's Chinese subjects. P39.

7137   *tsŭng-lĭng ... ts'ái-fù* 總領···財賦
SUNG: **Overseer-general of Revenues** in (place-name insert), a duty assignment at the Circuit (*lu*) level for an official responsible for collecting and transporting military supplies. SP: *directeur général des finances de ....*

7138   *tsŭng-lù* 總錄
N-S DIV: **Chief Overseer** of the Department of State Affairs (*shang-shu sheng*), variant of *lu* (Overseer); a concurrent appointment for a head of the developing Chancellery (*men-hsia sheng*) or Secretariat (*chung-shu sheng*), giving him supervisory authority over the principal administrative organ of the central government.

7139   *tsūng-miào* 宗廟
Ancestral Temple: throughout history a generic term for buildings in which ancestral spirits were honored or worshipped. See *t'ai-miao.* Cf. *ling* and *ling-ch'in* (Imperial Mausoleum). P28.

7140   *tsŭng-míng kuàn* 總明觀
N-S DIV (Sung): **Library for Complete Discernment,** established in 470 as a center of learning attached to the central government and the palace, with a staff of 20 selected Scholars (*hsüeh-shih*) apparently admitted by an Examiner (*fang-chü*) and supervised by the Chancellor of the Eastern Library (*tung-kuan chi-chiu*); organized in 5 Divisions (*pu*), one each for the study of Confucianism, Taoism, literature, history, and protoscience (*yin-yang*). One of the early antecedents of such famous state-sponsored institutions as the Hanlin Academy (*han-lin yüan*). P23.

7141   *tsŭng-mù* 總目
LIAO: **Supervisor-general,** designation of heads of some regional Tax Offices (*ch'ien-po ssu*). P52.

7142   *tsŭng-nŭ* 宗女
CH'ING: **Imperial Clanswoman,** official designation of daughters of nobles titled *pei-tzu, chen-kuo kung,* and *fu-kuo kung* by secondary wives. BH: daughter of a prince of the blood of rank below the 6th.

7143   *tsŭng-pă* 總把
YÜAN: **Assistant Battalion Commander,** until 1284 the senior aide to a Battalion Commander (*ch'ien-hu*) in the military hierarchy, rank not clear; in 1284 abolished.

7144   *tsŭng-pàn* 總辦
CH'ING: **Administrator,** designation of the head of an ad hoc, temporary agency established to deal with a specific problem; especially used in very late Ch'ing. BH: chief, senior secretary.

7145   *tsŭng-pàn láng-chūng* 總辦郎中
CH'ING: **Administrative Director,** 2, rank 5a, in charge of the Silver Vault (*yin-k'u*), with the special designation Managers of the Silver Vault (*kuan-li yin-k'u shih-wu*).

7146   *tsŭng-pīng kuān* 總兵官 or *tsung-pīng*
Regional Commander, military head of a territorial jurisdiction generically called a Defense Command (*chen*). (1) MING: an indefinite-tenure duty assignment, originally for eminent nobles and military Commissioners-in-chief (*tu-tu*), then during most of the dynasty for somewhat less eminent military officers, and in late Ming for civil officials and even eunuchs in ever larger numbers. In the mature Ming system, one assigned to each Province and one to each of the 9 Defense Commands created along the northern frontier, each normally supervising all military units in his ju-

risdiction with the help of Regional Vice Commanders (*fu tsung-ping kuan*), Assistant Regional Commanders (*ts'an-chiang*), and many varieties of local commanders; but under the authority of the appropriate civil service Grand Coordinators (*hsün-fu*) and Supreme Commanders (*tsung-tu*) as well as the Chief Military Commissions (*tu-tu fu*) and the Ministry of War (*ping-pu*) in the dynastic capital. (2) CH'ING: a regular position (*kuan*), rank 2a, in the Chinese military forces called the Green Standards (*lu-ying*); from 2 to 7 per Province, somewhat comparable to civil service Circuit Intendants (*tao-t'ai*); subordinate to Provincial Military Commanders (*t'i-tu*) and Provincial Governors (*hsün-fu*); each oversaw lesser officers and Green Standards garrisons in his jurisdiction. BH: brigade general. P57.

7147   *tsūng-pó* 宗伯
Lit., clansman Earl, or senior ceremonialist. (1) CHOU: variant reference to the *ta tsung-po* (**Minister of Rites**); also a collective reference to both the Minister of Rites and his Vice Minister (*hsiao tsung-po*). (2) HAN: from A.D. 4 to 25, the official variant of *tsung-cheng* (**Chamberlain for the Imperial Clan**). HB: elder of the imperial clan. P1. (3) N-S DIV–CH'ING: common unofficial reference to a **Chief Minister** (*ch'ing*) or **Director** (*ling*) **of the Court of the Imperial Clan** (*tsung-cheng ssu, tsung-jen fu*). (4) CH'ING: unofficial reference to the **Chief Minister** (*ch'ing*) **of the Court of Imperial Sacrifices** (*t'ai-ch'ang ssu*).

7148   *tsŭng-pù* 總部
MING: **General Bureau,** one of 3 or 4 major subsections in each of the early Ming Ministries (*pu;* see *liu pu*), each headed by a Director (*lang-chung*); all were gradually renamed in the 1380s and 1390s. P5, 6, 9, 12, 13, 15.

7149   *tsŭng-shèng hóu* 宗聖侯
N-S DIV (San-kuo Wei): **Marquis for Reverencing the Sage,** title of nobility (*chüeh*) awarded to each successive most direct male descendant of Confucius, responsible for presiding over the Confucian estate and temple in modern Shantung; granted the tax income from 100 households as emolument. See *pao-ch'eng hou, feng-sheng hou, ch'ung-sheng hou, kung-sheng hou, yen-sheng kung*. P66.

7150   *tsūng-shìh* 宗室
Imperial Clan: from antiquity the most common reference to the ruler's kinsmen, collectively and individually.

7151   *tsūng-shīh* 宗師
Monitor of Imperial Kinsmen. (1) HAN–N-S DIV (Chin): one ordered established in A.D. 5 in each Commandery (*chün*) and Princedom (*wang-kuo*), chosen from among resident members of the imperial clan; responsible for supervising the conduct of his kinsmen and reporting regularly to the Chamberlain for the Imperial Clan (*tsung-cheng, tsung-po*) in the central government all relevant data such as births, marriages, and deaths. Apparently terminated after the reign of Wang Mang if not earlier, then in 277 revived by Chin for the same purposes. HB: master of the imperial clan. (2) N-S DIV (Chou): a subordinate of the Grand Minister of State (*ta chung-tsai*), ranked as an Ordinary Grand Master (*chung ta-fu*; 5a); maintained the imperial genealogy, encouraged imperial clansmen toward proper behavior, etc.; a counterpart of the Court of the Imperial Clan (*tsung-cheng ssu, tsung-jen fu*) in other times. (3) T'ANG: briefly established as a subordinate in the Court of the Imperial Clan (*tsung-cheng ssu*) in 619; number, rank, and function not clear. RR: *maître de la cour des affaires de la famille impériale.* P1. (4) CH'ING: a fancy, unofficial reference to a Provincial Education Commissioner (*t'i-tu hsüeh-cheng*).

7152 *tsŭng-shìh kŭng* 宗室公
CH'ING: **Duke of the Imperial Clan,** a title of nobility (*chüeh*) awarded in perpetuity to Manchus descended in a direct line of inheritance from the dynastic founder, Nurhachi, as distinguished from Duke of the Collateral Line (*chüeh-lo kung*), awarded to heirs collaterally descended from Nurhachi, and Duke of the Eight Banners (*pa-ch'i kung*), awarded in perpetuity for great military merit.

7153 *tsŭng-shìh shìh-wèi* 宗室侍衛
CH'ING: **Imperial Clansmen Guards,** variant designation of the Imperial Clansmen Guards of the Three (Superior) Banners (*san-ch'i tsung-shih shih-wei*). BH: imperial clansmen corps of the imperial body-guard⌐

7154 *tsŭng-shŭ* 總署
CH'ING: common abbreviation of *tsung-li ko-kuo shih-wu ya-men* (**Foreign Office**).

7155 *tsŭng-tiĕn ch'ŭn-mù shĭh ssū* 總典羣牧使司
LIAO: **Chief Commission for Pasturages,** status in the governmental hierarchy not clear, but subordinate to the Court of the Imperial Stud (*t'ai-p'u ssu*) in the Southern Administration (*nan-mien*) of the central government; probably an intermediary agency below the Route (*lu*) level, directly subordinate to Commissioners of Herds (*ch'ün-mu shih*) of the various Routes. P18, 31.

7156 *tsŭng-ts'ái* 總裁
SUNG–CH'ING: **Director-general,** duty assignment for an eminent official to preside over an editorial project, a recruitment examination, a school, or the like. E.g., in Ch'ing used for the head of the Military Archive (*fang-lüeh kuan*), the Historiography Institute (*kuo-shih kuan*), and the Codification Office (*lü-li kuan*). Also see *ta tsung-ts'ai.* BH: director-general, director, reviser, president. P13, 23, 37.

7157 *tsŭng-tsuăn* 總纂
CH'ING: **Compiler-in-chief,** 4 Manchus and 6 Chinese on the staff of the Historiography Institute (*kuo-shih kuan*). BH: reviser.

7158 *tsŭng-tū* 總督
Lit., to be generally in charge; from Former Han on, occurs in a verbal sense and at times, especially in Ming and Ch'ing, as part of a verb–object title; see following entries. (1) MING: **Supreme Commander,** special duty assignment for a Minister (*shang-shu*) or Vice Minister (*shih-lang*) of the Ministry of War (*ping-pu*), normally with concurrent status as an executive official of the Censorate (*tu ch'a-yüan*), delegated to deal with military problems in a region overlapping regular provincial (*sheng*) jurisdictions; or delegated to supervise a multi-Province government enterprise such as the transport of tax grain from the Yangtze delta to North China (see *ts'ao-yün tsung-tu*). Originating in 1452 with the delegation of a Censor-in-chief (*tu yü-shih*) to supervise military operations in Kwangtung and Kwangsi, became steadily more common during the later 1400s and in the 1500s was standard throughout most of the country, the Supreme Commander becoming a long-term resident supervisor of Grand Coordinators (*hsün-fu*) in regional clusters of 2 or more Provinces. In the normal case, the Supreme Commander was himself Grand Coordinator of one of the Provinces under his supervision, which numbered as many as 5. Although he established a headquarters (see *k'ai-fu*), he was not authorized any official assistants; to the end of the dynasty, no matter how influential and powerful he was in fact, his status in the governmental hierarchy remained that of an ad hoc trouble-shooter with responsibilities and powers specified in each case. Late Ming Supreme Commanders began the practice of hiring non-official specialists as their personal aides in what came to be known as Private Secretariats (*mu-fu*). (2) CH'ING: **Governor-general,** an outgrowth of the Ming system, now a regular post (*kuan*) in the governmental hierarchy, rank 2a, being automatically a nominal concurrent Censor-in-chief (*tu yü-shih*) and sometimes also concurrent Minister of War (*ping-pu shang-shu*), in which case his rank rose to 1b; overall supervisor of both military and non-military affairs in a group of 2 or more neighboring Provinces, for one of which he normally served also as Governor (*hsün-fu*). In the mature Ch'ing system there were 9 such posts: one each for Chihli and Szechwan, combining Governorships; one for the 3 Manchurian Provinces of Fengtien, Kirin, and Heilungkiang combining the Governorship of Fengtien; one for Fukien and Chekiang combining the Governorship of Fukien; one for Hupei and Hunan combining the Governorship of Hupei; one for Shensi, Kansu, and eventually Sinkiang combining the Governorship of Kansu; one for Kwangtung and Kwangsi combining the Governorship of Kwangtung; one for Yunnan and Kweichow combining the Governorship of Yunnan; and one for Kiangsu, Kiangsi, and Anhwei without a combined Governorship. As in the case of his Ming predecessor, the Governor-general had no authorized official assistants; such agencies as Provincial Administration Commissions (*ch'eng-hsüan pu-cheng shih ssu*) and Provincial Surveillance Commissions (*t'i-hsing an-ch'a shih ssu*) provided principal administrative support for both Governors and Governors-general. However, Governors-general came to rely heavily on Private Secretariats (*mu-fu*), which gained quasiofficial status. P50.

7159 *tsŭng-tū hó-tào* 總督河道
Director-general of the Grand Canal. (1) MING: variant designation of the Director-general of Canal Transport (*ts'ao-yün tsung-tu*). (2) CH'ING: common transposition of *ho-tao tsung-tu.*

7160 *tsŭng-tū liáng-ch'ú* 總督糧儲
MING: **Director-general of Supplies** at the auxiliary capital, Nanking; duty assignment for a Vice Minister (*shih-lang*) of the Nanking Ministry of Revenue (*nan-ching hu-pu*), concurrently a Censor-in-chief (*tu yü-shih*), with overall supervisory responsibility for the reception and storage of tax grains at Nanking. P49.

7161 *tsŭng-tū ts'āng-ch'áng* 總督倉場
MING–CH'ING: **Director-general of the Capital Granaries,** duty assignment for a Minister of Revenue (*hu-pu shang-shu*) in Ming, for one Manchu and one Chinese Vice Minister of Revenue (*hu-pu shih-lang*) in Ch'ing; see under *ts'ang-ch'ang.* P8.

7162 *tsŭng-tū ts'áo-yùn* 總督漕運
MING–CH'ING: variant of *ts'ao-yün tsung-tu* (**Director-general of Grain Transport**).

7163 *tsŭng-t'ŭng* 總統
CH'ING: **Commander-general,** a distinguished duty assignment, normally for an Imperial Prince (*ch'in-wang*) or another noble, to head a special unit of the Eight Banners (*pa-ch'i*) military system made up of personnel of the Inner Banners (*nei-ch'i*) stationed at the dynastic capital, especially the Guards Brigade (*hu-chün ying*), the Vanguard Brigade (*ch'ien-feng ying*), the Firearms Brigade (*huo-ch'i ying*), or the Scouting Brigade (*chien-jui ying*). BH: general commandant.

7164 *tsŭng-tzŭ chēng* 宗子正

SUNG: **Provost of the School for the Imperial Family,** from 1102 a duty assignment for an imperial clansman to monitor the scholastic achievements of students in the School for the Imperial Family (*tsung-hsüeh*). SP: *chargé d'exécuter les règlements scolaires des fils de la famille impériale.*

7165 *tsūng-tzŭ hsüéh* 宗子學

SUNG: variant of *tsung-hsüeh* (**School for the Imperial Family**).

7166 *tsūng-wèi shuài-fŭ* 宗衛率府

SUI–T'ANG: **Clan Defense Guard Command,** 2 prefixed Left and Right, military units assigned to the establishment of the Heir Apparent; renamed Armed Attendants Guard Command (*wu-shih shuai-fu*) from c. 605 to 622, then Protective Guard Command (*ssu-yü shuai-fu*) from 662 to 705 and again from 711 on. P26.

7167 *tsŭng-yéh* 總爺

CH'ING: unofficial reference to a **Company Commander** (*ch'ien-tsung*) in the Chinese military forces called the Green Standards (*lu-ying*).

7168 *ts'úng* 從

N-S DIV–CH'ING: **Lower Class,** a subgrade of an official rank (*p'in*), in contrast to Upper Class (*cheng*); prefixed to a numeral. E.g., whereas *cheng-san p'in* means rank 3 upper class (here rendered 3a), *ts'ung-san p'in* means rank 3 lower class (here rendered 3b).

7169 *ts'úng-chēng* 從征

MING: lit., to follow along on a military expedition: **Old Campaigner,** a major category of hereditary soldiers in the regular military establishment, signifying those who early joined the forces of the Ming founder, or their descendants in service.

7170 *ts'úng-chèng láng* 從政郎

SUNG: **Gentleman for Governmental Participation,** prestige title (*san-kuan*) for rank 8b civil officials from c. 1117, superseding Gentleman for Thorough Service (*t'ung-shih lang*). P68.

7171 *ts'úng-ch'éng* 從丞

HAN: **Attendant Assistant,** a eunuch aide to the Director of Imperial Gatekeepers (*huang-men ling*) whose responsibility was to assure that the Emperor's private needs were always met only by eunuchs. HB: attendant assistant.

7172 *ts'úng chūn-shìh* 從軍士

Military Escort: common designation of members of the retinue of a traveling official.

7173 *ts'úng-ì àn* 從義案

SUNG: **Section for Rectitude** in the Bureau of Evaluations (*k'ao-kung ssu*) in the Ministry of Personnel (*li-pu*); staffing and specific functions not clear.

7174 *ts'úng-ì láng* 從義郎

SUNG: **Gentleman for Loyal Service,** from c. 1117 a prestige title (*san-kuan*) for civil officials of rank 8b.

7175 *ts'úng-kuān* 從官

Supporting Official: throughout history a categorical reference to petty personnel subordinate to whatever superior is indicated by the context, rather than an official title.

7176 *ts'úng-shìh* 從事

HAN–SUI: **Retainer,** unranked suboffical found on the staffs of various dignitaries of the central government such as the Han Metropolitan Commandant (*ssu-li hsiao-wei*) and especially those in units of territorial administration, most particularly Regional Inspectors (*tz'u-shih*); commonly headed the clerical Sections (*ts'ao*) among which staff members were distributed; terminated with the abolition of Regional Inspectors by Sui. Often preceded by a function-specifying prefix, e.g., *chi-chiu ts'ung-shih* (Libationer Retainer). HB: attendant. P32, 50, 52, 69.

7177 *ts'úng-shìh láng* 從事郎

SUNG: **Gentleman for Attendance,** from 1080 a prestige title (*san-kuan*) for civil officials of rank 8b. P68.

7178 *ts'úng-shìh láng* 從仕郎

CHIN–MING: **Gentleman for Service,** prestige title (*san-kuan*) for civil officials of rank 8b in Chin, 7b in Yüan and Ming; in Ming could be promoted to Gentleman for Summoning (*cheng-shih lang*) without a change of rank. P68.

7179 *ts'úng-shìh shǐh* 從事史

HAN–SUI: **Retainer Clerk,** common variant of *ts'ung-shih* (Retainer). HB: attendant clerk. P50, 52.

7180 *tū* 督

Supervisor: throughout imperial history a duty assignment for an eminent official, most commonly signifying that, without giving up his regular post (*kuan*), an official had been delegated to take temporary charge of another post; occasionally occurs as the title of a regular military post in lowly units of territorial administration.

7181 *tū* 都

(1) **Chief:** throughout history a prefix attached to titles or agency names to identify the superior in a group, commonly, of identically named offices, e.g., *tu yü-shih* (Censor-in-chief). (2) **Capital:** throughout history alternated with *ching* as the most common designation of a dynastic capital, normally with a geographic or hierarchic prefix, e.g., Tung-tu (Eastern Capital), Shang-tu (Supreme Capital). (3) CHOU: **Inherited Region,** generic reference to those Regions (*kuo*) into which the royal domain was divided that were hereditary fiefs of members of the royal family, in contrast to those that were administered by official delegates from the court (see *chia*); each supervised by 2 Justiciars of the Inherited Region (*tu-shih*), ranking as Ordinary Servicemen (*chung-shih*), who reported on all judicial matters to Justiciars of the Domain (*fang-shih*) in the Ministry of Justice (*ch'iu-kuan*). Cf. *chia-shih*. CL: *apanage*. (4) T'ANG: **Area Command,** from 881 the generic designation of 54 military units grouped geographically under the Ten Armies (*shih chün*) that constituted the New Army of Inspired Strategy (*shen-ts'e hsin-chün;* see *shen-ts'e chün*). RR: *groupe*. P43. (5) SUNG: **Troop,** a unit of 100 cavalrymen in the Metropolitan Cavalry Command (*ma-chün ssu;* cf. *shih-wei ch'in-chün ma-pu ssu*). SP: *troupe de cent soldats*. (6) SUNG, MING–CH'ING: **Sector,** a relatively uncommon designation for a unit of sub-District (*hsien*) organization of the populace, with regional as well as temporal variations in usage; in S. Sung a regional variant of *pao* (Security Group); in Ming–Ch'ing a regional variant of *fang* (Precinct) but also found as a customary designation of a rural territory including several Villages (*li*).

7182 *tū ch'á-ch'áng* 都茶場

SUNG: **Chief Tea Market,** several established in important tea-producing areas by the Department of State Affairs (*shang-shu sheng*), each headed by a delegated Controller (*t'i-hsia kuan*); issued certificates that authorized merchants to buy state-monopolized tea. SP: *administration des bons de thé, aire du thé.*

7183 tū ch'á-yüàn 都察院

MING–CH'ING: lit., chief surveillance bureau: **Censorate,** one of the major agencies of the central government, responsible directly to the Emperor for maintaining disciplinary surveillance over the entire officialdom, auditing fiscal accounts, checking judicial records, making regular and irregular inspections, impeaching officials for misconduct, recommending new policies and changes in old policies, etc.; counterpart of the earlier *yü-shih t'ai.* Created in 1382 after the early Ming *yü-shih t'ai* in traditional form had been stripped of all its executive posts in 1380, leaving only a *ch'a-yüan* (Investigation Bureau) staffed with Investigating Censors (*chien-ch'a yü-shih*), whose rank of 7a was soon dropped to 9a. In 1382 the Investigating Censors were reorganized into administrative groups called Circuits (*tao*), one for each Province bearing the provincial name as a prefix, each with 3, 4, or 5 Investigating Censors; and the whole aggregation was called Chief Surveillance Bureau and headed by 8 Chief Investigating Censors (*chien-ch'a tu yü-shih*), rank 7a. Further reorganizations in 1383 and 1384 brought the *tu ch'a-yüan* to its mature Ming form, with an executive staff of 2 Censors-in-chief (*tu yü-shih*), rank 2a, 2 Vice Censors-in-chief (*fu tu yü-shih*), 3a, and 4 Assistant Censors-in-chief (*ch'ien tu yü-shih*), 4a. The headquarters support agencies included a Registry (*ching-li ssu*), a General Services Office (*ssu-wu t'ing*), a Records Office (*chao-mo ssu*), and a Prison (*ssu-yü ssu*). Principal operational agents of the Censorate remained Investigating Censors (*chien-ch'a yü-shih*), restored to rank 7a, distributed among the Province-named Circuits, from 7 to 11 per Circuit, totaling 110 in the mature Ming structure. From 1421 to the end of Ming, a skeletal Censorate also existed among the agencies at Nanking, the auxiliary capital. The Censorate shared with the Ministry of Justice (*hsing-pu*) and the Court of Judicial Review (*ta-li ssu*) the collective designation Three Judicial Offices (*san fa-ssu*). The principal, Vice, and Assistant Censors-in-chief were among the most eminent dignitaries of the central government, and their titles came to be awarded also, as concurrent titles, to the provincial authorities called Grand Coordinators (*hsün-fu*) and Supreme Commanders (*tsung-tu*). Investigating Censors, while being under the general administrative jurisdiction of the various Censors-in-chief, were formally identified only with their Circuits, not as members of the Censorate; they reported individually to the Emperor and were popularly known as his "ears and eyes" (*t'ien-tzu erh-mu*); they were given a great variety of specialized duty assignments, most notably as Province-level Regional Inspectors (*hsün-an yü-shih*). Investigating Censors and independent Supervising Secretaries (*chi-shih-chung*) organized in Six Offices of Scrutiny (*liu k'o*) often collaborated on special investigatory missions and were commonly referred to by such collective designations as *k'o-tao* (Offices of Scrutiny and Circuits). Ch'ing in general perpetuated the Ming Censorate's pattern of organization and responsibilities but eliminated Assistant Censors-in-chief, reduced the number of Investigating Censors to 2 to 4 per Province-named Circuit, in 1661 terminated duty assignments as Regional Inspectors, in 1723 formally incorporated the Six Offices of Scrutiny into the Censorate, and made the Censorate the only agency of government in which Manchus and Chinese were appointed in exactly equal numbers to all principal posts—the executive offices, Investigating Censors, and Supervising Censors (a better rendering for post-1723 Supervising Secretaries). BH: censorate. P18.

7184 tú-chàn aò-t'oú 獨占鰲頭

SUNG–CH'ING: lit., to have taken a position alone atop the head of the leviathan that in mythology supports the earth: unofficial reference to the first-place passer of a major civil service recruitment examination, especially from Sung on the Palace Examination (*t'ing-shih, tien-shih*); i.e., **Principal Graduate** (*chuang-yüan*). Cf. *chan ao-t'ou.*

7185 tū chèn-fǔ ssū 都鎮撫司

MING: **Chief Prison** in the predynastic military structure; created in 1364 under the Chief Military Commission (*ta tu-tu fu*), headed by a Chief Judge (*tu chen-fu*), rank 5a; apparently terminated before 1368. P4.

7186 tū ch'éng-chǐh 都承旨

Chief Recipient of Edicts. (1) SUNG: one, rank 5a, in the Bureau of Military Affairs (*shu-mi yüan*); cf. *shu-mi ch'eng-chih.* SP: *transmetteur général des directives.* (2) LIAO: one, rank not clear, in the Southern Establishment (*nan-yüan*) in the Northern Administration (*pei-mien*) of the central government; apparently as in Sung a member of the Bureau of Military Affairs. P5.

7187 tú-ch'éng mì-mìng 獨承密命

T'ANG: **Sole Recipient of Secret Orders,** duty assignment for a regular member of the central government, a common stepping-stone to status as a Grand Councilor (*tsai-hsiang*). Apparently singled out to receive the Emperor's most important orders for distribution to central government agencies as directed.

7188 tū-ch'éng t'í-chǔ ssū 都城提舉司

CHIN: **Construction and Maintenance Office** in the Ministry of Works (*kung-pu*), responsible for building and repairing governmental offices, temples, etc., planting trees, and supervising government carpenters in the dynastic capital; headed by a Supervisor (*t'i-chü*), rank 6b; principal subordinates included 2 Capital Township Officials (*hsiang-kuan*) who managed conscripted laborers, 2 Monitors (*shou-chi kuan*) who received and distributed materials, and the Director (*ling*) of the Pottery Office (*chen-kuan shu*). Commonly abbreviated to *tu-ch'eng so.* P15.

7189 tū chǐ-shìh-chūng 都給事中

MING–CH'ING: **Chief Supervising Secretary,** rank 7a, the designated administrative leader of the Supervising Secretaries (*chi-shih-chung*) in each of the Six Offices of Scrutiny (*liu-k'o*); from 1391 to c. 1399 demoted to 8a; one in Ming, one each Manchu and Chinese in Ch'ing 'ill 1665, then abolished when each Office of Scrutiny was reduced to a staff of 2 Supervising Secretaries; replaced in 1666 with 2 Seal-holding (*chang-yin*) Supervising Secretaries as heads of each Office of Scrutiny. P18, 19.

7190 tū-chiàng chūng-láng 都匠中郎

N-S DIV (Chin): **Palace Attendant for Capital Craftsmen,** a post in a Princely Establishment (*wang-fu*). P60.

7191 tū chiào-lièn shǐh 都教練使

SUNG: **Chief Training Commissioner,** a post at the Prefecture (*chou*) level; status and functions not clear, but probably supervised militia training. SP: *instructeur général.*

7192 tū-chiēn 都監

T'ANG–YÜAN: **Director-in-chief.** (1) T'ANG, CHIN: a common eunuch title comparable to the Ming–Ch'ing title *t'ai-chien.* In late T'ang especially associated with the powerful palace eunuchs who dominated the Emperors and the imperial armies and struggled with regional authorities for control of the empire; sometimes exalted to *tu tu-chien* (Chief

Director-in-chief). In Chin especially concentrated in the Court Ceremonial Institute (*hsüan-hui yüan*). (2) From Sung on found in many agencies of both civil and military services, e.g., on the staffs of Supply Commissioners (*fa-yün shih*), Herds Offices (*ch'ün-mu ssu*), and Imperial Mausolea (*ling*) in Sung and Salt Commissions (*yen-shih ssu*) in Chin; normally lowly administrative or clerical personnel equivalent to office managers or chief clerks, often rank 9. (3) SUNG: also a common abbreviated reference to *ping-ma tu-chien* (Military Director-in-chief). (4) CHIN–YÜAN: hereditary specialists in charge of the Imperial Dispensary (*yü-yao yüan, yü-yao chien*), rank 9a.

7193 *tū chiěn-chēng* 都檢正
SUNG: **Chief Examiner,** one appointed c. 1068 as coordinator of the Examiners (*chien-cheng*) who headed the Five Offices (*wu fang*) into which the Secretariat (*chung-shu sheng*) was subdivided for routine administrative purposes; apparently a special duty assignment for an official of another central government agency. Such appointments seem to have been discontinued very quickly. SP: *contrôleur en chef.* P3.

7194 *tù-chīh* 度支
N-S DIV (San-kuo Wei)–T'ANG: lit., to measure and disburse: **Revenue Section** or **Ministry of Revenue,** from the 220s an important unit in the developing Department of State Affairs (*shang-shu sheng*), headed by one or more Ministers (*shang-shu*) and Vice Ministers (*lang-chung, lang*); generally responsible for managing state revenues other than land taxes and for the general state budget. Unlike some of its counterparts, only rarely suffixed *ts'ao* (Section) or *pu* (Ministry). By N. Wei presided over subsections identified by the title-prefixes of the Vice Ministers responsible for them: General Accounts (also *tu-chih*), Granaries (*ts'ang-pu*), Census (*tso-min*), Revenue (*yu-min*), Treasury (*chin-pu*), and Storehouse (*k'u-pu*). In Sui c. 583 the name *tu-chih* was changed to *min-pu* (Ministry of Revenue), but it was briefly revived in T'ang from 656 to 662. The name is easily confused with that of the Ministry's identically named subsection (see above), which from T'ang on was formally named *tu-chih ssu* (Bureau of General Accounts). P6.

7195 *tū-chīh* 都知
SUNG: **Office Manager,** normally rank 6a, found in a few eunuch and military agencies. SP: *intendant, administrateur général.*

7196 *tù-chīh àn* 度支案
SUNG: **Tax Section,** apparently originated as a subsidiary of the Tax Bureau (*tu-chih ssu*), one of the 3 agencies constituting the State Finance Commission (*san ssu*) of early Sung; then in 1005 reportedly merged with the Military Section (*ping-an*) of the Salt and Iron Monopoly Bureau (*yen-t'ieh ssu*) into a new Justice Section (*hsing-an*) subordinate jointly to the Tax Bureau and the Census Bureau (*hu-pu ssu; cf. hu-pu*), also a constituent unit of the State Finance Commission; subsequent history not clear, but in the 1080s transformed into the Tax Bureau (also *tu-chih ssu*) in the Ministry of Revenue (*hu-pu*). SP: *service des revenus publics.*

7197 *tù-chīh chiēn* 度支監
YÜAN: **Directorate for Animal Fodder,** an agency of the central government; hierarchical status and staffing not clear.

7198 *tū-chīh chiēn* 都知監
MING–CH'ING: **Directorate for Intimate Attendance,** one of 12 major Directorates (*chien*) in which palace eunuchs were organized; headed by a eunuch Director (*t'ai-chien*); originally responsible for communications among the palace Directorates, but in the 1440s gradually became a group of eunuch escorts for the Emperor's carriage. In Ch'ing existed only from 1656 to 1661; see under *shih-erh chien* (Twelve Directorates).

7199 *tū chǐh-hūi shǐh* 都指揮使
(1) SUNG: **Commander-in-chief,** a standard title for a military officer assigned to lead a campaigning Army (*chün*), an Army of the Provincial Armies (*hsiang-ping*), or any of the military units at the dynastic capital known collectively as the Two Commands (*erh ssu*) and the Three Capital Guards (*san wei*). The title was also sometimes awarded to chieftains of submissive southwestern aboriginal tribes. SP: *commandant général, commissaire général, commissaire en chef, commissaire-commandant.* (2) YÜAN: **Chief Military Commissioner,** duty assignment for Mongol nobles commanding units of the Imperial Guards (*shih-wei*) at the dynastic capital, or in posts of comparable importance. (3) MING: **Regional Military Commissioner,** rank 3a, one appointed for each Province (*sheng*) and additionally for each crucial zone along the northern frontier where general administration was almost entirely in military hands; an important member of the regular military hierarchy, controlling all resident military personnel in his jurisdiction, under the supervision of one of the Chief Military Commissions (*tu-tu fu*) at the dynastic capital and, from the 1440s, of a Province-level Grand Coordinator (*hsün-fu*) and a multi-Province Supreme Commander (*tsung-tu*). Shared with Provincial Administration Commissioners (*pu-cheng shih*) and Provincial Surveillance Commissioners (*an-ch'a shih*) the collective designation Three Provincial Offices (*san ssu*). His principal subordinates were a Vice Commissioner (*t'ung-chih*), rank 2b, and an Assistant Commissioner (*ch'ien-shih*), 3a; his administrative staff included a Registry (*ching-li ssu*), a Judicial Office (*tuan-shih ssu*), and a Prison Office (*ssu-yü ssu*). P56.

7200 *tū chǐh-hūi shǐh ssū* 都指揮使司
Lit., office of a *tu chih-hui shih.* (1) YÜAN: **Chief Military Commission.** (2) MING: **Regional Military Commission,** commonly abbreviated to *tu-ssu.*

7201 *tù-chīh k'ō* 度支科
MING: **General Accounts Section,** one of 4 clerical subdivisions of each Bureau (*pu*, then *ch'ing-li ssu*) into which the Ministry of Revenue (*hu-pu*) was divided from the 1390s. See *min-k'o, chin-k'o, ts'ang-k'o.*

7202 *tù-chīh láng-chūng* 度支郎中 or *tu-chih lang*
(1) N-S DIV–SUI: **Vice Minister of Revenue,** one or more principal assistants to the Minister (*shang-shu*) of the important fiscal agency known simply as *tu-chih* (Revenue Section, Ministry of Revenue). P6. (2) N-S DIV–SUI: **Vice Minister for General Accounts,** by N. Wei if not earlier the director of one of several subsections (sometimes called *ts'ao,* Section) of the Ministry of Revenue (*tu-chih*). P6. (3) T'ANG–SUNG: abbreviated reference to the **Director** (*lang-chung*), rank 5b or 6b, **of the Bureau of General Accounts** (*tu-chih ssu*), one of the major subdivisions of the Ministry of Revenue (*hu-pu*). P6.

7203 *tù-chīh pù* 度支部
(1) N-S DIV–SUI: may be encountered as a reference to the central government agency officially known simply as

tu-chih (**Revenue Section, Ministry of Revenue**). (2) MING: **Bureau of General Accounts,** one of 4 principal subsections of the Ministry of Revenue (*hu-pu*) from 1380 to 1390; headed by a Director (*lang-chung*); in 1390 terminated when the Ministry was reorganized into Bureaus (*ch'ing-li ssu*) prefixed with the names of Provinces. P6.

7204   *tù-chīh shàng-shū* 度支尚書
N-S DIV (San-kuo Wei)–T'ANG: **Minister of Revenue,** one of the chief fiscal officials under the developing Department of State Affairs (*shang-shu sheng*), head of the agency known simply as *tu-chih* (Revenue Section, Ministry of Revenue). P6.

7205   *tù-chīh ssū* 度支司
(1) T'ANG–SUNG: **Bureau of General Accounts,** one of 4 (T'ang) or 3 (Sung) principal subsections of the Ministry of Revenue (*hu-pu*), headed by one or 2 Directors (*lang-chung*), rank 5b in T'ang, 6b in Sung, assisted by one or 2 Vice Directors (*yüan-wai lang*), 6b in T'ang, 7a in Sung. In Sung subdivided into 5 Sections (*an*): Tax Section (*tu-chih an*), Transport Section (*fa-yün an*), Bursary Section (*chih-kung an*), Gifts Section (*shang-tz'u an*), and Miscellany Section (*chih-tsa an*). SP: *bureau des revenus publics*. P6. (2) T'ANG–5 DYN: **Tax Bureau,** one of 3 central government agencies created after mid-T'ang, collectively called the Three Fiscal Agencies (*san ssu*), to consolidate fiscal administration in those parts of the rebellion-shattered empire that remained under central government control; commonly headed by a Grand Councilor (*tsai-hsiang*) on special duty assignment. (3) SUNG: **Tax Bureau,** one of the early Sung agencies known in the aggregate as the State Finance Commission (*san ssu*); headed by a central government dignitary on duty assignment as Commissioner (*shih*). Given administrative support by 8 subsidiary Sections (*an*): Gifts and Presentations Section (*shang-chi an*), Coins and Silks Section (*ch'ien-po an*), Supplies Section (*liang-liao an*), Stabilization Fund Section (*ch'ang-p'ing an*), Transport Section (*fa-yün an*), State Horses Section (*chi-an*), State Grain Section (*hu-tou an*), and Officials Section (*po-kuan an*). At some unclear late date prior to its abolition in c. 1080, renamed Stabilization Fund Bureau (*ch'ang-p'ing ssu*). SP: *office des revenus publics*. P7. (4) LIAO: **Revenue Commission,** a fiscal agency based at the Central Capital (Chung-ching in southern Jehol), headed by a Commissioner (*shih*); functions not specifically described in the sources. P7.

7206   *tū chīh-tsá fáng* 都知雜房
SUNG: **Chief Miscellany Office,** a clerical subsection of the Department of State Affairs (*shang-shu sheng*); cf. *chih-tsa fang*. SP: *chambre des affaires diverses*.

7207   *tù-chīh ts'áo* 度支曹
N-S DIV: may be encountered as a reference to the central government agency officially known simply as *tu-chih* (**Revenue Section, Ministry of Revenue**). P6.

7208   *tū chìn-tsòu yüàn* 都進奏院
SUNG: **Chief Memorials Office,** variant designation of the *chin-tsou yüan* (Memorials Office) of the Chancellery (*men-hsia sheng*). SP: *bureau général de la réception des mémoires*. P21.

7209   *tū chù-ch'ién yüàn* 督鑄錢掾
HAN: **Supervisor of Coinage,** in Later Han an appointee of the Metropolitan Governor (*ching-chao yin*), actually to oversee transactions in the state market in the auxiliary capital, Ch'ang-an; whether he had any coinage responsibilities is not clear. P16.

7210   *tū chǔ-hsiá chīh-shoū ssū* 都主轄支收司
SUNG: **General Money Circulating Office,** one of many agencies serving the bureaus that constituted the State Finance Commission (*san ssu*) of early Sung; headed by an Administrative Assistant (*p'an-kuan*), rank 8a or 8b; oversaw the issuance of paper money to the Prefectures (*chou*), also reported all receipts. SP: *bureau général chargé d'administrer la sortie et la rentrée des objets publics*. P7.

7211   *tú-chù kuān* 讀祝官
CH'ING: **Prayer Reader,** numbers and ranks varying greatly, Manchu religious practitioners attached to the Ministry of Rites (*li-pu*), the Court of Imperial Sacrifices (*t'ai-ch'ang ssu*), the Office of Palace Ceremonial (*chang-i ssu*), and each of the Manchu Imperial Mausolea (*ling*). BH: reader of prayers at sacrifices. P27, 29.

7212   *tū chuán-yùn shīh* 都轉運使
(1) T'ANG: **Transport Commissioner-in-chief,** beginning in 734, an ad hoc duty assignment for a court official to expedite the transport of tax grain throughout the Chiang-Huai and Honan areas. P60. (2) SUNG–CHIN: **Fiscal Commissioner-in-chief,** in Sung and Liao a duty assignment for a court official to supervise tax transport and most other fiscal matters in 2 or more neighboring Circuits (*lu* or *tao*), in contrast to the normal case in which each Circuit had one Fiscal Commissioner (*chuan-yün shih*); in Chin a regular post (*kuan*), rank 3a, assigned to the Circuit administered from the Central Capital (Chung-tu, modern Peking), in contrast to the Fiscal Commissioners appointed in other Circuits. SP: *commissaire général du transport, commissaire général des finances, intendant général fiscal*. P52, 60. (3) MING: common variant designation of the **Salt Distribution Commissioner** (*tu chuan-yün yen shih*). (4) CH'ING: unofficial reference to the **Director-general of Grain Transport** (*ts'ao-yün tsung-tu*).

7213   *tū chuán-yùn yén shǐh* 都轉運鹽使
YÜAN–CH'ING: **Salt Distribution Commissioner** or **Salt Controller,** rank 3a in Yüan, 3b in Ming and Ch'ing; from 1277 appointed in each major salt-producing area to supervise the issuance of state salt to merchants for distribution throughout the empire; 3 in Yüan, 6 in Ming, 5 in Ch'ing. In Ming commonly abbreviated to *tu chuan-yün shih;* in Ch'ing also known as *yen-yün shih*. Also cf. *yen-k'o t'i-chü ssu, ch'a-yen chuan-yün shih, ch'a-yen t'i-chü ssu, yen-cheng*. P61.

7214   *tū-chuán* 都轉
(1) SUNG: abbreviation of *tu chuan-yün shih* (**Fiscal Commissioner-in-chief**). (2) MING–CH'ING: abbreviation of *tu chuan-yün yen shih* (**Salt Distribution Commissioner, Salt Controller**).

7215   *tū-ch'uán lìng* 都船令
HAN: **Director of the Capital Boats** under the Chamberlain for the Imperial Insignia (*chih chin-wu*), assisted by an Aide (*ch'eng*); status and functions not specified in the sources. HB: prefect director of boats.

7216   *tū-ch'uán yù* 都船獄
HAN: **Prison for the Capital Boatmen** under the early Han Chamberlain for the Imperial Insignia (*chung-wei*), headed by a Director (*ling*) and an Aide (*ch'eng*); status and functions not specified by the sources, but interpreted to be a jail for troublemakers among boatmen active on the rivers and canals of the dynastic capital or among state ship-builders at the capital. The Director was apparently coequal with

the Director of the Capital Boats (*tu-ch'uan ling*), but the post did not survive early Han. HB: prison of the director of boats. P13.

7217 *tū-chù* 都句
Common scribal variant of *tu-kou* (**Chief Administrative Clerk**).

7218 *tū chū-hsiá ssū* 都拘轄司
SUNG: **Chief Coordinating Office,** a headquarters unit of the Ministry of Revenue (*hu-pu*) with supervisory authority over the Ministry's functionally differentiated Bureaus (*ssu*); staffing not clear, but possibly headed by executive officials of the Ministry on a rotational basis. SP: *bureau général des finances.*

7219 *tū ch'ū-yüàn* 都麴院
SUNG: **Chief Fermentation Bureau,** a unit of the Court of the National Granaries (*ssu-nung ssu*) in charge of fermenting alcoholic beverages for palace and court use; headed by an official of the Court on duty assignment as Supervisor (*chien*). SP: *cour de la fabrication de levain.*

7220 *tú-chuǎn kuān* 讀卷官
MING: **Palace Examination Grader,** duty assignment for members of the Hanlin Academy (*han-lin yüan*) and other accomplished scholars serving in the central government; read and graded papers written in triennial Palace Examinations (*t'ing-shih*) in the civil service recruitment examination sequence.

7221 *tū-chūn* 督軍
N-S DIV (Chin): **Army Commander,** a military duty assignment normally particularized as *tu ... shih* (Commander of the ... Army); not as prestigious as *chien-chün* (Army Supervisor) or *tu-tu* (Commander-in-chief). P50.

7222 *tū chūn-liáng yù-shǐh* 督軍糧御史
N-S DIV (San-kuo Wei): **Censor Expediter of Army Supplies,** duty assignment for a Censor (*yü-shih*) to supervise the provisioning of field armies; also called *tu chün-liang chih-fa* (see *chih-fa,* variant of *yü-shih*). P18.

7223 *tú chūn-shǐh* 都軍使
SUNG: **Chief Military Commissioner,** duty assignment in S. Sung for a military officer to head a rotational Duty Group (*pan*) of troops on active service in the capital, under the Palace Command (*tien-ch'ien ssu*). SP: *commissaire général d'armée.*

7224 *tū-chūn yù-shǐh* 督軍御史
HAN–N-S DIV (San-kuo): **Army-supervising Censor,** an ad hoc duty assignment for a Censor (*yü-shih*) during the tumultuous years of fighting before and after the collapse of Han; an imperial delegate charged with helping to correct specific military problems and reporting back to the throne. P50.

7225 *tū fáng-yù shǐh* 都防禦使
SUNG: **Chief Defense Commissioner,** a title awarded to chiefs of some southwestern aboriginal tribes. P72.

7226 *tū-fēng ts'áo* 督烽曹
HAN: **Signal Beacon Section,** a unit commonly found in the headquarters of Commanderies (*chün*) in the vicinity of the northern frontier, which supervised the maintenance of emergency signaling systems. HB: bureau of the investigation of beacons.

7227 *tū-fǔ* 督撫
CH'ING: a combined, abbreviated reference to **Governors-general** (*tsung-tu*) **and Governors** (*hsün-fu*).

7228 *tū-fǔ* 都府
T'ANG: lit., office of a chief, i.e., a (regional) headquarters: unofficial reference to a **Military Commissioner** (*chieh-tu shih*). P50.

7229 *tū-fǔ-ssū-tào* 督撫司道
CH'ING: lit., a combined, abbreviated reference to *tsung-tu* (Governor-general), *hsün-fu* (Governor), and heads of the *pu-cheng ssu* (Provincial Administration Commission), the *an-ch'a ssu* (Provincial Surveillance Commission), the *yen-yün ssu* (Salt Distribution Commission), and the *liang-ch'u tao* (Grain Tax Circuit): i.e., the **Provincial Authorities,** who commonly met together as a deliberative and planning council in times of rebellions and other emergencies, especially from the 1850s.

7230 *tū-hsiá* 都轄
SUNG: **Administrator** of the Diplomacy Section (*kuo-hsin fang*) of the Bureau of Military Affairs (*shu-mi yüan*). SP: *administrateur.*

7231 *tū hsiāng-hóu* 都鄉侯
N-S DIV (San-kuo Wu): **Chief Township Marquis,** variant of the noble title *hsiang-hou* (Township Marquis), reserved for some members of the Sun family. P64.

7232 *tū-hsüéh shǐh-chě* 督學使者
CH'ING: **Education-supervising Commissioner,** variant designation of the Provincial Education Commissioner (*hsüeh-cheng*).

7233 *tū-hsüéh tào* 督學道
CH'ING: **Education Intendant Circuit,** one in supervisory control of education and civil service recruitment in each early Ch'ing Province, the Intendant being nominally an Assistant Commissioner (*ch'ien-shih*), rank 5a, of a Provincial Surveillance Commission (*t'i-hsing an-ch'a shih ssu*); in 1684 superseded by *t'i-tu hsüeh-cheng* (Provincial Education Commissioner). Also see *t'i-tu hsüeh-tao.* P51.

7234 *tū hsün-chiěn* 都巡檢
(1) SUNG: **Chief Military Inspector,** designation of the heads of some regional Military Inspectorates (*hsün-chien ssu*), more prestigious than *hsün-chien* (Military Inspector); also awarded to the chiefs of some southwestern aboriginal tribes. SP: *inspecteur général chargé d'entraîner les soldats et d'arrêter les bandits.* P54, 72. (2) CHIN: **Executive Police Chief** in a Prefecture (*chou*), rank 7a, supported by an Assistant (*fu*), 8a. Cf. *san hsün-chien shih* (Detached Police Chief). P54.

7235 *tū hsün-hó kuān* 都巡河官
CHIN: **Chief River Patroller,** rank 7b, a member of the Directorate of Waterways (*tu-shui chien*) in general charge of repairing river embankments and planting elm and willow trees on them; supervised scattered local River Patrollers (*hsün-ho kuan*). P59.

7236 *tū hsün-kuān* 都巡官 or *tū hsün-shǐh* 使
T'ANG–SUNG: **Chief Patrolling Inspector** (T'ang) or **Chief Capital Inspector** (Sung), rotating duty assignment for a member of the Censorate (*yü-shih t'ai*); supervised and coordinated the Patrolling Inspectors or Capital Inspectors (*hsün-shih;* also see *hsün*) who were responsible for maintaining order in the 2 sections into which the dynastic capitals, T'ang's Ch'ang-an and Sung's Kaifeng, were divided for local police administration. Cf. *hsün-ch'eng yü-shih.* P20.

7237 *tū-hù* 督護
HAN–YÜAN: **Protector-general,** a military duty assignment to preside over submitted alien peoples, especially in

modern Sinkiang, as an imperial delegate with viceregal powers; appears in many variations such as *shang tu-hu, ta tu-hu, hsi-yü tu-hu,* and *tu-hu chieh-tu shih* (Protector-general Military Commissioner), the latter being a T'ang assignment in modern Vietnam. Cf. *ts'an-chün tu-hu.*

7238 *tū-hù fŭ* 都護府
HAN–YÜAN: **Protectorate,** the jurisdiction of a Protector-general (*tu-hu*), or the designation of his headquarters.

7239 *tū-júng* 都戎
CH'ING: lit., chief militarist: unofficial reference to a **Brigade Vice Commander** (*tu-ssu*) in the Chinese military forces called the Green Standards (*lu-ying*).

7240 *tù-k'ō* 度科
YÜAN: **Accounts Section** in the Ministry of Revenue (*hu-pu*); see *nei-tu k'o* (Special Accounts Section) and *wai-tu k'o* (General Accounts Section).

7241 *tū k'ò-shĕng* 都客省
LIAO: variant of *k'o-sheng shih* (**Commissioner of the Visitors Bureau**); see *k'o-sheng.* P11.

7242 *tū-koū p'àn-kuān* 都勾判官
Clerical Administrative Assistant. (1) T'ANG: rank not clear and presumably very low; 2 staff members in each of the 2 Armies of Inspired Strategy (*shen-ts'e chün*). RR: *fonctionnaire chargé des affaires courantes pour les enquêtes générales.* (2) CHIN: rank 6b, record keepers on the staffs of Fiscal Commissioners (*chuan-yün shih*). P60.

7243 *tū koū-yā kuān* 都勾押官 or *tu-kou*
SUNG: **Chief Administrative Clerk,** unranked subofficials found in such agencies as the Court of Palace Attendants (*hsüan-hui yüan*), Herds Offices (*ch'ün-mu ssu*), etc. See *kou-ya kuan.* SP: *contrôleur général.* P38.

7244 *tū-kuān pù* 都官部 or *tu-kuan*
(1) N-S DIV: occasional variant of *tu-kuan ts'ao* (**Section for Justice**) in the Department of State Affairs (*shang-shu sheng*). (2) T'ANG–SUNG: variant of *tu-kuan ssu* (**Criminal Administration Bureau**) in the Ministry of Justice (*hsing-pu*). (3) MING: **Criminal Administration Bureau,** one of 4 functionally differentiated Bureaus in the Ministry of Justice (*hsing-pu*) from 1373 to 1390, when the Ministry was reorganized with one Bureau for each Province, named accordingly. P13.

7245 *tū-kuān ssū* 都官司 or *tu-kuan*
SUI–SUNG: **Criminal Administration Bureau,** one of the standard 4 Bureaus (*ssu*) that were the principal subsidiary units in the Ministry of Justice (*hsing-pu*); headed by a Director (*lang-chung*), rank 5b in T'ang, 6a or 6b in Sung; supervised the management of all prisoners of war and condemned criminals. RR+SP: *bureau des condamnés.* P13.

7246 *tū-kuān ts'áo* 都官曹 or *tu-kuan*
(1) HAN: **Capital Officials Section** under the Later Han Metropolitan Commandant (*ssu-li hsiao-wei*), staffed with Retainer Clerks (*ts'ung-shih shih*); exercised police and judicial authority over government personnel stationed in the dynastic capital. HB: bureau for the officials at the capital. (2) HAN–SUI: **Section for Justice,** originally one of the Six Sections (*liu ts'ao*) among which Imperial Secretaries (*shang-shu*) were distributed in the Later Han Imperial Secretariat (*shang-shu t'ai*); after Han gradually became a top-echelon unit in the developing Department of State Affairs (*shang-shu sheng*), normally headed by a Minister (*shang-shu*); in early Sui renamed *hsing-pu* (Ministry of Justice). In the era of N-S Division commonly subdivided into func-

tion-specific agencies including an identically named *tu-kuan* (Capital Officials Section). P13. (3) N-S DIV: **Capital Officials Section,** one of a varying number of agencies subordinate to the Section for Justice (#2 above), headed by a Director (*lang-chung*) and a Vice Director (*yüan-wai lang*). Comparable to the T'ang–Sung Criminal Administration Bureau (*tu-kuan ssu*). P13.

7247 *tū-kuān yù* 都官獄
HAN: **Capital Prison,** generic name for 26 or possibly 36 jails reportedly in existence from the time of Emperor Wu (r. 141–87 B.C.), each under a Director (*ling*); apparently had some relationship with the Metropolitan Commandant (*ssu-li hsiao-wei*) and the Section for Justice (*tu-kuan*) of the Imperial Secretariat (*shang-shu t'ai*), but details are not clear in the sources. HB: prison for officials at the capital.

7248 *tū-k'ŭn* 都閫
CH'ING: lit., chief pacifier (?): unofficial reference to a **Brigade Vice Commander** (*tu-ssu*) in the Chinese military forces called the Green Standards (*lu-ying*), presumably when he was in actual command of a Brigade (*ying*).

7249 *tū k'ŭng-mù kuān* 都孔目官
SUNG–CHIN: **Chief Clerk;** see under *k'ung-mu kuan.* SP: *fonctionnaire principal chargé de mettre en ordre les livres et les archives.*

7250 *tū lăo-yéh* 都老爺
CH'ING: **Chief Venerable,** unofficial reference to a Censor (*yü-shih*).

7251 *tū-lĭ ch'ién-fá shìh-láng* 督理錢法侍郎
MING–CH'ING: **Vice Minister Supervisory Manager of Coinage,** an official of the Ministry of Revenue (*hu-pu*), in Ch'ing jointly with a Vice Minister of Works (*kung-pu shih-lang*), assigned to supervise the Coinage Office (*ch'ien-fa t'ang*); first established in 1625. P16.

7252 *tū lĭ-ch'ièn ssū* 都理欠司
SUNG: **General Deficits Monitoring Office,** one of many agencies serving the 3 constituent bureaus of the State Finance Commission (*san ssu*) of early Sung; headed by an Administrative Assistant (*p'an-kuan*), rank 8a or 8b; responsible for expediting the remittance of tax arrearages from Prefectures (*chou*). Created in 987 by a consolidation of 3 separate Deficits Monitoring Offices (*li-ch'ien ssu*), one for each of the Commission's 3 bureaus. SP: *bureau général chargé de régler les dettes.* P7.

7253 *tū liáng-liào shìh* 都糧料使
SUNG: **Chief Commissioner of the Bursary** (*liang-liao yüan*) in the Court of the Imperial Treasury (*t'ai-fu ssu*). SP: *commissaire général des grains et des foins.*

7254 *tū-liáng tào* 督糧道
MING–CH'ING: **Tax Circuit Intendant,** one per Province; duty assignment for a Vice Commissioner (*ts'an-cheng*) or an Assistant Commissioner (*ts'an-i*) of a Provincial Administration Commission (*ch'eng-hsüan pu-cheng shih ssu*); coordinated Province-wide tax collecting and forwarding activities; counterpart of Grain Tax Circuits (*liang-ch'u tao*) established by Provincial Surveillance Commissions (*t'i-hsing an-ch'a shih ssu*) in Ch'ing, both then commonly simplified to *liang-tao.* From 1735 the Intendant (*tao-t'ai*) was transformed into an autonomous, regular office (*kuan*), rank 4a. BH: grain intendant. P60.

7255 *tū-lĭng shìh* 督領侍
CH'ING: **Supervising Attendant,** eunuch head, rank 4a, of the Directorate of Palace Domestic Service (*kung-tien chien*).

7256 *tū lìng-shǐh* 都令史
N-S DIV: **Chief Clerk,** a lowly official or unranked sub-official but superior to *ling-shih* (Clerk), found in the Department of State Affairs (*shang-shu sheng*) and its subsidiary units. P5, 6, 9, etc.

7257 *tū mièn-yüàn* 都麵院
SUNG: **Yeast Office** under the Office of Fine Wines (*liang-yün shu*) in the Court of Imperial Entertainments (*kuang-lu ssu*); staffed by non-official specialists. SP: *cour de la fabrication de levain.*

7258 *tū mò-k'àn ssū* 都磨勘司
SUNG: **General Accounting Office,** one of many agencies serving the 3 bureaus that constituted the State Finance Commission (*san ssu*) of early Sung; headed by an Administrative Assistant (*p'an-kuan*); created 996, terminated c. 1080. Cf. *mo-k'an.* SP: *bureau chargé de vérifier les comptes.* P7.

7259 *tū-mù* 都目
YÜAN: **Foreman,** apparently an unranked suboffical, found in agencies employing conscripted labor, such as the Superintendency of Tea Groves (*ch'a-yüan tu t'i-chü ssu*). P62.

7260 *tū-nèi* 都內
HAN: **Imperial Treasury,** a storehouse for such valuables as money and silk; under the Chamberlain for the National Treasury (*ta-nung ling,* then *ta ssu-nung*); headed by a Director (*ling*); by A.D. 82 abolished, its functions taken over by one of the Chamberlain's Aides (*ch'eng*). HB: imperial treasury.

7261 *tū-pàn* 督辦
CH'ING: variant of *tsung-pan* (**Administrator**).

7262 *tū-pǎo* 都保
SUNG: **Superior Security Group,** from the time of the reformer Wang An-shih a common unit of local self-government organization of the populace; an aggregation of 10 Large Security Groups (*ta-pao*) comprising 500 families under one Head (*cheng*). See *pao-chia.* SP: *groupe de 500 familles.*

7263 *tū-piāo* 督標
CH'ING: **Governor-general's Command,** designation of the total forces of Green Standards (*lu-ying*) troops controlled by a Governor-general (*tsung-tu*). See *piao.*

7264 *tū-pīng ts'áo* 都兵曹
N-S DIV: **Section in the Capital,** one of a varying number of top-echèlon units under the developing Ministry of War (*ch'i-ping ts'ao, wu-ping ts'ao*) in the Department of State Affairs (*shang-shu sheng*); headed by a Director (*lang, lang-chung*), rank 6a2 in N. Wei. P12.

7265 *tū p'íng-yú ssū* 都憑由司
SUNG: **General Wastage Monitoring Office,** one of many agencies serving the 3 bureaus that constituted the State Finance Commission (*san ssu*) of early Sung; headed by an Administrative Assistant (*p'an-kuan*), rank 8a or 8b; checked on wastage, breakage, or other deficiencies in goods issued to officials serving in the dynastic capital. SP: *bureau des certificats chargé des paiements officiels dans la capitale.* P7.

7266 *tū pò-chí-lièh* 都勃極烈
CHIN: **Supreme Chief,** Chinese rendering of a Jurchen word dating to predynastic times, when Jurchen tribal or other Chiefs (*po-chi-lieh*) were organized into a league under a Supreme Chief, who became the dynastic founder.

7267 *tū-pǔ ch'īng-lì ssū* 督捕清吏司
CH'ING: **Bureau of Arrests,** one among the mature 18 Bureaus in the Ministry of Justice (*hsing-pu*), headed by one Manchu and one Chinese Director (*lang-chung*), rank 5a. Whereas other Bureaus supervised judicial administration in specified Provinces and were named accordingly, this was responsible for bringing to justice deserters from the Banner (*ch'i*) military forces. Originally an Office of Arrests (*tu-pu ya-men*) under the Ministry of War (*ping-pu*), in 1699 it was reorganized under the Ministry of Justice as a cluster of agencies: Front Bureau of Arrests (*tu-pu ch'ien-ssu*), Rear Bureau of Arrests (*tu-pu hou-ssu*), and Police Office (*tu-pu t'ing*); then in 1734 consolidated into the single Bureau of Arrests. P12, 13.

7268 *tū-pù shǔ* 都部署
SUNG, LIAO: **Chief Administration Office,** common abbreviation of agencies, probably staffed with eunuchs, that prepared and maintained imperial quarters in auxiliary capitals or for Emperors in travel status, prefixed with *ta-nei* (Imperial Residence) or *hsing-kung* (Auxiliary Palace); apparently headed by a Chief Administrator (*tu-pu*) or a Vice Administrator (*fu-pu*). P38, 49.

7269 *tū pù shǔ-ssū* 都部署司
LIAO: **Tribal Chief,** designation of the heads of some Routes (*lu*) of tribal armies (*pu-tsu chün*).

7270 *tū sè-chǎng* 都色長
SUNG: **Chief Appearance Monitor,** 4 members of the Office of Musical Instruction (*ch'ien-hsia chiao-fang so*); see *se-chang* (Appearance Monitor). SP: *chef des sections.*

7271 *tū shāng-shùi wù* 都商稅務 or *tū shāng-shùi yüàn* 院
SUNG: **Commercial Tax Office for the Capital,** apparently variant designations of *shang-shui wu* (Commercial Tax Office). SP: *agence (cour) métropolitaine de la taxe commerciale.*

7272 *tū-shěng* 都省
(1) N-S DIV–SUNG: at times an official variant of, at others an unofficial reference to, *shang-shu sheng* (**Department of State Affairs**). (2) T'ANG: **Executive Office** of the Department of State Affairs, a collective reference to the Department's Director (*ling*), Vice Directors (*p'u-yeh*), and Assistant Directors (*ch'eng*).

7273 *tū-shìh* 都事
SUI–CH'ING: **Office Manager,** supervisor of an agency's internal clerical work, originating in the Six Ministries (*liu pu*) with Sui's retitling of *tu ling-shih* (Chief Clerk), gradually spreading into other central government agencies, then in Ming and Ch'ing retained only in the Censorate (*tu ch'a-yüan*) and Provincial Administration Offices (*ch'eng-hsüan pu-cheng shih ssu*); rank 8b2 in T'ang, 8a in Sung, 7a in Chin, 7b in Yüan, 7a or 7b in Ming, 6a or 7b in Ch'ing. Also see *tu-shih t'ing* (Office of the Office Manager). RR+SP: *surveillant.* BH: assistant secretary. P1, 4, 5, 6, 9, 13, 14, 18, etc.

7274 *tū-shìh* 都士
CHOU: **Justiciar of the Inherited Region,** 2 with rank as Ordinary Servicemen (*chung-shih*), responsible for judicial and penal administration in each Inherited Region (*tu,* q.v.); probably under the supervision of Justiciars of the Domain (*fang-shih*) in the Ministry of Justice (*ch'iu-kuan*), but possibly together with Justiciars of the Administrative Regions (*chia-shih*) known generically as Justiciars of the Domain. CL: *prévôt de justice de l'apanage.*

7275 *tū-shìh chūn-mǎ* 督視軍馬
SUNG: **Inspector of the Armies,** duty assignment for a Vice Grand Councilor (see *chih-cheng*) or comparable dignitary to assist in the management of a Superior Area Command (*ta tu-tu fu*) in a time of crisis; sometimes prefixed *tu* (Chief). SP: *inspecteur des armées et des chevaux, directeur-inspecteur des soldats et des chevaux.*

7276 *tū-shìh t'īng* 都事廳
CH'ING: **Office of the Office Manager** (*tu-shih*), also sometimes an unofficial reference to the incumbent Office Manager. BH: chancery.

7277 *tū-shǔi chǎng* 都水長
CH'IN–HAN: **Director of Waterways,** in charge of the maintenance and operation of irrigation canals and other waterways; status in Ch'in not clear; in Former Han proliferated under many central government agencies and units of territorial administration at least to the level of Commanderies (*chün*) and Princedoms (*wang-kuo*); under Emperor Ch'eng (r. 33–7 B.C.) placed under the coordination of 2 Commissioners of Waterways (*tu-shui shih-che*) in the central government; in Later Han those attached to the central government agencies seem mostly to have been abolished or transferred to units of territorial administration, where one of their responsibilities may have been to collect taxes from fishermen. Each Director was commonly assisted by one Aide (*ch'eng*); in Later Han the Directors were ranked from 300 to 400 bushels. Their functions were subsequently carried on by local administrations under supervision of such central government agencies as the Office of Waterways (*tu-shui t'ai*), the Directorate of Waterways (*tu-shui chien*), and the Bureau of Irrigation and Transportation (*tu-shui ch'ing-li ssu*). Cf. *shui-heng tu-wei* (Commandant of Waterways). HB: chief director of waters. P59.

7278 *tū-shǔi chiēn* 都水監
SUI–YÜAN: **Directorate of Waterways,** from mid-Sui on, under policy guidelines established by the Ministry of Works (*kung-pu*) or the early Sung State Finance Commission (*san ssu*), supervised the efforts of regional and local units of territorial administration in maintaining and operating irrigation systems and transport waterways, at times with regional branches (*tu-shui wai-chien* in Sung, *hsing tu-shui chien* in Yüan). In Sui headed by a Supervisor (*chien*), then a Director (*ling*); in T'ang and Sung by 2 Commissioners (*shih-che*), rank 5a1 in T'ang, 6a in Sung; in Liao by a Director (*ta-chien*); in Chin and Yüan by one or more Supervisors (*chien*), 4a in Chin, 3b in Yüan. From Sui through Sung commonly oversaw an Office of Boats and Boatmen (*chou-chi shu*) and an Office of Rivers and Canals (*ho-ch'ü shu*), each headed by a Director (*ling*). After Yüan the Directorate's functions were absorbed by the Bureau of Irrigation and Transportation (*tu-shui ch'ing-li ssu*) of the Ministry of Works and by such new dignitaries as the Director-general of the Grand Canal (*ho-tao tsung-tu*). RR+SP: *direction du contrôle des eaux.* P15, 59.

7279 *tū-shǔi ch'īng-lì ssū* 都水清吏司
MING–CH'ING: **Bureau of Irrigation and Transportation** in the Ministry of Works (*kung-pu*), headed by from one to 6 Directors (*lang-chung*), rank 5a; supervised the construction and maintenance of waterways throughout the empire, continuing the functions of the previous autonomous Directorate of Waterways (*tu-shui chien*). BH: department of waterways and dikes. P14, 15.

7280 *tū-shǔi kuān* 都水官
(1) **Waterways Officials:** throughout imperial history a generic reference to personnel of such agencies as the Office of Waterways (*tu-shui t'ai*), the Directorate of Waterways (*tu-shui chien*), and the Bureau of Irrigation and Transportation (*tu-shui ch'ing-li ssu*). (2) HAN: **Waterways Office,** common designation for agencies in all areas headed by Directors of Waterways (*tu-shui chang*). HB: office of the direction of waters. P14.

7281 *tū-shǔi lìng* 都水令
HAN: **Director-in-chief of Waterways,** in Later Han one ranked from 600 to 1,000 bushels appointed in each large Commandery (*chün*) and Princedom (*wang-kuo*), apparently supervising the lesser Directors of Waterways (*tu-shui chang*) in his jurisdiction. HB: prefect director of waters.

7282 *tū-shǔi shìh-chě* 都水使者
HAN–SUNG: **Commissioner of Waterways,** first established in the era 33–7 B.C., 2 prefixed Left and Right, as central government officials charged with coordinating the activities of Directors of Waterways (*tu-shui chang*) in many central government agencies as well as units of territorial administration; rank and organizational affiliation not clear. Not perpetuated in Later Han; but the title was revived by post-Han Chin for the head of the central government's Office of Waterways (*tu-shui t'ai*), thereafter alternating or coexisting with the post of Commandant of Waterways (*shui-heng tu-wei*); rank normally 4 or 5. In Sui the title alternated with Supervisor (*chien*) and Director (*ling*); T'ang stabilized it as the designation of the head of the Directorate of Waterways (*tu-shui chien*); normally 2 appointees, rank 5a1 in T'ang, 6a in Sung. RR: *commissaire chargé de la direction du contrôle des eaux.* SP: *commissaire du contrôle des eaux.* P14, 15, 59.

7283 *tū-shǔi t'ái* 都水臺
N-S DIV–SUI: **Office of Waterways,** in charge of the maintenance and operation of irrigation systems and of transport waterways and boats, from Chin on alternating or coexisting with the post of Commandant of Waterways (*shui-heng tu-wei*); variably under the Chamberlain for the Palace Revenues (*shao-fu*), the Chamberlain for the Palace Buildings (*chiang-tso ta-chiang*), and the developing Ministry of Works (*kung-pu*); consistently headed by a Commissioner (*shih-che*), rank 4 or 5, assisted by Administrators (*ts'an-chün-shih*), Aides (*ch'eng*), etc. Late in the Sui dynasty, reorganized as the Directorate of Waterways (*tu-shui chien*), which endured into Yüan times. P14, 40, 59.

7284 *tū-shǔi wèi* 都水尉
SUI: **Waterways Commandant,** 2, rank not clear, heads of the Water Transport Service (*chang-ch'uan chü*) in the Office of Waterways (*tu-shui t'ai*). P14.

7285 *tū-ssū* 都司
(1) SUI–CH'ING: occasional variant of *tu-shih* (**Office Manager**). (2) SUNG: **Headquarters Office,** generic reference to the Left and Right Offices (*tso-ssu, yu-ssu*) into which the Department of State Affairs (*shang-shu sheng*) was divided. (3) MING: common abbreviation of *tu chih-hui shih ssu* (**Regional Military Commission**). (4) CH'ING: **Brigade Vice Commander,** rank 4a, subordinate to a Brigade Commander (*yu-chi*) in the Chinese military forces called the Green Standards (*lu-ying*). BH: first captain.

7286 *tū ssū-k'ūng yù* 都司空獄
HAN: **Prison for Imperial Kinsmen,** a jail at the dynastic capital under the Chief Director of Convict Labor (*tu ssu-k'ung ling;* see *ssu-k'ung ling*), headed by a Director (*ling*). P13.

7287 *tū ssū-mǎ* 都司馬
CHOU: **Commandant of the Inherited Region,** 2 ranked as Senior Servicemen (*shang-shih*), 4 as Ordinary Servicemen (*chung-shih*), and 8 as Junior Servicemen (*hsia-shih*) authorized for each Region (*kuo*) within the royal domain that was an inherited fief (*tu*) of a member of the royal family; in charge of military matters in the domain. Not to be confused with *ta ssu-ma* (Minister of War). CL: *commandant de chevaux, chef militaire dans l'apanage.*

7288 *tū ssū yù-shìh fáng* 都司御史房
SUNG: **Office for Supervision of Censors** under the Department of State Affairs (*shang-shu sheng*), staffing not clear; specific functions also not clear, but apparently an agency of the Department that in some fashion monitored the activities of Censors (*yü-shih*). SP: *chambre chargée d'accuser les censeurs.*

7289 *tū-tà* 都大
SUNG: **Chief,** a prefix added, especially late in S. Sung, to titles of various dignitaries for prestige purposes, making such combinations as *tu-ta t'i-chü ch'a-ma* (Supervisor-in-chief of Horse Trading Offices), *tu-ta chih-chih* (Military Commissioner-in-chief), *tu-ta fa-yün shih* (Supply Commissioner-in-chief), *tu-ta t'i-chü ho-ch'ü shih* (Supervisor-in-chief of Waterways), etc. See under following terminology.

7290 *tū-t'ái* 都臺
(1) **Capital Pavilion,** from 685 to 696 the official variant name of the Department of State Affairs (*shang-shu sheng*). (2) MING–CH'ING: **Capital Minister,** unofficial reference to a Minister (*shang-shu*) of a Ministry (*pu*).

7291 *tū t'ài-shīh* 都太師
LIAO: **Supreme Grand Preceptor,** a dignitary of the Northern Administration (*pei-mien*) in the central government; supervised the various Hunting Preserves (*wei-ch'ang*) scattered about Manchuria and Jehol. P17.

7292 *tū t'ài-shǒu* 督太守
N-S DIV (Liang, Ch'en): **Supervisory Governor,** a title awarded to a Governor (*t'ai-shou*) of a Commandery (*chün*) of more than normal population, raising his rank from 5 to 4. Cf. *tu* and *tu-tu t'ai-shou*. P53.

7293 *tū-t'áng* 都堂
(1) T'ANG–SUNG, CHIN: **Executive Office** of the Department of State Affairs (*shang-shu sheng*), also a collective reference to the Department's executive officials. SP: *salle principale.* (2) MING: **Executive Censors,** collective reference to the executive officials of the Censorate (*tu ch'a-yüan*) and also to Grand Coordinators (*hsün-fu*) and Supreme Commanders (*tsung-tu*), who held executive posts in the Censorate on a concurrent basis.

7294 *tū t'í-chǔ* 都提舉
SUNG–YÜAN: **Supervisor-in-chief,** a prefix similar to, but somewhat less prestigious than, *tu-ta t'i-chü* (also Supervisor-in-chief; see under *tu-ta*). See under the following terminology.

7295 *tū t'í-chǔ kuān* 都提舉官
SUNG: **Supervisor-in-chief,** 8 authorized for each of the 2 Branch Directorates (*wai-chien*), Northern and Southern, of the Directorate of Waterways (*tu-shui chien*), subordinate to an Aide (*ch'eng*). SP: *intendant général.* P59.

7296 *tù-tiéh k'ù* 度牒庫
SUNG: **Repository of Monastic Certificates** in the Ministry of Rites (*lǐ-pu*), staffing not clear; maintained a stock of warrants that were sold to men wishing to escape various tax and service responsibilities that the state waived for monks. SP: *magasin des certificats de moines.*

7297 *tū tiěn-chiěn* 都點檢
Inspector-general. (1) 5 DYN: late in the era, a post created for the supreme commander of the Imperial Armies (*chin-chün*) or of a campaigning Army; it was from such a post that the Sung founder took the throne. (2) SUNG: occasionally used as a prestigious title for the head of the Palace Command (*tien-ch'ien ssu*) or the Capital Security Office (*huang-ch'eng ssu*). SP: *contrôleur général.* (3) LIAO: one of the titles given heads of regional Tax Offices (*ch'ien-po ssu*). P52.

7298 *tū-t'íng hóu* 都亭侯
N-S DIV: **Marquis of Metropolitan Residence,** a title of nobility (*chüeh*) used in the early post-Han years, presumably for imperial relatives or other dignitaries not awarded territorial fiefs. P64.

7299 *tū-t'íng ì-chiēn kuān* 都亭驛監官
SUNG: **Capital Translator,** duty assignment in the Court of State Ceremonial (*hung-lu ssu*) for an official versed in the languages of western frontier tribes with which the court had diplomatic relations; commonly abbreviated to *tu-t'ing.* SP (*tu-t'ing*): *poste des tributs payés par les tribus étrangères à l'ouest du fleuve jaune.* P11.

7300 *tū-t'óu* 都頭
(1) T'ANG: **Metropolitan Executive,** occasional unofficial reference to a Grand Councilor (*tsai-hsiang; see p'ing-chang*). (2) T'ANG: **Area Commander,** a quasiofficial designation for heads of some of the 54 Area Commands (*tu*) developed from 881 under the New Army of Inspired Strategy (*shen-ts'e hsin-chün*); equivalent to General (*chiang-chün*). (3) SUNG: **Troop Commandant,** leader of a Troop (*tu*) of 100 men in various units of the Palace Command (*tien-ch'ien ssu*) and the Metropolitan Command (*shih-wei ssu*). (4) MING–CH'ING: **District Agent,** generic reference to residents conscripted for menial service at the District (*hsien*) level.

7301 *tū-ts'áo* 都曹
(1) N-S DIV (N. Wei): **Capital Ministry,** a nominal office created in 488 for a palace eunuch favored by the Empress Dowager; see under *chung-ts'ao* (Palace Ministry). (2) SUNG: abbreviation of *tu chuan-yün shih* (**Fiscal Commissioner-in-chief**).

7302 *tū ts'áo-yün ssū* 都漕運司
CHIN–MING: **Chief Transport Office,** headed by one or 2 Commissioners (*shih*), rank 3a in Yüan; under supervision of the Ministry of Revenue (*hu-pu*), managed the transport of tax grains to the dynastic capital, supervising local Transport Offices (*ts'ao-yün ssu*). The principal Chief Transport Office was located at the dynastic capital and was responsible for transport from nearby T'ung-chou to Peking in Yüan times. Immediately after the Mongol conquest of South China, one counterpart was established in the South for control of the Yangtze and Huai River transport systems, and another was established in Shantung. As transport by sea became predominant, these agencies were abandoned; but a new counterpart was established outside Peking at Ho-hsi-wu, which controlled transport on the Yellow River plain and the receipt of sea-transported grain on the coast. In the first Ming reign a Chief Transport Office was briefly established at Nanking. P60.

7303 *tū-tsé* 都則

CHOU: **Monitor of the Inherited Region,** one ranked as an Ordinary Serviceman (*chung-shih*) and 2 as Junior Servicemen (*hsia-shih*), members of the Ministry of Justice (*ch'iu-kuan*) assigned to each of the Regions (*kuo*) within the royal domain that was an inherited fief (*tu*) of a member of the royal family; implemented special regulations concerning such fiefs, called *tse*. CL: *régulateur d'apanage*.

7304 *tū-ts'è tào* 督册道

MING: **Census Intendant Circuit,** one of the many Branch Offices (*fen-ssu*) maintained by Provincial Administration Commissions (*ch'eng-hsüan pu-cheng shih ssu*), staffed by an Administration Vice Commissioner (*ts'an-chang*) or an Assistant Administration Commissioner (*ts'an-i*); supervised the collection and maintenance of census data by territorial administrators in its jurisdiction. See *tao* (Circuit).

7305 *tú-tsò* 獨坐

T'ANG–CH'ING: lit., one who sits alone: **Venerable,** unofficial reference to a Censor-in-chief (*yü-shih ta-fu, tu yü-shih*). See *san tu-tso* (Three Venerables).

7306 *tū tsò-yüàn* 都作院

SUNG: **Chief Manufactory** under the Directorate for Armaments (*chün-ch'i chien*); staffing and specific functions not clear. SP: *cour générale de la fabrication des armes*.

7307 *tū tsūng-jén* 都宗人

CHOU: **Ritualist of the Inherited Region,** 2 ranked as Senior Servicemen (*shang-shih*) and 4 as Ordinary Servicemen (*chung-shih*), members of the Ministry of Rites (*ch'iu-kuan*) assigned to each of the Regions (*kuo*) within the royal domain that was an inherited fief (*tu*) of a member of the royal family. Cf. *tsung-jen*. CL: *officier des cérémonies sacrées dans l'apanage*.

7308 *tū tsǔng-kuǎn fǔ* 都總管府

(1) SUNG–CHIN: **Chief Area Command,** variant of *tsung-kuan fu* (Area Command) in particularly vital military regions; headed by a Commander-in-chief (*tu tsung-kuan*). P50. (2) YÜAN: **Chief Command,** a headquarters unit that shared control of military forces in Ta-tu Route (*lu*), in which the dynastic capital was located, with a Chief Military Commission (*tu chih-hui ssu*); headed by a Commander-in-chief (*tu tsung-kuan*), rank 3b then 3a. P32. (3) YÜAN: **Supreme Supervisorate-in-chief,** designation of some nonmilitary or semimilitary agencies headed by Supreme Commissioners-in-chief (*tu tsung-kuan*); see under prefixed terminology.

7309 *tū tsǔng-kuǎn ssū* 都總管司

SUNG: **Supreme Area Command,** a late S. Sung variant of Military Commission (*an-fu shih ssu*) in a Circuit (*lu*) or in military control of more than one Circuit; headed by a Commander-in-chief (*tu tsung-kuan*). SP: *bureau de commandment en chef*.

7310 *tū tsǔng-shǐh* 都總使

YÜAN: **Commandant-in-chief,** designation of the head of the Meritorious Brigade (*chao-kung wan-hu*), which served as the personal bodyguard of the Heir Apparent.

7311 *tū-tū* 都督

(1) HAN–SUNG: **Commander-in-chief,** eminent military title that probably originated in Later Han, possibly as early as the first Later Han reign, designating a man given overall command of the empire's military forces; after Han alternated with *tsung-kuan* (Area Commander-in-chief) as the designation of a powerful Regional Governor (*chou mu*) or Regional Inspector (*tz'u-shih*) who militarily dominated a cluster of neighboring Regions (*chou*); gradually displaced by the title *tsung-kuan*. Revived in T'ang for the chief of military forces in a Prefecture (*chou*), but soon yielded to the title *chieh-tu shih* (Military Commissioner). Occasionally revived in S. Sung for military commands encompassing more than one Circuit (*lu*), given to Grand Councilors (*tsai-hsiang*). Rank varied from 1 to 3. RR: *gouverneur-général*. SP: *gouverneur militaire, directeur-général*. P50. (2) SUI: **Commander-in-chief,** lowest of 11 merit titles (*hsün*) awarded for military distinction. P65. (3) T'ANG: **Supervisor-in-chief,** designation of 24 central government officials dispatched in 711 on duty assignments to provide censorial surveillance, each over a specified territory including several Prefectures (*chou*); one stage in the development of Surveillance Commissioners (*an-ch'a shih, kuan-ch'a shih*); not to be confused with the military dignitaries discussed under (1) above. RR: *gouverneur général*. (4) T'ANG: **Commander-in-chief,** a title awarded to some submissive aboriginal chieftains of South and Southwest China. P72. (5) MING–CH'ING: **Commissioner-in-chief,** number not prescribed, rank 1a, heads of the 5 Chief Military Commissions (*tu-tu fu*) in the central government, among which the military forces of the empire were distributed for operational supervision under guidelines established by the Ministry of War (*ping-pu*); together with Vice Commissioners-in-chief (*tu-tu t'ung-chih*), 1b, and Assistant Commissioners-in-chief (*tu-tu ch'ien-shih*), 2a, constituted a pool of general officers from which the Emperor chose men to command campaigns. Commonly awarded noble status (*chüeh*) as high as Duke (*kung*). The 5 Chief Military Commissions were created in 1380 in a fragmentation of the previous unitary Chief Military Commission (*ta tu-tu fu*). This form of military organization seems to have lasted into the earliest Ch'ing years, but not for long. Comparable to the Bureau of Military Affairs (*shu-mi yüan*) of earlier periods, superseded by the Ch'ing dynasty's Banner organization (see *ch'i, pa ch'i*).

7312 *tū-tū ch'iēn-shìh* 都督僉事

MING: **Assistant Commissioner-in-chief,** number unspecified, rank 2a, members of the 5 Chief Military Commissions (*tu-tu fu*) in the central government; see under *tu-tu* (Commissioner-in-chief).

7313 *tū tū-chǐh* 都都知

SUNG: **Chief Administrator,** rank 5b, eunuch head of the Palace Domestic Service (*ju-nei nei-shih sheng* or, after 1160, *nei-shih sheng*). SP: *administrateur général*.

7314 *tū-tū fǔ* 都督府

(1) HAN–SUNG: **Area Command,** designation of a regional military jurisdiction and its headquarters, headed by a Commander-in-chief (*tu-tu*); in T'ang for a time classified in 3 ways, as a Superior (*ta*) Area Command, an Ordinary (*chung*) Area Command, and a Lesser (*hsia*) Area Command. RR+SP: *gouvernement général*. P50. (2) MING: **Chief Military Commission,** 5 created in 1380 as central government agencies dividing among themselves control of the empire's military forces; each headed by an unspecified number of Commissioners-in-chief (*tu-tu*), rank 1a; prefixed with the directional terms Left, Right, Center, Front, and Rear; known collectively as *wu-chün tu-tu fu* (Five Chief Military Commissions), commonly abbreviated to *wu fu*.

7315 *tū tū-shìh chǖn-mǎ* 都督視軍馬

SUNG: **Chief Military Inspector,** a duty assignment for Vice Grand Councilors (*fu-hsiang;* also see *chih-cheng kuan, ts'an-chih cheng-shih*) to share in the management of Superior Area Commands (*ta tu-tu fu*) at critical times. SP: *surveillant-inspecteur général des soldats et des chevaux.*

7316 *tū-tū t'ài-shǒu* 都督太守
N-S DIV (Liang, Ch'en): **Supreme Governor,** title awarded to a Governor (*t'ai-shou*) of a Commandery (*chün*) of extraordinarily large population, raising his rank to 3 from rank 4 of Supervisory Governor (*tu t'ai-shou*) or rank 5 of ordinary Governor (*t'ai-shou*). P53.

7317 *tū-tū t'úng-chīh* 都督同知
MING: **Vice Commissioner-in-chief,** number unprescribed, rank 1b, members of the 5 Chief Military Commissions (*tu-tu fu*) in the central government, which divided among themselves control over the empire's military forces; see under *tu-tu* (Commissioner-in-chief).

7318 *tū-tū tz'ù-shǐh* 都督刺史
(1) N-S DIV: **Commander-in-chief and Regional Inspector,** combined title for a Regional Inspector (*tz'u-shih*) who, as Area Commander-in-chief (*tu-tu*), had military authority over Regions (*chou*) neighboring his principal base Region; the most important were those designated Commissioned with Extraordinary Powers (*shih ch'ih-chieh*), of greater prestige than those designated Commissioned with Special Powers (*ch'ih-chieh*). P50. (2) T'ANG: **Commander-Prefect,** combined title for a Prefect (*tz'u-shih*) who, as Area Commander-in-chief, had military power over Prefectures (*chou*) neighboring his principal base Prefecture, or for such a dignitary titled Superior Commander-in-chief (*ta tu-tu*). P50.

7319 *tū t'uán-lièn shǐh* 都團練使
T'ANG: **Chief Military Training Commissioner,** created c. 780 as officers of Mobile Brigades (*hsing-ying*) detached from the Armies of Inspired Strategy (*shen-ts'e chün*); concurrently, in accordance with the extent of their jurisdictions, served as Prefects (*tz'u-shih*) of Prefectures (*chou*), Aides (*chang-shih*) in Superior Area Commands (*ta tu-tu fu*), or Commanders-in-chief (*tu-tu*) in ordinary Area Commands (*tu-tu fu*). See *t'uan-lien shih*. RR: *commissaire impérial général aux milices locales.*

7320 *tū t'uán-lièn shǒu-chō shǐh* 都團練守捉使
T'ANG: **Chief Commissioner for Militiamen,** an unspecified number appointed in 758 to supervise the utilization of militiamen, some having jurisdiction over more than 10 Prefectures (*chou*). See *t'uan-lien shou-cho shih*. RR: *commissaire impérial général aux détachements militaires et aux milices locales.*

7321 *tū-t'ǔng* 都統
(1) N-S DIV (N. Ch'i): **Supervisor,** 2, rank 5, in charge of the Imperial Wardrobe Service (*chu-i chü*) of the Chancellery (*men-hsia sheng*). P37. (2) T'ANG–SUNG: **Campaign Commander,** one of several titles used for military leaders on active campaign; less prestigious than Marshal (*yüan-shuai*) or Vice Marshal (*fu yüan-shuai*). RR: *général en chef*. (3) CH'ING: **Commander-in-chief,** one in command of each Banner (*ch'i*) in the Eight Banners (*pa ch'i*) organization, rank 1b; in addition, one each in control of the tribal groups of Jehol and of Chahar. BH: lieutenant-general.

7322 *tū t'ǔng-chǎng* 都統長
N-S DIV (N. Wei): **Capital Commandant,** responsible for all guard troops within the palace; number, rank, and organizational affiliation not clear. P37.

7323 *tū t'ǔng-chìh* 都統制
SUNG: **Supreme Commandant,** appointed c. 1127 as head of the Imperial Defense Command (*yü-ying ssu*), in control of all the military forces in the empire; title subsequently borne by leaders of regional armies. SP: *directeur général militaire.*

7324 *tū t'úng hsǔn-chiěn* 都同巡檢 or *tu t'ung-hsün*
SUNG: **Assistant Chief Military Inspector** in a Route (*lu*; first form) or a Prefecture (*chou*; 2nd form); see *hsün-chien ssu*. SP: *inspecteur-examinateur général-adjoint, inspecteur général-adjoint.*

7325 *tū wàn-hù fǔ* 都萬戶府
YÜAN: **Chief Brigade,** a major supervisory unit of the Mongol Army (*meng-ku chün*); most commonly refers to the Chief Brigade headquartered at the dynastic capital, which administered all other Brigades (*wan-hu*) of the Mongol Army.

7326 *tū-wèi* 都尉
(1) **Commandant** or **Commander-in-chief:** throughout history a common military title, in later dynasties used mostly for merit titles (*hsün*); in all cases, specific identification is possible only by taking note of prefixes. E.g., see *fu-ma tu-wei* (Commandant-escort). HB: chief commandant. RR+SP: *officier surveillant.* (2) HAN: **Defender,** rank 2,000 bushels, head of the military forces in a Commandery (*chün*), a Region (*chou*), or a Dependent State (*shu-kuo*). HB: chief commandant. Cf. *wei*.

7327 *tū wéi-nā* 都維那
N-S DIV (N. Wei, N. Ch'i): **Chief Buddhist Deacon,** 3rd executive after a Controller-in-chief (*ta-t'ung*) and a Controller (*t'ung*) in the Office for the Clarification of Buddhist Profundities (*chao-hsüan ssu*). Also see *wei-na* (Buddhist Deacon). P17.

7328 *tū wēi-wèi shǐh ssū* 都威衛使司
YÜAN: **Metropolitan Guard Command,** 2 prefixed Right and Left, military units responsible for guarding the residence of the Heir Apparent, each headed by one or more Metropolitan Guard Commissioners (*tu wei-wei shih*).

7329 *tū yā-yá* 都押衙
SUNG: **Chief Lackey,** apparently a category of non-official hirelings for menial work in units of territorial administration. SP: *employé de 1ère classe.*

7330 *tū-yěh yüàn* 督冶掾
N-S DIV (Chin): **Coinage Clerk,** probably non-official specialists; supervised the minting of coins in workshops in the suburbs of the dynastic capital; prefixed East, West, North, and South; originally subordinates of the Chamberlain for the Palace Garrison (*wei-wei*), later of the Chamberlain for the Palace Revenues (*shao-fu*). P16.

7331 *tū-yén àn* 都鹽案 or *tū-yén yüàn* 院
SUNG: **Capital Salt Supply Section,** one of 8 Sections (*an*) in the Salt and Iron Monopoly Bureau (*yen-t'ieh ssu*) of early Sung, normally headed by an Administrative Assistant (*p'an-kuan, t'ui-kuan*); responsible for maintaining and distributing salt supplies in the capital city. SP: *service général du sel, cour de sel de la capitale chargée de recevoir le sel de Kiai-tcheou.*

7332 *tū-yú* 督郵
HAN–N-S DIV (S. Dyn.): **Local Inspector,** lowly staff members of Commanderies (*chün*) grouped into Inspection Sections (*tu-yu ts'ao*) headed by Administrators (*yüan-shih*);

toured and inspected activities of Districts (*hsien*) in the jurisdiction; prefixed East, West, South, North, and Center and known collectively as the Local Inspectors of the Five Sectors (*wu-pu tu-yü*). HB: investigator. P53.

7333 *tū-yù* 都尉
See under the romanization *tu-wei.*

7334 *tū yǔ-hóu* 都虞侯
Inspector-in-chief; see under *yü-hou.*

7335 *tū yù-shǐh* 都御史
MING–CH'ING: **Censor-in-chief,** 2 prefixed Left and Right in Ming, 2 Left and 2 Right in Ch'ing, in each Ch'ing case one each Manchu and Chinese; rank 3a from 1383, 2a from 1384 to 1730, thereafter 1b, chief executives of the Censorate (*tu ch'a-yüan*) and among the most influential officials of the central government. Originated in 1383 after reorganization of the old-style Censorate (*yü-shih t'ai*) beginning in 1380; aided by varying numbers of Vice Censors-in-chief (*fu tu yü-shih*), 3a, and in Ming but not Ch'ing by Assistant Censors-in-chief (*ch'ien tu yü-shih*), 4a. Because of the great prestige of the censorial titles, which warranted denunciation of anyone in government for misconduct and remonstrance with the Emperor about both public and personal matters, from 1453 Grand Coordinators (*hsün-fu*) of Provinces (*sheng*), and later multi-Province Supreme Commanders (*tsung-tu*) as well, were routinely given nominal concurrent appointments as executive officials of the Censorate. Because of the proliferation of nominal Censors-in-chief that resulted by the late Ming years, it became the practice to designate those executive censors who were actually on duty in the Censorate with the prefix "in charge of the affairs" (*chang ... shih*) of the Censorate; and in Ch'ing it became regularized that those officials serving in the Censorate were prefixed Left, and the prefix Right was awarded those who were only nominally Censors-in-chief or Vice Censors-in-chief. Cf. *yü-shih ta-fu, chien-ch'a tu yü-shih*. BH: president of the censorate. P18.

7336 *tū-yú ssū* 都虞司
CH'ING: **Office of the Imperial Hunt,** one of the major agencies of the Imperial Household Department (*nei-wu fu*), headed by Grand Ministers (*ta-ch'en*) of the Department; incorporated the Imperial Kennels (*kou-fang*), Imperial Falcon Cage (*ying-fang*), and Imperial Hawk Aviary (*hu-fang*); in addition, managed the pay and duty assignments of members of the Three Inner Banners (*neì. san ch'i*). BH: department of the household guard and the imperial hunt. P37.

7337 *tū yüán-shuài fǔ* 都元帥府
Chief Military Command. (1) LIAO: a central government agency in the Northern Administration (*pei-mien*), apparently with operational control of the military under administrative supervision of the Bureau of Military Affairs (*shu-mi yüan*); staffed with members of the nobility entitled Commander-in-chief (*tu yüan-shuai*), Vice Commander-in-chief (*fu tu yüan-shuai*), etc. See *t'ien-hsia ping-ma yüan-shuai.* (2) CHIN: a central government agency having operational control over active military campaigns, also under administrative supervision of the Bureau of Military Affairs; occasionally controlled one or more Branch (*fen*) Military Commands; staffed as in (1) above. In 1208 perhaps absorbed into, or superseded by, the Bureau of Military Affairs. (3) YÜAN: a military agency headed by a Commander-in-chief (*tu yüan-shuai*) often established for special campaigns or as equivalents of Pacification Offices (*hsüan-wei ssu*) for aboriginal tribes of South and Southwest China. P72.

7338 *tū-yùn* 都運
(1) SUNG: abbreviation of *tu chuan-yün shih* (**Fiscal Commissioner-in-chief**). (2) CH'ING: unofficial reference to a **Salt Controller** (*yen-yün shih*).

7339 *tū yùn-ts'áo yù-shǐh* 督運漕御史
HAN: **Transport-control Censor,** duty assignment for Attendant Censors (*shih yü-shih*); monitored the shipment of tax grain to the dynastic capital. P18.

7340 *tū-yùn yù-shǐh* 督運御史
N-S DIV (Chin): **Transport-control Censor,** a duty assignment from 381, equivalent to Han's *tu yün-ts'ao yü-shih.* P18, 60.

7341 *t'ú* 圖
MING–CH'ING: lit., a map, i.e., an area shown on a map: **Plat,** an uncommon term for an area (as distinct from a unit) of sub-District (*hsien*) organization of the populace, especially in urban areas; approximately equivalent to a Precinct (*fang*) or Community (*li*).

7342 *t'ǔ* 土
YÜAN–CH'ING: lit., the land, of the land: **Aboriginal,** a prefix attached to the designations of units of territorial administration that were in fact aboriginal tribes or comparable groups of minority peoples in South and Southwest China, whose chiefs or headmen were only nominally government officials and, so long as they were submissive, were allowed to manage their peoples' affairs in customary ways, e.g., as Aboriginal District Magistrates (*t'u chih-hsien*). At times members of the regular Chinese civil service were attached to such agencies in advisory roles. See *t'u-kuan, t'u-ssu.* BH: native. P72.

7343 *t'ú* 徒
CHOU: **Eighth Class Administrative Official,** lowest of 8 categories in which officials were classified in a hierarchy separate from the formal rank system called the Nine Honors (*chiu ming*); below those designated, in descending order of prestige, *cheng* (Principal), *shih* (Mentor), *ssu* (in charge of; office), *lü* (Functionary), *fu* (Storekeeper), *shih* (Scribe), and *hsü* (Assistant). CL: *huitième degré de la subordination administrative; suivant.*

7344 *t'ú-chě* 屠者
HAN: **Meat Trimmer,** 70-odd non-official specialists on the staff of the Great Sacrificial Butcher (*t'ai-tsai ling*). HB: meat trimmer.

7345 *t'ǔ-chūn* 土均
CHOU: **Outer Land Assessor,** 2 ranked as Senior Servicemen (*shang-shih*), 4 as Ordinary Servicemen (*chung-shih*), and 8 as Junior Servicemen (*hsia-shih*), members of the Ministry of Education (*ti-kuan*) who evaluated the territories of all Feudal Lords (*chu-hou*) and determined what taxes, services, and rites the King should require of each. Counterparts of the Land Assessors (*chün-jen*), who made such determinations for sectors of the royal domain. CL: *égaliseur territorial.*

7346 *t'ǔ-chūn* 土軍
SUNG: **Local Army,** apparently a term used for irregular forces raised for defense purposes by local dignitaries with state approval. Cf. *t'u-ping, chia-ping, kuan-ping.* SP: *armée locale pour se défendre contre des bandits.*

7347 *t'ǔ-fāng shìh* 土方氏
CHOU: **Surveyor,** 5 ranked as Senior Servicemen (*shang-shih*) and 10 as Junior Servicemen (*hsia-shih*), members of the Ministry of War (*hsia-kuan*) who mapped the borders

of feudal states, towns, and other settlements throughout the country, presumably to provide topographic data for military purposes. CL: *agent de mesurage des régions*.

7348　*t'ǔ-hsǜn* 土訓
CHOU: **Royal Scout,** 2 ranked as Ordinary Servicemen (*chung-shih*) and 4 as Junior Servicemen (*hsia-shih*), members of the Ministry of Education (*ti-kuan*) who briefed the King on the topography through which he planned to travel and, in some degree, advised the King about the appropriate kinds of labor and products he might requisition from different regions. CL: *démonstrateur des terres*.

7349　*t'ú-huà chú* 圖畫局
SUNG: **Painter Service,** one of 4 assemblages of non-official specialists in the Artisans Institute (*han-lin yüan*) of the Palace Domestic Service (*nei-shih sheng*); headed by a Manager (*kou-tang kuan*). Also see *hua-yüan*. SP: *office ou service de peinture*.

7350　*t'ú-huà shǔ* 圖畫署
CHIN: **Office for Drawing and Painting,** one of 6 workshops in the Directorate for Imperial Manufactories (*shao-fu chien*), headed by a Director (*ling*), rank 6b; in 1196 merged with the Office for Ornamentation (*wen-ssu shu*) into a Crafts Office (*chih-ying ssu*). P38.

7351　*t'ù-hún kuēi-míng* 吐渾歸明
SUNG: **Submitted T'ü-yü-hun,** members of a Western frontier tribe who served in the Palace Command (*tien-ch'ien shih-wei ssu*). SP: *armée des T'ou-houen (T'ou-yu-houen) soumis*.

7352　*t'ǔ-kuān* 土官
YÜAN–CH'ING: **Aboriginal Official,** generic term for chiefs or headmen of aboriginal tribes and other minority groups in South and Southwest China who were incorporated nominally into the structure of Chinese government with designations as Pacification Commissioner (*hsüan-fu shih, hsüan-wei shih, an-fu shih*) or, especially from Ming on, with regular local administrative titles prefixed with *t'u* (Aboriginal), e.g., *t'u chih-fu* (Aboriginal Prefect). From the 1500s on, the term *t'u-kuan* was restricted principally to Pacification Commissioners, who though subordinated to the Ministry of War (*ping-pu*) retained full customary control over their subjects. The term *t'u-ssu* (Aboriginal Office) came to refer principally to regular administrative units prefixed *t'u,* located in areas with predominantly aboriginal populations but staffed with combinations of aboriginal and Chinese officials under supervision of the Ministry of Personnel (*li-pu*). The Aboriginal Offices had less autonomy than the Pacification Commissioners. BH: administrators of native districts. P72.

7353　*t'ǔ-pīng* 土兵
MING: **Aboriginal Troops,** usually prefixed with a place-name, a reference to contingents of fighting men from aboriginal tribes of South and Southwest China (see *t'u-kuan, t'u-ssu*) requisitioned for service with regular government military units, e.g., in fighting Wakō coastal raiders in the 1500s and Manchu invaders from the north in the 1600s. Several such groups were notoriously savage fighters and were hard for the Chinese officialdom to keep under control, but many fought loyally for Ming against the Manchus. P72.

7354　*t'ú-shū shǐh* 圖書使
T'ANG: **Librarian,** number and status not clear, in the Palace Library (*pi-shu sheng*). P25.

7355　*t'ǔ-ssū* 土司
YÜAN–CH'ING: **Aboriginal Office,** generic reference to Prefectures (*fu*) and lesser units of territorial administration in areas of South and Southwest China where the population predominantly consisted of aboriginal tribes or comparable minority peoples. Although the term was used occasionally in Yüan, the *t'u-ssu* system became regularized in Ming times as a means of incorporating unassimilated peoples into the structure of Chinese government, by giving tribal chiefs and headmen nominal official status and titles (normally prefixed *t'u,* Aboriginal) while allowing them customary, autonomous authority over their peoples so long as they were submissive. From the 1500s on, the term *t'u-ssu* referred primarily to areas that had become relatively assimilated and whose peoples bore the obligations of normal Chinese subjects; local administrators were tribal chiefs and regular civil service officials intermixed, under supervision of the Ministry of Personnel (*li-pu*). Such peoples and areas were distinguished from those governed by *t'u-kuan* (Aboriginal Officials), predominantly entitled Pacification Commissioners (*hsüan-fu shih, hsüan-wei shih, an-fu shih*), who retained most of their traditional autonomy though nominally subordinate to the Ministry of War (*ping-pu*). BH: native tribes and their chieftains. P72.

7356　*t'ū-t'ún* 吐屯
T'ANG: occasional unofficial reference to a **Censor** (*yü-shih*), derived from the title's Turkic translation.

7357　*tuān* 端
Occasionally a quasiofficial or unofficial reference to an official or to his principal office or quarters, the meaning determined by a prefix; e.g., see *kung-tuan* and *ch'u-tuan* (both Supervisor of the Household of the Heir Apparent), *hsien-ssu tuan* (Censorate), *chou-tuan* (Regional Headquarters).

7358　*tuān-ch'éng* 斷丞
SUNG: **Sentencing Aide,** 6, rank not clear, recommended decisions in judicial cases submitted for review to the Court of Judicial Review (*ta-li ssu*). SP: *juge assistant*. P22.

7359　*tuān-ch'éng* 端丞
CH'ING: unofficial reference to a **Supervisor of the Household** (*chan-shih*) of the Heir Apparent.

7360　*tuǎn-fān chiàng* 短番匠
T'ANG: **Rotational Artisan,** more than 5,000 employed in the Directorate of Imperial Manufactories (*shao-fu chien*); the prefix *tuan-fan* denotes that they were private artisans called into state service on relatively brief rotational schedules rather than professional careerists in government or hereditary state employees. RR: *artisan prenant un tour de service bref*. P38.

7361　*tuǎn-fān sǎn-yüèh* 短番散樂
T'ANG: **Rotational Entertainer,** 1,000 authorized for the Imperial Music Office (*t'ai-yüeh shu*); the prefix *tuan-fan* denotes that they were private entertainers in popular forms of music and dance who were requisitioned from Prefectures (*chou*) for relatively short-term service in rotation, not professional careerists in government or hereditary state employees. RR: *musicien de musique profane prenant un tour de service bref*.

7362　*tuān-fēi* 端妃
MING: **Upright Consort,** one of many Consort (*fei*) titles used for secondary wives of Emperors.

7363 *tuàn-hsíng ssū* 斷刑司 or 斷刑寺
SUNG: variant of *tso-t'ing* (**Left Bureau** in the Court of Judicial Review, *ta-li ssu*).

7364 *tuàn-k'ù* 緞庫
CH'ING: **Silks Storehouse,** one of 6 Storehouses managed by the Storage Office (*kuang-ch'u ssu*) of the Imperial Household Department (*nei-wu fu*); also see *liu k'u*. Cf. *tuan-p'i k'u* (Silks and Furs Storehouse). BH: silk store.

7365 *tuàn-kuān* 斷官
SUNG: abbreviation of *hsiang-tuan kuan* (**Sentence Evaluator**).

7366 *tuān-k'uéi* 端揆
T'ANG–SUNG: lit., the prime mover and mastermind (in government), a combination of archaic terms with awesome overtones used as an unofficial reference to **Grand Councilors** (*tsai-hsiang*), most specifically the 2 Vice Directors (*p'u-yeh*) of the Department of State Affairs (*shang-shu sheng*), who from early T'ang were commonly the most important executive officials at court. The Vice Director of the Left (*tso p'u-yeh*) was called Left Mastermind (*tso-k'uei*); his counterpart of the Right was called Right Mastermind (*yu-k'uei*).

7367 *tuān-kūng* 端公
Lit., the very honorable(s). (1) T'ANG–SUNG: unofficial reference to **executive officials of the Censorate** (*yü-shih t'ai*), especially the **Vice Censor-in-chief** (*yü-shih chung-ch'eng*). RR: *messieurs les chefs; les premiers au tribunal des censeurs.* (2) T'ANG: unofficial reference to any or all **Attendant Censors** (*shih yü-shih*). Cf. *san-tuan, tsa-tuan.* P18.

7368 *tuàn-kūng* 鍛工
N-S DIV (Chou): **Foundryman,** number unspecified, ranked as Senior Servicemen (*shang-shih;* 7a), Ordinary Servicemen (*chung-shih;* 8a), and Junior Servicemen (*hsia-shih;* 9a), members of the Ministry of Works (*tung-kuan*). P14.

7369 *tuān-liáo* 端僚
Lit., assistant to an executive (?): occasional unofficial reference to an **Administrator** or **Aide** (both *chang-shih*) in a unit of territorial administration.

7370 *tuàn-mò t'í-lǐng sǒ* 斷沒提領所
YÜAN: **Superintendency of Fines and Confiscations,** a unit of the Ministry of Justice (*hsing-pu*); in 1283 renamed Office of Fines and Confiscations (*ssu-chi 'so*).

7371 *tuàn-p'ǐ k'ù* 段疋庫
CH'ING: **Silks and Furs Storehouse,** a unit of the Ministry of Revenue (*hu-pu*) headed by a Director (*lang-chung*), rank 5a, who like all his subalterns was always a Manchu; received goods produced in state manufactories and made purchases from private merchants. BH: silk and fur storehouse. Cf. *tuan-k'u* (Silks Storehouse). P7.

7372 *tuàn-shìh* 斷事
YÜAN: **Judge,** rank 6a, head of a Judicial Office (*tuan-shih ssu*) in a Regional Military Commission (*tu chih-hui shih ssu*). P56.

7373 *tuān-shíh* 端石
Lit., the foundation-stone (of the court), i.e., someone who wields paramount influence over the ruler and authority over the officialdom. (1) N-S DIV–SUNG: an unofficial, awed reference to a **Grand Councilor** (*tsai-hsiang*) or an antecedent, most particularly suggesting a Director (*ling*) or a Vice Director (*p'u-yeh*) of the Department of State Affairs (*shang-shu sheng*). (2) N-S DIV (Liang): unofficial reference to a **Censor** (*yü-shih*).

7374 *tuàn-shìh chīng-lì* 斷事經歷
MING: **Judicial Registrar,** rank 7a, an assistant to the Judicial Administrator (*ts'an-chün tuan-shih kuan*) in the pre-dynastic Secretariat (*chung-shu sheng*); established in 1364, apparently terminated in 1368. P4.

7375 *tuàn-shìh kuān* 斷事官
YÜAN: **Judge,** large numbers, rank 3a or 3b, placed in agencies throughout the government, e.g., the Secretariat (*chung-shu sheng*), the Bureau of Military Affairs (*shu-mi yüan*), the High Court of Justice (*ta tsung-cheng fu*), the Commission for Buddhist and Tibetan Affairs (*hsüan-cheng yüan*), and all Princely Establishments (*wang-fu*). P4, 17, 69.

7376 *tuàn-shìh ssū* 斷事司
MING: **Judicial Office** on the staff of a Regional Military Commissioner (*tu chih-hui shih*), staffed with a Judge (*tuan-shih*), rank 6a, and Assistant Judges (*fu tuan-shih*), 7a; supervised all judicial proceedings by military authorities in the jurisdiction. P56.

7377 *tuān-ssū* 端司
CH'ING: unofficial reference to the **Household Administration of the Heir Apparent** (*chan-shih fu*).

7378 *tuān-yǐn fǔ* 端尹府
T'ANG–CH'ING: from 662 to 670 the official redesignation of the **Household Administration of the Heir Apparent** (*chan-shih fu*), the Supervisor of the Household (*chan-shih*) also being retitled *tuan-yin;* thereafter both terms remained in use as unofficial references to the agency and the post, respectively. P26.

7379 *tuān-yù* 端右
Apparent scribal error for *tuan-shih* (lit., foundation-stone), q.v.

7380 *t'uán* 團
Lit., a lump; used with various prefixes and suffixes to designate a cohesive military unit. (1) SUI: **Company** in the early Sui Garrison Militia (*fu-ping*) system, then a **Division** of 1,000 cavalrymen or 2,000 infantrymen in the mercenary armies raised by Emperor Yang. (2) T'ANG: **Regiment** of 200 soldiers in the early T'ang Garrison Militia system; from the 700s a **Company** of 50 soldiers in the Permanent Palace Guard (*ch'ang-ts'ung su-wei*).

7381 *t'uán-chǔ* 團主
(1) SUI: **Company Commander** in the Garrison Militia (*fu-ping*) organization. (2) T'ANG: **Regimental Commander** in the Garrison Militia organization.

7382 *t'uán-kuān* 團官
T'ANG: **Herder,** lowly or unranked personnel in Horse Pasturages (*mu-chien*) under the Court of the Imperial Stud (*t'ai-p'u ssu*). P31.

7383 *t'uán-lièn* 團練
Lit., to gather together and train; from T'ang on a term used in titles and in other ways in reference to militia forces. (1) SUNG: **Militia,** prefix used with the designation Prefecture (*chou, fu, chün*), signifying that the area was within the jurisdiction of a Military Training Commissioner (*t'uan-lien shih*). (2) CH'ING: **Company** of 50 militiamen organized by a District Magistrate (*chih-hsien*). See *hsiang-yung, min-chuang, min-ping.* Cf. *kuan-ping.*

7384 *t'uán-lièn ān-fǔ ch'üàn-núng shǐh ssū* 團練安撫勸農使司
YÜAN: **Military Training, Pacification, and Agricultural Development Commission,** several established in disturbed areas in 1358, each under a Counselor (*ts'an-mou*)

delegated from the central government, who supervised Commissioners (*shih*) in every Circuit (*tao*) under his jurisdiction. P52.

7385 *t'uàn-lièn chūn-shìh t'ūi-kuān* 團練軍事推官
SUNG: **Military Judge** on the staff of a Military Training Commissioner (*t'uan-lien shih*). SP: *juge militaire du commissaire impérial aux milices.*

7386 *t'uán-lièn kuān-ch'á shǐh* 團練觀察使
T'ANG: **Surveillance Commissioner for Military Training,** one of many types of central government delegates with supervisory authority over a cluster of contiguous Prefectures (*chou*) called a Circuit (*tao*); presumably had special responsibility for operation of the Garrison Militia (*fu-ping*) organization.

7387 *t'uán-lièn shǐh* 團練使
Military Training Commissioner. (1) T'ANG: one of many types of military dignitaries delegated from the court to supervise clusters of Prefectures (*chou*) called Circuits (*tao*); normally subordinate to Surveillance Commissioners (*kuan-ch'a shih*) or equivalents. RR: *commissaire impérial aux milices locales.* P52. (2) SUNG, LIAO: a regular military post at the Prefecture (*chou*) level, rank 5b, in Sung; in Liao members of the Southern Administration (*nan-mien*) in the central government. SP: *commissaire impérial aux milices locales, commandant des milices.* P52.

7388 *t'uán-lièn shǒu-chō shǐh* 團練守捉使
T'ANG: **Commissioner for Militiamen,** in 758 an unspecified number appointed to supervise the utilization of militiamen in jurisdictions comprising 2 or 3 Prefectures (*chou*) each; in 773 made a concurrent duty assignment for every Prefect (*tz'u-shih*); in 777 suppressed except in 5 Prefectures. See *tu t'uan-lien shou-cho shih, shou-cho.* RR: *commissaire impérial aux milices locales et aux détachements militaires.*

7389 *t'uán-yíng* 團營
MING: **Integrated Division,** military units established at Peking and Nanking in 1450 to replace or supplement Capital Training Divisions (*ching-ying*) for the training and tactical use of troops rotated to the capitals from Guards (*wei*) throughout the empire; discontinued in 1550. A special characteristic was that while in the Integrated Divisions troops trained under the same officers who would lead them in combat if the need arose. See *san ta-ying, jung-cheng t'ing.*

7390 *tùi* 隊
Company: from high antiquity recurringly used as the designation of a basic military unit consisting of 100 men, with variations between infantry and cavalry; headed by a Commander (*cheng, chiang, shih*). BH: platoon. P26, 69.

7391 *tūi-shīh* 追師
CHOU: **Master of Adornments,** 2 ranked as Junior Servicemen (*hsia-shih*), members of the Ministry of State (*t'ien-kuan*) who prepared headgear for the Queen and other palace ladies to wear on ceremonial occasions. CL: *chef des joailliers.*

7392 *tùi-tú kuān* 對讀官
YÜAN: **Grader** in a civil service recruitment examination; a duty assignment rather than a regular post (*kuan*).

7393 *t'ūi* 推
(1) T'ANG: **Surveillance Jurisdiction:** see under *ssu-t'ui yü-shih* (Four Surveillance Censors). (2) SUNG: abbreviation of *t'ui-an* (**Investigative Section** in the Court of Ju-

dicial Review, *ta-li ssu*). See under *tso-t'ui an* and *yu-t'ui an.* SP: *réviseur judiciaire.*

7394 *t'ūi-ch'éng* 推丞
SUNG: **Investigatory Aide,** 4, rank not clear; participated in the review of judicial cases submitted to the Court of Judicial Review (*ta-li ssu*). SP: *juge-adjoint.* P22.

7395 *t'ūi-chíh kuān* 推直官 or *t'ui-chih*
SUNG: **Auxiliary Investigator,** 4, rank not clear, basic staff members of the Censorate (*yü-shih t'ai*) till c. 1080, then terminated; one also in charge of the Censorate prison. SP: *investigateur auxiliaire, investigateur auxiliaire censorial.*

7396 *t'ūi-k'àn chiěn-fǎ kuān* 推勘檢法官
SUNG: **Legal Researcher for Investigations,** created in 1088 in the Ministry of Revenue (*hu-pu*); number not clear, probably unranked subofficials; responsible for resolving disputes about prices in the state marketplaces. SP: *fonctionnaire chargé d'investigations et du contrôle judiciaire.* P6.

7397 *t'ūi-k'àn kuān* 推勘官 or *t'ui-k'an*
SUNG: **Investigator,** 10 or more, rank not clear; established in the 990s in the Censorate (*yü-shih t'ai*) to work with Auxiliary Investigators (*t'ui-chih kuan*) reviewing reports of judicial proceedings; apparently terminated c. 1080. SP: *chargé d'investigations.*

7398 *t'ūi-k'àn yüàn* 推勘院
SUNG: **Investigations Office** under the State Finance Commission (*san ssu*) of early Sung; responsible for resolving disputes about prices in the state marketplaces; terminated in 1070, its functions transferred to the Court of Judicial Review (*ta-li ssu*). SP: *cour d'investigation.*

7399 *t'ūi-kuān* 推官
(1) T'ANG–CH'ING: **Judge,** one or more on the staffs of T'ang–Sung regional authorities such as Military Commissioners (*chieh-tu shih*), Surveillance Commissioners (*kuan-ch'a shih*), etc.; from Sung till the late 1600s, normally the 3rd executive of a Prefecture or Superior Prefecture (*fu*), abolished in early Ch'ing; rank not specified in T'ang, commonly 8b in Sung, 6b in Chin, 6b or 7a in Ming and early Ch'ing. Responsible for supervising judicial proceedings in the jurisdiction. RR: *juge.* SP: *juge, juge militaire.* P32, 49, 52, 53, 60. (2) SUNG: **Administrative Assistant,** 3 briefly on the staff of the State Finance Commission (*san ssu*) in 993. P6.

7400 *t'ūi-p'àn* 推判
SUNG–MING: combined, abbreviated reference to **Judges** (*t'ui-kuan*) and **Assistant Prefects** (*p'an-kuan, t'ung-p'an*) in Prefectures and Superior Prefectures (*fu*).

7401 *t'ùi-ts'ái ch'áng* 退材場
SUNG: **Waste Retrieval Yard** under the Directorate for the Palace Buildings (*chiang-tso chien*); responsible for sifting through the Directorate's (?) cast-off materials and salvaging anything still useful for construction purposes or for fuel; headed by an unranked Supervisor (*chien-kuan*). SP: *bureau chargé de la réception des matériaux inutilisables de l'intérieur et de l'extérieur de la capitale.* P15.

7402 *tùn-tì shǐh* 頓遞使
SUNG: **Commissioner for Hostels and Postal Relay Stations,** number, rank, and organizational affiliation not clear; possibly duty assignments for personnel of units of territorial administration. SP: *commissaire chargé des approvisionnements et des relais en route.*

7403 *tūn-tsūng yüàn* 敦宗院
SUNG: **Hostel for Imperial Kinsmen**, one each maintained by the Southern Office and the Western Office of Imperial Clan Affairs (*nan-wai tsung-cheng ssu, hsi-wai tsung-cheng ssu*) at Yangchow and Loyang, respectively. SP: *cour de la surveillance et de l'éducation de la famille impériale.*

7404 *t'ún* 屯
HAN: lit., camp, settlement: **Company**, common designation for a small unit in a Campaigning Army (*ying*), headed by a Commander (*chang*); several such units commonly constituted a Regiment (*ch'ü*). HB: platoon.

7405 *t'ún-chì hsiào-wèi* 屯騎校尉
HAN–N-S DIV: **Commandant of Garrison Cavalry**, one of 8 Commandants (*hsiao-wei*) ranked at 2,000 bushels who were in charge of the Northern Army (*pei-chün*) at the dynastic capital in Han times; assisted by one or more Aides (*ch'eng*), Commanders (*ssu-ma*), and lesser officers. The post-Han S. Dynasties had as many as 7 officers with this title on the staff of the Heir Apparent. HB: colonel of garrison cavalry. P26.

7406 *t'ún-chì wèi* 屯騎尉
SUI: **Commandant of Garrison Cavalry**, 2nd highest of 8, later 16, prestige titles (*san-kuan*) awarded to military officers of rank 6a or 6b. P65.

7407 *t'ún-chiēn* 屯監
T'ANG–SUNG: **State Farm Directorate**, in charge of one of many State Farms (*t'un-t'ien*) that were scattered throughout the empire to help provision the military forces; each headed by a Supervisor (*chien*), rank 7b2 in T'ang; subordinate to the Court of the National Granaries (*ssu-nung ssu*). RR+SP: *direction de colonie militaire.*

7408 *t'ún-pù* 屯部
MING: **State Farms Bureau**, a major subdivision of the Ministry of Works (*kung-pu*); renamed from *t'un-t'ien pu* in 1380, then in 1396 renamed *t'un-t'ien ch'ing-li ssu*. P15.

7409 *t'ún-t'ién* 屯田
(1) HAN–CH'ING: **State Farm**, generic designation of tracts of state-owned agricultural land, or wilderness considered to have agricultural potentiality, that were assigned to soldiers, to landless peasants, or to resettled colonists; it was usually hoped that such assignees, if soldiers, might become self-sufficient by part-time farming or, if non-military personnel, might produce surpluses for special state uses, especially military; originated not later than 87 B.C. A common rendering is Agricultural Colony. See *chün-t'un* (Army Farm), *min-t'un* (Civilian State Farm), *shang-t'un* (Merchant Farm). HB: agricultural garrison. RR+SP: *colonie militaire.* BH: military-agricultural settlement. P14, 15, 52, 59. (2) N-S DIV: **State Farms Section** in the developing Department of State Affairs (*shang-shu sheng*), headed by a Minister (*shang-shu*) or a Director (*lang, lang-chung*), often more directly subordinate to the evolving Ministry of Rites (*i-ts'ao, tz'u-pu*); apparently not of special military significance. P14. (3) SUI–CH'ING: common abbreviated reference to the **State Farms Bureau** (*t'un-t'ien ssu, t'un-t'ien ch'ing-li ssu*) in the Ministry of Works (*kung-pu*). P14, 15.

7410 *t'ún-t'ién ch'iēn-hù sǒ* 屯田千戶所
YÜAN–MING: **State Farm Battalion**, a military unit assigned to full-time farming work on state-owned land. See *ch'ien-hu so.*

7411 *t'ún-t'ién ch'īng-lì ssū* 屯田清吏司
MING–CH'ING: **State Farms Bureau**, one of 4 principal agencies in the Ministry of Works (*kung-pu*), headed by a Director (*lang-chung*), rank 5a, in Ming, in Ch'ing by one Chinese and 4 Manchu Directors, 5a; supervised the management of State Farms (*t'un-t'ien*) throughout the empire, primarily to help provision the military establishment. P14, 15.

7412 *t'ún-t'ién kuǎn-kōu* 屯田管勾
CH'ING: **State Farms Clerk**, one, rank 7a, authorized for the Confucian family estate in Shantung presided over by the current most direct male descendant of Confucius, ennobled as Duke for Fulfilling the Sage (*yen-sheng kung*); responsible for receipts and expenditures concerning the estate's state-endowed lands and for providing sacrificial animals at times of major sacrifices. P66.

7413 *t'ún-t'ién shǐh ssū* 屯田使司
YÜAN: **State Farms Commission**, controlling both military and civilian personnel and accordingly sometimes prefixed *chün-min* (military-civilian), established in 1355 at P'ei-hsien in northern Kiangsu, headed by a Commissioner (*shih*), rank 3a; a response to natural calamities and popular unrest in the area. P52.

7414 *t'ún-t'ién ssū* 屯田司
(1) SUI–SUNG: **State Farms Bureau**, one of the major agencies in the Ministry of Works (*kung-pu*); headed by a Vice Minister (*shih-lang*) or Director (*lang-chung*) in Sui, by a Director thereafter, rank 5b in T'ang, 6b in Sung; supervised the management of State Farms (*t'un-t'ien*) throughout the empire in collaboration with the Court of the National Treasury (*ssu-nung ssu*), principally to produce supplementary provisions for the military establishment. RR+SP: *bureau des colonies militaires.* P14, 15. (2) SUNG: **State Farms Office**, apparently a regional supervisory agency headed by a Commissioner (*shih*). P59. (3) MING–CH'ING: common abbreviation of *t'un-t'ien ch'ing-li ssu* (**State Farms Bureau**).

7415 *t'ún-t'ién tǎ-pǔ tsǔng-kuǎn fǔ* 屯田打捕總管府
YÜAN: **Route Command for State Farms and Hunting**, designation of a unit of territorial administration prefixed with the regional name Huai-tung or Huai-hsi, based in Honan Province; directly subordinate to the Palace Provisions Commission (*hsüan-hui yüan*).

7416 *t'ún-t'ién tào* 屯田道
CH'ING: **State Farms Circuit**, one of the types of supervisory Circuits (see *tao*) established by Provincial Administration Commissions (*ch'eng-hsüan pu-cheng shih ssu*) in early Ch'ing; oversaw the functioning of State Farms (*t'un-t'ien*) in its jurisdiction. BH: taotai of agricultural settlements.

7417 *t'ún-t'ién wàn-hù fǔ* 屯田萬戶府
YÜAN: **State Farms Brigade**, a large military unit principally responsible for the functioning of State Farms (*t'un-t'ien*) in its jurisdiction, or whose soldiers were themselves principally engaged in farming.

7418 *t'ún-wèi* 屯衛
Encampment Guard. (1) HAN: collective reference to those soldiers under the jurisdiction of the Chamberlain for the Palace Garrison (*wei-wei*) who actively guarded all the entries into the imperial quarters, led by a total of 22 Commanders (*ssu-ma*) and Commandants (*hou*). HB: garrison guard. (2) SUI–SUNG: 2 prefixed Left and Right, among

the elite military units at the capital collectively called the Twelve Guards (*shih-erh wei*) or the Sixteen Guards (*shih-liu wei*); in T'ang renamed Awesome Guards (*wei-wei*) in 622 and so called thereafter except for the interval 705–711, when the name *t'un-wei* was revived. RR+SP: *garde de cantonnement*.

7419 *t'ún-yíng* 屯營
T'ANG: **Encampment,** 2 prefixed Left and Right, military units created in 638 under the Imperial Army of Original Followers (*yüan-ts'ung chin-chün*), consisting of troops called Flying Cavalrymen (*fei-chi*), including new recruits from elite families; commanded by Generals (*chiang-chün*) of the Southern Command (*nan-ya*); in 662 dissolved when the Imperial Army of Original Followers was transformed into the Left and Right Forest of Plumes Armies (*yü-lin chün*). RR: *cantonnement*.

7420 *tūng* 東
East: a common prefix in agency names and some official titles, ordinarily contrasting with West (*hsi*) but in other directional combinations as well; in addition to the following entries, look for entries formed by the characters that follow *tung* wherever encountered.

7421 *tūng-ch'ǎng* 東廠
MING: **Eastern Depot,** a palace eunuch agency created in 1420 to investigate treasonable offenses of any kind, gradually becoming a kind of imperial secret service headquarters not subject to the control of any regular governmental organization, and greatly feared; ordinarily headed by the powerful eunuch Director (*t'ai-chien*) of the eunuch Directorate of Ceremonial (*ssu-li chien*), who used personnel of the Imperial Bodyguard (*chin-i wei*) as the Depot's policemen. Also see *hsi-ch'ang* (Western Depot).

7422 *tūng-ch'áo* 東朝
Eastern Court: from Han on, a common unofficial reference to the chambers, and thus indirectly to the person, of either the Heir Apparent or the mother of the Emperor. Precise identification for any period seems possible only by inference from the context. See *tung-kung*.

7423 *tūng-chiēn* 東監
(1) SUI–T'ANG: **Directorate of the Eastern Parks,** one of 4 Directorates (*chien*) in charge of maintaining the building and grounds of imperial parks and gardens in the 4 quadrants of the dynastic capital city; in Sui under the supervision of the Directorate-general of the Imperial Parks (*yüan tsung-chien*), in T'ang under that of the Court of the National Granaries (*ssu-nung ssu*); in both periods headed by a Supervisor (*chien*), rank 6b2 in T'ang. Also see *ssu-mien chien*. P40. (2) CHIN: abbreviated reference to the **Eastern Directorate of Coinage** (*pao-yüan ch'ien-chien*).

7424 *tūng-chīh* 東織
HAN: **East Weaving Shop** under the Chamberlain for the Palace Revenues (*shao-fu*), headed by a Director (*ling*); eventually combined with a West Weaving Shop (*hsi-chih*) into a single Weaving Shop (*chih-shih*). HB: eastern weaving house. P37.

7425 *tūng-ch'īng* 冬卿
Winter Chamberlain, an archaic reference deriving from Chou usage of the term *tung-kuan*, q.v. (1) N-S DIV (Liang): generic or collective reference to 3 of the central government officials called the Twelve Chamberlains (*shih-erh ch'ing*). (2) SUI–CH'ING: unofficial reference to the Minister (*shang-shu*) or Vice Minister (*shih-lang*) of the Ministry of Works (*kung-pu*).

7426 *tùng-chǔ* 洞主
5 DYN–MING: lit., master of the grotto: **Dean,** a common designation of the head of an instructional Academy (*shu-yüan*), private or state-sponsored.

7427 *tūng-ch'ú* 東儲
N-S DIV–CH'ING: unofficial reference to the **Heir Apparent** (*t'ai-tzu*); see *ch'u, tung-kung*.

7428 *tūng-ch'üan* 東銓
T'ANG: **Selector of the East,** unofficial reference to one of the Vice Ministers (*shih-lang*) of the Ministry of Personnel (*li-pu*), contrasted with the other Vice Minister's unofficial designation as Selector of the West (*hsi-ch'üan*); reference is to the Ministry's role in selecting appointees for office. See *ch'üan, shang-shu ch'üan, chung-ch'üan*. Cf. *tung-hsüan*.

7429 *tūng-fǔ* 東府
SUNG: **East Administration,** unofficial reference to the major civil agencies in the central government, the Three Departments (*san sheng*)—especially the Secretariat (*chung-shu sheng*)—and the Grand Councilors (*tsai-hsiang, ch'eng-hsiang*), contrasted with the West Administration (*hsi-fu*), referring to the Bureau of Military Affairs (*shu-mi yüan*). These civil and military aggregations were known collectively as the Two Administrations (*erh fu*).

7430 *tūng-háng* 東行
T'ANG: **East Echelon** of Ministries (*pu*) in the Department of State Affairs (*shang-shu sheng*), specifically the Ministries of Personnel (*li-pu*), Revenue (*hu-pu*), and Rites (*li-pu*), contrasted with 3 others in a West Echelon (*hsi-hang*); supervised by the Left Assistant Director (*tso-ch'eng*) of the Department.

7431 *tūng-hó* 東河
CH'ING: unofficial reference to the **Director-general of the Grand Canal** (*ho-tao tsung-tu*) stationed at Chi-nan, Shantung; distinguished from the Director-general stationed at Huai-an, called *nan-ho*.

7432 *tūng-hsī k'ù* 東西庫
SUNG: **Eastern and Western Storehouses,** a combined reference to the 2 principal subsections of the Left Storehouse (*tso-tsang*) in the Court of the Imperial Treasury (*t'ai-fu ssu*). P7.

7433 *tūng-hsüǎn* 東選
T'ANG: **Appointer of the East,** unofficial reference to one of the Vice Ministers (*shih-lang*) of the Ministry of War (*ping-pu*), as distinguished from the Appointer of the West (*hsi-hsüan*); also see *hsüan, chung-hsüan*. The usage derives from the role played by the Vice Ministers in selecting appointees for military offices. Cf. *tung-ch'üan*.

7434 *tūng-í shìh-chě* 東夷使者
SUI: **Commissioner for Eastern Tributaries,** a member of the Court for Dependencies (*hung-lu ssu*) designated on an ad hoc basis to set up an Office (*shu*) to supervise arrangements for the treatment of envoys or chiefs from tribes on China's northeastern frontier; c. 610 superseded the consolidated Hostel for Tributary Envoys (*ssu-fang kuan*). P11.

7435 *tūng jǎn-yüàn* 東染院
SUNG: **East Dyeing Office,** a palace workshop headed by a Commissioner (*shih*). See *hsi jan-yüan*. SP: *cour orientale de teinturerie*.

7436 *tūng-kó chì-chiǔ* 東閣祭酒
SUI–T'ANG: **Master of Ceremonies in the East Hall,** a receptionist, rank 7b1, in a Princely Establishment (*wang-*

fu); difference from *hsi-ko chi-chiu* not clear. RR: *maître des cérémonies de la salle de l'est de la maison d'un prince*. P69.

7437 · *tŭng-k'ù* 東庫
SUNG: **Eastern Storehouse**, one of several storage facilities constituting the Left Storehouse (*tso-tsang*), which stored general state revenues under the supervision of the Court of the Imperial Treasury (*t'ai-fu ssu*).

7438 *tŭng-kuān* 冬官
(1) CHOU–CH'ING: **Ministry of Works:** in Chou the 6th of 6 top-echelon agencies in the central government, headed by a Minister of Works (*ssu-k'ung*) ranked as a Minister (*ch'ing*); responsible for 60 subordinate agencies or officials in charge of different sorts of provisioning activities. Revived by Chou of the N. Dynasties to replace what had been known as the *ch'i-pu* (Bureau of Public Construction); revived again in T'ang from 684 to 705 to replace the name *kung-pu* (Ministry of Works). In all later eras may be encountered as an unofficial, archaic reference to the *kung-pu*. CL: *ministère des travaux publics*. P14. (2) T'ANG–CH'ING: **Winter Office,** one of 5 seasonal Offices of calendrical specialists, including one for Mid-year (*chung*), in the T'ang Astrological Service (*t'ai-shih chü*) and later Bureau of Astronomy (*ssu-t'ien t'ai*), the Sung Astrological Service (*t'ai-shih chü*), the Sung–Ming Directorate of Astronomy (*ssu-t'ien chien*), and the Ming–Ch'ing Directorate of Astronomy (*ch'in-t'ien chien*); headed by a Director (*ling* in early T'ang, otherwise *cheng*), rank 5a except 8a in Sung and 6b in Ming and Ch'ing, in Ch'ing one Chinese and one Manchu appointee. RR+SP: *administration de l'hiver*. BH (*cheng*): astronomer for the winter. P35. (3) MING: **Winter Support,** from 1380 to 1382 one of 4 posts, each named after a season and open to more than one appointee, intended for the Emperor's closest and most trusted advisers; see *ssu fu-kuan* (Four Supports). P4, 67.

7439 *tŭng-kuān* 東觀
(1) HAN–N-S DIV (S. Dyn.): **Eastern Library,** designation of a group of scholarly officials summoned into the Later Han palace for historiographic and other editorial work; although lacking any formal organization, it was headed by a Chancellor (*chi-chiu*); perpetuated in the post-Han years, it was incorporated in 470 into the new Library for Complete Discernment (*tsung-ming kuan*). This was one of the earliest organized antecedents of the famous later Hanlin Academy (*han-lin yüan*). P23. (2) MING–CH'ING: an unofficial, archaic reference to the **Hanlin Academy.**

7440 *tŭng-kŭng* 東宮
Eastern Palace: throughout imperial history the designation of the residence of the Heir Apparent (*t'ai-tzu*), hence also a common indirect reference to the person of the Heir Apparent.

7441 *tŭng-kŭng chiŭ mù-chiēn* 東宮九牧監
T'ANG: **The Heir Apparent's Nine Directorates of Horse Pasturages,** apparently a single consolidated agency under the Court of the Imperial Stud (*t'ai-p'u ssu*) that maintained the herds of horses and cattle from which the establishment of the Heir Apparent was supplied; headed by 2 Aides (*ch'eng*), rank 8a; apparently established after the mid-700s, perhaps replacing the Stables Office (*chiu-mu shu*) of the Heir Apparent's staff. RR: *les neuf directions des élevages de l'héritier du trône*.

7442 *tŭng-kŭng liù-fú* 東宮六傅
Six Mentors of the Eastern Palace, an unofficial collective reference to the *t'ai-tzu san-shih* (Three Preceptors of

the Heir Apparent) and the *t'ai-tzu san-shao* (Three Junior Counselors of the Heir Apparent).

7443 *tŭng-kŭng pīn-k'ò* 東宮賓客
HAN–N-S DIV (Chin): **Adviser to the Eastern Palace,** a quasiofficial designation for an eminent court official, signifying his responsibility to counsel the Heir Apparent. Cf. *t'ai-tzu pin-k'o*. P67.

7444 *tŭng-kŭng sān-shǎo* 東宮三少
Common unofficial variant of *t'ai-tzu san-shao* (**Three Junior Counselors of the Heir Apparent**).

7445 *tŭng-kŭng sān-shīh* 東宮三師
Common unofficial variant of *t'ai-tzu san-shih* (**Three Preceptors of the Heir Apparent**).

7446 *tŭng-kŭng sān-t'ài* 東宮三太
Three Grand Attendants in the Eastern Palace: collective reference to the nominally substantive but actually honorific posts called Grand Preceptor of the Heir Apparent (*t'ai-tzu t'ai-shih*), Grand Mentor of the Heir Apparent (*t'ai-tzu t'ai-fu*), and Grand Guardian of the Heir Apparent (*t'ai-tzu t'ai-pao*).

7447 *tŭng-mén ch'ŭ-sŏ ssū* 東門取索司
SUNG: **Tolls Office at the East Gate** (?), a unit of the Palace Eunuch Service (*ju-nei nei-shih sheng*); function not clear. SP: *bureau de la réclamation de porte de l'est*.

7448 *tŭng-pù wèi* 東部尉
HAN: **Commandant of the Metropolitan Police, East Sector,** one, rank 400 bushels, under the Metropolitan Commandant (*ssu-li hsiao-wei*) in Later Han, responsible for police supervision of the eastern quadrant of the dynastic capital, Loyang. See *tso-pu* (Left Sector), *kuang-pu wei*. P20.

7449 *tŭng sān shĕng* 東三省
CH'ING: **Three Eastern Provinces,** quasiofficial collective reference to the Provinces of Feng-t'ien, Kirin, and Heilungkiang, comprising what Westerners commonly call Manchuria; administered by one Governor-general (*tsung-tu*) with status as Manchu General (*chiang-chün*).

7450 *tŭng shàng kó-mén* 東上閣門
SUNG–CHIN: **Palace Audience Gate of the East;** see under *shang ko-men* (Palace Audience Gate). SP: *porte du pavillon supérieur de l'est, bureau des cérémonies de félicitation*. P33.

7451 *tŭng-shĭh* 東使
(1) **East Commissioner:** may be found in any period referring to an east-west or a north-south-east-west differentiation among officials delegated from the dynastic capital with functions possibly clarified by prefixes. (2) T'ANG: **Commissioner for the Eastern Pasturages,** an official of the Court of the Imperial Stud (*t'ai-p'u ssu*) delegated to establish new horse pasturages or to inspect existing Directorates of Horse Pasturages (*mu-chien*) in the eastern parts of North China. This assignment was apparently discontinued in mid-T'ang. See *yen-chou shih*. RR: *commissaire impérial (aux élevages) de l'est*.

7452 *tŭng-ssū* 東司
CH'ING: **Eastern Office,** one of 8 units in the Rear Subsection (*hou-so*) of the Imperial Procession Guard (*luan-i wei*), headed by a Director (*chang-yin yün-hui shih*), rank 4a. BH: eastern section.

7453 *tŭng-t'ái* 東臺
T'ANG: **Eastern Tower,** official redesignation from 662 to

670 of the Chancellery (*men-hsia sheng*); also an unofficial reference to a Censor-in-chief (*yü-shih ta-fu*) stationed in the Eastern Capital, Loyang. See *liu-t'ai*. RR: *tribunal de l'est*. P3, 18.

7454 *tūng-t'ái shè-jén* 東臺舍人
T'ANG: **Supervising Secretary of the Chancellery** (*men-hsia sheng*), official redesignation from 661 to 670 of *chi-shih-chung* (Supervising Secretary), apparently to provide symmetry with the title Secretariat Drafter (*chung-shu she-jen*). P19.

7455 *tūng-t'óu* 東頭
SUNG: unofficial reference to the **Express Courier Office** (*ch'ü-shih yüan*) in the Institute of Academicians (*hsüeh-shih yüan*). P23.

7456 *tūng-tū yüàn* 東都苑
T'ANG: **Imperial Parks at the Eastern Capital** (Loyang), collective reference to 4 agencies of the Court of the National Granaries (*ssu-nung ssu*) that were so prefixed, namely, the Directorates of the West Imperial Park (*hsi-mien chien*) and the North, East, and South Imperial Parks. RR: *direction du côté ... des parcs de la capitale de l'est*.

7457 *tūng-ts'áo* 冬曹
T'ANG–CH'ING: lit., (member of) the winter section: unofficial reference to a **Vice Minister** (*shih-lang*) **of the Ministry of Works** (*kung-pu*); see *tung-kuan* (Ministry of Works).

7458 *tūng-ts'áo* 東曹
Eastern Section. (1) HAN: one of a dozen or more Sections (*ts'ao*) under the Defender-in-chief (*t'ai-wei*) and probably also under the Counselor-in-chief (*ch'eng-hsiang*) in the central government, headed by an Administrator (*yüan-shih*), rank =400 bushels; managed fiscal affairs for which their superiors were responsible. HB: bureau of the east. P12. (2) T'ANG: unofficial reference to the Ministry of Personnel (*li-pu*).

7459 *tūng-t'ūi* 東推
T'ANG: **East Surveillance Jurisdiction**, one of 2 jurisdictions defined for censorial surveillance; see under *ssu-t'ui yü-shih* (Four Surveillance Censors). RR: *examen judiciaire des affaires de l'est*.

7460 *tūng-yěh* 東冶
N-S DIV (S. Dyn.): **Eastern Mint**, one of several coin-producing agencies, each with a Director (*ling*) or an Aide (*ch'eng*) in charge, under the Chamberlain for the Palace Revenues (*shao-fu*); see *yeh*. P16.

7461 *tūng-yüàn* 東院
SUNG: **East Bureau.** (1) Abbreviation of *shen-kuan tung-yüan* (East Bureau of Personnel Evaluation); see under *shen-kuan yüan*. (2) A term apparently used in early Sung on some seals authorized for the Bureau of Military Affairs (*shu-mi yüan*) in contrast to others marked West Bureau (*hsi-yüan*), although the terms had no relevance to the organizational structure of the unified Bureau.

7462 *tūng-yüán chiàng* 東園匠
HAN–N-S DIV (Chin): **Carpenter of the Eastern Park**, number not clear; craftsmen specially skilled at making coffins and other goods for sacrificial and mourning uses, on the staff of the Chamberlain for the Palace Revenues (*shao-fu*); headed by a Director (*ling*) with an Aide (*ch'eng*). HB: artisans of the eastern garden. P14, 37.

7463 *tūng-yüán chǔ-chāng* 東園主章
HAN: **Woodsman of the Eastern Park**, number not clear;

craftsmen skilled at working with large timbers for construction, headed by a Director (*ling*) with an Aide (*ch'eng*); under the Chamberlain for the Palace Buildings (*chiang-tso shao-fu*). Redesignated *mu-kung* in 104 B.C. HB: prefect of large timbers for the eastern garden. P14.

7464 *t'úng* 同
T'ANG–CH'ING: **Associate** or **Jointly**, a prefix generally indicating that an official already serving in one post had been assigned, additionally, to take part in the work of another post; normally more prestigious than *fu* (Vice). SP: -*adjoint*.

7465 *t'ǔng* 統
N-S DIV (N. Ch'i): **Controller**, 2nd executive, after the Controller-in-chief (*ta-t'ung*), in the Office for the Clarification of Buddhist Profundities (*chao-hsüan yüan*). May be found in other offices of the era. P17.

7466 *t'ūng-chāng shǔ* 通章署
N-S DIV (Chin): **Communications Office**, apparently a palace agency that accepted memorials, headed by a military officer; but sources are not clear. P21.

7467 *t'ūng-chèng shǐh ssū* 通政使司
MING–CH'ING: **Office of Transmission**, an autonomous central government agency responsible for receiving, registering in ledgers, and presenting in audience all memorials submitted from throughout the empire; to some extent had "veto" (see *feng-po*) power to reject memorials considered improper either in form or in substance. Headed by a Commissioner (*shih*), rank 3a, in Ch'ing one each Manchu and Chinese. Principal aides were Vice Commissioners (*t'ung-cheng* till 1748, then *fu-shih*), 4a, and Assistant Commissioners (*ts'an-i*), 5a. For about a decade from 1379, the staff also incorporated Supervising Secretaries (*chi-shih-chung*). Also see *t'ung-chin ssu*. BH: transmission office. P21.

7468 *t'úng chēng-yüán* 同正員
T'ANG: lit., the same as a regular official: **Supplementary Official**, a category of officials with status between those designated Regular Officials (*cheng-yüan*) and those designated Supernumeraries (*yüan-wai*), Regular referring to those officials within the total staff quota of 730 (640? 643?) deemed sufficient early in the dynasty; created in the 650s with the provision that Supplementary Officials should draw the same pay as Regular Officials but receive no income from Office Lands (*chih-t'ien*). RR: *fonctionnaire assimilé aux réguliers*.

7469 *t'ūng-chèng yüàn* 通政院
YÜAN: **Bureau of Transmission**, an agency of the Ministry of War (*ping-pu*) that supervised operation of the postal relay system; created in 1276 through reorganization of the earlier office of the Controller-general of Postal Relay Stations (*chu-chan tu t'ung-ling shih*), subsequently one established at each capital, Ta-tu and Shang-tu; from 1292 to 1303 there was a Chiang-nan Branch Bureau (*fen-yüan*). Headed by one or more Commissioners (*shih*), rank 2b. P12, 17.

7470 *t'úng-ch'iēn* 同簽
SUNG–YÜAN: lit., cosignatory: **Deputy**, a variant of *t'ung* (Associate, Jointly). SP: *co-signataire*.

7471 *t'úng-chīh* 同知
(1) SUNG–MING: **Associate Administrator** or **Associate**, common designation for a secondary executive official in an agency headed by an Administrator (*chih*). SP: *chargé conjointement, assistant, administrateur-adjoint, coadmi-*

nistrateur. P1, 3, 5, 12, 21, etc. (2) YÜAN–CH'ING: **Vice Prefect,** 2nd executive in a Prefecture (*fu*, in Yüan also *chou*), assistant to a Prefect (*chih-fu*); rank 6a to 7a in Yüan, 5a in Ming and Ch'ing; in Ch'ing prefixed in many ways to indicate specialized functions. BH: first class sub-prefect. P32, 53, 60. (3) MING: **Vice Magistrate** in a Subprefecture (*chou*), rank 6b, assisting a Subprefectural Magistrate (*chih-chou*). P53, 54. (4) CH'ING: **Subprefectural Magistrate,** rank 5a, head of a Subprefecture (*t'ing*). BH: sub-prefect.

7472 *t'ŭng-chìh* 統制
SUNG: **Commander-general,** in S. Sung a common designation for leaders of armies; less prestigious than Supreme Commandant (*tu t'ung-chih*), more so than Commander-general (*t'ung-ling*). SP: *commandant général, gouverneur militaire général*.

7473 *t'ūng-chíh láng* 通直郎
SUI–SUNG: **Court Gentleman for Comprehensive Duty,** prestige title (*san-kuan*) for civil officials of rank 6b. P68.

7474 *t'ūng-chíh sǎn-chì ch'áng-shìh* 通直散騎常侍
N-S DIV (N. Ch'i, Chou): **Senior Recorder for Comprehensive Duty,** common designation for officials who, in addition to their regular functions, were specially assigned to participate in compilation of the Imperial Diary (*ch'i-chü chu*); a common variant was *t'ung-chih san-chi shih-lang*. Also see under *san-chi ch'ang-shih*. P24.

7475 *t'úng chìn-shìh ch'ū-shēn* 同進士出身
SUNG–CH'ING: lit., to enter service (*ch'u-shen*) with status equal to Presented Scholar or Metropolitan Graduate (both *chin-shih*): **Associate Metropolitan Graduate,** categorical designation of those new *chin-shih* who ranked in the lowest group (*chia*) of passers of the Palace Examination (*tien-shih, t'ing-shih*). Cf. *chin-shih chi-ti* (Metropolitan Graduate with Honors), *chin-shih ch'u-shen* (Regular Metropolitan Graduate).

7476 *t'ūng-chìn ssū* 通進司
SUNG–LIAO: **Memorial-forwarding Office,** an agency of the Chancellery (*men-hsia sheng*) staffed principally with Supervising Secretaries (*chi-shih-chung*), through whom memorials from throughout the empire were passed to the Emperor and his rescripts were distributed to appropriate agencies; also maintained the Emperor's files. Exercised "veto" (see *feng-po*) powers over both incoming and outgoing documents, returning them for reconsideration if deemed inappropriate either in form or in substance. Originally, in early Sung, separate from the Office of Transmission (*yin-t'ai ssu*), with which it shared its functions in some way not clear; soon the two were combined in the *t'ung-chin yin-t'ai ssu*, normally abbreviated as *t'ung-chin ssu*. Headed by an Administrator (*chih;* to know, etc.). SP: *office de la réception des rapports*. P21.

7477 *t'ūng-chìn yín-t'ái ssū* 通進銀臺司
SUNG: **Memorial-forwarding Office,** a combination of the names *t'ung-chin ssu* and *yin-t'ai ssu;* see under *t'ung-chin ssu*, the normal abbreviation. P21.

7478 *t'úng ch'ū-shēn* 同出身
SUNG: abbreviation of *t'ung chin-shih ch'u-shen* (**Associate Metropolitan Graduate**).

7479 *t'úng-chuǎn* 同轉
CH'ING: abbreviated reference to a **Deputy Salt Controller** (*yen-yün ssu yün-t'ung*); also see *chuan-yün shih*.

7480 *t'úng chūng-shū mén-hsià p'íng-chāng shìh* 同中書門下平章事
T'ANG–SUNG: **Jointly Manager of Affairs with the Secretariat-Chancellery,** designation of central government dignitaries who, in addition to their regular functions, participated in deliberations in the Administration Chamber (*cheng-shih t'ang*) as Grand Councilors (*tsai-hsiang*). Also see *p'ing-chang shih*. RR: *fonctionnaire chargé d'examiner et régler les affaires avec les présidents du département du grand secrétariat impérial et du département de la chancellerie impériale*. SP: *premier ministre chargé … (as RR)*. P3.

7481 *t'úng chūng-shū mén-hsià sán-p'ǐn* 同中書門下三品
T'ANG: **Cooperating with Third Rank Officials of the Secretariat-Chancellery,** designation added to the regular title of an official, usually an executive of the Department of State Affairs (*shang-shu sheng*), who additionally was assigned or authorized to participate in the deliberations at the Administration Chamber (*cheng-shih t'ang*) as a Grand Councilor (*tsai-hsiang*). RR: *l'égal des fonctionnaires du troisième degré des départements du grand secrétariat impérial et de la chancellerie impériale*. P2.

7482 *t'ŭng-chūn* 統軍 or *t'ŭng-chūn fǔ* 府
Commander-general. (1) T'ANG: head of the Personal Guard Garrison (*ch'in-chün fu*) in each Princely Establishment (*wang-fu*). (2) T'ANG: head of each Commander-general's Garrison (*t'ung-chün fu*), from 624 to 636 the basic unit in the Garrison Militia (*fu-ping*) organization; also see *fu* (Garrison). (3) T'ANG: from 787 (784?), 2nd executive officer in each of the Imperial Armies (*chin-chün*) that constituted the Northern Command (*pei-ya*), rank 3a1; under the 2 or 3 Generals-in-chief (*ta chiang-chün*), 2a2, and above the 3 Generals (*chiang-chün*), 3a2, in the normal command echelon. (4) SUNG: apparently perpetuated the nomenclature of T'ang's Imperial Armies, though not the reality except possibly in the earliest Sung years; the appointment seems to have been a sinecure for an imperial relative or favorite. See *liu chün, liu t'ung-chün*. RR+SP: *directeur d'armée*. P43.

7483 *t'ŭng-chūn shìh* 統軍使
LIAO: **Army Commander,** one of the titles used for hereditary chieftains of Tribal Armies (*pu-tsu chün*).

7484 *t'ūng-fèng tà-fū* 通奉大夫
SUNG–CH'ING: **Grand Master for Thorough Service,** prestige title (*san-kuan*) for civil officials of rank 3b in Sung and Chin, thereafter 2b. P68.

7485 *t'ūng-hóu* 通侯
HAN: lit., all-pervading Marquis: **Grandee of the Twentieth Order,** the highest of 20 titles of honorary nobility (*chüeh*) conferred on meritorious subjects; changed from *ch'e-hou* by Emperor Wu (r. 141–87 B.C.). P65.

7486 *t'ŭng-hsiá liǎng-ì mù-ch'áng tsŭng-kuǎn* 統轄兩翼牧場總管
CH'ING: **Supervisor-in-chief in Command of Pasturages in the Two Pasturelands,** general controller of the imperial horse herds in Mongolia; see under *liang-i* (Two Pasturelands). P31.

7487 *t'ūng-hsüán yüàn* 通玄院
T'ANG: **Office of Celestial Understanding,** from 758 a unit in the Bureau of Astronomy (*ssu-t'ien t'ai*) staffed with non-official specialists; its function was presumably to in-

terpret celestial irregularities as omens. RR: *cour de la pénétration céleste.*

7488   *t'ūng-ì láng* 通議郎
SUI: **Court Gentleman for Thorough Counsel,** prestige title (*san-kuan*) for rank 6b1 officials. P68.

7489   *t'úng-ì shěng-shìh* 同議省事
YÜAN: **Associate Consultant** in the Secretariat (*chung-shu sheng*) created temporarily in 1267; further details are not clear. P4.

7490   *t'ūng-ì tà-fū* 通議大夫
SUI–CH'ING: **Grand Master for Thorough Counsel,** prestige title (*san-kuan*) for civil officials of rank 4a through Chin, 3a in Ming and Ch'ing. P68.

7491   *t'ūng-k'ò ssū* 通課司
MING: early Ming variant of *shui-k'o ssu'* (**Commercial Tax Office**), attached to Prefectures (*fu*), Subprefectures (*chou*), and Districts (*hsien*). P53, 54, 62.

7492   *t'ūng-kuān* 通官
CH'ING: **Interpreter,** 8 ranging from ranks 6 to 8 on the staff of the Interpreters and Translators Institute (*hui-t'ung ssu-i kuan*). BH: interpreter. P11.

7493   *t'úng-kuān* 銅官
HAN: **Copper Factory,** a copper-producing agency located in Tan-yang Commandery, modern Anhwei Province; produced copper for coinage, presumably under the general supervision, successively, of the Chamberlain for the Palace Revenues (*shao-fu*), the Commandant of the Imperial Gardens (*shui-heng tu-wei*), and finally the Chamberlain for the National Treasury (*ta ssu-nung*). HB: office of copper. P16.

7494   *t'ǔng-lǐng* 統領
Commander-general. (1) SUNG: in S. Sung a common designation for leaders of armies; less prestigious than both *tu t'ung-chih* (Supreme Commandant) and *t'ung-chih* (also Commander-general). SP: *directeur militaire général.* (2) CH'ING: designation of the head of a Brigade (*ying*) comprised of members of the Inner Banners (*nei-ch'i*) who were not Imperial Guardsmen (*shih-wei ch'in-chün*); rank 3a then 2a. BH: captain-general.

7495   *t'ǔng-mǎ lìng* 挏馬令
HAN: **Director of the Imperial Mares,** one of the numerous subordinates of the Chamberlain for the Imperial Stud (*t'ai-p'u*), rank 600 bushels; title changed from *chia-ma ling* in 104 B.C. BH: prefect of the mare milkers. P31.

7496   *t'úng-p'àn* 同判
SUNG–CHIN: **Deputy** or **Vice Minister,** a variant of *t'ung* (Associate, Jointly). SP: *chargé de, chargé des affaires, vice-commissaire.*

7497   *t'ūng-p'àn* 通判
(1) SUNG: **Controller-general,** in early Sung decades a central government official delegated to serve as resident overseer of the work of a Prefect (*chih-chou*), with the right to submit memorials concerning prefectural affairs without the knowledge of the Prefect; no document issued by the Prefect was considered valid without being countersigned by the Controller-general. Some appointees were similarly delegated to Defense Commands (*chen*). Also known as a Prefectural Supervisor (*chien-chou*). After the earliest decades, the appointment became regularized as a Vice Prefect but remained a duty assignment rather than a regular post (*kuan*). SP: *administrateur, vice-administrateur, vice-préfet.*

P53. (2) MING–CH'ING: **Assistant Prefect,** number variable, rank 6a, 3rd executive official of a Prefecture (*fu*) after the Prefect (*chih-fu*) and Vice Prefects (*t'ung-chih*); commonly had narrowly specified functional assignment indicated by prefixes. BH: second class sub-prefect. P53. (3) CH'ING: **Subprefectural Magistrate,** head of a Subprefecture (*t'ing*), rank 6a. BH: assistant sub-prefect. P53. Cf. *t'ung-p'an* (Deputy, Vice Minister), *p'an-kuan* (Administrative Assistant).

7498   *t'úng p'íng-chāng chūn-kuó chùng-shìh* 同平章軍國重事
SUNG: **Jointly Manager of Important National Affairs,** one of many designations of central government dignitaries who, in addition to their regular functions, participated in deliberations at the Administration Chamber (*cheng-shih t'ang*) as Grand Councilors (*tsai-hsiang*). SP: *ministre des affaires d'état importantes.* P3.

7499   *t'úng p'íng-chāng shìh* 同平章事
T'ANG–SUNG: abbreviation of *t'ung chung-shu men-hsia p'ing-chang shih* (**Jointly Manager of Affairs with the Secretariat-Chancellery**); also see *p'ing-chang shih.* P3.

7500   *t'úng sán-p'ǐn* 同三品
T'ANG: abbreviation of *t'ung chung-shu men-hsia san-p'in* (**Cooperating with Third Rank Officials of the Secretariat-Chancellery**).

7501   *t'úng-shēng* 童生
MING–CH'ING: **Confucian Apprentice,** quasiofficial designation of a candidate for a civil service recruitment examination who had never been a student in a state school; in Ch'ing the status required certification in a preliminary examination given by a District Magistrate (*chih-hsien*). Cf. *ju-t'ung, wen-t'ung.*

7502   *t'úng-shìh* 彤史
T'ANG–SUNG: **Recorder of Imperial Intercourse** (?), one or 2 palace women, rank 6a in T'ang, 7a in Sung, attached to the Ritual Receptions Office (*ssu-tsan ssu*); functions are not clearly described in the sources, but attention has traditionally been drawn to commentaries on a passage concerning a red tube (*t'ung-kuan*) in the ancient *Classic of Songs* (*Shih-ching*), where it occurs as a love token, so that the *t'ung-shih* has been understood to be the keeper of records about which palace ladies slept with the Emperor at what times, and about the progress of their pregnancies. RR: *femme secrétaire au tube rouge.*

7503   *t'ūng-shìh* 通事
LIAO–CH'ING: **Interpreter-clerk,** normally unranked, found in both central government and territorial units of all sorts in Liao, Chin, and especially Yüan; thereafter regularly established only in the Interpreters Institute (*hui-t'ung kuan*). BH: interpreter. P5, 11, 12, 13, 15, 18, 19, etc.

7504   *t'ūng-shìh chiēn* 通市監
T'ANG: briefly in 685 the official variant of *hu-shih chien* (**Directorate of Tributary Trade**).

7505   *t'ūng-shìh láng* 通事郎
N-S DIV: **Vice Director** of the Secretariat (*chung-shu sheng*), a title alternating with *shih-lang* and *p'u-yeh,* qq.v. P2, 5.

7506   *t'ūng-shìh láng* 通仕郎
SUNG: **Gentleman for Thorough Service,** prestige title (*san-kuan*) for rank 8b civil officials till c. 1117, then replaced by Gentleman for Governmental Participation (*ts'ung-cheng lang*). P68.

7507 *t'ūng-shìh shè-jén* 通事舍人
N-S DIV (Chin)–MING: **Secretarial Receptionist,** middle or lower-level officials responsible principally for the handling of incoming memorials and outgoing imperial pronouncements in the early Secretariat (*chung-shu sheng*), co-existing or alternating with Secretariat Drafters (*chung-shu she-jen*). Especially powerful in Ch'i, when the 4 appointees were known collectively as the Four Households (*ssu hu*) and each controlled an office called a Department (*sheng*). In T'ang the title was increasingly attached to the function of introducing personages in court audience, and came into use in the establishment of the Heir Apparent as well as in the Secretariat. In Sung and Chin the title was also used in the Office for Audience Ceremonies (*ko-men*); in Yüan and early Ming it remained solely in use in the Palace Ceremonial Office (*shih-i ssu*). Rank 7b from T'ang to Yüan, 9b in early Ming. See *she-jen, t'ung-shih yeh-che*. RR: *introducteur des visiteurs et des affaires aux audiences*. SP: *introducteur des visiteurs et chargé des affaires aux audiences*. P2, 11, 21, 26, 33.

7508 *t'ūng-shìh shìh-láng* 通事侍郎
N-S DIV: variant of *t'ung-shih lang* (**Vice Director** in the developing Secretariat, *chung-shu sheng*).

7509 *t'ūng-shìh tū-wèi* 通事都尉
N-S DIV: variant of *t'ung-shih lang* (**Vice Director** in the developing Secretariat, *chung-shu sheng*).

7510 *t'ūng-shìh yèh-chě* 通事謁者
SUI–T'ANG: **Ceremonial Receptionist,** 20, rank not clear, established in the Tribunal of Receptions (*yeh-che t'ai*) by combining the prior posts of Receptionists (*yeh-che*) and Secretarial Receptionists (*t'ung-shih she-jen*); in 621 superseded in a revival of the title Secretarial Receptionist. P11, 21, 33.

7511 *t'ūng-shǒu* 通守
(1) SUI: **Vice Governor** of a Commandery (*chün*), principal assistant to the Governor (*t'ai-shou*); rank not clear. P49, 53. (2) CH'ING: unofficial reference to an **Assistant Prefect** (*t'ung-p'an*).

7512 *t'ǔng-şhǔ* 統署
MING–CH'ING: unofficial reference to an **Office Manager** (*ssu-wu; see ssu-wu t'ing*).

7513 *t'ūng-tào hsüéh* 通道學
T'ANG: lit., school for understanding the (Taoist) Way; in 743 a new name granted **Taoist Schools** (*ch'ung-hsüan hsüeh*) at the Prefecture (*chou*) level.

7514 *t'úng tūng-hsī t'ái sān-p'ǐn* 同東西臺三品
T'ANG: **Cooperating with Third Rank Officials of the Eastern and Western Towers,** briefly from 662 a variant of *t'ung chung-shu men-hsia san-p'in* (Cooperating with Third Rank Officials of the Secretariat-Chancellery), one of the designations used for Grand Councilors (*tsai-hsiang*), when the Chancellery and Secretariat were known, respectively, as the Eastern and Western Towers. RR: *l'égal des fonctionnaires du troisième degré des départements de la chancellerie impériale et du grand secrétariat impérial*.

7515 *t'úng-wén kuǎn* 同文館
SUNG: **Korean Relations Institute** in the Court of State Ceremonial (*hung-lu ssu*); headed by a Commissioner (*ta-shih*). SP: *bureau des relations diplomatiques avec la Corée*. P11.

7516 *t'úng-wén ssù* 同文寺
(1) T'ANG: **Court of Diplomatic Relations,** from 662 to

671 the official variant of *hung-lu ssu* (Court of State Ceremonial). P17, 33. (2) CH'ING: unofficial reference to the **Court of Colonial Affairs** (*li-fan yüan*).

7517 *t'úng-yěh ch'áng* 銅冶場
YÜAN: **Copper Smelter,** 3 established in copper-producing areas to prepare copper for being cast into coins, under the Supervisorate-in-chief of Coinage (*pao-ch'üan tu t'i-chü ssu*); each headed by a Superintendent (*t'i-ling*), rank 8a, with the aid of a Commissioner (*ta-shih*), 8b. P16.

7518 *t'ūng-yǐn ssū* 通引司
SUNG: **Reception Office** staffed by unranked subofficials in the Censorate (*yü-shih t'ai*), the headquarters of Kaifeng Prefecture (*fu*), and no doubt other agencies as well. SP: *bureau des huissiers*.

7519 *tzǔ* 子
Viscount: throughout history a title of nobility (*chüeh*), normally 5th highest of 6 standard titles, following Prince (*wang*), Duke (*kung*), Marquis (*hou*), and Earl (*po*) and preceding Baron (*nan*). See *chün-tzu, hsien-tzu, k'ai-kuo tzu*. Cf. *t'ai-tzu, shih-tzu*. RR+SP: *vicomte*. BH: viscount. P64, 65.

7520 *tzǔ-àn yù-shǐh* 紫案御史
T'ANG: lit., Censor (*yü-shih*) of the purple table; derivation not clear: unofficial reference to a **Palace Censor** (*tien-chung shih yü-shih*).

7521 *tzù-ch'én* 自陳
MING: **Self-appraisal,** designation of statements submitted by officials of the 4th and higher ranks during the capital evaluation (*ching-ch'a*) that was conducted every 6th year by the Ministry of Personnel (*lì-pu*); submitted in lieu of evaluations initiated by the Ministry, such statements often gave censorial and other officials opportunities to denounce powerful court dignitaries.

7522 *tzū-chèng ch'īng* 資政卿
MING: from 1398 to 1402 only, the official variant designation of **Ministers** (*shang-shu*) of Ministries (*pu*). P68.

7523 *tzū-chèng chung tà-fū* 資政中大夫
MING: from 1398 to 1402 only, the official variant of *lang-chung* (**Director**) in a Bureau (*ch'ing-li ssu*) of a Ministry (*pu*). P68.

7524 *tzū-chèng tà-fū* 資政大夫
(1) CHIN–CH'ING: **Grand Master for Assisting toward Good Governance,** prestige title (*san-kuan*) for civil officials of rank 3a in Chin, 2a thereafter. P68. (2) MING: from 1398 to 1402 only, the official variant of *yüan-wai lang* (**Vice Director**) in a Bureau (*ch'ing-li ssu*) of a Ministry (*pu*). P68.

7525 *tzū-chèng tièn* 資政殿
SUNG: **Hall for Aid in Governance,** a palace building to which former Grand Councilors (*tsai-hsiang*) and other dignitaries of long court service were appointed as Academicians (*hsüeh-shih*) and Grand Academicians (*ta hsüeh-shih*). P3, 23.

7526 *tzū-chèng yǎ-ch'īng* 資政亞卿
MING: from 1398 to 1402 only, the official variant designation of **Vice Ministers** (*shih-lang*) of Ministries (*pu*). P68.

7527 *tzū-chìh shǎo-yǐn* 資治少尹
MING: **Vice Governor Assisting in Administration,** a merit title (*hsün*) awarded to favored rank 3b officials. P65.

7528 *tzū-chìh yǐn* 資治尹
MING: **Governor Assisting in Administration,** a merit title (*hsün*) awarded to favored rank 3a officials. P65.

7529 *tzū-ì chūn-shìh* 諮議軍事
SUNG: **Military Consultant,** number not fixed, staff members in a Superior Area Command (*ta tu-tu fu*). SP: *conseiller des affaires militaires.*

7530 *tzū-ì kuān* 諮議官
Adviser. (1) CHIN: number not fixed, rank 9a, members of the Academy of Scholarly Worthies (*chi-hsien yüan*). P25. (2) MING: until 1376 a staff member in a Princely Establishment (*wang-fu*). P69. (3) May be encountered as a variant of *tzu-i ts'an-chün-shih* (Administrative Adviser).

7531 *tsū-ì ts'ān-chūn-shìh* 諮議參軍事 or *tzu-i*
N-S DIV (Chin)–YÜAN: **Administrative Adviser,** apparently a general assistant to the administrative head of a Princely Establishment (*wang-fu*); rank 5a1 in T'ang, 5b in Yüan, not clear for other periods. RR+SP: *administrateur conseiller d'un prince.* P69.

7532 *tzū-jèn àn* 資任案
SUNG: **Appointments Section** in the Bureau of Evaluations (*k'ao-kung ssu*) of the Ministry of Personnel (*lì-pu*); staffing not clear. SP: *bureau des états de service.*

7533 *tzū-k'ǎo ssū* 資考司
CHIN: **Bureau of Evaluations,** one of only 2 agencies that actively conducted the work of the Ministry of Personnel (*lì-pu*); headed by a Secretary (*chu-shih*), rank 7b. P5.

7534 *tzǔ-kó* 紫閣
T'ANG: **Purple Hall,** unofficial reference to the Secretariat (*chung-shu sheng*).

7535 *tzū-shàn* 資善
MING: **Assister toward Goodness;** see under *tzu-te yüan.*

7536 *tzū-shàn k'ù* 資善庫
YÜAN: lit., treasury for assisting toward (i.e., encouraging) goodness: **Treasury** for coins and silks in the Commission for Buddhist and Tibetan Affairs (*hsüan-cheng yüan*) at Peking, headed by an Overseer (*ta-lu-hua-ch'ih*) and a Supervisor (*t'i-chü*), rank 5b. P17.

7537 *tzū-shàn tà-fū* 資善大夫
CHIN–MING: **Grand Master for Assisting toward Goodness,** prestige title (*san-kuan*) for civil officials of rank 3a in Chin, 2a in Yüan and Ming. P68.

7538 *tzū-shàn t'áng* 資善堂
SUNG: lit., hall for assisting toward goodness: **School for the Heir Apparent,** part of the establishment called the Eastern Palace (*tung-kung*); included an Elementary School (*hsiao-hsüeh*); apparently educated all sons of the reigning Emperor. SP: *salle d'études de l'héritier du trône.*

7539 *tzū-shēng chiēn* 孳生監
SUNG: **Directorate of Horse Breeding** in the Court of the Imperial Stud (*t'ai-p'u ssu*); staffing not clear. SP: *direction d'élevage des chevaux.*

7540 *tzū-té* 資德
MING: **Assister toward Virtue;** see under *tzu-te yüan.*

7541 *tzū-té tà-fū* 資德大夫
CHIN–MING: **Grand Master for Assisting toward Virtue,** prestige title (*san-kuan*) for civil officials of rank 3a in Chin, 2a in Yüan and Ming. P68.

7542 *tzū-té yüàn* 資德院
MING: lit., office for assisting toward virtue: **School for the Heir Apparent** in the Household Administration of the Heir Apparent (*chan-shih fu*), headed by an Assister toward Virtue (*tzu-te*) and 2 Assisters toward Goodness (*tzu-shan*). P26.

7543 *tzǔ-wéi kó* 紫薇閣
CH'ING: lit., hall of the purple myrtle, deriving from the name of a celestial constellation considered favorable toward construction projects: unofficial reference to the **Central Drafting Office** (*chung-shu k'o*) attached to the Grand Secretariat (*nei-ko*).

7544 *tzǔ-wéi láng* 紫薇郎
CH'ING: unofficial reference to a **Drafter** (*chung-shu she-jen*) of the Central Drafting Office (*chung-shu k'o*); see under *tzu-wei ko.*

7545 *tzǔ-wéi shěng* 紫微省
Lit. meaning no doubt similar to that explained under *tzu-wei ko.* (1) T'ANG: from 713 to 717 the official variant designation of the **Secretariat** (*chung-shu sheng*). P3. (2) MING: unofficial reference to a **Provincial Administration Commission** (*ch'eng-hsüan pu-cheng shih ssu*).

7546 *tzū-wǔ k'ù* 資武庫
YÜAN: **Armory** in the Household Service of the Heir Apparent (*ch'u-cheng yüan*), headed by a Superintendent (*t'i-tien*) and a Commissioner-in-chief (*ta-shih*), rank not clear but low. P26.

7547 *tzù-yáng chù* 牸羊局
N-S DIV (N. Ch'i): **Ewes Service** in the Sheep Office (*ssu-yang shu*) of the Court of the Imperial Stud (*t'ai-p'u ssu*). See *t'e-yang chü* (Rams Service).

7548 *tzū-yùng k'ù* 資用庫
YÜAN: **Ready Access Storehouse** of furs and leather goods established in 1265 in the Directorate of the Imperial Treasury (*t'ai-fu chien*), in 1273 transferred to the Directorate for Leather and Fur Manufactures (*li-yung chien*); headed by a Superintendent (*t'i-tien*), rank 5a. P38.

7549 *tzǔ-yüán* 紫垣
T'ANG: lit., the purple wall, referring to the celestial constellation called the purple myrtle (see under *tzu-wei ko*): unofficial reference to the **Secretariat** (*chung-shu sheng*).

7550 *tz'ú-chì àn* 祠祭案 or *tz'ú-chì chù* 局
SUNG: **Sacrifices Section** (*an*) or **Sacrifices Service** (*chü*), a unit of the Court of Imperial Sacrifices (*t'ai-ch'ang ssu*); staffed largely with Provisioners (*kung-kuan*). SP: *service (an) des sacrifices, bureau (chü) des sacrifices.*

7551 *tz'ú-chì ch'īng-lì ssū* 祠祭清吏司
MING–CH'ING: **Bureau of Sacrifices,** one of 4 top-echelon Bureaus (*ch'ing-li ssu*) in the Ministry of Rites (*lǐ-pu*), in charge of arranging sacrificial rituals in conjunction with the Court of Imperial Sacrifices (*t'ai-ch'ang ssu*); headed by a Director (*lang-chung*), rank 5a. BH: department of sacrifices. P9.

7552 *tz'ú-chì shǔ* 祠祭署
MING–CH'ING: **Sacrificial Office** at each Imperial Mausoleum (*ling*) and at all major altars and temples in the dynastic capital, each headed by a Sacrificer (*feng-ssu*), rank 7b; charged with maintaining proper sacrificial practices on the Emperor's behalf, under supervision of the Bureau of Sacrifices (*tz'u-chi ch'ing-li ssu*) of the Ministry of Rites (*lǐ-pu*). P28, 29.

7553 *tz'ù-chīn hsü* 次金絞
HAN: lit. meaning not clear: **Estimator** of weights and sizes

(of receipts?); organizational affiliation and specific functions not clear. HB: appraiser. P14.

7554 *tz'ú-chǚ* 磁局
YÜAN: **Porcelain Service,** a manufactory of fine porcelains established in 1278 at modern Ching-te-chen in Kiangsi Province, under the Supervisorate-in-chief of Metal Workers and Jewelers (*chin-yü jen-chiang tsung-kuan fu*); staffed by non-official specialists, leadership not clear.

7555 *tz'ù-fēi* 伏飛
HAN: **Duck Hunter,** subordinates of the Chamberlain for the Palace Revenues (*shao-fu*) who shot ducks and geese in the capital parks for the Emperor's table and for sacrificial uses; headed by a Director (*ling*); created in 104 B.C. by renaming *tso-i*. HB: sharpshooter. P37.

7556 *tz'ù-fēi* 次妃
CHOU–N-S DIV: **Secondary Consort,** unofficial collective reference to the wives of rulers other than the Queen or Empress (*hou, huang-hou*), who was called the Principal Consort (*yüan-fei*).

7557 *tz'ú-fén sǒ* 祠墳所
SUNG: **Office for Sacrifices at the Grave,** one established at each Imperial Mausoleum (*ling*) by the Court of Imperial Sacrifices (*t'ai-ch'ang ssu*); particularly responsible for offerings to deceased imperial consorts and concubines. SP: *bureau des sacrifices pour les tombeaux impériaux*. P29.

7558 *tz'ù-fù* 次傅
Lit., secondary tutor: unofficial reference to a **Junior Mentor** (*shao-fu*).

7559 *tz'ù-fǔ* 次府
SUNG: **Superior Prefecture, Second Class,** categorical designation of Prefectures (ordinarily *chou*) in which principal Circuits (*lu*) were headquartered, as distinguished from regular Superior Prefectures (*fu*), where dynastic capitals and other major cities were located. SP: *capitale d'une province*.

7560 *tz'ù-fǔ* 次輔
Lit., secondary bulwark: unofficial reference to any of the **Three Solitaries** (*san ku*). Cf. *shou-fu* (Principal Bulwark), *t'ai-fu* (Chief Bulwark of State), *fu*.

7561 *tz'ù-hsiàng* 次相
Lit., secondary minister. (1) Unofficial reference to any of the **Three Solitaries** (*san ku*). (2) HAN–SUNG: unofficial reference to a **Censor-in-chief** (*yü-shih ta-fu*), deriving from his early Han status as general assistant to the Counselor-in-chief (*ch'eng-hsiang*). (3) SUNG: quasiofficial reference to a **Grand Academician of the Academy of Scholarly Worthies** (*chi-hsien tien ta hsüeh-shih*). SP: *conseiller de deuxième catégorie*.

7562 *tz'ú-k'ù* 磁庫
CH'ING: **Porcelain Storehouse,** one of 6 warehouses or vaults of valuables constituting the Storage Office (*kuang-ch'u ssu*) of the Imperial Household Department (*nei-wu fu*). BH: porcelain store.

7563 *tz'ú-lín* 詞林
SUNG–CH'ING: **Forest of Fine Phrases,** unofficial reference to the Hanlin Academy (*han-lin yüan*).

7564 *tz'ú-lù* 祠祿
SUNG: lit., stipend for worshipping: **Temple Salary,** designation of a category of appointments awarded to eminent court officials retiring from active service, carrying a stipend and at least nominal responsibility for being imperial

surrogates in worship at specified temples, monasteries, or other religious places. SP (*tz'u-lu kuan*): *poste donné aux hauts fonctionnaires pensionnés*.

7565 *tz'ú-miào shǔ* 祠廟署
T'ANG: **Office of Temple Worship,** one established at each of several imperial shrines devoted to culture heroes such as the legendary Yao, Shun, et al. of highest antiquity, the Chou dynasty's King Wen and King Wu, the founder of the Han dynasty, etc.; also one dedicated to the Fen River in Shansi, whose valley was the homeland of the T'ang ruling house. Each headed by a Director (*ling*), rank 7b or 6b; under the Court of Imperial Sacrifices (*t'ai-ch'ang ssu*). RR: *offices des temples et des temples des ancêtres*.

7566 *tz'ú-pù* 祠部
(1) N-S DIV: **Ministry of Sacrifices,** from San-kuo Wei through N. Ch'i a recurrent name, alternating principally with *i-ts'ao*, for what ultimately became the Ministry of Rites (*lǐ-pu*), one of the principal Ministries of the Department of State Affairs (*shang-shu sheng*); headed by a Minister (*shang-shu*); often called *tz'u-pu ts'ao* (Section for Sacrifices). Commonly incorporated 3 or 4 subsidiary Sections (*ts'ao*), e.g., the Liang dynasty's *tz'u-pu ts'ao* (as above), *i-ts'ao* (Section for Ministry Affairs), *chu-k'o ts'ao* (Section for Receptions), *tien-chung ts'ao* (Section for Palace Affairs). P9. (2) N-S DIV: **Section for Sacrifices,** recurrent name of a Section (*ts'ao* sometimes added as suffix) in the Ministry of Rites (*i-ts'ao*) or Ministry of Sacrifices (also *tz'u-pu*) in the developing Department of State Affairs; headed by a Director (*lang, lang-chung*). P9. (3) SUI–SUNG: **Bureau of Sacrifices,** one of a standard array of 4 Bureaus (*ssu* sometimes added as suffix) in the Ministry of Rites (*lǐ-pu*), headed by a Director (*lang-chung*), rank 5b in T'ang, 6b in Sung; antecedent of the Ming–Ch'ing Bureau of Sacrifices (*tz'u-chi ch'ing-li ssu*). RR+SP: *bureau des sacrifices*. P9. (4) MING–CH'ING: unofficial reference to the **Ministry of Rites** (*lǐ-pu*).

7567 *tz'ù-shǐh* 刺史
Lit., a clerk (*shih*, i.e., a Censor, *yü-shih*) who pokes, stimulates, criticizes. (1) HAN–SUI: **Regional Inspector,** from 106 B.C. a regular supervisory post intended to provide disciplinary surveillance over personnel in all units of territorial administration in a geographically prefixed Region (*pu* or *chou*); originally 13 delegated from among Attendant Censors (*shih yü-shih*) under supervision of the Palace Aide to the Censor-in-chief (*yü-shih chung-ch'eng*); from 7 B.C. appointed only irregularly, alternating with more prestigious Regional Governors (*mu*), but endured into Sui. During the era of N-S Division (still irregularly alternating with *mu*) became regular administrators in the territorial hierarchy, and proliferated so that at times a Region (*chou*) incorporated no more than 2 Commanderies (*chün*), which in turn incorporated no more than 2 Districts (*hsien*); and those Regional Inspectors who became locally powerful were able to dominate neighboring Regions as Area Commanders-in-chief (*tsung-kuan, tu-tu*). To simplify the multi-layered territorial hierarchy, the founder of Sui abolished Commanderies, leaving only the 2 levels of *chou* and *hsien*, here rendered Prefectures and Districts, respectively. Throughout Han and into the early post-Han years, the Regional Inspector ranked at 600 bushels; later in the era of N-S Division, he ranked from 2a down to 4a depending on the importance of his post. From Han times he had a staff of subordinates divided among function-specific Sections (*ts'ao*). HB: inspector. P50, 52, 53, 54. (2) N-S DIV–SUNG: **Regional Chief,** a title commonly awarded important heads

of aboriginal tribes in South and Southwest China. P72. (3) SUI–CHIN: **Prefect,** head of a Prefecture (*chou*); in T'ang ranked from 3b to 4a depending on the size and population of his jurisdiction; in Sung and Chin uncommon, mostly replaced by *chih-chou* (Prefect). RR+SP: *préfet.* P50, 52, 53, 54. (4) CH'ING: unofficial reference to a **Department Magistrate** (*chih-chou*).

7568   *tz'ù-shǐh chün* 刺史郡

CHIN: **Commandery,** designating an ordinary Commandery (*chün*) headed by a Prefect (*tz'u-shih*), as distinguished from a Defense Commandery (*fang-yü chün*) headed by a Defense Commissioner (*fang-yü shih*).

7569   *tz'ú-shǔ* 祠署

T'ANG: variant of *tz'u-miao shu* (**Office of Temple Worship**).

7570   *tz'ú-ssù* 祠祀

HAN: **Sacrificer,** ritual specialists found in various agencies; those most closely involved in palace rituals, headed by a Director (*ling*), were under the Chamberlain for Ceremonials (*t'ai-ch'ang*) in Former Han but in Later Han were transferred under the Chamberlain for the Palace Revenues (*shao-fu*); in Former Han the Director of Sacrificers was created in 144 B.C. to supersede the Great Supplicator (*t'ai-chu*), then in 104 B.C. was in turn superseded by the Director of Temple Sacrifices (*miao-ssu ling*), only to be revived in Later Han together with the Great Supplicator. The palace of the Empress also had a Director of Sacrificers, at least in Former Han; and Princedoms (*wang-kuo*) included Directors of Sacrificers (*tz'u-ssu chang*) on their staffs. The rank of such a Director ranged from 600 down to 400 bushels. HB (*ling*): prefect invocator, (*chang:*) chief invocator. P37, 69.

7571   *tz'ú-ts'áo* 辭曹

Complaints Section. (1) HAN: one of the clerical or administrative staff units under the Counselor-in-chief (*ch'eng-hsiang*) and the Defender-in-chief (*t'ai-wei*) in the central government; headed by an Administrator (*yüan-shih*), rank =400 bushels; also occasionally found in Commanderies (*chün*); functions not clear. Cf. *chüeh-ts'ao* (Judicial Section). HB: bureau of statements. (2) SUNG: occasional unofficial (derisive?) reference to a Revenue Section (*hu-ts'ao*) in a Prefecture (*chou*) headquarters.

7572   *tz'ù-tùi kuān* 次對官

T'ANG: lit., the next official to have a confrontation, i.e., imperial audience, after withdrawal of his superior: unofficial reference to a **Vice Censor-in-chief** (*yü-shih chung-ch'eng*). P18.

7573   *wài* 外

Outer, a prefix to official titles and agency names used throughout history in a pairing with (often implied) Inner (*nei*), to make distinctions between inside and outside the imperial palace, the dynastic capital, etc. In addition to the following entries, see under the nomenclature to which *wai* is prefixed.

7574   *wài-ch'á* 外察

MING: **Outer Evaluation,** an appraisal of all civil officials on duty outside the capital conducted every 3rd year, culminating in a great gathering of provincial and lower-level personnel in the capital for imperial audience, at which special promotions, demotions, dismissals, and various other punishments were announced on the basis of deliberations principally involving the Ministry of Personnel (*lì-pu*) and the Censorate (*tu ch'a-yüan*). See *ta-chi* (Great Reckoning).

7575   *wài-chàng hsiǎo-tǐ* 外帳小氐

CHIN: **Retainer of the Outer Chamber,** 30 or so on the staff of the Palace Inspectorate-general (*tien-ch'ien tu tien-chien ssu*), in 1172 retitled *feng-chih* (Steward). Also see *hsiao-ti.* P38.

7576   *wài-ch'áo* 外朝

Outer Court: from Former Han on, a common collective reference to the officialdom at large, originally under the unchallenged leadership of the Han Counselor-in-chief (*ch'eng-hsiang*), as distinguished from the Inner Court (*nei-ch'ao*) comprising the Emperor and his family, imperial in-laws, eunuchs, personal favorites, etc. For the importance of these concepts in history, see under *nei-ch'ao.* Also see *wai-t'ing, nei-t'ing.*

7577   *wài-ch'áo tà-jén kuān* 外朝大人官

N-S DIV (N. Wei): lit., officials (chosen for service) in the Outer Court (from among the younger brothers and sons of) regional dignitaries: **Attendants in the Outer Court,** no fixed number, junior members of powerful families serving in court attendance; commonly dispatched as imperial messengers or envoys; participated in all great court ceremonies. Subordinate to 4 Directors of Palace Attendants (*nei-shih chang*). P37.

7578   *wài-ch'éng* 外丞

HAN: variant of *yü-shih wai-ch'eng* (**Outer Aide of the Censor-in-chief**). Cf. *chung-ch'eng, yü-shih chung-ch'eng* (Palace Aide of the Censor-in-chief). P18.

7579   *wài chì-pīng ts'áo* 外騎兵曹

N-S DIV (N. Ch'i): **Outer Section,** designation of the cavalry, apparently in battle formation; distinguished from the Inner Section (*nei pu-ping ts'ao*) of infantry; presumably expected to enwrap the infantry in battle formation.

7580   *wài-ch'ì* 外戚

Imperial In-laws: throughout history a reference to relatives of rulers by marriage, ordinarily ennobled if not already of the nobility (*chüeh*). Considered members of the Inner Court (*nei-ch'ao, nei-t'ing*), sometimes exercised great influence on rulers or even usurped the throne to found new dynasties.

7581   *wài-ch'í* 外旗

CH'ING: **Outer Banners,** collective reference to all Metropolitan Bannermen (*ching-ch'i*) who were not members of the Imperial Bodyguard (*ch'in-chün ying*), also known as the Inner Banners (*nei-ch'i*); in early Ch'ing constituted a large Cavalry Brigade (*hsiao-chi ying*) that was the main striking force of the Manchu army; remained in garrisons in and around the dynastic capital, supervised in annual rotation by the Commanders-in-chief (*tu-t'ung*) of all the Banners (see *pa ch'i*). BH: outer banners, outer division. P44.

7582   *wài-chiā* 外家

HAN: variant of *wai-ch'i* (**Imperial In-laws**).

7583   *wài-chiàng* 外匠

N-S DIV (Chou): **Outer Artisan,** number not specified, ranked as Senior Servicemen (*shang-shih;* 7a) and Ordinary Servicemen (*chung-shih;* 8a), members of the Ministry of Works (*tung-kuan*) who were presumably in charge of carpentry work outside the imperial palace. P14.

7584   *wài-chiēn* 外監

(1) SUNG–CHIN: **Outer Directorate,** one or more branches of the Directorate of Waterways (*tu-shui chien*); in Chin one prefixed East and one prefixed West. SP: *direction extérieure.* P59. (2) CH'ING: **Outer Prison,** a section of

any prison (*chien-yü*) used for the detention of persons accused of lesser crimes. Cf. *nei-chien* (Inner Prison).

7585 *wài-chìh* 外制
Outer Drafter, generic designation of members of the Secretariat (*chung-shu sheng*) on duty assignment as secretarial assistants to Grand Councilors (*tsai-hsiang*) in the Administration Chamber (*cheng-shih t'ang*); see *nei-chih* (Inner Drafter) and *liang chih* (Two Drafting Groups). SP: *chargé de la rédaction des édits extérieurs.*

7586 *wài-chiù* 外厩
CH'ING: **Outer Stables** of the Palace Stud (*shang-ssu yüan*), a collective reference to a large aggregation of horse pasturages, corrals, and stables scattered throughout the empire, in contrast to those in or near the dynastic capital, called Inner Stables (*nei-chiu*); staffed with Chiefs of the Stables (*chiu-chang*), Pasturage Directors (*mu-chang*), etc. Not to be confused with units under the Court of the Imperial Stud (*t'ai-p'u ssu*). BH: provincial stables. P39.

7587 *wài-fŭ* 外府
(1) CHOU: **Outer Treasury,** an agency of the Ministry of State (*t'ien-kuan*) and the title of its 2 Directors, ranked as Ordinary Servicemen (*chung-shih*); stored money to be issued for preparation of the ruling family's clothing, as gifts presented by the King, and for use in sacrifices, funerals, court audiences, troop assemblies, etc. CL: *magasin extérieur.* (2) N-S DIV (Chou): **Outer Treasury,** organizational affiliation not clear, headed by one Senior Serviceman (*shang-shih*) and 2 Ordinary Servicemen (*chung-shih*); a storehouse of miscellaneous goods including silks, coins, furs, animal horns, etc. P7. (3) T'ANG: **Outer Garrisons,** collective reference to Garrisons (*fu*) of the Garrison Militia (*fu-ping*) organization that, in rotation, provided troops for service in the capital, in contrast to the Five Garrisons (*wu fu*) of such militiamen when on duty in the capital. RR: *milices de l'extérieur.*

7588 *wài-fŭ ssū* 外府司
T'ANG: from 662 to 671 (669?), the official variant designation of the **Court of the Imperial Treasury** (*t'ai-fu ssu*). P7.

7589 *wài-hàn* 外翰
CH'ING: lit., abbreviated suggestion of an outer counterpart of a member of the Hanlin Academy (*han-lin yüan*): unofficial reference to an **Instructor** (*chiao-shou*) in a Confucian School (*ju-hsüeh*) at the Prefecture (*fu*) level.

7590 *wài hàn-lín* 外翰林
MING: occasional unofficial reference to the **Ministry of Justice** (*hsing-pu*). Cf. *han-lin yüan* (Hanlin Academy).

7591 *wài-hsiāng* 外廂
SUNG: **Outer Capital Townships;** see under *ssu hsiang* (Four Capital Townships).

7592 *wài-kuān* 外官
Outer Officials, throughout history a collective reference to officials serving outside the dynastic capital; occasionally encountered in reference to officials considered members of the Outer Court (*wai-ch'ao, wai-t'ing*) in contrast to those considered members of the Inner Court (*nei-ch'ao, nei-t'ing*); occasionally also encountered specifying normal officials in contrast to eunuchs. For Han and Sui usage in the military, see *nei-kuan.*

7593 *wài-kuăn* 外館
CH'ING: **Outer Hostel,** one of 2 capital residences maintained by the Court of Colonial Affairs (*li-fan yüan*) to house visiting Mongolian dignitaries; see under *nei-kuan* (Inner Hostel). BH: outer inn. P17.

7594 *wài-láng* 外郎
(1) CH'IN: **Outer Gentleman,** one of the collective designations signified by the term Three Court Gentlemen (*san lang*, q.v.). (2) HAN: **Outer Gentleman,** a collective reference to expectant appointees serving as court attendants, similar to but not included among the Court Gentlemen (*lang*) organized into Three Corps (*san shu*) under the Chamberlain for Attendants (*lang-chung ling, kuang-lu-hsün*). (3) SUI–T'ANG: variant of *yüan-wai* (**Supernumerary Official**); also see *yüan-wai lang.*

7595 *wài-lién kuān* 外簾官 or *wài-lien*
YÜAN–CH'ING: **Outer Aides,** unofficial collective reference to provincial and lower-level officials who participated in Provincial Examinations (*hsiang-shih*) primarily as proctors, as distinguished from *nei-lien kuan* (Inner Examiners, Inner Aides), who primarily stayed in the private quarters of the examination hall and graded examination papers. Also see *lien-kuan, shih-kuan.*

7596 *wài mìng-fū* 外命夫
Variant form of *wai ming-nan* (**Outer Noblemen**).

7597 *wài mìng-fù* 外命婦
Outer Noblewoman. (1) CHOU: categorical designation of the wives of nobles and royal officials perhaps down to the rank of Serviceman (*shih*), in contrast to the secondary wives of the King, known collectively as Inner Noblewomen (*nei ming-fu*). CL: *femmes titrées de l'extérieur.* (2) T'ANG: collective reference to such relatives of the Emperor as aunts, sisters, and nieces, and to the wives of members of the nobility and of eminent officials. RR: *femmes titrées de l'extérieur.*

7598 *wài mìng-nán* 外命男
CHOU: **Outer Noblemen,** collective reference to royal officials serving outside the capital in the 6 Districts (*hsiang*) of the royal domain, in contrast to those serving in the dynastic capital, called Inner Noblemen (*nei ming-nan*). CL: *hommes titrés de l'extérieur.*

7599 *wài mìng-nŭ* 外命女
CHOU: variant of *wai ming-fu* (**Outer Noblewomen**).

7600 *wài-nŭ* 外女
CHOU: **Woman of Royal Relations,** generic reference to daughters of the King's aunts and sisters, who did not bear the royal surname; if appointed to office as attendants at sacrifices and funerals, called *wai-tsung* (Women of the Royal Clan) and subordinated to the Ministry of Rites (*ch'un-kuan*). CL: *femme de l'extérieur.*

7601 *wài pì-shū shĕng* 外祕書省
N-S DIV (N. Wei): **Outer Palace Library,** variant of what in other times was called simply the Palace Library (*pi-shu sheng*); also see under *nei pi-shu sheng* (Inner Palace Library).

7602 *wài-pīng ts'áo* 外兵曹 or *wai-ping*
N-S DIV: **Section for Outer Troops,** normally 2 prefixed Left and Right, commonly found in the upper echelon of subordinate units in the evolving Ministry of War (*wu-ping ts'ao, ch'i-ping ts'ao*) of the Department of State Affairs (*shang-shu sheng*); had administrative responsibility for all military forces stationed outside the environs of the dynastic capital; each headed by a Director (*lang, lang-chung*) or sometimes a Vice Minister (*shih-lang*); rank 6a2 in N. Wei. P12.

7603 *wài-shè* 外舍
(1) HAN: variant of *wai-ch'i* (**Imperial In-laws**). (2) SUNG: **Outer College** in the National University (*t'ai-hsüeh*) as reorganized by Wang An-shih c. 1070; was the entry-level section of the University, with a quota of 3,000 students, about 20% of whom graduated into an Inner College (*nei-she*). Also see *shang-she* (Superior College). SP: *collège extérieur*. P34.

7604 *wài-shǐh* 外史
Lit., outer scribe. (1) CHOU: **External Secretary,** 4 ranked as Senior Servicemen (*shang-shih*), 8 as Ordinary Servicemen (*chung-shih*), and 16 as Junior Servicemen (*hsia-shih*), subordinates of the Royal Secretaries (*nei-shih*) in the Ministry of Rites (*ch'un-kuan*) who drafted or recorded royal proclamations to be sent to the Feudal Lords (*chu-hou*); also reportedly responsible for preserving and writing histories; believed by some interpreters to have resided in the feudal states, reporting to the King about the conduct of his subjects. CL: *annaliste de l'extérieur*. (2) N-S DIV (Chou): **External Secretary,** ranked as a Junior Grand Master (*hsia ta-fu;* 6a), a member of the Ministry of Rites (*ch'un-kuan*) responsible for recording the activities of the Emperor. P23. (3) SUNG–CH'ING: occasional archaic reference to any **personnel of the Hanlin Academy** (*han-lin yüan*).

7605 *wài-t'ái* 外臺
Lit., outer pavilion or tower. (1) HAN: unofficial collective reference to **Receptionists** (*yeh-che*). (2) N-S DIV (Sankuo Wei): unofficial reference to the **Orchid Pavilion** (*lan-t'ai*), then the official name of what in other times was called the Censorate (*yü-shih t'ai*), in contrast to the Palace Library (*pi-shu;* see under *pi-shu chien*), then officially called *nei-ko* (Grand Secretariat). P18. (3) N-S DIV: common unofficial collective reference to **Regional Inspectors** (*tz'u-shih*) or **Regional Governors** (*chou mu*), both considered in some measure outer representatives of the Censorate (*yü-shih t'ai*). (4) T'ANG–SUNG: **Outer Censorate,** after 765 an unofficial collective reference to members of the Censorate (*yü-shih t'ai*) on important duty assignments outside the capital. RR: *tribunaux des censeurs des provinces*. P18. (5) MING–CH'ING: **Outer Censorate,** unofficial reference to a Provincial Surveillance Commission (*t'i-hsing an-ch'a shih ssu*). P18, 52.

7606 *wài-t'íng* 外廷
Variant of *wai-ch'ao* (**Outer Court**).

7607 *wài-ts'áo* 外曹
N-S DIV (N. Ch'i): abbreviation of *wai chi-p'ing ts'ao* (**Outer Section**).

7608 *wài-tsūng* 外宗
(1) CHOU: **Woman of the Royal Clan,** generic reference to the daughters of the King's aunts and sisters, i.e., Women of Royal Relations (*wai-nü*), when appointed to be attendants for the King's principal wives in sacrifices, funerals, etc., under direction of the Ministry of Rites (*ch'un-kuan*). CL: *honorables de l'extérieur*. (2) SUNG: abbreviated reference to an **Office of Imperial Clan Affairs** (*tsung-cheng ssu*).

7609 *wài-tù k'ō* 外度科
YÜAN: **General Accounts Section,** one of 6 Sections (*k'o*) through which the Ministry of Revenue (*hu-pu*) carried out its principal functions of gathering and expending the government's tax income; presumably supervised general government revenues rather than those earmarked for special palace purposes, in contrast to the Special Accounts Section

(*nei-tu k'o*). Headed by a Clerk (*ling-shih*), unranked. Cf. *tu-chih k'o*. P6.

7610 *wài-tz'ù tz'ù-chiēn* 外刺刺姦
HAN: lit., one who pries into treachery in the domains of outer Regional Inspectors (*tz'u-shih*) (?): **Security Officer of an Outer Region** (?), a military title in Later Han associated with the implementation of law; specific status and functions not clear. HB: inspector of treachery for outside inspection.

7611 *wài-wěi ch'iēn-tsǔng* 外委千總
CH'ING: **Detached Company Commander,** a regular post, rank 8a, in the Chinese military forces called the Green Standards (*lu-ying*), ranking beneath both Company Commanders (*ch'ien-tsung*) and Squad Leaders (*pa-tsung*); specific uses not clear. BH: ensign. P37.

7612 *wài-wěi pǎ-tsǔng* 外委把總
CH'ING: **Detached Squad Leader,** a regular post, rank 9a, in the Chinese military forces called the Green Standards (*lu-ying*), ranking beneath both Squad Leaders (*pa-tsung*) and Detached Company Commanders (*wai-wei ch'ien-tsung*); specific uses not clear. BH: colour-sergeant. P37.

7613 *wài-wù liào-k'ù* 外物料庫
SUNG: **Outer Storehouse** under the Court of Imperial Entertainments (*kuang-lu ssu*); staffing and specific uses not clear. Cf. *nei-wu liao-k'u* (Imperial Larder). SP: *magasin extérieur de denrées, riz, sel, huile et farine*.

7614 *wài yǎng-kǒu ch'ù* 外養狗處
CH'ING: **Outer Kennel** maintained by the Imperial Household Department (*nei-wu fu*); see *nei yang-kou ch'u* (Palace Kennel). P37.

7615 *wài-yung* 外饔
CHOU: **Grand Chef for External Ceremonies,** 4 ranked as Ordinary Servicemen (*chung-shih*) and 8 as Junior Servicemen (*hsia-shih*), members of the Ministry of State (*t'ien-kuan*) responsible for preparing food for sacrifices and other religious ceremonies conducted outside the royal palace; cf. *nei-yung* (Grand Chef of the Palace). CL: *cuisinier de l'extérieur*.

7616 *wài-yüàn* 外院
SUNG: **Outer Branch of the Palace Library** (*pi-shu sheng*), established in 1010; staffing and special purposes not clear. SP: *cour extérieure du département de la bibliothèque impériale*.

7617 *wàn ch'èng* 萬乘
Lit., 10,000 chariots: from antiquity an indirect reference to the supreme ruler, the **King** (*wang*) or **Emperor** (*huang-ti*).

7618 *wàn chì* 萬騎
T'ANG: **Myriad Cavaliers,** an elite group of mounted archers who escorted the Emperor on hunts and other outings; prior to 707 (710?) known successively as the Hundred Cavaliers (*po chi*) and the Thousand Cavaliers (*ch'ien chi*); in 710 transformed into the new Left and Right Militant as Dragons Armies (*lung-wu chün*) of the Northern Command (*pei-ya*). RR: *dix mille cavaliers*.

7619 *wàn-chiù* 萬廏
T'ANG: **Stable of Myriad Mounts,** one prefixed Left and one prefixed Right among the palace stable units collectively called the Six Stables (*liu chiu*). RR: *écurie des dix mille chevaux*.

7620 *wàn-fū* 萬夫
Occasional variant of *wan-hu* (**Brigade Commander**).

7621 *wàn-hù fǔ* 萬戶府
YÜAN: **Brigade,** a standard military unit theoretically comprising 10,000 soldiers under a Brigade Commander (*wan-hu*), rank variable from 2a to 3a; most commonly the military headquarters at the Route (*lu*) level of territorial administration, subordinate to a Circuit (*tao*) command of one of several types. In theory divided into 10 Battalions (*ch'ien-hu so*) of 1,000 soldiers each. Also used as a designation for some aboriginal tribes in the Southwest (see *chün-min wan-hu fu*). Also see *tu wan-hu fu* (Chief Brigade). Often rendered as myriarchy. P60, 72.

7622 *wàn-hù sǒ* 萬戶所
MING: **Brigade,** one of many designations conferred on southwestern aboriginal tribes, their chieftains being officially known as Brigade Commanders (*wan-hu*). See under *t'u-ssu, t'u-kuan*. P72.

7623 *wǎn-huá* 婉華
N-S DIV (N. Ch'i): **Lady of Kind Loveliness,** designation of one of 27 imperial wives collectively called *shih-fu* (Hereditary Consorts); rank =3b.

7624 *wǎn-í* 婉儀
T'ANG–SUNG: **Lady of Kind Deportment,** designation of a rank 2a imperial concubine; see *liu i* (Six Ladies of Deportment). RR+SP: *correction belle*.

7625 *wàn-ì ch'ǐ-yüán k'ù* 萬億綺源庫
YÜAN: lit., storehouse of ten thousand hundred thousands (of precious things from a) beautiful well: **Imperial Cloth Vault** under the Ministry of Revenue (*hu-pu*), which stored bolts of colored cloth; headed by a Supervisor-in-chief (*tu t'i-chü*), rank 4a. P7.

7626 *wàn-ì fù-yüán k'ù* 萬億賦源庫
YÜAN: lit., storehouse of ten thousand hundred thousands (of things from a) well endowed well: **Imperial Silk Vault** under the Ministry of Revenue (*hu-pu*), which stored precious silks, brocades, etc.; headed by a Supervisor-in-chief (*tu t'i-chü*), rank 4a. P7.

7627 *wàn-ì kuǎng-yüán k'ù* 萬億廣源庫
YÜAN: lit., storehouse of ten thousand hundred thousands (of treasures from a) vast well: **Imperial Treasures Vault** under the Ministry of Revenue (*hu-pu*), which stored incense, herbs, and precious papers; headed by a Supervisor-in-chief (*tu t'i-chü*), rank 4a. P7.

7628 *wàn-ì pǎo-yüán k'ù* 萬億寶源庫
YÜAN: lit., storehouse of ten thousand hundred thousands of coins: **Imperial Money Vault** under the Ministry of Revenue (*hu-pu*), which stored paper money and precious objects in jade; headed by a Supervisor-in-chief (*tu t'i-chü*), rank 4a. P7.

7629 *wǎn-júng* 婉容
SUNG: **Lady of Kind Manner,** designation of an imperial concubine, rank 1b; first appointed in 1008. SP: *femme titrée intérieure de 2ème rang*.

7630 *wǎn-láng* 挽郎
SUNG: lit., gentleman for funerary arrangements (?): **Tomb Attendant,** a duty assignment at some imperial mausolea (*ling*). SP: *chargé des affaires aux tombes impériales*.

7631 *wàn-lín nèi chiào-fāng* 萬林內教坊
T'ANG: **Palace School in the Grove,** briefly in 692 the official redesignation of the school for educating palace women, normally called Palace Institute of Literature (*nei wen-hsüeh kuan*). RR: *quartier de l'enseignement du palais intérieur des dix mille bosquets*.

7632 *wàn-nién kūng* 萬年宮
T'ANG: **Palace of Longevity,** from 651 to 667 the official redesignation of the Palace of the Perfect Cycle (*chiu-ch'eng kung*), the imperial summer resort in Shensi. See *chiu-ch'eng kung tsung-chien*.

7633 *wàn-sùi yéh* 萬歲爺
CH'ING: **Lord for Myriad Years,** one of the terms used for the Emperor in direct address. BH: lord of ten thousand years.

7634 *wáng* 王
Ety. uncertain; possibly an imposing human figure with arms outstretched standing on an extent of land. (1) CHOU: **King,** designation of the supreme ruler. After mid-Chou the title was usurped by Feudal Lords (*chu-hou*) so freely that in 221 B.C. the new unifier of China, Ch'in Shih-huang-ti, created the title *huang-ti* (Emperor) to replace it as the designation of a supreme ruler. Political theorists of late Chou times began the enduring custom of using *wang* in the sense of "a true king" who ruled by right and by virtue in contrast to one who ruled solely by force; see under *pa-wang* (Hegemons and Kings). CL: *empereur*. (2) HAN–CH'ING: **King,** title commonly used in reference to rulers of foreign states and alien peoples. (3) HAN–CH'ING: **Prince,** after disuse in Ch'in, revived in early Han as a title for the founding Emperor's most important military allies, who were granted large regions of the empire as semi-autonomous Princedoms (*wang-kuo*); from then on, the highest title of nobility (*chüeh*), awarded commonly to all sons of Emperors; occasionally throughout history conferred on unusually distinguished military officers. In some dynasties there were many gradations of Princes indicated by prefixes; e.g., see *ch'in-wang, chün-wang, i-tzu wang, liang-tzu wang, kuo-wang*. Cf. *wei-hsia, pei-lo*. HB: king. RR, SP, BH: prince.

7635 *wàng* 望
SUNG: lit., to gaze at from a distance, to admire, to expect: **Honored,** a prefix to the designation District (*hsien*) when the unit of territorial administration incorporated more than 4,000 registered households; may also be encountered as a prefix to *chou* (Prefecture), apparently the equivalent of *shang* (Large). Cf. the prefixes *ch'ih* (Imperial), *chi* (Metropolitan), *chin* (Important). SP: *remarquable*.

7636 *wáng ch'áng-shìh fǔ* 王常侍府
YÜAN: lit., office of Attendants-in-ordinary on a Prince: variant of *wang-fu* (**Princely Establishment**).

7637 *wàng-ch'ì* 望氣
HAN: **Observer of Air Currents,** one of several categories of duty assignments on the staff of the Grand Astrologer (*t'ai-shih ling*) for Expectant Officials (*tai-chao*). See *wang-lang* (Gentleman Observer). Cf. *hou-feng* (Wind Watcher). P35.

7638 *wáng-chǔ* 王主
HAN: **Grand Princess,** title awarded paternal aunts of a reigning Emperor.

7639 *wáng-fù* 王傅
SUNG–MING: **Princely Mentor,** either the head or the 2nd executive official of a Princely Establishment (*wang-fù*); an ad hoc duty assignment in Sung, rank 4a in Chin, 2a in Yüan, 2b in early Ming, when from 1370 to 1376 one Left and one Right appointee were outranked only by 2 Admin-

istrators (*hsiang*) on the staffs of Princes. In Yüan the title was changed in 1292 to *nei-shih* (Administrator). SP: *tuteur de prince*. P69.

7640 *wáng-fǔ* 王府
N-S DIV–CH'ING: **Princely Establishment,** a civil and military staff appointed for each imperial son other than the Heir Apparent (cf. *chan-shih fu*, Household Administration of the Heir Apparent). Prior to T'ang, occasionally established for Princes other than the Heir Apparent who were not enfeoffed with territories called Princedoms (*wang-kuo*). From T'ang on, established with territorial names commonly derived from ancient Chou feudal states when Princes reached maturity, but normally were not landed fiefs. In T'ang headed by a Mentor (*fu*), rank 3a2, and an Administrator (*chang-shih*), 4b1; thereafter normally by an Administrator, 5a in Ming, 3a in Ch'ing; in Liao and Yüan headed by an Administrator (*nei-shih*). The staff commonly included a military dignitary such as an Adjutant (*ssu-ma*) or the head of a Defense Brigade (*hu-chün fu*) or an Escort Guard (*hu-wei*); Record Keepers (*chi-shih*) or Archivists (*tien-pu*), etc. Through T'ang Princes commonly played significant roles in government, central or regional. In T'ang they were not regularly required to leave the dynastic capital on reaching maturity, but in native dynasties after T'ang they were commonly required to "go to their fiefs" (*chih-kuo*) on reaching maturity and had little influence on government at any level. RR+SP: *maison d'un prince*. BH: establishment (palace) of a prince of the blood. P69.

7641 *wáng-fǔ chǎng-shǐh ssū* 王府長史司
Lit., office of the Administrator (*chang-shih*) of a Princely Establishment (*wang-fu*): common variant of *wang-fu* (**Princely Establishment**).

7642 *wáng-fù fǔ* 王傅府
Lit., office of a Princely Mentor (*wang-fù*): common variant of *wang-fù* (**Princely Establishment**). P69.

7643 *wáng-hòu* 王后
HAN: variant of *huang-hou* (**Empress**).

7644 *wàng-hòu láng* 望候郎
N-S DIV (San-kuo Wei, Chin): **Gentleman for Astronomical Observation,** 20 observers and recorders of astronomical phenomena under the Grand Astrologer (*t'ai-shih ling*). P35.

7645 *wáng-hsiāng fǔ* 王相府
MING: lit., office of the Administrator (*hsiang*) for a Prince: 1370–1380 variant of *wang-fu* (**Princely Establishment**), headed by a Left and a Right Administrator (*hsiang*), rank 2a, and 2 Mentors (*fu*), 2b. P69.

7646 *wáng-hùi ssū* 王會司
CH'ING: **Inner Mongolian Reception Bureau** under the Court of Colonial Affairs (*li-fan yüan*) created in 1757 by renaming the Court's Receptions Bureau (*pin-k'o ssu*); headed by one Manchu and 2 Mongol Directors (*lang-chung*), rank 5a. BH: department for receiving princes of Inner Mongolia. P17.

7647 *wáng-kūng tà-hsiǎo hsüéh* 王宮大小學
SUNG: **School for the Princes** within the School for the Imperial Family (*tsung-hsüeh*); apparently a consolidated advanced (*ta*) and elementary (*hsiao*) school for the sons of Emperors as distinguished from other members of the imperial family, but possibly a combined reference to 2 separate schools; staffed with an Erudite (*po-shih*) and one or 2 Instructors (*chiao-shou*), ranks not clear. SP: *école supérieure et primaire du palais royal*.

7648 *wáng-kuó* 王國 or *wáng-kuó fǔ* 府
HAN–SUI: **Princedom,** in early Han a reference to territories allocated to the principal allies of the founding Emperor (cf. *hou-kuo*, Marquisate), thereafter primarily a reference to territories with which the sons of Emperors were enfeoffed; prefixed with territorial names mostly derived from the feudal states of Chou times. Prior to a revolt by the original Princes in 154 B.C., the Princedoms were virtually autonomous; each Prince appointed a staff that replicated the Emperor's central government, including a Counselor-in-chief (*ch'eng-hsiang*), a Censor-in-chief (*yü-shih ta-fu*), Nine Chamberlains (*chiu ch'ing*), etc.; and each Prince collected and used the revenue from his domain. Such autonomy was stripped away after the revolt was crushed. Thereafter the staff of each Princedom was reduced and was appointed by the central government; and the Princes were deprived of governmental powers in their domains. Each Princedom was managed for the Prince by a court-appointed Administrator (*hsiang*), with rank at 2,000 bushels equivalent to that of a Commandery Governor (*t'ai-shou*), assisted principally by an Aide (*chang-shih*). In early post-Han times Princedoms had staffs headed by such dignitaries as Preceptors (*shih*), Mentors (*fu*), or Companions (*yu*), but before Sui the *chang-shih* (now better rendered Administrator) rose into real executive authority, and Princedoms had begun to be called Princely Establishments (*wang-fu*). Through the era of N-S Division, the degree of autonomy enjoyed by Princedoms fluctuated with the strength or weakness of the central government; they were often seedbeds of rebellion and usurpation. From T'ang on, Princely Establishments (now the standard term) were more thoroughly dominated by the central government. Also see *kuo-wang*. HB: kingdom. P69.

7649 *wǎng-lái kuó-hsìn sǒ* 往來國信所
SUNG: **Office of Diplomatic Correspondence** in the Court of State Ceremonial (*hung-lu ssu*) in early Sung, responsible for diplomatic exchanges with the Khitan state of Liao; headed or jointly headed by a rank 6a eunuch assigned from the Palace Eunuch Service (*ju-nei nei-shih sheng*) as Concurrent Manager (*kuan-kou*); other staffing not clear. Cf. *kuo-hsin fang, kuan-kou wang-lai kuo-hsin so*. SP: *bureau des lettres de créance pour les relations diplomatiques avec les K'i-tan (Leao)*.

7650 *wàng-láng* 望郎
HAN: **Gentleman Observer,** 30 authorized for the staff of the Grand Astrologer (*t'ai-shih ling*); status not clear, but possibly men of official rank serving together with Expectant Officials (*tai-chao*) called Observers of Air Currents (*wang-ch'i*, q.v.); cf. *wang-hou lang* (Gentleman for Astronomical Observation). HB: gentleman of foresight. P35.

7651 *wáng pā-pā* 王妃妃
Princely Father-in-law: in late Ming and perhaps other times, a colloquialism apparently referring to the father of the consort of a Prince (*wang*).

7652 *wáng pāo-ī* 王包衣
CH'ING: **Bondservants of the Princes,** common reference to members of the Five Lesser Banners (*hsia wu ch'i*), the Manchu military units controlled by Imperial Princes (*ch'in-wang*). See *pao-i*. BH: bond-servants of princes of the blood.

7653 *wáng shìh-tzǔ* 王世子
N-S DIV–MING: **Princely Heir,** commonly the formal designation of the son of an Imperial Prince (*ch'in-wang*) chosen for preparation to succeed his father; usually the eldest son. See *shih-tzu*. P64.

7654   *wáng tà-ch'én* 王大臣

CH'ING: **Princes and Grand Ministers,** collective reference to the most eminent dignitaries of the imperial court, all commonly members of the Imperial Household Department (*nei-wu fu*); after 1861 a common reference to members of the Foreign Office (*tsung-li ko-kuo shih-wu ya-men, tsung-li ya-men*).

7655   *wáng-tǐ* 王邸

(1) **Princely Mansion:** throughout imperial history a reference to the residence in a dynastic capital of a Prince (*wang*) or of the liaison representative of a Prince based outside the capital; see *ti* (Liaison Hostel). P21. (2) CH'ING: indirect reference to an **Imperial Prince** (*ch'in-wang*).

7656   *wáng-yǔ* 王友

N-S DIV–SUNG: **Princely Companion,** variant of *yu* (Companion), a dignitary on the staff of a Prince (*wang*). SP: *conseiller princier.* P26.

7657   *wèi* 尉

(1) **Commandant:** throughout imperial history a common military title, sometimes honorific, sometimes with administrative responsibilities, not often suggesting active field command. See prefixed forms, e.g., *t'ai-wei, t'ing-wei, wei-wei, tu-wei, chih-su tu-wei, hsiao-wei, i-wei, cheng-i wei, hsiao-chi wei.* Traditionally pronounced *yü.* HB, RR, SP: commandant. (2) CH'IN–YÜAN: common abbreviated variant of *hsien-wei* (**District Defender**) or *chün-wei* (**Commandery Defender**).

7658   *wèi* 衛

(1) N-S DIV–MING: **Guard,** standard term for a large military organization normally in garrison but available for active defense duty, as contrasted with an Army (*chün*), the most common term for a large military organization on campaign. Through Yüan, the name Guard was generally reserved for units clustered in and around the dynastic capital, and they were distinguished by descriptive prefixes, e.g., Militant Guard (*wu-wei*), Awesome Guard (*wei-wei*), Protective Guard (*yü-wei*). This pattern persisted in Ming, but Guards were then also garrisoned throughout the empire, identified with place-name prefixes, e.g., Hangchow Guard. Through Sung, each Guard was commanded by one or more Generals (*chiang-chün*), rank 3a2 in T'ang, 3b or 4b in Sung, sometimes overshadowed by Generals-in-chief (*ta chiang-chün*), 3a1 in T'ang, 3a or 4a in Sung, and Generalissimos (*shang chiang-chün*), 2a2 in T'ang, from 2b to 3b in Sung. In Yüan each Guard was led by a Chief Military Commissioner (*tu chih-hui shih*), 3a, a capital counterpart of Brigade Commanders (*wan-hu*) in units away from the capital, Brigades (*wan-hu fu*). In Ming there were Guard Commanders (*chih-hui shih*), 3a. In Yüan and Ming times, Guards were divided into Battalions (*ch'ien-hu so*) and Companies (*po-hu so*), and in Ming the entire national military establishment was known by the term *wei-so* (Guards and Battalions). In all occurrences, with the exception of Guards with place-name prefixes, look under the preceding terminology, e.g., *shih-liu wei* (Sixteen Guards), *shih-erh wei* (Twelve Guards), *shih-wei* (Imperial Guard), *su-wei* (Capital Guard). RR+SP: *garde.* (2) CH'ING: **Transport Command,** designation of military units stationed along the Grand Canal, each with a Commandant (*shou-yü*), normally a rank 5b officer, supervising one segment of the Grand Canal tax-grain transport operation; supervised lesser military units called Transport Stations (*so,* with place-name prefix). See under *ts'ao-yün tsung-tu* (Director-general of Grain Transport). BH: first class transport station. P60.

7659   *wěi-ch'āi* 委差

YÜAN: **Courier,** 10 lowly officials or unranked subofficials on the staff of the Supervisorate of Land Transport to the Two Capitals (*liang-tu lu-yün t'i-chü ssu*). P60.

7660   *wéi-ch'áng* 圍場

Lit., an enclosure. (1) LIAO: **Hunting Preserve,** various areas for seasonal use located in different parts of the Manchurian plain and Jehol, all supervised by a Supreme Grand Preceptor (*tu t'ai-shih*), a member of the Northern Administration (*pei-mien*) of the central government. P17. (2) CH'ING: **Imperial Summer Resort,** a large tract at modern Ch'eng-te in Jehol to which the imperial court normally retreated in the 8th lunar month each year for hunting, relaxation, and receiving submissive chieftains from Mongolia, Central Asia, and Tibet; managed by a Supervisor-in-chief (*tsung-kuan*), rank 4 till 1748, then rank 3, under the jurisdiction of the Court of Colonial Affairs (*li-fan yüan*). BH: imperial hunting preserves. P17.

7661   *wèi chiàng-chūn* 衛將軍

General of the Guards. (1) HAN: in early Han one of many designations used for the leaders of military campaigns; from 87 B.C. awarded as honorific sinecures to court dignitaries, authorized a staff of subordinates organized into Sections (*ts'ao*). HB: general of the guards. (2) N-S DIV: one of the titles awarded to dignitaries to whom supervision of the inner quarters of the palace was entrusted. (3) CH'ING: unofficial reference to a Grand Minister of the Imperial Household Department Concurrently Controlling the Imperial Guardsmen (*ling shih-wei nei ta-ch'en*).

7662   *wēi chū-hóu* 猥諸侯

HAN: lit., rustic or humble Marquis: **Honorary Marquis,** a designation conferred on meritorious subjects; it did not confer the right to participate in regular court audiences or imperial sacrificial rituals and was not inheritable; whether or not it conferred a stipend is not clear. Cf. *hou, chu-hou, lieh-hou.*

7663   *wèi-fāng shuài* 衛坊率

N-S DIV (N. Ch'i): **Commandant of the Guards Office,** 2 prefixed Left and Right, rank not clear but apparently subordinate to a Commander (*ssu-ma*) for each of the Left and Right Guards (*tso-wei, yu-wei*); supervised the bodyguard troops of the Heir Apparent. P26.

7664   *wèi-fǔ* 衛府

T'ANG: **Guard,** prior to 622 the designation of *wei* (Guard), large military units at the dynastic capital.

7665   *wèi-hóu chíh tū chǐh-hūi shǐh ssū* 衛候直都指揮使司

YÜAN: **Office of the Household Guards** in the establishment of the Heir Apparent; headed by a Mongol nobleman designated Chief Military Commissioner (*tu chih-hui shih*). Commonly abbreviated to *wei-hou ssu.*

7666   *wèi-hsià* 位下

YÜAN: variant of *wang* (**Prince**).

7667   *wèi-hsiēn* 衛仙

T'ANG: **Escort Immortal,** from 662 to 670 the official designation of rank 6a imperial concubines, at other times known as Ladies of the Precious Bevy (*pao-lin*). RR: *femme qui escorte les immortels.*

7668   *wēi-í* 威儀

N-S DIV (Ch'i): **Disciplinarian,** 2 of low rank or unranked, on the staff of the School for the Sons of the State (*kuo-tzu hsüeh*). P34.

7669 wěi-jén 委人

CHOU: **Forager,** 2 ranked as Ordinary Servicemen (*chung-shih*) and 4 as Junior Servicemen (*hsia-shih*), members of the Ministry of Education (*ti-kuan*) responsible for supervising the collection of taxes in wood, fodder, and wild foodstuffs gathered in the mountains, riverways, and parklands in the remote areas of the royal domain, for use as imperial gifts, by visitors at court, and in sacrificial and funeral rituals. CL: *collecteur.*

7670 wèi jù liú 未入流

Lit., not yet entered the current: **Not Yet of Official Status,** a categorical reference to all persons in government service other than officials (*kuan*) with ranks (*p'in*), most abundantly including subofficial functionaries (*li, hsü-li*); equivalent to *liu-wai* (Outside the Current). Cf. *liu-nei.*

7671 wèi-kuān chün-wèi 衛官軍衛

SUNG: **Army Guard of Guard Officers;** see under *chün-wei* (Army Guard).

7672 wéi-nà 維那

Buddhist Deacon: Chinese transliteration of the Sanskrit term *karmadāna,* meaning an assigner of duties; commonly the 2nd most senior member of a Buddhist monastery. See *tu wei-na* (Chief Buddhist Deacon).

7673 wèi-shìh 尉氏

CHOU–HAN: unofficial reference to a **Jailor** or **Prison Guard,** or to any functionary who inflicted physical punishments on prisoners.

7674 wèi-shìh 衛士

HAN–T'ANG: **Guardsman,** common designation for an ordinary soldier, especially those on special duty in government offices, at temples and mausolea, etc., rather than in regular military units; in Han commonly led by a Director (*chang* or *ling*). HB: guard. RR: *garde.* P28, 30, 69, etc.

7675 wěi-shǔ 委署

CH'ING: **Deputy,** prefix to many titles, especially in the military service, usually of relatively lowly officers; also **Acting,** prefix appended to titles in units of territorial administration when appointments were made by provincial authorities, pending confirmation by the central government.

7676 wèi shuài-fǔ 衛率府

T'ANG–SUNG, CHIN: **Defense Guard Command,** 2 designated Left and Right, military units assigned to the establishment of the Heir Apparent, each headed by a Commandant (*shuai*), rank 4a in T'ang, 7b in Sung. Created in 622 by renaming former Attendant Guard Commands (*shih shuai-fu*); from 662 to 670 officially renamed *tien-jung wei* (Militant Guards). P26.

7677 wèi-ssū 尉司

N-S DIV (Chin): variant reference to the *liu-pu wei* (**Commandant of the Capital Patrol**). P20.

7678 wèi-ts'áo 尉曹

HAN: **Conscript Section,** one of a dozen or more Sections (*ts'ao*) subordinate to the Defender-in-chief (*t'ai-wei*) in the central government; headed by an Administrator (*yüan-shih*), rank =400 bushels; managed business concerning conscripts, criminals sent into military service, etc. HB: bureau of command.

7679 wéi-tzǔ-shǒu sǒ 圍子手所

MING: **Office of the Palace Guard,** 2, each headed by a Battalion Commander (*ch'ien-hu*); apparently active duty

stations for members of the Escort Guards (*hu-wei*) assigned to each Princely Establishment (*wang-fu*). P69.

7680 wēi-wèi 威衛

T'ANG: **Awesome Guard,** 2 prefixed Left and Right, included among the Sixteen Guards (*shih-liu wei*) at the dynastic capital, generally responsible for defense of the eastern sector of the capital city; created in 622 to replace the Left and Right Encampment Guards (*t'un-wei*) inherited with the Sui dynasty's Twelve Guards (*shih-erh wei*) organization; in 684 renamed Guards of the Leopard Strategy (*pao-t'ao wei*); in 705 briefly resumed the name Awesome Guards; from late 705 to 711 again called Encampment Guards; from 711 once again called Awesome Guards. There is an unlikely possibility that from 662 to 684 this name was replaced by Military and Awesome Guards (*wu-wei wei*). Members of the Awesome Guards were commonly called Fierce as Leopards Cavaliers (*pao-chi*). RR: *garde majestueuse.* P43.

7681 wèi-wèi 衛尉

CH'IN–N-S DIV: **Chamberlain for the Palace Garrison,** one of the Nine Chamberlains (*chiu ch'in*) in the central government, in Han ranked at 2,000 bushels; responsible for policing and defending the imperial palace. During the era of N-S Division gradually evolved into a Chief Minister (*ch'ing*) heading the Court for the Palace Garrison (*wei-wei ssu*). From Han on, subordinates were generally divided among Document Control Offices at the Gates (*kung-ch'e ssu-ma men*), a corps of patrolling Guardsmen (*wei-shih*), and a corps of Imperial Escorts (*lü-pen*). In Han the men under his command, totaling perhaps 3,000, were regular soldiers assigned by units of territorial administration to capital service in annual rotation; in the capital they were considered part of the Southern Army (*nan-chün*). After Han they were probably professional careerists, but the situation is not clear. HB: commandant of the guards. P21.

7682 wèi-wèi ch'īng 衛尉卿

(1) N-S DIV–SUI: **Chamberlain** (or **Chief Minister**) **of the Court for the Palace Garrison;** see *wei-wei ssu.* (2) T'ANG–SUNG: **Chief Minister of the Court of the Imperial Regalia;** see *wei-wei ssu, wei-wei yüan.* (3) CH'ING: unofficial reference to a **Commissioner** (*shih*) **of the Imperial Procession Guard** (*luan-i wei*).

7683 wèi-wèi ssù 衛尉寺

(1) N-S DIV–SUI: **Court for** (Sui: **Court of**) **the Palace Garrison,** headed by a Chief Minister (*ch'ing*); one of the Nine Courts (*chiu ssu*) in the central government; responsible for active patrolling and defense of the imperial palace, evolving from the Han dynasty Chamberlain for the Palace Garrison (*wei-wei*); the term was used perhaps as early as late Han. P21. (2) T'ANG–SUNG: **Court of the Imperial Regalia,** still one of the Nine Courts but no longer in charge of active military duty at the imperial palace, which was defended in T'ang by the Left and Right Palace Gate Guards (*chien-men wei*), in Sung by units of the Palace Command (*tien-ch'ien shih-wei ssu*); in T'ang was in charge of manufacturing and storing weapons, tents, insignia, and other kinds of military regalia; in Sung had practically no active function, its posts being sinecures for eminent officials. Headed by a Chief Minister (*ch'ing*), rank 3a1 in T'ang, 4b in Sung. RR+SP: *cour des insignes impériaux.* P21.

7684 wèi-wèi yüàn 衛尉院

YÜAN: **Court of the Imperial Regalia,** a central government agency responsible for arms, armor, saddlery, insignia, etc., required by the Emperor and his entourage; a continuation of the T'ang–Sung *wei-wei ssu*, headed by a Chief Minister (*ch'ing*), rank not clear.

7685 *wēi-wǔ chūn* 威武軍
T'ANG–SUNG: **Awesome and Militant Army,** originally appeared in 731 as a new name for the military force of a Defense Command (*chen*) based near modern Peking, previously identified by the place-name Yü-yang; likely disappeared in the great An Lu-shan rebellion of the 750s; headed by a Military Commissioner (*chieh-tu shih*). The name was revived during the rebellion to designate 2 new units, prefixed Left and Right, in the Northern Command (*pei-ya*) directly under imperial control, each headed by a General-in-chief (*ta chiang-chün*), rank 3a1; but very soon discontinued. Revived again in early Sung as the command of a Military Commissioner (*chieh-tu shih*), 2b, but apparently disappeared with the discontinuance of such posts very early in the dynasty. RR: *armée de Wei-wu, armée de la guerre majestueuse.* SP: *armée de Wei-wu.*

7686 *wèi wǔ-pù* 尉五部
N-S DIV (Chin): lit., commandant of 5 Troops (*pu*): variant reference to the **Commandant of the Capital Patrol** (*liu-pu wei*). P20.

7687 *wèi-yāng lìng* 未央令
HAN: **Director of the Inner Compound Stable,** one of numerous subordinates of the Chamberlain for the Imperial Stud (*t'ai-p'u*), rank 600 bushels; in charge of vehicles and horses used in the Forbidden City (*chin-ch'eng*), known as the Uncompleted Palace (*wei-yang kung*). HB: prefect of the stables of the eternal palace. P31.

7688 *wěi-yüán* 委員
CH'ING: **Special Delegate,** designation used for an Expectant Appointee (*hou-pu*) when on an ad hoc duty assignment. BH: deputy.

7689 *wěi-yüán chiàng* 葦園匠
T'ANG: **Craftsman of the Rattan Grove,** 100 non-official laborers and craft workers authorized on the staff of the Directorate of Bamboo Crafts (*ssu-chu chien*) in the Court of the Imperial Granaries (*ssu-nung ssu*). RR: *ouvrier pour les jardins de joncs.*

7690 *wén* 文
Lit., writing, literate, cultured, etc.: **Civil,** prefix sometimes attached to titles and other nomenclature to specify affiliation with the civil service rather than the military service, e.g., *wen-kuan* (Civil Official) as distinguished from *wu-kuan* (Military Officer). Also occurs as an element in more elegant nomenclature, e.g., *ch'ung-wen yüan* (Institute for the Veneration of Literature).

7691 *wén-àn* 文案
CH'ING: common abbreviation of *nei wen-an* (**Personal Staff**), q.v.

7692 *wén-ch'āng hsiāng* 文昌相
T'ANG: **Minister of the Pavilion of Culture and Prosperity,** one of the Left and one of the Right; from 684 to 705 the official redesignation of Vice Directors (*p'u-yeh*) of the Department of State Affairs (*shang-shu sheng*), apparently regardless of changes in the agency name from *wen-ch'ang t'ai* to *wen-ch'ang tu-sheng* in 684 or 685, then to *tu-t'ai* till 696, then back to *wen-ch'ang t'ai* till 703, then to *chung-t'ai* till 705, when the name *shang-shu sheng* was resumed.

7693 *wén-ch'āng t'ái* 文昌臺
T'ANG: **Pavilion of Culture and Prosperity:** briefly in 684

(–685?) and again from 696 to 703 the official redesignation of the *shang-shu sheng* (Department of State Affairs).

7694 *wén-ch'āng tū-shěng* 文昌都省
T'ANG: **Capital Department of Culture and Prosperity:** briefly in 684 (–685?) the official redesignation of the *shang-shu sheng* (Department of State Affairs).

7695 *wén-ch'én chǔn-pèi ch'āi-ch'iěn* 文臣準備差遣
SUNG: **Civil Official in Reserve for Special Assignment,** 5 authorized for each of 3 major Military Commissions (*an-fu ssu*) in the Yangtze Valley, and an unlimited number authorized for (all?) Fiscal Commissions (*chuan-yün ssu*). SP: *fonctionnaire civil en réserve pour être envoyé à une mission.*

7696 *wén-ch'ǐ chǘ* 紋綺局
YÜAN: **Adornment Service,** organizational affiliation not clear but most likely subordinate to the Palace Provisions Commission (*hsüan-hui yüan*); the staff included Embroiderers (*chih-chin*) who reportedly, among other things, produced brocaded portraits of ruling Emperors that were placed in every Buddhist temple and monastery (in the capital? in the empire?). P28.

7697 *wén-hàn kuǎn* 文翰館
MING: **Institute of Litterateurs,** in the period 1398–1402 only, a unit either supplementary or subordinate to the Hanlin Academy (*han-lin yüan*); details not clear. P23.

7698 *wēn-hsī tài-mèi chǘ* 溫犀玳瑁局
YÜAN: **Rhinoceros-horn and Tortoiseshell Service,** one of many craft workshops in the Supervisorate-in-chief of Metal Workers and Jewelers (*chin-yü jen-chiang tsung-kuan fu*); staffed with non-official craftsmen.

7699 *wén-hsiù shǔ* 文繡署
CHIN: **Embroidery Office,** one of 6 craft workshops under the Directorate for Imperial Manufactories (*shao-fu chien*), headed by a Director (*ling*), rank 6b; decorated clothing for the Emperor, his Empress, and his other wives. P38.

7700 *wén-hsiù yüàn* 文繡院
SUNG: **Embroidery Office,** one of 5 craft workshops under the Directorate of Imperial Manufactories (*shao-fu chien*), headed by a Supervisor (*chien-kuan*), probably unranked; prepared embroideries for use on the clothing, vehicle draperies, etc., of the Emperor and his wives. SP: *cour de broderie.* P38.

7701 *wén-hsüǎn* 文選
SUNG: variant of *tso-hsüan* (**Civil Appointments Process**). SP: *choix des fonctionnaires civils.*

7702 *wén-hsüǎn ch'īng-lì ssū* 文選清吏司 or *wén-hsüan ssū*
MING–CH'ING: **Bureau of Appointments,** one of the 4 principal subsections of the Ministry of Personnel (*lì-pu*); managed the appointments, rankings, promotions, demotions, transfers, etc., of all civil service personnel; headed by a Director (*lang-chung*), rank 5a, and one or more Vice Directors (*yüan-wai lang*), 5b. BH: department of selection. P5.

7703 *wén-hsüān kūng* 文宣公
T'ANG–SUNG: **Duke for the Propagation of Culture,** title of nobility (*chüeh*) conferred on the successive most direct male descendants of Confucius, with responsibility for presiding over the Confucian family estate, temple, and

cemetery in Shantung; in 739 changed from Marquis for Praising the Sage (*pao-sheng hou*), in 1055 changed to Duke for Fulfilling the Sage (*yen-sheng kung*). SP: *duc de la propagation littéraire*. P66.

7704   *wén-hsüéh* 文學
(1) HAN–YÜAN: **Instructor,** common designation of educational officials in units of territorial administration including Commanderies (*chün*), Princedoms (*wang-kuo*), Prefectures (*chou, fu*), and Districts (*hsien*), and in the establishment of the Heir Apparent; rank low, rising to 6a2 in the Secretariat of the Heir Apparent (*tso ch'un-fang*) in T'ang. HB: literary scholar. RR: *maître de l'art littéraire.* SP: *maître de l'art littéraire, inspecteur d'éducation, professor aux écoles préfectorales*. P26, 51, 69. (2) HAN: **Clerk** ranking from 100 to 200 bushels, found on the staffs of such central government dignitaries as the Chamberlains for the Palace Garrison (*wei-wei*), for Dependencies (*ta hung-lu*), for the National Treasury (*ta ssu-nung*), and for the Imperial Insignia (*chih chin-wu*); may refer to appointees who were recent graduates of the National University (*t'ai-hsüeh*), but the status is not entirely clear. P33.

7705   *wén-hsüéh chì-chiŭ* 文學祭酒
HAN–N-S DIV (S. Dyn.): **Director of Education** at the Commandery (*chün*) level; apparently interchangeable with *hsiao-kuan chi-chiu*. P51.

7706   *wén-hsüéh chíh-kuān* 文學直官 or *wen-hsüéh chih*
T'ANG: **Auxiliary Instructor,** a part-time duty assignment for a member of the central government with known literary and scholarly talents, to serve in rotation as a consultant to the Emperor in the Academy in the Hall of Elegance and Rectitude (*li-cheng tien hsiu-shu yüan*) or its successor Academy of Scholarly Worthies (*chi-hsien tien shu-yüan*). See under *chih* (Auxiliary). RR: *fonctionnaire auxiliaire de l'art littéraire*. P25.

7707   *wén-hsüéh chíh-kuăn* 文學直館
T'ANG: **Institute of Literary Attendants** affiliated with the Institute for the Veneration of Literature (*ch'ung-wen kuan*) in the establishment of the Heir Apparent; staffed on a rotational basis by distinguished members of the central government on duty assignments as Academicians (*hsüeh-shih*). RR: *collège auxiliaire des études littéraires*. P25.

7708   *wén-hsüéh kuăn* 文學館
LIAO: **Institute of Education** in the Secretariat of the Heir Apparent (*tso ch'un-fang*) and in each Princely Establishment (*wang-fu*); staffing not clear. P26, 69.

7709   *wén-hsüéh shŏu-chù yüàn* 文學守助掾
HAN: apparently a Later Han variant of *wen-hsüeh* (**Instructor**); 60 on the staff of the Governor (*yin*) of Ho-nan Commandery (*chün*), site of the dynastic capital. P32.

7710   *wén-hsüéh ts'ān-chūn* 文學參軍
SUNG: **Adjutant for Education,** rank 9b, at the Prefecture (*chou*) level, probably most commonly in Military Prefectures (*chün*) and Area Commands (*tu-tu fu*); responsible for encouraging education within the jurisdiction. Also see *ts'an-chün-shih*. SP: *inspecteur d'éducation*.

7711   *wén-hsüéh ts'úng-shìh* 文學從事
N-S DIV (San-kuo, S. Dyn.): **Educational Retainer,** personal aide to a Regional Inspector (*tz'u-shih*) charged with encouraging education in his Region (*chou*). See under *ts'ung-shih*. P51.

7712   *wén-hsüéh yŭ* 文學友
N-S DIV (San-kuo Wei): **Literatus Companion,** found on the staffs of Princedoms (*wang-kuo*), presumably in charge of fostering education. P69.

7713   *wén-hsüéh yüàn* 文學掾
N-S DIV (San-kuo Wei, Chin): **Instructor,** apparently a variant of *wen-hsüeh*). P51.

7714   *wén-kuān* 文官
Civil Official or **Civil Office,** the most common generic term throughout history for civil service personnel and their posts as distinguished from Military Officers or Military Offices (*wu-kuan*).

7715   *wén-kuăn* 文館
CH'ING: **Literary Institute,** predynastic antecedent of the Hanlin Academy (*han-lin yüan*), staffed with Academicians (*hsüeh-shih*); in 1635 transformed into the Three Palace Academies (*nei san yüan*). P23.

7716   *wén-lín kuăn* 文林館
Institute of Litterateurs. (1) N-S DIV (N. Ch'i)–SUI: agency for historical compilation apparently attached to the Palace Library (*pi-shu chien*), staffed with central government officials on duty assignments as Academicians (*hsüeh-shih*) and headed by a Supervisor (*p'an … shih*). P23. (2) CH'ING: unofficial reference to the Hanlin Academy (*han-lin yüan*).

7717   *wén-lín láng* 文林郎
SUI–CH'ING: **Gentleman-litterateur,** prestige title (*san-kuan*) for civil officials of rank 9b1 from Sui to Sung, 8a in Chin, 7a from Yüan to Ch'ing. P68.

7718   *wén-pù* 文部
T'ANG: from 752 to 758 the official redesignation of the *lì-pu* (**Ministry of Personnel**); may be encountered in later eras as an unofficial reference to the same Ministry. P5.

7719   *wén săn-kuān* 文散官
SUI–CH'ING: **Civil Service Prestige Title;** see under *san-kuan* (Prestige Title). SP: *mandarins civils portant un titre qui ne comporte pas de fonctions*. P68.

7720   *wèn-shìh* 問事
T'ANG: **Inquisitor,** designation of soldiers assigned to the Court of Judicial Review (*ta-li ssu*) and various units of territorial administration including Prefectures (*chou*); responsible for whipping prisoners with bamboo poles, probably to elicit confessions. RR: *satellite chargé de la bastonnade*. P53.

7721   *wén-shìh kuăn* 文史館
MING: **Institute of History:** in the period 1398–1402 only, a unit either supplementary or subordinate to the Hanlin Academy (*han-lin yüan*); details not clear. P23.

7722   *wén-shū fáng* 文書房
MING: **Palace Secretariat,** from the 1430s or 1440s manned by palace eunuchs handling the Emperor's paperwork as confidential secretaries. Also called *chung-shu fang*.

7723   *wén-ssù shŭ* 文思署
CHIN: **Office for Ornamentation,** one of 6 craft workshops under the Directorate for Imperial Manufactories (*shao-fu chien*), headed by a Director (*ling*), rank 6b; in 1196 merged with the Office for Drawing and Painting (*t'u-hua shu*) into a consolidated Crafts Office (*chih-ying ssu*). P15, 38.

7724 *wén-ssù yüàn* 文思院
T'ANG–SUNG, LIAO, MING: **Crafts Institute,** a eunuch-staffed workshop for the production of jewelry, fine brocades, etc., for use by the Emperor and his wives; in T'ang with a eunuch Commissioner (*shih*) apparently subordinate to the Palace Administration (*tien-chung sheng*), in Sung and Liao under the Directorate for Imperial Manufactories (*shao-fu chien*); in early Sung overseen by one civil and 2 military Supervisors (*chien-kuan*); in S. Sung came directly under the Ministry of Works (*kung-pu*) and split into 2 subsections (see *shang-chieh, hsia-chieh*) coordinated by a Controller (*t'i-hsia kuan*); in Liao headed by a Commissioner (*shih*); in Ming directly subordinate to the Ministry of Works, headed by a Commissioner-in-chief (*ta-shih*), rank 9a. SP: *cour des ornaments artistiques.* P15, 38, 49.

7725 *wén-té tài-chào shěng* 文德待詔省
N-S DIV (Liang): **Department of Learned and Virtuous Expectant Officials,** apparently a palace organization to which promising nominees for official appointments were assigned for participation in historical and other scholarly compilations. P23.

7726 *wén-tsūng* 文宗
CH'ING: unofficial reference to a **Provincial Education Commissioner** (*t'i-tu hsüeh-cheng*).

7727 *wén-t'úng* 文童
MING–CH'ING: variant of *t'ung-sheng* (**Confucian Apprentice**).

7728 *wén-wǔ èrh-wǔ láng* 文武二舞郎
T'ANG: **Performer of Both Civil and Military Dances,** 140 non-official specialists authorized for the Imperial Music Office (*t'ai-yüeh shu*); possibly a collective reference to 2 categories of dancers who performed in court entertainments, one for military and one for non-military types of dances. RR: *danseur pour les danses civiles ou guerrières.* P10.

7729 *wén-yüān kó* 文淵閣
MING–CH'ING: **Hall of Literary Profundity,** one of the palace buildings to which Ming dynasty Grand Secretaries (*ta hsüeh-shih*) were assigned; in Ch'ing served as a kind of imperial library, with a staff headed by a Supervisor (*t'i-chü*) delegated from the Imperial Household Department (*nei-wu fu*). P23, 25.

7730 *wēng-chǔ* 翁主
HAN: **Princess-ordinary,** designation of daughters of Princes (*wang*) not of the imperial family, differentiated from Imperial Princesses (*kung-chu*), the daughters of Imperial Princes (*ch'in-wang*); normally prefixed by the place-name of a Township (*hsiang*) or Neighborhood (*t'ing*). See *hsiang weng-chu, t'ing weng-chu.*

7731 *wò-lǔ-tǒ* 斡魯朵
LIAO: Chinese transliteration of the Khitan word *ordo,* translated into Chinese as *kung* (Palace), designation of the camp of a tribal chief including all his entourage, which moved wherever the chief moved and after his death continued as a cohesive living and fighting unit.

7732 *wǔ* 伍
(1) CHOU: **The Five,** abbreviated reference to the Five Grand Masters (*wu ta-fu*). CL: *les cinq.* (2) CHOU: **Squad,** a military unit of 5 soldiers headed by a Leader (*chang:* Head, etc.), 5 of which constituted a Platoon (*liang*) in an Army (*chün*). CL: *escouade.* (3) **Five,** designation of a local mutual-responsibility group of 5 neighboring households.

7733 *wū* 巫
CHOU: **Sorcerer** or **Sorceress,** generic reference to subordinates of the Directors of Sorcery (*ssu-wu*) in the Ministry of Rites (*ch'un-kuan*); see *nan-wu, nü-wu.* CL: *sorcier.*

7734 *wǔ* 武
Military: throughout history the standard prefix differentiating military officers and offices from those of the civil service (see *wen*).

7735 *wǔ-ch'én chǔn-pèi ch'āi-shǐ* 武臣準備差使
SUNG: **Military Officer in Reserve for Special Assignment,** 5 authorized for each of 3 major Military Commissions (*an-fu ssu*) in the Yangtze Valley, and an unlimited number authorized for (all?) Fiscal Commissions (*chuan-yün ssu*). SP: *fonctionnaire militaire en réserve pour être envoyé en mission.*

7736 *wǔ-ch'én t'í-hsíng* 武臣提刑
SUNG: **Military Judicial Commissioner,** a duty assignment for a military officer as Judicial Commissioner (*t'i-tien hsing-yü kung-shih*), among the Circuit Intendants (*chien-ssu*) of a Circuit (*lu*) in a region with a high density of military garrisons. SP: *intendant judiciaire militaire.*

7737 *wǔ ch'éng* 五城
MING–CH'ING: **Five Wards,** collective reference to the 5 police-administration districts into which the dynastic capital, Peking, was divided, as was also the Ming auxiliary capital, Nanking, in a complex relationship with but not subordinate to the 2 Districts (*hsien*) and the one Prefecture (*fu*) headquartered at the capital; differentiated with the directional prefixes Central, Eastern, Western, Southern, and Northern. Each Ward was the special jurisdiction of a Warden's Office (*ping-ma ssu*) under the supervision of a Ward-inspecting Censor (*hsün-ch'eng yü-shih*). BH: five cities. P20.

7738 *wǔ-ch'éng hsún-shíh yü-shǐh* 五城巡視御史 or *wu-ch'eng yü-shih*
MING–CH'ING: **Ward-inspecting Censors of the Five Wards** of the dynastic capital city; see *hsün-shih yü-shih.* P20.

7739 *wǔ-ch'éng pīng-mǎ ssū* 五城兵馬司
MING–CH'ING: **Wardens' Offices of the Five Wards** in the dynastic capital city; see *ping-ma ssu.* P20.

7740 *wù-chì hsiào-wèi* 戊己校尉
HAN: **Commandant of the Center** (?), rank =600 bushels, from 48 B.C. the designation of some commanders of military garrisons in Central Asia; the title seems to reflect the Taoist concept that the celestial symbols *wu* and *chi* represent the center (*chung*), but the relevance of this explanation is questionable. HB: Wu and Chi colonels.

7741 *wǔ-chì wèi* 武騎尉
SUI–MING: **Commandant of Militant Cavalry,** the least prestigious military merit title (*hsün*) awarded for military achievement, rank 7b through Chin, 6b in Yüan and Ming; in Ming awarded only to military officers. RR+SP: *directeur de la cavalerie guerrière.* P65.

7742 *wǔ-ch'ì chiēn* 武器監
T'ANG: early T'ang variant of *chün-ch'i chien* (**Directorate of Armaments**), discontinued in 632. RR: *direction des armes guerrières.*

7743 *wǔ-ch'ì shǒu-kūng* 武器守宮
T'ANG–SUNG: a combined reference to the **Office of Ar-**

maments (*wu-ch'i shu*) **and the Canopies Office** (*shou-kung shu*), both subordinate to the Court of the Imperial Regalia (*wei-wei ssu*) and perhaps combined in Sung times. P29.

7744 *wǔ-ch'ì shǔ* 武器署
T'ANG–SUNG: **Office of Armaments** under the Court of the Imperial Regalia (*wei-wei ssu*), responsible for over-seeing the use of arms taken from the Court's Armory (*wu-k'u shu*) for sacrificial ceremonies, imperial outings of various sorts, etc.; in T'ang headed by a Director (*ling*), rank 8a2. RR+SP: *office des armes guerrières*. P29.

7745 *wǔ-chiēh* 武階
SUI–CH'ING: **Military Rank,** specifically referring to the rank status of a military officer's prestige title (*san-kuan*).

7746 *wǔ chiēn* 五監
SUI–SUNG: **Five Directorates,** collective reference to 5 central government service agencies, in all periods including the Directorate of Waterways (*tu-shui chien*), Directorate for Imperial Manufactories (*shao-fu chien*), and Directorate for the Palace Buildings (*chiang-tso chien*); in Sui including the Directorate for Armaments (*chün-ch'i chien*) by one account, the Directorate of Palace Domestic Service (*ch'ang-ch'iu chien*) by another account; in Sui and T'ang also including the Directorate of Education (*kuo-tzu chien*); in T'ang and Sung also including the Directorate for Armaments; in Sung also including the Directorate of Astronomy (*ssu-t'ien chien*). Cf. *ssu chien* (Four Directorates).

7747 *wǔ-ch'iēn yíng* 五千營
MING: **Division of the Five Thousand,** variant name of the Firearms Division (*shen-chi ying*), one of the Three Great Training Divisions (*san ta-ying*) at Peking, with counter-parts at the auxiliary capital, Nanking. The term Five Thousand refers to horses of that total that were captured by a general on the northern frontier in the early 1400s.

7748 *wǔ chìh* 五畤
HAN: **Five Altars,** each supervised by a Commandant (*wei*) located at Yung District (*hsien*) outside the dynastic capital; established in early Han under the control of a Great Supplicator (*t'ai-chu ling*) and a Great Sacrificial Butcher (*t'ai-tsai ling*), both prefixed Yung and both under the Chamberlain for Ceremonials (*feng-ch'ang, t'ai-ch'ang*) in the central government; sources do not specify to which deities the altars were dedicated, but possibly dedicated to the legendary sage rulers of high antiquity known as the Five Ti; the altars appear to have been abandoned near the end of Former Han. HB: five sacred places. P28.

7749 *wǔ chǐh-hūi* 五指揮
SUNG: **Five Commanders,** collective reference to the military leaders, hence indirectly the total military force, of the Capital Security Office (*huang-ch'eng ssu*); the troops under the Office's jurisdiction reportedly totaled 2,970. SP: *cinq directions militaires*.

7750 *wǔ-chīng ch'ū-shēn* 五經出身
SUNG: **Graduate in the Five Classics,** status designation of successful candidates in the Metropolitan Examination (*sheng-shih*) of the civil service recruitment examination sequence who took the examination in the ancient works called the Five Classics. See *ch'u-shen*. SP: *docteur des cinq classiques*.

7751 *wǔ chīng-k'uéi* 五經魁
MING–CH'ING: **Five Notable Graduates;** see *ching-k'uei*.

7752 *wǔ-chīng pó-shìh* 五經博士
Erudite of the Five Classics. (1) From Han on, a generic

or specific designation of scholarly dignitaries who were principal staff members of the National University (*t'ai-hsüeh*), the School for the Sons of the State (*kuo-tzu hsüeh*), and counterparts that in Ming and Ch'ing were consolidated under the Directorate of Education (*kuo-tzu chien*); also at times found on the staff of the Hanlin Academy (*han-lin yüan*). Rank rose from 400 to 600 bushels in Han and was 5a in T'ang, 8b in Ming. HB: erudit. RR: *maître au vaste savoir des cinq classiques*. P34. (2) MING–CH'ING: hereditary title, rank 8a, awarded to various descendants of Confucius and notable Confucians, early and late. BH: doctor of the classics. P66.

7753 *wú ch'ū-shēn* 無出身
SUNG: **Without Formal Qualifications,** categorical reference to civil officials being considered for appointment or promotion who were second in prestige to men who had entered service by passing the Metropolitan Examination (*sheng-shih*) in the civil service recruitment examination sequence, those who had transferred into the civil service from comparable status in the military service, and some others who also were labeled With Formal Qualifications (*yu ch'u-shen*). Those Without Formal Qualifications principally included men of good standing who had not entered service via recruitment examinations; they in turn were more prestigious than men who had risen from status as subofficial functionaries (*li, hsü-li*), had purchased official status, etc. See *ch'u-shen*.

7754 *wǔ-chǔ* 武舉
SUNG: **Military Selectee,** from the mid-1000s the designation awarded men chosen for careers as military officers by virtue of having passed examinations in military skills.

7755 *wǔ-chǔ àn* 武舉案
SUNG: **Section for Military Selections,** a clerical unit in the Ministry of War (*ping-pu*); managed the examinations in military skills that were given to prospective military officers from the mid-1000s. SP: *service des examens militaires*.

7756 *wú-chüān* 無涓
HAN: **Lady Without Impurity,** title of a category of palace women, rank =100 bushels. HB: pure maid.

7757 *wǔ chūn-ssū shìh-shīh* 五均司市師
HAN: **Five Market Masters,** collective reference to the 5 Market Masters (*shih-shih*) established to collect mercantile taxes and control commodity prices in the official markets at the dynastic capital, Ch'ang-an, and in 5 other major cities—Loyang (modern Honan), Han-tan (Shansi), Lin-tzu (Shantung), Wan (Hopei), and Ch'eng-tu (Szechwan)—by Wang Mang (r. 9–23), replacing Former Han's Market Directors (*shih-ling*); their subordinates included Exchange Managers (*i*) and Tax and Credit Offices (*ch'ien-fu*).

7758 *wǔ-chūn tū-tū fǔ* 五軍都督府
MING: **Five Chief Military Commissions,** prefixed Front, Rear, Left, Right, and Center, each headed by unprescribed numbers of Commissioners-in-chief (*tu-tu*), rank 1a, Vice Commissioners-in-chief (*tu-tu t'ung-chih*), 1b, and Assistant Commissioners-in-chief (*tu-tu ch'ien-shih*), 2a, all commonly ennobled; a conglomeration of the empire's most eminent military leaders, who oversaw the professional military training of all military forces and led them on major campaigns. Each Commission was responsible for a designated group (not necessarily in geographical clusters) of the empire's military garrisons (see under *wei-so*), although strategic policies and general administrative controls were the business of the civil service Ministry of War

(*ping-pu*). The Five Commissions (commonly abbreviated to *wu fu*) were created in 1380 by a fragmentation of the previously consolidated Chief Military Commission (*tu-tu fu*) in an effort by the founding Emperor to secure total control of the government in his own hands. For internal clerical work, each Commission had a Registry (*ching-li ssu*) headed by a Registrar (*ching-li*), 5b. P4.

7759 *wǔ-chün t'ǔng-chìh* 五軍統制
SUNG: **Commander-general of the Five Armies,** head of the Imperial Defense Command (*yü-ying ssu*) established briefly in the South in the late 1120s during the Sung retreat from North China, when the empire's regular soldiery was reorganized into Five Inspired Armies (*shen-wu wu-chün*). This pattern, and probably the title, did not endure beyond 1130–1131. SP: *commandant général des cinq armées.*

7760 *wǔ-chün ying* 五軍營
MING: **Division of the Five Armies,** one of the Three Great Training Divisions (*san ta-ying*) at Peking, with counterparts at Nanking; originated as the principal military force at the dynastic capital in the founding reign. The term Five Armies refers to the fashion in which the Yung-lo Emperor (r. 1402–1424) organized his forces for campaigns against the Mongols.

7761 *wǔ fāng* 五坊
T'ANG: **Five Cages** of animals used in imperial hunts, under supervision of the Commissioner for the Imperial Stables (*hsien-chiu shih*) in the Palace Administration (*tien-chung sheng*): an Eagle Cage (*tiao-fang*), Hawk Cage (*hu-fang*), Kite Cage (*yao-fang*), Falcon Cage (*ying-fang*), and Dog Cage (*kou-fang*). RR: *cinq quartiers de vénerie.* P38.

7762 *wǔ fáng* 五房
Five Offices. (1) T'ANG: collective reference to the clerical units that conducted the business of the combined Secretariat-Chancellery (*chung-shu men-hsia*) from the 720s, each staffed with Secretariat Clerks (*t'ang-hou kuan*): a Personnel Office (*li-fang*), a Central Control Office (*shu-chi fang*), a War Office (*ping-fang*), a Revenue Office (*hu-fang*), and a combined Justice and Rites Office (*hsing-li fang*). In Sung this group was reorganized and known collectively as the Six Offices (*liu fang*). (2) SUNG: collective reference to subsections of the Proclamations Office (*chih-ch'ih yüan*) of the Secretariat (*chung-shu sheng*). SP: *cinq chambres du grand secrétariat.* P3.

7763 *wǔ fǔ* 五府
(1) T'ANG: **Five Garrisons,** collective reference to militiamen of the Garrison Militia organization (*fu-ping;* also see *fu*) on duty in the dynastic capital, distributed among the Sixteen Guards (*shih-liu wei*); derives from the 5 base areas in which they (or a select group, separate from the Sixteen Guards?) were quartered, each under a Commandant (*chung-lang chiang*), rank 4a2: a Bodyguard Garrison (*ch'in-fu*), a First and a Second Distinguished Garrison (*hsün i-fu, hsün erh-fu*), and a First and a Second Standby Garrison (*i i-fu, i erh-fu*). RR: *cinq milices.* P43. (2) T'ANG: a common though misleading reference to the **Three Garrisons** (*san fu*) in the establishment of the Heir Apparent. P26. (3) MING: abbreviated collective reference to the **Five Chief Military Commissions** (*wu-chün tu-tu fu*).

7764 *wū-fǔ* 烏府
Lit., blackbird office: from Han on, an unofficial reference to the **Censorate** (*yü-shih t'ai, tu ch'a-yüan*) or to its head, the **Censor-in-chief** (*yü-shih ta-fu, tu yü-shih*), because the Censorate's quarters in Han times were distinguished by a large cedar tree frequented by large numbers of birds. See *po-t'ai.*

7765 *wú-hài lì* 無害吏
HAN: lit., functionary (who makes sure there has been?) no harm: **Judicial Inspector,** designation of a delegate from a Commandery Governor (*t'ai-shou*) who in fall and winter toured the Districts (*hsien*) of the jurisdiction to determine whether District personnel had made any wrongful judicial decisions. HB: official who causes no harm. P53.

7766 *wǔ-hòu fǔ* 武候府
Occasional clerical error for or variant of *chien-hou fu* (**Office of Astronomical Observations**).

7767 *wǔ-hsiào pīng* 五校兵 or *wǔ-hsiào shìh* 五校士
HAN: **Troops of the Five Commandants,** a Later Han variant of the earlier name Northern Army (*pei-chün*), deriving from an original group of 5 leaders that subsequently fluctuated in number, each Commandant having a distinguishing prefix, e.g., Commandant of Infantry (*pu-ping hsiao-wei*). HB: troops of the five colonels.

7768 *wǔ-hsièn* 武憲
SUNG: variant of *wu-ch'en t'i-hsing* (**Military Judicial Commissioner**).

7769 *wǔ-hsièn chiàng-chün* 武顯將軍
CH'ING: **General of Military Brilliance,** prestige title (*feng-tseng*) for rank 2a military officers.

7770 *wǔ-hsìn chì-wèi* 武信騎尉
CH'ING: **Commandant of Military Trustworthiness,** prestige title (*feng-tseng*) for rank 7a military officers.

7771 *wǔ-hsìn tsǒ chì-wèi* 武信佐騎尉
CH'ING: **Assistant Commandant of Military Trustworthiness,** prestige title (*feng-tseng*) for rank 7b military officers.

7772 *wǔ-hsüǎn* 武選
Military Appointments Process: from Sung if not earlier, a reference to the institutional arrangements that dealt with the appointments, promotions, demotions, etc., of military officers. In early Sung managed by the West Bureau of Personnel Evaluation (*shen-kuan hsi-yüan;* see *shen-kuan yüan*) in conjunction with the Bureau of Lesser Military Assignments (*san-pan yüan*) in the Ministry of Personnel (*li-pu*), but from 1080 managed entirely by the Ministry of Personnel; see *hsüan, yu-hsüan, shih-lang yu-hsüan.* In Ming and Ch'ing such matters were handled by the Bureau of Military Appointments (*wu-hsüan ch'ing-li ssu*) in the Ministry of War (*ping-pu*). SP: *choix des fonctionnaires militaires.*

7773 *wǔ-hsüǎn ch'īng-lì ssū* 武選清吏司 or *wu-hsüan ssu*
MING–CH'ING: **Bureau of Military Appointments,** one of 4 principal agencies of the Ministry of War (*ping-pu*), responsible for managing the appointments, reappointments, promotions, demotions, retirements, etc., of military officers; headed by a Director (*lang-chung*), rank 5a, in Ming, in Ch'ing by one Chinese, one Mongol, and 3 Manchu Directors, also 5a. BH: department of selection. P12.

7774 *wǔ-hsüéh* 武學
Military School. (1) Common designation throughout history of educational units in large military garrisons, e.g., in Ming dynasty Guards (*wei*); staffed normally with Instructors (*chiao-shou*) in post-T'ang times. (2) SUNG: one of the several schools operated by the Directorate of Education (*kuo-tzu chien*), staffed with one or 2 Erudites (*po-*

shih), rank 8b, and after 1102 also with Instructors (*hsüeh-yü*), 9a. Like all other Military Schools, this trained principally in military skills such as horsemanship and archery, but in addition required some study of texts considered military classics, e.g., the ancient *Sun-tzu*. SP: *école militaire*.

7775　*wǔ-huā p'àn-shìh*　五花判事
N-S DIV–SUNG: lit., deciders of matters of all sorts: unofficial reference to **Secretariat Drafters** (*chung-shu she-jen*).

7776　*wǔ-ì*　武義
Militant Loyalty: prefix that occurs in prestige titles (*san-kuan*) for military officers, e.g., Sung's Gentleman of Militant Loyalty (*wu-i lang*, rank 7b) and Grand Master of Militant Loyalty (*wu-i ta-fu,*) and Ch'ing's Commandant-in-chief of Militant Loyalty (*wu-i tu-wei*, 3a).

7777　*wǔ-ì*　武翼
Militant Assistance: prefix that occurs in prestige titles (*san-kuan*) for military officers, e.g., Sung's Gentleman of Militant Assistance (*wu-i lang*, rank 7b) and Grand Master of Militant Assistance (*wu-i ta-fu*, 7a) and Ch'ing's Commandant-in-chief of Militant Assistance (*wu-i tu-wei*, 3b).

7778　*wǔ-k'ō*　武科
SUNG, MING: **Military Recruitment Examinations,** collective reference to examinations in military skills and ancient texts considered military classics, originated by Sung and revived by Ming in 1464, then in 1504 regularized in a 3-year cycle paralleling the civil service recruitment examination sequence, leading to such status as Military Provincial Graduate (*wu chü-jen*) and Military Metropolitan Graduate (*wu chin-shih*), which qualified men for appointments as regular military officers, supplementing the pool of hereditary officers (see under *wei-so*). Although the military examinations were theoretically open to all applicants, the normal graduates were the younger brothers and secondary sons of existing officers, who had the best opportunities for military training and experience. The Ming examinations did not significantly alter the hereditary character of the officer corps, producing only about 50 Military Metropolitan Graduates every 3 years. The examinations were managed by the Bureau of Military Appointments (*wu-hsüan ch'ing-li ssu*) in the Ministry of War (*ping-pu*). They were not continued in Ch'ing times.

7779　*wǔ-k'ù*　武庫
Armory: throughout history the common designation of an arms depot, particularly the most important one located at the dynastic capital; to be distinguished from agencies that manufactured arms such as the T'ang–Sung Directorate for Armaments (*chün-ch'i chien*) and the Ch'ing Court of Imperial Armaments (*wu-pei yüan*). In Han subordinate to the Chamberlain for the Imperial Insignia (*chih chin-wu*), headed by a Director (*ling*) ranked at 600 bushels; in the post-Han era of N-S Division, it was sometimes subordinate to the Chamberlain for the Palace Garrison (*wei-wei*), sometimes to the Storehouse Section (*k'u-pu*) of the Department of State Affairs (*shang-shu sheng*); in T'ang–Sung it was part of the Court of the Imperial Regalia (*wei-wei ssu*); in Ming–Ch'ing, it was the special responsibility of the Bureau of Provisions (*wu-k'u ch'ing-li ssu*) of the Ministry of War (*ping-pu*). SP: *magasin des armes militaires*. P12.

7780　*wǔ-k'ù ch'īng-lì ssū*　武庫清吏司　or *wu-k'u ssu*
MING–CH'ING: **Bureau of Provisions,** one of 4 major agencies in the Ministry of War (*ping-pu*), responsible for maintaining supplies of armaments and generally for logis-

tical support of the armed forces; headed by one Director (*lang-chung*), rank 5a, in Ming; in Ch'ing headed by one Chinese and 2 Manchu Directors of the same rank. BH: commissariat department. P12.

7781　*wǔ-k'ù lìng*　武庫令
(1) HAN–N-S DIV: **Director of the Armory,** in Han ranked at 600 bushels, under the Chamberlain for the Imperial Insignia (*chih chin-wu*), thereafter under either the Chamberlain for the Palace Garrison (*wei-wei*) or the Department of State Affairs (*shang-shu sheng*). HB: prefect of the arsenal. P12. (2) CH'ING: unofficial reference to the **Chief Minister** (*ch'ing*) **of the Court of Imperial Armaments** (*wu-pei yüan*).

7782　*wǔ-k'ù shǔ*　武庫署
T'ANG: **Armory,** one in the dynastic capital, Ch'ang-an, and another in the auxiliary capital, Loyang, both under the Court of the Imperial Regalia (*wei-wei ssu*), each headed by a Director (*ling*), rank 6b2; stored arms and other military gear. RR: *office du magasin des armes*. P12.

7783　*wǔ kuān*　五官
Lit., five offices, commonly used to suggest "various" or "miscellaneous" functions. (1) HAN: **Lady for Miscellaneous Uses,** designation of a category of palace women ranked at =300 bushels. HB: maid for all purposes. (2) N-S DIV: **General-purpose Clerk (?),** number and functions not clear; commonly unranked subofficials authorized in various agencies of both the central government and the hierarchy of territorial administration; interchangeable with *wu-kuan yüan*. P26, 27, 32, 33, 53, etc. (3) T'ANG–CH'ING: **Five Offices,** a cluster of 5 groups of calendrical specialists, each responsible for one season including Mid-year: Spring Office (*ch'un-kuan*), Summer Office (*hsia-kuan*), Autumn Office (*ch'iu-kuan*), Winter Office (*tung-kuan*), and Mid-year Office (*chung-kuan*), each headed by a Director (*ling* in early T'ang, otherwise *cheng*), rank 5a except 8a in Sung and 6b in Ming and Ch'ing; Ch'ing appointed one Manchu and one Chinese Director. The Offices were part of the T'ang Astrological Service (*t'ai-shih chü*) and later Bureau of Astronomy (*ssu-t'ien t'ai*), the Sung Astrological Service (*t'ai-shih chü*), the Sung–Ming Directorate of Astronomy (*ssu-t'ien chien*), and the Ming–Ch'ing Directorate of Astronomy (*ch'in-t'ien chien*). RR+SP: *cinq administrations*. BH: five astronomers. P35.

7784　*wǔ-kuān*　武官
Military Officer or **Military Office,** the most common generic term throughout history for military personnel or posts as distinguished from Civil Officials or Civil Offices (*wen-kuan*).

7785　*wǔ-kuān ch'ièh-hú chēng*　五官挈壺正
T'ANG–CH'ING: **Supervisors of Water Clocks in the Five Offices;** see *ch'ieh-hu cheng* and *wu kuan*.

7786　*wǔ-kuān chiēn-hòu*　五官監候
Astrological Observers in the Five Offices; see *chien-hou* and *wu kuan*.

7787　*wǔ-kuān chūng-láng chiāng*　五官中郎將
HAN–N-S DIV: **Leader of Court Gentlemen for Miscellaneous Uses,** one of 3 officials, rank =2,000 bushels, in charge of the expectant appointees serving as courtiers and called Court Gentlemen (*lang*); in Later Han each Leader controlled one of what were then called the Three Corps (*san shu*) of such personnel. See *chung-lang chiang*. HB: general of the gentlemen-of-the-household for all purposes.

7788　*wǔ-kuān láng-chūng*　五官郎中
HAN: **Gentleman of the Interior for Miscellaneous Uses,**

rank =300 bushels, one of the categories into which Gentlemen of the Interior (*lang-chung*) were divided.

7789 *wǔ-kuān líng-t'ái* 五官靈臺
T'ANG–CH'ING: variant reference to the **Imperial Observatory** (*ling-t'ai*).

7790 *wǔ-kuān pǎo-chāng chēng* 五官保章正
T'ANG–CH'ING: **Directors of Calendrical Calculations in the Five Offices**; see *pao-chang cheng* and *wu kuan*.

7791 *wǔ-kuān shìh-láng* 五官侍郎
HAN: **Attendant Gentleman for Miscellaneous Uses**, rank =400 bushels, one of the categories into which Attendant Gentlemen (*shih-lang*) were divided.

7792 *wǔ-kuān ssū-ch'én* 五官司辰
T'ANG–CH'ING: **Timekeepers in the Five Offices**; see *ssu-ch'en* and *wu kuan*.

7793 *wǔ-kuān ssū-lì* 五官司曆
(1) T'ANG–YÜAN: variant of *ssu-li* and *ssu-li wu-kuan* (both **Manager of the Calendar**). (2) MING: **Manager of the Calendar** in the Directorate of Astronomy (*ch'in-t'ien chien*), 2, rank 9a; a formal redesignation of *ssu-li*. P35.

7794 *wǔ-kuān ssū-shū* 五官司書
CH'ING: variant reference to a **Compiler** attached to the Five Offices (*wu kuan*) of calendrical specialists in the Directorate of Astronomy (*ch'in-t'ien chien*). BH: compiler. P35.

7795 *wǔ-kuān tà-fū* 五官大夫
SUNG: unofficial reference to *wu-kuan cheng* (**Directors of the Five Offices**): see under *wu kuan* (Five Offices). P35.

7796 *wǔ-kuān ts'áo* 五官曹
HAN: **General-purpose Section**, a clerical unit commonly found on the staffs of Commanderies (*chün*) and Districts (*hsien*), apparently for general administrative work. HB: bureau for all purposes.

7797 *wǔ-kuān yüàn* 五官掾
N-S DIV: variant of *wu kuan* (**General-purpose Clerk?**).

7798 *wǔ k'uéi* 五魁
MING–CH'ING: **Five Notable Graduates**; see *ching-k'uei* and *wu ching-k'uei*.

7799 *wǔ kùng* 五貢
CH'ING: **Five Categories of Tribute Students**, collective reference to the "regular path" (*cheng-t'u*) Tribute Students (*kung-sheng*) admitted to the National University (*t'ai-hsüeh*): Graduate by Grace (*en-kung*), Graduate for Preeminence (*pa-kung*), Certified Student Second Class (*fu kung-sheng*), Graduate for Excellence (*yu-kung*), and regular Tribute Student (*sui-kung*).

7800 *wǔ-kūng chiàng-chūn* 武功將軍
CH'ING: **General of Military Merit**, prestige title (*feng-tseng*) awarded to rank 2b military officers.

7801 *wǔ-láng* 舞郎
T'ANG: **Performer of Dances** in the Imperial Music Office (*t'ai-yüeh shu*); see under *wen-wu erh-wu lang*.

7802 *wù-liào k'ù* 物料庫
SUNG: **Warehouse**, general supply depot serving the Palace Workshops (*tso-fang ssu*) of the Directorate for the Palace Buildings (*chiang-tso chien*); see *tso-fang wu-liao k'u*. SP: *magasin des matériaux pour les ateliers de fabrication*. P15.

7803 *wū-lò-chì-k'ù* 烏呼濟庫
CHIN: variant of *wu-lu-ku* (**Herds Office**). P31.

7804 *wū-lǔ-kǔ* 烏魯古
CHIN: Chinese transliteration of a Jurchen word translated as *ch'ün-mu so* (**Herds Office**). See *t'i-k'ung wu-lu-ku*. P31.

7805 *wǔ-lüèh chì-wèi* 武略騎尉
CH'ING: **Commandant for Military Strategy**, prestige title (*feng-tseng*) for rank 6a military officers; also occurs with the prefix *tso* (Assistant) for rank 6b officers.

7806 *wǔ mǎ* 五馬
Lit., 5 horses: unofficial reference to a Han–Sui **Commandery Governor** (*t'ai-shou*) or a T'ang–Ch'ing **Prefect** (*tz'u-shih, chih-chou, chih-fu*), derivation a matter of controversy; by one account, whereas a team of 4 horses was standard for a chariot, a Han Commandery Governor was authorized to travel with a 5th horse in reserve.

7807 *wū-mǎ* 巫馬
CHOU: **Sorcerer for Horses**, 2 ranked as Junior Servicemen (*hsia-shih*), members of the Ministry of War (*hsia-kuan*) responsible for the care of sick horses; subordinate veterinarians were guided by their determinations of when particular horses were born and when they could be expected to die. CL: *sorcier de chevaux*.

7808 *wǔ-pèi fáng* 武備房
SUNG: **Defense Section**, a unit of the Bureau of Military Affairs (*shu-mi yüan*); staffing and duration not clear. Cf. *shih-erh fang* (Twelve Sections). SP: *chambre des préparatifs militaires*.

7809 *wǔ-pèi ssù* 武備寺
YÜAN: **Court of Imperial Armaments**, a central government agency headed by 4 Chief Ministers (*ch'ing*); supervised 39 subordinate agencies that manufactured and stored military gear for use by the Emperor and his entourage; created by promoting a former unit of the Court of the Imperial Regalia (*wei-wei yüan*), the Directorate of Armaments (*wu-pei chien*), a continuation of the T'ang–Sung Directorate for Armaments (*chün-ch'i chien*); date of change not clear.

7810 *wǔ-pèi yüàn* 武備院
CH'ING: **Court of Imperial Armaments**, originally created by renaming the Ming dynasty Palace Armory (*ping-chang chü*); in 1661 subordinated to the Imperial Household Department (*nei-wu fu*) with an unspecified number of the Department's Grand Ministers (*ta-ch'en*) in charge; in c. 1723 there were created posts of 2 Chief Ministers (*ch'ing*), rank 3a, one drawn from members of the Imperial Household Department, the other from officers of the Imperial Guardsmen (*shih-wei*). Principal subordinate units included Northern and Southern Storehouses (*pei-an k'u, nan-an k'u*). BH: imperial armory.

7811 *wǔ-pīng ts'áo* 五兵曹 or *wu-ping*
N-S DIV: lit. section of the 5 (categories of) troops: **Ministry of War** in the developing Department of State Affairs (*shang-shu sheng*), with administrative control over all armed forces; headed by a Minister (*shang-shu*); changed from *chia-pu* in the 280s, in N. Wei renamed *ch'i-ping* (7 troops) *ts'ao*; supervised a fluctuating number of Sections (*ts'ao*), from 2 to 7, the standard array including Sections for Inner Troops (*chung-ping*), Outer Troops (*wai-ping*), Cavalry (*chi-ping*), Allied Troops (*pieh-ping*), and Capital Troops (*tu-ping*); Sections headed by Directors (*lang, lang-chung*). P12.

7812 *wǔ-pù* 五部

HAN–N-S DIV (S. Dyn.): **Five Sectors,** collective reference to the East, West, South, North, and Center areas into which Commanderies (*chün*) were divided for administrative supervision by itinerant Local Inspectors (*tu-yu*), known collectively as Local Inspectors of the Five Sectors (*wu-pu tu-yu*). P53.

7813 *wǔ-pù* 武部

T'ANG: from 752 to 756 the official redesignation of the *ping-pu* (**Ministry of War**). RR: *ministère militaire*. P12.

7814 *wū-pù* 烏布

CH'ING: **Administrative Assistant,** Chinese transliteration of a Manchu word collectively designating personnel of Ministries (*pu*) below the rank of Bureau Director (*lang-chung*).

7815 *wǔ sǎn-kuān* 武散官

SUI–CH'ING: **Military Service Prestige Title;** see under *san-kuan* (Prestige Title). SP: *titre de prestige des fonctionnaires militaires*. P68.

7816 *wǔ shàng* 五尚

Five Chief Stewards. (1) HAN: collective designation of 5 subordinates of the Chamberlain for the Palace Revenues (*shao-fu*) who tended to the personal needs of the Emperor and the imperial household: Chief Stewards for Headgear (*shang-kuan*), for Accommodations (*shang-chang*), for Clothing (*shang-i*), for the Bedchamber (*shang-hsi*), and for Food (*shang-shih*). Cf. *liu shang* (Six Chief Stewards), *shang-shu*. P30. (2) SUNG: collective reference to 5 of the Six Chief Stewards (see under *liu chü*, Six Services), but which Chief Steward is omitted is not clear.

7817 *wǔ shěng* 五省

Five Departments, collective reference to major agencies of the central government. (1) N-S DIV (Liang): reference to the Department of State Affairs (*shang-shu sheng*), Chancellery (*men-hsia sheng*), Secretariat (*chung-shu sheng*), Palace Library (*pi-shu sheng*), and Department of Scholarly Counselors (*chi-shu sheng*). P28. (2) SUI: reference to the Department of State Affairs, Chancellery, Secretariat (*nei-shih sheng*, i.e., *chung-shu sheng*), Palace Library, and either Palace Domestic Service (*nei-shih sheng* in early Sui) or Palace Administration (*tien-nei sheng* in later Sui). (3) SUNG: reference to the Department of State Affairs, Chancellery, Secretariat, Palace Domestic Service (*nei-shih sheng*), and Palace Eunuch Service (*ju-nei nei-shih sheng*).

7818 *wǔ-shēng* 舞生

CH'ING: **Dance Performer,** 300 non-official specialists authorized for the Music Office (*ho-sheng shu*) in the Music Ministry (*yüeh-pu*). BH: posturer. P10.

7819 *wǔ shǐh* 五使

SUNG: **Five Commissioners,** collective reference to either of 2 groups: (1) Capital Inspectors of Left and Right (see under *hsün-shih*), Supervisor of Post-audience Banquets (*lang-hsia shih*), Commissioner Supervising the Sacrifices (*chien-chi shih*), and Supervisor of Incense Offerings (*chien-hsiang shih*), all duty assignments for Censors (*yü-shih*); or (2) Escort Carriage Rider (*lu-pu shih*), Imperial Regalia Commissioner (*i-chang shih*), Commissioner for Ceremonial Propriety (*li-i shih*), Commissioner for Grand Ceremonials (*ta-li shih*), and either Commissioner for Bridges and Roads (*ch'iao-tao shih*) or Commissioner for Hostels and Postal Relay Stations (*tun-ti shih*), common characteristics not clear. SP: *cinq commissaires*.

7820 *wǔ-shǐh* 舞師

Ceremonial Dancing Master. (1) CHOU: 2 ranked as Junior Servicemen (*hsia-shih*), members of the Ministry of Education (*ti-kuan*) responsible for preparing neophytes to fill vacancies in the ranks of Performing Dancers (*wu-t'u*) and for leading Performing Dancers in state ceremonies. CL: *maître des danses*. (2) N-S DIV (Chin): subordinate to the Grand Director of Music (*t'ai-yüeh ling*), number and rank status not clear. P10. (3) T'ANG: 15 non-official specialists authorized for the Imperial Divination Office (*t'ai-pu shu*). RR: *maître de la danse magique*.

7821 *wǔ-shǐh shuài-fǔ* 武侍率府

SUI–T'ANG: **Armed Attendants Guard Command,** 2 prefixed Left and Right, each headed by a Commandant (*shuai*); from c. 605 to 622 the official designation of military units assigned to the establishment of the Heir Apparent previously and later called Clan Defense Guard Commands (*tsung-wei shuai-fu*). P26.

7822 *wǔ ssū* 五司

SUNG: **Five Bureaus,** common collective reference to the major subsections of the Ministry of Revenue (*hu-pu*): Left Section (*tso-ts'ao*), Right Section (*yu-ts'ao*), Bureau of General Accounts (*tu-chih ssu*), Treasury Bureau (*chin-pu ssu*), and Granaries Bureau (*ts'ang-pu ssu*). SP: *cinq bureaux du ministère des finances*.

7823 *wǔ ssū-t'īng* 五司廳

SUNG: **Five Commissioners,** collective reference to early Sung Circuit (*tao*) dignitaries entitled Military Commissioner (*ching-lüeh*, *an-fu shih*, *chieh-tu shih*), Area Commander-in-chief (*tsung-kuan*), and Surveillance Commissioner (*kuan-ch'a shih*). P50.

7824 *wǔ tà-fū* 五大夫

CH'IN–HAN: lit., grand master of 5, i.e., of a Squad (?): **Grandee of the Ninth Order,** 12th highest of 20 titles of honorary nobility (*chüeh*) conferred on deserving subjects. P65.

7825 *wǔ tà-fū* 伍大夫

CHOU: **Five Grand Masters,** a vague collective reference to the principal assistants of the central government dignitaries called the Three Ministers (*san ch'ing*). Commonly abbreviated to *wu* (The Five). CL: *cinq préfets*.

7826 *wū-t'ái* 烏臺

Lit., blackbird pavilion: from Han on an unofficial reference to the **Censor-in-chief** (*yü-shih ta-fu*, *tu yü-shih*), because in Han times the Censorate's (*yü-shih t'ai*) quarters were distinguished by a large cedar tree frequented by large numbers of birds. See *po-t'ai*, *wu-fu*.

7827 *wū-t'ái shǐh-chūn* 烏臺使君

YÜAN: unofficial reference to a **Surveillance Commissioner** (*su-cheng lien-fang shih*), presumably deriving from the censorial character of his functions; see *wu-t'ai*.

7828 *wǔ-té chì-wèi* 武德騎尉

CH'ING: **Commandant of Military Virtue,** prestige title (*feng-tseng*) for rank 5a military officers; with the prefix *tso* (Assistant), for rank 5b officers.

7829 *wǔ t'í-hsíng* 武提刑

SUNG: abbreviation of *wu-ch'en t'i-hsing* (**Military Judicial Commissioner**). SP: *intendant judiciaire militaire*.

7830 *wǔ-tsàng* 武藏

N-S DIV (Chou): **Military Storehouse** in the Ministry of War (*hsia-kuan*); also the title of its head, the **Military**

Storekeeper, ranked as an Ordinary Grand Master (*chung ta-fu;* 5a). P12.

7831 wǔ ts'áo 五曹
(1) **Five Sections,** collective reference to 5 units, each headed by an Imperial Secretary (*shang-shu*), rank 600 bushels, that constituted what was informally called the Imperial Secretariat (*shang-shu t'ai*) from 29 B.C. into the early years of Later Han. Originally there were Four Sections (*ssu ts'ao*): Section for Attendants-in-ordinary (*ch'ang-shih ts'ao*), Section for Commandery Governors (*erh-ch'ien shih ts'ao*), Section for the People (*min-ts'ao*), and Section for Receptions (*chu-k'o ts'ao*); in 29 B.C. a Section for the Three Dukes (*san-kung ts'ao*) was added. The founder of Later Han reorganized the Imperial Secretariat into Six Sections (*liu ts'ao*). HB: five bureaus. (2) SUNG: **Five Lesser Ministries,** unofficial reference to the Ministries of Revenue (*hu-pu*), of Rites (*lǐ-pu*), of War (*ping-pu*), of Justice (*hsing-pu*), and of Works (*kung-pu*), i.e., all of the Six Ministries (*liu pu*) except the preeminent Ministry of Personnel (*li-pu*). SP: *cinq services.*

7832 wǔ-tū wáng 武都王
N-S DIV (S. Dyn.): lit. sense not clear: **Garrison Prince,** one of the honorary titles conferred on submissive chieftains of southwestern aboriginal tribes. P72.

7833 wǔ-t'ú 舞徒
CHOU: lit., 8th class administrative official (see under *t'u*) for dancing: **Performing Dancer,** 40 authorized as subordinates of the Ceremonial Dancing Masters (*wu-shih*) in the Ministry of Education (*ti-kuan*). CL: *suivant pour les danses.*

7834 wǔ-wèi 武衛
SUI-SUNG: **Militant Guard,** 2 military units prefixed Left and Right, created in 607 among the Twelve Guards (*shih-erh wei*) at the dynastic capital produced by reorganization of the earlier Left and Right Guards (*tso-wei, yu-wei*) and Palace Military Headquarters (*ling tso-yu fu*); retained when the Twelve Guards were reorganized into the Sixteen Guards (*shih-liu wei*), although from mid-T'ang all the Guards had only nominal existence, providing grandiose titles for members of the imperial family and other favored dignitaries; headed by a General (*chiang-chün*), normally rank 3a. RR+SP: *garde guerrière.* P20.

7835 wǔ-wèi chiàng-chūn 武衛將軍
(1) N-S DIV (San-kuo Wei): **Militant General,** one of 3 Generals who shared command of the Imperial Guard (*chin-lü*); see *ch'e-chi chiang-chün, p'iao-chi chiang-chün.* (2) SUI-T'ANG: **General of the Militant Guard,** leader of either the Left or the Right Militant Guard (*wu-wei*). P20.

7836 wǔ-wèi ch'īn-chūn tū chǐh-hūi shǐh ssū 武衛親軍都指揮使司
YÜAN: **Imperial Armies Support Commission,** an agency of the Bureau of Military Affairs (*shu-mi yüan*) in the central government, responsible for the construction and maintenance of military installations; headed by an Overseer (*ta-lu-hua-ch'ih*) and 3 Chief Military Commissioners (*tu chih-hui shih*).

7837 wǔ-wèi chūn tū chǐh-hūi shǐh ssū 武衛軍都指揮使司
CHIN: **Chief Military Commission for the Capital Guard,** a command unit responsible for defense of the dynastic capital and police patrols within the city; created in 1180 with a Chief Military Commissioner (*tu chih-hui shih*), rank 4a, in charge; in 1198 promoted to 3b. P20.

7838 wǔ-wēi wèi 武威衛
T'ANG: **Militant and Awesome Guard,** from 684 to 705 the name of 2 military units prefixed Left and Right, temporarily replacing the name Courageous Guard (*hsiao-wei*) in the array of Sixteen Guards (*shih-liu wei*) at the dynastic capital. There is an unlikely possibility, suggested by some sources, that this name also from 662 to 684 replaced the name Awesome Guard (*wei-wei*). P43.

7839 wǔ-yěh t'ài-shīh 五冶太師
LIAO: **Director of Mints** in supervisory charge of coinage processes throughout the empire; organizational affiliation and rank not clear. P16.

7840 wǔ-yīng tièn 武英殿
CH'ING: **Hall of Military Glory,** a palace building most noted for housing the Imperial Printing Office (*hsiu-shu ch'u*). BH: throne hall. P37.

7841 wǔ-yù 武諭
SUNG: abbreviation of *wu-hsüeh hsüeh-yü* (**Instructor in a Military School**).

7842 wǔ yüàn 五院
(1) SUNG: **Five Bureaus,** collective reference to the Institute of Academicians (*hsüeh-shih yüan*), the Bureau of Personnel Evaluation (*shen-kuan yüan*), the Judicial Control Office (*shen-hsing yüan*), the Public Petitioners Review Office (*teng-wen chien-yüan*), and the Public Petitioners Drum Office (*teng-wen ku-yüan*). These agencies seem to have had nothing in common other than the term *yüan* in their names; cf. *liu yüan* (Six Offices). SP: *cinq cours.* (2) LIAO: **Five Groups,** one of the categories into which the founding ruler, A-pao-chi, divided his followers; represented at court by the Office of the Grand Prince of the Five Groups (*wu-yüan ta-wang fu*). See *nan ta-wang fu, ssu ta-pu.* P17.

7843 yǎ 亞
Lit., inferior, lesser: **Vice,** found as a prefix to titles throughout history, signifying a secondary post, e.g., *ya-ch'ing* (Vice Minister).

7844 yā-chàng kuān 押仗官
SUNG: **Armed Escort,** designation of personnel of the Court of the Imperial Regalia (*wei-wei ssu*) when escorting the Emperor in state ceremonies. SP: *fonctionnaire d'escorte.*

7845 yá-chiàng 牙將
CH'ING: unofficial reference to a **Company Commander** (*ch'ien-tsung*) in the Chinese military forces called the Green Standards (*lu-ying*).

7846 yá-ch'ién 衙前
T'ANG–SUNG: lit., in front of the yamen or office, i.e., at the yamen. (1) Generic reference to menials hired by local units of territorial administration, or requisitioned from groups in the sub-District (*hsien*) organization of the populace. (2) Occasionally found as the equivalent of *tien-ch'ien;* e.g., see *tien-ch'ien chün* (Palace Army). SP: *agent public.*

7847 yá-ch'ién shè-shēng pīng 衙前射生兵
T'ANG: **Bowmen Shooters at Moving Targets,** a group of skilled archers organized in 757 into Left and Right Wings (*hsiang;* i.e., *ya-ch'ien tso-yu she-sheng hsiang*) as a special imperial bodyguard. Also known as *tien-ch'ien she-sheng shou* and *kung-feng she-sheng kuan.* Often referred to as the Left and Right Armies of Heroic Militancy (*ying-wu chün*). Promptly, perhaps in the very year of their activation, absorbed into the new Left and Right Armies of Inspired Militancy (*shen-wu chün*); but in 786 separated as

Left and Right Armies of Bowmen Shooters at Moving Targets (*tien-ch'ien she-sheng chün*). In 787 reorganized as the Left and Right Armies of Inspired Awesomeness (*shen-wei chün*), and in 813 absorbed into the Left and Right Armies of Inspired Strategy (*shen-ts'e chün*). RR: *archers habiles du devant du palais*. P43.

7848 *yá-chíh* 牙職
T'ANG–SUNG: **Local Subofficial,** apparently a reference to menials hired by local units of territorial administration or requisitioned for state service from groups in the sub-District (*hsien*) organization of the populace. P49, 72.

7849 *yǎ-ch'īng* 亞卿
T'ANG–CH'ING: unofficial reference to a **Vice Minister** (*shih-lang*) of a Ministry (*pu*).

7850 *yǎ chūng tà-fū* 亞中大夫
YÜAN–MING: **Lesser Grand Master of the Palace,** prestige title (*san-kuan*) for civil officials of rank 3b from c. 1314; changed from Junior Grand Master of the Palace (*shao chung ta-fu*). P68.

7851 *yá-chūn* 牙軍
T'ANG: lit., army (identified by) a flag with serrated edges: **Regional Army,** generic designation of armies controlled by Military Commissioners (*chieh-tu shih*) of the late T'ang decades.

7852 *yā-fān* 押番
SUNG: **Duty Group Leader,** apparently a common designation of the commander of a group of soldiers under the Metropolitan Cavalry Command (*ma-chün ssu*) or the Metropolitan Infantry Command (*pu-chün ssu*) on active rotational service; see *fan*. SP: *chef de troupe*.

7853 *yǎ-fù* 亞傅
Variant of *shao-fu* (**Junior Mentor**).

7854 *yǎ-hsiàng* 亞相
(1) HAN–N-S DIV: unofficial reference to a **Censor-in-chief** (*yü-shih ta-fu*), deriving from his status as assistant to the Counselor-in-chief (*ch'eng-hsiang*) in early Han times. (2) SUNG: unofficial reference to a **Grand Councilor of the Right** (*yu ch'eng-hsiang*). (3) CH'ING: unofficial reference to an **Assistant Grand Secretary** (*hsieh-pan ta hsüeh-shih*) in the Grand Secretariat (*nei-ko*).

7855 *yǔ hsiù kuān* 押宿官
YÜAN: **Constellation Watcher** (?), 2 non-official specialists in the Directorate of Astronomy (*ssu-t'ien chien*); specific functions not clear. P35.

7856 *yā-hù fáng* 鴉鶻房
CH'ING: **Imperial Hawk Aviary** maintained by the Office of the Imperial Hunt (*tu-yü ssu*); in 1746 renamed *yang ya-hu ch'u*. P37.

7857 *yā-kāng kuān* 押綱官
CHIN–CH'ING: **Convoy Leader,** large numbers attached to all agencies involved in grain transport by water, apparently lowly personnel on duty assignments from local units of territorial administration along the waterways; in charge of the requisitioned labor gangs that operated the boats in each grain convoy. P60.

7858 *yā-kuān* 押官
(1) T'ANG–SUNG: **Discipline Officer,** a duty assignment (?) for a military officer in a Garrison (*chen*) with 500 or more troops; on active campaign, followed in the rear to deal with deserters. RR+SP: *chef de la police des troupes*. (2) SUNG: **Prison Custodian** in a Mail and Prison Office (*mo-k'an ssu*).

7859 *yá-kuān* 牙官
T'ANG: lit., an officer bearing an animal-tooth (symbol of authority): **Military Specialist,** a military officer dispatched from the late T'ang court on duty assignment on the staff of each Military Commissioner (*chieh-tu shih*), Area Command (*chen*), and Prefecture (*chou, fu*); in later times used as a derogatory reference to military officers. P20.

7860 *yá-kuān* 衙官
T'ANG: lit., official (in charge of?) the office: **Headquarters Adjutant,** duty assignment for an official on the staff of a Prefect (*tz'u-shih*) with status as a Commissioner (*shih*) with military responsibilities; functions not clear. RR: *assesseur au tribunal*.

7861 *yá-lì* 牙吏 or 衙吏
Headquarters Functionary: in Sung and probably thereafter, an abbreviated reference to subofficial functionaries (*li*) employed in the office (*ya-men*) of a unit of territorial administration. P60.

7862 *yá-mén* 衙門 or 牙門
N-S DIV (San-kuo)–CH'ING: **Yamen,** i.e., the headquarters or office of the head of an agency, e.g., a District (*hsien*) Yamen. The term seems to have originated in the 2nd form above, designating the entrance to the tent or enclosure where a campaigning general was to be found, marked by his serrated flag (*ya*); how quickly the term came to refer to any government office is not clear. Especially in Ch'ing materials, look under prefixed terminology, e.g., *tsung-li ya-men* (Foreign Office).

7863 *yā-pān* 押班
SUNG: lit., to be in charge of a group on duty (*pan*); apparently an abbreviation of the eunuch designation *nei-shih ya-pan* (**Administrative Aide**), but perhaps not reserved for eunuchs alone. SP: *administrateur, chef, chef de compagnie*.

7864 *yǎ-pǎo* 亞保
Variant of *shao-pao* (**Junior Guardian**).

7865 *yá-pīng* 衙兵 or 牙兵
(1) T'ANG (first form only): **Troops of the Commands,** generic reference to soldiers of the Imperial Armies (*chǐn-chün*), divided into a Southern Command (*nan-ya*) and a Northern Command (*pei-ya*). (2) T'ANG–5 DYN (either form): **Headquarters Troops,** designation of the personal armies developed by late T'ang Military Commissioners (*chieh-tu shih*) and northern rulers in the Five Dynasties era.

7866 *yǎ-shīh* 亞師
Variant of *shao-shih* (**Junior Preceptor**).

7867 *yà-shìh* 訝士
CHOU: **Escort Guide,** 8 ranked as Ordinary Servicemen (*chung-shih*), members of the Ministry of Justice (*ch'iu-kuan*), principally responsible for escorting court visitors from afar; also reportedly concerned in some way not clear with criminal justice throughout the kingdom. CL: *prévôt-préveneur*.

7868 *yá-ssū* 衙司
SUNG: **Service Allocation Office,** one of many agencies that served the 3 bureaus that constituted the State Finance Commission (*san ssu*) of early Sung; headed by a Supervisor (*kuan-hsia kuan*) detached from the Commission's Mail Distribution Office (*k'ai-ch'ai ssu*) and a eunuch Administrative Aide (*ya-pan*) from the Palace Domestic Service (*nei-shih sheng*); tabulated the military achievements of general officers and allocated to them accordingly personal servants

chosen from among criminals sentenced to labor. From c. 1080, when the State Finance Commission was discontinued, reassigned to the Criminal Administration Bureau (*tu-kuan ssu*) in the Ministry of Justice (*hsing-pu*). SP: *bureau des registres des généraux*. P13.

7869 yā-ssū kuān 押司官 or **ya-ssu**
SUNG: (1) **Headquarters Clerk,** unranked subofficials found both in central government agencies and in units of territorial administration. SP: *clerc chargé de s'occuper des dossiers, registres, etc.; secrétaire inférieur, clerc.* (2) Variant of *ya-kuan* (**Prison Custodian**).

7870 yā-t'ái 亞臺
T'ANG: unofficial reference to a **Censor-in-chief** (*yü-shih ta-fu*).

7871 yā-tì 押遞
CHIN: **Transport Foreman,** from 30 to 50 unranked subofficials authorized for the staff of the Fiscal Commissioner (*chuan-yün shih*) of each Route (*lu*). P60.

7872 yá-t'ūi 衙推
T'ANG: **Associate Judge,** common duty assignment on the staffs of Prefects (*tz'u-shih*), Military Commissioners (*chieh-tu shih*), and Surveillance Commissioners (*kuan-ch'a shih*). Cf. *t'ui-kuan* (Judge). RR: *juge adjoint*. P52.

7873 yā-yá 押衙
SUNG: **Lackey,** categorical designation of non-official hirelings used for menial work in units of territorial administration. SP: *officier*.

7874 yā-yüàn chūng-shǐh 押院中使
T'ANG: **Eunuch Manager of the Academy,** i.e., the Academy in the Hall of Elegance and Rectitude (*li-cheng tien hsiu-shu yüan*) till 725, thereafter the Academy of Scholarly Worthies (*chi-hsien tien shu-yüan*); in charge of eunuchs assigned to the Academy, guards at the Academy gates, exit and entry, and communications between the Academy and the throne. RR: *commissaire impérial de l'intérieur du palais chargé de surveiller la bibliothèque*. P25.

7875 yái-kūng 崖公
Lit. sense not clear; from T'ang on, an unofficial reference to the **Emperor** (*huang-ti*).

7876 yáng-ch'ē hsiǎo-shǐh 羊車小史
T'ANG: **Goat-cart Driver,** 40 unranked subofficials authorized for the Office of the Imperial Coachman (*ch'eng-huang shu*). RR: *conducteur de voitures à chèvres*.

7877 yǎng-hsiàng sǒ 養象所
SUNG: **Office for Elephant Care** under the Court of the Imperial Stud (*t'ai-p'u ssu*), staffing not clear but probably unranked subofficials or non-official specialists. SP: *poste de l'entraînement des éléphants*. P31.

7878 yǎng-hsīn tièn tsào-pàn ch'ù 養心殿造辦處
CH'ING: **Workshop in the Hall of Moral Cultivation,** staffed with eunuchs who produced things needed in the ordinary service of the Emperor, an agency of the Imperial Household Department (*nei-wu fu*) headed by 3 Directors (*lang-chung*); till 1759 called *tsao-pan huo-chi ch'u* and supervised by an unspecified number of Managers (*kuan-li*). BH: workshop of the imperial household. P37.

7879 yáng-ī 瘍醫
CHOU: **Royal Surgeon,** 8 ranked as Junior Servicemen (*hsia-shih*), subordinate to the Master Physicians (*i-shih*) of

the Ministry of State (*t'ien-kuan*), responsible for treating wounds, fractures, and resulting swellings. CL: *médecin pour les ulcères, chirurgien*.

7880 yáng-jén 羊人
CHOU: **Keeper of Sacrificial Sheep,** 2 ranked as Junior Servicemen (*hsia-shih*), members of the Ministry of War (*hsia-kuan*) who provided sheep for all (military?) sacrificial ceremonies. CL: *officier du mouton*.

7881 yǎng-kóu ch'ù 養狗處
CH'ING: **Imperial Kennels** maintained by the Office of the Imperial Hunt (*tu-yü ssu*); also known as *kou-fang*. P37.

7882 yáng-kuān 陽官
CHOU: lit., sunshine official: variant reference to the **Ministry of Rites** (*ch'un-kuan*).

7883 yǎng-lién ó 養廉額
CH'ING: **Allowance to Encourage Honesty,** a salary supplement awarded to provincial officials to discourage corruption, varying according to rank, location, and the amount of official business transacted, from 20,000 taels down to 31 taels per year.

7884 yáng-lìn chú 楊藺局
YÜAN: **Service of Yang Lin** (of Yang and Lin possible but unlikely), a tailoring service for the Emperor aggregated with 7 other agencies into the Chief Office for the Imperial Costume (*pei-chang tsung-yüan*) in 1276; an example of an early Yüan practice of naming (minor?) governmental agencies after their incumbent heads or after officials who made appointments to them.

7885 yáng-pó 陽伯
CHOU: lit., sunshine Earl: variant reference to the **Minister of Rites** (*ta tsung-po*).

7886 yǎng yā-hù ch'ù 養鴉鶻處
CH'ING: **Imperial Hawk Aviary,** renamed from *ya-hu fang* in 1746; maintained by the Office of the Imperial Hunt (*tu-yü ssu*). P37.

7887 yǎng-yīng ch'ù 養鷹處
CH'ING: **Imperial Falcon Cage,** renamed from *ying-fang* in 1746; maintained by the Office of the Imperial Hunt (*tu-yü ssu*). P37.

7888 yǎng yīng-yào ch'ù 養鷹鶂處
CH'ING: **Gerfalcon and Hawk Aviary,** a unit in the Office of the Imperial Hunt (*tu-yü ssu*) headed by 3 Manchu noblemen serving as Managers (*kuan-li*); supervised the Imperial Kennels (*yang-kou ch'u*) as well as the Imperial Falcon Cage (*yang-ying ch'u*) and the Imperial Hawk Aviary (*yang ya-hu ch'u*). P37.

7889 yáo 徭
Forced Labor: see *ch'ai-yao, tsa-fan ch'ai-yao*.

7890 yáo-ch'áng 窰場
YÜAN: **Pottery Works,** 2 pottery production units, one under the Ministry of Works (*kung-pu*) and one under the Regency (*liu-shou ssu*) at the principal Mongol capital, Ta-tu (Peking); each headed by a Superintendent (*t'i-ling*), rank 8b and 6b, respectively, with subordinate Commissioners-in-chief (*ta-shih*). P15.

7891 yào-ch'éng 藥丞
HAN: **Pharmacist Aide** to the Imperial Physician (*t'ai-i ling*) on the staff of the Chamberlain for the Palace Revenues (*shao-fu*); possibly a practitioner of Taoist-type alchemical medicine. Cf. *fang-ch'eng* (Medical Treatment Aide). HB: assistant for medicines. P36.

7892　*yào-chí* 要籍
T'ANG: **Record Keeper,** duty assignment for a subaltern on the staff of a Military Commissioner (*chieh-tu shih*) or a Surveillance Commissioner (*kuan-ch'a shih*). RR: *fonctionnaire qui examine les registres nominatifs.* P52.

7893　*yào-chǘ* 藥局
SUNG: **Medical Service,** 7 offices under the Court of the Imperial Treasury (*t'ai-fu ssu*) and another in the Palace Administration (*tien-chung sheng*); staffing not clear, but presumably prepared medications and made medical diagnoses for residents of the palace and members of the central government. SP: *office de médecine.* P31.

7894　*yào-ch'üēh* 要缺
CH'ING: **Important,** categorical designation of the headships of units of territorial administration, less prestigious than Most Important (*tsui-yao*) but more so than Ordinary (*chung-ch'üeh*) and Simple (*chien-ch'üeh*); the agencies in the Important category were officially labeled with any 3 of 4 possible ratings: bustling, complex, exhausting, and difficult (see *ch'ung-fan-p'i-nan*). BH: important.

7895　*yáo-chǜn* 遙郡
SUNG: lit., distant or remote Commandery, suggesting posts over which the central government could exercise only limited control (?): **Adjunct,** categorical reference to officials who had not yet been awarded prestige titles (*san-kuan*), hence not yet fully regularized personnel; also a prefix to a title signifying that the post indicated was a supplementary one, not the appointee's principal (*cheng*) post. Cf. *cheng-jen* (Principal). SP: *irrégulier.*

7896　*yào-fāng* 鷂坊
T'ANG: **Kite Cage,** one of the Five Cages (*wu fang*) of animals used in imperial hunts, under supervision of the Commissioner for the Imperial Stables (*hsien-chiu shih*) in the Palace Administration (*tien-chung sheng*). RR: *le quartier des éperviers.* P38.

7897　*yào-í* 曜儀
N-S DIV (N. Ch'i): **Lady of Brilliant Deportment,** designation of one of 27 imperial wives collectively called Hereditary Consorts (*shih-fu*); rank =3b.

7898　*yáo-lǐng* 遙領
N-S DIV–T'ANG: **Remote Controiler,** prefix to a title or agency name, signifying that the indicated official, normally while continuing to hold his principal (*cheng*) post, was put concurrently in charge of another post to which he actually did not go (and was probably not expected to go)—a device by which an official's prestige, rank, and income might be increased without an actual change in his status. See *ling* (Concurrent, Concurrent Controller). P50.

7899　*yào-mì k'ù* 藥密庫
SUNG: **Medical Storehouse,** a unit common in local Herds Offices (*ch'ün-mu ssu*) in charge of state-owned horses; probably staffed by non-official specialists. SP: *magasin des médicaments pour les chevaux.*

7900　*yào-té* 曜德
N-S DIV (N. Ch'i): **Lady of Brilliant Virtue,** designation of one of 27 imperial wives collectively called Hereditary Consorts (*shih-fu*); rank =3b.

7901　*yào-tsàng chǘ* 藥藏局
N-S DIV (N. Ch'i)–T'ANG: **Pharmacy** in the Secretariat of the Heir Apparent (*men-hsia fang, tso ch'un-fang*); through Sui headed by one or 2 Supervisors (*chien*), in T'ang by 2 Directors (*lang*), rank 6b2. RR: *pharmacie de l'héritier du trône.* P26.

7902　*yào-t'úng* 藥童
T'ANG–SUNG: **Apprentice Pharmacist,** 14 authorized in the Imperial Medical Office (*t'ai-i shu*) and 30 in the Palace Medical Service (*shang-yao chü*) in T'ang, 11 in the Imperial Dispensary (*yü-yao yüan*) in Sung. RR+SP: *aide-pharmacien.* P36, 38.

7903　*yáo-wù* 窰務
SUNG: **Kiln Office** under the Directorate for the Palace Buildings (*chiang-tso chien*), headed by 3 Supervisors (*chien-kuan*); apparently a tile-producing agency. SP: *agence des fours à briques.* P15.

7904　*yào-wù yüàn* 藥物院
YÜAN: abbreviated reference to *hui-hui yao-wu yüan* (**Moslem Pharmacy**).

7905　*yào-yüán* 藥園
SUI–T'ANG: **Herbal Garden,** a unit of the Imperial Medical Office (*t'ai-i shu*), headed by 2 Herbal Gardeners (*yao-yüan shih*) and with Apprentice Herbalists (*yao-yüan sheng*) chosen from commoners from 15 through 19 years old. RR: *jardin des plantes médicinales.* P36.

7906　*yěh* 冶
N-S DIV (S. Dyn.): **Mint,** from 2 to 4 normally established to produce coins under supervision of the Chamberlain for the Palace Revenues (*shao-fu*), with directional prefixes, e.g., Northern, Southern, Western, Eastern; each headed by a Director (*ling*) or a Vice Director (*ch'eng*). Antecedents of the T'ang–Sung *chu-ch'ien chien* and the Ming–Ch'ing *pao-yüan chü,* etc. P16.

7907　*yèh-chě* 夜者
HAN: **Lady for Night Attendance,** designation of a palace woman with rank =100 bushels. HB: night attendant.

7908　*yèh-chě* 謁者
HAN–SUNG: **Receptionist,** designation of officials with functions resembling those of butlers, masters of ceremonies, ushers, messengers, stewards, etc.; in Han it was specified that they be chosen from among young court attendants who had fine beards and loud voices. In early times they were found at the imperial court, in the establishments of Heirs Apparent and Empresses, and in Princedoms (*wang-kuo*); they were commonly organized under one or more Supervisors (*p'u-yeh*) chosen from among their ranks; and their principal functions included welcoming and introducing visitors at court, receiving memorials addressed to the Emperor and transmitting imperial pronouncements to agencies of the central government, helping to manage major ceremonials, and taking the Emperor's condolences to the families of deceased officials. In early Han this was a eunuch post, but in 29 B.C. it was transformed into a post for regular civil officials; Later Han may have reappointed eunuchs. Receptionists were ordinarily subordinate to the Chamberlain for Attendants (*kuang-lu-hsün*), the Chamberlain for Dependencies (*ta hung-lu*), the Chamberlain for Ceremonials (*t'ai-ch'ang*), or the Chamberlain for the Palace Revenues (*shao-fu*); in Han their basic rank was 600 bushels. Those principally concerned with the management of visitors at court commonly constituted a Tribunal of Receptions (*yeh-che t'ai*). In Sui the Tribunal became an important autonomous agency of the central government charged, among other things, with making special ad hoc censorial investigations (see under *san t'ai,* Three Tribunals), but in 621 it was abolished and its staff of Ceremonial Receptionists (*t'ung-shih yeh-che*) was absorbed among the Secretarial Receptionists (*t'ung-shih she-jen*) in the Secretariat (*chung-shu sheng*). By Sung times Receptionists (*yeh-*

che) remained only in the establishment of the Heir Apparent. Also see *chung yeh-che, ch'ang-shih yeh-che, chi-shih yeh-che, kuan yeh-che lang-chung, ho-t'i yeh-che.* HB: internuncio. RR: *introducteur des visiteurs.* SP: *introducteur des visiteurs, huissier.* P27, 33, 37, 69.

7909 *yèh-chě t'ái* 謁者臺
HAN–T'ANG: **Tribunal of Receptions,** a central government agency with the principal function of managing the reception of important visitors at court, commonly in close association with or subordinate to the Chamberlain for Dependencies (*ta hung-lu*); staffed with Receptionists (*yeh-che*) under one or more Supervisors (*p'u-yeh*), rank 1,000 bushels in Later Han; at times headed by a Director (*ling*); in Sui at least partly an autonomous investigatory agency, one of a group of Three Tribunals (*san t'ai*), headed by a Grand Master (*ta-fu*). In 621 discontinued, its staff of Ceremonial Receptionists (*t'ung-shih yeh-che*) absorbed among the Secretarial Receptionists (*t'ung-shih she-jen*) of the Secretariat (*chung-shu sheng*). RR: *tribunal chargé d'introduire les visiteurs.* P33.

7910 *yěh-chiēn* 冶監
T'ANG–SUNG: **Foundry Directorate,** scattered establishments for the casting of weapons and agricultural tools under supervision of the Directorate for Imperial Manufactories (*shao-fu chien*), in T'ang each headed by a Director (*ling*), rank 7a2. Cf. *chu-ch'ien chien* (Directorate of Coinage). RR+SP: *direction de fonderie.*

7911 *yěh-chǖn* 夜君
HAN: variant of *yeh-che* (**Lady for Night Attendance**).

7912 *yěh-lǐ-k'ǒ-wēn chǎng-chiào ssū*
也理可溫掌教司
YÜAN: variant of *chang-chiao ssu* (**Religious Office**).

7913 *yěh-lú shìh* 野廬氏
CHOU: **Travel Patroller,** 6 ranked as Junior Servicemen (*hsia-shih*), members of the Ministry of Justice (*ch'iu-kuan*) who supervised a large staff that regularly patrolled roads and inspected hostels throughout the domain to assure the safety of travelers and to bring to punishment anyone who waylaid travelers. CL: *préposé aux baraques des campagnes.*

7914 *yěh-shìh* 夜士
CHOU: **Night Watchman** at the palace.

7915 *yěh-shǔ* 冶署
N-S DIV (Liang, Ch'en): **Mint Office,** 2 prefixed East and West, each with a Director (*ling*), under the Chamberlain for the Palace Revenues (*shao-fu*); comparable to the Mints (*yeh*) of other S. Dynasties. P16.

7916 *yěh-tào* 冶道
N-S DIV (N. Ch'i): **Coinage Circuit,** one designated Eastern (*yeh tung-tao*) and one Western (*yeh hsi-tao*) under the Court for the Palace Revenues (*t'ai-fu ssu*), each headed by a Director (*ling*); each supervised 3 or 4 local Services (*chü*). P37.

7917 *yèh-t'īng* 掖庭
See under *i-t'ing.*

7918 *yěn* 奄 or 闇
Ety., a combination of "great" and "stretch out," in 2nd form enclosed within a gate; significance not clear: throughout history one of the common terms for **eunuch.** See *huan-kuan, nei-shih.*

7919 *yèn-aň yüeh àn* 宴安樂案
SUNG: **Banquet Music Section,** one of 6 units in the Imperial Music Bureau (*ta-sheng fu*), staffed with non-official specialists. SP: *service de musique des banquets.*

7920 *yén-ch'á tà-shǐh* 鹽茶大使
CH'ING: **Commissioner-in-chief for Tea and Salt,** a non-official agent managing the taxation of state-monopolized tea and salt in a Prefecture (*fu*). BH: tea and salt examiner.

7921 *yén-ch'áng ssū* 鹽場司
YÜAN: **Saltern Office,** 29 scattered in salt-production areas of the Southeast to supervise operations of the state monopoly of salt under the Chief Tax Transport and Salt Monopoly Commission for Liang-Huai (*liang-huai tu chuan-yün-yen shih ssu;* see *chuan-yün-yen shih ssu*); each headed by a Director (*ling*), rank 7b. P61.

7922 *yén-ch'áng tà-shǐh* 鹽場大使
CH'ING: **Saltern Commissioner-in-chief,** variant of *yen-k'o ta-shih* (Salt Distribution Commissioner).

7923 *yén-ch'è kuān* 鹽掣官 or *yén-ch'è t'úng-chīh* 同知
CH'ING: **Salt Inspector,** 2 in Kiangsu and one in Shansi, rank 5a, under supervision of the Salt Controller (*yen-yün shih*) having jurisdiction in their areas; supervised and controlled the distribution of state-monopolized salt. BH: inspector of salt distribution. P61.

7924 *yén-chèng* 鹽政
(1) **Salt Administration,** throughout imperial history a general reference to the bureaucratic apparatus, the procedures, and the policies that governed the state monopoly of the production and distribution of salt. (2) CH'ING: **Salt Supervisor,** a duty assignment for members of the Censorate (*tu ch'a-yüan*), to maintain surveillance over the operation of the state salt monopoly; one each assigned to the major salt production regions, Ch'ang-lu in Hopei Province and the Liang-Huai area on the central east coast; in all other areas, a concurrent designation of Governors-general (*tsung-tu*) and Provincial Governors (*hsün-fu*). P61.

7925 *yén chīh-shìh* 鹽知事
CH'ING: **Administrative Clerk of a Salt Control Station** (*p'i-yen so*), rank 8b. P61.

7926 *yén-ch'íh chiēn* 鹽池監
T'ANG: **Salt Marsh Directorate,** one of many kinds of units under the Court of the National Granaries (*ssu-nung ssu*) that supervised the production of state-monopolized salt in particular localities, each headed by a Supervisor (*chien*), rank 7a2. RR: *direction de marais salant.* P61.

7927 *yén-ch'íh tsǔng-chiēn* 鹽池總監
SUI: **Director-general of Salt Marshes,** a central government official, rank =6b, in overall control of the production of state-monopolized salt; organizational affiliation not clear. Supervised 4 subordinate Directors (*chien*), rank =8a, prefixed East, West, North, and South, each overseeing operation of the state salt monopoly in a quadrant of the empire. P61.

7928 *yén-ch'ìng ssū* 延慶司
YÜAN: lit., office for the prolongation of blessings: **Office of Religion,** one authorized for each Princely Establishment (*wang-fu*) and one in the Household Service for the Heir Apparent (*ch'u-cheng yüan*), responsible for managing prayers and sacrifices; each headed by a Commissioner (*shih*), rank 3a. P26, 69.

7929 *yén-chiǔ shùi-wù* 鹽酒稅務
SUNG: **Salt and Wine Tax Office,** a unit in a Prefecture (*chou*), headed by a Supervisor (*chien*). SP: *gérant du service du monopole du sel et du vin.*

7930 *yén-chōu shǐh* 鹽州使
T'ANG: **Commissioner for the Pasturages of Yen Prefecture,** an official of the Court of the Imperial Stud (*t'ai-p'u ssu*) delegated to establish new horse pasturages or to inspect existing Directorates of Horse Pasturages (*mu-chien*) in Yen Prefecture (Yen-chou) in the vicinity of modern Ninghsia, Kansu Province. This commission was apparently not initiated until after mid-T'ang. See *tung-shih.* RR: *commissaire impérial (aux élevages) de Yen-tcheou.*

7931 *yén-chüēh shǐh* 鹽榷使
5 DYN (Later T'ang): **Commissioner for Salt Transit Taxes,** a concurrent duty assignment for a Prefect (*tz'u-shih*). P61.

7932 *yěn-fǎ* 演法
CH'ING: **Expounder,** 2 prefixed Left and Right, rank 6b, members of the state-recognized Taoist priesthood. BH: hierophant.

7933 *yén-fǎ liáng-wù tào* 鹽法糧務道
CH'ING: **Salt and Grain Tax Circuit,** an agency with combined responsibility for the collection of taxes on both salt and grain in a region of Honan, headquartered at Kaifeng; headed by a Circuit Intendant (*tao-t'ai*). See *yen-fa tao, liang-ch'u tao.* BH: salt and grain intendant.

7934 *yén-fǎ tào* 鹽法道
CH'ING: **Salt Control Circuit,** a specialized branch of provincial establishments in regions where the production of state-monopolized salt was an important industry; elsewhere combined into General Administration Circuits (*fen-shou tao*) and General Surveillance Circuits (*fen-hsün tao*); headed by a Circuit Intendant (*tao-t'ai*). Also see *tao* and *yen-cheng.* BH: salt taotai. P61.

7935 *yèn-fàng tà-ch'én* 驗放大臣
CH'ING: **Grand Minister for the Confirmation of Appointments,** an ad hoc duty assignment for eminent members of the central government, to approve newly appointed officials below rank 4, who were commonly excused from normal confirmation in imperial audience; the purpose was to check for physical infirmities, inappropriate demeanor, or other things that might disqualify an appointee. BH: controller for examinations of officials.

7936 *yèn-fēng ch'īng-lì ssū* 驗封清吏司 or *yen-feng ssu*
MING–CH'ING: **Bureau of Honors,** one of 4 Bureaus in the Ministry of Personnel (*li-pu*), responsible for processing enfeoffments, honorific titles, inheritance of official status, etc.; headed by a Director (*lang-chung*), rank 5a; in Ch'ing one Manchu and one Chinese appointee. BH: department of grants. P5.

7937 *yén-hsiāng ssū* 鹽香司
SUNG: **Salt and Incense Tax Office,** an agency for collecting taxes on state-monopolized commodities, probably at the District (*hsien*) level. SP: *bureau d'encens et du sel.*

7938 *yén hsǔn-chiěn* 鹽巡檢
CH'ING: **Salt Inspector,** rank 9b, a subordinate in a Salt Control Station (*p'i-yen so*), particularly responsible for guarding against illegal traffic in salt. BH: salt watcher. P61.

7939 *yèn-í* 豔儀
N-S DIV (N. Ch'i): **Lady of Captivating Deportment,** designation of one of 27 imperial wives collectively called Hereditary Consorts (*shih-fu*); rank =3b.

7940 *yěn-jén* 奄人
Variant of *yen* (**eunuch**).

7941 *yén-jén* 鹽人
CHOU: **Salt Steward,** 2 eunuchs on the staff of the Ministry of State (*t'ien-kuan*), responsible for selecting, classifying, and preparing salt for use by the royal family and in state ceremonies; supervised 20 Salt Maids (*nü-yen*). CL: *employé au sel.*

7942 *yēn-kō* 閹割
CH'ING: lit., a gatekeeper who has been wounded, i.e., castrated: an unofficial reference to a **eunuch** (*t'ai-chien*).

7943 *yén-k'ò ssū* 鹽課司
(1) Common abbreviation of *yen-k'o t'i-chü ssu* (**Salt Distribution Supervisorate**). (2) MING–CH'ING: **Salt Tax Office,** a local agency in the hierarchy of agencies that managed the state-monopolized trade in salt, overseen by a Salt Distribution Supervisorate or even directly by a Salt Distribution Commissioner or Salt Controller (*tu chuan-yün-yen shih*); normally headed by a Commissioner-in-chief (*ta-shih*), rank 8a or lower. BH (*yen-k'o ta-shih*): salt receiver. P61.

7944 *yén-k'ò t'í-chǔ ssū* 鹽課提舉司
YÜAN–CH'ING: **Salt Distribution Supervisorate,** an agency directing operation of the state-monopolized trade in salt in a large region, headed by a Supervisor (*t'i-chü*), rank 5b to 9a; supervised subordinate Saltern Offices (*yen-ch'ang ssu*), Salt Tax Offices (*yen-k'o ssu*), etc.; under the jurisdiction of Salt Distribution Commissioners or Salt Controllers (*tu chuan-yün-yen shih*). Numbers variable. BH (*t'i-chü*): salt inspector. P61.

7945 *yén-kuān* 言官
Speaking Official: generic reference to Grand Masters of Remonstrance (*chien-i ta-fu*), Supervising Secretaries (*chi-shih-chung*), and others whose principal and characteristic function was to monitor the making of policy decisions at court and to recommend or criticize policies, as differentiated from Surveillance Officials (*ch'a-kuan*), whose principal and characteristic function was to discover and impeach wayward officials. Also see *chien-kuan* (Remonstrance Official).

7946 *yén-kuān* 鹽官
HAN: **Salt Monopoly Office,** an agency commonly found in Commanderies (*chün*) and Princedoms (*wang-kuo*) for management of the state-controlled production and distribution of salt; headed by a Director (*ling, chang*), ranked from 600 to 1,000 bushels or from 300 to 400 bushels. HB: office of salt. P61.

7947 *yén-liào chú* 顏料局
MING: **Ornamentation Service,** a workshop in the Ministry of Works (*kung-pu*) headed by a Commissioner-in-chief (*ta-shih*), rank 9a; did not endure throughout the dynasty, but the date of discontinuance is not clear. P15.

7948 *yén-liào k'ù* 顏料庫
CH'ING: **Miscellany Vault,** one of 3 storehouses (see *san k'u*) supervised by the Ministry of Revenue (*hu-pu*); headed by a Director (*lang-chung*), rank 5a; stored various minerals, spices, and specialized items of local produce. P7.

7949 *yén-lù* 言路

Avenues of Criticism, a term traditionally used in reference both to Remonstrance Officials (*chien-kuan*), whose principal and characteristic function was to criticize governmental policies, and Surveillance Officials (*ch'a-kuan*), whose principal and characteristic function was to discover and impeach wayward officials and who were also relied upon to keep the ruler informed of general conditions and opinions among the people at large. Each Emperor, however tyrannical in fact, paid lip service to the ideal of keeping the Avenues of Criticism open; and at times officials with such responsibilities, by their silence, so isolated rulers from what was happening in the empire that rulers were effectively forced to change unpopular policies or reverse unpopular decisions. Rulers and eminent officials alike were readily criticized for blocking the Avenues of Criticism, the proper functioning of which was considered essential to good governance. Also see *yen-kuan*.

7950 *yén-mǎ ssū* 鹽馬司

MING: **Office for the Exchange of Salt and Horses,** 3 established in Szechwan in 1372 to exchange Chinese salt for horses belonging to aboriginal tribes; each with a Director (*ling*) till 1380, thereafter with a Commissioner-in-chief (*ta-shih*), but soon discontinued. P61.

7951 *yěn-shèng kūng* 衍聖公

SUNG–CH'ING: **Duke for Fulfilling the Sage,** designation awarded the successive most direct male descendants of Confucius, who presided over the Confucian family estate, temple, and cemetery at Ch'ü-fu, Shantung; in 1055 changed from Duke for the Propagation of Culture (*wen-hsüan kung*). BH: sacred prince. P66.

7952 *yén-shìh kuān* 言事官

SUNG: lit., official who speaks out about affairs: variant of *yen-shih yü-shih* (**Remonstrating Censor**). P18.

7953 *yén-shǐh ssū* 鹽使司

CHIN: **Salt Commission,** 7 scattered throughout the country to oversee operation of the state monopoly of the production and distribution of salt; each headed by a Commissioner (*shih*), rank 5a. P61.

7954 *yén-shìh yù-shǐh* 言事御史

SUNG: **Remonstrating Censor,** one or more established in the Censorate (*yü-shih t'ai*) in c. 1017 with the special responsibility of criticizing state policies, contrary to the traditional separation of censorial functions between Remonstrance Officials (*chien-kuan*) and Surveillance Officials (*ch'a-kuan*); in 1045 consolidated in an Office of Remonstrating Censors (*chien-kuan yü-shih t'ing*) in the Censorate; c. 1080 discontinued, absorbed into the staff of Palace Censors (*tien-chung yü-shih*). SP: *censeur politique.* P18.

7955 *yén-tào* 鹽道

CH'ING: abbreviation of *yen-fa tao* (**Salt Control Circuit**).

7956 *yén t'í-chǔ* 鹽提學

YÜAN–CH'ING: variant of *yen-k'o t'i-chü* (**Salt Distribution Supervisor**). P61.

7957 *yén-t'iěh p'àn-kuān* 鹽鐵判官

(1) SUNG: **Assistant Commissioner** in the Salt and Iron Monopoly Bureau (*yen-t'ieh ssu*) of early Sung. SP: *assistant à l'exploitation du sel et du fer.* (2) CHIN: **Assistant Commissioner for the Salt and Iron Monopoly,** rank 6b, one on the staff of each Fiscal Commissioner (*chuan-yün shih*). P60.

7958 *yén-t'iěh shǐh* 鹽鐵使

Lit., commissioner (supervising the state monopolies) of salt and iron. (1) T'ANG–5 DYN: **Salt Monopoly Commissioner,** from 758 an ad hoc duty assignment for an offical to supervise regional operation of the state monopoly of salt under the chief Salt Monopoly Commissioner (see *chüeh yen-t'ieh shih*); since iron was not monopolized in T'ang or early post-T'ang times, *t'ieh* in the title was an anachronism derived from Han usage (see under *ta ssu-nung*). The commission commonly carried combined responsibilities, most importantly as Salt and Transport Commissioner (*yen-t'ieh chuan-yün shih*) but also, e.g., as Salt and Coinage Commissioner (*yen-t'ieh chu-ch'ien shih*). (2) SUNG: **Salt and Iron Monopoly Commissioner,** head of the Salt and Iron Monopoly Bureau (*yen-t'ieh ssu*). (3) LIAO: **Salt Monopoly Commissioner,** a member of the Southern Administration (*nan-mien*) in the central government, supervising operation of the state monopoly of salt production and distribution. P61.

7959 *yén-t'iěh ssū* 鹽鐵司

(1) Designation of any Commission headed by a *yen-t'ieh shih* (Salt Monopoly Commissioner, Salt and Iron Monopoly Commissioner). (2) T'ANG–5 DYN: **Salt Monopoly Bureau** (see *san ssu*). (3) SUNG: **Salt and Iron Monopoly Bureau,** one of the 3 early Sung fiscal agencies collectively known as the State Finance Commission (*san ssu*), normally headed by an independent Commissioner (*shih*) on duty assignment from a nominal central government post, at times headed by a Commissioner controlling all 3 of the units constituting the State Finance Commission; the agency implemented state controls over the exploitation of all natural resources, supervised commerce and commercial taxation, provided essential military materials, etc., through 7 constituent Sections (*an*): Military Section (*ping-an*), Armaments Section (*chou-an*), Market Tax Section (*shang-shui an*), Capital Salt Supply Section (*tu-yen an*), Tea Section (*ch'a-an*), Iron Section (*t'ieh-an*), and Special Preparations Section (*she-an*). Transformed into a Tax Transport Bureau (*chuan-yün ssu*) in a reorganization prior to the abolition of the State Finance Commission in c. 1080, but date not clear. SP: *bureau de l'exploitation du fer et du sel.* P7.

7960 *yén-ts'āng tū* 鹽倉督

SUI: **Supervisor of the Salt Storehouse,** 2 subordinates of the Imperial Granaries Office (*t'ai-ts'ang tu*). P8.

7961 *yén-tzū k'ù* 延資庫

T'ANG–5 DYN: **Special Reserves Vault,** a storehouse in the dynastic capital for coins and other valuables used to provide for emergency military expenditures on the frontier; supervised by a Grand Councilor (*tsai-hsiang*) designated Commissioner (*shih*) of the Vault. Originated c. 845 as the *pei-pien k'u* (Frontier Defense Vault); renamed by 860. RR (*shih*): *commissaire impérial chargé de développer les ressources et les réserves de l'état.* P7.

7962 *yěn-yǐn* 奄尹

HAN: **Palace Doorman,** designation of or reference to the eunuch who controlled entry into the inner quarters of the palace.

7963 *yén-yǐn p'ī-yèn sǒ* 鹽引批驗所 or *yen-yin so*

MING–CH'ING: **Salt Control Station,** a local checkpoint to verify the certificates (*yin*) that were required to accompany all authorized commercial shipments of state-monopolized salt in transit; headed by a Commissioner-in-chief (*ta-shih*), rank 8a. See under *p'i-yen so*. P61.

7964 *yén-yüàn kuān* 鹽院官
T'ANG: **Salt Monopoly Official,** generic reference to officials in the hierarchy that supervised the state monopoly of salt production and distribution; see under *chüeh yen-t'ieh shih.* P61.

7965 *yén-yùn shǐh* 鹽運使
YÜAN–CH'ING: variant or unofficial abbreviation of *tu chuan-yün-yen shih* (**Salt Distribution Commissioner, Salt Controller**). BH: salt controller. P61.

7966 *yén-yùn ssū* 鹽運司
YÜAN–CH'ING: variant or unofficial abbreviation of *tu chuan-yün-yen shih ssu* (**Salt Distribution Commission**). P61.

7967 *yi*
See under the romanization *i.*

7968 *yìn* 印
Seal, an official's formal emblem of authority; its size, shape, and inscription varied according to the rank status of the office. See *chang-yin kuan, cheng-yin.*

7969 *yǐn* 尹
(1) HAN–SUI, SUNG–CH'ING: **Governor** of a Metropolitan Area (*ching-chao*) or of the Prefecture (*chou, fu*) in which a dynastic capital was located, distinguishing it from comparable units of territorial administration outside the capital, whose heads had less prestigious titles; rank 2,000 bushels in Han, 3b in Sung, 3a thereafter. HB: governor. SP: *préfet.* BH: prefect. P32. (2) T'ANG: **Administrator** of a Superior Prefecture (*fu*) and normally its active head, subordinate to an Imperial Prince (*ch'in-wang*) who was nominal Governor (*mu*). RR: *préfet.* P32. (3) 5 DYN–SUNG: **Governor** of a Superior Prefecture (*fu*), rank 3b. SP: *préfet.* P53. (4) YÜAN: **Prefect** of a Superior Prefecture (*fu*), rank 4a, or an ordinary Prefecture (*chou*), 4b, or a Military Prefecture (*chün*); also **Magistrate** of a District (*hsien*), 6b to 7b. P53, 54. (5) A common element in merit titles (*hsün*); see under preceding terminology, e.g., *tzu-chih yin.* P65.

7970 *yǐn* 殷
CHOU: lit., the many: a collective reference to all officials ranked as **Servicemen** (*shih*), of whatever grade.

7971 *yìn* 蔭 or 廕
Protection Privilege, the most common term throughout history, especially from T'ang on, for the process by which officials in service were rewarded with authorization for one or more sons to be qualified for official appointments when they matured without undergoing other qualification tests, or with exemptions from most other qualification tests. This was considered one of the "proper paths" (*cheng-t'u*) to attain official status in most dynasties and probably throughout history yielded half or more of the total civil service personnel.

7972 *yìn-ch'ào chǘ* 印鈔局
MING: **Plate Engraving Service** under the Ministry of Revenue (*hu-pu*), headed by a Commissioner-in-chief (*ta-shih*); prepared the engraved plates from which paper money was printed. P16.

7973 *yǐn-chià chàng* 引駕仗 or *yin-chia*
T'ANG: **Chariot Escort,** 60 (66?) members each of the Left and Right Imperial Insignia Guards (*chin-wu wei*) who were assigned to duty as intimate attendants at the palace and were considered part of the Three Capital Guards (*san wei*). Cf. *pieh-chia.* RR: *garde d'honneur chargé de guider les chars.*

7974 *yīn-chiēn* 音監
HAN: **Supervisor of Tones** in the Music Bureau (*yüeh-fu*); rank not clear. HB: inspector of tones.

7975 *yìn-chiēn* 蔭監
MING–CH'ING: **Student by Inheritance,** designation of a man entitled to official status by virtue of the Protection Privilege (*yin*) who, after preliminary testing by the Ministry of Personnel (*li-pu*), was admitted to the National University (*t'ai-hsüeh*); also see *chien-sheng* (National University Student).

7976 *yǐn-chièn ssū* 引見司
SUNG: **Office of Admittance** in the Palace Domestic Service (*nei-shih sheng*), which apparently regulated access to the Emperor; presumably staffed by eunuchs. SP: *bureau des registres des huissiers.*

7977 *yǐn-chìn fù-shǐh* 引進副使
(1) SUNG–CHIN: **Vice Commissioner of the Office of Presentations** (*yin-chin ssu*), rank 7b in Sung, 6b in Chin. SP: *vice-commissaire de la réception des présents offerts.* P11. (2) YÜAN: **Vice Commissioner for Presentations** in the Palace Ceremonial Office (*shih-i ssu*); discontinued in 1279. P33.

7978 *yǐn-chìn ssū* 引進司
SUNG–CHIN: **Office of Presentations,** a central government agency that managed the presentation to the throne of tribute gifts offered by foreign envoys, headed by one or 2 Commissioners (*shih*), rank 5b in Sung, 5a in Chin; in Sung under the Secretariat (*chung-shu sheng*), in Chin part of the Court Ceremonial Institute (*hsüan-hui yüan*). SP: *bureau de la réception des présents offerts par les pays étrangers.* P11.

7979 *yìn-chīng yüàn* 印經院
SUNG: **Classics Printing Bureau** under the Court of State Ceremonial (*hung-lu ssu*); probably a temporary agency established for a specific purpose not wholly clear. SP: *cour de l'impression des livres classiques.*

7980 *yín-ch'īng júng-lù tà-fū* 銀青榮祿大夫
CHIN–YÜAN: **Grand Master for Glorious Happiness with Silver Seal and Blue Ribbon,** prestige title (*san-kuan*) for civil officials of rank 2a2 in Chin, 1a in Yüan. Also see *jung-lu ta-fu.* P68.

7981 *yín-ch'īng kuāng-lù tà-fū* 銀青光祿大夫
SUI–SUNG: **Grand Master of Imperial Entertainments with Silver Seal and Blue Ribbon,** prestige title (*san-kuan*) for civil officials of rank 3a then 3b in Sui, thereafter 3b; in Sung especially used for all Ministers (*shang-shu*) except the Minister of Personnel (*li-pu shang-shu*). Also see *kuang-lu ta-fu.* P68.

7982 *yìn-fáng* 印房
CH'ING: **Seals Office** in the headquarters of the Manchu General (*chiang-chün*) of Ili in China's far Northwest, staffed with Clerks (*chang-ching*) who managed the paperwork of the headquarters.

7983 *yín-k'ù* 銀庫
Silver Vault. (1) MING: variant designation of the *t'ai-ts'ang k'u* (National Silver Vault). (2) CH'ING: one of 6 storehouses or vaults for valuables that constituted the Storage Office (*kuang-ch'u ssu*) of the Imperial Household Department (*nei-wu fu*). Also see *liu k'u.* BH: bullion vaults, state treasury. P7. (3) CH'ING: money-handling unit in the Court of Colonial Affairs (*li-fan yüan*), which principally disbursed funds to Mongols visiting Peking for their sustenance; established in 1707 with a staff headed by a Director

(*lang-chung*), rank 5a. BH: treasury of the court of colonial affairs. P17.

7984 *yìn-lǐ kuǎn-kōu* 印曆管勾
YÜAN: **Calendar Printing Clerk,** 2, rank 9b, in the Astrological Commission (*t'ai-shih yüan*). P35.

7985 *yǐn-lǐ shè-jén* 引禮舍人
MING: **Houseman Receptionist,** 3 eventually reduced to one, probably unranked, authorized for the staff of each Princely Establishment (*wang-fu*). P69.

7986 *yìn-lì sǒ* 印曆所
SUNG: **Calendar Printing Office** in the Palace Library (*pi-shu sheng*); early Sung staffing not clear; in S. Sung consolidated into the Palace Library without a separate identity. SP: *imprimerie du calendrier*. P35.

7987 *yín-p'ái t'iēn-shǐh* 銀牌天使
LIAO: lit., heavenly messenger with a silver badge: **Imperial Messenger,** designation of an ad hoc duty assignment.

7988 *yìn-pǔ* 蔭補
T'ANG–SUNG: lit., to be appointed to office (by virtue of) the protection privilege, i.e., on a hereditary basis: **Appointment by Protection,** a process whereby an official in service, on attaining a particular rank, was entitled to nominate one or more sons or other relatives for official status. After 1009 all "protected" nominees were required to study under the Directorate of Education (*kuo-tzu chien*) at the capital and pass an examination before they were fully qualified to be considered for appointment in the civil service. See *yin*. SP: *nomination de fonctionnaires par protection*.

7989 *yīn-shào-chiā kūng* 殷紹嘉公
HAN: **Duke for the Abundant Perpetuation of Excellence** (?), according to some sources the designation from A.D. 29 to 37 of the current most direct male descendant of Confucius; see under *pao-ch'eng hou*. P66.

7990 *yìn-shēng* 廕生
CH'ING: **Student by Inheritance,** a category of men with at least nominal status as students under the Directorate of Education (*kuo-tzu chien*), classified in 2 ways: as *en-yin chien-sheng* (National University Student Hereditary by Grace) and *nan-yin chien-sheng* (National University Student Hereditary by Heroism), qq.v. BH: honorary licentiate.

7991 *yīn-shēng jén* 音聲人
T'ANG: **Musician,** the most general term used for non-official specialists in the service of the Imperial Music Office (*t'ai-yüeh shu*), who reportedly numbered 10,000. RR: *musicien*.

7992 *yīn-shēng pó-shìh* 音聲博士
T'ANG: **Erudite of the Palace Music School** (*nei-chiao fang*), number unspecified, non-official specialists who taught within the palace. RR: *maître au vaste savoir des musiciens*.

7993 *yǐn-shìh shǐh* 引試使
SUNG: **Examination Commissioner,** designation of an eminent court official on duty assignment supervising a Metropolitan Examination (*sheng-shih*) in the civil service recruitment examination sequence. SP: *commissaire d'examen de doctorat*.

7994 *yìn-shòu chiēn* 印綬監
MING–CH'ING: **Directorate for Credentials,** one of 12 major Directorates (*chien*) in which palace eunuchs were organized; headed by a eunuch Director (*t'ai-chien*); in cooperation with the Directorate of Palace Seals (*shang-pao chien*) managed the seals and tallies with which imperial documents were authenticated; in Ch'ing existed only from 1656 to 1661. See under *shih-erh chien* (Twelve Directorates).

7995 *yìn-shù ch'ién-wù sǒ* 印書錢物所
SUNG: **Publications Office** in the Directorate of Education (*kuo-tzu chien*); staffing not clear. SP: *bureau pour le financement de l'impression des livres, presse de l'université*.

7996 *yín-t'ái* 銀臺
MING–CH'ING: **Silver Pavilion,** unofficial reference to the Office of Transmission (*t'ung-cheng shih ssu*), derived from the Sung *yin-t'ai ssu* (Office of Transmission). P21.

7997 *yín-t'ái ssū* 銀臺司
SUNG: **Office of Transmission,** in early Sung an agency of the Chancellery (*men-hsia sheng*) located at the Silver Pavilion Gate (*yin-t'ai men*) of the palace, charged with receiving, registering, and transmitting to the Emperor memorials submitted from throughout the empire, in some fashion cooperating with the Memorial-forwarding Office (*t'ung-chin ssu*), also in the Chancellery; soon combined with the latter into an agency called *t'ung-chin yin-t'ai ssu*, normally abbreviated as *t'ung-chin ssu*. Headed by an Administrator (*chih:* to know, etc.), often detached from regular duty in the Bureau of Military Affairs (*shu-mi yüan*). SP: *office de la réception et de la transmission des rapports*. P21.

7998 *yín-t'ái t'ūng-chìn ssū* 銀臺通進司
SUNG: variant of *t'ung-chin yin-t'ai ssu* (**Memorial-forwarding Office**); see under *t'ung-chin ssu*. P21.

7999 *yǐn-tsàn kuān* 引贊官
SUNG: **Receptionist,** 2 subofficial functionaries on the staff of the Censorate (*yü-shih t'ai*). SP: *huissier*.

8000 *yìn-tsào ch'ào-yǐn k'ù* 印造鈔引庫
CHIN: **Paper Money Repository,** headed by a Commissioner (*shih*); organizational affiliation not clear; relationship with the Ministry of Revenue's (*hu-pu*) Currency Printshop (*ch'ao-chih fang*) also not clear. P16.

8001 *yìn-tsào pǎo-ch'ào k'ù* 印造寶鈔庫
YÜAN: **Paper Money Printshop** under the Supervisorate of Paper Money (*pao-ch'ao t'i-chü ssu*), headed by an Overseer (*ta-lu-hua-ch'ih*) and one or more Commissioners-in-chief (*ta-shih*). P16.

8002 *yìn-ts'áo* 印曹
HAN–N-S DIV: **Seals Section,** one of 5 Sections among which Attendant Censors (*shih yü-shih*) were distributed in the Censorate (*yü-shih t'ai*); supervised the preparation of official seals (by eunuch workshops?). P9.

8003 *yín-tsò chú* 銀作局
MING: **Jewelry Service,** a minor agency of palace eunuchs that manufactured ornaments of gold and silver for palace use, headed by a eunuch Commissioner-in-chief (*ta-shih*) or Director (*t'ai-chien*). See *pa chü* (Eight Services).

8004 *yìn-tzǔ* 蔭子
Protection of Sons: variant reference to the process whereby officials in service were permitted to "protect" one or more sons or other dependents, i.e., exempt them from normal recruitment qualifications so that they expeditiously attained official status. See *jen-tzu* (Employment of Sons), *yin* (Protection Privilege).

8005 *yìn-wù chāng-chīng* 印務章京
CH'ING: **Correspondence Clerk,** rank 5b, in a Banner (*ch'i;* see *pa ch'i*) military unit. BH: adjutant.

8006 *yìn-wù ts'ān-lǐng* 印務參領
CH'ING: **Correspondence Supervisor,** 2 in each Banner (*ch'i;* see *pa ch'i*) military unit except for one in each Mongol Banner; chosen from among the ranks of the Commanders (*ts'an-ling*) of the Banners. BH: adjutant-general.

8007 *yìn-yáng hsüéh* 陰陽學
Yin-Yang School, a training unit in geomancy; from Ming if not earlier, established under the authorization of local units of territorial administration but without state subsidies, to train practitioners of geomancy and similar arts; in Ch'ing the nominal Principal (*cheng-shu*) at the Prefecture (*fu*) level was in fact supervisor of local fortune-tellers, entertainers, women dentists, midwives, etc., as a kind of licenser and inspector.

8008 *yín-yǔng pó-shìh* 吟詠博士
T'ANG: **Erudite of Recitation,** one of 18 Palace Erudites (*nei-chiao po-shih*) on the staff of the Palace Institute of Literature (*nei wen-hsüeh kuan*), where palace women were educated; from c. 741 a eunuch post. RR: *maître de poésie.*

8009 *yíng* 營
(1) HAN: **Campaigning Army,** common designation of an active tactical force commanded by a General-in-chief (*ta chiang-chün*), a General (*chiang-chün*), or perhaps a Deputy General (*p'ien chiang-chün*); normally consisted of several Divisions (*pu*) subdivided into Regiments (*ch'ü*). HB: division, encampment. (2) T'ANG: **Encampment,** 2 prefixed Left and Right created in 707 (710?) out of the prior Myriad Cavaliers (*wan chi*) of the Northern Command (*pei-ya*); in 710 transformed into Left and Right Militant as Dragons Armies (*lung-wu chün*). Also see *t'un-ying* (Encampment), *pei-ya ch'i ying* (Seven Encampments of the Northern Command). (3) SUNG: **Regiment,** basic garrison unit theoretically consisting of 500 soldiers, 5 such units comprising an Army (*chün*); the equivalent unit of a campaigning Army was called a *chen* (also Regiment). (4) MING: **Training Division;** see *ching-ying* (Capital Training Division) and *san ta-ying* (Three Great Training Divisions). (5) CH'ING: **Brigade,** basic operational unit of Bannermen (see *hsiao-chi ying, hu-chün ying, ch'ien-feng ying, huo-ch'i ying, chien-jui ying*), normally headed by an Imperial Prince (*ch'in-wang*) serving as Commander-general (*t'ung-ling, tsung-t'ung*); also the basic organizational unit of the Chinese military forces called the Green Standards (*lu-ying*), consisting of 500 men led by a Brigade Commander (*yu-chi*). BH: banner corps, battalion.

8010 *yǐng-chiàng* 郢匠
CH'ING: lit., the carpenter of Ying (place-name), derivation not clear: unofficial reference to a **Provincial Education Commissioner** (*t'i-tu hsüeh-yüan*).

8011 *yīng-fāng* 鷹坊
T'ANG: **Falcon Cage,** one of the Five Cages (*wu fang*) of animals used in imperial hunts; under the supervision of the Commissioner for the Imperial Stables (*hsien-chiu shih*) in the Palace Administration (*tien-chung sheng*). RR: *le quartier des faucons.* P38.

8012 *yīng-fáng* 鷹房
CH'ING: **Imperial Falcon Cage** maintained by the Office of the Imperial Hunt (*tu-yü ssu*); in 1746 retitled *yang-ying ch'u.* BH: imperial gerfalcon aviary. P37.

8013 *yīng-fèng* 應奉
SUNG–MING: **Provisioner,** a lowly member of the Hanlin Academy (*han-lin yüan*); rank 7b in Chin and Yüan, 5 appointees in Yüan; discontinued in 1381. P23.

8014 *yīng miěn-chiěh jén* 應免解人
SUNG: lit., someone who ought to be excused from being forwarded: variant of *mien-chieh jen* (**Already Certified Candidate**).

8015 *yíng-p'án* 營盤
YÜAN: **Land Grant,** one of several terms used to designate territories with which noblemen were enfeoffed; see *fen-ti* and *t'ou-hsia.*

8016 *yíng-pù* 營部
MING: **Building Bureau,** from 1389 to 1396 one of 4 major agencies in the Ministry of Works (*kung-pu*); replaced the prior General Bureau (*tsung-pu*), was superseded by the Bureau of Construction (*ying-shan ssu*).

8017 *yíng-shàn chiēn* 營繕監
T'ANG: **Directorate of Construction,** from 685 to 705 the official redesignation of the Directorate for the Palace Buildings (*chiang-tso chien*). P15.

8018 *yíng-shàn ch'īng-lì ssū* 營膳清吏司 or *ying-shan ssu*
MING–CH'ING: **Bureau of Construction,** one of 4 major agencies in the Ministry of Works (*kung-pu*), responsible for the construction and repair of palace buildings, altars and temples, city walls, granaries, storehouses, etc.; headed by a Director (*lang-chung*), rank 5a; 6 appointees in Ch'ing—4 Manchus, one Mongol, and one Chinese. BH: building department. P15.

8019 *yíng-shàn shǔ* 營繕署
T'ANG: from 684 to 685 only, the official redesignation of the **Center Construction Office** (*chung hsiao-shu;* see *hsiao-shu*).

8020 *yíng-shàn sǒ* 營繕所
(1) SUNG: **Construction Office,** a subsection of the Directorate for the Palace Buildings (*chiang-tso chien*); specific responsibilities not clear. SP: *bureau des travaux et des réparations.* (2) MING: **Work Project Office,** a subsection of the Ministry of Works (*kung-pu*) headed by a Director (*cheng*), rank 7a; superseded the Palace Buildings Office (*chiang-tso ssu*) in 1392; probably subject to the intermediary supervision of the Ministry's Bureau of Construction (*ying-shan ch'ing-li ssu*), but specific functions not clear. P15.

8021 *yǐng-t'áng* 影堂
YÜAN: **Image Hall** in a Buddhist monastery; see under *wen-ch'i chü* (Adornment Section). P28.

8022 *yíng-t'íen shǐh* 營田使
T'ANG: **Agriculture Commissioner,** after mid-T'ang one of the many kinds of regional Commissioners delegated from the central government to Circuits (*tao*) or comparable jurisdictions; supervised the development of state-owned lands such as State Farms (*t'un-t'ien*). RR: *commissaire impérial à l'administration d'une colonie agricole.*

8023 *yíng-tsào àn* 營造案
SUNG: **Construction Section,** a minor unit in the Ministry of Works (*kung-pu*); staffing and specific responsibilities not clear, but presumably related to the work of the Directorate of the Palace Buildings (*chiang-tso chien*). SP: *service de travaux de construction.*

8024 *yíng-tsào ssū* 營造司
CH'ING: **Office of Palace Construction,** one of the 7 principal agencies in the Imperial Household Department (*nei-wu fu*), generally responsible for all building and repairing work within the imperial palace; supervised by one or more Grand Ministers (*ta-ch'en*) of the Department in annual rotation. Created in 1677 to replace the earlier Palace Ministry of Works (*nei kung-pu*). For all or part of the dynasty, oversaw the Government Property Rental Agency (*kung-fang tsu-k'u*), the Imperial Library (*yü-shu ch'u*), the Imperial Printing Office (*hsiu-shu ch'u*), and the Workshop (*tsao-pan ch'u*) in the palace; more directly supervised various storage and workshop facilities. BH: department of works. P37.

8025 *yíng-tsào t'í-chǔ ssū* 營造提舉司
MING: **Supervisorate of Construction,** from 1373 to 1392 an agency under the Palace Buildings Office (*chiang-tso ssu*) of the Ministry of Works (*kung-pu*), headed by a Supervisor (*t'i-chü*), rank 7a (?); spawned one or more Branch Supervisorates (*fen-ssu*) with Supervisors of equal status; in 1392 apparently discontinued when the Ministry of Works was reorganized to include a Bureau of Construction (*ying-shan ch'ing-li ssu*). P15.

8026 *yíng-tsò chiàng* 營作將
N-S DIV (Liang, N. Ch'i): **Construction Supervisor,** an ad hoc duty assignment whenever a major construction project was undertaken under supervision of the Liang Chief Minister for the Palace Buildings (*ta-chiang ch'ing*) and the N. Ch'i Court for the Palace Buildings (*chiang-tso ssu; see under *chiang-tso ta-chiang*). P14.

8027 *yíng-tsǔng* 營總
CH'ING: **Brigade Commandant,** rank 3a, officers in various special detachments of Bannermen (see *ch'i, pa ch'i*), usually 2nd in command after a Commander-general (*tsung-t'ung*). BH: commandant.

8028 *yíng-wù ch'ù* 營務處
CH'ING: **Office of Military Affairs,** the military staff agency for a Provincial Governor (*hsün-fu*) or a multi-Province Governor-general (*tsung-tu*), headed by an Adjutant (*chung-chün*) normally with rank as a Vice General (*fu-chiang*), 2b. BH: military secretariat.

8029 *yīng-wǔ chūn* 英武軍
T'ANG: **Army of Heroic Militancy,** 2 prefixed Left and Right; variant designation of the Left and Right Wings (*hsiang*) of Bowmen Shooters at Moving Targets (*ya-ch'ien she-sheng ping*). RR: *armée brave et guerrière.*

8030 *yīng-yáng fǔ* 鷹揚府
SUI: **Soaring Hawk Garrison,** from 607 to the fall of Sui in 618 the formal designation of Garrison (*fu*) units in the Garrison Militia (*fu-ping*) organization; created by standardization of the 2 types called Cavalry Garrison (*p'iao-chi fu*) and Chariot and Horse Garrison (*ch'e-chi fu*); terminated when T'ang reinstituted these previous 2 types. Headed by a Commandant (*lang-chiang*), then in 618 briefly by a Military Chief (*chün-t'ou*). Especially see under *fu*. RR: *milice semblable à l'aigle qui vole.*

8031 *yīng-yáng wèi* 鷹揚衛
T'ANG: **Soaring Hawk Guard,** from 684 to 705 the official redesignation of Soaring Hawk Garrisons (*ying-yang fu*).

8032 *yǔ* 友
(1) CHOU: **Friend,** one of a number of designations for local leaders among the people collectively known as Unifying Agents (*ou*); specifically referred to the leader of a group of farming families using a common well. CL: *ami.* (2) N-S DIV–SUNG: **Companion,** one or more staff members of a Princely Establishment (*wang-fu*), in T'ang rank 5b2; responsible for giving moral guidance as well as companionship. RR: *compagnon.* SP: *conseiller, compagnon.* P69.

8033 *yù* 右
(1) **Right, of the Right, Junior:** throughout history (except as noted in #2 below) a common prefix to a title when a pair of appointees was authorized, both normally of the same rank, or to an agency name when a pair of identically named agencies existed; in prestige, Right yielded to Left (*tso*); geographically, Right indicated West whereas Left indicated East. (2) YÜAN: **Right, of the Right, Senior:** used as above but with reversed order of prestige among the Mongols.

8034 *yù-ch'éng* 右丞
(1) **Right Aide,** throughout history may be encountered in reference to a 2nd or 3rd executive official of an agency; see under *ch'eng*. (2) HAN: **Assistant Director of the Right,** one of a pair of 3rd-tier officials of the Imperial Secretariat (*shang-shu sheng*), rank 400 bushels, ranking behind the Director (*ling*) and Vice Director (*p'u-yeh*). HB: assistant of the right. P5. (3) N-S DIV–YÜAN: **Assistant Director of the Right** in the Department of State Affairs (*shang-shu sheng*), one of a pair normally ranking behind the Director and one or more Vice Directors (both titles as in #2 above), rank commonly 4a until Sung, then advanced to 2a; in T'ang had supervisory jurisdiction over the Ministries of War (*ping-pu*), of Justice (*hsing-pu*), and of Works (*kung-pu*); from Sung on commonly belonged to the elite central government group generically known as Grand Councilors (*tsai-hsiang*), with the specific added designation Participant in Determining Governmental Matters (*ts'an-chih cheng-shih*). RR: *assistant de droite.* SP: *grand conseiller-assistant de droite.* (4) T'ANG–CH'ING: common unofficial reference to the **Vice Minister** (*shih-lang*) of a Ministry (*pu*).

8035 *yù-chì* 右計
SUNG: **Right Account,** one of 2 large regional fiscal jurisdictions into which the empire was divided in 993–994, under a Commissioner of the Right Account (*yu chi-shih*), supervised by a Supreme Commissioner of Accounts (*tsung chi-shih*), in one stage in the development of the State Finance Commission (*san ssu*). SP: *comptes de droite.* P7.

8036 *yú-chī* 游擊
CH'ING: lit., to patrol and attack; see *yu-chi chiang-chün*: **Brigade Commander,** rank 3b, leader of a Brigade (*ying*), the basic organizational unit in the Chinese military establishment called the Green Standards (*lu-ying*); in theory, commanded 500 soldiers divided into 5 Companies (*shao*). BH: major.

8037 *yú-chī chiāng-chūn* 游擊將軍
Mobile Corps Commander. (1) T'ANG–SUNG: prestige title (*san-kuan*) for military officers of rank 5b2. RR+SP: *général qui attaque partout.* (2) MING: a tactical duty assignment for a regular officer of the hereditary Guard system (see *wei-so*), usually one under each Regional Commander (*tsung-ping kuan*) who maintained a kind of mobile reserve unit in a Province or comparable area, as distinguished from tactical officers with place-specific defense assignments.

8038 *yú-chì chiāng-chūn* 游騎將軍
T'ANG–SUNG: **General of Mobile Cavalry,** prestige title

(*san-kuan*) for military officers of rank 5b1. RR+SP: *général de la cavalerie mobile.*

8039 *yú-chì wèi*   游騎尉
SUI: **Commandant of Mobile Cavalry,** 4th highest of 8 Commandant titles conferred on inactive officials (*san-kuan*), rank 7b, beginning in 586; the practice terminated after 604. P65.

8040 *yù-chiàng*   右將
HAN: **Right Leader** of a group of Court Gentlemen (*lang*), distinguished from those led by the Center Leader (*chung-lang*) and the Left Leader (*tso-chiang*).

8041 *yú-chiǎo*   游徼
CH'IN–N-S DIV (Chin): **Patroller,** a local dignitary in the sub-District (*hsien*) organization of the populace who was responsible for police work in a Township (*hsiang*); also known as Township Guardian (*hsiang-li*). HB: patrol leader. P54.

8042 *yū chiēn-shēng*   優監生
CH'ING: **National University Student for Excellence,** a quasiofficial categorical reference to those state-subsidized students in the National University (*t'ai-hsüeh*) officially known as Supplementary Students (*fu-sheng*).

8043 *yǔ-chìh*   有秩
HAN: lit., to have rank status: **Petty Official with Rank,** a local dignitary in the sub-District (*hsien*) organization of the populace who was responsible for tax collection, requisitions of service, and even the administration of justice in a Township (*hsiang*) with 5,000 or more households; Townships with lesser populations commonly had Husbanders (*se-fu*) instead. In Later Han the *yu-chih* had the rank of 100 bushels. The title may have arisen to distinguish these from other sub-District dignitaries who had no rank status, but the derivation is not clear. HB: petty official with rank.

8044 *yù chìh-yù*   右治獄
SUNG: variant designation of the **Right Bureau** (*yu-t'ing*) of the Court of Judicial Review (*ta-li ssu*).

8045 *yù chīng-fǔ tū-wèi*   右京輔都尉
HAN: **Right Defender of the Capital,** one of the Three Defenders of the Metropolitan Area (*san-fu tu-wei*). HB: chief commandant of the western adjunct capital region.

8046 *yù chǔ-k'ò*   右主客
N-S DIV (N. Wei): **Right Section for Foreign Relations,** from c. 400 a component of the Ministry of Rites (*i-ts'ao*) in the evolving Department of State Affairs (*shang-shu sheng*), headed by a Director (*lang-chung*); shared dealings with foreign states (and dependencies?) with a Left Section for Foreign Relations (*tso chu-k'o*), but the basis for division is not clear.

8047 *yǔ ch'ū-shēn*   有出身
SUNG: **With Formal Qualifications,** categorical reference to civil officials being considered for appointment or promotion who were of highest esteem by virtue of having entered the service by passing the Metropolitan Examination (*sheng-shih*) in the civil service recruitment examination sequence, or by transfer from the military service with comparable status. Cf. *wu ch'u-shen* (Without Formal Qualifications), *ch'u-shen.*

8048 *yù-chūn*   右軍
Right Army. (1) Throughout history a common designation for one of 3 or 5 military forces in the field, others normally prefixed Left, Center, Front, and Rear. (2) HAN:

one of 8 special capital-defense forces organized at the end of Han; see *pa hsiao-wei* (Eight Commandants).

8049 *yù-fǔ*   右府
T'ANG: **Right Guard,** one of the Twelve Guards (*shih-erh wei*) at the dynastic capital; created in 622 by renaming the Right Personal Guard (see *pei-shen fu*), then in 660 renamed Right Personal Guard (see *ch'ien-niu wei*). Also cf. *yu-wei.* P43.

8050 *yú-fǔ*   游府
CH'ING: lit., mobile headquarters: unofficial reference to a **Brigade Commander** (*yu-chi*) in the Green Standards (*lu-ying*) military establishment.

8051 *yù fú-fēng*   右扶風
HAN: **Guardian of the Right,** ranked at 2,000 bushels, one of the Three Guardians (*san fu*) who administered the Metropolitan Area (*ching-shih*) from 104 B.C., after 89 B.C. under the domination of the Metropolitan Commandant (*ssu-li hsiao-wei*). Also see *chu-chüeh* (Commandant of the Nobles). HB: western sustainer. P18, 32.

8052 *yù-hsüǎn*   右選
SUNG: lit., selections of the left: **Military Appointments Process,** a reference to the Ministry of Personnel's (*li-pu*) appointments process (see *hsüan*), in which the selection of men for appointments and reappointments was delegated to different executive officials of the Ministry according to the ranks and services (civil or military) of the appointees. The term Right (*yu*) referred to military appointments. Also see *shang-shu yu-hsüan, shih-lang yu-hsüan, hsi-yüan, shen-kuan yüan.* P20.

8053 *yú-hsüān shǐh*   輶軒使
CHOU–HAN: lit., commissioner in (or with) a light chariot: **Royal Commissioner** (Chou) or **Imperial Commissioner** dispatched periodically from the dynastic capital to collect information about regional dialects, local folksongs, etc.; in Chou reportedly dispatched each year in the 8th month.

8054 *yù-hù ts'áo*   右戶曹 or *yu-hu*
HAN–N-S DIV: **Land Tax Section,** a unit in the developing Department of State Affairs (*shang-shu sheng*), perhaps originating very late in Han; headed by a Minister (*shang-shu*) or a Director (*lang, lang-chung*); principally responsible for processing reports of land tax collections from units of territorial administration; apparently a variant form of *yu-min ts'ao*, perhaps suggesting a tampering with the original terminology in T'ang times to avoid the tabooed personal name of Li Shih-min (T'ang T'ai-tsung). Also see *tso-hu ts'ao, hu-ts'ao, min-ts'ao.* P6.

8055 *yù-ì ch'ién-fēng*   右翼前鋒
CH'ING: **Vanguard Brigade Right Wing,** a seemingly transposed term commonly used as a prefix to the title of officers of the Brigade; see under *ch'ien-feng ying* and *i.*

8056 *yù-jén*   囿人
CHOU: **Animal Keeper,** 4 ranked as Ordinary Servicemen (*chung-shih*) and 8 as Junior Servicemen (*hsia-shih*), members of the Ministry of Education (*ti-kuan*) who tended quadrupeds in the royal park and provided them, dead or alive according to need, for sacrificial and funeral ceremonies and for various receptions and banquets. CL: *officier des parcs.*

8057 *yú-júng*   游戎
CH'ING: lit., a mobile soldier: unofficial reference to a **Brigade Commander** (*yu-chi*) in the Chinese military forces called the Green Standards (*lu-ying*).

8058 *yù-kēng* 右更
CH'IN–HAN: lit., member of the first watch: **Grandee of the Fourteenth Order,** 7th highest of 20 titles of honorary nobility (*chüeh*) conferred on meritorious subjects. P65.

8059 *yú-kuān* 油官
N-S DIV (Chin): **Sauceman** (?), unspecified number headed by an Aide (*ch'eng*) to the Chamberlain for the Palace Revenues (*shao-fu*); specific functions not clear. P37.

8060 *yú-kuān* 郵官
Lit., postal official: unofficial reference to the **Vice Director** (*ch'eng*) **of a Postal Relay Station** (*i*).

8061 *yù-k'uéi* 右揆
T'ANG–SUNG: lit., right mastermind: unofficial reference to the **Vice Director of the Right** (*yu p'u-yeh*) **of the Department of State Affairs** (*shang-shu sheng*), differentiated from his counterpart the Vice Director of the Left (*tso p'u-yeh, tso-k'uei*). Also see *tuan-k'uei.*

8062 *yū kùng-shēng* 憂貢生 or *yu-kung*
CH'ING: **Graduate for Excellence,** a status attained by a student in a local state school when he excelled on the regular annual examination administered by the Provincial Education Intendant (*hsüeh-cheng*), entitling the student to participate in the next Provincial Examination (*hsiang-shih*) in the civil service recruitment examination sequence and to be considered at least nominally a National University Student (*chien-sheng*) under the Directorate of Education (*kuo-tzu chien*), beyond the normal quota of Tribute Students (*kung-sheng*). BH: senior licentiate of the third class.

8063 *yù-mín ts'áo* 右民曹 or *yu-min*
N-S DIV: **Land Tax Section,** a unit repeatedly established in the developing Department of State Affairs (*shang-shu sheng*), sometimes headed by a Minister (*shang-shu*), sometimes by a Director (*lang, lang-chung*); apparently established only in a pair with a Census Section (*tso-min ts'ao*). Also see *yu-hu ts'ao, hu-ts'ao, m... :s'ao.* P6.

8064 *yù-pān tièn-chíh* 右班殿直
SUNG: **Palace Eunuch of the Right Duty Group,** 5th highest of 12 rank titles (*nei-shih chieh*) granted eunuchs from 1112. See *pan.* P68.

8065 *yù-pān tū-chīh* 右班都知
SUNG: **Office Manager for the Right Duty Group,** a rank 3 eunuch in the Palace Domestic Service (*nei-shih sheng*), aided by a rank 4 eunuch entitled Assistant Office Manager for the Right Duty Group (*yu-pan fu tu-chih*). See *pan.* SP: *administrateur général des compagnies de droite, intendant du palais de 3ème rang (eunuque).*

8066 *yù-păng* 右榜
YÜAN: **Non-Chinese Pass List** posted after the civil service recruitment examinations conducted in the dynastic capital; see *tso-pang* (Chinese Pass List).

8067 *yù-pì* 右弼
SUNG: **Supporter on the Right,** from 1113 to 1126 a variant designation of the Director (*ling*) of the Secretariat (*chung-shu sheng*). SP: *grand ministre de droite.*

8068 *yù-pì tū-wèi* 右弼都尉
N-S DIV (San-kuo Wu): **Commandant Supporter on the Right,** one of several Commandants (*tu-wei*) who served as advisers to the Heir Apparent. P26.

8069 *yù-pù* 右部
(1) HAN: **Right Sector,** collective designation of the west and north quadrants of the dynastic capitals, Ch'ang-an and Loyang; in Former Han the united jurisdiction of two Commandants of the Metropolitan Police, West and North (*ming-pu wei*); in Later Han the separate jurisdictions of the Commandant of the Metropolitan Police, West Sector (*hsi-pu wei*) and the Commandant of the Metropolitan Police, North Sector (*pei-pu wei*). Cf. *tso-pu* (Left Sector). P20. (2) YÜAN: **Ministries of the Right,** a variant of *yu san-pu* (Three Ministries of the Right).

8070 *yù sān-pù* 右三部
YÜAN: **Three Ministries of the Right,** from 1260 to 1264 and again from 1266 to 1268 a combination of the normally separate Ministries of War (*ping-pu*), of Justice (*hsing-pu*), and of Works (*kung-pu*) into a single agency, with 2 Ministers (*shang-shu*), rank 3a. Also see *ping-hsing-kung pu, tso san-pu.*

8071 *yù-shàng shǔ* 右尚署
T'ANG–SUNG: **Right Service Office** in the Directorate for Imperial Manufactories (*shao-fu chien*), principally responsible for preparing harnesses for horses used in the imperial palace; headed by 2 Directors (*ling*), rank 7b2. RR+SP: *office de l'atelier impérial de droite.* P38.

8072 *yù-shǐh* 右史
T'ANG–SUNG: **Right Scribe,** unofficial reference to Imperial Diarists (*ch'i-chü she-jen*) of the Secretariat (*chung-shu sheng*); in Sung also found on the staffs of Princely Establishments (*wang-fu*) of Imperial Princes (*ch'in-wang*). Cf. *tso-shih* (Left Scribe). SP: *annaliste de droite.*

8073 *yù-shīh* 右師
T'ANG: variant of *ssu-yeh* (**Director of Studies**).

8074 *yù shìh-chìn* 右侍禁
SUNG: **Right Palace Attendant,** 3rd highest ot 12 rank titles (*chieh*) granted to palace eunuchs from 1112; see *nei-shih chieh.* Cf. *tso shih-chin.* SP: *intendant du palais de 3ème rang (eunuque).* P68.

8075 *yù-shìh ts'áo* 右士曹
(1) N-S DIV: **Right Section of Servicemen,** a recurring unit in the developing Department of State Affairs (*shang-shu sheng*), apparently responsible for handling personnel matters relating to (military?) officials of middling to low rank; in N. Wei subordinate to the Department's Ministry of General Administration (*tu-kuan*), headed by a Director (*lang-chung*). Cf. *tso-shih ts'ao.* (2) N-S DIV (N. Wei): **Ministry of Justice** (?) in the developing Department of State Affairs, headed by a Minister (*shang-shu*); sources not clear.

8076 *yù shù-chǎng* 右庶長
CH'IN–HAN: lit., right chief of a host: **Grandee of the Eleventh Order,** 10th highest of 20 titles of honorary nobility (*chüeh*) conferred on meritorious subjects. P65.

8077 *yù-shǔ* 右署
HAN: **Right Corps,** variant reference to one of the Three Corps (*san shu*) in which Court Gentlemen (*lang*) were organized.

8078 *yù-sǒ* 右所
CH'ING: **Right Subsection** of the Imperial Procession Guard (*luan-i wei*), headed by a Director (*chang-yin kuan-chün shih*), rank 4a; subdivided into an Umbrella Office (*ch'ing-kai ssu*) and a Bow and Arrow Office (*kung-shih ssu*). BH: second department.

8079 *yù-ssū* 右司
Right Office, normally paired with a Left Office (*tso-ssu*). (1) N-S DIV–CH'ING: a common unofficial or quasiofficial collective reference to all personnel whose titles were

prefixed with Right in agencies of many sorts whose members were titled in Left and Right pairs. (2) N-S DIV–SUNG, CHIN: a common quasiofficial and sometimes official designation of the aggregation of Ministries of War (*ping-pu*), of Justice (*hsing-pu*), and of Works (*kung-pu*) in the Department of State Affairs (*shang-shu sheng*), commonly supervised by the Right Vice Director (*yu shih-lang*) of the Department with the support of a staff comparable to that of a Bureau (*ssu*) in a Ministry, especially including a Bureau Director (*lang-chung*) and a Vice Director (*yüan-wai lang*). RR+SP: *bureau de droite*. P5. (3) YÜAN: a variant reference to *yu-pu* (Ministries of the Right) or *yu san-pu* (Three Ministries of the Right) in the Secretariat (*chung-shu sheng*). (4) CH'ING: one of 8 units in the Rear Subsection (*hou-so*) of the Imperial Procession Guard (*luan-i wei*), headed by a Director (*chang-yin yün-hui shih*), rank 4a; also one of a pair of Offices into which the Court of the Imperial Clan (*tsung-jen fu*) and the Palace Stud (*shang-ssu yüan*) were each divided. BH: second department.

8080 *yù-ssù* 右寺
MING–CH'ING: **Right Court of Review,** one of a pair of subsections in the Court of Judicial Review (*ta-li ssu*), each staffed with Case Reviewers (*p'ing-shih*); until the 1690s (?) headed by a Director (*cheng*), rank 6a, thereafter by a Right Assistant Director (*yu-ch'eng*) of the Court, rank 5a or 6a. P22.

8081 *yǔ-ssū* 有司
Lit., (those who) have offices: **the authorities:** throughout history a vague reference to governmental officials in charge of activities at issue in particular contexts; probably most commonly used in reference to such local authorities as Prefects (*tz'u-shih, chih-chou, chih-fu*) and, most especially, District Magistrates (*hsien-ling, chih-hsien*), but also at times used in reference to officials in charge of civil service recruitment examinations. Cf. *so-ssu* (the responsible authorities), *cheng-fu* and *kuan-fu* (both The Administration, The Government).

8082 *yù-t'ái* 右臺
T'ANG: **Right Tribunal,** abbreviation of *yu yü-shih t'ai* or *yu su-cheng t'ai* from 684 to 712, when the traditionally unified Censorate (*yü-shih t'ai*) was split into Left and Right units; the Right Tribunal was principally responsible for maintaining disciplinary surveillance over units of territorial administration and observing local conditions throughout the empire, whereas the surveillance effort of the Left Tribunal was directed at the central government and the military establishment. RR: *tribunal de droite*. P18.

8083 *yù-t'áng* 右堂
CH'ING: unofficial reference to a **District Jailor** (*tien-shih*); cf. *tso-t'ang, t'ang.*

8084 *yù-t'īng* 右廳
SUNG: **Right Bureau,** one of 2 major subsections of the Court of Judicial Review (*ta-li ssu*), headed by a Vice Minister (*shao-ch'ing*), rank 6a; cf. *tso-t'ing* (Left Bureau). Also called *chih-yü ssu, yu chih-yü.* Supervised 4 lesser Sections (*an*) and 2 Offices (*ssu*): Sentence Fulfillment Section (*tso-yu ssu-an*), Internal Accounts Section (*ch'ü-mo an*), Legal Research Section (*chien-fa an*), Miscellany Section (*chih-tsa an*), Mail Distribution Office (*k'ai-ch'ai ssu*), and Memorializing Office (*piao-tsou ssu*). SP: *bureau judiciaire de droite chargé des révisions.* P22.

8085 *yú-t'íng* 郵亭
HAN: **Postal Relay Station** maintained by local units of sub-District (*hsien*) organization of the populace called

Neighborhoods (*t'ing*); staffed with runners or riders conscripted from the local residents; also served as hostels for traveling officials. HB: postal station.

8086 *yù-tsàng* 右藏
N-S DIV–YÜAN: **Right Storehouse** or **Right Vault,** one of a pair of major units under the early Chamberlain for the Palace Revenues (*t'ai-fu*) or later agency counterparts such as the Sui dynasty Court for the Palace Revenues (*t'ai-fu ssu*), the Sui–Sung Court of the Imperial Treasury (*t'ai-fu ssu*), and the Yüan Directorate of the Imperial Treasury (*t'ai-fu chien*). Normally headed by 2 or more Directors (*ling*), rank 8a in Sui, 7b in T'ang, or from Sung on by Commissioners (*shih*). Originally shared with the Palace Storehouse (*chung-huang tsang, nei-tsang*) or the Imperial Storehouse (*huang-tsang*) responsibility for the receipt, storage, and disbursement of valuables used in the palace; but from Sung on became principally responsible for handling general state revenues. In Ming superseded by clusters of storehouses under the Ministries of Revenue (*hu-pu*), War (*ping-pu*), and Works (*kung-pu*), collectively known as the Palace Storehouses (*nei-k'u*). See *tso-tsang, t'ai-tsang k'u, san k'u.* RR+SP: *trésor de droite.* P7.

8087 *yù-tsàng àn* 右藏案
SUNG: **Right Storage Section,** one of 6 Sections in the Treasury Bureau (*chin-pu ssu*) of the Ministry of Revenue (*hu-pu*), staffed with unranked subofficials; division of functions between this and the Left Storage Section (*tso-tsang an*) is not clear, but both presumably oversaw the receipt, storage, and issuance of the non-grain commodities with which the Treasury Bureau dealt; established c. 1080, when the State Finance Commission (*san ssu*) of early Sung was discontinued. SP: *service de trésor de droite.* P6.

8088 *yù tsàng k'ù* 右藏庫
SUNG–CHIN: variant of *yu-tsang* (**Right Storehouse** or **Right Vault**). P7.

8089 *yù-tsàng shǔ* 右藏署
N-S DIV–T'ANG: **Right Storehouse Office,** a unit of the Court for the Palace Revenues or the Court of the Imperial Revenues (both *t'ai-fu ssu*) in charge of the palace depot for valuables called the Right Storehouse (*yu-tsang*); headed by 2 Directors (*ling*), rank 8b in Sui, 6a1 in T'ang, except from c. 604 till the end of Sui, an interval when it was headed by a Supervisor (*chien*). See *yu-tsang, tso-tsang shu.* RR: *office du trésor de droite.* P7, 37.

8090 *yù-tsàng t'í-tiĕn* 右藏提點
YÜAN: **Superintendent of the Right Storehouse,** from 1282 4, rank not clear, appointed to oversee the 2 Commissioners-in-chief (*ta-shih*) who were nominal heads of the Right Storehouse, which shared with the Left Storehouse (*tso-tsang*) the receipt and disbursement of general government revenues. P7.

8091 *yù-ts'áo* 右曹
(1) HAN: **Head of the Right Section,** rank 2,000 bushels; nominally a subordinate of the Chamberlain for Attendants (*kuang-lu-hsün*); reportedly presented to the Emperor paperwork completed by the Imperial Secretaries (*shang-shu*), but apparently a sinecure for one or more favored companions of the Emperor; discontinued in Later Han. HB: bureau head of the right. (2) SUNG: **Right Section,** one of 5 Sections in the Ministry of Revenue (*hu-pu*) from the 1080s, when the Ministry was fully activated after being little more than a nominal office while its traditional fiscal functions were performed by the State Finance Commission (*san ssu*) of early Sung; headed by 2 Directors (*lang-chung*),

rank 6b, and 2 Vice Directors (*yüan-wai lang*), 7b. Consisted of 6 (originally 5?) subsidiary Sections (*an*), staffing not clear: Stabilization Fund Section (*ch'ang-p'ing an*), Section for Labor Exemptions (*mien-i an*), Shops and Yards Section (*fang-ch'ang an*), Price Stabilization Section (*p'ing-chun an*), Legal Research Section (*chien-fa an*), and Miscellany Section (*chih-tsa an*). See *tso-ts'ao, hu-pu ssu, chin-pu ssu, ts'ang-pu ssu*. SP: *bureau du droite chargé des exemptions de corvée et des greniers régulateurs*. (3) SUNG: **Right Section,** one of 2 Sections into which the Ministry of Justice (*hsing-pu*) was divided from 1103 (till the mid-1100s only?), presided over by the Right Vice Minister (*yu shih-lang*) of the Ministry; shared the work of the Ministry with a Left Section (*tso-ts'ao*) in some pattern not clear. SP: *service du droite*.

8092 *yú-ts'ù k'ù* 油醋庫
SUNG: **Oil and Vinegar Pantry** under the Court of Imperial Entertainments (*kuang-lu ssu*). SP: *magasin d'huile et de vinaigre*.

8093 *yù-t'ūi àn* 右推案
SUNG: **Investigative Section of the Right,** one of 5 Sections (*an*) constituting the Right Bureau (*yu-t'ing*) of the Court of Judicial Review (*ta-li ssu*); functions not clear. SP: *bureau judiciaire de droite (adresses au trône)*. P22.

8094 *yù-wèi* 右衛
SUI–SUNG: **Right Guard;** see *tso-yu wei, shih-erh wei, shih-liu wei, tso-wei*.

8095 *yù-yüàn* 右院
MING: **Right Tribunal,** one of a pair of units into which Investigating Censors (*chien-ch'a yü-shih*) were organized from 1400 to 1402, temporarily replacing the Circuits (*tao*) of the Censorate (*tu ch'a-yüan*). P18.

8096 *yúng* 榮
See under the romanization *jung*.

8097 *yǔng-hsiāng* 永巷
HAN: lit., the long lanes (in the palace): **Palace Discipline Service,** a eunuch agency with a Director (*ling*) subordinate to the Chamberlain for the Palace Revenues (*shao-fu*), responsible for monitoring the activities of the staff of palace women; in 104 B.C. renamed *i-t'ing*. Others found in Princedoms (*wang-kuo*) and the Establishments of Imperial Princesses (*kung-chu fu*) and of the Empress (*chung-kung*), headed by Directors (*chang*). HB (*ling*): prefect of the long lanes. P37, 69.

8098 *yǔng-lì k'ù* 永利庫
YÜAN: **Paper Money Treasury,** staffing not clear but head ranked 7b; a central government agency under the Supervisorate-in-chief of Coinage (*pao-ch'üan t'i-chü ssu*). P16.

8099 *yūng-shìh* 雍氏
CHOU: **Canal Patroller,** 2 ranked as Junior Servicemen (*hsia-shih*), members of the Ministry of Justice (*ch'iu-kuan*) who maintained police surveillance over transport canals (presumably in the environs of the royal capital) to ensure against their dikes being breached. CL: *préposé aux digues*.

8100 *yùng t'ài-chù lìng* 雍太祝令
HAN: **Great Supplicator at Yung,** a subordinate of the early Han Chamberlain for Ceremonials (*feng-ch'ang, t'ai-ch'ang*) delegated jointly with a Great Sacrificial Butcher at Yung (*yung t'ai-tsai ling*) to manage places of worship outside the dynastic capital known as the Five Altars (*wu chih*). HB: prefect grand supplicator in Yung. P28.

8101 *yùng t'ài-tsǎi lìng* 雍太宰令
HAN: **Great Sacrificial Butcher at Yung,** a subordinate of the early Han Chamberlain for Ceremonials (*feng-ch'ang, t'ai-ch'ang*) delegated jointly with a Great Supplicator at Yung (*yung t'ai-chu ling*) to manage places of worship outside the dynastic capital known as the Five Altars (*wu chih*). HB: prefect grand butcher in Yung. P28.

8102 *yù* 尉
Traditional pronunciation of *wèi* (**Commandant**).

8103 *yù* 獄
One of the common designations of a **Prison;** especially see *chao-yü* (Imperial Prison).

8104 *yú* 虞
See *shan-yü* (**Supervisor of Forestry and Hunting**).

8105 *yù ch'á-shàn ch'ù* 御茶膳處 or *fáng* 房
CH'ING: **Palace Larder** under the Imperial Household Department (*nei-wu fu*), staffed principally by Imperial Guardsmen (*shih-wei*) acting as Meal Servers (*shang-shan*), Tea Servers (*shang-ch'a*), etc., under Grand Ministers (*ta-ch'en*) of the Department serving as Managers (*kuan-li*) or Supervisors (*tsung-kuan*). BH: imperial buttery. P37.

8106 *yù-ch'én yüàn* 玉宸院
YÜAN: **Office for the Imperial Quarters,** original name of the Bureau of Imperial Ritual (*i-feng ssu*); date of change not clear.

8107 *yù-ch'éng* 獄丞
N-S DIV–YÜAN: **Prison Aide,** a lowly official or subofficial commonly found in central government agencies such as the early Department of State Affairs (*shang-shu sheng*), the Censorate (*yü-shih t'ai*), and the Court of Judicial Review (*ta-li ssu*); cf. *ssu-yü* (Warder). RR: *assistant chargé des prisons*. P13, 18, 20, 32.

8108 *yǔ-chì wèi* 羽騎尉
SUI: **Commandant of Plumed Cavalry,** the lowest of 8 Commandant titles conferred on inactive officials (*san-kuan*), rank 9b, beginning in 586; the practice was terminated after 604. P65.

8109 *yǔ-ch'ī* 御妻
Lesser Wife. (1) CHOU: generic designation of the lowest of 4 categories of palace women serving as consultants to the Queen (*hou*); 81 authorized, considered affiliated with the Ministry of State (*t'ien-kuan*), part of the group collectively known as Inner Noblewomen (*nei ming-fu*), and often considered a variant of *nü-yü* (Secondary Concubine). CL: *concubine impériale*. (2) N-S DIV (N. Ch'i): categorical reference to palace women of rank =4a, who bore 81 different titles.

8110 *yù-chiāng chǘ* 玉匠局
YÜAN: **Jade Crafts Service** under the Supervisorate-in-chief of Metal Workers and Jewelers (*chin-yü jen-chiang tsung-kuan fu*); title of head not clear, but rank 7a; in 1278 renamed Jade Crafts Supervisorate (*yü-chü t'i-chü ssu*).

8111 *yù-ch'ién chiǎ-k'ù* 御前甲庫
SUNG: **Palace Armory** at the S. Sung dynastic capital, modern Hangchow; stored military gear and records; staffing and organizational affiliation not clear. See *chia-k'u*.

8112 *yù-ch'ién chū-chūn tū t'ǔng-chìh*
御前諸軍都統制
SUNG: **Supreme Commandant of the Palace Armies,** appointed c. 1127 as head of the Imperial Defense Command (*yü-ying ssu*) and leader of all the military forces in

the empire during Sung's withdrawal from North China. Cf. *tu t'ung-chih.* SP: *directeur général des armées de la résidence impériale.*

8113   yǜ-ch'ién chuāng-kuǎn chī-shǎng k'ù 御前椿管激賞庫
SUNG: lit. meaning not clear; storehouse for ringing chimes to stimulate gifts (?): variant or unofficial designation of the **Southern Storehouse** (*nan-k'u*) of the Left Vault (*tso-tsang*) maintained by the Court of the Imperial Treasury (*t'ai-fu ssu*).

8114   yǜ-ch'ién chūn 御前軍
SUNG: **Palace Army,** generic designation of regional armies, originally consisting largely of irregular forces that rose to support the dynasty during the Sung withdrawal from North China after 1125; by about 1148 reorganized as regular forces under the Bureau of Military Affairs (*shu-mi yüan*) in the central government newly transplanted at modern Hangchow, each with a new commanding general and prefixed with place-names as Palace Armies Detached at such-and-such Prefectures (*chu-cha … chou yü-ch'ien chün*). Cf. *yü-ch'ien wu chün* (Five Imperial Armies). SP: *armée devant l'empereur.*

8115   yǜ-ch'ién chūn-ch'ì àn 御前軍器案 or **chiēn** 監 or **sǒ** 所
SUNG: **Section for (Directorate of, Office of) Imperial Armaments,** apparently different names for one agency subordinate to the Ministry of Works (*kung-pu*), probably the same as the Directorate of Armaments (*chün-ch'i chien*). SP: *service (direction, bureau) des armes de la résidence impériale.*

8116   yǜ-ch'ién fēng-chuāng 御前封椿
SUNG: **Imperial Emergency Reserves Storehouse (?),** apparently a variant of *feng-chuang k'u* (Emergency Reserves Storehouse); affiliated with Overseers-general (*tsung-ling*) of some areas in the Huai and Yangtze River basins. SP: *trésor impérial d'épargne pour les dépenses militaires et la famine.*

8117   yǜ-ch'ién hsíng-tsǒu 御前行走
CH'ING: **Imperial Attendant,** an honorific title granted some Mongolian chieftains. Cf. *hsing-tsou.* BH: attaché to the emperor's suite.

8118   yǜ-ch'ién kūng-mǎ tzǔ-tì sǒ 御前弓馬子弟所
SUNG: **Office for Military Training of Palace Youths,** an agency of the Bureau of Military Affairs (*shu-mi yüan*) apparently responsible for training youthful Princes (*wang*) and perhaps other young imperial kinsmen in archery and horsemanship; headed by a Supervisor (*t'i-chü*). SP: *bureau d'entraînement des jeunes cavaliers-archers de la résidence impériale.*

8119   yǜ-ch'ién shìh-wèi 御前侍衛
CH'ING: **Palace Guardsman,** number unspecified, chosen from among Imperial Guardsmen (*shih-wei*) for duty in the inner chambers of the palace. BH: guard of the ante-chamber.

8120   yǜ-ch'ién tà-ch'én 御前大臣
CH'ING: **Grand Minister in Attendance,** 4 members of the Emperor's most intimate bodyguard, chosen from among Princes (*wang*) and Grand Minister Supervisors of the Imperial Household Department (*tsung-kuan nei-wu fu ta-ch'en*); among other things, supervised the Office for Provincial Memorials (*tsou-shih ch'u*). BH: adjutant general.

8121   yǜ-ch'ién t'ǔng-lǐng kuān 御前統領官
SUNG: variant reference to the **Supreme Commandant of the Palace Armies** (*yü-ch'ien chu-chün tu t'ung-chih*). SP: *directeur militaire général de la résidence impériale.*

8122   yǜ-ch'iēn wèi 玉鈐衛
T'ANG: **Guard of the Jade Strategy,** 2 prefixed Left and Right, from 684 to 705 military units named after a plan in an ancient work on military strategy; included among the Sixteen Guards (*shih-liu wei*) at the dynastic capital, temporarily replacing the Left and Right Metropolitan Guards (*ling-chün wei*). P43.

8123   yǜ-ch'ién wǔ chūn 御前五軍
SUNG: **Five Imperial Armies,** briefly in 1129 the name of the imperial forces previously called the Five Armies of the Imperial Encampment (*yü-ying wu chün*) and later called the Five Inspired Armies (*shen-wu wu chün*). Cf. *yü-ch'ien chün* (Palace Army).

8124   yǜ-ch'ú ssū 御廚司 or *yü-ch'u*
SUNG: **Imperial Kitchen** maintained by the Court of Imperial Entertainments (*kuang-lu ssu*); subsidiary units included the Banquets Office (*ta-kuan shu*), Office of Delicacies (*chen-hsiu shu*), Office of Fine Wines (*liang-yün shu*), and Winery (*chang-yün shu*). SP: *cuisine impériale.* P30.

8125   yǜ-ch'uán ch'ù 御船處
CH'ING: **Office of the Palace Marina,** an agency of the Imperial Household Department (*nei-wu fu*) in charge of the boats used by palace personnel; supervised by one of the Department's Grand Ministers (*ta-ch'en*) as Manager (*kuan-li*). BH: imperial boats office.

8126   yǜ-chǘ t'í-chǔ ssū 玉局提舉司
YÜAN: **Jade Crafts Supervisorate** under the Supervisorate-in-chief of Metal Workers and Jewelers (*chin-yü jen-chiang tsung-kuan fu*), headed by a Supervisor (*t'i-chü*), rank 5b. Until 1278 called Jade Crafts Service (*yü-chiang chü*).

8127   yǜ-ch'üēh chì-pǔ 遇缺即補
CH'ING: lit., to be appointed when a vacancy occurs: **First Priority Expectant Appointee,** one of the categories of personnel in the Corps of Expectant Appointees (*hou-pu pan*) in an agency, indicating the member(s) with first claim on an opening on the staff. BH: candidate for the first vacancy.

8128   yǘ-chūn 餘軍
MING: lit., extra soldier: **Surplus Man,** designation of males of the immediate families of hereditary soldiers, especially younger brothers, who resided with the soldiers in garrisons of the *wei-so* military organization; such personnel constituted a kind of ready reserve from which replacements were sought when soldiers died, became overaged or disabled, etc. Also called *yü-ting.*

8129   yǜ-fǔ 御府
HAN–N-S DIV: **Palace Wardrobe,** a eunuch agency subordinate to the Chamberlain for the Palace Revenues (*shao-fu*) or, at times in the S. Dynasties, the Chamberlain for Attendants (*kuang-lu-hsün*); headed by a eunuch Director (*ling*), rank 600 bushels in Han; in Later Han also controlled by a eunuch Supervisor (*chien*) chosen from among Palace Attendants-in-ordinary (*chung ch'ang-shih*), also rank 600 bushels; the agency made and maintained the Emperor's clothing. HB: imperial wardrobe. P37.

8130   yǜ-fǔ 玉府
CHOU: **Storehouse of Treasures,** also **Storekeeper of Treasures,** in the Ministry of State (*t'ien-kuan*); the agency

stored jade, pearls, and precious metal objects that had been presented to the King or collected in taxes, to be used as personal adornments or items of ritual use or decor by the King; the Storekeepers included 2 ranked as Senior Servicemen (*shang-shih*) and 4 as Ordinary Servicemen (*chung-shih*). CL: (*chef de*) *magasin du jade*. P37.

8131 *yù-fū* 馭夫
CHOU: **Horse Team Supervisor,** 20 ranked as Ordinary Servicemen (*chung-shih*) and 40 as Junior Servicemen (*hsia-shih*), members of the Ministry of War (*hsia-kuan*) who drove special-purpose royal chariots in ceremonies, hunts, and military campaigns and chariots carrying special royal delegates. Cf. *ta-yü* (Grand Charioteer), *jung-p'u* (Royal Charioteer), *ch'i-p'u* (Ceremonial Charioteer), *t'ien-p'u* (Hunting Charioteer). CL: *aide-cocher*.

8132 *yǔ-héng* 虞衡
CHOU: lit., a combination of the titles *shan-yü* (Supervisor of Forestry and Hunting), *ch'uan-heng* (Guardian of the Waterways), *tse-yü* (Supervisor of Marshes), and *lin-heng* (Supervisor of Public Lands), used as a general designation of people who were regulated by such officials, as itinerant workers in the woodlands and waterways: **Foresters, Hunters, and Fishers.** CL: *bûcherons*.

8133 *yǔ-héng ch'īng-lì ssū* 虞衡清吏司 or *yü-heng ssu*
MING–CH'ING: **Bureau of Forestry and Crafts,** one of 4 Bureaus in the Ministry of Works (*kung-pu*), headed by a Director (*lang-chung*), rank 5a, one Chinese and 4 Manchu appointees in Ch'ing; supervised state forestry, pottery manufacture, marsh products, weights and measures, etc. Cf. the earlier *yü-pu* (Bureau of Forestry and Crafts). BH: department of weights and measures. P15.

8134 *yǔ-hòu* 虞候
Lit., to wait alertly, to keep under observation: (1) **Inspector,** a title normally used in the military service, originating in antiquity in reference to anyone put on watch duty against poachers, e.g., in small marshes; used especially from T'ang through Sung as a duty assignment for an officer in an active campaigning force, in a secondary staff role with the special responsibility of maintaining discipline among the troops. In Sung formally established in the Imperial Armies (*chin-chün*) of both the Palace Command (*tien-ch'ien ssu*) and the Metropolitan Command (*shih-wei ssu*), with such variant forms as *chiang yü-hou* (Inspector-general) and *tu yü-hou* (Inspector-in-chief); in some cases officers with such titles were in effect second in command to their Generals (*chiang-chün*), Marshals (*yüan-shuai*), etc. RR+SP: *officier de surveillance*. (2) SUI: **Palace Police Patrol,** 2 prefixed Left and Right on the staff of the Heir Apparent, to maintain discipline and order in his establishment; each led by a Commander (*k'ai-fu*) until c. 605, thereafter by a Commandant (*shuai*). P26.

8135 *yǔ-hóu shuài-fǔ* 虞候率府
T'ANG: **Police Patrol Guard Command,** 2 prefixed Left and Right, military units in the establishment of the Heir Apparent, each headed by a Commandant (*shuai*), rank 4a. In 662 the unit name was changed to *ch'ing-tao shuai-fu*. The units evolved out of the Sui units simply called *yü-hou* (Palace Police Patrol). RR: *la garde de l'héritier du trône chargée de la sécurité des routes*.

8136 *yù-hsì ts'āng* 御細倉
N-S DIV (N. Ch'i)–T'ANG: **Imperial Granary for Fine Grain** under the Office of Grain Supplies (*tao-kuan shu*);

headed by 2 Supervisors (*tu*), rank not clear; discontinued by 649. RR: *grenier des grains fins de l'empereur (?)*. P6.

8137 *yù-hsiāng chú* 御香局
YÜAN: **Imperial Perfume Service** in the Imperial Academy of Medicine (*t'ai-i yüan*), headed by a Director (*ling*), rank 5b, and a Superintendent (*t'i-tien*); founded in 1308–1309 to prepare all fragrances used by the Emperor and his women.

8138 *yù-hsiū* 御羞
HAN: **Imperial Garden of Delicacies** under the Commandant of the Imperial Gardens (*shui-heng tu-wei*), headed by a Director (*ling*); apparently cultivated special vegetables and fruits in the Imperial Forest Park (*shang-lin yüan*) for palace use. HB (*ling*): prefect of imperial delicacies.

8139 *yù-ī* 御醫
MING–CH'ING: **Imperial Physician** in the Imperial Academy of Medicine (*t'ai-i yüan*), from 4 to 18 in Ming, from 10 to 15 in Ch'ing; rank 8a in Ming, 8a then 7a in Ch'ing. BH: imperial physician. P36.

8140 *yù-ī chú* 御衣局
YÜAN: **Imperial Wardrobe Service,** a manufacturing agency under the Supervisorate-in-chief of Civilian Artisans (*min-chiang tsung-kuan fu*), established in 1263; headed by an Overseer (*ta-lu-hua-ch'ih*) and a Supervisor (*t'i-chü*), rank 5b; staffed with non-official personnel requisitioned from the general populace.

8141 *yù-ī shǐh tào-ān chú* 御衣史道安局
YÜAN: **Imperial Wardrobe Service of Shih Tao-an,** a manufacturing agency under the Supervisorate-in-chief of Civilian Artisans (*min-chiang tsung-kuan fu*), established in 1265 and named after the personage who originally controlled appointments in it, an early Mongol custom; headed by a Commissioner-in-chief (*ta-shih*), rank 6b. Relationship with the Imperial Wardrobe Service (*yü-i chü*) is not clear; probably was early absorbed into the latter. See *shih tao-an chü*.

8142 *yù-ī yüàn* 御衣院
T'ANG: **Office of Sacrificial Clothing,** one of 4 minor service agencies in the Court of Imperial Sacrifices (*t'ai-ch'ang ssu*); maintained the apparel worn by the Emperor in sacrificial ceremonies; apparently staffed solely by state slaves. RR: *service des vêtements impériaux*.

8143 *yù-ī yüàn* 御醫院
SUNG: variant reference to the *t'ai-i yüan* (**Imperial Academy of Medicine**).

8144 *yù-jén* 羽人
CHOU: **Plume Gatherer,** 2 ranked as Junior Servicemen (*hsia-shih*), members of the Ministry of Education (*ti-kuan*) who selected plumes for use on royal chariots and banners from among mountain and marsh products collected as taxes. CL: *officier des plumes*.

8145 *yù-jén* 鬱人
CHOU: **Gatherer of Aromatic Plants,** 2 ranked as Junior Servicemen (*hsia-shih*), members of the Ministry of Rites (*ch'un-kuan*) who collected special aromatic plants and mixed them in wine for use in royal sacrifices. CL: *officier des plantes aromatiques*.

8146 *yǔ-jén* 斂人
CHOU: **Fishing Supervisor,** 2 ranked as Ordinary Servicemen (*chung-shih*) and 4 as Junior Servicemen (*hsia-shih*), members of the Ministry of State (*t'ien-kuan*) who

regulated all fishing in the royal domain, oversaw the construction of weirs, and selected fish for the royal table, sacrifices, receptions, etc. CL: *pêcheur*.

8147 *yǔ-kào* 予告
CH'ING: lit., to grant a petition: **Retired Dignitary,** designation of a former eminent official whose request for retirement because of old age had been approved.

8148 *yú-kuān* 虞官
MING: **Forest Manager,** unofficial reference to personnel of the Imperial Forest Park (*shang-lin yüan*).

8149 *yù-liěn yüàn* 御輦院
SUNG: **Imperial Sedan-chair Office,** apparently not affiliated with any other agency, probably staffed by eunuchs. SP: *cour des voitures impériales*.

8150 *yù-lín chì* 羽林騎
HAN–N-S DIV (Chin): lit., cavalry of the forest of plumes or feathers, referring to a heavenly constellation called the celestial water bearer (*yü-lin*): **Palace Guard Cavalry,** created by Emperor Wu (r. 141–87 B.C.) as one of 5 military units charged with policing and defending the imperial palace and its immediate environs under supervision of the Chamberlain for Attendants (*lang-chung ling, kuang-lu-hsün*). Its members were called Palace Guards (*yü-lin*) or Gentlemen of the Palace Guard (*yü-lin lang*); they were originally commanded by a Director (*ling*), then by a Leader of Court Gentlemen (*chung-lang chiang*) with rank =2,000 bushels and a Commandant (*tu-wei*) of the same rank. Sources also refer to a Supervisor of the Palace Guard (*yü-lin chien, yü-lin lang chien*). HB: cavalry of the feathered forest.

8151 *yǔ-lín chūn* 羽林軍
(1) T'ANG: **Army of the Celestial Water Bearer,** one of the Twelve Armies (*shih-erh chün*) stationed at the capital, to which troops of the Garrison Militia (*fu-ping*) organization were rotated for periodic service; apparently discontinued in 636. (2) T'ANG–SUNG: **Forest of Plumes Army,** 2 prefixed Left and Right in the Northern Command (*pei-ya*) at the T'ang dynastic capital from 662; perpetuated among the Six Armies (*liu chün*) at the Sung capital, but with only nominal existence. RR+SP: *armée comme les plumes et la forêt*.

8152 *yǔ-lín kū-érh* 羽林孤兒
HAN: **Orphans of the Palace Guard Cavalry,** official designation of sons and grandsons of Han soldiers who died honorably in battle; given youthful training in the Palace Guard Cavalry (*yü-lin chi*) in the expectation of becoming career Gentlemen of the Palace Guard (*yü-lin lang*). HB: orphans of the feathered forest.

8153 *yǔ-lín láng* 羽林郎
(1) HAN: **Gentleman of the Palace Guard,** a career soldier rather than a courtier expecting an appointment or between appointments, as was generally the case with Court Gentlemen (*lang*); a member of the Palace Guard Cavalry (*yü-lin chi*). HB: gentleman of the feathered forest. (2) CH'ING: unofficial reference to an **Imperial Guardsman** (*shih-wei*).

8154 *yú-líng* 娛靈
HAN: **Lady Who Pleases the Spirit,** designation of a palace woman, rank =100 bushels. HB: pleasing maid.

8155 *yù-mǎ chiēn* 御馬監
MING–CH'ING: **Directorate of the Imperial Horses,** one of 12 major Directorates (*chien*) staffed with palace eunuchs; headed by a eunuch Director (*t'ai-chien*); in 1661 renamed *a-tun ya-men,* then in 1677 became the *shang-ssu yüan* (Palace Stud). Also see under *shih-erh chien* (Twelve Directorates). P39.

8156 *yù-mǎ ssū* 御馬司
MING: **Office of the Imperial Horses,** from 1367 to sometime after 1369 a eunuch agency headed by a Director (*cheng*); early renamed *yü-ma chien* (Directorate of the Imperial Horses). P39.

8157 *yù-mǎ ts'āng* 御馬倉
MING: **Imperial Hay Barn** under the Ministry of Revenue (*hu-pu*), headed by a Commissioner-in-chief (*ta-shih*), rank 9b. P6.

8158 *yù-mǎ yüàn* 御馬院
SUNG: **Imperial Horse Office;** organizational affiliation, staffing, and precise functions not clear. SP: *cour des chevaux impériaux*.

8159 *yù-mǐn chǘ* 裕民局 or *yù-mǐn ssū* 司
SUNG, MING: lit., service (*chü*) or office (*ssū*) for enriching the people; relevance not clear: **Horse Purchasing Service** (Sung) or **Horse Purchasing Office** (Ming), established in some units of territorial administration to buy horses for state use from southwestern aboriginal tribes; in Sung headed by a Supervisor (*t'i-chü*), in Ming by a Commissioner-in-chief (*ta-shih*), rank 8b. In Ming not established till 1374, then soon discontinued. SP: *bureau chargé d'enrichir le peuple*. P53.

8160 *yù niǎo-ch'iāng ch'ù* 御鳥槍處
CH'ING: variant of *niao-ch'iang ch'u* (**Imperial Game Preserve**).

8161 *yù-nǚ* 御女
Variant of *nü-yü* (**Secondary Concubine**).

8162 *yù-pó* 御伯
N-S DIV (Chou): **Imperial Adviser,** a member of the Ministry of State (*t'ien-kuan*) ranked as an Ordinary Grand Master (*chung ta-fu;* 5a); in 564 retitled *na-yen* (Adviser). P2.

8163 *yú-pù* 虞部
N-S DIV–SUNG, LIAO, MING: **Bureau of Forestry and Crafts,** evolving from the prior Section for Forestry and Crafts (*yü-ts'ao*), in N. Chou a principal agency in the Ministry of Education (*ti-kuan*) headed by a Minister (*shang-shu*) ranked as a Junior Grand Master (*hsia ta-fu;* 6a), from Sui one of a standard group of 4 Bureaus in the Ministry of Works (*kung-pu*) till Ming, when in 1396 it was retitled *yü-heng ch'ing-li ssu*. In Sui headed by a Vice Minister (*shih-lang*) of the Ministry, from T'ang on by a Director (*lang-chung*), rank 5b in T'ang, 6b in Sung, 5a in Ming. Principally regulated hunting and food-gathering in mountains, forests, etc., and provided the government with forest products. RR+SP: *bureau des forêts*. P15.

8164 *yù-p'ú* 御僕
CHOU: **Royal Attendant-in-ordinary,** 12 ranked as Junior Servicemen (*hsia-shih*), members of the Ministry of War (*hsia-kuan*) who received both officials and commoners at the palace, transmitted royal messages to them, and provided general assistance at sacrifices, funerals, etc. CL: *assistant particulier de l'empereur*.

8165 *yù-p'ú ssū* 馭僕寺
T'ANG: lit., court of the royal coachman: from 662 to 670 the official redesignation of *p'u-ssu* (**Livery Service of the Heir Apparent**); during this period its head was officially titled *yü-p'u ta-fu* (Grand Master of the ...).

8166 *yü-shĭh* 圉師
CHOU: **Chief Groom,** one without official rank assigned to each team of 4 horses in the royal stable, subordinate to the Ministry of War (*hsia-kuan*). CL: *chef palefrenier.*

8167 *yü-shĭh* 御史
Lit., royal or imperial scribe. (1) CHOU–CH'IN: **Royal Scribe,** in Chou 8 ranked as Ordinary Servicemen (*chung-shih*) and 16 as Junior Servicemen (*hsia-shih*), members of the Ministry of Rites (*ch'un-kuan*) who, with a reportedly authorized staff of 120 lesser Sixth Class Administrative Officials or Scribes (*shih*), assisted the Minister of State (*chung-tsai*) in writing out and keeping records of the King's and the Minister of State's pronouncements giving directions to the agencies and officials of the royal domain, including those of the central government, and to Feudal Lords (*chu-hou*). Although they no doubt were relied on to ensure that such orders were in proper form, they apparently had no authority to engage in any kind of censorial surveillance. The title seems to have been perpetuated in Ch'in times by some *yü-shih* who were in charge of the imperial library. CL: *secrétaire impérial.* P25. (2) CH'IN–CH'ING: **Censor,** throughout imperial history the standard generic designation of central government officials principally and characteristically responsible for maintaining disciplinary surveillance over the officialdom and impeaching wayward officials; they constituted an institution called the Censorate (*yü-shih fu, yü-shih t'ai, tu ch'a-yüan*), which was ordinarily an autonomous agency in the top echelon of the central government, answerable only to the Emperor. Individual Censors commonly were authorized to submit memorials, especially impeachments, directly to the Emperor and often were the only members of the officialdom who were authorized to submit memorials on any subject, since other officials were generally discouraged from submitting (if not forbidden to submit) memorials beyond the realms of their specified administrative responsibilities. Censors were commonly referred to by awesome quasiofficial terms such as "the ears and eyes of the Son of Heaven" (*t'ien-tzu erh-mu*) and were the most notable group in the larger category of personnel collectively called Surveillance Officials (*ch'a-kuan*). In addition to the following entries involving *yü-shih* + suffixes, note should be taken of entries involving the numerous prefixes that differentiated various kinds of Censors, e.g., *chien-ch'a yü-shih, shih yü-shih, chih-shu shih yü-shih, tien-chung shih yü-shih, yen-shih yü-shih.* Cf. *chi-shih-chung, yen-kuan, chien-kuan.* RR+SP: *censeur.* BH: provincial censor. P18, 19.

8168 *yü-shĭh* 御師
N-S DIV–SUI: **Imperial Physician,** equivalent to or variant of *i-shih* (Master Physician). Also cf. *yü-i.* P36, 37.

8169 *yü-shĭh* 御試
SUNG: variant of *t'ing-shih* or *tien-shih* (**Palace Examination**), presumably identifying a civil service recruitment examination at which the Emperor personally presided.

8170 *yü-shĭh* 獄史
Prison Clerk. (1) HAN: 27, probably unranked subofficials, on the staff of the Chamberlain for Law Enforcement (*t'ing-wei*); see *yü tsu-shih.* HB: judiciary clerk. P22. (2) T'ANG: 6 authorized to assist the Prison Aide (*yü-ch'eng*) in the Court of Judicial Review (*ta-li ssu*); apparently unranked subofficials. RR: *scribe pour les prisons.*

8171 *yü-shĭh chăng-shĭh* 御史長史
HAN: **Censor Aide,** rare variant of *yü-shih chung-ch'eng* (Palace Aide to the Censor-in-chief). HB: chief clerk secretary. P18.

8172 *yü-shĭh ch'éng* 御史丞
HAN: **Censor Aide,** abbreviated reference to one of the 2 Aides (*ch'eng*) authorized for the Censor-in-chief (*yü-shih ta-fu*), especially the Palace Aide to the Censor-in-chief (*yü-shih chung-ch'eng*). P18.

8173 *yü-shĭh chĭh-tsá* 御史知雜
SUNG: variant of *shih yü-shih chih tsa-shih* (**Associate Censor**). SP: *censeur des affaires diverses.*

8174 *yü-shĭh chŭng-ch'éng* 御史中丞
(1) CH'IN–N-S DIV: **Palace Aide to the Censor-in-chief,** 2nd in the hierarchy of central government Censors (*yü-shih*) only to the Censor-in-chief (*yü-shih ta-fu*) and actual head of the Censorate (*yü-shih fu, yü-shih t'ai*) during long periods beginning late in Former Han when the post of Censor-in-chief was discontinued; ranked at 1,000 bushels in Han and the S. Dynasties. In Ch'in and Former Han, from a palace headquarters called the Orchid Pavilion (*lan-t'ai*), controlled a staff of Attendant Censors (*shih yü-shih*) who scrutinized all memorials submitted to the throne to ensure that they contained nothing offensive in form or substance, distributed imperial pronouncements to central government agencies, and were sent out to tour units of territorial administration with duty assignment designations such as Supervising Censor (*chien yü-shih, chien-ch'a shih*) or Commandery-inspecting Censor (*chien-chün yü-shih*). From 106 B.C. disciplinary surveillance over territorial administration was entrusted to regular appointees called Regional Inspectors (*tz'u-shih*), but they reported to the Palace Aide to the Censor-in-chief. In Later Han, when the post of Censor-in-chief was not established and the Palace Aide presided over the Censorate, he was nominally made a subordinate of the Chamberlain for the Palace Revenues (*shao-fu*); but he and the Metropolitan Commandant (*ssu-li hsiao-wei*) were a powerful duo, the Palace Aide maintaining disciplinary surveillance over officials of the palace and central government and the Metropolitan Commandant exercising almost unlimited police powers throughout the capital region. This pattern generally persisted into the era of N-S Division, when it was sometimes said that the Palace Aide intimidated the whole officialdom and took on princely airs. N. Chou, in its revival of archaic titles, changed the Palace Aide's title to *ssu-hsien chung ta-fu* (Ordinary Grand Master of the Censorate), rank 5a. Sui re-established the post of Censor-in-chief and discontinued the title Palace Aide in avoidance of a personal name taboo. HB: palace assistant secretary. P18. (2) T'ANG–MING: **Vice Censor-in-chief,** 2nd executive official of the Censorate (*yü-shih t'ai*), no longer having any special relationship with the palace but occasionally in T'ang and commonly in Sung serving as actual head of the Censorate when the post of Censor-in-chief was left vacant; 2 appointees normal in T'ang, Yüan, and Ming; rank 5a then 4a in T'ang, 3b in Sung and Chin, 2a in Yüan and early Ming. In T'ang the title was commonly borne concurrently (*tai*) by such regional dignitaries as Surveillance Commissioners (*kuan-ch'a shih*), who gained prestige from it. It was finally discontinued in 1380, when the early Ming Censorate began a transformation that resulted in its being renamed *tu ch'a-yüan.* RR: *vice-président du tribunal des censeurs.* SP: *censeur en chef ou président (du tribunal des censeurs).* P18. (3) MING–CH'ING: unofficial, archaic reference to a **Grand Coordinator** or **Provincial Governor** (both *hsün-fu*), who normally had nominal status as a Vice Censor-in-chief (*fu tu yü-shih*).

8175 *yǔ-shǐh chūng chíh-fǎ* 御史中執法
HAN: lit., censor upholder of law in the palace: variant of *yü-shih chung-ch'eng* (**Palace Aide to the Censor-in-chief**). HB: palace secretary for the administration of laws. P18.

8176 *yǔ-shǐh chūng-wèi* 御史中尉
N-S DIV (N. Wei): **Palace Commandant of Censors:** official variant of *yü-shih chung-ch'eng* (Palace Aide to the Censor-in-chief). P18.

8177 *yǔ-shǐh fáng* 御史房
SUNG: **Section for Censors** in the Headquarters Office (*tu-ssu*) of the Department of State Affairs (*shang-shu sheng*); presumably an early Sung agency that handled the appointments, evaluations, etc., of personnel of the Censorate (*yü-shih t'ai*); staffing not clear. SP: *chambre des censeurs*.

8178 *yǔ-shǐh fǔ* 御史府
Lit., office of Censors. (1) HAN–N-S DIV: variant of *yü-shih t'ai* (**Censorate**). (2) MING: from 1400 to 1402 only, the official redesignation of the **Censorate** (*tu ch'a-yüan*). P18.

8179 *yǔ-shǐh hsǔn-àn* 御史巡按
T'ANG: **Censor on Tour,** designation of Investigating Censors (*chien-ch'a yü-shih*) who in early T'ang were dispatched on inspection tours of the Circuits (*tao*) into which the empire was divided, apparently to check on the effectiveness of local administration like later Regional Inspectors (*hsün-an yü-shih*); during the 8th century made concurrent inspectors of postal courier stations, and in 779 redesignated Postal Inspectors (*kuan-i shih*), an apparent indication that their earlier broader inspection powers had been restricted. P18.

8180 *yǔ-shǐh nèi-shǐh* 御史內史
HAN: variant of *yü-shih wai-ch'eng* (**Outer Aide of the Censor-in-chief**). P18.

8181 *yǔ-shǐh tà-fū* 御史大夫
CH'IN–MING: lit., grand master of Censors: **Censor-in-chief,** head of the Censorate (*yü-shih t'ai*) and one of the most eminent officials of the central government, in administrative charge of Censors (*yü-shih*) of many sorts who maintained disciplinary surveillance over the officialdom, freely impeaching any official for public or private misconduct. In Han ranked 2,000 bushels, in T'ang 3b, in Sung and Chin 2b, in Yüan 1a, in early Ming 1b; 2 appointees common in Sui, Yüan, and early Ming. In Ch'in and Former Han, while being responsible for censorial activities, he was also a general assistant to the Counselor-in-chief (*ch'eng-hsiang*), to which office he normally succeeded when it fell vacant. In 8 B.C. the post was discontinued and replaced by a Grand Minister of Works (*ta ssu-k'ung*). Although it was revived from A.D. 1 to 51, executive control of the Censorate shifted to the Censor-in-chief's former principal assistant, the Palace Aide to the Censor-in-chief (*yü-shih chung-ch'eng*), and through the post-Han era of N-S Division the title Censor-in-chief was revived only intermittently, the nominal Palace Aide remaining de facto head Censor. From Sui on, however, Censors-in-chief were again active heads of the Censorate, although to some extent in T'ang and especially in Sung appointments were not made and the *yü-shih chung-ch'eng* (now more appropriately rendered Vice Censor-in-chief) was again the de facto head Censor. In T'ang the title was commonly borne concurrently (*tai*) by regional dignitaries such as Military Commissioners (*chieh-tu shih*), who gained prestige from it. In 1380, when the early Ming central government was thoroughly reorganized, the title *yü-shih ta-fu* was finally dis-

continued, recurring thereafter only in unofficial, archaic references to the newly titled Censors-in-chief (*tu yü-shih*) in the newly named Censorate (*tu ch'a-yüan*). HB: grandee secretary. RR: *président du tribunal des censeurs*. SP: *censeur en chef*. P18.

8182 *yǔ-shǐh tà-fū ch'éng* 御史大夫丞
HAN: unofficial reference to the *yü-shih chung-ch'eng* (**Palace Aide to the Censor-in-chief**). P18.

8183 *yǔ-shǐh tà-fū ssū* 御史大夫寺
HAN: lit., court of the Censor-in-chief: variant reference to the **Censorate** (*yü-shih t'ai*). P18.

8184 *yǔ-shǐh t'ái* 御史臺
HAN–MING: lit., terrace or pavilion of imperial scribes, i.e., of Censors: **Censorate,** the standard name of an agency in the top echelon of the central government staffed by Censors (*yü-shih*) of various categories and headed by one or more Censors-in-chief (*yü-shih ta-fu*); generally free of routine administrative responsibilities except to participate with such agencies as the T'ang–Sung Ministry of Justice (*hsing-pu*) and Court of Judicial Review (*ta-li ssu*) in conducting major trials at court and reviewing important judicial cases reported from units of territorial administration, and with the paramount and characteristic responsibility of maintaining disciplinary surveillance over the whole officialdom, checking records and auditing accounts in government offices, accepting public complaints, and impeaching officials who in their private or public lives violated the law or otherwise conducted themselves improperly. Although most Han censorial titles were patterned after Ch'in antecedents, the name *yü-shih t'ai* probably originated in Han; thereafter into the early part of the era of N-S Division it was interchangeable with *yü-shih fu* (lit., Office of Censors); but from Sui into early Ming *yü-shih t'ai* was the standard name. In the Ming reorganization of the central government in 1380 the name was abolished, to be superseded from 1382 by the name *tu ch'a-yüan* (lit., chief surveillance bureau). In Yüan the Censorate shared its surveillance responsibilities with 2 Branch Censorates (*hsing yü-shih t'ai*), dividing China into 3 large surveillance jurisdictions. At times the Censorate had supervisory relationships with regional officials or agencies that imposed more intensive surveillance on local units of administration (especially, e.g., see the Yüan dynasty *t'i-hsing an-ch'a shih ssu*, Surveillance Commission); and from Ch'in on central government Censors were regularly or irregularly dispatched to tour and inspect units of territorial administration (see *chien-ch'a shih, chien yü-shih, yü-shih hsün-an*). In Han the censorial organization was headed by a Censor-in-chief (*yü-shih ta-fu*) until 8 B.C., thereafter by the nominal Palace Aide to the Censor-in-chief (*yü-shih chung-ch'eng*), ranked at 1,000 bushels and loosely subordinated to the Chamberlain for the Palace Revenues (*shao-fu*). There was also an Outer Aide to the Censor-in-chief (*yü-shih wai-ch'eng*) of the same rank, who presumably was a more general assistant to the Censor-in-chief. The principal staff consisted of 45 Attendant Censors (*shih yü-shih*), rank 600 bushels, of whom 2 were designated Secretarial Censors (*chih-shu shih yü-shih*) and charged to interpret the laws; 15 of the Attendant Censors were originally assigned to the Palace Aide, and all Attendant Censors were apparently organized in Sections (*ts'ao*) with some differentiation of functions that is not wholly clear. A principal underling was a Recorder (*chu-pu*), who seems to have been chief clerk of the agency. The Later Han organization, with the Palace Aide normally serving as active head, was perpetuated through the era of N-S Division. Sui re-established the office of

Censor-in-chief with 2 appointees, discontinued the post of Palace Aide, and appointed 2 Secretarial Censors as de facto assistant chiefs of the Censorate. The subordinate censorial staff then consisted of 8 Attendant Censors, 12 Palace Censors (*tien-chung shih yü-shih*), from 12 to 16 Investigating Censors (*chien-ch'a yü-shih*), a Recorder, and an Office Manager (*lu-shih*); ranks are not clear. From T'ang into early Ming the standard organization included one or 2 Censors-in-chief, rank from 3a to 1a; normally 2 Vice Censors-in-chief (*yü-shih chung-ch'eng*), 5a to 2a; a Headquarters Bureau (*t'ai-yüan*) staffed with Attendant Censors (discontinued after Sung), a Palace Bureau (*tien-yüan*) staffed with Palace Censors (*tien-chung shih yü-shih*), and an Investigation Bureau (*ch'a-yüan*) staffed with Investigating Censors (*chien-ch'a yü-shih*). RR+SP: *tribunal des censeurs*. P18.

8185   *yù-shíh wài-ch'éng* 御史外丞
HAN: **Outer Aide to the Censor-in-chief,** rank 1,000 bushels, a general assistant to the head of the Censorate (*yü-shih t'ai*), balancing the Palace Aide (*yü-shih chung-ch'eng*), who was stationed within the imperial palace; apparently supervised a group of Attendant Censors (*shih yü-shih*) organized in Sections (*ts'ao*), who were responsible for maintaining disciplinary surveillance over the central government officialdom. HB: assistant. P18.

8186   *yù-shǔ* 御屬
HAN: **Clerical Subordinate,** an unranked subofficial found in many agencies, normally under the supervision of a Clerk (*ling-shih*). HB: attendant. P2.

8187   *yù-shǔ* 玉署
T'ANG–CH'ING: lit., jade office: unofficial reference to the **Hanlin Academy** (*han-lin yüan*). P23.

8188   *yù-shū ch'ù* 御書處
CH'ING: **Imperial Library,** the Emperor's personal study and file room in the palace, staffed principally by Bannermen (see *pa ch'i*) under a Grand Minister of the Imperial Household Department (*nei-wu fu ta-ch'en*) designated Manager of the Imperial Library (*kuan-li yü-shu ch'u shih-wu*). BH: imperial library. P37.

8189   *yù-shū yüàn* 御書院
SUNG: abbreviation of *han-lin yü-shu yüan* (**Imperial Academy of Calligraphy**). SP: *cour de la calligraphie impériale, cour des livres impériaux.*

8190   *yǔ ssū-mǎ* 輿司馬
CHOU: **Commander of Chariots,** one of several Commanders (*ssu-ma*) serving under the Minister of War (*ta ssu-ma;* also see *hsia-kuan,* Ministry of War); 8 were authorized, with rank as Senior Servicemen (*shang-shih*). CL: *commandant des chevaux des chars.*

8191   *yù-t'áng* 玉堂
T'ANG–CH'ING: lit., jade hall: unofficial reference to the **Hanlin Academy** (*han-lin yüan*). P23.

8192   *yù-t'áng shǔ* 玉堂署
HAN: **Office of Imperial Portraiture** (?), a eunuch agency headed by a Director (*chang*). See *hua-shih shu.* HB: office of the jade hall.

8193   *yù-té* 諭德
T'ANG–CH'ING: lit., proclaimer of virtue: **Adviser** in the establishment of the Heir Apparent, commonly prefixed Left or Right; number variable; rank 4a in T'ang, 6a in Sung, 5b in Ming; discontinued in the 18th century. RR+SP: *grand conseiller de l'héritier du trône.* P26.

8194   *yù-tiéh sǒ* 玉牒所
(1) **Imperial Genealogy Office** in the Court of the Imperial Clan (*tsung-cheng ssu*), headed by one or 2 Grand Councilors (*tsai-hsiang*) serving as Supervisors (*t'i-chü*). SP: *bureau de la généalogie impériale.* (2) CH'ING: unofficial reference to the **Court of the Imperial Clan** (*tsung-jen fu*).

8195   *yù-tiéh tièn chǔ-kuǎn hsiāng-huǒ* 玉牒殿主管香火
SUNG: lit., manager of incense and (ceremonial) fires in the hall of the jade tablets, i.e., the imperial genealogy: early Sung title of the later **Building Administrators for the Imperial Genealogy Office** (*kan-pan yü-tieh so tien*). SP: *préposé aux encens de la salle du bureau de la généalogie impériale.*

8196   *yǚ-tīng* 餘丁
(1) SUNG: **Supplementary Security Guard,** a kind of reservist in the local self-defense system called *pao-chia,* as distinguished from principals in the system, called *pao-ting* (Security Guard). (2) MING: variant of *yü-chün* (**Surplus Man**) in the *wei-so* military organization.

8197   *yù-ts'áo* 獄曹
HAN: **Prison Section,** one of the clerical staff units found in the headquarters of some Districts (*hsien*). HB: bureau of litigation.

8198   *yǚ-ts'áo* 虞曹
N-S DIV: **Section for Forestry and Crafts,** a unit in the developing Department of State Affairs (*shang-shu sheng*) that managed hunting, fuel-gathering, weights and measures, and the taxation of forest and marsh products; sometimes directly subordinate to the Department, at other times part of the intermediary Ministry of Rites (*i-ts'ao, tz'u-pu*); commonly headed by a Director (*lang, lang-chung*), in N. Wei temporarily by a Minister (*shang-shu*). Cf. *yü-pu, yü-heng ch'ing-li ssu.* P14.

8199   *yù-ts'è yüàn* 玉冊院
SUNG: **Bureau of Nomination Certificates,** a unit attached to the Secretariat (*chung-shu sheng*) that presumably managed the preparation and issuance of warrants confirming imperial appointments, but specific functions and staffing are not clear. SP: *cour des certificats de nomination.*

8200   *yù tsú-shǐh* 獄卒史 or *yü-tsu*
HAN: **Prison Guard,** unranked suboffical found on the staff of the Chamberlain for Law Enforcement (*t'ing-wei*) and on the headquarters staffs of some Later Han Districts (*hsien*). HB: judiciary clerk.

8201   *yǚ-tzǔ* 餘子
CHOU: **Cadet,** categorical designation of young sons of court officials, who served as an intimate royal bodyguard under supervision of the Minister of Education (*ssu-t'u*). See *shu-tzu.* CL: *cadet.*

8202   *yù-wèi* 禦衛
SUI–T'ANG: **Protective Guard,** 2 prefixed Left and Right, units of the Garrison Militia (*fu-ping*) organization at the dynastic capital called the Twelve Guards (*shih-erh wei*); in 622 renamed Metropolitan Guards (*ling-chün wei*). RR: *garde guide des armées.*

8203   *yù wèi-hsià* 御位下
YÜAN: variant of *ch'in-wang* (**Imperial Prince**). See *wei-hsia.*

8204   *yù-yào chiēn* 御藥監
YÜAN: apparently a variant of *yü-yao chü* (**Imperial Dispensary**). P36.

8205 yù-yào chú 御藥局
YÜAN–MING: **Imperial Dispensary,** in Yüan a unit of the Imperial Academy of Medicine (*t'ai-i yüan*), headed by an Overseer (*ta-lu-hua-ch'ih*) and a Commissioner (*shih*), rank 5b; from 1305 or 1306 had a Branch Imperial Dispensary (*hsing yü-yao chü*) that provided medicines for the Emperor and his retinue in travel status; in Ming a eunuch agency, in 1536 renamed *sheng-chi tien*. P36.

8206 yù-yào fáng 御藥房
(1) MING: apparently a variant of *yü-yao chü* (**Imperial Dispensary**); in 1536 renamed *sheng-chi tien*. P36. (2) CH'ING: **Imperial Dispensary** under the Imperial Household Department (*nei-wu fu*), headed by a Grand Minister (*ta-ch'en*) of the Department serving as Manager (*kuan-li*). BH: imperial dispensary. P37.

8207 yù-yào yüàn 御藥院
SUNG–YÜAN: **Imperial Dispensary,** staffed by eunuchs at least in Sung, supervised jointly by the Palace Administration (*tien-chung sheng*) and the Palace Domestic Service (*nei-shih sheng*); in Chin headed by a Superintendent (*t'i-tien*), rank 5b, and subordinate to the Court of Palace Attendants (*hsüan-hui yüan*); in Yüan apparently a variant of *yü-yao chü*. SP: *cour de pharmacie impériale*. P36, 38.

8208 yù-yíng shǐh 御營使
5 DYN–SUNG: **Commissioner of the Imperial Encampment,** in the Five Dynasties era commonly the officer in charge of troops when an Emperor personally undertook a military campaign; in the Sung withdrawal to the South in the 1120s, the officer in command of the Imperial Defense Command (*yü-ying ssu*), normally the concurrent appointment of a Grand Councilor (*tsai-hsiang*). SP: *commissaire du camp impérial*.

8209 yù-yíng ssū 御營司
SUNG: **Imperial Defense Command,** an emergency military organization established to try to coordinate and control the Sung withdrawal to the South after 1125, headed by a Grand Councilor (*tsai-hsiang*) designated Commissioner of the Imperial Encampment (*yü-ying shih*). By 1130 absorbed into a reorganized Bureau of Military Affairs (*shu-mi yüan*). See *chi-su fang*. SP: *bureau du camp impérial*.

8210 yù-yíng sù-wèi shǐh 御營宿衛使
SUNG: lit., commissioner of the bodyguard in the imperial camp: variant of *yü-ying shih* (**Commissioner of the Imperial Encampment**). SP: *commissaire chargé d'assurer la garde du camp impérial*.

8211 yù-yíng wǔ chūn 御營五軍
SUNG: **Five Armies of the Imperial Encampment,** collective designation of the ragtag military units hastily organized during Sung's retreat from North China; activated in 1127 under an emergency Imperial Defense Command (*yü-ying ssu*) with directional differentiations: Left Army of the Imperial Encampment (*yü-ying tso-chün*) and others designated Right, Center, Front, and Rear; each led by a General (*chiang-chün*). In 1129 these units were redesignated the Five Imperial Armies (*yü-ch'ien wu chün*), changed before the end of the year to the Five Inspired Armies (*shen-wu wu chün*) and again in 1131 to the Four Field Defense Armies (*hsing-ying ssu hu-chün*). P43.

8212 yù-yùng ch'ì-wù chú 御用器務局
YÜAN: **Service of the Imperial Ornaments,** organizational affiliation not clear but apparently a counterpart of other periods' Directorate for Imperial Accouterments (*yü-yung chien*).

8213 yù-yùng chiēn 御用監
MING–CH'ING: **Directorate for Imperial Accouterments,** one of 12 major Directorates (*chien*) in which palace eunuchs were organized; headed by a eunuch Director (*t'ai-chien*); responsible for preparing fine wood and ivory objects for the Emperor's use and for presenting memorials for imperial attention that were submitted by the officialdom. In 1661 disbanded into various palace storehouses (*k'u*), which in 1667 were placed under the jurisdiction of the Storage Office (*kuang-ch'u ssu*) of the Imperial Household Department (*nei-wu fu*). See under *shih-erh chien* (Twelve Directorates). P37.

8214 yù-yüàn 獄掾
N-S DIV (N. Wei)–SUI: **Jail Warden,** members of the Section for Justice (*tu-kuan ts'ao*) in the Department of State Affairs (*shang-shu sheng*), 2 in N. Ch'i, 8 in Sui; rank 7b2 in N. Wei, otherwise not clear, probably unranked subofficials. P13.

8215 yù-yüàn t'ūng-chìn 御院通進
CHIN: **Ceremonial Receptionist,** 4, rank 7b, members of the Office for Audience Ceremonies (*ko-men*) in the Court Ceremonial Institute (*hsüan-hui yüan*); responsible for receiving memorials, tribute gifts, etc., in audience. P33.

8216 yǘ-yüèh 于越
LIAO: **Counselor,** one of the most eminent dignitaries in the Northern Administration (*pei-mien*) of the central government, also in separate tribes headed by Grand Princes (*ta-wang*).

8217 yüán 員
Official: one of the vaguest categorical terms for government personnel, most commonly occurring as an enumerating element, e.g., in listing the personnel of an agency to include a Director, 2 Vice Directors, 4 Assistant Directors, and 6 Secretaries, in all 13 *yüan;* but occasionally found as a component in particular titles. See under prefixes if any.

8218 yüán 園
(1) **Garden,** common designation of any park-like area; e.g., a garden under the supervision of an Aide (*ch'eng*) in the T'ang dynasty Granaries Office (*tien-ts'ang shu*) in the household of the Heir Apparent. (2) HAN–N-S DIV: **Funerary Park,** one established around each Imperial Mausoleum (*ling*), in Han supervised by a Director (*ling* or *chang* or *chien*) ranked at 600 bushels. The institution apparently originated in Later Han; how long it endured into the post-Han era is not clear. HB: funerary park.

8219 yüán 掾
(1) **Clerk:** lowly or unranked appointee found in many agencies, civil and military, at all levels of the governmental hierarchy; sometimes identifiable by a prefix. (2) **Administrator** of a clerical Section (*ts'ao*) in an agency at any level of government, equivalent to *yüan-shih* (Administrator), commonly of low rank or unranked. Rank 6a1 in T'ang. HB: division head. RR: *premier administrateur*.

8220 yüán 苑
Park: common designation of a hunting area or horse pasture, identifiable from preceding terminology; e.g., see *feng-ch'en yüan* (Imperial Parks Administration) of Ch'ing, *mu-shih yüan* (Imperial Horse Pasturage) of Han.

8221 yüán 院
(1) T'ANG–CH'ING: common final element in agency names, impossible to render consistently in English: **Office, Bureau, Court, Academy, Institute,** etc. See under

prefixes. (2) T'ANG: **Brokerage,** a regional salt control office in a major market center, where the distribution of state-monopolized salt was supervised and salt taxes were collected; headed by a Brokerage Official (*chih-yüan kuan*); subordinate to a regional Directorate (*chien*) and ultimately to the Salt Monopoly Commissioner (*chüeh yen-t'ieh shih*) headquartered at Yangchow. P61. (3) LIAO: **Establishment,** 2 prefixed North and South, groups of agencies into which the Northern Administration (*pei-mien*) of the central government was divided.

8222   *yüan-ch'ĭn*   園寢
CH'ING: **Mausoleum,** common designation of the tombs of imperial Consorts (*fei*); cf. *ling-ch'in.* P29.

8223   *yüan-ch'ú*   元儲
N-S DIV: unofficial reference to an **Heir Apparent** (*t'ai-tzu*).

8224   *yüan-fēi*   元妃
CHOU–N-S DIV: **Principal Consort:** from high antiquity a common unofficial reference to a Queen or Empress (*hou, huang-hou*), in contrast to all other wives of a ruler, known collectively as Secondary Consorts (*tz'u-fei*).

8225   *yüan-fŭ*   元輔
Principal Support: common unofficial reference to a paramount executive official of the central government such as a Counselor-in-chief (*ch'eng-hsiang*), a Grand Councilor (*tsai-hsiang*), or a senior Grand Secretary (*ta hsüeh-shih;* see *shou-fu*).

8226   *yüan-hòu*   元后
CH'ING: lit., principal ruler: unofficial reference to an **Emperor** (*huang-ti*).

8227   *yüan-í*   苑儀
N-S DIV (N. Ch'i), SUNG: **Lady of Elegant Deportment,** designation of a secondary imperial wife, in Sung rank 1b.

8228   *yüan-júng*   苑容
SUNG: **Lady of Elegant Appearance,** designation of a secondary imperial wife, rank 1b.

8229   *yüan-lăo*   元老
SUNG: lit., principal elder: reference to a **Grand Councilor** (*tsai-hsiang*) in direct address.

8230   *yüan-lì*   員吏
HAN: **Suboffici̇al Functionary,** generic designation of unranked (or very low-ranked) personnel found in agencies throughout the government. See *li, hsü-li.* P7, 30, 32, 36, 39, 59.

8231   *yüan-lì*   掾吏
HAN: variant of *yüan* (**Clerk**). P20.

8232   *yüan-liáng*   元良
Lit., principal one of excellence: unofficial reference to an **Heir Apparent** (*t'ai-tzu*).

8233   *yüan-luán hsién*   鵷鸞閑
T'ANG: **Pheasant Corral,** one of the Six Palace Corrals (*chang-nei liu hsien*) supervised by the Commissioner of the Palace Stables (*hsien-chiu shih*), where horses were bred and reared within the palace enclosure; *yüan-luan* (pheasant) apparently referred to a special breed of fine horses. RR: (*le parc des chevaux*) *du char du faisan.*

8234   *yüan-mă ssù*   苑馬寺
MING: **Pasturage Office,** 4 regional agencies under the direct control of the Ministry of War (*ping-pu*), counterparts of Branch Courts of the Imperial Stud (*hsing t'ai-p'u ssu*): one in the Northern Metropolitan Area (*pei chih-li*),

one in Liaotung, and 2 in Kansu, each headed by a Minister (*ch'ing*), rank 3b, who supervised variable numbers of local Directorates of Horse Pasturages (*mu-chien*). P31.

8235   *yüan-míng yüàn*   圓明園
CH'ING: **Garden of Total Clarity** or **Summer Palace,** imperial resort west of Peking, built in 1709 and greatly expanded in the Yung-cheng era (1723–1735), thereafter a common summer retreat for the Emperor and his courtiers; under the management of Guard Brigades (*hu-chün ying*) of the Inner Banners (*nei-ch'i*). BH: summer palace.

8236   *yüan-p'àn*   院判
YÜAN–CH'ING: **Administrative Assistant,** a middle-level headquarters official in various agencies called *yüan,* e.g., *t'ai-i yüan* (Imperial Academy of Medicine), *t'ai-shih yüan* (Astrological Commission), *ch'u-cheng yüan* (Household Service for the Heir Apparent), *t'ung-cheng yüan* (Bureau of Transmission); commonly 2 appointees, rank 5a in Yüan, 5a then 6a in Ming, 6a in Ch'ing. Cf. *p'an-kuan.* BH: vice-commissioner. P12, 35, 36.

8237   *yüan-shìh*   元士
Lit., paramount serviceman. (1) CHOU: variant of *shang-shih* (**Senior Serviceman**). (2) MING: for a short time in 1389 the official redesignation of **Supervising Secretaries** (*chi-shih-chung*). P19.

8238   *yüan-shìh*   掾史
(1) HAN–N-S DIV: **Administrator** of a clerical Section (*ts'ao*) in an agency at any level of government, commonly abbreviated to *yüan;* of low rank or unranked. HB: division head. P20, 52, 54. (2) LIAO–YÜAN: **Clerk,** numerous unranked suboffici̇als in various central government agencies, occasionally also in units of territorial administration. P5, 12, 23, 26, 69.

8239   *yüan-shìh*   源士
MING: briefly (only in 1389?) the official redesignation of **Supervising Secretaries** (*chi-shih-chung*), when the founding Emperor decided that the Six Offices of Scrutiny (*liu k'o*) in which Supervising Secretaries were organized constituted "the fundamental wellspring" (*pen-yüan*) of his officialdom. P19.

8240   *yüan-shĭh*   苑使
SUNG: **Park Commissioner,** 4, rank 6b2, each in charge of one of the 4 quadrants into which the imperial capital was divided for the purpose of exploiting parklands and gardens, his office known as the Office of Imperial Parks (*yüan-yüan ssu*); subordinate to the Court of the National Granaries (*ssu-nung ssu*). P40.

8241   *yüan-shīh*   邍師
CHOU: lit., mentor for plateaus: **Place-name Specialist,** 4 ranked as Ordinary Servicemen (*chung-shih*) and 8 as Junior Servicemen (*hsia-shih*), members of the Ministry of War (*hsia-kuan*) responsible for naming and recording the names of topographic features and natural products of wilderness areas between feudal domains. CL: *maître des plaines.*

8242   *yüan-shŏu*   元首
Lit., the paramount head or leader: **His Majesty,** from antiquity an indirect, unofficial reference to the ruler.

8243   *yüan-shŭ*   掾屬
Lesser Subordinates: a combined reference to *yüan* (Clerk, Administrator) and *shu* (Subsidiary Clerk, etc.).

8244   *yüan-shuài*   元帥
Lit., paramount leader: **Marshal,** throughout history, and

especially from T'ang on, a common designation for an eminent military officer on active campaign; usually has a place-
name or function-specific prefix. See *ta yüan-shuai, tu yüan-
shuai.* RR: *généralissime.* SP: *maréchal.*

8245 *yüán-shuài fǔ* 元帥府
(1) **Headquarters of a Marshal:** may be encountered in
any period, normally with a place-name or function-specific prefix, referring to the office or command post of a
yüan-shuai (Marshal). SP: *bureau du maréchal.* (2) CHIN:
Military Command, apparently from 1206 to 1208 the
official redesignation of the Bureau of Military Affairs (*shu-
mi yüan*) in the central government. (3) YÜAN: **Military
Command,** one of several designations given agencies in
control of Circuits (*tao*), all commonly known by the generic designation Pacification Commission (*hsüan-wei shih
ssu*). Also the designation given some southwestern aboriginal tribes. See *tu yüan-shuai fu.* P72.

8246 *yüán-t'án tà-yüèh lǐ-ch'ì k'ù*
圓壇大樂禮器庫
SUNG: **Storehouse of Musical and Ritual Gear for the
Altar of Heaven** under the Court of Imperial Sacrifices (*t'ai-
ch'ang ssu*); staffing not clear. SP: *magasin des objets rituels et de la musique suprême de l'autel céleste.*

8247 *yüàn-tsǒ* 掾佐
See separate entries for *yüan* (Administrator, Clerk) and *tso*
(Assistant).

8248 *yüàn tsǔng-chiēn* 苑總監
SUI–T'ANG: abbreviation of *kung-yüan tsung-chien* (**Directorate-general of the Imperial Parks**). P40.

8249 *yüán-ts'úng chìn-chūn* 元從禁軍
T'ANG: **Imperial Army of Original Followers,** designation of those soldiers who participated in the 617 uprising
of the T'ang founder against the Sui dynasty and, rather
than be distributed among various field armies, chose to
become the personal bodyguard of their leader when he took
the imperial throne in 618. They are reported to have constituted a force between 15,000 and 30,000; they were settled on abandoned land near the capital and became hereditary soldiers, colloquially referred to as the Hereditary Army
(*fu-tzu chün*). In 627 T'ai-tsung selected 100 of the most
skilled mounted archers in the group to be a special escort
unit on his hunting expeditions; designated the Hundred
Cavaliers (*po chi*), they served in 2 shifts as companions-
at-arms for the Emperor and were regularly called on to
demonstrate their prowess in archery, horsemanship, weight
lifting, etc. In 627 also, the Imperial Army of Original Followers, apparently without losing its identity and name, was
divided into Seven Encampments of the Northern Command (*pei-ya ch'i ying*), and each of the 7 units served on
active duty in the imperial entourage for one month in rotational sequence, alongside units of the militiamen called
into rotational service in the various Guards (*wei;* see *shih
liu wei*) of the Southern Command (*nan-ya*). In 638 the
original followers or their heirs were further reorganized
into 2 units called the Left and Right Encampments (*t'un-
ying*), to some extent supplemented with new volunteers
from elite families, commanded by Generals (*chiang-chün*)
of the Southern Command. Members of the Encampments
were now called Flying Cavalrymen (*fei-chi*), and the most
skilled among them were selected for the designation
Hundred Cavaliers, now formed into a Standby Guard (*i-
wei*) to accompany the Emperor on all his outings. Finally
in 662 the Imperial Army of Original Followers disappeared as an organization, transformed into a Left and a

Right Forest of Plumes Army (*yü-lin chün*). RR: *armée
chargée de la défense de l'empereur et qui suivit l'empereur
la première.*

8250 *yüán-wài* 員外
Supernumerary: throughout history used as a prefix to titles indicating appointees beyond the authorized quota for
the position; in T'ang such appointees received half the
standard stipend of a regular (*cheng*) appointee. Cf. *t'ung
cheng-yüan.* RR+SP: *auxiliaire.*

8251 *yüán-wài láng* 員外郎
(1) N-S DIV: abbreviation of *yüan-wai san-chi shih-lang*
(**Supernumerary Gentleman Cavalier Attendant** or **Supernumerary Senior Recorder;** see under *san-chi shih-
lang*). (2) SUI: **Supernumerary Vice Minister,** regular appointees assisting the Vice Ministers (*shih-lang*) who then
headed the Bureaus (*ssu*) in each Ministry (*pu;* see *liu pu*)
in the central government, and actively heading Bureaus
whenever appropriate Vice Ministers were not appointed.
P5. (3) T'ANG–CH'ING: **Vice Director** of a Bureau (*ssu,
ch'ing-li ssu*) in one of the Six Ministries (*liu pu*), a regular
appointee assisting the Bureau Director (*lang-chung*); rank
6b1 in T'ang, 6b or 7a in Sung, 6b in Chin and Yüan, 5b
in Ming and Ch'ing; normally one or 2 appointees, but in
Ch'ing highly variable, from one to 8; in Ch'ing also appointed in various agencies of the Imperial Household Department (*nei-wu fu*), the Court of the Imperial Stud (*t'ai-
p'u ssu*), etc. In all periods may be found with prefixes indicating specialized functions or temporary duty assignments, e.g., Vice Director (in the Ministry of Works serving as) Director of Coinage (*chien-chu yüan-wai lang*) in
Chin, Vice Director (in the Ministry of Works) in charge
of the Auditing Office (*chien-kuan chieh-shen k'u yüan-wai
lang;* see *chieh-shen k'u*) in Ming and Ch'ing, and Vice
Director (in the Ministry of Revenue) Supervisor of the
Capital Granaries (*chien-ts'ang yüan-wai lang;* see *ts'ang-
ch'ang*). RR: *secrétaire auxiliaire.* SP: *secrétaire auxiliaire, sous-directeur.* BH: assistant department director.
P5, 6, 9, 11, 12, 13, 14, 15, 31, 38, 39, 40.

8252 *yüàn-yú chūn* 苑游軍
T'ANG: **Army of the Celestial Parks and Gardens,** named
after an apparently unidentifiable group of stars or constellation; one of 12 regional supervisory headquarters for
militia Garrisons (*fu*) called the Twelve Armies (*shih-erh
chün*); existed only 620–623, 625–636. RR: *armée des parcs
et jardins.* P44.

8253 *yüàn-yù k'ù* 元祐庫
SUNG: lit., paramount protection storehouse, presumably
derived from the era-name Yüan-yu (1086–1094): variant
designation of the **Treasury Reserve Storehouse** (*feng-
chuang ch'ien-wu k'u*).

8254 *yüàn-yù* 苑圉
MING: **Horse Station,** a local horse pasturage headed by
a Director (*chang*), rank 9b, supervised by a regional Pasturage Office (*yüan-ma ssu*) in North China or Manchuria;
normally with a place-name prefix. P31.

8255 *yüán-yüàn chiēn* 園苑監
T'ANG: **Directorate of Imperial Parks,** one established
for each of the 4 quadrants of the dynastic capital for the
maintenance and exploitation of gardens and parklands, each
headed by a Supervisor (*chien*), rank 6b2; subordinate to
the Court of the National Granaries (*ssu-nung ssu*). P40.

8256 *yüán-yüàn ssū* 園苑司
SUNG: **Office of Imperial Parks,** one established for each

of the 4 quadrants of the dynastic capital for the maintenance and exploitation of gardens and parklands, each headed by a Park Commissioner (*yüan-shih*), rank 6b2; subordinate to the Court of National Granaries (*ssu-nung ssu*). SP: *bureau des jardins et des parcs impériaux*. P40.

8257 *yüeh-chāng* 籥章
Flutist. (1) CHOU: 2 ranked as Ordinary Servicemen (*chung-shih*) and 4 as Junior Servicemen (*hsia-shih*), members of the Ministry of Rites (*ch'un-kuan*) who played popular music on 3-holed flutes. See *yüeh-shih* (Flute Master). CL: *joueur de flûte à trois trous*. (2) N-S DIV (Chou): numbe. not clear, ranked as Ordinary Servicemen and Junior Servicemen (i.e., 8a and 9a), members of the Ministry of Rites (*ch'un-kuan*). P10.

8258 *yüeh-chēng* 樂正
SUI–SUNG: **Music Master,** 10 in Sui, 8 rank 9b2 in T'ang, and 5, rank not clear, in Sung; members of the Imperial Music Office (*t'ai-yüeh shu*) or Imperial Music Service (*t'ai-yüeh chü*) in the Court of Imperial Sacrifices (*t'ai-ch'ang ssu*). RR+SP: *directeur de musique*. P10.

8259 *yüeh-chì* 月計
MING: **Monthly Personnel Evaluation,** a report on cases of misconduct or incompetence that District and Subprefectural Magistrates (*chih-hsien, chih-chou*) were required to submit monthly to their Prefects (*chih-fu*), which contributed to the annual merit ratings (*sui-chi*) of all local government personnel submitted by Prefects to provincial authorities.

8260 *yüeh-ch'īng* 樂卿
T'ANG: **Chief Minister of Music,** unofficial reference to the Chief Minister (*ch'ing*) of the Court of Imperial Sacrifices (*t'ai-ch'ang ssu*).

8261 *yüeh-chüän tà-ch'én* 閱卷大臣
CH'ING: **Grand Minister Examiner,** designation of central government dignitaries who graded papers submitted in the Palace Examination (*tien-shih*) in the civil service recruitment examination sequence. BH: imperial reviser.

8262 *yüeh-fǔ* 樂府
HAN: **Music Bureau,** from 121 to 7 B.C. a unit under the Chamberlain for the Palace Revenues (*shao-fu*), headed by a Director (*ling*); had a staff of musicians swelling to 829, who performed at court entertainments, various state rituals, etc.; also reportedly dispatched agents throughout the empire to collect current folk songs, which were thought to reflect local socioeconomic conditions, popular morale, and thus the quality of governance. After 7 B.C. a reduced staff of musicians was transferred to the supervision of the Grand Director of Music (*t'ai-yüeh ling*) on the staff of the Chamberlain for Ceremonials (*t'ai-ch'ang*), under the direct leadership of 2 Supervisors (*p'u-yeh*). HB: bureau of music. P10, 37.

8263 *yüeh-hǎi kuān-pù* 粵海關部
CH'ING: **Kwangtung Customs Superintendent,** a duty assignment for a Grand Minister (*ta-ch'en*) of the Imperial Household Department (*nei-wu fu*) to manage China's trade with foreigners at Canton; known to Europeans as *Hoppo*. BH: superintendent of customs for the province of Kwangtung.

8264 *yüeh-hsién yüàn* 樂縣院
T'ANG: **Office of Sacrificial Music,** one of 4 minor service agencies in the Court of Imperial Sacrifices (*t'ai-ch'ang ssu*); maintained the various musical instruments used in imperial sacrificial ceremonies; apparently staffed solely by state slaves. RR: *service des instruments de musique et des supports d'instruments de musique*.

8265 *yüeh-hsǖ* 樂胥
N-S DIV (Chou): **Musician,** number not clear, ranked as Ordinary Servicemen (*chung-shih;* 8a) and Junior Servicemen (*hsia-shih;* 9a), subordinates of the Musicians-in-chief (*ta ssu-yüeh*) in the Ministry of Rites (*ch'un-kuan*). Also see *yüeh-shih* (Music Master). P10.

8266 *yüeh-lìng* 樂令
SUNG: variant of **Director of the Imperial Music Office** (see under *t'ai-yüeh ling*). SP: *assistant de musique*.

8267 *yüeh-lìng shīh* 月令師
HAN: **Master of Ordinances for the Months,** in Later Han a duty assignment for a Retainer Clerk (*ts'ung-shih shih*) on the staff of the Metropolitan Commandant (*ssu-li hsiao-wei*) and of each Regional Inspector (*tz'u-shih*) or Governor (*chou mu*); made sure that proper rituals were performed at proper times. The designation is derived from the *Yüeh-ling* chapter of the classical text *Li-chi* (*Ritual Records*). HB: master of the ordinances for the months.

8268 *yüeh-mù* 岳牧
Lit., mountain peaks and shepherds, stemming from legends that rulers of highest antiquity divided governmental authority geographically among 4 dignitaries called mountain peaks (*yüeh*) and their subordinates, called shepherds (*mu*): **Regional and Local Authorities,** throughout history a vague unofficial collective reference to the heads of units of territorial administration, in the later dynasties stretching from the Province (*sheng*) level down to Districts (*hsien*).

8269 *yüeh-pù* 樂部
CH'ING: **Music Ministry,** an autonomous central government agency created in 1729 to replace the former Music Office (*chiao-fang ssu*) of the Ministry of Rites (*lǐ-pu*), incorporating the new Music Office (*ho-sheng shu*) and the Imperial Music Office (*shen-yüeh shu*); supervised by Grand Ministers (*ta-ch'en*) of the Imperial Household Department (*nei-wu fu*) serving as Managers (*kuan-li*); responsible for all musical and dance performances in the palace and court. BH: board of state music. P10.

8270 *yüeh-shīh* 樂師
Music Master. (1) CHOU: 4 ranked as Junior Grand Masters (*hsia ta-fu*), 8 as Senior Servicemen (*shang-shih*), and 16 as Junior Servicemen (*hsia-shih*), members of the Ministry of Rites (*ch'un-kuan*) who, under the direction of Musicians-in-chief (*ta ssu-yüeh*), conducted music on state ritual occasions and instructed children of court officials in various musical instruments and dancing. CL: *chef ou maître de la musique*. (2) N-S DIV (Chou): number not clear, ranked as Ordinary Servicemen (*chung-shih;* 8a), subordinates of the Musicians-in-chief (*ta ssu-yüeh*) in the Ministry of Rites (*ch'un-kuan*). P10. (3) SUI: 8 in the Imperial Music Office (*t'ai-yüeh shu*) and 2 in the Office of Bell Music (*ch'ing-shang shu*), ranks and specific functions not clear; c. 604 retitled *yüeh-cheng* (also Music Master). P10.

8271 *yüeh-shīh* 籥師
CHOU: **Flute Master,** 4 ranked as Ordinary Servicemen (*chung-shih*), members of the Ministry of Rites (*ch'un-kuan*) who instructed dancing performers on 3-holed flutes and supervised their performances at state banquets and rituals. See *yüeh-chang* (Flutist). CL: *maître pour la flûte à trois trous*.

8272 *yǔn-chì wèi* 雲騎尉
SUI–CH'ING: **Commandant of Fleet-as-clouds Cavalry,**

prestige title (*san-kuan*) in Sui, merit title (*hsün*) from T'ang through Ming, title of hereditary nobility (*chüeh-yin*) in Ch'ing, for military officers of rank 9a in Sui, 7a from T'ang through Chin, 6a in Yüan and Ming, 5 in Ch'ing. RR+SP: *directeur de la cavalerie rapide comme les nuages.* P65.

8273   *yün-fù* 運副
CH'ING: abbreviation of *yen-yün fu-shih* (**Assistant Salt Controller**), rank 5b; see under *tu chuan-yün-yen shih.* BH: deputy assistant salt controller. P61.

8274   *yún-hó shǔ* 雲和署
YÜAN: **Office of Ancient Music,** established in 1275 under the Bureau of Musical Ritual (*i-feng ssu*), headed by 2 Directors (*ling*), rank 5b. P10.

8275   *yún-hó tào* 運河道
CH'ING: variant of *ho-tao* (**Waterways Circuit**).

8276   *yún-hūi chiāng-chūn* 雲麾將軍
T'ANG–SUNG: **General of the Cloud-like Flags,** merit title (*hsün*) for military officers of rank 3b1. RR: *général aux étendards nombreaux comme les nuages.* SP: *général aux étendards-nuages.* P65.

8277   *yún-hūi shǐh* 雲麾使
CH'ING: **Flag Assistant,** rank 4a subalterns in the Imperial Procession Guard (*luan-i wei*). BH: assistant marshal.

8278   *yün-k'ù* 運庫
CH'ING: **Salt Depot,** designation of regional and local storehouses for state-monopolized salt under the supervision of Salt Controllers (*tu chuan-yün-yen shih*); each headed by a Commissioner-in-chief (*ta-shih*), rank 8a.

8279   *yún-lěi chǎng* 雲壘長
HAN: **Director of the Cloudy Rampart Garrison,** commander of a capital defense force based north of the Wei River in Former Han, under jurisdiction of the Guardian of the Left (*tso p'ing-i*). HB: chief of the cloud rampart.

8280   *yün-liáng t'í-chǔ ssū* 運糧提擧司
YÜAN: **Supervisorate of Grain Tax Transport,** an agency of the Ministry of War (*ping-pu*) responsible for transporting tax grains from the Yangtze delta to the dynastic capital at Peking; in 1317 replaced by a Supervisorate of Land Transport to the Two Capitals (*liang-tu lu-yün t'i-chü ssu*). P60.

8281   *yün-liáng wàn-hù fǔ* 運糧萬戶府
YÜAN: **Grain Transport Brigade,** 3 military units activated in 1282 to operate the transport of tax grain from the Yangtze delta to the Peking area by coastal shipping; each under an Overseer (*ta-lu-hua-ch'ih*) and a Brigade Commander (*wan-hu*). Date of discontinuance is not clear.

8282   *yún-mù* 雲幕
T'ANG: unofficial reference to a **Private Secretary,** a nonofficial aide in the employ of a territorial dignitary; see *mu-fu* (Private Secretariat).

8283   *yün-p'àn* 運判
(1) YÜAN: **Transport Assistant,** a 3rd or 4th executive official in such agencies as Chief Transport Offices (*tu ts'ao-yün ssu*), Salt Distribution Commissions (*tu chuan-yün-yen shih ssu*), and Tea and Salt Monopoly and Tax Transport Commissions (*ch'a-yen chuan-yün-yen shih ssu*), rank normally 6a. P8, 60, 61. (2) CH'ING: **Second Assistant Salt Controller** in a Salt Distribution Commission (*tu chuan-yün-yen shih ssu*), rank 6b, below Deputy Salt Controllers (*yün-t'ung*) and Assistant Salt Controllers (*yün-fu*). BH: subassistant salt controller. P61.

8284   *yün-p'ǔ kuān* 運譜官
SUNG: **Musical Duty Roster Clerk** (?), rank not clear, in the Imperial Music Bureau (*ta-sheng fu*); responsible for keeping records (*p'u*) of rotational shifts (*yün*) of musical personnel on active duty? SP: *fonctionnaire chargé des notes de musiques.*

8285   *yún-sháo fǔ* 雲韶府 or *yún-sháo pù* 部
T'ANG–SUNG: **Bureau of Natural Harmony,** a school for training musicians in the Emperor's private apartments, staffed with eunuchs of the T'ang Palace Domestic Service (*nei-shih sheng*) and the Sung Palace Eunuch Service (*ju-nei nei-shih sheng*); in T'ang (*fu*) was a variant of *nei chiao-fang* (Palace Music School) from 692 to 714; the name derived from a type of popular tunes called *yün-shao* (cloud harmony). RR: *palace de la splendeur des nuages.* SP: *bureau de musique de la porte jaune.*

8286   *yün-shǐh* 運使
(1) YÜAN: abbreviation of *tu ts'ao-yün shih* (**Chief Transport Commissioner**). (2) CH'ING: abbreviation of *tu chuan-yün-yen shih* (**Salt Distribution Commissioner**).

8287   *yün-ssū* 運司
(1) SUNG: abbreviation of *chuan-yün ssu* (**Fiscal Commission**). (2) CH'ING: abbreviation of *tu chuan-yün-yen shih ssu* (**Salt Distribution Commission**).

8288   *yún-ssū* 雲司
T'ANG: lit., office of clouds, derivation not clear: unofficial reference to the **Court of Judicial Review** (*ta-li ssu*).

8289   *yún-t'ái* 芸臺
Lit., pavilion of rue, an insect-repelling plant, hence a good place for storing archives and books. (1) HAN: unofficial reference to the **Palace Library** (see under *pi-shu chien*). (2) CH'ING: unofficial reference to the **Hanlin Academy** (*han-lin yüan*).

8290   *yün-ts'áo* 運曹
N-S DIV (Chin): **Transport Section** under the developing Department of State Affairs (*shang-shu sheng*); responsible for the transport of tax grains to the capital; headed by a Director (*lang*). P6.

8291   *yün-t'úng* 運同
CH'ING: abbreviation of *yen-yün yün-t'ung* (**Deputy Salt Controller**), rank 4b, 2nd only to a Salt Controller (*tu chuan-yün-yen shih*). BH: assistant salt controller. P61.

Index to Suggested English Renderings

able-bodied male, 1510
aboriginal, 7342
Aboriginal Area, 6379
Aboriginal Chiefs' Offices, 3915
Aboriginal Office, 7355
Aboriginal Official, 7352
Aboriginal Troops, 7353
Abundant Classicist, 1226
Academician, 2704
Academician in Attendance, 2146
Academician Awaiting Instructions, 2151
Academician Awaiting Orders, 2150
Academician for Court Service, 3419
Academician on Duty in the Secretariat, 1045
Academician Editor, 2305
Academician of the Eight Solar Seasons, 4363
Academician Expositor-in-waiting, 5217
Academician Reader-in-waiting, 5326
Academician Recipient of Edicts, 465, 2707
Academicians, 3310
Academicians of the Grand Secretariat, 4195
Academies and Institutes, 3310
Academy: *kuan*, 3264; *shu-yüan*, 5471; *yüan*, 8221
Academy in the Hall of Elegance and Rectitude, 3593
Academy of Heaven, 932
Academy of Moslem Medicine, 3037
Academy of Scholarly Worthies, 553, 554
Academy for the Veneration of Literature, 4870
Accessory Clerk, 6989
Accommodations Service, 1989, 5035
Account Keeper: 180, 181, 943, 5561
Accountant, 5676, 6055, 6869
Accounting Commissioner, 598
Accounting Maid, 93
Accounting Office: *kou-pu ssu*, 3213; *kou-tso ssu*, 3217; *kuo-yung ts'an-chi so*, 3552; *shen-chi ssu*, 5144; *shen-chi yüan*, 5146
Account(s), 522
Accounts Assistant, 610, 4981

Accounts Clerk, 563, 565, 585, 4979
Accounts Office, 192, 5565
Accounts Section, 85, 604, 3261, 7240
Accounts Section for Imperial Envoys, 7082
Acting: *chia*, 647; *chieh*, 753; *chien-chiao*, 804; *hsing*, 2561; *she*, 5127; *shih*, 5204; *shou*, 5355; *shou-ch'üeh*, 5367; *shou-kuan*, 5380; *shu*, 5410; *wei-shu*, 7675
Acting Assistant, 684
Acting Concurrent, 5410
Acting Investigating Censor, 791
Active Duty Conscript, 5466
Acupuncture Master, 389, 2935
Acupuncture Student, 389
Acupuncturist, 380
Added Student, 6945
additional office, 666
adequate, 464
Adherents, 3367
Adjunct: *pi*, 4570; *shih liu-nei*, 5289; *tso-lang*, 6977; *yao-chün*, 7895
Adjunct Chamberlains, 4552
Adjunct Commandant, 4624
Adjunct Dukes, 4581
Adjunct Grand Master, 3700
Adjunct Marquis, 3698
Adjunct Student, 4558
Adjutant: *chang-ching*, 107; *chung-chün*, 1550; *chung-lang*, 1580; *fu-chiang*, 2041; *hsing-chün ssu-ma*, 2567; *ssu-ma*, 5713; *ts'an-chün-shih*, *ts'an-chün*, 6875
Adjutant for Education, 7710
Adjutant for Household Records, 1586
Adjutant-protector, 6877
Administering the Affairs of, 3639
Administration, 410, 3294
Administration Chamber, 441
Administration of the Heir Apparent, 3475
Administration Office, 3859
Administration of the Princess' Estate, 3411
Administration Vice Commissioner, 6868
Administrative Adviser, 7531
Administrative Aide: *ch'ien-hsia*, 898; *ch'ien-shu yüan-shih*, 925;

chu-shih, 1420; *kung-feng kung-yung*, 3421; *nei-shih ya-pan*, 4253; *pieh-chia*, 4623; *tsan-chih*, 6847; *tsan-wu*, 6862
Administrative Assistant: *fu-p'an*, 2089; *p'an-kuan*, 4425; *t'ui-kuan*, 7399; *wu-pu*, 7814; *yüan-p'an*, 8236
Administrative Assistant to the Military Commissioner, 776
Administrative Associates, 5677
Administrative Clerk: *chi-i kuan*, 558; *chih-shih*, 1050; *kan-shih*, 3138; *kou-ya kuan*, 3219; *kuan-kan*, 3306; *shu-tso*, 5464
Administrative Clerk of a Salt Control Station, 7925
Administrative Counselor, 4243
Administrative Director, 7145
Administrative Office, 5391
Administrative Office of the Empress, 1578
Administrative Official, 1055
Administrative Region, 649
Administrative Supervisor, 3860
Administrative Supervisor of the Hall, 6420
Administrator: *chang-shih*, 185; *chih*, 934; *hsiang*, 2303; *i-ling*, 2980; *kan-pan kung-shih*, 3136; *kan-tang*, *kan-tang kung-shih*, 3139; *li-shih kuan*, 3640; *nei-shih*, 4236; *p'ing-chang*, 4699; *pu-shu*, 4801; *ts'an-chang*, 6866; *ts'an-chün-shih*, *ts'an-chün*, 6876; *tsung-pan*, 7144; *tu-hsia*, 7230; *tu-pan*, 7261; *yin*, 7969; *'yüan*, 8219; *yüan-shih*, 8238
Administrator of the Bureau of Military Affairs, 1064
Administrator for Cavalry, 575
Administrator of the Censorate, 1073
Administrator of the Department of State Affairs, 1047
Administrator of the Hanlin Academy, 4423
Administrator (of local school), 3075
Administrator of the Ministry of Personnel Selections, 1029
Administrator of the Ministry of Rites Examinations, 1030
Administrator of the Office of Imperial Clan Affairs, 1087

Administrator of Personnel
  Selections, 994
Administrator for Public Order,
  5672, 5693, 5700
Administrator for Records, 5710
Administrator-general, 7093
Administrator-general of Court
  Rituals, 7094
Administrator-general of National
  Affairs, 7095
Administrators, 3739
Administrator's Office in a Princely
  Establishment, 186
Administrators of.the Various
  Sections, 1436
Admonisher, 6858
Admonishing Serviceman, 2751
Adornment Service, 7696
Adornments Maid, 183
Adornments Office, 5768
Adviser: i-sheng, 2994; na-yen,
  4079; tzu-i kuan, 7530; yü-te,
  8193
Adviser to the Eastern Palace, 7443
Adviser to the Heir Apparent, 6244
Adviser-Director, 4080
Advisory Office, 697
Agate Service, 3905
Agent, 3471, 7030
Aggregation, 3702
Aggregation Commandant, 687
Aggregation Leader, 3716
Agricultural Development
  Commissioner, 1711
Agricultural Inspector, 2750
Agriculture Commissioner, 8022
Agriculture Inspector, 1712
Agriculture Intendant, 1710
Agriculture Master, 4322
Agriculture Office, 6619
Agriculture Section, 4325, 4326
Aid Provider, 5366
Aide, 185, 457
Aide for Ceremonial in the
  Messenger Office, 5956
Aide for Fruits, 3506
Aide to the Imperial Physician, 6175
Aide to the Imperial Secretary, 5044
Aide for the Māhāsanghikāk Sect,
  4944
Aide for Mercantile Taxes, 1918
Aide for the Palace Walkways, 2104
Aide in the Royal Stud, 4821
Aide for Stone Quarries, 5269
Aide-Commander, 701
alien defector, 3373
alien soldier, 2986
all officials, 4739
All-encompassing Father, 2660
All-encompassing Sage, 2676
Allied Army, 6277
Allied Marquis, 3361, 3370
Allied Troops Section, 4628
allowance to encourage honesty,
  7883
Almoner, 2962

Already Certified Candidate, 3989,
  8014
Altar of Earth, 6385
Altar of Heaven, 6715
Altar of the Soil and Grain, 5133
Ancestral Attendant, 7104
Ancestral Temple, 7139
Ancillary, 4047
Animal Keeper, 8056
Animal Tamer, 2094
annual military subsidy, 4309
annual personnel evaluation, 5862
appanage, 1947, 4792; also see land
  grant
Appearance Monitor, 4938
appoint: ch'u, 1457; pai, 4388; pu,
  4763; pu-ch'üeh, 4777; shou, 5356
appoint to fill a vacancy: pu-shou,
  4800
Appointee on Punitive Probation,
  4737
Appointer of the East, 7433
Appointer of the West, 2240
Appointment Certificate, 3146
appointment by courtesy, 4415
appointment by protection, 7988
Appointment Verification Office,
  3309
Appointment Verification Service,
  3308
Appointments Process, 2653
Appointments Section: hsiao-li fang,
  2415; hsüan-pu, hsüan-pu ts'ao,
  2675; li-pu, li-pu ts'ao, 3630;
  tzu-jen an, 7532
Apprentice: hsi-hsüeh kuan, 2241;
  hsi-hsüeh kung-shih, 2242;
  hsüeh-hsi, 2695; hsüeh-shih, 2703;
  k'an-pan, 3142; pan-shih, 4412
Apprentice Audience Attendant,
  3142
Apprentice Pharmacist, 7902
Apprentice Physician, 3042
Apprentice Translator, 3025
Arbiter, 4698, 6775
Arbitrator, 6498
Archer on Duty, 3403
Archery Storehouse, 3404
Archive, 2092, 6285, 6627
Archive of the Heir Apparent, 6645
Archive of Personnel Records, 665
Archives, 663, 1109, 6527
Archives Section, 2839
Archives of the Six Ministries, 3806
Archivist: chia-ko kuan, 664;
  chih-shu kuan, 1062; chu-hsia
  shih, 1385; shou-chang, 5358;
  tien-chi, 6522; tien-pu, 6626;
  tien-shu ling, 6647
Area Command: tsung-kuan fu,
  7112; tsung-kuan ssu, 7116; tu,
  7181; tu-tu fu, 7314
Area Command for Hunting, 6010
Area Commander, 3101, 7300
Area Commander with Special
  Powers, 1106

Area Commander-in-chief, 5485,
  6096, 7110
Area General, 690
Armaments Office, 1743
Armaments Section, 1333
Armaments Storehouse, 1760
Armed Attendants Guard Command,
  7821
Armed Escort, 7844
armed forces, the, 4849
Armillary Sphere Office, 2890
Armor Section, 3126
Armorer, 2140, 5573, 5627
Armories of the Two Capitals, 3662
Armory: chia-chang k'u, 652;
  chia-k'u, 665; chün-fu, 1753;
  pa-tso yüan, 4382; tso-yüan, 7022;
  tzu-wu k'u, 7546; wu-k'u, 7779;
  wu-k'u shu, 7782
Armory for Bows and Lances, 1741
Armory for Crossbows, Arrows, and
  Swords, 1742
Armory of the Imperial Insignia
  Guard, 1163
Armory for Miscellaneous Weapons,
  1744
Armory Service, 142
Army, 1730, 3906, 6340
Army Aide, 2566
Army of Bowmen Shooters at
  Moving Targets, 6538
Army of the Celestial Black Lance,
  2668
Army of the Celestial Bull, 6691
Army of the Celestial Cornucopia,
  4714
Army of the Celestial Herdboy, 3225
Army of the Celestial Lion's Pelt,
  5147
Army of the Celestial Parks and
  Gardens, 8252
Army of the Celestial Serpent, 6688
Army of the Celestial Twins, 1253
Army of the Celestial Water Bearer,
  8151
Army of the Celestial Wolf, 564
Army of the Center, 890, 1550
Army Commander: chün-chu, 1749;
  kuan-chün, 3284; tu-chün, 7221;
  t'ung-chün shih, 7483
Army Counselor, 2568
Army Farm, 1799
Army of the Front, 890
Army of the Great Celestial Bear,
  308
Army Guard: chün-wei, 1802
Army Guard of Guard Officers, 7671
Army Headquarters, 1753
Army of Heavenly Awesomeness,
  6724
Army of Heroic Militancy, 8029
Army of Inspired Awesomeness,
  5167, 6541
Army of Inspired Militancy, 5169
Army of Inspired Power, 5149
Army of Inspired Strategy, 5163

Army of the Left, 890
Army Provisioning Commissioner, 5865
Army of the Rear, 890
Army of the Right, 890
Army Supervisor, 815, 1564
Army Wine Storehouse, 4953
Army-supervising Censor, 7224
array of, 3697
Arresting Agent (prefix), 2725
Arrow Maker, 5763
Artillery Lieutenant, 33zz
Artilleryman, 4509
artisan family, 696
Artisan Painter, 2809
Artisans Institute, 2154
Assault-resisting Garrison, 347
Assayer, 5555
Assembler, 95
Assessor of Lesser Penalties, 5095
Assignee, 1195
assignment: *chih*, 936
Assignment Section, 72
Assistant: *ch'ien*, 885; *ch'ien-shih*, 917; *chih-chung*, 967; *hsiang-fu kuan*, 2313; *hsieh*, 2460; *hsieh-t'ung kuan*, 2485; *hsü*, 2641; *p'an-kuan*, 4425; *ssu-ma*, 5713; *tso*, 6948; *tso-li*, 6978; *tso-tsa*, 7005
Assistant Administration Commissioner, 6881
Assistant Administrator, 6872
Assistant Administrator of the Hanlin Academy, 2480
Assistant Battalion Commander, 7143
Assistant Brigade Commander, 2203, 5393, 7110
Assistant Censor-in-chief, 929
Assistant Ceremonial Charioteer, 643
Assistant Chief Military Inspector, 7324
Assistant Clerk: *chu-shu*, 1429
Assistant Commandant, 2474, 6980
Assistant Commandant of Military Trustworthiness, 7771
Assistant Commander: *chih-hui ch'ien-shih*, 999; *fu-tu*, 2106; *po-chang*, 4719; *shuai tu-tu*, 5486
Assistant Commissioner, 931, 7857
Assistant Commissioner for the Salt and Iron Monopoly, 7857
Assistant Commissioner-in-chief: *tu-tu ch'ien-shih*, 7312
Assistant Construction Foreman, 3429
Assistant Construction Supervisor, 6835
Assistant Department Magistrate, 1343
Assistant Diarist, 621
Assistant Director, 516, 1003
Assistant Director of Astrology, 912
Assistant Director (of Bureau of Carpentry), 2442

Assistant Director (of Bureau of Convict Labor), 2440
Assistant Director (of Bureau of Equipment), 2385
Assistant Director (of Bureau of Excavation), 2448
Assistant Director (of Bureau of Gardens), 2437
Assistant Director (of Bureau of Metalwork), 2436
Assistant Director (of Bureau of Military Personnel), 2427
Assistant Director (of Bureau of Operations), 2390
Assistant Director (of Bureau of Punishments), 2402
Assistant Director (of Bureau of Waterways), 2447
Assistant Director of the Cattle Pasturage, 4073
Assistant Director of the Court of the Imperial Clan, 7104
Assistant Director of the Department of State Affairs, 5851
Assistant Director (of Imperial Secretariat, Department of State Affairs), 5044
Assistant Director of the Left, 6951
Assistant Director (of Office of Construction), 2386
Assistant Director of the Palace Library, 4587
Assistant Director of the Pass, 3273
Assistant Director of the Right, 8034
Assistant Director (of Section for Foreign Relations), 2399
Assistant Director (of Section for Tributary Relations), 2426
Assistant Director of the Standard-bearer Guard, 190
Assistant Director of a Subsection, 191
Assistant Duty Group Chief, 4441
Assistant Editorial Director, 1442
Assistant Gentleman for Ceremonial Service, 704
Assistant General, 4607
Assistant Grain Transport Commander, 2487
Assistant Grand Councilor: *ts'an-cheng*, 6868
Assistant Grand Secretary, 2479
Assistant Instructor, 2761
Assistant Magistrate, 1413, 4762
Assistant Manager, 2468
Assistant Gate Commandant, 5408
Assistant Market Director, 5211
Assistant Minister of State, 6816
Assistant Music Master, 2101
Assistant in the Palace Library, 4592
Assistant Palace Provisioner, 4230
Assistant for Pitchpipes, 2475
Assistant Prefect, 7497
Assistant Proofreader, 2464
Assistant Regional Commander, 6870

Assistant for the Resonant Pitchpipes, 2483
Assistant Supplementary Charioteer, 6326
Assistant Surveillance Commissioner, 9
Assistant for the Sweet Spring Palace and the Imperial Forest Park, 3130
Assistant for Sweets, 3128
Assistant for Tones, 2488
Assistant Transmission Commissioner, 6881
Assister toward Goodness, 7535, 7540
Associate: *hsieh*, 2460; *tso-erh*, 6962; *ts'ui-erh*, 7068; *t'ung*, 7464; *t'ung-chih*, 7471
Associate Administrator, 7471
Associate Censor, 8173
Associate Commander of the Army, 3907
Associate Consultant, 7489
Associate Director of the Court of the Imperial Clan, 7080
Associate Judge, 7872
Associate Metropolitan Graduate, 7475
Associate Military Superintendent, 6853
Astrologer, 2238, 3055, 3057
Astrologer Service, 6725
Astrological Apprentice, 2585
Astrological Commission, 6220
Astrological Observers in the Five Offices, 7786
Astrological Office, 6219
Astrological Section, 6214
Astrological Service, 4579, 6216
Astronomical College, 6728
Astronomical Observer, 824, 2221, 4709
Astronomical Official, 2578
Astronomical Officials, 5781
Astronomical Section, 6726
Attendant: *ch'eng-feng*, 477; *po-chih*, 4722; *shih*, 5198; *shih-chung*, 5229; *shih-ts'ung*, 5324
Attendant Academician, 5308
Attendant Assistant, 7171
Attendant Censor, 5350
Attendant for Elders, 2942
Attendant Gentleman, 5278
Attendant Gentleman for Miscellaneous Uses, 7791
Attendant Guard Command, 5312
Attendant Lecturer, 1121
Attendant Officer, 5864
Attendant in the Outer Court, 7577
Attendant of the Three Ranks, 4885, 4886
Attendant Tutor, 5218
Attendant-in-ordinary, 262, 273
Attendants, 7016
Attendants Section, 5244
Attending, 5198
Attending Physician, 5255

Attending Ritualist, 3613
Audience Attendant, 1954, 2681,
   3177
Audience Chamber, 6749
Audience Guide, 3178
Audience Monitor, 337
audience nomination, 6766
Audience Steward, 3170
Audience Usher, 3176
Auditing Office, 766
Augur, 5764
authorities, the, 8081
Autumn Chamberlain, 1321
Autumn Office, 1324
Autumn Park, 2804
Autumn Support, 1324
Auxiliary: *chih*, 934; *chih-kuan*,
   1016; *chih-yüan*, 1100; *hsing-tsai*,
   2601; *kung-feng*, 3418;
   nei kung-feng, 4210
Auxiliary Academician, 996
Auxiliary Academician in the Bureau
   of Military Affairs, 5449
Auxiliary in the Academy of
   Scholarly Worthies, 942
Auxiliary Capital, 4551, 4559
Auxiliary Censorate, 3815
Auxiliary Department of State
   Affairs, 4693
Auxiliary in the Hall of the Dragon
   Diagram, 1034
Auxiliary Illustrator, 2803
Auxiliary Instructor, 7706
Auxiliary Investigator, 7395
Auxiliary for Making Writing-
   brushes, 6914
Auxiliary Palace, 2580
Auxiliary Scribe, 5420
Avenues of Criticism, 7949
avoidance, 2887
avoidance examination, 4630
Awesome Guard, 7680
Awesome and Militant Army, 7685

Bachelor, 5419
Bailiff, 4940
Bamboo and Lumber Service, 1406
Bamboo-leaf Storehouse, 3060
Bandit-suppressing Censor, 2621,
   2622
Bandit-suppressing Commissioner,
   2621
Bandit-suppression Commission, 304
Bandit-suppression Commissioner,
   303
Banner, 611, 3237
Banner Commander, 3238, 3240
Banner Revenues Section, 1241
Banner Vice Commander, 3931
Banner Vice Commander-in-chief,
   107
Bannermen's School, 4359
Banquet Caterer, 3143
Banquet Music Section, 7919
Banquets Maid, 98
Banquets Office, 5572, 5973
Bark Grinder, 5803

Baron, 4082
Basket Handler, 4639
Bathing Office, 2900
Baton Holder, 1017
Battalion: *ch'ien-hu so*, 901; *lü*,
   3882; *meng-an*, 3956; *so*, 5523
Battalion Commander: *ch'ien-fu
   chang, ch'ien-fu*, 894; *ch'ien-hu*,
   901; *ch'ien-jen*, 903; *lü-shuai*,
   3894; *meng-an*, 3956
Battalion Head, 901
Battalion Vice Commander, 901
be in charge of, 5533
Bean Sauce Maker, 5216
Beard Trimmer, 6313
Bearer of Identification Certificates,
   480
Bearer of the Imperial Arms, 6133
Bearers of the Imperial Insignia,
   2932
Beauty, 3930
Beg (Moslem leader), 4738
Beile, 4526, 6789
Beile Prince, 3242, 4546
Bells and Drums Office, 1572
Belt and Leatherwork Service, 6763
Bey (Moslem leader), 4738
Bird Catcher, 5304
Bird Killer, 5140
Bird Netter, 3828
Bishbalik Service, 4629
Blind Musician, 3223, 3236
Blower of the Great Horn, 5927
Blue Collar Graduate, 1263
Blue Dye Shop, 3562
Bodyguard Garrison, 1180
Bondservant, 4482
Bondservants of the Princes, 7652
Bookbinding Service, 1511
Books Section, 1198
Border Monitor, 99
Border Section, 4829
Botanical Service, 2812
Bottom Graduate, 6272
Boundary Marker, 1994
Bow and Arrow Office, 3477
Bow and Arrow Workshop, 3455
Bowmaker, 5683
Bowman Shooter by Sound, 5142
Bowmen Leader, 3832
Bowmen Shooters at Moving
   Targets, 6540, 7847
Bows Office, 3454, 4318
boy eunuch, 2388
Branch, 1934, 2561
Branch Bureau of Military Affairs,
   2595
Branch Censorate, 2608, 3816
Branch Department of State Affairs,
   1637, 2591, 2598, 2599, 2600,
   5056
Branch Directorate of Waterways,
   1937
Branch Office, 1945, 1946
Branch Office for Provisions and
   Labor Services, 1936

Branch Secretariat, 2565
Brave as Tigers (prefix), 2787
Breeder of Sacrificial Animals, 4055
brevet rank, 2493
Bridge Tender, 752
Brigade, 7621, 7622, 8009
Brigade Commandant, 8027
Brigade Commander, 3331, 7620,
   7622, 8036
Brigade Vice Commander, 7285
Brocade Weaving and Dyeing
   Service, 3744
Brokerage, 8221
Brokerage Official, 1102
Broth Cook, 224
Buddhist authorities, 4947
Buddhist Chief, 4942
Buddhist Controller, 4949
Buddhist Deacon, 7672
Buddhist Patriarch, 4960
Buddhist Rectifier, 1717
Buddhist Registry for the Avenues of
   the Capital, 7017
Buddhist Superior, 4942
Budget Section, 5143
Building Administrator for the
   Imperial Genealogy Office, 3137
Building Administrators for the
   Imperial Genealogy Office, 8195
Building Bureau, 8016
Building Maintenance Office, 6517
Bulwark, 2035
Bulwark Duke, 1979, 2075
Bulwark of Government, 2039
Bulwark-commandant of the State,
   2074
Bulwark-general of the State, 2073
Bulwark-generalissimo of the State,
   2076
Bureau: *ch'ing-li ssu*, 1273; *ssu*,
   5533; *t'ing*, 6748; *yüan*, 8221
Bureau of Appointments, 3630,
   5704, 7702
Bureau of Arrests, 7267
Bureau of Astronomy, 5783, 6729
Bureau of Bells and Drums, 1573
Bureau of Capital and Court
   Officials, 4033
Bureau of Ceremonial Insignia and
   Arms for the Six Imperial Armies,
   3786
Bureau of Ceremonies, 2945, 2990
Bureau of Commissions, 68
Bureau of Communications, 355
Bureau of Compilation, 4638
Bureau of Construction, 8018
Bureau of Equipment, 676, 5575,
   5833
Bureau of Equipment and
   Communications, 355
Bureau of Evaluations: *k'ao-k'o ssu*,
   3152; *k'ao-kung ch'ing-li ssu*,
   3156; *k'ao-kung, k'ao-kung ssu*,
   3159; *ssu-chi*, 5560; *tzu-k'ao ssu*,
   7533
Bureau of Examination Copyists,
   6359

Bureau Executive in the Military Appointments Process, 5343
Bureau of Forestry and Crafts, 5832, 8133, 8163
Bureau for Functionaries, 3824
Bureau of General Accounts, 7203, 7205
Bureau of Granaries, 5604
Bureau of Honors: chu-chüeh, 1379; feng-hsün ssu, 1984; ssu-feng ssu, 5620; yen-feng ch'ing-li ssu, yen-feng ssu, 7936
Bureau of Irrigation and Transportation, 7279
Bureau of Joyful Music, 2572
Bureau of Judicial Administration, 2590, 5635
Bureau for Judicial Commissioners, 4034
Bureau of Judicial Investigation, 1288
Bureau of Judicial Investigation for the Capital, 1289
Bureau of Lesser Military Assignments, 4889
Bureau of Merit Titles, 5640, 5642
Bureau of Military Affairs, 5451
Bureau of Military Affairs in the Southern Establishment, 4120
Bureau of Military Appointments, 4691, 4692, 4696, 5664, 7773
Bureau of Military Personnel, 4691
Bureau of Ministry Affairs (in Ministry of Rites), 3017
Bureau of Minor Commissions, 4032
Bureau of Musical Ritual, 2953
Bureau of Natural Harmony, 8285
Bureau of Nomination Certificates, 8199
Bureau of Operations, 978, 979, 5549, 5827
Bureau of Personnel Assignments, 3153, 3803
Bureau of Personnel Evaluation, 5155
Bureau of Prisons: ssu-p'u, 5748
Bureau of Provisions: ching-shan ch'ing-li ssu, 1236; k'u-pu ssu, k'u-pu, 3249; ssu-chi, 5557; ssu-k'u, 5674; wu-k'u ch'ing-li ssu, wu-k'u ssu, 7780
Bureau of Punishments, 2528, 2590
Bureau of Records, 556
Bureau of Receptions: chu-k'o ch'ing-li ssu, 1394; chu-k'o ssu, chu-k'o, 1397; ch'ung-yüan shu, 1673; ssu-chi, 5559; ssu-fan, 5616; tien-k'o kuan, 6603
Bureau of Review, 4582, 5561
Bureau of Sacrifices: ssu-yin, 5824; tz'u-chi ch'ing-li ssu, 7551; tz'u-pu, 7566
Bureau of Sacrificial Music, 2315
Bureau of Standards, 4705
Bureau of Taoist Music, 1852, 2530
Bureau of Transmission, 7469
Bureau of Waterways, 5606

Bureau of Waterways and Irrigation, 5508, 5771
Burnt Vermillion Office, 5093
Bursar, 905, 995
Bursary, 1096, 3670
Bursary Section, 1019
Butcher, 6809
by courtesy, 4399
by purchase, 1701, 1703

Cadet, 5468, 8201
Cage, 1892
Calendar Clerk, 154
Calendar Clerk for the Metropolitan Area, 2079
Calendar Instructor, 3601
Calendar Maker, 6608
Calendar Preparation Office, 2623
Calendar Printing Clerk, 7984
Calendar Printing Office, 7986
Calendar Section, 5251
Calendrical Apprentice, 3635, 3636
Calligrapher Service, 5436
Calligraphy Clerk, 5309
Calligraphy Inspector, 6532
Calligraphy School, 5434
Camel and Cattle Office, 6793
Camel Corral, 6791
Camel Herd, 4071
Camp Supervisor, 121
Campaign Commander, 7321
Campaigning Army, 8009
Canal Patroller, 8099
Canal Transport-inspecting (prefix), 2755
Cancellations Office, 3211
Canopies Office, 5384
Capital: ching, 1188; ching-chao, 1190; ching-tu, 1243; chung, 1530; tu, 7181
Capital Army, 1550
Capital City, 1308
Capital Commandant, 1585, 7322
Capital Construction Office, 5687
Capital Department of Culture and Prosperity, 7693
Capital District, 1217
capital evaluation, 1189
Capital Governor, 1251
Capital Granaries, 6901
Capital Guards, 1248
Capital Inspector, 2752
Capital Liaison Office, 1156
Capital Liaison Representative, 1155, 3790
Capital Minister, 7290
Capital Ministry, 7301
Capital Officials, 1224
Capital Officials Section, 7246
Capital Pavilion, 7290
Capital Police Commissioner, 1209
Capital Prefecture, 1212
Capital Prison, 7247
Capital Protector, 1564, 2775
Capital Punishment Section, 1287
Capital Punishments Section, 2312
Capital Salt Supply Section, 7331

Capital Security Office, 2833
Capital Township Officials, 2326
Capital Training Divisions, 1252
Capital Translator, 7299
Capitulation Office, 299
Caps and Kerchiefs Service, 1133
Caretaker, 146, 787, 5401
Caretaker of the Altar Mound, 6279
Cargo Dispatcher, 4724
Carpenter of the Eastern Park, 7462
Carpentry Service, 2424, 5996
Carriage Attendant, 3072
Carriage Livery, 362
Carriage Master, 1418
Carriage Office, 3868
Case Review Section, 1009
Case Reviewer, 4712
Case Reviewer's Clerk, 4713
Castration Chamber, 6890
Caterer, 5279
Catering Bureau, 2429, 4959, 5752
Cattle and Sheep Office, 4315, 4316, 4317
Cavalier Attendant, 4833
Cavalier Attendant-in-ordinary, 4834
Cavalry, 548, 574
Cavalry Attendant-in-ordinary, 235
Cavalry Brigade, 2382
Cavalry Commandant, 456
Cavalry Commander of the Army, 1790
Cavalry Commander on Campaign, 2597
Cavalry Garrison, 4619
Cavalry General, 4618
Cavalry General-in-chief, 4620
Cavalry Section, 576, 4686
Cavalryman, 574
Censor, 973, 8167
Censor Aide, 8171, 8172
Censor Expediter of Army Supplies, 7222
Censor Inspecting ..., 2753
Censor on Tour, 8179
Censor-in-chief, 6033, 7335, 8181
Censorate: hsien-t'ai, 2540; ssu-hsien, 5632; su-cheng t'ai, 5850; tu ch'a-yüan, 7183; yü-shih fu, 8178; yü-shih ta-fu ssu, 8183; yü-shih t'ai, 8184
Censorate Physician, 6172
Censorial Gate Monitor, 863
Censorial Official, 2509
Censors and Remonstrators, 6149
Censors and Supervising Secretaries, 6211
Census Bureau, 2792, 3049, 5838
Census Intendant Circuit, 7304
Census Section: hu-k'ou an, 2785; jen-ts'ao, 3052; tso-hu ts'ao, tso-hu, 6971; tso-min ts'ao, tso-min, 6981
Center Construction Office, 8019
Center Leader, 1541
Center Leader of Court Gentlemen for Carriages, 361
Center Subsection, 1624

Central Appointer, 1562
Central Buddhist Registry, 4948
Central Control Office, 5418
Central Defense Army, 1564
Central Drafting Office, 1615
central government, the, 4806
Central Hall, 1631
Central Lumberyard, 4072
Central Office, 1607
Central Pavilion, 1629
Central Prison, 3061, 3776, 5687
Central Secretariat, 1619
Central Service Office, 1592, 1594, 1597, 4231
Central Taoist Registry, 6318
Centurion, *see* Company Commander
Cereals Chef, 628
Ceremonial Assistant, 431, 6854
Ceremonial Caps Section, 1233
Ceremonial Charioteer, 637
Ceremonial Companion, 2985
Ceremonial Dancer, 5125
Ceremonial Dancing Master, 7820
Ceremonial Escort, 1054, 6863
Ceremonial Guard, 3028
Ceremonial Horse Groom, 1132
Ceremonial Receptionist, 7510, 8215
Ceremonial Regalia Maid, 88
Ceremonial Regalia Office, 5539
Ceremonial Service, 5003
Ceremonials Office, 5660
Ceremonials Official, 5651
Ceremonies Office, 6594
Certificate Validation Office, 2201
Certification Clerk, 6522
Certification Clerk in the Grand Secretariat, 4200
Certification Office, 2025
Chamber Consort, 393
Chamberlain, 1255
Chamberlain for Attendants, 3570, 5609
Chamberlain for the Capital, 4236
Chamberlain for Ceremonials, 1088, 6137, 6138
Chamberlain of the Court for the Palace Garrison, 7682
Chamberlain for Dependencies, 5947, 6600
Chamberlain for the Imperial Clan, 7080, 7081, 7147
Chamberlain for the Imperial Insignia, 964
Chamberlain for the Imperial Stud, 6201, 6202
Chamberlain for Law Enforcement, 5984, 6767
Chamberlain for the National Treasury: *chih-su nei-shih*, 1069; *ssu-nung*, 5729; *ssu-nung ch'ing*, 5730; *su-k'o*, 5852; *ta-nung ling*, 6002; *ta ssu-nung*, 6042; *ta ssu-nung ch'ing*, 6043
Chamberlain for the Palace Buildings, 709, 712
Chamberlain for the Palace Bursary, 5940

Chamberlain for the Palace Garrison, 1628, 7681
Chamberlain for the Palace Revenues, 5097, 5099, 6159, 6162
Chamberlain for the Palace Stables, 1630
Chamberlain for Waterways, 5810
Chambermaid, 4348
Chancellery, 2846, 3867, 3939
Chancellery Office of Scrutiny, 3937
Chancellery Rear Section, 3938
Chancellor, 483, 542, 2704
Chancellor of Confucian Education, 3073
Chancellor of the Directorate of Education, 3540
Chancellor (of Directorate of Education), 6029
Chancellor of the Erudites, 4749
Chancellor of the Hanlin Academy, 226
Chancellor of the National University, 3540
Chancellor of the Palace Attendants, 5230
Changing the Frontier Guards, 3165
Charcoal Yard, 6274
Chariot Defenseman, 3097
Chariot Escort, 7973
Chariot and Horse Garrison, 353
Chariot and Horse General, 352
Chariot and Horse General Serving as Commander-in-chief, 6040
Chariot Lancer, 4697
Charioteer, 365
Chariots Section, 364
Charity Granary, 3016
Cherisher of Those Afar, 2817
Chief: *chang*, 84; *chang-kuan*, 143; *chih-chang*, 938; *i-li-chin*, 2974; *po-chi-lieh*, 4721; *tu*, 7181; *tu-ta*, 7289
Chief Administration Office, 7268
Chief Administration Office of the Imperial Residence, 6000
Chief Administrative Clerk, 3134, 7243
Chief Administrator, 4826, 7313
Chief Administrator of the Erudites, 4951
Chief Appearance Monitor, 7270
Chief Area Command, 7308
Chief Army Commander, 1749
Chief of Assistants, 2642, 2651
Chief of Attendants, 5628
Chief Brigade, 7325
Chief Buddhist Deacon, 7327
Chief Bulwark of the State, 6160
Chief Capital Inspector, 7236
Chief Ceremonial Minister, 2905
Chief Clerk: *kuan-ling*, 3318; *ling chu-shih*, 3751; *tu k'ung-mu kuan*, 7249; *tu ling-shih*, 7256
Chief Command, 7308
Chief Commandant-protector, 2779, 5671

Chief Commission for Pasturages, 7155
Chief Commissioner of the Bursary, 7253
Chief Commissioner for Militiamen, 7320
Chief Compiler of the Dynastic History, 829
Chief Coordinating Office, 7218
Chief Defense Commissioner, 7225
Chief of Domestic Service, 4271
Chief Eunuch, 3185
Chief Examiner, 151; *ssu kung-chi*, 5684; *tien kung-chü*, 6607; *tu chien-cheng*, 7193
Chief Executive, 4741
Chief Fermentation Bureau, 7219
Chief Gardener, 5647
Chief Groom, 8166
Chief of the Grotto, 1094
Chief of the Guard, 1138
Chief of Instruction, 2697, 2699
Chief of Interpreters, 2929
Chief Investigating Censor, 794
Chief Judge, 5299
Chief Lackey, 7329
Chief Librarian, 402
Chief on the List, 3383
Chief of Lumber Supplies, 1360
Chief Manufactory, 7306
Chief Memorials Office, 7208
Chief of the Miao Tribes, 3986
Chief Military Administrator of Infantry and Cavalry, 4688
Chief Military Command, 6097, 7337
Chief Military Commission, 7200, 7314
Chief Military Commission for the Capital Guard, 7837
Chief Military Commissioner, 7199, 7223
Chief Military Inspector, 6432, 7234, 7315
Chief Military and Naval Inspector, 5504
Chief Military Training Commissioner, 7319
Chief Minister, 406, 1255
Chief Minister for Administration, 403
Chief Minister of the Court for Dependencies, 2905
Chief Minister of the Court of the Imperial Clan, 6236, 7081
Chief Minister of the Court of the Imperial Regalia, 7682
Chief Minister of the Court of Imperial Sacrifices, 6138
Chief Minister of the Court of the Imperial Stud, 6202
Chief Minister of the Court of the Imperial Treasury, 6162
Chief Minister of the Court for the Palace Garrison, 7682
Chief Minister of the Court of State Ceremonial, 2905

Chief Minister for Dependencies, 2905
Chief Minister for Imperial Sacrifices, 5048
Chief Minister for Law Enforcement, 6770, 6771
Chief Minister of Music, 8260
Chief Minister for the Palace Buildings, 711, 712, 5896
Chief Minister for Visitors, 3192
Chief Ministers and Directors, 1262
Chief Miscellany Office, 7206
Chief Musician, 2477
Chief Office of Imperial Clan Affairs, 6083
Chief Office for the Imperial Costume, 4516
Chief Overseer, 7138
Chief Palace Commandant-protector, 2779
Chief of Palace Surveillance, 3397
Chief Paper Money Depository, 4459
Chief Patrolling Inspector, 7236
Chief of Physicians, 2971
Chief of Police, 3626
Chief Prison, 7185
Chief Prison Custodian, 1448
Chief Recipient of Edicts, 7186
Chief Recommendee, 3384
Chief River Patroller, 7235
Chief Secretary, 189
Chief of Service, 5221
Chief of the Stables, 1291
Chief Steward, 2026, 4971, 5663, 6676
Chief Steward for Accommodations, 4974
Chief Steward for the Bath, 5025
Chief Steward for the Bedchamber, 4997
Chief Steward for Food, 5038
Chief Steward for Headgear, 5009
Chief Steward of the Palace Medical Service, 1993
Chief Steward for the Wardrobe, 5000
Chief Steward for Writing, 5042
Chief Storehouse of Gauze, Gold, and Dyestuffs, 4950
Chief Supervising Secretary, 7189
Chief Tea Market, 7182
Chief of the Throne Steps, 4572
Chief Township Marquis, 7231
Chief Training Commissioner, 7191
Chief Transport Office, 7302
Chief's Office, 149
Chieftain, 2930, 2950
Child-bearing Concubine, 3083
Child Nurturess, 3070
Chiliarchy, see Battalion
Chinese Archive, 2160
Chinese Army, 2134
Chinese Assistant, 2139
Chinese Banners, 2134
Chinese Commissioner of the Imperial Procession Guard, 2155
Chinese Document Registry, 2157

Chinese Documents Section, 2156
Chinese Imperial Guardsman, 2159
Chinese Pass List, 6984
Chinese Soldiers Office, 2136
Chosen Attendant, 2679
Circuit, 3839, 6306
Circuit General, 3757, 3843
Circuit Intendant, 6322
Circuit Intendants, 6327
Circuit Intendants Evaluation Bureau, 1491
Circuit Supervisor, 864
Circuit Surveillance Official, 11
Circulating Offices, 3796
Civil (prefix), 7690
Civil Administration Command, 3320
Civil Appointments Process, 6970, 7701
civil office, 7714
civil official, 7714
Civil Official in Reserve for Imperial Assignment, 7695
civil service prestige title, 7719
civilian family, 3993
Civilian State Farm, 4003
Civilian Student, 4001
Civilizing General, 2818
Claims Section, 1260
Clan Defense Guard Command, 7166
Clan Leader, 4723
class (of rank), 520, 4400, 6344
Classicist, 4007
Classics Colloquium, 1249
Classics Instructor, 1219
Classics Printing Bureau, 7979
Classics Teacher, 1240
Classifications and Estimates Section, 4640
Clearer of the Way, 1276
Clerical Administrative Assistant, 7242
Clerical Aide, 684
Clerical Official, 3651
Clerical Scribe, 5446
Clerical Suboffical, 5452
Clerical Suboffcials of the Six Ministries, 4793
Clerical Subordinate, 8186
Clerical Supervisor, 5409
Clerk: *chang-ku*, 139, 140; *ch'ang-shih*, 263; *cheng ling-shih*, 427; *chu-shih ling-shih*, 1427; *fu-shih*, 2096; *kuan-kou*, 3312; *k'ung-mu, k'ung-mu kuan*, 3503; *li-mu*, 3626; *li-yüan*, 3651; *ling-shih*, 3768; *nei-yüan*, 4297; *pang-shih*, 4445; *pi-te-chen*, 4600; *pi-t'ieh-shih*, 4601; *pien-hsiu wen-tzu*, 4637; *shou-tang kuan*, 5399; *shu-li*, 5445; *shu-piao ssu, shu-piao*, 5454; *t'ieh-ssu*, 6512; *t'ieh-ssu*, 6513; *tien*, 6515; *tien-li*, 6609; *tien-shih*, 6638; *tsu-shih*, 7053; *wen-hsüeh*, 7704; *yüan*,

8219; *yüan-li*, 8231; *yüan-shih*, 8238
Clerk for the Chamberlain for Law Enforcement, 6777
Clerk in the Department of State Affairs, 5050
Clerk in the Imperial Secretariat, 5050
Clerk for Postal Relays in the West, 2245
Clerkly Calligrapher, 3121, 3122, 3124, 3125
Clerks Office, 3313, 4602
Cloth Storehouse, 4788
Clothier, 117, 6575
Clothing Maid, 127
Clothing Office, 5661
Clothing and Rations Section, 2978
Clothing Service, 2006, 5004
Clothing Storehouse, 2963
Clover Pasturage, 4068
Coachman, 679, 1098, 2011
Coachman of the Empress, 1577
Coachman of the Heir Apparent, 6245
Coalyard, 5316
Coastal Defense Circuit, 2126
Coastal Defense Commander, 2129
Coastal Patrol Circuit, 2734
Codification Office, 3886
Coiffure Attendant, 5220
Coinage Circuit, 7916
Coinage Clerk, 7330
Coinage Commissioner, 1373, 6472
Coinage Depot, 4471
Coinage Office, 891, 920, 3229
Coinage Service, 889, 2917, 4469
Coinage Service of the Ministry of Revenue, 4472
Coins and Silks Section, 913
Coins Officials, 1372
Collection Superintendent, 860
Collections Office, 5041
Collections Section, 2874
College, 5129, 6288
College for Broadening Academic Scope, 3353
College for Cultivating the Way, 2632
College for Guiding Human Nature, 5481
College for Making the Heart Sincere, 486
College for Moral Rectification, 418
College for Venerating Determination, 1647
Column Leader, 2163
Command, 4615
Command of the General-in-chief, 5898
Command of a Regional Vice Commander, 2482
Command of an Assistant Regional Commander, 2482
Commandant: *chung-lang chiang*, 1581; *hou*, 2205; *hsiao-wei*, 2456; *k'ua-lan-ta*, 3259; *lang-chiang*,

3564; *ling-chün,* 3753; *shou-pei,* 5393; *shou-yü,* 5406; *shuai,* 5476; *ssu-chün,* 5613; *t'i-hsia ssu,* 6444; *ts'an-ling,* 6888; *tu-wei,* 7326; *wei,* 7657

Commandant of an Administrative Region, 682

Commandant of Agriculture, 4328

Commandant at the Altar of Earth, 6386

Commandant of the Altar of Heaven, 6716

Commandant of Bamboo Crafts, 5603

Commandant of the Bodyguard of the Heir Apparent, 274

Commandant of Bondservants, 4483

Commandant Bulwark on the Left, 6966

Commandant Bulwark of Righteousness, 2065

Commandant of the Capital Gate, 503

Commandant of the Capital Gates, 504

Commandant of the Capital Patrol: *ch'i-pu wei,* 636; *liu-pu li-wei,* 3808; *liu-pu wei,* 3809; *wei-ssu,* 7677; *wei wu-pu,* 7686

Commandant of the Capital Street Patrol, 1245

Commandant of Cavalry, 606, 607

Commandant of Cavalry by Grace, 1813

Commandant of Cavalry Second Class, 6794

Commandant of the Center, 7740

Commandant of the City Gates, 2628

Commandant of Courageous Guards, 2381

Commandant of Fleet-as-clouds Cavalry, 8272

Commandant of Flying Cavalry, 1927

Commandant of Fortifications, 173

Commandant of Garrison Cavalry, 7405, 7406

Commandant of the Gates, 3954

Commandant of Granaries, 1404

Commandant of the Guard, 6666

Commandant of the Guard Command, 5479

Commandant of the Guards Office, 7663

Commandant of Horse Pasturages, 4056

Commandant at the Imperial Ancestral Temple, 6193

Commandant of the Imperial Escort, 5318

Commandant of the Imperial Gardens, 5497

Commandant of the Inherited Region, 7287

Commandant of Light Chariots, 1258

Commandant of the Metropolitan Police, East Sector, 7448

Commandant of the Metropolitan Police, East and South, 3350

Commandant of the Metropolitan Police, North Sector, 4536

Commandant of the Metropolitan Police, South Sector, 4115

Commandant of the Metropolitan Police, West and North, 4018

Commandant of the Metropolitan Police, West Sector, 2266

Commandant of Militant Cavalry, 7741

Commandant for Military Strategy, 7805

Commandant of Military Trustworthiness, 7770

Commandant of Military Virtue, 7828

Commandant of Mobile Cavalry, 8039

Commandant of the Nobles, 1379

Commandant of Plumed Cavalry, 8108

Commandant and Police Commissioner, 1757

Commandant for Rectitude, 2040

Commandant of the Royal Stud, 2409

Commandant of Southern Aborigines, 4105

Commandant of Standby Troops, 2951

Commandant Supporter on the Right, 8068

Commandant Tending the Western Frontier, 4554

Commandant of Waterways, 5496, 5497

Commandant-escort, 2083

Commandant-in-chief, 7310

Commandant-in-chief of Chariots, 1956

Commandant-in-chief of the Customs Barrier, 3333

Commandant-in-chief for Foraging, 5532

Commandant-in-chief of the Granaries, 1070, 5852

Commandant-in-ordinary, 1638

Commandant-steward, 4301

Commander: *chiang,* 690; *chih-hui,* 998; *chih-hui shih,* 1000; *chu-ssu li-tsai,* 1433; *hui-pan,* 2886; *k'ai-fu,* 3103; *o-chen,* 4352; *ping-ma shih,* 4684; *shuai,* 5475; *ssu-ma,* 5713; *ssu-ma tu,* 5717; *ta tu-tu,* 6096

Commander of the Alarm Gun, 861

Commander of the Capital Gates, 507

Commander of Chariots, 366, 8190

Commander Unequalled in Honor, 3105

Commander-general: *tsung-t'ung,* 7163; *t'ung-chih,* 7472; *t'ung-chün, t'ung-chün fu,* 7482; *t'ung-ling,* 7494

Commander-general of the Bondservants of the Three Banners, 4840

Commander-general of the Five Armies, 7759

Commander-in-chief: *ching-lüeh an-fu tu tsung-kuan,* 1233; *ta ssu-ma,* 6039; *ta tu-tu,* 6096; *tu chih-hui shih,* 7199; *tu-tu,* 7311; *tu-t'ung,* 7321; *tu-wei,* 7326

Commander-in-chief of the Alarm Guns, 2555

Commander-in-chief of the Armies, 3755

Commander-in-chief of Frontier Natives, 1873

Commander-in-chief of Infantry and Cavalry, 1774

Commander-in-chief and Regional Inspector, 7318

Commander-Prefect, 7318

Commanderies and Districts, 1758

Commandery, 1731, 7568

Commandery Aide, 1733

Commandery Assistant, 1797

Commandery Chief, 1782

Commandery Defender, 1803

Commandery Deputy, 1798

Commandery Duke, 1767

Commandery Earl, 1779

Commandery General, 1746

Commandery Governor, 1732, 1785

Commandery Grand Mistress, 1793

Commandery Marquis, 1756

Commandery Mistress, 1751, 1754

Commandery Prince, 1800, 6784

Commandery Princess, 1750, 1768, 7103

Commandery-inspecting Censor, 817

Commanding the Troops (prefix), 3286

Commercial Tax Office: *hsüan-k'o ssu, hsüan-k'o chü,* 2669; *shang-shui wu,* 5062; *shui-k'o ssu, shui-k'o chü,* 5498; *shui-k'u ssu,* 5499; *shui-wu ssu,* 5514; *t'ung-k'o ssu,* 7491

Commercial Tax Office for the Capital, 7271

Commissary, 1980, 4275

commission, 67

Commission for Buddhist and Tibetan Affairs, 2654

Commission for Militiamen, 7388

Commission for the Promotion of Religion, 1652

Commissioned with Extraordinary Powers, 5223

Commissioned with Special Powers, 1105

Commissioned with a Warrant, 655

Commissioner, 5197, 5208, 6017

Commissioner of Accounts, 584, 1474, 1475

Commissioner of the Armory, 1740

Commissioner for Arrangements, 1093

Commissioner of the Auxiliary Palace, 2582

Commissioner for Bridges and Roads, 751

Commissioner for Ceremonial Propriety, 3614

Commissioner for Ceremonies, 1244

Commissioner of Clear Proclamations, 284

Commissioner of the Crosswise Ranks, 2166

Commissioner for the Cultivation of Merit and Virtue, 2625

Commissioner of the Directorate of Palace Domestic Service, 7110

Commissioner of the Directorate of Waterways, 5497

Commissioner for the Eastern Pasturages, 7451

Commissioner for Eastern Tributaries, 7434

Commissioner for Estates and Residences, 1503

Commissioner for Fostering Propriety, 1660

Commissioner for Grand Ceremonials, 5985

Commissioner of the Hall of Abundant Happiness, 1215

Commissioner of Herds, 1806

Commissioner for Horse Pasturages, 3904

Commissioner for Hostels and Postal Relay Stations, 7402

Commissioner of the Imperial Encampment, 8208, 8210

Commissioner of the Imperial Granaries, 6231

Commissioner for Incense Offerings, 827

Commissioner for Interpretation and Embellishment, 1871

Commissioner of the Loyang Gardens, 3830

Commissioner of Merit and Virtue, 3485

Commissioner for the Northern Pasturages, 4541

Commissioner for Northern Tributaries, 4545

Commissioner for the Palace Corrals and Stables, 2499

Commissioner of Palace Halls and Parks, 3498

Commissioner of the Park of Broad Vistas, 4759

Commissioner Participating in Control of Military Affairs, 6867

Commissioner for the Pasturages of Yen Prefecture, 7930

Commissioner for Ritual Observances, 6140

Commissioner for Salt Transit Taxes, 7931

Commissioner of the Six Residences, 3780

Commissioner for the Southern Pasturages, 4118

Commissioner for Southern Tributaries, 4106

Commissioner for State Revenue, 7056

Commissioner Supervising the Left Storehouse, 7008

Commissioner Supervising the Sacrifices, 803

Commissioner of the Various Offices, 1435

Commissioner of the Visitors Bureau, 7241

Commissioner of Waterways, 5494, 7282

Commissioner for the Western Pasturages, 2270

Commissioner for Western Tributaries, 2249

Commissioner-Councilor, 5249

Commissioner-escort, 5876

Commissioner-general for Kaifeng, 6474

Commissioner-in-chief, 6017, 7311

Commissioner-in-chief for Tea and Salt, 7920

Commissioner's Agent, 1048

Commissioners of the Three Ranks, 4888

common people, the, 4780

commoner, 4745

Commoner Duke, 3995

Communications Clerk and Prison Aide, 474

Communications Office, 465, 5823, 7466

Communications Section, 1857

Communicator, 216

Community, 1675, 3587, 5128

Community Compact, 2373

Community Elder, 3624

community functionaries, 3609

Community Head, 3589, 5128

Community Self-defense System, 4465

Community Self-monitoring System, 3595

Companion: *chung-yün*, 1642; *nei-yün*, 4299; *p'ei-shih*, 4556; *pin-fu*, 4652; *pin-yu*, 4659; *yu*, 8032

Company: *hsiang-yung*, 2371; *mou-k'o*, 4039; *niu-lu*, 4314; *po-hu so*, 4735; *shao*, 5083; *so*, 5523; *tsu*, 7047; *t'uan*, 7380; *t'uan-lien*, 7383; *tui*, 7390; *t'un*, 7404

Company Commander: *chang-ching*, 107; *ch'ien-tsung*, 927; *fang-chu*, 1899; *mou-k'o*, 4039; *niu-lu*, 4314; *po-hu*, 4733; *po-hu chang*, 4734; *tso-ling*, 6980; *t'uan-chu*, 7381

Company Commander of Bondservants, 4485

Company of Crossbowmen, 4319

Compilation Clerk, 4645

Compiler: *chu*, 1356; *hsiu-tsuan*, 2636; *ssu-shu*, 5769; *tsuan-hsiu kuan, tsuan-hsiu*, 7058; *wu-kuan ssu-shu*, 7794

Compiler Academician, 2631

Compiler of the Imperial Genealogy, 2639

Compiler-in-chief, 7157

Complaint Drum Office, 3245

Complaint Review Office, 3597

Complaints Section, 7571

Complaisant Consort, 5517

Complete Consort, 476

completion of a tour of duty, 1876

Comptroller, 3220

Comptroller's Office, 4894

concurrent: *chien*, 785; *ling, ling ... shih*, 3735; *ling ... kuan*, 3760; *ling-shih*, 3767; *ling ... shih*, 3769; *tai*, 6126

Concurrent Assistant Director (of Hall of Literary Profundity), 3759

Concurrent Controller: *ling, ling ... shih*, 3735; *ling ... kuan*, 3760; *ling-shih*, 3767; *ling ... shih*, 3769

Concurrent Controller of the Directorate of Medication, 3742

Concurrent Controller of the Examination Office, 3762

Concurrent Court Gentleman for Fasting, 3736

Concurrent Manager of the Office of Diplomatic Correspondence, 3314

concurrent temporary appointment, 854

Concurrently Managing, 3312

Concurrently Serving, 2603

Concurrently Serving as (prefix), 3312

Condiments Service, 1319

Confectioner, 6290

Confidential Copier, 5433

Confirmation Test, 2099

Confucian, 3063

Confucian Apprentice, 3082, 7501; 7727

Confucian Official, 3071

Confucian School, 3067

Confucian Temple, 5185

Congratulatory Commissioner, 2656

conscript, 6782

Conscript Section, 7678

Conscripted Troops, 2987

Consolation Graduate, 2824

Consort: *fei*, 1925; *fu-jen*, 2066; *ku-lun o-fu*, 3235; *o-fu*, 4354; *pa-tzu*, 4385

Consort of a Commandery Mistress, 6788

Consort of a District Mistress, 3241

Consort of a District Princess, 6788

Consort Dowager, 6166

Consort of Fulfillment, 1651

Consort of the Imperial Princess, 2187

Consort of State, 3512

Consort-in-ordinary, 1925

Constellation Watcher, 7855

Construction Bureau, 635
Construction Foreman, 2164, 2375, 3398
Construction and Maintenance Office, 7188
Construction Office, 2375, 2434, 8020
Construction Section, 713, 8023
Construction Service, 6662
Construction Storehouse, 5361
Construction Supervisor, 6832, 8026
Consultant, 2324, 6880, 6881, 6884
Consultant in the Review of Sentences, 5152
Consultant in the Secretariat, 6883
Consultant-in-ordinary, 272
Consultation Section, 3018
Consultative Office, 6874
Control Army, 6568
Controller, 6442, 7465
Controller of Accounts, 1071
Controller of the Armies and Guards, 4429
Controller of Coinage, 6454
Controller of Herds Offices, 6455
Controller of Inspections, 6439
Controller of the Memorials Office, 6440
Controller of Military Training and Banditry Suppression, 6443
Controller of Waterways, 3295, 6456
Controller-general, 7497
Controller-general of Postal Relay Stations, 1359
Controller-in-chief, 6099
Convict Barracks at Sweet Spring Mountain, 3129
Convoy Leader, 7857
Cook, 1421, 5752
Cook for Sacrifices, 5795
Cooperating with Third Rank Officials in the Eastern and Western Towers, 7514
Cooperating with Third Rank Officials of the Secretariat-Chancellery, 7481
Copier, 5432
Copiers of Imperial Documents, 5423
Copper Factory, 7493
Copper Smelter, 7517
Copyist: *ch'ao-shih*, 336; *cheng-ming k'ai-shu*, 429; *cheng-ming t'ieh-fang*, 430; *shan-hsieh*, 4955; *shu-shou*, 5459
Copyist Clerk, 338
Copyist of Imperial Books, 2490
Copyreader, 3140
Corps of Expectant Appointees, 2222
Corps Leader, 1516
Correspondence Adjutant, 1972
Correspondence Clerk, 2158, 8005
Correspondence Supervisor, 8006
corvee, *see* requisitioned service
Cost-reduction Office, 5180
Council of State, 1735
Counselor: *chung-i*, 1567; *ssu-i*,

5653; *ts'an-mou kuan, ts'an-mou*, 6889; *yü-yüeh*, 8216
Counselor Duke, 3432
Counselor-delegate, 3510, 3514
Counselor-in-chief, 483, 2337
Counselors of the Heir Apparent, 3434
Courageous Garrison, 3522
Courageous Guard, 2378, 2379, 2457
Courier: *hsing-fu*, 2571; *hsüan-shih*, 2677; *ti-fu*, 6364; *wei-ch'ai*, 7659
Court: *fu*, 2034; *ssu*, 5534; *t'ing*, 6749; *yüan*, 8221
Court Attendant, 1147, 3571
court audience, 312
Court Calendar Office, 3058
Court Calligrapher, 2148, 5306
Court Ceremonial Institute, 2664
Court of Ceremonial Propriety, 3615
Court of Colonial Affairs, 3603, 5739
Court Conference, 2883, 6754
Court Diarist, 5283
Court of Diplomatic Relations, 7516
Court for Education, 3546
Court Examination, 327
Court for Dependencies, 2906
Court Gentleman, 3563, 3573; *also see* Gentleman
Court Gentleman at the Doors, 2786
Court Gentleman Consultant, 1991
Court Gentleman for Bells and Pipes, 1587
Court Gentleman for Carriages, 360
Court Gentleman for Ceremonial Service, 703
Court Gentleman for Ceremonials, 2002
Court Gentleman for Chariots, 1955
Court Gentleman for Comprehensive Duty, 7473
Court Gentleman for Consultation, 2972
Court Gentleman Driver of the Imperial Hand-drawn Carriage, 3711
Court Gentleman for Evaluations, 3449
Court Gentleman for Fasting, 63
Court Gentleman for Forthrightness, 1583
Court Gentleman of the Imperial Forest, 5020
Court Gentleman for the Imperial Livery, 2014, 6560
Court Gentleman for the Imperial Seals, 2058
Court Gentleman by Influence, 5213
Court Gentleman for Instruction, 2655
Court Gentleman for Lecturing, 700
Court Gentleman of Manifest Virtue, 2680
Court Gentleman for Manifesting Rightness, 2666

Court Gentleman for Medical Attendance, 2956
Court Gentleman for Medical Healing, 2949, 3040
Court Gentleman for Medical Practice, 2938
Court Gentleman for Medical Service, 2957
Court Gentleman for Personnel Evaluations, 3195
Court Gentleman for Promoted Service, 6347
Court Gentleman for Records Concerning the Western Barbarians, 1366
Court Gentleman for Regulating the Calendar, 1025
Court Gentleman for Regulating Rituals, 1026
Court Gentleman for Sacrifices and Fasting, 5680
Court Gentleman for Service, 2658
Court Gentleman for Thorough Counsel, 7488
Court Gentlemen of the Three Corps, 4910
Court Herald, 6846
Court of Imperial Armaments, 7809, 7810
Court of the Imperial Clan: *ssu-shu ssu*, 5770; *ssu-tsung ssu*, 5798; *ta mu-ch'in fu*, 5995; *ta t'e-li-kun ssu*, 6062; *ta tsung-cheng fu*, 6082; *t'e-li-kun ssu*, 6339; *tsung-cheng ssu*, 7085; *tsung-jen fu*, 7105
Court of Imperial Entertainments: *ch'ung-lu ssu*, 1666; *kuang-lu ssu*, 3348; *shang-yün shu*, 5082; *ssu-shan ssu*, 5754; *ssu-ting*, 5784; *ssu-tsai ssu*, 5785
Court of the Imperial Granaries, 5576
Court of the Imperial Mausoleum, 3773
Court of the Imperial Regalia, 5808, 7683, 7684
Court of Imperial Sacrifices: *feng-ch'ang ssu*, 1952; *ssu-ch'ang ssu*, 5541; *ssu-li ssu*, 5698; *t'ai-ch'ang ssu*, 6145
Court of the Imperial Saddlery, 4977
Court of the Imperial Stud, 5749, 5837, 6204
Court of the Imperial Treasury, 5626, 6165, 7588
Court of Judicial Inquiry, 42
Court of Judicial Review, 2320, 5637, 5986
Court Lady, 4013
Court of the National Granaries, 5731
Court for the National Treasury, 5731
Court Official, 328, 5177
Court of the Orchid Pavilion, 3561
Court Painter, 2814

Court of Palace Attendants, 2664, 5233
Court for the Palace Garrison, 7683
Court of the Palace Garrison, 7683
Court for the Palace Revenues, 5100, 6165
Court Physician, 5861
Court Scribe, 1837
Court Service Official on the East, 4288
Court Service Official on the West, 4179
Court of State Ceremonial, 2906, 5739
Court Theatrical Office, 4095, 5186
Court of the Watches, 3585, 5667
Court of the Women's Chambers, 238
courtesy, by, 4399
Courtier, 1589
Courtier for Memorials, 7041
Courtier of the Western Terrace, 2273
Courtier-attendant, 5347
Courtier-secretary, 1447
Courts and Directorates, 5583
Cowherd, 4313
Craft Workshop, 7002
Crafts Foreman, 3276
Crafts Institute, 7724
Crafts Office, 1097
Crafts Tax Supervisor, 5571
Craftsman of the Rattan Grove, 7689
Criminal Administration Bureau, 7244, 7245
Criminal Residency Section, 4555
Crossbows Office, 672
Crown Prince, 6968
Cultivated Talent, 2633, 3928
Cupbearer, 1969
Currency Printshop, 317
Currency Supply Service, 316
Custodian of Foreign Visitors, 6600
customs and regulations, 1963
Customs Collector, 689, 2495, 3147, 3271
Customs House, 329
Customs-collecting Censor, 1722

Dame-consort, 495, 2066
Dance Performer, 7818
Dancer, 5815
Dean, 4952, 7426
Deceased Imperial Father, 2837
Deceased Imperial Grandfather, 2871
Decision Expediting Office, 4616
Decorator, 6829
Decree Drafting Office, 2612
defector, 4766
Defender, 7327
Defender of the Capital, 1216
Defender of the Dependent State of …, 5443
Defender Duke, 384, 1977
Defender of the Fief, 3030
Defender of the Hall, 1907
Defender-general of the State, 382

Defender-generalissimo of the State, 385
Defender-in-chief, 3549, 6260, 6261
Defense Brigade, 2778
Defense Chief, 1900
Defense Command, 372, 757
Defense Commissioner, 1898, 1923, 5365
Defense Commissioners and Military Training Commissioners, 1916
Defense Detachment, 5364
Defense Guard Command, 7676
Defense (Prefecture), 1920
Defense Section, 7808
Defense and Security Commissioner, 1924
Defense and Surveillance Commissioner, 1922
Deficits Monitoring Office, 3598
degree (of rank), 6344; also see class
Deliberative Council, 2937
demote, 2288, 6955
Department, 1332, 5176
Department of Administration, 440
Department of Drafters, 5137
Department of Learned and Virtuous Expectant Officials, 7725
Department Magistrate, 965, 4041
Department of Palace Bondservants, Bannermen, and Secretaries, 4222
Department of Scholarly Counselors, 596, 4836
Department of State Affairs, 4263, 5053, 7272
Department Vice Magistrate, 1348
Departmental appointment, 6293, 6295
Departmental Buddhist Registry, 4943
Departmental Clerk, 5187
Dependent State, 5442
Depository, 6897
Depot, 231
Deputy: shu, 5410; ts'ui-che, 7064; t'ung-ch'ien, 7470; t'ung-p'an, 7496; wei-shu, 7675
Deputy Commander, 3790
Deputy General, 4648
Deputy Military and Surveillance Commissioner, 774
Deputy Surveillance Commissioner, 3268
Destroyer of Malicious Birds, 367
detached, 1412, 1934, 4831
detached at, 1458
Detached Company Commander, 7611
Detached Palace, 3622
Detached Police Chief, 4861
Detached as a Retinue Official, 4925
Detached Squad Leader, 7612
Diarist, 545
Dietician, 5257
different, 3697
Dike Supervisor, 851
Diplomacy Office, 3517
Diplomacy Section, 3515

directly attached, 1024
Director: chang, 84; chang-yin yün-hui shih, 222; cheng, 396; cheng-shih, 436; ch'eng-wu, 515; chi-chih chang, 540; chi-shih huang-men, 589; chien, 786; chien-ling, 842; chu-shih, 1420; hsiang, 2303; lang-chung, 3565; ling, 3733; ling-shih, 3767; ling-shih, 3768; ssu-cheng, 5548; ta-chien, 5899; t'ai-chien, 6148; tien-tso, 6661; tsung-li shih-wu kuan-chün shih, 7129; tzu-cheng chung ta-fu, 7523
Director of the Academy, 3281
Director of the Altar of the Soil and Grain, 6210
Director of the Armory, 7781
Director of Astronomy, 5780
Director of Bamboo Crafts, 5601
Director of Brick and Tile Making for the Imperial Mausolea, 3748
Director of the Bureau of Equipment, 676
Director of the Bureau of Evaluations, 5568
Director of the Bureau of Operations, 978
Director of the Bureau of Provisions, 5567
Director of the Bureau of Review, 5569
Director of Calendrical Calculations, 4452
Director of the Capital Boats, 7215
Director of the Capital Garrison, 1582
Director of the Catering Bureau, 5755
Director of Cavalry Mounts, 570
Director of Ceremonial Music, 3656
Director of the Chancellery: huang-men shih-lang, 2847; men-hsia shih-chung, 3941; shih-chung, 5229; shih-nei, 5293
Director of the Chariots Section, 363
Director of the Cloudy Rampart Garrison, 8279
Director of Coinage, 812, 1451
Director of Commerce, 5253, 6902
Director of Construction, 6833, 6834
Director of a Construction Office, 2422
Director of Convict Labor, 5689, 5695
Director of Corporal Punishments, 5635
Director of the Court of the Imperial Clan, 6339, 7106, 7133
Director of the Court of the Watches, 3584
Director of Courtiers, 1590
Director of Defense Works, 5633
Director of the Department of State Affairs, 5049
Director of the Directorate, 796

Director of the Directorate for the Palace Buildings, 5895
Director (of a District Justice Bureau), 2503
Director of Draperies, 4054
Director of Education, 2412, 2698, 7705
Director of Embankments, 6674
Director of Eunuch Attendants, 2844
Director of Eunuchs, 2823
Director of the Finest Steeds, 1772
Director of Fire Renewal, 4626
Director of Food Production, 4324
Director of Food Provisioners, 5276
Director of Grading and Sorting Raw Copper, 4646
Director of Granaries, 5789
Director of the Gun Room, 4302
Director of Hot Baths, 6291
Director of Hydraulic Works, 5511
Director of the Imperial Ancestral Temple, 6191
Director of the Imperial Forest, 5021
Director of the Imperial Granaries, 6230
Director of the Imperial Hunting Chariots, 3852
Director of the Imperial Mares, 670, 7495
Director of the Imperial Mausoleum, 3763
Director of Imperial Music, 2476, 2478
Director of the Imperial Music Office, 8266
Director of the Imperial Observatory, 5782
Director of the Imperial Secretariat, 5049
Director of the Inner Compound Stable, 7687
Director of the Institute, 3281
Director of Interpreters, 2966
Director of Labor, 702
Director of Lances and Shields, 5670
Director of the Livery Office, 357
Director of the Magnificent Iris Garden, 3743
Director of Markets, 5762
Director of Merit Awards, 5640
Director of Military Training, 2747
Director of Mints, 7839
Director of Minters, 1575
Director (of the Music Office), 2004
Director of the Palace, 6559
Director of the Palace Administration, 6558, 6615
Director of the Palace Attendance Service, 6558
Director of Palace Attendants, 4161, 4164, 4238
Director of the Palace Domestic Service, 4240, 5886
Director of Palace Entertainments, 490
Director of the Palace Library, 4588, 4593

Director of Palace Medications, 5075
Director of Palace Physicians, 6174
Director of the Palace Stable, 5907
Director of the Pass, 3317
Director (of a Pasturage), 3023
Director (of the Pasturage for Fine Steeds), 3003
Director of Provisions, 5039
Director of Public Petitions, 6354
Director of the Receipt of Grievances, 7043
Director of Receptions, 1395
Director of the Rosters Bureau, 4017
Director of the Sacred Fields, 602
Director of Sacrifices, 599
Director of Saddles, 5536
Director of the Secretariat, 4236
Director of the Section for Foreign Relations, 1881
Director of the Section for Tributary Relations, 4657
Director of Secular Music, 175
Director of Shields, 5665
Director of Sorcery, 5814
Director of the Ssu-hu, 5645
Director of the Stable, 1307
Director of Studies, 5115, 5821, 6991, 8073
Director of a Subsection, 220
Director of the Temple, 3981
Director of Temple Sacrifices, 3988
Director of Textile Production, 5586
Director of Tombs, 3738
Director of the Township Justice Bureau, 2311
Director of Translations from Afar, 1302
Director of Transport, 871
Director of the Treasury Bureau, 5545
Director of Tributary Trade, 2795
Director of Veterinarians, 4074
Director of the Wardrobe, 6576
Director of the Watches, 3584
Director of Waterways, 7277
Director of Waterways at the Sweet Spring Palace, 3132
Director of Woodcraft Production, 5725
Director of Works, 3446
Director-general, 7156
Director-general of the Capital Granaries, 7161
Director-general of Grain Transport, 6936, 7162
Director-general of the Grand Canal, 2193, 4096, 7159
Director-general of River Defense, 7096
Director-general of Salt Marshes, 7927
Director-general of Supplies, 7160
Director-in-chief, 3848, 7192
Director-in-chief of Brewing, 1699
Director-in-chief of Palaces and Temples, 3445
Director-in-chief of Waterways, 7281

Directorate, 786
Directorate of Agricultural Production for the Loyang Palace, 3829
Directorate for Animal Fodder, 7197
Directorate for Armaments, 1738
Directorate of Armaments, 7742
Directorate of the Armillary Sphere, 2897, 2901
Directorate of Astrology, 6215
Directorate of Astronomy, 1185, 5780
Directorate of Bamboo Crafts, 5602
Directorate of Ceremonial, 5696
Directorate of Ceremonial Propriety, 3612
Directorate of the Ch'eng-hua Horses, 489
Directorate of Coinage, 888, 1370, 3650
Directorate of Construction, 8017
Directorate for Credentials, 7994
Directorate for Documents, 5810
Directorate of the Dragon Horses, 3876
Directorate of the Eastern Parks, 7423
Directorate of Education, 3541, 5554
Directorate for Felt Manufactures, 1593
Directorate of Fine Steeds, 6713
Directorate of General Production, 4742
Directorate of Granaries and Commerce, 6902
Directorate of Herds, 3721, 5026
Directorate of Horse Breeding, 7539
Directorate of Horse Corrals, 2501
Directorate of Horse Pasturages, 4046, 4061
Directorate of Horses, 3896
Directorate for the Imperial Accessories, 169
Directorate for Imperial Accouterments, 8213
Directorate for Imperial Apparel, 5001
Directorate of Imperial Armaments, 8115
Directorate of the Imperial Horses, 8155
Directorate for Imperial Manufactories: *nei-fu chien*, 4176; *shang-fang*, 4992; *shang-fang chien*, 4993; *shao-fu chien*, 5098
Directorate of Imperial Medicine, 6177
Directorate of Imperial Parks, 5024, 8255
Directorate for Imperial Regalia, 5757
Directorate for Imperial Temples, 5156
Directorate of the Imperial Treasury, 6161
Directorate for Intimate Attendance, 7198

Directorate for Leather and Fur Manufactures, 3649
Directorate of Literature, 3031
Directorate of Medication, 129
Directorate of Medicine, 6591
Directorate of Money Circulation, 2111
Directorate for the Mongolian Pastures, 1194
Directorate of Moslem Astronomy, 2881
Directorate of the Northern Parks, 4518
Directorate of Palace Accounts, 3400
Directorate of Palace Attendants, 4241
Directorate of the Palace of Benevolence and Longevity, 3050
Directorate of the Palace of Bright Virtue, 4022
Directorate for the Palace Buildings, 708, 710, 4958
Directorate for Palace Delicacies, 5033
Directorate of Palace Domestic Service, 237, 3486
Directorate of Palace Eunuchs, 4205
Directorate of the Palace Kennels, 3205
Directorate of the Palace Library, 4588, 4598
Directorate of the Palace at Loyang, 1259
Directorate for Palace Maintenance, 1075
Directorate of the Palace Ruins Park, 1290
Directorate of Palace Seals, 5027
Directorate of the Park of Lasting Pleasure, 250
Directorate of Personnel Evaluation, 3155
Directorate for the Receipt of Edicts, 468
Directorate for the Reverence of Literature, 1669
Directorate of Sacrifices, 5825
Directorate of Salt Distribution, 5822
Directorate of the Southern Park, 4091
Directorate for the Temple to Chuang-tzu, 645
Directorate of the T'o-ch'üan Horses, 6790
Directorate of Tributary Trade, 738, 2795, 7504
Directorate of Water Crossings, 1377
Directorate of Waterways, 5493, 5593, 7278
Directorate of the Western Parks, 2233
Directorate of the Wild Horse Pasturage, 6329
Directorate-general of the Imperial Parks, 3499
Directorate-general of the Palace of the Perfect Cycle, 1293

Directorate-in-chief of Fruits, 3547
Directorates of Parks of the Four Quadrants, 5722
Directors of Calendrical Calculations in the Five Offices, 7790
Directors-in-chief Section, 3604
Directress of Accounts, 5561
Directress of Ceremonial Regalia, 5537
Directress of Clothing, 5652
Directress of Foods, 5752
Directress of Foodstuffs, 5605
Directress of the Inner Gates, 5649
Directress of the Inner Quarters, 5681
Directress of the Library, 5559
Directress of Music, 5844
Directress of Palace Surveillance, 5548
Directress of Rarities, 5543
Directress of Records, 5562
Directress of Standards, 5792
Directress of Transport, 5833
Directresses, 5533
Disciple, 3950
Disciple of the Son of Heaven, 6722
Disciplinarian, 6280, 7668
Disciplinarian of Attendants, 5732
Disciplinary Commissioner, 4965
Disciplinary Office, 5157, 5181
Discipline Officer, 7858
Discipline Section, 4966
Discussant of Secretariat Affairs, 5006
dismiss, 1457, 2694
Dispatcher and Expediter, 4725
Dissemination and Inquiry Official 100
Disseminator, 6276
Distinguished Garrison, 2730
Distinguished Imperial Relative, 2722
Distribution Office, 1853
District, 2304, 2492, 5859
District Agent, 7300
District Assistants, 2544
District Baron, 2524
District Buddhist Registry, 4945
District Commandant, 658
District Defender, 2549
District Duke, 2512
District Earl, 2345, 2526
District Elder, 2338
District Grand Master, 2353, 5874
District Grand Mistress, 2541
District Jailor, 6638
District Judge, 2350, 5872
District Justice Bureau, 2503
District Magistrate, 993, 2518, 3737
District Marquis, 2506
District Minister, 4008
District Mistress, 2502
District Official, 2510
District Preceptor, 2351, 5873
District Prince, 2548
District Princess, 2500, 7051
District Vice Magistrate, 3909

District Viscount, 2546
Divination Director, 4768
Divination Instructor, 4775
Divination Master, 4796
Divination Student, 4798
Diviner, 77, 4761, 4783
Diviner by the *Classic of Changes,* 2996
Diviner with Stalks, 5267
Division, 4764, 7380
Division Commander, 1790, 4648
Division of the Five Armies, 7760
Division of the Five Thousand, 7747
Division of the Three Thousand, 4845
Divisional Gatherer, 4773
Divisional Subaltern, 4774
Divisions and Companies, 4810
Divisions and Regiments, 4776
Divisions and Squads, 4812
doctoral degree, *see* Presented Scholar, Metropolitan Graduate
doctorate, *see* Presented Scholar, Metropolitan Graduate
Document Clerk, 6533
Document Drafting Office, 5138
Dog Cage, 3206
Domestic Customs-house, 3263
Domestic Servant, 668, 3633
Domestic Service of the Empress, 1531
Domestic Service of the Heir Apparent, 6243
Doorkeeper, 2899
Double Sewing Service, 5487
Dough Pantry Supervisor, 1694
Drafter: *chih-chih-kao,* 955; *chu-kao,* 1391; *chung-shu she-jen,* 1618; *she-jen,* 5136
Drafter on Duty in the Secretariat, 1046
Drafters in the Southern Department, 4117
Drafters in the Southern Palace, 4103
Dragon, 3873
Dragon Diagram Hall, 3878
Dragon Throne, 3879
Drum and Fife Section, 3230
Drum and Fife Service, 3230
Drummer, 5673
Ducal Establishment, 3426
Duck Hunter, 6972, 7555
Duke, 3388
Duke for the Abundant Perpetuation of Excellence, 7989
Duke of the Collateral Line, 1723
Duke of the Eight Banners, 4360
Duke for Fulfilling the Sage, 7951
Duke for Honoring the Sage, 2013
Duke of the Household, 2330
Duke of the Imperial Clan, 7152
Duke for the Propagation of Culture, 7703
Duke of State, 3525
Duke of Supreme Sageliness, 2673, 4463

Duke of Tsou, 7035
Dukedom, 3448
duty assignment, 67
Duty Attendant, 462, 6546
Duty Chief for Lamps and Water
   Clocks, 6346
Duty Group, 1862, 4400
Duty Group Chief, 3765
Duty Group Head, 1886
Duty Group Leader, 7852
duty pay, 947
Dyeing Office, 3044, 5662
Dyeing Service, 3045
Dyer, 3043
dynastic capital, 1188
Dynastic Elder, 3509
dynasty, 312, 340
Dynasty-founding (prefix), 3106
Dynasty-founding Baron, 3117
Dynasty-founding Commandery
   Duke, 3108
Dynasty-founding Commandery Earl,
   3109
Dynasty-founding Commandery
   Marquis, 3107
Dynasty-founding District Baron,
   3113
Dynasty-founding District Duke,
   3112
Dynasty-founding District Earl, 3114
Dynasty-founding District Marquis,
   3111
Dynasty-founding District Viscount,
   3115
Dynasty-founding Duke, 3116
Dynasty-founding Earl, 3118
Dynasty-founding Marquis, 3110
Dynasty-founding Viscount, 3119

Eagle Cage, 6494
Earl, 4718
Earl of Subordinate States, 4444
East (prefix), 7420
East Administration, 7429
East Bureau, 7461
East Commissioner, 7451
East Dyeing Office, 7435
East Echelon (of Ministries), 7430
East Surveillance Jurisdiction, 7459
East Weaving Shop, 7424
Eastern Court, 7422
Eastern Depot, 7421
Eastern Directorate of Coinage, 4505
Eastern Library, 7439
Eastern Mint, 7460
Eastern Office, 7452
Eastern Palace, 7440
Eastern Section, 7458
Eastern Storehouse, 7437
Eastern Tower, 7453
Eastern Turkestan Bureau, 3557
Eastern War Prisoner, 2973
Eastern and Western Storehouses,
   7432
Eccentric, 3358
Economic Overseer, 1354
Economic Stabilization Office, 1788
Edict Attendant, 6129

Edict Carrier, 1499
Editing Clerk, 741
Editor: *chia-cheng kuan*, 724;
   chiao-shu lang, 742; *ch'ou-chiao*,
   1349; *chu-tso chiao-shu lang*,
   1440; *hsiang-ting*, 2355;
   hsiang-ting kuan, 2358
Editor of Chinese, 723
Editorial (prefix), 1440
Editorial Assistant, 750, 4632, 6127
Editorial Assistant for Calligraphy,
   5460
Editorial Clerk, 1440
Editorial Director, 1442
Editorial Examiner, 883
Editorial Office, 826, 2360, 6128
Editorial Proofreader, 1440
Editorial Service: *chu-tso chü*, 1441;
   kuei-fang, 3365; *ssu-ching chü*,
   5595; *ssu-wen chü*, 5811;
   tien-ching chü, *tien-ching fang*,
   6549
Education Intendant, 6486
Education Intendant Circuit, 6451,
   6486, 7233
Education Official, 2411
Education-intendant Censor, 6452
Education-supervising Commissioner,
   7232
Educational Aide, 6585
Educational Assistant, 726, 1708
Educational Official, 733, 2696,
   2701
Educational Posts, 715
Educational Retainer, 7711
Eight Banners, 4358
Eight Chinese Banners, 2135
Eight Dukes, 4371
Eight Executives, 4381
Eight Grand Masters of the
   Ministries, 4376
Eight Great Families, 4378
Eight Manchu Banners, 3913
Eight Mongol Banners, 3967
Eight Privileges, 4366
Eight Review Sections, 4365
Eight Sabled Dignitaries, 4380
Eight Services, 4364
Eight Statesmen, 4373
Eight Tribal Overseers, 4377, 4379
eight-legged essay, 4370
Eighth Class Administrative Official,
   7343
Elder, 4876
Elders of the People, 5444
Elders of the State, 3526
Elegant Consort, 3606
Elegant Scholar, 1759
Elementary School, 2406
Elephant-training Office, 2738
elite, the, 5148, 5162, 5200
Elite Academy, 5287
Elite Army, 4991
Elite Guard, 5944
Elite Soldier, 5200
Elucidator, 767
Emblem Maker, 1202

Emblem Office, 1203
Embroidered-uniform Guard, 1127
Embroiderer, 961
Embroidery Office, 7699, 7700
Emergency Reserves Storehouse,
   1975
Emperor: *huang-ti*, 2866; *jen-chu*,
   3048; *t'ien-huang*, 6702
Emperor Emeritus, 6208
employment of sons, 3054
Empress: *hou*, 2206; *huang-hou*,
   2836; *t'ien-hou*, 6698; *wang-hou*,
   7643
Empress Dowager, 2860, 6698
Empress Dowager Regent, 2861
Empress and Four Chief Consorts,
   the, 2209
Empress's Usher, 695
Encampment, 7419, 8009
Encampment Guard, 7418
Endorsement-copying Office, 4611
enfeoff, 1967
Enfeoffed Beile, 2188
Enforcer of Agreements, 5845
Enlightenment Library, 508
Entertainers, 4935
Envelope Keeper, 119
Envoy: *hsin-shih*, 2556; *kung-shih*,
   3471; *shih-che*, 5208; *shih-ch'en*,
   5209; *shih-chieh*, 5219
Equitable Exchange Depot, 346
equitable exchange of grain for salt,
   3100
equitable exchange of rice for salt,
   1640
equivalent to, 4570, 5203
erase the name from the register,
   2694
Erudite, 2686, 2696, 4746, 5553
Erudite for Acupuncture, 388
Erudite of Astronomy, 6727
Erudite of the Calendar, 3628
Erudite of the Chamberlain for
   Ceremonials, 6143
Erudite of Chess, 634
Erudite of Chuang-tzu and Lao-tzu,
   1507
Erudite of the *Classic of Writings*,
   5051
Erudite of the Classics, 1220
Erudite of the Clerical Script, 3123
Erudite of the Court of Imperial
   Sacrifices, 6143
Erudite of Divination, 4795
Erudite Exalter of the Six Classics,
   4950
Erudite for Exorcism, 1338
Erudite for Exposition of the
   Classics, 692
Erudite of Fancy White Calligraphy,
   1932
Erudite for General Medicine, 2989
Erudite of History, the Masters,
   Belles Lettres, and Narrative, 5331
Erudite of Law, 3887
Erudite Literatus, 4732
Erudite for Massage, 24

Erudite of Mathematics, 5858
Erudite of the National University, 3543
Erudite for Palace Instruction, 3401
Erudite of the Palace Music School, 4154, 7992
Erudite of Promise, 4731
Erudite of Recitation, 8008
Erudite Scholasticus, 4730
Erudite of the Seal Script, 1489
Erudite Supervising Instruction, 830
Erudite of the Supreme Unity, 6181
Erudite of the True Word, 452
Erudite of Veterinary Medicine, 5378
Erudite of the Water Clock, 3834
Erudite of the Yellow Emperor's Classic of Medicine, 4165
Erudites of the Five Classics, 7752
Escort, 2739, 5871, 6670
Escort Brigade, 163
Escort Brigade Commander, 6568
Escort Carriage Rider, 3855
Escort Commissioner, 765
Escort for Court Audiences, 5860
Escort Guard, 2802
Escort Guide, 7867
Escort Immortal, 7667
Escort Office, 2354
Escort Officer, 1012
establish officials, 5139
Establishment, 8221
Estimator, 5799, 7553
eunuch: *chung-kuan,* 1574; *huan,* 2821; *huan-che,* 2822; *huan-jen, huan-kuan,* 2827; *nei-ch'en,* 4144; *nei-chien,* 4155; *nei-kuan,* 4203; *nei-shih, ssu-jen,* 5663; *yen,* 7918; *yen-jen,* 7940
eunuch (prefix), 3077
Eunuch Apprentice, 2380
Eunuch Attendant, 1
Eunuch Ceremonial Secretary, 4149
Eunuch Chief of Palace Attendants, 4148
Eunuch Commissioner of the Flying Dragon Corral, 4174
Eunuch Counselor-in-chief, 1538
Eunuch Director, 5390
Eunuch Director of Standards, 1546
Eunuch Duty Group, 4247
Eunuch Escort, 5663
Eunuch Fan-bearer, 4139
Eunuch of Fifth Rank, 6655
Eunuch Gate Monitor, 4150
Eunuch Grand Commandant, 5394
Eunuch of the High Duty Group, 4244
Eunuch of High Rank, 4245
Eunuch Huller, 1664
Eunuch Liquor Maker, 698
Eunuch Manager, 4156
Eunuch Manager of the Academy, 7874
Eunuch Master of the Wardrobe, 4260
Eunuch Musician, 1454

Eunuch Protector of the Mausoleum, 5389
Eunuch Protector-general of the Mausolea, 5394
eunuch rank titles, 4239
Eunuch Rectification Office, 4145
Eunuch Sacrificer, 2323
Eunuch School, 4257
Eunuch Seals Secretary, 4177
Eunuch Supervisor-in-chief, 7118
Eunuch Wine Maker, 1303
eunuchs, 4887
Eunuchs and Palace Women, 2828
evader, 4787
evaluation, 1705, 3149
evaluation for reassignment, 4030
Evaluations Clerk, 1707
Evaluations Section, 3202
Evaluations and Selections Office, 3150
Evaluator, 2324
Ever Full Granary, 252
Ever Full Haybarn, 278
Ever Normal Granary, 257
Ever Normal Granary Office, 258
Ewes Service, 7547
Exalter of the Six Classics, 3781
examination, 5204
Examination Administrator, 1020
Examination Aide, 6495
Examination Aides, 3710
Examination Candidate, 5329
Examination Casualty, 4490
Examination Commissioner, 7993
Examination Copyist, 6358
Examination by Grace, 1820
Examination Grader, 6389
Examination Graduate, 1848
Examination Graduates, 3190
Examination Manager, 6567
Examination Master, 6958
Examination Monitor, 5530
Examination Office, 3497
Examination Official, 5273
Examination Overseer, 858
Examination Sealer, 2005, 3976
Examiner: *chiao-shih lang,* 739; *chien-cheng kuan, chien-cheng,* 800; *chien-lin,* 841; *chu-k'ao,* 1392; *chu-ssu,* 1430; *fang-chü,* 1901; *fang-k'ao kuan,* 1906
Examining Editor, 868
Examining Official, 1426, 3154
Exchange Manager, 2922
Excoriator of Evil, 6499
Executioner, 157, 5805
Executive, 460, 3103
Executive Assistant, 583
Executive Assistant in the Ministry of State, 6705
Executive Attendant, 259
Executive Attendant-in-chief, 5887
Executive Censors, 7293
Executive Office (of Department of State Affairs), 7272, 7293
Executive Official, 423, 939

Executive Official of State, 6734, 6737, 6741, 6744
Executive Officials, 115
Executive Police Chief for the Southwest, 2261
Exemplar, 3381
Exhorter, 451
Exorcist, 6596
Expectant (prefix), 2177
Expectant Appointee, 2213, 2220
Expectant for Early Appointment, 1126
Expectant Examinee, 5526
Expectant Official, 6127
Expectant Physician, 3006
Expectant Star Watcher, 6582
expedited selection, 555
Expediter of Canal Transport Boats, 7072
Expediter of Shipment and Distribution, 7071
Expediter of Shipments, 7070
Expediting Office, 7066
Expediting Section, 7065
Expert Archer, 5134
Expositor-in-waiting, 3576, 5215
Expounder, 7932
Express Courier, 1696
Express Courier Office, 1697
Exterminator, 859, 1108
External Secretary, 7604
extraordinary promotion, 315, 335, 343

Facilitated Candidate. 6342
Fair Tax Office, 1766
Falcon Cage, 8011
Family Unifier, 7077
Fan Bearers Office, 4962
Fan Maker, 6628
Fast Courier, 536
Fattener of Sacrificial Animals, 1662
Favored Lady, 1658
Fear-proof Army, 350
Fellow (in School for the Sons of the State), 4419
Female Attendant, 4347
Female Banquet Caterer, 4339
Female Basket Handler, 4343
Female Cook, 4330
Female Huller, 4335
Female Liquor Maker, 4331
Female Palace Attendant, 4341
Female Provisioner of Sacrificial Wine Covers, 4342
Female Scribe, 4345
Female Storekeeper, 4336
Female Supplicant, 4334
Female Wine Maker, 4333
Feudal Lords, 1383
Feudatory Prince, 1384
fief, 2925, 6301; *also see* land grant
Field Investigator, 2596
Fierce as Leopards Cavaliers, 4464
Fifteen Circuits, 5340
Fifth Day Audience Officers, 3819
File (of soldiers), 5196

File Clerk, 86
File Leader, 4393, 5214
Finance Planning Commission, 956, 6500
Fineries Storehouse, 1140
Finished Leather Goods Service, 5453
Fire Captain, 2916
Fire Director, 5678
Firearms Brigade, 2915
Firearms Division, 5145
first, 650
First Category (of graduates), 2943
First Chosen, 3284
First Class Administrative Official, 396
First Distinguished Garrison, 2741
First Graduate, 770
First Manchu Duty Group, 3921
First Priority Expectant Appointee, 8127
First Section, 4972, 498?
First Scholar, 28
First Standby Garrison, 2960
First Veterinarian Directorate, 4984
First-class Prince, 3026
Fiscal Commission, 1492, 6929
Fiscal Commissioner, 1090, 1490
Fiscal Commissioner-in-chief, 7212
Fiscal Controller, 1363
Fiscal Secretary, 432
Fiscal and Supply Commissioner, 1204
Fishing Supervisor, 8146
Five, 7733
Five, the, 7732
Five Altars, 7748
Five Armies of the Imperial Encampment, 8211
Five Bureaus, 7822, 7842
Five Cages, 7761
Five Categories of Tribute Students, 7799
Five Chief Military Commissions, 7758
Five Chief Stewards, 7816
Five Commanders, 7749
Five Commissioners, 7819, 7823
Five Departments, 7817
Five Directorates, 7746
Five Garrisons, 7763
Five Grand Masters, 7825
Five Grand Ministers of the Deliberative Council, 2940
Five Groups, 7842
Five Imperial Armies, 8123
Five Inspired Armies, 5171
Five Lesser Banners, 2301
Five Lesser Ministries, 7831
Five Market Masters, 7757
Five Notable Graduates, 7751, 7798
Five Offices, 7762, 7783
Five Sections, 7831
Five Sections of the Ministry of Revenue, 2793
Five Sectors, 7812
Five Wards, 7737

Flag Assistant, 8277
Flag Assistant Serving as Assistant Director of the Imperial Procession Guard, 2473
Flute Master, 8271
Flutist, 5607, 8257
Fodder Section, 3685
Fodder Yard, 6924
Food Provisioner, 1882, 5274
Food Provisioners Office, 1882
Food Section, 1867
Food Service, 5040
Food Steward, 4954, 4967
Food Taster, 4661
Foods Office, 5753, 6632
Foods Service, 6631
Footwear Provisioner, 1681
for Court Service (prefix), 3418
Forager, 7669
forced labor, 73, 7889
forced labor for a minor offense, 6802
Ford Guardian, 1122
Ford Master, 1117
Foreign Language Student, 2995
Foreign Music-master, 6595
Foreign Office, 7127
Foreign Relations Office, 3627
Foreman: *cheng chien-tsao*, 401; *chih-chang*, 938; *li-ts'ung kuan*, 3646; *po-fu chang*, 4727; *tien-shih*, 6637; *ts'ui-chang*, 7063; *ts'ui-tsung*, 7073; *tsung-ling*, 7134, *tu-mu*, 7259
Foreman Curator of Calligraphy and Painting, 4422
Forest of Fine Phrases, 7563
Forest Manager, 8148
Forest of Plumes Army, 8151
Forest Tax Supervisor, 5725
Foresters, Hunters, and Fishers, 9132
Formation Monitor, 4394
Forward Scout, 897, 900
Foundry, 3166
Foundry Directorate, 7910
Foundry Office, 213
Foundryman, 7368
Four Appointments Processes, 5638
Four Artisan Services, 5611
Four Bureaus, 5745
Four Capital Townships, 5631
Four Categories of Troops, 5742
Four Circuit Supervisorates, 5484, 5584
Four Circuit Supervisors, 5584
Four Classifications, 5745
Four Controllers, 5629
Four Defenders, 5807
Four Departments, 5759
Four Directorates, 5581
Four Dragon Guard Wings, 3880
Four Duty Groups, 5587
Four Elite Armies, 5063
Four Field Defense Armies, 2606
Four Great Tribes, 5775
Four Households, 5644

Four Imperial Armies, 5614
Four Imperial Armies of the North Gates, 4528
Four Inspired Guard Wings, 5168
Four Luminaries, 5636
Four Offices, 5774
Four Offices of the Grand Princes, 5776
Four Principal Consorts, 5619
Four Sections, 5617, 5791
Four Sections of Imperial Secretaries, 5055
Four Sun-sustaining Wings, 4568
Four Supports, 5623
Four Surveillance Censors, 5804
Four Treasuries, 5675
Four Wings of Heaven-endowed Militancy, 6730
Fourth Class Administrative Official, 3882
Friend, 8032
Front Echelon (of Ministries), 895
Front Section (of Palace Domestic Service), 916
frontier, 4631
Frontier Defense Office, 1214
Frontier Defense Supply Commission, 1207
Frontier Defense Vault, 4534
Frontier Earl, 1879
Frontier Guardsmen, 3098
frontier pass, 3263
Frontier Post Commander, 5425
Frontier Prefecture, 1868
Frontier Tribal Troops, 1878
Frontier-defense Military Prefecture, 3556
Frontrider, 2519
Fruit Provisioner, 3524
Fruits Pantry, 3511
Fuels Service, 70
Full 2,000 Bushels, 1551
Fulminator, 7049
functional office, 1015
Functionary, 3882, 4940; *also see* Subofficial Functionary
functioning official, 1015, 1055
Fundamental laws, 2491
Fundamental Laws and Regulatory Principles, 2508, 2547
Funeral Director, 1042
Funerary Chanter, 4936
Funerary Park, 8218

Garden, 8218
Garden Service, 5841
Garden of Total Clarity, 8235
Gardener, 225, 247
Gardens Office, 5842
Garrison, 372, 1753, 2034
Garrison Commandant, 513
Garrison Commandant at the Sweet Spring Palace, 3131
Garrison of the Imperial Mausoleum, 3747
Garrison Militia, 2093
Garrison Prince, 7832

Gate Commandant, 506
Gate Commander, 2771
Gate Commissioner, 3326
Gate Gentleman-attendant, 27
Gate Guard, 843
Gate Guard Command, 846
Gate Guardsman, 629
Gate Tender, 845
Gate Tender for the Six Ministries, 3807
Gate Traffic Control Office, 3394
Gate Watcher, 4396
Gatekeeper: *chang-wei*, 209; *men-p'u*, 3949; *ssu-ko*, 5669; *ssu-men*, 5718
Gatekeepers Service, 3451
Gateman, 3953
Gatherer of Aromatic Plants, 8145
Gauze Service, 4951
Gauze Supervisorate, 4951
Genealogist, 1092
Genealogy Section, 5417
General: *cheng-chiang*, 398; *chiang*, 690; *chiang-chün*, 694; *hsiang-kun*, 2328; *hsiang-wen*, 2367; *ta-fang*, 5934
General Accounting Office, 7258
General Accounts Section, 7201, 7609
General Administration Circuit, 1943, 5400
General Administration Circuits and General Surveillance Circuits, 5375
General of the Army, 1745
General Bulwark of the Han, 2056
General Bureau, 4000, 7148
General Clerk, 1077
General of the Cloud-like Flags, 8276
General Commanding the Troops, 3287
General Deficits Monitoring Office, 7252
General by Grace, 1978
General of the Guards, 7661
General of Light Chariots, 1257
General Manager of Attendants, 479
General of the Militant Guard, 7835
General of Military Brilliance, 7769
General of Military Merit, 7800
General of Mobile Cavalry, 8038
General Money Circulating Office, 7210
General of the Pacification Army, 2053
General for Pacifying Faraway Lands, 6746
General of the Palace, 6557
General of the Palace Guard, 3754
General Palace Service, 5013
General of the Personal Guard, 908
General Purpose Censor, 5352
General Section, 7108
General Services Office, 5817
General Surveillance Circuit, 1941, 2762

General Surveillance and Military Defense Circuit, 1940
General Wastage Monitoring Office, 7265
General-in-chief, 5897
General-in-chief Commanding the Troops, 3291
General-in-chief Serving as Commander-in-chief, 6041
General-purpose Clerk, 7783, 7797
General-purpose Section, 7796
Generalissimo, 4982
Gentleman, 3563; *also see* Court Gentleman
Gentleman for Astronomical Observation, 7644
Gentleman for Attendance, 478, 7177
Gentleman Attendant at the Palace Gate, 2847, 5232
Gentleman Attendant-in-ordinary, 266, 275
Gentleman Brave as Tigers, 2788
Gentleman of the Capital Gates, 505
Gentleman Cavalier Attendant, 4835, 4837
Gentleman for Closing Court, 333
Gentleman Companion in Loyalty, 2463
Gentleman of Complete Loyalty, 469
Gentleman for Court Audiences, 318
Gentleman for Court Discussion, 325
Gentleman for Court Service, 321
Gentleman for Discussion, 498
Gentleman for Forthright Service, 1970
Gentleman for Fostering Temperance, 461
Gentleman for Fostering Uprightness, 467
Gentleman for Fostering Virtue, 514
Gentleman for Good Service, 2611
Gentleman for Governmental Participation, 7170
Gentleman of the Interior, 3565
Gentlemen of the Interior for Miscellaneous Uses, 7788
Gentleman of the Interior for Regulating the Calendar, 1027
Gentleman of the Interior Serving as Cavalry Commander, 3567
Gentleman of the Interior Serving as Chariot Commander, 3566
Gentleman of the Interior Serving as Director of Archivists, 3568
Gentleman of the Interior Serving as Gate Commander, 3569
Gentleman of the Interior Serving as Receptionist, 3335
Gentleman for Loyal Service, 7174
Gentleman for Managing Affairs, 511
Gentleman for Meritorious Achievement, 6374
Gentleman Observer, 7650
Gentleman for the Ordinary Wardrobe, 239

Gentleman of the Palace Gate, 2843
Gentleman of the Palace Guard, 8153
Gentleman for Perfect Health, 481
Gentleman for Proper Attendance, 439
Gentleman for Rendering Service, 516
Gentleman for Service, 590, 7178
Gentleman Summoned to Office, 407, 4708
Gentleman for Summoning, 438
Gentleman for Thorough Service, 7506
Gentleman of Trust, 485
Gentleman for Trustworthy Service, 1983
Gentleman-attendant, 3563
Gentleman-Confucian, 3074
Gentleman-litterateur, 7717
gentry, the, 1145, 5148, 5162
Gerfalcon and Hawk Aviary, 7888
Gifts and Presentations Section, 4978
Gifts Section, 5074
Glossy Paper Maker, 5421
Glossy Paper Maker and Mounter of Scrolls, 5422
Goat-cart Driver, 7876
Gold Factory, 1129
Gold and Silver Service, 1168
Gold and Silver Workshop, 1169, 4994
Gold Thread Service, 1152
Good Fortune Guard, 2029
Government, the, 410, 3294
Government Physician, 3300
Government Pottery Works, 6328
Government Property Rental Agency, 3293
Government School, 3298
government service, in, 5007
Government Student, 5193
Governmental Reform Service, 2610
Governor, 6111, 6221, 7969
Governor Assisting in Administration, 7528
Governor Companion in Rectitude, 2462
Governor Participating in Administration, 6849
Governor (of Province), 2731
Governor-general, 7158
Governor-general's Command, 7263
Governors-general and Governors, 7227
Gracious Consort, 2878
grade (of rank), 1482, 6344; *also see* class
Grader, 7392
Graduate for Excellence, 8062
Graduate in the Five Classics, 7750
Graduate in the Nine Classics, 1295
Graduate with Highest Honors, 2120
Graduate (of school), 2704
Grain Measurer, 5703
Grain Requisition Depot, 2195
Grain Tax Circuit, 3663, 3688

Grain Tax Supervisor, 5790
Grain Transactions Section, 6501
Grain Transport Brigade, 8281
Grain Transport Commander, 6935
Granaries Bureau, 5828, 6907
Granaries Office, 6659, 6950
Granaries Section, 6904, 6907, 6908, 6910
Granaries and Yards, 6901
Granary, 4327, 6899
Granary at Ao, 32
Granary Manager, 5705, 6903
Granary Master, 3725, 5789
Granary Section, 6900
Granary Supervisor, 6911
Granary at the Sweet Spring Palace, 3131
Granary-inspecting Censor, 49, 2763, 2764, 6483
Grand (prefix), 5878
Grand Academician, 4445, 5962
Grand Academician of the Academy of Scholarly Worthies, 7561
Grand Adjutant, 6891
Grand Agricultural Administration, 6044
Grand Astrologer, 6212, 6218
Grand Canal Storehouse Circuit, 2179
Grand Charioteer, 6115
Grand Chef for External Ceremonies, 7615
Grand Chef of the Palace, 4295
Grand Clansman, 6081
Grand Commandant, 5393
Grand Commissioner for Merit and Virtue, 5976
Grand Competition, 6006
Grand Coordinator, 2731
Grand Councilor: ch'eng-hsiang, 483; hsiang, 2303; hsiang-kuo, 2337; p'ing-chang, 4699; tsai-hsiang, 6819; yüan-lao, 8229
Grand Councilor in the Palace, 4181, 4274
Grand Councilor-in-chief, 5889
Grand Councilors of the Eight Palace Offices, 4219, 4367
Grand Counselor, 6117
Grand Counselor-in-chief, 5889
Grand Defender, 390
Grand Director of Music, 6262, 6268
Grand Diviner, 6008, 6197
Grand Empress Dowager, 6169, 6384
Grand Executive Attendant, 6142
Grand Guardian, 6195
Grand Guardian of the Heir Apparent, 6257
Grand Guardian of Herds, 1811
Grand Guest, 6007
Grand Imperial Secretary, 6013
Grand Lady of the Commandery, 1792
Grand Lord of the Commandery, 1792

Grand Marshal, 6026, 6120
Grand Marshal Military Commissioner, 6027
Grand Master, 2098, 5939
Grand Master Admonisher, 6859
Grand Master for Admonishment, 1985
Grand Master for Assisting toward Good Governance, 7524
Grand Master for Assisting toward Goodness, 7537
Grand Master for Assisting toward Virtue, 7541
Grand Master of Cemeteries, 4069
Grand Master for Closing Court, 334
Grand Master Companion in Loyalty, 2463
Grand Master for Complete Wholeness, 470
Grand Master for Consultation, 1992
Grand Master of Court Audience, 339
Grand Master for Court Audiences, 319
Grand Master for Court Discussion, 326
Grand Master for Court Precedence, 330
Grand Master for Court Service, 2659
Grand Master for Excellent Counsel, 660
Grand Master Exemplar, 1560
Grand Master for Forthright Service, 1971
Grand Master of Forthrightness, 1584
Grand Master of the Gates, 3951
Grand Master for Glorious Happiness, 3090
Grand Master for Glorious Happiness with Silver Seal and Blue Ribbon, 7980
Grand Master for Governance, 1961
Grand Master of Guests, 5740
Grand Master of Imperial Entertainments with Silver Seal and Blue Ribbon, 7981
Grand Master Inspector, 5942
Grand Master of the Livery, 1965
Grand Master of the Palace, 1627
Grand Master of Palace Accord, 1623
Grand Master for Palace Attendance, 1552
Grand Master of the Palace Corral, 1958
Grand Master for Palace Counsel, 1569
Grand Master of the Palace with Golden Seal and Purple Ribbon, 1159
Grand Master of Palace Leisure, 1591
Grand Master for Perfect Health, 482
Grand Master Preserver of the Emperor's Health, 4475

Grand Master for Proper Consultation, 417
Grand Master for Proper Service, 409
Grand Master of Remonstrance, 831, 865
Grand Master for Splendid Happiness, 3349
Grand Master of State, 3537
Grand Master for Thorough Counsel, 7490
Grand Master for Thorough Service, 7484
Grand Master for Venerating the Sage, 1667
Grand Master for Virtuous Service, 2021
Grand Mentor, 6158
Grand Mentor of the Heir Apparent, 6256
Grand Minister, 5888, 6150
Grand Minister Assistant Administrator of Tibet, 1438, 4443
Grand Minister Assistant Commander, 4846
Grand Minister Assistant Commander of the Imperial Guardsmen, 4262
Grand Minister in Attendance, 8120
Grand Minister in Charge of the Weaving and Dyeing Service, 3279
Grand Minister Commander, 1234
Grand Minister Commanding the Guard, 210
Grand Minister for the Confirmation of Appointments, 7935
Grand Minister Consultant, 6885, 6893
Grand Minister of Education, 6052
Grand Minister Examiner, 8261
Grand Minister of the Imperial Household Department, 4262
Grand Minister of the Imperial Household Department Concurrently Controlling the Imperial Guardsmen, 3771
Grand Minister Inspector of the Altars and Temples, 531
Grand Minister Inspector of the Central Drafting Office, 527
Grand Minister Instructor, 730
Grand Minister Preparer of the Altars and Temples, 4514
Grand Minister Protector of the Imperial Mausolea, 5376
Grand Minister of the Rear Watch, 2214
Grand Minister Resident of Tibet, 1438
Grand Minister serving as Assistant Director of the Official School in the Palace of Complete Contentment, 2472
Grand Minister for the Southern Seas, 4132

Grand Minister of State, 1737, 5925
Grand Minister Superintendent of Ch'ing-hai, 7123
Grand Minister Superintendent of the Music Ministry, 7132
Grand Minister Supervisor of the Imperial Household Department, 7115
Grand Minister Supervisor (of Palace Stud), 3327
Grand Minister of the Vanguard, 930, 933
Grand Minister of Works, 6037
Grand Ministers Commanding the Eight Banners, 4361
Grand National Commander-in-chief, 6700
Grand Physician, 5967
Grand Pillar of State, 5916
Grand Preceptor, 5250, 6213
Grand Preceptor of the Heir Apparent, 6258
Grand Prince, 6103
Grand Princess, 150, 7638
Grand Princess-cognate, 6206
Grand Protector, 6093, 6221
Grand Protectorate, 6094
Grand Scribe, 6018, 6212
Grand Secretariat, 4193, 6783
Grand Secretariat Academician Reader-in-waiting, 4197
Grand Secretariat Reader-in-waiting, 4196
Grand Secretary, 5962
Grand Secretary of the Grand Secretariat, 4199
Grand Steward, 6068, 6823
Grand Storekeeper, 6031, 6053
Grand Stylist, 6101
Grand Supplicator at Yung, 8100
Grand Treasurer, 5940
Grandee of the Eighteenth Order, 6021
Grandee of the Eighth Order, 3465
Grandee of the Eleventh Order, 8076
Grandee of the Fifteenth Order, 5111
Grandee of the Fifth Order, 5939
Grandee of the First Order, 3472, 3698
Grandee of the Fourteenth Order, 8057
Grandee of the Fourth Order, 4786
Grandee of the Nineteenth Order, *see* Marquis of Kuan-nei
Grandee of the Ninth Order, 7824
Grandee of the Second Order, 5067
Grandee Secretary, *see* Censor-in-chief (*yü-shih ta-fu*)
Grandee of the Seventeenth Order, 5542
Grandee of the Seventh Order, 3480
Grandee of the Sixteenth Order, 6014
Grandee of the Sixth Order, 3330
Grandee of the Tenth Order, 6997
Grandee of the Third Order, 4015, 6024, 6856

Grandee of the Thirteenth Order, 1571
Grandee of the Twelfth Order, 6974
Grandee of the Twentieth Order, 359, 7485
Grandson Successor, 6222
Grandson-heir, 5314
Grave Maker, 1570
Gravetender, 160
Great Border Prefecture, 5932
Great Consort, 6157
Great Court Conference, 5966
great reckoning, 5891
Great Sacrificial Butcher, 6226
Great Sacrificial Butcher at Yung, 8101
Great Steward, 6225
Great Supplicator, 6152, 6154
Great Tribal Chief, 6079
Great Within, 5998
Green Palace, 1270
Green Standards, 3862
Grievance Office, 3393
Groom, 123, 3039, 3502, 7055
Group, 6497
Group Leader, 5412
group of, 3697
guaranteed recommendation, 4450, 4468
guaranteed selection, 4480
Guard, 7658, 7664
Guard Command, 5478
Guard Commander, 2376
Guard Commander at the Customs House, 3290
Guard Honoring the Inner Apartments, 1661
Guard of the Jade Strategy, 8122
Guard of the Leopard Strategy, 4497
Guard in Personal Attendance, 4539
Guard of the Staircase, 5580
Guardian, 4450
Guardian of the Left, 6985
Guardian of Rectitude, 5359
Guardian of the Right, 8051
Guardian of the Waterways, 1497
Guardians of the Customs and Laws, 1982
Guards Brigade, 2780
Guards of the Hunting Preserve, 5405
Guardsman, 2775, 3637, 7674
Guest, 4650
Guides for Blind Musicians, 5285
Guides and Followers, 6325
Gunpowder Office, 2919

Halberd Office, 2124
Halberdier, 941
Half Company, 4406
Half Company Commander, 4406
Hall: *ko*, 3167; *tien*, 6516; *t'ing*, 6748
Hall for Aid in Governance, 7525
Hall for the Diffusion of Literature, 2114, 2684
Hall of Enlightened Rule, 4021

Hall of Heavenly Manifestations, 6686
Hall of Literary Profundity, 7729
Hall of Literature, 3382
Hall for Making Literature Illustrious, 2550
Hall of Military Glory, 7840
Hall for the Preservation of Harmony, 4478
Hall for Treasuring Culture, 4502
Hall for Treasuring the Heritage, 4492
Hall for the Veneration of Governance, 1645
Handler of Divination Bamboo, 1520
Handler of Imperial Edicts in the Northern Bureau of Military Affairs, 591
Hanlin, 2141
Hanlin Academician, 2142
Hanlin Academician Recipient of Edicts, 2143
Hanlin Academy, 2144, 2154
Hanlin Bachelor, 5419
Hanlin and Historiography Academy 2147
Harvesting Office, 6840
Hawk Cage, 2782
Hay Yard, 6918
Head: *chang*, 84; *cheng*, 396; *k'uei*, 3381; *t'ou-mu*, 6799
Head of the Censorate, 6136
Head Cook, 852
Head of Food Provisioners, 5275
Head of the Left Section, 7012
Head of the Livery Service, 4817
Head of Physician Families, 3302
Head of the Right Section, 8091
Headquarters: *cheng-t'ang*, 444; *fu-mu*, 2084; *fu-tuan*, 2110; *kung-t'ang*, 3484; *mu*, 4040; *ta-t'ang*, 6060; *t'ang*, 6288
Headquarters Aide, 6857
Headquarters Adjutant, 7860
Headquarters Bureau (in Censorate), 6263
Headquarters Bureau Director, 6299
Headquarters Bureau at the East Palace Gate, 4287
Headquarters Bureau (in Ministry of Rites), 3631, 5694, 5797
Headquarters Bureau (in Ministry of Works), 3462, 5744
Headquarters Bureau (in Palace Eunuch Service), 4284
Headquarters Clerk, 3940, 6302, 7869
Headquarters Clerk (in District), 6781
Headquarters Functionary, 7861
Headquarters of the General-in-chief, 5898
Headquarters of the Imperial Bodyguard, 3770, 5336
Headquarters of a Marshal, 8245
Headquarters Office, 7285
Headquarters Secretary, 6292

Headquarters Section (in Imperial Music Bureau), 6265
Headquarters Section (in Ministry of War), 633
Headquarters Supervisor, 3946
Headquarters Troops, 7865
Heavenly Horseman, 6687
Heavenly Horsemen of Inspired Militancy, 5170
Hegemon, 4357
Hegemons and Kings, 4386
Heir, 5328
Heir Apparent, 2863, 6239
Heir Apparent Once Removed, 2868
Heir Apparent Twice Removed, 2873
Heir Apparent's Nine Directorates of Horse Pasturages, the, 7441
Heir of a Commandery Prince, 206, 1801
Helmets Section, 1345
Herald, 4024
Herbal Garden, 7905
Herbs Repository, 5190
Herd Director, 1804
Herder, 7382
Herding Officials, 1808
Herds Office, 1807, 1808, 7803, 7804
hereditary, 499, 5247
Hereditary Army, 2112
Hereditary Consort, 5245
Hereditary by Grace, 1824
Hereditary Nobility, 1728
hereditary office, 5270
Hides Storehouse, 4610
High Court of Justice, 6082, 7083
high expectations, 1279
high repute, 1279
hired employee, 3469
His Eminence, 6003
His Honor, 3388, 3580, 5983, 6234
His Majesty: ch'eng-yü, 518; huang-shang, 2852; huang-t'a, 2856; shang, 4970; ta-tsun, 6080; ta-yeh, 6109; yüan-shou, 8242
Historiographer, 1488, 5271
Historiography Academy, 3536
Historiography Institute, 3534, 5272
Historiography and True Records Institute, 3535
History of the Dynasty, 3529
Holder of the Silks, 1041
Honor, 4004
Honorable, The, 3388
Honorable Failure, 2037
honorary, 647
Honorary Emperor, 6208
Honorary Marquis, 7662
Honorary Official, 2745
Honored (prefix), 7635
Honored Concubine, 3374
Honored Consort, 3366
Honored Ranks, 3362
Honored Student, 3579
honorific, 648
Honors Bureau, 3849

Honors Section, 1997
Horn Collector, 731
Horse Appraiser, 3898
Horse Herd, 4051
Horse Management Section, 1035
Horse Pasturage, 786, 3900
Horse Pasturage Section, 4062
Horse Pasturage Service, 5726
Horse Pasturage Supervisor, 848
Horse Purchasing Office, 1206, 8159
Horse Purchasing Service, 8159
Horse Recorder, 510
Horse Station, 8254
Horse Team Supervisor, 8131
Horse Trade Censor, 2715
Horse Trading Office, 48, 1282
Horse Trainer: hsi-ma hsiao-ti, 2260; hsi-yü, 2282; mu-shih, 4066; p'ai-ma, 4395; sou-jen, 5531; tsou-ma, 7036
Horse-skinning Office, 4612
Horse-training Office, 2748
Horses Office, 3903
Horses Section, 523
Hostel for Imperial Clansmen, 3339
Hostel for Imperial Kinsmen, 2226, 7403
Hostel for Tributary Envoys, 5618
Hostess, 171
Household Aide, 654
Household Administration of the Empress Dowager, 2875
Household Administration of the Heir Apparent, 80, 6240, 7378
Household Affairs Office, 6635
Household Affairs Service, 6634
Household Guard, 3502
Household of an Imperial Princess, 3005
Household Provisioner, 669, 5625
Household Provisioner for the Princess, 3409
Household Provisioner's Court, 3430
Household Sacrificer, 686
Household Service for the Empress, 1536
Household Service for the Heir Apparent, 1458
Household Serviceman, 678
Household Sorcerer, 688
Housekeeping Service, 4986
Houseman, 5136
Houseman Receptionist, 7985
Hsi Tribes, 2258
Humble Man, 2138
Humble Official, 2138
Hundred Bushels, 4747
Hundred Cavaliers, 4720
Hunter, 5379
Hunting Charioteer, 6710
Hunting Office, 6009
Hunting Preserve, 7660
Husbander, 4940

I-shih Tribes, 3001
Icehouse, 720, 4670
Image Hall, 8021

Imperial (rank prefix), 1104
Imperial Academy of Calligraphy, 2153
Imperial Academy of Medicine, 6184, 8143
Imperial Adviser, 8162
Imperial Agent, 630
Imperial Ancestral Temple, 6188
Imperial Ancestral Temple Office, 6192
Imperial Ancestral Temple Service, 6190
Imperial Archives, 4578
Imperial Armies, 1124, 1175, 6720
Imperial Armies Support Commission, 7836
Imperial Armies Tactical Defense Commission, 3874
Imperial Army of Original Followers, 8247
Imperial Arsenal, 1085
Imperial Attendant, 5259, 8117
Imperial Attendant Dietician, 5262
Imperial Bodyguard: ch'ieh-hsieh, 782; chin-i wei, 1127; ch'in-chün ying, 1178; kung-feng shih-wei, 3425; pei-shen, 4537; pei-shen fu, 4538; san-lang wei-shih, 4875; shih-wei ch'in-chün, 5334; su-wei, 5854
Imperial Bondservant, 2850, 4482
Imperial Brewery, 1700
Imperial Capital Park, 1904, 2891, 5166
Imperial Carriageman, 659
Imperial Chancellor, 483
Imperial Clan, 7150
Imperial Clan Prison, 3501
Imperial Clansmen, 2857
Imperial Clansmen Guards, 7153
Imperial Clansmen Guards of the Three (Superior) Banners, 4842
Imperial Clanswoman, 3172, 7142
Imperial Cloth Vault, 7625
Imperial Coachman, 491
Imperial Commissioner, 1256, 1600, 8053
Imperial Corral, 6692
Imperial Council, 2838
Imperial Councilor, 2838
Imperial Defense Command, 8209
Imperial Diarist, 620, 3575
Imperial Diarist and Rectifier of Omissions, 619
Imperial Diary, 617
Imperial Diary Office, 618, 624, 3056
Imperial Directorate of Medicine, 5002
Imperial Dispensary, 5178, 8204, 8205, 8206, 8207
Imperial Divination Office, 6200
Imperial Divination Service, 6198
Imperial Diviner, 6197, 6199
Imperial Documents Office, 5369
Imperial Editor, 5919

Imperial Emergency Reserves Storehouse, 8116
Imperial Entourage, 354
Imperial Escort, 3889
Imperial Falcon Cage, 7887, 8012
Imperial Family Monitor, 7080
Imperial Forest, 5016
Imperial Forest Park, 5023
Imperial Game Preserve, 4303, 8160
Imperial Garden, 1141
Imperial Garden of Delicacies, 8138
Imperial Gatekeeper, 2841
Imperial Genealogy Office, 8194
Imperial Genealogy Section, 2864
Imperial Granaries, 6227
Imperial Granaries Office, 6232
Imperial Granary for Fine Grain, 8136
Imperial Grandmother, 6194
Imperial Grandson-heir, 2862
Imperial Guard, 1177, 4985, 5333
Imperial Guard Duty Group Commander, 5338
Imperial Guards, 2830
Imperial Guardsmen, 1139, 1175, 5333
Imperial Guardsmen of the Three (Superior) Banners, 4841
Imperial Hairdresser, 5462
Imperial Hawk Aviary, 7856, 7886
Imperial Hay Barn, 8157
Imperial Heir Once Removed, 2832 2854
Imperial Honored Consort, 2840
Imperial Horse Office, 8158
Imperial Horse Pasturage, 4067
Imperial Household Department, 4291
Imperial Hunting Office, 5080
imperial in-law: *hung tai-tzu*, 2907; *kuo-yin*, 3550; *wai-ch'i*, 7580; *wai-chia*, 7582; *wai-she*, 7603
Imperial Insignia Guard, 1166
Imperial Kennels, 3207, 7881
Imperial Kitchen, 8124
Imperial Larder, 3459, 4292
Imperial Library, 8188
Imperial Lumber Depot, 2848
Imperial Manufactories Commission, 714
Imperial Marquises, 1383
Imperial Mausolea Administration, 509
Imperial Mausoleum, 3734, 3746
Imperial Medical Office, 6183
Imperial Medical Service, 6173, 6179
Imperial Medical Supervisor, 6177
Imperial Messenger, 7987
Imperial Money Vault, 7628
Imperial Mother: *huang t'ai fu-jen*, 2859; *t'ai-mu*, 6194; *t'ai-shang huang-hou*, 6207; *ti t'ai-hou*, 6383
Imperial Music Bureau, 6016
Imperial Music Office, 5172, 5173, 6269
Imperial Music Service, 6267

Imperial Nephew, 3528
Imperial Oarsman, 543
Imperial Observatory, 3774, 7789
Imperial Painting Academy, 2152
Imperial Palace, 1123, 5527
Imperial Parks Administration, 1960
Imperial Parks at the Eastern Capital, 7456
Imperial Perfume Service, 8137
Imperial Physician: *cheng feng-shang t'ai-i*, 408; *feng-shang t'ai-i*, 2010; *t'ai-i cheng*, 6174; *t'ai-i ling*, 6180; *yü-i*, 8139; *yü-shih*, 8168
Imperial Physician-in-attendance, 5348, 5351
Imperial Prince, 1186, 2184, 2872, 8203
Imperial Princess: *ho-shih kung-chu*, 2186; *jen*, 3047; *kung-chu*, 3408; *p'i-jen*, 4609; *ti-i*, 6368
Imperial Princess of the First Degree, 3234
Imperial Prison, 309
Imperial Prison in the Imperial Forest, 5017
Imperial Procession Guard, 3865, 3869
Imperial Regalia Commissioner, 2933
Imperial Regalia Office, 2983
Imperial Regalia Service, 2983
Imperial Seals Commission, 6598
Imperial Secretariat, 1619, 5057
Imperial Secretary, 5042
Imperial Sedan-chair Office, 8149
Imperial Silk Manufactory, 1083
Imperial Silk Vault, 7626
Imperial Son-in-law, 1939, 3519, 3521
Imperial Study, 1032
Imperial Summer Resort, 7660
Imperial Tomb, 3734, 3746
Imperial Treasures Vault, 7627
Imperial Treasury, 6696, 6717, 7260
Imperial Uncle, 2851, 2853
Imperial Wardrobe, 5005
Imperial Wardrobe Service, 1389, 8140
Imperial Wardrobe Service of Shih Tao-an, 8141
Imperial Winery, 1300, 5077
Imperial Workshop, 3157
Imperially Related Adjutant, 3508
Imperially Related Secretary, 3508
Important, 1116, 7894
impure, 1330
In Charge of, 1354
In Charge of the Affairs of, 3325
in government service, 5007
in rotation, 3871
In Translation (prefix), 1870
in unoccupied status, 4890
in-chief (prefix), 5878
inadequate (evaluation category), 4772
Incense Handler, 5630
Incorruptible, 3701

Independent, 1024
Independent Battalion, 5407
Industrial Prefecture, 786
Infantry Commandant, 4794
Inherited Region, 7181
Inner (prefix), 4137
Inner Aides, 4213
Inner Banners, 4151
Inner Branch of the Palace Library, 4595
Inner Capital Townships, 4180
Inner College, 4232
Inner Court, 1533, 4142, 4267
Inner Drafters, 4158
Inner Examiners, 4213
Inner Gates Office, 5809
Inner Gentleman, 1580
Inner Guard Command, 4258
Inner Hostel, 4204
Inner Mongolian Bureau, 614
Inner Mongolian Reception Bureau, 7646
Inner Nobleman, 4214, 4216
Inner Noblewoman, 4215, 4217
Inner Offices, 4259
Inner Officials, 4203
Inner Palace Doors, 5714
Inner Palace Library, 4223
Inner Posts, 4160
Inner Prison, 4155
Inner Quarters, 162, 4173
Inner Section, 4226
Inner Stables, 4167
Inner Storehouse of the Left, 4280
Inquiry Agent, 1450
Inquisitor, 7720
Insignia Office, 2934
Inspecting Censor, 807
Inspection Station, 5524
Inspector: *chi-ch'a*, 524; *chien . . . shih*, 857; *tien-chien kuan*, 6531; *yü-hou*, 8134
Inspector of the Armies, 3288, 7275
Inspector of the Four Quarters, 87
Inspector of Governmental Integrity, 3703
Inspector of the Imperial Granaries, 866, 6231
Inspector of Law Enforcement, 6769
Inspector of Medicine and Food, 6530
Inspector of Postal Relay Stations, 3301
Inspector of Provincial Coinage Services, 525
Inspector of Public Morality, 2019
Inspector of Receipts and Disbursements at the Imperial Granaries, 6228
Inspector of Regulations, 1091
Inspector-general, 717, 7297
Inspector-general of the Army, 3907
Inspector-in-chief, 7334
Inspector-in-chief of the Four Duty Groups, 5591
Institute, 8221
Institute of Advanced Study, 5415

Institute for the Advancement of Literature, 2911
Institute of Education, 7708
Institute of Eternal Splendor, 5381
Institute for the Extension of Literary Arts, 3352
Institute for the Glorification of Literature, 307
Institute of History, 7721
Institute of Imperial Diarists, 546
Institute for Improving Governance, 2941
Institute of Indulgences, 3069
Institute of Literary Attendants, 7707
Institute of Litterateurs, 3720, 7716, 7697
Institute for Propagation of the Tripitaka, 1496
Institute for Study of the Polite Arts, 2244
Institute for the Veneration of Literature, 1670, 1671
Institute for the Veneration of Worthies, 1653
Instructional Officials, 716
Instructor: chiang-shu, 705; chiang-shu chiao-shou, 706; chiao-hsi, 729; chiao-shou, 740; chiao-yü, 747; chih-shih chiao-yü, 1053; chu-chiao, 1367; wen-hsüeh, 7704; wen-hsüeh shou-chu yüan, 7709; wen-hsüeh yüan, 7713
Instructor for the Preparation of Presented Scholars, 963
Integrated Division, 7389
Intendant for Chahar, 3221
Interior Maintenance Maid, 178
Interior Maintenance Office, 5758
Internal Accounts Secretary in the Headquarters Section of the Ministry of Revenue, 4186
Internal Accounts Section, 1695
Interpreter, 2924, 5135, 7492
Interpreter of Dreams, 78
Interpreter-clerk, 2981, 3041, 3198, 7503
Interpreters Institute, 2889
Interpreters and Translators Institute, 2890
Interrogator, 4421
Intimate Minister, 4321
Inventory Office, 1686
Investigating Censor, 795
Investigating Commissioner, 792
Investigation Bureau, 56
Investigation Commissioner: ch'a-fang shih-che, 43; lien-fang shih, 3708; lien-shih, 3715; tsai-fang shih, 6826
Investigation Section, 8, 37, 39
Investigation Section for Certificates and Fees, 3209
Investigation and Supervisory Commissioner, 6825
Investigations Office, 7398
Investigative Section of the Left, 7014

Investigative Section of the Right, 8093
Investigator, 804, 3208, 7397
Investigator of Wrongs, 44
Investigatory Aide, 7394
Investigatory Official, 3707
Iron Market, 6510
Iron Monopoly Office, 6508
Iron Section, 6502
Iron Smelting Office, 6514
Iron-helmet Prince, 6509
Irregular Candidate, 4362
irregular functionary, 4878
irregular paths (into officialdom), 3022
irregular troops, 4892
Irrigation Chief, 1692
Irrigation Circuit, 5500
Irrigation Intendant, 5500

Jade Crafts Service, 8110
Jade Crafts Supervisorate, 8126
Jade Service, 3336
Jadeworker, 5830
Jail Warden, 8214
Jailor: chang-ch'iu, 110; jen-shu yüan, 3051; ta-shih, 6019; tien-yü, 6677
Jailor of the Central Prison, 5646
Jeweler, 89
Jewelry Service, 8003
Jewelry Storehouse, 1957
Joint Sacrificer, 2175
Jointly (prefix), 7464
Jointly Manager of Affairs with the Secretariat-Chancellery, 7480
Jointly Manager of Important National Affairs, 7498
Judge: chen-fu, 374; tuan-shih, 7372; tuan-shih kuan, 7375; t'ui-kuan, 7399
Judicial Administrator, 4413, 4813, 6878
Judicial Bureau, 3608
Judicial Clerk, 6757
Judicial Commission, 2537, 6447, 6449
Judicial Commissioner, 14, 6445, 6473
Judicial Control Office, 5154
Judicial Inspector, 7765
Judicial Intendant, 1033
Judicial Office, 1854, 2531, 7376
Judicial Offices Clerk, 1854
Judicial and Penal Administrator, 29
Judicial Registrar, 7374
judicial review, 4030
Judicial Secretary, 3647
Judicial Section, 1725
Judicial and Tea and Salt Commission, 6448
Junior, 5084, 6949, 8033
Junior Administrator, 3104
Junior Appointments Process, 5280
Junior Civil Appointments Process, 5281
Junior Clerk, 2211

Junior Compiler, 4635
Junior Dancing Master, 2403
junior eunuch, 4254
Junior Executive Attendant, 5086
Junior Grand Councilor, 2454
Junior Grand Master, 2299
Junior Grand Master of the Palace, 5094
Junior Guardian, 5110, 7864
Junior Guardian of the Heir Apparent, 6252
Junior Guardsman, 3558
Junior Guardsman-gamekeeper, 3559
Junior Lieutenant, 2375
Junior Maid, 5114
Junior Master, 5113
Junior Mentor, 5096, 7853
Junior Mentor of the Heir Apparent, 6251
Junior Messenger, 2401
Junior Military Appointments Process, 5282
Junior Minister, 2292
Junior Music Director, 2451
Junior Officials of the Two Departments, 2417
Junior Palace Attendant, 2443
Junior Preceptor, 2431, 5113, 7866
Junior Preceptor of the Heir Apparent, 6253
Junior Rectifier, 1534
Junior Remonstrator, 2389
Junior Scribe, 2430
Junior Serviceman, 2298
Junior Steward, 5122
Junior Subaltern, 5107
Junior Supplicator, 2394
Junior Three Judicial Offices, 2428
Junior Writer, 2395
Juniors, 5411
Jurchen, 3064, 3065
Justice and Rites Office, 2584
Justice Section, 2562, 2569, 2602
Justiciar, 579
Justiciar of the Administrative Region, 678
Justiciar of the Domain, 1912
Justiciar of the Inherited Region, 7274

Karluk Brigade, 2125
Keeper of Accounts, 7059
Keeper of the Altars, 201
Keeper of Charcoal, 193
Keeper of Clamshells, 179
Keeper of Consumables, 1037
Keeper of Dried Meats, 2247
Keeper of Dyes, 133
Keeper of Fibers, 136
Keeper of Fruits, 152
Keeper of Gems, 167
Keeper of Hides, 170
Keeper of Horse Herds, 6195
Keeper of Lumber, 197
Keeper of the Palace Keys, 5819
Keeper of the Peace, 1137
Keeper of Sacrificial Animals, 124

Keeper of Sacrificial Sheep, 7880
Keeper of Sacrificial Wines, 248
Keeper of the Seal, 102
Keeper of Seals, 167
Keeper of Security, 139
Keeper of Silks, 1040
Keeper of the Storehouse, 141
Keeper of the Temple Treasures, 6695
Keeper of Thistles, 205
Keeper of the Water Clock, 156, 3837
kesig, 782
Khan (of Hsiung-nu), 4968
Kiln Office, 7903
King, 3048, 7634
Kipchak Guard, 1174
Kitchen Director, 4508
Kitchen Helper, 1469
Kitchen Supervisor, 1478
Kite Cage, 7896
Korean Relations Institute, 7515
Kwangtung Customs Superintendent, 8263

Labor Crew Foreman, 3278
Labor Foreman, 4782
Labor Section, 3489, 3491
Lackey, 7873
Lady, 23, 640
Lady for Admonishment, 6860
Lady of Bright Beauty, 310
Lady of Bright Counsel, 3354
Lady of Bright Countenance, 289
Lady of Bright Deportment, 288
Lady of Bright Instruction, 3342
Lady of Bright Loveliness, 287
Lady of Bright Models, 4011
Lady of Bright Rectitude, 3337
Lady of Bright Tranquillity, 300
Lady of Bright Trustworthiness, 4016
Lady of Broad Instruction, 3343
Lady of Brilliant Deportment, 7897
Lady of Brilliant Models, 2877
Lady of Brilliant Patterns, 2892
Lady of Brilliant Virtue, 7900
Lady of Captivating Deportment, 7939
Lady of Chaste Beauty, 5472
Lady of Chaste Countenance, 5439
Lady of Chaste Deportment, 5435
Lady of Clear Instruction, 286
Lady of Clear Purity, 4020
Lady of Complaisant Constancy, 5515
Lady of Complaisant Countenance, 5520
Lady of Complaisant Deportment, 5519
Lady of Complaisant Loveliness, 5518
Lady of Complete Beauty, 1672
Lady of Complete Complaisance, 5516
Lady of Complete Countenance, 1665

Lady of Complete Deportment, 1659
Lady of Complete Loveliness, 1657
Lady of Cultivated Beauty, 2640
Lady of Cultivated Countenance, 2624
Lady of Cultivated Deportment, 2620
Lady of Cultivated Instruction, 2618
Lady of Cultivated Loveliness, 2619
Lady of Decorous Service, 1988
Lady of Elegance, 6839
Lady of Elegant Appearance, 8228
Lady of Elegant Brightness, 3924
Lady of Elegant Deportment, 8227
Lady of Esteemed Virtue, 1668
Lady of Exalted Excellence, 3875
Lady of Excellent Beauty, 3691
Lady of Excellent Employment, 3678
Lady of Fragrant Deportment, 1905
Lady of Fragrant Excellence, 1919
Lady of Fragrant Loveliness, 1903
Lady of Graceful Beauty, 2589
Lady of Handsome Fairness, 780
Lady of Harmonious Virtue, 2194
Lady of Inherent Excellence, 494
Lady of the Inner Chamber, 500
Lady of Kind Deportment, 7624
Lady of Kind Loveliness, 7623
Lady of Kind Manner, 7629
Lady of Lovely Countenance, 3089
Lady of Manifest Excellence, 2663
Lady of Manifest Intelligence, 2672
Lady of Manifest Rectitude, 2665
Lady for Miscellaneous Uses, 7783
Lady for Night Attendance, 7907, 7911
Lady of Noble Deportment, 3369
Lady in Palace Attendance, 4346
Lady of Perfect Loveliness, 4311
Lady of Perfect Radiance, 4312
Lady of the Precious Bevy, 4489
Lady of Proper Loveliness, 414
Lady of Proper Virtue, 445
Lady of Quiet Instruction, 1222
Lady of Respectful Instruction, 1221
Lady of Respectful Kindness, 1247
Lady of Respectful Trustworthiness, 1218
Lady of Reverent Gentleness, 3431
Lady for Service, 3418
Lady of Suitability, 2961
Lady of Supreme Deportment, 5965, 6170
Lady of Talents, 6830
Lady of True Models, 373
Lady of Vast Counsel, 2913
Lady of Vast Excellence, 2904
Lady of Vast Virtue, 2908
Lady of Virtue, 5438
Lady of Virtuous Deportment, 6332
Lady Who Could Comfort a Multitude, 4488
Lady Who Pleases the Spirit, 8154
Lady Without Impurity, 7756
Lady of Worthy Deportment, 2507
Lama Office, 3555

Land Assessor, 1763
Land Forces, 3853
land grant: *fen-ti*, 1947; *pu-lo*, 4792; *t'ang-mu i*, 6301; *t'ou-hsia*, 6797; *ying-p'an*, 8015; *also see* fief
land-grant nobles, 5258
Land Tax Section, 8054, 8063
Land Tax Supervisor, 5800
Lantern Keeper, 195
Lanterns Office, 5778
Large and Small Woodworking Service, 5950
Lattice and Trellis Factory, 3713
Law Clerk, 974, 4010, 6774
Law Code Office, 1112
Law Codification Section, 6738
Law Compliance Official, 5867
Law Examination, 4009
Law Graduate, 4009
Law Office, 4306, 5728
Law School, 3885
Law Section, 116, 1857
Law of Triple Avoidances, 4862
Laws Office, 1854
Leader, 690, 6798
Leader of Court Gentlemen, 1581, 3564
Leader of Court Gentlemen in Charge of Music, 5712
Leader of Court Gentlemen for Miscellaneous Uses, 7787
League, 7, 3955, 4764
Leather and Horns Warehouse, 4608
Leatherwork Service, 4613
Lecture Hall, 5522
Lecturer, 699, 944, 5521
Lecturer-companion, 4401
Left, 6949
Left Account, 6953
Left Aide, 6951
Left Army, 6961
Left Bureau, 7004, 7013, 7363
Left Charioteer, 7021
Left Defender of the Capital, 6957
Left Corps, 6996
Left Court of Review, 7000
Left Guard, 6965, 7015
Left Leader, 6954
Left Office, 6999
Left Office of the . . ., 6999
Left Palace Attendant, 6994
Left and Right, 7016
Left and Right Guard, 7020
Left and Right Guards, 7020
Left and Right Offices, 7018
Left Scribe, 6990
Left Section, 7012
Left Section for Foreign Relations, 6959
Left Section of Servicemen, 6995
Left Sector, 6986
Left Service Office, 6988
Left Storage Section, 7007
Left Storehouse, 6975, 7006, 7009
Left Storehouse Office, 7010
Left Subsection, 6998
Left Tribunal, 7001, 7023

Left Vault, 7006, 7009
Legal Counselor, 975
Legal Erudite, 3891
Legal Erudite for the Chamberlain for Law Enforcement, 6773
Legal Examiner, 1849
Legal Research Section, 820
Legal Researcher, 819, 821
Legal Researcher for Investigations, 7396
Legal Secretary, 2573, 2586, 2587
Lesser (prefix), 4785
Lesser Concubine, 2297
Lesser Grand Master of the Palace, 7850
Lesser Scholastics, 4025
Lesser Subordinates, 8243
Lesser Wife, 8109
Levied Service Section, 5320
Liaison Hostel, 6360, 6382
Liaison Hostel in the Capital, 6361
Liaison Hostel for the Commandery, 1794
Liaison Hosteler, 6372, 5376
Liao-Shen Circuit, 3694
Libationer, 542
Librarian: *chang-chi*, 92; *hsien-ma*, 2519; *ssu-ching*, 5594; *ssu-ching ta-fu*, 5596; *t'u-shu shih*, 7354
Library of the Academy of Scholarly Worthies, 552
Library for Complete Discernment, 7140
Library Clerk, 6642
Library (of Confucian estate), 3385
Library Office, 5564
Lieutenant, 2375
Lieutenant Chancellor, 483
Light Tender, 5639
List of Adequates, 4532
List Leader, 1500
List of Expectant Appointees, 1535
Literary Erudite, 862
Literary Institute, 7715
Literatus Companion, 7712
litterateur, 3351
Livery Office, 356, 358
Livery Service: *ch'e-yü chü*, 369; *feng-chia chü*, 1964; *shang-ch'eng chü*, 4976; *shang-chiu chü*, 4989
Livery Service for the Empress, 4227
Livery Service of the Heir Apparent, 6246, 8165
Living Buddha, 2801
Local Administrators, 3764
Local Agent, 2586
local army, 7346
Local Authority, 3492, 7052
Local Courier Station, 4825
Local Elder, 2338
Local Inspector, 7332
Local Militia, 2342
Local Militia Squad, 4503
Local Representative, 538, 551
local school, 4428
local school teacher, 4428

Local Student by Purchase, 3634
Local Subofficial, 7848
Local Units of Organization, 3731
Local Worthy, 2317, 2318, 2329
lodging, 3264
Long Flourishing Army, 243
Lord, 1729
Lord Advanced in Veneration, 1648
Lord Astrologer, 2955
Lord of the Golden Seal and Purple Ribbon, 1158
Lord of the Imperial Insignia, 1162
Lord for Myriad Years, 7633
Lord Praised for Fulfillment, Marquis of Kuan-nei, 4461
Lord Sacrificer, 2018
Lord Specially Advanced, 6335
Lower Army, 2294
lower class (of rank), 7168
Lumberyard, 4043, 4072

Magistrate: *chang*, 84; *ling*, 3733; *yin*, 7969
Mail Distribution Section, 3099
Mail and Prison Office, 4035
Maintaining Submission Commandant, 4496
Maintenance Director at the Imperial Mausoleum, 3749
Majestic Commander-in-chief, 2683
Majestic Guardsman, 5855
Manager: *chu-p'an kuan, chu-p'an*, 1411; *hui-pan*, 2886; *kou-kuan*, 3212; *kou-tang, kou-tang kuan*, 3214; *kuan-chu*, 3280; *kuan-li*, 3315; *ling*, 3733; *tien*, 6515; *tien-shih*, 6637; *tien-shu*, 6643
Manager of Accounts, 6523
Manager of the Accounts Office, 192
Manager of Adornments, 6639
Manager of Affairs, 940, 4703
Manager of Agriculture, 5729
Manager of Arms, 5741
Manager of Banquets, 6528
Manager of Bows and Arrows, 5685
Manager of the Bureau of Lesser Military Assignments, 3216
Manager of the Calendar, 5692, 5701, 7793
Manager for the Campaigning Army, 5866
Manager of Ceremonial Regalia, 6518
Manager of Ceremonies, 6587
Manager of Chariot Horses, 6636
Manager of Clothing, 6588
Manager of Coloring Processes, 5750
Manager of Combs, 5463
Manager of Communications, 6671
Manager of Credentials, 2042
Manager of Criminal Gear, 5690
Manager of Cultivated Marshes, 5529
Manager of Decorum, 214
Manager of Earthwork, 5800
Manager of Fish, 6680

Manager of Foods, 6629
Manager of Furnishings, 215
Manager of Furs, 5598
Manager of Gardens, 6681
Manager of Governmental Affairs, 3001, 4700
Manager of Granaries, 6658
Manager of Hay, 6660
Manager of Hemp, 6579
Manager of Herds, 6612
Manager of the Hostel, 3281
Manager of Important National Security Matters, 4701
Manager of the Inner Gates, 6665
Manager of Interior Maintenance, 6633
Manager of the Kitchen, 6622
Manager of Lances, 5668
Manager of Lanterns, 6653
Manager of Leatherwork, 5737
Manager of the Library, 6522
Manager of Long Lances, 5773
Manager of Mares, 6624
Manager of Medicines, 6668
Manager of Music, 6684
Manager of National Security Matters, 4702
Manager of Outer Garments, 5735
Manager of Palace Surveillance, 6521
Manager of Palace Women's Work, 6577
Manager of Postal Relay Stations, 76
Manager of Rarities, 6520
Manager of Receptions, 6604
Manager of Records, 6524
Manager of Registration, 6626
Manager of Requisitioned Labor, 5761
Manager of Rest Stations, 177
Manager of Ritual Receptions, 6657
Manager of the Royal Chariots, 6610
Manager of the Royal Flags, 5540
Manager of the Royal Lancers, 5826
Manager of Sacrifices, 6650, 6664
Manager of Seals, 6597, 6620
Manager of Security, 6586
Manager of Servicemen, 5761
Manager of Sewing, 6547
Manager of Silk, 6651
Manager of Silks, 6656
Manager of Stables, 6550
Manager of the State, 1235
Manager of Supplies, 6574
Manager of Swine, 6545
Manager of Swords and Shields, 5777
Manager of Tax Transport, 3316
Manager of Titles of Honor, 6611
Manager of Transport, 6679
Manager of Trophies, 6675
Manager of Visitors, 6623
Manager of the Water Clock, 3836
Manager of Waterways, 5771
Manager of the Wine Goblets, 5796
Manager of Wines, 6685
Manager of Writings, 5769

Managing Clerk, 6750
Managing Clerk at the Gate, 3952
Managing Clerk in the Palace, 3945
Manchu Archive, 3920
Manchu Document Registry, 3919
Manchu Documents Section, 3918
Manufactory, 6912
Maritime Trade Commissioner, 5295
Maritime Trade Superintendency,
   6433
Maritime Trade Supervisorate, 5296
Market Director, 5206, 5288
Market Exchange Mortgage
   Storehouse, 5265
Market Exchange Office, 5261;
   shih-i ssu, 5264; *shih-i wu*, 5266
Market Master, 5301
Market of Miscellanies, 6803
Market Office, 5307
Market Section, 5321
Market Shop Examiner, 5558
Market Shop Inspector, 5538
Market Shop Policeman, 5733
Market Shop Supervisor, 82
Market Tax Censor, 3257
Market Tax Supervisor, 5650
Marksmen, 4956
Marquis, 2205
Marquis Attending at Sacrifices,
   5332
Marquis for Audiences, 341
Marquis for Honoring the Sage,
   2012
Marquis of Kuan-chung, 3282
Marquis of Kuan-nei, 3321
Marquis of Kuan-wai, 3334
Marquis (for merit), 324
Marquis of Metropolitan Residence,
   7298
Marquis for Perpetuating the Sage,
   5112
Marquis for Praising the Sage, 4493
Marquis for Praising Virtue, 4498
Marquis for Reverencing the Sage,
   7149
Marquis for Revering the Sage, 3468
Marquis of State, 3513
Marquis for Venerating the Sage,
   1667
Marquis for Worshipping at the
   Temple (to Confucius), 4500
Marquis-consort, 3698
Marquisate, 2218
Marquises, 1755
Marriage Monitor, 3932
Marshal, 4689, 8244
Martial Guard, 3096
Master, 5207
Master of Adornments, 7391
Master of the Bells, 1602
Master of Ceremonies, 126
Master of Ceremonies in the East
   Hall, 7436
Master of Ceremonies in the West
   Hall, 2250
Master of the Chickens, 561

Master of Crickets, 3531
Master of Exorcism, 1339
Master of the Ford, 106
Master of Foreign Dances, 3923
Master of Foreign Music, 3933,
   6378
Master of the Hinterland, 6641
Master of Hounds, 1709
Master of Laws, 3888
Master of Masseurs, 25
Master of Medications, 6844
Master of Metal Bells, 4748
Master of Metals, 5592
Master of Mourning, 2300
Master of Musical Entertainments,
   3761
Master of the Musical Stones, 1275
Master of Ordinances for the
   Months, 8267
Master of the Palace Militia, 3461
Master of the Panpipe, 5189
Master Physician, 2998
Master of Protocol, 1039
Master of the Royal Chariots, 1118
Master of the Royal Headgear, 4644
Master of the Sacrifices, 5766
Master of State, 3538
Master of the Wardrobe, 5622
Master of the Waterways, 1501
Materials Yard, 5319
Materiel Storehouse, 5363
Mathematics School, 5856
Matron, 4971
Matron for Food, 5038
Maturer of Virtue, 194
Mausoleum, 8222
Mausoleum of the Heir Apparent,
   6241
Mausoleum Manager, 5386
Meal Allowance Office, 1889
Meal Server, 5032
Meat Server, 3464
Meat Trimmer, 7344
Medal for Merit, 3457
Medical Aide, 6589
Medical Apprentice, 2970
Medical Assistant, 3020
Medical Attendant, 128, 5349
Medical Erudite, 6182
Medical Institute, 2145
Medical Instructor, 4481, 6176,
   6178
Medical Office, 3666
Medical Official, 2964
Medical School, 2958
Medical Secretary, 3626
Medical Section, 3019
Medical Service, 7893
Medical Storehouse, 7899
Medical Supervisor, 2944
Medical Treatment Aide, 1897
Medication Maker, 2178
Medication Transport Service, 2563
Medicines Office, 5820
Member of the Regular Entourage,
   269

members of the imperial coterie,
   1119
Members of the Palace Theater,
   2867
Memorial Presenter, 4617
Memorial Processor, 1089
Memorial Processors, 7042
Memorial Reception Staff, 3175
Memorial Scribe, 5465
Memorial Transmitter, 1155
Memorial-forwarding Office, 7476,
   7477, 7998
Memorializing Section, 7038
Memorials Office, 202, 1156
Memorials Section, 7044
Men of the Three (Lesser)
   Categories, 4895
Menials Service, 2253
Mentor, 1563, 2031, 5468
Mentor of All Regions, 2728
Mentor of Labor, 6824
Mentor-commandant, 2113
Mercantile Controller, 1007
Mercenary Recruit, 4063
Merchant, 3224
Merchant Farm, 5073
Merchant Tax Office, 3197
Merchant Tax Section, 5061
merit rank, 1482
merit rating, 3148
Merit Recommendation Office,
   7032, 7033
merit title, 2711
Meritorious Brigade, 290
Meritorious Minister, 3395
Meritorious Ministers, 2718
Messenger, 2574, 4565
Messenger Awaiting Assignment,
   6753
Messenger Office, 2575, 5955
Metals and Jewels Workshop, 1170
metropolitan, 519
Metropolitan Area: *chi-fu*, 550;
   chi-nei, 573; *chih-li*, 1024; *ching*,
   1188; *ching-chao*, 1190;
   ching-shih, 1239; *fu-li*, 2078;
   ssu-chou, 5599
Metropolitan Area Justice Bureau,
   549
Metropolitan Area(s) and Provinces,
   1044
Metropolitan Bannermen, 1157,
   1200
Metropolitan Cavalry Command,
   3898
Metropolitan Cavalry Command and
   the Metropolitan Infantry
   Command, the, 5337
Metropolitan Circuit, 1199
Metropolitan Coinage Service, 4472,
   4506
Metropolitan Command, 5335
Metropolitan Commandant, 5697
Metropolitan Examination, 2888,
   5188
Metropolitan Examiner, 2432
Metropolitan Executive, 7300

Metropolitan Governor, 1192, 4041
Metropolitan Graduate, 1148
Metropolitan Graduate with
　Distinction, 2884, 5184
Metropolitan Graduate with Honors,
　1149
Metropolitan Graduate with Ritual
　Specialization, 3120
Metropolitan Granaries, 1246
Metropolitan Guard, 3756
Metropolitan Guard Command, 7328
Metropolitan Infantry Command,
　4778
Metropolitan Mint, 3227
Metropolitan Officials, 1193
Metropolitan Prefecture, 1191
Metropolitan Region, 1197
Mid-year Office, 1574
Middle Army, 1550
Middle Echelon, 1555
Middle Echelon Director, 1556
Middle Echelon Vice Director, 1557
Militant Assistance (prefix), 7777
Militant and Awesome Guard, 7838
Militant Commander-in-chief, 2685
Militant as Dragons Army, 3881
Militant General, 7835
Militant Guard, 6599, 7834
Militant Loyalty (prefix), 7776
Military, 1730, 5742, 7735
Military Administrator, 898, 3847
Military Administrator of Infantry
　and Cavalry, 4681
Military Affairs Commissioner, 5450
Military Appointments Process,
　7772, 8052
Military Archive, 1909
Military Artisans Section, 4669
Military Band, 1765
Military Ceremonial Mounts, 158,
　3590
Military Command, 1001, 1753,
　8245
Military Commandant, 4684
Military Commander, 1780, 1795
Military Commission, 18, 1068,
　5483
Military Commissioner: *chen-fu shih,*
　375; *chieh-fu shih,* 76C; *chieh-tu
　shih,* 777; *chih-chih shih,* 957;
　ching-lüeh, ching-lüeh shih, 1231;
　ching-lüeh an-fu shih, 1232; *fu-yü
　chün-ma,* 2117; *kuan-chün shih,*
　3289; *shuai-ch'en,* 5477
Military Commissioner for ·
　Participating in Sacrifices, 4557
Military Commissioner and
　Superintendent of Troops, 20
Military Commissioner-in-chief, 777,
　957
Military Consultant, 6892, 7529
Military Coroner, 5743
Military Defense Circuit, 4690
Military Defense and General
　Surveillance Circuit, 4675
Military Defense and Tax Intendant
　Circuit, 4678

Military Director-in-chief, 4687
Military Escort, 7172
military family, 1762
Military Headquarters, 3087
Military Inspector, 4683
Military Inspectorate, 2724
Military Judge, 1784, 7385
Military Judicial Commissioner,
　7736, 7768
Military Office, 3092, 7784
military officer, 7784
Military Officer in Reserve for
　Special Assignment, 7735
Military Prefecture, 1730
Military Protector, 2775
military rank, 7745
military recruitment examinations,
　7778
Military School, 7774
Military Section, 4666, 4696
military service prestige title, 7815
Military Service Section, 4696
Military Specialist, 7859
Military Storehouse, 7830
Military Storekeeper, 7830
Military Superintendent, 6484
Military Supervisor, 1783
Military Training Commissioner,
　7387
Military Training, Pacification, and
　Agricultural Development
　Commission, 7384
Military Vice Commissioner, 777
Militia (prefix), 7383
Militia Company, 3992
Militia General, 5412
Militia Guard Section, 3999
Militia Section, 3998
Militiaman, 685, 3997
Milk Products Office, 3076
Milk Provisioner, 1402
Mining Superintendent, 3438
Minister: *ch'en,* 392; *ch'ing,* 1255;
　hsiang, 2303; *shang-shu,* 5042;
　*also see under appropriate
　Ministry*
Minister of Agriculture, 6001
Minister Commissioner-in-chief,
　6022
Minister Duke, 2331
Minister of Education, 5801, 5802
Minister of Finance, 551
Minister of Hereditary Consorts,
　5246
Minister of Husbandry, 4939
Minister for Imperial Clansmen,
　7081
Minister of Justice, 2577, 5671, ·
　6036
Minister (of Ministry), 5042, 7522;
　*also see under appropriate
　Ministry*
Minister of the Pavilion of Culture
　and Prosperity, 7691
Minister Prince, 2365
Minister of Revenue, 7204

Minister of Rites: *ta ssu-li,* 6038; *ta
　tsung-po,* 6088; *t'ai-tsung,* 6235;
　tsung-po, 7147; *yang-po,* 7885
Minister of State, 1632, 2337
Minister of War, 6039
Minister of Works, 5687, 5688,
　6124
Ministerial Executives, 1266
ministerial selections, 5045
Ministries and the Censorate, 4814
Ministries of the Left, 6986
Ministries and Offices, 4801
Ministries of Personnel, of Revenue,
　and of Rites, 3610
Ministries of Personnel and of Rites,
　3625
Ministries of the Right, 8069
Ministries of War and of Justice,
　4674
Ministries of War, of Justice, and of
　Works, 4673
Ministry, 4764
Ministry of Education, 2789, 6371
Ministry Executive, 4802
Ministry of Heaven, 6709
Ministry of Justice: *ch'iu-kuan,* 1324;
　hsien-pu, 2528; *hsing-pu,* 2590;
　i-lo-hsi-pa yüan, 2982; *ssu-hsien,*
　5632; *ssu-hsing,* 5635; *yu-shih
　ts'ao,* 8075
Ministry of Justice and Works, 2581
Ministry of Northern Relations, 4535
Ministry Officials, 4767
Ministry of Palace Affairs, 6565
Ministry of Personnel: *li-pu,* 3630;
　li-ts'ao, 3644; *ssu-lieh,* 5704;
　t'ien-kuan, 6704; *wen-pu,* 7718
Ministry Physician, 4781
Ministry of Public Construction, 635
Ministry of Receptions, 1396
Ministry of Revenue: *chi-pu,* 577;
　hu-pu, 2789; *min-pu,* 4000;
　ssu-yüan, 5838; *ti-kuan,* 6371;
　tu-chih, 7194
Ministry of Rites: *ch'un-kuan,* 1525;
　i-ts'ao, 3017; *li-pu,* 3631;
　nan-sheng, 4116; *ssu-li,* 5694;
　yang-kuan, 7882
Ministry of Sacrifices, 5160, 7566
Ministry of Southern Relations, 4114
Ministry of State, 6704
Ministry of the Treasury, 1142
Ministry of War: *ch'i-ping, ch'i-ping
　ts'ao,* 633; *chia-pu,* 676;
　hsia-kuan, 2296; *ping-pu,* 4691;
　ssu-jung, 5664; *wu-ping ts'ao,*
　wu-ping, 7811; *wu-pu,* 7813
Ministry of Western Relations, 2265
Ministry of Works: *ch'i-pu,* 635;
　kung-pu, 3462; *ssu-p'ing,* 5744;
　tung-kuan, 7438
Minor Gifts Storehouse, 1182
Mint, 1371, 1374, 7906
Mint Office, 7915
Minting Directorate, 1369
Miscellaneous Manufactures Service, ·
　6805
Miscellaneous Storehouse, 6808

Miscellaneous Storehouse for the Southern Suburban and the Imperial Ancestral Temple Sacrifices, 4089
Miscellaneous Weaving and Dyeing Service, 1006
Miscellany Section, 1078, 1079
Miscellany Vault, 7948
Mistress, 2066
Mistress of the Ancestral Temple, 5159
Mistress of the Palace, 3479
Mistress of State, 3538
Mobile Brigade, 2605
Mobile Brigade of the Wing of Inspired Strategy, 5165
Mobile Corps Commander, 8037
Money Transactions Office, 1386
Mongol, 3957
Mongol Agency, 3972
Mongol Army, 3960
Mongol Official, 5971
Mongolian, 3957
Mongolian Clerk, 3969, 4576, 4584
Mongolian Directorate of Education, 3965
Mongolian Documents Section, 3968
Mongolian Executive, 3959
Mongolian Hanlin Academy, 3963
Mongolian Head Veterinarian, 3964
Mongolian School for the Sons of the State, 3966
Mongolian Scribe, 3970
Mongolian Secretary, 3958
Mongolian Translation Office, 3961
Monitor, 2689, 5360
Monitor of Imperial Kinsmen, 7151
Monitor of the Inherited Region, 7303
Monitor of Measurements, 5551
Monitoring Censor, 1125
Monitors Office at the East Palace Gate, 4286
Monopoly Exchange Bureau, 1721
Monopoly Exchange Commissioner, 1720
Monopoly Exchange Section, 1718
Monopoly Exchange Storehouse, 1719
Monopoly Tax Commission, 1716, 5260
monthly personnel evaluation, 8259
Moral Instructor, 3063
Moral Mentor, 580, 2991
Moslem, 2879
Moslem Clerk, 2880
Moslem Medical Office, 3344
Moslem Pharmacy, 2882
most important, 7061
Most Venerated, 1086
Mother of the State, 3527
Mount Prospect School, 1237
Mountain Tax Master, 4961
Mounted Attendant-in-ordinary, 264
Mounted Courier, 496, 3902, 7037
Mounted Escort, 4623
Mounter of Scrolls, 1504, 1506

Mounts Section, 605
Mounts Service, 615
Music Bureau, 8262
Music Director, 228, 5844, 5846
Music Master: chiao-shih, 737; ta-shih, 6020; t'ai yüeh-cheng, 6266; tsung-chang, 7078; yüeh-cheng, 8258; yüeh-shih, 8270
Music Ministry, 8269
Music Office, 728, 2183, 5847
Musical Duty Roster Clerk, 8284
Musician: chang-yüeh, 227; hsieh-yin lang, 2489; yin-sheng jen, 7991; yüeh-hsü, 8265
Musician-in-chief, 6056, 6264
Musk Storehouse, 2369
Musketeer, 4304
Musketeer Guardsman, 4305
Muslim, 2879
My Lord, 1729
Myriad Cavaliers, 7618
Myriarchy, see Brigade (wan-hu fu)

National Commander-in-chief, 6700
National Exemplar, 5243
National Silver Vault, 6229, 6233
National Temple, 6305
National University: kuo-hsüeh, 3520; kuo-tzu hsüeh, 3542; ta-hsüeh, 5961; t'ai-hsüeh, 6168
National University Student, 856, 3544, 4953
National University Student for Excellence, 8042
National University Student by Grace, 1819, 1822
National University Student Hereditary by Grace, 1825
National University Student Hereditary by Heroism, 4134
Naval Brigade, 5510
Naval Forces, 5509
Navy, 5492
Neighborhood: lin, 3717; lü, 3883; pi, 4570; p'u, 4816; t'ing, 6747
Neighborhood Earl, 6759
Neighborhood Head, 6750, 6751, 6780
Neighborhood Marquis, 6752
Neighborhood Princess, 6756
Neighborhood Princess-ordinary, 6779
New Grain Transport Supervisorate, 2559
New Music Office, 2558
New Official, 5303
New Script Academician, 2557
Newly Submitted Army, 2553
Night Patroller, 5813
Night Watchman, 3164, 7914
Nighttime Trapper, 4019
Nine Chamberlains, 1296
Nine Chief Ministers, 1296
Nine Concubines, 1314
Nine Courts, 1317
Nine Fiscal Agencies, 1301
Nine Frontiers, 1313

Nine Greater Chief Ministers, 5906
Nine Honors, 1310
Nine Lesser Chief Ministers, 2392
Nine Orders of Nobility, 1299
Nine Ranks, 1315
Nine Regions, 1297
Nine Sections, 1304
Nine Temples, 1309
nobility, 1715
noble scion, 3363, 3377, 3494
nominal office, 2493
nominal supernumerary appointment, 6503
Nominations Section, 1407, 4006
Nominations and Vacancies Section, 1408
Nominee for Office, 3474
Non-Chinese Pass List, 8066
Non-inheriting Son, 5468
North, 4512
North Commissioner, 4541
North Gate, 4527
North Palace, 4525
North Prison, 4542
North Township, 4522
North Visitors Bureau, 4523
Northeastern War Prisoner, 4036
Northern Administration, 4529
Northern Army, 4521
Northern Bureau of Military Affairs, 4548
Northern Command, 4548
Northern Court, 4550
Northern Defense Section, 4530
Northern Department, 4540
Northern Establishment, 4550
Northern Metropolitan Area, 4519
Northern Mint, 4549
Northern Office, 4543
Northern Office of the Grand Princes, 4544
Northern Residence Hall, 4515
Northern Storehouse, 4513, 4524
Northwestern Defense Section, 2176
not of official status, 3822
not yet of official status, 7670
Notable Graduate, 1225
Notary of the Administrative Assistant, 922
Notary of the Administrative Assistant to the Military Commissioner, 921
Notary of the Bureau of Military Affairs, 924
Notary of the Palace Domestic Service, 923
Novice, 3638
Novice Career Musician, 261, 6390
Number One Storehouse, 665

Observer, 3272
Observer of Air Currents, 2207, 7637
Observer of the Bell-like Pitchpipes, 2208
Observer of the Stars, 2212
Observer of the Sun, 2216

Observer of the Sundial, 2217
Observer of Winds, 2210
of the Left (prefix), 6949
of the Right (prefix), 8033
of official status, 3802
Offeror of Hunting Prayers, 6552
Office: *ch'u,* 1456; *fang,* 1892, 1893;
  fu, 2034; *kuan,* 3262; *kuan,* 3264;
  shu, 5410; *so,* 5523; *ssu,* 5533;
  t'ing, 6748; *yüan,* 8221
Office of the Administrative
  Assistant, 4427
Office of Admittance, 7976
Office for the Advancement of
  Literature, 2911
Office of Agriculture, 4323
Office for the Altar of the Soil and
  Grain, 5132
Office of Ancient Music, 8274
Office of Animal Offerings, 2268
Office of Armaments, 7744
Office of Armaments and the
  Canopies Office, 7743
Office of the Assistant Director for
  Northern Outer Waterways, 4547
Office of the Assistant Director of
  Southern Outer Waterways, 4129
Office of Astronomical Observation,
  825, 7766
Office Attendant, 857
Office for Audience Ceremonies,
  3180
Office of Bell Music, 1274
Office of Boats and Boatmen, 1336
Office Boy, 5853
Office of the Capital Granaries, 1230
Office of Capital Streets; 769
Office for the Care of Imperial
  Mausoleums, 790
Office of Celestial Understanding,
  7487
Office of the Chamberlain for
  Ceremonials, 6139
Office of the Chestnut Park, 3654
Office Chief, 5413
Office for the Clarification of
  Buddhist Profundities, 285
Office of Collected Regulations,
  2895
Office for the Compilation by
  Categories of Imperial
  Pronouncements, 4642
Office for the Compilation by
  Category of Imperial Policy
  Pronouncements, 4641
Office for the Compilation of
  Imperial Pronouncements, 4633
Office for the Compilation of
  Secretariat Regulations, 4634
Office of Contented Music, 21
Office of the Counselor-in-chief, 484
Office of Delicacies, 378, 2455,
  4975
Office of Dies, 135
Office of Diplomatic
  Correspondence, 7649
Office Director, 5416

Office for Distribution of Imperial
  Pronouncements, 526
Office of Domestic Affairs, 671
Office of Domestic Fowl, 1890
Office for Drawing and Painting,
  7350
Office for Dredging the Yellow
  River, 5426
Office of Drinks and Delicacies,
  6298
Office of Drums and Fifes, 3231
Office for Duty Assignments, 4397
Office for the Editing of Imperial
  Pronouncements, 2357
Office for the Editing of Regulations
  on the Officialdom, 2359
Office for Elephant Care, 7877
Office for Emergencies, 600
Office of Erudites, 4955
Office of Estimates, 3693
Office for the Evaluation of Capital
  and Court Officials, 3151
Office for the Exchange of Salt and
  Horses, 7950
Office of Female Services, 3012
office fields, 1076
Office of Fine Steeds, 2811
Office of Fine Wines, 3692
Office of Fines and Confiscations,
  5563
Office of Food Supplies for the Heir
  Apparent, 1476
Office of Foodstuffs, 5277
Office for Foreign Tribute Envoys,
  5658
Office of Fruits and Flowers, 3723
Office of Fruits and Tea, 2149
Office of Fuels, 71
Office of Grain Supplies, 6318
Office for Granaries and
  Storehouses, 6905
Office of Granary Repairs, 6441
Office of the Grand Clansman, 6063
Office of the Grand Councilors,
  6820
Office of the Grand Prince, 6104
Office of the Grand Prince of the
  Hsi Tribes, 2280
Office of Heavenly Mounts, 6689
Office of Herds, 6613
Office of History and the Calendar,
  3533
Office of the Household Guards,
  7665
Office of Husbandry, 3671
Office of Imperial Ancestral
  Worship, 6167
Office of Imperial Armaments, 8115
Office of the Imperial Clan, 6084,
  6237
Office of the Imperial Coachman,
  493, 6203
Office of the Imperial Descendants,
  2855
Office of the Imperial Horses, 8156
Office of the Imperial Mausoleum,
  3772

Office of Imperial Parks, 5022, 8256
Office of Imperial Parks Products,
  3218
Office of Imperial Pasturages, 1267
Office of Imperial Portraiture, 8192
Office for the Imperial Quarters,
  8106
Office of Imperial Sacrifices, 6144
Office of the Imperial Stables, 6551
Office of the Imperial Storehouse,
  2870
Office of Inspection, 6529
Office of Instruction, 1368
Office of Investigation and
  Remonstrance, 53
Office of Judicial Review, 4035
Office of Justice, 2569
Office for Law Enforcement, 6772
Office for Maintaining a Record of
  Current Policies, 4636
Office Manager: *chih-shih shih,*
  1056; *kan-pan, kan-pan kuan,*
  3135; *kou-tang kung-shih kuan,*
  3215; *lu-shih,* 3856; *lu,* 3857;
  nei-shih tu-chih, 4252; *tien-shih,*
  6637; *tu-chih,* 7195; *tu-shih,* 7273;
  tu-ssu, 7285
Office Manager for Ceremonial,
  6592
Office Manager of the Left Duty
  Group, 6983
Office Manager in the Northern
  Establishment, 168
Office Manager of the Right Duty
  Group, 8065
Office Manager in the Southern
  Establishment, 161
Office of Medication, 131, 6593
Office of Military Affairs, 8028
Office of Military Commanders,
  1796
Office for Military Training of
  Palace Youths, 8118
Office of Miscellaneous Purchases,
  5292, 6804
Office of Monopolized Goods, 874
Office of Moslem Music, 240
Office of Musical Instruction, 899
Office of Musical Supplies, 3356
Office of the National Altars, 736
Office of the Office Manager, 7276
Office for Ornamentation, 7723
Office of Palace Accounts, 3260
Office of Palace Attendants, 3944
Office of Palace Ceremonial, 132
Office of Palace Construction, 8024
Office of the Palace Guard, 7679
Office of Palace Justice, 4995, 5153
Office of the Palace Marina, 8125
Office of the Palace Paymaster, 502
Office of the Paymaster, 906
Office of Personnel Evaluation, 3158
Office of Presentations, 7978
Office of Produce Levies, 1352
Office of Public Order, 5702
Office for the Purchase of Cheap
  Grain, 6381

Office of Receptions, 6573, 6605
Office of Recommendation
    Evaluators, 2325
Office of Religion, 7928
Office for Religious Administration,
    5948
Office of Remonstrating Censors,
    839
Office of Rivers and Canals, 2171
Office for Sacrifices at the Fen
    River, 1949
Office for Sacrifices at the Grave,
    7557
Office of Sacrificial Animals, 5760
Office of Sacrificial Clothing, 8142
Office of Sacrificial Foods, 5150
Office of Sacrificial Grains and
    Animals, 3724
Office of Sacrificial Music, 8264
Office of Sacrificial Regalia for the
    Suburban Temple, 3307
Office of Sacrificial Treasures, 6697
Office of Sacrificial Utensils, 535
Office Scribe, 2097
Office of Scrutiny, 3187
Office of Scrutiny for Justice, 2576
Office of Scrutiny for Personnel,
    3616
Office of Scrutiny for Revenue, 2784
Office of Scrutiny for Rites, 3617
Office of Scrutiny for War, 4676
Office of Scrutiny for Works, 3440
Office of Sentence Evaluators, 2363
Office for Supervision of Censors,
    7288
Office of Tallies and Seals for
    Imperial Funerals, 1950
Office of Taoist Worship, 1656
Office of Tax Substitutes, 1787
Office of Temple Worship, 7565,
    7569
Office for Testing Armillary Spheres
    and Water Clocks, 6940
Office of Towered Warships, 3831
Office of Transmission, 7467, 7997
Office of Vegetables, 681
Office of the Vice Minister of
    Personnel, 2405
Office for War and Rites, 4677
Office of Waterways, 7283
Office of Western Medicine, 2283
Office of Western Music, 283, 6732
Office of Works, 3417
Officer Assignments Section, 4668
Officer in Charge of a Duty Group,
    4408
Officers of the Four Categories,
    5751
Officers of the Imperial Guards,
    2831
Offices of Assistant Directors for
    Southern and Northern Outer
    Waterways, 4112
Offices for Marketplaces in the Two
    Capitals, 3661
Official, 2821, 3262, 8217
Official at Leisure, 2511

official class, 1145, 5315
Official of the Domain, 3523
official duty, on, 6284, 6286
official elite, 1838
Official by Examination, 3191
Official on Rotational Duty, 1874
Official of the South Rank, 4108
official status, not of, 3822
official status, not yet of, 7670
official status, of, 3802
Official Student, 3299, 3324
officialdom, the, 4739
officials, 5327
officials of the establishment, 2069
Officials Section, 4740
officials of the various offices, 1432
Oil and Vinegar Pantry, 8092
Old Campaigner, 7169
on active duty, 2535
on annual duty, 1038
on Palace Duty (prefix or suffix),
    3405
on rotational duty, 1862
Operational Agents of the Two
    Offices, 4407
Orchid Pavilion, 3560
Order-promulgating Office, 1850
Order-promulgating Official, 1850
ordinary (rank), 1549
ordinary (evaluation category), 4704
Ordinary Appointee, 246
Ordinary Department, 4848
Ordinary Grand Master, 1627
Ordinary Imperial Clansman, 5467
Ordinary Lieutenant, 2375
Ordinary Minister, 1545
Ordinary Serviceman, 1601
Ordinary Subprefecture, 4923, 5461
ordo, 3389, 7731
Ornamentation Service, 794,
Ornaments Office, 6843
Orphans of the Palace Guard
    Cavalry, 8152
other, 1357, 3697
Our Dynasty, 3505
Outer (prefix), 7573
Outer Aide of the Censor-in-chief,
    7578, 8180, 8185
Outer Aides, 7595
Outer Artisan, 7583
Outer Banners, 7581
Outer Branch of the Palace Library,
    7616
Outer Capital Township, 7591
Outer Censorate, 7605
Outer Chancellery, 3947
Outer College, 7603
Outer Court, 7576, 7606
Outer Directorate, 7584
Outer Drafter, 7585
Outer Evaluation, 7574
Outer Garrisons, 7587
Outer Gentleman, 7594
Outer Hostel, 7593
Outer Kennel, 7614
Outer Land Assessor, 7345

Outer Mongolian Bureau, 6648
Outer Mongolian Reception Bureau,
    3062
Outer Noblemen, 7596, 7598
Outer Noblewomen, 7597, 7599
Outer Officials, 7592
Outer Palace Gates, 5715
Outer Palace Library, 7601
Outer Section, 7579
Outer Stables, 7586
Outer Storehouse, 7613
Outer Treasury, 7587
Overseer: *lu, lu ... shih*, 3857; *nei
    kuan-ling*, 4206; *ta-la-huo-ch'ih*,
    5982; *ta-lu-hua-ch'ih*, 5993
Overseer of Feudatories, 980
Overseer of Merchants, 3244
Overseer of Treasures, 962
Overseer-general, 7134
Overseer-general of Revenues, /137
Overseers Office, 4207
Oxtail-haired Cavalryman, 3926
Oxtail-haired Court Gentleman, 3926

Pacification Commission: *an-fu ssu*,
    18; *chao-t'ao ssu*, 304; *hsüan-fu
    ssu*, 2661; *hsüan-wei ssu*, 2682
Pacification Commissioner: *an-fu
    shih*, 17; *chao-an shih*, 279;
    chao-fu shih, 282; *chao-t'ao shih*,
    303; *ch'eng-hsüan shih*, 488;
    feng-shih hsüan-fu, 2016;
    fu-yü shih, 2118; *hsüan-fu shih*,
    2661; *hsüan-yü shih*, 2687; *hsün-
    fu shih*, 2732
Pacification Commissioner for the
    Suppression of Outlaws, 1331
Pacification Commissioner-in-chief,
    19, 2732
Pacification Office, 304, 2119, 2682
Pacification Official, 2687
Pacification and Supervisory
    Commissioner, 281
Pacifier of the Frontier, 6740
Paddy Supervisor, 6314
Paint Production Office, 6271
Painter Service, 7349
Painting Academy, 2816, 3069
Painting School, 2808
Painting Service, 2805
Palace, 1530, 3389
Palace Academy for the
    Advancement of Literature, 4189
Palace Administration: *tien-chung
    chü*, 6559; *tien-chung sheng*,
    6561; *tien-nei chü*, 6616; *tien-nei
    sheng*, 6617
Palace Administration Office, 6563
Palace Administrator, 4273, 6556
Palace Aide to the Censor-in-chief,
    8174, 8175
Palace Archery Storehouse, 4209
Palace Armory, 4667, 8111
Palace Army, 3412, 6534, 8114
Palace Army Duty Group, 6537
Palace Artisan, 4152, 4279
Palace Assistant, 6811

Palace Attendance Service, 4159, 4162, 6616
Palace Attendant: *chi-shih huang-men,* 589; *chih-hou nei-t'ing,* 989; *chung chi-shih-chung,* 1540; *chung huang-men,* 1565; *chung-lang,* 1580; *hsiao huang-men,* 2407; *kung-feng nei-t'ing,* 3422; *shih-chin,* 5226; *shih-chung,* 5229; *ssu-nei,* 5727; *nei ch'eng-chih,* 4146; *nei-chih,* 4159; *nei hsiao-ch'en,* 4182; *nei-shih,* 4237; *nei-shih kuan,* 4246; *nei-t'ing chih-hou,* 4268
Palace Attendant for Capital Craftsmen, 7190
Palace Attendant-in-ordinary, 1532
Palace Attendant-usher, 990
Palace Attendants Service, 1151
Palace Audience Gate, 5008
Palace Audience Gate of the East, 7450
Palace Audience Gate of the West, 2267
Palace Bandsman, 2842
Palace Bondservants, Bannermen, and Secretaries, 4222
Palace Branch of the Ministry of Works, 3487
Palace Buildings Office, 711
Palace Bureau, 6563, 6683
Palace Butcher, 4511
Palace Butchery, 4511
Palace Cadet, 1621
Palace Cavalry Brigade, 4183
Palace Cavalry and Infantry Armies, 6536
Palace Censor, 6562, 6618
Palace Ceremonial Office, 5263, 6654
Palace Clerk, 3943
Palace Command, 6542
Palace Commandant of Censors, 8176
Palace Commandant-protector, 2777
Palace Commander, 6564
Palace Companion, 3396
Palace Construction Commissioner, 4281
Palace Construction Office, 2635, 7128
Palace Construction Section, 2635
Palace Cook, 4510
Palace Courier, 4264
Palace Dancers, 2232
Palace Defense Section, 6812
Palace Depot, 4184
Palace Directorate, 6558
Palace Discipline Service, 8097
Palace Domestic Service: *ch'ang-ch'iu chien,* 237; *ch'eng-ying hsiao-ti chü,* 517; *nei-sheng,* 4234; *nei-shih chien,* 4240; *nei-shih sheng,* 4249; *shih-cheng fu,* 5210; *ssu-kung t'ai,* 5686

Palace Doorman, 4187, 4188, 4374, 7962
palace duty, on, 3405
Palace Duty Group, 4265
Palace Duty Officer, 4417
Palace Duty Officer-usher, 991
palace edict, 1543
Palace Editorial Assistant, 4272
Palace Erudite, 4154
palace establishment, 3466
palace eunuch: *kung-kuan,* 3442; *nei-p'in,* 4225; *t'ai-chien,* 6148; *tang,* 6281
Palace Eunuch Attendant-in-ordinary, 4141
Palace Eunuch of High Rank, 6535
Palace Eunuch of the Left Duty Group, 6982
Palace Eunuch of the North Rank, 4531
Palace Eunuch of the Right Duty Group, 8064
Palace Eunuch Service, 3078, 3079, 3080, 4170
Palace Eunuch Usher, 988
Palace Eunuch Usher of High Rank, 986
palace eunuchs, 6548
Palace Examination: *ko-shih,* 3183; *tien-shih,* 6640; *t'ing-shih,* 6762; *yü-shih,* 8169
Palace Examination Grader, 7220
Palace Examination Graduate, 3845
Palace Foreman, 6655
Palace Garden, 4296, 6323
Palace Gate Guard, 844, 847
Palace Gatekeeper, 3452
Palace Gates Guard Command, 3450
Palace Gates Office, 3453
Palace Gates Service, 3495
Palace Gentleman-usher, 985
Palace Governor for the Heir Apparent, 3496
Palace Granary, 4277
Palace Grazing Grounds, 3319
Palace Groom, 270, 2003
Palace Guard: *chin-nei shih-wei,* 1135; *chin-wei,* 1160; *ch'in-wei,* *ch'in-wei fu,* 1187; *kung-ts'ao,* 3489; *nei-chang,* 4138
Palace Guard Cavalry, 8150
Palace Guardian, 1058
Palace Guards, 5854
Palace Guards Brigade, 4185
Palace Guardsman, 8119
Palace Guide, 4198
Palace Gunpowder Depot, 4190
Palace Historiographic Academy, 4212
Palace Inspectorate-general, 6544
Palace Institute of Literature, 4290
Palace Isolation Building, 4797, 4799
Palace Kennel, 4293
Palace Larder, 8105
Palace Laundry Service, 2825

Palace Library, 3730, 4588, 4598, 4599
Palace Library Editor, 4575
Palace of Longevity, 7632
Palace Maintenance Office, 2629
Palace Manager, 4203, 6614
Palace Master, 5302, 6029
Palace Medical Service, 1990, 5076
Palace Memorial, 7031
Palace Mentor, 1553
Palace Military Headquarters, 3775
Palace Minister, 3407
Palace Ministry, 1634
Palace Ministry of Works, 4211
Palace Music School, 4153
Palace Park, 4298
Palace Patrolman, 1636
palace personnel, 3442
Palace Personnel Office, 4221
Palace Physician, 5654, 6171
Palace Police Patrol, 8134
Palace Presenter, 4266
Palace Prison, 1685, 2845, 4487
Palace Protector, 4494
Palace Provisioner, 1416, 1595, 4147, 4269
Palace Provisions Commission, 2664
Palace Receptionist, 1639, 4294
Palace Repository, 4220
Palace School, 3436, 3854
Palace School in the Grove, 7631
Palace Schools, 3298
Palace Secretariat, 1610, 5451, 7722
Palace Secretariat Academy, 4224
Palace Secretary: *chien-tien she-jen,* 869; *chung shang-shu,* 1596; *chung-shu,* 1606; *nei shu-mi shih,* 4255; *shu-mi shih,* 5450
Palace Security Service, 1604
Palace Sericulturist, 3013
Palace Servant, 3437, 4143
Palace Service Office, 4235
Palace Serving Woman, 5294
Palace Servitor, 3418
Palace Silk Worker, 4282
Palace Stationer, 5383
Palace Steward, 587, 3397
Palace Storehouse, 1566, 4276
Palace Storehouses, 4202
Palace Stud, 6, 5064
Palace Superintendent, 1603
Palace Supervisor, 3946
Palace Supplier, 4270
Palace Sweeper, 4937
Palace and Temple Custodian, 3444
Palace Theater, 3652
Palace Treasury, 4175
Palace Vanguard Brigade, 4157
Palace Vice Provisioner, 4230
Palace Visitors Bureau, 4201
Palace Wardrobe, 1641, 8129
Palace Weaving and Dyeing Service, 4163
Palace Winery, 4168
Palace Woman: *chang-shih,* 184; *ch'ang-tsai,* 271; *huan-nü,* 2828;

kung-kuan, 3442; *nei-jen,* 4192;
nei-kuan, 4203; *nü-kuan,* 4340
palace women: *chu chang-shih,*
1361; *i-t'ing,* 3010; *kung-jen,*
3437; *kung-nü,* 3456
Palace Workshop, 6915, 6963
Palace Writers, 4178
paper money, 721, 4454
Paper Money Incinerator, 5087
Paper Money Office, 745, 2893
Paper Money Printshop, 8001
Paper Money Repository, 746, 8000
Paper Money Storehouse, 722
Paper Money Treasury, 8098
Paper Office, 4457
Paragons, 6356
paramount ranks (of nobility), 331
Paramount Scribe, 6059
Park, 8220
Park Commissioner, 8240
Participant in the Classics
Colloquium, 1250
Participant in Deliberations about
Advantages and Disadvantages,
6886
Participant in Deliberations about
Court Policy, 6882, 6894
Participant in Determining
Governmental Matters:
ts'an-cheng, 6868; *ts'an-chih
cheng-shih,* 6872; *ts'an-chih
chi-wu,* 6873; *ts'an-yü cheng-shih,*
6895
Participant in the Drafting of
Proclamations, 955
Passed Scholar, 3474
Pasturage, 4044
Pasturage Office, 8234
Pasturage Director, 4042, 4045,
4046
Pasturage for Fine Steeds, 2810
Pasturage for Military Mounts, 1773
Patriotic Soldier, 2988
Patrol, 2712
Patrol Office of the Imperial Insignia
Guard, 1164
Patroller, 8041
Patrolling Inspector, 2712, 2752,
2768
Pavilion of Culture and Prosperity,
7692
Pavilion of Kinsmen, 3386
Pawnbroking Office, 6387
Paymaster, 569, 3682
Peers School, 1181
Penal Commissioner, 2607
Performer of Both Civil and Military
Dances, 7728
Performer of Dances, 7801
Performing Dancer, 7833
Permanent Academician, 3827
Permanent Palace Guard, 276, 3553
perpetual inheritance, 5248
Persian Priest, 4828
Personal Archer Guard, 3420
Personal Bodyguard, 1417

Personal Guard: *ch'ien-niu wei,*
ch'ien-nu fu, 910; *feng-ch'en wei,*
1959; *ko-shih, ko-shih-ha,* 3184;
pei-shen, 4537; *pei-shen fu,* 4538
Personal Guard Garrison, 1176,
1184, 6570
Personal Guard General, 908
Personal Staff, 4289
Personal Troops, 674
personally on active service, 5158
Personnel Evaluation Commissioner,
1462
Personnel Evaluation Section, 3489
Personnel Manager, 5682
Personnel Office, 3604
Personnel Paid in Pecks, 6796
Personnel Records Section, 3594
Personnel, Revenue, and Rites
Ministry, 3610
Personnel and Rites Ministry, 3625
Personnel Section, 3604, 3632, 3644
Personnel Selection Staff, 1268
Personnel Verification Section, 3053
Petition Box Commissioner, 1018,
2523, 3620
Petition Box Office, 3378
Petitioner, 5600
petty official, 4390
Petty Official with Rank, 8043
Pharmacist, 212, 1449, 6668
Pharmacist Aide, 7891
Pharmacy: *shu-yao so,* 5470;
t'ai-p'ing hui-min chü, 6196;
tien-yao chü, 6669; *yao-tsang chü,*
7901
Pharmacy Service, 2169
Pheasant Corral, 8233
Phoenix Hall, 1998
Phoenix Park, 2030
Physician, 2997
Physician Service, 2965
Pickler, 7050
Pillar of Heaven, 6693
Pillar of State, 1400
Pillar of State and General-in-chief,
1401
Pitchpipe Player, 22
Place-name Specialist, 8241
Placement Examination, 3161
Planting Manager, 6923
Plat, 7341
Plate Engraving Service, 7972
Platoon, 3657
Platoon Commander, 1920, 3680,
7089
Player (theatrical), 4729
Players (theatrical), 2269
Pleasure Girl, 6838
Plume Gatherer, 8144
Plume Maker, 6578
Plume-bearer, 120
Police Bureau, 1872
Police Chief, 2724
Police Clerk, 6941
Police Commission, 1223
Police Executive, 3476

Police Office, 1761, 2724
Police Patrol Guard Command,
1277, 8135
Police Section, 6942
Police Superintendent, 433
Policeman, 1510, 5209
Policy Adviser, 4834, 5212
Population Registrar, 5721
Porcelain Service, 3799, 7554
Porcelain Storehouse, 7562
Porcelain Works, 3800
Portraiture Office, 2815
Post Commandant, 1914
Post Station, 1791, 4816
Postal Inspector, 3303
Postal Relay Inspector, 6795
Postal Relay Station: *chan,* 74; *i,*
2926; *i-chan,* 2927; *ta-lo-ta,* 5991;
ta-ta, 6058; *t'ang,* 6289; *yu-t'ing,*
8084
Postal Service Circuit, 2948
posthumous enfeoffment, 1517
posthumous office, 6944
Potential Dignitary, 4736
Pottery Office, 379
Pottery Works, 7890
Praising Perfection Marquis, 4462
Prayer Reader, 7211
Prayer Tablet Section, 1410
Precedent Review Section, 2370
Preceptor, 5202
Preceptor of State, 3530
Precinct, 1892, 6845, 7048
Precinct Company, 1752
Precinct Mentor, 7054
Precinct Official, 3642
Preeminent Talent, 4383
Prefect, 965, 983, 7567, 7969
Prefect (of frontier Prefecture), 976
Prefect (of Industrial Prefecture), 946
Prefect (of Military Prefecture), 971
Prefects, 966
Prefects and District Magistrates,
5385
Prefectural Armies Section, 2343
Prefectural Army, 2341
Prefectural Buddhist Registry, 4946
Prefectural Examination, 768
Prefectural General, 3757
Prefectural Governor, 4041
Prefectural Graduate, 1682, 6330
Prefectural Graduate with Highest
Honors, 770, 781
Prefectural Judge, 778
Prefectural Nominee, 2333
Prefectural Remittances Section,
5011
Prefectural School, 2062
Prefectural Secretary, 773
Prefectural Supervisor, 811
Prefecture, 1332, 2034
Preparatory Branch of the National
University, 4604
Present Day Buddha, 6283
Presented Scholar, 1148
Preserver of Temperance, 4466

prestige title, 2023, 4868
Preventer of Crimes of Violence, 1144
Price Stabilization Agency, 4707
Price Stabilization Section, 4706
Priestess, 2067
Prime Horse Pasturage, 3387
Prime Mover at Court, 342
Prince: *a-ko,* 2; *tso hsien-wang,* 6968; *wang,* 7634; *wei-hsia,* 7666
Prince of the Deliberative Council, 2939
Prince Presumptive, 5806
Prince of the State, 3548
Princedom, 7648
Princely Administration, 4242
Princely Attendant, 5229
Princely Companion, 7656
Princely Establishment, 7636, 7640, 7641, 7642, 7645
Princely Father-in-law, 7651
Princely Heir, 7653
Princely Lady, 6938, 6939
Princely Mansion, 7655
Princely Mentor, 7639
Princes and Grand Ministers, 7654
Princess, 3408
Princess Supreme, 5882, 6151
Princess' Establishment, 3410
Princess-consort, 2044, 5438, 6365
Princess-ordinary, 7730
Principal (prefix), 396
Principal (appointee), 420
Principal Clerk, 447
Principal Consort, 8224
Principal of a Department Geomancy School, 6644
Principal of a Departmental Medical School, 6601
Principal of a District Geomancy School, 2759
Principal of a District Medical School, 2742
Principal Examiner, 421
Principal Expounder, 2947
Principal Functionary, 426
Principal Gentleman, 425
Principal Graduate: *ch'ih-t'ou,* 1114; *chuang-yüan,* 1515; *hsiang-yüan,* 2372; *hui-yüan,* 2896; *nan-kung ti-i jen,* 4104; *pang-yüan,* 4449; *sheng-yüan,* 5194; *ti-i jen,* 6369; *tien-chuan,* 6553; *tien-yüan,* 6682 *ting-yüan,* 6745; *tu-chan ao-t'ou,* 7184
Principal Grand Councilor, 5373
Principal Magistrate, 5374
Principal Official, 424
Principal Practitioner (medical), 2936
Principal Prefect, 5371
Principal of a Prefectural Geomancy School, 443
Principal of a Prefectural Medical School, 422
Principal Priest, 453
Principal Seal-holding Official, 454
Principal Support, 8225

Principal Territorial Aide, 5069
Principals and Assistants, 411
Prison, 376, 877, 5835, 8103
Prison Aide, 8107
Prison for the Capital Boatmen, 7216
Prison Clerk, 8170
Prison Custodian, 7858, 7869
Prison Guard, 8200
Prison for Imperial Kinsmen, 7286
Prison Office, 6457
Prison for Palace Women, 3011, 3014
Prison Section, 8197
Prison-inspecting (prefix), 2644
private academy, 5471
private army, 4776
private retainer, 4776
Private Secretariat, 3712, 4052
Private Secretary, 4075, 4656
Private Storehouse, 5624
Probationary: *ch'ang-chien,* 236; *ch'üan,* 1704; *li-hsing, li-hsing shih,* 3607; *shih,* 5204; *shou,* 5355
Probationary Ceremonial Assistant, 5724
Probationary Clerk, 244
Probationary Grand Minister of State, 1736, 6815
Probationary Physician, 245
probationary service, 3591
Probationer, 5345, 5723
Proclamation Carrier, 1495
Proclamation Drafter for Honors, 1976
Proclamation Drafting Section, 1010
Proclamations Archive, 959
Proclamations Office, 958, 960
Proctor, 802
Produce Levies Censor, 834
promote, 4970, 5174
Promoted Functionary, 3823
promoted to official status, 4769
promoted posthumously, 1154
Promoter of Culture, 1986
Promulgator of the Laws, 4779
Proofreader: *cheng-shu,* 442; *cheng-tzu,* 450; *chiao-k'an kuan,* 732; *chiao-tui,* 744; *chien-chiao,* 804; *ch'ou-chiao ts'o-wu,* 1350
Proofreader in the Academy, 3311
Proofreader in the Institute, 3311
protection privilege, 7971
protection of sons, 8004
Protective Guard, 8202
Protective Guard Command, 5834
Protector, 5831
Protector Commandant of the Center, 2777
Protector of Corpses, 36
Protector of the Palace, 6760
Protector of State, 1891
Protector-general, 2776, 7237
Protector-general of the Western Regions, 2284
Protectorate, 7238
Protocol Officer, 2007
Protocol Official, 2643

Province, 5176
Province (Tibetan), 4764
Provincial Administration Commission, 487
Provincial Arsenal, 1739
Provincial Authorities, 7229
Provincial Bannermen, 1381
Provincial Coinage Service, 889, 4472
Provincial Command, 6464
Provincial Courier, 6468
Provincial Education Commissioner, 6485, 6487
Provincial Examination, 2352
Provincial Examiner, 1392
Provincial Governor, 2731
Provincial Graduate, 1682, 2984
Provincial Graduate with Distinction, 2327
Provincial Graduate with Highest Honors, 770, 781
Provincial Graduates, 3187
Provincial Intendant, 864
Provincial Magnate, 1966
Provincial Military Commander, 6482
Provincial Military and Naval Commander, 5503
Provincial Surveillance Commission, 6446, 6447
Provisional, 1704
Provisional Government, 3729
Provisioner: *chang-shih,* 182; *kung-kuan,* 3441; *shan-kung,* 4957; *ta-kuan ling,* 5972; *t'ai-kuan ling, t'ai-kuan,* 6185; *tien-chi kuan, tien-chi,* 6525; *ying-feng,* 8013
Provisioner of Sacrificial Wine Covers, 3977
Provisioner of Sweets, 2579
Provisioner of Writing Brushes, 3406
Provisioning Office, 6554
Provisions Office, 6526
Provost, 2700
Provost of the School for the Imperial Family, 7164
Public Petitioners Drum, 6351
Public Petitioners Drum Office, 6352, 6353
Public Petitioners Office, 6355
Public Petitioners Review Office, 6350
Public Pharmacy, 2885
Public Welfare Granary, 3346
Public Worthy, 3472
Publications Office, 5441, 7995
Punishment Reviewing Office, 5153
pure, 1254
Pure Consort, 5427
pure and important, 1280
Purification Guide, 65
Purification Service, 66
Purple Hall, 7534

Qarluk Brigade, 2125
Quadruple First, 5840

Qualified by Contribution, 1134
Qualified by Special Examination,
   1816
Queen, 2206

raised to a ranking, 6349
Rams Service, 6343
rank: *chieh*, 754; *chuan*, 1482;
   hsien, 2493; *p'in*, 4660; *also see*
   class, degree
rank button, 6742
rank offices, 764
rank status, 4930
Rank-classified (prefix), 3081
ranks, 758
Rarities Office, 5544
ratings fulfilled, 3160
Reader-companion, 4419
Reader-in-waiting, 5325
Reading Assistant, 6861
Ready Access Storehouse, 7548
Rear Echelon, 2211
Rear Garden, 2228
Rear Ranks, 4037
Rear Section, 2224
Rear Subsection, 2225
recall (to active service), 612
recall and restore (to former post),
   626
Recall Section, 1680
Receipts and Payments Section, 572
Receiving Office, 5397
receiving salary, 6131
Reception Office, 7518
Reception Secretary, 6316
Reception Service, 6315
Receptionist: *chang-ya*, 211;
   ch'eng-shou kuan, 512; *pin-p'u*,
   4658; *yeh-che*, 7908; *yin-tsan*
   kuan, 7999
Receptionist for All Inquiries, 4757
Receptionist in Attendance, 594
Receptionist Attendant-in-ordinary,
   268
Receptionist Censor, 5398
Receptionist in the Empress's Palace,
   1579
Receptions Bureau, 4654
Recipient of Edicts, 463
Recipient of Edicts in the Bureau of
   Military Affairs, 5448
Recipient of Grace, 5368
Recitation Tutor, 707
Recommendation Evaluator, 2324
Recommendee, 1682
reconfirmation, 4030
Record Checking Censor, 5474
Record Checking Circuit, 5473
Record Keeper: *chang-chi*, 94;
   chao-mo, 291; *chi-shih*, 586;
   chih-shu, 1061; *ssu-lu*, 5707; *ssu
   lu-shih*, 5708; *t'i-kung an-tu*,
   t'i-kung, 6453; *yao-chi*, 7892
Record Keeper and Clerk, 294, 296
Record Keeper and Clerk-
   storekeeper, 295
Record Keeper and Storekeeper, 292

Recorder, 1413, 4643, 4762
Recorder of Imperial Intercourse,
   7502
Recorder of Misdeeds, 1261
Recorder's Office, 1414
Recording Secretary, 1365
Records Editing Office, 2356
Records Office: *chao-mo chien-chiao
   so*, 293; *chao-mo so*, 297; *ssu-chi
   ssu*, 5566; *ssu-lu ssu*, 5709
Records Reviewing Section, 4031
Records Section, 544, 4805
Records and Warrants Section, 97
Recruit Tor Office, 435
Recruiting Office, 302
Recruitment Bureau, 3463
recruitment by examination, 3193
recruitment (of mercenary soldiers),
   298
Recruitment Section, 3415
Rectification Clerk, 5589
Rectifier: *chang-cheng*, 90;
   chung-cheng, 1534; *k'uang-jen*,
   3359; *ssu-chih*, 5585; *ssu-chih
   lang*, 5588
Rectifier for the Chamberlain for
   Law Enforcement, 6778
Rectifier of Governance, 3357
Rectifier of Omissions, 4777
Rectifier-commandant of Decorum,
   419
Rector, 5550, 6029
Reed Storehouse, 6370
Regency, 3813, 5131
Regent: *chien-kuo*, 840; *chü-she*,
   1684; *lin-ch'ao*, 3718; *she-cheng*,
   5131
Regiment: *chia-la*, 667; *ch'ü*, 1690;
   shih, 5202; *t'uan*, 7380; *ying*,
   8009
Regimental Commander: *chang-
   ching*, 107; *shih-shuai*, 5311;
   ts'an-ling, 6888; *t'uan-chu*, 7381
Regimental Commander of
   Bondservants, 4484
Region: *chou*, 1332; *ch'u*, 1456; *kuo*,
   3504; *pu*, 4764
Region Unifier, 2173
Regional Administrator, 84
Regional Army, 7851
Regional Assistant, 4771
Regional Chief, 7567
Regional Command, 386
Regional Commander, 7146
Regional Commander for the
   Protection of Imperial Mausolea,
   5387
Regional Dance Director, 1917
Regional Earl, 1911
Regional Governor, 4041, 4060
Regional Headquarters, 1341, 1347
Regional Inspector: *hsün-an yü-shih*,
   2713; *hsün-ch'a k'o-tao*, 2714; *pu
   tz'u-shih*, 4811; *tz'u-shih*, 7567
Regional Investigator, 2717, 5612
Regional and Local Authorities,
   8268

Regional Mentor, 3360, 5202
Regional Military Commission, 7200
Regional Military Commissioner,
   7199
Regional Office, 1884
Regional Official, 1913
Regional Prince, 1888
Regional Rectifier, 1346
Regional Representative, 4041
Regional Retainer, 4809
Regional Supervisor, 1910, 3101
Regional Vice Commander, 2041
registered document, 2200
registered documents, 3141
Registered Documents Office, 1498
Registrar: *chang-pu*, 172; *chi-cheng*,
   533; *chih-hsüeh*, 995; *ching-li*,
   1227
Registrar of the Court ..., 5746
Registration Office, 5747
Registration Unit, 4391
Registration Unit Head, 4398
Registry, 1228, 4621
Registry Clerk, 562
Regular (title prefix), 371, 396
Regular Chamberlains, 406
Regular Metropolitan Graduate, 1150
Regular Official, 428, 455
regular paths (into officialdom), 449
regular recruitment, 3193
regular selection, 413, 5960
Regular Troops, 3285, 3323
Regularly Presented Graduates, 448
Regulator-general, 7092
Regulatory Official, 3618
Related Lady of Excellence, 3684
Relay Station for Cherishing Those
   Afar, 2820
released from the Institute, 4869
released into officialdom, 4869
Relief Commissioner, 7076
relieved of office, 1052
Religious Devotee, 5161
Religious Office, 101, 559, 7912
Religious Support Office, 3379
Reminder, 5256
Remonstrance Bureau, 882
Remonstrance Official, 836
Remonstrance Officials of the Two
   Departments, 3675
Remonstrance Secretary, 5659
Remonstrance Section, 837
Remonstrating Censor, 7952, 7854
Remote Controller, 7898
Remonstrator, 5582, 5657
Rent Collector, 5772
Rents Office for Lands of the Inner
   Banners, 4843
Repair Office, 4382
Replacement Clerk, 6132
Reporter of Ill Omens, 5227
Reports Office, 6466
Repository, 231
Repository of Monastic Certificates,
   7296
requisitioned service, 69, 2920
Reserve (prefix), 1522

Reserve Granary, 1973
Reserve Guard, 2227
resounding stone, 1933
Respectful Consort, 1211
Respectful Lady, 3439
Responder, 6113
responsible authorities, the, 5525
Restful Consort, 4310
Restorer of Frontier Defenses, 405
Restricted Regional Inspector, 6270
retained in the Institute, 3797
retained official, 3797
Retainer, 902, 2452, 7176
Retainer in the Bedchamber, 3066
Retainer Clerk, 7179
Retainer of the Outer Chamber, 7575
Retired Dignitary, 8147
Retired Helper, 4663
retired from office, 1052
Revenue Commission, 7205
Revenue Manager, 5643
Revenue Office, 2781
Revenue Section, 2781, 2798, 7194
Revenues Office, 6827
Revenues Section, 1153
Review Evaluator, 2314
Review of Probationers by Purchase,
    387
Review Section, 4583
Reviser, 3086, 4964
Rhinoceros-horn and Tortoiseshell
    Service, 7698
Right (prefix), 8033
Right Account, 8035
Right Aide, 8034
Right Army, 8048
Right Bureau, 8044, 8083
Right Corps, 8077
Right Court of Review, 8080
Right Defender of the Capital, 8045
Right Guard, 8049, 8094
Right Leader, 8040
Right Office, 8079
Right Palace Attendant, 8074
Right Scribe, 8072
Right Section, 8091
Right Section for Foreign Relations,
    8046
Right Section of Servicemen, 8075
Right Sector, 8069
Right Service Office, 8071
Right Storage Section, 8086
Right Storehouse, 8085, 8088
Right Storehouse Office, 8089
Right Subsection, 8078
Right Tribunal, 8082, 8095
Right Vault, 8085, 8088
Ringer of Bells and Musical Stones,
    5610
Rites Office, 3605
Rites Section, 3605, 3645
Ritual Academy, 3653, 6141
Ritual Apprentice, 3636
Ritual Attendant, 1028
Ritual Duty Official, 3600
Ritual and Music Section, 3655
Ritual Official, 2645, 7109

Ritual Receptionist, 199
Ritual Receptions Office, 5787
Ritual Regalia Section, 1858
Ritual Regalia Storehouse, 1858
Ritual Regulation Service, 3599
Ritual Revision Service, 2976
Ritual Service, 2975
Ritualist, 2992, 3017, 6377
Ritualist of the Inherited Region,
    7307
River Conservancy Commissioner,
    2196, 2800
River Controller, 6921
River Maintenance Circuit, 2202
River Patroller, 2735, 4710
River Tax Supervisor, 5771
River Transport Bureau, 4392
River Transport Office, 1335
River-patrol Censor, 2723
Rivers and Canals Section, 2171
Riverside Granary Office, 5513
Roaming Horse Pasturage, 3801
Roster of Lesser Scholastics, 4025
rotated down (or off), 1869
rotated up (or onto), 1881
rotation, in, 3871
Rotational Artisan, 7360
Rotational Entertainer, 7361
Rotational Troops, 4404
Route, 3840
Route Command, 7112
Route Command for State Farms and
    Hunting, 7415
Route Commander, 7110
Royal Archivist, 3368
Royal Astrologer, 4453
Royal Astronomer, 1981
Royal Attendant-in-ordinary, 8164
Royal Charioteer, 3091
Royal Clanswoman, 4218
Royal Coachman, 4815, 6202
Royal Commissioner, 8053
Royal Drummer, 3232
Royal Foot Escort, 3890
Royal Groom, 6011, 6201
Royal Guardsman, 2794
Royal Iceman, 3758
Royal Kinswoman, 4283
Royal Learning Retreat, 4604
Royal Physician, 557
Royal Progress, 2740
Royal Scout, 7348
Royal Scribe, 8167
Royal Secretary, 4236
Royal Surgeon, 7879
Royal Tailor, 1995
Royal Tour of Inspection, 2758
Royal Tutor, 1445
Royal Valet, 761
Rubbing Maker, 6125
Ruler, 1354
ruling class, the, 5148, 5162
Runner, 4789
rural elite, 2346
rural gentry, 2346

Saber-armed Guard, 948
sacred fields, 602

Sacred Fields Office, 602
Sacrificer, 2017, 7570
Sacrifices Section, 7550
Sacrifices Service, 7550
Sacrificial Aide, 578, 5552, 6851
Sacrificial Commissioner, 1088
Sacrificial Office, 2024, 7552
Sacrificial Priest, 1031
Sacrificing Official, 5793, 5794
Saddlery Service, 26
Saddlery Storehouse, 27, 609
Salaried Apprentice Physician, 5284
salary office, 569
salary ranks, 568
Salt Administration, 7924
Salt Aide, 7025
Salt Commission, 7953
Salt Commissioner, 1726
Salt Control Circuit, 7934
Salt Control Station, 7963
Salt Controller, 7213
Salt Depot, 8278
Salt Distribution Commissioner,
    7212, 7213
Salt Distribution Supervisor, 7856
Salt Distribution Supervisorate, 7944
Salt and Grain Tax Circuit, 7933
Salt and Incense Tax Office, 7937
Salt Inspector, 7923, 7938
Salt and Iron Monopoly Bureau,
    7859
Salt and Iron Monopoly
    Commissioner, 7858
Salt Maid, 4350
Salt Marsh Directorate, 7926
Salt Monopoly Bureau, 7859
Salt Monopoly Commissioner, 1727,
    7858
Salt Monopoly Office, 7946
Salt Monopoly Official, 7964
Salt Steward, 7941
Salt Supervisor, 7924
Salt Tax Office, 7943
Salt and Wine Tax Office, 7929
Salt-control Censor, 2756, 2767
Saltern Commissioner-in-chief, 7922
Saltern Office, 7921
Sanctifier of Covenants, 5720
Sand Gathering Office, 6841
Sauce Maker, 691
Sauceman, 6058
Savant, 4882
Scents Service, 6061
Scholar, 2704
scholar-officials, see elite, official
    class
School of the Four Gates, 5719
School of the Four Sage Clans, 5767
School at the Gate of the Great
    Capital, 2909
School for the Heir Apparent, 7538,
    7542
School for the Imperial Family,
    7102, 7165
School at the Palace of Universal
    Peace, 2494
School for the Princes, 7647

School for the Sons of the State, 3542

Schools of the Three Sage Clans, 4905

Scions of State, 3539

Scout, 2215

Scouting Brigade, 832

Scribbler, 6320

Scribe: *chu-shu*, 1428; *shih*, 5199; *shu-shih*, 5457; *t'ieh-hsieh chung-shu*, 6506

Scrollbinder, 1508, 1512

Sea Transport Brigade, 2130

Sea Transport Defense Battalion, 2128

Sea Transport Defense Brigade, 1921

seal, 7968

Seal Keeper, 6580, 6673

Seal Maker, 1452

Seal Office, 6287

Seal-holder, 144

Seal-holding, 217

Seal-holding Director, 218, 221

Seal-holding Official, 146, 219

Seal-keeper, 1095

Seals Office: *shang-pao ssu*, 5029; *ssu-pao ssu*, 5734; *tien-pao so*, 6621; *yin-fang*, 7982

Seals Secretary, 2058, 2091

Seals Section, 8002

Seals Service, 1453, 5028

Seamstress, 104

seasonal camp, 4078

Seasons Section, 5322

Second, 1826

Second Assistant Salt Controller, 8283

Second Category, 1827

Second Chinese Duty Group, 2137

Second Class Administrative Official, 5202

Second Cook, 853

Second Distinguished Garrison, 2726

Second Manchu Duty Group, 3914

Second Section, 2289, 2290

Second Standby Garrison, 2952

Second Veterinarian Directorate, 2291

Second-class Prince, 3687

Secondary Army, 6960

Secondary Concubine, 4351, 8161

Secondary Concubines, 1320

Secondary Consort, 7556

Secondary Gentleman for Meritorious Achievement, 6375

Secondary Gentleman for Promoted Service, 6348

Secretarial Academy, 5989

Secretarial Aide, 593

Secretarial Censor, 1065, 5310

Secretarial Clerk, 1063

Secretarial Court Gentlemen, 5047

Secretarial Receptionist, 3181, 7507

Secretarial Section, 1066

Secretariat: *chung-shu sheng*, 1619; *nei-shu sheng*, 4256; *pi-shu chien*, 4588; *tzu-wei sheng*, 7545

Secretariat Clerk, 5195

Secretariat Director, 1616

Secretariat Drafter, 1618

Secretariat Examiner, 1609

Secretariat of the Heir Apparent, 1524, 3936

Secretariat Mentor, 3182

Secretariat Rear Section, 1612

Secretariat Supervisor, 1608

Secretariat-Chancellery, 1617

Secretaries in the Grand Secretariat, 4194

Secretary: *chang-ching*, 107; *chang-shu*, 188; *chih-shih*, 1049; *chih-shu*, 1059, 1060; *chu-shih*, 1420; *chung she-jen*, 1599; *chung-shu*, 1606; *hsiao chün-chi*, 2398; *kuan-chi she-jen*, 3274; *lin-ya*, 3732; *lu-shih shih*, 3858; *nei she-jen*, 4233; *she-jen*, 5136; *ssu-yüan*, 5839

Secretary in the Council of State, 1734

Secretary of the Council of State Concurrently Serving as Assistant Duty Group Chief, 4442

Secretary of the Council of State Concurrently Serving as Duty Group Chief, 3766

Secretary for Native Affairs, 2946

Secretary-companion, 4416

Secretary's Office, 1425

Section: *an*, 8; *fang*, 1893; *k'o*, 3187; *ts'ao*, 6916

Section for Administrators, 3740

Section for Altars and Temples, 6278

Section for the Arrest of Bandits, 4803

Section for Astrological Interpretation, 4906

Section for Attendants-in-ordinary, 267

Section for Building Materials, 6837

Section for Calendrical Calculations, 5857

Section in the Capital, 7264

Section for Censors, 8177

Section for Ceremonial Propriety, 3611

Section Chief, 177, 3188

Section Clerk, 6931

Section for Commandery Governors, 1829

Section for Communication with the Nobility, 2022

Section for Communications and Horse-breeding, 676

Section for Confirmations, 6458

Section for Cultivated Fields, 6718

Section for the Cultivation of Militancy, 2638

Section for Eighth Rank Personnel, 4375

Section for Fines and Confiscations, 1518

Section for Foreign Relations, 1880

Section for Forestry and Crafts, 8198

Section for Grand Masters, 5941

Section for the History of the Dynasty, 3532

Section for Honors and Enfeoffments, 2729

Section for Imperial Armaments, 8115

Section for Inner Troops, 1588

Section for Judicial Offices, 1856

Section for Justice, 7244, 7246

Section for Labor Exemptions, 3990

Section for Laws, 6572

Section for Major Trials, 2894

Section for Memorials Requesting Judicial Decisions, 7045

Section for Military Selections, 7755

Section for Ministry Affairs (in Ministry of Rites), 3017

Section for the Ninth Rank, 1316

Section for Northern Relations, 4520

Section for Outer Troops, 7602

Section for Palace Affairs, 6565

Section for Palace Service, 1057

Section for the People, 4002

Section for Personnel Registers, 4410

Section for Promulgations, 4402

Section for Public Construction, 635

Section for Receptions, 1398, 3204

Section for Rectitude, 7173

Section for Rites, 3017

Section for Roads and Bridges, 6309

Section for Sacrifices, 7566

Section of Sacrificial Grains and Animals, 3724

Section for Section Clerks, 6932

Section for the Seventh Rank, 632

Section for the Sixth Rank, 3804

Section for Southern Relations, 4092

Section for Submission of Recommendations, 1136

Section for Submitted Tribes, 1875

Section Supervising Fords and Drainways, 810

Section for Terminations, 6743

Section for the Three Dukes, 4872

Section for Tributary Relations, 4657

Section for Vice Commissioners, 2100

Section for Water Transport, 6928

Sector, 7181

Secular Palace Musician, 165

Security Group, 4450

Security Group Head, 4451, 4460

Security Group Horses, 4491

Security Guard, 4499

Security Officer of an Outer Region, 7610

Security Official, 529

Sedan-chair Bearer, 2027

Sedan-chair Foreman, 5014

Sedan-chair Master, 155

Sedan-chair Service, 2028, 5015

Sedan-chair Supervisor, 1409

Sedate Consort, 1505

Seed Specialist, 5574

Selected Student, 2670
selection, 2653
Selection of Subofficial
   Functionaries, 3824
selection by substitution, 6367
Selectman, 2667
Selector of the East, 7428
Selector of the West, 2235
self-appraisal, 7521
Semiannual Taxes Subsection, 1845
send down, 2288
Senior, 6949
Senior Adjutant, 4991
Senior Appointments Process, 5046
Senior Censor, 4093, 4125
Senior Civil Appointments Process,
   5058
Senior Commandant of Light
   Chariots, 4988
Senior Commandant-in-chief of
   Cavalry, 4980
Senior Compiler, 2614
Senior Compiler of the Academy,
   6583
Senior Dancing Master, 5959
Senior General-in-chief, 5065
Senior Grand Master, 5066
Senior Grand Secretary, 5372
Senior Lieutenant, 2375
Senior Messenger, 5957
Senior Military Appointments
   Process, 5060
Senior Military Protector, 4999
Senior Minister, 4987
Senior Official, 143, 6297, 6303
Senior Palace Attendant, 2344
Senior Recorder, 4834, 4837
Senior Recorder for Comprehensive
   Duty, 7474
Senior Rectifier, 1534
Senior Serviceman, 5037, 8237
Senior Steward, 4261
Senior Subalterns, 153
Senior Supervising Secretary, 588,
   1540
Senior Supplicator, 5913
Senior Three Judicial Offices, 6012
Senior Writer, 5914
Sentence Evaluator, 2362, 4715
Sentence Evaluators Section, 2361
Sentence Fulfillment Section, 7019
Sentence Promulgating Section, 2662
Sentence Review Section, 2319
Sentenced Soldiers, 348
Sentencing Aide, 7358
Sentry, 3027
separate, 3697
Separating and Registering Section,
   1942
Servant, 2377
Service, 1674
Service Allocation Office, 7868
Service for the Altars of the Soil and
   Grain, 6209
Service for the Capital Approaches,
   4671
Service of the Imperial Ornaments,
   8212

Service of the Imperial Stud, 7136
Service of the Imperial Utensils, 641
Service of Rare Embroideries, 3034
Service of Rare Textiles, 3033
Service of Sacrificial Animals, 5760
Service of Shih Tao-an, 5317
Service of Yang Lin, 7884
Serviceman, 5200
Servicemen, 7970
serving in his titular office, 5395
Settlement, 7074
Settlement Head, 7075
Seven Chief Ministers, 616
Seven Encampments, 642
Seventh Class Administrative
   Official, 2641
Sewing Office, 5590
Sewing Service, 381
Shaman, 1902
Shamaness, 4827
Shamanism Office, 5151
Sheep Office, 5818
Shop, 1892
Shops and Yards Section, 1894
Shouter of Warnings, 2170
Shouting Guide, 2190
Signal Beacon Section, 7226
Silencer, 2521
Silk Brocade Office, 3745
Silk Brocade Workshop, 3745
Silk Worker, 198
Silks and Furs Storehouse, 7371
Silks Office, 5786
Silks Storehouse, 7364
Silver Pavilion, 7996
Silver Vault, 7983
simple (ranking prefix), 814
Singer, 3173, 5668
Single Classic Specialist, 2693
Sino-Manchu Translation Office,
   4172
Six Categories, 3793
Six Chief Stewards, 3810
Six Colleges, 3817
Six Commander-generals, 3821
Six Directresses, 3814
Six Groups, 3826
Six Herds, 3787
Six Hsi Tribes, 2258
Six Imperial Armies, 3785
Six Investigators, 3779
Six Ladies of Deportment, 3792
Six Managers, 3818
Six Matrons, 3810
Six Mentors of the Eastern Palace,
   7442
Six Ministers, 3812
Six Ministries, 3795, 3805
Six Offices, 3788, 3826
Six Offices of Scrutiny, 3793
Six Palace Corrals, 164
Six Palace Services, 3784, 3811
Six Principal Wives, 3798
Six Sections, 3820
Six Services, 3784
Six Stables, 3783
Six Storehouses, 3794

Six Tax Supervisors, 3789
Six Troops, 3805
Sixteen Guards, 5290
Sixth Class Administrative Official,
   5199
Skilled Archer, 6836
Skilled Soldier, 6831
Skilled Workman, 537
Slave, 4320
Small Security Group, 2425
Soaring Hawk Garrison, 8030
Soaring Hawk Guard, 8031
Social Exemplar, 2453
Soft Leather Service, 3084
soldier, 4665, 7047
Sole Recipient of Secret Orders,
   7187
Solitaries, 3222
Son of Heaven, 6719
Son by the Principal Wife, 5330
Son by a Secondary Wife, 5468
Sorcerer, 4130, 7734
Sorceror for Horses, 7807
Sorceress, 4349, 7734
South Commissioner, 4118
South Prison, 4121
South Township, 4097
South Visitors Bureau, 4100
Southeastern War Prisoner, 3996
Southern Administration, 4107
Southern Army, 4094
Southern Chinese, 3922
Southern Command, 4131
Southern Court, 4136
Southern Establishment, 4136
Southern Mint, 4133
Southern and Northern Bureaus,
   4113
Southern and Northern Granaries of
   the Department of State Affairs,
   4111
Southern and Northern Residence
   Halls, 4109
Southern and Northern Storehouses,
   4110
Southern Office of the Grand
   Princes, 4124
Southern Office of Imperial Clan
   Affairs, 4128
Southern Offices, 4122, 4131
Southern Palace, 4102
Southern Park, 4135
Southern Residence Hall, 4085
Southern Storehouse, 4084
Southern Storehouse of the Left
   Vault, 8113
Southern Study, 4119
Southern War Prisoner, 3917
Southerner, 4099
Southwestern Defense Section, 3341
Speaking Official, 7945
Spears Office, 3169
Special Accounts Section, 1128,
   1142, 4285
Special Category Men, 4941
Special Commissioner, 6341
Special Control Office, 1486

Special Delegate, 7688
special edict, 6333
special examination, 1011
Special Gifts Storehouse, 4191
Special Preparations Section, 5130
special reappointment, 6969
special recruitment, 969
Special Reserves Vault, 7961
Special Stable, 3842
Special Supply Commissioner, 7056
Specially Established (prefix), 6334
Specially Gifted Artisan, 4026
Specially Promoted Grand Master for Glorious Happiness, 6336
Specially Promoted Grand Master for Splendid Happiness, 6337
Specially Promoted Senior Minister for Aid in Governance, 6338
Specially-appointed Administrator, 1484
Specially-appointed Examining Editor of Imperial Writings, 1485
Spell Chanter, 1337
Spice Keeper, 1382
Spice Pantry, 118
Spiceman, 2127
Spicewoman, 4337
Splendid Consort, 2807
Spokesman for the Ruler, 2223
sponsored appointment, 4486
Spring Chamberlain, 1523
Spring Office, 1525
Spring Support, 1525
Squad: *chia*, 650; *huo*, 2914; *p'ai*, 4391; *p'eng*, 4566; *ssu*, 5533; *wu*, 7732
Squad Commander, 651, 2383, 4398
Squad Leader, 4384
Squadron, 4647
Stabilization Fund Bureau, 256
Stabilization Fund Office, 255
Stabilization Fund Section, 253
Stabilization Fund Supervisorate, 6402, 6403
Stable, 1285
Stable for Ceremonial Mounts, 5992
Stable of Flying Mounts, 1929
Stable of the Imperial Coachman, 492
Stable for Imperial Processions, 7069
Stable Keeper, 2497
Stable Manager, 109
Stable Master, 1311
Stable of Myriad Mounts, 7619
Stables of Meteoric Mounts, 4562
Stables Office, 1312
Stables of the Palace Colts, 4171
Stables of Trustworthy Mounts, 108
Staff Administrator, 6980
Staff Foreman, 5691
Staff Officers, 3695
Staff Supervisor, 5388
Staff Supervisors Office, 5391
Standard Script Calligrapher for the Dynastic History, 2467
Standard-bearer Guard, 638
Standby Garrison, 2954

Standby Gentleman, 4874
Standby Guard, 3029
Star Watcher, 6582
State, 3504
State Councilor, 6810
State Courier-envoy, 3516
State Farm, 7409
State Farm Battalion, 7410
State Farm Directorate, 7407
State Farms Brigade, 7417
State Farms Bureau, 5779, 7408, 7411, 7414
State Farms Circuit, 7416
State Farms Clerk, 7412
State Farms Commission, 7413
State Farms Office, 7414
State Farms Section, 7409
State Finance Commission, 4912
State Finance Commission Accounting Office, 4914
State Finance Commissioner, 1022, 4915
State Finance Office, 3551
State Fiscal Commission, 798
State Fiscal Commissioner, 3507, 4915
State Grain Section, 2797
State Historiographer, 2626, 3529
state laborer, 3443
state land, 3332
State Monopoly Agent, 867
State Properties Subsection, 1915
State Refuge, 4820
State Salt Monopoly, 7026
Station Master, 6468
Statistics Section, 3994
Steward: *chang-k'o*, 137; *feng-chih*, 1968; *fu-ling*, 2081; *tsai*, 6809
Steward of the Empress Dowager, 241, 242, 251
Steward-bulwark of State, 6817
Steward-regulator of State, 6818
Stipend Student, 3727, 3728, 4791
Stipends Office, 2020
Stock Clerk, 4564
Stockade, 58
Stockade Commander, 62
Stoneyard, 5268
Storage Monitoring Office, 7067
Storage Office, 3340
Storehouse: *fu*, 2034; *k'u*, 3248; *tsang*, 6896; *tsang-fu*, 6898
Storehouse Commissioner, 3251
Storehouse Commissioner-in-chief, 3253
Storehouse for Court Ritual Regalia, 323
Storehouse for Drugs Acquired by Redemption, 5469
Storehouse of Gifts, 987
Storehouse (of Interpreters Institute), 5362
Storehouse Keeper, 3252
Storehouse of Leather and Metal, 1084
Storehouse Manager, 3254
Storehouse of Musical and Ritual

Gear for the Altar of Heaven, 8246
Storehouse for Musical and Sacrificial Instruments, 6731
Storehouse of New Clothes, 2554
Storehouse Office, 5788
Storehouse for Precious Valuables, 631
Storehouse Section, 3250
Storehouse of Silk Bolts, 5392
Storehouse of Spices and Silks, 547
Storehouse of Treasures, 8130
Storehouse of Utensils for the Imperial Ancestral Temple, 6189
Storehouse-inspecting (prefix), 2744
Storehouseman, 3258
Storekeeper, 200, 473
Storekeeper of Treasures, 8130
Stores Office, 2034
Stove Attendant, 4567
straightforward and upright, 1896
Straight-pointer, 951
Street Patrolman, 771
Striped Hides Service, 2481
Student, 2702, 5175
Student Calendar Binder, 1509
Student by Contribution, 4077
Student of General Medicine, 2992
Student by Grace, 1815
Student by Inheritance, 7975, 7990
Student by Purchase, 1702, 2348, 3596
Student by Purchase, First Class, 3719
Student by Purchase, Fourth Class, 856
Student by Purchase, Second Class, 6943
Student by Purchase, Third Class, 2043
students, 1419
Study Hall, 59
Subeditor, 735
subject, 392
subject to rotational duty, 1862
submit (a memorial), 4970
Submitted T'u-yü-hun, 7351
Suboffical Functionary: *hsiao-li*, 2413; *hsü-li*, 2648; *hsü-shih*, 2 0; *hsü-tso*, 2652; *li*, 3586; *shu-jen*, 5437; *yüan-li*, 8230
suboffical post, 6801
subordinate to, 5409
Subordinated Prefecture, 571
Subprecinct, 4391
Subprefectural Buddhist Registry, 4943
Subprefectural Magistrate, 965, 7471, 7497
Subprefecture, 1332, 6748
Subsection, 3187, 5523
Subsidiary Clerk, 5409
substantive, 5201
substantive appointment, 5305
substantively appointed to fill a vacancy, 5234
subtribe, 5286

Suburban Sacrifices Office, 743
Summer Chamberlain, 2293
Summer Office, 2296
Summer Palace, 8235
Summer Support, 2296
Summer Tax Section, 2796
summon (for appointment), 394
Sun Time Specialist, 3059
Superintendency, 6461, 6479
Superintendency of Buddhist
  Happiness, 823
Superintendency of Court Clothing
  and Regalia, 6471
Superintendency of Fines and
  Confiscations, 7370
Superintendency of Medicine, 3036
Superintendency of Ordination
  Certificates, 6463
Superintendency of Palace
  Gardening, 6324
Superintendency of Physician
  Families, 3305
Superintendency-in-chief for
  Artisans, 3277
Superintendent: chien-tu, 873;
  t'i-ling, 6459; t'i-tien kuan,
  t'i-tien. 6475; tsung-li, 7121
Superintendent of the Capital
  Granaries, 6480
Superintendent of Ceremonies, 7126
Superintendent of Coinage, 1375
Superintendent of the Directorate of
  Astronomy, 7122
Superintendent of the Directorate
  of Horses, 6477
Superintendent of the Disposition of
  the Ministry of Revenue's Monies,
  6462
Superintendent of Domestic Customs
  Barriers, 3328
Superintendent of the Five Offices,
  6481
Superintendent of Grain Supplies,
  3892
Superintendent of the Grand Canal,
  7124
Superintendent of the Grand Canal
  and of Grain Transport, 7125
Superintendent of the Imperial
  Calendar, 1110
Superintendent of Imperial Silk
  Manufacturing, 1081, 1082
Superintendent of the Interpreters
  Institute, 6488
Superintendent of the Interpreters
  and Translators Institute, 6489
Superintendent of the Left
  Storehouse, 7011
Superintendent of the Mausoleum,
  6478
Superintendent of Medical
  Education, 2692
Superintendent of Mints, 6460
Superintendent of the ... Palace,
  6476
Superintendent of Postal Relay
  Stations, 3329

Superintendent of the Right
  Storehouse, 8090
Superintendent of Salt Distribution,
  7131
Superintendent of Seals, 876
Superintendent of the ... Taoist
  Temple, 6476
Superintendent of Training, 6450
Superintendent of the Translators
  Institute, 6491
Superior Area Command, 6087,
  6097
Superior Chamberlains, 4987
Superior College, 5034
Superior Concubines, 5030
Superior Duke Grand Mentor, 6164
Superior Dukes, 5010
Superior Grand Master of the Palace,
  6155
Superior Prefecture, 2034, 4853
Superior Prefecture, Second Class,
  7559
Superior Protectorate, 5072
Superior Security Group, 7262
Supernumerary, 4355, 8250
Supernumerary Director, 2514
Supernumerary Follower, 3094
Supernumerary Official, 7594
Supernumerary Palace Eunuch
  Usher, 6504
Supernumerary Vice Minister, 8251
Supervising (prefix), 3318
Supervising Attendant, 7255
Supervising Censor, 587, 793, 878
Supervising Secretaries and Censors,
  3201
Supervising Secretary:
  chi-shih-chung, 587; chi-shih lang,
  590; chung chi-shih, 1539; hsiao
  men-hsia, 2423; yüan-shih, 8237,
  8239
Supervising Secretary of the
  Chancellery, 7454
Supervisor: cheng, 396; chien, 786;
  chien-cheng, 801; chien ... shih,
  857; chih-chih, 949; kuan-hsia
  kuan, 3297; kuan-ling, 3318;
  kung-shih, 3470; ling-hsia, 3757;
  p'an, p'an-shih, 4436; p'an-yüan,
  p'an yüan-shih, 4438; p'u-yeh,
  4826; t'i-chü, 6395; t'i-tiao kuan,
  t'i-tiao, 6470; tu, 7180; tu-t'ung,
  7321
Supervisor of Administrative Clerks,
  6421
Supervisor of the Advisory Office,
  6404
Supervisor of the Affairs of ...,
  4438
Supervisor of the Alum Monopoly,
  954
Supervisor of Archives, 6394
Supervisor of the Buddhist Clergy,
  5556
Supervisor of the Bureau, 4437
Supervisor of the Bureau of
  Personnel Assignments, 4430

Supervisor of the Capital Security
  Office, 6417
Supervisor of the Cereals Granary,
  3246
Supervisor of Ceremonial Seating,
  5570
Supervisor of Ceremonies, 6590
Supervisor of the Chancellery, 4431
Supervisor of Coinage, 7209
Supervisor of Confucian Schools,
  3068
Supervisor of the Court, 4437
Supervisor of Court Gentlemen,
  3574
Supervisor of Craftsmen, 5577
Supervisor of Customs Duties, 5679
Supervisor of Dependencies, 6602
Supervisor of Dependent Countries,
  6646
Supervisor of the Directorate of
  Astrology, 6215
Supervisor of the Dynastic History,
  6425
Supervisor of Education, 6422, 6469
Supervisor of the Entourage, 3095
Supervisor of Exterior Districts,
  5868
Supervisor of Food, 5222
Supervisor of Foods, 6630
Supervisor of Forestry and Hunting,
  4969
Supervisor of Foundries, 6419
Supervisor of Foundries and
  Maritime Trade, 6418
Supervisor of the Four Imperial
  Parks, 5843
Supervisor of Grain and Salt
  Exchange and of Community Self-
  defense, 6405
Supervisor of Granaries and
  Agriculture, 6906
Supervisor of Grooms, 7039
Supervisor of Horse Purchases, 6427
Supervisor of the Household, 79,
  7378
Supervisor of Hunting, 2706
Supervisor of the Imperial Ancestral
  Temple, 1036
Supervisor of the Imperial Clan,
  5071
Supervisor of the Imperial
  Manufactories, 4993
Supervisor of Law Enforcement,
  6768
Supervisor of Marshes, 6937
Supervisor of Medicine Tasting, 277
Supervisor of the Memorials Office,
  6407
Supervisor of the Military, 6431
Supervisor of Militia, 875
Supervisor of the Ministry, 4433
Supervisor of Mongolian Schools,
  3971
Supervisor of the Office, 4437
Supervisor of the ... Palace, 6424
Supervisor of the Palace Attendants,
  5231

Supervisor of the Palace Maintenance Office, 6414
Supervisor of Police, 3296
Supervisor of Post-audience Banquets, 3572
Supervisor of Postal Relay Stations, 2737, 2749
Supervisor of Preparation of the Dynastic Administrative Regulations, 6430
Supervisor of the Prisoner Cart, 799
Supervisor of Public Lands, 3722
Supervisor of Receptionists, 6110
Supervisor of Residences for Commandery and District Princesses, 6410
Supervisor of the Rice Granary, 3978
Supervisor of Rites, 6587
Supervisor of Sacrifices to the Soil, 5756
Supervisor of the Salt Storehouse, 7960
Supervisor of the School for the Imperial Family, 6437
Supervisor of Schools, 6415
Supervisor of the Six Palace Services and of Administrative Clerks, 6426
Supervisor of the State Finance Commission, 4434
Supervisor of the Suburban Sacrifices, 5579
Supervisor of the ... Taoist Temple, 6424
Supervisor of the Tea Monopoly, 952
Supervisor of a Tea and Salt Supervisorate, 6397
Supervisor of the Ten Ponds in the Imperial Forest, 5019
Supervisor of Territories, 2570
Supervisor of the Three Fiscal Agencies, 4434
Supervisor of Tones, 7974
Supervisor of Transactions, 809
Supervisor of Transport, 808, 884
Supervisor of Tribute Goods, 822
Supervisor of the T'ung-chou Terminus of the Grand Canal, 6979
Supervisor of Umbrella-making, 174
Supervisor of Villages, 3893
Supervisor of Water Clocks, 784
Supervisor of Wines, 1292
Supervisor of the Yellow River Conservancy Office, 6413
Supervisor-general, 7091, 7141
Supervisor-in-chief: tsung-kuan, 7110; tu t'i-chü, 7294; tu t'i-chü kuan, 7295; tu-tu, 7311
Supervisor-in-chief in Command of Pasturages in the Two Pasturelands, 7486
Supervisor-in-chief of the Imperial Mausolea Administration, 3750
Supervisor-in-chief of the Six Storehouses, 7114

Supervisorate, 6395
Supervisorate of Accounts, 6400
Supervisorate of Agriculture, 6813
Supervisorate of Archery, 6423
Supervisorate of Brocade Weaving and Dyeing, 3744
Supervisorate for Capital Construction, 6438
Supervisorate of Coinage, 4473
Supervisorate of Community Self-defense, 6429
Supervisorate of Construction, 8025
Supervisorate of Education, 6416
Supervisorate of Gold and Silver Utensils, 1167
Supervisorate of Grain and Salt Exchange, 6406
Supervisorate of Grain Supplies, 6436
Supervisorate of Grain Tax Transport, 8280 .
Supervisorate of Horse Trading, 6396
Supervisorate of Incense, Tea, and Alum, 6412
Supervisorate of Land Transport, 3864
Supervisorate of Land Transport to the Two Capitals, 3686
Supervisorate of Medical Relief, 3338
Supervisorate of Medical Schools, 2959
Supervisorate of Medicines, 3035
Supervisorate of Monasteries, 6652
Supervisorate of Monopoly Taxes, 6409
Supervisorate of Physicians, 3304
Supervisorate of the Pien River Dikes, 6428
Supervisorate of Paper Money, 4458
Supervisorate of River Defense, 2174
Supervisorate of Storehouses in the Capital Agencies, 6435
Supervisorate of Tea Groves, 57
Supervisorate of the T'ung-chou Terminus of the Grand Canal, 6979
Supervisorate of the Various State Storehouses, 6408
Supervisorate of Waterways, 6411
Supervisorate-in-chief, 7112
Supervisorate-in-chief of All Classes of Artisans, 1415
Supervisorate-in-chief of Civilian Artisans, 3991
Supervisorate-in-chief of Coinage, 4474
Supervisorate-in-chief of Metal Workers and Jewelers, 1171
Supervisorate-in-chief of Migratory Hunters, Falconers, and All Classes of Artisans, 5870
Supervisorate-in-chief of Palace Schools, 7113
Supervisors of Water Clocks in the Five Offices, 7785

Supervisory Commissioner, 1461
Supervisory Director, 838
Supervisory Governor, 7292
Supervisory Inspector of the Inner Hostel, 530
Supervisory Inspector of the Outer Hostel, 532
Supervisory Office, 864
Supervisory Official, 835
Supervisory Service, 1605
Supervisory Superintendent of Coinage, 6434
supplemental assignment, 656
Supplemental Tribute Student by Grace, 1818
supplementary (prefix), 6711
Supplementary Appointee, 4800
Supplementary Charioteer, 6321
Supplementary List, 2090
Supplementary Official, 6694, 7468
Supplementary Secondary Wives, 4651
Supplementary Security Guard, 8196
supplementary selection, 45
Supplementary Student, 2063, 2095
Supplicant, 1355
Supplicant for Rain, 1281
Supplication Scribe, 1424
Supplies Section, 3669
Supply Commission, 1861, 6909
Supply Commissioner: ch'ang-p'ing kuan, 254; chieh-tu shih, 777; ching-chih ... kan-pan ch'ang-p'ing kung-shih, 1205; fa-ün shih, 1860; shui-lu fa-yün shih, 5502
Supply and Printing Office, 2604
Support Army, 1380
Supporter on the Right, 8067
Supporter-commandant of the State, 2000
Supporter-general of the State, 1999
Supporter-generalissimo of the State, 2001
Supporting Official, 7175
Supreme Area Command, 7309
Supreme Chief, 7266
Supreme Chief Minister for Administration, 404
Supreme Commandant, 7323
Supreme Commandant of the Palace Armies, 8112, 8121
Supreme Commander, 7158
Supreme Commissioner of Accounts, 7088
Supreme Control Commission, 7097
Supreme Councilor, 4998
Supreme Governor, 7316
Supreme Grand Preceptor, 7291
Supreme National Commander-in-chief, 6700
Supreme Pillar of State, 4990
Supreme Supervisorate-in-chief, 7308
Supreme Supervisorate-in-chief of All Classes of Artisans, 1415
Supreme Supervisorate-in-chief for Revenues, 6828

Surname of State, 3435, 3518
Surplus Man, 8128
Surrendered Forces, 3373
Surrendered Po-hai and Khitan
  Forces, 4728
Surveillance (prefix), 3265
Surveillance Agent, 2826
Surveillance Circuit Judge, 3270
Surveillance Commission. 13. 5849,
  6447
Surveillance Commissioner, 12,
  3269
Surveillance Commissioner for
  Military Training, 7386
Surveillance Commissioner's Agent,
  3266
Surveillance Commissioners, 864
Surveillance Commissions, 864
Surveillance, Investigation, and
  Supervisory Commissioner, 15
Surveillance Jurisdiction, 7393
Surveillance Official, 47
Surveillance and Supervisory
  Commissioner, 3267
Surveillance Vice Commissioner, 10
Surveyor, 3668, 7347
Swords Office, 657, 4403
Swordsman, 5537
Swordsman in Attendance, 5537
Swordsman Guard, 909

Table Maid, 176
Tai-chou Directorate of Coinage,
  6130
Tailoring Shop, 377
tally, 2200
Tangutan School, 6296
Taoist Administrator, 5838
Taoist Affairs Service, 1654
Taoist offices, 6317
Taoist Patriarch, 415, 416
Taoist posts, 6310
Taoist Recruit, 6311
Taoist Registry, 6307, 6308, 6312
Taoist School, 1655, 7513
Tapestry Weaver, 4065
Targets and Arrows Section, 280
Tax Assistant, 2770
Tax Bureau, 5799, 7205
Tax Captain, 3658
Tax Circuit, 3683
Tax Circuit Intendant, 7254
Tax Collector, 2105
Tax Commission, 2791
Tax and Credit Office, 893
Tax Manager, 3316
Tax Office, 914
Tax Section, 7196
Tax Transport Bureau, 1492
Tax Transport Leader, 4384
Tax Transport and Salt Monopoly
  Commission, 1493
Tea Control Station, 55
Tea and Salt Control Station, 4614
Tea and Salt Inspector, 805
Tea and Salt Monopoly and
  Supervisory Commissioner, 51

Tea and Salt Monopoly and Tax
  Transport Commissioner, 52
Tea and Salt Supervisor, 6398, 6401
Tea and Salt Supervisorate, 54, 6399
Tea Section, 40
Tea Server, 4973
Tea Storehouse, 46
Teacher, 2761
Teaching Aide, 6584
Temple, 1173, 3980
Temple Attendant, 3982
Temple Clerk, 3984
Temple Director, 3985, 5205
Temple of the Empress, 2219
Temple of the Heir Apparent, 6242
Temple Maintenance Office, 5816
Temple Registrar, 3987
temple salary, 7564
Temple School, 3983
Ten (group of families), 5196
Ten Grand Ministers Administering
  Affairs, 3641
Ten Guard Commands, 5313
Ten Imperial Armies, 5236
Tender of the Water Clock, 3838
Tent Handler, 207
Tentmaker, 5812
Tents Office, 6667
term of service, 1862
Territorial Administrator, 759, 5402
Territorial Official, 6363
Territorial Representative, 314, 551
Third Category, 4844
Third Class Administrative Official,
  5533
Third Day Audience Officers, 1318
Third Graduate, 6275
Third Ranking Metropolitan
  Graduate, 6739
Thirteen Bureaus, 5297
Thirteen Circuits, 5298
This Weakling, 1663
Thousand Cavaliers, 887
Three, the, 4830
Three Adjutants, 4849
Three Area Commanders-in-chief,
  4926
Three Armies, 4849
Three Bureaus, 4934
Three Capital Guards, 4929
Three Chamberlains of the Heir
  Apparent, 6247
Three Circuits, 4881
Three Colleges, 4899
Three Commandants, 4859
Three Commands, 4931
Three Commissioners, 4902
Three Communicating Agencies,
  4922
Three Companions, 4883
Three Concubines, 4891
Three Consorts, 4851, 4855
Three Corps, 4909
Three Court Gentlemen, 4873
Three Courts, 4913
Three Defenders of the Metropolitan
  Area, 4857

Three Departments, 4852, 4900,
  6211
Three Departments and the Bureau
  of Military Affairs, the, 4901
Three Dignitaries, 4912
Three Dukes, 4871
Three Eastern Provinces, 7449
Three Elders, 4832
Three Fiscal Agencies, 4912
Three Garrisons, 4852
Three Grand Attendants in the
  Eastern Palace, 7446
Three Great Administrations, 4918
Three Great Training Divisions,
  4920
Three Greats, 4917
Three Guardians, 4854
Three Inner Banners, 4228
Three Institutes, 4867
Three Judicial Agencies, 4912
Three Judicial Commissioners, 4915
Three Judicial Offices, 4850
Three Junior Counselors of the Heir
  Apparent, 6248
Three Juniors, 4898
Three Law Enforcement Aides, 6776
Three Marshals, 4911
Three Ministers, 4847, 4858
Three Ministries of the Left, 6987
Three Ministries of the Right, 8070
Three Money Managers of the Court
  of the Imperial Gardens, 5495
Three Monitoring Offices, 4912
Three Monitoring Surrogates, 4915
Three ... Officials, the, 4866
Three Palace Academies, 4229
Three Preceptors, 4903
Three Preceptors of the Heir
  Apparent, 6249
Three Provincial Authorities, 4919
Three Provincial Offices, 4912
Three Ranks, 4884
Three Seasonal Tailoring Groups,
  4856
Three Service Offices, 4897
Three Service Officials, 4896
Three Solitaries, 4864
Three Special Agencies, 4934
Three Storehouses, 4865
Three Superior Banners, 5031
Three Superior Duke Preceptors,
  4907
Three Supremes, 4921
Three Venerables, 4927
Three Wardens of Chien-k'ang, 833
Threshing Office, 3911
Tibetan School, 6296
Tiger-hunting Brigade, 2772
Time Drummer, 6606
Time Keeper, 6555
Timekeeper, 5546, 5547
Timekeepers in the Five Offices,
  7792
Tithing, 650
Tithing Chief, 680, 683
Titular Office, 4563
Tolls Office at the East Gate, 7447

Tomb Attendant, 7630
Tone Monitor, 6663
Tortoise Keeper, 3372
Tortoiseshell Diviner, 3375
Touring Brokerage, 2769
Touring Censor, 2717
Touring Censorial Inspector, 2713
Touring Surveillance Commissioner, 2716
Towel Attendant, 5225
Township: *chou,* 1332; *hsiang,* 2302, 2303; *hsiang,* 2304; *hsien,* 2492; *tang,* 6282
Township Company, 2364
Township Duke, 2332
Township Guardian, 2340
Township Head, 1334
Township Justice Bureau, 2311
Township Justiciar, 2533
Township Marquis, 2316
Township Mistress, 2309
Township Officials, 2326
Township Preceptor, 2534
Township Princess, 2334
Township Princess-ordinary, 2368
Township School, 2322
Township Supervisor, 2335
Tracker, 560
Training and Monitoring Section, 749
Training Division, 8009
Transit Authorization Bureau, 5679, 5718
Translator, 2999, 3032
Translator of Foreign Writings, 1883
Translators Institute, 5656
Transmission Secretary, 2671
Transmission Commissioner for the Capital Gates, 1306
Transport Assistant, 8283
Transport Censor-in-chief, 6922
Transport Clerk, 6926
Transport Command, 6925, 7658
Transport Commander, 6927
Transport Commission, 1492
Transport Commissioner, 1490, 1860, 6933
Transport Commissioner-in-chief, 7212
Transport Director, 6920
Transport Foreman, 7871
Transport Intendant, 6919
Transport Maid, 223
Transport Office, 5836, 6392, 6934
Transport and Salt Control Circuit, 3038
Transport Section, 1859, 8290
Transport Service, 1103
Transport Station, 5523
Transport Station Commandant, 3778
Transport Supervision Section, 7135
Transport-control Censor: *hsün-ho yü-shih,* 2736; *hsün-ts'ao yü-shih, hsün-ts'ao k'o-tao,* 2765; *tsan-yün yü-shih,* 6864; *tu yün-ts'ao yü-shih,* 7339; *tu-yün yü-shih,* 7340

Transporters, 762
Travel Guide, 5875
Travel Patroller, 7913
Treasurer for Market Taxes, 1706
Treasury, 7536
Treasury for the Benevolent Issuance of Paper Money, 4456
Treasury Bureau, 1142, 5543, 5592
Treasury of the Chamberlain for the National Treasury, 6304
Treasury Reserve Storehouse, 1974, 8253
Treasury Section, 1128
Tribal Chief, 1387, 3916, 4057, 7269
Tribal Command, 1777, 1778
tribal domain, 4792
Tribal Judge, 2977
Tribal Office, 1776
Tribal Overseer, 5969
tribe: *ai-ma,* 7; *chih-erh,* 972; *mu-k'un,* 4057; *pu,* 4764; *pu-lo,* 4792; *pu-tsu,* 4808; *tsu,* 7048
Tribunal of Censors, *see* Censorate (*yü-shih t'ai*)
Tribunal of Inspectors, 5699
Tribunal of Receptions, 7909
tributary envoy, 3424
Tribute Monitor, 125
Tribute Student, 3467, 5869
Tribute Student by Grace, 1817, 1823
Tribute Student for Merit, 3447
Tribute Student by Purchase, 3623
Tribute Student by Purchase, First Class, 3726
Tribute Student by Purchase, Fourth Class, 3623
Tribute Student by Purchase, Second Class, 6946
Tribute Student by Purchase, Third Class, 2072
Tribute Student, Second Class, 2071
Triple First, 4924, 4933
Troop, 7181
Troop Commandant, 7300
Troop Commander, 4774, 6625
Troop Disposition Section, 937
troop purification, 1264, 1272
Troop Purification Circuit, 1265
Troops, 3882
Troops of the Commands, 7865
Troops of the Five Commandants, 7767
true (salary-level prefix), 371
True Records Institute, 5291
tümen, see Army (*t'e-man*)
Turtle Catcher, 4627
Tutor of the Young, 3973
Tutorial Companion, 5342
Twelve Armies, 5239
Twelve Chamberlains, 5238
Twelve Directorates, 5237
Twelve Guards, 5242
Twelve Military Circuits, 5241
Twelve Sections, 5240
Twenty-four Agencies, 1825

Twenty-four Bureaus, 1841
Twenty-four Directresses, 1841
Twenty-four Handlers, 1840
Twenty-four Managers, 1842
Twenty-four Offices, 1841
Two Administrations, 1834, 3664
Two Administrators, 3664
Two Categories of Diarists, 3677
Two Censorates, 3681
Two Censorial Offices, 3689
Two Commands, 1846, 3679
Two Commissioners, 3676
Two Departments, 3674
Two Drafting Groups, 3660
Two Editors, 1831
Two Magnates, 3690
Two Mentors, 1832
Two Ministries, 1833
Two Offices, 3679
Two Pasturelands, 3665
Two Provincial Offices, 1877, 3679
Two Ranks, 3672
Two Scribes, 1839
Two Stables of the Palace, 3659
Two Thousand Bushel Official, 1828

Uighur, *see* Moslem
Umbrella Office, 1269
Umbrella-bearer of the Palace Guard, 1996
Unassigned Bannerman, 2529
Understanding and Knowledge Both Excellent, 6842
Unequaled in Honor, 3024
Unifying Agent, 3657, 4356
University Student-initiate, 1677
Unloading Office, 2295
Unoccupied Placeman, 4879
unoccupied status, in, 4890
Upper Army, 4991
Upper Class (rank), 396
upright, 396
Upright Consort, 7362
Uprooter of Trees, 6993
Usher, 984, 2649
Utensil Storehouse for the Southern Suburban Sacrifices, 4088

Vacancies Section, 114
Valet, 1388
Valeting Office, 2967
Vanguard Brigade, 892
Vanguard Brigade Left Wing, 6973
Vanguard Brigade Right Wing, 8055
various, 3697
various Directresses, 1434
various functionaries, 1403
various Managers (palace women), 1437
various offices, 1431
Various Palace Commissioners, the, 4169
various Prefectures, 1340
various Routes, 1405
Vault of Imperial Abundance, 2087
Venerable, 7305
Venerable Sir, 3581
Verification Office, 528, 2102

Verifier, 434
Veterinarian, 3000, 5377
Veterinarian Directorate, 4074
Vice (prefix): chih-chung, 967; fu, 2032; hsieh, 2460; ssu-ma, 5713; ya, 7843
Vice Censor-in-chief, 2108, 5634, 8174
Vice Chancellor of the National University, 2433
Vice Commandant, 2486, 2775, 3564
Vice Commandant Tending the Western Frontier, 4553
Vice Commander, 1002
Vice Commander-general, 6980
Vice Commander-in-chief, 2107
Vice Commissioner of the Office of Presentations, 7977
Vice Commissioner of the Right for Imperial Warrants, 6357
Vice Commissioner of the Right Superintending Imperial Warrants, 6492
Vice Commissioner-in-chief, 7317
Vice Director: fu-cheng, 2038; hsiao chiang-shih, 2386; hsiao chih-fang, 2390; hsiao fan-pu, 2399; hsiao hsing-pu, 2402; hsiao pin-pu, 2426; hsiao ping-pu, 2427; hsiao ssu-chin, 2436; hsiao ssu-hui, 2437; hsiao ssu-li, 2440; hsiao ssu-mu, 2442; hsiao ssu-shui, 2447; hsiao ssu-t'u, 2448; hsieh-li kuan-fang shih-wu, 2470; ssu-fu, 5621
Vice Director of Astrology, 912
Vice Director of the Astronomical College in the Directorate of Astronomy, 2469
Vice Director of the Bureau of Appointments, 2416
Vice Director of the Bureau of Forestry, 2459
Vice Director of the Bureau of Jade Work, 2450
Vice Director of the Bureau of Leatherwork, 2444
Vice Director (of Bureau in Ministry), 8251
Vice Director of the Bureau of Paints, 2445
Vice Director of the Bureau of Provisions, 2458
Vice Director of the Bureau of Textiles, 2435
Vice Director for Ceremonials, 2002
Vice Director of the Chancellery, 2847, 3942
Vice Director of the Department of State Affairs, 4826, 6124
Vice Director of the Markets Office, 2446
Vice Director (of Palace Ceremonial Office), 1054
Vice Director of the Palace Library, 4587, 4596, 4597
Vice Director for Rituals, 1026

Vice Director (of Secretariat), 5278, 7505, 7508, 7509
Vice Director of the Secretariat-Chancellery, 3935
Vice Director serving as Assistant Director of the Summer Palace, 2471
Vice Director of the Township Justice Bureau, 2311
Vice Directors, 2393
Vice Directors of the Department of State Affairs, 2303
Vice General, 2041, 2400
Vice Governor Assisting in Administration, 7527
Vice Governor (of Commandery), 7511
Vice Governor Participating in Administration, 6848
Vice Grand Councilor, 6872
Vice Lieutenant, 2375
Vice Magistrate (in Subprefecture), 7471
Vice Minister, 5278, 5621, 6868, 7496, 7526
Vice Minister of Education, 2449
Vice Minister for General Accounts, 7202
Vice Minister of Justice, 2438
Vice Minister in the Military Appointments Process, 5344
Vice Minister (of Ministry), 7526
Vice Minister of Revenue, 7202
Vice Minister Supervisory Manager of Coinage, 7251
Vice Minister of War, 2441
Vice Minister of Works, 2439
Vice Ministerial Sections, 1548
Vice Ministers of the Front Echelon, 896
Vice Ministers of the Three Appointments Processes, 4860
Vice Prefect, 968, 7471
Vice Prefect for Militia, 5480
Vice Rectifier, 2109
Vice Superintendent, 1013
Vice Supervisor of the Household of the Heir Apparent, 6250
Victualler's Office, 112
Victualling Office, 2256
Village, 3587, 3883
Village Assistant, 3884
Village Commandant, 677
village elder, 3624
village functionaries, 3609
Village Head, 3592, 3621, 3643
Vinegar Maker, 7024
Vinegar Woman, 4338
Vinegarman, 2248
Virtuous Consort, 6331
Virtuous Lady, 3667
Viscount, 7519
Visitor, 3186
Visitors Bureau, 3194, 3200
Visitors Office, 5738

Wagon Camp, 368
Waiter, 1416

War and Justice Ministry, 4674
War, Justice, and Works Ministry, 4673
War Office, 4672
war prisoners, 7060
War Section, 4696
Ward, 2304, 4571, 6282
Ward Preceptor, 4585
Ward-inspecting Censor, 2721
Ward-inspecting Censor for the . . . Ward, 2757
Ward-inspecting Censors, 2720
Ward-inspecting Censors of the Five Wards, 7738
Ward-inspecting Censors of the Imperial Capital Wards, 2754
Warden of Banished Criminals, 204
Warden of Captive Eastern Barbarians, 130
Warden of Captive Northern Barbarians, 196
Warden of Captive Southern Barbarians, 159
Warden of Captive Western Barbarians, 134
Warden of Convicted Criminals, 203
Warden's Office, 4682, 4685
Wardens' Offices of the Five Wards, 7739
Warder, 5829
Wardrobe Attendant, 497
Wardrobe Service, 4996
Warehouse, 7802
Warehouse for the Palace Workshops, 6964
Warehouseman, 5674
Waste Retrieval Yard, 7401
Watch Officer, 1558
Water Clock Office, 3835
Water Clock Section, 3833
Water Clock Supervisor, 105
Water and Land Transport Commissioner, 5501, 5502, 5505
Water Mill Office, 5506
Water Sprinkler, 2774
Water Transport Service, 113
Water-tester, 783
Waterways Circuit, 2191, 8275
Waterways Command, 2181
Waterways Commandant, 7284
Waterways Manager, 3283
Waterways Office, 3210, 7280
Waterways Officials, 7280
Waterways Section, 5512
Waterways Supervisor, 5901
Waterways Supervisorate, 2192
Weaver, 935
Weaving and Dyeing Office, 1005
Weaving and Dyeing Service, 1004
Weaving Shop, 1051
Weed Burner, 6465
Weighmaster, 2167, 5608
Welfare Supervisor, 5597
West Administration, 2236
West Bureau, 2287
West Chamber, 2243
West Commissioner, 2270

West Dyeing Office, 2246
West Echelon (of Ministries), 2237
West Garden, 2285
West Office of Embroidery, 2257
West Palace Dyeing Office, 2262
West Residence, 2274
West Surveillance Jurisdiction, 2278
West Weaving Shop, 2234
Western Depot, 2231
Western Directorate of Coinage,
  4476
Western Mint, 2281
Western Office, 2271
Western Office of Imperial Clan
  Affairs, 2279
Western Palace, 2254
Western Section, 2276
Western Storehouse, 2251
Whip-cracker, 6855
whole governmental establishment,
  the, 4756
Wine Steward, 229
Wine Stewards Office, 5082
Wine Stewards Service, 5081
Wine Tax Subsection, 3196
Winery, 230, 1851
Wines Office, 5848

Wing, 2302, 2923
Wing of Bowmen Shooters at
  Moving Targets, 6539
Wing Commander, 2928, 2979,
  7134
Wing of Inspired Strategy, 5164
Winter Chamberlain, 7425
Winter Office, 7438
Winter Support, 7438
with formal qualifications, 8047
without formal qualifications, 7753
Woman of the Household, 661
Woman of the Royal Clan, 7608
Woman of Royal Relations, 7600
Woodsman of the Eastern Park, 7463
Woodworker, 4058
Woodworking Service, 4050, 6496
Work Project Office, 8020
Work Superintendent, 870
Work Supervisor, 872
Works Section, 3390, 3490
Workshop, 1892, 6913
Workshop in the Hall of Moral
  Cultivation, 7878
Workshop Service, 5012
Worm Specialist, 5456
Worthy Consort, 2504

Worthy and Excellent, 2516
Worthy, Excellent, and Learned,
  2517
Worthy and Excellent,
  Straightforward and Upright, 2516
Worthy Lady, 3371
Writer, 6511
Writing-brush Maker, 4574

Yamen, 7862
Yeast Office, 7257
Yeast Section, 1691
Yellow River Conservation Office,
  2615
Yellow-helmeted Gentleman, 2869
Yin-Yang School, 8007
your disciple, 3948
Your Eminence, 6003
Your Honor, 5983, 6234, 6300
your humble servant, 392
Your Majesty: chai-chia, 60; pi-hsia,
  4577; shang, 4970; ta-chia, 5894;
  tien-hsia, 6581
your minister, 392
your slave, 4320
Youthful Talent, 1679

Index to Chinese Terms

1 一

一丈夫 2931
一甲 2943
一字王 3026
一第滬子 3008
一點青 3009
丁 6733
七子 640
七兵曹 633
七品案 632
七部尉 636
七卿 616
七營 642
下 2288
下士 2298
下大夫 2299
下五旗 2301
下卸司 2295
下界 2290
下軍 2294
下案 2289
下卿 2292
下監 2291
下嬪 2297
三 4830
三千營 4845
三大 4917
三大政 4918
三大營 4920
三大憲 4919
三元 4933
三公 4871
三公郎 4872
三太 4921
三夫人 4855
三互法 4862
三氏學 4905
三司 4912
三司使 4915
三司條例司 4916
三司會計司 4914

三少 4898
三尹 4932
三甲 4844
三吏 4877
三寺 4913
三妃 4851
三式科 4906
三老 4876
三色人 4895
三伴 4883
三事 4902
三事大夫 4908
三使 4903
三孤 4864
三官 4866
三尚方 4896
三尚署 4897
三府 4852
三服 4856
三服官 4856
三法司 4850
三舍 4899
三長 4832
三帥 4911
三昧 4882
三省 4900
三省樞密院 4901
三相 4858
三軍 4849
三郎 4873
三郎衛士 4875
三院 4934
三師 4904
三師上公 4907
三庫 4865
三校尉 4859
三班 4884
三班內侍 4887
三班使臣 4888
三班奉職 4886
三班院 4889
三班借職 4885

三部 4893
三部勾院 4894
三卿 4847
三衙 4931
三路 4881
三都督 4926
三輩 4890
三旗 4838
三旗包衣統領 4840
三旗侍衛 4841
三旗宗室侍衛 4842
三旗莊頭處 4839
三旗銀糧莊頭處 4843
三槐 4863
三署 4909
三署郎 4910
三臺 4922
三輔 4854
三輔都尉 4857
三獨坐 4927
三衛 4929
三選侍郎 4860
三頭 4924
三嬪 4891
三館 4867
三館書院 4870
上 4970
上三旗 5031
上士 5037
上大夫 5066
上大將軍 5065
上公 5010
上四軍 5063
上佐 5069
上佐官 5069
上供案 5011
上宗 5071
上林 5016

上林中十池監 5019
上林令 5021
上林郎 5020
上林苑 5023
上林苑監 5024
上林詔獄 5017
上林監 5018
上林署 5022
上直衛 4985
上舍 5034
上柱國 4990
上界 4983
上相 4998
上計吏 4979
上計掾 4981
上軍 4991
上案 4972
上卿 4987
上將軍 4982
上造 5067
上都護府 5072
上虞備用處 5080
上閤門 5008
上監 4984
上綱 5007
上輕車都尉 4988
上駟院 5064
上嬪 5030
上騎都尉 4980
上護軍 4999
不入八分 4785
不入寢殿小氐 4784
不更 4786
不稱職 4772
世子 5328
世官 5270
世孫 5314
世婦 5245
世婦卿 5246
世爵 5234

世襲 5247
世襲罔替 5248
丞 457
丞直 462
丞郎 501
丞相 483
丞相府 484
丞簿 510

2 丨

中 1530
中二千石 1551
中士 1601
中大夫 1627
中大夫令 1628
中允 1642
中太僕 1630
中外府 1637
中司 1625
中尚 1592
中正 1534
中正榜 1535
中丞 1537
中丞相 1538
中寺中 1626
中旨 1543
中行 1555
中行平博 1561
中行郎中 1556
中行員外郎 1557
中兵 1588
中兵曹 1588
中更 1571
中使 1600
中使局 1605
中侍中 1603
中侍中省 1604
中奉大夫 1552
中官 1574
中尚方署 1594
中尚食 1595

中尚書 1596
中尚監 1593
中尚署 1597
中所 1624
中舍 1598
中舍人 1599
中長秋 1531
中亮大夫 1584
中亮郎 1583
中政院 1536
中盾 1636
中軍 1550
中郎 1580
中郎將 1581
中候 1558
中卿 1545
中宮 1576
中宮署 1578
中宮僕 1577
中宮謁者 1579
中書 1606
中書令 1616
中書外省 1622
中書行省 1613
中書侍郎 1620
中書府 1611
中書房 1610
中書舍人 1618
中書後省 1612
中書門下 1617
中書省 1619
中書科 1615
中書監 1608
中書學 1614
中書檢正 1609
中曹 1634
中校 1559
中缺 1549
中堂 1631
中執法 1544
中尉 1638
中常侍 1532

中庶子 1621
中御府 1641
中將 1541
中都官曹 1635
中都曹 1635
中傅 1553
中散 1589
中散大夫 1591
中散令 1590
中朝 1533
中給事 1539
中給事中 1540
中順大夫 1623
中黃門 1565
中黃藏 1566
中黃藏府 1566
中準令 1546
中署 1607
中臺 1629
中銓 1548
中領軍 1585
中儀 1567
中憲大夫 1560
中翰 1554
中舉 1547
中諫 1542
中謁者 1639
中選 1562
中錄事參軍 1586
中壘令 1582
中藏府 1633
中議 1568
中議大夫 1569
中鹽 1640
中護 1563
中護軍 1564

3 丶

丹粉所 6271
主 1354
主子 1444
主戶 1387
主文 1446
主文中散 1447
主司 1430
主司里宰 1433
主考 1392
主衣 1388
主衣局 1389
主判 1411
主判官 1411
主事 1420

主事令史 1427
主事房 1425
主押官 1448
主食 1421
主客 1396,
　1397, 1398
主客令 1395
主客司 1397
主客部 1396
主客曹 1398
主客清吏司 1394
主政 1362
主計 1363
主乘 1418
主射左右 1417
主書 1428
主羌夷吏民尚書
　郎 1366
主記史 1364
主記室 1364
主記室史 1365
主曹 1439
主章長 1360
主酪 1402
主試官 1426
主管 1399
主樂內品 1454
主稿 1391
主璽 1409
主廩 1404
主膳 1416
主轄收支司 1386
主簿 1413
主簿廳 1414
主醢 1382
主爵 1379
主藥 1449

4 丿

之國 1021
乘黃 491
乘黃廄 492
乘黃署 493
乘輿 518
乘驛 496

5 乙

乙榜 2984
九寺 1317
九州 1297
九成宮總監 1293

九命 1310
九府 1301
九門 1308
九品 1315
九品案 1316
九科 1304
九重 1298
九卿 1296
九參官 1318
九御 1320
九棘 1294
九經出身 1295
九廟 1309
九嬪 1314
九關通事使 1306
九爵 1299
九譯令 1302
九邊 1313
也理可溫掌教司 7912
乳酪院 3076
乾元院 932

6 亅

予告 8147
事材場 5319

7 二

二十四司 1841
二十四典 1842
二十四掌 1840
二十四衙門 1843
二千石 1828
二千石曹 1829
二史 1839
二司 1846
二甲 1827
二府 1833
二品 1838
二傅 1832
二稅科 1845
二著 1831
于越 8216
互市監 2795
井田科 1241
井鈇軍 1253
五千營 7747
五大夫 7824
五司 7822
五司廳 7823
五兵 7811

五兵曹 7811
五冶太師 7839
五坊 7761
五坊司市師 7757
五使 7819
五官 7783
五官大夫 7795
五官中郎將 7787
五官司辰 7792
五官司事 7794
五官司曆 7793
五官侍郎 7791
五官保章正 7790
五官郎中 7788
五官挈壺正 7785
五官曹 7796
五官掾 7797
五官監候 7786
五官靈臺 7789
五尚 7816
五府 7763
五房 7762
五花判事 7775
五指揮 7749
五省 7817
五貢 7799
五軍都督府 7758
五軍統制 7759
五軍營 7760
五院 7842
五城 7737
五城巡視御史 7738
五城兵馬司 7739
五城御史 7738
五校兵 7767
五校士 7767
五部 7812
五馬 7806
五曹 7831
五時 7748
五經出身 7750
五經博士 7752
五經魁 7751
五監 7746
五魁 7798
亞 7843
亞中大夫 7850
亞保 7864
亞相 7855
亞師 7866
亞卿 7849
亞傅 7853

亞臺 7870

8 一

交子務 745
交引庫 746
交市監 738
交鈔 721
交鈔庫 722
京 1188
京尹 1251
京兆 1190
京兆尹 1192
京兆府 1191
京局 1210
京城游徼 1196
京官 1224
京府 1212
京師 1239
京通倉 1246
京都 1243
京朝官 1193
京察 1189
京旗 1200
京輔 1213
京輔都尉 1216
京畿 1197
京畿道 1199
京衛 1248
京營 1252
京縣 1217
京糧廳 1230
京警巡使 1209
亭 6747
亭公主 6756
亭父 6751
亭伯 6759
亭長 6750
亭侯 6752
亭員 6780
亭翁主 6779

9 人

人主 3048
人部 3049
人從看詳案 3053
人曹 3052
仇香 1353
仁恕掾 3051
仁壽宮監 3050
什 5196
什將 5214

仗內 162
仗內散樂 165
仗庫局 142
仗馬 158
仗廄 108
付事 2096
令 3733
令史 3768
令丞 3739
令丞案 3740
令君 3752
令事 3767
令長 3737
令貢院 3762
令錄 3764
仕途 5327
仕進 5224
仙郎 2514
仙曹 2543
仙韶院 2530
代人令史 6132
代州錢監 6130
价藩 759
伊勒希巴院 2982
伊耆氏 2942
伊實部 3002
任 3047
任子 3054
伍 7732
伍大夫 7825
伶官師 3761
伴書 4416
伴講 4401
伴讀 4419
伻 4565
伯 4718
伯克 4738
佐 6948
佐史 6989
佐吏 6978
佐軍 6960
佐郎 6977
佐棘 6952
佐貳 6962
佐領 6980
佐雜 7005
作坊司 6963
作坊物料庫 6964
作院 7022
作堂 7002
位下 7666
供事 3469

供奉 3418
供奉弓箭備身 3420
供奉內廷 3422
供奉侍衛 3425
供奉供用 3421
供奉官 3418
供奉射生官 3423
供奉學士 3419
供官 3441
供進筆 3406
供備庫 3459
供膳 3464
來遠軍 3556
例生 3634
例貢生 3623
例部 3629
例監 3596
例監生 3596
侍 5198
侍巾 5225
侍中 5229
侍中寺 5233
侍中侍郎 5232
侍中祭酒 5230
侍中僕射 5231
侍內 5293
侍右 5342
侍右侍郎 5344
侍右郎官 5343
侍左 5323
侍正府 5210
侍立修注官 5283
侍奉曹 5244
侍祠侯 5332
侍郎 5278
侍郎右選 5282
侍郎左選 5281
侍郎選 5280
侍書 5306
侍書侍御史 5310
侍書學士 5308
侍從 5324
侍御 5346
侍御中散 5347
侍御史 5350
侍御史知雜事 5352
侍御尚醫 5349
侍御師 5351
侍御醫 5348
侍教 5218
侍率府 5312

侍極 5212
侍禁 5226
侍監 5221
侍儀 5254
侍儀司 5263
侍儀奉御 5259
侍衛 5333
侍衛司 5339
侍衛班領 5338
侍衛馬軍步軍司 5337
侍衛處 5336
侍衛親軍 5334
侍衛親軍馬步司 5335
侍講 5215
侍講學士 5217
侍醫 5255
侍櫛 5220
侍讀 5325
侍讀學士 5326
使 5197
使女 5294
使臣 5209
使持節 5223
使星 5252
使相 5249
使者 5208
使院 5353
使節 5219
依飛 7555
佾生 2992
侯 2205
侯國 2218
保 4450
保丁 4499
保氏 4494
保正 4460
保甲 4465
保任 4486
保伍 4503
保沖大夫 4475
保和殿 4478
保林 4488
保長 4451
保相 4479
保宮 4487
保馬 4491
保章正 4452
保章氏 4453
保傅 4477
保順郎將 4496
保節 4466

保學醫 4481
保舉 4468
保選 4480
信 2552
信使 2556
信礮總管 2555
俊秀 1759
值年 1038
俸餉處 1980
俸檔房 2020
候人 2215
候日 2216
候星 2212
候風 2210
候部史 2221
候部郎 2221
候氣 2207
候晷影 2217
候補 2220
候補班 2222
候衛 2227
候選 2213
候鐘律 2208
俳長 4393
修內司 2629
修日曆所 2623
修文館 2637
修玉牒官 2639
修合司藥司 2617
修武案 2638
修注 2613
修河司 2616
修政局 2610
修倉所 2634
修容 2624
修書處 2630
修書學士 2631
修訓 2618
修國史 2626
修敕令司 2612
修造司 2635
修造案 2635
修媛 2640
修華 2619
修道堂 2632
修儀 2620
修撰 2614
修撰官 2614
修濬黃河司 2615
修職郎 2611
修類譜官 2627
修纂 2636
倉 6899

倉人 6903
倉司 6909
倉科 6904
倉庫署 6905
倉案 6900
倉部 6907
倉部司 6907
倉部曹 6908
倉曹 6910
倉貨監 6902
倉場 6901
倉農監 6906
倉督 6911
借 753
倅 7062
倅車 7064
倅貳 7068
健仔 780
假 647
假士 677
假五 687
假伍 687
假佐 684
假候 658
假節 655
健銳營 832
偶 4356
偏 4647
偏將 4648
偏將軍 4648
側室 6939
側福晉 6938
傳 2031
傳令 2081
傳尉 2113
備身 4537
備身左右 4539
備身府 4538
備查壇廟大臣 4514
備章總院 4516
備榜 4532
備邊庫 4534
傛僕 3089
傔人 902
傔從 928
傳令 1499
傳車 1494
傳法院 1496
傳制 1495
傳舍 1487
傳宣合同司 1498
傳宰 1502

傳臚 1500
僉 885
僉判太史監事 912
僉院 931
僉都御史 929
僉事 917
催長 7063
催綱官 7070
催綱撥發 7071
催總 7073
催驅司 7067
催驅房 7066
催驅案 7065
催攢運船 7072
僚屬 3695
僕 4815
僕人師 4822
僕夫 4821
僕正 4819
僕寺 4824
僕臣 4818
僕長 4817
僕射 4823
僧正 4942
僧正司 4943
僧官 4947
僧祇部丞 4944
僧統 4949
僧會司 4945
僧綱司 4946
僧錄司 4948
儀仗勾當 2932
儀仗司 2934
儀仗使 2933
儀司 3003
儀同 3023
儀同三司 3024
儀制司 2945
儀制清吏司 2945
儀注 2947
儀部 2990
儀曹 3017
儀賓 2985
儀臺 3007
儀衛 3028
儀鳳司 2953
儀禮局 2975
儀鸞司 2983
儀鸞局 2983
儒 3063
儒官 3071
儒林郎 3074

儒林參軍 3075
儒林祭酒 3073
儒童 3082
儒學 3067
儒學提舉 3068
盡先補用 1126
優監生 8042
儲 1455
儲妃 1466
儲君 1464
儲兩 1472
儲政院 1458
儲皇 1468
儲宮 1471
儲副 1467
儲貳 1465
儲嫡 1479
儲極 1459
儲端 1480
儲膳司 1476
儲慶使司 1463
儲闈 1481
儹運御史 6864

10 儿

元士 8237
元后 8226
元妃 8224
元老 8229
元帥 8244
元帥府 8245
元戎 8232
元首 8242
元祐庫 8253
元從禁軍 8249
元輔 8225
元儲 8223
充 1643
充人 1662
充妃 1651
充依 1658
充容 1665
充媛 1672
充華 1657
充儀 1659
光正 3337
光訓 3342
光祿大夫 3349
光祿寺 3348
光祿勳 3347
光獻 3354
先民 2522

先馬 2519
先輩 2525
克埒穆爾齊 3198
免役案 3990
免解人 3989

11 入

入內 3077
入內內侍省 3080
入內內班院 3079
入內省 3080
入內黃門班院 3078
入品 3081
入等 3081
入寢殿小氐 3066
入輦祗應 3072
內 4137
內人 4192
內八府宰相 4219
內三旗 4228
內三院 4229
內大臣 4262
內女 4218
內小臣 4182
內工部 4211
內弓箭庫 4209
內中高品班院 4170
內仗 4138
內允 4299
內文案 4289
內文學館 4290
內火藥庫 4190
內包衣牛象章京 4222
內史 4236
內史府 4242
內史省 4250
內史相 4243
內史監 4241
內司 4259
內司服 4260
內命女 4217
內命夫 4214
內命男 4216
內命婦 4215
內弘文院 4189
內正司 4145
內匠 4152
內寺伯 4261
內左庫 4280

內臣 4144
內行廠 4184
內衣物庫 4191
內西頭供奉官 4179
內作巧兒 4279
內作使 4281
內作使綾匠 4282
內坊 4173
內廷 4267
內廷供用 4270
內廷供奉 4269
內廷侍 4271
內廷待詔 4272
內廷祗候 4268
內步兵曹 4226
內供奉 4210
內使省 4249
內侍 4237
內侍伯 4248
內侍官 4246
內侍押班 4253
內侍班 4247
內侍長 4238
內侍高品 4245
內侍高班 4244
內侍都知 4252
內侍階 4239
內侍監 4240
內侍殿頭 4251
內典引 4266
內制 4158
內官 4203
內官監 4205
內宗 4283
內尚方署 4231
內府 4175
內府監 4176
內承奉 4147
內承奉班押班 4148
內承直 4146
內東門司 4286
內東門取索司 4286
內東門都知司 4287
內東頭供奉官 4288
內物料庫 4292
內直 4159
內直局 4162
內直郎 4164

內直監 4161
內省 4234
內省司 4235
內相 4181
內祕書院 4224
內祕書省 4223
內舍 4232
內舍人 4233
內前鋒營 4157
內飛龍使 4174
內品 4225
內客省 4201
內度科 4285
內率府 4258
內班院 4221
內者 4143
內苑 4298
內倉 4277
內務府 4291
內宮 4208
內宰 4273
內宰司 4275
內宰相 4274
內庫 4202
內書省 4256
內書堂 4257
內酒坊 4168
內國史院 4212
內常侍 4141
內教坊 4153
內教博士 4154
內曹 4278
內符寶郎 4177
內都知司 4284
內卿 4166
內廂 4180
內掌侍 4140
內掌扇 4139
內掾 4297
內朝 4142
內給事 4149
內給使 4150
內園 4296
內會總科主事 4186
內殿承制 4264
內殿直 4265
內經博士 4165
內養狗處 4293
內僕局 4227
內閣 4193
內閣大學士 4199
內閣中書 4194

內閣侍讀 4196
內閣侍讀學士 4197
內閣典籍 4200
內閣帥 4198
內閣學士 4195
內廄 4167
內旗 4151
內監 4155
內監管理 4156
內管領 4206
內管領處 4207
內臺 4263
內樞密使 4255
內辦事廳 4220
內豎 4254
內駒廄 4171
內翰 4178
內膳 4230
內諸司使 4169
內謁者 4294
內闈史 4188
內闈官 4187
內館 4204
內繙書房 4172
內織染局 4163
內職 4160
內藏 4276
內藏庫 4276
內廉 4213
內廉官 4213
內護軍營 4185
內驍騎營 4183
內饔 4295
兩 3657
兩仗內 3659
兩史 3677
兩司 3679
兩司馬 3680
兩字王 3687
兩京武庫署 3662
兩京諸市署 3661
兩使 3676
兩制 3660
兩制官 3660
兩府 3664
兩省 3674
兩省官 3675
兩院 3690
兩班 3672
兩都陸運提舉司 3686
兩衙門 3689

兩榜 3673
兩臺 3681
兩翼 3665

12 八

八大人官 4379
八大家 4378
八子 4385
八公 4371
八分 4366
分付宰相 4367
八作司 4382
八作院 4382
八局 4364
八房 4365
八股文 4370
八品案 4375
八座 4381
八校尉 4368
八部大人 4377
八部大夫 4376
八國 4373
八貂 4380
八旗 4358
八旗公 4360
八旗官學 4359
八旗總管大臣 4361
八節學士 4263
公 3388
公士 3472
公大夫 3480
公子 3494
公主 3408
公主府 3410
公主邑 3411
公主邑司 3411
公主家令 3409
公車 3392
公車司馬門 3394
公車署 3393
公事 3470
公事幹當官 3476
公使 3471
公姓 3435
公府 3426
公相 3432
公祖 3492
公乘 3465
公國 3448
公堂 3484
六司 3814

六宅使 3780
六局 3784
六典 3818
六官 3795
六尚 3810
六尚局 3811
六尚書 3812
六府 3789
六房 3788
六押 3825
六品案 3804
六軍 3785
六軍儀仗司 3786
六院 3826
六宮 3798
六科 3793
六庫 3794
六部 3805
六部里尉 3808
六部架閣 3806
六部尉 3809
六部監門 3807
六參 3819
六參官 3819
六堂 3817
六曹 3820
六卿 3782
六統軍 3821
六閑 3791
六經祭酒 3781
六群 3787
六察 3779
六廄 3783
六儀 3792
共工 3446
共和 3431
兵 4665
兵仗局 4667
兵右 4697
兵刑工部 4673
兵刑部 4674
兵匠案 4669
兵巡道 4675
兵房 4672
兵科 4676
兵案 4666
兵部 4691
兵部司 4692
兵馬 4679
兵馬元帥 4689
兵馬司 4685
兵馬巡檢 4683
兵馬使 4684

兵馬指揮司 4682
兵馬曹 4686
兵馬都鈐轄 4688
兵馬都監 4687
兵馬鈐轄 4681
兵馬監押 4680
兵曹 4696
兵備道 4690
兵署 4694
兵禮房 4677
兵糧道 4678
兵籍房 4668
典 6515
典內 6614
典仗 6518
典史 6638
典正 6521
典印 6673
典吏 6609
典同 6663
典夷樂 6595
典寺署 6652
典戎衛 6599
典牝 6624
典艸 6660
典衣 6588
典作 6661
典作局 6662
典兵 6625
典庖 6622
典牡 6612
典祀 6650
典言 6671
典事 6637
典命 6611
典府 6574
典服 6575
典服正 6576
典法大臣 6571
典法曹 6572
典牧署 6613
典直 6546
典客 6600
典客令 6604
典客監 6602
典客署 6605
典客館 6603
典庸器 6675
典星 6582
典枲 6579
典珍 6520
典祠令 6664
典科 6601

典苑 6681
典計 6523
典軍 6568
典軍司 6570
典郡 6569
典乘 6636
典倉令 6658
典倉署 6659
典扇 6628
典書 6642
典書令 6647
典書坊 6645
典記 6524
典貢舉 6607
典婦功 6577
典御 6676
典術 6644
典設 6633
典設局 6634
典設署 6635
典魚 6680
典幄署 6667
典巂 6545
典掌儀衛 6519
典給 6525
典給官 6525
典給署 6526
典絲 6651
典瑞 6597
典瑞院 6598
典經坊 6549
典經局 6549
典虞 6678
典路 6610
典農署 6619
典飾 6639
典鼓 6606
典庖 6550
典庖署 6551
典獄 6677
典綵 6656
典署 6643
典製 6547
典賓 6623
典儀 6587
典儀所 6594
典儀監 6590
典儀錄事 6592
典樂 6684
典衛 6666
典衛令 6666
典雍 6674
典學 6584

典學從事 6585
典曆 6608
典燈 6653
典翰 6578
典膳 6629
典膳局 6631
典膳所 6632
典膳監 6630
典舉 6567
典蕃署 6573
典謁 6670
典醞 6685
典輿 6679
典闈 6665
典醫丞 6589
典醫監 6591
典醫署 6593
典璽 6580
典簿 6626
典簿廳 6627
典藥 6668
典藥局 6669
典贊 6657
典寶 6620
典寶所 6621
典籍 6522
典籍廳 6527
典鐘 6555
典饎 6528
典饌廳 6554
典屬司 6648
典屬國 6646
典禳 6596
典護 6586
典籤 6533
兼 785
兼判 849
兼攝 854
冀用庫 609

13 冂

岡卿 1328
岡臺 1329

14 宀

冠軍 3284
冠軍大將軍 3291
冠軍使 3289
冠軍將軍 3287
冢人 1570
冢宰 1632

冥氏 4019
冪人 3977

15 冫

冬官 7438
冬卿 7425
冬曹 7457
冲人 1663
冰井務 4671
冰窖 4670
冰廳 4695
冶 7906
冶道 7916
冶監 7910
冶署 7915
凌人 3758
凌玉 3777
凝華 4311
凝暉 4312

16 几

17 凵

出身 1477
出納使 1475
出納錢物使 1474
出閣 1470
出閤 1470
函工 2140
函使 2158

18 刀

刀人 6313
刀筆吏 6320
分 1934
分司 1945
分地 1947
分守道 1943
分巡兵備道 1940
分巡道 1941
分府 1938
分治監 1937
分差粮料院 1936
分條 1948
分察使 1935
分臺 1946
分簿案 1942
刊正 3140
刊正官 3140

刑工部 2581
刑名 2586
刑官 2577
刑房 2569
刑科 2576
刑席 2573
刑部 2590
刑案 2562
刑曹 2602
刑獄按察使 2607
刑幕 2587
刑禮房 2584
列 3697
列大夫 3700
列侯 3698
列宮 3699
利用監 3649
利用錢監 3650
判 4436
判三司 4434
判六軍諸衛事
　　4429
判司 4437
判司官 4438
判台 4439
判寺 4437
判…事 4436
判官 4425
判官司 4427
判門下省事 4431
判南衙 4432
判省事 4435
判院 4440
判院事 4440
判流內銓事 4430
判部 4433
判部事 4433
判館事 4426
別火令 4626
別失八里局 4629
別兵曹 4628
別教院 4625
別將 4624
別駕 4623
別頭 4630
刪定使 4965
刪定官 4964
刪定曹 4966
制司 1068
制府 982
制勅房 958
制勅院 960
制度掾 1091

制科 1011
制軍 970
制書令史 1063
制勘案 1009
制國用使 1022
制敕庫房 959
制置 949
制置三司條例司
　　956
制置大使 957
制置使 957
制置茶事 952
制置發通使 953
制臺 1072
制誥案 1010
制憲 992
制舉 969
制置鹽稅 954
刻漏 3199
刺史 7567
刺史郡 7568
刷卷御史 5474
刷卷道 5473
削除名籍 2694
前引大臣 930
前行 895
前行引 897, 900
前行正郎 896
前省 916
前軍 890
前馬 907
前鋒營 892
副 2032
副正 2038
副主 2046
副本庫 2092
副后 2057
副戎 2068
副君 2050
副車 2037
副京兆 2045
副使正 2101
副使案 2100
副兩 2080
副相 2059
副郎 2077
副馬 2082
副將 2041
副貢生 2071
副都 2106
副都御史 2108
副都統 2107
副爺 2115

副榜 2090
副端 2109
副憲 2060
副齋 2036
副轉 2048
剩員 5192
劇曹 1688

19 力

加 648
加官 666
加職 656
功臣 3395
功貢 3447
功曹 3489
功牌 3457
功論郎 3449
功德使 3485
助軍 1380
助書 1429
助教 1367
助教廳 1368
勃菫 4723
勃極烈 4721
勘合 3141
勢家郎 5213
募兵 4063
勳 2711
勳一府 2741
勳二府 2726
勳臣 2718
勳官 2745
勳府 2730
勳府右闈 2733
勳封科 2729
勳戚 2722
勸農公事 1710
勸農使 1711
勸農掾 1712
勸學從事 1708

20 勹

勾押官 3219
勾院判官 3220
勾當 3214
勾當三班院 3216
勾當公事官 3215
勾當官 3214
勾管 3212
勾銷房 3211
勾簿司 3213

勾覆官 3208
勾覆理欠憑由案 3209
勾鑿司 3217
包衣 4482
包衣佐領 4485
包衣昂邦 4483
包衣參領 4484

21 匕

北 4512
北大王院 4544
北丞 4517
北主客曹 4520
北司 4543
北外都水丞司 4547
北宅 4515
北冶 4549
北使 4541
北所 4542
北狄使者 4545
北直隸 4519
北門 4527
北門四軍 4528
北客館 4523
北省 4540
北軍 4521
北院 4550
北面 4529
北面房 4530
北宮 4525
北庫 4524
北班內品 4531
北部 4535
北部尉 4536
北廂 4522
北衙 4548
北鞍庫 4513
北監 4518

22 匚

匡人 3359
匡政 3357
匠戶 696
匠師 702
匠卿 693
甌使 3376
甌院 3378

23 匸

24 十

十二房 5240
十二軍 5239
十二卿 5238
十二道 5241
十二監 5237
十二衛 5242
十二衛府 5242
十三司 5297
十三道 5298
十五道 5340
十六衛 5290
十六衛府 5290
十軍 5236
十率府 5313
千人 903
千夫 894
千夫長 894
千牛 909
千牛府 910
千牛備身 909
千牛將軍 908
千牛衛 910
千戶所 901
千總 927
千騎 887
升 5174
升朝官 5177
半刺 4420
半箇佐領 4406
協 2460
協台 2484
協正庶尹 2462
協同守備 2486
協同官 2485
協同督運參將 2487
協戎 2465
協忠大夫 2463
協忠郎 2463
協律 2475
協律郎 2477
協律校尉 2476
協律都尉 2478
協音 2488
協脩 2464
協理 2468
協理事務大臣 2472

協理事務郎史 2471
協理事務雲麾使 2473
協理欽天監天文算學事務 2469
協理關防事務 2470
協揆 2466
協領 2474
協標 2482
協辦大學士 2479
協辦院事 2480
協聲律官 2483
協鎮 2461
卒 7047
卒史 7053
卒騶 7055
南 4081
南人 4099
南大王院 4124
南主客曹 4092
南北外都水丞司 4112
南北宅 4109
南北省倉 4111
南北院 4113
南北庫 4110
南司 4122
南外宗正司 4128
南外都水丞司 4129
南丞 4087
南宅 4085
南寺 4123
南使 4118
南冶 4133
南巫 4130
南府 4095
南所 4121
南河 4096
南琳 4093
南郊什物庫 4089
南郊太廟祭器庫 4090
南郊祭器庫 4088
南客館 4100
南洋大臣 4132
南省 4116
南省舍人 4117
南軍 4094
南院 4136
南面 4107

南宮 4102
南宮舍人 4103
南宮第一人 4104
南庫 4101
南書房 4119
南班官 4108
南苑 4135
南部 4114
南部尉 4115
南曹 4127
南廂 4097
難蔭監生 4134
南衙 4131
南榻 4125
南監 4091
南臺 4126
南鞍庫 4084
南樞密院 4120
南選曹 4098
南齋 4086
南蠻使者 4106
南蠻校尉 4105
博士 4746
博士六經祭酒 4750
博士弟子 4753
博士弟子員 4754
博士師 4752
博士祭酒 4749
博士僕射 4751
博士廳 4755
博望苑使 4759
博學宏材 4731
博學宏詞 4732
博學鴻詞 4732
博學鴻儒 4730

25 卜

卜 4761
卜人 4783
卜正 4768
卜助教 4775
卜師 4796
卜博士 4795
卜筮生 4798
占人 77
占夢 78
占龜頭 75
卡官 689
卡倫侍衛 3098

26 卩

印 7968
印房 7982
印書錢物所 7995
印務章京 8005
印務參領 8006
印曹 8002
印造鈔引庫 8000
印造寶鈔庫 8001
印鈔局 7972
印經院 7979
印綬監 7994
印曆所 7986
印曆管勾 7984
卿 1255
卿貳 1266
卿監 1262

27 厂

厚宗院 2226
廠 231

28 厶

參 6865
參戎 6887
參府 6879
參知 6871
參知政事 6872
參知機務 6873
參政 6868
參計官 6869
參軍 6876
參軍事 6876
參軍都護 6877
參軍斷事官 6878
參酌院 6874
參將 6870
參掌 6866
參掌樞密事 6867
參與政事 6895
參詳官 6880
參預朝政 6894
參旗軍 5147, 6875
參領 6888
參謀 6889
參謀官 6889
參贊大臣 6893
參贊軍事 6892
參贊機務 6891

參議 6881
參議大臣 6885
參議中書省事 6883
參議官 6884
參議得失 6886
參議朝政 6882

29 又

及第 601
友 8032
受事司 5397
受事御史 5398
受恩 5368
受納匹段庫 5392
受給 5360
受給官 5360
受給庫 5361

30 口

口北道 3221
古諸侯 3228
句司 1687
史 5199
史子集綴文博士 5331
史官 5271
史院 5354
史書令史 5309
史道安局 5317
史館 5272
司 5533
司儿筵 5570
司刀盾 5777
司土 5800
司士 5761
司川 5606
司干 5665
司弓 5683
司弓矢 5685
司中 5609
司元·5838
司內 5727
司天官 5781
司天監 5780
司天臺 5783
司天靈臺郎 5782
司戈 5667
司戈盾 5670
司戶 5643
司文局 5811

司文監 5810
司木 5725
司水 5771
司伏 5537
司伏司 5539
司令 5706
司功 5682
司卉 5647
司右 5826
司市 5762
司平 5744
司正 5548
司民 5721
司玉 5830
司田 5779
司甲 5573
司皮 5737
司矢 5763
司刑 5635
司刑寺 5637
司列 5704
司匠 5577
司吏 5691
司州 5599
司戎 5664
司竹監 5602
司竹長 5601
司竹都尉 5603
司羊署 5818
司衣 5652
司衣司 5661
司兵 5741
司判 5732
司吹 5607
司巫 5814
司成 5550
司成宣業 5553
司成館 5554
司更寺 5666
司社 5756
司色 5750
司言司 5823
司辰 5546
司辰師 5547
司函 5627
司刺 5805
司官 5677
司宗 5797
司宗寺 5798
司府令 5625
司府寺 5626
司服 5622
司法 5615

司牧局 5726
司直 5585
司直史 5589
司直郎 5588
司空 5687
司空公 5688
司空令 5689
司郊 5579
司金 5592
司門 5718
司俎官 5794
司則 5792
司城 5549
司封司 5620
司度 5799
司律中郎將 5712
司牲司 5760
司牲局 5760
司珍 5543
司珍 5544
司珍大夫 5545
司祝 5600
司約 5845
司胙官 5793
司苑司 5842
司苑局 5841
司計 5561
司計大夫 5569
司計司 5565
司軍 5613
司香 5630
司候 5628
司倉 5789
司員 5839
司宰寺 5785
司宮臺 5686
司庫 5674
司書 5769
司烜氏 5639
司病官 5743
司桌 5728
司草 5790
司袍襖 5735
司記 5562
司記司 5566
司訓 5641
司貢籍 5684
司賓大夫 5740
司賓司 5738

司賓寺 5739
司馬 5713
司馬大夫 5716
司馬中 5714
司馬門 5715
司馬督 5717
司副 5621
司務廳 5817
司域 5827
司寂 5556
司寇 5671
司寇參軍 5672
司常 5540
司常寺 5541
司庾 5828
司教 5578
司救 5597
司晨 5546
司烹大夫 5736
司理 5693
司理參軍 5700
司理院 5702
司狷 5773
司裒 5598
司設司 5758
司設監 5757
司貨 5650
司階 5580
司尊彝 5796
司幄 5812
司戟 5557
司戟大夫 5567
司會 5676
司程 5551
司稅 5772
司程官 5555
司量 5703
司馭寺 5837
司業 5821
司準 5608
司獄 5829
司獄司 5835
司盟 5720
司碓 5803
司禋 5824
司禋監 5825
司笚 5764
司經 5594
司經大夫 5596
司經局 5595
司虞 5832
司農 5729
司農寺 5731

司農卿 5730
司鞍長 5536
司鼎 5784
司鼓 5673
司僕 5748
司僕寺 5749
司瘠 5813
司歌 5668
司綵司 5786
司舞 5815
司製司 5590
司閣 5669
司闈 5681
司飾司 5768
司儀 5651
司儀長 5655
司儀署 5660
司屬 5690
司樂 5844
司樂司 5847
司樂郎 5846
司稼 5574
司稼寺 5576
司簙 5616
司衛寺 5808
司險 5633
司駕 5575
司勳 5640
司勳司 5642
司器 5571
司圜 5646
司廩 5705
司憲 5632
司憲大夫 5634
司曆 5692
司曆五官 5701
司燈司 5778
司禦 5831
司禦率府 5834
司稽 5558
司膳 5753
司膳大夫 5755
司膳寺 5754
司覛 5733
司諫 5582
司錄 5707
司錄司 5709
司錄事 5708
司錄參軍 5710
司錄參軍事 5710
司闔 5649
司隸 5695
司隸校尉 5697

司隸臺 5699
司禮 5694
司禮寺 5698
司禮監 5696
司績 5560
司績大夫 5568
司舉從事 5612
司興 5833
司興司 5836
司醯司 5848
司闌司 5809
司織 5586
司儲 5604
司藏 5788
司藏署 5788
司醫 5654
司鹽監 5822
司簿司 5747
司藥司 5820
司贊司 5787
司關 5679
司寶司 5734
司籍 5559
司籍司 5564
司籍所 5563
司議 5653
司議官 5657
司議郎 5659
司鐘磬 5610
司屬寺 5770
司饌 5605
司饎司 5572
司爟 5678
司鑰長 5819
司爨 5795
台宰 6224
台輔 6160
右 8033
右三部 8070
右土曹 8075
右戶 8054
右戶曹 8054
右主客 8046
右史 8072
右司 8079
右民 8063
右民曹 8063
右丞 8034
右寺 8080
右扶風 8051
右更 8058
右京輔都尉 8045
右侍禁 8074

右尙署 8071
右府 8049
右所 8078
右治獄 8044
右計 8035
右軍 8048
右院 8095
右師 8073
右班都知 8065
右班殿直 8064
右部 8069
右堂 8083
右庶長 8076
右推案 8093
右曹 8091
右將 8040
右弼 8067
右弼都尉 8068
右揆 8061
右榜 8066
右署 8077
右臺 8082
右翼前鋒 8055
右衛 8094
右選 8052
右藏 8086
右藏庫 8088
右藏案 8087
右藏提點 8090
右藏署 8089
右廳 8084
后 2206
后妃四星 2209
后廟 2219
合入 2177
合口脂匠 2178
合方氏 2173
合同 2200
合同憑由司 2201
合奉祀 2175
吏 3586
吏士 3637
吏戶禮部 3610
吏目 3626
吏房 3604
吏科 3616
吏部 3630
吏部曹 3632
吏員 3651
吏從官 3646
吏曹 3644
吏禮部 3625
吏籍案 3594

名表郎 4017
名號侯 4015
名藩 4012
名籍案 4006
吐屯 7356
吐渾歸明 7351
同 7464
同三品 7500
同中書門下三品 7481
同中書門下平章事 7480
同文寺 7516
同文館 7515
同出身 7478
同平章事 7499
同平章軍國重事 7498
同正員 7468
同判 7496
同東西臺三品 7514
同知 7471
同進士出身 7475
同轉 7479
同簽 7470
同議省事 7489
告身 3146
君 1729
君主 1748
君侯 1755
吟詠博士 8008
呼圖克圖 2801
呵止 2170
呵導 2190
和用監 2204
和德 2194
和碩公主 2186
和碩貝勒 2188
和碩格格 2185
和碩親王 2184
和碩額駙 2187
和劑局 2169
和聲署 2183
和羅場 2195
命 4004
命夫 4013
命婦 4013
命卿 4008
咒禁工 1337
咒禁師 1339
咒禁博士 1338
咸安宮官學 2494

哈喇魯萬戶府 2125
品 4660
品子 4664
品郎 4662
品管官 4661
哲簇氏 367
哨 5083
唐古忞學 6296
員 8217
員外 8250
員外郎 8251
員吏 8230
啓心郎 627
商屯 5073
商稅院 5061
商稅案 5061
商稅務 5062
商議省事 5006
問事 7720
喜起舞 2232
喉舌 2223
喇嘛印務處 3555
喪祝 4936
善世 4960
單于 4968
單車刺史 6270
嗇夫 4940
嗣王 5806
嗣適 5765
嘗藥監 277
嘉政 653
嘉蔬署 681
嘉議大夫 660
器物局 641
器備庫 631
嚮導處 2354

31 口

四大王府 5776
四大部 5775
四元 5840
四戶 5644
四方館 5618
四氏學 5767
四司 5774
四夷貢奉司 5658
四夷館 5656
四妃 5619
四色官 5751
四兵 5742
四局 5611

四房 5617
四直 5587
四直都虞候 5591
四門學 5719
四星 5636
四省 5759
四軍 5614
四面監 5722
四庫 5675
四部 5745
四尉 5807
四推御史 5804
四曹 5791
四廂 5631
四園苑提舉官 5843
四監 5581
四監司 5584
四輔 5623
四輔官 5623
四膳 5752
四選 5638
四轄 5629
四譯館 5656
回回 2879
回回令史 2880
回回司天監 2881
回回藥物院 2882
固山 3237
固山大 3243
固山貝子 3242
固山昂邦 3238
固山格格 3239
固山額眞 3240
固山額駙 3241
固倫 3233
固倫公主 3234
固倫額駙 3235
囹圄 3776
囿人 8056
國 3504
國大夫 3537
國子 3539
國子生 3544
國子寺 3546
國子師 3545
國子博士 3543
國子祭酒 3540
國子監 3541
國子學 3542
國公 3525
國夫人 3512
國太夫人 3538

國王 3548
國史 3529
國史日曆所 3533
國史院 3536
國史實錄院 3535
國史案 3532
國史館 3534
國母 3527
國用司 3551
國用參計所 3552
國老 3526
國君 3510
國姓 3518
國姓阿 3518
國官 3523
國侯 3513
國信司 3517
國信使 3516
國信房 3515
國信所 3517
國姻 3550
國相 3514
國計使 3507
國師 3530
國婚 3521
國尉 3549
國威章京 3508
國甥 3528
國舅 3509
國壻 3519
國朝 3505
國學 3520
圉師 8166
圈子手所 7679
圍場 7660
圓明園 8235
圓壇大樂禮器庫 8246
園 8218
園苑司 8256
園苑監 8255
園囿 8222
圖 7341
圖書使 7354
圖畫局 7349
圖畫署 7350
團 7380
團主 7381
團官 7382
團營 7389
團練 7383
團練安撫勸農使司 7384

團練守捉使 7387
團練使 7388
團練軍事推官 7385
團練觀察使 7386

32 土

土 7342
土方氏 7347
土司 7355
土兵 7353
土均 7345
土官 7352
土軍 7346
土訓 7348
地方官 6363
地官 6371
地官卿 6373
地面 6379
地曹 6388
地卿 6362
地壇 6385
地壇尉 6386
在京人事 6811
在京房 6812
在軍機大臣上學習行走 6815
坊 1892
坊主 1899
坊官 1908
坊場案 1894
坊郭丞 1918
坑冶司 3166
圻父 625
均人 1763
均司 1788
均官 1766
均輸 1787
坐廠廳 6950
坐衙 6967
坐選 6970
坐糧廳 6979
垂簾 1521
城 458
城守尉 513
城門司馬 507
城門郎 505
城門侯 503
城門校尉 504
城門領 506
垜集 6782

執千牛刀備身 948
執方 977
執守侍 1058
執事侍 1056
執帛 1041
執法 973
執法郎 975
執金吾 964
執政 939
執政官 939
執書 1059
執珪 1017
執秩 950
執戟 941
執馭 1098
堂 6288
堂上 6303
堂子 6305
堂老 6300
堂主事 6292
堂官 6297
堂郎中 6299
堂除 6293
堂後官 6294
堂筆帖式 6302
堂選 6295
場人 247
報羅使 4490
堤岸司 6393
塞曹 4829
塘 6289
墓大夫 4069
墨曹 4038
增生 6947
增貢生 6946
增廣生員 6945
增監生 6943
壇廟案 6278
壇墠 6279
壕寨 2164

33 士

士 5200
士大夫 5315
士子 5329
士林館 5287
士郎 5279
士師 5299
士曹 5320
士卿 5228
壯丁 1510

壺涿氏 2774
壽光省 5381
壽光殿 5381

34 夂

35 夊

夏官 2296
夏采 2300
夏卿 2293

36 夕

夕拜 2263
夕郎 2255
外 7573
外丞 7578
外女 7600
外史 7604
外匠 7583
外兵 7602
外兵曹 7602
外廷 7606
外制 7585
外刺刺姦 7610
外命女 7599
外命夫 7596
外命男 7598
外命婦 7597
外委千總 7611
外委把總 7612
外官 7592
外宗 7608
外府 7587
外府司 7588
外物料庫 7613
外舍 7603
外度科 7609
外祕書省 7601
外郎 7594
外院 7616
外家 7582
外帳小氏 7575
外戚 7580
外曹 7607
外廂 7591
外朝 7576
外朝大人官 7577
外厩 7586
外察 7574
外旗 7581

外監 7584
外臺 7605
外養狗處 7614
外翰 7589
外翰林 7590
外館 7593
外騎兵曹 7579
外廉 7595
外廉官 7595
外饔 7615
多爾吉衙門 6783
多羅 6784
多羅貝勒 6789
多羅格格 6786
多羅郡王 6785
多羅額駙 6788
多囉倫穆騰 6787
夜士 7914
夜君 7911
夜者 7907

37 大

大 5878
大九卿 5906
大人 5969
大卜 6008
大三司 6012
大上造 6014
大于越 6117
大士 6019
大小彫木局 5950
大世長 6021
大中丞 5923
大中護 5924
大元侯 6119
大元帥 6120
大元宰 6121
大元輔 6118
大內 5998
大內史 5999
大內都部署 6000
大分麾 5937
大夫 5939
大天 6065
大太史 6059
大夫案 5941
大夫監 5942
大少府 6015
大尹 6111
大文宗 6107
大文衡 6106
大方 5934

大方伯 5935
大方岳 5936
大木局 5996
大比 6006
大王 6103
大王府 6104
大主考 5915
大主禋 5920
大令 5990
大功曹 5978
大功德使 5976
大史 6018
大司元 6055
大司允 6057
大司天 6048
大司平 6045
大司巡 6034
大司成 6029
大司宗 6051
大司空 6037
大司城 6028
大司徒 6052
大司馬 6039
大司馬大將軍 6041
大司馬車騎將軍 6040
大司寇 6036
大司庚 6053
大司戚 6030
大司族 6050
大司農 6042
大司農司 6044
大司農卿 6043
大司僕 6046
大司漕 6049
大司儀 6035
大司樂 6056
大司賦 6032
大司憲 6033
大司膳 6047
大司禮 6038
大司儲 6031
大司籥 6054
大外翰 6102
大守侯 6023
大州牧 5911
大州幕 5912
大戎伯 5970
大旬宣 5964
大老爺 5983
大臣 5888

大舟 5910
大舟卿 5910
大行 5955
大行人 5957
大行治禮丞 5956
大行臺 5958
大邦伯 6004
大佐賦 6076
大匠 5895
大匠卿 5896
大辰相 5987
大角手 5927
大邑宰 5968
大京兆 5905
大使 6017
大使臣 6022
大典禮 6064
大岡伯 5909
大和羹 5946
大宗 6081
大宗正司 6083
大宗正府 6082
大宗正院 6084
大宗伯 6088
大宗師 6089
大官令 5972
大官署 5973
大尚書 6013
大岳牧 6123
大府 5940
大林牙院 5989
大牧正 5994
大直指 5902
大金吾 5904
大長公主 5882
大長侯 5881
大長秋 5886
大保釐 6005
大威衛 6105
大帥 6026
大拜 6003
大柱史 5917
大柱石 5918
大柱國 5916
大相臺 5949
大祝 5913
大秋臺 5908
大胥 5959
大計 5891
大軍機 5928
大郡伯 5930
大郡侯 5929
大冢宰 5925

大家 5894
大宰 6068
大宮允 5980
大宮輔 5975
大宮端 5979
大宮贊 5977
大師 6020
大烏臺 6108
大特哩袞司 6062
大率節度使 6027
犬秩宗 5903
大納言 5997
大訓翰 5963
大參 6073
大參戎 6074
大國醫 5981
大堂 6060
大將 5897
大將軍 5897
大將軍府 5898
大庶長 6024
大常伯 5887
大族軍主 6079
大晟府 6016
大理 5984
大理寺 5986
大都督 6096
大都督府 6097
大都閫 6095
大都憲 6092
大都護 6093
大都護府 6094
大馭 6115
大魁 5974
大罍 6080
大惕隱司 6063
大掌術 5885
大掌樞 5884
大掌翰 5880
大掌籙 5883
大棘 5890
大統 6099
大給諫 5892
大詞翰 6101
大貳侯 5931
大傳經 5922
大廐令 5907
大廉憲 5988
大業 6109
大督河 6091
大睦親府 5995
大著 5914
大著作 5919

大虞卿 6116　　太 6134　　太宗 6235　　太學 6168　　天章閣 6686　　奉聖公 2013
大資 6100　　太一博士 6181　　太宗正 6236　　太樂 6264　　天廄坊 6692　　奉聖侯 2012
大輅廄 5992　　太卜 6197　　太宗正院 6237　　太樂令 6268　　天駟監 6713　　奉聖亭侯 2015
大農 6001　　太卜令 6199　　太官令 6185　　太樂正 6266　　天節軍 6691　　奉蓋羽林郎 1996
大農令 6002　　太卜局 6198　　太官署 6186　　太樂局 6267　　天壇 6715　　奉儀 1988
大遊戎 6114　　太卜署 6200　　太府 6159　　太樂案 6265　　天壇尉 6716　　奉德大夫 2021
大鼎相 6066　　太上 6205　　太府寺 6165　　太樂署 6269　　天樂祭器庫 6731　　奉輦祗應 2003
大僕 6011　　太上君 6206　　太府卿 6162　　太禧宗禋院 6167　　天樂署 6732　　奉駕大夫 1965
大樂案 6122　　太上皇 6208　　太府監 6161　　太醫 6171　　天藏府 6717　　奉駕局 1964
大漕 6075　　太上皇后 6207　　太保 6195　　太醫令 6180　　天騎 6687　　奉膳局 2009
大漢將軍 5944　　太上皇帝 6208　　太皇太后 6169　　太醫正 6174　　天驥府 6689　　奉禮郎 2002
大監 5899　　太予樂令 6262　　太祝 6152　　太醫丞 6175　　夷兵 2986　　奉職 1968
大監部 5901　　太子 6239　　太祝令 6154　　太醫助教 6178　　夷离董 2974　　奉醫大夫 1993
大端佐 6098　　太子三少 6248　　太倉 6227　　太醫局 6179　　夷离畢 2977　　奉醫局 1990
大賓客 6007　　太子三師 6249　　太倉令 6230　　太醫院 6184　　夷情章京 2946　　奉觶 1969
大銀臺 6112　　太子三卿 6247　　太倉出納使 6228　　太醫案 6173　　夷隸 2973　　奉議大夫 1992
大銓衡 5926　　太子內坊局 6243　　太倉使 6231　　太醫教官 6176　　夸蘭大 3259　　奉議郎 1991
大鳳 5938　　太子太保 6257　　太倉庫 6229　　太醫博士 6182　　奉上太醫 2010　　奉爨 2027
大儀 5965　　太子太師 6258　　太倉署 6232　　太醫署 6183　　奉化 1986　　奉爨局 2028
大樞臺 6025　　太子太傅 6256　　太倉銀庫 6233　　太醫監 6177　　奉安符寶所 1950　　奉孿 2004
大畿牧 5893　　太子少保 6252　　太卿 6150　　天下母 6699　　奉旨參軍 1972　　奄 7918
大學 5961　　太子少師 6253　　太孫 6222　　天下兵馬元帥 6700　　奉祀 2017　　奄人 7940
大學士 5962　　太子少傅 6251　　太宰 6225　　　　　　　　　奉祀君 2018　　奄尹 7962
大禪宗 5879　　太子少詹事 6250　　太宰令 6226　　天下宗師 6701　　奉車郎 1955　　奎文閣 3385
大禧宗禋院 5948　　太子帥更令 6254　　太師 6213　　天女 6708　　奉車都尉 1956　　奎章閣 3382
大翰博 5945　　太子賓客 6244　　太晟府 6147　　天子 6719　　奉使宣撫 2016　　奔星廄 4562
大諫 5900　　太子宮傅府 6240　　太尉 6260　　天子耳目 6721　　奉信郎 1983　　奏事中散 7041
大謁者 6110　　太子陵 6241　　太尉公 6261　　天子門生 6722　　奉政大夫 1961　　奏事令 7043
大選 5960　　太子率更寺 6255　　太常 6137　　天子禁軍 6720　　奉直大夫 1971　　奏事官 7042
大憲副 5952　　太子僕 6245　　太常司 6144　　天公 6706　　奉直郎 1970　　奏事處 7040
大憲僉 5951　　太子僕寺 6246　　太常寺 6145　　天文局 6725　　奉祠所 2024　　奏表案 7038
大憲臺 5954　　太子廟 6242　　太常伯 6142　　天文科 6726　　奉乘 2011　　奏差 7030
大禮使 5985　　太子樂令 6259　　太常府 6139　　天文院 6729　　奉乘郎 2014　　奏曹 7044
大總侯 6086　　太中大夫 6155　　太常卿 6138　　天文博士 6727　　奉宸大夫 1958　　奏摺 7031
大總制 6085　　太夫人 6163　　太常博士 6143　　天文算學 6728　　奉宸庫 1957　　奏蔭 7046
大總裁 6090　　太主 6151　　太常禮院 6141　　天王 6723　　奉宸苑 1960　　奏薦賞功司 7033
大總管府 6087　　太史 6212　　太常禮儀院 6140　　天生仙 6712　　奉宸衛 1959　　奏薦賞功案 7032
大鴻臚 5947　　太史令 6218　　太傅 6158　　天后 6698　　奉恩將軍 1978　　奏讞曹 7045
大儲端 5921　　太史公 6217　　太傅上公 6164　　天老 6707　　奉恩輔國公 1979　　奚 2229
大醫 5967　　太史局 6216　　太尊 6234　　天官 6704　　奉恩鎮國公 1977　　奚六部 2258
大獻納 5953　　太史院 6220　　太僕 6201　　天府 6695　　奉宸局 1989　　奚王府 2280
大藩府 5932　　太史案 6214　　太僕司 6203　　天武四廂 6730　　奉班都知 2007　　奚官府 2253
大藩侯 5933　　太史曹 6219　　太僕寺 6204　　天官給事 6705　　奉訓大夫 1985
大贊府 6071　　太史監 6215　　太僕卿 6202　　天府院 6697　　奉晃局 2006　　**38 女**
大贊治 6070　　太守 6221　　太監 6148　　天府藏 6696　　奉國上將軍 2001
大贊侯 6072　　太平惠民局 6196　　太儀 6170　　天柱 6693　　奉國中尉 2000　　女史 4345
大贊政 6069　　太母 6194　　太廟 6188　　天皇 6702　　奉國將軍 1999　　女巫 4349
大臝藏 5943　　太后 6166　　太廟令 6191　　天紀軍 6688　　奉常 1951　　女侍中 4346
大議 5966　　太妃 6157　　太廟局 6190　　天威軍 6724　　奉常大夫 1953　　女侍史 4347
大醮侯 6077　　太君 6156　　太廟尉 6193　　天姬 6703　　奉常寺 1952　　女官 4340
大醮憲 6078　　太社令 6210　　太廟祭器法物庫 6189　　天孫 6714　　奉御 2026　　女尚書 4344
大聽 6067　　太社局 6209　　　　　　　　　天家 6690　　奉裕衛 2029　　女府 4336
夫人 2066　　太官 6185　　太廟署 6192　　天部 6709　　奉朝請 1954　　女直 3065, 4332

女祝 4334
女宮 4341
女酒 4333
女眞 3064, 4329
女桃 4348
女春扤 4335
女御 4351
女漿 4331
女稾 4339
女冪 4342
女醢 4337
女醯 4338
女餳 4330
女邊 4343
女鹽 4350
奴才 4320
妃 1925
如意館 3069
委人 7669
委員 7688
委差 7659
委署 7675
威武軍 7685
威儀 7668
威衛 7680
嫛娒 2589
娘娘 4300
娛靈 8154
婦 2033
婦人 2067
婕妤 780
婉容 7629
婉華 7623
婉儀 7624
媒氏 3932
嫡福晉 6365
嬪 4649
嬪婦 4651
嬢嬢 4300

39 子

子 7519
孔目 3503
孔目官 3503
存撫使 7076
孝弟力田 2453
孝廉 2418
孝廉方正 2419
孝廉右尉 2421
孝廉左尉 2421
孝廉郎 2420
孝經師 2391

孤 3222
孤卿 3226
孳生監 7539
學士 2704
學士承旨 2707
學士院 2708
學正 2691
學正官醫提領 2692
學生 2702
學事 2703
學究 2693
學官 2696
學官令 2699
學官長 2697
學官祭酒 2698
學長 2689
學政 2690
學院 2709
學師 2705
學習 2695
學博 2701
學道 2709
學臺 2709
學諭 2710
學錄 2700
孺人 3070
孺子 3083

40 宀

穴從 3094
穴從僕射 3095
安人 23
安和署 21
安撫大使 19
安撫司 18
安撫使 17
安撫使司 18
安撫制置使 16
安撫提轄兵甲 20
守 5355
守令 5385
守本官 5395
守正 5359
守巡道 5375
守助像 5366
守府 5370
守屏 5396
守倅 5404
守宰 5402
守宮令 5383

守宮署 5384
守捉 5364
守捉使 5365
守祧 5401
守陵 5386
守陵太監 5389
守陵寢總兵官 5387
守備 5393
守備太監 5394
守圍場兵 5405
守當官 5399
守道 5400
守禦 5406
守禦千戶所 5407
守禦千總 5408
守關 5367
守關 5380
守護陵寢大臣 5376
宅 344
宅家 60
宅家子 61
宏父 2903
宏文院 2912
宏詞 2910
宏猷 2913
宏德 2908
宏徽 2904
宜人 2961
官 3262
官大夫 3330
官生 3324
官田 3332
官兵 3323
官告局 3308
官告院 3309
官府 3294
官房租庫 3293
官軍 3285
官家 3275
官馬坊 3319
官學 3298
官學生 3299
官誥局 3308
官誥院 3309
官醫 3300
官醫提領所 3305
官醫提舉司 3304
定科曹 6738
定奪案 6743
定遠將軍 6746
定課曹 6738

定邊 6740
宗 7077
宗人 7104
宗人令 7106
宗人府 7105
宗女 7142
宗子學 7165
宗子正 7164
宗工 7120
宗令 7133
宗正 7080
宗正司 7084
宗正寺 7085
宗正奉使帳案 7082
宗正府 7083
宗正卿 7081
宗丞 7086
宗伯 7147
宗官 7109
宗姬 7103
宗室 7150
宗室公 7152
宗室侍衛 7153
宗師 7151
宗卿 7098
宗理監務 7122
宗聖侯 7149
宗廟 7139
宗衛率府 7166
宗學 7102
宗憲 7101
臣 2821
臣人 2827
臣女 2828
臣寺 2829
臣官 2827
臣者 2822
臣者令 2823
客 3186
客省 3200
客曹 3204
客卿 3192
客館 3194
室史 5300
室長 5205
宣文閣 2684
宣父 2660
宣令舍人 2671
宣尼公 2673
宣判 2674
宣奉大夫 2659
宣奉郎 2658

宣使 2677
宣明 2672
宣武都指揮使 2685
宣室 2678
宣政院 2654
宣威都指揮使 2683
宣教郎 2655
宣黃案 2662
宣聖 2676
宣業 2686
宣義郎 2666
宣儀 2665
宣德郎 2680
宣慶使 2656
宣慰司 2682
宣撫司 2661
宣撫使 2661
宣課司 2669
宣課局 2669
宣諭使 2687
宣諭官 2687
宣徽 2663
宣徽院 2664
宣藩 2657
宣贊舍人 2681
宣議郎 2666
宸妃 393
家 649
家人子 661
家內司 671
家士 678
家令 669
家司馬 682
家丞 654
家吏 668
家兵 674
家宗人 686
家巫 688
家馬令 670
宮 3389
宮人 3437
宮女 3456
宮中官 3413
宮允 3500
宮太保 3482
宮太師 3483
宮太傅 3481
宮尹 3496
宮正 3397
宮司令 3479
宮臣賓客 3396

宮伯 3461
宮坊 3416
宮使 3470
宮官 3442
宮府寺 3430
宮直 3405
宮門司 3453
宮門局 3451
宮門將府 3450
宮門僕 3452
宮保 3458
宮相 3433
宮省 3466
宮師 3473
宮師府 3475
宮苑使 3498
宮苑總監 3499
宮庶 3478
宮教博士 3401
宮傅 3427
宮卿 3407
宮衆 3412
宮殿府行工部 3487
宮殿監 3486
宮詹 3391
宮端 3493
宮輔 3428
宮衛 3434
宮學 3436
宮嬪 3460
宮闈局 3495
宮贊 3488
宮籍監 3400
宮觀使 3444
宮觀都監 3445
宰 6809
宰夫 6816
宰君 6814
宰相 6819
宰相判官 6821
宰相府 6820
宰執 6810
宰歷 6823
宰輔 6817
宰縣 6822
宰衡 6818
容華 3089
容卿 3088
容臺 3093
宴安樂案 7919
寄祿官 569
寄祿格 568

寄祿階 568
寄椿庫 547
密院 3979
宿衛 5854
富寧庫 2087
寒人 2138
寒官 2138
察 37
察官 47
察言司 53
察非掾 44
察院 56
察案 39
察案御史 41
察推 50
察訪使 43
察訪使者 43
寨 58
寨主 62
寧妃 4310
實 5201
實缺 5235
實授 5305
實錄院 5291
寢 1173
審刑司 5153
審刑院 5154
審刑議官 5152
審官院 5155
審計司 5144
審計科 5143
審計院 5146
審理所 5157
寫國史楷書 2467
寫御書人 2490
寵主 1649
寶文閣 4502
寶抄 4454
寶…局 4469
寶林 4489
寶泉 4470
寶泉局 4472
寶泉都提舉司 4474
寶泉提舉司 4473
寶泉廠 4471
寶鈔 4454
寶鈔司 4457
寶鈔提舉司 4458
寶鈔廣惠軍 4455
寶鈔廣惠庫 4456
寶鈔總庫 4459
寶源 4504

寶源局 4506
寶源庫 4507
寶源錢監 4505
寶謨閣 4492
寶豐錢監 4476

41 寸

寺 5534
寺人 5663
寺互令 5645
寺副 5621
寺務司 5816
寺監 5583
寺簿 5746
封人 1994
封印院 2025
封册表奏案 2022
封建 1967
封諡科 1997
封勳司 1984
封椿庫 1975
封椿錢物庫 1974
封駁 2008
封彌官 2005
封爵制誥 1976
封疆大吏 1966
封贈 2023
射人 5134
射生 5141
射鳥氏 5140
射聲 5142
專勾司 1486
專知 1484
專知御書檢討 1485
專城伯 1483
將 690
將仕佐郎 704
將仕郎 703
將行 695
將作大匠 712
將作少府 709
將作少府監 710
將作司 711
將作院 714
將作曹 713
將作監 708
將兵長史 701
將軍 694
將虞候 717
尉 7657
尉五部 7686

尉氏 7673
尉司 7677
尉曹 7678
對讀官 7392
導官 6318
導官署 6318
導客局 6315
導客舍人 6316
導從 6325

42 小

小 2374
小九卿 2392
小三司 2428
小方 2400
小木局 2424
小史 2430
小司土 2448
小司內 2443
小司木 2442
小司水 2447
小司卉 2437
小司市 2446
小司玉 2450
小司皮 2444
小司色 2445
小司空 2439
小司金 2436
小司徒 2449
小司馬 2441
小司寇 2438
小司樂 2451
小司隸 2440
小司織 2435
小刑部 2402
小匠師 2386
小吏 2413
小吏房 2415
小吏部 2416
小臣 2377
小行人 2401
小兵部 2427
小底 2452
小兩省官 2417
小官 2410
小武藏 2458
小門下 2423
小保 2425
小祝 2394
小秋 2393
小胥 2403
小軍機 2398

小宰相 2454
小師 2431
小師氏 2433
小教習 2387
小給使學生 2380
小黃門 2407
小著 2395
小虞部 2459
小試官 2432
小旗 2383
小監 2388
小賓部 2426
小銓 2397
小儀 2408
小學 2406
小駕部 2385
小膳部 2429
小蕃部 2399
小諫 2389
小選 2404
小選院 2405
小職方 2390
少 5084
少上造 5111
少中大夫 5094
少內 5109
少公 5106
少尹 5126
少仙 5102
少令 5108
少司成 5115
少司徒 5121
少司馬 5117
少司農 5118
少司僕 5119
少司膳 5120
少司禮 5116
少匠 5088
少吏 5107
少行人 5103
少使 5114
少府 5097
少府寺 5100
少府卿 5099
少府監 5098
少保 5110
少師 5113
少參 5123
少宰 5122
少秩 5090
少尉 5124
少常伯 5086
少傅 5096

少卿 5091
少卿監 5092
少詹事 5085
少監 5089
少儀 5104
少鵰司 5101
尚 4971
尚方 4992
尚方司 4995
尚方院 4995
尚方監 4993
尚方署 4994
尚功局 5012
尚右 5078
尚右郎官 5079
尚左 5068
尚左郎官 5070
尚收所 5041
尚衣 5000
尚衣局 5004
尚衣庫 5005
尚衣監 5001
尚沐 5025
尚牧監 5026
尚服局 4996
尚舍局 5035
尚乘寺 4977
尚乘局 4976
尚冠 5009
尚席 4997
尚珍署 4975
尚食 5038
尚食局 5040
尚食監 5039
尚宮局 5013
尚書 5042
尚書大行臺 5056
尚書丞 5044
尚書令 5049
尚書令史 5050
尚書右選 5060
尚書四曹 5055
尚書左選 5058
尚書寺 5054
尚書省 5053
尚書郎 5047
尚書博士 5051
尚書都省 5059
尚書裏行 5048
尚書僕射 5052
尚書臺 5057
尚書銓 5045
尚書選 5046

尚茶 4973
尚帳 4974
尚飲局 5077
尚寢局 4986
尚廄局 4989
尚署 5043
尚儀局 5003
尚輦 5014
尚輦局 5015
尚膳 5032
尚膳監 5033
尚醞局 5081
尚醞署 5082
尚醫監 5002
尚藥 5075
尚藥局 5076
尚藥監 5075
尚寶司 5029
尚寶局 5028
尚寶監 5027

43 兀

44 尸

尹 7969
局 1674
居室 1685
居攝 1684
屠者 7344
履人 1681
屬 5409
屬州 5424
屬國 5442
屬國都尉 5443
屬籍案 5417
屬廳 5461

45 屮

屯 7404
屯田 7409
屯田千戶所 7410
屯田司 7414
屯田打捕總管府 7415
屯田使司 7413
屯田清吏司 7411
屯田萬戶府 7417
屯田道 7416
屯田管勾 7412
屯部 7408

屯監 7407
屯衛 7418
屯營 7419
屯騎校尉 7405
屯騎尉 7406

46 山

山長 4952
山師 4961
山虞 4969
岳牧 8268
崇元署 1673
崇文院 1671
崇文監 1669
崇文館 1670
崇文觀 1670
崇玄署 1656
崇玄學 1655
崇志堂 1647
崇政院 1646
崇政殿 1645
崇掖衛 1661
崇虛局 1654
崇祿寺 1666
崇進 1648
崇福司 1652
崇聖侯 1667
崇儀使 1660
崇德 1668
崇賢館 1653
崖公 7875

47 巛

川師 1501
川衡 1497
州 1332
州同 1348
州判 1343
州牧 1342
州長 1334
州軍監 1340
州宰 1344
州都 1346
州端 1347
州幕 1341
巡 2712
巡史 2752
巡司 2760
巡守 2758
巡江御史 2723
巡防官 2727

巡使 2752
巡官 2746
巡幸 2740
巡河 2735
巡河官 2735
巡河御史 2736
巡城科道 2720
巡城御史 2721
巡按 2713
巡按御史 2713
巡政廳 2719
巡查御史 2717
巡狩 2758
巡院 2769
巡倉御史 2764
巡倉科道 2763
巡庫 2744
巡御史 2768
巡捉 2725
巡海道 2734
巡茶馬御史 2715
巡馬遞鋪 2749
巡視 2753
巡視皇城御史
　2754
巡視…御史 2757
巡視…漕務 2755
巡視鹽政御史
　2756
巡察 2714
巡察使 2716
巡察科道 2714
巡察御史 2717
巡農御史 2750
巡道 2762
巡漕科道 2765
巡漕御史 2765
巡撫 2731
巡撫大使 2732
巡撫使 2732
巡檢司 2724
巡轄馬遞鋪 2737
巡轄馬鋪 2737
巡鹽 2766
巡鹽直指 2766
巡鹽御史 2767

48 工

工正 3398
工作案 3491
工官 3443
工房 3417

工科 3440
工案 3390
工部 3462
工副 3429
工曹 3490
左 6949
左三部 6987
左士曹 6995
左弋 6972
左戶 6971
左戶曹 6971
左主客 6959
左史 6990
左司 6999
左右 7016
左右司 7018
左右寺案 7019
左右街僧錄司
　7017
左右衛 7020
左寺 7000
左民 6981
左民曹 6981
左丞 6951
左更 6974
左京輔都尉 6957
左侍禁 6994
左尚署 6988
左府 6965
左所 6998
左班都知 6983
左班殿直 6982
左計 6953
左軍 6961
左院 7023
左師 6991
左庫 6975
左御 7021
左部 6986
左堂 7003
左執法 6956
左將 6954
左庶長 6997
左推案 7014
左曹 7012
左揆 6976
左馮翊 6985
左榜 6984
左署 6996
左輔都尉 6966
左賢王 6968
左遷 6955
左選 6969

左翼前鋒 6973
左衛 7015
左斷刑 7013
左臺 7001
左藏 7006
左藏出納使 7008
左藏庫 7009
左藏案 7007
左藏提點 7011
左藏署 7010
左廳 7004
巫 7733
巫馬 7807
差 38
差役 69
差次案 72
差徭 73
差遣 67
差遣院 68

49 己

巷伯 2344

50 巾

巾車 1118
巾帽局 1133
布衣 4780
布政司 4770
布政使 4770
布庫 4788
布憲 4779
市令 5288
市丞 5211
市易上界 5261
市易下界 5260
市易司 5264
市易抵當庫 5265
市易務 5266
市長 5206
市師 5301
市曹 5321
市舶使 5295
市舶提舉司 5296
市買司 5292
市署 5307
帑藏 6304
帖司 6512
帥 5475
帥司 5483
帥府通判 5480
帥臣 5477

帥都督 5485
帥漕憲倉 5484
帝匹 6380
帝太太后 6384
帝太后 6383
帝姬 6368
帮領班 4441
帮領班章京上行
　走 4442
帮辦大臣 4443
師 5202
師氏 5302
師友 5341
師長 5207
師帥 5311
師相 5250
師範 5243
帳下督 121
帳內六閑 164
帳內府 163
帳史 180
帳司 192
帳案 85
帳籍告身案 97
帳籍案 96
常 232
常平司 256
常平官 254
常平倉 257
常平倉司 258
常平案 253
常平署 255
常在 271
常臣 234
常伯 259
常侍 262
常侍府 265
常侍郎 266
常侍曹 267
常侍謁者 268
常侍騎 264
常服郎 239
常和署 240
常盈庫 278
常參官 272
常從 273
常從虎賁督 274
常從郎 275
常滿倉 252
常選官 246
常騎侍 235
帶 6126
帶俸 6131

帶御器械 6133
幕 4040
幕人 4054
幕士 4065
幕友 4075
幕府 4052
幕職 4047
幕職官 4047
幢將 1516

51 干

平 4698
平事 4711
平常 4704
平章 4699
平章事 4703
平章政事 4700
平章軍國事 4702
平章軍國重事
　4701
平準 4705
平道軍 4714
平準案 4706
平準務 4707
年例 4309
并省 4693
幸 2560
幹 3127
幹事 3138
幹官長 3134
幹當 3139
幹當公事 3139
幹辦 3135
幹辦公事 3136
幹辦玉牒所殿
　3137
幹辦官 3135

52 幺

53 广

序客 2646
序班 2649
府 2034
府元 2120
府公 2070
府尹 2116
府主 2047
府史 2097
府兵 2093

府判 2089
府官 2069
府牧 2085
府郡 2051
府院法直官 2122
府尉 2113
府端 2110
府學 2062
府幕 2084
庖人 4510
庖正 4508
店宅務 6517
庠生 2347
度支 7194
度支司 7205
度支尚書 7204
度支科 7201
度支郎 7202
度支郎中 7202
度支案 7196
度支部 7203
度支曹 7207
度支監 7197
度科 7240
度牒庫 7296
庫 3248
庫大使 3253
庫子 3258
庫守 3252
庫使 3251
庫典 3254
庫部 3249, 3250
庫部司 3249
庫部曹 3250
庫曹 3256
庫曹御史 3257
庫廳 3255
庭氏 6760
座主 6958
座師 6992
庶人 5437
庶子 5468
庶氏 5456
庶吉士 5419
庶老 5444
庶宗 5467
庶長 5412
庶常 5414
庶常館 5415
廂 2302
廂公 2330
廂吏 2339
廂兵 2341

廂兵案 2343
廂官 2326
廊下使 3572
廊下食使 3572
廉 3701
廉車 3704
廉使 3715
廉捕 3714
廉訪 3706
廉訪使 3708
廉訪官 3707
廉察 3703
廉察使 3703
廉憲 3709
廉鎮 3705
慶人 5531
廐 1285
廐令 1307
廐牧 1311
廐牧署 1312
廐長 1291
廕 7971
廕生 7990
塵人 82
尉史 1478
尉役 1469
廣文 3351
廣文館 3352
廣西房 3341
廣訓 3343
廣部尉 3350
廣惠司 3345
廣惠倉 3346
廣惠庫 3344
廣業堂 3353
廣源庫 3355
廣濟提舉司 3338
廣樂庫 3356
廣親睦親宅 3339
廣儲司 3340
廟 3980
廟令 3985
廟祀令 3988
廟直官 3982
廟長 3981
廟幹 3984
廟學 3983
廟簿 3987
廩人 3725
廩生 3728
廩貢生 3726
廩監生 3719
廩膳生 3727

廩犧 3724
廳 6748

54 夂

廷 6749
廷史 6761
廷平 6758
廷吏文學 6757
廷則 6764
廷尉 6767
廷尉三官 6776
廷尉史 6777
廷尉司直 6778
廷尉平 6775
廷尉府 6772
廷尉正 6768
廷尉明法掾 6774
廷尉律博士 6773
廷尉秋卿 6771
廷尉卿 6770
廷尉評 6775
廷尉監 6769
廷推 6766
廷掾 6781
廷評 6758
廷試 6762
廷對 6765
廷魁 6755
廷議 6754
延資庫 7961
延慶司 7928
廸功佐郎 6375
廸功郎 6374
廻避 2887
建昌院 798
建康三官 833

55 卄

卄人 3438
弁師 4644

56 弋

式道侯 5318

57 弓

弓矢司 3477
弓弩院 3455
弓弩造箭院 3455
弓弩署 3454

弓箭直 3403
弓箭庫 3404
引見司 7976
引進司 7978
引進副使 7977
引試使 7993
引駕 7973
引駕仗 7973
引禮舍人 7985
引贊官 7999
弘文館 2911
弟子長教者 6390
弟子員 6391
駕手班 4319
弩坊署 4318
弼 4569
彈壓 6280
彌封官 3976
彍騎 3553

58 彐

59 彡

形方氏 2570
形史 7502
彫木局 6496
彩女 6838
彩畫官 6829
影堂 8021

60 彳

役 2920
役兵 2987
往來國信所 7649
後所 2225
後行 2211
後省 2224
後苑 2228
後扈大臣 2214
律令師 3888
律令博士 3887
律例館 3886
律博士 3891
律學 3885
待詔 6127
待詔廳 6128
待制 6129
待制官 6129
徒 7343
徠遠司 3557

徠遠軍 3556
得解 6330
得解舉人 6330
從 7168
從仕郎 7178
從丞 7171
從事 7176
從事史 7179
從事郎 7177
從官 7175
從征 7169
從政郎 7170
從軍士 7172
從義郎 7174
從義案 7173
御女 8161
御史 8167
御史大夫 8181
御史大夫丞 8182
御史大夫寺 8183
御史中丞 8174
御史中執法 8175
御史中尉 8176
御史內史 8180
御史外丞 8185
御史丞 8172
御史巡按 8179
御史府 8178
御史房 8177
御史知雜 8173
御史長史 8171
御史臺 8184
御用監 8213
御用器務局 8212
御衣史道安局 8141
御衣局 8140
御衣院 8142
御伯 8162
御位下 8203
御妻 8109
御府 8129
御前大臣 8120
御前弓馬子弟所 8118
御前五軍 8123
御前甲庫 8111
御前行走 8117
御前侍衛 8119
御前封椿 8116
御前軍 8114
御前軍器所 8115
御前軍器案 8115

御前軍器監 8115
御前椿管激賞庫 8113
御前諸軍都統制 8112
御院通進 8215
御香局 8137
御師 8168
御書處 8188
御書院 8189
御茶膳房 8105
御茶膳處 8105
御馬司 8156
御馬院 8158
御馬倉 8157
御馬監 8155
御細倉 8136
御羞 8138
御船處 8125
御鳥槍處 8160
御試 8169
御僕 8164
御廚 8124
御廚司 8124
御輦院 8149
御營五軍 8211
御營司 8209
御營使 8208
御營宿衛使 821
御醫 8139
御醫院 8143
御藥局 8205
御藥房 8206
御藥院 8207
御藥監 8204
御屬 8186
復訓 2064
循行 2739
徭 7889
徵 394
徹侯 359
徵士 435
徵比 432
徵仕郎 438
徵君 407
徵事 434
徵事郎 438
德妃 6331
德儀 6332
徽政院 2875

61 心

必闍赤 4584
念珠曹 4308
怯薛 782
急選 555
急腳遞 536
恭人 3439
恩生 1819
恩地 1821
恩取監生 1815
恩科出身 1816
恩貢 1817
恩貢生 1817
恩戚家人 1814
御前統領官 812
恩補貢生 1818
恩廕 1824
恩廕監生 1825
恭聖侯 3468
恩試 1820
恩賜貢生 1823
恩賜監生 1822
恩騎尉 1813
恤刑 2644
惠民局 2885
惠民藥局 2885
惠妃 2878
惜薪司 2239
愛馬 7
愛瑪克 7
慶豐司 1267
慶遠裕民司 1282
憂貢 8062
憂貢生 8062
憲 2491
憲司 2537
憲司端 2538
憲司幕 2538
憲臣 2496
憲官 2509
憲府 2505
憲長 2496
憲部 2528
憲綱 2508
憲網 2547
憲臺 2540
憑由司 4716
應免解人 8014
應奉 8013
懷化將軍 2818
懷方氏 2817
懷遠驛 2820

62 戈

戈什 3184
戈什哈 3184
戈戟司 3169
戊己校尉 7740
成全大夫 470
成妃 476
成均祭酒 471
成均監 472
成忠郎 469
成和大夫 482
成和郎 481
成務郎 516
成婚 495
戈司 3092
戈右 3097
戈政府 3087
戈政廳 3087
戈僕 3091
戈衛 3096
戍主 5425
戍卒 5466
戲師 2269

63 戶

戶口案 2785
戶房 2781
戶直郎 2773
戶科 2784
戶郎 2786
戶部 2789
戶部五科 2793
戶部司 2792
戶部使司 2791
戶部局 2790
戶將 2771
戶曹 2798
戶稅案 2796
戶籍判官 2770
房 1893
房地科 1915
房考官 1906
所 5523
所司 5525
所由 5528
扁手司 4962

64 手

才人 6830
才識兼茂 6842

打套局 6061
打捕所 6009
打捕總管府 6010
托克托和斯 6792
抄事 336
抄事公使 338
抄紙局 316
折中倉 346
折威軍 350
折桂人 349
折衝府 347
承旨 463
承旨閣子 466
承衣 497
承事郎 511
承制學士 465
承受 512
承受官 512
承奉 477
承奉郎 478
承奉班都知 479
承明廬 508
承直郎 467
承信郎 485
承勅監 468
承宣布政使司 487
承宣使 488
承政 460
承務 515
承務郎 516
承差 459
承祿署 502
承符 480
承發司 475
承發架閣庫 473
承發管勾兼獄丞 474
承華令 490
承華監 489
承節郎 461
承管 499
承閣 500
承德郎 514
承應小底局 517
承辦事務衙門 509
承徽 494
承議郎 498
扶風 2055
技巧 537
把戈 4369
把門 4374

把總 4384
批本處 4611
批驗所 4614
投下 6797
招安使 279
招收部署 302
招納司 299
招討司 304
招討使 303
招搖軍 308
招募 298
招撫使 282
招撫處置使 281
招箭班 280
抽分竹木局 1352
抽分局 1352
抽分場提領所 1351
拘收司 1686
拔貢 4372
拔貢生 4372
拔萃 4383
拔解 4362
拜 4388
抵當免行所 6387
抵當所 6387
抵選 6367
拖沙喇哈番 6794
押伏官 7844
押司 7869
押司官 7869
押官 7858
押院中使 7874
押班 7863
押宿官 7856
押番 7852
押衙 7873
押綱官 7857
押遞 7871
指省 1043
指揮 998
指揮司 1001
指揮同知 1002
指揮使 1000
指揮使司 1001
指揮僉事 999
持書侍御史 1113
持節 1105
持節督 1106
挈壺 783
挈壺正 784
捌馬令 7495
按协聲律官 22

按察司 13
按察使 12
按察官 11
按察副使 10
按察採訪處置使 15
按察…道刑獄使 14
按察僉事 9
按察簽事 9
按摩師 25
按摩博士 24
拾遺 5256
捉賊招安安撫使 1331
捐 1701
捐貢 1702
捐輸 1703
捕盜案 4803
捕賊官 4807
捕廳 4804
挽郎 7630
掌 83
掌伏 88
掌北院頭子 168
掌印 217
掌印太監 221
掌印官 219
掌印冠軍使 220
掌印雲麾使 222
掌印監督太監 218
掌史 181
掌囚 110
掌正 90
掌皮 170
掌交 100
掌戎隸 134
掌次 207
掌衣 127
掌冶署 213
掌夷隸 130
掌材 197
掌狄隸 196
掌言 216
掌…事大臣 187
掌函 119
掌固 139
掌所事冠軍使 190
掌所事雲麾使 191
掌津 106

掌法案 116
掌知刻漏 105
掌舍 177
掌南院頭子 161
掌客 137
掌故 140
掌果 152
掌炭 193
掌珍 89
掌…科 138
掌計 93
掌院學士 226
掌食 182
掌庫 141
掌座 201
掌徒 204
掌御湯藥 224
掌書 188
掌書記 189
掌染草 133
掌案 86
掌畜 124
掌記 94
掌貢部 151
掌貢舉 151
掌教司 101
掌船局 113
掌茶 205
掌設 178
掌訝 211
掌貨賄 125
掌傘總領 174
掌麻 154
掌散樂 175
掌閑 123
掌集 95
掌園 225
掌察四方 87
掌廄都轄 109
掌節 102
掌罪隸 203
掌葛 136
掌蜃 179
掌飾 183
掌墓 160
掌橋司 135
掌漏 156
掌筵 215
掌綵 198
掌製 104
掌賓 171
掌儀 126
掌儀司 132

掌戮 157
掌樂 227
掌樂官 228
掌燈 195
掌衛事大臣 210
掌輦 155
掌嚴 214
掌憲 122
掌曆 154
掌翰 120
掌膳 176
掌醖 229
掌醖署 230
掌輿 223
掌醢署 118
掌闈 209
掌關防 144
掌關防事務 148
掌關防官 146
掌關防處 145
掌關防管理內管
　領事務處 147
掌縫 117
掌藏 200
掌醫 128
掌醫監 129
掌醫署 131
掌疆 99
掌簿 172
掌藥 212
掌贊 199
掌寶 167
掌籍 92
掌闕案 114
掌饎 98
掌饌廳 112
掌蠻隸 159
捧日四廂 4568
控鶴 3502
捹鉢 4078
排岸司 4392
排門人 4396
排陣使 4394
排馬 4395
掃洒院子 4937
授 5356
探花 6275
探花郎 6275
探馬赤軍 6277
推 7393
推丞 7394
推判 7400
推官 7399

推直 7395
推直官 7395
推勘 7397
推勘官 7397
推勘院 7398
推勘檢法官 7396
採沙所 6841
採捕衙門 6840
採訪使 6826
採訪處置使 6825
採藥師 6844
接伴使 765
措置羅便司 7057
掖庭 3010
掖庭局 3012
掖庭祕獄 3014
掖庭詔獄 3011
掖庭綾匠 3013
插選 45
揀發 818
揆 3380
掾 8219
掾史 8238
掾吏 8231
掾佐 8247
掾屬 8243
提刑 6445
提刑司 6449
提刑按察司 6447
提刑按察使司
　6446
提刑茶鹽司 6448
提台 6467
提牢廳 6457
提控 6453
提控案牘 6453
提控漕河事 6456
提控諸烏魯古
　6455
提控鑄錢監 6454
提塘 6468
提督 6482
提督四夷館 6491
提督京通二倉御
　史 6483
提督軍務 6484
提督會同四譯館
　6489
提督會同館 6488
提督學政 6485
提督學院 6487
提督學道 6486
提督館務 6490

提督膳黃右通政
　6492
提領 6459
提領司 6461
提領所 6461
提領度牒所 6463
提領措置戶部財
　用 6462
提領鑄錢司 6460
提標 6464
提學 6450
提學御史 6452
提學道 6451
提舉 6395
提舉弓箭手司
　6423
提舉六尙局及管
　幹官 6426
提舉市舶司 6433
提舉在京諸司庫
　務司 6435
提舉兵馬 6431
提舉兵馬巡檢都
　監 6432
提舉坑冶司 6419
提舉坑冶市舶
　6418
提舉汴堤岸司
　6428
提舉制置解鹽司
　6406
提舉宗子學事
　6437
提舉河渠司 6411
提舉保甲司 6429
提舉皇城司 6417
提舉郡縣主等宅
　官 6410
提舉香茶礬事司
　6412
提舉修內司 6414
提舉修河司 6413
提舉倉場司 6436
提舉…宮 6424
提舉茶馬司 6396
提舉茶鹽公事
　6398
提舉茶鹽司 6399
提舉茶鹽常平等
　公事 6397
提舉國史 6425
提舉帳司 6400
提舉常平司 6402

提舉常平倉司
　6403
提舉常平茶鹽公
　事 6401
提舉都城所 6438
提舉提點鑄錢等
　公事 6434
提舉解鹽保甲
　6405
提舉買馬 6427
提舉進奏院 6407
提舉權貨司 6409
提舉管勾學事
　6422
提舉管幹官 6421
提舉閣事 6420
提舉編修國朝會
　要 6430
提舉學事司 6416
提舉學校所 6415
提舉諸司庫務司
　6408
提舉講義司 6404
提舉…觀 6424
提調 6470
提調官 6470
提調學校官 6469
提檢案牘 6374
提轄 6442
提轄司 6444
提轄兵甲盜賊公
　事 6443
提轄官 6442
提轄修倉所 6441
提轄進奏院 6440
提轄檢察官 6439
提點 6475
提點山陵 6478
提點五房 6481
提點司 6479
提點刑獄公事
　6473
提點在京倉場所
　6480
提點官 6475
提點所 6479
提點…宮 6476
提點馬監 6477
提點朝廷法物庫
　所 6471
提點開封界公
　事 6474
提點鑄錢事 6472

提點…觀 6476
搜檢懷挾官 5530
搨書手 6125
搢紳 1145
撰史學士 1488
撫軍 2052
撫軍將軍 2053
撫院 2121
撫臺 2103
撫憲 2061
撫諭司 2119
撫諭使 2118
撫諭軍馬 2117
撥發船運官 4724
撥發催綱 4725
撢人 6276
擎蓋司 1269
撻林 6124
擔榜壯元 6272
操江 6921
擬 2921
攝 5127
攝政 5131
攢典 7059

65 支

支使 1048
支供案 1019
支度使 1090
支差房 937
支計官 943
支馬房 1035
支應局 1096
絞儀 2645
絞職 2643

66 攵

攷工 3157
攷工室 3157
收支庫 5363
收支諸物庫 5362
收掌 5358
收發紅本處 5369
政 395
政事省 440
政事堂 441
政官 423
政府 410
政治上卿 404
政治卿 403
政選 413

敕令局 1112
敕令所 1112
敕庫 1109
敕頭 1114
教坊 728
教坊司 728
教助 726
教官 733
教師 737
教授 740
教習 729
教習大臣 730
教閱房 749
教諭 747
教職 725
救 1286
赦倉 32
散 4831
散令 4880
散吏 4878
散州 4848
散巡檢 4861
散巡檢使 4861
散位 4930
散兵 4892
散官 4868, 4869
散府 4853
散郎 4874
散秩大臣 4846
散從官 4925
散僚 4879
散端 4928
散樂 4935
散館 4869
散騎 4833
散騎侍郎 4837
散騎省 4836
散騎郎 4835
散騎常侍 4834
散廳 4923
敵史 263
敦宗院 7403
敬妃 1211
敬信 1218
敬訓 1221
敬婉 1247
敷文閣 2114
敵烈麻都 6377
整宜尉 419
整飭…邊備 405
整儀尉 419

67 文

文 7690
文史館 7721
文臣準備差遣 7695
文官 7714
文宗 7726
文散官 7719
文書房 7722
文昌相 7692
文昌都省 7694
文昌臺 7693
文林郎 7717
文林館 7716
文武二舞郎 7728
文宣公 7703
文思院 7724
文思署 7723
文案 7691
文部 7718
文淵閣 7729
文童 7727
文德待詔省 7725
文學 7704
文學友 7712
文學守助教 7709
文學直 7706
文學直官 7706
文學直館 7707
文學參軍 7710
文學從事 7711
文學祭酒 7705
文學掾 7713
文學館 7708
文翰館 7697
文選 7701
文選清吏司 7702
文館 7715
文繡院 7700
文繡署 7699

68 斗

斗食 6796
料估所 3693
料院 3696
斛斗案 2797
斜皮局 2481
斡魯朵 7731

69 斤

斧鉞司 2124
新字學士 2557
新衣庫 2554
新附軍 2553
新運糧提舉司 2559
新樂府 2558
斷丞 7358
斷刑司 7363
斷刑寺 7363
斷沒提領所 7370
斷事 7372
斷事司 7376
斷事官 7375
斷事經歷 7374
斷官 7365

70 方

方士 1912
方氏 1913
方正 1896
方丞 1897
方伯 1911
方相氏 1902
方面 1910
方略館 1909
方舞郎 1917
方鎮 1895
旅 3882
旅帥 3894
旅師 3892
旅賁 3889
旅賁氏 3890
庀人 3923
庀頭郎 3926
庀頭騎 3926
族 7048
族姬 7051
族師 7054
旌節司 1203
旌節官 1202
旗 611
旗手衛 638
旗牌官 630
旗籍司 614
旛幢司 1887

71 无

72 日

日官 3057
日者 3055
日時 3059
日曆所 3058
日講起居注館 3056
曳剌 3027
易 2922
易筮 2996
明安 4005
明廷 4023
明法 4009
明法掾 4010
明府 4014
明信 4016
明部尉 4018
明堂 4021
明淑 4020
明通榜 4025
明經 4007
明德宮監 4022
明範 4011
明資匠 4026
昇平署 5186
昭元寺 311
昭功萬戶 290
昭文學士 306
昭文館 307
昭玄寺 285
昭和署 283
昭宣使 284
昭苑 310
昭容 289
昭訓 286
昭媛 310
昭寶 300
昭華 287
昭儀 288
春司 1527
春坊 1524
春官 1525
春官大夫 1526
春卿 1523
春曹 1529
春臺 1528
星使 2593
星官 2578
星郎 2583

星置 2564
星曆生 2585
昂邦 30
時曹 5322
時憲科 5251
晉贈 1154
景山官學 1237
景福殿使 1215
普濟院 4820
普濟堂 4820
暉則 2892
暉範 2877
暴室 4797
暴室獄 4799
曆生 3635
曆助教 3601
曆博士 3628
曜儀 7897
曜德 7900

73 曰

曲 1690
曲臺 1698
更人 3164
更戍 3165
昆臺 3386
書手 5459
書令史 5446
書史 5457
書吏 5445
書奏 5465
書佐 5464
書直 5420
書直寫御書手 5423
書表 5454
書表司 5454
書待詔 5460
書院 5471
書庫 5441
書寫 5432
書寫機宜文字 5433
書辦 5452
書學 5434
書藝局 5436
曹 6916
曹長 6917
曹掾 6931
曹掾案 6932
最要 7061
會子務 2893

會子監 2893
會元 2896
會同四譯館 2890
會同館 2889
會要所 2895
會計司 3260
會問案 2894
會曹 3261
會通苑 2891
會場案 2874
會試 2888
會魁 2884
會辦 2886
會議 2883

74 月

月令師 8267
月計 8259
有出身 8047
有司 8081
有秩 8043
服不氏 2094
朕 370
望 7635
望郎 7650
望候郎 7644
望氣 7637
朝 312
朝士 337
朝大夫 339
朝代 340
朝列大夫 330
朝廷侯 341
朝奉大夫 322
朝奉郎 321
朝官 328
朝服法物庫 323
朝侯 324
朝散大夫 334
朝散郎 333
朝集使 314
朝端 342
朝請大夫 319
朝請郎 318
朝簿廳 332
朝議大夫 326
朝議郎 325
期門 629
期門郎 629

75 木

木工 4058
木天 4070
木局 4050
木倉 4072
木場 4043
木蘭 4059
札爾呼齊 33
札魯呼齊 34
札薩克 35
末班 4037
本 4560
本官 4563
本把 4564
本房 4561
未入流 7670
未央令 7687
朱衣使者 1390
村 7074
村長官 7075
材官 6831
材官令 6833
材官司馬 6835
材官挽强 6836
材官校令 6833
材官校尉 6834
材官將軍 6832
材料案 6837
枝兒 972
果子都監 3547
果丞 3506
果官 3524
果房 3511
果毅府 3522
林牙 3732
林啇 3732
林衡 3722
林衡署 3723
板 4399
板授 4415
東 7420
東上閤門 7450
東三省 7449
東司 7452
東西庫 7432
東行 7430
東夷使者 7534
東冶 7460
東門取索司 7447
東河 7431
東府 7429
東使 7451

東院 7461
東染院 7435
東宮 7440
東宮九牧監 7441
東宮三太 7446
東宮三少 7444
東宮三師 7445
東宮六傅 7442
東宮賓客 7443
東庫 7437
東部尉 7448
東都苑 7456
東推 7459
東曹 7458
東朝 7422
東園主章 7463
東園匠 7462
東廠 7421
東監 7423
東臺 7453
東臺舍人 7454
東銓 7428
東閣祭酒 7436
東選 7433
東頭 7455
東儲 7427
東織 7424
東觀 7439
查法臺 42
查倉御史 49
柴炭司 71
柴炭局 70
桂下史 1385
桂史 1422
桂石 1423
桂國 1400
桂國大將軍 1401
染人 3043
染院 3045
染署 3044
柔遠司 3062
架閣官 664
架閣庫 663
柏府 4726
柏臺 4758
柞氏 6993
校 2375
校人 2409
校正 724
校正官 724
校正漢文官 723
校令 2422
校長 2376

校官 2411
校官祭酒 2412
校事郎 739
校書 741
校書郎 742
校勘 732
校勘官 732
校尉 2456
校理 735
校對 744
校署 2434
校閱官 750
格格 3172
桂下史 3368
桂坊 3365
栗園司 3654
案 8
案首 28
案獄掾 29
栢府 4726
栢臺 4758
條 6497
條例司 6500
條狼氏 6499
黎園 3652
梅勒額眞 3931
梳頭夫人 5462
梳頭管理 5463
棘丞 534
棘寺 597
棘庭 603
棘卿 541
棘路 567
棘署 595
棚 4566
椒房 727
椒蘭班 734
楷書 3121
楷書手 3124
楷書郎 3122
楷書員 3125
楷書博士 3123
楊蘭局 7884
槐廳 2819
榜元 4449
榜式 4445
榜首 4446
榜眼 4448
榮祿大夫 3090
樞使 5458
樞府 5429
樞副 5428
樞相 5431

樞省 5455
樞輔 5430
樞密 5447
樞密承旨 5448
樞密使 5450
樞密直學士 5449
樞密院 5451
樞機房 5418
權易使 1720
權易院 1721
權易庫 1719
權易案 1718
權部 1724
權貨務 1716
權關御史 1722
權鹽使 1726
權鹽鐵使 1727
樓船官 3831
樓煩將 3832
樂令 8266
樂正 8258
樂府 8262
樂胥 8265
樂師 8270
樂部 8269
樂卿 8260
樂縣院 8264
標 4615
機速房 600
橫行使 2166
橋丁 752
橋道使 751
槖泉監長 6790
檢正 800
檢正官 800
檢法 819
檢法官 821
檢法案 820
檢院 879
檢討 868
檢討官 868
檢校 804
檢校所 806
檢校批驗官 805
檢校御史 807
檢詳所 826
檢詳房 826
檢察承受 788
檢察宮陵所 790
檢閱 883
檢閱官 883
檔房 6285
檻車督 799
權 1704

76 欠

次妃 7556
次府 7559
次金綬 7553
次相 7561
次傅 7558
次輔 7560
次對官 7572
欽天監 1185
欽奉上諭事件處 1179
欽察衛 1174
歌工 3173

77 止

正 396
正一 415
正一眞人 416
正一嗣教眞人 416
正令史 427
正印 453
正印官 454
正平監 433
正任 420
正吏 426
正名 428
正名帖房 430
正名貼房 430
正名楷書 429
正名贊者 431
正字 450
正考官 421
正言 451
正言博士 452
正侍 436
正侍郎 439
正奉上太醫 408
正奉大夫 409
正奏名 448
正官 424
正治卿 403
正郎 425
正相 412
正科 422
正卿 406
正員 455
正員司馬 456
正書 442

正副 411
正堂 444
正將 398
正術 443
正途 449
正華 414
正貼司 447
正義堂 418
正監平 399
正監造 401
正監造司庫 402
正德 445
正適 437
正諫大夫 400
正選 413
正議大夫 417
正齋 397
正體 446
步兵校尉 4794
步快 4789
步軍司 4778
武 7734
武功將軍 7800
武臣提刑 7735
武臣準備差使 7736
武侍率府 7821
武官 7784
武信佐騎尉 7771
武信騎尉 7770
武威衛 7838
武科 7778
武英殿 7840
武候府 7766
武備寺 7809
武備房 7808
武備院 7810
武庫 7779
武庫令 7781
武庫司 7780
武庫清吏司 7780
武庫署 7782
武部 7813
武略騎尉 7805
武都王 7832
武階 7745
武提刑 7829
武散官 7815
武義 7776
武德騎尉 7828
武衛 7834
武衛軍都指揮使司 7837

武衛將軍 7835
武衛親軍都指揮使司 7836
武器守宮 7743
武器監 7742
武器署 7744
武學 7774
武憲 7768
武舉 7754
武舉案 7755
武諭 7841
武選 7772
武選司 7773
武選清吏司 7773
武翼 7777
武藏 7830
武騎尉 7741
武顯將軍 7769
歲貢生 5869
歲貢 5869
歲計 5862
歲進士 5863
歷事 3638
歷政 3591
歸安侯 3361
歸附 3367
歸明 3373
歸義侯 3370

78 歹

79 殳

段疋庫 7371
殷 7970
殷紹嘉公 7989
殿 6516
殿下 6581
殿中 6556
殿中司 6563
殿中司馬督 6564
殿中侍御史 6562
殿中奉乘郎 6560
殿中局 6559
殿中省 6561
殿中將軍 6557
殿中御史 6566
殿中曹 6565
殿中監 6558
殿元 6682
殿內侍御史 6618
殿內局 6616

殿內省 6617
殿內監 6615
殿直 6548
殿前司 6543
殿前侍衛司 6542
殿前神威軍 6541
殿前軍 6534
殿前射生手 6540
殿前射生軍 6538
殿前射生廂 6539
殿前班 6537
殿前馬步軍 6536
殿前高品 6535
殿前都點檢司 6544
殿帥 6649
殿院 6683
殿修撰 6583
殿庭儀禮司 6654
殿試 6640
殿撰 6553
殿頭 6655
殿嚴 6672

80 母

母后 4053

81 比

比 4570
比公 4581
比部 4582
比部司 4582
比部曹 4583
比德眞 4600

82 毛

83 氏

民公 3995
民屯 4003
民戶 3993
民生 4001
民兵 3997
民兵房 3998
民兵衛案 3999
民匠總管府 3991
民壯 3992
民科 3994
民部 4000
民曹 4002

84 气

85 水

水司空長 5511
水正 5490
水次倉署 5513
水利道 5500
水軍 5492
水師 5509
水師營 5510
水部 5507
水部司 5508
水部曹 5508
水陸師持督 5503
水陸都巡檢使 5504
水陸發運使 5502
水陸運使 5505
水陸轉運使 5501
水曹 5512
水磨務 5506
水衡三官 5495
水衡令 5494
水衡典虞 5496
水衡都尉 5497
水衡監 5493
永利庫 8098
永巷 8097
汾祠署 1949
決曹 1725
治中 967
治中曹 968
治宜正 1003
治官 1014
治書 1060
治書侍御史 1065
治書御史 1067
治書曹 1066
治粟內史 1069
治粟都尉 1070
治獄司 1099
治曆 1023
治曆郎 1025
治曆郎中 1027
治儀正 1003
治禮吏 1028
治禮郎 1026
注擬案 1407

注擬掌關 1408
法司 1854
法司案 1856
法寺 1855
法曲所處院 1852
法直官 1849
法物案 1858
法物庫 1858
法酒庫 1851
法曹 1857
河台 2189
河防提舉司 2174
河西房 2176
河泊所 2182
河庫道 2179
河務道 2202
河隄使 2196
河隄謁者 2196
河渠署 2171
河督 2199
河道 2191
河道提舉司 2192
河道總督 2193
河臺 2189
河標 2181
河營參將 2203
河廳 2197
泠官師 3761
泮宮 4428
泉布 1713
泉府 1706
油官 8059
油醋庫 8092
洛苑使 3830
洛陳宮農圃監 3829
派辦處 4397
洗馬 2519
洞主 7426
津主 1122
津長 1117
海子 2131
海防道 2126
海道巡防千戶所 2128
海道巡防官 2129
海道糧運萬戶府 2130
浣衣局 2825
流內 3802
流內銓 3803
流外 3822
流外出身 3823

流外銓 3824
流官 3796
流馬苑 3801
混堂司 2900
淑人 5438
淑妃 5427
淑容 5439
淑媛 5472
淑儀 5435
添注官 6694
添設 6711
清 1254
清吏司 1273
清郎 1271
清軍 1264
清軍道 1265
清紀郎 1261
清要 1280
清城宮監 1259
清望 1279
清理軍務 1272
清商 1274
清商署 1274
清詔使 1256
清道 1276
清道率府 1277
清道衛 1278
清選 1268
渾天監 2901
渾儀台 2898
渾儀監 2897
渠長 1692
渤海契丹歸明 4728
湯木邑 6301
湯沐邑 6301
湯官 6298
湯監 6291
測驗渾儀刻漏所 6940
溫犀玳瑁局 7698
游戎 8057
游府 8050
游徼 8041
游擊 8036
游擊將軍 8037
游騎將軍 8038
游騎尉 8039
準備 1522
溝河司 3210
源士 8239
漢 2132
漢人司 2139

漢二班 2137
漢本房 2156
漢侍衛 2159
漢軍 2134
漢軍八旗 2135
漢軍堂 2136
漢票籤處 2157
漢頭班 2161
漢檔房 2160
漢蠻輿使 2155
漏刻典事 3836
漏刻所 3835
漏刻科 3833
漏刻博士 3834
漏郎 3837
漏郎將 3837
漏童 3838
滿 3912
滿二班 3914
滿本房 3918
滿洲八旗 3913
滿票籤處 3919
滿頭班 3921
滿檔房 3920
漕水曹 6928
漕正 6920
漕司 6929
漕史 6926
漕臣 6919
漕帥 6927
漕督 6930
漕運司 6934
漕運使 6933
漕運總兵官 6935
漕運總督 6936
漕標 6925
漕憲 6922
槳人 698
漆園監 645
演法 7932
濁 1330
澤虞 6937
灌謁者郎中 3335

86 火

火 2914
火甲 2916
火坡 2918
火器營 2915
火藥司 2919
炭場 6274

烏布 7814
烏府 7764
烏呼濟庫 7803
烏臺 7826
烏臺使君 7827
烏魯古 7804
烹人 4567
無出身 7753
無害吏 7765
無涓 7756
照磨 291
照磨所 297
照磨兼承發架閣庫 292
照磨兼管勾 294
照磨兼管勾承發架閣 295
照磨管勾 296
照磨檢校所 293
照廳 305
煖卿 4321
熟皮局 5453
熟紙匠 5421
熟紙裝潢匠 5422
熟藥所 5470
燒朱所 5093
燒鈔庫 5087
燈漏直長 6346
營 8009
營田使 8022
營作將 8026
營部 8016
營務處 8028
營造司 8024
營造案 8023
營造提舉司 8025
營盤 8015
營膳司 8018
營繕所 8020
營膳清吏司 8018
營繕監 8017
營繕署 8019
營總 8027

87 爪

爪士 301
爵 1715
爵廳 1728

88 父

父子軍 2112

父母官 2086
父師 2098

89 爻

爽鳩氏 5486

90 爿

91 片

版 4399
版戶 4405
版使 4411
版部 4409
版授 4415
版曹 4418
牌 4391
牌子頭 4398
牌頭 4398

92 牙

牙吏 7861
牙兵 7865
牙官 7859
牙門 7862
牙軍 7851
牙將 7845
牙職 7848

93 牛

牛人 4313
牛羊司 4317
牛羊供應所 4315
牛羊署 4316
牛錄 4314
牧 4041
牧人 4055
牧正 4045
牧伯 4064
牧長 4042
牧官都尉 4056
牧馬房 4062
牧馬監 4061
牧師 4066
牧師苑 4067
牧尉 4073
牧圉 4076
牧場 4044
牧羣 4051

牧監 4046
牧領 4060
牧養監 4074
牧槖 4071
物料庫 7802
特旨 6333
特羊局 6343
特派差使 6341
特哩袞司 6339
特進 6335
特進光祿大夫 6337
特進資政上卿 6338
特進榮祿大夫 6336
特置 6334
特滿 6340
牪羊局 7547
犀部 2264
犧牲所 2268

94 犬

犬人 1709
狀元 1515
狀頭 1512
狂夫 3358
狗坊 3206
狗房 3207
狗監 3205
狩 5357
猛安 3956
猥諸侯 7662
獄 8103
獄史 8170
獄丞 8107
獄卒 8200
獄卒史 8200
獄曹 8197
獄掾 8214
獨占籠頭 7184
獨坐 7305
獨承密命 7187
獸人 5379
獸醫 5377
獸醫博士 5378
獻納使 2523

95 玄

玄戈軍 2668
率 5476

率更 5482
率更令 3584
率更寺 3585
率府 5478
率府率 5479
率性堂 5481

96 玉

玉册院 8199
玉匠局 8110
玉局提舉司 8126
玉府 8130
玉宸院 8106
玉堂 8191
玉堂署 8192
玉牒所 8194
玉牒殿主管香火 8195
玉鈐衛 8122
玉署 8187
王 7634
王大臣 7654
王世子 7653
王友 7656
王主 7638
王包衣 7652
王后 7643
王妃妃 7651
王邸 7655
王府 7640
王府長史司 7641
特奏名 6342
王相府 7645
王宮大小學 7647
王國 7648
王國府 7648
王常侍府 7636
王傅 7639
王傅府 7642
王會司 7646
珍羞署 378
珍饈署 378
班 4400
班軍 4404
班殿直 4417
班領 4408
班劍司 4403
班簿房 4410
珥筆 1837
現食俸祿 2535
現審司 2532
現審處 2531

理欠司 3598
理刑司 3608
理…事 3639
理事十大臣 3641
理事官 3640
理…事務 3639
理官 3618
理匭使 3620
理問 3648
理檢院 3597
理藩 3602
理藩院 3603
琉璃局 3799
琉璃窰 3800
瑞錦窨 3085
瑪瑙局 3905
瑣闥 5527
瑣闥 5526
環人 2826
環衛 2830
環衛官 2831
璫 6281
瓘玉局 3336

97 瓜

98 瓦

甄別 387
甄官署 379

99 甘

甘丞 3128
甘泉上林丞 3130
甘泉居室 3129
甘泉倉 3131
甘泉都水長 3132
甘泉衛尉 3133

100 生

生 5175
生員 5193
生藥庫 5190

101 用

102 田

田曹 6718

田僕 6710
甲 650
甲仗庫 652
甲坊署 657
甲卒 685
甲弩坊署 672
甲長 651
甲首 680
甲庫 665
甲喇 667
甲榜 673
甲頭 683
甲鎧署 662
男 4082
甸祝 6552
甸師 6641
留司御史臺 3815
留守司 3813
留官 3797
留後 3790
留後使 3790
留院官 3827
留臺 3816
留館 3797
異途 3022
異樣局 3033
異樣紋綉局 3034
番 1862
番下 1869
番上 1881
番夷都指揮使 1873
番役處 1872
番官 1874
番滿 1876
番頭 1886
畫士 2814
畫工 2809
畫局 2805
畫直 2803
畫室署 2815
畫省 2813
畫院 2816
畫學 2808
當今佛爺 6283
當月處 6287
當軸 6284
當路 6286
當路子 6286
畿 519
畿內 573
畿法 549
畿輔 550

103 疋

疏濬黃河司 5426

104 疒

疲 4606
疾醫 557
瘍 7879
癡林 1107

105 癶

登仕佐郎 6348
登仕郎 6347
登第 6349
登聞令 6354
登聞院 6355
登聞鼓 6351
登聞鼓院 6353
登聞鼓廳 6352
登聞檢院 6350
登賢書 6345
登瀛洲 6356
發放司 1853
發敕官 1850
發解 1848
發運司 1861
發運使 1860
發運案 1859

106 白

白士 4745
白衣卿相 4736
白衣領職 4737
白身 4745
白直 4722
白袍子 4744
白雲 4760
百工監 4742
百夫長 4727
百戶 4733
百戶所 4735
百戶長 4734
百司庶府 4756
百司問事謟者 4757
百石 4747
百里 4743
百官 4739
百官案 4740
百長 4719

百揆 4741
百戲師 4729
百騎 4720
皇上 2852
皇女 2849
皇子 2872
皇元孫 2873
皇太子 2863
皇太夫人 2859
皇太后 2860
皇太后臨朝 2861
皇太妃 2858
皇太孫 2862
皇木廠 2848
皇包衣 2850
皇后 2836
皇伯 2851
皇叔 2853
皇城司 2833
皇長孫 2832
皇帝 2866
皇帝梨園弟子 2867
皇祖 2871
皇孫 2854
皇孫府 2855
皇貴妃 2840
皇嫡孫 2868
皇儲 2834

107 皮

皮作局 4613
皮角場 4608
皮剝所 4612
皮庫 4610

108 皿

益政院 2941
盟 3955
監 786
監太倉使 866
監支納官 809
監令 842
監印 876
監司 864
監平 850
監正 801
監生 856
監丞 802
監守信藏官 861
監收 860

監州 811
監作 872
監事 857
監官 835
監官提領 838
監府 822
監押 875
監牧 848
監牧使 848
監物務 874
監長 796
監門 843
監門官 845
監門府 844
監門率府 846
監門衛 847
監候 824
監候府 825
監修 829
監修國史 829
監津渠曹 810
監軍 815
監郡 816
監郡御史 817
監院 880
監香使 827
監國 840
監書博士 862
監祭使 803
監埽官 851
監御史 878
監搜御史 863
監造 870
監殿舍人 869
監當 867
監當官 867
監督 873
監福曹 823
監置 808
監試 858
監運 884
監察史 793
監察使 792
監察官 789
監察御史 795
監察都御史 794
監察裏行使 791
監漕 871
監獄 877
監課御史 834
監學博士 830
監膳 852
監膳史 853

監臨 841
監鑄 812

109 目

直 933
直史 1049
直事曹 1057
直侍儀使 1054
直官 1016
直長 938
直指 951
直省 1044
直省舍人 1046
直省學士 1045
直院 1100
直院學士 1101
直集賢院 942
直殿監 1075
直學 995
直學士 996
直學士院 997
直舘 1016
直隸 1024
直館 1016
直講 944
直龍圖閣 1034
直廬 1032
看班 3142
省 5176
省元 5194
省事 5187
省眼 5191
省掾 5195
省減司 5180
省試 5188
省魁 5184
相 2303
相公 2331
相王 2365
相室 2349
相副官 2313
相國 2337
眂祲 5227
眂瞭 5285
眞 371
睦親宅 4048
睦親廣親宅 4049
睡卿 5491
督 7180
督太守 7292
督册道 7304
督辦 7261

督冶掾 7330
督軍 7221
督軍御史 7224
督軍糧御史 7222
督捕清吏司 7267
督烽曹 7226
督理錢法侍郎 7251
督視軍馬 7275
督郵 7332
督運御史 7340
督運漕御史 7339
督領侍 7255
督撫 7227
督撫司道 7229
督標 7263
督學使者 7232
督學道 7233
督糧道 7254
督護 7237
督鑄錢掾 7209
瞽 3223
瞽矇 3236

110 矛

111 矢

知 934
知印 1095
知吏部選事 1029
知州 965
知州軍事 966
知事 1050
知侍儀事 1054
知制誥 955
知宗 1087
知宗子表疏官 1089
知府 983
知法 974
知客押衙 1012
知峒 1094
知政事 940
知洞 1094
知省事 1047
知軍 971
知軍使 971
知院官 1102
知書 1061
知書官 1062
知班 1039

知貢舉 1020
知甌事 1018
知甌使 1018
知進士助教 963
知頓使 1093
知監 946
知監事 946
知臺事 1073
知臺襍 1074
知圖譜官 1092
知廟少卿 1036
知樞密院事 1064
知縣 993
知選事 994
知錄 1033
知禮部貢舉 1030
知雜 1077
知雜房 1079
知雜案 1078
知雜御史 1080
知藩府 976
知觀 1013
短番匠 7360
短番散樂 7361

112 石

石炭場 5316
石庫 5268
石烈 5286
石窟丞 5269
砦 58
砦主 62
碁博士 634
磁局 7554
磁庫 7562
磬師 1275
磨勘 4030
磨勘司 4035
磨勘京朝官院 4033
磨勘案 4031
磨勘差遣院 4032
磨勘諸路提點刑獄司 4034
礉驍騎 4509

113 示

社 5128
社稷署 5132
社稷壇 5133
祀丞 5552

祀官齋郎 5680
祈父 625
祗候 984
祗候內廷 989
祗候內品 988
祗候侍禁 990
祗候高品 986
祗候庫 987
祗候黃門 985
祗候殿直 991
祗應司 1097
祝 1355
祝史 1424
祝版案 1410
祝禁… 1376
祝鳩氏 1378
祕書 4586
祕書中散 4589
祕書內省 4595
祕書少令 4597
祕書少監 4596
祕書丞 4587
祕書令 4593
祕書令史 4594
祕書寺 4599
祕書省 4598
祕書郎 4592
祕書監 4588
祕書閣 4590
祕書閣局 4591
祕校 4575
祕獄 4603
祕閣令 4580
祕閣局 4579
神士 5161
神房 5151
神武天軍 5171
神武天騎 5170
神武軍 5169
神勁軍 5149
神宮監 5156
神威軍 5167
神部 5160
神策行營 5165
神策軍 5163
神策廂 5164
神都苑 5166
神廟夫人 5159
神廚院 5150
神樂所 5173
神樂署 5173
神樂觀 5172
神衛四廂 5168

神機營 5145
祖公 7052
祠祀 7570
祠部 7566
祠祭局 7550
祠祭案 7550
祠祭清吏司 7551
祠祭署 7552
祠祿 7564
祠署 7569
祠廟署 7565
祠墳所 7557
票客 4622
票簽處 4621
祥刑寺 2320
祥和署 2315
祭祀供應官 599
祭酒 542
祭僕 578
祭器司 535
禁中 1123
禁內侍衛 1135
禁防御史 1125
禁兵 1139
禁林 1130
禁省 1146
禁軍 1124
禁圃 1141
禁殺戮 1144
禁族八旗 1157
禁備史 1138
禁暴氏 1137
禁衛 1160
禁衛所 1161
禁臠 1131
祿臣 3841
福晉 2044
禦衛 8202
禮生 3636
禮制局 3599
禮官 3619
禮房 3605
禮直 3600
禮直官 3600
禮長 3588
禮科 3617
禮院 3653
禮部 3631
禮曹 3645
禮賓院 3627
禮儀使 3614
禮儀直 3613
禮儀院 3615

禮儀案 3611
禮儀監 3612
禮樂長 3656
禮樂案 3655

114 内

115 禾

禾絹 2172
秀才 2633
私名 5723
私名贊者 5724
私府 5624
科 3187
科甲 3190
科甲出身 3191
科長 3188
科參 3203
科道 3201
科舉 3193
秋坊 1322
秋典 1326
秋官 1324
秋官大夫 1325
秋曹 1327
秋卿 1321
秋憲 1323
秩宗 1088
秘書 4586
秘閣 4578
租庸使 7056
稍人 5105
稍法 5095
稅務司 5514
稅庫司 5499
稅課司 5498
稅課局 5498
稗官 4390
稱職 464
穀倉督 3246
槀人 3143
稽查中書科事務
　大臣 527
稽查壇廟大臣
　531
稽查錢局 525
稽察 524
稽察內館監督
　530
稽察外館監督
　532

稽察房 528
稽察欽奉上諭事
　件處 526
稽疑司 559
稽勳司 556
稽勳清吏司 556
稼部 675
稻人 6314
稻田場 6323
稻田提領所 6324
穆昆 4057
蘗官 6318
蘗官署 6318
稽臣 4939

116 穴

穴氏 2706
空房 3501
窨廠 720
窰務 7903
窰場 7890

117 立

立伕馬 3590
站 74
站赤 76
站齊 76
章京 107
章佩監 169
章奏房 202
童生 7501
端 7357
端公 7367
端尹府 7378
端司 7377
端右 7379
端石 7373
端丞 7359
端妃 7362
端揆 7366
端僚 7369

118 竹

竹木務 1406
符節令 2042
符璽郎 2058
符寶郎 2091
笙師 5189
第一人 6369
第下 6366

第策官 6389
筆且齊 4576
筆匠 4574
筆帖式 4601
筆帖式署 4602
筆政 4573
答剌火赤 5982
答應 6113
等 6344
筮人 5267
筮仕 5303
笲氏 1520
管千丁 3278
管勾 3312
管勾司 3313
管勾…事 3312
管勾往來國信所
　3314
管主 3280
管民總管府 3320
管匠 3276
管匠都提領所
　3277
管…事 3325
管事務大臣 3327
管河 3295
管帶 3331
管泉主事 3283
管軍 3286
管記舍人 3274
管理 3315
管領 3318
管領…官 3318
管幹 3306
管幹郊廟祭器所
　3307
管轄官 3297
管轄番役 3296
管糧 3316
管織染局大臣
　3279
管醫人頭目 3302
管礮驍騎校 3322
算博士 5858
算曆科 5857
算學 5856
篆書博士 1489
籥庫 3060
節下 762
節府使 760
節服氏 761
節度 772
節度判官 776

節度使 777
節度推官 778
節度掌書記 773
節度幕 775
節度端 775
節度觀察留後
　774
節政鎮 757
節推 779
節慎庫 766
節察 755
節鎮 756
簡缺 814
廉官 3710
廉箔場 3713
簿 4762
簿曹 4805
簽 885
簽判 911
簽事 917
簽院 931
簽書 918
簽書判官廳公事
　922
簽書省事 923
簽書院事 925
簽書樞密院事
　924
簽書節度判官廳
　公事 921
簽樞 919
簽廳 926
簽廳官 926
籍勾管 562
籍田 602
籍直長 540
簪褭 6856
籭師 8271
籭章 8257
籩人 4639

119 米

米稟督 3978
粉侯 1939
粉署 1944
粧釘局 1511
粟客 5852
粤海關部 8263
精奇尼哈番 1201
精膳司 1238
精膳清吏司 1236
糧台 3682

糧長 3658
糧務道 3688
糧料院 3670
糧料案 3669
糧草科 3685
糧臺 3682
糧道 3683
糧儲道 3663
糧便司 6381
糧糴案 6501

120 糸

糾察司 1288
糾察刑獄司 1288
糾察在京刑獄司
　1289
糾察案 1287
紅帶子 2907
紀善 580
級 520
納言 4079
納言令 4080
納貢 4077
紗金顏料總庫
　4950
紗羅局 4951
紋綺局 7696
紳士 5162
紳衿 5148
紹聖侯 5112
細作署 2277
紫垣 7549
紫案御史 7520
紫微省 7545
紫閣 7534
紫薇郎 7544
紫薇閣 7543
給 521
給事 583
給事中 587
給事中給事 588
給事北院知聖旨
　頭子事 591
給事舍人 592
給事郎 590
給事黃門 589
給事謁者 594
給舍 581
給納案 572
給諫 539
絲綸閣 5711
統 7465

統制 7472
統軍 7482
統軍使 7483
統軍府 7482
統署 7512
統領 7494
統轄兩翼牧場總
　管 7486
經正監 1194
經邦 1235
經制司 1208
經制買馬司 1206
經制…幹辦常平
　公事 1205
經制發運使 1204
經制邊防財用司
　1207
經度制置使 1244
經承 1195
經郎 1226
經師 1240
經途尉 1245
經略 1231
經略大臣 1234
經略安撫使 1232
經略安撫都總管
　1233
經略使 1231
經筵 1249
經筵官 1250
經魁 1225
經學助教 1219
經學博士 1220
經撫房 1214
經歷 1227
經歷司 1228
經歷廳 1229
經籍案 1198
經廳 1242
綠營 3862
綺源庫 646
緊 1116
綾錦坊 3745
綾錦院 3745
綾綿織染局 3744
綾綿織染提舉司
　3744
綸閣 3872
維那 7672
編定書籍官 4645
編估局 4640
編修 4635

編修中書條例所
　4634
編修文字 4637
編修官 4635
編修勅令所 4633
編修院 4638
編修時政記房
　4636
編校 4632
編校官 4632
編錄官 4643
編類御筆所 4642
編類聖政所 4641
緞庫 7364
縣 2492
縣士 2533
縣大夫 2539
縣子 2546
縣公 2512
縣公主 2513
縣太君 2541
縣尹 2551
縣文閣 2550
縣王 2548
縣主 2500
縣佐 2544
縣男 2524
縣令 2518
縣伯 2526
縣君 2502
縣官 2510
縣法 2503
縣侯 2506
縣宰 2542
縣師 2534
縣馬 2520
縣尉 2549
縣尊 2545
縣簿 2527
縉紳 1145
縉雲 1172
縉雲司 1172
繁 1863
縫人 1995
總甲 7090
總目 7141
總戎 7107
總兵 7146
總兵官 7146
總把 7143
總明觀 7140
總河 7100
總治河防使 7096

總典轝牧使司
　7155
總制 7092
總制院 7097
總官 7110
總府 7099
總承 7087
總知 7093
總知軍國事 7095
總科 7108
總裁 7156
總計使 7088
總部 7148
總理 7121
總理工程處 7128
總理各國事務衙
　門 7127
總理事務冠軍使
　7129
總理河道 7124
總理河漕 7125
總理青海事務大
　臣 7123
總理衙門 7130
總理樂部大臣
　7132
總理鹽政 7131
總章 7078
總知朝廷禮儀
　7094
總統 7163
總爺 7167
總督 7158
總督河道 7159
總督倉場 7161
總督漕運 7162
總督糧儲 7160
總旗 7089
總監 7091
總管 7110
總管大臣 7117
總管內務府大臣
　7115
總管六庫事務
　7114
總管太監 7118
總管司 7116
總管官學事務
　7113
總管府 7112
總管鈐轄司 7111
總署 7154
總領 7134

總領內外廄馬局
　7136
總領房 7135
總領…財賦 7137
總辦 7144
總辦郎中 7145
總錄 7138
總閫 7119
總禮儀事 7126
總鎮 7079
總纂 7157
織 935
織室 1051
織染局 1004
織染所雜造局
　1006
織染署 1005
織造 1081
織造局 1083
織造監督 1082
織錦 961
繙譯 1870
繞殿雷 3046
繢人 4956
繢寫 4955
繢工監 4958
繡衣使 2621
繡衣直指 2621
繡衣御史 2622
繩愆廳 5181
纂修 7058
纂修官 7058

121 缶

122 网

置將 945
置將法 945
置頓使 1093
罪隸 7060
署 5410
署正 5416
署長 5413
羅氏 3828
羈縻州 571
羈縻府州 571

123 羊

羊人 7880
羊車小史 7876

美人 3930
義兵 2988
義和 2955
義倉 3016
羣太保 1811
羣牧司 1808
羣牧使 1806
羣牧所 1807
羣長 1804
群牧制置使 1805
義和 2238

124 羽

羽人 8144
羽林孤兒 8152
羽林軍 8151
羽林郎 8153
羽林騎 8150
羽騎尉 8108
翁主 7730
習馬小底 2260
習馭 2282
習學公事 2242
習學官 2241
習藝館 2244
翊一府 2960
翊二府 2952
翊府 2954
翊軍校尉 2951
翊善 2991
翊衛 3029
翦氏 859
是氏 5304
翰林 2141
翰林司 2149
翰林供奉 2146
翰林侍書 2148
翰林待制 2151
翰林待詔 2150
翰林院 2154
翰林國史院 2147
翰林御書院 2153
翰林圖書院 2152
翰林學士 2142
翰林學士承旨
　2143
翰林學士院 2144
翰林醫官院 2145
翰長 2133
翰苑 2162
翼 2923
翼長 2928

翼領 2979
翼馭 3039
翻譯經潤文使
　1871

125 老

老公 3580
老家 3577
老秀才 3579
老爺 3581
老鳳 3578
考 3148
考功司 3159
考功所 3158
考功清吏司 3156
考功監 3155
考官 3154
考試 3161
考察 3149
考滿 3160
考課司 3152
考課京朝官院
　3151
考課院 3153
考選科 3150

126 而

127 耒

耤 4356

128 耳

耳目官 1836
聘君 4708
聖主 5182
聖廟 5185
聖裔 5183
聖濟院 5179
聖濟殿 5178
聚 1675
職 936
職內 1037
職方 978
職方氏 980
職方司 981
職方清吏司 979
職田 1076
職事官 1055
職事教諭 1053

職官 1015
職金 962
職喪 1042
職歲 1071
職幣 1040
職錢 947
聽候差使 6753

129 聿

肆長 5538
肆師 5766
肅政臺 5850
肅政廉訪司 5849
肅衛 5855
肅機 5851

130 肉

肺石 1933
胄案 1333
胄曹 1345
胞人 4511
胥 2641
胥史 2650
胥吏 2648
胥佐 2652
胥長 2642
胥師 2651
胥魁 2647
脩功德使 2625
脩閭氏 2628
脫脫禾孫 6795
腊人 2247
腹裏 2078
腹裏印曆管勾 2079
膳工 4957
膳夫 4954
膳司 4963
膳宰 4967
膳部 4959
臚人 3850
臚傳 3845

131 臣

臣 392
臨時政府 3729
臨朝 3718
臨漢監 3721

132 自

自陳 7521
臬司 4306
臬府 4306
臬臺 4306

133 至

至尊 1086
至靈 1031
致仕 1052
致遠務 1103
臺 6135
臺主 6153
臺丞 6146
臺長 6136
臺省 6211
臺郎 6187
臺院 6263
臺端 6238
臺諫 6149
臺醫 6172
臺雜 6223

134 臼

春人 1664
興文署 2604
興和署 2572
舉人 1682
舉子 1689
舉紋案 1680
舉監 1677
舊宅監 1290
舊故宅監 1305

135 舌

舌人 5135
舍 5129
舍人 5136
舍人省 5137
舍人院 5138
舖 4816
舖司 4825

136 舛

舞生 7818
舞郎 7801
舞師 7820
舞徒 7833

137 舟

舟楫河渠署 1335
舟楫署 1336
般押推司 4421

138 艮

艮人 3667
艮使 3678
艮牧署 3671
艮娣 3684
艮媛 3691
艮醞署 3692
艮醫所 3666

139 色

色目人 4941
色長 4938

140 艸

芳華 1903
芳華苑 1904
芳猷 1919
芳儀 1905
花木局 2812
芸臺 8289
若廬獄 3061
茂才 3927
茂光 3924
茂材異等 3928
苗民官 3986
苜蓿苑 4068
英武軍 8029
苑 8220
苑使 8240
苑容 8228
苑馬寺 8334
苑圃 8254
苑游軍 8252
苑儀 8227
苑總監 8248
茶引所 55
茶引批驗所 55
茶庫 46
茶案 40
茶馬司 48
茶園都提舉司 57
茶鹽制置使 51
茶鹽提舉司 54

茶鹽轉運使 52
草人 6923
草料場 6924
草場 6918
莊妃 1505
莊宅使 1503
莊老博士 1507
莊頭處 1513
莫府 4029
荻庫 6370
華妃 2807
華坊 2806
華秋苑 2804
萍氏 4710
菹醢匠 7050
著 1356
著作 1440
著作局 1441
著作郎 1442
著作省 1443
著作曹 1443
萬夫 7620
萬戶府 7621
萬戶所 7622
萬年宮 7632
萬林內教坊 7631
萬乘 7617
萬歲爺 7633
萬廐 7619
萬億廣源庫 7627
萬億賦源庫 7626
萬億綺源庫 7625
萬億寶源庫 7628
萬騎 7618
葦園匠 7689
蒙古 3957
蒙古八旗 3967
蒙古本房 3968
蒙古房 3962
蒙古承政 3959
蒙古軍 3960
蒙古書寫 3970
蒙古國子監 3965
蒙古國子學 3966
蒙古章京 3958
蒙古衙門 3972
蒙古提舉學校官 3971
蒙古筆且齊 3969
蒙古翰林院 3963
蒙古繙譯房 3961
蒙古醫生頭目 3964

蒙養 3973
蓮幕 3712
藍 7971
藍子 8004
藍補 7988
藍監 7975
蕃兵 1878
蕃官案 1875
蕃育署 1890
蕃部 1880
蕃書譯語 1883
雍氏 6465
薩滿太太 4827
薩寶 4828
薦紳 855
薦舉 813
藍翎侍衛 3558
藍翎總承 3559
藍靛廠 3562
藏 6896
藏府 6898
藩 1864
藩王 1888
藩司 1884
藩伯 1879
藩岳 1891
藩府 1868
藩房 1866
藩垣 1891
藩臬兩司 1877
藩臺 1885
藩鎮 1865
藝文監 3031
藪 5529
藥丞 7891
藥局 7893
藥物院 7904
藥密庫 7899
藥童 7902
藥園 7905
藥藏局 7901
蘇拉 5853
蘭臺 3560
蘭臺寺 3561

141 虍

虎士 2794
虎賁 2787
虎賁郎 2788
虎槍營 2772
處 1456
處置使 1461

虞 8104
虞官 8148
虞候 8134
虞候率府 8135
虞部 8163
虞曹 8198
虞衡 8132
虞衡司 8133
虞衡清吏司 8133

142 虫

蜡氏 36
螭頭 115
蜩氏 3531
蠶室 6890
蠻子 3922
蠻夷官 3916
蠻夷長官司 3915
蠻隸 3917

143 血

144 行

行 2561
行人 2574
行人司 2575
行中書省 2565
行內 2588
行夫 2571
行司馬 2597
行在 2601
行走 2603
行…事 2561
行尚書省 2591
行省 2592
行軍 2567
行軍司馬 2567
行軍長史 2566
行軍參謀 2568
行院 2609
行首 2163
行宮 2580
行宮使 2582
行御史臺 2608
行書佐 2596
行臺 2598
行臺尚書省 2599
行臺省 2600
行樞密院 2595
行簾司藥局 2563

行營 2605
行營四護軍 2606
衍聖公 7951
街卒 771
街道司 769
街道廳 769
衙司 7868
衙吏 7861
衙兵 7865
衙官 7860
衙門 7862
衙前 7846
衙前射生兵 7847
衙推 7872
衝 1644
衝繁疲難 1650
衛 7658
衛士 7674
衛仙 7667
衛坊率 7663
衛官軍衛 7671
衛府 7664
衛候直都指揮使
　司 7665
衛尉 7681
衛尉寺 7683
衛尉院 7684
衛尉卿 7682
衛將軍 7661
衛率府 7676
衡 2165
衡官 2167
衡宰 2168

145 衣

衣冠署 2967
衣庫 2963 、
衣糧案 2978
表奏官 4617
表奏議司 4616
裁造院 6843
裁造署 6843
裁種提舉司 6813
裝制敕匠 1504
裝書直 1508
裝書曆生 1509
裝裁匠 1514
裝潢匠 1506
裙帶官 1810
裙帶親 1809
裏行 3607
裏行使 3607

補 4763
補正名 4769
補袞 4790
補授 4800
補廩 4791
補闕 4777
裕民司 8159
裕民局 8159
製造庫 1084
製造御前軍器局
　1085
裨將 4607
複道丞 2104
襄成君關內侯
　4461
襄成侯 4462
襄成宣尼公 4463
襄亭侯 4500
襄聖侯 4493
襄德侯 4498

146 西

西 2230
西上閤門 2267
西內染院 2262
西司 2271
西外宗正司 2279
西戎使者 2249
西行 2237
西冶 2281
西邸 2274
西使 2270
西官 2252
西府 2236
西南都巡檢（使）
　2261
西垣 2286
西染院 2246
西院 2287
西宮 2254
西庫 2251
西部 2265
西部尉 2266
西域都護 2284
西域醫藥司 2283
西掖 2243
西推 2278
西曹 2276
西園 2285
西廠 2231
西監 2233
西綾錦（司）2257

西臺 2272
西臺中散 2273
西銓 2235
西閣祭酒 2250
西選 2240
西頭 2275
西織 2234
西驛管勾官 2245
要缺 7894
要籍 7892
覆試 2099
覆實司 2102

147 見

規運司 3379
覓舉 3975
視 5203
視流內 5289
親王 1186
親衣庫 1182
親事府 1184
親府 1180
親軍 1175
親軍府 1176
親軍衛 1177
親軍營 1178
親試 1183
親衛 1187
親衛府 1187
親賢宅 1181
覺義 1717
覺羅公 1723
觀政 3272
觀察 3265
觀察支使 3266
觀察使 3269
觀察留後 3268
觀察推官 3270
觀察處置使 3267

148 角

角人 731
解元 781
解戶 763
解事 767
解試 768
解頭 770

149 言

言事官 7952

言事御史 7954
言官 7945
言路 7949
計 522
計史 585
計司 598
計吏 566
計使 584
計官 563
計省 582
計相 551
計部 577
計偕 538
計掾 610
計議官 558
訓士 2751
訓方氏 2728
訓科 2742
訓術 2759
訓練鈐轄 2747
訓課 2743
訓導 2761
記注官 545
記注院 546
記注案 544
記郎 565
記室 586
記室參軍 593
記室參軍事 593
訪舉 1901
設官 5139
設案 5130
訝士 7867
詔獄 309
詛祝 7049
評 4698
評事 4712
評事史 4713
評斷官 4715
詞林 7563
詹事 79
詹事府 80
詹事院 81
試 5204
試用 5345
試官 5273
詳正學士 2305
詳刑寺 2320
詳刑案 2319
詳定 2355
詳定所 2360
詳定官 2358
詳定官制所 2359

詳定勅令所 2357
詳定帳籍所 2356
詳袞 2328
詳斷司 2363
詳斷官 2362
詳斷案 2361
詳覆官 2314
詳覆案 2312
詳穩 2367
詳議 2324
詳議司 2325
詳議官 2324
詳讞案 2370
詮寫 1707
誠心堂 486
說書 5521
說書所 5522
說書宮 5522
誦訓 5875
課功郎中 3195
課利司 3197
課利科 3196
課第曹 3202
課績院 3189
調人 6498
調簾 6495
請雨 1281
請給案 1260
諸 1357
諸子 1445
諸司 1431
諸司使 1435
諸司事 1434
諸司官 1432
諸司參軍 1436
諸生 1419
諸吏 1403
諸色人匠總管府
　1415
諸冶署令 1451
諸典事 1437
諸侯 1383
諸侯王 1384
諸津監 1377
諸科 1393
諸站都統領使
　1359
諸掌事 1361
諸路 1405
諸音郎 2489
諫 787
諫大夫 865
諫垣 881

諫官 836
諫官御史廳 839
諫官案 837
諫長 797
諫院 882
諫議大夫 831
謀克 4039
諮議 7531
諮議官 7530
諮議軍事 7529
謁者 7908
謁者臺 7909
諗德 8193
講官 699
講郎 700
講書 705
講書教授 706
講書說書 707
講經博士 692
講義司 697
講讀 715
講讀官 716
謄黃右通政 6357
謄錄官 6358
謄錄院 6359
謫發 348
譏察官 529
議司 3004
議生 2994
議事平章 3001
議政五大臣 2940
議政王 2939
議政處 2937
議郎 2972
議曹 3018
議禮局 2976
警巡院 1223
譯 2924
譯文官 3032
譯令史 2981
譯史 2999
譯生 2995
譯字生 3025
譯官令 2966
譯長 2929
譯語通事 3041
讚議參軍事 7531
護軍 2775
護軍中尉 2777
護軍府 2778
護軍將軍 2776
護軍都尉 2779
護軍營 2780

護都水使 2800
護漕都尉 2799
護衛 2802
讀卷官 7220
讀祝官 7211
讎校 1349
讎校錯誤 1350

150 谷

151 豆

豉匠 5216
豎 5411
豐儲倉 1973
豔儀 7939

152 豕

象胥 2321

153 豸

豹騎 4464
豹韜衛 4497
貂 6493
貉隸 4036
貓食 3925

154 貝

貝子 4546
貝勒 4526
貞範 373
負弩 2088
貢士 3474
貢生 3467
貢奉使 3424
貢院 3497
貢部 3463
貢監 3402
貢學案 3415
財賦司 6827
財賦都總管府 6828
貨泉局 2917
貧倅 4663
貴 3360
貴人 3371
貴主 3364
貴介公子 3363
貴妃 3366

貴階 3362
貴遊子弟 3377
貴儀 3369
貴嬪 3374
貳 1826
貳尹 1847
貳令 1835
貳守 1844
貳府 1834
貳卿 1830
貼司 6513
貼刑官 6507
貼祗候內品 6504
貼書 6511
貼寫中書 6506
貼職 6503
賈 3224
賈師 3244
賊捕掾 6941
賊曹 6942
資用庫 7548
資任案 7532
資考司 7533
資武庫 7546
資治少尹 7527
資治尹 7528
資政大夫 7524
資政中大夫 7523
資政亞卿 7526
資政卿 7522
資政殿 7525
資善 7535
資善大夫 7537
資善庫 7536
資善堂 7538
資德 7540
資德大夫 7541
資德院 7542
賓 4650
賓友 4659
賓客 4653
賓客司 4654
賓部 4657
賓僚 4655
賓僕 4658
賓幕 4656
賓輔 4652
質人 1007
賦曹 2105
賦源庫 2123
賢妃 2504
賢良 2515
賢良文學 2517

賢良方正 2516
賢書 2536
賢察 2495
賢儀 2507
賞給案 4978
賞賜案 5074
贊公 6852
贊引 6863
贊引使 6863
贊府 6850
贊治 6847
贊治少尹 6848
贊治尹 6849
贊者 6846
贊部 6857
贊務 6862
贊理軍務 6853
贊善 6858
贊善大夫 6859
贊鳴鞭 6855
贊德 6860
贊禮郎 6854
贊饗 6851
贊讀 6861
贈官 6944
贍軍酒庫 4953
贓罰庫 6897
贖藥庫 5469

155 赤

赤 1104
赤令 1111
赤犮氏 1108
赤曆提領官 1110

156 走

走馬承受公事 7037
走卿 7034
起 612
起居令史 621
起居注 617
起居注補闕 619
起居注館 618
起居舍人 622
起居省 623
起居郎 620
起居院 624
起部 635
起部曹 635
起曹 639

起復 626
超 313
超升 335
超品 331
超陞 335
超越 343
超遷 315
趣馬 7036

157 足

路 3839
路分 3846
路分都監 3848
路分鈐轄 3847
路將 3843
路輪令 3852
路鈐 3844

158 身

身列仕版 5158

159 車

車 351
車司馬 366
車府 356
車府令 357
車府署 358
車郎 360
車郎中將 361
車部郎 363
車部曹 364
車輅院 362
車僕 365
車駕 354
車駕司 355
車駕清吏司 355
車營 368
車輿局 369
車騎 1676
車騎府 353
車騎將軍 352
軍 1730
軍屯 1799
軍戶 1762
軍主 1749
軍司 1789
軍司馬 1790
軍民府 1776
軍民萬戶府 1778
軍民總管府 1777

軍坊 1752
軍巡院 1761
軍事推官 1784
軍事監判官 1783
軍使 1780
軍府 1753
軍門 1775
軍容 1764
軍師 1781
軍馬牧 1773
軍馬都督 1774
軍國 1769
軍將 1745
軍監 1747
軍需庫 1760
軍機大臣 1737
軍機行走 1736
軍機章京 1734
軍機處 1735
軍衛 1802
軍器弓槍庫 1741
軍器弩箭劍庫 1742
軍器所 1743
軍器局 1739
軍器庫使 1740
軍器監 1738
軍器雜物庫 1744
軍頭 1795
軍頭司 1796
軍轄兼巡捕使 1757
軟皮局 3084
輅輪令 3852
載師 6824
輔 2035
輔正都尉 2040
輔政 2039
輔國上將軍 2076
輔國中尉 2074
輔國公 2075
輔國將軍 2073
輔義都尉 2065
輔漢將軍 2056
輔轉 2049
輔藩 2054
輕車將軍 1257
輕車都尉 1258
輦郎 3711
輪 3871
輩輩 4533
輜濯 543
輶軒使 8053

輿司馬 8190
轉 1482
轉運司 1492
轉運使 1490
轉運使副提點形
　獄課續院 1491
轉運鹽使司 1493

160 辛

辟任 4609
辟雍 4604
辟雍省 4605
辨銅令 4646
辦事 4412
辦事大臣 4414
辦事司員 4413
辦院事 4423
辦理二司事務 4407
辦驗書畫直長 4422
辭曹 7571
辯銅令 4646

161 辰

農父 4322
農田案 4326
農官 4323
農倉 4327
農圃監 4324
農部 4325
農部曹 4325
農都尉 4328

162 辵

近臣 1119
近侍 1147
近侍局 1151
述古殿直學士 5440
追封 1517
追師 7391
追毀案 1518
送伴使 5876
退材場 7401
迹人 560
逐要 1450
連 3702
連帥 3716
連率 3716

逋臣 4766
逋客 4787
通引司 7518
通仕郎 7506
通市監 7504
通玄院 7487
通守 7511
通判 7497
通事 7503
通事侍郎 7508
通事舍人 7507
通事郎 7505
通事都尉 7509
通事謁者 7510
通奉大夫 7484
通官 7492
通直郎 7473
通直散騎常侍 7474
通侯 7485
通政使司 7467
通政院 7469
通進司 7476
通進銀臺司 7477
通道學 7513
通課司 7491
通議大夫 7490
通議郎 7488
通章署 7466
造作所 6915
造局 6912
造筆直 6914
造辦活計處 6913
進士 1148
進士及第 1149
進士出身 1150
進奏官 1155
進奏院 1156
進納出身 1134
進馬 1132
進講 1121
進擬案 1136
逡 5859
逡人 5868
逡士 5872
逡大夫 5874
逡法 5867
逡師 5873
達官 5971
達勒達 5991
達達 6058
達魯花赤 5993
道 6306

道右 6326
道正司 6307
道官 6317
道紀司 6308
道員 6327
道會司 6312
道僕 6321
道臺 6322
道橋曹 6309
道舉 6311
道錄司 6319
道職 6310
遇缺即補 8127
運司 8287
運同 8291
運判 8283
運使 8286
運河道 8275
運庫 8278
運副 8273
運曹 8290
運糧萬戶府 8281
運糧提舉司 8280
運譜官 8284
遞夫 6364
遞運所 6392
遙郡 7895
遙領 7898
適子 5330
遺人 2962
遺公 2969
遼瀋道 3694
選 2653
選人 2667
選侍 2679
選院 2688
選貢 2670
選部 2675
選部曹 2675
還魂秀才 2824
邊 4631
邊師 8241

163 邑

邑 2925
邑令 2980
邑司 3005
邑君 2950
邑長 2930
邑宰 3015
邑尉 3030
邑尊 3021

邦佐 4447
邦伯 4444
邸 6360
邸吏 6376
邸京師 6361
邸官 6372
邸舍 6382
郊社局 736
郊社署 736
郊祀署 743
郡 1731
郡公 1767
郡公主 1768
郡夫人 1754
郡太夫人 1793
郡太君 1792
郡王 1800
郡王世子 1801
郡主 1750
郡台 1791
郡丞 1733
郡佐 1797
郡伯 1779
郡君 1751
郡邸 1794
郡使 1782
郡長 1732
郡侯 1756
郡首 1786
郡倅 1798
郡馬 1771
郡國 1770
郡尉 1803
郡將 1746
郡將軍 1746
郡縣 1758
郎 3563
郎中 3565
郎中戶將 3569
郎中令 3570
郎中車將 3566
郎中柱下令 3568
郎中騎將 3567
郎君 3571
郎侍講 3576
郎官 3573
郎舍人 3575
郎將 3564
郎僕射 3574
郔匠 8010
部 4764
部丞 4771

部伍 4812
部曲 4776
部臣 4767
部役 4782
部役官 4782
部刺史 4811
部長 4765
部院 4814
部員 4813
部堂 4802
部將 4774
部隊 4810
部從事 4809
部族 4808
部曹 4806
部集 4773
部署 4801
部落 4792
部辦 4793
部醫 4781
郵官 8060
郵亭 8085
都 7181
都士 7274
都大 7289
都元帥府 7337
都內 7260
都勾 7243
都勾判官 7242
都勾押官 7243
都太師 7291
都孔目官 7249
都水令 7281
都水使者 7282
都水官 7280
都水長 7277
都水尉 7284
都水清吏司 7279
都水監 7278
都水臺 7283
都主轄支收司 7210
都令史 7256
都句 7217
都司 7285
都司空獄 7286
都司馬 7287
都司御史房 7288
都目 7259
都匠中郎 7190
都同巡 7324
都同巡檢 7324
都巡使 7236

都巡官 7236
都巡河官 7235
都巡檢 7234
都戎 7239
都老爺 7250
都色長 7270
都防禦使 7225
都兵曹 7264
都作院 7306
都事 7273
都事廳 7276
都官 7244, 7245, 7246
都官司 7245
都官部 7244
都官曹 7246
都官獄 7247
都宗人 7307
都府 7228
都承旨 7186
都押衙 7329
都拘轄司 7218
都知 7195
都知監 7198
都知雜房 7206
都亭侯 7298
都亭驛監官 7299
都保 7262
都則 7303
都勃極烈 7266
都威衛使司 7328
都客省 7241
都指揮使 7199
都指揮使司 7200
都省 7272
都軍使 7223
都城提舉司 7188
都茶場 7182
都部署 7268
都部署司 7269
都都知 7313
都商稅院 7271
都商稅務 7271
都堂 7293
都尉 7326
都御史 7335
都教練使 7191
都曹 7301
都理欠司 7252
都船令 7215
都船獄 7216
都提舉 7294
都提舉官 7295

都統 7321
都統長 7322
都統制 7323
都給事中 7189
都萬戶府 7325
都進奏院 7208
都鄉侯 7231
都察院 7183
都督 7311
都督太守 7316
都督府 7314
都督同知 7317
都督刺史 7318
都督視軍馬 7315
都督僉事 7312
都粮料使 7253
都虞司 7336
都虞侯 7334
都運 7338
都團練使 7319
都團練守捉使 7320
都漕運司 7302
都監 7192
都維那 7327
都臺 7290
都麵院 7257
都憑由司 7265
都磨勘司 7258
都闈 7248
都頭 7300
都檢正 7193
都總使 7310
都總管司 7309
都總管府 7308
都轄 7230
都点檢 7297
都轉 7214
都轉運使 7212
都轉運鹽使 7213
都鎮撫司 7185
都麴院 7219
都護府 7238
都鹽院 7331
都鹽案 7331
鄉 2304
鄉士 2350
鄉大夫 2353
鄉元 2372
鄉公 2332
鄉公主 2334
鄉先生 2318
鄉先達 2318

鄉吏 2340
鄉老 2338
鄉伯 2345
鄉兵 2342
鄉君 2309
鄉法 2311
鄉侯 2316
鄉勇 2371
鄉約 2373
鄉軍 2310
鄉師 2351
鄉翁主 2368
鄉衰 2329
鄉貢 2333
鄉貢郎 2335
鄉貢首 2336
鄉紳 2346
鄉進士 2307
鄉試 2352
鄉團 2364
鄉魁 2327
鄉學 2322
鄉賢 2317
鄉舉 2308
鄉薦 2306
鄒國公 7035
鄙 4571
鄙師 4585
鄰 3717
鄰伍 3731
鄭 6845

16　酉

配隷案 4555
酒人 1303
酒正 1292
酒坊 1300
酒醋麵局 1319
酢匠 7024
醢人 2127
醫士 2997
醫工 2970
醫工長 2971
醫正 2936
醫正郎 2938
醫生 2993
醫佐 3020
醫佐員 3020
醫官 2964
醫官局 2965
醫官院 2968
醫侯郎 2956

醫待詔 3006
醫員 3042
醫師 2998
醫師長 3000
醫效郎 2957
醫針博士 2935
醫博士 2989
醫曹 3019
醫痊郎 2949
醫愈郎 3040
醫監 2944
醫學 2958
醫學提舉司 2959
醫藥院 3037
醫藥提領所 3036
醫藥提舉司 3035
醫匠 691
醯人 2248
釀食典軍 4301

165　朵

朵女 6839

166　里

里 3587
里司官 3642
里正 3592
里甲 3595
里老 3624
里長 3589
里胥 3609
里宰 3643
里尉 3647
里魁 3621
野廬氏 7913
量人 3668

167　金

金正 1120
金玉人匠總管府 1171
金玉府 1170
金吾 1162
金吾仗司 1163
金吾司 1165
金吾街司 1164
金吾衛 1166
金官 1129
金帛府帑 1140
金科 1128

金部 1142
金部司 1142
金部曹 1143
金曹 1153
金紫 1158
金紫光祿大夫 1159
金絲子局 1152
金銀作坊院 1169
金銀局 1168
金銀器盒提舉司 1167
針工 380
針師 389
針博士 388
針線院 377
鈔法 320
鈔紙坊 317
鈔紙局 316
鈔關 329
鈎盾 3218
鈎盾署 3218
鈐 886
鈐轄 898
鈐轄教坊所 899
鈞容直 1765
鉅公 1683
鈴下 3757
鈴轄 3757
鉋盾 4501
鉛部 915
衡 2493
衡枚氏 2521
銅冶場 7517
銅官 7493
銓 1705
銓部 1714
銓寫 1707
銀作局 8003
銀庫 7983
銀青光祿大夫 7981
銀青榮祿大夫 7980
銀牌天使 7987
銀臺 7996
銀臺司 7997
銀臺通進司 7998
錦衣衛 1127
錄 3857
錄公 3851
錄事 3856
錄…事 3857

錄事史 3858
錄事司 3859
錄事參軍 3860
錄事參軍事 3860
錄參 3861
錄勳司 3849
錢官 904
錢府 893
錢局 889
錢帛司 914
錢帛案 913
錢法堂 891
錢粮官 905
錢監 888
錢署 920
錢糧衙門 906
鍼工局 381
鍛工 7368
鎮 372
鎮台 391
鎮守 390
鎮國上將軍 385
鎮國中尉 383
鎮國公 384
鎮國將軍 382
鎮撫 374
鎮撫司 376
鎮撫使 375
鎮標 386
鎧曹 3126
鎖 5524
鏄師 4748
鐘官令 1575
鐘律郎 1587
鐘師 1602
鐘鼓司 1572
鐘鼓院 1573
鐵市 6510
鐵冶所 6514
鐵官 6508
鐵柱 6505
鐵案 6502
鐵帽子王 6509
鑄印局 1453
鑄印篆文官 1452
鑄監 1369
鑄錢司 1374
鑄錢坊 1371
鑄錢使 1373
鑄錢官 1372
鑄錢都將 1375
鑄錢監 1370
鑾坡 3866

鑾臺 3867
鑾儀衛 3865
鑾輿司 3868
鑾輿衛 3869

168　長

長 84
長上 260
長上弟子 261
長子 206
長公主 150
長王 208
長史 185
長史司 186
長丞 91
長吏 153
長行人 244
長行太醫 245
長使 184
長官 143
長官司 149
長信少府 242
長信詹事 241
長秋寺 238
長秋監 237
長兼 236
長流 249
長從宿衛 276
長貳 115
長德 194
長樂少府 251
長樂監 250
長隨 269
長隨奉御 270
長興軍 243

169　門

門下 3934
門下中書使郎 3935
門下史 3940
門下司 3944
門下外省 3947
門下坊 3936
門下侍中 3941
門下侍郎 3942
門下亭長 3945
門下省 3939
門下封駁司 3937
門下後省 3938
門下書佐 3943

門下晚生 3948
門下督 3946
門大夫 3951
門生 3950
門卒 3953
門亭長 3952
門尉 3954
門僕 3949
閑長 2497
閑散 2529
閑廄使 2499
閑駒監長 2501
閑職 2498
閒官 2511
開中 3100
開坊 3102
開府 3103
開府祭酒 3104
開府儀同三司 3105
開拆案 3099
開國 3106
開國子 3119
開國公 3116
開國男 3117
開國伯 3118
開國侯 3110
開國郡公 3108
開國郡伯 3109
開國郡侯 3107
開國縣子 3115
開國縣公 3112
開國縣男 3113
開國縣伯 3114
開國縣侯 3111
開藩 3101
開寶通禮 3120
閣 3167
閣老 3174
閣長 3168
閣門司 3180
閣門舍 3178
閣門宣贊舍人 3177
閣門祗候 3176
閣門通事舍人 3181
閣師 3182
閣試 3183
閣學 3171
閣職 3170
閣門 3175
閣門舍人 3179

閣帥 3185
閣隸 3996
閽 3883
閽胥 3884
閽師 3893
閱卷大臣 8261
閹人 2899
闈 7918
闈割 7942
關 3263
關中侯 3282
關內侯 3321
關外侯 3334
關丞 3273
關令 3317
關防事務處 3292
關防處 3292
關使 3326
關差 3271
關軍使 3290
關軍容宣尉處置
　使 3288
關都尉 3333
關稅監督 3328

170 阜

阜通錢監 2111
防主 1900
防守尉 1914
防禁使 1898
防團 1916
防閤 1907
防禦 1920
防禦守捉使 1924
防禦使 1923
防禦海道運糧萬
　戶府 1921
防禦觀察使 1922
附生 2095
附貢生 2072
防監生 2043
附學生 2063
阿哥 2
阿思哈尼哈番
　3
阿格 2
阿敦侍衛 5
阿敦衙門 6
阿達哈哈番 4
阿監 1
除 1457
除名 1473

除籍 1460
陛下 4577
陛長 4572
院 8221
院判 8236
陵 3734
陵令 3763
陵長 3738
陵寢 3746
陵寢司工匠 3749
陵寢管理燒造磚
　瓦官 3748
陵寢駐防 3747
陵寢總管 3750
陵臺 3773
陵監 3741
陵署 3772
陸路 3853
陸運使 3863
陸運提舉司 3864
陪戎校尉 4554
陪戎副尉 4553
陪祀冠軍使 4557
陪京 4551
陪侍 4556
陪卿 4552
陪堂生 4558
陪都 4559
陶官瓦署 6328
陰陽學 8007
隊 7390
階 754
階官 764
階級 758
隆徽 3875
隆鎮衛親軍都指
　揮司 3874
陽伯 7885
陽官 7882
障塞尉 173
隨身 5871
隨軍 5864
隨軍幹辦官 5866
隨軍轉運使 5865
隨朝太醫 5861
隨朝伴官 5860
隨路打捕鷹房諸
　色民匠總管府
　5870

171 隶

隸僕 3633

172 隹

集正 533
集書省 596
集曹 604
集賢院 554
集賢書庫 552
集賢殿書院 553
集賽 579
雍太祝令 8100
雍太宰令 8101
雍氏 8099
雎鳩氏 1678
雜人 561
雙線局 5487
雜犯差徭 6802
雜物庫 6808
雜造局 6805
雜買務 6804
雜端 6806
雜端諫議 6807
雜賣場 6803
雜職 6801
離宮 3622
難 4083

173 雨

雲司 8288
雲和署 8274
雲幕 8282
雲韶府 8285
雲韶部 8285
雲暈長 8279
雲麾使 8277
雲麾將軍 8276
雲騎尉 8272
雷封 3583
霜臺 5488
露門學 3854
露門館 3854
霸 4357
霸王 4386
靈芝園監 3743
靈臺 3774

174 青

青衿子 1263
青宮 1270
青雲 1283
靜訓 1222

175 非

176 面

177 革

鞍轡局 26
鞍轡庫 27
輕帶斜皮局 6763
鞠秀才 1679
鞮鞻氏 6378

178 韋

韎師 3933

179 韭

180 音

音監 7974
音聲人 7991
音聲博士 7992
韶舞 5125

181 頁

頂子 6742
頂戴 6742
順妃 5517
順成 5516
順容 5520
順常 5515
順華 5518
順儀 5519
頒降案 4402
頓遞使 7402
領 3735
領主事 3751
領左右府 3775
領…事 3735, 3769
領侍衛內大臣
　3771
領侍衛府 3770
領…官 3760
領軍 3753
領軍大都督 3755
領軍將軍 3754
領軍衛 3756
領班 3765

領班章京上行走
　3766
領運 3778
領監官 3742
領閣事 3759
領齋郎 3736
頭上尹 6800
頭目 6799
頭領 6798
額外 4355
額真 4352
額爾奇木 4353
額駙 4354
題署 6466
顏料局 7947
顏料庫 7948

182 風

風俗使 2019
風紀 1963
風憲 1982
風憲官 1982

183 飛

飛白書博士 1932
飛廄 1929
飛錢 1928
飛龍使 1931
飛龍院 1930
飛龍廄 1930
飛騎 1926
飛騎尉 1927

184 食

食 5535
食邑 5258
食官 5274
食官令 5276
食官長 5275
食官署 5277
食貨監 5253
食監 5222
食糧醫員 5284
食醫 5257
食醫侍御 5262
飯上人委署 1882
飯房 1867
飯銀處 1889
飽卿 4467
餉生 2348

養心殿造辦處
　7878
養狗處 7881
養象所 7877
養廉額 7883
養鴉鶻處 7886
養鷹鷂處 7888
養鷹處 7887
餘丁 8196
餘子 8201
餘軍 8128
餚藏署 2455
館 3264
館主 3281
館所監督 3329
館閣 3310
館閣校勘 3311
館驛巡官 3301
館驛使 3303
錫匠 6290
錫官 2579
錫官吏 2579
廩廩司 2256
饍人 628

185 首

首令太監 5390
首府 5371
首相 5373
首參 5403
首揆 5382
首輔 5372
首領官 5388
首領廳 5391
首縣 5374

186 香

香火內使 2323
香尉 2366
香藥庫 2369

187 馬

馬 3895
馬先 3901
馬快 3902
馬牧使 3904
馬步軍 3906
馬步院 3908
馬步都虞候 3907
馬前 3897

馬軍司 3899
馬曹 3910
馬羣司 3900
馬監 3896
馬質 3898
馬館 3903
馮相氏 1981, 4709
馭夫 8131
馭僕寺 8165
馴馬司 2748
馴象所 2738
駐防 1381
駐防八旗 1381
駐泊 1412
駐箚 1358
駐藏大臣 1438
駙馬都尉 2083
駕士 679
駕相 659
駕部 676
馴車庶長 5542
駝牛署 6793
駝坊 6791
駿馬令 1772
騏驥院 615
騎 613
騎兵 574
騎兵參軍事 575
騎兵曹 576
騎官軍 564
騎軍 548
騎案 523
騎馬令 570
騎尉 607
騎尉府 608
騎曹 605
騎都尉 606
駒駼監 6329
駃騠廄 3842
駿粟都尉 5532
駃蹄苑 3387
騶僕射 7039
驅使官 1696
驅使院 1697
驅磨案 1695
驃騎大將軍 4620
驃騎府 4619
驃騎將軍 4618
驍衛 2457
驍衛府 2457
驍騎 2378
驍騎府 2379

驍騎尉 2381
驍騎衛府 2379
驍騎營 2382
驊騮牧 2810
驊騮署 2811
驗放大臣 7935
驗封司 7936
驗封清吏司 7936
驛 2926
驛站 2927
驛傳道 2948
驛鹽道 3038

188 骨

體量案 6458

189 高

高品 3145
高班 3144
高第 3147

190 髟

191 鬥

192 鬯

鬯人 248
鬱人 8145

193 鬲

194 鬼

魁 3381
魁甲 3383
魁薦 3384

195 魚

鮌人 8146

196 鳥

鳥槍長 4302
鳥槍處 4303
鳥槍護軍 4305
鳥槍驍騎 4304

鳳苑 2030
鳳凰池 1987
鳳閣 1998
鳴贊 4024
鴉鶻房 7854
鴻臣 2902
鴻都門學 2909
鴻臚寺 2906
鴻臚卿 2905
鵬坊 6494
鵁鵃閑 8233
鶴廳 2198
鶡坊 2782
鶡房 2783
鶵坊 7896
鷹坊 8011
鷹房 8012
鷹揚府 8030
鷹揚衛 8031

197 鹵

鹵簿 3855
鹵簿使 3855
鹺尹 7029
鹺任 7026
鹺使 7027
鹺務 7028
鹺貳 7025
鹽人 7941
鹽引所 7963
鹽引批驗所 7963
鹽州使 7930
鹽巡檢 7938
鹽池監 7926
鹽池總監 7927
鹽使司 7953
鹽官 7946
鹽法道 7934
鹽法糧務道 7933
鹽知事 7925
鹽政 7924
鹽院官 7964
鹽香司 7937
鹽倉督 7960
鹽酒稅務 7929
鹽茶大使 7920
鹽馬司 7950
鹽場大使 7922
鹽場司 7921
鹽掣同知 7923
鹽掣官 7923
鹽提舉 7956

鹽運司 7966
鹽運使 7965
鹽道 7955
鹽榷使 7931
鹽課司 7943
鹽課提舉司 7944
鹽鐵司 7959
鹽鐵判官 7957
鹽鐵使 7958

198 鹿

麗正修書院 3593
麗正殿修書院 3593
麗妃 3606
麟趾殿 3720
麟臺 3730

199 麥

麥麴場 3911
麪物都監 1699
麪院 1700
麪案 1691
麪麴倉督 1694

200 麻

麻普 3909

201 黃

黃考 2837
黃門 2841
黃門北寺 2845
黃門令 2844
黃門侍郎 2847
黃門省 2846
黃門郎 2843
黃門鼓吹 2842
黃帶子 2857
黃堂 2865
黃犀 2835
黃閣 2838
黃閣曹 2839
黃頭郎 2869
黃檔房 2864
黃藏署 2870
黃闥 2856

202 黍

203 黑

黜陟使 1462
點檢文字 6532
點檢官 6531
點檢房 6529
點檢醫藥飯食 6530
黨 6282

204 黹

205 黽

鼀峯 31
黽人 4627

206 鼎

鼎元 6745
鼎司 6741
鼎甲 6735
鼎臣 6734
鼎位 6744
鼎席 6737
鼎輔 6736
鼎魁 6739

207 鼓

鼓人 3232
鼓司 3245
鼓吹局 3230
鼓吹案 3230
鼓吹署 3231
鼓院 3247
鼓旗軍 3225
鼓鑄公署 3229
鼓鑄局 3227

208 鼠

209 鼻

210 齊

齊右 643
齊僕 637
齋 59
齋帥 65

齋帥局 66
齋郎 63
齋師 64

211 齒

212 龍

龍 3873
龍位 3879
龍武軍 3881
龍首 3877
龍馬監 3876
龍圖閣 3878
龍衛四廂 3880
龍頭 3877

213 龜

龜人 3372
龜卜 3375

214 龠

Conversion Table: Pinyin to Wade-Giles

Pinyin	Wade-Giles	Pinyin	Wade-Giles	Pinyin	Wade-Giles	Pinyin	Wade-Giles
a	a	cui	ts'ui	gun	kun	kun	k'un
ai	ai	cun	ts'un	guo	kuo	kuo	k'uo
an	an	cuo	ts'o	ha	ha	la	la
ang	ang	da	ta	hai	hai	lai	lai
ao	ao	dai	tai	han	han	lan	lan
ba	pa	dan	tan	hang	hang	lang	lang
bai	pai	dang	tang	hao	hao	lao	lao
ban	pan	dao	tao	he	ho	le	le
bang	pang	de	te	hei	hei	lei	lei
bao	pao	deng	teng	hen	hen	leng	leng
bei	pei	di	ti	heng	heng	li	li
ben	pen	dian	tien	hong	hung	lian	lien
beng	per	diao	tiao	hou	hou	liang	liang
bi	pi	die	tieh	hu	hu	liao	liao
bian	pien	ding	ting	hua	hua	lie	lieh
biao	piao	diu	tiu	huai	huai	lin	lin
bie	pieh	dong	tung	huan	huan	ling	ling
bin	pin	dou	tou	huang	huang	liu	liu
bing	ping	du	tu	hui	hui	long	lung
bo	po	duan	tuan	hun	hun	lou	lou
bu	pu	dui	tui	huo	huo	lu	lu
ca	ts'a	dun	tun	ji	chi	luan	luan
cai	ts'ai	duo	to	jia	chia	lun	lun
can	ts'an	e	o, a	jian	chien	luo	lo
cang	ts'ang	en	en	jiang	chiang	lü	lü
cao	ts'ao	eng	eng	jiao	chiao	lüe	lüeh
ce	ts'e	er [r]	erh	jie	chieh	ma	ma
cen	ts'en	fa	fa	jin	chin	mai	mai
ceng	ts'eng	fan	fan	jing	ching	man	man
cha	ch'a	fang	fang	jiong	chiung	mang	mang
chai	ch'ai	fei	fei	jiu	chiu	mao	mao
chan	ch'an	fen	fen	ju	chü	mei	mei
chang	ch'ang	feng	feng	juan	chüan	men	men
chao	ch'ao	fo	fo	jue	chüeh	meng	meng
che	ch'e	fou	fou	jun	chün	mi	mi
chen	ch'en	fu	fu	ka	k'a	mian	mien
cheng	ch'eng	ga	ka	kai	k'ai	miao	miao
chi	ch'ih	gai	kai	kan	k'an	mie	mieh
chong	ch'ung	gan	kan	kang	k'ang	min	min
chou	ch'ou	gang	kang	kao	k'ao	ming	ming
chu	ch'u	gao	kao	ke	k'o	miu	miu
chuai	ch'uai	ge	ko	ken	k'en	mo	mo
chuan	ch'uan	gen	ken	keng	k'eng	mou	mou
chuang	ch'uang	geng	keng	kong	k'ung	mu	mu
chui	ch'ui	gong	kung	kou	k'ou	na	na
chun	ch'un	gou	kou	ku	k'u	nai	nai
chuo	ch'o	gu	ku	kua	k'ua	nan	nan
ci	tz'u	gua	kua	kuai	k'uai	nang	nang
cong	ts'ung	guai	kuai	kuan	k'uan	nao	nao
cou	ts'ou	guan	kuan	kuang	k'uang	nei	nei
cu	ts'u	guang	kuang	kui	k'uei	nen	nun
cuan	ts'uan	gui	kuei				

Pinyin	Wade-Giles	Pinyin	Wade-Giles	Pinyin	Wade-Giles	Pinyin	Wade-Giles
neng	neng	quan	ch'üan	sun	sun	yao	yao
ni	ni	que	ch'üeh	suo	so	ye	yeh
nian	nien	qun	ch'ün			yi	i
niang	niang			ta	t'a	yin	yin
niao	niao	ran	jan	tai	t'ai	ying	ying
nie	nieh	rang	jang	tan	t'an	yo	yüeh
nin	nin	rao	jao	tang	t'ang	yong	yung
ning	ning	re	je	tao	t'ao	you	yu
niu	niu	ren	jen	te	t'e	yu	yü
nong	nung	reng	jeng	teng	t'eng	yuan	yüan
nou	nou	ri	jih	ti	t'i	yue	yüeh
nu	nu	rong	jung	tian	t'ien	yun	yün
nuan	nuan	rou	jou	tiao	t'iao		
nun	nun	ru	ju	tie	t'ieh	za	tsa
nuo	no	ruan	juan	ting	t'ing	zai	tsai
nü	nü	rui	jui	tong	t'ung	zan	tsan
nüe	nüeh	run	jun	tou	t'ou	zang	tsang
		ruo	jo	tu	t'u	zao	tsao
o	o			tuan	t'uan	ze	tse
ou	ou	sa	sa	tui	t'ui	zei	tsei
		sai	sai	tun	t'un	zen	tsen
pa	p'a	san	san	tuo	t'o	zeng	tseng
pai	p'ai	sang	sang				
pan	p'an	sao	sao	wa	wa	zha	cha
pang	p'ang	se	se	wai	wai	zhai	chai
pao	p'ao	sen	sen	wan	wan	zhan	chan
pei	p'ei	seng	seng	wang	wang	zhang	chang
pen	p'en	sha	sha	wei	wei	zhao	chao
peng	p'eng	shai	shai	wen	wen	zhe	che
pi	p'i	shan	shan	weng	weng	zhen	chen
pian	p'ien	shang	shang	wo	wo	zheng	cheng
piao	p'iao	shao	shao	wu	wu	zhi	chih
pie	p'ieh	she	she			zhong	chung
pin	p'in	shen	shen	xi	hsi	zhou	chou
ping	p'ing	sheng	sheng	xia	hsia	zhu	chu
po	p'o	shi	shih	xian	hsien	zhua	chua
pou	p'ou	shou	shou	xiang	hsiang	zhuai	chuai
pu	p'u	shu	shu	xiao	hsiao	zhuan	chuan
		shua	shua	xie	hsieh	zhuang	chuang
qi	ch'i	shuai	shuai	xin	hsin	zhui	chui
qia	ch'ia	shuan	shuan	xing	hsing	zhun	chun
qian	ch'ien	shuang	shuang	xiong	hsiung	zhuo	cho
qiang	ch'iang	shui	shui	xiu	hsiu		
qiao	ch'iao	shun	shun	xu	hsü	zi	tzu
qie	ch'ieh	shuo	shuo	xuan	hsüan	zong	tsung
qin	ch'in	si	ssu	xue	hsüeh	zou	tsou
qing	ch'ing	song	sung	xun	hsün	zu	tsu
qiong	ch'iung	sou	sou			zuan	tsuan
qiu	ch'iu	su	su	ya	ya	zui	tsui
qu	ch'ü	suan	suan	(yai)	yai	zun	tsun
		sui	sui	yan	yen	zuo	tso
				yang	yang		